RCL

RESOURCES *for* COLLEGE LIBRARIES

2007

This Edition of *Resources for College Libraries* was prepared by:

ACRL & Choice:
Project Editor: Marcus Elmore
Editorial Director, Choice: Francine Graf
Editor & Publisher, Choice: Irving Rockwood

Special Thanks to Our Proofreaders:
Monika Maslowski, Jinna Anderson, Chris Sullivan, Jennifer Donahue, Judith Douville,
Rebecca Bartlett, and Carolyn Wilcox

Record Entry Completed By:
Monika Maslowski, Laurie Trulock, and Sheila Laverty

R. R. Bowker LLC:
John Krafty: Product Manager, RCL
Ashley Ludwig: Managing Editor, RCL
Frank Morris: IT Director
Minh Huynh: Senior Programmer Analyst
Robert Zeisler: Senior Programmer Analyst

Editorial Staff:
Ian Singer: Vice President, Data Services
Roy Crego: Senior Managing Director, Editorial
Eleanor Schubauer: Managing Editor
Michael Olenick: Managing Editor
Beverly Palacio: Associate Editor

Production Department:
Doreen Gravesande: Senior Director, Production
Ralph Coviello, Manager, Manufacturing Services
Myriam Nunez: Project Manager, Product Development & Content Integrity
Kennard McGill: Production Consultant

Research Completed By:
Pat Diaz, Bobbie Ferraro, Kathy Griner, Becky Housel, and Diane Johnson.

Record Entry Completed By:
Jenny Marie DeJesus, Dorothy Perry-Gilchrist, Anthony Giuffra, and Steven Zaffuto

2007

Volume 1:
Humanities

Mary Ellen Davis, Executive Director, ACRL

Published by
R. R. Bowker LLC
630 Central Avenue, New Providence
New Jersey 07974

Annie Callanan, President and CEO

URL: http://www.rclweb.net
E-mail address: rclfeedback@bowker.com

Readers may send any corrections and/or updates to the information in this work to:
rclfeedback@bowker.com

International Standard Book Number:

7 Volume Set:	ISBN: 0-8352-4855-0
	ISBN13: 978-0-8352-4855-6
Vol. 1: Humanities:	ISBN: 0-8352-4856-9
	ISBN13: 978-0-8352-4856-3
Vol. 2: Language & Literature:	ISBN: 0-8352-4857-7
	ISBN13: 978-0-8352-4857-0
Vol. 3: History:	ISBN: 0-8352-4858-5
	ISBN13: 978-0-8352-4858-7
Vol. 4: Social Sciences:	ISBN: 0-8352-4859-3
	ISBN13: 978-0-8352-4859-4
Vol. 5: Science and Technology:	ISBN: 0-8352-4860-7
	ISBN13: 978-0-8352-4860-0
Vol. 6: Interdisciplinary & Area Studies:	ISBN: 0-8352-4861-5
	ISBN13: 978-0-8352-4861-7
Vol. 7: Indexes:	ISBN: 0-8352-4862-3
	ISBN13: 978-0-8352-4862-4

Printed and bound in the United States of America

Table of Contents

Resources for College Libraries: General Introduction

Like its predecessors, the three editions of *Books for College Libraries* (BCL) that appeared in 1988, 1975, and 1964, *Resources for College Libraries* (RCL) is a bibliography of carefully selected works spanning the college curriculum and comprising a recommended core collection for all academic libraries. In the tradition of its predecessors, which drew on the such sources as the published catalog of Harvard's Lamont Library (1954), the shelflist of the undergraduate library of the University of Michigan, and, crucially, Charles Shaw's *List of Books for College Libraries* (1931), RCL attempts to balance multiple, often contradictory demands. It seeks to provide a balanced set of recommendations that take note of the weight of the various academic disciplines within the undergraduate curriculum, the degree to which those various disciplines depend on book materials for their essential teaching and research resources, and the extensive pattern of changes that have reshaped the academic curriculum since 1988, the year in which BCL3, the most recent edition of *Books for College Libraries,* appeared.

Of necessity, RCL also embodies a paradox identified by the late Virginia Clark, editor of BCL3: it "can fully succeed only by failing. It would be disastrous should the collection it suggests serve perfectly to ratify the finished work of book selection in any library."[1] Not only will individual institutions create collections significantly larger than the roughly 65,000 titles recommended by RCL, but they will tailor those collections to reflect the size and strength of their own individual departments, majors, and programs. RCL attempts to make general recommendations, within individual subject areas, of those titles most necessary for teaching the subject to undergraduates. In many cases, this means a foundation to which the smallest institutions should aspire but which larger collections will far surpass.

We describe RCL as a successor to, rather than a new edition of, BCL for two reasons. The first is formal, and lies behind the change in nomenclature: RCL includes in its recommendations a variety of electronic resources, including Web sites, subscription databases, e-books, and other electronic materials. The second, procedural reason follows from this: unlike its predecessors, RCL will appear as both a multivolume print edition and a searchable, continuously updated electronic database. In addition, there is a third, tacit distinction which may be made between RCL and the various editions of BCL: although bibliographers compiling subject lists for RCL often took the titles listed in BCL3 as a starting point, our bibliographic work emphasized building a comprehensive, retrospective list of titles by reference to the current undergraduate curriculum, and thus much of the work on RCL was from scratch. In contrast, the relationship between the various editions of BCL was demonstrably that of revision; from one edition to the next, there was an expectation that a title would be retained unless it was actively removed (if, for instance, it had been superseded by a more recent work). Because so much more time had passed between the appearance of BCL3 and the development of RCL than between any successive editions of BCL, bibliographers faced the simultaneously daunting and liberating prospect of creating a subject list *de novo.* That this same period (1988-2006) has seen momentous sea changes in many of the academic disciplines in the humanities and the sciences, as well as the growth of interdisciplinary study across all the academic disciplines, made this an opportunity to take measure of the way subjects are taught to undergraduates, as well as the sorts of subjects which are taught, when developing our core list.

One result of this reassessment was the decision to recognize and include as separate subject divisions in RCL a number of interdisciplinary fields, e.g., Environmental Studies and Gender Studies. The decision about which fields to include was based primarily on the degree to which those subjects function as areas of formal study at undergraduate institutions in the U.S., whether as major programs, academic minors, or areas of concentration housed within another department (film studies, for instance, is often offered as a program or concentration within the departments of English, Comparative Literature, or Theater). We recognized that the lists of titles recommended for teaching interdisciplinary subjects, e.g., Asian American Studies, might overlap significantly with the corresponding title lists for related traditional fields, e.g., American Literature. At the same time, we were confident that many of the recommended interdisciplinary titles would be unique, and so it has proved. The degree of overlap between the various sections of RCL is, throughout, fortuitous and reflects actual overlap between various undergraduate curricula. Effort was made to regularize the editions selected, but the work of compiling the various subject lists proceeded on an independent basis.

---

1. Virginia Clark, "Introduction," *Books for College Libraries: A Core Collection of 50,000 Titles,* (3rd ed., Chicago: American Library Association, 1988), vii.

The other dramatic difference between RCL and BCL is the decision to move away from Library of Congress classification as the primary framework for the selection and classification of titles. Though this is bound to be regarded by many librarians as a controversial decision, we are confident that it will prove in retrospect to be a sound one. The rationale for doing so is the desire to have titles classified in a fashion which closely follows the contours of the undergraduate curriculum. While LC accomplishes this for some subjects (for instance, British or American Literature, which are taught by chronological periods, and within periods by major authors and by forms such as poetry or drama), other curricula fail to mesh well with LC classification: Business Administration, for example, is responsible for the largest portion of baccalaureate degrees conferred by U.S. colleges and universities,[2] yet the classification of materials in the business curriculum in LC class HB-HJ, while sufficient for cataloging purposes, offers no insight on the relationship between materials so classified and the curriculum in which they are used. It is, furthermore, an arrangement which makes perfect sense to, but only to, librarians. Not all copies of BCL resided in technical services departments, but it seems unlikely that they were much consulted by students or faculty. Our hope is that the new classification scheme will work to the advantage of all the academic library's constituencies: librarians, especially those lacking strong background in a given subject, will be able to see not only the recommended titles but also, in the subject taxonomy, a map of the undergraduate curriculum; faculty will find recommendations of essential works in a form more accessible than LC, and bearing a closer correspondence to the way their courses and departments are organized; students, searching for a place to begin research on a particular topic, will also be able to recognize in the classification scheme something corresponding to their own encounter with the subject matter in the classroom and laboratory. Finally, since each entry in RCL retains its LC classification, those who prefer to search for materials in this fashion will still be able to.

RCL is the result of the collaborative efforts of 332 contributors, almost exclusively teaching faculty or librarians at U.S. colleges and universities. There were three kinds of contributors: subject editors, bibliographers, and referees. Subject editors were selected on the basis of their subject expertise and teaching or collection development experience: eighteen hold doctorates, four are members of the teaching faculty at research universities, two are independent scholars, and the remainder are academic librarians. Many have previously contributed to or authored major bibliographies in their subject areas. They were responsible for developing the subject classification taxonomy for their respective subject areas, for recruiting bibliographers and coordinating their efforts, and for reviewing the results. The subject editors represented a change from the various editions of BCL, where the bibliographers (mainly Choice reviewers) dealt directly with the project editor. By inserting a layer of subject experts we sought to ensure that the titles selected and the taxonomies in which they were classified reflected as much as possible the realities of the contemporary undergraduate curriculum. The second class of RCL contributors, bibliographers, was responsible for the bulk of the actual selection of titles. Like the subject editors, they were faculty and librarians selected for their subject knowledge, often with particular expertise in one specific aspect of a field. Finally, a pool of sixty-four referees, senior faculty or subject-specialist librarians, provided independent assessment of the initial lists developed by the bibliographers; the subject editors used this feedback to further refine their lists prior to publication.

The development of RCL had presumed from the beginning that bibliographers would be manipulating electronic bibliographic records in some sort of online environment, but the decision of the Association of College and Research Libraries (ACRL) Board of Directors to partner with publisher R. R. Bowker to produce RCL allowed us access to Bowker's massive database of bibliographic records, as well as the extensive technical support and expertise Bowker deployed on behalf of the project. Bibliographers selected titles in Bowker's *booksinprint.com* database, in a particular edition, and then imported them to the online RCL Authoring System, where they assigned subject headings and recommended audience levels. In those instances where no bibliographic record existed for a desired title, one was created from a reliable source (preferably with book in hand, though this was not always possible). At the same time, bibliographers submitted corrections to Bowker records when they identified errors or inconsistencies. While this system allowed us to avoid much of the brute effort which was expended on the creation of bibliographic records for the various editions of BCL, it also meant that bibliographers spent thousands of person-hours in the *booksinprint.com* database, identifying the most recent and reliable edition of particular works; in some cases, editors elected to include multiple editions, especially where the differences between them are significant for undergraduate teaching (see, for instance, the decision to include multiple, equally worthwhile translations of Dante's *Divine Comedy* in the Italian literature section).

The use of an online system for the manipulation of electronic bibliographic records was in part a matter of efficiency, but more importantly, it finally addresses one longstanding issue faced by BCL, that of obsolescence.

---

2. http://nces.ed.gov/fastfacts/display.asp?id=37: U.S. Department of Education, National Center for Education Statistics. (2006). *Digest of Education Statistics, 2005* (NCES 2006-030), chapter 3.

When *Choice* magazine was founded in 1964, it was envisioned as, among other things, an ongoing supplement to BCL1. This approach did not prove practical, and the second and third editions of BCL were required. In contrast, RCL will be updated on an ongoing basis beginning almost immediately after its initial publication; bibliographic records will reflect changes in print status, and new titles will be introduced at regular intervals, to supplement or replace extant titles.

In addition to the tireless efforts of the contributors, on whom I cannot lavish sufficient praise, special thanks to the ACRL Board of Directors and Mary Ellen Davis, ACRL Executive Director, without whose approval and generous support this project would not have been possible. Oversight and advice were provided throughout the project by the RCL Editorial Board: Carolyn Sheehy, North Central College, Chair; and other members Joan Ellen Broome, Georgia Southern University; Barbara Burd, College Misericordia; Brian E. Coutts, Western Kentucky University; Bradford Lee Eden, University of California, Santa Barbara; Stacey Marien, American University; and Richard Shaw, Technical College of the Lowcountry.

Thanks are also due the editorial staff of *Choice*, all of whom contributed effort and advice to the production of this work in varying degrees (and all of whom exhibited tremendous kindness in their efforts, especially in the final days): Becky Bartlett, Judith Douville, Fran Graf, Lisa Mitten, and Carolyn Wilcox. Fran Graf and Irv Rockwood, the Publisher of *Choice*, deserve another helping of praise for their advice, encouragement, and

oversight of the project, as well as for handling negotiations of our partnership with R. R. Bowker. Judith Douville made superhuman contributions to a number of subject areas in addition to her own responsibilities in Chemistry. Although almost every member of the *Choice* office staff contributed to this work, Sheila Laverty deserves special praise for her work on the Dance section. Finally, the work would not have been completed if it had not been for the tireless effort of a small cadre of freelance staff, namely Jennifer Donahue, Monika Maslowski, Teri Staab, and Laurie Trulock, who proofread and edited subject headings and section notes, entered titles, cataloged records, and helped maintain communication with subject editors, with extraordinary care, intelligence, and persistence.

With our partners at R. R. Bowker, we enjoyed the highest degree of collegiality and cooperation. Special thanks are due to Angela D'Agostino, Vice-President of Marketing; John Krafty, Product Manager of *Books In Print*; Ashley Ludwig, Managing Editor; Todd Rudloff, Project Manager of *Books In Print*; Frank Morris, Senior Programmer; Minh Huynh, Senior Programmer Analyst, all of whom made significant contributions to bringing this work to the light of day.

Finally, my deep thanks to my family, Colleen and Graham, for their patience and support throughout this project.

Marcus Elmore,

Editor

A Note on the RCL Subject Taxonomy

One of the distinctive features of *Resources for College Libraries* is the subject taxonomy used to organize the titles included in RCL. Developed specifically for RCL by the RCL editorial team, and in particular by the subject editors, the RCL taxonomy reflects the contours of today's undergraduate curriculum. The RCL taxonomy's major headings, therefore, generally correspond to academic majors, departments, or courses of study, e.g., anthropology, business administration, or physics. (In some cases an academic discipline has been further subdivided in order to create sections of manageable size, e.g., the subdivision of History by geographical region.) The goal is a classification scheme, which organizes materials as they would be taught by faculty and encountered in the classroom and the laboratory by undergraduate students.

In some subject areas, e.g. British and American literature, the RCL subject taxonomy closely resembles the Library of Congress classification scheme used in *Books for College Libraries,* 3rd edition. In most cases, however, the differences between LC and today's undergraduate curriculum, have been so substantial as to require the development of a new taxonomy from scratch. This has been especially true for the interdisciplinary subjects such as African American Studies, Criminal Justice, and Native American Studies, which draw upon materials from a dizzying range of LC classes. Gender Studies, for example, draws from a large array of academic disciplines, including (but not limited to) psychology, sociology, literature, philosophy, political science, medicine, and history.

The coverage of interdisciplinary subjects in RCL is another of its distinguishing features, and one deemed essential from the very inception of the project. Although there is some overlap between the interdisciplinary title lists and those of related traditional subjects, e.g., American literature and Chicano/a literature (a subsection of Latino Studies), the interdisciplinary sections inevitably include many unique titles. In addition, the inclusion of the interdisciplinary subjects makes it possible to distinguish those titles which have been selected as essential resources for a traditional subject such as American literature (e.g., Carson McCullers' *Collected Novels*), from those selected for an interdisciplinary area (e.g., Pat Mora's *Communion,* selected for Latino Studies > Humanities > Literature > Chicano/a Literature), and also from those selected for both (e.g., Mora's *Borders*).

By making the ways in which titles are actually used in the classroom the focus for our classification of titles in RCL, we hope to both dramatically increase its usefulness to students and faculty members and also to underscore the extent to which titles were selected on the basis of their importance to undergraduate study and teaching.

RCL Contributors

John Abbott, Graduate Student, GSLIS, University of Illinois, Urbana-Champaign.
Subject Editor: European History.

Randy Abbott, Head Reference Librarian, University of Evansville.
Referee.

Anthony Adam, Assistant Director, John B. Coleman Library, Prairie View A&M University.
Bibliographer: GLBT Studies.

Jan Adamczyk, Slavic Reference Service, University of Illinois.
Bibliographer: Russian Languages and Literatures.

Michael Adams, Librarian, CUNY Graduate Center.
Bibliographer: American Literature.

Paulita Aguilar, Curator, Indigenous Nations Library Program, University of New Mexico.
Bibliographer: Native American Studies.

Flavia Alaya, Professor of English, Ramapo College of New Jersey.
Referee.

Jean Alexander, Head of Reference, Hunt Library, Carnegie Mellon University.
Referee.

Duncan Alford, Head of Reference, Law Library, Georgetown University.
Bibliographer: Law.

Karen Antell, Head, Reference Department, University of Oklahoma.
Bibliographer: Technology and Engineering.

Ralph Arcari, Director Emeritus, Health Center Library, University of Connecticut.
Subject Editor: Medicine.

Susan Ariew, University Librarian, University of South Florida.
Bibliographer: Education.

Jan Armstrong, Professor of Education, University of New Mexico.
Referee.

Teresa Arrington, Associate Professor of Modern Languages, Blue Mountain College.
Bibliographer: Spanish Language and Literature.

Susan Awe, Director of Parish Memorial Library, University of New Mexico.
Referee.

David Azzolina, Reference librarian, University of Pennsylvania.
Bibliographer: General Language and Literature.

Pete Banholzer, Technical Information Specialist, NASA.
Bibliographer: Geology.

Ron Banks, Human Subjects Coordinator, Institutional Review Board, University of Illinois.
Bibliographer: Education.

David Bantz, Chief Information Architect, University of Alaska.
Referee.

Adele Barsh, Business and Economics Librarian, Carnegie Mellon University.
Bibliographer: Business Administration.

Jennifer Bartlett, Head of Research & Instructional Services, Murray State University.
Bibliographer: American Literature.

Edwin Battistella, Dean of Arts and Letters and Professor of English, University of Southern Oregon.
Bibliographer: General Language and Literature.

Frederic Baumgartner, Professor of History, Virginia Tech University.
Bibliographer: European History.

Robert Beauregard, Professor, Urban Policy Analysis and Management, New School University.
Referee.

Linda Behrend, Cataloging Librarian, University of Tennessee, Knoxville.
Bibliographer: American Literature.

Penny Beile, Head, Curriculum Materials Center, University of Central Florida.
Bibliographer: Education.

Dean Bell, Dean and Chief Academic Officer, Spertus Institute of Jewish Studies.
Bibliographer: European History.

Dennis Benamati, Director, Ryan-Matura Library, Sacred Heart University.
Referee.

Riva Berleant-Schiller, Professor emerita of Anthropology, University of Connecticut, emerita.
Subject Editor: Anthropology.

Jay Bernstein, Reader Services Librarian, Kingsborough Community College.
Referee.

John Berry, Native American Studies Librarian, University of California, Berkeley.
Subject Editor: Native American Studies.

Sharon Black, Librarian, Annenberg School for Communication, University of Pennsylvania.
Bibliographer: Journalism and Communication.

Steve Blackburn, Library Director, Hartford Seminary.
Referee.

Robert Bland, Associate University Librarian
Automation and Technical Services, University of North
Carolina, Asheville.
Bibliographer: Philosophy.

Richard Bleiler, Humanities Bibliographer, University of
Connecticut.
Bibliographer: General Language and Literature.

Laurel Blewett, Manager of Library Services,
Edward Hospital.
Referee.

Christopher Bloss, Instructional Services Librarian,
University of South Dakota.
Bibliographer: American Literature.

Ellen Bosman, Head of Technical Services, New Mexico
State University.
Subject Editor: GLBT Studies.

Jesús Bottaro, Instructor, CUNY / Medgar Evers
College.
Bibliographer: Spanish Language and Literature.

Steven Botterill, Professor of Italian, University of
California, Berkeley.
Referee.

Sally Bowdoin, Head of Serials, Brooklyn College.
Subject Editor: British Literature.

Linda Bowles-Adarkwa, Subject Specialist, Black
Studies and Women Studies, San Francisco State
University.
Bibliographer: African American Studies.

James Boxall, Director, GIS Centre, Dalhousie University.
Subject Editor: Geography.

James Bracken, Assistant Director for Main Library
Research and Reference Services, Ohio State University.
Subject Editor: Other Literatures in English.

Laura Braunstein, Research and Reference Services,
Dartmouth University.
Bibliographer: General Language and Literature.

Tony Bremholm, Life Sciences Librarian, Texas
A&M University.
Referee.

Karl Bridges, Coordinator of Electronic Instruction
Resources, University of Vermont.
Bibliographer: U.S. and Canadian History.

JoEllen Broome, Reference Specialist, Georgia Southern
University.
Subject Editor: Environmental Studies.

Mitchell Brown, Research Librarian for Chemistry and
Earth System Sciences, University of California,
Irvine.
Referee.

Mary Jane Brustman, Bibliographer for Social Welfare
and Criminal Justice, SUNY Albany.
Subject Editor: Criminal Justice.

Mark Bullock, Graduate Student, History Department,
University of Illinois at Chicago.
Bibliographer: European History.

Merry Burlingham, Chief Bibliographer and Collections
Officer, University of Texas.
**Bibliographer: Asian History, Languages, and
Literatures.**

Angela Cannon, Reference Librarian, Library of
Congress.
**Bibliographer: Russian Languages and
Literatures.**

Karen Cary, Head, Collection Management, Virginia
Commonwealth University.
Bibliographer: Sociology.

Melissa Cast, Reference Librarian and Subject Specialist
for Education, University of Nebraska Omaha.
Bibliographer: Education.

Rafaela Castro, Bibliographer, University of California,
Davis.
Subject Editor: Latino Studies.

Tina Ching, Reference Librarian, Arizona State
University.
Referee.

Diana Chlebek, English and Modern Languages and
Literature Bibliographer, University of Akron.
Bibliographer: French Language and Literature.

Michael Chromey, Humanities Librarian, Atlanta
University Center.
Bibliographer: African American Studies.

Hui Hua Chua, US Documents Librarian, Michigan
State University.
Bibliographer: Journalism and Communication.

Alan Church, Professor of English, University of
Texas at Brownsville.
Referee.

Janet Clarke, Asian American Studies Selector, Stony
Brook University.
Bibliographer: Asian American Studies.

Kim Clarke, Assistant Librarian, Selector for Women's
Studies, University of Minnesota, Twin Cities.
Subject Editor: Gender Studies.

Rudolph Clay, Subject Librarian, African and
African-American Studies, Washington University.
Bibliographer: African American Studies.

Ana Maria Cobos, Library Department Chair, Saddleback
College.
Subject Editor: Latino Studies.

Francesca Colecchia, Professor of Spanish, Duquesne
University.
Referee.

Gerardo Colmenar, Associate Librarian, Asian American Studies, University of California, Santa Barbara.
Subject Editor: Asian American Studies.

Mark Connell, Director, Center for Advancement of Technology in Education, SUNY College at Cortland.
Referee.

Paul Connors, Research Analyst, Michigan Legislative Service Bureau.
Bibliographer: U.S. and Canadian History.

Miriam Conteh-Morgan, Collection Manager for African Studies, Ohio State University.
Bibliographer: African American Studies.

Kate Corby, Education and Psychology Bibliographer, Michigan State University.
Subject Editor: Education.

Ronald Cormier, Professor of French, Longwood College.
Referee.

Alice Crosetto, Acquisitions Librarian, University of Toledo.
Bibliographer: British Literature.

Cynthia Crosser, Social Sciences and Humanities Librarian, University of Maine.
Bibliographer: Education.

Gwyneth Crowley, Coordinator of Collection Development, Social Science Libraries, Yale University.
Subject Editor: Economics.

Alice Daugherty, Reference Librarian, Louisiana State University.
Bibliographer: American Literature.

Stephanie Davis, Librarian, Spring Arbor University.
Bibliographer: Education.

Judith de Luce, Professor of Classics, Miami University of Ohio.
Referee.

Kathy Dean, Humanities Bibliographer, Ohio State University.
Bibliographer: Other Literatures in English.

Louise Deis, Science & Technology Reference Librarian, Princeton University.
Subject Editor: Environmental Sciences; General Science.

JoAnn DeVries, Associate Librarian, Reference/Bibliographer, University of Minnesota.
Bibliographer: Agriculture.

Jan Dixon, Reference Librarian, University of Arkansas.
Bibliographer: Geology.

Deborah Dolan, Social Science Librarian, Hofstra University.
Bibliographer: Psychology.

Travis Dolence, Instruction Librarian, Minnesota State University Moorhead.
Referee.

Michael Doorley, Associate Lecturer in Humanities, American College, Dublin.
Bibliographer: European History.

Judith Douville, Visual Arts, Science and Technology Editor, CHOICE.
Subject Editor: Chemistry.

Bill Drew, Associate Librarian, Systems and Reference, SUNY – Morrisville.
Referee.

Heather Dubnick, Field Bibliographer, Modern Language Assoc.
Subject Editor: Spanish Language and Literature.

Dana Dunn, Professor of Psychology, Moravian College.
Referee.

Lisa Dunn, Head of Reference, Colorado School of Mines.
Bibliographer: Geology.

Karin Durán, Teacher Curriculum Center Librarian, California State University Northridge.
Bibliographer: Latino Studies.

David Eastman, Doctoral Candidate, Department of Religious Studies, Yale University.
Bibliographer: Religion.

Mary Edsall, Professor of Library and Information Science, Catholic University of America.
Subject Editor: Dance.

Marcus Elmore, CHOICE.
Subject Editor: General Language and Literature.

Robert Elsie, Independent scholar.
Bibliographer: European History.

Kimberly Embelton, Literature and Languages Librarian, California State University Northridge.
Bibliographer: British Literature.

Michael Emery, Professor of English, Cottey College.
Bibliographer: GLBT Studies.

Mark Emmons, Head, Instruction Services, University of New Mexico.
Subject Editor: Film.

Carlene Engstrom, Director, D'Arcy McNickle Library, Salish Kootenai College.
Bibliographer: Native American Studies.

Pam Enrici, Associate Librarian, University of Maryland.
Bibliographer: Technology and Engineering.

Robert Entenmann, Professor of History, St. Olaf College.
Referee.

Isabel Espinal, Librarian for Afro American Studies, Anthropology, Native American Indian Studies, University of Massachussetts.
Bibliographer: African American Studies.

James Allan Evans, Professor Emeritus of Classical
Near Eastern and Religious Studies, University of British
Columbia.
Bibliographer: European History.

Angel Falcon, Harvard University, formerly.
Bibliographer: African American Studies.

David Feldman, Professor of Mathematics, University of
New Hampshire.
Referee.

Robert Fernekes, Information Services Librarian,
Business Specialist, Georgia Southern University.
Bibliographer: Business Administration.

Anne Fields, OSU Libraries Coordinator for Research
and Reference, Ohio State University.
Bibliographer: Education.

Jenifer Flaxbart, Head Librarian, Reference and
Information Services, University of Texas, Austin.
Bibliographer: Journalism and Communication.

Adonna Fleming, GIS / Maps Librarian,
University of Nebraska – Lincoln.
Bibliographer: Geology.

Nicole Fluhr, Professor of English, Southern Connecticut
State University.
Referee.

Michael Fosmire, Science Librarian, Purdue University.
Subject Editor: Physics.

Stephen Foster, University Librarian, Wright State
University.
Referee.

Gerri Foudy, Government and Politics, Public Affairs,
and Law Librarian, University of Maryland.
Bibliographer: Political Science.

Kathleen Fountain, Political Science and Social Work
Librarian, California State University, Chico.
Bibliographer: Political Science.

Kristine Fowler, Mathematics Librarian, University of
Minnesota, Twin Cities.
Subject Editor: Mathematics.

Stephen Fowlkes, Bibliographer for Sociology, Social
Work and Reference, Tulane University.
Bibliographer: Sociology.

Ann Fox, Professor of English, Davidson College.
Referee.

Joe Fugate, Professor of German, Kalamazoo College.
Referee.

Steve Fullwood, Manuscripts Librarian, Schomburg
Center for Research in Black Culture, New York Public
Library.
Bibliographer: African American Studies.

Ronald Ganze, Professor of English, Valparaiso
University.
Bibliographer: Medieval Studies.

Bill Gargan, Reference Librarian and Bibliographer,
Brooklyn College.
Bibliographer: British Literature.

Meryle Gaston, Islamic and Middle Eastern Studies
Librarian, University of California, Santa Barbara.
**Subject Editor: Middle Eastern History, Languages,
and Literatures.**

Cameron Gearen, Lecturer in English, Yale University.
**Bibliographer: General Language and
Literature.**

Caroline Geck, Librarian, Kean University.
Referee.

Jennifer Geddes, Research Associate Professor of
Religious Studies, University of Virginia.
Bibliographer: General Language and Literature.

Mary Gilles, Business Reference Librarian,
Washington State University.
Subject Editor: Law.

David Giovacchini, Arabic Librarian, Middle East
Collection, Stanford University.
Referee.

Ed Goedeken, Humanities Bibliographer, Iowa State
University.
Subject Editor: U.S. and Canadian History.

Melissa Goldsmith, Lecturer, Louisiana State University.
Referee.

Millie Gonzalez, Reference Librarian, Framingham
State College.
Bibliographer: Business Administration.

Olympia Gonzalez, Professor of Spanish, Loyola
University of Chicago.
Referee.

David Goodman, Professor of Library and Information
Science, Long Island University.
Subject Editor: Biology.

Candice Goucher, Professor of History, Washington State
University, Vancouver.
Referee.

Malaika Grant, Reference/Instruction Librarian,
University of Minnesota, Twin Cities.
Bibliographer: Gender Studies.

Laura Graves, Professor of History, South Plains
College.
Bibliographer: Native American Studies.

Chip Green, Professor of Geology, University of South
Carolina Upstate.
Referee.

Susan Green, Professor of History, California State
University, Chico.
Referee.

Cheryl Grossman, Electronic Services Supervisor, LearningWork Connection, Ohio State University.
Bibliographer: Education.

Anna Marie Guengerich, Librarian, College of Education, University of Iowa.
Bibliographer: Psychology.

Richard Hacken, European Studies Bibliographer, Brigham Young University.
Referee.

Michael Handis, Associate Librarian for Collection Management, CUNY Graduate Center.
Bibliographer: European History.

Shaun Hardy, Librarian, Carnegie Institution of Washington.
Bibliographer: Geology.

Sara Harrington, Art Librarian, Rutgers University.
Referee.

Jon Harrison, Social Sciences Collections Coordinator, Missouri State University.
Bibliographer: Criminal Justice.

Elizabeth Hartung, Professor of Sociology, California Sate University Channel Islands.
Bibliographer: Sociology.

Laurence Hauptman, Professor of History, SUNY New Paltz.
Bibliographer: Native American Studies.

Peter Hayes, Professor of History, Northwestern University.
Bibliographer: European History.

Charles Hayford, Research Fellow, Department of History, Northwestern University.
Subject Editor: Asian History, Languages, and Literatures.

Jeremy Hein, Professor of Sociology, University of Wisconsin – Eau Claire.
Referee.

Eileen Herring, Agriculture Librarian, University of Hawaii.
Bibliographer: Agriculture.

Martin Hewitt, Head of History Department, Trinity and All Saints College, University of Leeds.
Referee.

Terry Hill, Customer Representative for North America, OTTO HARRASSOWITZ GmbH & Co. KG.
Bibliographer: Political Science.

Baraba Hillson, Public and International Affairs and Psychology Liaison Librarian, George Mason University.
Referee.

Lee Hilyer, Mathematics Subject Librarian, University of Houston.
Bibliographer: Education.

Keith Hitchins, Professor of History, University of Illinois.
Bibliographer: European History.

Adrian Ho, Assistant Librarian, University of Houston.
Bibliographer: Journalism and Communication.

David Hogg, Astronomer, National Radio Astronomy Observatory.
Referee.

Jane Holmquist, Astrophysics Librarian, Princeton University.
Subject Editor: Astronomy.

Emily Horning, Librarian for Philosophy, Religious Studies and Anthropology, Yale University.
Subject Editor: Religion.

John Hunter, Science/Engineering Librarian, Rice University.
Bibliographer: Geology.

Carol Hutchins, Head Librarian, Courant Institute of Mathematical Sciences, New York University.
Subject Editor: Computing.

Robin Imhof, Reference Librarian, University of the Pacific.
Bibliographer: GLBT Studies.

Richard Irving, Associate Librarian, SUNY Albany.
Bibliographer: Criminal Justice.

Kristin Jacobi, Head, Catologing Department, Eastern Connecticut State University.
Bibliographer: Native American Studies.

James Jaffe, Professor of History, University of Wisconsin – Whitewater.
Bibliographer: European History.

Arif Jamal, Social Sciences Bibliographer, University of Pittsburgh.
Bibliographer: African American Studies.

Sylvia James, Sylvia James Consultancy.
Bibliographer: Business Administration.

Fred Jenkins, Head of Collection Management, University of Dayton.
Subject Editor: Ancient History; Classics.

Donald Clay Johnson, Curator, Ames Library of South Asia, University of Minnesota.
Bibliographer: Asian History, Languages, and Literatures.

Melissa Johnson, Reference and Instruction Librarian, Lynn University.
Bibliographer: European History.

Sarah Johnson, Librarian, Eastern Illinois University.
Bibliographer: General Language and Literature.

Lisa Johnston, Head of Public Services, Sweet Briar College.
Bibliographer: British Literature.

Scott Johnston, Librarian, CUNY Graduate Center.
Subject Editor: Urban Studies.

David P. Jordan, Professor of History, University of Illinois at Chicago.
Bibliographer: European History.

Jonathan Judaken, Professor of History, University of Memphis.
Bibliographer: European History.

Jeannie Kamerman, Director, Curriculum Materials Library, University of West Florida.
Bibliographer: Education.

James Kelly, Humanities Bibliographer, University of Massachussetts.
Subject Editor: American Literature.

Marcia Keyser, Instruction and Reference Librarian, Drake University.
Bibliographer: Education.

Shayee Khanaka, Librarian, Middle Eastern Collection, University of California Berkeley.
Bibliographer: Middle Eastern History, Languages, and Literatures.

Sherise Kimura, Reference Librarian, University of San Francisco.
Bibliographer: Asian American Studies.

Douglas King, Librarian, University of South Carolina.
Bibliographer: American Literature.

Laura Kinner, Coordinator, Cataloging Services, University of Toledo.
Bibliographer: British Literature.

Harold Kirkwood, Librarian, Purdue University.
Bibliographer: Business Administration.

Patricia Kirkwood, Science Librarian, University of Arkansas.
Bibliographer: Technology and Engineering.

Sheila Kirven, Education Services Librarian, New Jersey City University.
Bibliographer: Education.

Linda Klein, Reference Librarian, Eastern Kentucky University.
Bibliographer: British Literature.

Michael Knee, Science Bibliographer and Reference Librarian, University of Albany.
Bibliographer: Computing.

Norma Kobzina, Head of Information Services, Marian Koshland Bioscience and Natural Resources Library, University of California, Berkeley.
Subject Editor: Agriculture.

David Koenigstein, Librarian, Brooklyn College.
Bibliographer: British Literature.

Gayla Koerting, Special Collections Librarian, University of South Dakota.
Bibliographer: U.S. and Canadian History.

Laura Koltutsky, Information Services Librarian, University of Houston.
Bibliographer: Education.

Kwasi Konadu, Professor of History, Winston Salem State University.
Bibliographer: African History, Languages, and Literatures.

Svetlana Korolev, Science Librarian, University of Wisconsin, Madison.
Referee.

Wade Kotter, Social Sciences Librarian, Weber State University.
Bibliographer: Criminal Justice.

Joe Kraus, Science Librarian, University of Denver.
Referee.

Eiko Kuwana, Professor of History, University of the Sacred Heart, Tokyo.
Bibliographer: European History.

Sharon Ladenson, Gender Studies and Communications Bibliographer, Michigan State University.
Bibliographer: Journalism and Communication.

Carolyn Laffoon, Earth and Atmospheric Sciences Librarian, Purdue University.
Bibliographer: Geology.

Blake Landor, Bibliographer for Philosophy, Classics, and Religion, University of Florida.
Subject Editor: Philosophy.

Jeffry Larson, Librarian for Romance Languages and Literatures, Linguistics, and Classics, Yale University.
Subject Editor: French Language and Literature; Italian Language and Literature.

Jason E. Lavery, Professor of History, Oklahoma State University.
Bibliographer: European History.

Bernadette Lear, Behavioral Sciences and Education Librarian, Pennsylvania State University.
Bibliographer: Psychology.

Patrick Leary, Research Fellow, Department of History, Northwestern University.
Subject Editor: Victorian Studies.

Richard S. Levy, Professor of History, University of Illinois at Chicago.
Bibliographer: European History.

Kevin Lindstrom, Behavioral Sciences and Education Librarian, University of British Columbia.
Bibliographer: Geology.

Ken Liss, Communication Librarian, Boston College.
Bibliographer: Journalism and Communication.

Carol Loranger, Professor of English, Wright
State University.
Referee.

Jack Lynch, Professor of English, Rutgers University.
Bibliographer: British Literature.

Karen MacDonald, Business Subject Specialist
Librarian, Texas A&M University.
Bibliographer: Business Administration.

Peter Magierski, Librarian for the Middle East Studies,
New York University.
**Bibliographer: Middle Eastern History, Languages,
and Literatures.**

Diane Maher, University Archivist, University of San
Diego.
**Bibliographer: American Literature; British
Literature.**

Janice Mathews, Librarian for Urban Studies and Social
Work, University of Connecticut.
Referee.

Rhonda McGinnis, Business and Economics Librarian,
Wayne State University.
Bibliographer: Business Administration.

Glenn McGuigan, Business Reference Librarian, Penn
State University.
Subject Editor: Business Administration.

Peter McKay, Business Librarian, University of Florida.
Bibliographer: Business Administration.

Paula McMillen, Social Sciences Librarian, Oregon State
University.
Bibliographer: Education.

Lori Mestre, Digital Learning Librarian, University of
Illinois.
Bibliographer: Education.

Sue Metcalf, Social Sciences Librarian, New Mexico
State University.
Referee.

Marion Miller, Professor of History, University of Illinois
at Chicago, emerita.
Bibliographer: European History.

Lisa Mitten, CHOICE.
Subject Editor: Native American Studies.

Sandy Mooney, Design Librarian, Louisiana State
University.
Referee.

Fred Muratori, Bibliographer for Anglo-American and
Comparative Literature and Film, Cornell
University.
Bibliographer: Drama and Theater.

Paula Murphy, Library Consultant.
Referee.

Linda Musser, Head, Fletcher L. Byrom Earth and
Mineral Sciences Library, Pennsylvania State University.
Bibliographer: Geology.

Theodore Natsoulas, Professor of History, University of
Toledo.
Bibliographer: European History.

Sharon Naylor, Education, Psychology and TMC
Division Head, Illinois State University.
Bibliographer: Education.

Antoinette Nelson, Branch Manager, Science and
Engineering Library, University of Texas Arlington.
Subject Editor: Technology and Engineering.

Jan Newberry, Professor of Anthropology, University of
Lethbridge.
Referee.

Shawn Nicholson, Bibliographer for Sociology, Social
Work, Urban Planning, Michigan State University.
Referee.

Jim Niessen, World History Librarian, Rutgers
University.
Bibliographer: European History.

Byron Nordstrom, Professor of History, Gustavus
Adolphus University.
Bibliographer: European History.

Akilah Nosakhere, Manager, Reference and Research
Division, Auburn Avenue Research Library of
African American Culture and History.
Subject Editor: African American Studies.

Nancy O'Brien, Head, Education and Social Science
Library, University of Illinois.
Subject Editor: Education.

Darby Orcutt, Collection Manager for the Humanities
and Data Analysis, North Carolina State
University.
Bibliographer: Journalism and Communication.

Harriet Ottenheimer, Professor of Anthropology,
Kansas State University.
Bibliographer: Anthropology.

Mark Padnos, Coordinator of Public Services, Bronx
Community College.
**Subject Editor: Germanic Languages and
Literatures.**

John Page, Associate Dean, Learning Resources
Division, University of the District of Columbia.
Bibliographer: African American Studies.

Tim Parrish, Professor of English, Southern Connecticut
State University.
Bibliographer: General Language and Literature.

Lucy Patrick, Head of Special Collections, Florida
State University.
Referee.

Christopher Peebles, Associate Vice President for Information Technology and Professor of Anthropology, Indiana University.
Bibliographer: Anthropology.

Ed Peters, Professor of History, University of Pennsylvania.
Bibliographer: European History.

Carmelita Pickett, African American Studies Librarian, Emory University.
Bibliographer: African American Studies.

Lisa Pillow, Collection Development Librarian, University of Wisconsin – River Falls.
Bibliographer: African American Studies.

Chestalene Pintozzi, Science-Engineering Librarian, University of Arizona.
Bibliographer: Geology.

Don Polzella, Professor of Psychology and Associate Dean for Faculty Development and Graduate Programs, University of Dayton.
Subject Editor: Psychology.

Diethelm Prowe, Professor of History, Carleton College.
Bibliographer: European History.

Eleanor Randall, Reference Librarian, Edinboro University of Pennsylvania.
Bibliographer: Biology.

Brenda Reed, Public Services Librarian, Education Library, Queen's University.
Bibliographer: Education.

Ira Revels, Instruction Librarian, Cornell University.
Bibliographer: African American Studies.

Leslie Reynolds, Director of Policy Sciences and Economics Library, Texas A&M University.
Bibliographer: Business Administration.

Amy Robb, Field Librarian for Women's Studies and Communication, University of Michigan.
Bibliographer: Journalism and Communication.

Gloria Roberson, Reference Librarian, Adelphi University.
Bibliographer: African American Studies.

Beth Roberts, Earth and Mineral Sciences Librarian, Pennsylvania State University.
Bibliographer: Geology.

Elizabeth Robertson, Professor of English, University of Colorado.
Bibliographer: British Literature.

Martin Roden, Professor emeritus of Engineering, UCLA.
Bibliographer: Technology and Engineering.

Raquel Rodriguez, Librarian for the African American Collection, University of Pittsburgh.
Bibliographer: African American Studies.

Lisa Romero, Communications Librarian, University of Illinois.
Subject Editor: Journalism and Communication.

Lana Kay Rosenberg, Director, Dance Theatre, Miami University of Ohio.
Referee.

Tony Rosso, Professor of English, Southern Connecticut State University.
Bibliographer: British Literature.

Dana Roth, Chemistry Librarian, Caltech.
Bibliographer: Chemistry.

Linda Salem, Education Librarian, San Diego State University.
Bibliographer: British Literature.

Mark Sanders, Student Outreach Reference Librarian, East Carolina University.
Bibliographer: Environmental Studies.

Rachel Sandoval, Historical Records Project Archivist, University of California, Irvine.
Bibliographer: Latino Studies.

Victoria Santana, Electronic Services Librarian, Oklahoma City University.
Bibliographer: Native American Studies.

Román Santillán, Reference/Instruction Librarian, CUNY / College of Staten Island.
Bibliographer: Spanish Language and Literature.

Vernon Schlotzhauer, Social Science Librarian, Pennsylvania State University.
Bibliographer: Psychology.

Geoff Schmidt, Professor of English, Illinois State University – Edwardsville.
Bibliographer: General Language and Literature.

Alan Schroeder, Business Librarian, California State University Northridge.
Bibliographer: Business Administration.

Kate Schroeder, Doctoral Candidate, History Department, Indiana University.
Subject Editor: African History, Languages, and Literatures.

Friedrich Schuler, Professor of History, Portland State University.
Subject Editor: Latin American History.

Katrin Schultheiss, Professor of History, University of Illinois at Chicago.
Bibliographer: European History.

Jason Schultz, Communications Librarian, Georgia State University.
Bibliographer: African American Studies.

Catherine Shreve, Librarian for Public Policy and Political Science, Duke University.
Subject Editor: Political Science.

Jack Shreve, Professor of English, Allegany College.
Bibliographer: GLBT Studies.

Adam Siegel, Reference Librarian, University of California, Davis.
Bibliographer: Native American Studies.

Dorothy Siles, Librarian, Taylorville Public Library.
Bibliographer: Native American Studies.

Jane Sloan, Media Librarian, Rutgers University.
Subject Editor: Film.

Becky Smith, Head, Business and Economics Library, University of Illinois.
Bibliographer: Business Administration.

Helen Smith, Life Sciences Librarian, Penn State University.
Bibliographer: Agriculture.

Michael Smith, Business Librarian, Texas A&M University.
Bibliographer: Business Administration.

Jacqueline Snider, Librarian, ACT.
Bibliographer: Education.

Doug Southard, DRA International.
Bibliographer: Business Administration.

Roland Spickermann, Professor of History, University of Texas, Permian Basin.
Bibliographer: European History.

Jill Spreitzer, Assistant Librarian, Public Services, University of Detroit Mercy.
Bibliographer: Technology and Engineering.

Jennifer Stevens, Humanities Liaison Librarian, George Mason University.
Bibliographer: Other Literatures in English.

David Stoloff, Professor of Education, Eastern Connecticut State University.
Referee.

Fred Stoss, Biological Science Librarian, SUNY Buffalo.
Subject Editor: Biology.

Stephen Stratton, Head of Collection Development, California State University, Channel Islands.
Subject Editor: Sociology.

Cindy Stretch, Professor of English, Southern Connecticut State University.
Referee.

Leanne Strum, Library Liaison to the School of Business, Regent University.
Bibliographer: Business Administration.

Mila Su, Coordinator of Reference Services, Pennsylvania State University.
Subject Editor: Sport and Recreation.

Helen Sullivan, Head, Slavic Reference Service, University of Illinois.
Subject Editor: Russian Languages and Literatures.

Sarah Sussman, Curator, French and Italian Collections, Stanford University.
Bibliographer: European History.

Marek Suszko, Professor of History, Purdue University North Central.
Bibliographer: European History.

Laura Taddeo, Reference Librarian, SUNY Buffalo.
Bibliographer: British Literature.

Kornelia Tancheva, Director of Instructional Services, Cornell University.
Subject Editor: Drama and Theater.

Wendy Tann, Librarian, Federal Reserve Bank.
Bibliographer: Business Administration.

Cornelia Akins Taylor, Special Collections Librarian, Florida A & M University.
Bibliographer: African American Studies.

Betty Taylor-Thompson, Professor of English, Texas Southern University.
Referee.

Edward Teague, Head, Architecture & Allied Arts Library, University of Oregon.
Subject Editor: Visual Arts.

Samantha Teplitzky, Earth Sciences Librarian and Bibliographer, Stanford University.
Bibliographer: Geology.

Stephen Thompson, Co-Leader, Technical Services Department, Brown University.
Bibliographer: American Literature.

Erik Thomson, Collegiate Assistant Professor, Social Sciences, University of Chicago.
Bibliographer: European History.

Charles Thurston, Reference Librarian and Bibliographer, University of Texas at San Antonio.
Bibliographer: Education.

Judie Triplehorn, Librarian, Geophysical Institute, University of Alaska.
Bibliographer: Geology.

Markel Tumlin, English and American Literature Librarian, San Diego State University.
Bibliographer: American Literature.

Andrea Twiss-Brooks, Bibliographer for Chemical and Geophysical Sciences, University of Chicago.
Subject Editor: Geology.

Kent Underwood, Music Librarian, New York University.
Subject Editor: Music.

Alan Unsworth, Reference Librarian, University of Rochester.
Referee.

David Vaccari, Professor of Engineering, Stevens Institute of Technology.
Bibliographer: Technology and Engineering.

Susan Vega Garcia, Reference & Instruction Librarian, Bibliographer, Iowa State University.
Bibliographer: Latino Studies.

Tom Volkening, Engineering Librarian, Michigan State University.
Bibliographer: Technology and Engineering.

Heather Ward, University of Oregon, formerly.
Subject Editor: Medieval Studies.

Diane Warner, Monographs and Special Formats Cataloger, Texas Tech University.
Bibliographer: American Literature.

Gary Wasdin, Library Director, New School University.
Referee.

Matthew Wayman, Instruction Coordinator, Penn State University.
Bibliographer: U.S. and Canadian History.

Jeneen Willemssen, Librarian, Conserve School.
Bibliographer: Education.

Wendy Williamson, Economics Librarian, University of Minnesota.
Referee.

Suzanne Wise, Collection Development Librarian, Appalachia State University.
Referee.

Ada Woods, Reference Librarian, Towson University.
Bibliographer.

Peng Xu, Reference Librarian, Michigan State University.
Bibliographer: Business Administration.

Lisa Yuro, Reference Librarian/Humanities and Social Sciences Coordinator, University of Alabama.
Bibliographer: Journalism and Communication.

Ann Zawistoski, Reference and Instruction Librarian, Carleton College.
Bibliographer: Geology.

Linda Zellmer, Head, Geology Library, Indiana University.
Subject Editor: Geology.

HOW TO USE
RESOURCES FOR COLLEGE LIBRARIES

Resources for College Libraries (RCL) was designed to be easily searchable by author, title, and the RCL subject taxonomy. The set consists of seven volumes, Volumes 1-6 arranged by RCL Subject, and sorted alphabetically by author. Volume 7 is a comprehensive author, title and subject index. The volumes are arranged by *Resources for College Library* Subject Headings, a full listing of which is present in the Subject Headings Index in volume 7.

Each title in *Resources for College Libraries* has been classified with a specific RCL Subject and/or subjects. Titles can and often do appear within more than one RCL Subject area. Titles have been given a specific readership level through audience code: g=general, l=lower-division undergraduate, u=upper-division undergraduate graduate, and/or f=faculty level resources. Titles previously mentioned in *Books for College Libraries, 3rd Edition*, have been noted with a specific BCL3 icon 𝕭. Non-book entries can be easily identified with the icons for Web ▢, Ebook 𝖊, or CD/DVD-ROM ✇.

Classification Number, Dewey Decimal Number, Library of Congress Control Number, Audience Code, and whether it has been reviewed in Choice Magazine.

Entries in the Author Index can include the following bibliographic information when available: author, co-author, editor, co-editor, translator, co-translator, along with page number(s) and volume number(s) of the selected works within the 6-volume set. Entries are not cross-referenced by other than primary author and/or first contributor. Entries in the Title Index include the title, page number(s) and volume number(s) of the selected works within the 6-volume set.

Titles in *Resources for College Libraries* have been alphabetized using the following rules:

- Initial articles of titles in English, French, German, Italian, and Spanish are not included for sorting purposes.

- Titles beginning with acronyms appear before those

SAMPLE RCL ENTRY

❶ DRAMA AND THEATER ❯ Western Drama ❯ United States

❷ **Wilmeth, Don B. & Bigsby,** PN2221
Christopher (Editors)
❸ The Cambridge History of American Theater: ❹ 1870-1945. ❺ Ed. 2
❻ Don B. Wilmeth & Christopher Bigsby (Contribution by). ❼ Trade Paper.
❽ Cambridge University Press. ❾ New York, NY. ❿ 2006. ⓫ 608p.
⓬ Cambridge History of American Theater Ser. ⓭ ISBN: 0-521-67984-2,
ISBN13: 978-0-521-67984-8. ⓮ Dewey:792/.0973.
⓯ LCCN: 00-000000
⓰ Audience: l,u,f. ⓱ *Choice*, 2005 𝕭

1. RCL Subject Heading
2. Author/First Contributor
3. Title
4. Subtitle
5. Ed. Info
6. Additional Contributors
7. Binding Type
8. Publisher
9. Publisher Location
10. Publication Date
11. Number of Pages
12. Series Title
13. ISBN, ISBN-13
14. Dewey
15. LCCN
16. Audience Code
17. Choice Review and Date

Title entries can include the following bibliographic information, when available: author, co-author, editor, co-editor, translator, co-translator, title, number of volumes, edition, series information, binding type, publisher, publisher location, date of publication, number of pages, ISBN, ISBN-13, Library of Congress

beginning with words. For example, B E A M A Directory would precede Baal, Babylon.

- As a general rule, U.S. and UN are filed in strict alphabetical order.

- Numeric Titles may be found near the end of the Title Index

Authors in *Resources for College Libraries* have been alphabetized using the following rules:

- Proper names beginning with "Mc" and "Mac" are filed in strict alphabetical order. For example, entries for contributors' names such as MacAdam, MacAvory, and MacCarthy are located prior to the pages with entries for names such as McAdam, McCoy, and McDermott.

- When author names are represented with initials, they are alphabetized before author first names. For example, Smith, H. C. appears before Smith, Harold A.

Any errors in bibliographic data should be E-mailed directly to: rclwebfeedback@bowker.com

ABBREVIATIONS AND CODE LIST:

BCL3	*Books for College Libraries, 3rd Edition*
Bk.(s.)	Book(s)
Ed.	Edition
F	Faculty
G	General
Inc.	Incorporated
Jr.	Junior
ISBN	International Standard Book Number
L	Lower-Division Undergraduate
LCCN	Library of Congress Control Number
p.	Pages
RCL	Resources for College Libraries
Ser.	Series
Sr.	Senior
U	Upper-Division Undergraduate

Geographical Abbreviations

AL	Alabama	NJ	New Jersey
AK	Alaska	NM	New Mexico
AB	Alberta	NSW	New South Wales
AE	American Europe	NY	New York
AS	American Samoa	NF	Newfoundland
AZ	Arizona	NC	North Carolina
AR	Arkansas	ND	North Dakota
ACT	Australian Capital Territory	NP	Northern Marianas
BC	British Columbia	N.T.	Northern Territory (Australia)
CA	California	NT	Northwest Territory
CM	Central Marianas	NS	Nova Scotia
CO	Colorado	NU	Nunavut
CT	Connecticut	OH	Ohio
DE	Delaware	OK	Oklahoma
DC	District Of Columbia	ON	Ontario
FM	Federated States Of Micronesia	OR	Oregon
FL	Florida	TT	Pacific Territories
GA	Georgia	PW	Pacific West
GU	Guam	PA	Pennsylvania
HI	Hawaii	PE	Prince Edward Island
ID	Idaho	PR	Puerto Rico
IL	Illinois	PQ	Quebec
IN	Indiana	QLD	Queensland
IA	Iowa	RI	Rhode Island
KS	Kansas	SK	Saskatchewan
KY	Kentucky	SA	South Australia
LA	Louisiana	SC	South Carolina
ME	Maine	SD	South Dakota
MB	Manitoba	TAS	Tasmania
MH	Marshall Islands	TN	Tennessee
MD	Maryland	TX	Texas
MA	Massachusetts	UT	Utah
MI	Michigan	VT	Vermont
MP	Middle Pacific	VIC	Victoria
MN	Minnesota	VI	Virgin Islands
MS	Mississippi	VA	Virginia
MO	Missouri	WA	Washington
MT	Montana	WV	West Virginia
NE	Nebraska	W.A.	Western Australia
NV	Nevada	WI	Wisconsin
NB	New Brunswick	WY	Wyoming
NH	New Hampshire	YT	Yukon Territory

DANCE

This section on dance represents a core selection of the most authoritative and noteworthy works of print and non-print literature from an emergent field of scholarship. It is appropriate for use by librarians, faculty, and students in an undergraduate college setting, in building and evaluating library collections that support broad-based curricula in dance. This listing can also be used as a point of departure in developing collections to support more focused curricula. Although juvenile literature is not included, secondary education materials can be located through a specific selection process.

Because the interdisciplinary nature of dance has made the categorization quite challenging, many of the works are cross-referenced in more than one category. However, the majority of titles are individually placed in the section most relevant to the major emphasis of the work.

—Mary Edsall

General Reference Works

GV1623

Dance Magazine College Guide, 1998-1999. Ed. 3. Trade Paper. Dance Magazine, Inc. Oakland, CA. 1998. 98p. ISBN:0-930036-29-8, ISBN13: 978-0-930036-29-4. Dewey:793.31973.

Audience: **l,u.**

Balanchine, George & Mason, Francis **GV1790.A1**

101 Stories of the Great Ballets: The Scene-by-Scene Stories of the Most Popular Ballets, Old and New. UK-Trade Paper. Doubleday Publishing. New York, NY. 1975. 560p. ISBN:0-385-03398-2, ISBN13: 978-0-385-03398-5. Dewey:792.8/4. LCCN:73-009140.

Audience: **g,l.**

Balanchine, George, et al. **MT95.B31977**

Balanchine's Complete Stories of the Great Ballets. Francis Mason & Jeffrey Bairstow (Authors). Trade Cloth. Doubleday Publishing. New York, NY. 1977. xxvi, 838p. ISBN:0-385-11381-1, ISBN13: 978-0-385-11381-6. Dewey:792.8/4. LCCN:76-055684.

Audience: **g,l,u,f.** *B*

Beaumont, Cyril W. **GV1790.A1 B4**

Complete Book of Ballets: A Guide to the Principal Ballets of the Nineteenth and Twentieth Centuries. Grosset and Dunlap. 1956.

Audience: **g,l,u,f.**

Beaumont, Cyril W. **GV1790.A1**

Complete Book of Ballets: Ballets Past and Present. Putnam. 1955.

Audience: **g,l,u,f.**

Billman, Larry **GV1779.B55 1997**

Film Choreographers and Dance Directors: An Illustrated Biographical Encyclopedia, with a History and Filmographies, 1893 Through 1995. Cloth Text. McFarland & Company, Incorporated Publishers. Jefferson, NC. 1997. 664p. ISBN:0-89950-868-5, ISBN13: 978-0-89950-868-9. Dewey:792.6/2/0922. LCCN:96-31756.

Audience: **g,l,u,f.** *Choice, 1998.*

Bopp, Mary S. **Z7514.D2.B6 1994**

Research in Dance: A Guide to Resources. Trade Cloth. Macmillan Publishing Company, Inc. Old Tappan, NJ. 1993. 304p. Reference Ser. ISBN:0-8161-9065-8, ISBN13: 978-0-8161-9065-2. Dewey:016.7928. LCCN:92-042508.

Audience: **g,l,u.** *Choice, 1994.*

Bremser, Martha **GV1785.A1B74 1999**

Fifty Contemporary Choreographers. Trade Paper. Routledge. New York, NY. 1999. 240p. ISBN:0-415-10364-9, ISBN13: 978-0-415-10364-0. Dewey:792.8/2/0922. LCCN:00-700459.

Audience: **g,l,u.**

Bremser, Martha (Editor) **GV1585.I57 1993**

International Dictionary of Ballet, Set. Trade Cloth. Thomson Gale. Farmington Hills, MI. 1993. 1600p. ISBN:1-55862-084-2, ISBN13: 978-1-55862-084-1. Dewey:792.803. LCCN:93-025051.

Audience: **g,l,u,f.** *Choice, 1994.*

Chujoy, Anatole & Manchester, P. W. **GV1585**

The Dance Encyclopedia. Lincoln Kerstein (Introduction by). Trade Paper. Simon & Schuster. New York, NY. 1978. ISBN:0-671-24027-7, ISBN13: 978-0-671-24027-1. Dewey:793.3/03.

Audience: **g,l,u,f.**

Clarke, Mary & Vaughn, David (Editors) **GV1585**

The Encyclopedia of Dance and Ballet. Other. Penguin Group (USA) Inc. New York, NY. 1977. 376p. ISBN:0-399-11955-8, ISBN13: 978-0-399-11955-2. Dewey:793.3/2/03. LCCN:76-052325.

Audience: **g,l,u,f.**

Cohen, Selma Jeanne & Dorris, George (Editors) **GV1585.I586 1998**

International Encyclopedia of Dance. Thomas F. Kelly (Contribution by). Trade Cloth. Oxford University Press, Inc. New York, NY. 1998. ISBN:0-19-512307-7, ISBN13: 978-0-19-512307-4. Dewey:792.8/03. LCCN:97-036562.

Audience: **l,u,f.**

Cohen-Stratyner, Barbara **GV1785.A1**

Biographical Dictionary of Dance. Trade Cloth. Thomson Gale. Farmington Hills, MI. 1982. vi, 970p. ISBN:0-02-870260-3, ISBN13: 978-0-02-870260-5. Dewey:793.3/092/2. LCCN:81-086153.

Audience: **g,l,u,f.**

Craine, Debra & Mackrell, Judith **GV1585.C78 2000**

The Oxford Dictionary of Dance. Trade Cloth. Oxford University Press, Inc. New York, NY. 2000. 536p. ISBN:0-19-860106-9, ISBN13: 978-0-19-860106-7. Dewey:792.8/03. LCCN:2001-274422.

Audience: **g,l,u,f.** *Choice, 2001.*

Greskovic, Robert **GV1787.G74 2005**

Ballet 101: A Complete Guide to Learning and Loving the Ballet. Trade Paper, Perfect. Hal Leonard Corporation. Milwaukee, WI. 2005. 634p. ISBN:0-87910-325-6, ISBN13: 978-0-87910-325-5. Dewey:792.8. LCCN:2005-025425.

Audience: **g,l.**

Knowles, Mark **GV1794.K66 1998**

The Tap Dance Dictionary. Cloth Text. McFarland & Company, Incorporated Publishers. Jefferson, NC. 1998. 264p. ISBN:0-7864-0352-7, ISBN13: 978-0-7864-0352-3. Dewey:792.7/8. LCCN:97-50281.

Audience: **g,l,u,f.**

Audience: g=general, l=lower division undergraduate, u=upper division undergraduate, f=faculty.

3

Love, Paul   GV1585
Modern Dance Terminology: The ABC's of Modern Dance as
Defined by Its Originators. Eleanor King (Introduction by).
Trade Paper. Princeton Book Company Publishers. Hightstown,
NJ. 1997. 96p. ISBN:0-87127-206-7, ISBN13:
978-0-87127-206-5. Dewey:793.303. LCCN:96-071976.
                                          Audience: **g,l,u,f.**

Malkin, Mary Ann O'Brian   GV1643
Dancing by the Book: a Catalogue of Books, 1531-1804, in the
Collection of Mary Ann O'Brian Malkin. Privately printed :
[Distributed by the Pennsylvania State University Libraries].
2003.
                                          Audience: **u,f.**

Mapp, Edward   PN1590.B53M3 1990
Directory of Blacks in the Performing Arts. Ed. 2. Earle Hyman
(Foreword by). Trade Cloth. Scarecrow Press, Inc. Lanham,
MD. 1990. 612p. ISBN:0-8108-2222-9, ISBN13:
978-0-8108-2222-1. Dewey:791/.08996073. LCCN:89-030477.
                              Audience: **g,l,u,f.** *Choice, 1990.*

McCormack, Allen E.   GV1580.D247
Stern's Performing Arts Directory 2000. Trade Paper. Dance
Magazine, Inc. Oakland, CA. 1999. ISBN:0-930036-31-X,
ISBN13: 978-0-930036-31-7. Dewey:791/.025.
                                          Audience: **g,l,u,f.**

McDonagh, Don   GV1783.M26
The Complete Guide to Modern Dance. Trade Cloth. Doubleday
Publishing. New York, NY. 1976. 576p. ISBN:0-385-05055-0,
ISBN13: 978-0-385-05055-5. Dewey:793.3/2. LCCN:75-021235.
                                          Audience: **g,l.**

National Dance Association   GV1589.N38 1994
  Staff
National Standards for Dance Education. Trade Paper. Princeton
Book Company Publishers. Hightstown, NJ. 1994. 48p.
ISBN:0-87127-200-8, ISBN13: 978-0-87127-200-3.
Dewey:792.8/07. LCCN:94-046773.
                                          Audience: **u,f.**

New York Public Library   PN1584
  Staff
New York Public Library Desk Reference to the Performing
Arts. Trade Cloth. Macmillan Publishing Company, Inc. Old
Tappan, NJ. 1996. 432p. ISBN:0-02-861447-X, ISBN13:
978-0-02-861447-2. Dewey:791/.03.
                                          Audience: **g,l,u,f.**

Odell, George C.   PN2277.N5.O4 1970
Annals of the New York Stage. Trade Cloth. A M S Press, Inc.
New York, NY. 1970. ISBN:0-404-07830-3, ISBN13:
978-0-404-07830-0. Dewey:792/.097471. LCCN:77-116018.
                                          Audience: **g.** *B*

Preston-Dunlop, Valerie   GV1585.P74 1995
  (Compiled by)
Dance Words. Cloth Text. Gordon & Breach Publishing Group.
New York, NY. 1995. 707p. Choreography and Dance Studies,

Vol. 8 ISBN:3-7186-5601-9, ISBN13: 978-3-7186-5601-1.
Dewey:793.303. LCCN:99-521798.
                              Audience: **g,l,u,f.** *Choice, 1996.*

Raffe, Walter George   GV1585.R3
Dictionary of the Dance. Barnes. 1964. ISBN:0-498-01643-9,
ISBN13: 978-0-498-01643-1.
                                          Audience: **l,u,f.**

Ray Ollie M.   GV1768.R39 1992
Encyclopedia of Line Dances: The Steps that Came and Stayed.
National Dance Association. 1992. ISBN:0-88314-500-6,
ISBN13: 978-0-88314-500-5.
                                          Audience: **l,u,f.**

Ryman, Rhonda   GV1585
Dictionary of Classical Ballet Terminology: Royal Academy of
Dancing. Ed. 2. Trade Paper. Royal Academy of Dancing.
London, 1998. 92p. ISBN:0-9524848-0-3, ISBN13:
978-0-9524848-0-6. Dewey:792.803.
                                          Audience: **g,l,u,f.**

Schlundt, Christina L.   GV1781.S35 1989
Dance in the Musical Theater: Jerome Robbins and His Peers,
1934-1965, A Guide. Paper over Boards. Garland Publishing,
Inc. New York, NY. 1989. 272p. ISBN:0-8240-5547-0, ISBN13:
978-0-8240-5547-9. Dewey:792.8/2. LCCN:89-001117.
                              Audience: **g,l,u,f.** *Choice, 1989.*

Spain, Louise   GV1595.D342 1997
Dance on Camera: A Guide to Dance Films and Videos. Trade
Cloth. Scarecrow Press, Inc. Lanham, MD. 1998. 272p.
ISBN:0-8108-3303-4, ISBN13: 978-0-8108-3303-6.
Dewey:792.8/0216. LCCN:96-053236.
                              Audience: **g,l,u,f.** *Choice, 1998.*

St. James Press Staff   GV1585.B46 1998
International Dictionary of Modern Dance. Taryn
Benbow-Pfalzgraf (Editor), Glynis Benbow-Niemier
(Contribution by). Trade Cloth. Thomson Gale. Farmington
Hills, MI. 1998. 900p. ISBN:1-55862-359-0, ISBN13:
978-1-55862-359-0. Dewey:792.803. LCCN:98-009853.
                              Audience: **g,l,u,f.** *Choice, 1999.*

Steinfirst, Susan   Z5981.S74 1992
Folklore and Folklife: A Guide to English-Language Sources.
Paper over Boards. Garland Publishing, Inc. New York, NY.
1992. 1236p. Folklore Bibliographies Ser., Vol. 16
ISBN:0-8153-0068-9, ISBN13: 978-0-8153-0068-7.
Dewey:016.398. LCCN:92-013594.
                              Audience: **g,l,u,f.** *Choice, 1993.*

Ulrich, Paul S., et.al   PN1584
SIBMAS International Directory of Performing Arts Collections.
Freydank, Ruth; Rennenberg, Roger (Authors). Emmett
Publishing. 1996. ISBN:1-869934-73-3, ISBN13:
978-1-869934-73-6.
                                          Audience: **u,f.**

Historical Overviews

Adshead-Lansdale, Janet GV1787
(Editor)
Dance History: Introduction. Ed. 2. Trade Paper. Routledge.
New York, NY. 1994. 304p. ISBN:0-415-09030-X, ISBN13:
978-0-415-09030-8. Dewey:792.8. LCCN:93-043265.

Audience: **g,l.**

Anderson, Jack GV1787
Ballet and Modern Dance: A Concise History. Ed. 2. Trade
Paper. Princeton Book Company Publishers. Hightstown, NJ.
1992. 299p. ISBN:0-87127-172-9, ISBN13: 978-0-87127-172-3.
Dewey:792.8/09.

Audience: **g,l,u.** *Choice, 1986.*

Au, Susan GV1787.A79 1988
Ballet and Modern Dance: A Concise History. Selma J. Cohen
(Introduction by). Trade Paper. Thames & Hudson. New York,
NY. 1988. 200p. World of Art Ser. ISBN:0-500-20219-2,
ISBN13: 978-0-500-20219-7. Dewey:792.8/09.
LCCN:87-050193.

Audience: **g,l,u.**

Carreiro, Assis GV1619
Ballet and Dance in the 1940's: An Historical Retrospective:
The War Years and Beyond. DanceXchange. 1995.

Audience: **l,u,f.**

Chazin-Bennahum, Judith GV1649.C48 1988
Dance in the Shadow of the Guillotine. Selma J. Cohen
(Introduction by). Cloth Text. Southern Illinois University Press.
Carbondale, IL. 1988. 244p. ISBN:0-8093-1487-8, ISBN13:
978-0-8093-1487-4. Dewey:792.8/0944. LCCN:88-012199.

Audience: **u,f.** *Choice, 1989.*

Clarke, Mary & Crisp, GV1601.C71 981
Clement
The History of Dance. Crown. 1981. ISBN:0-517-54282-X,
ISBN13: 978-0-517-54282-8.

Audience: **g,l.**

De Mille, Agnes GV1601.D4
The Book of Dance. Golden Press. 1963.

Audience: **g,l,u,f.**

Kirstein, Lincoln GV1781.K5 1987
Dance: A Short History of Classic Theatrical Dancing. Trade
Paper. Princeton Book Company Publishers. Hightstown, NJ.
1987. 414p. ISBN:0-87127-019-6, ISBN13: 978-0-87127-019-1.
Dewey:793.3/2/09. LCCN:70-077179.

Audience: **l,u,f.**

Kraus, Richard & GV1601
Charman, Sarah
A History of the Dance in Art and Education. Ed. 2. Cloth Text.
Prentice Hall PTR. Upper Saddle River, NJ. 1980. 432p.
ISBN:0-13-390021-5, ISBN13: 978-0-13-390021-7.
Dewey:793.3/09. LCCN:80-016188.

Audience: **g,l,u.**

Martin, John GV1783.M33
Introduction to the Dance. Trade Paper. Princeton Book
Company Publishers. Hightstown, NJ. 1986. 363p.
ISBN:0-87127-002-1, ISBN13: 978-0-87127-002-3.
Dewey:793.3. LCCN:65-024216.

Audience: **g,l.**

Reynolds, Nancy & GV1619.R49 2003
McCormick, Malcolm
No Fixed Points: Dance in the Twentieth Century. Cloth over
Boards. Yale University Press. Cumberland, RI. 2003. 928p.
ISBN:0-300-09366-7, ISBN13: 978-0-300-09366-7.
Dewey:792.8/09/04. LCCN:2003-010754.

Audience: **g,l,u,f.** *Choice, 2004.*

Sachs, Curt GV1601.S2613
World History of the Dance. Bessie Schonberg (Translator).
Trade Cloth. W. W. Norton & Company, Inc. New York, NY.
1963. ISBN:0-393-02205-6, ISBN13: 978-0-393-02205-6.
Dewey:793.3/09.

Audience: **g,l.**

Wagner, Ann L. GV1623.W25 1997
Adversaries of Dance: From the Puritans to the Present. Trade
Cloth. University of Illinois Press. Champaign, IL. 1997. 464p.
ISBN:0-252-06590-5, ISBN13: 978-0-252-06590-3.
Dewey:792.8/0973. LCCN:96-025187.

Audience: **l,u,f.** *Choice, 1997.*

Dance Biographies and Autobiographies

Acocella, Joan R. GV1785.M635 A27 1993
Mark Morris. Cloth over Boards. Farrar, Straus & Giroux. New
York, NY. 1993. 308p. ISBN:0-374-20295-8, ISBN13:
978-0-374-20295-8. Dewey:792.8/2/092. LCCN:93-013697.

Audience: **u,f.**

Ailey, Alvin Jr. & Bailey, A. GV1785.A38A3 1994
Peter
Revelations: The Autobiography of Alvin Ailey. Trade Cloth.
Carol Publishing Group. Secaucus, NJ. 1994. 256p.
ISBN:1-55972-255-X, ISBN13: 978-1-55972-255-1.
Dewey:792.8/2/092. LCCN:94-016684.

Audience: **g,l,u,f.** *Choice, 1995.*

Anawalt, Sasha GV1623
The Joffrey Ballet: Robert Joffrey and the Making of an
American Dance Company. Trade Cloth. DIANE Publishing
Company. Collingdale, PA. 2000. 464p. ISBN:0-7881-9335-X,
ISBN13: 978-0-7881-9335-4. Dewey:792.8/0973.

Audience: **g,l,u,f.**

Aschenbrenner, Joyce GV1785.D82A73 2002
Katherine Dunham: Dancing a Life. Trade Cloth. University of
Illinois Press. Champaign, IL. 2002. 304p. ISBN:0-252-02759-0,
ISBN13: 978-0-252-02759-8. Dewey:792.8/028/092 B.
LCCN:2001-007541.

Audience: **g,l,u,f.** *Choice, 2003.*

Ashley, Merrill & Kaplan, Larry GV1785.A78 A34 1984
Dancing for Balanchine. Trade Cloth. Penguin Group (USA) Inc. New York, NY. 1984. 256p. ISBN:0-525-24280-5, ISBN13: 978-0-525-24280-2. Dewey:792.8/2/0922.

Audience: **l,u,f.**

Astaire, Fred GV1580
Steps in Time. Ginger Rogers (Introduction by). Trade Paper. Da Capo Press, Inc. Cambridge, MA. 1981. 327p. Quality Paperbacks Ser. ISBN:0-306-80141-8, ISBN13: 978-0-306-80141-9. Dewey:793.3/2/0924. LCCN:80-028725.

Audience: **g,l,u,f.**

Atkins, Cholly & Malone, Jacqui GV1785.A84A3 2003
Class Act: The Jazz Life of Choreographer Cholly Atkins. Trade Paper. Columbia University Press. New York, NY. 2003. 280p. ISBN:0-231-12365-5, ISBN13: 978-0-231-12365-5. Dewey:792.8/2/092.

Audience: **g,l,u,f.**

Baker, Jean-Claude & Chase, Chris GV1785.B3B35 2001
Josephine: The Hungry Heart. Trade Paper. Cooper Square Publishers, Inc. New York, NY. 2001. 592p. ISBN:0-8154-1172-3, ISBN13: 978-0-8154-1172-7. Dewey:792.8/028/092 B. LCCN:2001-028685.

Audience: **g,l,u,f.** *Choice, 1994.*

Barker, Barbara GV1790.A38.A67 1983
Ballet or Ballyhoo: The American Careers of Maria Bonfanti, Rita Sangalli, and Giuseppina Morlachi. Trade Cloth. Princeton Book Company Publishers. Hightstown, NJ. 1984. 269p. ISBN:0-87127-136-2, ISBN13: 978-0-87127-136-5. Dewey:792.842. LCCN:82-083629.

Audience: **u,f.**

Beckford, Ruth GV1785.D82
Katherine Dunham: A Biography. Arthur Mitchell (Introduction by). Trade Cloth. Marcel Dekker Inc. New York, NY. 1979. ISBN:0-8247-6828-0, ISBN13: 978-0-8247-6828-7. Dewey:793.3/2/0924. LCCN:79-004577.

Audience: **u,f.**

Bennahum, Ninotchka D. GV1785.A673B46 2000
Antonia Merce, la Argentina: Flamenco and the Spanish Avant Garde. Library Binding. Wesleyan University Press. Middletown, CT. 2000. 282p. ISBN:0-8195-6383-8, ISBN13: 978-0-8195-6383-5. Dewey:792.8/028/092 B. LCCN:99-035663.

Audience: **u,f.**

Blair, Fredrika GV1785.D8B56 1986
Isadora: Portrait of the Artist As a Woman. Cloth Text. McGraw-Hill Companies, The. New York, NY. 1985. ISBN:0-07-005598-X, ISBN13: 978-0-07-005598-8. Dewey:793.3/2/0924. LCCN:85-012808.

Audience: **g,l,u,f.** *Choice, 1987.*

Bland, Alexander GV1785.A1
Fonteyn and Nureyev: The Story of a Partnership. Trade Cloth.

Crown Publishing Group. New York, NY. 1979. ISBN:0-8129-0860-0, ISBN13: 978-0-8129-0860-2. Dewey:792.8/092/2. LCCN:79-064452.

Audience: **g,l,u.**

Bournonville, August GV1785.B64A3
My Theatre Life. Patricia N. McAndrew (Translator), Svend Kragh-Jacobsen (Introduction by). Trade Paper. Books on Demand. Ann Arbor, MI. 759p. ISBN:0-598-05291-7, ISBN13: 978-0-598-05291-9. Dewey:792.8/092/4. LCCN:78-027349.

Audience: **u,f.**

Bremser, Martha GV1785.A1B74 1999
Fifty Contemporary Choreographers. Trade Paper. Routledge. New York, NY. 1999. 240p. ISBN:0-415-10364-9, ISBN13: 978-0-415-10364-0. Dewey:792.8/2/0922. LCCN:00-700459.

Audience: **g,l,u.**

Buckle, Richard GV1785.D5.B79 1979
Diaghilev. Trade Cloth. Simon & Schuster. New York, NY. 1979. xxiv, 616p. ISBN:0-689-10952-0, ISBN13: 978-0-689-10952-2. Dewey:792.8/092/4. LCCN:78-073084.

Audience: **g,l,u,f.**

Buckle, Richard GV1785.D5
Nijinsky. Trade Paper. HarperCollins Publishers. New York, NY. 1975. ISBN:0-380-00459-3, ISBN13: 978-0-380-00459-1. Dewey:792.8/0924.

Audience: **l,u,f.**

Buckle, Richard & Taras, John GV1785.B32B83 1988
George Balanchine: Ballet Master. Trade Cloth. Random House, Inc. New York, NY. 1988. 432p. ISBN:0-394-53906-0, ISBN13: 978-0-394-53906-5. Dewey:792.8/2/0924 B. LCCN:87-042667.

Audience: **g,l,u,f.** *Choice, 1988.*

Caldwell, Helen GV1785.I86
Michio Ito: The Dancer and His Dances. Trade Cloth. University of California Press. Berkeley, CA. 1977. xi, 184p. ISBN:0-520-03219-5, ISBN13: 978-0-520-03219-4. Dewey:793.3/2/0924. LCCN:76-007756.

Audience: **u,f.**

Castle, Irene GV1785.C37
Castles in the Air. Ginger Rogers (Introduction by). Paper Text. Da Capo Press, Inc. Cambridge, MA. 1980. 264p. ISBN:0-306-80122-1, ISBN13: 978-0-306-80122-8. Dewey:793.3/092/2.

Audience: **g,l,u,f.**

Chazin-Bennahum, Judith GV1785.B32
The Ballets of Antony Tudor: Studies in Psyche and Satire. Trade Cloth. Replica Books. Bridgewater, NJ. 2000. 326p. ISBN:0-7351-0297-X, ISBN13: 978-0-7351-0297-2. Dewey:792.8/2/092.

Audience: **u,f.** *Choice, 1994.*

Cherniavsky, Felix   GV1785.A6 C47 1991
The Salome Dancer: The Life and Times of Maud Allan.
McClelland & Stewart. 1991. ISBN:0-7710-1957-2, ISBN13:
978-0-7710-1957-9.

Audience: **u,f.**

Conrad, Christine   GV1785.R52
Jerome Robbins: That Broadway Man. Trade Cloth.
Booth-Clibborn Editions. London, 2000. 304p.
ISBN:1-86154-173-2, ISBN13: 978-1-86154-173-4.
Dewey:792.8.

Audience: **g,l,u.**

Coton, A.V.   GV1785.J57 C67 1946
The New Ballet: Kurt Jooss and His Work. Dennis Dobson.
1946.

Audience: **u,f.**

Cunningham, Merce &   GV1783
  Lesschaeve, Jacqueline
The Dancer and the Dance: Merce Cunningham in Conversation
with Jacqueline Lesschaeve. Trade Paper. Marion Boyars
Publishers, Inc. New York, NY. 1991. 238p.
ISBN:0-7145-2931-1, ISBN13: 978-0-7145-2931-8.
Dewey:792.8/092.

Audience: **u,f.** *Choice, 1986.*

Current, Richard Nelson &   GV1785.F8C87 1997
  Current, Marcia E.
Loie Fuller: Goddess of Light. Cloth Text. Northeastern
University Press. Boston, MA. 1997. 400p.
ISBN:1-55553-309-4, ISBN13: 978-1-55553-309-0.
Dewey:792.8/028/092 B. LCCN:96-052659.

Audience: **u,f.** *Choice, 1997.*

Daly, Ann   GV1785.D8D35 1995
Done into Dance: Isadora Duncan in America. Cloth Text.
Indiana University Press. Bloomington, IN. 1995. 352p.
ISBN:0-253-32924-8, ISBN13: 978-0-253-32924-0.
Dewey:792.8/028/092 B. LCCN:95-011633.

Audience: **u,f.** *Choice, 1996.*

Danilova, Alexandra   GV1785.D24A3 1988
Choura: The Memoirs of Alexandra Danilova. Trade Paper.
Fromm International Publishing Corporation. New York, NY.
1987. 213p. ISBN:0-88064-103-7, ISBN13: 978-0-88064-103-6.
Dewey:792.8/2/0924 B. LCCN:87-027496.

Audience: **u,f.** *Choice, 1987.*

De Mille, Agnes   GV1785.G7
Martha: The Life and Work of Martha Graham. Trade Cloth.
Random House, Inc. New York, NY. 1991. 509p.
ISBN:0-394-55643-7, ISBN13: 978-0-394-55643-7.
Dewey:792.8/028/092.

Audience: **g,l,u,f.** *Choice, 1992.*

De Mille, Agnes   GV1785.D36
Dance to the Piper and Promenade Home: A Two-Part
Autobiography. Cynthia Gregory (Introduction by). Paper Text.

Da Capo Press, Inc. Cambridge, MA. 1982. 492p. Quality
Paperbacks Ser. ISBN:0-306-80161-2, ISBN13:
978-0-306-80161-7. Dewey:793.3/092/4.

Audience: **l,u,f.**

De Valois, Ninette   GV1785.D4
Come Dance with Me, a Memoir 1898: 1956. Paper Text.
Textbook Publishers. Temecula, CA. 2003. 254p.
ISBN:0-7581-0261-5, ISBN13: 978-0-7581-0261-4.
Dewey:927.93.

Audience: **l,u,f.**

Donloe, Darlene   GV1785.D82D67 1993
Katherine Dunham: Dancer and Choreographer. Trade Cloth.
Holloway House Publishing Company. Los Angeles, CA. 1993.
192p. Black American Ser. ISBN:0-87067-775-6, ISBN13:
978-0-87067-775-5. Dewey:792.8/028/092 B. LCCN:94-126776.

Audience: **u,f.**

Drummond, John   GV1785.D5
Speaking of Diaghiley. Trade Paper. DIANE Publishing
Company. Collingdale, PA. 1997. 382p. ISBN:0-7567-6151-4,
ISBN13: 978-0-7567-6151-6. Dewey:792.8.

Audience: **l,u,f.**

Duncan, Isadora   GV1785.K3
My Life. Library Binding. Reprint Services Company. Temecula,
CA. 1991. 376p. American Biography Ser. ISBN:0-7812-8115-6,
ISBN13: 978-0-7812-8115-7. Dewey:792.8/092.

Audience: **g,l,u,f.**

Dunning, Jennifer   GV1785.A38D85 1996
Alvin Ailey: A Life in Dance. Cloth Text. Perseus Books Group.
New York, NY. 1996. 480p. ISBN:0-201-62607-1, ISBN13:
978-0-201-62607-0. Dewey:792.8/028/092 B. LCCN:96-015167.

Audience: **l,u,f.** *Choice, 1997.*

Easton, Carol   GV1785.T32
No Intermissions: The Life of Agnes De Mille. Trade Paper.
DIANE Publishing Company. Collingdale, PA. 1996. 548p.
ISBN:0-7567-6103-4, ISBN13: 978-0-7567-6103-5.
Dewey:792.8/028/092 B.

Audience: **g,l,u,f.**

Farrell, Suzanne & Bentley,   GV1785
  Toni
Holding on to the Air: An Autobiography. Trade Cloth.
University Press of Florida. Gainesville, FL. 2002. 322p.
ISBN:0-8130-2593-1, ISBN13: 978-0-8130-2593-3.
Dewey:792.8/092 B. LCCN:2002-020448.

Audience: **u,f.**

Flatley, Michael   GV1785.A3F583 2006
Lord of the Dance: My Story. Douglas Thompson (As told to).
Trade Cloth. Simon & Schuster. New York, NY. 2006. 352p.
ISBN:0-7432-9179-4, ISBN13: 978-0-7432-9179-8.
Dewey:793.3/19415. LCCN:2005-057517.

Audience: **u,f.**

Fokine, Michel   GV1785.F6
Fokine: Memoirs of a Ballet Master. Paper Text. Textbook
Publishers. Temecula, CA. 2003. 318p. ISBN:0-7581-9725-X,
ISBN13: 978-0-7581-9725-2. Dewey:792.809.

Audience: **u,f.**

Fonteyn, Margot   GV1785.F63
Margot Fonteyn: Autobiography. Trade Cloth. Alfred A. Knopf
Inc. New York, NY. 1976. ISBN:0-394-48570-X, ISBN13:
978-0-394-48570-6. Dewey:792.8/028/0924.

Audience: **g,l,u,f.**

Garcia-Marquez, Vicente   GV1785.M35G37 1995
Massine: A Biography. Trade Cloth. Alfred A. Knopf Inc. New
York, NY. 1995. 456p. ISBN:0-394-51003-8, ISBN13:
978-0-394-51003-3. Dewey:792.8/028/092. LCCN:93-035666.

Audience: **g,l,u,f.** *Choice, 1996.*

Geva, Tamara   GV1785.G44.A37 1972
Split Seconds; a Remembrance. Trade Cloth. Harper & Row
Ltd. London, 1972. 358p. ISBN:0-06-011512-2, ISBN13:
978-0-06-011512-8. Dewey:792.8/2/0924. LCCN:72-079666.

Audience: **u,f.**

Glover, Savion & Weber,   GV1785.G56A3 2000
   Bruce
Savion!: My Life in Tap. Gregory Hines (Foreword by). Trade
Cloth. HarperCollins Publishers. New York, NY. 2000. 80p.
ISBN:0-688-15629-0, ISBN13: 978-0-688-15629-9.
Dewey:729.7/8 B. LCCN:98-031517.

Audience: **g,l,u.**

Gottfried, Martin   PN2287.F
All His Jazz: The Life and Death of Bob Fosse. Ed. 2. Trade
Paper. Da Capo Press, Inc. Cambridge, MA. 2003. 512p.
ISBN:0-306-81284-3, ISBN13: 978-0-306-81284-2.
Dewey:792.82092 B. LCCN:2004-556213.

Audience: **g,l,u,f.**

Gottfried, Martin   PN2287.R74
Nobody's Fool. Trade Paper. Simon & Schuster. New York, NY.
2002. 352p. ISBN:0-7432-4476-1, ISBN13: 978-0-7432-4476-3.
Dewey:792.7/028/092 B.

Audience: **g,l,u.**

Gottlieb, Robert   GV1785.B32G68 2004
George Balanchine: The Ballet Maker. Trade Cloth.
HarperCollins Publishers. New York, NY. 2004. 224p. Eminent
Lives Ser. ISBN:0-06-075070-7, ISBN13: 978-0-06-075070-1.
Dewey:792.8/2/092 B. LCCN:2004-048856.

Audience: **g,l,u,f.** *Choice, 2005.*

Graham, Martha   GV1785.G7A3 1991
Blood Memory: An Autobiography. Trade Cloth. Doubleday
Publishing. New York, NY. 1991. 288p. ISBN:0-385-26503-4,
ISBN13: 978-0-385-26503-4. Dewey:792.8/028/092 B.
LCCN:91-015444.

Audience: **g,l,u,f.**

Grubb, Kevin B.   GV1785.F67G78 1991
Razzle Dazzle: The Life and Work of Bob Fosse. Trade Cloth.
St. Martin's Press. Gordonville, VA. 1991. 8p.
ISBN:0-312-05502-1, ISBN13: 978-0-312-05502-8.
Dewey:792.8/2/092 B. LCCN:90-019225.

Audience: **g,l,u,f.**

Gruen, John   GV1785.B78 G78
Erik Bruhn: Danseur Noble. Trade Cloth. Penguin Group (USA)
Inc. New York, NY. 1979. ISBN:0-670-29771-2, ISBN13:
978-0-670-29771-9. Dewey:792.8/092/4.

Audience: **u,f.**

Gruen, John   GV1785.A1
People Who Dance. Trade Cloth. Princeton Book Company
Publishers. Hightstown, NJ. 1988. 176p. ISBN:0-916622-74-6,
ISBN13: 978-0-916622-74-9. Dewey:792.8/092/2.
LCCN:88-060952.

Audience: **g,l,u,f.**

Guest, Ivor   GV1785.C43 G8 1974
Fanny Cerrito: The Life of a Romantic Ballerina. Dance Books.
1974. ISBN:0-903102-09-9, ISBN13: 978-0-903102-09-4.

Audience: **u,f.**

Guest, Ivor F.   GV1785.Z82G8
The Divine Virginia: A Biography of Virginia Zucchi. Trade
Paper. Books on Demand. Ann Arbor, MI. 206p. The Dance
Program Ser., Vol. 1 ISBN:0-608-16848-3, ISBN13:
978-0-608-16848-7. Dewey:792.80924. LCCN:76-020006.

Audience: **u,f.**

Guest, Ivor F.   GV1785.E4.G8 1970
Fanny Elssler. Trade Cloth. Wesleyan University Press.
Middletown, CT. 1970. 284p. ISBN:0-8195-4022-6, ISBN13:
978-0-8195-4022-5. Dewey:792.8/0924. LCCN:74-105507.

Audience: **u,f.**

Guest, Ivor F.   GV1785.P417G84 1984
Jules Perrot: Master of the Romantic Ballet. Trade Cloth.
Princeton Book Company Publishers. Hightstown, NJ. 1984.
383p. ISBN:0-87127-140-0, ISBN13: 978-0-87127-140-2.
Dewey:792.8/2/0924 B. LCCN:83-073636.

Audience: **u,f.**

Guest, Ivor F.   GV1649
The Romantic Ballet in Paris. Ed. 2. Lillian C. Moore
(Foreword by). Trade Cloth. Dance Books, Ltd. Alton, 1980.
xix, 314p. ISBN:0-903102-45-5, ISBN13: 978-0-903102-45-2.
Dewey:792.8/0944.

Audience: **u,f.**

Haskins, James S.   GV1785.D82 H38 1982
Katherine Dunham. Trade Cloth. Penguin Group (USA) Inc.
New York, NY. 1982. 176p. ISBN:0-698-20549-9, ISBN13:
978-0-698-20549-9. Dewey:793.3/2/0924.

Audience: **l,u,f.**

Haygood, Wil   PN2287.D322
In Black and White: The Life of Sammy Davis, Jr. Knopf. 2003.
ISBN:0-375-40354-X, ISBN13: 978-0-375-40354-5.

Audience: **g,l,u,f.**

Hickenlooper Sowell, Debra   GV1785.A1
The Christensen Brothers: An American Dance Epic. Cloth Text.
Gordon & Breach Publishing Group. New York, NY. 1998.
604p. Choreography and Dance Studies ISBN:90-5755-028-8,
ISBN13: 978-90-5755-028-7. Dewey:792.8/0922.
Audience: **u,f.**

Hirschhorn, Clive   PN2287.C5
Gene Kelly. Trade Cloth. Thomson Gale. Farmington Hills, MI.
1985. General Ser. ISBN:0-8161-3915-6, ISBN13:
978-0-8161-3915-6. Dewey:791.43/028/0924 B.
Audience: **g,l,u.**

Horosko, Marian   GV1785.O42H67 2005
May O'Donnell: Modern Dance Pioneer. Jennifer Dunning
(Foreword by). Trade Paper, Perfect. University Press of Florida.
Gainesville, FL. 2005. 136p. ISBN:0-8130-2857-4, ISBN13:
978-0-8130-2857-6. Dewey:792.8/0929aB. LCCN:2005-048565.
Audience: **g,l,u.**

Horwitz, Dawn L.   GV1785.F65H67 1985
Michel Fokine. Trade Cloth. Thomson Gale. Farmington Hills,
MI. 1985. Dance Ser. ISBN:0-8057-9603-7, ISBN13:
978-0-8057-9603-2. Dewey:792.8/2/0924 B. LCCN:85-000928.
Audience: **u,f.** *Choice, 1986.*

Humphrey, Doris   GV1785.H8.A3
Doris Humphrey: An Artist First. Trade Cloth. Wesleyan
University Press. Middletown, CT. 1972. xiv, 305p.
ISBN:0-8195-4054-4, ISBN13: 978-0-8195-4054-6.
Dewey:793.3/2. LCCN:72-003695.
Audience: **u,f.**

Ingber, Judith B.   GV1785.B443
Victory Dances: The Story of Fred Berk, a Modern Day Jewish
Dancing Master. Trade Paper. Emmett Publishing Company.
Minneapolis, MN. 225p. ISBN:0-934682-11-9, ISBN13:
978-0-934682-11-4. Dewey:793.3/2/0924.
Audience: **u,f.**

Jamison, Judith & Kaplan,   GV1785.T32
  Howard
Dancing Spirit: An Autobiography. Trade Cloth. Doubleday
Publishing. New York, NY. 1993. ISBN:0-385-42557-0,
ISBN13: 978-0-385-42557-5. Dewey:792.8/028/092 B.
LCCN:93-025480.
Audience: **g,l,u,f.**

Jones, Bill T.   GV1785.J55A3 1995
Last Night on Earth. Peggy Gillespie (Contribution by). Trade
Cloth. Knopf Publishing Group. New York, NY. 1995. 304p.
ISBN:0-679-43926-9, ISBN13: 978-0-679-43926-4.
Dewey:792.8/2/092 B. LCCN:95-002962.
Audience: **u,f.**

Jones, Bill T. & Zane, Arnie   GV1785.A1J66 1989
Body Against Body: The Dance and Other Collaborations of
Bill T. Jones and Arnie Zane. Elizabeth Zimmer (Text by).
Trade Paper. Barrytown/Station Hill Press. Barrytown, NY.
1989. 128p. ISBN:0-88268-064-1, ISBN13: 978-0-88268-064-4.
Dewey:792.8/2/0922 B. LCCN:88-004930.
Audience: **u,f.**

Jowitt, Deborah   GV1785.R52J69 2004
Jerome Robbins: His Life, His Theater, His Dance. Trade Cloth.
Simon & Schuster, Inc. New York, NY. 2004. 640p.
ISBN:0-684-86985-3, ISBN13: 978-0-684-86985-8.
Dewey:792.8/2/092 B. LCCN:2004-045440.
Audience: **l,u,f.** *Choice, 2005.*

Jowitt, Deborah (Editor)   ML410.M72M47 1997
Meredith Monk. Trade Cloth. Johns Hopkins University Press.
Baltimore, MD. 1997. 224p. PAJ Bks., :Art and Performance
ISBN:0-8018-5539-X, ISBN13: 978-0-8018-5539-9.
Dewey:700/.92. LCCN:97-006597.
Audience: **l,u,f.**

Kahn, Albert E.   GV1785.U4 K3 1980
Days with Ulanova. Library Binding. Ayer Company Publishers,
Inc. Manchester, NH. 1980. Dance Ser. ISBN:0-8369-9297-0,
ISBN13: 978-0-8369-9297-7. Dewey:792.8/092/4.
LCCN:79-007770.
Audience: **u,f.**

Karsavina, Tamara   GV1785.K3
Theatre Street. Library Binding. Ayer Company Publishers, Inc.
Manchester, NH. 1980. Dance Ser. ISBN:0-8369-9298-9,
ISBN13: 978-0-8369-9298-4. Dewey:792.8/092/4.
LCCN:79-007771.
Audience: **u,f.**

Kendall, Elizabeth   GV1623 .K46 1979
Where She Danced . . .: American Dancing, 1880-1930. Trade
Cloth. Alfred A. Knopf Inc. New York, NY. 1979.
ISBN:0-394-40029-1, ISBN13: 978-0-394-40029-7.
Dewey:793.3/1973. LCCN:78-020544.
Audience: **g,l,u,f.**

Kent, Allegra   GV1785.A1
Once a Dancer: An Autobiography. Trade Paper. St. Martin's
Press. Gordonville, VA. 1998. 352p. ISBN:0-312-18750-5,
ISBN13: 978-0-312-18750-7. Dewey:792.8/028/092 B.
Audience: **g,l,u.**

Kirkland, Gelsey &   GV1785.K49A3 1986
  Lawrence, D. H.
Dancing on My Grave. Trade Cloth. Doubleday Publishing.
New York, NY. 1986. ISBN:0-385-19964-3, ISBN13:
978-0-385-19964-3. Dewey:792.8/2/0924 B. LCCN:86-008857.
Audience: **g,l,u,f.**

Kirstein, Lincoln   GV1785.B32
Portrait of Mr. B: Photographs of George Balanchine with an
Essay. Jonathan Cott & Edwin Derby (Photographers), Peter
Martins (Foreword by). Trade Cloth. Penguin Group (USA) Inc.
New York, NY. 1984. 144p. ISBN:0-670-56632-2, ISBN13:
978-0-670-56632-7. Dewey:792.8/2/0924.
Audience: **g,l,u,f.**

Klosty, James (Editor)   GV1785.C85M47 1986
Merce Cunningham. Trade Paper. Hal Leonard Corporation.
Milwaukee, WI. 1987. 218p. ISBN:0-87910-055-9, ISBN13:
978-0-87910-055-1. Dewey:793.3/2/0924 B. LCCN:86-002807.
Audience: **l,u,f.**

Koner, Pauline   GV1785.K596A3 1989
Solitary Song: An Autobiography. Cloth Text. Duke University
Press. Durham, NC. 1989. xi, 306p. ISBN:0-8223-0878-9,
ISBN13: 978-0-8223-0878-2. Dewey:793.3/2/0924 B.
LCCN:89-001546.
                                    Audience: **u,f.** *Choice, 1989.*

Kurth, Peter   GV1785.K3
Isadora: A Sensational Life. Trade Paper. Little Brown &
Company. New York, NY. 2002. 704p. ISBN:0-316-05713-4,
ISBN13: 978-0-316-05713-4. Dewey:792.8/092.
                                    Audience: **g,l,u,f.** *Choice, 2002.*

Laban, Rudolf   GV1580
A Life for Dance: The Autobiography of Rudolf Laban. Lisa
Ullman (Translator). Trade Cloth. Princeton Book Company
Publishers. Hightstown, NJ. 1975. 193p. ISBN:0-7121-1231-6,
ISBN13: 978-0-7121-1231-4. Dewey:793.3/2/0924.
                                                    Audience: **u,f.**

Levinson, Andre   GV1785.T3
Marie Taglioni (1804-1884). Cyril W. Beaumont (Translator).
Trade Paper. Princeton Book Company Publishers. Hightstown,
NJ. 1977. 111p. ISBN:0-903102-33-1, ISBN13:
978-0-903102-33-9. Dewey:792.8/092/4.
                                                    Audience: **u,f.**

Limon, Jose   GV1785.T32
Jose Limon: An Unfinished Memoir. Lynn Garafola (Editor).
Trade Paper. Wesleyan University Press. Middletown, CT. 2001.
245p. ISBN:0-8195-6505-9, ISBN13: 978-0-8195-6505-1.
Dewey:792.8/028/092.
                                                    Audience: **u,f.**

Livingston, Lili Cockerille   GV1785.A1L526 1997
American Indian Ballerinas. Trade Cloth. University of
Oklahoma Press. Norman, OK. 1997. 348p.
ISBN:0-8061-2896-8, ISBN13: 978-0-8061-2896-2.
Dewey:792.8. LCCN:96-032307.
                                    Audience: **u,f.** *Choice, 1997.*

Loewenthal, Lillian   GV1785.D8.L64 1993
The Search for Isadora Duncan: The Legend and Legacy of
Isadora Duncan. Trade Cloth. Princeton Book Company
Publishers. Hightstown, NJ. 1993. 225p. ISBN:0-87127-179-6,
ISBN13: 978-0-87127-179-2. Dewey:792.8/092.
LCCN:92-050754.
                                    Audience: **g,l,u,f.** *Choice, 1993.*

Loney, Glenn   GV1785.C63L66 1984
Unsung Genius: The Passion of Dancer-Choreographer Jack
Cole. Trade Cloth. Scholastic Library Publishing. Danbury, CT.
1984. 384p. ISBN:0-531-09765-X, ISBN13: 978-0-531-09765-6.
Dewey:793.3/2/0924 B. LCCN:84-007447.
                                               Audience: **g,l,u,f.**

Louis, Murray   GV1785.L68A3 1992
Murray Louis on Dance. Trade Cloth. A Cappella Books.
Chicago, IL. 1992. 180p. ISBN:1-55652-147-2, ISBN13:
978-1-55652-147-8. Dewey:792.8/028/092. LCCN:92-006468.
                                    Audience: **u,f.** *Choice, 1992.*

Lynham, Deryck   GV1785.N7 L9 1972
The Chevalier Noverre: Father of Modern Ballet, a Biography.
Dance Books. 1972. ISBN:0-903102-01-3, ISBN13:
978-0-903102-01-8.
                                                    Audience: **u,f.**

Makarova, Natalia   GV1785.M26
A Dance Autobiography. Gennady Smakov (Editor), Dina
Makarova (Photographer). Trade Cloth. Alfred A. Knopf Inc.
New York, NY. 1979. ISBN:0-394-50141-1, ISBN13:
978-0-394-50141-3. Dewey:792.8/092/4. LCCN:78-020621.
                                                    Audience: **u,f.**

Manning, Susan   GV1785.K3
Ecstasy and Demon: The Dances of Mary Wigman. Ed. 2. Trade
Paper. University of Minnesota Press. Minneapolis, MN. 2006.
376p. ISBN:0-8166-3802-0, ISBN13: 978-0-8166-3802-4.
Dewey:792.8092 B. LCCN:2006-016452.
                                                    Audience: **u,f.**

Martin, John   GV1785P26
Ruth Page: An Intimate Biography. Trade Cloth. Marcel Dekker
Inc. New York, NY. 1977. 350p. ISBN:0-8247-6490-0, ISBN13:
978-0-8247-6490-6. Dewey:792.8/092/4.
                                                    Audience: **u,f.**

Martins, Peter & Cornfield,   GV1785.M34 A34 1982
  Robert
Far from Denmark. Trade Cloth. Little Brown & Company. New
York, NY. 1982. ISBN:0-316-54855-3, ISBN13:
978-0-316-54855-7. Dewey:792.8/2/0924.
                                               Audience: **g,l,u,f.**

Mason, Francis   GV1785.B32M36 1991
I Remember Balanchine: Recollections of the Ballet Master by
Those Who Knew Him Best. Trade Cloth. Doubleday
Publishing. New York, NY. 1991. 624p. ISBN:0-385-26610-3,
ISBN13: 978-0-385-26610-9. Dewey:792.8/2/092 B.
LCCN:90-003732.
                                                    Audience: **u,f.**

Massine, Leonide   GV1785.M35A3 1968
My Life in Ballet. St. Martin's Press. 1968.
                                                    Audience: **u,f.**

McDonagh, Don   GV1785.B32M38 1983
George Balanchine. Trade Cloth. Thomson Gale. Farmington
Hills, MI. 1983. Dance Ser. ISBN:0-8057-9601-0, ISBN13:
978-0-8057-9601-8. Dewey:792.8/2/0924 B. LCCN:84-153760.
                                               Audience: **g,l,u,f.**

McDonagh, Don   GV1785.G7 M32
Martha Graham. Praeger. 1973.
                                               Audience: **l,u,f.**

Miller, Norma   GV1784.M556 1996
Swingin' at the Savoy: The Memoir of a Jazz Dancer. Evette
Jensen (Contribution by). Trade Cloth. Temple University Press.
Philadelphia, PA. 1996. 310p. ISBN:1-56639-494-5, ISBN13:
978-1-56639-494-9. Dewey:792.8. LCCN:96-020104.
                                               Audience: **g,l,u,f.**

Money, Keith   GV1785.P3
Anna Pavlova: Her Life and Art. Trade Cloth. Alfred A. Knopf
Inc. New York, NY. 1982. 440p. ISBN:0-394-42786-6, ISBN13:
978-0-394-42786-7. Dewey:792.8/2/0924. LCCN:81-047502.
Audience: **l,u,f.**

Money, Keith   GV1785.F63 M65 1974
Fonteyn: The Making of a Legend. Reynall. 1974.
ISBN:0-688-61163-X, ISBN13: 978-0-688-61163-7.
Audience: **l,u,f.**

Newman, Barbara   GV1785.A1
Striking a Balance: Dancers Talk About Dancing. Trade Cloth.
Houghton Mifflin Company. New York, NY. 1982. 416p.
ISBN:0-395-31325-2, ISBN13: 978-0-395-31325-1.
Dewey:792.8/2/0922.
Audience: **u,f.**

Nijinska, Bronislava   GV1785.N59A3
Bronislava Nijinska: Early Memoirs. Ed. 2. Irina Nijinska &
Jean Rawlinson (Editors), Irina Nijinska & Jean Rawlinson
(Translators), Anna Kisselgoff (Introduction by). Paper Text.
Duke University Press. Durham, NC. 1992. 576p.
ISBN:0-8223-1295-6, ISBN13: 978-0-8223-1295-6.
Dewey:792.8092247. LCCN:92-013666.
Audience: **u,f.**

Nijinsky, Vaslav   GV1785.K3
The Diary of Vaslav Nijinsky. Joan R. Acocella (Editor), Kyril
FitzLyon (Translator), Joan R. Acocella (Introduction by). Trade
Paper. Farrar, Straus & Giroux. New York, NY. 2000. 320p.
ISBN:0-374-52685-0, ISBN13: 978-0-374-52685-6.
Dewey:792.8/092.
Audience: **u,f.**

Olatunji, Babatunde &   ML419.O385A3 2005
  Atkinson, Robert
The Beat of My Drum: An Autobiography. Joan Baez (Foreword
by), Eric Charry (Introduction by). Trade Paper. Temple
University Press. Philadelphia, PA. 2005. 272p.
ISBN:1-59213-354-1, ISBN13: 978-1-59213-354-3.
Dewey:786.9/163/092 B. LCCN:2004-053726.
Audience: **u,f.** *Choice, 2005.*

Osato, Sono   GV1785.O6.A33 1980
Distant Dances. Trade Cloth. Alfred A. Knopf Inc. New York,
NY. 1980. xi, 301p. ISBN:0-394-50891-2, ISBN13:
978-0-394-50891-7. Dewey:792.8/092/4. LCCN:79-003487.
Audience: **u,f.**

Perlmutter, Donna   GV1785.T83P47 1995
Shadowplay: The Life of Antony Tudor. Trade Paper. Hal
Leonard Corporation. Milwaukee, WI. 1995. 420p.
ISBN:0-87910-189-X, ISBN13: 978-0-87910-189-3.
Dewey:792.8/2/092 B. LCCN:94-039957.
Audience: **l,u,f.**

Perron, Wendy (Editor)   GV1786.J82
Judson Dance Theater: 1962-1966. Bennington College. 1981.
Audience: **l,u,f.**

Petipa, Marius   GV1785.P42 A313
Russian Ballet Master: the Memories of Marius Petipa. Adam &
Charles Black. 1958.
Audience: **u,f.**

Prevots, Naima   GV1785.A1P74
Dancing in the Sun: Hollywood Choreographers, 1915-1937.
Oscar G. Brockett (Editor). Trade Paper. Books on Demand.
Ann Arbor, MI. 1987. 290p. Theater and Dramatic Studies, Vol.
44 ISBN:0-8357-1825-5, ISBN13: 978-0-8357-1825-7.
Dewey:792.8/2/0922 B. LCCN:87-013859.
Audience: **u,f.** *Choice, 1988.*

Racster, Olga   GV1785.C4
The Master of the Russian Ballet: The Memoirs of Cav. Enrico
Cecchetti. Paper Text. Da Capo Press, Inc. Cambridge, MA.
1978. 362p. Series in Dance ISBN:0-306-77589-1, ISBN13:
978-0-306-77589-5. Dewey:792.8/092/4. LCCN:78-018777.
Audience: **u,f.**

Rainer, Yvonne   GV1785.R25 A38
Work, 1961-1973. Trade Cloth. New York University Press.
New York, NY. 1974. 338p. The Nova Scotia Ser.
ISBN:0-8147-7360-5, ISBN13: 978-0-8147-7360-4.
Dewey:793.3/2/0924. LCCN:73-087480.
Audience: **u,f.**

Ramazani, Nesta   GV1785.R34A3 2001
The Dance of the Rose and the Nightingale. Trade Cloth.
Syracuse University Press. Syracuse, NY. 2001. 272p. Gender,
Culture, and Politics in the Middle East Ser.
ISBN:0-8156-0727-X, ISBN13: 978-0-8156-0727-4.
Dewey:792.8/028/092 B. LCCN:2001-054940.
Audience: **u,f.** *Choice, 2002.*

Rambert, Marie   GV1785.R36.A36
Quicksilver: The Autobiography of Marie Rambert. Trade Cloth.
Macmillan Publishing Company, Inc. Old Tappan, NJ. 1972.
231p. ISBN:0-333-08942-1, ISBN13: 978-0-333-08942-2.
Dewey:792.8/092/4. LCCN:72-083628.
Audience: **u,f.**

Rose, Phyllis   GV1785.B3R66 1989
Jazz cleopatra Rose: Josephine Baker in Her Time. Trade Cloth.
Doubleday Publishing. New York, NY. 1989. 384p.
ISBN:0-385-24891-1, ISBN13: 978-0-385-24891-4.
LCCN:88-035585.
Audience: **g,l,u,f.** *Choice, 1990.*

Roslavleva, Natalia   GV1785.P55 R62
Maya Plisetskaya. Foreign Language Publishing House. 1956.
Audience: **u,f.**

Ross, Janice
Anna Halprin: Experience as Dance. Richard Schechner
(Foreword by). Trade Cloth. University of California Press.
Berkeley, CA. 2007. 448p. ISBN:0-520-24757-4, ISBN13:
978-0-520-24757-4.
Audience: **u,f.**

Sagolla, Lisa Jo GV1785.M23S35 2003
The Girl Who Fell Down: A Biography of Joan Mccracken.
Trade Cloth. Northeastern University Press. Boston, MA. 2005.
320p. ISBN:1-55553-573-9, ISBN13: 978-1-55553-573-5.
Dewey:792.8/092 B. LCCN:2003-006557.
Audience: **u,f.** *Choice, 2004.*

Servos, Norbert GV1782.5.S47 1984
Pina Bausch Wuppertal Dance Theater: On the Art of Training a
Goldfish--Excursions into Dance. Ballet-Buhnen Verlag. 1984.
ISBN:3-922224-05-9, ISBN13: 978-3-922224-05-1.
Audience: **u,f.**

Seymour, Bruce DA565.S34
Lola Montez: A Life. Trade Paper. Yale University Press.
Cumberland, RI. 1998. 480p. ISBN:0-300-07439-5, ISBN13:
978-0-300-07439-0. Dewey:941/.08/092.
Audience: **u,f.** *Choice, 1996.*

Shawn, Ted GV1785.S5.A3 1979
One Thousand and One Night Stands. Paper Text. Da Capo
Press, Inc. Cambridge, MA. 1979. 622p. Quality Paperbacks
Ser. ISBN:0-306-80095-0, ISBN13: 978-0-306-80095-5.
Dewey:792.8/092/4. LCCN:78-020818.
Audience: **l,u,f.**

Shelton, Suzanne GV1785.S3.S53
Divine Dancer: A Biography of Ruth St. Denis. Trade Cloth.
Doubleday Publishing. New York, NY. 1981. 360p.
ISBN:0-385-14159-9, ISBN13: 978-0-385-14159-8.
Dewey:793.3/2/0924. LCCN:80-002442.
Audience: **g,l,u.**

Sherman, Jane GV1785.S553.A37
Soaring: The Diary and Letters of a Denishawn Dancer in the
Far East, 1925-1926. Trade Cloth. Wesleyan University Press.
Middletown, CT. 1976. 288p. ISBN:0-8195-4093-5, ISBN13:
978-0-8195-4093-5. Dewey:793.3/2/0924. LCCN:75-034445.
Audience: **u,f.**

Sherman, Jane & Mumaw, GV1785.M77S54 2000
Barton
Barton Mumaw, Dancer: From Denishawn to Jacob's Pillow and
Beyond. David Gere (Foreword by). Trade Paper. Wesleyan
University Press. Middletown, CT. 2000. 392p.
ISBN:0-8195-6453-2, ISBN13: 978-0-8195-6453-5.
Dewey:792.8/028/92 B. LCCN:00-105411.
Audience: **l,u,f.** *Choice, 1986.*

Shloss, Carol Loeb PR6019.O9
Lucia Joyce: To Dance in the Wake. Trade Paper. Picador. New
York, NY. 2005. 576p. ISBN:0-312-42269-5, ISBN13:
978-0-312-42269-1. Dewey:823/.912 B.
Audience: **u,f.** *Choice, 2004.*

Siegel, Marcia GV1785.T43S54 2006
Howling Near Heaven: Twyla Tharp and the Reinvention of
Modern Dance. Trade Cloth. Palgrave Macmillan. New York,
NY. 2006. 336p. ISBN:0-312-23294-2, ISBN13:
978-0-312-23294-8. Dewey:792.8/2092. LCCN:2005-044685.
Audience: **u,f.**

Siegel, Marcia B. GV.1580
Days on Earth: The Dance of Doris Humphrey. Trade Paper.
Princeton Book Company Publishers. Hightstown, NJ. 1993.
351p. ISBN:0-8223-1346-4, ISBN13: 978-0-8223-1346-5.
Dewey:793.3/2/0924 B. LCCN:92-033367.
Audience: **u,f.**

Smakov, Gennady GV1785.P3
Baryshnikov: From Russia to the West. Trade Cloth. Farrar,
Straus & Giroux. New York, NY. 1981. 244p.
ISBN:0-374-10908-7, ISBN13: 978-0-374-10908-0.
Dewey:792.8/2/0924.
Audience: **g,l,u,f.**

Soares, Janet M. ML410.H86S5 1992
Louis Horst: Musician in a Dancer's World. Trade Cloth. Duke
University Press. Durham, NC. 1992. 296p.
ISBN:0-8223-1226-3, ISBN13: 978-0-8223-1226-0.
Dewey:792.8092. LCCN:91-032933.
Audience: **u,f.** *Choice, 1992.*

Solway, Diane GV1785.N8S66 1998
Nureyev: His Life. Trade Cloth. HarperCollins Publishers. New
York, NY. 1999. 625p. ISBN:0-688-12873-4, ISBN13:
978-0-688-12873-9. Dewey:792.8/092. LCCN:98-013483.
Audience: **g,l,u,f.** *Choice, 1999.*

Sommer, Sally & Harris,
Margaret
LaLoie: The Life and Art of Loie Fuller. Putnam. 1986.
Audience: **l,u,f.**

Sorell, Walter GV1785.H6 S6
Hanya Holm: The Biography of an Artist. Trade Cloth.
Wesleyan University Press. Middletown, CT. 1969. 238p.
ISBN:0-8195-3096-4, ISBN13: 978-0-8195-3096-7.
Dewey:792.8/2/092. LCCN:69-017796.
Audience: **u,f.**

Sorell, Walter GV1785.W5 A35
The Mary Wigman Book. Wesleyan University Press. 1975.
Audience: **u,f.**

Souritz, Elizabeth GV1785.A1S7813 1990
Soviet Choreographers in the 1920s. Sally Banes (Editor,
Translator), Lynn Visson (Translator). Cloth Text. Duke
University Press. Durham, NC. 1990. 384p.
ISBN:0-8223-0952-1, ISBN13: 978-0-8223-0952-9.
Dewey:792.8/2/0922 B. LCCN:89-016877.
Audience: **u,f.** *Choice, 1990.*

Spector, Irwin ML429.J2S6 1990
Rhythm and Life: The Work of Emile Jaques-Dalcroze. Cloth
Text. Pendragon Press. Hillsdale, NY. 1989. 400p. Dance and
Music Ser., No. 3 ISBN:0-945193-00-9, ISBN13:
978-0-945193-00-5. Dewey:780/.92 B. LCCN:89-028139.
Audience: **u,f.** *Choice, 1991.*

St. Denis, Ruth GV1785.S3
An Unfinished Life: An Autobiography. Library Binding.

Reprint Services Company. Temecula, CA. 1991. 391p. American Biography Ser. ISBN:0-7812-8335-3, ISBN13: 978-0-7812-8335-9. Dewey:927.933.

Audience: **u,f.**

Steegmuller, Francis PQ2605.O15Z86 1986
Cocteau: A Biography. Trade Paper. David R. Godine Publisher. Boston, MA. 1986. 608p. Nonpareil Bks., Vol. 40 ISBN:0-87923-606-X, ISBN13: 978-0-87923-606-9. Dewey:848/.9/1209. LCCN:76-117039.

Audience: **g,l,u.** 𝓑

Steegmuller, Francis GV1785.D8
(Editor)
Your Isadora: The Love Story of Isadora Duncan and Gordon Craig Told Through Letters and Diaries. Trade Paper. Random House, Inc. New York, NY. 1982. Giant Ser. ISBN:0-394-72078-4, ISBN13: 978-0-394-72078-4. Dewey:793.3/2/0924.

Audience: **g,l,u.**

Sullivan, Lawrence CT25
Elisabeth Anderson-Ivantsova: A Bolshoi Ballerina Abroad. Xlibris Corporation. 2006. ISBN:1-59926-362-9, ISBN13: 978-1-59926-362-5.

Audience: **u,f.**

Swift, Mary G. GV1785.D54
A Loftier Flight. Trade Cloth. Wesleyan University Press. Middletown, CT. 1974. 230p. De la Torre Bueno Prize Book, 1973 ISBN:0-8195-4070-6, ISBN13: 978-0-8195-4070-6. Dewey:792.8/092/4. LCCN:73-015007.

Audience: **u,f.**

Tallchief, Maria & Kaplan, GV1785.T32A3 1997
Larry
Maria Tallchief: America's Prima Ballerina. Trade Cloth. Henry Holt & Company. New York, NY. 1997. 368p. ISBN:0-8050-3302-5, ISBN13: 978-0-8050-3302-1. Dewey:792.8/092 B. LCCN:96-045271.

Audience: **l,u,f.**

Taylor, Paul GV1785.T39A3 1987
Private Domain: An Autobiography. Trade Cloth. Alfred A. Knopf Inc. New York, NY. 1987. ISBN:0-394-51683-4, ISBN13: 978-0-394-51683-7. Dewey:792.8/2/092. LCCN:86-045366.

Audience: **u,f.** *Choice, 1987.*

Teachout, Terry GV1785.B32T43 2004
All in the Dances: A Brief Life of George Balanchine. Cloth over Boards. Harcourt Trade Publishers. New York, NY. 2004. 208p. ISBN:0-15-101088-9, ISBN13: 978-0-15-101088-2. Dewey:792.8/2/092 B. LCCN:2004-009226.

Audience: **g,l.**

Tharp, Twyla GV1785.T43
Push Comes to Shove: An Autobiography. Trade Cloth. Bantam Books. New York, NY. 1992. 352p. ISBN:0-553-07306-0, ISBN13: 978-0-553-07306-5. Dewey:792.8/2/092. LCCN:92-017977.

Audience: **u,f.**

Thorpe, Edward GV1785.M252T47 1985
Kenneth MacMillan: The Man and the Ballets. Ninette De Valois (Foreword by). Cloth Text. Trafalgar Square. North Pomfret, VT. 1986. 239p. ISBN:0-241-11694-5, ISBN13: 978-0-241-11694-4. Dewey:792.8/092/4 B. LCCN:86-126949.

Audience: **u,f.**

Tomalonis, Alexandra GV1785
Henning Kronstam: Portrait of a Danish Dancer. Trade Cloth. University Press of Florida. Gainesville, FL. 2002. 572p. ISBN:0-8130-2546-X, ISBN13: 978-0-8130-2546-9. Dewey:792.8028092. LCCN:2002-020447.

Audience: **u,f.**

Unger, Craig CT275.H3834U64 1988
Blue Blood: How Rebekah Harkness, One of the Richest Women in the World, Destroyed a Great American Family. Trade Cloth. HarperCollins Publishers. New York, NY. 1988. 388p. ISBN:0-688-05081-6, ISBN13: 978-0-688-05081-8. Dewey:973.92/092/4 B. LCCN:87-034761.

Audience: **g,l,u,f.**

Vaughan, David GV1788
Frederick Ashton and His Ballets. Ed. 2. Trade Cloth. Princeton Book Company Publishers. Hightstown, NJ. 570p. ISBN:1-85273-062-5, ISBN13: 978-1-85273-062-8. Dewey:792.8/2.

Audience: **u,f.**

Vaughan, David & Harris, GV1785.C85V38 1997
Melissa
Merce Cunningham: Fifty Years. Ed. 1. Trade Cloth. Aperture Foundation, Inc. New York, NY. 1997. 315p. ISBN:0-89381-767-8, ISBN13: 978-0-89381-767-1. Dewey:792.8092. LCCN:97-070518.

Audience: **u,f.**

Villella, Edward & Kaplan, GV1785.V56 A3
Larry
Prodigal Son: Dancing for Balanchine in a World of Pain and Magic. Trade Paper. Simon & Schuster. New York, NY. 1993. 320p. ISBN:0-671-79717-4, ISBN13: 978-0-671-79717-1. Dewey:792.8/028/092.

Audience: **u,f.**

Warren, Larry GV1580
Lester Horton: Modern Dance Pioneer. John Martin (Foreword by). Trade Paper. Princeton Book Company Publishers. Hightstown, NJ. 1992. 265p. ISBN:0-87127-165-6, ISBN13: 978-0-87127-165-5. Dewey:793.3/2/0924.

Audience: **g,l,u,f.**

Warren, Larry GV1785.S59W37 1990
Anna Sokolow: The Rebellious Spirit. Jerome Robbins (Introduction by). Trade Cloth. Princeton Book Company Publishers. Hightstown, NJ. 1991. 432p. ISBN:0-87127-162-1, ISBN13: 978-0-87127-162-4. Dewey:792.8/2/092 B. LCCN:90-063072.

Audience: **u,f.** *Choice, 1991.*

Weaver, John   GV1785.W39 R34 1985
The Life and Works of John Weaver: An Account of His Life,
Writings and Theatrical Productions, with an Annotated Reprint
of His Complete Publications. Dance Horizons. 1985.
ISBN:0-87127-139-7, ISBN13: 978-0-87127-139-6.
                                             Audience: **u,f.**

Wiley, Roland J.   GV1785.I88W55 1997
The Life and Ballets of Lev Ivanov: Choreographer of the
Nutcracker and Swan Lake. Trade Cloth. Oxford University
Press, Inc. New York, NY. 1997. 326p. ISBN:0-19-816567-6,
ISBN13: 978-0-19-816567-5. Dewey:792.8/2/092.
LCCN:96-024978.
                                     Audience: **u,f.** *Choice, 1998.*

Woolf, Vicki   GV1799.4
Dancing in the Vortex: The Story of Ida Rubinstein. Cloth Text.
Gordon & Breach Publishing Group. New York, NY. 1999.
204p. Choreography and Dance Studies, Vol. 20
ISBN:90-5755-087-3, ISBN13: 978-90-5755-087-4.
Dewey:792.8/092.
                                             Audience: **u,f.**

Yudkoff, Alvin   PN2287.M69
Gene Kelly: A Life of Dance and Dreams. Trade Cloth.
Watson-Guptill Publications, Inc. New York, NY. 2001. 240p.
ISBN:0-8230-8819-7, ISBN13: 978-0-8230-8819-5.
Dewey:791.43/028/092 B.
                                   Audience: **g,l,u.** *Choice, 2000.*

Dance Styles, Forms, and Traditions > Geographical Traditions > Africa

Ajayi, Omofolabo S.   GV1713.N6A53 1997
Yoruba Dance: Semiotics, Movement and Yoruba Body Attitude
in Communication. Trade Cloth. Africa World Press. Trenton,
NJ. 1998. 196p. ISBN:0-86543-563-4, ISBN13:
978-0-86543-563-6. Dewey:394.3. LCCN:97-013295.
                                             Audience: **u,f.**

Aschenbrenner, Joyce   GV1785.D82A73 2002
Katherine Dunham: Dancing a Life. Trade Cloth. University of
Illinois Press. Champaign, IL. 2002. 304p. ISBN:0-252-02759-0,
ISBN13: 978-0-252-02759-8. Dewey:792.8/028/092 B.
LCCN:2001-007541.
                                   Audience: **g,l,u,f.** *Choice, 2003.*

Emery, Lynne Fauley   GV1624.7.A34
Black Dance: From 1619 to Today. Trade Cloth. Princeton Book
Company Publishers. Hightstown, NJ. 1988. xii, 397p.
ISBN:0-916622-61-4, ISBN13: 978-0-916622-61-9.
Dewey:793.3089/96073. LCCN:88-061031.
                                             Audience: **g,l,u.**

Gorer, Geoffrey   GV1705
Africa Dances. Trade Paper. Eland Books. London, 2004. 292p.
ISBN:0-907871-18-6, ISBN13: 978-0-907871-18-7.
Dewey:793.31966.
                                             Audience: **g,l.**

Olatunji, Babatunde &   ML419.O385A3 2005
  Atkinson, Robert
The Beat of My Drum: An Autobiography. Joan Baez (Foreword
by), Eric Charry (Introduction by). Trade Paper. Temple
University Press. Philadelphia, PA. 2005. 272p.
ISBN:1-59213-354-1, ISBN13: 978-1-59213-354-3.
Dewey:786.9/163/092 B. LCCN:2004-053726.
                                     Audience: **u,f.** *Choice, 2005.*

Welsh-Asante, Kariamu   BH221
  (Editor)
The African Aesthetic: Keeper of the Traditions. Trade Cloth.
Greenwood Publishing Group, Inc. Portsmouth, NH. 1993. 280p.
Contributions in Afro-American and African Studies Ser., No.
153 ISBN:0-313-26549-6, ISBN13: 978-0-313-26549-5.
Dewey:111.8508996. LCCN:92-005438.
                                             Audience: **u,f.**

Welsh-Asante, Kariamu   GV1705.A47 1996
  (Editor)
African Dance: An Artistic, Historical and Philosophical Inquiry.
Trade Cloth. Africa World Press. Trenton, NJ. 1994. 350p.
ISBN:0-86543-197-3, ISBN13: 978-0-86543-197-3.
Dewey:792.8/096. LCCN:94-041598.
                                             Audience: **u,f.**

Dance Styles, Forms, and Traditions > Geographical Traditions > Americas

Browner, Tara   E98
Heartbeat of the People: Music and Dance of the Northern
Pow-Wow. Trade Paper. University of Illinois Press. Champaign,
IL. 2004. 200p. ISBN:0-252-07186-7, ISBN13:
978-0-252-07186-7. Dewey:781.62/97.
                                   Audience: **u,f.** *Choice, 2003, 2002.*

Downey, Greg   GV1796.C145D69 2005
Learning Capoeira: Lessons in Cunning from an Afro-Brazilian
Art. Trade Cloth. Oxford University Press, Inc. New York, NY.
2005. 286p. ISBN:0-19-517698-7, ISBN13: 978-0-19-517698-8.
Dewey:793.3/1981. LCCN:2004-054797.
                                             Audience: **u,f.**

Fergusson, Erna   E78.N65F42 1988
Dancing Gods: Indian Ceremonials of New Mexico and
Arizona. Tony Hillerman (Foreword by). Trade Paper. University
of New Mexico Press. Albuquerque, NM. 1988. 286p.
ISBN:0-8263-1050-8, ISBN13: 978-0-8263-1050-7.
Dewey:299/.74. LCCN:87-019231.
                                             Audience: **u,f.**

Fletcher, Alice C.   E98.G2F6 1994
Indian Games and Dances with Native Songs: Arranged from
American Indian Ceremonies and Sports. Helen Myers
(Introduction by). Paper Text. University of Nebraska Press.
Lincoln, NE. 1994. 139p. ISBN:0-8032-6886-6, ISBN13:
978-0-8032-6886-9. Dewey:394/.3/09701. LCCN:94-031508.
                                             Audience: **l,u,f.**

Groppa, Carlos G.   GV1796.T3G76 2003
The Tango in the United States: A History. Cloth Text.
McFarland & Company, Incorporated Publishers. Jefferson, NC.
2003. 239p. ISBN:0-7864-1406-5, ISBN13: 978-0-7864-1406-2.
Dewey:784.18/885/0973. LCCN:2003-009260.
Audience: **g,l,u,f.** *Choice, 2004.*

Heth, Charlotte (Editor)   E59.D35
Native American Dance: Ceremonies and Social Traditions.
Trade Paper. Fulcrum Publishing. Golden, CO. 1993. 208p.
ISBN:1-56373-021-9, ISBN13: 978-1-56373-021-4.
Dewey:394.3/0897. LCCN:92-034969.
Audience: **u,f.** *Choice, 1993.*

Kurath, Gertrude P.   ML3557.K87 2000
Iroquois Music and Dance: Ceremonial Arts of Two Seneca
Longhouses. Tara Browner (Introduction by). Trade Paper.
Dover Publications, Inc. Mineola, NY. 2000. 320p.
ISBN:0-486-41469-8, ISBN13: 978-0-486-41469-0.
Dewey:781.62/9755. LCCN:00-056982.
Audience: **u,f.**

Sandmel, Ben   ML3560.C25S26 1999
Zydeco!. Rick Olivier (Photographer). Trade Cloth. University
Press of Mississippi. Jackson, MS. 1999. 182p.
ISBN:1-57806-115-6, ISBN13: 978-1-57806-115-0.
Dewey:781.62/410763. LCCN:98-048793.
Audience: **g,l,u,f.**

Savigliano, Marta   PS3619.A86A85 2003
Angora Matta: Fatal Acts of North-South Translation = Actos
Fatales de Traduccion Norte-Sur. Library Binding. Wesleyan
University Press. Middletown, CT. 2003. 264p. Music/Culture
Ser. ISBN:0-8195-6598-9, ISBN13: 978-0-8195-6598-3.
Dewey:812/.6. LCCN:2003-041187.
Audience: **u,f.**

Savigliano, Marta E.   GV1796.T3S28 1995
Tango and the Political Economy of Passion. Trade Paper.
Westview Press. Boulder, CO. 1994. 312p. Institutional
Structures of Feeling Ser. ISBN:0-8133-1638-3, ISBN13:
978-0-8133-1638-3. Dewey:784.18/885. LCCN:94-032610.
Audience: **u,f.** *Choice, 1995.*

Speck, Frank G.   E98.P86
Cherokee Dance and Drama. Trade Paper. University of
Oklahoma Press. Norman, OK. 1993. 138p. Civilization of the
American Indian Ser. ISBN:0-8061-2580-2, ISBN13:
978-0-8061-2580-0. Dewey:793.3108997. LCCN:83-047839.
Audience: **u,f.**

Tembeck, Iro   GV1625.5.Q3
Dancing in Montreal: Seeds of a Choreographic History. Perfect.
Wesleyan University Press. Middletown, CT. 1994. 160p.
Studies in Dance History Ser. ISBN:0-9653519-3-9, ISBN13:
978-0-9653519-3-5. Dewey:792.8/09714.
Audience: **u,f.**

Dance Styles, Forms, and Traditions > Geographical Traditions > Asia

Banerji, Sures Chandra   ML120.I5 B36 1990
A Companion to Indian Music and Dance. Sri Satguru
Publications. 1990. ISBN:81-7030-240-4, ISBN13:
978-81-7030-240-7.
Audience: **g,l,u,f.**

Fraleigh, Sondra Horton   GV1783.2.B87F73 1999
Dancing into Darkness: Butoh, Zen, and Japan. Cloth Text.
University of Pittsburgh Press. Pittsburgh, PA. 1999. 192p.
ISBN:0-8229-4098-1, ISBN13: 978-0-8229-4098-2.
Dewey:792.8/0952. LCCN:98-058109.
Audience: **u,f.** *Choice, 2000.*

Gaston, Anne-Marie   GV1796.B4G38 1996
Bharata Natyam from Temple to Theatre. Trade Cloth. Manohar
Publications. New Delhi, 1996. 403p. ISBN:81-7304-146-6,
ISBN13: 978-81-7304-146-4. Dewey:793.31954.
LCCN:97-904128.
Audience: **u,f.** *Choice, 1998.*

Ginn, Victoria & Rizzoli   GV1588.6.G56 1990
The Spirited Earth. Keri Hulmer (Foreword by). Trade Cloth.
Rizzoli International Publications, Inc. New York, NY. 1990.
192p. ISBN:0-8478-1167-0, ISBN13: 978-0-8478-1167-0.
Dewey:793.3. LCCN:90-034682.
Audience: **u,f.**

Hesselink, Nathan   ML3752.7.C5
P'ungmul: South Korean Drumming and Dance. University of
Chicago Press. 2006. Chicago Studies in Ethnomusicology
ISBN:0-226-33093-1, ISBN13: 978-0-226-33093-8.
Audience: **u,f.**

Hoffman, Ethan   GV1783.2.B87 1987
(Photographer)
Butoh: Dance of the Dark Soul. Mark Holburn, Tatsumi Hijikata
& Yukio Mishima (Contribution by), Haven O'More (Afterword
by). Trade Cloth. Aperture Foundation, Inc. New York, NY.
1987. 128p. ISBN:0-89381-216-1, ISBN13: 978-0-89381-216-4.
Dewey:792.8/022/2. LCCN:85-052457.
Audience: **u,f.** *Choice, 1988.*

Lorrick, Peter   ML1751.C4S58 1997
Chinese Opera: Images and Stories. Siu Wang-Ngai
(Photographer). Trade Cloth. University of British Columbia
Press. Vancouver, BC. 1997. 250p. ISBN:0-7748-0592-7,
ISBN13: 978-0-7748-0592-6. Dewey:782.1/0951.
LCCN:96-910495.
Audience: **u,f.**

Massey, Reginald & Massey,   GV1693
Jamila
The Dances of India: A General Guide and a Users' Handbook.
Trade Cloth. Asia Publishing House, Inc. Cincinnati, OH. 1992.
xix, 164p. ISBN:0-317-05152-0, ISBN13: 978-0-317-05152-0.
Dewey:793.31/954.
Audience: **l,u,f.**

Matida, Kasyo   **GV1695**
Odori: Japanese Dance. Trade Cloth. Kegan Paul International,
Ltd. London, 2005. 70p. ISBN:0-7103-1019-6, ISBN13:
978-0-7103-1019-4. Dewey:793.31952.

Audience: **g,l.** *Choice, 2006.*

Schwartz, Susan L.   **PN2881.R29 2004**
Rasa: Performing the Divine in India. Trade Cloth. Kegan Paul
International, Ltd. London, 2004. 160p. ISBN:0-231-13144-5,
ISBN13: 978-0-231-13144-5. Dewey:791/.0954.
LCCN:2003-062701.

Audience: **u,f.** *Choice, 2005.*

Shay, Anthony &   **GV1798.5.B45 2005**
Sellers-Young, Barbara (Editors)
Belly Dance: Orientalism, Transnationalism, and Harem Fantasy.
Paper Text. Mazda Publishers, Inc. Costa Mesa, CA. 2005.
296p. Bibliotheca Iranica Ser., Vol. 6:Performing Arts Ser.
ISBN:1-56859-183-7, ISBN13: 978-1-56859-183-4.
Dewey:793.3. LCCN:2005-050852.

Audience: **u,f.**

Singer, Noel F.   **GV1703.B95S46 1995**
Burmese Dance and Theatre. Cloth Text. Oxford University
Press, Inc. New York, NY. 1996. 106p. Images of Asia Ser.
ISBN:967-65-3086-7, ISBN13: 978-967-65-3086-8.
Dewey:792/.09591. LCCN:94-041033.

Audience: **g,l,u.** *Choice, 1996.*

Van Zile, Judy   **GV1703.K7V36 2001**
Perspectives on Korean Dance. Library Binding. Wesleyan
University Press. Middletown, CT. 2001. 392p.
ISBN:0-8195-6493-1, ISBN13: 978-0-8195-6493-1.
Dewey:793.3/19519. LCCN:2001-002709.

Audience: **u,f.**

Wong, Deborah A.   **GN635.T4W66 2001**
Sounding the Center: History and Aesthetics in Thai Buddhist
Performance. Trade Cloth. University of Chicago Press.
Chicago, IL. 2001. 336p. Chicago Studies in Ethnomusicology
ISBN:0-226-90585-3, ISBN13: 978-0-226-90585-3.
Dewey:306.48409593. LCCN:00-033775.

Audience: **u,f.**

Dance Styles, Forms, and Traditions > Geographical Traditions > Europe

Brooks, Lynn Matluck & de   **GV1673.B76 2002**
Esquivel Navarro, Juan
The Art of Dancing in Seventeenth-Century Spain: Juan de
Esquivel Navarro and His World. Trade Cloth. Bucknell
University Press. Cranbury, NJ. 2003. 336p.
ISBN:0-8387-5531-3, ISBN13: 978-0-8387-5531-0.
Dewey:792.6/2/094609032. LCCN:2002-074511.

Audience: **u,f.**

Gitelman, Claudia (Editor,   **GV1785**
Compiled by)
Liebe Hanya: Mary Wigman's Letters to Hanya Holm. Hedwig
Müller (Introduction by). Trade Paper. University of Wisconsin
Press. Chicago, IL. 2004. 272p. Studies in Dance History
ISBN:0-299-19074-9, ISBN13: 978-0-299-19074-3.
Dewey:792.8 B. LCCN:2003-005657.

Audience: **u,f.**

Sharp, Cecil J.   **GV1796.S9 S52**
Sword Dances of Northern England Together with the Horn
Dance of Abbots Bromley. Trade Paper. Kessinger Publishing,
LLC. Whitefish, MT. 2003. ISBN:0-7661-7443-3, ISBN13:
978-0-7661-7443-6. Dewey:793.35.

Audience: **u,f.**

Torp, Lisbet   **GV1743.T67 1990**
Chain and Round Dance Patterns. Trade Cloth. Museum
Tusculanum Press. Copenhagen S, 1990. 511p.
ISBN:87-7289-101-7, ISBN13: 978-87-7289-101-9.
Dewey:793.3. LCCN:95-222565.

Audience: **l,u.**

Dance Styles, Forms, and Traditions > Geographical Traditions > Mediterranean and the Near East

Al-Zayer, Penni   **GV1704.A52 2003**
Middle Eastern Dance. Trade Paper. Facts On File, Inc. New
York, NY. 2004. 112p. World of Dance Ser.
ISBN:0-7910-7775-6, ISBN13: 978-0-7910-7775-7.
Dewey:793.3/1953. LCCN:2003-016808.

Audience: **g,l.**

Berk, Fred   **BM198**
Chasidic Dance. Trade Paper. URJ Press. New York, NY. 1975.
ISBN:0-8074-0083-1, ISBN13: 978-0-8074-0083-8.
Dewey:793.3.

Audience: **u,f.**

Cowan, Jane K.   **GV1588.6.C69 1990**
Dance and the Body Politic in Northern Greece. Trade Paper.
Princeton University Press. Princeton, NJ. 1990. 310p. Princeton
Modern Greek Studies ISBN:0-691-02854-0, ISBN13:
978-0-691-02854-5. Dewey:792.8/09495. LCCN:90-030232.

Audience: **u,f.**

Lawler, Lillian B.   **GV1611.L37**
The Dance in Ancient Greece. Trade Paper. Books on Demand.
Ann Arbor, MI. 1984. 160p. Dance 657 Ser.
ISBN:0-7837-8196-2, ISBN13: 978-0-7837-8196-9.
Dewey:793.31938. LCCN:65-013203.

Audience: **u,f.**

Mishkin, Julie Russo &   **GV1798**
Schill, Marta
The Compleat Belly Dancer. Mass Market. Doubleday
Publishing. New York, NY. 1973. 160p. ISBN:0-385-03556-X,
ISBN13: 978-0-385-03556-9. Dewey:793.3. LCCN:72-092407.

Audience: **g,l,u,f.**

Ramazani, Nesta   GV1785.R34A3 2001
The Dance of the Rose and the Nightingale. Trade Cloth.
Syracuse University Press. Syracuse, NY. 2001. 272p. Gender,
Culture, and Politics in the Middle East Ser.
ISBN:0-8156-0727-X, ISBN13: 978-0-8156-0727-4.
Dewey:792.8/028/092 B. LCCN:2001-054940.
Audience: **u,f.** *Choice, 2002.*

Richards, Tazz (Editor)   GV1798.5
The Belly Dance Book: Rediscovering the Oldest Dance. Kajira
Djoumahna (Introduction by). Trade Paper. Backbeat Press.
Concord, CA. 2000. 208p. ISBN:0-9700247-0-3, ISBN13:
978-0-9700247-0-1. Dewey:793.3.
Audience: **g,l,u.**

Shay, Anthony   GV1588.45.S5 2002
Choreographic Politics: State Folk Companies, Representation
and Power. Library Binding. University Press of New England.
Lebanon, NH. 2002. 252p. ISBN:0-8195-6520-2, ISBN13:
978-0-8195-6520-4. Dewey:793.3/1. LCCN:2001-008180.
Audience: **u,f.** *Choice, 2003.*

Shay, Anthony   GV1588.6.S53 1999
Choreophobia: Solo Improvised Dance in the Iranian World.
Trade Cloth. Mazda Publishers, Inc. Costa Mesa, CA. 1999.
266p. Bibliotheca Iranica Ser., Vol. 5 ISBN:1-56859-083-0,
ISBN13: 978-1-56859-083-7. Dewey:792.8. LCCN:99-028112.
Audience: **u,f.**

Shay, Anthony &   GV1798.5.B45 2005
  Sellers-Young, Barbara (Editors)
Belly Dance: Orientalism, Transnationalism, and Harem Fantasy.
Paper Text. Mazda Publishers, Inc. Costa Mesa, CA. 2005.
296p. Bibliotheca Iranica Ser., Vol. 6:Performing Arts Ser.
ISBN:1-56859-183-7, ISBN13: 978-1-56859-183-4.
Dewey:793.3. LCCN:2005-050852.
Audience: **u,f.**

Dance Styles, Forms, and Traditions > Geographical Traditions > Oceania

Alejandro, Reynaldo G.   GV1703.P4 A43
Philippine Dance: Mainstream and Crosscurrents. Vera-Reyes.
1978.
Audience: **l,u,f.**

Allen, Thomas   GV1796.F35T56 1996
New Song and Dance from the Central Pacific: Creating and
Performing the Fatele of Tokelau in the Islands and in New
Zealand. Trade Cloth. Pendragon Press. Hillsdale, NY. 1996.
180p. Dance and Music Ser., No. 9 ISBN:0-945193-77-7,
ISBN13: 978-0-945193-77-7. Dewey:793.3/1. LCCN:96-012561.
Audience: **u,f.**

Kaeppler, Adrienne L.   GV1728.T66 K34 1993
Poetry in Motion: Studies in Tongan Dance. Vava'u Press. 1993.
ISBN:982-213-003-1, ISBN13: 978-982-213-003-4.
Audience: **u,f.**

Kaeppler, Adrienne L.   GV1796.H8 H85 1993
Hula Pahu: Hawaiian Drum Dances: Ha'a and Hula Pahu Sacred
Movements. Kaupena Wong (Introduction by). Trade Paper.
Bishop Museum Press. Honolulu, HI. 1992. 290p. Bulletins in
Anthropology Ser., No. 3 ISBN:0-930897-55-2, ISBN13:
978-0-930897-55-0. Dewey:793.3/19969.
Audience: **u,f.**

Malinowski, Bronislaw   DU740.42
Argonauts of the Western Pacific: An Account of Native
Enterprise and Adventure in the Archipelagoes of Melanesian
New Guinea. James George Frazer (Preface by). Trade Cloth.
Library Reprints, Inc. Temecula, CA. 1922. 527p.
ISBN:0-7222-2643-8, ISBN13: 978-0-7222-2643-8.
Dewey:306/.0899912.
Audience: **u,f.**

Ness, Sally Ann   GV1796.S57N47 1992
ⓔ Body, Movement, and Culture: Kinesthetic and Visual
Symbolism in a Philippine Community. E-Book. NetLibrary,
Inc. Boulder, CO. 1992. ISBN:0-585-17279-X, ISBN13:
978-0-585-17279-8. Dewey:793.3/19599.
Audience: **u,f.**

Stillman, Amy K.   GV1796.H8S75 1998
Sacred Hula: The Hula Ala Apapa. Trade Paper. Bishop
Museum Press. Honolulu, HI. 1998. Bulletin in Anthropology
Ser., No. 8 ISBN:0-930897-73-0, ISBN13: 978-0-930897-73-4.
Dewey:793.3/19969. LCCN:97-052344.
Audience: **u,f.**

Van Zile, Judy A.   GV1624.H3
The Japanese Bon Dance in Hawaii. Ellen Schroeder
(Illustrator). Trade Paper. Press Pacifica, Ltd. Kailua, HI. 1982.
96p. ISBN:0-916630-27-7, ISBN13: 978-0-916630-27-0.
Dewey:793.3/1952.
Audience: **u,f.**

Dance Styles, Forms, and Traditions > African American Dance

Adamczyk, Alice J.   Z7514.D2A33 1989
Black Dance: An Annotated Bibliography. Library Binding.
Garland Publishing, Inc. New York, NY. 1989. 250p. Books on
Music ISBN:0-8240-8808-5, ISBN13: 978-0-8240-8808-8.
Dewey:016.7933/2. LCCN:84-048403.
Audience: **g,l,u,f.** *Choice, 1989.*

Aschenbrenner, Joyce   GV1785.D82A73 2002
Katherine Dunham: Dancing a Life. Trade Cloth. University of
Illinois Press. Champaign, IL. 2002. 304p. ISBN:0-252-02759-0,
ISBN13: 978-0-252-02759-8. Dewey:792.8/028/092 B.
LCCN:2001-007541.
Audience: **g,l,u,f.** *Choice, 2003.*

Aschenbrenner, Joyce   GV1624.7.A34 A83
Katherine Dunham: Reflections on the Social and Political
Contexts of Afro-American Dance. CORD Inc. 1981.
Audience: **u,f.**

Bogle, Donald   PN1995.9.N4B59 2005
Bright Boulevards, Bold Dreams: The Story of Black
Hollywood. Trade Cloth. Ballantine Books. New York, NY.
2005. 432p. ISBN:0-345-45418-9, ISBN13: 978-0-345-45418-8.
Dewey:791.4302/8/092396073. LCCN:2004-054781.
                                          Audience: **l,u.**

DeFrantz, Thomas (Editor)   GV1624.7.A34.D38
Dancing Many Drums: Excavations in African American Dance.
Trade Paper. University of Wisconsin Press. Chicago, IL. 2001.
xiii, 366p. ISBN:0-299-17314-3, ISBN13: 978-0-299-17314-2.
Dewey:793.3/089/96073. LCCN:2001-001943.
                              Audience: **u,f.** *Choice, 2002.*

DeFrantz, Thomas F.   GV1785.T32
Dancing Revelations: Alvin Ailey's Embodiment of African
American Culture. Trade Paper. Oxford University Press, Inc.
New York, NY. 2006. 318p. ISBN:0-19-530171-4, ISBN13:
978-0-19-530171-7. Dewey:792.8/028/092 B.
                                          Audience: **u,f.**

Dixon Gottschild, Brenda   GV1624.7.A34 G68
The Black Dancing Body: A Geography from Coon to Cool.
Trade Paper, Perfect. Palgrave Macmillan. New York, NY. 2005.
352p. ISBN:1-4039-7121-8, ISBN13: 978-1-4039-7121-0.
Dewey:793.3/089/96073.
                                          Audience: **u,f.**

Dunham, Katherine   GV1785.D82K35 2006
Kaiso!: Writings by and about Katherine Dunham. VeVe A.
Clark & Sarah East Johnson (Editors). Trade Cloth. University
of Wisconsin Press. Chicago, IL. 2006. 718p. Studies in Dance
History ISBN:0-299-21270-X, ISBN13: 978-0-299-21270-4.
Dewey:792.8/028/092 B. LCCN:2005-008258.
                              Audience: **u,f.** *Choice, 2006.*

Dunning, Jennifer   NX512.H64D86 2001
Geoffrey Holder: A Life in Theater, Dance and Art. Trade Cloth.
Harry N. Abrams, Inc. New York, NY. 2001. 238p.
ISBN:0-8109-1392-5, ISBN13: 978-0-8109-1392-9.
Dewey:700/.92 B. LCCN:2001-004552.
                                          Audience: **u,f.**

Emery, Lynne Fauley   GV1624.7.A34
Black Dance: From 1619 to Today. Trade Cloth. Princeton Book
Company Publishers. Hightstown, NJ. 1988. xii, 397p.
ISBN:0-916622-61-4, ISBN13: 978-0-916622-61-9.
Dewey:793.3089/96073. LCCN:88-061031.
                                          Audience: **g,l,u.**

Fine, Elizabeth C.   GV1624.7.A34F56 2003
Soulstepping: African American Step Shows. Trade Cloth.
University of Illinois Press. Champaign, IL. 2002. 208p.
ISBN:0-252-02475-3, ISBN13: 978-0-252-02475-7.
Dewey:793.3/089/96073. LCCN:2002-004789.
                              Audience: **u,f.** *Choice, 2003.*

Fishman, Katharine Davis   GV1786.A35F57 2004
Attitude!: Eight Young Dancers Come of Age at the Ailey

School. Trade Cloth. Penguin Group (USA) Inc. New York, NY.
2004. 304p. ISBN:1-58542-355-6, ISBN13: 978-1-58542-355-2.
Dewey:792.8/09747/1. LCCN:2004-049847.
                                          Audience: **g,l.**

Gottschild, Brenda D.   PN1590
Digging the Africanist Presence in American Performance:
Dance and Other Contexts. Trade Cloth. Greenwood Publishing
Group, Inc. Portsmouth, NH. 1996. 224p. Contributions in
Afro-American and African Studies Ser., No. 179
ISBN:0-313-29684-7, ISBN13: 978-0-313-29684-0.
Dewey:791/.08996/073. LCCN:95-020558.
                              Audience: **u,f.** *Choice, 1997.*

Gottschild, Brenda Dixon   GV1785.W393
Waltzing in the Dark: African American Vaudeville and Race
Politics in the Swing Era. Cloth over Boards. Palgrave
Macmillan. New York, NY. 1999. 288p. ISBN:0-312-21418-9,
ISBN13: 978-0-312-21418-0. Dewey:792.808996.
                              Audience: **u,f.** *Choice, 2000.*

Graves, Nadine George   GV1785.A1G46 2000
The Royalty of Negro Vaudeville: The Whitman Sisters and the
Negotiation of Race, Gender and Class in African American
Theater 1900-1940. Cloth over Boards. Palgrave Macmillan.
New York, NY. 2000. 208p. ISBN:0-312-22562-8, ISBN13:
978-0-312-22562-9. Dewey:792.7/092/396073 B.
LCCN:99-088103.
                              Audience: **u,f.** *Choice, 2001.*

Haskins, James   GV1624.7.A34H37 1990
Black Dance in America: A History Through Its People. Trade
Cloth. HarperCollins Publishers. New York, NY. 1990. 240p.
ISBN:0-690-04659-6, ISBN13: 978-0-690-04659-5.
Dewey:792.8/089/96073. LCCN:89-035529.
                                          Audience: **g,l,u.**

Manning, Susan   GV1627.7.A34M36 2004
Modern Dance, Negro Dance: Race in Motion. Trade Cloth.
University of Minnesota Press. Minneapolis, MN. 2004. 296p.
ISBN:0-8166-3736-9, ISBN13: 978-0-8166-3736-2.
Dewey:792.8/089/96073. LCCN:2003-022003.
                                          Audience: **u,f.**

Mr. Fresh and the Supreme   GV1796.B74F74 1984
**   Rockers Staff**
Breakdancing. Trade Paper. HarperCollins Publishers. New
York, NY. 1984. 128p. ISBN:0-380-88153-5, ISBN13:
978-0-380-88153-6. Dewey:793.3. LCCN:84-006332.
                                          Audience: **g,l,u,f.**

Perpener, John O. III   GV1603
African-American Concert Dance: The Harlem Renaissance and
Beyond. Trade Paper. University of Illinois Press. Champaign,
IL. 2005. 336p. ISBN:0-252-07261-8, ISBN13:
978-0-252-07261-1. Dewey:792.8/089/96073.
                              Audience: **u,f.** *Choice, 2002.*

Semmes, Clovis E.   PN2277.C42R44 2006
The Regal Theater and Black Culture. Cloth over Boards.

Palgrave Macmillan. New York, NY. 2006. 304p.
ISBN:1-4039-7171-4, ISBN13: 978-1-4039-7171-5.
Dewey:792.089/96073077311. LCCN:2005-054435.

Audience: **u,f.**

Stearns, Jean & Stearns,   GV1624.7.A34S74 1994
Marshall W.
Jazz Dance: The Story of American Vernacular Dance. Ed. 2.
Brenda Bufalino (Introduction by). Trade Paper. Da Capo Press,
Inc. Cambridge, MA. 1994. 508p. ISBN:0-306-80553-7,
ISBN13: 978-0-306-80553-0. Dewey:793.3/089/96073.
LCCN:93-040957.

Audience: **g,l,u.**

Tracy, Robert   GV1786.A42T73 2004
Ailey Spirit: The Journey of an American Dance Company.
Trade Cloth. Stewart, Tabori & Chang. New York, NY. 2004.
168p. ISBN:1-58479-364-3, ISBN13: 978-1-58479-364-9.
Dewey:792.8/0973. LCCN:2004-005580.

Audience: **g,l,u,f.**

White, Shane & White,   E185.86.W4388 1998
Graham J.
Stylin': African American Expressive Culture from Its
Beginnings to the Zoot Suit. Book, Other. Cornell University
Press. Ithaca, NY. 1998. 320p. ISBN:0-8014-3179-4, ISBN13:
978-0-8014-3179-1. Dewey:305.896/073. LCCN:97-038507.

Audience: **l,u,f.** *Choice, 1998.*

Dance Styles, Forms, and Traditions > African Caribbean Dance

Aschenbrenner, Joyce   GV1785.D82A73 2002
Katherine Dunham: Dancing a Life. Trade Cloth. University of
Illinois Press. Champaign, IL. 2002. 304p. ISBN:0-252-02759-0,
ISBN13: 978-0-252-02759-8. Dewey:792.8/028/092 B.
LCCN:2001-007541.

Audience: **g,l,u,f.** *Choice, 2003.*

Browning, Barbara   GV1637.B76 1995
e Samba: Resistance in Motion. E-Book. NetLibrary, Inc.
Boulder, CO. 1995. ISBN:0-585-00131-6, ISBN13:
978-0-585-00131-9. Dewey:306.4/84.

Audience: **u,f.**

Daniel, Yvonne   GV1769.R8D32 1995
Rumba: Dance and Social Change in Contemporary Cuba. Trade
Cloth. Indiana University Press. Bloomington, IN. 1995. 208p.
Blacks in the Diaspora Ser. ISBN:0-253-31605-7, ISBN13:
978-0-253-31605-9. Dewey:784.18/88. LCCN:94-034363.

Audience: **u,f.** *Choice, 1996.*

Delgado, Celeste F. &   GV1626.E84 1997
Munoz, Jose E. (Editors)
Everynight Life: Culture and Dance in Latino America. Library
Binding. Duke University Press. Durham, NC. 1997. 368p. Latin
America Otherwise Ser. ISBN:0-8223-1926-8, ISBN13:
978-0-8223-1926-9. Dewey:792.8/098. LCCN:96-043796.

Audience: **u,f.** *Choice, 1998.*

Dunham, Katherine   F1916.D8 1994
Island Possessed. Trade Paper. University of Chicago Press.
Chicago, IL. 1994. 287p. ISBN:0-226-17113-2, ISBN13:
978-0-226-17113-5. Dewey:972.94. LCCN:93-046117.

Audience: **u,f.**

Dunham, Katherine   GV1785.D82K35 2006
Kaiso!: Writings by and about Katherine Dunham. VeVe A.
Clark & Sarah East Johnson (Editors). Trade Cloth. University
of Wisconsin Press. Chicago, IL. 2006. 718p. Studies in Dance
History ISBN:0-299-21270-X, ISBN13: 978-0-299-21270-4.
Dewey:792.8/028/092 B. LCCN:2005-008258.

Audience: **u,f.** *Choice, 2006.*

Dunham, Katherine   GV1632.H2
The Dances of Haiti. Patricia Cummings (Photographer). Trade
Cloth. C A A S Publications. Los Angeles, CA. 1983. 78p.
Special Publications, Vol. 2 ISBN:0-934934-17-7, ISBN13:
978-0-934934-17-6. Dewey:793.3/19729/4.

Audience: **g,l,u,f.**

Emery, Lynne Fauley   GV1624.7.A34
Black Dance: From 1619 to Today. Trade Cloth. Princeton Book
Company Publishers. Hightstown, NJ. 1988. xii, 397p.
ISBN:0-916622-61-4, ISBN13: 978-0-916622-61-9.
Dewey:793.3089/96073. LCCN:88-061031.

Audience: **g,l,u.**

Lekis, Lisa   GV1626
Folk Dances of Latin America. Trade Paper. Books on Demand.
Ann Arbor, MI. 312p. ISBN:0-598-45934-0, ISBN13:
978-0-598-45934-3. Dewey:793.31. LCCN:58-007802.

Audience: **g,l.**

Nettleford, Rex   GV1786.N26N39 1985
Dance Jamaica: Cultural Definition and Artistic Discovery, the
National Dance Theatre Company of Jamaica 1962-1983. Trade
Cloth. Grove/Atlantic, Inc. New York, NY. 1985. 320p.
ISBN:0-394-54316-5, ISBN13: 978-0-394-54316-1.
Dewey:793.3/2/097292. LCCN:84-048415.

Audience: **u,f.** *Choice, 1985.*

Savigliano, Marta E.   GV1796.T3S28 1995
Tango and the Political Economy of Passion. Trade Paper.
Westview Press. Boulder, CO. 1994. 312p. Institutional
Structures of Feeling Ser. ISBN:0-8133-1638-3, ISBN13:
978-0-8133-1638-3. Dewey:784.18/885. LCCN:94-032610.

Audience: **u,f.** *Choice, 1995.*

Vega, Marta Moreno   F128.9.P85V438 2004
When the Spirits Dance Mambo: Growing up Nuyorican in el
Barrio. Trade Paper. Crown Publishing Group. New York, NY.
2004. 288p. ISBN:1-4000-4924-5, ISBN13: 978-1-4000-4924-0.
Dewey:974.7/004687295/0922. LCCN:2003-027912.

Audience: **l,u.**

Dance Styles, Forms, and Traditions > Latin American Dance

Browning, Barbara   GV1637.B76 1995
e Samba: Resistance in Motion. E-Book. NetLibrary, Inc.
Boulder, CO. 1995. ISBN:0-585-00131-6, ISBN13:
978-0-585-00131-9. Dewey:306.4/84.

Audience: **u,f.**

Collier, Simon, et al.   GV1796.T3
Tango!: The Dance, the Song, the Story. Artemis Cooper, Maria
S. Azzi & Richard Martin (Authors). Trade Paper. Thames &
Hudson. New York, NY. 1997. 208p. ISBN:0-500-27979-9,
ISBN13: 978-0-500-27979-3. Dewey:793.3/1982.
LCCN:95-006078.

Audience: **g,l,u,f.**

Delgado, Celeste F. &   GV1626.E84 1997
  Munoz, Jose E. (Editors)
Everynight Life: Culture and Dance in Latino America. Library
Binding. Duke University Press. Durham, NC. 1997. 368p. Latin
America Otherwise Ser. ISBN:0-8223-1926-8, ISBN13:
978-0-8223-1926-9. Dewey:792.8/098. LCCN:96-043796.
Audience: **u,f.** *Choice, 1998.*

Guillermoprieto, Alma   F1765.3.G85 2004
Dancing with Cuba: A Memoir of the Revolution. Trade Cloth.
Knopf Publishing Group. New York, NY. 2004. 304p.
ISBN:0-375-42093-2, ISBN13: 978-0-375-42093-1.
Dewey:972.9106/4. LCCN:2003-044200.

Audience: **u,f.**

Lekis, Lisa   GV1626
Folk Dances of Latin America. Trade Paper. Books on Demand.
Ann Arbor, MI. 312p. ISBN:0-598-45934-0, ISBN13:
978-0-598-45934-3. Dewey:793.31. LCCN:58-007802.

Audience: **g,l.**

Lewis, J. Lowell   GV1796.C145.L48 1992
Ring of Liberation: Deceptive Discourse in Brazilian Capoeira.
Robert F. Thompson (Foreword by). Trade Cloth. University of
Chicago Press. Chicago, IL. 1992. 294p. ISBN:0-226-47682-0,
ISBN13: 978-0-226-47682-7. Dewey:793.31981.
LCCN:92-003749.

Audience: **u,f.** *Choice, 1993.*

Savigliano, Marta E.   GV1796.T3S28 1995
Tango and the Political Economy of Passion. Trade Paper.
Westview Press. Boulder, CO. 1994. 312p. Institutional
Structures of Feeling Ser. ISBN:0-8133-1638-3, ISBN13:
978-0-8133-1638-3. Dewey:784.18/885. LCCN:94-032610.
Audience: **u,f.** *Choice, 1995.*

Vianna, Hermano   98-22170 [ML]
The Mystery of Samba: Popular Music and National Identity in
Brazil. John C. Chasteen (Translator). Trade Paper. University of
North Carolina Press. Chapel Hill, NC. 1999. 168p. Latin
America in Translation Ser. ISBN:0-8078-4766-6, ISBN13:
978-0-8078-4766-4. Dewey:784.18/88. LCCN:98-022170.
Audience: **l,u,f.** *Choice, 1999.*

Dance Styles, Forms, and Traditions > Spanish Dance

Brooks, Lynn Matluck   GV1783.5.B76 1988
The Dances of the Processions of Seville in Spain's Golden
Age. Ed. Reichenberger. 1988. ISBN:3-923593-65-1, ISBN13:
978-3-923593-65-1.

Audience: **u,f.**

Brooks, Lynn Matluck & de   GV1673.B76 2002
  Esquivel Navarro, Juan
The Art of Dancing in Seventeenth-Century Spain: Juan de
Esquivel Navarro and His World. Trade Cloth. Bucknell
University Press. Cranbury, NJ. 2003. 336p.
ISBN:0-8387-5531-3, ISBN13: 978-0-8387-5531-0.
Dewey:792.6/2/094609032. LCCN:2002-074511.

Audience: **u,f.**

Dolmetsch, Mabel   GV1618
Dances of Spain and Italy from 1400-1600. Paper Text. Da
Capo Press, Inc. Cambridge, MA. 1975. xii, 174p. Series in
Dance ISBN:0-306-70726-8, ISBN13: 978-0-306-70726-1.
Dewey:793.3/1. LCCN:74-028450.

Audience: **u,f.**

Grut, Marina   GV1673
The Bolero School: an illustrated history of the Bolero, the
Seguidillas and the Escuela Bolera : syllabus and dances. Lorca,
Alberto (Prologue). [Alton, Hampshire, UK] : Dance Books.
2002. ISBN:1-85273-081-1, ISBN13: 978-1-85273-081-9.

Audience: **u,f.**

Haas, Ken (Photographer)   GV1796.F55H33 2000
Flamenco!. Gwynne Edwards (Text by). Trade Cloth. Thames &
Hudson. New York, NY. 2000. 176p. ISBN:0-500-51018-0,
ISBN13: 978-0-500-51018-6. Dewey:793.3/1946.
LCCN:00-101121.

Audience: **g,l,u,f.**

Hughes, Russell Meriwether   GV1673
Spanish Dancing. Trade Paper. Books on Demand. Ann Arbor,
MI. 208p. ISBN:0-598-55498-X, ISBN13: 978-0-598-55498-7.
Dewey:793.31. LCCN:48-006696.

Audience: **g,l,u,f.**

Ivanova, Anna   GV1673.I9
The Dance in Spain. Praeger Publishers. 1970.
Audience: **g,l,u,f.**

Lewis, Daniel (Editor)   GV1626
Dance in Hispanic Cultures. UK-B Format Paperback. Gordon
& Breach Publishing Group. New York, NY. 1994. 136p.
Choreography and Dance Studies, Vol. 3, Pt. 4
ISBN:3-7186-5534-9, ISBN13: 978-3-7186-5534-2.
Dewey:792.8205.

Audience: **u,f.**

Pohren, D. E.   GV1674.A6
The Art of Flamenco. Cloth Text. Society of Spanish Studies. 1990. 225p. ISBN:0-933224-10-9, ISBN13: 978-0-933224-10-0. Dewey:793.319468.

Audience: **u,f.**

Saura, Carlos   PN1998.3.S28A5 2003
Carlos Saura: Interviews. Linda M. Willem (Editor). Trade Cloth. University Press of Mississippi. Jackson, MS. 2003. 208p. Conversations with Filmmakers Ser. ISBN:1-57806-494-5, ISBN13: 978-1-57806-494-6. Dewey:791.43/0233/092. LCCN:2002-003009.

Audience: **u,f.**

Schreiner, Claus   ML3712.F613 1990
Flamenco: Gypsy Dance and Music from Andalusia. Mollie Comerford Peters (Translator). Trade Cloth. Hal Leonard Corporation. Milwaukee, WI. 1990. 178p. ISBN:0-931340-25-X, ISBN13: 978-0-931340-25-3. Dewey:784.1/882. LCCN:89-048450.

Audience: **u,f.**

Taylor, Julie   GV1796.T3T39 1998
Paper Tangos. Trade Paper. Duke University Press. Durham, NC. 1998. 160p. Public Planet Bks. ISBN:0-8223-2191-2, ISBN13: 978-0-8223-2191-0. Dewey:793.3/3. LCCN:97-031240.

Audience: **u,f.**

Vittucci, Matteo M. & Goya,   GV1673
Carola
The Language of Spanish Dance. Louis Gioial (Illustrator), Richard Cragun (Foreword by). Trade Paper. University of Oklahoma Press. Norman, OK. 1993. 320p. ISBN:0-8061-2532-2, ISBN13: 978-0-8061-2532-9. Dewey:793.3/1946/014. LCCN:89-048953.

Audience: **u,f.** *Choice, 1991.*

Dance Styles, Forms, and Traditions > Sacred and Liturgical Dance

Adams, Doug &   GV1741.D24 1990
Apostolos-Cappadona, Diane (Editors)
Dance As Religious Studies. Trade Paper. Crossroad Publishing Company. New York, NY. 1990. 256p. ISBN:0-8245-0988-9, ISBN13: 978-0-8245-0988-0. Dewey:792.8. LCCN:89-028388.

Audience: **u,f.** *Choice, 1990.*

Arbeau, Thoinot   GV1590
Orchesographie. Trade Cloth. Georg Olms Verlag AG. Hildesheim, 1989. 104p. ISBN:3-487-06697-1, ISBN13: 978-3-487-06697-4. Dewey:793.3.

Audience: **u,f.**

Bandem, I. Made & DeBoer,   GV1703.I532B34322
Frederick E.
Balinese Dance in Transition: Kaja and Kelod. Ed. 2. Trade Cloth. Oxford University Press, Inc. New York, NY. 1996. 180p. ISBN:967-65-3071-9, ISBN13: 978-967-65-3071-4. Dewey:793.3/19598/6. LCCN:94-041032.

Audience: **u,f.** *Choice, 1996.*

Davies, J.G.   GV1783.5.D38 1984
Liturgical Dance: An Historical, Theological, and Practical Handbook. SCM. 1984. ISBN:0-334-00905-7, ISBN13: 978-0-334-00905-4.

Audience: **u,f.**

Fleurant, Gerdes   ML3197
Dancing Spirits: Rhythms and Rituals of Haitian Vodun, the Rada Rite. Trade Cloth. Greenwood Publishing Group, Inc. Portsmouth, NH. 1996. 240p. Contributions to the Study of Music and Dance Ser., Vol. 42 ISBN:0-313-29718-5, ISBN13: 978-0-313-29718-2. Dewey:781.7/96. LCCN:95-046061.

Audience: **u,f.** *Choice, 1997.*

Jones, Evan John   BF1572.M37J66 1997
Sacred Mask, Sacred Dance: Evan John Jones and Chas Clifton. Charles Clifton (Editor). Trade Paper. Llewellyn Publications. Woodbury, MN. 1997. 0p. Craft Ser. ISBN:1-56718-373-5, ISBN13: 978-1-56718-373-3. Dewey:291.3/7. LCCN:96-040945.

Audience: **u,f.**

Laude, Jean, et al.   GV1705.H8313 1978
The Dance, Art, and Ritual of Africa. Jean-Louis Paudrat & Michelle Huet (Authors). Trade Cloth. Knopf Publishing Group. New York, NY. 1978. 241p. ISBN:0-394-50272-8, ISBN13: 978-0-394-50272-4. Dewey:793.3/196. LCCN:78-054705.

Audience: **u,f.**

Oesterley, W. O. E.   BL605.O4 2002
Sacred Dance in the Ancient World. Trade Paper. Dover Publications, Inc. Mineola, NY. 2002. 256p. ISBN:0-486-42494-4, ISBN13: 978-0-486-42494-1. Dewey:291.3/7. LCCN:2002-031296.

Audience: **u,f.**

Rust, E. Gardner   ML128
The Music and Dance of the World's Religions: A Comprehensive, Annotated Bibliography of Materials in the English Language. Cloth Text. Greenwood Publishing Group, Inc. Portsmouth, NH. 1996. 504p. Music Reference Collection, Vol. 54 ISBN:0-313-29561-1, ISBN13: 978-0-313-29561-4. Dewey:016.7817. LCCN:96-018212.

Audience: **g,l,u,f.** *Choice, 1997.*

Troxell, Kay   Z7514.D2.R38 1991
Resources in Sacred Dance, 1991: Annotated Bibliography from Christian and Jewish Traditions. Trade Paper. Sacred Dance Guild, Inc. Lancaster, PA. 1991. 56p. ISBN:0-9623137-1-8, ISBN13: 978-0-9623137-1-4. Dewey:016.7933. LCCN:91-187899.

Audience: **u,f.** *Choice, 1992.*

Dance Styles, Forms, and Traditions > Western European Renaissance and Baroque Dance

Cunningham, James P.   GV1646.E6 C8
Dancing in the Inns of Court. Jordan and Sons. 1965.

Audience: **u,f.**

Davies, John   **PR2358**
Orchestra: or a Poem of Dancing. Library Binding. Reprint
Services Company. Temecula, CA. 1988. ISBN:0-7812-0025-3,
ISBN13: 978-0-7812-0025-7. Dewey:821/.3.

Audience: **u,f.**

Fletcher, Ifan K., et al.   **GV1646.E6 F55 1980**
Famed for Dance. Selma J. Cohen & Roger Lonsdalef
(Authors). Library Binding. Ayer Company Publishers, Inc.
Manchester, NH. 1980. Dance Ser. ISBN:0-8369-9291-1,
ISBN13: 978-0-8369-9291-5. Dewey:793.3/2/0924.
LCCN:79-007762.

Audience: **u,f.**

Hilton, Wendy   **GV1649.H54 1997**
Dance of Court and Theater: Selected Writings of Wendy
Hilton. Ed. 2. Cloth Text. Pendragon Press. Hillsdale, NY. 1997.
469p. Dance and Music Ser., Vol. 10 ISBN:0-945193-98-X,
ISBN13: 978-0-945193-98-2. Dewey:793.3/1944.
LCCN:97-019359.

Audience: **u,f.**

Lehner, Marcus   **GV1655**
Manual of Sixteenth-Century Italian Dance Steps. fa-gisis. 1997.
ISBN:3-931344-01-0, ISBN13: 978-3-931344-01-6.

Audience: **u,f.**

Marks, Joseph E. (Editor)   **GV1740**
The Mathers on Dancing. Trade Cloth. Princeton Book
Company Publishers. Hightstown, NJ. 1976. 99p.
ISBN:0-87127-063-3, ISBN13: 978-0-87127-063-4.
Dewey:793.3/01/3. LCCN:75-009156.

Audience: **u,f.**

Mather, Betty B. & Karns,   **ML3427.M37 1987**
Dean M.
Dance Rhythms of the French Baroque: A Handbook for
Performance. Trade Cloth. Indiana University Press.
Bloomington, IN. 1988. 352p. Music, :Scholarship and
Performance Ser. ISBN:0-253-31606-5, ISBN13:
978-0-253-31606-6. Dewey:785.4/1/0944. LCCN:86-045991.

Audience: **u,f.**

Playford, John   **PN1584**
The English Dancing Master (Sixteen Fifty-One). Margaret
Dean-Smith (Editor). Trade Cloth. European American Music
Distributors Corporation. New York, NY. 1957.
ISBN:0-901938-44-0, ISBN13: 978-0-901938-44-2.
Dewey:791.31941.

Audience: **u,f.**

Ralph, Richard   **GV1785.W39**
The Life and Works of John Weaver: An Account of His Life,
Writings and Theatrical Productions, with an Annotated Reprint
of His Complete Publications. Cloth over Boards. Princeton
Book Company Publishers. Hightstown, NJ. 1985. 1075p.
ISBN:0-87127-139-7, ISBN13: 978-0-87127-139-6.
Dewey:792.8/2/0924. LCCN:82-083649.

Audience: **u,f.**

Schwartz, Judith L. &   **Z7514.D2S3 1987**
Schlundt, Christina L.
French Court Dance and Music: A Guide to Primary Source
Writings 1643-1789. Cloth Text. Pendragon Press. Hillsdale, NY.
1987. Dance and Music Ser., Vol. 1 ISBN:0-918728-72-X,
ISBN13: 978-0-918728-72-2. Dewey:016.7923/0944.
LCCN:87-014888.

Audience: **u,f.**

Van Orden, Kate   **DC33.3.V36 2005**
Music, Discipline, and Arms in Early Modern France. Trade
Cloth. University of Chicago Press. Chicago, IL. 2005. 344p.
ISBN:0-226-84976-7, ISBN13: 978-0-226-84976-8.
Dewey:944/.03. LCCN:2004-020976.

Audience: **u,f.**

Winter, Marian Hannah   **GV1787.W58 1974**
The Pre-Romantic Ballet. Pitman Publishing. 1974.
ISBN:0-273-00334-8, ISBN13: 978-0-273-00334-2.

Audience: **g,l,u.**

Dance Styles, Forms, and Traditions > Ballet

Anawalt, Sasha   **GV1623**
The Joffrey Ballet: Robert Joffrey and the Making of an
American Dance Company. Trade Cloth. DIANE Publishing
Company. Collingdale, PA. 2000. 464p. ISBN:0-7881-9335-X,
ISBN13: 978-0-7881-9335-4. Dewey:792.8/0973.

Audience: **g,l,u,f.**

Barringer, Janice &   **GV1788.B37 2004**
Schlesinger, Sarah
The Pointe Book: Shoes, Training and Technique. Ed. 2. David
Howard (Foreword by). Trade Paper. Princeton Book Company
Publishers. Hightstown, NJ. 2004. 304p. ISBN:0-87127-261-X,
ISBN13: 978-0-87127-261-4. Dewey:794.8.
LCCN:2004-050366.

Audience: **l,u,f.**   *Choice, 2005.*

Beaumont, Cyril W.   **ML410.C4**
The Ballet Called Swan Lake. Trade Paper. Princeton Book
Company Publishers. Hightstown, NJ. 1982. 176p.
ISBN:0-87127-128-1, ISBN13: 978-0-87127-128-0.
Dewey:782.9/5/0924. LCCN:81-070094.

Audience: **u,f.**

Beaumont, Cyril W.   **GV1785.B32**
Michel Fokine and His Ballets. Trade Paper. Princeton Book
Company Publishers. Hightstown, NJ. 1996. 170p.
ISBN:1-85273-050-1, ISBN13: 978-1-85273-050-5.
Dewey:792.8/2/092.

Audience: **u,f.**

Beaumont, Cyril W.   **GV1790.G5**
The Ballet Called Giselle. Selma J. Cohen (Introduction by).
Trade Paper. Princeton Book Company Publishers. Hightstown,
NJ. 1987. 141p. ISBN:1-85273-004-8, ISBN13:
978-1-85273-004-8. Dewey:792.8/42. LCCN:72-077185.

Audience: **u,f.**

Beaumont, Cyril W. &   **GV1783.B397 2003**
  Idzikowski, Stanislas
The Cecchetti Method of Classical Ballet Theory and Technique.
Trade Paper. Dover Publications, Inc. Mineola, NY. 2003. 272p.
ISBN:0-486-43177-0, ISBN13: 978-0-486-43177-2.
Dewey:792.8. LCCN:2003-051300.
                               Audience: **u,f.**

Bennahum, Judith   **GV1789.2.C59 2005**
Lure of Perfection: Fashion and Ballet, 1780-1830. Paper over
Boards. Routledge. New York, NY. 2004. 304p.
ISBN:0-415-97037-7, ISBN13: 978-0-415-97037-2.
Dewey:792.8/4. LCCN:2004-019194.
                               Audience: **l,u,f.**

Bland, Alexander   **GV1786.R6**
The Royal Ballet. Trade Cloth. Doubleday Publishing. New
York, NY. 1981. 288p. ISBN:0-385-17043-2, ISBN13:
978-0-385-17043-7. Dewey:792.8/0942. LCCN:80-002403.
                               Audience: **g,l,u,f.**

Bruhn, Erik   **GV1788.B63 B7**
Bournonville and Ballet Technique: Studies and Comments on
August Bournonville's Etudes Choregraphiques. Paper Text.
Textbook Publishers. Temecula, CA. 2003. 70p.
ISBN:0-7581-9307-6, ISBN13: 978-0-7581-9307-0.
Dewey:792.8/2/0924.
                               Audience: **u,f.**

Chazin-Bennahum, Judith   **GV1785.B32**
The Ballets of Antony Tudor: Studies in Psyche and Satire.
Trade Cloth. Replica Books. Bridgewater, NJ. 2000. 326p.
ISBN:0-7351-0297-X, ISBN13: 978-0-7351-0297-2.
Dewey:792.8/2/092.
                     Audience: **u,f.** *Choice, 1994.*

Clarke, Mary & Crisp,   **GV1787**
  Clement
Ballet: An Illustrated History. Ed. 2. Antoinette Sibley
(Introduction by). Trade Cloth. Penguin Group (USA) Inc. New
York, NY. 1993. 320p. ISBN:0-241-13068-9, ISBN13:
978-0-241-13068-1. Dewey:792.8/09.
                               Audience: **g,l,u.**

Cohen, Selma J. (Editor)   **GV1751**
Next Week, Swan Lake: Reflections on Dance and Dances.
Trade Paper. Wesleyan University Press. Middletown, CT. 1982.
207p. ISBN:0-8195-6110-X, ISBN13: 978-0-8195-6110-7.
Dewey:793.3. LCCN:82-002614.
                               Audience: **u,f.**

Daneman, Meredith   **GV1785**
Margot Fonteyn Biography: A Life. Trade Paper. Penguin Group
(USA) Inc. New York, NY. 2005. 672p. ISBN:0-14-016530-4,
ISBN13: 978-0-14-016530-2. Dewey:792.8028092.
                               Audience: **g,l,u.**

Devonyar, Jill, et al.   **N6853.D33A4 2002**
Degas and the Dance. Edgar Degas & Richard Kendall
(Authors), Detroit Institute of Arts Staff & Philadelphia Museum
of Art Staff (Contribution by). Trade Paper. Harry N. Abrams,
Inc. New York, NY. 2002. p. cm.p. ISBN:0-8109-9077-6,
ISBN13: 978-0-8109-9077-7. Dewey:759.4.
LCCN:2002-018230.
                     Audience: **g,l,u.** *Choice, 2003.*

Dunning, Jennifer   **GV1788.6.S36D86 1985**
But First a School: The First Fifty Years of the School of
American Ballet. Trade Cloth. Penguin Group (USA) Inc. New
York, NY. 1985. 304p. ISBN:0-670-80407-X, ISBN13:
978-0-670-80407-8. Dewey:792.8/07/107471. LCCN:85-007625.
                     Audience: **g,l,u.** *Choice, 1986.*

Fairfax, Edmund   **GV1787.F35 2003**
The Styles of Eighteenth Century Ballet. Trade Cloth. Scarecrow
Press, Inc. Lanham, MD. 2003. 392p. ISBN:0-8108-4698-5,
ISBN13: 978-0-8108-4698-2. Dewey:792.8/09/033.
LCCN:2002-154137.
                     Audience: **u,f.** *Choice, 2004.*

Fisher, Jennifer   **GV1790.N8F57 2003**
Nutcracker Nation: How an Old World Ballet Became a
Christmas Tradition in the New World. Cloth over Boards. Yale
University Press. Cumberland, RI. 2003. 256p.
ISBN:0-300-09746-8, ISBN13: 978-0-300-09746-7.
Dewey:792.8/4. LCCN:2003-005866.
                               Audience: **g,l,u.**

Garafola, Lynn   **GV1786.B355G37 1989**
Diaghilev's Ballets Russes. Trade Cloth. Oxford University
Press, Inc. New York, NY. 1989. 576p. ISBN:0-19-505701-5,
ISBN13: 978-0-19-505701-0. Dewey:792.8/0947.
LCCN:89-009365.
                     Audience: **u,f.** *Choice, 1990.*

Garafola, Lynn   **GV1594**
Legacies of Twentieth-Century Dance. Library Binding.
Wesleyan University Press. Middletown, CT. 2005. 464p.
ISBN:0-8195-6673-X, ISBN13: 978-0-8195-6673-7.
Dewey:792.8/09/04. LCCN:2004-019057.
                     Audience: **u,f.** *Choice, 2005.*

Garafola, Lynn (Editor)   **GV1643**
Rethinking the Sylph: New Perspectives on the Romantic Ballet.
University Press of New England. 1997. Studies in Dance
History ISBN:0-8195-6325-0, ISBN13: 978-0-8195-6325-5.
                               Audience: **u,f.**

Garis, Robert   **GV1785.B32G37 1995**
Following Balanchine. Cloth over Boards. Yale University Press.
Cumberland, RI. 1995. 272p. ISBN:0-300-06178-1, ISBN13:
978-0-300-06178-9. Dewey:792.8/2/092. LCCN:94-034826.
                     Audience: **u,f.** *Choice, 1996.*

Gottlieb, Robert   **GV1785.B32G68 2004**
George Balanchine: The Ballet Maker. Trade Cloth.
HarperCollins Publishers. New York, NY. 2004. 224p. Eminent
Lives Ser. ISBN:0-06-075070-7, ISBN13: 978-0-06-075070-1.
Dewey:792.8/2/092 B. LCCN:2004-048856.
                   Audience: **g,l,u,f.** *Choice, 2005.*

Greskovic, Robert   **GV1787.G74 2005**
Ballet 101: A Complete Guide to Learning and Loving the
Ballet. Trade Paper, Perfect. Hal Leonard Corporation.
Milwaukee, WI. 2005. 634p. ISBN:0-87910-325-6, ISBN13:
978-0-87910-325-5. Dewey:792.8. LCCN:2005-025425.
                                                    Audience: **g,l.**

Guest, Ivor F.   **GV1646.E6G78 1992**
Ballet in Leicester Square. Cloth Text. Dance Books, Ltd. Alton,
1992. 202p. ISBN:1-85273-034-X, ISBN13: 978-1-85273-034-5.
Dewey:792.8/09421. LCCN:94-162698.
                                                    Audience: **u,f.**

Guest, Ivor F.   **GV1787**
The Ballet of the Enlightenment: The Establishment of the
Ballet d'Action in France, 1770-1793. Trade Cloth. Princeton
Book Company Publishers. Hightstown, NJ. 1997. 520p.
ISBN:1-85273-049-8, ISBN13: 978-1-85273-049-9.
Dewey:792.809443609033.
                                                    Audience: **u,f.**

Guest, Ivor F.   **GV1649**
The Ballet of the Second Empire. Trade Cloth. Wesleyan
University Press. Middletown, CT. 1974. 313p.
ISBN:0-8195-4067-6, ISBN13: 978-0-8195-4067-6.
Dewey:792.8/0944. LCCN:73-015010.
                                                    Audience: **u,f.**

Guest, Ivor F.   **GV1646.E6.G8 1972**
The Romantic Ballet in England: Its Development, Fulfillment
and Decline. Ed. 2. Trade Cloth. Wesleyan University Press.
Middletown, CT. 1972. 176p. ISBN:0-8195-4050-1, ISBN13:
978-0-8195-4050-8. Dewey:792.8. LCCN:77-172138.
                                                    Audience: **u,f.**

Guest, Ivor F.   **GV1649**
The Romantic Ballet in Paris. Ed. 2. Lillian C. Moore
(Foreword by). Trade Cloth. Dance Books, Ltd. Alton, 1980.
xix, 314p. ISBN:0-903102-45-5, ISBN13: 978-0-903102-45-2.
Dewey:792.8/0944.
                                                    Audience: **u,f.**

Joseph, Charles M.   **ML410.S932J665 2002**
Stravinsky and Balanchine: A Journey of Invention. Cloth over
Boards. Yale University Press. Cumberland, RI. 2002. 464p.
ISBN:0-300-08712-8, ISBN13: 978-0-300-08712-3.
Dewey:781.5/56/092. LCCN:2001-007130.
                                                    Audience: **l,u,f.**

Karsavina, Tamara   **GV1788**
Classical Ballet: The Flow of Movement. Trade Cloth.
Routledge. New York, NY. 1974. ISBN:0-87830-028-7, ISBN13:
978-0-87830-028-0. Dewey:792.8/2. LCCN:73-075919.
                                                    Audience: **u,f.**

Kirstein, Lincoln   **GV1781.K5 1987**
Dance: A Short History of Classic Theatrical Dancing. Trade
Paper. Princeton Book Company Publishers. Hightstown, NJ.
1987. 414p. ISBN:0-87127-019-6, ISBN13: 978-0-87127-019-1.
Dewey:793.3/2/09. LCCN:70-077179.
                                                    Audience: **l,u,f.**

Kirstein, Lincoln   **GV1787.K513 1984**
Four Centuries of Ballet: Fifty Masterworks. Dover Publications.
1984. ISBN:0-486-24631-0, ISBN13: 978-0-486-24631-4.
                                                    Audience: **l,u,f.**

Kostrovitskaya, Vera S. &   **GV1589**
  Pisarev, Alexei
School of Classical Dance. John Barker (Retold by). Paper Text.
Dance Books, Ltd. Alton, 1995. 488p. ISBN:1-85273-044-7,
ISBN13: 978-1-85273-044-4. Dewey:792.807.
                                                    Audience: **u,f.**

Lopukhov, Fedor Vasil'evich   **GV1787.L63 2002**
Writings on Ballet and Music. Stephanie Jordan (Editor),
Dorinda Offord (Translator), Stephanie Jordan (Introduction by).
Trade Cloth. University of Wisconsin Press. Chicago, IL. 2003.
184p. ISBN:0-299-18270-3, ISBN13: 978-0-299-18270-0.
Dewey:792.8. LCCN:2002-002339.
                                 Audience: **u,f.** *Choice, 2003.*

Martins, Peter   **GV1786.N4T75 1998**
Tributes: Celebrating 50 Years of New York City Ballet.
Christopher Ramsey (Editor), Mikhail Baryshnikov (Foreword
by), George Plimpton, Susan Cheever, Nikki Giovanni, Dianne
Wiest, Eric Carle, Marc Chagall & Elleworth Kelly
(Contribution by). Trade Cloth. HarperCollins Publishers. New
York, NY. 1998. 176p. ISBN:0-688-15751-3, ISBN13:
978-0-688-15751-7. Dewey:792.8/09747/1. LCCN:98-013671.
                                                    Audience: **g,l,u,f.**

Norton, Leslie   **GV1785.M283N67 2004**
Léonide Massine and the 20th Century Ballet. Paper Text.
McFarland & Company, Incorporated Publishers. Jefferson, NC.
2004. 380p. ISBN:0-7864-1752-8, ISBN13: 978-0-7864-1752-0.
Dewey:792.8/2/092 B. LCCN:2004-002721.
                                                    Audience: **u,f.**

Payne, Charles   **GV1786.A43.A44**
The American Ballet Theatre. Trade Cloth. Alfred A. Knopf Inc.
New York, NY. 1978. 380p. ISBN:0-394-49835-6, ISBN13:
978-0-394-49835-5. Dewey:792.8/4. LCCN:77-075002.
                                                    Audience: **g,l,u.**

Press, Stephen D.   **ML410.P865P74 2002**
Prokofiev's Ballets for Diaghilev. Trade Cloth. Ashgate
Publishing Company. Williston, VT. 2005. 328p.
ISBN:0-7546-0402-0, ISBN13: 978-0-7546-0402-0.
Dewey:781.5/56/092. LCCN:2002-074723.
                                 Audience: **u,f.** *Choice, 2006.*

Reynolds, Nancy   **GV1786.N4**
Repertory in Review: 40 Years of the New York City Ballet.
Trade Cloth. Penguin Group (USA) Inc. New York, NY. 1977.
352p. ISBN:0-385-27100-X, ISBN13: 978-0-385-27100-4.
Dewey:792.8/4/097471.
                                                    Audience: **l,u,f.**

Scholl, Tim   **GV1787**
From Petipa to Balanchine: Classical Revival and the
Modernization of Ballet. Paper over Boards. Routledge. New

York, NY. 1994. 180p. ISBN:0-415-09222-1, ISBN13:
978-0-415-09222-7. Dewey:792.809. LCCN:93-002102.

Audience: **u,f.** *Choice, 1994.*

Scholl, Tim   GV1790.S55S35 2004
Sleeping Beauty: A Legend in Progress. Cloth over Boards. Yale
University Press. Cumberland, RI. 2004. 256p.
ISBN:0-300-09956-8, ISBN13: 978-0-300-09956-0.
Dewey:792.8/42. LCCN:2003-017368.

Audience: **g,l,u,f.** *Choice, 2004.*

Schorer, Suki   GV1788.S288 1999
Suki Schorer on Balanchine Technique. Trade Cloth. David
McKay Company, Inc. New York, NY. 1999. 448p.
ISBN:0-679-45060-2, ISBN13: 978-0-679-45060-3.
Dewey:792.8/2. LCCN:98-016012.

Audience: **u,f.**

Schorer, Suki   GV1788
Balanchine Pointework. Lynn Garafola (Editor), Martha Swope
& Carol Rosegg (Photographers), Robert Greskovic (Afterword
by). Trade Paper. Society of Dance History Scholars.
Minneapolis, MN. 1995. 77p. Studies in Dance History, Vol. 11
ISBN:0-9653519-0-4, ISBN13: 978-0-9653519-0-4.
Dewey:792.8.

Audience: **u,f.**

Serebrennikov, Nikolai   GV1788.2.P37
  Nikolaevich & Horosko, Marian
Pas de Deux: A Textbook on Partnering. Ed. 2. University Press
of Florida. 2000. ISBN:0-8130-1768-8, ISBN13:
978-0-8130-1768-6.

Audience: **l,u,f.**

Smith, Marian   ML1727.8.P2S65 2000
Ballet and Opera in the Age of Giselle. Trade Cloth. Princeton
University Press. Princeton, NJ. 2000. 328p. Studies in Opera
ISBN:0-691-04994-7, ISBN13: 978-0-691-04994-6.
Dewey:782.1/09/034. LCCN:00-060622.

Audience: **u,f.** *Choice, 2001.*

Van Norman Baer, Nancy   GV1786.B355B35 1999
The Ballets Russes and Its World. Lynn Garafola (Editor). Cloth
over Boards. Yale University Press. Cumberland, RI. 1999.
432p. ISBN:0-300-06176-5, ISBN13: 978-0-300-06176-5.
Dewey:792.8/0947. LCCN:98-051002.

Audience: **u,f.**

Vaughan, David   GV1785.A8.V38 1977
Frederick Ashton and His Ballets. Trade Cloth. Alfred A. Knopf
Inc. New York, NY. 1977. xx, 522p. ISBN:0-394-41085-8,
ISBN13: 978-0-394-41085-2. Dewey:792.8/2. LCCN:76-047939.

Audience: **l,u,f.**

Vaughan, David &   GV1787.6
  Chapman, John V. (Editors)
Looking at Ballet: Ashton and Balanchine, 1926-1936. Jane B.
Roberts & David Vaughan (Contribution by, Compiled by),
Bruce Fleming, Robert Greskovic, Alastair Macaulay, Jane

Pritchard & Constance Valis-Hill (Contribution by). Perfect.
Wesleyan University Press. Middletown, CT. 1992. 69p. Studies
in Dance History Ser. ISBN:0-9653519-7-1, ISBN13:
978-0-9653519-7-3. Dewey:792.8.

Audience: **u,f.**

Wiley, Roland J.   ML410.C4.W53 1985
Tchaikovsky's Ballets: Swan Lake, Sleeping Beauty, Nutcracker.
Trade Cloth. Oxford University Press, Inc. New York, NY. 1985.
448p. ISBN:0-19-315314-9, ISBN13: 978-0-19-315314-1.
Dewey:782.9/5/0924. LCCN:83-023843.

Audience: **u,f.** *Choice, 1985.*

Wiley, Ronald John   GV1785.I88 W55 1997
The Life and Ballets of Lev Ivanov: Choreographer of the
Nutcracker and Swan Lake. Clarendon Press. 1997.
ISBN:0-19-816567-6, ISBN13: 978-0-19-816567-5.

Audience: **u,f.**

Woodcock, Sarah C.   GV1787
The Sadler's Wells Royal Ballet: Now the Birmingham Royal
Ballet. Trade Cloth. Trafalgar Square. North Pomfret, VT. 1991.
338p. ISBN:1-85619-034-X, ISBN13: 978-1-85619-034-3.
Dewey:792.80942.

Audience: **l,u,f.**

Dance Styles, Forms, and Traditions > Contemporary Dance Traditions

Anderson, Jack   GV1783.A53 1997
Art Without Boundaries: The World of Modern Dance. Trade
Cloth. University of Iowa Press. Iowa City, IA. 1997. 346p.
ISBN:0-87745-583-X, ISBN13: 978-0-87745-583-7.
Dewey:792.8. LCCN:96-052226.

Audience: **g,l,u,f.** *Choice, 1998.*

Banes, Sally   GV1783
Democracy's Body: Judson Dance Theater, 1962-1964. Paper
Text. Duke University Press. Durham, NC. 1993. 288p.
ISBN:0-8223-1399-5, ISBN13: 978-0-8223-1399-1.
Dewey:793.3/2. LCCN:93-021760.

Audience: **u,f.**

Banes, Sally   NX511.N4.B26 1993
Greenwich Village, 1963: Avant-Garde Performance and the
Effervescent Body. Cloth Text. Duke University Press. Durham,
NC. 1993. 352p. ISBN:0-8223-1357-X, ISBN13:
978-0-8223-1357-1. Dewey:700.97471. LCCN:93-018393.

Audience: **u,f.** *Choice, 1994.*

Banes, Sally   GV1623 .B36 1994
Writing Dancing in the Age of Postmodernism. Trade Paper.
Wesleyan University Press. Middletown, CT. 1994. 428p.
ISBN:0-8195-6268-8, ISBN13: 978-0-8195-6268-5.
Dewey:792.8/0973. LCCN:93-008225.

Audience: **u,f.**

Baral, Robert   ML1711.8.N3
Revue. Trade Cloth. Fleet Press Corporation. New York, NY.
1970. ISBN:0-8303-0091-0, ISBN13: 978-0-8303-0091-4.
Dewey:782.8/1/097471. LCCN:62-007579.

Audience: **g,l,u,f.**

Brown, Jean (Editor), et al.   GV1783.V57 1997
The Vision of Modern Dance: In the Words of Its Creators. Ed.
2. Charles H. Woodford & Naomi Mindlin (Editors). Trade
Paper. Princeton Book Company Publishers. Hightstown, NJ.
1998. 230p. ISBN:0-87127-205-9, ISBN13: 978-0-87127-205-8.
Dewey:792.8/092/2. LCCN:97-028330.

Audience: **u,f.**

Cohen, Selma J. (Editor,   GV1783
  Introduction by)
The Modern Dance: Seven Statements of Belief. Trade Paper.
Wesleyan University Press. Middletown, CT. 1966. 112p.
ISBN:0-8195-6003-0, ISBN13: 978-0-8195-6003-2.
Dewey:793.32. LCCN:66-014663.

Audience: **l,u,f.**

Cunningham, Merce   GV1785.C85V38 1997
Merce Cunningham: Fifty Years. David Vaughan (Commentaries
by). Trade Cloth. Aperture Foundation, Inc. New York, NY.
1997. 320p. ISBN:0-89381-624-8, ISBN13: 978-0-89381-624-7.
Dewey:792.8092. LCCN:97-070518.

Audience: **u,f.** *Choice, 1998.*

Daly, Ann   GV1785.D8D35 1995
Done into Dance: Isadora Duncan in America. Cloth Text.
Indiana University Press. Bloomington, IN. 1995. 352p.
ISBN:0-253-32924-8, ISBN13: 978-0-253-32924-0.
Dewey:792.8/028/092 B. LCCN:95-011633.

Audience: **u,f.** *Choice, 1996.*

Duncan, Doree (Editor), et   GV1785.D8.L54 1993
  al.
Life into Art: Isadora Duncan and Her World. Carol Pratl &
Cynthia Splatt (Editors), Agnes De Mille (Foreword by). Trade
Cloth. W. W. Norton & Company, Inc. New York, NY. 1993.
200p. ISBN:0-393-03507-7, ISBN13: 978-0-393-03507-0.
Dewey:792.8/028/092 B. LCCN:93-001737.

Audience: **g,l,u,f.** *Choice, 1994.*

Fraleigh, Sondra Horton   GV1783.2.B87F73 1999
Dancing into Darkness: Butoh, Zen, and Japan. Cloth Text.
University of Pittsburgh Press. Pittsburgh, PA. 1999. 192p.
ISBN:0-8229-4098-1, ISBN13: 978-0-8229-4098-2.
Dewey:792.8/0952. LCCN:98-058109.

Audience: **u,f.** *Choice, 2000.*

Graff, Ellen   GV1624.5.N4G73 1997
Stepping Left: Dance and Politics in New York City, 1928-1942.
Library Binding. Duke University Press. Durham, NC. 1997.
280p. ISBN:0-8223-1953-5, ISBN13: 978-0-8223-1953-5.
Dewey:792.8/09747/109043. LCCN:96-050908.

Audience: **u,f.**

Greenfield, Lois   TR817.5
Airborne: The New Dance Photography of Lois Greenfield.
William A. Ewing (Preface by), Daniel Girardin (Afterword by).

Trade Cloth. Chronicle Books LLC. San Francisco, CA. 1998.
112p. ISBN:0-8118-2171-4, ISBN13: 978-0-8118-2171-1.
Dewey:779/.97928. LCCN:98-195307.

Audience: **u,f.**

Helpern, Alice   GV1785.G7 H45
The Technique of Martha Graham. Society of Dance History
Scholars. 1992.

Audience: **u,f.**

Horst, Louis & Russell,   GV1783.H65 1987
  Carroll
Modern Dance Forms: In Relation to the Other Modern Arts.
Janet Soares (Preface by), Martha Graham (Foreword by). Trade
Paper. Princeton Book Company Publishers. Hightstown, NJ.
1987. 152p. ISBN:0-916622-52-5, ISBN13: 978-0-916622-52-7.
Dewey:793.3/2. LCCN:61-011421.

Audience: **u,f.**

Jackson, Naomi M.   GV1783.J33 2000
Converging Movements: Modern Dance and Jewish Culture at
the 92nd Street Y. Library Binding. Wesleyan University Press.
Middletown, CT. 2000. 302p. ISBN:0-8195-6419-2, ISBN13:
978-0-8195-6419-1. Dewey:792.8/089/92407471.
LCCN:00-011313.

Audience: **u,f.**

Jowitt, Deborah (Editor)   ML410.M72M47 1997
Meredith Monk. Trade Cloth. Johns Hopkins University Press.
Baltimore, MD. 1997. 224p. PAJ Bks., :Art and Performance
ISBN:0-8018-5539-X, ISBN13: 978-0-8018-5539-9.
Dewey:700/.92. LCCN:97-006597.

Audience: **l,u,f.**

Kendall, Elizabeth   GV1623 .K46 1979
Where She Danced . . .: American Dancing, 1880-1930. Trade
Cloth. Alfred A. Knopf Inc. New York, NY. 1979.
ISBN:0-394-40029-1, ISBN13: 978-0-394-40029-7.
Dewey:793.3/1973. LCCN:78-020544.

Audience: **g,l,u,f.**

Kriegsman, Sali A.   GV1786.B38.K74
Modern Dance in America: The Bennington Years. Trade Cloth.
Macmillan Publishing Company, Inc. Old Tappan, NJ. 1981. xiv,
357p. ISBN:0-8161-8528-X, ISBN13: 978-0-8161-8528-3.
Dewey:793.3/2/097438. LCCN:81-013332.

Audience: **u,f.**

Lloyd, Margaret   GV1785.A1
Borzoi Book of Modern Dance. Trade Paper. Princeton Book
Company Publishers. Hightstown, NJ. 1970. 356p.
ISBN:0-87127-023-4, ISBN13: 978-0-87127-023-8.
Dewey:792.8. LCCN:78-077181.

Audience: **g,l.**

Manning, Susan A.   GV1785.W5.M36 1993
Ecstasy and the Demon: Feminism and Nationalism in the
Dances of Mary Wigman. Trade Cloth. University of California
Press. Berkeley, CA. 1993. 353p. ISBN:0-520-08193-5, ISBN13:
978-0-520-08193-2. Dewey:792.8028092. LCCN:92-032232.

Audience: **u,f.** *Choice, 1994.*

Formats: Web: ☐ Ebook: **e** CD/DVD-ROM: 🐟 BCL3: **B**

Martin, John   **GV1783**
The Modern Dance. Trade Paper. Princeton Book Company Publishers. Hightstown, NJ. 1989. 128p. ISBN:0-87127-001-3, ISBN13: 978-0-87127-001-6. Dewey:792.8. LCCN:65-024217.
          Audience: **l,u,f.**

McDonagh, Don   **GV1783.M26**
The Complete Guide to Modern Dance. Trade Cloth. Doubleday Publishing. New York, NY. 1976. 576p. ISBN:0-385-05055-0, ISBN13: 978-0-385-05055-5. Dewey:793.3/2. LCCN:75-021235.
          Audience: **g,l.**

McDonagh, Don   **GV1783.M27 1990**
The Rise and Fall and Rise of Modern Dance. Trade Paper. A Cappella Books. Chicago, IL. 1990. 240p. ISBN:1-55652-089-1, ISBN13: 978-1-55652-089-1. Dewey:792.8. LCCN:90-037637.
          Audience: **g,l,u,f.**

Morgan, Barbara   **GV1785.G7.M6 1980**
Martha Graham: Sixteen Dances in Photographs. Trade Cloth. Morgan & Morgan, Inc. Essex, NY. 1980. 168p. ISBN:0-87100-176-4, ISBN13: 978-0-87100-176-4. Dewey:793.3/2/0924. LCCN:80-081766.
          Audience: **g,l,u.**

Perces, Marjorie, et al. **GV1783.P46 1992**
The Dance Technique of Lester Horton. Ana M. Forsythe & Cheryl Bell (Authors), Alvin Ailey Jr. (Foreword by). Trade Paper. Princeton Book Company Publishers. Hightstown, NJ. 1992. 205p. ISBN:0-87127-164-8, ISBN13: 978-0-87127-164-8. Dewey:792.8. LCCN:92-000241.
      Audience: **u,f.** *Choice, 1993.*

Preston-Dunlop, Valerie   **GV1651.S36**
 (Editor)
Schrifttanz: German Moden Dance Writings of the 1920s and 1930s. Princeton Book Company. 1990. ISBN:1-85273-016-1, ISBN13: 978-1-85273-016-1.
          Audience: **u,f.**

Ramsay, Burt   **GV1783.B87 1998**
Alien Bodies: Representations of Modernity, "Race" and Nation in Early Modern Dance. Paper over Boards. Routledge. New York, NY. 1998. 240p. ISBN:0-415-14594-5, ISBN13: 978-0-415-14594-7. Dewey:792.8. LCCN:97-023360.
          Audience: **u,f.**

Ruyter, Nancy L.   **GV1623**
Reformers and Visionaries: The Americanization of the Art of Dance. Trade Cloth. Princeton Book Company Publishers. Hightstown, NJ. 1980. 153p. ISBN:0-87127-101-X, ISBN13: 978-0-87127-101-3. Dewey:793.3/0973. LCCN:77-081990.
          Audience: **u,f.**

Shawn, Ted   **GV463 .S46**
Every Little Movement: A Book about Delsarte. Trade Paper. Princeton Book Company Publishers. Hightstown, NJ. 1985. 127p. ISBN:0-87127-015-3, ISBN13: 978-0-87127-015-3. Dewey:793.3/0924. LCCN:68-028049.
          Audience: **u,f.**

Siegel, Marcia B.   **GV1623**
The Shapes of Change: Images of American Dance. Trade Paper. University of California Press. Berkeley, CA. 1985. 386p. ISBN:0-520-04212-3, ISBN13: 978-0-520-04212-4. Dewey:792.8/0973. LCCN:78-023669.
          Audience: **u,f.**

Tracy, Robert (Editor) **GV1785.G7T73 1997**
Goddess: Martha Graham's Dancers Remember. Trade Cloth. Hal Leonard Corporation. Milwaukee, WI. 1997. 320p. ISBN:0-87910-086-9, ISBN13: 978-0-87910-086-5. Dewey:792.8/028/092 B. LCCN:96-031310.
     Audience: **g,l,u,f.** *Choice, 1997.*

Trager, Philip   **TR817.5.T73 1996**
Persephone. Eavan Boland & Rita Dove (Contribution by), Ralph Lemon & Andrew Szegedy-Maszak (Text by). Library Binding. Wesleyan University Press. Middletown, CT. 1996. 40p. ISBN:0-8195-5303-4, ISBN13: 978-0-8195-5303-4. Dewey:292.13. LCCN:96-068503.
          Audience: **u,f.**

Dance Styles, Forms, and Traditions > Contemporary Dance Traditions > Modern Dance

Albright, Ann Cooper & **GV1781.2.T35 2003**
 Gere, David (Editors)
Taken by Surprise: A Dance Improvisation Reader. Library Binding. Wesleyan University Press. Middletown, CT. 2003. 304p. ISBN:0-8195-6647-0, ISBN13: 978-0-8195-6647-8. Dewey:792.8. LCCN:2003-012767.
     Audience: **g,l,u,f.** *Choice, 2004.*

Anderson, Janet   **GV1783.A55 2004**
Modern Dance. Trade Paper. Facts On File, Inc. New York, NY. 2004. 112p. World of Dance Ser. ISBN:0-7910-7774-8, ISBN13: 978-0-7910-7774-0. Dewey:792.8. LCCN:2003-009478.
          Audience: **g,l.**

Banes, Sally   **NX511.N4**
Subversive Expectations: Performance Art and Paratheater in New York, 1976-85. Trade Paper. University of Michigan Press. Chicago, IL. 1998. 312p. ISBN:0-472-06678-1, ISBN13: 978-0-472-06678-0. Dewey:709/.747/1. LCCN:98-006969.
          Audience: **u,f.**

Banes, Sally (Editor)   **GV1783.R44 2003**
Reinventing Dance in the 1960s: Everything Was Possible. Mikhail Baryshnikov (Foreword by), Andrea Harris (Contribution by). Trade Cloth. University of Wisconsin Press. Chicago, IL. 2003. 248p. ISBN:0-299-18010-7, ISBN13: 978-0-299-18010-2. Dewey:792.8. LCCN:2002-152195.
     Audience: **g,l,u,f.** *Choice, 2004.*

Bentley, Toni   **GV1785.A1B47 2005**
Sisters of Salome. Trade Paper. University of Nebraska Press. Lincoln, NE. 2005. 233p. ISBN:0-8032-6241-8, ISBN13: 978-0-8032-6241-6. Dewey:792.8/092/2 B. LCCN:2004-028372.
     Audience: **l,u,f.** *Choice, 2003.*

Bird, Dorothy & Greenberg,   **GV1787**
   Joyce
Bird's Eye View: Dancing with Martha Graham and on
Broadway. Trade Paper. University of Pittsburgh Press.
Pittsburgh, PA. 2002. 296p. ISBN:0-8229-5791-4, ISBN13:
978-0-8229-5791-1. Dewey:792.8.

         Audience: **u,f.**

Buonaventura, Wendy   **GV1588.6.B87 2004**
Something in the Way She Moves: Dancing Women from
Salome to Madonna. Trade Cloth. Da Capo Press, Inc.
Cambridge, MA. 2004. 312p. ISBN:0-306-81348-3, ISBN13:
978-0-306-81348-1. Dewey:792.8/082. LCCN:2004-050025.

     Audience: **g,l,u,f.** *Choice, 2005.*

Carr, C   **GV1794**
On Edge: Performance at the End of the Twentieth Century.
Trade Paper. Wesleyan University Press. Middletown, CT. 1993.
357p. ISBN:0-8195-6269-6, ISBN13: 978-0-8195-6269-2.
Dewey:792.76543. LCCN:93-008182.

         Audience: **u,f.**

Chatterjea, Ananya   **GV1588.6.C53 2004**
Butting Out: Reading Resistive Choreographies Through Works
by Jawole Willa Jo Zollar and Chandralekha. Trade Paper.
Wesleyan University Press. Middletown, CT. 2004. 400p.
ISBN:0-8195-6733-7, ISBN13: 978-0-8195-6733-8.
Dewey:792.8/2. LCCN:2004-019055.

         Audience: **u,f.**

Copeland, Roger   **GV1785.C85**
Merce Cunningham: The Modernizing of Modern Dance. Paper
over Boards. Routledge. New York, NY. 2004. 320p.
ISBN:0-415-96574-8, ISBN13: 978-0-415-96574-3.
Dewey:792.8/2/092 B.

     Audience: **g,l,u.** *Choice, 2004.*

Escoffier, Jeffrey & Lore,   **GV1790.L35M37 2001**
   Matthew (Editors)
Mark Morris's L'Allegro, il Pensorosco, ed il Moderato: A
Celebration. Trade Cloth. Avalon Publishing Group. New York,
NY. 2001. 160p. ISBN:1-56924-631-9, ISBN13:
978-1-56924-631-3. Dewey:792.8/2. LCCN:00-052098.

         Audience: **u,f.**

Fishman, Katharine Davis   **GV1786.A35F57 2004**
Attitude!: Eight Young Dancers Come of Age at the Ailey
School. Trade Cloth. Penguin Group (USA) Inc. New York, NY.
2004. 304p. ISBN:1-58542-355-6, ISBN13: 978-1-58542-355-2.
Dewey:792.8/09747/1. LCCN:2004-049847.

         Audience: **g,l.**

Foulkes, Julia L.   **2001059758 [GV]**
Modern Bodies: Dance and American Modernism from Martha
Graham to Alvin Ailey. Trade Paper. University of North
Carolina Press. Chapel Hill, NC. 2002. 272p. Cultural Studies of
the United States ISBN:0-8078-5367-4, ISBN13:
978-0-8078-5367-2. Dewey:792.8. LCCN:2001-059758.

     Audience: **u,f.** *Choice, 2003.*

Franko, Mark   **GV1783.F72 1995**
Dancing Modernism - Performing Politics. Trade Cloth. Indiana
University Press. Bloomington, IN. 1995. 240p.
ISBN:0-253-32432-7, ISBN13: 978-0-253-32432-0.
Dewey:792.8. LCCN:94-031788.

         Audience: **u,f.**

Gere, David   **GV1588.6.G47 2004**
How to Make Dances in an Epidemic: Tracking Choreography
in the Age of AIDS. Trade Cloth. University of Wisconsin Press.
Chicago, IL. 2004. 352p. ISBN:0-299-20080-9, ISBN13:
978-0-299-20080-0. Dewey:306.4/84. LCCN:2004-005184.
     Audience: **l,u,f.** *Choice, 2005.*

Gitelman, Claudia (Editor,   **GV1785**
   Compiled by)
Liebe Hanya: Mary Wigman's Letters to Hanya Holm. Hedwig
Müller (Introduction by). Trade Paper. University of Wisconsin
Press. Chicago, IL. 2004. 272p. Studies in Dance History
ISBN:0-299-19074-9, ISBN13: 978-0-299-19074-3.
Dewey:792.8 B. LCCN:2003-005657.

         Audience: **u,f.**

Goldberg, Roselee   **NX456.5.P38**
Performance Art: from Futurism to the Present. Thames &
Hudson. 2001. World of Art ISBN:0-500-20339-3, ISBN13:
978-0-500-20339-2.

         Audience: **u,f.**

Guillermoprieto, Alma   **F1765.3.G85 2004**
Dancing with Cuba: A Memoir of the Revolution. Trade Cloth.
Knopf Publishing Group. New York, NY. 2004. 304p.
ISBN:0-375-42093-2, ISBN13: 978-0-375-42093-1.
Dewey:972.9106/4. LCCN:2003-044200.

         Audience: **u,f.**

Hay, Deborah   **GV1783.H37 2000**
My Body, the Buddhist. Susan Foster (Introduction by). Library
Binding. Wesleyan University Press. Middletown, CT. 2000.
133p. ISBN:0-8195-6436-2, ISBN13: 978-0-8195-6436-8.
Dewey:792.8/2. LCCN:00-008647.

         Audience: **u,f.**

Horosko, Marian   **GV1785.G7M27 2002**
Martha Graham: The Evolution of Her Dance Theory and
Training. Ed. 2. Trade Cloth. University Press of Florida.
Gainesville, FL. 2002. 304p. ISBN:0-8130-2473-0, ISBN13:
978-0-8130-2473-8. Dewey:792.8/2/092 B. LCCN:2002-016565.
         Audience: **u,f.**

King, Kenneth   **GV1600.K56 2003**
Writing in Motion. Trade Paper. University Press of New
England. Lebanon, NH. 2003. 224p. ISBN:0-8195-6614-4,
ISBN13: 978-0-8195-6614-0. Dewey:792.8/09.
LCCN:2003-015186.

     Audience: **u,f.** *Choice, 2004.*

Lemon, Ralph   **GV1785.L385**
Tree: Belief/Culture/Balance. Wesleyan University Press. 2004.
ISBN:0-8195-6699-3, ISBN13: 978-0-8195-6699-7.

         Audience: **u,f.**

Manning, Susan   GV1627.7.A34M36 2004
Modern Dance, Negro Dance: Race in Motion. Trade Cloth.
University of Minnesota Press. Minneapolis, MN. 2004. 296p.
ISBN:0-8166-3736-9, ISBN13: 978-0-8166-3736-2.
Dewey:792.8/089/96073. LCCN:2003-022003.

Audience: **u,f.**

Morgan, Barbara &   TR653.M652 1999
Patnaik, Deba P.
Barbara Morgan. Lesley Martin (Editor). Trade Cloth. Aperture
Foundation, Inc. New York, NY. 1999. 96p. Aperture Masters of
Photography Ser. ISBN:0-89381-825-9, ISBN13:
978-0-89381-825-8. Dewey:779/.092. LCCN:98-086911.

Audience: **u,f.**

Morris, Gay   GV1619.M67 2006
Game for Dancers: Performing Modernism in the Postwar Years,
1945-1960. Library Binding. Wesleyan University Press.
Middletown, CT. 2006. 288p. ISBN:0-8195-6804-X, ISBN13:
978-0-8195-6804-5. Dewey:792.809/045. LCCN:2006-000181.

Audience: **l,u,f.**

Prevots, Naima   GV1601
Dance for Export: Cultural Diplomacy and the Cold War. Eric
Foner (Introduction by). Trade Paper. Wesleyan University
Press. Middletown, CT. 2001. 188p. ISBN:0-8195-6464-8,
ISBN13: 978-0-8195-6464-1. Dewey:792.809.

Audience: **u,f.**

Ross, Janice
Anna Halprin: Experience as Dance. Richard Schechner
(Foreword by). Trade Cloth. University of California Press.
Berkeley, CA. 2007. 448p. ISBN:0-520-24757-4, ISBN13:
978-0-520-24757-4.

Audience: **u,f.**

Siegel, Marcia   GV1785.T43S54 2006
Howling Near Heaven: Twyla Tharp and the Reinvention of
Modern Dance. Trade Cloth. Palgrave Macmillan. New York,
NY. 2006. 336p. ISBN:0-312-23294-2, ISBN13:
978-0-312-23294-8. Dewey:792.8/2092. LCCN:2005-044685.

Audience: **u,f.**

Teicher, Hendel   GV1785.B76T75 2003
Trisha Brown: Dance and Art in Dialogue, 1961-2001. Trade
Cloth. MIT Press. Cambridge, MA. 2002. 340p.
ISBN:0-262-20139-9, ISBN13: 978-0-262-20139-1.
Dewey:792.8/2/0973. LCCN:2002-016500.

Audience: **u,f.**   *Choice, 2003.*

Tracy, Robert   GV1786.A42T73 2004
Ailey Spirit: The Journey of an American Dance Company.
Trade Cloth. Stewart, Tabori & Chang. New York, NY. 2004.
168p. ISBN:1-58479-364-3, ISBN13: 978-1-58479-364-9.
Dewey:792.8/0973. LCCN:2004-005580.

Audience: **g,l,u,f.**

Vaughan, David   GV1785.K3.C85 M47
Merce Cunningham: Fifty Forward. Cunningham Dance
Foundation. 2005. ISBN:0-9769537-0-6, ISBN13:
978-0-9769537-0-8.

Audience: **l,u,f.**

Dance Styles, Forms, and Traditions > Contemporary Dance Traditions > Postmodern Dance

Albright, Ann Cooper &   GV1781.2.T35 2003
Gere, David (Editors)
Taken by Surprise: A Dance Improvisation Reader. Library
Binding. Wesleyan University Press. Middletown, CT. 2003.
304p. ISBN:0-8195-6647-0, ISBN13: 978-0-8195-6647-8.
Dewey:792.8. LCCN:2003-012767.

Audience: **g,l,u,f.**   *Choice, 2004.*

Anderson, Janet   GV1783.A55 2004
Modern Dance. Trade Paper. Facts On File, Inc. New York, NY.
2004. 112p. World of Dance Ser. ISBN:0-7910-7774-8, ISBN13:
978-0-7910-7774-0. Dewey:792.8. LCCN:2003-009478.

Audience: **g,l.**

Banes, Sally   NX511.N4
Subversive Expectations: Performance Art and Paratheater in
New York, 1976-85. Trade Paper. University of Michigan Press.
Chicago, IL. 1998. 312p. ISBN:0-472-06678-1, ISBN13:
978-0-472-06678-0. Dewey:709/.747/1. LCCN:98-006969.

Audience: **u,f.**

Banes, Sally (Editor)   GV1783.R44 2003
Reinventing Dance in the 1960s: Everything Was Possible.
Mikhail Baryshnikov (Foreword by), Andrea Harris
(Contribution by). Trade Cloth. University of Wisconsin Press.
Chicago, IL. 2003. 248p. ISBN:0-299-18010-7, ISBN13:
978-0-299-18010-2. Dewey:792.8. LCCN:2002-152195.

Audience: **g,l,u,f.**   *Choice, 2004.*

Bentley, Toni   GV1785.A1B47 2005
Sisters of Salome. Trade Paper. University of Nebraska Press.
Lincoln, NE. 2005. 233p. ISBN:0-8032-6241-8, ISBN13:
978-0-8032-6241-6. Dewey:792.8/092/2 B. LCCN:2004-028372.

Audience: **l,u,f.**   *Choice, 2003.*

Bird, Dorothy & Greenberg,   GV1787
Joyce
Bird's Eye View: Dancing with Martha Graham and on
Broadway. Trade Paper. University of Pittsburgh Press.
Pittsburgh, PA. 2002. 296p. ISBN:0-8229-5791-4, ISBN13:
978-0-8229-5791-1. Dewey:792.8.

Audience: **u,f.**

Buonaventura, Wendy   GV1588.6.B87 2004
Something in the Way She Moves: Dancing Women from
Salome to Madonna. Trade Cloth. Da Capo Press, Inc.
Cambridge, MA. 2004. 312p. ISBN:0-306-81348-3, ISBN13:
978-0-306-81348-1. Dewey:792.8/082. LCCN:2004-050025.

Audience: **g,l,u,f.**   *Choice, 2005.*

Carr, C   GV1794
On Edge: Performance at the End of the Twentieth Century.
Trade Paper. Wesleyan University Press. Middletown, CT. 1993.
357p. ISBN:0-8195-6269-6, ISBN13: 978-0-8195-6269-2.
Dewey:792.76543. LCCN:93-008182.

Audience: **u,f.**

Chatterjea, Ananya   **GV1588.6.C53 2004**
Butting Out: Reading Resistive Choreographies Through Works
by Jawole Willa Jo Zollar and Chandralekha. Trade Paper.
Wesleyan University Press. Middletown, CT. 2004. 400p.
ISBN:0-8195-6733-7, ISBN13: 978-0-8195-6733-8.
Dewey:792.8/2. LCCN:2004-019055.

Audience: **u,f.**

Copeland, Roger   **GV1785.C85**
Merce Cunningham: The Modernizing of Modern Dance. Paper
over Boards. Routledge. New York, NY. 2004. 320p.
ISBN:0-415-96574-8, ISBN13: 978-0-415-96574-3.
Dewey:792.8/2/092 B.

Audience: **g,l,u.** *Choice, 2004.*

Escoffier, Jeffrey & Lore,   **GV1790.L35M37 2001**
  Matthew (Editors)
Mark Morris's L'Allegro, il Pensorosco, ed il Moderato: A
Celebration. Trade Cloth. Avalon Publishing Group. New York,
NY. 2001. 160p. ISBN:1-56924-631-9, ISBN13:
978-1-56924-631-3. Dewey:792.8/2. LCCN:00-052098.

Audience: **u,f.**

Fishman, Katharine Davis   **GV1786.A35F57 2004**
Attitude!: Eight Young Dancers Come of Age at the Ailey
School. Trade Cloth. Penguin Group (USA) Inc. New York, NY.
2004. 304p. ISBN:1-58542-355-6, ISBN13: 978-1-58542-355-2.
Dewey:792.8/09747/1. LCCN:2004-049847.

Audience: **g,l.**

Foulkes, Julia L.   **2001059758 [GV]**
Modern Bodies: Dance and American Modernism from Martha
Graham to Alvin Ailey. Trade Paper. University of North
Carolina Press. Chapel Hill, NC. 2002. 272p. Cultural Studies of
the United States ISBN:0-8078-5367-4, ISBN13:
978-0-8078-5367-2. Dewey:792.8. LCCN:2001-059758.

Audience: **u,f.** *Choice, 2003.*

Franko, Mark   **GV1783.F72 1995**
Dancing Modernism - Performing Politics. Trade Cloth. Indiana
University Press. Bloomington, IN. 1995. 240p.
ISBN:0-253-32432-7, ISBN13: 978-0-253-32432-0.
Dewey:792.8. LCCN:94-031788.

Audience: **u,f.**

Gere, David   **GV1588.6.G47 2004**
How to Make Dances in an Epidemic: Tracking Choreography
in the Age of AIDS. Trade Cloth. University of Wisconsin Press.
Chicago, IL. 2004. 352p. ISBN:0-299-20080-9, ISBN13:
978-0-299-20080-0. Dewey:306.4/84. LCCN:2004-005184.

Audience: **l,u,f.** *Choice, 2005.*

Gitelman, Claudia (Editor,   **GV1785**
  Compiled by)
Liebe Hanya: Mary Wigman's Letters to Hanya Holm. Hedwig
Müller (Introduction by). Trade Paper. University of Wisconsin
Press. Chicago, IL. 2004. 272p. Studies in Dance History
ISBN:0-299-19074-9, ISBN13: 978-0-299-19074-3.
Dewey:792.8 B. LCCN:2003-005657.

Audience: **u,f.**

Goldberg, Roselee   **NX456.5.P38**
Performance Art: from Futurism to the Present. Thames &
Hudson. 2001. World of Art ISBN:0-500-20339-3, ISBN13:
978-0-500-20339-2.

Audience: **u,f.**

Guillermoprieto, Alma   **F1765.3.G85 2004**
Dancing with Cuba: A Memoir of the Revolution. Trade Cloth.
Knopf Publishing Group. New York, NY. 2004. 304p.
ISBN:0-375-42093-2, ISBN13: 978-0-375-42093-1.
Dewey:972.9106/4. LCCN:2003-044200.

Audience: **u,f.**

Hay, Deborah   **GV1783.H37 2000**
My Body, the Buddhist. Susan Foster (Introduction by). Library
Binding. Wesleyan University Press. Middletown, CT. 2000.
133p. ISBN:0-8195-6436-2, ISBN13: 978-0-8195-6436-8.
Dewey:792.8/2. LCCN:00-008647.

Audience: **u,f.**

Horosko, Marian   **GV1785.G7M27 2002**
Martha Graham: The Evolution of Her Dance Theory and
Training. Ed. 2. Trade Cloth. University Press of Florida.
Gainesville, FL. 2002. 304p. ISBN:0-8130-2473-0, ISBN13:
978-0-8130-2473-8. Dewey:792.8/2/092 B. LCCN:2002-016565.
Audience: **u,f.**

King, Kenneth   **GV1600.K56 2003**
Writing in Motion. Trade Paper. University Press of New
England. Lebanon, NH. 2003. 224p. ISBN:0-8195-6614-4,
ISBN13: 978-0-8195-6614-0. Dewey:792.8/09.
LCCN:2003-015186.

Audience: **u,f.** *Choice, 2004.*

Lemon, Ralph   **GV1785.L385**
Tree: Belief/Culture/Balance. Wesleyan University Press. 2004.
ISBN:0-8195-6699-3, ISBN13: 978-0-8195-6699-7.

Audience: **u,f.**

Manning, Susan   **GV1627.7.A34M36 2004**
Modern Dance, Negro Dance: Race in Motion. Trade Cloth.
University of Minnesota Press. Minneapolis, MN. 2004. 296p.
ISBN:0-8166-3736-9, ISBN13: 978-0-8166-3736-2.
Dewey:792.8/089/96073. LCCN:2003-022003.

Audience: **u,f.**

Morgan, Barbara &   **TR653.M652 1999**
  Patnaik, Deba P.
Barbara Morgan. Lesley Martin (Editor). Trade Cloth. Aperture
Foundation, Inc. New York, NY. 1999. 96p. Aperture Masters of
Photography Ser. ISBN:0-89381-825-9, ISBN13:
978-0-89381-825-8. Dewey:779/.092. LCCN:98-086911.

Audience: **u,f.**

Morris, Gay   **GV1619.M67 2006**
Game for Dancers: Performing Modernism in the Postwar Years,
1945-1960. Library Binding. Wesleyan University Press.
Middletown, CT. 2006. 288p. ISBN:0-8195-6804-X, ISBN13:
978-0-8195-6804-5. Dewey:792.809/045. LCCN:2006-000181.

Audience: **l,u,f.**

Prevots, Naima　　　　　　　　　　**GV1601**
Dance for Export: Cultural Diplomacy and the Cold War. Eric Foner (Introduction by). Trade Paper. Wesleyan University Press. Middletown, CT. 2001. 188p. ISBN:0-8195-6464-8, ISBN13: 978-0-8195-6464-1. Dewey:792.809.

Audience: **u,f.**

Ross, Janice
Anna Halprin: Experience as Dance. Richard Schechner (Foreword by). Trade Cloth. University of California Press. Berkeley, CA. 2007. 448p. ISBN:0-520-24757-4, ISBN13: 978-0-520-24757-4.

Audience: **u,f.**

Siegel, Marcia　　　　　**GV1785.T43S54 2006**
Howling Near Heaven: Twyla Tharp and the Reinvention of Modern Dance. Trade Cloth. Palgrave Macmillan. New York, NY. 2006. 336p. ISBN:0-312-23294-2, ISBN13: 978-0-312-23294-8. Dewey:792.8/2092. LCCN:2005-044685.

Audience: **u,f.**

Teicher, Hendel　　　　　**GV1785.B76T75 2003**
Trisha Brown: Dance and Art in Dialogue, 1961-2001. Trade Cloth. MIT Press. Cambridge, MA. 2002. 340p. ISBN:0-262-20139-9, ISBN13: 978-0-262-20139-1. Dewey:792.8/2/0973. LCCN:2002-016500.

Audience: **u,f.** *Choice, 2003.*

Tracy, Robert　　　　　**GV1786.A42T73 2004**
Ailey Spirit: The Journey of an American Dance Company. Trade Cloth. Stewart, Tabori & Chang. New York, NY. 2004. 168p. ISBN:1-58479-364-3, ISBN13: 978-1-58479-364-9. Dewey:792.8/0973. LCCN:2004-005580.

Audience: **g,l,u,f.**

Vaughan, David　　　　　**GV1785.K3.C85 M47**
Merce Cunningham: Fifty Forward. Cunningham Dance Foundation. 2005. ISBN:0-9769537-0-6, ISBN13: 978-0-9769537-0-8.

Audience: **l,u,f.**

Dance Styles, Forms, and Traditions > Jazz Dance

Atkins, Cholly & Malone,　　　**GV1785.A84A3 2003**
Jacqui
Class Act: The Jazz Life of Choreographer Cholly Atkins. Trade Paper. Columbia University Press. New York, NY. 2003. 280p. ISBN:0-231-12365-5, ISBN13: 978-0-231-12365-5. Dewey:792.8/2/092.

Audience: **g,l,u,f.**

Bordman, Gerald　　　　　**ML1711.B67 2001**
American Musical Theater: A Chronicle. Ed. 3. Trade Cloth. Oxford University Press, Inc. New York, NY. 2001. 840p. ISBN:0-19-513074-X, ISBN13: 978-0-19-513074-4. Dewey:782.1/4/0973. LCCN:00-059812.

Audience: **g,l,u,f.**

Cayou, Dolores K.　　　　　**GV1753**
Modern Jazz Dance. Trade Paper. Mayfield Publishing Company. San Francisco, CA. 1971. 148p. ISBN:0-87484-139-9, ISBN13: 978-0-87484-139-8. Dewey:793.3/2. LCCN:70-126056.

Audience: **g,l,u.**

Croce, Arlene　　　　　**PN1998.A2**
The Fred Astaire and Ginger Rogers Book. Trade Paper. Penguin Group (USA) Inc. New York, NY. 1987. ISBN:0-525-48371-3, ISBN13: 978-0-525-48371-7. Dewey:791.43/028/0922.

Audience: **g,l,u.**

Dodge, Pryor (Editor)　　　　　**ML3507**
Hot Jazz and Jazz Dance: Roger Pryor Dodge Collected Writings 1929-1964. Trade Cloth. Replica Books. Bridgewater, NJ. 2000. 382p. ISBN:0-7351-0375-5, ISBN13: 978-0-7351-0375-7. Dewey:781.65/09.

Audience: **u,f.**

Emery, Lynne Fauley　　　　　**GV1624.7.A34**
Black Dance: From 1619 to Today. Trade Cloth. Princeton Book Company Publishers. Hightstown, NJ. 1988. xii, 397p. ISBN:0-916622-61-4, ISBN13: 978-0-916622-61-9. Dewey:793.3089/96073. LCCN:88-061031.

Audience: **g,l,u.**

Giordano, Gus　　　　　**GV1753.A57**
Anthology of American Jazz Dance. Orion Publishing House. 1975.

Audience: **g,l,u.**

Giordano, Gus　　　　　**GV1751**
Jazz Dance Class: Beginning Thru Advanced. Trade Paper. Princeton Book Company Publishers. Hightstown, NJ. 1992. 209p. ISBN:0-87127-182-6, ISBN13: 978-0-87127-182-2. Dewey:793.3.

Audience: **l,u,f.**

Gottfried, Martin　　　　　**GV1785.F67G68 1990**
All His Jazz: The Life and Death of Bob Fosse. Trade Cloth. Bantam Books. New York, NY. 1990. 496p. ISBN:0-553-07038-X, ISBN13: 978-0-553-07038-5. Dewey:792.82092 B. LCCN:90-038650.

Audience: **u,f.**

Hazzard-Gordon, Katrina　　　**GV1624.7.A34H39 1990**
Jookin': The Rise of Social Dance Formations in African-American Culture. Trade Paper. Temple University Press. Philadelphia, PA. 1992. xiii, 226p. ISBN:0-87722-956-2, ISBN13: 978-0-87722-956-8. Dewey:793.3/089/96073.

Audience: **u,f.** *Choice, 1990.*

Kislan, Richard　　　　　**GV1623.K57 1987**
Hoofing on Broadway: A History of Show Dancing. Trade Cloth. Prentice Hall PTR. Upper Saddle River, NJ. 1987. 208p. ISBN:0-13-809484-5, ISBN13: 978-0-13-809484-3. Dewey:793.30973. LCCN:86-018757.

Audience: **l,u,f.**

Kriegel, Lorraine P. &   GV1784.K75 1994
  Chandler-Vaccaro, Kimberly
Jazz Dance Today. Clyde Perlee (Editor). Paper Text.
Brooks/Cole. Pacific Grove, CA. 1994. 176p.
ISBN:0-314-02717-3, ISBN13: 978-0-314-02717-7.
Dewey:793.3. LCCN:93-041158.

                           Audience: **l,u,f.**

Kriegel, Lorraine, et al.   GV1784.L85 1997
Luigi's Jazz Warm Up: An Introduction to Jazz Style and
Technique. Francis Roach & Luigi (Authors). Trade Paper.
Princeton Book Company Publishers. Hightstown, NJ. 1997.
181p. ISBN:0-87127-202-4, ISBN13: 978-0-87127-202-7.
Dewey:613.7/1. LCCN:96-032734.

                           Audience: **l,u.**

Loney, Glenn   GV1785.C63L66 1984
Unsung Genius: The Passion of Dancer-Choreographer Jack
Cole. Trade Cloth. Scholastic Library Publishing. Danbury, CT.
1984. 384p. ISBN:0-531-09765-X, ISBN13: 978-0-531-09765-6.
Dewey:793.3/2/0924 B. LCCN:84-007447.

                         Audience: **g,l,u,f.**

Loney, Glenn Meredith   ML1711.C66
Musical Theater in America. Greenwood Press. 1981.

                         Audience: **g,l,u.**

Long, Richard A.   GV1624.7.A34
Black Tradition in American Dance. Trade Cloth. Smithmark
Publishers, Inc. New York, NY. 1995. 192p.
ISBN:0-8317-0763-1, ISBN13: 978-0-8317-0763-7.
Dewey:793.3.

                         Audience: **l,u,f.**

Malone, Jacqui   GV1624.7.A34M35 1996
Steppin' on the Blues: The Visible Rhythms of African
American Dance. Trade Paper. University of Illinois Press.
Champaign, IL. 1996. 312p. Folklore and Society Ser.
ISBN:0-252-06508-5, ISBN13: 978-0-252-06508-8.
Dewey:793.3/1973. LCCN:95-004413.

                Audience: **u,f.** *Choice, 1997.*

Mates, Julian   ML1711
America's Musical Stage: Two Hundred Years of Musical
Theatre. Trade Cloth. Greenwood Publishing Group, Inc.
Portsmouth, NH. 1985. 252p. Contributions in Drama and
Theatre Studies Ser., No. 18 ISBN:0-313-23948-7, ISBN13:
978-0-313-23948-9. Dewey:782.81/0973. LCCN:85-000935.

           Audience: **u,f.** *B̶* *Choice, 1986.*

Yudkoff, Alvin   PN2287.M69
Gene Kelly: A Life of Dance and Dreams. Trade Cloth.
Watson-Guptill Publications, Inc. New York, NY. 2001. 240p.
ISBN:0-8230-8819-7, ISBN13: 978-0-8230-8819-5.
Dewey:791.43/028/092 B.

           Audience: **g,l,u.** *Choice, 2000.*

Dance Styles, Forms, and Traditions > Tap Dance

Atkins, Cholly & Malone,   GV1785.A84A3 2003
  Jacqui
Class Act: The Jazz Life of Choreographer Cholly Atkins. Trade
Paper. Columbia University Press. New York, NY. 2003. 280p.
ISBN:0-231-12365-5, ISBN13: 978-0-231-12365-5.
Dewey:792.8/2/092.

                         Audience: **g,l,u,f.**

Bogle, Donald   PN1995.9.N4B59 2005
Bright Boulevards, Bold Dreams: The Story of Black
Hollywood. Trade Cloth. Ballantine Books. New York, NY.
2005. 432p. ISBN:0-345-45418-9, ISBN13: 978-0-345-45418-8.
Dewey:791.4302/8/092396073. LCCN:2004-054781.

                         Audience: **l,u.**

Feldman, Anita   GV1794.F39 1995
Inside Tap: Technique and Improvisation for Today's Tap
Dancer. Trade Paper. Princeton Book Company Publishers.
Hightstown, NJ. 1996. 218p. ISBN:0-87127-199-0, ISBN13:
978-0-87127-199-0. Dewey:792.7. LCCN:95-014823.

           Audience: **u,f.** *Choice, 1996.*

Frank, Rusty E.   GV1785.A1
Tap!: The Greatest Tap Dance Stars and Their Stories,
1900-1955. Ed. 2. Gregor Hines (Introduction by). Trade Paper.
Da Capo Press, Inc. Cambridge, MA. 1995. 358p.
ISBN:0-306-80635-5, ISBN13: 978-0-306-80635-3.
Dewey:792.8/028/0922.

                         Audience: **g,l.**

Glover, Savion & Weber,   GV1785.G56A3 2000
  Bruce
Savion!: My Life in Tap. Gregory Hines (Foreword by). Trade
Cloth. HarperCollins Publishers. New York, NY. 2000. 80p.
ISBN:0-688-15629-0, ISBN13: 978-0-688-15629-9.
Dewey:729.7/8 B. LCCN:98-031517.

                         Audience: **g,l,u.**

Hill, Constance Valis   GV1794
Brotherhood in Rhythm: The Jazz Tap Dancing of the Nicholas
Brothers. Trade Paper. Cooper Square Publishers, Inc. New
York, NY. 2002. 352p. ISBN:0-8154-1215-0, ISBN13:
978-0-8154-1215-1. Dewey:792.7/8 B.

           Audience: **u,f.** *Choice, 2000.*

Kislan, Richard   GV1623.K57 1987
Hoofing on Broadway: A History of Show Dancing. Trade
Cloth. Prentice Hall PTR. Upper Saddle River, NJ. 1987. 208p.
ISBN:0-13-809484-5, ISBN13: 978-0-13-809484-3.
Dewey:793.30973. LCCN:86-018757.

                         Audience: **l,u,f.**

Knowles, Mark   GV1794.K66 1998
The Tap Dance Dictionary. Cloth Text. McFarland & Company,

Incorporated Publishers. Jefferson, NC. 1998. 264p.
ISBN:0-7864-0352-7, ISBN13: 978-0-7864-0352-3.
Dewey:792.7/8. LCCN:97-50281.

Audience: **g,l,u,f.**

Stearns, Jean & Stearns,   **GV1624.7.A34S74 1994**
   Marshall W.
Jazz Dance: The Story of American Vernacular Dance. Ed. 2.
Brenda Bufalino (Introduction by). Trade Paper. Da Capo Press,
Inc. Cambridge, MA. 1994. 508p. ISBN:0-306-80553-7,
ISBN13: 978-0-306-80553-0. Dewey:793.3/089/96073.
LCCN:93-040957.

Audience: **g,l,u.**

Dance Styles, Forms, and Traditions > European and American Social Dance Traditions > Folk Dancing

Barrand, Anthony G.   **GV1796.M7**
Six Fools and a Dancer: The Timeless Way of the Morris.
Northern Harmony Publishing Company. 1991.
ISBN:0-9627554-1-9, ISBN13: 978-0-9627554-1-5.

Audience: **u,f.**

Buckman, Peter   **GV1601 .B83 1979**
Let's Dance: Social, Ballroom and Folk Dancing. Trade Paper.
Penguin Group (USA) Inc. New York, NY. 1979.
ISBN:0-14-005325-5, ISBN13: 978-0-14-005325-8.
Dewey:793.3/09.

Audience: **g,l.**

Corrsin, Stephen D.   **GV1796.S9C67 1996**
Sword Dancing: A History. Trade Paper. Hisarlik Press. Enfield,
1996. 256p. ISBN:1-874312-25-7, ISBN13: 978-1-874312-25-3.
Dewey:793.35094. LCCN:96-196483.

Audience: **u,f.**

Flett, T. M. & Flett, J. P.   **GV1646.S35**
Traditional Dancing in Scotland. Trade Paper. Routledge. New
York, NY. 1985. 313p. ISBN:0-7102-0731-X, ISBN13:
978-0-7102-0731-9. Dewey:793.319411.

Audience: **u,f.**

Frost, Helen   **MT950**
Clog and Character Dances. Trade Paper. Kessinger Publishing,
LLC. Whitefish, MT. 2004. ISBN:1-4179-0871-8, ISBN13:
978-1-4179-0871-4. Dewey:793.32.

Audience: **g,l,u.**

Greene, Hank   **GV1763.G69 1984**
Square and Folk Dancing. Manosalvas (Illustrator). Trade Cloth.
HarperCollins Publishers. New York, NY. 1984. 416p.
ISBN:0-06-015325-3, ISBN13: 978-0-06-015325-0.
Dewey:793.3/4. LCCN:84-047575.

Audience: **g,l.**

Lekis, Lisa   **GV1626**
Folk Dances of Latin America. Trade Paper. Books on Demand.
Ann Arbor, MI. 312p. ISBN:0-598-45934-0, ISBN13:
978-0-598-45934-3. Dewey:793.31. LCCN:58-007802.

Audience: **g,l.**

Sharp, Cecil J. & Karpeles,   **GV1763.S52**
   Maud
The Country Dance Book. EP Publishing. 1976.

Audience: **l,u,f.**

Ysursa, John M.   **GV1674.P35Y78 1995**
Basque Dance. Trade Paper. Tamarack Books, Inc. Boise, ID.
1995. 120p. ISBN:1-886609-03-9, ISBN13: 978-1-886609-03-7.
Dewey:793.3/1/09466. LCCN:96-133734.

Audience: **u,f.**

Dance Styles, Forms, and Traditions > European and American Social Dance Traditions > Square, Old Time, Contra, and Round Dancing

Casey, Betty   **GV1763**
The Complete Book of Square Dancing and Round Dancing.
Trade Cloth. Doubleday Publishing. New York, NY. 1976. 394p.
ISBN:0-385-03603-5, ISBN13: 978-0-385-03603-0.
Dewey:793.3/4. LCCN:75-040718.

Audience: **g,l,u.**

Dart, Mary M.   **GV1763.D37 1995**
Contra Dance Choreography: A Reflection of Social Change.
Cloth Text. Garland Publishing, Inc. New York, NY. 1995. 271p.
Garland Studies in American Popular History and Culture
ISBN:0-8153-1984-3, ISBN13: 978-0-8153-1984-9.
Dewey:793.3/4. LCCN:94-049557.

Audience: **g,l,u,f.**

Spalding, Susan E. &   **GV1624**
   Woodside, Jane H.
Communities in Motion: Dance, Community and Tradition in
America's Southeast and Beyond. Trade Cloth. Greenwood
Publishing Group, Inc. Portsmouth, NH. 1995. 288p.
Contributions to the Study of Music and Dance Ser., Vol. 60
ISBN:0-313-29428-3, ISBN13: 978-0-313-29428-0.
Dewey:793.3/1974. LCCN:94-030928.

Audience: **u,f.**

Tolman, Beth & Page,   **GV1763**
   Ralph
The Country Dance Book. F. W. Tolman (Illustrator). Trade
Paper. Penguin Group (USA) Inc. New York, NY. 1976.
ISBN:0-8289-0274-7, ISBN13: 978-0-8289-0274-8.
Dewey:793.3/4. LCCN:75-041877.

Audience: **g,l,u.**

Dance Styles, Forms, and Traditions > European and American Social Dance Traditions > Ballroom, Club Dancing, Competition Dancing, and Dance Sport

GV1751

Ballroom Dance Music: A Reference Guide. Library Binding. Gordon Press Publishers. New York, NY. 1994. ISBN:0-8490-9068-7, ISBN13: 978-0-8490-9068-4. Dewey:793.33.

Audience: **g,l,u,f.**

Aldrich, Elizabeth   **GV1619.A43 1991**

From the Ballroom to Hell: Grace and Folly in Nineteenth-Century Dance. Mina Mulvey (Foreword by). Trade Paper. Northwestern University Press. Evanston, IL. 1991. 225p. ISBN:0-8101-0913-1, ISBN13: 978-0-8101-0913-1. Dewey:792.8. LCCN:91-003225.

Audience: **u,f.**

Castle, Vernon & Castle,   **GV1746**
Irene

Modern Dancing. Paper Text. Da Capo Press, Inc. Cambridge, MA. 1980. 186p. Series in Dance ISBN:0-306-76050-9, ISBN13: 978-0-306-76050-1. Dewey:793.3/3. LCCN:80-017215.

Audience: **g,l,u.**

Groppa, Carlos G.   **GV1796.T3G76 2003**

The Tango in the United States: A History. Cloth Text. McFarland & Company, Incorporated Publishers. Jefferson, NC. 2003. 239p. ISBN:0-7864-1406-5, ISBN13: 978-0-7864-1406-2. Dewey:784.18/885/0973. LCCN:2003-009260.

Audience: **g,l,u,f.** *Choice, 2004.*

Leisner, Tony   **GV1763**

The Official Guide to Country Dance Steps. Trade Cloth. Quality Books, Inc. Oregon, IL. 1980. 96p. ISBN:0-89196-062-7, ISBN13: 978-0-89196-062-1. Dewey:793.3/1. LCCN:79-067001.

Audience: **g,l,u.**

Malbon, Ben   **HQ799.8.G7M35 2002**

🄴 Clubbing: Dancing, Ecstasy and Vitality. E-Book. Routledge. New York, NY. 1999. ISBN:0-203-25735-9, ISBN13: 978-0-203-25735-7. Dewey:305.242/0941.

Audience: **l,u,f.**

Malnig, Julie   **GV1746**

Dancing till Dawn: A Century of Exhibition Ballroom Dance. Trade Cloth. Greenwood Publishing Group, Inc. Portsmouth, NH. 1992. 192p. Contributions to the Study of Music and Dance Ser., No. 25 ISBN:0-313-27647-1, ISBN13: 978-0-313-27647-7. Dewey:793.33. LCCN:91-033482.

Audience: **l,u,f.** *Choice, 1993.*

Pener, Degen   **ML3518.P46 1999**

The Swing Book. Trade Paper. Little Brown & Company. New York, NY. 1999. 256p. ISBN:0-316-69802-4, ISBN13: 978-0-316-69802-3. Dewey:781.65/4. LCCN:99-042126.

Audience: **g,l,u.**

Stephenson, Richard M.   **GV1751.S77**

The Complete Book of Ballroom Dancing. Joseph Iaccarino (Contribution by). UK-Trade Paper. Doubleday Publishing. New York, NY. 1992. 256p. ISBN:0-385-42416-7, ISBN13: 978-0-385-42416-5. Dewey:793.3/3. LCCN:78-022648.

Audience: **g,l,u,f.**

Thornton, Sarah   **HN383.5.T43 1996**

Club Cultures: Music, Media, and Subcultural Capital. Trade Paper. Wesleyan University Press. Middletown, CT. 1996. 201p. Music Culture Ser. ISBN:0-8195-6297-1, ISBN13: 978-0-8195-6297-5. Dewey:306/.0941. LCCN:95-061500.

Audience: **u,f.** *Choice, 1996.*

Wright, Judy   **GV1753.5.W75 2003**

Social Dance: Steps to Success. Ed. 2. Trade Paper. Human Kinetics Publishers. Champaign, IL. 2002. 24p. ISBN:0-7360-4505-8, ISBN13: 978-0-7360-4505-6. Dewey:793.3/3. LCCN:2002-010840.

Audience: **g,l,u.**

Dance Styles, Forms, and Traditions > Variety Dance > Minstrel

Courlander, Harold   **ML3556**

Negro Folk Music U. S. A. Trade Paper. Dover Publications, Inc. Mineola, NY. 1998. 324p. ISBN:0-486-27350-4, ISBN13: 978-0-486-27350-1. Dewey:781.6296073. LCCN:92-035475.

Audience: **u,f.**

Emery, Lynne Fauley   **GV1624.7.A34**

Black Dance: From 1619 to Today. Trade Cloth. Princeton Book Company Publishers. Hightstown, NJ. 1988. xii, 397p. ISBN:0-916622-61-4, ISBN13: 978-0-916622-61-9. Dewey:793.3089/96073. LCCN:88-061031.

Audience: **g,l,u.**

Fletcher, Tom   **ML3556**

One Hundred Years of the Negro in Show Business. Thomas L. Riis (Introduction by). Paper Text. Da Capo Press, Inc. Cambridge, MA. 1984. 337p. Music Reprint Ser. ISBN:0-306-76219-6, ISBN13: 978-0-306-76219-2. Dewey:782.81/08996073.

Audience: **g,l,u,f.**

Hughes, Langston &   **PN2286.H75 1990**
Meltzer, Milton

Black Magic: A Pictorial History of the African-American in the Performing Arts. Ossie Davis (Introduction by). Trade Paper. Da Capo Press, Inc. Cambridge, MA. 1990. 384p. Quality Paperbacks Ser. ISBN:0-306-80406-9, ISBN13: 978-0-306-80406-9. Dewey:791/.08996073. LCCN:90-039145.

Audience: **g,l,u,f.**

Minsky, Morton & Machlin, Milt   **PN1948.U6**
Minsky's Burlesque. Trade Cloth. HarperCollins Publishers. New York, NY. 1986. 256p. ISBN:0-87795-743-6, ISBN13: 978-0-87795-743-0. Dewey:792.7/0973.
> Audience: **l,u,f.**

Nathan, Hans   **ML410.E5**
Dan Emmett and the Rise of Early Negro Minstrelsy. Trade Cloth. University of Oklahoma Press. Norman, OK. 1977. 496p. ISBN:0-8061-0540-2, ISBN13: 978-0-8061-0540-6. Dewey:780.0712.
> Audience: **u,f.**

Sampson, Henry T.   **ML1711**
Blacks in Blackface: A Source Book on Early Black Musical Shows. Trade Cloth. Scarecrow Press, Inc. Lanham, MD. 1980. 562p. ISBN:0-8108-1318-1, ISBN13: 978-0-8108-1318-2. Dewey:782.81/092/2. LCCN:80-015048.
> Audience: **g,l,u,f.**

Toll, Robert C.   **PN1969.M5**
Blacking Up: The Minstrel Show in Nineteenth-Century America. Trade Paper. Oxford University Press, Inc. New York, NY. 1977. 340p. ISBN:0-19-502172-X, ISBN13: 978-0-19-502172-1. Dewey:791.1/2/0973. LCCN:74-083992.
> Audience: **u,f.**

Toll, Robert C.   **PN2245.T58**
On with the Show!: The First Century of American Show Business. Trade Cloth. Oxford University Press, Inc. New York, NY. 1976. 374p. ISBN:0-19-502057-X, ISBN13: 978-0-19-502057-1. Dewey:790.2/0973. LCCN:75-046355.
> Audience: **g,l,u,f.**

Wittke, Carl F.   **PN3195**
Tambo and Bones: A History of the American Minstrel Stage. Trade Cloth. Greenwood Publishing Group, Inc. Portsmouth, NH. 1971. 269p. ISBN:0-8371-0276-6, ISBN13: 978-0-8371-0276-4. Dewey:791.1/2/0973. LCCN:69-010174.
> Audience: **l,u,f.**

Dance Styles, Forms, and Traditions > Variety Dance > Vaudeville

DiMeglio, John E.   **PN1968.U5 D5**
Vaudeville U.S.A. Bowling Green University Popular Press. 1973. ISBN:0-87972-053-0, ISBN13: 978-0-87972-053-7.
> Audience: **g,l,u,f.**

Gilbert, Douglas   **PN1967**
American Vaudeville, Its Life and Times. Trade Paper. Dover Publications, Inc. Mineola, NY. 1940. ISBN:0-486-20999-7, ISBN13: 978-0-486-20999-9. Dewey:792.20973.
> Audience: **g,l,u,f.**

Graves, Nadine George   **GV1785.A1G46 2000**
The Royalty of Negro Vaudeville: The Whitman Sisters and the Negotiation of Race, Gender and Class in African American Theater 1900-1940. Cloth over Boards. Palgrave Macmillan.

New York, NY. 2000. 208p. ISBN:0-312-22562-8, ISBN13: 978-0-312-22562-9. Dewey:792.7/092/396073 B. LCCN:99-088103.
> Audience: **u,f.** *Choice, 2001.*

Laurie, Joe   **PN1967.L3**
Vaudeville: From the Honky-Tonks to the Palace. Trade Cloth. Henry Holt & Company. New York, NY. 1953. 561p. ISBN:0-8046-1535-7, ISBN13: 978-0-8046-1535-8. Dewey:792.2. LCCN:53-009590.
> Audience: **g,l.**

Seldes, Gilbert   **PN1584.S45**
The 7 Lively Arts. Paper Text. Textbook Publishers. Temecula, CA. 2003. 306p. ISBN:0-7581-4228-5, ISBN13: 978-0-7581-4228-3. Dewey:791.
> Audience: **l,u.**

Smith, Bill   **PN1968.U5 S4**
The Vaudevillians. MacMillan. 1976. ISBN:0-02-611890-4, ISBN13: 978-0-02-611890-3.
> Audience: **g,l,u,f.**

Snyder, Robert W.   **PN1968.U5S68 1989**
Voice of the City: Vaudeville and Popular Culture in New York. Trade Cloth. Oxford University Press, Inc. New York, NY. 1989. 244p. ISBN:0-19-505285-4, ISBN13: 978-0-19-505285-5. Dewey:792.7/09747/1. LCCN:89-016143.
> Audience: **u,f.** *Choice, 1990.*

Sobel, Bernard   **PN1968.U5S69 2002**
A Pictorial History of Vaudeville. Trade Paper. Barricade Books, Inc. Fort Lee, NJ. 2002. 224p. ISBN:1-56980-237-8, ISBN13: 978-1-56980-237-3. Dewey:792.7/0973. LCCN:2002-026100.
> Audience: **g,l,u.** *B*

Stein, Charles W.   **PN1968.U5A4 1984**
American Vaudeville As Seen by Its Contemporaries. Trade Cloth. Alfred A. Knopf Inc. New York, NY. 1984. 335p. ISBN:0-394-53743-2, ISBN13: 978-0-394-53743-6. Dewey:792.7/0973. LCCN:84-047526.
> Audience: **g,l,u.**

Stratyner, Barbara   **GV1785.W39C64**
Ned Wayburn and the Dance Routine: From Vaudeville to the Ziegfeld Follies. Perfect. Society of Dance History Scholars. Minneapolis, MN. 1996. 141p. Studies in Dance History, Vol. 13 ISBN:0-9653519-2-0, ISBN13: 978-0-9653519-2-8. Dewey:792.820924. LCCN:96-070657.
> Audience: **u,f.**

Toll, Robert C.   **PN2245.T58**
On with the Show!: The First Century of American Show Business. Trade Cloth. Oxford University Press, Inc. New York, NY. 1976. 374p. ISBN:0-19-502057-X, ISBN13: 978-0-19-502057-1. Dewey:790.2/0973. LCCN:75-046355.
> Audience: **g,l,u,f.**

Dance Styles, Forms, and Traditions > Variety Dance > Burlesque

Baldwin, Michelle   **PN1942.B35 2004**
Burlesque and the New Bump-N-Grind. Trade Paper. Speck Press. Denver, CO. 2004. 168p. ISBN:0-9725776-2-9, ISBN13: 978-0-9725776-2-5. Dewey:792.7/0973/0904. LCCN:2004-001149.
Audience: **g,l,u,f.**

Lee, Gypsy Rose   **PN2287.L29 A3**
Gypsy. Futura. 1988.
Audience: **g,l,u,f.**

Minsky, Morton & Machlin,   **PN1948.U6**
  Milt
Minsky's Burlesque. Trade Cloth. HarperCollins Publishers. New York, NY. 1986. 256p. ISBN:0-87795-743-6, ISBN13: 978-0-87795-743-0. Dewey:792.7/0973.
Audience: **l,u,f.**

Shteir, Rachel   **PN1949.S7**
Striptease: The Untold History of the Girlie Show. Trade Paper. Oxford University Press, Inc. New York, NY. 2005. 448p. ISBN:0-19-530076-9, ISBN13: 978-0-19-530076-5. Dewey:792.7. LCCN:2004-014760.
Audience: **g,l,u,f.** *Choice, 2005.*

Sobel, Bernard   **PN1947.S6**
A Pictorial History of Burlesque. G.P. Putnam's Sons. 1956.
Audience: **g,l,u.**

Zeidman, Irving   **PN1948.U6 Z4**
American Burlesque Show. Hawthorne. 1967.
Audience: **g,l,u,f.**

Dance Styles, Forms, and Traditions > Dance in Commercial Theater and Movies

Bird, Dorothy & Greenberg,   **GV1787**
  Joyce
Bird's Eye View: Dancing with Martha Graham and on Broadway. Trade Paper. University of Pittsburgh Press. Pittsburgh, PA. 2002. 296p. ISBN:0-8229-5791-4, ISBN13: 978-0-8229-5791-1. Dewey:792.8.
Audience: **u,f.**

Bogle, Donald   **PN1995.9.N4B59 2005**
Bright Boulevards, Bold Dreams: The Story of Black Hollywood. Trade Cloth. Ballantine Books. New York, NY. 2005. 432p. ISBN:0-345-45418-9, ISBN13: 978-0-345-45418-8. Dewey:791.4302/8/092396073. LCCN:2004-054781.
Audience: **l,u.**

Dodds, Sherril   **GV1594**
Dance on Screen: Genres and Media from Hollywood to Experimental Art. Ed. 2. Trade Paper. Palgrave Macmillan. New York, NY. 2005. 224p. ISBN:1-4039-4145-9, ISBN13: 978-1-4039-4145-9. Dewey:791.43/655.
Audience: **u,f.** *Choice, 2002.*

Haygood, Wil   **PN2287.D322**
In Black and White: The Life of Sammy Davis, Jr. Knopf. 2003. ISBN:0-375-40354-X, ISBN13: 978-0-375-40354-5.
Audience: **g,l,u,f.**

Jowitt, Deborah   **GV1785.R52J69 2004**
Jerome Robbins: His Life, His Theater, His Dance. Trade Cloth. Simon & Schuster, Inc. New York, NY. 2004. 640p. ISBN:0-684-86985-3, ISBN13: 978-0-684-86985-8. Dewey:792.8/2/092 B. LCCN:2004-045440.
Audience: **l,u,f.** *Choice, 2005.*

Long, Robert Emmet   **GV1785.A1L65 2001**
Broadway, the Golden Years: Jerome Robbins and the Great Choreographer-Directors, 1940 to the Present. Trade Cloth. Continuum International Publishing Group, Ltd. London, 2003. 312p. ISBN:0-8264-1347-1, ISBN13: 978-0-8264-1347-5. Dewey:792.8/2/09227471 B. LCCN:2001-032570.
Audience: **g,l,u,f.** *Choice, 2002.*

Parker, David, & Siegel,   **GV1779.P37**
  Esther
Guide to Dance in Film. Gale Research Company. 1978.
Audience: **g,l,u,f.**

Saura, Carlos   **PN1998.3.S28A5 2003**
Carlos Saura: Interviews. Linda M. Willem (Editor). Trade Cloth. University Press of Mississippi. Jackson, MS. 2003. 208p. Conversations with Filmmakers Ser. ISBN:1-57806-494-5, ISBN13: 978-1-57806-494-6. Dewey:791.43/0233/092. LCCN:2002-003009.
Audience: **u,f.**

Stratyner, Barbara   **GV1785.W39C64**
Ned Wayburn and the Dance Routine: From Vaudeville to the Ziegfeld Follies. Perfect. Society of Dance History Scholars. Minneapolis, MN. 1996. 141p. Studies in Dance History, Vol. 13 ISBN:0-9653519-2-0, ISBN13: 978-0-9653519-2-8. Dewey:792.820924. LCCN:96-070657.
Audience: **u,f.**

Dance Styles, Forms, and Traditions > Television, Video, and New Media Dance

Dodds, Sherril   **GV1594**
Dance on Screen: Genres and Media from Hollywood to Experimental Art. Ed. 2. Trade Paper. Palgrave Macmillan. New York, NY. 2005. 224p. ISBN:1-4039-4145-9, ISBN13: 978-1-4039-4145-9. Dewey:791.43/655.
Audience: **u,f.** *Choice, 2002.*

Choreography

Billman, Larry   GV1779.B55 1997
Film Choreographers and Dance Directors: An Illustrated
Biographical Encyclopedia, with a History and Filmographies,
1893 Through 1995. Cloth Text. McFarland & Company,
Incorporated Publishers. Jefferson, NC. 1997. 664p.
ISBN:0-89950-868-5, ISBN13: 978-0-89950-868-9.
Dewey:792.6/2/0922. LCCN:96-31756.
Audience: **g,l,u,f.** *Choice, 1998.*

Delamater, Jerome   GV1779
Dance in the Hollywood Musical. Diane Kirkpatrick (Editor).
Trade Cloth. U M I Research Press. Ann Arbor, MI. 1981. 324p.
Studies in Cinema, No. 4 ISBN:0-8357-1198-6, ISBN13:
978-0-8357-1198-2. Dewey:793.3/2. LCCN:81-007513.
Audience: **g,l,u,f.**

Gere, David   GV1588.6.G47 2004
How to Make Dances in an Epidemic: Tracking Choreography
in the Age of AIDS. Trade Cloth. University of Wisconsin Press.
Chicago, IL. 2004. 352p. ISBN:0-299-20080-9, ISBN13:
978-0-299-20080-0. Dewey:306.4/84. LCCN:2004-005184.
Audience: **l,u,f.** *Choice, 2005.*

Hewitt, Andrew   GV1782.5.H49 2005
Social Choreography: Ideology As Performance in Dance and
Everyday Movement. Trade Cloth. Duke University Press.
Durham, NC. 2005. 264p. Post-Contemporary Interventions Ser.
ISBN:0-8223-3502-6, ISBN13: 978-0-8223-3502-3.
Dewey:792.8/2. LCCN:2004-022037.
Audience: **u,f.**

Jordan, Stephanie & Allen,   GV1787
  Dave (Editors)
Parallel Lines: Media Representation of Dance. Trade Paper.
University of Luton Press. Luton, 2003. 256p.
ISBN:0-86196-371-7, ISBN13: 978-0-86196-371-3.
Dewey:792.8.
Audience: **u,f.**

Lawson, Joan   GV1782.5.L38 1991
Ballet-Maker's Handbook: Sources, Vocabulary, Styles.
Routledge/Theatre Arts Books. 1991. ISBN:0-7136-3246-1,
ISBN13: 978-0-7136-3246-0.
Audience: **g,l.**

Mueller, John   PN1995.9.F54
Astaire Dancing: The Musical Films. Trade Cloth. Alfred A.
Knopf Inc. New York, NY. 1985. 448p. ISBN:0-394-51654-0,
ISBN13: 978-0-394-51654-7. Dewey:791.43/655.
LCCN:84-047874.
Audience: **g,l,u.**

Nagrin, Daniel   GV1595.N35 1997
The Six Questions: Acting Techniques for Dance Performance.
Trade Paper. University of Pittsburgh Press. Pittsburgh, PA.
1997. 221p. ISBN:0-8229-5624-1, ISBN13: 978-0-8229-5624-2.
Dewey:792.7/8. LCCN:96-051277.
Audience: **l,u,f.**

Newman, Barbara   GV1787
Grace under Pressure: Passing Dance Through Time. Trade
Paper. Hal Leonard Corporation. Milwaukee, WI. 2004. 480p.
ISBN:0-87910-995-5, ISBN13: 978-0-87910-995-0.
Dewey:792.8/092/2 B. LCCN:2003-019294.
Audience: **u,f.** *Choice, 2004.*

Prevots, Naima   GV1785.A1P74
Dancing in the Sun: Hollywood Choreographers, 1915-1937.
Oscar G. Brockett (Editor). Trade Paper. Books on Demand.
Ann Arbor, MI. 1987. 290p. Theater and Dramatic Studies, Vol.
44 ISBN:0-8357-1825-5, ISBN13: 978-0-8357-1825-7.
Dewey:792.8/2/0922 B. LCCN:87-013859.
Audience: **u,f.** *Choice, 1988.*

Schlundt, Christina L.   GV1781.S35 1989
Dance in the Musical Theater: Jerome Robbins and His Peers,
1934-1965, A Guide. Paper over Boards. Garland Publishing,
Inc. New York, NY. 1989. 272p. ISBN:0-8240-5547-0, ISBN13:
978-0-8240-5547-9. Dewey:792.8/2. LCCN:89-001117.
Audience: **g,l,u,f.** *Choice, 1989.*

Tharp, Twyla   BF408.T415 2006
The Creative Habit: Learn It and Use It for Life. Trade Paper.
Simon & Schuster, Inc. New York, NY. 2005. 256p.
ISBN:0-7432-3527-4, ISBN13: 978-0-7432-3527-3.
Dewey:153.3/5. LCCN:2005-285389.
Audience: **g,l,u,f.** *Choice, 2004.*

Dance Production and Administration

Clarke, Mary & Crisp,   GV1782.C56 1978
  Clement
Design for Ballet. Hawthorn Books. 1978. ISBN:0-8015-2020-7,
ISBN13: 978-0-8015-2020-4.
Audience: **u,f.**

Cooper, Susan   GV1782.C66 1998
Staging Dance. Trade Paper. Routledge. New York, NY. 1998.
128p. Theatre Arts Ser. ISBN:0-87830-081-3, ISBN13:
978-0-87830-081-5. Dewey:792.8/4. LCCN:97-035293.
Audience: **u,f.**

Pecktal, Lynn   TT507.P39 1999
Costume Design: Techniques of Modern Masters. Trade Cloth.
Watson-Guptill Publications, Inc. New York, NY. 1999. 256p.
ISBN:0-8230-8812-X, ISBN13: 978-0-8230-8812-6.
Dewey:792/.026/0922. LCCN:98-049867.
Audience: **u,f.**

Schlaich, Joan & DuPont,   GV1782.D35 1998
  Betty (Editors)
Dance: The Art of Production. Ed. 3. Trade Paper. Princeton
Book Company Publishers. Hightstown, NJ. 1988. 191p.
ISBN:0-87127-207-5, ISBN13: 978-0-87127-207-2.
Dewey:793.3/2. LCCN:98-050077.
Audience: **u,f.**

Sherbon, Elizabeth   GV1753.5.S48 1990
On the Count of One: The Art, Craft, and Science of Teaching
Modern Dance. Ed. 4. Trade Paper. A Cappella Books. Chicago,
IL. 1990. 224p. ISBN:1-55652-090-5, ISBN13:
978-1-55652-090-7. Dewey:792.8. LCCN:90-037649.
                                                          Audience: **u,f.**

White, David R.   GV1596.5
Poor Dancer's Almanac: Managing Life and Work in the
Performing Arts. Lise Friedman & Tia T. Levinson (Editors).
Trade Cloth. Duke University Press. Durham, NC. 1993. 380p.
ISBN:0-8223-1305-7, ISBN13: 978-0-8223-1305-2.
Dewey:792.802373. LCCN:92-021499.
                                                          Audience: **l,u.**

Williams, Peter   GV1782.W54 1981
Masterpieces of Ballet Design. Phaidon Press. 1981.
ISBN:0-7148-2042-3, ISBN13: 978-0-7148-2042-2.
                                                          Audience: **u,f.**

Dance Notation

Beck, Jill & Reiser, Joseph   GV1788
C.
Moving Notation: A Handbook of Musical Rhythm and
Elementary Labanotation for the Dancer. Cloth Text. Gordon &
Breach Publishing Group. New York, NY. 1998. 396p.
Performing Arts Studies ISBN:90-5702-178-1, ISBN13:
978-90-5702-178-7. Dewey:792.8/2.
                                                          Audience: **g,l,u.**

Benesh, Rudolf; Benesh,   GV1587.B44 1977
   Joan
Reading Dance: the Birth of Choreology. Souvenir Press (E. &
A.) Ltd. 1977. ISBN:0-285-62291-9, ISBN13:
978-0-285-62291-3.
                                                          Audience: **l,u,f.**

Dell, Cecily   BF295
Primer for Movement Description Using Effort/Shape. Ed. 2.
Paper Text. Dance Notation Bureau, Inc. New York, NY. 1970.
123p. ISBN:0-932582-03-6, ISBN13: 978-0-932582-03-4.
Dewey:792.8071. LCCN:78-111086.
                                                          Audience: **l,u,f.**

Guest, Ann Hutchinson   GV1587.G82 1989
Choreo-Graphics: A Comparison of Dance Notation Systems
from the Fifteenth Century to the Present. Gordon and Breach.
1989. ISBN:2-88124-714-8, ISBN13: 978-2-88124-714-9.
                                                          Audience: **u,f.**

Guest, Ann Hutchinson   GV1587.G83 1984
Dance Notation: The Process of Recording Movement on Paper.
Trade Cloth. Princeton Book Company Publishers. Hightstown,
NJ. 1984. 224p. ISBN:0-87127-141-9, ISBN13:
978-0-87127-141-9. Dewey:793.3/2. LCCN:84-070511.
                                                          Audience: **l,u,f.**

Guest, Ann Hutchinson   GV1587.H8
Labanotation or Kinetography Laban: The System of Analyzing
and Recording Movement. Routledge. 1987.
                                                          Audience: **l,u,f.**

Guest, Ann Hutchinson   GV452.G83 1983 SUPPL
🄴 Your Move: A New Approach to the Study of Movement and
Dance : Teacher's Guide. E-Book. Taylor & Francis Group.
Philadelphia, PA. ISBN:0-203-98527-3, ISBN13:
978-0-203-98527-4. Dewey:372.86.
                                                          Audience: **l,u,f.**

Miles, Alan   GV1587
Dictionary of Classical Ballet in Labanotation. Princeton Book
Company. 1976.
                                                          Audience: **g,l,u,f.**

Topaz, Muriel   GV1587
Elementary Labanotation. Trade Paper. Princeton Book
Company Publishers. Hightstown, NJ. 1997. 209p.
ISBN:0-87127-203-2, ISBN13: 978-0-87127-203-4.
Dewey:792.82.
                                                          Audience: **l,u,f.**

Dance Criticism

Anderson, Jack   GV1782.5.A53 1987
Choreography Observed. Cloth Text. University of Iowa Press.
Iowa City, IA. 1987. 304p. ISBN:0-87745-172-9, ISBN13:
978-0-87745-172-3. Dewey:792.8/2. LCCN:87-006021.
                                            Audience: **l,u,f.** *Choice, 1988.*

Banes, Sally   NX511.N4
Subversive Expectations: Performance Art and Paratheater in
New York, 1976-85. Trade Paper. University of Michigan Press.
Chicago, IL. 1998. 312p. ISBN:0-472-06678-1, ISBN13:
978-0-472-06678-0. Dewey:709/.747/1. LCCN:98-006969.
                                                          Audience: **u,f.**

Banes, Sally   GV1623 .B36 1994
Writing Dancing in the Age of Postmodernism. Trade Paper.
Wesleyan University Press. Middletown, CT. 1994. 428p.
ISBN:0-8195-6268-8, ISBN13: 978-0-8195-6268-5.
Dewey:792.8/0973. LCCN:93-008225.
                                                          Audience: **u,f.**

Buckle, Richard   GV1787.6.B82 1980
Buckle at the Ballet: Selected Ballet Writings. Trade Cloth.
Simon & Schuster. New York, NY. 1980. 416p.
ISBN:0-689-11085-5, ISBN13: 978-0-689-11085-6.
Dewey:792.8/4. LCCN:80-066015.
                                                          Audience: **u,f.**

Carr, C   GV1794
On Edge: Performance at the End of the Twentieth Century.
Trade Paper. Wesleyan University Press. Middletown, CT. 1993.
357p. ISBN:0-8195-6269-6, ISBN13: 978-0-8195-6269-2.
Dewey:792.76543. LCCN:93-008182.
                                                          Audience: **u,f.**

Croce, Arlene   GV1624.5.N4.C76 1977
Afterimages. Trade Cloth. Knopf Publishing Group. New York,
NY. 1977. 466p. ISBN:0-394-41093-9, ISBN13:
978-0-394-41093-7. Dewey:792.8/0973. LCCN:78-004592.
                                    Audience: **u,f.**

Croce, Arlene   GV1599 .C76 1982
Going to the Dance. Trade Paper. Alfred A. Knopf Inc. New
York, NY. 1982. ISBN:0-394-70826-1, ISBN13:
978-0-394-70826-3. Dewey:793.3. LCCN:81-048110.
                                    Audience: **u,f.**

Croce, Arlene   GV1624.5.N4
Sight Lines. Trade Cloth. Alfred A. Knopf Inc. New York, NY.
1988. ISBN:0-317-68135-4, ISBN13: 978-0-317-68135-2.
Dewey:793.3/2/097471.
                        Audience: **u,f.** *Choice, 1988.*

Croce, Arlene   GV1624.5.N4C79 2000
Writing in the Dark, Dancing in the New Yorker: An Arlene
Croce Reader. Cloth over Boards. Farrar, Straus & Giroux. New
York, NY. 2000. 720p. ISBN:0-374-10455-7, ISBN13:
978-0-374-10455-9. Dewey:792.8/09747/1. LCCN:00-035448.
                                    Audience: **l,u,f.**

Daly, Ann   GV1783.D35 2002
Critical Gestures: Writings on Dance and Culture. Library
Binding. University Press of New England. Lebanon, NH. 2002.
320p. ISBN:0-8195-6565-2, ISBN13: 978-0-8195-6565-5.
Dewey:792.8. LCCN:2002-010172.
                                    Audience: **u,f.**

Denby, Edwin   GV1599.D393 1998
Dance Writings and Poetry. Robert Cornfield (Editor). Trade
Paper. Yale University Press. Cumberland, RI. 1998. 336p.
ISBN:0-300-06985-5, ISBN13: 978-0-300-06985-3.
Dewey:793.3. LCCN:98-002517.
                        Audience: **u,f.** *Choice, 1999.*

Foster, Susan L.   GV1623
Reading Dancing: Bodies and Subjects in Contemporary
American Dance. Trade Cloth. University of California Press.
Berkeley, CA. 1988. 224p. ISBN:0-520-06333-3, ISBN13:
978-0-520-06333-4.
                                    Audience: **u,f.**

Gere, David (Editor), et al.   GV1600.L66 1995
Looking Out: Perspectives on Dance and Criticism in a
Multicultural World. Lewis Segal, Patrice Koelsch & Elizabeth
Zimmer (Editors). Trade Cloth. Thomson Gale. Farmington
Hills, MI. 1995. 242p. ISBN:0-02-870683-8, ISBN13:
978-0-02-870683-2. Dewey:792.82. LCCN:95-098941.
                                    Audience: **g,l.**

Guest, Ivor F. (Editor,   GV1649
 Translator)
Gautier on Dance. Trade Cloth. Dance Books, Ltd. Alton, 1995.
350p. ISBN:0-903102-94-3, ISBN13: 978-0-903102-94-0.
Dewey:792.8/45.
                                    Audience: **u,f.**

Johnston, Jill   PS3568.O243
Marmalade Me. Deborah Jowitt (Introduction by), Sally Banes
(Afterword by). Trade Paper. Wesleyan University Press.
Middletown, CT. 1998. 343p. ISBN:0-8195-6314-5, ISBN13:
978-0-8195-6314-9. Dewey:813/.5/4. LCCN:97-021727.
                                    Audience: **l,u,f.**

Jowitt, Deborah   GV1624.5.N4J
Dance Beat: Selected Views and Reviews, 1967-1976. Trade
Paper. Books on Demand. Ann Arbor, MI. 222p.
ISBN:0-608-13601-8, ISBN13: 978-0-608-13601-1.
Dewey:793.32. LCCN:76-044564.
                                    Audience: **u,f.**

Jowitt, Deborah   GV1599.J66 1985
The Dance in Mind: Profiles and Reviews, 1977-83. Lois
Greenfield (Photographer). Trade Cloth. David R. Godine
Publisher. Boston, MA. 1985. 320p. ISBN:0-87923-534-9,
ISBN13: 978-0-87923-534-5. Dewey:793.3. LCCN:84-047654.
                                    Audience: **u,f.**

Martin, John   GV1783.M328 1989
The Dance in Theory. Jack Anderson (Introduction by). Trade
Paper. Princeton Book Company Publishers. Hightstown, NJ.
1989. 96p. ISBN:0-916622-90-8, ISBN13: 978-0-916622-90-9.
Dewey:792.8/0973. LCCN:89-024192.
                                    Audience: **u,f.**

Morris, Gay (Editor)   GV1600.M68 1996
Moving Words: Re-Writing Dance. Paper over Boards.
Routledge. New York, NY. 1996. 360p. ISBN:0-415-12542-1,
ISBN13: 978-0-415-12542-0. Dewey:792.8. LCCN:95-039924.
                        Audience: **u,f.** *Choice, 1997.*

Siegel, M. B.   GV1623.S53
At the Vanishing Point. Trade Cloth. Penguin Group (USA) Inc.
New York, NY. 1985. ix, 320p. ISBN:0-8415-0174-2, ISBN13:
978-0-8415-0174-4. Dewey:793.3/08. LCCN:72-079040.
                                    Audience: **u,f.**

Siegel, Marcia B.   GV1623.S54
Watching the Dance Go By. Trade Cloth. Houghton Mifflin
Company. New York, NY. 1977. xvii, 345p.
ISBN:0-395-25173-7, ISBN13: 978-0-395-25173-7.
Dewey:793.3/2. LCCN:76-058029.
                                    Audience: **l,u,f.**

Siegel, Marcia B.   GV1783.S53 1991
The Tail of the Dragon: New Dance, 1976-1982. Nathaniel
Tileston (Photographer). Cloth Text. Duke University Press.
Durham, NC. 1991. 251p. ISBN:0-8223-1156-9, ISBN13:
978-0-8223-1156-0. Dewey:792.8. LCCN:91-000522.
                        Audience: **u,f.** *Choice, 1992.*

Sorell, Walter   GV1785.S64A35 1986
Looking Back in Wonder: Diary of a Dance Critic. Trade Cloth.
Columbia University Press. New York, NY. 1986. 284p.
ISBN:0-231-06278-8, ISBN13: 978-0-231-06278-7.
Dewey:793.3/2/0924 B. LCCN:85-031380.
                        Audience: **u,f.** *Choice, 1987.*

Theodores, Diana   **GV1588.5**
First We Take Manhattan: Four American Women and the New
York School of Dance Criticism. Library Binding. Gordon &
Breach Publishing Group. New York, NY. 1996. 180p.
Choreography and Dance Studies ISBN:3-7186-5876-3,
ISBN13: 978-3-7186-5876-3. Dewey:792.8/015.
                                                         Audience: **u.**

Van Vechten, Carl   **GV1781.V32 1974**
The Dance Writings of Carl Van Vechten. Trade Cloth.
Princeton Book Company Publishers. Hightstown, NJ. 1974.
xxi, 182p. ISBN:0-87127-052-8, ISBN13: 978-0-87127-052-8.
Dewey:792.8/4. LCCN:74-081412.
                                                       Audience: **u,f.**

Dance Theory

Bachelard, Gaston   **B2430.B253**
The Poetics of Space. John R. Stilgoe (Foreword by). Trade
Paper. Beacon Press. Boston, MA. 1994. 288p.
ISBN:0-8070-6473-4, ISBN13: 978-0-8070-6473-3. Dewey:114.
LCCN:93-027874.
                                              Audience: **g,u,f.** *B*

Banes, Sally   **GV1783**
Democracy's Body: Judson Dance Theater, 1962-1964. Paper
Text. Duke University Press. Durham, NC. 1993. 288p.
ISBN:0-8223-1399-5, ISBN13: 978-0-8223-1399-1.
Dewey:793.3/2. LCCN:93-021760.
                                                       Audience: **u,f.**

Banes, Sally   **NX511.N4.B26 1993**
Greenwich Village, 1963: Avant-Garde Performance and the
Effervescent Body. Cloth Text. Duke University Press. Durham,
NC. 1993. 352p. ISBN:0-8223-1357-X, ISBN13:
978-0-8223-1357-1. Dewey:700.97471. LCCN:93-018393.
                                  Audience: **u,f.** *Choice, 1994.*

Banes, Sally   **GV1623 .B36 1994**
Writing Dancing in the Age of Postmodernism. Library Binding.
Wesleyan University Press. Middletown, CT. 1994. 428p.
ISBN:0-8195-5266-6, ISBN13: 978-0-8195-5266-2.
Dewey:792.8/0973. LCCN:93-008225.
                                                       Audience: **u,f.**

Battock, Gregory   **NX600.P47**
Performance Art. Trade Paper. Penguin Group (USA) Inc. New
York, NY. 1984. 344p. ISBN:0-525-48039-0, ISBN13:
978-0-525-48039-6. Dewey:700/.9/04.
                                                       Audience: **l,u,f.**

Birringer, Johannes   **PN2039.B57 1991**
Theatre, Theory, Postmodernism. Trade Cloth. Indiana
University Press. Bloomington, IN. 1991. 256p. Drama and
Performance Studies ISBN:0-253-31195-0, ISBN13:
978-0-253-31195-5. Dewey:792/.01. LCCN:90-024442.
                                  Audience: **u,f.** *Choice, 1992.*

Birringer, Johannes H.   **NX212.B57 1998**
Media and Performance: Along the Border. Trade Paper. Johns
Hopkins University Press. Baltimore, MD. 1998. 400p. PAJ
Bks., :Art and Performance ISBN:0-8018-5852-6, ISBN13:
978-0-8018-5852-9. Dewey:700/.9/04. LCCN:98-012702.
                                  Audience: **u,f.** *Choice, 1999.*

Brown, Jean (Editor), et al.   **GV1783.V57 1997**
The Vision of Modern Dance: In the Words of Its Creators. Ed.
2. Charles H. Woodford & Naomi Mindlin (Editors). Trade
Paper. Princeton Book Company Publishers. Hightstown, NJ.
1998. 230p. ISBN:0-87127-205-9, ISBN13: 978-0-87127-205-8.
Dewey:792.8/092/2. LCCN:97-028330.
                                                       Audience: **u,f.**

Buonaventura, Wendy   **GV1588.6.B87 2004**
Something in the Way She Moves: Dancing Women from
Salome to Madonna. Trade Cloth. Da Capo Press, Inc.
Cambridge, MA. 2004. 312p. ISBN:0-306-81348-3, ISBN13:
978-0-306-81348-1. Dewey:792.8/082. LCCN:2004-050025.
                                  Audience: **g,l,u,f.** *Choice, 2005.*

Burt, Ramsey   **GV1595.B87 1995**
The Male Dancer: Bodies, Spectacle and Sexualities. Trade
Paper. Routledge. New York, NY. 1995. 240p.
ISBN:0-415-08900-X, ISBN13: 978-0-415-08900-5.
Dewey:792.8/081. LCCN:94-032793.
                                                       Audience: **l,u,f.**

Calabria, Frank M.   **GV1623.C25 1993**
Dance of the Sleepwalkers: The Dance Marathon Fad. Trade
Cloth. University of Wisconsin Press. Chicago, IL. 1993. 215p.
ISBN:0-87972-569-9, ISBN13: 978-0-87972-569-3.
Dewey:793.3/1973. LCCN:92-073976.
                                  Audience: **g,l,u,f.** *Choice, 1993.*

Chatterjea, Ananya   **GV1588.6.C53 2004**
Butting Out: Reading Resistive Choreographies Through Works
by Jawole Willa Jo Zollar and Chandralekha. Trade Paper.
Wesleyan University Press. Middletown, CT. 2004. 400p.
ISBN:0-8195-6733-7, ISBN13: 978-0-8195-6733-8.
Dewey:792.8/2. LCCN:2004-019055.
                                                       Audience: **u,f.**

Cohen, Selma J. (Editor)   **GV1751**
Next Week, Swan Lake: Reflections on Dance and Dances.
Trade Paper. Wesleyan University Press. Middletown, CT. 1982.
207p. ISBN:0-8195-6110-X, ISBN13: 978-0-8195-6110-7.
Dewey:793.3. LCCN:82-002614.
                                                       Audience: **u,f.**

Cohen, Selma J. (Editor,   **GV1783**
  Introduction by)
The Modern Dance: Seven Statements of Belief. Trade Paper.
Wesleyan University Press. Middletown, CT. 1966. 112p.
ISBN:0-8195-6003-0, ISBN13: 978-0-8195-6003-2.
Dewey:793.32. LCCN:66-014663.
                                                       Audience: **l,u,f.**

Cohen, Selma J. (Editor)   GV1781
Dance As a Theatre Art: Source Readings in Dance History
from 1851 to Present. Ed. 2. Katy Matheson (Contribution by).
Trade Paper. Princeton Book Company Publishers. Hightstown,
NJ. 1991. 271p. ISBN:0-87127-173-7, ISBN13:
978-0-87127-173-0. Dewey:792.8/09. LCCN:92-116094.
Audience: **u,f.**

Copeland, Roger & Cohen,   GV1594
  Marshall
What Is Dance?: Readings in Theory and Criticism. Trade
Cloth. Oxford University Press, Inc. New York, NY. 1983. 600p.
ISBN:0-19-503217-9, ISBN13: 978-0-19-503217-8.
Dewey:793.3. LCCN:82-014366.
Audience: **u,f.**

Davies, Eden   GV1587.D38 2006
Beyond Dance: Laban's Legacy of Movement Analysis. Cloth
Text. Routledge. New York, NY. 2005. 264p.
ISBN:0-415-97727-4, ISBN13: 978-0-415-97727-2.
Dewey:792.8/2. LCCN:2006-295022.
Audience: **u,f.**

DeFrantz, Thomas (Editor)   GV1624.7.A34.D38
Dancing Many Drums: Excavations in African American Dance.
Trade Paper. University of Wisconsin Press. Chicago, IL. 2001.
xiii, 366p. ISBN:0-299-17314-3, ISBN13: 978-0-299-17314-2.
Dewey:793.3/089/96073. LCCN:2001-001943.
Audience: **u,f.**   *Choice, 2002.*

DeFrantz, Thomas F.   GV1785.T32
Dancing Revelations: Alvin Ailey's Embodiment of African
American Culture. Trade Paper. Oxford University Press, Inc.
New York, NY. 2006. 318p. ISBN:0-19-530171-4, ISBN13:
978-0-19-530171-7. Dewey:792.8/028/092 B.
Audience: **u,f.**

Desmond, Jane C. (Editor)   GV1588.6.D395 2001
Dancing Desires: Choreographing Sexualities on and off the
Stage. Trade Cloth. University of Wisconsin Press. Chicago, IL.
2001. x, 475p. Studies in Dance History ISBN:0-299-17050-0,
ISBN13: 978-0-299-17050-9. Dewey:792.8. LCCN:00-010661.
Audience: **l,u,f.**   *Choice, 2002.*

Desmond, Jane C.   GV1588.6.M43 1997
Meaning in Motion: New Cultural Studies of Dance. Trade
Cloth. Duke University Press. Durham, NC. 1997. 408p.
Post-Contemporary Interventions Ser. ISBN:0-8223-1936-5,
ISBN13: 978-0-8223-1936-8. Dewey:306.4/84.
LCCN:96-043776.
Audience: **u,f.**

Dils, Ann & Albright, Ann   GV1601.M86 2001
  Cooper (Editors)
Moving History: Dancing Cultures: A Dance History Reader.
Library Binding. Wesleyan University Press. Middletown, CT.
2001. 544p. ISBN:0-8195-6412-5, ISBN13: 978-0-8195-6412-2.
Dewey:792.8/09. LCCN:2001-023549.
Audience: **l,u,f.**

Fancher, Gordon & Myers,   GV1588.3
  Gerald (Editors)
Philosophical Essays on Dance: With Responses from
Choreographers, Critics and Dancers. Trade Paper. Princeton
Book Company Publishers. Hightstown, NJ. 1981. 178p.
ISBN:0-87127-126-5, ISBN13: 978-0-87127-126-6.
Dewey:793.3/01. LCCN:81-067061.
Audience: **u,f.**

Foster, Susan L. (Editor)   GN298.C48 1995
Choreographing History. Trade Cloth. Indiana University Press.
Bloomington, IN. 1995. 272p. Unnatural Acts, :Theorizing the
Performative Ser. ISBN:0-253-32411-4, ISBN13:
978-0-253-32411-5. Dewey:306.4. LCCN:94-003622.
Audience: **u,f.**

Foster, Susan Leigh   GV1785.B834F67 2002
Dances That Describe Themselves: The Improvised
Choreography of Richard Bull. Library Binding. Wesleyan
University Press. Middletown, CT. 2002. 352p.
ISBN:0-8195-6550-4, ISBN13: 978-0-8195-6550-1.
Dewey:792.8/2/092 B. LCCN:2002-006149.
Audience: **u,f.**   *Choice, 2003.*

Foulkes, Julia L.   2001059758 [GV]
Modern Bodies: Dance and American Modernism from Martha
Graham to Alvin Ailey. Trade Paper. University of North
Carolina Press. Chapel Hill, NC. 2002. 272p. Cultural Studies of
the United States ISBN:0-8078-5367-4, ISBN13:
978-0-8078-5367-2. Dewey:792.8. LCCN:2001-059758.
Audience: **u,f.**   *Choice, 2003.*

Fraleigh, Sondra   GV1588.3.F724 2004
Dancing Identity: Metaphysics in Motion. Trade Cloth.
University of Pittsburgh Press. Pittsburgh, PA. 2004. 256p.
ISBN:0-8229-4239-9, ISBN13: 978-0-8229-4239-9.
Dewey:792.8/01. LCCN:2004-013584.
Audience: **u,f.**

Fraleigh, Sondra Horton   GV1783
Dance and the Lived Body. Trade Paper. University of
Pittsburgh Press. Pittsburgh, PA. 1996. 328p.
ISBN:0-8229-5579-2, ISBN13: 978-0-8229-5579-5.
Dewey:793.3/2. LCCN:86-019288.
Audience: **u,f.**   *Choice, 1987.*

Fraleigh, Sondra Horton   GV1589.R47 1999
Researching Dance: Evolving Modes of Inquiry. Cloth Text.
University of Pittsburgh Press. Pittsburgh, PA. 1999. 450p.
ISBN:0-8229-4084-1, ISBN13: 978-0-8229-4084-5.
Dewey:792.8/072. LCCN:98-040181.
Audience: **u,f.**   *Choice, 1999.*

Franko, Mark   GV1649
Dance As Text: Ideologies of the Baroque Body. Trade Cloth.
Cambridge University Press. New York, NY. 1993. 260p. RES
Monographs on Anthropology and Aesthetics
ISBN:0-521-43392-4, ISBN13: 978-0-521-43392-1.
Dewey:792.80944. LCCN:92-023437.
Audience: **u,f.**

Franko, Mark   GV1783.F72 1995
Dancing Modernism - Performing Politics. Trade Cloth. Indiana
University Press. Bloomington, IN. 1995. 240p.
ISBN:0-253-32432-7, ISBN13: 978-0-253-32432-0.
Dewey:792.8. LCCN:94-031788.

Audience: **u,f.**

Franko, Mark & Richards,   NX212.A25 2000
Annette (Editors)
Acting on the Past: Historical Performance Across the
Disciplines. Library Binding. Wesleyan University Press.
Middletown, CT. 2000. 253p. ISBN:0-8195-6394-3, ISBN13:
978-0-8195-6394-1. Dewey:790.2. LCCN:99-043625.

Audience: **u,f.** *Choice, 2000.*

Friedler, Sharon E. &   GV1799.4
Glazer, Susan B. (Editors)
Dancing Female: Lives and Issues of Women in Contemporary
Dance. Trade Paper. Gordon & Breach Publishing Group. New
York, NY. 1997. 336p. Choreography and Dance Studies
ISBN:90-5702-026-2, ISBN13: 978-90-5702-026-1.
Dewey:792.8/082.

Audience: **u,f.** *Choice, 1998.*

Gere, David   GV1588.6.G47 2004
How to Make Dances in an Epidemic: Tracking Choreography
in the Age of AIDS. Trade Cloth. University of Wisconsin Press.
Chicago, IL. 2004. 352p. ISBN:0-299-20080-9, ISBN13:
978-0-299-20080-0. Dewey:306.4/84. LCCN:2004-005184.

Audience: **l,u,f.** *Choice, 2005.*

Gere, David (Editor), et al.   GV1600.L66 1995
Looking Out: Perspectives on Dance and Criticism in a
Multicultural World. Lewis Segal, Patrice Koelsch & Elizabeth
Zimmer (Editors). Trade Cloth. Thomson Gale. Farmington
Hills, MI. 1995. 242p. ISBN:0-02-870683-8, ISBN13:
978-0-02-870683-2. Dewey:792.82. LCCN:95-098941.

Audience: **g,l.**

Goldberg, Rosalee   NX456.5.P38G66 1998
Performance: Live Art Since 1960. Trade Cloth. Harry N.
Abrams, Inc. New York, NY. 1998. 240p. ISBN:0-8109-4360-3,
ISBN13: 978-0-8109-4360-5. Dewey:700/.9/045.
LCCN:98-022775.

Audience: **l,u,f.**

Goldberg, Roselee   NX456.5.P38
Performance Art: from Futurism to the Present. Thames &
Hudson. 2001. World of Art ISBN:0-500-20339-3, ISBN13:
978-0-500-20339-2.

Audience: **u,f.**

Hewitt, Andrew   GV1782.5.H49 2005
Social Choreography: Ideology As Performance in Dance and
Everyday Movement. Trade Cloth. Duke University Press.
Durham, NC. 2005. 264p. Post-Contemporary Interventions Ser.
ISBN:0-8223-3502-6, ISBN13: 978-0-8223-3502-3.
Dewey:792.8/2. LCCN:2004-022037.

Audience: **u,f.**

Highwater, Jamake   GV1787
Dance: Rituals of Experience. Ed. 3. Trade Paper. Princeton
Book Company Publishers. Hightstown, NJ. 1992. 288p.
ISBN:0-87127-174-5, ISBN13: 978-0-87127-174-7.
Dewey:792.8/09.

Audience: **u,f.**

Hodgins, Paul   ML3858
Relationships Between Score and Choreography in
Twentieth-Century Dance: Music, Movement and Metaphor.
Trade Cloth. Edwin Mellen Press, The. Lewiston, NY. 1992.
240p. ISBN:0-7734-9552-5, ISBN13: 978-0-7734-9552-4.
Dewey:792.8/2. LCCN:92-010794.

Audience: **u,f.**

Horosko, Marian   GV1785.G7M27 2002
Martha Graham: The Evolution of Her Dance Theory and
Training. Ed. 2. Trade Cloth. University Press of Florida.
Gainesville, FL. 2002. 304p. ISBN:0-8130-2473-0, ISBN13:
978-0-8130-2473-8. Dewey:792.8/2/092 B. LCCN:2002-016565.

Audience: **u,f.**

Huxley, Michael & Witts,   PN1584.T84 1996
Noel (Compiled by)
The Twentieth Century Performance Reader. Trade Paper.
Routledge. New York, NY. 1996. 448p. ISBN:0-415-11628-7,
ISBN13: 978-0-415-11628-2. Dewey:791/.0904.
LCCN:95-021772.

Audience: **g,l,u.**

Jordan, Stephanie   GV1783.J66 1992
Striding Out: Aspects of Contemporary and New Dance in
Britain. Trade Paper. Dance Books, Ltd. Alton, 1992. 224p.
ISBN:1-85273-032-3, ISBN13: 978-1-85273-032-1.
Dewey:792.8/0941. LCCN:94-159888.

Audience: **u,f.**

Jordan, Stephanie & Allen,   GV1787
Dave (Editors)
Parallel Lines: Media Representation of Dance. Trade Paper.
University of Luton Press. Luton, 2003. 256p.
ISBN:0-86196-371-7, ISBN13: 978-0-86196-371-3.
Dewey:792.8.

Audience: **u,f.**

King, Kenneth   GV1600.K56 2003
Writing in Motion. Trade Paper. University Press of New
England. Lebanon, NH. 2003. 224p. ISBN:0-8195-6614-4,
ISBN13: 978-0-8195-6614-0. Dewey:792.8/09.
LCCN:2003-015186.

Audience: **u,f.** *Choice, 2004.*

Kirstein, Lincoln   NX456.K56 1991
By with to and From: A Lincoln Kirstein Reader. Nicholas
Jenkins (Editor). Cloth over Boards. Farrar, Straus & Giroux.
New York, NY. 1991. 423p. ISBN:0-374-18765-7, ISBN13:
978-0-374-18765-1. LCCN:90-048226.

Audience: **u,f.**

Laws, Kenneth & Laws,   QP310.D35L388 2002
Kenneth L.
Physics and the Art of Dance: Understanding Movement. Trade

Paper. Oxford University Press, Inc. New York, NY. 2005. 256p. ISBN:0-19-514916-5, ISBN13: 978-0-19-514916-6. Dewey:612/.044. LCCN:2001-035077.

Audience: **l,u,f.** *Choice, 2002.*

Lepecki, Andre   **GV1588.6.O4 2004**
Of the Presence of the Body: Essays on Dance and Performance Theory. Library Binding. Wesleyan University Press. Middletown, CT. 2004. 192p. ISBN:0-8195-6611-X, ISBN13: 978-0-8195-6611-9. Dewey:306.4/84. LCCN:2003-023913.

Audience: **u,f.**

Louis, Murray   **GV1785.L68A3 1992**
Murray Louis on Dance. Trade Cloth. A Cappella Books. Chicago, IL. 1992. 180p. ISBN:1-55652-147-2, ISBN13: 978-1-55652-147-8. Dewey:792.8/028/092. LCCN:92-006468.

Audience: **u,f.** *Choice, 1992.*

Martin, Randy   **GV1588.6.M37 1998**
Critical Moves: Dance Studies in Theory and Politics. Trade Paper. Duke University Press. Durham, NC. 1998. 296p. ISBN:0-8223-2219-6, ISBN13: 978-0-8223-2219-1. Dewey:792.8. LCCN:97-049360.

Audience: **u,f.**

McFee, Graham   **GV1589**
The Concept of Dance Education. Trade Cloth. Routledge. New York, NY. 1993. 240p. ISBN:0-415-08376-1, ISBN13: 978-0-415-08376-8. Dewey:792.807. LCCN:93-009997.

Audience: **u,f.**

McFee, Graham   **GV1588.3.M37 1992**
Understanding Dance. Cloth Text. Routledge. New York, NY. 1992. 352p. ISBN:0-415-07809-1, ISBN13: 978-0-415-07809-2. Dewey:792.8. LCCN:91-044620.

Audience: **l,u,f.** *Choice, 1993.*

Morris, Gay   **GV1619.M67 2006**
Game for Dancers: Performing Modernism in the Postwar Years, 1945-1960. Library Binding. Wesleyan University Press. Middletown, CT. 2006. 288p. ISBN:0-8195-6804-X, ISBN13: 978-0-8195-6804-5. Dewey:792.809/045. LCCN:2006-000181.

Audience: **l,u,f.**

Morris, Gay (Editor)   **GV1600.M68 1996**
Moving Words: Re-Writing Dance. Trade Paper. Routledge. New York, NY. 1996. 360p. ISBN:0-415-12543-X, ISBN13: 978-0-415-12543-7. Dewey:792.8. LCCN:95-039924.

Audience: **u,f.** *Choice, 1997.*

Nagrin, Daniel   **GV1787**
Dance and the Specific Image: Improvisation. Cloth Text. University of Pittsburgh Press. Pittsburgh, PA. 1993. 256p. ISBN:0-8229-3776-X, ISBN13: 978-0-8229-3776-0. Dewey:792.8. LCCN:93-027793.

Audience: **u,f.** *Choice, 1994.*

Novack, Cynthia J.   **GV1781.2.N68 1990**
Sharing the Dance: Contact Improvisation and American Culture. Cloth Text. University of Wisconsin Press. Chicago, IL. 1990. 272p. New Directions in Anthropological Writing Ser.

ISBN:0-299-12440-1, ISBN13: 978-0-299-12440-3. Dewey:792.8. LCCN:89-040534.

Audience: **u,f.** *Choice, 1991.*

Pavis, Patrice   **PN1584.P3813 2003**
Analyzing Performance: Theater, Dance, and Film. A. David Williams (Translator). Trade Cloth. University of Michigan Press. Chicago, IL. 2003. 362p. ISBN:0-472-09689-3, ISBN13: 978-0-472-09689-3. Dewey:791. LCCN:2002-005533.

Audience: **u,f.**

Pegg, Carole   **ML3758.M6P45 2001**
Mongolian Music, Dance and Oral Narrative: Performing Diverse Identities. Trade Cloth. University of Washington Press. Seattle, WA. 2001. xvii, 376p. ISBN:0-295-98030-3, ISBN13: 978-0-295-98030-0. Dewey:781.62/00951/7. LCCN:00-042308.

Audience: **u,f.** *Choice, 2002.*

Preston-Dunlop, Valerie   **GV1783**
  Monthland & Sanchez-Colberg, Ana
Dance and the Performative: A Choreological Perspective : Laban and Beyond. Verve. 2002. ISBN:0-9509859-2-9, ISBN13: 978-0-9509859-2-3.

Audience: **u,f.**

Royce, Anya   **GV1788.R69**
Movement and Meaning: Creativity and Interpretation in Ballet and Mime. Trade Paper. Books on Demand. Ann Arbor, MI. 1984. 254p. ISBN:0-608-05042-3, ISBN13: 978-0-608-05042-3. Dewey:792.8. LCCN:83-048526.

Audience: **u,f.**

Savigliano, Marta   **PS3619.A86A85 2003**
Angora Matta: Fatal Acts of North-South Translation = Actos Fatales de Traduccion Norte-Sur. Library Binding. Wesleyan University Press. Middletown, CT. 2003. 264p. Music/Culture Ser. ISBN:0-8195-6598-9, ISBN13: 978-0-8195-6598-3. Dewey:812/.6. LCCN:2003-041187.

Audience: **u,f.**

Shawn, Ted   **GV463 .S46**
Every Little Movement: A Book about Delsarte. Trade Paper. Princeton Book Company Publishers. Hightstown, NJ. 1985. 127p. ISBN:0-87127-015-3, ISBN13: 978-0-87127-015-3. Dewey:793.3/0924. LCCN:68-028049.

Audience: **u,f.**

Shay, Anthony   **GV1588.45.S5 2002**
Choreographic Politics: State Folk Companies, Representation and Power. Library Binding. University Press of New England. Lebanon, NH. 2002. 252p. ISBN:0-8195-6520-2, ISBN13: 978-0-8195-6520-4. Dewey:793.3/1. LCCN:2001-008180.

Audience: **u,f.** *Choice, 2003.*

Sheets-Johnstone, Maxine   **GV1595**
The Phenomenology of Dance. Library Binding. Ayer Company Publishers, Inc. Manchester, NH. 1980. Dance Ser. ISBN:0-8369-9304-7, ISBN13: 978-0-8369-9304-2. Dewey:793.3/01. LCCN:79-007779.

Audience: **u,f.**

Siegel, Marcia B.   GV1783.S53 1991
The Tail of the Dragon: New Dance, 1976-1982. Nathaniel
Tileston (Photographer). Cloth Text. Duke University Press.
Durham, NC. 1991. 251p. ISBN:0-8223-1156-9, ISBN13:
978-0-8223-1156-0. Dewey:792.8. LCCN:91-000522.
                                   Audience: **u,f.** *Choice, 1992.*

Sorell, Walter (Editor)   GV1781
Dance Has Many Faces. Ed. 2. Cloth Text. Columbia University
Press. New York, NY. 1966. ISBN:0-231-02968-3, ISBN13:
978-0-231-02968-1. Dewey:793.3. LCCN:66-025457.
                                              Audience: **u,f.**

Sparshott, Francis   GV1588.S64 1995
A Measured Pace: Toward a Philosophical Understanding of the
Arts of Dance. Cloth over Boards. University of Toronto Press.
Toronto, ON. 1995. 580p. Studies in Philosophy
ISBN:0-8020-0510-1, ISBN13: 978-0-8020-0510-6.
Dewey:792.8/01. LCCN:95-165446.
                                              Audience: **u,f.**

Taplin, D.T. (Editor)   GV1594.D373 1982
Dance Spectrum: Critical and Philosophical Enquiry. University
of Waterloo. 1982.
                                              Audience: **u,f.**

Taplin, D.T. (Editor)   GV1583.D35 1979
New Directions in Dance. Pergamon. 1979.
ISBN:0-08-024773-3, ISBN13: 978-0-08-024773-1.
                                              Audience: **u,f.**

Tharp, Twyla   BF408.T415 2006
The Creative Habit: Learn It and Use It for Life. Trade Paper.
Simon & Schuster, Inc. New York, NY. 2005. 256p.
ISBN:0-7432-3527-4, ISBN13: 978-0-7432-3527-3.
Dewey:153.3/5. LCCN:2005-285389.
                                   Audience: **g,l,u,f.** *Choice, 2004.*

Thomas, Helen   GV1588.6.T44 2003
The Body, Dance and Cultural Theory. Cloth over Boards.
Palgrave Macmillan. New York, NY. 2003. 256p.
ISBN:0-333-72431-3, ISBN13: 978-0-333-72431-6.
Dewey:306.4/84. LCCN:2003-042928.
                                   Audience: **u,f.** *Choice, 2004.*

Thomas, Helen   GV1588.6.D38 1997
Dance in the City. Trade Paper. Palgrave Macmillan. New York,
NY. 1997. 272p. ISBN:0-312-17454-3, ISBN13:
978-0-312-17454-5. Dewey:306.4/84/091732/0904.
LCCN:97-001717.
                                              Audience: **g,l,u,f.**

Thomas, Helen (Editor)   GV1588.6.D37 1993
Dance, Gender, and Culture. Cloth Text. Palgrave Macmillan.
New York, NY. 1993. 272p. ISBN:0-312-08881-7, ISBN13:
978-0-312-08881-1. Dewey:306.4/84. LCCN:92-027878.
                                   Audience: **u,f.** *Choice, 1993.*

Thomas, Helen   GV1588.6.T46 1995
Dance, Modernity and Culture: Explorations in the Sociology of

Dance. Trade Paper. Routledge. New York, NY. 1995. 232p.
ISBN:0-415-08794-5, ISBN13: 978-0-415-08794-0.
Dewey:792.8. LCCN:94-037061.
                                              Audience: **u,f.**

Dance and Related Arts

Aloff, Mindy (Editor)   GV1594.A46 2006
Dance Anecdotes: Stories from the Worlds of Ballet, Broadway,
the Ballroom, and Modern Dance. Trade Cloth. Oxford
University Press, Inc. New York, NY. 2006. 284p.
ISBN:0-19-505411-3, ISBN13: 978-0-19-505411-8.
Dewey:792.8. LCCN:2005-024553.
                                              Audience: **g,l,u,f.**

Bennahum, Judith   GV1789.2.C59 2005
Lure of Perfection: Fashion and Ballet, 1780-1830. Paper over
Boards. Routledge. New York, NY. 2004. 304p.
ISBN:0-415-97037-7, ISBN13: 978-0-415-97037-2.
Dewey:792.8/4. LCCN:2004-019194.
                                              Audience: **l,u,f.**

Brissenden, Alan   PR3034
Shakespeare and the Dance. Trade Paper. Princeton Book
Company Publishers. Hightstown, NJ. 2001. 148p.
ISBN:1-85273-083-8, ISBN13: 978-1-85273-083-3.
Dewey:822.3/3.
                                              Audience: **u,f.**

Cage, John M.   ML3845
Silence: Lectures and Writings. Trade Paper. Wesleyan
University Press. Middletown, CT. 1961. 288p.
ISBN:0-8195-6028-6, ISBN13: 978-0-8195-6028-5.
Dewey:780.1. LCCN:61-014238.
                                              Audience: **g,l,u,f.**

Cavalli, Harriet   MT950.C38 2001
Dance and Music: A Guide to Dance Accompaniment for
Musicians and Dance Teachers. Trade Cloth. University Press of
Florida. Gainesville, FL. 2001. xvii, 425p. ISBN:0-8130-1887-0,
ISBN13: 978-0-8130-1887-4. Dewey:781.5/54143.
LCCN:2001-027588.
                                              Audience: **l,u,f.**

Deren, Maya   PN1998.A3 D4573 1988
The Legend of Maya Deren: A Documented Biography and
Collected Works, Vol. 1, Part II. Clark, Verve A. (Editor);
Hodson, Millicent (Editor); Neiman, Catrina (Editor). Anthology
Film Archives. 1988. ISBN:0-911689-17-6, ISBN13:
978-0-911689-17-4.
                                              Audience: **u,f.**

Deren, Maya   PN1998.A3 D4573 1984
The Legend of Maya Deren: A Documented Biography and
Collected Works: Vol. 1, Signatures (1917-42). Clark, Verve A.
(Editor); Hodson, Millicent (Editor); Neiman, Catrina (Editor).
Anthology Film Archives/Film Culture. 1985.
ISBN:0-911689-16-8, ISBN13: 978-0-911689-16-7.
                                              Audience: **u,f.**

Devonyar, Jill, et al. N6853.D33A4 2002
Degas and the Dance. Edgar Degas & Richard Kendall
(Authors), Detroit Institute of Arts Staff & Philadelphia Museum
of Art Staff (Contribution by). Trade Paper. Harry N. Abrams,
Inc. New York, NY. 2002. p. cm.p. ISBN:0-8109-9077-6,
ISBN13: 978-0-8109-9077-7. Dewey:759.4.
LCCN:2002-018230.

Audience: **g,l,u.** *Choice, 2003.*

Dunning, Jennifer NX512.H64D86 2001
Geoffrey Holder: A Life in Theater, Dance and Art. Trade Cloth.
Harry N. Abrams, Inc. New York, NY. 2001. 238p.
ISBN:0-8109-1392-5, ISBN13: 978-0-8109-1392-9.
Dewey:700/.92 B. LCCN:2001-004552.

Audience: **u,f.**

Eichenbaum, Rose GV1785.A1E53 2004
Masters of Movement: Portraits of America's Great
Choreographers. Trade Cloth. Smithsonian Institution Press.
Washington, DC. 2004. 288p. ISBN:1-58834-185-2, ISBN13:
978-1-58834-185-3. Dewey:792.8/2/0922 B.
LCCN:2004-048246.

Audience: **g,l,u,f.**

Ewing, William A. GV1595
Dance and Photography. Trade Cloth. Random House Value
Publishing. New York, NY. 1990. ISBN:0-517-03178-7,
ISBN13: 978-0-517-03178-0. Dewey:793.3/022/2.

Audience: **g,l,u,f.**

Ewing, William A. TR817.5.E945 1992
Breaking Bounds: The Dance Photography of Lois Greenfield.
Lois Greenfield (Photographer). Trade Cloth. Chronicle Books
LLC. San Francisco, CA. 1992. 120p. ISBN:0-8118-0210-8,
ISBN13: 978-0-8118-0210-9. Dewey:779.97928.
LCCN:92-004553.

Audience: **u,f.**

Goeliner, Ellen W. & GV1600.B63 1995
  Murphy, Jacqueline S. (Editors)
Bodies of the Text: Dance As Theory, Literature As Dance.
Cloth Text. Rutgers University Press. Piscataway, NJ. 1995.
280p. ISBN:0-8135-2126-2, ISBN13: 978-0-8135-2126-8.
Dewey:792.8/015. LCCN:94-014738.

Audience: **u,f.** *Choice, 1995.*

Guest, Ann H., et al. GV1790.A38
Afternoon of a Faun: Mallarme, Debussy, Nijinsky. Claudia
Jeschke, Philippe Neagu & Jean-Michel Nectoux (Authors).
Trade Cloth. Vendome Press, The. New York, NY. 1989. 144p.
ISBN:0-86565-116-7, ISBN13: 978-0-86565-116-6.
Dewey:792.8/42.

Audience: **u,f.**

Haring, Keith NC139.H3A2 1999
Dance. Trade Cloth. Little Brown & Company. New York, NY.
1999. 80p. ISBN:0-8212-2555-3, ISBN13: 978-0-8212-2555-4.
Dewey:741.973. LCCN:98-056464.

Audience: **g,l,u,f.**

Holmberg, Arthur PN2287.W494 H65 1996
The Theatre of Robert Wilson. Christopher Innes (Contribution
by). Trade Cloth. Cambridge University Press. New York, NY.
1997. 249p. Directors in Perspective Ser. ISBN:0-521-36492-2,
ISBN13: 978-0-521-36492-8. Dewey:792/.0233/092.
LCCN:95-051227.

Audience: **u,f.** *Choice, 1998.*

Hoskins, Jim PR3091.H66 2005
The Dances of Shakespeare. UK-B Format Paperback.
Routledge. New York, NY. 2005. 168p. ISBN:0-415-97434-8,
ISBN13: 978-0-415-97434-9. Dewey:822.3/3.
LCCN:2005-001699.

Audience: **g,l,u,f.**

Jordan, Stephanie & Allen, GV1787
  Dave (Editors)
Parallel Lines: Media Representation of Dance. Trade Paper.
University of Luton Press. Luton, 2003. 256p.
ISBN:0-86196-371-7, ISBN13: 978-0-86196-371-3.
Dewey:792.8.

Audience: **u,f.**

Kendall, Richard N6853.D33
Degas Dancers. Trade Cloth. Vendome Press, The. New York,
NY. 1996. 80p. Universe of Art Ser. ISBN:0-7893-0060-5,
ISBN13: 978-0-7893-0060-7. Dewey:709/.2. LCCN:96-060680.

Audience: **u,f.**

Kirstein, Lincoln N5220.K57
Quarry: A Collection in Lieu of Memoirs by Lincoln Kirstein.
Trade Cloth. Twelvetrees Press. Santa Fe, NM. 1986. 112p.
ISBN:0-942642-27-9, ISBN13: 978-0-942642-27-8.
Dewey:708.1.

Audience: **u,f.**

Leong, Roger GV1789.2.F76 1998
From Russia with Love: Costumes for the Ballets Russes,
1909-1933. Paper Text. Australian Government Publishing
Service. Canberra, ACT. 2000. 96p. ISBN:0-642-54116-7,
ISBN13: 978-0-642-54116-1. Dewey:792.8026094709041.
LCCN:00-272596.

Audience: **u,f.**

Little, Meredith & Jenne, ML410.B13L52 2001
  Natalie (Editors)
Dance and the Music of J. S. Bach. Ed. 2. Trade Cloth. Indiana
University Press. Bloomington, IN. 2001. 288p.
Music--Scholarship and Performance Ser. ISBN:0-253-33936-7,
ISBN13: 978-0-253-33936-2. Dewey:784.18/82/092.
LCCN:2001-016944.

Audience: **u,f.** *Choice, 2002.*

Lopukhov, Fedor Vasil'evich GV1787.L63 2002
Writings on Ballet and Music. Stephanie Jordan (Editor),
Dorinda Offord (Translator), Stephanie Jordan (Introduction by).
Trade Cloth. University of Wisconsin Press. Chicago, IL. 2003.
184p. ISBN:0-299-18270-3, ISBN13: 978-0-299-18270-0.
Dewey:792.8. LCCN:2002-002339.

Audience: **u,f.** *Choice, 2003.*

McCann, Colum   **PR6015.I3**
Dancer: A Novel. Trade Paper. Picador. New York, NY. 2004.
352p. ISBN:0-312-42318-7, ISBN13: 978-0-312-42318-6.
Dewey:823/.914.

Audience: **g,l,u.**

Mester, Terri A.   **PR478.D35M47 1997**
Movement and Modernism: Yeats, Eliot, Williams and Early
Twentieth-Century Dance. Cloth Text. University of Arkansas
Press. Fayetteville, AR. 1997. 192p. ISBN:1-55728-455-5,
ISBN13: 978-1-55728-455-6. Dewey:820.9/357.
LCCN:96-029802.

Audience: **u,f.** *Choice, 1997.*

Morgan, Barbara &   **TR653.M652 1999**
Patnaik, Deba P.
Barbara Morgan. Lesley Martin (Editor). Trade Cloth. Aperture
Foundation, Inc. New York, NY. 1999. 96p. Aperture Masters of
Photography Ser. ISBN:0-89381-825-9, ISBN13:
978-0-89381-825-8. Dewey:779/.092. LCCN:98-086911.

Audience: **u,f.**

Mueller, John   **PN1995.9.F54**
Astaire Dancing: The Musical Films. Trade Cloth. Alfred A.
Knopf Inc. New York, NY. 1985. 448p. ISBN:0-394-51654-0,
ISBN13: 978-0-394-51654-7. Dewey:791.43/655.
LCCN:84-047874.

Audience: **g,l,u.**

Pavis, Patrice   **PN1584.P3813 2003**
Analyzing Performance: Theater, Dance, and Film. A. David
Williams (Translator). Trade Cloth. University of Michigan
Press. Chicago, IL. 2003. 362p. ISBN:0-472-09689-3, ISBN13:
978-0-472-09689-3. Dewey:791. LCCN:2002-005533.

Audience: **u,f.**

Schouvaloff, Alexander   **PN2096.B337.S36 1991**
Leon Bakst: The Theater Art. Trade Cloth. Sotheby's
Publications. New York, NY. 1991. 272p. ISBN:0-85667-391-9,
ISBN13: 978-0-85667-391-7. Dewey:792.025092.
LCCN:91-060246.

Audience: **u,f.** *Choice, 1992.*

Schouvaloff, Alexander &   **GV1789.2.S36 1997**
Wadsworth, Atheneum
The Ballets Russes: The Serge Lifar Collection of Theater
Designs, Costumes, and Paintings at the Wadsworth Atheneum.
Cloth over Boards. Yale University Press. Cumberland, RI.
1998. 352p. ISBN:0-300-07484-0, ISBN13: 978-0-300-07484-0.
Dewey:792.8/0947. LCCN:97-042146.

Audience: **u,f.**

Shloss, Carol Loeb   **PR6019.O9**
Lucia Joyce: To Dance in the Wake. Trade Paper. Picador. New
York, NY. 2005. 576p. ISBN:0-312-42269-5, ISBN13:
978-0-312-42269-1. Dewey:823/.912 B.

Audience: **u,f.** *Choice, 2004.*

Solomon, Deborah   **N6537.C66S64 1997**
Utopia Parkway: The Life and Work of Joseph Cornell. Trade

Cloth. Farrar, Straus & Giroux. New York, NY. 1997. 426p.
ISBN:0-374-18012-1, ISBN13: 978-0-374-18012-6.
Dewey:759.1/3. LCCN:95-018258.

Audience: **l,u,f.**

Teachout, Terry   **NX504.T43 2004**
A Terry Teachout Reader. Cloth over Boards. Yale University
Press. Cumberland, RI. 2004. 464p. ISBN:0-300-09894-4,
ISBN13: 978-0-300-09894-5. Dewey:700/.973.
LCCN:2003-016561.

Audience: **l,u,f.**

Volkov, Solomon   **ML410.C4**
Balanchine's Tchaikovsky: Interviews with George Balanchine.
Antonina W. Bouis (Translator). Trade Cloth. Simon & Schuster.
New York, NY. 1985. 208p. ISBN:0-671-49875-4, ISBN13:
978-0-671-49875-7. Dewey:792.8/092.

Audience: **u,f.**

Zane, Arnie   **TR647.Z36 1999**
Continuous Replay: The Photographs of Arnie Zane. Jonathan
Green (Editor), Bill T. Jones (Introduction by). Trade Paper.
MIT Press. Cambridge, MA. 1999. 200p. ISBN:0-262-57127-7,
ISBN13: 978-0-262-57127-2. Dewey:779/.2/092.
LCCN:98-045351.

Audience: **u,f.**

Dance Education

Adshead-Lansdale, Janet   **GV1787**
(Editor)
Dance History: Introduction. Ed. 2. Trade Paper. Routledge.
New York, NY. 1994. 304p. ISBN:0-415-09030-X, ISBN13:
978-0-415-09030-8. Dewey:792.8. LCCN:93-043265.

Audience: **g,l.**

Benari, Naomi   **GV1799.2**
Inner Rhythm: Dance Training for the Deaf. Cloth Text. Gordon
& Breach Publishing Group. New York, NY. 1995. 81p.
Performing Arts Studies, Vol. 3 ISBN:3-7186-5611-6, ISBN13:
978-3-7186-5611-0. Dewey:792.8/0872.

Audience: **u,f.**

Bennahum, Judith   **GV1589**
Teaching Dance Studies. Paper over Boards. Routledge. New
York, NY. 2005. 272p. ISBN:0-415-97035-0, ISBN13:
978-0-415-97035-8. Dewey:792.8/071/1. LCCN:2005-001224.

Audience: **l,u,f.**

Boas, Franziska   **GV1595**
The Function of Dance in Human Society. Trade Paper.
Princeton Book Company Publishers. Hightstown, NJ. 1986.
52p. ISBN:0-87127-032-3, ISBN13: 978-0-87127-032-0.
Dewey:793.3. LCCN:71-181478.

Audience: **g,l,u,f.**

Brinson, Peter   **GV1589.B75 1991**
Dance As Education. Trade Cloth. Taylor & Francis Group.
Philadelphia, PA. 1991. 246p. ISBN:1-85000-716-0, ISBN13:
978-1-85000-716-6. Dewey:792.807/041. LCCN:90-046270.

Audience: **g,l,u,f.**

Brinson, Peter   GV1645
Dance Education and Training in Britain. Calouste Gulbenkian
Foundation. 1994.

Audience: **u,f.**

Cavalli, Harriet   MT950.C38 2001
Dance and Music: A Guide to Dance Accompaniment for
Musicians and Dance Teachers. Trade Cloth. University Press of
Florida. Gainesville, FL. 2001. xvii, 425p. ISBN:0-8130-1887-0,
ISBN13: 978-0-8130-1887-4. Dewey:781.5/54143.
LCCN:2001-027588.

Audience: **l,u,f.**

Dunning, Jennifer   GV1788.6.S36D86 1985
But First a School: The First Fifty Years of the School of
American Ballet. Trade Cloth. Penguin Group (USA) Inc. New
York, NY. 1985. 304p. ISBN:0-670-80407-X, ISBN13:
978-0-670-80407-8. Dewey:792.8/07/107471. LCCN:85-007625.

Audience: **g,l,u.** *Choice, 1986.*

Hanna, Judith Lynne   GV1589.H35 1999
Partnering Dance and Education: Intelligent Moves for
Changing Times. Trade Paper. Human Kinetics Publishers.
Champaign, IL. 1998. 272p. ISBN:0-88011-511-4, ISBN13:
978-0-88011-511-7. Dewey:792.8/071/073. LCCN:98-034340.

Audience: **u,f.** *Choice, 1999.*

Hawkins, Alma M.   GV1782.5.H39 1988
Creating Through Dance. Trade Cloth. Princeton Book Company
Publishers. Hightstown, NJ. 1988. 164p. ISBN:0-916622-65-7,
ISBN13: 978-0-916622-65-7. Dewey:792.8/2. LCCN:87-063489.

Audience: **l,u.**

H'Doubler, Margaret N.   GV1751
Dance: A Creative Art Experience. Ed. 2. G. E. Johnson
(Foreword by). Trade Cloth. University of Wisconsin Press.
Chicago, IL. 1957. 200p. ISBN:0-299-01520-3, ISBN13:
978-0-299-01520-6. Dewey:793.3.

Audience: **l,u,f.**

Jaques-Dalcroze, Emile   MT22
Rhythm, Music and Education. Trade Cloth. Ayer Company
Publishers, Inc. Manchester, NH. 1972. ISBN:0-405-08666-0,
ISBN13: 978-0-405-08666-3. Dewey:780.7. LCCN:77-187829.

Audience: **l,u,f.**

King, Bruce   GV1799
Creative Dance: Experience for Learning. Montana State
University. 1968.

Audience: **l,u,f.**

Kraus, Richard &   GV1601
  Charman, Sarah
A History of the Dance in Art and Education. Ed. 2. Cloth Text.
Prentice Hall PTR. Upper Saddle River, NJ. 1980. 432p.
ISBN:0-13-390021-5, ISBN13: 978-0-13-390021-7.
Dewey:793.3/09. LCCN:80-016188.

Audience: **g,l,u.**

Laban, Rudolf   GV1587
The Language of Movement. Trade Cloth. Kalmbach Publishing
Company, Books Division. Waukesha, WI. 1974.
ISBN:0-8238-0159-4, ISBN13: 978-0-8238-0159-6.
Dewey:793.3. LCCN:73-013552.

Audience: **l,u.**

Laban, Rudolf   PN2071.M6 L3
Mastery of Movement. Trade Cloth. Kalmbach Publishing
Company, Books Division. Waukesha, WI. 1971.
ISBN:0-8238-0123-3, ISBN13: 978-0-8238-0123-7.
Dewey:792.028. LCCN:73-155889.

Audience: **l,u.**

Laban, Rudolf   GV1580
A Life for Dance: The Autobiography of Rudolf Laban. Lisa
Ullman (Translator). Trade Cloth. Princeton Book Company
Publishers. Hightstown, NJ. 1975. 193p. ISBN:0-7121-1231-6,
ISBN13: 978-0-7121-1231-4. Dewey:793.3/2/0924.

Audience: **u,f.**

Laban, Rudolf   GV1783
Modern Educational Dance. Ed. 3. Lisa Ullman (Translator).
Paper Text. Princeton Book Company Publishers. Hightstown,
NJ. 1988. 121p. ISBN:0-7121-1381-9, ISBN13:
978-0-7121-1381-6. Dewey:793.3/2/071.

Audience: **u,f.**

Lavender, Larry   GV1600.L38 1996
Dancers Talking Dance: Critical Evaluation in the Choreography
Class. Trade Paper. Human Kinetics Publishers. Champaign, IL.
1996. 16p. ISBN:0-87322-667-4, ISBN13: 978-0-87322-667-7.
Dewey:792.82. LCCN:95-049233.

Audience: **u.**

Lerman, Liz   GV1753.5
Teaching Dance to Senior Adults. Cloth Text. Charles C Thomas
Publisher, Ltd. Springfield, IL. 1984. 190p.
ISBN:0-398-04903-3, ISBN13: 978-0-398-04903-4.
Dewey:793.3/2.

Audience: **l,u,f.**

McFee, Graham   GV1589
The Concept of Dance Education. Trade Cloth. Routledge. New
York, NY. 1993. 240p. ISBN:0-415-08376-1, ISBN13:
978-0-415-08376-8. Dewey:792.807. LCCN:93-009997.

Audience: **u,f.**

Mertz, Annelise (Editor)   GV1589.B63 2002
The Body Can Speak: Essays on Creative Movement Education
with Emphasis on Dance and Drama. Trade Cloth. Southern
Illinois University Press. Carbondale, IL. 2002. 224p.
ISBN:0-8093-2418-0, ISBN13: 978-0-8093-2418-7.
Dewey:792.8/071. LCCN:2001-049021.

Audience: **u,f.** *Choice, 2002.*

Mettler, Barbara   GV1785.M48
Dance As an Element of Life. Trade Cloth. Mettler Studios, Inc.
Tucson, AZ. 1985. ISBN:0-912536-12-8, ISBN13:
978-0-912536-12-5. Dewey:793.3/2/0924.

Audience: **g,l,u,f.**

Murray, Ruth L.   GV1799
Dance in Elementary Education: A Program for Boys and Girls.
Ed. 3. Cloth Text. Addison-Wesley Educational Publishers, Inc.
Boston, MA. 1975. 574p. School and Education Physical
Education and Recreation Ser. ISBN:0-06-044681-1, ISBN13:
978-0-06-044681-9. Dewey:372.8/6. LCCN:74-011386.
Audience: **u,f.**

Preston-Dunlop, Valerie   GV1587
Practical Kinetography Laban. Trade Cloth. Princeton Book
Company Publishers. Hightstown, NJ. 1972. 224p.
ISBN:0-7121-1609-5, ISBN13: 978-0-7121-1609-1.
Dewey:793.32.
Audience: **l,u.**

Preston-Dunlop, Valerie M.   GV1799.P7 1969
A Handbook for Modern Educational Dance. Trade Cloth.
International Publications Service. Levittown, PA. 1977. 198p.
ISBN:0-7121-0801-7, ISBN13: 978-0-7121-0801-0.
Dewey:793.3/2. LCCN:73-016341.
Audience: **l,u,f.**

Rogers, Frederick R.   GV1595
Dance: A Basic Educational Technique. Trade Paper. Princeton
Book Company Publishers. Hightstown, NJ. 1980. 351p.
ISBN:0-87127-108-7, ISBN13: 978-0-87127-108-2.
Dewey:792.8. LCCN:79-051364.
Audience: **l,u.**

Ross, Janice   GV1785.H37R68 2000
Moving Lessons: Margaret H'Doubler and the Beginning of
Dance in American Education. Trade Paper. University of
Wisconsin Press. Chicago, IL. 2000. xxii, 276p.
ISBN:0-299-16934-0, ISBN13: 978-0-299-16934-3.
Dewey:792.8/0973. LCCN:00-008344.
Audience: **u,f.**

Ruyter, Nancy Lee Chalfa   GV463
The Cultivation of Body and Mind in Nineteenth-Century
American Delsartism. Trade Cloth. Greenwood Publishing
Group, Inc. Portsmouth, NH. 1999. 200p. Contributions to the
Study of Music and Dance Ser., Vol. 56 ISBN:0-313-31042-4,
ISBN13: 978-0-313-31042-3. Dewey:792/.028.
LCCN:99-010076.
Audience: **u,f.**   *Choice, 2000.*

Serebrennikov, Nikolai   GV1788.2.P37
Nikolaevich & Horosko, Marian
Pas de Deux: A Textbook on Partnering. Ed. 2. University Press
of Florida. 2000. ISBN:0-8130-1768-8, ISBN13:
978-0-8130-1768-6.
Audience: **l,u,f.**

Shapiro, Sherry   LC196.S54 1999
Pedagogy and the Politics of the Body: A Critical Praxis. Cloth
Text. Garland Publishing, Inc. New York, NY. 1998. 208p.
Critical Education Practice Ser., Vol. 16 ISBN:0-8153-2781-1,
ISBN13: 978-0-8153-2781-3. Dewey:370.11/5.
LCCN:98-033338.
Audience: **u,f.**

Shapiro, Sherry B. (Editor)   GV1589.D387 1998
Dance, Power, and Difference: Critical and Feminist
Perspectives on Dance Education. Trade Paper. Human Kinetics
Publishers. Champaign, IL. 1998. 20p. ISBN:0-88011-747-8,
ISBN13: 978-0-88011-747-0. Dewey:792.8/071.
LCCN:98-002675.
Audience: **u,f.**

Smith-Autard, Jacqueline   GV1589.S65 1994
M.
The Art of Dance in Education. Trade Paper. A & C Black.
London, 1998. 160p. ISBN:0-7136-3897-4, ISBN13:
978-0-7136-3897-4. Dewey:792.8/071. LCCN:95-148917.
Audience: **l,u.**

Dance Ethnology and Anthropology

Boas, Franziska   GV1595
The Function of Dance in Human Society. Trade Paper.
Princeton Book Company Publishers. Hightstown, NJ. 1986.
52p. ISBN:0-87127-032-3, ISBN13: 978-0-87127-032-0.
Dewey:793.3. LCCN:71-181478.
Audience: **g,l,u,f.**

Buckland, Theresa J.   GV1588.6.D39 1999
(Editor)
Dance in the Field: Theory, Methods and Issues in Dance
Ethnography. Cloth over Boards. Palgrave Macmillan. New
York, NY. 1999. 241p. ISBN:0-312-22378-1, ISBN13:
978-0-312-22378-6. Dewey:306.4/84. LCCN:99-021778.
Audience: **u,f.**

Cowan, Jane K. (Editor)   GV1588.6.C69 1990
Dance and the Body Politic in Northern Greece. Trade Cloth.
Princeton University Press. Princeton, NJ. 1990. 310p. Modern
Greek Studies ISBN:0-691-09449-7, ISBN13:
978-0-691-09449-6. Dewey:792.8/09495. LCCN:90-030232.
Audience: **u,f.**

Hanna, Judith L.   GV1595.H33 1988
Dance, Sex, and Gender: Signs of Identity, Dominance,
Defiance, and Desire. Library Binding. University of Chicago
Press. Chicago, IL. 1988. xx, 312p. ISBN:0-226-31550-9,
ISBN13: 978-0-226-31550-8. Dewey:793.3/2. LCCN:87-023784.
Audience: **u,f.**   *Choice, 1988.*

Hanna, Judith Lynn   GV1588.6
To Dance Is Human: A Theory of Nonverbal Communication.
Cloth Text. University of Texas Press. Austin, TX. 1979. 343p.
ISBN:0-292-78032-X, ISBN13: 978-0-292-78032-3.
Dewey:306/.484. LCCN:78-021612.
Audience: **l,u,f.**

Kaeppler, Adrienne Lois   GV1728.T66 K34 1993
Poetry in Motion: Studies of Tongan Dance. Vava'u Press. 1993.
ISBN:982-213-003-1, ISBN13: 978-982-213-003-4.
Audience: **u,f.**

Kurath, Gertrude Prokosch;   ML3557.K875
 Garcia, Antonio
Music and Dance of the Tewa Pueblos. Museum of New
Mexico Press. 1970.
Audience: **u,f.**

Ness, Sally Ann   GV1796.S57N47 1992
e Body, Movement, and Culture: Kinesthetic and Visual
Symbolism in a Philippine Community. E-Book. NetLibrary,
Inc. Boulder, CO. 1992. ISBN:0-585-17279-X, ISBN13:
978-0-585-17279-8. Dewey:793.3/19599.
Audience: **u,f.**

Royce, Anya Peterson   GV1588.6.R7 1977
The Anthropology of Dance. University of Indiana Press. 1977.
ISBN:0-253-30752-X, ISBN13: 978-0-253-30752-1.
Audience: **g,l,u.**

Royce, Anya Peterson   PN1590.A58R68 2004
Anthropology of Performing Arts: Artistry, Virtuosity, and
Interpretation in a Cross-Cultural Perspective. Trade Cloth.
AltaMira Press. Walnut Creek, CA. 2004. 272p.
ISBN:0-7591-0223-6, ISBN13: 978-0-7591-0223-1.
Dewey:791/.01/03. LCCN:2003-025785.
Audience: **u,f.** *Choice, 2005.*

Sachs, Curt   GV1601.S2613
World History of the Dance. Bessie Schonberg (Translator).
Trade Cloth. W. W. Norton & Company, Inc. New York, NY.
1963. ISBN:0-393-02205-6, ISBN13: 978-0-393-02205-6.
Dewey:793.3/09.
Audience: **g,l.**

Solomon, John & Solomon,   GV1703.E18 E28 1995
 Ruth (Editors)
East Meets West in Dance: Voices in the Cross-Cultural
Dialogue. UK-B Format Paperback. Gordon & Breach
Publishing Group. New York, NY. 1995. 332p. Choreography
and Dance Studies, Vol. 9 ISBN:3-7186-5604-3, ISBN13:
978-3-7186-5604-2. Dewey:792.8.
Audience: **u,f.**

Spencer, Paul (Editor)   GV1588.6 .S63 1985
Society and the Dance: The Social Anthropology of Process and
Performance. Cloth Text. Cambridge University Press. New
York, NY. 1986. 235p. ISBN:0-521-30521-7, ISBN13:
978-0-521-30521-1. Dewey:306.4/84. LCCN:84-029212.
Audience: **u,f.** *Choice, 1986.*

Taylor, Julie   GV1796.T3T39 1998
Paper Tangos. Trade Paper. Duke University Press. Durham,
NC. 1998. 160p. Public Planet Bks. ISBN:0-8223-2191-2,
ISBN13: 978-0-8223-2191-0. Dewey:793.3/3. LCCN:97-031240.
Audience: **u,f.**

Williams, Drid   GV1595.W53 2000
Anthropology and Human Movement: Searching for Origins.
Ed. 2. Trade Cloth. Scarecrow Press, Inc. Lanham, MD. 2000.
320p. Readings in Anthropology and Human Movement, Vol. 2
ISBN:0-8108-3707-2, ISBN13: 978-0-8108-3707-2.
Dewey:306.4/84. LCCN:99-033951.
Audience: **u,f.**

Williams, Drid   GV1588.6.W55 2003
Anthropology and the Dance: Ten Lectures. Ed. 2. Brenda
Farnell (Foreword by). Trade Cloth. University of Illinois Press.
Champaign, IL. 2004. 328p. ISBN:0-252-02855-4, ISBN13:
978-0-252-02855-7. Dewey:306.4/84. LCCN:2002-155965.
Audience: **u,f.** *Choice, 2005.*

Dance Science and Medicine

Arnheim, Daniel D.   RD93
Dance Injuries. Trade Paper. Princeton Book Company
Publishers. Hightstown, NJ. 1989. ISBN:0-916622-80-0,
ISBN13: 978-0-916622-80-0. Dewey:617/.1.
Audience: **l,u,f.**

Clarkson, Priscilla M. &   RC1220.D35S25 1988
 Skrinar, Margaret (Editors)
Science of Dance Training. Cloth Text. Human Kinetics
Publishers. Champaign, IL. 1988. 312p. ISBN:0-87322-122-2,
ISBN13: 978-0-87322-122-1. Dewey:617/.1. LCCN:87-003370.
Audience: **l,u,f.**

Dowd, Irene   QP303
Taking Root to Fly. Ed. 2. Trade Paper. Contact Editions.
Northampton, MA. 1990. 48p. ISBN:0-937645-00-1, ISBN13:
978-0-937645-00-0. Dewey:793.3.
Audience: **u,f.**

Fitt, Sally S.   QP310.D35F58 1996
Dance Kinesiology. Ed. 2. Cloth Text. Thomson Wadsworth.
Belmont, CA. 1996. 504p. ISBN:0-02-864507-3, ISBN13:
978-0-02-864507-0. Dewey:612/.7. LCCN:96-032649.
Audience: **l,u,f.** *Choice, 1997.*

Howse, Justin, et al.   RC1220.D35.H68 1988
Dance Technique and Injury Prevention. Shirley Hancock &
Ninette De Valois (Authors). Trade Cloth. Routledge. New York,
NY. 1988. 216p. ISBN:0-87830-985-3, ISBN13:
978-0-87830-985-6. Dewey:617/.1. LCCN:88-016094.
Audience: **u,f.**

Laws, Kenneth   GV1788
The Physics of Dance. Martha Swope (Photographer). Trade
Cloth. Thomson Gale. Farmington Hills, MI. 1984. 200p.
ISBN:0-02-872030-X, ISBN13: 978-0-02-872030-2.
Dewey:612/.76. LCCN:83-020462.
Audience: **g,l,u,f.**

McCarren, Felicia M.   GV1588.5.M33 1998
Dance Pathologies: Performance, Poetics, Medicine. Trade
Cloth. Stanford University Press. Palo Alto, CA. 1998. 296p.
Writing Science Ser. ISBN:0-8047-2989-1, ISBN13:
978-0-8047-2989-5. Dewey:792.8/01/9. LCCN:98-011386.
Audience: **u,f.**

Paskevska, Anna   GV1788
Both Sides of the Mirror: The Science and Art of Ballet. Ed. 2.
Trade Paper. Princeton Book Company Publishers. Hightstown,
NJ. 1992. 224p. ISBN:0-87127-180-X, ISBN13:
978-0-87127-180-8. Dewey:792.8/2. LCCN:79-051362.
Audience: **u,f.**

Ryan, Allan J. & Stephens,   RC1220.D35
  Robert E. (Editors)
Dance Medicine: A Comprehensive Guide. Trade Cloth. Precept
Press. Chicago, IL. 1987. 375p. ISBN:0-931028-92-2, ISBN13:
978-0-931028-92-2. Dewey:617/.102. LCCN:87-060404.

Audience: **u,f.**

Ryan, Allan J. & Stephens,   RC1220.D35D36 1989
  Robert E.
The Healthy Dancer: Dance Medicine for Dancers. Trade Paper.
Princeton Book Company Publishers. Hightstown, NJ. 1989.
234p. ISBN:0-916622-86-X, ISBN13: 978-0-916622-86-2.
Dewey:617.1/02. LCCN:89-060616.

Audience: **u,f.**

Sataloff, Robert Thayer   RC965.P46 T48
  (Editor)
Textbook of Performing Arts Medicine. Trade Cloth. Thomson
Delmar Learning. Albany, NY. 1991. 448p.
ISBN:1-56593-743-0, ISBN13: 978-1-56593-743-7.
Dewey:616.9/802.

Audience: **u,f.**

Spilken, Terry L.   RD560
The Dancer's Foot Book. Trade Paper. Princeton Book
Company Publishers. Hightstown, NJ. 1990. 152p.
ISBN:0-916622-96-7, ISBN13: 978-0-916622-96-1.
Dewey:617.5/85. LCCN:89-064299.

Audience: **l,u,f.**

Watkins, Andrea &   GV1588.W38 1990
  Clarkson, Priscilla
Dancing Longer, Dancing Stronger: A Dancer's Guide to
Improving Technique and Preventing Injury. Trade Paper.
Princeton Book Company Publishers. Hightstown, NJ. 1990.
296p. ISBN:0-916622-98-3, ISBN13: 978-0-916622-98-5.
Dewey:792.8. LCCN:89-064300.

Audience: **l,u,f.**   *Choice, 1990.*

Dance Therapy

Bartenieff, Irmgard &   GV1595
  Davis, Martha Ann
Effort-Shape Analysis of Movement: The Unity of Expression
and Function. Yeshiva University. 1965.

Audience: **u,f.**

Bartenieff, Irmgard, et al.   GV1587 .B35
Four Adaptations of Effort Theory in Research and Teaching.
Martha Davis & Forrestine Paulay (Authors). Paper Text. Dance
Notation Bureau, Inc. New York, NY. 1970. viii, 72p.
ISBN:0-932582-06-0, ISBN13: 978-0-932582-06-5.
Dewey:792.8/2. LCCN:73-047570.

Audience: **u,f.**

Bartenieff, Irmgard &   GV1587
  Lewis, D.
Body Movement: Coping with the Environment. Paper over

Boards. Gordon & Breach Publishing Group. New York, NY.
1980. 304p. ISBN:0-677-05500-5, ISBN13: 978-0-677-05500-8.
Dewey:793.3/2. LCCN:80-007454.

Audience: **u,f.**

Berardi, Gigi   GV1595.B47 2004
Finding Balance: Fitness, Training, and Health for a Lifetime in
Dance. Ed. 2. Paper over Boards. Routledge. New York, NY.
2004. 304p. ISBN:0-415-94338-8, ISBN13: 978-0-415-94338-3.
Dewey:792.8. LCCN:2004-017293.

Audience: **l,u,f.**

Chodorow, Joan   RC489.D3C53 1990
Dance Therapy and Depth Psychology: The Moving
Imagination. Trade Cloth. Routledge. New York, NY. 1991.
208p. ISBN:0-415-05301-3, ISBN13: 978-0-415-05301-3.
Dewey:616.89/1655. LCCN:90-008434.

Audience: **u,f.**

Drake, Alexander   RA781.5.D73 1996
The Alexander Technique in Everyday Life. Thorsons. 1996.
ISBN:0-7225-3290-3, ISBN13: 978-0-7225-3290-4.

Audience: **l,u,f.**

Earl, William L.   GV1588.5.E25 1988
A Dancer Takes Flight: Psychological Concerns in the
Development of the American Male Dancer. Trade Cloth.
University Press of America, Inc. Lanham, MD. 1988. 180p.
ISBN:0-8191-6947-1, ISBN13: 978-0-8191-6947-1.
Dewey:792.8/2/088041. LCCN:88-005445.

Audience: **u,f.**

Espenak, Liljan   RC489.D3
Dance Therapy: Theory and Application. Trade Cloth. Charles C
Thomas Publisher, Ltd. Springfield, IL. 1981. 210p.
ISBN:0-398-04110-5, ISBN13: 978-0-398-04110-6.
Dewey:616.89/1655.

Audience: **u,f.**

Exiner, Johanna & Kelynak,   RC489.D3E94 1994
  Denis
Dance Therapy Redefined: A Body Approach to Therapeutic
Dance. Lisa Roberts (Illustrator), Naomi Aitchison & Jenny
Czulak (Contribution by). Cloth Text. Charles C Thomas
Publisher, Ltd. Springfield, IL. 1994. 130p.
ISBN:0-398-05913-6, ISBN13: 978-0-398-05913-2.
Dewey:615.8/5155. LCCN:94-008556.

Audience: **u,f.**

Feldenkrais, Moshe   RA781
Awareness Through Movement: Health Exercises for Personal
Growth. Trade Cloth. HarperCollins Publishers. New York, NY.
1972. 192p. ISBN:0-06-062345-4, ISBN13: 978-0-06-062345-6.
Dewey:613.7. LCCN:74-184419.

Audience: **g,l,u,f.**

Feldenkrais, Moshe   RA781
Elusive Obvious. Trade Cloth. M E T A Publications. Capitola,
CA. 1981. 158p. ISBN:0-916990-09-5, ISBN13:
978-0-916990-09-1. Dewey:613.71. LCCN:81-082159.

Audience: **u,f.**

Feldenkrais, Moshe   QP360.F46 2005
Body and Mature Behavior: A Study of Anxiety, Sex,
Gravitation, and Learning. Carl Ginsburg (Foreword by). Trade
Paper, Perfect. Frog, Ltd. Berkeley, CA. 2005. 233p.
ISBN:1-58394-115-0, ISBN13: 978-1-58394-115-7. Dewey:152.
LCCN:2005-011825.

Audience: **u,f.**

Franklin, Eric N.   RC1220.D35 F73 1996
Dynamic Alignment Through Imagery. Human Kinetics. 1996.
ISBN:0-87322-475-2, ISBN13: 978-0-87322-475-8.

Audience: **u,f.**

Levy, Fran J. (Editor)   RC489.D3D34 1995
Dance and Other Expressive Art Therapies: When Words Are
Not Enough. UK-B Format Paperback. Routledge. New York,
NY. 1995. 288p. ISBN:0-415-91229-6, ISBN13:
978-0-415-91229-7. Dewey:616.89/1655. LCCN:95-016839.

Audience: **l,u,f.**

Levy, Fran J.   RC489.D3 L48 1992
Dance Movement Therapy: A Healing Art. Elissa Q. White
(Foreword by). Perfect. American Alliance for Health, Physical
Education, Recreation & Dance. Oxon Hill, MD. 2005. 377p.
ISBN:0-88314-531-6, ISBN13: 978-0-88314-531-9.
Dewey:615.8/5155.

Audience: **u,f.**

Payne, Helen   RM931.D35
Creative Movement and Dance in Groupwork. Spiral.
Speechmark Publishing Ltd. Bicester, 282p.
ISBN:0-86388-473-3, ISBN13: 978-0-86388-473-3.
Dewey:615.8/5155.

Audience: **l,u,f.**

Payne, Helen (Editor)   RC489.D3D36 1991
Dance Movement Therapy: Theory and Practice. Cloth Text.
Routledge. New York, NY. 1992. 272p. ISBN:0-415-05659-4,
ISBN13: 978-0-415-05659-5. Dewey:615.8/5155.
LCCN:91-022938.

Audience: **u,f.**

Payne, Helen (Editor)   RC489.D3
Dance Movement Therapy: Theory, Research and Practice. Ed.
2. Routledge. 2006. ISBN:1-58391-702-0, ISBN13:
978-1-58391-702-2.

Audience: **u,f.**

Rosen, Elizabeth   RC489.D3 R6 1974
Dance in Psychotherapy. Dance Horizons Republication. 1974.

Audience: **u,f.**

Salkin, J.   RC489.D3
Body Ego Technique: An Educational and Therapeutic Approach
to Body Image and Self Identity. Trade Cloth. Charles C
Thomas Publisher, Ltd. Springfield, IL. 1973. 224p.
ISBN:0-398-02826-5, ISBN13: 978-0-398-02826-8.
Dewey:616.8/916/5.

Audience: **u,f.**

Schoop, Trudi & Mitchell,   RC489.D3 S33
  Peggy
Won't You Join the Dance?: A Dancer's Essay into the
Treatment of Psychosis. Hedi Schoop (Illustrator). Paper Text.
Mayfield Publishing Company. San Francisco, CA. 1974. 206p.
ISBN:0-87484-228-X, ISBN13: 978-0-87484-228-9.
Dewey:616.8/916/5. LCCN:73-087475.

Audience: **l,u,f.**

Siegel, Elaine V.   RC489.D3
Dance-Movement Therapy: Mirror of Ourselves: The
Psychoanalytic Approach. Trade Cloth. Springer. New York, NY.
1984. 216p. ISBN:0-89885-157-2, ISBN13: 978-0-89885-157-1.
Dewey:616.89/1655.

Audience: **u,f.**

Sweigard, Lulu E.   QP303
Human Movement Potential: Its Ideokinetic Facilitation. Cloth
Text. Addison-Wesley Educational Publishers, Inc. Boston, MA.
1974. 352p. ISBN:0-06-046521-2, ISBN13: 978-0-06-046521-6.
Dewey:612/.76.

Audience: **u,f.**

Wethered, Audrey G.   RC489.D3
Movement and Drama in Therapy. Ed. 2. Trade Paper. Jessica
Kingsley Ltd. London, 1993. 128p. ISBN:1-85302-199-7,
ISBN13: 978-1-85302-199-2. Dewey:615.85155.

Audience: **u,f.**

Somatic Studies

Bainbridge-Cohen, Bonnie;   RM725.M542 1979
  Mills, Margaret
Developmental Movement Therapy. The School for Body-Mind
Centering. 1986.

Audience: **u,f.**

Bartenieff, Irmgard &   GV1587
  Lewis, D.
Body Movement: Coping with the Environment. Paper over
Boards. Gordon & Breach Publishing Group. New York, NY.
1980. 304p. ISBN:0-677-05500-5, ISBN13: 978-0-677-05500-8.
Dewey:793.3/2. LCCN:80-007454.

Audience: **u,f.**

Calais-Germain, Blandine   QP301.C2313 1993
Anatomy of Movement. Paper Text. Eastland Press. Seattle, WA.
1995. 289p. ISBN:0-939616-17-3, ISBN13: 978-0-939616-17-6.
Dewey:612.7/6. LCCN:93-071669.

Audience: **u,f.**

Cohen, Bonnie B.   QP301
Sensing Feeling and Action: The Experiential Anatomy of
Body-Mind Centering. Robert Tobey (Photographer). Trade
Paper. Contact Editions. Northampton, MA. 1993. 171p.
ISBN:0-937645-03-6, ISBN13: 978-0-937645-03-1.
Dewey:612.04.

Audience: **u,f.**

Feldenkrais, Moshe   RC489.F44F44213 1993
Body Awareness As Healing Therapy: The Case of Nora. Trade
Paper. Frog, Ltd. Berkeley, CA. 1993. 73p.
ISBN:1-883319-08-0, ISBN13: 978-1-883319-08-3.
Dewey:616.8109. LCCN:93-025025.

Audience: **u,f.**

Gomez, Ninoska   QP301.G6 1988
Movement, Body and Awareness: Exploring Somatic Processes.
N. Gomez. 1988.

Audience: **u,f.**

Hanna, Thomas   RM724
The Body of Life. Trade Cloth. Alfred A. Knopf Inc. New York,
NY. 1980. ISBN:0-394-42383-6, ISBN13: 978-0-394-42383-8.
Dewey:615.8/2. LCCN:79-003503.

Audience: **g,l,u,f.**

Macdonald, Glynn   RA781.5
Alexander Technique. Trade Paper. Hodder General Publishing
Division. London, 1995. 94p. Headway Lifeguides Ser.
ISBN:0-340-59680-5, ISBN13: 978-0-340-59680-7.
Dewey:613.78.

Audience: **g,l,u.**

McGowan, Danny &   BF145 .A57 1997
  Alexander, F. M. (Editors)
Alexander Technique: Original Writings of F. M. Alexander -
Constructive Conscious Control. Danny McGowan (Selected
by). Trade Paper. Larson Publications. Burdett, NY. 1997. 189p.
ISBN:0-943914-78-7, ISBN13: 978-0-943914-78-7.
Dewey:615.8/2. LCCN:96-076393.

Audience: **u,f.**

Rywerant, Yochanan &   RM724
  Feldenkrais, Moshe
The Feldenkrais Method: Teaching by Handling, A Technique
for Individuals. Trade Cloth. HarperCollins Publishers. New
York, NY. 1983. 256p. Giniger Book Ser. ISBN:0-06-250750-8,
ISBN13: 978-0-06-250750-1. Dewey:615.8/2. LCCN:83-047734.

Audience: **u,f.**

Sweigard, Lulu E.   QP303
Human Movement Potential: Its Ideokinetic Facilitation. Cloth

Text. Addison-Wesley Educational Publishers, Inc. Boston, MA.
1974. 352p. ISBN:0-06-046521-2, ISBN13: 978-0-06-046521-6.
Dewey:612/.76.

Audience: **u,f.**

Todd, Mabel E.   QP88.2
The Thinking Body: A Study of the Balancing Forces of
Dynamic Man. Lulu E. Sweigard (Foreword by). Trade Paper.
Princeton Book Company Publishers. Hightstown, NJ. 1968.
314p. ISBN:0-87127-014-5, ISBN13: 978-0-87127-014-6.
Dewey:612.7/5. LCCN:68-028048.

Audience: **u,f.**

Dance Documentation and Preservation

GV1623
Sustaining America's Dance Legacy: How the Field of Dance
Heritage Can Build Capacity and Broaden Awareness to Dance
in the Next Ten Years. Dance Heritage Coalition. 2000.

Audience: **u,f.**

Deputy, Janice (Editor)   GV1595
Frames of Reference: A Resource Guide from the National
Initiative to Preserve America's Dance. Marian A. Godfrey
(Introduction by), Andrea E. Snyder (Foreword by). Spiral.
Dance/U S A. Washington, DC. 2001. 80p.
ISBN:1-931683-00-X, ISBN13: 978-1-931683-00-5.
Dewey:793.3.

Audience: **u,f.**

Johnson, Catherine J. &   GV1595.J58 1999
  Snyder, Allegra F.
Securing Our Dance Heritage: Issues in the Documentation and
Preservation of Dance. Trade Paper. Council on Library &
Information Resources. Washington, DC. 1999. 43p.
ISBN:1-887334-69-6, ISBN13: 978-1-887334-69-3.
Dewey:793.3. LCCN:99-233666.

Audience: **u,f.**

Newman, Barbara   GV1787
Grace under Pressure: Passing Dance Through Time. Trade
Paper. Hal Leonard Corporation. Milwaukee, WI. 2004. 480p.
ISBN:0-87910-995-5, ISBN13: 978-0-87910-995-0.
Dewey:792.8/092/2 B. LCCN:2003-019294.

Audience: **u,f.** *Choice, 2004.*

DRAMA AND THEATER

This section attempts to breach the traditional (and unfortunate) gap between the study of drama and theater and bring them together as a single heading, reserving the heading of Theater Production for works which focus explicitly on the art of theatrical production and its many aspects, including how-to works. As a rule, the Theater Production heading does not include broad historical overviews of theater, unless they focus on stagecraft, while the Drama and Theater heading is used for all aspects of drama and theater except those explicitly concerned with stagecraft and how-to resources.

The underlying philosophy of the section is that of inclusion of non-Western and non-traditional works, even though major traditional works and authors have also been included. An attempt has been made to balance canonical works with those by emerging or previously neglected periods, genres, countries, and authors. Some specific scope considerations include the following: The subheadings of Individual Works are used for single works by one author, while collected plays by one author are included under Country, Period, or Genre. Collections of Plays is used for collections of works by multiple authors. Periods is used for critical works and anthologies encompassing multiple periods in the development of Western or non-Western drama and theater. The Avant-garde is used for both the historical European avant-garde of the early 20th century and the mid-20th century American avant-garde.

—Kornelia Tancheva

General

Hartnoll, Phyllis (Editor)   **PN2035.O9 1983**
Oxford Companion to the Theatre. Ed. 4. Trade Cloth. Oxford
University Press, Inc. New York, NY. 1983. 640p.
ISBN:0-19-211546-4, ISBN13: 978-0-19-211546-1.
Dewey:792/.03/21. LCCN:83-235664.

Audience: **g.** *B*

Styan, John L.   **PN1655.S75**
The Elements of Drama. Paper Text. Textbook Publishers.
Temecula, CA. 2003. 306p. ISBN:0-7581-1323-4, ISBN13:
978-0-7581-1323-8. Dewey:792.01.

Audience: **g.**

General > History

Bentley, Eric   **PN1851.B4**
The Playwright As Thinker: A Study of Drama in Modern
Times. Paper Text. Textbook Publishers. Temecula, CA. 2003.
314p. ISBN:0-7581-8320-8, ISBN13: 978-0-7581-8320-0.
Dewey:809.2.

Audience: **g.** *B*

Brockett, Oscar Gross &   **PN2101.B68 2003**
  Hildy, Franklin J.
History of the Theatre. Ed. 9. Trade Cloth. Allyn & Bacon, Inc.
Boston, MA. 2002. 720p. ISBN:0-205-35878-0, ISBN13:
978-0-205-35878-6. Dewey:792/.09. LCCN:2002-025352.

Audience: **l,u,f.**

Fischer-Lichte, Erika   **PN1731.F513 2001**
History of European Drama and Theatre. Trade Paper.
Routledge. New York, NY. 2004. 416p. ISBN:0-415-18060-0,
ISBN13: 978-0-415-18060-3. Dewey:809.2.
LCCN:2001-034969.

Audience: **u,f.** *Choice, 2002.*

Gassner, John & Quinn,   **PN1625**
  Edward (Editors)
The Readers Encyclopedia of World Drama. Trade Paper. Dover
Publications, Inc. Mineola, NY. 2002. 1040p.
ISBN:0-486-42064-7, ISBN13: 978-0-486-42064-6.
Dewey:808.82009.

Audience: **g.**

International Theatre   **PN2037.W725 2000**
  Institute Staff
The World of Theatre: 2000 Edition. Ian Herbert & Nicole
Leclercq (Editors). Paper over Boards. Routledge. New York,
NY. 2000. 328p. ISBN:0-415-23866-8, ISBN13:
978-0-415-23866-3. Dewey:792. LCCN:00-044649.

Audience: **g.**

Majumadara, Ramendu   **PN2037**
  (Editor)
The World of Theatre. Theatre Communications Group, Inc.
2005. ISBN:1-55936-264-2, ISBN13: 978-1-55936-264-1.

Audience: **g.**

Odell, George C.   **PN2277.N5.O4 1970**
Annals of the New York Stage. Trade Cloth. A M S Press, Inc.
New York, NY. 1970. ISBN:0-404-07830-3, ISBN13:
978-0-404-07830-0. Dewey:792/.097471. LCCN:77-116018.

Audience: **g.** *B*

Postlewait, Thomas   **PN2115.I54 1989**
Interpreting the Theatrical Past: Essays in the Historiography of
Performance. University of Iowa Press. 1989.
ISBN:0-87745-238-5, ISBN13: 978-0-87745-238-6.

Audience: **l,u,f.**

Styan, John L.   **PR3091**
Drama Stage and Audience. Trade Paper. Cambridge University
Press. New York, NY. 1975. 264p. ISBN:0-521-09869-6,
ISBN13: 978-0-521-09869-4. Dewey:792.9/5. LCCN:74-076948.

Audience: **l,u,f.** *B*

Turner, Victor W.   **GN473.T84 1982**
From Ritual to Theatre: The Human Seriousness of Play. Trade
Paper. P A J Publications. New York, NY. 1982. 127p.
ISBN:0-933826-17-6, ISBN13: 978-0-933826-17-5.
Dewey:306.4/84. LCCN:81-083751.

Audience: **g,u,f.**

General > Theory

Artaud, Antonin   **PN2021.A713 1993**
Theatre and Its Double. Victor Corti (Translator). Trade Paper.
Riverrun Press, Inc. Flemington, NJ. 2002. 102p.
ISBN:0-7145-4234-2, ISBN13: 978-0-7145-4234-8. Dewey:792.

Audience: **u,f.**

Baker, George P.   **PN1661**
Dramatic Technique. Trade Cloth. Greenwood Publishing Group,
Inc. Portsmouth, NH. 1970. 531p. ISBN:0-8371-3005-0,
ISBN13: 978-0-8371-3005-7. Dewey:808.2. LCCN:74-100220.

Audience: **l,u.** *B*

Birringer, Johannes   **PN2039**
Theatre, Theory, Postmodernism. Paper Text. Indiana University
Press. Bloomington, IN. 1993. 256p. Drama and Performance
Studies ISBN:0-253-20845-9, ISBN13: 978-0-253-20845-3.
Dewey:792/.01. LCCN:90-024442.

Audience: **u,f.** *Choice, 1992.*

Brandt, George W.   **PN1655.M59 1997**
Modern Theories of Drama: A Selection of Writings on Drama
and Theatre, 1850-1990. Paper Text. Oxford University Press,
Inc. New York, NY. 1999. 356p. ISBN:0-19-871139-5, ISBN13:
978-0-19-871139-1. Dewey:809.2. LCCN:97-027188.

Audience: **l,u,f.**

Brecht, Bertolt   **PN2037**
Brecht on Theatre: The Development of an Aesthetic. Ed. 2.
Trade Paper. Methuen Publishing Ltd. London, 2003.
ISBN:0-413-38800-X, ISBN13: 978-0-413-38800-1. Dewey:792.
LCCN:63-018479.

Audience: **l,u,f.** *B*

Carlson, Marvin   **PN2039.C26 1993**
Theories of the Theatre: A Historical and Critical Survey from the Greeks to the Present. Trade Paper. Cornell University Press. Ithaca, NY. 1993. 552p. ISBN:0-8014-8154-6, ISBN13: 978-0-8014-8154-3. Dewey:792/.01. LCCN:93-030778.
Audience: **u,f.** _B_

Craig, Edward Gordon   **PN2091.S8**
On the Art of the Theatre. Paper Text. Textbook Publishers. Temecula, CA. 2003. 295p. ISBN:0-7581-3150-X, ISBN13: 978-0-7581-3150-8. Dewey:792.
Audience: **l,u,f.** _B_

Dolan, Jill   **PN2270.F45D64 1988**
The Feminist Spectator As Critic. UMI Research Press. 1988. ISBN:0-8357-1874-3, ISBN13: 978-0-8357-1874-5.
Audience: **l,u,f.**

Dukore, B. F.   **PN1621.D8**
Dramatic Theory and Criticism. Cloth Text. Harcourt College Publishers. Fort Worth, TX. 1974. 1003p. ISBN:0-03-091152-4, ISBN13: 978-0-03-091152-1. Dewey:808.2. LCCN:73-009778.
Audience: **l,u.** _B_

Fei, Faye Chunfang (Editor)   **PN2871.C535**
Chinese Theories of Theater and Performance from Confucius to the Present. Trade Paper. University of Michigan Press. Chicago, IL. 2002. 232p. ISBN:0-472-08923-4, ISBN13: 978-0-472-08923-9. Dewey:792.0951. LCCN:99-017404.
Audience: **u,f.**

Fortier, Mark   **PN2039.F67 1997**
Theory/Theatre: An Introduction. Routledge. 1997. ISBN:0-415-16165-7, ISBN13: 978-0-415-16165-7.
Audience: **l,u,f.**

Hsu, Tao-Ching   **PN2871**
The Chinese Conception of the Theatre. Cloth Text. University of Washington Press. Seattle, WA. 1985. 676p. ISBN:0-295-96034-5, ISBN13: 978-0-295-96034-0. Dewey:792/.0951. LCCN:83-005964.
Audience: **u,f.**

James, Henry   **PN2021**
The Scenic Art: Notes and Acting and the Drama. Allan Wade (Editor). Trade Paper. Books on Demand. Ann Arbor, MI. 420p. ISBN:0-598-27634-3, ISBN13: 978-0-598-27634-6. Dewey:792.04.
Audience: **u,f.**

Matthews, Brander (Editor)   **PN1661.M29 1970**
Papers on Playmaking. Trade Cloth. Ayer Company Publishers, Inc. Manchester, NH. 1977. 312p. Essay Index Reprint Ser. ISBN:0-8369-1890-8, ISBN13: 978-0-8369-1890-8. Dewey:809.2. LCCN:75-111852.
Audience: **g.** _B_

Nicoll, Allardyce   **PN1631**
The Theory of Drama. Trade Cloth. Ayer Company Publishers, Inc. Manchester, NH. 1972. ISBN:0-405-08818-3, ISBN13: 978-0-405-08818-6. Dewey:809.2. LCCN:66-029422.
Audience: **l,u,f.**

Postlewait, Thomas   **PN2115.I54 1989**
Interpreting the Theatrical Past: Essays in the Historiography of Performance. University of Iowa Press. 1989. ISBN:0-87745-238-5, ISBN13: 978-0-87745-238-6.
Audience: **l,u,f.**

Reinelt, Janelle G. and   **PN2039**
Joseph R. Roach
Critical Theory and Performance. University of Michigan Press. 1992. ISBN:0-472-09458-0, ISBN13: 978-0-472-09458-5.
Audience: **u,f.**

Shaw, George Bernard   **PR5366**
Shaw on Theatre: A Half Century of Advices. Mary C. Stratton (Editor), Stephen Kraft (Illustrator), Stanley Weintraub (Introduction by). Trade Cloth. Press of Appletree Alley, The. Lewisburg, PA. 1998. 72p. Ellen Clarke Bertrand Library Limited Edition Ser. ISBN:0-916375-24-2, ISBN13: 978-0-916375-24-9. Dewey:826.912.
Audience: **l,u,f.**

General > Theory > Genre Studies

Aristotle   **PN1040.A513 2001**
Aristotle on Poetics. Seth Benardete (Translator), Michael Davis (Translator, Introduction by). Cloth Text. Saint Augustine's Press, Inc. South Bend, IN. 2002. 144p. ISBN:1-58731-025-2, ISBN13: 978-1-58731-025-6. Dewey:808.2. LCCN:2001-005879.
Audience: **u,f.**

Goldman, Michael   **PN1631.G59 2000**
On Drama: Boundaries of Genre, Borders of Self. Trade Cloth. University of Michigan Press. Chicago, IL. 2000. 144p. Theater Ser., :Theory - Text - Performance ISBN:0-472-11011-X, ISBN13: 978-0-472-11011-7. Dewey:808.2. LCCN:00-008697.
Audience: **u,f.** _Choice, 2001._

Hokenson, Jan   **PN56.C66H65 2006**
The Idea of Comedy: History, Theory, Critique. Trade Cloth. Fairleigh Dickinson University Press. Cranbury, NJ. 2006. 288p. ISBN:0-8386-4096-6, ISBN13: 978-0-8386-4096-8. Dewey:809/.917. LCCN:2005-018161.
Audience: **g.** _Choice, 2006._

Kelly, Henry Ansgar   **PN1891.K45 1993**
Ideas and Forms of Tragedy from Aristotle to the Middle Ages. Alastair Minnis, Patrick Boyde, John Burrow, Rita Copeland, Alan Deyermond, Peter Dronke, Nigel Palmer & Winthrop Wetherbee (Contribution by). Trade Paper. Cambridge University Press. New York, NY. 2005. 275p. Cambridge Studies in Medieval Literature Ser., Vol. 18 ISBN:0-521-02377-7, ISBN13: 978-0-521-02377-1. Dewey:809.2512.
Audience: **l,u,f.**

Nietzsche, Friedrich   **BH39**
The Birth of Tragedy. Douglas Smith (Editor). Trade Paper.

Oxford University Press, Inc. New York, NY. 2000. 218p. Oxford World's Classics Ser. ISBN:0-19-283292-1, ISBN13: 978-0-19-283292-4. Dewey:111.8/5.

Audience: **u,f.**

Orr, John   **PN1907.O7 1991**
Tragicomedy and Contemporary Culture: Play and Performance from Beckett to Shepard. Trade Cloth. University of Michigan Press. Chicago, IL. 1991. 176p. Theater Ser., :Theory - Text - Performance ISBN:0-472-10262-1, ISBN13: 978-0-472-10262-4. Dewey:809.2/523. LCCN:91-009736.

Audience: **g,l.**

Palmer, Richard H.   **PN1892**
Tragedy and Tragic Theory: An Analytical Guide. Cloth Text. Greenwood Publishing Group, Inc. Portsmouth, NH. 1992. 252p. ISBN:0-313-28203-X, ISBN13: 978-0-313-28203-4. Dewey:809.916. LCCN:91-046861.

Audience: **l,u,f.**

Schmidt, Dennis J.   **PA3131.S366 2001**
On Germans and Other Greeks: Tragedy and Ethical Life. E-Book. Indiana University Press. Bloomington, IN. 2001. 432p. Studies in Continental Thought ISBN:0-253-33868-9, ISBN13: 978-0-253-33868-6. Dewey:882/.0109. LCCN:00-050642.

Audience: **u,f.**

Worthen, William B.   **PR736.W64 1992**
Modern Drama and the Rhetoric of Theater. Trade Cloth. University of California Press. Berkeley, CA. 1991. 240p. ISBN:0-520-07468-8, ISBN13: 978-0-520-07468-2. Dewey:822/.9109. LCCN:91-017677.

Audience: **l,u,f.** *Choice, 1992.*

Reference

                                                  PN2285.C58
Contemporary Theatre, Film, and Television, Vol. 71. Trade Cloth. Thomson Gale. Farmington Hills, MI. 2006. 500p. ISBN:0-7876-9044-9, ISBN13: 978-0-7876-9044-1. Dewey:791/.092/2 B.

Audience: **g.**

                                                  PN2035.E52 1977
The Encyclopedia of World Theater: With 420 Illustrations and an Index of Play Titles. Trade Cloth. Simon & Schuster. New York, NY. 1977. 320p. ISBN:0-684-14834-X, ISBN13: 978-0-684-14834-2. Dewey:792/.03. LCCN:76-019741.

Audience: **g.** *B*

                                                  PN2035.I49
International Dictionary of Theatre, Set. Ed. 2. Trade Cloth. Thomson Gale. Farmington Hills, MI. 2005. ISBN:1-55862-344-2, ISBN13: 978-1-55862-344-6. Dewey:792/.03.

Audience: **g.**

                                                  PN2277.N5
Internet Broadway Database.
http://www.ibdb.com/

Audience: **g,l,u,f.**

                                                  PS3525.A24785
Office of the Revels: The Dramatic Records of Sir Henry Herbert, Master of the Revels, 1623-1673. Paper Text. Classic Books. Murrieta, CA. 2001. 155p. ISBN:0-7426-9229-9, ISBN13: 978-0-7426-9229-9. Dewey:704.

Audience: **u,f.**

Alexander Street Press   **PN6119.7**
Black Drama 1850 to Present.
http://www.alexanderstreet2.com/BLDRLive/
Alexander Street Press.

Audience: **g,l,u,f.**

Alexander, Catherine   **PR2976.C3 2003**
  (Editor)
The Cambridge Shakespeare Library: Shakespeare's Times, Texts, and Stages; Shakespeare Criticism; Shakespeare Performance, Set. Quantity Pack, Trade Cloth. Cambridge University Press. New York, NY. 2003. 1416p. ISBN:0-521-82433-8, ISBN13: 978-0-521-82433-0. Dewey:822.3/3. LCCN:2002-031457.

Audience: **l,u,f.**

Aston, Elaine & Reinelt,   **PR739.F45C36 2000**
  Janelle (Editors)
The Cambridge Companion to Modern British Women Playwrights. Cloth Text. Cambridge University Press. New York, NY. 2000. 296p. Companions to Literature Ser. ISBN:0-521-59422-7, ISBN13: 978-0-521-59422-6. Dewey:822/.91099282. LCCN:99-036626.

Audience: **g.** *Choice, 2001.*

Banham, Martin (Editor)   **PN2035.C27 1995**
The Cambridge Guide to Theatre. Ed. 2. Trade Cloth. Cambridge University Press. New York, NY. 1995. 1247p. ISBN:0-521-43437-8, ISBN13: 978-0-521-43437-9. Dewey:792/.09. LCCN:95-001011.

Audience: **g.** *Choice, 1996.*

Banham, Martin (Editor), et   **PN2969.C36 1994**
  al.
The Cambridge Guide to African and Caribbean Theatre. Errol Hill & George Woodyard (Editors). Trade Paper. Cambridge University Press. New York, NY. 2005. 269p. ISBN:0-521-61207-1, ISBN13: 978-0-521-61207-4. Dewey:792/.096/03. LCCN:2005-279353.

Audience: **g.**

Barnet, Sylvan   **PN1621.B3**
Aspects of the Drama: A Handbook. Paper Text. Textbook Publishers. Temecula, CA. 2003. 270p. ISBN:0-7581-9702-0, ISBN13: 978-0-7581-9702-3. Dewey:809.2.

Audience: **g.**

Beadle, Richard (Editor)　　　　PN2587.C36 1994
The Cambridge Companion to Medieval English Theatre. Trade
Paper. Cambridge University Press. New York, NY. 1994. 394p.
Companions to Literature Ser. ISBN:0-521-45916-8, ISBN13:
978-0-521-45916-7. Dewey:792.0942. LCCN:93-004397.
　　　　　　　　　　　　　　　Audience: **g,u,f.**

Benson, Eugene & Conolly,　　　　PN2300.O94 1989
　L. W. (Editors)
The Oxford Companion to Canadian Theatre. Trade Cloth.
Oxford University Press, Inc. New York, NY. 1990. 680p.
ISBN:0-19-540672-9, ISBN13: 978-0-19-540672-6.
Dewey:792.0971. LCCN:90-126294.
　　　　　　　　　　　　Audience: **g.** *Choice, 1990.*

Bigsby, Christopher (Editor)　　　　PS3563.A4345Z59 2004
The Cambridge Companion to David Mamet. Cloth Text.
Cambridge University Press. New York, NY. 2004. 266p.
Cambridge Companions to Literature Ser. ISBN:0-521-81557-6,
ISBN13: 978-0-521-81557-4. Dewey:812/.54.
LCCN:2003-063279.
　　　　　　　　　　　　Audience: **g.** *Choice, 2005.*

Bordman, Gerald Martin &　　　　PN2220.B6 2004
　Hischak, Thomas S.
The Oxford Companion to American Theatre. Ed. 3. Trade
Cloth. Oxford University Press, Inc. New York, NY. 2004. 394p.
ISBN:0-19-516986-7, ISBN13: 978-0-19-516986-7.
Dewey:792/.0973/03. LCCN:2003-021367.
　　　　　　　　　　　　Audience: **g.** *Choice, 2004.*

Bowman, Walter Parker　　　　PN2035.R28
Theatre Language: A Dictionary of Terms in English of the
Drama and Stage from Medieval to Modern Times,. Paper Text.
Textbook Publishers. Temecula, CA. 2003. 428p.
ISBN:0-7581-3147-X, ISBN13: 978-0-7581-3147-8.
Dewey:792.03.
　　　　　　　　　　　　　　　　Audience: **g.**

Brandon, James R. (Editor)　　　　PN2860.C35 1997
The Cambridge Guide to Asian Theatre. Ed. 2. Trade Paper.
Cambridge University Press. New York, NY. 1997. 261p.
ISBN:0-521-58822-7, ISBN13: 978-0-521-58822-5.
Dewey:792.095.
　　　　　　　　　　　　　　　　Audience: **g.**

Braunmuller, A. R. &　　　　PR651.C36 2003
　Hattaway, Michael (Editors)
The Cambridge Companion to English Renaissance Drama. Ed.
2. Cloth Text. Cambridge University Press. New York, NY.
2003. 484p. Cambridge Companions to Literature Ser.
ISBN:0-521-82115-0, ISBN13: 978-0-521-82115-5.
Dewey:822/.309. LCCN:2002-035073.
　　　　　　Audience: **g,l,u,f.** *Choice, 2004, 1991.*

Bushnell, Rebecca W.　　　　PN1892.C56 2004
　(Editor)
A Companion to Tragedy. Blackwell Publishing, Inc. 2005.
ISBN:1-4051-0735-9, ISBN13: 978-1-4051-0735-8.
　　　　　　　　　　　　　　　Audience: **u,f.**

Chambers, Colin　　　　PN2035.C65 2002
Continuum Companion to Twentieth Century Theatre. Trade
Cloth. Continuum International Publishing Group, Ltd. London,
2004. 896p. ISBN:0-8264-4959-X, ISBN13: 978-0-8264-4959-7.
Dewey:792/.0904/03. LCCN:2002-025931.
　　　　　　　　　　　Audience: **g.** *Choice, 2003, 2002.*

Charney, Maurice (Editor)　　　　PN6147
Comedy: A Geographic and Historical Guide. Cloth Text.
Greenwood Publishing Group, Inc. Portsmouth, NH. 2005. 688p.
ISBN:0-313-32706-8, ISBN13: 978-0-313-32706-3.
Dewey:809/.7. LCCN:2005-008410.
　　　　　　　　　　　　Audience: **g.** *Choice, 2006.*

Chaturvedi, Ravi (Editor),　　　　PN2974
　et al.
Asia/Pacific. Ramendu Majumdar, Chua Soo Pong, Minoru
Tanokura & Katherine Brisbane (Editors). Paper over Boards.
Routledge. New York, NY. 2001. 544p. World Encyclopedia of
Contemporary Theatre Ser., Vol. 5 ISBN:0-415-05933-X,
ISBN13: 978-0-415-05933-6. Dewey:792/.096/03.
　　　　　　　　　　　　Audience: **g.** *Choice, 1999.*

Cortes, Eladio &　　　　PQ7082
　Barrea-Marlys, Mirta (Editors)
Encyclopedia of Latin American Theater. Cloth Text.
Greenwood Publishing Group, Inc. Portsmouth, NH. 2003. 552p.
ISBN:0-313-29041-5, ISBN13: 978-0-313-29041-1.
Dewey:862.009/98/03. LCCN:2003-049135.
　　　　　　　　　　　　Audience: **g.** *Choice, 2004.*

Craig, Carolyn Casey　　　　PS338.W6C73 2004
Women Pulitzer Playwrights: Biographical Profiles and Analyses
of the Plays. Paper Text. McFarland & Company, Incorporated
Publishers. Jefferson, NC. 2004. 347p. ISBN:0-7864-1881-8,
ISBN13: 978-0-7864-1881-7. Dewey:812/.5099287.
LCCN:2004-020165.
　　　　　　　　　　　　　　　Audience: **l,u.**

Cullen, Frank　　　　PN1962
Vaudeville, Old and New: An Encyclopedia of Variety
Performers. Paper over Boards. Routledge. New York, NY.
2006. 1376p. ISBN:0-415-93853-8, ISBN13:
978-0-415-93853-2. Dewey:792.7097303. LCCN:2005-030588.
　　　　　　　　　　　　　　　Audience: **g.**

Demastes, William W.　　　　PS351
　(Editor)
American Playwrights, 1880-1945: A Research and Production
Sourcebook. Cloth Text. Greenwood Publishing Group, Inc.
Portsmouth, NH. 1994. 512p. ISBN:0-313-28638-8, ISBN13:
978-0-313-28638-4. Dewey:016.812/409. LCCN:94-013690.
　　　　　　　　　　　　Audience: **g.** *Choice, 1995.*

Dunton, Chris　　　　Z2014.D7
Nigerian Theatre in English. Trade Cloth. R. R. Bowker LLC.
East Grinstead, 1998. 400p. ISBN:1-873836-71-6, ISBN13:
978-1-873836-71-2. Dewey:016.8/22/0099669.
LCCN:97-038650.
　　　　　　　　　　　　Audience: **g.** *Choice, 1999.*

Easterling, P. E. (Editor)   PA3131 .C29 1997
The Cambridge Companion to Greek Tragedy. Trade Paper.
Cambridge University Press. New York, NY. 1997. 410p.
Companions to Literature Ser. ISBN:0-521-42351-1, ISBN13:
978-0-521-42351-9. Dewey:882/.01/09. LCCN:96-037392.
                              Audience: **g,l,u,f.** *Choice, 1998.*

Everett, William & Laird,   ML2054.C35 2002
  Paul R. (Editors)
The Cambridge Companion to the Musical. Cloth Text.
Cambridge University Press. New York, NY. 2002. 328p.
Cambridge Companions to Music Ser. ISBN:0-521-79189-8,
ISBN13: 978-0-521-79189-2. Dewey:302.2/244/0945.
LCCN:2002-023788.
                              Audience: **g.** *Choice, 2003.*

Fiske, Deborah Payne   PR691.C35 2000
  (Editor)
The Cambridge Companion to English Restoration Theatre.
Cloth Text. Cambridge University Press. New York, NY. 2000.
322p. Companions to Literature Ser. ISBN:0-521-58215-6,
ISBN13: 978-0-521-58215-5. Dewey:822/.409.
LCCN:99-015230.
                              Audience: **g.** *Choice, 2001.*

Granville, Wilfred   KF4575.B55
The Theater Dictionary: British and American Terms in the
Drama, Opera, and Ballet. Paper Text. Textbook Publishers.
Temecula, CA. 2003. 227p. ISBN:0-7581-6428-9, ISBN13:
978-0-7581-6428-5. Dewey:347.9973.
                              Audience: **g.**

Griffiths, Trevor R.   PN2035.G73 2004
The Ivan R. Dee Guide to Plays and Playwrights. Trade Paper.
Ivan R. Dee Publisher. Blue Ridge Summit, PA. 2004. 384p.
ISBN:1-56663-566-7, ISBN13: 978-1-56663-566-0.
Dewey:809.2/0003. LCCN:2003-070127.
                              Audience: **g.** *Choice, 2004.*

Gänzl, Kurt   ML102.M88G3 2001
The Encyclopedia of the Musical Theatre. Trade Cloth.
Thomson Gale. Farmington Hills, MI. 2001.
ISBN:0-02-865574-5, ISBN13: 978-0-02-865574-1.
Dewey:782.1/4/03. LCCN:2001-018361.
                              Audience: **g.**

Harrison, Martin   PN2041.S45
The Language of Theatre. Trade Cloth. Shelfmark. Chicago, IL.
2003. 225p. ISBN:0-9743318-2-1, ISBN13: 978-0-9743318-2-9.
Dewey:792/.014.
                              Audience: **g.**

Hartnoll, Phyllis (Editor)   PN2035.O9 1983
Oxford Companion to the Theatre. Ed. 4. Trade Cloth. Oxford
University Press, Inc. New York, NY. 1983. 640p.
ISBN:0-19-211546-4, ISBN13: 978-0-19-211546-1.
Dewey:792/.03/21. LCCN:83-235664.
                              Audience: **g.** *B*

Hawkins, Frederick William   PN2621
Annals of the French Stage from Its Origin to the Death of

Racine. Paper Text. Classic Books. Murrieta, CA. 2001.
ISBN:0-7426-9245-0, ISBN13: 978-0-7426-9245-9.
Dewey:792/.0944.
                              Audience: **u,f.** *B*

Hischak, Thomas S.   ML102
Stage It with Music: An Encyclopedic Guide to the American
Musical Theatre. Cloth Text. Greenwood Publishing Group, Inc.
Portsmouth, NH. 1993. 328p. ISBN:0-313-28708-2, ISBN13:
978-0-313-28708-4. Dewey:792.60973. LCCN:92-035321.
                              Audience: **l,u.** *Choice, 1993.*

Hughes, Derek & Todd,   PR3317.Z5C36 2004
  Janet (Editors)
The Cambridge Companion to Aphra Behn. Trade Paper,
Perfect. Cambridge University Press. New York, NY. 2004.
274p. Cambridge Companions to Literature Ser.
ISBN:0-521-52720-1, ISBN13: 978-0-521-52720-0.
Dewey:822/.4. LCCN:2004-049740.
                              Audience: **g,l,u,f.** *Choice, 2005.*

Kennedy, Dennis (Editor)   PN1655
The Oxford Encyclopedia of Theatre and Performance, Set.
Trade Cloth. Oxford University Press, Inc. New York, NY. 2003.
1,618p. ISBN:0-19-860174-3, ISBN13: 978-0-19-860174-6.
Dewey:792.03. LCCN:2003-266308.
                              Audience: **g.** *Choice, 2003.*

Lal, Ananda (Editor)   PN2881.O95 2004
The Oxford Companion to Indian Theatre. Trade Cloth. Oxford
University Press, Inc. New York, NY. 2004. 600p.
ISBN:0-19-564446-8, ISBN13: 978-0-19-564446-3.
Dewey:792.0954. LCCN:2004-312160.
                              Audience: **g.** *Choice, 2005.*

Langhans, Edward A.   PN2035
  (Editor), et al.
An International Dictionary of Theatre Language. James R.
Brandon & June V. Gibson (Editors), Joel Trapido (Contribution
by). Cloth Text. Greenwood Publishing Group, Inc. Portsmouth,
NH. 1985. 1032p. ISBN:0-313-22980-5, ISBN13:
978-0-313-22980-0. Dewey:792/.03/21. LCCN:83-022756.
                              Audience: **g.** *Choice, 1986.*

Law, Jonathan   PN2035.N49 2001
Penguin Dictionary of the Theatre. Trade Paper. Penguin Group
(USA) Inc. New York, NY. 2001. 576p. ISBN:0-14-051454-6,
ISBN13: 978-0-14-051454-4. Dewey:792/.03.
LCCN:2001-280241.
                              Audience: **g.**

Leiter, Samuel L.   PN2277
The Encyclopedia of the New York Stage, 1930-1940. Cloth
Text. Greenwood Publishing Group, Inc. Portsmouth, NH. 1989.
1339p. ISBN:0-313-25509-1, ISBN13: 978-0-313-25509-0.
Dewey:792.9/5/09471. LCCN:88-005668.
                              Audience: **g.** *Choice, 1990.*

Leiter, Samuel L.   PN2277
The Encyclopedia of the New York Stage, 1940-1950. Cloth
Text. Greenwood Publishing Group, Inc. Portsmouth, NH. 1992.

1000p. ISBN:0-313-27510-6, ISBN13: 978-0-313-27510-4.
Dewey:792/.097471. LCCN:92-007397.

Audience: **g.** *Choice, 1993.*

Leiter, Samuel L.   **PN2921.L45 2006**
Historical Dictionary of Japanese Traditional Theatre. Trade
Cloth. Scarecrow Press, Inc. Lanham, MD. 2006. 632p.
Historical Dictionaries of Literature and the Arts Ser., No. 4
ISBN:0-8108-5527-5, ISBN13: 978-0-8108-5527-4.
Dewey:792/.0952/03. LCCN:2005-019419.

Audience: **g.**

Leiter, Samuel L. & Hill,   **PN2277**
  Holly (Contribution by)
The Encyclopedia of the New York Stage, 1920-1930, Set. Cloth
Text. Greenwood Publishing Group, Inc. Portsmouth, NH. 1985.
1331p. ISBN:0-313-23615-1, ISBN13: 978-0-313-23615-0.
Dewey:792.9/5/097471. LCCN:84-006558.

Audience: **g.** *B* *Choice, 1986.*

Leiter, Samuel L. & Hill,   **PN2277.N5L361985**
  Holly (Contribution by)
The Encyclopedia of the New York Stage, 1920-1930, Vol. 1.
Cloth Text. Greenwood Publishing Group, Inc. Portsmouth, NH.
1985. 1331p. ISBN:0-313-25037-5, ISBN13:
978-0-313-25037-8. Dewey:792.9/5/097471. LCCN:84-006558.

Audience: **g.** *B* *Choice, 1986.*

Liu, Miles Xian (Editor)   **PS338**
Asian American Playwrights: A Bio-Bibliographical Critical
Sourcebook. Cloth Text. Greenwood Publishing Group, Inc.
Portsmouth, NH. 2002. 424p. ISBN:0-313-31455-1, ISBN13:
978-0-313-31455-1. Dewey:812/.509895/03 B.
LCCN:2001-037680.

Audience: **g,l,u,f.** *Choice, 2003.*

Maleh, Ghassan (Editor), et   **PN1861.W67 1994**
al.
The Arab World. Samir Sirhan, Ahmed Zaki & Farouk Ohan
(Editors). Paper over Boards. Routledge. New York, NY. 1999.
336p. World Encyclopedia of Contemporary Theatre Ser., Vol. 4
ISBN:0-415-05932-1, ISBN13: 978-0-415-05932-9.
Dewey:792.0917492703.

Audience: **g.** *Choice, 2000.*

Manheim, Michael (Editor)   **PS3529.N5Z575 1998**
The Cambridge Companion to Eugene O'Neill. Cloth Text.
Cambridge University Press. New York, NY. 1998. 274p.
Companions to Literature Ser. ISBN:0-521-55389-X, ISBN13:
978-0-521-55389-6. Dewey:812/.52. LCCN:97-042228.

Audience: **g,l,u,f.** *Choice, 1999.*

McGraw-Hill Staff   **PN1625.M3 1984**
McGraw-Hill Encyclopedia of World Drama, Vol. 99. Ed. 2.
Daniel Gerould (Preface by). Trade Cloth. McGraw-Hill
Professional Publishing. New York, NY. 1984. 2900p.
ISBN:0-07-079169-4, ISBN13: 978-0-07-079169-5.
Dewey:809.2. LCCN:83-009919.

Audience: **g.** *B*

Murphy, Brenda (Editor)   **PS338.W6C36 1999**
The Cambridge Companion to American Women Playwrights.
Trade Paper. Cambridge University Press. New York, NY. 1999.
324p. Companions to Literature Ser. ISBN:0-521-57680-6,
ISBN13: 978-0-521-57680-2. Dewey:812.009/9287.
LCCN:98-036593.

Audience: **g,l,u,f.**

Partnow, Elaine & Hyatt,   **PN471.P37 1998**
  Lesley
The Female Dramatists: Profiles of Women Playwrights from the
Middle Ages to the Contemporary Times. Trade Cloth. Facts On
File, Inc. New York, NY. 1998. 304p. ISBN:0-8160-3015-4,
ISBN13: 978-0-8160-3015-6. Dewey:809.2/082.
LCCN:97-026501.

Audience: **g.** *Choice, 1998.*

Pavis, Patrice   **PN2035.P2913 1998**
Dictionary of the Theatre: Terms, Concepts, and Analysis.
Christine Shantz (Translator), Marvin Carlson (Preface by).
Trade Cloth. University of Toronto Press. Toronto, ON. 1998.
1024p. ISBN:0-8020-4342-9, ISBN13: 978-0-8020-4342-9.
Dewey:792/.03. LCCN:00-703934.

Audience: **g.** *Choice, 1999.*

Pavis, Patrice   **PN2035.P2913 1998**
Dictionary of the Theatre: Terms, Concepts and Analysis.
Christine Shantz (Translator), Marvin Carlson (Preface by).
Trade Paper. University of Toronto Press. Toronto, ON. 1998.
864p. ISBN:0-8020-8163-0, ISBN13: 978-0-8020-8163-6.
Dewey:792/.03. LCCN:00-703934.

Audience: **g.** *Choice, 1999.*

Peterson, Bernard L.   **ML102**
A Century of Musicals in Black and White: An Encyclopedia of
Musical Stage Works by, About, or Involving Black Americans.
Cloth Text. Greenwood Publishing Group, Inc. Portsmouth, NH.
1993. 560p. ISBN:0-313-26657-3, ISBN13: 978-0-313-26657-7.
Dewey:782.1408996073. LCCN:92-041976.

Audience: **g.** *Choice, 1994.*

Powell, Kerry (Editor)   **PN2594**
The Cambridge Companion to Victorian and Edwardian Theatre.
Trade Cloth. Cambridge University Press. New York, NY. 2004.
308p. Cambridge Companions to Literature Ser.
ISBN:0-521-79157-X, ISBN13: 978-0-521-79157-1.
Dewey:792/.0942/09034. LCCN:2002-041552.

Audience: **g,l,u,f.** *Choice, 2004.*

Raby, Peter (Editor)   **PR6066.I53Z625520**
The Cambridge Companion to Harold Pinter. Cloth Text.
Cambridge University Press. New York, NY. 2001. 292p.
Companions to Literature Ser. ISBN:0-521-65123-9, ISBN13:
978-0-521-65123-3. Dewey:822/.914. LCCN:2001-022302.

Audience: **g,l,u,f.** *Choice, 2002.*

Richmond, Hugh Macrae   **PR3095.R53 2004**
Shakespeare's Theatre. Trade Paper. Continuum International
Publishing Group, Ltd. London, 2005. 584p.
ISBN:0-8264-7776-3, ISBN13: 978-0-8264-7776-7.
Dewey:822.33.

Audience: **l,u.**

Roudani, Matthew   PS3569.H394Z65 2002
The Cambridge Companion to Sam Shepard. Cloth Text.
Cambridge University Press. New York, NY. 2002. 352p.
Cambridge Companions to Literature Ser. ISBN:0-521-77158-7,
ISBN13: 978-0-521-77158-0. Dewey:812/.54 B.
LCCN:2001-043211.
                                          Audience: **g.** *Choice, 2003.*

Rouyer, Philippe & Nagy,   **PN1861**
  Peter (Editors)
Europe, Vol. 1. Trade Paper. Routledge. New York, NY. 2001.
1072p. World Encyclopedia of Contemporary Theatre Ser.
ISBN:0-415-25157-5, ISBN13: 978-0-415-25157-0.
Dewey:912.4.
                                          Audience: **g.**

Rubin, Don   PJ7565.W67 1999
e The World Encyclopedia of Contemporary Theatre. E-Book.
Taylor & Francis Group. Philadelphia, PA. ISBN:0-203-16804-6,
ISBN13: 978-0-203-16804-2. Dewey:792.0917492703.
                                          Audience: **g.**

Rubin, Don (Editor)   **PN1861.W67**
World Encyclopedia of Contemporary Theatre, Set. Paper over
Boards. Routledge. New York, NY. 2000. 3500p. World
Encyclopedia of Contemporary Theatre Ser.
ISBN:0-415-23205-8, ISBN13: 978-0-415-23205-0.
Dewey:792/.03.
                                          Audience: **g.**

Rubin, Don (Editor), et al.   **PN1861**
Africa. Ousmane Diakhate & Hansel Ndumbe Eyoh (Editors).
Trade Paper. Routledge. New York, NY. 2000. 448p. World
Encyclopedia of Contemporary Theatre Ser., Vol. 3
ISBN:0-415-22746-1, ISBN13: 978-0-415-22746-9.
Dewey:792.09603.
                                          Audience: **g.**

Sell, Michael   NA6840.G7T48 2000
The Theatres Trust Guide to British Theatres, 1750-1950. Trade
Paper. A & C Black. London, 2004. 304p. ISBN:0-7136-5688-3,
ISBN13: 978-0-7136-5688-6. Dewey:792/.0941.
LCCN:2001-326143.
                                          Audience: **g.**

Solorzano, Carlos (Editor)   PA6073.B44
The Americas. Trade Paper. Routledge. New York, NY. 2000.
640p. World Encyclopedia of Contemporary Theatre Ser., Vol. 2
ISBN:0-415-22745-3, ISBN13: 978-0-415-22745-2.
Dewey:792.03.
                                          Audience: **g.** *Choice, 1996.*

Wells, Stanley & Stanton,   PR3091.C36 2002
  Sarah (Editors)
The Cambridge Companion to Shakespeare on Stage. Trade
Paper. Cambridge University Press. New York, NY. 2002. 338p.
Cambridge Companions to Literature Ser. ISBN:0-521-79711-X,
ISBN13: 978-0-521-79711-5. Dewey:792.9/5.
LCCN:2001-052447.
                                          Audience: **g,l,u,f.**

White, Edmund   PQ2605.O28
Genet: A Biography. Book, Other. Knopf Publishing Group.
New York, NY. 1994. 800p. ISBN:0-679-75479-2, ISBN13:
978-0-679-75479-4. Dewey:848/.91209 B.
                                          Audience: **g,l,u,f.** *Choice, 1994.*

Woll, Allen L.   **PN2270**
Dictionary of the Black Theatre: Broadway, Off-Broadway, and
Selected Harlem Theatre. Cloth Text. Greenwood Publishing
Group, Inc. Portsmouth, NH. 1983. 359p. ISBN:0-313-22561-3,
ISBN13: 978-0-313-22561-1. Dewey:792/.08996073.
LCCN:82-021090.
                                          Audience: **g.** *B*

Zung, Cecilia S. L.   PL2357.Z8
Secrets of the Chinese Drama: A Complete Explanatory Guide
to Actions and Symbols as Seen in the Performance of Chinese
Dramas. Trade Cloth. Kegan Paul International, Ltd. London,
2005. 300p. ISBN:0-7103-1208-3, ISBN13: 978-0-7103-1208-2.
Dewey:792.0951.
                                          Audience: **l,u.**

Western Drama and Theater

                                          PN2035.E52 1977
The Encyclopedia of World Theater: With 420 Illustrations and
an Index of Play Titles. Trade Cloth. Simon & Schuster. New
York, NY. 1977. 320p. ISBN:0-684-14834-X, ISBN13:
978-0-684-14834-2. Dewey:792/.03. LCCN:76-019741.
                                          Audience: **g.** *B*

Banham, Martin (Editor)   PN2035.C27 1995
The Cambridge Guide to Theatre. Ed. 2. Trade Cloth.
Cambridge University Press. New York, NY. 1995. 1247p.
ISBN:0-521-43437-8, ISBN13: 978-0-521-43437-9.
Dewey:792/.09. LCCN:95-001011.
                                          Audience: **g.** *Choice, 1996.*

Hartnoll, Phyllis (Editor)   PN2035.O9 1983
Oxford Companion to the Theatre. Ed. 4. Trade Cloth. Oxford
University Press, Inc. New York, NY. 1983. 640p.
ISBN:0-19-211546-4, ISBN13: 978-0-19-211546-1.
Dewey:792/.03/21. LCCN:83-235664.
                                          Audience: **g.** *B*

International Theatre   PN2037.W725 2000
  Institute Staff
The World of Theatre: 2000 Edition. Ian Herbert & Nicole
Leclercq (Editors). Paper over Boards. Routledge. New York,
NY. 2000. 328p. ISBN:0-415-23866-8, ISBN13:
978-0-415-23866-3. Dewey:792. LCCN:00-044649.
                                          Audience: **g.**

Majumadara, Ramendu   **PN2037**
  (Editor)
The World of Theatre. Theatre Communications Group, Inc.
2005. ISBN:1-55936-264-2, ISBN13: 978-1-55936-264-1.
                                          Audience: **g.**

Pinter, Harold   PR6066.I53 1990
Complete Works: Birthday Party. Trade Paper. Grove/Atlantic,
Inc. New York, NY. 1994. 256p. ISBN:0-8021-5096-9, ISBN13:
978-0-8021-5096-7. Dewey:822/.914. LCCN:90-013933.

Audience: **g,l,u,f.**

Western Drama and Theater > Individual Works

Fugard, Athol, et al.   PR9369.3.F8 M3 1997
Master Harold. Laurie G. Kirszner & Stephen R. Mandell
(Authors). Paper Text. Thomson Heinle. Boston, MA. 1997.
192p. Harcourt Brace Casebook Series in Literature Ser.
ISBN:0-15-505483-X, ISBN13: 978-0-15-505483-7. Dewey:822.
LCCN:97-070035.

Audience: **l,u,f.**

Goethe, Johann Wolfgang   PT2026.F2M84 2004
  von & Mueller, Carl Richard
Faust: Parts One and Two. Trade Paper. Smith and Kraus
Publishers, Inc. Lyme, NH. 2005. 640p. ISBN:1-57525-360-7,
ISBN13: 978-1-57525-360-2. Dewey:832/.6.
LCCN:2004-045378.

Audience: **l,u,f.**

Hrotsvitha   PR2065
Dulcitius, a Mediaeval Comedy. Trade Paper. Books on
Demand. Ann Arbor, MI. 20p. ISBN:0-598-75592-6, ISBN13:
978-0-598-75592-6. Dewey:872. LCCN:17-006632.

Audience: **u,f.**

Kushner, Tony   PS3561.U778A85 2003
Angels in America: A Gay Fantasia on National Themes. Trade
Paper. Theatre Communications Group, Inc. New York, NY.
2003. 304p. ISBN:1-55936-231-6, ISBN13: 978-1-55936-231-3.
Dewey:812/.54. LCCN:2003-017904.

Audience: **g,l,u.**

Mamet, David   PS3545.I5365
American Buffalo. Library Binding. Sagebrush Education
Resources. Caledonia, MN. 1996. ISBN:0-613-29186-7,
ISBN13: 978-0-613-29186-6. Dewey:812.5/4.

Audience: **l,u,f.**

Mamet, David   PS3545.I5365
Glengarry Glen Ross. Trade Paper. Grove/Atlantic, Inc. New
York, NY. 1984. 112p. ISBN:0-8021-3091-7, ISBN13:
978-0-8021-3091-4. Dewey:812.5/4. LCCN:83-049380.

Audience: **g,l,u,f.**

Mamet, David   PS3563.A4345O4 1993
Oleanna. UK-Trade Paper. Knopf Publishing Group. New York,
NY. 1993. 96p. ISBN:0-679-74536-X, ISBN13:
978-0-679-74536-5. Dewey:812.5/4. LCCN:92-050638.

Audience: **l,u,f.**

Mamet, David   PS3563.A4345S64 1988
Speed-the-Plow. Trade Paper. Grove/Atlantic, Inc. New York,
NY. 1988. 96p. ISBN:0-8021-3046-1, ISBN13:
978-0-8021-3046-4. Dewey:812.5/4. LCCN:87-037252.

Audience: **l,u,f.**

Vogel, Paula   PS3572.O296H88 1997
How I Learned to Drive. Trade Paper. Dramatists Play Service,
Inc. New York, NY. 1997. 60p. ISBN:0-8222-1623-X, ISBN13:
978-0-8222-1623-0. Dewey:812/.54. LCCN:98-128331.

Audience: **g,l,u,f.**

Western Drama and Theater > Collections of Plays

                                                    PN6112
The Best Plays of 1932-1933. Trade Cloth. Ayer Company
Publishers, Inc. Manchester, NH. 1975. The Best Plays Ser.
ISBN:0-405-07647-9, ISBN13: 978-0-405-07647-3.
Dewey:812.508. LCCN:75-019860.

Audience: **l,u.**

                                                    PS634
Best Plays Series. Trade Cloth. Ayer Company Publishers, Inc.
Manchester, NH. 1976. ISBN:0-405-07637-1, ISBN13:
978-0-405-07637-4. Dewey:812.5408. LCCN:75-019860.

Audience: **l,u.**

                                                    PN6112
Best Plays, 1963-1964. Trade Cloth. Ayer Company Publishers,
Inc. Manchester, NH. 1981. ISBN:0-405-13215-8, ISBN13:
978-0-405-13215-5. Dewey:812.08.

Audience: **l,u.**

                                                    PS634
Best Plays, 1964-1965. Trade Cloth. Ayer Company Publishers,
Inc. Manchester, NH. 1981. ISBN:0-405-13216-6, ISBN13:
978-0-405-13216-2. Dewey:808.82.

Audience: **l,u.**

                                                    PN6112
Best Plays, 1966-1967. Trade Cloth. Ayer Company Publishers,
Inc. Manchester, NH. 1981. ISBN:0-405-13217-4, ISBN13:
978-0-405-13217-9. Dewey:808.82.

Audience: **l,u.**

                                                    PR1269
Eighteenth Century Plays. Paper Text. Textbook Publishers.
Temecula, CA. 2003. 484p. ISBN:0-7581-8086-1, ISBN13:
978-0-7581-8086-5. Dewey:822.5.

Audience: **l,u,f.**

Aboff, Marcie   PZ7.A164GIA 2004
The Giant Jellybean Jar. Michael Benedikt & George E.
Wellwarth (Editors), Paige Billin Frye (Illustrator). Trade Cloth.
Penguin Group (USA) Inc. New York, NY. 2004. 32p. Dutton
Easy Reader Ser. ISBN:0-525-47236-3, ISBN13:
978-0-525-47236-0. Dewey:[E]. LCCN:2004-300475.

Audience: **l,u,f.**

Aeschylus, et al.   **PA3463.S59 2002**
Six Greek Tragedies: Aeschylus: Persians, Prometheus Bound;
Sophocles: Women of Trachi, Philoctetes; Euripides: Trojan
Women, Bacchae. Sophocles & Euripides (Authors), Marianne
McDonald & J. Michael Walton (Editors), Marianne McDonald
& J. Michael Walton (Translators). Trade Paper. Methuen
Publishing Ltd. London, 2004. Methuen Drama Ser.
ISBN:0-413-77256-X, ISBN13: 978-0-413-77256-5.
Dewey:882/.01/08. LCCN:2004-426593.
Audience: l,u,f.

Baines, Paul & Burns,   **PR1271.F59 2000**
  Edward (Editors)
Five Romantic Plays, 1768-1821. Trade Paper. Oxford
University Press, Inc. New York, NY. 2000. 432p. Oxford
World's Classics Ser. ISBN:0-19-283316-2, ISBN13:
978-0-19-283316-7. Dewey:822/.6080145. LCCN:00-699989.
Audience: l,u,f.

Barker, Simon & Hinds,   **PR1263.R68 2002**
  Hilary (Editors)
Routledge Anthology of Renaissance Drama. Paper over Boards.
Routledge. New York, NY. 2002. 480p. ISBN:0-415-18733-8,
ISBN13: 978-0-415-18733-6. Dewey:822/.308.
LCCN:2002-026872.
Audience: l,u,f.

Barr, Alan (Editor)   **PN6119.8.M65 2001**
Modern Women Playwrights of Europe. Paper Text. Oxford
University Press, Inc. New York, NY. 2000. 608p.
ISBN:0-19-513536-9, ISBN13: 978-0-19-513536-7.
Dewey:808.82/0082/094. LCCN:99-086027.
Audience: l,u,f.

Bentley, Eric   **PN6112.B43**
The Play, a Critical Anthology. Paper Text. Textbook Publishers.
Temecula, CA. 2003. 774p. ISBN:0-7581-6026-7, ISBN13:
978-0-7581-6026-3. Dewey:808.82.
Audience: l. *B*

Bergh, Albert Ellery   **PN6111**
Classic Drama Plays by Greek, Spanish, French, German and
English Dramatists, Vol. 1. The World's Great Classics (Editor).
Trade Paper. Kessinger Publishing, LLC. Whitefish, MT. 2004.
ISBN:1-4179-4186-3, ISBN13: 978-1-4179-4186-5.
Dewey:808.82.
Audience: l,u.

Berkowitz, Joel (Editor,   **PJ5191.E5L34 2006**
  Translator)
Landmark Yiddish Plays: A Critical Anthology. Jeremy Dauber
(Introduction by). Book, Other. State University of New York
Press. Albany, NY. 2006. 336p. SUNY Series on Modern Jewish
Literature and Culture ISBN:0-7914-6779-1, ISBN13:
978-0-7914-6779-4. Dewey:839/.12008. LCCN:2005-023939.
Audience: l,u,f.

Bevington, David   **PR1263.E56 2003**
English Renaissance Drama: A Norton Anthology. Lars Engle,
Katharine Eisaman Maus & Eric Rasmussen (Editors). Trade

Cloth. W. W. Norton & Company, Inc. New York, NY. 2002.
2400p. ISBN:0-393-97655-6, ISBN13: 978-0-393-97655-7.
Dewey:822/.308. LCCN:2002-025074.
Audience: l,u,f.

Branch, William B. (Editor)   **PS628.N4C76 1993**
Crosswinds: An Anthology of Black Dramatists in the Diaspora.
Trade Paper. Indiana University Press. Bloomington, IN. 1993.
448p. Blacks in the Diaspora Ser. ISBN:0-253-20778-9,
ISBN13: 978-0-253-20778-4. Dewey:808.82/008996.
LCCN:92-026648.
Audience: l,u,f.

Brogyanyi, Eugene   **PH3166.D73 1991**
Drama Contemporary: Hungary. Cloth Text. P A J Publications.
New York, NY. 1991. 247p. ISBN:1-55554-053-8, ISBN13:
978-1-55554-053-1. Dewey:894/.5112308. LCCN:94-222019.
Audience: u,f.

Cardullo, Bert & Knopf,   **PN6112.T42 2001**
  Robert (Editors)
Theater of the Avant-Garde, 1890-1950: A Critical Anthology.
Cloth over Boards. Yale University Press. Cumberland, RI.
2001. 546p. ISBN:0-300-08525-7, ISBN13: 978-0-300-08525-9.
Dewey:808.82/911. LCCN:00-043891.
Audience: u,f.

Chapman, John (Editor)   **PN6112**
Burns Mantle Best Plays of Nineteen Forty-Nine to Nineteen
Fifty. Trade Cloth. Ayer Company Publishers, Inc. Manchester,
NH. 1978. The Best Plays Ser. ISBN:0-405-09177-X, ISBN13:
978-0-405-09177-3. Dewey:812.5082. LCCN:75-019860.
Audience: l,u.

Coldewey, John C. (Editor)   **PR1260.E27 1993**
Early English Drama: An Anthology. Cloth Text. Garland
Publishing, Inc. New York, NY. 1993. 392p.
ISBN:0-8240-4699-4, ISBN13: 978-0-8240-4699-6.
Dewey:822.208. LCCN:92-007686.
Audience: u,f.

Conlon, Raymond (Editor)   **PN820.A835 2003**
An Anthology of Renaissance Plays in Translation: Works from
the Italian, Spanish, and Portuguese Traditions. Trade Cloth.
Edwin Mellen Press, The. Lewiston, NY. 2002. 516p. Studies in
Renaissance Literature, Vol. 23 ISBN:0-7734-6905-2, ISBN13:
978-0-7734-6905-1. Dewey:852/.208. LCCN:2002-033753.
Audience: l,u,f.

Corneille, Pierre   **PS758.A8**
Chief Plays. Paper Text. Textbook Publishers. Temecula, CA.
2003. 386p. ISBN:0-7581-5803-3, ISBN13: 978-0-7581-5803-1.
Dewey:811/.2.
Audience: l,u,f. *B*

Corneille, Pierre, et al.   **PQ1220**
Landmarks of French Classical Drama. Jean Racine, Moliere,
Marivaux & Beaumarchais (Authors), David Bryer, Robert D.
MacDonald, Christopher Hampton & John Fowles (Translators),

David Bradby (Introduction by). Trade Paper. Heinemann. Portsmouth, NH. 1991. 393p. ISBN:0-413-63100-1, ISBN13: 978-0-413-63100-8. Dewey:842.4/08.

Audience: **l,u,f.**

Corrigan, Robert W.   **PA3629.C5 1987**
Classical Comedy - Greek and Roman: Six Plays. Trade Paper. Applause Theatre Book Publishers. New York, NY. 1987. 492p. ISBN:0-936839-85-6, ISBN13: 978-0-936839-85-1. Dewey:882/.01/08. LCCN:87-017442.

Audience: **l,u,f.**

Corrigan, Robert W.   **PA3626.A2C67 1990**
(Editor)
Classical Tragedy Greek and Roman: Eight Plays with Critical Essays. Hal Leonard Corporation Staff (Created by). Trade Paper. Applause Theatre Book Publishers. New York, NY. 1990. 576p. ISBN:1-55783-046-0, ISBN13: 978-1-55783-046-3. Dewey:882/.0108. LCCN:90-030152.

Audience: **l,u,f.**

Cox, Jeffrey N. & Gamer,   **PR1271.B72 2003**
Michael (Editors)
The Broadview Anthology of Romantic Drama. Trade Paper. Broadview Press. Peterborough, ON. 2003. 432p. Broadview Anthologies of English Literature Ser. ISBN:1-55111-298-1, ISBN13: 978-1-55111-298-5. Dewey:822/.7080145. LCCN:2003-446769.

Audience: **l,u,f.**

Day, Barbara (Editor)   **PG5145.E5C94 1994**
Czech Plays: Modern Czech Drama. Trade Paper. Theatre Communications Group, Inc. New York, NY. 1998. 256p. ISBN:1-85459-074-X, ISBN13: 978-1-85459-074-9. Dewey:891.8625. LCCN:94-127607.

Audience: **u,f.**

Delgado, Ramon (Editor)   **PN6111**
The Best American Short Plays 1989. Trade Cloth. Applause Theatre Book Publishers. New York, NY. 1989. 264p. The Best American Short Plays Ser. ISBN:1-55783-045-2, ISBN13: 978-1-55783-045-6. Dewey:808.82.

Audience: **l,u.**

Delgado, Ramon (Editor)   **PN6112**
The Best Short Plays: 1984. Trade Cloth. NP/Chilton. West Chester, PA. 1984. 251p. Plays and Play Collections ISBN:0-8019-7411-9, ISBN13: 978-0-8019-7411-3. Dewey:808.8241. LCCN:38-008006.

Audience: **l,u.**

Delgado, Ramon (Editor)   **PN6111**
The Best Short Plays: 1983. Trade Cloth. NP/Chilton. West Chester, PA. 1983. 251p. Plays and Play Collections ISBN:0-8019-7296-5, ISBN13: 978-0-8019-7296-6. Dewey:812.508. LCCN:38-008006.

Audience: **l,u.**

Delgado, Ramon   **PN6111**
The Best Short Plays: 1988-1989. Trade Cloth. Applause

Theatre Book Publishers. New York, NY. 1989. 540p. Best Short Plays Ser. ISBN:1-55783-187-4, ISBN13: 978-1-55783-187-3. Dewey:808.82.

Audience: **l,u.**

Delgado, Ramon (Editor)   **PN6120.A4**
The Best Short Plays: 1987. Trade Cloth. Applause Theatre Book Publishers. New York, NY. 1987. 282p. Best Short Plays Ser. ISBN:0-936839-94-5, ISBN13: 978-0-936839-94-3. Dewey:808.82.

Audience: **g,l,u,f.**

Delgado, Ramon (Editor)   **PN6120.A4**
The Best Short Plays: 1985. Trade Cloth. Empire Publishing Service. Studio City, CA. 1985. 243p. Best Short Plays Ser. ISBN:0-8019-7541-7, ISBN13: 978-0-8019-7541-7. Dewey:812.08. LCCN:38-008006.

Audience: **l,u.**

Delgado, Ramon   **PN6111**
The Best Short Plays of 1986. Trade Paper. Applause Theatre Book Publishers. New York, NY. 1986. 258p. ISBN:0-936839-13-9, ISBN13: 978-0-936839-13-4. Dewey:812.08.

Audience: **l,u.**

Dickinson, Thomas H.   **PN6112.D5**
Chief Contemporary Dramatists: Twenty-Two Plays from the Recent Drama of England, Ireland, America, Germany, France, Belgium, Norway, Sweden and Russia. Library Binding. Richard West. Philadelphia, PA. 1979. ISBN:0-8492-4207-X, ISBN13: 978-0-8492-4207-6. Dewey:808.82.

Audience: **l,u,f.**

Dickinson, Thomas H.   **PN6112.D52**
Chief Contemporary Dramatists. Trade Paper. Kessinger Publishing, LLC. Whitefish, MT. 2005. ISBN:1-4179-8690-5, ISBN13: 978-1-4179-8690-3. Dewey:808.82.

Audience: **l,u,f.**

Dickinson, Thomas H.   **PN6112.D52**
(Editor)
Chief Contemporary Dramatists, Second Series: Eighteen Plays from the Recent Drama of England, Ireland, America, France, Germany, Austria, Italy, Spain, Russia, and Scandinavia. Library Binding. Darby Books. Darby, PA. 1985. 734p. ISBN:0-317-17328-6, ISBN13: 978-0-317-17328-4. Dewey:808.82/041.

Audience: **l,u,f.**

Dodgson, Elyse (Editor)   **PT1258**
German Plays 2. Trade Paper. Theatre Communications Group, Inc. New York, NY. 2000. 256p. ISBN:1-85459-479-6, ISBN13: 978-1-85459-479-2. Dewey:832.9/14/08.

Audience: **u,f.**

Dodgson, Elyse   **PT2685.E5**
German Plays. Anna Langhoff, Dea Loher, Klaus Pohl & D. Rust (Contribution by). Trade Paper. Theatre Communications

Group, Inc. New York, NY. 1998. 208p. International Collection ISBN:1-85459-338-2, ISBN13: 978-1-85459-338-2. Dewey:832.9/14.

Audience: **u,f.**

Elam, Harry J. Jr. &   **PS628.N4C65 1996**
  Alexander, Robert (Editors)
Colored Contradictions: An Anthology of Contemporary African-American Plays. Trade Paper. Penguin Group (USA) Inc. New York, NY. 1996. 656p. ISBN:0-452-27497-4, ISBN13: 978-0-452-27497-6. Dewey:812/.54080896073. LCCN:96-015948.

Audience: **l,u,f.**

Fisk, Deborah Payne   **PR1266.F675 2005**
  (Editor)
Four Restoration Libertine Plays. Trade Paper, Perfect. Oxford University Press, Inc. New York, NY. 2005. 468p. Oxford World's Classics Ser. ISBN:0-19-283294-8, ISBN13: 978-0-19-283294-8. Dewey:822/.408. LCCN:2004-027977.

Audience: **l,u,f.**

Gassner, John (Introduction   **PS634.B4**
  by)
Best American Plays: Third Series, 1945-51. Trade Cloth. Crown Publishing Group. New York, NY. 1987. 736p. ISBN:0-517-50950-4, ISBN13: 978-0-517-50950-0. Dewey:812.08.

Audience: **l,u.**

Gassner, John (Editor)   **PS625.B47 2000**
Best Plays of the Early American Theatre, 1787-1911. Trade Paper. Dover Publications, Inc. Mineola, NY. 2000. 768p. ISBN:0-486-41098-6, ISBN13: 978-0-486-41098-2. Dewey:812.008. LCCN:00-027931.

Audience: **g,l,u,f.** *B*

Gassner, John   **PR1262.M43 1987**
Medieval and Tudor Drama: Twenty-Four Plays. Trade Paper. Applause Theatre Book Publishers. New York, NY. 1995. 462p. ISBN:0-936839-84-8, ISBN13: 978-0-936839-84-4. Dewey:822/.2/08. LCCN:87-018836.

Audience: **l,u,f.**

Geiogamah, Hanay (Editor)   **PS3545.I5365**
New Native American Drama: Three Plays. Jeffrey Huntsman (Introduction by). Trade Paper. University of Oklahoma Press. Norman, OK. 1980. 158p. ISBN:0-8061-1697-8, ISBN13: 978-0-8061-1697-6. Dewey:812/.54. LCCN:79-004733.

Audience: **l,u,f.** *B*

Goetz-Stankiewicz, Marketa   **PG5145.E5**
  (Editor)
Drama Contemporary: Czechoslovakia. Trade Paper. P A J Publications. New York, NY. 1985. 222p. Drama Contemporary Ser. ISBN:0-933826-76-1, ISBN13: 978-0-933826-76-2. Dewey:891.8/62/5.

Audience: **u,f.**

Griffiths, Trevor (Editor)   **PR1248**
Restoration Comedy. Trade Paper. Theatre Communications Group, Inc. New York, NY. 2005. 352p. ISBN:1-85459-848-1, ISBN13: 978-1-85459-848-6. Dewey:822.4/08017.

Audience: **l,u,f.**

Guernsey, Otis L. Jr.   **PN6112.B45**
  (Editor)
The Best Plays of 1998-1999: The Otis Guernsey-Burns Mantle Theatre Yearbook. Trade Cloth. Hal Leonard Corporation. Milwaukee, WI. 2004. 556p. The Otis Guernsey-Burns Mantle Theater Yearbook Ser., Vol. 80:Best Plays ISBN:0-87910-290-X, ISBN13: 978-0-87910-290-6. Dewey:808.82.

Audience: **l,u.**

Guernsey, Otis L. Jr.   **PN2266.A2**
  (Editor)
The Otis Guernsey-Burns Mantle Theater Yearbook: The Best Plays of 1996-1997. Ed. 78. Trade Cloth. Hal Leonard Corporation. Milwaukee, WI. 1997. 496p. The Otis Guernsey-Burns Mantle Theater Yearbook Ser., No. 78:Best Plays ISBN:0-87910-097-4, ISBN13: 978-0-87910-097-1. Dewey:812.508.

Audience: **l,u.**

Guernsey, Otis L. Jr.   **PN2266.A2**
The Best Plays of 1999-2000: The Otis Guernsey-Burns Mantle Theatre Yearbook, Set. Ed. 81. Al Hirschfeld (Illustrator). Trade Cloth. Hal Leonard Corporation. Milwaukee, WI. 2004. 516p. The Otis Guernsey-Burns Mantle Theater Yearbook Ser., :Best Plays ISBN:0-87910-955-6, ISBN13: 978-0-87910-955-4. Dewey:808.82.

Audience: **l,u.**

Guernsey, Otis L. Jr.   **PN6112**
  (Editor)
The Otis Guernsey-Burns Mantle Theater Yearbook: The Best Plays of 1997-1998. Ed. 79. Al Hirschfeld (Illustrator). Trade Cloth. Hal Leonard Corporation. Milwaukee, WI. 1998. 496p. The Otis Guernsey-Burns Mantle Theater Yearbook Ser., :Best Plays ISBN:0-87910-271-3, ISBN13: 978-0-87910-271-5. Dewey:812.

Audience: **l,u.**

Guernsey, Otis L. Jr. &   **PN6112**
  Sweet, Jeffrey (Editors)
The Applause-Best Plays Theater Yearbook, 1990-1991: The Complete Broadway and Off-Broadway Sourcebook. Trade Cloth. Applause Theatre Book Publishers. New York, NY. 1991. 564p. ISBN:1-55783-106-8, ISBN13: 978-1-55783-106-4. Dewey:808.2.

Audience: **l,u.**

Guernsey, Otis L. Jr. &   **PN6112.B45**
  Sweet, Jeffrey (Editors)
The Otis Guernsey-Burns Mantle Theater Yearbook: The Best Plays of 1995-1996. Ed. 77. Trade Cloth. Hal Leonard Corporation. Milwaukee, WI. 1996. 587p. ISBN:0-87910-089-3, ISBN13: 978-0-87910-089-6. Dewey:812.508.

Audience: **l,u.**

Guernsey, Otis L. Jr. &   **PN6112**
  Sweet, Jeffrey (Editors)
The Applause-Best Plays Theater Yearbook, 1991-1992: Featuring the Ten Best Plays of the Year. Al Hirschfeld (Illustrator). Trade Paper. Applause Theatre Book Publishers. New York, NY. 1992. 549p. Best Plays Ser. ISBN:1-55783-147-5, ISBN13: 978-1-55783-147-7. Dewey:808.82.

Audience: **l,u.**

Guernsey, Otis L. Jr. &   **PN2266**
  Sweet, Jeffrey (Editors)
The Best Plays of 1987-1987. Al Hirschfeld (Illustrator). Trade Cloth. W. Clement Stone, P M A Communications, Inc. Northbrook, IL. 1989. ISBN:0-396-09077-X, ISBN13: 978-0-396-09077-9. Dewey:808.822.

Audience: **l,u.**

Guernsey, Otis L. Jr. &   **PN6112**
  Sweet, Jeffrey (Editors)
The Best Plays of 1988-1989. Ed. 70. Al Hirschfeld (Illustrator). Trade Cloth. Applause Theatre Book Publishers. New York, NY. 1989. 676p. The Burns Mantle Theater Yearbook Ser. ISBN:1-55783-056-8, ISBN13: 978-1-55783-056-2. Dewey:808.82.

Audience: **l,u.**

Guernsey, Otis L. Jr. &   **PN6112**
  Sweet, Jeffrey (Editors)
The Best Plays of 1989-1990. Al Hirschfeld (Illustrator). Trade Cloth. Applause Theatre Book Publishers. New York, NY. 1990. 676p. The Burns Mantle Theatre Yearbook Ser. ISBN:1-55783-091-6, ISBN13: 978-1-55783-091-3. Dewey:808.2.

Audience: **l,u.**

Guernsey, Otis L. Jr. &   **PN6112**
  Sweet, Jeffrey (Editors)
The Otis Guernsey-Burns Mantle Theater Yearbook: The Best Plays of 1992-1993. Al Hirschfeld (Illustrator). Trade Cloth. Hal Leonard Corporation. Milwaukee, WI. 1993. 648p. ISBN:0-87910-173-3, ISBN13: 978-0-87910-173-2. Dewey:812.508.

Audience: **l,u.**

Guernsey, Otis L. Jr. &   **PN6112**
  Sweet, Jeffrey (Editors)
The Otis Guernsey-Burns Mantle Theater Yearbook: The Best Plays of 1993-1994. Al Hirschfeld (Illustrator). Trade Cloth. Hal Leonard Corporation. Milwaukee, WI. 1994. 661p. ISBN:0-87910-183-0, ISBN13: 978-0-87910-183-1. Dewey:812.508.

Audience: **l,u.**

Guernsey, Otis L. Jr. &   **TK454.D44**
  Sweet, Jeffrey (Editors)
The Otis Guernsey-Burns Mantle Theater Yearbook: The Best Plays of 1994-1995. Al Hirschfeld (Contribution by). Trade Cloth. Hal Leonard Corporation. Milwaukee, WI. 1995. 608p. ISBN:0-87910-196-2, ISBN13: 978-0-87910-196-1. Dewey:621.319/2.

Audience: **l,u.**

Guernsey, Otis L. Jr. &   **PN6112**
  Sweet, Jeffrey (Editors)
Best Plays of 1987-1988. Al Hirshfeld (Illustrator). Trade Cloth. Applause Theatre Book Publishers. New York, NY. 1989. 592p. The Burns Mantle Theater Yearbook Ser. ISBN:1-55783-040-1, ISBN13: 978-1-55783-040-1. Dewey:812.508.

Audience: **l,u.**

Hamalian, Leo & Hatch,   **PS628.N4**
  James V. (Editors)
Roots of African American Drama: An Anthology of Early Plays, 1858-1938. George C. Wolfe (Introduction by). Trade Paper. Wayne State University Press. Detroit, MI. 1992. 456p. African American Life Ser. ISBN:0-8143-2142-9, ISBN13: 978-0-8143-2142-3. Dewey:812.008/0896073. LCCN:90-012002.
Audience: **l,u,f.** *Choice, 1991.*

Hill, Philip G. (Editor)   **PN6111**
Our Dramatic Heritage: The Golden Age. Trade Cloth. Fairleigh Dickinson University Press. Cranbury, NJ. 1985. 624p. ISBN:0-8386-3107-X, ISBN13: 978-0-8386-3107-2. Dewey:808.82. LCCN:81-065294.

Audience: **l,u,f.**

Hill, Philip G. (Editor)   **PN6111 .O87**
Our Dramatic Heritage: Romanticism and Realism. Trade Cloth. Fairleigh Dickinson University Press. Cranbury, NJ. 1989. 504p. ISBN:0-8386-3267-X, ISBN13: 978-0-8386-3267-3. Dewey:808.82. LCCN:81-065294.

Audience: **l,u,f.**

Hill, Philip G. (Editor)   **PN6111 .O87**
Our Dramatic Heritage: The 18th Century, Vol. 3. Trade Cloth. Fairleigh Dickinson University Press. Cranbury, NJ. 1987. ISBN:0-8386-3108-8, ISBN13: 978-0-8386-3108-9. Dewey:808.82. LCCN:81-065294.

Audience: **l,u,f.**

Hill, Philip G. (Editor)   **PN6111 .O87**
Our Dramatic Heritage: Reactions to Realism, Vol. 5. Trade Cloth. Fairleigh Dickinson University Press. Cranbury, NJ. 1991. 384p. ISBN:0-8386-3411-7, ISBN13: 978-0-8386-3411-0. Dewey:808.82. LCCN:81-065294.

Audience: **l,u,f.**

Hill, Philip G. (Editor)   **PN6111 .O87**
Our Dramatic Heritage: Expressing the Inexpressible, Vol. 6. Trade Cloth. Fairleigh Dickinson University Press. Cranbury, NJ. 1992. 336p. ISBN:0-8386-3421-4, ISBN13: 978-0-8386-3421-9. Dewey:809.2. LCCN:81-065294.

Audience: **l,u,f.**

Hill, Philip G. (Editor)   **PN6111.O87 1983**
Our Dramatic Heritage, Vol. 1. Trade Cloth. Fairleigh Dickinson University Press. Cranbury, NJ. 1983. 368p. ISBN:0-8386-3106-1, ISBN13: 978-0-8386-3106-5. Dewey:808.82. LCCN:81-065294.

Audience: **l,u.** *B*

Holt, Marion P. (Editor)   **PQ6267.E6**
Drama Contemporary: Spain. Trade Paper. P A J Publications. New York, NY. 1985. 232p. Drama Contemporary Ser.

ISBN:0-933826-86-9, ISBN13: 978-0-933826-86-1.
Dewey:862.6408.

Audience: **u,f.** *Choice, 1986.*

House, Jane & Attisani,   PQ4244.E5T83 1994
  Antonio (Editors)
Twentieth-Century Italian Drama: An Anthology, the First Fifty
Years. Trade Cloth. Columbia University Press. New York, NY.
1995. 622p. ISBN:0-231-07118-3, ISBN13: 978-0-231-07118-5.
Dewey:852/.91208. LCCN:94-029111.

Audience: **l,u,f.**

Houston, Velina H. (Editor)   PS628.A85S75 1997
But Still, Like Air, I'll Rise: New Asian American Plays. Trade
Cloth. Temple University Press. Philadelphia, PA. 1997. 512p.
Asian American History and Culture Ser. ISBN:1-56639-537-2,
ISBN13: 978-1-56639-537-3. Dewey:812/.54080895073.
LCCN:96-048729.

Audience: **l,u,f.** *Choice, 1997.*

Houston, Velina H. (Editor,   PS628.A85
  Introduction by)
The Politics of Life: Four Plays by Asian American Women.
Trade Cloth. Temple University Press. Philadelphia, PA. 1993.
288p. Asian American History and Culture Ser.
ISBN:1-56639-000-1, ISBN13: 978-1-56639-000-2.
Dewey:812/.540809287. LCCN:92-013090.

Audience: **l,u,f.**

Jacobus, Lee A.   PN6112.B36 2004
The Bedford Introduction to Drama. Ed. 5. Trade Paper.
Bedford/Saint Martin's. New York, NY. 2004. 1872p.
ISBN:0-312-41441-2, ISBN13: 978-0-312-41441-2.
Dewey:808.2. LCCN:2004-101200.

Audience: **l,u.**

Jenkins, Jeffrey Eric   PQ4287.L5
The Best Plays of 2000-2001: The Otis Guernsey-Burns Mantle
Theatre Yearbook. Ed. 82. Al Hirschfeld (Illustrator). Trade
Cloth. Hal Leonard Corporation. Milwaukee, WI. 2004. 444p.
Theater Yearbook Ser. ISBN:0-87910-968-8, ISBN13:
978-0-87910-968-4. Dewey:853.15.

Audience: **l,u.**

Kermode, Frank   PR1265.5.D83 2005
The Duchess of Malfi: Eight Masterpieces of Jacobean Drama.
Trade Paper. Random House Adult Trade Publishing Group.
New York, NY. 2005. 688p. The Modern Library Classics
ISBN:0-679-64243-9, ISBN13: 978-0-679-64243-5.
Dewey:822/.308. LCCN:2004-061004.

Audience: **l,u,f.**

King, Woodie Jr. (Editor)   PS628.N4N38 1995
The National Black Drama Anthology: Eleven Plays from
America's Leading African-American Theaters. Trade Paper.
Applause Theatre Book Publishers. New York, NY. 2000. 528p.
ISBN:1-55783-219-6, ISBN13: 978-1-55783-219-1.
Dewey:812.5/4/08/0896. LCCN:95-034945.

Audience: **l,u,f.** *Choice, 1996.*

Kinney, Arthur F. (Editor)   PR1263.R45 2004
Renaissance Drama: An Anthology of Plays and Entertainments.
Ed. 2. Trade Paper. Blackwell Publishing, Inc. Malden, MA.
2004. 928p. Blackwell Anthologies Ser. ISBN:1-4051-1967-5,
ISBN13: 978-1-4051-1967-2. Dewey:822/.308.
LCCN:2004-047626.

Audience: **l,u,f.**

Lamont, Rosette C. (Editor)   PS628.W6.W664 1993
Women on the Verge: Seven Avant-Garde American Plays. Trade
Paper. Applause Theatre Book Publishers. New York, NY. 1992.
416p. ISBN:1-55783-148-3, ISBN13: 978-1-55783-148-4.
Dewey:812.540809287. LCCN:93-011557.

Audience: **u,f.** *Choice, 1994.*

Langen, Timothy & Weir,   PG3245.E38 2000
  Justin (Editors)
Eight Twentieth-Century Russian Plays. Trade Paper.
Northwestern University Press. Evanston, IL. 2000. 354p.
European Drama Classics Ser. ISBN:0-8101-1374-0, ISBN13:
978-0-8101-1374-9. Dewey:891.72/408. LCCN:00-008680.

Audience: **g,l,u,f.**

Lewis, Victoria   PS628.P46B49 2005
Beyond Victims and Villains: Contemporary Plays by Disabled
Playwrights. Theatre Communication Group. 2005.
ISBN:1-55936-250-2, ISBN13: 978-1-55936-250-4.

Audience: **g,l,u,f.**

Lifson, David S. (Translator)   PJ5191.E5 L5
Epic and Folk Plays from the Yiddish Theatre. Trade Cloth.
Fairleigh Dickinson University Press. Cranbury, NJ. 1975. 224p.
ISBN:0-8386-1082-X, ISBN13: 978-0-8386-1082-4.
Dewey:839/.09/2008. LCCN:73-002899.

Audience: **l,u,f.**

Loomis, Roger S. & Wells,   PN6112 .L57 1970
  Henry W. (Editors)
Representative Medieval and Tudor Plays. Trade Cloth. Ayer
Company Publishers, Inc. Manchester, NH. 1977. Play
Anthology Reprint Ser. ISBN:0-8369-8202-9, ISBN13:
978-0-8369-8202-2. Dewey:808.82/51. LCCN:77-111109.

Audience: **l,u,f.**

Lyons, Paddy & Morgan,   PR1266
  Fideles (Editors)
Female Playwrights of the Restoration: Five Comedies. Ed. 2.
Paddy Lyons & Fideles Morgan (Introduction by). Trade Paper.
Tuttle Publishing. Boston, MA. 1994. 365p.
ISBN:0-460-87427-6, ISBN13: 978-0-460-87427-4.
Dewey:822.40809287.

Audience: **l,u,f.**

Machiavelli, Niccolo &   PQ4244.E5T48 1996
  Ariosto, Ludovico
Three Italian Renaissance Comedies: Ariosto's The Supposes;
Machiavelli's The Mandrake; Intronati's The Deceived.
Christopher Cairns & Accademia Senese Degli Intronati Staff
(Editors), Jennifer Lorch (Translator, Introduction by). Trade

Cloth. Edwin Mellen Press, The. Lewiston, NY. 1996. 452p.
ISBN:0-7734-8821-9, ISBN13: 978-0-7734-8821-2.
Dewey:852/.309. LCCN:96-019456.

Audience: **l,u,f.**

Mantle, Burns (Editor)   **PN2266.A2**
The Best Plays of 1919-1920. Trade Cloth. Ayer Company
Publishers, Inc. Manchester, NH. 1978. The Best Plays Ser.
ISBN:0-405-09168-0, ISBN13: 978-0-405-09168-1.
Dewey:808.82. LCCN:75-019860.

Audience: **l,u.**

Mantle, Burns (Editor)   **PN2266.A2**
The Best Plays of 1929-1930. Trade Cloth. Ayer Company
Publishers, Inc. Manchester, NH. 1975. The Best Plays Ser.
ISBN:0-405-09170-2, ISBN13: 978-0-405-09170-4.
Dewey:812.08. LCCN:75-019860.

Audience: **l,u.**

Matthews, Brander   **PN6112**
The Chief European Dramatists: Twenty-One Plays from the
Drama of Greece, Rome, Spain, France, Italy, Germany,
Denmark, and Norway from 500 B. C. to 1879 A. D. Trade
Paper. University Press of the Pacific. Miami, FL. 2004. 800p.
ISBN:1-4102-1454-0, ISBN13: 978-1-4102-1454-6.
Dewey:808.82.

Audience: **l,u.**

Miles, Julia   **PS628.W6H47 1997**
Here to Stay: Five Plays from the Women's Project. Applause.
1997. ISBN:1-55783-315-X, ISBN13: 978-1-55783-315-0.

Audience: **g,l,u,f.**

Nelson, Brian (Editor)   **PS628.A85A88 1997**
Asian American Drama: 9 Plays from the Multiethnic
Landscape. David Henry Hwang (Foreword by). Trade Paper.
Applause Theatre Book Publishers. New York, NY. 2000. 432p.
ISBN:1-55783-314-1, ISBN13: 978-1-55783-314-3.
Dewey:812/.54080895. LCCN:97-027054.

Audience: **l,u,f.**

Ostrow, Eileen J. (Editor)   **PS628.N4C4 1991**
Center Stage: An Anthology of Twenty-One Contemporary
Black-American Plays. Sandra L. Richards (Introduction by).
Trade Paper. University of Illinois Press. Champaign, IL. 1991.
328p. ISBN:0-252-06178-0, ISBN13: 978-0-252-06178-3.
Dewey:812/.54080896073. LCCN:90-022631.

Audience: **l,u,f.**

Perkins, Kathy A. (Editor)   **PS628.N4**
🄴 Black Female Playwrights: An Anthology of Plays Before
1950. E-Book. Indiana University Press. Bloomington, IN. 1990.
298p. Blacks in the Diaspora Ser. ISBN:0-253-20623-5,
ISBN13: 978-0-253-20623-7. Dewey:812/.008/09287.
LCCN:88-046040.

Audience: **g,l,u,f.** *Choice, 1990.*

Perkins, Kathy A. & Uno,   **PS627.M5C66 1996**
  Roberta (Editors)
Contemporary Plays by Women of Color: An Anthology. Paper
over Boards. Routledge. New York, NY. 1996. 336p.

ISBN:0-415-11377-6, ISBN13: 978-0-415-11377-9.
Dewey:812/.540809287. LCCN:95-007465.

Audience: **g,l,u,f.** *Choice, 1996.*

Posnick, Michael & Schiff,   **PS628.J47N56 2005**
  Ellen (Editors)
9 Contemporary Jewish Plays: From the New Play Commission
of the National Foundation for Jewish Culture. Theodore Bikel
(Foreword by). Trade Paper, Perfect. University of Texas Press.
Austin, TX. 2005. 587p. ISBN:0-292-71290-1, ISBN13:
978-0-292-71290-4. Dewey:812/.60808924. LCCN:2005-007621.

Audience: **l,u,f.**

Roberts, Peter (Editor)   **PN2595**
The Best of Plays and Players: 1969-1983, Vol. 2. Donald
Cooper (Illustrator). Trade Cloth. Heinemann. Portsmouth, NH.
1989. 272p. ISBN:0-413-62150-2, ISBN13: 978-0-413-62150-4.
Dewey:792.0941.

Audience: **l,u.** *Choice, 1990.*

Roberts, Peter (Editor)   **PN2595 .B47 1988**
The Best of Plays and Players 1953-1968, Vol. 1. Zoe Dominic
(Illustrator). Trade Paper. Heinemann. Portsmouth, NH. 1990.
254p. ISBN:0-413-52970-3, ISBN13: 978-0-413-52970-1.
Dewey:792/.0941. LCCN:88-140018.

Audience: **l,u.**

Russell, Douglas A. (Editor,   **PT3826.D8**
  Introduction by)
An Anthology of Austrian Drama. Trade Cloth. Fairleigh
Dickinson University Press. Cranbury, NJ. 1982. 450p.
ISBN:0-8386-2003-5, ISBN13: 978-0-8386-2003-8.
Dewey:832/.008/09436. LCCN:76-019836.

Audience: **u,f.** 🅱

Sandoval-Sanchez, Alberto   **PS628.H57P87 2000**
  & Sternbach, Nancy S. (Editors)
Puro Teatro, a Latina Anthology: A Latina Anthology. Trade
Paper. University of Arizona Press. Tucson, AZ. 2000. 440p.
ISBN:0-8165-1827-0, ISBN13: 978-0-8165-1827-2.
Dewey:812/.540809287/08968. LCCN:99-006567.

Audience: **l,u,f.**

Schurer, Ernst (Editor)   **PT1258.G46 1997**
German Expressionist Plays. Trade Paper. Continuum
International Publishing Group, Ltd. London, 1997. 344p.
German Library, Vol. 66 ISBN:0-8264-0950-4, ISBN13:
978-0-8264-0950-8. Dewey:832.9/12/08/0115.
LCCN:94-038092.

Audience: **l,u,f.**

Segel, Harold B. (Editor)   **PG7445.E5**
Polish Romantic Drama: Three Plays in English Translation. Ed.
2. Trade Paper. Gordon & Breach Publishing Group. New York,
NY. 1997. 304p. Polish Theatre Archive Ser.
ISBN:90-5702-088-2, ISBN13: 978-90-5702-088-9.
Dewey:891.8/5/2/6/08.

Audience: **g,l,u,f.** 🅱

Shaughnessy, Robert   **PR1248.F68 2003**
Four Renaissance Comedies. Trade Paper. Palgrave Macmillan.
New York, NY. 2004. 368p. ISBN:0-333-97365-8, ISBN13:
978-0-333-97365-3. Dewey:822/.05230803. LCCN:2003-053655.
Audience: **l,u.**

Simonarson, Olafur H.   **PT7094**
Drama Contemporary: Scandinavia. Trade Cloth. P A J
Publications. New York, NY. 1990. 215p. ISBN:1-55554-050-3,
ISBN13: 978-1-55554-050-0. Dewey:839.52/4.
Audience: **g,u,f.**

Sokel, Walter H. (Editor)   **PT1258.A57 1984**
Anthology of German Expressionist Drama. Book, Other.
Cornell University Press. Ithaca, NY. 1984. 336p.
ISBN:0-8014-9296-3, ISBN13: 978-0-8014-9296-9.
Dewey:832/.912/0801. LCCN:84-045197.
Audience: **l,u,f.**

Stein, Howard & Young,   **PN6111**
  Glenn (Editors)
The Best American Short Plays 1990. Trade Paper. Applause
Theatre Book Publishers. New York, NY. 1991. 208p. The Best
American Short Plays Ser. ISBN:1-55783-085-1, ISBN13:
978-1-55783-085-2. Dewey:812.08.
Audience: **l,u.**

The World's Great Classics   **PN6111**
  (Editor)
Classic Drama Plays by Greek, Spanish, French, German and
English Dramatists, Vol. 2. Albert Ellery Bergh (Illustrator).
Trade Paper. Kessinger Publishing, LLC. Whitefish, MT. 2004.
ISBN:0-7661-9942-8, ISBN13: 978-0-7661-9942-2.
Dewey:808.82.
Audience: **l,u.**

Uno, Roberta (Editor)   **PS628.W6**
Unbroken Thread: An Anthology of Plays by Asian American
Women. Trade Paper. University of Massachusetts Press.
Amherst, MA. 1993. 336p. ISBN:0-87023-856-6, ISBN13:
978-0-87023-856-7. Dewey:812/.540809287. LCCN:93-021858.
Audience: **l,u,f.** *Choice, 1994.*

Upor, Laszlo (Editor)   **PH3166**
Hungarian Plays. Peter Karpati, Andras Nagy, Akos Nemeth &
Andor Szilagyi (Contribution by). Trade Paper. Nick Hern
Books, Ltd. London, 1996. 256p. International Collection
ISBN:1-85459-244-0, ISBN13: 978-1-85459-244-6.
Dewey:894.5/1123/08.
Audience: **u,f.**

Vega, Lope de & Zorrilla,   **PQ6438**
  Rojas
Three Spanish Golden Age Plays: The Duchess of Amalfi's
Steward/The Capulets and Montagues/Cleopatra. Gwynne
Edwards (Translator). Trade Paper, Perfect. Methuen Publishing
Ltd. London, 2005. 337p. ISBN:0-413-77475-9, ISBN13:
978-0-413-77475-0. Dewey:862.308.
Audience: **l,u,f.**

Weber, Carl (Editor)   **PT1258**
Drama Contemporary: Germany. Trade Paper. Theatre
Communications Group, Inc. New York, NY. 2005. 282p.
ISBN:1-55554-063-5, ISBN13: 978-1-55554-063-0.
Dewey:832/.91408.
Audience: **u,f.**

Wehle, Philippa (Editor)   **PQ1223**
Drama Contemporary: France. Trade Paper. P A J Publications.
New York, NY. 1986. 234p. ISBN:0-933826-94-X, ISBN13:
978-0-933826-94-6. Dewey:842.9108.
Audience: **l,u,f.**

Worthen, W. B.   **PN6112.H28**
The Wadsworth Anthology of Drama. Ed. 5. Paper Text.
Thomson Heinle. Boston, MA. 2006. 1728p.
ISBN:1-4130-1767-3, ISBN13: 978-1-4130-1767-0.
Dewey:808.82.
Audience: **g.**

Western Drama and Theater > Periods

Bieber, Margarete   **PA3201.B52**
The History of the Greek and Roman Theater. Paper Text.
Textbook Publishers. Temecula, CA. 2003. 343p.
ISBN:0-7581-5775-4, ISBN13: 978-0-7581-5775-1.
Dewey:882.09.
Audience: **l,u,f.** *B*

Corrigan, Robert W.   **PA3629.C5 1987**
Classical Comedy - Greek and Roman: Six Plays. Trade Paper.
Applause Theatre Book Publishers. New York, NY. 1987. 492p.
ISBN:0-936839-85-6, ISBN13: 978-0-936839-85-1.
Dewey:882/.01/08. LCCN:87-017442.
Audience: **l,u,f.**

Corrigan, Robert W.   **PA3626.A2C67 1990**
  (Editor)
Classical Tragedy Greek and Roman: Eight Plays with Critical
Essays. Hal Leonard Corporation Staff (Created by). Trade
Paper. Applause Theatre Book Publishers. New York, NY. 1990.
576p. ISBN:1-55783-046-0, ISBN13: 978-1-55783-046-3.
Dewey:882/.0108. LCCN:90-030152.
Audience: **l,u,f.**

Gassner, John   **PR1262.M43 1987**
Medieval and Tudor Drama: Twenty-Four Plays. Trade Paper.
Applause Theatre Book Publishers. New York, NY. 1995. 462p.
ISBN:0-936839-84-8, ISBN13: 978-0-936839-84-4.
Dewey:822/.2/08. LCCN:87-018836.
Audience: **l,u,f.**

Hill, Philip G. (Editor)   **PN6111 .O87**
Our Dramatic Heritage: Romanticism and Realism. Trade Cloth.
Fairleigh Dickinson University Press. Cranbury, NJ. 1989. 504p.
ISBN:0-8386-3267-X, ISBN13: 978-0-8386-3267-3.
Dewey:808.82. LCCN:81-065294.
Audience: **l,u,f.**

Hill, Philip G. (Editor)   PN6111 .O87
Our Dramatic Heritage: Reactions to Realism, Vol. 5. Trade
Cloth. Fairleigh Dickinson University Press. Cranbury, NJ.
1991. 384p. ISBN:0-8386-3411-7, ISBN13: 978-0-8386-3411-0.
Dewey:808.82. LCCN:81-065294.

                                        Audience: **l,u,f.**

Hill, Philip G. (Editor)   PN6111.O87 1983
Our Dramatic Heritage, Vol. 1. Trade Cloth. Fairleigh Dickinson
University Press. Cranbury, NJ. 1983. 368p.
ISBN:0-8386-3106-1, ISBN13: 978-0-8386-3106-5.
Dewey:808.82. LCCN:81-065294.

                                Audience: **l,u.** *B*

Kelly, Henry Ansgar   PN1891.K45 1993
Ideas and Forms of Tragedy from Aristotle to the Middle Ages.
Alastair Minnis, Patrick Boyde, John Burrow, Rita Copeland,
Alan Deyermond, Peter Dronke, Nigel Palmer & Winthrop
Wetherbee (Contribution by). Trade Paper. Cambridge
University Press. New York, NY. 2005. 275p. Cambridge
Studies in Medieval Literature Ser., Vol. 18
ISBN:0-521-02377-7, ISBN13: 978-0-521-02377-1.
Dewey:809.2512.

                                        Audience: **l,u,f.**

Loomis, Roger S. & Wells,   PN6112 .L57 1970
  Henry W. (Editors)
Representative Medieval and Tudor Plays. Trade Cloth. Ayer
Company Publishers, Inc. Manchester, NH. 1977. Play
Anthology Reprint Ser. ISBN:0-8369-8202-9, ISBN13:
978-0-8369-8202-2. Dewey:808.82/51. LCCN:77-111109.

                                        Audience: **l,u,f.**

Worthen, William B.   PR736.W64 1992
Modern Drama and the Rhetoric of Theater. Trade Cloth.
University of California Press. Berkeley, CA. 1991. 240p.
ISBN:0-520-07468-8, ISBN13: 978-0-520-07468-2.
Dewey:822/.9109. LCCN:91-017677.

                        Audience: **l,u,f.** *Choice, 1992.*

Western Drama and Theater > Periods > Ancient Greek Drama and Theater

Aeschylus   PA3978
Aeschylus: Plays Two. Frederic Raphael & Kenneth McLeish
(Translators), J. Michael Walton (Introduction by). Trade Paper.
Methuen Publishing Ltd. London, 2004. 129p. Methuen's World
Dramatists Ser. ISBN:0-413-65480-X, ISBN13:
978-0-413-65480-9. Dewey:882/.01.

                                        Audience: **l,u,f.**

Aeschylus   PA3978
Aeschylus: Plays One. Frederic Raphael & Kenneth McLeish
(Translators), J. Michael Walton (Introduction by). Trade Paper.
Methuen Publishing Ltd. London, 2004. 153p. Methuen World
Dramatists Ser. ISBN:0-413-65190-8, ISBN13:
978-0-413-65190-7. Dewey:882/.01.

                                        Audience: **l,u,f.**

Aeschylus, et al.   PA3463.S59 2002
Six Greek Tragedies: Aeschylus: Persians, Prometheus Bound;
Sophocles: Women of Trachi, Philoctetes; Euripides: Trojan
Women, Bacchae. Sophocles & Euripides (Authors), Marianne
McDonald & J. Michael Walton (Editors), Marianne McDonald
& J. Michael Walton (Translators). Trade Paper. Methuen
Publishing Ltd. London, 2004. Methuen Drama Ser.
ISBN:0-413-77256-X, ISBN13: 978-0-413-77256-5.
Dewey:882/.01/08. LCCN:2004-426593.

                                        Audience: **l,u,f.**

Allen, James T.   PA3202.A5
Greek Theatre of the Fifth Century Before Christ. Library
Binding. M. S. G. Haskell House. Brooklyn, NY. 1969. Studies
in Drama, No. 39 ISBN:0-8383-0647-0, ISBN13:
978-0-8383-0647-5. Dewey:792.0938. LCCN:68-002221.

                                        Audience: **l,u,f.**

Aristophanes   PA3978
Aristophanes: Plays One. Trade Paper. Methuen Publishing Ltd.
London, 2004. 264p. ISBN:0-413-66900-9, ISBN13:
978-0-413-66900-1. Dewey:882/.01.

                                        Audience: **l,u,f.**

Aristophanes   PA3978
Aristophanes: Plays Two. Trade Paper. Methuen Publishing Ltd.
London, 2004. ISBN:0-413-66910-6, ISBN13:
978-0-413-66910-0. Dewey:882/.01.

                                        Audience: **l,u,f.**

Aristotle   PN1040.A513 2001
Aristotle on Poetics. Seth Benardete (Translator), Michael Davis
(Translator, Introduction by). Cloth Text. Saint Augustine's
Press, Inc. South Bend, IN. 2002. 144p. ISBN:1-58731-025-2,
ISBN13: 978-1-58731-025-6. Dewey:808.2.
LCCN:2001-005879.

                                        Audience: **u,f.**

Arnott, Peter D.   PA3201 .A76
An Introduction to the Greek Theatre. Paper Text. Textbook
Publishers. Temecula, CA. 2003. 239p. ISBN:0-7581-8855-2,
ISBN13: 978-0-7581-8855-7. Dewey:792.0938.

                                        Audience: **l,u.**

Arnott, Peter D.   PA3201
Public and Performance in the Greek Theatre. Trade Paper.
Routledge. New York, NY. 1991. 216p. ISBN:0-415-06299-3,
ISBN13: 978-0-415-06299-2. Dewey:792/.0938.
LCCN:88-032156.

                        Audience: **l,u,f.** *Choice, 1990.*

Bieber, Margarete   PA3201.B52
The History of the Greek and Roman Theater. Paper Text.
Textbook Publishers. Temecula, CA. 2003. 343p.
ISBN:0-7581-5775-4, ISBN13: 978-0-7581-5775-1.
Dewey:882.09.

                                Audience: **l,u,f.** *B*

Corrigan, Robert W.   PA3629.C5 1987
Classical Comedy - Greek and Roman: Six Plays. Trade Paper.

Applause Theatre Book Publishers. New York, NY. 1987. 492p.
ISBN:0-936839-85-6, ISBN13: 978-0-936839-85-1.
Dewey:882/.01/08. LCCN:87-017442.

Audience: **l,u,f.**

Corrigan, Robert W.   **PA3626.A2C67 1990**
  (Editor)
Classical Tragedy Greek and Roman: Eight Plays with Critical
Essays. Hal Leonard Corporation Staff (Created by). Trade
Paper. Applause Theatre Book Publishers. New York, NY. 1990.
576p. ISBN:1-55783-046-0, ISBN13: 978-1-55783-046-3.
Dewey:882/.0108. LCCN:90-030152.

Audience: **l,u,f.**

Easterling, P. E. (Editor)   **PA3131 .C29 1997**
The Cambridge Companion to Greek Tragedy. Trade Paper.
Cambridge University Press. New York, NY. 1997. 410p.
Companions to Literature Ser. ISBN:0-521-42351-1, ISBN13:
978-0-521-42351-9. Dewey:882/.01/09. LCCN:96-037392.

Audience: **g,l,u,f.** *Choice, 1998.*

Euripides   **PA3978**
Plays Two: Hecuba, the Women of Troy, Iphigenia at Aulis,
Cyclops. Peter D. Arnott & Don Taylor (Translators), J. Michael
Walton (Translator, Introduction by). Trade Paper. Methuen
Publishing Ltd. London, 2004. Methuen World Dramatists Ser.
ISBN:0-413-16420-9, ISBN13: 978-0-413-16420-9.
Dewey:882/.01.

Audience: **l,u,f.**

Euripides   **PA3975.A2 1997**
Plays Four. Kenneth McLeish (Translator, Introduction by), J.
Michael Walton (Introduction by). Trade Paper. Methuen
Publishing Ltd. London, 2004. Methuen Classical Greek
Dramatists Ser. ISBN:0-413-71630-9, ISBN13:
978-0-413-71630-9. Dewey:882/.01. LCCN:98-133592.

Audience: **l,u,f.**

Euripides   **PA3975.A2**
Plays 1. David Thompson (Translator), J. Michael Walton
(Introduction by). Trade Paper. Methuen Publishing Ltd.
London, 2004. Methuen Classical Greek Dramatists Ser.
ISBN:0-413-75280-1, ISBN13: 978-0-413-75280-2.
Dewey:882/.01.

Audience: **l,u,f.**

Euripides   **PA3975.A2 1997**
Plays Five. J. Michael Walton & Kenneth McLeish (Introduction
by). Trade Paper. Methuen Publishing Ltd. London, 2004.
Methuen Classical Greek Dramatists Ser. ISBN:0-413-71640-6,
ISBN13: 978-0-413-71640-8. Dewey:882/.01. LCCN:98-194780.

Audience: **l,u,f.**

Gregory, Justina (Editor)   **PA3131.C56 2006**
A Companion to Greek Tragedy. Trade Cloth. Blackwell
Publishing, Inc. Malden, MA. 2005. 576p. Blackwell
Companions to the Ancient World Ser. ISBN:1-4051-0770-7,
ISBN13: 978-1-4051-0770-9. Dewey:882/.0109.
LCCN:2004-024920.

Audience: **u,f.** *Choice, 2006.*

Hill, Philip G. (Editor)   **PN6111.O87 1983**
Our Dramatic Heritage, Vol. 1. Trade Cloth. Fairleigh Dickinson
University Press. Cranbury, NJ. 1983. 368p.
ISBN:0-8386-3106-1, ISBN13: 978-0-8386-3106-5.
Dewey:808.82. LCCN:81-065294.

Audience: **l,u.** *B*

Izenour, George C.   **PA3201.I97 1992**
Roofed Theaters of Classical Antiquity. Cloth over Boards. Yale
University Press. Cumberland, RI. 1992. 258p.
ISBN:0-300-04685-5, ISBN13: 978-0-300-04685-4.
Dewey:792/.0938. LCCN:91-012010.

Audience: **u,f.** *Choice, 1992.*

Kelly, Henry Ansgar   **PN1891.K45 1993**
Ideas and Forms of Tragedy from Aristotle to the Middle Ages.
Alastair Minnis, Patrick Boyde, John Burrow, Rita Copeland,
Alan Deyermond, Peter Dronke, Nigel Palmer & Winthrop
Wetherbee (Contribution by). Trade Paper. Cambridge
University Press. New York, NY. 2005. 275p. Cambridge
Studies in Medieval Literature Ser., Vol. 18
ISBN:0-521-02377-7, ISBN13: 978-0-521-02377-1.
Dewey:809.2512.

Audience: **l,u,f.**

McLeish, Kenneth &   **PA3201**
  Griffiths, Trevor
Guide to Greek Theatre and Drama. Trade Paper. Methuen
Publishing Ltd. London, 2004. Methuen Drama Ser.
ISBN:0-413-72030-6, ISBN13: 978-0-413-72030-6.
Dewey:882/.0109. LCCN:2003-447738.

Audience: **l,u,f.**

Menander   **PA4246.E4B35 2002**
Menander, the Plays and Fragments. Maurice Balme
(Translator), Peter Brown (Introduction by). Trade Paper. Oxford
University Press, Inc. New York, NY. 2002. 346p. Oxford
World's Classics Ser. ISBN:0-19-283983-7, ISBN13:
978-0-19-283983-1. Dewey:822/.01. LCCN:2002-025760.

Audience: **g,l,u.**

Rehm, Rush   **PA3131.R38**
Greek Tragic Theatre. Trade Paper. Routledge. New York, NY.
1994. 184p. Theatre Production Ser. ISBN:0-415-11894-8,
ISBN13: 978-0-415-11894-1. Dewey:882.0109.
LCCN:91-033611.

Audience: **u,f.** *Choice, 1993.*

Schmidt, Dennis J.   **PA3131.S366 2001**
On Germans and Other Greeks: Tragedy and Ethical Life.
E-Book. Indiana University Press. Bloomington, IN. 2001. 432p.
Studies in Continental Thought ISBN:0-253-33868-9, ISBN13:
978-0-253-33868-6. Dewey:882/.0109. LCCN:00-050642.

Audience: **u,f.**

Smith, Helaine   **PA3131**
Masterpieces of Classic Greek Drama. Trade Cloth. Greenwood
Publishing Group, Inc. Portsmouth, NH. 2005. 232p. Greenwood
Introduces Literary Masterpieces Ser. ISBN:0-313-33268-1,
ISBN13: 978-0-313-33268-5. Dewey:882/.0109.
LCCN:2005-019210.

Audience: **l.** *Choice, 2006.*

Sophocles PA4414.A1 C3
Sophocles the Seven Plays in English Ver. Trade Paper.
Kessinger Publishing, LLC. Whitefish, MT. 2005.
ISBN:1-4179-0075-X, ISBN13: 978-1-4179-0075-6. Dewey:882.
Audience: **u,f.**

Walton, J. Michael, et al. PA3975
Plays 3, Vol. 3. Kenneth McLeish & Euripides (Authors). Trade
Paper. Methuen Publishing Ltd. London, 2004.
ISBN:0-413-71620-1, ISBN13: 978-0-413-71620-0.
Dewey:882/.01.
Audience: **l,u,f.**

Wetmore, Kevin J. PS338.N4W48 2003
Black Dionysus: Greek Tragedy and African American Theatre.
Paper Text. McFarland & Company, Incorporated Publishers.
Jefferson, NC. 2003. 272p. ISBN:0-7864-1545-2, ISBN13:
978-0-7864-1545-8. Dewey:812.009/896073.
LCCN:2002-156684.
Audience: **u,f.** *Choice, 2003.*

Wiles, David PA3201 .W53 2000
Greek Theatre Performance: An Introduction. Trade Paper.
Cambridge University Press. New York, NY. 2000. 256p.
ISBN:0-521-64857-2, ISBN13: 978-0-521-64857-8.
Dewey:792/.0938. LCCN:99-043723.
Audience: **l,u.**

Western Drama and Theater > Periods > Roman Drama and Theater

Beacham, Richard C. PA6073
The Roman Theatre and Its Audience. Trade Paper. Harvard
University Press. Cambridge, MA. 1996. 279p.
ISBN:0-674-77914-2, ISBN13: 978-0-674-77914-3.
Dewey:792/.0937/6.
Audience: **u,f.** *Choice, 1992.*

Beacham, Richard C. PA6073.B44
Roman Theatre and Its Audience. Trade Paper. Routledge. New
York, NY. 1999. 288p. ISBN:0-415-12163-9, ISBN13:
978-0-415-12163-7. Dewey:792.0937.
Audience: **u,f.**

Bieber, Margarete PA3201.B52
The History of the Greek and Roman Theater. Paper Text.
Textbook Publishers. Temecula, CA. 2003. 343p.
ISBN:0-7581-5775-4, ISBN13: 978-0-7581-5775-1.
Dewey:882.09.
Audience: **l,u,f.** *B*

Corrigan, Robert W. PA3629.C5 1987
Classical Comedy - Greek and Roman: Six Plays. Trade Paper.
Applause Theatre Book Publishers. New York, NY. 1987. 492p.
ISBN:0-936839-85-6, ISBN13: 978-0-936839-85-1.
Dewey:882/.01/08. LCCN:87-017442.
Audience: **l,u,f.**

Corrigan, Robert W. PA3626.A2C67 1990
(Editor)
Classical Tragedy Greek and Roman: Eight Plays with Critical
Essays. Hal Leonard Corporation Staff (Created by). Trade
Paper. Applause Theatre Book Publishers. New York, NY. 1990.
576p. ISBN:1-55783-046-0, ISBN13: 978-1-55783-046-3.
Dewey:882/.0108. LCCN:90-030152.
Audience: **l,u,f.**

Duckworth, George Eckel PA6069.D8
The Nature of Roman Comedy, A Study in Popular
Entertainment. Paper Text. Textbook Publishers. Temecula, CA.
2003. 501p. ISBN:0-7581-5789-4, ISBN13: 978-0-7581-5789-8.
Dewey:872.09.
Audience: **u,f.**

Hill, Philip G. (Editor) PN6111.O87 1983
Our Dramatic Heritage, Vol. 1. Trade Cloth. Fairleigh Dickinson
University Press. Cranbury, NJ. 1983. 368p.
ISBN:0-8386-3106-1, ISBN13: 978-0-8386-3106-5.
Dewey:808.82. LCCN:81-065294.
Audience: **l,u.** *B*

Izenour, George C. PA3201.I97 1992
Roofed Theaters of Classical Antiquity. Cloth over Boards. Yale
University Press. Cumberland, RI. 1992. 258p.
ISBN:0-300-04685-5, ISBN13: 978-0-300-04685-4.
Dewey:792/.0938. LCCN:91-012010.
Audience: **u,f.** *Choice, 1992.*

Kelly, Henry Ansgar PN1891.K45 1993
Ideas and Forms of Tragedy from Aristotle to the Middle Ages.
Alastair Minnis, Patrick Boyde, John Burrow, Rita Copeland,
Alan Deyermond, Peter Dronke, Nigel Palmer & Winthrop
Wetherbee (Contribution by). Trade Paper. Cambridge
University Press. New York, NY. 2005. 275p. Cambridge
Studies in Medieval Literature Ser., Vol. 18
ISBN:0-521-02377-7, ISBN13: 978-0-521-02377-1.
Dewey:809.2512.
Audience: **l,u,f.**

Plautus, Titus Maccius & PA6137.3
Terence
Four Roman Comedies: The Haunted House, Casina, or A
Funny Thing Happened on the Way to the Wedding, the Eunuch,
Brothers. J. Michael Walton (Editor, Introduction by). Trade
Paper. Methuen Publishing Ltd. London, 2003. 320p. Methuen
Classical Drama Ser. ISBN:0-413-77296-9, ISBN13:
978-0-413-77296-1. Dewey:872/.0108. LCCN:2003-430388.
Audience: **u,f.**

Sear, Frank NA325.T5
Roman Theatres: An Architectural Study. Trade Cloth. Oxford
University Press, Inc. New York, NY. 2006. 534p. Oxford
Monographs on Classical Archaeology Ser.
ISBN:0-19-814469-5, ISBN13: 978-0-19-814469-4.
Dewey:725.8220937.
Audience: **u,f.**

Seneca, Lucius Annaeus   PA6666.A1 1992
Seneca: The Tragedies. David R. Slavitt (Translator). Trade
Paper. Johns Hopkins University Press. Baltimore, MD. 1992.
224p. Seneca Ser., Vol. 1 ISBN:0-8018-4309-X, ISBN13:
978-0-8018-4309-9. Dewey:872.01. LCCN:91-036347.
                                         Audience: **u,f.**

Slater, Niall W.   PA6585.S55 2000
Plautus in Performance: The Theatre of the Mind. Ed. 2. Cloth
Text. Gordon & Breach Publishing Group. New York, NY. 2000.
228p. Greek and Roman Theatre Ser., Vol. 2
ISBN:90-5755-037-7, ISBN13: 978-90-5755-037-9.
Dewey:872/.01. LCCN:2002-405986.
                                    Audience: **u,f.** 𝐵

Slavitt, David R.   PA6569.S55 1995
Plautus: The Comedies. Palmer Bovie & T. Maccius Plautus
(Editors). Trade Paper. Johns Hopkins University Press.
Baltimore, MD. 1990. 360p. Plautus Ser., Vol. 4
ISBN:0-8018-5073-8, ISBN13: 978-0-8018-5073-8.
Dewey:872/.01. LCCN:94-045317.
                            Audience: **u,f.** *Choice, 1996.*

Western Drama and Theater > Periods > Medieval Drama and Theatre in Europe

Beadle, Richard (Editor)   PN2587.C36 1994
The Cambridge Companion to Medieval English Theatre. Trade
Paper. Cambridge University Press. New York, NY. 1994. 394p.
Companions to Literature Ser. ISBN:0-521-45916-8, ISBN13:
978-0-521-45916-7. Dewey:792.0942. LCCN:93-004397.
                                       Audience: **g,u,f.**

Chambers, E. K.   PN2152
The Medieval Stage. Paper Text. Classic Books. Murrieta, CA.
2001. ISBN:0-7426-9205-1, ISBN13: 978-0-7426-9205-3.
Dewey:792.094.
                                          Audience: **u,f.**

Coldewey, John C. (Editor)   PR1260.E27 1993
Early English Drama: An Anthology. Cloth Text. Garland
Publishing, Inc. New York, NY. 1993. 392p.
ISBN:0-8240-4699-4, ISBN13: 978-0-8240-4699-6.
Dewey:822.208. LCCN:92-007686.
                                          Audience: **u,f.**

Cox, John D. & Kastan,   PR641.N49 1997
  David S.
A New History of Early English Drama. Cloth Text. Columbia
University Press. New York, NY. 1997. 580p.
ISBN:0-231-10242-9, ISBN13: 978-0-231-10242-1.
Dewey:822/.009. LCCN:96-029670.
                            Audience: **l,u,f.** *Choice, 1997.*

Davidson, Clifford   PN2587.D38 1996
Technology, Guilds, and Early English Drama. Trade Cloth, Box
or Slipcased. Medieval Institute Publications. Kalamazoo, MI.
1996. 128p. Early Drama, Art and Music Monograph Ser.

ISBN:1-879288-79-6, ISBN13: 978-1-879288-79-9.
Dewey:792/.0942/0902. LCCN:96-032689.
                            Audience: **l,u,f.** *Choice, 1997.*

Gassner, John   PR1262.M43 1987
Medieval and Tudor Drama: Twenty-Four Plays. Trade Paper.
Applause Theatre Book Publishers. New York, NY. 1995. 462p.
ISBN:0-936839-84-8, ISBN13: 978-0-936839-84-4.
Dewey:822/.2/08. LCCN:87-018836.
                                        Audience: **l,u,f.**

Hill, Philip G. (Editor)   PN6111.O87 1983
Our Dramatic Heritage, Vol. 1. Trade Cloth. Fairleigh Dickinson
University Press. Cranbury, NJ. 1983. 368p.
ISBN:0-8386-3106-1, ISBN13: 978-0-8386-3106-5.
Dewey:808.82. LCCN:81-065294.
                                    Audience: **l,u.** 𝐵

Hrotsvitha   PR2065
Dulcitius, a Mediaeval Comedy. Trade Paper. Books on
Demand. Ann Arbor, MI. 20p. ISBN:0-598-75592-6, ISBN13:
978-0-598-75592-6. Dewey:872. LCCN:17-006632.
                                          Audience: **u,f.**

Kelly, Henry Ansgar   PN1891.K45 1993
Ideas and Forms of Tragedy from Aristotle to the Middle Ages.
Alastair Minnis, Patrick Boyde, John Burrow, Rita Copeland,
Alan Deyermond, Peter Dronke, Nigel Palmer & Winthrop
Wetherbee (Contribution by). Trade Paper. Cambridge
University Press. New York, NY. 2005. 275p. Cambridge
Studies in Medieval Literature Ser., Vol. 18
ISBN:0-521-02377-7, ISBN13: 978-0-521-02377-1.
Dewey:809.2512.
                                        Audience: **l,u,f.**

Loomis, Roger S. & Wells,   PN6112 .L57 1970
  Henry W. (Editors)
Representative Medieval and Tudor Plays. Trade Cloth. Ayer
Company Publishers, Inc. Manchester, NH. 1977. Play
Anthology Reprint Ser. ISBN:0-8369-8202-9, ISBN13:
978-0-8369-8202-2. Dewey:808.82/51. LCCN:77-111109.
                                        Audience: **l,u,f.**

Muir, Lynette R.   PN1880 .M85 1995
The Biblical Drama of Medieval Europe. Trade Paper.
Cambridge University Press. New York, NY. 2003. 344p.
ISBN:0-521-54210-3, ISBN13: 978-0-521-54210-4.
Dewey:809.2/516.
                            Audience: **u,f.** *Choice, 1996.*

Tydeman, William   PN2570
The Theatre in the Middle Ages: Western European Stage
Conditions, C. 800-1576. Trade Paper. Cambridge University
Press. New York, NY. 1979. 310p. ISBN:0-521-29304-9,
ISBN13: 978-0-521-29304-4. Dewey:792/.094.
LCCN:77-085683.
                                          Audience: **u,f.**

Tydeman, William (Editor)   PN2570 .M39 2001
The Medieval European Stage, 500-1550. W. D. Howarth, John
Northam & Glynne W. Wickham (Contribution by). Trade Cloth.
Cambridge University Press. New York, NY. 2001. 782p.

Theatre in Europe Ser. ISBN:0-521-24609-1, ISBN13: 978-0-521-24609-5. Dewey:792/.094/0902. LCCN:00-067610.

Audience: **u,f.** *Choice, 2002.*

Wickham, Glynne W.　　　　　　　　　**PN2152 .W5 1987**
The Medieval Theatre. Ed. 3. Trade Paper. Cambridge University Press. New York, NY. 1987. 276p. ISBN:0-521-31248-5, ISBN13: 978-0-521-31248-6. Dewey:792/.094. LCCN:86-020742.

Audience: **l,u,f.** *B Choice, 1988.*

Williams, Arnold　　　　　　　　　　　　**PR641.W55**
The Drama of Medieval England. Paper Text. Textbook Publishers. Temecula, CA. 2003. 186p. ISBN:0-7581-8137-X, ISBN13: 978-0-7581-8137-4. Dewey:822.109.

Audience: **l,u,f.**

Western Drama and Theater > Periods > European Renaissance Drama

PQ6105
A Society on Stage: Essays on Spanish Golden Age. Paper Text. University Press of the South, Inc. New Orleans, LA. 1997. Iberian Studies, Vol. 15 ISBN:1-889431-19-2, ISBN13: 978-1-889431-19-2. Dewey:862.309.

Audience: **u,f.**

Barker, Simon & Hinds,　　　　　　**PR1263.R68 2002**
Hilary (Editors)
Routledge Anthology of Renaissance Drama. Paper over Boards. Routledge. New York, NY. 2002. 480p. ISBN:0-415-18733-8, ISBN13: 978-0-415-18733-6. Dewey:822/.308. LCCN:2002-026872.

Audience: **l,u,f.**

Bevington, David　　　　　　　　　　**PR1263.E56 2003**
English Renaissance Drama: A Norton Anthology. Lars Engle, Katharine Eisaman Maus & Eric Rasmussen (Editors). Trade Cloth. W. W. Norton & Company, Inc. New York, NY. 2002. 2400p. ISBN:0-393-97655-6, ISBN13: 978-0-393-97655-7. Dewey:822/.308. LCCN:2002-025074.

Audience: **l,u,f.**

Braunmuller, A. R. &　　　　　　　　**PR651.C36 2003**
Hattaway, Michael (Editors)
The Cambridge Companion to English Renaissance Drama. Ed. 2. Cloth Text. Cambridge University Press. New York, NY. 2003. 484p. Cambridge Companions to Literature Ser. ISBN:0-521-82115-0, ISBN13: 978-0-521-82115-5. Dewey:822/.309. LCCN:2002-035073.

Audience: **g,l,u,f.** *Choice, 2004, 1991.*

Cairns, Christopher (Editor)　　　　　**PR653.R46**
Renaissance Theatre: Texts, Performance and Design, Vol. 2. Trade Cloth. Ashgate Publishing, Ltd. Aldershot, 1999. 358p. ISBN:0-7546-0008-4, ISBN13: 978-0-7546-0008-4. Dewey:822/.309.

Audience: **l,u,f.**

Cairns, Christopher (Editor)　　　　**PR653.R46 1999**
The Renaissance Theatre - Texts, Performance and Design: English and Italian Theatre. Trade Cloth. Ashgate Publishing, Ltd. Aldershot, 1999. 200p. ISBN:0-7546-0006-8, ISBN13: 978-0-7546-0006-0. Dewey:822/.309. LCCN:99-029487.

Audience: **l,u,f.**

Cairns, Christopher (Editor)　　　　**PN2091.S8S292 1996**
Scenery, Set and Staging in the Italian Renaissance: Studies in the Practice of Theatre. Trade Cloth. Edwin Mellen Press, The. Lewiston, NY. 1996. 340p. ISBN:0-7734-8814-6, ISBN13: 978-0-7734-8814-4. Dewey:792/.025/0945. LCCN:96-003909.

Audience: **l,u,f.**

Calderón de la Barca, Pedro　　　　**PQ6292.A1**
Calderon: Plays One. Gwynne Edwards (Translator, Introduction by). Trade Paper. Methuen Publishing Ltd. London, 2004. Methuen World Classics Ser., Vol. 1 ISBN:0-413-63460-4, ISBN13: 978-0-413-63460-3. Dewey:862.3.

Audience: **l,u,f.**

Cerasano, Susan P. &　　　　　　　**PR658.W6R43 1998**
Wynne-Davies, Marion
Readings in Renaissance Women's Drama: Criticism, History, and Performance, 1594-1998. Trade Paper. Routledge. New York, NY. 1998. 336p. ISBN:0-415-16443-5, ISBN13: 978-0-415-16443-6. Dewey:822/.3099287. LCCN:98-006670.

Audience: **l,u,f.** *Choice, 1999.*

Cohen, Walter　　　　　　　　　　　　**PR651**
Drama of a Nation: Public Theater in Renaissance England and Spain. Book, Other. Cornell University Press. Ithaca, NY. 1988. 416p. ISBN:0-8014-9494-X, ISBN13: 978-0-8014-9494-9. Dewey:822/.3/09. LCCN:85-002633.

Audience: **l,u,f.**

Conlon, Raymond (Editor)　　　　　**PN820.A835 2003**
An Anthology of Renaissance Plays in Translation: Works from the Italian, Spanish, and Portuguese Traditions. Trade Cloth. Edwin Mellen Press, The. Lewiston, NY. 2002. 516p. Studies in Renaissance Literature, Vol. 23 ISBN:0-7734-6905-2, ISBN13: 978-0-7734-6905-1. Dewey:852/.208. LCCN:2002-033753.

Audience: **l,u,f.**

Di Maria, Salvatore　　　　　　　　　**PQ4147.D5 2002**
The Italian Tragedy in the Renaissance: Cultural Realities and Theatrical Innovations. Trade Cloth. Bucknell University Press. Cranbury, NJ. 2002. 272p. ISBN:0-8387-5490-2, ISBN13: 978-0-8387-5490-0. Dewey:852/.05120903. LCCN:2001-035662.

Audience: **l,u,f.**

Hill, Philip G. (Editor)　　　　　　　**PN6111**
Our Dramatic Heritage: The Golden Age. Trade Cloth. Fairleigh Dickinson University Press. Cranbury, NJ. 1985. 624p. ISBN:0-8386-3107-X, ISBN13: 978-0-8386-3107-2. Dewey:808.82. LCCN:81-065294.

Audience: **l,u,f.**

Kermode, Frank　　　　　　　　　　　**PR1265.5.D83 2005**
The Duchess of Malfi: Eight Masterpieces of Jacobean Drama. Trade Paper. Random House Adult Trade Publishing Group.

New York, NY. 2005. 688p. The Modern Library Classics
ISBN:0-679-64243-9, ISBN13: 978-0-679-64243-5.
Dewey:822/.308. LCCN:2004-061004.

Audience: **l,u,f.**

Kinney, Arthur F. (Editor)   **PR1263.R45 2004**
Renaissance Drama: An Anthology of Plays and Entertainments.
Ed. 2. Trade Paper. Blackwell Publishing, Inc. Malden, MA.
2004. 928p. Blackwell Anthologies Ser. ISBN:1-4051-1967-5,
ISBN13: 978-1-4051-1967-2. Dewey:822/.308.
LCCN:2004-047626.

Audience: **l,u,f.**

Machiavelli, Niccolo &   **PQ4244.E5T48 1996**
Ariosto, Ludovico
Three Italian Renaissance Comedies: Ariosto's The Supposes;
Machiavelli's The Mandrake; Intronati's The Deceived.
Christopher Cairns & Accademia Senese Degli Intronati Staff
(Editors), Jennifer Lorch (Translator, Introduction by). Trade
Cloth. Edwin Mellen Press, The. Lewiston, NY. 1996. 452p.
ISBN:0-7734-8821-9, ISBN13: 978-0-7734-8821-2.
Dewey:852/.309. LCCN:96-019456.

Audience: **l,u,f.**

McRae, Andrew   **PR646**
Renaissance Drama. Trade Paper. Oxford University Press, Inc.
New York, NY. 2003. 192p. Context Ser. ISBN:0-340-76347-7,
ISBN13: 978-0-340-76347-6. Dewey:822/.309.
LCCN:2004-297099.

Audience: **u,f.**

Nicoll, Allardyce (Editor)   **PR2900**
Elizabethan Theatre. Jonathan Bate, Margreta De Grazia,
Michael Dobson, Inga-Stina Ewbank, R. A. Foakes, Andrew
Gurr, Lena Cowen Orlin, Terence Hawkes, John Jowett & A. D.
Nuttall (Contribution by). Trade Paper. Cambridge University
Press. New York, NY. 2002. 182p. Shakespeare Survey Ser.,
Vol. 12 ISBN:0-521-52348-6, ISBN13: 978-0-521-52348-6.
Dewey:822.3/3.

Audience: **u,f.**

Prouty, Charles Tyler   **PN2596**
Studies in the Elizabethan Theatre. Paper Text. Textbook
Publishers. Temecula, CA. 2003. 198p. ISBN:0-7581-3918-7,
ISBN13: 978-0-7581-3918-4. Dewey:792.0942.

Audience: **u,f.** *B*

Serlio, Sebastiano   **PN2221.H76**
The Renaissance Stage: Documents of Serlio, Sabbattini and
Furttenbach. Paper Text. Textbook Publishers. Temecula, CA.
2003. 256p. ISBN:0-7581-2129-6, ISBN13: 978-0-7581-2129-5.
Dewey:792.

Audience: **u,f.** *B*

Shaughnessy, Robert   **PR1248.F68 2003**
Four Renaissance Comedies. Trade Paper. Palgrave Macmillan.
New York, NY. 2004. 368p. ISBN:0-333-97365-8, ISBN13:
978-0-333-97365-3. Dewey:822/.05230803. LCCN:2003-053655.

Audience: **l,u.**

Sullivan, Garrett A., et al.   **PR653.E17 2006**
Early Modern English Drama: A Critical Companion. Patrick
Gerard Cheney & Andrew Hadfield (Authors). Trade Paper.
Oxford University Press, Inc. New York, NY. 2005. 351p.
ISBN:0-19-515386-3, ISBN13: 978-0-19-515386-6.
Dewey:822/.309. LCCN:2004-066273.

Audience: **g,l,u,f.**

Vega, Lope de & Zorrilla,   **PQ6438**
Rojas
Three Spanish Golden Age Plays: The Duchess of Amalfi's
Steward/The Capulets and Montagues/Cleopatra. Gwynne
Edwards (Translator). Trade Paper, Perfect. Methuen Publishing
Ltd. London, 2005. 337p. ISBN:0-413-77475-9, ISBN13:
978-0-413-77475-0. Dewey:862.308.

Audience: **l,u,f.**

Worthen, W. B.   **PR647**
Renaissance Drama, Vol. 34. Wendy Wall & Jeffrey Masten
(Editors). Trade Cloth. Northwestern University Press. Evanston,
IL. 2006. 224p. Renaissance Drama Ser. ISBN:0-8101-2308-8,
ISBN13: 978-0-8101-2308-3. Dewey:822.309.

Audience: **u,f.**

Western Drama and Theater > Periods > European Renaissance Drama > Shakespeare

Adams, Joseph Quincy   **PN2596.L6A55**
Shakespearean Playhouses: A History of English Theatres from
the Beginnings to the Restoration. Paper Text. Textbook
Publishers. Temecula, CA. 2003. 473p. ISBN:0-7581-6786-5,
ISBN13: 978-0-7581-6786-6. Dewey:792.09421.

Audience: **l,u,f.** *B*

Alexander, Catherine   **PR2976.C3 2003**
(Editor)
The Cambridge Shakespeare Library: Shakespeare's Times,
Texts, and Stages; Shakespeare Criticism; Shakespeare
Performance, Set. Quantity Pack, Trade Cloth. Cambridge
University Press. New York, NY. 2003. 1416p.
ISBN:0-521-82433-8, ISBN13: 978-0-521-82433-0.
Dewey:822.3/3. LCCN:2002-031457.

Audience: **l,u,f.**

Bristol, Michael D. &   **PR3100.S52 2001**
McLuskie, Kathleen (Editors)
Shakespeare and Modern Theatre: The Performance of
Modernity. Paper over Boards. Routledge. New York, NY. 2001.
224p. Accents on Shakespeare Ser. ISBN:0-415-21984-1,
ISBN13: 978-0-415-21984-6. Dewey:792.9/5. LCCN:00-065307.

Audience: **u,f.**

Callaghan, Dympna (Editor)   **PR2976**
A Feminist Companion to Shakespeare. Trade Paper. Blackwell
Publishing, Inc. Malden, MA. 2001. 416p. Companions to
Literature and Culture Ser. ISBN:0-631-20807-0, ISBN13:
978-0-631-20807-5. Dewey:822.3/3.

Audience: **l,u,f.** *Choice, 2000.*

Chambers, Colin PN2596.S82R684 2004
Inside the Royal Shakespeare Company: Creativity and the
Institution. Paper over Boards. Routledge. New York, NY. 2004.
280p. ISBN:0-415-21202-2, ISBN13: 978-0-415-21202-1.
Dewey:792/.0942. LCCN:2003-015745.
Audience: **l,u,f.**

Foakes, R. A. PN2589.F6 1985
Illustrations of the English Stage, 1580-1642. Trade Cloth.
Stanford University Press. Palo Alto, CA. 1985. 180p.
ISBN:0-8047-1236-0, ISBN13: 978-0-8047-1236-1.
Dewey:792/.0941. LCCN:83-040517.
Audience: **l,u,f.** 𝕭

Gale Editors (Editor) PR2976
Shakespearean Criticism. Trade Cloth. Thomson Gale.
Farmington Hills, MI. 2006. ISBN:0-7876-8838-X, ISBN13:
978-0-7876-8838-7. Dewey:822.33.
Audience: **l,u,f.**

Gibson, H. N. PR2937
The Shakespeare Claimants: A Critical Survey of the Four
Principal Theories Concerning the Authorship of the
Shakespearean Plays. Paper over Boards. Routledge. New York,
NY. 2005. 336p. ISBN:0-415-35290-8, ISBN13:
978-0-415-35290-1. Dewey:822.33.
Audience: **u,f.**

Gurr, Andrew PR3095.G86 2004
The Shakespeare Company, 1594-1642. Trade Cloth. Cambridge
University Press. New York, NY. 2004. 356p.
ISBN:0-521-80730-1, ISBN13: 978-0-521-80730-2.
Dewey:792/.09421. LCCN:2003-055895.
Audience: **u,f.** *Choice, 2005.*

Hoenselaars, Ton (Editor) PR2982.S475 2004
Shakespeare's History Plays: Performance, Translation and
Adaptation in Britain and Abroad. Dennis Kennedy (Foreword
by). Trade Cloth. Cambridge University Press. New York, NY.
2004. 302p. ISBN:0-521-82902-X, ISBN13: 978-0-521-82902-1.
Dewey:822.3/3. LCCN:2004-040752.
Audience: **u,f.** *Choice, 2005.*

Kennedy, Dennis (Editor) PR2971.F66 F66 1993
Foreign Shakespeare: Contemporary Performance. Trade Paper.
Cambridge University Press. New York, NY. 2004. 329p.
ISBN:0-521-61708-1, ISBN13: 978-0-521-61708-6.
Dewey:792.95.
Audience: **l,u,f.** *Choice, 1994.*

Kermode, Frank PR3095
The Age of Shakespeare. Trade Paper. Random House Adult
Trade Publishing Group. New York, NY. 2005. 240p.
ISBN:0-8129-7433-6, ISBN13: 978-0-8129-7433-1.
Dewey:822.33.
Audience: **l,u,f.**

Massai, Sonia (Editor) PR2880.A1W67 2005
World-Wide Shakespeares. Paper over Boards. Routledge. New
York, NY. 2005. 216p. ISBN:0-415-32455-6, ISBN13:
978-0-415-32455-7. Dewey:822.3/3. LCCN:2004-028867.
Audience: **l,u,f.**

McDonald, Russ (Editor) PR2970.S495 2004
Shakespeare: An Anthology of Criticism and Theory, 1945-2000.
Trade Cloth. Blackwell Publishing, Inc. Malden, MA. 2004.
952p. ISBN:0-631-23487-X, ISBN13: 978-0-631-23487-6.
Dewey:822.3/3. LCCN:2003-012197.
Audience: **u,f.** *Choice, 2004.*

McEachern, Claire (Editor) PR2983.C28 2002
The Cambridge Companion to Shakespearean Tragedy. Cloth
Text. Cambridge University Press. New York, NY. 2003. 292p.
Cambridge Companions to Literature Ser. ISBN:0-521-79009-3,
ISBN13: 978-0-521-79009-3. Dewey:822.3//3.
LCCN:2002-067262.
Audience: **u,f.** *Choice, 2003.*

McEachern, Claire (Editor) PR2983.C28 2002
The Cambridge Companion to Shakespearean Tragedy. Trade
Paper. Cambridge University Press. New York, NY. 2003. 292p.
Cambridge Companions to Literature Ser. ISBN:0-521-79359-9,
ISBN13: 978-0-521-79359-9. Dewey:822.3//3.
LCCN:2002-067262.
Audience: **u,f.** *Choice, 2003.*

Nicoll, Allardyce PH3281.K85P313
Shakespeare: An Introduction. Paper Text. Textbook Publishers.
Temecula, CA. 2003. 181p. ISBN:0-7581-7198-6, ISBN13:
978-0-7581-7198-6. Dewey:894/.51133.
Audience: **l,u.**

Novy, Marianne (Editor) PR116
Transforming Shakespeare: Contemporary Women's Re-Visions
in Literature and Performance. Trade Paper. Palgrave
Macmillan. New York, NY. 2000. 272p. ISBN:0-312-23509-7,
ISBN13: 978-0-312-23509-3. Dewey:820.9/9287/0904.
Audience: **u,f.** *Choice, 1999.*

Occhiogrosso, Frank PR3091.S3627 2002
(Editor)
Shakespeare in Performance: A Collection of Essays. Trade
Cloth. University of Delaware Press. Newark, DE. 2003. 152p.
ISBN:0-87413-776-4, ISBN13: 978-0-87413-776-7.
Dewey:792.9/5. LCCN:2002-018093.
Audience: **l,u.**

Orgel, Stephen PR2965.O74 2003
Imagining Shakespeare. Cloth over Boards. Palgrave Macmillan.
New York, NY. 2003. 192p. ISBN:1-4039-1177-0, ISBN13:
978-1-4039-1177-3. Dewey:822.3/3. LCCN:2003-051778.
Audience: **u,f.** *Choice, 2003.*

Proudfoot, Richard, et al. PR2754
The Arden Shakespeare Complete Works. Ann Thompson &
David Scott Kastan (Authors). Trade Cloth. Thomson Learning
EMEA, Ltd. London, 2000. 1352p. ISBN:1-903436-39-7,
ISBN13: 978-1-903436-39-4. Dewey:822.33.
Audience: **l,u,f.**

Richmond, Hugh Macrae PR3095.R53 2004
Shakespeare's Theatre. Trade Paper. Continuum International

Publishing Group, Ltd. London, 2005. 584p.
ISBN:0-8264-7776-3, ISBN13: 978-0-8264-7776-7.
Dewey:822.33.

Audience: **l,u.**

Shakespeare, William &   **PR2754.B4 2003**
  Bevington, David
The Complete Works of Shakespeare. Ed. 5. Trade Cloth.
Longman Publishing. Boston, MA. 2003. 2016p.
ISBN:0-321-09333-X, ISBN13: 978-0-321-09333-2.
Dewey:822.3/3. LCCN:2003-045975.

Audience: **l,u,f.**

Shaughnessy, Robert   **PR3091.S363 2000**
  (Editor)
Shakespeare in Performance. Trade Paper. Palgrave Macmillan.
New York, NY. 2000. 240p. New Casebooks Ser.
ISBN:0-312-23312-4, ISBN13: 978-0-312-23312-9.
Dewey:822.3/3. LCCN:99-086321.

Audience: **u,f.**

Smallwood, Robert (Editor)   **PR3112.P556 2004**
Players of Shakespeare 6: Essays in the Performance of
Shakespeare's History Plays. Trade Cloth. Cambridge University
Press. New York, NY. 2004. 236p. Players of Shakespeare Ser.
ISBN:0-521-84088-0, ISBN13: 978-0-521-84088-0.
Dewey:792.950941. LCCN:2005-273797.

Audience: **u,f.**

Styan, John L.   **PR3091.S79 1999**
Perspectives on Shakespeare in Performance. Paper Text. Peter
Lang Publishing, Inc. New York, NY. 2000. 183p. Studies in
Shakespeare, Vol. 11 ISBN:0-8204-4426-X, ISBN13:
978-0-8204-4426-0. Dewey:792.9/5. LCCN:98-053181.

Audience: **u,f.**

Thaler, Alwin   **PN2585.T5**
Shakespeare to Sheridan. Trade Cloth. Ayer Company
Publishers, Inc. Manchester, NH. 1972. ISBN:0-405-09025-0,
ISBN13: 978-0-405-09025-7. Dewey:792.0941.
LCCN:63-023190.

Audience: **l,u.**

Wells, Stanley & Stanton,   **PR3091.C36 2002**
  Sarah (Editors)
The Cambridge Companion to Shakespeare on Stage. Trade
Paper. Cambridge University Press. New York, NY. 2002. 338p.
Cambridge Companions to Literature Ser. ISBN:0-521-79711-X,
ISBN13: 978-0-521-79711-5. Dewey:792.9/5.
LCCN:2001-052447.

Audience: **g,l,u,f.**

Werner, Sarah   **PR3106.W47 2001**
Shakespeare and Feminist Performance: Ideology on Stage.
Paper over Boards. Routledge. New York, NY. 2001. 144p.
Accents on Shakespeare Ser. ISBN:0-415-22729-1, ISBN13:
978-0-415-22729-2. Dewey:822.3/3. LCCN:2001-018088.

Audience: **u,f.**

Worthen, W. B.   **PR3091 .W67 1997**
Shakespeare and the Authority of Performance. Trade Cloth.
Cambridge University Press. New York, NY. 1997. 265p.

ISBN:0-521-55134-X, ISBN13: 978-0-521-55134-2.
Dewey:822.3/3. LCCN:96-045571.

Audience: **u,f.** *Choice, 1998.*

Worthen, W. B.   **PR3100.W67 2003**
Shakespeare and the Force of Modern Performance. Trade
Cloth. Cambridge University Press. New York, NY. 2003. 282p.
ISBN:0-521-81030-2, ISBN13: 978-0-521-81030-2.
Dewey:792.9/5. LCCN:2002-031061.

Audience: **u,f.**

Western Drama and Theater > Periods > Restoration Drama and Theater

Behn, Aphra   **PR3317 .A19 1990**
Behn: Five Plays. Maureen Duffy (Introduction by). Trade
Paper. Methuen Publishing Ltd. London, 2004. 474p. Methuen
World Dramatists Ser. ISBN:0-413-17090-X, ISBN13:
978-0-413-17090-3. Dewey:822/.4. LCCN:92-146508.

Audience: **l,u,f.**

Fisk, Deborah Payne   **PR1266.F675 2005**
  (Editor)
Four Restoration Libertine Plays. Trade Paper, Perfect. Oxford
University Press, Inc. New York, NY. 2005. 468p. Oxford
World's Classics Ser. ISBN:0-19-283294-8, ISBN13:
978-0-19-283294-8. Dewey:822/.408. LCCN:2004-027977.

Audience: **l,u,f.**

Fiske, Deborah Payne   **PR691.C35 2000**
  (Editor)
The Cambridge Companion to English Restoration Theatre.
Cloth Text. Cambridge University Press. New York, NY. 2000.
322p. Companions to Literature Ser. ISBN:0-521-58215-6,
ISBN13: 978-0-521-58215-5. Dewey:822/.409.
LCCN:99-015230.

Audience: **g.** *Choice, 2001.*

Griffiths, Trevor (Editor)   **PR1248**
Restoration Comedy. Trade Paper. Theatre Communications
Group, Inc. New York, NY. 2005. 352p. ISBN:1-85459-848-1,
ISBN13: 978-1-85459-848-6. Dewey:822.4/08017.

Audience: **l,u,f.**

Hotson, Leslie   **PN2596.L6S49**
The Commonwealth and Restoration Stage. Paper Text.
Textbook Publishers. Temecula, CA. 2003. 424p.
ISBN:0-7581-4432-6, ISBN13: 978-0-7581-4432-4.
Dewey:792.094212.

Audience: **g.** *B*

Hughes, Derek & Todd,   **PR3317.Z5C36 2004**
  Janet (Editors)
The Cambridge Companion to Aphra Behn. Trade Paper,
Perfect. Cambridge University Press. New York, NY. 2004.
274p. Cambridge Companions to Literature Ser.
ISBN:0-521-52720-1, ISBN13: 978-0-521-52720-0.
Dewey:822/.4. LCCN:2004-049740.

Audience: **g,l,u,f.** *Choice, 2005.*

Lyons, Paddy & Morgan,   **PR1266**
  Fideles (Editors)
Female Playwrights of the Restoration: Five Comedies. Ed. 2.
Paddy Lyons & Fideles Morgan (Introduction by). Trade Paper.
Tuttle Publishing. Boston, MA. 1994. 365p.
ISBN:0-460-87427-6, ISBN13: 978-0-460-87427-4.
Dewey:822.40809287.

                Audience: **l,u,f.**

Orgel, Stephen   **PN2592**
The Illusion of Power: Political Theater in the English
Renaissance. Trade Paper. University of California Press.
Berkeley, CA. 1991. 95p. Quantum Bks. ISBN:0-520-02741-8,
ISBN13: 978-0-520-02741-1. Dewey:792/.0942.
LCCN:73-080827.

             Audience: **u,f.** *B*

Western Drama and Theater > Periods > Neoclassical Drama and Theater

Corneille, Pierre   **PS758.A8**
Chief Plays. Paper Text. Textbook Publishers. Temecula, CA.
2003. 386p. ISBN:0-7581-5803-3, ISBN13: 978-0-7581-5803-1.
Dewey:811/.2.

             Audience: **l,u,f.** *B*

Corneille, Pierre, et al.   **PQ1220**
Landmarks of French Classical Drama. Jean Racine, Moliere,
Marivaux & Beaumarchais (Authors), David Bryer, Robert D.
MacDonald, Christopher Hampton & John Fowles (Translators),
David Bradby (Introduction by). Trade Paper. Heinemann.
Portsmouth, NH. 1991. 393p. ISBN:0-413-63100-1, ISBN13:
978-0-413-63100-8. Dewey:842.4/08.

             Audience: **l,u,f.**

Hill, Philip G. (Editor)   **PN6111 .O87**
Our Dramatic Heritage: The 18th Century, Vol. 3. Trade Cloth.
Fairleigh Dickinson University Press. Cranbury, NJ. 1987.
ISBN:0-8386-3108-8, ISBN13: 978-0-8386-3108-9.
Dewey:808.82. LCCN:81-065294.

             Audience: **l,u,f.**

Howarth, William D.   **PN2621.F73 1997**
  (Editor)
French Theatre in the Neo-Classical Era: 1550-1789. Trade
Cloth. Cambridge University Press. New York, NY. 1997. 760p.
Theatre in Europe Ser., :A Documentary History
ISBN:0-521-23013-6, ISBN13: 978-0-521-23013-1.
Dewey:792/.0944/0903. LCCN:96-013074.

             Audience: **l,u,f.**

Racine, Jean   **PR3071.B6**
Three Plays: Andromache, Britannicus [and] Phaedra. Paper
Text. Textbook Publishers. Temecula, CA. 2003. 183p.
ISBN:0-7581-2580-1, ISBN13: 978-0-7581-2580-4.
Dewey:822.33.

             Audience: **l,u,f.**

Vince, Ronald W.   **PN1841**
Neoclassical Theatre: A Historiographical Handbook. Cloth Text.
Greenwood Publishing Group, Inc. Portsmouth, NH. 1988. 239p.
ISBN:0-313-24445-6, ISBN13: 978-0-313-24445-2.
Dewey:792/.09. LCCN:87-017803.

        Audience: **g.** *Choice, 1988.*

Western Drama and Theater > Periods > Romanticism

Baines, Paul & Burns,   **PR1271.F59 2000**
  Edward (Editors)
Five Romantic Plays, 1768-1821. Trade Paper. Oxford
University Press, Inc. New York, NY. 2000. 432p. Oxford
World's Classics Ser. ISBN:0-19-283316-2, ISBN13:
978-0-19-283316-7. Dewey:822/.6080145. LCCN:00-699989.

             Audience: **l,u,f.**

Cox, Jeffrey N. & Gamer,   **PR1271.B72 2003**
  Michael (Editors)
The Broadview Anthology of Romantic Drama. Trade Paper.
Broadview Press. Peterborough, ON. 2003. 432p. Broadview
Anthologies of English Literature Ser. ISBN:1-55111-298-1,
ISBN13: 978-1-55111-298-5. Dewey:822/.7080145.
LCCN:2003-446769.

             Audience: **l,u,f.**

Finkel, Alicia   **PN2087.G7**
Romantic Stages: Set and Costume Design in Victorian England.
Trade Paper, Perfect. McFarland & Company, Incorporated
Publishers. Jefferson, NC. 2005. 215p. ISBN:0-7864-2336-6,
ISBN13: 978-0-7864-2336-1. Dewey:792/.025/0942.
LCCN:96-000639.

        Audience: **u,f.** *Choice, 1996.*

Finkel, Alicia   **PN2087.G7F56 1996**
Romantic Stages: Set and Costume Design in Victorian England.
Cloth Text. McFarland & Company, Incorporated Publishers.
Jefferson, NC. 1996. 215p. ISBN:0-7864-0234-2, ISBN13:
978-0-7864-0234-2. Dewey:792/.025/0942. LCCN:96-639.

        Audience: **l,u,f.** *Choice, 1996.*

Gillespie, Gerald (Editor)   **PN1851.R66 1994**
Romantic Drama. Library Binding. John Benjamins Publishing
Company. Philadelphia, PA. 1993. 516p. Comparative History of
Literatures in European Languages Ser., Vol. No. 9
ISBN:1-55619-600-8, ISBN13: 978-1-55619-600-3.
Dewey:809.2/9145. LCCN:93-034838.

             Audience: **l,u,f.**

Goethe, Johann Wolfgang   **PT2026.F2M84 2004**
  von & Mueller, Carl Richard
Faust: Parts One and Two. Trade Paper. Smith and Kraus
Publishers, Inc. Lyme, NH. 2005. 640p. ISBN:1-57525-360-7,
ISBN13: 978-1-57525-360-2. Dewey:832/.6.
LCCN:2004-045378.

             Audience: **l,u,f.**

Goethe, Johann Wolfgang   **PT2026.A5 1993**
  von
Plays: Egmont, Iphigenia in Tauris, Torquato Tasso. Frank G.
Ryder (Introduction by). Trade Paper. Continuum International
Publishing Group, Ltd. London, 1992. 276p. German Library,
Vol. 20 ISBN:0-8264-0717-X, ISBN13: 978-0-8264-0717-7.
Dewey:832/.6. LCCN:92-025103.

                                              Audience: **u,f.**

Hill, Philip G. (Editor)   **PN6111 .O87**
Our Dramatic Heritage: Romanticism and Realism. Trade Cloth.
Fairleigh Dickinson University Press. Cranbury, NJ. 1989. 504p.
ISBN:0-8386-3267-X, ISBN13: 978-0-8386-3267-3.
Dewey:808.82. LCCN:81-065294.

                                              Audience: **l,u,f.**

Powell, Kerry (Editor)   **PN2594**
The Cambridge Companion to Victorian and Edwardian Theatre.
Trade Cloth. Cambridge University Press. New York, NY. 2004.
308p. Cambridge Companions to Literature Ser.
ISBN:0-521-79157-X, ISBN13: 978-0-521-79157-1.
Dewey:792/.0942/09034. LCCN:2002-041552.
                           Audience: **g,l,u,f.** *Choice, 2004.*

Von Kleist, Heinrich   **PT2378.A2**
Plays. Trade Paper. Theatre Communications Group, Inc. New
York, NY. 2000. 259p. Absolute Classics Ser.
ISBN:1-84002-123-3, ISBN13: 978-1-84002-123-3.
Dewey:832/.6.

                                              Audience: **l,u,f.**

Western Drama and Theater > Periods > Realism

Alexander, Doris   **PS3529.N5Z555 1992**
Eugene O'Neill's Creative Struggle: The Decisive Decade,
1924-1933. Trade Cloth. Pennsylvania State University Press.
University Park, PA. 1992. 384p. ISBN:0-271-00813-X,
ISBN13: 978-0-271-00813-4. Dewey:812/.52 B.
LCCN:91-029976.
                               Audience: **l,u,f.** *Choice, 1992.*

Bigsby, Christopher   **PS3525.I5156Z5445**
Arthur Miller: A Critical Study. Trade Paper. Cambridge
University Press. New York, NY. 2004. 524p.
ISBN:0-521-60553-9, ISBN13: 978-0-521-60553-3.
Dewey:812/.52 B. LCCN:2004-045813.
                                              Audience: **l,u,f.**

Black, Cheryl   **PN2297.P7B58 2002**
The Women of Provincetown, 1915-1922. Trade Cloth.
University of Alabama Press. Tuscaloosa, AL. 2001. 273p.
ISBN:0-8173-1112-2, ISBN13: 978-0-8173-1112-4.
Dewey:792/.082/0974492. LCCN:2001-003850.
                               Audience: **u,f.** *Choice, 2002.*

Demastes, William W.   **PS338**
Beyond Naturalism: A New Realism in American Theatre. Trade
Cloth. Greenwood Publishing Group, Inc. Portsmouth, NH.
1988. 182p. Contributions in Drama and Theatre Studies Ser.,

No. 27 ISBN:0-313-26320-5, ISBN13: 978-0-313-26320-0.
Dewey:812/.54/0912. LCCN:88-017787.
                                    Audience: **l,u,f.** *Choice, 1989.*

Demastes, William W.   **PS338.R42R43 1996**
  (Editor)
Realism and the American Dramatic Tradition. Trade Paper.
University of Alabama Press. Tuscaloosa, AL. 1996. 312p.
ISBN:0-8173-0837-7, ISBN13: 978-0-8173-0837-7.
Dewey:812/.50912. LCCN:96-004682.
                                    Audience: **l,u,f.** *Choice, 1997.*

Dickinson, Thomas H.   **PN6112.D5**
Chief Contemporary Dramatists: Twenty-Two Plays from the
Recent Drama of England, Ireland, America, Germany, France,
Belgium, Norway, Sweden and Russia. Library Binding. Richard
West. Philadelphia, PA. 1979. ISBN:0-8492-4207-X, ISBN13:
978-0-8492-4207-6. Dewey:808.82.

                                              Audience: **l,u,f.**

Dickinson, Thomas H.   **PN6112.D52**
Chief Contemporary Dramatists. Trade Paper. Kessinger
Publishing, LLC. Whitefish, MT. 2005. ISBN:1-4179-8690-5,
ISBN13: 978-1-4179-8690-3. Dewey:808.82.

                                              Audience: **l,u,f.**

Dickinson, Thomas H.   **PN6112.D52**
  (Editor)
Chief Contemporary Dramatists, Second Series: Eighteen Plays
from the Recent Drama of England, Ireland, America, France,
Germany, Austria, Italy, Spain, Russia, and Scandinavia. Library
Binding. Darby Books. Darby, PA. 1985. 734p.
ISBN:0-317-17328-6, ISBN13: 978-0-317-17328-4.
Dewey:808.82/041.

                                              Audience: **l,u,f.**

Egan, Leona Rust   **PS3529.N5Z6294 1994**
Provincetown as a Stage: Provincetown, the Provincetown
Players, and the Discovery of Eugene O'Neill. Trade Cloth.
Parnassus Imprints. Marstons Mills, MA. 1994. 296p.
ISBN:0-940160-57-9, ISBN13: 978-0-940160-57-6.
Dewey:792.097. LCCN:93-087449.

                                              Audience: **l,u,f.**

Fleche, Anne   **PS338.R42F58 1997**
Mimetic Disillusion: Eugene O'Neill, Tennessee Williams and
U. S. Dramatic Realism. Trade Paper. University of Alabama
Press. Tuscaloosa, AL. 1997. 152p. ISBN:0-8173-0838-5,
ISBN13: 978-0-8173-0838-4. Dewey:812/.5209.
LCCN:96-024510.
                                    Audience: **l,u,f.** *Choice, 1997.*

Hill, Philip G. (Editor)   **PN6111 .O87**
Our Dramatic Heritage: Romanticism and Realism. Trade Cloth.
Fairleigh Dickinson University Press. Cranbury, NJ. 1989. 504p.
ISBN:0-8386-3267-X, ISBN13: 978-0-8386-3267-3.
Dewey:808.82. LCCN:81-065294.

                                              Audience: **l,u,f.**

Hill, Philip G. (Editor)   **PN6111 .O87**
Our Dramatic Heritage: Reactions to Realism, Vol. 5. Trade

Cloth. Fairleigh Dickinson University Press. Cranbury, NJ. 1991. 384p. ISBN:0-8386-3411-7, ISBN13: 978-0-8386-3411-0. Dewey:808.82. LCCN:81-065294.

Audience: **l,u,f.**

Ibsen, Henrik   **PT8854**
Ibsen's Selected Plays. Trade Paper. W. W. Norton & Company, Inc. New York, NY. 2003. 612p. A Norton Critical Edition Ser. ISBN:0-393-92404-1, ISBN13: 978-0-393-92404-6. Dewey:839.8/226. LCCN:2003-051293.

Audience: **l,u,f.**

Ibsen, Henrik   **PT8854**
The Complete Major Prose Plays. Rolf Fjelde (Translator), Henrik Ibsen (Illustrator), Rolf Fjelde (Foreword by). Trade Paper. Penguin Group (USA) Inc. New York, NY. 1978. 1152p. Plume Book Ser. ISBN:0-452-26205-4, ISBN13: 978-0-452-26205-8. Dewey:839.8. LCCN:78-050714.

Audience: **l,u,f.**

Lacey, Stephen   **PR739.R37L33 1995**
British Realist Theatre: The New Wave in Its Context, 1956-1965. Paper over Boards. Routledge. New York, NY. 1995. 216p. ISBN:0-415-07782-6, ISBN13: 978-0-415-07782-8. Dewey:792/.0941. LCCN:94-044677.

Audience: **l,u,f.** *Choice, 1996.*

MacGowan, Kenneth   **PN2570**
Continental Stagecraft. Paper Text. Classic Books. Murrieta, CA. 2001. 233p. ISBN:0-7426-9204-3, ISBN13: 978-0-7426-9204-6. Dewey:792.094.

Audience: **l,u,f.** *B*

Mamet, David   **PS3545.I5365**
Glengarry Glen Ross. Trade Paper. Grove/Atlantic, Inc. New York, NY. 1984. 112p. ISBN:0-8021-3091-7, ISBN13: 978-0-8021-3091-4. Dewey:812.5/4. LCCN:83-049380.

Audience: **g,l,u,f.**

Manheim, Michael   **PN1851.M25 2002**
Vital Contradictions: Characterization in the Plays of Ibsen, Strindberg, Chekhov, and O'Neill. Trade Cloth. Peter Lang Publishing, Inc. New York, NY. 2002. 208p. Dramaturgies Ser., No. 6 ISBN:90-5201-991-6, ISBN13: 978-90-5201-991-8. Dewey:809.2/927. LCCN:2002-075251.

Audience: **l,u,f.**

Murphy, Brenda   **PS338.R42 M87 1987**
American Realism and American Drama, 1880-1940. Albert Gelpi & Ross Posnock (Contribution by). Trade Cloth. Cambridge University Press. New York, NY. 1987. 248p. Studies in American Literature and Culture, No. 22 ISBN:0-521-32711-3, ISBN13: 978-0-521-32711-4. Dewey:812/.52/0912. LCCN:86-013694.

Audience: **l,u,f.** *Choice, 1987.*

Murphy, Brenda   **PN2277**
Provincetown Players and the Culture of Modernity. Don B. Wilmeth (Contribution by). Trade Cloth. Cambridge University Press. New York, NY. 2005. 302p. Cambridge Studies in

American Theatre and Drama Ser., Vol. 23 ISBN:0-521-83852-5, ISBN13: 978-0-521-83852-8. Dewey:792.0974492. LCCN:2006-296175.

Audience: **u,f.** *Choice, 2006.*

Osborne, John   **PR6066.I53**
John Osborne Plays 1: Look Back in Anger; Epitaph for George Dillion; the World of Paul... Trade Paper. Faber & Faber, Inc. New York, NY. 1996. 289p. ISBN:0-571-17766-2, ISBN13: 978-0-571-17766-0. Dewey:822.9/14.

Audience: **g,l,u,f.**

Powell, Kerry (Editor)   **PN2594**
The Cambridge Companion to Victorian and Edwardian Theatre. Trade Cloth. Cambridge University Press. New York, NY. 2004. 308p. Cambridge Companions to Literature Ser. ISBN:0-521-79157-X, ISBN13: 978-0-521-79157-1. Dewey:792/.0942/09034. LCCN:2002-041552.

Audience: **g,l,u,f.** *Choice, 2004.*

Roose-Evans, James   **PN2189**
Experimental Theatre: From Stanislavsky to Peter Brook. Ed. 4. Trade Paper. Routledge. New York, NY. 1996. 260p. ISBN:0-415-00963-4, ISBN13: 978-0-415-00963-8. Dewey:792/.022.

Audience: **l,u,f.** *B*

Sarlos, Robert K.   **PN2297.P7.S27 1982**
Jig Cook and the Provincetown Players: Theatre in Ferment. Library Binding. University of Massachusetts Press. Amherst, MA. 1982. 280p. ISBN:0-87023-349-1, ISBN13: 978-0-87023-349-4. Dewey:792/.09744/92. LCCN:81-016104.

Audience: **l,u,f.** *B*

Shaw, George Bernard   **PR5360**
Bernard Shaw's the Quintessence of Ibsenism and Related Writings. Paper Text. Classic Books. Murrieta, CA. 2001. Collected Works of Bernard Shaw ISBN:0-7426-8213-7, ISBN13: 978-0-7426-8213-9. Dewey:822.

Audience: **u,f.**

Shaw, George Bernard   **PN2638.B5A3**
Plays: Pleasant and Pleasant. Paper Text. Classic Books. Murrieta, CA. 2001. Collected Works of Bernard Shaw ISBN:0-7426-8216-1, ISBN13: 978-0-7426-8216-0. Dewey:792.0924.

Audience: **l,u,f.**

Shaw, George Bernard   **PN2287.A457M37**
Plays and Players: Essays on the Theatre. Paper Text. Textbook Publishers. Temecula, CA. 2003. 350p. ISBN:0-7581-7268-0, ISBN13: 978-0-7581-7268-6. Dewey:792/.028/092.

Audience: **l,u,f.**

Shaw, George Bernard   **PR5363**
Three Plays for Puritans by Bernard Shaw Being the Third Volume of His Collected Plays. Trade Paper. Kessinger Publishing, LLC. Whitefish, MT. 2004. ISBN:1-4179-1317-7, ISBN13: 978-1-4179-1317-6. Dewey:822/.912.

Audience: **l,u.**

Styan, John L.　　　　　　**PN1861.S76 1983**
Modern Drama in Theory and Practice: Realism and Naturalism,
Vol. 1. Trade Paper. Cambridge University Press. New York,
NY. 1983. 217p. ISBN:0-521-29628-5, ISBN13:
978-0-521-29628-1. Dewey:809.2. LCCN:79-015947.
　　　　　　　　　　　　　　　　Audience: **l,u,f.**

Timberlake, Craig　　　　　　**PN2587.W532**
The Bishop of Broadway: The Life and Work of David Belasco.
Paper Text. Textbook Publishers. Temecula, CA. 2003. 291p.
ISBN:0-7581-9867-1, ISBN13: 978-0-7581-9867-9.
Dewey:792/.0942.
　　　　　　　　　　　　　　　　Audience: **l,u,f.**

Tornqvist, Egil　　　　　　**PS3529.N5**
Eugene O'Neill: A Playwright's Theatre. Paper Text. McFarland
& Company, Incorporated Publishers. Jefferson, NC. 2004.
268p. ISBN:0-7864-1713-7, ISBN13: 978-0-7864-1713-1.
Dewey:812/.52. LCCN:2003-025325.
　　　　　　　　　Audience: **l,u,f.** *Choice, 2004.*

Waxman, Samuel M.　　　　　　**PN2636.P4T75**
Antoine and the Theatre Libre. Trade Cloth. Ayer Company
Publishers, Inc. Manchester, NH. 1972. ISBN:0-405-09056-0,
ISBN13: 978-0-405-09056-1. Dewey:792.0944361.
LCCN:63-023192.
　　　　　　　　　　　　　　　　Audience: **l,u,f.**

Winter, William　　　　　　**PN2287.B4 W5 1970**
Life of David Belasco, Set. Trade Cloth. Ayer Company
Publishers, Inc. Manchester, NH. 1977. Select Bibliographies
Reprint Ser. ISBN:0-8369-5202-2, ISBN13: 978-0-8369-5202-5.
Dewey:792/.0924. LCCN:72-107837.
　　　　　　　　　　　　　　　　Audience: **g.**

Worrall, Nick　　　　　　**PN2726.M62M73 1996**
The Moscow Art Theatre. Paper over Boards. Routledge. New
York, NY. 1996. 256p. Theatre Production Studies
ISBN:0-415-05598-9, ISBN13: 978-0-415-05598-7.
Dewey:792.9/5/0947312. LCCN:95-045724.
　　　　　　　　　　　　　　　　Audience: **l,u,f.**

Western Drama and Theater > Periods > Modernism

Alexander, Doris　　　　　　**PS3529.N5Z555 1992**
Eugene O'Neill's Creative Struggle: The Decisive Decade,
1924-1933. Trade Cloth. Pennsylvania State University Press.
University Park, PA. 1992. 384p. ISBN:0-271-00813-X,
ISBN13: 978-0-271-00813-4. Dewey:812/.52 B.
LCCN:91-029976.
　　　　　　　　　Audience: **l,u,f.** *Choice, 1992.*

Beckett, Samuel　　　　　　**PR6003.E282**
Samuel Beckett: Waiting for Godot-Endgame. Peter Boxall
(Editor). Trade Paper. Palgrave Macmillan. New York, NY.
2003. 206p. Readers' Guides to Essential Criticism Ser.
ISBN:1-84046-082-2, ISBN13: 978-1-84046-082-7.
Dewey:822.912.
　　　　　　　　　　　　　　Audience: **g,l,u,f.**

Black, Cheryl　　　　　　**PN2297.P7B58 2002**
The Women of Provincetown, 1915-1922. Trade Cloth.
University of Alabama Press. Tuscaloosa, AL. 2001. 273p.
ISBN:0-8173-1112-2, ISBN13: 978-0-8173-1112-4.
Dewey:792/.082/0974492. LCCN:2001-003850.
　　　　　　　　　Audience: **u,f.** *Choice, 2002.*

Brecht, Bertolt　　　　　　**PT2603.R397A27 1997**
Plays: The Threepenny Opera, the Measures Taken, Galileo,
Mother Courage and Her Children, Baal. Reinhold Grimm &
Caroline Molina y Vedia (Editors). Trade Cloth. Continuum
International Publishing Group, Ltd. London, 1999. 324p.
German Library, Vol. 75 ISBN:0-8264-0736-6, ISBN13:
978-0-8264-0736-8. Dewey:832/.912. LCCN:76-020409.
　　　　　　　　　　　　　　　　Audience: **l,u,f.**

Bristol, Michael D. &　　　　　　**PR3100.S52 2001**
　McLuskie, Kathleen (Editors)
Shakespeare and Modern Theatre: The Performance of
Modernity. Paper over Boards. Routledge. New York, NY. 2001.
224p. Accents on Shakespeare Ser. ISBN:0-415-21984-1,
ISBN13: 978-0-415-21984-6. Dewey:792.9/5. LCCN:00-065307.
　　　　　　　　　　　　　　　　Audience: **u,f.**

Brustein, Robert　　　　　　**PN2189.B7 1991**
The Theatre of Revolt: Studies in Modern Drama from Ibsen to
Genet. Trade Paper. Ivan R. Dee Publisher. Blue Ridge Summit,
PA. 1991. 435p. ISBN:0-929587-53-7, ISBN13:
978-0-929587-53-0. Dewey:809.2/04. LCCN:90-023644.
　　　　　　　　　　　　　　　　Audience: **l,u.**

Carter, Huntly　　　　　　**PN2658.R4C3**
The Theatre of Max Reinhardt. Paper Text. Classic Books.
Murrieta, CA. 2001. 332p. ISBN:0-7426-9203-5, ISBN13:
978-0-7426-9203-9. Dewey:792.0943.
　　　　　　　　　　　　　　　　Audience: **l,u,f.**

Cheney, Sheldon　　　　　　**PR9199.2.R43**
The Art Theatre: A Discussion of Its Ideals, Its Organization,
and Its Promise As a Corrective for Present Evils in the
Commercial Theatre. Paper Text. Classic Books. Murrieta, CA.
2001. 249p. ISBN:0-7426-9207-8, ISBN13: 978-0-7426-9207-7.
Dewey:813/.3.
　　　　　　　　　　　　　　　　Audience: **l,u,f.**

Cheney, Sheldon　　　　　　**PN2189.C5**
The New Movement in the Theatre. Paper Text. Classic Books.
Murrieta, CA. 2001. 303p. ISBN:0-7426-9195-0, ISBN13:
978-0-7426-9195-7. Dewey:792/.08.
　　　　　　　　　　　　　　　　Audience: **l,u.**

Craig, Edward Gordon　　　　　　**PN2091.S8**
On the Art of the Theatre. Paper Text. Textbook Publishers.
Temecula, CA. 2003. 295p. ISBN:0-7581-3150-X, ISBN13:
978-0-7581-3150-8. Dewey:792.
　　　　　　　　　　　　　Audience: **l,u,f.** *B*

Dickinson, Thomas H.　　　　　　**PN6112.D5**
Chief Contemporary Dramatists: Twenty-Two Plays from the
Recent Drama of England, Ireland, America, Germany, France,

Belgium, Norway, Sweden and Russia. Library Binding. Richard West. Philadelphia, PA. 1979. ISBN:0-8492-4207-X, ISBN13: 978-0-8492-4207-6. Dewey:808.82.

Audience: **l,u,f.**

Dickinson, Thomas H. PN6112.D52
Chief Contemporary Dramatists. Trade Paper. Kessinger Publishing, LLC. Whitefish, MT. 2005. ISBN:1-4179-8690-5, ISBN13: 978-1-4179-8690-3. Dewey:808.82.

Audience: **l,u,f.**

Dickinson, Thomas H. PN6112.D52
  (Editor)
Chief Contemporary Dramatists, Second Series: Eighteen Plays from the Recent Drama of England, Ireland, America, France, Germany, Austria, Italy, Spain, Russia, and Scandinavia. Library Binding. Darby Books. Darby, PA. 1985. 734p. ISBN:0-317-17328-6, ISBN13: 978-0-317-17328-4. Dewey:808.82/041.

Audience: **l,u,f.**

Dodgson, Elyse PT2685.E5
German Plays. Anna Langhoff, Dea Loher, Klaus Pohl & D. Rust (Contribution by). Trade Paper. Theatre Communications Group, Inc. New York, NY. 1998. 208p. International Collection ISBN:1-85459-338-2, ISBN13: 978-1-85459-338-2. Dewey:832.9/14.

Audience: **u,f.**

Egan, Leona Rust PS3529.N5Z6294 1994
Provincetown as a Stage: Provincetown, the Provincetown Players, and the Discovery of Eugene O'Neill. Trade Cloth. Parnassus Imprints. Marstons Mills, MA. 1994. 296p. ISBN:0-940160-57-9, ISBN13: 978-0-940160-57-6. Dewey:792.097. LCCN:93-087449.

Audience: **l,u,f.**

Fleche, Anne PS338.R42F58 1997
Mimetic Disillusion: Eugene O'Neill, Tennessee Williams and U. S. Dramatic Realism. Trade Paper. University of Alabama Press. Tuscaloosa, AL. 1997. 152p. ISBN:0-8173-0838-5, ISBN13: 978-0-8173-0838-4. Dewey:812/.5209. LCCN:96-024510.

Audience: **l,u,f.** *Choice, 1997.*

Gewirtz, Arthur & Kolb, PS351
  James J. (Editors)
Experimenters, Rebels and Disparate Voices: The Theatre of the 1920s Celebrates American Diversity. Trade Cloth. Greenwood Publishing Group, Inc. Portsmouth, NH. 2003. 216p. Contributions in Drama and Theatre Studies, Vol. 99 ISBN:0-313-32466-2, ISBN13: 978-0-313-32466-6. Dewey:812/.5209920693. LCCN:2002-072543.

Audience: **l,u,f.** *Choice, 2004.*

Gilman, Richard PN1851.G5 1999
The Making of Modern Drama: A Study of Bhuchner, Ibsen, Strindberg, Chekhov, Pirandello, Brecht, Handke. Trade Paper. Yale University Press. Cumberland, RI. 2000. 320p. ISBN:0-300-07902-8, ISBN13: 978-0-300-07902-9. Dewey:809.2/0094. LCCN:99-045334.

Audience: **u,f.**

Graver, David NX456.5.M64G73 1995
The Aesthetics of Disturbance: Anti-Art in Avant-Garde Drama. Trade Cloth. University of Michigan Press. Chicago, IL. 1995. 272p. Theater Ser., :Theory - Text - Performance ISBN:0-472-10507-8, ISBN13: 978-0-472-10507-6. Dewey:700/.1. LCCN:95-016289.

Audience: **u,f.** *Choice, 1996.*

Grossvogel, David I. PN1861 .G7 1975
Four Playwrights and a Postscript: Brecht, Ionesco, Beckett, Genet. Trade Cloth. Greenwood Publishing Group, Inc. Portsmouth, NH. 1976. 209p. ISBN:0-8371-8438-X, ISBN13: 978-0-8371-8438-8. Dewey:809.2/04. LCCN:75-027654.

Audience: **l,u,f.** *B*

Harrison, Elizabeth J. PR478.M6U53 1997
  (Editor)
Unmanning Modernism: Gendered Re-Readings. Peterson, Shirley (Editor). University of Tennessee Press. 1997. ISBN:0-87049-985-8, ISBN13: 978-0-87049-985-2.

Audience: **u,f.**

Hill, Philip G. (Editor) PN6111 .O87
Our Dramatic Heritage: Reactions to Realism, Vol. 5. Trade Cloth. Fairleigh Dickinson University Press. Cranbury, NJ. 1991. 384p. ISBN:0-8386-3411-7, ISBN13: 978-0-8386-3411-0. Dewey:808.82. LCCN:81-065294.

Audience: **l,u,f.**

Hill, Philip G. (Editor) PN6111 .O87
Our Dramatic Heritage: Expressing the Inexpressible, Vol. 6. Trade Cloth. Fairleigh Dickinson University Press. Cranbury, NJ. 1992. 336p. ISBN:0-8386-3421-4, ISBN13: 978-0-8386-3421-9. Dewey:809.2. LCCN:81-065294.

Audience: **l,u,f.**

Hostetter, Anthony PN2656.B42G764 2003
Max Reinhardt's Grosses Schauspielhaus: Its Artistic Goals, Planning, and Operation, 1910-1933. Trade Cloth. Edwin Mellen Press, The. Lewiston, NY. 2003. 224p. Studies in Theatre Arts, Vol. 20 ISBN:0-7734-6802-1, ISBN13: 978-0-7734-6802-3. Dewey:330 /945/58. LCCN:2003-042163.

Audience: **l,u,f.**

Ibsen, Henrik PT8854
Ibsen's Selected Plays. Trade Paper. W. W. Norton & Company, Inc. New York, NY. 2003. 612p. A Norton Critical Edition Ser. ISBN:0-393-92404-1, ISBN13: 978-0-393-92404-6. Dewey:839.8/226. LCCN:2003-051293.

Audience: **l,u,f.**

Ibsen, Henrik PT8854
The Complete Major Prose Plays. Rolf Fjelde (Translator), Henrik Ibsen (Illustrator), Rolf Fjelde (Foreword by). Trade Paper. Penguin Group (USA) Inc. New York, NY. 1978. 1152p. Plume Book Ser. ISBN:0-452-26205-4, ISBN13: 978-0-452-26205-8. Dewey:839.8. LCCN:78-050714.

Audience: **l,u,f.**

Innes, Christopher   PN2598.C85I562 1998
Edward Gordon Craig: A Vision of Theatre. Ed. 2. Trade Paper.
Gordon & Breach Publishing Group. New York, NY. 1998.
352p. Contemporary Theatre Studies ISBN:90-5702-125-0,
ISBN13: 978-90-5702-125-1. Dewey:792/.0233/092.
LCCN:99-521846.

Audience: **l,u,f.**

MacGowan, Kenneth   PN2570
Continental Stagecraft. Paper Text. Classic Books. Murrieta, CA.
2001. 233p. ISBN:0-7426-9204-3, ISBN13: 978-0-7426-9204-6.
Dewey:792.094.

Audience: **l,u,f.** *B*

Manheim, Michael   PN1851.M25 2002
Vital Contradictions: Characterization in the Plays of Ibsen,
Strindberg, Chekhov, and O'Neill. Trade Cloth. Peter Lang
Publishing, Inc. New York, NY. 2002. 208p. Dramaturgies Ser.,
No. 6 ISBN:90-5201-991-6, ISBN13: 978-90-5201-991-8.
Dewey:809.2/927. LCCN:2002-075251.

Audience: **l,u,f.**

Marker, F. J. & Innes,   PN1851.M64 1998
  Christopher (Editors)
Modernism in European Drama: Ibsen, Strindberg, Pirandello,
Beckett: Essays from Modern Drama. Cloth over Boards.
University of Toronto Press. Toronto, ON. 1998. 336p.
ISBN:0-8020-4399-2, ISBN13: 978-0-8020-4399-3.
Dewey:809.2. LCCN:99-170702.

Audience: **l,u.**

Murphy, Brenda   PN2277
Provincetown Players and the Culture of Modernity. Don B.
Wilmeth (Contribution by). Trade Cloth. Cambridge University
Press. New York, NY. 2005. 302p. Cambridge Studies in
American Theatre and Drama Ser., Vol. 23 ISBN:0-521-83852-5,
ISBN13: 978-0-521-83852-8. Dewey:792.0974492.
LCCN:2006-296175.

Audience: **u,f.** *Choice, 2006.*

Pirandello, Luigi   PQ4835.I7
Three Plays by Luigi Pirandello: Six Characters in Search of an
Author; Henry IV and Right You Are. Trade Paper. Kessinger
Publishing, LLC. Whitefish, MT. 2005. ISBN:1-4179-1825-X,
ISBN13: 978-1-4179-1825-6. Dewey:852.89.

Audience: **l,u,f.**

Roose-Evans, James   PN2189
Experimental Theatre: From Stanislavsky to Peter Brook. Ed. 4.
Trade Paper. Routledge. New York, NY. 1996. 260p.
ISBN:0-415-00963-4, ISBN13: 978-0-415-00963-8.
Dewey:792/.022.

Audience: **l,u,f.** *B*

Sarlos, Robert K.   PN2297.P7.S27 1982
Jig Cook and the Provincetown Players: Theatre in Ferment.
Library Binding. University of Massachusetts Press. Amherst,
MA. 1982. 280p. ISBN:0-87023-349-1, ISBN13:
978-0-87023-349-4. Dewey:792/.09744/92. LCCN:81-016104.

Audience: **l,u,f.** *B*

Sayler, Oliver M. (Editor)   PN2658.R4
Max Reinhardt and His Theatre. Trade Cloth. Ayer Company
Publishers, Inc. Manchester, NH. 1972. 381p.
ISBN:0-405-08926-0, ISBN13: 978-0-405-08926-8.
Dewey:792/.0924 B. LCCN:68-020245.

Audience: **l,u.**

Sokel, Walter H. (Editor)   PT1258.A57 1984
Anthology of German Expressionist Drama. Book, Other.
Cornell University Press. Ithaca, NY. 1984. 336p.
ISBN:0-8014-9296-3, ISBN13: 978-0-8014-9296-9.
Dewey:832/.912/0801. LCCN:84-045197.

Audience: **l,u,f.**

Strindberg, August   PT9811.A3S635 1997
Strindberg: Other Sides: Seven Plays. Joseph Martin
(Translator). Paper Text. Peter Lang Publishing, Inc. New York,
NY. 1998. 382p. ISBN:0-8204-3691-7, ISBN13:
978-0-8204-3691-3. Dewey:839.72/6. LCCN:96-054508.

Audience: **u,f.**

Strindberg, August   PT9811.A3
Plays Three. Michael Meyer (Translator). Trade Paper. Methuen
Publishing Ltd. London, 2004. Methuen World Dramatists Ser.
ISBN:0-413-64840-0, ISBN13: 978-0-413-64840-2.
Dewey:839.7/26.

Audience: **u,f.**

Strindberg, August   PT9811.A3M4
Plays Two. Michael Meyer (Translator, Introduction by). Trade
Paper. Methuen Publishing Ltd. London, 2004. Methuen World
Classics Ser. ISBN:0-413-49750-X, ISBN13:
978-0-413-49750-5. Dewey:839.72.

Audience: **u,f.**

Strindberg, August   PT9811.A3
Strindberg: Plays One. Michael Meyer (Translator, Introduction
by). Trade Paper. Heinemann. Portsmouth, NH. 2004. 192p.
Methuen World Dramatists Ser. ISBN:0-413-52160-5, ISBN13:
978-0-413-52160-6. Dewey:839.7/2/6.

Audience: **u,f.**

Styan, John L. (Editor)   PN1861 .S76
Modern Drama in Theory and Practice: Symbolism, Surrealism
and the Absurd. Trade Paper. Cambridge University Press. New
York, NY. 1983. 235p. ISBN:0-521-29629-3, ISBN13:
978-0-521-29629-8. Dewey:809.2. LCCN:79-015947.

Audience: **l,u.**

Tornqvist, Egil   PS3529.N5
Eugene O'Neill: A Playwright's Theatre. Paper Text. McFarland
& Company, Incorporated Publishers. Jefferson, NC. 2004.
268p. ISBN:0-7864-1713-7, ISBN13: 978-0-7864-1713-1.
Dewey:812/.52. LCCN:2003-025325.

Audience: **l,u,f.** *Choice, 2004.*

Walker, Julia   PS351
Expressionism and Modernism in the American Theatre: Bodies,
Voices, Words. Don B. Wilmeth (Contribution by). Trade Cloth.
Cambridge University Press. New York, NY. 2005. 312p.

Cambridge Studies in American Theatre and Drama Ser., Vol. 21 ISBN:0-521-84747-8, ISBN13: 978-0-521-84747-6. Dewey:812/.5209115. LCCN:2005-047508.

Audience: **u,f.**

Willinger, David   **PQ3858.E3T48 2002**
Theatrical Gestures of Belgian Modernism: Dada, Surrealism, Futurism, and Pure Plastic in the Twentieth Century Belgian Theatre. Luc Deneulin (Translator). Trade Cloth. Peter Lang Publishing, Inc. New York, NY. 2002. 198p. Belgian Francophone Library, Vol. 14 ISBN:0-8204-5503-2, ISBN13: 978-0-8204-5503-7. Dewey:842/.910809493. LCCN:2002-002231.

Audience: **f.**

Worrall, Nick   **PN2726.M62M73 1996**
The Moscow Art Theatre. Paper over Boards. Routledge. New York, NY. 1996. 256p. Theatre Production Studies ISBN:0-415-05598-9, ISBN13: 978-0-415-05598-7. Dewey:792.9/5/0947312. LCCN:95-045724.

Audience: **l,u,f.**

Western Drama and Theater > Periods > The Avant-garde

Aronson, Arnold   **PN2193.E86A88 2000**
American Avant-Garde Theatre. Paper over Boards. Routledge. New York, NY. 2000. 256p. Theatre Production Ser. ISBN:0-415-02580-X, ISBN13: 978-0-415-02580-5. Dewey:792/.022. LCCN:00-032215.

Audience: **u,f.** *Choice, 2001.*

Berghaus, Günter   **PN2193.E86B47 2005**
Avant-Garde Performance. Cloth over Boards. Palgrave Macmillan. New York, NY. 2005. 352p. ISBN:1-4039-4644-2, ISBN13: 978-1-4039-4644-7. Dewey:792.02/23. LCCN:2004-065797.

Audience: **u,f.**

Berghaus, Günter   **PN2684**
Italian Futurist Theatre, 1909-1944. Trade Cloth. Oxford University Press, Inc. New York, NY. 1998. 610p. ISBN:0-19-815898-X, ISBN13: 978-0-19-815898-1. Dewey:792/.0945/0904. LCCN:97-027694.

Audience: **f.**

Berghaus, Günter   **PN2193.E86B475 2005**
Theatre, Performance, and the Historical Avant-Garde. Cloth over Boards. Palgrave Macmillan. New York, NY. 2006. 400p. Palgrave Studies in Theatre and Performance History Ser. ISBN:1-4039-6955-8, ISBN13: 978-1-4039-6955-2. Dewey:792.02/9. LCCN:2005-054609.

Audience: **u,f.**

Boyer, Patricia E.   **NC1002.P7B68 1998**
Artists and the Avant-Garde: Theatre in Paris, 1887-1900. Trade Paper. Ashgate Publishing, Ltd. Aldershot, 1999. 180p. The

Martin and Liane W. Atlas Collection Ser. ISBN:0-89468-274-1, ISBN13: 978-0-89468-274-2. Dewey:792/.09443/6109034. LCCN:97-044775.

Audience: **u,f.**

Cardullo, Bert & Knopf,   **PN6112.T42 2001**
Robert (Editors)
Theater of the Avant-Garde, 1890-1950: A Critical Anthology. Cloth over Boards. Yale University Press. Cumberland, RI. 2001. 546p. ISBN:0-300-08525-7, ISBN13: 978-0-300-08525-9. Dewey:808.82/911. LCCN:00-043891.

Audience: **u,f.**

Carter, Huntly   **PN2658.R4C3**
The Theatre of Max Reinhardt. Paper Text. Classic Books. Murrieta, CA. 2001. 332p. ISBN:0-7426-9203-5, ISBN13: 978-0-7426-9203-9. Dewey:792.0943.

Audience: **l,u,f.**

Cate, Phillip D.   **NX549.P2S67 1996**
The Spirit of Montmartre: Cabarets, Humor, and the Avant-Garde, 1875-1905. Mary Shaw (Editor). Trade Paper. Rutgers University Press. Piscataway, NJ. 1996. 240p. ISBN:0-8135-2324-9, ISBN13: 978-0-8135-2324-8. Dewey:792.7/0944/36109034. LCCN:95-081835.

Audience: **f.** *Choice, 1996.*

Dukore, Bernard F. &   **PN6112 .D8 1976**
Gerould, Daniel C.
Avant Garde Drama: A Casebook. Trade Paper. HarperCollins Publishers. New York, NY. 1976. ISBN:0-690-00848-1, ISBN13: 978-0-690-00848-7. Dewey:808.82/04. LCCN:75-027237.

Audience: **u,f.**

García Lorca, Federico   **PQ6613.A763A2265**
Four Major Plays. John Edmunds (Translator), Nicholas Round (Introduction by), Ann MacLaren (Notes by). Trade Paper. Oxford University Press, Inc. New York, NY. 2000. 288p. Oxford World's Classics Ser. ISBN:0-19-283938-1, ISBN13: 978-0-19-283938-1. Dewey:862/.62. LCCN:00-703215.

Audience: **l,u,f.**

Gewirtz, Arthur & Kolb,   **PS351**
James J. (Editors)
Experimenters, Rebels and Disparate Voices: The Theatre of the 1920s Celebrates American Diversity. Trade Cloth. Greenwood Publishing Group, Inc. Portsmouth, NH. 2003. 216p. Contributions in Drama and Theatre Studies, Vol. 99 ISBN:0-313-32466-2, ISBN13: 978-0-313-32466-6. Dewey:812/.5209920693. LCCN:2002-072543.

Audience: **l,u,f.** *Choice, 2004.*

Graver, David   **NX456.5.M64G73 1995**
The Aesthetics of Disturbance: Anti-Art in Avant-Garde Drama. Trade Cloth. University of Michigan Press. Chicago, IL. 1995. 272p. Theater Ser., :Theory - Text - Performance ISBN:0-472-10507-8, ISBN13: 978-0-472-10507-6. Dewey:700/.1. LCCN:95-016289.

Audience: **u,f.** *Choice, 1996.*

Grossvogel, David I.   **PN1861 .G7 1975**
Four Playwrights and a Postscript: Brecht, Ionesco, Beckett,
Genet. Trade Cloth. Greenwood Publishing Group, Inc.
Portsmouth, NH. 1976. 209p. ISBN:0-8371-8438-X, ISBN13:
978-0-8371-8438-8. Dewey:809.2/04. LCCN:75-027654.
Audience: **l,u,f.** B

Grotowski, Jerzy   **PN2061.G75 2002**
Towards Poor Theatre. Eugenio Barba (Editor), Peter Brook
(Introduction by, Preface by). Trade Paper. Routledge. New
York, NY. 2002. 272p. ISBN:0-87830-155-0, ISBN13:
978-0-87830-155-3. Dewey:792.02/8. LCCN:2004-266663.
Audience: **u,f.**

Harding, James M. (Editor)   **PN2193.E86C66 2000**
Contours of the Theatrical Avant-Garde: Performance and
Textuality. Trade Paper. University of Michigan Press. Chicago,
IL. 2000. 312p. Theater Ser., :Theory - Text - Performance
ISBN:0-472-06727-3, ISBN13: 978-0-472-06727-5.
Dewey:792/.022. LCCN:00-008540.
Audience: **u,f.** *Choice, 2001.*

Harrison, Elizabeth J.   **PR478.M6U53 1997**
(Editor)
Unmanning Modernism: Gendered Re-Readings. Peterson,
Shirley (Editor). University of Tennessee Press. 1997.
ISBN:0-87049-985-8, ISBN13: 978-0-87049-985-2.
Audience: **u,f.**

Hostetter, Anthony   **PN2656.B42G764 2003**
Max Reinhardt's Grosses Schauspielhaus: Its Artistic Goals,
Planning, and Operation, 1910-1933. Trade Cloth. Edwin Mellen
Press, The. Lewiston, NY. 2003. 224p. Studies in Theatre Arts,
Vol. 20 ISBN:0-7734-6802-1, ISBN13: 978-0-7734-6802-3.
Dewey:330 /945/58. LCCN:2003-042163.
Audience: **l,u,f.**

Innes, Christopher   **PN1861.I5 1993**
Avant-Garde Theatre: 1892-1992. Ed. 2. Trade Paper. Routledge.
New York, NY. 1993. 272p. ISBN:0-415-06518-6, ISBN13:
978-0-415-06518-4. Dewey:792.09. LCCN:92-016204.
Audience: **u,f.**

Kleberg, Lars   **NX556.A1K5813**
Theatre As Action: Soviet Russian Avant-Garde Aesthetics.
Trade Paper. New York University Press. New York, NY. 1993.
168p. ISBN:0-333-56817-6, ISBN13: 978-0-333-56817-0.
Dewey:792.01.
Audience: **u,f.**

Maeterlinck, Maurice, et al.   **PQ1240.E5T63 1997**
Three Pre-Surrealist Plays. Alfred Jarry & Guillaume Apollinaire
(Authors), Maya Slater (Translator, Introduction by, Notes by).
Trade Paper. Oxford University Press, Inc. New York, NY. 1997.
272p. Oxford World's Classics Ser. ISBN:0-19-283217-4,
ISBN13: 978-0-19-283217-7. Dewey:842/.808.
LCCN:96-052367.
Audience: **u,f.**

Pronko, Leonard C.   **PQ558 .P7 1978**
Avant Garde: The Experimental Theater in France. Trade Cloth.
Greenwood Publishing Group, Inc. Portsmouth, NH. 1978. 225p.
ISBN:0-313-20096-3, ISBN13: 978-0-313-20096-0.
Dewey:842/.9/1409. LCCN:77-026017.
Audience: **u,f.**

Roose-Evans, James   **PN2189**
Experimental Theatre: From Stanislavsky to Peter Brook. Ed. 4.
Trade Paper. Routledge. New York, NY. 1996. 260p.
ISBN:0-415-00963-4, ISBN13: 978-0-415-00963-8.
Dewey:792/.022.
Audience: **l,u,f.** B

Rudnitsky, Konstantin   **PN2724.R76 2000**
Russian and Soviet Theatre: Tradition and the Avant-Garde.
Trade Paper. Thames & Hudson. New York, NY. 2000. 320p.
ISBN:0-500-28195-5, ISBN13: 978-0-500-28195-6.
Dewey:792/.0947/09041. LCCN:99-066013.
Audience: **l,u,f.**

Sayler, Oliver M. (Editor)   **PN2658.R4**
Max Reinhardt and His Theatre. Trade Cloth. Ayer Company
Publishers, Inc. Manchester, NH. 1972. 381p.
ISBN:0-405-08926-0, ISBN13: 978-0-405-08926-8.
Dewey:792/.0924 B. LCCN:68-020245.
Audience: **l,u.**

Schurer, Ernst (Editor)   **PT1258.G46 1997**
German Expressionist Plays. Trade Paper. Continuum
International Publishing Group, Ltd. London, 1997. 344p.
German Library, Vol. 66 ISBN:0-8264-0950-4, ISBN13:
978-0-8264-0950-8. Dewey:832.9/12/08/0115.
LCCN:94-038092.
Audience: **l,u,f.**

Segel, Harold B.   **PN1972.S43 1995**
Pinocchio's Progeny: Puppets, Marionettes, Automatons, and
Robots in Modernist and Avant-Garde Drama. Trade Cloth.
Johns Hopkins University Press. Baltimore, MD. 1995. 424p.
PAJ Bks. ISBN:0-8018-5031-2, ISBN13: 978-0-8018-5031-8.
Dewey:812/.54. LCCN:95-075204.
Audience: **l,u,f.** *Choice, 1996.*

Sell, Mike   **PN2297.L5S45 2005**
Avant-Garde Performance and the Limits of Criticism:
Approaching the Living Theatre, Happenings/Fluxus and the
Black Arts Movement. Trade Cloth. University of Michigan
Press. Chicago, IL. 2005. 336p. Theater Ser.,
:Theory/Text/Performance Ser. ISBN:0-472-11495-6, ISBN13:
978-0-472-11495-5. Dewey:792/.09747/1. LCCN:2005-016628.
Audience: **l,u,f.**

Sokel, Walter H. (Editor)   **PT1258.A57 1984**
Anthology of German Expressionist Drama. Book, Other.
Cornell University Press. Ithaca, NY. 1984. 336p.
ISBN:0-8014-9296-3, ISBN13: 978-0-8014-9296-9.
Dewey:832/.912/0801. LCCN:84-045197.
Audience: **l,u,f.**

Styan, John L.   **PN1861.S76**
Modern Drama in Theory and Practice: Expressionism and Epic Theatre, Vol. 3. Trade Paper. Cambridge University Press. New York, NY. 1983. 242p. ISBN:0-521-29630-7, ISBN13: 978-0-521-29630-4. Dewey:792/.0904. LCCN:79-015947.

Audience: **l,u,f.**

Walker, Julia   **PS351**
Expressionism and Modernism in the American Theatre: Bodies, Voices, Words. Don B. Wilmeth (Contribution by). Trade Cloth. Cambridge University Press. New York, NY. 2005. 312p. Cambridge Studies in American Theatre and Drama Ser., Vol. 21 ISBN:0-521-84747-8, ISBN13: 978-0-521-84747-6. Dewey:812/.5209115. LCCN:2005-047508.

Audience: **u,f.**

Willinger, David   **PQ3858.E3T48 2002**
Theatrical Gestures of Belgian Modernism: Dada, Surrealism, Futurism, and Pure Plastic in the Twentieth Century Belgian Theatre. Luc Deneulin (Translator). Trade Cloth. Peter Lang Publishing, Inc. New York, NY. 2002. 198p. Belgian Francophone Library, Vol. 14 ISBN:0-8204-5503-2, ISBN13: 978-0-8204-5503-7. Dewey:842/.910809493. LCCN:2002-002231.

Audience: **f.**

Western Drama and Theater > Periods > Postmodernism

Albee, Edward   **PS3545.I5365**
The Collected Plays of Edward Albee, Vol. 1. Trade Cloth. Overlook Press, The. New York, NY. 2004. 356p. ISBN:1-58567-529-6, ISBN13: 978-1-58567-529-6. Dewey:812/.54.

Audience: **l,u,f.**

Albee, Edward   **PS3545.I5365**
The Collected Plays of Edward Albee: 1978-2003. Trade Cloth. Overlook Press, The. New York, NY. 2006. 656p. ISBN:1-58567-777-9, ISBN13: 978-1-58567-777-1. Dewey:812/.54.

Audience: **l,u,f.**

Albee, Edward   **PS3551.L25**
The Collected Plays of Edward Albee, 1966-1977, Vol. 2. Trade Cloth. Overlook Press, The. New York, NY. 2005. 608p. ISBN:1-58567-617-9, ISBN13: 978-1-58567-617-0. Dewey:812.54.

Audience: **l,u,f.**

Auslander, Philip   **NX220**
Presence and Resistance: Postmodernism and Cultural Politics in Contemporary American Performance. Trade Paper. University of Michigan Press. Chicago, IL. 1994. 216p. Theater Ser., :Theory - Text - Performance ISBN:0-472-08278-7, ISBN13: 978-0-472-08278-0. Dewey:700.9/73/09048.

Audience: **u,f.** *Choice, 1993.*

Birringer, Johannes   **PN2039**
Theatre, Theory, Postmodernism. Paper Text. Indiana University Press. Bloomington, IN. 1993. 256p. Drama and Performance Studies ISBN:0-253-20845-9, ISBN13: 978-0-253-20845-3. Dewey:792/.01. LCCN:90-024442.

Audience: **u,f.** *Choice, 1992.*

Bristol, Michael D. &   **PR3100.S52 2001**
  McLuskie, Kathleen (Editors)
Shakespeare and Modern Theatre: The Performance of Modernity. Paper over Boards. Routledge. New York, NY. 2001. 224p. Accents on Shakespeare Ser. ISBN:0-415-21984-1, ISBN13: 978-0-415-21984-6. Dewey:792.9/5. LCCN:00-065307.

Audience: **u,f.**

Callaghan, Dympna (Editor)   **PR2976**
A Feminist Companion to Shakespeare. Trade Paper. Blackwell Publishing, Inc. Malden, MA. 2001. 416p. Companions to Literature and Culture Ser. ISBN:0-631-20807-0, ISBN13: 978-0-631-20807-5. Dewey:822.3/3.

Audience: **l,u,f.** *Choice, 2000.*

Carlson, Marvin   **PR739.D48C36 1993**
Deathtraps: The Postmodern Comedy Thriller. Trade Cloth. Indiana University Press. Bloomington, IN. 1993. 224p. ISBN:0-253-31305-8, ISBN13: 978-0-253-31305-8. Dewey:822/.052709. LCCN:92-045237.

Audience: **u,f.**

Fahy, Thomas; King,   **PS338.P4P44 2001**
  Kimball
Peering Behind the Curtain: Cisability, Illness, and the Extraordinary Body in Contemporary Theater. Routledge. 2002. ISBN:0-415-92997-0, ISBN13: 978-0-415-92997-4.

Audience: **g.**

Gainor, J. Ellen (Editor)   **PN2049.I47 1995**
Imperialism and Theatre: Essays on World Theatre, Drama and Performance. Trade Paper. Routledge. New York, NY. 1995. 280p. ISBN:0-415-10641-9, ISBN13: 978-0-415-10641-2. Dewey:792/.013. LCCN:94-035439.

Audience: **l,u,f.** *Choice, 1996.*

Kaye, Nick   **PN2037.K35 1994**
Postmodernism and Performance. Trade Paper. Palgrave Macmillan. New York, NY. 1994. 188p. New Directions in Theatre Ser. ISBN:0-312-12024-9, ISBN13: 978-0-312-12024-5. Dewey:792. LCCN:93-032470.

Audience: **u,f.** *Choice, 1994.*

Kostelanetz, Richard   **PN3203**
The Theatre of Mixed Means. Trade Paper. Archae Editions. New York, NY. 1981. 336p. ISBN:0-932360-28-9, ISBN13: 978-0-932360-28-1. Dewey:792/.02. LCCN:68-010828.

Audience: **l,u.**

Kuppers, Petra   **HV1568.K87 2003**
Disability and Contemporary Performance: Bodies on Edge. Routledge. 2003. ISBN:0-415-30238-2, ISBN13: 978-0-415-30238-8.

Audience: **u,f.**

Lamont, Rosette C. (Editor)   **PS628.W6.W664 1993**
Women on the Verge: Seven Avant-Garde American Plays. Trade
Paper. Applause Theatre Book Publishers. New York, NY. 1992.
416p. ISBN:1-55783-148-3, ISBN13: 978-1-55783-148-4.
Dewey:812.540809287. LCCN:93-011557.
Audience: **u,f.** *Choice, 1994.*

Mamet, David   **PS3563.A4345O4 1993**
Oleanna. UK-Trade Paper. Knopf Publishing Group. New York,
NY. 1993. 96p. ISBN:0-679-74536-X, ISBN13:
978-0-679-74536-5. Dewey:812.5/4. LCCN:92-050638.
Audience: **l,u,f.**

Mamet, David   **PS3563.A4345**
Sexual Perversity in Chicago and the Duck Variations. Trade
Paper. Grove/Atlantic, Inc. New York, NY. 1978. 128p.
ISBN:0-8021-5011-X, ISBN13: 978-0-8021-5011-0. Dewey:812.
LCCN:77-091885.
Audience: **l,u,f.**

Mann, Bruce J. (Editor)   **PS3551.L25Z655 2003**
Edward Albee: A Casebook. Paper over Boards. Routledge. New
York, NY. 2002. 168p. Casebooks on Modern Dramatists, Vol.
29 ISBN:0-8153-3165-7, ISBN13: 978-0-8153-3165-0.
Dewey:812/.54. LCCN:2002-011279.
Audience: **l,u,f.** *Choice, 2003.*

Maufort, Marc (Editor)   **PS352.S73 1995**
Staging Difference: Cultural Pluralism in American Theatre and
Drama. Cloth Text. Peter Lang Publishing, Inc. New York, NY.
1996. 396p. American University Studies, Vol. 25:Theatre Arts
ISBN:0-8204-2732-2, ISBN13: 978-0-8204-2732-4.
Dewey:812/.5409920693. LCCN:94-043336.
Audience: **l,u,f.** *Choice, 1996.*

Orr, John   **PN1907.O7 1991**
Tragicomedy and Contemporary Culture: Play and Performance
from Beckett to Shepard. Trade Cloth. University of Michigan
Press. Chicago, IL. 1991. 176p. Theater Ser., :Theory - Text -
Performance ISBN:0-472-10262-1, ISBN13: 978-0-472-10262-4.
Dewey:809.2/523. LCCN:91-009736.
Audience: **g,l.**

Roose-Evans, James   **PN2189**
Experimental Theatre: From Stanislavsky to Peter Brook. Ed. 4.
Trade Paper. Routledge. New York, NY. 1996. 260p.
ISBN:0-415-00963-4, ISBN13: 978-0-415-00963-8.
Dewey:792/.022.
Audience: **l,u,f.** *B*

Schmidt, Kerstin   **PS352 .S35 2005**
The Theater of Transformation: Postmodernism in American
Drama. Trade Paper. Rodopi. Kenilworth, NY. 2005. 230p.
Postmodern Studies, 37 ISBN:90-420-1895-X, ISBN13:
978-90-420-1895-2. Dewey:812.609.
Audience: **u,f.**

Seller, Maxine S. (Editor)   **PN2226**
Ethnic Theatre in the United States. Book, Other. Greenwood

Publishing Group, Inc. Portsmouth, NH. 1983. 606p.
ISBN:0-313-21230-9, ISBN13: 978-0-313-21230-7.
Dewey:792/.0973. LCCN:81-013494.
Audience: **l,u,f.** *B*

Shaughnessy, Robert   **PR3091.S363 2000**
   (Editor)
Shakespeare in Performance. Trade Paper. Palgrave Macmillan.
New York, NY. 2000. 240p. New Casebooks Ser.
ISBN:0-312-23312-4, ISBN13: 978-0-312-23312-9.
Dewey:822.3/3. LCCN:99-086321.
Audience: **u,f.**

Stoppard, Tom   **PR6066.I53**
Tom Stoppard: Arcadia, The Real Thing, Night and Day, Indian
Ink, Hapgood. Trade Paper. Faber & Faber, Inc. New York, NY.
2000. 608p. ISBN:0-571-19751-5, ISBN13: 978-0-571-19751-4.
Dewey:822.9/14.
Audience: **l,u,f.**

Stoppard, Tom   **PR6066.I53**
Tom Stoppard: The Real Inspector Hound; Dirty Linen; Dogg's
Hamlet; Cahoot's MacBeth... Trade Paper. Faber & Faber, Inc.
New York, NY. 1996. 224p. ISBN:0-571-17765-4, ISBN13:
978-0-571-17765-3. Dewey:822.9/14.
Audience: **l,u,f.**

Turner, J.   **PN2688.B33T87 2004**
Eugenio Barba. Paper over Boards. Routledge. New York, NY.
2005. 192p. Routledge Performance Practitioners Ser.
ISBN:0-415-27327-7, ISBN13: 978-0-415-27327-5.
Dewey:792.02/33/092. LCCN:2004-004779.
Audience: **u,f.**

Werner, Sarah   **PR3106.W47 2001**
Shakespeare and Feminist Performance: Ideology on Stage.
Paper over Boards. Routledge. New York, NY. 2001. 144p.
Accents on Shakespeare Ser. ISBN:0-415-22729-1, ISBN13:
978-0-415-22729-2. Dewey:822.3/3. LCCN:2001-018088.
Audience: **u,f.**

Western Drama and Theater > Genres, Styles, and Types

Nicoll, Allardyce   **PN1631**
The Theory of Drama. Trade Cloth. Ayer Company Publishers,
Inc. Manchester, NH. 1972. ISBN:0-405-08818-3, ISBN13:
978-0-405-08818-6. Dewey:809.2. LCCN:66-029422.
Audience: **l,u,f.**

Western Drama and Theater > Genres, Styles, and Types > Tragedy, Tragicomedy, Melodrama

Aeschylus   **PA3978**
Aeschylus: Plays Two. Frederic Raphael & Kenneth McLeish
(Translators), J. Michael Walton (Introduction by). Trade Paper.

Methuen Publishing Ltd. London, 2004. 129p. Methuen's World Dramatists Ser. ISBN:0-413-65480-X, ISBN13: 978-0-413-65480-9. Dewey:882/.01.

Audience: **l,u,f.**

Aeschylus   **PA3978**
Aeschylus: Plays One. Frederic Raphael & Kenneth McLeish (Translators), J. Michael Walton (Introduction by). Trade Paper. Methuen Publishing Ltd. London, 2004. 153p. Methuen World Dramatists Ser. ISBN:0-413-65190-8, ISBN13: 978-0-413-65190-7. Dewey:882/.01.

Audience: **l,u,f.**

Aeschylus, et al.   **PA3463.S59 2002**
Six Greek Tragedies: Aeschylus: Persians, Prometheus Bound; Sophocles: Women of Trachi, Philoctetes; Euripides: Trojan Women, Bacchae. Sophocles & Euripides (Authors), Marianne McDonald & J. Michael Walton (Editors), Marianne McDonald & J. Michael Walton (Translators). Trade Paper. Methuen Publishing Ltd. London, 2004. Methuen Drama Ser. ISBN:0-413-77256-X, ISBN13: 978-0-413-77256-5. Dewey:882/.01/08. LCCN:2004-426593.

Audience: **l,u,f.**

Aristotle   **PN1040.A513 2001**
Aristotle on Poetics. Seth Benardete (Translator), Michael Davis (Translator, Introduction by). Cloth Text. Saint Augustine's Press, Inc. South Bend, IN. 2002. 144p. ISBN:1-58731-025-2, ISBN13: 978-1-58731-025-6. Dewey:808.2. LCCN:2001-005879.

Audience: **u,f.**

Arnott, Peter D.   **PA3201 .A76**
An Introduction to the Greek Theatre. Paper Text. Textbook Publishers. Temecula, CA. 2003. 239p. ISBN:0-7581-8855-2, ISBN13: 978-0-7581-8855-7. Dewey:792.0938.

Audience: **l,u.**

Bushnell, Rebecca W.   **PN1892.C56 2004**
(Editor)
A Companion to Tragedy. Blackwell Publishing, Inc. 2005. ISBN:1-4051-0735-9, ISBN13: 978-1-4051-0735-8.

Audience: **u,f.**

Corrigan, Robert W.   **PA3626.A2C67 1990**
(Editor)
Classical Tragedy Greek and Roman: Eight Plays with Critical Essays. Hal Leonard Corporation Staff (Created by). Trade Paper. Applause Theatre Book Publishers. New York, NY. 1990. 576p. ISBN:1-55783-046-0, ISBN13: 978-1-55783-046-3. Dewey:882/.0108. LCCN:90-030152.

Audience: **l,u,f.**

Disher, Maurice Willson   **PN1917.D5**
Melodrama: Plots That Thrilled. Paper Text. Textbook Publishers. Temecula, CA. 2003. 210p. ISBN:0-7581-4775-9, ISBN13: 978-0-7581-4775-2. Dewey:808.2.

Audience: **l,u.**

Easterling, P. E. (Editor)   **PA3131 .C29 1997**
The Cambridge Companion to Greek Tragedy. Trade Paper. Cambridge University Press. New York, NY. 1997. 410p.

Companions to Literature Ser. ISBN:0-521-42351-1, ISBN13: 978-0-521-42351-9. Dewey:882/.01/09. LCCN:96-037392.

Audience: **g,l,u,f.** *Choice, 1998.*

Euripides   **PA3978**
Plays Two: Hecuba, the Women of Troy, Iphigenia at Aulis, Cyclops. Peter D. Arnott & Don Taylor (Translators), J. Michael Walton (Translator, Introduction by). Trade Paper. Methuen Publishing Ltd. London, 2004. Methuen World Dramatists Ser. ISBN:0-413-16420-9, ISBN13: 978-0-413-16420-9. Dewey:882/.01.

Audience: **l,u,f.**

Euripides   **PA3975.A2 1997**
Plays Four. Kenneth McLeish (Translator, Introduction by), J. Michael Walton (Introduction by). Trade Paper. Methuen Publishing Ltd. London, 2004. Methuen Classical Greek Dramatists Ser. ISBN:0-413-71630-9, ISBN13: 978-0-413-71630-9. Dewey:882/.01. LCCN:98-133592.

Audience: **l,u,f.**

Euripides   **PA3975.A2**
Plays 1. David Thompson (Translator), J. Michael Walton (Introduction by). Trade Paper. Methuen Publishing Ltd. London, 2004. Methuen Classical Greek Dramatists Ser. ISBN:0-413-75280-1, ISBN13: 978-0-413-75280-2. Dewey:882/.01.

Audience: **l,u,f.**

Euripides   **PA3975.A2 1997**
Plays Five. J. Michael Walton & Kenneth McLeish (Introduction by). Trade Paper. Methuen Publishing Ltd. London, 2004. Methuen Classical Greek Dramatists Ser. ISBN:0-413-71640-6, ISBN13: 978-0-413-71640-8. Dewey:882/.01. LCCN:98-194780.

Audience: **l,u,f.**

Hays, Michael &   **PN1922**
  Nikolopoulou, Anastasia (Editors)
Melodrama: The Cultural Emergence of a Genre. Trade Paper. Palgrave Macmillan. New York, NY. 1999. 304p. ISBN:0-312-22127-4, ISBN13: 978-0-312-22127-0. Dewey:809.2/52.

Audience: **u,f.** *Choice, 1997.*

Kelly, Henry Ansgar   **PN1891.K45 1993**
Ideas and Forms of Tragedy from Aristotle to the Middle Ages. Alastair Minnis, Patrick Boyde, John Burrow, Rita Copeland, Alan Deyermond, Peter Dronke, Nigel Palmer & Winthrop Wetherbee (Contribution by). Trade Paper. Cambridge University Press. New York, NY. 2005. 275p. Cambridge Studies in Medieval Literature Ser., Vol. 18 ISBN:0-521-02377-7, ISBN13: 978-0-521-02377-1. Dewey:809.2512.

Audience: **l,u,f.**

Nietzsche, Friedrich   **BH39**
The Birth of Tragedy. Douglas Smith (Editor). Trade Paper. Oxford University Press, Inc. New York, NY. 2000. 218p. Oxford World's Classics Ser. ISBN:0-19-283292-1, ISBN13: 978-0-19-283292-4. Dewey:111.8/5.

Audience: **u,f.**

Orr, John   PN1907.O7 1991
Tragicomedy and Contemporary Culture: Play and Performance from Beckett to Shepard. Trade Cloth. University of Michigan Press. Chicago, IL. 1991. 176p. Theater Ser., :Theory - Text - Performance ISBN:0-472-10262-1, ISBN13: 978-0-472-10262-4. Dewey:809.2/523. LCCN:91-009736.
         Audience: **g,l.**

Palmer, Richard H.   PN1892
Tragedy and Tragic Theory: An Analytical Guide. Cloth Text. Greenwood Publishing Group, Inc. Portsmouth, NH. 1992. 252p. ISBN:0-313-28203-X, ISBN13: 978-0-313-28203-4. Dewey:809.916. LCCN:91-046861.
         Audience: **l,u,f.**

Schmidt, Dennis J.   PA3131.S366 2001
ⓔ On Germans and Other Greeks: Tragedy and Ethical Life. E-Book. Indiana University Press. Bloomington, IN. 2001. 432p. Studies in Continental Thought ISBN:0-253-33868-9, ISBN13: 978-0-253-33868-6. Dewey:882/.0109. LCCN:00-050642.
         Audience: **u,f.**

Seneca, Lucius Annaeus   PA6666.A1 1992
Seneca: The Tragedies. David R. Slavitt (Translator). Trade Paper. Johns Hopkins University Press. Baltimore, MD. 1992. 224p. Seneca Ser., Vol. 1 ISBN:0-8018-4309-X, ISBN13: 978-0-8018-4309-9. Dewey:872.01. LCCN:91-036347.
         Audience: **u,f.**

Sophocles   PA4414.A1 C3
Sophocles the Seven Plays in English Ver. Trade Paper. Kessinger Publishing, LLC. Whitefish, MT. 2005. ISBN:1-4179-0075-X, ISBN13: 978-1-4179-0075-6. Dewey:882.
         Audience: **u,f.**

Steiner, George   PN1892
The Death of Tragedy. Trade Paper. Yale University Press. Cumberland, RI. 1996. 382p. ISBN:0-300-06916-2, ISBN13: 978-0-300-06916-7. Dewey:809.2/512.
         Audience: **u,f.**

Von Kleist, Heinrich   PT2378.A2
Plays. Trade Paper. Theatre Communications Group, Inc. New York, NY. 2000. 259p. Absolute Classics Ser. ISBN:1-84002-123-3, ISBN13: 978-1-84002-123-3. Dewey:832/.6.
         Audience: **l,u,f.**

Walton, J. Michael, et al.   PA3975
Plays 3, Vol. 3. Kenneth McLeish & Euripides (Authors). Trade Paper. Methuen Publishing Ltd. London, 2004. ISBN:0-413-71620-1, ISBN13: 978-0-413-71620-0. Dewey:882/.01.
         Audience: **l,u,f.**

Western Drama and Theater > Genres, Styles, and Types > Comedy, Burlesque, Vaudeville

Aristophanes   PA3978
Aristophanes: Plays One. Trade Paper. Methuen Publishing Ltd. London, 2004. 264p. ISBN:0-413-66900-9, ISBN13: 978-0-413-66900-1. Dewey:882/.01.
         Audience: **l,u,f.**

Aristophanes   PA3978
Aristophanes: Plays Two. Trade Paper. Methuen Publishing Ltd. London, 2004. ISBN:0-413-66910-6, ISBN13: 978-0-413-66910-0. Dewey:882/.01.
         Audience: **l,u,f.**

Aristotle   PN1040.A513 2001
Aristotle on Poetics. Seth Benardete (Translator), Michael Davis (Translator, Introduction by). Cloth Text. Saint Augustine's Press, Inc. South Bend, IN. 2002. 144p. ISBN:1-58731-025-2, ISBN13: 978-1-58731-025-6. Dewey:808.2. LCCN:2001-005879.
         Audience: **u,f.**

Arnott, Peter D.   PA3201 .A76
An Introduction to the Greek Theatre. Paper Text. Textbook Publishers. Temecula, CA. 2003. 239p. ISBN:0-7581-8855-2, ISBN13: 978-0-7581-8855-7. Dewey:792.0938.
         Audience: **l,u.**

Bermel, Albert   PN1942.B4 1990
Farce: A History from Aristophanes to Woody Allen. Trade Paper. Southern Illinois University Press. Carbondale, IL. 1990. 464p. ISBN:0-8093-1645-5, ISBN13: 978-0-8093-1645-8. Dewey:809.2/523. LCCN:89-021846.
         Audience: **l,u,f.**

Calder, Andrew   PQ1860.C3
Moliere: The Theory and Practice of Comedy. Trade Paper. Continuum International Publishing Group, Ltd. London, 1996. 244p. ISBN:0-485-12127-1, ISBN13: 978-0-485-12127-8. Dewey:842.4.
         Audience: **l,u,f.** *Choice, 1993.*

Carlson, Marvin   PR739.D48C36 1993
Deathtraps: The Postmodern Comedy Thriller. Trade Cloth. Indiana University Press. Bloomington, IN. 1993. 224p. ISBN:0-253-31305-8, ISBN13: 978-0-253-31305-8. Dewey:822/.052709. LCCN:92-045237.
         Audience: **u,f.**

Charney, Maurice (Editor)   PN6147
Comedy: A Geographic and Historical Guide. Cloth Text. Greenwood Publishing Group, Inc. Portsmouth, NH. 2005. 688p.

ISBN:0-313-32706-8, ISBN13: 978-0-313-32706-3.
Dewey:809/.7. LCCN:2005-008410.

Audience: **g.** *Choice, 2006.*

Corrigan, Robert W.   **PA3629.C5 1987**
Classical Comedy - Greek and Roman: Six Plays. Trade Paper.
Applause Theatre Book Publishers. New York, NY. 1987. 492p.
ISBN:0-936839-85-6, ISBN13: 978-0-936839-85-1.
Dewey:882/.01/08. LCCN:87-017442.

Audience: **l,u,f.**

Cullen, Frank   **PN1962**
Vaudeville, Old and New: An Encyclopedia of Variety
Performers. Paper over Boards. Routledge. New York, NY.
2006. 1376p. ISBN:0-415-93853-8, ISBN13:
978-0-415-93853-2. Dewey:792.7097303. LCCN:2005-030588.

Audience: **g.**

Davis, Jessica Milner   **PN1942.D3 2002**
Farce. Trade Paper. Transaction Publishers. Somerset, NJ. 2002.
191p. Classics in Communication and Mass Culture Ser.
ISBN:0-7658-0887-0, ISBN13: 978-0-7658-0887-5.
Dewey:809/.25232. LCCN:2002-028629.

Audience: **g,l,u.**

Duckworth, George Eckel   **PA6069.D8**
The Nature of Roman Comedy, A Study in Popular
Entertainment. Paper Text. Textbook Publishers. Temecula, CA.
2003. 501p. ISBN:0-7581-5789-4, ISBN13: 978-0-7581-5789-8.
Dewey:872.09.

Audience: **u,f.**

Fisk, Deborah Payne   **PR1266.F675 2005**
(Editor)
Four Restoration Libertine Plays. Trade Paper, Perfect. Oxford
University Press, Inc. New York, NY. 2005. 468p. Oxford
World's Classics Ser. ISBN:0-19-283294-8, ISBN13:
978-0-19-283294-8. Dewey:822/.408. LCCN:2004-027977.

Audience: **l,u,f.**

Fredrick, Edna C.   **PQ538 .F7 1973**
The Plot and Its Construction in Eighteenth Century Criticism of
French Comedy: A Study of the Theory with Relation to the
Practice of Beaumarchais. Library Binding. Burt Franklin
Publisher. New York, NY. 1973. 132p. ISBN:0-8337-4118-7,
ISBN13: 978-0-8337-4118-9. Dewey:842/.052.
LCCN:72-082001.

Audience: **u,f.**

Griffiths, Trevor (Editor)   **PR1248**
Restoration Comedy. Trade Paper. Theatre Communications
Group, Inc. New York, NY. 2005. 352p. ISBN:1-85459-848-1,
ISBN13: 978-1-85459-848-6. Dewey:822.4/08017.

Audience: **l,u,f.**

Hokenson, Jan   **PN56.C66H65 2006**
The Idea of Comedy: History, Theory, Critique. Trade Cloth.
Fairleigh Dickinson University Press. Cranbury, NJ. 2006. 288p.
ISBN:0-8386-4096-6, ISBN13: 978-0-8386-4096-8.
Dewey:809/.917. LCCN:2005-018161.

Audience: **g.** *Choice, 2006.*

Janko, Richard   **PN1924**
Aristotle on Comedy: Towards a Reconstruction of "Poetics II".
Ed. 2. Trade Paper. Gerald Duckworth & Company, Ltd.
London, 320p. ISBN:0-7156-3169-1, ISBN13:
978-0-7156-3169-0. Dewey:882/.01.

Audience: **u,f.**

Lyons, Paddy & Morgan,   **PR1266**
Fideles (Editors)
Female Playwrights of the Restoration: Five Comedies. Ed. 2.
Paddy Lyons & Fideles Morgan (Introduction by). Trade Paper.
Tuttle Publishing. Boston, MA. 1994. 365p.
ISBN:0-460-87427-6, ISBN13: 978-0-460-87427-4.
Dewey:822.40809287.

Audience: **l,u,f.**

Menander   **PA4246.E4B35 2002**
Menander, the Plays and Fragments. Maurice Balme
(Translator), Peter Brown (Introduction by). Trade Paper. Oxford
University Press, Inc. New York, NY. 2002. 346p. Oxford
World's Classics Ser. ISBN:0-19-283983-7, ISBN13:
978-0-19-283983-1. Dewey:822/.01. LCCN:2002-025760.

Audience: **g,l,u.**

Plautus, Titus Maccius &   **PA6137.3**
Terence
Four Roman Comedies: The Haunted House, Casina, or A
Funny Thing Happened on the Way to the Wedding, the Eunuch,
Brothers. J. Michael Walton (Editor, Introduction by). Trade
Paper. Methuen Publishing Ltd. London, 2003. 320p. Methuen
Classical Drama Ser. ISBN:0-413-77296-9, ISBN13:
978-0-413-77296-1. Dewey:872/.0108. LCCN:2003-430388.

Audience: **u,f.**

Rogers, Will & Day, Donald   **PN2287.R74A3 1998**
The Autobiography of Will Rogers. Trade Cloth. Transaction
Publishers. Somerset, NJ. 1998. 528p. ISBN:1-56000-526-2,
ISBN13: 978-1-56000-526-1. Dewey:792.7/028/092 B.
LCCN:98-030710.

Audience: **g.**

Slater, Niall W.   **PA6585.S55 2000**
Plautus in Performance: The Theatre of the Mind. Ed. 2. Cloth
Text. Gordon & Breach Publishing Group. New York, NY. 2000.
228p. Greek and Roman Theatre Ser., Vol. 2
ISBN:90-5755-037-7, ISBN13: 978-90-5755-037-9.
Dewey:872/.01. LCCN:2002-405986.

Audience: **u,f.** *B*

Slavitt, David R.   **PA6569.S55 1995**
Plautus: The Comedies. Palmer Bovie & T. Maccius Plautus
(Editors). Trade Paper. Johns Hopkins University Press.
Baltimore, MD. 1990. 360p. Plautus Ser., Vol. 4
ISBN:0-8018-5073-8, ISBN13: 978-0-8018-5073-8.
Dewey:872/.01. LCCN:94-045317.

Audience: **u,f.** *Choice, 1996.*

Sobel, Bernard   **PN1968.U5S69 2002**
A Pictorial History of Vaudeville. Trade Paper. Barricade Books,
Inc. Fort Lee, NJ. 2002. 224p. ISBN:1-56980-237-8, ISBN13:
978-1-56980-237-3. Dewey:792.7/0973. LCCN:2002-026100.

Audience: **g,l,u.** *B*

Western Drama and Theater > Genres, Styles, and Types > Commedia del'arte

PN2018.T64 1993
ⓔ Commedia Dell'Arte Performance: Context and Contents.
E-Book. NetLibrary, Inc. Boulder, CO. 1993.
ISBN:0-585-35791-9, ISBN13: 978-0-585-35791-1. Dewey:792.

Audience: **u,f.**

Andrews, Richard   **PQ4149 .A48 1993**
Scripts and Scenarios: The Performance of Comedy in
Renaissance Italy. Cloth Text. Cambridge University Press. New
York, NY. 1993. 312p. ISBN:0-521-35357-2, ISBN13:
978-0-521-35357-1. Dewey:852.05230903. LCCN:92-023446.

Audience: **l,u,f.**

Cairns, Christopher (Editor)   **PQ4155.C63 1989**
The Commedia Dell'arte from the Renaissance to Dario Fo: The
Italian Origins of European Theatre VI. Trade Cloth. Edwin
Mellen Press, The. Lewiston, NY. 1989. 362p.
ISBN:0-88946-080-9, ISBN13: 978-0-88946-080-5.
Dewey:852/.052309. LCCN:89-013576.

Audience: **l,u,f.** *Choice, 1990.*

Cairns, Christopher (Editor)   **PN2091.S8S292 1996**
Scenery, Set and Staging in the Italian Renaissance: Studies in
the Practice of Theatre. Trade Cloth. Edwin Mellen Press, The.
Lewiston, NY. 1996. 340p. ISBN:0-7734-8814-6, ISBN13:
978-0-7734-8814-4. Dewey:792/.025/0945. LCCN:96-003909.

Audience: **l,u,f.**

Castagno, Paul C.   **PQ4155.C35 1994**
The Early Commedia Dell'arte (1550-1621): The Mannerist
Context. Cloth Text. Peter Lang Publishing, Inc. New York, NY.
1994. 290p. American University Studies, Vol. 13:Theatre Arts
ISBN:0-8204-1794-7, ISBN13: 978-0-8204-1794-3.
Dewey:852/.0523/09031. LCCN:91-039538.

Audience: **u,f.** *Choice, 1995.*

Fisher, James   **PQ4155.F57 1992**
The Theatre of Yesterday and Tomorrow: Commedia Dell'Arte
on the Modern Stage. Trade Cloth. Edwin Mellen Press, The.
Lewiston, NY. 1992. 424p. ISBN:0-7734-9529-0, ISBN13:
978-0-7734-9529-6. Dewey:792.2. LCCN:92-014529.

Audience: **l,u,f.**

Henke, Robert   **PQ4155**
Performance and Literature in the Commedia Dell'Arte. Trade
Cloth. Cambridge University Press. New York, NY. 2002. 278p.
ISBN:0-521-64324-4, ISBN13: 978-0-521-64324-5.
Dewey:792.2 /3/0945. LCCN:2003-268759.

Audience: **u,f.**

Nicoll, Allardyce   **PN2071.G4 N5**
Masks, Mimes and Miracles. Trade Cloth. Cooper Square
Publishers, Inc. New York, NY. 1981. ISBN:0-8154-0163-9,
ISBN13: 978-0-8154-0163-6. Dewey:792.09. LCCN:63-017895.

Audience: **l,u,f.**

Rudlin, John   **PQ4155.R83 1994**
The Commedia Dell'Arte in the Twentieth Century. Trade Paper.
Routledge. New York, NY. 1994. 296p. ISBN:0-415-04770-6,
ISBN13: 978-0-415-04770-8. Dewey:792.209.
LCCN:93-013426.

Audience: **l,u,f.**

Western Drama and Theater > Genres, Styles, and Types > Theater of the Absurd

Albee, Edward   **PS3545.I5365**
The Collected Plays of Edward Albee, Vol. 1. Trade Cloth.
Overlook Press, The. New York, NY. 2004. 356p.
ISBN:1-58567-529-6, ISBN13: 978-1-58567-529-6.
Dewey:812/.54.

Audience: **l,u,f.**

Albee, Edward   **PS3545.I5365**
The Collected Plays of Edward Albee: 1978-2003. Trade Cloth.
Overlook Press, The. New York, NY. 2006. 656p.
ISBN:1-58567-777-9, ISBN13: 978-1-58567-777-1.
Dewey:812/.54.

Audience: **l,u,f.**

Albee, Edward   **PS3551.L25**
The Collected Plays of Edward Albee, 1966-1977, Vol. 2. Trade
Cloth. Overlook Press, The. New York, NY. 2005. 608p.
ISBN:1-58567-617-9, ISBN13: 978-1-58567-617-0.
Dewey:812.54.

Audience: **l,u,f.**

Beckett, Samuel   **PR6003.E282**
Dramatic Works and Dialogues, Vol. 2. Trade Paper. Riverrun
Press, Inc. Flemington, NJ. 1999. 80p. Beckett Shorts Ser., 2
ISBN:0-7145-4214-8, ISBN13: 978-0-7145-4214-0.
Dewey:822.912.

Audience: **l,u,f.**

Beckett, Samuel   **PR6003.E282A6 2006**
The Dramatic Works of Samuel Beckett: Volume III of the
Grove Centenary Editions. Paul Auster (Editor), Edward Albee
(Introduction by). Cloth over Boards. Grove/Atlantic, Inc. New
York, NY. 2006. 520p. ISBN:0-8021-1819-4, ISBN13:
978-0-8021-1819-6. Dewey:848/.81409. LCCN:2005-055078.

Audience: **g,l,u,f.**

Beckett, Samuel, et al.   **PR6003.E282Z57188**
Beckett Remembering, Remembering Beckett: A Centenary
Celebration. James Knowlson & Elizabeth Knowlson (Authors).
Trade Cloth. Arcade Publishing, Inc. New York, NY. 2006.
336p. ISBN:1-55970-772-0, ISBN13: 978-1-55970-772-5.
Dewey:848/.91409. LCCN:2005-010308.

Audience: **u,f.**

Erskine, Robb   **PQ2617.O6Z6785 2002**
Eugene Ionesco. Harold Bloom (Editor, Introduction by). Trade

Cloth. Facts On File, Inc. New York, NY. 2002. 120p. Bloom's Major Dramatists Ser. ISBN:0-7910-7037-9, ISBN13: 978-0-7910-7037-6. Dewey:842/.914. LCCN:2002-012506.

Audience: **u,f.**

Esslin, Martin   **PN1861**
The Theatre of the Absurd. Ed. 3. Trade Paper. Knopf Publishing Group. New York, NY. 2004. 480p. ISBN:1-4000-7523-8, ISBN13: 978-1-4000-7523-2. Dewey:809.2/045. LCCN:2004-268174.

Audience: **l,u,f.** $\mathcal{B}$

Grossvogel, David I.   **PN1861 .G7 1975**
Four Playwrights and a Postscript: Brecht, Ionesco, Beckett, Genet. Trade Cloth. Greenwood Publishing Group, Inc. Portsmouth, NH. 1976. 209p. ISBN:0-8371-8438-X, ISBN13: 978-0-8371-8438-8. Dewey:809.2/04. LCCN:75-027654.

Audience: **l,u,f.** $\mathcal{B}$

Mann, Bruce J. (Editor)   **PS3551.L25Z655 2003**
Edward Albee: A Casebook. Paper over Boards. Routledge. New York, NY. 2002. 168p. Casebooks on Modern Dramatists, Vol. 29 ISBN:0-8153-3165-7, ISBN13: 978-0-8153-3165-0. Dewey:812/.54. LCCN:2002-011279.

Audience: **l,u,f.** *Choice, 2003.*

Orr, John   **PN1907.O7 1991**
Tragicomedy and Contemporary Culture: Play and Performance from Beckett to Shepard. Trade Cloth. University of Michigan Press. Chicago, IL. 1991. 176p. Theater Ser., :Theory - Text - Performance ISBN:0-472-10262-1, ISBN13: 978-0-472-10262-4. Dewey:809.2/523. LCCN:91-009736.

Audience: **g,l.**

Pattie, David   **PR6003.E282Z7858**
The Complete Critical Guide to Samuel Beckett. Trade Paper. Routledge. New York, NY. 2004. 240p. Routledge Guides to Literature Ser. ISBN:0-415-20254-X, ISBN13: 978-0-415-20254-1. Dewey:848/.91409. LCCN:00-055819.

Audience: **g.**

Pinter, Harold   **PR6066.I53 1990**
Complete Works: Birthday Party. Trade Paper. Grove/Atlantic, Inc. New York, NY. 1994. 256p. ISBN:0-8021-5096-9, ISBN13: 978-0-8021-5096-7. Dewey:822/.914. LCCN:90-013933.

Audience: **g,l,u,f.**

Pinter, Harold   **PR6066.I53 1990**
Complete Works: The Homecoming, Vol. 3. Trade Paper. Grove/Atlantic, Inc. New York, NY. 1994. 256p. ISBN:0-8021-5049-7, ISBN13: 978-0-8021-5049-3. Dewey:822/.914. LCCN:90-013933.

Audience: **g,l,u,f.**

Pinter, Harold   **PR6066.I53 1990**
Complete Works: The Caretaker, Vol. 2. Trade Paper. Grove/Atlantic, Inc. New York, NY. 1994. 256p. ISBN:0-8021-3237-5, ISBN13: 978-0-8021-3237-6. Dewey:822/.914. LCCN:90-013933.

Audience: **g,l,u,f.**

Pinter, Harold   **PR6066.I53 1990**
Complete Works: Betrayal. Trade Paper. Grove/Atlantic, Inc. New York, NY. 1994. 384p. ISBN:0-8021-5050-0, ISBN13: 978-0-8021-5050-9. Dewey:822/.914. LCCN:90-013933.

Audience: **g,l,u,f.**

Raby, Peter (Editor)   **PR6066.I53Z625520**
The Cambridge Companion to Harold Pinter. Cloth Text. Cambridge University Press. New York, NY. 2001. 292p. Companions to Literature Ser. ISBN:0-521-65123-9, ISBN13: 978-0-521-65123-3. Dewey:822/.914. LCCN:2001-022302.

Audience: **g,l,u,f.** *Choice, 2002.*

White, Edmund   **PQ2605.O28**
Genet: A Biography. Book, Other. Knopf Publishing Group. New York, NY. 1994. 800p. ISBN:0-679-75479-2, ISBN13: 978-0-679-75479-4. Dewey:848/.91209 B.

Audience: **g,l,u,f.** *Choice, 1994.*

Western Drama and Theater > Genres, Styles, and Types > Musical Theater

                                                    PN2277.N5
☐ Internet Broadway Database.
http://www.ibdb.com/

Audience: **g,l,u,f.**

Everett, William & Laird,   **ML2054.C35 2002**
Paul R. (Editors)
The Cambridge Companion to the Musical. Cloth Text. Cambridge University Press. New York, NY. 2002. 328p. Cambridge Companions to Music Ser. ISBN:0-521-79189-8, ISBN13: 978-0-521-79189-2. Dewey:302.2/244/0945. LCCN:2002-023788.

Audience: **g.** *Choice, 2003.*

Gänzl, Kurt   **ML102.M88G3 2001**
The Encyclopedia of the Musical Theatre. Trade Cloth. Thomson Gale. Farmington Hills, MI. 2001. ISBN:0-02-865574-5, ISBN13: 978-0-02-865574-1. Dewey:782.1/4/03. LCCN:2001-018361.

Audience: **g.**

Hischak, Thomas S.   **ML102**
Stage It with Music: An Encyclopedic Guide to the American Musical Theatre. Cloth Text. Greenwood Publishing Group, Inc. Portsmouth, NH. 1993. 328p. ISBN:0-313-28708-2, ISBN13: 978-0-313-28708-4. Dewey:792.60973. LCCN:92-035321.

Audience: **l,u.** *Choice, 1993.*

Lamb, Andrew   **ML2054.L35 2000**
150 Years of Popular Musical Theatre. Cloth over Boards. Yale University Press. Cumberland, RI. 2001. 400p. ISBN:0-300-07538-3, ISBN13: 978-0-300-07538-0. Dewey:782.1/09/034. LCCN:00-025281.

Audience: **g.**

Peterson, Bernard L.　　　　　**ML102**
A Century of Musicals in Black and White: An Encyclopedia of Musical Stage Works by, About, or Involving Black Americans. Cloth Text. Greenwood Publishing Group, Inc. Portsmouth, NH. 1993. 560p. ISBN:0-313-26657-3, ISBN13: 978-0-313-26657-7. Dewey:782.1408996073. LCCN:92-041976.
Audience: **g.**　*Choice, 1994.*

Porter, Steven　　　　　**ML1950.P68 1997**
The American Musical Theatre: A Complete Musical Theatre Course. Ed. 2. Trade Paper. Players Press, Inc. Studio City, CA. 2003. 152p. Musical Theatre Ser. ISBN:0-88734-686-3, ISBN13: 978-0-88734-686-6. Dewey:782.81. LCCN:97-039626.
Audience: **l,u,f.**

Smith, Cecil & Litton,　　　　**ML1711.S6 1981**
Glenn
Musical Comedy in America: From the Black Crook Through Sweeney Todd. Ed. 2. Trade Paper. Routledge. New York, NY. 1987. 367p. ISBN:0-87830-564-5, ISBN13: 978-0-87830-564-3. Dewey:782.81/0973. LCCN:80-051638.
Audience: **l,u,f.**　*B*

Thelen, Lawrence　　　　**PN2285.T48 2000**
The Show Makers: Great Directors of American Musical Theatre. UK-B Format Paperback. Routledge. New York, NY. 2002. 264p. ISBN:0-415-92347-6, ISBN13: 978-0-415-92347-7. Dewey:792.6/0233/092273 B. LCCN:99-029455.
Audience: **l,u,f.**　*Choice, 2000.*

Western Drama and Theater > Genres, Styles, and Types > Puppet Theater

Blumenthal, Eileen　　　　**PN1972.B57 2005**
Puppetry: A World History. Trade Cloth. Harry N. Abrams, Inc. New York, NY. 2005. 272p. ISBN:0-8109-5587-3, ISBN13: 978-0-8109-5587-5. Dewey:791.5/3. LCCN:2004-029349.
Audience: **g,l,u,f.**　*Choice, 2005.*

Currell, David　　　　**TT174.7.C8716 1999**
Puppets and Puppet Theatre. Trade Cloth. Crowood Press, Limited, The. Wiltshire, 1999. 176p. ISBN:1-86126-135-7, ISBN13: 978-1-86126-135-9. Dewey:791.5.
Audience: **l,u,f.**

Jurkowski, Henryk　　　　**PN1978.E85 J87 1996**
A History of European Puppetry: The Twentieth Century. Trade Cloth. Edwin Mellen Press, The. Lewiston, NY. 1998. 740p. ISBN:0-7734-8322-5, ISBN13: 978-0-7734-8322-4. Dewey:791.5/3/094. LCCN:96-007208.
Audience: **l,u,f.**

Jurkowski, Henryk　　　　**PN1978.E85H57 1996**
A History of European Puppetry from Its Origins to the End of the 19th Century. Penny Francis (Editor). Trade Cloth. Edwin Mellen Press, The. Lewiston, NY. 1996. 480p. ISBN:0-7734-8803-0, ISBN13: 978-0-7734-8803-8. Dewey:791.5/3/094. LCCN:96-007208.
Audience: **l,u,f.**

McCormick, John　　　　**PN1978.G7M38 2004**
The Victorian Marionette Theatre. Clodagh McCormick & John Phillips (Contribution by). Trade Paper. University of Iowa Press. Iowa City, IA. 2004. 292p. Studies in Theatre History and Culture ISBN:0-87745-912-6, ISBN13: 978-0-87745-912-5. Dewey:791.5/094109034. LCCN:2004-048015.
Audience: **u,f.**　*Choice, 2005.*

McCormick, John &　　　　**PN1978.E85 M38 1998**
Pratasik, Bennie
Popular Puppet Theatre in Europe, 1800-1914. Trade Paper. Cambridge University Press. New York, NY. 2005. 266p. ISBN:0-521-61615-8, ISBN13: 978-0-521-61615-7. Dewey:791.5/3.
Audience: **l,u.**　*Choice, 1998.*

Segel, Harold B.　　　　**PN1972.S43 1995**
Pinocchio's Progeny: Puppets, Marionettes, Automatons, and Robots in Modernist and Avant-Garde Drama. Trade Cloth. Johns Hopkins University Press. Baltimore, MD. 1995. 424p. PAJ Bks. ISBN:0-8018-5031-2, ISBN13: 978-0-8018-5031-8. Dewey:812/.54. LCCN:95-075204.
Audience: **l,u,f.**　*Choice, 1996.*

Tillis, Steve　　　　**PN1972**
Toward an Aesthetics of the Puppet: Puppetry As a Theatrical Art. Trade Cloth. Greenwood Publishing Group, Inc. Portsmouth, NH. 1992. 200p. Contributions in Drama and Theatre Studies Ser., No. 47 ISBN:0-313-28359-1, ISBN13: 978-0-313-28359-8. Dewey:791.5301. LCCN:91-043366.
Audience: **u,f.**

Western Drama and Theater > Genres, Styles, and Types > Pantomime

Aubert, Charles & Sears,　　　　**PN1985.A83 2003**
Edith
The Art of Pantomime. Trade Paper. Dover Publications, Inc. Mineola, NY. 2003. 224p. Performing Arts: Drama, Film and Dance Ser. ISBN:0-486-42857-5, ISBN13: 978-0-486-42857-4. Dewey:792.3. LCCN:2003-041459.
Audience: **l,u,f.**

Broadbent, R. J.　　　　**PN1985 .B7**
A History of Pantomime. Paper Text. Classic Books. Murrieta, CA. 2001. 226p. ISBN:0-7426-9200-0, ISBN13: 978-0-7426-9200-8. Dewey:792.309.
Audience: **l,u,f.**　*B*

Harris, Paul　　　　**PN1985.H35 1996**
The Pantomime. Trade Paper. Peter Owen Ltd. London, 1996. 144p. ISBN:0-7206-1013-3, ISBN13: 978-0-7206-1013-0. Dewey:822/.914. LCCN:96-223583.
Audience: **l,u,f.**

Nicoll, Allardyce　　　　**PN2071.G4 N5**
Masks, Mimes and Miracles. Trade Cloth. Cooper Square Publishers, Inc. New York, NY. 1981. ISBN:0-8154-0163-9, ISBN13: 978-0-8154-0163-6. Dewey:792.09. LCCN:63-017895.
Audience: **l,u,f.**

O'Brien, John   **PN1987.G7O27 2004**
Harlequin Britain: Pantomime and Entertainment, 1690-1760.
Trade Cloth. Johns Hopkins University Press. Baltimore, MD.
2004. 304p. ISBN:0-8018-7910-8, ISBN13: 978-0-8018-7910-4.
Dewey:792.3/8/09033. LCCN:2003-021417.

                                     Audience: **u,f.** *Choice, 2005.*

Western Drama and Theater > Genres, Styles, and Types > Drama and Theater for Special Purposes

Crook, Tim   **PN1991.65.C66 1999**
Radio Drama. Paper over Boards. Routledge. New York, NY.
1999. 312p. ISBN:0-415-21602-8, ISBN13: 978-0-415-21602-9.
Dewey:809.2/22. LCCN:99-026899.

                                 Audience: **l,u,f.** *Choice, 2000.*

Drakakis, John (Editor)   **PN1991.65 .B74**
British Radio Drama. Trade Paper. Cambridge University Press.
New York, NY. 1981. 296p. ISBN:0-521-29383-9, ISBN13:
978-0-521-29383-9. Dewey:822/.02/09. LCCN:80-040678.

                                     Audience: **l,u,f.**

Fahy, Thomas; King,   **PS338.P4P44 2001**
   Kimball
Peering Behind the Curtain: Cisability, Illness, and the
Extraordinary Body in Contemporary Theater. Routledge. 2002.
ISBN:0-415-92997-0, ISBN13: 978-0-415-92997-4.

                                     Audience: **g.**

Grams, Martin Jr.   **PN1991.9.G73 2000**
Radio Drama: A Comprehensive Chronicle of American
Network Programs, 1932-1962. Cloth Text. McFarland &
Company, Incorporated Publishers. Jefferson, NC. 2000. 584p.
ISBN:0-7864-0051-X, ISBN13: 978-0-7864-0051-5.
Dewey:016.79144/75/0973. LCCN:99-29879.

                       Audience: **l,u,f.** *Choice, 2000.*

Jennings, Sue   **RC489.P7J453 1998**
Introduction to Dramatherapy: Ariadne's Ball of Thread. Trade
Paper. Jessica Kingsley Ltd. London, 1998. 200p.
ISBN:1-85302-115-6, ISBN13: 978-1-85302-115-2.
Dewey:616.89/1523. LCCN:98-114033.

                                     Audience: **u,f.**

Lewis, Penny & Johnson,   **RC489.P7C86 2000**
   David Read (Editors)
Current Approaches in Drama Therapy. Trade Paper. Charles C
Thomas Publisher, Ltd. Springfield, IL. 2000. 502p.
ISBN:0-398-07083-0, ISBN13: 978-0-398-07083-0.
Dewey:616.89/1523. LCCN:00-032612.

                                     Audience: **u,f.**

Pitruzzella, Salvo   **RC489.P7P587 2004**
Introduction to Dramatherapy: Person and Threshold. Paper over
Boards. Brunner-Routledge. Philadelphia, PA. 2004. 208p.
ISBN:1-58391-974-0, ISBN13: 978-1-58391-974-3.
Dewey:616.89/1523. LCCN:2003-019903.

                                     Audience: **u,f.**

Thompson, James   **HV8861.P47 1998**
Perspectives and Practices in Prison Theatre. Trade Paper.
Jessica Kingsley Ltd. London, 1998. 247p. Forensic Focus Ser.
ISBN:1-85302-417-1, ISBN13: 978-1-85302-417-7.
Dewey:365/.66. LCCN:96-032681.

                                     Audience: **l,u,f.**

Western Drama and Theater > Europe

Barker, Simon & Hinds,   **PR1263.R68 2002**
   Hilary (Editors)
Routledge Anthology of Renaissance Drama. Paper over Boards.
Routledge. New York, NY. 2002. 480p. ISBN:0-415-18733-8,
ISBN13: 978-0-415-18733-6. Dewey:822/.308.
LCCN:2002-026872.

                                     Audience: **l,u,f.**

Barr, Alan (Editor)   **PN6119.8.M65 2001**
Modern Women Playwrights of Europe. Paper Text. Oxford
University Press, Inc. New York, NY. 2000. 608p.
ISBN:0-19-513536-9, ISBN13: 978-0-19-513536-7.
Dewey:808.82/0082/094. LCCN:99-086027.

                                     Audience: **l,u,f.**

Beckett, Samuel   **PR6003.E282**
Dramatic Works and Dialogues, Vol. 2. Trade Paper. Riverrun
Press, Inc. Flemington, NJ. 1999. 80p. Beckett Shorts Ser., 2
ISBN:0-7145-4214-8, ISBN13: 978-0-7145-4214-0.
Dewey:822.912.

                                     Audience: **l,u,f.**

Beckett, Samuel   **PR6003.E282A6 2006**
The Dramatic Works of Samuel Beckett: Volume III of the
Grove Centenary Editions. Paul Auster (Editor), Edward Albee
(Introduction by). Cloth over Boards. Grove/Atlantic, Inc. New
York, NY. 2006. 520p. ISBN:0-8021-1819-4, ISBN13:
978-0-8021-1819-6. Dewey:848/.81409. LCCN:2005-055078.

                                     Audience: **g,l,u,f.**

Beckett, Samuel   **PR6003.E282**
Samuel Beckett: Waiting for Godot-Endgame. Peter Boxall
(Editor). Trade Paper. Palgrave Macmillan. New York, NY.
2003. 206p. Readers' Guides to Essential Criticism Ser.
ISBN:1-84046-082-2, ISBN13: 978-1-84046-082-7.
Dewey:822.912.

                                     Audience: **g,l,u,f.**

Beckett, Samuel, et al.   **PR6003.E282Z57188**
Beckett Remembering, Remembering Beckett: A Centenary
Celebration. James Knowlson & Elizabeth Knowlson (Authors).
Trade Cloth. Arcade Publishing, Inc. New York, NY. 2006.
336p. ISBN:1-55970-772-0, ISBN13: 978-1-55970-772-5.
Dewey:848/.91409. LCCN:2005-010308.

                                     Audience: **u,f.**

Bentley, Eric   **PN6112.B43**
The Play, a Critical Anthology. Paper Text. Textbook Publishers.
Temecula, CA. 2003. 774p. ISBN:0-7581-6026-7, ISBN13:
978-0-7581-6026-3. Dewey:808.82.

                                     Audience: **l.** *B*

Bergh, Albert Ellery　　　　　　　　　　**PN6111**
Classic Drama Plays by Greek, Spanish, French, German and
English Dramatists, Vol. 1. The World's Great Classics (Editor).
Trade Paper. Kessinger Publishing, LLC. Whitefish, MT. 2004.
ISBN:1-4179-4186-3, ISBN13: 978-1-4179-4186-5.
Dewey:808.82.

Audience: **l,u.**

Berghaus, Günter　　　　　　　　**PN2193.E86B47 2005**
Avant-Garde Performance. Cloth over Boards. Palgrave
Macmillan. New York, NY. 2005. 352p. ISBN:1-4039-4644-2,
ISBN13: 978-1-4039-4644-7. Dewey:792.02/23.
LCCN:2004-065797.

Audience: **u,f.**

Berghaus, Günter　　　　　　　**PN2193.E86B475 2005**
Theatre, Performance, and the Historical Avant-Garde. Cloth
over Boards. Palgrave Macmillan. New York, NY. 2006. 400p.
Palgrave Studies in Theatre and Performance History Ser.
ISBN:1-4039-6955-8, ISBN13: 978-1-4039-6955-2.
Dewey:792.02/9. LCCN:2005-054609.

Audience: **u,f.**

Boyer, Patricia E.　　　　　　　　**NC1002.P7B68 1998**
Artists and the Avant-Garde: Theatre in Paris, 1887-1900. Trade
Paper. Ashgate Publishing, Ltd. Aldershot, 1999. 180p. The
Martin and Liane W. Atlas Collection Ser. ISBN:0-89468-274-1,
ISBN13: 978-0-89468-274-2. Dewey:792/.09443/6109034.
LCCN:97-044775.

Audience: **u,f.**

Branch, William B. (Editor)　　　　　**PS628.N4C76 1993**
Crosswinds: An Anthology of Black Dramatists in the Diaspora.
Trade Paper. Indiana University Press. Bloomington, IN. 1993.
448p. Blacks in the Diaspora Ser. ISBN:0-253-20778-9,
ISBN13: 978-0-253-20778-4. Dewey:808.82/008996.
LCCN:92-026648.

Audience: **l,u,f.**

Brustein, Robert　　　　　　　　　**PN2189.B7 1991**
The Theatre of Revolt: Studies in Modern Drama from Ibsen to
Genet. Trade Paper. Ivan R. Dee Publisher. Blue Ridge Summit,
PA. 1991. 435p. ISBN:0-929587-53-7, ISBN13:
978-0-929587-53-0. Dewey:809.2/04. LCCN:90-023644.

Audience: **l,u.**

Cairns, Christopher (Editor)　　　　　　**PR653.R46**
Renaissance Theatre: Texts, Performance and Design, Vol. 2.
Trade Cloth. Ashgate Publishing, Ltd. Aldershot, 1999. 358p.
ISBN:0-7546-0008-4, ISBN13: 978-0-7546-0008-4.
Dewey:822/.309.

Audience: **l,u,f.**

Cairns, Christopher (Editor)　　　　　**PR653.R46 1999**
The Renaissance Theatre - Texts, Performance and Design:
English and Italian Theatre. Trade Cloth. Ashgate Publishing,
Ltd. Aldershot, 1999. 200p. ISBN:0-7546-0006-8, ISBN13:
978-0-7546-0006-0. Dewey:822/.309. LCCN:99-029487.

Audience: **l,u,f.**

Cardullo, Bert & Knopf,　　　　　**PN6112.T42 2001**
　Robert (Editors)
Theater of the Avant-Garde, 1890-1950: A Critical Anthology.
Cloth over Boards. Yale University Press. Cumberland, RI.
2001. 546p. ISBN:0-300-08525-7, ISBN13: 978-0-300-08525-9.
Dewey:808.82/911. LCCN:00-043891.

Audience: **u,f.**

Cate, Phillip D.　　　　　　　　**NX549.P2S67 1996**
The Spirit of Montmartre: Cabarets, Humor, and the
Avant-Garde, 1875-1905. Mary Shaw (Editor). Trade Paper.
Rutgers University Press. Piscataway, NJ. 1996. 240p.
ISBN:0-8135-2324-9, ISBN13: 978-0-8135-2324-8.
Dewey:792.7/0944/36109034. LCCN:95-081835.

Audience: **f.** *Choice, 1996.*

Cheney, Sheldon　　　　　　　　　**PR9199.2.R43**
The Art Theatre: A Discussion of Its Ideals, Its Organization,
and Its Promise As a Corrective for Present Evils in the
Commercial Theatre. Paper Text. Classic Books. Murrieta, CA.
2001. 249p. ISBN:0-7426-9207-8, ISBN13: 978-0-7426-9207-7.
Dewey:813/.3.

Audience: **l,u,f.**

Cheney, Sheldon　　　　　　　　　**PN2189.C5**
The New Movement in the Theatre. Paper Text. Classic Books.
Murrieta, CA. 2001. 303p. ISBN:0-7426-9195-0, ISBN13:
978-0-7426-9195-7. Dewey:792/.08.

Audience: **l,u.**

Cohen, Walter　　　　　　　　　　　**PR651**
Drama of a Nation: Public Theater in Renaissance England and
Spain. Book, Other. Cornell University Press. Ithaca, NY. 1988.
416p. ISBN:0-8014-9494-X, ISBN13: 978-0-8014-9494-9.
Dewey:822/.3/09. LCCN:85-002633.

Audience: **l,u,f.**

Conlon, Raymond (Editor)　　　　　**PN820.A835 2003**
An Anthology of Renaissance Plays in Translation: Works from
the Italian, Spanish, and Portuguese Traditions. Trade Cloth.
Edwin Mellen Press, The. Lewiston, NY. 2002. 516p. Studies in
Renaissance Literature, Vol. 23 ISBN:0-7734-6905-2, ISBN13:
978-0-7734-6905-1. Dewey:852/.208. LCCN:2002-033753.

Audience: **l,u,f.**

Dickinson, Thomas H.　　　　　　　**PN6112.D5**
Chief Contemporary Dramatists: Twenty-Two Plays from the
Recent Drama of England, Ireland, America, Germany, France,
Belgium, Norway, Sweden and Russia. Library Binding. Richard
West. Philadelphia, PA. 1979. ISBN:0-8492-4207-X, ISBN13:
978-0-8492-4207-6. Dewey:808.82.

Audience: **l,u,f.**

Dickinson, Thomas H.　　　　　　　**PN6112.D52**
Chief Contemporary Dramatists. Trade Paper. Kessinger
Publishing, LLC. Whitefish, MT. 2005. ISBN:1-4179-8690-5,
ISBN13: 978-1-4179-8690-3. Dewey:808.82.

Audience: **l,u,f.**

Dickinson, Thomas H.   PN6112.D52
  (Editor)
Chief Contemporary Dramatists, Second Series: Eighteen Plays
from the Recent Drama of England, Ireland, America, France,
Germany, Austria, Italy, Spain, Russia, and Scandinavia. Library
Binding. Darby Books. Darby, PA. 1985. 734p.
ISBN:0-317-17328-6, ISBN13: 978-0-317-17328-4.
Dewey:808.82/041.

Audience: **l,u,f.**

Dukore, Bernard F. &   PN6112 .D8 1976
  Gerould, Daniel C.
Avant Garde Drama: A Casebook. Trade Paper. HarperCollins
Publishers. New York, NY. 1976. ISBN:0-690-00848-1, ISBN13:
978-0-690-00848-7. Dewey:808.82/04. LCCN:75-027237.

Audience: **u,f.**

Erskine, Robb   PQ2617.O6Z6785 2002
Eugene Ionesco. Harold Bloom (Editor, Introduction by). Trade
Cloth. Facts On File, Inc. New York, NY. 2002. 120p. Bloom's
Major Dramatists Ser. ISBN:0-7910-7037-9, ISBN13:
978-0-7910-7037-6. Dewey:842/.914. LCCN:2002-012506.

Audience: **u,f.**

Esslin, Martin   PN1861
The Theatre of the Absurd. Ed. 3. Trade Paper. Knopf
Publishing Group. New York, NY. 2004. 480p.
ISBN:1-4000-7523-8, ISBN13: 978-1-4000-7523-2.
Dewey:809.2/045. LCCN:2004-268174.

Audience: **l,u,f.** *B*

Fischer-Lichte, Erika   PN1731.F513 2001
History of European Drama and Theatre. Trade Paper.
Routledge. New York, NY. 2004. 416p. ISBN:0-415-18060-0,
ISBN13: 978-0-415-18060-3. Dewey:809.2.
LCCN:2001-034969.

Audience: **u,f.** *Choice, 2002.*

Gillespie, Gerald (Editor)   PN1851.R66 1994
Romantic Drama. Library Binding. John Benjamins Publishing
Company. Philadelphia, PA. 1993. 516p. Comparative History of
Literatures in European Languages Ser., Vol. No. 9
ISBN:1-55619-600-8, ISBN13: 978-1-55619-600-3.
Dewey:809.2/9145. LCCN:93-034838.

Audience: **l,u,f.**

Graver, David   NX456.5.M64G73 1995
The Aesthetics of Disturbance: Anti-Art in Avant-Garde Drama.
Trade Cloth. University of Michigan Press. Chicago, IL. 1995.
272p. Theater Ser., :Theory - Text - Performance
ISBN:0-472-10507-8, ISBN13: 978-0-472-10507-6.
Dewey:700/.1. LCCN:95-016289.

Audience: **u,f.** *Choice, 1996.*

Grossvogel, David I.   PN1861 .G7 1975
Four Playwrights and a Postscript: Brecht, Ionesco, Beckett,
Genet. Trade Cloth. Greenwood Publishing Group, Inc.
Portsmouth, NH. 1976. 209p. ISBN:0-8371-8438-X, ISBN13:
978-0-8371-8438-8. Dewey:809.2/04. LCCN:75-027654.

Audience: **l,u,f.** *B*

Harding, James M. (Editor)   PN2193.E86C66 2000
Contours of the Theatrical Avant-Garde: Performance and
Textuality. Trade Paper. University of Michigan Press. Chicago,
IL. 2000. 312p. Theater Ser., :Theory - Text - Performance
ISBN:0-472-06727-3, ISBN13: 978-0-472-06727-5.
Dewey:792/.022. LCCN:00-008540.

Audience: **u,f.** *Choice, 2001.*

Harrison, Elizabeth J.   PR478.M6U53 1997
  (Editor)
Unmanning Modernism: Gendered Re-Readings. Peterson,
Shirley (Editor). University of Tennessee Press. 1997.
ISBN:0-87049-985-8, ISBN13: 978-0-87049-985-2.

Audience: **u,f.**

Hays, Michael &   PN1922
  Nikolopoulou, Anastasia (Editors)
Melodrama: The Cultural Emergence of a Genre. Trade Paper.
Palgrave Macmillan. New York, NY. 1999. 304p.
ISBN:0-312-22127-4, ISBN13: 978-0-312-22127-0.
Dewey:809.2/52.

Audience: **u,f.** *Choice, 1997.*

Innes, Christopher   PN1861.I5 1993
Avant-Garde Theatre: 1892-1992. Ed. 2. Trade Paper. Routledge.
New York, NY. 1993. 272p. ISBN:0-415-06518-6, ISBN13:
978-0-415-06518-4. Dewey:792.09. LCCN:92-016204.

Audience: **u,f.**

Jurkowski, Henryk   PN1978.E85 J87 1996
A History of European Puppetry: The Twentieth Century. Trade
Cloth. Edwin Mellen Press, The. Lewiston, NY. 1998. 740p.
ISBN:0-7734-8322-5, ISBN13: 978-0-7734-8322-4.
Dewey:791.5/3/094. LCCN:96-007208.

Audience: **l,u,f.**

Jurkowski, Henryk   PN1978.E85H57 1996
A History of European Puppetry from Its Origins to the End of
the 19th Century. Penny Francis (Editor). Trade Cloth. Edwin
Mellen Press, The. Lewiston, NY. 1996. 480p.
ISBN:0-7734-8803-0, ISBN13: 978-0-7734-8803-8.
Dewey:791.5/3/094. LCCN:96-007208.

Audience: **l,u,f.**

Kullman, Colby H. &   PN2256
  Young, William C. (Editors)
Theatre Companies of the World: Africa, Asia, Australia, and
New Zealand, Canada, Eastern Europe, Latin America, the
Middle East, Scandinavia, Vol. 1. Cloth Text. Greenwood
Publishing Group, Inc. Portsmouth, NH. 1986. 1024p.
ISBN:0-313-25667-5, ISBN13: 978-0-313-25667-7.
Dewey:792/.09. LCCN:84-000539.

Audience: **g.**

Lee, Briant H.   NA6840.E85L44 1996
European Post-Baroque Neoclassical Theatre Architecture. Trade
Cloth. Edwin Mellen Press, The. Lewiston, NY. 1996. 248p.
Studies in Theatre Arts, Vol. 3 ISBN:0-7734-8845-6, ISBN13:
978-0-7734-8845-8. Dewey:725/.822/09409033.
LCCN:95-041058.

Audience: **u,f.**

Leiter, Samuel L.   **PN2597**
From Belasco to Brook: Representative Directors of the
English-Speaking Stage. Trade Cloth. Greenwood Publishing
Group, Inc. Portsmouth, NH. 1991. 320p. Contributions in
Drama and Theatre Studies Ser., No. 33 ISBN:0-313-27662-5,
ISBN13: 978-0-313-27662-0. Dewey:792/.0233/0922 B.
LCCN:90-045350.

Audience: **l,u,f.** *Choice, 1991.*

MacGowan, Kenneth   **PN2570**
Continental Stagecraft. Paper Text. Classic Books. Murrieta, CA.
2001. 233p. ISBN:0-7426-9204-3, ISBN13: 978-0-7426-9204-6.
Dewey:792.094.

Audience: **l,u,f.** *B*

Marker, F. J. & Innes,   **PN1851.M64 1998**
Christopher (Editors)
Modernism in European Drama: Ibsen, Strindberg, Pirandello,
Beckett: Essays from Modern Drama. Cloth over Boards.
University of Toronto Press. Toronto, ON. 1998. 336p.
ISBN:0-8020-4399-2, ISBN13: 978-0-8020-4399-3.
Dewey:809.2. LCCN:99-170702.

Audience: **l,u.**

Matthews, Brander   **PN6112**
The Chief European Dramatists: Twenty-One Plays from the
Drama of Greece, Rome, Spain, France, Italy, Germany,
Denmark, and Norway from 500 B. C. to 1879 A. D. Trade
Paper. University Press of the Pacific. Miami, FL. 2004. 800p.
ISBN:1-4102-1454-0, ISBN13: 978-1-4102-1454-6.
Dewey:808.82.

Audience: **l,u.**

McCormick, John &   **PN1978.E85 M38 1998**
Pratasik, Bennie
Popular Puppet Theatre in Europe, 1800-1914. Trade Paper.
Cambridge University Press. New York, NY. 2005. 266p.
ISBN:0-521-61615-8, ISBN13: 978-0-521-61615-7.
Dewey:791.5/3.

Audience: **l,u.** *Choice, 1998.*

Muir, Lynette R.   **PN1880 .M85 1995**
The Biblical Drama of Medieval Europe. Trade Paper.
Cambridge University Press. New York, NY. 2003. 344p.
ISBN:0-521-54210-3, ISBN13: 978-0-521-54210-4.
Dewey:809.2/516.

Audience: **u,f.** *Choice, 1996.*

Nicoll, Allardyce   **PN2071.G4 N5**
Masks, Mimes and Miracles. Trade Cloth. Cooper Square
Publishers, Inc. New York, NY. 1981. ISBN:0-8154-0163-9,
ISBN13: 978-0-8154-0163-6. Dewey:792.09. LCCN:63-017895.

Audience: **l,u,f.**

Pattie, David   **PR6003.E282Z7858**
The Complete Critical Guide to Samuel Beckett. Trade Paper.
Routledge. New York, NY. 2004. 240p. Routledge Guides to
Literature Ser. ISBN:0-415-20254-X, ISBN13:
978-0-415-20254-1. Dewey:848/.91409. LCCN:00-055819.

Audience: **g.**

Rouyer, Philippe & Nagy,   **PN1861**
Peter (Editors)
Europe, Vol. 1. Trade Paper. Routledge. New York, NY. 2001.
1072p. World Encyclopedia of Contemporary Theatre Ser.
ISBN:0-415-25157-5, ISBN13: 978-0-415-25157-0.
Dewey:912.4.

Audience: **g.**

Sandrow, Nahma   **PN3035.S25 1996**
Vagabond Stars: A World History of Yiddish Theater. Trade
Cloth. Syracuse University Press. Syracuse, NY. 1995. 448p.
Judaic Traditions in Literature, Music and Art Ser.
ISBN:0-8156-0329-0, ISBN13: 978-0-8156-0329-0.
Dewey:792/.089924. LCCN:95-035166.

Audience: **l,u,f.** *B*

Styan, John L.   **PN1861.S76 1983**
Modern Drama in Theory and Practice: Realism and Naturalism,
Vol. 1. Trade Paper. Cambridge University Press. New York,
NY. 1983. 217p. ISBN:0-521-29628-5, ISBN13:
978-0-521-29628-1. Dewey:809.2. LCCN:79-015947.

Audience: **l,u,f.**

Styan, John L. (Editor)   **PN1861 .S76**
Modern Drama in Theory and Practice: Symbolism, Surrealism
and the Absurd. Trade Paper. Cambridge University Press. New
York, NY. 1983. 235p. ISBN:0-521-29629-3, ISBN13:
978-0-521-29629-8. Dewey:809.2. LCCN:79-015947.

Audience: **l,u.**

Styan, John L.   **PN1861.S76**
Modern Drama in Theory and Practice: Expressionism and Epic
Theatre, Vol. 3. Trade Paper. Cambridge University Press. New
York, NY. 1983. 242p. ISBN:0-521-29630-7, ISBN13:
978-0-521-29630-4. Dewey:792/.0904. LCCN:79-015947.

Audience: **l,u,f.**

The World's Great Classics   **PN6111**
(Editor)
Classic Drama Plays by Greek, Spanish, French, German and
English Dramatists, Vol. 2. Albert Ellery Bergh (Illustrator).
Trade Paper. Kessinger Publishing, LLC. Whitefish, MT. 2004.
ISBN:0-7661-9942-8, ISBN13: 978-0-7661-9942-2.
Dewey:808.82.

Audience: **l,u.**

Tydeman, William   **PN2570**
The Theatre in the Middle Ages: Western European Stage
Conditions, C. 800-1576. Trade Paper. Cambridge University
Press. New York, NY. 1979. 310p. ISBN:0-521-29304-9,
ISBN13: 978-0-521-29304-4. Dewey:792/.094.
LCCN:77-085683.

Audience: **u,f.**

Tydeman, William (Editor)   **PN2570 .M39 2001**
The Medieval European Stage, 500-1550. W. D. Howarth, John
Northam & Glynne W. Wickham (Contribution by). Trade Cloth.
Cambridge University Press. New York, NY. 2001. 782p.
Theatre in Europe Ser. ISBN:0-521-24609-1, ISBN13:
978-0-521-24609-5. Dewey:792/.094/0902. LCCN:00-067610.

Audience: **u,f.** *Choice, 2002.*

Western Drama and Theater > Europe > Britain

PN2596.L7.R515 1981
At the Royal Court: 25 Years of the English Stage Company. Trade Cloth. Bow Historical Books. New Providence, NJ. 1981. 201, [56]p. ISBN:0-8021-0211-5, ISBN13: 978-0-8021-0211-9. Dewey:792/.09421/34. LCCN:80-085375.

Audience: **u,f.** 𝐵

PR1269
Eighteenth Century Plays. Paper Text. Textbook Publishers. Temecula, CA. 2003. 484p. ISBN:0-7581-8086-1, ISBN13: 978-0-7581-8086-5. Dewey:822.5.

Audience: **l,u,f.**

PS3525.A24785
Office of the Revels: The Dramatic Records of Sir Henry Herbert, Master of the Revels, 1623-1673. Paper Text. Classic Books. Murrieta, CA. 2001. 155p. ISBN:0-7426-9229-9, ISBN13: 978-0-7426-9229-9. Dewey:704.

Audience: **u,f.**

Adams, Joseph Quincy   **PN2596.L6A55**
Shakespearean Playhouses: A History of English Theatres from the Beginnings to the Restoration. Paper Text. Textbook Publishers. Temecula, CA. 2003. 473p. ISBN:0-7581-6786-5, ISBN13: 978-0-7581-6786-6. Dewey:792.09421.

Audience: **l,u,f.** 𝐵

Alexander, Catherine   **PR2976.C3 2003**
(Editor)
The Cambridge Shakespeare Library: Shakespeare's Times, Texts, and Stages; Shakespeare Criticism; Shakespeare Performance, Set. Quantity Pack, Trade Cloth. Cambridge University Press. New York, NY. 2003. 1416p. ISBN:0-521-82433-8, ISBN13: 978-0-521-82433-0. Dewey:822.3/3. LCCN:2002-031457.

Audience: **l,u,f.**

Arundell, Dennis   **PN2596.L7S3**
The Story of Sadler's Wells, 1683-1977. Ed. 2. Trade Cloth. David & Charles Publishers. Newton Abbot, 1978. 352p. ISBN:0-7153-7620-9, ISBN13: 978-0-7153-7620-1. Dewey:792/.09421/43. LCCN:78-316129.

Audience: **u,f.** 𝐵

Aston, Elaine   **PR739.F45A77 2003**
Feminist Views on the English Stage: Women Playwrights, 1990-2000. David Bradby (Contribution by). Trade Cloth. Cambridge University Press. New York, NY. 2003. 248p. Cambridge Studies in Modern Theatre Ser. ISBN:0-521-80003-X, ISBN13: 978-0-521-80003-7. Dewey:822/.914099287. LCCN:2003-051551.

Audience: **u,f.**

Aston, Elaine & Reinelt,   **PR739.F45C36 2000**
Janelle (Editors)
The Cambridge Companion to Modern British Women Playwrights. Cloth Text. Cambridge University Press. New York,

NY. 2000. 296p. Companions to Literature Ser. ISBN:0-521-59422-7, ISBN13: 978-0-521-59422-6. Dewey:822/.91099282. LCCN:99-036626.

Audience: **g.** *Choice, 2001.*

Baines, Paul & Burns,   **PR1271.F59 2000**
Edward (Editors)
Five Romantic Plays, 1768-1821. Trade Paper. Oxford University Press, Inc. New York, NY. 2000. 432p. Oxford World's Classics Ser. ISBN:0-19-283316-2, ISBN13: 978-0-19-283316-7. Dewey:822/.6080145. LCCN:00-699989.

Audience: **l,u,f.**

Baker, Herschel C.   **PN2598**
John Philip Kemble: The Actor in His Theatre. Trade Cloth. Greenwood Publishing Group, Inc. Portsmouth, NH. 1970. 414p. ISBN:0-8371-2279-1, ISBN13: 978-0-8371-2279-3. Dewey:792/.028/0924. LCCN:76-090701.

Audience: **l,u,f.** 𝐵

Barton, Margaret   **PN2598.G3 B3 1978**
Garrick. Trade Cloth. Greenwood Publishing Group, Inc. Portsmouth, NH. 1978. 312p. ISBN:0-313-20270-2, ISBN13: 978-0-313-20270-4. Dewey:792/.028/0924. LCCN:78-000612.

Audience: **g,l,u,f.** 𝐵

Beadle, Richard (Editor)   **PN2587.C36 1994**
The Cambridge Companion to Medieval English Theatre. Trade Paper. Cambridge University Press. New York, NY. 1994. 394p. Companions to Literature Ser. ISBN:0-521-45916-8, ISBN13: 978-0-521-45916-7. Dewey:792.0942. LCCN:93-004397.

Audience: **g,u,f.**

Behn, Aphra   **PR3317 .A19 1990**
Behn: Five Plays. Maureen Duffy (Introduction by). Trade Paper. Methuen Publishing Ltd. London, 2004. 474p. Methuen World Dramatists Ser. ISBN:0-413-17090-X, ISBN13: 978-0-413-17090-3. Dewey:822/.4. LCCN:92-146508.

Audience: **l,u,f.**

Bevington, David   **PR1263.E56 2003**
English Renaissance Drama: A Norton Anthology. Lars Engle, Katharine Eisaman Maus & Eric Rasmussen (Editors). Trade Cloth. W. W. Norton & Company, Inc. New York, NY. 2002. 2400p. ISBN:0-393-97655-6, ISBN13: 978-0-393-97655-7. Dewey:822/.308. LCCN:2002-025074.

Audience: **l,u,f.**

Braunmuller, A. R. &   **PR651.C36 2003**
Hattaway, Michael (Editors)
The Cambridge Companion to English Renaissance Drama. Ed. 2. Cloth Text. Cambridge University Press. New York, NY. 2003. 484p. Cambridge Companions to Literature Ser. ISBN:0-521-82115-0, ISBN13: 978-0-521-82115-5. Dewey:822/.309. LCCN:2002-035073.

Audience: **g,l,u,f.** *Choice, 2004, 1991.*

Bridges-Adams, William   **PN2589.C7**
The Irresistible Theatre. Paper Text. Textbook Publishers. Temecula, CA. 2003. 446p. ISBN:0-7581-0244-5, ISBN13: 978-0-7581-0244-7. Dewey:822.309.

Audience: **l,u.**

Bristol, Michael D. &   **PR3100.S52 2001**
  McLuskie, Kathleen (Editors)
Shakespeare and Modern Theatre: The Performance of
Modernity. Paper over Boards. Routledge. New York, NY. 2001.
224p. Accents on Shakespeare Ser. ISBN:0-415-21984-1,
ISBN13: 978-0-415-21984-6. Dewey:792.9/5. LCCN:00-065307.
                                 Audience: **u,f.**

Burnim, Kalman A.   **PN2638.S27A5**
David Garrick, Director. Paper Text. Textbook Publishers.
Temecula, CA. 2003. 234p. ISBN:0-7581-1616-0, ISBN13:
978-0-7581-1616-1. Dewey:792.081.
                                 Audience: **l,u,f.** ℬ

Callaghan, Dympna (Editor)   **PR2976**
A Feminist Companion to Shakespeare. Trade Paper. Blackwell
Publishing, Inc. Malden, MA. 2001. 416p. Companions to
Literature and Culture Ser. ISBN:0-631-20807-0, ISBN13:
978-0-631-20807-5. Dewey:822.3/3.
                  Audience: **l,u,f.** *Choice, 2000.*

Cerasano, Susan P. &   **PR658.W6R43 1998**
  Wynne-Davies, Marion
Readings in Renaissance Women's Drama: Criticism, History,
and Performance, 1594-1998. Trade Paper. Routledge. New
York, NY. 1998. 336p. ISBN:0-415-16443-5, ISBN13:
978-0-415-16443-6. Dewey:822/.3099287. LCCN:98-006670.
                  Audience: **l,u,f.** *Choice, 1999.*

Chambers, Colin   **PN2596.S82R684 2004**
Inside the Royal Shakespeare Company: Creativity and the
Institution. Paper over Boards. Routledge. New York, NY. 2004.
280p. ISBN:0-415-21202-2, ISBN13: 978-0-415-21202-1.
Dewey:792/.0942. LCCN:2003-015745.
                                Audience: **l,u,f.**

Churchill, Caryl   **PR6053.H786A19 1985**
Plays. Trade Paper. Methuen Publishing Ltd. London, 2004.
Methuen Paperback Ser. ISBN:0-413-56670-6, ISBN13:
978-0-413-56670-6. Dewey:822.9/14. LCCN:85-186277.
                        Audience: **g,l,u,f.** ℬ

Churchill, Caryl   **PR6066.I53**
Plays Two, Vol. 2. Trade Paper. Methuen Publishing Ltd.
London, 2004. Methuen World Dramatists Ser.
ISBN:0-413-62270-3, ISBN13: 978-0-413-62270-9.
Dewey:822.9/14.
                                 Audience: **l,u,f.**

Coldewey, John C. (Editor)   **PR1260.E27 1993**
Early English Drama: An Anthology. Cloth Text. Garland
Publishing, Inc. New York, NY. 1993. 392p.
ISBN:0-8240-4699-4, ISBN13: 978-0-8240-4699-6.
Dewey:822.208. LCCN:92-007686.
                                 Audience: **u,f.**

Cox, Jeffrey N. & Gamer,   **PR1271.B72 2003**
  Michael (Editors)
The Broadview Anthology of Romantic Drama. Trade Paper.
Broadview Press. Peterborough, ON. 2003. 432p. Broadview

Anthologies of English Literature Ser. ISBN:1-55111-298-1,
ISBN13: 978-1-55111-298-5. Dewey:822/.7080145.
LCCN:2003-446769.
                                 Audience: **l,u,f.**

Cox, John D. & Kastan,   **PR641.N49 1997**
  David S.
A New History of Early English Drama. Cloth Text. Columbia
University Press. New York, NY. 1997. 580p.
ISBN:0-231-10242-9, ISBN13: 978-0-231-10242-1.
Dewey:822/.009. LCCN:96-029670.
                  Audience: **l,u,f.** *Choice, 1997.*

Craik, T. W.   **PN2596.L6R6**
The Tudor Interlude: Stage, Costume, and Acting. Paper Text.
Textbook Publishers. Temecula, CA. 2003. 158p.
ISBN:0-7581-1342-0, ISBN13: 978-0-7581-1342-9.
Dewey:792.09421.
                                Audience: **u,f.** ℬ

Daniels, Sarah   **PR6066.I53**
Plays One. Trade Paper. Methuen Publishing Ltd. London, 2004.
0p. Methuen World Dramatists Ser. ISBN:0-413-64930-X,
ISBN13: 978-0-413-64930-0. Dewey:822.9/14.
                                 Audience: **l,u,f.**

Davidson, Clifford   **PN2587.D38 1996**
Technology, Guilds, and Early English Drama. Trade Cloth, Box
or Slipcased. Medieval Institute Publications. Kalamazoo, MI.
1996. 128p. Early Drama, Art and Music Monograph Ser.
ISBN:1-879288-79-6, ISBN13: 978-1-879288-79-9.
Dewey:792/.0942/0902. LCCN:96-032689.
                  Audience: **l,u,f.** *Choice, 1997.*

Dent, Edward J.   **PN2596.L7 O73 1979**
A Theatre for Everybody: The Story of the Old Vic and Sadler's
Wells. Kay Ambrose (Illustrator). Trade Cloth. Hyperion Press,
Inc. Westport, CT. 1979. ISBN:0-88355-691-X, ISBN13:
978-0-88355-691-7. Dewey:792/.09421/2. LCCN:78-010887.
                                 Audience: **l,u,f.**

Doran   **PN2581**
Their Majesties' Servants or Annals of the English Stage from
Thomas Betterton tc Edmund Kean; Actors, Authors, Audiences.
Trade Paper. Kessinger Publishing, LLC. Whitefish, MT. 2004.
ISBN:1-4179-4578-8, ISBN13: 978-1-4179-4578-8. Dewey:792.
                                 Audience: **g.**

Drakakis, John (Editor)   **PN1991.65 .B74**
British Radio Drama. Trade Paper. Cambridge University Press.
New York, NY. 1981. 296p. ISBN:0-521-29383-9, ISBN13:
978-0-521-29383-9. Dewey:822/.02/09. LCCN:80-040678.
                                 Audience: **l,u,f.**

Finkel, Alicia   **PN2087.G7**
Romantic Stages: Set and Costume Design in Victorian England.
Trade Paper, Perfect. McFarland & Company, Incorporated
Publishers. Jefferson, NC. 2005. 215p. ISBN:0-7864-2336-6,
ISBN13: 978-0-7864-2336-1. Dewey:792/.025/0942.
LCCN:96-000639.
                  Audience: **u,f.** *Choice, 1996.*

Finkel, Alicia   **PN2087.G7F56 1996**
Romantic Stages: Set and Costume Design in Victorian England.
Cloth Text. McFarland & Company, Incorporated Publishers.
Jefferson, NC. 1996. 215p. ISBN:0-7864-0234-2, ISBN13:
978-0-7864-0234-2. Dewey:792/.025/0942. LCCN:96-639.
Audience: **l,u,f.** *Choice, 1996.*

Fisk, Deborah Payne   **PR1266.F675 2005**
  (Editor)
Four Restoration Libertine Plays. Trade Paper, Perfect. Oxford
University Press, Inc. New York, NY. 2005. 468p. Oxford
World's Classics Ser. ISBN:0-19-283294-8, ISBN13:
978-0-19-283294-8. Dewey:822/.408. LCCN:2004-027977.
Audience: **l,u,f.**

Fiske, Deborah Payne   **PR691.C35 2000**
  (Editor)
The Cambridge Companion to English Restoration Theatre.
Cloth Text. Cambridge University Press. New York, NY. 2000.
322p. Companions to Literature Ser. ISBN:0-521-58215-6,
ISBN13: 978-0-521-58215-5. Dewey:822/.409.
LCCN:99-015230.
Audience: **g.** *Choice, 2001.*

Foakes, R. A.   **PN2589.F6 1985**
Illustrations of the English Stage, 1580-1642. Trade Cloth.
Stanford University Press. Palo Alto, CA. 1985. 180p.
ISBN:0-8047-1236-0, ISBN13: 978-0-8047-1236-1.
Dewey:792/.0941. LCCN:83-040517.
Audience: **l,u,f.** $\mathcal{B}$

Gale Editors (Editor)   **PR2976**
Shakespearean Criticism. Trade Cloth. Thomson Gale.
Farmington Hills, MI. 2006. ISBN:0-7876-8838-X, ISBN13:
978-0-7876-8838-7. Dewey:822.33.
Audience: **l,u,f.**

Gassner, John   **PR1262.M43 1987**
Medieval and Tudor Drama: Twenty-Four Plays. Trade Paper.
Applause Theatre Book Publishers. New York, NY. 1995. 462p.
ISBN:0-936839-84-8, ISBN13: 978-0-936839-84-4.
Dewey:822/.2/08. LCCN:87-018836.
Audience: **l,u,f.**

Gibson, H. N.   **PR2937**
The Shakespeare Claimants: A Critical Survey of the Four
Principal Theories Concerning the Authorship of the
Shakespearean Plays. Paper over Boards. Routledge. New York,
NY. 2005. 336p. ISBN:0-415-35290-8, ISBN13:
978-0-415-35290-1. Dewey:822.33.
Audience: **u,f.**

Goodwin, John (Editor)   **PN2091.S8**
British Theatre Design. Trade Paper. Phoenix House. London,
1997. 208p. ISBN:0-7538-0129-9, ISBN13: 978-0-7538-0129-1.
Dewey:792/.025/0941.
Audience: **l,u,f.** *Choice, 1997.*

Griffiths, Trevor (Editor)   **PR1248**
Restoration Comedy. Trade Paper. Theatre Communications
Group, Inc. New York, NY. 2005. 352p. ISBN:1-85459-848-1,
ISBN13: 978-1-85459-848-6. Dewey:822.4/08017.
Audience: **l,u,f.**

Gurr, Andrew   **PR3095.G86 2004**
The Shakespeare Company, 1594-1642. Trade Cloth. Cambridge
University Press. New York, NY. 2004. 356p.
ISBN:0-521-80730-1, ISBN13: 978-0-521-80730-2.
Dewey:792/.09421. LCCN:2003-055895.
Audience: **u,f.** *Choice, 2005.*

Hare, David   **PR6058.A678.A6 1997**
David Hare: Fanshen; A Map of the World; Saigonp; The Bay at
Nice; The Secret Rapture. Trade Paper. Faber & Faber, Inc. New
York, NY. 1997. 280p. ISBN:0-571-17835-9, ISBN13:
978-0-571-17835-3. Dewey:822/.914. LCCN:99-230984.
Audience: **l,u,f.**

Hare, David   **PR6066.I53**
David Hare: Slag, Teeth 'n' Smiles, Knuckle, Licking Hitler,
Plenty. Trade Paper. Faber & Faber, Inc. New York, NY. 1996.
224p. Contemporary Classics Ser. ISBN:0-571-17741-7,
ISBN13: 978-0-571-17741-7. Dewey:822.9/14.
Audience: **l,u,f.**

Highfill, Philip H., et al.   **PN2597.H54 1993**
🄴 A Biographical Dictionary of Actors, Actresses, Musicians,
Dancers, Managers and Other Stage Personnel in London,
1660-1800. Kalman A. Burnim & Edward A. Langhans
(Authors). E-Book. NetLibrary, Inc. Boulder, CO. 1993.
ISBN:0-585-03033-2, ISBN13: 978-0-585-03033-3.
Dewey:790.2/092/2.
Audience: **g.**

Hillebrand, Harold N.   **PN2598.K3H5**
Edmund Kean. Trade Cloth. A M S Press, Inc. New York, NY.
ISBN:0-404-03269-9, ISBN13: 978-0-404-03269-2.
Dewey:792/.028/0924. LCCN:77-181904.
Audience: **l,u,f.**

Hodges, Ben   **PN6120.G43F67 2003**
Forbidden Acts: Pioneering Gay and Lesbian Plays of the
Twentieth Century. Trade Paper. Applause Theatre Book
Publishers. New York, NY. 2003. 741p. ISBN:1-55783-587-X,
ISBN13: 978-1-55783-587-1. Dewey:808.82/0086/640904.
LCCN:2003-014043.
Audience: **g,l,u,f.**

Hoenselaars, Ton (Editor)   **PR2982.S475 2004**
Shakespeare's History Plays: Performance, Translation and
Adaptation in Britain and Abroad. Dennis Kennedy (Foreword
by). Trade Cloth. Cambridge University Press. New York, NY.
2004. 302p. ISBN:0-521-82902-X, ISBN13: 978-0-521-82902-1.
Dewey:822.3/3. LCCN:2004-040752.
Audience: **u,f.** *Choice, 2005.*

Hogan, Charles Beecher   **PN2592.L58 1968**
🄴 The London Stage, 1660-1800: A Calendar of Plays,
Entertainments and Afterpieces Together with Casts,

Box-Receipts and Contemporary Comment. E-Book. NetLibrary, Inc. Boulder, CO. 1968. ISBN:0-585-29412-7, ISBN13: 978-0-585-29412-4. Dewey:792/.09421.

Audience: **g.**

Hotson, Leslie   PN2596.L6S49
The Commonwealth and Restoration Stage. Paper Text. Textbook Publishers. Temecula, CA. 2003. 424p. ISBN:0-7581-4432-6, ISBN13: 978-0-7581-4432-4. Dewey:792.094212.

Audience: **g.** *B*

Hughes, Derek & Todd,   PR3317.Z5C36 2004
  Janet (Editors)
The Cambridge Companion to Aphra Behn. Trade Paper, Perfect. Cambridge University Press. New York, NY. 2004. 274p. Cambridge Companions to Literature Ser. ISBN:0-521-52720-1, ISBN13: 978-0-521-52720-0. Dewey:822/.4. LCCN:2004-049740.

Audience: **g,l,u,f.** *Choice, 2005.*

Innes, Christopher   PN2598.C85I562 1998
Edward Gordon Craig: A Vision of Theatre. Ed. 2. Trade Paper. Gordon & Breach Publishing Group. New York, NY. 1998. 352p. Contemporary Theatre Studies ISBN:90-5702-125-0, ISBN13: 978-90-5702-125-1. Dewey:792/.0233/092. LCCN:99-521846.

Audience: **l,u,f.**

Joseph, Bertram Leon   PN2598.G3B8
The Tragic Actor. Paper Text. Textbook Publishers. Temecula, CA. 2003. 415p. ISBN:0-7581-4543-8, ISBN13: 978-0-7581-4543-7. Dewey:792/.028/0924.

Audience: **l,u,f.** *B*

Kennedy, Dennis (Editor)   PR2971.F66 F66 1993
Foreign Shakespeare: Contemporary Performance. Trade Paper. Cambridge University Press. New York, NY. 2004. 329p. ISBN:0-521-61708-1, ISBN13: 978-0-521-61708-6. Dewey:792.95.

Audience: **l,u,f.** *Choice, 1994.*

Kermode, Frank   PR3095
The Age of Shakespeare. Trade Paper. Random House Adult Trade Publishing Group. New York, NY. 2005. 240p. ISBN:0-8129-7433-6, ISBN13: 978-0-8129-7433-1. Dewey:822.33.

Audience: **l,u,f.**

King, Kimball   PR736.M56 2001
Modern Dramatists: A Casebook of the Major British and American Playwrights. Cloth Text. Garland Publishing, Inc. New York, NY. 2001. 325p. Studies in Modern Drama, Vol. 14 ISBN:0-8153-2349-2, ISBN13: 978-0-8153-2349-5. Dewey:822/.9109. LCCN:00-065297.

Audience: **l,u,f.**

Lacey, Stephen   PR739.R37L33 1995
British Realist Theatre: The New Wave in Its Context, 1956-1965. Paper over Boards. Routledge. New York, NY. 1995.

216p. ISBN:0-415-07782-6, ISBN13: 978-0-415-07782-8. Dewey:792/.0941. LCCN:94-044677.

Audience: **l,u,f.** *Choice, 1996.*

Leacroft, Richard   NA6840.G7L4 1988
The Development of the English Playhouse. Ed. 2. Trade Paper. Heinemann. Portsmouth, NH. 1988. 354p. ISBN:0-413-60600-7, ISBN13: 978-0-413-60600-6. Dewey:725/.822/0942. LCCN:88-156431.

Audience: **l,u,f.** *B*

Loomis, Roger S. & Wells,   PN6112 .L57 1970
  Henry W. (Editors)
Representative Medieval and Tudor Plays. Trade Cloth. Ayer Company Publishers, Inc. Manchester, NH. 1977. Play Anthology Reprint Ser. ISBN:0-8369-8202-9, ISBN13: 978-0-8369-8202-2. Dewey:808.82/51. LCCN:77-111109.

Audience: **l,u,f.**

Lyons, Paddy & Morgan,   PR1266
  Fideles (Editors)
Female Playwrights of the Restoration: Five Comedies. Ed. 2. Paddy Lyons & Fideles Morgan (Introduction by). Trade Paper. Tuttle Publishing. Boston, MA. 1994. 365p. ISBN:0-460-87427-6, ISBN13: 978-0-460-87427-4. Dewey:822.40809287.

Audience: **l,u,f.**

Mander, Raymond &   PN2596
  Mitchenson, Joe
The Theatres of London. Trade Cloth. Greenwood Publishing Group, Inc. Portsmouth, NH. 1979. 292p. ISBN:0-313-21227-9, ISBN13: 978-0-313-21227-7. Dewey:792/.09421. LCCN:78-011868.

Audience: **l,u,f.** *B*

Massai, Sonia (Editor)   PR2880.A1W67 2005
World-Wide Shakespeares. Paper over Boards. Routledge. New York, NY. 2005. 216p. ISBN:0-415-32455-6, ISBN13: 978-0-415-32455-7. Dewey:822.3/3. LCCN:2004-028867.

Audience: **l,u,f.**

McCormick, John   PN1978.G7M38 2004
The Victorian Marionette Theatre. Clodagh McCormick & John Phillips (Contribution by). Trade Paper. University of Iowa Press. Iowa City, IA. 2004. 292p. Studies in Theatre History and Culture ISBN:0-87745-912-6, ISBN13: 978-0-87745-912-5. Dewey:791.5/094109034. LCCN:2004-048015.

Audience: **u,f.** *Choice, 2005.*

McDonald, Russ (Editor)   PR2970.S495 2004
Shakespeare: An Anthology of Criticism and Theory, 1945-2000. Trade Cloth. Blackwell Publishing, Inc. Malden, MA. 2004. 952p. ISBN:0-631-23487-X, ISBN13: 978-0-631-23487-6. Dewey:822.3/3. LCCN:2003-012197.

Audience: **u,f.** *Choice, 2004.*

McRae, Andrew   PR646
Renaissance Drama. Trade Paper. Oxford University Press, Inc.

New York, NY. 2003. 192p. Context Ser. ISBN:0-340-76347-7, ISBN13: 978-0-340-76347-6. Dewey:822/.309. LCCN:2004-297099.

Audience: **u,f.**

Melville, Joy   **PN2598**
Ellen Terry. Book, Other. Haus Publishing. London, 2005. 192p. ISBN:1-904950-14-0, ISBN13: 978-1-904950-14-1. Dewey:792.028092.

Audience: **l,u,f.**

Milhous, Judith & Hume,   **PN2596.L6.V5**
Robert D. (Editors)
Vice Chamberlain Coke's Theatrical Papers, 1706-1715. Trade Cloth. Southern Illinois University Press. Carbondale, IL. 1982. 319p. ISBN:0-8093-1024-4, ISBN13: 978-0-8093-1024-1. Dewey:792/.09421/2. LCCN:81-005616.

Audience: **u,f.** *B*

Nicoll, Allardyce   **PN2581**
English Theatre: A Short History. Trade Cloth. Greenwood Publishing Group, Inc. Portsmouth, NH. 1971. 252p. ISBN:0-8371-3133-2, ISBN13: 978-0-8371-3133-7. Dewey:792/.09421. LCCN:75-098861.

Audience: **u.** *B*

Nicoll, Allardyce   **PH3281.K85P313**
Shakespeare: An Introduction. Paper Text. Textbook Publishers. Temecula, CA. 2003. 181p. ISBN:0-7581-7198-6, ISBN13: 978-0-7581-7198-6. Dewey:894/.51133.

Audience: **l,u.**

Nicoll, Allardyce (Editor)   **PR2900**
Elizabethan Theatre. Jonathan Bate, Margreta De Grazia, Michael Dobson, Inga-Stina Ewbank, R. A. Foakes, Andrew Gurr, Lena Cowen Orlin, Terence Hawkes, John Jowett & A. D. Nuttall (Contribution by). Trade Paper. Cambridge University Press. New York, NY. 2002. 182p. Shakespeare Survey Ser., Vol. 12 ISBN:0-521-52348-6, ISBN13: 978-0-521-52348-6. Dewey:822.3/3.

Audience: **u,f.**

Novy, Marianne (Editor)   **PR116**
Transforming Shakespeare: Contemporary Women's Re-Visions in Literature and Performance. Trade Paper. Palgrave Macmillan. New York, NY. 2000. 272p. ISBN:0-312-23509-7, ISBN13: 978-0-312-23509-3. Dewey:820.9/9287/0904.

Audience: **u,f.** *Choice, 1999.*

O'Brien, John   **PN1987.G7O27 2004**
Harlequin Britain: Pantomime and Entertainment, 1690-1760. Trade Cloth. Johns Hopkins University Press. Baltimore, MD. 2004. 304p. ISBN:0-8018-7910-8, ISBN13: 978-0-8018-7910-4. Dewey:792.3/8/09033. LCCN:2003-021417.

Audience: **u,f.** *Choice, 2005.*

Occhiogrosso, Frank   **PR3091.S3627 2002**
(Editor)
Shakespeare in Performance: A Collection of Essays. Trade

Cloth. University of Delaware Press. Newark, DE. 2003. 152p. ISBN:0-87413-776-4, ISBN13: 978-0-87413-776-7. Dewey:792.9/5. LCCN:2002-018093.

Audience: **l,u.**

Orgel, Stephen   **PN2592**
The Illusion of Power: Political Theater in the English Renaissance. Trade Paper. University of California Press. Berkeley, CA. 1991. 95p. Quantum Bks. ISBN:0-520-02741-8, ISBN13: 978-0-520-02741-1. Dewey:792/.0942. LCCN:73-080827.

Audience: **u,f.** *B*

Orgel, Stephen   **PR2965.O74 2003**
Imagining Shakespeare. Cloth over Boards. Palgrave Macmillan. New York, NY. 2003. 192p. ISBN:1-4039-1177-0, ISBN13: 978-1-4039-1177-3. Dewey:822.3/3. LCCN:2003-051778.

Audience: **u,f.** *Choice, 2003.*

Osborne, John   **PR6066.I53**
John Osborne Plays 1: Look Back in Anger; Epitaph for George Dillion; the World of Paul... Trade Paper. Faber & Faber, Inc. New York, NY. 1996. 289p. ISBN:0-571-17766-2, ISBN13: 978-0-571-17766-0. Dewey:822.9/14.

Audience: **g,l,u,f.**

Pearson, Hesketh   **PN2597.P4 1971**
Last Actor-Managers. Trade Cloth. Ayer Company Publishers, Inc. Manchester, NH. 1977. 83p. Biography Index Reprint Ser. ISBN:0-8369-8072-7, ISBN13: 978-0-8369-8072-1. Dewey:792/.028/0922. LCCN:77-148225.

Audience: **l,u,f.** *B*

Pinter, Harold   **PR6066.I53 1990**
Complete Works: Birthday Party. Trade Paper. Grove/Atlantic, Inc. New York, NY. 1994. 256p. ISBN:0-8021-5096-9, ISBN13: 978-0-8021-5096-7. Dewey:822/.914. LCCN:90-013933.

Audience: **g,l,u,f.**

Pinter, Harold   **PR6066.I53 1990**
Complete Works: The Homecoming, Vol. 3. Trade Paper. Grove/Atlantic, Inc. New York, NY. 1994. 256p. ISBN:0-8021-5049-7, ISBN13: 978-0-8021-5049-3. Dewey:822/.914. LCCN:90-013933.

Audience: **g,l,u,f.**

Pinter, Harold   **PR6066.I53 1990**
Complete Works: The Caretaker, Vol. 2. Trade Paper. Grove/Atlantic, Inc. New York, NY. 1994. 256p. ISBN:0-8021-3237-5, ISBN13: 978-0-8021-3237-6. Dewey:822/.914. LCCN:90-013933.

Audience: **g,l,u,f.**

Pinter, Harold   **PR6066.I53 1990**
Complete Works: Betrayal. Trade Paper. Grove/Atlantic, Inc. New York, NY. 1994. 384p. ISBN:0-8021-5050-0, ISBN13: 978-0-8021-5050-9. Dewey:822/.914. LCCN:90-013933.

Audience: **g,l,u,f.**

Powell, Kerry (Editor)   **PN2594**
The Cambridge Companion to Victorian and Edwardian Theatre.
Trade Paper. Cambridge University Press. New York, NY. 2004.
308p. Cambridge Companions to Literature Ser.
ISBN:0-521-79536-2, ISBN13: 978-0-521-79536-4.
Dewey:792/.0942/09034. LCCN:2002-041552.

Audience: **u,f.** *Choice, 2004.*

Proudfoot, Richard, et al.   **PR2754**
The Arden Shakespeare Complete Works. Ann Thompson &
David Scott Kastan (Authors). Trade Cloth. Thomson Learning
EMEA, Ltd. London, 2000. 1352p. ISBN:1-903436-39-7,
ISBN13: 978-1-903436-39-4. Dewey:822.33.

Audience: **l,u,f.**

Prouty, Charles Tyler   **PN2596**
Studies in the Elizabethan Theatre. Paper Text. Textbook
Publishers. Temecula, CA. 2003. 198p. ISBN:0-7581-3918-7,
ISBN13: 978-0-7581-3918-4. Dewey:792.0942.

Audience: **u,f.** *B*

Raby, Peter (Editor)   **PR6066.I53Z625520**
The Cambridge Companion to Harold Pinter. Cloth Text.
Cambridge University Press. New York, NY. 2001. 292p.
Companions to Literature Ser. ISBN:0-521-65123-9, ISBN13:
978-0-521-65123-3. Dewey:822/.914. LCCN:2001-022302.

Audience: **g,l,u,f.** *Choice, 2002.*

Richmond, Hugh Macrae   **PR3095.R53 2004**
Shakespeare's Theatre. Trade Paper. Continuum International
Publishing Group, Ltd. London, 2005. 584p.
ISBN:0-8264-7776-3, ISBN13: 978-0-8264-7776-7.
Dewey:822.33.

Audience: **l,u.**

Rosenfeld, Sybil Marion   **PN2597.J6**
The Theatre of the London Fairs in the 18th Century. Paper
Text. Textbook Publishers. Temecula, CA. 2003. 194p.
ISBN:0-7581-1301-3, ISBN13: 978-0-7581-1301-6.
Dewey:792.1028.

Audience: **u,f.** *B*

Rowell, George & Jackson,   **PN2595.3 .R68 1984**
Anthony
The Repertory Movement: A History of Regional Theatre in
Britain. Trade Paper. Cambridge University Press. New York,
NY. 1984. 234p. ISBN:0-521-31919-6, ISBN13:
978-0-521-31919-5. Dewey:792/.0941. LCCN:84-009522.

Audience: **u,f.**

Schneider, Ben R. Jr.   **PN2596.L6**
(Compiled by)
Index to "The London Stage, 1660-1800". George W. Stone
(Foreword by). Trade Cloth. Southern Illinois University Press.
Carbondale, IL. 1979. 960p. ISBN:0-8093-0907-6, ISBN13:
978-0-8093-0907-8. Dewey:792/.09421. LCCN:79-102595.

Audience: **l,u,f.** *B*

Sell, Michael   **NA6840.G7T48 2000**
The Theatres Trust Guide to British Theatres, 1750-1950. Trade

Paper. A & C Black. London, 2004. 304p. ISBN:0-7136-5688-3,
ISBN13: 978-0-7136-5688-6. Dewey:792/.0941.
LCCN:2001-326143.

Audience: **g.**

Shakespeare, William &   **PR2754.B4 2003**
Bevington, David
The Complete Works of Shakespeare. Ed. 5. Trade Cloth.
Longman Publishing. Boston, MA. 2003. 2016p.
ISBN:0-321-09333-X, ISBN13: 978-0-321-09333-2.
Dewey:822.3/3. LCCN:2003-045975.

Audience: **l,u,f.**

Shaughnessy, Robert   **PR1248.F68 2003**
Four Renaissance Comedies. Trade Paper. Palgrave Macmillan.
New York, NY. 2004. 368p. ISBN:0-333-97365-8, ISBN13:
978-0-333-97365-3. Dewey:822/.05230803. LCCN:2003-053655.

Audience: **l,u.**

Shaughnessy, Robert   **PR3091.S363 2000**
(Editor)
Shakespeare in Performance. Trade Paper. Palgrave Macmillan.
New York, NY. 2000. 240p. New Casebooks Ser.
ISBN:0-312-23312-4, ISBN13: 978-0-312-23312-9.
Dewey:822.3/3. LCCN:99-086321.

Audience: **u,f.**

Shaw, George Bernard   **PR5360**
Bernard Shaw's the Quintessence of Ibsenism and Related
Writings. Paper Text. Classic Books. Murrieta, CA. 2001.
Collected Works of Bernard Shaw ISBN:0-7426-8213-7,
ISBN13: 978-0-7426-8213-9. Dewey:822.

Audience: **u,f.**

Shaw, George Bernard   **PN2638.B5A3**
Plays: Pleasant and Pleasant. Paper Text. Classic Books.
Murrieta, CA. 2001. Collected Works of Bernard Shaw
ISBN:0-7426-8216-1, ISBN13: 978-0-7426-8216-0.
Dewey:792.0924.

Audience: **l,u,f.**

Shaw, George Bernard   **PN2287.A457M37**
Plays and Players: Essays on the Theatre. Paper Text. Textbook
Publishers. Temecula, CA. 2003. 350p. ISBN:0-7581-7268-0,
ISBN13: 978-0-7581-7268-6. Dewey:792/.028/092.

Audience: **l,u,f.**

Shaw, George Bernard   **PR5363**
Three Plays for Puritans by Bernard Shaw Being the Third
Volume of His Collected Plays. Trade Paper. Kessinger
Publishing, LLC. Whitefish, MT. 2004. ISBN:1-4179-1317-7,
ISBN13: 978-1-4179-1317-6. Dewey:822/.912.

Audience: **l,u.**

Shaw, George Bernard   **PR5366**
Shaw on Theatre: A Half Century of Advices. Mary C. Stratton
(Editor), Stephen Kraft (Illustrator), Stanley Weintraub
(Introduction by). Trade Cloth. Press of Appletree Alley, The.
Lewisburg, PA. 1998. 72p. Ellen Clarke Bertrand Library
Limited Edition Ser. ISBN:0-916375-24-2, ISBN13:
978-0-916375-24-9. Dewey:826.912.

Audience: **l,u,f.**

Smallwood, Robert (Editor)   PR3112.P556 2004
Players of Shakespeare 6: Essays in the Performance of
Shakespeare's History Plays. Trade Cloth. Cambridge University
Press. New York, NY. 2004. 236p. Players of Shakespeare Ser.
ISBN:0-521-84088-0, ISBN13: 978-0-521-84088-0.
Dewey:792.950941. LCCN:2005-273797.

Audience: **u,f.**

Stone, George W. Jr. &   PN2598.G3.S67
  Kahrl, George M.
David Garrick: A Critical Biography. Trade Cloth. Southern
Illinois University Press. Carbondale, IL. 1979. 791p.
ISBN:0-8093-0931-9, ISBN13: 978-0-8093-0931-3.
Dewey:792/.028/0924. LCCN:79-009476.

Audience: **g,l,u,f.** *B*

Stoppard, Tom   PR6066.I53
Tom Stoppard: Arcadia, The Real Thing, Night and Day, Indian
Ink, Hapgood. Trade Paper. Faber & Faber, Inc. New York, NY.
2000. 608p. ISBN:0-571-19751-5, ISBN13: 978-0-571-19751-4.
Dewey:822.9/14.

Audience: **l,u,f.**

Stoppard, Tom   PR6066.I53
Tom Stoppard: The Real Inspector Hound; Dirty Linen; Dogg's
Hamlet; Cahoot's MacBeth... Trade Paper. Faber & Faber, Inc.
New York, NY. 1996. 224p. ISBN:0-571-17765-4, ISBN13:
978-0-571-17765-3. Dewey:822.9/14.

Audience: **l,u,f.**

Styan, John L.   PN2581 .S89 1996
The English Stage: A History of Drama and Performance. Trade
Paper. Cambridge University Press. New York, NY. 1996. 448p.
A Canto Book Ser. ISBN:0-521-55636-8, ISBN13:
978-0-521-55636-1. Dewey:792/.0942. LCCN:95-040921.

Audience: **l,u,f.** *Choice, 1997.*

Styan, John L.   PR3091.S79 1999
Perspectives on Shakespeare in Performance. Paper Text. Peter
Lang Publishing, Inc. New York, NY. 2000. 183p. Studies in
Shakespeare, Vol. 11 ISBN:0-8204-4426-X, ISBN13:
978-0-8204-4426-0. Dewey:792.9/5. LCCN:98-053181.

Audience: **u,f.**

Sullivan, Garrett A., et al.   PR653.E17 2006
Early Modern English Drama: A Critical Companion. Patrick
Gerard Cheney & Andrew Hadfield (Authors). Trade Paper.
Oxford University Press, Inc. New York, NY. 2005. 351p.
ISBN:0-19-515386-3, ISBN13: 978-0-19-515386-6.
Dewey:822/.309. LCCN:2004-066273.

Audience: **g,l,u,f.**

Thaler, Alwin   PN2585.T5
Shakespeare to Sheridan. Trade Cloth. Ayer Company
Publishers, Inc. Manchester, NH. 1972. ISBN:0-405-09025-0,
ISBN13: 978-0-405-09025-7. Dewey:792.0941.
LCCN:63-023190.

Audience: **l,u.**

Watson, Ernest Bradlee   PN2596.L6
Sheridan to Robertson: A Study of the Nineteenth-Century
London Stage. Trade Paper. Kessinger Publishing, LLC.
Whitefish, MT. 2005. ISBN:1-4179-1875-6, ISBN13:
978-1-4179-1875-1. Dewey:792.0942.

Audience: **l,u,f.**

Wearing, J. P.   PN2596.L6 W37
The London Stage, 1890-1899: A Calendar of Plays and Players.
Trade Cloth. Scarecrow Press, Inc. Lanham, MD. 1976. 1242p.
ISBN:0-8108-0910-9, ISBN13: 978-0-8108-0910-9.
Dewey:792/.09421/2. LCCN:76-001825.

Audience: **l,u,f.** *B*

Wearing, J. P.   PN2596.L6
The London Stage, 1900-1909: A Calendar of Plays and Players,
Set. Trade Cloth. Scarecrow Press, Inc. Lanham, MD. 1981.
1202p. ISBN:0-8108-1403-X, ISBN13: 978-0-8108-1403-5.
Dewey:792/.09421. LCCN:80-028353.

Audience: **l,u,f.** *B*

Wearing, J. P.   PN2596.L6
The London Stage, 1910-1919: A Calendar of Plays and Players,
Set. Trade Cloth. Scarecrow Press, Inc. Lanham, MD. 1982.
1370p. ISBN:0-8108-1596-6, ISBN13: 978-0-8108-1596-4.
Dewey:792/.09421. LCCN:82-019190.

Audience: **l,u,f.** *B*

Wearing, J. P.   PN2596.L6
The London Stage, 1920-1929: A Calendar of Plays and Players,
Set. Trade Cloth. Scarecrow Press, Inc. Lanham, MD. 1984.
1808p. ISBN:0-8108-1715-2, ISBN13: 978-0-8108-1715-9.
Dewey:792/.09421. LCCN:84-010665.

Audience: **l,u,f.** *B*

Wearing, J. P.   PN2596.L6W3845 1990
The London Stage, 1930-1939: A Calender of Plays and Players,
Set. Trade Cloth. Scarecrow Press, Inc. Lanham, MD. 1990.
1999p. ISBN:0-8108-2349-7, ISBN13: 978-0-8108-2349-5.
Dewey:792/.09421. LCCN:90-008883.

Audience: **l,u,f.** *Choice, 1991.*

Wearing, J. P.   PN2596.L6.W3846 1991
The London Stage, 1940-1949: A Calendar of Plays and Players.
Trade Cloth. Scarecrow Press, Inc. Lanham, MD. 1991. 1284p.
ISBN:0-8108-2500-7, ISBN13: 978-0-8108-2500-0.
Dewey:792.0942109044. LCCN:91-036206.

Audience: **l,u,f.** *Choice, 1992.*

Wearing, J. P.   PN2596.L6W3847 1993
The London Stage, 1950-1959: A Calendar of Plays and Players.
Trade Cloth. Scarecrow Press, Inc. Lanham, MD. 1993. 1807p.
ISBN:0-8108-2690-9, ISBN13: 978-0-8108-2690-8.
Dewey:792.0942109045. LCCN:93-017179.

Audience: **l,u,f.**

Wells, Stanley & Stanton,   PR3091.C36 2002
  Sarah (Editors)
The Cambridge Companion to Shakespeare on Stage. Trade
Paper. Cambridge University Press. New York, NY. 2002. 338p.

Cambridge Companions to Literature Ser. ISBN:0-521-79711-X, ISBN13: 978-0-521-79711-5. Dewey:792.9/5. LCCN:2001-052447.

Audience: **g,l,u,f.**

Werner, Sarah   **PR3106.W47 2001**
Shakespeare and Feminist Performance: Ideology on Stage. Paper over Boards. Routledge. New York, NY. 2001. 144p. Accents on Shakespeare Ser. ISBN:0-415-22729-1, ISBN13: 978-0-415-22729-2. Dewey:822.3/3. LCCN:2001-018088.

Audience: **u,f.**

Wickham, Glynne W.   **PN2592.H6**
Early English Stages, 1300 To 1660. Paper Text. Textbook Publishers. Temecula, CA. 2003. ISBN:0-7581-4524-1, ISBN13: 978-0-7581-4524-6. Dewey:792.094212.

Audience: **u,f.**

Williams, Arnold   **PR641.W55**
The Drama of Medieval England. Paper Text. Textbook Publishers. Temecula, CA. 2003. 186p. ISBN:0-7581-8137-X, ISBN13: 978-0-7581-8137-4. Dewey:822.109.

Audience: **l,u,f.**

Worthen, W. B.   **PR3091 .W67 1997**
Shakespeare and the Authority of Performance. Trade Cloth. Cambridge University Press. New York, NY. 1997. 265p. ISBN:0-521-55134-X, ISBN13: 978-0-521-55134-2. Dewey:822.3/3. LCCN:96-045571.

Audience: **u,f.** *Choice, 1998.*

Worthen, W. B.   **PR3100.W67 2003**
Shakespeare and the Force of Modern Performance. Trade Cloth. Cambridge University Press. New York, NY. 2003. 282p. ISBN:0-521-81030-2, ISBN13: 978-0-521-81030-2. Dewey:792.9/5. LCCN:2002-031061.

Audience: **u,f.**

Worthen, William B.   **PR736.W64 1992**
Modern Drama and the Rhetoric of Theater. Trade Cloth. University of California Press. Berkeley, CA. 1991. 240p. ISBN:0-520-07468-8, ISBN13: 978-0-520-07468-2. Dewey:822/.9109. LCCN:91-017677.

Audience: **l,u,f.** *Choice, 1992.*

Western Drama and Theater > Europe > France

Barrault, Jean-Louis   **PN2638.B27 A313**
Reflections on the Theatre. Paper Text. Textbook Publishers. Temecula, CA. 2003. 185p. ISBN:0-7581-4777-5, ISBN13: 978-0-7581-4777-6. Dewey:792/.092/4.

Audience: **l,u,f.** *B*

Bernhardt, Sarah   **PN2592.A5**
Memories of My Life, Being My Personal, Professional, and Social Recollections As Woman and Artist. Paper Text. Classic Books. Murrieta, CA. 2001. 456p. ISBN:0-7426-9244-2, ISBN13: 978-0-7426-9244-2. Dewey:792.0942.

Audience: **l,u,f.** *B*

Bernhardt, Sarah   **PN2061.B4**
The Art of the Theatre. H. J. Stenning (Translator), James Agate (Preface by). Trade Cloth. Ayer Company Publishers, Inc. Manchester, NH. 1972. ISBN:0-405-08264-9, ISBN13: 978-0-405-08264-1. Dewey:792.028. LCCN:70-082819.

Audience: **l,u,f.**

Calder, Andrew   **PQ1860.C3**
Moliere: The Theory and Practice of Comedy. Trade Paper. Continuum International Publishing Group, Ltd. London, 1996. 244p. ISBN:0-485-12127-1, ISBN13: 978-0-485-12127-8. Dewey:842.4.

Audience: **l,u,f.** *Choice, 1993.*

Cardy, Michael & Connon,   **PQ556.A7 2000**
  Derek F. (Editors)
Aspects of Twentieth-Century Theatre in French. Trade Cloth. Peter Lang Publishing, Inc. New York, NY. 2000. 243p. ISBN:3-906764-45-1, ISBN13: 978-3-906764-45-0. Dewey:842/.9109. LCCN:00-022411.

Audience: **l,u,f.**

Corneille, Pierre   **PS758.A8**
Chief Plays. Paper Text. Textbook Publishers. Temecula, CA. 2003. 386p. ISBN:0-7581-5803-3, ISBN13: 978-0-7581-5803-1. Dewey:811/.2.

Audience: **l,u,f.** *B*

Corneille, Pierre, et al.   **PQ1220**
Landmarks of French Classical Drama. Jean Racine, Moliere, Marivaux & Beaumarchais (Authors), David Bryer, Robert D. MacDonald, Christopher Hampton & John Fowles (Translators), David Bradby (Introduction by). Trade Paper. Heinemann. Portsmouth, NH. 1991. 393p. ISBN:0-413-63100-1, ISBN13: 978-0-413-63100-8. Dewey:842.4/08.

Audience: **l,u,f.**

Fowlie, Wallace   **PQ556.F6**
Dionysus in Paris: A Guide to Contemporary French Theatre. Trade Cloth. Peter Smith Publisher, Inc. Magnolia, MA. 1990. ISBN:0-8446-0096-2, ISBN13: 978-0-8446-0096-3. Dewey:842/.9/109.

Audience: **u,f.** *B*

Fredrick, Edna C.   **PQ538 .F7 1973**
The Plot and Its Construction in Eighteenth Century Criticism of French Comedy: A Study of the Theory with Relation to the Practice of Beaumarchais. Library Binding. Burt Franklin Publisher. New York, NY. 1973. 132p. ISBN:0-8337-4118-7, ISBN13: 978-0-8337-4118-9. Dewey:842/.052. LCCN:72-082001.

Audience: **u,f.**

Hawkins, Frederick William   **PN2621**
Annals of the French Stage from Its Origin to the Death of Racine. Paper Text. Classic Books. Murrieta, CA. 2001. ISBN:0-7426-9245-0, ISBN13: 978-0-7426-9245-9. Dewey:792/.0944.

Audience: **u,f.** *B*

Hawkins, Frederick William   PN2636.P3H3
The French Stage in the Eighteenth Century. Paper Text. Classic
Books. Murrieta, CA. 2001. ISBN:0-7426-9246-9, ISBN13:
978-0-7426-9246-6. Dewey:792/.09443/6.
                                        Audience: **l,u,f.**

Howarth, William D.   PN2621.F73 1997
 (Editor)
French Theatre in the Neo-Classical Era: 1550-1789. Trade
Cloth. Cambridge University Press. New York, NY. 1997. 760p.
Theatre in Europe Ser., :A Documentary History
ISBN:0-521-23013-6, ISBN13: 978-0-521-23013-1.
Dewey:792/.0944/0903. LCCN:96-013074.
                                        Audience: **l,u,f.**

Knapp, Bettina   PN2634.K5 1988
The Reign of the Theatrical Director: French Theatre:
1887-1924. Trade Cloth. Whitston Publishing Company, Inc.
Albany, NY. 1988. 273p. ISBN:0-87875-358-3, ISBN13:
978-0-87875-358-1. Dewey:792/.0233/0922. LCCN:87-051204.
                              Audience: **l,u,f.** *Choice, 1989.*

Pronko, Leonard C.   PQ558 .P7 1978
Avant Garde: The Experimental Theater in France. Trade Cloth.
Greenwood Publishing Group, Inc. Portsmouth, NH. 1978. 225p.
ISBN:0-313-20096-3, ISBN13: 978-0-313-20096-0.
Dewey:842/.9/1409. LCCN:77-026017.
                                        Audience: **u,f.**

Racine, Jean   PR3071.B6
Three Plays: Andromache, Britannicus [and] Phaedra. Paper
Text. Textbook Publishers. Temecula, CA. 2003. 183p.
ISBN:0-7581-2580-1, ISBN13: 978-0-7581-2580-4.
Dewey:822.33.
                                        Audience: **l,u,f.**

Vince, Ronald W.   PN1841
Neoclassical Theatre: A Historiographical Handbook. Cloth Text.
Greenwood Publishing Group, Inc. Portsmouth, NH. 1988. 239p.
ISBN:0-313-24445-6, ISBN13: 978-0-313-24445-2.
Dewey:792/.09. LCCN:87-017803.
                              Audience: **g.** *Choice, 1988.*

Ward, Simon   PT2621.O46
French 'Classical' Theatre Today: Teaching, Research,
Performance. Trade Paper. Rodopi. Kenilworth, NY. 2001. 307p.
Faux Titre, Vol. 205 ISBN:90-420-1576-4, ISBN13:
978-90-420-1576-0. Dewey:833.912.
                                        Audience: **u,f.**

Waxman, Samuel M.   PN2636.P4T75
Antoine and the Theatre Libre. Trade Cloth. Ayer Company
Publishers, Inc. Manchester, NH. 1972. ISBN:0-405-09056-0,
ISBN13: 978-0-405-09056-1. Dewey:792.0944361.
LCCN:63-023192.
                                        Audience: **l,u,f.**

Wehle, Philippa (Editor)   PQ1223
Drama Contemporary: France. Trade Paper. P A J Publications.
New York, NY. 1986. 234p. ISBN:0-933826-94-X, ISBN13:
978-0-933826-94-6. Dewey:842.9108.
                                        Audience: **l,u,f.**

White, Edmund   PQ2605.O28
Genet: A Biography. Book, Other. Knopf Publishing Group.
New York, NY. 1994. 800p. ISBN:0-679-75479-2, ISBN13:
978-0-679-75479-4. Dewey:848/.91209 B.
                          Audience: **g,l,u,f.** *Choice, 1994.*

Wiley, William L.   PN2625 .W5 1972
The Early Public Theatre in France. Trade Cloth. Greenwood
Publishing Group, Inc. Portsmouth, NH. 1973. 326p.
ISBN:0-8371-6449-4, ISBN13: 978-0-8371-6449-6.
Dewey:792/.0944. LCCN:72-006190.
                                        Audience: **u,f.**

Western Drama and Theater > Europe > Italy

                                              PN2018.T64 1993
🄴 Commedia Dell'Arte Performance: Context and Contents.
E-Book. NetLibrary, Inc. Boulder, CO. 1993.
ISBN:0-585-35791-9, ISBN13: 978-0-585-35791-1. Dewey:792.
                                        Audience: **u,f.**

Andrews, Richard   PQ4149 .A48 1993
Scripts and Scenarios: The Performance of Comedy in
Renaissance Italy. Cloth Text. Cambridge University Press. New
York, NY. 1993. 312p. ISBN:0-521-35357-2, ISBN13:
978-0-521-35357-1. Dewey:852.05230903. LCCN:92-023446.
                                        Audience: **l,u,f.**

Berghaus, Günter   PN2684
Italian Futurist Theatre, 1909-1944. Trade Cloth. Oxford
University Press, Inc. New York, NY. 1998. 610p.
ISBN:0-19-815898-X, ISBN13: 978-0-19-815898-1.
Dewey:792/.0945/0904. LCCN:97-027694.
                                        Audience: **f.**

Cairns, Christopher (Editor)   PQ4155.C63 1989
The Commedia Dell'arte from the Renaissance to Dario Fo: The
Italian Origins of European Theatre VI. Trade Cloth. Edwin
Mellen Press, The. Lewiston, NY. 1989. 362p.
ISBN:0-88946-080-9, ISBN13: 978-0-88946-080-5.
Dewey:852/.052309. LCCN:89-013576.
                              Audience: **l,u,f.** *Choice, 1990.*

Cairns, Christopher (Editor)   PN2091.S8S292 1996
Scenery, Set and Staging in the Italian Renaissance: Studies in
the Practice of Theatre. Trade Cloth. Edwin Mellen Press, The.
Lewiston, NY. 1996. 340p. ISBN:0-7734-8814-6, ISBN13:
978-0-7734-8814-4. Dewey:792/.025/0945. LCCN:96-003909.
                                        Audience: **l,u,f.**

Di Maria, Salvatore   PQ4147.D5 2002
The Italian Tragedy in the Renaissance: Cultural Realities and
Theatrical Innovations. Trade Cloth. Bucknell University Press.
Cranbury, NJ. 2002. 272p. ISBN:0-8387-5490-2, ISBN13:
978-0-8387-5490-0. Dewey:852/.05120903. LCCN:2001-035662.
                                        Audience: **l,u,f.**

Farrell, Joseph PQ4699.C2835 1997
Carlo Goldoni and Eighteenth-Century Theatre. Trade Cloth.
Edwin Mellen Press, The. Lewiston, NY. 1997. 272p.
ISBN:0-7734-8465-5, ISBN13: 978-0-7734-8465-8.
Dewey:792.094509033. LCCN:97-053176.
Audience: **l,u,f.**

Fisher, James PQ4155.F57 1992
The Theatre of Yesterday and Tomorrow: Commedia Dell'Arte
on the Modern Stage. Trade Cloth. Edwin Mellen Press, The.
Lewiston, NY. 1992. 424p. ISBN:0-7734-9529-0, ISBN13:
978-0-7734-9529-6. Dewey:792.2. LCCN:92-014529.
Audience: **l,u,f.**

Fo, Dario PQ4866.O2
Plays 1. Trade Paper. Methuen Publishing Ltd. London, 2004.
ISBN:0-413-15420-3, ISBN13: 978-0-413-15420-0.
Dewey:852.9/14.
Audience: **l,u,f.**

Goldoni, Carlo PQ4692
Goldoni, Vol. 2. Robert D. MacDonald (Translator). Trade
Paper. Theatre Communications Group, Inc. New York, NY.
1999. 193p. Absolute Classics Ser., Vol. 2 ISBN:1-870259-37-8,
ISBN13: 978-1-870259-37-8. Dewey:852.6.
Audience: **l,u,f.**

Goldoni, Carlo PQ4695
Goldoni, Vol. 1. Robert D. MacDonald (Translator). Trade
Paper. Theatre Communications Group, Inc. New York, NY.
1997. 139p. Oberon Bks. ISBN:1-870259-48-3, ISBN13:
978-1-870259-48-4. Dewey:852.6.
Audience: **l,u,f.**

House, Jane & Attisani, PQ4244.E5T83 1994
  Antonio (Editors)
Twentieth-Century Italian Drama: An Anthology, the First Fifty
Years. Trade Cloth. Columbia University Press. New York, NY.
1995. 622p. ISBN:0-231-07118-3, ISBN13: 978-0-231-07118-5.
Dewey:852/.91208. LCCN:94-029111.
Audience: **l,u,f.**

Luciani, Vincent PQ4134 .L8
A Concise History of the Italian Theatre. Paper Text. Textbook
Publishers. Temecula, CA. 2003. 81p. ISBN:0-7581-4249-8,
ISBN13: 978-0-7581-4249-8. Dewey:852.009.
Audience: **l,u,f.**

Machiavelli, Niccolo & PQ4244.E5T48 1996
  Ariosto, Ludovico
Three Italian Renaissance Comedies: Ariosto's The Supposes;
Machiavelli's The Mandrake; Intronati's The Deceived.
Christopher Cairns & Accademia Senese Degli Intronati Staff
(Editors), Jennifer Lorch (Translator, Introduction by). Trade
Cloth. Edwin Mellen Press, The. Lewiston, NY. 1996. 452p.
ISBN:0-7734-8821-9, ISBN13: 978-0-7734-8821-2.
Dewey:852/.309. LCCN:96-019456.
Audience: **l,u,f.**

Pirandello, Luigi PQ4835.I7
Three Plays by Luigi Pirandello: Six Characters in Search of an

Author; Henry IV and Right You Are. Trade Paper. Kessinger
Publishing, LLC. Whitefish, MT. 2005. ISBN:1-4179-1825-X,
ISBN13: 978-1-4179-1825-6. Dewey:852.89.
Audience: **l,u,f.**

Street, Jack D. & Umlas, PQ4244.E6S874 2003
  Rod (Editors)
The Italian Theater of the Grotesque: A New Theater for the
Twentieth Century: An Anthology. Jack D. Street & Rod Umlas
(Translators). Trade Cloth. Edwin Mellen Press, The. Lewiston,
NY. 2003. 420p. ISBN:0-7734-6738-6, ISBN13:
978-0-7734-6738-5. Dewey:852/.9108. LCCN:2003-043641.
Audience: **u,f.**

Turner, J. PN2688.B33T87 2004
Eugenio Barba. Paper over Boards. Routledge. New York, NY.
2005. 192p. Routledge Performance Practitioners Ser.
ISBN:0-415-27327-7, ISBN13: 978-0-415-27327-5.
Dewey:792.02/33/092. LCCN:2004-004779.
Audience: **u,f.**

Western Drama and Theater > Europe > Spain

PQ6105
A Society on Stage: Essays on Spanish Golden Age. Paper Text.
University Press of the South, Inc. New Orleans, LA. 1997.
Iberian Studies, Vol. 15 ISBN:1-889431-19-2, ISBN13:
978-1-889431-19-2. Dewey:862.309.
Audience: **u,f.**

Aboff, Marcie PZ7.A164GIA 2004
The Giant Jellybean Jar. Michael Benedikt & George E.
Wellwarth (Editors), Paige Billin Frye (Illustrator). Trade Cloth.
Penguin Group (USA) Inc. New York, NY. 2004. 32p. Dutton
Easy Reader Ser. ISBN:0-525-47236-3, ISBN13:
978-0-525-47236-0. Dewey:[E]. LCCN:2004-300475.
Audience: **l,u,f.**

Calderón de la Barca, Pedro PQ6292.A1
Calderon: Plays One. Gwynne Edwards (Translator, Introduction
by). Trade Paper. Methuen Publishing Ltd. London, 2004.
Methuen World Classics Ser., Vol. 1 ISBN:0-413-63460-4,
ISBN13: 978-0-413-63460-3. Dewey:862.3.
Audience: **l,u,f.**

Delgado, Maria (Editor) PN2784
Spanish Theatre, 1920-1995: Strategies in Protest and
Imagination 3. Ed. 3. Trade Paper. Gordon & Breach Publishing
Group. New York, NY. 1998. 88p. Contemporary Theatre
Review Ser. ISBN:90-5702-116-1, ISBN13: 978-90-5702-116-9.
Dewey:792.09460904.
Audience: **u,f.**

García Lorca, Federico PQ6613.A763A2265
Four Major Plays. John Edmunds (Translator), Nicholas Round
(Introduction by), Ann MacLaren (Notes by). Trade Paper.

Oxford University Press, Inc. New York, NY. 2000. 288p. Oxford World's Classics Ser. ISBN:0-19-283938-1, ISBN13: 978-0-19-283938-1. Dewey:862/.62. LCCN:00-703215.

Audience: **l,u,f.**

Hill, Philip G. (Editor)   **PN6111**
Our Dramatic Heritage: The Golden Age. Trade Cloth. Fairleigh Dickinson University Press. Cranbury, NJ. 1985. 624p. ISBN:0-8386-3107-X, ISBN13: 978-0-8386-3107-2. Dewey:808.82. LCCN:81-065294.

Audience: **l,u,f.**

Holt, Marion P. (Editor)   **PQ6267.E6**
Drama Contemporary: Spain. Trade Paper. P A J Publications. New York, NY. 1985. 232p. Drama Contemporary Ser. ISBN:0-933826-86-9, ISBN13: 978-0-933826-86-1. Dewey:862.6408.

Audience: **u,f.** *Choice, 1986.*

Vega, Lope de & Zorrilla,   **PQ6438**
  Rojas
Three Spanish Golden Age Plays: The Duchess of Amalfi's Steward/The Capulets and Montagues/Cleopatra. Gwynne Edwards (Translator). Trade Paper, Perfect. Methuen Publishing Ltd. London, 2005. 337p. ISBN:0-413-77475-9, ISBN13: 978-0-413-77475-0. Dewey:862.308.

Audience: **l,u,f.**

Western Drama and Theater > Europe > Other European Countries

Brecht, Bertolt   **PT2603.R397A27 1997**
Plays: The Threepenny Opera, the Measures Taken, Galileo, Mother Courage and Her Children, Baal. Reinhold Grimm & Caroline Molina y Vedia (Editors). Trade Cloth. Continuum International Publishing Group, Ltd. London, 1999. 324p. German Library, Vol. 75 ISBN:0-8264-0736-6, ISBN13: 978-0-8264-0736-8. Dewey:832/.912. LCCN:76-020409.

Audience: **l,u,f.**

Brogyanyi, Eugene   **PH3166.D73 1991**
Drama Contemporary: Hungary. Cloth Text. P A J Publications. New York, NY. 1991. 247p. ISBN:1-55554-053-8, ISBN13: 978-1-55554-053-1. Dewey:894/.5112308. LCCN:94-222019.

Audience: **u,f.**

Byrne, Dawson   **PN2602.D82**
The Story of Ireland's National Theatre: The Abbey Theatre Dublin. Trade Paper. Kessinger Publishing, LLC. Whitefish, MT. 2005. ISBN:1-4179-0749-5, ISBN13: 978-1-4179-0749-6. Dewey:792/.09418/3.

Audience: **u,f.**

Carter, Huntly   **PN2658.R4C3**
The Theatre of Max Reinhardt. Paper Text. Classic Books. Murrieta, CA. 2001. 332p. ISBN:0-7426-9203-5, ISBN13: 978-0-7426-9203-9. Dewey:792.0943.

Audience: **l,u,f.**

Chekhov, Anton   **PG3455**
The Complete Plays. Laurence Senelick (Editor). Trade Cloth. W. W. Norton & Company, Inc. New York, NY. 2005. 992p. ISBN:0-393-04885-3, ISBN13: 978-0-393-04885-8. Dewey:891.72/3. LCCN:2005-024362.

Audience: **g,l,u,f.**

Clark, William S.   **PN2601 .C6 1973**
The Early Irish Stage, the Beginnings to 1720. Trade Cloth. Greenwood Publishing Group, Inc. Portsmouth, NH. 1973. 227p. ISBN:0-8371-7004-4, ISBN13: 978-0-8371-7004-6. Dewey:792/.09415. LCCN:73-009262.

Audience: **u,f.**

Day, Barbara (Editor)   **PG5145.E5C94 1994**
Czech Plays: Modern Czech Drama. Trade Paper. Theatre Communications Group, Inc. New York, NY. 1998. 256p. ISBN:1-85459-074-X, ISBN13: 978-1-85459-074-9. Dewey:891.8625. LCCN:94-127607.

Audience: **u,f.**

Delgado, Maria M.   **PN2784**
'Other' Spanish Theatres: Erasure and Inscription on the Twentieth-Century Spanish Stage. Cloth over Boards. Manchester University Press. Manchester, 2003. 384p. ISBN:0-7190-5975-5, ISBN13: 978-0-7190-5975-9. Dewey:792/.0946/0904. LCCN:2003-059570.

Audience: **u,f.** *Choice, 2004.*

Dodgson, Elyse (Editor)   **PT1258**
German Plays 2. Trade Paper. Theatre Communications Group, Inc. New York, NY. 2000. 256p. ISBN:1-85459-479-6, ISBN13: 978-1-85459-479-2. Dewey:832.9/14/08.

Audience: **u,f.**

Dodgson, Elyse   **PT2685.E5**
German Plays. Anna Langhoff, Dea Loher, Klaus Pohl & D. Rust (Contribution by). Trade Paper. Theatre Communications Group, Inc. New York, NY. 1998. 208p. International Collection ISBN:1-85459-338-2, ISBN13: 978-1-85459-338-2. Dewey:832.9/14.

Audience: **u,f.**

Goethe, Johann Wolfgang   **PT2026.F2M84 2004**
  von & Mueller, Carl Richard
Faust: Parts One and Two. Trade Paper. Smith and Kraus Publishers, Inc. Lyme, NH. 2005. 640p. ISBN:1-57525-360-7, ISBN13: 978-1-57525-360-2. Dewey:832/.6. LCCN:2004-045378.

Audience: **l,u,f.**

Goethe, Johann Wolfgang   **PT2026.A5 1993**
  von
Plays: Egmont, Iphigenia in Tauris, Torquato Tasso. Frank G. Ryder (Introduction by). Trade Paper. Continuum International Publishing Group, Ltd. London, 1992. 276p. German Library, Vol. 20 ISBN:0-8264-0717-X, ISBN13: 978-0-8264-0717-7. Dewey:832/.6. LCCN:92-025103.

Audience: **u,f.**

Goetz-Stankiewicz, Marketa   **PG5145.E5**
  (Editor)
Drama Contemporary: Czechoslovakia. Trade Paper. P A J
Publications. New York, NY. 1985. 222p. Drama Contemporary
Ser. ISBN:0-933826-76-1, ISBN13: 978-0-933826-76-2.
Dewey:891.8/62/5.

Audience: **u,f.**

Grotowski, Jerzy   **PN2061.G75 2002**
Towards Poor Theatre. Eugenio Barba (Editor), Peter Brook
(Introduction by, Preface by). Trade Paper. Routledge. New
York, NY. 2002. 272p. ISBN:0-87830-155-0, ISBN13:
978-0-87830-155-3. Dewey:792.02/8. LCCN:2004-266663.

Audience: **u,f.**

Handke, Peter   **PT2685.E5**
Handke Plays One. Trade Paper. Heinemann. Portsmouth, NH.
1996. 304p. Methuen Contemporary Dramatists Ser.
ISBN:0-413-68090-8, ISBN13: 978-0-413-68090-7.
Dewey:832.9/14.

Audience: **u,f.**

Hostetter, Anthony   **PN2656.B42G764 2003**
Max Reinhardt's Grosses Schauspielhaus: Its Artistic Goals,
Planning, and Operation, 1910-1933. Trade Cloth. Edwin Mellen
Press, The. Lewiston, NY. 2003. 224p. Studies in Theatre Arts,
Vol. 20 ISBN:0-7734-6802-1, ISBN13: 978-0-7734-6802-3.
Dewey:330 /945/58. LCCN:2003-042163.

Audience: **l,u,f.**

Hrotsvitha   **PR2065**
Dulcitius, a Mediaeval Comedy. Trade Paper. Books on
Demand. Ann Arbor, MI. 20p. ISBN:0-598-75592-6, ISBN13:
978-0-598-75592-6. Dewey:872. LCCN:17-006632.

Audience: **u,f.**

Ibsen, Henrik   **PT8854**
Ibsen's Selected Plays. Trade Paper. W. W. Norton & Company,
Inc. New York, NY. 2003. 612p. A Norton Critical Edition Ser.
ISBN:0-393-92404-1, ISBN13: 978-0-393-92404-6.
Dewey:839.8/226. LCCN:2003-051293.

Audience: **l,u,f.**

Ibsen, Henrik   **PT8854**
The Complete Major Prose Plays. Rolf Fjelde (Translator),
Henrik Ibsen (Illustrator), Rolf Fjelde (Foreword by). Trade
Paper. Penguin Group (USA) Inc. New York, NY. 1978. 1152p.
Plume Book Ser. ISBN:0-452-26205-4, ISBN13:
978-0-452-26205-8. Dewey:839.8. LCCN:78-050714.

Audience: **l,u,f.**

Kantor, Tadeusz   **PN2859.P6.K36 1993**
A Journey Through Other Spaces: Essays and Manifestos,
1944-1990. Michal Kobialka (Editor, Translator). Trade Cloth.
University of California Press. Berkeley, CA. 1993. 451p.
ISBN:0-520-07911-6, ISBN13: 978-0-520-07911-3.
Dewey:792.09438. LCCN:92-036296.

Audience: **u,f.** *Choice, 1994.*

Kleberg, Lars   **NX556.A1K5813**
Theatre As Action: Soviet Russian Avant-Garde Aesthetics.
Trade Paper. New York University Press. New York, NY. 1993.
168p. ISBN:0-333-56817-6, ISBN13: 978-0-333-56817-0.
Dewey:792.01.

Audience: **u,f.**

Langen, Timothy & Weir,   **PG3245.E38 2000**
  Justin (Editors)
Eight Twentieth-Century Russian Plays. Trade Paper.
Northwestern University Press. Evanston, IL. 2000. 354p.
European Drama Classics Ser. ISBN:0-8101-1374-0, ISBN13:
978-0-8101-1374-9. Dewey:891.72/408. LCCN:00-008680.

Audience: **g,l,u,f.**

Leach, Robert & Borovsky,   **PN2721.H57 1999**
  Victor
A History of Russian Theatre. Catriona Kelly, A. P. Briggs,
Anatoly Altschuller, Cynthia Marsh, Inna Solovyova, Kate
Sealey & Andy Adamson (Contribution by). Trade Cloth.
Cambridge University Press. New York, NY. 1999. 462p.
ISBN:0-521-43220-0, ISBN13: 978-0-521-43220-7.
Dewey:792/.0947. LCCN:97-035232.

Audience: **l,u,f.**

Leach, Robert   **PN2728.M4**
Vsevolod Meyerhold. Christopher Innes (Contribution by). Trade
Paper. Cambridge University Press. New York, NY. 1993. 237p.
Directors in Perspective Ser. ISBN:0-521-31843-2, ISBN13:
978-0-521-31843-3. Dewey:792/.0233/0924.

Audience: **l,u,f.** *Choice, 1990.*

Maeterlinck, Maurice, et al.   **PQ1240.E5T63 1997**
Three Pre-Surrealist Plays. Alfred Jarry & Guillaume Apollinaire
(Authors), Maya Slater (Translator, Introduction by, Notes by).
Trade Paper. Oxford University Press, Inc. New York, NY. 1997.
272p. Oxford World's Classics Ser. ISBN:0-19-283217-4,
ISBN13: 978-0-19-283217-7. Dewey:842/.808.
LCCN:96-052367.

Audience: **u,f.**

Manheim, Michael   **PN1851.M25 2002**
Vital Contradictions: Characterization in the Plays of Ibsen,
Strindberg, Chekhov, and O'Neill. Trade Cloth. Peter Lang
Publishing, Inc. New York, NY. 2002. 208p. Dramaturgies Ser.,
No. 6 ISBN:90-5201-991-6, ISBN13: 978-90-5201-991-8.
Dewey:809.2/927. LCCN:2002-075251.

Audience: **l,u,f.**

Mitter, Shomit   **PN2071.R45 M57**
Systems of Rehearsal: Stanislavsky, Brecht, Grotowski and Peter
Brook. Trade Paper. Routledge. New York, NY. 1992. 192p.
ISBN:0-415-06784-7, ISBN13: 978-0-415-06784-3.
Dewey:792.028. LCCN:92-000043.

Audience: **l,u,f.**

Morash, Christopher   **PN2601 .M64 2002**
A History of Irish Theatre, 1601-2000. Trade Paper. Cambridge
University Press. New York, NY. 2004. 342p.
ISBN:0-521-64682-0, ISBN13: 978-0-521-64682-6.
Dewey:792/.09415. LCCN:2001-035894.

Audience: **u,f.** *Choice, 2002.*

Richards, Thomas PN2859.P66G7713 1995
At Work with Grotowski on Physical Actions. Jerzy Grotowski
(Preface by). Trade Paper. Routledge. New York, NY. 1995.
152p. ISBN:0-415-12492-1, ISBN13: 978-0-415-12492-8.
Dewey:792/.0233/092. LCCN:94-023889.

Audience: **l,u,f.**

Roberts, J. W. PN2287.B484 R6 1981
Richard Boleslavsky: His Life and Work in the Theatre. Trade
Paper. Books on Demand. Ann Arbor, MI. 298p. Theater and
Dramatic Studies, Vol. 7 ISBN:0-8357-1250-8, ISBN13:
978-0-8357-1250-7. Dewey:792/.0233/0924. LCCN:81-016411.

Audience: **l,u,f.**

Rudnitsky, Konstantin PN2724.R76 2000
Russian and Soviet Theatre: Tradition and the Avant-Garde.
Trade Paper. Thames & Hudson. New York, NY. 2000. 320p.
ISBN:0-500-28195-5, ISBN13: 978-0-500-28195-6.
Dewey:792/.0947/09041. LCCN:99-066013.

Audience: **l,u,f.**

Russell, Douglas A. (Editor, PT3826.D8
 Introduction by)
An Anthology of Austrian Drama. Trade Cloth. Fairleigh
Dickinson University Press. Cranbury, NJ. 1982. 450p.
ISBN:0-8386-2003-5, ISBN13: 978-0-8386-2003-8.
Dewey:832/.008/09436. LCCN:76-019836.

Audience: **u,f.** ℬ

Sayler, Oliver Martin PN2724.S3
The Russian Theatre. Paper Text. Classic Books. Murrieta, CA.
2001. 346p. ISBN:0-7426-9249-3, ISBN13: 978-0-7426-9249-7.
Dewey:792.

Audience: **l,u,f.**

Schurer, Ernst (Editor) PT1258.G46 1997
German Expressionist Plays. Trade Paper. Continuum
International Publishing Group, Ltd. London, 1997. 344p.
German Library, Vol. 66 ISBN:0-8264-0950-4, ISBN13:
978-0-8264-0950-8. Dewey:832.9/12/08/0115.
LCCN:94-038092.

Audience: **l,u,f.**

Segel, Harold B. (Editor) PG7445.E5
Polish Romantic Drama: Three Plays in English Translation. Ed.
2. Trade Paper. Gordon & Breach Publishing Group. New York,
NY. 1997. 304p. Polish Theatre Archive Ser.
ISBN:90-5702-088-2, ISBN13: 978-90-5702-088-9.
Dewey:891.8/5/2/6/08.

Audience: **g,l,u,f.** ℬ

Simonarson, Olafur H. PT7094
Drama Contemporary: Scandinavia. Trade Cloth. P A J
Publications. New York, NY. 1990. 215p. ISBN:1-55554-050-3,
ISBN13: 978-1-55554-050-0. Dewey:839.52/4.

Audience: **g,u,f.**

Slonim, Marc PN3354.J3
Russian Theater, from the Empire to the Soviets. Paper Text.

Textbook Publishers. Temecula, CA. 2003. 354p.
ISBN:0-7581-0245-3, ISBN13: 978-0-7581-0245-4.
Dewey:808.3.

Audience: **u,f.** ℬ

Sokel, Walter H. (Editor) PT1258.A57 1984
Anthology of German Expressionist Drama. Book, Other.
Cornell University Press. Ithaca, NY. 1984. 336p.
ISBN:0-8014-9296-3, ISBN13: 978-0-8014-9296-9.
Dewey:832/.912/0801. LCCN:84-045197.

Audience: **l,u,f.**

Strindberg, August PT9811.A3S635 1997
Strindberg: Other Sides: Seven Plays. Joseph Martin
(Translator). Paper Text. Peter Lang Publishing, Inc. New York,
NY. 1998. 382p. ISBN:0-8204-3691-7, ISBN13:
978-0-8204-3691-3. Dewey:839.72/6. LCCN:96-054508.

Audience: **u,f.**

Strindberg, August PT9811.A3
Plays Three. Michael Meyer (Translator). Trade Paper. Methuen
Publishing Ltd. London, 2004. Methuen World Dramatists Ser.
ISBN:0-413-64840-0, ISBN13: 978-0-413-64840-2.
Dewey:839.7/26.

Audience: **u,f.**

Strindberg, August PT9811.A3M4
Plays Two. Michael Meyer (Translator, Introduction by). Trade
Paper. Methuen Publishing Ltd. London, 2004. Methuen World
Classics Ser. ISBN:0-413-49750-X, ISBN13:
978-0-413-49750-5. Dewey:839.72.

Audience: **u,f.**

Strindberg, August PT9811.A3
Strindberg: Plays One. Michael Meyer (Translator, Introduction
by). Trade Paper. Heinemann. Portsmouth, NH. 2004. 192p.
Methuen World Dramatists Ser. ISBN:0-413-52160-5, ISBN13:
978-0-413-52160-6. Dewey:839.7/2/6.

Audience: **u,f.**

Upor, Laszlo (Editor) PH3166
Hungarian Plays. Peter Karpati, Andras Nagy, Akos Nemeth &
Andor Szilagyi (Contribution by). Trade Paper. Nick Hern
Books, Ltd. London, 1996. 256p. International Collection
ISBN:1-85459-244-0, ISBN13: 978-1-85459-244-6.
Dewey:894.5/1123/08.

Audience: **u,f.**

Von Kleist, Heinrich PT2378.A2
Plays. Trade Paper. Theatre Communications Group, Inc. New
York, NY. 2000. 259p. Absolute Classics Ser.
ISBN:1-84002-123-3, ISBN13: 978-1-84002-123-3.
Dewey:832/.6.

Audience: **l,u,f.**

Weber, Carl (Editor) PT1258
Drama Contemporary: Germany. Trade Paper. Theatre
Communications Group, Inc. New York, NY. 2005. 282p.
ISBN:1-55554-063-5, ISBN13: 978-1-55554-063-0.
Dewey:832/.91408.

Audience: **u,f.**

Willinger, David   **PQ3858.E3T48 2002**
Theatrical Gestures of Belgian Modernism: Dada, Surrealism,
Futurism, and Pure Plastic in the Twentieth Century Belgian
Theatre. Luc Deneulin (Translator). Trade Cloth. Peter Lang
Publishing, Inc. New York, NY. 2002. 198p. Belgian
Francophone Library, Vol. 14 ISBN:0-8204-5503-2, ISBN13:
978-0-8204-5503-7. Dewey:842/.910809493.
LCCN:2002-002231.

Audience: **f.**

Wolford, Lisa & Schechner,   **PN2598.B69**
    Richard (Editors)
The Grotowski Sourcebook. Trade Paper. Routledge. New York,
NY. 2001. 544p. Worlds of Performance Ser.
ISBN:0-415-13111-1, ISBN13: 978-0-415-13111-7.
Dewey:792/.0233/092.

Audience: **l,u,f.**

Worrall, Nick   **PN2726.M62M73 1996**
The Moscow Art Theatre. Paper over Boards. Routledge. New
York, NY. 1996. 256p. Theatre Production Studies
ISBN:0-415-05598-9, ISBN13: 978-0-415-05598-7.
Dewey:792.9/5/0947312. LCCN:95-045724.

Audience: **l,u,f.**

Western Drama and Theater > United States

PN6112
The Best Plays of 1932-1933. Trade Cloth. Ayer Company
Publishers, Inc. Manchester, NH. 1975. The Best Plays Ser.
ISBN:0-405-07647-9, ISBN13: 978-0-405-07647-3.
Dewey:812.508. LCCN:75-019860.

Audience: **l,u.**

PS634
Best Plays Series. Trade Cloth. Ayer Company Publishers, Inc.
Manchester, NH. 1976. ISBN:0-405-07637-1, ISBN13:
978-0-405-07637-4. Dewey:812.5408. LCCN:75-019860.

Audience: **l,u.**

PN6112
Best Plays, 1963-1964. Trade Cloth. Ayer Company Publishers,
Inc. Manchester, NH. 1981. ISBN:0-405-13215-8, ISBN13:
978-0-405-13215-5. Dewey:812.08.

Audience: **l,u.**

PS634
Best Plays, 1964-1965. Trade Cloth. Ayer Company Publishers,
Inc. Manchester, NH. 1981. ISBN:0-405-13216-6, ISBN13:
978-0-405-13216-2. Dewey:808.82.

Audience: **l,u.**

PN6112
Best Plays, 1966-1967. Trade Cloth. Ayer Company Publishers,
Inc. Manchester, NH. 1981. ISBN:0-405-13217-4, ISBN13:
978-0-405-13217-9. Dewey:808.82.

Audience: **l,u.**

PN2277.N5
☐ Internet Broadway Database.
http://www.ibdb.com/

Audience: **g,l,u,f.**

PN1581
The New York Times Theater Reviews, 1870-1990. Trade Cloth.
Garland Publishing, Inc. New York, NY. 1992.
ISBN:0-318-69660-6, ISBN13: 978-0-318-69660-7.
Dewey:792.950973.

Audience: **l,u,f.**

PN2266
The New York Times Theater Reviews, 1995-1996. Cloth Text.
Garland Publishing, Inc. New York, NY. 1998. 456p. New York
Times Theater Review Ser., Vol. 29 ISBN:0-8153-0645-8,
ISBN13: 978-0-8153-0645-0.

Audience: **l,u,f.**

Albee, Edward   **PS3545.I5365**
The Collected Plays of Edward Albee, Vol. 1. Trade Cloth.
Overlook Press, The. New York, NY. 2004. 356p.
ISBN:1-58567-529-6, ISBN13: 978-1-58567-529-6.
Dewey:812/.54.

Audience: **l,u,f.**

Albee, Edward   **PS3545.I5365**
The Collected Plays of Edward Albee: 1978-2003. Trade Cloth.
Overlook Press, The. New York, NY. 2006. 656p.
ISBN:1-58567-777-9, ISBN13: 978-1-58567-777-1.
Dewey:812/.54.

Audience: **l,u,f.**

Albee, Edward   **PS3551.L25**
The Collected Plays of Edward Albee, 1966-1977, Vol. 2. Trade
Cloth. Overlook Press, The. New York, NY. 2005. 608p.
ISBN:1-58567-617-9, ISBN13: 978-1-58567-617-0.
Dewey:812.54.

Audience: **l,u,f.**

Alexander, Doris   **PS3529.N5Z555 1992**
Eugene O'Neill's Creative Struggle: The Decisive Decade,
1924-1933. Trade Cloth. Pennsylvania State University Press.
University Park, PA. 1992. 384p. ISBN:0-271-00813-X,
ISBN13: 978-0-271-00813-4. Dewey:812/.52 B.
LCCN:91-029976.

Audience: **l,u,f.** *Choice, 1992.*

Aronson, Arnold   **PN2193.E86A88 2000**
American Avant-Garde Theatre. Paper over Boards. Routledge.
New York, NY. 2000. 256p. Theatre Production Ser.
ISBN:0-415-02580-X, ISBN13: 978-0-415-02580-5.
Dewey:792/.022. LCCN:00-032215.

Audience: **u,f.** *Choice, 2001.*

Atkinson, Brooks   **PN2277.N5.A78 1974**
Broadway. Trade Cloth. Macmillan Publishing Company, Inc.
Old Tappan, NJ. 1974. ix, 564p. ISBN:0-02-504180-0, ISBN13:
978-0-02-504180-6. Dewey:792/.097471. LCCN:74-012077.

Audience: **l,u,f.** *B*

Auslander, Philip NX220
Presence and Resistance: Postmodernism and Cultural Politics in Contemporary American Performance. Trade Paper. University of Michigan Press. Chicago, IL. 1994. 216p. Theater Ser., :Theory - Text - Performance ISBN:0-472-08278-7, ISBN13: 978-0-472-08278-0. Dewey:700.9/73/09048.

Audience: **u,f.** *Choice, 1993.*

Berkowitz, Gerald M. PS350.B47 1992
American Drama of the Twentieth Century. Trade Paper. Addison-Wesley Longman, Inc. Boston, MA. 1995. 312p. Longman Literature in English Ser. ISBN:0-582-01601-0, ISBN13: 978-0-582-01601-9. Dewey:812.509. LCCN:92-009396.

Audience: **l,u,f.**

Bigsby, Christopher PS3525.I5156Z5445
Arthur Miller: A Critical Study. Trade Paper. Cambridge University Press. New York, NY. 2004. 524p. ISBN:0-521-60553-9, ISBN13: 978-0-521-60553-3. Dewey:812/.52 B. LCCN:2004-045813.

Audience: **l,u,f.**

Bigsby, Christopher (Editor) PS3563.A4345Z59 2004
The Cambridge Companion to David Mamet. Cloth Text. Cambridge University Press. New York, NY. 2004. 266p. Cambridge Companions to Literature Ser. ISBN:0-521-81557-6, ISBN13: 978-0-521-81557-4. Dewey:812/.54. LCCN:2003-063279.

Audience: **g.** *Choice, 2005.*

Bigsby, Christopher PS352 .B54 1999
Contemporary American Playwrights. Cloth Text. Cambridge University Press. New York, NY. 2000. 450p. ISBN:0-521-66108-0, ISBN13: 978-0-521-66108-9. Dewey:812.5409. LCCN:98-050378.

Audience: **l,u,f.**

Bordman, Gerald PN2266.3.B67 1995
American Theatre: A Chronicle of Comedy and Drama, 1914-1930. Trade Cloth. Oxford University Press, Inc. New York, NY. 1995. 454p. ISBN:0-19-509078-0, ISBN13: 978-0-19-509078-9. Dewey:792/.0973/09034. LCCN:94-013842.

Audience: **l,u,f.** *Choice, 1996.*

Bordman, Gerald Martin & PN2220.B6 2004
Hischak, Thomas S.
The Oxford Companion to American Theatre. Ed. 3. Trade Cloth. Oxford University Press, Inc. New York, NY. 2004. 394p. ISBN:0-19-516986-7, ISBN13: 978-0-19-516986-7. Dewey:792/.0973/03. LCCN:2003-021367.

Audience: **g.** *Choice, 2004.*

Chapman, John (Editor) PN6112
Burns Mantle Best Plays of Nineteen Forty-Nine to Nineteen Fifty. Trade Cloth. Ayer Company Publishers, Inc. Manchester, NH. 1978. The Best Plays Ser. ISBN:0-405-09177-X, ISBN13: 978-0-405-09177-3. Dewey:812.5082. LCCN:75-019860.

Audience: **l,u.**

Clapp, William Warland PN2277.B6
A Record of the Boston Stage. Trade Cloth. Scholarly Publishing Office, University of Michigan Library. Ann Arbor, MI. 2004. ISBN:1-4181-2043-X, ISBN13: 978-1-4181-2043-6.

Audience: **u,f.**

Clurman, Harold PN2297.G7 C5 1983
Fervent Years: The Group Theatre and the Thirties. Stella Adler (Introduction by). Trade Paper. Da Capo Press, Inc. Cambridge, MA. 1983. 352p. Quality Paperbacks Ser. ISBN:0-306-80186-8, ISBN13: 978-0-306-80186-0. Dewey:792/.0973. LCCN:82-025239.

Audience: **l,u,f.**

Coad, Oral E178.5
American Stage. Library Binding. Reprint Services Company. Temecula, CA. 1993. 362p. ISBN:0-7812-5268-7, ISBN13: 978-0-7812-5268-3. Dewey:973.

Audience: **l,u.**

Cohen-Stratyner, Barbara Z6935 .P46
(Introduction by)
Performing Arts Resources: The Drews and the Barrymores, a Dynasty of Actors. Warren Kliewer (Foreword by). Trade Cloth. Theatre Library Association. New York, NY. 1988. 161p. ISBN:0-932610-10-2, ISBN13: 978-0-932610-10-2. Dewey:016.7902/08. LCCN:75-646287.

Audience: **g.**

Delgado, Ramon (Editor) PN6111
The Best American Short Plays 1989. Trade Cloth. Applause Theatre Book Publishers. New York, NY. 1989. 264p. The Best American Short Plays Ser. ISBN:1-55783-045-2, ISBN13: 978-1-55783-045-6. Dewey:808.82.

Audience: **l,u.**

Delgado, Ramon (Editor) PN6112
The Best Short Plays: 1984. Trade Cloth. NP/Chilton. West Chester, PA. 1984. 251p. Plays and Play Collections ISBN:0-8019-7411-9, ISBN13: 978-0-8019-7411-3. Dewey:808.8241. LCCN:38-008006.

Audience: **l,u.**

Delgado, Ramon (Editor) PN6111
The Best Short Plays: 1983. Trade Cloth. NP/Chilton. West Chester, PA. 1983. 251p. Plays and Play Collections ISBN:0-8019-7296-5, ISBN13: 978-0-8019-7296-6. Dewey:812.508. LCCN:38-008006.

Audience: **l,u.**

Delgado, Ramon PN6111
The Best Short Plays: 1988-1989. Trade Cloth. Applause Theatre Book Publishers. New York, NY. 1989. 540p. Best Short Plays Ser. ISBN:1-55783-187-4, ISBN13: 978-1-55783-187-3. Dewey:808.82.

Audience: **l,u.**

Delgado, Ramon (Editor) PN6120.A4
The Best Short Plays: 1987. Trade Cloth. Applause Theatre

Formats: Web: ☐   Ebook: 🄴   CD/DVD-ROM: 🌠   BCL3: 𝓑

Book Publishers. New York, NY. 1987. 282p. Best Short Plays Ser. ISBN:0-936839-94-5, ISBN13: 978-0-936839-94-3. Dewey:808.82.

Audience: **g,l,u,f.**

Delgado, Ramon (Editor)   **PN6120.A4**
The Best Short Plays: 1985. Trade Cloth. Empire Publishing Service. Studio City, CA. 1985. 243p. Best Short Plays Ser. ISBN:0-8019-7541-7, ISBN13: 978-0-8019-7541-7. Dewey:812.08. LCCN:38-008006.

Audience: **l,u.**

Delgado, Ramon   **PN6111**
The Best Short Plays of 1986. Trade Paper. Applause Theatre Book Publishers. New York, NY. 1986. 258p. ISBN:0-936839-13-9, ISBN13: 978-0-936839-13-4. Dewey:812.08.

Audience: **l,u.**

Demastes, William W. (Editor)   **PS351**
American Playwrights, 1880-1945: A Research and Production Sourcebook. Cloth Text. Greenwood Publishing Group, Inc. Portsmouth, NH. 1994. 512p. ISBN:0-313-28638-8, ISBN13: 978-0-313-28638-4. Dewey:016.812/409. LCCN:94-013690.

Audience: **g.** *Choice, 1995.*

Demastes, William W.   **PS338**
Beyond Naturalism: A New Realism in American Theatre. Trade Cloth. Greenwood Publishing Group, Inc. Portsmouth, NH. 1988. 182p. Contributions in Drama and Theatre Studies Ser., No. 27 ISBN:0-313-26320-5, ISBN13: 978-0-313-26320-0. Dewey:812/.54/0912. LCCN:88-017787.

Audience: **l,u,f.** *Choice, 1989.*

Demastes, William W. (Editor)   **PS338.R42R43 1996**
Realism and the American Dramatic Tradition. Trade Paper. University of Alabama Press. Tuscaloosa, AL. 1996. 312p. ISBN:0-8173-0837-7, ISBN13: 978-0-8173-0837-7. Dewey:812/.50912. LCCN:96-004682.

Audience: **l,u,f.** *Choice, 1997.*

Dickinson, Thomas H.   **PN6112.D5**
Chief Contemporary Dramatists: Twenty-Two Plays from the Recent Drama of England, Ireland, America, Germany, France, Belgium, Norway, Sweden and Russia. Library Binding. Richard West. Philadelphia, PA. 1979. ISBN:0-8492-4207-X, ISBN13: 978-0-8492-4207-6. Dewey:808.82.

Audience: **l,u,f.**

Dickinson, Thomas H.   **PN6112.D52**
Chief Contemporary Dramatists. Trade Paper. Kessinger Publishing, LLC. Whitefish, MT. 2005. ISBN:1-4179-8690-5, ISBN13: 978-1-4179-8690-3. Dewey:808.82.

Audience: **l,u,f.**

Dickinson, Thomas H. (Editor)   **PN6112.D52**
Chief Contemporary Dramatists, Second Series: Eighteen Plays from the Recent Drama of England, Ireland, America, France,

Germany, Austria, Italy, Spain, Russia, and Scandinavia. Library Binding. Darby Books. Darby, PA. 1985. 734p. ISBN:0-317-17328-6, ISBN13: 978-0-317-17328-4. Dewey:808.82/041.

Audience: **l,u,f.**

Dillon, Jim & Naylor, David   **NA6830.N38 1997**
American Theaters: Performance Halls of the Nineteenth Century. Trade Cloth. John Wiley & Sons, Inc. Hoboken, NJ. 1997. 224p. ISBN:0-471-14393-6, ISBN13: 978-0-471-14393-2. Dewey:725/.822/097309034. LCCN:96-043764.

Audience: **l,u,f.**

Dunlap, William   **PN2221**
History of American Theatre from Its Origins to 1832. Tice L. Miller (Introduction by). Trade Paper. University of Illinois Press. Champaign, IL. 2005. 472p. ISBN:0-252-07285-5, ISBN13: 978-0-252-07285-7. Dewey:792.0973. LCCN:2005-302019.

Audience: **l,u,f.** *Choice, 2006.*

Eaton, Walter P.   **PN2295.T5.E3 1970**
Theatre Guild, the First Ten Years, with Articles by the Directors. Trade Cloth. Ayer Company Publishers, Inc. Manchester, NH. 1977. 299p. Select Bibliographies Reprint Ser. ISBN:0-8369-5180-8, ISBN13: 978-0-8369-5180-6. Dewey:792/.0973. LCCN:75-107799.

Audience: **l,u,f.** *B*

Egan, Leona Rust   **PS3529.N5Z6294 1994**
Provincetown as a Stage: Provincetown, the Provincetown Players, and the Discovery of Eugene O'Neill. Trade Cloth. Parnassus Imprints. Marstons Mills, MA. 1994. 296p. ISBN:0-940160-57-9, ISBN13: 978-0-940160-57-6. Dewey:792.097. LCCN:93-087449.

Audience: **l,u,f.**

Engle, Ron & Miller, Tice L. (Editors)   **PN2226 .A5 1993**
The American Stage: Social and Economic Issues from the Colonial Period to the Present. Cloth Text. Cambridge University Press. New York, NY. 1993. 342p. ISBN:0-521-41238-2, ISBN13: 978-0-521-41238-4. Dewey:306.4840973. LCCN:92-022016.

Audience: **l,u,f.** *Choice, 1994.*

Fleche, Anne   **PS338.R42F58 1997**
Mimetic Disillusion: Eugene O'Neill, Tennessee Williams and U. S. Dramatic Realism. Trade Paper. University of Alabama Press. Tuscaloosa, AL. 1997. 152p. ISBN:0-8173-0838-5, ISBN13: 978-0-8173-0838-4. Dewey:812/.5209. LCCN:96-024510.

Audience: **l,u,f.** *Choice, 1997.*

Gardner, Bonnie Milne   **PS352.G37 2001**
The Emergence of the Playwright-Director in American Theatre, 1960-1983. Trade Cloth. Edwin Mellen Press, The. Lewiston, NY. 2001. 236p. Studies in Theatre Arts, Vol. 15 ISBN:0-7734-7470-6, ISBN13: 978-0-7734-7470-3. Dewey:892.4/2608. LCCN:00-065373.

Audience: **l,u,f.**

Gassner, John (Introduction by)   **PS634.B4**
Best American Plays: Third Series, 1945-51. Trade Cloth. Crown Publishing Group. New York, NY. 1987. 736p. ISBN:0-517-50950-4, ISBN13: 978-0-517-50950-0. Dewey:812.08.

Audience: **l,u.**

Gassner, John (Editor)   **PS625.B47 2000**
Best Plays of the Early American Theatre, 1787-1911. Trade Paper. Dover Publications, Inc. Mineola, NY. 2000. 768p. ISBN:0-486-41098-6, ISBN13: 978-0-486-41098-2. Dewey:812.008. LCCN:00-027931.

Audience: **g,l,u,f.** 𝓑

Gewirtz, Arthur & Kolb, James J. (Editors)   **PS351**
Experimenters, Rebels and Disparate Voices: The Theatre of the 1920s Celebrates American Diversity. Trade Cloth. Greenwood Publishing Group, Inc. Portsmouth, NH. 2003. 216p. Contributions in Drama and Theatre Studies, Vol. 99 ISBN:0-313-32466-2, ISBN13: 978-0-313-32466-6. Dewey:812/.5209920693. LCCN:2002-072543.

Audience: **l,u,f.** *Choice, 2004.*

Graham, Philip   **PN2293.S4 G7**
Showboats: The History of an American Institution. Paper Text. Textbook Publishers. Temecula, CA. 2003. 224p. ISBN:0-7581-1538-5, ISBN13: 978-0-7581-1538-6. Dewey:792.

Audience: **g.** 𝓑

Grams, Martin Jr.   **PN1991.9.G73 2000**
Radio Drama: A Comprehensive Chronicle of American Network Programs, 1932-1962. Cloth Text. McFarland & Company, Incorporated Publishers. Jefferson, NC. 2000. 584p. ISBN:0-7864-0051-X, ISBN13: 978-0-7864-0051-5. Dewey:016.79144/75/0973. LCCN:99-29879.

Audience: **l,u,f.** *Choice, 2000.*

Guernsey, Otis L. Jr. (Editor)   **PN6112.B45**
The Best Plays of 1998-1999: The Otis Guernsey-Burns Mantle Theatre Yearbook. Trade Cloth. Hal Leonard Corporation. Milwaukee, WI. 2004. 556p. The Otis Guernsey-Burns Mantle Theater Yearbook Ser., Vol. 80:Best Plays ISBN:0-87910-290-X, ISBN13: 978-0-87910-290-6. Dewey:808.82.

Audience: **l,u.**

Guernsey, Otis L. Jr. (Editor)   **PN2266.A2**
The Otis Guernsey-Burns Mantle Theater Yearbook: The Best Plays of 1996-1997. Ed. 78. Trade Cloth. Hal Leonard Corporation. Milwaukee, WI. 1997. 496p. The Otis Guernsey-Burns Mantle Theater Yearbook Ser., No. 78:Best Plays ISBN:0-87910-097-4, ISBN13: 978-0-87910-097-1. Dewey:812.508.

Audience: **l,u.**

Guernsey, Otis L. Jr.   **PN2266.A2**
The Best Plays of 1999-2000: The Otis Guernsey-Burns Mantle Theatre Yearbook, Set. Ed. 81. Al Hirschfeld (Illustrator). Trade Cloth. Hal Leonard Corporation. Milwaukee, WI. 2004. 516p.

The Otis Guernsey-Burns Mantle Theater Yearbook Ser., :Best Plays ISBN:0-87910-955-6, ISBN13: 978-0-87910-955-4. Dewey:808.82.

Audience: **l,u.**

Guernsey, Otis L. Jr. (Editor)   **PN6112**
The Otis Guernsey-Burns Mantle Theater Yearbook: The Best Plays of 1997-1998. Ed. 79. Al Hirschfeld (Illustrator). Trade Cloth. Hal Leonard Corporation. Milwaukee, WI. 1998. 496p. The Otis Guernsey-Burns Mantle Theater Yearbook Ser., :Best Plays ISBN:0-87910-271-3, ISBN13: 978-0-87910-271-5. Dewey:812.

Audience: **l,u.**

Guernsey, Otis L. Jr. & Sweet, Jeffrey (Editors)   **PN6112**
The Applause-Best Plays Theater Yearbook, 1990-1991: The Complete Broadway and Off-Broadway Sourcebook. Trade Cloth. Applause Theatre Book Publishers. New York, NY. 1991. 564p. ISBN:1-55783-106-8, ISBN13: 978-1-55783-106-4. Dewey:808.2.

Audience: **l,u.**

Guernsey, Otis L. Jr. & Sweet, Jeffrey (Editors)   **PN6112.B45**
The Otis Guernsey-Burns Mantle Theater Yearbook: The Best Plays of 1995-1996. Ed. 77. Trade Cloth. Hal Leonard Corporation. Milwaukee, WI. 1996. 587p. ISBN:0-87910-089-3, ISBN13: 978-0-87910-089-6. Dewey:812.508.

Audience: **l,u.**

Guernsey, Otis L. Jr. & Sweet, Jeffrey (Editors)   **PN6112**
The Applause-Best Plays Theater Yearbook, 1991-1992: Featuring the Ten Best Plays of the Year. Al Hirschfeld (Illustrator). Trade Paper. Applause Theatre Book Publishers. New York, NY. 1992. 549p. Best Plays Ser. ISBN:1-55783-147-5, ISBN13: 978-1-55783-147-7. Dewey:808.82.

Audience: **l,u.**

Guernsey, Otis L. Jr. & Sweet, Jeffrey (Editors)   **PN2266**
The Best Plays of 1987-1987. Al Hirschfeld (Illustrator). Trade Cloth. W. Clement Stone, P M A Communications, Inc. Northbrook, IL. 1989. ISBN:0-396-09077-X, ISBN13: 978-0-396-09077-9. Dewey:808.822.

Audience: **l,u.**

Guernsey, Otis L. Jr. & Sweet, Jeffrey (Editors)   **PN6112**
The Best Plays of 1988-1989. Ed. 70. Al Hirschfeld (Illustrator). Trade Cloth. Applause Theatre Book Publishers. New York, NY. 1989. 676p. The Burns Mantle Theater Yearbook Ser. ISBN:1-55783-056-8, ISBN13: 978-1-55783-056-2. Dewey:808.82.

Audience: **l,u.**

Guernsey, Otis L. Jr. & Sweet, Jeffrey (Editors)   **PN6112**
The Best Plays of 1989-1990. Al Hirschfeld (Illustrator). Trade

Cloth. Applause Theatre Book Publishers. New York, NY. 1990. 676p. The Burns Mantle Theatre Yearbook Ser. ISBN:1-55783-091-6, ISBN13: 978-1-55783-091-3. Dewey:808.2.

Audience: **l,u.**

Guernsey, Otis L. Jr. &   **PN6112**
Sweet, Jeffrey (Editors)
The Otis Guernsey-Burns Mantle Theater Yearbook: The Best Plays of 1992-1993. Al Hirschfeld (Illustrator). Trade Cloth. Hal Leonard Corporation. Milwaukee, WI. 1993. 648p. ISBN:0-87910-173-3, ISBN13: 978-0-87910-173-2. Dewey:812.508.

Audience: **l,u.**

Guernsey, Otis L. Jr. &   **PN6112**
Sweet, Jeffrey (Editors)
The Otis Guernsey-Burns Mantle Theater Yearbook: The Best Plays of 1993-1994. Al Hirschfeld (Illustrator). Trade Cloth. Hal Leonard Corporation. Milwaukee, WI. 1994. 661p. ISBN:0-87910-183-0, ISBN13: 978-0-87910-183-1. Dewey:812.508.

Audience: **l,u.**

Guernsey, Otis L. Jr. &   **TK454.D44**
Sweet, Jeffrey (Editors)
The Otis Guernsey-Burns Mantle Theater Yearbook: The Best Plays of 1994-1995. Al Hirschfeld (Contribution by). Trade Cloth. Hal Leonard Corporation. Milwaukee, WI. 1995. 608p. ISBN:0-87910-196-2, ISBN13: 978-0-87910-196-1. Dewey:621.319/2.

Audience: **l,u.**

Guernsey, Otis L. Jr. &   **PN6112**
Sweet, Jeffrey (Editors)
Best Plays of 1987-1988. Al Hirshfeld (Illustrator). Trade Cloth. Applause Theatre Book Publishers. New York, NY. 1989. 592p. The Burns Mantle Theater Yearbook Ser. ISBN:1-55783-040-1, ISBN13: 978-1-55783-040-1. Dewey:812.508.

Audience: **l,u.**

Harrison, Elizabeth J.   **PR478.M6U53 1997**
(Editor)
Unmanning Modernism: Gendered Re-Readings. Peterson, Shirley (Editor). University of Tennessee Press. 1997. ISBN:0-87049-985-8, ISBN13: 978-0-87049-985-2.

Audience: **u,f.**

Hays, Michael &   **PN1922**
Nikolopoulou, Anastasia (Editors)
Melodrama: The Cultural Emergence of a Genre. Trade Paper. Palgrave Macmillan. New York, NY. 1999. 304p. ISBN:0-312-22127-4, ISBN13: 978-0-312-22127-0. Dewey:809.2/52.

Audience: **u,f.** *Choice, 1997.*

Henderson, Mary C.   **PN2277.N5**
The City and the Theatre: The History of New York Playhouses: A 250 Year Journey from Bowling Green to Times Square. Gerald Schoenfield (Foreword by). Trade Cloth. Watson-Guptill

Publications, Inc. New York, NY. 2004. 384p. ISBN:0-8230-0637-9, ISBN13: 978-0-8230-0637-3. Dewey:792.097471.

Audience: **u,f.** *Choice, 2005.*

Hewitt, Barnard   **PN2285.F8**
Theatre USA, 1668 to 1957. Paper Text. Textbook Publishers. Temecula, CA. 2003. 528p. ISBN:0-7581-8614-2, ISBN13: 978-0-7581-8614-0. Dewey:792.028.

Audience: **l,u,f.**

Hischak, Thomas S.   **PN2277.N5H57 2000**
American Theatre: A Chronicle of Comedy and Drama, 1969-2000. Trade Cloth. Oxford University Press, Inc. New York, NY. 2001. 514p. ISBN:0-19-512347-6, ISBN13: 978-0-19-512347-0. Dewey:792/.09747/1. LCCN:00-028287.

Audience: **l,u,f.** *Choice, 2001.*

Hischak, Thomas S.   **ML102**
Stage It with Music: An Encyclopedic Guide to the American Musical Theatre. Cloth Text. Greenwood Publishing Group, Inc. Portsmouth, NH. 1993. 328p. ISBN:0-313-28708-2, ISBN13: 978-0-313-28708-4. Dewey:792.60973. LCCN:92-035321.

Audience: **l,u.** *Choice, 1993.*

Hodge, Francis   **PN2248**
Yankee Theatre: The Image of America on the Stage, 1825-1850. Cloth Text. Ayer Company Publishers, Inc. Manchester, NH. 1977. ISBN:0-8369-8198-7, ISBN13: 978-0-8369-8198-8. Dewey:792.2/0973.

Audience: **l,u,f.** ℬ

Hornblow, Arthur   **PN2221.H6**
A History of the Theatre in America from Its Beginnings to the Present Time. Paper Text. Classic Books. Murrieta, CA. 2001. ISBN:0-7426-9210-8, ISBN13: 978-0-7426-9210-7. Dewey:792.0973.

Audience: **l,u,f.** ℬ

Hughes, Glenn   **PN511.B54**
A History of the American Theatre 1700: 1950. Paper Text. Textbook Publishers. Temecula, CA. 2003. 562p. ISBN:0-7581-4245-5, ISBN13: 978-0-7581-4245-0. Dewey:804.

Audience: **l,u,f.** ℬ

Jenkins, Jeffrey Eric   **PQ4287.L5**
The Best Plays of 2000-2001: The Otis Guernsey-Burns Mantle Theatre Yearbook. Ed. 82. Al Hirschfeld (Illustrator). Trade Cloth. Hal Leonard Corporation. Milwaukee, WI. 2004. 444p. Theater Yearbook Ser. ISBN:0-87910-968-8, ISBN13: 978-0-87910-968-4. Dewey:853.15.

Audience: **l,u.**

King, Kimball   **PR736.M56 2001**
Modern Dramatists: A Casebook of the Major British and American Playwrights. Cloth Text. Garland Publishing, Inc. New York, NY. 2001. 325p. Studies in Modern Drama, Vol. 14 ISBN:0-8153-2349-2, ISBN13: 978-0-8153-2349-5. Dewey:822/.9109. LCCN:00-065297.

Audience: **l,u,f.**

Kinne, Wisner P. PN2287
George Pierce Baker and the American Theatre. Trade Cloth.
Greenwood Publishing Group, Inc. Portsmouth, NH. 1969. 348p.
ISBN:0-8371-0129-8, ISBN13: 978-0-8371-0129-3.
Dewey:927.92. LCCN:68-008741.

Audience: l,u,f. *B*

Kolin, Philip C. (Editor) PS3545
Tennessee Williams: A Guide to Research and Performance.
Book, Other. Greenwood Publishing Group, Inc. Portsmouth,
NH. 1998. 296p. ISBN:0-313-30306-1, ISBN13:
978-0-313-30306-7. Dewey:812/.54. LCCN:98-013972.

Audience: l,u,f. *Choice, 1999.*

Krasner, David (Editor) PS350.C655 2005
A Companion to Twentieth Century American Drama. Trade
Cloth. Blackwell Publishing, Inc. Malden, MA 2004. 600p.
Blackwell Companions to Literature and Culture Ser.
ISBN:1-4051-1088-0, ISBN13: 978-1-4051-1088-4.
Dewey:812/.509. LCCN:2004-007690.

Audience: l,u,f. *Choice, 2005.*

Langley, Stephen PN2291 .L29
Theatre Management and Production in America: Commercial,
Stock, Resident, College, Community, Theatre, and Presenting
Organizations. Trade Paper. Quite Specific Media Group, Ltd.
Hollywood, CA. 1990. 702p. ISBN:0-89676-143-6, ISBN13:
978-0-89676-143-8. Dewey:792/.068.

Audience: l,u,f.

Leiter, Samuel L. PN2277
The Encyclopedia of the New York Stage, 1930-1940. Cloth
Text. Greenwood Publishing Group, Inc. Portsmouth, NH. 1989.
1339p. ISBN:0-313-25509-1, ISBN13: 978-0-313-25509-0.
Dewey:792.9/5/09471. LCCN:88-005668.

Audience: g. *Choice, 1990.*

Leiter, Samuel L. PN2277
The Encyclopedia of the New York Stage, 1940-1950. Cloth
Text. Greenwood Publishing Group, Inc. Portsmouth, NH. 1992.
1000p. ISBN:0-313-27510-6, ISBN13: 978-0-313-27510-4.
Dewey:792/.097471. LCCN:92-007397.

Audience: g. *Choice, 1993.*

Leiter, Samuel L. PN2597
From Belasco to Brook: Representative Directors of the
English-Speaking Stage. Trade Cloth. Greenwood Publishing
Group, Inc. Portsmouth, NH. 1991. 320p. Contributions in
Drama and Theatre Studies Ser., No. 33 ISBN:0-313-27662-5,
ISBN13: 978-0-313-27662-0. Dewey:792/.0233/0922 B.
LCCN:90-045350.

Audience: l,u,f. *Choice, 1991.*

Leiter, Samuel L. & Hill, PN2277
Holly (Contribution by)
The Encyclopedia of the New York Stage, 1920-1930, Set. Cloth
Text. Greenwood Publishing Group, Inc. Portsmouth, NH. 1985.
1331p. ISBN:0-313-23615-1, ISBN13: 978-0-313-23615-0.
Dewey:792.9/5/097471. LCCN:84-006558.

Audience: g. *B Choice, 1986.*

Leiter, Samuel L. & Hill, PN2277.N5L361985
Holly (Contribution by)
The Encyclopedia of the New York Stage, 1920-1930, Vol. 1.
Cloth Text. Greenwood Publishing Group, Inc. Portsmouth, NH.
1985. 1331p. ISBN:0-313-25037-5, ISBN13:
978-0-313-25037-8. Dewey:792.9/5/097471. LCCN:84-006558.

Audience: g. *B Choice, 1986.*

Mamet, David PS3545.I5365
American Buffalo. Library Binding. Sagebrush Education
Resources. Caledonia, MN. 1996. ISBN:0-613-29186-7,
ISBN13: 978-0-613-29186-6. Dewey:812.5/4.

Audience: l,u,f.

Mamet, David PS3545.I5365
Glengarry Glen Ross. Trade Paper. Grove/Atlantic, Inc. New
York, NY. 1984. 112p. ISBN:0-8021-3091-7, ISBN13:
978-0-8021-3091-4. Dewey:812.5/4. LCCN:83-049380.

Audience: g,l,u,f.

Mamet, David PS3563.A4345O4 1993
Oleanna. UK-Trade Paper. Knopf Publishing Group. New York,
NY. 1993. 96p. ISBN:0-679-74536-X, ISBN13:
978-0-679-74536-5. Dewey:812.5/4. LCCN:92-050638.

Audience: l,u,f.

Mamet, David PS3563.A4345
Sexual Perversity in Chicago and the Duck Variations. Trade
Paper. Grove/Atlantic, Inc. New York, NY. 1978. 128p.
ISBN:0-8021-5011-X, ISBN13: 978-0-8021-5011-0. Dewey:812.
LCCN:77-091885.

Audience: l,u,f.

Mamet, David PS3563.A4345S64 1988
Speed-the-Plow. Trade Paper. Grove/Atlantic, Inc. New York,
NY. 1988. 96p. ISBN:0-8021-3046-1, ISBN13:
978-0-8021-3046-4. Dewey:812.5/4. LCCN:87-037252.

Audience: l,u,f.

Manheim, Michael (Editor) PS3529.N5Z575 1998
The Cambridge Companion to Eugene O'Neill. Cloth Text.
Cambridge University Press. New York, NY. 1998. 274p.
Companions to Literature Ser. ISBN:0-521-55389-X, ISBN13:
978-0-521-55389-6. Dewey:812/.52. LCCN:97-042228.

Audience: g,l,u,f. *Choice, 1999.*

Mann, Bruce J. (Editor) PS3551.L25Z655 2003
Edward Albee: A Casebook. Paper over Boards. Routledge. New
York, NY. 2002. 168p. Casebooks on Modern Dramatists, Vol.
29 ISBN:0-8153-3165-7, ISBN13: 978-0-8153-3165-0.
Dewey:812/.54. LCCN:2002-011279.

Audience: l,u,f. *Choice, 2003.*

Mantle, Burns (Editor) PN2266.A2
The Best Plays of 1919-1920. Trade Cloth. Ayer Company
Publishers, Inc. Manchester, NH. 1978. The Best Plays Ser.
ISBN:0-405-09168-0, ISBN13: 978-0-405-09168-1.
Dewey:808.82. LCCN:75-019860.

Audience: l,u.

Mantle, Burns (Editor)   **PN2266.A2**
The Best Plays of 1929-1930. Trade Cloth. Ayer Company
Publishers, Inc. Manchester, NH. 1975. The Best Plays Ser.
ISBN:0-405-09170-2, ISBN13: 978-0-405-09170-4.
Dewey:812.08. LCCN:75-019860.

Audience: **l,u.**

McArthur, Benjamin   **PN2256.M39 2000**
Actors and American Culture, 1880-1920. Trade Paper.
University of Iowa Press. Iowa City, IA. 2000. 304p. Studies in
Theatre History and Culture ISBN:0-87745-710-7, ISBN13:
978-0-87745-710-7. Dewey:792/.028/097309034.
LCCN:00-268718.

Audience: **l,u,f.**

Miller, Arthur   **PS3525.I5156A6 2006**
Arthur Miller: Collected Plays, 1944-1961. Tony Kushner
(Editor). Trade Cloth. Library of America, The. New York, NY.
2006. 864p. The Library of America, Vol. 163
ISBN:1-931082-91-X, ISBN13: 978-1-931082-91-4.
Dewey:812/.52. LCCN:2005-049442.

Audience: **g,l,u,f.**

Murphy, Brenda   **PS338.R42 M87 1987**
American Realism and American Drama, 1880-1940. Albert
Gelpi & Ross Posnock (Contribution by). Trade Cloth.
Cambridge University Press. New York, NY. 1987. 248p.
Studies in American Literature and Culture, No. 22
ISBN:0-521-32711-3, ISBN13: 978-0-521-32711-4.
Dewey:812/.52/0912. LCCN:86-013694.

Audience: **l,u,f.** *Choice, 1987.*

Murphy, Brenda   **PN2277**
Provincetown Players and the Culture of Modernity. Don B.
Wilmeth (Contribution by). Trade Cloth. Cambridge University
Press. New York, NY. 2005. 302p. Cambridge Studies in
American Theatre and Drama Ser., Vol. 23 ISBN:0-521-83852-5,
ISBN13: 978-0-521-83852-8. Dewey:792.0974492.
LCCN:2006-296175.

Audience: **u,f.** *Choice, 2006.*

New York Times Staff   **PR3091**
  (Contribution by)
The New York Times Theatre Reviews, 1999-2000. Paper over
Boards. Routledge. New York, NY. 2002. 500p. The New York
Times Theater Reviews Ser. ISBN:0-415-93697-7, ISBN13:
978-0-415-93697-2. Dewey:792.9/5/05.

Audience: **l,u,f.**

Odell, George C.   **PN2277.N5.O4 1970**
Annals of the New York Stage. Trade Cloth. A M S Press, Inc.
New York, NY. 1970. ISBN:0-404-07830-3, ISBN13:
978-0-404-07830-0. Dewey:792/.097471. LCCN:77-116018.

Audience: **g.** *B*

O'Neill, Eugene   **PS3529.N5 1988**
O'Neill Complete Plays, 1913-1920, Vol. 1. Travis Bogard
(Editor). Trade Cloth. Library of America, The. New York, NY.
1988. 1100p. ISBN:0-940450-48-8, ISBN13:
978-0-940450-48-6. Dewey:812/.52. LCCN:88-050685.

Audience: **g,l,u,f.** *Choice, 1989.*

O'Neill, Eugene   **PS3529.N5 1988**
O'Neill Complete Plays, 1920-1931, Vol. 2. Travis Bogard
(Editor). Trade Cloth. Library of America, The. New York, NY.
1988. 1072p. ISBN:0-940450-49-6, ISBN13:
978-0-940450-49-3. Dewey:812/.52. LCCN:88-050685.

Audience: **g,l,u,f.** *Choice, 1989.*

O'Neill, Eugene   **PS3529.N5 1988**
O'Neill Complete Plays, 1933-1943, Vol. 3. Travis Bogard
(Editor). Trade Cloth. Library of America, The. New York, NY.
1988. 1000p. Library of Congress Classics
ISBN:0-940450-50-X, ISBN13: 978-0-940450-50-9.
Dewey:812/.52. LCCN:88-050685.

Audience: **g,l,u,f.** *Choice, 1989.*

Owen, Bobbi   **PN2096**
Scenic Design on Broadway: Designers and Their Credits,
1915-1990. Cloth Text. Greenwood Publishing Group, Inc.
Portsmouth, NH. 1991. 320p. Bibliographies and Indexes in the
Performing Arts Ser., No. 10 ISBN:0-313-26534-8, ISBN13:
978-0-313-26534-1. Dewey:792.02509227471.
LCCN:91-025254.

Audience: **l,u,f.** *Choice, 1992.*

Porter, Steven   **ML1950.P68 1997**
The American Musical Theatre: A Complete Musical Theatre
Course. Ed. 2. Trade Paper. Players Press, Inc. Studio City, CA.
2003. 152p. Musical Theatre Ser. ISBN:0-88734-686-3, ISBN13:
978-0-88734-686-6. Dewey:782.81. LCCN:97-039626.

Audience: **l,u,f.**

Postlewait, Thomas   **PN2115.I54 1989**
Interpreting the Theatrical Past: Essays in the Historiography of
Performance. University of Iowa Press. 1989.
ISBN:0-87745-238-5, ISBN13: 978-0-87745-238-6.

Audience: **l,u,f.**

Random House Staff   **PN1581**
The New York Times Theatre Reviews, 1991-92. Library
Binding. Garland Publishing, Inc. New York, NY. 1994. New
York Times Theater Reviews Ser., Vol. 27 ISBN:0-8153-0643-1,
ISBN13: 978-0-8153-0643-6. Dewey:792.950973.

Audience: **l,u,f.**

Roberts, Peter (Editor)   **PN2595**
The Best of Plays and Players: 1969-1983, Vol. 2. Donald
Cooper (Illustrator). Trade Cloth. Heinemann. Portsmouth, NH.
1989. 272p. ISBN:0-413-62150-2, ISBN13: 978-0-413-62150-4.
Dewey:792.0941.

Audience: **l,u.** *Choice, 1990.*

Roberts, Peter (Editor)   **PN2595 .B47 1988**
The Best of Plays and Players 1953-1968, Vol. 1. Zoe Dominic
(Illustrator). Trade Paper. Heinemann. Portsmouth, NH. 1990.
254p. ISBN:0-413-52970-3, ISBN13: 978-0-413-52970-1.
Dewey:792/.0941. LCCN:88-140018.

Audience: **l,u.**

Rogers, Will & Day, Donald   **PN2287.R74A3 1998**
The Autobiography of Will Rogers. Trade Cloth. Transaction

Publishers. Somerset, NJ. 1998. 528p. ISBN:1-56000-526-2, ISBN13: 978-1-56000-526-1. Dewey:792.7/028/092 B. LCCN:98-030710.

Audience: **g.**

Roudani, Matthew   PS3569.H394Z65 2002
The Cambridge Companion to Sam Shepard. Cloth Text. Cambridge University Press. New York, NY. 2002. 352p. Cambridge Companions to Literature Ser. ISBN:0-521-77158-7, ISBN13: 978-0-521-77158-0. Dewey:812/.54 B. LCCN:2001-043211.

Audience: **g.** *Choice, 2003.*

Ruggles, Eleanor   PN2287.B5 R9
Prince of Players: Edwin Booth. Paper Text. Textbook Publishers. Temecula, CA. 2003. 401p. ISBN:0-7581-7575-2, ISBN13: 978-0-7581-7575-5. Dewey:792/.028/0924.

Audience: **l,u,f.** 🅱

Sarlos, Robert K.   PN2297.P7.S27 1982
Jig Cook and the Provincetown Players: Theatre in Ferment. Library Binding. University of Massachusetts Press. Amherst, MA. 1982. 280p. ISBN:0-87023-349-1, ISBN13: 978-0-87023-349-4. Dewey:792/.09744/92. LCCN:81-016104.

Audience: **l,u,f.** 🅱

Schmidt, Kerstin   PS352 .S35 2005
The Theater of Transformation: Postmodernism in American Drama. Trade Paper. Rodopi. Kenilworth, NY. 2005. 230p. Postmodern Studies, 37 ISBN:90-420-1895-X, ISBN13: 978-90-420-1895-2. Dewey:812.609.

Audience: **u,f.**

Seilhamer, George O.   PN2221 .S4
History of the American Theatre. Paper Text. Classic Books. Murrieta, CA. 2001. ISBN:0-7426-9216-7, ISBN13: 978-0-7426-9216-9. Dewey:792.

Audience: **l,u,f.** 🅱

Seldes, Gilbert   PN1584.S45
The 7 Lively Arts. Paper Text. Textbook Publishers. Temecula, CA. 2003. 306p. ISBN:0-7581-4228-5, ISBN13: 978-0-7581-4228-3. Dewey:791.

Audience: **l,u.**

Sell, Mike   PN2297.L5S45 2005
Avant-Garde Performance and the Limits of Criticism: Approaching the Living Theatre, Happenings/Fluxus and the Black Arts Movement. Trade Cloth. University of Michigan Press. Chicago, IL. 2005. 336p. Theater Ser., :Theory/Text/Performance Ser. ISBN:0-472-11495-6, ISBN13: 978-0-472-11495-5. Dewey:792/.09747/1. LCCN:2005-016628.

Audience: **l,u,f.**

Shelton, Lewis E.   PN2256.S54 2005
Ideas of Theatre: The Five Directorial Perspectives of the American Stage. Library Binding. Academica Press, LLC. Bethesda, MD. 2005. 364p. ISBN:1-933146-04-4, ISBN13: 978-1-933146-04-1. Dewey:792.02/33/092273. LCCN:2005-002998.

Audience: **l,u,f.**

Shepard, Sam   PS3545.I5365
Sam Shepard: Seven Plays. Mass Market. Bantam Books. New York, NY. 1999. ISBN:0-553-23401-3, ISBN13: 978-0-553-23401-5. Dewey:812.5/4.

Audience: **l,u,f.**

Smith, C. S.   PN2881.G3
The New York Times Theater Reviews 1997-1998. Cloth Text. Taylor & Francis Group. Philadelphia, PA. 2001. 496p. The New York Times Theater Reviews Ser. ISBN:0-8153-3341-2, ISBN13: 978-0-8153-3341-8. Dewey:792.0954.

Audience: **l,u,f.**

Smith, Cecil & Litton,   ML1711.S6 1981
  Glenn
Musical Comedy in America: From the Black Crook Through Sweeney Todd. Ed. 2. Trade Paper. Routledge. New York, NY. 1987. 367p. ISBN:0-87830-564-5, ISBN13: 978-0-87830-564-3. Dewey:782.81/0973. LCCN:80-051638.

Audience: **l,u,f.** 🅱

Solorzano, Carlos (Editor)   PA6073.B44
The Americas. Trade Paper. Routledge. New York, NY. 2000 640p. World Encyclopedia of Contemporary Theatre Ser., Vol. 2 ISBN:0-415-22745-3, ISBN13: 978-0-415-22745-2. Dewey:792.03.

Audience: **g.** *Choice, 1996.*

Thelen, Lawrence   PN2285.T48 2000
The Show Makers: Great Directors of American Musical Theatre. UK-B Format Paperback. Routledge. New York, NY. 2002. 264p. ISBN:0-415-92347-6, ISBN13: 978-0-415-92347-7. Dewey:792.6/0233/092273 B. LCCN:99-029455.

Audience: **l,u,f.** *Choice, 2000.*

Tompkins, Eugene   PN2277.B7B77
The History of the Boston Theatre, 1854-1901. Paper Text. Classic Books. Murrieta, CA. 2001. 550p. ISBN:0-7426-9217-5, ISBN13: 978-0-7426-9217-6. Dewey:792/.09744/61.

Audience: **f.** 🅱

Tornqvist, Egil   PS3529.N5
Eugene O'Neill: A Playwright's Theatre. Paper Text. McFarland & Company, Incorporated Publishers. Jefferson, NC. 2004. 268p. ISBN:0-7864-1713-7, ISBN13: 978-0-7864-1713-1. Dewey:812/.52. LCCN:2003-025325.

Audience: **l,u,f.** *Choice, 2004.*

Waldau, Roy S.   PN2295.T5.W3
Vintage Years of the Theatre Guild, 1928-1939. Trade Cloth. Press of Case Western Reserve University. Cleveland, OH. 1972. 519p. ISBN:0-8295-0203-3, ISBN13: 978-0-8295-0203-9. Dewey:792/.0973. LCCN:79-141463.

Audience: **l,u,f.** 🅱

Walker, Julia   PS351
Expressionism and Modernism in the American Theatre: Bodies, Voices, Words. Don B. Wilmeth (Contribution by). Trade Cloth. Cambridge University Press. New York, NY. 2005. 312p.

Cambridge Studies in American Theatre and Drama Ser., Vol. 21
ISBN:0-521-84747-8, ISBN13: 978-0-521-84747-6.
Dewey:812/.5209115. LCCN:2005-047508.

Audience: **u,f.**

Watt, Stephen &   **PS625.A5 1995**
  Richardson, Gary A.
American Drama: From the Colonial to the Contemporary.
Paper Text. Thomson Heinle. Boston, MA. 1994. 850p.
ISBN:0-15-500003-9, ISBN13: 978-0-15-500003-2.
Dewey:812.008. LCCN:93-081045.

Audience: **l,u,f.**

Williams, Tennessee   **PS3545.I5365A6 2000**
Tennessee Williams: Plays 1957-1980. Mel Gussow & Kenneth
Holditch (Editors). Trade Cloth. Library of America, The. New
York, NY. 2000. 975p. Library of America, Vol. 119
ISBN:1-883011-87-6, ISBN13: 978-1-883011-87-1.
Dewey:812/.54. LCCN:00-030190.

Audience: **g,l,u,f.**

Williams, Tennessee   **PS3545.I5365A6 2000**
Tennessee Williams: Plays 1937-1955. Mel Gussow & Kenneth
Holditch (Editors). Trade Cloth. Library of America, The. New
York, NY. 2000. 975p. Library of America, Vol. 119
ISBN:1-883011-86-8, ISBN13: 978-1-883011-86-4.
Dewey:812/.54. LCCN:00-030190.

Audience: **g,l,u,f.**

Wilmeth, Don B. & Bigsby,   **PN2221**
  Christopher (Editors)
The Cambridge History of American Theatre: 1870-1945. Don
B. Wilmeth & Christopher Bigsby (Contribution by). Trade
Paper. Cambridge University Press. New York, NY. 2006. 608p.
Cambridge History of American Theatre Ser.
ISBN:0-521-67984-2, ISBN13: 978-0-521-67984-8.
Dewey:792/.0973.

Audience: **l,u,f.**   *Choice, 2000.*

Wilmeth, Don B. & Bigsby,   **PN2221.C37 1998**
  Christopher (Editors)
The Cambridge History of American Theatre: Beginnings to
1870. Don B. Wilmeth & Christopher Bigsby (Contribution by).
Trade Paper. Cambridge University Press. New York, NY. 2006.
544p. Cambridge History of American Theatre Ser.
ISBN:0-521-67983-4, ISBN13: 978-0-521-67983-1.
Dewey:792/.0973.

Audience: **l,u,f.**   *Choice, 1998.*

Wilmeth, Don B. & Bigsby,   **PN2221.C37 2006**
  Christopher (Editors)
The Cambridge History of American Theatre: Post-World War II
to The 1990s. Don B. Wilmeth & Christopher Bigsby
(Contribution by). Trade Paper. Cambridge University Press.
New York, NY. 2006. 600p. Cambridge History of American
Theatre Ser. ISBN:0-521-67985-0, ISBN13: 978-0-521-67985-5.
Dewey:792.0973.

Audience: **l,u,f.**

Winter, William   **PR6005.A77Z63**
Life and Art of Edwin Booth. Trade Paper. Kessinger
Publishing, LLC. Whitefish, MT. 2005. ISBN:0-7661-9557-0,
ISBN13: 978-0-7661-9557-8. Dewey:823.912.

Audience: **u.**

Winter, William   **PN2287.B4 W5 1970**
Life of David Belasco, Set. Trade Cloth. Ayer Company
Publishers, Inc. Manchester, NH. 1977. Select Bibliographies
Reprint Ser. ISBN:0-8369-5202-2, ISBN13: 978-0-8369-5202-5.
Dewey:792/.0924. LCCN:72-107837.

Audience: **g.**

Witham, Barry B.   **PN2270.F43**
The Federal Theatre Project: A Case Study. Don B. Wilmeth
(Contribution by). Trade Cloth. Cambridge University Press.
New York, NY. 2003. 204p. Cambridge Studies in American
Theatre and Drama Ser., Vol. 20 ISBN:0-521-82259-9, ISBN13:
978-0-521-82259-6. Dewey:792.0973. LCCN:2004-299872.

Audience: **l,u,f.**   *Choice, 2004.*

Wood, William Burke   **PN2277**
Old Drury of Philadelphia: A History of the Philadelphia Stage,
1800-1835. Trade Cloth. Greenwood Publishing Group, Inc.
Portsmouth, NH. 1968. 694p. ISBN:0-8371-0115-8, ISBN13:
978-0-8371-0115-6. Dewey:792/.09748/11. LCCN:69-010108.

Audience: **u,f.** *B*

Worthen, William B.   **PR736.W64 1992**
Modern Drama and the Rhetoric of Theater. Trade Cloth.
University of California Press. Berkeley, CA. 1991. 240p.
ISBN:0-520-07468-8, ISBN13: 978-0-520-07468-2.
Dewey:822/.9109. LCCN:91-017677.

Audience: **l,u,f.**   *Choice, 1992.*

Western Drama and Theater > United States > Minstrel Shows

Bean, Annemarie (Editor),   **PN3195.I58 1996**
  et al.
Inside the Minstrel Mask: Readings in Nineteenth-Century
Blackface Minstrelsy. James V. Hatch & Brooks McNamara
(Editors), Mel Watkins (Foreword by). Trade Paper. Wesleyan
University Press. Middletown, CT. 1996. 324p.
ISBN:0-8195-6300-5, ISBN13: 978-0-8195-6300-2.
Dewey:791/.12/097309034. LCCN:96-016572.

Audience: **l,u,f.**

Cockrell, Dale   **ML1711 .C63 1997**
Demons of Disorder: Early Blackface Minstrels and Their
World. Don B. Wilmeth (Contribution by). Trade Cloth.
Cambridge University Press. New York, NY. 1997. 256p.
Studies in American Theatre and Drama, Vol. 8
ISBN:0-521-56074-8, ISBN13: 978-0-521-56074-0.
Dewey:791.1/2/0973. LCCN:96-045566.

Audience: **u,f.**   *Choice, 1998.*

Riis, Thomas L. ML1711 .R54 1992
More Than Just Minstrel Shows: The Rise of Black Musical Theatre at the Turn of the Century. Trade Paper. Institute for Studies in American Music. Brooklyn, NY. 1992. 72p. I.S.A.M. Monographs, No. 33 ISBN:0-914678-36-1, ISBN13: 978-0-914678-36-6. Dewey:792.6/089/96073. LCCN:92-072055.
Audience: **l,u,f.**

Sweet, Frank W. PN3195
A History of the Minstrel Show. Paper Text. Boxes & Arrows, Inc. Palm Coast, FL. 2000. 36p. ISBN:0-939479-21-4, ISBN13: 978-0-939479-21-4. Dewey:791.12.
Audience: **l,u,f.**

Wittke, Carl F. PN3195
Tambo and Bones: A History of the American Minstrel Stage. Trade Cloth. Greenwood Publishing Group, Inc. Portsmouth, NH. 1971. 269p. ISBN:0-8371-0276-6, ISBN13: 978-0-8371-0276-4. Dewey:791.1/2/0973. LCCN:69-010174.
Audience: **l,u,f.**

Western Drama and Theater > United States > Ethnic/Minority Drama and Theater in the U.S.

Ellis, Roger & Zapel, PS627.M5M85 1998
Theodore O. (Editors)
Multicultural Theatre II: Contemporary Hispanic, Asian and African-American Plays. Trade Paper. Meriwether Publishing, Ltd. Colorado Springs, CO. 1998. 392p. Ser. ISBN:1-56608-042-8, ISBN13: 978-1-56608-042-2. Dewey:812/.54080920693. LCCN:98-028515.
Audience: **l,u,f.** *Choice, 1999.*

Maufort, Marc (Editor) PS352.S73 1995
Staging Difference: Cultural Pluralism in American Theatre and Drama. Cloth Text. Peter Lang Publishing, Inc. New York, NY. 1996. 396p. American University Studies, Vol. 25:Theatre Arts ISBN:0-8204-2732-2, ISBN13: 978-0-8204-2732-4. Dewey:812/.5409920693. LCCN:94-043336.
Audience: **l,u,f.** *Choice, 1996.*

Seller, Maxine S. (Editor) PN2226
Ethnic Theatre in the United States. Book, Other. Greenwood Publishing Group, Inc. Portsmouth, NH. 1983. 606p. ISBN:0-313-21230-9, ISBN13: 978-0-313-21230-7. Dewey:792/.0973. LCCN:81-013494.
Audience: **l,u,f.** 𝕭

Swanson, Meg (Editor) PS627.M5P57 1999
Playwrights of Color. Robin Murray (Contribution by). Paper Text. Intercultural Press, Inc. Yarmouth, ME. 1999. 714p. ISBN:1-877864-35-8, ISBN13: 978-1-877864-35-3. Dewey:812/.54080920693. LCCN:99-014126.
Audience: **l,u,f.**

Western Drama and Theater > United States > Ethnic/Minority Drama and Theater in the U.S. > Female-Authored Drama and Theater

Allen, Carol PS338.N4A425 2005
Peculiar Passages: Black Women Playwrights, 1875 to 2000. Trade Cloth. Peter Lang Publishing, Inc. New York, NY. 2005. 295p. ISBN:0-8204-7620-X, ISBN13: 978-0-8204-7620-9. Dewey:812/.4099287. LCCN:2004-020875.
Audience: **l,u,f.**

Allen, Carol PS338.N4A425 2005
Peculiar Passages: Black Women Playwrights, 1875 to 2000. Trade Paper. Peter Lang Publishing, Inc. New York, NY. 2005. 295p. ISBN:0-8204-7619-6, ISBN13: 978-0-8204-7619-3. Dewey:812/.4099287. LCCN:2004-020875.
Audience: **l,u,f.**

Barlow, Judith E. (Editor) PS628.W6
Plays by American Women, 1930-1960. Hal Leonard Corporation Staff (Created by). Trade Paper. Applause Theatre Book Publishers. New York, NY. 2001. 576p. ISBN:1-55783-446-6, ISBN13: 978-1-55783-446-1. Dewey:812/.50809287.
Audience: **l,u,f.**

Black, Cheryl PN2297.P7B58 2002
The Women of Provincetown, 1915-1922. Trade Cloth. University of Alabama Press. Tuscaloosa, AL. 2001. 273p. ISBN:0-8173-1112-2, ISBN13: 978-0-8173-1112-4. Dewey:792/.082/0974492. LCCN:2001-003850.
Audience: **u,f.** *Choice, 2002.*

Burke, Sally PS338.W6
American Feminist Playwrights. Trade Paper. Thomson Gale. Farmington Hills, MI. 1997. Twayne's Critical History of American Drama Ser. ISBN:0-8057-1620-3, ISBN13: 978-0-8057-1620-7. Dewey:812.009/9287. LCCN:96-010832.
Audience: **l,u,f.** *Choice, 1998.*

Case, Sue-Ellen (Editor) PS627.L48S65 1996
Split Britches: Lesbian Practice - Feminist Performance. Trade Paper. Routledge. New York, NY. 1996. 288p. ISBN:0-415-12766-1, ISBN13: 978-0-415-12766-0. Dewey:812.5/4/08/09287. LCCN:95-047164.
Audience: **l,u,f.**

Chavez, Denise & Feyder, PS628.H57 S5 1992
Linda (Editors)
Shattering the Myth: Plays by Hispanic Women. Trade Paper. Arte Publico Press. Houston, TX. 2003. 256p. Latin-American Play Anthologies Ser. ISBN:1-55885-041-4, ISBN13: 978-1-55885-041-5. Dewey:812/.540809287. LCCN:91-040997.
Audience: **g,l,u.**

Chinoy, Helen Krich & PN1590.W64
Jenkins, Linda Walsh (Editors)
Women in American Theatre. Trade Paper. Theatre

Communications Group, Inc. New York, NY. 2005. 600p.
ISBN:1-55936-263-4, ISBN13: 978-1-55936-263-4.
Dewey:792/.082/0973.

Audience: **l,u,f.**

Craig, Carolyn Casey   **PS338.W6C73 2004**
Women Pulitzer Playwrights: Biographical Profiles and Analyses
of the Plays. Paper Text. McFarland & Company, Incorporated
Publishers. Jefferson, NC. 2004. 347p. ISBN:0-7864-1881-8,
ISBN13: 978-0-7864-1881-7. Dewey:812/.5099287.
LCCN:2004-020165.

Audience: **l,u.**

Darby, Jaye T. & Fitzgerald,   **PS628.I53**
  Stephanie (Editors)
Keepers of the Morning Star: An Anthology of Native Women's
Theater. Trade Cloth. University of California, American Indian
Studies Center. Los Angeles, CA. 2004. 386p. Native American
Theater Ser. ISBN:0-935626-56-5, ISBN13: 978-0-935626-56-8.
Dewey:812/.54080897. LCCN:2003-100128.

Audience: **l,u,f.**   *Choice, 2004.*

Desti-Demanti, Zoe   **PS338.W6D48 1998**
Early American Women Dramatists, 1780-1860. Trade Cloth.
Garland Publishing, Inc. New York, NY. 1998. 240p. Studies in
American Popular History and Culture Ser.
ISBN:0-8153-3304-8, ISBN13: 978-0-8153-3304-3.
Dewey:812/.2099287. LCCN:98-045560.

Audience: **u,f.**

Dolan, Jill   **PN2270.F45D64 1988**
The Feminist Spectator As Critic. UMI Research Press. 1988.
ISBN:0-8357-1874-3, ISBN13: 978-0-8357-1874-5.

Audience: **l,u,f.**

Flores, Yolanda   **PQ7082.D7F65 2000**
The Drama of Gender: Feminist Theater by Women of the
Americas. Cloth Text. Peter Lang Publishing, Inc. New York,
NY. 2000. 144p. Worlds of Change Ser., Vol. 38:Latin-American
and Iberian Literature ISBN:0-8204-3958-4, ISBN13:
978-0-8204-3958-7. Dewey:862. LCCN:99-026923.

Audience: **l,u,f.**

Glancy, Diane   **PS3557.L294A84 2002**
American Gypsy: Six Native American Plays. Trade Cloth.
University of Oklahoma Press. Norman, OK. 2002. 224p.
American Indian Literature and Critical Studies, Vol. 45
ISBN:0-8061-3456-9, ISBN13: 978-0-8061-3456-7.
Dewey:812/.54. LCCN:2002-018870.

Audience: **l,u,f.**

Greene, Alexis (Editor)   **PS352.W66 2001**
Women Who Write Plays: Interviews with Contemporary
American Dramatists. Trade Paper. Smith and Kraus Publishers,
Inc. Lyme, NH. 2001. 543p. An Art of Theater Book Ser.
ISBN:1-57525-262-7, ISBN13: 978-1-57525-262-9.
Dewey:812/.54099287. LCCN:2001-032200.

Audience: **l,u,f.**

Hellman, Lillian   **PS3515.E343 A6 1979**
Six Plays by Lillian Hellman: The Children's Hour, Days to
Come, The Little Foxes, Watch on the Rhine, Another Part of
the Forest, The Autumn Garden. Book, Other. Knopf Publishing
Group. New York, NY. 1979. 512p. ISBN:0-394-74112-9,
ISBN13: 978-0-394-74112-3. Dewey:812/.5/2.
LCCN:79-002160.

Audience: **l,u,f.**

Kennedy, Adrienne   **PS3561.E4252**
The Alexander Plays. University of Minnesota Press. 1992.
ISBN:0-8166-2077-6, ISBN13: 978-0-8166-2077-7.

Audience: **g,l,u,f.**

Kritzer, Amelia H. (Editor,   **PS628.W6P595 1995**
  Compiled by)
Plays by Early American Women, 1775-1850. Trade Paper.
University of Michigan Press. Chicago, IL. 1995. 448p.
ISBN:0-472-06598-X, ISBN13: 978-0-472-06598-1.
Dewey:812/.20809287. LCCN:94-045115.

Audience: **g,l,u,f.**   *Choice, 1995.*

Lamont, Rosette C. (Editor)   **PS628.W6.W664 1993**
Women on the Verge: Seven Avant-Garde American Plays. Trade
Paper. Applause Theatre Book Publishers. New York, NY. 1992.
416p. ISBN:1-55783-148-3, ISBN13: 978-1-55783-148-4.
Dewey:812.540809287. LCCN:93-011557.

Audience: **u,f.**   *Choice, 1994.*

Miles, Julia   **PS628.W6H47 1997**
Here to Stay: Five Plays from the Women's Project. Applause.
1997. ISBN:1-55783-315-X, ISBN13: 978-1-55783-315-0.

Audience: **g,l,u,f.**

Murphy, Brenda (Editor)   **PS338.W6C36 1999**
The Cambridge Companion to American Women Playwrights.
Trade Paper. Cambridge University Press. New York, NY. 1999.
324p. Companions to Literature Ser. ISBN:0-521-57680-6,
ISBN13: 978-0-521-57680-2. Dewey:812.009/9287.
LCCN:98-036593.

Audience: **g,l,u,f.**

Norman, Marsha   **PS3564.O623A6 1997**
Marsha Norman: Collected Plays Works. Trade Paper. Smith and
Kraus Publishers, Inc. Lyme, NH. 1997. 336p. Contemporary
American Playwrights Ser., :Anthologies ISBN:1-57525-029-2,
ISBN13: 978-1-57525-029-8. Dewey:812/.54. LCCN:97-007665.

Audience: **l,u,f.**

Perkins, Kathy A. (Editor)   **PS628.N4**
🄴 Black Female Playwrights: An Anthology of Plays Before
1950. E-Book. Indiana University Press. Bloomington, IN. 1990.
298p. Blacks in the Diaspora Ser. ISBN:0-253-20623-5,
ISBN13: 978-0-253-20623-7. Dewey:812/.008/09287.
LCCN:88-046040.

Audience: **g,l,u,f.**   *Choice, 1990.*

Perkins, Kathy A. & Uno,   **PS627.M5C66 1996**
  Roberta (Editors)
Contemporary Plays by Women of Color: An Anthology. Paper
over Boards. Routledge. New York, NY. 1996. 336p.

ISBN:0-415-11377-6, ISBN13: 978-0-415-11377-9.
Dewey:812/.540809287. LCCN:95-007465.
Audience: **g,l,u,f.** *Choice, 1996.*

Ramirez, Elizabeth C.   **PN2270.H57R36 2000**
Chicanas - Latinas in American Theatre: A History of
Performance. Library Binding. Indiana University Press.
Bloomington, IN. 2000. 188p. ISBN:0-253-33714-3, ISBN13:
978-0-253-33714-6. Dewey:792/.082/0973. LCCN:00-029578.
Audience: **l,u,f.**

Schleuter, June (Editor)   **PS338.W6 M6**
Modern American Drama: The Female Canon. Trade Paper.
Fairleigh Dickinson University Press. Cranbury, NJ. 1996. 312p.
ISBN:0-8386-3707-8, ISBN13: 978-0-8386-3707-4.
Dewey:812.009/9287. LCCN:89-045579.
Audience: **l,u,f.**

Shafer, Yvonne   **PS338.W6S48 1995**
American Women Playwrights from 1900 to 1950. Paper Text.
Peter Lang Publishing, Inc. New York, NY. 1995. 546p.
ISBN:0-8204-2142-1, ISBN13: 978-0-8204-2142-1.
Dewey:812/.5099287. LCCN:93-018357.
Audience: **l,u,f.** *Choice, 1996.*

Smith, Anna Deavere   **PS3569.M465T95 1994**
Twilight--Los Angeles, 1992: On the Road: A Search for
American Character. Anchor Books. 1994. ISBN:0-385-47375-3,
ISBN13: 978-0-385-47375-0.
Audience: **g,l,u,f.**

Uno, Roberta (Editor)   **PS628.W6**
Unbroken Thread: An Anthology of Plays by Asian American
Women. Trade Paper. University of Massachusetts Press.
Amherst, MA. 1993. 336p. ISBN:0-87023-856-6, ISBN13:
978-0-87023-856-7. Dewey:812/.540809287. LCCN:93-021858.
Audience: **l,u,f.** *Choice, 1994.*

Vogel, Paula   **PS3572.O296H88 1997**
How I Learned to Drive. Trade Paper. Dramatists Play Service,
Inc. New York, NY. 1997. 60p. ISBN:0-8222-1623-X, ISBN13:
978-0-8222-1623-0. Dewey:812/.54. LCCN:98-128331.
Audience: **g,l,u,f.**

Wasserstein, Wendy   **PS3573.A798H4 1991**
The Heidi Chronicles and Other Plays. Trade Paper. Alfred A.
Knopf Inc. New York, NY. 1991. 272p. ISBN:0-679-73499-6,
ISBN13: 978-0-679-73499-4. Dewey:812.54. LCCN:90-055681.
Audience: **l,u,f.**

Western Drama and Theater > United States > Ethnic/Minority Drama and Theater in the U.S. > African American Drama and Theater

Alexander Street Press   **PN6119.7**
☐ Black Drama 1850 to Present.
http://www.alexanderstreet2.com/BLDRLive/
Alexander Street Press.
Audience: **g,l,u,f.**

Allen, Carol   **PS338.N4A425 2005**
Peculiar Passages: Black Women Playwrights, 1875 to 2000.
Trade Cloth. Peter Lang Publishing, Inc. New York, NY. 2005.
295p. ISBN:0-8204-7620-X, ISBN13: 978-0-8204-7620-9.
Dewey:812/.4099287. LCCN:2004-020875.
Audience: **l,u,f.**

Allen, Carol   **PS338.N4A425 2005**
Peculiar Passages: Black Women Playwrights, 1875 to 2000.
Trade Paper. Peter Lang Publishing, Inc. New York, NY. 2005.
295p. ISBN:0-8204-7619-6, ISBN13: 978-0-8204-7619-3.
Dewey:812/.4099287. LCCN:2004-020875.
Audience: **l,u,f.**

Branch, William B. (Editor)   **PS628.N4C76 1993**
Crosswinds: An Anthology of Black Dramatists in the Diaspora.
Trade Paper. Indiana University Press. Bloomington, IN. 1993.
448p. Blacks in the Diaspora Ser. ISBN:0-253-20778-9,
ISBN13: 978-0-253-20778-4. Dewey:808.82/008996.
LCCN:92-026648.
Audience: **l,u,f.**

Elam, Harry J. Jr. &   **PS628.N4C65 1996**
  Alexander, Robert (Editors)
Colored Contradictions: An Anthology of Contemporary
African-American Plays. Trade Paper. Penguin Group (USA)
Inc. New York, NY. 1996. 656p. ISBN:0-452-27497-4, ISBN13:
978-0-452-27497-6. Dewey:812/.54080896073.
LCCN:96-015948.
Audience: **l,u,f.**

Hamalian, Leo & Hatch,   **PS628.N4**
  James V. (Editors)
Roots of African American Drama: An Anthology of Early
Plays, 1858-1938. George C. Wolfe (Introduction by). Trade
Paper. Wayne State University Press. Detroit, MI. 1992. 456p.

African American Life Ser. ISBN:0-8143-2142-9, ISBN13: 978-0-8143-2142-3. Dewey:812.008/0896073. LCCN:90-012002.
　　　　　　　　　　　　　　Audience: **l,u,f.** *Choice, 1991.*

Hatch, James V., et al.　　　　　　**PR9272.9.H55H55 2005**
A History of African American Theatre. Errol Hill & Errol G. Hill (Authors), Don B. Wilmeth (Contribution by). Trade Paper. Cambridge University Press. New York, NY. 2005. 632p. Cambridge Studies in American Theatre and Drama Ser. ISBN:0-521-62472-X, ISBN13: 978-0-521-62472-5. Dewey:792/.089/96073. LCCN:2002-034991.
　　　　　　　　　　　　　　Audience: **l,u,f.** *Choice, 2004.*

Hay, Samuel A.　　　　　　　　**PN2270.A35 H39**
African American Theatre: An Historical and Critical Analysis. Don B. Wilmeth (Contribution by). Trade Paper. Cambridge University Press. New York, NY. 1994. 303p. Studies in American Theatre and Drama, No. 1 ISBN:0-521-46585-0, ISBN13: 978-0-521-46585-4. Dewey:792/.08996073.
　　　　　　　　　　　　　　Audience: **l,u,f.**

King, Woodie Jr. (Editor)　　　　　**PS628.N4N38 1995**
The National Black Drama Anthology: Eleven Plays from America's Leading African-American Theaters. Trade Paper. Applause Theatre Book Publishers. New York, NY. 2000. 528p. ISBN:1-55783-219-6, ISBN13: 978-1-55783-219-1. Dewey:812.5/4/08/0896. LCCN:95-034945.
　　　　　　　　　　　　　　Audience: **l,u,f.** *Choice, 1996.*

Krasner, David　　　　　　　　**PS338.N4**
A Beautiful Pageant: African American Theatre, Drama, and Performance in the Harlem Renaissance, 1910-1927. Trade Paper. Palgrave Macmillan. New York, NY. 2004. 400p. ISBN:1-4039-6541-2, ISBN13: 978-1-4039-6541-7. Dewey:812/.5209896073.
　　　　　　　　　　　　　　Audience: **l,u,f.** *Choice, 2003.*

Krasner, David　　　　　　　　**PN2270.A35**
Resistance, Parody and Double Consciousness in African American Theatre, 1895-1910. Trade Paper. Palgrave Macmillan. New York, NY. 1998. 252p. ISBN:0-312-21925-3, ISBN13: 978-0-312-21925-3. Dewey:792/.08996073.
　　　　　　　　　　　　　　Audience: **l,u,f.** *Choice, 1999.*

Marshall, Herbert　　　　　　　**PN2598.R42A3**
Ira Aldridge, the Negro Tragedian. Paper Text. Textbook Publishers. Temecula, CA. 2003. 355p. ISBN:0-7581-3677-3, ISBN13: 978-0-7581-3677-0. Dewey:927.92.
　　　　　　　　　　　　　　Audience: **l,u,f.** *B*

Ostrow, Eileen J. (Editor)　　　　　**PS628.N4C4 1991**
Center Stage: An Anthology of Twenty-One Contemporary Black-American Plays. Sandra L. Richards (Introduction by). Trade Paper. University of Illinois Press. Champaign, IL. 1991. 328p. ISBN:0-252-06178-0, ISBN13: 978-0-252-06178-3. Dewey:812/.54080896073. LCCN:90-022631.
　　　　　　　　　　　　　　Audience: **l,u,f.**

Perkins, Kathy A. (Editor)　　　　　**PS628.N4**
🄴 Black Female Playwrights: An Anthology of Plays Before 1950. E-Book. Indiana University Press. Bloomington, IN. 1990.

298p. Blacks in the Diaspora Ser. ISBN:0-253-20623-5, ISBN13: 978-0-253-20623-7. Dewey:812/.008/09287. LCCN:88-046040.
　　　　　　　　　　　　　　Audience: **g,l,u,f.** *Choice, 1990.*

Perkins, Kathy A. & Uno,　　　　　**PS627.M5C66 1996**
Roberta (Editors)
Contemporary Plays by Women of Color: An Anthology. Paper over Boards. Routledge. New York, NY. 1996. 336p. ISBN:0-415-11377-6, ISBN13: 978-0-415-11377-9. Dewey:812/.540809287. LCCN:95-007465.
　　　　　　　　　　　　　　Audience: **g,l,u,f.** *Choice, 1996.*

Peterson, Bernard L. Jr.　　　　　**PN2286**
Profiles of African American Stage Performers and Theatre People, 1816-1960. James V. Hatch (Foreword by). Cloth Text. Greenwood Publishing Group, Inc. Portsmouth, NH. 2000. 440p. ISBN:0-313-29534-4, ISBN13: 978-0-313-29534-8. Dewey:791/.089/96073 B. LCCN:99-088456.
　　　　　　　　　　　　　　Audience: **l,u,f.** *Choice, 2001.*

Wetmore, Kevin J.　　　　　　　**PS338.N4W48 2003**
Black Dionysus: Greek Tragedy and African American Theatre. Paper Text. McFarland & Company, Incorporated Publishers. Jefferson, NC. 2003. 272p. ISBN:0-7864-1545-2, ISBN13: 978-0-7864-1545-8. Dewey:812.009/896073. LCCN:2002-156684.
　　　　　　　　　　　　　　Audience: **u,f.** *Choice, 2003.*

Wilson, August　　　　　　　　**PS338.N4 W55**
Cultivating the Ground on Which We Stand: African-American Theater. Trade Cloth. Palgrave Macmillan. New York, NY. 2003. ISBN:0-312-22308-0, ISBN13: 978-0-312-22308-3. Dewey:812/.5409896073.
　　　　　　　　　　　　　　Audience: **l,u,f.**

Wilson, August　　　　　　　　**PS3573.I45677F4**
Fences: A Play. Library Binding. Sagebrush Education Resources. Caledonia, MN. 1986. ISBN:0-7857-9611-8, ISBN13: 978-0-7857-9611-4. Dewey:812.54.
　　　　　　　　　　　　　　Audience: **g,l,u,f.**

Wilson, August　　　　　　　　**PS3545.I5365**
The Piano Lesson. Library Binding. Sagebrush Education Resources. Caledonia, MN. 1990. ISBN:0-613-03323-X, ISBN13: 978-0-613-03323-7. Dewey:812.5/4.
　　　　　　　　　　　　　　Audience: **g,l,u,f.**

Wilson, August (Preface by)　　　**PS3573.I45677A6 1991**
Three Plays. Paul C. Harrison (Afterword by). Trade Cloth. University of Pittsburgh Press. Pittsburgh, PA. 1991. 336p. ISBN:0-8229-3666-6, ISBN13: 978-0-8229-3666-4. Dewey:812/.54. LCCN:90-044105.
　　　　　　　　　　　　　　Audience: **l,u,f.** *Choice, 1992.*

Woll, Allen L.　　　　　　　　**PN2270**
Dictionary of the Black Theatre: Broadway, Off-Broadway, and Selected Harlem Theatre. Cloth Text. Greenwood Publishing Group, Inc. Portsmouth, NH. 1983. 359p. ISBN:0-313-22561-3, ISBN13: 978-0-313-22561-1. Dewey:792/.08996073. LCCN:82-021090.
　　　　　　　　　　　　　　Audience: **g.** *B*

Western Drama and Theater > United States > Ethnic/Minority Drama and Theater in the U.S. > Native American Drama and Theater

D'Aponte, Mimi G. (Editor)   **PS628.I53S48 1999**
Seventh Generation: An Anthology of Native American Plays.
Trade Paper. Theatre Communications Group, Inc. New York,
NY. 1998. 300p. ISBN:1-55936-147-6, ISBN13:
978-1-55936-147-7. Dewey:812/.54080897. LCCN:98-004449.
Audience: **l,u,f.**

Darby, Jaye T. & Fitzgerald,   **PS628.I53**
Stephanie (Editors)
Keepers of the Morning Star: An Anthology of Native Women's
Theater. Trade Cloth. University of California, American Indian
Studies Center. Los Angeles, CA. 2004. 386p. Native American
Theater Ser. ISBN:0-935626-56-5, ISBN13: 978-0-935626-56-8.
Dewey:812/.54080897. LCCN:2003-100128.
Audience: **l,u,f.** *Choice, 2004.*

Geiogamah, Hanay &   **PN2270.I53A48 2000**
Darby, Jaye T. (Editors)
American Indian Theater in Performance: A Reader. Trade
Paper. University of California, American Indian Studies Center.
Los Angeles, CA. 2000. 414p. ISBN:0-935626-52-2, ISBN13:
978-0-935626-52-0. Dewey:792/.089/97073. LCCN:99-067670.
Audience: **l,u,f.** *Choice, 2001.*

Geiogamah, Hanay &   **PS628.I53**
Darby, Jaye T. (Editors)
Stories of Our Way: An Anthology of American Indian Plays.
Trade Paper. University of California, American Indian Studies
Center. Los Angeles, CA. 1999. 503p. Native American Theater
Ser., No. 1 ISBN:0-935626-50-6, ISBN13: 978-0-935626-50-6.
Dewey:812/.5080897.
Audience: **l,u,f.** *Choice, 1999.*

Geiogamah, Hanay (Editor)   **PS3545.I5365**
New Native American Drama: Three Plays. Jeffrey Huntsman
(Introduction by). Trade Paper. University of Oklahoma Press.
Norman, OK. 1980. 158p. ISBN:0-8061-1697-8, ISBN13:
978-0-8061-1697-6. Dewey:812/.54. LCCN:79-004733.
Audience: **l,u,f.** *B*

Glancy, Diane   **PS3557.L294A84 2002**
American Gypsy: Six Native American Plays. Trade Cloth.
University of Oklahoma Press. Norman, OK. 2002. 224p.
American Indian Literature and Critical Studies, Vol. 45
ISBN:0-8061-3456-9, ISBN13: 978-0-8061-3456-7.
Dewey:812/.54. LCCN:2002-018870.
Audience: **l,u,f.**

Perkins, Kathy A. & Uno,   **PS627.M5C66 1996**
Roberta (Editors)
Contemporary Plays by Women of Color: An Anthology. Paper
over Boards. Routledge. New York, NY. 1996. 336p.

ISBN:0-415-11377-6, ISBN13: 978-0-415-11377-9.
Dewey:812/.540809287. LCCN:95-007465.
Audience: **g,l,u,f.** *Choice, 1996.*

Warmbrunn, Erika   **DS798.2.W37 2001**
Where the Pavement Ends: One Woman's Bicycle Trip Through
Mongolia, China and Vietnam. Cloth Text. Mountaineers Books,
The. Seattle, WA. 2001. 280p. Barbara Savage Award Bks.
ISBN:0-89886-684-7, ISBN13: 978-0-89886-684-1.
Dewey:915.104/59. LCCN:2001-000035.
Audience: **l,u,f.**

Yellow Robe, William S.   **PS3575.E46W48 2000**
Where the Pavement Ends: Five Native American Plays. Trade
Cloth. University of Oklahoma Press. Norman, OK. 2000. 192p.
American Indian Literature and Critical Studies Ser., Vol. 37
ISBN:0-8061-3265-5, ISBN13: 978-0-8061-3265-5.
Dewey:812/.6. LCCN:00-023468.
Audience: **l,u,f.**

Western Drama and Theater > United States > Ethnic/Minority Drama and Theater in the U.S. > Hispanic/Latino Drama and Theater

Broyles-González, Yolanda   **PN3307.U6B76 1994**
El Teatro Campesino: Theater in the Chicano Movement. Trade
Paper. University of Texas Press. Austin, TX. 1994. 304p.
ISBN:0-292-70801-7, ISBN13: 978-0-292-70801-3.
Dewey:792/.022. LCCN:94-000935.
Audience: **l,u.** *Choice, 1995.*

Chavez, Denise & Feyder,   **PS628.H57 S5 1992**
Linda (Editors)
Shattering the Myth: Plays by Hispanic Women. Trade Paper.
Arte Publico Press. Houston, TX. 2003. 256p. Latin-American
Play Anthologies Ser. ISBN:1-55885-041-4, ISBN13:
978-1-55885-041-5. Dewey:812/.540809287. LCCN:91-040997.
Audience: **g,l,u.**

Kanellos, Nicolás   **PN2270.H57 H57 1984**
Hispanic Theatre in the United States. Trade Paper. Arte Publico
Press. Houston, TX. 2003. 80p. Latin-American Play
Anthologies Ser. ISBN:0-934770-44-1, ISBN13:
978-0-934770-44-6. Dewey:792/.08968073. LCCN:89-164046.
Audience: **l,u,f.**

Kanellos, Nicolás   **PN2270.M48 M49 1989**
Mexican American Theatre: Then and Now. Trade Paper. Arte
Publico Press. Houston, TX. 2003. 120p. Latin-American Play
Anthologies Ser. ISBN:0-934770-22-0, ISBN13:
978-0-934770-22-4. Dewey:792/.0896872073. LCCN:83-070675.
Audience: **l,u.**

Perkins, Kathy A. & Uno,   **PS627.M5C66 1996**
Roberta (Editors)
Contemporary Plays by Women of Color: An Anthology. Paper
over Boards. Routledge. New York, NY. 1996. 336p.

ISBN:0-415-11377-6, ISBN13: 978-0-415-11377-9.
Dewey:812/.540809287. LCCN:95-007465.

Audience: **g,l,u,f.** *Choice, 1996.*

Ramirez, Elizabeth C.   **PN2270.H57R36 2000**
Chicanas - Latinas in American Theatre: A History of
Performance. Library Binding. Indiana University Press.
Bloomington, IN. 2000. 188p. ISBN:0-253-33714-3, ISBN13:
978-0-253-33714-6. Dewey:792/.082/0973. LCCN:00-029578.

Audience: **l,u,f.**

Sandoval-Sanchez, Alberto   **PS628.H57P87 2000**
& Sternbach, Nancy S. (Editors)
Puro Teatro, a Latina Anthology: A Latina Anthology. Trade
Paper. University of Arizona Press. Tucson, AZ. 2000. 440p.
ISBN:0-8165-1827-0, ISBN13: 978-0-8165-1827-2.
Dewey:812/.540809287/08968. LCCN:99-006567.

Audience: **l,u,f.**

Valdez, Luis   **PS3572.A387 Z6 1992**
Zoot Suit and Other Plays. Trade Paper. Arte Publico Press.
Houston, TX. 2003. 216p. Latin-American Play Anthologies Ser.
ISBN:1-55885-048-1, ISBN13: 978-1-55885-048-4.
Dewey:812/.54. LCCN:91-041789.

Audience: **g,l,u.**

Western Drama and Theater > United States > Ethnic/Minority Drama and Theater in the U.S. > Asian American Drama and Theater

Houston, Velina H. (Editor)   **PS628.A85S75 1997**
But Still, Like Air, I'll Rise: New Asian American Plays. Trade
Cloth. Temple University Press. Philadelphia, PA. 1997. 512p.
Asian American History and Culture Ser. ISBN:1-56639-537-2,
ISBN13: 978-1-56639-537-3. Dewey:812/.54080895073.
LCCN:96-048729.

Audience: **l,u,f.** *Choice, 1997.*

Houston, Velina H. (Editor,   **PS628.A85**
Introduction by)
The Politics of Life: Four Plays by Asian American Women.
Trade Cloth. Temple University Press. Philadelphia, PA. 1993.
288p. Asian American History and Culture Ser.
ISBN:1-56639-000-1, ISBN13: 978-1-56639-000-2.
Dewey:812/.540809287. LCCN:92-013090.

Audience: **l,u,f.**

Lee, Esther Kim   **PN2297**
A History of Asian American Theatre. Don B. Wilmeth
(Contribution by). Trade Cloth. Cambridge University Press.
New York, NY. 2006. 282p. Cambridge Studies in American
Theatre and Drama Ser. ISBN:0-521-85051-7, ISBN13:
978-0-521-85051-3. Dewey:792.08995073.

Audience: **l,u,f.**

Liu, Miles Xian (Editor)   **PS338**
Asian American Playwrights: A Bio-Bibliographical Critical
Sourcebook. Cloth Text. Greenwood Publishing Group, Inc.
Portsmouth, NH. 2002. 424p. ISBN:0-313-31455-1, ISBN13:
978-0-313-31455-1. Dewey:812/.509895/03 B.
LCCN:2001-037680.

Audience: **g,l,u,f.** *Choice, 2003.*

Nelson, Brian (Editor)   **PS628.A85A88 1997**
Asian American Drama: 9 Plays from the Multiethnic
Landscape. David Henry Hwang (Foreword by). Trade Paper.
Applause Theatre Book Publishers. New York, NY. 2000. 432p.
ISBN:1-55783-314-1, ISBN13: 978-1-55783-314-3.
Dewey:812/.54080895. LCCN:97-027054.

Audience: **l,u,f.**

Perkins, Kathy A. & Uno,   **PS627.M5C66 1996**
Roberta (Editors)
Contemporary Plays by Women of Color: An Anthology. Paper
over Boards. Routledge. New York, NY. 1996. 336p.
ISBN:0-415-11377-6, ISBN13: 978-0-415-11377-9.
Dewey:812/.540809287. LCCN:95-007465.

Audience: **g,l,u,f.** *Choice, 1996.*

Uno, Roberta (Editor)   **PS628.W6**
Unbroken Thread: An Anthology of Plays by Asian American
Women. Trade Paper. University of Massachusetts Press.
Amherst, MA. 1993. 336p. ISBN:0-87023-856-6, ISBN13:
978-0-87023-856-7. Dewey:812/.540809287. LCCN:93-021858.

Audience: **l,u,f.** *Choice, 1994.*

Western Drama and Theater > United States > Ethnic/Minority Drama and Theater in the U.S. > Gay and Lesbian Drama and Theater

Case, Sue-Ellen (Editor)   **PS627.L48S65 1996**
Split Britches: Lesbian Practice - Feminist Performance. Trade
Paper. Routledge. New York, NY. 1996. 288p.
ISBN:0-415-12766-1, ISBN13: 978-0-415-12766-0.
Dewey:812.5/4/08/09287. LCCN:95-047164.

Audience: **l,u,f.**

Dolan, Jill   **PN2270.G39D65 2001**
Geographies of Learning: Theory and Practice, Activism and
Performance. Wesleyan University Press. 2001.
ISBN:0-8195-6468-0, ISBN13: 978-0-8195-6468-9.

Audience: **u,f.**

Dolan, Jill   **PN2270.F45D65 1993**
Presence and Desire: Essays on Gender, Sexuality, Performance.
University of Michigan Press. 1993. ISBN:0-472-09530-7,
ISBN13: 978-0-472-09530-8.

Audience: **u,f.**

Hodges, Ben PN6120.G43F67 2003
Forbidden Acts: Pioneering Gay and Lesbian Plays of the
Twentieth Century. Trade Paper. Applause Theatre Book
Publishers. New York, NY. 2003. 741p. ISBN:1-55783-587-X,
ISBN13: 978-1-55783-587-1. Dewey:808.82/0086/640904.
LCCN:2003-014043.

Audience: **g,l,u,f.**

Kushner, Tony PS3561.U778A85 2003
Angels in America: A Gay Fantasia on National Themes. Trade
Paper. Theatre Communications Group, Inc. New York, NY.
2003. 304p. ISBN:1-55936-231-6, ISBN13: 978-1-55936-231-3.
Dewey:812/.54. LCCN:2003-017904.

Audience: **g,l,u.**

Schanke, Robert A. & PN2286.5
 Marra, Kimberely Bell (Editors)
Passing Performances: Queer Readings of Leading Players in
American Theater History. Trade Paper. University of Michigan
Press. Chicago, IL. 1998. 352p. Triangulations Ser.
ISBN:0-472-06681-1, ISBN13: 978-0-472-06681-0.
Dewey:792/.028/08664 B. LCCN:98-019710.
Audience: **l,u,f.** *Choice, 1999.*

Schanke, Robert A. & PS338.H66S73 2001
 Marra, Kimberley B. (Editors)
Staging Desire: Queer Readings of American Theater History.
Trade Paper. University of Michigan Press. Chicago, IL. 2002.
416p. Triangulations Ser., :Lesbian - Gay - Queer Theater -
Drama - Performance ISBN:0-472-06749-4, ISBN13:
978-0-472-06749-7. Dewey:812.009/353. LCCN:2001-006446.
Audience: **g,l,u,f.** *Choice, 2003.*

Schanke, Robert A. (Editor), PN2286.5.G38 2005
 et al.
The Gay and Lesbian Theatrical Legacy: A Biographical
Dictionary of Major Figures in American Stage History in the
Pre-Stonewall Era. Kimberley Bell Marra & Billy J. Harbin
(Editors). Trade Cloth. University of Michigan Press. Chicago,
IL. 2005. 440p. Triangulations Ser., :Lesbian/Gay/Queer
Theater/Drama/Performance Ser. ISBN:0-472-09858-6, ISBN13:
978-0-472-09858-3. Dewey:792/.092/273 B.
LCCN:2004-020338.
Audience: **g,l.** *Choice, 2005.*

Western Drama and Theater > United States > Ethnic/Minority Drama and Theater in the U.S. > Jewish Drama and Theater

Berkowitz, Joel (Editor) PN3035.Y475 2003
The Yiddish Theatre: New Approaches. Trade Cloth. Littman
Library of Jewish Civilization, The. London, 2003. 269p.
ISBN:1-874774-81-1, ISBN13: 978-1-874774-81-5.
Dewey:792/.089/924. LCCN:2003-040264.
Audience: **l,u,f.** *Choice, 2004.*

Berkowitz, Joel (Editor, PJ5191.E5L34 2006
 Translator)
Landmark Yiddish Plays: A Critical Anthology. Jeremy Dauber
(Introduction by). Book, Other. State University of New York
Press. Albany, NY. 2006. 336p. SUNY Series on Modern Jewish
Literature and Culture ISBN:0-7914-6779-1, ISBN13:
978-0-7914-6779-4. Dewey:839/.12008. LCCN:2005-023939.
Audience: **l,u,f.**

Lifson, David S. (Translator) PJ5191.E5 L5
Epic and Folk Plays from the Yiddish Theatre. Trade Cloth.
Fairleigh Dickinson University Press. Cranbury, NJ. 1975. 224p.
ISBN:0-8386-1082-X, ISBN13: 978-0-8386-1082-4.
Dewey:839/.09/2008. LCCN:73-002899.
Audience: **l,u,f.**

Nahshon, Edna PN3035
Yiddish Proletarian Theatre: The Art and Politics of the Artef,
1925-1940. Trade Cloth. Greenwood Publishing Group, Inc.
Portsmouth, NH. 1998. 288p. Contributions in Drama and
Theatre Studies Ser., Vol. 85 ISBN:0-313-29063-6, ISBN13:
978-0-313-29063-3. Dewey:792/.089/92407471.
LCCN:98-015599.

Audience: **l,u,f.**

Posnick, Michael & Schiff, PS628.J47N56 2005
 Ellen (Editors)
9 Contemporary Jewish Plays: From the New Play Commission
of the National Foundation for Jewish Culture. Theodore Bikel
(Foreword by). Trade Paper, Perfect. University of Texas Press.
Austin, TX. 2005. 587p. ISBN:0-292-71290-1, ISBN13:
978-0-292-71290-4. Dewey:812/.60808924. LCCN:2005-007621.
Audience: **l,u,f.**

Sandrow, Nahma PN3035.S25 1996
Vagabond Stars: A World History of Yiddish Theater. Trade
Cloth. Syracuse University Press. Syracuse, NY. 1995. 448p.
Judaic Traditions in Literature, Music and Art Ser.
ISBN:0-8156-0329-0, ISBN13: 978-0-8156-0329-0.
Dewey:792/.089924. LCCN:95-035166.
Audience: **l,u,f.** *B*

Western Drama and Theater > Canada

Bains, Yashdip S. PN2301.B25 1998
English Canadian Theatre, 1765-1826, Vol. 27. Cloth Text. Peter
Lang Publishing, Inc. New York, NY. 1998. 244p. American
University Studies, :Theatre Arts ISBN:0-8204-3822-7, ISBN13:
978-0-8204-3822-1. Dewey:792/.0971/09033. LCCN:97-014021.
Audience: **g,l,u,f.**

Benson, Eugene & Conolly, PN2300.O94 1989
 L. W. (Editors)
The Oxford Companion to Canadian Theatre. Trade Cloth.
Oxford University Press, Inc. New York, NY. 1990. 680p.
ISBN:0-19-540672-9, ISBN13: 978-0-19-540672-6.
Dewey:792.0971. LCCN:90-126294.
Audience: **g.** *Choice, 1990.*

Cardy, Michael & Connon,   PQ556.A7 2000
  Derek F. (Editors)
Aspects of Twentieth-Century Theatre in French. Trade Cloth.
Peter Lang Publishing, Inc. New York, NY. 2000. 243p.
ISBN:3-906764-45-1, ISBN13: 978-3-906764-45-0.
Dewey:842/.9109. LCCN:00-022411.

           Audience: **l,u,f.**

Glaap, Albert-Reiner &   PR9191.5.P47 2003
  Grace, Sherrill E. (Editors)
Performing National Identities: International Perspectives on
Contemporary Canadian Theatre. Trade Paper. Talonbooks, Ltd.
Vancouver, BC. 2003. 288p. ISBN:0-88922-475-7, ISBN13:
978-0-88922-475-9. Dewey:812/.5409. LCCN:2003-464855.

           Audience: **g.**

Rubin, Don (Editor)   PN2301
Canadian Theatre History: Selected Readings. Ed. 2. Trade
Paper. Theatre Communications Group, Inc. New York, NY.
2004. ISBN:0-88754-744-3, ISBN13: 978-0-88754-744-7.
Dewey:792/.0971/09.

           Audience: **g.**

Solorzano, Carlos (Editor)   PA6073.B44
The Americas. Trade Paper. Routledge. New York, NY. 2000.
640p. World Encyclopedia of Contemporary Theatre Ser., Vol. 2
ISBN:0-415-22745-3, ISBN13: 978-0-415-22745-2.
Dewey:792.03.

           Audience: **g.** *Choice, 1996.*

Western Drama and Theater > Latin America

Boon, Richard & Plastow,   PN2049 .T44 1998
  Jane (Editors)
Theatre Matters: Performance and Culture on the World Stage.
Wole Soyinka (Foreword by), Ferni Osofisan, Solomon Tsehaye,
Ian Steadman, Christopher Innes, Carole-Anne Upton, Jatinder
Verma & David Bradby (Contribution by). Cloth Text.
Cambridge University Press. New York, NY. 1998. 225p.
Cambridge Studies in Modern Theatre ISBN:0-521-63054-1,
ISBN13: 978-0-521-63054-2. Dewey:792. LCCN:97-046774.

           Audience: **g.**

Branch, William B. (Editor)   PS628.N4C76 1993
Crosswinds: An Anthology of Black Dramatists in the Diaspora.
Trade Paper. Indiana University Press. Bloomington, IN. 1993.
448p. Blacks in the Diaspora Ser. ISBN:0-253-20778-9,
ISBN13: 978-0-253-20778-4. Dewey:808.82/008996.
LCCN:92-026648.

           Audience: **l,u,f.**

Cortes, Eladio &   PQ7082
  Barrea-Marlys, Mirta (Editors)
Encyclopedia of Latin American Theater. Cloth Text.
Greenwood Publishing Group, Inc. Portsmouth, NH. 2003. 552p.
ISBN:0-313-29041-5, ISBN13: 978-0-313-29041-1.
Dewey:862.009/98/03. LCCN:2003-049135.

           Audience: **g.** *Choice, 2004.*

Dauster, Frank (Editor)   AP2; PQ7082.D7
Perspectives on Contemporary Spanish American Theatre. Trade
Cloth. Bucknell University Press. Cranbury, NJ. 1997. 160p.
Review Ser., Vol. XL, No. 2 ISBN:0-8387-5345-0, ISBN13:
978-0-8387-5345-3. Dewey:860. LCCN:55-058217.

           Audience: **g.**

Flores, Yolanda   PQ7082.D7F65 2000
The Drama of Gender: Feminist Theater by Women of the
Americas. Cloth Text. Peter Lang Publishing, Inc. New York,
NY. 2000. 144p. Worlds of Change Ser., Vol. 38:Latin-American
and Iberian Literature ISBN:0-8204-3958-4, ISBN13:
978-0-8204-3958-7. Dewey:862. LCCN:99-026923.

           Audience: **l,u,f.**

George, David   PN2471.G455 1999
Flash and Crash Days: Brazilian Theater in the Post-Dictatorship
Period. Cloth Text. Garland Publishing, Inc. New York, NY.
1999. 200p. Latin American Studies, Vol. 19
ISBN:0-8153-3360-9, ISBN13: 978-0-8153-3360-9.
Dewey:792/.0981/09045. LCCN:99-044208.

           Audience: **g.**

Graham-Jones, Jean   PQ7689.G73 2000
Exorcising History: Argentine Theater under Dictatorship. Trade
Cloth. Bucknell University Press. Cranbury, NJ. 2000. 259p.
ISBN:0-8387-5424-4, ISBN13: 978-0-8387-5424-5. Dewey:862.
LCCN:99-024478.

           Audience: **g.** *Choice, 2000.*

Kullman, Colby H. &   PN2256
  Young, William C. (Editors)
Theatre Companies of the World: Africa, Asia, Australia, and
New Zealand, Canada, Eastern Europe, Latin America, the
Middle East, Scandinavia, Vol. 1. Cloth Text. Greenwood
Publishing Group, Inc. Portsmouth, NH. 1986. 1024p.
ISBN:0-313-25667-5, ISBN13: 978-0-313-25667-7.
Dewey:792/.09. LCCN:84-000539.

           Audience: **g.**

Rodriguez del Pino,   PQ7271.E5S58 2001
  Salvador (Editor)
Six Plays in Translation from Mexican Contemporary Theatre: A
New Golden Age. Trade Cloth. Edwin Mellen Press, The.
Lewiston, NY. 2001. 304p. Hispanic Literature Ser., Vol. 42
ISBN:0-7734-8274-1, ISBN13: 978-0-7734-8274-6. Dewey:862.
LCCN:98-040428.

           Audience: **l,u,f.**

Solorzano, Carlos (Editor)   PA6073.B44
The Americas. Trade Paper. Routledge. New York, NY. 2000.
640p. World Encyclopedia of Contemporary Theatre Ser., Vol. 2
ISBN:0-415-22745-3, ISBN13: 978-0-415-22745-2.
Dewey:792.03.

           Audience: **g.** *Choice, 1996.*

Thomas, Charles   PR4659.E7
🄴 Latin American Theatre in Translation: An Anthology of
Work from Mexico, the Caribbean and the Southern Cone.

E-Book. Xlibris Corporation. Philadelphia, PA. 2000. 540p. ISBN:0-7388-8550-9, ISBN13: 978-0-7388-8550-6. Dewey:824. LCCN:00-190399.

Audience: l,u,f.

Western Drama and Theater > Australia

Fensham, Rachel &   **PN2860.D57 1999**
Eckersall, Peter (Editors)
Disorientations: Cultural Praxis in Theatre: Asia, Pacific, and Australia. Trade Cloth. Monash University Press. Monash University, VIC. 1999. 194p. Monash Theatre Papers, Vol. 1 ISBN:0-7326-2049-X, ISBN13: 978-0-7326-2049-3. Dewey:791/.095. LCCN:00-361252.

Audience: l,u,f.

Kullman, Colby H. &   **PN2256**
Young, William C. (Editors)
Theatre Companies of the World: Africa, Asia, Australia, and New Zealand, Canada, Eastern Europe, Latin America, the Middle East, Scandinavia, Vol. 1. Cloth Text. Greenwood Publishing Group, Inc. Portsmouth, NH. 1986. 1024p. ISBN:0-313-25667-5, ISBN13: 978-0-313-25667-7. Dewey:792/.09. LCCN:84-000539.

Audience: g.

Williamson, David (Editor),   **PR9611.5**
et al.
Contemporary Australian Plays. Hannie Rayson, Keith Robinson, Tony Taylor, Wesley Enoch, Deborah Mailman & Russell Vanderbroucke (Editors). Trade Paper. Methuen Publishing Ltd. London, 2004. ISBN:0-413-76760-4, ISBN13: 978-0-413-76760-8. Dewey:822.

Audience: g,l,u,f.

Non-Western Drama and Theater

PN2035.E52 1977
The Encyclopedia of World Theater: With 420 Illustrations and an Index of Play Titles. Trade Cloth. Simon & Schuster. New York, NY. 1977. 320p. ISBN:0-684-14834-X, ISBN13: 978-0-684-14834-2. Dewey:792/.03. LCCN:76-019741.

Audience: g. *B*

Banham, Martin (Editor)   **PN2035.C27 1995**
The Cambridge Guide to Theatre. Ed. 2. Trade Cloth. Cambridge University Press. New York, NY. 1995. 1247p. ISBN:0-521-43437-8, ISBN13: 978-0-521-43437-9. Dewey:792/.09. LCCN:95-001011.

Audience: g. *Choice, 1996.*

Banham, Martin (Editor), et   **PN2969.C36 1994**
al.
The Cambridge Guide to African and Caribbean Theatre. Errol Hill & George Woodyard (Editors). Trade Paper. Cambridge University Press. New York, NY. 2005. 269p. ISBN:0-521-61207-1, ISBN13: 978-0-521-61207-4. Dewey:792/.096/03. LCCN:2005-279353.

Audience: g.

Boon, Richard & Plastow,   **PN2049 .T44 1998**
Jane (Editors)
Theatre Matters: Performance and Culture on the World Stage. Wole Soyinka (Foreword by), Ferni Osofisan, Solomon Tsehaye, Ian Steadman, Christopher Innes, Carole-Anne Upton, Jatinder Verma & David Bradby (Contribution by). Cloth Text. Cambridge University Press. New York, NY. 1998. 225p. Cambridge Studies in Modern Theatre ISBN:0-521-63054-1, ISBN13: 978-0-521-63054-2. Dewey:792. LCCN:97-046774.

Audience: g.

Gainor, J. Ellen (Editor)   **PN2049.I47 1995**
Imperialism and Theatre: Essays on World Theatre, Drama and Performance. Trade Paper. Routledge. New York, NY. 1995. 280p. ISBN:0-415-10641-9, ISBN13: 978-0-415-10641-2. Dewey:792/.013. LCCN:94-035439.

Audience: l,u,f. *Choice, 1996.*

Hartnoll, Phyllis (Editor)   **PN2035.O9 1983**
Oxford Companion to the Theatre. Ed. 4. Trade Cloth. Oxford University Press, Inc. New York, NY. 1983. 640p. ISBN:0-19-211546-4, ISBN13: 978-0-19-211546-1. Dewey:792/.03/21. LCCN:83-235664.

Audience: g. *B*

International Theatre   **PN2037.W725 2000**
Institute Staff
The World of Theatre: 2000 Edition. Ian Herbert & Nicole Leclercq (Editors). Paper over Boards. Routledge. New York, NY. 2000. 328p. ISBN:0-415-23866-8, ISBN13: 978-0-415-23866-3. Dewey:792. LCCN:00-044649.

Audience: g.

Majumadara, Ramendu   **PN2037**
(Editor)
The World of Theatre. Theatre Communications Group, Inc. 2005. ISBN:1-55936-264-2, ISBN13: 978-1-55936-264-1.

Audience: g.

Non-Western Drama and Theater > Individual Works

Fugard, Athol, et al.   **PR9369.3.F8 M3 1997**
Master Harold. Laurie G. Kirszner & Stephen R. Mandell (Authors). Paper Text. Thomson Heinle. Boston, MA. 1997. 192p. Harcourt Brace Casebook Series in Literature Ser. ISBN:0-15-505483-X, ISBN13: 978-0-15-505483-7. Dewey:822. LCCN:97-070035.

Audience: l,u,f.

Soyinka, Wole   **PR9387.9.S6 J4 1973**
Jero Plays. Trade Paper. Methuen Publishing Ltd. London, 2003. ISBN:0-413-29240-1, ISBN13: 978-0-413-29240-7. Dewey:822.

Audience: l,u,f.

Sudraka, et al.   **PK3798.S91M713 1994**
e The Little Clay Cart: An English Translation of the Mrcchakatika of Sudraka, As Adapted for the Stage. A. L.

Basham & Arvind Sharma (Authors). E-Book. NetLibrary, Inc. Boulder, CO. 1994. ISBN:0-585-04427-9, ISBN13: 978-0-585-04427-9. Dewey:891/.22.

Audience: **l,u,f.**

Tang, Xianzu　　　　　　　　　　**PL2695.M8E5 2002**
The Peony Pavilion. Ed. 2. Trade Paper. Indiana University Press. Bloomington, IN. 2002. 400p. ISBN:0-253-21527-7, ISBN13: 978-0-253-21527-7. Dewey:895.1/24. LCCN:2002-068779.

Audience: **l,u,f.**　*Choice, 2002.*

Tendulkar, Vijay　　　　　　　　　　　**PK5461**
Collected Plays in Translation. Trade Paper. Oxford University Press, Inc. New York, NY. 2004. 650p. Oxford India Paperbacks Ser. ISBN:0-19-566913-4, ISBN13: 978-0-19-566913-8. Dewey:891.4/6271.

Audience: **l,u,f.**

Vasudeva, Somadeva　　　　　**PK3796.S4V37 2005**
(Editor)
The Recognition of Shakuntala. Trade Cloth. New York University Press. New York, NY. 2006. 450p. The Clay Sanskrit Library ISBN:0-8147-8815-7, ISBN13: 978-0-8147-8815-8. Dewey:891/.22 2 22. LCCN:2004-029513.

Audience: **l,u,f.**

Non-Western Drama and Theater > Collections of Plays

PZ3.I235
The Noh Drama: Ten Plays from the Japanese Selected and Translated by the Special Noh Committee, Japanese Classics Translation Committee, Nippon Gakujutsu Shinkokai. Paper Text. Textbook Publishers. Temecula, CA. 2003. 192p. ISBN:0-7581-3049-X, ISBN13: 978-0-7581-3049-5. Dewey:895.63.

Audience: **u,f.**

Brandon, James R. (Editor)　　　　　**PN1979.S5**
On Thrones of Gold: Three Javanese Shadow Plays. Trade Cloth. University of Hawaii Press. Honolulu, HI. 1993. 426p. ISBN:0-8248-1425-8, ISBN13: 978-0-8248-1425-0. Dewey:899/.222/2. LCCN:93-014879.

Audience: **l,u,f.** *B*

Brandon, James R. &　　　　　　　　**PL782**
Leiter, Samuel L. (Editors)
Masterpieces of Kabuki: Eighteen Plays on Stage. Trade Cloth. University of Hawaii Press. Honolulu, HI. 2004. 368p. ISBN:0-8248-2788-0, ISBN13: 978-0-8248-2788-5. Dewey:895.62008. LCCN:2004-553320.

Audience: **l,u,f.** *Choice, 2005.*

Brazell, Karen　　　　　　　**PL782.E5T73 1998**
Traditional Japanese Theater: An Anthology of Plays. James T. Araki (Translator). Trade Paper. Columbia University Press. New York, NY. 1999. 464p. Translations from the Asian

Classics ISBN:0-231-10873-7, ISBN13: 978-0-231-10873-7. Dewey:895.6/2008. LCCN:97-023964.

Audience: **l,u,f.** *Choice, 1998.*

Chen, Xiaomei (Editor,　　　　　**PL2658.E5R43 2003**
Introduction by)
Reading the Right Text: An Anthology of Contemporary Chinese Drama. Trade Cloth. University of Hawaii Press. Honolulu, HI. 2003. 480p. ISBN:0-8248-2505-5, ISBN13: 978-0-8248-2505-8. Dewey:895.1/2508. LCCN:2002-155363.

Audience: **l,u,f.**

Leiter, Samuel L.　　　　　　　**PN2924.5.K3A7 1999**
Art of Kabuki: Five Famous Plays. Ed. 2. Trade Paper. Dover Publications, Inc. Mineola, NY. 1999. 300p. ISBN:0-486-40872-8, ISBN13: 978-0-486-40872-9. Dewey:895.6/2008. LCCN:99-046425.

Audience: **l,u,f.**

Mee, Erin (Editor)　　　　　　　　　　　**PK5437**
Drama Contemporary: India. Trade Paper. Theatre Communications Group, Inc. New York, NY. 2005. 362p. ISBN:1-55554-064-3, ISBN13: 978-1-55554-064-7. Dewey:808.82/00954/09045.

Audience: **l,u,f.**

Plastow, Jane & Banham,　　　　　**PR9347.C65 1999**
Martin (Editors)
Contemporary African Plays. Jane Plastow & Martin Banham (Introduction by). Trade Paper. Methuen Publishing Ltd. London, 2003. ISBN:0-413-72330-5, ISBN13: 978-0-413-72330-7. Dewey:822/.91409896. LCCN:00-300722.

Audience: **l,u,f.**

Pound, Ezra & Fenollosa,　　　　　**PN2924.5.N6F46 2004**
Ernest
The Noh Theatre of Japan: With Complete Texts of 15 Classic Plays. Trade Paper. Dover Publications, Inc. Mineola, NY. 2004. 288p. ISBN:0-486-43699-3, ISBN13: 978-0-486-43699-9. Dewey:895.6/2008. LCCN:2004-050239.

Audience: **l,u,f.**

Worthen, W. B.　　　　　　　　　　　**PN6112.H28**
The Wadsworth Anthology of Drama. Ed. 5. Paper Text. Thomson Heinle. Boston, MA. 2006. 1728p. ISBN:1-4130-1767-3, ISBN13: 978-1-4130-1767-0. Dewey:808.82.

Audience: **g.**

Non-Western Drama and Theater > Countries

Maleh, Ghassan (Editor), et　　　　　**PN1861.W67 1994**
al.
The Arab World. Samir Sirhan, Ahmed Zaki & Farouk Ohan (Editors). Paper over Boards. Routledge. New York, NY. 1999.

336p. World Encyclopedia of Contemporary Theatre Ser., Vol. 4
ISBN:0-415-05932-1, ISBN13: 978-0-415-05932-9.
Dewey:792.0917492703.

Audience: **g.** *Choice, 2000.*

Non-Western Drama and Theater > Countries > Africa

Banham, Martin (Editor)　　　**PN2969.H57 2003**
A History of Theatre in Africa. Trade Cloth. Cambridge
University Press. New York, NY. 2004. 496p.
ISBN:0-521-80813-8, ISBN13: 978-0-521-80813-2.
Dewey:792/.096. LCCN:2003-055280.

Audience: **l,u.** *Choice, 2004.*

Banham, Martin (Editor), et　　　**PN2969.C36 1994**
al.
The Cambridge Guide to African and Caribbean Theatre. Errol
Hill & George Woodyard (Editors). Trade Paper. Cambridge
University Press. New York, NY. 2005. 269p.
ISBN:0-521-61207-1, ISBN13: 978-0-521-61207-4.
Dewey:792/.096/03. LCCN:2005-279353.

Audience: **g.**

Branch, William B. (Editor)　　　**PS628.N4C76 1993**
Crosswinds: An Anthology of Black Dramatists in the Diaspora.
Trade Paper. Indiana University Press. Bloomington, IN. 1993.
448p. Blacks in the Diaspora Ser. ISBN:0-253-20778-9,
ISBN13: 978-0-253-20778-4. Dewey:808.82/008996.
LCCN:92-026648.

Audience: **l,u,f.**

Conteh-Morgan, John　　　**PQ3983 .C66 1994**
Theatre and Drama in Francophone Africa: A Critical
Introduction. Trade Cloth. Cambridge University Press. New
York, NY. 1994. 255p. ISBN:0-521-43453-X, ISBN13:
978-0-521-43453-9. Dewey:842.00996. LCCN:93-006070.

Audience: **l,u,f.** *Choice, 1995.*

Dunton, Chris　　　**Z2014.D7**
Nigerian Theatre in English. Trade Cloth. R. R. Bowker LLC.
East Grinstead, 1998. 400p. ISBN:1-873836-71-6, ISBN13:
978-1-873836-71-2. Dewey:016.8/22/0099669.
LCCN:97-038650.

Audience: **g.** *Choice, 1999.*

Fugard, Athol, et al.　　　**PR9369.3.F8 M3 1997**
Master Harold. Laurie G. Kirszner & Stephen R. Mandell
(Authors). Paper Text. Thomson Heinle. Boston, MA. 1997.
192p. Harcourt Brace Casebook Series in Literature Ser.
ISBN:0-15-505483-X, ISBN13: 978-0-15-505483-7. Dewey:822.
LCCN:97-070035.

Audience: **l,u,f.**

Jeyifo, Biodun　　　**PR9347.M63 2001**
Modern African Drama. Trade Paper. W. W. Norton &
Company, Inc. New York, NY. 2002. 608p. A Norton Critical
Edition Ser. ISBN:0-393-97529-0, ISBN13: 978-0-393-97529-1.
Dewey:822.008/096. LCCN:2001-044667.

Audience: **g,l,u,f.**

Kerr, David (Editor)　　　**PN3000.S6**
African Theatre: Southern Africa. Trade Paper. Africa World
Press. Trenton, NJ. 2003. 192p. ISBN:1-59221-143-7, ISBN13:
978-1-59221-143-2. Dewey:792.0968.

Audience: **l,u,f.**

Kullman, Colby H. &　　　**PN2256**
Young, William C. (Editors)
Theatre Companies of the World: Africa, Asia, Australia, and
New Zealand, Canada, Eastern Europe, Latin America, the
Middle East, Scandinavia, Vol. 1. Cloth Text. Greenwood
Publishing Group, Inc. Portsmouth, NH. 1986. 1024p.
ISBN:0-313-25667-5, ISBN13: 978-0-313-25667-7.
Dewey:792/.09. LCCN:84-000539.

Audience: **g.**

Losambe, Lokangaka &　　　**PL8010.5.P74 2001**
Sarinjeive, Devi (Editors)
Precolonial and Postcolonial Drama and Theatre in Africa. Trade
Cloth. Africa World Press. Trenton, NJ. 2001. 168p.
ISBN:0-86543-968-0, ISBN13: 978-0-86543-968-9.
Dewey:809.2/0096. LCCN:2001-003780.

Audience: **l,u,f.**

Plastow, Jane & Banham,　　　**PR9347.C65 1999**
Martin (Editors)
Contemporary African Plays. Jane Plastow & Martin Banham
(Introduction by). Trade Paper. Methuen Publishing Ltd.
London, 2003. ISBN:0-413-72330-5, ISBN13:
978-0-413-72330-7. Dewey:822/.91409896. LCCN:00-300722.

Audience: **l,u,f.**

Rubin, Don (Editor), et al.　　　**PN1861**
Africa. Ousmane Diakhate & Hansel Ndumbe Eyoh (Editors).
Trade Paper. Routledge. New York, NY. 2000. 448p. World
Encyclopedia of Contemporary Theatre Ser., Vol. 3
ISBN:0-415-22746-1, ISBN13: 978-0-415-22746-9.
Dewey:792.09603.

Audience: **g.**

Soyinka, Wole　　　**PR9387.9.S6 J4 1973**
Jero Plays. Trade Paper. Methuen Publishing Ltd. London, 2003.
ISBN:0-413-29240-1, ISBN13: 978-0-413-29240-7. Dewey:822.

Audience: **l,u,f.**

Non-Western Drama and Theater > Countries > Asia

PN2860.C35
Asian Theatre. Spiral. Scholargy Publishing, Inc. Phoenix, AZ.
2003. ISBN:1-59247-214-1, ISBN13: 978-1-59247-214-7.
Dewey:792/.095.

Audience: **l,u,f.**

Brandon, James R. (Editor)　　　**PN2860.C35 1997**
The Cambridge Guide to Asian Theatre. Ed. 2. Trade Paper.
Cambridge University Press. New York, NY. 1997. 261p.
ISBN:0-521-58822-7, ISBN13: 978-0-521-58822-5.
Dewey:792.095.

Audience: **g.**

Chaturvedi, Ravi (Editor),   **PN2974**
   et al.
Asia/Pacific. Ramendu Majumdar, Chua Soo Pong, Minoru
Tanokura & Katherine Brisbane (Editors). Paper over Boards.
Routledge. New York, NY. 2001. 544p. World Encyclopedia of
Contemporary Theatre Ser., Vol. 5 ISBN:0-415-05933-X,
ISBN13: 978-0-415-05933-6. Dewey:792/.096/03.

               Audience: **g.** *Choice, 1999.*

Non-Western Drama and Theater > Countries > Asia > India

Chattopadhyay, Siddheswar   **PK2931.C48 1993**
Theatre in Ancient India. Trade Cloth. Manohar Publications.
New Delhi, 1993. ISBN:81-7304-016-8, ISBN13:
978-81-7304-016-0. Dewey:891.22. LCCN:93-907776.

               Audience: **l,u,f.**

Dharwadker, Aparna   **PN2884.D49 2005**
   Bhargava
Theatres of Independence: Drama, Theory, and Urban
Performance in India since 1947. Trade Cloth. University of
Iowa Press. Iowa City, IA. 2005. 456p. Studies Theatre Hist and
Culture Ser. ISBN:0-87745-961-4, ISBN13: 978-0-87745-961-3.
Dewey:792/.0954/09045. LCCN:2005-043936.

               Audience: **l,u,f.**

Garagi, Balawanta   **PN3451.H6**
Theatre in India. Paper Text. Textbook Publishers. Temecula,
CA. 2003. 245p. ISBN:0-7581-3152-6, ISBN13:
978-0-7581-3152-2. Dewey:809.3.

               Audience: **l,u,f.** *B*

Lal, Ananda (Editor)   **PN2881.O95 2004**
The Oxford Companion to Indian Theatre. Trade Cloth. Oxford
University Press, Inc. New York, NY. 2004. 600p.
ISBN:0-19-564446-8, ISBN13: 978-0-19-564446-3.
Dewey:792.0954. LCCN:2004-312160.

               Audience: **g.** *Choice, 2005.*

Mahta, Tarla   **PN2882.M43 1995**
Sanskrit Play Production in Ancient India. Trade Cloth. Motilal
Banarsidass Publishers (Pvt. Ltd). New Delhi, 1999. 446p.
Music and Dance Ser. ISBN:81-208-1057-0, ISBN13:
978-81-208-1057-0. Dewey:791.0954. LCCN:95-901716.

               Audience: **l,u,f.**

Mee, Erin (Editor)   **PK5437**
Drama Contemporary: India. Trade Paper. Theatre
Communications Group, Inc. New York, NY. 2005. 362p.
ISBN:1-55554-064-3, ISBN13: 978-1-55554-064-7.
Dewey:808.82/00954/09045.

               Audience: **l,u,f.**

Sudraka, et al.   **PK3798.S91M713 1994**
🄴 The Little Clay Cart: An English Translation of the
Mrcchakatika of Sudraka, As Adapted for the Stage. A. L.

Basham & Arvind Sharma (Authors). E-Book. NetLibrary, Inc.
Boulder, CO. 1994. ISBN:0-585-04427-9, ISBN13:
978-0-585-04427-9. Dewey:891/.22.

               Audience: **l,u,f.**

Tendulkar, Vijay   **PK5461**
Collected Plays in Translation. Trade Paper. Oxford University
Press, Inc. New York, NY. 2004. 650p. Oxford India Paperbacks
Ser. ISBN:0-19-566913-4, ISBN13: 978-0-19-566913-8.
Dewey:891.4/6271.

               Audience: **l,u,f.**

Vasudeva, Somadeva   **PK3796.S4V37 2005**
   (Editor)
The Recognition of Shakuntala. Trade Cloth. New York
University Press. New York, NY. 2006. 450p. The Clay Sanskrit
Library ISBN:0-8147-8815-7, ISBN13: 978-0-8147-8815-8.
Dewey:891/.22 2 22. LCCN:2004-029513.

               Audience: **l,u,f.**

Non-Western Drama and Theater > Countries > Asia > China

Broman, Sven   **PN1979.S5 B68 1981**
Chinese Shadow Theatre. Trade Paper. Almqvist & Wiksell
International. Stockholm, 1981. 250p. Ethnographical Museum
of Sweden Monograph Ser. ISBN:91-85344-01-X, ISBN13:
978-91-85344-01-7. Dewey:791.5. LCCN:85-118648.

               Audience: **u,f.**

Chen, Xiaomei (Editor,   **PL2658.E5R43 2003**
   Introduction by)
Reading the Right Text: An Anthology of Contemporary
Chinese Drama. Trade Cloth. University of Hawaii Press.
Honolulu, HI. 2003. 480p. ISBN:0-8248-2505-5, ISBN13:
978-0-8248-2505-8. Dewey:895.1/2508. LCCN:2002-155363.

               Audience: **l,u,f.**

Fei, Faye Chunfang (Editor)   **PN2871.C535**
Chinese Theories of Theater and Performance from Confucius to
the Present. Trade Paper. University of Michigan Press. Chicago,
IL. 2002. 232p. ISBN:0-472-08923-4, ISBN13:
978-0-472-08923-9. Dewey:792.0951. LCCN:99-017404.

               Audience: **u,f.**

Hsu, Tao-Ching   **PN2871**
The Chinese Conception of the Theatre. Cloth Text. University
of Washington Press. Seattle, WA. 1985. 676p.
ISBN:0-295-96034-5, ISBN13: 978-0-295-96034-0.
Dewey:792/.0951. LCCN:83-005964.

               Audience: **u,f.**

Menglin, Zhao & Jiqing,   **TN414.C6W4**
   Yan
Peking Opera Painted Faces with Notes on 200 Operas. Trade
Cloth. Morning Glory Press. Beijing, 1996. 142p.
ISBN:7-5054-0412-1, ISBN13: 978-7-5054-0412-0.
Dewey:622.3421.

               Audience: **u,f.**

Riley, Jo   PN2871.5 .R56 1997
Chinese Theatre and the Actor in Performance. David Bradby
(Contribution by). Trade Cloth. Cambridge University Press.
New York, NY. 1997. 360p. Studies in Modern Theatre, Vol. 3
ISBN:0-521-57090-5, ISBN13: 978-0-521-57090-9.
Dewey:792/.0951. LCCN:96-031554.

Audience: **l,u,f.** *Choice, 1998.*

Scott, A. C. (Author,   PN2871.S4 2001
   Illustrator)
The Classical Theatre of China. Trade Paper. Dover
Publications, Inc. Mineola, NY. 2001. 260p.
ISBN:0-486-41579-1, ISBN13: 978-0-486-41579-6.
Dewey:792/.0951. LCCN:00-065907.

Audience: **u,f.**

Shen, Grant   PN2871.S484 2005
Elite Theatre in Ming China, 1368-1644. Trade Cloth.
Routledge. New York, NY. 2005. 256p. RoutledgeCurzon
Studies on the Early History of Asia ISBN:0-415-34326-7,
ISBN13: 978-0-415-34326-8. Dewey:792/.0951.
LCCN:2004-015323.

Audience: **u,f.**

Tang, Xianzu   PL2695.M8E5 2002
The Peony Pavilion. Ed. 2. Trade Paper. Indiana University
Press. Bloomington, IN. 2002. 400p. ISBN:0-253-21527-7,
ISBN13: 978-0-253-21527-7. Dewey:895.1/24.
LCCN:2002-068779.

Audience: **l,u,f.** *Choice, 2002.*

Zung, Cecilia S. L.   PL2357.Z8
Secrets of the Chinese Drama: A Complete Explanatory Guide
to Actions and Symbols as Seen in the Performance of Chinese
Dramas. Trade Cloth. Kegan Paul International, Ltd. London,
2005. 300p. ISBN:0-7103-1208-3, ISBN13: 978-0-7103-1208-2.
Dewey:792.0951.

Audience: **l,u.**

Non-Western Drama and Theater >
Countries > Asia > Japan

                                                 PZ3.I235
The Noh Drama: Ten Plays from the Japanese Selected and
Translated by the Special Noh Committee, Japanese Classics
Translation Committee, Nippon Gakujutsu Shinkokai. Paper
Text. Textbook Publishers. Temecula, CA. 2003. 192p.
ISBN:0-7581-3049-X, ISBN13: 978-0-7581-3049-5.
Dewey:895.63.

Audience: **u,f.**

Brandon, James R. &   PL782
   Leiter, Samuel L. (Editors)
Masterpieces of Kabuki: Eighteen Plays on Stage. Trade Cloth.
University of Hawaii Press. Honolulu, HI. 2004. 368p.
ISBN:0-8248-2788-0, ISBN13: 978-0-8248-2788-5.
Dewey:895.62008. LCCN:2004-553320.

Audience: **l,u,f.** *Choice, 2005.*

Brazell, Karen   PL782.E5T73 1998
Traditional Japanese Theater: An Anthology of Plays. James T.
Araki (Translator). Trade Paper. Columbia University Press.
New York, NY. 1999. 464p. Translations from the Asian
Classics ISBN:0-231-10873-7, ISBN13: 978-0-231-10873-7.
Dewey:895.6/2008. LCCN:97-023964.

Audience: **l,u,f.** *Choice, 1998.*

Coldiron, Margaret   PN2058.C65 2004
Trance and Transformation of the Actor in Japanese Noh and
Balinese Masked Dance-Drama. Trade Cloth. Edwin Mellen
Press, The. Lewiston, NY. 2004. 360p. Studies in Theatre Arts,
Vol. 30 ISBN:0-7734-6341-0, ISBN13: 978-0-7734-6341-7.
Dewey:792.02/8/019. LCCN:2004-054145.

Audience: **u,f.**

Ernst, Earle   PN2924.5.K3E76 1974
e The Kabuki Theatre. E-Book. NetLibrary, Inc. Boulder, CO.
1974. ISBN:0-585-31288-5, ISBN13: 978-0-585-31288-0.
Dewey:792/.0952.

Audience: **l,u,f.** *B*

Fenollosa, Ernest Francisco   PL2307.L57
The Classic Noh Theatre of Japan. Paper Text. Textbook
Publishers. Temecula, CA. 2003. 163p. ISBN:0-7581-7796-8,
ISBN13: 978-0-7581-7796-4. Dewey:895.1109.

Audience: **l,u,f.**

Keene, Donald   PN2924.5.N6K38 1990
No and Bunraku: Two Forms of Japanese Theatre. Trade Paper.
Columbia University Press. New York, NY. 1990. 199p.
ISBN:0-231-07419-0, ISBN13: 978-0-231-07419-3.
Dewey:895.6/2009. LCCN:90-002319.

Audience: **u,f.**

Leiter, Samuel L.   PN2924.5.K3A7 1999
Art of Kabuki: Five Famous Plays. Ed. 2. Trade Paper. Dover
Publications, Inc. Mineola, NY. 1999. 300p.
ISBN:0-486-40872-8, ISBN13: 978-0-486-40872-9.
Dewey:895.6/2008. LCCN:99-046425.

Audience: **l,u,f.**

Leiter, Samuel L.   PN2921.L45 2006
Historical Dictionary of Japanese Traditional Theatre. Trade
Cloth. Scarecrow Press, Inc. Lanham, MD. 2006. 632p.
Historical Dictionaries of Literature and the Arts Ser., No. 4
ISBN:0-8108-5527-5, ISBN13: 978-0-8108-5527-4.
Dewey:792/.0952/03. LCCN:2005-019419.

Audience: **g.**

Mico International   PN1978.J3
   (Produced by)
Bunraku: Masters of Japanese Puppet Theater. Video, VHS
Format. Films Media Group. Princeton, NJ. 2001.
ISBN:0-7365-4532-8, ISBN13: 978-0-7365-4532-7.
Dewey:792.0952.

Audience: **l,u,f.**

Mitchell, John D. &   PN2924 .M58
   Watanabe, Miyoko
Staging Japanese Theatre: Noh and Kabuki. Michael Cooper

(Illustrator). Paper Text. Institute for Advanced Studies in the Theatre Arts (I A S T A). Key West, FL. 245p. ISBN:1-882763-06-8, ISBN13: 978-1-882763-06-1. Dewey:895.6.

Audience: **u,f.**

Ortolani, Benito   PN2921.O78 1995
The Japanese Theatre: From Shamanistic Ritual to Contemporary Pluralism. Ed. 2. Trade Paper. Princeton University Press. Princeton, NJ. 1995. 390p. ISBN:0-691-04333-7, ISBN13: 978-0-691-04333-3. Dewey:792/.0952. LCCN:94-023504.

Audience: **u,f.** *Choice, 1991.*

Pound, Ezra & Fenollosa,   PN2924.5.N6F46 2004
  Ernest
The Noh Theatre of Japan: With Complete Texts of 15 Classic Plays. Trade Paper. Dover Publications, Inc. Mineola, NY. 2004. 288p. ISBN:0-486-43699-3, ISBN13: 978-0-486-43699-9. Dewey:895.6/2008. LCCN:2004-050239.

Audience: **l,u,f.**

Scott, A. C.   PN2924.5.K3S265 1999
The Kabuki Theatre of Japan. Trade Paper. Dover Publications, Inc. Mineola, NY. 1999. 320p. ISBN:0-486-40645-8, ISBN13: 978-0-486-40645-9. Dewey:792/.0952. LCCN:98-043894.

Audience: **l,u,f.** *B*

Non-Western Drama and Theater > Countries > Asia > Other Asian Countries

Brandon, James R. (Editor)   PN1979.S5
On Thrones of Gold: Three Javanese Shadow Plays. Trade Cloth. University of Hawaii Press. Honolulu, HI. 1993. 426p. ISBN:0-8248-1425-8, ISBN13: 978-0-8248-1425-0. Dewey:899/.222/2. LCCN:93-014879.

Audience: **l,u,f.** *B*

Fensham, Rachel &   PN2860.D57 1999
  Eckersall, Peter (Editors)
Disorientations: Cultural Praxis in Theatre: Asia, Pacific, and Australia. Trade Cloth. Monash University Press. Monash University, VIC. 1999. 194p. Monash Theatre Papers, Vol. 1 ISBN:0-7326-2049-X, ISBN13: 978-0-7326-2049-3. Dewey:791/.095. LCCN:00-361252.

Audience: **l,u,f.**

Miettinen, Jukka O.   PN2860.M538 1992
Classical Dance and Theatre in South-East Asia. Cloth Text. Oxford University Press, Inc. New York, NY. 1993. 196p. ISBN:0-19-588595-3, ISBN13: 978-0-19-588595-8. Dewey:792.0959. LCCN:92-010946.

Audience: **l,u,f.**

Mrazek, Jan (Editor)   PN1979.S5
Puppet Theater in Contemporary Indonesia: New Approaches to Performance-Events. Trade Cloth. University of Michigan, Center for South & Southeast Asian Studies. Ann Arbor, MI.

2002. 392p. Michigan Papers on South and Southeast Asia, No. 50 ISBN:0-89148-083-8, ISBN13: 978-0-89148-083-9. Dewey:791.53.

Audience: **l,u,f.**

Singer, Noel F.   GV1703.B95S46 1995
Burmese Dance and Theatre. Cloth Text. Oxford University Press, Inc. New York, NY. 1996. 106p. Images of Asia Ser. ISBN:967-65-3086-7, ISBN13: 978-967-65-3086-8. Dewey:792/.09591. LCCN:94-041033.

Audience: **g,l,u.** *Choice, 1996.*

Non-Western Drama and Theater > Periods, Genres, Styles, Types

                                        PZ3.I235
The Noh Drama: Ten Plays from the Japanese Selected and Translated by the Special Noh Committee, Japanese Classics Translation Committee, Nippon Gakujutsu Shinkokai. Paper Text. Textbook Publishers. Temecula, CA. 2003. 192p. ISBN:0-7581-3049-X, ISBN13: 978-0-7581-3049-5. Dewey:895.63.

Audience: **u,f.**

Blumenthal, Eileen   PN1972.B57 2005
Puppetry: A World History. Trade Cloth. Harry N. Abrams, Inc. New York, NY. 2005. 272p. ISBN:0-8109-5587-3, ISBN13: 978-0-8109-5587-5. Dewey:791.5/3. LCCN:2004-029349.

Audience: **g,l,u,f.** *Choice, 2005.*

Brandon, James R. &   PL782
  Leiter, Samuel L. (Editors)
Masterpieces of Kabuki: Eighteen Plays on Stage. Trade Cloth. University of Hawaii Press. Honolulu, HI. 2004. 368p. ISBN:0-8248-2788-0, ISBN13: 978-0-8248-2788-5. Dewey:895.62008. LCCN:2004-553320.

Audience: **l,u,f.** *Choice, 2005.*

Brazell, Karen   PL782.E5T73 1998
Traditional Japanese Theater: An Anthology of Plays. James T. Araki (Translator). Trade Paper. Columbia University Press. New York, NY. 1999. 464p. Translations from the Asian Classics ISBN:0-231-10873-7, ISBN13: 978-0-231-10873-7. Dewey:895.6/2008. LCCN:97-023964.

Audience: **l,u,f.** *Choice, 1998.*

Chattopadhyay, Siddheswar   PK2931.C48 1993
Theatre in Ancient India. Trade Cloth. Manohar Publications. New Delhi, 1993. ISBN:81-7304-016-8, ISBN13: 978-81-7304-016-0. Dewey:891.22. LCCN:93-907776.

Audience: **l,u,f.**

Chen, Xiaomei (Editor,   PL2658.E5R43 2003
  Introduction by)
Reading the Right Text: An Anthology of Contemporary Chinese Drama. Trade Cloth. University of Hawaii Press. Honolulu, HI. 2003. 480p. ISBN:0-8248-2505-5, ISBN13: 978-0-8248-2505-8. Dewey:895.1/2508. LCCN:2002-155363.

Audience: **l,u,f.**

Dharwadker, Aparna   **PN2884.D49 2005**
Bhargava
Theatres of Independence: Drama, Theory, and Urban
Performance in India since 1947. Trade Cloth. University of
Iowa Press. Iowa City, IA. 2005. 456p. Studies Theatre Hist and
Culture Ser. ISBN:0-87745-961-4, ISBN13: 978-0-87745-961-3.
Dewey:792/.0954/09045. LCCN:2005-043936.

Audience: **l,u,f.**

Ernst, Earle   **PN2924.5.K3E76 1974**
🄴 The Kabuki Theatre. E-Book. NetLibrary, Inc. Boulder, CO.
1974. ISBN:0-585-31288-5, ISBN13: 978-0-585-31288-0.
Dewey:792/.0952.

Audience: **l,u,f.** 𝓑

Fenollosa, Ernest Francisco   **PL2307.L57**
The Classic Noh Theatre of Japan. Paper Text. Textbook
Publishers. Temecula, CA. 2003. 163p. ISBN:0-7581-7796-8,
ISBN13: 978-0-7581-7796-4. Dewey:895.1109.

Audience: **l,u,f.**

Keene, Donald   **PN2924.5.N6K38 1990**
No and Bunraku: Two Forms of Japanese Theatre. Trade Paper.
Columbia University Press. New York, NY. 1990. 199p.
ISBN:0-231-07419-0, ISBN13: 978-0-231-07419-3.
Dewey:895.6/2009. LCCN:90-002319.

Audience: **u,f.**

Leiter, Samuel L.   **PN2924.5.K3A7 1999**
Art of Kabuki: Five Famous Plays. Ed. 2. Trade Paper. Dover
Publications, Inc. Mineola, NY. 1999. 300p.
ISBN:0-486-40872-8, ISBN13: 978-0-486-40872-9.
Dewey:895.6/2008. LCCN:99-046425.

Audience: **l,u,f.**

Mahta, Tarla   **PN2882.M43 1995**
Sanskrit Play Production in Ancient India. Trade Cloth. Motilal
Banarsidass Publishers (Pvt. Ltd). New Delhi, 1999. 446p.
Music and Dance Ser. ISBN:81-208-1057-0, ISBN13:
978-81-208-1057-0. Dewey:791.0954. LCCN:95-901716.

Audience: **l,u,f.**

Mico International   **PN1978.J3**
(Produced by)
🗗 Bunraku: Masters of Japanese Puppet Theater. Video, VHS
Format. Films Media Group. Princeton, NJ. 2001.
ISBN:0-7365-4532-8, ISBN13: 978-0-7365-4532-7.
Dewey:792.0952.

Audience: **l,u,f.**

Miettinen, Jukka O.   **PN2860.M538 1992**
Classical Dance and Theatre in South-East Asia. Cloth Text.
Oxford University Press, Inc. New York, NY. 1993. 196p.
ISBN:0-19-588595-3, ISBN13: 978-0-19-588595-8.
Dewey:792.0959. LCCN:92-010946.

Audience: **l,u,f.**

Mrazek, Jan (Editor)   **PN1979.S5**
Puppet Theater in Contemporary Indonesia: New Approaches to
Performance-Events. Trade Cloth. University of Michigan,
Center for South & Southeast Asian Studies. Ann Arbor, MI.

2002. 392p. Michigan Papers on South and Southeast Asia, No.
50 ISBN:0-89148-083-8, ISBN13: 978-0-89148-083-9.
Dewey:791.53.

Audience: **l,u,f.**

Pound, Ezra & Fenollosa,   **PN2924.5.N6F46 2004**
Ernest
The Noh Theatre of Japan: With Complete Texts of 15 Classic
Plays. Trade Paper. Dover Publications, Inc. Mineola, NY. 2004.
288p. ISBN:0-486-43699-3, ISBN13: 978-0-486-43699-9.
Dewey:895.6/2008. LCCN:2004-050239.

Audience: **l,u,f.**

Scott, A. C.   **PN2924.5.K3S265 1999**
The Kabuki Theatre of Japan. Trade Paper. Dover Publications,
Inc. Mineola, NY. 1999. 320p. ISBN:0-486-40645-8, ISBN13:
978-0-486-40645-9. Dewey:792/.0952. LCCN:98-043894.

Audience: **l,u,f.** 𝓑

Scott, A. C. (Author,   **PN2871.S4 2001**
Illustrator)
The Classical Theatre of China. Trade Paper. Dover
Publications, Inc. Mineola, NY. 2001. 260p.
ISBN:0-486-41579-1, ISBN13: 978-0-486-41579-6.
Dewey:792/.0951. LCCN:00-065907.

Audience: **u,f.**

Shen, Grant   **PN2871.S484 2005**
Elite Theatre in Ming China, 1368-1644. Trade Cloth.
Routledge. New York, NY. 2005. 256p. RoutledgeCurzon
Studies on the Early History of Asia ISBN:0-415-34326-7,
ISBN13: 978-0-415-34326-8. Dewey:792/.0951.
LCCN:2004-015323.

Audience: **u,f.**

Theater Production

Banham, Martin (Editor)   **PN2035.C27 1995**
The Cambridge Guide to Theatre. Ed. 2. Trade Cloth.
Cambridge University Press. New York, NY. 1995. 1247p.
ISBN:0-521-43437-8, ISBN13: 978-0-521-43437-9.
Dewey:792/.09. LCCN:95-001011.

Audience: **g.** *Choice, 1996.*

Gillette, J. Michael   **PN2085.G5 2004**
Theatrical Design and Production: An Introduction to Scene
Design and Construction, Lighting, Sound, Costume, and
Makeup. Ed. 5. Cloth Text. McGraw-Hill Companies, The. New
York, NY. 2004. 640p. ISBN:0-07-256262-5, ISBN13:
978-0-07-256262-0. Dewey:792/.025. LCCN:2004-049902.

Audience: **l,u,f.**

Theater Production > Performance Studies

Bial, Henry (Compiled by)   **PN2041.A57P49 2003**
The Performance Studies Reader. Trade Paper. Routledge. New
York, NY. 2003. 352p. ISBN:0-415-30241-2, ISBN13:
978-0-415-30241-8. Dewey:791. LCCN:2003-005708.

Audience: **l,u,f.**

Case, Sue-Ellen (Editor)　　　　**PS627.L48S65 1996**
Split Britches: Lesbian Practice - Feminist Performance. Trade
Paper. Routledge. New York, NY. 1996. 288p.
ISBN:0-415-12766-1, ISBN13: 978-0-415-12766-0.
Dewey:812.5/4/08/09287. LCCN:95-047164.

Audience: **l,u,f.**

Dolan, Jill　　　　**PN2270.G39D65 2001**
Geographies of Learning: Theory and Practice, Activism and
Performance. Wesleyan University Press. 2001.
ISBN:0-8195-6468-0, ISBN13: 978-0-8195-6468-9.

Audience: **u,f.**

Dolan, Jill　　　　**PN2270.F45D65 1993**
Presence and Desire: Essays on Gender, Sexuality, Performance.
University of Michigan Press. 1993. ISBN:0-472-09530-7,
ISBN13: 978-0-472-09530-8.

Audience: **u,f.**

Gainor, J. Ellen (Editor)　　　　**PN2049.I47 1995**
Imperialism and Theatre: Essays on World Theatre, Drama and
Performance. Trade Paper. Routledge. New York, NY. 1995.
280p. ISBN:0-415-10641-9, ISBN13: 978-0-415-10641-2.
Dewey:792/.013. LCCN:94-035439.

Audience: **l,u,f.**　*Choice, 1996.*

Henke, Robert　　　　**PQ4155**
Performance and Literature in the Commedia Dell'Arte. Trade
Cloth. Cambridge University Press. New York, NY. 2002. 278p.
ISBN:0-521-64324-4, ISBN13: 978-0-521-64324-5.
Dewey:792.2 /3/0945. LCCN:2003-268759.

Audience: **u,f.**

Hoenselaars, Ton (Editor)　　　　**PR2982.S475 2004**
Shakespeare's History Plays: Performance, Translation and
Adaptation in Britain and Abroad. Dennis Kennedy (Foreword
by). Trade Cloth. Cambridge University Press. New York, NY.
2004. 302p. ISBN:0-521-82902-X, ISBN13: 978-0-521-82902-1.
Dewey:822.3/3. LCCN:2004-040752.

Audience: **u,f.**　*Choice, 2005.*

Kaye, Nick　　　　**PN2037.K35 1994**
Postmodernism and Performance. Trade Paper. Palgrave
Macmillan. New York, NY. 1994. 188p. New Directions in
Theatre Ser. ISBN:0-312-12024-9, ISBN13: 978-0-312-12024-5.
Dewey:792. LCCN:93-032470.

Audience: **u,f.**　*Choice, 1994.*

Kennedy, Dennis (Editor)　　　　**PR2971.F66 F66 1993**
Foreign Shakespeare: Contemporary Performance. Trade Paper.
Cambridge University Press. New York, NY. 2004. 329p.
ISBN:0-521-61708-1, ISBN13: 978-0-521-61708-6.
Dewey:792.95.

Audience: **l,u,f.**　*Choice, 1994.*

Kuppers, Petra　　　　**HV1568.K87 2003**
Disability and Contemporary Performance: Bodies on Edge.
Routledge. 2003. ISBN:0-415-30238-2, ISBN13:
978-0-415-30238-8.

Audience: **u,f.**

Massai, Sonia (Editor)　　　　**PR2880.A1W67 2005**
World-Wide Shakespeares. Paper over Boards. Routledge. New
York, NY. 2005. 216p. ISBN:0-415-32455-6, ISBN13:
978-0-415-32455-7. Dewey:822.3/3. LCCN:2004-028867.

Audience: **l,u,f.**

Mitchell, John D. &　　　　**PN2924 .M58**
　Watanabe, Miyoko
Staging Japanese Theatre: Noh and Kabuki. Michael Cooper
(Illustrator). Paper Text. Institute for Advanced Studies in the
Theatre Arts (I A S T A). Key West, FL. 245p.
ISBN:1-882763-06-8, ISBN13: 978-1-882763-06-1.
Dewey:895.6.

Audience: **u,f.**

Novy, Marianne (Editor)　　　　**PR116**
Transforming Shakespeare: Contemporary Women's Re-Visions
in Literature and Performance. Trade Paper. Palgrave
Macmillan. New York, NY. 2000. 272p. ISBN:0-312-23509-7,
ISBN13: 978-0-312-23509-3. Dewey:820.9/9287/0904.

Audience: **u,f.**　*Choice, 1999.*

Occhiogrosso, Frank　　　　**PR3091.S3627 2002**
　(Editor)
Shakespeare in Performance: A Collection of Essays. Trade
Cloth. University of Delaware Press. Newark, DE. 2003. 152p.
ISBN:0-87413-776-4, ISBN13: 978-0-87413-776-7.
Dewey:792.9/5. LCCN:2002-018093.

Audience: **l,u.**

Rudlin, John　　　　**PQ4155.R83 1994**
The Commedia Dell'Arte in the Twentieth Century. Trade Paper.
Routledge. New York, NY. 1994. 296p. ISBN:0-415-04770-6,
ISBN13: 978-0-415-04770-8. Dewey:792.209.
LCCN:93-013426.

Audience: **l,u,f.**

Schanke, Robert A. &　　　　**PN2286.5**
　Marra, Kimberely Bell (Editors)
Passing Performances: Queer Readings of Leading Players in
American Theater History. Trade Paper. University of Michigan
Press. Chicago, IL. 1998. 352p. Triangulations Ser.
ISBN:0-472-06681-1, ISBN13: 978-0-472-06681-0.
Dewey:792/.028/08664 B. LCCN:98-019710.

Audience: **l,u,f.**　*Choice, 1999.*

Schanke, Robert A. &　　　　**PS338.H66S73 2001**
　Marra, Kimberley B. (Editors)
Staging Desire: Queer Readings of American Theater History.
Trade Paper. University of Michigan Press. Chicago, IL. 2002.
416p. Triangulations Ser., :Lesbian - Gay - Queer Theater -
Drama - Performance ISBN:0-472-06749-4, ISBN13:
978-0-472-06749-7. Dewey:812.009/353. LCCN:2001-006446.

Audience: **g,l,u,f.**　*Choice, 2003.*

Schechner, Richard　　　　**PN2039**
The Future of Ritual: Writings on Culture and Performance.
Trade Paper. Routledge. New York, NY. 1995. 296p.
ISBN:0-415-04690-4, ISBN13: 978-0-415-04690-9.
Dewey:792/.01.

Audience: **u,f.**

Schechner, Richard   PN2041.A57S34 2002
Performance Studies: An Introduction. Paper over Boards.
Routledge. New York, NY. 2002. 304p. ISBN:0-415-14620-8,
ISBN13: 978-0-415-14620-3. Dewey:792. LCCN:2001-048687.

Audience: **l,u,f.**

Schechner, Richard   PN2039.S37 2003
Performance Theory. Ed. 2. Trade Paper. Routledge. New York,
NY. 2003. 432p. Classics Ser. ISBN:0-415-31455-0, ISBN13:
978-0-415-31455-8. Dewey:306/.484.

Audience: **u,f.**

Schechner, Richard &   PN2049.R5
  Schuman, Mady (Editors)
Ritual, Play, and Performance: Readings in the Social
Sciences/Theatre. Trade Cloth. The Seabury Press, Inc. New
York, NY. 1976. 230p. A Continuum Book Ser.
ISBN:0-8164-9285-9, ISBN13: 978-0-8164-9285-5.
Dewey:301.5/7. LCCN:76-006910.

Audience: **l,u,f.** *B*

Shaughnessy, Robert   PR3091.S363 2000
  (Editor)
Shakespeare in Performance. Trade Paper. Palgrave Macmillan.
New York, NY. 2000. 240p. New Casebooks Ser.
ISBN:0-312-23312-4, ISBN13: 978-0-312-23312-9.
Dewey:822.3/3. LCCN:99-086321.

Audience: **u,f.**

Smallwood, Robert (Editor)   PR3112.P556 2004
Players of Shakespeare 6: Essays in the Performance of
Shakespeare's History Plays. Trade Cloth. Cambridge University
Press. New York, NY. 2004. 236p. Players of Shakespeare Ser.
ISBN:0-521-84088-0, ISBN13: 978-0-521-84088-0.
Dewey:792.950941. LCCN:2005-273797.

Audience: **u,f.**

Striff, Erin (Editor)   PN2041.A57P47 2002
Performance Studies. Cloth over Boards. Palgrave Macmillan.
New York, NY. 2003. 224p. Readers in Cultural Criticism Ser.
ISBN:0-333-78673-4, ISBN13: 978-0-333-78673-4. Dewey:791.
LCCN:2002-026750.

Audience: **l,u,f.**

Stucky, Nathan & Wimmer,   PN1576.T43 2002
  Cynthia (Editors)
Teaching Performance Studies. Trade Cloth. Southern Illinois
University Press. Carbondale, IL. 2002. 304p. Theater in the
Americas Ser. ISBN:0-8093-2465-2, ISBN13:
978-0-8093-2465-1. Dewey:791/.071. LCCN:2002-018757.

Audience: **l,u,f.**

Turner, Victor W.   GN473.T84 1982
From Ritual to Theatre: The Human Seriousness of Play. Trade
Paper. P A J Publications. New York, NY. 1982. 127p.
ISBN:0-933826-17-6, ISBN13: 978-0-933826-17-5.
Dewey:306.4/84. LCCN:81-083751.

Audience: **g,u,f.**

Watson, Ian (Editor)   PN2061
Performer Training: Developments Across Cultures. Trade Paper.

Routledge. New York, NY. 2002. 252p. Harwood Contemporary
Theatre Studies, Vol. 38 ISBN:0-415-27019-7, ISBN13:
978-0-415-27019-9. Dewey:792/.028.

Audience: **g.**

Worthen, W. B.   PR3091 .W67 1997
Shakespeare and the Authority of Performance. Trade Cloth.
Cambridge University Press. New York, NY. 1997. 265p.
ISBN:0-521-55134-X, ISBN13: 978-0-521-55134-2.
Dewey:822.3/3. LCCN:96-045571.

Audience: **u,f.** *Choice, 1998.*

Worthen, W. B.   PR3100.W67 2003
Shakespeare and the Force of Modern Performance. Trade
Cloth. Cambridge University Press. New York, NY. 2003. 282p.
ISBN:0-521-81030-2, ISBN13: 978-0-521-81030-2.
Dewey:792.9/5. LCCN:2002-031061.

Audience: **u,f.**

Worthen, W. B.   PR647
Renaissance Drama, Vol. 34. Wendy Wall & Jeffrey Masten
(Editors). Trade Cloth. Northwestern University Press. Evanston,
IL. 2006. 224p. Renaissance Drama Ser. ISBN:0-8101-2308-8,
ISBN13: 978-0-8101-2308-3. Dewey:822.309.

Audience: **u,f.**

Theater Production > General

Chambers, Colin   PN2596.S82R684 2004
Inside the Royal Shakespeare Company: Creativity and the
Institution. Paper over Boards. Routledge. New York, NY. 2004.
280p. ISBN:0-415-21202-2, ISBN13: 978-0-415-21202-1.
Dewey:792/.0942. LCCN:2003-015745.

Audience: **l,u,f.**

James, Henry   PN2021
The Scenic Art: Notes and Acting and the Drama. Allan Wade
(Editor). Trade Paper. Books on Demand. Ann Arbor, MI. 420p.
ISBN:0-598-27634-3, ISBN13: 978-0-598-27634-6.
Dewey:792.04.

Audience: **u,f.**

Kullman, Colby H. &   PN2256
  Young, William C. (Editors)
Theatre Companies of the World: Africa, Asia, Australia, and
New Zealand, Canada, Eastern Europe, Latin America, the
Middle East, Scandinavia, Vol. 1. Cloth Text. Greenwood
Publishing Group, Inc. Portsmouth, NH. 1986. 1024p.
ISBN:0-313-25667-5, ISBN13: 978-0-313-25667-7.
Dewey:792/.09. LCCN:84-000539.

Audience: **g.**

Matthews, Brander (Editor)   PN1661.M29 1970
Papers on Playmaking. Trade Cloth. Ayer Company Publishers,
Inc. Manchester, NH. 1977. 312p. Essay Index Reprint Ser.
ISBN:0-8369-1890-8, ISBN13: 978-0-8369-1890-8.
Dewey:809.2. LCCN:75-111852.

Audience: **g.** *B*

Postlewait, Thomas   PN2115.I54 1989
Interpreting the Theatrical Past: Essays in the Historiography of
Performance. University of Iowa Press. 1989.
ISBN:0-87745-238-5, ISBN13: 978-0-87745-238-6.
                                        Audience: **l,u,f.**

Theater Production > General > History

                                        PN1581
The New York Times Theater Reviews, 1870-1990. Trade Cloth.
Garland Publishing, Inc. New York, NY. 1992.
ISBN:0-318-69660-6, ISBN13: 978-0-318-69660-7.
Dewey:792.950973.
                                        Audience: **l,u,f.**

                                        PN2266
The New York Times Theater Reviews, 1995-1996. Cloth Text.
Garland Publishing, Inc. New York, NY. 1998. 456p. New York
Times Theater Review Ser., Vol. 29 ISBN:0-8153-0645-8,
ISBN13: 978-0-8153-0645-0.
                                        Audience: **l,u,f.**

Arnott, Peter D.   **PA3201**
Public and Performance in the Greek Theatre. Trade Paper.
Routledge. New York, NY. 1991. 216p. ISBN:0-415-06299-3,
ISBN13: 978-0-415-06299-2. Dewey:792/.0938.
LCCN:88-032156.
                              Audience: **l,u,f.** *Choice, 1990.*

Benedetti, Jean (Editor)   **PN2122**
The Art of the Actor: The Essential History of Acting from
Classical Times to the Present Day. Paper over Boards.
Routledge. New York, NY. 2006. 256p. ISBN:0-87830-203-4,
ISBN13: 978-0-87830-203-1. Dewey:792.02809.
                                        Audience: **l,u,f.**

Braun, E.   **PN2053**
Director and the Stage. Trade Paper. Methuen Publishing Ltd.
London, 2003. ISBN:0-413-46300-1, ISBN13:
978-0-413-46300-5. Dewey:792/.0233/094/09034.
                                        Audience: **l,u,f.**

Brockett, Oscar Gross &   PN2101.B68 2003
  Hildy, Franklin J.
History of the Theatre. Ed. 9. Trade Cloth. Allyn & Bacon, Inc.
Boston, MA. 2002. 720p. ISBN:0-205-35878-0, ISBN13:
978-0-205-35878-6. Dewey:792/.09. LCCN:2002-025352.
                                        Audience: **l,u,f.**

Cohen-Stratyner, Barbara   Z6935 .P46
  (Introduction by)
Performing Arts Resources: The Drews and the Barrymores, a
Dynasty of Actors. Warren Kliewer (Foreword by). Trade Cloth.
Theatre Library Association. New York, NY. 1988. 161p.
ISBN:0-932610-10-2, ISBN13: 978-0-932610-10-2.
Dewey:016.7902/08. LCCN:75-646287.
                                        Audience: **g.**

Frome, Shelly   PN2078.U62
The Actors Studio: A History. Paper Text. McFarland &
Company, Incorporated Publishers. Jefferson, NC. 2005. 224p.
ISBN:0-7864-2320-X, ISBN13: 978-0-7864-2320-0.
Dewey:792/.028/097471. LCCN:2001-031610.
                                        Audience: **l,u,f.**

Gardner, Bonnie Milne   PS352.G37 2001
The Emergence of the Playwright-Director in American Theatre,
1960-1983. Trade Cloth. Edwin Mellen Press, The. Lewiston,
NY. 2001. 236p. Studies in Theatre Arts, Vol. 15
ISBN:0-7734-7470-6, ISBN13: 978-0-7734-7470-3.
Dewey:892.4/2608. LCCN:00-065373.
                                        Audience: **l,u,f.**

Langley, Stephen   PN2291 .L29
Theatre Management and Production in America: Commercial,
Stock, Resident, College, Community, Theatre, and Presenting
Organizations. Trade Paper. Quite Specific Media Group, Ltd.
Hollywood, CA. 1990. 702p. ISBN:0-89676-143-6, ISBN13:
978-0-89676-143-8. Dewey:792/.068.
                                        Audience: **l,u,f.**

New York Times Staff   **PR3091**
  (Contribution by)
The New York Times Theatre Reviews, 1999-2000. Paper over
Boards. Routledge. New York, NY. 2002. 500p. The New York
Times Theater Reviews Ser. ISBN:0-415-93697-7, ISBN13:
978-0-415-93697-2. Dewey:792.9/5/05.
                                        Audience: **l,u,f.**

Odell, George C.   PN2277.N5.O4 1970
Annals of the New York Stage. Trade Cloth. A M S Press, Inc.
New York, NY. 1970. ISBN:0-404-07830-3, ISBN13:
978-0-404-07830-0. Dewey:792/.097471. LCCN:77-116018.
                                        Audience: **g.**

Random House Staff   **PN1581**
The New York Times Theatre Reviews, 1991-92. Library
Binding. Garland Publishing, Inc. New York, NY. 1994. New
York Times Theater Reviews Ser., Vol. 27 ISBN:0-8153-0643-1,
ISBN13: 978-0-8153-0643-6. Dewey:792.950973.
                                        Audience: **l,u,f.**

Rehm, Rush   PA3131.R38
Greek Tragic Theatre. Trade Paper. Routledge. New York, NY.
1994. 184p. Theatre Production Ser. ISBN:0-415-11894-8,
ISBN13: 978-0-415-11894-1. Dewey:882.0109.
LCCN:91-033611.
                              Audience: **u,f.** *Choice, 1993.*

Richmond, Hugh Macrae   PR3095.R53 2004
Shakespeare's Theatre. Trade Paper. Continuum International
Publishing Group, Ltd. London, 2005. 584p.
ISBN:0-8264-7776-3, ISBN13: 978-0-8264-7776-7.
Dewey:822.33.
                                        Audience: **l,u.**

Roose-Evans, James   **PN2189**
Experimental Theatre: From Stanislavsky to Peter Brook. Ed. 4.

Trade Paper. Routledge. New York, NY. 1996. 260p.
ISBN:0-415-00963-4, ISBN13: 978-0-415-00963-8.
Dewey:792/.022.

Audience: **l,u,f.** *B*

Serlio, Sebastiano   **PN2221.H76**
The Renaissance Stage: Documents of Serlio, Sabbattini and
Furttenbach. Paper Text. Textbook Publishers. Temecula, CA.
2003. 256p. ISBN:0-7581-2129-6, ISBN13: 978-0-7581-2129-5.
Dewey:792.

Audience: **u,f.** *B*

Smith, C. S.   **PN2881.G3**
The New York Times Theater Reviews 1997-1998. Cloth Text.
Taylor & Francis Group. Philadelphia, PA. 2001. 496p. The
New York Times Theater Reviews Ser. ISBN:0-8153-3341-2,
ISBN13: 978-0-8153-3341-8. Dewey:792.0954.

Audience: **l,u,f.**

Stanislavsky, Constantin   **PN2728.S78A32 1950Z**
My Life in Art. Trade Paper. Kessinger Publishing, LLC.
Whitefish, MT. 2005. ISBN:1-4179-2577-9, ISBN13:
978-1-4179-2577-3. Dewey:792.092.

Audience: **l,u,f.**

Timberlake, Craig   **PN2587.W532**
The Bishop of Broadway: The Life and Work of David Belasco.
Paper Text. Textbook Publishers. Temecula, CA. 2003. 291p.
ISBN:0-7581-9867-1, ISBN13: 978-0-7581-9867-9.
Dewey:792/.0942.

Audience: **l,u,f.**

Wiles, David   **PA3201 .W53 2000**
Greek Theatre Performance: An Introduction. Trade Paper.
Cambridge University Press. New York, NY. 2000. 256p.
ISBN:0-521-64857-2, ISBN13: 978-0-521-64857-8.
Dewey:792/.0938. LCCN:99-043723.

Audience: **l,u.**

Worrall, Nick   **PN2726.M62M73 1996**
The Moscow Art Theatre. Paper over Boards. Routledge. New
York, NY. 1996. 256p. Theatre Production Studies
ISBN:0-415-05598-9, ISBN13: 978-0-415-05598-7.
Dewey:792.9/5/0947312. LCCN:95-045724.

Audience: **l,u,f.**

Worthen, William B.   **PR736.W64 1992**
Modern Drama and the Rhetoric of Theater. Trade Cloth.
University of California Press. Berkeley, CA. 1991. 240p.
ISBN:0-520-07468-8, ISBN13: 978-0-520-07468-2.
Dewey:822/.9109. LCCN:91-017677.

Audience: **l,u,f.** *Choice, 1992.*

Theater Production > General > Theory

Appia, Adolphe   **PN2081.O6S6**
The Work of Living Art: A Theory of the Theatre. Paper Text.
Textbook Publishers. Temecula, CA. 2003. 131p.
ISBN:0-7581-2132-6, ISBN13: 978-0-7581-2132-5.
Dewey:792.025.

Audience: **l,u,f.** *B*

Artaud, Antonin   **PN2021.A713 1993**
Theatre and Its Double. Victor Corti (Translator). Trade Paper.
Riverrun Press, Inc. Flemington, NJ. 2002. 102p.
ISBN:0-7145-4234-2, ISBN13: 978-0-7145-4234-8. Dewey:792.

Audience: **u,f.**

Benedetti, Robert L.   **PN2061.B39 2001**
Actor at Work. Ed. 8. Cloth Text. Allyn & Bacon, Inc. Boston,
MA. 2000. 256p. ISBN:0-205-31888-6, ISBN13:
978-0-205-31888-9. Dewey:792/.028. LCCN:99-056676.

Audience: **l,u,f.**

Bennett, Susan   **PN1590.A9B48 1998**
Theatre Audiences: A Theory of Production and Reception. Ed.
2. Trade Paper. Routledge. New York, NY. 1997. 264p.
ISBN:0-415-15723-4, ISBN13: 978-0-415-15723-0. Dewey:792.
LCCN:97-011461.

Audience: **u,f.** *Choice, 1990.*

Brecht, Bertolt   **PN2037**
Brecht on Theatre: The Development of an Aesthetic. Ed. 2.
Trade Paper. Methuen Publishing Ltd. London, 2003.
ISBN:0-413-38800-X, ISBN13: 978-0-413-38800-1. Dewey:792.
LCCN:63-018479.

Audience: **l,u,f.** *B*

Brook, Peter   **PN1655.B75 2005**
The Open Door. UK-Trade Paper. Knopf Publishing Group.
New York, NY. 2005. 160p. ISBN:1-4000-7787-7, ISBN13:
978-1-4000-7787-8. Dewey:792. LCCN:2004-059494.

Audience: **l,u,f.**

Carlson, Marvin   **PN2039.C26 1993**
Theories of the Theatre: A Historical and Critical Survey from
the Greeks to the Present. Trade Paper. Cornell University Press.
Ithaca, NY. 1993. 552p. ISBN:0-8014-8154-6, ISBN13:
978-0-8014-8154-3. Dewey:792/.01. LCCN:93-030778.

Audience: **u,f.** *B*

Craig, Edward Gordon   **PN2091.S8**
On the Art of the Theatre. Paper Text. Textbook Publishers.
Temecula, CA. 2003. 295p. ISBN:0-7581-3150-X, ISBN13:
978-0-7581-3150-8. Dewey:792.

Audience: **l,u,f.** *B*

Demastes, William W.   **PR635.C69D46 2002**
Staging Consciousness: Theater and the Materialization of Mind.
Trade Cloth. University of Michigan Press. Chicago, IL. 2002.
208p. Theater Ser., :Theory, Text and Performance
ISBN:0-472-11202-3, ISBN13: 978-0-472-11202-9.
Dewey:822.009/384. LCCN:2001-003754.

Audience: **u,f.** *Choice, 2003.*

Grotowski, Jerzy   **PN2061.G75 2002**
Towards Poor Theatre. Eugenio Barba (Editor), Peter Brook
(Introduction by, Preface by). Trade Paper. Routledge. New
York, NY. 2002. 272p. ISBN:0-87830-155-0, ISBN13:
978-0-87830-155-3. Dewey:792.02/8. LCCN:2004-266663.

Audience: **u,f.**

Hall, Peter   **PN2101**
The Necessary Theatre. Trade Paper. Nick Hern Books, Ltd. London, 2002. 64p. ISBN:1-85459-402-8, ISBN13: 978-1-85459-402-0. Dewey:792/.09.

Audience: **l,u,f.**

Homan, Sidney   **PN2053.H63 2003**
Staging Modern Playwrights. Trade Cloth. Bucknell University Press. Cranbury, NJ. 2003. 144p. ISBN:0-8387-5563-1, ISBN13: 978-0-8387-5563-1. Dewey:792/.0233. LCCN:2003-007542.

Audience: **l,u.** *Choice, 2004.*

Jones, Robert Edmond   **PN2091.S8**
The Dramatic Imagination: Reflections and Speculations on the Art of the Theatre. Ed. 2. UK-B Format Paperback. Routledge. New York, NY. 2004. 176p. A Theatre Arts Book Ser. ISBN:0-87830-184-4, ISBN13: 978-0-87830-184-3. Dewey:792. LCCN:2004-011710.

Audience: **l,u,f.**

Krasner, David (Editor)   **PN2062.M48 2000**
Method Acting Reconsidered: Theory, Practice, Future. Trade Paper. Palgrave Macmillan. New York, NY. 2000. 288p. ISBN:0-312-22309-9, ISBN13: 978-0-312-22309-0. Dewey:792/.028. LCCN:00-035269.

Audience: **l,u,f.** *Choice, 2001.*

Leach, Robert   **PN2728.M4**
Vsevolod Meyerhold. Christopher Innes (Contribution by). Trade Paper. Cambridge University Press. New York, NY. 1993. 237p. Directors in Perspective Ser. ISBN:0-521-31843-2, ISBN13: 978-0-521-31843-3. Dewey:792/.0233/0924.

Audience: **l,u,f.** *Choice, 1990.*

Longman, Stanley Vincent   **PN1707.L66 2004**
Page and Stage: An Approach to Script Analysis. Trade Paper. Allyn & Bacon, Inc. Boston, MA. 2003. 160p. ISBN:0-205-37822-6, ISBN13: 978-0-205-37822-7. Dewey:808.2. LCCN:2003-049610.

Audience: **l,u.**

Reid, Francis   **PN2037**
The Staging Handbook. Trade Paper. Routledge. New York, NY. 2002. 96p. Globe Quartos Ser. ISBN:0-87830-160-7, ISBN13: 978-0-87830-160-7. Dewey:792/.02.

Audience: **l,u,f.**

Reinelt, Janelle G. and   **PN2039**
  Joseph R. Roach
Critical Theory and Performance. University of Michigan Press. 1992. ISBN:0-472-09458-0, ISBN13: 978-0-472-09458-5.

Audience: **u,f.**

Rousseau, Jean-Jacques   **PN2051**
Politics and the Arts: Letter to M. D'Alembert on the Theatre. Allan Bloom (Translator). Trade Paper. Cornell University Press. Ithaca, NY. 1968. 196p. ISBN:0-8014-9071-5, ISBN13: 978-0-8014-9071-2. Dewey:792.013.

Audience: **l,u,f.**

Simonson, Lee   **PN2091.S8 S536 1975**
The Stage Is Set. Trade Cloth. Ayer Company Publishers, Inc. Manchester, NH. 1977. New Reprints in Essay and General Literature Index Ser. ISBN:0-518-10206-8, ISBN13: 978-0-518-10206-9. Dewey:792. LCCN:75-014368.

Audience: **l,u,f.** *B*

Stanislavski, Constantin   **PN2062.S7613 1989**
An Actor Prepares. Elizabeth Reynolds Hapgood (Translator). Trade Paper. Routledge. New York, NY. 1989. 336p. ISBN:0-87830-983-7, ISBN13: 978-0-87830-983-2. Dewey:792/.028. LCCN:89-146170.

Audience: **l,u,f.**

Stanislavsky, Constantin   **PN2085.B6**
Creating a Role. Paper Text. Textbook Publishers. Temecula, CA. 2003. 271p. ISBN:0-7581-3141-0, ISBN13: 978-0-7581-3141-6. Dewey:792/.028.

Audience: **l,u,f.** *B*

Stanislavsky, Constantin   **PN2728.S78A32 1950Z**
My Life in Art. Trade Paper. Kessinger Publishing, LLC. Whitefish, MT. 2005. ISBN:1-4179-2577-9, ISBN13: 978-1-4179-2577-3. Dewey:792.092.

Audience: **l,u,f.**

Willett, John   **PN2658.P5.W55 1979**
The Theatre of Erwin Piscator: Half a Century of Politics in the Theatre. Trade Cloth. Holmes & Meier Publishers, Inc. Teaneck, NJ. 1979. 224p. ISBN:0-8419-0501-0, ISBN13: 978-0-8419-0501-6. Dewey:792/.0233/0924. LCCN:79-011941.

Audience: **u,f.** *B*

Theater Production > Reference

    PN1581
The New York Times Theater Reviews, 1870-1990. Trade Cloth. Garland Publishing, Inc. New York, NY. 1992. ISBN:0-318-69660-6, ISBN13: 978-0-318-69660-7. Dewey:792.950973.

Audience: **l,u,f.**

    PN2266
The New York Times Theater Reviews, 1995-1996. Cloth Text. Garland Publishing, Inc. New York, NY. 1998. 456p. New York Times Theater Review Ser., Vol. 29 ISBN:0-8153-0645-8, ISBN13: 978-0-8153-0645-0.

Audience: **l,u,f.**

    PS3525.A24785
Office of the Revels: The Dramatic Records of Sir Henry Herbert, Master of the Revels, 1623-1673. Paper Text. Classic Books. Murrieta, CA. 2001. 155p. ISBN:0-7426-9229-9, ISBN13: 978-0-7426-9229-9. Dewey:704.

Audience: **u,f.**

Alexander Street Press   **PN6119.7**
▢ Black Drama 1850 to Present.
http://www.alexanderstreet2.com/BLDRLive/
Alexander Street Press.

Audience: **g,l,u,f.**

Chambers, Colin   PN2035.C65 2002
Continuum Companion to Twentieth Century Theatre. Trade Cloth. Continuum International Publishing Group, Ltd. London, 2004. 896p. ISBN:0-8264-4959-X, ISBN13: 978-0-8264-4959-7. Dewey:792/.0904/03. LCCN:2002-025931.
     Audience: **g.** *Choice, 2003, 2002.*

Clapp, William Warland   PN2277.B6
A Record of the Boston Stage. Trade Cloth. Scholarly Publishing Office, University of Michigan Library. Ann Arbor, MI. 2004. ISBN:1-4181-2043-X, ISBN13: 978-1-4181-2043-6.
     Audience: **u,f.**

Cohen-Stratyner, Barbara   Z6935 .P46
   (Introduction by)
Performing Arts Resources: The Drews and the Barrymores, a Dynasty of Actors. Warren Kliewer (Foreword by). Trade Cloth. Theatre Library Association. New York, NY. 1988. 161p. ISBN:0-932610-10-2, ISBN13: 978-0-932610-10-2. Dewey:016.7902/08. LCCN:75-646287.
     Audience: **g.**

Dessen, Alan C. &   PR658.S59 D47 1999
   Thomson, Leslie
A Dictionary of Stage Directions in English Drama, 1580-1642. Trade Paper. Cambridge University Press. New York, NY. 2001. 306p. ISBN:0-521-00029-7, ISBN13: 978-0-521-00029-1. Dewey:822/.3003.
     Audience: **g.** *Choice, 2000.*

Doran   PN2581
Their Majesties' Servants or Annals of the English Stage from Thomas Betterton to Edmund Kean; Actors, Authors, Audiences. Trade Paper. Kessinger Publishing, LLC. Whitefish, MT. 2004. ISBN:1-4179-4578-8, ISBN13: 978-1-4179-4578-8. Dewey:792.
     Audience: **g.**

Guthrie, Tyrone   PN2658.P5
A Life in the Theatre. Paper Text. Textbook Publishers. Temecula, CA. 2003. 357p. ISBN:0-7581-8744-0, ISBN13: 978-0-7581-8744-4. Dewey:792/.0233/0924.
     Audience: **g,l,u,f.** *B*

Harrison, Martin   PN2041.S45
The Language of Theatre. Trade Cloth. Shelfmark. Chicago, IL. 2003. 225p. ISBN:0-9743318-2-1, ISBN13: 978-0-9743318-2-9. Dewey:792/.014.
     Audience: **g.**

Hawkins, Frederick William   PN2621
Annals of the French Stage from Its Origin to the Death of Racine. Paper Text. Classic Books. Murrieta, CA. 2001. ISBN:0-7426-9245-0, ISBN13: 978-0-7426-9245-9. Dewey:792/.0944.
     Audience: **u,f.** *B*

Highfill, Philip H., et al.   PN2597.H54 1993
ⓔ A Biographical Dictionary of Actors, Actresses, Musicians, Dancers, Managers and Other Stage Personnel in London,

1660-1800. Kalman A. Burnim & Edward A. Langhans (Authors). E-Book. NetLibrary, Inc. Boulder, CO. 1993. ISBN:0-585-03033-2, ISBN13: 978-0-585-03033-3. Dewey:790.2/092/2.
     Audience: **g.**

Hogan, Charles Beecher   PN2592.L58 1968
ⓔ The London Stage, 1660-1800: A Calendar of Plays, Entertainments and Afterpieces Together with Casts, Box-Receipts and Contemporary Comment. E-Book. NetLibrary, Inc. Boulder, CO. 1968. ISBN:0-585-29412-7, ISBN13: 978-0-585-29412-4. Dewey:792/.09421.
     Audience: **g.**

Jowers, Sidney Jackson   Z5691.J68 2000
Theatrical Costume, Masks, Make-Up and Wigs: A Bibliography and Iconography. John Cavanagh (Editor). Paper over Boards. Routledge. New York, NY. 2000. 542p. Motley Bibliographies Ser., Vol. 4 ISBN:0-415-24774-8, ISBN13: 978-0-415-24774-0. Dewey:792/.026. LCCN:00-062573.
     Audience: **g.** *Choice, 2001.*

Kennedy, Dennis (Editor)   PN1655
The Oxford Encyclopedia of Theatre and Performance, Set. Trade Cloth. Oxford University Press, Inc. New York, NY. 2003. 1,618p. ISBN:0-19-860174-3, ISBN13: 978-0-19-860174-6. Dewey:792.03. LCCN:2003-266308.
     Audience: **g.** *Choice, 2003.*

Lounsbury, Warren C. &   PN2091.M3L68 1999
   Boulanger, Norman C.
Theatre Backstage from A to Z. Ed. 4. Trade Cloth. University of Washington Press. Seattle, WA. 1998. xxix, 231p. ISBN:0-295-97717-5, ISBN13: 978-0-295-97717-1. Dewey:792/.025/03. LCCN:98-004854.
     Audience: **g.** *Choice, 1990.*

Menglin, Zhao & Jiqing,   TN414.C6W4
   Yan
Peking Opera Painted Faces with Notes on 200 Operas. Trade Cloth. Morning Glory Press. Beijing, 1996. 142p. ISBN:7-5054-0412-1, ISBN13: 978-7-5054-0412-0. Dewey:622.3421.
     Audience: **u,f.**

Mikotowicz, Tom (Editor)   PN2096
Theatrical Designers: An International Biographical Dictionary. Cloth Text. Greenwood Publishing Group, Inc. Portsmouth, NH. 1992. 408p. ISBN:0-313-26270-5, ISBN13: 978-0-313-26270-8. Dewey:792/.025/03 B. LCCN:91-028086.
     Audience: **g.** *Choice, 1993.*

Mobley, Jonnie P.   PN2035
NTC's Dictionary of Theatre and Drama Terms. Trade Cloth. McGraw-Hill Companies, The. New York, NY. 1992. 176p. ISBN:0-8442-5345-6, ISBN13: 978-0-8442-5345-9. Dewey:792/.03.
     Audience: **g.**

Molin, Donald H.   P367
Actor's Encyclopedia of Dialects. Ed. 2. Trade Paper. Bragi
Press. Van Nuys, CA. 1991. 256p. ISBN:0-9628545-0-6,
ISBN13: 978-0-9628545-0-7. Dewey:417/.2.

Audience: **u,f.**

New York Times Staff   PR3091
  (Contribution by)
The New York Times Theatre Reviews, 1999-2000. Paper over
Boards. Routledge. New York, NY. 2002. 500p. The New York
Times Theater Reviews Ser. ISBN:0-415-93697-7, ISBN13:
978-0-415-93697-2. Dewey:792.9/5/05.

Audience: **l,u,f.**

Owen, Bobbi   PN2091
Lighting Design on Broadway: Designers and Their Credits,
1915-1990. Cloth Text. Greenwood Publishing Group, Inc.
Portsmouth, NH. 1991. 176p. Bibliographies and Indexes in the
Performing Arts Ser., No. 11 ISBN:0-313-26533-X, ISBN13:
978-0-313-26533-4. Dewey:792/.025/09227471 B.
LCCN:91-024007.

Audience: **g.**

Peterson, Bernard L. Jr.   PN2286
Profiles of African American Stage Performers and Theatre
People, 1816-1960. James V. Hatch (Foreword by). Cloth Text.
Greenwood Publishing Group, Inc. Portsmouth, NH. 2000. 440p.
ISBN:0-313-29534-4, ISBN13: 978-0-313-29534-8.
Dewey:791.089/96073 B. LCCN:99-088456.

Audience: **l,u,f.** *Choice, 2001.*

Pickering, David (Editor)   PN2035.I49 1992
International Dictionary of Theatre: Actors, Directors and
Designers. Trade Cloth. Thomson Gale. Farmington Hills, MI.
1995. 830p. ISBN:1-55862-097-4, ISBN13: 978-1-55862-097-1.
Dewey:792/.03. LCCN:92-215736.

Audience: **g.** *Choice, 1996.*

Rae, Kenneth   HQ759
An International Vocabulary of Technical Theatre Terms, in
Eight Languages: American, Dutch, English, French, German,
Italian, Spanish, Swedish. Paper Text. Textbook Publishers.
Temecula, CA. 2003. 139p. ISBN:0-7581-3145-3, ISBN13:
978-0-7581-3145-4. Dewey:306.874/3.

Audience: **g.** *B*

Random House Staff   PN1581
The New York Times Theatre Reviews, 1991-92. Library
Binding. Garland Publishing, Inc. New York, NY. 1994. New
York Times Theater Reviews Ser., Vol. 27 ISBN:0-8153-0643-1,
ISBN13: 978-0-8153-0643-6. Dewey:792.950973.

Audience: **l,u,f.**

Reed, Francis   PN2091.E4
The ABC of Stage Lighting. Paper Text. Quite Specific Media
Group, Ltd. Hollywood, CA. 1992. 144p. ISBN:0-89676-119-3,
ISBN13: 978-0-89676-119-3. Dewey:792.025.

Audience: **g.** *Choice, 1993.*

Rees, James   PN2287.F6
Life of Edwin Forrest with Reminiscences and Personal
Recollections. Library Binding. Reprint Services Company.
Temecula, CA. 1993. 524p. ISBN:0-7812-5285-7, ISBN13:
978-0-7812-5285-0. Dewey:B.

Audience: **g.**

Riggs, Thomas (Editor)   PN2285 .C58
Contemporary Theatre, Film and Television: A Biographical
Guide Featuring Performers, Directors, Writers, Producers,
Designers, Managers, Choreographers, Technicians, Composers,
Executives, Dancers, and Critics in the United States, Canada,
Great Britain and the World, Vol. 65. Perfect, Paper over
Boards. Thomson Gale. Farmington Hills, MI. 2005. 482p.
Contemporary Theatre, Film and Television Ser.
ISBN:0-7876-9038-4, ISBN13: 978-0-7876-9038-0.
Dewey:791/.092/2 B.

Audience: **g.**

Schneider, Ben R. Jr.   PN2596.L6
  (Compiled by)
Index to "The London Stage, 1660-1800". George W. Stone
(Foreword by). Trade Cloth. Southern Illinois University Press.
Carbondale, IL. 1979. 960p. ISBN:0-8093-0907-6, ISBN13:
978-0-8093-0907-8. Dewey:792/.09421. LCCN:79-102595.

Audience: **l,u,f.** *B*

Sheehy, Helen   PN2688.D8S48 2002
Eleonora Duse: A Biography. Trade Cloth. Alfred A. Knopf Inc.
New York, NY. 2003. 400p. ISBN:0-375-40017-6, ISBN13:
978-0-375-40017-9. Dewey:792/.028/092 B.
LCCN:2002-033997.

Audience: **l,u,f.**

Smith, C. S.   PN2881.G3
The New York Times Theater Reviews 1997-1998. Cloth Text.
Taylor & Francis Group. Philadelphia, PA. 2001. 496p. The
New York Times Theater Reviews Ser. ISBN:0-8153-3341-2,
ISBN13: 978-0-8153-3341-8. Dewey:792.0954.

Audience: **l,u,f.**

Stone, George W. Jr. &   PN2598.G3.S67
  Kahrl, George M.
David Garrick: A Critical Biography. Trade Cloth. Southern
Illinois University Press. Carbondale, IL. 1979. 791p.
ISBN:0-8093-0931-9, ISBN13: 978-0-8093-0931-3.
Dewey:792/.028/0924. LCCN:79-009476.

Audience: **g,l,u,f.** *B*

Timberlake, Craig   PN2587.W532
The Bishop of Broadway: The Life and Work of David Belasco.
Paper Text. Textbook Publishers. Temecula, CA. 2003. 291p.
ISBN:0-7581-9867-1, ISBN13: 978-0-7581-9867-9.
Dewey:792/.0942.

Audience: **l,u,f.**

Tumielewicz, P. J. & Lyons,   PN2078.U6
  Peg (Editors)
Directory of Theatre Training Programs, 2003-05. Ed. 9. Trade

Paper. Theatre Directories Inc. Dorset, VT. 2004. 295p.
ISBN:0-933919-55-7, ISBN13: 978-0-933919-55-6.
Dewey:792/.071/173; 792.

Audience: **g.**

Watson, Ian (Editor)   **PN2061**
Performer Training: Developments Across Cultures. Trade Paper.
Routledge. New York, NY. 2002. 252p. Harwood Contemporary
Theatre Studies, Vol. 38 ISBN:0-415-27019-7, ISBN13:
978-0-415-27019-9. Dewey:792/.028.

Audience: **g.**

Wearing, J. P.   **PN2596.L6 W37**
The London Stage, 1890-1899: A Calendar of Plays and Players.
Trade Cloth. Scarecrow Press, Inc. Lanham, MD. 1976. 1242p.
ISBN:0-8108-0910-9, ISBN13: 978-0-8108-0910-9.
Dewey:792/.09421/2. LCCN:76-001825.

Audience: **l,u,f.** *B*

Wearing, J. P.   **PN2596.L6**
The London Stage, 1900-1909: A Calendar of Plays and Players,
Set. Trade Cloth. Scarecrow Press, Inc. Lanham, MD. 1981.
1202p. ISBN:0-8108-1403-X, ISBN13: 978-0-8108-1403-5.
Dewey:792/.09421. LCCN:80-028353.

Audience: **l,u,f.** *B*

Wearing, J. P.   **PN2596.L6**
The London Stage, 1910-1919: A Calendar of Plays and Players,
Set. Trade Cloth. Scarecrow Press, Inc. Lanham, MD. 1982.
1370p. ISBN:0-8108-1596-6, ISBN13: 978-0-8108-1596-4.
Dewey:792/.09421. LCCN:82-019190.

Audience: **l,u,f.** *B*

Wearing, J. P.   **PN2596.L6**
The London Stage, 1920-1929: A Calendar of Plays and Players,
Set. Trade Cloth. Scarecrow Press, Inc. Lanham, MD. 1984.
1808p. ISBN:0-8108-1715-2, ISBN13: 978-0-8108-1715-9.
Dewey:792/.09421. LCCN:84-010665.

Audience: **l,u,f.** *B*

Wearing, J. P.   **PN2596.L6W3845 1990**
The London Stage, 1930-1939: A Calender of Plays and Players,
Set. Trade Cloth. Scarecrow Press, Inc. Lanham, MD. 1990.
1999p. ISBN:0-8108-2349-7, ISBN13: 978-0-8108-2349-5.
Dewey:792/.09421. LCCN:90-008883.

Audience: **l,u,f.** *Choice, 1991.*

Wearing, J. P.   **PN2596.L6.W3846 1991**
The London Stage, 1940-1949: A Calendar of Plays and Players.
Trade Cloth. Scarecrow Press, Inc. Lanham, MD. 1991. 1284p.
ISBN:0-8108-2500-7, ISBN13: 978-0-8108-2500-0.
Dewey:792.0942109044. LCCN:91-036206.

Audience: **l,u,f.** *Choice, 1992.*

Wearing, J. P.   **PN2596.L6W3847 1993**
The London Stage, 1950-1959: A Calendar of Plays and Players.
Trade Cloth. Scarecrow Press, Inc. Lanham, MD. 1993. 1807p.
ISBN:0-8108-2690-9, ISBN13: 978-0-8108-2690-8.
Dewey:792.0942109045. LCCN:93-017179.

Audience: **l,u,f.**

Winter, William   **PN2287.B4 W5 1970**
Life of David Belasco, Set. Trade Cloth. Ayer Company
Publishers, Inc. Manchester, NH. 1977. Select Bibliographies
Reprint Ser. ISBN:0-8369-5202-2, ISBN13: 978-0-8369-5202-5.
Dewey:792/.0924. LCCN:72-107837.

Audience: **g.**

Theater Production > Performance

Condee, William F.   **PN2091.S8**
Theatrical Space: A Guide for Directors and Designers. Trade
Paper. Scarecrow Press, Inc. Lanham, MD. 2002. 248p.
ISBN:0-8108-4211-4, ISBN13: 978-0-8108-4211-3.
Dewey:792/.025. LCCN:95-003311.

Audience: **l,u,f.**

Gillette, J. Michael   **PN2085.G5 2000**
Theatrical Design and Production: An Introduction to Scene
Design and Construction, Lighting, Sound, Costume, and
Makeup. Ed. 4. Cloth Text. McGraw-Hill Higher Education.
Burr Ridge, IL. 1999. 604p. ISBN:0-7674-1191-9, ISBN13:
978-0-7674-1191-2. Dewey:792/.025. LCCN:99-028595.

Audience: **l,u,f.**

Highfill, Philip H., et al.   **PN2597.H54 1993**
e A Biographical Dictionary of Actors, Actresses, Musicians,
Dancers, Managers and Other Stage Personnel in London,
1660-1800. Kalman A. Burnim & Edward A. Langhans
(Authors). E-Book. NetLibrary, Inc. Boulder, CO. 1993.
ISBN:0-585-03033-2, ISBN13: 978-0-585-03033-3.
Dewey:790.2/092/2.

Audience: **g.**

Moussinac, Leon (Compiled   **PN2091.S8 M76**
by)
The New Movement in the Theatre. Trade Cloth. Ayer Company
Publishers, Inc. Manchester, NH. 1972. ISBN:0-405-08808-6,
ISBN13: 978-0-405-08808-7. Dewey:792/.02. LCCN:65-019619.

Audience: **l,u,f.**

Peterson, Bernard L. Jr.   **PN2286**
Profiles of African American Stage Performers and Theatre
People, 1816-1960. James V. Hatch (Foreword by). Cloth Text.
Greenwood Publishing Group, Inc. Portsmouth, NH. 2000. 440p.
ISBN:0-313-29534-4, ISBN13: 978-0-313-29534-8.
Dewey:791/.089/96073 B. LCCN:99-088456.

Audience: **l,u,f.** *Choice, 2001.*

Styan, John L.   **PR3091.S79 1999**
Perspectives on Shakespeare in Performance. Paper Text. Peter
Lang Publishing, Inc. New York, NY. 2000. 183p. Studies in
Shakespeare, Vol. 11 ISBN:0-8204-4426-X, ISBN13:
978-0-8204-4426-0. Dewey:792.9/5. LCCN:98-053181.

Audience: **u,f.**

Watson, Ernest Bradlee   **PN2596.L6**
Sheridan to Robertson: A Study of the Nineteenth-Century
London Stage. Trade Paper. Kessinger Publishing, LLC.
Whitefish, MT. 2005. ISBN:1-4179-1875-6, ISBN13:
978-1-4179-1875-1. Dewey:792.0942.

Audience: **l,u,f.**

Watson, Ian (Editor)   **PN2061**
Performer Training: Developments Across Cultures. Trade Paper.
Routledge. New York, NY. 2002. 252p. Harwood Contemporary
Theatre Studies, Vol. 38 ISBN:0-415-27019-7, ISBN13:
978-0-415-27019-9. Dewey:792/.028.

Audience: **g.**

Theater Production > Performance > Actors and Acting

PN2596.L7.R515 1981
At the Royal Court: 25 Years of the English Stage Company.
Trade Cloth. Bow Historical Books. New Providence, NJ. 1981.
201, [56]p. ISBN:0-8021-0211-5, ISBN13: 978-0-8021-0211-9.
Dewey:792/.09421/34. LCCN:80-085375.

Audience: **u,f.** 🅑

Arundell, Dennis   **PN2596.L7S3**
The Story of Sadler's Wells, 1683-1977. Ed. 2. Trade Cloth.
David & Charles Publishers. Newton Abbot, 1978. 352p.
ISBN:0-7153-7620-9, ISBN13: 978-0-7153-7620-1.
Dewey:792/.09421/43. LCCN:78-316129.

Audience: **u,f.** 🅑

Asher, Sandra Fenichel, et al.   **PN2080.A65 2003**
125 Original Audition Monologues. Kent R. Brown & Joseph
Robinette (Authors). Trade Paper. Dramatic Publishing
Company. Woodstock, IL. 2003. 307p. ISBN:1-58342-148-3,
ISBN13: 978-1-58342-148-2. Dewey:812/.54.
LCCN:2005-272325.

Audience: **l,u.**

Aubert, Charles & Sears, Edith   **PN1985.A83 2003**
The Art of Pantomime. Trade Paper. Dover Publications, Inc.
Mineola, NY. 2003. 224p. Performing Arts: Drama, Film and
Dance Ser. ISBN:0-486-42857-5, ISBN13: 978-0-486-42857-4.
Dewey:792.3. LCCN:2003-041459.

Audience: **l,u,f.**

Baker, Herschel C.   **PN2598**
John Philip Kemble: The Actor in His Theatre. Trade Cloth.
Greenwood Publishing Group, Inc. Portsmouth, NH. 1970. 414p.
ISBN:0-8371-2279-1, ISBN13: 978-0-8371-2279-3.
Dewey:792/.028/0924. LCCN:76-090701.

Audience: **l,u,f.** 🅑

Barrault, Jean-Louis   **PN2638.B27 A313**
Reflections on the Theatre. Paper Text. Textbook Publishers.
Temecula, CA. 2003. 185p. ISBN:0-7581-4777-5, ISBN13:
978-0-7581-4777-6. Dewey:792/.092/4.

Audience: **l,u,f.** 🅑

Benedetti, Jean (Editor)   **PN2122**
The Art of the Actor: The Essential History of Acting from
Classical Times to the Present Day. Paper over Boards.
Routledge. New York, NY. 2006. 256p. ISBN:0-87830-203-4,
ISBN13: 978-0-87830-203-1. Dewey:792.02809.

Audience: **l,u,f.**

Benedetti, Robert L.   **PN2061.B39 2001**
Actor at Work. Ed. 8. Cloth Text. Allyn & Bacon, Inc. Boston,
MA. 2000. 256p. ISBN:0-205-31888-6, ISBN13:
978-0-205-31888-9. Dewey:792/.028. LCCN:99-056676.

Audience: **l,u,f.**

Bernhardt, Sarah   **PN2592.A5**
Memories of My Life, Being My Personal, Professional, and
Social Recollections As Woman and Artist. Paper Text. Classic
Books. Murrieta, CA. 2001. 456p. ISBN:0-7426-9244-2,
ISBN13: 978-0-7426-9244-2. Dewey:792.0942.

Audience: **l,u,f.** 🅑

Bernhardt, Sarah   **PN2061.B4**
The Art of the Theatre. H. J. Stenning (Translator), James Agate
(Preface by). Trade Cloth. Ayer Company Publishers, Inc.
Manchester, NH. 1972. ISBN:0-405-08264-9, ISBN13:
978-0-405-08264-1. Dewey:792.028. LCCN:70-082819.

Audience: **l,u,f.**

Boleslavsky, Richard   **PN2061.B55 2003**
Acting: The First Six Lessons. Paper over Boards. Routledge.
New York, NY. 1987. 152p. A Theatre Arts Book Ser.
ISBN:0-87830-000-7, ISBN13: 978-0-87830-000-6.
Dewey:792/.028. LCCN:2002-153023.

Audience: **u,f.** 🅑

Calder, Andrew   **PQ1860.C3**
Moliere: The Theory and Practice of Comedy. Trade Paper.
Continuum International Publishing Group, Ltd. London, 1996.
244p. ISBN:0-485-12127-1, ISBN13: 978-0-485-12127-8.
Dewey:842.4.

Audience: **l,u,f.** *Choice, 1993.*

Chekhov, Michael   **PN2061**
To the Actor: On Technique of Acting. Ed. 2. Simon Callow
(Foreword by). Paper over Boards. Routledge. New York, NY.
2002. 288p. ISBN:0-415-25875-8, ISBN13: 978-0-415-25875-3.
Dewey:792/.028.

Audience: **l,u,f.**

Clurman, Harold   **PN2297.G7 C5 1983**
Fervent Years: The Group Theatre and the Thirties. Stella Adler
(Introduction by). Trade Paper. Da Capo Press, Inc. Cambridge,
MA. 1983. 352p. Quality Paperbacks Ser. ISBN:0-306-80186-8,
ISBN13: 978-0-306-80186-0. Dewey:792/.0973.
LCCN:82-025239.

Audience: **l,u,f.**

Coad, Oral   **E178.5**
American Stage. Library Binding. Reprint Services Company.
Temecula, CA. 1993. 362p. ISBN:0-7812-5268-7, ISBN13:
978-0-7812-5268-3. Dewey:973.

Audience: **l,u.**

Cohen-Stratyner, Barbara (Introduction by)   **Z6935 .P46**
Performing Arts Resources: The Drews and the Barrymores, a
Dynasty of Actors. Warren Kliewer (Foreword by). Trade Cloth.

Theatre Library Association. New York, NY. 1988. 161p.
ISBN:0-932610-10-2, ISBN13: 978-0-932610-10-2.
Dewey:016.7902/08. LCCN:75-646287.

Audience: **g.**

Coldiron, Margaret   **PN2058.C65 2004**
Trance and Transformation of the Actor in Japanese Noh and
Balinese Masked Dance-Drama. Trade Cloth. Edwin Mellen
Press, The. Lewiston, NY. 2004. 360p. Studies in Theatre Arts,
Vol. 30 ISBN:0-7734-6341-0, ISBN13: 978-0-7734-6341-7.
Dewey:792.02/8/019. LCCN:2004-054145.

Audience: **u,f.**

Cole, Toby (Editor)   **PN2065.C55 1995**
Actors on Acting: The Theories, Techniques, and Practices of
the World's Great Actors, Told in Their Own Words. Ed. 4.
Trade Paper. Random House Value Publishing. New York, NY.
1995. 736p. ISBN:0-517-88478-X, ISBN13: 978-0-517-88478-2.
Dewey:792/.028. LCCN:95-220939.

Audience: **l,u,f.** 𝓑

Craik, T. W.   **PN2596.L6R6**
The Tudor Interlude: Stage, Costume, and Acting. Paper Text.
Textbook Publishers. Temecula, CA. 2003. 158p.
ISBN:0-7581-1342-0, ISBN13: 978-0-7581-1342-9.
Dewey:792.09421.

Audience: **u,f.** 𝓑

Dent, Edward J.   **PN2596.L7 O73 1979**
A Theatre for Everybody: The Story of the Old Vic and Sadler's
Wells. Kay Ambrose (Illustrator). Trade Cloth. Hyperion Press,
Inc. Westport, CT. 1979. ISBN:0-88355-691-X, ISBN13:
978-0-88355-691-7. Dewey:792/.09421/2. LCCN:78-010887.

Audience: **l,u,f.**

Doran   **PN2581**
Their Majesties' Servants or Annals of the English Stage from
Thomas Betterton to Edmund Kean; Actors, Authors, Audiences.
Trade Paper. Kessinger Publishing, LLC. Whitefish, MT. 2004.
ISBN:1-4179-4578-8, ISBN13: 978-1-4179-4578-8. Dewey:792.

Audience: **g.**

Eaton, Walter P.   **PN2295.T5.E3 1970**
Theatre Guild, the First Ten Years, with Articles by the
Directors. Trade Cloth. Ayer Company Publishers, Inc.
Manchester, NH. 1977. 299p. Select Bibliographies Reprint Ser.
ISBN:0-8369-5180-8, ISBN13: 978-0-8369-5180-6.
Dewey:792/.0973. LCCN:75-107799.

Audience: **l,u,f.** 𝓑

Egan, Leona Rust   **PS3529.N5Z6294 1994**
Provincetown as a Stage: Provincetown, the Provincetown
Players, and the Discovery of Eugene O'Neill. Trade Cloth.
Parnassus Imprints. Marstons Mills, MA. 1994. 296p.
ISBN:0-940160-57-9, ISBN13: 978-0-940160-57-6.
Dewey:792.097. LCCN:93-087449.

Audience: **l,u,f.**

Fowler, Gene Jr.   **PN2287.B35 F6**
Good Night, Sweet Prince. Trade Cloth. Buccaneer Books, Inc.
Cutchogue, NY. 1978. ISBN:0-89966-095-9, ISBN13:
978-0-89966-095-0. Dewey:927.92. LCCN:80-070166.

Audience: **l,u.** 𝓑

Frome, Shelly   **PN2078.U62**
The Actors Studio: A History. Paper Text. McFarland &
Company, Incorporated Publishers. Jefferson, NC. 2005. 224p.
ISBN:0-7864-2320-X, ISBN13: 978-0-7864-2320-0.
Dewey:792/.028/097471. LCCN:2001-031610.

Audience: **l,u,f.**

Funke, Lewis   **PN511.C42**
Actors Talk about Acting: Fourteen Interviews with Stars of the
Theatre. Paper Text. Textbook Publishers. Temecula, CA. 2003.
469p. ISBN:0-7581-5073-3, ISBN13: 978-0-7581-5073-8.
Dewey:824.91.

Audience: **l,u.**

Gielgud, John   **PN2598.G45**
Stage Directions. Trade Cloth. Greenwood Publishing Group,
Inc. Portsmouth, NH. 1979. 146p. ISBN:0-313-21035-7,
ISBN13: 978-0-313-21035-8. Dewey:792. LCCN:78-023580.

Audience: **l,u,f.** 𝓑

Gurr, Andrew   **PR3095.G86 2004**
The Shakespeare Company, 1594-1642. Trade Cloth. Cambridge
University Press. New York, NY. 2004. 356p.
ISBN:0-521-80730-1, ISBN13: 978-0-521-80730-2.
Dewey:792/.09421. LCCN:2003-055895.

Audience: **u,f.** *Choice, 2005.*

Hagen, Uta & Frankel,   **PN2061**
Haskel
Respect for Acting. Trade Cloth. John Wiley & Sons, Inc.
Hoboken, NJ. 1973. 240p. ISBN:0-02-547390-5, ISBN13:
978-0-02-547390-4. Dewey:792/.028. LCCN:72-002328.

Audience: **u,f.** 𝓑

Henke, Robert   **PQ4155**
Performance and Literature in the Commedia Dell'Arte. Trade
Cloth. Cambridge University Press. New York, NY. 2002. 278p.
ISBN:0-521-64324-4, ISBN13: 978-0-521-64324-5.
Dewey:792.2 /3/0945. LCCN:2003-268759.

Audience: **u,f.**

Hillebrand, Harold N.   **PN2598.K3H5**
Edmund Kean. Trade Cloth. A M S Press, Inc. New York, NY.
ISBN:0-404-03269-9, ISBN13: 978-0-404-03269-2.
Dewey:792/.028/0924. LCCN:77-181904.

Audience: **l,u,f.**

Hotson, Leslie   **PN2596.L6S49**
The Commonwealth and Restoration Stage. Paper Text.
Textbook Publishers. Temecula, CA. 2003. 424p.
ISBN:0-7581-4432-6, ISBN13: 978-0-7581-4432-4.
Dewey:792.094212.

Audience: **g.** 𝓑

Joseph, Bertram Leon   PN2598.G3B8
The Tragic Actor. Paper Text. Textbook Publishers. Temecula,
CA. 2003. 415p. ISBN:0-7581-4543-8, ISBN13:
978-0-7581-4543-7. Dewey:792/.028/0924.

Audience: **l,u,f.** *B*

Krasner, David (Editor)   PN2062.M48 2000
Method Acting Reconsidered: Theory, Practice, Future. Trade
Paper. Palgrave Macmillan. New York, NY. 2000. 288p.
ISBN:0-312-22309-9, ISBN13: 978-0-312-22309-0.
Dewey:792/.028. LCCN:00-035269.

Audience: **l,u,f.** *Choice, 2001.*

Marshall, Herbert   PN2598.R42A3
Ira Aldridge, the Negro Tragedian. Paper Text. Textbook
Publishers. Temecula, CA. 2003. 355p. ISBN:0-7581-3677-3,
ISBN13: 978-0-7581-3677-0. Dewey:927.92.

Audience: **l,u,f.** *B*

McArthur, Benjamin   PN2256.M39 2000
Actors and American Culture, 1880-1920. Trade Paper.
University of Iowa Press. Iowa City, IA. 2000. 304p. Studies in
Theatre History and Culture ISBN:0-87745-710-7, ISBN13:
978-0-87745-710-7. Dewey:792/.028/097309034.
LCCN:00-268718.

Audience: **l,u,f.**

Melville, Joy   PN2598
Ellen Terry. Book, Other. Haus Publishing. London, 2005. 192p.
ISBN:1-904950-14-0, ISBN13: 978-1-904950-14-1.
Dewey:792.028092.

Audience: **l,u,f.**

Mitter, Shomit   PN2071.R45 M57
Systems of Rehearsal: Stanislavsky, Brecht, Grotowski and Peter
Brook. Trade Paper. Routledge. New York, NY. 1992. 192p.
ISBN:0-415-06784-7, ISBN13: 978-0-415-06784-3.
Dewey:792.028. LCCN:92-000043.

Audience: **l,u,f.**

Pearson, Hesketh   PN2597.P4 1971
Last Actor-Managers. Trade Cloth. Ayer Company Publishers,
Inc. Manchester, NH. 1977. 83p. Biography Index Reprint Ser.
ISBN:0-8369-8072-7, ISBN13: 978-0-8369-8072-1.
Dewey:792/.028/0922. LCCN:77-148225.

Audience: **l,u,f.** *B*

Pickering, David (Editor)   PN2035.I49 1992
International Dictionary of Theatre: Actors, Directors and
Designers. Trade Cloth. Thomson Gale. Farmington Hills, MI.
1995. 830p. ISBN:1-55862-097-4, ISBN13: 978-1-55862-097-1.
Dewey:792/.03. LCCN:92-215736.

Audience: **g.** *Choice, 1995.*

Redgrave, Michael   PN2061
The Actor's Ways and Means. Paper Text. Textbook Publishers.
Temecula, CA. 2003. 90p. ISBN:0-7581-3153-4, ISBN13:
978-0-7581-3153-9. Dewey:792/.028.

Audience: **g,l,u.** *B*

Redgrave, Michael   PR4021.S8
Mask or Face: Reflections in an Actor's Mirror. Paper Text.
Textbook Publishers. Temecula, CA. 2003. 188p.
ISBN:0-7581-3142-9, ISBN13: 978-0-7581-3142-3.
Dewey:824.8.

Audience: **g,l,u.**

Rees, James   PN2287.F6
Life of Edwin Forrest with Reminiscences and Personal
Recollections. Library Binding. Reprint Services Company.
Temecula, CA. 1993. 524p. ISBN:0-7812-5285-7, ISBN13:
978-0-7812-5285-0. Dewey:B.

Audience: **g.**

Richards, Thomas   PN2859.P66G7713 1995
At Work with Grotowski on Physical Actions. Jerzy Grotowski
(Preface by). Trade Paper. Routledge. New York, NY. 1995.
152p. ISBN:0-415-12492-1, ISBN13: 978-0-415-12492-8.
Dewey:792/.0233/092. LCCN:94-023889.

Audience: **l,u,f.**

Riley, Jo   PN2871.5 .R56 1997
Chinese Theatre and the Actor in Performance. David Bradby
(Contribution by). Trade Cloth. Cambridge University Press.
New York, NY. 1997. 360p. Studies in Modern Theatre, Vol. 3
ISBN:0-521-57090-5, ISBN13: 978-0-521-57090-9.
Dewey:792/.0951. LCCN:96-031554.

Audience: **l,u,f.** *Choice, 1998.*

Ruggles, Eleanor   PN2287.B5 R9
Prince of Players: Edwin Booth. Paper Text. Textbook
Publishers. Temecula, CA. 2003. 401p. ISBN:0-7581-7575-2,
ISBN13: 978-0-7581-7575-5. Dewey:792/.028/0924.

Audience: **l,u,f.** *B*

Sheehy, Helen   PN2688.D8S48 2002
Eleonora Duse: A Biography. Trade Cloth. Alfred A. Knopf Inc.
New York, NY. 2003. 400p. ISBN:0-375-40017-6, ISBN13:
978-0-375-40017-9. Dewey:792/.028/092 B.
LCCN:2002-033997.

Audience: **l,u,f.**

Stanislavski, Constantin   PN2062.S7613 1977
Building a Character. UK-B Format Paperback. Routledge. New
York, NY. 1989. 352p. ISBN:0-87830-982-9, ISBN13:
978-0-87830-982-5. Dewey:792/.028. LCCN:89-145827.

Audience: **l,u,f.**

Stanislavski, Constantin   PN2062.S7613 1989
An Actor Prepares. Elizabeth Reynolds Hapgood (Translator).
Trade Paper. Routledge. New York, NY. 1989. 336p.
ISBN:0-87830-983-7, ISBN13: 978-0-87830-983-2.
Dewey:792/.028. LCCN:89-146170.

Audience: **l,u,f.**

Stanislavski, Constantin   PN2062.S7513 1987
Creating a Role. Hermine I. Popper (Editor), Elizabeth R.
Hapgood (Translator). Cloth Text. Routledge. New York, NY.
1987. 306p. ISBN:0-87830-024-4, ISBN13: 978-0-87830-024-2.
Dewey:792. LCCN:60-010494.

Audience: **l,u,f.**

Stanislavsky, Constantin   **PN2085.B6**
Creating a Role. Paper Text. Textbook Publishers. Temecula, CA. 2003. 271p. ISBN:0-7581-3141-0, ISBN13: 978-0-7581-3141-6. Dewey:792/.028.

Audience: **l,u,f.** *B*

Waldau, Roy S.   **PN2295.T5.W3**
Vintage Years of the Theatre Guild, 1928-1939. Trade Cloth. Press of Case Western Reserve University. Cleveland, OH. 1972. 519p. ISBN:0-8295-0203-3, ISBN13: 978-0-8295-0203-9. Dewey:792/.0973. LCCN:79-141463.

Audience: **l,u,f.** *B*

Winter, William   **PR6005.A77Z63**
Life and Art of Edwin Booth. Trade Paper. Kessinger Publishing, LLC. Whitefish, MT. 2005. ISBN:0-7661-9557-0, ISBN13: 978-0-7661-9557-8. Dewey:823.912.

Audience: **u.**

Witham, Barry B.   **PN2270.F43**
The Federal Theatre Project: A Case Study. Don B. Wilmeth (Contribution by). Trade Cloth. Cambridge University Press. New York, NY. 2003. 204p. Cambridge Studies in American Theatre and Drama Ser., Vol. 20 ISBN:0-521-82259-9, ISBN13: 978-0-521-82259-6. Dewey:792.0973. LCCN:2004-299872.

Audience: **l,u,f.** *Choice, 2004.*

Wolford, Lisa & Schechner, Richard (Editors)   **PN2598.B69**
The Grotowski Sourcebook. Trade Paper. Routledge. New York, NY. 2001. 544p. Worlds of Performance Ser. ISBN:0-415-13111-1, ISBN13: 978-0-415-13111-7. Dewey:792/.0233/092.

Audience: **l,u,f.**

Theater Production > Performance > Designers and Design

Aronson, Arnold   **PN2091.S8A73 2005**
Looking into the Abyss: Essays on Scenography. Trade Cloth. University of Michigan Press. Chicago, IL. 2005. 248p. Theater-Theory/Text/Performance Ser. ISBN:0-472-09888-8, ISBN13: 978-0-472-09888-0. Dewey:792.02/5. LCCN:2004-027782.

Audience: **l,f.**

Baker, Hendrik   **PN2085**
Stage Management and Theatrecraft: A Stage Manager's Handbook. Ed. 4. Margaret Woodward (Illustrator), Basil Dean (Foreword by). Trade Paper. J. Garnet Miller Ltd. Malvern, 2003. 392p. ISBN:0-85343-556-1, ISBN13: 978-0-85343-556-3. Dewey:792/.02. LCCN:68-016449.

Audience: **l,u.**

Baugh, Christopher   **PN2091.S8**
Theatre, Performance and Technology: The Development of Scenography in the Twentieth Century. Trade Paper, Saddle Stitched. Palgrave Macmillan. New York, NY. 2005. 272p.

Theatre and Performance Practices Ser. ISBN:1-4039-1697-7, ISBN13: 978-1-4039-1697-6. Dewey:792.02/5. LCCN:2005-047457.

Audience: **l,u,f.**

Baugh, Christopher   **PN2091.S8**
Theatre Performance and Technology: The Development of Scenography in the Twentieth Century. Graham Ley & Jane Milling (Editors). Cloth over Boards. Palgrave Macmillan. New York, NY. 2005. 272p. Theatre and Performance Practices Ser. ISBN:1-4039-1696-9, ISBN13: 978-1-4039-1696-9. Dewey:792.02/5. LCCN:2005-047457.

Audience: **l,u,f.**

Cairns, Christopher (Editor)   **PR653.R46**
Renaissance Theatre: Texts, Performance and Design, Vol. 2. Trade Cloth. Ashgate Publishing, Ltd. Aldershot, 1999. 358p. ISBN:0-7546-0008-4, ISBN13: 978-0-7546-0008-4. Dewey:822/.309.

Audience: **l,u,f.**

Cairns, Christopher (Editor)   **PR653.R46 1999**
The Renaissance Theatre - Texts, Performance and Design: English and Italian Theatre. Trade Cloth. Ashgate Publishing, Ltd. Aldershot, 1999. 200p. ISBN:0-7546-0006-8, ISBN13: 978-0-7546-0006-0. Dewey:822/.309. LCCN:99-029487.

Audience: **l,u,f.**

Cairns, Christopher (Editor)   **PN2091.S8S292 1996**
Scenery, Set and Staging in the Italian Renaissance: Studies in the Practice of Theatre. Trade Cloth. Edwin Mellen Press, The. Lewiston, NY. 1996. 340p. ISBN:0-7734-8814-6, ISBN13: 978-0-7734-8814-4. Dewey:792/.025/0945. LCCN:96-003909.

Audience: **l,u,f.**

Carter, Huntly   **PN2658.R4C3**
The Theatre of Max Reinhardt. Paper Text. Classic Books. Murrieta, CA. 2001. 332p. ISBN:0-7426-9203-5, ISBN13: 978-0-7426-9203-9. Dewey:792.0943.

Audience: **l,u,f.**

Cassin-Scott, Jack   **PN2067.C63 2004**
Costumes and Settings for Historical Plays: The Classical Period: Ancient Through Early Middle Ages. Trade Paper. Players Press, Inc. Studio City, CA. 2004. 98p. ISBN:0-88734-951-X, ISBN13: 978-0-88734-951-5. Dewey:792.02/6. LCCN:2004-044398.

Audience: **l,u,f.**

Condee, William F.   **PN2091.S8**
Theatrical Space: A Guide for Directors and Designers. Trade Paper. Scarecrow Press, Inc. Lanham, MD. 2002. 248p. ISBN:0-8108-4211-4, ISBN13: 978-0-8108-4211-3. Dewey:792/.025. LCCN:95-003311.

Audience: **l,u,f.**

Finkel, Alicia   **PN2087.G7F56 1996**
Romantic Stages: Set and Costume Design in Victorian England. Cloth Text. McFarland & Company, Incorporated Publishers. Jefferson, NC. 1996. 215p. ISBN:0-7864-0234-2, ISBN13: 978-0-7864-0234-2. Dewey:792/.025/0942. LCCN:96-639.

Audience: **l,u,f.** *Choice, 1996.*

Holloway, John   **PN2037**
Illustrated Theatre Production Guide. Paper Text. Elsevier
Science & Technology Books. Saint Louis, MO. 2002. 336p.
ISBN:0-240-80493-7, ISBN13: 978-0-240-80493-4.
Dewey:792/.02.

Audience: **l,u.**

Ingham, Rosemary   **PN2091.S8I45 1998**
From Page to Stage: How Theatre Designers Make Connections
Between Scripts and Images. Trade Paper. Heinemann.
Portsmouth, NH. 1998. 192p. ISBN:0-435-07042-8, ISBN13:
978-0-435-07042-7. Dewey:792/.025. LCCN:97-22412.

Audience: **l,u,f.**

Innes, Christopher   **PN2598.C85I562 1998**
Edward Gordon Craig: A Vision of Theatre. Ed. 2. Trade Paper.
Gordon & Breach Publishing Group. New York, NY. 1998.
352p. Contemporary Theatre Studies ISBN:90-5702-125-0,
ISBN13: 978-90-5702-125-1. Dewey:792/.0233/092.
LCCN:99-521846.

Audience: **l,u,f.**

James, Thurston   **PN2091.S8J34 2000**
The Theatre Props Handbook. Ed. 2. Trade Paper. Players Press,
Inc. Studio City, CA. 2003. 272p. ISBN:0-88734-934-X,
ISBN13: 978-0-88734-934-8. Dewey:792/.025.
LCCN:99-085744.

Audience: **l,u,f.**

Jones, Robert Edmond   **PN2091.S8**
The Dramatic Imagination: Reflections and Speculations on the
Art of the Theatre. Ed. 2. UK-B Format Paperback. Routledge.
New York, NY. 2004. 176p. A Theatre Arts Book Ser.
ISBN:0-87830-184-4, ISBN13: 978-0-87830-184-3. Dewey:792.
LCCN:2004-011710.

Audience: **l,u,f.**

Larson, Orville K.   **PN2091.S8S48**
Scene Design for Stage and Screen: Readings on the Aesthetics
and Methodology of Scene Design for Drama, Opera, Musical
Comedy, Ballet, Motion Pictures, Television and Arena Theatre.
Paper Text. Textbook Publishers. Temecula, CA. 2003. 334p.
ISBN:0-7581-8140-X, ISBN13: 978-0-7581-8140-4.
Dewey:792.025.

Audience: **l,u,f.**

Mikotowicz, Tom (Editor)   **PN2096**
Theatrical Designers: An International Biographical Dictionary.
Cloth Text. Greenwood Publishing Group, Inc. Portsmouth, NH.
1992. 408p. ISBN:0-313-26270-5, ISBN13: 978-0-313-26270-8.
Dewey:792/.025/03 B. LCCN:91-028086.

Audience: **g.** *Choice, 1993.*

Moody, James L.   **PN2086.M66 2002**
The Business of Theatrical Design. Trade Paper. Allworth Press.
New York, NY. 2002. 288p. ISBN:1-58115-248-5, ISBN13:
978-1-58115-248-7. Dewey:792/.025/023. LCCN:2002-013999.

Audience: **l,u.** *Choice, 2003.*

Orton, Keith   **PN2091.S8**
Model Making for the Stage: A Practical Guide. Trade Cloth.
Crowood Press, Limited, The. Wiltshire, 2005. 160p.
ISBN:1-86126-690-1, ISBN13: 978-1-86126-690-3.
Dewey:792/.025.

Audience: **l,u.** *Choice, 2005.*

Owen, Bobbi   **PN2091**
Lighting Design on Broadway: Designers and Their Credits,
1915-1990. Cloth Text. Greenwood Publishing Group, Inc.
Portsmouth, NH. 1991. 176p. Bibliographies and Indexes in the
Performing Arts Ser., No. 11 ISBN:0-313-26533-X, ISBN13:
978-0-313-26533-4. Dewey:792/.025/09227471 B.
LCCN:91-024007.

Audience: **g.**

Owen, Bobbi   **PN2096**
Scenic Design on Broadway: Designers and Their Credits,
1915-1990. Cloth Text. Greenwood Publishing Group, Inc.
Portsmouth, NH. 1991. 320p. Bibliographies and Indexes in the
Performing Arts Ser., No. 10 ISBN:0-313-26534-8, ISBN13:
978-0-313-26534-1. Dewey:792.02509227471.
LCCN:91-025254.

Audience: **l,u,f.** *Choice, 1992.*

Parker, W. Oren, et al.   **PN2091.S8**
Scene Design and Stage Lighting. Ed. 8. R. Craig Wolf & Dick
Block (Authors). Cloth Text. Thomson Wadsworth. Belmont,
CA. 2002. 672p. ISBN:0-15-506114-3, ISBN13:
978-0-15-506114-9. Dewey:792/.025. LCCN:2002-103124.

Audience: **l,u,f.**

Parker, W. Oren, et al.   **PN2091.S8P3 2003**
Scene Design and Stage Lighting. Ed. 8. R. Craig Wolf & Dick
Block (Authors). Cloth Text. Thomson Wadsworth. Belmont,
CA. 2002. 608p. ISBN:0-534-25985-5, ISBN13:
978-0-534-25985-3. Dewey:792/.025. LCCN:2002-103124.

Audience: **l,u,f.**

Pecktal, Lynn   **PN2091.S8P36 1995**
Designing and Drawing for the Theater. Cloth Text.
McGraw-Hill Higher Education. Burr Ridge, IL. 1994. 608p.
ISBN:0-07-557232-X, ISBN13: 978-0-07-557232-9.
Dewey:792/.025. LCCN:94-021038.

Audience: **l,u.**

Pickering, David (Editor)   **PN2035.I49 1992**
International Dictionary of Theatre: Actors, Directors and
Designers. Trade Cloth. Thomson Gale. Farmington Hills, MI.
1995. 830p. ISBN:1-55862-097-4, ISBN13: 978-1-55862-097-1.
Dewey:792/.03. LCCN:92-215736.

Audience: **g.** *Choice, 1996.*

Reid, Francis   **PN2037**
The Staging Handbook. Trade Paper. Routledge. New York, NY.
2002. 96p. Globe Quartos Ser. ISBN:0-87830-160-7, ISBN13:
978-0-87830-160-7. Dewey:792/.02.

Audience: **l,u,f.**

Sayler, Oliver M. (Editor) PN2658.R4
Max Reinhardt and His Theatre. Trade Cloth. Ayer Company
Publishers, Inc. Manchester, NH. 1972. 381p.
ISBN:0-405-08926-0, ISBN13: 978-0-405-08926-8.
Dewey:792/.0924 B. LCCN:68-020245.
Audience: **l,u.**

Schlemmer, Oskar PN2221.H4
The Theater of the Bauhaus. Paper Text. Textbook Publishers.
Temecula, CA. 2003. 109p. ISBN:0-7581-0604-1, ISBN13:
978-0-7581-0604-9. Dewey:792.0973.
Audience: **l,u,f.**

Serlio, Sebastiano PN2221.H76
The Renaissance Stage: Documents of Serlio, Sabbattini and
Furttenbach. Paper Text. Textbook Publishers. Temecula, CA.
2003. 256p. ISBN:0-7581-2129-6, ISBN13: 978-0-7581-2129-5.
Dewey:792.
Audience: **u,f.** *B*

Simonson, Lee PN2091.S8 S536 1975
The Stage Is Set. Trade Cloth. Ayer Company Publishers, Inc.
Manchester, NH. 1977. New Reprints in Essay and General
Literature Index Ser. ISBN:0-518-10206-8, ISBN13:
978-0-518-10206-9. Dewey:792. LCCN:75-014368.
Audience: **l,u,f.** *B*

Sofer, Andrew PN2091.S8S616 2003
The Stage Life of Props. Trade Paper. University of Michigan
Press. Chicago, IL. 2003. 272p. Theater Ser.,
:Theory/Text/Performance ISBN:0-472-06839-3, ISBN13:
978-0-472-06839-5. Dewey:792/.025. LCCN:2002-154228.
Audience: **l,u.** *Choice, 2004.*

Stell, W. Joseph PN2091.S8S73 2001
Scenery: Design and Fabrication. Trade Paper. Players Press,
Inc. Studio City, CA. 2003. 256p. Technical Theatre, Film and
Television Ser. ISBN:0-88734-663-4, ISBN13:
978-0-88734-663-7. Dewey:792/.025. LCCN:2001-036371.
Audience: **l,u.** *Choice, 2002.*

Todd, Andrew & Lecat, PN2598.B69T63 2003
Jean Guys
The Open Circle: The Theater Environment of Peter Brook.
Cloth over Boards. Palgrave Macmillan. New York, NY. 2003.
160p. ISBN:1-4039-6362-2, ISBN13: 978-1-4039-6362-8.
Dewey:792.02/33/092. LCCN:2003-060829.
Audience: **l,u,f.**

White, Christine A. & PN2091.S8
Carver, Gavin
Computer Visualization for the Theatre: 3D Modelling for
Designers. Trade Paper. Elsevier Science & Technology Books.
Saint Louis, MO. 2003. 240p. ISBN:0-240-51617-6, ISBN13:
978-0-240-51617-2. Dewey:792/.025/0285. LCCN:2003-052765.
Audience: **l,u,f.**

Theater Production > Performance > Lighting, Sets, Scenery

Boulanger, Norman C. PN2091.E4.B59 1992
Theatre Lighting from A to Z. Trade Paper. University of
Washington Press. Seattle, WA. 1992. 206p.
ISBN:0-295-97214-9, ISBN13: 978-0-295-97214-5.
Dewey:792/.023/03. LCCN:92-014620.
Audience: **l,u,f.** *Choice, 1993.*

Carter, Huntly PN2658.R4C3
The Theatre of Max Reinhardt. Paper Text. Classic Books.
Murrieta, CA. 2001. 332p. ISBN:0-7426-9203-5, ISBN13:
978-0-7426-9203-9. Dewey:792.0943.
Audience: **l,u,f.**

Finkel, Alicia PN2087.G7
Romantic Stages: Set and Costume Design in Victorian England.
Trade Paper, Perfect. McFarland & Company, Incorporated
Publishers. Jefferson, NC. 2005. 215p. ISBN:0-7864-2336-6,
ISBN13: 978-0-7864-2336-1. Dewey:792/.025/0942.
LCCN:96-000639.
Audience: **u,f.** *Choice, 1996.*

Finkel, Alicia PN2087.G7F56 1996
Romantic Stages: Set and Costume Design in Victorian England.
Cloth Text. McFarland & Company, Incorporated Publishers.
Jefferson, NC. 1996. 215p. ISBN:0-7864-0234-2, ISBN13:
978-0-7864-0234-2. Dewey:792/.025/0942. LCCN:96-639.
Audience: **l,u,f.** *Choice, 1996.*

Fraser, Neil PN2091.S6
Lighting and Sound. Trade Paper. Phaidon Press. London, 1994.
132p. Theatre Manuals Ser. ISBN:0-7148-2514-X, ISBN13:
978-0-7148-2514-4. Dewey:792/.025.
Audience: **l,u,f.**

McCandless, Stanley PN2091.S8S3313
A Method of Lighting the Stage. Paper Text. Textbook
Publishers. Temecula, CA. 2003. 143p. ISBN:0-7581-3143-7,
ISBN13: 978-0-7581-3143-0. Dewey:792/.025.
Audience: **l,u,f.**

Owen, Bobbi PN2091
Lighting Design on Broadway: Designers and Their Credits,
1915-1990. Cloth Text. Greenwood Publishing Group, Inc.
Portsmouth, NH. 1991. 176p. Bibliographies and Indexes in the
Performing Arts Ser., No. 11 ISBN:0-313-26533-X, ISBN13:
978-0-313-26533-4. Dewey:792/.025/09227471 B.
LCCN:91-024007.
Audience: **g.**

Parker, W. Oren, et al. PN2091.S8
Scene Design and Stage Lighting. Ed. 8. R. Craig Wolf & Dick
Block (Authors). Cloth Text. Thomson Wadsworth. Belmont,
CA. 2002. 672p. ISBN:0-15-506114-3, ISBN13:
978-0-15-506114-9. Dewey:792/.025. LCCN:2002-103124.
Audience: **l,u,f.**

Parker, W. Oren, et al.   PN2091.S8P3 2003
Scene Design and Stage Lighting. Ed. 8. R. Craig Wolf & Dick Block (Authors). Cloth Text. Thomson Wadsworth. Belmont, CA. 2002. 608p. ISBN:0-534-25985-5, ISBN13: 978-0-534-25985-3. Dewey:792/.025. LCCN:2002-103124.

Audience: **l,u,f.**

Pilbrow, Richard   PN2091.E4P52 1997
Stage Lighting Design: The Art - The Craft - The Life. Paper Text. Quite Specific Media Group, Ltd. Hollywood, CA. 1997. 528p. ISBN:0-89676-235-1, ISBN13: 978-0-89676-235-0. Dewey:792/.025. LCCN:92-026071.

Audience: **l,u,f.**

Reed, Francis   PN2091.E4
The ABC of Stage Lighting. Paper Text. Quite Specific Media Group, Ltd. Hollywood, CA. 1992. 144p. ISBN:0-89676-119-3, ISBN13: 978-0-89676-119-3. Dewey:792.025.

Audience: **g.** *Choice, 1993.*

Simonson, Lee   PN2091.S8 S536 1975
The Stage Is Set. Trade Cloth. Ayer Company Publishers, Inc. Manchester, NH. 1977. New Reprints in Essay and General Literature Index Ser. ISBN:0-518-10206-8, ISBN13: 978-0-518-10206-9. Dewey:792. LCCN:75-014368.

Audience: **l,u,f.** *B*

Swift, Charles I.   PN2091.E4S95 2004
Introduction to Stage Lighting: The Fundamentals of Theatre Lighting Design. Trade Paper. Meriwether Publishing, Ltd. Colorado Springs, CO. 2004. 161p. New Fall Titles Ser. ISBN:1-56608-098-3, ISBN13: 978-1-56608-098-9. Dewey:792.02/5. LCCN:2004-014999.

Audience: **l,u.** *Choice, 2005.*

Theater Production > Performance > Management and Production

     PN2596.L7.R515 1981
At the Royal Court: 25 Years of the English Stage Company. Trade Cloth. Bow Historical Books. New Providence, NJ. 1981. 201, [56]p. ISBN:0-8021-0211-5, ISBN13: 978-0-8021-0211-9. Dewey:792/.09421/34. LCCN:80-085375.

Audience: **u,f.** *B*

Aaron, Melissa D.   PR3095.A15 2005
Global Economics: A History of the Theater Business, the Chamberlain's/King's Men, and Their Plays, 1599-1642. Trade Cloth. University of Delaware Press. Newark, DE. 2005. 256p. ISBN:0-87413-877-9, ISBN13: 978-0-87413-877-1. Dewey:792.9/5/0942109031. LCCN:2004-029998.

Audience: **l,f.**

Arundell, Dennis   PN2596.L7S3
The Story of Sadler's Wells, 1683-1977. Ed. 2. Trade Cloth. David & Charles Publishers. Newton Abbot, 1978. 352p. ISBN:0-7153-7620-9, ISBN13: 978-0-7153-7620-1. Dewey:792/.09421/43. LCCN:78-316129.

Audience: **u,f.** *B*

Baker, Hendrik   PN2085
Stage Management and Theatrecraft: A Stage Manager's Handbook. Ed. 4. Margaret Woodward (Illustrator), Basil Dean (Foreword by). Trade Paper. J. Garnet Miller Ltd. Malvern, 2003. 392p. ISBN:0-85343-556-1, ISBN13: 978-0-85343-556-3. Dewey:792/.02. LCCN:68-016449.

Audience: **l,u.**

Brecht, Bertolt   PN2037
Brecht on Theatre: The Development of an Aesthetic. Ed. 2. Trade Paper. Methuen Publishing Ltd. London, 2003. ISBN:0-413-38800-X, ISBN13: 978-0-413-38800-1. Dewey:792. LCCN:63-018479.

Audience: **l,u,f.** *B*

Celentano, Suzanne C. &   PN2053.C354 1998
  Marshall, Kevin
Theatre Management: A Successful Guide to Producing Plays on Commercial and Non-Profit Stages. Trade Paper. Players Press, Inc. Studio City, CA. 2003. 208p. ISBN:0-88734-684-7, ISBN13: 978-0-88734-684-2. Dewey:792/.068. LCCN:98-005835.

Audience: **l,u.**

Chambers, Colin   PN2596.S82R684 2004
Inside the Royal Shakespeare Company: Creativity and the Institution. Paper over Boards. Routledge. New York, NY. 2004. 280p. ISBN:0-415-21202-2, ISBN13: 978-0-415-21202-1. Dewey:792/.0942. LCCN:2003-015745.

Audience: **l,u,f.**

Dean, Peter   PN2053
Production Management: Making Shows Happen. Trade Paper. Crowood Press, Limited, The. Wiltshire, 2002. 192p. ISBN:1-86126-451-8, ISBN13: 978-1-86126-451-0. Dewey:792/.0232.

Audience: **l,u.**

Dent, Edward J.   PN2596.L7 O73 1979
A Theatre for Everybody: The Story of the Old Vic and Sadler's Wells. Kay Ambrose (Illustrator). Trade Cloth. Hyperion Press, Inc. Westport, CT. 1979. ISBN:0-88355-691-X, ISBN13: 978-0-88355-691-7. Dewey:792/.09421/2. LCCN:78-010887.

Audience: **l,u,f.**

Eaton, Walter P.   PN2295.T5.E3 1970
Theatre Guild, the First Ten Years, with Articles by the Directors. Trade Cloth. Ayer Company Publishers, Inc. Manchester, NH. 1977. 299p. Select Bibliographies Reprint Ser. ISBN:0-8369-5180-8, ISBN13: 978-0-8369-5180-6. Dewey:792/.0973. LCCN:75-107799.

Audience: **l,u,f.** *B*

Egan, Leona Rust   PS3529.N5Z6294 1994
Provincetown as a Stage: Provincetown, the Provincetown Players, and the Discovery of Eugene O'Neill. Trade Cloth. Parnassus Imprints. Marstons Mills, MA. 1994. 296p. ISBN:0-940160-57-9, ISBN13: 978-0-940160-57-6. Dewey:792.097. LCCN:93-087449.

Audience: **l,u,f.**

Grippo, Charles   **PN2053.G696 2002**
The Stage Producer's Business and Legal Guide. Trade Paper.
Allworth Press. New York, NY. 2002. 256p.
ISBN:1-58115-241-8, ISBN13: 978-1-58115-241-8.
Dewey:792/.0232. LCCN:2002-006264.

Audience: **l,u,f.**

Guinn, David E. &   **KF4290 .O74**
  Orenstein, Harold
Entertainment Law and Business. Ringbound, 3.5 Diskette. Juris
Publishing, Inc. Huntington, NY. 2004. 750p.
ISBN:1-57823-148-5, ISBN13: 978-1-57823-148-5.
Dewey:343.73/0787902 347.3.

Audience: **l,u,f.**

Maccoy, Peter   **PN2053**
Essentials of Stage Management. Nicholas Hytner (Foreword
by). UK-B Format Paperback. Routledge. New York, NY. 2004.
256p. ISBN:0-87830-199-2, ISBN13: 978-0-87830-199-7.
Dewey:792/.023.

Audience: **l,u.**

Moody, James L.   **PN2086.M66 2002**
The Business of Theatrical Design. Trade Paper. Allworth Press.
New York, NY. 2002. 288p. ISBN:1-58115-248-5, ISBN13:
978-1-58115-248-7. Dewey:792/.025/023. LCCN:2002-013999.

Audience: **l,u.** *Choice, 2003.*

Pearson, Hesketh   **PN2597.P4 1971**
Last Actor-Managers. Trade Cloth. Ayer Company Publishers,
Inc. Manchester, NH. 1977. 83p. Biography Index Reprint Ser.
ISBN:0-8369-8072-7, ISBN13: 978-0-8369-8072-1.
Dewey:792/.028/0922. LCCN:77-148225.

Audience: **l,u,f.** *B*

Schneider, Richard E. &   **PN2073.S35**
  Ford, Mary Jo
Theater Management Handbook. Trade Paper. F & W
Publications, Inc. Cincinnati, OH. 1999. 128p.
ISBN:1-55870-620-8, ISBN13: 978-1-55870-620-0.
Dewey:792.068.

Audience: **l,u.**

Stern, Lawrence   **PN2085.S77 2005**
Stage Management. Ed. 8. Trade Paper. Allyn & Bacon, Inc.
Boston, MA. 2005. 352p. ISBN:0-205-44973-5, ISBN13:
978-0-205-44973-6. Dewey:792/.068. LCCN:2005-049980.

Audience: **l,u.**

Waldau, Roy S.   **PN2295.T5.W3**
Vintage Years of the Theatre Guild, 1928-1939. Trade Cloth.
Press of Case Western Reserve University. Cleveland, OH. 1972.
519p. ISBN:0-8295-0203-3, ISBN13: 978-0-8295-0203-9.
Dewey:792/.0973. LCCN:79-141463.

Audience: **l,u,f.** *B*

Webb, Duncan M.   **PN2053.W36 2004**
Running Theaters: Best Practices for Leaders and Managers.
Michael Kaiser (Foreword by). Trade Paper. Allworth Press.
New York, NY. 2005. 256p. ISBN:1-58115-393-7, ISBN13:
978-1-58115-393-4. Dewey:792/.068. LCCN:2004-021394.

Audience: **l,u,f.**

Witham, Barry B.   **PN2270.F43**
The Federal Theatre Project: A Case Study. Don B. Wilmeth
(Contribution by). Trade Cloth. Cambridge University Press.
New York, NY. 2003. 204p. Cambridge Studies in American
Theatre and Drama Ser., Vol. 20 ISBN:0-521-82259-9, ISBN13:
978-0-521-82259-6. Dewey:792.0973. LCCN:2004-299872.

Audience: **l,u,f.** *Choice, 2004.*

Theater Production > Performance > Costume and Make-up

Barton, Lucy   **GT525**
Historic Costume for the Stage. D. Sarvis (Illustrator). Trade
Cloth. Baker's Plays. Quincy, MA. 1961. ISBN:0-87440-002-3,
ISBN13: 978-0-87440-002-1. Dewey:391.

Audience: **l,u,f.** *B*

Bicat, Tina   **PN2067**
Period Costume for the Stage: A Practical Guide. Trade Paper.
Crowood Press, Limited, The. Wiltshire, 2003. 160p.
ISBN:1-86126-589-1, ISBN13: 978-1-86126-589-0.
Dewey:792.02/6. LCCN:2005-360221.

Audience: **l,u.**

Brooke, Iris & Landes,   **GT720.B733 1993**
  William-Alan
Western European Costume Thirteenth to Seventeenth Century.
Trade Paper. Players Press, Inc. Studio City, CA. 2003. 192p.
ISBN:0-88734-635-9, ISBN13: 978-0-88734-635-4.
Dewey:391/.0094. LCCN:93-036612.

Audience: **l,u,f.**

Cassin-Scott, Jack   **PN2067.C63 2004**
Costumes and Settings for Historical Plays: The Classical
Period: Ancient Through Early Middle Ages. Trade Paper.
Players Press, Inc. Studio City, CA. 2004. 98p.
ISBN:0-88734-951-X, ISBN13: 978-0-88734-951-5.
Dewey:792.02/6. LCCN:2004-044398.

Audience: **l,u,f.**

Corson, Richard   **PN2068 .C65**
Stage Makeup: Special Edition. Ed. 8. Trade Cloth. Prentice
Hall PTR. Upper Saddle River, NJ. 1992. 416p.
ISBN:0-13-840174-8, ISBN13: 978-0-13-840174-0.
Dewey:792/.027.

Audience: **l,u.**

Corson, Richard & Glavan,   **PN2068.C65 2000**
  James
Stage Makeup. Ed. 9. Cloth Text. Allyn & Bacon, Inc. Boston,
MA. 2000. 432p. ISBN:0-13-606153-2, ISBN13:
978-0-13-606153-3. Dewey:792/.027. LCCN:00-046879.

Audience: **l,u.**

Craik, T. W.   **PN2596.L6R6**
The Tudor Interlude: Stage, Costume, and Acting. Paper Text.
Textbook Publishers. Temecula, CA. 2003. 158p.
ISBN:0-7581-1342-0, ISBN13: 978-0-7581-1342-9.
Dewey:792.09421.

Audience: **u,f.** *B*

Finkel, Alicia   **PN2087.G7**
Romantic Stages: Set and Costume Design in Victorian England.
Trade Paper, Perfect. McFarland & Company, Incorporated
Publishers. Jefferson, NC. 2005. 215p. ISBN:0-7864-2336-6,
ISBN13: 978-0-7864-2336-1. Dewey:792/.025/0942.
LCCN:96-000639.

Audience: **u,f.** *Choice, 1996.*

Finkel, Alicia   **PN2087.G7F56 1996**
Romantic Stages: Set and Costume Design in Victorian England.
Cloth Text. McFarland & Company, Incorporated Publishers.
Jefferson, NC. 1996. 215p. ISBN:0-7864-0234-2, ISBN13:
978-0-7864-0234-2. Dewey:792/.025/0942. LCCN:96-639.
Audience: **l,u,f.** *Choice, 1996.*

Hunnisett, Jean   **TT520.H93 1990**
Period Costume for Stage and Screen: Patterns for Women's
Dress, 1500-1800. Trade Cloth. Players Press, Inc. Studio City,
CA. 2003. 176p. ISBN:0-88734-610-3, ISBN13:
978-0-88734-610-1. Dewey:646.4/7804/0903. LCCN:90-050385.
Audience: **l,u,f.**

Hunnisett, Jean   **TT520.H933 1990**
Period Costume for Stage and Screen: Patterns for Women's
Dress, 1800-1909. Trade Cloth. Players Press, Inc. Studio City,
CA. 2003. 192p. ISBN:0-88734-609-X, ISBN13:
978-0-88734-609-5. Dewey:646.4/7804/09034.
LCCN:90-043905.

Audience: **l,u,f.**

Hunnisett, Jean   **TT633**
Period Costume for Stage and Screen: Dominos, Dolmans,
Coats, Pelisses, Spencers, Callashes, Hoods and Bonnets. Fiona
Foulkes, Kathryn Turner & Jill Spanner (Illustrators). Trade
Cloth. Players Press, Inc. Studio City, CA. 2003. 176p.
ISBN:0-88734-670-7, ISBN13: 978-0-88734-670-5.
Dewey:646.478.

Audience: **l,u,f.** *Choice, 2004.*

Hunnisett, Jean   **TT530.H86 2001**
Period Costume for Stage and Screen: Patterns for Outer
Garments: Cloaks, Capes, Stoles and Wadded Mantles.
William-Alan Landes (Editor). Trade Cloth. Players Press, Inc.
Studio City, CA. 2003. 176p. ISBN:0-88734-665-0, ISBN13:
978-0-88734-665-1. Dewey:646.4/78. LCCN:00-053733.
Audience: **l,u,f.**

Hunnisett, Jean   **TT520.H933 1996**
Period Costume for Stage and Screen: Medieval-1500. Kathryn
Turner (Illustrator). Trade Cloth. Players Press, Inc. Studio City,
CA. 2003. 192p. ISBN:0-88734-653-7, ISBN13:
978-0-88734-653-8. Dewey:646.4/7804/0902. LCCN:95-050302.
Audience: **l,u,f.**

Jowers, Sidney Jackson   **Z5691.J68 2000**
Theatrical Costume, Masks, Make-Up and Wigs: A Bibliography
and Iconography. John Cavanagh (Editor). Paper over Boards.
Routledge. New York, NY. 2000. 542p. Motley Bibliographies
Ser., Vol. 4 ISBN:0-415-24774-8, ISBN13: 978-0-415-24774-0.
Dewey:792/.026. LCCN:00-062573.
Audience: **g.** *Choice, 2001.*

Laver, James   **PN2091.S8L29**
Drama, Its Costume and Decor. Paper Text. Textbook
Publishers. Temecula, CA. 2003. 276p. ISBN:0-7581-3367-7,
ISBN13: 978-0-7581-3367-0. Dewey:792.025.

Audience: **l,u.**

Menglin, Zhao & Jiqing,   **TN414.C6W4**
 Yan
Peking Opera Painted Faces with Notes on 200 Operas. Trade
Cloth. Morning Glory Press. Beijing, 1996. 142p.
ISBN:7-5054-0412-1, ISBN13: 978-7-5054-0412-0.
Dewey:622.3421.

Audience: **u,f.**

O'Donnol, Shirley M.   **PN2067.O3 1982**
American Costume, 1915-1970: A Source Book for the Stage
Costumer. Lucy Barton (Foreword by). Trade Cloth. Indiana
University Press. Bloomington, IN. 1982. 286p.
ISBN:0-253-30589-6, ISBN13: 978-0-253-30589-3.
Dewey:792/.026. LCCN:81-048390.

Audience: **l,u,f.**

Swinfield, Rosemarie   **PN2068**
Period Make-Up for the Stage. Trade Cloth. F & W
Publications, Inc. Cincinnati, OH. 1997. 128p.
ISBN:1-55870-468-X, ISBN13: 978-1-55870-468-8.
Dewey:792.027.

Audience: **l,u,f.**

Thudium, Laura   **PN2068.T48 1999**
Stage Makeup: The Actor's Complete Guide to Today's
Techniques and Materials. Trade Cloth. Watson-Guptill
Publications, Inc. New York, NY. 1999. 160p.
ISBN:0-8230-8839-1, ISBN13: 978-0-8230-8839-3.
Dewey:792/.027. LCCN:98-053214.

Audience: **l,u,f.**

Theater Production > Performance > Directors

Barba, Eugenio & Savarese,   **PN2041.A57A5313 2005**
 Nicola (Editors)
A Dictionary of Theatre Anthropology: The Secret Art of the
Performer. Ed. 2. Paper Text. Routledge. New York, NY. 2006.
288p. ISBN:0-415-37861-3, ISBN13: 978-0-415-37861-1.
Dewey:795/.03. LCCN:2005-051690.

Audience: **u,f.**

Barrault, Jean-Louis   **PN2638.B27 A313**
Reflections on the Theatre. Paper Text. Textbook Publishers.
Temecula, CA. 2003. 185p. ISBN:0-7581-4777-5, ISBN13:
978-0-7581-4777-6. Dewey:792/.092/4.

Audience: **l,u,f.** *B*

Barton, Margaret   **PN2598.G3 B3 1978**
Garrick. Trade Cloth. Greenwood Publishing Group, Inc.
Portsmouth, NH. 1978. 312p. ISBN:0-313-20270-2, ISBN13:
978-0-313-20270-4. Dewey:792/.028/0924. LCCN:78-000612.
Audience: **g,l,u,f.** *B*

Bogart, Anne   **PN2053.B59 2001**
A Director Prepares: Seven Essays on Art and Theatre.
Routledge. 2001. ISBN:0-415-23831-5, ISBN13:
978-0-415-23831-1.

Audience: **g,l,u,f.**

Braun, E.   **PN2053**
Director and the Stage. Trade Paper. Methuen Publishing Ltd.
London, 2003. ISBN:0-413-46300-1, ISBN13:
978-0-413-46300-5. Dewey:792/.0233/094/09034.

Audience: **l,u,f.**

Brecht, Bertolt   **PN2037**
Brecht on Theatre: The Development of an Aesthetic. Ed. 2.
Trade Paper. Methuen Publishing Ltd. London, 2003.
ISBN:0-413-38800-X, ISBN13: 978-0-413-38800-1. Dewey:792.
LCCN:63-018479.

Audience: **l,u,f.** *B*

Brook, Peter   **PN1655.B75 2005**
The Open Door. UK-Trade Paper. Knopf Publishing Group.
New York, NY. 2005. 160p. ISBN:1-4000-7787-7, ISBN13:
978-1-4000-7787-8. Dewey:792. LCCN:2004-059494.

Audience: **l,u,f.**

Burnim, Kalman A.   **PN2638.S27A5**
David Garrick, Director. Paper Text. Textbook Publishers.
Temecula, CA. 2003. 234p. ISBN:0-7581-1616-0, ISBN13:
978-0-7581-1616-1. Dewey:792.081.

Audience: **l,u,f.** *B*

Carter, Huntly   **PN2658.R4C3**
The Theatre of Max Reinhardt. Paper Text. Classic Books.
Murrieta, CA. 2001. 332p. ISBN:0-7426-9203-5, ISBN13:
978-0-7426-9203-9. Dewey:792.0943.

Audience: **l,u,f.**

Chekhov, Michael   **PN2053**
To the Director and Playwright. Charles Leonard (Compiled by).
Trade Cloth. Greenwood Publishing Group, Inc. Portsmouth,
NH. 1977. 329p. ISBN:0-8371-9615-9, ISBN13:
978-0-8371-9615-2. Dewey:792/.0233. LCCN:77-008158.

Audience: **l,u.** *B*

Clurman, Harold   **PN2053.C54 1997**
On Directing. Trade Paper. Simon & Schuster. New York, NY.
1997. 336p. ISBN:0-684-82622-4, ISBN13: 978-0-684-82622-6.
Dewey:792/.0233. LCCN:96-046762.

Audience: **l,u,f.** *B*

Cole, Susan   **PN2071.R45.C64 1992**
Directors in Rehearsal: A Hidden World. Cloth Text. Routledge.
New York, NY. 1992. 352p. ISBN:0-87830-018-X, ISBN13:
978-0-87830-018-1. Dewey:792.02330922. LCCN:92-000059.

Audience: **l,u,f.** *Choice, 1993.*

Cole, Toby & Chinoy, Helen   **PN2053**
  Krich
Directors on Directing: A Source Book of the Modern Theatre.

Ed. 1. Trade Paper. Allyn & Bacon, Inc. Boston, MA. 1963.
440p. ISBN:0-02-323300-1, ISBN13: 978-0-02-323300-5.
Dewey:792/.0232/08.

Audience: **l,u,f.** *B*

Condee, William F.   **PN2091.S8**
Theatrical Space: A Guide for Directors and Designers. Trade
Paper. Scarecrow Press, Inc. Lanham, MD. 2002. 248p.
ISBN:0-8108-4211-4, ISBN13: 978-0-8108-4211-3.
Dewey:792/.025. LCCN:95-003311.

Audience: **l,u,f.**

Eaton, Walter P.   **PN2295.T5.E3 1970**
Theatre Guild, the First Ten Years, with Articles by the
Directors. Trade Cloth. Ayer Company Publishers, Inc.
Manchester, NH. 1977. 299p. Select Bibliographies Reprint Ser.
ISBN:0-8369-5180-8, ISBN13: 978-0-8369-5180-6.
Dewey:792/.0973. LCCN:75-107799.

Audience: **l,u,f.** *B*

Gardner, Bonnie Milne   **PS352.G37 2001**
The Emergence of the Playwright-Director in American Theatre,
1960-1983. Trade Cloth. Edwin Mellen Press, The. Lewiston,
NY. 2001. 236p. Studies in Theatre Arts, Vol. 15
ISBN:0-7734-7470-6, ISBN13: 978-0-7734-7470-3.
Dewey:892.4/2608. LCCN:00-065373.

Audience: **l,u,f.**

Guthrie, Tyrone   **PN2658.P5**
A Life in the Theatre. Paper Text. Textbook Publishers.
Temecula, CA. 2003. 357p. ISBN:0-7581-8744-0, ISBN13:
978-0-7581-8744-4. Dewey:792/.0233/0924.

Audience: **g,l,u,f.** *B*

Hall, Peter   **PN2101**
The Necessary Theatre. Trade Paper. Nick Hern Books, Ltd.
London, 2002. 64p. ISBN:1-85459-402-8, ISBN13:
978-1-85459-402-0. Dewey:792/.09.

Audience: **l,u,f.**

Hostetter, Anthony   **PN2656.B42G764 2003**
Max Reinhardt's Grosses Schauspielhaus: Its Artistic Goals,
Planning, and Operation, 1910-1933. Trade Cloth. Edwin Mellen
Press, The. Lewiston, NY. 2003. 224p. Studies in Theatre Arts,
Vol. 20 ISBN:0-7734-6802-1, ISBN13: 978-0-7734-6802-3.
Dewey:330 /945/58. LCCN:2003-042163.

Audience: **l,u,f.**

Kantor, Tadeusz   **PN2859.P6.K36 1993**
A Journey Through Other Spaces: Essays and Manifestos,
1944-1990. Michal Kobialka (Editor, Translator). Trade Cloth.
University of California Press. Berkeley, CA. 1993. 451p.
ISBN:0-520-07911-6, ISBN13: 978-0-520-07911-3.
Dewey:792.09438. LCCN:92-036296.

Audience: **u,f.** *Choice, 1994.*

Knapp, Bettina   **PN2634.K5 1988**
The Reign of the Theatrical Director: French Theatre:
1887-1924. Trade Cloth. Whitston Publishing Company, Inc.
Albany, NY. 1988. 273p. ISBN:0-87875-358-3, ISBN13:
978-0-87875-358-1. Dewey:792/.0233/0922. LCCN:87-051204.

Audience: **l,u,f.** *Choice, 1989.*

Leach, Robert   **PN2728.M4**
Vsevolod Meyerhold. Christopher Innes (Contribution by). Trade
Paper. Cambridge University Press. New York, NY. 1993. 237p.
Directors in Perspective Ser. ISBN:0-521-31843-2, ISBN13:
978-0-521-31843-3. Dewey:792/.0233/0924.
                              Audience: **l,u,f.** *Choice, 1990.*

Leiter, Samuel L.   **PN2597**
From Belasco to Brook: Representative Directors of the
English-Speaking Stage. Trade Cloth. Greenwood Publishing
Group, Inc. Portsmouth, NH. 1991. 320p. Contributions in
Drama and Theatre Studies Ser., No. 33 ISBN:0-313-27662-5,
ISBN13: 978-0-313-27662-0. Dewey:792/.0233/0922 B.
LCCN:90-045350.
                              Audience: **l,u,f.** *Choice, 1991.*

Pickering, David (Editor)   **PN2035.I49 1992**
International Dictionary of Theatre: Actors, Directors and
Designers. Trade Cloth. Thomson Gale. Farmington Hills, MI.
1995. 830p. ISBN:1-55862-097-4, ISBN13: 978-1-55862-097-1.
Dewey:792/.03. LCCN:92-215736.
                              Audience: **g.** *Choice, 1996.*

Richards, Thomas   **PN2859.P66G7713 1995**
At Work with Grotowski on Physical Actions. Jerzy Grotowski
(Preface by). Trade Paper. Routledge. New York, NY. 1995.
152p. ISBN:0-415-12492-1, ISBN13: 978-0-415-12492-8.
Dewey:792/.0233/092. LCCN:94-023889.
                              Audience: **l,u,f.**

Roberts, J. W.   **PN2287.B484 R6 1981**
Richard Boleslavsky: His Life and Work in the Theatre. Trade
Paper. Books on Demand. Ann Arbor, MI. 298p. Theater and
Dramatic Studies, Vol. 7 ISBN:0-8357-1250-8, ISBN13:
978-0-8357-1250-7. Dewey:792/.0233/0924. LCCN:81-016411.
                              Audience: **l,u,f.**

Saint-Denis, Michel   **DT30.5**
Theatre, the Rediscovery of Style. Paper Text. Textbook
Publishers. Temecula, CA. 2003. 110p. ISBN:0-7581-3148-8,
ISBN13: 978-0-7581-3148-5. Dewey:320.96.
                              Audience: **l,u,f.**

Sayler, Oliver M. (Editor)   **PN2658.R4**
Max Reinhardt and His Theatre. Trade Cloth. Ayer Company
Publishers, Inc. Manchester, NH. 1972. 381p.
ISBN:0-405-08926-0, ISBN13: 978-0-405-08926-8.
Dewey:792/.0924 B. LCCN:68-020245.
                              Audience: **l,u.**

Shelton, Lewis E.   **PN2256.S54 2005**
Ideas of Theatre: The Five Directorial Perspectives of the
American Stage. Library Binding. Academica Press, LLC.
Bethesda, MD. 2005. 364p. ISBN:1-933146-04-4, ISBN13:
978-1-933146-04-1. Dewey:792.02/33/092273.
LCCN:2005-002998.
                              Audience: **l,u,f.**

Stone, George W. Jr. &   **PN2598.G3.S67**
  Kahrl, George M.
David Garrick: A Critical Biography. Trade Cloth. Southern
Illinois University Press. Carbondale, IL. 1979. 791p.
ISBN:0-8093-0931-9, ISBN13: 978-0-8093-0931-3.
Dewey:792/.028/0924. LCCN:79-009476.
                              Audience: **g,l,u,f.** *B*

Thelen, Lawrence   **PN2285.T48 2000**
The Show Makers: Great Directors of American Musical
Theatre. UK-B Format Paperback. Routledge. New York, NY.
2002. 264p. ISBN:0-415-92347-6, ISBN13: 978-0-415-92347-7.
Dewey:792.6/0233/092273 B. LCCN:99-029455.
                              Audience: **l,u,f.** *Choice, 2000.*

Todd, Andrew & Lecat,   **PN2598.B69T63 2003**
  Jean Guys
The Open Circle: The Theater Environment of Peter Brook.
Cloth over Boards. Palgrave Macmillan. New York, NY. 2003.
160p. ISBN:1-4039-6362-2, ISBN13: 978-1-4039-6362-8.
Dewey:792.02/33/092. LCCN:2003-060829.
                              Audience: **l,u,f.**

Turner, J.   **PN2688.B33T87 2004**
Eugenio Barba. Paper over Boards. Routledge. New York, NY.
2005. 192p. Routledge Performance Practitioners Ser.
ISBN:0-415-27327-7, ISBN13: 978-0-415-27327-5.
Dewey:792.02/33/092. LCCN:2004-004779.
                              Audience: **u,f.**

Waldau, Roy S.   **PN2295.T5.W3**
Vintage Years of the Theatre Guild, 1928-1939. Trade Cloth.
Press of Case Western Reserve University. Cleveland, OH. 1972.
519p. ISBN:0-8295-0203-3, ISBN13: 978-0-8295-0203-9.
Dewey:792/.0973. LCCN:79-141463.
                              Audience: **l,u,f.** *B*

Waxman, Samuel M.   **PN2636.P4T75**
Antoine and the Theatre Libre. Trade Cloth. Ayer Company
Publishers, Inc. Manchester, NH. 1972. ISBN:0-405-09056-0,
ISBN13: 978-0-405-09056-1. Dewey:792.0944361.
LCCN:63-023192.
                              Audience: **l,u,f.**

Willett, John   **PN2658.P5.W55 1979**
The Theatre of Erwin Piscator: Half a Century of Politics in the
Theatre. Trade Cloth. Holmes & Meier Publishers, Inc. Teaneck,
NJ. 1979. 224p. ISBN:0-8419-0501-0, ISBN13:
978-0-8419-0501-6. Dewey:792/.0233/0924. LCCN:79-011941.
                              Audience: **u,f.** *B*

Winter, William   **PN2287.B4 W5 1970**
Life of David Belasco, Set. Trade Cloth. Ayer Company
Publishers, Inc. Manchester, NH. 1977. Select Bibliographies
Reprint Ser. ISBN:0-8369-5202-2, ISBN13: 978-0-8369-5202-5.
Dewey:792/.0924. LCCN:72-107837.
                              Audience: **g.**

Theater Production > Performance > Buildings and Spaces

PN2596.L7.R515 1981

At the Royal Court: 25 Years of the English Stage Company. Trade Cloth. Bow Historical Books. New Providence, NJ. 1981. 201, [56]p. ISBN:0-8021-0211-5, ISBN13: 978-0-8021-0211-9. Dewey:792/.09421/34. LCCN:80-085375.

Audience: **u,f.** *B*

Adams, Joseph Quincy   **PN2596.L6A55**

Shakespearean Playhouses: A History of English Theatres from the Beginnings to the Restoration. Paper Text. Textbook Publishers. Temecula, CA. 2003. 473p. ISBN:0-7581-6786-5, ISBN13: 978-0-7581-6786-6. Dewey:792.09421.

Audience: **l,u,f.** *B*

Allen, James T.   **PA3202.A5**

Greek Theatre of the Fifth Century Before Christ. Library Binding. M. S. G. Haskell House. Brooklyn, NY. 1969. Studies in Drama, No. 39 ISBN:0-8383-0647-0, ISBN13: 978-0-8383-0647-5. Dewey:792.0938. LCCN:68-002221.

Audience: **l,u,f.**

Arundell, Dennis   **PN2596.L7S3**

The Story of Sadler's Wells, 1683-1977. Ed. 2. Trade Cloth. David & Charles Publishers. Newton Abbot, 1978. 352p. ISBN:0-7153-7620-9, ISBN13: 978-0-7153-7620-1. Dewey:792/.09421/43. LCCN:78-316129.

Audience: **u,f.** *B*

Boyle, Walden P.   **PN2091.E4M3**

Central and Flexible Staging: A New Theater in the Making. Paper Text. Textbook Publishers. Temecula, CA. 2003. 117p. ISBN:0-7581-2806-1, ISBN13: 978-0-7581-2806-5. Dewey:792.025.

Audience: **l,u,f.**

Carlson, Marvin   **NA6821.C36 1993**

Places of Performance: The Semiotics of Theatre Architecture. Trade Paper. Cornell University Press. Ithaca, NY. 1993. 224p. ISBN:0-8014-8094-9, ISBN13: 978-0-8014-8094-2. Dewey:725/.822. LCCN:88-047936.

Audience: **u,f.** *Choice, 1989.*

Chambers, E. K.   **PN2152**

The Medieval Stage. Paper Text. Classic Books. Murrieta, CA. 2001. ISBN:0-7426-9205-1, ISBN13: 978-0-7426-9205-3. Dewey:792.094.

Audience: **u,f.**

Condee, William F.   **PN2091.S8**

Theatrical Space: A Guide for Directors and Designers. Trade Paper. Scarecrow Press, Inc. Lanham, MD. 2002. 248p. ISBN:0-8108-4211-4, ISBN13: 978-0-8108-4211-3. Dewey:792/.025. LCCN:95-003311.

Audience: **l,u,f.**

Craik, T. W.   **PN2596.L6R6**

The Tudor Interlude: Stage, Costume, and Acting. Paper Text. Textbook Publishers. Temecula, CA. 2003. 158p. ISBN:0-7581-1342-0, ISBN13: 978-0-7581-1342-9. Dewey:792.09421.

Audience: **u,f.** *B*

Dent, Edward J.   **PN2596.L7 O73 1979**

A Theatre for Everybody: The Story of the Old Vic and Sadler's Wells. Kay Ambrose (Illustrator). Trade Cloth. Hyperion Press, Inc. Westport, CT. 1979. ISBN:0-88355-691-X, ISBN13: 978-0-88355-691-7. Dewey:792/.09421/2. LCCN:78-010887.

Audience: **l,u,f.**

Diderot, Denis & Alembert,   **NA6820**
Jean L.

Theatre Architecture and Stage Machines: Engravings from the Encyclopedie, ou Dictionnaire Raisonne des Sciences, des Arts, et des Metiers. Trade Cloth. Ayer Company Publishers, Inc. Manchester, NH. 1972. ISBN:0-405-09139-7, ISBN13: 978-0-405-09139-1. Dewey:725.822.

Audience: **l,u,f.**

Dillon, Jim & Naylor, David   **NA6830.N38 1997**

American Theaters: Performance Halls of the Nineteenth Century. Trade Cloth. John Wiley & Sons, Inc. Hoboken, NJ. 1997. 224p. ISBN:0-471-14393-6, ISBN13: 978-0-471-14393-2. Dewey:725/.822/097309034. LCCN:96-043764.

Audience: **l,u,f.**

Foakes, R. A.   **PN2589.F6 1985**

Illustrations of the English Stage, 1580-1642. Trade Cloth. Stanford University Press. Palo Alto, CA. 1985. 180p. ISBN:0-8047-1236-0, ISBN13: 978-0-8047-1236-1. Dewey:792/.0941. LCCN:83-040517.

Audience: **l,u,f.** *B*

Goodwin, John (Editor)   **PN2091.S8**

British Theatre Design. Trade Paper. Phoenix House. London, 1997. 208p. ISBN:0-7538-0129-9, ISBN13: 978-0-7538-0129-1. Dewey:792/.025/0941.

Audience: **l,u,f.** *Choice, 1997.*

Hardin, Terri   **NA6821**

Theatres and Opera Houses. Trade Cloth. New Line Books. New York, NY. 2000. 80p. ISBN:1-57717-145-4, ISBN13: 978-1-57717-145-4. Dewey:725.8/22.

Audience: **l,u,f.**

Henderson, Mary C.   **PN2277.N5**

The City and the Theatre: The History of New York Playhouses: A 250 Year Journey from Bowling Green to Times Square. Gerald Schoenfield (Foreword by). Trade Cloth. Watson-Guptill Publications, Inc. New York, NY. 2004. 384p. ISBN:0-8230-0637-9, ISBN13: 978-0-8230-0637-3. Dewey:792.097471.

Audience: **u,f.** *Choice, 2005.*

Hostetter, Anthony   **PN2656.B42G764 2003**

Max Reinhardt's Grosses Schauspielhaus: Its Artistic Goals, Planning, and Operation, 1910-1933. Trade Cloth. Edwin Mellen

Press, The. Lewiston, NY. 2003. 224p. Studies in Theatre Arts, Vol. 20 ISBN:0-7734-6802-1, ISBN13: 978-0-7734-6802-3. Dewey:330 /945/58. LCCN:2003-042163.

Audience: **l,u,f.**

Izenour, George C.   PA3201.I97 1992
Roofed Theaters of Classical Antiquity. Cloth over Boards. Yale University Press. Cumberland, RI. 1992. 258p. ISBN:0-300-04685-5, ISBN13: 978-0-300-04685-4. Dewey:792/.0938. LCCN:91-012010.

Audience: **u,f.** *Choice, 1992.*

Leacroft, Richard   NA6840.G7L4 1988
The Development of the English Playhouse. Ed. 2. Trade Paper. Heinemann. Portsmouth, NH. 1988. 354p. ISBN:0-413-60600-7, ISBN13: 978-0-413-60600-6. Dewey:725/.822/0942. LCCN:88-156431.

Audience: **l,u,f.** *B*

Lee, Briant H.   NA6840.E85L44 1996
European Post-Baroque Neoclassical Theatre Architecture. Trade Cloth. Edwin Mellen Press, The. Lewiston, NY. 1996. 248p. Studies in Theatre Arts, Vol. 3 ISBN:0-7734-8845-6, ISBN13: 978-0-7734-8845-8. Dewey:725/.822/09409033. LCCN:95-041058.

Audience: **u,f.**

Mander, Raymond &   PN2596
  Mitchenson, Joe
The Theatres of London. Trade Cloth. Greenwood Publishing Group, Inc. Portsmouth, NH. 1979. 292p. ISBN:0-313-21227-9, ISBN13: 978-0-313-21227-7. Dewey:792/.09421. LCCN:78-011868.

Audience: **l,u,f.** *B*

Morrison, Craig   NA6830.M67 2005
Theaters. Trade Cloth, Mixed Media, Compact Disc. W. W. Norton & Company, Inc. New York, NY. 2006. 384p. Norton/Library of Congress Visual Sourcebooks in Architecture, Design, and Engineering ISBN:0-393-73108-1, ISBN13: 978-0-393-73108-8. Dewey:725/.822/0973. LCCN:2005-048839.

Audience: **l,u,f.**

Mulryne, Ronnie (Editor), et   NA6840.G72 L668 1997
  al.
Shakespeare's Globe Rebuilt. Margaret Shewring & J. R. Mulryne (Editors). Trade Paper. Cambridge University Press. New York, NY. 1997. 192p. ISBN:0-521-59988-1, ISBN13: 978-0-521-59988-7. Dewey:725.8/22/09421. LCCN:97-178719.

Audience: **g,l,u,f.**

Sachs, Edwin O. &   NA6821 .S22
  Woodrow, Ernest A.
Modern Opera Houses and Theatres, Set. Trade Cloth. Ayer Company Publishers, Inc. Manchester, NH. 1972. ISBN:0-405-08904-X, ISBN13: 978-0-405-08904-6. Dewey:725/.822/094. LCCN:67-012461.

Audience: **l,u,f.**

Sear, Frank   NA325.T5
Roman Theatres: An Architectural Study. Trade Cloth. Oxford University Press, Inc. New York, NY. 2006. 534p. Oxford Monographs on Classical Archaeology Ser. ISBN:0-19-814469-5, ISBN13: 978-0-19-814469-4. Dewey:725.8220937.

Audience: **u,f.**

Serlio, Sebastiano   PN2221.H76
The Renaissance Stage: Documents of Serlio, Sabbattini and Furttenbach. Paper Text. Textbook Publishers. Temecula, CA. 2003. 256p. ISBN:0-7581-2129-6, ISBN13: 978-0-7581-2129-5. Dewey:792.

Audience: **u,f.** *B*

Silverman, Maxwell &   NA6821 .S55
  Bowman, Ned A.
Contemporary Theatre Architecture: An Illustrated Survey. George Freedley (Foreword by). Trade Cloth. DIANE Publishing Company. Collingdale, PA. 2001. 144p. ISBN:0-7881-9903-X, ISBN13: 978-0-7881-9903-5. Dewey:725.822.

Audience: **l,u.**

Southern, Richard W.   PN2085.L3
The Open Stage and the Modern Theatre in Research and Practice. Paper Text. Textbook Publishers. Temecula, CA. 2003. 125p. ISBN:0-7581-3144-5, ISBN13: 978-0-7581-3144-7. Dewey:792.

Audience: **l,u,f.**

Tydeman, William   PN2570
The Theatre in the Middle Ages: Western European Stage Conditions, C. 800-1576. Trade Paper. Cambridge University Press. New York, NY. 1979. 310p. ISBN:0-521-29304-9, ISBN13: 978-0-521-29304-4. Dewey:792/.094. LCCN:77-085683.

Audience: **u,f.**

Tydeman, William (Editor)   PN2570 .M39 2001
The Medieval European Stage, 500-1550. W. D. Howarth, John Northam & Glynne W. Wickham (Contribution by). Trade Cloth. Cambridge University Press. New York, NY. 2001. 782p. Theatre in Europe Ser. ISBN:0-521-24609-1, ISBN13: 978-0-521-24609-5. Dewey:792/.094/0902. LCCN:00-067610.

Audience: **u,f.** *Choice, 2002.*

Wickham, Glynne W.   PN2592.H6
Early English Stages, 1300 To 1660. Paper Text. Textbook Publishers. Temecula, CA. 2003. ISBN:0-7581-4524-1, ISBN13: 978-0-7581-4524-6. Dewey:792.094212.

Audience: **u,f.**

Wood, William Burke   PN2277
Old Drury of Philadelphia: A History of the Philadelphia Stage, 1800-1835. Trade Cloth. Greenwood Publishing Group, Inc. Portsmouth, NH. 1968. 694p. ISBN:0-8371-0115-8, ISBN13: 978-0-8371-0115-6. Dewey:792/.09748/11. LCCN:69-010108.

Audience: **u,f.** *B*

MUSIC

This selection describes a collection to support the study and teaching of music — the music of all peoples, places, and times, in all its historical, cultural, technical, and critical dimensions — at an undergraduate level.

Emphasis is on current and recent scholarship, with some classic works included for historical depth even when subsequent writings have superceded them. Textbooks and popular-level books are excluded except when indispensable as introductions to the topic. Notated scores and recorded performances (audio or video) are excluded except as an integral supplement to a book. For scores and recordings please refer to A Basic Music Library, 3rd ed. (Chicago: ALA, 1996).

— Kent Underwood

Reference Resources > Dictionaries and Encyclopedias

ML100

☐ Grove Music Online.
http://www.grovemusic.com/
Oxford University Press.

Audience: **g,l,u,f.**

Ammer, Christine **ML108**
The A to Z of Foreign Musical Terms: From Adagio to Zierlich
- A Dictionary for Performers and Students. Paper Text. E. C.
Schirmer Music Company, Inc. Boston, MA. 1989.
ISBN:0-911318-15-1, ISBN13: 978-0-911318-15-9.
Dewey:780.3.

Audience: **g,l,u,f.**

Bachmann, Alberto **ML800.B13**
An Encyclopedia of the Violin. Trade Cloth. Library Reprints,
Inc. Temecula, CA. 2001. 470p. ISBN:0-7222-5990-5, ISBN13:
978-0-7222-5990-0. Dewey:787.1.

Audience: **l,u,f.** *B*

Barlow, Harold & **ML100**
  Morgenstern, Sam
A Dictionary of Musical Themes. Library Binding. Reprint
Services Company. Temecula, CA. 1990. 642p.
ISBN:0-7812-9266-2, ISBN13: 978-0-7812-9266-5.
Dewey:780.3.

Audience: **l,u,f.**

Barlow, Harold **ML128.V7B3 1976**
Dictionary of Opera and Song Themes. Sam Morgenstern
(Compiled by). Trade Cloth. Crown Publishing Group. New
York, NY. 1976. 500p. ISBN:0-517-52503-8, ISBN13:
978-0-517-52503-6. Dewey:016.784. LCCN:75-030751.

Audience: **l,u,f.**

Berkowitz, Freda P. **ML113.B39 1975**
Popular Titles and Subtitles of Musical Compositions. Ed. 2.
Trade Cloth. Scarecrow Press, Inc. Lanham, MD. 1975. 217p.
ISBN:0-8108-0806-4, ISBN13: 978-0-8108-0806-5.
Dewey:016.78. LCCN:75-004751.

Audience: **g,l,u,f.**

Boccagna, David (Composed **ML108.B55 1999**
  by)
Musical Terminology: A Practical Compendium in Four
Languages. Trade Paper. Pendragon Press. Hillsdale, NY. 1999.
243p. ISBN:1-57647-015-6, ISBN13: 978-1-57647-015-2.
Dewey:780/.3. LCCN:99-031743.

Audience: **g,l,u,f.** *Choice, 2000.*

Cary, Tristram **ML102**
Dictionary of Musical Technology. Cloth Text. Greenwood
Publishing Group, Inc. Portsmouth, NH. 1992. 576p.
ISBN:0-313-28694-9, ISBN13: 978-0-313-28694-0.
Dewey:780/.3. LCCN:92-014583.

Audience: **g,l,u,f.** *Choice, 1993.*

Craggs, Stewart R. **ML102.M68C73 1998**
Soundtracks: An International Dictionary of Film Music
Composers. Trade Cloth. Ashgate Publishing, Ltd. Aldershot,
1998. 360p. ISBN:1-85928-189-3, ISBN13: 978-1-85928-189-5.
Dewey:781.5/42/0922 B. LCCN:97-019854.

Audience: **g,l,u,f.** *Choice, 1998.*

Crofton, Ian & Fraser, Don **ML60**
A Dictionary of Musical Quotations. Trade Paper. Music Sales
Corporation. New York, NY. 1989. 192p. ISBN:0-8256-7175-2,
ISBN13: 978-0-8256-7175-3. Dewey:780. LCCN:85-005051.

Audience: **g,l,u,f.** *Choice, 1986.*

Eakin, Nathan **F490**
☐ Gaylord Music Library Necrology.
http://library.wustl.edu/units.music/necro/
Hahn, Paul. Gaylord Music Library, Washington University.

Audience: **g,l,u,f.**

Feather, Leonard **ML102.J3F4 1984**
Encyclopedia of Jazz. Trade Paper. Da Capo Press, Inc.
Cambridge, MA. 1984. 527p. Paperback Ser.
ISBN:0-306-80214-7, ISBN13: 978-0-306-80214-0.
Dewey:785.42/03/21. LCCN:83-026164.

Audience: **g,l,u,f.**

Feather, Leonard **ML105**
Encyclopedia of Jazz in the Sixties. Trade Cloth. Horizon Press.
Tucson, AZ. 1967. ISBN:0-8180-1205-6, ISBN13:
978-0-8180-1205-1. Dewey:785.420922.

Audience: **g,l,u,f.**

Feather, Leonard & Gitler, **ML102.J3F39 1999**
  Ira (Editors)
The Biographical Encyclopedia of Jazz. Ed. 2. Trade Cloth.
Oxford University Press, Inc. New York, NY. 1999. 738p.
ISBN:0-19-507418-1, ISBN13: 978-0-19-507418-5.
Dewey:781.65/092/2 B. LCCN:98-015485.

Audience: **g,l,u,f.** *Choice, 2000.*

Feather, Leonard & Gitler, **ML105.F36**
  Ira
The Encyclopedia of Jazz in the Seventies. Quincy Jones
(Introduction by). Trade Cloth. Horizon Press. Tucson, AZ.
1976. 393p. ISBN:0-8180-1215-3, ISBN13: 978-0-8180-1215-0.
Dewey:785.4/2/0922. LCCN:76-021196.

Audience: **g,l,u,f.**

Floyd, Samuel A. Jr. **ML105.I5 1999**
  (Editor)
International Dictionary of Black Composers, Set. Trade Cloth.
Fitzroy Dearborn Publishers, Inc. Chicago, IL. 1999. 1600p.
ISBN:1-884964-27-3, ISBN13: 978-1-884964-27-5.
Dewey:780/.92/396 B. LCCN:99-214303.

Audience: **g,l,u,f.** *Choice, 1999.*

Fradkin, Robert A. **ML109.F73 1996**
The Well-Tempered Announcer: A Pronunciation Guide to
Classical Music. Trade Paper. Indiana University Press.
Bloomington, IN. 1996. 256p. ISBN:0-253-21064-X, ISBN13:
978-0-253-21064-7. Dewey:780/.14. LCCN:95-000360.

Audience: **g,l,u,f.** *Choice, 1997.*

Audience: g=general, l=lower division undergraduate, u=upper division undergraduate, f=faculty.

159

Fuld, James J.   **ML113.F8 2000**
The Book of World-Famous Music: Classical, Popular and Folk.
Ed. 5. Trade Paper. Dover Publications, Inc. Mineola, NY. 2000.
752p. ISBN:0-486-41475-2, ISBN13: 978-0-486-41475-1.
Dewey:016.78. LCCN:00-702558.
                                  Audience: **g,l,u,f.**

Ganzl, Kurt   **ML102.M88G3 2001**
Encyclopedia of Musical Theater. Ed. 2. Trade Cloth. Thomson
Gale. Farmington Hills, MI. 1905. 2274p. ISBN:0-02-864970-2,
ISBN13: 978-0-02-864970-2. Dewey:782.1/4/03.
LCCN:2001-018361.
                    Audience: **g,l,u,f.** *Choice, 2001.*

Green, Jeff   **ML156.4.P6G73 2002**
The Green Book of Songs by Subject: The Thematic Guide to
Popular Music. Ed. 5. Trade Cloth. Professional Desk
References, Inc. Nashville, TN. 2002. xxi, 1569p.
ISBN:0-939735-10-5, ISBN13: 978-0-939735-10-5.
Dewey:016.78242164/0266. LCCN:2001-099825.
          Audience: **g,l,u,f.** *Choice, 2002, 1995.*

Grigg, Carolyn D.   **ML108**
  (Compiled by)
Music Translation Dictionary: An English, Czech, Danish,
Dutch, French, German, Hungarian, Italian, Polish, Portuguese,
Russian, Spanish, Swedish Vocabulary of Music. Cloth Text.
Greenwood Publishing Group, Inc. Portsmouth, NH. 1978. 336p.
ISBN:0-313-20559-0, ISBN13: 978-0-313-20559-0.
Dewey:780.3. LCCN:78-060526.
                                  Audience: **g,l,u,f.**

Gänzl, Kurt   **ML102.M88G3 2001**
The Encyclopedia of the Musical Theatre. Trade Cloth.
Thomson Gale. Farmington Hills, MI. 2001.
ISBN:0-02-865574-5, ISBN13: 978-0-02-865574-1.
Dewey:782.1/4/03. LCCN:2001-018361.
                                  Audience: **g.**

Hinson, Maurice   **ML102.P5H46 2004**
The Pianist's Dictionary. Trade Paper. Indiana University Press.
Bloomington, IN. 2004. 160p. ISBN:0-253-21682-6, ISBN13:
978-0-253-21682-3. Dewey:786.2/03. LCCN:2003-025350.
          Audience: **g,l,u,f.** *Choice, 2004.*

Hitchcock, H. Wiley &   **ML100**
  Sadie, Stanley (Editors)
The New Grove Dictionary of American Music. Trade Cloth.
Oxford University Press, Inc. New York, NY. 1986. 2736p.
ISBN:0-943818-36-2, ISBN13: 978-0-943818-36-8.
Dewey:781.773/03/21. LCCN:86-000404.
          Audience: **g,l,u,f.** *Choice, 1987.*

Hixon, Don L. & Hennessee,   **ML105.H6 1993**
  Don A.
Women in Music: An Encyclopedic Biobibliography. Ed. 2.
Trade Cloth. Scarecrow Press, Inc. Lanham, MD. 1993. 772p.
ISBN:0-8108-2769-7, ISBN13: 978-0-8108-2769-1.
Dewey:016.78/0922. LCCN:93-034731.
                                  Audience: **g,l,u,f.**

Hixon, Donald L.   **ML100.H45 2005**
Music Abbreviations: A Reverse Dictionary. Trade Paper.
Scarecrow Press, Inc. Lanham, MD. 2005. 234p.
ISBN:0-8108-4834-1, ISBN13: 978-0-8108-4834-4.
Dewey:780/.1/4. LCCN:2004-021561.
                                  Audience: **g,l,u,f.**

Hoffmann, Frank W.   **ML102.S67E5 2004**
  (Editor)
Encyclopedia of Recorded Sound. Ed. 2. Paper over Boards.
Routledge. New York, NY. 2004. 1320p. ISBN:0-415-93835-X,
ISBN13: 978-0-415-93835-8. Dewey:384. LCCN:2003-026491.
          Audience: **g,l,u,f.** *Choice, 2005.*

Jackson, Roland   **ML100.J29 2004**
Performance Practice: A Dictionary Guide for Musicians. Paper
over Boards. Routledge. New York, NY. 2005. 544p.
ISBN:0-415-94139-3, ISBN13: 978-0-415-94139-6.
Dewey:781.4/3/09. LCCN:2004-026541.
          Audience: **g,l,u,f.** *Choice, 2005.*

Jasen, David A.   **ML102.P66J37 2003**
Tin Pan Alley: An Encyclopedia of the Golden Age of American
Song. Paper over Boards. Routledge. New York, NY. 2003.
384p. ISBN:0-415-93877-5, ISBN13: 978-0-415-93877-8.
Dewey:782.42164/0973. LCCN:2003-002699.
                                  Audience: **g,l,u,f.**

Jenkins, Todd S.   **ML102**
Free Jazz and Free Improvisation: An Encyclopedia. Cloth Text.
Greenwood Publishing Group, Inc. Portsmouth, NH. 2004. 468p.
ISBN:0-313-29881-5, ISBN13: 978-0-313-29881-3.
Dewey:781.65/136/03. LCCN:2004-047531.
          Audience: **g,l,u,f.** *Choice, 2005.*

Kernfeld, Barry D. &   **ML102.J3N48 2001**
  Kernfeld, Barry (Editors)
The New Grove Dictionary of Jazz. Ed. 2. Trade Cloth. Oxford
University Press, Inc. New York, NY. 2001. 3000p.
ISBN:1-56159-284-6, ISBN13: 978-1-56159-284-5.
Dewey:781.65/03. LCCN:2001-040794.
          Audience: **g,l,u,f.** *Choice, 2002, 1989.*

Kingsbury, Paul (Editor)   **ML102.C7E54**
The Encyclopedia of Country Music: The Ultimate Guide to the
Music. The Country Music Foundation (Compiled by). Trade
Paper. Oxford University Press, Inc. New York, NY. 2004. 648p.
ISBN:0-19-517608-1, ISBN13: 978-0-19-517608-7.
Dewey:781.642/03. LCCN:2003-000144.
                                  Audience: **g,l,u,f.**

Komara, Edward (Editor)   **ML102.B6**
Encyclopedia of the Blues. Paper over Boards. Routledge. New
York, NY. 2005. 1440p. ISBN:0-415-92699-8, ISBN13:
978-0-415-92699-7. Dewey:781.643/03. LCCN:2005-044346.
          Audience: **g,l,u,f.** *Choice, 2006.*

Larkin, Colin (Editor)   **ML102.P66G84**
The Encyclopedia of Popular Music, Set. Ed. 3. Library
Binding. Groves Dictionaries, Inc. New York, NY. 1998. 8000p.

ISBN:1-56159-237-4, ISBN13: 978-1-56159-237-1.
Dewey:782.4/2/164/03. LCCN:98-037439.
Audience: **g,l,u,f.** *Choice, 1999.*

Latham, Alison (Editor)   ML100.S37 2002
The Oxford Companion to Music. Trade Cloth. Oxford
University Press, Inc. New York, NY. 2002. 1,444p.
ISBN:0-19-866212-2, ISBN13: 978-0-19-866212-9.
Dewey:780/.3. LCCN:2002-537302.
Audience: **g,l,u,f.** *Choice, 2002.*

Loewenberg, Alfred   ML1700
Annals of Opera, Fifteen Ninety-Seven to Nineteen Forty, Set.
Library Binding. Reprint Services Company. Temecula, CA.
1988. ISBN:0-7812-0999-4, ISBN13: 978-0-7812-0999-1.
Dewey:782.1/09.
Audience: **g,l,u,f.**

McNeil, W. K.   ML102.G6E63 2005
Encyclopedia of American Gospel Music. Paper over Boards.
Routledge. New York, NY. 2005. 512p. ISBN:0-415-94179-2,
ISBN13: 978-0-415-94179-2. Dewey:782.25/4/03.
LCCN:2005-044994.
Audience: **g,l,u,f.** *Choice, 2006.*

Moskowitz, David V.   ML102
Caribbean Popular Music: An Encyclopedia of Reggae, Mento,
Ska, Rocksteady, and Dancehall. Trade Cloth. Greenwood
Publishing Group, Inc. Portsmouth, NH. 2005. 368p.
ISBN:0-313-33158-8, ISBN13: 978-0-313-33158-9.
Dewey:781.64/09729/03. LCCN:2005-018629.
Audience: **g,l,u,f.**

Nettl, Bruno (Editor), et al.   ML100.G16
The Garland Encyclopedia of World Music Set. Ruth M. Stone,
James Porter & Timothy Rice (Editors). Library Binding.
Garland Publishing, Inc. New York, NY. 1999. 1000p. Garland
Encyclopedia of World Music Ser. ISBN:0-8153-1865-0,
ISBN13: 978-0-8153-1865-1. Dewey:780.9. LCCN:97-009671.
Audience: **g,l,u,f.**

Olsen, Eric, et al.   ML105.E53 1999
The Encyclopedia of Record Producers. Carlo Wolff & Paul
Verna (Authors). Trade Paper. Watson-Guptill Publications, Inc.
New York, NY. 1999. 912p. ISBN:0-8230-7607-5, ISBN13:
978-0-8230-7607-9. Dewey:781.64/092/2 B. LCCN:99-032191.
Audience: **g,l,u,f.** *Choice, 2000.*

Palmieri, Robert &   ML102.P5E53 2003
  Palmieri, Margaret W. (Editors)
The Piano: An Encyclopedia. Ed. 2. Paper over Boards.
Routledge. New York, NY. 2003. 576p. Encyclopedia of
Keyboard Instruments Ser. ISBN:0-415-93796-5, ISBN13:
978-0-415-93796-2. Dewey:786.203. LCCN:2003-002696.
Audience: **g,l,u,f.** *Choice, 2004.*

Powell, Mark Allan   ML102.C66P68 2002
Encyclopedia of Contemporary Christian Music. CD-ROM,
Trade Paper. Hendrickson Publishers, Inc. Peabody, MA. 2004.
1088p. ISBN:1-56563-679-1, ISBN13: 978-1-56563-679-8.
Dewey:782.25. LCCN:2002-008473.
Audience: **g,l,u,f.** *Choice, 2003.*

Randel, Don M. (Editor)   ML105.H38 1996
The Harvard Biographical Dictionary of Music. Trade Cloth.
Harvard University Press. Cambridge, MA. 1996. 1032p.
Harvard University Press Reference Library
ISBN:0-674-37299-9, ISBN13: 978-0-674-37299-3.
Dewey:780/.92/2 B. LCCN:96-016456.
Audience: **g,l,u,f.** *Choice, 1997.*

Randel, Don Michael   ML100.H37 2003
  (Editor)
The Harvard Dictionary of Music. Ed. 4. Trade Cloth. Harvard
University Press. Cambridge, MA. 2003. 1008p. Harvard
University Press Reference Library ISBN:0-674-01163-5,
ISBN13: 978-0-674-01163-2. Dewey:780/.3.
LCCN:2003-058262.
Audience: **g,l,u,f.** *Choice, 2004.*

Rehrig, William H.   ML102.B35
Supplement to the Heritage Encyclopedia of Band Music. Paul
E. Bierley (Editor). Trade Cloth. Integrity Press. Westerville,
OH. 1996. 1056p. ISBN:0-918048-12-5, ISBN13:
978-0-918048-12-7. Dewey:16.784. LCCN:96-077526.
Audience: **l,u,f.**

Rehrig, William H.   ML102.B35.R4 1991
The Heritage Encyclopedia of Band Music: Composers and
Their Music, Set. Paul E. Bierley (Editor), Alfred Reed (Preface
by). Trade Cloth. Integrity Press. Westerville, OH. 1991. 1087p.
ISBN:0-918048-08-7, ISBN13: 978-0-918048-08-0.
Dewey:016.784. LCCN:91-073637.
Audience: **l,u,f.** *Choice, 1992.*

Reid, Cornelius L.   ML102.V6 R4
A Dictionary of Vocal Terminology. Cloth Text. Recital
Publications. Huntsville, TX. 1994. 480p. ISBN:0-9663862-0-5,
ISBN13: 978-0-9663862-0-2. Dewey:784.9/03/21.
Audience: **g,l,u,f.**

Romanowksi, Patricia   ML102.R6R64 2001
  (Editor), et al.
The Rolling Stone Encyclopedia of Rock and Roll: Revised and
Updated for the 21st Century. Ed. 3. Holly George-Warren &
John Pareles (Editors). Trade Paper. Simon & Schuster. New
York, NY. 2001. 1136p. ISBN:0-7432-0120-5, ISBN13:
978-0-7432-0120-9. Dewey:781.66/03. LCCN:2001-040285.
Audience: **g,l,u,f.**

Sadie, Julie Anne & Samuel,   ML105
  Rhian (Editors)
New Grove Dictionary of Women Composers. Trade Cloth.
Oxford University Press, Inc. New York, NY. 1994. 592p.
ISBN:0-333-51598-6, ISBN13: 978-0-333-51598-3.
Dewey:780.9203.
Audience: **g,l,u,f.**

Sadie, Stanley   ML102.I5
The New Grove Dictionary of Musical Instruments. Trade Cloth.
Oxford University Press, Inc. New York, NY. 1985.
ISBN:0-333-37878-4, ISBN13: 978-0-333-37878-6.
Dewey:781.91/03/21.
Audience: **g,l,u,f.**

Sadie, Stanley (Editor)   ML102.O6
The New Grove Dictionary of Opera, Set. Trade Paper. Oxford
University Press, Inc. New York, NY. 1992. 5,426p.
ISBN:0-19-522186-9, ISBN13: 978-0-19-522186-2.
Dewey:782.1/03.
                             Audience: **g,l,u,f.** *Choice, 1993.*

Sadie, Stanley & Tyrrell,   ML100
  John (Editors)
The New Grove Dictionary of Music and Musicians. Ed. 2.
Trade Cloth. Oxford University Press, Inc. New York, NY. 2001.
25000p. ISBN:0-19-517067-9, ISBN13: 978-0-19-517067-2.
Dewey:780/.3.
                             Audience: **g,l,u,f.** *Choice, 2001.*

Shepherd, John (Editor)   ML102.P66C66 2003
Continuum Encyclopedia of Popular Music of the World: Media,
Industry and Society, Vol. 1. Trade Cloth. Continuum
International Publishing Group, Ltd. London, 2003. 832p.
ISBN:0-8264-6321-5, ISBN13: 978-0-8264-6321-0.
Dewey:781.63/09. LCCN:2002-074146.
                             Audience: **g,l,u,f.** *Choice, 2004.*

Shepherd, John (Editor)   ML102.P66C66 2003
Continuum Encyclopedia of Popular Music of the World:
Performance and Production, Vol. 2. Trade Cloth. Continuum
International Publishing Group, Ltd. London, 2003. 712p.
ISBN:0-8264-6322-3, ISBN13: 978-0-8264-6322-7.
Dewey:781.63/09. LCCN:2002-074146.
                             Audience: **g,l,u,f.** *Choice, 2004.*

Shepherd, John   ML102.P66
Encyclopedia of Popular Music of the World, Vols 3-7. Trade
Cloth. Continuum International Publishing Group, Ltd. London,
2005. 1,984p. ISBN:0-8264-7436-5, ISBN13:
978-0-8264-7436-0. Dewey:781.6/3/03.
                             Audience: **g,l,u,f.** *Choice, 2005.*

Shuker, Roy   ML102.P66S58 2005
Popular Music: The Key Concepts. Ed. 2. Paper over Boards.
Routledge. New York, NY. 2005. XVIII, 326p. Routledge Key
Guides ISBN:0-415-34770-X, ISBN13: 978-0-415-34770-9.
Dewey:781.64/03. LCCN:2004-027956.
                             Audience: **g,l,u,f.**

Slonimsky, Nicolas   ML105.B16 2001
Baker's Biographical Dictionary of Musicians, Vol. 6. Ed. 10.
Trade Cloth. Thomson Gale. Farmington Hills, MI. 2000.
ISBN:0-02-865571-0, ISBN13: 978-0-02-865571-0.
Dewey:780/.92/2. LCCN:00-046375.
                             Audience: **g,l,u,f.**

Slonimsky, Nicolas (Editor)   ML105.B16 2001
Baker's Biographical Dictionary of Musicians: Centennial
Edition. Ed. 9. Trade Cloth. Thomson Gale. Farmington Hills,
MI. 1905. 4220p. ISBN:0-02-865525-7, ISBN13:
978-0-02-865525-3. Dewey:780/.92/2 B. LCCN:00-046375.
                             Audience: **g,l,u,f.** *Choice, 2001.*

Slonimsky, Nicolas   ML105.B16 2001
Baker's Biographical Dictionary of Musicians, Vol. 4. Ed. 10.
Trade Cloth. Thomson Gale. Farmington Hills, MI. 2000.
ISBN:0-02-865529-X, ISBN13: 978-0-02-865529-1.
Dewey:780/.92/2. LCCN:00-046375.
                             Audience: **g,l,u,f.**

Slonimsky, Nicolas   ML105.B16 2001
Baker's Biographical Dictionary of Musicians, Vol. 3. Ed. 10.
Trade Cloth. Thomson Gale. Farmington Hills, MI. 2000.
ISBN:0-02-865528-1, ISBN13: 978-0-02-865528-4.
Dewey:780/.92/2. LCCN:00-046375.
                             Audience: **g,l,u,f.**

Slonimsky, Nicolas   ML105.B16 2001
Baker's Biographical Dictionary of Musicians, Vol. 1. Ed. 10.
Trade Cloth. Thomson Gale. Farmington Hills, MI. 2000.
ISBN:0-02-865526-5, ISBN13: 978-0-02-865526-0.
Dewey:780/.92/2. LCCN:00-046375.
                             Audience: **g,l,u,f.**

Slonimsky, Nicolas   ML105.B16 2001
Baker's Biographical Dictionary of Musicians, Vol. 2. Ed. 10.
Trade Cloth. Thomson Gale. Farmington Hills, MI. 2000.
ISBN:0-02-865527-3, ISBN13: 978-0-02-865527-7.
Dewey:780/.92/2. LCCN:00-046375.
                             Audience: **g,l,u,f.**

Slonimsky, Nicolas   ML105.B16 2001
Baker's Biographical Dictionary of Musicians, Vol. 5. Ed. 10.
Trade Cloth. Thomson Gale. Farmington Hills, MI. 2000.
ISBN:0-02-865530-3, ISBN13: 978-0-02-865530-7.
Dewey:780/.92/2. LCCN:00-046375.
                             Audience: **g,l,u,f.**

Slonimsky, Nicolas &   ML100.S635 1997
  Kassell, Richard (Editors)
Baker's Dictionary of Music. Trade Cloth. Thomson Gale.
Farmington Hills, MI. 1997. 1171p. ISBN:0-02-864791-2,
ISBN13: 978-0-02-864791-3. Dewey:780/.3. LCCN:97-021923.
                             Audience: **g,l,u,f.** *Choice, 1998.*

Southern, Eileen   ML105
Biographical Dictionary of Afro-American and African
Musicians. Cloth Text. Greenwood Publishing Group, Inc.
Portsmouth, NH. 1982. 496p. Encyclopedia of Black Music Ser.
ISBN:0-313-21339-9, ISBN13: 978-0-313-21339-7.
Dewey:780/.92/2 B. LCCN:81-002586.
                             Audience: **g,l,u,f.**

Stambler, Irwin & Stambler,   ML102.F66S73 2001
  Lyndon
Folk and Blues: The Premier Encyclopedia of American Roots
Music. Cloth over Boards. St. Martin's Press. Gordonville, VA.
2001. 816p. ISBN:0-312-20057-9, ISBN13: 978-0-312-20057-2.
Dewey:781.64/0973/03. LCCN:2001-273473.
                             Audience: **g,l,u,f.**

Townley, Eric   ML156.4.J3
Tell Your Story: A Dictionary of Jazz and Blues Recordings 1917-1950, Vol. 1. Chigwell, Eng.: Storyville Publications. 1976.

Audience: **g,l,u,f.**

Townley, Eric   ML156.4.J3
Tell Your Story: A Dictionary of Jazz and Blues Recordings 1951-1975, Vol. 2. Chigwell, Essex, England: Storyville Publications. 1987. ISBN:0-902391-09-7, ISBN13: 978-0-902391-09-3.

Audience: **g,l,u,f.**

Vallely, Fintan   ML101.I73.V35 1999
Companion to Irish Traditional Music. Trade Cloth. Cork University Press. Cork, 1998. 560p. ISBN:1-85918-148-1, ISBN13: 978-1-85918-148-5. Dewey:781.62/9162/003. LCCN:99-197930.

Audience: **g,l,u,f.**

Wadhams, Wayne   ML102.M85W3 1988
Dictionary of Music Production and Engineering Terminology. Cloth Text. Thomson Gale. Farmington Hills, MI. 1987. 288p. ISBN:0-02-872691-X, ISBN13: 978-0-02-872691-5. Dewey:338.4/778/0321. LCCN:87-030988.

Audience: **g,l,u,f.** *Choice, 1989*

Westbrook, Paul &   ML102.R27W47 2002
  Westbrook, Alonzo T.
Hip Hoptionary (TM): The Dictionary of Hip Hop Terminology. Trade Paper. Broadway Books. New York, NY. 2002. 240p. ISBN:0-7679-0924-0, ISBN13: 978-0-7679-0924-2. Dewey:306/.1. LCCN:2003-555627.

Audience: **g,l,u,f.**

White, Glenn D. & Louie,   TK7881.4.W48 2004
  Gary J.
The Audio Dictionary. Ed. 3. Trade Paper, Perfect. University of Washington Press. Seattle, WA. 2005. 516p. ISBN:0-295-98498-8, ISBN13: 978-0-295-98498-8. Dewey:621.389/3. LCCN:2004-029425.

Audience: **g,l,u,f.** *Choice, 2005, 1992.*

Whitsett, Tim   ML3790
Dictionary of Music Business Terms. Sarah Jones (Editor). Trade Paper. artistpro.com, LLC. Vallejo, CA. 1998. 159p. ISBN:0-87288-684-0, ISBN13: 978-0-87288-684-1. Dewey:780.25. LCCN:98-067691.

Audience: **g,l,u,f.**

Reference Resources > Indexes and Abstracts

ML113
☐ International Index to Music Periodicals: IIMP Full Text.
http://iimpft.chadwyck.com/home
Chadwyck-Healey, Inc.

Audience: **l,u,f.**

ML118
☐ Music Index.
http://www.harmonieparkpress.com/MusicIndex.asp
Harmonie Park Press.

Audience: **g,l,u,f.**

ML5
☐ RILM Abstracts of Music Literature = International Repertory of Music Literature.
http://www.rilm.org
RILM International Center.

Audience: **u,f.**

Reference Resources > Bibliographies and Catalogs > Individual Composers

Antokoletz, Elliott   ML134.B18A7 1997
Bela Bartok: A Guide to Research. Ed. 2. Guy A. Marco (Editor). Cloth Text. Garland Publishing, Inc. New York, NY. 1997. 536p. Composer Resource Manuals Ser., Vol. 40 ISBN:0-8153-2088-4, ISBN13: 978-0-8153-2088-3. Dewey:016.78/092. LCCN:96-039298.

Audience: **l,u,f.** *Choice, 1997, 1988.*

Ayotte, Benjamin   ML134.S25A95 2003
Heinrich Schenker: A Guide to Research. Paper over Boards. Routledge. New York, NY. 2003. 368p. Routledge Music Bibliographies Ser. ISBN:0-415-94071-0, ISBN13: 978-0-415-94071-9. Dewey:016.78/092. LCCN:2003-008616.

Audience: **u,f.**

Briscoe, James R.   ML134.D26B7 1990
Claude Debussy: A Guide to Research. Cloth Text. Garland Publishing, Inc. New York, NY. 1990. 526p. Composer Resource Manuals Ser., Vol. 27 ISBN:0-8240-5795-3, ISBN13: 978-0-8240-5795-4. Dewey:016.78/092. LCCN:89-023691.

Audience: **l,u,f.** *Choice, 1990.*

Cooper, John M.   ML134.M53C6 2001
Felix Mendelssohn Bartholdy: Guide to Research with Introduction to Research Concerning Fanny. Cloth Text. Garland Publishing, Inc. New York, NY. 2001. 272p. Composer Resource Manuals, Vol. 54 ISBN:0-8153-1513-9, ISBN13: 978-0-8153-1513-1. Dewey:016.78/092. LCCN:00-045737.

Audience: **l,u,f.**

Earp, Lawrence   ML134.G956E3 1995
Guillaume de Machaut: A Guide to Research. Library Binding. Garland Publishing, Inc. New York, NY. 1995. 696p. Composer Resource Manuals Ser., Vol. 36 ISBN:0-8240-2323-4, ISBN13: 978-0-8240-2323-2. Dewey:016.841/1. LCCN:95-035044.

Audience: **u,f.** *Choice, 1996.*

Grave, Floyd K. & Grave,   ML134.H272G74 1990
  Margaret G.
Franz Joseph Haydn: A Guide to Research. Cloth Text. Garland Publishing, Inc. New York, NY. 1990. 464p. Composer Resource Manuals Ser., Vol. 31 ISBN:0-8240-8487-X, ISBN13: 978-0-8240-8487-5. Dewey:016.78/092. LCCN:90-003533.

Audience: **l,u,f.** *Choice, 1991.*

Harwood, Gregory W.   ML134.V47H37 1998
Giuseppe Verdi: A Guide to Research. Cloth Text. Garland
Publishing, Inc. New York, NY. 1998. 426p. Composer
Resource Manuals Ser., Vol. 42 ISBN:0-8240-4117-8, ISBN13:
978-0-8240-4117-5. Dewey:782.1/092. LCCN:98-012194.
                                          Audience: **l,u,f.** *Choice, 1998.*

Hastings, Baird   ML134.M9H34 1989
Wolfgang Amadeus Mozart: A Guide to Research. Trade Cloth.
Garland Publishing, Inc. New York, NY. 1989. 500p. Composer
Resource Manuals Ser. ISBN:0-8240-8347-4, ISBN13:
978-0-8240-8347-2. Dewey:016.78/092/4. LCCN:88-021294.
                                          Audience: **l,u,f.** *Choice, 1989.*

Kiel, Dyke & Adams, K.   ML134.M66A5 1989
  Gary
Claudio Monteverdi: A Guide to Research. Cloth Text. Garland
Publishing, Inc. New York, NY. 1989. 292p. Composer
Resource Manuals Ser., Vol. 23 ISBN:0-8240-7743-1, ISBN13:
978-0-8240-7743-3. Dewey:016.782/0092. LCCN:89-033040.
                                          Audience: **l,u,f.** *Choice, 1989.*

Köchel, Ludwig   ML134.M8
Chronologisch-thematisches Verzeichnis sämtlicher Tonwerke
Wolfgang Amadé Mozarts: nebst Angabe der
verlorengegangenen, angefangenen, von fremder Hand
bearbeiteten, zweifelhaften und unterschobenen Kompositionen.
Ed. 8. Geigling, Franz; Weinmann, Alexander; Sievers, Gerd.
Wiesbaden: Breitkopf & Härtel; New York: C. F. Peters, sole
agents in USA. 1983.

                                          Audience: **u,f.**

Marvin, Clara   ML134.P2M37 2001
Giovanni Pierluigi da Palestrina: A Research Guide. Cloth Text.
Garland Publishing, Inc. New York, NY. 2002. 350p. Composer
Resource Manuals Ser., Vol. 56 ISBN:0-8153-2351-4, ISBN13:
978-0-8153-2351-8. Dewey:016.7822/2/092. LCCN:00-068435.
                                          Audience: **l,u,f.**

Melamed, Daniel R. &   ML134.B1M45 1998
  Marissen, Michael
An Introduction to Bach Studies. Cloth Text. Oxford University
Press, Inc. New York, NY. 1998. 208p. ISBN:0-19-512231-3,
ISBN13: 978-0-19-512231-2. Dewey:016.780/92.
LCCN:97-040406.
                                          Audience: **l,u,f.** *Choice, 1998.*

Mozart, Wolfgang Amadeus   ML134.M9A17 1990
Mozart's "Thematic Catalogue". Ed. 2. Albi Rosenthal & Alan
Tyson (Editors), Albi Rosenthal & Alan Tyson (Introduction by).
Book, Other. Cornell University Press. Ithaca, NY. 1990. 160p.
ISBN:0-8014-2545-X, ISBN13: 978-0-8014-2545-5.
Dewey:780/.92. LCCN:90-002486.
                                          Audience: **l,u,f.** *Choice, 1992.*

Parker, Mary Ann   ML134.H16P37 2005
G. F. Handel: A Guide to Research. Ed. 2. Paper over Boards.
Routledge. New York, NY. 2005. 408p. Routledge Music
Bibliographies Ser. ISBN:0-415-94323-X, ISBN13:
978-0-415-94323-9. Dewey:016.78/092. LCCN:2005-006736.
                                          Audience: **l,u,f.**

Ping-Robbins, Nancy R. &   ML134.J75P56 1998
  Marco, Guy (Editors)
Scott Joplin: A Guide to Research. Cloth Text. Garland
Publishing, Inc. New York, NY. 1998. 426p. Composer
Resource Manuals Ser., Vol. 7 ISBN:0-8240-8399-7, ISBN13:
978-0-8240-8399-1. Dewey:016.78/092. LCCN:98-010988.
                                          Audience: **l,u,f.** *Choice, 1999.*

Platt, Heather (Editor)   ML134
Johannes Brahms. Paper over Boards. Routledge. New York,
NY. 2003. 416p. Routledge Music Bibliographies Ser.
ISBN:0-8153-3850-3, ISBN13: 978-0-8153-3850-5.
Dewey:016.78/092. LCCN:2003-271627.
                                          Audience: **l,u,f.** *Choice, 2004.*

Poznansky, Alexander &   ML134.C42P69 2001
  Langston, Brett
The Tchaikovsky Handbook: Catalogue of Letters, Bibliography.
Trade Cloth. Indiana University Press. Bloomington, IN. 2002.
730p. Russian Music Studies ISBN:0-253-33947-2, ISBN13:
978-0-253-33947-8. Dewey:780/.92 B. LCCN:2001-039546.
                                          Audience: **u,f.** *Choice, 2002.*

Poznansky, Alexander &   ML134.C42P69 2001
  Langston, Brett
The Tchaikovsky Handbook: Thematic Catalogue of Works,
Catalogue of Photographs, Autobiography. Trade Cloth. Indiana
University Press. Bloomington, IN. 2002. 730p. Russian Music
Studies ISBN:0-253-33921-9, ISBN13: 978-0-253-33921-8.
Dewey:780/.92 B. LCCN:2001-039546.
                                          Audience: **u,f.** *Choice, 2002.*

Saffle, Michael   ML134.L7S2 2003
Franz Liszt: A Guide to Research. Ed. 2. Paper over Boards.
Routledge. New York, NY. 2004. 536p. Routledge Music
Bibliographies Ser. ISBN:0-415-94011-7, ISBN13:
978-0-415-94011-5. Dewey:016.78/092. LCCN:2003-026223.
                                          Audience: **l,u,f.** *Choice, 1992.*

Saffle, Michael   ML134.W1S24 2002
Richard Wagner: A Guide to Research. Paper over Boards.
Garland Publishing, Inc. New York, NY. 2002. 352p. Routledge
Musical Bibliographies Ser. ISBN:0-8240-5695-7, ISBN13:
978-0-8240-5695-7. Dewey:016.7821/092. LCCN:2001-048162.
                                          Audience: **l,u,f.**

Schmieder, Wolfgang   ML134.B155
Thematisch-systematisches Verzeichnis der musikalischen Werke
von Johann Sebastian Bach: Bach-Werke-Verzeichnis (BWV).
Ed. 2. Wiesbaden : Breitkopf & Härtel. 1990.

                                          Audience: **u,f.**

Sherwood, Gayle   ML134.I9S44 2002
Charles Ives: Guide to Research. Paper over Boards. Garland
Publishing, Inc. New York, NY. 2002. 176p. Routledge Musical
Bibliographies Ser. ISBN:0-8153-3821-X, ISBN13:
978-0-8153-3821-5. Dewey:016.780/92. LCCN:2002-075204.
                                          Audience: **l,u,f.**

Smialek, William   ML134.C54S65 2000
Frederic Chopin: A Guide to Research. Guy A. Marco (Editor).
Cloth Text. Garland Publishing, Inc. New York, NY. 1999. 300p.

Composer Resource Manuals Ser., Vol. 50 ISBN:0-8153-2180-5, ISBN13: 978-0-8153-2180-4. Dewey:016.7862/092. LCCN:99-042566.

Audience: **l,u,f.** *Choice, 2000.*

Turbet, Richard   **ML134.B96T9 2005**
William Byrd: A Guide to Research. Ed. 2. Paper over Boards. Routledge. New York, NY. 2006. 352p. Routledge Music Bibliographies Ser. ISBN:0-415-94301-9, ISBN13: 978-0-415-94301-7. Dewey:016.78/092. LCCN:2005-013599.

Audience: **l,u,f.** *Choice, 1988.*

Zaslaw, Neal & Fiel, Fiona   **ML134.M9M83 1991**
M. (Editors)
The Mozart Repertory: A Guide for Musicians, Programmers, and Researchers. Book, Other. Cornell University Press. Ithaca, NY. 1991. 176p. ISBN:0-8014-9937-2, ISBN13: 978-0-8014-9937-1. Dewey:016.78/092. LCCN:91-007459.

Audience: **g,l,u,f.**

Zimmerman, Franklin B.   **ML134.P95**
Henry Purcell: A Guide to Research. New York : Garland Pub. 1989. Garland Composer Resource Manuals; Vol. 18 ISBN:0-8240-7786-5, ISBN13: 978-0-8240-7786-0.

Audience: **l,u,f.**

Reference Resources > Bibliographies and Catalogs > Topical

Arnold, Ben   **ML128.W2.A75 1993**
Music and War: A Research and Information Guide. Paper over Boards. Garland Publishing, Inc. New York, NY. 1993. 464p. Music Research and Information Guides Ser., Vol. 17 ISBN:0-8153-0826-4, ISBN13: 978-0-8153-0826-3. Dewey:016.781599. LCCN:93-024938.

Audience: **l,u,f.** *Choice, 1994.*

Baron, John H.   **ML128.O5**
Chamber Music: A Research and Information Guide. Ed. 2. Paper over Boards. Routledge. New York, NY. 2002. 680p. Routledge Music Bibliographies Ser. ISBN:0-415-93736-1, ISBN13: 978-0-415-93736-8. Dewey:016.7/85.

Audience: **l,u,f.** *Choice, 1988.*

Bloom, Kenneth   **ML128.M78.B6 1996**
American Song: The Complete Musical Theatre Companion, 1877-1995, Vol. 1 & 2. Ed. 2. Trade Cloth. Thomson Gale. Farmington Hills, MI. 1905. 2093p. ISBN:0-02-870484-3, ISBN13: 978-0-02-870484-5. Dewey:782.1/4/0973. LCCN:95-049840.

Audience: **g,l,u,f.** *Choice, 1996.*

Bloom, Kenneth   **ML128.M7B6 1995**
Hollywood Song: The Complete Film and Musical Companion. Trade Cloth. Facts On File, Inc. New York, NY. 1995. ISBN:0-8160-3231-9, ISBN13: 978-0-8160-3231-0. Dewey:016.7821/4/0973. LCCN:90-022261.

Audience: **g,l,u,f.**

Bradley, Carol June   **ML156.9**
Index to Poetry in Music. Paper over Boards. Routledge. New York, NY. 2003. 1008p. ISBN:0-415-94302-7, ISBN13: 978-0-415-94302-4. Dewey:016.782. LCCN:2003-271638.

Audience: **g,l,u,f.** *Choice, 2003.*

Brook, Barry S. & Viano,   **ML113.B86 1997**
Richard J.
Thematic Catalogues in Music: An Annotated Bibliography. Ed. 2. Trade Cloth. Pendragon Press. Hillsdale, NY. 1997. 602p. Rilm Retro Ser., No. 5 ISBN:0-918728-86-X, ISBN13: 978-0-918728-86-9. Dewey:016.78. LCCN:97-002411.

Audience: **u,f.** *Choice, 1997.*

Carner, Gary (Compiled by)   **ML128**
Jazz Performers: An Annotated Bibliography of Biographical Materials. Cloth Text. Greenwood Publishing Group, Inc. Portsmouth, NH. 1990. 384p. Music Reference Collection, No. 26 ISBN:0-313-26250-0, ISBN13: 978-0-313-26250-0. Dewey:016.78165/092/2. LCCN:90-031765.

Audience: **g,l,u,f.** *Choice, 1990.*

Coffin, Berton   **PE1128.A2R454 2002**
Singer's Repertoire: Mezzo Soprano and Contralto. Ed. 2. Trade Paper. Scarecrow Press, Inc. Lanham, MD. 2002. 234p. ISBN:0-8108-4190-8, ISBN13: 978-0-8108-4190-1. Dewey:428/.0071. LCCN:2001-054168.

Audience: **l,u,f.**

Coffin, Berton   **ML128.V7 C67**
Singer's Repertoire: Coloratura Soprano, Lyric Soprano, and Dramatic Soprano. Ed. 2. Trade Paper. Scarecrow Press, Inc. Lanham, MD. 2003. 313p. ISBN:0-8108-4526-1, ISBN13: 978-0-8108-4526-8. Dewey:781.97.

Audience: **u,f.**

Coffin, Berton & Singer,   **ML128.V7 C67**
Werner
Program Notes for the Singer's Repertoire. Trade Cloth. Scarecrow Press, Inc. Lanham, MD. 1962. 230p. ISBN:0-8108-0169-8, ISBN13: 978-0-8108-0169-1. Dewey:781.97. LCCN:60-007265.

Audience: **u,f.**

Damschroder, David &   **ML128.T5D27 1990**
Williams, David R.
Music Theory from Zarlino to Schenker: A Bibliography and Guide. Library Binding. Pendragon Press. Hillsdale, NY. 1991. 550p. Harmonologia Ser., No. 4 ISBN:0-918728-99-1, ISBN13: 978-0-918728-99-9. Dewey:016.781. LCCN:90-006952.

Audience: **u,f.**

Daniels, David   **ML128.O5D3 2005**
Orchestral Music: A Handbook. Ed. 4. Trade Cloth. Scarecrow Press, Inc. Lanham, MD. 2005. 618p. ISBN:0-8108-5674-3, ISBN13: 978-0-8108-5674-5. Dewey:016.7842. LCCN:2005-021983.

Audience: **u,f.**

Davis, Deta S.   **ML128.C62D4 1988**
Computer Applications in Music: A Bibliography. Trade Cloth. A-R Editions, Inc. Middleton, WI. 1988. 537p. Computer Music

and Digital Audio Ser., Vol. 4 ISBN:0-89579-225-7, ISBN13: 978-0-89579-225-9. Dewey:016.780285. LCCN:88-070079.

Audience: **u,f.** *Choice, 1989.*

Davis, Deta S. ML128.C62
Computer Applications in Music: A Bibliography, Supplement 1. John Strawn (Preface by). Trade Cloth. A-R Editions, Inc. Middleton, WI. 1993. 600p. Computer Music and Digital Audio Ser., Vol. 10 ISBN:0-89579-267-2, ISBN13: 978-0-89579-267-9. Dewey:016.780285. LCCN:92-013289.

Audience: **u,f.** *Choice, 1989.*

Davis, Elizabeth A. & Music ML113.B3 1997
 Library Association Staff
A Basic Music Library: Essential Scores and Sound Recordings. Ed. 3. Trade Cloth. American Library Association. Chicago, IL. 1997. 650p. ISBN:0-8389-3461-7, ISBN13: 978-0-8389-3461-6. Dewey:016.78026. LCCN:96-047351.

Audience: **g,l,u,f.** *Choice, 1997.*

Diamond, Harold J. ML128.A7D5 1991
Music Analyses: An Annotated Guide to the Literature. Trade Cloth. Thomson Gale. Farmington Hills, MI. 1991. 716p. ISBN:0-02-870110-0, ISBN13: 978-0-02-870110-3. Dewey:016.781. LCCN:90-013432.

Audience: **l,u,f.** *Choice, 1991.*

Duckles, Vincent H., et al. ML113.D83 1997
Music Reference and Research Materials: An Annotated Bibliography. Ed. 5. Michael A. Keller & Ida Reed (Authors). Cloth Text. Thomson Wadsworth. Belmont, CA. 1997. 832p. ISBN:0-02-870821-0, ISBN13: 978-0-02-870821-8. Dewey:016.78. LCCN:97-011148.

Audience: **g,l,u,f.** *Choice, 1998, 1989.*

Everett, William ML128.M78E84 2004
The Musical: A Research Guide to Musical Theater and Film. Paper over Boards. Routledge. New York, NY. 2004. 248p. Routledge Music Bibliographies Ser. ISBN:0-415-94295-0, ISBN13: 978-0-415-94295-9. Dewey:016.7821/4. LCCN:2004-016007.

Audience: **l,u,f.**

Figueroa, Rafael (Compiled ML128
 by)
Salsa and Related Genres: A Bibliographical Guide. Cloth Text. Greenwood Publishing Group, Inc. Portsmouth, NH. 1992. 128p. Music Reference Collection, No. 38 ISBN:0-313-27883-0, ISBN13: 978-0-313-27883-9. Dewey:016.7816268. LCCN:92-023778.

Audience: **g,l,u,f.**

Floyd, James Michael & ML128.C54
 Sharp, Avery T.
Church and Worship Music: A Research and Information Guide. Paper over Boards. Routledge. New York, NY. 2005. 344p. Routledge Music Bibliographies Ser. ISBN:0-415-96647-7, ISBN13: 978-0-415-96647-4. Dewey:016.7817100973. LCCN:2005-562113.

Audience: **g,l,u,f.**

Foreman, Lewis ML113.I53 2003
Information Sources in Music. Trade Cloth. K. G. Saur Verlag GmbH & Company. Munchen 70, 2002. xx; 445p. ISBN:3-598-24441-X, ISBN13: 978-3-598-24441-4. Dewey:16.78098. LCCN:2003-551750.

Audience: **g,l,u,f.**

Gooch, Bryan N. & ML120.G7
 Thatcher, David (Editors)
A Shakespeare Music Catalogue: Bibliography. Trade Cloth. Oxford University Press, Inc. New York, NY. 1991. 314p. ISBN:0-19-812945-9, ISBN13: 978-0-19-812945-5. Dewey:16.78.

Audience: **u,f.**

Gooch, Bryan N. & ML5
 Thatcher, David (Editors)
A Shakespeare Music Catalogue: Indices. Trade Cloth. Oxford University Press, Inc. New York, NY. 1991. 356p. ISBN:0-19-812944-0, ISBN13: 978-0-19-812944-8. Dewey:780/.903.

Audience: **u,f.**

Gooch, Bryan N. & ML134.5.S52G6 1991
 Thatcher, David (Editors)
A Shakespeare Music Catalogue: The Catalogue of Music: Macbeth--The Taming of the Shrew. Trade Cloth. Oxford University Press, Inc. New York, NY. 1991. 804p. ISBN:0-19-812942-4, ISBN13: 978-0-19-812942-4. Dewey:016.78/00822. LCCN:89-009270.

Audience: **u,f.**

Gooch, Bryan N. & ML120.G7
 Thatcher, David (Editors)
A Shakespeare Music Catalogue: The Tempest--The Two Noble Kinsmen, the Sonnets, the Poems, Commemorative Pieces. Trade Cloth. Oxford University Press, Inc. New York, NY. 1991. 686p. ISBN:0-19-812943-2, ISBN13: 978-0-19-812943-1. Dewey:16.78.

Audience: **u,f.**

Gooch, Bryan N. & ML134.5.S52G6 1991
 Thatcher, David (Editors)
A Shakespeare Music Catalogue: The Catalogue of Music: All's Well That Ends Well--Love's Labour's Lost. Trade Cloth. Oxford University Press, Inc. New York, NY. 1991. 798p. ISBN:0-19-812941-6, ISBN13: 978-0-19-812941-7. Dewey:016.78/00822. LCCN:89-009270.

Audience: **u,f.**

Gray, John ML120
African Music: A Bibliographical Guide to the Traditional, Popular, Art, and Liturgical Musics of Sub-Saharan Africa. Cloth Text. Greenwood Publishing Group, Inc. Portsmouth, NH. 1991. 504p. African Special Bibliographic Ser., No. 14 ISBN:0-313-27769-9, ISBN13: 978-0-313-27769-6. Dewey:016.78/0967. LCCN:90-024517.

Audience: **l,u,f.** *Choice, 1991.*

Heintze, James R. ML120.U5H46 1990
Early American Music, 1620-1820: A Research and Information Guide. Trade Cloth. Garland Publishing, Inc. New York, NY.

Formats: Web: ☐ Ebook: 🄮 CD/DVD-ROM: 🖫 BCL3: *B*

1990. 524p. Music Research and Information Guides Ser., Vol. 13 ISBN:0-8240-4119-4, ISBN13: 978-0-8240-4119-9. Dewey:016.78/0973/09033. LCCN:89-016904.

Audience: **l,u,f.** *Choice, 1990.*

Hemmasi, Harriette &   **ML111.H36 1998**
   Rowley, Fred (Compiled by)
Music Subject Headings, Compiled from Library of Congress Subject Headings. Ed. 2. Richard P. Smiraglia (Foreword by), Bradford J. Young (Introduction by). Perfect. Soldier Creek Press, Inc. Belle Plain, MN. 1998. 610p. Soldier Creek Music Ser., Vol. 4 ISBN:0-936996-76-5, ISBN13: 978-0-936996-76-9. Dewey:025.49/78. LCCN:98-039597.

Audience: **g,l,u,f.**

Heskes, Irene (Compiled by)   **ML128**
The Resource Book of Jewish Music: A Bibliographical and Topical Guide to the Book and Journal Literature and Program Materials. Cloth Text. Greenwood Publishing Group, Inc. Portsmouth, NH. 1985. 302p. Music Reference Collection, No. 3 ISBN:0-313-23251-2, ISBN13: 978-0-313-23251-0. Dewey:016.7817/2924. LCCN:84-022435.

Audience: **g,l,u,f.** *Choice, 1985.*

Heyer, Anna H.   **ML113.H52 1980**
Historical Sets, Collected Editions, and Monuments of Music: A Guide to Their Contents. Ed. 3. Trade Cloth. American Library Association. Chicago, IL. 1980. ISBN:0-8389-0288-X, ISBN13: 978-0-8389-0288-2. Dewey:016.78. LCCN:80-022893.

Audience: **u,f.**

Hill, George R. & Stephens,   **ML113.H55 1997**
   Norris L.
Collected Editions, Historical Series and Sets, and Monuments of Music: A Bibliography. Trade Cloth. Scarecrow Press, Inc. Lanham, MD. 1997. 1349p. Reference Books in Music, No. 14 ISBN:0-914913-22-0, ISBN13: 978-0-914913-22-1. Dewey:016.78. LCCN:96-045419.

Audience: **u,f.** *Choice, 1997.*

Hinson, Maurice   **ML128.P3H5 2000**
🖳 Guide to the Pianist's Repertoire. Ed. 3. E-Book. Indiana University Press. Bloomington, IN. 2000. 992p. ISBN:0-253-33646-5, ISBN13: 978-0-253-33646-0. Dewey:016.7862/0263. LCCN:99-058594.

Audience: **l,u,f.** *Choice, 1987.*

Hinson, Maurice   **ML128.P3H534 1998**
The Pianist's Bookshelf: A Practical Guide to Books, Videos, and Other Resources. Trade Paper. Indiana University Press. Bloomington, IN. 1998. 352p. ISBN:0-253-21145-X, ISBN13: 978-0-253-21145-3. Dewey:016.7862. LCCN:97-047307.

Audience: **l,u,f.**

Hoffmann, Frank   **ML128.R6**
The Literature of Rock, 1954-1978. Trade Cloth. Scarecrow Press, Inc. Lanham, MD. 1981. 349p. ISBN:0-8108-1371-8, ISBN13: 978-0-8108-1371-7. Dewey:016.7845/4/009. LCCN:80-023459.

Audience: **u,f.**

Hoffmann, Frank & Cooper,   **ML128.R6**
   B. Lee
The Literature of Rock III, 1984-1990: With Additional Material for the Period 1954-1983. Trade Cloth. Scarecrow Press, Inc. Lanham, MD. 1995. 1003p. ISBN:0-8108-2762-X, ISBN13: 978-0-8108-2762-2. Dewey:016.78242166. LCCN:93-036263.

Audience: **u,f.**

Hoffmann, Frank & Cooper,   **ML128.R6**
   B. Lee
The Literature of Rock II: Including an Exhaustive Survey of the Literature from 1979-1983 and Incorporating Supplementary Material from 1954-1978 Not Covered in the First Volume. Ann Hoffmann (Contribution by). Trade Cloth. Scarecrow Press, Inc. Lanham, MD. 1986. 1114p. ISBN:0-8108-1821-3, ISBN13: 978-0-8108-1821-7. Dewey:016.7845/4. LCCN:85-008384.

Audience: **u,f.**

Horn, David   **ML120.U5.H7**
The Literature of American Music in Books and Folk Music Collections: A Fully Annotated Bibliography. Trade Cloth. Scarecrow Press, Inc. Lanham, MD. 1977. 570p. ISBN:0-8108-0996-6, ISBN13: 978-0-8108-0996-3. Dewey:016.781773. LCCN:76-013160.

Audience: **u,f.** *Choice, 1989.*

Horn, David & Jackson,   **ML120.U5.H7SUPPL.1**
   Richard
The Literature of American Music in Books and Folk Music Collections: A Fully Annotated Bibliography. Trade Cloth. Scarecrow Press, Inc. Lanham, MD. 1988. 586p. ISBN:0-8108-1997-X, ISBN13: 978-0-8108-1997-9. Dewey:016.781773. LCCN:87-009630.

Audience: **u,f.** *Choice, 1989.*

Jacobs, Dick & Jacobs,   **ML120.U5J23 1994**
   Harriet
Who Wrote That Song? Ed. 2. Trade Paper. F & W Publications, Inc. Cincinnati, OH. 1994. 448p. ISBN:0-89879-639-3, ISBN13: 978-0-89879-639-1. Dewey:784.5/00973. LCCN:93-048545.

Audience: **g,l,u,f.** *Choice, 1989.*

Katz, Mark   **ML128.V4K38 2006**
The Violin: A Research and Information Guide. Trade Cloth. Routledge. New York, NY. 2005. 336p. Music Research and Information Guides ISBN:0-8153-3637-3, ISBN13: 978-0-8153-3637-2. Dewey:016.7872. LCCN:2005-030659.

Audience: **u,f.**

Keeling, Richard   **ML128.F75K44 1997**
North American Indian Music: A Guide to Published Sources and Selected Recordings. Cloth Text. Garland Publishing, Inc. New York, NY. 1997. 472p. Library of Music Ethnology, Vol. 5 ISBN:0-8153-0232-0, ISBN13: 978-0-8153-0232-2. Dewey:016.78/089/97. LCCN:96-041847.

Audience: **u,f.** *Choice, 1997.*

Krummel, Donald W.   **ML200**
   (Editor), et al.
Resources of American Music History: A Directory of Source Materials from Colonial Times to World War II. Jean Geil,

Doris J. Dyen & Deane L. Root (Editors). Trade Cloth. University of Illinois Press. Champaign, IL. 1981. 463p. Music in American Life Ser. ISBN:0-252-00828-6, ISBN13: 978-0-252-00828-3. Dewey:026/.781773. LCCN:80-014873.

Audience: **u,f.**

Krummel, Donald W. &   **ML112.M86 1990**
  Sadie, Stanley (Editors)
Music Printing and Publishing. Trade Cloth. W. W. Norton & Company, Inc. New York, NY. 1990. xiv, 615p. Grove Handbooks in Music Ser. ISBN:0-393-02809-7, ISBN13: 978-0-393-02809-6. Dewey:070.5/794. LCCN:90-178838.

Audience: **u,f.**

Lax, Roger & Smith,   **ML128.S3L4 1989**
  Frederick
The Great Song Thesaurus. Ed. 2. Cloth Text. Oxford University Press, Inc. New York, NY. 1989. 792p. ISBN:0-19-505408-3, ISBN13: 978-0-19-505408-8. Dewey:784.5/0016. LCCN:88-031267.

Audience: **g,l,u,f.**

Lems-Dworkin, Carol   **ML120.A35.L4 1991**
African Music: A Pan African Annotated Bibliography. Trade Cloth. Carol Lems-Dworkin Publishers. Evanston, IL. 1991. 400p. ISBN:0-905450-91-4, ISBN13: 978-0-905450-91-9. Dewey:016.780967. LCCN:91-033581.

Audience: **u,f.** *Choice, 1992.*

Lewine, Richard, et al.   **ML128.S3**
Songs of the Theater. Simon, Alfred (Author). New York: H.W. Wilson Co.. 1984.

Audience: **l,u,f.**

Limbacher, James L.   **ML128.M7**
Keeping Score: Film Music, 1972-1979. Trade Cloth. Scarecrow Press, Inc. Lanham, MD. 1981. 519p. ISBN:0-8108-1390-4, ISBN13: 978-0-8108-1390-8. Dewey:016.7828/55. LCCN:80-026474.

Audience: **u,f.**

Limbacher, James L. &   **ML128.M7L5 1991**
  Wright, H. Stephen
Keeping Score: Film and Television Music, 1980-1988 (with Additional Coverage of 1921-1979). Trade Cloth. Scarecrow Press, Inc. Lanham, MD. 1991. 928p. ISBN:0-8108-2453-1, ISBN13: 978-0-8108-2453-9. Dewey:016.7815/42. LCCN:91-021180.

Audience: **u,f.**

Marco, Guy A.   **ML120.U5M133 1996**
Checklist of Writings on American Music, 1640-1992, Vols. 1-3. Trade Cloth. Scarecrow Press, Inc. Lanham, MD. 1996. 248p. ISBN:0-8108-3133-3, ISBN13: 978-0-8108-3133-9. Dewey:016.7/8/0973. LCCN:95-026773.

Audience: **u,f.** *Choice, 1997.*

Marco, Guy A. et al.   **ML120.U5**
Literature of American Music III, 1983-1992. Horn, David (Author). Lanham, Md.: Scarecrow Press. 1996. ISBN:0-8108-3132-5, ISBN13: 978-0-8108-3132-2.

Audience: **u,f.**

Marco, Guy A.   **ML128.O4M28 2001**
Opera: A Research and Information Guide. Ed. 2. Edward O. D. Downes (Foreword by). Cloth Text. Garland Publishing, Inc. New York, NY. 2000. 624p. Music Research and Information Guides Ser., Vol. 21 ISBN:0-8153-3516-4, ISBN13: 978-0-8153-3516-0. Dewey:016.7821. LCCN:00-050302.

Audience: **g,l,u,f.** *Choice, 2001.*

Marill, Alvin H.   **ML128.M7M28 1998**
Keeping Score: Film and Television Music, 1988-1997. Trade Cloth. Scarecrow Press, Inc. Lanham, MD. 1998. 370p. Keeping Score Ser. ISBN:0-8108-3416-2, ISBN13: 978-0-8108-3416-3. Dewey:016.7815/42. LCCN:98-028712.

Audience: **u,f.**

Mattfeld, Julius   **ML128.V7**
Variety Music Cavalcade, 1620-1969; A Chronology of Vocal and Instrumental Music Popular in the United States. Ed. 3. Englewood Cliffs, N.J., Prentice-Hall. 1971. ISBN:0-13-940718-9, ISBN13: 978-0-13-940718-5.

Audience: **g,l,u,f.**

McCoy, Judy   **ML128.R28.M3 1992**
Rap Music in the 1980s: A Reference Guide. Trade Cloth. Scarecrow Press, Inc. Lanham, MD. 1992. 275p. ISBN:0-8108-2649-6, ISBN13: 978-0-8108-2649-6. Dewey:782.42164. LCCN:92-039684.

Audience: **g,l,u,f.** *Choice, 1993.*

McTyre, Ruthann B.   **ML128**
  (Compiled by)
Library Resources for Singers, Coaches and Accompanists: An Annotated Bibliography, 1970-1997. Cloth Text. Greenwood Publishing Group, Inc. Portsmouth, NH. 1998. 176p. Music Reference Collection, Vol. 71 ISBN:0-313-30266-9, ISBN13: 978-0-313-30266-4. Dewey:016.783. LCCN:98-023959.

Audience: **l,u,f.** *Choice, 1998.*

Meade, Guthrie Jr.   **2002022360 [ML]**
Country Music Sources: A Biblio-Discography of Commercially Recorded Traditional Music. Trade Cloth. University of North Carolina Press. Chapel Hill, NC. 2002. 1024p. Southern Folklife Collection ISBN:0-8078-2723-1, ISBN13: 978-0-8078-2723-9. Dewey:016.78162/13/00266. LCCN:2002-022360.

Audience: **u,f.** *Choice, 2003.*

Meadows, Eddie S.   **ML128.J3**
Jazz Scholarship and Pedagogy: A Research and Information Guide. Ed. 3. Routledge. 2006. Routledge Music Bibliographies ISBN:0-415-93965-8, ISBN13: 978-0-415-93965-2.

Audience: **l,u,f.**

Miller, Terry E.   **ML128.F74M5 1986**
Folk Music in America: A Reference Guide. Library Binding. Garland Publishing, Inc. New York, NY. 1986. 448p. Music Research and Information Guides Ser., Vol. 5 ISBN:0-8240-8935-9, ISBN13: 978-0-8240-8935-1. Dewey:016.781773. LCCN:84-048014.

Audience: **l,u,f.** *Choice, 1987.*

O'Brien, Robert F. (Editor)   ML128
School Songs of America's Colleges and Universities: A
Directory. Cloth Text. Greenwood Publishing Group, Inc.
Portsmouth, NH. 1991. 208p. ISBN:0-313-27890-3, ISBN13:
978-0-313-27890-7. Dewey:782.42/159. LCCN:91-011337.
Audience: **g,l,u,f.**

Parker, Mara E.   ML128.S68P37 2005
String Quartets: A Research and Information Guide. Perfect,
Paper over Boards. Routledge. New York, NY. 2005. 384p.
Routledge Music Bibliographies Ser. ISBN:0-415-94176-8,
ISBN13: 978-0-415-94176-1. Dewey:16.7857.
LCCN:2005-561917.
Audience: **u,f.**

Pendle, Karin   ML128.W7P46 2005
Women in Music Guide to Research. Paper over Boards.
Routledge. New York, NY. 2005. 728p. Routledge Music
Bibliographies Ser. ISBN:0-415-94354-X, ISBN13:
978-0-415-94354-3. Dewey:016.78/082. LCCN:2005-023054.
Audience: **l,u,f.**

Post, Jennifer C.   ML128.E8
Ethnomusicology: A Guide to Research. Routledge. 2004.
Routledge Music Bibliographies ISBN:0-415-93834-1, ISBN13:
978-0-415-93834-1.
Audience: **u,f.**

Rust, E. Gardner   ML128
The Music and Dance of the World's Religions: A
Comprehensive, Annotated Bibliography of Materials in the
English Language. Cloth Text. Greenwood Publishing Group,
Inc. Portsmouth, NH. 1996. 504p. Music Reference Collection,
Vol. 54 ISBN:0-313-29561-1, ISBN13: 978-0-313-29561-4.
Dewey:016.7817. LCCN:96-018212.
Audience: **g,l,u,f.** *Choice, 1997*

Seaton, Douglas   ML128.S3S33 1987
The Art Song: A Reference and Information Guide. Library
Binding. Garland Publishing, Inc. New York, NY. 1987. 300p.
Reference Library of the Humanities ISBN:0-8240-8554-X,
ISBN13: 978-0-8240-8554-4. Dewey:016.7843.
LCCN:86-033553.
Audience: **l,u,f.** *Choice, 1987.*

Sharp, Avery T. & Floyd,   ML128.C48S53 2001
James Michael
Choral Music: A Research and Information Guide. Cloth Text.
Garland Publishing, Inc. New York, NY. 2001. 498p. Routledge
Music Bibliographies Ser. ISBN:0-8240-5944-1, ISBN13:
978-0-8240-5944-6. Dewey:016.7825. LCCN:2001-019115.
Audience: **l,u,f.** *Choice, 2002.*

Skowronski, JoAnn   ML128.B45
Black Music in America: A Bibliography. Trade Cloth.
Scarecrow Press, Inc. Lanham, MD. 1981. 733p.
ISBN:0-8108-1443-9, ISBN13: 978-0-8108-1443-1.
Dewey:016.7817/296073. LCCN:81-005609.
Audience: **l,u,f.**

Vander Weg, etval.   ML128.T9
Serial Music and Serialism: A Research and Information Guide.
John Dean (Author). New York; London: Routledge. 2001.
ISBN:0-8153-3528-8, ISBN13: 978-0-8153-3528-3.
Audience: **u,f.**

Wenk, Arthur B.   ML113.W45 1987
Analyses of Nineteenth- and Twentieth-Century Music,
1940-1985. Trade Paper. Music Library Association. Canton,
MA. 1987. 370p. Music Library Association Index and
Bibliography Ser., No. 25 ISBN:0-914954-36-9, ISBN13:
978-0-914954-36-1. Dewey:016.78/0903/4. LCCN:87-005675.
Audience: **l,u,f.**

Reference Resources > Discographies

ML156.4.P6
Allmusic = All Music Guide.
http://www.allmusic.com
All Media Guide.
Audience: **g,l,u,f.**

Ackelson, Richard W.   ML156.7.S56
Frank Sinatra: A Complete Recording History of Technqiues,
Songs, Composers, Lyricists, Arrangers, Sessions and First-Issue
Albums, 1939-1984. Library Binding. McFarland & Company,
Incorporated Publishers. Jefferson, NC. 1991. 480p.
ISBN:0-89950-554-6, ISBN13: 978-0-89950-554-1.
Dewey:016.78242163092. LCCN:91-052629.
Audience: **u,f.**

Barrow, Steve & Dalton,   ML3532.B37 2004
Peter
The Rough Guide to Reggae. Ed. 3. Trade Paper. Rough Guides,
Ltd. London, 2004. 528p. Rough Guide Music Guides Ser.
ISBN:1-84353-329-4, ISBN13: 978-1-84353-329-0.
Dewey:781.646. LCCN:2004-558939.
Audience: **g,l,u,f.**

Bogdanov, Vladimir   ML1630.18
(Editor), et al.
All Music Guide to Country: The Definitive Guide to Country
Music. Ed. 2. Chris Woodstra & Stephen Thomas Erlewine
(Editors). Trade Paper. Backbeat Books. San Francisco, CA.
2003. 700p. ISBN:0-87930-760-9, ISBN13: 978-0-87930-760-8.
Dewey:782.4/21642/0266. LCCN:90-024517.
Audience: **g,l,u,f.** *Choice, 2004.*

Bogdanov, Vladimir   ML102.U53A55 2001
(Editor), et al.
All Music Guide to Electronica: The Expert's Guide to the Best
Electronic Recordings. Ed. 4. Chris Woodstra & Stephen
Thomas Erlewine (Editors). Trade Paper. Backbeat Books. San
Francisco, CA. 2001. 688p. All Music Guides
ISBN:0-87930-628-9, ISBN13: 978-0-87930-628-1.
Dewey:781.64. LCCN:2001-025514.
Audience: **g,l,u,f.**

Bogdanov, Vladimir   ML156.4.J3A45 2002
(Editor), et al.
All Music Guide to Jazz: The Definitive Guide to Jazz. Ed. 4.
Chris Woodstra & Stephen Thomas Erlewine (Editors). Trade
Paper. Backbeat Books. San Francisco, CA. 2002. 1400p. AMG
All Music Guide Ser. ISBN:0-87930-717-X, ISBN13:
978-0-87930-717-2. Dewey:781.65/0266. LCCN:2002-028031.

                                     Audience: **g,l,u,f.**

Bogdanov, Vladimir   ML156.9.A39 2002
(Editor), et al.
All Music Guide to Rock: The Definitive Guide to Rock, Pop
and Soul. Ed. 3. Chris Woodstra & Stephen Thomas Erlewine
(Editors). Trade Paper. Backbeat Books. San Francisco, CA.
2002. 1399p. AMG All Media Guide Ser. ISBN:0-87930-653-X,
ISBN13: 978-0-87930-653-3. Dewey:016.78164/0266.
LCCN:2002-018397.

                                     Audience: **g,l,u,f.**

Bogdanov, Vladimir, et al.   ML156.4.B6A45 2003
All Music Guide to the Blues: The Definitive Guide to the
Blues. Ed. 3. Chris Woodstra & Stephen Thomas Erlewine
(Authors). Trade Paper. Backbeat Books. San Francisco, CA.
2003. 800p. AMG All Media Guide Ser. ISBN:0-87930-736-6,
ISBN13: 978-0-87930-736-3. Dewey:016.781643/0266.
LCCN:2003-040408.

                                     Audience: **g,l,u,f.**

Bogdanov, Vladimir   ML3531
(Editor), et al.
All Music Guide to Hip-Hop: The Definitive Guide to Rap and
Hip-Hop. Chris Woodstra, Stephen Thomas Erlewine & John
Bush (Editors). Trade Paper. Backbeat Books. San Francisco,
CA. 2003. 640p. AMG All Media Guide Ser.
ISBN:0-87930-759-5, ISBN13: 978-0-87930-759-2.
Dewey:782.421649. LCCN:2003-057799.

                                     Audience: **g,l,u,f.**

Brackett, Nathan & Hoard,   ML156.4.P6R62 2004
Christian (Editors)
The New Rolling Stone Album Guide. Ed. 4. Trade Paper.
Simon & Schuster, Inc. New York, NY. 2004. 944p.
ISBN:0-7432-0169-8, ISBN13: 978-0-7432-0169-8.
Dewey:781.66/026/6. LCCN:2004-058905.

                                     Audience: **g,l,u,f.**

Bronson, Fred   ML156.4.P6B76 2004
The Billboard Book of Number One Hits. Ed. 5. Trade Paper.
Watson-Guptill Publications, Inc. New York, NY. 2003. 1,008p.
Ser. ISBN:0-8230-7677-6, ISBN13: 978-0-8230-7677-2.
Dewey:016.78164/0973. LCCN:2003-016910.

                       Audience: **l,u,f.** *Choice, 2004.*

Broughton, Simon et al.   ML102.W67W67 1999
Rough Guide to World Music, Vol. 1: Africa, Europe, and the
Middle East. Ellingham, Mark; Trillo, Richard (Authors) Duane,
Orla; Dowell, Vanessa. Rough Guides, Ltd. 2000.
ISBN:1-85828-635-2, ISBN13: 978-1-85828-635-8.

                                     Audience: **g,l,u,f.**

Broughton, Simon, et al.   ML160
Rough Guide to World Music, Vol. 2: Latin and North America,
the Caribbean, Asia, and the Pacific. Ellingham, Mark; Trillo,
Richard (Authors) Duane, Orla; Dowell, Vanessa. Rough
Guides, Ltd. 2000. ISBN:1-85828-636-0, ISBN13:
978-1-85828-636-5.

                                     Audience: **g,l,u,f.**

Cowley, John & Oliver, Paul   ML156.4.B6B6 1996
The New Blackwell Guide to Recorded Blues. Ed. 2. Trade
Cloth. Blackwell Publishing, Inc. Malden, MA. 1996. 448p.
ISBN:0-631-20163-7, ISBN13: 978-0-631-20163-2.
Dewey:782.4/2/1643/0266. LCCN:96-012140.

                                     Audience: **g,l,u,f.**

Fujioka, Yasuhiro   ML156.7.C58F85 1995
John Coltrane: A Discography and Musical Biography. Lewis
Porter & Yoh-Ichi Hamada (Preface by). Trade Cloth. Scarecrow
Press, Inc. Lanham, MD. 1995. 416p. Studies in Jazz, No. 20
ISBN:0-8108-2986-X, ISBN13: 978-0-8108-2986-2.
Dewey:016.7887/165/092. LCCN:94-048457.

                                     Audience: **u,f.**

Green, Jeff   ML156.4.P6G73 2002
The Green Book of Songs by Subject: The Thematic Guide to
Popular Music. Ed. 5. Trade Cloth. Professional Desk
References, Inc. Nashville, TN. 2002. xxi, 1569p.
ISBN:0-939735-10-5, ISBN13: 978-0-939735-10-5.
Dewey:016.78242164/0266. LCCN:2001-099825.

                    Audience: **g,l,u,f.** *Choice, 2002, 1995.*

Kernfeld, Barry D.   ML156.4.J3B66 1995
The Blackwell Guide to Recorded Jazz. Ed. 2. Trade Paper.
Blackwell Publishing, Inc. Malden, MA. 1995. 588p. Music
Guides Ser. ISBN:0-631-19552-1, ISBN13: 978-0-631-19552-8.
Dewey:016.78165/026/6. LCCN:95-000762.

                            Audience: **g,l,u,f.** *Choice, 1996.*

Koch, Lawrence O.   ML156.7.P35K6 1999
Yardbird Suite: A Compendium of the Music and Life of Charlie
Parker. Ed. 2. Cloth Text. Northeastern University Press. Boston,
MA. 1999. 416p. ISBN:1-55553-385-X, ISBN13:
978-1-55553-385-4. Dewey:788.7/3165/092. LCCN:99-019348.

                            Audience: **u,f.** *Choice, 1999, 1989.*

Lewisohn, Mark   ML156.7.B4
The Beatles Recording Sessions. Harmony Books. 1988.
ISBN:0-517-57066-1, ISBN13: 978-0-517-57066-1.

                                     Audience: **u,f.**

Meade, Guthrie Jr.   2002022360 [ML]
Country Music Sources: A Biblio-Discography of Commercially
Recorded Traditional Music. Trade Cloth. University of North
Carolina Press. Chapel Hill, NC. 2002. 1024p. Southern Folklife
Collection ISBN:0-8078-2723-1, ISBN13: 978-0-8078-2723-9.
Dewey:016.78162/13/00266. LCCN:2002-022360.

                            Audience: **u,f.** *Choice, 2003.*

Pruter, Robert   ML156.4.S6
The Blackwell Guide to Soul Recordings. Oxford, UK;
Cambridge, Mass.: Blackwell Publishers. 1993. Blackwell
Reference ISBN:0-631-18595-X, ISBN13: 978-0-631-18595-6.

Audience: **g,l,u,f.**

Raymond, Jack   ML156.4.M8R4 1992
Show Music on Record: The First One Hundred Years. Trade
Cloth. Smithsonian Institution Press. Washington, DC. 1992.
440p. ISBN:1-56098-151-2, ISBN13: 978-1-56098-151-0.
Dewey:016.7821/4/0266. LCCN:91-023483.

Audience: **g,l,u,f.**

Spottswood, Richard K.   ML156.4.F5 S69
Ethnic Music on Records - A Discography of Ethnic Recordings
Produced in the United States, 1893-1942: Eastern Europe.
Trade Cloth. University of Illinois Press. Champaign, IL. 1990.
504p. Music in American Life Ser., Vol. 3 ISBN:0-252-01721-8,
ISBN13: 978-0-252-01721-6. Dewey:016.78162/0026/6.

Audience: **u,f.**

Spottswood, Richard K.   ML156.4.F5 S69
Ethnic Music on Records - A Discography of Ethnic Recordings
Produced in the United States, 1893-1942: Spanish, Portuguese,
Philippines, Basque. Trade Cloth. University of Illinois Press.
Champaign, IL. 1990. 904p. Music in American Life Ser., Vol. 4
ISBN:0-252-01722-6, ISBN13: 978-0-252-01722-3.
Dewey:016.78162/0026/6.

Audience: **u,f.**

Spottswood, Richard K.   ML156.4.F5 S69
Ethnic Music on Records - A Discography of Ethnic Recordings
Produced in the United States, 1893-1942: Record Number
Index, Matrix Number Index. Trade Cloth. University of Illinois
Press. Champaign, IL. 1990. 640p. Music in American Life Ser.
Vol. 7 ISBN:0-252-01725-0, ISBN13: 978-0-252-01725-4.
Dewey:016.78162/0026/6.

Audience: **u,f.**

Spottswood, Richard K.   ML156.4.F5 S69
Ethnic Music on Records - A Discography of Ethnic Recordings
Produced in the United States, 1893-1942: Western Europe.
Trade Cloth. University of Illinois Press. Champaign, IL. 1991.
682p. Music in American Life Ser. ISBN:0-252-01719-6,
ISBN13: 978-0-252-01719-3. Dewey:016.78162/0026/6.

Audience: **u,f.**

Spottswood, Richard K.   ML156.4.F5 S69
Ethnic Music on Records - A Discography of Ethnic Recordings
Produced in the United States, 1893-1942: Slavic. Trade Cloth.
University of Illinois Press. Champaign, IL. 1990. 552p. Music
in American Life Ser., Vol. 2 ISBN:0-252-01720-X, ISBN13:
978-0-252-01720-9. Dewey:016.78162/0026/6.

Audience: **u,f.**

Spottswood, Richard K.   ML156.4.F5 S69
Ethnic Music on Records - A Discography of Ethnic Recordings
Produced in the United States, 1893-1942: Artist Index, Title
Index. Trade Cloth. University of Illinois Press. Champaign, IL.

1990. 760p. Music in American Life Ser., Vol. 6
ISBN:0-252-01724-2, ISBN13: 978-0-252-01724-7.
Dewey:016.78162/0026/6.

Audience: **u.**

Spottswood, Richard K.   ML156.4.F5 S69
Ethnic Music on Records - A Discography of Ethnic Recordings
Produced in the United States, 1893-1942: Middle East, Far
East, Scandinavian, English Language, American Indian,
International. Trade Cloth. University of Illinois Press.
Champaign, IL. 1990. 512p. Music in American Life Ser., Vol. 5
ISBN:0-252-01723-4, ISBN13: 978-0-252-01723-0.
Dewey:016.78162/0026/6.

Audience: **u,f.**

Strong, Martin C.   ML156.4.R6
The Great Rock Discography: Complete Discographies Listing
Every Track Recorded by More Than 1,200 Artists. Ed. 7. John
Peel (Foreword by). Trade Paper. Canongate Books. Edinburgh,
2004. 1,120p. ISBN:1-84195-615-5, ISBN13:
978-1-84195-615-2. Dewey:781.660166.

Audience: **l,u,f.**

Townley, Eric   ML156.4.J3
Tell Your Story: A Dictionary of Jazz and Blues Recordings
1917-1950, Vol. 1. Chigwell, Eng.: Storyville Publications.
1976.

Audience: **g,l,u,f.**

Townley, Eric   ML156.4.J3
Tell Your Story: A Dictionary of Jazz and Blues Recordings
1951-1975, Vol. 2. Chigwell, Essex, England: Storyville
Publications. 1987. ISBN:0-902391-09-7, ISBN13:
978-0-902391-09-3.

Audience: **g,l,u,f.**

Wallis, Geoff & Wilson, Sue   ML3654
The Rough Guide to Irish Music. Trade Paper. Rough Guides,
Ltd. London, 2001. 400p. Travel Ser. ISBN:1-85828-642-5,
ISBN13: 978-1-85828-642-6. Dewey:781.6/2/9162.

Audience: **g,l,u,f.**

Whitburn, Joel   ML156.4.P6
Joel Whitburn Presents a Century of Pop Music: Year-by-Year
Top 40 Rankings of the Songs and Artists That Shaped a
Century: Compiled from America's Popular Music Charts,
Surveys, and Record Listings 1900-1939, and Billboard's Pop
Singles Charts, 1940-1999. Menomonee Falls, Wis.: Record
Research. 1999. ISBN:0-89820-135-7, ISBN13:
978-0-89820-135-2.

Audience: **g,l,u,f.**

Whitburn, Joel   ML146.4.P6
Joel Whitburn Presents Top 10 Singles Charts: Chart Data
Compiled from Billboard's Best Sellers in Stores and Hot 100
Charts, 1955-2000. Menomonee Falls, WI: Record Research.
2001. ISBN:0-89820-145-4, ISBN13: 978-0-89820-145-1.

Audience: **g,l,u,f.**

Whitburn, Joel   ML156.4.B6W25 2004
Joel Whitburn Presents Top R & B/Hip-Hop Singles, 1942-2004.
Trade Cloth. Record Research, Inc. Menomonee Falls, WI.
2005. 818p. ISBN:0-89820-160-8, ISBN13: 978-0-89820-160-4.
Dewey:016.781643/0266. LCCN:2005-297809.
                                      Audience: **g,l,u,f.**

Whitburn, Joel   ML156.4.P6
Joel Whitburn's Top Pop Albums, 1955-2001. Menomonee
Falls, Wis.: Record Research. 2001. ISBN:0-89820-147-0,
ISBN13: 978-0-89820-147-5.
                                      Audience: **g,l,u,f.**

Whitburn, Joel   ML156.4.C7
Top Country Singles, 1944 to 2001: Chart Data Compiled from
Billboard's Country Singles Charts, 1944-2001. Ed. 5.
Menomonee Falls, Wis.: Record Research. 2002.
ISBN:0-89820-151-9, ISBN13: 978-0-89820-151-2.
                                      Audience: **g,l,u,f.**

Whitburn, Joel   ML156.4.P6
Top Pop Singles 1955-2002. Ed. 10. Record Research, Inc.
2004. ISBN:0-89820-155-1, ISBN13: 978-0-89820-155-0.
                                      Audience: **u,f.**

Woodstra, Chris, et al.   ML156
All Music Guide to Classical Music: The Definitive Guide to
Classical Music. Gerald Brennan & Allen Schrott (Authors).
Trade Paper, Perfect. Backbeat Books. San Francisco, CA. 2005.
1607p. ISBN:0-87930-865-6, ISBN13: 978-0-87930-865-0.
Dewey:016.78026/6. LCCN:2005-023988.
                            Audience: **g,l,u,f.** *Choice, 2006.*

Reference Resources > Directories and Information Sites

                                                ML105.I54
International Who's Who in Classical Music. Europa
Publications Ltd. 2002.
                                      Audience: **g,l,u,f.**

                                                    ML66
International Who's Who in Popular Music. Europa Publications
Ltd. 2002.
                                      Audience: **g,l,u,f.**

                                                    ML12
Musical America Worldwide. Commonwealth Business Media
Inc. 2006.
                                      Audience: **g,l,u,f.**

                                                  ML3790
Recording Industry Sourcebook. Anscona Communications.
1990.
                                      Audience: **g,l,u,f.**

American Musicological   ML3797
  Society
☐ WWW Sites of Interest to Musicologists.

http://www.ams-net.org/musicology_www.html
American Musicological Society.
                                      Audience: **g,l,u,f.**

American Society of   ML27.U5
  Composers, Authors and Publishers
☐ ASCAP: The American Society of Composers, Authors and
Publishers.
http://www.ascap.com/index.html
American Society of Composers, Authors and Publishers.
                                      Audience: **l,u,f.**

Axford, Elizabeth C.   ML74.7.A94 2004
Song Sheets to Software: A Guide to Print Music, Software, and
Web Sites for Musicians. Ed. 2. Trade Paper. Scarecrow Press,
Inc. Lanham, MD. 2004. 274p. ISBN:0-8108-5027-3, ISBN13:
978-0-8108-5027-9. Dewey:780.26. LCCN:2004-002488.
                            Audience: **l,u,f.** *Choice, 2005.*

Broadcast Music Inc.   ML27.U5 B65
☐ BMI = Broadcast Music Inc.
http://www.bmi.com/
Broadcast Music Inc.
                                      Audience: **l,u,f.**

College Music Society   ML13
Directory of Music Faculties in Colleges and Universities, U.S.
and Canada. College Music Society. 2006.
                                      Audience: **g,l,u,f.**

Harry Fox Agency
☐ HFA = Harry Fox Agency.
http://www.harryfox.com/
Harry Fox Agency.
                                      Audience: **u,f.**

International Alliance for   ML128.W7
  Women in Music
☐ IAWM = International Alliance for Women in Music.
http://www.iawm.org
International Alliance for Women in Music.
                                      Audience: **g,l,u,f.**

Music Publishers'   ML112 M73
  Association of the United States
☐ MPA = Music Publisher's Association of the United States.
http://www.mpa.org
Music Publisher's Association of the United States.
                                      Audience: **u,f.**

National Music Publishers'   ML27
  Association
☐ NMPA = National Music Publishers' Association.
http://www.nmpa.org/
National Music Publishers' Association.
                                      Audience: **u,f.**

Recording Industry   ML3790
  Association of America
☐ RIAA = Recording Industry Association of America.

http://www.riaa.com
Recording Industry Association of America.

Audience: **g,l,u,f.**

Sibelius Academy   **ML63**
◻ Music Resources.
http://www2.siba.fi/Kulttuuripalvelut/music.html
Sibelius Academy.

Audience: **g,l,u,f.**

Society of European Stage   **Z653 .N2**
  Authors and Composers
◻ SESAC = Society of European Stage Authors and
Composers.
http://www.sesac.com
Society of European Stage Authors and Composers.

Audience: **u,f.**

William and Gayle Cook   **ML100**
  Music Library, Indiana University School of Music
◻ Worldwide Internet Music Resources.
http://library.music.indiana.edu/music_resources/
William and Gayle Cook Music Library, Indiana University
School of Music.

Audience: **g,l,u,f.**

Disciplines and Methodologies of Music Scholarship

Allen, W. D.   **ML3800.A43 P5**
Philosophies of Music History: A Study of General Histories of
Music, 1600-1960. Trade Cloth. Peter Smith Publisher, Inc.
Magnolia, MA. 1988. ISBN:0-8446-1529-3, ISBN13:
978-0-8446-1529-5. Dewey:780.01.

Audience: **u,f.**

Beard, David & Gloag,   **ML3797.B35 2005**
  Kenneth
Musicology: The Key Concepts. Paper over Boards. Routledge.
New York, NY. 2005. XIV, 242p. Routledge Key Guides
ISBN:0-415-31693-6, ISBN13: 978-0-415-31693-4.
Dewey:780/.72. LCCN:2004-017044.

Audience: **u,f.**

Bellman, Jonathan   **ML3797.B4 1999**
A Short Guide to Writing about Music. Trade Paper. Longman
Publishing. Boston, MA. 1999. 174p. ISBN:0-321-01577-0,
ISBN13: 978-0-321-01577-8. Dewey:808/.06678.
LCCN:99-014759.

Audience: **g,l,u,f.**

Bohlman, Philip V.   **ML3545.B64 1988**
The Study of Folk Music in the Modern World. Trade Cloth.
Indiana University Press. Bloomington, IN. 1988. 182p.
ISBN:0-253-35555-9, ISBN13: 978-0-253-35555-3.
Dewey:781.7/09. LCCN:87-045401.

Audience: **l,u,f.** *Choice, 1989.*

Clarke, Eric & Cook,   **ML3797**
  Nicholas (Editors)
Empirical Musicology: Aims, Methods, Prospects. Trade Paper.
Oxford University Press, Inc. New York, NY. 2004. 238p.
ISBN:0-19-516750-3, ISBN13: 978-0-19-516750-4.
Dewey:780/.72. LCCN:2004-012210.

Audience: **u,f.**

Crabtree, Phillip D., et al.   **ML113.C68 2005**
Sourcebook for Research in Music. Ed. 2. Donald H. Foster &
Scott Allen (Authors). Trade Cloth. Indiana University Press.
Bloomington, IN. 2005. 352p. ISBN:0-253-21780-6, ISBN13:
978-0-253-21780-6. Dewey:016.7. LCCN:2005-282480.

Audience: **l,u,f.** *Choice, 2006, 1994.*

Dahlhaus, Carl   **ML3797.D2313 1983**
Foundations of Music History. J. Bradford Robinson
(Translator). Trade Paper. Cambridge University Press. New
York, NY. 1983. 182p. ISBN:0-521-29890-3, ISBN13:
978-0-521-29890-2. Dewey:780/.9. LCCN:82-009591.

Audience: **u,f.** ℬ

Hood, Mantle   **ML3798.H66**
The Ethnomusicologist. Trade Paper. Books on Demand. Ann
Arbor, MI. 430p. ISBN:0-7837-0577-8, ISBN13:
978-0-7837-0577-4. Dewey:780.89. LCCN:82-014828.

Audience: **u,f.**

Irvine, Demar   **ML3797.I79 1999**
Irvine's Writing about Music. Ed. 3. Mark A. Radice (Revised
by). Trade Paper. Hal Leonard Corporation. Milwaukee, WI.
2003. 260p. ISBN:1-57467-049-2, ISBN13: 978-1-57467-049-3.
Dewey:808/.06678. LCCN:98-045510.

Audience: **g,l,u,f.**

Kerman, Joseph   **ML3791.1**
Contemplating Music: Challenges to Musicology. Trade Paper.
Harvard University Press. Cambridge, MA. 1986. 256p.
ISBN:0-674-16678-7, ISBN13: 978-0-674-16678-3.
Dewey:780/.01.

Audience: **u,f.** ℬ *Choice, 1985.*

Myers, Helen (Editor)   **ML3798**
Ethnomusicology : An Introduction. W.W. Norton. 1992. The
Norton/Grove Handbooks in Music

Audience: **l,u,f.**

Nettl, Bruno   **ML3798.N47 2005**
The Study of Ethnomusicology: Thirty-One Issues and
Concepts. Ed. 2. Trade Cloth. University of Illinois Press.
Champaign, IL. 2005. 528p. ISBN:0-252-03033-8, ISBN13:
978-0-252-03033-8. Dewey:780/.89. LCCN:2005-011181.

Audience: **u,f.** *Choice, 2006.*

Phelps, Roger P., et al.   **MT1.P5 2005**
A Guide to Research in Music Education. Ed. 5. Ronald Sadoff,
Edward C. Warburton & Lawrence Ferrara (Authors). Trade
Cloth. Scarecrow Press, Inc. Lanham, MD. 2004. 288p.
ISBN:0-8108-5240-3, ISBN13: 978-0-8108-5240-2.
Dewey:780/.7. LCCN:2004-010739.

Audience: **u,f.**

Poultney, David   **ML161.P8 1995**
Studying Music History: Learning, Reasoning, and Writing
about Music History and Literature. Ed. 2. Trade Paper. Prentice
Hall PTR. Upper Saddle River, NJ. 1995. 262p.
ISBN:0-13-190224-5, ISBN13: 978-0-13-190224-4.
Dewey:780/.9. LCCN:95-013540.

Audience: **g,l,u,f.**

Wingell, Richard   **ML3797.W54 2002**
Writing about Music: An Introductory Guide. Ed. 3. Trade
Paper. Prentice Hall PTR. Upper Saddle River, NJ. 2001. 171p.
ISBN:0-13-040603-1, ISBN13: 978-0-13-040603-3.
Dewey:808/.06678. LCCN:2001-045945.

Audience: **g,l,u,f.**

Studies in Music History, Criticism, Analysis, and Appreciation > Western Classical Literature by Period > General Histories

Burney, Charles   **ML159**
A General History of Music, from the Earliest Ages to the
Present Period (1789). Mercer, Frank (Editor). Classic
Textbooks. 1935. ISBN:1-4047-9540-5, ISBN13:
978-1-4047-9540-2.

Audience: **u,f.**

Haas, Robert, et al.   **ML89**
A History of Music in Pictures. Schnoor, Hans (Author) Kinsky,
Georg (Editor). Classic Textbooks. 1951. ISBN:1-4047-9214-7,
ISBN13: 978-1-4047-9214-2.

Audience: **g,l,u,f.**

Hall, Charles John   **ML240.O3**
Chronology of Western Classical Music, 1751-2000, Set. Paper
over Boards. Routledge. New York, NY. 2002. 800p.
ISBN:0-415-93878-3, ISBN13: 978-0-415-93878-5.
Dewey:781.6/8/094.

Audience: **g,l,u,f.**

Hawkins, John   **ML159**
A General History of the Science and Practice of Music. Trade
Cloth. Library Reprints, Inc. Temecula, CA. 2001.
ISBN:0-7222-5029-0, ISBN13: 978-0-7222-5029-7.
Dewey:780.9.

Audience: **u,f.** B

Kelly, Thomas Forrest   **ML63.K44 2000**
First Nights: Five Musical Premieres. Cloth over Boards. Yale
University Press. Cumberland, RI. 2000. 416p.
ISBN:0-300-07774-2, ISBN13: 978-0-300-07774-2.
Dewey:780/.78/09. LCCN:99-050265.
Audience: **g,l,u,f.** *Choice, 2000.*

Lang, Paul Henry   **ML160.L25 1997**
Music in Western Civilization. Trade Cloth. W. W. Norton &
Company, Inc. New York, NY. 1997. 1100p.

ISBN:0-393-04074-7, ISBN13: 978-0-393-04074-6.
Dewey:780/.9. LCCN:97-005883.

Audience: **g,l,u,f.** B

Lang, Paul Henry   **ML89**
A Pictorial History of Music. Paper Text. Textbook Publishers.
Temecula, CA. 2003. vii, 242p. ISBN:0-7581-7569-8, ISBN13:
978-0-7581-7569-4. Dewey:780.9.

Audience: **g,l,u,f.**

Machlis, Joseph & Forney,   **MT90.M23 2003**
Kristine
The Enjoyment of Music: An Introduction to Perceptive
Listening. Ed. 9. Trade Cloth. W. W. Norton & Company, Inc.
New York, NY. 2003. 680p. ISBN:0-393-97878-8, ISBN13:
978-0-393-97878-0. Dewey:780. LCCN:2002-044852.

Audience: **g,l,f.**

Morgenstern, Sam (Editor)   **ML90.M6 1969**
Composers on Music: An Anthology of Composers Writings
from Palestrina to Copland. Library Binding. Greenwood
Publishing Group, Inc. Portsmouth, NH. 1985. xxiii, 584p.
ISBN:0-8371-1147-1, ISBN13: 978-0-8371-1147-6.
Dewey:780/.8. LCCN:69-014005.

Audience: **g,l,u,f.** B

Palisca, Claude V., et al.   **ML160.G872 2005**
A History of Western Music. Ed. 7. J. Peter Burkholder &
Donald Jay Grout (Authors). Cloth Text. W. W. Norton &
Company, Inc. New York, NY. 2005. 965p.
ISBN:0-393-97991-1, ISBN13: 978-0-393-97991-6.
Dewey:780/.9. LCCN:2005-048797.

Audience: **g,l,u,f.**

Reese, Gustave   **ML160.R33 1970**
Fourscore Classics of Music Literature. Paper Text. Da Capo
Press, Inc. Cambridge, MA. 1970. Music Reprint Ser.
ISBN:0-306-71620-8, ISBN13: 978-0-306-71620-1.
Dewey:780.9. LCCN:78-087616.

Audience: **u,f.**

Stolba, K. Marie   **ML160**
Development of Western Music. Trade Cloth, Compact Disc.
McGraw-Hill Higher Education. Burr Ridge, IL. 1999.
ISBN:0-697-41767-0, ISBN13: 978-0-697-41767-1.
Dewey:780/.9.

Audience: **g,l,u,f.**

Strunk, Oliver & Treitler,   **ML160.S89 1998**
Leo (Editors)
Source Readings in Music History. Trade Cloth. W. W. Norton
& Company, Inc. New York, NY. 1998. 1572p.
ISBN:0-393-03752-5, ISBN13: 978-0-393-03752-4.
Dewey:780/.9. LCCN:94-034569.

Audience: **g,l,u,f.**

Taruskin, Richard   **ML160**
The Oxford History of Western Music, Set. Trade Cloth. Oxford
University Press, Inc. New York, NY. 2005. 4,250p.
ISBN:0-19-516979-4, ISBN13: 978-0-19-516979-9.
Dewey:780/.9. LCCN:2004-017897.

Audience: **g,l,u,f.**

Taruskin, Richard F.   ML160.M865
Music in the Western World. Cloth Text. Thomson Gale.
Farmington Hills, MI. 1996. 816p. ISBN:0-02-872543-3,
ISBN13: 978-0-02-872543-7. Dewey:780/.9.

Audience: **g,l,u,f.**

Van der Merwe, Peter   MT6
Roots of the Classical: The Popular Origins of Western Music.
Trade Cloth. Oxford University Press, Inc. New York, NY. 2005.
576p. ISBN:0-19-816647-8, ISBN13: 978-0-19-816647-4.
Dewey:781.

Audience: **u,f.** *Choice, 2005.*

Weiss, Piero   ML90.W44
Letters of Composers Through Six Centuries. Trade Cloth.
Reprint Services Company. Temecula, CA. 1986.
ISBN:0-685-14779-7, ISBN13: 978-0-685-14779-5.
Dewey:780/.922.

Audience: **g,l,u,f.** *B*

Winternitz, Emanuel   ML96.4.W5
Musical Autographs from Monteverdi to Hindemith. Trade
Cloth. Peter Smith Publisher, Inc. Magnolia, MA. 1980.
ISBN:0-8446-3197-3, ISBN13: 978-0-8446-3197-4.
Dewey:781.969.

Audience: **l,u,f.**

Studies in Music History, Criticism, Analysis, and Appreciation > Western Classical Literature by Period > Antiquity

Anderson, Warren D.   ML169.A66 1994
Music and Musicians in Ancient Greece. Book, Other. Cornell
University Press. Ithaca, NY. 1995. 256p. ISBN:0-8014-3083-6,
ISBN13: 978-0-8014-3083-1. Dewey:780/.9/01.
LCCN:94-028507.

Audience: **g,l,u,f.** *Choice, 1995.*

Barker, Andrew (Editor)   ML167.G73 1984
Greek Musical Writings: Harmonic and Acoustic Theory. John
Stevens & Peter le Huray (Contribution by). Trade Paper.
Cambridge University Press. New York, NY. 2004. 589p.
Cambridge Readings in the Literature of Music Ser., Vol. 2
ISBN:0-521-61697-2, ISBN13: 978-0-521-61697-3.
Dewey:780.938. LCCN:2006-271704.

Audience: **u,f.**

Barker, Andrew (Editor)   ML167.G73
Greek Musical Writings: The Musician and His Art. John
Stevens & Peter Le Huray (Contribution by). Trade Paper.
Cambridge University Press. New York, NY. 1989. 348p.
Cambridge Readings in the Literature of Music Ser.
ISBN:0-521-38911-9, ISBN13: 978-0-521-38911-2.
Dewey:781/.0938. LCCN:83-020924.

Audience: **u,f.**

Buckley, Ann I (Editor)   ML3797.7
Hearing the Past : Essays in Historical Ethnomusicology and the
Archaeology of Sound. Liège: Université de Liège. 1998.
E.R.A.U.L.; 86

Audience: **u,f.**

Galpin, Francis W.   ML164 .G17M9 1970C
The Music of the Sumerians and Their Immediate Successors,
the Babylonians and Assyrians. Trade Cloth. Greenwood
Publishing Group, Inc. Portsmouth, NH. 1970. 110p.
ISBN:0-8371-3928-7, ISBN13: 978-0-8371-3928-9.
Dewey:781.7/35. LCCN:75-104273.

Audience: **u,f.**

Landels, John G.   ML169.L24 1998
Music in Ancient Greece and Rome. Paper over Boards.
Routledge. New York, NY. 1998. 312p. ISBN:0-415-16776-0,
ISBN13: 978-0-415-16776-5. Dewey:780/.938.
LCCN:98-003051.

Audience: **g,l,u,f.** *Choice, 1999.*

Lippman, Edward A.   ML169.L68
Musical Thought in Ancient Greece. Paper Text. Da Capo Press,
Inc. Cambridge, MA. 1975. Music Reprint Ser.
ISBN:0-306-70669-5, ISBN13: 978-0-306-70669-1.
Dewey:780/.1/0938. LCCN:74-023415.

Audience: **u,f.**

Maas, Martha & Snyder,   ML169.M2 1989
Jane M.
Stringed Instruments of Ancient Greece. Cloth over Boards. Yale
University Press. Cumberland, RI. 1989. 288p.
ISBN:0-300-03686-8, ISBN13: 978-0-300-03686-2.
Dewey:787/.00938. LCCN:87-002103.

Audience: **u,f.** *Choice, 1989.*

Manniche, Lise   ML164
Music and Musicians in Ancient Egypt. London, England:
British Museum Press. 1991. ISBN:0-7141-0949-5, ISBN13:
978-0-7141-0949-7.

Audience: **u,f.**

Mathiesen, Thomas J.   ML169.M39 2000
Apollo's Lyre: Greek Music and Music Theory in Antiquity and
the Middle Ages. Cloth Text. University of Nebraska Press.
Lincoln, NE. 2000. 807p. Publications of the Center for the
History of Music Theory and Literature Ser., Vol. 2
ISBN:0-8032-3079-6, ISBN13: 978-0-8032-3079-8.
Dewey:780/.938. LCCN:99-035248.

Audience: **u,f.**

McKinnon, James W.   ML162
(Editor)
Music in Early Christian Literature. John Stevens & Peter le
Huray (Contribution by). Trade Paper. Cambridge University
Press. New York, NY. 1989. 192p. Cambridge Readings in the
Literature of Music Ser. ISBN:0-521-37624-6, ISBN13:
978-0-521-37624-2. Dewey:780/.901.

Audience: **g,l,u,f.** *Choice, 1987.*

Michaelides, Solon   **ML167.M5**
The Music of Ancient Greece. Trade Cloth. Faber & Faber, Ltd.
London, 1978. 382p. ISBN:0-571-10021-X, ISBN13:
978-0-571-10021-7. Dewey:781.7/38. LCCN:78-308507.
Audience: **u,f.**

Montagu, Jeremy   **ML166.M66 2002**
Musical Instruments of the Bible. Trade Cloth. Scarecrow Press,
Inc. Lanham, MD. 2002. 192p. ISBN:0-8108-4282-3, ISBN13:
978-0-8108-4282-3. Dewey:220.8/78419. LCCN:2002-021202.
Audience: **g,l,u,f.**

Pohlmann, Egert & West,   **ML169.P587D63 2001**
  Martin L.
Documents of Ancient Greek Music: The Extant Melodies and
Fragments. Trade Cloth. Oxford University Press, Inc. New
York, NY. 2001. 232p. ISBN:0-19-815223-X, ISBN13:
978-0-19-815223-1. Dewey:780/.937. LCCN:2001-275658.
Audience: **u,f.**

Pérez Arroyo, Rafael   **ML164**
Egypt: Music in the Age of the Pyramids. Hare, Dorothy; Hill,
Guy (Translators). Madrid: Editorial Centro de Estudios
Egipcios. 2003. ISBN:84-932796-1-7, ISBN13:
978-84-932796-1-5.
Audience: **g,l,u,f.**

Sachs, Curt   **ML162**
Rise of Music in the Ancient World. Trade Cloth. W. W. Norton
& Company, Inc. New York, NY. 1943. ISBN:0-393-09718-8,
ISBN13: 978-0-393-09718-4. Dewey:781.8.
Audience: **g,l,u,f.**

Scott, William C.   **ML169**
Musical Design in Aeschylean Theater. Library Binding.
University Press of New England. Lebanon, NH. 1984. 252p.
ISBN:0-87451-291-3, ISBN13: 978-0-87451-291-5.
Dewey:782.8/3/0938. LCCN:83-040560.
Audience: **u,f.** *B*

Scott, William C.   **ML169.S38 1996**
Musical Design in Sophoclean Theater. Trade Cloth. University
Press of New England. Lebanon, NH. 1996. 352p.
ISBN:0-87451-739-7, ISBN13: 978-0-87451-739-2.
Dewey:781.5/52/0938. LCCN:95-021611.
Audience: **u,f.** *Choice, 1996.*

West, M. L.   **ML169**
Ancient Greek Music. Trade Paper. Oxford University Press,
Inc. New York, NY. 1994. 424p. ISBN:0-19-814975-1, ISBN13:
978-0-19-814975-0. Dewey:780.9/38. LCCN:91-005170.
Audience: **u,f.** *Choice, 1993.*

Studies in Music History, Criticism, Analysis, and Appreciation > Western Classical Literature by Period > Middle Ages

Apel, Willi   **ML431.A6**
Notation of Polyphonic Music, 900-1600. Ed. 5. Trade Cloth.
Medieval Academy of America. Cambridge, MA. 1961.
Medieval Academy Bks., No. 38 ISBN:0-910956-15-4, ISBN13:
978-0-910956-15-4. Dewey:781.24. LCCN:61-012067.
Audience: **u,f.**

Aubrey, Elizabeth   **ML182**
The Music of the Troubadours. Trade Paper. Indiana University
Press. Bloomington, IN. 2000. 352p. Music Ser., :Scholarship
and Performance ISBN:0-253-21389-4, ISBN13:
978-0-253-21389-1. Dewey:782.4/3/0944809021.
LCCN:96-010358.
Audience: **u,f.** *Choice, 1997.*

Berger, Anna Maria Busse   **ML172 .B43 2005**
Medieval Music and the Art of Memory. Trade Cloth. University
of California Press. Berkeley, CA. 2005. 386p.
ISBN:0-520-24028-6, ISBN13: 978-0-520-24028-5.
Dewey:780/.9/02. LCCN:2004-016542.
Audience: **u,f.** *Choice, 2005.*

Boethius   **MT5.5**
Fundamentals of Music. Bower, Calvin M. (Translator); Palisca,
Claude V. (Editor). New Haven : Yale University Press. 1989.
Music Theory Translation ISBN:0-300-03943-3, ISBN13:
978-0-300-03943-6.
Audience: **u,f.**

Brown, Howard Mayer &   **ML5**
  Sadie, Stanley (Editors)
Performance Practice: Music Before 1600. Trade Cloth. W. W.
Norton & Company, Inc. New York, NY. 1990. Grove
Handbooks in Music Ser. ISBN:0-393-02807-0, ISBN13:
978-0-393-02807-2. Dewey:780/.903.
Audience: **u,f.**

Crocker, Richard L.   **ML3082.C73 2000**
An Introduction to Gregorian Chant. Cloth over Boards. Yale
University Press. Cumberland, RI. 2000. 256p.
ISBN:0-300-08310-6, ISBN13: 978-0-300-08310-1.
Dewey:782.32/22. LCCN:99-088603.
Audience: **l,u,f.** *Choice, 2000.*

Crocker, Richard & Hiley, David (Editors)   ML160.N44 1990
The New Oxford History of Music: The Early Middle Ages to 1300. Ed. 2. Trade Cloth. Oxford University Press, Inc. New York, NY. 1990. 816p. New Oxford History of Music Ser. ISBN:0-19-316329-2, ISBN13: 978-0-19-316329-4. Dewey:780/.9. LCCN:88-022471.

Audience: **g,l,u,f.**

Duffin, Ross W.   ML457.P475 2000
A Performer's Guide to Medieval Music. Trade Cloth. Indiana University Press. Bloomington, IN. 2000. xi, 599p. Publications of the Early Music Institute ISBN:0-253-33752-6, ISBN13: 978-0-253-33752-8. Dewey:781.4/3/0902. LCCN:00-040968.

Audience: **u,f.**

Earp, Lawrence   ML134.G956E3 1995
Guillaume de Machaut: A Guide to Research. Library Binding. Garland Publishing, Inc. New York, NY. 1995. 696p. Composer Resource Manuals Ser., Vol. 36 ISBN:0-8240-2323-4, ISBN13: 978-0-8240-2323-2. Dewey:016.841/1. LCCN:95-035044.

Audience: **u,f.** *Choice, 1996.*

Everist, Mark   ML2927.E94 1994
French Motets in the Thirteenth Century: Music, Poetry and Genre. Iain Fenlon, Thomas Forrest Kelly & John Stevens (Contribution by). Trade Paper. Cambridge University Press. New York, NY. 2004. 213p. Cambridge Studies in Medieval and Renaissance Music Ser. ISBN:0-521-61204-7, ISBN13: 978-0-521-61204-3. Dewey:782.260944.

Audience: **u,f.**

Flanagan, Sabina   BX4700.J7
Hildegard of Bingen: A Visionary Life. Ed. 2. Trade Paper. Routledge. New York, NY. 1998. 244p. ISBN:0-415-18551-3, ISBN13: 978-0-415-18551-6. Dewey:248.2/2/092. LCCN:98-012847.

Audience: **u,f.**

Goldin, Frederick (Editor, Translator)   PC3322
Lyrics of the Troubadours and Trouveres: An Anthology and a History. Trade Cloth. Peter Smith Publisher, Inc. Magnolia, MA. 1990. ISBN:0-8446-5036-6, ISBN13: 978-0-8446-5036-4. Dewey:849.104.

Audience: **u,f.**

Haines, John   ML182
Eight Centuries of Troubadours and Trouvéres: The Changing Identity of Medieval Music. John Butt & Laurence Dreyfus (Contribution by). Trade Cloth. Cambridge University Press. New York, NY. 2004. 360p. Musical Performance and Reception Ser. ISBN:0-521-82672-1, ISBN13: 978-0-521-82672-3. Dewey:782.4/3/09. LCCN:2005-297125.

Audience: **u,f.** *Choice, 2005.*

Hiley, David   ML3082.H54 1995
Western Plainchant: A Handbook. Paper Text. Oxford University Press, Inc. New York, NY. 1995. 758p. ISBN:0-19-816572-2, ISBN13: 978-0-19-816572-9. Dewey:782.32/22. LCCN:95-015755.

Audience: **u,f.**

Hoppin, Richard H.   ML172.H8
Medieval Music. Trade Cloth. W. W. Norton & Company, Inc. New York, NY. 1978. 566p. Norton Introduction to Music History Ser. ISBN:0-393-09090-6, ISBN13: 978-0-393-09090-1. Dewey:780/.902. LCCN:78-007010.

Audience: **g,l,u,f.** *B*

Jeffery, Peter   ML3082 .J34
Re-Envisioning Past Musical Cultures: Ethnomusicology in the Study of Gregorian Chant. Trade Paper. University of Chicago Press. Chicago, IL. 1995. 222p. Chicago Studies in Ethnomusicology Ser. ISBN:0-226-39580-4, ISBN13: 978-0-226-39580-7. Dewey:782.3222009.

Audience: **u,f.**

Karp, Theodore   ML174.K33 1992
The Polyphony of Saint Martial and Santiago de Compostela. Trade Cloth. University of California Press. Berkeley, CA. 1993. 710p. ISBN:0-520-04744-3, ISBN13: 978-0-520-04744-0. Dewey:781.2/84/0902. LCCN:91-002873.

Audience: **u,f.**

Knighton, Tess & Fallows, David (Editors)   ML172.C65 1992
Companion to Medieval and Renaissance Music. Trade Cloth. Thomson Gale. Farmington Hills, MI. 1992. 428p. ISBN:0-02-871221-8, ISBN13: 978-0-02-871221-5. Dewey:780/.9/02. LCCN:92-032213.

Audience: **g,l,u,f.** *Choice, 1993.*

Leech-Wilkinson, Daniel   ML410.G966L3 1990
Machaut's Mass: An Introduction. Trade Cloth. Oxford University Press, Inc. New York, NY. 1990. 224p. ISBN:0-19-316333-0, ISBN13: 978-0-19-316333-1. Dewey:782.32/32. LCCN:89-023005.

Audience: **l,u,f.** *Choice, 1991.*

Leech-Wilkinson, Daniel   ML172.L483 2002
The Modern Invention of Medieval Music: Scholarship, Ideology, Performance. John Butt & Laurence Dreyfus (Contribution by). Trade Cloth. Cambridge University Press. New York, NY. 2002. 348p. Musical Performance and Reception Ser. ISBN:0-521-81870-2, ISBN13: 978-0-521-81870-4. Dewey:780/.9/02. LCCN:2003-268355.

Audience: **u,f.** *Choice, 2003.*

McGee, Timothy J. (Editor)   ML430.7.I46 2003
Improvisation in the Arts of the Middle Ages and Renaissance. Trade Cloth. Medieval Institute Publications. Kalamazoo, MI. 2005. xii, 331p. Early Drama, Art, and Music Monograph Ser., Vol. 30 ISBN:1-58044-044-4, ISBN13: 978-1-58044-044-8. Dewey:791/.094/0902. LCCN:2002-015087.

Audience: **u,f.**

McGee, Timothy J. & Rosenfield, Randall A.   ML172.M44 1998
The Sound of Medieval Song: Ornamentation and Vocal Style According to the Treatises. Cloth Text. Oxford University Press, Inc. New York, NY. 1998. 216p. Oxford Monographs on Music ISBN:0-19-816619-2, ISBN13: 978-0-19-816619-1. Dewey:782.04/3/0902. LCCN:97-002770.

Audience: **u,f.**

McKinnon, James   **ML160**
Antiquity and the Middle Ages: From Ancient Greece to the Middle Ages. Paper Text. Prentice Hall PTR. Upper Saddle River, NJ. 1990. 400p. ISBN:0-13-036161-5, ISBN13: 978-0-13-036161-5. Dewey:780.9034.

Audience: **g,l,u,f.**

Page, Christopher   **ML497.2.P33 1990**
The Owl and the Nightingale: Musical Life and Ideas in France, 1100-1300. Trade Cloth. University of California Press. Berkeley, CA. 1990. 291p. ISBN:0-520-06944-7, ISBN13: 978-0-520-06944-2. Dewey:780/.944/0902. LCCN:89-040538.

Audience: **u,f.** *Choice, 1990.*

Palisca, Claude V. (Editor)   **MT5.5.M8713 1995**
Musica Enchiriadis: And Scolica Enchiriadis. Raymond Erickson (Translator, Introduction by, Notes by). Cloth over Boards. Yale University Press. Cumberland, RI. 1995. 160p. Music Theory Translation Ser. ISBN:0-300-05818-7, ISBN13: 978-0-300-05818-5. Dewey:781/.09/02. LCCN:94-034601.

Audience: **u,f.**

Pesce, Dolores (Editor)   **ML3275.H4 1998**
Hearing the Motet: Essays on the Motet of the Middle Ages and Renaissance. Trade Paper. Oxford University Press, Inc. New York, NY. 1998. 392p. ISBN:0-19-512905-9, ISBN13: 978-0-19-512905-2. Dewey:782.2/6/092.

Audience: **u,f.** *Choice, 1997.*

Phillips, Elizabeth B. &   **ML430.5.P52 1986**
  Jackson, John-Paul C.
Performing Medieval and Renaissance Music: An Introductory Guide. Trade Cloth. Thomson Gale. Farmington Hills, MI. 1986. 240p. ISBN:0-02-871790-2, ISBN13: 978-0-02-871790-6. Dewey:780/.902. LCCN:85-018419.

Audience: **u,f.**

Reaney, Gilbert   **ML410.G966 R4**
Guillaume de Machaut. Trade Cloth. Oxford University Press, Inc. New York, NY. 1971. 76p. Oxford Studies of Composers ISBN:0-19-315218-5, ISBN13: 978-0-19-315218-2. Dewey:780/.924. LCCN:79-032092.

Audience: **u,f.**

Robertson, Anne W.   **ML410.G966.R63 2002**
Guillaume de Machaut and Reims: Context and Meaning in His Musical Works. Trade Cloth. Cambridge University Press. New York, NY. 2002. 476p. ISBN:0-521-41876-3, ISBN13: 978-0-521-41876-8. Dewey:782.2/6/092. LCCN:2001-043949.

Audience: **u,f.** *Choice, 2003.*

Stevens, John E.   **ML172.S86 1986**
Words and Music in the Middle Ages: Song, Narrative, Dance and Drama, 1050-1350. Trade Cloth. Cambridge University

Press. New York, NY. 1986. 576p. Cambridge Studies in Music ISBN:0-521-24507-9, ISBN13: 978-0-521-24507-4. Dewey:784/.09/02. LCCN:85-025496.

Audience: **u,f.** *Choice, 1987.*

Treitler, Leo   **ML1402.T73 2003**
With Voice and Pen: Coming to Know Medieval Song and How it Was Made. Trade Cloth. Oxford University Press, Inc. New York, NY. 2003. 536p. ISBN:0-19-816644-3, ISBN13: 978-0-19-816644-3. Dewey:782.42/09/02. LCCN:2002-192579.

Audience: **u,f.**

Wellesz, Egon   **ML188.W363**
History of Byzantine Music and Hymnography. Ed. 2. Trade Cloth. Oxford University Press, Inc. New York, NY. 1961. 476p. ISBN:0-19-816111-5, ISBN13: 978-0-19-816111-0. Dewey:781.7495.

Audience: **u,f.**

Williams, Peter   **ML553.W54 1993**
The Organ in Western Culture, 750-1250. Iain Fenlon, Thomas Forrest Kelly & John Stevens (Contribution by). Trade Paper. Cambridge University Press. New York, NY. 2005. 415p. Cambridge Studies in Medieval and Renaissance Music Ser. ISBN:0-521-61707-3, ISBN13: 978-0-521-61707-9. Dewey:786.5/1909. LCCN:2005-284177.

Audience: **u,f.**

Wilson, David F.   **ML172.W6 1990**
Music of the Middle Ages: Style and Structure. Trade Cloth. Thomson Wadsworth. Belmont, CA. 1990. 403p. ISBN:0-02-872951-X, ISBN13: 978-0-02-872951-0. Dewey:780/.9/02. LCCN:90-038155.

Audience: **l,u,f.**

Wright, Craig   **ML3027.8.P2W7 1989**
Music and Ceremony at Notre Dame of Paris, 500-1550. Trade Cloth. Cambridge University Press. New York, NY. 1989. 420p. Cambridge Studies in Music ISBN:0-521-24492-7, ISBN13: 978-0-521-24492-3. Dewey:783.2/00944/361. LCCN:88-029924.

Audience: **u,f.** *Choice, 1990.*

Yardley, Anne Bagnall   **ML3003**
Performing Piety: Musical Cultures in Medieval English Nunneries. Cloth over Boards. Palgrave Macmillan. New York, NY. 2006. 344p. The New Middle Ages Ser. ISBN:1-4039-6299-5, ISBN13: 978-1-4039-6299-7. Dewey:781.71/24200902. LCCN:2005-045614.

Audience: **u,f.**

Yudkin, Jeremy   **ML171.Y8 1989**
Music in Medieval Europe. Ed. 1. Trade Paper. Prentice Hall

Formats: Web: ☐   Ebook: **ⓔ**   CD/DVD-ROM: 💾   BCL3: *B*

PTR. Upper Saddle River, NJ. 1989. 640p. Prentice Hall History of Music Ser. ISBN:0-13-608192-4, ISBN13: 978-0-13-608192-0. Dewey:780/.902. LCCN:88-032495.

Audience: **g,l,u,f.**

Studies in Music History, Criticism, Analysis, and Appreciation > Western Classical Literature by Period > Renaissance

Apel, Willi   **ML431.A6**
Notation of Polyphonic Music, 900-1600. Ed. 5. Trade Cloth. Medieval Academy of America. Cambridge, MA. 1961. Medieval Academy Bks., No. 38 ISBN:0-910956-15-4, ISBN13: 978-0-910956-15-4. Dewey:781.24. LCCN:61-012067.

Audience: **u,f.**

Arnold, Denis   **ML410.G11 A8**
Giovanni Gabrieli and the Music of the Venetian High Renaissance. Trade Cloth. Oxford University Press, Inc. New York, NY. 1980. 334p. ISBN:0-19-315232-0, ISBN13: 978-0-19-315232-8. Dewey:780/.92/4. LCCN:77-030382.

Audience: **u,f.**

Atlas, Allan W.   **ML172.A84 1998**
Renaissance Music. Trade Paper. W. W. Norton & Company, Inc. New York, NY. 1998. 600p. Norton Introduction to Music History Ser. ISBN:0-393-97169-4, ISBN13: 978-0-393-97169-9. Dewey:780/.9/02. LCCN:97-019816.

Audience: **g,l,u,f.**

Bent, Margaret   **ML410.D933**
Dunstaple. London; New York: Oxford University Press. 1981. Oxford Studies of Composers; 17 ISBN:0-19-315225-8, ISBN13: 978-0-19-315225-0.

Audience: **u,f.**

Bizzarini, Marco & Chater,   **ML410.M326B5813 2002**
James (Translators)
Luca Marenzio: The Career of a Musician Between the Renaissance and the Counter-Reformation. Trade Cloth. Ashgate Publishing, Ltd. Aldershot, 2003. 400p. ISBN:0-7546-0516-7, ISBN13: 978-0-7546-0516-4. Dewey:782.4/3/092 B. LCCN:2002-027917.

Audience: **u,f.**

Blackburn, Bonnie J.   **ML171.C75 1990**
(Editor), et al.
A Correspondence of Renaissance Musicians. Edward E. Lowinsky & Clement Miller (Editors). Trade Cloth. Oxford University Press, Inc. New York, NY. 1991. 1, 112p. ISBN:0-19-315153-7, ISBN13: 978-0-19-315153-6. Dewey:780/.92/245. LCCN:90-014197.

Audience: **u,f**

Brown, Howard Mayer   **ML270.2.B8**
Music in the French Secular Theater, 1400-1550. Harvard University Press. 1963.

Audience: **u,f.**

Brown, Howard Mayer &   **ML5**
Sadie, Stanley (Editors)
Performance Practice: Music Before 1600. Trade Cloth. W. W. Norton & Company, Inc. New York, NY. 1990. Grove Handbooks in Music Ser. ISBN:0-393-02807-0, ISBN13: 978-0-393-02807-2. Dewey:780/.903.

Audience: **u,f.**

Carpenter, Nan Cooke   **ML80.R2**
Rabelais and Music. University of North Carolina Press. 1954.

Audience: **u,f.**

Duffin, Ross W.   **ML80.S5D85 2004**
Shakespeare's Songbook. Stephen Orgel (Foreword by). Trade Cloth. W. W. Norton & Company, Inc. New York, NY. 2004. 496p. ISBN:0-393-05889-1, ISBN13: 978-0-393-05889-5. Dewey:782.42/0942. LCCN:2003-070217.

Audience: **g,l,u,f.** *Choice, 2004.*

Einstein, Alfred   **ML2633**
The Italian Madrigal. Krappe, Alexander Haggerty (Translator); Sessions, Roger (Translator); Strunk, W. Oliver; (William Oliver) (Translator). Princeton University Press. 1971. ISBN:0-691-09112-9, ISBN13: 978-0-691-09112-9.

Audience: **u,f.**

Fallows, David   **ML410.D83**
Dufay. Cloth Text. J. M. Dent & Sons. London, 1982. viii, 321p. ISBN:0-460-03180-5, ISBN13: 978-0-460-03180-6. Dewey:780/.92/4 B. LCCN:82-200447.

Audience: **u,f.**

Fenlon, Iain   **ML172.R44 1989**
The Renaissance: From the 1470's to the End of the 16th Century. Paper Text. Prentice Hall PTR. Upper Saddle River, NJ. 1990. 400p. ISBN:0-13-773417-4, ISBN13: 978-0-13-773417-7. Dewey:780/.9/031. LCCN:90-224619.

Audience: **g,l,u,f.**

Galilei, Vincenzo   **MT5.5.G313 2003**
Dialogue on Ancient and Modern Music. Claude V. Palisca (Translator, Introduction by, Notes by). Cloth over Boards. Yale University Press. Cumberland, RI. 2003. 464p. Music Theory Translation Ser. ISBN:0-300-09045-5, ISBN13: 978-0-300-09045-1. Dewey:781. LCCN:2002-191087.

Audience: **u,f.** *Choice, 2004.*

Gooch, Bryan N. &   **ML120.G7**
Thatcher, David (Editors)
A Shakespeare Music Catalogue: Bibliography. Trade Cloth. Oxford University Press, Inc. New York, NY. 1991. 314p. ISBN:0-19-812945-9, ISBN13: 978-0-19-812945-5. Dewey:16.78.

Audience: **u,f.**

Gooch, Bryan N. &   **ML5**
Thatcher, David (Editors)
A Shakespeare Music Catalogue: Indices. Trade Cloth. Oxford University Press, Inc. New York, NY. 1991. 356p. ISBN:0-19-812944-0, ISBN13: 978-0-19-812944-8. Dewey:780/.903.

Audience: **u,f.**

Gooch, Bryan N. &   **ML134.5.S52G6 1991**
  Thatcher, David (Editors)
A Shakespeare Music Catalogue: The Catalogue of Music:
Macbeth--The Taming of the Shrew. Trade Cloth. Oxford
University Press, Inc. New York, NY. 1991. 804p.
ISBN:0-19-812942-4, ISBN13: 978-0-19-812942-4.
Dewey:016.78/00822. LCCN:89-009270.

Audience: **u,f.**

Gooch, Bryan N. &   **ML120.G7**
  Thatcher, David (Editors)
A Shakespeare Music Catalogue: The Tempest--The Two Noble
Kinsmen, the Sonnets, the Poems, Commemorative Pieces.
Trade Cloth. Oxford University Press, Inc. New York, NY. 1991.
686p. ISBN:0-19-812943-2, ISBN13: 978-0-19-812943-1.
Dewey:16.78.

Audience: **u,f.**

Gooch, Bryan N. &   **ML134.5.S52G6 1991**
  Thatcher, David (Editors)
A Shakespeare Music Catalogue: The Catalogue of Music: All's
Well That Ends Well--Love's Labour's Lost. Trade Cloth.
Oxford University Press, Inc. New York, NY. 1991. 798p.
ISBN:0-19-812941-6, ISBN13: 978-0-19-812941-7.
Dewey:016.78/00822. LCCN:89-009270.

Audience: **u,f.**

Harley, John   **ML410.B996H37 1997**
William Byrd: Gentleman of the Chapel Royal. Trade Cloth.
Ashgate Publishing, Ltd. Aldershot, 1997. 504p.
ISBN:1-85928-165-6, ISBN13: 978-1-85928-165-9.
Dewey:780.9/2. LCCN:96-037221.

Audience: **u,f.** *Choice, 1997.*

Harran, Don   **ML410.R78H37 1999**
Salamone Rossi: Jewish Musician in Late Renaissance Mantua.
Trade Cloth. Oxford University Press, Inc. New York, NY. 1999.
320p. Oxford Monographs on Music ISBN:0-19-816271-5,
ISBN13: 978-0-19-816271-1. Dewey:780/.92 B.
LCCN:98-007974.

Audience: **u,f.**

Higgins, Paula (Editor)   **ML410.B9798A58 1996**
Antoine Busnois: Method, Meaning, and Context in Late
Medieval Music. Trade Cloth. Oxford University Press, Inc.
New York, NY. 2000. 622p. ISBN:0-19-816406-8, ISBN13:
978-0-19-816406-7. Dewey:780/.92. LCCN:95-045522.

Audience: **u,f.**

Holman, Peter   **ML410.D808H651999**
Dowland: Lachrimae (1604). Julian Rushton (Contribution by).
Cloth Text. Cambridge University Press. New York, NY. 1999.
116p. Music Handbks. ISBN:0-521-58196-6, ISBN13:
978-0-521-58196-7. Dewey:784.1882. LCCN:98-054374.

Audience: **u,f.**

Jeppesen, Knud   **ML3003.J362 2005**
The Style of Palestrina and the Dissonance. Trade Paper. Dover
Publications, Inc. Mineola, NY. 2005. 320p.
ISBN:0-486-44268-3, ISBN13: 978-0-486-44268-6.
Dewey:782.2/2/092. LCCN:2004-065738.

Audience: **u,f.**

Kirkman, Andrew & Slavin,   **ML410.B5885B56 2000**
  Dennis (Editors)
Binchois Studies. Trade Cloth. Oxford University Press, Inc.
New York, NY. 2001. 372p. ISBN:0-19-816668-0, ISBN13:
978-0-19-816668-9. Dewey:780/.92. LCCN:00-028823.

Audience: **u,f.**

Kite-Powell, Jeffery T.   **ML457.P48 1994**
  (Editor)
A Performer's Guide to Renaissance Music. Trade Cloth.
Thomson Wadsworth. Belmont, CA. 1994. 400p. Performer's
Guides to Early Music Ser. ISBN:0-02-871231-5, ISBN13:
978-0-02-871231-4. Dewey:781.4/3/09031. LCCN:93-048544.

Audience: **u,f.** *Choice, 1995.*

Marvin, Clara   **ML134.P2M37 2001**
Giovanni Pierluigi da Palestrina: A Research Guide. Cloth Text.
Garland Publishing, Inc. New York, NY. 2002. 350p. Composer
Resource Manuals Ser., Vol. 56 ISBN:0-8153-2351-4, ISBN13:
978-0-8153-2351-8. Dewey:016.7822/2/092. LCCN:00-068435.

Audience: **l,u,f.**

McClary, Susan   **ML2633.2.M332004**
Modal Subjectivities: Self-Fashioning in the Italian Madrigal.
Trade Cloth. University of California Press. Berkeley, CA. 2004.
380p. ISBN:0-520-23493-6, ISBN13: 978-0-520-23493-2.
Dewey:782.4/3/0945. LCCN:2003-025287.

Audience: **u,f.**

Meconi, Honey   **ML410.L287**
Pierre de la Rue and Musical Life at the Habsburg-Burgundian
Court. Trade Cloth. Oxford University Press, Inc. New York,
NY. 2003. 416p. ISBN:0-19-816554-4, ISBN13:
978-0-19-816554-5. Dewey:781.71/2/0092 B.
LCCN:2002-038106.

Audience: **u,f.**

Morley, Thomas   **MT6.M86P69**
A Plain and Easy Introduction to Practical Music. Paper Text.
Textbook Publishers. Temecula, CA. 2003. xxix, 326p.
ISBN:0-7581-7562-0, ISBN13: 978-0-7581-7562-5. Dewey:781.

Audience: **u,f.** *B*

Owens, Jessie Ann   **ML430.O94**
Composers at Work: The Craft of Musical Composition
1450-1600. Trade Paper. Oxford University Press, Inc. New
York, NY. 1998. 368p. ISBN:0-19-512904-0, ISBN13:
978-0-19-512904-5. Dewey:781/.3/09031.

Audience: **u,f.**

Palisca, Claude V.   **MT5.5.F63 1989**
The Florentine Camerata: Documentary Studies and
Translations. Trade Cloth. Yale University Press. Cumberland,
RI. 1989. 240p. ISBN:0-300-03916-6, ISBN13:
978-0-300-03916-0. Dewey:781. LCCN:88-001711.

Audience: **u,f.** *Choice, 1989.*

Palisca, Claude V.   **ML290.2.P34 1986**
Humanism in Italian Renaissance Musical Thought. Trade Cloth.

Yale University Press. Cumberland, RI. 1986. 448p.
ISBN:0-300-03302-8, ISBN13: 978-0-300-03302-1.
Dewey:781.745. LCCN:85-008190.

Audience: **u,f.** ℬ

Palisca, Claude   **ML174.P35 2006**
Music and Ideas in the Sixteenth and Seventeenth Centuries.
Thomas J. Mathiesen (Editor). Trade Cloth. University of
Illinois Press. Champaign, IL. 2006. 312p. Studies in the
History of Music Theory and Literature, Vol. 1
ISBN:0-252-03156-3, ISBN13: 978-0-252-03156-4.
Dewey:780.9/031. LCCN:2005-046749.

Audience: **u,f.** *Choice, 2006.*

Perkins, Leeman L.   **ML172.P47 1998**
Music in the Age of the Renaissance. Trade Cloth. W. W.
Norton & Company, Inc. New York, NY. 1999. 750p.
ISBN:0-393-04608-7, ISBN13: 978-0-393-04608-3.
Dewey:780/.9/031. LCCN:98-028961.

Audience: **g,l,u,f.**

Phillips, Elizabeth B. &   **ML430.5.P52 1986**
 Jackson, John-Paul C.
Performing Medieval and Renaissance Music: An Introductory
Guide. Trade Cloth. Thomson Gale. Farmington Hills, MI. 1986.
240p. ISBN:0-02-871790-2, ISBN13: 978-0-02-871790-6.
Dewey:780/.902. LCCN:85-018419.

Audience: **u,f.**

Phillips, Peter   **ML2931.2**
English Sacred Music 1549-1649. Gimell. 1991.
ISBN:0-9515784-0-5, ISBN13: 978-0-9515784-0-7.

Audience: **u,f.**

Poulton, Diana   **ML410.B4**
John Dowland. Ed. 2. Trade Cloth. University of California
Press. Berkeley, CA. 1982. 550p. ISBN:0-520-04687-0, ISBN13:
978-0-520-04687-0. Dewey:780/.92/4.

Audience: **l,u,f.**

Reese, Gustave   **ML172.R42**
Music in the Renaissance. Ed. 2. Trade Cloth. W. W. Norton &
Company, Inc. New York, NY. 1959. 17p. ISBN:0-393-09530-4,
ISBN13: 978-0-393-09530-2. Dewey:780.94.

Audience: **u,f.** ℬ

Roche, Jerome   **ML2600.R63 1990**
The Madrigal. Ed. 2. Trade Cloth. Oxford University Press, Inc.
New York, NY. 1991. 192p. ISBN:0-19-313131-5, ISBN13:
978-0-19-313131-6. Dewey:784/.1. LCCN:90-031147.

Audience: **u,f.**

Sherr, Richard (Editor)   **ML410.J815J68 2000**
The Josquin Companion. Trade Cloth. Oxford University Press,
Inc. New York, NY. 2001. 732p. ISBN:0-19-816335-5, ISBN13:
978-0-19-816335-0. Dewey:782.2/2/092. LCCN:00-056654.

Audience: **l,u,f.** *Choice, 2001.*

Sternfeld, F. W.   **PR3034**
Music in Shakespearean Tragedy. Perfect, Paper over Boards.
Routledge. New York, NY. 2005. 384p. ISBN:0-415-35327-0,
ISBN13: 978-0-415-35327-4. Dewey:822.33.

Audience: **u,f.**

Stevenson, Robert   **ML3047.S83 1976**
Spanish Cathedral Music in the Golden Age. Trade Cloth.
Greenwood Publishing Group, Inc. Portsmouth, NH. 1976. 523p.
ISBN:0-8371-8744-3, ISBN13: 978-0-8371-8744-0.
Dewey:783/.026/2. LCCN:76-001013.

Audience: **u,f.**

Stevenson, Robert   **ML315.2 .S74 1979**
Spanish Music in the Age of Columbus. Trade Cloth. Hyperion
Press, Inc. Westport, CT. 1986. Encore Music Editions Ser.
ISBN:0-88355-872-6, ISBN13: 978-0-88355-872-0.
Dewey:781.7/46. LCCN:78-020496.

Audience: **g,l,u,f.**

Turbet, Richard   **ML134.B96T9 2005**
William Byrd: A Guide to Research. Ed. 2. Paper over Boards.
Routledge. New York, NY. 2006. 352p. Routledge Music
Bibliographies Ser. ISBN:0-415-94301-9, ISBN13:
978-0-415-94301-7. Dewey:016.78/092. LCCN:2005-013599.

Audience: **l,u,f.** *Choice, 1988.*

Watkins, Glenn   **ML410.G29 W4 1991**
Gesualdo: The Man and His Music. Ed. 2. Igor Stravinsky
(Preface by). Trade Paper. Oxford University Press, Inc. New
York, NY. 1991. 438p. ISBN:0-19-816197-2, ISBN13:
978-0-19-816197-4. Dewey:782.430. LCCN:92-212547.

Audience: **l,u,f.**

Wegman, Rob C.   **ML410.O27W44 1996**
Born for the Muses: The Life and Masses of Jacob Obrecht.
Trade Paper. Oxford University Press, Inc. New York, NY. 1997.
432p. Oxford Monographs on Music ISBN:0-19-816650-8,
ISBN13: 978-0-19-816650-4. Dewey:780.9/2. LCCN:96-023052.

Audience: **u,f.** *Choice, 1995.*

Zarlino, Gioseffo   **MT55**
Art of Counterpoint: Part Three of "Le Institution Harmoniche",
1558. Guy A. Marco & Claude V. Palisco (Translators). Trade
Cloth. Yale University Press. Cumberland, RI. 1969. iii, 294p.
Music Theory Translation Ser., No. 2 ISBN:0-300-01084-2,
ISBN13: 978-0-300-01084-8. Dewey:781.42. LCCN:68-013923.

Audience: **u,f.**

Zarlino, Gioseffo   **ML3809**
On the Modes: Part Four of le Istitutioni Armoniche, 1558.
Claude V. Palisca (Introduction by). Trade Cloth. Yale
University Press. Cumberland, RI. 1983. 152p. Yale Music
Theory Translation Ser. ISBN:0-300-02937-3, ISBN13:
978-0-300-02937-6. Dewey:781/.22. LCCN:83-002477.

Audience: **u,f.** ℬ

Studies in Music History, Criticism, Analysis, and Appreciation > Western Classical Literature by Period > Baroque

Agricola, Johann Friedrich   MT892 .T6713 1995
& Tosi, Pier Francesco
Introduction to the Art of Singing by Johann Friedrich Agricola. John Butt & Laurence Dreyfus (Contribution by), Julianne C. Baird (Edited and Translated by). Trade Cloth. Cambridge University Press. New York, NY. 1995. 308p. Cambridge Musical Texts and Monographs ISBN:0-521-45428-X, ISBN13: 978-0-521-45428-5. Dewey:783/.043. LCCN:94-011416.
Audience: **u,f.**

Allsop, Peter   ML410.C78A8 1998
Arcangelo Corelli: New Orpheus of Our Times. Trade Cloth. Oxford University Press, Inc. New York, NY. 1999. 272p. Oxford Monographs on Music ISBN:0-19-816562-5, ISBN13: 978-0-19-816562-0. Dewey:787.2/092 B. LCCN:98-007973.
Audience: **u,f.** *Choice, 2000.*

Allsop, Peter   ML1156.A44I8 1992
The Italian "Trio" Sonata: From Its Origins until Corelli. Trade Cloth. Oxford University Press, Inc. New York, NY. 1992. 352p. Oxford Monographs on Music ISBN:0-19-816229-4, ISBN13: 978-0-19-816229-2. Dewey:785/.13183/0945. LCCN:92-001001.
Audience: **u,f.** *Choice, 1993.*

Anthony, James R.   ML270.2.A6 1997
French Baroque Music from Beaujoyeulx to Rameau. Ed. 2. Trade Cloth. Hal Leonard Corporation. Milwaukee, WI. 1997. 590p. ISBN:1-57467-021-2, ISBN13: 978-1-57467-021-9. Dewey:780/.944/09032. LCCN:96-038352.
Audience: **g,l,u,f.** *Choice, 1998.*

Arnold, F. T.   ML442.A7 2003
The Art of Accompaniment from a Thorough-Bass, Vol. 2. Trade Paper. Dover Publications, Inc. Mineola, NY. 2003. 448p. American Musicological Society-Music Library Association Reprint ISBN:0-486-43195-9, ISBN13: 978-0-486-43195-6. Dewey:781.47. LCCN:2003-048966.
Audience: **u,f.**

Arnold, F. T.   ML442.A7 2003
The Art of Accompaniment from a Thorough-Bass, Vol. 1. Trade Paper. Dover Publications, Inc. Mineola, NY. 2003. 512p. American Musicological Society-Music Library Association Reprint ISBN:0-486-43188-6, ISBN13: 978-0-486-43188-8. Dewey:781.47. LCCN:2003-048966.
Audience: **u,f.**

Ashbee, Andrew (Editor)   ML410.L334W55 1998
William Lawes (1602-1645): Essays on His Life, Times and Work. Trade Cloth. Ashgate Publishing, Ltd. Aldershot, 1998. 380p. ISBN:1-85928-354-3, ISBN13: 978-1-85928-354-7. Dewey:780/.92 B. LCCN:97-077628.
Audience: **u,f.**

Beaussant, Phillippe   ML410.C855B413 1990
Francois Couperin. Alexandra Land (Translator). Trade Cloth. Hal Leonard Corporation. Milwaukee, WI. 1990. 426p. ISBN:0-931340-27-6, ISBN13: 978-0-931340-27-7. Dewey:780/.92 B. LCCN:89-028729.
Audience: **u,f.** *Choice, 1991.*

Boyd, Malcolm   ML410.B1
Bach. Ed. 3. Trade Paper. Oxford University Press, Inc. New York, NY. 2006. 320p. Master Musicians Ser. ISBN:0-19-530771-2, ISBN13: 978-0-19-530771-9. Dewey:780/.92 B.
Audience: **g,l,u,f.**

Boyd, Malcolm   ML410.S221B7 1987
Domenico Scarlatti: Master of Music. Trade Cloth. Music Sales Corporation. New York, NY. 1987. 302p. ISBN:0-02-870291-3, ISBN13: 978-0-02-870291-9. Dewey:780/.92/4. LCCN:86-021743.
Audience: **l,u,f.** *Choice, 1987.*

Boyd, Malcolm   ML410.B1J15 1999
The Oxford Companion to Bach. Trade Cloth. Oxford University Press, Inc. New York, NY. 1999. 656p. Oxford Composer Companion Ser. ISBN:0-19-866208-4, ISBN13: 978-0-19-866208-2. Dewey:780/.92. LCCN:98-019587.
Audience: **g,l,u,f.** *Choice, 2000.*

Brown, Howard Mayer &   ML5
Sadie, Stanley (Editors)
Performance Practice: Music after 1600. Trade Cloth. W. W. Norton & Company, Inc. New York, NY. 1990. xi, 533p. Grove Handbooks in Music Ser. ISBN:0-393-02808-9, ISBN13: 978-0-393-02808-9. Dewey:780/.903. LCCN:91-110857.
Audience: **u,f.**

Buelow, George J.   ML193.B76 2004
A History of Baroque Music: Music in the Seventeenth and First Half of the Eighteenth Centuries. Trade Cloth. Indiana University Press. Bloomington, IN. 2004. 752p. ISBN:0-253-34365-8, ISBN13: 978-0-253-34365-9. Dewey:780/.9/032. LCCN:2003-025348.
Audience: **g,l,u,f.** *Choice, 2005.*

Buelow, George J. (Editor)   ML193
The Late Baroque Era: From the 1680s to 1740. Prentice Hall. 1994. ISBN:0-13-104340-4, ISBN13: 978-0-13-104340-4.
Audience: **g,l,u,f.**

Burden, Michael (Editor)   ML410.P93P86 1995
The Purcell Companion. Trade Cloth. Hal Leonard Corporation. Milwaukee, WI. 1995. 514p. ISBN:0-931340-93-4, ISBN13: 978-0-931340-93-2. Dewey:780/.92 B. LCCN:95-169070.
Audience: **g,l,u,f.** *Choice, 1995.*

Burrows, Donald   ML410.H13
Handel. New York: Schirmer Books: Maxwell Macmillan International. 1994. The Master Musicians Ser.: Variation ISBN:0-02-870327-8, ISBN13: 978-0-02-870327-5.
Audience: **g,l,u,f.**

Burrows, Donald (Editor)   **ML410.H13 C2 1997**
The Cambridge Companion to Handel. Jonathan Cross
(Contribution by). Trade Paper. Cambridge University Press.
New York, NY. 1997. 365p. Cambridge Companions to Music
Ser. ISBN:0-521-45613-4, ISBN13: 978-0-521-45613-5.
Dewey:780/.92 B. LCCN:96-050935.

Audience: **g,l,u,f.**

Burrows, Donald   **ML410.H13 B95 1991**
Handel: Messiah. Julian Rushton (Contribution by). Trade Paper.
Cambridge University Press. New York, NY. 1991. 137p. Music
Handbks. ISBN:0-521-37620-3, ISBN13: 978-0-521-37620-4.
Dewey:782.23. LCCN:90-002566.

Audience: **g,l,u,f.** *Choice, 1992.*

Butt, John (Editor)   **ML410.M9**
The Cambridge Companion to Bach. Jonathan Cross
(Contribution by). Trade Paper. Cambridge University Press.
New York, NY. 1997. 342p. Cambridge Companions to Music
Ser. ISBN:0-521-58780-8, ISBN13: 978-0-521-58780-8.
Dewey:780.9/2. LCCN:96-022581.

Audience: **g,l,u,f.** *Choice, 1998.*

Butt, John   **ML410.B1B193 1992**
Bach: Mass in B Minor. Julian Rushton (Contribution by). Trade
Paper. Cambridge University Press. New York, NY. 1991. 126p.
Music Handbks. ISBN:0-521-38716-7, ISBN13:
978-0-521-38716-3. Dewey:782.32/32. LCCN:90-002286.

Audience: **u,f.** *Choice, 1992.*

Carter, Stewart   **ML457.P49 1997**
A Performer's Guide to Seventeenth-Century Music. Trade
Cloth. Thomson Wadsworth. Belmont, CA. 1997. Early Music
America Ser. ISBN:0-02-870492-4, ISBN13:
978-0-02-870492-0. Dewey:781.4/3/09032. LCCN:97-001310.

Audience: **u,f.**

Carter, Tim   **ML410.M77C37 2002**
Monteverdi's Musical Theatre. Cloth over Boards. Yale
University Press. Cumberland, RI. 2002. 336p.
ISBN:0-300-09676-3, ISBN13: 978-0-300-09676-7.
Dewey:782.1/092. LCCN:2002-109930.

Audience: **u,f.**

Cessac, Catherine   **ML410.C433C4713 1995**
Marc-Antoine Charpentier. E. Thomas Glasow (Translator).
Trade Cloth. Hal Leonard Corporation. Milwaukee, WI. 1995.
566p. ISBN:0-931340-80-2, ISBN13: 978-0-931340-80-2.
Dewey:782.1/092 B. LCCN:94-029786.

Audience: **u,f.** *Choice, 1995.*

Chafe, Eric   **ML410.B13C38 2000**
Analyzing Bach Cantatas. Trade Cloth. Oxford University Press,
Inc. New York, NY. 2000. 304p. ISBN:0-19-512099-X, ISBN13:
978-0-19-512099-8. Dewey:782.2/4/092. LCCN:98-015109.

Audience: **u,f.** *Choice, 2000.*

David, Hans T.   **ML410.B1**
J. S. Bach's Musical Offering: History, Interpretation and

Analysis. Trade Paper. Dover Publications, Inc. Mineola, NY.
1972. 190p. ISBN:0-486-22768-5, ISBN13: 978-0-486-22768-9.
Dewey:785.7. LCCN:72-165391.

Audience: **u,f.**

David, Hans T.   **ML410.M9**
The New Bach Reader: A Life of Johann Sebastian Bach in
Letters and Documents. Trade Paper. W. W. Norton & Company,
Inc. New York, NY. 1999. 608p. ISBN:0-393-31956-3, ISBN13:
978-0-393-31956-9. Dewey:780/.92 B.

Audience: **g,l,u,f.** *Choice, 1998.*

Dean, Winton   **ML410.B13**
Handel's Dramatic Oratorios and Masques. Paper Text.
Textbook Publishers. Temecula, CA. 2003. xii, 694p.
ISBN:0-7581-7050-5, ISBN13: 978-0-7581-7050-7.
Dewey:782.23.

Audience: **u,f.**

Dean, Winton & Knapp,   **ML410.H13D37 1987**
John M.
Handel's Operas Seventeen Four to Seventeen Twenty-Six.
Trade Cloth. Oxford University Press, Inc. New York, NY. 1987.
772p. ISBN:0-19-315219-3, ISBN13: 978-0-19-315219-9.
Dewey:782.1/092/4. LCCN:85-011580.

Audience: **u,f.** *Choice, 1987.*

Dent, Edward J.   **ML410.S22**
Alessandro Scarlatti: His Life and Works. Paper Text. Classic
Textbooks. Murrieta, CA. 1960. 172p. ISBN:1-4047-0141-9,
ISBN13: 978-1-4047-0141-0. Dewey:927.8.

Audience: **u,f.**

Deutsch, Otto Erich   **ML0410.H13D4**
Handel: A Documentary Biography. Trade Paper. Books on
Demand. Ann Arbor, MI. 1028p. ISBN:0-598-63419-3, ISBN13:
978-0-598-63419-1. Dewey:ML0410.H13D4. LCCN:55-006770.

Audience: **g,l,u,f.**

Dixon, Graham   **ML410.C3/**
Carissimi. Trade Cloth. Oxford University Press, Inc. New York,
NY. 1986. 96p. Studies of Composers ISBN:0-19-315249-5,
ISBN13: 978-0-19-315249-6. Dewey:783/.092/4.

Audience: **u,f.**

Dreyfus, Laurence   **ML410.B1D63 1996**
Bach and the Patterns of Invention. Trade Cloth. Harvard
University Press. Cambridge, MA. 1997. 288p.
ISBN:0-674-06005-9, ISBN13: 978-0-674-06005-0.
Dewey:780/.92 B. LCCN:96-032275.

Audience: **u,f.** *Choice, 1997.*

Durr, Alfred   **ML410.B13D87 2003**
The Cantatas of J. S. Bach. Richard Jones (Translator). Trade
Cloth. Oxford University Press, Inc. New York, NY. 2005. 984p.
ISBN:0-19-816707-5, ISBN13: 978-0-19-816707-5.
Dewey:782.2/4092. LCCN:2005-299548.

Audience: **u,f.** *Choice, 2006.*

Eggebrecht, Hans H.   MT145.B14.E4513 1993
J. S. Bach's "The Art of the Fugue": The Work and Its
Interpretation. Jeffrey L. Praeter (Translator). Cloth Text.
Blackwell Publishing Professional. Ames, IA. 1993. 160p.
ISBN:0-8138-1489-8, ISBN13: 978-0-8138-1489-6.
Dewey:786/.1872. LCCN:93-001281.
                                   Audience: **u,f.** *Choice, 1994.*

Everett, Paul   ML410.V82 E84 1996
Vivaldi: The Four Seasons and Other Concertos, Op. 8. Julian
Rushton (Contribution by). Cloth Text. Cambridge University
Press. New York, NY. 1996. 128p. Music Handbks.
ISBN:0-521-40499-1, ISBN13: 978-0-521-40499-0.
Dewey:780/.92. LCCN:95-018173.
                                            Audience: **u,f.**

Geiringer, Karl   ML410.B1
The Bach Family: Seven Generations of Creative Genius. Paper
Text. Textbook Publishers. Temecula, CA. 2003. xiv, 514p.
ISBN:0-7581-7209-5, ISBN13: 978-0-7581-7209-9.
Dewey:780/.92/2 B.
                                        Audience: **g,l,u,f.**

Gianturco, Carolyn   ML410.S87
Alessandro Stradella, 1639-1682: His Life and Music. Oxford:
Clarendon Press; New York: Oxford University Press. 1994.
Oxford Monographs on Music ISBN:0-19-816138-7, ISBN13:
978-0-19-816138-7.
                                            Audience: **u,f.**

Girdlestone, Cuthbert M.   ML410.R2 G5
Jean-Philippe Rameau: His Life and Work. Trade Paper. Dover
Publications, Inc. Mineola, NY. 1990. 631p.
ISBN:0-486-26200-6, ISBN13: 978-0-486-26200-0.
Dewey:780/.924.
                                        Audience: **g,l,u,f.**

Glixon, Beth Lise, et al.   ML1733.8.V4
Inventing the Business of Opera: The Impresario and His World
in Seventeenth-Century Venice. Glixon, Jonathan Emmanuel
(Author). Oxford University Press. 2006. AMS Studies in Music
ISBN:0-19-515416-9, ISBN13: 978-0-19-515416-0.
                                            Audience: **u,f.**

Glover, Jane   ML410.B4
Cavalli. Cloth Text. Palgrave Macmillan. New York, NY. 1978.
ISBN:0-312-12546-1, ISBN13: 978-0-312-12546-2.
Dewey:780/.92/4. LCCN:77-023638.
                                            Audience: **u,f.**

Hammond, Frederick   ML0410.F85H3
Girolamo Frescobaldi. Trade Paper. Books on Demand. Ann
Arbor, MI. 424p. ISBN:0-7837-6085-X, ISBN13:
978-0-7837-6085-8. Dewey:786.5/092/4. LCCN:82-011938.
                                            Audience: **u,f.**

Harran, Don   ML410.R78H37 1999
Salamone Rossi: Jewish Musician in Late Renaissance Mantua.
Trade Cloth. Oxford University Press, Inc. New York, NY. 1999.

320p. Oxford Monographs on Music ISBN:0-19-816271-5,
ISBN13: 978-0-19-816271-1. Dewey:780/.92 B.
LCCN:98-007974.
                                            Audience: **u,f.**

Heyer, John Hajdu (Editor)   ML410.L95 L96 2000
Lully Studies. Trade Cloth. Cambridge University Press. New
York, NY. 2000. 331p. Cambridge Composer Studies
ISBN:0-521-62183-6, ISBN13: 978-0-521-62183-0.
Dewey:780/.92. LCCN:00-020313.
                                   Audience: **u,f.** *Choice, 2001.*

Hill, John Walter   ML193.H54 2004
Baroque Music. Trade Cloth. W. W. Norton & Company, Inc.
New York, NY. 2004. xx, 525p. Norton Introduction to Music
History Ser. ISBN:0-393-97800-1, ISBN13: 978-0-393-97800-1.
Dewey:780/.9/032. LCCN:2004-058144.
                                        Audience: **g,l,u,f.**

Hill, William H., et al.   ML424.S8
Antonio Stradivari, His Life and Work (1644-1739). Ed. 2.
Arthur F. Hill, Alfred E. Hill & Frances A. Davis (Authors).
Trade Paper. Dover Publications, Inc. Mineola, NY. 1963. 315p.
ISBN:0-486-20425-1, ISBN13: 978-0-486-20425-3.
Dewey:787.12.
                                        Audience: **g,l,u,f.**

Hogwood, Christopher   ML410.M9
Handel. Trade Paper. Thames & Hudson. New York, NY. 1996.
312p. ISBN:0-500-27498-3, ISBN13: 978-0-500-27498-9.
Dewey:780.9/2. LCCN:84-072765.
                                   Audience: **g,l,u,f.** *Choice, 1985.*

Holman, Peter   ML410.P93H63 1994
Henry Purcell. Trade Paper. Oxford University Press, Inc. New
York, NY. 1995. 268p. Oxford Studies of Composers
ISBN:0-19-816341-X, ISBN13: 978-0-19-816341-1.
Dewey:780.9/2. LCCN:94-031870.
                                   Audience: **u,f.** *Choice, 1995.*

Johnson, Theodore O.   MT145.B14J56 1986
An Analytical Survey of the 15 Sinfonias: Three-Part Inventions
by J. S. Bach. Trade Paper. University Press of America, Inc.
Lanham, MD. 1986. 190p. ISBN:0-8191-5378-8, ISBN13:
978-0-8191-5378-4. Dewey:786.1/092/4. LCCN:86-009091.
                                   Audience: **l,u,f.** *Choice, 1986.*

Keller, Hermann   MT49.K2952 1990
Thoroughbass Method. Cloth Text. Columbia University Press.
New York, NY. 1990. 112p. A Morningside Bk.
ISBN:0-231-07320-8, ISBN13: 978-0-231-07320-2.
Dewey:781.47. LCCN:89-071221.
                                            Audience: **u,f.**

Kendrick, Robert L.   ML290.8.M4K46 1996
Celestial Sirens: Nuns and Their Music in Early Modern Milan.
Cloth Text. Oxford University Press, Inc. New York, NY. 1996.
577p. Monographs on Music ISBN:0-19-816408-4, ISBN13:
978-0-19-816408-1. Dewey:781.71/2/0082. LCCN:95-044937.
                                   Audience: **u,f.** *Choice, 1997.*

Kerman, Joseph   **MT59 .K49 2005**
The Art of Fugue: Bach Fugues for Keyboard, 1715-1750.
Davitt Moroney & Karen Rosenak (Performed by). Mixed
Media, Trade Cloth, Compact Disc. University of California
Press. Berkeley, CA. 2005. 208p. ISBN:0-520-24358-7, ISBN13:
978-0-520-24358-3. Dewey:786/.1872/092. LCCN:2005-004045.
                                              Audience: **u,f.**

Kiel, Dyke & Adams, K.   **ML134.M66A5 1989**
  Gary
Claudio Monteverdi: A Guide to Research. Cloth Text. Garland
Publishing, Inc. New York, NY. 1989. 292p. Composer
Resource Manuals Ser., Vol. 23 ISBN:0-8240-7743-1, ISBN13:
978-0-8240-7743-3. Dewey:016.782/0092. LCCN:89-033040.
                                   Audience: **l,u,f.** *Choice, 1989.*

Kirkpatrick, Ralph   **ML410.S221 K5 1983**
Domenico Scarlatti. Trade Paper. Princeton University Press.
Princeton, NJ. 1983. 496p. ISBN:0-691-02708-0, ISBN13:
978-0-691-02708-1. Dewey:[B]. LCCN:53-006387.
                                              Audience: **l,u,f.**

Kurtzman, Jeffrey   **ML410.M77K87 1999**
The Monteverdi Vespers of 1610: Music, Context, and
Performance. Trade Cloth. Oxford University Press, Inc. New
York, NY. 2000. 624p. ISBN:0-19-816409-2, ISBN13:
978-0-19-816409-8. Dewey:782.32/4. LCCN:98-015026.
                                   Audience: **u,f.** *Choice, 2000.*

Larsen, Jens P.   **ML410**
Handel's Messiah: Origins, Composition, Sources. Ed. 2. Trade
Cloth. Greenwood Publishing Group, Inc. Portsmouth, NH.
1990. 336p. ISBN:0-313-24426-X, ISBN13: 978-0-313-24426-1.
Dewey:783.3/092/4. LCCN:88-010128.
                                              Audience: **u,f.**

Ledbetter, David   **ML410.B13**
Bach's Well-Tempered Clavier: The 48 Preludes and Fugues.
Cloth over Boards. Yale University Press. Cumberland, RI.
2002. 432p. ISBN:0-300-09707-7, ISBN13: 978-0-300-09707-8.
Dewey:786/.1872. LCCN:2002-109926.
                                              Audience: **l,u,f.**

Lester, Joel   **ML418.P2**
Bach's Works for Solo Violin: Style, Structure, Performance.
Trade Paper. Oxford University Press, Inc. New York, NY. 2003.
196p. ISBN:0-19-517144-6, ISBN13: 978-0-19-517144-0.
Dewey:787.2/092.
                                   Audience: **u,f.** *Choice, 2000.*

Little, Meredith & Jenne,   **ML410.B13L52 2001**
  Natalie (Editors)
Dance and the Music of J. S. Bach. Ed. 2. Trade Cloth. Indiana
University Press. Bloomington, IN. 2001. 288p.
Music--Scholarship and Performance Ser. ISBN:0-253-33936-7,
ISBN13: 978-0-253-33936-2. Dewey:784.18/82/092.
LCCN:2001-016944.
                                   Audience: **u,f.** *Choice, 2002.*

Mann, Alfred   **ML410.H13M36 1996**
Handel: The Orchestral Music. Cloth Text. Thomson
Wadsworth. Belmont, CA. 1995. 182p. Monuments of Western

Music Ser. ISBN:0-02-871382-6, ISBN13: 978-0-02-871382-3.
Dewey:784.2/092. LCCN:95-010441.
                                   Audience: **u,f.** *Choice, 1996.*

Marshall, Robert L.   **ML410.B1.M285**
The Compositional Process of J. S. Bach. Trade Cloth. Princeton
University Press. Princeton, NJ. 1972. 177p. Studies in Music,
No. 4 ISBN:0-691-09113-7, ISBN13: 978-0-691-09113-6.
Dewey:783/.092/4. LCCN:76-113005.
                                              Audience: **u,f.**

Marshall, Robert L.   **ML410.B13M28 1989**
The Music of Johann Sebastian Bach: The Sources, the Style,
the Significance. Trade Cloth. Thomson Gale. Farmington Hills,
MI. 1989. 375p. ISBN:0-02-871781-3, ISBN13:
978-0-02-871781-4. Dewey:780.9/2. LCCN:88-023921.
                                   Audience: **l,u,f.** *Choice, 1989.*

Mather, Betty B. & Karns,   **ML3427.M37 1987**
  Dean M.
Dance Rhythms of the French Baroque: A Handbook for
Performance. Trade Cloth. Indiana University Press.
Bloomington, IN. 1988. 352p. Music, :Scholarship and
Performance Ser. ISBN:0-253-31606-5, ISBN13:
978-0-253-31606-6. Dewey:785.4/1/0944. LCCN:86-045991.
                                              Audience: **u,f.**

McVeigh, Simon &   **ML1263.M28 2005**
  Hirshberg, Jehoash
The Italian Solo Concerto, 1700-1760: Rhetorical Strategies and
Style History. Trade Cloth. Boydell & Brewer, Ltd. Woodbridge,
2004. 384p. ISBN:1-84383-092-2, ISBN13: 978-1-84383-092-4.
Dewey:784.18/6. LCCN:2004-004670.
                                              Audience: **u,f.**

Melamed, Daniel R.   **MT115.B2M43 2005**
Hearing Bach's Passions. Trade Cloth. Oxford University Press,
Inc. New York, NY. 2005. 190p. ISBN:0-19-516933-6, ISBN13:
978-0-19-516933-1. Dewey:782.23. LCCN:2004-013785.
                                   Audience: **l,u,f.** *Choice, 2005.*

Melamed, Daniel R. &   **ML134.B1M45 1998**
  Marissen, Michael
An Introduction to Bach Studies. Cloth Text. Oxford University
Press, Inc. New York, NY. 1998. 208p. ISBN:0-19-512231-3,
ISBN13: 978-0-19-512231-2. Dewey:016.780/92.
LCCN:97-040406.
                                   Audience: **l,u,f.** *Choice, 1998.*

Mellers, Wilfrid   **ML410.C855**
Francois Couperin and the French Classical Tradition. Ed. 2.
Trade Cloth. Faber & Faber, Inc. New York, NY. 1987. 544p.
ISBN:0-571-13983-3, ISBN13: 978-0-571-13983-5.
Dewey:780/.92/4.
                                   Audience: **u,f.** *Choice, 1988.*

Monteverdi, Claudio   **ML410.V4**
Operas of Monteverdi: Includes Orfeo, Return of Ulysses,
Coronation of Poppea. Anne Ridler (Translator). Trade Paper.
Riverrun Press, Inc. Flemington, NJ. 1992. 208p. English

National Opera Guide Series: Bilingual Libretto, Articles, No. 45 ISBN:0-7145-4207-5, ISBN13: 978-0-7145-4207-2. Dewey:782.1092.

Audience: **g,l,u,f.**

Newman, William S.   **ML1156.N4S6**
The Sonata in the Baroque Era. Paper Text. Textbook Publishers. Temecula, CA. 2003. 447p. ISBN:0-7581-1883-X, ISBN13: 978-0-7581-1883-7. Dewey:781/.52/09.

Audience: **u,f.** *B*

Palisca, Claude V.   **ML193.P34 1991**
Baroque Music. Ed. 3. Trade Paper. Prentice Hall PTR. Upper Saddle River, NJ. 1990. 368p. Prentice Hall History of Music Ser. ISBN:0-13-058496-7, ISBN13: 978-0-13-058496-0. Dewey:780/.9/032. LCCN:90-046900.

Audience: **g,l,u,f.** *B*

Parker, Mary Ann   **ML134.H16P37 2005**
G. F. Handel: A Guide to Research. Ed. 2. Paper over Boards. Routledge. New York, NY. 2005. 408p. Routledge Music Bibliographies Ser. ISBN:0-415-94323-X, ISBN13: 978-0-415-94323-9. Dewey:016.78/092. LCCN:2005-006736.

Audience: **l,u,f.**

Parrott, Andrew   **ML410.B13P29 2000**
The Essential Bach Choir. Trade Paper, Trade Cloth. Boydell & Brewer, Ltd. Woodbridge, 2002. 240p. ISBN:0-85115-786-6, ISBN13: 978-0-85115-786-3. Dewey:782.2/4/092. LCCN:99-087035.

Audience: **u,f.** *Choice, 2000.*

Price, Curtis (Editor)   **ML193**
The Early Baroque Era. Cloth Text. Prentice Hall PTR. Upper Saddle River, NJ. 1993. ISBN:0-13-223835-7, ISBN13: 978-0-13-223835-9. Dewey:780.9032.

Audience: **g,l,u,f.**

Price, Curtis   **ML410.P93**
Henry Purcell and the London Stage. Trade Cloth. Cambridge University Press. New York, NY. 1984. 394p. ISBN:0-521-23831-5, ISBN13: 978-0-521-23831-1. Dewey:780/.92/4. LCCN:83-015170.

Audience: **u,f.**

Rosand, Ellen   **ML1733.8.V4R67 1991**
Opera in Seventeenth-Century Venice: The Creation of a Genre. Trade Cloth. University of California Press. Berkeley, CA. 1990. 710p. ISBN:0-520-06808-4, ISBN13: 978-0-520-06808-7. Dewey:782.1/0945/3109032. LCCN:90-040399.

Audience: **u,f.** *Choice, 1991.*

Sadie, Julie Anne   **ML193.C56 1998**
  (Contribution by)
Companion to Baroque Music. Trade Paper. Oxford University Press, Inc. New York, NY. 1998. 568p. ISBN:0-19-816704-0, ISBN13: 978-0-19-816704-4. Dewey:780/.9/032. LCCN:98-014755.

Audience: **g,l,u,f.**

Sadler, Graham & Wood,   **ML1727.W64 2000**
  Caroline
French Baroque Opera: A Reader. Trade Cloth. Ashgate Publishing, Ltd. Aldershot, 2000. ix, 160p. ISBN:1-84014-241-3, ISBN13: 978-1-84014-241-9. Dewey:782.1/0944/09032. LCCN:99-054365.

Audience: **u,f.**

Schmieder, Wolfgang   **ML134.B155**
Thematisch-systematisches Verzeichnis der musikalischen Werke von Johann Sebastian Bach: Bach-Werke-Verzeichnis (BWV). Ed. 2. Wiesbaden : Breitkopf & Härtel. 1990.

Audience: **u,f.**

Schulenberg, David   **MT145.B14S415 1992**
The Keyboard Music of J. S. Bach. Trade Cloth. Thomson Gale. Farmington Hills, MI. 1992. 475p. ISBN:0-02-873275-8, ISBN13: 978-0-02-873275-6. Dewey:786/.092. LCCN:91-039348.

Audience: **l,u,f.** *Choice, 1993.*

Smallman, Basil   **ML410.S35S6 2000**
Schutz. Cloth Text. Oxford University Press, Inc. New York, NY. 2000. 236p. Master Musicians Ser. ISBN:0-19-816674-5, ISBN13: 978-0-19-816674-0. Dewey:782.2/2/092 B. LCCN:99-042131.

Audience: **l,u,f.** *Choice, 2001.*

Smither, Howard E.   **76-43980**
The Oratorio in the Baroque Era: Italy, Vienna, Paris. Trade Cloth. University of North Carolina Press. Chapel Hill, NC. 1977. 507p. History of the Oratorio Ser. ISBN:0-8078-1274-9, ISBN13: 978-0-8078-1274-7. Dewey:782.8/2/09. LCCN:76-043980.

Audience: **u,f.** *B* *Choice, 1987.*

Smither, Howard E.   **76-43980**
The Oratorio in the Baroque Era: Protestant Germany and England. Trade Cloth. University of North Carolina Press. Chapel Hill, NC. 1977. 415p. History of the Oratorio Ser., Vol. 2 ISBN:0-8078-1294-3, ISBN13: 978-0-8078-1294-5. Dewey:782.2/3/09033. LCCN:76-043980.

Audience: **u,f.**

Smithers, Don L.   **ML960.S63 1988**
The Music and History of the Baroque Trumpet Before 1721. Cloth Text. Southern Illinois University Press. Carbondale, IL. 1989. 356p. ISBN:0-8093-1497-5, ISBN13: 978-0-8093-1497-3. Dewey:788/.1/09. LCCN:88-023804.

Audience: **u,f.** *B*

Snyder, Kerala J.   **ML410.B4**
Dietrich Buxtehude: Organist in Lubeck. Trade Cloth. Thomson Wadsworth. Belmont, CA. 1993. 551p. ISBN:0-02-872455-0, ISBN13: 978-0-02-872455-3. Dewey:780/.92/4 B. LCCN:87-018505.

Audience: **u,f.** *Choice, 1988.*

Spitzer, John & Zaslaw,   **ML1200**
  Neal
The Birth of the Orchestra: History of an Institution, 1650-1815. Trade Paper, Perfect. Oxford University Press, Inc. New York,

NY. 2005. 640p. ISBN:0-19-518955-8, ISBN13: 978-0-19-518955-1. Dewey:784.2/09.

Audience: **u,f.** *Choice, 2005.*

Stauffer, George B.   **ML410.B13S75 1997**
Bach: The Mass in B Minor. Cloth Text. Thomson Wadsworth. Belmont, CA. 1996. 309p. Monuments of Western Music Ser. ISBN:0-02-872475-5, ISBN13: 978-0-02-872475-1. Dewey:782.32/32. LCCN:96-027495.

Audience: **l,u,f.**

Stein, Louise K.   **ML1747.2.S84 1993**
Songs of Mortals, Dialogues of the Gods: Music and Theatre in Seventeenth-Century Spain. Trade Cloth. Oxford University Press, Inc. New York, NY. 1993. 586p. Oxford Monographs on Music ISBN:0-19-816273-1, ISBN13: 978-0-19-816273-5. Dewey:781.5520946. LCCN:92-038274.

Audience: **u,f.**

Sternfeld, F. W.   **ML1733.2**
The Birth of Opera. Trade Cloth. Oxford University Press, Inc. New York, NY. 1993. 280p. ISBN:0-19-816130-1, ISBN13: 978-0-19-816130-1. Dewey:782.1/0945/09031. LCCN:92-030841.

Audience: **u.** *Choice, 1993.*

Stevens, Denis   **ML410.M77A4 1995**
The Letters of Claudio Monteverdi. Ed. 2. Cloth Text. Oxford University Press, Inc. New York, NY. 1995. 480p. ISBN:0-19-816414-9, ISBN13: 978-0-19-816414-2. Dewey:782/.0092 B. LCCN:94-040349.

Audience: **u,f.** *Choice, 1996.*

Stinson, Russell   **ML410.B13S87 1996**
Bach: The Orgelbuchlein. Trade Cloth. Thomson Gale. Farmington Hills, MI. 1996. xv, 208p. Monuments of Western Music Ser. ISBN:0-02-872505-0, ISBN13: 978-0-02-872505-5. Dewey:786.5/18992/092. LCCN:96-024581.

Audience: **u,f.** *Choice, 1997.*

Sutcliffe, W. Dean   **ML410.S22S88 2003**
The Keyboard Sonatas of Domenico Scarlatti and Eighteenth-Century Musical Style. Trade Cloth. Cambridge University Press. New York, NY. 2003. 412p. ISBN:0-521-48140-6, ISBN13: 978-0-521-48140-3. Dewey:786/.183/092. LCCN:2002-035012.

Audience: **u,f.** *Choice, 2004.*

Talbot, Michael   **ML410.A315T37 1990**
Tomaso Albinoni: The Venetian Composer and His World. Trade Cloth. Oxford University Press, Inc. New York, NY. 1990. 304p. ISBN:0-19-315245-2, ISBN13: 978-0-19-315245-8. Dewey:780/.92 B. LCCN:89-049221.

Audience: **u,f.** *Choice, 1991.*

Talbot, Michael   **ML410.V82**
Vivaldi. New York: Schirmer Books: Maxwell Macmillan International. 199. The Master Musicians ISBN:0-02-872665-0, ISBN13: 978-0-02-872665-6.

Audience: **l,u,f.**

Tatlow, Ruth   **ML410.B1 T18 1990**
Bach and the Riddle of the Number Alphabet. Trade Cloth. Cambridge University Press. New York, NY. 1991. 200p. ISBN:0-521-36191-5, ISBN13: 978-0-521-36191-0. Dewey:780/.92. LCCN:90-001550.

Audience: **l,u,f.** *Choice, 1991.*

Tomlinson, Gary   **ML410.B4**
Monteverdi and the End of the Renaissance. Trade Paper. University of California Press. Berkeley, CA. 1990. 292p. ISBN:0-520-06980-3, ISBN13: 978-0-520-06980-0. Dewey:780/.92/4.

Audience: **u,f.** *Choice, 1987.*

Troeger, Richard   **MT179.T76 2003**
Playing Bach on the Keyboard: A Practical Guide. Trade Cloth. Hal Leonard Corporation. Milwaukee, WI. 2003. 300p. ISBN:1-57467-084-0, ISBN13: 978-1-57467-084-4. Dewey:786/.092. LCCN:2003-012791.

Audience: **l,u,f.** *Choice, 2004.*

Whenham, John   **ML410.M77**
Monteverdi, Vespers (1610). Cambridge University Press. 1997. Cambridge music handbooks ISBN:0-521-45377-1, ISBN13: 978-0-521-45377-6.

Audience: **u,f.**

Whenham, John   **ML410.M77 C55 1986**
Claudio Monteverdi: Orfeo. Richard Wagner (Contribution by). Trade Paper. Cambridge University Press. New York, NY. 1986. 230p. Cambridge Opera Handbooks Ser. ISBN:0-521-28477-5, ISBN13: 978-0-521-28477-6. Dewey:782.1/092/4. LCCN:85-009923.

Audience: **l,u,f.** *Choice, 1986.*

Williams, Peter F.   **MT145.B14W53 2002**
The Organ Music of J. S. Bach. Ed. 2. Cloth Text. Cambridge University Press. New York, NY. 2003. 634p. ISBN:0-521-81416-2, ISBN13: 978-0-521-81416-4. Dewey:786.5/092. LCCN:2002-067368.

Audience: **l,u,f.** *Choice, 2004.*

Williams, Peter F.   **MT145.B14 W55 2001**
Bach: The Goldberg Variations. Julian Rushton (Contribution by). Cloth Text. Cambridge University Press. New York, NY. 2001. 118p. Music Handbks. ISBN:0-521-80735-2, ISBN13: 978-0-521-80735-7. Dewey:786.4/1825. LCCN:2001-025616.

Audience: **u,f.**

Wolff, Christoph   **ML410.B1W793 2000**
Johann Sebastian Bach: The Learned Musician. Trade Cloth. W. W. Norton & Company, Inc. New York, NY. 2000. 544p. ISBN:0-393-04825-X, ISBN13: 978-0-393-04825-4. Dewey:780.9/2. LCCN:99-054364.

Audience: **l,u,f.** *Choice, 2000.*

Zimmerman, Franklin B.   **ML134.P95**
Henry Purcell: A Guide to Research. New York : Garland Pub. 1989. Garland Composer Resource Manuals; Vol. 18 ISBN:0-8240-7786-5, ISBN13: 978-0-8240-7786-0.

Audience: **l,u,f.**

Studies in Music History, Criticism, Analysis, and Appreciation > Western Classical Literature by Period > Classical

Allanbrook, Wye J.   **ML410.M9**
Rhythmic Gesture in Mozart: "Le Nozze Di Figaro" and "Don Giovanni". Trade Cloth. University of Chicago Press. Chicago, IL. 1984. xii, 396p. ISBN:0-226-01403-7, ISBN13: 978-0-226-01403-6. Dewey:782.1/092/4. LCCN:83-009184.

Audience: **u,f.**

Bach, Carl Philipp Emanuel   **MT224.B132**
Essay on the True Art of Playing Keyboard Instruments. William J. Mitchell (Editor). Trade Cloth. W. W. Norton & Company, Inc. New York, NY. 1948. 449p. ISBN:0-393-09716-1, ISBN13: 978-0-393-09716-0. Dewey:786.193.

Audience: **u,f.** *B*

Bauman, Thomas   **ML410.M9B185 1987**
W. A. Mozart: Die Entführung aus dem Serail. Richard Wagner (Contribution by). Trade Paper. Cambridge University Press. New York, NY. 1988. 156p. Cambridge Opera Handbooks Ser. ISBN:0-521-31060-1, ISBN13: 978-0-521-31060-4. Dewey:782.1/092/4. LCCN:87-010326.

Audience: **u,f.** *Choice, 1988.*

Branscombe, Peter   **ML410.M9 B76 1991**
W. A. Mozart: Die Zauberflöte. Richard Wagner (Contribution by). Trade Paper. Cambridge University Press. New York, NY. 1991. 263p. Cambridge Opera Handbooks Ser. ISBN:0-521-31916-1, ISBN13: 978-0-521-31916-4. Dewey:782.1. LCCN:90-040403.

Audience: **u,f.**

Braunbehrens, Volkmar   **ML410.S16B713 1992**
Maligned Master: The Real Story of Antonio Salieri. Eveline L. Kanes (Translator). Trade Cloth. Fromm International Publishing Corporation. New York, NY. 1993. 264p. ISBN:0-88064-140-1, ISBN13: 978-0-88064-140-1. Dewey:780/.92. LCCN:92-028067.

Audience: **u,f.** *Choice, 1993.*

Brown, A. Peter   **ML1255.B87**
The First Golden Age of the Viennese Symphony: Haydn, Mozart, Beethoven and Schubert. Trade Cloth. Indiana University Press. Bloomington, IN. 2002. 816p. ISBN:0-253-33487-X, ISBN13: 978-0-253-33487-9. Dewey:784.2/184 s 784.2. LCCN:98-026549.

Audience: **g,l,u,f.** *Choice, 2003.*

Brown, Bruce Alan   **ML410.M9B8191995**
W. A. Mozart: Così Fan Tutte. Richard Wagner (Contribution by). Trade Paper. Cambridge University Press. New York, NY. 1995. 220p. Opera Handbooks Ser. ISBN:0-521-43735-0, ISBN13: 978-0-521-43735-6. Dewey:782.1. LCCN:95-009885.

Audience: **u,f.** *Choice, 1997.*

Brown, Clive   **ML457**
Classical and Romantic Performing Practice 1750-1900. Trade Paper. Oxford University Press, Inc. New York, NY. 2004. 676p. ISBN:0-19-516665-5, ISBN13: 978-0-19-516665-1. Dewey:781.4309033. LCCN:97-050572.

Audience: **u,f.**

Brown, Howard Mayer &   **ML5**
  Sadie, Stanley (Editors)
Performance Practice: Music after 1600. Trade Cloth. W. W. Norton & Company, Inc. New York, NY. 1990. xi, 533p. Grove Handbooks in Music Ser. ISBN:0-393-02808-9, ISBN13: 978-0-393-02808-9. Dewey:780/.903. LCCN:91-110857.

Audience: **u,f.**

Burney, Charles   **ML195 .B961 1976**
The Present State of Music in France and Italy. Ed. 2. Trade Cloth. A M S Press, Inc. New York, NY. 1976. ISBN:0-404-12875-0, ISBN13: 978-0-404-12875-3. Dewey:780/.944. LCCN:74-024263.

Audience: **u,f.**

Burney, Charles   **ML195 .B962**
The Present State of Music in Germany, The Netherlands and United Provinces. Library Binding. Broude Brothers, Ltd. Williamstown, MA. 1969. Monuments of Music and Music Literature in Facsimile Ser., Series II, Vol. 117 ISBN:0-8450-2317-9, ISBN13: 978-0-8450-2317-4. Dewey:780/.943.

Audience: **u,f.**

Burton, Anthony (Editor)   **ML457**
A Performer's Guide to Music of the Classical Period. London: Associated Board of the Royal Schools of Music. 2002. Performer's Guides ISBN:1-86096-193-2, ISBN13: 978-1-86096-193-9.

Audience: **l,u,f.**

Carter, Tim   **ML410.M9 C33 1987**
Le Nozze Di Figaro. Richard Wagner (Contribution by). Trade Paper. Cambridge University Press. New York, NY. 1988. 192p. Cambridge Opera Handbooks Ser. ISBN:0-521-31606-5, ISBN13: 978-0-521-31606-4. Dewey:782.109. LCCN:87-011597.

Audience: **u,f.** *Choice, 1988.*

Clark, Caryl (Editor)   **ML410.H4C17 2005**
The Cambridge Companion to Haydn. Jonathan Cross (Contribution by). Cloth Text. Cambridge University Press. New York, NY. 2005. 338p. Cambridge Companions to Music Ser. ISBN:0-521-83347-7, ISBN13: 978-0-521-83347-9. Dewey:780/.92 B. LCCN:2005-003945.

Audience: **g,l,u,f.** *Choice, 2006.*

Da Ponte, Lorenzo   **ML423.D15A3 2000**
Memoirs of Lorenzo Da Ponte. Elisabeth Abbott (Translator), Charles Rosen (Introduction by). Trade Paper. New York Review of Books, Incorporated, The. New York, NY. 2000. 472p. New York Review Books Classics Ser. ISBN:0-940322-35-8, ISBN13: 978-0-940322-35-6. LCCN:99-046014.

Audience: **u,f.**

Davidson, Michael   **MT220**
Mozart and the Pianist: A Guide for Performers and Teachers to Mozart's Major Works for Solo Piano. Ed. 2. Trade Paper. Kahn & Averill Publishers. London, 2001. 384p. ISBN:1-871082-76-5, ISBN13: 978-1-871082-76-0. Dewey:786.2143.

       Audience: **l,u,f.**

Deutsch, Otto Erich   **ML410.M9 D4782**
Mozart: A Documentary Biography. Trade Cloth. Stanford University Press. Palo Alto, CA. 1965. xii, 680p. ISBN:0-8047-0233-0, ISBN13: 978-0-8047-0233-1. Dewey:780.924.

       Audience: **g,l,u,f.**

Downs, Philip G   **ML195**
Classical Music: The Era of Haydn, Mozart, and Beethoven. W.W. Norton. 1992. The Norton Introduction to Music History ISBN:0-393-95191-X, ISBN13: 978-0-393-95191-2.

       Audience: **g,l,u,f.**

Eisen, Cliff   **ML410.M9.D4782**
New Mozart Documents: A Supplement to O. E. Deutsch's Documentary Biography. Trade Cloth. Stanford University Press. Palo Alto, CA. 1991. 192p. ISBN:0-8047-1955-1, ISBN13: 978-0-8047-1955-1. Dewey:016.78/092. LCCN:91-065554.

       Audience: **u,f.** *Choice, 1992.*

Fubini, Enrico   **ML240.3.M8613 1994**
Music and Culture in Eighteenth-Century Europe: A Source Book. Bonnie J. Blackburn (Editor), Wolfgang Freis, Lisa Gasbarrone & Michael L. Leone (Translators). Trade Cloth. University of Chicago Press. Chicago, IL. 1994. 432p. ISBN:0-226-26731-8, ISBN13: 978-0-226-26731-9. Dewey:780/.9/033. LCCN:93-036066.

       Audience: **u,f.** *Choice, 1995.*

Glover, Jane   **ML410.M9G645 2004**
Mozart's Women: His Family, His Friends, His Music. Trade Cloth. HarperCollins Publishers. New York, NY. 2006. 416p. ISBN:0-06-056350-8, ISBN13: 978-0-06-056350-9. Dewey:780/.92 B. LCCN:2005-052699.

       Audience: **g,l,u,f.**

Grave, Floyd K. & Grave, Margaret G.   **ML134.H272G74 1990**
Franz Joseph Haydn: A Guide to Research. Cloth Text. Garland Publishing, Inc. New York, NY. 1990. 464p. Composer Resource Manuals Ser., Vol. 31 ISBN:0-8240-8487-X, ISBN13: 978-0-8240-8487-5. Dewey:016.78/092. LCCN:90-003533.

       Audience: **l,u,f.** *Choice, 1991.*

Grave, Floyd K. & Grave, Margaret G.   **ML410.H4G69 2006**
The String Quartets of Joseph Haydn. Trade Cloth. Oxford University Press, Inc. New York, NY. 2006. 492p. ISBN:0-19-517357-0, ISBN13: 978-0-19-517357-4. Dewey:785/.7194/092. LCCN:2005-047784.

       Audience: **u,f.**

Guede, Alain   **DC137.5.S35G8413**
Monsieur de Saint-George: Virtuoso, Swordsman, Revolutionary: A Legendary Life Rediscovered. Gilda M.

Roberts (Translator). Cloth over Boards. Picador. New York, NY. 2003. 240p. ISBN:0-312-30927-9, ISBN13: 978-0-312-30927-5. Dewey:944/.00496/0092 B. LCCN:2003-049888.

       Audience: **g,l,u,f.** *Choice, 2004.*

Gärtner, Heinz   **ML410.B15**
John Christian Bach: Mozart's Friend and Mentor. Pauly, Reinhard G. (Translator). Amadeus Press. 1994. ISBN:0-931340-79-9, ISBN13: 978-0-931340-79-6.

       Audience: **u,f.**

Haimo, Ethan   **MT130.H4H35 1995**
Haydn's Symphonic Forms: Essays in Compositional Logic. Trade Cloth. Oxford University Press, Inc. New York, NY. 1995. 310p. Oxford Monographs on Music ISBN:0-19-816392-4, ISBN13: 978-0-19-816392-3. Dewey:784.2/184/092. LCCN:94-049097.

       Audience: **u,f.** *Choice, 1996.*

Hall, Charles J. (Compiled by)   **ML195.H28 1990**
An Eighteenth-Century Musical Chronicle: Events 1750-1799, 25. Library Binding. Greenwood Publishing Group, Inc. Portsmouth, NH. 1990. 176p. Music Reference Collection, No. 25 ISBN:0-313-26576-3, ISBN13: 978-0-313-26576-1. Dewey:780/.9/033. LCCN:89-071527.

       Audience: **u,f.** *Choice, 1990.*

Halliwell, Ruth   **ML410.M91H35 1998**
The Mozart Family: Four Lives in a Social Context. Trade Cloth. Oxford University Press, Inc. New York, NY. 1998. 784p. ISBN:0-19-816371-1, ISBN13: 978-0-19-816371-8. Dewey:780.9/22. LCCN:97-009676.

       Audience: **u,f.** *Choice, 1998.*

Harrison, Bernard   **ML410.H4 H314 1998**
Haydn: The 'Paris' Symphonies. Julian Rushton (Contribution by). Trade Paper. Cambridge University Press. New York, NY. 1998. 134p. Music Handbks. ISBN:0-521-47743-3, ISBN13: 978-0-521-47743-7. Dewey:784.2/184/092. LCCN:97-042606.

       Audience: **u,f.** *Choice, 1999.*

Hastings, Baird   **ML134.M9H34 1989**
Wolfgang Amadeus Mozart: A Guide to Research. Trade Cloth. Garland Publishing, Inc. New York, NY. 1989. 500p. Composer Resource Manuals Ser. ISBN:0-8240-8347-4, ISBN13: 978-0-8240-8347-2. Dewey:016.78/092/4. LCCN:88-021294.

       Audience: **l,u,f.** *Choice, 1989.*

Haydn, Joseph   **ML410.H4**
The Collected Correspondence and London Notebooks of Joseph Haydn. Landon, Howard Chandler Robbins (Editor) (Translator). London, Barrie and Rockliff. 1959.

       Audience: **u,f.**

Heartz, Daniel   **ML246.8.V6H4 1994**
Haydn, Mozart and the Viennese School 1740-1780. Paper Text. W. W. Norton & Company, Inc. New York, NY. 1994. ISBN:0-393-96533-3, ISBN13: 978-0-393-96533-9. Dewey:780/.9436/1309033. LCCN:93-047001.

       Audience: **u,f.**

Heartz, Daniel   **ML410.V4**
Mozart's Operas. Trade Paper. University of California Press.
Berkeley, CA. 1992. 382p. ISBN:0-520-07872-1, ISBN13:
978-0-520-07872-7. Dewey:782.1/092. LCCN:89-020435.
Audience: **u,f.** *Choice, 1991.*

Heartz, Daniel   **ML240.3.H43 2003**
Music in European Capitals: The Galant Style 1720 to 1780.
Trade Cloth. W. W. Norton & Company, Inc. New York, NY.
2003. 1062p. ISBN:0-393-05080-7, ISBN13:
978-0-393-05080-6. Dewey:780/.9/032. LCCN:2002-015693.
Audience: **u,f.**

Honolka, Kurt   **ML423.S346H613 1990**
Papageno: Emanuel Schikaneder - Man of the Theater in
Mozart's Time. Jane M. Wilde (Translator). Trade Cloth. Hal
Leonard Corporation. Milwaukee, WI. 1990. 236p.
ISBN:0-931340-21-7, ISBN13: 978-0-931340-21-5.
Dewey:782.1/092 B. LCCN:89-017574.
Audience: **u,f.** *Choice, 1990.*

Howard, Patricia   **ML410.G5H668 1995**
Gluck: An Eighteenth-Century Portrait in Letters and
Documents. Trade Cloth. Oxford University Press, Inc. New
York, NY. 1995. 286p. ISBN:0-19-816385-1, ISBN13:
978-0-19-816385-5. Dewey:782.1/092. LCCN:95-017332.
Audience: **u,f.** *Choice, 1996.*

Howard, Patricia   **ML410.G5 C2 1981**
Orfeo. Richard Wagner (Contribution by). Trade Paper.
Cambridge University Press. New York, NY. 1981. 152p.
Cambridge Opera Handbooks Ser. ISBN:0-521-29664-1,
ISBN13: 978-0-521-29664-9. Dewey:782.1. LCCN:80-049734.
Audience: **l,u,f.**

Hutchings, Arthur   **MT130.M8H8 1998**
A Companion to Mozart's Piano Concertos. Ed. 2. Cliff Eisen
(Introduction by). Trade Paper. Oxford University Press, Inc.
New York, NY. 1999. 228p. ISBN:0-19-816708-3, ISBN13:
978-0-19-816708-2. Dewey:784.2/62/092. LCCN:98-039904.
Audience: **l,u,f.**

Irving, John   **ML410.M9 I73 1998**
Mozart: The 'Haydn' Quartets. Julian Rushton (Contribution
by). Cloth Text. Cambridge University Press. New York, NY.
1998. 113p. Music Handbks. ISBN:0-521-58475-2, ISBN13:
978-0-521-58475-3. Dewey:785/.7194/092. LCCN:97-007268.
Audience: **u,f.**

Keefe, Simon P. (Editor)   **ML410.M9C255 2003**
The Cambridge Companion to Mozart. Jonathan Cross
(Contribution by). Trade Paper. Cambridge University Press.
New York, NY. 2003. 312p. Cambridge Companions to Music
Ser. ISBN:0-521-00192-7, ISBN13: 978-0-521-00192-2.
Dewey:780/.92 B. LCCN:2002-034926.
Audience: **g,l,u,f.** *Choice, 2004.*

Kuster, Konrad   **ML410.M9K9813 1996**
Mozart: A Musical Biography. Mary Whittall (Translator). Trade
Cloth. Oxford University Press, Inc. New York, NY. 1996. 428p.

ISBN:0-19-816339-8, ISBN13: 978-0-19-816339-8.
Dewey:780.9/2. LCCN:95-035042.
Audience: **l,u,f.** *Choice, 1997.*

Köchel, Ludwig   **ML134.M8**
Chronologisch-thematisches Verzeichnis sämtlicher Tonwerke
Wolfgang Amadé Mozarts: nebst Angabe der
verlorengegangenen, angefangenen, von fremder Hand
bearbeiteten, zweifelhaften und unterschobenen Kompositionen.
Ed. 8. Geigling, Franz; Weinmann, Alexander; Sievers, Gerd.
Wiesbaden: Breitkopf & Härtel; New York: C. F. Peters, sole
agents in USA. 1983.
Audience: **u,f.**

Landon, H. C. Robbins   **ML410.M9L236 1999**
1791: Mozart's Last Year. Trade Paper. Thames & Hudson. New
York, NY. 1999. 240p. ISBN:0-500-28107-6, ISBN13:
978-0-500-28107-9. Dewey:780/.92 B. LCCN:98-061442.
Audience: **g,l,u,f.**

Landon, H. C. Robbins   **ML410.H4**
Haydn: The Early Years, 1732-1765. Trade Cloth. Thames &
Hudson. New York, NY. 1995. 656p. Haydn, :Chronicle and
Works ISBN:0-500-01169-9, ISBN13: 978-0-500-01169-0.
Dewey:780.924. LCCN:94-061473.
Audience: **l,u,f.**

Landon, H. C. Robbins   **ML410.H4**
Haydn: The Late Years, 1801-1809. Trade Cloth. Thames &
Hudson. New York, NY. 1995. 504p. Haydn, :Chronicle and
Works ISBN:0-500-01167-2, ISBN13: 978-0-500-01167-6.
Dewey:780/.92/4. LCCN:94-061478.
Audience: **l,u,f.**

Landon, H. C. Robbins   **ML410.H4**
Haydn: The Years of Creation, 1796-1800. Trade Cloth. Thames
& Hudson. New York, NY. 1995. 676p. Haydn, :Chronicle and
Works ISBN:0-500-01166-4, ISBN13: 978-0-500-01166-9.
Dewey:780/.92/4. LCCN:94-061477.
Audience: **l,u,f.**

Landon, H. C. Robbins   **ML410.H4**
Haydn at Eszterhaza, 1766-1790. Trade Cloth. Thames &
Hudson. New York, NY. 1995. 819p. Haydn, :Chronicle and
Works ISBN:0-500-01168-0, ISBN13: 978-0-500-01168-3.
Dewey:780/.92/4. LCCN:94-061475.
Audience: **l,u,f.**

Landon, H. C. Robbins   **ML410.H4**
Haydn in England, 1791-1795. Trade Cloth. Thames & Hudson.
New York, NY. 1995. 648p. Haydn, :Chronicle and Works
ISBN:0-500-01164-8, ISBN13: 978-0-500-01164-5.
Dewey:780/.92/4. LCCN:94-061476.
Audience: **l,u,f.**

Landon, H. C. Robbins   **ML410.H4**
The Symphonies of Joseph Haydn. Paper Text. Textbook
Publishers. Temecula, CA. 2003. xvii, 862p.
ISBN:0-7581-2881-9, ISBN13: 978-0-7581-2881-2.
Dewey:785.110924.
Audience: **l,u,f.**

Landon, H. C. & Wyn   ML410.H4L265 1988
Jones, David
Haydn: His Life and Music. Cloth Text. Indiana University
Press. Bloomington, IN. 1988. 384p. ISBN:0-253-37265-8,
ISBN13: 978-0-253-37265-9. Dewey:780/.92/4 B.
LCCN:88-002685.

Audience: **g,l,u,f.** *Choice, 1989.*

Lawson, Colin J.   ML410.M9 L26 1996
Mozart: Clarinet Concerto. Julian Rushton (Contribution by).
Cloth Text. Cambridge University Press. New York, NY. 1996.
123p. Music Handbks. ISBN:0-521-47384-5, ISBN13:
978-0-521-47384-2. Dewey:784.2/862. LCCN:95-022790.

Audience: **u,f.**

Lester, Joel   ML430
Compositional Theory in the 18th Century. Trade Paper. Harvard
University Press. Cambridge, MA. 1994. 368p.
ISBN:0-674-15523-8, ISBN13: 978-0-674-15523-7. Dewey:781.

Audience: **u,f.**

MacIntyre, Bruce   ML410.H4M13 1998
Haydn: The Creation. Trade Cloth. Thomson Wadsworth.
Belmont, CA. 1997. Monuments of Western Music Ser.
ISBN:0-02-871375-3, ISBN13: 978-0-02-871375-5.
Dewey:782.23. LCCN:97-025759.

Audience: **u,f.**

Marshall, Robert L. (Editor)   ML705.E37 1994
Eighteenth Century Keyboard Music. Trade Cloth. Thomson
Wadsworth. Belmont, CA. 1994. 384p. Studies in Musical
Genres and Repertoires ISBN:0-02-871355-9, ISBN13:
978-0-02-871355-7. Dewey:786/.09/033. LCCN:93-045594.

Audience: **u,f.** *Choice, 1995.*

Morrow, Mary S.   ML246.8.V6M87 1989
Concert Life in Haydn's Vienna: Aspects of a Developing
Musical and Social Institution. Library Binding. Pendragon
Press. Hillsdale, NY. 1989. 500p. Sociology of Music Ser., No.
7 ISBN:0-918728-83-5, ISBN13: 978-0-918728-83-8.
Dewey:780/.7/30943613. LCCN:88-023385.

Audience: **u,f.** *Choice, 1989.*

Mozart, Wolfgang Amadeus   ML49.M83 M42 1991
The Metropolitan Opera Book of Mozart Operas. Metropolitan
Opera Guild Staff & Paul Gruber (Editors), Judyth Schaubhut
Smith, David Stivender & Susan Webb (Translators). Trade
Paper. HarperCollins Publishers. New York, NY. 1991. 640p.
ISBN:0-06-273051-7, ISBN13: 978-0-06-273051-0.
Dewey:782.1/026/8. LCCN:91-055003.

Audience: **g,l,u,f.**

Newman, Ernest   ML410.G5 N3 1976
Gluck and the Opera: A Study in Musical History. Trade Cloth.
Greenwood Publishing Group, Inc. Portsmouth, NH. 1976. 300p.
ISBN:0-8371-8849-0, ISBN13: 978-0-8371-8849-2.
Dewey:782.1/092/4. LCCN:76-007579.

Audience: **u,f.**

Newman, William S.   ML1156
The Sonata in the Classic Era. Ed. 3. Trade Cloth. W. W. Norton
& Company, Inc. New York, NY. 1983. 958p.
ISBN:0-393-95286-X, ISBN13: 978-0-393-95286-5.
Dewey:781/.52/09. LCCN:82-024575.

Audience: **u,f.** *B*

Ottenberg, Hans-Gunter   ML410.B16O873 1987
C. P. E. Bach. Philip J. Whitmore (Translator). Trade Cloth.
Oxford University Press, Inc. New York, NY. 1988. 296p.
ISBN:0-19-315246-0, ISBN13: 978-0-19-315246-5.
Dewey:780/.92/4 B. LCCN:86-023904.

Audience: **l,u,f.**

Parker, Mara E.   ML1160.P37 2002
The String Quartet, 1750-1797: Four Types of Musical
Conversation. Trade Cloth. Ashgate Publishing, Ltd. Aldershot,
2002. 330p. ISBN:1-84014-682-6, ISBN13: 978-1-84014-682-0.
Dewey:785/.7194/09033. LCCN:2002-019634.

Audience: **u,f.**

Pauly, Reinhard G.   ML195.P38 2000
Music in the Classic Period. Ed. 4. Trade Paper. Prentice Hall
PTR. Upper Saddle River, NJ. 1999. 272p. Prentice Hall History
of Music Ser. ISBN:0-13-011502-9, ISBN13:
978-0-13-011502-7. Dewey:780/.903/3. LCCN:99-030849.

Audience: **g,l,u,f.** *B*

Plantinga, Leon   ML410.C64.P5
Clementi: His Life and Music. Trade Cloth. Oxford University
Press, Inc. New York, NY. 1977. xiii, 346p.
ISBN:0-19-315227-4, ISBN13: 978-0-19-315227-4.
Dewey:786.1/092/4 B. LCCN:77-359247.

Audience: **l,u,f.**

Ratner, Leonard G.   ML240.3
Classic Music: Expression, Form and Style. Trade Paper.
Thomson Wadsworth. Belmont, CA. 1985. 496p.
ISBN:0-02-872690-1, ISBN13: 978-0-02-872690-8.
Dewey:780/.903/3. LCCN:76-057808.

Audience: **l,u,f.**

Richards, Annette   ML3849 .R48 2001
The Free Fantasia and the Musical Picturesque. Jeffrey Kallberg,
Anthony Newcomb & Ruth Solie (Contribution by). Trade
Cloth. Cambridge University Press. New York, NY. 2001. 263p.
New Perspectives in Music History and Criticism Ser., No. 6
ISBN:0-521-64077-6, ISBN13: 978-0-521-64077-0.
Dewey:784.18/94. LCCN:00-028944.

Audience: **u,f.**

Rosen, Charles   ML195.R68 1997
Classical Style: Haydn, Mozart, Beethoven. Ed. 2. Trade Cloth.
W. W. Norton & Company, Inc. New York, NY. 1997. 548p.
ISBN:0-393-04020-8, ISBN13: 978-0-393-04020-3.
Dewey:780/.9/033. LCCN:96-027335.

Audience: **l,u,f.** *B Choice, 1997.*

Rosselli, John   ML410.M9 R847 1998
The Life of Mozart. Trade Paper. Cambridge University Press.
New York, NY. 1998. 183p. Musical Lives Ser.

ISBN:0-521-58744-1, ISBN13: 978-0-521-58744-0.
Dewey:780/.92 B. LCCN:97-033013.
Audience: **g,l,u,f.** *Choice, 1998.*

Rushton, Julian   **ML410.M9 R88 1981**
Don Giovanni. Richard Wagner (Contribution by). Trade Paper.
Cambridge University Press. New York, NY. 1981. 176p.
Cambridge Opera Handbooks Ser. ISBN:0-521-29663-3,
ISBN13: 978-0-521-29663-2. Dewey:782.1/092/4.
LCCN:80-041534.
Audience: **l,u,f.**

Rushton, Julian   **ML410.M9 R89 1993**
W. A. Mozart: Idomeneo. Richard Wagner (Contribution by).
Trade Paper. Cambridge University Press. New York, NY. 1993.
197p. Cambridge Opera Handbooks Ser. ISBN:0-521-43741-5,
ISBN13: 978-0-521-43741-7. Dewey:782.1. LCCN:92-025833.
Audience: **u,f.**

Schroeder, David P.   **ML410.H4S45 1997**
Haydn and the Enlightenment: The Late Symphonies and Their
Audience. Trade Paper. Oxford University Press, Inc. New York,
NY. 1998. 230p. Oxford Monographs on Music
ISBN:0-19-816682-6, ISBN13: 978-0-19-816682-5.
Dewey:784.2/184/092. LCCN:97-025754.
Audience: **u,f.**

Sisman, Elaine Rochelle   **ML410.M9S561993**
Mozart, the "Jupiter" Symphony, No. 41 in C Major, K. 551.
Julian Rushton (Editor, Contribution by). Trade Paper.
Cambridge University Press. New York, NY. 1993. 122p.
Cambridge Music Handbooks Ser. ISBN:0-521-40924-1,
ISBN13: 978-0-521-40924-7. Dewey:784.184092.
LCCN:92-039074.
Audience: **u,f.**

Smither, Howard E.   **76-43980**
The Oratorio in the Classical Era. Trade Cloth. University of
North Carolina Press. Chapel Hill, NC. 1987. 736p. History of
the Oratorio Ser., Vol. 3 ISBN:0-8078-1731-7, ISBN13:
978-0-8078-1731-5. Dewey:782.8/2/09. LCCN:76-043980.
Audience: **u.**

Solomon, Maynard   **ML410.M9**
Mozart: A Life. Trade Paper. HarperCollins Publishers. New
York, NY. 2006. 656p. ISBN:0-06-088344-8, ISBN13:
978-0-06-088344-7. Dewey:780.9/2.
Audience: **g,l,u,f.**

Spaethling, Robert (Editor,   **ML410.M9A4 2000**
Translator)
Mozart's Letters, Mozart's Life. Trade Cloth. W. W. Norton &
Company, Inc. New York, NY. 2000. 416p.
ISBN:0-393-04719-9, ISBN13: 978-0-393-04719-6.
Dewey:780/.92 B. LCCN:00-025530.
Audience: **u,f.** *Choice, 2001.*

Spitzer, John & Zaslaw,   **ML1200**
Neal
The Birth of the Orchestra: History of an Institution, 1650-1815.
Trade Paper, Perfect. Oxford University Press, Inc. New York,

NY. 2005. 640p. ISBN:0-19-518955-8, ISBN13:
978-0-19-518955-1. Dewey:784.2/09.
Audience: **u,f.** *Choice, 2005.*

Steblin, Rita   **ML3838.S8 2002**
A History of Key Characteristics in the 18th and Early 19th
Centuries. Ed. 2. Trade Cloth. University of Rochester Press.
Rochester, NY. 2005. 420p. ISBN:1-58046-041-0, ISBN13:
978-1-58046-041-5. Dewey:781.1/1/09033. LCCN:2002-020679.
Audience: **u,f.**

Strohm, Reinhard   **ML1733.3.S87 1997**
Dramma per Musica: Italian Opera Seria of the Eighteenth
Century. Cloth over Boards. Yale University Press. Cumberland,
RI. 1997. 336p. ISBN:0-300-06454-3, ISBN13:
978-0-300-06454-4. Dewey:782.1/0945/09033.
LCCN:97-027576.
Audience: **u,f.** *Choice, 1998.*

Temperley, Nicholas   **ML410.H4 T36 1991**
Haydn: The Creation. Julian Rushton (Contribution by). Trade
Paper. Cambridge University Press. New York, NY. 1991. 143p.
Music Handbks. ISBN:0-521-37865-6, ISBN13:
978-0-521-37865-9. Dewey:782.23. LCCN:90-001859.
Audience: **u,f.** *Choice, 1992.*

Von Dittersdorf, Karl D.   **ML410.D6**
The Autobiography of Karl Von Dittersdorf. Trade Cloth.
Library Reprints, Inc. Temecula, CA. 2001. 316p.
ISBN:0-7222-5403-2, ISBN13: 978-0-7222-5403-5.
Dewey:780/.924.
Audience: **u,f.**

Wheelock, Gretchen A.   **ML410.H4W47 1992**
Haydn's Ingenious Jesting with Art: Contexts of Musical Wit
and Humor. Trade Cloth. Thomson Gale. Farmington Hills, MI.
1992. 269p. ISBN:0-02-872855-6, ISBN13: 978-0-02-872855-1.
Dewey:784/.092. LCCN:91-046730.
Audience: **u,f.** *Choice, 1993.*

Wolff, Christoph   **ML410.M9**
Mozart's Requiem: Historical and Analytical Studies,
Documents, Score. Trade Paper. University of California Press.
Berkeley, CA. 1998. 190p. ISBN:0-520-21389-0, ISBN13:
978-0-520-21389-0. Dewey:782.32/38.
Audience: **u,f.**

Wyn Jones, David, et al.   **ML410.H4**
Haydn. Biba, Otto (Author). Oxford; New York: Oxford
University Press. 2002. Oxford Composer Companions
ISBN:0-19-866216-5, ISBN13: 978-0-19-866216-7.
Audience: **l,u,f.**

Zaslaw, Neal   **ML195.C595 1989**
The Classical Era: From the 1740's to the End of the 18th
Century. Paper Text. Prentice Hall PTR. Upper Saddle River,
NJ. 1989. 400p. ISBN:0-13-136938-5, ISBN13:
978-0-13-136938-2. Dewey:780/.9/033. LCCN:90-224637.
Audience: **g,l,u,f.**

Zaslaw, Neal (Editor) **ML410.M9M875 1996**
Mozart's Piano Concertos: Text, Context, Interpretation. Trade
Cloth. University of Michigan Press. Chicago, IL. 1997. 496p.
ISBN:0-472-10314-8, ISBN13: 978-0-472-10314-0.
Dewey:784.2/62/092. LCCN:96-004416.
    Audience: **l,u,f.**

Zaslaw, Neal **ML410.B5**
Mozart's Symphonies: Context, Performance Practice,
Reception. Paper Text. Oxford University Press, Inc. New York,
NY. 1991. 642p. ISBN:0-19-816286-3, ISBN13:
978-0-19-816286-5. Dewey:785.1/1/0924.
    Audience: **l,u,f.** *Choice, 1990.*

Zaslaw, Neal & Cowdery, **MT145.M7Z4 1990**
 William
The Compleat Mozart: A Guide to the Musical Works of
Wolfgang Amadeus Mozart. Trade Cloth. W. W. Norton &
Company, Inc. New York, NY. 1991. 368p.
ISBN:0-393-02886-0, ISBN13: 978-0-393-02886-7.
Dewey:780/.92. LCCN:90-030833.
    Audience: **g,l,u,f.** *Choice, 1991.*

Zaslaw, Neal & Fiel, Fiona **ML134.M9M83 1991**
 M. (Editors)
The Mozart Repertory: A Guide for Musicians, Programmers,
and Researchers. Book, Other. Cornell University Press. Ithaca,
NY. 1991. 176p. ISBN:0-8014-9937-2, ISBN13:
978-0-8014-9937-1. Dewey:016.78/092. LCCN:91-007459.
    Audience: **g,l,u,f.**

Studies in Music History, Criticism, Analysis, and Appreciation > Western Classical Literature by Period > Romantic

Abbate, Carolyn **ML3858.A2 1996**
Unsung Voices: Opera and Musical Narrative in the Nineteenth
Century. Trade Paper. Princeton University Press. Princeton, NJ.
1996. 304p. Princeton Studies in Opera ISBN:0-691-02608-4,
ISBN13: 978-0-691-02608-4. Dewey:782.1/09/034.
    Audience: **u,f.** *Choice, 1991.*

Abbate, Carolyn & Parker, **MT95.A59 1989**
 Roger (Editors)
Analyzing Opera: Verdi and Wagner. Trade Cloth. University of
California Press. Berkeley, CA. 1989. 250p. California Studies
in 19th Century Music, No. 6 ISBN:0-520-06157-8, ISBN13:
978-0-520-06157-6. Dewey:782.1/092/2. LCCN:88-021072.
    Audience: **u,f.** *Choice, 1990.*

Abraham, Gerald E. **ML5**
 (Editor)
The New Oxford History of Music: Romanticism (1830-1890).
Trade Cloth. Oxford University Press, Inc. New York, NY. 1990.

956p. New Oxford History of Music Ser. ISBN:0-19-316309-8,
ISBN13: 978-0-19-316309-6. Dewey:780.9/034.
LCCN:54-012578.
    Audience: **g,l,u,f.** *Choice, 1991.*

Abraham, Gerald E. **ML410.R52 A62 1976**
Rimsky-Korsakov. Trade Cloth. A M S Press, Inc. New York,
NY. BCL Ser., No. II ISBN:0-404-14500-0, ISBN13:
978-0-404-14500-2. Dewey:780/.92/4. LCCN:75-041002.
    Audience: **l,u,f.**

Anderson, Emily (Editor) **ML410.B4**
The Letters of Beethoven. Trade Cloth. W. W. Norton &
Company, Inc. New York, NY. 1986. ISBN:0-393-02247-1,
ISBN13: 978-0-393-02247-6. Dewey:780.92.
    Audience: **g,l,u,f.**

Arnold, Denis, et. al **ML410.B4**
The Beethoven Reader. Fortune, Nigel (Author). W. W. Norton.
1971.
    Audience: **l,u,f.**

Ashbrook, William **ML410.D7**
Donizetti. London, Cassell. 1965.
    Audience: **l,u,f.**

Ashbrook, William **MT100.P95A8 1985**
The Operas of Puccini. Roger Parker (Foreword by). Trade
Paper. Cornell University Press. Ithaca, NY. 1985. 288p. Cornell
Paperbacks Ser. ISBN:0-8014-9309-9, ISBN13:
978-0-8014-9309-6. Dewey:782.1/092/4. LCCN:84-072674.
    Audience: **g,l,u,f.**

Balthazar, Scott L. (Editor) **ML410**
The Cambridge Companion to Verdi. Jonathan Cross
(Contribution by). Cloth Text. Cambridge University Press. New
York, NY. 2004. 364p. Cambridge Companions to Music Ser.
ISBN:0-521-63228-5, ISBN13: 978-0-521-63228-7.
Dewey:782.1092 B. LCCN:2005-280590.
    Audience: **g,l,u,f.**

Barzun, Jacques **ML410.B5.B2 1969**
Berlioz and the Romantic Century. Ed. 3. Trade Cloth.
Columbia University Press. New York, NY. 1969. 1088p.
ISBN:0-231-03135-1, ISBN13: 978-0-231-03135-6.
Dewey:780/.924. LCCN:77-097504.
    Audience: **g,u,f.**

Beckerman, Michael **ML410.M9**
 (Editor)
Dvorak and His World. Trade Paper. Princeton University Press.
Princeton, NJ. 1993. 294p. The Bard Music Festival Ser.
ISBN:0-691-00097-2, ISBN13: 978-0-691-00097-8.
Dewey:780/.92. LCCN:93-004037.
    Audience: **g,l,u,f.** *Choice, 1994.*

Beckerman, Michael B. **ML410.D99B42 2003**
New Worlds of Dvorak: Searching in America for the
Composers Inner Life. Trade Cloth. W. W. Norton & Company,
Inc. New York, NY. 2003. 200p. ISBN:0-393-04706-7, ISBN13:
978-0-393-04706-6. Dewey:780/.92 B. LCCN:2002-026590.
    Audience: **g,l,u,f.**

Beckerman, Michael Brim   ML410
  (Editor)
Janacek and His World. Trade Cloth. Princeton University Press.
Princeton, NJ. 2003. 320p. The Bard Music Festival Ser.
ISBN:0-691-11675-X, ISBN13: 978-0-691-11675-4.
Dewey:780.9/2.

Audience: **g,l,u,f.**

Beckett, Lucy   ML410.W17.B37
Richard Wagner: "Parsifal". Cloth Text. Cambridge University
Press. New York, NY. 1981. 173p. Cambridge Opera Handbooks
Ser. ISBN:0-521-22825-5, ISBN13: 978-0-521-22825-1.
Dewey:782.1/092/4. LCCN:80-040870.

Audience: **u,f.**

Beethoven, Ludwig van   ML410.B4
Fidelio. Nicholas John (Editor), Tom Hammond (Translator).
Trade Paper. Riverrun Press, Inc. Flemington, NJ. 1981. 96p.
English National Opera Guide Ser., No. 4:Bilingual Libretto,
Articles ISBN:0-7145-3823-X, ISBN13: 978-0-7145-3823-5.
Dewey:782.1.

Audience: **g,l,u,f.**

Benestad, Finn &   ML410.G9B413 1988
  Schjelderup-Ebbe, Dag
Edvard Grieg: The Man and the Artist. William H. Halverson &
Leland B. Sateren (Translators). Trade Cloth. University of
Nebraska Press. Lincoln, NE. 1988. 441p. ISBN:0-8032-1202-X,
ISBN13: 978-0-8032-1202-2. Dewey:780/.92/4 B.
LCCN:87-020608.

Audience: **g,l,u,f.** *Choice, 1989.*

Berlioz, Hector   ML410.B5A533 1999
Evenings with the Orchestra. Jacques Barzen (Translator). Trade
Paper. University of Chicago Press. Chicago, IL. 1999. 408p.
ISBN:0-226-04374-6, ISBN13: 978-0-226-04374-6.
Dewey:780/.944/36109034. LCCN:98-054094.

Audience: **u,f.** *B*

Berlioz, Hector   ML270
The Musical Madhouse: An English Translation of Berlioz's les
Grotesques de la Musique. Alastair Bruce (Editor), Hugh
Macdonald (Introduction by). Trade Cloth. University of
Rochester Press. Rochester, NY. 2004. 264p. Eastman Studies in
Music ISBN:1-58046-132-8, ISBN13: 978-1-58046-132-0.
Dewey:780/.9. LCCN:2003-001049.

Audience: **u,f.** *Choice, 2003.*

Berlioz, Hector   ML410.B5A3 2002
The Memoirs of Hector Berlioz. David Cairns (Editor,
Translator, Introduction by). Trade Cloth. Alfred A. Knopf Inc.
New York, NY. 2002. 720p. Everyman's Library
ISBN:0-375-41391-X, ISBN13: 978-0-375-41391-9.
Dewey:780/.92 B. LCCN:2002-283060.

Audience: **u,f.**

Berlioz, Hector   ML410.B42B49 2000
A Critical Study of Beethoven's Nine Symphonies. Edwin
Evans (Translator), Kern Holoman (Introduction by). Trade

Paper. University of Illinois Press. Champaign, IL. 2000. 192p.
ISBN:0-252-06942-0, ISBN13: 978-0-252-06942-0.
Dewey:784.2/184/092. LCCN:00-047939.

Audience: **u,f.**

Bizet, Georges   ML50.B625C22 1982
Carmen. Nicholas John (Editor), Nell Moody & John Moody
(Translators). Trade Paper. Beekman Books, Inc. Wappingers
Falls, NY. 1982. 128p. English National Opera Guide Ser., No.
13:Bilingual Libretto, Articles ISBN:0-7145-3937-6, ISBN13:
978-0-7145-3937-9. Dewey:782.1/2. LCCN:83-107621.

Audience: **g,l,u,f.**

Block, Adrienne F.   ML410.B36B56 1998
Amy Beach, Passionate Victorian: The Life and Works of an
American Composer, 1867-1944. Trade Cloth. Oxford
University Press, Inc. New York, NY. 1998. 426p.
ISBN:0-19-507408-4, ISBN13: 978-0-19-507408-6.
Dewey:780.9/2. LCCN:97-002710.

Audience: **g,l,u,f.** *Choice, 1999.*

Bloom, Peter (Editor)   ML410 .B5 C27 2000
The Cambridge Companion to Berlioz. Trade Paper. Cambridge
University Press. New York, NY. 2000. 326p. Cambridge
Companions to Music Ser. ISBN:0-521-59638-6, ISBN13:
978-0-521-59638-1. Dewey:780/.92. LCCN:99-054359.

Audience: **g,l,u,f.** *Choice, 2001.*

Botstein, Leon (Editor)   ML410.B8C64 1999
The Compleat Brahms: A Guide to the Musical Works of
Johannes Brahms. Trade Cloth. W. W. Norton & Company, Inc.
New York, NY. 1999. 350p. ISBN:0-393-04708-3, ISBN13:
978-0-393-04708-0. Dewey:780/.92. LCCN:98-043968.

Audience: **g,l,u,f.**

Brahms, Johannes   ML410.B8A4 1997
Johannes Brahms: Life and Letters. Styra Avins (Editor,
Translator), Josef Eisinger (Translator). Trade Cloth. Oxford
University Press, Inc. New York, NY. 1998. 886p.
ISBN:0-19-816234-0, ISBN13: 978-0-19-816234-6.
Dewey:780.9/2. LCCN:97-005417.

Audience: **u,f.** *Choice, 1998.*

Brown, A. Peter   ML1255.B87
The First Golden Age of the Viennese Symphony: Haydn,
Mozart, Beethoven and Schubert. Trade Cloth. Indiana
University Press. Bloomington, IN. 2002. 816p.
ISBN:0-253-33487-X, ISBN13: 978-0-253-33487-9.
Dewey:784.2/184 s 784.2. LCCN:98-026549.

Audience: **g,l,u,f.** *Choice, 2003.*

Brown, A. Peter   ML1255.B87
The Symphonic Repertoire: The Second Golden Age of the
Viennese Symphony. Cloth Text. Indiana University Press.
Bloomington, IN. 2003. 816p. ISBN:0-253-33488-8, ISBN13:
978-0-253-33488-6. Dewey:784.2/184. LCCN:2003-551931.

Audience: **g,l,u,f.** *Choice, 2004.*

Brown, Clive   ML457
Classical and Romantic Performing Practice 1750-1900. Trade

Paper. Oxford University Press, Inc. New York, NY. 2004. 676p. ISBN:0-19-516665-5, ISBN13: 978-0-19-516665-1. Dewey:781.4309033. LCCN:97-050572.

Audience: **u,f.**

Brown, Clive   **ML410.M5B76 2003**
A Portrait of Mendelssohn. Cloth over Boards. Yale University Press. Cumberland, RI. 2003. 586p. ISBN:0-300-09539-2, ISBN13: 978-0-300-09539-5. Dewey:780/.92 B. LCCN:2002-012154.

Audience: **u,f.** *Choice, 2004.*

Brown, David   **ML410.M97B75 2002**
Musorgsky: His Life and Works. Trade Cloth. Oxford University Press, Inc. New York, NY. 2002. 410p. Master Musicians Ser. ISBN:0-19-816587-0, ISBN13: 978-0-19-816587-3. Dewey:780/.92 B. LCCN:2002-020154.

Audience: **g,l,u,f.**

Brown, David   **ML390**
Tchaikovsky Remembered. Paper Text. DIANE Publishing Company. Collingdale, PA. 1999. 248p. ISBN:0-7881-6785-5, ISBN13: 978-0-7881-6785-0. Dewey:780/.92 B.

Audience: **u,f.**

Budden, Julian   **ML410.V4**
The Operas of Verdi: From Il Trovatore to la Forza Del Destino. Vol. 2. Ed. 2. Trade Paper. Oxford University Press, Inc. New York, NY. 1992. 542p. ISBN:0-19-816262-6, ISBN13: 978-0-19-816262-9. Dewey:782.1/092.

Audience: **g,l,u,f.**

Budden, Julian   **ML410.V4**
The Operas of Verdi: From Oberto to Rigoletto, Vol. 1. Ed. 2. Trade Paper. Oxford University Press, Inc. New York, NY. 1992. 538p. ISBN:0-19-816261-8, ISBN13: 978-0-19-816261-2. Dewey:782.1092.

Audience: **g,l,u,f.**

Budden, Julian (Editor)   **ML410.V4 B88 1991**
The Operas of Verdi: From Don Carlos to Falstaff, Vol. 3. Ed. 2. Trade Paper. Oxford University Press, Inc. New York, NY. 1992. 550p. ISBN:0-19-816263-4, ISBN13: 978-0-19-816263-6. Dewey:782.1/092. LCCN:91-036272.

Audience: **g,l,u,f.**

Budden, Julian   **ML410.V4**
Puccini: His Life and Works. Trade Paper, Perfect. Oxford University Press, Inc. New York, NY. 2005. 538p. Master Musicians Ser. ISBN:0-19-517974-9, ISBN13: 978-0-19-517974-3. Dewey:782.1/092 B.

Audience: **g,l,u,f.**

Budden, Julian   **ML410.V4**
Verdi. New York: Schirmer Books. 1996. Master Musicians Ser. ISBN:0-02-864616-9, ISBN13: 978-0-02-864616-9.

Audience: **g,l,u,f.**

Burbidge, Peter & Sutton,   **ML410.V4**
Richard (Editors)

The Wagner Companion. Trade Cloth. Cambridge University Press. New York, NY. 1979. ISBN:0-521-22787-9, ISBN13: 978-0-521-22787-2. Dewey:782.1/092/4. LCCN:79-050099.

Audience: **u,f.**

Burton, Anthony (Editor)   **ML457**
A Performer's Guide to Music of the Romantic Period. London; Associated Board of the Royal Schools of Music. 2002. Performer's Guides ISBN:1-86096-194-0, ISBN13: 978-1-86096-194-6.

Audience: **l,u,f.**

Caballero, Carlo   **ML410.F27 C33 2001**
Fauré and French Musical Aesthetics. Arnold Whittall (Contribution by). Trade Paper. Cambridge University Press. New York, NY. 2004. 345p. Music in the Twentieth Century Ser., Vol. 13 ISBN:0-521-54398-3, ISBN13: 978-0-521-54398-9. Dewey:780/.92.

Audience: **u,f.** *Choice, 2002.*

Cairns, David   **ML410.B5C25 1999**
The Making of an Artist, 1803-1832. Trade Cloth. University of California Press. Berkeley, CA. 2000. 672p. Berlioz Ser., Vol. 1 ISBN:0-520-22199-0, ISBN13: 978-0-520-22199-4. Dewey:780/.92. LCCN:99-053825.

Audience: **l,u,f.**

Cairns, David   **ML410.B5 C25 1999**
Servitude and Greatness. Trade Cloth. University of California Press. Berkeley, CA. 2000. 907p. Berlioz Ser., Vol. 2 ISBN:0-520-22200-8, ISBN13: 978-0-520-22200-7. Dewey:780/.92 B. LCCN:99-053825.

Audience: **g,l,u,f.**

Campbell, Stuart (Editor)   **ML300.4 .R87 1994**
Russians on Russian Music, 1830-1880: An Anthology in Translation. Trade Cloth. Cambridge University Press. New York, NY. 1994. 317p. ISBN:0-521-40267-0, ISBN13: 978-0-521-40267-5. Dewey:780.94709034. LCCN:93-017690.

Audience: **u,f.** *Choice, 1995.*

Carner, Mosco   **ML410.P89 C25 1985**
Giacomo Puccini: Tosca. Cloth Text. Cambridge University Press. New York, NY. 1985. 174p. Cambridge Opera Handbooks Ser. ISBN:0-521-22824-7, ISBN13: 978-0-521-22824-4. Dewey:782.1/092/4.

Audience: **u,f.** *Choice, 1986.*

Clark, Walter Aaron   **ML410.C54**
Isaac Albeniz: Portrait of a Romantic. Trade Paper. Oxford University Press, Inc. New York, NY. 2002. 342p. ISBN:0-19-925052-9, ISBN13: 978-0-19-925052-3. Dewey:786.2/092. LCCN:97-032612.

Audience: **u,f.**

Cook, Nicholas   **ML410.B42 C66 1993**
Beethoven "Symphony No. 9". Cloth Text. Cambridge University Press. New York, NY. 1993. 143p. Music Handbks. ISBN:0-521-39039-7, ISBN13: 978-0-521-39039-2. Dewey:784.2184. LCCN:92-020451.

Audience: **l,u,f.**

Cooper, Barry   ML410.M9
Beethoven and the Creative Process. Paper Text. Oxford
University Press, Inc. New York, NY. 1993. 336p.
ISBN:0-19-816353-3, ISBN13: 978-0-19-816353-4.
Dewey:780/.92. LCCN:89-032325.
                                  Audience: **u,f.** *Choice, 1991.*

Cooper, Barry (Editor)   ML410.B4.B2813 1992
The Beethoven Compendium. Trade Cloth. Thames & Hudson.
New York, NY. 1991. 336p. ISBN:0-500-01523-6, ISBN13:
978-0-500-01523-0. Dewey:780.92. LCCN:91-065423.
                                  Audience: **g,l,u,f.** *Choice, 1992.*

Cooper, John M.   ML134.M53C6 2001
Felix Mendelssohn Bartholdy: Guide to Research with
Introduction to Research Concerning Fanny. Cloth Text. Garland
Publishing, Inc. New York, NY. 2001. 272p. Composer
Resource Manuals, Vol. 54 ISBN:0-8153-1513-9, ISBN13:
978-0-8153-1513-1. Dewey:016.78/092. LCCN:00-045737.
                                  Audience: **l,u,f.**

Cooper, John Michael   MT130.M35C66 2003
Mendelssohn's 'Italian' Symphony. Trade Cloth. Oxford
University Press, Inc. New York, NY. 2003. 252p. Studies in
Musical Genesis and Structure ISBN:0-19-816653-2, ISBN13:
978-0-19-816653-5. Dewey:784.2/184. LCCN:2002-030842.
                                  Audience: **u,f.**

Cooper, John Michael &   ML410
 Prandi, Julie D. (Editors)
The Mendelssohns: Their Music in History. Trade Cloth. Oxford
University Press, Inc. New York, NY. 2003. 404p.
ISBN:0-19-816723-7, ISBN13: 978-0-19-816723-5.
Dewey:780.922. LCCN:2003-275059.
                                  Audience: **g,l,u,f.** *Choice, 2003.*

Cooper, Martin   ML410.B4.C75
Beethoven; the Last Decade 1817-1827. Trade Cloth. Oxford
University Press, Inc. New York, NY. 1970. x, 483p.
ISBN:0-19-315310-6, ISBN13: 978-0-19-315310-3.
Dewey:780/.924. LCCN:76-116137.
                                  Audience: **l,u,f.**

Crittenden, Camille   ML410.S91 C75 2000
Johann Strauss and Vienna: Operetta and the Politics of Popular
Culture. Trade Cloth. Cambridge University Press. New York,
NY. 2000. 336p. Cambridge Studies in Opera
ISBN:0-521-77121-8, ISBN13: 978-0-521-77121-4.
Dewey:782.1/2/094361309034. LCCN:99-088871.
                                  Audience: **u,f.**

Dahlhaus, Carl   ML196
Nineteenth-Century Music. J. Bradford Robinson (Translator).
Trade Paper. University of California Press. Berkeley, CA. 1991.
427p. California Studies in 19th-Century Music Ser.
ISBN:0-520-07644-3, ISBN13: 978-0-520-07644-0.
Dewey:780/.903/4.
                                  Audience: **u,f.** *Choice, 1989.*

Dahlhaus, Carl   ML410.W13
Richard Wagner's Music Dramas. Mary Whittall (Translator).
Trade Cloth. Cambridge University Press. New York, NY. 1979.
174p. ISBN:0-521-22397-0, ISBN13: 978-0-521-22397-3.
Dewey:782.1092. LCCN:78-068359.
                                  Audience: **u,f.**

Darcy, Warren   MT100.W26D33 1996
Wagner's das Rheingold. Paper Text. Oxford University Press,
Inc. New York, NY. 1996. 274p. Studies in Musical Genesis and
Structure ISBN:0-19-816603-6, ISBN13: 978-0-19-816603-0.
Dewey:782.1. LCCN:96-033659.
                                  Audience: **u,f.**

Daverio, John   ML390.D335 2002
Crossing Paths: Schubert, Schumann, and Brahms. Trade Cloth.
Oxford University Press, Inc. New York, NY. 2002. 328p.
ISBN:0-19-513296-3, ISBN13: 978-0-19-513296-0.
Dewey:780/.92/243. LCCN:2001-038744.
                                  Audience: **u,f.** *Choice, 2003.*

Daverio, John   ML410.S4D38 1997
Robert Schumann: Herald of a New Poetic Age. Trade Cloth.
Oxford University Press, Inc. New York, NY. 1997. 618p.
ISBN:0-19-509180-9, ISBN13: 978-0-19-509180-9.
Dewey:780/.92 B. LCCN:96-023177.
                                  Audience: **g,l,u,f.** *Choice, 1997.*

Daverio, John J.   ML275 .D38 1993
Nineteenth-Century Music and the German Romantic Ideology.
Trade Cloth. Thomson Gale. Farmington Hills, MI. 1993. 274p.
ISBN:0-02-870675-7, ISBN13: 978-0-02-870675-7.
Dewey:780/.943/09034. LCCN:92-042513.
                                  Audience: **u,f.**

Davies, Peter J.   ML410
The Character of a Genius: Beethoven in Perspective. Trade
Cloth. Greenwood Publishing Group, Inc. Portsmouth, NH.
2001. 376p. Contributions to the Study of Music and Dance
Ser., Vol. 60 ISBN:0-313-31913-8, ISBN13: 978-0-313-31913-6.
Dewey:780/.92 B. LCCN:2001-018022.
                                  Audience: **u,f.** *Choice, 2002.*

Dean, Winton   ML410.B62
Georges Bizet: His Life and Work. J.M. Dent. 1965.
                                  Audience: **g,l,u,f.**

Deutsch, Otto Erich   ML410.S3
The Schubert Reader. Paper Text. Classic Textbooks. Murrieta,
CA. 1947. 1039p. ISBN:1-4047-9618-5, ISBN13:
978-1-4047-9618-8. Dewey:927.8.
                                  Audience: **g,l,u,f.**

Donington, Robert   ML410.W15
Wagner's 'Ring' and Its Symbols: The Music and the Myth. Ed.
3. Trade Paper. Faber & Faber, Inc. New York, NY. 1974. 304p.
ISBN:0-571-04818-8, ISBN13: 978-0-571-04818-2.
Dewey:782.154. LCCN:74-164583.
                                  Audience: **u,f.**

Drabkin, William   ML410.B42 D8 1991
Beethoven: Missa Solemnis. Julian Rushton (Contribution by). Trade Paper. Cambridge University Press. New York, NY. 1991. 132p. Music Handbks. ISBN:0-521-37831-1, ISBN13: 978-0-521-37831-4. Dewey:782.32/32. LCCN:91-011383.
        Audience: **u,f.**

Einstein, Alfred   ML196
Music in the Romantic Era. Trade Cloth. W. W. Norton & Company, Inc. New York, NY. 1947. 371p. ISBN:0-393-09733-1, ISBN13: 978-0-393-09733-7. Dewey:780.903.
        Audience: **u,f.** 𝐵

Emerson, Caryl   ML410.M97 E42 1999
The Life of Musorgsky. Trade Paper. Cambridge University Press. New York, NY. 1999. 216p. Musical Lives Ser. ISBN:0-521-48507-X, ISBN13: 978-0-521-48507-4. Dewey:780/.92 B. LCCN:98-047948.
        Audience: **g,l,u,f.** *Choice, 2000.*

Erickson, Raymond (Editor)   ML410.S3S29975 1997
Schubert's Vienna. Cloth over Boards. Yale University Press. Cumberland, RI. 1997. 304p. ISBN:0-300-07080-2, ISBN13: 978-0-300-07080-4. Dewey:780/.92 B. LCCN:97-010707.
        Audience: **u,f.** *Choice, 1998.*

Finson, Jon W.   ML196.F56 2002
Nineteenth-Century Music: The Western Classical Tradition. Trade Paper. Prentice Hall PTR. Upper Saddle River, NJ. 2001. 336p. ISBN:0-13-927179-1, ISBN13: 978-0-13-927179-3. Dewey:780/.9/034. LCCN:2001-036166.
        Audience: **g,l,u,f.**

Friedland, Bea   ML0410.F227F7
Louise Farrenc, 1804-1875: Composer, Performer, Scholar. George J. Buelow (Editor). Trade Paper. Books on Demand. Ann Arbor, MI. 1980. 283p. Studies in Musicology, Vol. 32 ISBN:0-8357-1111-0, ISBN13: 978-0-8357-1111-1. Dewey:780/.92/4. LCCN:80-022465.
        Audience: **l,u,f.**

Frisch, Walter   ML410.B8F75 1996
Brahms: The Four Symphonies. Spiral. Thomson Wadsworth. Belmont, CA. 1996. 226p. Monuments of Western Music Ser. ISBN:0-02-870765-6, ISBN13: 978-0-02-870765-5. Dewey:780.9/2. LCCN:96-022951.
        Audience: **l,u,f.** *Choice, 1997.*

Frisch, Walter   ML410.M9
Brahms and the Principle of Developing Variation. Trade Paper University of California Press. Berkeley, CA. 1984. 232p. California Studies in 19th Century Music, No. 2 ISBN:0-520-06958-7, ISBN13: 978-0-520-06958-9. Dewey:780.9/2. LCCN:82-013675.
        Audience: **u,f.**

Gammond, Peter   ML410.O41
Offenbach: His Life and Times. Tunbridge Wells, Kent: Midas Books. 1980. ISBN:0-85936-231-0, ISBN13: 978-0-85936-231-3.
        Audience: **u,f.**

Gibbs, Christopher H.   ML410.M9
The Life of Schubert. Trade Paper. Cambridge University Press. New York, NY. 2000. 226p. Musical Lives Ser. ISBN:0-521-59512-6, ISBN13: 978-0-521-59512-4. Dewey:780/.92 B.
        Audience: **g,l,u,f.** *Choice, 2000.*

Gibbs, Christopher H.   ML410.S3 C18 1997
(Editor)
The Cambridge Companion to Schubert. Jonathan Cross (Contribution by). Trade Paper. Cambridge University Press. New York, NY. 1997. 354p. Cambridge Companions to Music Ser. ISBN:0-521-48424-3, ISBN13: 978-0-521-48424-4. Dewey:780.9/2. LCCN:96-014260.
        Audience: **g,l,u,f.** *Choice, 1998.*

Gottschalk, Louis M.   ML410.C54
Notes of a Pianist. Jeanne Behrend (Editor), Frederick S. Starr (Foreword by). Trade Paper. Princeton University Press. Princeton, NJ. 2006. 504p. ISBN:0-691-12716-6, ISBN13: 978-0-691-12716-3. Dewey:786.1/092/4.
        Audience: **u,f.**

Gregor-Dellin, Martin   ML410.W1 G73413 1983
Richard Wagner: His Life, His Work, His Century. J. Maxwell Brownjohn (Translator). Trade Cloth. Harcourt Trade Publishers. New York, NY. 1983. 592p. A Helen and Kurt Wolff Bk. ISBN:0-15-177151-0, ISBN13: 978-0-15-177151-6. Dewey:782.1/092/4. LCCN:82-015421.
        Audience: **g,l,u,f.**

Grey, Thomas S. (Editor)   ML410.W132 .R48 2000
Richard Wagner: Der Fliegende Holländer. Trade Paper. Cambridge University Press. New York, NY. 2000. 240p. Cambridge Opera Handbooks Ser. ISBN:0-521-58763-8, ISBN13: 978-0-521-58763-1. Dewey:782.1. LCCN:99-059951.
        Audience: **u,f.**

Grimley, Daniel M. &   ML410.E41C36 2004
Rushton, Julian (Editors)
The Cambridge Companion to Elgar. Cloth Text. Cambridge University Press. New York, NY. 2005. 276p. Cambridge Companions to Music Ser. ISBN:0-521-82623-3, ISBN13: 978-0-521-82623-5. Dewey:780/.92 B. LCCN:2004-047286.
        Audience: **u,f.** *Choice, 2005.*

Groos, Arthur & Parker,   ML410.P89 G76 1986
Roger (Editors)
Giacomo Puccini: La Bohème. Trade Cloth. Cambridge University Press. New York, NY. 1986. 224p. Cambridge Opera Handbooks Ser. ISBN:0-521-26489-8, ISBN13: 978-0-521-26489-1. Dewey:782.1. LCCN:85-028076.
        Audience: **u,f.** *Choice, 1987.*

Hall, Charles J. (Compiled   ML196.H34 1989
by)
A Nineteenth-Century Musical Chronicle: Events, 1800-1899, 21B. Library Binding. Greenwood Publishing Group, Inc. Portsmouth, NH. 1989. 374p. Music Reference Collection, No. 21 ISBN:0-313-26578-X, ISBN13: 978-0-313-26578-5. Dewey:780/.9/034. LCCN:89-017201.
        Audience: **u,f.** *Choice, 1990.*

Hall, Michael (Editor)   MT121.S36H35 2003
Schubert's Song Sets. Trade Cloth. Ashgate Publishing, Ltd.
Aldershot, 2003. 300p. ISBN:0-7546-0798-4, ISBN13:
978-0-7546-0798-4. Dewey:782.4/7/092. LCCN:2001-099668.

Audience: **l,u,f.**

Hamilton, Kenneth (Editor)   ML410.L7
The Cambridge Companion to Liszt. Trade Paper, Perfect.
Cambridge University Press. New York, NY. 2005. 300p.
Cambridge Companions to Music Ser. ISBN:0-521-64462-3,
ISBN13: 978-0-521-64462-4. Dewey:780/.92 B.
LCCN:2004-040793.

Audience: **g,l,u,f.**

Hamilton, Kenneth & Liszt,   ML410.L7 H258 1996
  Franz
Liszt: Sonata in B Minor. Julian Rushton (Contribution by).
Cloth Text. Cambridge University Press. New York, NY. 1996.
101p. Music Handbks. ISBN:0-521-46570-2, ISBN13:
978-0-521-46570-0. Dewey:786.2/183. LCCN:95-049839.

Audience: **u,f.**

Hanslick, Eduard   ML246.8.V6 H242 1988
Hanslick's Music Criticisms. Trade Paper. Dover Publications,
Inc. Mineola, NY. 1988. ISBN:0-486-25739-8, ISBN13:
978-0-486-25739-6. Dewey:780. LCCN:88-010932.

Audience: **u.**

Harwood, Gregory W.   ML134.V47H37 1998
Giuseppe Verdi: A Guide to Research. Cloth Text. Garland
Publishing, Inc. New York, NY. 1998. 426p. Composer
Resource Manuals Ser., Vol. 42 ISBN:0-8240-4117-8, ISBN13:
978-0-8240-4117-5. Dewey:782.1/092. LCCN:98-012194.

Audience: **l,u,f.** *Choice, 1998.*

Hefling, Stephen   ML1104.N56 2003
19th-Century Chamber Music. Ed. 2. UK-B Format Paperback.
Routledge. New York, NY. 2003. 392p. Studies in Musical
Genres ISBN:0-415-96650-7, ISBN13: 978-0-415-96650-4.
Dewey:785/.009/034. LCCN:2003-047187.

Audience: **u,f.**

Hepokoski, James A.   ML410.V4 H46 1983
Giuseppe Verdi: Falstaff. Richard Wagner (Contribution by).
Trade Paper. Cambridge University Press. New York, NY. 1983.
192p. Cambridge Opera Handbooks Ser. ISBN:0-521-28016-8,
ISBN13: 978-0-521-28016-7. Dewey:782.1/092/4.
LCCN:83-023493.

Audience: **u,f.**

Hepokoski, James A.   ML410.V4 H48 1987
Giuseppe Verdi: Otello. Richard Wagner (Contribution by).
Trade Paper. Cambridge University Press. New York, NY. 1987.
226p. Cambridge Opera Handbooks Ser. ISBN:0-521-27749-3,
ISBN13: 978-0-521-27749-5. Dewey:782.1/092/4.
LCCN:86-017189.

Audience: **u,f.**

Hoffmann, E. T. A. (Ernst   ML196
  Theodor Amadeus)
E. T. A. Hoffmann's Musical Writings: Kreisleriana, The Poet
and the Composer, Music Criticism. Charlton, David (Editor)

(Annotated by) (Introduced by) ; Clarke, Martyn (Translator).
Cambridge University Press. 2003. ISBN:0-521-54339-8,
ISBN13: 978-0-521-54339-2.

Audience: **u,f.**

Holman, J. K.   ML1700
Wagner's Ring: A Listener's Companion and Concordance.
Trade Paper. Hal Leonard Corporation. Milwaukee, WI. 2003.
440p. ISBN:1-57467-070-0, ISBN13: 978-1-57467-070-7.
Dewey:782.1.

Audience: **g,l,u,f.**

Holoman, D. Kern   ML410.B5H58 1989
Berlioz. Trade Cloth. Harvard University Press. Cambridge,
MA. 1989. 704p. Smith Fund Ser. ISBN:0-674-06778-9,
ISBN13: 978-0-674-06778-3. Dewey:780/.92/4 B.
LCCN:88-035788.

Audience: **l,u,f.** *Choice, 1990.*

Holoman, D. Kern   ML1255.N5 1996
The Nineteenth Century Symphony. Cloth Text. Thomson
Wadsworth. Belmont, CA. 1996. 468p. Studies in Musical
Genres and Repertories ISBN:0-02-871105-X, ISBN13:
978-0-02-871105-8. Dewey:784.2/184/09034. LCCN:96-024580.

Audience: **g,l,u,f.** *Choice, 1997.*

Hopkins, Anthony   MT130.B43H67 1996
The Seven Concertos of Beethoven. Trade Cloth. Ashgate
Publishing, Ltd. Aldershot, 1996. 110p. ISBN:1-85928-245-8,
ISBN13: 978-1-85928-245-8. Dewey:784.2/3/092.
LCCN:96-024729.

Audience: **l,u,f.**

Irvine, Demar   ML410.M41I8 1994
Massenet: A Chronicle of His Life and Times. Trade Cloth. Hal
Leonard Corporation. Milwaukee, WI. 1994. 400p.
ISBN:0-931340-63-2, ISBN13: 978-0-931340-63-5.
Dewey:782.1/092. LCCN:93-024443.

Audience: **u,f.** *Choice, 1994.*

Jackson, Timothy L.   ML410.C4 J33 1999
Tchaikovsky: Symphony No. 6 (Pathétique). Cloth Text.
Cambridge University Press. New York, NY. 1999. 164p. Music
Handbks. ISBN:0-521-64111-X, ISBN13: 978-0-521-64111-1.
Dewey:784.2/184. LCCN:98-039930.

Audience: **u,f.**

Jensen, Eric Frederick   ML410
Schumann. Trade Paper. Oxford University Press, Inc. New
York, NY. 2005. 408p. Master Musicians Ser.
ISBN:0-19-518297-9, ISBN13: 978-0-19-518297-2.
Dewey:780/.92 B. LCCN:00-027866.

Audience: **l,u,f.**

Johnson, Douglas, et al.   ML410.B4.J58 1985
The Beethoven Sketchbooks: History, Reconstruction, Inventory.
Alan Tyson & Robert Winter (Authors). Trade Cloth. University
of California Press. Berkeley, CA. 1985. 500p. California
Studies in 19th Century Music, No. 4 ISBN:0-520-04835-0,
ISBN13: 978-0-520-04835-5. Dewey:780/.92/4.
LCCN:82-025920.

Audience: **u,f.** *Choice, 1986.*

Jones, David Wyn (Editor)   ML410.B4 W96 1995
Beethoven: The Pastoral Symphony. Cloth Text. Cambridge
University Press. New York, NY. 1995. 113p. Music Handbks.
ISBN:0-521-45074-8, ISBN13: 978-0-521-45074-4.
Dewey:784.2/184. LCCN:95-009937.

Audience: **u,f.**

Jones, Timothy   ML410.B42 J66 1999
Beethoven: The 'Moonlight' and Other Sonatas, Op. 27 and Op.
31. Julian Rushton (Contribution by). Cloth Text. Cambridge
University Press. New York, NY. 1999. 158p. Music Handbks.
ISBN:0-521-59136-8, ISBN13: 978-0-521-59136-2.
Dewey:786.2/183. LCCN:98-045826.

Audience: **l,u,f.**

Kallberg, Jeffrey   ML410.C54
Chopin at the Boundaries: Sex, History, and Musical Genre.
Trade Paper. Harvard University Press. Cambridge, MA. 1998.
320p. Convergences Ser., :Inventories of the Present Ser.
ISBN:0-674-12791-9, ISBN13: 978-0-674-12791-3.
Dewey:786.2092.

Audience: **u,f.** *Choice, 1996.*

Katz, Jacob   ML410.W19K3313 1986
The Darker Side of Genius: Richard Wagner's Anti-Semitism.
Trade Cloth. University Press of New England. Lebanon, NH.
1986. 172p. Tauber Institute Ser., No. 5 ISBN:0-87451-368-5,
ISBN13: 978-0-87451-368-4. Dewey:782.1/092/4.
LCCN:85-040935.

Audience: **u,f.** *Choice, 1986.*

Kearney, Leslie (Editor)   ML410.C4T36 1998
Tchaikovsky and His World. Cloth Text. Princeton University
Press. Princeton, NJ. 1998. 350p. The Bard Music Festival Ser.
ISBN:0-691-00429-3, ISBN13: 978-0-691-00429-7.
Dewey:780/.92. LCCN:98-025777.

Audience: **g,l,u,f.** *Choice, 1999.*

Kemp, Ian (Editor)   ML410.B5H3 1988
Hector Berlioz: "Les Troyens". Trade Cloth. Cambridge
University Press. New York, NY. 1989. 256p. Cambridge Opera
Handbooks Ser. ISBN:0-521-34280-5, ISBN13:
978-0-521-34280-3. Dewey:782.1/092/4. LCCN:88-002719.

Audience: **u,f.**

Kennedy, Michael   ML410.E41K48 2004
The Life of Elgar. Cloth Text. Cambridge University Press. New
York, NY. 2004. 238p. Musical Lives Ser. ISBN:0-521-81076-0,
ISBN13: 978-0-521-81076-0. Dewey:780/.92 B.
LCCN:2003-055733.

Audience: **u,f.**

Kimbell, David R. B.   ML410.B44 K56 1998
Vincenzo Bellini: Norma. Richard Wagner (Contribution by).
Trade Paper. Cambridge University Press. New York, NY. 1998.
154p. Opera Handbooks Ser. ISBN:0-521-48514-2, ISBN13:
978-0-521-48514-2. Dewey:782.1. LCCN:97-032615.

Audience: **u,f.** *Choice, 1999.*

Kinderman, William   ML410.B42B425 1991
   (Editor)
Beethoven's Compositional Process. Cloth Text. University of
Nebraska Press. Lincoln, NE. 1991. 195p. North American
Beethoven Studies, Vol. 1 ISBN:0-8032-1222-4, ISBN13:
978-0-8032-1222-0. Dewey:780/.92. LCCN:90-024227.

Audience: **u,f.** *Choice, 1992.*

Kinderman, William   ML410.S4
Beethoven's Diabelli Variations. Paper Text. Oxford University
Press, Inc. New York, NY. 1989. 246p. Studies in Musical
Genesis and Structure ISBN:0-19-816198-0, ISBN13:
978-0-19-816198-1. Dewey:786.2/1825. LCCN:86-008590.

Audience: **u,f.** *Choice, 1988.*

Kinderman, William &   ML3811.S43 1996
   Krebs, Harald (Editors)
The Second Practice of Nineteenth Century Tonality. Cloth Text.
University of Nebraska Press. Lincoln, NE. 1996. 281p.
ISBN:0-8032-2724-8, ISBN13: 978-0-8032-2724-8.
Dewey:781.2/6/09034. LCCN:95-016160.

Audience: **u,f.**

Kitcher, Philip & Schacht,   ML410.W15K57 2004
   Richard
Finding an Ending: Reflections on Wagner's Ring. Trade Cloth.
Oxford University Press, Inc. New York, NY. 2004. 253p.
ISBN:0-19-517359-7, ISBN13: 978-0-19-517359-8.
Dewey:782.1. LCCN:2004-041478.

Audience: **u,f.** *Choice, 2005.*

Kohler, Joachim   ML410.W1K8313 2004
Richard Wagner: The Last of the Titans. Stewart Spencer
(Translator). Cloth over Boards. Yale University Press.
Cumberland, RI. 2004. 704p. ISBN:0-300-10422-7, ISBN13:
978-0-300-10422-6. Dewey:782.1/092 B. LCCN:2004-110664.

Audience: **u,f.** *Choice, 2005.*

Korstvedt, Benjamin M.   ML410.B88 K67 2000
Bruckner: Symphony No. 8. Julian Rushton (Contribution by).
Cloth Text. Cambridge University Press. New York, NY. 2000.
146p. Music Handbks., No. 8 ISBN:0-521-63226-9, ISBN13:
978-0-521-63226-3. Dewey:784.2184. LCCN:99-031880.

Audience: **u,f.**

Kramer, Lawrence   ML3849
Music and Poetry: The Nineteenth Century and After. Trade
Cloth. University of California Press. Berkeley, CA. 1984. 300p.
California Studies in 19th Century Music, No. 3
ISBN:0-520-04873-3, ISBN13: 978-0-520-04873-7.
Dewey:780/.08. LCCN:83-001173.

Audience: **u,f.** B

Kramer, Lawrence   ML3880.K7 1990
Music As Cultural Practice, 1800-1900. Trade Cloth. University
of California Press. Berkeley, CA. 1990. 241p. California
Studies in 19th Century Music, No. 8 ISBN:0-520-06857-2,
ISBN13: 978-0-520-06857-5. Dewey:780/.9/034.
LCCN:89-020445.

Audience: **u,f.** *Choice, 1991.*

Krebs, Harald   ML410.S4K68 1999
Fantasy Pieces: Metrical Dissonance in the Music of Robert
Schumann. Trade Cloth. Oxford University Press, Inc. New
York, NY. 1999. 304p. ISBN:0-19-511623-2, ISBN13:
978-0-19-511623-6. Dewey:781.2/26/092. LCCN:98-012647.
                                   Audience: **u,f.** *Choice, 2000.*

Landon, H. C.   ML410.M9
Beethoven: His Life, Work and World. Ed. 2. Trade Cloth.
Thames & Hudson. New York, NY. 1993. 248p.
ISBN:0-500-01540-6, ISBN13: 978-0-500-01540-7.
Dewey:780.92. LCCN:92-064271.
                                        Audience: **g,l,u,f.**

Levy, Alan H.   ML410.M12L48 1998
Edward MacDowell: An American Master. Book, Other.
Scarecrow Press, Inc. Lanham, MD. 1999. 281p.
ISBN:0-8108-3463-4, ISBN13: 978-0-8108-3463-7.
Dewey:780/.92 b. LCCN:98-007958.
                                   Audience: **u,f.** *Choice, 1999.*

Levy, David Benjamin   ML410.B42L48 2003
Beethoven: The Ninth Symphony. Ed. 2. Trade Paper. Yale
University Press. Cumberland, RI. 2003. 256p. Yale Music
Masterworks Ser. ISBN:0-300-09964-9, ISBN13:
978-0-300-09964-5. Dewey:784.2/184.
                                   Audience: **u,f.** *Choice, 1995.*

Liebert, Georges   ML423.N56L5413 2004
Nietzsche and Music. David Pellauer & Graham Parkes
(Translators). Trade Cloth. University of Chicago Press.
Chicago, IL. 2004. 304p. ISBN:0-226-48087-9, ISBN13:
978-0-226-48087-9. Dewey:780/.92. LCCN:2003-012778.
                                        Audience: **u,f.**

Lockwood, Lewis   ML410.B4L597 2002
Beethoven: The Music and the Life. Trade Cloth. W. W. Norton
& Company, Inc. New York, NY. 2002. 480p.
ISBN:0-393-05081-5, ISBN13: 978-0-393-05081-3.
Dewey:780/.92 B. LCCN:2002-075397.
                                   Audience: **g,l,u,f.** *Choice, 2003.*

Lockwood, Lewis & Kroll,   MT145.B422B4 2004
Mark (Editors)
The Beethoven Violin Sonatas: History, Criticism, Performance.
Trade Cloth. University of Illinois Press. Champaign, IL. 2004.
176p. ISBN:0-252-02932-1, ISBN13: 978-0-252-02932-5.
Dewey:787.2/183/092. LCCN:2003-026966.
                                   Audience: **l,u,f.** *Choice, 2005.*

MacDonald, Hugh (Editor)   ML410.B5A33 1997
Selected Letters of Berlioz. Roger Nichols (Translator). Trade
Cloth. W. W. Norton & Company, Inc. New York, NY. 1997.
496p. ISBN:0-393-04062-3, ISBN13: 978-0-393-04062-3.
Dewey:780/.92 B. LCCN:96-047015.
                                   Audience: **u,f.** *Choice, 1997.*

MacDonald, Malcolm   ML410.B8M113 1990
Brahms. Trade Cloth. Music Sales Corporation. New York, NY.
1990. 490p. ISBN:0-02-871393-1, ISBN13: 978-0-02-871393-9.
Dewey:780.9/2. LCCN:90-008545.
                                   Audience: **l,u,f.** *Choice, 1990.*

Magee, Bryan   ML410.W19M14 2001
The Tristan Chord: Wagner and Philosophy. Cloth over Boards.
Henry Holt & Company. New York, NY. 2001. 416p.
ISBN:0-8050-6788-4, ISBN13: 978-0-8050-6788-0.
Dewey:782.1/092. LCCN:2001-030779.
                                        Audience: **u,f.**

Marston, Nicholas   ML410.S4 M37 1992
Schumann: Fantasie, Op. 17. Julian Rushton (Contribution by).
Trade Paper. Cambridge University Press. New York, NY. 1992.
131p. Music Handbks. ISBN:0-521-39892-4, ISBN13:
978-0-521-39892-3. Dewey:786.2189. LCCN:91-039602.
                                   Audience: **u,f.** *Choice, 1993.*

Mayer, Anton   ML410.S91 M3913 1999
Johann Strauss: A Nineteenth Century Pop-Idol. Steblin, Rita.
Wien: Bohlau. 1999. ISBN:3-205-99061-7, ISBN13:
978-3-205-99061-1.
                                        Audience: **u,f.**

McClary, Susan   ML410.B62 M25 1992
Georges Bizet: Carmen. Richard Wagner (Contribution by).
Trade Paper. Cambridge University Press. New York, NY. 1992.
175p. Cambridge Opera Handbooks Ser. ISBN:0-521-39897-5,
ISBN13: 978-0-521-39897-8. Dewey:782.1. LCCN:91-032840.
                                   Audience: **l,u,f.** *Choice, 1993.*

Mercer-Taylor, Peter   ML410.M5C36 2004
(Editor)
The Cambridge Companion to Mendelssohn. Jonathan Cross
(Contribution by). Trade Paper. Cambridge University Press.
New York, NY. 2004. 332p. Cambridge Companions to Music
Ser. ISBN:0-521-53342-2, ISBN13: 978-0-521-53342-3.
Dewey:780/.92 B. LCCN:2003-069735.
                                   Audience: **g,l,u,f.** *Choice, 2005.*

Miller, Richard   MT121.S38M55 1999
Singing Schumann: An Interpretive Guide for Performers. Trade
Cloth. Oxford University Press, Inc. New York, NY. 1999. 260p.
ISBN:0-19-511904-5, ISBN13: 978-0-19-511904-6.
Dewey:782.42168/092. LCCN:98-031645.
                                   Audience: **u,f.** *Choice, 2000.*

Millington, Barry (Editor)   ML410.M9
The Wagner Compendium: A Guide to Wagner's Life and
Music. Trade Paper. Thames & Hudson. New York, NY. 2001.
432p. ISBN:0-500-28274-9, ISBN13: 978-0-500-28274-8.
Dewey:780.9/2.
                                   Audience: **g,l,u,f.** *Choice, 1993.*

Muller, Ulrich (Editor), et   ML410.W131R41613
al.
Wagner Handbook. Peter Wapnewski & John Deathridge
(Editors). Trade Cloth. Harvard University Press. Cambridge,
MA. 1992. 728p. ISBN:0-674-94530-1, ISBN13:
978-0-674-94530-2. Dewey:782.1/092. LCCN:91-042202.
                                   Audience: **l,u,f.** *Choice, 1993.*

Musgrave, Michael   **ML410.M9**
A Brahms Reader. Trade Paper. Yale University Press.
Cumberland, RI. 2001. 400p. ISBN:0-300-09199-0, ISBN13:
978-0-300-09199-1. Dewey:780.9/2.

Audience: **l,u,f.**

Musgrave, Michael (Editor)   **ML410.B8 C36 1999**
The Cambridge Companion to Brahms. Jonathan Cross
(Contribution by). Trade Paper. Cambridge University Press.
New York, NY. 1999. 348p. Cambridge Companions to Music
Ser. ISBN:0-521-48581-9, ISBN13: 978-0-521-48581-4.
Dewey:780/.92 B. LCCN:98-003057.

Audience: **g,l,u,f.**

Musgrave, Michael   **ML410.B8M86 1996**
Brahms: A German Requiem. Julian Rushton (Contribution by).
Trade Paper. Cambridge University Press. New York, NY. 1996.
109p. Music Handbks. ISBN:0-521-40995-0, ISBN13:
978-0-521-40995-7. Dewey:782.3/238. LCCN:95-051987.

Audience: **u,f.** *Choice, 1997.*

Musgrave, Michael &   **MT92**
  Sherman, Bernard D. (Editors)
Performing Brahms: Early Evidence of Performance Style. John
Butt & Laurence Dreyfus (Contribution by). Trade Cloth.
Cambridge University Press. New York, NY. 2003. 412p.
Musical Performance and Reception Ser. ISBN:0-521-65273-1,
ISBN13: 978-0-521-65273-5. Dewey:781.4/3/09034.
LCCN:2004-272942.

Audience: **u,f.**

Mussorgsky, Modest   **ML410.M97**
Boris Godunov. Nicholas John (Editor), David Lloyd-Jones
(Translator). Trade Paper. Riverrun Press, Inc. Flemington, NJ.
1982. 128p. English National Opera Guide Ser., No.
11:Bilingual Libretto, Articles ISBN:0-7145-3922-8, ISBN13:
978-0-7145-3922-5. Dewey:782.1/092/4.

Audience: **g,l,u,f.**

Newbould, Brian   **ML410.M9**
Schubert: The Music and the Man. Trade Paper. University of
California Press. Berkeley, CA. 1999. 465p.
ISBN:0-520-21957-0, ISBN13: 978-0-520-21957-1.
Dewey:780.9/2. LCCN:96-049876.

Audience: **u,f.** *Choice, 1997.*

Newman, Ernest   **ML410.W1**
The Life of Richard Wagner. Trade Paper. Cambridge University
Press. New York, NY. 1976. ISBN:0-521-29149-6, ISBN13:
978-0-521-29149-1. Dewey:782.1/092/4. LCCN:76-022682.

Audience: **l,u,f.**

Newman, William S.   **ML410.C54**
Beethoven on Beethoven: Playing His Piano Music His Way.
Trade Paper. W. W. Norton & Company, Inc. New York, NY.
1991. 336p. ISBN:0-393-30719-0, ISBN13: 978-0-393-30719-1.
Dewey:786.1/092/4.

Audience: **l,u,f.** *Choice, 1989.*

Newman, William S.   **ML1156**
The Sonata since Beethoven. Ed. 3. Trade Cloth. W. W. Norton
& Company, Inc. New York, NY. 1983. xxvi, 870p.
ISBN:0-393-95290-8, ISBN13: 978-0-393-95290-2.
Dewey:781/.52/09. LCCN:82-024573.

Audience: **u,f.**

Orlova, Alexandra   **ML410.C4.A3 1990**
Tchaikovsky: A Self-Portrait. R. M. Davison (Translator), David
B. Brown (Foreword by). Trade Cloth. Oxford University Press,
Inc. New York, NY. 1990. 476p. ISBN:0-19-315319-X, ISBN13:
978-0-19-315319-6. Dewey:780.92. LCCN:91-123364.

Audience: **u,f.** *Choice, 1991.*

Orlova, Alexandra (Editor)   **ML410.M97M2213 1991**
Musorgsky Remembered. Veronique Zaytzeff & Frederick
Morrison (Translators). Trade Cloth. Indiana University Press.
Bloomington, IN. 1991. 212p. Russian Music Studies
ISBN:0-253-34264-3, ISBN13: 978-0-253-34264-5.
Dewey:780/.92 B. LCCN:90-025310.

Audience: **u,f.** *Choice, 1992.*

Osborne, Charles   **ML390.O82 1994**
The Bel Canto Operas: A Guide to the Operas of Rossini,
Bellini, and Donizetti. Trade Cloth. Hal Leonard Corporation.
Milwaukee, WI. 1994. 378p. ISBN:0-931340-71-3, ISBN13:
978-0-931340-71-0. Dewey:782.1/0945/09034.
LCCN:94-168756.

Audience: **g,l,u,f.** *Choice, 1994.*

Osborne, Charles   **ML410.V4**
The Complete Operas of Richard Wagner. Trade Paper. Da Capo
Press, Inc. Cambridge, MA. 1993. 288p. ISBN:0-306-80522-7,
ISBN13: 978-0-306-80522-6. Dewey:782.1/092.
LCCN:92-034417.

Audience: **l,u,f.** *Choice, 1991.*

Osborne, Richard   **ML410.R8O9 2001**
Rossini. Ed. 3. Trade Paper. Oxford University Press, Inc. New
York, NY. 2002. 360p. Master Musicians Ser.
ISBN:0-19-816490-4, ISBN13: 978-0-19-816490-6.
Dewey:782.1/092/4. LCCN:00-057106.

Audience: **l,u,f.**

Ostwald, Peter F.   **ML410.S4**
Schumann: The Inner Voices of a Musical Genius. Paper Text.
Northeastern University Press. Boston, MA. 1987. 390p.
ISBN:1-55553-014-1, ISBN13: 978-1-55553-014-3.
Dewey:780/.92/4.

Audience: **l,u,f.**

Phillips-Matz, Mary Jane   **ML410.P89P52 2002**
Puccini: A Biography. William Weaver (Foreword by). Trade
Cloth. Northeastern University Press. Boston, MA. 2005. 384p.
ISBN:1-55553-530-5, ISBN13: 978-1-55553-530-8.
Dewey:782.1/092 B. LCCN:2002-009017.

Audience: **l,u,f.** *Choice, 2003.*

Phillips-Matz, Mary J.   **ML410.V4P43 1993**
Verdi: A Biography. Andrew Porter (Foreword by). Trade Cloth.
Oxford University Press, Inc. New York, NY. 1993. 994p.

ISBN:0-19-313204-4, ISBN13: 978-0-19-313204-7.
Dewey:782.1/092. LCCN:92-037841.

Audience: **l,u,f.** *Choice, 1994.*

Pike, Lionel   **MT125 .P55**
Beethoven, Sibelius and "The Profound Logic": Studies in
Symphonic Analysis. Cloth Text. Continuum International
Publishing Group, Ltd. London, 1978. 240p.
ISBN:0-485-11178-0, ISBN13: 978-0-485-11178-1.
Dewey:785.1/1/0922. LCCN:79-309070.

Audience: **u,f.**

Plantinga, Leon   **ML410.B42P6 1998**
Beethoven Concertos: History, Style, Performance. Trade Cloth.
W. W. Norton & Company, Inc. New York, NY. 1999. 416p.
ISBN:0-393-04691-5, ISBN13: 978-0-393-04691-5.
Dewey:784.2/3/092. LCCN:98-022552.

Audience: **l,u,f.** *Choice, 2000.*

Plantinga, Leon   **ML196.P6 1984**
Romantic Music. Trade Paper. W. W. Norton & Company, Inc.
New York, NY. 1985. 523p. Norton Introduction to Music
History Ser. ISBN:0-393-95196-0, ISBN13: 978-0-393-95196-7.
Dewey:780/.903/4. LCCN:83-042653.

Audience: **g,l,u,f.** *Choice, 1985.*

Platt, Heather (Editor)   **ML134**
Johannes Brahms. Paper over Boards. Routledge. New York,
NY. 2003. 416p. Routledge Music Bibliographies Ser.
ISBN:0-8153-3850-3, ISBN13: 978-0-8153-3850-5.
Dewey:016.78/092. LCCN:2003-271627.

Audience: **l,u,f.** *Choice, 2004.*

Poznansky, Alexander   **ML410.C4P856 1996**
Tchaikovsky's Last Days: A Documentary Study. Trade Cloth.
Oxford University Press, Inc. New York, NY. 1996. 254p.
ISBN:0-19-816596-X, ISBN13: 978-0-19-816596-5.
Dewey:780.9/2. LCCN:96-013332.

Audience: **l,u,f.** *Choice, 1997.*

Poznansky, Alexander &   **ML134.C42P69 2001**
Langston, Brett
The Tchaikovsky Handbook: Catalogue of Letters, Bibliography.
Trade Cloth. Indiana University Press. Bloomington, IN. 2002.
730p. Russian Music Studies ISBN:0-253-33947-2, ISBN13:
978-0-253-33947-8. Dewey:780/.92 B. LCCN:2001-039546.

Audience: **u,f.** *Choice, 2002.*

Poznansky, Alexander &   **ML134.C42P69 2001**
Langston, Brett
The Tchaikovsky Handbook: Thematic Catalogue of Works,
Catalogue of Photographs, Autobiography. Trade Cloth. Indiana
University Press. Bloomington, IN. 2002. 730p. Russian Music
Studies ISBN:0-253-33921-9, ISBN13: 978-0-253-33921-8.
Dewey:780/.92 B. LCCN:2001-039546.

Audience: **u,f.** *Choice, 2002.*

Puccini, Giacomo   **ML410.P89.A23 1971**
Letters of Giacomo Puccini. Ena Makin (Editor). Trade Cloth. A

M S Press, Inc. New York, NY. 1971. 335p.
ISBN:0-404-05149-9, ISBN13: 978-0-404-05149-5.
Dewey:782.1/0924. LCCN:71-140038.

Audience: **u,f.**

Puccini, Giacomo   **ML49.P75**
Seven Puccini Librettos. William Weaver (Translator). Trade
Paper. W. W. Norton & Company, Inc. New York, NY. 1981.
ISBN:0-393-00930-0, ISBN13: 978-0-393-00930-9.
Dewey:782.1/2.

Audience: **g,l,u,f.**

Ratner, Leonard G.   **ML196.R27 1992**
Romantic Music: Sound and Syntax. Trade Cloth. Thomson
Gale. Farmington Hills, MI. 1992. 348p. ISBN:0-02-872065-2,
ISBN13: 978-0-02-872065-4. Dewey:781/.09/034.
LCCN:92-010566.

Audience: **g,l,u,f.** *Choice, 1993.*

Reed, John   **ML410.S3R265 1997**
The Schubert Song Companion. Norma Deane & Celia Larner
(Translators), Janet Baker (Foreword by). Trade Paper.
Manchester University Press. Manchester, 1997. 528p.
ISBN:1-901341-00-3, ISBN13: 978-1-901341-00-3.
Dewey:784.3/0092/4. LCCN:98-179605.

Audience: **l,u,f.** *Choice, 1985.*

Reich, Nancy B.   **ML417.S4R4 2001**
Clara Schumann: The Artist and the Woman. Ed. 2. Book,
Other. Cornell University Press. Ithaca, NY. 2001. 408p.
ISBN:0-8014-8637-8, ISBN13: 978-0-8014-8637-1.
Dewey:786.2/092 B. LCCN:00-011932.

Audience: **l,u,f.** *Choice, 1985.*

Reinhard, Thilo (Editor)   **ML54.6.S4 R413 1989**
The Singer's Schumann. Library Binding. Rosen Publishing
Group, Incorporated, The. New York, NY. 1989. 423p.
ISBN:0-8239-0673-6, ISBN13: 978-0-8239-0673-4.
Dewey:784.3/05. LCCN:88-028387.

Audience: **u,f.**

Ringer, Alexander   **ML196 .E2 1991**
The Early Romantic Era. Cloth Text. Prentice Hall PTR. Upper
Saddle River, NJ. 1990. 325p. ISBN:0-13-222399-6, ISBN13:
978-0-13-222399-7. Dewey:780/.9/034.

Audience: **g,l,u,f.**

Rink, John   **ML410.C54RR54 1997**
Chopin: The Piano Concertos. Julian Rushton (Editor,
Contribution by). Cloth Text. Cambridge University Press. New
York, NY. 1997. 149p. Music Handbks. ISBN:0-521-44109-9,
ISBN13: 978-0-521-44109-4. Dewey:784.2/62/092.
LCCN:97-006905.

Audience: **u,f.**

Robinson, Paul (Editor)   **ML410.B4 R46 1996**
Ludwig Van Beethoven: Fidelio. Richard Wagner (Contribution
by). Trade Paper. Cambridge University Press. New York, NY.
1996. 203p. Cambridge Opera Handbooks Ser.
ISBN:0-521-45852-8, ISBN13: 978-0-521-45852-8.
Dewey:780.9/2. LCCN:95-046935.

Audience: **u,f.** *Choice, 1997.*

Rosen, Charles   MT145.B42R67 2002
Beethoven's Piano Sonatas: A Short Companion. Cloth over
Boards. Yale University Press. Cumberland, RI. 2002. 272p.
ISBN:0-300-09070-6, ISBN13: 978-0-300-09070-3.
Dewey:786.2/183/092. LCCN:2001-093745.
                            Audience: **l,u,f.** *Choice, 2003, 2002.*

Rosen, Charles   ML196
The Romantic Generation. Harvard University Press. 1995.
ISBN:0-674-77933-9, ISBN13: 978-0-674-77933-4.
                            Audience: **g,l,u,f.**

Rosen, David   ML410.V4 R73 1995
Verdi: Requiem. Julian Rushton (Contribution by). Trade Paper.
Cambridge University Press. New York, NY. 1995. 125p. Music
Handbks. ISBN:0-521-39767-7, ISBN13: 978-0-521-39767-4.
Dewey:782.3/238. LCCN:94-033380.
                            Audience: **u,f.** *Choice, 1996.*

Rosselli, John   ML410.B44 R77 1996
The Life of Bellini. Trade Paper. Cambridge University Press.
New York, NY. 1997. 194p. Musical Lives Ser.
ISBN:0-521-46781-0, ISBN13: 978-0-521-46781-0.
Dewey:780.9/2. LCCN:95-039270.
                            Audience: **u,f.**

Rosselli, John   ML290.4
Music and Musicians in Nineteenth Century Italy. Trade Cloth.
Hal Leonard Corporation. Milwaukee, WI. 1991. 162p.
ISBN:0-931340-40-3, ISBN13: 978-0-931340-40-6.
Dewey:780.92.
                            Audience: **u,f.**

Rossini, Gioacchino Antonio   ML50.P965
The Barber of Seville and Moses. Nicholas John (Editor),
Edward J. Dent, John Moody & Nell Moody (Translators).
Trade Paper. Riverrun Press, Inc. Flemington, NJ. 1986. 160p.
English National Opera Guide Ser., No. 36:Bilingual Libretto,
Articles ISBN:0-7145-4080-3, ISBN13: 978-0-7145-4080-1.
Dewey:782.1/2. LCCN:85-052162.
                            Audience: **g,l,u,f.**

Rushton, Julian   ML410.B5 R85 1994
Berlioz: Romeo et Juliette. Trade Paper. Cambridge University
Press. New York, NY. 1994. 129p. Music Handbks.
ISBN:0-521-37767-6, ISBN13: 978-0-521-37767-6.
Dewey:784.2/2. LCCN:93-032505.
                            Audience: **u,f.**

Rushton, Julian   ML410.B5R87 2001
The Music of Berlioz. Trade Paper. Oxford University Press,
Inc. New York, NY. 2001. 380p. ISBN:0-19-816738-5, ISBN13:
978-0-19-816738-9. Dewey:780/.92. LCCN:00-045299.
                            Audience: **l,u,f.** *Choice, 2002.*

Rushton, Julian (Author,   ML410.E41 R87 1999
  Contribution by)
Elgar: Enigma Variations. Cloth Text. Cambridge University
Press. New York, NY. 1999. 124p. Music Handbks.
ISBN:0-521-63175-0, ISBN13: 978-0-521-63175-4.
Dewey:784.2/1825. LCCN:98-022042.
                            Audience: **u,f.** *Choice, 1999.*

Russ, Michael   ML410.M97 R9 1992
Musorgsky: Pictures at an Exhibition. Julian Rushton
(Contribution by). Trade Paper. Cambridge University Press.
New York, NY. 1992. 110p. Music Handbks.
ISBN:0-521-38607-1, ISBN13: 978-0-521-38607-4.
Dewey:786.21896. LCCN:91-032687.
                            Audience: **l,u,f.** *Choice, 1993.*

Sadie, Stanley (Editor)   ML410.W13W114 2000
Wagner and His Operas. Trade Cloth. St. Martin's Press.
Gordonville, VA. 2000. xv, 219p. The New Grove Composers
Ser. ISBN:0-333-79021-9, ISBN13: 978-0-333-79021-2.
Dewey:782.1/092. LCCN:00-701304.
                            Audience: **l,u,f.**

Saffle, Michael   ML134.L7S2 2003
Franz Liszt: A Guide to Research. Ed. 2. Paper over Boards.
Routledge. New York, NY. 2004. 536p. Routledge Music
Bibliographies Ser. ISBN:0-415-94011-7, ISBN13:
978-0-415-94011-5. Dewey:016.78/092. LCCN:2003-026223.
                            Audience: **l,u,f.** *Choice, 1992.*

Saffle, Michael   ML134.W1S24 2002
Richard Wagner: A Guide to Research. Paper over Boards.
Garland Publishing, Inc. New York, NY. 2002. 352p. Routledge
Musical Bibliographies Ser. ISBN:0-8240-5695-7, ISBN13:
978-0-8240-5695-7. Dewey:016.7821/092. LCCN:2001-048162.
                            Audience: **l,u,f.**

Sams, Eric   MT115.S38
The Songs of Robert Schumann. Ed. 3. Gerald Moore
(Foreword by). Bloomington: Indiana University Press. 1993.
ISBN:0-253-35065-4, ISBN13: 978-0-253-35065-7.
                            Audience: **l,u,f.**

Samson, Jim (Editor)   ML196 .C36 2001
The Cambridge History of Nineteenth-Century Music. Cloth
Text. Cambridge University Press. New York, NY. 2001. 788p.
History of Music Ser. ISBN:0-521-59017-5, ISBN13:
978-0-521-59017-4. Dewey:780.9034. LCCN:00-067469.
                            Audience: **g,l,u,f.** *Choice, 2002.*

Samson, Jim   ML410.C54S1865 1998
Chopin. Trade Paper. Oxford University Press, Inc. New York,
NY. 2006. 334p. Master Musicians Ser. ISBN:0-19-816703-2,
ISBN13: 978-0-19-816703-7. Dewey:786.2/092 B.
LCCN:98-008653.
                            Audience: **l,u,f.** *Choice, 1997.*

Samson, Jim (Editor)   ML196 .L37 1991
The Late Romantic Era. Cloth Text. Prentice Hall PTR. Upper
Saddle River, NJ. 1991. x, 463p. ISBN:0-13-524174-X,
ISBN13: 978-0-13-524174-5. Dewey:780/.9/034.
LCCN:92-100988.
                            Audience: **g,l,u,f.**

Samson, Jim   ML410.C54S188 1994
The Music of Chopin. Trade Paper. Oxford University Press,
Inc. New York, NY. 1994. 252p. ISBN:0-19-816402-5, ISBN13:
978-0-19-816402-9. Dewey:786.2/092. LCCN:93-030977.
                            Audience: **l,u,f.** *Choice, 1986.*

Samson, Jim (Editor)   **ML410.C54**
The Cambridge Companion to Chopin. Jonathan Cross
(Contribution by). Trade Paper. Cambridge University Press.
New York, NY. 1994. 353p. Cambridge Companions to Music
Ser. ISBN:0-521-47752-2, ISBN13: 978-0-521-47752-9.
Dewey:786.2/092. LCCN:91-024533.
                                    Audience: **g,l,u,f.** *Choice, 1993.*

Samson, Jim   **ML410.C54 S187 1992**
Chopin: The Four Ballades. Julian Rushton (Contribution by).
Trade Cloth. Cambridge University Press. New York, NY. 1992.
114p. Music Handbks. ISBN:0-521-38461-3, ISBN13:
978-0-521-38461-2. Dewey:786.21896. LCCN:91-002542.
                                                    Audience: **u,f.**

Schenker, Heinrich   **ML410.B42**
Beethoven's Ninth Symphony: A Portrayal of Its Musical
Content, with Running Commentary on Performance and
Literature As Well. John Rothgeb (Editor, Translator). Trade
Cloth. Yale University Press. Cumberland, RI. 1992. 350p.
ISBN:0-300-05459-9, ISBN13: 978-0-300-05459-0.
Dewey:784.2184. LCCN:91-036684.
                                    Audience: **u,f.** *Choice, 1993.*

Schindler, Anton F. &   **ML410.B4S3333 1996**
  Macardle, Donald W.
Beethoven As I Knew Him. Ed. 3. Trade Paper. Dover
Publications, Inc. Mineola, NY. 1996. 560p.
ISBN:0-486-29232-0, ISBN13: 978-0-486-29232-8.
Dewey:780/.92. LCCN:96-022901.
                                                    Audience: **u,f.**

Schumann, Robert   **ML410.S4 A124 1983**
On Music and Musicians. Konrad Wolff (Editor), Paul Rosenfeld
(Translator). Trade Paper. University of California Press.
Berkeley, CA. 1982. 274p. ISBN:0-520-04685-4, ISBN13:
978-0-520-04685-6. Dewey:780. LCCN:82-070650.
                                                    Audience: **g,l,u,f.**

Self, Geoffrey   **ML410.C74S45 1995**
The Hiawatha Man: The Life and Music of Samuel
Coleridge-Taylor. Trade Cloth. Ashgate Publishing, Ltd.
Aldershot, 1995. 328p. ISBN:0-85967-983-7, ISBN13:
978-0-85967-983-1. Dewey:780/.92 B. LCCN:94-045001.
                                    Audience: **l,u,f.** *Choice, 1996.*

Senici, Emanuele (Editor)   **ML410.R8C17 2003**
The Cambridge Companion to Rossini. Trade Cloth. Cambridge
University Press. New York, NY. 2004. 280p. Cambridge
Companions to Music Ser. ISBN:0-521-80736-0, ISBN13:
978-0-521-80736-4. Dewey:782.1/092 B. LCCN:2003-048560.
                                                    Audience: **l,u,f.**

Simpson, Robert   **ML410.B88S46 1992**
The Essence of Bruckner. Ed. 2. Trade Paper. Victor Gollancz
Ltd. London, 1992. 256p. ISBN:0-575-05221-X, ISBN13:
978-0-575-05221-5. Dewey:784.2/184/092. LCCN:93-183982.
                                                    Audience: **u,f.**

Sipe, Thomas   **ML410.B42 S57 1998**
Beethoven: Eroica Symphony. Julian Rushton (Contribution by).
Trade Paper. Cambridge University Press. New York, NY. 1998.
158p. Music Handbks. ISBN:0-521-47562-7, ISBN13:
978-0-521-47562-4. Dewey:784.2/184. LCCN:97-033020.
                                    Audience: **u,f.** *Choice, 1999.*

Smaczny, Jan   **MT130.D9 S6 1999**
Dvořák: Cello Concerto. Cloth Text. Cambridge University
Press. New York, NY. 1999. 130p. Music Handbks.
ISBN:0-521-66050-5, ISBN13: 978-0-521-66050-1.
Dewey:784.2/74. LCCN:98-052746.
                                                    Audience: **u,f.**

Smialek, William   **ML134.C54S65 2000**
Frederic Chopin: A Guide to Research. Guy A. Marco (Editor).
Cloth Text. Garland Publishing, Inc. New York, NY. 1999. 300p.
Composer Resource Manuals Ser., Vol. 50 ISBN:0-8153-2180-5,
ISBN13: 978-0-8153-2180-4. Dewey:016.7862/092.
LCCN:99-042566.
                                    Audience: **l,u,f.** *Choice, 2000.*

Smither, Howard E.   **ML3201 .S6**
The Oratorio in the Nineteenth and Twentieth Centuries. Trade
Cloth. University of North Carolina Press. Chapel Hill, NC.
2000. 856p. History of the Oratorio Ser., Vol. 4
ISBN:0-8078-2511-5, ISBN13: 978-0-8078-2511-2.
Dewey:782.2309034. LCCN:76-043980.
                                                    Audience: **u,f.**

Solomon, Maynard   **ML410.B4**
Beethoven. Ed. 2. Trade Paper. Music Sales Corporation. New
York, NY. 2004. 554p. ISBN:0-8256-7268-6, ISBN13:
978-0-8256-7268-2. Dewey:780/.92/4.
                                                    Audience: **g,l,u,f.**

Sonneck, Oscar G. (Editor)   **ML410.B4**
Beethoven: Impressions by His Contemporaries. Trade Paper.
Dover Publications, Inc. Mineola, NY. 1967. 231p.
ISBN:0-486-21770-1, ISBN13: 978-0-486-21770-3.
Dewey:780.924.
                                                    Audience: **u,f.**

Stanley, Glenn (Editor)   **ML410.B4 C24 2000**
The Cambridge Companion to Beethoven. Trade Paper.
Cambridge University Press. New York, NY. 2000. 387p.
Cambridge Companions to Music Ser. ISBN:0-521-58934-7,
ISBN13: 978-0-521-58934-5. Dewey:780/.92. LCCN:98-042732.
                                    Audience: **l,u,f.** *Choice, 2000.*

Starr, S. Frederick   **ML410.G68S7 2000**
Louis Moreau Gottschalk. Trade Paper. University of Illinois
Press. Champaign, IL. 2000. 592p. Music in American Life Ser.
ISBN:0-252-06876-9, ISBN13: 978-0-252-06876-8.
Dewey:780/.92 B. LCCN:99-088040.
                                                    Audience: **l,u,f.**

Stowell, Robin (Editor)   **ML410.B42 P47 1994**
Performing Beethoven. Trade Paper. Cambridge University
Press. New York, NY. 2005. 260p. Cambridge Studies in

Performance Practice Ser., Vol. 4 ISBN:0-521-02374-2, ISBN13: 978-0-521-02374-0. Dewey:780.92. LCCN:2006-276118.

Audience: **l,u,f.** *Choice, 1995.*

Stowell, Robin   **ML410.B4 S76 1998**
Beethoven: Violin Concerto. Julian Rushton (Contribution by). Cloth Text. Cambridge University Press. New York, NY. 1998. 138p. Music Handbks. ISBN:0-521-45159-0, ISBN13: 978-0-521-45159-8. Dewey:784.2/72. LCCN:97-014035.

Audience: **u,f.**

Tanner, Michael   **ML410.V4**
Wagner. Trade Paper. Princeton University Press. Princeton, NJ. 2002. 248p. ISBN:0-691-10290-2, ISBN13: 978-0-691-10290-0. Dewey:782.1/092.

Audience: **u,f.** *Choice, 1997.*

Taub, Robert   **MT145.B42T38 2002**
Playing the Beethoven Piano Sonatas. Trade Cloth. Hal Leonard Corporation. Milwaukee, WI. 2003. 258p. ISBN:1-57467-071-9, ISBN13: 978-1-57467-071-4. Dewey:786.2/183/092. LCCN:2001-046126.

Audience: **l,u,f.** *Choice, 2003, 2002.*

Thayer, Alexander Wheelock   **ML410.B4**
Thayer's Life of Beethoven, Vol. 1. Forbes, Elliot (Editor); Deiters, Hermann (Editor); Riemann, Hugo (Editor); Krehbiel, Henry Edward (Editor). Princeton University Press. 1991. ISBN:0-691-02717-X, ISBN13: 978-0-691-02717-3.

Audience: **u,f.**

Thayer, Alexander Wheelock   **ML410.B4**
Thayer's Life of Beethoven, Vol. 2. Forbes, Elliot (Editor); Deiters, Hermann (Editor); Riemann, Hugo (Editor); Krehbiel, Henry Edward (Editor). Princeton University Press. 1991. ISBN:0-691-02718-8, ISBN13: 978-0-691-02718-0.

Audience: **u,f.**

Tillard, Francoise   **ML410.H482T513 1996**
Fanny Mendelssohn. Camille Naish (Translator). Trade Cloth. Hal Leonard Corporation. Milwaukee, WI. 1996. 402p. ISBN:0-931340-96-9, ISBN13: 978-0-931340-96-3. Dewey:786.2/092 B. LCCN:95-017336.

Audience: **l,u,f.** *Choice, 1996.*

Todd, Larry   **ML706.N56 2003**
19th-Century Piano Music. Ed. 2. Trade Paper. Routledge. New York, NY. 2003. 460p. Studies in Musical Genres ISBN:0-415-94362-0, ISBN13: 978-0-415-94362-8. Dewey:786.2/09/034. LCCN:2003-058687.

Audience: **u,f.**

Todd, Larry (Editor)   **ML410.S4S323 1994**
Schumann and His World. Trade Cloth. Princeton University Press. Princeton, NJ. 1994. 408p. ISBN:0-691-03697-7, ISBN13: 978-0-691-03697-7. Dewey:780/.92. LCCN:94-009686.

Audience: **g,l,u,f.** *Choice, 1995.*

Todd, R. Larry   **ML410**
Mendelssohn: A Life in Music. Trade Paper. Oxford University Press, Inc. New York, NY. 2005. 712p. ISBN:0-19-517988-9, ISBN13: 978-0-19-517988-0. Dewey:780/.92 B.

Audience: **l,u,f.**

Todd, R. Larry   **ML410.M5M47 1991**
Mendelssohn and His World by Todd. Trade Paper. Princeton University Press. Princeton, NJ. 1991. 428p. The Bard Music Festival Ser. ISBN:0-691-02715-3, ISBN13: 978-0-691-02715-9. LCCN:91-016124.

Audience: **g,l,u,f.** *Choice, 1992.*

Todd, R. Larry   **ML410.M5**
Mendelssohn: The Hebrides and Other Overtures. Julian Rushton (Contribution by). Trade Paper. Cambridge University Press. New York, NY. 1993. 129p. Music Handbks. ISBN:0-521-40764-8, ISBN13: 978-0-521-40764-9. Dewey:784.218926092. LCCN:92-036005.

Audience: **u,f.** *Choice, 1994.*

Verdi, Giuseppe   **ML49.V45**
Seven Verdi Librettos. William Weaver (Translator). Trade Paper. W. W. Norton & Company, Inc. New York, NY. 1977. ISBN:0-393-00852-5, ISBN13: 978-0-393-00852-4. Dewey:782.5.

Audience: **g,l,u,f.**

Von Westernhagen, Curt   **ML410.W15**
The Forging of the Ring: Richard Wagner's Composition Sketches for Der Ring des Nibelungen. Arnold Whittall & Mary Whittall (Translators). Trade Cloth. Cambridge University Press. New York, NY. 1976. 248p. ISBN:0-521-21293-6, ISBN13: 978-0-521-21293-9. Dewey:782.1/092/4. LCCN:76-007140.

Audience: **u,f.**

Wagner, Richard   **ML410.W1 A1434**
The Art Work of the Future. Trade Paper. Kessinger Publishing, LLC. Whitefish, MT. 2004. ISBN:1-4191-5273-4, ISBN13: 978-1-4191-5273-3. Dewey:700/.1.

Audience: **u,f.**

Wagner, Richard   **ML410.V4**
My Life. Library Binding. Reprint Services Company. Temecula, CA. 1988. ISBN:0-7812-0537-9, ISBN13: 978-0-7812-0537-5. Dewey:782.1/092 B.

Audience: **u,f.**

Wagner, Richard   **ML410.W1A246 1989**
Wagner on Conducting. Trade Paper. Dover Publications, Inc. Mineola, NY. 1989. 128p. ISBN:0-486-25932-3, ISBN13: 978-0-486-25932-1. Dewey:781.6/35. LCCN:88-026827.

Audience: **u,f.**

Wagner, Richard   **ML410.W1A1266 1995**
Actors and Singers. William A. Ellis (Translator). Trade Cloth. University of Nebraska Press. Lincoln, NE. 1995. 441p. ISBN:0-8032-9773-4, ISBN13: 978-0-8032-9773-9. Dewey:780. LCCN:95-030854.

Audience: **u,f.**

Wagner, Richard   **ML410.W1A12663 1995**
Art and Politics. William A. Ellis (Translator). Paper Text.
University of Nebraska Press. Lincoln, NE. 1995. 415p.
ISBN:0-8032-9774-2, ISBN13: 978-0-8032-9774-6. Dewey:780.
LCCN:95-024316.

Audience: **u,f.**

Wagner, Richard   **ML410.W1A1268 1995**
Opera and Drama. William Ashton Ellis (Translator). Trade
Paper. University of Nebraska Press. Lincoln, NE. 1995. 416p.
ISBN:0-8032-9765-3, ISBN13: 978-0-8032-9765-4.
Dewey:782.1. LCCN:95-005263.

Audience: **u,f.**

Wagner, Richard   **ML50.M939**
Lohengrin. Nicholas John (Editor). Trade Paper. Riverrun Press,
Inc. Flemington, NJ. 1994. 128p. English National Opera Guide
Series: Bilingual Libretto, Articles, No. 47 ISBN:0-7145-3852-3,
ISBN13: 978-0-7145-3852-5. Dewey:782.10268.

Audience: **g,l,u,f.**

Wagner, Richard   **ML50.W14T22 1988**
Tannhauser. Nicholas John (Editor). Trade Paper. Riverrun Press,
Inc. Flemington, NJ. 1988. 96p. English National Opera Guide
Series: Bilingual Libretto, Articles, No. 39 ISBN:0-7145-4147-8,
ISBN13: 978-0-7145-4147-1. Dewey:782.1/2. LCCN:88-006443.

Audience: **g,l,u,f.**

Wagner, Richard   **ML410.W16**
The Mastersingers of Nuremberg. Nicholas John (Editor), F.
Jameson & Feasey Kember (Translators). Trade Paper. Riverrun
Press, Inc. Flemington, NJ. 2003. 128p. English National Opera
Guide Ser., No. 19:Bilingual Libretto, Articles
ISBN:0-7145-3961-9, ISBN13: 978-0-7145-3961-4.
Dewey:782.1/092/4.

Audience: **g,l,u,f.**

Wagner, Richard   **ML410.W17**
Parsifal. Nicholas John (Editor), Andrew Porter (Translator).
Trade Paper. Riverrun Press, Inc. Flemington, NJ. 1986. 128p.
English National Opera Guide Series: Bilingual Libretto,
Articles, No. 34 ISBN:0-7145-4079-X, ISBN13:
978-0-7145-4079-5. Dewey:782.1/092/4. LCCN:85-052160.

Audience: **g,l,u,f.**

Wagner, Richard   **ML50.B422**
Tristan and Isolde. Nicholas John (Editor), Andrew Porter
(Translator). Trade Paper. Riverrun Press, Inc. Flemington, NJ.
1981. 96p. English National Opera Guide Ser., No. 6:Bilingual
Libretto, Articles ISBN:0-7145-3849-3, ISBN13:
978-0-7145-3849-5. Dewey:782.1/2.

Audience: **g,l,u,f.**

Wagner, Richard   **ML50.W14**
The Ring of the Nibelung. Andrew Porter (Translator). Trade
Paper. W. W. Norton & Company, Inc. New York, NY. 1977.
ISBN:0-393-00867-3, ISBN13: 978-0-393-00867-8.
Dewey:782.12.

Audience: **g,l,u,f.**

Walker, Alan   **ML410.L7**
Franz Liszt: The Final Years, 1861-1886. Ed. 2. Trade Paper.
Cornell University Press. Ithaca, NY. 1997. 624p.
ISBN:0-8014-8453-7, ISBN13: 978-0-8014-8453-7.
Dewey:780.92.

Audience: **l,u,f.**

Walker, Alan   **ML410.L7W27 1987**
Franz Liszt: The Virtuoso Years, 1811-1847. Ed. 3. Trade Paper.
Cornell University Press. Ithaca, NY. 1987. 512p.
ISBN:0-8014-9421-4, ISBN13: 978-0-8014-9421-5.
Dewey:780/.92/4 B. LCCN:82-047821.

Audience: **l,u,f.**

Walker, Alan   **ML410.L7 W27 1987**
Franz Liszt: The Weimar Years, 1848-1861. Ed. 2. Book, Other.
Cornell University Press. Ithaca, NY. 1993. 656p.
ISBN:0-8014-9721-3, ISBN13: 978-0-8014-9721-6.
Dewey:780/.92/4.

Audience: **l,u,f.**

Walker, Alan   **ML410.L7W296 2005**
Reflections on Liszt. Book, Other. Cornell University Press.
Ithaca, NY. 2005. 272p. ISBN:0-8014-4363-6, ISBN13:
978-0-8014-4363-3. Dewey:780/.92. LCCN:2004-030467.

Audience: **l,u,f.**

Wallace, Robin   **ML410.B4**
Beethoven's Critics: Aesthetic Dilemmas and Resolutions
During the Composer's Lifetime. Trade Paper. Cambridge
University Press. New York, NY. 1990. 192p.
ISBN:0-521-38634-9, ISBN13: 978-0-521-38634-0.
Dewey:780/.92/4.

Audience: **u,f.** *Choice, 1987.*

Warrack, John   **ML410.W3**
Carl Maria Von Weber. Ed. 2. Trade Cloth. Cambridge
University Press. New York, NY. 1976. 411p.
ISBN:0-521-21354-1, ISBN13: 978-0-521-21354-7.
Dewey:780.92. LCCN:76-012915.

Audience: **u,f.**

Warrack, John   **ML410.W1 A286 1994**
Richard Wagner: Die Meistersinger von Nürnberg. Richard
Wagner (Contribution by). Cloth Text. Cambridge University
Press. New York, NY. 1994. 185p. Opera Handbooks Ser.
ISBN:0-521-44444-6, ISBN13: 978-0-521-44444-6.
Dewey:782.1. LCCN:93-039615.

Audience: **u,f.**

Watson, Derek   **ML410.B88**
Bruckner. New York: Schirmer Books; London: Prentice Hall
International. 1997. Master Musicians Ser. ISBN:0-02-864626-6,
ISBN13: 978-0-02-864626-8.

Audience: **l,u,f.**

Watson, Derek   **ML410.W1.W38 1981**
Richard Wagner: A Biography. Trade Cloth. Music Sales
Corporation. New York, NY. 1981. 384p. ISBN:0-02-872700-2,
ISBN13: 978-0-02-872700-4. Dewey:782.1/092/4.
LCCN:81-001161.

Audience: **g,l,u,f.**

Weaver, William & Puccini,   ML410.P89
  Simonetta
The Puccini Companion. Ed. 1. New York: W.W. Norton. 1994.
ISBN:0-393-02930-1, ISBN13: 978-0-393-02930-7.

Audience: **g,l,u,f.**

Weaver, William & Chusid,   ML410.V4
  Martin (Editors)
The Verdi Companion. Ed. 2. Trade Paper. W. W. Norton &
Company, Inc. New York, NY. 1988. 384p.
ISBN:0-393-30443-4, ISBN13: 978-0-393-30443-5.
Dewey:782.1/092/4.

Audience: **g,l,u,f.**

Weber, Carl M.   ML275.4
Writings on Music. John Warrack (Editor), Martin Cooper
(Translator). Trade Cloth. Cambridge University Press. New
York, NY. 1981. 413p. ISBN:0-521-22892-1, ISBN13:
978-0-521-22892-3. Dewey:781.743. LCCN:76-012915.

Audience: **u,f.**

Weiner, Marc A.   ML410.W19W23 1997
Richard Wagner and the Anti-Semetic Imagination. Cloth Text.
University of Nebraska Press. Lincoln, NE. 1995. 447p. Texts
and Contexts Ser. ISBN:0-8032-4775-3, ISBN13:
978-0-8032-4775-8. Dewey:782.1/092. LCCN:94-012187.

Audience: **u,f.** *Choice, 1995.*

Wenk, Arthur B.   ML113.W45 1987
Analyses of Nineteenth- and Twentieth-Century Music,
1940-1985. Trade Paper. Music Library Association. Canton,
MA. 1987. 370p. Music Library Association Index and
Bibliography Ser., No. 25 ISBN:0-914954-36-9, ISBN13:
978-0-914954-36-1. Dewey:016.78/0903/4. LCCN:87-005675.

Audience: **l,u,f.**

Wigmore, Richard   ML54.6.S39.W53 1988
  (Translator)
Schubert: The Complete Song Texts. Trade Cloth. Thomson
Gale. Farmington Hills, MI. 1988. 380p. ISBN:0-02-872911-0,
ISBN13: 978-0-02-872911-4. Dewey:784.3/05.
LCCN:88-011653.

Audience: **l,u,f.** *Choice, 1989.*

Williams, Adrian   ML410.L7W55 1990
Portrait of Liszt: By Himself and His Contemporaries. Cloth
Text. Oxford University Press, Inc. New York, NY. 1990. 784p.
ISBN:0-19-816150-6, ISBN13: 978-0-19-816150-9.
Dewey:780/.92 B. LCCN:89-009333.

Audience: **l,u,f.** *Choice, 1991.*

Williamson, John (Editor)   ML410.B88C36 2003
The Cambridge Companion to Bruckner. Jonathan Cross
(Contribution by). Cloth Text. Cambridge University Press. New
York, NY. 2004. 326p. Cambridge Companions to Music Ser.
ISBN:0-521-80404-3, ISBN13: 978-0-521-80404-2.
Dewey:780/.92 B. LCCN:2002-038785.

Audience: **u,f.** *Choice, 2005.*

Williamson, John   ML410.S93 W55 1993
Strauss: Also Sprach Zarathustra. Julian Rushton (Contribution

by). Cloth Text. Cambridge University Press. New York, NY.
1993. 136p. Music Handbks. ISBN:0-521-40076-7, ISBN13:
978-0-521-40076-3. Dewey:784.2184. LCCN:92-020457.

Audience: **u,f.**

Winter, Robert & Martin,   MT145.B425.B4 1994
  Robert (Editors)
The Beethoven Quartet Companion. Trade Cloth. University of
California Press. Berkeley, CA. 1994. 300p.
ISBN:0-520-08211-7, ISBN13: 978-0-520-08211-3.
Dewey:785.7/194/092. LCCN:92-040668.

Audience: **l,u,f.** *Choice, 1995.*

Yastrebtsev, V. V. & Jonas,   ML410.R52I233 1985
  Florence
Reminiscences of Rimsky-Korsakov. Trade Cloth. Columbia
University Press. New York, NY. 1985. 578p.
ISBN:0-231-05260-X, ISBN13: 978-0-231-05260-3.
Dewey:780/.92/4 B. LCCN:84-016967.

Audience: **l,u,f.** *Choice, 1986.*

Youens, Susan   ML410.W8.Y7 1992
Hugo Wolf: The Vocal Music. Cloth Text. Princeton University
Press. Princeton, NJ. 1992. 412p. ISBN:0-691-09145-5, ISBN13:
978-0-691-09145-7. Dewey:782.42168/092. LCCN:91-045446.

Audience: **u,f.** *Choice, 1993.*

Youens, Susan   ML410.S3
Retracing a Winter's Journey: Schubert's Winterreise. Book,
Other. Cornell University Press. Ithaca, NY. 1991. 320p.
ISBN:0-8014-9966-6, ISBN13: 978-0-8014-9966-1.
Dewey:782.4/7. LCCN:91-055234.

Audience: **u,f.** *Choice, 1992.*

Youens, Susan   ML410.S3 Y7 1992
Schubert: Die Schone Mullerin. Julian Rushton (Contribution
by). Trade Paper. Cambridge University Press. New York, NY.
1992. 129p. Music Handbks. ISBN:0-521-42279-5, ISBN13:
978-0-521-42279-6. Dewey:782.42168. LCCN:91-028960.

Audience: **u,f.**

Studies in Music History, Criticism, Analysis, and Appreciation > Western Classical Literature by Period > Modern and Postmodern

Johnson, Steven (Editor)   ML3849
The New York Schools of Music and Visual Arts : John Cage,
Morton Feldman, Edgard Varèse, Willem De Kooning, Jasper
Johns, Robert Rauschenberg. . Routledge. 2002. Studies in
Contemporary Music and Culture ISBN:0-8153-3364-1,
ISBN13: 978-0-8153-3364-7.

Audience: **u,f.**

Adlington, Robert   ML410.A6326
Louis Andriessen: De Staat. Trade Cloth, Compact Disc.
Ashgate Publishing, Ltd. Aldershot, 2004. 180p. Landmarks in

Music since 1950 Ser. ISBN:0-7546-0925-1, ISBN13: 978-0-7546-0925-4. Dewey:782.4/8. LCCN:2003-059519.

Audience: **u,f.** *Choice, 2005.*

Adlington, Robert **ML410.B605 A35 2000**
The Music of Harrison Birtwistle. Arnold Whittall (Contribution by). Cloth Text. Cambridge University Press. New York, NY. 2000. 256p. Music in the Twentieth Century Ser., No. 12 ISBN:0-521-63082-7, ISBN13: 978-0-521-63082-5. Dewey:780/.92. LCCN:99-022678.

Audience: **u,f.** *Choice, 2000.*

Adorno, Theodor W. **ML197**
Quasi una Fantasia: Essays on Modern Music. Ed. 2. Trade Paper. Analytical Psychology Club of San Francisco, Inc. San Francisco, CA. 1998. 336p. Classics Ser., Vol. 17 ISBN:1-85984-159-7, ISBN13: 978-1-85984-159-4. Dewey:780.9/04.

Audience: **u,f.** *Choice, 1993.*

Albright, Daniel (Editor, **ML197.M58 2004**
 Commentaries by)
Modernism and Music: An Anthology of Sources. Trade Cloth. University of Chicago Press. Chicago, IL. 2004. 440p. ISBN:0-226-01266-2, ISBN13: 978-0-226-01266-7. Dewey:780/.9/04. LCCN:2003-017899.

Audience: **u,f.**

Anderson, Donna K. **ML410.G9134.A8 1993**
Charles T. Griffes: A Life in Music. Trade Cloth. Smithsonian Institution Press. Washington, DC. 1993. 272p. Studies of American Musicians ISBN:1-56098-191-1, ISBN13: 978-1-56098-191-6. Dewey:780.92. LCCN:92-021844.

Audience: **u,f.** *Choice, 1993.*

Anderson, Laurie **NX512.A54**
Stories from the Nerve Bible: A Twenty-Year Retrospective. Trade Cloth. HarperCollins Canada, Ltd. Scarborough, ON. 1993. ISBN:0-06-016606-1, ISBN13: 978-0-06-016606-9. Dewey:700/.92.

Audience: **u,f.**

Andriessen, Louis & **ML410.B4**
 Schonberger, Elmer
The Apollonian Clockwork: On Stravinsky. Trade Paper. Amsterdam University Press. Amsterdam, 2006. ISBN:90-5356-856-5, ISBN13: 978-90-5356-856-9. Dewey:780/.92/4.

Audience: **u,f.** *Choice, 1990.*

Antheil, George **ML410.A638A3 1990**
Bad Boy of Music. Trade Cloth. Samuel French Trade. Hollywood, CA. 1990. 378p. ISBN:0-573-60604-8, ISBN13: 978-0-573-60604-5. Dewey:780/.92 B. LCCN:90-003331.

Audience: **g,l,u,f.**

Antokoletz, Elliott **ML410.M9**
The Music of Bela Bartok: A Study of Tonality and Progression in Twentieth Century Music. Trade Paper. University of

California Press. Berkeley, CA. 1984. 472p. ISBN:0-520-06747-9, ISBN13: 978-0-520-06747-9. Dewey:780.92. LCCN:82-017352.

Audience: **u,f.**

Antokoletz, Elliott **ML197.A63 1992**
Twentieth Century Music. Ed. 1. Cloth Text. Prentice Hall PTR. Upper Saddle River, NJ. 1991. 512p. ISBN:0-13-934126-9, ISBN13: 978-0-13-934126-7. Dewey:780/.9/04. LCCN:90-019651.

Audience: **u,f.**

Antokoletz, Elliott (Editor), **ML410.B26B284 2000**
 et al.
Bartok Perspectives: Man, Composer, and Ethnomusicologist. Victoria Fischer & Benjamin Suchoff (Editors). Trade Cloth. Oxford University Press, Inc. New York, NY. 2000. 332p. ISBN:0-19-512562-2, ISBN13: 978-0-19-512562-7. Dewey:780/.92. LCCN:99-022696.

Audience: **l,u,f.**

Antokoletz, Elliott **ML134.B18A7 1997**
Bela Bartok: A Guide to Research. Ed. 2. Guy A. Marco (Editor). Cloth Text. Garland Publishing, Inc. New York, NY. 1997. 536p. Composer Resource Manuals Ser., Vol. 40 ISBN:0-8153-2088-4, ISBN13: 978-0-8153-2088-3. Dewey:016.78/092. LCCN:96-039298.

Audience: **l,u,f.** *Choice, 1997, 1988.*

Appleby, David P. **ML410.V76A67 2002**
Heitor Villa-Lobos: A Life (1887-1959). Trade Cloth. Scarecrow Press, Inc. Lanham, MD. 2002. 288p. ISBN:0-8108-4149-5, ISBN13: 978-0-8108-4149-9. Dewey:780/.92 B. LCCN:2001-049887.

Audience: **g,l,u,f.** *Choice, 2002.*

Ashby, Arved (Editor) **ML197.P57 2004**
The Pleasure of Modernist Music: Listening, Meaning, Intention, Ideology. Trade Cloth. University of Rochester Press. Rochester, NY. 2004. 416p. Eastman Studies in Music Ser., Vol. 29 ISBN:1-58046-143-3, ISBN13: 978-1-58046-143-6. Dewey:780/.9/04. LCCN:2004-011370.

Audience: **g,l,u,f.** *Choice, 2005.*

Auner, Joseph Henry **ML410.S283A97 2003**
A Schoenberg Reader: Documents of a Life. Cloth over Boards. Yale University Press. Cumberland, RI. 2003. 460p. ISBN:0-300-09540-6, ISBN13: 978-0-300-09540-1. Dewey:780/.92. LCCN:2002-154114.

Audience: **l,u,f.** *Choice, 2004.*

Auner, Joseph & Lochhead, **ML3845.P74 2002**
 Judy (Editors)
Postmodern Music/Postmodern Thought. Cloth Text. Garland Publishing, Inc. New York, NY. 2001. 350p. Studies in Contemporary Music and Culture, Vol. 4 ISBN:0-8153-3819-8, ISBN13: 978-0-8153-3819-2. Dewey:780/.9/05. LCCN:2002-514829.

Audience: **g,l,u,f.**

Babbitt, Milton   **ML60.B12 2003**
The Collected Essays of Milton Babbitt. Stephen Peles, Stephen Dembski, Andrew Mead & Joseph N. Straus (Editors). Trade Cloth. Princeton University Press. Princeton, NJ. 2003. 504p. ISBN:0-691-08966-3, ISBN13: 978-0-691-08966-9. Dewey:780. LCCN:2003-044496.
           Audience: **u,f.** *Choice, 2004.*

Bailey, Kathryn   **ML410.W33 B32 1998**
The Life of Webern. Trade Paper. Cambridge University Press. New York, NY. 1998. 237p. Musical Lives Ser. ISBN:0-521-57566-4, ISBN13: 978-0-521-57566-9. Dewey:780/.92 B. LCCN:97-025751.
           Audience: **g,l,u,f.** *Choice, 1998.*

Bailey, Kathryn   **ML410.U33**
The Twelve-Note Music of Anton Webern: Old Forms in a New Language. Arnold Whittall (Contribution by). Trade Paper. Cambridge University Press. New York, NY. 2004. 474p. Music in the Twentieth Century Ser., Vol. 2 ISBN:0-521-54796-2, ISBN13: 978-0-521-54796-3. Dewey:781.2/68092. LCCN:2006-277394.
           Audience: **u,f.** *Choice, 1992.*

Baker, James M.   **ML410.S5988B33 1986**
The Music of Alexander Scriabin. Cloth over Boards. Yale University Press. Cumberland, RI. 1986. 291p. ISBN:0-300-03337-0, ISBN13: 978-0-300-03337-3. Dewey:786.1/092/4. LCCN:85-002494.
           Audience: **u,f.** *Choice, 1986.*

Bayley, Amanda (Editor)   **ML410.B26 C35 2001**
The Cambridge Companion to Bartók. Trade Paper. Cambridge University Press. New York, NY. 2001. 285p. Cambridge Companions to Music Ser. ISBN:0-521-66958-8, ISBN13: 978-0-521-66958-0. Dewey:780/.92.
           Audience: **l,u,f.** *Choice, 2001.*

Bazzana, Kevin   **ML417.G68B393 2004**
Wondrous Strange: The Life and Art of Glenn Gould. Trade Cloth. Oxford University Press, Inc. New York, NY. 2004. 558p. ISBN:0-19-517440-2, ISBN13: 978-0-19-517440-3. Dewey:786.2/092 B. LCCN:2004-300097.
           Audience: **g,l,u,f.**

Beckerman, Michael Brim (Editor)   **ML410**
Janacek and His World. Trade Cloth. Princeton University Press. Princeton, NJ. 2003. 320p. The Bard Music Festival Ser. ISBN:0-691-11675-X, ISBN13: 978-0-691-11675-4. Dewey:780.9/2.
           Audience: **g,l,u,f.**

Berg, Alban   **ML50.B491W62 1990**
Wozzeck. Nicholas John (Editor), Eric Blocknel & Vicki Hartfold (Translators). Trade Paper. Beekman Books, Inc. Wappingers Falls, NY. 1990. 116p. English National Opera Guide Series: Bilingual Libretto, Articles, No. 42 ISBN:0-7145-4201-6, ISBN13: 978-0-7145-4201-0. Dewey:782.1/0268. LCCN:90-044450.
           Audience: **g,l,u,f.**

Berger, Arthur V.   **ML410.C756B4 1990**
Aaron Copland. Leonard Burkat (Introduction by). Paper Text. Da Capo Press, Inc. Cambridge, MA. 1990. 496p. Music Reprint Ser. ISBN:0-306-76266-8, ISBN13: 978-0-306-76266-6. Dewey:780/.92/4 B. LCCN:85-000462.
           Audience: **u,f.**

Bernard, Jonathan W.   **ML410.V27B5 1987**
The Music of Edgard Varese. Trade Cloth. Yale University Press. Cumberland, RI. 1987. 304p. ISBN:0-300-03515-2, ISBN13: 978-0-300-03515-5. Dewey:780/.92/4. LCCN:86-022431.
           Audience: **u,f.** *Choice, 1987.*

Bertensson, Sergei & Leyda, Jay   **ML410.R12B47 2001**
Sergei Rachmaninoff: A Lifetime in Music. David Butler Cannata (Introduction by). Trade Paper. Indiana University Press. Bloomington, IN. 2001. 480p. Russian Music Studies ISBN:0-253-21421-1, ISBN13: 978-0-253-21421-8. Dewey:780/.92 B. LCCN:2001-016765.
           Audience: **g,l,u,f.**

Betz, Albrecht   **ML410.E37 B43 1982**
Hanns Eisler: Political Musician. Bill Hopkins (Translator). Trade Cloth. Cambridge University Press. New York, NY. 1982. 336p. ISBN:0-521-24022-0, ISBN13: 978-0-521-24022-2. Dewey:780/.92/4. LCCN:81-012260.
           Audience: **u,f.**

Bird, John   **ML410.M9**
Percy Grainger. Ed. 2. Trade Cloth. Oxford University Press, Inc. New York, NY. 1999. 404p. ISBN:0-19-816652-4, ISBN13: 978-0-19-816652-8. Dewey:780.9/2. LCCN:98-009603.
           Audience: **u,f.** *Choice, 1999.*

Block, Geoffrey Holden   **ML410.I94**
Ives, Concord Sonata: Piano Sonata No. 2. Cambridge University Press. 1996. Cambridge Music Handbooks ISBN:0-521-49656-X, ISBN13: 978-0-521-49656-8.
           Audience: **u,f.**

Born, Georgina   **ML3795**
Rationalizing Culture: IRCAM, Boulez, and the Institutionalisation of the Avant-Garde. Trade Paper. University of California Press. Berkeley, CA. 1995. 406p. ISBN:0-520-20216-3, ISBN13: 978-0-520-20216-0. Dewey:306.4/84. LCCN:93-039386.
           Audience: **u,f.**

Boulez, Pierre   **ML197.B7213**
Boulez on Music Today. Trade Cloth. Harvard University Press. Cambridge, MA. 1971. 144p. ISBN:0-674-08006-8, ISBN13: 978-0-674-08006-5. Dewey:781. LCCN:74-142073.
           Audience: **u,f.**

Boulez, Pierre   **ML60.B796**
Orientations: Collected Writings. Jean-Jacques Nattiez (Editor), Martin Cooper (Translator). Trade Paper. Harvard University Press. Cambridge, MA. 1990. 544p. ISBN:0-674-64376-3, ISBN13: 978-0-674-64376-5. Dewey:780.
           Audience: **u,f.**

Boulez, Pierre ML60.B71313 1991
Stocktakings from an Apprenticeship. Stephen Walsh
(Translator). Trade Cloth. Oxford University Press, Inc. New
York, NY. 1991. 348p. ISBN:0-19-311210-8, ISBN13:
978-0-19-311210-0. Dewey:780/.9. LCCN:90-007655.
Audience: **u,f.** *Choice, 1992.*

Braun, Hans-Joachim ML197.I2 2002
Music and Technology in the Twentieth Century. International
Committee for the History of Technology (Contribution by).
Trade Cloth. Johns Hopkins University Press. Baltimore, MD.
2002. 256p. ISBN:0-8018-6885-8, ISBN13: 978-0-8018-6885-6.
Dewey:780/.06. LCCN:2001-042490.
Audience: **u,f.**

Briscoe, James R. ML134.D26B7 1990
Claude Debussy: A Guide to Research. Cloth Text. Garland
Publishing, Inc. New York, NY. 1990. 526p. Composer
Resource Manuals Ser., Vol. 27 ISBN:0-8240-5795-3, ISBN13:
978-0-8240-5795-4. Dewey:016.78/092. LCCN:89-023691.
Audience: **l,u,f.** *Choice, 1990.*

Brown, Malcolm Hamrick ML410.S53S46 2004
(Editor)
A Shostakovich Casebook. Trade Cloth. Indiana University
Press. Bloomington, IN. 2004. 392p. ISBN:0-253-34364-X,
ISBN13: 978-0-253-34364-2. Dewey:780/.92 B.
LCCN:2003-017153.
Audience: **g,l,u,f.** *Choice, 2004.*

Brown, Matthew MT130.D4B76 2002
Debussy's Iberia. Trade Cloth. Oxford University Press, Inc.
New York, NY. 2003. 194p. Studies in Musical Genesis and
Structure ISBN:0-19-816199-9, ISBN13: 978-0-19-816199-8.
Dewey:784.2/1896. LCCN:2002-192554.
Audience: **u,f.**

Burge, David ML707.B87 1990
Twentieth Century Piano Music, Vol. 132. Trade Cloth.
Thomson Wadsworth. Belmont, CA. 1990. 284p.
ISBN:0-02-870321-9, ISBN13: 978-0-02-870321-3.
Dewey:786.2/09/04. LCCN:90-008663.
Audience: **u,f.** *Choice, 1991.*

Burkholder, J. Peter ML410.M9
All Made of Tunes: Charles Ives and the Uses of Musical
Borrowing. Trade Paper. Yale University Press. Cumberland, RI.
2004. 568p. ISBN:0-300-10212-7, ISBN13: 978-0-300-10212-3.
Dewey:780.9/2.
Audience: **u,f.** *Choice, 1996.*

Burkholder, J. Peter ML410.I94C33 1996
(Editor)
Charles Ives and His World. Cloth Text. Princeton University
Press. Princeton, NJ. 1996. 464p. The Bard Music Festival Ser.
ISBN:0-691-01164-8, ISBN13: 978-0-691-01164-6.
Dewey:780.92. LCCN:96-021393.
Audience: **g,l,u,f.** *Choice, 1997.*

Burt, Peter ML410.T134 B87 2001
The Music of Toru Takemitsu. Arnold Whittall (Contribution
by). Trade Cloth. Cambridge University Press. New York, NY.

2001. 306p. Music in the Twentieth Century Ser.
ISBN:0-521-78220-1, ISBN13: 978-0-521-78220-3.
Dewey:780/.92. LCCN:00-045505.
Audience: **u,f.** *Choice, 2002.*

Burton, Humphrey ML410.B566B9 1994
Leonard Bernstein. Trade Cloth. Doubleday Publishing. New
York, NY. 1994. 608p. ISBN:0-385-42345-4, ISBN13:
978-0-385-42345-8. Dewey:780.9/2. LCCN:93-040278.
Audience: **l,u,f.**

Burton, William W. (Editor) ML410.M9
Conversations about Bernstein. Cloth Text. DIANE Publishing
Company. Collingdale, PA. 1999. 198p. ISBN:0-7881-6100-8,
ISBN13: 978-0-7881-6100-1. Dewey:780.9/2.
Audience: **l,u,f.**

Caballero, Carlo ML410.F27 C33 2001
Fauré and French Musical Aesthetics. Arnold Whittall
(Contribution by). Trade Paper. Cambridge University Press.
New York, NY. 2004. 345p. Music in the Twentieth Century
Ser., Vol. 13 ISBN:0-521-54398-3, ISBN13: 978-0-521-54398-9.
Dewey:780/.92.
Audience: **u,f.** *Choice, 2002.*

Cage, John M. ML60
Empty Words: Writings, '73 -'78. Trade Paper. Wesleyan
University Press. Middletown, CT. 1979. 199p.
ISBN:0-8195-6067-7, ISBN13: 978-0-8195-6067-4. Dewey:780.
LCCN:78-027212.
Audience: **u,f.**

Cage, John M. PS3553.A32
M: Writings '67-'72. Trade Paper. Wesleyan University Press.
Middletown, CT. 1973. 233p. ISBN:0-8195-6035-9, ISBN13:
978-0-8195-6035-3. Dewey:818.54. LCCN:72-011051.
Audience: **u,f.**

Cage, John M. ML3845
Silence: Lectures and Writings. Trade Paper. Wesleyan
University Press. Middletown, CT. 1961. 288p.
ISBN:0-8195-6028-6, ISBN13: 978-0-8195-6028-5.
Dewey:780.1. LCCN:61-014238.
Audience: **g,l,u,f.**

Cale, John & Bockris, ML420.P96
Victor
What's Welsh for Zen: The Autobiography of John Cale. Trade
Paper. Bloomsbury Publishing. New York, NY. 2000. 272p.
ISBN:1-58234-068-4, ISBN13: 978-1-58234-068-5.
Dewey:782.4/2/166/092.
Audience: **u,f.**

Carley, Lionel ML410.D35F74 1998
Frederick Delius: Music, Art and Literature. Trade Cloth.
Ashgate Publishing, Ltd. Aldershot, 1997. 350p.
ISBN:1-85928-222-9, ISBN13: 978-1-85928-222-9.
Dewey:780/.92. LCCN:97-003005.
Audience: **u,f.**

Carpenter, Humphrey   ML410.B853C37 1993
Benjamin Britten: A Biography. Trade Cloth. Thomson Gale.
Farmington Hills, MI. 1993. 677p. ISBN:0-684-19569-0,
ISBN13: 978-0-684-19569-8. Dewey:780.92. LCCN:93-018146.
Audience: **g,l,u,f.** *Choice, 1993.*

Carroll, Mark   ML3795.C34 2003
Music and Ideology in Cold War Europe. Arnold Whittall
(Contribution by). Trade Cloth. Cambridge University Press.
New York, NY. 2003. 256p. Music in the Twentieth Century
Ser., Vol. 18 ISBN:0-521-82072-3, ISBN13: 978-0-521-82072-1.
Dewey:780/.9/04. LCCN:2002-031245.
Audience: **u,f.**

Carter, Elliott   ML197
Elliott Carter: Collected Essays and Lectures, 1937-1995.
Jonathan W. Bernard (Editor). Trade Paper. University of
Rochester Press. Rochester, NY. 1998. 392p. Eastman Studies in
Music, No. 7 ISBN:1-58046-025-9, ISBN13:
978-1-58046-025-5. Dewey:780.9/04. LCCN:96-026355.
Audience: **u,f.** *Choice, 1997.*

Chadabe, Joel   ML1380.C43 1997
Electric Sound: The Past and Promise of Electronic Music.
Trade Paper. Prentice Hall PTR. Upper Saddle River, NJ. 1996.
370p. ISBN:0-13-303231-0, ISBN13: 978-0-13-303231-4.
Dewey:786.7. LCCN:96-029349.
Audience: **g,l,u,f.**

Cheek, Timothy   ML49.J36O62 2003
The Janacek Opera Libretti: Kat'a Kabanova Translations and
Pronunciation. Trade Paper. Scarecrow Press, Inc. Lanham, MD.
2004. 280p. ISBN:0-8108-5014-1, ISBN13: 978-0-8108-5014-9.
Dewey:782.1/0268. LCCN:2002-153032.
Audience: **u,f.**

Cone, Edward T.   ML60.C773M9 1989
Music: A View from Delft. Selected Essays. Robert P. Morgan
(Editor). Trade Paper. University of Chicago Press. Chicago, IL.
1989. 344p. ISBN:0-226-11470-8, ISBN13: 978-0-226-11470-5.
Dewey:780.9. LCCN:88-020659.
Audience: **u,f.**

Cook, Nicholas & Pople,   ML197.C26 2004
  Anthony (Editors)
The Cambridge History of Twentieth-Century Music. Cloth Text.
Cambridge University Press. New York, NY. 2004. 836p. The
Cambridge History of Music Ser. ISBN:0-521-66256-7, ISBN13:
978-0-521-66256-7. Dewey:780/.9/04. LCCN:2003-055131.
Audience: **g,l,u,f.** *Choice, 2005.*

Cooke, Mervyn   ML410.B853 C76 1996
Britten: War Requiem. Cloth Text. Cambridge University Press.
New York, NY. 1996. 125p. Music Handbks.
ISBN:0-521-44089-0, ISBN13: 978-0-521-44089-9.
Dewey:782.3/238. LCCN:96-006338.
Audience: **u,f.**

Cooke, Mervyn (Editor)   ML1706
The Cambridge Companion to Twentieth-Century Opera. Trade
Paper. Cambridge University Press. New York, NY. 2005. 424p.

Cambridge Companions to Music Ser. ISBN:0-521-78393-3,
ISBN13: 978-0-521-78393-4. Dewey:782.109/04.
LCCN:2006-295723.
Audience: **g,l,u,f.**

Cooke, Mervyn (Editor)   ML410.B853 C36 1999
The Cambridge Companion to Benjamin Britten. Jonathan Cross
(Contribution by). Trade Paper. Cambridge University Press.
New York, NY. 1999. 368p. Cambridge Companions to Music
Ser. ISBN:0-521-57476-5, ISBN13: 978-0-521-57476-1.
Dewey:780/.92 B. LCCN:98-030683.
Audience: **g,l,u,f.** *Choice, 2000.*

Cooper, David   ML410.B26 C66 1996
Bartók: Concerto for Orchestra. Cloth Text. Cambridge
University Press. New York, NY. 1996. 111p. Music Handbks.
ISBN:0-521-48004-3, ISBN13: 978-0-521-48004-8.
Dewey:784.2/3/092. LCCN:95-021614.
Audience: **u,f.**

Cope, David   ML197.C757 2001
New Directions in Music. Ed. 7. Paper Text. Waveland Press,
Inc. Prospect Heights, IL. 2000. 259p. ISBN:1-57766-108-7,
ISBN13: 978-1-57766-108-5. Dewey:780/.9/04.
LCCN:2001-266343.
Audience: **g,l,u,f.**

Copland, Aaron   ML63
Copland on Music. Paper Text. Classic Textbooks. Murrieta,
CA. 1960. 280p. ISBN:1-4047-9255-4, ISBN13:
978-1-4047-9255-5. Dewey:780.8.
Audience: **u,f.** *B*

Copland, Aaron   ML197 .C76
The New Music, 1900-1960. Library Binding. Reprint Services
Company. Temecula, CA. 194p. ISBN:0-685-14848-3, ISBN13:
978-0-685-14848-8. Dewey:780/.904.
Audience: **u,f.** *B*

Copland, Aaron   ML410.C756
Aaron Copland A Reader: Selected Writings 1923-1972.
Kostelanetz, Richard (Editor) (Introduction by); Silverstein,
Steven (Assistant Editor). Routledge. 2004.
ISBN:0-415-93940-2, ISBN13: 978-0-415-93940-9.
Audience: **u,f.**

Copland, Aaron & Perlis,   ML410.C756A3 1987
  Vivian
Copland: 1900 Through 1942. Trade Paper. St. Martin's Press.
Gordonville, VA. 1999. 402p. ISBN:0-312-01149-0, ISBN13:
978-0-312-01149-9. Dewey:[B]. LCCN:84-011703.
Audience: **g,l,u,f.**

Copland, Aaron & Perlis,   ML410.C756A3 1990
  Vivian
Copland: Since 1943. Trade Paper. St. Martin's Press.
Gordonville, VA. 1990. 480p. ISBN:0-312-05066-6, ISBN13:
978-0-312-05066-5. Dewey:780/.92 B. LCCN:90-036888.
Audience: **g,l,u,f.**

Cowell, Henry   **ML60.C85 2000**
Essential Cowell: Selected Writings on Music. Dick Higgins
(Editor). Trade Cloth. McPherson & Company. Kingston, NY.
2003. 347p. ISBN:0-929701-63-1, ISBN13: 978-0-929701-63-9.
Dewey:780. LCCN:00-055904.

Audience: **u,f.**

Cowell, Henry   **MT6.C7895 N4 1996**
New Musical Resources. David Nicholls (Notes by). Cloth Text.
Cambridge University Press. New York, NY. 1996. 195p.
ISBN:0-521-49651-9, ISBN13: 978-0-521-49651-3.
Dewey:784.1. LCCN:95-031529.

Audience: **u,f.**

Craft, Robert   **ML410.B4**
Stravinsky: Selected Correspondence, Vol. II. Trade Cloth.
Alfred A. Knopf Inc. New York, NY. 1984. 559p.
ISBN:0-394-52813-1, ISBN13: 978-0-394-52813-7.
Dewey:780/.92/4. LCCN:81-047495.

Audience: **u,f.** *Choice, 1985.*

Craft, Robert   **ML410.S932C8 1994**
Stravinsky: Chronicle of a Friendship. Ed. 2. Trade Cloth.
Vanderbilt University Press. Nashville, TN. 1994. 608p.
ISBN:0-8265-1258-5, ISBN13: 978-0-8265-1258-1.
Dewey:780/.92 B. LCCN:94-012666.

Audience: **u,f.** *Choice, 1995.*

Craft, Robert (Editor)   **ML410.B4**
Stravinsky: Selected Correspondence, Vol. I. Trade Cloth. Alfred
A. Knopf Inc. New York, NY. 1982. 416p. ISBN:0-394-51870-5,
ISBN13: 978-0-394-51870-1. Dewey:780/.92/4.
LCCN:81-047495.

Audience: **u,f.** *Choice, 1985.*

Craft, Robert   **ML410.B4**
Stravinsky: Selected Correspondence. Robert Gottlieb & Eva
Resnikova (Editors). Trade Cloth. Alfred A. Knopf Inc. New
York, NY. 1985. 521p. ISBN:0-394-54220-7, ISBN13:
978-0-394-54220-1. Dewey:780/.92/4. LCCN:81-047495.

Audience: **u,f.** *Choice, 1985.*

Cross, Jonathan (Editor)   **ML410.S932**
The Cambridge Companion to Stravinsky. Cloth Text.
Cambridge University Press. New York, NY. 2003. 344p.
Cambridge Companions to Music Ser. ISBN:0-521-66330-X,
ISBN13: 978-0-521-66330-4. Dewey:780/.92.
LCCN:2003-279769.

Audience: **g,l,u,f.** *Choice, 2004.*

Cross, Jonathan   **ML410.B605C76 2000**
Harrison Birtwistle: Man, Mind, Music. Book, Other. Cornell
University Press. Ithaca, NY. 2000. 304p. ISBN:0-8014-8672-6,
ISBN13: 978-0-8014-8672-2. Dewey:780/.92 B.
LCCN:00-020553.

Audience: **u,f.** *Choice, 2000.*

Cross, Jonathan   **ML410.S932 C87 1998**
The Stravinsky Legacy. Arnold Whittall (Contribution by). Trade
Cloth. Cambridge University Press. New York, NY. 1998. 294p.
Music in the Twentieth Century Ser., No. 8

ISBN:0-521-56365-8, ISBN13: 978-0-521-56365-9.
Dewey:780/.92. LCCN:2006-562076.

Audience: **u,f.** *Choice, 1999.*

de La Grange, Henry L.   **ML410.M23L3413 1995**
Gustav Mahler: Vienna: The Years of Challenge (1897-1904).
Trade Cloth. Oxford University Press, Inc. New York, NY. 1995.
912p. ISBN:0-19-315159-6, ISBN13: 978-0-19-315159-8.
Dewey:780/.92 B. LCCN:94-018322.

Audience: **u,f.** *Choice, 1995.*

de La Grange, Henry L.   **ML410.M23L3413 1995**
Gustav Mahler: Vienna: Triumph and Disillusion (1904-1907).
Trade Cloth. Oxford University Press, Inc. New York, NY. 2000.
1,016p. ISBN:0-19-315160-X, ISBN13: 978-0-19-315160-4.
Dewey:780.9/2. LCCN:94-018322.

Audience: **u,f.**

Debussy, Claude, et al.   **ML90**
Three Classics in the Aesthetic of Music. Ferruccio Busoni &
Charles Ives (Authors). Trade Paper. Dover Publications, Inc.
Mineola, NY. 1962. 188p. ISBN:0-486-20320-4, ISBN13:
978-0-486-20320-1. Dewey:780.922.

Audience: **u,f.**

Debussy, Claude   **ML410.D28**
Pelleas and Melisande. Nicholas John (Editor), Hugh
MacDonald (Translator). Trade Paper. Riverrun Press, Inc.
Flemington, NJ. 1982. 128p. English National Opera Guide Ser.,
No. 9:Bilingual Libretto, Articles ISBN:0-7145-3906-6, ISBN13:
978-0-7145-3906-5. Dewey:782.1/092/4.

Audience: **g,l,u,f.**

DeLio, Thomas   **ML410**
The Music of Morton Feldman. Book, Other. Greenwood
Publishing Group, Inc. Portsmouth, NH. 1996. 260p.
Contributions to the Study of Music and Dance Ser., Vol. 36
ISBN:0-313-29803-3, ISBN13: 978-0-313-29803-5.
Dewey:780/.92. LCCN:95-024022.

Audience: **u,f.** *Choice, 1996.*

Duckworth, William   **ML197.D84**
20/20: 20 New Sounds of the 20th Century. Digital, Other.
Thomson Wadsworth. Belmont, CA. 1999. 240p.
ISBN:0-02-864864-1, ISBN13: 978-0-02-864864-4.
Dewey:780/.9/04. LCCN:98-045504.

Audience: **g,l,u,f.**

Duckworth, William &   **ML390**
  Fleming, Richard (Editors)
Sound and Light: La Monte Young Marian Zazeela. Trade
Cloth. Bucknell University Press. Cranbury, NJ. 1997. 232p.
Review Ser., Vol. 40, No. 1 ISBN:0-8387-5346-9, ISBN13:
978-0-8387-5346-0. Dewey:780.922. LCCN:55-058217.

Audience: **u,f.**

Duckworth, William &   **ML390**
  Jansen, David A.
Talking Music: Conversations with John Cage, Philip Glass,
Laurie Anderson and Five Generations of American

Experimental Composers. Trade Cloth. Music Sales Corporation. New York, NY. 1995. 489p. ISBN:0-8256-7230-9, ISBN13: 978-0-8256-7230-9. Dewey:780/.92/273 B.

Audience: **g,l,u,f.**

Dufallo, Richard   **ML390**
Trackings: Composers Speak with Richard Dufallo. Oxford University Press. 1989. ISBN:0-7351-0368-2, ISBN13: 978-0-7351-0368-9.

Audience: **u,f.**

Dunsby, Jonathan   **ML410.S283 D83 1992**
Schoenberg: Pierrot Lunaire. Julian Rushton (Contribution by). Trade Paper. Cambridge University Press. New York, NY. 1992. 94p. Music Handbks. ISBN:0-521-38715-9, ISBN13: 978-0-521-38715-6. Dewey:782.47. LCCN:91-036068.

Audience: **u,f.**

Emmerson, Simon (Editor)   **ML1380.M86 2000**
Music, Electronic Media and Culture. Trade Cloth. Ashgate Publishing, Ltd. Aldershot, 2000. 262p. ISBN:0-7546-0109-9, ISBN13: 978-0-7546-0109-8. Dewey:786.7. LCCN:00-059415.

Audience: **l,u,f.**

Evans, Peter   **ML410.B853E9 1995**
The Music of Benjamin Britten. Ed. 2. Paper Text. Oxford University Press, Inc. New York, NY. 1996. 602p. ISBN:0-19-816590-0, ISBN13: 978-0-19-816590-3. Dewey:780/.92. LCCN:95-047363.

Audience: **u,f.**

Farneth, David   **ML410.W395F37 1999**
Kurt Weill: A Life in Pictures and Documents. Trade Cloth. Overlook Press, The. New York, NY. 1999. 312p. ISBN:0-87951-721-2, ISBN13: 978-0-87951-721-2. Dewey:782.1/092 B. LCCN:99-033577.

Audience: **g,l,u,f.** *Choice, 2000.*

Fassett, Agatha   **ML410.B26**
The Naked Face of Genius: Béla Bartók's American Years. Houghton Mifflin. 1968.

Audience: **u,f.**

Fay, Laurel   **ML410.S53F39 2000**
Shostakovich: A Life. Trade Cloth. Oxford University Press, Inc. New York, NY. 1999. 480p. ISBN:0-19-513438-9, ISBN13: 978-0-19-513438-4. Dewey:780/.92 B. LCCN:99-025255.

Audience: **g,l,u,f.** *Choice, 2000.*

Fay, Laurel E. (Editor)   **ML410.S53**
Shostakovich and His World. Trade Cloth. Princeton University Press. Princeton, NJ. 2004. 432p. The Bard Music Festival Ser. ISBN:0-691-12068-4, ISBN13: 978-0-691-12068-3. Dewey:780.9/2. LCCN:2004-104803.

Audience: **g,l,u,f.**

Fearn, Raymond   **ML410.D138F43 2003**
The Music of Luigi Dallapiccola. Trade Cloth. University of Rochester Press. Rochester, NY. 2005. 324p. Eastman Studies in Music ISBN:1-58046-078-X, ISBN13: 978-1-58046-078-1. Dewey:780/.92. LCCN:2003-007367.

Audience: **u,f.** *Choice, 2004.*

Feder, Stuart   **ML410.I94 F42 1999**
The Life of Charles Ives. Cloth Text. Cambridge University Press. New York, NY. 1999. 214p. Musical Lives Ser. ISBN:0-521-59072-8, ISBN13: 978-0-521-59072-3. Dewey:780/.92 B. LCCN:98-049662.

Audience: **g,l,u,f.**

Feldman, Morton   **ML410.M9**
Give My Regards to Eighth Street: Collected Writings of Morton Feldman. B. H. Friedman (Editor), Frank O'Hara (Foreword by). Trade Paper. Exact Change. Cambridge, MA. 2003. 256p. ISBN:1-878972-31-6, ISBN13: 978-1-878972-31-6. Dewey:780.9/2.

Audience: **u,f.**

Forte, Allen   **ML410.W33F67 1998**
The Atonal Music of Anton Webern. Cloth over Boards. Yale University Press. Cumberland, RI. 1999. 416p. Composers of the Twentieth Century Ser. ISBN:0-300-07352-6, ISBN13: 978-0-300-07352-2. Dewey:780/.92. LCCN:97-049645.

Audience: **u,f.** *Choice, 1999.*

Forte, Allen   **MT100.S968 F7**
The Harmonic Organization of the Rite of Spring. Trade Paper. Yale University Press. Cumberland, RI. 1978. 160p. ISBN:0-300-10537-1, ISBN13: 978-0-300-10537-7. Dewey:782.9/5/0924.

Audience: **u,f.**

Franklin, Peter   **ML410.M23 F69 1997**
The Life of Mahler. Trade Paper. Cambridge University Press. New York, NY. 1997. 238p. Musical Lives Ser. ISBN:0-521-46761-6, ISBN13: 978-0-521-46761-2. Dewey:780/.92 B. LCCN:96-025105.

Audience: **g,l,u,f.**

Frisch, Walter (Editor)   **ML410.S283S36 1999**
Schoenberg and His World. Cloth Text. Princeton University Press. Princeton, NJ. 1999. 350p. The Bard Music Festival Ser. ISBN:0-691-04860-6, ISBN13: 978-0-691-04860-4. Dewey:780/.92. LCCN:99-031792.

Audience: **g,l,u,f.** *Choice, 2000.*

Fulcher, Jane F. (Editor)   **ML410.D28D37 2001**
Debussy and His World. Trade Cloth. Princeton University Press. Princeton, NJ. 2001. 350p. The Bard Music Festival Ser. ISBN:0-691-09041-6, ISBN13: 978-0-691-09041-2. Dewey:780/.92. LCCN:2001-027840.

Audience: **g,l,u,f.** *Choice, 2002.*

Gagne, Cole   **ML390.S6682 1993**
Soundpieces Two: Interviews with American Composers. Trade Cloth. Scarecrow Press, Inc. Lanham, MD. 1993. 568p. ISBN:0-8108-2710-7, ISBN13: 978-0-8108-2710-3. Dewey:780/.92/273. LCCN:93-034663.

Audience: **u,f.** *Choice, 1994.*

Gagne, Cole & Caras, Tracy   **ML390**
Soundpieces: Interviews with American Composers. Gene Bagnato (Photographer), Nicolas Slonimsky & Gilbert Chase

(Introduction by). Trade Cloth. Scarecrow Press, Inc. Lanham, MD. 1982. 436p. ISBN:0-8108-1474-9, ISBN13: 978-0-8108-1474-5. Dewey:780/.92/2. LCCN:81-013520.

Audience: **u,f.**

Gann, Kyle   ML200.5.G36 1997
American Music in the Twentieth Century. Cloth Text. Thomson Wadsworth. Belmont, CA. 1997. 416p. ISBN:0-02-864655-X, ISBN13: 978-0-02-864655-8. Dewey:780/.973/0904. LCCN:97-019863.

Audience: **g,l,u,f.** *Choice, 1998.*

Gann, Kyle   MT92.N36 G36 1995
The Music of Conlon Nancarrow. Arnold Whittall (Contribution by). Trade Cloth. Cambridge University Press. New York, NY. 1995. 316p. Music in the Twentieth Century Ser., No. 7 ISBN:0-521-46534-6, ISBN13: 978-0-521-46534-2. Dewey:786.2/092. LCCN:94-029969.

Audience: **u,f.**

Gilbert, Steven E.   ML410.G288G55 1995
The Music of Gershwin. Cloth over Boards. Yale University Press. Cumberland, RI. 1995. 268p. Composers of the Twentieth Century Ser. ISBN:0-300-06233-8, ISBN13: 978-0-300-06233-5. Dewey:780.9/2. LCCN:95-012086.

Audience: **u,f.** *Choice, 1996.*

Gilliam, Bryan   ML410.S93 G53 1999
The Life of Richard Strauss. Trade Paper. Cambridge University Press. New York, NY. 1999. 210p. Musical Lives Ser. ISBN:0-521-57895-7, ISBN13: 978-0-521-57895-0. Dewey:780/.92 B. LCCN:98-047947.

Audience: **g,l,u,f.** *Choice, 2000.*

Gilliam, Bryan (Editor)   ML410.S93 R44 1992
Richard Strauss and His World. Trade Paper. Princeton University Press. Princeton, NJ. 1992. 438p. Princeton Paperbacks Ser. ISBN:0-691-02762-5, ISBN13: 978-0-691-02762-3. Dewey:780.9/2. LCCN:92-015748.

Audience: **g,l,u,f.** *Choice, 1993.*

Gilliam, Bryan   ML410.S93G54 1996
Richard Strauss's Elektra. Trade Paper. Oxford University Press, Inc. New York, NY. 1996. 284p. Studies in Musical Genesis and Structure ISBN:0-19-816602-8, ISBN13: 978-0-19-816602-3. Dewey:782.1/092. LCCN:95-049506.

Audience: **u,f.** *Choice, 1992.*

Gillies, Malcolm (Editor)   ML410.B26B274 1994
The Bartok Companion. Trade Cloth. Hal Leonard Corporation. Milwaukee, WI. 1994. 592p. ISBN:0-931340-74-8, ISBN13: 978-0-931340-74-1. Dewey:780/.92 B. LCCN:94-193114.

Audience: **g,l,u,f.**

Gillies, Malcolm   ML410.B26.G463 1990
Bartok Remembered. Trade Cloth. W. W. Norton & Company, Inc. New York, NY. 1991. xl, 238p. ISBN:0-393-02971-9, ISBN13: 978-0-393-02971-0. Dewey:780.92. LCCN:91-188227.

Audience: **g,l,u,f.** *Choice, 1991.*

Gillies, Malcolm & Pear,   ML410.G75G55 2002
  David (Editors)
Portrait of Percy Grainger. Trade Cloth. University of Rochester Press. Rochester, NY. 2002. 242p. Eastman Studies in Music ISBN:1-58046-087-9, ISBN13: 978-1-58046-087-3. Dewey:780/.92 B. LCCN:2001-048100.

Audience: **u,f.**

Gillmor, Alan M.   ML410.S196G54 1988
Erik Satie. Trade Cloth. Macmillan Publishing Company, Inc. Old Tappan, NJ. 1988. 408p. Twayne's Music Ser. ISBN:0-8057-9472-7, ISBN13: 978-0-8057-9472-4. Dewey:780/.92/4 B. LCCN:87-037381.

Audience: **g,l,u,f.** *Choice, 1988.*

Gilmore, Bob   ML410.P176G55 1998
Harry Partch: A Biography. Cloth over Boards. Yale University Press. Cumberland, RI. 1998. 480p. ISBN:0-300-06521-3, ISBN13: 978-0-300-06521-3. Dewey:[B]. LCCN:97-039140.

Audience: **g,l,u,f.**

Giroud, Francoise   DB844.M34G5713 1991
Alma Mahler: Or the Art of Being Loved. R. M. Stock (Editor, Translator). Trade Cloth. Oxford University Press, Inc. New York, NY. 1992. 176p. ISBN:0-19-816156-5, ISBN13: 978-0-19-816156-1. Dewey:780/.92 B. LCCN:91-003678.

Audience: **u,f.**

Glass, Philip   ML410.G398A3 1995
Music by Philip Glass. Robert T. Jones (Editor). Paper Text. Da Capo Press, Inc. Cambridge, MA. 1995. 432p. ISBN:0-306-80636-3, ISBN13: 978-0-306-80636-0. Dewey:780/.92/4 B. LCCN:95-005009.

Audience: **u,f.** *Choice, 1988.*

Glinsky, Albert   ML429.T43G6 2000
Theremin: Ether Music and Espionage. Robert Moog (Foreword by). Trade Cloth. University of Illinois Press. Champaign, IL. 2000. 480p. Music in American Life Ser. ISBN:0-252-02582-2, ISBN13: 978-0-252-02582-2. Dewey:786.7/3 B. LCCN:00-008024.

Audience: **g,l,u,f.** *Choice, 2001.*

Goldberg, Roselee &   NX512.A54G65 2000
  Anderson, Laurie
Laurie Anderson. Trade Cloth. Harry N. Abrams, Inc. New York, NY. 2000. 204p. ISBN:0-8109-3582-1, ISBN13: 978-0-8109-3582-2. Dewey:709.2. LCCN:99-044944.

Audience: **l,u,f.**

Gordon, Eric A.   ML410.B6515
Mark the Music: The Life and Work of Marc Blitzstein. Trade Paper. iUniverse, Inc. Lincoln, NE. 2000. 644p. ISBN:0-595-09248-9, ISBN13: 978-0-595-09248-2. Dewey:780/.92/4 B.

Audience: **g,l,u,f.**

Gould, Glenn & Page, Tim   ML60.G68 1984
The Glenn Gould Reader. Trade Cloth. Alfred A. Knopf Inc. New York, NY. 1984. 441p. ISBN:0-394-54067-0, ISBN13: 978-0-394-54067-2. Dewey:780. LCCN:84-047819.

Audience: **u,f.** *B*

Grainger, Percy   **ML60.G74 1999**
Grainger on Music. Malcolm Gillies & Bruce Ross (Editors).
Trade Cloth. Oxford University Press, Inc. New York, NY. 1999.
416p. ISBN:0-19-816665-6, ISBN13: 978-0-19-816665-8.
Dewey:780. LCCN:98-045828.

Audience: **u,f.**

Greene, Richard   **ML410.H748 G74 1995**
Holst: The Planets. Julian Rushton (Contribution by). Cloth
Text. Cambridge University Press. New York, NY. 1995. 110p.
Music Handbks. ISBN:0-521-45000-4, ISBN13:
978-0-521-45000-3. Dewey:784.2/1858. LCCN:94-017175.

Audience: **u,f.** *Choice, 1995.*

Griffiths, Paul   **ML410.M9**
Gyorgy Ligeti: Contemporary Composer. Trade Paper. Anova
Books. London, 1997. 160p. ISBN:1-86105-058-5, ISBN13:
978-1-86105-058-8. Dewey:780.9/2.

Audience: **u,f.**

Griffiths, Paul   **ML197.G76 1995**
Modern Music and After. Ed. 2. Paper Text. Oxford University
Press, Inc. New York, NY. 1996. 388p. ISBN:0-19-816511-0,
ISBN13: 978-0-19-816511-8. Dewey:780.9/04.
LCCN:95-013369.

Audience: **g,l,u,f.** *Choice, 1996.*

Grimley, Daniel M. (Editor)   **ML410.S54C36 2003**
The Cambridge Companion to Sibelius. Cloth Text. Cambridge
University Press. New York, NY. 2004. 294p. Cambridge
Companions to Music Ser. ISBN:0-521-81552-5, ISBN13:
978-0-521-81552-9. Dewey:780/.92. LCCN:2003-051521.

Audience: **g,l,u,f.** *Choice, 2004.*

Haimo, Ethan   **ML410.S283H33 1990**
Schoenberg's Serial Odyssey: The Evolution of His
Twelve-Tone Method, 1914-1928. Trade Cloth. Oxford
University Press, Inc. New York, NY. 1990. 208p.
ISBN:0-19-315260-6, ISBN13: 978-0-19-315260-1.
Dewey:781.3. LCCN:88-019617.

Audience: **u,f.** *Choice, 1991.*

Hall, Charles J. (Compiled   **ML197.H15 1989**
by)
A Twentieth-Century Musical Chronicle: Events, 1900-1988, 20.
Library Binding. Greenwood Publishing Group, Inc. Portsmouth,
NH. 1989. 358p. ISBN:0-313-26577-1, ISBN13:
978-0-313-26577-8. Dewey:780/.9/04. LCCN:89-002138.

Audience: **u,f.** *Choice, 1990.*

Harley, James   **ML410.X45H37 2004**
Xenakis: His Life in Music. Paper over Boards. Routledge. New
York, NY. 2004. 296p. ISBN:0-415-97145-4, ISBN13:
978-0-415-97145-4. Dewey:780/.92 B. LCCN:2004-002283.

Audience: **u,f.**

Harris, Donald (Editor), et   **ML410.B47A4 1987**
al.
The Berg-Schoenberg Correspondence: Selected Letters.
Christopher Hailey & Juliane Brand (Editors). Trade Cloth. W.

W. Norton & Company, Inc. New York, NY. 1987. xxviii, 497p.
ISBN:0-393-01919-5, ISBN13: 978-0-393-01919-3.
Dewey:780/.92/2. LCCN:86-008346.

Audience: **u,f.** *Choice, 1988.*

Headlam, Dave   **ML410.B47H43 1996**
The Music of Alban Berg. Cloth over Boards. Yale University
Press. Cumberland, RI. 1996. 472p. Composers of the Twentieth
Century Ser. ISBN:0-300-06400-4, ISBN13: 978-0-300-06400-1.
Dewey:780.9/2. LCCN:95-046936.

Audience: **u,f.** *Choice, 1997.*

Heffley, Mike   **ML410**
The Music of Anthony Braxton. Trade Cloth. Greenwood
Publishing Group, Inc. Portsmouth, NH. 1996. 504p.
Contributions to the Study of Music and Dance Ser., No. 43
ISBN:0-313-29956-0, ISBN13: 978-0-313-29956-8.
Dewey:781.65/092. LCCN:95-043113.

Audience: **u,f.**

Hefling, Stephen E.   **MT121.M34 H44 2000**
Mahler: Das Lied Von der Erde (The Song of the Earth). Cloth
Text. Cambridge University Press. New York, NY. 2000. 173p.
Music Handbks. ISBN:0-521-47534-1, ISBN13:
978-0-521-47534-1. Dewey:782.4/7. LCCN:99-023189.

Audience: **u,f.**

Henze, Hans W. & Spencer,   **ML410.H483A3 1998**
Stewart
Bohemian Fifths: An Autobiography. Cloth Text. Princeton
University Press. Princeton, NJ. 1999. 520p.
ISBN:0-691-00683-0, ISBN13: 978-0-691-00683-3.
Dewey:780/.92 B. LCCN:98-037783.

Audience: **u,f.**

Hepokoski, James A.   **ML410.S54 H4 1993**
Sibelius: Symphony No. 5. Julian Rushton (Contribution by).
Cloth Text. Cambridge University Press. New York, NY. 1993.
121p. Music Handbks. ISBN:0-521-40143-7, ISBN13:
978-0-521-40143-2. Dewey:784.2184. LCCN:92-021614.

Audience: **u,f.**

Hess, Carol A. (Contribution   **ML410.F215H48 2004**
by)
Sacred Passions: The Life and Music of Manuel de Falla. Trade
Cloth. Oxford University Press, Inc. New York, NY. 2004. 368p.
ISBN:0-19-514561-5, ISBN13: 978-0-19-514561-8.
Dewey:780/.92 B. LCCN:2004-041472.

Audience: **u,f.** *Choice, 2005.*

Heyman, Barbara B.   **ML410.M9**
Samuel Barber: The Composer and His Music. Trade Paper.
Oxford University Press, Inc. New York, NY. 1994. 608p.
ISBN:0-19-509058-6, ISBN13: 978-0-19-509058-1.
Dewey:780/.92. LCCN:91-002454.

Audience: **l,u,f.** *Choice, 1993.*

Hicks, Michael   **ML410.C859H53 2002**
Henry Cowell, Bohemian. Trade Cloth. University of Illinois
Press. Champaign, IL. 2002. 240p. Music in American Life Ser.

ISBN:0-252-02751-5, ISBN13: 978-0-252-02751-2. Dewey:780/.92 B. LCCN:2001-007064.

Audience: **g,l,u,f.**   *Choice, 2003.*

Hill, Peter (Editor)   **ML410.M595M48 1995**
The Messiaen Companion. Trade Paper. Hal Leonard Corporation. Milwaukee, WI. 1995. 584p. ISBN:0-931340-94-2, ISBN13: 978-0-931340-94-9. Dewey:780/.92. LCCN:95-170368.

Audience: **l,u,f.**   *Choice, 1995.*

Hill, Peter   **ML410.S932 H55 2000**
Stravinsky: The Rite of Spring. Julian Rushton (Contribution by). Cloth Text. Cambridge University Press. New York, NY. 2000. 180p. Music Handbks. ISBN:0-521-62221-2, ISBN13: 978-0-521-62221-9. Dewey:784.2/1556. LCCN:00-023703.

Audience: **l,u,f.**

Hill, Peter & Simeone, Nigel   **ML410**
Messiaen. Saddle Stitched, Cloth over Boards, Dust Jacket. Yale University Press. Cumberland, RI. 2005. 352p. ISBN:0-300-10907-5, ISBN13: 978-0-300-10907-8. Dewey:780.92.

Audience: **u,f.**   *Choice, 2006.*

Hillier, Paul   **ML410.P1755H55 1997**
Arvo Part. Trade Paper. Oxford University Press, Inc. New York, NY. 1997. 232p. Oxford Studies of Composers ISBN:0-19-816616-8, ISBN13: 978-0-19-816616-0. Dewey:780.9/2. LCCN:96-026035.

Audience: **u,f.**

Ho, Allan & Feofanov, Dmitry   **ML410.S53H58 1998**
Shostakovich Reconsidered. Allan Ho & Dmitry Feofanov (Editors), Vladimir Ashkenazy (Translator). Trade Cloth. Toccata Press. London, 1998. 788p. ISBN:0-907689-56-6, ISBN13: 978-0-907689-56-0. Dewey:780/.92. LCCN:98-221223.

Audience: **g,l,u,f.**   *Choice, 1999.*

Holmes, Thom   **ML1380**
Electronic and Experimental Music: Pioneers in Technology and Composition. Ed. 2. Paper over Boards. Routledge. New York, NY. 2002. 336p. ISBN:0-415-93643-8, ISBN13: 978-0-415-93643-9. Dewey:781.69.

Audience: **l,u,f.**

Howat, Roy   **ML410.M9**
Debussy in Proportion: A Musical Analysis. Trade Paper. Cambridge University Press. New York, NY. 1986. 246p. ISBN:0-521-31145-4, ISBN13: 978-0-521-31145-8. Dewey:780.9/2.

Audience: **u,f.**

Hyland, William G.   **ML410**
George Gershwin: A New Biography. Trade Cloth. Greenwood Publishing Group, Inc. Portsmouth, NH. 2003. 312p. ISBN:0-275-98111-8, ISBN13: 978-0-275-98111-2. Dewey:780/.92 B. LCCN:2003-046303.

Audience: **l,u,f.**   *Choice, 2004.*

Jablonski, Edward   **ML410.G288J29 1998**
Gershwin: A Biography. Trade Paper. Da Capo Press, Inc. Cambridge, MA. 1998. 460p. ISBN:0-306-80847-1, ISBN13: 978-0-306-80847-0. Dewey:780/.92 B. LCCN:98-011830.

Audience: **l,u,f.**   *Choice, 1988.*

Jaffe, Daniel   **ML410.M9**
Sergey Prokofiev. Trade Paper. Phaidon Press. London, 1998. 240p. Twentieth-Century Composers Ser. ISBN:0-7148-3513-7, ISBN13: 978-0-7148-3513-6. Dewey:780.9/2.

Audience: **l,u,f.**

Jameux, Dominique   **ML410.B773J313 1990**
Pierre Boulez. Susan Bradshaw (Translator). Trade Cloth. Harvard University Press. Cambridge, MA. 1990. 436p. ISBN:0-674-66740-9, ISBN13: 978-0-674-66740-2. Dewey:781.3092. LCCN:90-004715.

Audience: **l,u,f.**   *Choice, 1991.*

Janacek, Leos & Cheek, Timothy   **ML49.J36J37 2003**
The Janacek Opera Libretti: Translations and Pronunciation. Trade Cloth. Scarecrow Press, Inc. Lanham, MD. 2003. 224p. ISBN:0-8108-4671-3, ISBN13: 978-0-8108-4671-5. Dewey:782.1/0268. LCCN:2002-153032.

Audience: **u,f.**

Jarman, Douglas (Editor)   **ML410.B47J28 1991**
Alban Berg: "Lulu". Cloth Text. Cambridge University Press. New York, NY. 1991. 160p. Cambridge Opera Handbooks Ser. ISBN:0-521-24150-2, ISBN13: 978-0-521-24150-2. Dewey:782.1. LCCN:90-001637.

Audience: **u,f.**   *Choice, 1991.*

Jarman, Douglas (Editor)   **ML410.B47B53 1990**
The Berg Companion. Cloth Text. Northeastern University Press. Boston, MA. 1990. 301p. ISBN:1-55553-068-0, ISBN13: 978-1-55553-068-6. Dewey:780/.92. LCCN:89-008581.

Audience: **l,u,f.**   *Choice, 1990.*

Jarman, Douglas   **ML410.B47.J33**
The Music of Alban Berg. Trade Cloth. University of California Press. Berkeley, CA. 1979. xii, 266p. ISBN:0-520-03485-6, ISBN13: 978-0-520-03485-3. Dewey:780/.92/4. LCCN:77-076687.

Audience: **l,u,f.**

Jarman, Douglas   **ML410.B47 J3 1989**
Alban Berg: Wozzeck. Richard Wagner (Contribution by). Trade Paper. Cambridge University Press. New York, NY. 1989. 192p. Cambridge Opera Handbooks Ser. ISBN:0-521-28481-3, ISBN13: 978-0-521-28481-3. Dewey:782.109. LCCN:88-015965.

Audience: **l,u,f.**   *Choice, 1990.*

Jefferson, Alan   **ML410.S93**
Richard Strauss, Der Rosenkavalier. Cambridge; New York: Cambridge University Press. 1985. Cambridge Opera Handbooks ISBN:0-521-26036-1, ISBN13: 978-0-521-26036-7.

Audience: **l,u,f.**

Joseph, Charles M.   ML410.S932J665 2002
Stravinsky and Balanchine: A Journey of Invention. Cloth over
Boards. Yale University Press. Cumberland, RI. 2002. 464p.
ISBN:0-300-08712-8, ISBN13: 978-0-300-08712-3.
Dewey:781.5/56/092. LCCN:2001-007130.

Audience: **l,u,f.**

Joseph, Charles M.   ML410.S932J68 2001
Stravinsky Inside Out. Cloth over Boards. Yale University Press.
Cumberland, RI. 2001. 352p. ISBN:0-300-07537-5, ISBN13:
978-0-300-07537-3. Dewey:780/.92 B. LCCN:2001-000913.

Audience: **l,u,f.** *Choice, 2002.*

Jowitt, Deborah (Editor)   ML410.M72M47 1997
Meredith Monk. Trade Cloth. Johns Hopkins University Press.
Baltimore, MD. 1997. 224p. PAJ Bks., :Art and Performance
ISBN:0-8018-5539-X, ISBN13: 978-0-8018-5539-9.
Dewey:700/.92. LCCN:97-006597.

Audience: **l,u,f.**

Kallir, Jane   NS511.5.S37
Arnold Schoenberg's Vienna. Trade Paper. Rizzoli International
Publications, Inc. New York, NY. 1985. 120p.
ISBN:0-8478-0580-8, ISBN13: 978-0-8478-0580-8.
Dewey:759.36.

Audience: **l,u,f.**

Kelly, Barbara L.   ML410.M674K45 2002
Tradition and Style in the Works of Darius Milhaud 1912-1939.
Trade Cloth. Ashgate Publishing, Ltd. Aldershot, 2003. 228p.
ISBN:0-7546-3033-1, ISBN13: 978-0-7546-3033-3.
Dewey:780/.92. LCCN:2002-074468.

Audience: **u,f.** *Choice, 2004.*

Kennedy, Michael   ML410.S93 K46 1999
Richard Strauss: Man, Musician, Enigma. Trade Cloth.
Cambridge University Press. New York, NY. 1999. 472p.
ISBN:0-521-58173-7, ISBN13: 978-0-521-58173-8.
Dewey:780/.92 B. LCCN:98-035860.

Audience: **g,l,u,f.** *Choice, 1999.*

Kennedy, Michael   ML410.B4
The Works of Ralph Vaughan Williams. Ed. 2. Paper Text.
Oxford University Press, Inc. New York, NY. 1994. 464p.
ISBN:0-19-816330-4, ISBN13: 978-0-19-816330-5.
Dewey:780/.92/4.

Audience: **u,f.**

Kirkpatrick, John & Ives,   ML410.M9
  Charles
Charles E. Ives: Memos. Trade Paper. W. W. Norton &
Company, Inc. New York, NY. 1991. 355p.
ISBN:0-393-30756-5, ISBN13: 978-0-393-30756-6.
Dewey:780.92.

Audience: **u,f.**

Kostelanetz, Richard   ML410.C24K68 2003
Conversing with Cage. Ed. 2. Paper over Boards. Routledge.
New York, NY. 2002. 344p. ISBN:0-415-93791-4, ISBN13:
978-0-415-93791-7. Dewey:780.92. LCCN:2003-555574.

Audience: **u,f.** *Choice, 1988.*

Kostelanetz, Richard   ML420.P96
The Frank Zappa Companion: Four Decades of Commentary.
Trade Paper. Music Sales Corporation. New York, NY. 1997.
300p. Companion Ser. ISBN:0-8256-7181-7, ISBN13:
978-0-8256-7181-4. Dewey:782.4/2/166/092. LCCN:96-041352.

Audience: **g,l,u,f.**

Kostelanetz, Richard   ML410.M9
  (Editor)
Virgil Thomson Reader: Selected Writings, 1924-1984. Paper
over Boards. Routledge. New York, NY. 2002. 304p.
ISBN:0-415-93795-7, ISBN13: 978-0-415-93795-5.
Dewey:780.9/2.

Audience: **l,u,f.**

Kostelanetz, Richard   ML410.M9
  (Editor)
Writings about John Cage. Trade Cloth. University of Michigan
Press. Chicago, IL. 1993. 376p. ISBN:0-472-10348-2, ISBN13:
978-0-472-10348-5. Dewey:780.9/2. LCCN:92-032218.

Audience: **g,l,u,f.** *Choice, 1994.*

Kostelanetz, Richard   ML410.G398
Writings on Glass: Essays, Interviews, Criticism. New York:
Schirmer Books. 1997. ISBN:0-02-864657-6, ISBN13:
978-0-02-864657-2.

Audience: **u,f.**

Kostelanetz, Richard   ML55
  (Editor)
Classic Essays on Twentieth-Century Music : A Continuing
Symposium. Darby, Joseph (Editor). Schirmer Books. 1996.
ISBN:0-02-864581-2, ISBN13: 978-0-02-864581-0.

Audience: **g,l,u,f.**

Kurtz, Michael   ML410.M9
Stockhausen: A Biography. Richard Toop (Translator). Trade
Paper. Faber & Faber, Inc. New York, NY. 1994. 270p.
ISBN:0-571-17146-X, ISBN13: 978-0-571-17146-0.
Dewey:780.92.

Audience: **l,u,f.**

La Grange, Henry-Louis de   ML410.M23
Mahler. London, Victor Gollancz Ltd. 1974.
ISBN:0-575-01672-8, ISBN13: 978-0-575-01672-9.

Audience: **l,u,f.**

Laki, Peter   ML410.B26B272 1995
Bartok and His World. Cloth Text. Princeton University Press.
Princeton, NJ. 1995. 250p. The Bard Music Festival Ser.
ISBN:0-691-00634-2, ISBN13: 978-0-691-00634-5.
Dewey:780.9/2. LCCN:95-013368.

Audience: **g,l,u,f.** *Choice, 1996.*

Lambert, Philip   ML410.M9
The Music of Charles Ives. Trade Paper. Yale University Press.
Cumberland, RI. 1997. 256p. Composers of the Twentieth
Century Serie Ser. ISBN:0-300-10534-7, ISBN13:
978-0-300-10534-6. Dewey:780/.92 B.

Audience: **u,f.** *Choice, 1998.*

Lawson, Jack ML410.M9
Carl Nielsen. Trade Paper. Phaidon Press. London, 1997. 240p.
Twentieth-Century Composers Ser. ISBN:0-7148-3507-2,
ISBN13: 978-0-7148-3507-5. Dewey:780.9/2.

Audience: **u,f.**

Lee, Douglas ML1255
Masterworks of 20th-Century Music: The Modern Repertory of
the Symphony Orchestra. UK-B Format Paperback. Routledge.
New York, NY. 2002. 528p. ISBN:0-415-93847-3, ISBN13:
978-0-415-93847-1. Dewey:784.1/84.

Audience: **g,l,u,f.**

Lysloff, Rene T. A. & Gay, ML197.M78 2003
  Leslie C. (Editors)
Music and Technoculture. Library Binding. Wesleyan University
Press. Middletown, CT. 2003. 416p. Music/Culture Ser.
ISBN:0-8195-6513-X, ISBN13: 978-0-8195-6513-6.
Dewey:780/.06. LCCN:2003-004628.

Audience: **u,f.** *Choice, 2004.*

MacDonald, Ian ML410.S53
The New Shostakovich. Cloth Text. Northeastern University
Press. Boston, MA. 1990. 352p. ISBN:1-55553-089-3, ISBN13:
978-1-55553-089-1. Dewey:780/.92.

Audience: **l,u,f.** *Choice, 1991.*

MacDonald, Malcolm ML410
Varese: Astronomer in Sound. Trade Paper. Kahn & Averill
Publishers. London, 2003. 448p. ISBN:1-871082-79-X, ISBN13:
978-1-871082-79-1. Dewey:780.9/2.

Audience: **l,u,f.**

Maconie, Robin ML410.S858M29 2005
Other Planets: The Music of Karlheinz Stockhausen. Book,
Other. Scarecrow Press, Inc. Lanham, MD. 2005. 592p.
ISBN:0-8108-5356-6, ISBN13: 978-0-8108-5356-0.
Dewey:780/.92. LCCN:2004-062109.

Audience: **u,f.** *Choice, 2005.*

Mallach, Alan ML410.M39M25 2002
Pietro Mascagni and His Operas. Trade Cloth. Northeastern
University Press. Boston, MA. 2002. 320p.
ISBN:1-55553-524-0, ISBN13: 978-1-55553-524-7.
Dewey:782.1/092 B. LCCN:2001-059191.

Audience: **l,u,f.** *Choice, 2003, 2002.*

Manning, Peter D. ML1380.M36 2004
Electronic and Computer Music. Trade Paper. Oxford University
Press, Inc. New York, NY. 2004. 484p. ISBN:0-19-517085-7,
ISBN13: 978-0-19-517085-6. Dewey:786.7/09.
LCCN:2002-155278.

Audience: **u,f.**

Martin, George MT95.M253 1999
Twentieth Century Opera: A Guide. Trade Paper. Hal Leonard
Corporation. Milwaukee, WI. 1998. 703p. ISBN:0-87910-275-6,
ISBN13: 978-0-87910-275-3. Dewey:782.1/09/04.
LCCN:99-027953.

Audience: **u,f.**

Maurice, Donald G. ML410.B26
Bartok's Viola Concerto: The Remarkable Story of His
Swansong. Trade Cloth. Oxford University Press, Inc. New
York, NY. 2004. 234p. Studies in Musical Genesis and Structure
ISBN:0-19-515690-0, ISBN13: 978-0-19-515690-4.
Dewey:784.2/73. LCCN:2003-026914.

Audience: **u,f.** *Choice, 2004.*

Mawer, Deborah (Editor) ML410.R23 C36 2000
The Cambridge Companion to Ravel. Trade Paper. Cambridge
University Press. New York, NY. 2000. 310p. Cambridge
Companions to Music Ser. ISBN:0-521-64856-4, ISBN13:
978-0-521-64856-1. Dewey:780/.92 B. LCCN:99-047568.

Audience: **g,l,u,f.** *Choice, 2001.*

McCalla, James ML1106
Twentieth-Century Chamber Music. Ed. 2. Routledge. 2002.
ISBN:0-415-96695-7, ISBN13: 978-0-415-96695-5.

Audience: **u,f.**

McGregor, Richard (Editor) ML410.D254P47 2000
Perspectives on Peter Maxwell Davies. Trade Cloth. Ashgate
Publishing, Ltd. Aldershot, 2000. 194p. ISBN:1-84014-298-7,
ISBN13: 978-1-84014-298-3. Dewey:780/.92. LCCN:00-107423.

Audience: **u,f.**

Mead, Andrew ML410.M9
An Introduction to the Music of Milton Babbit. Cloth Text.
Princeton University Press. Princeton, NJ. 1994. 264p.
ISBN:0-691-03314-5, ISBN13: 978-0-691-03314-3.
Dewey:780.92. LCCN:92-037178.

Audience: **u,f.** *Choice, 1995.*

Mellers, Wilfrid ML410.M9
Francis Poulenc. Paper Text. Oxford University Press, Inc. New
York, NY. 1995. 204p. Oxford Studies of Composers
ISBN:0-19-816338-X, ISBN13: 978-0-19-816338-1.
Dewey:780/.92.

Audience: **l,u,f.** *Choice, 1994.*

Messiaen, Oliver MT6
The Technique of My Musical Language. Library Binding.
Reprint Services Company. Temecula, CA. 1987.
ISBN:0-685-14827-0, ISBN13: 978-0-685-14827-3. Dewey:781.

Audience: **u,f.**

Messiaen, Olivier, et al. ML410.M595
Music and Color: Conversations with Claude Samuel. Samuel,
Claude (Author); Glasow, E. Thomas (Translator). Portland, Or.:
Amadeus Press. 1994. ISBN:0-931340-67-5, ISBN13:
978-0-931340-67-3.

Audience: **u,f.**

Metzer, David Joel ML197.M38Q68 2003
Quotation and Cultural Meaning in Twentieth-Century Music.
Jeffrey Kallberg, Anthony Newcomb & Ruth Solie (Contribution
by). Trade Cloth. Cambridge University Press. New York, NY.
2003. 238p. New Perspectives in Music History and Criticism
Ser. ISBN:0-521-82509-1, ISBN13: 978-0-521-82509-2.
Dewey:781.3. LCCN:2002-031365.

Audience: **u,f.** *Choice, 2004.*

Miles, Barry   ML410.Z285.M49 2004
Zappa: A Biography. Trade Cloth. Grove/Atlantic, Inc. New
York, NY. 2004. 464p. ISBN:0-8021-1783-X, ISBN13:
978-0-8021-1783-0. Dewey:782.42166/092 B.
LCCN:2004-051805.

Audience: **l,u,f.**

Milhaud, Darius   ML410.M674A3 1994
My Happy Life. Donald Evans (Translator), Christopher Palmer
(Translator, Introduction by). Trade Paper. Marion Boyars
Publishers, Inc. New York, NY. 1994. 380p.
ISBN:0-7145-2957-5, ISBN13: 978-0-7145-2957-8.
Dewey:780/.92 B. LCCN:94-009018.

Audience: **u,f.**

Miller, Leta E. &   ML410.H2066M55 2004
  Lieberman, Fredric
Composing a World: Lou Harrison, Musical Wayfarer. Ed. 2.
Trade Paper. University of Illinois Press. Champaign, IL. 2004.
416p. Music in American Life Ser. ISBN:0-252-07188-3,
ISBN13: 978-0-252-07188-1. Dewey:780/.92 B.
LCCN:2004-042201.

Audience: **u,f.**

Minturn, Neil   ML410.P865M56 1997
The Music of Sergei Prokofiev. Cloth over Boards. Yale
University Press. Cumberland, RI. 1997. 256p. Composers of
the Twentieth Century Ser. ISBN:0-300-06366-0, ISBN13:
978-0-300-06366-0. Dewey:780.92. LCCN:96-027064.

Audience: **u,f.** *Choice, 1998.*

Mitchell, Donald   ML410.M23M48 2002
Gustav Mahler: Songs and Symphonies of Life and Death -
Interpretations and Annotations. Trade Paper. Boydell & Brewer,
Ltd. Woodbridge, 2005. 664p. ISBN:0-85115-908-7, ISBN13:
978-0-85115-908-9. Dewey:780.92. LCCN:2002-036674.

Audience: **l,u,f.**

Mitchell, Donald   ML410.B4978
Gustav Mahler: the Wunderhorn Years: Chronicles and
Commentaries. Ed. 3. Trade Paper. Boydell & Brewer, Ltd.
Woodbridge, 2005. 528p. ISBN:1-84383-003-5, ISBN13:
978-1-84383-003-0. Dewey:780.92.

Audience: **l,u,f.**

Mitchell, Donald   ML410.M23
Gustav Mahler: The Early Years. Ed. 3. Paul Banks & Donald
Matthews (Revised by). Trade Paper. Boydell & Brewer, Ltd.
Woodbridge, 2003. 372p. ISBN:1-84383-002-7, ISBN13:
978-1-84383-002-3. Dewey:780/.92 B. LCCN:2004-269960.

Audience: **l,u,f.**

Mitchell, Donald (Author,   ML410.M9
  Editor)
The Mahler Companion. Andrew Nicholson (Editor). Trade
Paper. Oxford University Press, Inc. New York, NY. 2002. 668p.
ISBN:0-19-924965-2, ISBN13: 978-0-19-924965-7.
Dewey:780/.92.

Audience: **g,l,u,f.** *Choice, 2000.*

Moldenhauer, Hans &   ML410.W33.M55 1979
  Moldenhauer, Rosaleen
Anton Von Webern: A Chronicle of His Life and Work. Trade
Cloth. Alfred A. Knopf Inc. New York, NY. 1979. 803p.
ISBN:0-394-47237-3, ISBN13: 978-0-394-47237-9.
Dewey:780/.92/4. LCCN:77-020370.

Audience: **u,f.**

Morgan, Robert P.   ML197
Modern Times: From World War I to the Present. Ed. 1.
Prentice Hall. 1994. ISBN:0-13-590159-6, ISBN13:
978-0-13-590159-5.

Audience: **u,f.**

Morgan, Robert P.   ML197
Twentieth-Century Music : A History of Musical Style in
Modern Europe and America. Ed. 1. Norton. 1991. The Norton
Introduction to Music History ISBN:0-393-95272-X, ISBN13:
978-0-393-95272-8.

Audience: **g,l,u,f.**

Myers, Paul   ML410.B566M84 1998
Leonard Bernstein. Trade Paper. Phaidon Press. London, 1998.
240p. Twentieth-Century Composers Ser. ISBN:0-7148-3701-6,
ISBN13: 978-0-7148-3701-7. Dewey:780/.92 B.
LCCN:99-182081.

Audience: **l,u,f.**

Nectoux, Jean-Michel   ML410.F27 N413 1991
Gabriel Fauré: A Musical Life. Roger Nichols (Translator).
Trade Paper. Cambridge University Press. New York, NY. 2004.
672p. ISBN:0-521-61695-6, ISBN13: 978-0-521-61695-9.
Dewey:780.92 B. LCCN:2005-280639.

Audience: **u,f.** *Choice, 1992.*

Neumeyer, David   ML410.H685N5 1986
The Music of Paul Hindemith. Trade Cloth. Yale University
Press. Cumberland, RI. 1986. 312p. ISBN:0-300-03287-0,
ISBN13: 978-0-300-03287-1. Dewey:780/.92/4.
LCCN:85-014495.

Audience: **u,f.** *Choice, 1986.*

Newman, William S.   ML1156
The Sonata since Beethoven. Ed. 3. Trade Cloth. W. W. Norton
& Company, Inc. New York, NY. 1983. xxvi, 870p.
ISBN:0-393-95290-8, ISBN13: 978-0-393-95290-2.
Dewey:781/.52/09. LCCN:82-024573.

Audience: **u,f.**

Nice, David   ML410.P865
Prokofiev: A Biography: From Russia to the West, 1891-1935.
Cloth over Boards. Yale University Press. Cumberland, RI.
2003. 416p. ISBN:0-300-09914-2, ISBN13: 978-0-300-09914-0.
Dewey:780/.92 B. LCCN:2004-296430.

Audience: **u,f.** *Choice, 2004.*

Nicholls, David (Editor)   ML410.C24 C36 2002
The Cambridge Companion to John Cage. Jonathan Cross
(Contribution by). Trade Paper. Cambridge University Press.
New York, NY. 2002. 302p. Cambridge Companions to Music

Ser. ISBN:0-521-78968-0, ISBN13: 978-0-521-78968-4.
Dewey:780/.92 B. LCCN:2001-052401.

Audience: **l,u,f.** *Choice, 2003.*

Nichols, Roger   **ML410.D28 N55 1998**
The Life of Debussy. Trade Paper. Cambridge University Press.
New York, NY. 1998. 192p. Musical Lives Ser.
ISBN:0-521-57887-6, ISBN13: 978-0-521-57887-5.
Dewey:780/.92 B. LCCN:97-025666.

Audience: **g,l,u,f.** *Choice, 1998.*

Nichols, Roger   **ML410.M9**
Debussy Remembered. Claude Debussy (Composed by). Trade
Cloth. Hal Leonard Corporation. Milwaukee, WI. 1992. 264p.
ISBN:0-931340-41-1, ISBN13: 978-0-931340-41-3.
Dewey:780.92. LCCN:92-226956.

Audience: **l,u,f.**

Nichols, Roger & Smith,   **ML410.D28 N48 1989**
  Richard Langham
Claude Debussy: Pelléas et Mélisande. Richard Wagner
(Contribution by). Trade Paper. Cambridge University Press.
New York, NY. 1989. 224p. Cambridge Opera Handbooks Ser.
ISBN:0-521-31446-1, ISBN13: 978-0-521-31446-6.
Dewey:782.1. LCCN:88-016172.

Audience: **u,f.** *Choice, 1989.*

Norris, Geoffrey   **ML410.R12N67 2000**
Rachmaninoff. Ed. 2. Trade Paper. Oxford University Press, Inc.
New York, NY. 2006. 216p. Master Musicians Ser.
ISBN:0-19-816488-2, ISBN13: 978-0-19-816488-3.
Dewey:780.9/2. LCCN:00-057115.

Audience: **u,f.** *Choice, 1994.*

Noss, Luther   **ML410.H685N7 1989**
Paul Hindemith in the United States. Trade Cloth. University of
Illinois Press. Champaign, IL. 1989. 248p. Music in American
Life Ser. ISBN:0-252-01563-0, ISBN13: 978-0-252-01563-2.
Dewey:780/.92/4 B. LCCN:88-010694.

Audience: **u,f.** *Choice, 1989.*

Nyman, Michael   **ML197 .N85 1999**
Experimental Music: Cage and Beyond. Ed. 2. Robert Worby
(Contribution by), Brian Eno (Foreword by), Arnold Whittall
(Contribution by). Trade Paper. Cambridge University Press.
New York, NY. 1999. 216p. Music in the Twentieth Century Ser.
ISBN:0-521-65383-5, ISBN13: 978-0-521-65383-1.
Dewey:780/.904. LCCN:98-031731.

Audience: **g,l,u,f.**

Oja, Carol J.   **ML200.8.N5O43 2000**
Making Music Modern: New York in the 1920s. Trade Cloth.
Oxford University Press, Inc. New York, NY. 2000. 507p.
ISBN:0-19-505849-6, ISBN13: 978-0-19-505849-9.
Dewey:780/.9747/109042. LCCN:99-052604.

Audience: **u,f.**

Oja, Carol J. & Tick, Judith   **ML410**
  (Editors)
Aaron Copland and His World. Trade Paper, Perfect. Princeton

University Press. Princeton, NJ. 2005. 328p. The Bard Music
Festival Ser. ISBN:0-691-12470-1, ISBN13: 978-0-691-12470-4.
Dewey:780.92.

Audience: **g,l,u,f.**

Oliveros, Pauline   **ML60**
Software for People. Trade Cloth. Printed Editions. West Glover,
VT. 1985. 320p. Music Ser. ISBN:0-914162-59-4, ISBN13:
978-0-914162-59-9. Dewey:780.

Audience: **u,f.**

Orenstein, Arbie   **ML410.R23O73 1991**
Ravel: Man and Musician. Trade Paper. Dover Publications, Inc.
Mineola, NY. 1991. 352p. ISBN:0-486-26633-8, ISBN13:
978-0-486-26633-6. Dewey:780/.92 B. LCCN:91-002789.

Audience: **g,l,u,f.**

Orledge, Robert   **ML410.M9**
Satie Remembered. Trade Cloth. Hal Leonard Corporation.
Milwaukee, WI. 1995. 272p. ISBN:1-57467-000-X, ISBN13:
978-1-57467-000-4. Dewey:780.9/2. LCCN:95-198285.

Audience: **u,f.** *Choice, 1996.*

Orledge, Robert   **ML410.S196O74 1990**
Satie the Composer. Trade Cloth. Cambridge University Press.
New York, NY. 1990. 437p. Music in the Twentieth Century
Ser., No. 1 ISBN:0-521-35037-9, ISBN13: 978-0-521-35037-2.
Dewey:780/.92. LCCN:89-022309.

Audience: **u,f.** *Choice, 1991.*

Osmond-Smith, David   **ML410.B4968O55 1990**
Berio. Trade Cloth. Oxford University Press, Inc. New York,
NY. 1991. 176p. Oxford Studies of Composers, No. 20
ISBN:0-19-315478-1, ISBN13: 978-0-19-315478-0.
Dewey:780/.92 B. LCCN:90-007368.

Audience: **l,u,f.** *Choice, 1991.*

Osmond-Smith, David   **MT115.B58 O8 1985**
Playing on Words: A Guide to Luciano Berio's Sinfonia. Trade
Cloth. Ashgate Publishing, Ltd. Aldershot, 1985. 104p. Royal
Musical Association Monographs ISBN:0-947854-00-2, ISBN13:
978-0-947854-00-3. Dewey:785.1/1/0924. LCCN:85-154370.

Audience: **u,f.**

Painter, Karen (Editor)   **ML410.M23**
Mahler and His World. Trade Paper. Princeton University Press.
Princeton, NJ. 2002. 408p. The Bard Music Festival Ser.
ISBN:0-691-09244-3, ISBN13: 978-0-691-09244-7.
Dewey:780/.92.

Audience: **g,l,u,f.** *Choice, 2003.*

Parks, Richard S.   **ML410.D28P24 1989**
The Music of Claude Debussy. Cloth over Boards. Yale
University Press. Cumberland, RI. 1990. 360p. Composers of
the Twentieth Century Ser. ISBN:0-300-04439-9, ISBN13:
978-0-300-04439-3. Dewey:780/.92/4. LCCN:89-031406.

Audience: **u,f.** *Choice, 1990.*

Partch, Harry   **MT7**
Genesis of a Music: An Account of a Creative Work, Its Roots,
and Its Fulfillments. Ed. 2. Trade Paper. Da Capo Press, Inc.

Cambridge, MA. 1979. 544p. Music Reprint Ser. ISBN:0-306-80106-X, ISBN13: 978-0-306-80106-8. Dewey:781. LCCN:76-087373.

Audience: **u,f.**

Partch, Harry   ML410.M9
Bitter Music: Collected Journals, Essays, Introductions and Librettos. Thomas McGeary (Editor, Introduction by). Trade Paper. University of Illinois Press. Champaign, IL. 2000. 520p. Music in American Life Ser. ISBN:0-252-06913-7, ISBN13: 978-0-252-06913-0. Dewey:780/.92 B.

Audience: **u,f.** *Choice, 1991.*

Perle, George   ML410.B47
The Operas of Alban Berg: Lulu. Trade Cloth. University of California Press. Berkeley, CA. 1984. 352p. ISBN:0-520-04502-5, ISBN13: 978-0-520-04502-6. Dewey:782.1092. LCCN:76-052033.

Audience: **u,f.** *Choice, 1985.*

Perle, George   ML410.B47
The Operas of Alban Berg: Wozzeck. Trade Cloth. University of California Press. Berkeley, CA. 1980. 325p. ISBN:0-520-03440-6, ISBN13: 978-0-520-03440-2. Dewey:782.1/092/4. LCCN:76-052033.

Audience: **u,f.**

Perle, George & Berg,   MT145.B47P47 2001
 Alban
Style and Idea in the Lyric Suite of Alban Berg. Ed. 2. Trade Cloth. Pendragon Press. Hillsdale, NY. 2001. xv, 112p. ISBN:1-57647-085-7, ISBN13: 978-1-57647-085-5. Dewey:785/.7194. LCCN:2001-052345.

Audience: **u,f.**

Perlis, Vivian   ML410.I94P5 2002
Charles Ives Remembered: An Oral History. Trade Paper. University of Illinois Press. Champaign, IL. 2002. 264p. Music in American Life Ser. ISBN:0-252-07078-X, ISBN13: 978-0-252-07078-5. Dewey:780/.92 B. LCCN:2001-055532.

Audience: **l,u,f.**

Pike, Lionel   MT125 .P55
Beethoven, Sibelius and "The Profound Logic": Studies in Symphonic Analysis. Cloth Text. Continuum International Publishing Group, Ltd. London, 1978. 240p. ISBN:0-485-11178-0, ISBN13: 978-0-485-11178-1. Dewey:785.1/1/0922. LCCN:79-309070.

Audience: **u,f.**

Pike, Lionel   ML422.K22
Vaughan Williams and the Symphony. Cloth over Boards. Toccata Press. London, 2003. 352p. ISBN:0-907689-54-X, ISBN13: 978-0-907689-54-6. Dewey:784.2092.

Audience: **u,f.**

Pople, Anthony (Editor)   ML410.B47 C38 1997
The Cambridge Companion to Berg. Jonathan Cross (Contribution by). Cloth Text. Cambridge University Press. New York, NY. 1997. 320p. Cambridge Companions to Music Ser.

ISBN:0-521-56374-7, ISBN13: 978-0-521-56374-1. Dewey:780/.92 B. LCCN:96-039727.

Audience: **l,u,f.** *Choice, 1998.*

Pople, Anthony   ML410.B47 P6 1991
Berg: Violin Concerto. Julian Rushton (Contribution by). Trade Paper. Cambridge University Press. New York, NY. 1991. 130p. Music Handbks. ISBN:0-521-39976-9, ISBN13: 978-0-521-39976-0. Dewey:784.2/72. LCCN:90-002542.

Audience: **u,f.**

Pople, Anthony   ML410.M595 P58 1998
Messiaen: Quatuor Pour la Fin du Temps. Julian Rushton (Contribution by). Cloth Text. Cambridge University Press. New York, NY. 1998. 126p. Music Handbks. ISBN:0-521-58497-3, ISBN13: 978-0-521-58497-5. Dewey:785/.24194. LCCN:98-023937.

Audience: **u,f.** *Choice, 1999.*

Potter, Caroline   ML410.D965P68 1997
Henri Dutilleux: His Life and Works. Trade Cloth. Ashgate Publishing, Ltd. Aldershot, 1997. 272p. ISBN:1-85928-330-6, ISBN13: 978-1-85928-330-1. Dewey:[B]. LCCN:96-040411.

Audience: **u,f.**

Potter, Keith   N/A
Four Musical Minimalists: La Monte Young, Terry Riley, Steve Reich, Philip Glass. Arnold Whittall (Contribution by). Cloth Text. Cambridge University Press. New York, NY. 2000. 406p. Music in the Twentieth Century Ser., No. 11 ISBN:0-521-48250-X, ISBN13: 978-0-521-48250-9. Dewey:780/.92/273. LCCN:99-011736.

Audience: **u,f.** *Choice, 2001.*

Pritchett, James   ML410.M9
The Music of John Cage. Arnold Whittall (Contribution by). Trade Paper. Cambridge University Press. New York, NY. 1996. 237p. Music in the Twentieth Century Ser., No. 5 ISBN:0-521-56544-8, ISBN13: 978-0-521-56544-8. Dewey:780.9/2.

Audience: **u,f.**

Prokofiev, Sergei   ML410.P865
Prokofiev by Prokofiev: A Composer's Memoir. Trade Cloth. Doubleday Publishing. New York, NY. 1979. ISBN:0-385-09960-6, ISBN13: 978-0-385-09960-8. Dewey:780/.92/4. LCCN:77-025605.

Audience: **l,u,f.**

Prokofiev, Sergei   ML410.P865.A3 1992
Soviet Diary, 1927 and Other Writings. Oleg Prokofiev & Christopher Palmer (Editors), Oleg Prokofiev (Translator). Cloth Text. Northeastern University Press. Boston, MA. 1992. 290p. ISBN:1-55553-120-2, ISBN13: 978-1-55553-120-1. Dewey:780.92. LCCN:91-045921.

Audience: **u,f.** *Choice, 1993.*

Puffett, Derrick (Editor)   ML410.S93R485 1989
Richard Strauss: "Elektra". Cloth Text. Cambridge University Press. New York, NY. 1990. 187p. Cambridge Opera Handbooks

Ser. ISBN:0-521-35173-1, ISBN13: 978-0-521-35173-7.
Dewey:782.1/092/4. LCCN:89-000499.

Audience: **u,f.** *Choice, 1990.*

Puffett, Derrick (Editor)   ML410.S93 R52 1989
Richard Strauss: Salome. Richard Wagner (Contribution by).
Trade Paper. Cambridge University Press. New York, NY. 1989.
224p. Cambridge Opera Handbooks Ser. ISBN:0-521-35970-8,
ISBN13: 978-0-521-35970-2. Dewey:782.109.
LCCN:89-000500.

Audience: **u,f.** *Choice, 1990.*

Radano, Ronald M.   ML419.B735.R3 1993
New Musical Figurations: Anthony Braxton's Cultural Critique.
Trade Cloth. University of Chicago Press. Chicago, IL. 1994.
336p. ISBN:0-226-70195-6, ISBN13: 978-0-226-70195-0.
Dewey:788.7165092. LCCN:93-001878.

Audience: **u,f.** *Choice, 1994.*

Rae, Charles B.   ML410.M9
The Music of Lutoslawski. Ed. 3. Trade Cloth. Omnibus Press.
New York, NY. 1999. 318p. ISBN:0-7119-6910-8, ISBN13:
978-0-7119-6910-0. Dewey:780.92.

Audience: **u,f.**

Ravel, Maurice   ML410.R23A4 2003
A Ravel Reader: Correspondence, Articles, Interviews. Arbie
Orenstein (Editor). Trade Paper. Dover Publications, Inc.
Mineola, NY. 2003. 704p. ISBN:0-486-43078-2, ISBN13:
978-0-486-43078-2. Dewey:780/.92 B. LCCN:2003-047259.

Audience: **l,u,f.**

Reich, Steve   ML60.R352 2002
Writings on Music, 1965-2000. Paul Hillier (Editor, Introduction
by). Trade Paper. Oxford University Press, Inc. New York, NY.
2004. 270p. ISBN:0-19-515115-1, ISBN13: 978-0-19-515115-2.
Dewey:789/.9/04. LCCN:2001-037477.

Audience: **l,u,f.**

Reynolds Roger   ML197.R5 2005
Mind Models: New Forms of Musical Experience. Ed. 2. Paper
over Boards. Routledge. New York, NY. 2005. 208p.
ISBN:0-415-97428-3, ISBN13: 978-0-415-97428-8.
Dewey:780/.9/04. LCCN:2005-013083.

Audience: **u,f.**

Rickards, Guy   ML410.S54
Jean Sibelius. London: Phaidon Press. 1997.
ISBN:0-7148-3581-1, ISBN13: 978-0-7148-3581-5.

Audience: **l,u,f.**

Rischin, Rebecca   ML410.M595R57 2003
For the End of Time: The Story of the Messiaen Quartet. Book,
Other. Cornell University Press. Ithaca, NY. 2003. 184p.
ISBN:0-8014-4136-6, ISBN13: 978-0-8014-4136-3.
Dewey:785/.24194. LCCN:2003-011589.

Audience: **u,f.** *Choice, 2004.*

Roads, Curtis   MT723
The Music Machine: Selected Readings from Computer Music

Journal. Trade Paper. MIT Press. Cambridge, MA. 1992. 739p.
ISBN:0-262-68078-5, ISBN13: 978-0-262-68078-3.
Dewey:786.7/6.

Audience: **u,f.**

Roberts, Paul   ML410.C54
Images: The Piano Music of Claude Debussy. Trade Paper. Hal
Leonard Corporation. Milwaukee, WI. 2003. 372p.
ISBN:1-57467-068-9, ISBN13: 978-1-57467-068-4.
Dewey:786.2/092.

Audience: **l,u,f.** *Choice, 1996.*

Robinson, Harlow (Author,   ML410.P865R55 2002
  Foreword by, Afterword by)
Sergei Prokofiev: A Biography. Trade Paper. Northeastern
University Press. Boston, MA. 2005. 632p.
ISBN:1-55553-517-8, ISBN13: 978-1-55553-517-9.
Dewey:780/.92/4. LCCN:2002-070919.

Audience: **l,u,f.** *Choice, 1987.*

Rochberg, George   ML60.R62 2004
The Aesthetics of Survival: A Composer's View of
Twentieth-Century Music. Trade Paper. University of Michigan
Press. Chicago, IL. 2005. 288p. ISBN:0-472-03026-4, ISBN13:
978-0-472-03026-2. Dewey:780/.9/04. LCCN:2004-051645.

Audience: **u,f.**

Rosenstiel, Leonie   ML410.B4
Nadia Boulanger: A Life in Music. Trade Paper. W. W. Norton
& Company, Inc. New York, NY. 1998. 440p.
ISBN:0-393-31713-7, ISBN13: 978-0-393-31713-8.
Dewey:780/.92/4. LCCN:81-018811.

Audience: **l,u,f.**

Russolo, Luigi   ML3877.R8713 1986
The Art of Noises. Barclay Brown (Translator). Library Binding.
Pendragon Press. Hillsdale, NY. 1987. 87p. Monographs in
Musicology, No. 6 ISBN:0-918728-57-6, ISBN13:
978-0-918728-57-9. Dewey:789.9/8. LCCN:85-028413.

Audience: **u,f.**

Salzman, Eric   ML197.S17 2002
Twentieth Century Music: An Introduction. Ed. 4. Trade Paper.
Prentice Hall PTR. Upper Saddle River, NJ. 2001. 337p.
Prentice-Hall History of Music Ser. ISBN:0-13-095941-3,
ISBN13: 978-0-13-095941-6. Dewey:780/.9/04.
LCCN:2001-021466.

Audience: **g,l,u,f.**

Samson, Jim   ML3809
Music in Transition: A Study of Tonal Expansion and Atonality,
1900-1920. Paper Text. Oxford University Press, Inc. New York,
NY. 1995. 256p. ISBN:0-460-86150-6, ISBN13:
978-0-460-86150-2. Dewey:781/.22.

Audience: **u,f.**

Satie, Erik   ML410.M9
A Mammal's Notebook: Collected Writings of Erik Satie.
Ornella Volta (Editor), Anthony Melville (Translator). Trade

Cloth. Atlas Press. London, 1997. 208p. Atlas Arkhive Ser., Vol. 5 ISBN:0-947757-92-9, ISBN13: 978-0-947757-92-2. Dewey:780.92.

Audience: **u,f.**

Schebera, Jurgen   ML410.W395S3513 1995
Kurt Weill: An Illustrated Life. Caroline Murphy (Translator). Cloth over Boards. Yale University Press. Cumberland, RI. 1995. 400p. ISBN:0-300-06055-6, ISBN13: 978-0-300-06055-3. Dewey:780.9/2. LCCN:94-041444.

Audience: **l,u,f.** *Choice, 1996.*

Schiff, David   ML410.C3293S34 1998
The Music of Elliott Carter. Ed. 2. Elliott Carter (Foreword by). Trade Cloth. Cornell University Press. Ithaca, NY. 1998. 356p. ISBN:0-8014-3612-5, ISBN13: 978-0-8014-3612-3. Dewey:780/.92. LCCN:98-033956.

Audience: **u,f.** *Choice, 1999.*

Schiff, David   ML410.G288 S27 1997
Gershwin: Rhapsody in Blue. Julian Rushton (Contribution by). Cloth Text. Cambridge University Press. New York, NY. 1997. 132p. Music Handbks. ISBN:0-521-55077-7, ISBN13: 978-0-521-55077-2. Dewey:784.2/62. LCCN:96-047439.

Audience: **l,u,f.**

Schloezer, Boris   ML410.S5988S313 1987
Scriabin: Artist and Mystic. Nicolas Slonimsky (Translator), Marina Scriabine (Introduction by). Trade Cloth. University of California Press. Berkeley, CA. 1987. 336p. ISBN:0-520-04384-7, ISBN13: 978-0-520-04384-8. Dewey:780/.92/4 B. LCCN:86-040109.

Audience: **l,u,f.** *Choice, 1988.*

Schneider, Wayne (Editor)   ML410.G288.G49 1999
The Gershwin Style: New Looks at the Music of George Gershwin. Trade Cloth. Oxford University Press, Inc. New York, NY. 1999. 304p. ISBN:0-19-509020-9, ISBN13: 978-0-19-509020-8. Dewey:780.9/2. LCCN:97-050590.

Audience: **u,f.** *Choice, 1999.*

Schnittke, Alfred   ML197.S2627 2002
e A Schnittke Reader. John Goodliffe (Translator), Mstislav Rostropovich (Preface by). E-Book. Indiana University Press. Bloomington, IN. 2002. 352p. Russian Music Studies ISBN:0-253-33818-2, ISBN13: 978-0-253-33818-1. Dewey:780/.92. LCCN:2001-005133.

Audience: **u,f.**

Schoenberg, Arnold   ML60.S374S8 1985
Style and Idea: Selected Writings of Arnold Schoenberg. Leonard Stein (Editor), Leo Black (Translator). Trade Paper. University of California Press. Berkeley, CA. 1984. 560p. ISBN:0-520-05294-3, ISBN13: 978-0-520-05294-9. Dewey:780. LCCN:84-002604.

Audience: **l,u,f.** *B*

Schuller, Gunther   ML60.S392 1999
Musings: The Musical Worlds of Gunther Schuller. Trade Paper.

Da Capo Press, Inc. Cambridge, MA. 1999. 416p. ISBN:0-306-80902-8, ISBN13: 978-0-306-80902-6. Dewey:780. LCCN:98-048220.

Audience: **u,f.**

Schwartz, Elliott   ML1092.S37 1989
Electronic Music: A Listener's Guide. Paper Text. Da Capo Press, Inc. Cambridge, MA. 1989. 306p. Music Reprint Ser. ISBN:0-306-76260-9, ISBN13: 978-0-306-76260-4. Dewey:789.9/9. LCCN:84-021508.

Audience: **g,l,u,f.**

Schwartz, Elliott, et al.   ML197.C7512 1998
Contemporary Composers on Contemporary Music. Ed. 2. Barney Childs & Jim Fox (Authors). Trade Paper. Da Capo Press, Inc. Cambridge, MA. 1998. 510p. ISBN:0-306-80819-6, ISBN13: 978-0-306-80819-7. Dewey:780/.9/04. LCCN:97-045587.

Audience: **g,l,u,f.** *B*

Schwartz, Elliott & Godfrey,   ML197 .S35 1992
Daniel
Music since 1945: Issues, Materials, and Literature. Cloth Text. Thomson Wadsworth. Belmont, CA. 1993. 560p. ISBN:0-02-873040-2, ISBN13: 978-0-02-873040-0. Dewey:780/.9/04. LCCN:92-011959.

Audience: **g,l,u,f.**

Schwinger, Wolfram   ML410.B4
Krzysztof Penderecki: His Life and Work. William Mann (Translator). Trade Paper. European American Music Distributors Corporation. New York, NY. 1989. 292p. ISBN:0-946535-11-6, ISBN13: 978-0-946535-11-8. Dewey:780/.92/4.

Audience: **u,f.**

Secrest, Meryle   ML410.M9
Leonard Bernstein: A Life. Trade Cloth. Random House Value Publishing. New York, NY. 1997. RHVP-Remainder Ser. ISBN:0-517-19882-7, ISBN13: 978-0-517-19882-7. Dewey:780.9/2.

Audience: **l,u,f.** *Choice, 1995.*

Sessions, Roger & Cone,   ML60.S514
Edward T. (Editors)
Roger Sessions on Music: Collected Essays. Trade Cloth. Princeton University Press. Princeton, NJ. 1979. 400p. ISBN:0-691-09126-9, ISBN13: 978-0-691-09126-6. Dewey:780/.8. LCCN:78-051190.

Audience: **u,f.** *B*

Sherwood, Gayle   ML134.I9S44 2002
Charles Ives: Guide to Research. Paper over Boards. Garland Publishing, Inc. New York, NY. 2002. 176p. Routledge Musical Bibliographies Ser. ISBN:0-8153-3821-X, ISBN13: 978-0-8153-3821-5. Dewey:016.780/92. LCCN:2002-075204.

Audience: **l,u,f.**

Shostakovich, Dmitrii   ML410.S53
Dmitrievich
Testimony: The Memoirs of Dmitri Shostakovich. Volkov,

Solomon (Editor); Ashkenazy, Vladimir (Foreword by); Bouis, Antonina W. (Translator). New York: Limelight Editions. 2004. ISBN:0-87910-998-X, ISBN13: 978-0-87910-998-1.

Audience: **u,f.**

Simms, Bryan R.   ML410.S283S45 2000
The Atonal Music of Arnold Schoenberg, 1908-1923. Trade Cloth. Oxford University Press, Inc. New York, NY. 2000. 274p. ISBN:0-19-512826-5, ISBN13: 978-0-19-512826-0. Dewey:780/.92. LCCN:99-035938.

Audience: **u,f.** *Choice, 2001.*

Simms, Bryan R.   ML197.C748 1999
Composers on Modern Music Culture: An Anthology of Source Readings on Twentieth-Century Music. Paper Text. Thomson Wadsworth. Belmont, CA. 1999. 286p. ISBN:0-02-864751-3, ISBN13: 978-0-02-864751-7. Dewey:780/.9/04. LCCN:98-014757.

Audience: **u,f.** *Choice, 1999.*

Simms, Bryan R.   ML197
Music of the Twentieth Century: Style and Structure. Ed. 2. Digital, Other. Thomson Wadsworth. Belmont, CA. 1996. ISBN:0-02-864602-9, ISBN13: 978-0-02-864602-2. Dewey:780/.904.

Audience: **g,l,u,f.** *Choice, 1997.*

Simoni, Mary   ML1380.A53 2005
Analytical Methods of Electroacoustic Music. Cloth Text. Routledge. New York, NY. 2005. 312p. Studies on New Music Research ISBN:0-415-97629-4, ISBN13: 978-0-415-97629-9. Dewey:781.2. LCCN:2005-014484.

Audience: **u,f.**

Sitsky, Larry (Editor)   ML390
Music of the Twentieth-Century Avant-Garde: A Biocritical Sourcebook. Cloth Text. Greenwood Publishing Group, Inc. Portsmouth, NH. 2002. 680p. ISBN:0-313-29689-8, ISBN13: 978-0-313-29689-5. Dewey:780/.9/04. LCCN:2002-276826.

Audience: **u,f.** *Choice, 2003.*

Skelton, Geoffrey   ML410.H685 S6
Paul Hindemith: The Man Behind the Music. Trade Cloth. Taplinger Publishing Company, Inc. Marlboro, NJ. 1977. ISBN:0-87597-107-5, ISBN13: 978-0-87597-107-0. Dewey:780/.92/4.

Audience: **l,u,f.**

Slonimsky, Nicolas, et al.   ML197
Music since 1900. Ed. 6. Kuhn, Laura Diane (Author). Schirmer Reference. 2001. ISBN:0-02-864787-4, ISBN13: 978-0-02-864787-6.

Audience: **g,l,u,f.**

Smith, Catherine P.   ML410.S855 S65 2000
William Grant Still: A Study in Contradictions. D. G. Murchison & Willard Gatewood (Contribution by). Trade Cloth. University of California Press. Berkeley, CA. 2000. 384p. Music of the African Diaspora Ser., Vol. 2 ISBN:0-520-21542-7, ISBN13: 978-0-520-21542-9. Dewey:780/.92. LCCN:99-043232.

Audience: **l,u,f.**

Smith, Stuart S. & DeLio, Thomas (Editors)   ML197.W77 1989
Words and Spaces: An Anthology of Twentieth Century Musical Experiments in Language and Sonic Environments. Trade Paper. University Press of America, Inc. Lanham, MD. 1989. 280p. ISBN:0-8191-7426-2, ISBN13: 978-0-8191-7426-0. Dewey:780/.904. LCCN:89-005609.

Audience: **u,f.** *Choice, 1990.*

Smither, Howard E.   ML3201 .S6
The Oratorio in the Nineteenth and Twentieth Centuries. Trade Cloth. University of North Carolina Press. Chapel Hill, NC. 2000. 856p. History of the Oratorio Ser., Vol. 4 ISBN:0-8078-2511-5, ISBN13: 978-0-8078-2511-2. Dewey:782.2309034. LCCN:76-043980.

Audience: **u,f.**

Steinitz, Richard   ML410.L645S84 2003
Gyorgy Ligeti: Music of the Imagination. Trade Cloth. Northeastern University Press. Boston, MA. 2005. 416p. ISBN:1-55553-551-8, ISBN13: 978-1-55553-551-3. Dewey:780/.92. LCCN:2002-035896.

Audience: **l,u,f.** *Choice, 2003.*

Stevens, Halsey   ML410.M9
The Life and Music of Bela Bartok. Ed. 3. Trade Paper. Oxford University Press, Inc. New York, NY. 1993. 382p. ISBN:0-19-816349-5, ISBN13: 978-0-19-816349-7. Dewey:780.92.

Audience: **l,u,f.**

Stivender, David   ML410.M393
Mascagni: An Autobiography Compiled, Edited and Translated from Original Sources. Trade Cloth. Bold Strummer, Limited, The. Westport, CT. 1988. 388p. ISBN:0-912483-06-7, ISBN13: 978-0-912483-06-1. Dewey:782.1092.

Audience: **u,f.** *Choice, 1989.*

Stockhausen, Karlheinz   ML3845
Stockhausen on Music: Lectures and Interviews. Robin Maconie (Compiled by). Trade Paper. Marion Boyars Publishers, Inc. New York, NY. 2000. 220p. ISBN:0-7145-2918-4, ISBN13: 978-0-7145-2918-9. Dewey:780.1.

Audience: **l,u,f.** *Choice, 1989.*

Straus, Joseph N.   ML197.S767 1990
Remaking the Past: Musical Modernism and the Influence of the Tonal Tradition. Trade Cloth. Harvard University Press. Cambridge, MA. 1990. 264p. ISBN:0-674-75990-7, ISBN13: 978-0-674-75990-9. Dewey:780/.9/04. LCCN:89-024721.

Audience: **u,f.** *Choice, 1990.*

Straus, Joseph N.   ML410.S932 S72 2001
Stravinsky's Late Music. Ian Bent (Contribution by). Trade Paper. Cambridge University Press. New York, NY. 2004. 278p. Cambridge Studies in Music Theory and Analysis Ser., Vol. 16 ISBN:0-521-60288-2, ISBN13: 978-0-521-60288-4. Dewey:780/.92.

Audience: **u,f.**

Straus, Joseph N.   ML410.S4446S77 1995
The Music of Ruth Crawford Seeger. Arnold Whittall
(Contribution by). Trade Paper. Cambridge University Press.
New York, NY. 2003. 272p. Music in the Twentieth Century
Ser., Vol. 6 ISBN:0-521-54818-7, ISBN13: 978-0-521-54818-2.
Dewey:780/.92.
                              Audience: **u,f.** *Choice, 1996.*

Strauss, Richard   ML50.S918S32 1988
Salome and Elektra. Nicholas John (Editor). Trade Paper.
Riverrun Press, Inc. Flemington, NJ. 1989. 144p. English
National Opera Guide Ser., No. 37:Bilingual Libretto, Articles
ISBN:0-7145-4131-1, ISBN13: 978-0-7145-4131-0.
Dewey:782.1/2. LCCN:88-006444.
                                        Audience: **g,l,u,f.**

Strauss, Richard   ML50.M939
Der Rosenkavalier. Nicholas John (Editor), Alfred Kalisch
(Translator). Trade Paper. Riverrun Press, Inc. Flemington, NJ.
1982. English National Opera Guide Series: Bilingual Libretto,
Articles, No. 8 ISBN:0-7145-3851-5, ISBN13:
978-0-7145-3851-8. Dewey:782.10268.
                                        Audience: **g,l,u,f.**

Stravinsky, Igor   ML410.M9
Stravinsky: An Autobiography. Trade Paper. W. W. Norton &
Company, Inc. New York, NY. 1998. 192p.
ISBN:0-393-31856-7, ISBN13: 978-0-393-31856-2.
Dewey:780.92.
                                        Audience: **u,f.**

Stravinsky, Igor, et al.   ML410.S932
Conversations with Igor Stravinsky. Craft, Robert (Author).
Garden City, N.Y., Doubleday. 1977.
                                        Audience: **u,f.**

Stravinsky, Igor, et al.   ML410.S932
Themes and Episodes. Craft, Robert (Author). New York, A.A.
Knopf. 1966.
                                        Audience: **u,f.**

Stravinsky, Igor & Craft,   ML0410.S932A
  Robert
Dialogues. Trade Paper. Books on Demand. Ann Arbor, MI.
152p. ISBN:0-7837-4848-5, ISBN13: 978-0-7837-4848-1.
Dewey:780/.92/4. LCCN:82-050247.
                                        Audience: **u,f.**

Stravinsky, Igor & Craft,   ML410.S932
  Robert
Expositions and Developments. Trade Paper. University of
California Press. Berkeley, CA. 1981. ISBN:0-520-04403-7,
ISBN13: 978-0-520-04403-6. Dewey:784.092.
                                        Audience: **u,f.**

Stravinsky, Igor & Craft,   ML410.S932 A35
  Robert
Memories and Commentaries, Vol. 1. Trade Paper. Faber &
Faber, Inc. New York, NY. 2003. 320p. ISBN:0-571-21163-1,
ISBN13: 978-0-571-21163-0. Dewey:780/.92/4.
                                        Audience: **u,f.**

Stravinsky, Igor   ML49.S77O32 1991
Oedipus Rex and the Rake's Progress. Nicholas John (Editor).
Trade Paper. Riverrun Press, Inc. Flemington, NJ. 1991. 112p.
English National Opera Guide Series: Bilingual Libretto,
Articles, No. 43 ISBN:0-7145-4193-1, ISBN13:
978-0-7145-4193-8. Dewey:782.1. LCCN:90-026770.
                                        Audience: **g,l,u,f.**

Stravinsky, Igor   MT7
Poetics of Music in the Form of Six Lessons. George Seferis
(Preface by). Trade Paper. Harvard University Press. Cambridge,
MA. 1993. 160p. The Charles Eliot Norton Lectures
ISBN:0-674-67856-7, ISBN13: 978-0-674-67856-9. Dewey:781.
LCCN:79-099520.
                                        Audience: **g,l,u,f.** *B*

Stravinsky, Vera & Craft,   ML410.S932.S787
  Robert
Stravinsky: In Pictures and Documents. Trade Cloth. Simon &
Schuster. New York, NY. 1979. 688p. ISBN:0-671-24382-9,
ISBN13: 978-0-671-24382-1. Dewey:780/.92/4.
LCCN:78-015375.
                                        Audience: **u,f.**

Strickland, Edward   ML390.S942 1991
American Composers: Dialogues on Contemporary Music. Trade
Paper. Indiana University Press. Bloomington, IN. 1991. 236p.
ISBN:0-253-20643-X, ISBN13: 978-0-253-20643-5.
Dewey:780/.92/273. LCCN:90-046787.
                              Audience: **u,f.** *Choice, 1992.*

Strickland, Edward   NX504
Minimalism: Origins. Trade Paper. Indiana University Press.
Bloomington, IN. 2000. 320p. ISBN:0-253-21388-6, ISBN13:
978-0-253-21388-4. Dewey:780.904.
                                        Audience: **u,f.**

Stuckenschmidt, Hans Heinz   ML410.S283
Schoenberg: His Life, World, and Work. Searle, Humphrey
(Translator). New York: Schirmer Books. 1978.
ISBN:0-02-872480-1, ISBN13: 978-0-02-872480-5.
                                        Audience: **u,f.**

Suchoff, Benjamin   ML410.B26S83 1995
Bartok: Concerto for Orchestra: Understanding Bartok's World.
Cloth Text. Thomson Wadsworth. Belmont, CA. 1995. 266p.
Monuments of Western Music Ser. ISBN:0-02-872495-X,
ISBN13: 978-0-02-872495-9. Dewey:784.2/186.
LCCN:95-010440.
                              Audience: **u,f.** *Choice, 1996.*

Takemitsu, Toru   ML60.T258713 1995
Confronting Silence: Selected Writings. Glenn Glasow &
Yoshiko Kakudo (Translators), Seiji Ozawa (Foreword by),
Glenn Glasow & Yoshiko Kakudo (Preface by). Trade Cloth.
Scarecrow Press, Inc. Lanham, MD. 1995. 730p. Fallen Leaf
Monographs on Contemporary Composers, No. 1
ISBN:0-914913-31-X, ISBN13: 978-0-914913-31-3. Dewey:780.
LCCN:95-009884.
                                        Audience: **u,f.**

Taruskin, Richard F.   ML410.S932.T38 1996
Stravinsky and the Russian Traditions: A Biography of the
Works Through "Mavra". Trade Cloth. University of California
Press. Berkeley, CA. 1996. 1800p. ISBN:0-520-07099-2,
ISBN13: 978-0-520-07099-8. Dewey:780/.92. LCCN:93-028500.
Audience: **l,u,f.** *Choice, 1997.*

Tavener, John   ML410.M9
The Music of Silence: A Composer's Testament. Brian Keeble
(Editor). Trade Paper. Faber & Faber, Inc. New York, NY. 2000.
208p. ISBN:0-571-20088-5, ISBN13: 978-0-571-20088-7.
Dewey:780.9/2.
Audience: **u,f.**

Tick, Judith   ML410.S4446T5 1997
Ruth Crawford Seeger: A Composer's Search for American
Music. Trade Cloth. Oxford University Press, Inc. New York,
NY. 1997. 472p. ISBN:0-19-506509-3, ISBN13:
978-0-19-506509-1. Dewey:780.9/2. LCCN:95-030085.
Audience: **l,u,f.** *Choice, 1998.*

Toop, David   ML63.G624
Haunted Weather: Resonant Spaces, Silence and Memory. Trade
Paper. Serpent's Tail Ltd. London, 2004. 352p.
ISBN:1-85242-812-0, ISBN13: 978-1-85242-812-9.
Dewey:780/.9/05. LCCN:2004-100908.
Audience: **u,f.**

Toop, David   ML197
Ocean of Sound: Aether Talk, Ambient Sound and Imaginary
Worlds. Trade Cloth. Serpent's Tail Ltd. London, 2001. 320p.
ISBN:1-85242-743-4, ISBN13: 978-1-85242-743-6.
Dewey:780.9/04.
Audience: **u,f.**

Toop, Richard   ML410.L645T66 1999
Gyorgy Ligeti. Trade Paper. Phaidon Press. London, 1999. 238p.
Twentieth-Century Composers Ser. ISBN:0-7148-3795-4,
ISBN13: 978-0-7148-3795-6. Dewey:780/.92 B.
LCCN:00-363647.
Audience: **l,u,f.**

Treib, Marc   NA6750.B7P497 1996
Space Calculated in Seconds: The Philips Pavilion, le Corbusier,
Edgard Varese. Trade Cloth. Princeton University Press.
Princeton, NJ. 1996. 302p. ISBN:0-691-02137-6, ISBN13:
978-0-691-02137-9. Dewey:725/.91/0949332. LCCN:96-004114.
Audience: **u,f.**

Trezise, Simon (Editor)   ML410.D28C26 2002
The Cambridge Companion to Debussy. Cloth Text. Cambridge
University Press. New York, NY. 2003. 346p. Cambridge
Companions to Music Ser. ISBN:0-521-65243-X, ISBN13:
978-0-521-65243-8. Dewey:780/.92 B. LCCN:2001-043703.
Audience: **g,l,u,f.** *Choice, 2004.*

Trezise, Simon   ML410.D28 T7 1994
Debussy: La Mer. Julian Rushton (Contribution by). Trade
Paper. Cambridge University Press. New York, NY. 1995. 121p.
Music Handbks. ISBN:0-521-44656-2, ISBN13:
978-0-521-44656-3. Dewey:784.2/1896. LCCN:93-042789.
Audience: **u,f.** *Choice, 1995.*

Trochimczyk, Maja (Editor)   ML410.A6326A5 2002
The Music of Louis Andriessen. Paper over Boards. Routledge.
New York, NY. 2002. 344p. Studies in Contemporary Music and
Culture, No. 7 ISBN:0-8153-3789-2, ISBN13:
978-0-8153-3789-8. Dewey:780/.92 B. LCCN:2001-041855.
Audience: **u,f.**

Tyrrell, John   ML410.J18 A4 1992
Janacek Operas. Cloth Text. Princeton University Press.
Princeton, NJ. 1992. 436p. ISBN:0-691-09148-X, ISBN13:
978-0-691-09148-8. Dewey:782.1/092. LCCN:92-016091.
Audience: **u,f.** *Choice, 1993.*

Tyrrell, John (Editor)   ML410.J18 L49 1982
Leos Janacek: Kat'a Kabanova. Richard Wagner (Contribution
by). Trade Paper. Cambridge University Press. New York, NY.
1982. 248p. Cambridge Opera Handbooks Ser.
ISBN:0-521-29853-9, ISBN13: 978-0-521-29853-7.
Dewey:782.1/092/4. LCCN:81-038505.
Audience: **u,f.**

Van den Toorn, Pieter C.   ML410.S932
The Music of Igor Stravinsky. Trade Cloth. Yale University
Press. Cumberland, RI. 1987. 512p. Composers of the Twentieth
Century Ser. ISBN:0-300-02693-5, ISBN13: 978-0-300-02693-1.
Dewey:780/.92/4. LCCN:82-002560.
Audience: **l,u,f.**

Van den Toorn, Pieter C.   ML410.S932.V38 1988
Stravinsky and the "Rite of Spring": The Beginnings of a
Musical Language. Trade Cloth. University of California Press.
Berkeley, CA. 1987. 200p. ISBN:0-520-05958-1, ISBN13:
978-0-520-05958-0. Dewey:785.3/2/0924. LCCN:86-031778.
Audience: **l,u,f.** *Choice, 1988.*

Varese, Louise   ML410.V27 V272
Varese: A Looking-Glass Diary. Trade Cloth. W. W. Norton &
Company, Inc. New York, NY. 1972. ISBN:0-393-07461-7,
ISBN13: 978-0-393-07461-1. Dewey:785/.0924.
LCCN:74-139392.
Audience: **u,f.**

Von Gunden, Heidi   ML410.O5834
The Music of Pauline Oliveros. Trade Cloth. Scarecrow Press,
Inc. Lanham, MD. 1983. 195p. ISBN:0-8108-1600-8, ISBN13:
978-0-8108-1600-8. Dewey:780/.92/4. LCCN:82-021443.
Audience: **u,f.**

Walsh, Stephen   ML410.B4
The Music of Stravinsky. Trade Paper. Oxford University Press,
Inc. New York, NY. 1993. 326p. ISBN:0-19-816375-4, ISBN13:
978-0-19-816375-6. Dewey:780/.92/4. LCCN:87-012896.
Audience: **l,u,f.**

Walsh, Stephen   ML410.S932W345 1999
Stravinsky: A Creative Spring: Russia and France, 1882-1934.
Trade Cloth. Alfred A. Knopf Inc. New York, NY. 1999. 720p.
ISBN:0-679-41484-3, ISBN13: 978-0-679-41484-1.
Dewey:780/.92 B. LCCN:99-462433.
Audience: **l,u,f.**

Walsh, Stephen   ML410.S932W355 2006
Stravinsky: The Second Exile: France and America, 1934-1971.
Alfre. 2006. ISBN:0-375-40752-9, ISBN13: 978-0-375-40752-9.
         Audience: **l,u,f.**

Walsh, Stephen   ML410.S932 W35 1993
Stravinsky: Oedipus Rex. Julian Rushton (Contribution by).
Cloth Text. Cambridge University Press. New York, NY. 1993.
130p. Music Handbks. ISBN:0-521-40431-2, ISBN13:
978-0-521-40431-0. Dewey:782.1092. LCCN:92-030088.
         Audience: **u,f.**

Wenk, Arthur B.   ML113.W45 1987
Analyses of Nineteenth- and Twentieth-Century Music,
1940-1985. Trade Paper. Music Library Association. Canton,
MA. 1987. 370p. Music Library Association Index and
Bibliography Ser., No. 25 ISBN:0-914954-36-9, ISBN13:
978-0-914954-36-1. Dewey:016.78/0903/4. LCCN:87-005675.
         Audience: **l,u,f.**

White, Eric W.   ML410.B4
Stravinsky: The Composer and His Works. Ed. 2. Trade Cloth.
University of California Press. Berkeley, CA. 1980. 656p.
ISBN:0-520-03985-8, ISBN13: 978-0-520-03985-8.
Dewey:780.9/2. LCCN:66-027667.
         Audience: **l,u,f.**

Whittall, Arnold   ML197.W54 2003
Exploring Twentieth-Century Music: Tradition and Innovation.
Trade Paper. Cambridge University Press. New York, NY. 2003.
250p. ISBN:0-521-01668-1, ISBN13: 978-0-521-01668-1.
Dewey:780/.9/04. LCCN:2002-073825.
         Audience: **u,f.** *Choice, 2003.*

Wightman, Alistair   ML410.S99W54 1999
Karol Szymanowski: His Life and Work. Trade Cloth. Ashgate
Publishing, Ltd. Aldershot, 1999. 492p. ISBN:1-85928-391-8,
ISBN13: 978-1-85928-391-2. Dewey:780/.92 B.
LCCN:99-022690.
         Audience: **u,f.**

Williams, Ralph Vaughan   ML60.V288 1996
National Music and Other Essays. Ed. 2. Ursula Vaughan
Williams (Preface by), Michael Kennedy (Introduction by).
Paper Text. Oxford University Press, Inc. New York, NY. 1996.
328p. ISBN:0-19-816593-5, ISBN13: 978-0-19-816593-4.
Dewey:780/.9. LCCN:95-042483.
         Audience: **u,f.**

Wilson, Paul   ML410.B26W5 1992
The Music of Bela Bartok. Cloth over Boards. Yale University
Press. Cumberland, RI. 1992. 224p. Composers of the Twentieth
Century Ser. ISBN:0-300-05111-5, ISBN13: 978-0-300-05111-7.
Dewey:780.92. LCCN:91-036107.
         Audience: **u,f.** *Choice, 1992.*

Wingfield, Paul   ML410.J18 W56 1992
Janacek: Glagolitic Mass. Julian Rushton (Contribution by).
Cloth Text. Cambridge University Press. New York, NY. 1992.
146p. Music Handbks. ISBN:0-521-38013-8, ISBN13:
978-0-521-38013-3. Dewey:782.32/3. LCCN:91-016986.
         Audience: **u,f.** *Choice, 1993.*

Wyatt, Robert & Johnson,   ML410.G288G47 2004
John Andrew (Editors)
The George Gershwin Reader. Trade Cloth. Oxford University
Press, Inc. New York, NY. 2004. 368p. Readers on American
Musicians Ser. ISBN:0-19-513019-7, ISBN13:
978-0-19-513019-5. Dewey:780/.92. LCCN:2003-016160.
         Audience: **l,u,f.**

Xenakis, Iannis   ML3800.X4 1991
Formalized Music: Thought and Mathematics in Composition.
Library Binding. Pendragon Press. Hillsdale, NY. 1992. 402p.
Harmonologia Ser., No. 6 ISBN:0-945193-24-6, ISBN13:
978-0-945193-24-1. Dewey:781.3. LCCN:90-041022.
         Audience: **u,f.** *Choice, 1992.*

Zemanová, Mirka   ML410.J18
Janácek. Boston : Northeastern University Press. 2002.
ISBN:1-55553-549-6, ISBN13: 978-1-55553-549-0.
         Audience: **l,u,f.**

Zychowicz, James L.   ML410.B42
Mahler's Fourth Symphony. Trade Cloth. Oxford University
Press, Inc. New York, NY. 2000. 206p. Studies in Musical
Genesis, Structure, and Interpretation ISBN:0-19-816206-5,
ISBN13: 978-0-19-816206-3. Dewey:784.2/184.
         Audience: **u,f.**

Studies in Music History, Criticism, Analysis, and Appreciation > Western Classical Literature by Genre > Opera and Ballet

         ML100
☐ Grove Music Online.
http://www.grovemusic.com/
Oxford University Press.
         Audience: **g,l,u,f.**

Abbate, Carolyn   ML3858.A2 1996
Unsung Voices: Opera and Musical Narrative in the Nineteenth
Century. Trade Paper. Princeton University Press. Princeton, NJ.
1996. 304p. Princeton Studies in Opera ISBN:0-691-02608-4,
ISBN13: 978-0-691-02608-4. Dewey:782.1/09/034.
         Audience: **u,f.** *Choice, 1991.*

Abbate, Carolyn & Parker,   MT95.A59 1989
Roger (Editors)
Analyzing Opera: Verdi and Wagner. Trade Cloth. University of
California Press. Berkeley, CA. 1989. 250p. California Studies
in 19th Century Music, No. 6 ISBN:0-520-06157-8, ISBN13:
978-0-520-06157-6. Dewey:782.1/092/2. LCCN:88-021072.
         Audience: **u,f.** *Choice, 1990.*

Allanbrook, Wye J.   ML410.M9
Rhythmic Gesture in Mozart: "Le Nozze Di Figaro" and "Don
Giovanni". Trade Cloth. University of Chicago Press. Chicago,
IL. 1984. xii, 396p. ISBN:0-226-01403-7, ISBN13:
978-0-226-01403-6. Dewey:782.1/092/4. LCCN:83-009184.
         Audience: **u,f.**

Alpert, Hollis   ML410.G288A35 1990
The Life and Times of Porgy and Bess: The Story of an
American Classic. Trade Cloth. Alfred A. Knopf Inc. New York,
NY. 1990. ISBN:0-394-58339-6, ISBN13: 978-0-394-58339-6.
Dewey:782.1. LCCN:89-043367.
Audience: **g,l,u,f.**

Ashbrook, William   ML410.D7
Donizetti. London, Cassell. 1965.
Audience: **l,u,f.**

Ashbrook, William   MT100.P95A8 1985
The Operas of Puccini. Roger Parker (Foreword by). Trade
Paper. Cornell University Press. Ithaca, NY. 1985. 288p. Cornell
Paperbacks Ser. ISBN:0-8014-9309-9, ISBN13:
978-0-8014-9309-6. Dewey:782.1/092/4. LCCN:84-072674.
Audience: **g,l,u,f.**

Balanchine, George, et al.   MT95.B31977
Balanchine's Complete Stories of the Great Ballets. Francis
Mason & Jeffrey Bairstow (Authors). Trade Cloth. Doubleday
Publishing. New York, NY. 1977. xxvi, 838p.
ISBN:0-385-11381-1, ISBN13: 978-0-385-11381-6.
Dewey:792.8/4. LCCN:76-055684.
Audience: **g,l,u,f.** *B*

Balthazar, Scott L. (Editor)   ML410
The Cambridge Companion to Verdi. Jonathan Cross
(Contribution by). Cloth Text. Cambridge University Press. New
York, NY. 2004. 364p. Cambridge Companions to Music Ser.
ISBN:0-521-63228-5, ISBN13: 978-0-521-63228-7.
Dewey:782.1092 B. LCCN:2005-280590.
Audience: **g,l,u,f.**

Barlow, Harold   ML128.V7B3 1976
Dictionary of Opera and Song Themes. Sam Morgenstern
(Compiled by). Trade Cloth. Crown Publishing Group. New
York, NY. 1976. 500p. ISBN:0-517-52503-8, ISBN13:
978-0-517-52503-6. Dewey:016.784. LCCN:75-030751.
Audience: **l,u,f.**

Bauman, Thomas   ML410.M9B185 1987
W. A. Mozart: Die Entführung aus dem Serail. Richard Wagner
(Contribution by). Trade Paper. Cambridge University Press.
New York, NY. 1988. 156p. Cambridge Opera Handbooks Ser.
ISBN:0-521-31060-1, ISBN13: 978-0-521-31060-4.
Dewey:782.1/092/4. LCCN:87-010326.
Audience: **u,f.** *Choice, 1988.*

Beckett, Lucy   ML410.W17.B37
Richard Wagner: "Parsifal". Cloth Text. Cambridge University
Press. New York, NY. 1981. 173p. Cambridge Opera Handbooks
Ser. ISBN:0-521-22825-5, ISBN13: 978-0-521-22825-1.
Dewey:782.1/092/4. LCCN:80-040870.
Audience: **u,f.**

Beethoven, Ludwig van   ML410.B4
Fidelio. Nicholas John (Editor), Tom Hammond (Translator).
Trade Paper. Riverrun Press, Inc. Flemington, NJ. 1981. 96p.

English National Opera Guide Ser., No. 4:Bilingual Libretto,
Articles ISBN:0-7145-3823-X, ISBN13: 978-0-7145-3823-5.
Dewey:782.1.
Audience: **g,l,u,f.**

Berg, Alban   ML50.B491W62 1990
Wozzeck. Nicholas John (Editor), Eric Blocknel & Vicki
Hartfold (Translators). Trade Paper. Beekman Books, Inc.
Wappingers Falls, NY. 1990. 116p. English National Opera
Guide Series: Bilingual Libretto, Articles, No. 42
ISBN:0-7145-4201-6, ISBN13: 978-0-7145-4201-0.
Dewey:782.1/0268. LCCN:90-044450.
Audience: **g,l,u,f.**

Bizet, Georges   ML50.B625C22 1982
Carmen. Nicholas John (Editor), Nell Moody & John Moody
(Translators). Trade Paper. Beekman Books, Inc. Wappingers
Falls, NY. 1982. 128p. English National Opera Guide Ser., No.
13:Bilingual Libretto, Articles ISBN:0-7145-3937-6, ISBN13:
978-0-7145-3937-9. Dewey:782.1/2. LCCN:83-107621.
Audience: **g,l,u,f.**

Branscombe, Peter   ML410.M9 B76 1991
W. A. Mozart: Die Zauberflöte. Richard Wagner (Contribution
by). Trade Paper. Cambridge University Press. New York, NY.
1991. 263p. Cambridge Opera Handbooks Ser.
ISBN:0-521-31916-1, ISBN13: 978-0-521-31916-4.
Dewey:782.1. LCCN:90-040403.
Audience: **u,f.**

Brown, Bruce Alan   ML410.M9B8191995
W. A. Mozart: Così Fan Tutte. Richard Wagner (Contribution
by). Trade Paper. Cambridge University Press. New York, NY.
1995. 220p. Opera Handbooks Ser. ISBN:0-521-43735-0,
ISBN13: 978-0-521-43735-6. Dewey:782.1. LCCN:95-009885.
Audience: **u,f.** *Choice, 1997.*

Budden, Julian   ML410.V4
The Operas of Verdi: From Il Trovatore to la Forza Del Destino,
Vol. 2. Ed. 2. Trade Paper. Oxford University Press, Inc. New
York, NY. 1992. 542p. ISBN:0-19-816262-6, ISBN13:
978-0-19-816262-9. Dewey:782.1/092.
Audience: **g,l,u,f.**

Budden, Julian   ML410.V4
The Operas of Verdi: From Oberto to Rigoletto, Vol. 1. Ed. 2.
Trade Paper. Oxford University Press, Inc. New York, NY. 1992.
538p. ISBN:0-19-816261-8, ISBN13: 978-0-19-816261-2.
Dewey:782.1092.
Audience: **g,l,u,f.**

Budden, Julian (Editor)   ML410.V4 B88 1991
The Operas of Verdi: From Don Carlos to Falstaff, Vol. 3. Ed. 2.
Trade Paper. Oxford University Press, Inc. New York, NY. 1992.
550p. ISBN:0-19-816263-4, ISBN13: 978-0-19-816263-6.
Dewey:782.1/092. LCCN:91-036272.
Audience: **g,l,u,f.**

Carner, Mosco   ML410.P89 C25 1985
Giacomo Puccini: Tosca. Cloth Text. Cambridge University
Press. New York, NY. 1985. 174p. Cambridge Opera Handbooks

Ser. ISBN:0-521-22824-7, ISBN13: 978-0-521-22824-4.
Dewey:782.1/092/4.

Audience: **u,f.** *Choice, 1986.*

Carter, Tim   **ML410.M77C37 2002**
Monteverdi's Musical Theatre. Cloth over Boards. Yale
University Press. Cumberland, RI. 2002. 336p.
ISBN:0-300-09676-3, ISBN13: 978-0-300-09676-7.
Dewey:782.1/092. LCCN:2002-109930.

Audience: **u,f.**

Carter, Tim   **ML410.M9 C33 1987**
Le Nozze Di Figaro. Richard Wagner (Contribution by). Trade
Paper. Cambridge University Press. New York, NY. 1988. 192p.
Cambridge Opera Handbooks Ser. ISBN:0-521-31606-5,
ISBN13: 978-0-521-31606-4. Dewey:782.109.
LCCN:87-011597.

Audience: **u,f.** *Choice, 1988.*

Celletti, Rodolfo   **ML1460.C413 1996**
A History of Bel Canto. Frederick Fuller (Translator). Trade
Paper. Oxford University Press, Inc. New York, NY. 1997. 224p.
ISBN:0-19-816641-9, ISBN13: 978-0-19-816641-2.
Dewey:782.1/0945. LCCN:96-028219.

Audience: **u,f.** *Choice, 1992.*

Charlton, David (Editor)   **ML1700.C16 2002**
The Cambridge Companion to Grand Opera. Cloth Text.
Cambridge University Press. New York, NY. 2003. 518p.
Cambridge Companions to Music Ser. ISBN:0-521-64118-7,
ISBN13: 978-0-521-64118-0. Dewey:782.1.
LCCN:2002-074190.

Audience: **g,l,u,f.** *Choice, 2004.*

Cheek, Timothy   **ML49.J36O62 2003**
The Janacek Opera Libretti: Kat'a Kabanova Translations and
Pronunciation. Trade Paper. Scarecrow Press, Inc. Lanham, MD.
2004. 280p. ISBN:0-8108-5014-1, ISBN13: 978-0-8108-5014-9.
Dewey:782.1/0268. LCCN:2002-153032.

Audience: **u,f.**

Cooke, Mervyn (Editor)   **ML1706**
The Cambridge Companion to Twentieth-Century Opera. Trade
Paper. Cambridge University Press. New York, NY. 2005. 424p.
Cambridge Companions to Music Ser. ISBN:0-521-78393-3,
ISBN13: 978-0-521-78393-4. Dewey:782.109/04.
LCCN:2006-295723.

Audience: **g,l,u,f.**

Dahlhaus, Carl   **ML410.W13**
Richard Wagner's Music Dramas. Mary Whittall (Translator).
Trade Cloth. Cambridge University Press. New York, NY. 1979.
174p. ISBN:0-521-22397-0, ISBN13: 978-0-521-22397-3.
Dewey:782.1092. LCCN:78-068359.

Audience: **u,f.**

Darcy, Warren   **MT100.W26D33 1996**
Wagner's das Rheingold. Paper Text. Oxford University Press,
Inc. New York, NY. 1996. 274p. Studies in Musical Genesis and
Structure ISBN:0-19-816603-6, ISBN13: 978-0-19-816603-0.
Dewey:782.1. LCCN:96-033659.

Audience: **u,f.**

Dean, Winton & Knapp,   **ML410.H13D37 1987**
John M.
Handel's Operas Seventeen Four to Seventeen Twenty-Six.
Trade Cloth. Oxford University Press, Inc. New York, NY. 1987.
772p. ISBN:0-19-315219-3, ISBN13: 978-0-19-315219-9.
Dewey:782.1/092/4. LCCN:85-011580.

Audience: **u,f.** *Choice, 1987.*

Debussy, Claude   **ML410.D28**
Pelleas and Melisande. Nicholas John (Editor), Hugh
MacDonald (Translator). Trade Paper. Riverrun Press, Inc.
Flemington, NJ. 1982. 128p. English National Opera Guide Ser.,
No. 9:Bilingual Libretto, Articles ISBN:0-7145-3906-6, ISBN13:
978-0-7145-3906-5. Dewey:782.1/092/4.

Audience: **g,l,u,f.**

Dizikes, John   **ML1711**
Opera in America: A Cultural History. Trade Paper. Yale
University Press. Cumberland, RI. 1995. 622p.
ISBN:0-300-06101-3, ISBN13: 978-0-300-06101-7.
Dewey:782.10973.

Audience: **u,f.** *Choice, 1994.*

Donington, Robert   **ML1700**
Opera and Its Symbols: The Unity of Words, Music, and
Staging. Trade Paper. Yale University Press. Cumberland, RI.
1992. 256p. ISBN:0-300-05661-3, ISBN13: 978-0-300-05661-7.
Dewey:782.1.

Audience: **u,f.** *Choice, 1991.*

Donington, Robert   **ML410.W15**
Wagner's 'Ring' and Its Symbols: The Music and the Myth. Ed.
3. Trade Paper. Faber & Faber, Inc. New York, NY. 1974. 304p.
ISBN:0-571-04818-8, ISBN13: 978-0-571-04818-2.
Dewey:782.154. LCCN:74-164583.

Audience: **u,f.**

Gilliam, Bryan   **ML410.S93G54 1996**
Richard Strauss's Elektra. Trade Paper. Oxford University Press,
Inc. New York, NY. 1996. 284p. Studies in Musical Genesis and
Structure ISBN:0-19-816602-8, ISBN13: 978-0-19-816602-3.
Dewey:782.1/092. LCCN:95-049506.

Audience: **u,f.** *Choice, 1992.*

Glixon, Beth Lise, et al.   **ML1733.8.V4**
Inventing the Business of Opera: The Impresario and His World
in Seventeenth-Century Venice. Glixon, Jonathan Emmanuel
(Author). Oxford University Press. 2006. AMS Studies in Music
ISBN:0-19-515416-9, ISBN13: 978-0-19-515416-0.

Audience: **u,f.**

Grey, Thomas S. (Editor)   **ML410.W132 .R48 2000**
Richard Wagner: Der Fliegende Holländer. Trade Paper.
Cambridge University Press. New York, NY. 2000. 240p.
Cambridge Opera Handbooks Ser. ISBN:0-521-58763-8,
ISBN13: 978-0-521-58763-1. Dewey:782.1. LCCN:99-059951.

Audience: **u,f.**

Groos, Arthur & Parker,   **ML410.P89 G76 1986**
Roger (Editors)
Giacomo Puccini: La Bohème. Trade Cloth. Cambridge
University Press. New York, NY. 1986. 224p. Cambridge Opera

Handbooks Ser. ISBN:0-521-26489-8, ISBN13:
978-0-521-26489-1. Dewey:782.1. LCCN:85-028076.

Audience: **u,f.** *Choice, 1987.*

Groos, Arthur & Parker,   **ML2110.R4 1988**
  Roger (Editors)
Reading Opera. Cloth Text. Princeton University Press.
Princeton, NJ. 1988. 381p. ISBN:0-691-09132-3, ISBN13:
978-0-691-09132-7. Dewey:782.1/2. LCCN:88-025984.

Audience: **u,f.** *Choice, 1989.*

Grout, Donald Jay &   **ML1700.G83 2003**
  Williams, Hermine Weigel
A Short History of Opera. Ed. 4. Trade Cloth. Columbia
University Press. New York, NY. 2003. 992p.
ISBN:0-231-11958-5, ISBN13: 978-0-231-11958-0.
Dewey:782.1/09. LCCN:2002-041470.

Audience: **g,l,u,f.** B

Heartz, Daniel   **ML410.V4**
Mozart's Operas. Trade Paper. University of California Press.
Berkeley, CA. 1992. 382p. ISBN:0-520-07872-1, ISBN13:
978-0-520-07872-7. Dewey:782.1/092. LCCN:89-020435.

Audience: **u,f.** *Choice, 1991.*

Hepokoski, James A.   **ML410.V4 H46 1983**
Giuseppe Verdi: Falstaff. Richard Wagner (Contribution by).
Trade Paper. Cambridge University Press. New York, NY. 1983.
192p. Cambridge Opera Handbooks Ser. ISBN:0-521-28016-8,
ISBN13: 978-0-521-28016-7. Dewey:782.1/092/4.
LCCN:83-023493.

Audience: **u,f.**

Hepokoski, James A.   **ML410.V4 H48 1987**
Giuseppe Verdi: Otello. Richard Wagner (Contribution by).
Trade Paper. Cambridge University Press. New York, NY. 1987.
226p. Cambridge Opera Handbooks Ser. ISBN:0-521-27749-3,
ISBN13: 978-0-521-27749-5. Dewey:782.1/092/4.
LCCN:86-017189.

Audience: **u,f.**

Heriot, Angus   **ML400**
The Castrati in Opera. Paper Text. Textbook Publishers.
Temecula, CA. 2003. 243p. ISBN:0-7581-3973-X, ISBN13:
978-0-7581-3973-3. Dewey:782.1/092/2.

Audience: **u,f.** B

Holman, J. K.   **ML1700**
Wagner's Ring: A Listener's Companion and Concordance.
Trade Paper. Hal Leonard Corporation. Milwaukee, WI. 2003.
440p. ISBN:1-57467-070-0, ISBN13: 978-1-57467-070-7.
Dewey:782.1.

Audience: **g,l,u,f.**

Howard, Patricia   **ML410.G5 C2 1981**
Orfeo. Richard Wagner (Contribution by). Trade Paper.
Cambridge University Press. New York, NY. 1981. 152p.
Cambridge Opera Handbooks Ser. ISBN:0-521-29664-1,
ISBN13: 978-0-521-29664-9. Dewey:782.1. LCCN:80-049734.

Audience: **l,u,f.**

Hutcheon, Linda &   **ML2100.H88 2004**
  Hutcheon, Michael
Opera: The Art of Dying. Trade Cloth. Harvard University
Press. Cambridge, MA. 2004. 256p. Convergences Ser.,
:Inventories of the Present Ser. ISBN:0-674-01326-3, ISBN13:
978-0-674-01326-1. Dewey:782.1. LCCN:2003-058737.

Audience: **u,f.** *Choice, 2004.*

Janacek, Leos & Cheek,   **ML49.J36J37 2003**
  Timothy
The Janacek Opera Libretti: Translations and Pronunciation.
Trade Cloth. Scarecrow Press, Inc. Lanham, MD. 2003. 224p.
ISBN:0-8108-4671-3, ISBN13: 978-0-8108-4671-5.
Dewey:782.1/0268. LCCN:2002-153032.

Audience: **u,f.**

Jarman, Douglas (Editor)   **ML410.B47J28 1991**
Alban Berg: "Lulu". Cloth Text. Cambridge University Press.
New York, NY. 1991. 160p. Cambridge Opera Handbooks Ser.
ISBN:0-521-24150-2, ISBN13: 978-0-521-24150-2.
Dewey:782.1. LCCN:90-001637.

Audience: **u,f.** *Choice, 1991.*

Jarman, Douglas   **ML410.B47 J3 1989**
Alban Berg: Wozzeck. Richard Wagner (Contribution by). Trade
Paper. Cambridge University Press. New York, NY. 1989. 192p.
Cambridge Opera Handbooks Ser. ISBN:0-521-28481-3,
ISBN13: 978-0-521-28481-3. Dewey:782.109.
LCCN:88-015965.

Audience: **l,u,f.** *Choice, 1990.*

Jefferson, Alan   **ML410.S93**
Richard Strauss, Der Rosenkavalier. Cambridge; New York:
Cambridge University Press. 1985. Cambridge Opera
Handbooks ISBN:0-521-26036-1, ISBN13: 978-0-521-26036-7.

Audience: **l,u,f.**

Kelly, Thomas Forrest   **ML1720.K45 2004**
First Nights at the Opera. Cloth over Boards. Yale University
Press. Cumberland, RI. 2004. 464p. ISBN:0-300-10044-2,
ISBN13: 978-0-300-10044-0. Dewey:782.1/09.
LCCN:2004-006932.

Audience: **g,l,u,f.** *Choice, 2005.*

Kemp, Ian (Editor)   **ML410.B5H3 1988**
Hector Berlioz: "Les Troyens". Trade Cloth. Cambridge
University Press. New York, NY. 1989. 256p. Cambridge Opera
Handbooks Ser. ISBN:0-521-34280-5, ISBN13:
978-0-521-34280-3. Dewey:782.1/092/4. LCCN:88-002719.

Audience: **u,f.**

Kerman, Joseph   **ML3858 .K4**
Opera As Drama. Ed. 50. Trade Paper, Perfect. University of
California Press. Berkeley, CA. 2005. 249p.
ISBN:0-520-24692-6, ISBN13: 978-0-520-24692-8.
Dewey:782.1.

Audience: **u,f.** B *Choice, 1989.*

Kimbell, David R. B.   **ML410.B44 K56 1998**
Vincenzo Bellini: Norma. Richard Wagner (Contribution by).
Trade Paper. Cambridge University Press. New York, NY. 1998.

154p. Opera Handbooks Ser. ISBN:0-521-48514-2, ISBN13: 978-0-521-48514-2. Dewey:782.1. LCCN:97-032615.

Audience: **u,f.** *Choice, 1999.*

Kimbell, David R. B. **ML733.K55 1994**
Italian Opera. John Warrack (Contribution by). Trade Paper. Cambridge University Press. New York, NY. 1994. 702p. National Tradition of Opera Ser. ISBN:0-521-46643-1, ISBN13: 978-0-521-46643-1. Dewey:782.1/0945.

Audience: **u,f.**

Kitcher, Philip & Schacht, **ML410.W15K57 2004**
Richard
Finding an Ending: Reflections on Wagner's Ring. Trade Cloth. Oxford University Press, Inc. New York, NY. 2004. 253p. ISBN:0-19-517359-7, ISBN13: 978-0-19-517359-8. Dewey:782.1. LCCN:2004-041478.

Audience: **u,f.** *Choice, 2005.*

Loewenberg, Alfred **ML1700**
Annals of Opera, Fifteen Ninety-Seven to Nineteen Forty, Set. Library Binding. Reprint Services Company. Temecula, CA. 1988. ISBN:0-7812-0999-4, ISBN13: 978-0-7812-0999-1. Dewey:782.1/09.

Audience: **g,l,u,f.**

Mallach, Alan **ML410.M39M25 2002**
Pietro Mascagni and His Operas. Trade Cloth. Northeastern University Press. Boston, MA. 2002. 320p. ISBN:1-55553-524-0, ISBN13: 978-1-55553-524-7. Dewey:782.1/092 B. LCCN:2001-059191.

Audience: **l,u,f.** *Choice, 2003, 2002.*

Marco, Guy A. **ML128.O4M28 2001**
Opera: A Research and Information Guide. Ed. 2. Edward O. D. Downes (Foreword by). Cloth Text. Garland Publishing, Inc. New York, NY. 2000. 624p. Music Research and Information Guides Ser., Vol. 21 ISBN:0-8153-3516-4, ISBN13: 978-0-8153-3516-0. Dewey:016.7821. LCCN:00-050302.

Audience: **g,l,u,f.** *Choice, 2001.*

Martin, George **MT95.M253 1999**
Twentieth Century Opera: A Guide. Trade Paper. Hal Leonard Corporation. Milwaukee, WI. 1998. 703p. ISBN:0-87910-275-6, ISBN13: 978-0-87910-275-3. Dewey:782.1/09/04. LCCN:99-027953.

Audience: **u,f.**

McClary, Susan **ML410.B62 M25 1992**
Georges Bizet: Carmen. Richard Wagner (Contribution by). Trade Paper. Cambridge University Press. New York, NY. 1992. 175p. Cambridge Opera Handbooks Ser. ISBN:0-521-39897-5, ISBN13: 978-0-521-39897-8. Dewey:782.1. LCCN:91-032840.

Audience: **l,u,f.** *Choice, 1993.*

Monteverdi, Claudio **ML410.V4**
Operas of Monteverdi: Includes Orfeo, Return of Ulysses, Coronation of Poppea. Anne Ridler (Translator). Trade Paper. Riverrun Press, Inc. Flemington, NJ. 1992. 208p. English

National Opera Guide Series: Bilingual Libretto, Articles, No. 45 ISBN:0-7145-4207-5, ISBN13: 978-0-7145-4207-2. Dewey:782.1092.

Audience: **g,l,u,f.**

Mozart, Wolfgang Amadeus **ML49.M83 M42 1991**
The Metropolitan Opera Book of Mozart Operas. Metropolitan Opera Guild Staff & Paul Gruber (Editors), Judyth Schaubhut Smith, David Stivender & Susan Webb (Translators). Trade Paper. HarperCollins Publishers. New York, NY. 1991. 640p. ISBN:0-06-273051-7, ISBN13: 978-0-06-273051-0. Dewey:782.1/026/8. LCCN:91-055003.

Audience: **g,l,u,f.**

Mussorgsky, Modest **ML410.M97**
Boris Godunov. Nicholas John (Editor), David Lloyd-Jones (Translator). Trade Paper. Riverrun Press, Inc. Flemington, NJ. 1982. 128p. English National Opera Guide Ser., No. 11:Bilingual Libretto, Articles ISBN:0-7145-3922-8, ISBN13: 978-0-7145-3922-5. Dewey:782.1/092/4.

Audience: **g,l,u,f.**

Newman, Ernest **ML410.G5 N3 1976**
Gluck and the Opera: A Study in Musical History. Trade Cloth. Greenwood Publishing Group, Inc. Portsmouth, NH. 1976. 300p. ISBN:0-8371-8849-0, ISBN13: 978-0-8371-8849-2. Dewey:782.1/092/4. LCCN:76-007579.

Audience: **u,f.**

Nichols, Roger & Smith, **ML410.D28 N48 1989**
Richard Langham
Claude Debussy: Pelléas et Mélisande. Richard Wagner (Contribution by). Trade Paper. Cambridge University Press. New York, NY. 1989. 224p. Cambridge Opera Handbooks Ser. ISBN:0-521-31446-1, ISBN13: 978-0-521-31446-6. Dewey:782.1. LCCN:88-016172.

Audience: **u,f.** *Choice, 1989.*

Osborne, Charles **ML390.O82 1994**
The Bel Canto Operas: A Guide to the Operas of Rossini, Bellini, and Donizetti. Trade Cloth. Hal Leonard Corporation. Milwaukee, WI. 1994. 378p. ISBN:0-931340-71-3, ISBN13: 978-0-931340-71-0. Dewey:782.1/0945/09034. LCCN:94-168756.

Audience: **g,l,u,f.** *Choice, 1994.*

Osborne, Charles **ML410.V4**
The Complete Operas of Richard Wagner. Trade Paper. Da Capo Press, Inc. Cambridge, MA. 1993. 288p. ISBN:0-306-80522-7, ISBN13: 978-0-306-80522-6. Dewey:782.1/092. LCCN:92-034417.

Audience: **l,u,f.** *Choice, 1991.*

Parker, Roger (Editor) **ML1700**
The Oxford Illustrated History of Opera. Trade Paper. Oxford University Press, Inc. New York, NY. 2001. 558p. Oxford Illustrated Histories Ser. ISBN:0-19-285445-3, ISBN13: 978-0-19-285445-2. Dewey:782.1/09.

Audience: **g,l,u,f.** *Choice, 1995.*

Peattie, Antony   **MT95.K52 1997**
The New Kobbe's Opera Book. Earl of Harewood Staff (Editor).
Trade Cloth. Penguin Group (USA) Inc. New York, NY. 1997.
1032p. ISBN:0-399-14332-7, ISBN13: 978-0-399-14332-8.
Dewey:782.1/0269. LCCN:97-010981.

Audience: **g,l,u,f.**

Perle, George   **ML410.B47**
The Operas of Alban Berg: Lulu. Trade Cloth. University of
California Press. Berkeley, CA. 1984. 352p.
ISBN:0-520-04502-5, ISBN13: 978-0-520-04502-6.
Dewey:782.1092. LCCN:76-052033.

Audience: **u,f.** *Choice, 1985.*

Perle, George   **ML410.B47**
The Operas of Alban Berg: Wozzeck. Trade Cloth. University of
California Press. Berkeley, CA. 1980. 325p.
ISBN:0-520-03440-6, ISBN13: 978-0-520-03440-2.
Dewey:782.1/092/4. LCCN:76-052033.

Audience: **u,f.**

Pleasants, Henry   **ML400**
The Great Singers: From the Dawn of Opera to Our Own Time.
London: Macmillan. 1983. ISBN:0-333-34854-0, ISBN13:
978-0-333-34854-3.

Audience: **g,l,u,f.**

Price, Curtis   **ML410.P93**
Henry Purcell and the London Stage. Trade Cloth. Cambridge
University Press. New York, NY. 1984. 394p.
ISBN:0-521-23831-5, ISBN13: 978-0-521-23831-1.
Dewey:780/.92/4. LCCN:83-015170.

Audience: **u,f.**

Puccini, Giacomo   **ML49.P75**
Seven Puccini Librettos. William Weaver (Translator). Trade
Paper. W. W. Norton & Company, Inc. New York, NY. 1981.
ISBN:0-393-00930-0, ISBN13: 978-0-393-00930-9.
Dewey:782.1/2.

Audience: **g,l,u,f.**

Puffett, Derrick (Editor)   **ML410.S93R485 1989**
Richard Strauss: "Elektra". Cloth Text. Cambridge University
Press. New York, NY. 1990. 187p. Cambridge Opera Handbooks
Ser. ISBN:0-521-35173-1, ISBN13: 978-0-521-35173-7.
Dewey:782.1/092/4. LCCN:89-000499.

Audience: **u,f.** *Choice, 1990.*

Puffett, Derrick (Editor)   **ML410.S93 R52 1989**
Richard Strauss: Salome. Richard Wagner (Contribution by).
Trade Paper. Cambridge University Press. New York, NY. 1989.
224p. Cambridge Opera Handbooks Ser. ISBN:0-521-35970-8,
ISBN13: 978-0-521-35970-2. Dewey:782.109.
LCCN:89-000500.

Audience: **u,f.** *Choice, 1990.*

Radice, Mark A.   **MT955.O54 1998**
Opera in Context: Essays on Historical Staging from the Late
Renaissance to the Time of Puccini. Trade Cloth. Hal Leonard
Corporation. Milwaukee, WI. 2003. 410p. ISBN:1-57467-032-8,

ISBN13: 978-1-57467-032-5. Dewey:792.5/023.
LCCN:97-002712.

Audience: **u,f.** *Choice, 1998.*

Robinson, Paul (Editor)   **ML410.B4 R46 1996**
Ludwig Van Beethoven: Fidelio. Richard Wagner (Contribution
by). Trade Paper. Cambridge University Press. New York, NY.
1996. 203p. Cambridge Opera Handbooks Ser.
ISBN:0-521-45852-8, ISBN13: 978-0-521-45852-8.
Dewey:780.9/2. LCCN:95-046935.

Audience: **u,f.** *Choice, 1997.*

Rosand, Ellen   **ML1733.8.V4R67 1991**
Opera in Seventeenth-Century Venice: The Creation of a Genre.
Trade Cloth. University of California Press. Berkeley, CA. 1990.
710p. ISBN:0-520-06808-4, ISBN13: 978-0-520-06808-7.
Dewey:782.1/0945/3109032. LCCN:90-040399.

Audience: **u,f.** *Choice, 1991.*

Rosselli, John   **ML1733.R78 1984**
The Opera Industry in Italy from Cimarosa to Verdi: The Role
of the Impresario. Trade Cloth. Cambridge University Press.
New York, NY. 1984. 224p. ISBN:0-521-25732-8, ISBN13:
978-0-521-25732-9. Dewey:782.1/0945. LCCN:83-007688.

Audience: **u,f.** *B*

Rosselli, John   **ML460.R68 1995**
Singers of Italian Opera: The History of a Profession. Trade
Paper. Cambridge University Press. New York, NY. 1995. 288p.
ISBN:0-521-42697-9, ISBN13: 978-0-521-42697-8.
Dewey:782.1023.

Audience: **u,f.** *Choice, 1993.*

Rossini, Gioacchino Antonio   **ML50.P965**
The Barber of Seville and Moses. Nicholas John (Editor),
Edward J. Dent, John Moody & Nell Moody (Translators).
Trade Paper. Riverrun Press, Inc. Flemington, NJ. 1986. 160p.
English National Opera Guide Ser., No. 36:Bilingual Libretto,
Articles ISBN:0-7145-4080-3, ISBN13: 978-0-7145-4080-1.
Dewey:782.1/2. LCCN:85-052162.

Audience: **g,l,u,f.**

Rushton, Julian   **ML410.M9 R88 1981**
Don Giovanni. Richard Wagner (Contribution by). Trade Paper.
Cambridge University Press. New York, NY. 1981. 176p.
Cambridge Opera Handbooks Ser. ISBN:0-521-29663-3,
ISBN13: 978-0-521-29663-2. Dewey:782.1/092/4.
LCCN:80-041534.

Audience: **l,u,f.**

Rushton, Julian   **ML410.M9 R89 1993**
W. A. Mozart: Idomeneo. Richard Wagner (Contribution by).
Trade Paper. Cambridge University Press. New York, NY. 1993.
197p. Cambridge Opera Handbooks Ser. ISBN:0-521-43741-5,
ISBN13: 978-0-521-43741-7. Dewey:782.1. LCCN:92-025833.

Audience: **u,f.**

Sadie, Stanley (Editor)   **ML102.O6**
The New Grove Dictionary of Opera, Set. Trade Paper. Oxford
University Press, Inc. New York, NY. 1992. 5,426p.

ISBN:0-19-522186-9, ISBN13: 978-0-19-522186-2.
Dewey:782.1/03.

Audience: **g,l,u,f.** *Choice, 1993.*

Sadie, Stanley (Editor)   **ML410.W13W114 2000**
Wagner and His Operas. Trade Cloth. St. Martin's Press.
Gordonville, VA. 2000. xv, 219p. The New Grove Composers
Ser. ISBN:0-333-79021-9, ISBN13: 978-0-333-79021-2.
Dewey:782.1/092. LCCN:00-701304.

Audience: **l,u,f.**

Sadler, Graham & Wood,   **ML1727.W64 2000**
  Caroline
French Baroque Opera: A Reader. Trade Cloth. Ashgate
Publishing, Ltd. Aldershot, 2000. ix, 160p. ISBN:1-84014-241-3,
ISBN13: 978-1-84014-241-9. Dewey:782.1/0944/09032.
LCCN:99-054365.

Audience: **u,f.**

Schmidgall, Gary   **ML3858 .S37**
Literature As Opera. Trade Cloth. Oxford University Press, Inc.
New York, NY. 1977. 446p. ISBN:0-19-502213-0, ISBN13:
978-0-19-502213-1. Dewey:782.1/3. LCCN:76-057264.

Audience: **u,f.** *B*

Steane, J. B.   **ML400.S83 1996**
Singers of the Century. Trade Cloth. Hal Leonard Corporation.
Milwaukee, WI. 2003. 288p. Singers of the Century Ser., Vol. 2
ISBN:1-57467-040-9, ISBN13: 978-1-57467-040-0.
Dewey:782/.00922. LCCN:96-016827.

Audience: **u,f.** *Choice, 1997.*

Steane, J. B.   **ML400.S83 1996**
Singers of the Century. Trade Cloth. Hal Leonard Corporation.
Milwaukee, WI. 1996. 288p. ISBN:1-57467-009-3, ISBN13:
978-1-57467-009-7. Dewey:782/.00922. LCCN:96-016827.

Audience: **u,f.** *Choice, 1997.*

Steane, J. B.   **ML400.S83 1996**
Singers of the Century. Trade Cloth. Hal Leonard Corporation.
Milwaukee, WI. 2003. 275p. Singers of the Century Ser., Vol. 3
ISBN:1-57467-057-3, ISBN13: 978-1-57467-057-8.
Dewey:782/.00922. LCCN:96-016827.

Audience: **u,f.** *Choice, 1997.*

Sternfeld, F. W.   **ML1733.2**
The Birth of Opera. Trade Cloth. Oxford University Press, Inc.
New York, NY. 1993. 280p. ISBN:0-19-816130-1, ISBN13:
978-0-19-816130-1. Dewey:782.1/0945/09031.
LCCN:92-030841.

Audience: **u.** *Choice, 1993.*

Strauss, Richard   **ML50.S918S32 1988**
Salome and Elektra. Nicholas John (Editor). Trade Paper.
Riverrun Press, Inc. Flemington, NJ. 1989. 144p. English
National Opera Guide Ser., No. 37:Bilingual Libretto, Articles
ISBN:0-7145-4131-1, ISBN13: 978-0-7145-4131-0.
Dewey:782.1/2. LCCN:88-006444.

Audience: **g,l,u,f.**

Strauss, Richard   **ML50.M939**
Der Rosenkavalier. Nicholas John (Editor), Alfred Kalisch
(Translator). Trade Paper. Riverrun Press, Inc. Flemington, NJ.
1982. English National Opera Guide Series: Bilingual Libretto,
Articles, No. 8 ISBN:0-7145-3851-5, ISBN13:
978-0-7145-3851-8. Dewey:782.10268.

Audience: **g,l,u,f.**

Stravinsky, Igor   **ML49.S77O32 1991**
Oedipus Rex and the Rake's Progress. Nicholas John (Editor).
Trade Paper. Riverrun Press, Inc. Flemington, NJ. 1991. 112p.
English National Opera Guide Series: Bilingual Libretto,
Articles, No. 43 ISBN:0-7145-4193-1, ISBN13:
978-0-7145-4193-8. Dewey:782.1. LCCN:90-026770.

Audience: **g,l,u,f.**

Strohm, Reinhard   **ML1733.3.S87 1997**
Dramma per Musica: Italian Opera Seria of the Eighteenth
Century. Cloth over Boards. Yale University Press. Cumberland,
RI. 1997. 336p. ISBN:0-300-06454-3, ISBN13:
978-0-300-06454-4. Dewey:782.1/0945/09033.
LCCN:97-027576.

Audience: **u,f.** *Choice, 1998.*

Sturman, Janet Lynn   **ML1950.S78 2000**
Zarzuela: Spanish Operetta, American Stage. Trade Cloth.
University of Illinois Press. Champaign, IL. 2000. 256p. Music
in American Life Ser. ISBN:0-252-02596-2, ISBN13:
978-0-252-02596-9. Dewey:782.1/2. LCCN:00-008032.

Audience: **u,f.**

Traubner, Richard   **ML1900.T7 2003**
Operetta: A Theatrical History. Ed. 2. UK-B Format Paperback.
Routledge. New York, NY. 2003. 496p. ISBN:0-415-96641-8,
ISBN13: 978-0-415-96641-2. Dewey:782.81/09.
LCCN:2003-054800.

Audience: **u,f.** *B*

Tyrrell, John   **ML410.J18 A4 1992**
Janacek Operas. Cloth Text. Princeton University Press.
Princeton, NJ. 1992. 436p. ISBN:0-691-09148-X, ISBN13:
978-0-691-09148-8. Dewey:782.1/092. LCCN:92-016091.

Audience: **u,f.** *Choice, 1993.*

Tyrrell, John (Editor)   **ML410.J18 L49 1982**
Leos Janacek: Kat'a Kabanova. Richard Wagner (Contribution
by). Trade Paper. Cambridge University Press. New York, NY.
1982. 248p. Cambridge Opera Handbooks Ser.
ISBN:0-521-29853-9, ISBN13: 978-0-521-29853-7.
Dewey:782.1/092/4. LCCN:81-038505.

Audience: **u,f.**

Van den Toorn, Pieter C.   **ML410.S932.V38 1988**
Stravinsky and the "Rite of Spring": The Beginnings of a
Musical Language. Trade Cloth. University of California Press.
Berkeley, CA. 1987. 200p. ISBN:0-520-05958-1, ISBN13:
978-0-520-05958-0. Dewey:785.3/2/0924. LCCN:86-031778.

Audience: **l,u,f.** *Choice, 1988.*

Van Witsen, Leo   **MT955**
Costuming for Opera: Who Wears What and Why. Trade Cloth.
Scarecrow Press, Inc. Lanham, MD. 1994. 256p.
ISBN:0-8108-2933-9, ISBN13: 978-0-8108-2933-6.
Dewey:792.5026. LCCN:93-029999.
Audience: **u,f.** *Choice, 1995.*

Verdi, Giuseppe   **ML49.V45**
Seven Verdi Librettos. William Weaver (Translator). Trade
Paper. W. W. Norton & Company, Inc. New York, NY. 1977.
ISBN:0-393-00852-5, ISBN13: 978-0-393-00852-4.
Dewey:782.5.
Audience: **g,l,u,f.**

Von Westernhagen, Curt   **ML410.W15**
The Forging of the Ring: Richard Wagner's Composition
Sketches for Der Ring des Nibelungen. Arnold Whittall & Mary
Whittall (Translators). Trade Cloth. Cambridge University Press.
New York, NY. 1976. 248p. ISBN:0-521-21293-6, ISBN13:
978-0-521-21293-9. Dewey:782.1/092/4. LCCN:76-007140.
Audience: **u,f.**

Wagner, Richard   **ML50.M939**
Lohengrin. Nicholas John (Editor). Trade Paper. Riverrun Press,
Inc. Flemington, NJ. 1994. 128p. English National Opera Guide
Series: Bilingual Libretto, Articles, No. 47 ISBN:0-7145-3852-3,
ISBN13: 978-0-7145-3852-5. Dewey:782.10268.
Audience: **g,l,u,f.**

Wagner, Richard   **ML50.W14T22 1988**
Tannhauser. Nicholas John (Editor). Trade Paper. Riverrun Press,
Inc. Flemington, NJ. 1988. 96p. English National Opera Guide
Series: Bilingual Libretto, Articles, No. 39 ISBN:0-7145-4147-8,
ISBN13: 978-0-7145-4147-1. Dewey:782.1/2. LCCN:88-006443.
Audience: **g,l,u,f.**

Wagner, Richard   **ML410.W16**
The Mastersingers of Nuremberg. Nicholas John (Editor), F.
Jameson & Feasey Kember (Translators). Trade Paper. Riverrun
Press, Inc. Flemington, NJ. 2003. 128p. English National Opera
Guide Ser., No. 19:Bilingual Libretto, Articles
ISBN:0-7145-3961-9, ISBN13: 978-0-7145-3961-4.
Dewey:782.1/092/4.
Audience: **g,l,u,f.**

Wagner, Richard   **ML410.W17**
Parsifal. Nicholas John (Editor), Andrew Porter (Translator).
Trade Paper. Riverrun Press, Inc. Flemington, NJ. 1986. 128p.
English National Opera Guide Series: Bilingual Libretto,
Articles, No. 34 ISBN:0-7145-4079-X, ISBN13:
978-0-7145-4079-5. Dewey:782.1/092/4. LCCN:85-052160.
Audience: **g,l,u,f.**

Wagner, Richard   **ML50.B422**
Tristan and Isolde. Nicholas John (Editor), Andrew Porter
(Translator). Trade Paper. Riverrun Press, Inc. Flemington, NJ.
1981. 96p. English National Opera Guide Ser., No. 6:Bilingual
Libretto, Articles ISBN:0-7145-3849-3, ISBN13:
978-0-7145-3849-5. Dewey:782.1/2.
Audience: **g,l,u,f.**

Wagner, Richard   **ML50.W14**
The Ring of the Nibelung. Andrew Porter (Translator). Trade
Paper. W. W. Norton & Company, Inc. New York, NY. 1977.
ISBN:0-393-00867-3, ISBN13: 978-0-393-00867-8.
Dewey:782.12.
Audience: **g,l,u,f.**

Warrack, John   **ML1729 .W37 2001**
German Opera: From the Beginnings to Wagner. Tim Carter,
John Deathridge, Arthur Groos, James Hepokoski, Paul
Robinson & Ellen Rosand (Contribution by). Trade Cloth.
Cambridge University Press. New York, NY. 2001. 464p.
Cambridge Studies in Opera Ser. ISBN:0-521-23532-4, ISBN13:
978-0-521-23532-7. Dewey:792.10943. LCCN:00-062127.
Audience: **u,f.** *Choice, 2002.*

Warrack, John   **ML410.W1 A286 1994**
Richard Wagner: Die Meistersinger von Nürnberg. Richard
Wagner (Contribution by). Cloth Text. Cambridge University
Press. New York, NY. 1994. 185p. Opera Handbooks Ser.
ISBN:0-521-44444-6, ISBN13: 978-0-521-44444-6.
Dewey:782.1. LCCN:93-039615.
Audience: **u,f.**

Warren, Raymond   **ML1700.W3 1995**
Opera Workshop. Trade Cloth. Ashgate Publishing, Ltd.
Aldershot, 1995. 288p. ISBN:0-85967-970-5, ISBN13:
978-0-85967-970-1. Dewey:782.1/143. LCCN:94-013604.
Audience: **u,f.** *Choice, 1995.*

Weiss, Piero (Author,   **ML1700.O644 2002**
Compiled by)
Opera: A History in Documents. Trade Paper. Oxford University
Press, Inc. New York, NY. 2002. 342p. ISBN:0-19-511638-0,
ISBN13: 978-0-19-511638-0. Dewey:782.1/09.
LCCN:2001-032179.
Audience: **g,l,u,f.**

Whenham, John   **ML410.M77 C55 1986**
Claudio Monteverdi: Orfeo. Richard Wagner (Contribution by).
Trade Paper. Cambridge University Press. New York, NY. 1986.
230p. Cambridge Opera Handbooks Ser. ISBN:0-521-28477-5,
ISBN13: 978-0-521-28477-6. Dewey:782.1/092/4.
LCCN:85-009923.
Audience: **l,u,f.** *Choice, 1986.*

White, Eric W.   **ML1700**
A History of English Opera. Trade Cloth. Faber & Faber, Ltd.
London, 1983. 472p. ISBN:0-571-10788-5, ISBN13:
978-0-571-10788-9. Dewey:782.1/0942. LCCN:83-001599.
Audience: **u,f.** *B*

Woodstra, Chris, et al.   **ML156**
All Music Guide to Classical Music: The Definitive Guide to
Classical Music. Gerald Brennan & Allen Schrott (Authors).
Trade Paper, Perfect. Backbeat Books. San Francisco, CA. 2005.
1607p. ISBN:0-87930-865-6, ISBN13: 978-0-87930-865-0.
Dewey:016.78026/6. LCCN:2005-023988.
Audience: **g,l,u,f.** *Choice, 2006.*

Studies in Music History, Criticism, Analysis, and Appreciation > Western Classical Literature by Genre > Vocal Concert Genres

Barlow, Harold   ML128.V7B3 1976
Dictionary of Opera and Song Themes. Sam Morgenstern (Compiled by). Trade Cloth. Crown Publishing Group. New York, NY. 1976. 500p. ISBN:0-517-52503-8, ISBN13: 978-0-517-52503-6. Dewey:016.784. LCCN:75-030751.
Audience: **l,u,f.**

Blume, Friedrich   ML3100.B5913
Protestant Church Music. Paul H. Lang (Foreword by). Trade Cloth. W. W. Norton & Company, Inc. New York, NY. 1975. 912p. ISBN:0-393-02176-9, ISBN13: 978-0-393-02176-9. Dewey:783/.026. LCCN:74-008392.
Audience: **u,f.** *B*

Burrows, Donald   ML410.H13 B95 1991
Handel: Messiah. Julian Rushton (Contribution by). Trade Paper. Cambridge University Press. New York, NY. 1991. 137p. Music Handbks. ISBN:0-521-37620-3, ISBN13: 978-0-521-37620-4. Dewey:782.23. LCCN:90-002566.
Audience: **g,l,u,f.** *Choice, 1992.*

Butt, John   ML410.B1B193 1992
Bach: Mass in B Minor. Julian Rushton (Contribution by). Trade Paper. Cambridge University Press. New York, NY. 1991. 126p. Music Handbks. ISBN:0-521-38716-7, ISBN13: 978-0-521-38716-3. Dewey:782.32/32. LCCN:90-002286.
Audience: **u,f.** *Choice, 1992.*

Chafe, Eric   ML410.B13C38 2000
Analyzing Bach Cantatas. Trade Cloth. Oxford University Press, Inc. New York, NY. 2000. 304p. ISBN:0-19-512099-X, ISBN13: 978-0-19-512099-8. Dewey:782.2/4/092. LCCN:98-015109.
Audience: **u,f.** *Choice, 2000.*

Chase, Robert   ML3088.C43 2003
Dies Irae: A Guide to Requiem Music. Trade Cloth. Scarecrow Press, Inc. Lanham, MD. 2003. 736p. ISBN:0-8108-4664-0, ISBN13: 978-0-8108-4664-7. Dewey:782.32/38. LCCN:2002-152105.
Audience: **u,f.** *Choice, 2004.*

Cook, Nicholas   ML410.B42 C66 1993
Beethoven "Symphony No. 9". Cloth Text. Cambridge University Press. New York, NY. 1993. 143p. Music Handbks. ISBN:0-521-39039-7, ISBN13: 978-0-521-39039-2. Dewey:784.2184. LCCN:92-020451.
Audience: **l,u,f.**

Cooke, Mervyn   ML410.B853 C76 1996
Britten: War Requiem. Cloth Text. Cambridge University Press. New York, NY. 1996. 125p. Music Handbks. ISBN:0-521-44089-0, ISBN13: 978-0-521-44089-9. Dewey:782.3/238. LCCN:96-006338.
Audience: **u,f.**

Dean, Winton   ML410.B13
Handel's Dramatic Oratorios and Masques. Paper Text. Textbook Publishers. Temecula, CA. 2003. xii, 694p. ISBN:0-7581-7050-5, ISBN13: 978-0-7581-7050-7. Dewey:782.23.
Audience: **u,f.**

Drabkin, William   ML410.B42 D8 1991
Beethoven: Missa Solemnis. Julian Rushton (Contribution by). Trade Paper. Cambridge University Press. New York, NY. 1991. 132p. Music Handbks. ISBN:0-521-37831-1, ISBN13: 978-0-521-37831-4. Dewey:782.32/32. LCCN:91-011383.
Audience: **u,f.**

Dunsby, Jonathan   ML410.S283 D83 1992
Schoenberg: Pierrot Lunaire. Julian Rushton (Contribution by). Trade Paper. Cambridge University Press. New York, NY. 1992. 94p. Music Handbks. ISBN:0-521-38715-9, ISBN13: 978-0-521-38715-6. Dewey:782.47. LCCN:91-036068.
Audience: **u,f.**

Durr, Alfred   ML410.B13D87 2003
The Cantatas of J. S. Bach. Richard Jones (Translator). Trade Cloth. Oxford University Press, Inc. New York, NY. 2005. 984p. ISBN:0-19-816707-5, ISBN13: 978-0-19-816707-5. Dewey:782.2/4092. LCCN:2005-299548.
Audience: **u,f.** *Choice, 2006.*

Hall, Michael (Editor)   MT121.S36H35 2003
Schubert's Song Sets. Trade Cloth. Ashgate Publishing, Ltd. Aldershot, 2003. 300p. ISBN:0-7546-0798-4, ISBN13: 978-0-7546-0798-4. Dewey:782.4/7/092. LCCN:2001-099668.
Audience: **l,u,f.**

Hefling, Stephen E.   MT121.M34 H44 2000
Mahler: Das Lied Von der Erde (The Song of the Earth). Cloth Text. Cambridge University Press. New York, NY. 2000. 173p. Music Handbks. ISBN:0-521-47534-1, ISBN13: 978-0-521-47534-1. Dewey:782.4/7. LCCN:99-023189.
Audience: **u,f.**

Larsen, Jens P.   ML410
Handel's Messiah: Origins, Composition, Sources. Ed. 2. Trade Cloth. Greenwood Publishing Group, Inc. Portsmouth, NH. 1990. 336p. ISBN:0-313-24426-X, ISBN13: 978-0-313-24426-1. Dewey:783.3/092/4. LCCN:88-010128.
Audience: **u,f.**

Leech-Wilkinson, Daniel   ML410.G966L3 1990
Machaut's Mass: An Introduction. Trade Cloth. Oxford University Press, Inc. New York, NY. 1990. 224p. ISBN:0-19-316333-0, ISBN13: 978-0-19-316333-1. Dewey:782.32/32. LCCN:89-023005.
Audience: **l,u,f.** *Choice, 1991.*

Levy, David Benjamin   ML410.B42L48 2003
Beethoven: The Ninth Symphony. Ed. 2. Trade Paper. Yale University Press. Cumberland, RI. 2003. 256p. Yale Music Masterworks Ser. ISBN:0-300-09964-9, ISBN13: 978-0-300-09964-5. Dewey:784.2/184.
Audience: **u,f.** *Choice, 1995.*

MacIntyre, Bruce   ML410.H4M13 1998
Haydn: The Creation. Trade Cloth. Thomson Wadsworth.
Belmont, CA. 1997. Monuments of Western Music Ser.
ISBN:0-02-871375-3, ISBN13: 978-0-02-871375-5.
Dewey:782.23. LCCN:97-025759.

Audience: **u,f.**

Melamed, Daniel R.   MT115.B2M43 2005
Hearing Bach's Passions. Trade Cloth. Oxford University Press,
Inc. New York, NY. 2005. 190p. ISBN:0-19-516933-6, ISBN13:
978-0-19-516933-1. Dewey:782.23. LCCN:2004-013785.

Audience: **l,u,f.** *Choice, 2005.*

Miller, Philip L.   ML54.6.M5 R5 1973
    (Introduction by)
The Ring of Words: An Anthology of Song Texts. Trade Paper.
W. W. Norton & Company, Inc. New York, NY. 1973. 544p.
Norton Library ISBN:0-393-00677-8, ISBN13:
978-0-393-00677-3. Dewey:781.9/6. LCCN:72-010270.

Audience: **g,l,u,f.**

Miller, Phillip L. (Editor), et   ML54.6.G275 1990
    al.
German Lieder. Brahms & Gustav Mahler (Editors). Trade
Paper. Continuum International Publishing Group, Ltd. London,
1990. German Library, Vol. 42 ISBN:0-8264-0328-X, ISBN13:
978-0-8264-0328-5. Dewey:782.4/3/0943. LCCN:89-039980.

Audience: **g,l,u,f.**

Miller, Richard   MT121.S38M55 1999
Singing Schumann: An Interpretive Guide for Performers. Trade
Cloth. Oxford University Press, Inc. New York, NY. 1999. 260p.
ISBN:0-19-511904-5, ISBN13: 978-0-19-511904-6.
Dewey:782.42168/092. LCCN:98-031645.

Audience: **u,f.** *Choice, 2000.*

Musgrave, Michael   ML410.B8M86 1996
Brahms: A German Requiem. Julian Rushton (Contribution by).
Trade Paper. Cambridge University Press. New York, NY. 1996.
109p. Music Handbks. ISBN:0-521-40995-0, ISBN13:
978-0-521-40995-7. Dewey:782.3/238. LCCN:95-051987.

Audience: **u,f.** *Choice, 1997.*

Osmond-Smith, David   MT115.B58 O8 1985
Playing on Words: A Guide to Luciano Berio's Sinfonia. Trade
Cloth. Ashgate Publishing, Ltd. Aldershot, 1985. 104p. Royal
Musical Association Monographs ISBN:0-947854-00-2, ISBN13:
978-0-947854-00-3. Dewey:785.1/1/0924. LCCN:85-154370.

Audience: **u,f.**

Parsons, James (Editor)   ML2829.C36 2003
The Cambridge Companion to the Lied. Jonathan Cross
(Contribution by). Trade Cloth. Cambridge University Press.
New York, NY. 2004. 438p. Cambridge Companions to Music
Ser. ISBN:0-521-80027-7, ISBN13: 978-0-521-80027-3.
Dewey:782.42168/0943. LCCN:2003-051229.

Audience: **u,f.**

Potter, John (Editor)   ML1460 .C28 2000
The Cambridge Companion to Singing. Trade Paper. Cambridge
University Press. New York, NY. 2000. 296p. Cambridge

Companions to Music Ser. ISBN:0-521-62709-5, ISBN13:
978-0-521-62709-2. Dewey:782/.009. LCCN:99-032948.

Audience: **g,l,u,f.** *Choice, 2000.*

Reed, John   ML410.S3R265 1997
The Schubert Song Companion. Norma Deane & Celia Larner
(Translators), Janet Baker (Foreword by). Trade Paper.
Manchester University Press. Manchester, 1997. 528p.
ISBN:1-901341-00-3, ISBN13: 978-1-901341-00-3.
Dewey:784.3/0092/4. LCCN:98-179605.

Audience: **l,u,f.** *Choice, 1985.*

Reinhard, Thilo (Editor)   ML54.6.S4 R413 1989
The Singer's Schumann. Library Binding. Rosen Publishing
Group, Incorporated, The. New York, NY. 1989. 423p.
ISBN:0-8239-0673-6, ISBN13: 978-0-8239-0673-4.
Dewey:784.3/05. LCCN:88-028387.

Audience: **u,f.**

Rosen, David   ML410.V4 R73 1995
Verdi: Requiem. Julian Rushton (Contribution by). Trade Paper.
Cambridge University Press. New York, NY. 1995. 125p. Music
Handbks. ISBN:0-521-39767-7, ISBN13: 978-0-521-39767-4.
Dewey:782.3/238. LCCN:94-033380.

Audience: **u,f.** *Choice, 1996.*

Rushton, Julian   ML410.B5 R85 1994
Berlioz: Romeo et Juliette. Trade Paper. Cambridge University
Press. New York, NY. 1994. 129p. Music Handbks.
ISBN:0-521-37767-6, ISBN13: 978-0-521-37767-6.
Dewey:784.2/2. LCCN:93-032505.

Audience: **u,f.**

Sams, Eric   MT115.S38
The Songs of Robert Schumann. Ed. 3. Gerald Moore
(Foreword by). Bloomington: Indiana University Press. 1993.
ISBN:0-253-35065-4, ISBN13: 978-0-253-35065-7.

Audience: **l,u,f.**

Scott, Michael   ML1460
The Record of Singing. Paper Text. Northeastern University
Press. Boston, MA. 1993. 505p. ISBN:1-55553-163-6, ISBN13:
978-1-55553-163-8. Dewey:783.009. LCCN:92-046984.

Audience: **u,f.**

Seaton, Douglas   ML128.S3S33 1987
The Art Song: A Reference and Information Guide. Library
Binding. Garland Publishing, Inc. New York, NY. 1987. 300p.
Reference Library of the Humanities ISBN:0-8240-8554-X,
ISBN13: 978-0-8240-8554-4. Dewey:016.7843.
LCCN:86-033553.

Audience: **l,u,f.** *Choice, 1987.*

Sharp, Avery T. & Floyd,   ML128.C48S53 2001
    James Michael
Choral Music: A Research and Information Guide. Cloth Text.
Garland Publishing, Inc. New York, NY. 2001. 498p. Routledge
Music Bibliographies Ser. ISBN:0-8240-5944-1, ISBN13:
978-0-8240-5944-6. Dewey:016.7825. LCCN:2001-019115.

Audience: **l,u,f.** *Choice, 2002.*

Smither, Howard E.   **76-43980**
The Oratorio in the Baroque Era: Italy, Vienna, Paris. Trade
Cloth. University of North Carolina Press. Chapel Hill, NC.
1977. 507p. History of the Oratorio Ser. ISBN:0-8078-1274-9,
ISBN13: 978-0-8078-1274-7. Dewey:782.8/2/09.
LCCN:76-043980.

Audience: **u,f.** *B̶ Choice, 1987.*

Smither, Howard E.   **76-43980**
The Oratorio in the Baroque Era: Protestant Germany and
England. Trade Cloth. University of North Carolina Press.
Chapel Hill, NC. 1977. 415p. History of the Oratorio Ser., Vol.
2 ISBN:0-8078-1294-3, ISBN13: 978-0-8078-1294-5.
Dewey:782.2/3/09033. LCCN:76-043980.

Audience: **u,f.**

Smither, Howard E.   **76-43980**
The Oratorio in the Classical Era. Trade Cloth. University of
North Carolina Press. Chapel Hill, NC. 1987. 736p. History of
the Oratorio Ser., Vol. 3 ISBN:0-8078-1731-7, ISBN13:
978-0-8078-1731-5. Dewey:782.8/2/09. LCCN:76-043980.

Audience: **u.**

Smither, Howard E.   **ML3201 .S6**
The Oratorio in the Nineteenth and Twentieth Centuries. Trade
Cloth. University of North Carolina Press. Chapel Hill, NC.
2000. 856p. History of the Oratorio Ser., Vol. 4
ISBN:0-8078-2511-5, ISBN13: 978-0-8078-2511-2.
Dewey:782.2309034. LCCN:76-043980.

Audience: **u,f.**

Stauffer, George B.   **ML410.B13S75 1997**
Bach: The Mass in B Minor. Cloth Text. Thomson Wadsworth.
Belmont, CA. 1996. 309p. Monuments of Western Music Ser.
ISBN:0-02-872475-5, ISBN13: 978-0-02-872475-1.
Dewey:782.32/32. LCCN:96-027495.

Audience: **l,u,f.**

Steane, J. B.   **ML400.S83 1996**
Singers of the Century. Trade Cloth. Hal Leonard Corporation.
Milwaukee, WI. 2003. 288p. Singers of the Century Ser., Vol. 2
ISBN:1-57467-040-9, ISBN13: 978-1-57467-040-0.
Dewey:782/.00922. LCCN:96-016827.

Audience: **u,f.** *Choice, 1997.*

Steane, J. B.   **ML400.S83 1996**
Singers of the Century. Trade Cloth. Hal Leonard Corporation.
Milwaukee, WI. 1996. 288p. ISBN:1-57467-009-3, ISBN13:
978-1-57467-009-7. Dewey:782/.00922. LCCN:96-016827.

Audience: **u,f.** *Choice, 1997.*

Steane, J. B.   **ML400.S83 1996**
Singers of the Century. Trade Cloth. Hal Leonard Corporation.
Milwaukee, WI. 2003. 275p. Singers of the Century Ser., Vol. 3
ISBN:1-57467-057-3, ISBN13: 978-1-57467-057-8.
Dewey:782/.00922. LCCN:96-016827.

Audience: **u,f.** *Choice, 1997.*

Stevens, Denis   **ML460**
A History of Song. Paper Text. Textbook Publishers. Temecula,

CA. 2003. 491p. ISBN:0-7581-0723-4, ISBN13:
978-0-7581-0723-7. Dewey:784/.09.

Audience: **g,l,u,f.** *B̶*

Studwell, William E.   **ML1400.S78 1996**
The National and Religious Song Reader: Patriotic, Traditional
and Sacred Songs from Around the World. Trade Cloth.
Haworth Press, Incorporated, The. Binghamton, NY. 1996. 150p.
ISBN:0-7890-0099-7, ISBN13: 978-0-7890-0099-6.
Dewey:781.5/99. LCCN:96-005944.

Audience: **u,f.**

Temperley, Nicholas   **ML410.H4 T36 1991**
Haydn: The Creation. Julian Rushton (Contribution by). Trade
Paper. Cambridge University Press. New York, NY. 1991. 143p.
Music Handbks. ISBN:0-521-37865-6, ISBN13:
978-0-521-37865-9. Dewey:782.23. LCCN:90-001859.

Audience: **u,f.** *Choice, 1992.*

Thomson, Virgil   **ML1406.T5 1989**
Music with Words: A Composer's View. Cloth over Boards. Yale
University Press. Cumberland, RI. 1989. 112p.
ISBN:0-300-04505-0, ISBN13: 978-0-300-04505-5.
Dewey:784/.028. LCCN:89-030709.

Audience: **u,f.** *Choice, 1989.*

Walsh, Stephen   **ML410.S932 W35 1993**
Stravinsky: Oedipus Rex. Julian Rushton (Contribution by).
Cloth Text. Cambridge University Press. New York, NY. 1993.
130p. Music Handbks. ISBN:0-521-40431-2, ISBN13:
978-0-521-40431-0. Dewey:782.1092. LCCN:92-030088.

Audience: **u,f.**

Whenham, John   **ML410.M77**
Monteverdi, Vespers (1610). Cambridge University Press. 1997.
Cambridge music handbooks ISBN:0-521-45377-1, ISBN13:
978-0-521-45377-6.

Audience: **u,f.**

Wigmore, Richard   **ML54.6.S39.W53 1988**
(Translator)
Schubert: The Complete Song Texts. Trade Cloth. Thomson
Gale. Farmington Hills, MI. 1988. 380p. ISBN:0-02-872911-0,
ISBN13: 978-0-02-872911-4. Dewey:784.3/05.
LCCN:88-011653.

Audience: **l,u,f.** *Choice, 1989.*

Wingfield, Paul   **ML410.J18 W56 1992**
Janacek: Glagolitic Mass. Julian Rushton (Contribution by).
Cloth Text. Cambridge University Press. New York, NY. 1992.
146p. Music Handbks. ISBN:0-521-38013-8, ISBN13:
978-0-521-38013-3. Dewey:782.32/3. LCCN:91-016986.

Audience: **u,f.** *Choice, 1993.*

Wolff, Christoph   **ML410.M9**
Mozart's Requiem: Historical and Analytical Studies,
Documents, Score. Trade Paper. University of California Press.
Berkeley, CA. 1998. 190p. ISBN:0-520-21389-0, ISBN13:
978-0-520-21389-0. Dewey:782.32/38.

Audience: **u,f.**

Woodstra, Chris, et al.   **ML156**
All Music Guide to Classical Music: The Definitive Guide to
Classical Music. Gerald Brennan & Allen Schrott (Authors).
Trade Paper, Perfect. Backbeat Books. San Francisco, CA. 2005.
1607p. ISBN:0-87930-865-6, ISBN13: 978-0-87930-865-0.
Dewey:016.78026/6. LCCN:2005-023988.
Audience: **g,l,u,f.** *Choice, 2006.*

Youens, Susan   **ML410.W8.Y7 1992**
Hugo Wolf: The Vocal Music. Cloth Text. Princeton University
Press. Princeton, NJ. 1992. 412p. ISBN:0-691-09145-5, ISBN13:
978-0-691-09145-7. Dewey:782.42168/092. LCCN:91-045446.
Audience: **u,f.** *Choice, 1993.*

Youens, Susan   **ML410.S3**
Retracing a Winter's Journey: Schubert's Winterreise. Book,
Other. Cornell University Press. Ithaca, NY. 1991. 320p.
ISBN:0-8014-9966-6, ISBN13: 978-0-8014-9966-1.
Dewey:782.4/7. LCCN:91-055234.
Audience: **u,f.** *Choice, 1992.*

Youens, Susan   **ML410.S3 Y7 1992**
Schubert: Die Schone Mullerin. Julian Rushton (Contribution
by). Trade Paper. Cambridge University Press. New York, NY.
1992. 129p. Music Handbks. ISBN:0-521-42279-5, ISBN13:
978-0-521-42279-6. Dewey:782.42168. LCCN:91-028960.
Audience: **u,f.**

Studies in Music History, Criticism, Analysis, and Appreciation > Western Classical Literature by Genre > Instrumental Genres

Arnold, Corliss Richard   **ML600**
Organ Literature : A Comprehensive Survey. Ed. 3. Scarecrow
Press. 1995. ISBN:0-8108-2970-3, ISBN13: 978-0-8108-2970-1.
Audience: **u,f.**

Baron, John H.   **ML128.O5**
Chamber Music: A Research and Information Guide. Ed. 2.
Paper over Boards. Routledge. New York, NY. 2002. 680p.
Routledge Music Bibliographies Ser. ISBN:0-415-93736-1,
ISBN13: 978-0-415-93736-8. Dewey:016.7/85.
Audience: **l,u,f.** *Choice, 1988.*

Berger, Melvin   **ML1100.B45 2001**
Guide to Chamber Music. Ed. 3. Trade Paper. Dover
Publications, Inc. Mineola, NY. 2001. 480p.
ISBN:0-486-41879-0, ISBN13: 978-0-486-41879-7.
Dewey:785.7/009. LCCN:2001-028648.
Audience: **g,l,u,f.** *Choice, 1986.*

Berger, Melvin   **ML1156.B46 1991**
Guide to Sonatas: Music for One or Two Instruments. Trade
Paper. Alfred A. Knopf Inc. New York, NY. 1990. 224p.
ISBN:0-385-41302-5, ISBN13: 978-0-385-41302-2.
Dewey:784.18/3. LCCN:90-000982.
Audience: **g,l,u,f.**

Brown, A. Peter   **ML1255.B87**
The First Golden Age of the Viennese Symphony: Haydn,
Mozart, Beethoven and Schubert. Trade Cloth. Indiana
University Press. Bloomington, IN. 2002. 816p.
ISBN:0-253-33487-X, ISBN13: 978-0-253-33487-9.
Dewey:784.2/184 s 784.2. LCCN:98-026549.
Audience: **g,l,u,f.** *Choice, 2003.*

Brown, A. Peter   **ML1255.B87**
The Symphonic Repertoire: The Second Golden Age of the
Viennese Symphony. Cloth Text. Indiana University Press.
Bloomington, IN. 2003. 816p. ISBN:0-253-33488-8, ISBN13:
978-0-253-33488-6. Dewey:784.2/184. LCCN:2003-551931.
Audience: **g,l,u,f.** *Choice, 2004.*

Cohn, Arthur   **ML1100**
The Literature of Chamber Music. Chapel Hill, N.C. : Hinshaw
Music. 1997. ISBN:0-937276-16-2, ISBN13:
978-0-937276-16-7.
Audience: **u,f.**

Cook, Nicholas   **ML410.B42 C66 1993**
Beethoven "Symphony No. 9". Cloth Text. Cambridge
University Press. New York, NY. 1993. 143p. Music Handbks.
ISBN:0-521-39039-7, ISBN13: 978-0-521-39039-2.
Dewey:784.2184. LCCN:92-020451.
Audience: **l,u,f.**

Cooper, David   **ML410.B26 C66 1996**
Bartók: Concerto for Orchestra. Cloth Text. Cambridge
University Press. New York, NY. 1996. 111p. Music Handbks.
ISBN:0-521-48004-3, ISBN13: 978-0-521-48004-8.
Dewey:784.2/3/092. LCCN:95-021614.
Audience: **u,f.**

Cooper, John Michael   **MT130.M35C66 2003**
Mendelssohn's 'Italian' Symphony. Trade Cloth. Oxford
University Press, Inc. New York, NY. 2003. 252p. Studies in
Musical Genesis and Structure ISBN:0-19-816653-2, ISBN13:
978-0-19-816653-5. Dewey:784.2/184. LCCN:2002-030842.
Audience: **u,f.**

Daniels, David   **ML128.O5D3 2005**
Orchestral Music: A Handbook. Ed. 4. Trade Cloth. Scarecrow
Press, Inc. Lanham, MD. 2005. 618p. ISBN:0-8108-5674-3,
ISBN13: 978-0-8108-5674-5. Dewey:016.7842.
LCCN:2005-021983.
Audience: **u,f.**

David, Hans T.   **ML410.B1**
J. S. Bach's Musical Offering: History, Interpretation and
Analysis. Trade Paper. Dover Publications, Inc. Mineola, NY.
1972. 190p. ISBN:0-486-22768-5, ISBN13: 978-0-486-22768-9.
Dewey:785.7. LCCN:72-165391.
Audience: **u,f.**

Davidson, Michael   **MT220**
Mozart and the Pianist: A Guide for Performers and Teachers to
Mozart's Major Works for Solo Piano. Ed. 2. Trade Paper. Kahn
& Averill Publishers. London, 2001. 384p. ISBN:1-871082-76-5,
ISBN13: 978-1-871082-76-0. Dewey:786.2143.
Audience: **l,u,f.**

Eggebrecht, Hans H.   MT145.B14.E4513 1993
J. S. Bach's "The Art of the Fugue": The Work and Its
Interpretation. Jeffrey L. Praeter (Translator). Cloth Text.
Blackwell Publishing Professional. Ames, IA. 1993. 160p.
ISBN:0-8138-1489-8, ISBN13: 978-0-8138-1489-6.
Dewey:786/.1872. LCCN:93-001281.

        Audience: **u,f.** *Choice, 1994.*

Everett, Paul   ML410.V82 E84 1996
Vivaldi: The Four Seasons and Other Concertos, Op. 8. Julian
Rushton (Contribution by). Cloth Text. Cambridge University
Press. New York, NY. 1996. 128p. Music Handbks.
ISBN:0-521-40499-1, ISBN13: 978-0-521-40499-0.
Dewey:780/.92. LCCN:95-018173.

        Audience: **u,f.**

Forte, Allen   MT100.S968 F7
The Harmonic Organization of the Rite of Spring. Trade Paper.
Yale University Press. Cumberland, RI. 1978. 160p.
ISBN:0-300-10537-1, ISBN13: 978-0-300-10537-7.
Dewey:782.9/5/0924.

        Audience: **u,f.**

Frisch, Walter   ML410.B8F75 1996
Brahms: The Four Symphonies. Spiral. Thomson Wadsworth.
Belmont, CA. 1996. 226p. Monuments of Western Music Ser.
ISBN:0-02-870765-6, ISBN13: 978-0-02-870765-5.
Dewey:780.9/2. LCCN:96-022951.

        Audience: **l,u,f.** *Choice, 1997.*

Gordon, Stewart   ML700.G65 1996
A History of Keyboard Literature: Music for the Piano and Its
Forerunners. Cloth Text. Thomson Wadsworth. Belmont, CA.
1996. 576p. ISBN:0-02-870965-9, ISBN13: 978-0-02-870965-9.
Dewey:786. LCCN:95-031762.

        Audience: **g,l,u,f.** *Choice, 1996.*

Grave, Floyd K. & Grave,   ML410.H4G69 2006
  Margaret G.
The String Quartets of Joseph Haydn. Trade Cloth. Oxford
University Press, Inc. New York, NY. 2006. 492p.
ISBN:0-19-517357-0, ISBN13: 978-0-19-517357-4.
Dewey:785/.7194/092. LCCN:2005-047784.

        Audience: **u,f.**

Grayson, David   ML410.M9 G82 1998
Mozart: Piano Concertos. Julian Rushton (Contribution by).
Cloth Text. Cambridge University Press. New York, NY. 1999.
155p. Cambridge Music Handbooks Ser. ISBN:0-521-48156-2,
ISBN13: 978-0-521-48156-4. Dewey:784.262092.
LCCN:97-050598.

        Audience: **u,f.** *Choice, 1999.*

Greene, Richard   ML410.H748 G74 1995
Holst: The Planets. Julian Rushton (Contribution by). Cloth
Text. Cambridge University Press. New York, NY. 1995. 110p.
Music Handbks. ISBN:0-521-45000-4, ISBN13:
978-0-521-45000-3. Dewey:784.2/1858. LCCN:94-017175.

        Audience: **u,f.** *Choice, 1995.*

Haimo, Ethan   MT130.H4H35 1995
Haydn's Symphonic Forms: Essays in Compositional Logic.
Trade Cloth. Oxford University Press, Inc. New York, NY. 1995.
310p. Oxford Monographs on Music ISBN:0-19-816392-4,
ISBN13: 978-0-19-816392-3. Dewey:784.2/184/092.
LCCN:94-049097.

        Audience: **u,f.** *Choice, 1996.*

Hamilton, Kenneth & Liszt,   ML410.L7 H258 1996
  Franz
Liszt: Sonata in B Minor. Julian Rushton (Contribution by).
Cloth Text. Cambridge University Press. New York, NY. 1996.
101p. Music Handbks. ISBN:0-521-46570-2, ISBN13:
978-0-521-46570-0. Dewey:786.2/183. LCCN:95-049839.

        Audience: **u,f.**

Harrison, Bernard   ML410.H4 H314 1998
Haydn: The 'Paris' Symphonies. Julian Rushton (Contribution
by). Trade Paper. Cambridge University Press. New York, NY.
1998. 134p. Music Handbks. ISBN:0-521-47743-3, ISBN13:
978-0-521-47743-7. Dewey:784.2/184/092. LCCN:97-042606.

        Audience: **u,f.** *Choice, 1999.*

Hefling, Stephen   ML1104.N56 2003
19th-Century Chamber Music. Ed. 2. UK-B Format Paperback.
Routledge. New York, NY. 2003. 392p. Studies in Musical
Genres ISBN:0-415-96650-7, ISBN13: 978-0-415-96650-4.
Dewey:785/.009/034. LCCN:2003-047187.

        Audience: **u,f.**

Hepokoski, James A.   ML410.S54 H4 1993
Sibelius: Symphony No. 5. Julian Rushton (Contribution by).
Cloth Text. Cambridge University Press. New York, NY. 1993.
121p. Music Handbks. ISBN:0-521-40143-7, ISBN13:
978-0-521-40143-2. Dewey:784.2184. LCCN:92-021614.

        Audience: **u,f.**

Hill, Peter   ML410.S932 H55 2000
Stravinsky: The Rite of Spring. Julian Rushton (Contribution
by). Cloth Text. Cambridge University Press. New York, NY.
2000. 180p. Music Handbks. ISBN:0-521-62221-2, ISBN13:
978-0-521-62221-9. Dewey:784.2/1556. LCCN:00-023703.

        Audience: **l,u,f.**

Hinson, Maurice   ML128.P3H5 2000
🄴 Guide to the Pianist's Repertoire. Ed. 3. E-Book. Indiana
University Press. Bloomington, IN. 2000. 992p.
ISBN:0-253-33646-5, ISBN13: 978-0-253-33646-0.
Dewey:016.7862/0263. LCCN:99-058594.

        Audience: **l,u,f.** *Choice, 1987.*

Hinson, Maurice   ML128.P3H534 1998
The Pianist's Bookshelf: A Practical Guide to Books, Videos,
and Other Resources. Trade Paper. Indiana University Press.
Bloomington, IN. 1998. 352p. ISBN:0-253-21145-X, ISBN13:
978-0-253-21145-3. Dewey:016.7862. LCCN:97-047307.

        Audience: **l,u,f.**

Holman, Peter   ML410.D808H651999
Dowland: Lachrimae (1604). Julian Rushton (Contribution by).

Cloth Text. Cambridge University Press. New York, NY. 1999.
116p. Music Handbks. ISBN:0-521-58196-6, ISBN13:
978-0-521-58196-7. Dewey:784.1882. LCCN:98-054374.
Audience: **u,f.**

Holoman, D. Kern   **MT125.H62 1992**
Evenings with the Orchestra: A Norton Companion for
Concert-Goers. Trade Cloth. W. W. Norton & Company, Inc.
New York, NY. 1992. 752p. ISBN:0-393-02936-0, ISBN13:
978-0-393-02936-9. Dewey:784.2. LCCN:91-003441.
Audience: **g,l,u,f.**

Holoman, D. Kern   **ML1255.N5 1996**
The Nineteenth Century Symphony. Cloth Text. Thomson
Wadsworth. Belmont, CA. 1996. 468p. Studies in Musical
Genres and Repertories ISBN:0-02-871105-X, ISBN13:
978-0-02-871105-8. Dewey:784.2/184/09034. LCCN:96-024580.
Audience: **g,l,u,f.** *Choice, 1997.*

Hopkins, Anthony   **MT130.B43H67 1996**
The Seven Concertos of Beethoven. Trade Cloth. Ashgate
Publishing, Ltd. Aldershot, 1996. 110p. ISBN:1-85928-245-8,
ISBN13: 978-1-85928-245-8. Dewey:784.2/3/092.
LCCN:96-024729.
Audience: **l,u,f.**

Hutcheson, Ernest & Ganz,   **MT140**
  Rudolph
Literature of the Piano: A Guide for Amateur and Student. Trade
Cloth. Random House Children's Books. New York, NY. 1965.
ISBN:0-394-40830-6, ISBN13: 978-0-394-40830-9.
Dewey:786.4/09. LCCN:63-009130.
Audience: **g,l,u,f.** *B*

Hutchings, Arthur   **MT130.M8H8 1998**
A Companion to Mozart's Piano Concertos. Ed. 2. Cliff Eisen
(Introduction by). Trade Paper. Oxford University Press, Inc.
New York, NY. 1999. 228p. ISBN:0-19-816708-3, ISBN13:
978-0-19-816708-2. Dewey:784.2/62/092. LCCN:98-039904.
Audience: **l,u,f.**

Irving, John   **ML410.M9 I73 1998**
Mozart: The 'Haydn' Quartets. Julian Rushton (Contribution
by). Cloth Text. Cambridge University Press. New York, NY.
1998. 113p. Music Handbks. ISBN:0-521-58475-2, ISBN13:
978-0-521-58475-3. Dewey:785/.7194/092. LCCN:97-007268.
Audience: **u,f.**

Jackson, Timothy L.   **ML410.C4 J33 1999**
Tchaikovsky: Symphony No. 6 (Pathétique). Cloth Text.
Cambridge University Press. New York, NY. 1999. 164p. Music
Handbks. ISBN:0-521-64111-X, ISBN13: 978-0-521-64111-1.
Dewey:784.2/184. LCCN:98-039930.
Audience: **u,f.**

Johnson, Theodore O.   **MT145.B14J56 1986**
An Analytical Survey of the 15 Sinfonias: Three-Part Inventions
by J. S. Bach. Trade Paper. University Press of America, Inc.
Lanham, MD. 1986. 190p. ISBN:0-8191-5378-8, ISBN13:
978-0-8191-5378-4. Dewey:786.1/092/4. LCCN:86-009091.
Audience: **l,u,f.** *Choice, 1986.*

Jones, David Wyn (Editor)   **ML410.B4 W96 1995**
Beethoven: The Pastoral Symphony. Cloth Text. Cambridge
University Press. New York, NY. 1995. 113p. Music Handbks.
ISBN:0-521-45074-8, ISBN13: 978-0-521-45074-4.
Dewey:784.2/184. LCCN:95-009937.
Audience: **u,f.**

Jones, Timothy   **ML410.B42 J66 1999**
Beethoven: The 'Moonlight' and Other Sonatas, Op. 27 and Op.
31. Julian Rushton (Contribution by). Cloth Text. Cambridge
University Press. New York, NY. 1999. 158p. Music Handbks.
ISBN:0-521-59136-8, ISBN13: 978-0-521-59136-2.
Dewey:786.2/183. LCCN:98-045826.
Audience: **l,u,f.**

Keefe, Simon P. (Editor)   **ML1263**
The Cambridge Companion to the Concerto. Jonathan Cross
(Contribution by). Cloth Text. Cambridge University Press. New
York, NY. 2005. 338p. Cambridge Companions to Music Ser.
ISBN:0-521-83483-X, ISBN13: 978-0-521-83483-4.
Dewey:784.2/3. LCCN:2006-295568.
Audience: **u,f.** *Choice, 2006.*

Kerman, Joseph   **MT59 .K49 2005**
The Art of Fugue: Bach Fugues for Keyboard, 1715-1750.
Davitt Moroney & Karen Rosenak (Performed by). Mixed
Media, Trade Cloth, Compact Disc. University of California
Press. Berkeley, CA. 2005. 208p. ISBN:0-520-24358-7, ISBN13:
978-0-520-24358-3. Dewey:786/.1872/092. LCCN:2005-004045.
Audience: **u,f.**

Kinderman, William   **ML410.S4**
Beethoven's Diabelli Variations. Paper Text. Oxford University
Press, Inc. New York, NY. 1989. 246p. Studies in Musical
Genesis and Structure ISBN:0-19-816198-0, ISBN13:
978-0-19-816198-1. Dewey:786.2/1825. LCCN:86-008590.
Audience: **u,f.** *Choice, 1988.*

Kirby, F. E.   **ML700.K45 1995**
Music for Piano: A Short History. Maurice Hinson (Foreword
by). Trade Cloth. Hal Leonard Corporation. Milwaukee, WI.
1995. 468p. ISBN:0-931340-86-1, ISBN13: 978-0-931340-86-4.
Dewey:786.2/09. LCCN:94-042642.
Audience: **u,f.** *Choice, 1996.*

Korstvedt, Benjamin M.   **ML410.B88 K67 2000**
Bruckner: Symphony No. 8. Julian Rushton (Contribution by).
Cloth Text. Cambridge University Press. New York, NY. 2000.
146p. Music Handbks., No. 8 ISBN:0-521-63226-9, ISBN13:
978-0-521-63226-3. Dewey:784.2184. LCCN:99-031880.
Audience: **u,f.**

Kramer, Jonathan D.   **MT125.K72 1988**
Listen to the Music: A Self-Guided Tour Through the Orchestral
Repertoire. Trade Cloth. Music Sales Corporation. New York,
NY. 1988. 815p. ISBN:0-02-871841-0, ISBN13:
978-0-02-871841-5. Dewey:785/.01/5. LCCN:88-009248.
Audience: **g,l,u,f.** *Choice, 1989.*

Landon, H. C. Robbins   **ML410.H4**
The Symphonies of Joseph Haydn. Paper Text. Textbook
Publishers. Temecula, CA. 2003. xvii, 862p.
ISBN:0-7581-2881-9, ISBN13: 978-0-7581-2881-2.
Dewey:785.110924.
Audience: **l,u,f.**

Lawson, Colin J.   **ML410.M9 L26 1996**
Mozart: Clarinet Concerto. Julian Rushton (Contribution by).
Cloth Text. Cambridge University Press. New York, NY. 1996.
123p. Music Handbks. ISBN:0-521-47384-5, ISBN13:
978-0-521-47384-2. Dewey:784.2/862. LCCN:95-022790.
Audience: **u,f.**

Layton, Robert (Editor)   **ML1263.C64 1989**
A Companion to the Concerto. Cloth Text. Thomson Gale.
Farmington Hills, MI. 1989. 369p. ISBN:0-02-871961-1,
ISBN13: 978-0-02-871961-0. Dewey:785.6. LCCN:88-026417.
Audience: **g,l,u,f.** *Choice, 1989.*

Ledbetter, David   **ML410.B13**
Bach's Well-Tempered Clavier: The 48 Preludes and Fugues.
Cloth over Boards. Yale University Press. Cumberland, RI.
2002. 432p. ISBN:0-300-09707-7, ISBN13: 978-0-300-09707-8.
Dewey:786/.1872. LCCN:2002-109926.
Audience: **l,u,f.**

Lee, Douglas   **ML1255**
Masterworks of 20th-Century Music: The Modern Repertory of
the Symphony Orchestra. UK-B Format Paperback. Routledge.
New York, NY. 2002. 528p. ISBN:0-415-93847-3, ISBN13:
978-0-415-93847-1. Dewey:784.1/84.
Audience: **g,l,u,f.**

Lester, Joel   **ML418.P2**
Bach's Works for Solo Violin: Style, Structure, Performance.
Trade Paper. Oxford University Press, Inc. New York, NY. 2003.
196p. ISBN:0-19-517144-6, ISBN13: 978-0-19-517144-0.
Dewey:787.2/092.
Audience: **u,f.** *Choice, 2000.*

Levy, David Benjamin   **ML410.B42L48 2003**
Beethoven: The Ninth Symphony. Ed. 2. Trade Paper. Yale
University Press. Cumberland, RI. 2003. 256p. Yale Music
Masterworks Ser. ISBN:0-300-09964-9, ISBN13:
978-0-300-09964-5. Dewey:784.2/184.
Audience: **u,f.** *Choice, 1995.*

Lockwood, Lewis & Kroll,   **MT145.B422B4 2004**
Mark (Editors)
The Beethoven Violin Sonatas: History, Criticism, Performance.
Trade Cloth. University of Illinois Press. Champaign, IL. 2004.
176p. ISBN:0-252-02932-1, ISBN13: 978-0-252-02932-5.
Dewey:787.2/183/092. LCCN:2003-026966.
Audience: **l,u,f.** *Choice, 2005.*

Mann, Alfred   **ML410.H13M36 1996**
Handel: The Orchestral Music. Cloth Text. Thomson
Wadsworth. Belmont, CA. 1995. 182p. Monuments of Western
Music Ser. ISBN:0-02-871382-6, ISBN13: 978-0-02-871382-3.
Dewey:784.2/092. LCCN:95-010441.
Audience: **u,f.** *Choice, 1996.*

Marshall, Robert L. (Editor)   **ML705.E37 1994**
Eighteenth Century Keyboard Music. Trade Cloth. Thomson
Wadsworth. Belmont, CA. 1994. 384p. Studies in Musical
Genres and Repertoires ISBN:0-02-871355-9, ISBN13:
978-0-02-871355-7. Dewey:786/.09/033. LCCN:93-045594.
Audience: **u,f.** *Choice, 1995.*

Marston, Nicholas   **ML410.S4 M37 1992**
Schumann: Fantasie, Op. 17. Julian Rushton (Contribution by).
Trade Paper. Cambridge University Press. New York, NY. 1992.
131p. Music Handbks. ISBN:0-521-39892-4, ISBN13:
978-0-521-39892-3. Dewey:786.2189. LCCN:91-039602.
Audience: **u,f.** *Choice, 1993.*

Maurice, Donald G.   **ML410.B26**
Bartok's Viola Concerto: The Remarkable Story of His
Swansong. Trade Cloth. Oxford University Press, Inc. New
York, NY. 2004. 234p. Studies in Musical Genesis and Structure
ISBN:0-19-515690-0, ISBN13: 978-0-19-515690-4.
Dewey:784.2/73. LCCN:2003-026914.
Audience: **u,f.** *Choice, 2004.*

McCalla, James   **ML1106**
Twentieth-Century Chamber Music. Ed. 2. Routledge. 2002.
ISBN:0-415-96695-7, ISBN13: 978-0-415-96695-5.
Audience: **u,f.**

Newman, William S.   **ML1156**
The Sonata since Beethoven. Ed. 3. Trade Cloth. W. W. Norton
& Company, Inc. New York, NY. 1983. xxvi, 870p.
ISBN:0-393-95290-8, ISBN13: 978-0-393-95290-2.
Dewey:781/.52/09. LCCN:82-024573.
Audience: **u,f.**

Parker, Mara E.   **ML1160.P37 2002**
The String Quartet, 1750-1797: Four Types of Musical
Conversation. Trade Cloth. Ashgate Publishing, Ltd. Aldershot,
2002. 330p. ISBN:1-84014-682-6, ISBN13: 978-1-84014-682-0.
Dewey:785/.7194/09033. LCCN:2002-019634.
Audience: **u,f.**

Parker, Mara E.   **ML128.S68P37 2005**
String Quartets: A Research and Information Guide. Perfect,
Paper over Boards. Routledge. New York, NY. 2005. 384p.
Routledge Music Bibliographies Ser. ISBN:0-415-94176-8,
ISBN13: 978-0-415-94176-1. Dewey:16.7857.
LCCN:2005-561917.
Audience: **u,f.**

Perle, George & Berg,   **MT145.B47P47 2001**
Alban
Style and Idea in the Lyric Suite of Alban Berg. Ed. 2. Trade
Cloth. Pendragon Press. Hillsdale, NY. 2001. xv, 112p.
ISBN:1-57647-085-7, ISBN13: 978-1-57647-085-5.
Dewey:785/.7194. LCCN:2001-052345.
Audience: **u,f.**

Pike, Lionel   **MT125 .P55**
Beethoven, Sibelius and "The Profound Logic": Studies in
Symphonic Analysis. Cloth Text. Continuum International

Publishing Group, Ltd. London, 1978. 240p.
ISBN:0-485-11178-0, ISBN13: 978-0-485-11178-1.
Dewey:785.1/1/0922. LCCN:79-309070.

Audience: **u,f.**

Pike, Lionel   **ML422.K22**
Vaughan Williams and the Symphony. Cloth over Boards.
Toccata Press. London, 2003. 352p. ISBN:0-907689-54-X,
ISBN13: 978-0-907689-54-6. Dewey:784.2092.

Audience: **u,f.**

Plantinga, Leon   **ML410.B42P6 1998**
Beethoven Concertos: History, Style, Performance. Trade Cloth.
W. W. Norton & Company, Inc. New York, NY. 1999. 416p.
ISBN:0-393-04691-5, ISBN13: 978-0-393-04691-5.
Dewey:784.2/3/092. LCCN:98-022552.

Audience: **l,u,f.** *Choice, 2000.*

Pople, Anthony   **ML410.B47 P6 1991**
Berg: Violin Concerto. Julian Rushton (Contribution by). Trade
Paper. Cambridge University Press. New York, NY. 1991. 130p.
Music Handbks. ISBN:0-521-39976-9, ISBN13:
978-0-521-39976-0. Dewey:784.2/72. LCCN:90-002542.

Audience: **u,f.**

Pople, Anthony   **ML410.M595 P58 1998**
Messiaen: Quatuor Pour la Fin du Temps. Julian Rushton
(Contribution by). Cloth Text. Cambridge University Press. New
York, NY. 1998. 126p. Music Handbks. ISBN:0-521-58497-3,
ISBN13: 978-0-521-58497-5. Dewey:785/.24194.
LCCN:98-023937.

Audience: **u,f.** *Choice, 1999.*

Rink, John   **ML410.C54RR54 1997**
Chopin: The Piano Concertos. Julian Rushton (Editor,
Contribution by). Cloth Text. Cambridge University Press. New
York, NY. 1997. 149p. Music Handbks. ISBN:0-521-44109-9,
ISBN13: 978-0-521-44109-4. Dewey:784.2/62/092.
LCCN:97-006905.

Audience: **u,f.**

Rischin, Rebecca   **ML410.M595R57 2003**
For the End of Time: The Story of the Messiaen Quartet. Book,
Other. Cornell University Press. Ithaca, NY. 2003. 184p.
ISBN:0-8014-4136-6, ISBN13: 978-0-8014-4136-3.
Dewey:785/.24194. LCCN:2003-011589.

Audience: **u,f.** *Choice, 2004.*

Roberts, Paul   **ML410.C54**
Images: The Piano Music of Claude Debussy. Trade Paper. Hal
Leonard Corporation. Milwaukee, WI. 2003. 372p.
ISBN:1-57467-068-9, ISBN13: 978-1-57467-068-4.
Dewey:786.2/092.

Audience: **l,u,f.** *Choice, 1996.*

Roeder, Michael T.   **ML1263.R64 1994**
A History of the Concerto. Trade Cloth. Hal Leonard
Corporation. Milwaukee, WI. 1994. 484p. ISBN:0-931340-61-6,
ISBN13: 978-0-931340-61-1. Dewey:784.2/3/09.
LCCN:92-041967.

Audience: **u,f.** *Choice, 1994.*

Rosen, Charles   **MT145.B42R67 2002**
Beethoven's Piano Sonatas: A Short Companion. Cloth over
Boards. Yale University Press. Cumberland, RI. 2002. 272p.
ISBN:0-300-09070-6, ISBN13: 978-0-300-09070-3.
Dewey:786.2/183/092. LCCN:2001-093745.

Audience: **l,u,f.** *Choice, 2003, 2002.*

Rosen, Charles   **ML1156**
The Sonata Forms. Ed. 2. Trade Paper. W. W. Norton &
Company, Inc. New York, NY. 1988. 426p.
ISBN:0-393-30219-9, ISBN13: 978-0-393-30219-6.
Dewey:781/.52/09. LCCN:79-027538.

Audience: **l,u,f.**

Rushton, Julian (Author,   **ML410.E41 R87 1999**
Contribution by)
Elgar: Enigma Variations. Cloth Text. Cambridge University
Press. New York, NY. 1999. 124p. Music Handbks.
ISBN:0-521-63175-0, ISBN13: 978-0-521-63175-4.
Dewey:784.2/1825. LCCN:98-022042.

Audience: **u,f.** *Choice, 1999.*

Russ, Michael   **ML410.M97 R9 1992**
Musorgsky: Pictures at an Exhibition. Julian Rushton
(Contribution by). Trade Paper. Cambridge University Press.
New York, NY. 1992. 110p. Music Handbks.
ISBN:0-521-38607-1, ISBN13: 978-0-521-38607-4.
Dewey:786.21896. LCCN:91-032687.

Audience: **l,u,f.** *Choice, 1993.*

Samson, Jim   **ML410.C54 S187 1992**
Chopin: The Four Ballades. Julian Rushton (Contribution by).
Trade Cloth. Cambridge University Press. New York, NY. 1992.
114p. Music Handbks. ISBN:0-521-38461-3, ISBN13:
978-0-521-38461-2. Dewey:786.21896. LCCN:91-002542.

Audience: **u,f.**

Schiff, David   **ML410.G288 S27 1997**
Gershwin: Rhapsody in Blue. Julian Rushton (Contribution by).
Cloth Text. Cambridge University Press. New York, NY. 1997.
132p. Music Handbks. ISBN:0-521-55077-7, ISBN13:
978-0-521-55077-2. Dewey:784.2/62. LCCN:96-047439.

Audience: **l,u,f.**

Schroeder, David P.   **ML410.H4S45 1997**
Haydn and the Enlightenment: The Late Symphonies and Their
Audience. Trade Paper. Oxford University Press, Inc. New York,
NY. 1998. 230p. Oxford Monographs on Music
ISBN:0-19-816682-6, ISBN13: 978-0-19-816682-5.
Dewey:784.2/184/092. LCCN:97-025754.

Audience: **u,f.**

Schulenberg, David   **MT145.B14S415 1992**
The Keyboard Music of J. S. Bach. Trade Cloth. Thomson Gale.
Farmington Hills, MI. 1992. 475p. ISBN:0-02-873275-8,
ISBN13: 978-0-02-873275-6. Dewey:786/.092.
LCCN:91-039348.

Audience: **l,u,f.** *Choice, 1993.*

Sipe, Thomas   ML410.B42 S57 1998
Beethoven: Eroica Symphony. Julian Rushton (Contribution by).
Trade Paper. Cambridge University Press. New York, NY. 1998.
158p. Music Handbks. ISBN:0-521-47562-7, ISBN13:
978-0-521-47562-4. Dewey:784.2/184. LCCN:97-033020.
                                        Audience: **u,f.** *Choice, 1999.*

Sisman, Elaine Rochelle   ML410.M9S561993
Mozart, the "Jupiter" Symphony, No. 41 in C Major, K. 551.
Julian Rushton (Editor, Contribution by). Trade Paper.
Cambridge University Press. New York, NY. 1993. 122p.
Cambridge Music Handbooks Ser. ISBN:0-521-40924-1,
ISBN13: 978-0-521-40924-7. Dewey:784.184092.
LCCN:92-039074.
                                        Audience: **u,f.**

Smaczny, Jan   MT130.D9 S6 1999
Dvorák: Cello Concerto. Cloth Text. Cambridge University
Press. New York, NY. 1999. 130p. Music Handbks.
ISBN:0-521-66050-5, ISBN13: 978-0-521-66050-1.
Dewey:784.2/74. LCCN:98-052746.
                                        Audience: **u,f.**

Smallman, Basil   ML128.C4
The Piano Trio: Its History, Technique, and Repertoire. Paper
Text. Oxford University Press, Inc. New York, NY. 1992. 238p.
ISBN:0-19-816304-5, ISBN13: 978-0-19-816304-6.
Dewey:785/.28193.
                                        Audience: **u,f.** *Choice, 1991.*

Steinberg, Michael   ML1263.S74 1998
The Concerto: A Listener's Guide. Trade Cloth. Oxford
University Press, Inc. New York, NY. 1998. 522p.
ISBN:0-19-510330-0, ISBN13: 978-0-19-510330-4.
Dewey:784.2/3/015. LCCN:97-042678.
                                        Audience: **g,l,u,f.**

Steinberg, Michael   MT125
The Symphony: A Listener's Guide. Trade Paper. Oxford
University Press, Inc. New York, NY. 1998. 696p.
ISBN:0-19-512665-3, ISBN13: 978-0-19-512665-5.
Dewey:784.2/184/015.
                                        Audience: **g,l,u,f.**

Stinson, Russell   ML410.B13S87 1996
Bach: The Orgelbuchlein. Trade Cloth. Thomson Gale.
Farmington Hills, MI. 1996. xv, 208p. Monuments of Western
Music Ser. ISBN:0-02-872505-0, ISBN13: 978-0-02-872505-5.
Dewey:786.5/18992/092. LCCN:96-024581.
                                        Audience: **u,f.** *Choice, 1997.*

Stowell, Robin (Editor)   ML1160
The Cambridge Companion to the String Quartet. Jonathan
Cross (Contribution by). Cloth Text. Cambridge University
Press. New York, NY. 2003. 390p. Cambridge Companions to
Music Ser. ISBN:0-521-80194-X, ISBN13: 978-0-521-80194-2.
Dewey:785.7/194. LCCN:2003-043508.
                                        Audience: **u,f.** *Choice, 2004.*

Stowell, Robin   ML410.B4 S76 1998
Beethoven: Violin Concerto. Julian Rushton (Contribution by).
Cloth Text. Cambridge University Press. New York, NY. 1998.
138p. Music Handbks. ISBN:0-521-45159-0, ISBN13:
978-0-521-45159-8. Dewey:784.2/72. LCCN:97-014035.
                                        Audience: **u,f.**

Suchoff, Benjamin   ML410.B26S83 1995
Bartok: Concerto for Orchestra: Understanding Bartok's World.
Cloth Text. Thomson Wadsworth. Belmont, CA. 1995. 266p.
Monuments of Western Music Ser. ISBN:0-02-872495-X,
ISBN13: 978-0-02-872495-9. Dewey:784.2/186.
LCCN:95-010440.
                                        Audience: **u,f.** *Choice, 1996.*

Sutcliffe, W. Dean   ML410.S22S88 2003
The Keyboard Sonatas of Domenico Scarlatti and
Eighteenth-Century Musical Style. Trade Cloth. Cambridge
University Press. New York, NY. 2003. 412p.
ISBN:0-521-48140-6, ISBN13: 978-0-521-48140-3.
Dewey:786/.183/092. LCCN:2002-035012.
                                        Audience: **u,f.** *Choice, 2004.*

Taub, Robert   MT145.B42T38 2002
Playing the Beethoven Piano Sonatas. Trade Cloth. Hal Leonard
Corporation. Milwaukee, WI. 2003. 258p. ISBN:1-57467-071-9,
ISBN13: 978-1-57467-071-4. Dewey:786.2/183/092.
LCCN:2001-046126.
                                        Audience: **l,u,f.** *Choice, 2003, 2002.*

Todd, Larry   ML706.N56 2003
19th-Century Piano Music. Ed. 2. Trade Paper. Routledge. New
York, NY. 2003. 460p. Studies in Musical Genres
ISBN:0-415-94362-0, ISBN13: 978-0-415-94362-8.
Dewey:786.2/09/034. LCCN:2003-058687.
                                        Audience: **u,f.**

Todd, R. Larry   ML410.M5
Mendelssohn: The Hebrides and Other Overtures. Julian
Rushton (Contribution by). Trade Paper. Cambridge University
Press. New York, NY. 1993. 129p. Music Handbks.
ISBN:0-521-40764-8, ISBN13: 978-0-521-40764-9.
Dewey:784.218926092. LCCN:92-036005.
                                        Audience: **u,f.** *Choice, 1994.*

Trezise, Simon   ML410.D28 T7 1994
Debussy: La Mer. Julian Rushton (Contribution by). Trade
Paper. Cambridge University Press. New York, NY. 1995. 121p.
Music Handbks. ISBN:0-521-44656-2, ISBN13:
978-0-521-44656-3. Dewey:784.2/1896. LCCN:93-042789.
                                        Audience: **u,f.** *Choice, 1995.*

Troeger, Richard   MT179.T76 2003
Playing Bach on the Keyboard: A Practical Guide. Trade Cloth.
Hal Leonard Corporation. Milwaukee, WI. 2003. 300p.
ISBN:1-57467-084-0, ISBN13: 978-1-57467-084-4.
Dewey:786/.092. LCCN:2003-012791.
                                        Audience: **l,u,f.** *Choice, 2004.*

Williams, Peter F.   MT145.B14W53 2002
The Organ Music of J. S. Bach. Ed. 2. Cloth Text. Cambridge
University Press. New York, NY. 2003. 634p.
ISBN:0-521-81416-2, ISBN13: 978-0-521-81416-4.
Dewey:786.5/092. LCCN:2002-067368.
                                  Audience: **l,u,f.** *Choice, 2004.*

Williams, Peter F.   MT145.B14 W55 2001
Bach: The Goldberg Variations. Julian Rushton (Contribution
by). Cloth Text. Cambridge University Press. New York, NY.
2001. 118p. Music Handbks. ISBN:0-521-80735-2, ISBN13:
978-0-521-80735-7. Dewey:786.4/1825. LCCN:2001-025616.
                                           Audience: **u,f.**

Williamson, John   ML410.S93 W55 1993
Strauss: Also Sprach Zarathustra. Julian Rushton (Contribution
by). Cloth Text. Cambridge University Press. New York, NY.
1993. 136p. Music Handbks. ISBN:0-521-40076-7, ISBN13:
978-0-521-40076-3. Dewey:784.2184. LCCN:92-020457.
                                           Audience: **u,f.**

Winter, Robert & Martin,   MT145.B425.B4 1994
  Robert (Editors)
The Beethoven Quartet Companion. Trade Cloth. University of
California Press. Berkeley, CA. 1994. 300p.
ISBN:0-520-08211-7, ISBN13: 978-0-520-08211-3.
Dewey:785.7/194/092. LCCN:92-040668.
                                  Audience: **l,u,f.** *Choice, 1995.*

Wolff, Konrad   ML705.W64 1990
Masters of the Keyboard: Individual Style Elements in the Piano
Music of Bach, Haydn, Mozart, Beethoven, and Schubert. Trade
Cloth. Indiana University Press. Bloomington, IN. 1990. 328p.
ISBN:0-253-36458-2, ISBN13: 978-0-253-36458-6.
Dewey:786.2/09/033. LCCN:89-045570.
                          Audience: **u,f.** *B* *Choice, 1991.*

Woodstra, Chris, et al.   ML156
All Music Guide to Classical Music: The Definitive Guide to
Classical Music. Gerald Brennan & Allen Schrott (Authors).
Trade Paper, Perfect. Backbeat Books. San Francisco, CA. 2005.
1607p. ISBN:0-87930-865-6, ISBN13: 978-0-87930-865-0.
Dewey:016.78026/6. LCCN:2005-023988.
                                  Audience: **g,l,u,f.** *Choice, 2006.*

Zaslaw, Neal (Editor)   ML410.M9M875 1996
Mozart's Piano Concertos: Text, Context, Interpretation. Trade
Cloth. University of Michigan Press. Chicago, IL. 1997. 496p.
ISBN:0-472-10314-8, ISBN13: 978-0-472-10314-0.
Dewey:784.2/62/092. LCCN:96-004416.
                                           Audience: **l,u,f.**

Zaslaw, Neal   ML410.B5
Mozart's Symphonies: Context, Performance Practice,
Reception. Paper Text. Oxford University Press, Inc. New York,
NY. 1991. 642p. ISBN:0-19-816286-3, ISBN13:
978-0-19-816286-5. Dewey:785.1/1/0924.
                                  Audience: **l,u,f.** *Choice, 1990.*

Zychowicz, James L.   ML410.B42
Mahler's Fourth Symphony. Trade Cloth. Oxford University
Press, Inc. New York, NY. 2000. 206p. Studies in Musical
Genesis, Structure, and Interpretation ISBN:0-19-816206-5,
ISBN13: 978-0-19-816206-3. Dewey:784.2/184.
                                           Audience: **u,f.**

Studies in Music History, Criticism, Analysis, and Appreciation > Western Classical Literature by Genre > Electroacoustic

Braun, Hans-Joachim   ML197.I2 2002
Music and Technology in the Twentieth Century. International
Committee for the History of Technology (Contribution by).
Trade Cloth. Johns Hopkins University Press. Baltimore, MD.
2002. 256p. ISBN:0-8018-6885-8, ISBN13: 978-0-8018-6885-6.
Dewey:780/.06. LCCN:2001-042490.
                                           Audience: **u,f.**

Chadabe, Joel   ML1380.C43 1997
Electric Sound: The Past and Promise of Electronic Music.
Trade Paper. Prentice Hall PTR. Upper Saddle River, NJ. 1996.
370p. ISBN:0-13-303231-0, ISBN13: 978-0-13-303231-4.
Dewey:786.7. LCCN:96-029349.
                                           Audience: **g,l,u,f.**

Emmerson, Simon (Editor)   ML1380.M86 2000
Music, Electronic Media and Culture. Trade Cloth. Ashgate
Publishing, Ltd. Aldershot, 2000. 262p. ISBN:0-7546-0109-9,
ISBN13: 978-0-7546-0109-8. Dewey:786.7. LCCN:00-059415.
                                           Audience: **l,u,f.**

Glinsky, Albert   ML429.T43G6 2000
Theremin: Ether Music and Espionage. Robert Moog (Foreword
by). Trade Cloth. University of Illinois Press. Champaign, IL.
2000. 480p. Music in American Life Ser. ISBN:0-252-02582-2,
ISBN13: 978-0-252-02582-2. Dewey:786.7/3 B.
LCCN:00-008024.
                                  Audience: **g,l,u,f.** *Choice, 2001.*

Holmes, Thom   ML1380
Electronic and Experimental Music: Pioneers in Technology and
Composition. Ed. 2. Paper over Boards. Routledge. New York,
NY. 2002. 336p. ISBN:0-415-93643-8, ISBN13:
978-0-415-93643-9. Dewey:781.69.
                                           Audience: **l,u,f.**

Manning, Peter D.   ML1380.M36 2004
Electronic and Computer Music. Trade Paper. Oxford University
Press, Inc. New York, NY. 2004. 484p. ISBN:0-19-517085-7,
ISBN13: 978-0-19-517085-6. Dewey:786.7/09.
LCCN:2002-155278.
                                           Audience: **u,f.**

Roads, Curtis   **MT723**
The Music Machine: Selected Readings from Computer Music
Journal. Trade Paper. MIT Press. Cambridge, MA. 1992. 739p.
ISBN:0-262-68078-5, ISBN13: 978-0-262-68078-3.
Dewey:786.7/6.
Audience: **u,f.**

Schwartz, Elliott   **ML1092.S37 1989**
Electronic Music: A Listener's Guide. Paper Text. Da Capo
Press, Inc. Cambridge, MA. 1989. 306p. Music Reprint Ser.
ISBN:0-306-76260-9, ISBN13: 978-0-306-76260-4.
Dewey:789.9/9. LCCN:84-021508.
Audience: **g,l,u,f.**

Simoni, Mary   **ML1380.A53 2005**
Analytical Methods of Electroacoustic Music. Cloth Text.
Routledge. New York, NY. 2005. 312p. Studies on New Music
Research ISBN:0-415-97629-4, ISBN13: 978-0-415-97629-9.
Dewey:781.2. LCCN:2005-014484.
Audience: **u,f.**

Wierzbicki, James Eugene   **ML410.B258W54 2005**
Louis and Bebe Barron's Forbidden Planet: A Film Score Guide.
Trade Paper. Scarecrow Press, Inc. Lanham, MD. 2005. 200p.
Scarecrow Film Score Guides Ser., No. 4 ISBN:0-8108-5670-0,
ISBN13: 978-0-8108-5670-7. Dewey:781.5/42.
LCCN:2005-008132.
Audience: **u,f.**

Studies in Music History, Criticism, Analysis, and Appreciation > Western Classical Literature by European Nationality

Applegate, Celia & Potter,   **ML275.M933 2002**
   Pamela Maxine
Music and German National Identity. Trade Cloth. University of
Chicago Press. Chicago, IL. 2002. 329p. ISBN:0-226-02130-0,
ISBN13: 978-0-226-02130-0. Dewey:780/.943.
LCCN:2001-007534.
Audience: **u,f.**

Bellman, Jonathan   **ML240.B37 1993**
The Style Hongrois in the Music of Western Europe. Cloth Text.
Northeastern University Press. Boston, MA. 1993. 224p.
ISBN:1-55553-169-5, ISBN13: 978-1-55553-169-0.
Dewey:780/.9/033. LCCN:93-010150.
Audience: **u,f.** *Choice, 1994.*

Brinkmann, Reinhold &   **ML198.5 .D75 1999**
   Wolff, Christoph
Driven into Paradise: The Musical Migration from Nazi
Germany to the United States. Trade Cloth. University of
California Press. Berkeley, CA. 1999. 388p.
ISBN:0-520-21413-7, ISBN13: 978-0-520-21413-2.
Dewey:780/.943/0973. LCCN:98-028956.
Audience: **u,f.** *Choice, 2000.*

Caldwell, John   **ML286.C28**
The Oxford History of English Music: C. 1715 to the Present
Day, Vol. II. Trade Cloth. Oxford University Press, Inc. New
York, NY. 1999. 636p. ISBN:0-19-816288-X, ISBN13:
978-0-19-816288-9. Dewey:780.9/42. LCCN:90-014229.
Audience: **u,f.** *Choice, 2000.*

Caldwell, John   **ML286.C28 1991**
The Oxford History of English Music: From the Beginnings to
c. 1715. Trade Cloth. Oxford University Press, Inc. New York,
NY. 1992. 708p. Oxford History of English Music Ser.
ISBN:0-19-816129-8, ISBN13: 978-0-19-816129-5.
Dewey:780.9/42. LCCN:90-014229.
Audience: **u,f.** *Choice, 1992.*

Campbell, Stuart (Editor)   **ML300.4 .R87 1994**
Russians on Russian Music, 1830-1880: An Anthology in
Translation. Trade Cloth. Cambridge University Press. New
York, NY. 1994. 317p. ISBN:0-521-40267-0, ISBN13:
978-0-521-40267-5. Dewey:780.94709034. LCCN:93-017690.
Audience: **u,f.** *Choice, 1995.*

Chase, Gilbert   **ML315**
Music of Spain. Ed. 2. Trade Paper. Dover Publications, Inc.
Mineola, NY. 1960. ISBN:0-486-20549-5, ISBN13:
978-0-486-20549-6. Dewey:780.946.
Audience: **u,f.** *B*

Daverio, John J.   **ML275 .D38 1993**
Nineteenth-Century Music and the German Romantic Ideology.
Trade Cloth. Thomson Gale. Farmington Hills, MI. 1993. 274p.
ISBN:0-02-870675-7, ISBN13: 978-0-02-870675-7.
Dewey:780/.943/09034. LCCN:92-042513.
Audience: **u,f.**

Dobszay, Laszlo   **ML248 .D5813 1993**
A History of Hungarian Music. Trade Paper. Corvina Books.
1999. 236p. ISBN:963-13-3498-8, ISBN13: 978-963-13-3498-2.
Dewey:780/.9439. LCCN:98-193377.
Audience: **u,f.**

Gilliam, Bryan Randolph   **ML457 .M86 1994**
   (Editor)
Music and Performance During the Weimar Republic. Cloth
Text. Cambridge University Press. New York, NY. 1994. 234p.
Cambridge Studies in Performance Practice Ser., Vol. 3
ISBN:0-521-42012-1, ISBN13: 978-0-521-42012-9.
Dewey:780.9/43/09042. LCCN:93-031382.
Audience: **u,f.** *Choice, 1995.*

Johnson, James H.   **ML270.J64 1995**
Listening in Paris: A Cultural History. Trade Cloth. University
of California Press. Berkeley, CA. 1995. 363p. Studies on the
History of Society and Culture, Vol. 21 ISBN:0-520-08564-7,
ISBN13: 978-0-520-08564-0. Dewey:780.9/44361.
LCCN:94-006492.
Audience: **u,f.** *Choice, 1995.*

Karas, Joza   **ML247.8.T47**
Music in Terezin, 1941-1945. Trade Paper. Pendragon Press.
Hillsdale, NY. 1985. 212p. ISBN:0-918728-34-7, ISBN13:
978-0-918728-34-0. Dewey:780/.9437/1. LCCN:84-024411.
Audience: **u,f.**

Kater, Michael H.   **ML275.5.K38 1997**
The Twisted Muse: Musicians and Their Music in the Third
Reich. Trade Cloth. Oxford University Press, Inc. New York,
NY. 1997. 342p. ISBN:0-19-509620-7, ISBN13:
978-0-19-509620-0. Dewey:780/.943/09043. LCCN:96-006339.
Audience: **u,f.** *Choice, 1997.*

Kimbell, David R. B.   **ML733.K55 1994**
Italian Opera. John Warrack (Contribution by). Trade Paper.
Cambridge University Press. New York, NY. 1994. 702p.
National Tradition of Opera Ser. ISBN:0-521-46643-1, ISBN13:
978-0-521-46643-1. Dewey:782.1/0945.
Audience: **u,f.**

Mason, Laura   **ML3621.R48M37 1996**
Singing the French Revolution: Popular Culture and Politics,
1787-1799. Trade Cloth. Cornell University Press. Ithaca, NY.
1996. 280p. ISBN:0-8014-3233-2, ISBN13: 978-0-8014-3233-0.
Dewey:781.5/99/094409033. LCCN:96-017694.
Audience: **u,f.** *Choice, 1997.*

Miller, Phillip L. (Editor), et **ML54.6.G275 1990**
al.
German Lieder. Brahms & Gustav Mahler (Editors). Trade
Paper. Continuum International Publishing Group, Ltd. London,
1990. German Library, Vol. 42 ISBN:0-8264-0328-X, ISBN13:
978-0-8264-0328-5. Dewey:782.4/3/0943. LCCN:89-039980.
Audience: **g,l,u,f.**

Newmarch, Rosa H.   **ML247**
The Music of Czechoslovakia. Library Binding. Reprint Services
Company. Temecula, CA. 1992. 244p. Music Book Index Ser.
ISBN:0-7812-9510-6, ISBN13: 978-0-7812-9510-9.
Dewey:780/.9437.
Audience: **u,f.**

Parsons, James (Editor)   **ML2829.C36 2003**
The Cambridge Companion to the Lied. Jonathan Cross
(Contribution by). Trade Cloth. Cambridge University Press.
New York, NY. 2004. 438p. Cambridge Companions to Music
Ser. ISBN:0-521-80027-7, ISBN13: 978-0-521-80027-3.
Dewey:782.42168/0943. LCCN:2003-051229.
Audience: **u,f.**

Rosand, Ellen   **ML1733.8.V4R67 1991**
Opera in Seventeenth-Century Venice: The Creation of a Genre.
Trade Cloth. University of California Press. Berkeley, CA. 1990.
710p. ISBN:0-520-06808-4, ISBN13: 978-0-520-06808-7.
Dewey:782.1/0945/3109032. LCCN:90-040399.
Audience: **u,f.** *Choice, 1991.*

Rosselli, John   **ML290.4**
Music and Musicians in Nineteenth Century Italy. Trade Cloth.

Hal Leonard Corporation. Milwaukee, WI. 1991. 162p.
ISBN:0-931340-40-3, ISBN13: 978-0-931340-40-6.
Dewey:780.92.
Audience: **u,f.**

Rosselli, John   **ML1733.R78 1984**
The Opera Industry in Italy from Cimarosa to Verdi: The Role
of the Impresario. Trade Cloth. Cambridge University Press.
New York, NY. 1984. 224p. ISBN:0-521-25732-8, ISBN13:
978-0-521-25732-9. Dewey:782.1/0945. LCCN:83-007688.
Audience: **u,f.** *B*

Sachs, Harvey   **ML290.5 .S23 1988**
Music in Fascist Italy. Trade Cloth. W. W. Norton & Company,
Inc. New York, NY. 1988. ISBN:0-393-02563-2, ISBN13:
978-0-393-02563-7. Dewey:780.945. LCCN:2004-366524.
Audience: **u,f.**

Sadler, Graham & Wood,   **ML1727.W64 2000**
Caroline
French Baroque Opera: A Reader. Trade Cloth. Ashgate
Publishing, Ltd. Aldershot, 2000. ix, 160p. ISBN:1-84014-241-3,
ISBN13: 978-1-84014-241-9. Dewey:782.1/0944/09032.
LCCN:99-054365.
Audience: **u,f.**

Schwarz, Boris   **ML300.5.S37 1983**
Music and Musical Life in Soviet Russia, 1917-1981. Trade
Cloth. Indiana University Press. Bloomington, IN. 1983. 736p.
ISBN:0-253-33956-1, ISBN13: 978-0-253-33956-0.
Dewey:780/.947. LCCN:82-048267.
Audience: **u,f.** *B*

Slobin, Mark (Editor)   **ML240.5.R48 1996**
Retuning Culture: Musical Changes in Central and Eastern
Europe. Trade Cloth. Duke University Press. Durham, NC.
1996. 320p. ISBN:0-8223-1855-5, ISBN13: 978-0-8223-1855-2.
Dewey:780/.947/0904. LCCN:96-027983.
Audience: **u,f.** *Choice, 1997.*

Smith, Frederick Key   **ML310**
Nordic Art Music: From the Middle Ages to the Third
Millennium. Trade Cloth. Greenwood Publishing Group, Inc.
Portsmouth, NH. 2002. 216p. ISBN:0-275-97399-9, ISBN13:
978-0-275-97399-5. Dewey:780/.948. LCCN:2001-058947.
Audience: **u,f.** *Choice, 2003.*

Strohm, Reinhard   **ML1733.3.S87 1997**
Dramma per Musica: Italian Opera Seria of the Eighteenth
Century. Cloth over Boards. Yale University Press. Cumberland,
RI. 1997. 336p. ISBN:0-300-06454-3, ISBN13:
978-0-300-06454-4. Dewey:782.1/0945/09033.
LCCN:97-027576.
Audience: **u,f.** *Choice, 1998.*

Sturman, Janet Lynn   **ML1950.S78 2000**
Zarzuela: Spanish Operetta, American Stage. Trade Cloth.
University of Illinois Press. Champaign, IL. 2000. 256p. Music
in American Life Ser. ISBN:0-252-02596-2, ISBN13:
978-0-252-02596-9. Dewey:782.1/2. LCCN:00-008032.
Audience: **u,f.**

Taruskin, Richard F.   ML300.T37 2000
Defining Russia Musically: Historical and Hermeneutical
Essays. Trade Paper. Princeton University Press. Princeton, NJ.
2000. 594p. ISBN:0-691-07065-2, ISBN13: 978-0-691-07065-0.
Dewey:780/.947.

> Audience: **u,f.** *Choice, 1997.*

Warrack, John   ML1729 .W37 2001
German Opera: From the Beginnings to Wagner. Tim Carter,
John Deathridge, Arthur Groos, James Hepokoski, Paul
Robinson & Ellen Rosand (Contribution by). Trade Cloth.
Cambridge University Press. New York, NY. 2001. 464p.
Cambridge Studies in Opera Ser. ISBN:0-521-23532-4, ISBN13:
978-0-521-23532-7. Dewey:792.10943. LCCN:00-062127.

> Audience: **u,f.** *Choice, 2002.*

White, Eric W.   ML1700
A History of English Opera. Trade Cloth. Faber & Faber, Ltd.
London, 1983. 472p. ISBN:0-571-10788-5, ISBN13:
978-0-571-10788-9. Dewey:782.1/0942. LCCN:83-001599.

> Audience: **u,f.** *B*

Studies in Music History, Criticism, Analysis, and Appreciation > Western Classical Literature: Miscellaneous Studies and Essays

Bellman, Jonathan (Editor)   ML55.E9 1998
The Exotic in Western Music. Cloth Text. Northeastern
University Press. Boston, MA. 1997. 416p.
ISBN:1-55553-320-5, ISBN13: 978-1-55553-320-5. Dewey:780.
LCCN:97-016407.

> Audience: **u,f.** *Choice, 1998.*

Bernstein, Leonard   ML60
The Joy of Music. Paper Text. Textbook Publishers. Temecula,
CA. 2003. 303p. ISBN:0-7581-3834-2, ISBN13:
978-0-7581-3834-7. Dewey:780.

> Audience: **g,l,u,f.**

Copland, Aaron   MT6
What to Listen for in Music. Library Binding. Sagebrush
Education Resources. Caledonia, MN. 1999.
ISBN:0-613-18082-8, ISBN13: 978-0-613-18082-5.
Dewey:780/.1/5.

> Audience: **l,u,f.** *B*

Dower, Catherine   ML60
Alfred Einstein on Music: Selected Music Criticisms. Trade
Cloth. Greenwood Publishing Group, Inc. Portsmouth, NH.
1991. 328p. Contributions to the Study of Music and Dance
Ser., No. 21 ISBN:0-313-27363-4, ISBN13: 978-0-313-27363-6.
Dewey:780/.9. LCCN:90-013997.

> Audience: **u,f.**

Gould, Glenn & Page, Tim   ML60.G68 1984
The Glenn Gould Reader. Trade Cloth. Alfred A. Knopf Inc.
New York, NY. 1984. 441p. ISBN:0-394-54067-0, ISBN13:
978-0-394-54067-2. Dewey:780. LCCN:84-047819.

> Audience: **u,f.** *B*

Grainger, Percy   ML60.G74 1999
Grainger on Music. Malcolm Gillies & Bruce Ross (Editors).
Trade Cloth. Oxford University Press, Inc. New York, NY. 1999.
416p. ISBN:0-19-816665-6, ISBN13: 978-0-19-816665-8.
Dewey:780. LCCN:98-045828.

> Audience: **u,f.**

Hollander, John   ML3849
The Untuning of the Sky: Ideas of Music in English Poetry,
1500-1700. Trade Cloth. Shoe String Press, Inc. North Haven,
CT. 1992. 498p. ISBN:0-208-02351-8, ISBN13:
978-0-208-02351-3. Dewey:821.009/357. LCCN:92-007084.

> Audience: **u,f.**

Kerman, Joseph   ML60
Write All These Down: Essays on Music. Trade Paper.
University of California Press. Berkeley, CA. 1998. 374p.
ISBN:0-520-21377-7, ISBN13: 978-0-520-21377-7. Dewey:780.
LCCN:93-001876.

> Audience: **u,f.**

McClary, Susan   ML60
Conventional Wisdom: The Content of Musical Form. Trade
Paper. University of California Press. Berkeley, CA. 2001. 220p.
Ernest Bloch Lectures ISBN:0-520-23208-9, ISBN13:
978-0-520-23208-2. Dewey:780. LCCN:99-029428.

> Audience: **u,f.**

Morgenstern, Sam (Editor)   ML90.M6 1969
Composers on Music: An Anthology of Composers Writings
from Palestrina to Copland. Library Binding. Greenwood
Publishing Group, Inc. Portsmouth, NH. 1985. xxiii, 584p.
ISBN:0-8371-1147-1, ISBN13: 978-0-8371-1147-6.
Dewey:780/.8. LCCN:69-014005.

> Audience: **g,l,u,f.** *B*

Page, Tim   ML60.P143 2002
Tim Page on Music: Views and Reviews. Anthony Tommasini
(Foreword by). Trade Cloth. Hal Leonard Corporation.
Milwaukee, WI. 2003. 364p. ISBN:1-57467-076-X, ISBN13:
978-1-57467-076-9. Dewey:780. LCCN:2002-066534.

> Audience: **u,f.**

Rorem, Ned   ML60.R78425 2001
A Ned Rorem Reader. Cloth over Boards. Yale University Press.
Cumberland, RI. 2001. 320p. ISBN:0-300-08984-8, ISBN13:
978-0-300-08984-4. Dewey:780. LCCN:2001-033334.

> Audience: **g,l,u,f.**

Rosen, Charles   ML60.R7848 2000
Critical Entertainments: Music Old and New. Trade Cloth.
Harvard University Press. Cambridge, MA. 2000. 336p.
ISBN:0-674-17730-4, ISBN13: 978-0-674-17730-7. Dewey:780.
LCCN:99-088602.

> Audience: **g,l,u,f.**

Audience: g=general, l=lower division undergraduate, u=upper division undergraduate, f=faculty.

247

Shaw, George Bernard ML286.8.L5S32 1995
Shaw on Music. Eric Bentley (Editor). Trade Paper. Applause
Theatre Book Publishers. New York, NY. 2000. 310p.
ISBN:1-55783-149-1, ISBN13: 978-1-55783-149-1. Dewey:780.
LCCN:95-005376.
Audience: **u,f.**

Slonimsky, Nicolas ML3785.S5 2000
Lexicon of Musical Invective: Critical Assaults on Composers
since Beethoven's Time. Trade Paper. W. W. Norton &
Company, Inc. New York, NY. 2000. 325p.
ISBN:0-393-32009-X, ISBN13: 978-0-393-32009-1.
Dewey:780/.9. LCCN:2001-266586.
Audience: **g,l,u,f.**

Slonimsky, Nicolas ML60
Nicolas Slonimsky: The First Hundred Years. Kostelanetz,
Richard (Editor) (Introduction by); Darby, Joseph (Assistant
Editor). Schirmer Books. 1994. ISBN:0-02-871845-3, ISBN13:
978-0-02-871845-3.
Audience: **u,f.**

Winn, James Anderson ML3849
Unsuspected Eloquence: A History of the Relations Between
Poetry and Music. Trade Cloth. Yale University Press.
Cumberland, RI. 1981. xiv, 381p. ISBN:0-300-02615-3,
ISBN13: 978-0-300-02615-3. Dewey:780/.08. LCCN:80-027055.
Audience: **u,f.** *B*

Studies in Music History, Criticism, Analysis, and Appreciation > Musical Theatre

Ainger, Michael ML410.S95A77 2002
Gilbert and Sullivan: A Dual Biography. Trade Cloth. Oxford
University Press, Inc. New York, NY. 2002. 528p.
ISBN:0-19-514769-3, ISBN13: 978-0-19-514769-8.
Dewey:782.1/2/0922 B. LCCN:2001-056046.
Audience: **g,l,u,f.** *Choice, 2003.*

Alpert, Hollis ML410.G288A35 1990
The Life and Times of Porgy and Bess: The Story of an
American Classic. Trade Cloth. Alfred A. Knopf Inc. New York,
NY. 1990. ISBN:0-394-58339-6, ISBN13: 978-0-394-58339-6.
Dewey:782.1. LCCN:89-043367.
Audience: **g,l,u,f.**

Bergreen, Laurence ML410.B499B5 1996
As Thousands Cheer: The Life of Irving Berlin. Trade Paper. Da
Capo Press, Inc. Cambridge, MA. 1996. 702p.
ISBN:0-306-80675-4, ISBN13: 978-0-306-80675-9.
Dewey:782.1/4/092 B. LCCN:95-049847.
Audience: **g,l,u,f.** *Choice, 1991.*

Black, Don & Hampton, ML50.Z99
Christopher
Sunset Boulevard. Trade Paper. Faber & Faber, Inc. New York,
NY. 1993. 128p. ISBN:0-571-17214-8, ISBN13:
978-0-571-17214-6. Dewey:782.140268.
Audience: **g,l,u,f.**

Block, Geoffrey ML410.S6872
The Richard Rodgers Reader. Trade Paper. Oxford University
Press, Inc. New York, NY. 2006. 368p. Readers on American
Musicians Ser. ISBN:0-19-531343-7, ISBN13:
978-0-19-531343-7. Dewey:782.1/4/092.
Audience: **g,l,u,f.**

Block, Geoffrey Holden ML410.R6315B56 2003
Richard Rodgers. Cloth over Boards. Yale University Press.
Cumberland, RI. 2003. 336p. Yale Broadway Masters Ser.
ISBN:0-300-09747-6, ISBN13: 978-0-300-09747-4.
Dewey:782.1/4/092 B. LCCN:2003-002412.
Audience: **g,l,u,f.** *Choice, 2004.*

Bloom, Kenneth ML128.M78.B6 1996
American Song: The Complete Musical Theatre Companion,
1877-1995, Vol. 1 & 2. Ed. 2. Trade Cloth. Thomson Gale.
Farmington Hills, MI. 1905. 2093p. ISBN:0-02-870484-3,
ISBN13: 978-0-02-870484-5. Dewey:782.1/4/0973.
LCCN:95-049840.
Audience: **g,l,u,f.** *Choice, 1996.*

Bloom, Kenneth ML128.M7B6 1995
Hollywood Song: The Complete Film and Musical Companion.
Trade Cloth. Facts On File, Inc. New York, NY. 1995.
ISBN:0-8160-3231-9, ISBN13: 978-0-8160-3231-0.
Dewey:016.7821/4/0973. LCCN:90-022261.
Audience: **g,l,u,f.**

Bordman, Gerald ML1711.B67 2001
American Musical Theater: A Chronicle. Ed. 3. Trade Cloth.
Oxford University Press, Inc. New York, NY. 2001. 840p.
ISBN:0-19-513074-X, ISBN13: 978-0-19-513074-4.
Dewey:782.1/4/0973. LCCN:00-059812.
Audience: **g,l,u,f.**

Bordman, Gerald ML410.K385.B7
Jerome Kern: His Life and Music. Trade Cloth. Oxford
University Press, Inc. New York, NY. 1980. 448p.
ISBN:0-19-502649-7, ISBN13: 978-0-19-502649-8.
Dewey:782.8/1/0924. LCCN:79-013826.
Audience: **l,u,f.**

Bradley, Ian (Editor) ML49.S9A1 1996
The Complete Annotated Gilbert and Sullivan. Trade Cloth.
Oxford University Press, Inc. New York, NY. 1996. 1, 212p.
ISBN:0-19-816503-X, ISBN13: 978-0-19-816503-3.
Dewey:782.1/2/0268. LCCN:95-051813.
Audience: **g,l,u,f.** *Choice, 1997.*

Brecht, Bertolt PT2603.R397
The Threepenny Opera. Eric Bentley & Desmond Vesey
(Translators), Lotte Lenya (Foreword by). Trade Paper.
Grove/Atlantic, Inc. New York, NY. 1964. ISBN:0-394-17472-0,
ISBN13: 978-0-394-17472-3. Dewey:832/.912.
Audience: **g,l,u,f.**

Citron, Stephen ML410.H5624C58 2004
Jerry Herman: Poet of the Showtune. Cloth over Boards. Yale

University Press. Cumberland, RI. 2004. 352p.
ISBN:0-300-10082-5, ISBN13: 978-0-300-10082-2.
Dewey:782.1/4/092 B. LCCN:2003-027632.

Audience: **g,l,u,f.**

Citron, Stephen   **ML390.C586 2001**
Stephen Sondheim and Andrew Lloyd Webber: The New
Musical. Trade Cloth. Oxford University Press, Inc. New York,
NY. 2001. 464p. The Great Songwriters Ser.
ISBN:0-19-509601-0, ISBN13: 978-0-19-509601-9.
Dewey:782.1/4/0922. LCCN:2001-031408.

Audience: **u,f.**

Citron, Stephen   **ML403.C56 1995**
The Wordsmiths: Oscar Hammerstein II and Alan Jay Lerner.
Trade Cloth. Oxford University Press, Inc. New York, NY. 1995.
464p. The Great Songwriters Ser. ISBN:0-19-508386-5,
ISBN13: 978-0-19-508386-6. Dewey:782.1/4/0922 B.
LCCN:94-020279.

Audience: **u,f.**

Cohan, Steven (Editor)   **ML2075.H65 2002**
Hollywood Musicals, the Film Reader. Paper over Boards.
Routledge. New York, NY. 2001. 224p. In Focus Ser.
ISBN:0-415-23559-6, ISBN13: 978-0-415-23559-4.
Dewey:791.436. LCCN:2001-058919.

Audience: **u,f.**

Comden, Betty & Green,   **ML48.N49 1997**
  Adolph
The New York Musicals of Comden and Green: On the Town,
Wonderful Town, Bells Are Ringing. Trade Cloth. Applause
Theatre Book Publishers. New York, NY. 1996. 298p.
ISBN:1-55783-242-0, ISBN13: 978-1-55783-242-9.
Dewey:782.1/4/0268. LCCN:96-032626.

Audience: **g,l,u,f.**

Coward, Noel   **ML54.6.C83N64 1998**
Noel Coward: The Complete Illustrated Lyrics. Barry Day
(Editor). Trade Cloth. Overlook Press, The. New York, NY.
1998. 367p. ISBN:0-87951-896-0, ISBN13: 978-0-87951-896-7.
Dewey:782.42164/0268. LCCN:98-017414.

Audience: **g,l,u,f.** *Choice, 1999.*

Darion, Joe & Wasserman,   **ML50.L536M32**
  Dale
Man of La Mancha. Trade Paper. Random House, Inc. New
York, NY. 1966. 112p. ISBN:0-394-40619-2, ISBN13:
978-0-394-40619-0. Dewey:782.81028.

Audience: **g,l,u,f.**

Davison, Richard A. (Editor)   **ML1711.A77 2005**
The Art of the American Musical: Conversations with the
Creators. Saddle Stitched, Cloth over Boards. Rutgers University
Press. Piscataway, NJ. 2005. 308p. ISBN:0-8135-3612-X,
ISBN13: 978-0-8135-3612-5. Dewey:782.1/4/092273.
LCCN:2004-025319.

Audience: **g,l,u,f.**

Eliot, T. S.   **ML50.L804**
Cats: The Book of the Musical. John Napier (Photographer).

Trade Paper. Harcourt Trade Publishers. New York, NY. 1983.
112p. Harvest Book Ser. ISBN:0-15-615582-6, ISBN13:
978-0-15-615582-3. Dewey:782.81/2. LCCN:82-048026.

Audience: **g,l,u,f.**

Everett, William   **ML128.M78E84 2004**
The Musical: A Research Guide to Musical Theater and Film.
Paper over Boards. Routledge. New York, NY. 2004. 248p.
Routledge Music Bibliographies Ser. ISBN:0-415-94295-0,
ISBN13: 978-0-415-94295-9. Dewey:016.7821/4.
LCCN:2004-016007.

Audience: **l,u,f.**

Everett, William A. &   **ML2054.C35 2002**
  Laird, Paul R. (Editors)
The Cambridge Companion to the Musical. Jonathan Cross
(Contribution by). Trade Paper. Cambridge University Press.
New York, NY. 2002. 328p. Cambridge Companions to Music
Ser., Vol. 4 ISBN:0-521-79639-3, ISBN13: 978-0-521-79639-2.
Dewey:302.2/244/0945. LCCN:2002-031052.

Audience: **g,l,u,f.**

Farneth, David   **ML410.W395F37 1999**
Kurt Weill: A Life in Pictures and Documents. Trade Cloth.
Overlook Press, The. New York, NY. 1999. 312p.
ISBN:0-87951-721-2, ISBN13: 978-0-87951-721-2.
Dewey:782.1/092 B. LCCN:99-033577.

Audience: **g,l,u,f.** *Choice, 2000.*

Finn, William & Lapine,   **ML49.F55 R5 1993**
  James
Falsettos: In Trousers, Falsettoland and March of the Falsettos.
Frank Rich (Afterword by). Trade Paper. Penguin Group (USA)
Inc. New York, NY. 1993. 256p. Drama Ser.
ISBN:0-452-27072-3, ISBN13: 978-0-452-27072-5.
Dewey:782.1/4/0268.

Audience: **g,l,u,f.**

Furia, Philip   **ML410.M9**
Ira Gershwin: The Art of the Lyricist. Trade Paper. Oxford
University Press, Inc. New York, NY. 1997. 288p.
ISBN:0-19-511570-8, ISBN13: 978-0-19-511570-3.
Dewey:780.9/2. LCCN:94-045715.

Audience: **u,f.** *Choice, 1996.*

Furth, George   **ML50.S705C6 1996**
Company: Music and Lyrics by Stephen Sondheim. Ed. 25.
Trade Paper. Theatre Communications Group, Inc. New York,
NY. 1995. 128p. ISBN:1-55936-108-5, ISBN13:
978-1-55936-108-8. Dewey:782.1/4. LCCN:95-045985.

Audience: **g,l,u,f.**

Gammond, Peter   **ML410.O41**
Offenbach: His Life and Times. Tunbridge Wells, Kent: Midas
Books. 1980. ISBN:0-85936-231-0, ISBN13:
978-0-85936-231-3.

Audience: **u,f.**

Ganzl, Kurt   **ML102.M88G3 2001**
Encyclopedia of Musical Theater. Ed. 2. Trade Cloth. Thomson
Gale. Farmington Hills, MI. 1905. 2274p. ISBN:0-02-864970-2,

ISBN13: 978-0-02-864970-2. Dewey:782.1/4/03.
LCCN:2001-018361.

Audience: **g,l,u,f.** *Choice, 2001.*

Ganzl, Kurt   **ML1700.G322 1997**
The Musical: A Concise History. Trade Cloth. Northeastern
University Press. Boston, MA. 1997. 448p.
ISBN:1-55553-311-6, ISBN13: 978-1-55553-311-3.
Dewey:782.1/4/09. LCCN:97-003008.

Audience: **g,l,u,f.** *Choice, 1998.*

Ganzl, Kurt   **ML410.L78**
The Complete Aspects of Love. Clive Barda (Photographer).
Trade Cloth. Penguin Group (USA) Inc. New York, NY. 1990.
176p. ISBN:0-670-83192-1, ISBN13: 978-0-670-83192-0.
Dewey:782.1/4. LCCN:89-040452.

Audience: **g,l,u,f.** *Choice, 1990.*

Garebian, Keith   **ML1711**
The Making of Cabaret. Trade Paper. Mosaic Press. Niagara
Falls, NY. 2004. 152p. The Making of the Great Broadway
Musicals Ser. ISBN:0-88962-651-0, ISBN13:
978-0-88962-651-5. Dewey:782.1/4/0973.

Audience: **l,u,f.**

Garebian, Keith   **ML50.F49678**
The Making of Guys and Dolls. Trade Paper. Mosaic Press.
Niagara Falls, NY. 2004. 154p. The Making of the Great
Broadway Musicals Ser. ISBN:0-88962-764-9, ISBN13:
978-0-88962-764-2. Dewey:782.1/4.

Audience: **l,u,f.**

Garebian, Keith   **ML1711**
The Making of Gypsy. Trade Paper. Mosaic Press. Niagara
Falls, NY. 2004. 160p. The Making of the Great Broadway
Musicals Ser. ISBN:0-88962-654-5, ISBN13:
978-0-88962-654-6. Dewey:782.1/4/0973.

Audience: **l,u,f.**

Garebian, Keith   **ML1711**
The Making of My Fair Lady. Trade Paper. Mosaic Press.
Niagara Falls, NY. 2004. 160p. The Making of the Great
Broadway Musicals Ser. ISBN:0-88962-653-7, ISBN13:
978-0-88962-653-9. Dewey:782.1/4/0973.

Audience: **l,u,f.**

Garebian, Keith   **ML1711**
The Making of West Side Story. Trade Paper. Mosaic Press.
Niagara Falls, NY. 2004. 160p. The Making of the Great
Broadway Musicals Ser. ISBN:0-88962-652-9, ISBN13:
978-0-88962-652-2. Dewey:782.1/4/0973.

Audience: **l,u,f.**

Gay, John   **ML50.7.B43 1999**
The Beggar's Opera. Trade Paper. Dover Publications, Inc.
Mineola, NY. 1999. 64p. Thrift Editions Ser.
ISBN:0-486-40888-4, ISBN13: 978-0-486-40888-0.
Dewey:782.1/40268. LCCN:99-015104.

Audience: **g,l,u,f.**

Gelbart, Larry, et al.   **ML50.C688C6 1990**
City of Angels. Cy Coleman & David Zippel (Authors). Trade
Paper. Applause Theatre Book Publishers. New York, NY. 1990.
204p. Applause Musical Library ISBN:1-55783-081-9, ISBN13:
978-1-55783-081-4. Dewey:782.1/4/0268. LCCN:90-001207.

Audience: **g,l,u,f.**

Gershwin, Ira & Kimball,   **PZ8.3**
  Robert
The Complete Lyrics of Ira Gershwin. Trade Cloth. Alfred A.
Knopf Inc. New York, NY. 1993. 448p. ISBN:0-394-55651-8,
ISBN13: 978-0-394-55651-2. Dewey:782.42. LCCN:93-012175.

Audience: **g,l,u,f.**

Gilbert, Steven E.   **ML410.G288G55 1995**
The Music of Gershwin. Cloth over Boards. Yale University
Press. Cumberland, RI. 1995. 268p. Composers of the Twentieth
Century Ser. ISBN:0-300-06233-8, ISBN13: 978-0-300-06233-5.
Dewey:780.9/2. LCCN:95-012086.

Audience: **u,f.** *Choice, 1996.*

Hamlisch, Marvin   **ML410.H1745 A3 1992**
The Way I Was. Trade Cloth. Simon & Schuster. New York, NY.
1992. ISBN:0-684-19327-2, ISBN13: 978-0-684-19327-4.
Dewey:780/.92. LCCN:92-020094.

Audience: **g,l,u,f.**

Hammerstein, Oscar II   **ML49.H12H3 1985**
  (Lyrics by)
Lyrics by Oscar Hammerstein II. Ed. 2. Stephen Sondheim
(Foreword by). Trade Cloth. Hal Leonard Corporation.
Milwaukee, WI. 1985. 292p. Biographies and Commentary Ser.,
:Musicals/Classical/Folk/Religious Music Ser.
ISBN:0-88188-379-4, ISBN13: 978-0-88188-379-4.
Dewey:782.81/2. LCCN:85-050895.

Audience: **g,l,u,f.**

Hart, Lorenz   **ML54.6.H4H4 1995**
The Complete Lyrics of Lorenz Hart. Dorothy Hart & Robert
Kimball (Editors). Trade Paper. Da Capo Press, Inc. Cambridge,
MA. 1995. 208p. ISBN:0-306-80667-3, ISBN13:
978-0-306-80667-4. Dewey:782.1/4/0268. LCCN:95-021606.

Audience: **g,l,u,f.**

Hausam, Wiley (Editor)   **ML48.N485 2001**
The New American Musical: An Anthology from the End of the
20th Century. Trade Paper. Theatre Communications Group, Inc.
New York, NY. 2001. 450p. ISBN:1-55936-200-6, ISBN13:
978-1-55936-200-9. Dewey:782.1/40268. LCCN:2001-027192.

Audience: **g,l,u,f.**

Herman, Jerry & Stasio,   **ML410.H5624H47 1996**
  Marilyn
Showtune: A Memoir by Jerry Herman. Trade Cloth. Penguin
Group (USA) Inc. New York, NY. 1996. 288p.
ISBN:1-55611-502-4, ISBN13: 978-1-55611-502-8.
Dewey:782.1/4/092 B. LCCN:96-034210.

Audience: **g,l,u,f.**

Hinton, Stephen (Editor)   **ML410.W395**
Kurt Weill: "The Threepenny Opera". Trade Paper. Cambridge
University Press. New York, NY. 1990. 245p. Cambridge Opera

Handbooks Ser. ISBN:0-521-33888-3, ISBN13: 978-0-521-33888-2. Dewey:780/.92/4. LCCN:91-109557.

Audience: **u,f.** *Choice, 1991.*

Hirsch, Foster   **ML429.P78H6 2005**
Harold Prince and the American Musical Theater. Trade Paper. Applause Theatre Book Publishers. New York, NY. 2005. 288p. ISBN:1-55783-617-5, ISBN13: 978-1-55783-617-5. Dewey:792.602/3/092. LCCN:2005-003597.

Audience: **g,l,u,f.** *Choice, 2005, 1989.*

Houghton, Norris   **PR2831.A2**
Romeo and Juliet and West Side Story. Mass Market. Random House Children's Books. New York, NY. 1965. 256p. ISBN:0-440-97483-6, ISBN13: 978-0-440-97483-3. Dewey:822.3/3.

Audience: **g,l,u,f.**

Jablonski, Edward   **ML423.L3J3 1996**
Alan Jay Lerner: A Biography. Trade Cloth. Henry Holt & Company. New York, NY. 1996. 88p. ISBN:0-8050-4076-5, ISBN13: 978-0-8050-4076-0. Dewey:782.1/4/092 B. LCCN:95-037656.

Audience: **g,l,u,f.** *Choice, 1996.*

Jablonski, Edward   **ML410.A76J33 1996**
Harold Arlen: Rhythm, Rainbows, and Blues. Cloth Text. Northeastern University Press. Boston, MA. 1996. 490p. ISBN:1-55553-263-2, ISBN13: 978-1-55553-263-5. Dewey:782.42164/092 B. LCCN:95-044708.

Audience: **g,l,u,f.** *Choice, 1996.*

Jablonski, Edward   **ML410.B499J33 1998**
Irving Berlin: American Troubadour. Cloth over Boards. Henry Holt & Company. New York, NY. 1999. 406p. Irving Berlin Collection, Vol. 1 ISBN:0-8050-4077-3, ISBN13: 978-0-8050-4077-7. Dewey:782.42164/092 B. LCCN:98-003058.

Audience: **g,l,u,f.** *Choice, 1999.*

Jablonski, Edward &   **ML410.G288J3 1996**
  Stewart, Lawrence D.
The Gershwin Years: George and Ira. Ed. 3. Trade Paper. Da Capo Press, Inc. Cambridge, MA. 1996. 400p. ISBN:0-306-80739-4, ISBN13: 978-0-306-80739-8. Dewey:780.9/22. LCCN:96-022950.

Audience: **u,f.**

Jacobs, Dick & Jacobs,   **ML120.U5J23 1994**
  Harriet
Who Wrote That Song? Ed. 2. Trade Paper. F & W Publications, Inc. Cincinnati, OH. 1994. 448p. ISBN:0-89879-639-3, ISBN13: 978-0-89879-639-1. Dewey:784.5/00973. LCCN:93-048545.

Audience: **g,l,u,f.** *Choice, 1989.*

Jones, John Bush   **ML1711.J65 2003**
Our Musicals, Ourselves: A Social History of the American Musical Theater. Trade Cloth. University Press of New England. Lebanon, NH. 2003. 256p. ISBN:1-58465-311-6, ISBN13: 978-1-58465-311-0. Dewey:782.1/4/0973. LCCN:2003-000240.

Audience: **u,f.**

Kimball, Robert & Berlin,   **ML54.6.B464K55 2000**
  Irving
Complete Lyrics of Irving Berlin. Trade Cloth. Alfred A. Knopf Inc. New York, NY. 2001. 560p. ISBN:0-679-41943-8, ISBN13: 978-0-679-41943-3. Dewey:782.42164/0268. LCCN:00-062890.

Audience: **g,l,u,f.**

Kimball, Robert & Nelson,   **ML54.6.L64 2003**
  Steve
The Complete Lyrics of Frank Loesser. Trade Cloth. David McKay Company, Inc. New York, NY. 2003. 352p. ISBN:0-679-45059-9, ISBN13: 978-0-679-45059-7. Dewey:782.4216403. LCCN:2003-109481.

Audience: **g,l,u,f.**

Kirkwood, James, et al.   **ML50.H2397C5 1995**
A Chorus Line: The Complete Book of the Musical. Nicholas Dante & Edward Kleban (Authors), Michael Bennett (Created by). Trade Cloth. Applause Theatre Book Publishers. New York, NY. 2000. 150p. Musical Library ISBN:1-55783-131-9, ISBN13: 978-1-55783-131-6. Dewey:782.1/4/0268. LCCN:95-021617.

Audience: **g,l,u,f.**

Knapp, Raymond   **ML1711.K6 2004**
The American Musical and the Formation of National Identity. Trade Cloth. Princeton University Press. Princeton, NJ. 2004. 360p. ISBN:0-691-11864-7, ISBN13: 978-0-691-11864-2. Dewey:782.1/4/0973. LCCN:2004-041469.

Audience: **u,f.** *Choice, 2005.*

Kotis, Greg & Hollmann,   **ML50.K8785U75 2002**
  Mark
Urinetown: The Musical. David Auburn (Preface by). Trade Paper. Faber & Faber, Inc. New York, NY. 2003. 144p. ISBN:0-571-21182-8, ISBN13: 978-0-571-21182-1. Dewey:782.1/4/0268. LCCN:2002-033875.

Audience: **g,l,u,f.**

Lapine, James & Sondheim,   **ML50.S705I5 1989**
  Stephen
Into the Woods. Trade Paper. Theatre Communications Group, Inc. New York, NY. 1998. 160p. ISBN:0-930452-93-3, ISBN13: 978-0-930452-93-3. Dewey:782.81/2. LCCN:89-004402.

Audience: **g,l,u,f.**

Lax, Roger & Smith,   **ML128.S3L4 1989**
  Frederick
The Great Song Thesaurus. Ed. 2. Cloth Text. Oxford University Press, Inc. New York, NY. 1989. 792p. ISBN:0-19-505408-3, ISBN13: 978-0-19-505408-8. Dewey:784.5/0016. LCCN:88-031267.

Audience: **g,l,u,f.**

Lees, Gene   **ML410.L7986L4 1990**
Inventing Champagne: The Worlds of Lerner and Loewe. Trade Cloth. St. Martin's Press. Gordonville, VA. 1990. ISBN:0-312-05136-0, ISBN13: 978-0-312-05136-5. Dewey:782.1/4/0922 B. LCCN:90-037200.

Audience: **u,f.**

Lerner, Alan J.   ML423.L3A3 1994
Street Where I Live. Trade Paper. Da Capo Press, Inc.
Cambridge, MA. 1994. 333p. ISBN:0-306-80602-9, ISBN13:
978-0-306-80602-5. Dewey:782.1/4/092. LCCN:94-012693.
Audience: **l,u,f.**

Lerner, Alan J. & Green,   PS3523.E76H96 1987
Benny
A Hymn to Him: The Lyrics of Alan Jay Lerner. Al Hirschfeld
(Illustrator). Trade Cloth. Hal Leonard Corporation. Milwaukee,
WI. 1987. 319p. ISBN:0-87910-109-1, ISBN13:
978-0-87910-109-1. Dewey:782.81/2. LCCN:87-405427.
Audience: **g,l,u,f.**

Lewine, Richard, et al.   ML128.S3
Songs of the Theater. Simon, Alfred (Author). New York: H.W.
Wilson Co.. 1984.
Audience: **l,u,f.**

Lloyd Webber, Andrew &   ML50.L804
Rice, Tim
Evita. Trade Cloth. Quite Specific Media Group, Ltd.
Hollywood, CA. 1979. 128p. ISBN:0-89676-030-8, ISBN13:
978-0-89676-030-1. Dewey:782.81/2. LCCN:79-053888.
Audience: **g,l,u,f.**

Loesser, Susan   ML410.L7984L6 1993
A Most Remarkable Fella: Frank Loesser and the Guys and
Dolls in His Life: A Portrait by His Daughter. Trade Cloth.
Penguin Group (USA) Inc. New York, NY. 1993. 320p.
ISBN:1-55611-364-1, ISBN13: 978-1-55611-364-2.
Dewey:782.1/4/092 B. LCCN:92-054985.
Audience: **l,u,f.** *Choice, 1994.*

MacDermot, Galt, et al.   ML50.M1229
Hair: The American Tribal Love-Rock Musical. Ragni, Gerome;
Rado, James (Authors). Pocket Books. 1969.
ISBN:0-671-77060-8, ISBN13: 978-0-671-77060-0.
Audience: **g,l,u,f.**

Masteroff, Joe, et al.   ML410.H1745
Cabaret: The Illustrated Book and Lyrics. John Kander & Fred
Ebb (Authors), Linda Sunshine (Editor), Rivka Katvan & Joan
Marcus (Photographers). Trade Cloth. Newmarket Press. New
York, NY. 2004. 128p. ISBN:1-55704-383-3, ISBN13:
978-1-55704-383-2. Dewey:792.6/42. LCCN:99-022945.
Audience: **g,l,u,f.**

Mates, Julian   ML1711
America's Musical Stage: Two Hundred Years of Musical
Theatre. Trade Cloth. Greenwood Publishing Group, Inc.
Portsmouth, NH. 1985. 252p. Contributions in Drama and
Theatre Studies Ser., No. 18 ISBN:0-313-23948-7, ISBN13:
978-0-313-23948-9. Dewey:782.81/0973. LCCN:85-000935.
Audience: **u,f.** *B̶ Choice, 1986.*

McBrien, William   ML410.P7844M33 1998
Cole Porter: A Biography. Trade Cloth. Alfred A. Knopf Inc.
New York, NY. 1998. 480p. ISBN:0-394-58235-7, ISBN13:
978-0-394-58235-1. Dewey:782.1/4/092 B. LCCN:97-046116.
Audience: **l,u,f.** *Choice, 1999.*

Mitchell, John Cameron &   ML50.T769H4 2003
Trask, Stephen
Hedwig and the Angry Inch. Trade Paper. Dramatists Play
Service, Inc. New York, NY. 2003. 42p. ISBN:0-8222-1901-8,
ISBN13: 978-0-8222-1901-9. Dewey:782.1/4/0268.
LCCN:2005-560193.
Audience: **g,l,u,f.**

Mordden, Ethan   ML1711.8.N3 M768
Beautiful Mornin': The Broadway Musical in The 1940s. Trade
Cloth. DIANE Publishing Company. Collingdale, PA. 2005.
278p. ISBN:0-7567-9672-5, ISBN13: 978-0-7567-9672-3.
Dewey:782.1/4/0973.
Audience: **g,l,u,f.**

Mordden, Ethan   ML1711.8.N3
Coming up Roses: The Broadway Musical in the 1950s. Trade
Paper. Oxford University Press, Inc. New York, NY. 2000. 272p.
ISBN:0-19-514058-3, ISBN13: 978-0-19-514058-3.
Dewey:782.1/4/097471.
Audience: **g,l,u,f.**

Mordden, Ethan   ML2054.M66 2004
The Happiest Corpse I've Ever Seen: The Last Twenty-Five
Years of the Broadway Musical. Cloth over Boards. Palgrave
Macmillan. New York, NY. 2004. 320p. ISBN:0-312-23954-8,
ISBN13: 978-0-312-23954-1. Dewey:782.1/4/0973.
LCCN:2004-044304.
Audience: **g,l,u,f.** *Choice, 2005.*

Mordden, Ethan   ML1711.8.N3M78 1997
Make-Believe: The Broadway Musical in the 1920s. Trade
Cloth. Oxford University Press, Inc. New York, NY. 1997. 272p.
ISBN:0-19-510594-X, ISBN13: 978-0-19-510594-0.
Dewey:782.1/4/09747109042. LCCN:96-040962.
Audience: **g,l,u,f.**

Mordden, Ethan   ML1711
One More Kiss: The Broadway Musical in the 1970s. Trade
Paper. Palgrave Macmillan. New York, NY. 2004. 288p.
ISBN:1-4039-6539-0, ISBN13: 978-1-4039-6539-4.
Dewey:782.1/4/097471.
Audience: **g,l,u,f.** *Choice, 2004.*

Mordden, Ethan   ML2054.M67 2001
Open a New Window: The Broadway Musical in the 1960s.
Cloth over Boards. Palgrave Macmillan. New York, NY. 2001.
288p. The Golden Age of the Broadway Musical Ser.
ISBN:0-312-23952-1, ISBN13: 978-0-312-23952-7.
Dewey:782.1/4/097471. LCCN:2001-019453.
Audience: **g,l,u,f.** *Choice, 2002.*

Mordden, Ethan   ML2054.M69 2005
Sing for Your Supper: The Broadway Musical in the 1930s.
Trade Cloth. Palgrave Macmillan. New York, NY. 2005. 288p.
ISBN:0-312-23951-3, ISBN13: 978-0-312-23951-0.
Dewey:782.1/4/097471. LCCN:2004-053477.
Audience: **g,l,u,f.** *Choice, 2005.*

Most, Andrea   ML1711.M74 2003
Making Americans: Jews and the Broadway Musical. Trade
Cloth. Harvard University Press. Cambridge, MA. 2004. 272p.
ISBN:0-674-01165-1, ISBN13: 978-0-674-01165-6.
Dewey:782.1/4/089924073. LCCN:2003-056636.

Audience: **u,f.**

Norton, Richard C. (Editor)   ML1711.8.N3N67 2002
A Chronology of American Musical Theater, Set. Trade Cloth.
Oxford University Press, Inc. New York, NY. 2002. 3,074p.
ISBN:0-19-508888-3, ISBN13: 978-0-19-508888-5.
Dewey:782.14097471. LCCN:2001-055710.

Audience: **u,f.** *Choice, 2003.*

Perry, George   ML1950
The Complete Phantom of the Opera. Clive Barda
(Photographer). Trade Paper. DIANE Publishing Company.
Collingdale, PA. 2005. 167p. ISBN:0-7567-8833-1, ISBN13:
978-0-7567-8833-9. Dewey:782.81.

Audience: **g,l,u,f.**

Porter, Cole & Kimball,   ML50.Z99
  Robert
The Complete Lyrics of Cole Porter. John Updike (Foreword
by). Trade Cloth. Alfred A. Knopf Inc. New York, NY. 1983.
354p. ISBN:0-394-53214-7, ISBN13: 978-0-394-53214-1.
Dewey:782.1/4/0268. LCCN:83-048101.

Audience: **g,l,u,f.**

Porter, Susan L.   ML1711.P67 1991
With an Air Debonair: Musical Theatre in America, 1785-1815.
Trade Cloth. Smithsonian Institution Press. Washington, DC.
1991. 648p. ISBN:1-56098-063-X, ISBN13: 978-1-56098-063-6.
Dewey:792.6/0973/09034. LCCN:90-024921.

Audience: **g,l,u,f.** *Choice, 1992.*

Raymond, Jack   ML156.4.M8R4 1992
Show Music on Record: The First One Hundred Years. Trade
Cloth. Smithsonian Institution Press. Washington, DC. 1992.
440p. ISBN:1-56098-151-2, ISBN13: 978-1-56098-151-0.
Dewey:016.7821/4/0266. LCCN:91-023483.

Audience: **g,l,u,f.**

Rice, Tim   ML50.Z99
Joseph and the Amazing Technicolor Dreamcoat. Quentin Blake
(Illustrator), Andrew Lloyd Webber (Composed by). Trade
Cloth. Henry Holt & Company. New York, NY. 1982. 48p.
ISBN:0-03-061517-8, ISBN13: 978-0-03-061517-7.
Dewey:782.81/2. LCCN:81-023722.

Audience: **g,l,u,f.**

Richards, Stanley   ML48.R5 1976
Great Musicals of the American Theatre. Trade Cloth. Chilton
Book Publishing Company. Southborough, MA. 1976.
ISBN:0-8019-5731-1, ISBN13: 978-0-8019-5731-4.
Dewey:782.8/1/2. LCCN:78-113020.

Audience: **g,l,u,f.**

Richards, Stanley   ML48.G7
Great Rock Musicals. Trade Cloth. Henry Holt & Company.
New York, NY. 1979. x, 562p. ISBN:0-8128-2509-8, ISBN13:
978-0-8128-2509-1. Dewey:782.8/1/2. LCCN:78-007005.

Audience: **g,l,u,f.**

Rodgers, Richard &   ML48
  Hammerstein, Oscar II
Six Plays. Trade Cloth. Random House, Inc. New York, NY.
1959. ISBN:0-394-60200-5, ISBN13: 978-0-394-60200-4.
Dewey:812.

Audience: **g,l,u,f.**

Rodgers, Richard   ML410.S95
Musical Stages: An Autobiography. Ed. 2. Mary Rodgers
(Introduction by), John Lahr (Afterword by). Trade Paper. Da
Capo Press, Inc. Cambridge, MA. 2002. 384p.
ISBN:0-306-81134-0, ISBN13: 978-0-306-81134-0.
Dewey:782.8/1/0924.

Audience: **g,l,u,f.**

Rosenberg, Deena   ML410.G288R67 1997
Fascinating Rhythm: The Collaboration of George and Ira
Gershwin. Trade Paper. University of Michigan Press. Chicago,
IL. 1998. 560p. ISBN:0-472-08469-0, ISBN13:
978-0-472-08469-2. Dewey:780.922. LCCN:97-041926.

Audience: **l,u,f.** *Choice, 1992.*

Schebera, Jurgen   ML410.W395S3513 1995
Kurt Weill: An Illustrated Life. Caroline Murphy (Translator).
Cloth over Boards. Yale University Press. Cumberland, RI.
1995. 400p. ISBN:0-300-06055-6, ISBN13: 978-0-300-06055-3.
Dewey:780.9/2. LCCN:94-041444.

Audience: **l,u,f.** *Choice, 1996.*

Schmidt, Harvey & Jones,   ML50.S347F42 1990
  Tom
The Fantasticks. Ed. 30. Trade Cloth. Applause Theatre Book
Publishers. New York, NY. 1990. 170p. Musical Library
ISBN:1-55783-074-6, ISBN13: 978-1-55783-074-6.
Dewey:782.1/4. LCCN:90-033931.

Audience: **g,l,u,f.** *Choice, 1990.*

Schulman, Sarah   ML410.L2857S38 1998
Stagestruck: Theater, AIDS and Marketing of Gay America.
Trade Cloth. Duke University Press. Durham, NC. 1998. 152p.
ISBN:0-8223-2132-7, ISBN13: 978-0-8223-2132-3.
LCCN:98-012053.

Audience: **g,l,u,f.** *Choice, 1999.*

Secrest, Meryle   ML410.S6872S42 1999
Stephen Sondheim: A Life. Trade Paper. Dell Publishing. New
York, NY. 1999. 480p. ISBN:0-385-33412-5, ISBN13:
978-0-385-33412-9. Dewey:780.9/2.

Audience: **g,l,u,f.** *Choice, 1999.*

Shaw, George Bernard &   PR5363
  Lerner, Alan Jay
Pygmalion and My Fair Lady. Ed. 50. Mass Market. Penguin

Group (USA) Inc. New York, NY. 2006. 240p.
ISBN:0-451-53009-8, ISBN13: 978-0-451-53009-7.
Dewey:822.912.

Audience: **g,l,u,f.**

Smalls, Charlie (Music by,   **ML50.S618**
 Lyrics by)
The Wiz. L. Frank Baum & William F. Brown (Based on a book
by). Trade Paper. Samuel French Inc. New York, NY. 1979.
ISBN:0-573-68091-4, ISBN13: 978-0-573-68091-5.
Dewey:782.81/2.

Audience: **g,l,u,f.**

Snelson, John   **ML410.L78S64 2004**
Andrew Lloyd Webber. Geoffrey Holden Block (Foreword by).
Cloth over Boards. Yale University Press. Cumberland, RI.
2004. 288p. Yale Broadway Masters Ser. ISBN:0-300-10459-6,
ISBN13: 978-0-300-10459-2. Dewey:782.1/4/092.
LCCN:2004-004311.

Audience: **g,l,u,f.** *Choice, 2005.*

Sondheim, Stephen &   **ML50.S705F65 2001**
 Goldman, James
Follies. Trade Paper. Theatre Communications Group, Inc. New
York, NY. 2000. 128p. ISBN:1-55936-196-4, ISBN13:
978-1-55936-196-5. Dewey:782.1/4/0268. LCCN:00-068276.

Audience: **g,l,u,f.**

Sondheim, Stephen &   **ML410.S6872A5 2002**
 Horowitz, Mark Eden
Sondheim on Music: Minor Details and Major Decisions. Trade
Cloth. Scarecrow Press, Inc. Lanham, MD. 2003. 416p.
ISBN:0-8108-4437-0, ISBN13: 978-0-8108-4437-7.
Dewey:782.1/4/092. LCCN:2002-010564.

Audience: **l,u,f.** *Choice, 2003.*

Sondheim, Stephen &   **ML50.S955G9 1994**
 Laurents, Arthur
Gypsy. Jules Styne (Contribution by). Trade Paper. Theatre
Communications Group, Inc. New York, NY. 1994. 120p.
ISBN:1-55936-086-0, ISBN13: 978-1-55936-086-9.
Dewey:782.1/4/0268. LCCN:94-002588.

Audience: **g,l,u,f.**

Sondheim, Stephen (Lyrics   **ML50.Z99**
 by, Music by)
Four by Sondheim: Wheeler, Lapine, Shevelove, Gelbart. Trade
Cloth. Applause Theatre Book Publishers. New York, NY. 2000.
772p. ISBN:1-55783-407-5, ISBN13: 978-1-55783-407-2.
Dewey:782.1/40268. LCCN:00-100279.

Audience: **g,l,u,f.**

Stein, Joseph, et al.   **ML50.B6745F52 1990**
Fiddler on the Roof: Based on Sholom Aleichem's Stories. Jerry
Bock, Sheldon Harnick & Sholem Aleichem (Authors). Trade
Paper. Hal Leonard Corporation. Milwaukee, WI. 1990. 154p.
ISBN:0-87910-136-9, ISBN13: 978-0-87910-136-7.
Dewey:782.1/4/0268. LCCN:89-049701.

Audience: **g,l,u,f.**

Swain, Joseph Peter   **ML2054.S93 2002**
The Broadway Musical: A Critical and Musical Survey. Ed. 2.
Trade Cloth. Scarecrow Press, Inc. Lanham, MD. 2002. 464p.
ISBN:0-8108-4375-7, ISBN13: 978-0-8108-4375-2.
Dewey:782.1/4/0973. LCCN:2002-004981.

Audience: **g,l,u,f.**

Traubner, Richard   **ML1900.T7 2003**
Operetta: A Theatrical History. Ed. 2. UK-B Format Paperback.
Routledge. New York, NY. 2003. 496p. ISBN:0-415-96641-8,
ISBN13: 978-0-415-96641-2. Dewey:782.81/09.
LCCN:2003-054800.

Audience: **u,f.** *B*

Weidman, John &   **ML50.S705**
 Sondheim, Stephen
Pacific Overtures. Trade Paper. Theatre Communications Group,
Inc. New York, NY. 1991. 144p. ISBN:1-55936-026-7, ISBN13:
978-1-55936-026-5. Dewey:782.1/4/0268. LCCN:90-029041.

Audience: **g,l,u,f.**

Woll, Allen L.   **ML1711.W64 1989**
Black Musical Theatre: From Coontown to Dreamgirls. Trade
Cloth. Louisiana State University Press. Baton Rouge, LA.
1989. xiv, 301p. ISBN:0-8071-1469-3, ISBN13:
978-0-8071-1469-8. Dewey:782.81/08996073. LCCN:88-008904.

Audience: **u,f.** *Choice, 1989.*

Wyatt, Robert & Johnson, **ML410.G288G47 2004**
 John Andrew (Editors)
The George Gershwin Reader. Trade Cloth. Oxford University
Press, Inc. New York, NY. 2004. 368p. Readers on American
Musicians Ser. ISBN:0-19-513019-7, ISBN13:
978-0-19-513019-5. Dewey:780/.92. LCCN:2003-016160.

Audience: **l,u,f.**

Studies in Music History, Criticism, Analysis, and Appreciation > Film, Television, and Video Music

Adorno, Theodor W. &   **MT40.E35 1994**
 Eisler, Hanns
Composing for the Films. Graham McCann (Introduction by).
Trade Cloth. Continuum International Publishing Group, Ltd.
London, 1994. 171p. ISBN:0-485-11454-2, ISBN13:
978-0-485-11454-6. Dewey:781.5/4213. LCCN:94-017469.

Audience: **u,f.**

Bazelon, Irwin   **ML2075**
Knowing the Score : Notes on Film Music. Arco Pub.. 1981.
ISBN:0-668-05132-9, ISBN13: 978-0-668-05132-3.

Audience: **u,f.**

Bloom, Kenneth   **ML128.M7B6 1995**
Hollywood Song: The Complete Film and Musical Companion.
Trade Cloth. Facts On File, Inc. New York, NY. 1995.
ISBN:0-8160-3231-9, ISBN13: 978-0-8160-3231-0.
Dewey:016.7821/4/0973. LCCN:90-022261.

Audience: **g,l,u,f.**

Brown, Royal S.   ML2075.B76 1994
Overtones and Undertones: Reading Film Music. Trade Paper.
University of California Press. Berkeley, CA. 1994. 406p.
ISBN:0-520-08544-2, ISBN13: 978-0-520-08544-2.
Dewey:781.5/42/09. LCCN:93-046924.

Audience: **u,f.** *Choice, 1995.*

Burt, George D.   ML2075
The Art of Film Music. Paper Text. Northeastern University
Press. Boston, MA. 1994. 280p. ISBN:1-55553-270-5, ISBN13:
978-1-55553-270-3. Dewey:781.5/42.

Audience: **u,f.** *Choice, 1995.*

Cohan, Steven (Editor)   ML2075.H65 2002
Hollywood Musicals, the Film Reader. Paper over Boards.
Routledge. New York, NY. 2001. 224p. In Focus Ser.
ISBN:0-415-23559-6, ISBN13: 978-0-415-23559-4.
Dewey:791.436. LCCN:2001-058919.

Audience: **u,f.**

Cooper, David   ML410.H562C64 2005
Bernard Herrmann's the Ghost and Mrs. Muir: A Film Score
Guide. Trade Paper. Scarecrow Press, Inc. Lanham, MD. 2005.
192p. Scarecrow Film Score Guides Ser., No. 5
ISBN:0-8108-5679-4, ISBN13: 978-0-8108-5679-0.
Dewey:781.5/42. LCCN:2005-007726.

Audience: **u,f.**

Cooper, David   ML410
Bernard Herrmann's Vertigo: A Film Score Handbook. Book,
Other. Greenwood Publishing Group, Inc. Portsmouth, NH.
2001. 176p. Film Score Guides Ser., No. 2
ISBN:0-313-31490-X, ISBN13: 978-0-313-31490-2.
Dewey:781.5/42. LCCN:00-049501.

Audience: **u,f.**

Darby, William & Du Bois,   ML2075
 Jack
American Film Music: Major Composers, Techniques, Trends,
1915-1990. Perfect. McFarland & Company, Incorporated
Publishers. Jefferson, NC. 1999. 399p. ISBN:0-7864-0753-0,
ISBN13: 978-0-7864-0753-8. Dewey:781.5/42/0973.
LCCN:89-43658.

Audience: **g,l,u,f.** *Choice, 1991.*

Daubney, Kate   ML410
Max Steiner's Now, Voyager: A Film Score Guide. Cloth Text.
Greenwood Publishing Group, Inc. Portsmouth, NH. 2000. 136p.
Film Score Guides Ser., Vol. 1 ISBN:0-313-31253-2, ISBN13:
978-0-313-31253-3. Dewey:781.5/42. LCCN:99-088601.

Audience: **u,f.**

Davison, Annette   ML2075
Hollywood Theory, Non-Hollywood Practice: Cinema
Soundtracks in the 1980s and 1990s. Trade Cloth. Ashgate
Publishing, Ltd. Aldershot, 2004. 232p. Ashgate Popular and
Folk Music Ser. ISBN:0-7546-0582-5, ISBN13:
978-0-7546-0582-9. Dewey:781.5/42. LCCN:2003-041873.

Audience: **u,f.** *Choice, 2004.*

Goodwin, Andrew   PN1992.8.M87
Dancing in the Distraction Factory: Music Television and
Popular Culture. Trade Paper. University of Minnesota Press.
Minneapolis, MN. 1992. 320p. ISBN:0-8166-2063-6, ISBN13:
978-0-8166-2063-0. Dewey:791.45/657. LCCN:92-013861.

Audience: **l,u,f.** *Choice, 1993.*

Gorbman, Claudia   ML2075.G67 1987
Unheard Melodies: Narrative Film Music. Trade Cloth. Indiana
University Press. Bloomington, IN. 1987. 200p.
ISBN:0-253-33987-1, ISBN13: 978-0-253-33987-4.
Dewey:782.8/5. LCCN:86-045941.

Audience: **u,f.** *Choice, 1988.*

Grossberg, Lawrence   PN1992.8.M87
 (Editor), et al.
Sound and Vision: The Music Video Reader. Simon Frith &
Andrew Goodwin (Editors). Trade Paper. Routledge. New York,
NY. 1993. 228p. ISBN:0-415-09431-3, ISBN13:
978-0-415-09431-3. Dewey:791.45/75. LCCN:92-025419.

Audience: **l,u,f.**

Halfyard, Janet K.   ML410.E396H35 2004
Danny Elfman's Batman: A Film Score Guide. Ed. 2. Trade
Paper. Scarecrow Press, Inc. Lanham, MD. 2004. 192p.
Scarecrow Film Score Guides Ser., No. 2 ISBN:0-8108-5126-1,
ISBN13: 978-0-8108-5126-9. Dewey:781.5/42.
LCCN:2004-006852.

Audience: **u,f.**

Kalinak, Kathryn   ML2075
Settling the Score: Music and the Classical Hollywood Film.
Trade Paper. University of Wisconsin Press. Chicago, IL. 1992.
266p. Wisconsin Studies in Film ISBN:0-299-13364-8, ISBN13:
978-0-299-13364-1. Dewey:781.5/42/0973. LCCN:92-006853.

Audience: **u,f.**

Karlin, Fred   ML2075.K37 1994
Listening to Movies: Film Lover's Guide to Film Music. Trade
Cloth. Thomson Wadsworth. Belmont, CA. 1994. 400p.
ISBN:0-02-873315-0, ISBN13: 978-0-02-873315-9.
Dewey:781.542. LCCN:93-014304.

Audience: **g,l,u,f.**

Karlin, Fred & Wright,   MT64.M65K3 2003
 Rayburn
On the Track: A Guide to Contemporary Film Scoring. Ed. 2.
John Williams (Foreword by). Paper over Boards. Routledge.
New York, NY. 2004. 560p. ISBN:0-415-94135-0, ISBN13:
978-0-415-94135-8. Dewey:781.5/4213. LCCN:2003-011579.

Audience: **u,f.**

Leinberger, Charles   ML410.M79L45 2004
Ennio Morricone's the Good, the Bad and the Ugly: A Film
Score Guide. Trade Paper. Scarecrow Press, Inc. Lanham, MD.
2004. 153p. Scarecrow Film Score Guides Ser., No. 3
ISBN:0-8108-5132-6, ISBN13: 978-0-8108-5132-0.
Dewey:781.5/42. LCCN:2004-008692.

Audience: **u,f.**

Limbacher, James L.   ML128.M7
Keeping Score: Film Music, 1972-1979. Trade Cloth. Scarecrow
Press, Inc. Lanham, MD. 1981. 519p. ISBN:0-8108-1390-4,
ISBN13: 978-0-8108-1390-8. Dewey:016.7828/55.
LCCN:80-026474.

Audience: **u,f.**

Limbacher, James L. &   ML128.M7L5 1991
 Wright, H. Stephen
Keeping Score: Film and Television Music, 1980-1988 (with
Additional Coverage of 1921-1979). Trade Cloth. Scarecrow
Press, Inc. Lanham, MD. 1991. 928p. ISBN:0-8108-2453-1,
ISBN13: 978-0-8108-2453-9. Dewey:016.7815/42.
LCCN:91-021180.

Audience: **u,f.**

MacDonald, Laurence E.   ML2075
The Invisible Art of Film Music: A Comprehensive History.
Trade Paper. Rowman & Littlefield Publishers, Inc. Lanham,
MD. 1998. 431p. ISBN:1-880157-56-X, ISBN13:
978-1-880157-56-5. Dewey:781.54/2.

Audience: **g,l,u,f.**

Mancini, Henry   ML410
Did They Mention the Music?: The Autobiography of Henry
Mancini. Gene Lees (Author, Afterword by, Foreword by). Trade
Paper. Cooper Square Publishers, Inc. New York, NY. 2002.
312p. ISBN:0-8154-1175-8, ISBN13: 978-0-8154-1175-8.
Dewey:780.92.

Audience: **g,l,u,f.**

Marill, Alvin H.   ML128.M7M28 1998
Keeping Score: Film and Television Music, 1988-1997. Trade
Cloth. Scarecrow Press, Inc. Lanham, MD. 1998. 370p. Keeping
Score Ser. ISBN:0-8108-3416-2, ISBN13: 978-0-8108-3416-3.
Dewey:016.7815/42. LCCN:98-028712.

Audience: **u,f.**

McGrath, Tom   HE8700.72.U6
MTV: The Making of a Revolution. Cloth Text. DIANE
Publishing Company. Collingdale, PA. 1999. 208p.
ISBN:0-7881-6664-6, ISBN13: 978-0-7881-6664-8.
Dewey:384.5/55/0973.

Audience: **g,l,u,f.**

Mundy, John H.   ML2075
Popular Music on Screen: From Hollywood Musical to Music
Video. Trade Paper. Manchester University Press. Manchester,
1999. 256p. Music and Society Ser. ISBN:0-7190-4029-9,
ISBN13: 978-0-7190-4029-0. Dewey:781.5/42/09.

Audience: **l,u,f.** *Choice, 2000.*

Nasta, Dominique   PN1995
Meaning in Film: Relevant Structures in Soundtrack and
Narrative. Trade Paper. Herbert Lang Et Compagnie AG,
Buchhandlung, Antiquariat. Bern, 1992. 180p. Regards sur
L'Image Ser. ISBN:3-261-04482-9, ISBN13:
978-3-261-04482-2. Dewey:791.43/01.

Audience: **u,f.**

Prendergast, Roy M.   ML2075.P73 1991
Film Music: A Neglected Art. Ed. 2. Trade Paper. W. W. Norton
& Company, Inc. New York, NY. 1992. 352p.
ISBN:0-393-30874-X, ISBN13: 978-0-393-30874-7.
Dewey:781.5/42/09. LCCN:90-021393.

Audience: **g,l,u,f.**

Rona, Jeff   MT64.M65R66 2000
The Reel World: Scoring for Pictures. Trade Paper. Backbeat
Books. San Francisco, CA. 2000. 272p. ISBN:0-87930-591-6,
ISBN13: 978-0-87930-591-8. Dewey:781.5/4213.
LCCN:00-056058.

Audience: **u,f.**

Shoilevska, Sanya   ML410
Alex North, Film Composer: A Biography. Cloth Text.
McFarland & Company, Incorporated Publishers. Jefferson, NC.
2003. 278p. ISBN:0-7864-1470-7, ISBN13: 978-0-7864-1470-3.
Dewey:781.5/42/092 B. LCCN:2003-007867.

Audience: **u,f.**

Smith, Jeff   ML2075.S65 1998
The Sounds of Commerce: Marketing Popular Film Music.
Trade Paper. Columbia University Press. New York, NY. 1998.
304p. Film and Culture Ser. ISBN:0-231-10863-X, ISBN13:
978-0-231-10863-8. Dewey:781.5/42/0688. LCCN:98-017923.

Audience: **l,u,f.** *Choice, 1999.*

Smith, Steven C.   ML410.H562S6 1991
A Heart at Fire's Center: The Life and Music of Bernard
Herrmann. Trade Cloth. University of California Press. Berkeley,
CA. 1991. 400p. ISBN:0-520-07123-9, ISBN13:
978-0-520-07123-0. Dewey:780/.92 B. LCCN:90-036861.

Audience: **l,u,f.** *Choice, 1991.*

Vernallis, Carol   PN1992.8.M87V47 2004
Experiencing Music Video: Aesthetics and Cultural Context.
Trade Paper. Edinburgh University Press. Edinburgh, 2004.
480p. ISBN:0-231-11799-X, ISBN13: 978-0-231-11799-9.
Dewey:780.26/7. LCCN:2003-064605.

Audience: **l,u,f.** *Choice, 2004.*

Wierzbicki, James Eugene   ML410.B258W54 2005
Louis and Bebe Barron's Forbidden Planet: A Film Score Guide.
Trade Paper. Scarecrow Press, Inc. Lanham, MD. 2005. 200p.
Scarecrow Film Score Guides Ser., No. 4 ISBN:0-8108-5670-0,
ISBN13: 978-0-8108-5670-7. Dewey:781.5/42.
LCCN:2005-008132.

Audience: **u,f.**

Studies in Music History, Criticism, Analysis, and Appreciation > Jazz and Blues

                                                        ML100
☐ Grove Music Online.
http://www.grovemusic.com/
Oxford University Press.

Audience: **g,l,u,f.**

Albertson, Chris   **ML420.S667A7 2003**
Bessie. Ed. 2. Cloth over Boards. Yale University Press.
Cumberland, RI. 2003. 336p. ISBN:0-300-09902-9, ISBN13:
978-0-300-09902-7. Dewey:784/.092/4. LCCN:2002-155414.
                    Audience: **g,l,u,f.** *Choice, 2004.*

Armstrong, Louis   **ML419.A75A3**
Louis Armstrong, in His Own Words: Selected Writings. Ed. 2.
Thomas Brothers (Editor). Trade Paper. Oxford University Press,
Inc. New York, NY. 2001. 274p. ISBN:0-19-514046-X, ISBN13:
978-0-19-514046-0. Dewey:781.65/092 B.
                    Audience: **g,l,u,f.** *Choice, 2000.*

Balmer, Paul   **ML418.G7**
Stéphane Grappelli: With and Without Django. London :
Sanctuary. 2003. ISBN:1-86074-453-2, ISBN13:
978-1-86074-453-2.
                              Audience: **g,l,u,f.**

Basie, Count & Murray,   **ML417.M846**
   Albert
Good Morning Blues: An Autobiography of Count Basie. Ed. 2.
Trade Paper. Da Capo Press, Inc. Cambridge, MA. 2002. 432p.
ISBN:0-306-81107-3, ISBN13: 978-0-306-81107-4.
Dewey:786.2/165/092.
                              Audience: **g,l,u,f.**

Bechet, Sidney   **ML419**
Treat It Gentle: An Autobiography. Trade Paper. Da Capo Press,
Inc. Cambridge, MA. 2002. 280p. ISBN:0-306-81108-1,
ISBN13: 978-0-306-81108-1. Dewey:780.924.
                              Audience: **g,l,u,f.**

Berger, Morroe, et al.   **ML419.C4B5 2002**
Benny Carter: A Life in American Music, Set. Ed. 2. Edward
Berger & James Patrick (Authors), Benny Carter (Foreword by).
Trade Cloth. Scarecrow Press, Inc. Lanham, MD. 2002. 1440p.
Studies in Jazz, No. 40 ISBN:0-8108-4111-8, ISBN13:
978-0-8108-4111-6. Dewey:781.65/092 B. LCCN:2001-049082.
                              Audience: **u,f.**

Berlin, Edward A.   **ML419.J7**
King of Ragtime: Scott Joplin and His Era. Trade Paper. Oxford
University Press, Inc. New York, NY. 1995. 352p.
ISBN:0-19-810408-1, ISBN13: 978-0-19-810408-7.
Dewey:781.6/4/092.
                              Audience: **g,l,u,f.**

Berlin, Edward A.   **ML3530**
Ragtime: A Musical and Cultural History. Trade Paper.
iUniverse, Inc. Lincoln, NE. 2002. 274p. ISBN:0-595-26158-2,
ISBN13: 978-0-595-26158-1. Dewey:781/.572/09041.
                    Audience: **g,l,u,f.** *B*

Berliner, Paul F.   **ML3506.B475 1994**
Thinking in Jazz: The Infinite Art of Improvisation. Trade Paper.
University of Chicago Press. Chicago, IL. 1994. 904p. Chicago
Studies in Ethnomusicology ISBN:0-226-04381-9, ISBN13:
978-0-226-04381-4. Dewey:781.6/5/136. LCCN:93-034660.
                          Audience: **u,f.** *Choice, 1995.*

Berrett, Joshua   **ML419.A75B46 2004**
Louis Armstrong and Paul Whiteman: Two Kings of Jazz. Cloth
over Boards. Yale University Press. Cumberland, RI. 2004.
256p. ISBN:0-300-10384-0, ISBN13: 978-0-300-10384-7.
Dewey:781.65/092/2 B. LCCN:2004-004217.
                              Audience: **u,f.**

Berrett, Joshua   **ML410.E44**
The Louis Armstrong Companion: Eight Decades of
Commentary. Trade Paper. Music Sales Corporation. New York,
NY. 1999. 300p. ISBN:0-8256-7193-0, ISBN13:
978-0-8256-7193-7. Dewey:781.65/092 B. LCCN:98-029206.
                    Audience: **g,l,u,f.** *Choice, 2000.*

Bogdanov, Vladimir   **ML156.4.J3A45 2002**
   (Editor), et al.
All Music Guide to Jazz: The Definitive Guide to Jazz. Ed. 4.
Chris Woodstra & Stephen Thomas Erlewine (Editors). Trade
Paper. Backbeat Books. San Francisco, CA. 2002. 1400p. AMG
All Music Guide Ser. ISBN:0-87930-717-X, ISBN13:
978-0-87930-717-2. Dewey:781.65/0266. LCCN:2002-028031.
                          Audience: **g,l,u,f.**

Bogdanov, Vladimir, et al.   **ML156.4.B6A45 2003**
All Music Guide to the Blues: The Definitive Guide to the
Blues. Ed. 3. Chris Woodstra & Stephen Thomas Erlewine
(Authors). Trade Paper. Backbeat Books. San Francisco, CA.
2003. 800p. AMG All Media Guide Ser. ISBN:0-87930-736-6,
ISBN13: 978-0-87930-736-3. Dewey:016.781643/0266.
LCCN:2003-040408.
                          Audience: **g,l,u,f.**

Brown, Scott & Hilbert,   **ML417.J62B76 1986**
   Robert
James P. Johnson: A Case of Mistaken Identity. Dan
Morgenstern (Foreword by). Trade Cloth. Scarecrow Press, Inc.
Lanham, MD. 1986. 522p. Studies in Jazz, No. 4
ISBN:0-8108-1887-6, ISBN13: 978-0-8108-1887-3.
Dewey:786.1/092/4 B. LCCN:86-003830.
                    Audience: **g,l,u,f.** *Choice, 1987.*

Carner, Gary (Compiled by)   **ML128**
Jazz Performers: An Annotated Bibliography of Biographical
Materials. Cloth Text. Greenwood Publishing Group, Inc.
Portsmouth, NH. 1990. 384p. Music Reference Collection, No.
26 ISBN:0-313-26250-0, ISBN13: 978-0-313-26250-0.
Dewey:016.78165/092/2. LCCN:90-031765.
                    Audience: **g,l,u,f.** *Choice, 1990.*

Carr, Ian   **ML417.J35C4 1992**
Keith Jarrett: The Man and His Music. Trade Paper. Da Capo
Press, Inc. Cambridge, MA. 1992. 272p. ISBN:0-306-80478-6,
ISBN13: 978-0-306-80478-6. Dewey:786.2/165/092.
                              Audience: **g,l,u,f.**

Carr, Ian   **ML419.D39**
Miles Davis: The Definitive Biography. Trade Paper. DIANE
Publishing Company. Collingdale, PA. 2004. 658p.
ISBN:0-7567-8375-5, ISBN13: 978-0-7567-8375-4.
Dewey:788.9/2165/092 B.
                              Audience: **g,l,u,f.**

Charters, Samuel B.   ML3521.C49 1991
The Blues Makers. Trade Paper. Da Capo Press, Inc.
Cambridge, MA. 1991. 186p. Quality Paperbacks Ser.
ISBN:0-306-80438-7, ISBN13: 978-0-306-80438-0.
Dewey:781.643/0973/09041. LCCN:91-006978.

Audience: **g,l,u,f.**

Charters, Samuel B.   ML3521.C5 1991
The Roots of the Blues: An African Search. Trade Paper. Da
Capo Press, Inc. Cambridge, MA. 1991. 168p.
ISBN:0-306-80445-X, ISBN13: 978-0-306-80445-8.
Dewey:781.643/09. LCCN:91-020452.

Audience: **g,l,u,f.**

Chilton, John   ML419.H35C5 1990
The Song of the Hawk: The Life and Recordings of Coleman
Hawkins. Trade Paper. University of Michigan Press. Chicago,
IL. 1990. 460p. The American Music Ser. ISBN:0-472-08201-9,
ISBN13: 978-0-472-08201-8. Dewey:788.7/165/092 B.
LCCN:90-047644.

Audience: **u,f.** *Choice, 1991.*

Cooke, Mervyn & Horn,   ML3506.C29 2002
  David (Editors)
The Cambridge Companion to Jazz. Jonathan Cross
(Contribution by). Cloth Text. Cambridge University Press. New
York, NY. 2003. 426p. Cambridge Companions to Music Ser.
ISBN:0-521-66320-2, ISBN13: 978-0-521-66320-5.
Dewey:781.65. LCCN:2001-052671.

Audience: **g,l,u,f.** *Choice, 2003.*

Cowley, John & Oliver, Paul   ML156.4.B6B6 1996
The New Blackwell Guide to Recorded Blues. Ed. 2. Trade
Cloth. Blackwell Publishing, Inc. Malden, MA. 1996. 448p.
ISBN:0-631-20163-7, ISBN13: 978-0-631-20163-2.
Dewey:782.4/2/1643/0266. LCCN:96-012140.

Audience: **g,l,u,f.**

Dance, Stanley   ML417.H5 D4 1983
The World of Earl Hines. Paper Text. Da Capo Press, Inc.
Cambridge, MA. 1983. 262p. Quality Paperbacks Ser.
ISBN:0-306-80182-5, ISBN13: 978-0-306-80182-2.
Dewey:785.42/092/4. LCCN:82-025252.

Audience: **u,f.**

Davis, Francis   ML3521
History of the Blues: The Roots, the Music, the People. Ed. 2.
Trade Paper. Da Capo Press, Inc. Cambridge, MA. 2003. 320p.
ISBN:0-306-81296-7, ISBN13: 978-0-306-81296-5.
Dewey:781.643/09. LCCN:2004-559601.

Audience: **g,l,u,f.**

Davis, Miles & Troupe,   ML419.D39A3 1990
  Quincy
Miles: The Autobiography. Trade Paper. Simon & Schuster. New
York, NY. 1990. 448p. ISBN:0-671-72582-3, ISBN13:
978-0-671-72582-2. Dewey:788.9/2165/092 B.
LCCN:90-037501.

Audience: **g,l,u,f.** *Choice, 1990.*

De Veaux, Scott   ML3506
The Birth of Bebop: A Social and Musical History. Trade Paper.
University of California Press. Berkeley, CA. 1999. 587p.
ISBN:0-520-21665-2, ISBN13: 978-0-520-21665-5.
Dewey:781.6/55. LCCN:96-046887.

Audience: **u,f.**

Dregni, Michael   ML419.R44D74 2004
Django: The Life and Music of a Gypsy Legend. Trade Cloth.
Oxford University Press, Inc. New York, NY. 2004. 344p.
ISBN:0-19-516752-X, ISBN13: 978-0-19-516752-8.
Dewey:787.87/165/092 B. LCCN:2004-006214.

Audience: **u,f.**

Ellington, Duke   ML419.A75
Music Is My Mistress. Trade Cloth. Doubleday Publishing. New
York, NY. 1973. 544p. ISBN:0-385-02235-2, ISBN13:
978-0-385-02235-4. Dewey:785.4/2/0924 B. LCCN:73-083189.

Audience: **g,l,u,f.**

Feather, Leonard   ML105
Encyclopedia of Jazz in the Sixties. Trade Cloth. Horizon Press.
Tucson, AZ. 1967. ISBN:0-8180-1205-6, ISBN13:
978-0-8180-1205-1. Dewey:785.420922.

Audience: **g,l,u,f.**

Feather, Leonard & Gitler,   ML102.J3F39 1999
  Ira (Editors)
The Biographical Encyclopedia of Jazz. Ed. 2. Trade Cloth.
Oxford University Press, Inc. New York, NY. 1999. 738p.
ISBN:0-19-507418-1, ISBN13: 978-0-19-507418-5.
Dewey:781.65/092/2 B. LCCN:98-015485.

Audience: **g,l,u,f.** *Choice, 2000.*

Feather, Leonard & Gitler,   ML105.F36
  Ira
The Encyclopedia of Jazz in the Seventies. Quincy Jones
(Introduction by). Trade Cloth. Horizon Press. Tucson, AZ.
1976. 393p. ISBN:0-8180-1215-3, ISBN13: 978-0-8180-1215-0.
Dewey:785.4/2/0922. LCCN:76-021196.

Audience: **g,l,u,f.**

Fernandez, Raul A.   ML3506.F46 2002
Latin Jazz: The Perfect Combination - La Combinacion Perfecta.
Trade Paper. Chronicle Books LLC. San Francisco, CA. 2002.
400p. ISBN:0-8118-3608-8, ISBN13: 978-0-8118-3608-1.
Dewey:781.65/7. LCCN:2002-067229.

Audience: **g,l,u,f.**

Firestone, Ross   ML410.E44
Swing, Swing, Swing: The Life and Times of Benny Goodman.
Trade Paper. W. W. Norton & Company, Inc. New York, NY.
1994. ISBN:0-393-31168-6, ISBN13: 978-0-393-31168-6.
Dewey:781.65092.

Audience: **g,l,u,f.** *Choice, 1993.*

Friedwald, Will   ML3508.F74 1996
Jazz Singing: America's Great Voices from Bessie Smith to
Bebop and Beyond. Trade Paper. Da Capo Press, Inc.
Cambridge, MA. 1996. 540p. ISBN:0-306-80712-2, ISBN13:
978-0-306-80712-1. Dewey:782.4165092273. LCCN:96-023837.

Audience: **g,l,u,f.** *Choice, 1990.*

Fujioka, Yasuhiro   ML156.7.C58F85 1995
John Coltrane: A Discography and Musical Biography. Lewis
Porter & Yoh-Ichi Hamada (Preface by). Trade Cloth. Scarecrow
Press, Inc. Lanham, MD. 1995. 416p. Studies in Jazz, No. 20
ISBN:0-8108-2986-X, ISBN13: 978-0-8108-2986-2.
Dewey:016.7887/165/092. LCCN:94-048457.

Audience: **u,f.**

Giddins, Gary   ML3507.G5 2000
Rhythm-a-Ning: Jazz Tradition and Innovation. Ed. 80. Trade
Paper. Da Capo Press, Inc. Cambridge, MA. 2000. 320p.
ISBN:0-306-80987-7, ISBN13: 978-0-306-80987-3.
Dewey:781.65/5. LCCN:00-064461.

Audience: **g,l,u,f.** *Choice, 1985.*

Giddins, Gary   ML3506
Riding on a Blue Note: Jazz and American Pop. Trade Paper.
DIANE Publishing Company. Collingdale, PA. 2000. 313p.
ISBN:0-7567-6671-0, ISBN13: 978-0-7567-6671-9.
Dewey:781.65.

Audience: **g,l,u,f.** *B*

Giddins, Gary   ML410.E44
Satchmo. Trade Paper. Doubleday Publishing. New York, NY.
1992. 240p. ISBN:0-385-24429-0, ISBN13: 978-0-385-24429-9.
Dewey:781.6/5/092. LCCN:92-008584.

Audience: **g,l,u,f.**

Giddins, Gary   ML3507.G53 2004
Weather Bird: Jazz at the Dawn of Its Second Century. Trade
Cloth. Oxford University Press, Inc. New York, NY. 2004. 656p.
ISBN:0-19-515607-2, ISBN13: 978-0-19-515607-2.
Dewey:781.65. LCCN:2004-000654.

Audience: **g,l,u,f.**

Gillespie, Dizzy & Fraser, Al   ML419.G54.A3
To Be or Not to Bop: Memoirs. Trade Cloth. Doubleday
Publishing. New York, NY. 1979. xix, 552p.
ISBN:0-385-12052-4, ISBN13: 978-0-385-12052-4.
Dewey:785.420924. LCCN:77-076237.

Audience: **g,l,u,f.**

Gioia, Ted   ML3506.G54 1997
The History of Jazz. Trade Cloth. Oxford University Press, Inc.
New York, NY. 1997. 480p. ISBN:0-19-509081-0, ISBN13:
978-0-19-509081-9. Dewey:781.6/5/09. LCCN:97-000102.

Audience: **g,l,u,f.** *Choice, 1998.*

Gottlieb, Robert (Editor)   ML3507
Reading Jazz: A Gathering of Autobiography, Reportage, and
Criticism from 1919 to Now. Trade Paper. Knopf Publishing
Group. New York, NY. 1999. 1088p. ISBN:0-679-78111-0,
ISBN13: 978-0-679-78111-0. Dewey:781.6/5/0904.

Audience: **u,f.**

Gourse, Leslie   ML419
Art Blakey: Jazz Messenger. Trade Cloth. Music Sales
Corporation. New York, NY. 2004. 209p. ISBN:0-8256-7272-4,
ISBN13: 978-0-8256-7272-9. Dewey:786.9/165/092 B.
LCCN:2003-279376.

Audience: **g,l,u,f.**

Gourse, Leslie   ML420.H58
The Billie Holiday Companion: 7 Decades of Commentary.
Trade Paper. Music Sales Corporation. New York, NY. 1997.
300p. ISBN:0-8256-7165-5, ISBN13: 978-0-8256-7165-4.
Dewey:782.42165/092. LCCN:96-031528.

Audience: **g,l,u,f.**

Gourse, Leslie   ML420.F52
The Ella Fitzgerald Companion: Seven Decades of Commentary.
Schirmer Books. 1998. ISBN:0-02-864625-8, ISBN13:
978-0-02-864625-1.

Audience: **u,f.**

Gourse, Leslie   ML417.M846
Straight, No Chaser: The Life and Genius of Thelonious Monk.
Trade Paper. Music Sales Corporation. New York, NY. 1998.
400p. ISBN:0-8256-7229-5, ISBN13: 978-0-8256-7229-3.
Dewey:786.2/1/65/092. LCCN:97-010509.

Audience: **g,l,u,f.**

Gourse, Leslie   ML420.C63G7 2000
Unforgettable: The Life and Mystique of Nat King Cole. Trade
Paper. Cooper Square Publishers, Inc. New York, NY. 2000.
352p. ISBN:0-8154-1082-4, ISBN13: 978-0-8154-1082-9.
Dewey:782.42164/092 B. LCCN:00-057000.

Audience: **g,l,u,f.**

Graham, Charles &   ML87.G79 2000
Morgenstern, Dan
Great Jazz Day. Art Kane, Milt Hinton & Dizzy Gillespie
(Photographers). Trade Paper. Woodford Publishing, Inc.
Emeryville, CA. 1999. 144p. ISBN:0-942627-35-0, ISBN13:
978-0-942627-35-0. Dewey:781.65/092/2. LCCN:99-066152.

Audience: **g,l,u,f.**

Gridley, Mark C.   ML3506.G74 2005
Jazz Styles: History and Analysis. Ed. 9. Trade Paper. Prentice
Hall PTR. Upper Saddle River, NJ. 2005. 432p.
ISBN:0-13-193115-6, ISBN13: 978-0-13-193115-2.
Dewey:781.65. LCCN:2004-060027.

Audience: **g,l,u,f.**

Groves, Alan & Shipton,   ML417.P73G76 2001
Alyn
The Glass Enclosure: The Life of Bud Powell. Trade Paper.
Continuum International Publishing Group, Ltd. London, 2001.
144p. A Bayou Book Ser. ISBN:0-8264-4746-5, ISBN13:
978-0-8264-4746-3. Dewey:786.2/165/092 B.
LCCN:2001-028002.

Audience: **g,l,u,f.**

Guralnick, Peter   ML420.J735G8 1989
Searching for Robert Johnson. Trade Cloth. Penguin Group
(USA) Inc. New York, NY. 1989. 9p. ISBN:0-525-24801-3,
ISBN13: 978-0-525-24801-9. Dewey:781.643092.
LCCN:89-007912.

Audience: **l,u,f.**

Hajdu, David   ML410.S9325H35 1996
Lush Life: A Biography of Billy Strayhorn. Cloth over Boards.
Farrar, Straus & Giroux. New York, NY. 1996. 305p.

ISBN:0-374-19438-6, ISBN13: 978-0-374-19438-3.
Dewey:781.6/55/092. LCCN:95-044707.

Audience: ■,f. *Choice, 1996.*

Hall, Fred M.   **ML410.B868H35 1996**
It's about Time: The Dave Brubeck Story. Cloth Text.
University of Arkansas Press. Fayetteville, AR. 1996. 240p.
ISBN:1-55728-404-0, ISBN13: 978-1-55728-404-4.
Dewey:781.65/092 B. LCCN:95-038531.

Audience: ι,f. *Choice, 1996.*

Hampton, Lionel & Haskins,   **ML419.H26 A3 1993**
  James
Hamp: An Autobiography. Trade Paper. HarperCollins
Publishers. New York, NY. 1999. 320p. ISBN:_-56743-019-8,
ISBN13: 978-1-56743-019-6. Dewey:786.8/43/092.
LCCN:93-000102.

Audience: g,l,u,f. *Choice, 1990.*

Handy, W. C.   **ML410.H18A3 1991**
Father of the Blues: An Autobiography. Arna Bontemps (Editor),
Abbe Niles (Introduction by). Trade Paper. Da Capo Press, Inc.
Cambridge, MA. 1991. 340p. Quality Paperbacks Ser.
ISBN:0-306-80421-2, ISBN13: 978-0-306-80421-2.
Dewey:784.5/3/00924 B. LCCN:90-026262.

Audience: g,l,u,f.

Heffley, Mike   **ML410**
The Music of Anthony Braxton. Trade Cloth. Greenwood
Publishing Group, Inc. Portsmouth, NH. 1996. 504p.
Contributions to the Study of Music and Dance Ser., No. 43
ISBN:0-313-29956-0, ISBN13: 978-0-313-29956-8.
Dewey:781.65/092. LCCN:95-043113.

Audience: u,f.

Jasen, David A. & Jones,   **ML3530.J38**
  Gene
That American Rag: The Story of Ragtime in the United States.
Trade Cloth. Music Sales Corporation. New York, NY. 1999.
350p. ISBN:0-8256-7233-3, ISBN13: 978-0-8256-7233-0.
Dewey:781.6/45/0973. LCCN:99-031803.

Audience: g,l,u,f.

Jenkins, Todd S.   **ML102**
Free Jazz and Free Improvisation: An Encyclopedia. Cloth Text.
Greenwood Publishing Group, Inc. Portsmouth, NH. 2004. 468p.
ISBN:0-313-29881-5, ISBN13: 978-0-313-29881-3.
Dewey:781.65/136/03. LCCN:2004-047531.

Audience: g,l,u,f. *Choice, 2005.*

Jost, Ekkehard   **ML3506.J67 1994**
Free Jazz: The Roots of Jazz. Trade Paper. Da Capo Press, Inc.
Cambridge, MA. 1994. 214p. Roots of Jazz Ser.
ISBN:0-306-80556-1, ISBN13: 978-0-306-80556-1.
Dewey:781.65/5. LCCN:93-034779.

Audience: u,f.

Kahn, Ashley   **ML419.C645**
A Love Supreme: The Story of John Coltrane's Signature

Album. Trade Paper. Penguin Group (USA) Inc. New York, NY.
2003. 288p. ISBN:0-14-200352-2, ISBN13: 978-0-14-200352-7.
Dewey:785/.34165.

Audience: u,f.

Kahn, Ashley   **ML419.D39**
Kind of Blue: The Making of the Miles Davis Masterpiece.
Jimmy Cobb (Foreword by). Trade Paper. Da Capo Press, Inc.
Cambridge, MA. 2001. 224p. ISBN:0-306-81067-0, ISBN13:
978-0-306-81067-1. Dewey:785/.32196165.

Audience: u,f.

Keil, Charles   **ML3521**
Urban Blues. University of Chicago Press. 1991.
ISBN:0-226-42960-1, ISBN13: 978-0-226-42960-1.

Audience: u,f.

Kernfeld, Barry D.   **ML156.4.J3B66 1995**
The Blackwell Guide to Recorded Jazz. Ed. 2. Trade Paper.
Blackwell Publishing, Inc. Malden, MA. 1995. 588p. Music
Guides Ser. ISBN:0-631-19552-1, ISBN13: 978-0-631-19552-8.
Dewey:016.78165/026/6. LCCN:95-000762.

Audience: g,l,u,f. *Choice, 1996.*

Kernfeld, Barry D. &   **ML102.J3N48 2001**
  Kernfeld, Barry (Editors)
The New Grove Dictionary of Jazz. Ed. 2. Trade Cloth. Oxford
University Press, Inc. New York, NY. 2001. 3000p.
ISBN:1-56159-284-6, ISBN13: 978-1-56159-284-5.
Dewey:781.65/03. LCCN:2001-040794.

Audience: g,l,u,f. *Choice, 2002, 1989.*

Kernodle, Tammy L.   **ML410.W7134K46 2004**
Soul on Soul: The Life and Music of Mary Lou Williams. Trade
Cloth. Northeastern University Press. Boston, MA. 2005. 348p.
ISBN:1-55553-606-9, ISBN13: 978-1-55553-606-0.
Dewey:786.2/165/092 B. LCCN:2003-021871.

Audience: l,u,f. *Choice, 2004.*

King, B. B. & Ritz, David   **ML420.K473**
Blues All Around Me: The Autobiography of B. B. King. Trade
Paper. HarperCollins Publishers. New York, NY. 1999. 360p.
ISBN:0-380-80760-2, ISBN13: 978-0-380-80760-4.
Dewey:781.643/092 B. LCCN:96-027773.

Audience: g,l,u,f.

Kirchner, Bill (Editor)   **ML419.D39M55 1997**
A Miles Davis Reader. Trade Cloth. Smithsonian Institution
Press. Washington, DC. 1997. 278p. ISBN:1-56098-774-X,
ISBN13: 978-1-56098-774-1. Dewey:788.9/2165/092.
LCCN:97-012802.

Audience: g,l,u,f.

Kirchner, Bill (Editor)   **ML3507.J32 2005**
The Oxford Companion to Jazz. Trade Paper. Oxford University
Press, Inc. New York, NY. 2005. 852p. ISBN:0-19-518359-2,
ISBN13: 978-0-19-518359-7. Dewey:781.65/09.

Audience: g,l,u,f. *Choice, 2001.*

Koch, Lawrence O.   **ML156.7.P35K6 1999**
Yardbird Suite: A Compendium of the Music and Life of Charlie
Parker. Ed. 2. Cloth Text. Northeastern University Press. Boston,
MA. 1999. 416p. ISBN:1-55553-385-X, ISBN13:
978-1-55553-385-4. Dewey:788.7/3165/092. LCCN:99-019348.
                          Audience: **u,f.** *Choice, 1999, 1989.*

Kofsky, Frank   **ML3508.K64 1998**
John Coltrane and the Jazz Revolution of The 1960s. Ed. 2.
Trade Paper. Pathfinder Press. New York, NY. 1998. 500p.
ISBN:0-87348-857-1, ISBN13: 978-0-87348-857-0.
Dewey:781.65/5/08996073. LCCN:97-069548.
                                      Audience: **u,f.**

Komara, Edward (Editor)   **ML102.B6**
Encyclopedia of the Blues. Paper over Boards. Routledge. New
York, NY. 2005. 1440p. ISBN:0-415-92699-8, ISBN13:
978-0-415-92699-7. Dewey:781.643/03. LCCN:2005-044346.
                          Audience: **g,l,u,f.** *Choice, 2006.*

Kostelanetz, Richard   **ML420.K473B3 2005**
   (Editor)
The B. B. King Reader: Six Decades of Commentary. Ed. 2.
Trade Paper. Hal Leonard Corporation. Milwaukee, WI. 2005.
256p. ISBN:0-634-09927-2, ISBN13: 978-0-634-09927-4.
Dewey:781.643/092 B. LCCN:2005-023200.
                                  Audience: **g,l,u,f.**

Kubik, Gerhard   **ML3521.K83 1999**
Africa and the Blues. Trade Cloth. University Press of
Mississippi. Jackson, MS. 1999. xviii, 240p. American Made
Music Ser. ISBN:1-57806-146-6, ISBN13: 978-1-57806-146-4.
Dewey:781.643/096. LCCN:99-024343.
                          Audience: **u,f.** *Choice, 2000.*

Lambert, Eddie &   **ML410.E44L33 1999**
  Norsworthy, Elaine
Duke Ellington: A Listener's Guide. Trade Cloth. Scarecrow
Press, Inc. Lanham, MD. 1998. 396p. Studies in Jazz, Vol. 26
ISBN:0-8108-3161-9, ISBN13: 978-0-8108-3161-2.
Dewey:781.65/092. LCCN:98-036431.
                          Audience: **g,l,u,f.** *Choice, 1999.*

Lester, James   **ML417.M846**
Too Marvelous for Words: The Life and Genius of Art Tatum.
Trade Paper. Oxford University Press, Inc. New York, NY. 1995.
254p. ISBN:0-19-509640-1, ISBN13: 978-0-19-509640-8.
Dewey:786.2/165/092.
                          Audience: **u,f.** *Choice, 1995.*

Lion, Jean Pierre   **ML419.B25**
Bix: The Definitive Biography of Jazz Legend Leon "Bix"
Beiderbecke. Gabriella Page-Fort (Translator). Trade Cloth.
Continuum International Publishing Group, Ltd. London, 2005.
356p. ISBN:0-8264-1699-3, ISBN13: 978-0-8264-1699-5.
Dewey:788.9/6165/092 B. LCCN:2005-010509.
                          Audience: **u,f.** *Choice, 2006.*

Litweiler, John   **ML3506.L57 1990**
The Freedom Principle: Jazz after 1958. Trade Paper. Da Capo
Press, Inc. Cambridge, MA. 1990. 324p. Quality Paperbacks

Ser. ISBN:0-306-80377-1, ISBN13: 978-0-306-80377-2.
Dewey:781.65/5. LCCN:89-026054.
                                      Audience: **g,l,u,f.** ℬ

Lomax, Alan   **ML3521**
The Land Where the Blues Began. Trade Paper, Compact Disc.
New Press, The. New York, NY. 2002. 560p.
ISBN:1-56584-739-3, ISBN13: 978-1-56584-739-2.
Dewey:781.6/43/09762. LCCN:2004-268632.
                          Audience: **g,l,u,f.** *Choice, 1994.*

Lomax, Alan   **ML410.M82 L6 2001**
Mister Jelly Roll: The Fortunes of Jelly Roll Morton, New
Orleans Creole and "Inventor of Jazz". Trade Paper. University
of California Press. Berkeley, CA. 2001. 368p.
ISBN:0-520-22530-9, ISBN13: 978-0-520-22530-5.
Dewey:781.65/092 B. LCCN:00-064430.
                                  Audience: **g,l,u,f.**

Magee, Jeffrey   **ML422.H44M34 2004**
The Uncrowned King of Swing: Fletcher Henderson and Big
Band Jazz. Trade Cloth. Oxford University Press, Inc. New
York, NY. 2005. 352p. ISBN:0-19-509022-5, ISBN13:
978-0-19-509022-2. Dewey:781.65/092 B. LCCN:2004-004727.
                                      Audience: **u,f.**

Maggin, Donald L.   **ML419.C645**
Stan Getz: A Life in Jazz. Trade Cloth. HarperCollins
Publishers. New York, NY. 1996. ISBN:0-614-95806-7, ISBN13:
978-0-614-95806-5. Dewey:788.7/165/092.
                                  Audience: **g,l,u,f.**

Mandell, Howard   **ML3506**
Future Jazz. Trade Paper. Oxford University Press, Inc. New
York, NY. 2000. 240p. ISBN:0-19-514121-0, ISBN13:
978-0-19-514121-4. Dewey:781.65.
                                      Audience: **u,f.**

Marquis, Donald M.   **ML419.B65M4 2005**
In Search of Buddy Bolden: First Man of Jazz. Trade Cloth.
Louisiana State University Press. Baton Rouge, LA. 2005. 256p.
ISBN:0-8071-3093-1, ISBN13: 978-0-8071-3093-3.
Dewey:788.9/6165/092 B. LCCN:2005-002004.
                                      Audience: **u,f.**

Martin, Henry   **ML419.P4M37**
Charlie Parker and Thematic Improvisation. Trade Paper.
Scarecrow Press, Inc. Lanham, MD. 1996. 170p. Studies in
Jazz, No. 24 ISBN:0-8108-4155-X, ISBN13:
978-0-8108-4155-0. Dewey:781.6/136/092. LCCN:86-003830.
                                      Audience: **u,f.**

Meadows, Eddie S.   **ML3508**
Bebop to Cool: Context, Ideology, and Musical Identity. Trade
Cloth. Greenwood Publishing Group, Inc. Portsmouth, NH.
2003. 416p. Jazz Companions Ser. ISBN:0-313-30071-2,
ISBN13: 978-0-313-30071-4. Dewey:781.65/5.
LCCN:2002-070036.
                          Audience: **u,f.** *Choice, 2004.*

Meadows, Eddie S. ML128.J3
Jazz Scholarship and Pedagogy: A Research and Information Guide. Ed. 3. Routledge. 2006. Routledge Music Bibliographies ISBN:0-415-93965-8, ISBN13: 978-0-415-93965-2.
Audience: l,u,f.

Mercer, Michelle ML419.S55M47 2004
Footprints: The Life and Music of Wayne Shorter. Trade Cloth. Penguin Group (USA) Inc. New York, NY. 2004. 320p. ISBN:1-58542-353-X, ISBN13: 978-1-58542-353-8. Dewey:788.7/165/092 B. LCCN:2004-058845.
Audience: l,u,f.

Mingus, Charles ML410.M6795
Beneath the Underdog. Nel Kinh (Editor). Trade Paper. Penguin Group (USA) Inc. New York, NY. 1980. 272p. ISBN:0-14-003880-9, ISBN13: 978-0-14-003880-4. Dewey:781.6/5/092. LCCN:80-016132.
Audience: g,l,u,f.

Monson, Ingrid ML3506.M64 1996
Saying Something: Jazz Improvisation and Interaction. Trade Cloth. University of Chicago Press. Chicago, IL. 1997. 261p. Chicago Studies in Ethnomusicology ISBN:0-226-53477-4, ISBN13: 978-0-226-53477-0. Dewey:781.65/136. LCCN:96-023224.
Audience: u,f. *Choice, 1997.*

Moore, Allan (Editor) ML3521
The Cambridge Companion to Blues and Gospel Music. Jonathan Cross (Contribution by). Cloth Text. Cambridge University Press. New York, NY. 2003. 234p. Cambridge Companions to Music Ser. ISBN:0-521-80635-6, ISBN13: 978-0-521-80635-0. Dewey:781.643. LCCN:2003-544910.
Audience: g,l,u,f. *Choice, 2003.*

Nicholson, Stuart ML410.E44N53 1999
Reminiscing in Tempo: A Portrait of Duke Ellington. Trade Cloth. Northeastern University Press. Boston, MA. 1999. 560p. ISBN:1-55553-380-9, ISBN13: 978-1-55553-380-9. Dewey:781.65/092 B. LCCN:99-010873.
Audience: l,u,f. *Choice, 1999.*

Nisenson, Eric ML419.D39N58 2000
Kind of Blue: The Making of the Miles Davis Masterpiece. Trade Cloth. St. Martin's Press. Gordonville, VA. 2000. xv, 236p. ISBN:0-312-26617-0, ISBN13: 978-0-312-26617-2. Dewey:781.65/026/6. LCCN:00-044170.
Audience: u,f.

Nisenson, Eric ML419.C645
Open Sky: Sonny Rollins and His World of Improvisation. Sonny Rollins (Foreword by). Trade Cloth. DIANE Publishing Company. Collingdale, PA. 2006. 216p. ISBN:1-4223-5032-0, ISBN13: 978-1-4223-5032-4. Dewey:788.7/165/092 B.
Audience: u,f.

Oliver, Paul ML3521.O46 1998
The Story of the Blues. Cloth Text. Northeastern University Press. Boston, MA. 1998. 288p. ISBN:1-55553-355-8, ISBN13: 978-1-55553-355-7. Dewey:784.7. LCCN:98-012192.
Audience: g,l,u,f.

Oliver, Paul ML3521 .O42 1990
Blues Fell This Morning: Meaning in the Blues. Ed. 2. Richard Wright (Foreword by). Trade Paper. Cambridge University Press. New York, NY. 1990. 372p. ISBN:0-521-37793-5, ISBN13: 978-0-521-37793-5. Dewey:781.643. LCCN:89-025402.
Audience: u,f. *Choice, 1990.*

Pearson, Barry Lee & McCulloch, Bill ML420.J735P4 2003
Robert Johnson: Lost and Found. Trade Cloth. University of Illinois Press. Champaign, IL. 2003. 160p. Music in American Life Ser. ISBN:0-252-02835-X, ISBN13: 978-0-252-02835-9. Dewey:782.421643/092 B. LCCN:2002-012714.
Audience: l,u,f. *Choice, 2004.*

Peterson, Oscar ML417.A46A3 2002
A Jazz Odyssey: The Life of Oscar Peterson. Richard Palmer (Editor). Trade Cloth. Continuum International Publishing Group, Ltd. London, 2002. 400p. ISBN:0-8264-5807-6, ISBN13: 978-0-8264-5807-0. Dewey:786.2/165/092 B. LCCN:2002-073362.
Audience: l,u,f. *Choice, 2003.*

Pettinger, Peter ML417.E9P53 1998
Bill Evans: How My Heart Sings. Cloth over Boards. Yale University Press. Cumberland, RI. 1998. 362p. ISBN:0-300-07193-0, ISBN13: 978-0-300-07193-1. Dewey:[B]. LCCN:97-049991.
Audience: l,u,f. *Choice, 1998.*

Pond, Steven F. ML417.H23P66 2005
Head Hunters: The Making of Jazz's First Platinum Album. Trade Cloth. University of Michigan Press. Chicago, IL. 2005. 288p. Jazz Perspectives Ser. ISBN:0-472-11417-4, ISBN13: 978-0-472-11417-7. Dewey:781.65/7. LCCN:2005-014482.
Audience: u,f.

Porter, Eric ML3508 .P67 2002
What Is This Thing Called Jazz? Trade Paper. University of California Press. Berkeley, CA. 2002. 428p. Music of the African Diaspora Ser., Vol. 6 ISBN:0-520-23296-8, ISBN13: 978-0-520-23296-9. Dewey:781.65/089/96073. LCCN:2001-044408.
Audience: u,f.

Porter, Lewis ML156.7.C58P65 1999
John Coltrane: His Life and Music. Trade Paper. University of Michigan Press. Chicago, IL. 2000. 448p. The Michigan American Music Ser. ISBN:0-472-08643-X, ISBN13: 978-0-472-08643-6. Dewey:[B]. LCCN:97-041995.
Audience: g,l,u,f.

Porter, Lewis ML419.Y7P7 2005
Lester Young. Trade Paper, Perfect. University of Michigan Press. Chicago, IL. 2005. 176p. Jazz Perspectives Ser. ISBN:0-472-08922-6, ISBN13: 978-0-472-08922-2. Dewey:788.7/165/092 B. LCCN:2004-065835.
Audience: l,u,f. *Choice, 1986.*

Formats: Web: ☐ Ebook: **e** CD/DVD-ROM: 🎵 BCL3: **B**

Porter, Lewis (Editor)   ML419.Y7L47 1991
A Lester Young Reader. Trade Cloth. Smithsonian Institution
Press. Washington, DC. 1991. 344p. Smithsonian Readers in
American Music Ser. ISBN:1-56098-064-8, ISBN13:
978-1-56098-064-3. Dewey:788.7/165/092 B. LCCN:90-024922.
> Audience: **l,u,f.** *Choice, 1992.*

Radano, Ronald M.   ML419.B735.R3 1993
New Musical Figurations: Anthony Braxton's Cultural Critique.
Trade Cloth. University of Chicago Press. Chicago, IL. 1994.
336p. ISBN:0-226-70195-6, ISBN13: 978-0-226-70195-0.
Dewey:788.7165092. LCCN:93-001878.
> Audience: **u,f.** *Choice, 1994.*

Rattenbury, Ken   ML410.E44
Duke Ellington, Jazz Composer. Trade Paper. Yale University
Press. Cumberland, RI. 1993. 339p. ISBN:0-300-05507-2,
ISBN13: 978-0-300-05507-8. Dewey:781.6/5/092.
LCCN:89-016544.
> Audience: **u,f.** *Choice, 1991.*

Rayno, Don   ML422.W4R38 2003
Paul Whiteman: Pioneer in American Music, Vol. 1. William H.
Youngren (Foreword by). Trade Cloth. Scarecrow Press, Inc.
Lanham, MD. 2003. 840p. Studies in Jazz, No. 43
ISBN:0-8108-4579-2, ISBN13: 978-0-8108-4579-4.
Dewey:784.4/8165/092 B. LCCN:2002-012943.
> Audience: **u,f.**

Russell, Tony   ML3521
The Blues: From Robert Johnson to Robert Cray. Trade Cloth.
Thomson Gale. Farmington Hills, MI. 1997. 224p.
ISBN:0-02-864862-5, ISBN13: 978-0-02-864862-0.
Dewey:781.6/43. LCCN:97-067479.
> Audience: **g,l,u,f.**

Santoro, Gene   ML410.E44
Myself When I Am Real: The Life and Music of Charles
Mingus. Ed. 2. Trade Paper. Oxford University Press, Inc. New
York, NY. 2001. 462p. ISBN:0-19-514711-1, ISBN13:
978-0-19-514711-7. Dewey:781.65/092 B.
> Audience: **l,u,f.** *Choice, 2001.*

Schroeder, Patricia R.   ML420.J735S37 2004
Robert Johnson, Mythmaking, and Contemporary American
Culture. Trade Cloth. University of Illinois Press. Champaign,
IL. 2004. 216p. Music in American Life Ser.
ISBN:0-252-02915-1, ISBN13: 978-0-252-02915-8.
Dewey:782.421643/092. LCCN:2003-020027.
> Audience: **g,l,u,f.** *Choice, 2005.*

Schuller, Gunther   ML60.S392 1999
Musings: The Musical Worlds of Gunther Schuller. Trade Paper.
Da Capo Press, Inc. Cambridge, MA. 1999. 416p.
ISBN:0-306-80902-8, ISBN13: 978-0-306-80902-6. Dewey:780.
LCCN:98-048220.
> Audience: **u,f.**

Schuller, Gunther A.   ML3506.S35 1986
Early Jazz: Its Roots and Musical Development. Trade Paper.

Oxford University Press, Inc. New York, NY. 1986. 416p.
ISBN:0-19-504043-0, ISBN13: 978-0-19-504043-2.
Dewey:781.6/52. LCCN:86-002403.
> Audience: **u,f.**

Schuller, Gunther A.   ML3506.S36
The Swing Era: The Development of Jazz, 1930-1945. Trade
Cloth. Oxford University Press, Inc. New York, NY. 1989. 944p.
History of Jazz Ser., Vol. 2 ISBN:0-19-504312-X, ISBN13:
978-0-19-504312-9. Dewey:781/.57 s. LCCN:87-001664.
> Audience: **u,f.** *Choice, 1989.*

Shaughnessy, Mary Angela   ML419.P47S5 1993
Les Paul: An American Original. Trade Cloth. HarperCollins
Publishers. New York, NY. 1993. 347p. ISBN:0-688-08467-2,
ISBN13: 978-0-688-08467-7. Dewey:781.64/092.
LCCN:92-035832.
> Audience: **l,u,f.**

Shipton, Alyn   ML417.W15S5 2002
Fats Waller: The Cheerful Little Earful. Ed. 2. Trade Cloth.
Continuum International Publishing Group, Ltd. London, 2002.
192p. Bayou Jazz Lives Ser. ISBN:0-8264-5796-7, ISBN13:
978-0-8264-5796-7. Dewey:786.2/165/092 B.
LCCN:2001-047404.
> Audience: **l,u,f.** *Choice, 2002.*

Shipton, Alyn   ML419.D39
Groovin' High: The Life of Dizzy Gillespie. Trade Paper.
DIANE Publishing Company. Collingdale, PA. 2004. 422p.
ISBN:0-7567-7598-1, ISBN13: 978-0-7567-7598-8.
Dewey:788.9/2165/092 B.
> Audience: **g,l,u,f.** *Choice, 2000.*

Silvester, Peter J.   ML747.S54 1989
A Left Hand Like God: A History of Boogie Woogie Piano.
Paper Text. Da Capo Press, Inc. Cambridge, MA. 1989. 558p.
Quality Paperbacks Ser. ISBN:0-306-80359-3, ISBN13:
978-0-306-80359-8. Dewey:786.2/1655. LCCN:89-012057.
> Audience: **u,f.**

Simosko, Vladimir &   ML419.D646
Tepperman, Barry
Eric Dolphy: A Musical Biography and Discography. Trade
Paper. Da Capo Press, Inc. Cambridge, MA. 1996. 200p.
Quality Paperbacks Ser. ISBN:0-306-80524-3, ISBN13:
978-0-306-80524-0. Dewey:788/.0092/4. LCCN:79-015117.
> Audience: **u,f.**

Snowden, Don & Dixon,   ML410.D68A3 1989
Willie
I Am the Blues: The Willie Dixon Story. Trade Paper. Da Capo
Press, Inc. Cambridge, MA. 1990. 264p. ISBN:0-306-80415-8,
ISBN13: 978-0-306-80415-1. Dewey:781.643/092 B.
LCCN:90-038862.
> Audience: **l,u,f.**

Stambler, Irwin & Stambler,   ML102.F66S73 2001
Lyndon
Folk and Blues: The Premier Encyclopedia of American Roots

Music. Cloth over Boards. St. Martin's Press. Gordonville, VA. 2001. 816p. ISBN:0-312-20057-9, ISBN13: 978-0-312-20057-2. Dewey:781.64/0973/03. LCCN:2001-273473.

Audience: **g,l,u,f.**

Summerfield, Maurice J.   **ML399**
The Jazz Guitar. Ed. 4. Trade Paper. Ashley Mark Publishing. Blaydon On Tyne, 1998. 404p. ISBN:1-872639-31-3, ISBN13: 978-1-872639-31-4. Dewey:787.61.

Audience: **g,l,u,f.**

Szwed, John F.   **ML410.S978S73 1998**
Space Is the Place: The Lives and Times of Sun Ra. Trade Paper. Da Capo Press, Inc. Cambridge, MA. 1998. 496p. ISBN:0-306-80855-2, ISBN13: 978-0-306-80855-5. Dewey:781.65/092 B. LCCN:98-015303.

Audience: **u,f.**

Taft, Michael   **PS591.N4T35 2005**
Talkin' to Myself: Blues Lyrics, 1921-1942. Trade Paper. Routledge. New York, NY. 2005. 744p. ISBN:0-415-97378-3, ISBN13: 978-0-415-97378-6. Dewey:811/.52080357. LCCN:2005-006740.

Audience: **g,l,u,f.**

Taylor, Arthur   **ML394 .T4 1993**
Notes and Tones: Musician-to-Musician Interviews. Ed. 2. Trade Paper. Da Capo Press, Inc. Cambridge, MA. 1993. 320p. ISBN:0-306-80526-X, ISBN13: 978-0-306-80526-4. Dewey:781.65/092/2. LCCN:93-025111.

Audience: **u,f.**

Taylor, Billy   **ML700**
Jazz Piano: A Jazz History. W.C. Brown Co. Publishers. 1983. ISBN:0-697-09959-8, ISBN13: 978-0-697-09959-4.

Audience: **g,l,u,f.**

Titon, Jeff Todd   **94-6953 [ML]**
Early Downhome Blues: A Musical and Cultural Analysis. Ed. 2. Trade Paper. University of North Carolina Press. Chapel Hill, NC. 1995. 340p. Cultural Studies of the United States ISBN:0-8078-4482-9, ISBN13: 978-0-8078-4482-3. Dewey:781.643/09. LCCN:94-006953.

Audience: **u,f.**

Townley, Eric   **ML156.4.J3**
Tell Your Story: A Dictionary of Jazz and Blues Recordings 1917-1950, Vol. 1. Chigwell, Eng.: Storyville Publications. 1976.

Audience: **g,l,u,f.**

Townley, Eric   **ML156.4.J3**
Tell Your Story: A Dictionary of Jazz and Blues Recordings 1951-1975, Vol. 2. Chigwell, Essex, England: Storyville Publications. 1987. ISBN:0-902391-09-7, ISBN13: 978-0-902391-09-3.

Audience: **g,l,u,f.**

Tucker, Mark (Editor)   **ML410.E44**
The Duke Ellington Reader. Trade Paper. Oxford University

Press, Inc. New York, NY. 1995. 560p. ISBN:0-19-509391-7, ISBN13: 978-0-19-509391-9. Dewey:781.6/5/092.

Audience: **g,l,u,f.** *Choice, 1994.*

van de Leur, Walter   **ML410.S9325L48 2002**
Something to Live For: The Music of Billy Strayhorn. Trade Paper. Oxford University Press, Inc. New York, NY. 2002. 352p. ISBN:0-19-512448-0, ISBN13: 978-0-19-512448-4. Dewey:781.65/092. LCCN:2001-037040.

Audience: **u,f.**

Van Der Bliek, Rob (Editor)   **ML417.M846T54 2001**
The Thelonious Monk Reader. Ed. 2. Trade Cloth. Oxford University Press, Inc. New York, NY. 2001. 286p. Readers in American Music Ser. ISBN:0-19-512166-X, ISBN13: 978-0-19-512166-7. Dewey:786.2165/092 B. LCCN:00-037475.

Audience: **g,l,u,f.**

Vigeland, Carl & Marsalis,   **ML419.D39**
    Wynton
Jazz in the Bittersweet Blues of Life. Trade Paper. Da Capo Press, Inc. Cambridge, MA. 2002. 256p. ISBN:0-306-81127-8, ISBN13: 978-0-306-81127-2. Dewey:788.9/2165/092.

Audience: **g,l,u,f.**

Wald, Elijah   **ML420.J735W35 2004**
Escaping the Delta: Robert Johnson and the Invention of the Blues. Trade Cloth. HarperCollins Publishers. New York, NY. 2004. 368p. ISBN:0-06-052423-5, ISBN13: 978-0-06-052423-4. Dewey:782.421643/092 B. LCCN:2003-052287.

Audience: **g,l,u,f.**

Walser, Robert (Editor)   **ML3507.K4 1999**
Keeping Time: Readings in Jazz History. Paper Text. Oxford University Press, Inc. New York, NY. 1998. 464p. ISBN:0-19-509173-6, ISBN13: 978-0-19-509173-1. Dewey:781.65/09. LCCN:97-042484.

Audience: **u,f.**

Weissman, Dick   **ML3521.W45 2004**
Blues Basics. Paper over Boards. Routledge. New York, NY. 2004. 224p. The Basics Ser. ISBN:0-415-97067-9, ISBN13: 978-0-415-97067-9. Dewey:781.643/09. LCCN:2004-019116.

Audience: **g,l,u,f.** *Choice, 2006.*

Wilson, Peter N.   **ML419.C63W513 1999**
Ornette Coleman: His Life and Music. Robert Dobbin (Translator). Trade Paper. Berkeley Hills Books. Berkeley, CA. 1999. 216p. ISBN:1-893163-04-0, ISBN13: 978-1-893163-04-1. Dewey:788.7/165/092 B. LCCN:99-021581.

Audience: **l,u,f.**

Woideck, Carl   **ML419.P4W65 2005**
Charlie Parker: His Music and Life. Trade Paper. University of Michigan Press. Chicago, IL. 1998. 304p. The Michigan American Music Ser. ISBN:0-472-08555-7, ISBN13: 978-0-472-08555-2. Dewey:788.7/165/092 B. LCCN:96-030211.

Audience: **g,l,u,f.** *Choice, 1997.*

Woideck, Carl   **ML420.H58**
The Charlie Parker Companion: Six Decades of Commentary.
Trade Paper. Music Sales Corporation. New York, NY. 1998.
300p. ISBN:0-8256-7170-1, ISBN13: 978-0-8256-7170-8.
Dewey:782.4/2/165/092. LCCN:97-041859.
                              Audience: **g,l,u,f.**

Woideck, Carl   **ML419.C645**
John Coltrane Companion: Four Decades of Commentary. Trade
Paper. Music Sales Corporation. New York, NY. 1998. 300p.
ISBN:0-8256-7189-2, ISBN13: 978-0-8256-7189-0.
Dewey:788.7/165/092.
                              Audience: **g,l,u,f.**

Yanow, Scott   **ML3508**
Jazz: A Regional Exploration. Cloth Text. Greenwood
Publishing Group, Inc. Portsmouth, NH. 2005. 320p. Greenwood
Guides to American Roots Music Ser. ISBN:0-313-32871-4,
ISBN13: 978-0-313-32871-8. Dewey:781.65/0973.
LCCN:2004-018158.
               Audience: **g,l,u,f.** *Choice, 2005.*

Studies in Music History, Criticism, Analysis, and Appreciation > Rock, Pop, Rhythm and Blues, Soul, Hip Hop, and Country

                              ML156.4.P6
⊡ Allmusic = All Music Guide.
http://www.allmusic.com
All Media Guide.
                              Audience: **g,l,u,f.**

Ackelson, Richard W.   **ML156.7.S56**
Frank Sinatra: A Complete Recording History of Technqiues,
Songs, Composers, Lyricists, Arrangers, Sessions and First-Issue
Albums, 1939-1984. Library Binding. McFarland & Company,
Incorporated Publishers. Jefferson, NC. 1991. 480p.
ISBN:0-89950-554-6, ISBN13: 978-0-89950-554-1.
Dewey:016.78242163092. LCCN:91-052629.
                              Audience: **u,f.**

Akenson, James E.   **ML394.W65 2003**
The Women of Country Music: A Reader. Charles K. Wolfe
(Editor). Trade Cloth. University Press of Kentucky. Lexington,
KY. 2003. 224p. ISBN:0-8131-2280-5, ISBN13:
978-0-8131-2280-9. Dewey:782.421642/082.
LCCN:2003-005310.
                              Audience: **u,f.**

Altschuler, Glenn C.   **ML3534**
All Shook Up: How Rock 'n' Roll Changed America. Trade
Paper. Oxford University Press, Inc. New York, NY. 2004. 240p.
Pivotal Moments in American History Ser. ISBN:0-19-517749-5,
ISBN13: 978-0-19-517749-7. Dewey:781.66/0973.
LCCN:2003-001214.
                              Audience: **u,f.**

Auslander, Philip   **ML3534.A9 2006**
Performing Glam Rock: Gender and Theatricality in Popular
Music. Trade Cloth. University of Michigan Press. Chicago, IL.
2006. 272p. ISBN:0-472-09868-3, ISBN13: 978-0-472-09868-2.
Dewey:781.66. LCCN:2005-017928.
                              Audience: **u,f.**

Averill, Gage   **ML3516.A94 2002**
Four Parts, No Waiting: A Social History of American
Barbershop Harmony. Cloth Text. Oxford University Press, Inc.
New York, NY. 2003. 248p. American Musicspheres Ser., Vol. 1
ISBN:0-19-511672-0, ISBN13: 978-0-19-511672-4.
Dewey:782.8/0973. LCCN:2002-000696.
                 Audience: **u.** *Choice, 2003.*

Bangs, Lester   **ML3534.B315 1988**
Psychotic Reactions and Carburetor Dung: The Work of a
Legendary Critic: Rock 'N' Roll As Literature and Literature As
Rock 'N' Roll. Greil Marcus (Editor). Trade Paper. Knopf
Publishing Group. New York, NY. 1988. 416p.
ISBN:0-679-72045-6, ISBN13: 978-0-679-72045-4.
Dewey:784.5/4/009. LCCN:88-040180.
                              Audience: **u,f.**

Bangs, Lester   **ML3534.B314 2003**
Mainlines, Blood Feasts, Bad Taste: A Lester Bangs Reader.
John Morthland (Editor, Introduction by). UK-Trade Paper.
Knopf Publishing Group. New York, NY. 2003. 432p.
ISBN:0-375-71367-0, ISBN13: 978-0-375-71367-5.
Dewey:781.66/09. LCCN:2003-040392.
                              Audience: **u,f.**

Beatles, The (Performed by)   **ML54.6.B4**
The Beatles Lyrics: The Songs of Lennon, McCartney, Harrison
and Starr. Trade Paper. Hal Leonard Corporation. Milwaukee,
WI. 1992. 256p. Songwriting and Lyrics Ser.
ISBN:0-7935-1537-8, ISBN13: 978-0-7935-1537-0.
Dewey:782.42166.
                              Audience: **g,l,u,f.**

Bego, Mark   **ML420**
Aretha Franklin: The Queen of Soul. Trade Paper. Da Capo
Press, Inc. Cambridge, MA. 2001. 448p. ISBN:0-306-80935-4,
ISBN13: 978-0-306-80935-4. Dewey:782.4/2/1644/092.
                            Audience: **g,l,u,f.**

Bennett, Andy   **ML38.W66**
Remembering Woodstock. Trade Cloth. Ashgate Publishing, Ltd.
Aldershot, 2004. 182p. Ashgate Popular and Folk Music Ser.
ISBN:0-7546-0713-5, ISBN13: 978-0-7546-0713-7.
Dewey:781.66/079/74735. LCCN:2003-062698.
             Audience: **g,l,u,f.** *Choice, 2005.*

Benson, Carl   **ML420.D98**
Bob Dylan Companion: Four Decades of Commentary. Trade
Paper. Music Sales Corporation. New York, NY. 1998. 300p.
ISBN:0-8256-7169-8, ISBN13: 978-0-8256-7169-2.
Dewey:782.42164/092. LCCN:98-035862.
                            Audience: **g,l,u,f.**

Berkenstadt, Jim & Cross,   ML421.N57B4 2004
Charles R.
Nevermind: Nirvana. Trade Paper. Music Sales Corporation.
New York, NY. 2004. 172p. ISBN:0-8256-7286-4, ISBN13:
978-0-8256-7286-6. Dewey:782.4/2166/0922. LCCN:97-051361.
Audience: **g,l,u,f.**

Berry, Chuck   ML420.B365
Chuck Berry: The Autobiography. Faber and Faber. 2001.
ISBN:0-571-20754-5, ISBN13: 978-0-571-20754-1.
Audience: **g,l,u,f.**

Bertrand, Michael T.   ML3918.R63B47 2000
Race, Rock and Elvis. Trade Cloth. University of Illinois Press.
Champaign, IL. 2000. 352p. Music in American Life Ser.
ISBN:0-252-02586-5, ISBN13: 978-0-252-02586-0.
Dewey:781.66/0975. LCCN:99-050895.
Audience: **u,f.** *Choice, 2001.*

Bogdanov, Vladimir   ML1630.18
(Editor), et al.
All Music Guide to Country: The Definitive Guide to Country
Music. Ed. 2. Chris Woodstra & Stephen Thomas Erlewine
(Editors). Trade Paper. Backbeat Books. San Francisco, CA.
2003. 700p. ISBN:0-87930-760-9, ISBN13: 978-0-87930-760-8.
Dewey:782.4/21642/0266. LCCN:90-024517.
Audience: **g,l,u,f.** *Choice, 2004.*

Bogdanov, Vladimir   ML102.U53A55 2001
(Editor), et al.
All Music Guide to Electronica: The Expert's Guide to the Best
Electronic Recordings. Ed. 4. Chris Woodstra & Stephen
Thomas Erlewine (Editors). Trade Paper. Backbeat Books. San
Francisco, CA. 2001. 688p. All Music Guides
ISBN:0-87930-628-9, ISBN13: 978-0-87930-628-1.
Dewey:781.64. LCCN:2001-025514.
Audience: **g,l,u,f.**

Bogdanov, Vladimir   ML156.9.A39 2002
(Editor), et al.
All Music Guide to Rock: The Definitive Guide to Rock, Pop
and Soul. Ed. 3. Chris Woodstra & Stephen Thomas Erlewine
(Editors). Trade Paper. Backbeat Books. San Francisco, CA.
2002. 1399p. AMG All Media Guide Ser. ISBN:0-87930-653-X,
ISBN13: 978-0-87930-653-3. Dewey:016.78164/0266.
LCCN:2002-018397.
Audience: **g,l,u,f.**

Bogdanov, Vladimir   ML3531
(Editor), et al.
All Music Guide to Hip-Hop: The Definitive Guide to Rap and
Hip-Hop. Chris Woodstra, Stephen Thomas Erlewine & John
Bush (Editors). Trade Paper. Backbeat Books. San Francisco,
CA. 2003. 640p. AMG All Media Guide Ser.
ISBN:0-87930-759-5, ISBN13: 978-0-87930-759-2.
Dewey:782.421649. LCCN:2003-057799.
Audience: **g,l,u,f.**

Bordowitz, Hank   ML3532
Every Little Thing Gonna Be Alright: The Bob Marley Reader.

Trade Paper. Da Capo Press, Inc. Cambridge, MA. 2004. 336p.
ISBN:0-306-81340-8, ISBN13: 978-0-306-81340-5.
Dewey:782.421646/092 B. LCCN:2004-009767.
Audience: **g,l,u,f.**

Brackett, David   ML3470 .B73 2000
Interpreting Popular Music. Trade Paper. University of
California Press. Berkeley, CA. 2000. 276p.
ISBN:0-520-22541-4, ISBN13: 978-0-520-22541-1.
Dewey:781.64. LCCN:00-042611.
Audience: **u,f.**

Brackett, David   ML3470.B75 2004
The Pop, Rock, and Soul Reader: Histories and Debates. Trade
Cloth. Oxford University Press, Inc. New York, NY. 2004. 544p.
ISBN:0-19-512570-3, ISBN13: 978-0-19-512570-2.
Dewey:781.64/09. LCCN:2004-041598.
Audience: **g,l,u,f.**

Brackett, Nathan & Hoard,   ML156.4.P6R62 2004
Christian (Editors)
The New Rolling Stone Album Guide. Ed. 4. Trade Paper.
Simon & Schuster, Inc. New York, NY. 2004. 944p.
ISBN:0-7432-0169-8, ISBN13: 978-0-7432-0169-8.
Dewey:781.66/026/6. LCCN:2004-058905.
Audience: **g,l,u,f.**

Brewster, Bill & Broughton,   ML3470.B75 2000
Frank
Last Night a DJ Saved My Life: The History of the Disc
Jockey. Trade Paper. Grove/Atlantic, Inc. New York, NY. 2000.
x, 435p. ISBN:0-8021-3688-5, ISBN13: 978-0-8021-3688-6.
Dewey:791.4/4. LCCN:00-023968.
Audience: **g,l,u,f.**

Brody, James & Campbell,   ML3534.C26 1999
Michael
Rock and Roll: An Introduction. Paper Text. Thomson
Wadsworth. Belmont, CA. 1999. 464p. ISBN:0-02-864727-0,
ISBN13: 978-0-02-864727-2. Dewey:781.66. LCCN:99-010095.
Audience: **g,l,u,f.**

Bronson, Fred   ML156.4.P6B76 2004
The Billboard Book of Number One Hits. Ed. 5. Trade Paper.
Watson-Guptill Publications, Inc. New York, NY. 2003. 1,008p.
Ser. ISBN:0-8230-7677-6, ISBN13: 978-0-8230-7677-2.
Dewey:016.78164/0973. LCCN:2003-016910.
Audience: **l,u,f.** *Choice, 2004.*

Brown, James & Tucker,   ML420
Bruce
James Brown: The Godfather of Soul. Trade Paper. Avalon
Publishing Group. New York, NY. 2002. 384p.
ISBN:1-56025-388-6, ISBN13: 978-1-56025-388-4.
Dewey:784.5/5/00924. LCCN:2004-270602.
Audience: **g,l,u,f.**

Buchanan, Scott (Editor)   ML54.6.R58 1994
Rock 'n Roll: The Famous Lyrics. Trade Paper. HarperCollins

Publishers. New York, NY. 1994. 320p. ISBN:0-06-273235-8, ISBN13: 978-0-06-273235-4. Dewey:782.42166/0268. LCCN:94-010112.

Audience: **g,l,u,f.**

**Bufwack, Mary A. &   ML3524.B83 2003
Oermann, Robert K.**
Finding Her Voice: Women in Country Music, 1800-2000. Trade Cloth. Vanderbilt University Press. Nashville, TN. 2003. 616p. ISBN:0-8265-1432-4, ISBN13: 978-0-8265-1432-5. Dewey:781.642/082. LCCN:2003-002519.

Audience: **u,f.** *Choice, 2004.*

Butler, Mark J.   MT146.B88 2005
Unlocking the Groove: Rhythm, Meter, and Musical Design in Electronic Dance Music. Trade Paper. Indiana University Press. Bloomington, IN. 2006. 272p. Profiles in Popular Music Ser. ISBN:0-253-21804-7, ISBN13: 978-0-253-21804-9. Dewey:786.7/164. LCCN:2005-020156.

Audience: **l,u,f.**

**Cale, John & Bockris,   ML420.P96
Victor**
What's Welsh for Zen: The Autobiography of John Cale. Trade Paper. Bloomsbury Publishing. New York, NY. 2000. 272p. ISBN:1-58234-068-4, ISBN13: 978-1-58234-068-5. Dewey:782.4/2/166/092.

Audience: **u,f.**

Campbell, Michael   ML3477.C36 2005
Popular Music in America: And the Beat Goes On. Ed. 2. Paper Text. Thomson Wadsworth. Belmont, CA. 2005. 440p. ISBN:0-534-55534-9, ISBN13: 978-0-534-55534-4. Dewey:781.64/0973. LCCN:2004-112306.

Audience: **g,l,u,f.**

**Cash, Johnny & Carr,   ML420.C265A3 1998
Patrick**
Cash: The Autobiography. Mass Market. HarperCollins Publishers. New York, NY. 2005. 448p. ISBN:0-06-101357-9, ISBN13: 978-0-06-101357-7. Dewey:782.4/2/1642/092. LCCN:98-227899.

Audience: **g,l,u,f.**

Cepeda, Raquel (Editor)   ML3531.A53 2004
And It Don't Stop: The Best American Hip-Hop Journalism of the Last 25 Years. Nelson George (Foreword by). Trade Paper. Faber & Faber, Inc. New York, NY. 2004. 384p. ISBN:0-571-21159-3, ISBN13: 978-0-571-21159-3. Dewey:782.421649. LCCN:2004-004920.

Audience: **g,l,u,f.**

Charles, Ray & Ritz, David   ML420.C46A3 2004
Brother Ray: Ray Charles' Own Story. Paper Text. Da Capo Press, Inc. Cambridge, MA. 2004. 384p. ISBN:0-306-81431-5, ISBN13: 978-0-306-81431-0. Dewey:782.4/21644/092.

Audience: **g,l,u,f.**

Cohen, Rich   ML405.C63 2004
Machers and Rockers: Chess Records and the Business of Rock

and Roll. Trade Cloth. W. W. Norton & Company, Inc. New York, NY. 2004. 160p. ISBN:0-393-05280-X, ISBN13: 978-0-393-05280-0. Dewey:781.66/0973. LCCN:2004-011792.

Audience: **l,u,f.**

Covach, John   ML3534.C7 2006
What's That Sound?: Intoduction to Rock and Its History. Trade Paper. W. W. Norton & Company, Inc. New York, NY. 2006. 450p. ISBN:0-393-97575-4, ISBN13: 978-0-393-97575-8. Dewey:781.6609. LCCN:2006-002220.

Audience: **g,l,u,f.**

**Covach, John & Boone,   ML3534.U53 1997
Graeme (Editors)**
Understanding Rock: Essays in Musical Analysis. Trade Paper. Oxford University Press, Inc. New York, NY. 1997. 236p. ISBN:0-19-510005-0, ISBN13: 978-0-19-510005-1. Dewey:781.66/0973. LCCN:96-053475.

Audience: **u,f.**

Cox, Jim   ML68.C8 2005
Music Radio: The Great Performers and Programs of the 1920s Through Early 1960s. Cloth Text. McFarland & Company, Incorporated Publishers. Jefferson, NC. 2005. 380p. ISBN:0-7864-2047-2, ISBN13: 978-0-7864-2047-6. Dewey:781.5/44/097309041. LCCN:2005-001716.

Audience: **u,f.**

Cusic, Don   ML3187.C88 1990
The Sound of Light: A History of Gospel Music. Trade Cloth. University of Wisconsin Press. Chicago, IL. 1990. 282p. ISBN:0-87972-497-8, ISBN13: 978-0-87972-497-9. Dewey:782.25. LCCN:90-082744.

Audience: **g,l,u,f.** *Choice, 1991.*

**Dauncey, Hugh & Cannon,   ML3489.P67 2003
Steve (Editors)**
Popular Music in France from Chanson to Techno: Culture, Identity and Society. Trade Cloth. Ashgate Publishing, Ltd. Aldershot, 2003. 294p. Ashgate Popular and Folk Music Ser. ISBN:0-7546-0849-2, ISBN13: 978-0-7546-0849-3. Dewey:781.64/0944. LCCN:2002-028149.

Audience: **u,f.**

**DeCurtis, Anthony &   ML3534.R64 1992
Rolling Stone Magazine Staff**
The Rolling Stone Illustrated History of Rock and Roll: The Definitive History of the Most Important Artists and Their Music. Ed. 3. Trade Paper. Random House, Inc. New York, NY. 1992. 720p. ISBN:0-679-73728-6, ISBN13: 978-0-679-73728-5. Dewey:781.66/09. LCCN:92-006339.

Audience: **l,u,f.**

**Dettmar, Kevin J. & Richey,   ML3534.R3844 1999
William (Editors)**
Reading Rock and Roll: Authenticity, Appropriation and Aesthetics. Anthony DeCurtis (Foreword by). Trade Cloth. Columbia University Press. New York, NY. 1999. 352p. ISBN:0-231-11398-6, ISBN13: 978-0-231-11398-4. Dewey:781.66. LCCN:99-011659.

Audience: **u,f.** *Choice, 2000.*

Dodd, David & Spaulding,   **ML421.B4**
Diana (Editors)
The Grateful Dead Reader. Trade Paper. Oxford University Press, Inc. New York, NY. 2002. 353p. Readers on American Musicians Ser. ISBN:0-19-514706-5, ISBN13: 978-0-19-514706-3. Dewey:782.42166/092/2.

                     Audience: **g,l,u,f.**

Doggett, Peter   **ML421.B4**
Abbey Road - Let It Be: The Beatles. Trade Cloth. Music Sales Corporation. New York, NY. 1998. ISBN:0-8256-7150-7, ISBN13: 978-0-8256-7150-0. Dewey:782.42166/0922. LCCN:97-029051.

                     Audience: **g,l,u,f.**

Doss, Erika   **ML420.P96D68 1999**
Elvis Culture: Fans, Faith, and Image. Trade Cloth. University Press of Kansas. Lawrence, KS. 1999. xiv, 290p. CultureAmerica Ser. ISBN:0-7006-0948-2, ISBN13: 978-0-7006-0948-2. Dewey:782.42166/092. LCCN:97-034373.

           Audience: **g,l,u,f.** *Choice, 1999.*

Dylan, Bob   **ML420.D98A3 2004**
Chronicles, Vol. 1. Trade Cloth. Simon & Schuster. New York, NY. 2004. 304p. ISBN:0-7432-2815-4, ISBN13: 978-0-7432-2815-2. Dewey:782.42164/092 B. LCCN:2004-056454.

          Audience: **g,l,u,f.** *Choice, 2005.*

Dylan, Bob   **ML54.6.D94S62 2002**
Lyrics: 1962-2001. Trade Cloth. Simon & Schuster. New York, NY. 2004. 624p. ISBN:0-7432-2827-8, ISBN13: 978-0-7432-2827-5. Dewey:782.42164/0268. LCCN:2002-042823.

                     Audience: **g,l,u,f.**

Eberly, Phillip K.   **ML68 .E23**
Music in the Air: America's Changing Taste in Popular Music, 1920-1980. Trade Paper. Hastings House Daytrips Publishers. Winter Park, FL. 1982. 448p. Communication Arts Bks. ISBN:0-8038-4742-4, ISBN13: 978-0-8038-4742-2. Dewey:780/.973.

                     Audience: **g,l,u,f.**

Ennis, Philip H.   **ML3534.E551992**
The Seventh Stream: The Emergence of Rock N Roll in American Popular Music. Trade Paper. Wesleyan University Press. Middletown, CT. 1992. 460p. ISBN:0-8195-6257-2, ISBN13: 978-0-8195-6257-9. Dewey:781.66/0973. LCCN:92-053859.

                     Audience: **u,f.**

Ertegun, Ahmet   **ML427.A85**
What'd I Say?: The Atlantic Story, 50 Years of Music. Greil Marcus, Lenny Kaye & Robert Christgau (Contribution by). Trade Cloth. Welcome Rain Publishers. New York, NY. 2001. 528p. ISBN:1-56649-048-0, ISBN13: 978-1-56649-048-1. Dewey:781.660973.

                     Audience: **l,u,f.**

Escott, Colin, et al.   **ML420.W55E83 2004**
Hank Williams: The Biography. George Merritt & William MacEwen (Authors). Trade Paper. Little Brown & Company. New York, NY. 2004. 388p. ISBN:0-316-73497-7, ISBN13: 978-0-316-73497-4. Dewey:782.42/1642/092 B. LCCN:2003-026510.

                     Audience: **g,l,u,f.**

Everett, Walter   **ML421.B4**
The Beatles As Musicians: Revolver Through the Anthology. Trade Paper. Oxford University Press, Inc. New York, NY. 1999. 416p. ISBN:0-19-512941-5, ISBN13: 978-0-19-512941-0. Dewey:782.42166/092/2. LCCN:98-023704.

          Audience: **g,l,u,f.** *Choice, 1999.*

Ewbank, Alison J. &   **ML3470**
Papageorgiou, Fouli T. (Editors)
Whose Master's Voice?: The Development of Popular Music in Thirteen Cultures, 41. Trade Cloth. Greenwood Publishing Group, Inc. Portsmouth, NH. 1997. 272p. Contributions to the Study of Music and Dance Ser., No. 41 ISBN:0-313-27772-9, ISBN13: 978-0-313-27772-6. Dewey:781.63/09. LCCN:95-046060.

                     Audience: **u,f.**

Ewing, Tom   **ML420.M5595B55 2000**
The Bill Monroe Reader. Trade Cloth. University of Illinois Press. Champaign, IL. 2000. 336p. Music in American Life Ser. ISBN:0-252-02500-8, ISBN13: 978-0-252-02500-6. Dewey:781.642/092. LCCN:00-008015.

          Audience: **g,l,u,f.** *Choice, 2001.*

Fast, Susan   **ML421.L4F37 2001**
In the Houses of the Holy: Led Zeppelin and the Power of Rock Music. Trade Paper. Oxford University Press, Inc. New York, NY. 2001. 258p. ISBN:0-19-514723-5, ISBN13: 978-0-19-514723-0. Dewey:782.42166/092/2. LCCN:00-048367.

                     Audience: **g,l,u,f.**

Fikentscher, Kai   **ML3540.5.F55 2000**
You Better Work!: Underground Dance Music in New York. Library Binding. Wesleyan University Press. Middletown, CT. 2000. 176p. Music Culture Ser. ISBN:0-8195-6403-6, ISBN13: 978-0-8195-6403-0. Dewey:781.5/54. LCCN:00-009088.

          Audience: **u,f.** *Choice, 2001.*

Forman, Murray   **ML3918.R37M67 2002**
The 'Hood Comes First: Race, Space, and Place in Rap and Hip-Hop. Library Binding. Wesleyan University Press. Middletown, CT. 2002. 400p. Music Culture Ser. ISBN:0-8195-6396-X, ISBN13: 978-0-8195-6396-5. Dewey:782.421649. LCCN:2001-055920.

                     Audience: **u,f.**

Forte, Allen, et al.   **ML3477.F672 2001**
Listening to Classic American Popular Songs. Richard Lalli & Gary Chapman (Authors). Cloth over Boards. Yale University Press. Cumberland, RI. 2001. 240p. ISBN:0-300-08338-6, ISBN13: 978-0-300-08338-5. Dewey:782.42164/0973. LCCN:00-011309.

                     Audience: **u,f.**

Fouz-Hernandez, Santiago   ML420.M1387
  & Jarman-Ivens, Freya
Madonna's Drowned Worlds: New Approaches to Her
Subcultural Transformations, 1983-2003. Trade Cloth. Ashgate
Publishing, Ltd. Aldershot, 2004. 246p. Ashgate Popular and
Folk Music Ser. ISBN:0-7546-3371-3, ISBN13:
978-0-7546-3371-6. Dewey:782.42166/092. LCCN:2003-062883.

Audience: **u,f.**

Friedwald, Will   ML420.S565F78 1997
Sinatra! The Song Is You: A Singer's Art. Trade Paper. Da Capo
Press, Inc. Cambridge, MA. 1997. 560p. ISBN:0-306-80742-4,
ISBN13: 978-0-306-80742-8. Dewey:782.4/2/164/092.
LCCN:96-043855.

Audience: **u,f.**

Frith, Simon   ML3534.F75 1988
Music for Pleasure: Essays in the Sociology of Pop. Trade
Cloth. Routledge. New York, NY. 1988. 208p.
ISBN:0-415-90051-4, ISBN13: 978-0-415-90051-5.
Dewey:784.5/4/009. LCCN:88-006678.

Audience: **u,f.** *Choice, 1989.*

Frith, Simon   ML3795.F738 1996
Performing Rites: On the Value of Popular Music. Trade Cloth.
Harvard University Press. Cambridge, MA. 1996. 360p.
ISBN:0-674-66195-8, ISBN13: 978-0-674-66195-0.
Dewey:306.4/84. LCCN:96-001121.

Audience: **u,f.** *Choice, 1997.*

Frith, Simon (Editor,   ML3470
  Translator, Introduction by)
Popular Music. Paper over Boards. Routledge. New York, NY.
2004. 1752p. Critical Concepts in Media and Cultural Studies
ISBN:0-415-29905-5, ISBN13: 978-0-415-29905-3.
Dewey:781.64. LCCN:2003-058481.

Audience: **u,f.**

Frith, Simon & Horne,   ML3470
  Howard
Art into Pop. Trade Paper. Routledge. New York, NY. 1988.
192p. ISBN:0-416-41540-7, ISBN13: 978-0-416-41540-7.
Dewey:780/.42. LCCN:87-011308.

Audience: **u,f.** *Choice, 1988.*

Frith, Simon (Editor), et al.   ML3470 .C36 2001
The Cambridge Companion to Pop and Rock. Will Straw &
John Street (Editors), Jonathan Cross (Contribution by). Trade
Paper. Cambridge University Press. New York, NY. 2001. 322p.
Companions to Music Ser. ISBN:0-521-55660-0, ISBN13:
978-0-521-55660-6. Dewey:781.64. LCCN:00-068908.

Audience: **g,l,u,f.**

Gaar, Gillian G.   ML394
She's a Rebel: The History of Women in Rock and Roll. Ed. 2.
Yoko Ono (Preface by). Trade Paper. Avalon Publishing Group.
New York, NY. 2002. 496p. ISBN:1-58005-078-6, ISBN13:
978-1-58005-078-4. Dewey:781.66/092/2 B.
LCCN:2003-267936.

Audience: **g,l,u,f.** *Choice, 1993.*

Gendron, Bernard   ML3470.G48 2002
Between Montmartre and the Mudd Club: Popular Music and
the Avant-Garde. Trade Cloth. University of Chicago Press.
Chicago, IL. 2002. 400p. ISBN:0-226-28735-1, ISBN13:
978-0-226-28735-5. Dewey:781.64/09/04. LCCN:2001-042791.

Audience: **u,f.**

George, Nelson   ML3479
Buppies, B-Boys, Baps, and Bohos: Notes on Post-Soul Black
Culture. Ed. 2. Trade Paper. Da Capo Press, Inc. Cambridge,
MA. 2001. 384p. ISBN:0-306-81027-1, ISBN13:
978-0-306-81027-5. Dewey:306/.08996/073.

Audience: **u,f.**

George, Nelson   ML3556
The Death of Rhythm and Blues. Trade Paper. Penguin Group
(USA) Inc. New York, NY. 2003. 256p. ISBN:0-14-200408-1,
ISBN13: 978-0-14-200408-1. Dewey:781.7/296073.

Audience: **u,f.**

George, Nelson   ML3531.G46 2005
Hip Hop America. Trade Paper. Penguin Group (USA) Inc. New
York, NY. 2005. 256p. ISBN:0-14-303515-0, ISBN13:
978-0-14-303515-2. Dewey:782.421649. LCCN:2005-273978.

Audience: **g,l,u,f.**

George, Nelson   ML3537.G46 1987
Where Did Our Love Go?: The Rise and Fall of the Motown
Sound. Trade Paper. St. Martin's Press. Gordonville, VA. 1987.
256p. ISBN:0-312-01109-1, ISBN13: 978-0-312-01109-3.
Dewey:784.5/5/00973. LCCN:87-016283.

Audience: **g,l,u,f.**

Giddins, Gary   ML420.C93G53 2001
Bing Crosby: A Pocketful of Dreams - The Early Years,
1903-1940. Trade Cloth. Little Brown & Company. New York,
NY. 2000. 736p. ISBN:0-316-88188-0, ISBN13:
978-0-316-88188-3. Dewey:782.42164092. LCCN:00-044403.

Audience: **g,l,u,f.** *Choice, 2001.*

Giuliano, Geoffrey   ML410.M115G58 1997
Blackbird: The Life and Times of Paul McCartney. Ed. 2.
Denny Laine (Foreword by). Trade Paper. Da Capo Press, Inc.
Cambridge, MA. 1997. 440p. ISBN:0-306-80781-5, ISBN13:
978-0-306-80781-7. Dewey:782.42166/092 B. LCCN:97-021945.

Audience: **g,l,u,f.**

Goldsmith, Thomas (Editor)   ML3520.B54 2004
The Bluegrass Reader. Trade Cloth. University of Illinois Press.
Champaign, IL. 2004. 376p. Music in American Life Ser.
ISBN:0-252-02914-3, ISBN13: 978-0-252-02914-1.
Dewey:781.642. LCCN:2003-019686.

Audience: **g,l,u,f.**

Gordy, Berry Jr.   ML429.G67A3 1994
To Be Loved: The Music, the Magic, the Memories of Motown
an Autobiography. Trade Cloth. Warner Books, Inc. New York,
NY. 1994. 448p. ISBN:0-446-51523-X, ISBN13:
978-0-446-51523-8. Dewey:781.644/092 B. LCCN:94-029067.

Audience: **l,u,f.**

Gracyk, Theodore   ML3534.G7 1996
Rhythm and Noise: An Aesthetics of Rock. Cloth Text. Duke
University Press. Durham, NC. 1996. 304p.
ISBN:0-8223-1734-6, ISBN13: 978-0-8223-1734-0.
Dewey:781.6/6. LCCN:95-044601.

Audience: **u,f.**

Green, Douglas B.   ML3524
Singing in the Saddle: The History of the Singing Cowboy.
Trade Paper. Vanderbilt University Press. Nashville, TN. 2005.
392p. ISBN:0-8265-1506-1, ISBN13: 978-0-8265-1506-3.
Dewey:781.642/0973.

Audience: **u,f.** *Choice, 2003.*

Guralnick, Peter   ML420.P96
Last Train to Memphis: The Rise of Elvis Presley. Trade Cloth.
DIANE Publishing Company. Collingdale, PA. 2000. 560p.
ISBN:0-7881-9347-3, ISBN13: 978-0-7881-9347-7.
Dewey:782.4/2/166/092.

Audience: **g,l,u,f.** *Choice, 1995.*

Hedin, Benjamin   ML420.D98H44 2004
Studio A: The Bob Dylan Reader. Trade Cloth. W. W. Norton &
Company, Inc. New York, NY. 2004. 288p.
ISBN:0-393-05844-1, ISBN13: 978-0-393-05844-4.
Dewey:782.42164/092. LCCN:2004-013616.

Audience: **g,l,u,f.**

Herbst, Peter (Editor)   ML394 .R65
Rolling Stone Interviews: Talking with the Legends of Rock &
Roll, 1967-1980. Rolling Stone Magazine Staff (Contribution
by), Ben Fong-Torres (Instructed by). Trade Cloth. St. Martin's
Press. Gordonville, VA. 1981. 426p. ISBN:0-312-68954-3,
ISBN13: 978-0-312-68954-4. Dewey:784.5/4/00922.

Audience: **g,l,u,f.**

Heylin, Clinton   ML3534
From the Velvets to the Voidoids: The Birth of American Punk
Rock. Trade Paper. Chicago Review Press, Inc. Chicago, IL.
2005. 432p. ISBN:1-55652-575-3, ISBN13: 978-1-55652-575-9.
Dewey:781.66.

Audience: **g,l,u,f.**

Heylin, Clinton   ML421.S4
Never Mind the Bollocks, Here's the Sex Pistols: The Sex
Pistols. New York: Schirmer Books; London: Prentice Hall
International. 1998. Classic Rock Albums ISBN:0-02-864726-2,
ISBN13: 978-0-02-864726-5.

Audience: **g,l,u,f.**

Hoffmann, Frank   ML128.R6
The Literature of Rock, 1954-1978. Trade Cloth. Scarecrow
Press, Inc. Lanham, MD. 1981. 349p. ISBN:0-8108-1371-8,
ISBN13: 978-0-8108-1371-7. Dewey:016.7845/4/009.
LCCN:80-023459.

Audience: **u,f.**

Hoffmann, Frank & Cooper,   ML128.R6
B. Lee
The Literature of Rock III, 1984-1990: With Additional Material

for the Period 1954-1983. Trade Cloth. Scarecrow Press, Inc.
Lanham, MD. 1995. 1003p. ISBN:0-8108-2762-X, ISBN13:
978-0-8108-2762-2. Dewey:016.78242166. LCCN:93-036263.

Audience: **u,f.**

Hoffmann, Frank & Cooper,   ML128.R6
B. Lee
The Literature of Rock II: Including an Exhaustive Survey of
the Literature from 1979-1983 and Incorporating Supplementary
Material from 1954-1978 Not Covered in the First Volume. Ann
Hoffmann (Contribution by). Trade Cloth. Scarecrow Press, Inc.
Lanham, MD. 1986. 1114p. ISBN:0-8108-1821-3, ISBN13:
978-0-8108-1821-7. Dewey:016.7845/4. LCCN:85-008384.

Audience: **u,f.**

Jackson, Jerma A.   ML3187.J23 2004
Singing in My Soul. Trade Cloth. University of North Carolina
Press. Chapel Hill, NC. 2004. 256p. ISBN:0-8078-2860-2,
ISBN13: 978-0-8078-2860-1. Dewey:782.25/4.
LCCN:2003-024973.

Audience: **u,f.** *Choice, 2004.*

Jacobs, Dick & Jacobs,   ML120.U5J23 1994
Harriet
Who Wrote That Song? Ed. 2. Trade Paper. F & W Publications,
Inc. Cincinnati, OH. 1994. 448p. ISBN:0-89879-639-3, ISBN13:
978-0-89879-639-1. Dewey:784.5/00973. LCCN:93-048545.

Audience: **g,l,u,f.** *Choice, 1989.*

Jasen, David A.   ML102.P66J37 2003
Tin Pan Alley: An Encyclopedia of the Golden Age of American
Song. Paper over Boards. Routledge. New York, NY. 2003.
384p. ISBN:0-415-93877-5, ISBN13: 978-0-415-93877-8.
Dewey:782.42164/0973. LCCN:2003-002699.

Audience: **g,l,u,f.**

Jenness, David & Velsey,   ML3477.J46 2005
Donald
Classic American Popular Song: The Second Half-Century,
1950-2000. Paper over Boards. Routledge. New York, NY. 2005.
408p. ISBN:0-415-97056-3, ISBN13: 978-0-415-97056-3.
Dewey:782.42164/0973/09045. LCCN:2005-008175.

Audience: **u,f.**

Jones, Quincy   ML419.J7
Q: The Autobiography of Quincy Jones. Trade Paper. Broadway
Books. New York, NY. 2002. 432p. ISBN:0-7679-0510-5,
ISBN13: 978-0-7679-0510-7. Dewey:781.64/092 B.

Audience: **g,l,u,f.**

Keyes, Cheryl L.   ML3531
Rap Music and Street Consciousness. Trade Paper. University of
Illinois Press. Champaign, IL. 2004. 336p. Music in American
Life Ser. ISBN:0-252-07201-4, ISBN13: 978-0-252-07201-7.
Dewey:782.4/21649.

Audience: **u,f.**

Kingsbury, Paul (Editor)   ML102.C7E54
The Encyclopedia of Country Music: The Ultimate Guide to the
Music. The Country Music Foundation (Compiled by). Trade

Paper. Oxford University Press, Inc. New York, NY. 2004. 648p. ISBN:0-19-517608-1, ISBN13: 978-0-19-517608-7. Dewey:781.642/03. LCCN:2003-000144.

Audience: **g,l,u,f.**

Kostelanetz, Richard   **ML420.P96**
The Frank Zappa Companion: Four Decades of Commentary. Trade Paper. Music Sales Corporation. New York, NY. 1997. 300p. Companion Ser. ISBN:0-8256-7181-7, ISBN13: 978-0-8256-7181-4. Dewey:782.4/2/166/092. LCCN:96-041352.

Audience: **g,l,u,f.**

Kozinn, Allan   **ML421.B4**
The Beatles. Trade Paper. Phaidon Press. London, 1995. 240p. Twentieth-Century Composers Ser. ISBN:0-7148-3203-0, ISBN13: 978-0-7148-3203-6. Dewey:782.4/2166/0922. LCCN:99-495142.

Audience: **g,l,u,f.**

Kureishi, M.   **ML3470.F2 1995**
The Faber Book of Pop. Trade Cloth. Faber & Faber, Inc. New York, NY. 1995. xxxiii, 862p. ISBN:0-571-16992-9, ISBN13: 978-0-571-16992-4. Dewey:781.64/09/045. LCCN:95-223012.

Audience: **u,f.**

Laing, Dave   **ML3534.L34 1985**
One Chord Wonders: Power and Meaning in Punk Rock. Trade Cloth. McGraw-Hill Education. Maidenhead, 1985. 192p. ISBN:0-335-15065-9, ISBN13: 978-0-335-15065-6. Dewey:784.5/4. LCCN:85-010542.

Audience: **u,f.** *Choice, 1986.*

Larkin, Colin (Editor)   **ML102.P66G84**
The Encyclopedia of Popular Music, Set. Ed. 3. Library Binding. Groves Dictionaries, Inc. New York, NY. 1998. 8000p. ISBN:1-56159-237-4, ISBN13: 978-1-56159-237-1. Dewey:782.4/2/164/03. LCCN:98-037439.

Audience: **g,l,u,f.** *Choice, 1999.*

Lawrence, Tim   **ML3411.5.L38 2003**
Love Saves the Day: A History of American Dance Music Culture 1970-1979. Trade Cloth. Duke University Press. Durham, NC. 2003. 456p. ISBN:0-8223-3185-3, ISBN13: 978-0-8223-3185-8. Dewey:306.4/84. LCCN:2003-010839.

Audience: **u,f.** *Choice, 2004.*

Lawrence, Tim   **ML3411.5.L38 2003**
Love Saves the Day: A History of American Dance Music Culture, 1970-1979. Trade Paper. Duke University Press. Durham, NC. 2003. 456p. ISBN:0-8223-3198-5, ISBN13: 978-0-8223-3198-8. Dewey:306.4/84. LCCN:2003-010839.

Audience: **l,u,f.** *Choice, 2004.*

Lax, Roger & Smith,   **ML128.S3L4 1989**
  Frederick
The Great Song Thesaurus. Ed. 2. Cloth Text. Oxford University Press, Inc. New York, NY. 1989. 792p. ISBN:0-19-505408-3, ISBN13: 978-0-19-505408-8. Dewey:784.5/0016. LCCN:88-031267.

Audience: **g,l,u,f.**

Luftig, Stacy   **ML420.S565**
The Joni Mitchell Companion: Four Decades of Commentary. Trade Paper. Music Sales Corporation. New York, NY. 1999. 300p. Classic Rock Albums Ser. ISBN:0-8256-7190-6, ISBN13: 978-0-8256-7190-6. Dewey:782.42164/092.

Audience: **g,l,u,f.**

Luftig, Stacy   **ML420.S563**
The Paul Simon Companion: 4 Decades of Commentary. Trade Paper. Music Sales Corporation. New York, NY. 1997. 300p. Companion Ser. ISBN:0-8256-7207-4, ISBN13: 978-0-8256-7207-1. Dewey:782.42164/092.

Audience: **g,l,u,f.**

Lydon, Michael   **ML420.C46L93 2004**
Ray Charles: Man and Music. Ed. 2. UK-B Format Paperback. Routledge. New York, NY. 2004. 472p. ISBN:0-415-97043-1, ISBN13: 978-0-415-97043-3. Dewey:782.42164/092 B. LCCN:2003-058684.

Audience: **g,l,u,f.**

Makower, Joel   **ML38.W66M34 1989**
Woodstock: Oral History. Trade Cloth. Doubleday Publishing. New York, NY. 1989. 360p. ISBN:0-385-24716-8, ISBN13: 978-0-385-24716-0. Dewey:784.5/4/007974734. LCCN:89-001593.

Audience: **g,l,u,f.**

Malone, Bill C.   **ML3524.M34 2002**
Country Music, U. S. A. Ed. 3. Trade Paper. University of Texas Press. Austin, TX. 2002. 646p. ISBN:0-292-75262-8, ISBN13: 978-0-292-75262-7. Dewey:781.642/0973. LCCN:2002-004792.

Audience: **g,l,u,f.** *Choice, 1985.*

Malone, Bill C. & Stricklin,   **ML3551**
  David
Southern Music/American Music. Trade Cloth. University Press of Kentucky. Lexington, KY. 2003. 240p. ISBN:0-8131-9055-X, ISBN13: 978-0-8131-9055-6. Dewey:781.64/0975. LCCN:2003-269675.

Audience: **u,f.** *Choice, 2003.*

Manuel, Peter   **ML3470**
Popular Musics of the Non-Western World: An Introductory Survey. Paper Text. Oxford University Press, Inc. New York, NY. 1990. 314p. ISBN:0-19-506334-1, ISBN13: 978-0-19-506334-9. Dewey:780/.42. LCCN:87-034861.

Audience: **g,l,u,f.** *Choice, 1989.*

Marcus, Greil   **ML3534.M362 1999**
In the Fascist Bathroom: Punk in Pop Music, 1977-1992. Trade Paper. Harvard University Press. Cambridge, MA. 1999. 448p. ISBN:0-674-44577-5, ISBN13: 978-0-674-44577-2. Dewey:781.66. LCCN:98-043708.

Audience: **u,f.**

Marcus, Greil   **ML3534.M36 1997**
The Mystery Train: Images of America in Rock-n-Roll. Ed. 4. Trade Paper. Penguin Group (USA) Inc. New York, NY. 1997. 336p. ISBN:0-452-27836-8, ISBN13: 978-0-452-27836-3. Dewey:781.66/0973. LCCN:96-053338.

Audience: **u,f.**

Marsh, Dave   **ML420.S77M335 2003**
Bruce Springsteen: Two Hearts. Trade Paper. Routledge. New
York, NY. 2003. 696p. ISBN:0-415-96928-X, ISBN13:
978-0-415-96928-4. Dewey:782.42166/092 B.
LCCN:2003-054801.

Audience: **g,l,u,f.**

Marsh, Dave   **ML420.S565**
Elvis. Trade Paper. Avalon Publishing Group. New York, NY.
1993. 272p. ISBN:1-56025-038-0, ISBN13: 978-1-56025-038-8.
Dewey:784.5/0092/4.

Audience: **g,l,u,f.**

McCoy, Judy   **ML128.R28.M3 1992**
Rap Music in the 1980s: A Reference Guide. Trade Cloth.
Scarecrow Press, Inc. Lanham, MD. 1992. 275p.
ISBN:0-8108-2649-6, ISBN13: 978-0-8108-2649-6.
Dewey:782.42164. LCCN:92-039684.

Audience: **g,l,u,f.** *Choice, 1993.*

McGrath, Tom   **HE8700.72.U6**
MTV: The Making of a Revolution. Cloth Text. DIANE
Publishing Company. Collingdale, PA. 1999. 208p.
ISBN:0-7881-6664-6, ISBN13: 978-0-7881-6664-8.
Dewey:384.5/55/0973.

Audience: **g,l,u,f.**

McKeen, William (Editor)   **ML3534.R613 2000**
Rock and Roll Is Here to Stay: An Anthology. Trade Cloth. W.
W. Norton & Company, Inc. New York, NY. 2000. 800p.
ISBN:0-393-04700-8, ISBN13: 978-0-393-04700-4.
Dewey:781.66. LCCN:99-031759.

Audience: **g,l,u,f.** *Choice, 2001.*

McNeil, Legs & McCain,   **PQ2625.A716**
  Gillian
Please Kill Me: The Uncensored Oral History of Punk. Trade
Paper. Grove/Atlantic, Inc. New York, NY. 2006. 488p.
ISBN:0-8021-4264-8, ISBN13: 978-0-8021-4264-1.
Dewey:843/.9/12. LCCN:79-002333.

Audience: **g,l,u,f.**

Meade, Guthrie Jr.   **2002022360 [ML]**
Country Music Sources: A Biblio-Discography of Commercially
Recorded Traditional Music. Trade Cloth. University of North
Carolina Press. Chapel Hill, NC. 2002. 1024p. Southern Folklife
Collection ISBN:0-8078-2723-1, ISBN13: 978-0-8078-2723-9.
Dewey:016.78162/13/00266. LCCN:2002-022360.

Audience: **u,f.** *Choice, 2003.*

Meltzer, Richard   **ML3877.M45 1987**
The Aesthetics of Rock. Greil Marcus (Introduction by). Trade
Paper. Da Capo Press, Inc. Cambridge, MA. 1987. 384p.
ISBN:0-306-80287-2, ISBN13: 978-0-306-80287-4.
Dewey:784.5/4/009. LCCN:87-000518.

Audience: **u,f.**

Metz, A. & Benson, C.   **ML420.P96**
The Madonna Companion: Two Decades of Commentary. Trade

Paper. Music Sales Corporation. New York, NY. 1999. xiv,
346p. ISBN:0-8256-7194-9, ISBN13: 978-0-8256-7194-4.
Dewey:782.4/2/166/092.

Audience: **g,l,u,f.**

Middleton, Richard (Editor)   **ML3470.R418 1999**
Reading Pop: Approaches to Textual Analysis in Popular Music.
Trade Paper. Oxford University Press, Inc. New York, NY. 2000.
400p. ISBN:0-19-816611-7, ISBN13: 978-0-19-816611-5.
Dewey:781.64. LCCN:98-039903.

Audience: **u,f.**

Middleton, Richard   **ML3470.M5 1990**
Studying Popular Music. Paper Text. McGraw-Hill Education.
Maidenhead, 1990. 336p. ISBN:0-335-15275-9, ISBN13:
978-0-335-15275-9. Dewey:781.64/09. LCCN:89-034686.

Audience: **u,f.**

Miles, Barry   **ML410.Z285.M49 2004**
Zappa: A Biography. Trade Cloth. Grove/Atlantic, Inc. New
York, NY. 2004. 464p. ISBN:0-8021-1783-X, ISBN13:
978-0-8021-1783-0. Dewey:782.42166/092 B.
LCCN:2004-051805.

Audience: **l,u,f.**

Mitchell, Tony (Editor)   **ML3531.G56 2001**
Global Noise: Rap and Hip Hop Outside the U. S. A. Trade
Paper. Wesleyan University Press. Middletown, CT. 2002. 352p.
Music Culture Ser. ISBN:0-8195-6502-4, ISBN13:
978-0-8195-6502-0. Dewey:782.421649/09. LCCN:2001-046705.

Audience: **u,f.**

Mitsui, Toru & Hosokawa,   **ML3795.K22 1998**
  Shuhei
Karaoke Around the World: Global Technology, Local Singing.
Paper over Boards. Routledge. New York, NY. 1998. 224p.
Research in Cultural and Media Studies ISBN:0-415-16371-4,
ISBN13: 978-0-415-16371-2. Dewey:306.4/84.
LCCN:97-019902.

Audience: **u,f.**

Moore, Allan F.   **ML3534.M66 2001**
Rock, the Primary Text: Developing a Musicology of Rock. Ed.
2. Trade Cloth. Ashgate Publishing, Ltd. Aldershot, 2001. 270p.
Popular and Folk Music Ser. ISBN:0-7546-0298-2, ISBN13:
978-0-7546-0298-9. Dewey:781.66/09. LCCN:2001-022836.

Audience: **u,f.** *Choice, 1993.*

Moorefield, Virgil   **ML3470.M66 2005**
The Producer as Composer: Shaping the Sounds of Popular
Music. Trade Cloth. MIT Press. Cambridge, MA. 2005. 143p.
ISBN:0-262-13457-8, ISBN13: 978-0-262-13457-6.
Dewey:781.49. LCCN:2005-041588.

Audience: **l,u,f.** *Choice, 2006.*

Murray, Charles Shaar   **ML410.H476**
Crosstown Traffic: Jimi Hendrix and Post-War Pop. London:
Faber. 2001. ISBN:0-571-20749-9, ISBN13: 978-0-571-20749-7.

Audience: **g,l,u,f.**

Negus, Keith   **ML3470.N44 1997**
Popular Music in Theory: An Introduction. Trade Paper.
Wesleyan University Press. Middletown, CT. 1996. 249p. Music
Culture Ser. ISBN:0-8195-6310-2, ISBN13: 978-0-8195-6310-1.
Dewey:781.64. LCCN:96-061301.
     Audience: **u,f.** *Choice, 1997.*

Neises, Charles P.   **ML421.B4**
The Beatles Reader: A Selection of Contemporary Views, News
and Reviews of the Beatles in Their Heyday. Trade Cloth.
Popular Culture, Ink. Harbor Springs, MI. 1991. 232p. Rock and
Roll Remembrances Ser., No. 6 ISBN:1-56075-024-3, ISBN13:
978-1-56075-024-6. Dewey:784.5/4/00922. LCCN:84-060267.
     Audience: **g,l,u,f.**

Olsen, Eric, et al.   **ML105.E53 1999**
The Encyclopedia of Record Producers. Carlo Wolff & Paul
Verna (Authors). Trade Paper. Watson-Guptill Publications, Inc.
New York, NY. 1999. 912p. ISBN:0-8230-7607-5, ISBN13:
978-0-8230-7607-9. Dewey:781.64/092/2 B. LCCN:99-032191.
     Audience: **g,l,u,f.** *Choice, 2000.*

Perone, James E.   **ML3918**
Music of the Counterculture Era. Cloth Text. Greenwood
Publishing Group, Inc. Portsmouth, NH. 2004. 240p. American
History Through Music Ser. ISBN:0-313-32689-4, ISBN13:
978-0-313-32689-9. Dewey:781.64/0973/09046.
LCCN:2004-040432.
     Audience: **g,l,u,f.** *Choice, 2004.*

Perry, John   **ML421.R64**
Exile on Main Street: Rolling Stones. Trade Paper. Music Sales
Corporation. New York, NY. 1999. 172p. Classic Rock Albums
Ser. ISBN:0-8256-7180-9, ISBN13: 978-0-8256-7180-7.
Dewey:782.42166/092/2.
     Audience: **g,l,u,f.**

Peterson, Richard A.   **ML3524.P48 1997**
Creating Country Music: Fabricating Authenticity. Trade Cloth.
University of Chicago Press. Chicago, IL. 1997. 320p.
ISBN:0-226-66284-5, ISBN13: 978-0-226-66284-8.
Dewey:781.642/09. LCCN:97-009675.
     Audience: **u,f.** *Choice, 1998.*

Petkov, Steven & Mustazza,   **ML420.S565F74 1995**
   Leonard (Editors)
The Frank Sinatra Reader. Trade Cloth. Oxford University Press,
Inc. New York, NY. 1995. 336p. ISBN:0-19-509531-6, ISBN13:
978-0-19-509531-9. Dewey:782.4/2/164/092. LCCN:95-000197.
     Audience: **g,l,u,f.**

Platt, John   **ML421.C74**
Disraeli Gears: Cream. New York: Schirmer Books; London:
Prentice Hall International. 1998. Classic Rock Albums
ISBN:0-02-864774-2, ISBN13: 978-0-02-864774-6.
     Audience: **l,u,f.**

Potash, Chris   **ML420.P96**
The Jimi Hendrix Companion: Three Decades of Commentary.

Trade Paper. Music Sales Corporation. New York, NY. 1996.
300p. ISBN:0-8256-7237-6, ISBN13: 978-0-8256-7237-8.
Dewey:782.4/2/166/092. LCCN:96-031526.
     Audience: **g,l,u,f.**

Powell, Mark Allan   **ML102.C66P68 2002**
Encyclopedia of Contemporary Christian Music. CD-ROM,
Trade Paper. Hendrickson Publishers, Inc. Peabody, MA. 2004.
1088p. ISBN:1-56563-679-1, ISBN13: 978-1-56563-679-8.
Dewey:782.25. LCCN:2002-008473.
     Audience: **g,l,u,f.** *Choice, 2003.*

Pratt, Ray   **ML3470**
Rhythm and Resistance: Explorations in the Political Uses of
Popular Music. Trade Cloth. Greenwood Publishing Group, Inc.
Portsmouth, NH. 1990. 256p. Media and Society Ser.
ISBN:0-275-92624-9, ISBN13: 978-0-275-92624-3.
Dewey:306.4/84. LCCN:89-016197.
     Audience: **u,f.** *Choice, 1991.*

Pruter, Robert   **ML156.4.S6**
The Blackwell Guide to Soul Recordings. Oxford, UK;
Cambridge, Mass.: Blackwell Publishers. 1993. Blackwell
Reference ISBN:0-631-18595-X, ISBN13: 978-0-631-18595-6.
     Audience: **g,l,u,f.**

Quain, Kevin   **ML420.P96 E44 1992**
The Elvis Reader: Texts and Sources on the King of Rock 'n'
Roll. Trade Paper. St. Martin's Press. Gordonville, VA. 1991.
352p. ISBN:0-312-06966-9, ISBN13: 978-0-312-06966-7.
Dewey:782.42166/092. LCCN:91-033832.
     Audience: **g,l,u,f.**

Reynolds, Simon   **ML3540.R49 1999**
Generation Ecstasy: Into the World of Techno and Rave Culture.
Trade Paper. Routledge. New York, NY. 1999. 504p.
ISBN:0-415-92373-5, ISBN13: 978-0-415-92373-6.
Dewey:781.64. LCCN:99-022695.
     Audience: **g,l,u,f.**

Ribowsky, Mark   **ML429**
He's a Rebel: Phil Spector - Rock and Roll's Legendary
Producer. Trade Paper. Da Capo Press, Inc. Cambridge, MA.
2006. 384p. ISBN:0-306-81471-4, ISBN13: 978-0-306-81471-6.
Dewey:782.42166092.
     Audience: **l,u,f.**

Rocco, John   **ML421.D66**
The Doors Companion: Four Decades of Commentary. Trade
Paper. Music Sales Corporation. New York, NY. 1997. 300p.
ISBN:0-8256-7235-X, ISBN13: 978-0-8256-7235-4.
Dewey:782.42166/092/2. LCCN:94-045692.
     Audience: **l,u,f.**

Rocco, John   **ML421.N57**
The Nirvana Companion: Two Decades of Commentary. Trade
Paper. Music Sales Corporation. New York, NY. 1998. 300p.
ISBN:0-8256-7203-1, ISBN13: 978-0-8256-7203-3.
Dewey:782.42166/092/2. LCCN:98-016171.
     Audience: **g,l,u,f.**

Rolling Stones   ML421.R64
According to the Rolling Stones. Dora Loewenstein & Philip
Dodd (Editors). Trade Cloth. Chronicle Books LLC. San
Francisco, CA. 2003. 360p. ISBN:0-8118-4060-3, ISBN13:
978-0-8118-4060-6. Dewey:782.42166092/2.

Audience: **g,l,u,f.**

Romanowksi, Patricia   ML102.R6R64 2001
(Editor), et al.
The Rolling Stone Encyclopedia of Rock and Roll: Revised and
Updated for the 21st Century. Ed. 3. Holly George-Warren &
John Pareles (Editors). Trade Paper. Simon & Schuster. New
York, NY. 2001. 1136p. ISBN:0-7432-0120-5, ISBN13:
978-0-7432-0120-9. Dewey:781.66/03. LCCN:2001-040285.

Audience: **g,l,u,f.**

Rose, Tricia   ML3531.R67 1994
Black Noise: Rap Music and Black Culture in Contemporary
America. Trade Paper. Wesleyan University Press. Middletown,
CT. 1994. 257p. Music Culture Ser. ISBN:0-8195-6275-0,
ISBN13: 978-0-8195-6275-3. Dewey:782.42164.
LCCN:93-041386.

Audience: **u,f.** *Choice, 1994.*

Rosenberg, Neil V.   ML3524
Bluegrass: A History. Ed. 20. Trade Paper, Perfect. University of
Illinois Press. Champaign, IL. 2005. 512p. Music in American
Life (MAL) Ser. ISBN:0-252-07245-6, ISBN13:
978-0-252-07245-1. Dewey:781.642.

Audience: **g,l,u,f.** *Choice, 1986.*

Santoro, Gene   ML3477.S21 2004
Highway 61 Revisited: The Tangled Roots of American Jazz,
Blues, Rock, and Country Music. Trade Cloth. Oxford
University Press, Inc. New York, NY. 2004. 320p.
ISBN:0-19-515481-9, ISBN13: 978-0-19-515481-8.
Dewey:781.64/0973. LCCN:2003-024872.

Audience: **g,l,u,f.**

Savage, Jon   ML421.S47S3 2002
England's Dreaming: Anarchy, Sex Pistols, Punk Rock, and
Beyond. Trade Paper. St. Martin's Press. Gordonville, VA. 2002.
656p. ISBN:0-312-28822-0, ISBN13: 978-0-312-28822-8.
Dewey:306.4/84. LCCN:2001-048360.

Audience: **g,l,u,f.**

Sawyers, June Skinner   ML420.S77R33 2004
(Author, Editor)
Racing in the Street: The Bruce Springsteen Reader. Martin
Scorsese (Foreword by). Trade Paper. Penguin Group (USA)
Inc. New York, NY. 2004. 464p. ISBN:0-14-200354-9, ISBN13:
978-0-14-200354-1. Dewey:782.42166/092 B.
LCCN:2003-062414.

Audience: **g,l,u,f.**

Scheurer, Timothy E.   ML3477.S33 1991
Born in the U. S. A.: The Myth of America in Popular Music
from Colonial Times to the Present. Trade Cloth. University
Press of Mississippi. Jackson, MS. 1991. xi, 280p. Studies in
Popular Culture ISBN:0-87805-496-0, ISBN13:
978-0-87805-496-1. Dewey:782.42164/1599. LCCN:90-029114.
Audience: **g,l,u,f.** *Choice, 1991.*

Schloss, Joseph G.   ML3531.S35 2004
Making Beats: The Art of Sample-Based Hip-Hop. Library
Binding. Wesleyan University Press. Middletown, CT. 2004.
240p. Music/Culture Ser. ISBN:0-8195-6695-0, ISBN13:
978-0-8195-6695-9. Dewey:782.421649/149.
LCCN:2004-043013.

Audience: **g,l,u,f.** *Choice, 2005.*

Shaughnessy, Mary Angela   ML419.P47S5 1993
Les Paul: An American Original. Trade Cloth. HarperCollins
Publishers. New York, NY. 1993. 347p. ISBN:0-688-08467-2,
ISBN13: 978-0-688-08467-7. Dewey:781.64/092.
LCCN:92-035832.

Audience: **l,u,f.**

Shepherd, John (Editor)   ML102.P66C66 2003
Continuum Encyclopedia of Popular Music of the World: Media,
Industry and Society, Vol. 1. Trade Cloth. Continuum
International Publishing Group, Ltd. London, 2003. 832p.
ISBN:0-8264-6321-5, ISBN13: 978-0-8264-6321-0.
Dewey:781.63/09. LCCN:2002-074146.

Audience: **g,l,u,f.** *Choice, 2004.*

Shepherd, John (Editor)   ML102.P66C66 2003
Continuum Encyclopedia of Popular Music of the World:
Performance and Production, Vol. 2. Trade Cloth. Continuum
International Publishing Group, Ltd. London, 2003. 712p.
ISBN:0-8264-6322-3, ISBN13: 978-0-8264-6322-7.
Dewey:781.63/09. LCCN:2002-074146.

Audience: **g,l,u,f.** *Choice, 2004.*

Shepherd, John   ML102.P66
Encyclopedia of Popular Music of the World, Vols 3-7. Trade
Cloth. Continuum International Publishing Group, Ltd. London,
2005. 1,984p. ISBN:0-8264-7436-5, ISBN13:
978-0-8264-7436-0. Dewey:781.6/3/03.

Audience: **g,l,u,f.** *Choice, 2005.*

Shuker, Roy   ML102.P66S58 2005
Popular Music: The Key Concepts. Ed. 2. Paper over Boards.
Routledge. New York, NY. 2005. XVIII, 326p. Routledge Key
Guides ISBN:0-415-34770-X, ISBN13: 978-0-415-34770-9.
Dewey:781.64/03. LCCN:2004-027956.

Audience: **g,l,u,f.**

Stanley, Lawrence A.   ML3531
(Editor)
Rap - The Lyrics: The Words to Rap's 175 Greatest Hits.
Jefferson Morley (Introduction by). Trade Paper. Penguin Group
(USA) Inc. New York, NY. 1992. 400p. ISBN:0-14-014788-8,
ISBN13: 978-0-14-014788-9. Dewey:782.42164.
LCCN:91-047632.

Audience: **g,l,u,f.**

Starr, Larry, et al.   ML3477.S73 2002
American Popular Music: From Minstrelsy to MTV. Christopher
Alan Waterman, Lawrence Starr & Christopher Waterman
(Authors). Trade Paper. Oxford University Press, Inc. New York,
NY. 2002. 512p. ISBN:0-19-510854-X, ISBN13:
978-0-19-510854-5. Dewey:781.640973. LCCN:2002-000699.

Audience: **g,l,u,f.**

Stephenson, Ken   **MT146.S74 2002**
What to Listen for in Rock: A Stylistic Analysis. Cloth over
Boards. Yale University Press. Cumberland, RI. 2002. 272p.
ISBN:0-300-09239-3, ISBN13: 978-0-300-09239-4.
Dewey:781.66/117. LCCN:2001-006564.
Audience: **g,l,u,f.** *Choice, 2003.*

Streissguth, Michael   **ML420.C265**
Ring of Fire: The Johnny Cash Reader. Trade Paper. Da Capo
Press, Inc. Cambridge, MA. 2003. 336p. ISBN:0-306-81225-8,
ISBN13: 978-0-306-81225-5. Dewey:782.4/21642/092.
Audience: **g,l,u,f.**

Streissguth, Michael   **ML394.S87 2004**
Voices of the Country: Interviews with Classic Country
Performers. Paper over Boards. Routledge. New York, NY.
2004. 232p. ISBN:0-415-97041-5, ISBN13: 978-0-415-97041-9.
Dewey:781.642/092/2 B. LCCN:2003-024530.
Audience: **u,f.**

Strong, Martin C.   **ML156.4.R6**
The Great Rock Discography: Complete Discographies Listing
Every Track Recorded by More Than 1,200 Artists. Ed. 7. John
Peel (Foreword by). Trade Paper. Canongate Books. Edinburgh,
2004. 1,120p. ISBN:1-84195-615-5, ISBN13:
978-1-84195-615-2. Dewey:781.660166.
Audience: **l,u,f.**

Sylvan, Robin   **ML3918.U53S95 2005**
Trance Formation: The Spiritual and Religious Dimensions of
Global Rave Culture. UK-B Format Paperback. Routledge. New
York, NY. 2005. 224p. ISBN:0-415-97091-1, ISBN13:
978-0-415-97091-4. Dewey:306/.1. LCCN:2005-022969.
Audience: **l,u,f.**

Szatmary, David P.   **ML3534.S94 2006**
Rockin' in Time: A Social History of Rock and Roll. Ed. 6.
Trade Paper. Prentice Hall PTR. Upper Saddle River, NJ. 2006.
400p. ISBN:0-13-188790-4, ISBN13: 978-0-13-188790-9.
Dewey:781.660973. LCCN:2005-034618.
Audience: **g,l,u,f.**

Tamm, Eric   **ML410.E58T3 1995**
Brian Eno: His Music and the Vertical Color of Sound. Trade
Paper. Da Capo Press, Inc. Cambridge, MA. 1995. 246p.
ISBN:0-306-80649-5, ISBN13: 978-0-306-80649-0.
Dewey:780/.92/4 B. LCCN:95-021602.
Audience: **l,u,f.** *Choice, 1990.*

Tawa, Nicholas E.   **ML3477.T39 2005**
Supremely American: Popular Song in the 20th Century: Styles,
Singers, and Milieus, and How They Reflected American
Society. Trade Paper. Scarecrow Press, Inc. Lanham, MD. 2005.
352p. ISBN:0-8108-5295-0, ISBN13: 978-0-8108-5295-2.
Dewey:782.42164/0973/0904. LCCN:2004-022882.
Audience: **u,f.** *Choice, 2005.*

Tawa, Nicholas E.   **ML3477.T42 1990**
The Way to Tin Pan Alley: American Popular Song, 1866-1920.
Trade Cloth. Thomson Gale. Farmington Hills, MI. 1990. 296p.

ISBN:0-02-872541-7, ISBN13: 978-0-02-872541-3.
Dewey:782.42164/0973/09034. LCCN:89-038174.
Audience: **u,f.** *Choice, 1990.*

Thomson, Elizabeth, et al.   **ML420.L38**
The Lennon Companion: Twenty-Five Years of Comment.
Gutman, David (Author). Cambridge, MA: Da Capo Press.
2004. ISBN:0-306-81270-3, ISBN13: 978-0-306-81270-5.
Audience: **g,l,u,f.**

Thomson, Elizabeth &   **ML420.B754B69 1996**
  Gutman, David
The Bowie Companion. Trade Paper. Da Capo Press, Inc.
Cambridge, MA. 1996. 300p. ISBN:0-306-80707-6, ISBN13:
978-0-306-80707-7. Dewey:782.4/2/166/092. LCCN:96-021685.
Audience: **g,l,u,f.**

Toop, David   **ML3531.T66 2000**
Rap Attack 3: From African Jive to Global Hip-hop. Ed. 3.
Trade Paper. Serpent's Tail Ltd. London, 1999. 224p.
ISBN:1-85242-627-6, ISBN13: 978-1-85242-627-9.
Dewey:782.421649. LCCN:98-089857.
Audience: **u,f.**

Tribe, Ivan M.   **ML3524**
Country: A Regional Exploration. Trade Cloth. Greenwood
Publishing Group, Inc. Portsmouth, NH. 2006. 312p. Greenwood
Guides to American Roots Music Ser. ISBN:0-313-33026-3,
ISBN13: 978-0-313-33026-1. Dewey:781.64209.
LCCN:2005-034851.
Audience: **g,l,u,f.** *Choice, 2006.*

Van der Merwe, Peter   **ML3470**
Origins of the Popular Style: The Antecedents of
Twentieth-Century Popular Music. Trade Paper. Oxford
University Press, Inc. New York, NY. 1992. 366p.
ISBN:0-19-816305-3, ISBN13: 978-0-19-816305-3.
Dewey:781.6409034.
Audience: **g,l,u,f.**

Waksman, Steve   **ML1015.G9W24 1999**
Instruments of Desire: The Electric Guitar and the Shaping of
Musical Experience. Trade Cloth. Harvard University Press.
Cambridge, MA. 2000. 384p. ISBN:0-674-00065-X, ISBN13:
978-0-674-00065-0. Dewey:787.87/19. LCCN:99-039764.
Audience: **u,f.** *Choice, 2000.*

Walser, Robert   **ML3534**
Running with the Devil: Power, Gender, and Madness in Heavy
Metal Music. Trade Paper. Wesleyan University Press.
Middletown, CT. 1993. 254p. Music Culture Ser.
ISBN:0-8195-6260-2, ISBN13: 978-0-8195-6260-9.
Dewey:781.6/6. LCCN:92-056911.
Audience: **u,f.** *Choice, 1993.*

Warner, Timothy   **ML3470.W38 2002**
Pop Music - Technology and Creativity: Trevor Horn and the
Digital Revolution. Trade Cloth. Ashgate Publishing, Ltd.
Aldershot, 2003. 186p. Ashgate Popular and Folk Music Ser.
ISBN:0-7546-3131-1, ISBN13: 978-0-7546-3131-6.
Dewey:786.7/164. LCCN:2002-074728.
Audience: **u,f.** *Choice, 2004.*

Westbrook, Paul &　　　　　**ML102.R27W47 2002**
　Westbrook, Alonzo T.
Hip Hoptionary (TM): The Dictionary of Hip Hop Terminology.
Trade Paper. Broadway Books. New York, NY. 2002. 240p.
ISBN:0-7679-0924-0, ISBN13: 978-0-7679-0924-2.
Dewey:306/.1. LCCN:2003-555627.
　　　　　　　　　　　　　　　　　Audience: **g,l,u,f.**

Whitburn, Joel　　　　　　　**ML156.4.P6**
Joel Whitburn Presents a Century of Pop Music: Year-by-Year
Top 40 Rankings of the Songs and Artists That Shaped a
Century: Compiled from America's Popular Music Charts,
Surveys, and Record Listings 1900-1939, and Billboard's Pop
Singles Charts, 1940-1999. Menomonee Falls, Wis.: Record
Research. 1999. ISBN:0-89820-135-7, ISBN13:
978-0-89820-135-2.
　　　　　　　　　　　　　　　　　Audience: **g,l,u,f.**

Whitburn, Joel　　　　　　　**ML146.4.P6**
Joel Whitburn Presents Top 10 Singles Charts: Chart Data
Compiled from Billboard's Best Sellers in Stores and Hot 100
Charts, 1955-2000. Menomonee Falls, WI: Record Research.
2001. ISBN:0-89820-145-4, ISBN13: 978-0-89820-145-1.
　　　　　　　　　　　　　　　　　Audience: **g,l,u,f.**

Whitburn, Joel　　　　　　**ML156.4.B6W25 2004**
Joel Whitburn Presents Top R & B/Hip-Hop Singles, 1942-2004.
Trade Cloth. Record Research, Inc. Menomonee Falls, WI.
2005. 818p. ISBN:0-89820-160-8, ISBN13: 978-0-89820-160-4.
Dewey:016.781643/0266. LCCN:2005-297809.
　　　　　　　　　　　　　　　　　Audience: **g,l,u,f.**

Whitburn, Joel　　　　　　　**ML156.4.P6**
Joel Whitburn's Top Pop Albums, 1955-2001. Menomonee
Falls, Wis.: Record Research. 2001. ISBN:0-89820-147-0,
ISBN13: 978-0-89820-147-5.
　　　　　　　　　　　　　　　　　Audience: **g,l,u,f.**

Whitburn, Joel　　　　　　　**ML156.4.C7**
Top Country Singles, 1944 to 2001: Chart Data Compiled from
Billboard's Country Singles Charts, 1944-2001. Ed. 5.
Menomonee Falls, Wis.: Record Research. 2002.
ISBN:0-89820-151-9, ISBN13: 978-0-89820-151-2.
　　　　　　　　　　　　　　　　　Audience: **g,l,u,f.**

Whitburn, Joel　　　　　　　**ML156.4.P6**
Top Pop Singles 1955-2002. Ed. 10. Record Research, Inc.
2004. ISBN:0-89820-155-1, ISBN13: 978-0-89820-155-0.
　　　　　　　　　　　　　　　　　Audience: **u,f.**

White, Timothy　　　　　　　**ML420.M3313**
Catch a Fire: The Life of Bob Marley. Ed. 4. Trade Paper.
Henry Holt & Company. New York, NY. 2006. 576p.
ISBN:0-8050-8086-4, ISBN13: 978-0-8050-8086-5.
Dewey:784.5/0092/4.
　　　　　　　　　　　　　　　　　Audience: **g,l,u,f.**

Wilder, Alec　　　　　　　　**ML3477**
American Popular Song: The Great Innovators, 1900-1950.
James T. Maher (Introduction by). Cloth Text. Oxford University

Press, Inc. New York, NY. 1972. 576p. ISBN:0-19-501445-6,
ISBN13: 978-0-19-501445-7. Dewey:782.421640973.
LCCN:70-159643.
　　　　　　　　　　　　　　　　　Audience: **l,u,f.**

Zak, Albin　　　　　　　　　**ML421.V44**
The Velvet Underground Companion: 4 Decades of
Commentary. Trade Paper. Music Sales Corporation. New York,
NY. 1997. 300p. Companion Ser. ISBN:0-8256-7242-2, ISBN13:
978-0-8256-7242-2. Dewey:782.42166/092/2. LCCN:97-009247.
　　　　　　　　　　　　　　　　　Audience: **g,l,u,f.**

Zappa, Frank　　　　　　　　**ML420.P96**
Real Frank Zappa Book. Trade Paper. Simon & Schuster. New
York, NY. 1990. 352p. ISBN:0-671-70572-5, ISBN13:
978-0-671-70572-5. Dewey:784.5/4/00924 B.
　　　　　　　　　　　　　　　　　Audience: **l,u,f.**

Zwonitzer, Mark &　　　　**ML421.C33Z86 2002**
　Hirshberg, Charles
Will You Miss Me When I'm Gone?: The Carter Family and
Their Legacy in American Music. Trade Cloth. Simon &
Schuster. New York, NY. 2002. 432p. ISBN:0-684-85763-4,
ISBN13: 978-0-684-85763-3. Dewey:781.642/092/2.
LCCN:2002-022395.
　　　　　　　　　　　　Audience: **g,l,u,f.** *Choice, 2002.*

Studies in Music History, Criticism, Analysis, and Appreciation > Music In the United States and Canada

Alexander, James Heywood　　　**ML200.T67 2002**
To Stretch Our Ears: A Documentary History of America's
Music. Trade Paper. W. W. Norton & Company, Inc. New York,
NY. 2002. xix, 508p. ISBN:0-393-97411-1, ISBN13:
978-0-393-97411-9. Dewey:780/.973. LCCN:2001-044816.
　　　　　　　　　　　　　　　　　Audience: **g,l,u,f.**

Austin, William W.　　　　　**ML410.F78A9 1989**
Susanna, "Jeanie," and "The Old Folks at Home": The Songs of
Stephen C. Foster from His Time to Ours. Ed. 2. Trade Cloth.
University of Illinois Press. Champaign, IL. 1988. 456p. Music
in American Life Ser. ISBN:0-252-01476-6, ISBN13:
978-0-252-01476-5. Dewey:784/.092/4. LCCN:87-013931.
　　　　　　　　　　　　　　　　　Audience: **l,u,f.**

Bierley, Paul E.　　　　　　　**ML410.S688**
John Philip Sousa: American Phenomenon. Trade Cloth. Warner
Bros. Publications. Miami, FL. 2001. 270p.
ISBN:0-7579-0612-5, ISBN13: 978-0-7579-0612-1.
Dewey:785/.092.
　　　　　　　　　　　　　　　　　Audience: **g,l,u,f.**

Bohlman, Philip V. (Editor),　　　**ML2911.M87 2005**
　et al.
Music in American Religious Experience. Edith Blumhofer &
Maria Chow (Editors). Trade Paper. Oxford University Press,
Inc. New York, NY. 2005. 368p. ISBN:0-19-517304-X, ISBN13:
978-0-19-517304-8. Dewey:201/.678/0973. LCCN:2005-052304.
　　　　　　　　　　　　Audience: **g,l,u,f.** *Choice, 2006.*

Broyles, Michael   ML390.B862 2004
Mavericks and Other Traditions in American Music. Cloth over
Boards. Yale University Press. Cumberland, RI. 2004. 400p.
ISBN:0-300-10045-0, ISBN13: 978-0-300-10045-7.
Dewey:780/.973. LCCN:2003-021090.
             Audience: **u,f.** *Choice, 2004.*

Chase, Gilbert   ML200.1
America's Music: From the Pilgrims to the Present. Ed. 3. Trade
Paper. University of Illinois Press. Champaign, IL. 1992. 744p.
Music in American Life Ser. ISBN:0-252-06275-2, ISBN13:
978-0-252-06275-9. Dewey:781.773. LCCN:86-030795.
             Audience: **g,l,u,f.** *Choice, 1988.*

Cornelius, Steven   ML3551
Music of the Civil War Era. Cloth Text. Greenwood Publishing
Group, Inc. Portsmouth, NH. 2004. 320p. American History
Through Music Ser. ISBN:0-313-32081-0, ISBN13:
978-0-313-32081-1. Dewey:780/.973/09034.
LCCN:2004-042531.
             Audience: **u,f.** *Choice, 2005.*

Crawford, Richard   ML200
Introduction to American Music. Paper Text, Compact Disc. W.
W. Norton & Company, Inc. New York, NY. 2001.
ISBN:0-393-94407-7, ISBN13: 978-0-393-94407-5.
Dewey:780.973.
             Audience: **g,l,u,f.**

DeVenney, David P.   ML1511
(Annotations by, Compiled by)
Source Readings in American Choral Music: Composers'
Writings, Interviews, and Reviews. Trade Cloth. College Music
Society, The. Missoula, MT. 1996. xiv, 258p. Monographs and
Bibliographics in American Music Ser. ISBN:0-9650647-0-0,
ISBN13: 978-0-9650647-0-5. Dewey:782.5.
             Audience: **u,f.**

Dizikes, John   ML1711
Opera in America: A Cultural History. Trade Paper. Yale
University Press. Cumberland, RI. 1995. 622p.
ISBN:0-300-06101-3, ISBN13: 978-0-300-06101-7.
Dewey:782.10973.
             Audience: **u,f.** *Choice, 1994.*

Ellinwood, Leonard   ML200 .E4 1970
History of American Church Music. Paper Text. Da Capo Press,
Inc. Cambridge, MA. 1970. Music Reprint Ser.
ISBN:0-306-71233-4, ISBN13: 978-0-306-71233-3.
Dewey:783/.026/0973. LCCN:69-012683.
             Audience: **u,f.**

Emerson, Ken   ML410.F78E46 1997
Doo-Dah!: Stephen Foster and the Rise of American Popular
Culture. Trade Cloth. Simon & Schuster. New York, NY. 1997.
400p. ISBN:0-684-81010-7, ISBN13: 978-0-684-81010-2.
Dewey:782.42164/092 B. LCCN:96-029816.
             Audience: **g,l,u,f.** *Choice, 1998.*

Grant, Mark N.   ML3915.G73 1998
Maestros of the Pen: A History of Classical Music Criticism in
America. Eric Friedheim (Editor). Cloth Text. Northeastern
University Press. Boston, MA. 1998. 416p.
ISBN:1-55553-363-9, ISBN13: 978-1-55553-363-2.
Dewey:781.6/8/0973. LCCN:98-028959.
             Audience: **u,f.** *Choice, 1999.*

Gura, Philip F. & Bollman,   98-46164 [ML]
    James F.
America's Instrument: The Banjo in the Nineteenth Century.
Trade Cloth. University of North Carolina Press. Chapel Hill,
NC. 1999. 400p. ISBN:0-8078-2484-4, ISBN13:
978-0-8078-2484-9. Dewey:787.8/81973/09034.
LCCN:98-046164.
             Audience: **l,u,f.** *Choice, 2000.*

Hall, Charles J.   ML200.H15 1996
A Chronicle of American Music, 1700-1995. Trade Cloth.
Thomson Gale. Farmington Hills, MI. 1996. 825p.
ISBN:0-02-860296-X, ISBN13: 978-0-02-860296-7.
Dewey:780/.973. LCCN:96-016458.
             Audience: **u,f.** *Choice, 1997.*

Hamm, Charles   ML200
Music in the New World. Trade Cloth. W. W. Norton &
Company, Inc. New York, NY. 1983. 736p.
ISBN:0-393-95193-6, ISBN13: 978-0-393-95193-6.
Dewey:781.773. LCCN:82-006481.
             Audience: **g,l,u,f.**

Hazen, Margaret H. &   ML1311
    Hazen, Robert M.
The Music Men: An Illustrated History of Brass Bands in
America, 1800-1920. Trade Cloth. Smithsonian Institution Press.
Washington, DC. 1987. 272p. ISBN:0-87474-546-2, ISBN13:
978-0-87474-546-7. Dewey:785.06/71. LCCN:86-020376.
             Audience: **u,f.** *Choice, 1987.*

Heintze, James R.   ML120.U5H46 1990
Early American Music, 1620-1820: A Research and Information
Guide. Trade Cloth. Garland Publishing, Inc. New York, NY.
1990. 524p. Music Research and Information Guides Ser., Vol.
13 ISBN:0-8240-4119-4, ISBN13: 978-0-8240-4119-9.
Dewey:016.78/0973/09033. LCCN:89-016904.
             Audience: **l,u,f.** *Choice, 1990.*

Hicks, Michael   ML3174
Mormonism and Music: A History. Trade Paper. University of
Illinois Press. Champaign, IL. 2003. 280p. Music in American
Life Ser. ISBN:0-252-07147-6, ISBN13: 978-0-252-07147-8.
Dewey:782.32/293/009. LCCN:2004-268009.
             Audience: **u,f.** *Choice, 1990.*

Hitchcock, H. Wiley   ML200.H58 2000
Music in the United States: A Historical Introduction. Ed. 4.
Trade Paper. Prentice Hall PTR. Upper Saddle River, NJ. 1999.
413p. History of Music Ser. ISBN:0-13-907643-3, ISBN13:
978-0-13-907643-5. Dewey:780.9/73. LCCN:99-042121.
             Audience: **g,l,u,f.**

Hitchcock, H. Wiley &   **ML100**
Sadie, Stanley (Editors)
The New Grove Dictionary of American Music. Trade Cloth.
Oxford University Press, Inc. New York, NY. 1986. 2736p.
ISBN:0-943818-36-2, ISBN13: 978-0-943818-36-8.
Dewey:781.773/03/21. LCCN:86-000404.
                           Audience: **g,l,u,f**. *Choice, 1987.*

Horn, David   **ML120.U5.H7**
The Literature of American Music in Books and Folk Music
Collections: A Fully Annotated Bibliography. Trade Cloth.
Scarecrow Press, Inc. Lanham, MD. 1977. 570p.
ISBN:0-8108-0996-6, ISBN13: 978-0-8108-0996-3.
Dewey:016.781773. LCCN:76-013160.
                           Audience: **u,f**. *Choice, 1989.*

Horn, David & Jackson,   **ML120.U5.H7SUPPL.1**
Richard
The Literature of American Music in Books and Folk Music
Collections: A Fully Annotated Bibliography. Trade Cloth.
Scarecrow Press, Inc. Lanham, MD. 1988. 586p.
ISBN:0-8108-1997-X, ISBN13: 978-0-8108-1997-9.
Dewey:016.781773. LCCN:87-009630.
                           Audience: **u,f**. *Choice, 1989.*

Kingman, Daniel   **ML200.K55 1990**
American Music: A Panorama. Ed. 2. Cloth Text. Thomson
Wadsworth. Belmont, CA. 1990. 684p. ISBN:0-02-873370-3,
ISBN13: 978-0-02-873370-8. Dewey:780/.973.
LCCN:89-034119.
                           Audience: **l,u,f**.

Koskoff, Ellen   **ML3917.U6M87 2005**
Music Cultures in the United States: An Introduction. Paper
over Boards. Routledge. New York, NY. 2005. 448p.
ISBN:0-415-96588-8, ISBN13: 978-0-415-96588-0.
Dewey:306.4/842/0973. LCCN:2004-019853.
                           Audience: **g,l,u,f**.

Krummel, Donald W.   **ML200**
(Editor), et al.
Resources of American Music History: A Directory of Source
Materials from Colonial Times to World War II. Jean Geil,
Doris J. Dyen & Deane L. Root (Editors). Trade Cloth.
University of Illinois Press. Champaign, IL. 1981. 463p. Music
in American Life Ser. ISBN:0-252-00828-6, ISBN13:
978-0-252-00828-3. Dewey:026/.781773. LCCN:80-014873.
                           Audience: **u,f**.

Lawrence, Vera B.   **ML200.8.N5**
Strong on Music: Resonances, 1836-1849. Trade Paper.
University of Chicago Press. Chicago, IL. 1995. 742p.
ISBN:0-226-47009-1, ISBN13: 978-0-226-47009-2.
Dewey:780.97471. LCCN:94-205956.
                           Audience: **u,f**.

Lawrence, Vera B.   **ML200.8.N5L4 1995**
Strong on Music: Reverberations, 1850-1856, Vol. 2. Trade
Cloth. University of Chicago Press. Chicago, IL. 1995. 886p.
ISBN:0-226-47010-5, ISBN13: 978-0-226-47010-8.
Dewey:780/.9747/109034. LCCN:94-205956.
                           Audience: **u,f**.

Lawrence, Vera Brodsky   **ML200.8.N5L4**
Strong on Music: Repercussions, 1857-1862. Trade Cloth.
University of Chicago Press. Chicago, IL. 1999. 658p. Strong
on Music Ser., Vol. 3 ISBN:0-226-47015-6, ISBN13:
978-0-226-47015-3. Dewey:780/.9747/109034.
LCCN:2001-547651.
                           Audience: **u,f**.

Lichtenstein, Grace &   **ML200.8.N48L5 1993**
Dankner, Laura
Musical Gumbo: The Music of New Orleans. Trade Cloth. W.
W. Norton & Company, Inc. New York, NY. 1993. 352p.
ISBN:0-393-03468-2, ISBN13: 978-0-393-03468-4.
Dewey:780/.9763/35. LCCN:92-030690.
                           Audience: **g,l,u,f**. *Choice, 1993.*

Linn, Karen   **ML1015.B3L5 1994**
That Half-Barbaric Twang: The Banjo in American Popular
Culture. Trade Paper. University of Illinois Press. Champaign,
IL. 1994. 208p. Music in American Life Ser.
ISBN:0-252-06433-X, ISBN13: 978-0-252-06433-3.
Dewey:787.8/80973. LCCN:95-168823.
                           Audience: **u,f**. *Choice, 1992.*

Marco, Guy A.   **ML120.U5M133 1996**
Checklist of Writings on American Music, 1640-1992, Vols. 1-3.
Trade Cloth. Scarecrow Press, Inc. Lanham, MD. 1996. 248p.
ISBN:0-8108-3133-3, ISBN13: 978-0-8108-3133-9.
Dewey:016.7/8/0973. LCCN:95-026773.
                           Audience: **u,f**. *Choice, 1997.*

Marco, Guy A. et al.   **ML120.U5**
Literature of American Music III, 1983-1992. Horn, David
(Author). Lanham, Md.: Scarecrow Press. 1996.
ISBN:0-8108-3132-5, ISBN13: 978-0-8108-3132-2.
                           Audience: **u,f**.

Marini, Stephen A.   **ML2911.M37 2003**
Sacred Song in America: Religion, Music, and Public Culture.
Trade Cloth. University of Illinois Press. Champaign, IL. 2003.
416p. Public Expressions of Religion in America Ser.
ISBN:0-252-02800-7, ISBN13: 978-0-252-02800-7.
Dewey:782.25/0973. LCCN:2002-008741.
                           Audience: **u,f**. *Choice, 2004.*

Mattfeld, Julius   **ML128.V7**
Variety Music Cavalcade, 1620-1969; A Chronology of Vocal
and Instrumental Music Popular in the United States. Ed. 3.
Englewood Cliffs, N.J., Prentice-Hall. 1971.
ISBN:0-13-940718-9, ISBN13: 978-0-13-940718-5.
                           Audience: **g,l,u,f**.

McGee, Timothy J.   **ML205 .M37 1985**
The Music of Canada. Ed. 2. Trade Paper. W. W. Norton &
Company, Inc. New York, NY. 1985. 257p.
ISBN:0-393-95376-9, ISBN13: 978-0-393-95376-3.
Dewey:781.771. LCCN:84-027318.
                           Audience: **u,f**.

McKay, David P. &   **ML0410.B588M**
  Crawford, Richard
William Billings of Boston: Eighteenth-Century Composer.
Trade Paper. Books on Demand. Ann Arbor, MI. 1975. 314p.
ISBN:0-608-02501-1, ISBN13: 978-0-608-02501-8.
Dewey:783.0924. LCCN:74-019035.

                 Audience: **u,f.**

Nicholls, David (Editor)   **ML200 .C36 1998**
The Cambridge History of American Music. Victoria L. Levine,
William Brooks, Kate V. Keller, John Koegel, Nym Cooke,
Jacqueline Cogdell DjeDje, Michael Broyles & Dale Cockrell
(Contribution by). Cloth Text. Cambridge University Press. New
York, NY. 1998. 653p. The Cambridge History of Music Ser.
ISBN:0-521-45429-8, ISBN13: 978-0-521-45429-2.
Dewey:780/.973. LCCN:98-003814.

           Audience: **l,u,f.**   *Choice, 1999.*

Ochse, Orpha C.   **ML561**
The History of the Organ in the United States. Trade Paper.
Indiana University Press. Bloomington, IN. 1988. 512p.
ISBN:0-253-20495-X, ISBN13: 978-0-253-20495-0.
Dewey:786.6/273. LCCN:73-022644.

                 Audience: **u,f.**

Oja, Carol J.   **ML200.8.N5O43 2000**
Making Music Modern: New York in the 1920s. Trade Cloth.
Oxford University Press, Inc. New York, NY. 2000. 507p.
ISBN:0-19-505849-6, ISBN13: 978-0-19-505849-9.
Dewey:780/.9747/109042. LCCN:99-052604.

                 Audience: **u,f.**

Pelletier, Theo   **ML200.7.M73W35 1998**
  (Photographer)
River of Song: A Musical Journey down the Mississippi. John
Junkerman & Elijah Wald (Text by). Trade Cloth. St. Martin's
Press. Gordonville, VA. 1998. 352p. ISBN:0-312-20059-5,
ISBN13: 978-0-312-20059-6. Dewey:780/.977.
LCCN:98-045508.

               Audience: **g,l,u,f.**

Perone, James E.   **ML3918**
Music of the Counterculture Era. Cloth Text. Greenwood
Publishing Group, Inc. Portsmouth, NH. 2004. 240p. American
History Through Music Ser. ISBN:0-313-32689-4, ISBN13:
978-0-313-32689-9. Dewey:781.64/0973/09046.
LCCN:2004-040432.

           Audience: **g,l,u,f.**   *Choice, 2004.*

Reyes, Adelaida   **ML200.R48 2004**
Music in America: Experiencing Music, Expressing Culture.
Cloth Text. Oxford University Press, Inc. New York, NY. 2004.
144p. Global Music Ser. ISBN:0-19-514666-2, ISBN13:
978-0-19-514666-0. Dewey:780/.973. LCCN:2004-050099.

                Audience: **l,u,f.**

Roell, Craig H.   **ML661.R64 1989**
The Piano in America, 1890-1940. Cloth Text. University of
North Carolina Press. Chapel Hill, NC. 1991. xx, 396p.
ISBN:0-8078-1802-X, ISBN13: 978-0-8078-1802-2.
Dewey:381/.4568181621/0973. LCCN:88-014326.

          Audience: **u,f.**   *Choice, 1989.*

Sablosky, Irving   **ML200.4.W5 1986**
What They Heard: Music in America, 1852-1881, from the
Pages of "Dwight's Journal of Music". Cloth Text. Louisiana
State University Press. Baton Rouge, LA. 1986. x, 317p.
ISBN:0-8071-1258-5, ISBN13: 978-0-8071-1258-8.
Dewey:780/.973. LCCN:85-013016.

                 Audience: **u,f.**

Sanjek, Russell   **ML200.S26 1988**
American Popular Music and Its Business: The First Four
Hundred Years: From 1790 to 1909, Vol. II. Cloth Text. Oxford
University Press, Inc. New York, NY. 1988. 494p.
ISBN:0-19-504310-3, ISBN13: 978-0-19-504310-5.
Dewey:780/.42/0973. LCCN:87-018605.

           Audience: **g,l,u,f.**   *Choice, 1989.*

Sanjek, Russell   **ML200.S26 1988**
American Popular Music and Its Business: The First Four
Hundred Years, 1790-1909. Cloth Text. Oxford University Press,
Inc. New York, NY. 1988. 494p. ISBN:0-19-504028-7, ISBN13:
978-0-19-504028-9. Dewey:780/.42/0973. LCCN:87-018605.

           Audience: **g,l,u,f.**   *Choice, 1989.*

Sanjek, Russell   **ML200.S26 1988**
American Popular Music and Its Business: The First Four
Hundred Years, 1900-1984, Vol. 3. Cloth Text. Oxford
University Press, Inc. New York, NY. 1988. 750p.
ISBN:0-19-504311-1, ISBN13: 978-0-19-504311-2.
Dewey:780/.42/0973. LCCN:87-018605.

           Audience: **g,l,u,f.**   *Choice, 1989.*

Spottswood, Richard K.   **ML156.4.F5 S69**
Ethnic Music on Records - A Discography of Ethnic Recordings
Produced in the United States, 1893-1942: Eastern Europe.
Trade Cloth. University of Illinois Press. Champaign, IL. 1990.
504p. Music in American Life Ser., Vol. 3 ISBN:0-252-01721-8,
ISBN13: 978-0-252-01721-6. Dewey:016.78162/0026/6.

                 Audience: **u,f.**

Spottswood, Richard K.   **ML156.4.F5 S69**
Ethnic Music on Records - A Discography of Ethnic Recordings
Produced in the United States, 1893-1942: Spanish, Portuguese,
Philippines, Basque. Trade Cloth. University of Illinois Press.
Champaign, IL. 1990. 904p. Music in American Life Ser., Vol. 4
ISBN:0-252-01722-6, ISBN13: 978-0-252-01722-3.
Dewey:016.78162/0026/6.

                 Audience: **u,f.**

Spottswood, Richard K.   **ML156.4.F5 S69**
Ethnic Music on Records - A Discography of Ethnic Recordings
Produced in the United States, 1893-1942: Record Number
Index, Matrix Number Index. Trade Cloth. University of Illinois
Press. Champaign, IL. 1990. 640p. Music in American Life Ser.,
Vol. 7 ISBN:0-252-01725-0, ISBN13: 978-0-252-01725-4.
Dewey:016.78162/0026/6.

                 Audience: **u,f.**

Spottswood, Richard K.   **ML156.4.F5 S69**
Ethnic Music on Records - A Discography of Ethnic Recordings
Produced in the United States, 1893-1942: Western Europe.

Trade Cloth. University of Illinois Press. Champaign, IL. 1991. 682p. Music in American Life Ser. ISBN:0-252-01719-6, ISBN13: 978-0-252-01719-3. Dewey:016.78162/0026/6.

Audience: **u,f.**

Spottswood, Richard K.   **ML156.4.F5 S69**
Ethnic Music on Records - A Discography of Ethnic Recordings Produced in the United States, 1893-1942: Slavic. Trade Cloth. University of Illinois Press. Champaign, IL. 1990. 552p. Music in American Life Ser., Vol. 2 ISBN:0-252-01720-X, ISBN13: 978-0-252-01720-9. Dewey:016.78162/0026/6.

Audience: **u,f.**

Spottswood, Richard K.   **ML156.4.F5 S69**
Ethnic Music on Records - A Discography of Ethnic Recordings Produced in the United States, 1893-1942: Artist Index, Title Index. Trade Cloth. University of Illinois Press. Champaign, IL. 1990. 760p. Music in American Life Ser., Vol. 6 ISBN:0-252-01724-2, ISBN13: 978-0-252-01724-7. Dewey:016.78162/0026/6.

Audience: **u.**

Spottswood, Richard K.   **ML156.4.F5 S69**
Ethnic Music on Records - A Discography of Ethnic Recordings Produced in the United States, 1893-1942: Middle East, Far East, Scandinavian, English Language, American Indian, International. Trade Cloth. University of Illinois Press. Champaign, IL. 1990. 512p. Music in American Life Ser., Vol. 5 ISBN:0-252-01723-4, ISBN13: 978-0-252-01723-0. Dewey:016.78162/0026/6.

Audience: **u,f.**

Stevenson, Robert Murrell   **ML3111**
Protestant Church Music in America: A Short Survey of Men and Movements from 1564 to the Present. W.W. Norton. 1966.

Audience: **u,f.**

Stowe, David W.   **ML2911.S76 2004**
How Sweet the Sound: Music in the Spiritual Lives of Americans. Trade Cloth. Harvard University Press. Cambridge, MA. 2004. 352p. ISBN:0-674-01290-9, ISBN13: 978-0-674-01290-5. Dewey:781.7/00973. LCCN:2003-067543.

Audience: **u,f.** *Choice, 2004.*

Tawa, Nicholas E.   **ML200.7.N3T39 2001**
From Psalm to Symphony: A History of Music in New England. Trade Cloth. Northeastern University Press. Boston, MA. 2005. 416p. ISBN:1-55553-491-0, ISBN13: 978-1-55553-491-2. Dewey:780/.974. LCCN:2001-034529.

Audience: **u,f.** *Choice, 2002.*

Tawa, Nicholas E.   **ML200**
Mainstream Music of Early Twentieth Century America: The Composers, Their Times, and Their Works, 28. Trade Cloth. Greenwood Publishing Group, Inc. Portsmouth, NH. 1992. 224p. Contributions to the Study of Music and Dance Ser., No. 28 ISBN:0-313-28563-2, ISBN13: 978-0-313-28563-9. Dewey:780/.973/09041. LCCN:92-010676.

Audience: **u,f.** *Choice, 1993.*

Tawa, Nicholas E.   **ML200.5.T38 1984**
Serenading the Reluctant Eagle: American Musical Life During Crisis, 1925-1945. Trade Cloth. Thomson Wadsworth. Belmont, CA. 1984. 272p. ISBN:0-02-871760-0, ISBN13: 978-0-02-871760-9. Dewey:780/.973. LCCN:84-005438.

Audience: **u,f.**

Studies in Music History, Criticism, Analysis, and Appreciation > African American and African Diaspora

Anderson, Marian   **ML420.A6A3 2001**
My Lord, What a Morning: An Autobiography. James Anderson DePreist (Foreword by). Trade Paper. University of Illinois Press. Champaign, IL. 2002. 352p. Music in American Life Ser. ISBN:0-252-07053-4, ISBN13: 978-0-252-07053-2. Dewey:782.1/092 B. LCCN:2001-040980.

Audience: **g,l,u,f.**

Badger, R. Reid   **ML422.E87B2 1995**
A Life in Ragtime: A Biography of James Reese Europe. Trade Cloth. Oxford University Press, Inc. New York, NY. 1995. 338p. ISBN:0-19-506044-X, ISBN13: 978-0-19-506044-7. Dewey:781.65/092 B. LCCN:93-042407.

Audience: **g,l,u,f.** *Choice, 1995.*

Baraka, Amiri Imamu   **ML3556.B15 1998**
Black Music. Paper Text. Da Capo Press, Inc. Cambridge, MA. 1998. 224p. ISBN:0-306-80814-5, ISBN13: 978-0-306-80814-2. Dewey:780/.89/96073. LCCN:97-041725.

Audience: **u,f.**

Baraka, Amiri & Jones,   **ML3556.B16 1999**
LeRoi
Blues People: Negro Music in White America. Trade Paper. HarperCollins Publishers. New York, NY. 1999. 256p. ISBN:0-688-18474-X, ISBN13: 978-0-688-18474-2. Dewey:780/.89/96073. LCCN:98-049663.

Audience: **g,l,u,f.** *B*

Behague, Gerard H. (Editor)   **ML3549.M87 1994**
Music and Black Ethnicity: The Caribbean and South America. Trade Paper. University of Miami, North/South Center Press. Coral Gables, FL. 1998. 352p. ISBN:1-56000-708-7, ISBN13: 978-1-56000-708-1. Dewey:780/.899608. LCCN:94-000503.

Audience: **g,l,u,f.** *Choice, 1995.*

Brooks, Tim & Spottswood,   **ML3479.B76 2004**
Richard K.
Lost Sounds: Blacks and the Birth of the Recording Industry, 1890-1919. Trade Cloth. University of Illinois Press. Champaign, IL. 2004. 656p. Music in American Life Ser. ISBN:0-252-02850-3, ISBN13: 978-0-252-02850-2. Dewey:781.64/149/08996073. LCCN:2003-001102.

Audience: **u,f.** *Choice, 2004.*

Cockrell, Dale   **ML1711 .C63 1997**
Demons of Disorder: Early Blackface Minstrels and Their
World. Don B. Wilmeth (Contribution by). Trade Cloth.
Cambridge University Press. New York, NY. 1997. 256p.
Studies in American Theatre and Drama, Vol. 8
ISBN:0-521-56074-8, ISBN13: 978-0-521-56074-0.
Dewey:791.1/2/0973. LCCN:96-045566.
Audience: **u,f.** *Choice, 1998.*

Courlander, Harold   **ML3556**
Negro Folk Music U. S. A. Trade Paper. Dover Publications,
Inc. Mineola, NY. 1998. 324p. ISBN:0-486-27350-4, ISBN13:
978-0-486-27350-1. Dewey:781.6296073. LCCN:92-035475.
Audience: **u,f.**

Cruz, Jon   **ML3556.C78 1999**
Culture on the Margins: The Black Spiritual and the Rise of
American Cultural Interpretation. Trade Paper. Princeton
University Press. Princeton, NJ. 1999. 300p.
ISBN:0-691-00474-9, ISBN13: 978-0-691-00474-7.
Dewey:782.25/3. LCCN:98-043567.
Audience: **u,f.**

Epstein, Dena J.   **ML3556**
Sinful Tunes and Spirituals: Black Folk Music to the Civil War.
Trade Cloth. University of Illinois Press. Champaign, IL. 1981.
460p. Music in American Life Ser. ISBN:0-252-00520-1,
ISBN13: 978-0-252-00520-6. Dewey:784.756009.
LCCN:77-006315.
Audience: **g,l,u,f.**

Floyd, Samuel A. Jr.   **ML105.I5 1999**
  (Editor)
International Dictionary of Black Composers, Set. Trade Cloth.
Fitzroy Dearborn Publishers, Inc. Chicago, IL. 1999. 1600p.
ISBN:1-884964-27-3, ISBN13: 978-1-884964-27-5.
Dewey:780/.92/396 B. LCCN:99-214303.
Audience: **g,l,u,f.** *Choice, 1999.*

Gourse, Leslie   **ML420.C63G7 2000**
Unforgettable: The Life and Mystique of Nat King Cole. Trade
Paper. Cooper Square Publishers, Inc. New York, NY. 2000.
352p. ISBN:0-8154-1082-4, ISBN13: 978-0-8154-1082-9.
Dewey:782.42164/092 B. LCCN:00-057000.
Audience: **g,l,u,f.**

Gray, John   **ML120**
African Music: A Bibliographical Guide to the Traditional,
Popular, Art, and Liturgical Musics of Sub-Saharan Africa.
Cloth Text. Greenwood Publishing Group, Inc. Portsmouth, NH.
1991. 504p. African Special Bibliographic Ser., No. 14
ISBN:0-313-27769-9, ISBN13: 978-0-313-27769-6.
Dewey:016.78/0967. LCCN:90-024517.
Audience: **l,u,f.** *Choice, 1991.*

Guede, Alain   **DC137.5.S35G8413**
Monsieur de Saint-George: Virtuoso, Swordsman,
Revolutionary: A Legendary Life Rediscovered. Gilda M.
Roberts (Translator). Cloth over Boards. Picador. New York,

NY. 2003. 240p. ISBN:0-312-30927-9, ISBN13:
978-0-312-30927-5. Dewey:944/.00496/0092 B.
LCCN:2003-049888.
Audience: **g,l,u,f.** *Choice, 2004.*

Lott, Eric   **ML1711.L67 1993**
Love and Theft: Blackface Minstrelsy and the American
Working Class. Trade Paper. Oxford University Press, Inc. New
York, NY. 1995. 322p. Race and American Culture Ser.
ISBN:0-19-509641-X, ISBN13: 978-0-19-509641-5.
Dewey:791/.12/097309034.
Audience: **u,f.** *Choice, 1994.*

Lovell, John Jr.   **ML3556.L69 1986**
Black Song: The Forge and the Flame. Trade Paper. Paragon
House Publishers. Saint Paul, MN. 1986. 686p.
ISBN:0-913729-53-1, ISBN13: 978-0-913729-53-3.
Dewey:783.6/7/09. LCCN:86-018699.
Audience: **g,l,u,f.**

Mahar, William J.   **ML1711.M34 1999**
Behind the Burnt Cork Mask: Early Blackface Minstrelsy and
Antebellum American Popular Culture. Trade Paper. University
of Illinois Press. Champaign, IL. 1998. 472p. Music in
American Life Ser. ISBN:0-252-06696-0, ISBN13:
978-0-252-06696-2. Dewey:791/.12/0973. LCCN:97-033851.
Audience: **u,f.** *Choice, 1999.*

McCoy, Judy   **ML128.R28.M3 1992**
Rap Music in the 1980s: A Reference Guide. Trade Cloth.
Scarecrow Press, Inc. Lanham, MD. 1992. 275p.
ISBN:0-8108-2649-6, ISBN13: 978-0-8108-2649-6.
Dewey:782.42164. LCCN:92-039684.
Audience: **g,l,u,f.** *Choice, 1993.*

Monson, Ingrid   **ML3760.1.A37 2000**
The African Diaspora: A Musical Perspective. Cloth Text.
Garland Publishing, Inc. New York, NY. 2000. 366p. Conceptual
Issues in Ethnomusicology Ser., Vol. 3 ISBN:0-8153-2382-4,
ISBN13: 978-0-8153-2382-2. Dewey:780/.89/96.
LCCN:99-045341.
Audience: **u,f.** *Choice, 2001.*

Oliver, Paul   **ML3556 .O466 1984**
Songsters and Saints: Vocal Traditions on Race Records. Trade
Paper. Cambridge University Press. New York, NY. 1984. 346p.
ISBN:0-521-26942-3, ISBN13: 978-0-521-26942-1.
Dewey:784.500. LCCN:84-001699.
Audience: **u,f.**

Peters, Erskine   **ML54.6**
Lyrics of the Afro-American Spiritual: A Documentary
Collection. Cloth Text. Greenwood Publishing Group, Inc.
Portsmouth, NH. 1993. 480p. Encyclopedia of Black Music Ser.
ISBN:0-313-26238-1, ISBN13: 978-0-313-26238-8.
Dewey:782.25. LCCN:92-027574.
Audience: **g,l,u,f.**

Ping-Robbins, Nancy R. &   **ML134.J75P56 1998**
  Marco, Guy (Editors)
Scott Joplin: A Guide to Research. Cloth Text. Garland
Publishing, Inc. New York, NY. 1998. 426p. Composer

Resource Manuals Ser., Vol. 7 ISBN:0-8240-8399-7, ISBN13: 978-0-8240-8399-1. Dewey:016.78/092. LCCN:98-010988.
Audience: **l,u,f.** *Choice, 1999.*

Radano, Ronald M.   **ML3556.R25 2003**
Lying up a Nation: Race and Black Music. Trade Cloth. University of Chicago Press. Chicago, IL. 1998. 440p. ISBN:0-226-70197-2, ISBN13: 978-0-226-70197-4. Dewey:780/.89/96073. LCCN:2003-001142.
Audience: **u,f.** *Choice, 2004.*

Radano, Ronald M. &   **ML3795.M782 2000**
  Bohlman, Philip V. (Editors)
Music and the Racial Imagination. Trade Cloth. University of Chicago Press. Chicago, IL. 2000. 703p. Chicago Studies in Ethnomusicology ISBN:0-226-70199-9, ISBN13: 978-0-226-70199-8. Dewey:780/.89. LCCN:00-023672.
Audience: **u,f.**

Ramsey, Guthrie P.   **ML3556 .R32 2003**
Race Music: Black Cultures from Bebop to Hip-Hop. Trade Cloth. University of California Press. Berkeley, CA. 2003. 288p. Music of the African Diaspora Ser., Vol. 7 ISBN:0-520-21048-4, ISBN13: 978-0-520-21048-6. Dewey:781.64/089/96073. LCCN:2002-068455.
Audience: **u,f.** *Choice, 2004.*

Roberts, John S.   **ML3556.R6 1998**
Black Music of Two Worlds: African, Caribbean, Latin, and African-American Traditions. Ed. 2. Paper Text. Thomson Wadsworth. Belmont, CA. 1998. 368p. ISBN:0-02-864929-X, ISBN13: 978-0-02-864929-0. Dewey:780/.89/96. LCCN:98-006587.
Audience: **g,l,u,f.**

Sacks, Howard L. & Sacks,   **ML3556.S2 2003**
  Judith Rose
Way up North in Dixie: A Black Family's Claim to the Confederate Anthem. Trade Paper. University of Illinois Press. Champaign, IL. 2003. 288p. Music in American Life Ser. ISBN:0-252-07160-3, ISBN13: 978-0-252-07160-7. Dewey:780/.92/2771 B. LCCN:2003-007169.
Audience: **g,l,u,f.** *Choice, 1994.*

Sampson, Henry T.   **ML1711**
Blacks in Blackface: A Source Book on Early Black Musical Shows. Trade Cloth. Scarecrow Press, Inc. Lanham, MD. 1980. 562p. ISBN:0-8108-1318-1, ISBN13: 978-0-8108-1318-2. Dewey:782.81/092/2. LCCN:80-015048.
Audience: **g,l,u,f.**

Schroeder, Patricia R.   **ML420.J735S37 2004**
Robert Johnson, Mythmaking, and Contemporary American Culture. Trade Cloth. University of Illinois Press. Champaign, IL. 2004. 216p. Music in American Life Ser. ISBN:0-252-02915-1, ISBN13: 978-0-252-02915-8. Dewey:782.421643/092. LCCN:2003-020027.
Audience: **g,l,u,f.** *Choice, 2005.*

Self, Geoffrey   **ML410.C74S45 1995**
The Hiawatha Man: The Life and Music of Samuel Coleridge-Taylor. Trade Cloth. Ashgate Publishing, Ltd.

Aldershot, 1995. 328p. ISBN:0-85967-983-7, ISBN13: 978-0-85967-983-1. Dewey:780/.92 B. LCCN:94-045001.
Audience: **l,u,f.** *Choice, 1996.*

Skowronski, JoAnn   **ML128.B45**
Black Music in America: A Bibliography. Trade Cloth. Scarecrow Press, Inc. Lanham, MD. 1981. 733p. ISBN:0-8108-1443-9, ISBN13: 978-0-8108-1443-1. Dewey:016.7817/296073. LCCN:81-005609.
Audience: **l,u,f.**

Smith, Catherine P.   **ML410.S855 S65 2000**
William Grant Still: A Study in Contradictions. D. G. Murchison & Willard Gatewood (Contribution by). Trade Cloth. University of California Press. Berkeley, CA. 2000. 384p. Music of the African Diaspora Ser., Vol. 2 ISBN:0-520-21542-7, ISBN13: 978-0-520-21542-9. Dewey:780/.92. LCCN:99-043232.
Audience: **l,u,f.**

Southern, Eileen   **ML105**
Biographical Dictionary of Afro-American and African Musicians. Cloth Text. Greenwood Publishing Group, Inc. Portsmouth, NH. 1982. 496p. Encyclopedia of Black Music Ser. ISBN:0-313-21339-9, ISBN13: 978-0-313-21339-7. Dewey:780/.92/2 B. LCCN:81-002586.
Audience: **g,l,u,f.**

Southern, Eileen   **ML3556**
The Music of Black Americans: A History. Ed. 3. W.W. Norton. 1997. ISBN:0-393-03843-2, ISBN13: 978-0-393-03843-9.
Audience: **g,l,u,f.**

Southern, Eileen   **ML3556**
Readings in Black American Music. Ed. 2. Trade Paper. W. W. Norton & Company, Inc. New York, NY. 1983. 338p. ISBN:0-393-95280-0, ISBN13: 978-0-393-95280-3. Dewey:781.7/296073. LCCN:83-004192.
Audience: **l,u,f.**

Southern, Eileen & Wright,   **ML3556.S738 2000**
  Josephine
Images: Iconography of Music and Musicians in African-American Culture 1770s-1920s. Cloth Text. Garland Publishing, Inc. New York, NY. 2000. 288p. Music in African American Culture Ser., Vol. 1 ISBN:0-8153-2875-3, ISBN13: 978-0-8153-2875-9. Dewey:780/.89/96073. LCCN:00-029362.
Audience: **g,l,u,f.** *Choice, 2001.*

Stewart, Earl L.   **ML3556.S87 1998**
African-American Music: An Introduction. Cloth Text. Thomson Wadsworth. Belmont, CA. 1998. 400p. ISBN:0-02-860294-3, ISBN13: 978-0-02-860294-3. Dewey:780/.89/96073. LCCN:97-042487.
Audience: **g,l,u,f.**

Walker-Hill, Helen   **ML390.W16 2002**
From Spirituals to Symphonies: African-American Women Composers and Their Music. Cloth Text. Greenwood Publishing Group, Inc. Portsmouth, NH. 2002. 432p. Jazz Companions Ser. ISBN:0-313-29947-1, ISBN13: 978-0-313-29947-6. Dewey:780.89/96073. LCCN:2001-040600.
Audience: **g,l,u,f.** *Choice, 2003.*

Woll, Allen L.   ML1711.W64 1989
Black Musical Theatre: From Coontown to Dreamgirls. Trade
Cloth. Louisiana State University Press. Baton Rouge, LA.
1989. xiv, 301p. ISBN:0-8071-1469-3, ISBN13:
978-0-8071-1469-8. Dewey:782.81/08996073. LCCN:88-008904.
Audience: **u,f.** *Choice, 1989.*

Studies in Music History, Criticism, Analysis, and Appreciation > Folk and Traditional Music > General and Intercontinental Studies

Bohlman, Philip V.   ML3545.B64 1988
The Study of Folk Music in the Modern World. Trade Cloth.
Indiana University Press. Bloomington, IN. 1988. 182p.
ISBN:0-253-35555-9, ISBN13: 978-0-253-35555-3.
Dewey:781.7/09. LCCN:87-045401.
Audience: **l,u,f.** *Choice, 1989.*

Bohlman, Philip V.   ML3470.B68 2002
World Music: A Very Short Introduction. Trade Paper. Oxford
University Press, Inc. New York, NY. 2002. 198p. Very Short
Introductions Ser., Vol. 65 ISBN:0-19-285429-1, ISBN13:
978-0-19-285429-2. Dewey:780/.9. LCCN:2002-512787.
Audience: **g,l,u,f.**

Campbell, Patricia Shehan   MT1
& Wade, Bonnie C.
Teaching Music Globally. Trade Paper. Oxford University Press,
Inc. New York, NY. 2004. 286p. Global Music Ser.
ISBN:0-19-517143-8, ISBN13: 978-0-19-517143-3.
Dewey:780.7/1. LCCN:2003-054900.
Audience: **u,f.**

Greene, Paul D. & Porcello,   ML3545.W57 2004
Thomas
Wired for Sound: Engineering and Technologies in Sonic
Cultures. Library Binding. Wesleyan University Press.
Middletown, CT. 2004. 304p. Music/Culture Ser.
ISBN:0-8195-6516-4, ISBN13: 978-0-8195-6516-7.
Dewey:780/.9/05. LCCN:2004-016021.
Audience: **u,f.** *Choice, 2005.*

Malm, William P.   ML330.M3 1996
Music Cultures of the Pacific, the Near East and Asia. Ed. 3.
Trade Paper. Prentice Hall PTR. Upper Saddle River, NJ. 1995.
278p. Prentice Hall History of Music Ser. ISBN:0-13-182387-6,
ISBN13: 978-0-13-182387-7. Dewey:780/.95. LCCN:94-048578.
Audience: **g,l,u,f.**

Manuel, Peter   ML3470
Popular Musics of the Non-Western World: An Introductory
Survey. Paper Text. Oxford University Press, Inc. New York,
NY. 1990. 314p. ISBN:0-19-506334-1, ISBN13:
978-0-19-506334-9. Dewey:780/.42. LCCN:87-034861.
Audience: **g,l,u,f.** *Choice, 1989.*

Mitsui, Toru & Hosokawa,   ML3795.K22 1998
Shuhei
Karaoke Around the World: Global Technology, Local Singing.
Paper over Boards. Routledge. New York, NY. 1998. 224p.
Research in Cultural and Media Studies ISBN:0-415-16371-4,
ISBN13: 978-0-415-16371-2. Dewey:306.4/84.
LCCN:97-019902.
Audience: **u,f.**

Nettl, Bruno (Editor)   ML3795
Eight Urban Musical Cultures: Tradition and Change. Trade
Cloth. University of Illinois Press. Champaign, IL. 1978. 336p.
ISBN:0-252-00208-3, ISBN13: 978-0-252-00208-3.
Dewey:780/.9173/2. LCCN:77-025041.
Audience: **u,f.**

Nettl, Bruno   MT90.E95 2004
Excursions in World Music. Ed. 4. Trade Paper. Prentice Hall
PTR. Upper Saddle River, NJ. 2004. 384p.
ISBN:0-13-140305-2, ISBN13: 978-0-13-140305-5.
Dewey:780/.9. LCCN:2003-048683.
Audience: **g,l,u,f.**

Nettl, Bruno   ML3798 .N48
The Western Impact on World Music: Change, Adaptation, and
Survival. Trade Cloth. Macmillan Publishing Company, Inc. Old
Tappan, NJ. 1985. 232p. ISBN:0-317-46649-6, ISBN13:
978-0-317-46649-2. Dewey:780/.07.
Audience: **u,f.**

Nettl, Bruno & Russell,   ML430.7.I47 1998
Melinda (Editors)
In the Course of Performance: Studies in the World of Musical
Improvisation. Trade Cloth. University of Chicago Press.
Chicago, IL. 1998. 424p. Chicago Studies in Ethnomusicology
Ser. ISBN:0-226-57410-5, ISBN13: 978-0-226-57410-3.
Dewey:781.3/6. LCCN:98-003640.
Audience: **u,f.**

Nettl, Bruno (Editor), et al.   ML100.G16
The Garland Encyclopedia of World Music Set. Ruth M. Stone,
James Porter & Timothy Rice (Editors). Library Binding.
Garland Publishing, Inc. New York, NY. 1999. 1000p. Garland
Encyclopedia of World Music Ser. ISBN:0-8153-1865-0,
ISBN13: 978-0-8153-1865-1. Dewey:780.9. LCCN:97-009671.
Audience: **g,l,u,f.**

Nidel, Richard   ML3545.N54 2005
World Music: The Basics. Paper over Boards. Routledge. New
York, NY. 2004. 424p. The Basics Ser. ISBN:0-415-96800-3,
ISBN13: 978-0-415-96800-3. Dewey:780/.9.
LCCN:2004-019817.
Audience: **g,l,u,f.**

Post, Jennifer C.   ML128.E8
Ethnomusicology: A Guide to Research. Routledge. 2004.
Routledge Music Bibliographies ISBN:0-415-93834-1, ISBN13:
978-0-415-93834-1.
Audience: **u,f.**

Ralls-Mcleod, Karen & Harvey, Graham (Editors)   ML2900.I53 2000
Indigenous Religious Musics. Trade Cloth. Ashgate Publishing, Ltd. Aldershot, 2001. xi, 238p. SOAS Musicology Ser. ISBN:0-7546-0249-4, ISBN13: 978-0-7546-0249-1. Dewey:781.7. LCCN:00-135320.

Audience: **u,f.**

Rust, E. Gardner   ML128
The Music and Dance of the World's Religions: A Comprehensive, Annotated Bibliography of Materials in the English Language. Cloth Text. Greenwood Publishing Group, Inc. Portsmouth, NH. 1996. 504p. Music Reference Collection, Vol. 54 ISBN:0-313-29561-1, ISBN13: 978-0-313-29561-4. Dewey:016.7817. LCCN:96-018212.

Audience: **g,l,u,f.** *Choice, 1997.*

Shelemay, Kay Kaufman   MT90.S53 2006
Soundscapes: Exploring Music in a Changing World. Ed. 2. Trade Paper. W. W. Norton & Company, Inc. New York, NY. 2006. li, 471p. ISBN:0-393-92567-6, ISBN13: 978-0-393-92567-8. Dewey:780.9. LCCN:2006-040017.

Audience: **g,l,u,f.**

Shepherd, John (Editor)   ML102.P66C66 2003
Continuum Encyclopedia of Popular Music of the World: Media, Industry and Society, Vol. 1. Trade Cloth. Continuum International Publishing Group, Ltd. London, 2003. 832p. ISBN:0-8264-6321-5, ISBN13: 978-0-8264-6321-0. Dewey:781.63/09. LCCN:2002-074146.

Audience: **g,l,u,f.** *Choice, 2004.*

Shepherd, John (Editor)   ML102.P66C66 2003
Continuum Encyclopedia of Popular Music of the World: Performance and Production, Vol. 2. Trade Cloth. Continuum International Publishing Group, Ltd. London, 2003. 712p. ISBN:0-8264-6322-3, ISBN13: 978-0-8264-6322-7. Dewey:781.63/09. LCCN:2002-074146.

Audience: **g,l,u,f.** *Choice, 2004.*

Shepherd, John   ML102.P66
Encyclopedia of Popular Music of the World, Vols 3-7. Trade Cloth. Continuum International Publishing Group, Ltd. London, 2005. 1,984p. ISBN:0-8264-7436-5, ISBN13: 978-0-8264-7436-0. Dewey:781.6/3/03.

Audience: **g,l,u,f.** *Choice, 2005.*

Slobin, Mark   ML3798 .S46 1993
Subcultural Sounds: Micromusics of the West. Trade Paper. Wesleyan University Press. Middletown, CT. 1993. 139p. Music Culture Ser. ISBN:0-8195-6261-0, ISBN13: 978-0-8195-6261-6. Dewey:780/.89. LCCN:92-034289.

Audience: **u,f.**

Titon, Jeff Todd (General Editor)   ML3545
Worlds of Music: An Introduction to the Music of the World's Peoples. Ed. 3. Schirmer. 1996. ISBN:0-02-872612-X, ISBN13: 978-0-02-872612-0.

Audience: **g,l,u,f.**

Wade, Bonnie C.   ML3798.W33 2003
Thinking Musically: Experiencing Music, Expressing Culture. Trade Cloth. Oxford University Press, Inc. New York, NY. 2003. 206p. Global Music Ser., Vol. 1 ISBN:0-19-513663-2, ISBN13: 978-0-19-513663-0. Dewey:780/.8. LCCN:2003-041940.

Audience: **g,l,u,f.**

Wallin, Nils L. (Editor), et al.   ML3800.O74 2000
The Origins of Music. Bjorn Merker & Steven Brown (Editors). Trade Paper. MIT Press. Cambridge, MA. 2001. 512p. Bradford Bks. ISBN:0-262-73143-6, ISBN13: 978-0-262-73143-0. Dewey:781/.1.

Audience: **u,f.**

Studies in Music History, Criticism, Analysis, and Appreciation > Folk and Traditional Music > Sub-Saharan Africa

Agawu, Kofi   ML3760.7.G4A3 1995
African Rhythm: A Northern Ewe Perspective. Trade Cloth, Compact Disc, Mixed Media. Cambridge University Press. New York, NY. 1995. 237p. ISBN:0-521-48084-1, ISBN13: 978-0-521-48084-0. Dewey:781.62/96337401224. LCCN:94-031648.

Audience: **u,f.**

Agawu, Kofi   ML350.A355 2003
Representing African Music: Postcolonial Notes, Queries, Positions. Paper over Boards. Routledge. New York, NY. 2003. 288p. ISBN:0-415-94389-2, ISBN13: 978-0-415-94389-5. Dewey:780/.67. LCCN:2002-153450.

Audience: **u,f.**

Askew, Kelly Michelle   ML3760.A84 2002
Performing the Nation: Swahili Music and Cultural Politics in Tanzania. Trade Cloth, Compact Disc. University of Chicago Press. Chicago, IL. 2002. 392p. Chicago Studies in Ethnomusicology ISBN:0-226-02980-8, ISBN13: 978-0-226-02980-1. Dewey:306.4/84. LCCN:2001-008414.

Audience: **u,f.**

Barz, Gregory F.   ML350.B37 2004
Music in East Africa: Experiencing Music, Expressing Culture. Trade Cloth. Oxford University Press, Inc. New York, NY. 2004. 160p. Global Music Ser. ISBN:0-19-514151-2, ISBN13: 978-0-19-514151-1. Dewey:781.62/9676. LCCN:2003-060848.

Audience: **l,u,f.**

Bebey, Francis   ML3760
African Music: A People's Art. Josephine Bennett (Revised by). Trade Paper. Chicago Review Press, Inc. Chicago, IL. 1975. 192p. ISBN:1-55652-128-6, ISBN13: 978-1-55652-128-7. Dewey:781.7/1/6. LCCN:74-009348.

Audience: **l,u,f.**

Bender, Wolfgang   ML3502.5.B4613 1991
Sweet Mother: Modern African Music. Wolfgang Freis
(Translator). Trade Cloth. University of Chicago Press. Chicago,
IL. 1991. 256p. Chicago Studies in Ethnomusicology
ISBN:0-226-04253-7, ISBN13: 978-0-226-04253-4.
Dewey:780/.96. LCCN:90-020316.

Audience: **u,f.** *Choice, 1991.*

Berliner, Paul F.   ML350
The Soul of Mbira: Music and Traditions of the Shona People
of Zimbabwe. Trade Paper. University of Chicago Press.
Chicago, IL. 1993. 334p. ISBN:0-226-04379-7, ISBN13:
978-0-226-04379-1. Dewey:786.8/5. LCCN:92-041356.

Audience: **u,f.**

Blacking, John   ML3760.B62 1995
Venda Children's Songs: A Study in Ethnomusicological
Analysis. Trade Cloth. University of Chicago Press. Chicago,
IL. 1995. 210p. ISBN:0-226-05510-8, ISBN13:
978-0-226-05510-7. Dewey:782.42162/96397. LCCN:94-036465.

Audience: **u,f.**

Broughton, Simon et al.   ML102.W67W67 1999
Rough Guide to World Music, Vol. 1: Africa, Europe, and the
Middle East. Ellingham, Mark; Trillo, Richard (Authors) Duane,
Orla; Dowell, Vanessa. Rough Guides, Ltd. 2000.
ISBN:1-85828-635-2, ISBN13: 978-1-85828-635-8.

Audience: **g,l,u,f.**

Charry, Eric S.   ML3760.C38 2000
Mande Music: Traditional and Modern Music of the Maninka
and Mandinka of Western Africa. Trade Cloth. University of
Chicago Press. Chicago, IL. 2000. 531p. Chicago Studies in
Ethnomusicology ISBN:0-226-10161-4, ISBN13:
978-0-226-10161-3. Dewey:781.62/9634. LCCN:99-046011.

Audience: **u,f.** *Choice, 2001.*

Ebron, Paulla A.   ML3760.E27 2002
Performing Africa. Trade Paper. Princeton University Press.
Princeton, NJ. 2002. 272p. ISBN:0-691-07489-5, ISBN13:
978-0-691-07489-4. Dewey:781.62/96345. LCCN:2001-055408.

Audience: **u,f.** *Choice, 2003.*

Erlmann, Veit   ML350.E77 1991
African Stars: Studies in Black South African Performance.
Trade Cloth. University of Chicago Press. Chicago, IL. 1991.
238p. Chicago Studies in Ethnomusicology
ISBN:0-226-21722-1, ISBN13: 978-0-226-21722-2.
Dewey:780/.89/968. LCCN:91-013927.

Audience: **u,f.** *Choice, 1992.*

Erlmann, Veit   ML3760.E75 1999
Music, Modernity, and the Global Imagination: South Africa and
the West. Trade Cloth. Oxford University Press, Inc. New York,
NY. 1999. 320p. ISBN:0-19-512367-0, ISBN13:
978-0-19-512367-8. Dewey:780/.968. LCCN:98-007806.

Audience: **u,f.**

Erlmann, Veit   ML3760.E76 1995
Nightsong: Performance, Power, and Practice in South Africa.
Joseph Shabalala (Introduction by). Trade Cloth. University of
Chicago Press. Chicago, IL. 1996. 462p. Chicago Studies in

Ethnomusicology ISBN:0-226-21720-5, ISBN13:
978-0-226-21720-8. Dewey:782.42162/963986068.
LCCN:94-024977.

Audience: **u,f.** *Choice, 1996.*

Eyre, Banning   ML3760.E9 2000
In Griot Time: An American Guitarist in Mali. Trade Cloth.
Temple University Press. Philadelphia, PA. 2000. 280p.
ISBN:1-56639-758-8, ISBN13: 978-1-56639-758-2.
Dewey:780.9/6623. LCCN:99-045338.

Audience: **u,f.**

Gray, John   ML120
African Music: A Bibliographical Guide to the Traditional,
Popular, Art, and Liturgical Musics of Sub-Saharan Africa.
Cloth Text. Greenwood Publishing Group, Inc. Portsmouth, NH.
1991. 504p. African Special Bibliographic Ser., No. 14
ISBN:0-313-27769-9, ISBN13: 978-0-313-27769-6.
Dewey:016.78/0967. LCCN:90-024517.

Audience: **l,u,f.** *Choice, 1991.*

Herbst, Anri (Editor)   MT3.A28M87 2003
Musical Arts in Africa : Theory, Practice, and Education. Ed. 1.
Nzewi, Meki. (Editor); Agawu, V. Kofi (Editor). Unisa Press.
2003. ISBN:1-86888-279-9, ISBN13: 978-1-86888-279-3.

Audience: **u,f.**

Lems-Dworkin, Carol   ML120.A35.L4 1991
African Music: A Pan African Annotated Bibliography. Trade
Cloth. Carol Lems-Dworkin Publishers. Evanston, IL. 1991.
400p. ISBN:0-905450-91-4, ISBN13: 978-0-905450-91-9.
Dewey:016.780967. LCCN:91-033581.

Audience: **u,f.** *Choice, 1992.*

Meintjes, Louise   ML3503.S6M45 2003
Sound of Africa!: Making Music Zulu in a South African
Studio. Trade Cloth. Duke University Press. Durham, NC. 2003.
344p. ISBN:0-8223-3027-X, ISBN13: 978-0-8223-3027-1.
Dewey:781.63/0968. LCCN:2002-010220.

Audience: **u,f.** *Choice, 2003.*

Merriam, Alan P.   ML350.1 .M47 1982
African Music in Perspective. Library Binding. Garland
Publishing, Inc. New York, NY. 1982. ISBN:0-8240-9461-1,
ISBN13: 978-0-8240-9461-4. Dewey:780/.96. LCCN:80-008523.

Audience: **u,f.**

Muller, Carol Ann   ML350.5
South African Music: A Century of Traditions in
Transformation. Michael B. Bakan (Editor). Library Binding.
ABC-CLIO, Inc. Santa Barbara, CA. 2004. 300p. World Music
Ser. ISBN:1-57607-276-2, ISBN13: 978-1-57607-276-9.
Dewey:780/.968. LCCN:2004-006533.

Audience: **u,f.** *Choice, 2004.*

Nketia, Joseph H. Kwabena   ML350.N595
The Music of Africa. Paper Text. W. W. Norton & Company,
Inc. New York, NY. 1974. 278p. ISBN:0-393-09249-6, ISBN13:
978-0-393-09249-3. Dewey:780/.96.

Audience: **g,l,u,f.**

Olaniyan, Tejumola   **ML420.F333O43 2004**
🄴 Arrest the Music!: Fela and His Rebel Art and Politics.
E-Book. Indiana University Press. Bloomington, IN. 2004. 248p.
African Expressive Cultures Ser. ISBN:0-253-34461-1, ISBN13:
978-0-253-34461-8. Dewey:781.63/092 B. LCCN:2004-002138.
Audience: **g,l,u,f.** *Choice, 2005.*

Studies in Music History, Criticism, Analysis, and Appreciation > Folk and Traditional Music > North Africa, Middle East, and Central Asia

Schoonmaker, Trevor   **ML410.F2955F45 2003**
  (Editor)
Fela: From West Africa to West Broadway. Cloth over Boards.
Palgrave Macmillan. New York, NY. 2003. 224p.
ISBN:1-4039-6209-X, ISBN13: 978-1-4039-6209-6.
Dewey:781.63/092 B. LCCN:2003-545361.
Audience: **l,u,f.** *Choice, 2004.*

Baily, John   **ML3758.A3B3 1988**
Music of Afghanistan: Professional Musicians in the City of
Herat. Trade Cloth. Cambridge University Press. New York, NY.
1988. 200p. Cambridge Studies in Ethnomusicology
ISBN:0-521-25000-5, ISBN13: 978-0-521-25000-9.
Dewey:780/.958/1. LCCN:87-035525.
Audience: **u,f.** *Choice, 1989.*

Stewart, Gary   **ML3503.C66S74 2001**
Rumba on the River: A History of the Popular Music of Two
Congos. Trade Cloth. Verso Books. London, 2004. 400p.
ISBN:1-85984-368-9, ISBN13: 978-1-85984-368-0.
Dewey:781.6/3/096751.
Audience: **u,f.**

Broughton, Simon et al.   **ML102.W67W67 1999**
Rough Guide to World Music, Vol. 1: Africa, Europe, and the
Middle East. Ellingham, Mark; Trillo, Richard (Authors) Duane,
Orla; Dowell, Vanessa. Rough Guides, Ltd. 2000.
ISBN:1-85828-635-2, ISBN13: 978-1-85828-635-8.
Audience: **g,l,u,f.**

Stone, Ruth M. (Editor)   **ML350.G54 1999**
The Garland Handbook of African Music. Paper Text. Garland
Publishing, Inc. New York, NY. 1999. 432p. Paperbacks Ser., :
ISBN:0-8153-3473-7, ISBN13: 978-0-8153-3473-6.
Dewey:780/.96. LCCN:99-040652.
Audience: **g,l,u,f.**

Cohen, Dalia & Katz, Ruth   **ML3754.C632 2005**
Palestinian Arab Music: A Maqam Tradition in Practice. Trade
Cloth. University of Chicago Press. Chicago, IL. 2006. 416p.
Chicago Studies in Ethnomusicology ISBN:0-226-11298-5,
ISBN13: 978-0-226-11298-5. Dewey:782.42162/927405694.
LCCN:2004-023148.
Audience: **u,f.**

Stone, Ruth M.   **ML350.S76 2004**
Music in West Africa: Experiencing Music, Expressing Culture.
Paper Text. Oxford University Press, Inc. New York, NY. 2004.
128p. Global Music Ser. ISBN:0-19-514500-3, ISBN13:
978-0-19-514500-7. Dewey:780/.966. LCCN:2003-070153.
Audience: **u,f.**

Danielson, Virginia   **ML420.U46D36 1997**
The Voice of Egypt: Umm Kulthum, Arabic Song, and Egyptian
Society in the Twentieth Century. Trade Paper. University of
Chicago Press. Chicago, IL. 1998. 288p. Chicago Studies in
Ethnomusicology ISBN:0-226-13612-4, ISBN13:
978-0-226-13612-7. Dewey:[B]. LCCN:96-045394.
Audience: **g,l,u,f.**

Turino, Thomas   **ML3503.Z55T87 2000**
Nationalists, Cosmopolitans, and Popular Music in Zimbabwe.
Trade Cloth. University of Chicago Press. Chicago, IL. 2000.
352p. Chicago Studies in Ethnomusicology
ISBN:0-226-81701-6, ISBN13: 978-0-226-81701-9.
Dewey:781.63/096891. LCCN:00-008067.
Audience: **u,f.** *Choice, 2001.*

Davis, Ruth Frances   **ML350.5.D38 2004**
Ma'luf: Reflections on the Arab Andalusian Music of Tunisia.
Trade Cloth. Scarecrow Press, Inc. Lanham, MD. 2005. 136p.
ISBN:0-8108-5138-5, ISBN13: 978-0-8108-5138-2.
Dewey:781.62/927061. LCCN:2004-052130.
Audience: **u,f.** *Choice, 2005.*

Waterman, Christopher A.   **ML3503.N6W4 1990**
Juju: A Social History and Ethnography of an African Popular
Music. Trade Paper. University of Chicago Press. Chicago, IL.
1990. 285p. Chicago Studies in Ethnomusicology
ISBN:0-226-87465-6, ISBN13: 978-0-226-87465-4.
Dewey:781.63/09669/2. LCCN:89-028691.
Audience: **u,f.** *Choice, 1991.*

During, Jean, et al.   **ML344.D86 1991**
The Art of Persian Music. Zia Mirabdolbaghi & Dariush Safvat
(Authors). Trade Cloth. Mage Publishers, Inc. Washington, DC.
1991. 1192p. ISBN:0-934211-22-1, ISBN13: 978-0-934211-22-2.
Dewey:780/.955. LCCN:90-043217.
Audience: **u,f.** *Choice, 1991.*

El-Mallah, Issam   **ML345.O5**
Omani Traditional Music. Tutzing: H. Schneider. 1998.
Publications of the Oman Centre for Traditional Music; Vol. 5;
Variation: Matbuʻat Markaz ʻUman lil-Musiqá al-Taqlidiyah
ISBN:3-7952-0914-5, ISBN13: 978-3-7952-0914-8.
Audience: **u,f.**

Farhat, Hormoz   **ML344.F32 2004**
The Dastgah Concept in Persian Music. John Blacking
(Contribution by). Trade Paper. Cambridge University Press.
New York, NY. 2004. 213p. Cambridge Studies in
Ethnomusicology Ser. ISBN:0-521-54206-5, ISBN13:
978-0-521-54206-7. Dewey:780/.955.
Audience: **u,f.** *Choice, 1991.*

Farmer, Henry G.   **ML189.F3**
A History of Arabian Music to the XIIIth Century. Trade Cloth.
Luzac Oriental Ltd. Corsham, 1996. 264p. ISBN:1-898942-01-3,
ISBN13: 978-1-898942-01-6. Dewey:780.917671.
Audience: **u,f.**

Lems-Dworkin, Carol   **ML120.A35.L4 1991**
African Music: A Pan African Annotated Bibliography. Trade
Cloth. Carol Lems-Dworkin Publishers. Evanston, IL. 1991.
400p. ISBN:0-905450-91-4, ISBN13: 978-0-905450-91-9.
Dewey:016.780967. LCCN:91-033581.
Audience: **u,f.** *Choice, 1992.*

Malm, William P.   **ML330.M3 1996**
Music Cultures of the Pacific, the Near East and Asia. Ed. 3.
Trade Paper. Prentice Hall PTR. Upper Saddle River, NJ. 1995.
278p. Prentice Hall History of Music Ser. ISBN:0-13-182387-6,
ISBN13: 978-0-13-182387-7. Dewey:780/.95. LCCN:94-048578.
Audience: **g,l,u,f.**

Naroditskaya, Inna   **ML315**
Song from the Land of Fire: Continuity and Change in
Azerbaijanian Mugham. Paper over Boards. Routledge. New
York, NY. 2003. 290p. Current Research in Ethnomusicology
Ser., Vol. 6:Outstanding Dissertations ISBN:0-415-94021-4,
ISBN13: 978-0-415-94021-4. Dewey:782.42162/94361/009.
LCCN:2002-154338.
Audience: **u,f.**

Nettl, Bruno (Editor)   **ML344**
The Radif of Persian Music : Studies of Structure and Cultural
Context in the Classical Music of Iran. Elephant & Cat. 1992.
Audience: **u,f.**

Nettl, Bruno, et al.   **ML3545.N285 1990**
Folk and Traditional Music of the Western Continents. Ed. 3.
Gerard Behaque & Valerie Goertzen (Authors). Paper Text.
Prentice Hall PTR. Upper Saddle River, NJ. 1989. 304p.
ISBN:0-13-323247-6, ISBN13: 978-0-13-323247-9.
Dewey:781.7/09182/1. LCCN:89-034653.
Audience: **g,l,u,f.**

Racy, A. J.   **ML348**
Making Music in the Arab World: The Culture and Artistry of
Tarab. Julia A. Clancy-Smith, Israel Gershoni, Roger Owen,
Yezid Sayigh, Charles Tripp & Judith E. Tucker (Contribution
by). Trade Paper. Cambridge University Press. New York, NY.

2004. 264p. Cambridge Middle East Studies
ISBN:0-521-31685-5, ISBN13: 978-0-521-31685-9.
Dewey:780/.917/4927.
Audience: **u,f.** *Choice, 2003.*

Sakata, Hiromi Lorraine   **ML345.A35S24 2002**
Music in the Mind: The Concepts of Music and Musician in
Afghanistan. Ed. 2. Margaret Mills (Foreword by). Trade Cloth.
Smithsonian Institution Press. Washington, DC. 2002. 288p.
ISBN:1-58834-090-2, ISBN13: 978-1-58834-090-0.
Dewey:780/.9581. LCCN:2002-026923.
Audience: **u,f.**

Shannon, Jonathan Holt   **ML3795.S415 2006**
Among the Jasmine Trees: Music and Modernity in
Contemporary Syria. Library Binding. Wesleyan University
Press. Middletown, CT. 2006. 292p. Music/Culture Ser.
ISBN:0-8195-6798-1, ISBN13: 978-0-8195-6798-7.
Dewey:780.95691. LCCN:2005-028912.
Audience: **u,f.**

Shiloah, Amnon   **ML189 .S5 1993**
The Dimension of Music in Islamic and Jewish Culture. Trade
Cloth. Ashgate Publishing, Ltd. Aldershot, 1993. 320p. Collected
Studies, No. CS 393 ISBN:0-86078-352-9, ISBN13:
978-0-86078-352-7. Dewey:780/.8/82971. LCCN:93-000585.
Audience: **u,f.**

Shiloah, Amnon   **ML3545.S486 1995**
Music in the World of Islam: A Socio-Cultural Study. Cloth
Text. Wayne State University Press. Detroit, MI. 1995. 262p.
ISBN:0-8143-2589-0, ISBN13: 978-0-8143-2589-6.
Dewey:780/.917/671. LCCN:94-047620.
Audience: **g,l,u,f.** *Choice, 1995.*

Simms, Rob   **ML3758.I7S56 2004**
The Repertoire of Iraqi Maqam. Trade Cloth. Scarecrow Press,
Inc. Lanham, MD. 2003. 208p. ISBN:0-8108-4758-2, ISBN13:
978-0-8108-4758-3. Dewey:780/.9567. LCCN:2003-013957.
Audience: **u,f.**

Stokes, Martin   **ML345.T8**
The Arabesk Debate: Music and Musicians in Modern Turkey.
Trade Cloth. Oxford University Press, Inc. New York, NY. 1993.
288p. Oxford Studies in Social and Cultural Anthropology -
Cultural Forms ISBN:0-19-827367-3, ISBN13:
978-0-19-827367-7. Dewey:780.949618. LCCN:91-039946.
Audience: **u,f.**

Touma, Habib Hassan   **ML348**
The Music of the Arabs. Trade Paper, Compact Disc, Mixed
Media. Hal Leonard Corporation. Milwaukee, WI. 2003. 260p.
ISBN:1-57467-081-6, ISBN13: 978-1-57467-081-3.
Dewey:780.9/174927.
Audience: **g,l,u,f.**

Studies in Music History, Criticism, Analysis, and Appreciation > Folk and Traditional Music > South Asia, Northeast Asia, Southeast Asia, and Oceania

Baranovitch, Nimrod　　　**ML3918.P67 B36 2003**
China's New Voices: Popular Music, Ethnicity, Gender, and Politics, 1978-1997. Trade Cloth. University of California Press. Berkeley, CA. 2003. 336p. ISBN:0-520-23449-9, ISBN13: 978-0-520-23449-9. Dewey:306.4/84. LCCN:2002-068452.
Audience: **u,f**.

Broughton, Simon, et al.　　　**ML160**
Rough Guide to World Music, Vol. 2: Latin and North America, the Caribbean, Asia, and the Pacific. Ellingham, Mark; Trillo, Richard (Authors) Duane, Orla; Dowell, Vanessa. Rough Guides, Ltd. 2000. ISBN:1-85828-636-0, ISBN13: 978-1-85828-636-5.
Audience: **g,l,u,f**.

De Ferranti, Hugh　　　**ML535.D4 2000**
Japanese Musical Instruments. Trade Cloth. Oxford University Press, Inc. New York, NY. 2000. 112p. Images of Asia Ser. ISBN:0-19-590500-8, ISBN13: 978-0-19-590500-7. Dewey:784.1952. LCCN:00-021246.
Audience: **u,f**.

Farrell, Gerry　　　**ML338**
Indian Music and the West. Trade Paper. Oxford University Press, Inc. New York, NY. 2000. 254p. ISBN:0-19-816717-2, ISBN13: 978-0-19-816717-4. Dewey:780.9/54.
Audience: **u,f**. *Choice, 1998.*

Galliano, Luciana　　　**ML240.5.G35 2002**
Yogaku: Japanese Music in the 20th Century. Trade Cloth. Scarecrow Press, Inc. Lanham, MD. 2002. 368p. ISBN:0-8108-4325-0, ISBN13: 978-0-8108-4325-7. Dewey:780/.952/0904. LCCN:2002-003145.
Audience: **u,f**.

Gold, Lisa　　　**ML345.I5G65 2004**
Music in Bali: Experiencing Music, Expressing Culture. Trade Cloth. Oxford University Press, Inc. New York, NY. 2004. 208p. Global Music Ser. ISBN:0-19-514150-4, ISBN13: 978-0-19-514150-4. Dewey:780/.9598/6. LCCN:2004-041563.
Audience: **u,f**.

Guy, Nancy　　　**ML1751.T25G89 2005**
Peking Opera and Politics in Taiwan. Trade Cloth. University of Illinois Press. Champaign, IL. 2005. 256p. ISBN:0-252-02973-9, ISBN13: 978-0-252-02973-8. Dewey:306.4/84/0951156. LCCN:2004-023670.
Audience: **u,f**. *Choice, 2006.*

Hesselink, Nathan (Editor)　　　**ML3752.5.C66 2002**
Contemporary Directions: Korean Folk Music Engaging the Twentieth Century and Beyond. Trade Cloth. University of California, Institute of East Asian Studies. Berkeley, CA. 2002.

262p. Korea Research Monograph Ser., Vol. 27 ISBN:1-55729-074-1, ISBN13: 978-1-55729-074-8. Dewey:781.62/957. LCCN:2002-020745.
Audience: **u,f**.

Howard, Keith　　　**ML537.H68 1995**
Korean Musical Instruments. Trade Cloth. Oxford University Press, Inc. New York, NY. 1996. 80p. Images of Asia Ser. ISBN:0-19-586177-9, ISBN13: 978-0-19-586177-8. Dewey:784.1/9/519. LCCN:95-031765.
Audience: **u,f**.

Jones, Stephen　　　**ML3746**
Folk Music of China: Living Instrumental Traditions. Paper Text. Oxford University Press, Inc. New York, NY. 1999. 456p. ISBN:0-19-816718-0, ISBN13: 978-0-19-816718-1. Dewey:781.6/2/00951. LCCN:98-033455.
Audience: **u,f**. *Choice, 1996.*

Kanahele, George S. (Editor)　　　**ML200.7.H4 H45**
Hawaiian Music and Musicians: An Illustrated History. Trade Cloth. University of Hawaii Press. Honolulu, HI. 1979. 576p. ISBN:0-8248-0578-X, ISBN13: 978-0-8248-0578-4. Dewey:781.7/969. LCCN:79-014233.
Audience: **u,f**.

Lee, Yuan-Yuan & Shen, Sinyan　　　**ML531.L43 1999**
Chinese Musical Instruments. Yuan-Yuan Lee & Sinyan Shen (Editors). Paper Text. Chinese Music Society of North America. Woodridge, IL. 1999. vi, 200p. Chinese Music Monograph Ser. ISBN:1-880464-03-9, ISBN13: 978-1-880464-03-8. Dewey:784.1951. LCCN:99-031752.
Audience: **u,f**.

Liang, David Mingyue　　　**ML336**
Music of the Billion: An Introduction to Chinese Musical Culture. New York: Heinrichshofen Edition: Sole Selling Agents for USA and Canada, C.F. Peters. 1985. Paperbacks on Musicology ; 8 ISBN:3-7959-0474-9, ISBN13: 978-3-7959-0474-6.
Audience: **g,l,u,f**.

Lovrick, Peter　　　**ML1751.C4S58 1997**
Chinese Opera: Images and Stories. Siu Wang-Ngai (Illustrator). Trade Cloth. University of Washington Press. Seattle, WA. 1997. 160p. ISBN:0-295-97610-1, ISBN13: 978-0-295-97610-5. Dewey:782.1/0951. LCCN:96-039595.
Audience: **u,f**.

Mackerras, Colin　　　**ML1751.C4M32 1997**
Peking Opera. Trade Cloth. Oxford University Press, Inc. New York, NY. 1997. 80p. Images of Asia Ser. ISBN:0-19-587729-2, ISBN13: 978-0-19-587729-8. Dewey:782.1/0951. LCCN:97-006887.
Audience: **u,f**. *Choice, 1998.*

Malm, William P.　　　**ML330.M3 1996**
Music Cultures of the Pacific, the Near East and Asia. Ed. 3.

Trade Paper. Prentice Hall PTR. Upper Saddle River, NJ. 1995. 278p. Prentice Hall History of Music Ser. ISBN:0-13-182387-6, ISBN13: 978-0-13-182387-7. Dewey:780/.95. LCCN:94-048578.

Audience: **g,l,u,f.**

Malm, William P.   **ML340 .M34 1986**
Six Hidden Views of Japanese Music. Trade Cloth. University of California Press. Berkeley, CA. 1986. 200p. Ernest Bloch Lectures, No. 6 ISBN:0-520-05045-2, ISBN13: 978-0-520-05045-7. Dewey:781.752. LCCN:83-017984.

Audience: **u,f.** *Choice, 1986.*

Malm, William P.   **ML340**
Traditional Japanese Music and Musical Instruments. Ed. 2. Trade Cloth. Kodansha International. Tokyo, 2001. 356p. ISBN:4-7700-2395-2, ISBN13: 978-4-7700-2395-7. Dewey:780.9/52.

Audience: **u,f.**

Marrett, Allan   **ML3770.M27 2005**
Songs, Dreaming, and Ghosts: The Wangga of North Australia. Library Binding. Wesleyan University Press. Middletown, CT. 2005. 320p. Music/Culture Ser. ISBN:0-8195-6617-9, ISBN13: 978-0-8195-6617-1. Dewey:781.62/9915094295. LCCN:2005-042261.

Audience: **u,f.**

Matusky, Patricia & Tan,   **ML3758.M4**
Sooi Beng (Editors)
The Music of Malaysia: The Classical, Folk and Syncretic Traditions. University of London, School of Oriental and African Studies Staff (Contribution by). Trade Cloth. Ashgate Publishing, Ltd. Aldershot, 2004. 494p. SOAS Musicology Ser. ISBN:0-7546-0831-X, ISBN13: 978-0-7546-0831-8. Dewey:780/.9595. LCCN:2002-027782.

Audience: **u,f.**

McLean, Mervyn   **ML3770.M35 1996**
Maori Music. Trade Cloth. Auckland University Press. Auckland, 1997. 480p. ISBN:1-86940-144-1, ISBN13: 978-1-86940-144-3. Dewey:781.62/99442. LCCN:96-232016.

Audience: **u,f.** *Choice, 1997.*

McLean, Mervyn   **ML360.M28 1999**
Weavers of Song: Polynesian Music and Dance. Trade Cloth, CD-ROM. University of Hawaii Press. Honolulu, HI. 2000. 560p. ISBN:0-8248-2271-4, ISBN13: 978-0-8248-2271-2. Dewey:780/.996. LCCN:99-034404.

Audience: **u,f.** *Choice, 2000.*

McPhee, Colin   **ML345.B3 M25 1976**
Music in Bali. Paper Text. Da Capo Press, Inc. Cambridge, MA. 1976. xviii, 430p. Music Reprint Ser. ISBN:0-306-70778-0, ISBN13: 978-0-306-70778-0. Dewey:781.7/598/6. LCCN:76-004979.

Audience: **u,f.**

Miller, Terry E.   **ML345**
Traditional Music of the Lao: Kaen Playing and Mawlum Singing in Northeast Thailand, 13. Trade Cloth. Greenwood Publishing Group, Inc. Portsmouth, NH. 1985. 333p.

Contributions in Intercultural and Comparative Studies Ser., No. 13 ISBN:0-313-24765-X, ISBN13: 978-0-313-24765-1. Dewey:781.7/29591. LCCN:84-022538.

Audience: **u,f.**

Morton, David   **ML345.T/**
The Traditional Music of Thailand. Trade Cloth. University of California Press. Berkeley, CA. 1976. xv, 258p. ISBN:0-520-01876-1, ISBN13: 978-0-520-01876-1. Dewey:781.7/593. LCCN:70-142048.

Audience: **u,f.**

Myers, John E. B.   **ML1015.P5.M9 1992**
The Way of the Pipa: Structure and Imagery in Chinese Lute Music. Trade Cloth. Kent State University Press. Kent, OH. 1992. 152p. World Music Ser. ISBN:0-87338-455-5, ISBN13: 978-0-87338-455-1. Dewey:787.820951. LCCN:91-033965.

Audience: **u,f.** *Choice, 1993.*

Pratt, Keith   **ML342.P7 1987**
Korean Music: Its History and Performance. Trade Cloth. Faber & Faber, Inc. New York, NY. 1987. 275p. ISBN:0-571-10081-3, ISBN13: 978-0-571-10081-1. Dewey:781.7519. LCCN:86-032769.

Audience: **u,f.**

Qureshi, Regula B.   **ML3197**
Sufi Music of India and Pakistan: Sound, Context and Meaning in Qawwali. Trade Paper. Kazi Publications, Inc. Chicago, IL. 1996. 266p. ISBN:0-614-21357-6, ISBN13: 978-0-614-21357-7. Dewey:783/.02/9740954.

Audience: **u,f.**

Rees, Helen   **ML3746.7.Y8R44 2000**
Echoes of History: Naxi Music in Modern China. Trade Paper. Oxford University Press, Inc. New York, NY. 2000. 293p. ISBN:0-19-512950-4, ISBN13: 978-0-19-512950-2. Dewey:781.62/95. LCCN:99-054366.

Audience: **u,f.**

Ruckert, George E.   **ML338.R83 2003**
Music in North India: Experiencing Music, Expressing Culture. Bonnie C. Wade (Editor). Trade Cloth. Oxford University Press, Inc. New York, NY. 2003. 112p. Global Music Ser., Vol. 4 ISBN:0-19-513992-5, ISBN13: 978-0-19-513992-1. Dewey:780/.954. LCCN:2003-053588.

Audience: **l,u,f.**

Shankar, Ravi   **ML1015.S6**
Raga Mala: The Autobiography of Ravi Shankar. Yehudi Menuhin (Afterword by), George Harrison (Foreword by). Trade Paper. Welcome Rain Publishers. New York, NY. 2001. 352p. ISBN:1-56649-217-3, ISBN13: 978-1-56649-217-1. Dewey:787.8/2.

Audience: **g,l,u,f.**

Shen, Sin-Yan   **ML336**
Chinese Music and Orchestration: A Primer on Principles and Practice. Trade Paper. Chinese Music Society of North America.

Woodridge, IL. 1991. 196p. Chinese Music Monograph Ser. ISBN:1-880464-00-4, ISBN13: 978-1-880464-00-7. Dewey:784/.0951.

Audience: **u,f.**

Shen, Sin-Yan   ML336.5.S54 2001
Chinese Music in the 20th Century. Yuan-Yuan Lee (Editor). Trade Paper. Chinese Music Society of North America. Woodridge, IL. 2001. 250p. Chinese Music Monograph Ser., Vol. 4 ISBN:1-880464-04-7, ISBN13: 978-1-880464-04-5. Dewey:780/.951/0904. LCCN:00-065668.

Audience: **g,l,u,f.**

Shen, Sinyan   ML336
China: A Journey into Its Musical Art. Yuan-Yuan Lee (Editor). Paper Text. Chinese Music Society of North America. Woodridge, IL. 1999. 200p. Chinese Music Monograph Ser. ISBN:1-880464-07-1, ISBN13: 978-1-880464-07-6. Dewey:780/.951.

Audience: **g,l,u,f.**

So, Jenny F.   ML462.W33A78 2000
Music in the Age of Confucius. Trade Cloth. University of Washington Press. Seattle, WA. 2000. 152p. ISBN:0-295-97953-4, ISBN13: 978-0-295-97953-3. Dewey:780/.951/0901. LCCN:99-056011.

Audience: **u,f.** *Choice, 2001.*

Song, Bang-song   ML342
Korean Music: Historical and Other Aspects. Seoul, Korea: Jimoondang Pub. Co.. 2000. Korean Studies Series: Chimundang Seoul, Korea; No. 13 ISBN:89-88095-13-8, ISBN13: 978-89-88095-13-3.

Audience: **u,f.**

Sorrell, Neil   M1628
A Guide to the Gamelan. Martin Hatch (Illustrator). Trade Paper. Society for Asian Music. Ithaca, NY. 2000. A Society for Asian Music Edition ISBN:0-9669915-0-8, ISBN13: 978-0-9669915-0-5. Dewey:784.6.

Audience: **g,l,u,f.** *Choice, 1991.*

Sumarsam   ML345.I5S86 1995
Gamelan: Cultural Interaction and Musical Development in Central Java. Trade Cloth. University of Chicago Press. Chicago, IL. 1995. 368p. Chicago Studies in Ethnomusicology ISBN:0-226-78010-4, ISBN13: 978-0-226-78010-8. Dewey:780/.9598/2. LCCN:94-043013.

Audience: **u,f.** *Choice, 1996.*

Sutton, R. Anderson   ML1251.I53S93 1991
Traditions of Gamelan Music in Java: Musical Pluralism and Regional Identity. John Blacking (Contribution by). Trade Cloth. Cambridge University Press. New York, NY. 1991. 313p. Studies in Ethnomusicology ISBN:0-521-36153-2, ISBN13: 978-0-521-36153-8. Dewey:784.2/09598/2. LCCN:90-040031.

Audience: **u,f.** *Choice, 1992.*

Tenzer, Michael   ML1251.I53
Gamelan Gong Kebyar : The Art of Twentieth-Century Balinese Music. University of Chicago Press. 2000. ISBN:0-226-79281-1, ISBN13: 978-0-226-79281-1.

Audience: **u,f.**

Thielemann, Selina   ML330.T54 1999
The Music of South Asia. Trade Cloth. Ashish Publishing House. New Delhi, 1999. v, 690p. ISBN:81-7648-057-6, ISBN13: 978-81-7648-057-4. Dewey:780/.954. LCCN:99-940514.

Audience: **g,l,u,f.**

Thrasher, Alan R.   ML531.T47 2000
Chinese Musical Instruments. Cloth Text. Oxford University Press, Inc. New York, NY. 2001. 124p. Images of Asia Ser. ISBN:0-19-590777-9, ISBN13: 978-0-19-590777-3. Dewey:784.1951. LCCN:00-067752.

Audience: **u,f.**

Viswanathan, T., et al.   ML338
Music in South India : Tthe Karnatak Concert Tradition and Beyond : Experiencing Music, Expressing Culture. Allen, Matthew Harp (Author). Oxford University Press. 2004. Global Music Ser. ISBN:0-19-514590-9, ISBN13: 978-0-19-514590-8.

Audience: **u,f.**

Wade, Bonnie C.   ML1451.I5W3 1984
Khyal: Creativity Within North India's Classical Music Tradition. Trade Cloth. Cambridge University Press. New York, NY. 1985. 334p. Cambridge Studies in Ethnomusicology ISBN:0-521-25659-3, ISBN13: 978-0-521-25659-9. Dewey:784.3/00954. LCCN:84-001755.

Audience: **u,f.**

Wade, Bonnie C.   ML338
Music in India: The Classical Traditions. Trade Cloth. Manohar Publications. New Delhi, 2001. 262p. ISBN:81-7304-395-7, ISBN13: 978-81-7304-395-6. Dewey:781.754.

Audience: **g,l,u,f.**

Wade, Bonnie C.   ML340.W22 2004
Music in Japan: Experiencing Music, Expressing Culture. Trade Paper. Oxford University Press, Inc. New York, NY. 2004. 206p. Global Music Ser. ISBN:0-19-514488-0, ISBN13: 978-0-19-514488-8. Dewey:780/.952. LCCN:2004-041486.

Audience: **g,l,u,f.**

Witzleben, J. Lawrence   ML3746.8.S5W57 1995
Silk and Bamboo Music in Shanghai: The Jiangnan Sizhu Instrumental Ensemble Tradition. Trade Cloth. Kent State University Press. Kent, OH. 1995. 224p. World Music Ser. ISBN:0-87338-499-7, ISBN13: 978-0-87338-499-5. Dewey:781.62/951051132. LCCN:94-009092.

Audience: **u,f.**

Studies in Music History, Criticism, Analysis, and Appreciation > Folk and Traditional Music > South America and the Caribbean

Aparicio, Frances R.   ML3535.5.A63 1998
Listening to Salsa: Gender, Latin Popular Music, and Puerto Rican Cultures. Library Binding. Wesleyan University Press. Middletown, CT. 1998. 302p. Music Culture Ser. ISBN:0-8195-5306-9, ISBN13: 978-0-8195-5306-5. Dewey:781.64. LCCN:97-009121.
Audience: **u,f.** *Choice, 1998.*

Appleby, David P.   ML232 .A74 1983
The Music of Brazil. Cloth Text. University of Texas Press. Austin, TX. 1983. 223p. ISBN:0-292-75068-4, ISBN13: 978-0-292-75068-5. Dewey:781.781. LCCN:82-013613.
Audience: **g,l,u,f.**

Austerlitz, Paul   ML3465.A95 1997
Merengue: Dominican Music and Dominican Identity. Robert F. Thompson (Foreword by). Trade Cloth. Temple University Press. Philadelphia, PA. 1997. 224p. ISBN:1-56639-483-X, ISBN13: 978-1-56639-483-3. Dewey:784.18/88. LCCN:96-024778.
Audience: **u,f.** *Choice, 1997.*

Averill, Gage   ML3486.H3A94 1997
A Day for the Hunter, a Day for the Prey: Popular Music and Power in Haiti. Trade Cloth. University of Chicago Press. Chicago, IL. 1997. 306p. Chicago Studies in Ethnomusicology ISBN:0-226-03291-4, ISBN13: 978-0-226-03291-7. Dewey:781.63/097294. LCCN:96-034209.
Audience: **u,f.** *Choice, 1997.*

Azzi, Maria Susana &   ML410.P579A99 2000
Collier, Simon
Le Grand Tango: The Life and Music of Astor Piazzolla. Trade Cloth. Oxford University Press, Inc. New York, NY. 2000. 344p. ISBN:0-19-512777-3, ISBN13: 978-0-19-512777-5. Dewey:780/.92 B. LCCN:99-031795.
Audience: **g,l,u,f.**

Barrow, Steve & Dalton,   ML3532.B37 2004
Peter
The Rough Guide to Reggae. Ed. 3. Trade Paper. Rough Guides, Ltd. London, 2004. 528p. Rough Guide Music Guides Ser. ISBN:1-84353-329-4, ISBN13: 978-1-84353-329-0. Dewey:781.646. LCCN:2004-558939.
Audience: **g,l,u,f.**

Behague, Gerard   ML199
Music in Latin America: An Introduction. Cloth Text. Prentice Hall PTR. Upper Saddle River, NJ. 1979. xiv, 369p. History of Music Ser. ISBN:0-13-608919-4, ISBN13: 978-0-13-608919-3. Dewey:780/.98. LCCN:78-017264.
Audience: **g,l,u,f.**

Bordowitz, Hank   ML3532
Every Little Thing Gonna Be Alright: The Bob Marley Reader. Trade Paper. Da Capo Press, Inc. Cambridge, MA. 2004. 336p. ISBN:0-306-81340-8, ISBN13: 978-0-306-81340-5. Dewey:782.421646/092 B. LCCN:2004-009767.
Audience: **g,l,u,f.**

Bradley, Lloyd   ML3532
Bass Culture: When Reggae Was King. London: Viking. 2000. ISBN:0-670-85563-4, ISBN13: 978-0-670-85563-6.
Audience: **u,f.**

Broughton, Simon, et al.   ML160
Rough Guide to World Music, Vol. 2: Latin and North America, the Caribbean, Asia, and the Pacific. Ellingham, Mark; Trillo, Richard (Authors) Duane, Orla; Dowell, Vanessa. Rough Guides, Ltd. 2000. ISBN:1-85828-636-0, ISBN13: 978-1-85828-636-5.
Audience: **g,l,u,f.**

Carpentier, Alejo   ML207.C8
Music in Cuba. Timothy Brennan (Editor) (Introduction by); Alan West-Durán (Translator). Minneapolis: University of Minnesota Press. 2001. Cultural Studies of the Americas; Vol. 5 ISBN:0-8166-3229-4, ISBN13: 978-0-8166-3229-9.
Audience: **u,f.**

Chang, Kevin O. & Chen,   ML3532.C45 1998
Wayne
Reggae Routes: The Story of Jamaican Music. Trade Paper. Temple University Press. Philadelphia, PA. 1997. 250p. ISBN:1-56639-629-8, ISBN13: 978-1-56639-629-5. Dewey:781.646/097292. LCCN:98-164555.
Audience: **g,l,u,f.**

Clark, Walter Aaron   ML3475.F76 2002
(Editor)
From Tejano to Tango: Latin American Popular Music. Paper over Boards. Garland Publishing, Inc. New York, NY. 2002. 320p. Perspectives in Global Pop Ser. ISBN:0-8153-3639-X, ISBN13: 978-0-8153-3639-6. Dewey:781.64/098. LCCN:2001-048174.
Audience: **g,l,u,f.**

Courlander, Harold   ML3565.H3 C7 1973
Haiti Singing. Trade Cloth. Cooper Square Publishers, Inc. New York, NY. 1973. 274p. ISBN:0-8154-0461-1, ISBN13: 978-0-8154-0461-3. Dewey:784.4/97294. LCCN:72-095270.
Audience: **u,f.**

Crook, Larry   ML232
Brazilian Music: Northeastern Traditions and the Heartbeat of a Modern Nation. Michael B. Bakan (Editor). Library Binding. ABC-CLIO, Inc. Santa Barbara, CA. 2005. 350p. World Music Ser. ISBN:1-57607-287-8, ISBN13: 978-1-57607-287-5. Dewey:780/.981/1. LCCN:2005-021774.
Audience: **u,f.**

Dudley, Shannon & Wade,   ML207.T759
Bonnie C.
Carnival Music In Trinidad: Experiencing Music, Expressing Culture. Trade Cloth. Oxford University Press, Inc. New York,

NY. 2003. 128p. Global Music Ser., Vol. 2 ISBN:0-19-513832-5, ISBN13: 978-0-19-513832-0. Dewey:781.5/5. LCCN:2003-041941.

Audience: **u,f.**

Dunn, Christopher   2001035148 [ML]

Brutality Garden: Tropicalia and the Emergence of a Brazilian Counterculture. Trade Paper. University of North Carolina Press. Chapel Hill, NC. 2001. 276p. ISBN:0-8078-4976-6, ISBN13: 978-0-8078-4976-7. Dewey:306.4/84. LCCN:2001-035148.

Audience: **u,f.** *Choice, 2002.*

Fernandez, Raul A.   ML3506.F46 2002

Latin Jazz: The Perfect Combination - La Combinacion Perfecta. Trade Paper. Chronicle Books LLC. San Francisco, CA. 2002. 400p. ISBN:0-8118-3608-8, ISBN13: 978-0-8118-3608-1. Dewey:781.65/7. LCCN:2002-067229.

Audience: **g,l,u,f.**

Figueroa, Rafael (Compiled by)   ML128

Salsa and Related Genres: A Bibliographical Guide. Cloth Text. Greenwood Publishing Group, Inc. Portsmouth, NH. 1992. 128p. Music Reference Collection, No. 38 ISBN:0-313-27883-0, ISBN13: 978-0-313-27883-9. Dewey:016.7816268. LCCN:92-023778.

Audience: **g,l,u,f.**

Fleurant, Gerdes   ML3197

Dancing Spirits: Rhythms and Rituals of Haitian Vodun, the Rada Rite. Trade Cloth. Greenwood Publishing Group, Inc. Portsmouth, NH. 1996. 240p. Contributions to the Study of Music and Dance Ser., Vol. 42 ISBN:0-313-29718-5, ISBN13: 978-0-313-29718-2. Dewey:781.7/96. LCCN:95-046061.

Audience: **u,f.** *Choice, 1997.*

Fryer, Peter   ML232

Rhythms of Resistance: African Musical Heritage in Brazil. Library Binding. Wesleyan University Press. Middletown, CT. 2000. 281p. ISBN:0-8195-6417-6, ISBN13: 978-0-8195-6417-7. Dewey:780.9/81. LCCN:00-100046.

Audience: **u,f.**

Guilbault, Jocelyne, et al.   ML3485.5.G84 1993

Zouk: World Music in the West Indies. Gage Averill, Edouard Benoit & Gregory Rabess (Authors). Trade Cloth, Mixed Media, Compact Disc. University of Chicago Press. Chicago, IL. 1993. 306p. Chicago Studies in Ethnomusicology ISBN:0-226-31041-8, ISBN13: 978-0-226-31041-1. Dewey:781.6209729. LCCN:92-027432.

Audience: **u,f.** *Choice, 1994.*

Hagedorn, Katherine J.   ML3565.H34 2001

Divine Utterances: The Performance of Afro-Cuban Santeria. Trade Paper, Compact Disc. Smithsonian Institution Press. Washington, DC. 2001. 320p. ISBN:1-56098-947-5, ISBN13: 978-1-56098-947-9. Dewey:781.7/96. LCCN:2001-020698.

Audience: **g,l,u,f.**

Hill, Donald R.   ML3470

Calypso Calaloo: Early Carnival Music of Trinidad. Trade Cloth. University Press of Florida. Gainesville, FL. 1993. 352p. ISBN:0-8130-1221-X, ISBN13: 978-0-8130-1221-6. Dewey:781.64. LCCN:93-014862.

Audience: **u,f.**

Katz, David & Spillman, Rob   ML3532.K38 2003

Solid Foundation: An Oral History of Reggae. Trade Paper. Bloomsbury Publishing. New York, NY. 2003. 448p. ISBN:1-58234-143-5, ISBN13: 978-1-58234-143-9. Dewey:781.646/09. LCCN:2003-041879.

Audience: **u,f.**

King, Stephen A.   ML3532.K55 2002

Reggae, Rastafari, and the Rhetoric of Social Control. Barry T. Bays & P. Rene Foster (Contribution by). Trade Cloth. University Press of Mississippi. Jackson, MS. 2006. 176p. ISBN:1-57806-489-9, ISBN13: 978-1-57806-489-2. Dewey:781.646/097292. LCCN:2002-001734.

Audience: **u,f.**

Kuss, Malena (Editor)   ML199.M858 2004

Music in Latin America and the Caribbean: Performing Beliefs: Indigenous Peoples of South America, Central America, and Mexico. Trade Cloth, Compact Disc. University of Texas Press. Austin, TX. 2004. 448p. Joe R. and Teresa Lozano Long Series in Latin American and Latino Art and Culture Ser. ISBN:0-292-70298-1, ISBN13: 978-0-292-70298-1. Dewey:780/.98. LCCN:2004-012481.

Audience: **g,l,u,f.**

Larkin, Colin   ML3532

The Virgin Encyclopedia of Reggae. Trade Paper. Virgin Books Ltd. London, 1998. 352p. Virgin Encyclopedias of Popular Music Ser. ISBN:0-7535-0242-9, ISBN13: 978-0-7535-0242-6. Dewey:782.4/2/1646/03.

Audience: **g,l,u,f.**

Leymarie, Isabelle   ML3486.C8

Cuban Fire: The Story of Salsa and Latin Jazz. Trade Paper. Continuum International Publishing Group, Ltd. London, 2003. 400p. ISBN:0-8264-6566-8, ISBN13: 978-0-8264-6566-5. Dewey:781.6/4/097291.

Audience: **g,l,u,f.**

List, George   ML3575.C7 L55 1983

Music and Poetry in a Colombian Village: A Tri-Cultural Heritage. Trade Cloth. Indiana University Press. Bloomington, IN. 1983. 640p. ISBN:0-253-33951-0, ISBN13: 978-0-253-33951-5. Dewey:781.7861/1. LCCN:82-048534.

Audience: **u,f.**

Livingston-Isenhour, Tamara Elena & Garcia, Thomas George Caracas   ML3487.L58 2005

Choro: A Social History of a Brazilian Popular Music. Trade Cloth, Compact Disc. Indiana University Press. Bloomington, IN. 2005. 304p. Profiles in Popular Music Ser. ISBN:0-253-34541-3, ISBN13: 978-0-253-34541-7. Dewey:781.64/0981. LCCN:2004-026035.

Audience: **u,f.** *Choice, 2006.*

Loza, Steven J.   ML419.P82L6 1999
Tito Puente and the Making of Latin Music. Trade Paper.
University of Illinois Press. Champaign, IL. 1999. 312p. Music
in American Life Ser. ISBN:0-252-06778-9, ISBN13:
978-0-252-06778-5. Dewey:784.4/81888/092 B.
LCCN:98-025507.

         Audience: **l,u,f.** *Choice, 2000.*

Manuel, Peter, et al.   ML3565.M36 2006
Caribbean Currents: Caribbean Music from Rumba to Reggae.
Ed. 2. Kenneth Bilby & Michael Largey (Authors). Trade Cloth.
Temple University Press. Philadelphia, PA. 2006. 336p.
ISBN:1-59213-462-9, ISBN13: 978-1-59213-462-5.
Dewey:780/.9729. LCCN:2005-050676.

         Audience: **g,l,u,f.** *Choice, 1996.*

McAlister, Elizabeth A.   ML3565 .M384 2002
Rara!: Vodou, Power, and Performance in Haiti and Its
Diaspora. Trade Cloth. University of California Press. Berkeley,
CA. 2002. 280p. ISBN:0-520-22822-7, ISBN13:
978-0-520-22822-1. Dewey:394.265/96897294.
LCCN:2001-005016.

         Audience: **u,f.** *Choice, 2002.*

McCann, Bryan   ML3487.B7M39 2004
Hello, Hello Brazil: Popular Music in the Making of Modern
Brazil. Trade Cloth, Pictures or Photographs. Duke University
Press. Durham, NC. 2004. 312p. ISBN:0-8223-3284-1, ISBN13:
978-0-8223-3284-8. Dewey:781.64/0981. LCCN:2003-024989.
         Audience: **u,f.** *Choice, 2004.*

Morales, Ed   ML3475.M67 2003
The Latin Beat: The Rhythms and Roots of Latin Music, from
Bossa Nova to Salsa and Beyond. Trade Paper. Da Capo Press,
Inc. Cambridge, MA. 2003. 400p. ISBN:0-306-81018-2,
ISBN13: 978-0-306-81018-3. Dewey:781.64/098.
LCCN:2003-016423.

         Audience: **g,l,u,f.** *Choice, 2004.*

Moskowitz, David V.   ML102
Caribbean Popular Music: An Encyclopedia of Reggae, Mento,
Ska, Rocksteady, and Dancehall. Trade Cloth. Greenwood
Publishing Group, Inc. Portsmouth, NH. 2005. 368p.
ISBN:0-313-33158-8, ISBN13: 978-0-313-33158-9.
Dewey:781.64/09729/03. LCCN:2005-018629.

         Audience: **g,l,u,f.**

Myers, Helen   ML3565.M94 1998
Music of Hindu Trinidad: Songs from the India Diaspora. Trade
Cloth. University of Chicago Press. Chicago, IL. 1999. 542p.
Chicago Studies in Ethnomusicology ISBN:0-226-55451-1,
ISBN13: 978-0-226-55451-8. Dewey:781.62/914072983.
LCCN:97-025692.

         Audience: **u,f.**

Nettl, Bruno, et al.   ML3545.N285 1990
Folk and Traditional Music of the Western Continents. Ed. 3.
Gerard Behaque & Valerie Goertzen (Authors). Paper Text.
Prentice Hall PTR. Upper Saddle River, NJ. 1989. 304p.
ISBN:0-13-323247-6, ISBN13: 978-0-13-323247-9.
Dewey:781.7/09182/1. LCCN:89-034653.

         Audience: **g,l,u,f.**

Nevin, Jeff   ML3485.N48 2001
Virtuoso Mariachi. Trade Paper. University Press of America,
Inc. Lanham, MD. 2001. 274p. ISBN:0-7618-2173-2, ISBN13:
978-0-7618-2173-1. Dewey:784.4/164/0972.
LCCN:2001-055506.

         Audience: **u,f.**

Olsen, Dale A.   ML3575.A2O57 2001
Music of El Dorado: The Ethnomusicology of Ancient South
American Cultures. Trade Cloth. University Press of Florida.
Gainesville, FL. 2002. xxii, 290p. ISBN:0-8130-2440-4,
ISBN13: 978-0-8130-2440-0. Dewey:780/.98.
LCCN:2001-034780.

         Audience: **u,f.** *Choice, 2002.*

Olsen, Dale A.   ML3575.V3O47 1996
Music of the Warao of Venezuela: Song People of the Rain
Forest. Compact Disc, Trade Cloth. University Press of Florida.
Gainesville, FL. 1996. 432p. ISBN:0-8130-1390-9, ISBN13:
978-0-8130-1390-9. Dewey:781.62/98. LCCN:95-046549.
         Audience: **u,f.** *Choice, 1996.*

Olsen, Dale A. & Sheehy,   ML199.G36 2000
Daniel E. (Editors)
The Garland Handbook of Latin American Music. Paper Text.
Garland Publishing, Inc. New York, NY. 2000. 454p. Reference
Library of the Humanities ISBN:0-8153-3833-3, ISBN13:
978-0-8153-3833-8. Dewey:780/.98. LCCN:00-061754.
         Audience: **g,l,u,f.**

Pacini-Hernandez, Deborah   ML3486.D65P3 1995
Bachata: Social History of a Dominican Popular Music. Paper
Text. Temple University Press. Philadelphia, PA. 1995. 288p.
ISBN:1-56639-300-0, ISBN13: 978-1-56639-300-3.
Dewey:781.64/097293. LCCN:94-029477.

         Audience: **u,f.**

Pedelty, Mark   ML210.8.M4P43 2004
Musical Ritual in Mexico City: From the Aztec to NAFTA.
Trade Cloth. University of Texas Press. Austin, TX. 2004. 352p.
ISBN:0-292-70231-0, ISBN13: 978-0-292-70231-8.
Dewey:780/.972/53. LCCN:2003-018269.

         Audience: **u,f.**

Perrone, Charles A. &   ML3487.B7B76 2001
Dunn, Christopher
Brazilian Popular Music and Globalization. Trade Cloth.
University Press of Florida. Gainesville, FL. 2001. xii, 288p.
ISBN:0-8130-1821-8, ISBN13: 978-0-8130-1821-8.
Dewey:781.64/0981. LCCN:00-069055.
         Audience: **u,f.** *Choice, 2001.*

Peña, Manuel H.   ML3481
Música Tejana : The Cultural Economy of Artistic
Transformation. College Station : Texas A & M University
Press. 1999. University of Houston series in Mexican American
studies; no. 1 ISBN:0-89096-877-2, ISBN13:
978-0-89096-877-2.

         Audience: **u,f.**

Potash, Chris   ML3532
Reggae, Rasta Revolution: Jamaican Music from Ska to Dub.
Trade Paper. Music Sales Corporation. New York, NY. 1997.
250p. ISBN:0-8256-7212-0, ISBN13: 978-0-8256-7212-5.
Dewey:781.6/46/097292. LCCN:97-019893.
                                              Audience: **g,l,u,f.**

Reymundo, Ana Cristina &   ML420.C957A3 2044
  Cruz, Celia
Celia: My Life. Jose Lucas Badue (Translator). Trade Cloth.
HarperCollins Publishers. New York, NY. 2004. 304p.
ISBN:0-06-072553-2, ISBN13: 978-0-06-072553-2.
Dewey:782.42164/092 B. LCCN:2004-046868.
                                              Audience: **g,l,u,f.**

Roberts, John S.   ML3556.R6 1998
Black Music of Two Worlds: African, Caribbean, Latin, and
African-American Traditions. Ed. 2. Paper Text. Thomson
Wadsworth. Belmont, CA. 1998. 368p. ISBN:0-02-864929-X,
ISBN13: 978-0-02-864929-0. Dewey:780/.89/96.
LCCN:98-006587.
                                              Audience: **g,l,u,f.**

Roberts, John S.   ML3477.R63 1998
The Latin Tinge: The Impact of Latin American Music on the
United States. Ed. 2. Trade Cloth. Oxford University Press, Inc.
New York, NY. 1999. 288p. ISBN:0-19-512101-5, ISBN13:
978-0-19-512101-8. Dewey:780/.89/68073. LCCN:98-019580.
                                              Audience: **l,u,f.**

Roberts, John Storm   ML3506
Latin Jazz : The First of the Fusions, 1880s to Today. Schirmer
Books. 1999. ISBN:0-02-864681-9, ISBN13:
978-0-02-864681-7.
                                              Audience: **g,l,u,f.**

Romero, Raul R.   ML236.R66 2001
Debating the Past: Music, Memory, and Identity in the Andes.
Trade Cloth. Oxford University Press, Inc. New York, NY. 2001.
200p. ISBN:0-19-513881-3, ISBN13: 978-0-19-513881-8.
Dewey:780/.985. LCCN:00-047825.
                                    Audience: **u,f.** *Choice, 2002.*

Roy, Maya   ML3486.C8R69 2002
Cuban Music: From Son and Rumba to the Buena Vista Social
Club and Timba Cubana. Denise Afar & Gabriel Asfar
(Translators). Trade Cloth. Markus Wiener Publishers, Inc.
Princeton, NJ. 2002. 260p. ISBN:1-55876-281-7, ISBN13:
978-1-55876-281-7. Dewey:780/.97291. LCCN:2001-056846.
                                              Audience: **g,l,u,f.**

Salazar, Max   ML3411.8.N48
Mambo Kingdom: Latin Music in New York, 1926-1990. Trade
Cloth. Music Sales Corporation. New York, NY. 2002. 350p.
ISBN:0-8256-7277-5, ISBN13: 978-0-8256-7277-4.
Dewey:784.18/88/097471.
                                              Audience: **g,l,u,f.**

Schechter, John Mendell   ML199.M86 1999
Music in Latin American Culture: Regional Traditions. Cloth
Text. Thomson Wadsworth. Belmont, CA. 1999. 512p.

ISBN:0-02-864750-5, ISBN13: 978-0-02-864750-0.
Dewey:780/.98. LCCN:99-013859.
                                    Audience: **g,l,u,f.** *Choice, 1999.*

Schreiner, Claus   ML3575.B7
Musica Brasileira: A History of Popular Music and the People
of Brazil. Weinstein, Mark (Translator). New York: Marion
Boyars. 2002. ISBN:0-7145-3066-2, ISBN13:
978-0-7145-3066-6.
                                              Audience: **u,f.**

Seeger, Anthony   ML3575.B7S36 2004
Why Suya Sing: A Musical Anthropology of an Amazonian
People. Trade Paper. University of Illinois Press. Champaign,
IL. 2004. 170p. ISBN:0-252-07202-2, ISBN13:
978-0-252-07202-4. Dewey:780/.89/984. LCCN:2004-007220.
                                    Audience: **u,f.** *Choice, 1988.*

Shaw, Lisa   ML3417.S53 1999
The Social History of the Brazilian Samba. Trade Cloth.
Ashgate Publishing, Ltd. Aldershot, 1999. 211p. Studies in
Ethnomusicology ISBN:1-84014-289-8, ISBN13:
978-1-84014-289-1. Dewey:784.18/88. LCCN:98-036992.
                                    Audience: **u,f.** *Choice, 1999.*

Sheehy, Daniel   ML3485.S54 2005
Mariachi Music in America: Experiencing Music, Expressing
Culture. Trade Cloth, Compact Disc. Oxford University Press,
Inc. New York, NY. 2005. 110p. Global Music Ser.
ISBN:0-19-514145-8, ISBN13: 978-0-19-514145-0.
Dewey:781.64/089/6872073. LCCN:2004-065663.
                                              Audience: **u,f.**

Simonett, Helena   ML3485.7.S56S55 2001
Banda: Mexican Musical Life Across Borders. Library Binding.
Wesleyan University Press. Middletown, CT. 2001. 336p. Music
Culture Ser. ISBN:0-8195-6429-X, ISBN13: 978-0-8195-6429-0.
Dewey:784.4/164/089/6872. LCCN:2001-026897.
                                              Audience: **u,f.**

Stevenson, Robert   ML3549
Music in Aztec and Inca Territory. Trade Cloth. University of
California Press. Berkeley, CA. 1977. ISBN:0-520-03169-5,
ISBN13: 978-0-520-03169-2. Dewey:781.772.
                                              Audience: **g,l,u,f.**

Stolzoff, Norman C.   ML3486.J3S76 2000
  (Contribution by)
Wake the Town and Tell the People: Dancehall Culture in
Jamaica. Trade Cloth. Duke University Press. Durham, NC.
2000. 360p. ISBN:0-8223-2478-4, ISBN13: 978-0-8223-2478-2.
Dewey:306.4/84. LCCN:99-050028.
                                              Audience: **u,f.**

Stuempfle, Stephen   ML3486.T7S78 1995
The Steelband Movement: The Forging of a National Art in
Trinidad and Tobago. Trade Cloth. University of Pennsylvania
Press. Philadelphia, PA. 1996. 312p. ISBN:0-8122-3329-8,
ISBN13: 978-0-8122-3329-2. Dewey:784.6/8. LCCN:95-038564.
                                    Audience: **u,f.** *Choice, 1996.*

Sublette, Ned   ML207.C8S83 2004
Cuba and Its Music: From the First Drums to the Mambo. Cloth
over Boards. Chicago Review Press, Inc. Chicago, IL. 2004.
688p. ISBN:1-55652-516-8, ISBN13: 978-1-55652-516-2.
Dewey:780/.97291. LCCN:2003-022097.
Audience: **g,l,u,f.** *Choice, 2004.*

Thompson, Donald (Editor,   ML207.P81M87 2002
Translator)
Music in Puerto Rico: A Reader's Anthology. Trade Cloth.
Scarecrow Press, Inc. Lanham, MD. 2002. 160p.
ISBN:0-8108-3914-8, ISBN13: 978-0-8108-3914-4.
Dewey:780/.97295. LCCN:2002-019510.
Audience: **u,f.**

Turino, Thomas   ML3575.P4.T87 1993
Moving Away from Silence: Music of the Peruvian Altiplano
and the Experience of Urban Migration. Trade Cloth. University
of Chicago Press. Chicago, IL. 1993. 331p. Chicago Studies in
Ethnomusicology ISBN:0-226-81699-0, ISBN13:
978-0-226-81699-9. Dewey:781.62688508536.
LCCN:92-026935.
Audience: **u,f.** *Choice, 1993.*

Veloso, Caetano   ML3487.B7V4513 2002
Tropical Truth: A Story of Music and Revolution in Brazil.
Isabel De Sena & Barbara Einzig (Translators). Trade Cloth.
Alfred A. Knopf Inc. New York, NY. 2002. 368p.
ISBN:0-375-40788-X, ISBN13: 978-0-375-40788-8.
Dewey:781.64/0981. LCCN:2002-066147.
Audience: **g,l,u,f.**

Vianna, Hermano   98-22170 [ML]
The Mystery of Samba: Popular Music and National Identity in
Brazil. John C. Chasteen (Translator). Trade Paper. University of
North Carolina Press. Chapel Hill, NC. 1999. 168p. Latin
America in Translation Ser. ISBN:0-8078-4766-6, ISBN13:
978-0-8078-4766-4. Dewey:784.18/88. LCCN:98-022170.
Audience: **l,u,f.** *Choice, 1999.*

Wade, Peter   ML3487.C7W33 2000
Music, Race, and Nation: Musica Tropical in Colombia. Trade
Cloth. University of Chicago Press. Chicago, IL. 2000. 331p.
Chicago Studies in Ethnomusicology ISBN:0-226-86844-3,
ISBN13: 978-0-226-86844-8. Dewey:781.6409861.
LCCN:99-088600.
Audience: **u,f.** *Choice, 2001.*

Studies in Music History, Criticism, Analysis, and Appreciation > Folk and Traditional Music > North America

Averill, Gage   ML3516.A94 2002
Four Parts, No Waiting: A Social History of American
Barbershop Harmony. Cloth Text. Oxford University Press, Inc.
New York, NY. 2003. 248p. American Musicspheres Ser., Vol. 1
ISBN:0-19-511672-0, ISBN13: 978-0-19-511672-4.
Dewey:782.8/0973. LCCN:2002-000696.
Audience: **u.** *Choice, 2003.*

Broughton, Simon, et al.   ML160
Rough Guide to World Music, Vol. 2: Latin and North America,
the Caribbean, Asia, and the Pacific. Ellingham, Mark; Trillo,
Richard (Authors) Duane, Orla; Dowell, Vanessa. Rough
Guides, Ltd. 2000. ISBN:1-85828-636-0, ISBN13:
978-1-85828-636-5.
Audience: **g,l,u,f.**

Cantwell, Robert S.   ML3551.C36 1996
When We Were Good: The Folk Revival. Trade Cloth. Harvard
University Press. Cambridge, MA. 1996. 432p.
ISBN:0-674-95132-8, ISBN13: 978-0-674-95132-7.
Dewey:781.62/13/00904. LCCN:95-020954.
Audience: **u,f.** *Choice, 1996.*

Cohen, Norm   ML3551
Folk Music: A Regional Exploration. Cloth Text. Greenwood
Publishing Group, Inc. Portsmouth, NH. 2005. 376p. Greenwood
Guides to American Roots Music Ser. ISBN:0-313-32872-2,
ISBN13: 978-0-313-32872-5. Dewey:781.62/00973.
LCCN:2004-017425.
Audience: **g,l,u,f.** *Choice, 2005.*

Cohen, Norm   ML3551.C57 2000
Long Steel Rail: The Railroad in American Folksong. Ed. 2.
Trade Paper. University of Illinois Press. Champaign, IL. 2000.
768p. Music in American Life Ser. ISBN:0-252-06881-5,
ISBN13: 978-0-252-06881-2. Dewey:782.42/162130159.
LCCN:00-269272.
Audience: **u,f.**

Courlander, Harold   ML3556
Negro Folk Music U. S. A. Trade Paper. Dover Publications,
Inc. Mineola, NY. 1998. 324p. ISBN:0-486-27350-4, ISBN13:
978-0-486-27350-1. Dewey:781.6296073. LCCN:92-035475.
Audience: **u,f.**

Cray, Ed   ML419.G852C73 2004
Ramblin Man: The Life and Times of Woody Guthrie. Trade
Cloth. W. W. Norton & Company, Inc. New York, NY. 2004.
384p. ISBN:0-393-04759-8, ISBN13: 978-0-393-04759-2.
Dewey:782.42162/13/0092 B. LCCN:2003-021071.
Audience: **g,l,u,f.** *Choice, 2004.*

Densmore, Frances   ML3557
The American Indians and Their Music. New York, Johnson
Reprint Corp.. 1976. Series in American Studies
Audience: **g,l,u,f.**

Densmore, Frances   ML3557.D36 S7
The Study of Indian Music in the Nineteenth Century. Paper
Text. Classic Textbooks. Murrieta, CA. 1999.
ISBN:1-4047-9514-6, ISBN13: 978-1-4047-9514-3.
Dewey:781.71.
Audience: **u,f.**

Diamond, Beverley, et al.   ML3557.D5 1994
Visions of Sound: Musical Instruments of First Nations
Communities in Northeastern America. M. Sam Cronk &
Franziska Von Rosen (Authors). Trade Paper. University of

Chicago Press. Chicago, IL. 1995. 240p. Chicago Studies in Ethnomusicology ISBN:0-226-14476-3, ISBN13: 978-0-226-14476-4. Dewey:784.1974/08997. LCCN:94-010337.

Audience: **g,l,u,f.**

Dunaway, David K.   **ML420.S445D8 1990**
How Can I Keep from Singing: Pete Seeger. Trade Paper. Da Capo Press, Inc. Cambridge, MA. 1990. 416p. Quality Paperbacks Ser. ISBN:0-306-80399-2, ISBN13: 978-0-306-80399-4. Dewey:782.42162/0092 B. LCCN:89-071394.

Audience: **u,f.**

Guthrie, Woody   **ML410**
Pastures of Plenty: A Self-Portrait. Dave Marsh & Harold Leventhal (Editors). Trade Paper. HarperCollins Publishers. New York, NY. 1992. 288p. ISBN:0-06-098419-8, ISBN13: 978-0-06-098419-9. Dewey:781.62092. LCCN:89-046547.

Audience: **l,u,f.**

Kanahele, George S.   **ML200.7.H4 H45**
(Editor)
Hawaiian Music and Musicians: An Illustrated History. Trade Cloth. University of Hawaii Press. Honolulu, HI. 1979. 576p. ISBN:0-8248-0578-X, ISBN13: 978-0-8248-0578-4. Dewey:781.7/969. LCCN:79-014233.

Audience: **u,f.**

Keeling, Richard   **ML128.F75K44 1997**
North American Indian Music: A Guide to Published Sources and Selected Recordings. Cloth Text. Garland Publishing, Inc. New York, NY. 1997. 472p. Library of Music Ethnology, Vol. 5 ISBN:0-8153-0232-0, ISBN13: 978-0-8153-0232-2. Dewey:016.78/089/97. LCCN:96-041847.

Audience: **u,f.** *Choice, 1997.*

Keil, Charles, et al.   **GV1796.P55K45 1992**
Polka Happiness. Angeliki Keil & Dick Blau (Authors). Trade Cloth. Temple University Press. Philadelphia, PA. 1992. 288p. Visual Studies ISBN:0-87722-819-1, ISBN13: 978-0-87722-819-6. Dewey:793.3/3. LCCN:91-045224.

Audience: **u,f.** *Choice, 1993.*

Koskoff, Ellen   **ML3917.U6M87 2005**
Music Cultures in the United States: An Introduction. Paper over Boards. Routledge. New York, NY. 2005. 448p. ISBN:0-415-96588-8, ISBN13: 978-0-415-96588-0. Dewey:306.4/842/0973. LCCN:2004-019853.

Audience: **g,l,u,f.**

Lankford, Ronald D. Jr. &   **ML3551.L28 2005**
Lankford, Ronald D.
Folk Music U. S. A.: The Changing Voice of Protest. Trade Paper, Perfect. Music Sales Corporation. New York, NY. 2005. 208p. ISBN:0-8256-7300-3, ISBN13: 978-0-8256-7300-9. Dewey:781.62/00973/09045. LCCN:2004-028955.

Audience: **g,l,u.**

Lomax, Alan   **ML3545.L63**
Folk Song Style and Culture. Trade Paper. Books on Demand. Ann Arbor, MI. 383p. American Association for the

Advancement of Science, Publication No. 88 Ser. ISBN:0-598-21930-7, ISBN13: 978-0-598-21930-5. LCCN:68-021545.

Audience: **u,f.**

Lomax, Alan   **ML3551.L65 2003**
Alan Lomax: Selected Writings, 1934-1997. Ronald D. Cohen (Editor). Paper over Boards. Routledge. New York, NY. 2003. 376p. ISBN:0-415-93854-6, ISBN13: 978-0-415-93854-9. Dewey:781.62/00973. LCCN:2005-412046.

Audience: **g,l,u,f.** *Choice, 2003.*

Lornell, Kip   **ML3551.L67 2002**
Introducing American Folk Music: Ethnic and Grassroot Traditions in the United States. Ed. 2. Trade Paper. McGraw-Hill Higher Education. Burr Ridge, IL. 2001. 320p. ISBN:0-07-241421-9, ISBN13: 978-0-07-241421-9. Dewey:781.62/13. LCCN:2001-044320.

Audience: **g,l,u,f.**

Lornell, Kip & Rasmussen,   **ML3477.M88 1997**
Anne K.
Musics of Multicultural America. Paper Text. Thomson Wadsworth. Belmont, CA. 1997. 368p. ISBN:0-02-864585-5, ISBN13: 978-0-02-864585-8. Dewey:780/.973. LCCN:97-019860.

Audience: **g,l,u,f.**

McNeil, W. K.   **ML102.G6E63 2005**
Encyclopedia of American Gospel Music. Paper over Boards. Routledge. New York, NY. 2005. 512p. ISBN:0-415-94179-2, ISBN13: 978-0-415-94179-2. Dewey:782.25/4/03. LCCN:2005-044994.

Audience: **g,l,u,f.** *Choice, 2006.*

Miller, Terry E.   **ML128.F74M5 1986**
Folk Music in America: A Reference Guide. Library Binding. Garland Publishing, Inc. New York, NY. 1986. 448p. Music Research and Information Guides Ser., Vol. 5 ISBN:0-8240-8935-9, ISBN13: 978-0-8240-8935-1. Dewey:016.781773. LCCN:84-048014.

Audience: **l,u,f.** *Choice, 1987.*

Moon, Krystyn R.   **ML3477.M66 2005**
Yellowface: Creating the Chinese in American Popular Music and Performance, 1850s-1920s. Trade Cloth. Rutgers University Press. Piscataway, NJ. 2005. 224p. ISBN:0-8135-3506-9, ISBN13: 978-0-8135-3506-7. Dewey:780/.89/951073. LCCN:2004-007534.

Audience: **u,f.**

Nettl, Bruno   **ML3557.N38 1989**
Blackfoot Musical Thought: Comparative Perspectives. Trade Cloth. Kent State University Press. Kent, OH. 1989. 210p. World Music Ser. ISBN:0-87338-370-2, ISBN13: 978-0-87338-370-7. Dewey:781.7/297. LCCN:88-028450.

Audience: **u,f.** *Choice, 1989.*

Patterson, Daniel W.   ML3178.S5P4 2000
The Shaker Spiritual. Ed. 2. Trade Paper. Dover Publications,
Inc. Mineola, NY. 2000. 592p. ISBN:0-486-41375-6, ISBN13:
978-0-486-41375-4. Dewey:782.27/088/288. LCCN:00-063851.
Audience: **u,f.**

Reyes, Adelaida   ML200.R48 2004
Music in America: Experiencing Music, Expressing Culture.
Cloth Text. Oxford University Press, Inc. New York, NY. 2004.
144p. Global Music Ser. ISBN:0-19-514666-2, ISBN13:
978-0-19-514666-0. Dewey:780/.973. LCCN:2004-050099.
Audience: **l,u,f.**

Reyes, Adelaida   ML3560.V5R49 1999
Songs of the Caged, Songs of the Free: Music and the
Vietnamese Refugee Experience. Trade Cloth. Temple
University Press. Philadelphia, PA. 1999. 248p.
ISBN:1-56639-685-9, ISBN13: 978-1-56639-685-1.
Dewey:780/.89/9592073. LCCN:98-054778.
Audience: **l,u.** *Choice, 1999.*

Riddle, Ronald   ML200
Flying Dragons, Flowing Streams: Music in the Life of San
Francisco's Chinese. Trade Cloth. Greenwood Publishing Group,
Inc. Portsmouth, NH. 1983. 349p. Contributions in Intercultural
and Comparative Studies Ser., No. 7 ISBN:0-313-23682-8,
ISBN13: 978-0-313-23682-2. Dewey:781.7/2951079461.
LCCN:82-012005.
Audience: **u,f.**

Seeger, Pete   ML3545 .S43 1992
The Incompleat Folksinger. Jo M. Schwartz (Editor). Trade
Paper. University of Nebraska Press. Lincoln, NE. 1992. 596p.
ISBN:0-8032-9216-3, ISBN13: 978-0-8032-9216-1.
Dewey:782.42162. LCCN:92-031574.
Audience: **g,l,u,f.**

Seeger, Ruth Crawford   ML3551.1.S44 2001
The Music of American Folk Song and Selected Other Writings
on American Folk Music. Larry Polansky (Editor), Judith Tick
(Editor, Introduction by). Trade Cloth. University of Rochester
Press. Rochester, NY. 2002. 210p. Eastman Studies in Music
ISBN:1-58046-095-X, ISBN13: 978-1-58046-095-8.
Dewey:782.42162/13. LCCN:2001-035576.
Audience: **u,f.** *Choice, 2002.*

Stambler, Irwin & Stambler,   ML102.F66S73 2001
Lyndon
Folk and Blues: The Premier Encyclopedia of American Roots
Music. Cloth over Boards. St. Martin's Press. Gordonville, VA.
2001. 816p. ISBN:0-312-20057-9, ISBN13: 978-0-312-20057-2.
Dewey:781.64/0973/03. LCCN:2001-273473.
Audience: **g,l,u,f.**

Titon, Jeff Todd   94-6953 [ML]
Early Downhome Blues: A Musical and Cultural Analysis. Ed.
2. Trade Paper. University of North Carolina Press. Chapel Hill,
NC. 1995. 340p. Cultural Studies of the United States
ISBN:0-8078-4482-9, ISBN13: 978-0-8078-4482-3.
Dewey:781.643/09. LCCN:94-006953.
Audience: **u,f.**

Titon, Jeff Todd & Carlin,   ML3551.A53 2001
Bob (Editors)
American Musical Traditions. Ed. 5. Trade Cloth. Thomson
Gale. Farmington Hills, MI. 2001. 1064p. ISBN:0-02-864624-X,
ISBN13: 978-0-02-864624-4. Dewey:781.62/00973.
LCCN:2001-042050.
Audience: **g,l,u,f.** *Choice, 2002.*

Vander, Judith   ML3557.V34 1997
Shoshone Ghost Dance Religion: Poetry Songs and Great Basin
Context. Trade Cloth. University of Illinois Press. Champaign,
IL. 1997. 688p. Music in American Life Ser.
ISBN:0-252-02214-9, ISBN13: 978-0-252-02214-2.
Dewey:782.42162/974. LCCN:95-041755.
Audience: **u,f.**

Wolfe, Charles & Lornell,   ML420.L277W6 1999
Kip
Life and Legend of Leadbelly. Trade Paper. Da Capo Press, Inc.
Cambridge, MA. 1999. 360p. ISBN:0-306-80896-X, ISBN13:
978-0-306-80896-8. Dewey:782.42162/0092 B.
LCCN:99-010989.
Audience: **l,u,f.**

Wong, Deborah Anne   ML3560.A85W66 2004
Speak It Louder: Asian Americans Making Music. Paper over
Boards. Routledge. New York, NY. 2004. 400p.
ISBN:0-415-97039-3, ISBN13: 978-0-415-97039-6.
Dewey:780/.89/95073. LCCN:2003-024527.
Audience: **u,f.**

Studies in Music History, Criticism, Analysis, and Appreciation > Folk and Traditional Music > Europe

Atkinson, David   ML3650.A86 2002
The English Traditional Ballad: Theory, Method, and Practice.
Trade Cloth. Ashgate Publishing, Ltd. Aldershot, 2002. 326p.
Ashgate Popular and Folk Music Ser. ISBN:0-7546-0634-1,
ISBN13: 978-0-7546-0634-5. Dewey:782.4/3/0941.
LCCN:2002-018209.
Audience: **u,f.**

Bartok, Bela   ML3580.B37 1997
Bela Bartok Studies in Ethnomusicology. Benjamin Suchoff
(Editor). Cloth Text. University of Nebraska Press. Lincoln, NE.
1997. 295p. ISBN:0-8032-4247-6, ISBN13: 978-0-8032-4247-0.
Dewey:781.62/0094. LCCN:96-026380.
Audience: **u,f.**

Bohlman, Philip V.   ML3580.B64 2004
The Music of European Nationalism:Cultural Identity and
Modern History. Michael B. Bakan (Editor). Library Binding.
ABC-CLIO, Inc. Santa Barbara, CA. 2004. 325p. World Music
Ser. ISBN:1-57607-270-3, ISBN13: 978-1-57607-270-7.
Dewey:781.5/99/094. LCCN:2004-005429.
Audience: **u,f.** *Choice, 2005.*

Brocken, Michael　　　　　　　　**ML3580**
The British Folk Revival: 1944-2002. Trade Cloth. Ashgate
Publishing, Ltd. Aldershot, 2003. 248p. Ashgate Popular and
Folk Music Ser. ISBN:0-7546-3281-4, ISBN13:
978-0-7546-3281-8. Dewey:781.62/21. LCCN:2002-043960.
　　　　　　　　　　　　　　　Audience: **u,f.** *Choice, 2004.*

Bronson, Bertrand Harris,　　　　　**ML3650**
　et al.
The Traditional Tunes of the Child Ballads: With Their Texts,
According to the Extant Records of Great Britain and America.
Child, Francis James (Author). Princeton University Press. 1980.
ISBN:0-691-09104-8, ISBN13: 978-0-691-09104-4.
　　　　　　　　　　　　　　　Audience: **u,f.**

Broughton, Simon et al.　　　　**ML102.W67W67 1999**
Rough Guide to World Music, Vol. 1: Africa, Europe, and the
Middle East. Ellingham, Mark; Trillo, Richard (Authors) Duane,
Orla; Dowell, Vanessa. Rough Guides, Ltd. 2000.
ISBN:1-85828-635-2, ISBN13: 978-1-85828-635-8.
　　　　　　　　　　　　　　　Audience: **g,l,u,f.**

Czekanowska, Anna　　　　　　**ML3677 .C9 1990**
Polish Folk Music: Slavonic Heritage - Polish Tradition -
Contemporary Trends. John Blacking (Contribution by). Trade
Paper. Cambridge University Press. New York, NY. 2006. 238p.
Cambridge Studies in Ethnomusicology Ser.
ISBN:0-521-02797-7, ISBN13: 978-0-521-02797-7.
Dewey:781.62/9185.
　　　　　　　　　　　　Audience: **u,f.** *Choice, 1992.*

Feld, Steven　　　　　　　**ML3611.M3K45 2002**
Bright Balkan Morning: Romani Lives and the Power of Music
in Greek Macedonia. Dick Blau (Photographer), Charles Keil &
Angeliki V. Keil (Text by). Trade Paper, Compact Disc.
Wesleyan University Press. Middletown, CT. 2002. 352p. Music
Culture Ser. ISBN:0-8195-6488-5, ISBN13: 978-0-8195-6488-7.
Dewey:781.62/914970495. LCCN:2002-016785.
　　　　　　　　　　　　Audience: **u,f.** *Choice, 2003.*

Goertzen, Chris　　　　　　**ML3704.G64 1997**
Fiddling for Norway: Revival and Identity. Trade Cloth.
University of Chicago Press. Chicago, IL. 1997. 364p. Chicago
Studies in Ethnomusicology ISBN:0-226-30049-8, ISBN13:
978-0-226-30049-8. Dewey:787.2/1623982. LCCN:97-007385.
　　　　　　　　　　　　　　　Audience: **u,f.**

Holst, Gail　　　　　　　　**ML3499.G8**
Road to Rembetika. Ed. 5. Mass Market. Cosmos Publishing
Company, Inc. River Vale, NJ. 1994. 182p.
ISBN:960-7120-07-8, ISBN13: 978-960-7120-07-6.
Dewey:782.42162/893.
　　　　　　　　　　　　　　　Audience: **u,f.**

Ling, Jan　　　　　　　　**ML3580.L5613 1997**
A History of European Folk Music. Linda Schenck & Robert
Schenck (Translators). Trade Cloth. University of Rochester
Press. Rochester, NY. 1998. 256p. ISBN:1-878822-77-2,
ISBN13: 978-1-878822-77-2. Dewey:781.62/0094.
LCCN:97-001136.
　　　　　　　　　　　　　　Audience: **g,l,u,f.**

MacFadyen, David　　　　　**ML3497.M3 2002**
Estrada?!: Grand Narratives and the Philosophy of the Russian
Popular Song since Perestroika. Cloth Text. McGill-Queen's
University Press. Montreal, PQ. 2002. 260p.
ISBN:0-7735-2371-5, ISBN13: 978-0-7735-2371-5.
Dewey:782.42164/0947/0904. LCCN:2003-446311.
　　　　　　　　　　　　Audience: **u,f.** *Choice, 2003.*

MacFadyen, David　　　　　**ML3497.M33 2001**
Red Stars: Personality and the Soviet Popular Song, 1955-1991.
Cloth Text. McGill-Queen's University Press. Montreal, PQ.
2001. xi, 319p. ISBN:0-7735-2106-2, ISBN13:
978-0-7735-2106-3. Dewey:782.42164/0947/0904.
LCCN:2002-511352.
　　　　　　　　　　　　　　　Audience: **u,f.**

MacFadyen, David　　　　　　　**ML3497**
Songs for Fat People: Affect, Emotion, and Celebrity in the
Russian Popular Song, 1900-1955. Cloth Text. McGill-Queen's
University Press. Montreal, PQ. 2002. 408p.
ISBN:0-7735-2441-X, ISBN13: 978-0-7735-2441-5.
Dewey:782.42164/0947/0904. LCCN:2001-008590.
　　　　　　　　　　　　Audience: **u,f.** *Choice, 2003.*

O'Sullivan, Donal　　　　　　**ML419.C35**
Carolan: The Life Times and Music of an Irish Harper. Ed. 2.
Trade Paper. Ossian Publications Limited. Incorporating. Cork,
2004. 384p. ISBN:1-900428-71-7, ISBN13: 978-1-900428-71-2.
Dewey:787.5092.
　　　　　　　　　　　　　　　Audience: **u,f.**

Prokhorov, Vadim　　　　　　**ML3680.P77 2001**
Russian Folk Songs: Musical Genres and History. Trade Cloth.
Scarecrow Press, Inc. Lanham, MD. 2002. 208p.
ISBN:0-8108-4127-4, ISBN13: 978-0-8108-4127-7.
Dewey:782.42162/9171. LCCN:2001-042911.
　　　　　　　　　　　　Audience: **u,f.** *Choice, 2002.*

Rice, Timothy　　　　　　　**ML3602.R5 1994**
May It Fill Your Soul: Experiencing Bulgarian Music. Trade
Cloth. University of Chicago Press. Chicago, IL. 1994. 386p.
Chicago Studies in Ethnomusicology ISBN:0-226-71121-8,
ISBN13: 978-0-226-71121-8. Dewey:781.62/91811.
LCCN:93-034083.
　　　　　　　　　　　　Audience: **u,f.** *Choice, 1995.*

Rice, Timothy & Wade,　　　　**ML252.R53 2003**
　Bonnie C.
Music in Bulgaria: Experiencing Music, Expressing Culture.
Trade Cloth. Oxford University Press, Inc. New York, NY. 2003.
144p. Global Music Ser., Vol. 6 ISBN:0-19-514147-4, ISBN13:
978-0-19-514147-4. Dewey:780/.9499. LCCN:2003-041943.
　　　　　　　　　　　　　　　Audience: **u,f.**

Sawyers, June Skinner　　　　　　**ML3654**
Celtic Music: The Complete Guide. Trade Paper. Da Capo Press,
Inc. Cambridge, MA. 2001. 384p. ISBN:0-306-81007-7,
ISBN13: 978-0-306-81007-7. Dewey:781.62/916.
　　　　　　　　　　　　　　Audience: **g,l,u,f.**

Schreiner, Claus   ML3712
Flamenco: Gypsy Dance and Music from Andalusia. Mollie C. Peters (Translator). Trade Paper. Hal Leonard Corporation. Milwaukee, WI. 1996. 176p. ISBN:1-57467-013-1, ISBN13: 978-1-57467-013-4. Dewey:784.1/882.

Audience: **g,l,u,f.**

Scott, Stanley, et al.   ML3654.H35 2004
Music in Ireland: Experiencing Music, Expressing Culture. Dora Hast & Dorothea E. Hast (Authors), Bonnie C. Wade & Patricia S. Campbell (Editors). Trade Cloth. Oxford University Press, Inc. New York, NY. 2004. 174p. Global Music Ser. ISBN:0-19-514554-2, ISBN13: 978-0-19-514554-0. Dewey:781.62/91620415. LCCN:2003-065467.

Audience: **g,l,u,f.**

Slobin, Mark (Editor)   ML240.5.R48 1996
Retuning Culture: Musical Changes in Central and Eastern Europe. Trade Cloth. Duke University Press. Durham, NC. 1996. 320p. ISBN:0-8223-1855-5, ISBN13: 978-0-8223-1855-2. Dewey:780/.947/0904. LCCN:96-027983.

Audience: **u,f.** *Choice, 1997.*

Stokes, Martin & Bohlman,   ML3580.C36 2003
Philip Vilas (Editors)
Celtic Modern: Music at the Global Fringe. Trade Cloth. Scarecrow Press, Inc. Lanham, MD. 2003. 302p. Europea Ser., No. 1 ISBN:0-8108-4780-9, ISBN13: 978-0-8108-4780-4. Dewey:780/.89/916. LCCN:2003-045637.

Audience: **u,f.** *Choice, 2004.*

Totton, Robin   ML3712.T67 2003
Song of the Outcasts: An Introduction to Flamenco. Trade Cloth, Compact Disc, Mixed Media. Hal Leonard Corporation. Milwaukee, WI. 2003. 224p. ISBN:1-57467-079-4, ISBN13: 978-1-57467-079-0. Dewey:781.62/610468. LCCN:2002-029919.

Audience: **u,f.**

Vallely, Fintan   ML101.I73.V35 1999
Companion to Irish Traditional Music. Trade Cloth. Cork University Press. Cork, 1998. 560p. ISBN:1-85918-148-1, ISBN13: 978-1-85918-148-5. Dewey:781.62/9162/003. LCCN:99-197930.

Audience: **g,l,u,f.**

Vargyas, Lajos   ML3593 .V37413
Folk Music of the Hungarians. CD-ROM, Trade Cloth. Akademiai Kiado. Budapest, 2005. 844p. ISBN:963-05-8162-0, ISBN13: 978-963-05-8162-2. Dewey:781.62/94511. LCCN:2006-276345.

Audience: **u,f.**

Vernon, Paul   ML3719.V47 1998
A History of the Portuguese Fado. Trade Cloth, Compact Disc. Ashgate Publishing, Ltd. Aldershot, 1998. 156p. ISBN:1-85928-377-2, ISBN13: 978-1-85928-377-6. Dewey:782.42162/691. LCCN:97-045087.

Audience: **u,f.**

Wallis, Geoff & Wilson, Sue   ML3654
The Rough Guide to Irish Music. Trade Paper. Rough Guides, Ltd. London, 2001. 400p. Travel Ser. ISBN:1-85828-642-5, ISBN13: 978-1-85828-642-6. Dewey:781.6/2/9162.

Audience: **g,l,u,f.**

Studies in Music History, Criticism, Analysis, and Appreciation > Folk and Traditional Music > Jewish Diaspora and Israel

Bohlman, Philip V.   ML345.I8B6 1989
The Land Where Two Streams Flow: Music in the German-Jewish Community of Israel. Trade Cloth. University of Illinois Press. Champaign, IL. 1989. 280p. ISBN:0-252-01596-7, ISBN13: 978-0-252-01596-0. Dewey:781.75694. LCCN:88-025902.

Audience: **u,f.** *Choice, 1990.*

Brinkmann, Reinhold &   ML198.5 .D75 1999
Wolff, Christoph
Driven into Paradise: The Musical Migration from Nazi Germany to the United States. Trade Cloth. University of California Press. Berkeley, CA. 1999. 388p. ISBN:0-520-21413-7, ISBN13: 978-0-520-21413-2. Dewey:780/.943/0973. LCCN:98-028956.

Audience: **u,f.** *Choice, 2000.*

Gilbert, Shirli   ML3776.G54 2
Music and Holocaust: Confronting Life in the Nazi Ghettos and Camps. Trade Cloth. Oxford University Press, Inc. New York, NY. 2005. 264p. Oxford Historical Monographs ISBN:0-19-927797-4, ISBN13: 978-0-19-927797-1. Dewey:940.53/18. LCCN:2005-277352.

Audience: **u,f.** *Choice, 2006.*

Gottlieb, Jack   ML3776.G65 2004
Funny, It Doesn't Sound Jewish: How Yiddish Songs and Synagogue Melodies Influenced Tin Pan Alley, Broadway, and Hollywood. Trade Cloth, Compact Disc. Library of Congress. Washington, DC. 2004. 306p. SUNY Series on Modern Jewish Literature and Culture ISBN:0-8444-1130-2, ISBN13: 978-0-8444-1130-9. Dewey:781.64/089/924073. LCCN:2003-044257.

Audience: **u,f.** *Choice, 2004.*

Gradenwitz, Peter E.   ML345.I5G73 1996
The Music of Israel: From the Biblical Era to Modern Times. Ed. 2. Leonard Bernstein (Foreword by), Yehudi Menuhin (Preface by). Trade Cloth. Hal Leonard Corporation. Milwaukee, WI. 1996. 420p. ISBN:1-57467-012-3, ISBN13: 978-1-57467-012-7. Dewey:780/.89/924. LCCN:95-047994.

Audience: **g,l,u,f.** *Choice, 1997.*

Harran, Don   ML410.R78H37 1999
Salamone Rossi: Jewish Musician in Late Renaissance Mantua. Trade Cloth. Oxford University Press, Inc. New York, NY. 1999.

320p. Oxford Monographs on Music ISBN:0-19-816271-5,
ISBN13: 978-0-19-816271-1. Dewey:780/.92 B.
LCCN:98-007974.

Audience: **u,f.**

Heskes, Irene   **ML3776**
Passport to Jewish Music: Its History, Traditions and Culture.
Trade Cloth. Greenwood Publishing Group, Inc. Portsmouth,
NH. 1994. 368p. Contributions to the Study of Music and
Dance Ser., No. 33 ISBN:0-313-28035-5, ISBN13:
978-0-313-28035-1. Dewey:780/.89924. LCCN:93-035835.

Audience: **u,f.** *Choice, 1994.*

Heskes, Irene (Compiled by)   **ML128**
The Resource Book of Jewish Music: A Bibliographical and
Topical Guide to the Book and Journal Literature and Program
Materials. Cloth Text. Greenwood Publishing Group, Inc.
Portsmouth, NH. 1985. 302p. Music Reference Collection, No. 3
ISBN:0-313-23251-2, ISBN13: 978-0-313-23251-0.
Dewey:016.7817/2924. LCCN:84-022435.

Audience: **g,l,u,f.** *Choice, 1985.*

Hirshberg, Jehoash   **ML345.P3H57 1996**
Music in the Jewish Community of Palestine 1880-1948: A
Social History. Trade Paper. Oxford University Press, Inc. New
York, NY. 1996. 310p. ISBN:0-19-816651-6, ISBN13:
978-0-19-816651-1. Dewey:780.8/9924/05694.
LCCN:96-035559.

Audience: **u,f.** *Choice, 1995.*

Idelsohn, A. Z.   **ML3776**
Jewish Music in Its Historical Development. Paper Text.
Textbook Publishers. Temecula, CA. 2003. xi, 535p.
ISBN:0-7581-4152-1, ISBN13: 978-0-7581-4152-1.
Dewey:781.7/2924.

Audience: **g,l,u,f.**

Karas, Joza   **ML247.8.T47**
Music in Terezin, 1941-1945. Trade Paper. Pendragon Press.
Hillsdale, NY. 1985. 212p. ISBN:0-918728-34-7, ISBN13:
978-0-918728-34-0. Dewey:780/.9437/1. LCCN:84-024411.

Audience: **u,f.**

Katz, Jacob   **ML410.W19K3313 1986**
The Darker Side of Genius: Richard Wagner's Anti-Semitism.
Trade Cloth. University Press of New England. Lebanon, NH.
1986. 172p. Tauber Institute Ser., No. 5 ISBN:0-87451-368-5,
ISBN13: 978-0-87451-368-4. Dewey:782.1/092/4.
LCCN:85-040935.

Audience: **u,f.** *Choice, 1986.*

Levin, Theodore   **ML3758.A783L48 1996**
The Hundred Thousand Fools of God: Musical Travels in
Central Asia (& Queens, New York). Compact Disc, Cloth Text.
Indiana University Press. Bloomington, IN. 1997. 346p.
ISBN:0-253-33206-0, ISBN13: 978-0-253-33206-6.
Dewey:780/.958. LCCN:96-007607.

Audience: **u,f.** *Choice, 1997.*

Most, Andrea   **ML1711.M74 2003**
Making Americans: Jews and the Broadway Musical. Trade
Cloth. Harvard University Press. Cambridge, MA. 2004. 272p.
ISBN:0-674-01165-1, ISBN13: 978-0-674-01165-6.
Dewey:782.1/4/089924073. LCCN:2003-056636.

Audience: **u,f.**

Regev, Motti & Seroussi,   **ML3502.I75 R44 2004**
Edwin
Popular Music and National Culture in Israel. Trade Cloth.
University of California Press. Berkeley, CA. 2004. 304p.
ISBN:0-520-23652-1, ISBN13: 978-0-520-23652-3.
Dewey:306.4/8423/095694. LCCN:2003-022856.

Audience: **u,f.** *Choice, 2004.*

Rothmüller, Aron Marko   **ML166**
The Music of the Jews: An Historical Appreciation. South
Brunswick, T. Yoseloff. 1967.

Audience: **u,f.**

Rubin, Ruth   **ML3776.R77 2000**
Voices of a People: The Story of Yiddish Folksong. Trade Paper.
University of Illinois Press. Champaign, IL. 2000. 560p.
ISBN:0-252-06918-8, ISBN13: 978-0-252-06918-5.
Dewey:782.42162/924. LCCN:00-039216.

Audience: **u,f.**

Sapoznik, Henry   **ML3528.8.S26 2005**
Klezmer!: Jewish Music from Old World to Our World. Ed. 2.
Trade Paper, Compact Disc. Music Sales Corporation. New
York, NY. 2005. 350p. ISBN:0-8256-7324-0, ISBN13:
978-0-8256-7324-5. Dewey:781.62/924. LCCN:2005-015522.

Audience: **g,l,u,f.** *Choice, 2000.*

Shelemay, Kay Kaufman   **ML3776.S53 1998**
Let Jasmine Rain Down: Song and Remembrance among Syrian
Jews. Trade Cloth. University of Chicago Press. Chicago, IL.
1998. 310p. Chicago Studies in Ethnomusicology Ser.
ISBN:0-226-75211-9, ISBN13: 978-0-226-75211-2.
Dewey:782.42162/92405691. LCCN:98-010938.

Audience: **u,f.**

Shiloah, Amnon   **ML3195.S4 1992**
Jewish Musical Traditions. Trade Cloth. Wayne State University
Press. Detroit, MI. 1995. 274p. Jewish Folklore and
Anthropology Ser. ISBN:0-8143-2235-2, ISBN13:
978-0-8143-2235-2. Dewey:781.6/2924.

Audience: **u,f.** *Choice, 1993.*

Slobin, Mark   **ML3528.8**
American Klezmer : Its Roots and Offshoots. University of
California Press. 2002. ISBN:0-520-22717-4, ISBN13:
978-0-520-22717-0.

Audience: **u,f.**

Slobin, Mark   **ML3195**
Chosen Voices: The Story of the American Cantorate. Trade
Paper. University of Illinois Press. Champaign, IL. 2002. 368p.
Music in American Life Ser. ISBN:0-252-07089-5, ISBN13:
978-0-252-07089-1. Dewey:782.3/6/00973. LCCN:2002-284122.

Audience: **u,f.** *Choice, 1989.*

Slobin, Mark   ML3776 .S6
Tenement Songs: The Popular Music of the Jewish Immigrants. Audio Cassette, Trade Paper. University of Illinois Press. Champaign, IL. 1996. 256p. ISBN:0-252-06563-8, ISBN13: 978-0-252-06563-7. Dewey:784.5/0089924.

Audience: **u,f.**

Weiner, Marc A.   ML410.W19W23 1997
Richard Wagner and the Anti-Semetic Imagination. Cloth Text. University of Nebraska Press. Lincoln, NE. 1995. 447p. Texts and Contexts Ser. ISBN:0-8032-4775-3, ISBN13: 978-0-8032-4775-8. Dewey:782.1/092. LCCN:94-012187.

Audience: **u,f.** *Choice, 1995.*

Werner, Eric   ML166
The Sacred Bridge; The Interdependence of Liturgy and Music in Synagogue and Church During the First Millennium. London, D. Dobson; New York, Columbia University Press. 1959. ISBN:0-88125-052-X, ISBN13: 978-0-88125-052-7.

Audience: **u,f.**

Biographies and Studies of Composers and Performers > A > Albeniz, Isaac

Clark, Walter Aaron   ML410.C54
Isaac Albeniz: Portrait of a Romantic. Trade Paper. Oxford University Press, Inc. New York, NY. 2002. 342p. ISBN:0-19-925052-9, ISBN13: 978-0-19-925052-3. Dewey:786.2/092. LCCN:97-032612.

Audience: **u,f.**

Biographies and Studies of Composers and Performers > A > Albinoni, Tomaso

Talbot, Michael   ML410.A315T37 1990
Tomaso Albinoni: The Venetian Composer and His World. Trade Cloth. Oxford University Press, Inc. New York, NY. 1990. 304p. ISBN:0-19-315245-2, ISBN13: 978-0-19-315245-8. Dewey:780/.92 B. LCCN:89-049221.

Audience: **u,f.** *Choice, 1991.*

Biographies and Studies of Composers and Performers > A > Anderson, Laurie

Anderson, Laurie   NX512.A54
Stories from the Nerve Bible: A Twenty-Year Retrospective. Trade Cloth. HarperCollins Canada, Ltd. Scarborough, ON. 1993. ISBN:0-06-016606-1, ISBN13: 978-0-06-016606-9. Dewey:700/.92.

Audience: **u,f.**

Goldberg, Roselee &   NX512.A54G65 2000
  Anderson, Laurie
Laurie Anderson. Trade Cloth. Harry N. Abrams, Inc. New York, NY. 2000. 204p. ISBN:0-8109-3582-1, ISBN13: 978-0-8109-3582-2. Dewey:709.2. LCCN:99-044944.

Audience: **l,u,f.**

Biographies and Studies of Composers and Performers > A > Anderson, Marian

Anderson, Marian   ML420.A6A3 2001
My Lord, What a Morning: An Autobiography. James Anderson DePreist (Foreword by). Trade Paper. University of Illinois Press. Champaign, IL. 2002. 352p. Music in American Life Ser. ISBN:0-252-07053-4, ISBN13: 978-0-252-07053-2. Dewey:782.1/092 B. LCCN:2001-040980.

Audience: **g,l,u,f.**

Biographies and Studies of Composers and Performers > A > Andriessen, Louis

Adlington, Robert   ML410.A6326
Louis Andriessen: De Staat. Trade Cloth, Compact Disc. Ashgate Publishing, Ltd. Aldershot, 2004. 180p. Landmarks in Music since 1950 Ser. ISBN:0-7546-0925-1, ISBN13: 978-0-7546-0925-4. Dewey:782.4/8. LCCN:2003-059519.

Audience: **u,f.** *Choice, 2005.*

Trochimczyk, Maja (Editor)   ML410.A6326A5 2002
The Music of Louis Andriessen. Paper over Boards. Routledge. New York, NY. 2002. 344p. Studies in Contemporary Music and Culture, No. 7 ISBN:0-8153-3789-2, ISBN13: 978-0-8153-3789-8. Dewey:780/.92 B. LCCN:2001-041855.

Audience: **u,f.**

Biographies and Studies of Composers and Performers > A > Antheil, George

Antheil, George   ML410.A638A3 1990
Bad Boy of Music. Trade Cloth. Samuel French Trade. Hollywood, CA. 1990. 378p. ISBN:0-573-60604-8, ISBN13: 978-0-573-60604-5. Dewey:780/.92 B. LCCN:90-003331.

Audience: **g,l,u,f.**

Biographies and Studies of Composers and Performers > A > Arlen, Harold

Jablonski, Edward   ML410.A76J33 1996
Harold Arlen: Rhythm, Rainbows, and Blues. Cloth Text. Northeastern University Press. Boston, MA. 1996. 490p.

ISBN:1-55553-263-2, ISBN13: 978-1-55553-263-5.
Dewey:782.42164/092 B. LCCN:95-044708.
Audience: **g,l,u,f.** *Choice, 1996.*

Biographies and Studies of Composers and Performers > A > Armstrong, Louis

Armstrong, Louis   **ML419.A75A3**
Louis Armstrong, in His Own Words: Selected Writings. Ed. 2.
Thomas Brothers (Editor). Trade Paper. Oxford University Press,
Inc. New York, NY. 2001. 274p. ISBN:0-19-514046-X, ISBN13:
978-0-19-514046-0. Dewey:781.65/092 B.
Audience: **g,l,u,f.** *Choice, 2000.*

Berrett, Joshua   **ML419.A75B46 2004**
Louis Armstrong and Paul Whiteman: Two Kings of Jazz. Cloth
over Boards. Yale University Press. Cumberland, RI. 2004.
256p. ISBN:0-300-10384-0, ISBN13: 978-0-300-10384-7.
Dewey:781.65/092/2 B. LCCN:2004-004217.
Audience: **u,f.**

Berrett, Joshua   **ML410.E44**
The Louis Armstrong Companion: Eight Decades of
Commentary. Trade Paper. Music Sales Corporation. New York,
NY. 1999. 300p. ISBN:0-8256-7193-0, ISBN13:
978-0-8256-7193-7. Dewey:781.65/092 B. LCCN:98-029206.
Audience: **g,l,u,f.** *Choice, 2000.*

Giddins, Gary   **ML410.E44**
Satchmo. Trade Paper. Doubleday Publishing. New York, NY.
1992. 240p. ISBN:0-385-24429-0, ISBN13: 978-0-385-24429-9.
Dewey:781.6/5/092. LCCN:92-008584.
Audience: **g,l,u,f.**

Biographies and Studies of Composers and Performers > B > Babbitt, Milton

Babbitt, Milton   **ML60.B12 2003**
The Collected Essays of Milton Babbitt. Stephen Peles, Stephen
Dembski, Andrew Mead & Joseph N. Straus (Editors). Trade
Cloth. Princeton University Press. Princeton, NJ. 2003. 504p.
ISBN:0-691-08966-3, ISBN13: 978-0-691-08966-9. Dewey:780.
LCCN:2003-044496.
Audience: **u,f.** *Choice, 2004.*

Mead, Andrew   **ML410.M9**
An Introduction to the Music of Milton Babbit. Cloth Text.
Princeton University Press. Princeton, NJ. 1994. 264p.
ISBN:0-691-03314-5, ISBN13: 978-0-691-03314-3.
Dewey:780.92. LCCN:92-037178.
Audience: **u,f.** *Choice, 1995.*

Biographies and Studies of Composers and Performers > B > Bach, Carl Philipp Emanuel

Geiringer, Karl   **ML410.B1**
The Bach Family: Seven Generations of Creative Genius. Paper
Text. Textbook Publishers. Temecula, CA. 2003. xiv, 514p.
ISBN:0-7581-7209-5, ISBN13: 978-0-7581-7209-9.
Dewey:780/.92/2 B.
Audience: **g,l,u,f.**

Ottenberg, Hans-Gunter   **ML410.B16O873 1987**
C. P. E. Bach. Philip J. Whitmore (Translator). Trade Cloth.
Oxford University Press, Inc. New York, NY. 1988. 296p.
ISBN:0-19-315246-0, ISBN13: 978-0-19-315246-5.
Dewey:780/.92/4 B. LCCN:86-023904.
Audience: **l,u,f.**

Biographies and Studies of Composers and Performers > B > Bach, Johann Christian

Geiringer, Karl   **ML410.B1**
The Bach Family: Seven Generations of Creative Genius. Paper
Text. Textbook Publishers. Temecula, CA. 2003. xiv, 514p.
ISBN:0-7581-7209-5, ISBN13: 978-0-7581-7209-9.
Dewey:780/.92/2 B.
Audience: **g,l,u,f.**

Gärtner, Heinz   **ML410.B15**
John Christian Bach: Mozart's Friend and Mentor. Pauly,
Reinhard G. (Translator). Amadeus Press. 1994.
ISBN:0-931340-79-9, ISBN13: 978-0-931340-79-6.
Audience: **u,f.**

Biographies and Studies of Composers and Performers > B > Bach, Johann Sebastian

Boyd, Malcolm   **ML410.B1**
Bach. Ed. 3. Trade Paper. Oxford University Press, Inc. New
York, NY. 2006. 320p. Master Musicians Ser.
ISBN:0-19-530771-2, ISBN13: 978-0-19-530771-9.
Dewey:780/.92 B.
Audience: **g,l,u,f.**

Boyd, Malcolm   **ML410.B1J15 1999**
The Oxford Companion to Bach. Trade Cloth. Oxford
University Press, Inc. New York, NY. 1999. 656p. Oxford
Composer Companion Ser. ISBN:0-19-866208-4, ISBN13:
978-0-19-866208-2. Dewey:780/.92. LCCN:98-019587.
Audience: **g,l,u,f.** *Choice, 2000.*

Butt, John (Editor)   **ML410.M9**
The Cambridge Companion to Bach. Jonathan Cross
(Contribution by). Trade Paper. Cambridge University Press.
New York, NY. 1997. 342p. Cambridge Companions to Music
Ser. ISBN:0-521-58780-8, ISBN13: 978-0-521-58780-8.
Dewey:780.9/2. LCCN:96-022581.
Audience: **g,l,u,f.** *Choice, 1998.*

Butt, John   **ML410.B1B193 1992**
Bach: Mass in B Minor. Julian Rushton (Contribution by). Trade
Paper. Cambridge University Press. New York, NY. 1991. 126p.
Music Handbks. ISBN:0-521-38716-7, ISBN13:
978-0-521-38716-3. Dewey:782.32/32. LCCN:90-002286.
Audience: **u,f.** *Choice, 1992.*

Chafe, Eric   **ML410.B13C38 2000**
Analyzing Bach Cantatas. Trade Cloth. Oxford University Press,
Inc. New York, NY. 2000. 304p. ISBN:0-19-512099-X, ISBN13:
978-0-19-512099-8. Dewey:782.2/4/092. LCCN:98-015109.
Audience: **u,f.** *Choice, 2000.*

David, Hans T.   **ML410.B1**
J. S. Bach's Musical Offering: History, Interpretation and
Analysis. Trade Paper. Dover Publications, Inc. Mineola, NY.
1972. 190p. ISBN:0-486-22768-5, ISBN13: 978-0-486-22768-9.
Dewey:785.7. LCCN:72-165391.
Audience: **u,f.**

David, Hans T.   **ML410.M9**
The New Bach Reader: A Life of Johann Sebastian Bach in
Letters and Documents. Trade Paper. W. W. Norton & Company,
Inc. New York, NY. 1999. 608p. ISBN:0-393-31956-3, ISBN13:
978-0-393-31956-9. Dewey:780/.92 B.
Audience: **g,l,u,f.** *Choice, 1998.*

Dreyfus, Laurence   **ML410.B1D63 1996**
Bach and the Patterns of Invention. Trade Cloth. Harvard
University Press. Cambridge, MA. 1997. 288p.
ISBN:0-674-06005-9, ISBN13: 978-0-674-06005-0.
Dewey:780/.92 B. LCCN:96-032275.
Audience: **u,f.** *Choice, 1997.*

Durr, Alfred   **ML410.B13D87 2003**
The Cantatas of J. S. Bach. Richard Jones (Translator). Trade
Cloth. Oxford University Press, Inc. New York, NY. 2005. 984p.
ISBN:0-19-816707-5, ISBN13: 978-0-19-816707-5.
Dewey:782.2/4092. LCCN:2005-299548.
Audience: **u,f.** *Choice, 2006.*

Eggebrecht, Hans H.   **MT145.B14.E4513 1993**
J. S. Bach's "The Art of the Fugue": The Work and Its
Interpretation. Jeffrey L. Praeter (Translator). Cloth Text.
Blackwell Publishing Professional. Ames, IA. 1993. 160p.
ISBN:0-8138-1489-8, ISBN13: 978-0-8138-1489-6.
Dewey:786/.1872. LCCN:93-001281.
Audience: **u,f.** *Choice, 1994.*

Geiringer, Karl   **ML410.B1**
The Bach Family: Seven Generations of Creative Genius. Paper

Text. Textbook Publishers. Temecula, CA. 2003. xiv, 514p.
ISBN:0-7581-7209-5, ISBN13: 978-0-7581-7209-9.
Dewey:780/.92/2 B.
Audience: **g,l,u,f.**

Johnson, Theodore O.   **MT145.B14J56 1986**
An Analytical Survey of the 15 Sinfonias: Three-Part Inventions
by J. S. Bach. Trade Paper. University Press of America, Inc.
Lanham, MD. 1986. 190p. ISBN:0-8191-5378-8, ISBN13:
978-0-8191-5378-4. Dewey:786.1/092/4. LCCN:86-009091.
Audience: **l,u,f.** *Choice, 1986.*

Kerman, Joseph   **MT59 .K49 2005**
The Art of Fugue: Bach Fugues for Keyboard, 1715-1750.
Davitt Moroney & Karen Rosenak (Performed by). Mixed
Media, Trade Cloth, Compact Disc. University of California
Press. Berkeley, CA. 2005. 208p. ISBN:0-520-24358-7, ISBN13:
978-0-520-24358-3. Dewey:786/.1872/092. LCCN:2005-004045.
Audience: **u,f.**

Ledbetter, David   **ML410.B13**
Bach's Well-Tempered Clavier: The 48 Preludes and Fugues.
Cloth over Boards. Yale University Press. Cumberland, RI.
2002. 432p. ISBN:0-300-09707-7, ISBN13: 978-0-300-09707-8.
Dewey:786/.1872. LCCN:2002-109926.
Audience: **l,u,f.**

Lester, Joel   **ML418.P2**
Bach's Works for Solo Violin: Style, Structure, Performance.
Trade Paper. Oxford University Press, Inc. New York, NY. 2003.
196p. ISBN:0-19-517144-6, ISBN13: 978-0-19-517144-0.
Dewey:787.2/092.
Audience: **u,f.** *Choice, 2000.*

Little, Meredith & Jenne,   **ML410.B13L52 2001**
Natalie (Editors)
Dance and the Music of J. S. Bach. Ed. 2. Trade Cloth. Indiana
University Press. Bloomington, IN. 2001. 288p.
Music--Scholarship and Performance Ser. ISBN:0-253-33936-7,
ISBN13: 978-0-253-33936-2. Dewey:784.18/82/092.
LCCN:2001-016944.
Audience: **u,f.** *Choice, 2002.*

Marshall, Robert L.   **ML410.B1.M285**
The Compositional Process of J. S. Bach. Trade Cloth. Princeton
University Press. Princeton, NJ. 1972. 177p. Studies in Music,
No. 4 ISBN:0-691-09113-7, ISBN13: 978-0-691-09113-6.
Dewey:783/.092/4. LCCN:76-113005.
Audience: **u,f.**

Marshall, Robert L.   **ML410.B13M28 1989**
The Music of Johann Sebastian Bach: The Sources, the Style,
the Significance. Trade Cloth. Thomson Gale. Farmington Hills,
MI. 1989. 375p. ISBN:0-02-871781-3, ISBN13:
978-0-02-871781-4. Dewey:780.9/2. LCCN:88-023921.
Audience: **l,u,f.** *Choice, 1989.*

Melamed, Daniel R.   **MT115.B2M43 2005**
Hearing Bach's Passions. Trade Cloth. Oxford University Press,
Inc. New York, NY. 2005. 190p. ISBN:0-19-516933-6, ISBN13:
978-0-19-516933-1. Dewey:782.23. LCCN:2004-013785.
Audience: **l,u,f.** *Choice, 2005.*

Melamed, Daniel R. &   **ML134.B1M45 1998**
  Marissen, Michael
An Introduction to Bach Studies. Cloth Text. Oxford University Press, Inc. New York, NY. 1998. 208p. ISBN:0-19-512231-3, ISBN13: 978-0-19-512231-2. Dewey:016.780/92. LCCN:97-040406.

                 Audience: **l,u,f.** *Choice, 1998.*

Parrott, Andrew   **ML410.B13P29 2000**
The Essential Bach Choir. Trade Paper, Trade Cloth. Boydell & Brewer, Ltd. Woodbridge, 2002. 240p. ISBN:0-85115-786-6, ISBN13: 978-0-85115-786-3. Dewey:782.2/4/092. LCCN:99-087035.

                 Audience: **u,f.** *Choice, 2000.*

Schmieder, Wolfgang   **ML134.B155**
Thematisch-systematisches Verzeichnis der musikalischen Werke von Johann Sebastian Bach: Bach-Werke-Verzeichnis (BWV). Ed. 2. Wiesbaden : Breitkopf & Härtel. 1990.

                 Audience: **u,f.**

Schulenberg, David   **MT145.B14S415 1992**
The Keyboard Music of J. S. Bach. Trade Cloth. Thomson Gale. Farmington Hills, MI. 1992. 475p. ISBN:0-02-873275-8, ISBN13: 978-0-02-873275-6. Dewey:786/.092. LCCN:91-039348.

                 Audience: **l,u,f.** *Choice, 1993.*

Stauffer, George B.   **ML410.B13S75 1997**
Bach: The Mass in B Minor. Cloth Text. Thomson Wadsworth. Belmont, CA. 1996. 309p. Monuments of Western Music Ser. ISBN:0-02-872475-5, ISBN13: 978-0-02-872475-1. Dewey:782.32/32. LCCN:96-027495.

                 Audience: **l,u,f.**

Stinson, Russell   **ML410.B13S87 1996**
Bach: The Orgelbuchlein. Trade Cloth. Thomson Gale. Farmington Hills, MI. 1996. xv, 208p. Monuments of Western Music Ser. ISBN:0-02-872505-0, ISBN13: 978-0-02-872505-5. Dewey:786.5/18992/092. LCCN:96-024581.

                 Audience: **u,f.** *Choice, 1997.*

Tatlow, Ruth   **ML410.B1 T18 1990**
Bach and the Riddle of the Number Alphabet. Trade Cloth. Cambridge University Press. New York, NY. 1991. 200p. ISBN:0-521-36191-5, ISBN13: 978-0-521-36191-0. Dewey:780/.92. LCCN:90-001550.

                 Audience: **l,u,f.** *Choice, 1991.*

Troeger, Richard   **MT179.T76 2003**
Playing Bach on the Keyboard: A Practical Guide. Trade Cloth. Hal Leonard Corporation. Milwaukee, WI. 2003. 300p. ISBN:1-57467-084-0, ISBN13: 978-1-57467-084-4. Dewey:786/.092. LCCN:2003-012791.

                 Audience: **l,u,f.** *Choice, 2004.*

Williams, Peter F.   **MT145.B14W53 2002**
The Organ Music of J. S. Bach. Ed. 2. Cloth Text. Cambridge University Press. New York, NY. 2003. 634p. ISBN:0-521-81416-2, ISBN13: 978-0-521-81416-4. Dewey:786.5/092. LCCN:2002-067368.

                 Audience: **l,u,f.** *Choice, 2004.*

Williams, Peter F.   **MT145.B14 W55 2001**
Bach: The Goldberg Variations. Julian Rushton (Contribution by). Cloth Text. Cambridge University Press. New York, NY. 2001. 118p. Music Handbks. ISBN:0-521-80735-2, ISBN13: 978-0-521-80735-7. Dewey:786.4/1825. LCCN:2001-025616.

                 Audience: **u,f.**

Wolff, Christoph   **ML410.B1W793 2000**
Johann Sebastian Bach: The Learned Musician. Trade Cloth. W. W. Norton & Company, Inc. New York, NY. 2000. 544p. ISBN:0-393-04825-X, ISBN13: 978-0-393-04825-4. Dewey:780.9/2. LCCN:99-054364.

                 Audience: **l,u,f.** *Choice, 2000.*

Biographies and Studies of Composers and Performers > B > Barber, Samuel

Heyman, Barbara B.   **ML410.M9**
Samuel Barber: The Composer and His Music. Trade Paper. Oxford University Press, Inc. New York, NY. 1994. 608p. ISBN:0-19-509058-6, ISBN13: 978-0-19-509058-1. Dewey:780/.92. LCCN:91-002454.

                 Audience: **l,u,f.** *Choice, 1993.*

Biographies and Studies of Composers and Performers > B > Bartok, Bela

Antokoletz, Elliott   **ML410.M9**
The Music of Bela Bartok: A Study of Tonality and Progression in Twentieth Century Music. Trade Paper. University of California Press. Berkeley, CA. 1984. 472p. ISBN:0-520-06747-9, ISBN13: 978-0-520-06747-9. Dewey:780.92. LCCN:82-017352.

                 Audience: **u,f.**

Antokoletz, Elliott (Editor),   **ML410.B26B284 2000**
  et al.
Bartok Perspectives: Man, Composer, and Ethnomusicologist. Victoria Fischer & Benjamin Suchoff (Editors). Trade Cloth. Oxford University Press, Inc. New York, NY. 2000. 332p. ISBN:0-19-512562-2, ISBN13: 978-0-19-512562-7. Dewey:780/.92. LCCN:99-022696.

                 Audience: **l,u,f.**

Antokoletz, Elliott   **ML134.B18A7 1997**
Bela Bartok: A Guide to Research. Ed. 2. Guy A. Marco (Editor). Cloth Text. Garland Publishing, Inc. New York, NY. 1997. 536p. Composer Resource Manuals Ser., Vol. 40 ISBN:0-8153-2088-4, ISBN13: 978-0-8153-2088-3. Dewey:016.78/092. LCCN:96-039298.

                 Audience: **l,u,f.** *Choice, 1997, 1988.*

Bayley, Amanda (Editor)   ML410.B26 C35 2001
The Cambridge Companion to Bartók. Trade Paper. Cambridge
University Press. New York, NY. 2001. 285p. Cambridge
Companions to Music Ser. ISBN:0-521-66958-8, ISBN13:
978-0-521-66958-0. Dewey:780/.92.

Audience: **l,u,f.** *Choice, 2001.*

Cooper, David   ML410.B26 C66 1996
Bartók: Concerto for Orchestra. Cloth Text. Cambridge
University Press. New York, NY. 1996. 111p. Music Handbks.
ISBN:0-521-48004-3, ISBN13: 978-0-521-48004-8.
Dewey:784.2/3/092. LCCN:95-021614.

Audience: **u,f.**

Fassett, Agatha   ML410.B26
The Naked Face of Genius: Béla Bartók's American Years.
Houghton Mifflin. 1968.

Audience: **u,f.**

Gillies, Malcolm (Editor)   ML410.B26B274 1994
The Bartok Companion. Trade Cloth. Hal Leonard Corporation.
Milwaukee, WI. 1994. 592p. ISBN:0-931340-74-8, ISBN13:
978-0-931340-74-1. Dewey:780/.92 B. LCCN:94-193114.

Audience: **g,l,u,f.**

Gillies, Malcolm   ML410.B26.G463 1990
Bartok Remembered. Trade Cloth. W. W. Norton & Company,
Inc. New York, NY. 1991. xl, 238p. ISBN:0-393-02971-9,
ISBN13: 978-0-393-02971-0. Dewey:780.92. LCCN:91-188227.

Audience: **g,l,u,f.** *Choice, 1991.*

Laki, Peter   ML410.B26B272 1995
Bartok and His World. Cloth Text. Princeton University Press.
Princeton, NJ. 1995. 250p. The Bard Music Festival Ser.
ISBN:0-691-00634-2, ISBN13: 978-0-691-00634-5.
Dewey:780.9/2. LCCN:95-013368.

Audience: **g,l,u,f.** *Choice, 1996.*

Maurice, Donald G.   ML410.B26
Bartok's Viola Concerto: The Remarkable Story of His
Swansong. Trade Cloth. Oxford University Press, Inc. New
York, NY. 2004. 234p. Studies in Musical Genesis and Structure
ISBN:0-19-515690-0, ISBN13: 978-0-19-515690-4.
Dewey:784.2/73. LCCN:2003-026914.

Audience: **u,f.** *Choice, 2004.*

Stevens, Halsey   ML410.M9
The Life and Music of Bela Bartok. Ed. 3. Trade Paper. Oxford
University Press, Inc. New York, NY. 1993. 382p.
ISBN:0-19-816349-5, ISBN13: 978-0-19-816349-7.
Dewey:780.92.

Audience: **l,u,f.**

Suchoff, Benjamin   ML410.B26S83 1995
Bartok: Concerto for Orchestra: Understanding Bartok's World.
Cloth Text. Thomson Wadsworth. Belmont, CA. 1995. 266p.
Monuments of Western Music Ser. ISBN:0-02-872495-X,
ISBN13: 978-0-02-872495-9. Dewey:784.2/186.
LCCN:95-010440.

Audience: **u,f.** *Choice, 1996.*

Wilson, Paul   ML410.B26W5 1992
The Music of Bela Bartok. Cloth over Boards. Yale University
Press. Cumberland, RI. 1992. 224p. Composers of the Twentieth
Century Ser. ISBN:0-300-05111-5, ISBN13: 978-0-300-05111-7.
Dewey:780.92. LCCN:91-036107.

Audience: **u,f.** *Choice, 1992.*

Biographies and Studies of Composers and Performers > B > Basie, Count

Basie, Count & Murray,   ML417.M846
  Albert
Good Morning Blues: An Autobiography of Count Basie. Ed. 2.
Trade Paper. Da Capo Press, Inc. Cambridge, MA. 2002. 432p.
ISBN:0-306-81107-3, ISBN13: 978-0-306-81107-4.
Dewey:786.2/165/092.

Audience: **g,l,u,f.**

Biographies and Studies of Composers and Performers > B > Beach, Amy

Block, Adrienne F.   ML410.B36B56 1998
Amy Beach, Passionate Victorian: The Life and Works of an
American Composer, 1867-1944. Trade Cloth. Oxford
University Press, Inc. New York, NY. 1998. 426p.
ISBN:0-19-507408-4, ISBN13: 978-0-19-507408-6.
Dewey:780.9/2. LCCN:97-002710.

Audience: **g,l,u,f.** *Choice, 1999.*

Biographies and Studies of Composers and Performers > B > Beatles

Beatles, The (Performed by)   ML54.6.B4
The Beatles Lyrics: The Songs of Lennon, McCartney, Harrison
and Starr. Trade Paper. Hal Leonard Corporation. Milwaukee,
WI. 1992. 256p. Songwriting and Lyrics Ser.
ISBN:0-7935-1537-8, ISBN13: 978-0-7935-1537-0.
Dewey:782.42166.

Audience: **g,l,u,f.**

Doggett, Peter   ML421.B4
Abbey Road - Let It Be: The Beatles. Trade Cloth. Music Sales
Corporation. New York, NY. 1998. ISBN:0-8256-7150-7,
ISBN13: 978-0-8256-7150-0. Dewey:782.42166/0922.
LCCN:97-029051.

Audience: **g,l,u,f.**

Everett, Walter   ML421.B4
The Beatles As Musicians: Revolver Through the Anthology.
Trade Paper. Oxford University Press, Inc. New York, NY. 1999.
416p. ISBN:0-19-512941-5, ISBN13: 978-0-19-512941-0.
Dewey:782.42166/092/2. LCCN:98-023704.

Audience: **g,l,u,f.** *Choice, 1999.*

Kozinn, Allan   **ML421.B4**
The Beatles. Trade Paper. Phaidon Press. London, 1995. 240p.
Twentieth-Century Composers Ser. ISBN:0-7148-3203-0,
ISBN13: 978-0-7148-3203-6. Dewey:782.4/2166/0922.
LCCN:99-495142.

Audience: **g,l,u,f.**

Lewisohn, Mark   **ML156.7.B4**
The Beatles Recording Sessions. Harmony Books. 1988.
ISBN:0-517-57066-1, ISBN13: 978-0-517-57066-1.

Audience: **u,f.**

Neises, Charles P.   **ML421.B4**
The Beatles Reader: A Selection of Contemporary Views, News
and Reviews of the Beatles in Their Heyday. Trade Cloth.
Popular Culture, Ink. Harbor Springs, MI. 1991. 232p. Rock and
Roll Remembrances Ser., No. 6 ISBN:1-56075-024-3, ISBN13:
978-1-56075-024-6. Dewey:784.5/4/00922. LCCN:84-060267.

Audience: **g,l,u,f.**

Biographies and Studies of Composers and Performers > B > Bechet, Sidney

Bechet, Sidney   **ML419**
Treat It Gentle: An Autobiography. Trade Paper. Da Capo Press,
Inc. Cambridge, MA. 2002. 280p. ISBN:0-306-81108-1,
ISBN13: 978-0-306-81108-1. Dewey:780.924.

Audience: **g,l,u,f.**

Biographies and Studies of Composers and Performers > B > Beethoven, Ludwig van

Anderson, Emily (Editor)   **ML410.B4**
The Letters of Beethoven. Trade Cloth. W. W. Norton &
Company, Inc. New York, NY. 1986. ISBN:0-393-02247-1,
ISBN13: 978-0-393-02247-6. Dewey:780.92.

Audience: **g,l,u,f.**

Arnold, Denis, et. al   **ML410.B4**
The Beethoven Reader. Fortune, Nigel (Author). W. W. Norton.
1971.

Audience: **l,u,f.**

Beethoven, Ludwig van   **ML410.B4**
Fidelio. Nicholas John (Editor), Tom Hammond (Translator).
Trade Paper. Riverrun Press, Inc. Flemington, NJ. 1981. 96p.
English National Opera Guide Ser., No. 4:Bilingual Libretto,
Articles ISBN:0-7145-3823-X, ISBN13: 978-0-7145-3823-5.
Dewey:782.1.

Audience: **g,l,u,f.**

Berlioz, Hector   **ML410.B42B49 2000**
A Critical Study of Beethoven's Nine Symphonies. Edwin
Evans (Translator), Kern Holoman (Introduction by). Trade
Paper. University of Illinois Press. Champaign, IL. 2000. 192p.
ISBN:0-252-06942-0, ISBN13: 978-0-252-06942-0.
Dewey:784.2/184/092. LCCN:00-047939.

Audience: **u,f.**

Brown, A. Peter   **ML1255.B87**
The First Golden Age of the Viennese Symphony: Haydn,
Mozart, Beethoven and Schubert. Trade Cloth. Indiana
University Press. Bloomington, IN. 2002. 816p.
ISBN:0-253-33487-X, ISBN13: 978-0-253-33487-9.
Dewey:784.2/184 s 784.2. LCCN:98-026549.

Audience: **g,l,u,f.**   *Choice, 2003.*

Cook, Nicholas   **ML410.B42 C66 1993**
Beethoven "Symphony No. 9". Cloth Text. Cambridge
University Press. New York, NY. 1993. 143p. Music Handbks.
ISBN:0-521-39039-7, ISBN13: 978-0-521-39039-2.
Dewey:784.2184. LCCN:92-020451.

Audience: **l,u,f.**

Cooper, Barry   **ML410.M9**
Beethoven and the Creative Process. Paper Text. Oxford
University Press, Inc. New York, NY. 1993. 336p.
ISBN:0-19-816353-3, ISBN13: 978-0-19-816353-4.
Dewey:780/.92. LCCN:89-032325.

Audience: **u,f.**   *Choice, 1991.*

Cooper, Barry (Editor)   **ML410.B4.B2813 1992**
The Beethoven Compendium. Trade Cloth. Thames & Hudson.
New York, NY. 1991. 336p. ISBN:0-500-01523-6, ISBN13:
978-0-500-01523-0. Dewey:780.92. LCCN:91-065423.

Audience: **g,l,u,f.**   *Choice, 1992.*

Cooper, Martin   **ML410.B4.C75**
Beethoven; the Last Decade 1817-1827. Trade Cloth. Oxford
University Press, Inc. New York, NY. 1970. x, 483p.
ISBN:0-19-315310-6, ISBN13: 978-0-19-315310-3.
Dewey:780/.924. LCCN:76-116137.

Audience: **l,u,f.**

Davies, Peter J.   **ML410**
The Character of a Genius: Beethoven in Perspective. Trade
Cloth. Greenwood Publishing Group, Inc. Portsmouth, NH.
2001. 376p. Contributions to the Study of Music and Dance
Ser., Vol. 60 ISBN:0-313-31913-8, ISBN13: 978-0-313-31913-6.
Dewey:780/.92 B. LCCN:2001-018022.

Audience: **u,f.**   *Choice, 2002.*

Drabkin, William   **ML410.B42 D8 1991**
Beethoven: Missa Solemnis. Julian Rushton (Contribution by).
Trade Paper. Cambridge University Press. New York, NY. 1991.
132p. Music Handbks. ISBN:0-521-37831-1, ISBN13:
978-0-521-37831-4. Dewey:782.32/32. LCCN:91-011383.

Audience: **u,f.**

Hopkins, Anthony   **MT130.B43H67 1996**
The Seven Concertos of Beethoven. Trade Cloth. Ashgate

Publishing, Ltd. Aldershot, 1996. 110p. ISBN:1-85928-245-8,
ISBN13: 978-1-85928-245-8. Dewey:784.2/3/092.
LCCN:96-024729.

Audience: **l,u,f.**

Johnson, Douglas, et al.   ML410.B4.J58 1985
The Beethoven Sketchbooks: History, Reconstruction, Inventory.
Alan Tyson & Robert Winter (Authors). Trade Cloth. University
of California Press. Berkeley, CA. 1985. 500p. California
Studies in 19th Century Music, No. 4 ISBN:0-520-04835-0,
ISBN13: 978-0-520-04835-5. Dewey:780/.92/4.
LCCN:82-025920.

Audience: **u,f.**   *Choice, 1986.*

Jones, David Wyn (Editor)   ML410.B4 W96 1995
Beethoven: The Pastoral Symphony. Cloth Text. Cambridge
University Press. New York, NY. 1995. 113p. Music Handbks.
ISBN:0-521-45074-8, ISBN13: 978-0-521-45074-4.
Dewey:784.2/184. LCCN:95-009937.

Audience: **u,f.**

Jones, Timothy   ML410.B42 J66 1999
Beethoven: The 'Moonlight' and Other Sonatas, Op. 27 and Op.
31. Julian Rushton (Contribution by). Cloth Text. Cambridge
University Press. New York, NY. 1999. 158p. Music Handbks.
ISBN:0-521-59136-8, ISBN13: 978-0-521-59136-2.
Dewey:786.2/183. LCCN:98-045826.

Audience: **l,u,f.**

Kinderman, William   ML410.B42B425 1991
  (Editor)
Beethoven's Compositional Process. Cloth Text. University of
Nebraska Press. Lincoln, NE. 1991. 195p. North American
Beethoven Studies, Vol. 1 ISBN:0-8032-1222-4, ISBN13:
978-0-8032-1222-0. Dewey:780/.92. LCCN:90-024227.

Audience: **u,f.**   *Choice, 1992.*

Kinderman, William   ML410.S4
Beethoven's Diabelli Variations. Paper Text. Oxford University
Press, Inc. New York, NY. 1989. 246p. Studies in Musical
Genesis and Structure ISBN:0-19-816198-0, ISBN13:
978-0-19-816198-1. Dewey:786.2/1825. LCCN:86-008590.

Audience: **u,f.**   *Choice, 1988.*

Landon, H. C.   ML410.M9
Beethoven: His Life, Work and World. Ed. 2. Trade Cloth.
Thames & Hudson. New York, NY. 1993. 248p.
ISBN:0-500-01540-6, ISBN13: 978-0-500-01540-7.
Dewey:780.92. LCCN:92-064271.

Audience: **g,l,u,f.**

Levy, David Benjamin   ML410.B42L48 2003
Beethoven: The Ninth Symphony. Ed. 2. Trade Paper. Yale
University Press. Cumberland, RI. 2003. 256p. Yale Music
Masterworks Ser. ISBN:0-300-09964-9, ISBN13:
978-0-300-09964-5. Dewey:784.2/184.

Audience: **u,f.**   *Choice, 1995.*

Lockwood, Lewis   ML410.B4L597 2002
Beethoven: The Music and the Life. Trade Cloth. W. W. Norton
& Company, Inc. New York, NY. 2002. 480p.

ISBN:0-393-05081-5, ISBN13: 978-0-393-05081-3.
Dewey:780/.92 B. LCCN:2002-075397.

Audience: **g,l,u,f.**   *Choice, 2003.*

Lockwood, Lewis & Kroll,   MT145.B422B4 2004
  Mark (Editors)
The Beethoven Violin Sonatas: History, Criticism, Performance.
Trade Cloth. University of Illinois Press. Champaign, IL. 2004.
176p. ISBN:0-252-02932-1, ISBN13: 978-0-252-02932-5.
Dewey:787.2/183/092. LCCN:2003-026966.

Audience: **l,u,f.**   *Choice, 2005.*

Newman, William S.   ML410.C54
Beethoven on Beethoven: Playing His Piano Music His Way.
Trade Paper. W. W. Norton & Company, Inc. New York, NY.
1991. 336p. ISBN:0-393-30719-0, ISBN13: 978-0-393-30719-1.
Dewey:786.1/092/4.

Audience: **l,u,f.**   *Choice, 1989.*

Pike, Lionel   MT125 .P55
Beethoven, Sibelius and "The Profound Logic": Studies in
Symphonic Analysis. Cloth Text. Continuum International
Publishing Group, Ltd. London, 1978. 240p.
ISBN:0-485-11178-0, ISBN13: 978-0-485-11178-1.
Dewey:785.1/1/0922. LCCN:79-309070.

Audience: **u,f.**

Plantinga, Leon   ML410.B42P6 1998
Beethoven Concertos: History, Style, Performance. Trade Cloth.
W. W. Norton & Company, Inc. New York, NY. 1999. 416p.
ISBN:0-393-04691-5, ISBN13: 978-0-393-04691-5.
Dewey:784.2/3/092. LCCN:98-022552.

Audience: **l,u,f.**   *Choice, 2000.*

Robinson, Paul (Editor)   ML410.B4 R46 1996
Ludwig Van Beethoven: Fidelio. Richard Wagner (Contribution
by). Trade Paper. Cambridge University Press. New York, NY.
1996. 203p. Cambridge Opera Handbooks Ser.
ISBN:0-521-45852-8, ISBN13: 978-0-521-45852-8.
Dewey:780.9/2. LCCN:95-046935.

Audience: **u,f.**   *Choice, 1997.*

Rosen, Charles   MT145.B42R67 2002
Beethoven's Piano Sonatas: A Short Companion. Cloth over
Boards. Yale University Press. Cumberland, RI. 2002. 272p.
ISBN:0-300-09070-6, ISBN13: 978-0-300-09070-3.
Dewey:786.2/183/092. LCCN:2001-093745.

Audience: **l,u,f.**   *Choice, 2003, 2002.*

Rosen, Charles   ML195.R68 1997
Classical Style: Haydn, Mozart, Beethoven. Ed. 2. Trade Cloth.
W. W. Norton & Company, Inc. New York, NY. 1997. 548p.
ISBN:0-393-04020-8, ISBN13: 978-0-393-04020-3.
Dewey:780/.9/033. LCCN:96-027335.

Audience: **l,u,f.**   *Choice, 1997.*

Schenker, Heinrich   ML410.B42
Beethoven's Ninth Symphony: A Portrayal of Its Musical
Content, with Running Commentary on Performance and
Literature As Well. John Rothgeb (Editor, Translator). Trade

Cloth. Yale University Press. Cumberland, RI. 1992. 350p.
ISBN:0-300-05459-9, ISBN13: 978-0-300-05459-0.
Dewey:784.2184. LCCN:91-036684.

Audience: **u,f.** *Choice, 1993.*

Schindler, Anton F. &　　　　　　**ML410.B4S3333 1996**
　Macardle, Donald W.
Beethoven As I Knew Him. Ed. 3. Trade Paper. Dover
Publications, Inc. Mineola, NY. 1996. 560p.
ISBN:0-486-29232-0, ISBN13: 978-0-486-29232-8.
Dewey:780/.92. LCCN:96-022901.

Audience: **u,f.**

Sipe, Thomas　　　　　　　　　　**ML410.B42 S57 1998**
Beethoven: Eroica Symphony. Julian Rushton (Contribution by).
Trade Paper. Cambridge University Press. New York, NY. 1998.
158p. Music Handbks. ISBN:0-521-47562-7, ISBN13:
978-0-521-47562-4. Dewey:784.2/184. LCCN:97-033020.

Audience: **u,f.** *Choice, 1999.*

Solomon, Maynard　　　　　　　　　　**ML410.B4**
Beethoven. Ed. 2. Trade Paper. Music Sales Corporation. New
York, NY. 2004. 554p. ISBN:0-8256-7268-6, ISBN13:
978-0-8256-7268-2. Dewey:780/.92/4.

Audience: **g,l,u,f.**

Sonneck, Oscar G. (Editor)　　　　　　　**ML410.B4**
Beethoven: Impressions by His Contemporaries. Trade Paper.
Dover Publications, Inc. Mineola, NY. 1967. 231p.
ISBN:0-486-21770-1, ISBN13: 978-0-486-21770-3.
Dewey:780.924.

Audience: **u,f.**

Stanley, Glenn (Editor)　　　　　　　**ML410.B4 C24 2000**
The Cambridge Companion to Beethoven. Trade Paper.
Cambridge University Press. New York, NY. 2000. 387p.
Cambridge Companions to Music Ser. ISBN:0-521-58934-7,
ISBN13: 978-0-521-58934-5. Dewey:780/.92. LCCN:98-042732.

Audience: **l,u,f.** *Choice, 2000.*

Stowell, Robin (Editor)　　　　　　　**ML410.B42 P47 1994**
Performing Beethoven. Trade Paper. Cambridge University
Press. New York, NY. 2005. 260p. Cambridge Studies in
Performance Practice Ser., Vol. 4 ISBN:0-521-02374-2, ISBN13:
978-0-521-02374-0. Dewey:780.92. LCCN:2006-276118.

Audience: **l,u,f.** *Choice, 1995.*

Stowell, Robin　　　　　　　　　　**ML410.B4 S76 1998**
Beethoven: Violin Concerto. Julian Rushton (Contribution by).
Cloth Text. Cambridge University Press. New York, NY. 1998.
138p. Music Handbks. ISBN:0-521-45159-0, ISBN13:
978-0-521-45159-8. Dewey:784.2/72. LCCN:97-014035.

Audience: **u,f.**

Taub, Robert　　　　　　　　　　**MT145.B42T38 2002**
Playing the Beethoven Piano Sonatas. Trade Cloth. Hal Leonard
Corporation. Milwaukee, WI. 2003. 258p. ISBN:1-57467-071-9,
ISBN13: 978-1-57467-071-4. Dewey:786.2/183/092.
LCCN:2001-046126.

Audience: **l,u,f.** *Choice, 2003, 2002.*

Thayer, Alexander Wheelock　　　　　　**ML410.B4**
Thayer's Life of Beethoven, Vol. 1. Forbes, Elliot (Editor);
Deiters, Hermann (Editor); Riemann, Hugo (Editor); Krehbiel,
Henry Edward (Editor). Princeton University Press. 1991.
ISBN:0-691-02717-X, ISBN13: 978-0-691-02717-3.

Audience: **u,f.**

Thayer, Alexander Wheelock　　　　　　**ML410.B4**
Thayer's Life of Beethoven, Vol. 2. Forbes, Elliot (Editor);
Deiters, Hermann (Editor); Riemann, Hugo (Editor); Krehbiel,
Henry Edward (Editor). Princeton University Press. 1991.
ISBN:0-691-02718-8, ISBN13: 978-0-691-02718-0.

Audience: **u,f.**

Wallace, Robin　　　　　　　　　　**ML410.B4**
Beethoven's Critics: Aesthetic Dilemmas and Resolutions
During the Composer's Lifetime. Trade Paper. Cambridge
University Press. New York, NY. 1990. 192p.
ISBN:0-521-38634-9, ISBN13: 978-0-521-38634-0.
Dewey:780/.92/4.

Audience: **u,f.** *Choice, 1987.*

Winter, Robert & Martin,　　　　　　**MT145.B425.B4 1994**
　Robert (Editors)
The Beethoven Quartet Companion. Trade Cloth. University of
California Press. Berkeley, CA. 1994. 300p.
ISBN:0-520-08211-7, ISBN13: 978-0-520-08211-3.
Dewey:785.7/194/092. LCCN:92-040668.

Audience: **l,u,f.** *Choice, 1995.*

Biographies and Studies of Composers and Performers > B > Beiderbecke, Bix

Lion, Jean Pierre　　　　　　　　　　**ML419.B25**
Bix: The Definitive Biography of Jazz Legend Leon "Bix"
Beiderbecke. Gabriella Page-Fort (Translator). Trade Cloth.
Continuum International Publishing Group, Ltd. London, 2005.
356p. ISBN:0-8264-1699-3, ISBN13: 978-0-8264-1699-5.
Dewey:788.9/6165/092 B. LCCN:2005-010509.

Audience: **u,f.** *Choice, 2006.*

Biographies and Studies of Composers and Performers > B > Bellini, Vincenzo

Kimbell, David R. B.　　　　　　　　**ML410.B44 K56 1998**
Vincenzo Bellini: Norma. Richard Wagner (Contribution by).
Trade Paper. Cambridge University Press. New York, NY. 1998.
154p. Opera Handbooks Ser. ISBN:0-521-48514-2, ISBN13:
978-0-521-48514-2. Dewey:782.1. LCCN:97-032615.

Audience: **u,f.** *Choice, 1999.*

Osborne, Charles   ML390.O82 1994
The Bel Canto Operas: A Guide to the Operas of Rossini,
Bellini, and Donizetti. Trade Cloth. Hal Leonard Corporation.
Milwaukee, WI. 1994. 378p. ISBN:0-931340-71-3, ISBN13:
978-0-931340-71-0. Dewey:782.1/0945/09034.
LCCN:94-168756.

Audience: **g,l,u,f.** *Choice, 1994.*

Rosselli, John   ML410.B44 R77 1996
The Life of Bellini. Trade Paper. Cambridge University Press.
New York, NY. 1997. 194p. Musical Lives Ser.
ISBN:0-521-46781-0, ISBN13: 978-0-521-46781-0.
Dewey:780.9/2. LCCN:95-039270.

Audience: **u,f.**

Biographies and Studies of Composers and Performers > B > Berg, Alban

Berg, Alban   ML50.B491W62 1990
Wozzeck. Nicholas John (Editor), Eric Blocknel & Vicki
Hartfold (Translators). Trade Paper. Beekman Books, Inc.
Wappingers Falls, NY. 1990. 116p. English National Opera
Guide Series: Bilingual Libretto, Articles, No. 42
ISBN:0-7145-4201-6, ISBN13: 978-0-7145-4201-0.
Dewey:782.1/0268. LCCN:90-044450.

Audience: **g,l,u,f.**

Harris, Donald (Editor), et al.   ML410.B47A4 1987
The Berg-Schoenberg Correspondence: Selected Letters.
Christopher Hailey & Juliane Brand (Editors). Trade Cloth. W.
W. Norton & Company, Inc. New York, NY. 1987. xxviii, 497p.
ISBN:0-393-01919-5, ISBN13: 978-0-393-01919-3.
Dewey:780/.92/2. LCCN:86-008346.

Audience: **u,f.** *Choice, 1988.*

Headlam, Dave   ML410.B47H43 1996
The Music of Alban Berg. Cloth over Boards. Yale University
Press. Cumberland, RI. 1996. 472p. Composers of the Twentieth
Century Ser. ISBN:0-300-06400-4, ISBN13: 978-0-300-06400-1.
Dewey:780.9/2. LCCN:95-046936.

Audience: **u,f.** *Choice, 1997.*

Jarman, Douglas (Editor)   ML410.B47J28 1991
Alban Berg: "Lulu". Cloth Text. Cambridge University Press.
New York, NY. 1991. 160p. Cambridge Opera Handbooks Ser.
ISBN:0-521-24150-2, ISBN13: 978-0-521-24150-2.
Dewey:782.1. LCCN:90-001637.

Audience: **u,f.** *Choice, 1991.*

Jarman, Douglas (Editor)   ML410.B47B53 1990
The Berg Companion. Cloth Text. Northeastern University
Press. Boston, MA. 1990. 301p. ISBN:1-55553-068-0, ISBN13:
978-1-55553-068-6. Dewey:780/.92. LCCN:89-008581.

Audience: **l,u,f.** *Choice, 1990.*

Jarman, Douglas   ML410.B47.J33
The Music of Alban Berg. Trade Cloth. University of California
Press. Berkeley, CA. 1979. xii, 266p. ISBN:0-520-03485-6,
ISBN13: 978-0-520-03485-3. Dewey:780/.92/4.
LCCN:77-076687.

Audience: **l,u,f.**

Jarman, Douglas   ML410.B47 J3 1989
Alban Berg: Wozzeck. Richard Wagner (Contribution by). Trade
Paper. Cambridge University Press. New York, NY. 1989. 192p.
Cambridge Opera Handbooks Ser. ISBN:0-521-28481-3,
ISBN13: 978-0-521-28481-3. Dewey:782.109.
LCCN:88-015965.

Audience: **l,u,f.** *Choice, 1990.*

Perle, George   ML410.B47
The Operas of Alban Berg: Lulu. Trade Cloth. University of
California Press. Berkeley, CA. 1984. 352p.
ISBN:0-520-04502-5, ISBN13: 978-0-520-04502-6.
Dewey:782.1092. LCCN:76-052033.

Audience: **u,f.** *Choice, 1985.*

Perle, George   ML410.B47
The Operas of Alban Berg: Wozzeck. Trade Cloth. University of
California Press. Berkeley, CA. 1980. 325p.
ISBN:0-520-03440-6, ISBN13: 978-0-520-03440-2.
Dewey:782.1/092/4. LCCN:76-052033.

Audience: **u,f.**

Perle, George & Berg, Alban   MT145.B47P47 2001
Style and Idea in the Lyric Suite of Alban Berg. Ed. 2. Trade
Cloth. Pendragon Press. Hillsdale, NY. 2001. xv, 112p.
ISBN:1-57647-085-7, ISBN13: 978-1-57647-085-5.
Dewey:785/.7194. LCCN:2001-052345.

Audience: **u,f.**

Pople, Anthony (Editor)   ML410.B47 C38 1997
The Cambridge Companion to Berg. Jonathan Cross
(Contribution by). Cloth Text. Cambridge University Press. New
York, NY. 1997. 320p. Cambridge Companions to Music Ser.
ISBN:0-521-56374-7, ISBN13: 978-0-521-56374-1.
Dewey:780/.92 B. LCCN:96-039727.

Audience: **l,u,f.** *Choice, 1998.*

Pople, Anthony   ML410.B47 P6 1991
Berg: Violin Concerto. Julian Rushton (Contribution by). Trade
Paper. Cambridge University Press. New York, NY. 1991. 130p.
Music Handbks. ISBN:0-521-39976-9, ISBN13:
978-0-521-39976-0. Dewey:784.2/72. LCCN:90-002542.

Audience: **u,f.**

Biographies and Studies of Composers and Performers > B > Berio, Luciano

Osmond-Smith, David   ML410.B4968O55 1990
Berio. Trade Cloth. Oxford University Press, Inc. New York,
NY. 1991. 176p. Oxford Studies of Composers, No. 20

ISBN:0-19-315478-1, ISBN13: 978-0-19-315478-0.
Dewey:780/.92 B. LCCN:90-007368.

Audience: **l,u,f.** *Choice, 1991.*

Osmond-Smith, David   MT115.B58 O8 1985
Playing on Words: A Guide to Luciano Berio's Sinfonia. Trade
Cloth. Ashgate Publishing, Ltd. Aldershot, 1985. 104p. Royal
Musical Association Monographs ISBN:0-947854-00-2, ISBN13:
978-0-947854-00-3. Dewey:785.1/1/0924. LCCN:85-154370.

Audience: **u,f.**

Biographies and Studies of Composers and Performers > B > Berlin, Irving

Bergreen, Laurence   ML410.B499B5 1996
As Thousands Cheer: The Life of Irving Berlin. Trade Paper. Da
Capo Press, Inc. Cambridge, MA. 1996. 702p.
ISBN:0-306-80675-4, ISBN13: 978-0-306-80675-9.
Dewey:782.1/4/092 B. LCCN:95-049847.

Audience: **g,l,u,f.** *Choice, 1991.*

Jablonski, Edward   ML410.B499J33 1998
Irving Berlin: American Troubadour. Cloth over Boards. Henry
Holt & Company. New York, NY. 1999. 406p. Irving Berlin
Collection, Vol. 1 ISBN:0-8050-4077-3, ISBN13:
978-0-8050-4077-7. Dewey:782.42164/092 B. LCCN:98-003058.

Audience: **g,l,u,f.** *Choice, 1999.*

Kimball, Robert & Berlin,   ML54.6.B464K55 2000
Irving
Complete Lyrics of Irving Berlin. Trade Cloth. Alfred A. Knopf
Inc. New York, NY. 2001. 560p. ISBN:0-679-41943-8, ISBN13:
978-0-679-41943-3. Dewey:782.42164/0268. LCCN:00-062890.

Audience: **g,l,u,f.**

Biographies and Studies of Composers and Performers > B > Berlioz, Hector

Barzun, Jacques   ML410.B5.B2 1969
Berlioz and the Romantic Century. Ed. 3. Trade Cloth.
Columbia University Press. New York, NY. 1969. 1088p.
ISBN:0-231-03135-1, ISBN13: 978-0-231-03135-6.
Dewey:780/.924. LCCN:77-097504.

Audience: **g,u,f.**

Berlioz, Hector   ML410.B5A533 1999
Evenings with the Orchestra. Jacques Barzen (Translator). Trade
Paper. University of Chicago Press. Chicago, IL. 1999. 408p.
ISBN:0-226-04374-6, ISBN13: 978-0-226-04374-6.
Dewey:780/.944/36109034. LCCN:98-054094.

Audience: **u,f.** *B*

Berlioz, Hector   ML270
The Musical Madhouse: An English Translation of Berlioz's les
Grotesques de la Musique. Alastair Bruce (Editor), Hugh
Macdonald (Introduction by). Trade Cloth. University of
Rochester Press. Rochester, NY. 2004. 264p. Eastman Studies in
Music ISBN:1-58046-132-8, ISBN13: 978-1-58046-132-0.
Dewey:780/.9. LCCN:2003-001049.

Audience: **u,f.** *Choice, 2003.*

Berlioz, Hector   ML410.B5A3 2002
The Memoirs of Hector Berlioz. David Cairns (Editor,
Translator, Introduction by). Trade Cloth. Alfred A. Knopf Inc.
New York, NY. 2002. 720p. Everyman's Library
ISBN:0-375-41391-X, ISBN13: 978-0-375-41391-9.
Dewey:780/.92 B. LCCN:2002-283060.

Audience: **u,f.**

Bloom, Peter (Editor)   ML410 .B5 C27 2000
The Cambridge Companion to Berlioz. Trade Paper. Cambridge
University Press. New York, NY. 2000. 326p. Cambridge
Companions to Music Ser. ISBN:0-521-59638-6, ISBN13:
978-0-521-59638-1. Dewey:780/.92. LCCN:99-054359.

Audience: **g,l,u,f.** *Choice, 2001.*

Cairns, David   ML410.B5C25 1999
The Making of an Artist, 1803-1832. Trade Cloth. University of
California Press. Berkeley, CA. 2000. 672p. Berlioz Ser., Vol. 1
ISBN:0-520-22199-0, ISBN13: 978-0-520-22199-4.
Dewey:780/.92. LCCN:99-053825.

Audience: **l,u,f.**

Cairns, David   ML410.B5 C25 1999
Servitude and Greatness. Trade Cloth. University of California
Press. Berkeley, CA. 2000. 907p. Berlioz Ser., Vol. 2
ISBN:0-520-22200-8, ISBN13: 978-0-520-22200-7.
Dewey:780/.92 B. LCCN:99-053825.

Audience: **g,l,u,f.**

Holoman, D. Kern   ML410.B5H58 1989
Berlioz. Trade Cloth. Harvard University Press. Cambridge,
MA. 1989. 704p. Smith Fund Ser. ISBN:0-674-06778-9,
ISBN13: 978-0-674-06778-3. Dewey:780/.92/4 B.
LCCN:88-035788.

Audience: **l,u,f.** *Choice, 1990.*

Kemp, Ian (Editor)   ML410.B5H3 1988
Hector Berlioz: "Les Troyens". Trade Cloth. Cambridge
University Press. New York, NY. 1989. 256p. Cambridge Opera
Handbooks Ser. ISBN:0-521-34280-5, ISBN13:
978-0-521-34280-3. Dewey:782.1/092/4. LCCN:88-002719.

Audience: **u,f.**

MacDonald, Hugh (Editor)   ML410.B5A33 1997
Selected Letters of Berlioz. Roger Nichols (Translator). Trade
Cloth. W. W. Norton & Company, Inc. New York, NY. 1997.
496p. ISBN:0-393-04062-3, ISBN13: 978-0-393-04062-3.
Dewey:780/.92 B. LCCN:96-047015.

Audience: **u,f.** *Choice, 1997.*

Rushton, Julian　　　　　　　**ML410.B5 R85 1994**
Berlioz: Romeo et Juliette. Trade Paper. Cambridge University
Press. New York, NY. 1994. 129p. Music Handbks.
ISBN:0-521-37767-6, ISBN13: 978-0-521-37767-6.
Dewey:784.2/2. LCCN:93-032505.

Audience: **u,f.**

Rushton, Julian　　　　　　　**ML410.B5R87 2001**
The Music of Berlioz. Trade Paper. Oxford University Press,
Inc. New York, NY. 2001. 380p. ISBN:0-19-816738-5, ISBN13:
978-0-19-816738-9. Dewey:780/.92. LCCN:00-045299.

Audience: **l,u,f.** *Choice, 2002.*

Biographies and Studies of Composers and Performers > B > Bernstein, Leonard

Bernstein, Leonard　　　　　　　　　　　　**ML60**
The Joy of Music. Paper Text. Textbook Publishers. Temecula,
CA. 2003. 303p. ISBN:0-7581-3834-2, ISBN13:
978-0-7581-3834-7. Dewey:780.

Audience: **g,l,u,f.**

Burton, Humphrey　　　　　　**ML410.B566B9 1994**
Leonard Bernstein. Trade Cloth. Doubleday Publishing. New
York, NY. 1994. 608p. ISBN:0-385-42345-4, ISBN13:
978-0-385-42345-8. Dewey:780.9/2. LCCN:93-040278.

Audience: **l,u,f.**

Burton, William W. (Editor)　　　　　**ML410.M9**
Conversations about Bernstein. Cloth Text. DIANE Publishing
Company. Collingdale, PA. 1999. 198p. ISBN:0-7881-6100-8,
ISBN13: 978-0-7881-6100-1. Dewey:780.9/2.

Audience: **l,u,f.**

Comden, Betty & Green,　　　　　**ML48.N49 1997**
　Adolph
The New York Musicals of Comden and Green: On the Town,
Wonderful Town, Bells Are Ringing. Trade Cloth. Applause
Theatre Book Publishers. New York, NY. 1996. 298p.
ISBN:1-55783-242-0, ISBN13: 978-1-55783-242-9.
Dewey:782.1/4/0268. LCCN:96-032626.

Audience: **g,l,u,f.**

Garebian, Keith　　　　　　　　　　　**ML1711**
The Making of West Side Story. Trade Paper. Mosaic Press.
Niagara Falls, NY. 2004. 160p. The Making of the Great
Broadway Musicals Ser. ISBN:0-88962-652-9, ISBN13:
978-0-88962-652-2. Dewey:782.1/4/0973.

Audience: **l,u,f.**

Houghton, Norris　　　　　　　　　　　**PR2831.A2**
Romeo and Juliet and West Side Story. Mass Market. Random
House Children's Books. New York, NY. 1965. 256p.
ISBN:0-440-97483-6, ISBN13: 978-0-440-97483-3.
Dewey:822.3/3.

Audience: **g,l,u,f.**

Myers, Paul　　　　　　　　**ML410.B566M84 1998**
Leonard Bernstein. Trade Paper. Phaidon Press. London, 1998.
240p. Twentieth-Century Composers Ser. ISBN:0-7148-3701-6,
ISBN13: 978-0-7148-3701-7. Dewey:780/.92 B.
LCCN:99-182081.

Audience: **l,u,f.**

Secrest, Meryle　　　　　　　　　　　**ML410.M9**
Leonard Bernstein: A Life. Trade Cloth. Random House Value
Publishing. New York, NY. 1997. RHVP-Remainder Ser.
ISBN:0-517-19882-7, ISBN13: 978-0-517-19882-7.
Dewey:780.9/2.

Audience: **l,u,f.** *Choice, 1995.*

Biographies and Studies of Composers and Performers > B > Berry, Chuck

Berry, Chuck　　　　　　　　　　　**ML420.B365**
Chuck Berry: The Autobiography. Faber and Faber. 2001.
ISBN:0-571-20754-5, ISBN13: 978-0-571-20754-1.

Audience: **g,l,u,f.**

Biographies and Studies of Composers and Performers > B > Billings, William

McKay, David P. &　　　　　　**ML0410.B588M**
　Crawford, Richard
William Billings of Boston: Eighteenth-Century Composer.
Trade Paper. Books on Demand. Ann Arbor, MI. 1975. 314p.
ISBN:0-608-02501-1, ISBN13: 978-0-608-02501-8.
Dewey:783.0924. LCCN:74-019035.

Audience: **u,f.**

Biographies and Studies of Composers and Performers > B > Binchois, Gilles

Kirkman, Andrew & Slavin,　　**ML410.B5885B56 2000**
　Dennis (Editors)
Binchois Studies. Trade Cloth. Oxford University Press, Inc.
New York, NY. 2001. 372p. ISBN:0-19-816668-0, ISBN13:
978-0-19-816668-9. Dewey:780/.92. LCCN:00-028823.

Audience: **u,f.**

Biographies and Studies of Composers and Performers > B > Birtwistle, Harrison

Adlington, Robert　　　　　　**ML410.B605 A35 2000**
The Music of Harrison Birtwistle. Arnold Whittall (Contribution
by). Cloth Text. Cambridge University Press. New York, NY.

2000. 256p. Music in the Twentieth Century Ser., No. 12
ISBN:0-521-63082-7, ISBN13: 978-0-521-63082-5.
Dewey:780/.92. LCCN:99-022678.

Audience: **u,f.** *Choice, 2000.*

Cross, Jonathan　　　　　　　**ML410.B605C76 2000**
Harrison Birtwistle: Man, Mind, Music. Book, Other. Cornell
University Press. Ithaca, NY. 2000. 304p. ISBN:0-8014-8672-6,
ISBN13: 978-0-8014-8672-2. Dewey:780/.92 B.
LCCN:00-020553.

Audience: **u,f.** *Choice, 2000.*

Biographies and Studies of Composers and Performers > B > Bizet, Georges

Bizet, Georges　　　　　　　**ML50.B625C22 1982**
Carmen. Nicholas John (Editor), Nell Moody & John Moody
(Translators). Trade Paper. Beekman Books, Inc. Wappingers
Falls, NY. 1982. 128p. English National Opera Guide Ser., No.
13:Bilingual Libretto, Articles ISBN:0-7145-3937-6, ISBN13:
978-0-7145-3937-9. Dewey:782.1/2. LCCN:83-107621.

Audience: **g,l,u,f.**

Dean, Winton　　　　　　　**ML410.B62**
Georges Bizet: His Life and Work. J.M. Dent. 1965.

Audience: **g,l,u,f.**

McClary, Susan　　　　　　　**ML410.B62 M25 1992**
Georges Bizet: Carmen. Richard Wagner (Contribution by).
Trade Paper. Cambridge University Press. New York, NY. 1992.
175p. Cambridge Opera Handbooks Ser. ISBN:0-521-39897-5,
ISBN13: 978-0-521-39897-8. Dewey:782.1. LCCN:91-032840.

Audience: **l,u,f.** *Choice, 1993.*

Biographies and Studies of Composers and Performers > B > Blakey, Art

Gourse, Leslie　　　　　　　**ML419**
Art Blakey: Jazz Messenger. Trade Cloth. Music Sales
Corporation. New York, NY. 2004. 209p. ISBN:0-8256-7272-4,
ISBN13: 978-0-8256-7272-9. Dewey:786.9/165/092 B.
LCCN:2003-279376.

Audience: **g,l,u,f.**

Biographies and Studies of Composers and Performers > B > Blitzstein, Marc

Gordon, Eric A.　　　　　　　**ML410.B6515**
Mark the Music: The Life and Work of Marc Blitzstein. Trade
Paper. iUniverse, Inc. Lincoln, NE. 2000. 644p.
ISBN:0-595-09248-9, ISBN13: 978-0-595-09248-2.
Dewey:780/.92/4 B.

Audience: **g,l,u,f.**

Biographies and Studies of Composers and Performers > B > Bolden, Buddy

Marquis, Donald M.　　　　　　　**ML419.B65M4 2005**
In Search of Buddy Bolden: First Man of Jazz. Trade Cloth.
Louisiana State University Press. Baton Rouge, LA. 2005. 256p.
ISBN:0-8071-3093-1, ISBN13: 978-0-8071-3093-3.
Dewey:788.9/6165/092 B. LCCN:2005-002004.

Audience: **u,f.**

Biographies and Studies of Composers and Performers > B > Boulanger, Nadia

Rosenstiel, Leonie　　　　　　　**ML410.B4**
Nadia Boulanger: A Life in Music. Trade Paper. W. W. Norton
& Company, Inc. New York, NY. 1998. 440p.
ISBN:0-393-31713-7, ISBN13: 978-0-393-31713-8.
Dewey:780/.92/4. LCCN:81-018811.

Audience: **l,u,f.**

Biographies and Studies of Composers and Performers > B > Boulez, Pierre

Boulez, Pierre　　　　　　　**ML197.B7213**
Boulez on Music Today. Trade Cloth. Harvard University Press.
Cambridge, MA. 1971. 144p. ISBN:0-674-08006-8, ISBN13:
978-0-674-08006-5. Dewey:781. LCCN:74-142073.

Audience: **u,f.** *B*

Boulez, Pierre　　　　　　　**ML60.B796**
Orientations: Collected Writings. Jean-Jacques Nattiez (Editor),
Martin Cooper (Translator). Trade Paper. Harvard University
Press. Cambridge, MA. 1990. 544p. ISBN:0-674-64376-3,
ISBN13: 978-0-674-64376-5. Dewey:780.

Audience: **u,f.**

Boulez, Pierre　　　　　　　**ML60.B71313 1991**
Stocktakings from an Apprenticeship. Stephen Walsh
(Translator). Trade Cloth. Oxford University Press, Inc. New
York, NY. 1991. 348p. ISBN:0-19-311210-8, ISBN13:
978-0-19-311210-0. Dewey:780/.9. LCCN:90-007655.

Audience: **u,f.** *Choice, 1992.*

Jameux, Dominique　　　　　　　**ML410.B773J313 1990**
Pierre Boulez. Susan Bradshaw (Translator). Trade Cloth.
Harvard University Press. Cambridge, MA. 1990. 436p.
ISBN:0-674-66740-9, ISBN13: 978-0-674-66740-2.
Dewey:781.3092. LCCN:90-004715.

Audience: **l,u,f.** *Choice, 1991.*

Biographies and Studies of Composers and Performers > B > Bowie, David

Thomson, Elizabeth & Gutman, David   ML420.B754B69 1996
The Bowie Companion. Trade Paper. Da Capo Press, Inc. Cambridge, MA. 1996. 300p. ISBN:0-306-80707-6, ISBN13: 978-0-306-80707-7. Dewey:782.4/2/166/092. LCCN:96-021685.
Audience: **g,l,u,f.**

Biographies and Studies of Composers and Performers > B > Brahms, Johannes

Botstein, Leon (Editor)   ML410.B8C64 1999
The Compleat Brahms: A Guide to the Musical Works of Johannes Brahms. Trade Cloth. W. W. Norton & Company, Inc. New York, NY. 1999. 350p. ISBN:0-393-04708-3, ISBN13: 978-0-393-04708-0. Dewey:780/.92. LCCN:98-043968.
Audience: **g,l,u,f.**

Brahms, Johannes   ML410.B8A4 1997
Johannes Brahms: Life and Letters. Styra Avins (Editor, Translator), Josef Eisinger (Translator). Trade Cloth. Oxford University Press, Inc. New York, NY. 1998. 886p. ISBN:0-19-816234-0, ISBN13: 978-0-19-816234-6. Dewey:780.9/2. LCCN:97-005417.
Audience: **u,f.** *Choice, 1998.*

Daverio, John   ML390.D335 2002
Crossing Paths: Schubert, Schumann, and Brahms. Trade Cloth. Oxford University Press, Inc. New York, NY. 2002. 328p. ISBN:0-19-513296-3, ISBN13: 978-0-19-513296-0. Dewey:780/.92/243. LCCN:2001-038744.
Audience: **u,f.** *Choice, 2003.*

Frisch, Walter   ML410.B8F75 1996
Brahms: The Four Symphonies. Spiral. Thomson Wadsworth. Belmont, CA. 1996. 226p. Monuments of Western Music Ser. ISBN:0-02-870765-6, ISBN13: 978-0-02-870765-5. Dewey:780.9/2. LCCN:96-022951.
Audience: **l,u,f.** *Choice, 1997.*

Frisch, Walter   ML410.M9
Brahms and the Principle of Developing Variation. Trade Paper. University of California Press. Berkeley, CA. 1984. 232p. California Studies in 19th Century Music, No. 2 ISBN:0-520-06958-7, ISBN13: 978-0-520-06958-9. Dewey:780.9/2. LCCN:82-013675.
Audience: **u,f.**

MacDonald, Malcolm   ML410.B8M113 1990
Brahms. Trade Cloth. Music Sales Corporation. New York, NY. 1990. 490p. ISBN:0-02-871393-1, ISBN13: 978-0-02-871393-9. Dewey:780.9/2. LCCN:90-008545.
Audience: **l,u,f.** *Choice, 1990.*

Musgrave, Michael   ML410.M9
A Brahms Reader. Trade Paper. Yale University Press. Cumberland, RI. 2001. 400p. ISBN:0-300-09199-0, ISBN13: 978-0-300-09199-1. Dewey:780.9/2.
Audience: **l,u,f.**

Musgrave, Michael (Editor)   ML410.B8 C36 1999
The Cambridge Companion to Brahms. Jonathan Cross (Contribution by). Trade Paper. Cambridge University Press. New York, NY. 1999. 348p. Cambridge Companions to Music Ser. ISBN:0-521-48581-9, ISBN13: 978-0-521-48581-4. Dewey:780/.92 B. LCCN:98-003057.
Audience: **g,l,u,f.**

Musgrave, Michael   ML410.B8M86 1996
Brahms: A German Requiem. Julian Rushton (Contribution by). Trade Paper. Cambridge University Press. New York, NY. 1996. 109p. Music Handbks. ISBN:0-521-40995-0, ISBN13: 978-0-521-40995-7. Dewey:782.3/238. LCCN:95-051987.
Audience: **u,f.** *Choice, 1997.*

Musgrave, Michael & Sherman, Bernard D. (Editors)   MT92
Performing Brahms: Early Evidence of Performance Style. John Butt & Laurence Dreyfus (Contribution by). Trade Cloth. Cambridge University Press. New York, NY. 2003. 412p. Musical Performance and Reception Ser. ISBN:0-521-65273-1, ISBN13: 978-0-521-65273-5. Dewey:781.4/3/09034. LCCN:2004-272942.
Audience: **u,f.**

Platt, Heather (Editor)   ML134
Johannes Brahms. Paper over Boards. Routledge. New York, NY. 2003. 416p. Routledge Music Bibliographies Ser. ISBN:0-8153-3850-3, ISBN13: 978-0-8153-3850-5. Dewey:016.78/092. LCCN:2003-271627.
Audience: **l,u,f.** *Choice, 2004.*

Swafford, Jan   ML410.M9
Johannes Brahms: A Biography. UK-Trade Paper. Knopf Publishing Group. New York, NY. 1999. 752p. ISBN:0-679-74582-3, ISBN13: 978-0-679-74582-2. Dewey:780.9/2.
Audience: **g,l,u,f.**

Biographies and Studies of Composers and Performers > B > Braxton, Anthony

Heffley, Mike   ML410
The Music of Anthony Braxton. Trade Cloth. Greenwood Publishing Group, Inc. Portsmouth, NH. 1996. 504p. Contributions to the Study of Music and Dance Ser., No. 43 ISBN:0-313-29956-0, ISBN13: 978-0-313-29956-8. Dewey:781.65/092. LCCN:95-043113.
Audience: **u,f.**

Radano, Ronald M.   **ML419.B735.R3 1993**
New Musical Figurations: Anthony Braxton's Cultural Critique.
Trade Cloth. University of Chicago Press. Chicago, IL. 1994.
336p. ISBN:0-226-70195-6, ISBN13: 978-0-226-70195-0.
Dewey:788.7165092. LCCN:93-001878.

Audience: **u,f.**   *Choice, 1994.*

Biographies and Studies of Composers and Performers > B > Britten, Benjamin

Carpenter, Humphrey   **ML410.B853C37 1993**
Benjamin Britten: A Biography. Trade Cloth. Thomson Gale.
Farmington Hills, MI. 1993. 677p. ISBN:0-684-19569-0,
ISBN13: 978-0-684-19569-8. Dewey:780.92. LCCN:93-018146.

Audience: **g,l,u,f.**   *Choice, 1993.*

Cooke, Mervyn   **ML410.B853 C76 1996**
Britten: War Requiem. Cloth Text. Cambridge University Press.
New York, NY. 1996. 125p. Music Handbks.
ISBN:0-521-44089-0, ISBN13: 978-0-521-44089-9.
Dewey:782.3/238. LCCN:96-006338.

Audience: **u,f.**

Cooke, Mervyn (Editor)   **ML410.B853 C36 1999**
The Cambridge Companion to Benjamin Britten. Jonathan Cross
(Contribution by). Trade Paper. Cambridge University Press.
New York, NY. 1999. 368p. Cambridge Companions to Music
Ser. ISBN:0-521-57476-5, ISBN13: 978-0-521-57476-1.
Dewey:780/.92 B. LCCN:98-030683.

Audience: **g,l,u,f.**   *Choice, 2000.*

Evans, Peter   **ML410.B853E9 1995**
The Music of Benjamin Britten. Ed. 2. Paper Text. Oxford
University Press, Inc. New York, NY. 1996. 602p.
ISBN:0-19-816590-0, ISBN13: 978-0-19-816590-3.
Dewey:780/.92. LCCN:95-047363.

Audience: **u,f.**

Biographies and Studies of Composers and Performers > B > Brown, James

Brown, James & Tucker,   **ML420**
  Bruce
James Brown: The Godfather of Soul. Trade Paper. Avalon
Publishing Group. New York, NY. 2002. 384p.
ISBN:1-56025-388-6, ISBN13: 978-1-56025-388-4.
Dewey:784.5/5/00924. LCCN:2004-270602.

Audience: **g,l,u,f.**

Biographies and Studies of Composers and Performers > B > Brubeck, Dave

Hall, Fred M.   **ML410.B868H35 1996**
It's about Time: The Dave Brubeck Story. Cloth Text.
University of Arkansas Press. Fayetteville, AR. 1996. 240p.
ISBN:1-55728-404-0, ISBN13: 978-1-55728-404-4.
Dewey:781.65/092 B. LCCN:95-038531.

Audience: **u,f.**   *Choice, 1996.*

Biographies and Studies of Composers and Performers > B > Bruckner, Anton

Korstvedt, Benjamin M.   **ML410.B88 K67 2000**
Bruckner: Symphony No. 8. Julian Rushton (Contribution by).
Cloth Text. Cambridge University Press. New York, NY. 2000.
146p. Music Handbks., No. 8 ISBN:0-521-63226-9, ISBN13:
978-0-521-63226-3. Dewey:784.2184. LCCN:99-031880.

Audience: **u,f.**

Simpson, Robert   **ML410.B88S46 1992**
The Essence of Bruckner. Ed. 2. Trade Paper. Victor Gollancz
Ltd. London, 1992. 256p. ISBN:0-575-05221-X, ISBN13:
978-0-575-05221-5. Dewey:784.2/184/092. LCCN:93-183982.

Audience: **u,f.**

Watson, Derek   **ML410.B88**
Bruckner. New York: Schirmer Books; London: Prentice Hall
International. 1997. Master Musicians Ser. ISBN:0-02-864626-6,
ISBN13: 978-0-02-864626-8.

Audience: **l,u,f.**

Williamson, John (Editor)   **ML410.B88C36 2003**
The Cambridge Companion to Bruckner. Jonathan Cross
(Contribution by). Cloth Text. Cambridge University Press. New
York, NY. 2004. 326p. Cambridge Companions to Music Ser.
ISBN:0-521-80404-3, ISBN13: 978-0-521-80404-2.
Dewey:780/.92 B. LCCN:2002-038785.

Audience: **u,f.**   *Choice, 2005.*

Biographies and Studies of Composers and Performers > B > Busnois, Antoine

Higgins, Paula (Editor)   **ML410.B9798A58 1996**
Antoine Busnois: Method, Meaning, and Context in Late
Medieval Music. Trade Cloth. Oxford University Press, Inc.
New York, NY. 2000. 622p. ISBN:0-19-816406-8, ISBN13:
978-0-19-816406-7. Dewey:780/.92. LCCN:95-045522.

Audience: **u,f.**

Biographies and Studies of Composers and Performers > B > Buxtehude, Dietrich

Snyder, Kerala J.   **ML410.B4**
Dietrich Buxtehude: Organist in Lubeck. Trade Cloth. Thomson Wadsworth. Belmont, CA. 1993. 551p. ISBN:0-02-872455-0, ISBN13: 978-0-02-872455-3. Dewey:780/.92/4 B. LCCN:87-018505.

Audience: **u,f.**   *Choice, 1988.*

Biographies and Studies of Composers and Performers > B > Byrd, William

Harley, John   **ML410.B996H37 1997**
William Byrd: Gentleman of the Chapel Royal. Trade Cloth. Ashgate Publishing, Ltd. Aldershot, 1997. 504p. ISBN:1-85928-165-6, ISBN13: 978-1-85928-165-9. Dewey:780.9/2. LCCN:96-037221.

Audience: **u,f.**   *Choice, 1997.*

Turbet, Richard   **ML134.B96T9 2005**
William Byrd: A Guide to Research. Ed. 2. Paper over Boards. Routledge. New York, NY. 2006. 352p. Routledge Music Bibliographies Ser. ISBN:0-415-94301-9, ISBN13: 978-0-415-94301-7. Dewey:016.78/092. LCCN:2005-013599.

Audience: **l,u,f.**   *Choice, 1988.*

Biographies and Studies of Composers and Performers > C > Cage, John

Cage, John M.   **ML60**
Empty Words: Writings, '73 -'78. Trade Paper. Wesleyan University Press. Middletown, CT. 1979. 199p. ISBN:0-8195-6067-7, ISBN13: 978-0-8195-6067-4. Dewey:780. LCCN:78-027212.

Audience: **u,f.**

Cage, John M.   **PS3553.A32**
M: Writings '67-'72. Trade Paper. Wesleyan University Press. Middletown, CT. 1973. 233p. ISBN:0-8195-6035-9, ISBN13: 978-0-8195-6035-3. Dewey:818.54. LCCN:72-011051.

Audience: **u,f.**

Cage, John M.   **ML3845**
Silence: Lectures and Writings. Trade Paper. Wesleyan University Press. Middletown, CT. 1961. 288p. ISBN:0-8195-6028-6, ISBN13: 978-0-8195-6028-5. Dewey:780.1. LCCN:61-014238.

Audience: **g,l,u,f.**

Kostelanetz, Richard   **ML410.C24K68 2003**
Conversing with Cage. Ed. 2. Paper over Boards. Routledge. New York, NY. 2002. 344p. ISBN:0-415-93791-4, ISBN13: 978-0-415-93791-7. Dewey:780.92. LCCN:2003-555574.

Audience: **u,f.**   *Choice, 1988.*

Kostelanetz, Richard (Editor)   **ML410.M9**
Writings about John Cage. Trade Cloth. University of Michigan Press. Chicago, IL. 1993. 376p. ISBN:0-472-10348-2, ISBN13: 978-0-472-10348-5. Dewey:780.9/2. LCCN:92-032218.

Audience: **g,l,u,f.**   *Choice, 1994.*

Nicholls, David (Editor)   **ML410.C24 C36 2002**
The Cambridge Companion to John Cage. Jonathan Cross (Contribution by). Trade Paper. Cambridge University Press. New York, NY. 2002. 302p. Cambridge Companions to Music Ser. ISBN:0-521-78968-0, ISBN13: 978-0-521-78968-4. Dewey:780/.92 B. LCCN:2001-052401.

Audience: **l,u,f.**   *Choice, 2003.*

Pritchett, James   **ML410.M9**
The Music of John Cage. Arnold Whittall (Contribution by). Trade Paper. Cambridge University Press. New York, NY. 1996. 237p. Music in the Twentieth Century Ser., No. 5 ISBN:0-521-56544-8, ISBN13: 978-0-521-56544-8. Dewey:780.9/2.

Audience: **u,f.**

Biographies and Studies of Composers and Performers > C > Cale, John

Cale, John & Bockris, Victor   **ML420.P96**
What's Welsh for Zen: The Autobiography of John Cale. Trade Paper. Bloomsbury Publishing. New York, NY. 2000. 272p. ISBN:1-58234-068-4, ISBN13: 978-1-58234-068-5. Dewey:782.4/2/166/092.

Audience: **u,f.**

Biographies and Studies of Composers and Performers > C > Callas, Maria

Levine, Robert   **ML420.C18L48 2003**
Maria Callas: A Musical Biography. Mixed Media. Black Dog & Leventhal Publishers, Inc. New York, NY. 2003. 224p. ISBN:1-57912-283-3, ISBN13: 978-1-57912-283-6. Dewey:782.1/092 B. LCCN:2003-004173.

Audience: **g,l,u,f.**

Biographies and Studies of Composers and Performers > C > Carolan, Turlough

O'Sullivan, Donal   **ML419.C35**
Carolan: The Life Times and Music of an Irish Harper. Ed. 2. Trade Paper. Ossian Publications Limited. Incorporating. Cork, 2004. 384p. ISBN:1-900428-71-7, ISBN13: 978-1-900428-71-2. Dewey:787.5092.

Audience: **u,f.**

Biographies and Studies of Composers and Performers > C > Carissimi, Giacomo

Dixon, Graham   **ML410.C3/**
Carissimi. Trade Cloth. Oxford University Press, Inc. New York, NY. 1986. 96p. Studies of Composers ISBN:0-19-315249-5, ISBN13: 978-0-19-315249-6. Dewey:783/.092/4.

Audience: **u,f.**

Biographies and Studies of Composers and Performers > C > Carter, Benny

Berger, Morroe, et al.   **ML419.C4B5 2002**
Benny Carter: A Life in American Music, Set. Ed. 2. Edward Berger & James Patrick (Authors), Benny Carter (Foreword by). Trade Cloth. Scarecrow Press, Inc. Lanham, MD. 2002. 1440p. Studies in Jazz, No. 40 ISBN:0-8108-4111-8, ISBN13: 978-0-8108-4111-6. Dewey:781.65/092 B. LCCN:2001-049082.

Audience: **u,f.**

Biographies and Studies of Composers and Performers > C > Carter, Elliott

Carter, Elliott   **ML197**
Elliott Carter: Collected Essays and Lectures, 1937-1995. Jonathan W. Bernard (Editor). Trade Paper. University of Rochester Press. Rochester, NY. 1998. 392p. Eastman Studies in Music, No. 7 ISBN:1-58046-025-9, ISBN13: 978-1-58046-025-5. Dewey:780.9/04. LCCN:96-026355.

Audience: **u,f.** *Choice, 1997.*

Schiff, David   **ML410.C3293S34 1998**
The Music of Elliott Carter. Ed. 2. Elliott Carter (Foreword by). Trade Cloth. Cornell University Press. Ithaca, NY. 1998. 356p. ISBN:0-8014-3612-5, ISBN13: 978-0-8014-3612-3. Dewey:780/.92. LCCN:98-033956.

Audience: **u,f.** *Choice, 1999.*

Biographies and Studies of Composers and Performers > C > Carter Family

Zwonitzer, Mark & Hirshberg, Charles   **ML421.C33Z86 2002**
Will You Miss Me When I'm Gone?: The Carter Family and Their Legacy in American Music. Trade Cloth. Simon & Schuster. New York, NY. 2002. 432p. ISBN:0-684-85763-4, ISBN13: 978-0-684-85763-3. Dewey:781.642/092/2. LCCN:2002-022395.

Audience: **g,l,u,f.** *Choice, 2002.*

Biographies and Studies of Composers and Performers > C > Cash, Johnny

Cash, Johnny & Carr, Patrick   **ML420.C265A3 1998**
Cash: The Autobiography. Mass Market. HarperCollins Publishers. New York, NY. 2005. 448p. ISBN:0-06-101357-9, ISBN13: 978-0-06-101357-7. Dewey:782.4/2/1642/092. LCCN:98-227899.

Audience: **g,l,u,f.**

Streissguth, Michael   **ML420.C265**
Ring of Fire: The Johnny Cash Reader. Trade Paper. Da Capo Press, Inc. Cambridge, MA. 2003. 336p. ISBN:0-306-81225-8, ISBN13: 978-0-306-81225-5. Dewey:782.4/21642/092.

Audience: **g,l,u,f.**

Biographies and Studies of Composers and Performers > C > Cavalli, Pier Francesco

Glover, Jane   **ML410.B4**
Cavalli. Cloth Text. Palgrave Macmillan. New York, NY. 1978. ISBN:0-312-12546-1, ISBN13: 978-0-312-12546-2. Dewey:780/.92/4. LCCN:77-023638.

Audience: **u,f.**

Biographies and Studies of Composers and Performers > C > Charles, Ray

Charles, Ray & Ritz, David   **ML420.C46A3 2004**
Brother Ray: Ray Charles' Own Story. Paper Text. Da Capo Press, Inc. Cambridge, MA. 2004. 384p. ISBN:0-306-81431-5, ISBN13: 978-0-306-81431-0. Dewey:782.4/21644/092.

Audience: **g,l,u,f.**

Lydon, Michael　　　　　　　　　ML420.C46L93 2004
Ray Charles: Man and Music. Ed. 2. UK-B Format Paperback. Routledge. New York, NY. 2004. 472p. ISBN:0-415-97043-1, ISBN13: 978-0-415-97043-3. Dewey:782.42164/092 B. LCCN:2003-058684.

Audience: **g,l,u,f.**

Biographies and Studies of Composers and Performers > C > Charpentier, Marc-Antoine

Cessac, Catherine　　　　　　　ML410.C433C4713 1995
Marc-Antoine Charpentier. E. Thomas Glasow (Translator). Trade Cloth. Hal Leonard Corporation. Milwaukee, WI. 1995. 566p. ISBN:0-931340-80-2, ISBN13: 978-0-931340-80-2. Dewey:782.1/092 B. LCCN:94-029786.

Audience: **u,f.**　*Choice, 1995.*

Biographies and Studies of Composers and Performers > C > Chopin, Frederic

Kallberg, Jeffrey　　　　　　　　　　　ML410.C54
Chopin at the Boundaries: Sex, History, and Musical Genre. Trade Paper. Harvard University Press. Cambridge, MA. 1998. 320p. Convergences Ser., :Inventories of the Present Ser. ISBN:0-674-12791-9, ISBN13: 978-0-674-12791-3. Dewey:786.2092.

Audience: **u,f.**　*Choice, 1996.*

Rink, John　　　　　　　　　　ML410.C54RR54 1997
Chopin: The Piano Concertos. Julian Rushton (Editor, Contribution by). Cloth Text. Cambridge University Press. New York, NY. 1997. 149p. Music Handbks. ISBN:0-521-44109-9, ISBN13: 978-0-521-44109-4. Dewey:784.2/62/092. LCCN:97-006905.

Audience: **u,f.**

Samson, Jim　　　　　　　　ML410.C54S1865 1998
Chopin. Trade Paper. Oxford University Press, Inc. New York, NY. 2006. 334p. Master Musicians Ser. ISBN:0-19-816703-2, ISBN13: 978-0-19-816703-7. Dewey:786.2/092 B. LCCN:98-008653.

Audience: **l,u,f.**　*Choice, 1997.*

Samson, Jim　　　　　　　　ML410.C54S188 1994
The Music of Chopin. Trade Paper. Oxford University Press, Inc. New York, NY. 1994. 252p. ISBN:0-19-816402-5, ISBN13: 978-0-19-816402-9. Dewey:786.2/092. LCCN:93-030977.

Audience: **l,u,f.**　*Choice, 1986.*

Samson, Jim (Editor)　　　　　　　　ML410.C54
The Cambridge Companion to Chopin. Jonathan Cross (Contribution by). Trade Paper. Cambridge University Press. New York, NY. 1994. 353p. Cambridge Companions to Music Ser. ISBN:0-521-47752-2, ISBN13: 978-0-521-47752-9. Dewey:786.2/092. LCCN:91-024533.

Audience: **g,l,u,f.**　*Choice, 1993.*

Samson, Jim　　　　　　　　ML410.C54 S187 1992
Chopin: The Four Ballades. Julian Rushton (Contribution by). Trade Cloth. Cambridge University Press. New York, NY. 1992. 114p. Music Handbks. ISBN:0-521-38461-3, ISBN13: 978-0-521-38461-2. Dewey:786.21896. LCCN:91-002542.

Audience: **u,f.**

Smialek, William　　　　　　　ML134.C54S65 2000
Frederic Chopin: A Guide to Research. Guy A. Marco (Editor). Cloth Text. Garland Publishing, Inc. New York, NY. 1999. 300p. Composer Resource Manuals Ser., Vol. 50 ISBN:0-8153-2180-5, ISBN13: 978-0-8153-2180-4. Dewey:016.7862/092. LCCN:99-042566.

Audience: **l,u,f.**　*Choice, 2000.*

Biographies and Studies of Composers and Performers > C > Clementi, Muzio

Plantinga, Leon　　　　　　　　　ML410.C64.P5
Clementi: His Life and Music. Trade Cloth. Oxford University Press, Inc. New York, NY. 1977. xiii, 346p. ISBN:0-19-315227-4, ISBN13: 978-0-19-315227-4. Dewey:786.1/092/4 B. LCCN:77-359247.

Audience: **l,u,f.**

Biographies and Studies of Composers and Performers > C > Cole, Nat King

Gourse, Leslie　　　　　　　　ML420.C63G7 2000
Unforgettable: The Life and Mystique of Nat King Cole. Trade Paper. Cooper Square Publishers, Inc. New York, NY. 2000. 352p. ISBN:0-8154-1082-4, ISBN13: 978-0-8154-1082-9. Dewey:782.42164/092 B. LCCN:00-057000.

Audience: **g,l,u,f.**

Biographies and Studies of Composers and Performers > C > Coleman, Ornette

Wilson, Peter N.　　　　　　　ML419.C63W513 1999
Ornette Coleman: His Life and Music. Robert Dobbin (Translator). Trade Paper. Berkeley Hills Books. Berkeley, CA. 1999. 216p. ISBN:1-893163-04-0, ISBN13: 978-1-893163-04-1. Dewey:788.7/165/092 B. LCCN:99-021581.

Audience: **l,u,f.**

Biographies and Studies of Composers and Performers > C > Coleridge-Taylor, Samuel

Self, Geoffrey   ML410.C74S45 1995
The Hiawatha Man: The Life and Music of Samuel
Coleridge-Taylor. Trade Cloth. Ashgate Publishing, Ltd.
Aldershot, 1995. 328p. ISBN:0-85967-983-7, ISBN13:
978-0-85967-983-1. Dewey:780/.92 B. LCCN:94-045001.
                                Audience: **l,u,f.** *Choice, 1996.*

Biographies and Studies of Composers and Performers > C > Coltrane, John

Fujioka, Yasuhiro   ML156.7.C58F85 1995
John Coltrane: A Discography and Musical Biography. Lewis
Porter & Yoh-Ichi Hamada (Preface by). Trade Cloth. Scarecrow
Press, Inc. Lanham, MD. 1995. 416p. Studies in Jazz, No. 20
ISBN:0-8108-2986-X, ISBN13: 978-0-8108-2986-2.
Dewey:016.7887/165/092. LCCN:94-048457.
                                                Audience: **u,f.**

Kahn, Ashley   ML419.C645
A Love Supreme: The Story of John Coltrane's Signature
Album. Trade Paper. Penguin Group (USA) Inc. New York, NY.
2003. 288p. ISBN:0-14-200352-2, ISBN13: 978-0-14-200352-7.
Dewey:785/.34165.
                                                Audience: **u,f.**

Kofsky, Frank   ML3508.K64 1998
John Coltrane and the Jazz Revolution of The 1960s. Ed. 2.
Trade Paper. Pathfinder Press. New York, NY. 1998. 500p.
ISBN:0-87348-857-1, ISBN13: 978-0-87348-857-0.
Dewey:781.65/5/08996073. LCCN:97-069548.
                                                Audience: **u,f.**

Porter, Lewis   ML156.7.C58P65 1999
John Coltrane: His Life and Music. Trade Paper. University of
Michigan Press. Chicago, IL. 2000. 448p. The Michigan
American Music Ser. ISBN:0-472-08643-X, ISBN13:
978-0-472-08643-6. Dewey:[B]. LCCN:97-041995.
                                                Audience: **g,l,u,f.**

Woideck, Carl   ML419.C645
John Coltrane Companion: Four Decades of Commentary. Trade
Paper. Music Sales Corporation. New York, NY. 1998. 300p.
ISBN:0-8256-7189-2, ISBN13: 978-0-8256-7189-0.
Dewey:788.7/165/092.
                                                Audience: **g,l,u,f.**

Biographies and Studies of Composers and Performers > C > Copland, Aaron

Berger, Arthur V.   ML410.C756B4 1990
Aaron Copland. Leonard Burkat (Introduction by). Paper Text.
Da Capo Press, Inc. Cambridge, MA. 1990. 496p. Music
Reprint Ser. ISBN:0-306-76266-8, ISBN13: 978-0-306-76266-6.
Dewey:780/.92/4 B. LCCN:85-000462.
                                                Audience: **u,f.**

Copland, Aaron   ML63
Copland on Music. Paper Text. Classic Textbooks. Murrieta,
CA. 1960. 280p. ISBN:1-4047-9255-4, ISBN13:
978-1-4047-9255-5. Dewey:780.8.
                                                Audience: **u,f.** *B*

Copland, Aaron   ML197 .C76
The New Music, 1900-1960. Library Binding. Reprint Services
Company. Temecula, CA. 194p. ISBN:0-685-14848-3, ISBN13:
978-0-685-14848-8. Dewey:780/.904.
                                                Audience: **u,f.** *B*

Copland, Aaron   MT6
What to Listen for in Music. Library Binding. Sagebrush
Education Resources. Caledonia, MN. 1999.
ISBN:0-613-18082-8, ISBN13: 978-0-613-18082-5.
Dewey:780/.1/5.
                                                Audience: **l,u,f.** *B*

Copland, Aaron   ML410.C756
Aaron Copland A Reader: Selected Writings 1923-1972.
Kostelanetz, Richard (Editor) (Introduction by); Silverstein,
Steven (Assistant Editor). Routledge. 2004.
ISBN:0-415-93940-2, ISBN13: 978-0-415-93940-9.
                                                Audience: **u,f.**

Copland, Aaron & Perlis,   ML410.C756A3 1987
  Vivian
Copland: 1900 Through 1942. Trade Paper. St. Martin's Press.
Gordonville, VA. 1999. 402p. ISBN:0-312-01149-0, ISBN13:
978-0-312-01149-9. Dewey:[B]. LCCN:84-011703.
                                                Audience: **g,l,u,f.**

Copland, Aaron & Perlis,   ML410.C756A3 1990
  Vivian
Copland: Since 1943. Trade Paper. St. Martin's Press.
Gordonville, VA. 1990. 480p. ISBN:0-312-05066-6, ISBN13:
978-0-312-05066-5. Dewey:780/.92 B. LCCN:90-036888.
                                                Audience: **g,l,u,f.**

Oja, Carol J. & Tick, Judith   ML410
  (Editors)
Aaron Copland and His World. Trade Paper, Perfect. Princeton
University Press. Princeton, NJ. 2005. 328p. The Bard Music
Festival Ser. ISBN:0-691-12470-1, ISBN13: 978-0-691-12470-4.
Dewey:780.92.
                                                Audience: **g,l,u,f.**

Biographies and Studies of Composers and Performers > C > Corelli, Arcangelo

Allsop, Peter ML410.C78A8 1998
Arcangelo Corelli: New Orpheus of Our Times. Trade Cloth.
Oxford University Press, Inc. New York, NY. 1999. 272p.
Oxford Monographs on Music ISBN:0-19-816562-5, ISBN13:
978-0-19-816562-0. Dewey:787.2/092 B. LCCN:98-007973.
Audience: **u,f.** *Choice, 2000.*

Biographies and Studies of Composers and Performers > C > Couperin, Francois

Beaussant, Phillippe ML410.C855B413 1990
Francois Couperin. Alexandra Land (Translator). Trade Cloth.
Hal Leonard Corporation. Milwaukee, WI. 1990. 426p.
ISBN:0-931340-27-6, ISBN13: 978-0-931340-27-7.
Dewey:780/.92 B. LCCN:89-028729.
Audience: **u,f.** *Choice, 1991.*

Mellers, Wilfrid ML410.C855
Francois Couperin and the French Classical Tradition. Ed. 2.
Trade Cloth. Faber & Faber, Inc. New York, NY. 1987. 544p.
ISBN:0-571-13983-3, ISBN13: 978-0-571-13983-5.
Dewey:780/.92/4.
Audience: **u,f.** *Choice, 1988.*

Biographies and Studies of Composers and Performers > C > Cowell, Henry

Cowell, Henry ML60.C85 2000
Essential Cowell: Selected Writings on Music. Dick Higgins
(Editor). Trade Cloth. McPherson & Company. Kingston, NY.
2003. 347p. ISBN:0-929701-63-1, ISBN13: 978-0-929701-63-9.
Dewey:780. LCCN:00-055904.
Audience: **u,f.**

Hicks, Michael ML410.C859H53 2002
Henry Cowell, Bohemian. Trade Cloth. University of Illinois
Press. Champaign, IL. 2002. 240p. Music in American Life Ser.
ISBN:0-252-02751-5, ISBN13: 978-0-252-02751-2.
Dewey:780/.92 B. LCCN:2001-007064.
Audience: **g,l,u,f.** *Choice, 2003.*

Biographies and Studies of Composers and Performers > C > Cream

Platt, John ML421.C74
Disraeli Gears: Cream. New York: Schirmer Books; London:
Prentice Hall International. 1998. Classic Rock Albums
ISBN:0-02-864774-2, ISBN13: 978-0-02-864774-6.
Audience: **l,u,f.**

Biographies and Studies of Composers and Performers > C > Crosby, Bing

Giddins, Gary ML420.C93G53 2001
Bing Crosby: A Pocketful of Dreams - The Early Years,
1903-1940. Trade Cloth. Little Brown & Company. New York,
NY. 2000. 736p. ISBN:0-316-88188-0, ISBN13:
978-0-316-88188-3. Dewey:782.42164092. LCCN:00-044403.
Audience: **g,l,u,f.** *Choice, 2001.*

Biographies and Studies of Composers and Performers > C > Cruz, Celia

Reymundo, Ana Cristina & ML420.C957A3 2044
 Cruz, Celia
Celia: My Life. Jose Lucas Badue (Translator). Trade Cloth.
HarperCollins Publishers. New York, NY. 2004. 304p.
ISBN:0-06-072553-2, ISBN13: 978-0-06-072553-2.
Dewey:782.42164/092 B. LCCN:2004-046868.
Audience: **g,l,u,f.**

Biographies and Studies of Composers and Performers > D > Dallapiccola, Luigi

Fearn, Raymond ML410.D138F43 2003
The Music of Luigi Dallapiccola. Trade Cloth. University of
Rochester Press. Rochester, NY. 2005. 324p. Eastman Studies in
Music ISBN:1-58046-078-X, ISBN13: 978-1-58046-078-1.
Dewey:780/.92. LCCN:2003-007367.
Audience: **u,f.** *Choice, 2004.*

Biographies and Studies of Composers and Performers > D > Da Ponte, Lorenzo

Da Ponte, Lorenzo ML423.D15A3 2000
Memoirs of Lorenzo Da Ponte. Elisabeth Abbott (Translator),
Charles Rosen (Introduction by). Trade Paper. New York
Review of Books, Incorporated, The. New York, NY. 2000.
472p. New York Review Books Classics Ser.
ISBN:0-940322-35-8, ISBN13: 978-0-940322-35-6.
LCCN:99-046014.
Audience: **u,f.**

Biographies and Studies of Composers and Performers > D > Davies, Peter Maxwell

McGregor, Richard (Editor) ML410.D254P47 2000
Perspectives on Peter Maxwell Davies. Trade Cloth. Ashgate
Publishing, Ltd. Aldershot, 2000. 194p. ISBN:1-84014-298-7,
ISBN13: 978-1-84014-298-3. Dewey:780/.92. LCCN:00-107423.
Audience: **u,f.**

Biographies and Studies of Composers and Performers > D > Davis, Miles

Carr, Ian ML419.D39
Miles Davis: The Definitive Biography. Trade Paper. DIANE
Publishing Company. Collingdale, PA. 2004. 658p.
ISBN:0-7567-8375-5, ISBN13: 978-0-7567-8375-4.
Dewey:788.9/2165/092 B.
Audience: **g,l,u,f.**

Davis, Miles & Troupe, ML419.D39A3 1990
  Quincy
Miles: The Autobiography. Trade Paper. Simon & Schuster. New
York, NY. 1990. 448p. ISBN:0-671-72582-3, ISBN13:
978-0-671-72582-2. Dewey:788.9/2165/092 B.
LCCN:90-037501.
Audience: **g,l,u,f.** *Choice, 1990.*

Kahn, Ashley ML419.D39
Kind of Blue: The Making of the Miles Davis Masterpiece.
Jimmy Cobb (Foreword by). Trade Paper. Da Capo Press, Inc.
Cambridge, MA. 2001. 224p. ISBN:0-306-81067-0, ISBN13:
978-0-306-81067-1. Dewey:785/.32196165.
Audience: **u,f.**

Kirchner, Bill (Editor) ML419.D39M55 1997
A Miles Davis Reader. Trade Cloth. Smithsonian Institution
Press. Washington, DC. 1997. 278p. ISBN:1-56098-774-X,
ISBN13: 978-1-56098-774-1. Dewey:788.9/2165/092.
LCCN:97-012802.
Audience: **g,l,u,f.**

Nisenson, Eric ML419.D39N58 2000
Kind of Blue: The Making of the Miles Davis Masterpiece.
Trade Cloth. St. Martin's Press. Gordonville, VA. 2000. xv,
236p. ISBN:0-312-26617-0, ISBN13: 978-0-312-26617-2.
Dewey:781.65/026/6. LCCN:00-044170.
Audience: **u,f.**

Biographies and Studies of Composers and Performers > D > Debussy, Claude

Briscoe, James R. ML134.D26B7 1990
Claude Debussy: A Guide to Research. Cloth Text. Garland
Publishing, Inc. New York, NY. 1990. 526p. Composer
Resource Manuals Ser., Vol. 27 ISBN:0-8240-5795-3, ISBN13:
978-0-8240-5795-4. Dewey:016.78/092. LCCN:89-023691.
Audience: **l,u,f.** *Choice, 1990.*

Brown, Matthew MT130.D4B76 2002
Debussy's Iberia. Trade Cloth. Oxford University Press, Inc.
New York, NY. 2003. 194p. Studies in Musical Genesis and
Structure ISBN:0-19-816199-9, ISBN13: 978-0-19-816199-8.
Dewey:784.2/1896. LCCN:2002-192554.
Audience: **u,f.**

Debussy, Claude, et al. ML90
Three Classics in the Aesthetic of Music. Ferruccio Busoni &
Charles Ives (Authors). Trade Paper. Dover Publications, Inc.
Mineola, NY. 1962. 188p. ISBN:0-486-20320-4, ISBN13:
978-0-486-20320-1. Dewey:780.922.
Audience: **u,f.**

Fulcher, Jane F. (Editor) ML410.D28D37 2001
Debussy and His World. Trade Cloth. Princeton University
Press. Princeton, NJ. 2001. 350p. The Bard Music Festival Ser.
ISBN:0-691-09041-6, ISBN13: 978-0-691-09041-2.
Dewey:780/.92. LCCN:2001-027840.
Audience: **g,l,u,f.** *Choice, 2002.*

Howat, Roy ML410.M9
Debussy in Proportion: A Musical Analysis. Trade Paper.
Cambridge University Press. New York, NY. 1986. 246p.
ISBN:0-521-31145-4, ISBN13: 978-0-521-31145-8.
Dewey:780.9/2.
Audience: **u,f.**

Nichols, Roger ML410.D28 N55 1998
The Life of Debussy. Trade Paper. Cambridge University Press.
New York, NY. 1998. 192p. Musical Lives Ser.
ISBN:0-521-57887-6, ISBN13: 978-0-521-57887-5.
Dewey:780/.92 B. LCCN:97-025666.
Audience: **g,l,u,f.** *Choice, 1998.*

Nichols, Roger ML410.M9
Debussy Remembered. Claude Debussy (Composed by). Trade
Cloth. Hal Leonard Corporation. Milwaukee, WI. 1992. 264p.
ISBN:0-931340-41-1, ISBN13: 978-0-931340-41-3.
Dewey:780.92. LCCN:92-226956.
Audience: **l,u,f.**

Nichols, Roger & Smith, ML410.D28 N48 1989
  Richard Langham
Claude Debussy: Pelléas et Mélisande. Richard Wagner
(Contribution by). Trade Paper. Cambridge University Press.

New York, NY. 1989. 224p. Cambridge Opera Handbooks Ser.
ISBN:0-521-31446-1, ISBN13: 978-0-521-31446-6.
Dewey:782.1. LCCN:88-016172.
Audience: **u,f.** *Choice, 1989.*

Parks, Richard S. **ML410.D28P24 1989**
The Music of Claude Debussy. Cloth over Boards. Yale
University Press. Cumberland, RI. 1990. 360p. Composers of
the Twentieth Century Ser. ISBN:0-300-04439-9, ISBN13:
978-0-300-04439-3. Dewey:780/.92/4. LCCN:89-031406.
Audience: **u,f.** *Choice, 1990.*

Roberts, Paul **ML410.C54**
Images: The Piano Music of Claude Debussy. Trade Paper. Hal
Leonard Corporation. Milwaukee, WI. 2003. 372p.
ISBN:1-57467-068-9, ISBN13: 978-1-57467-068-4.
Dewey:786.2/092.
Audience: **l,u,f.** *Choice, 1996.*

Trezise, Simon (Editor) **ML410.D28C26 2002**
The Cambridge Companion to Debussy. Cloth Text. Cambridge
University Press. New York, NY. 2003. 346p. Cambridge
Companions to Music Ser. ISBN:0-521-65243-X, ISBN13:
978-0-521-65243-8. Dewey:780/.92 B. LCCN:2001-043703.
Audience: **g,l,u,f.** *Choice, 2004.*

Trezise, Simon **ML410.D28 T7 1994**
Debussy: La Mer. Julian Rushton (Contribution by). Trade
Paper. Cambridge University Press. New York, NY. 1995. 121p.
Music Handbks. ISBN:0-521-44656-2, ISBN13:
978-0-521-44656-3. Dewey:784.2/1896. LCCN:93-042789.
Audience: **u,f.** *Choice, 1995.*

Biographies and Studies of Composers and Performers > D > Delius, Frederick

Carley, Lionel **ML410.D35F74 1998**
Frederick Delius: Music, Art and Literature. Trade Cloth.
Ashgate Publishing, Ltd. Aldershot, 1997. 350p.
ISBN:1-85928-222-9, ISBN13: 978-1-85928-222-9.
Dewey:780/.92. LCCN:97-003005.
Audience: **u,f.**

Biographies and Studies of Composers and Performers > D > Dittersdorf, Karl Ditters von

Von Dittersdorf, Karl D. **ML410.D6**
The Autobiography of Karl Von Dittersdorf. Trade Cloth.
Library Reprints, Inc. Temecula, CA. 2001. 316p.
ISBN:0-7222-5403-2, ISBN13: 978-0-7222-5403-5.
Dewey:780/.924.
Audience: **u,f.**

Biographies and Studies of Composers and Performers > D > Dixon, Willie

Snowden, Don & Dixon, **ML410.D68A3 1989**
 Willie
I Am the Blues: The Willie Dixon Story. Trade Paper. Da Capo
Press, Inc. Cambridge, MA. 1990. 264p. ISBN:0-306-80415-8,
ISBN13: 978-0-306-80415-1. Dewey:781.643/092 B.
LCCN:90-038862.
Audience: **l,u,f.**

Biographies and Studies of Composers and Performers > D > Dolphy, Eric

Simosko, Vladimir & **ML419.D646**
 Tepperman, Barry
Eric Dolphy: A Musical Biography and Discography. Trade
Paper. Da Capo Press, Inc. Cambridge, MA. 1996. 200p.
Quality Paperbacks Ser. ISBN:0-306-80524-3, ISBN13:
978-0-306-80524-0. Dewey:788/.0092/4. LCCN:79-015117.
Audience: **u,f.**

Biographies and Studies of Composers and Performers > D > Donizetti, Gaetano

Ashbrook, William **ML410.D7**
Donizetti. London, Cassell. 1965.
Audience: **l,u,f.**

Osborne, Charles **ML390.O82 1994**
The Bel Canto Operas: A Guide to the Operas of Rossini,
Bellini, and Donizetti. Trade Cloth. Hal Leonard Corporation.
Milwaukee, WI. 1994. 378p. ISBN:0-931340-71-3, ISBN13:
978-0-931340-71-0. Dewey:782.1/0945/09034.
LCCN:94-168756.
Audience: **g,l,u,f.** *Choice, 1994.*

Biographies and Studies of Composers and Performers > D > Doors

Rocco, John · **ML421.D66**
The Doors Companion: Four Decades of Commentary. Trade
Paper. Music Sales Corporation. New York, NY. 1997. 300p.
ISBN:0-8256-7235-X, ISBN13: 978-0-8256-7235-4.
Dewey:782.42166/092/2. LCCN:94-045692.
Audience: **l,u,f.**

Biographies and Studies of Composers and Performers > D > Dowland, John

Holman, Peter   **ML410.D808H651999**
Dowland: Lachrimae (1604). Julian Rushton (Contribution by). Cloth Text. Cambridge University Press. New York, NY. 1999. 116p. Music Handbks. ISBN:0-521-58196-6, ISBN13: 978-0-521-58196-7. Dewey:784.1882. LCCN:98-054374.
Audience: **u,f.**

Poulton, Diana   **ML410.B4**
John Dowland. Ed. 2. Trade Cloth. University of California Press. Berkeley, CA. 1982. 550p. ISBN:0-520-04687-0, ISBN13: 978-0-520-04687-0. Dewey:780/.92/4.
Audience: **l,u,f.**

Biographies and Studies of Composers and Performers > D > Dufay, Guillaume

Fallows, David   **ML410.D83**
Dufay. Cloth Text. J. M. Dent & Sons. London, 1982. viii, 321p. ISBN:0-460-03180-5, ISBN13: 978-0-460-03180-6. Dewey:780/.92/4 B. LCCN:82-200447.
Audience: **u,f.**

Biographies and Studies of Composers and Performers > D > Dunstable, John

Bent, Margaret   **ML410.D933**
Dunstaple. London; New York: Oxford University Press. 1981. Oxford Studies of Composers; 17 ISBN:0-19-315225-8, ISBN13: 978-0-19-315225-0.
Audience: **u,f.**

Biographies and Studies of Composers and Performers > D > Dutilleux, Henri

Potter, Caroline   **ML410.D965P68 1997**
Henri Dutilleux: His Life and Works. Trade Cloth. Ashgate Publishing, Ltd. Aldershot, 1997. 272p. ISBN:1-85928-330-6, ISBN13: 978-1-85928-330-1. Dewey:[B]. LCCN:96-040411.
Audience: **u,f.**

Biographies and Studies of Composers and Performers > D > Dvorak, Antonin

Beckerman, Michael   **ML410.M9**
(Editor)
Dvorak and His World. Trade Paper. Princeton University Press. Princeton, NJ. 1993. 294p. The Bard Music Festival Ser. ISBN:0-691-00097-2, ISBN13: 978-0-691-00097-8. Dewey:780/.92. LCCN:93-004037.
Audience: **g,l,u,f.**   *Choice, 1994.*

Beckerman, Michael B.   **ML410.D99B42 2003**
New Worlds of Dvorak: Searching in America for the Composers Inner Life. Trade Cloth. W. W. Norton & Company, Inc. New York, NY. 2003. 200p. ISBN:0-393-04706-7, ISBN13: 978-0-393-04706-6. Dewey:780/.92 B. LCCN:2002-026590.
Audience: **g,l,u,f.**

Smaczny, Jan   **MT130.D9 S6 1999**
Dvorák: Cello Concerto. Cloth Text. Cambridge University Press. New York, NY. 1999. 130p. Music Handbks. ISBN:0-521-66050-5, ISBN13: 978-0-521-66050-1. Dewey:784.2/74. LCCN:98-052746.
Audience: **u,f.**

Biographies and Studies of Composers and Performers > D > Dylan, Bob

Benson, Carl   **ML420.D98**
Bob Dylan Companion: Four Decades of Commentary. Trade Paper. Music Sales Corporation. New York, NY. 1998. 300p. ISBN:0-8256-7169-8, ISBN13: 978-0-8256-7169-2. Dewey:782.42164/092. LCCN:98-035862.
Audience: **g,l,u,f.**

Dylan, Bob   **ML420.D98A3 2004**
Chronicles, Vol. 1. Trade Cloth. Simon & Schuster. New York, NY. 2004. 304p. ISBN:0-7432-2815-4, ISBN13: 978-0-7432-2815-2. Dewey:782.42164/092 B. LCCN:2004-056454.
Audience: **g,l,u,f.**   *Choice, 2005.*

Dylan, Bob   **ML54.6.D94S62 2002**
Lyrics: 1962-2001. Trade Cloth. Simon & Schuster. New York, NY. 2004. 624p. ISBN:0-7432-2827-8, ISBN13: 978-0-7432-2827-5. Dewey:782.42164/0268. LCCN:2002-042823.
Audience: **g,l,u,f.**

Hedin, Benjamin   **ML420.D98H44 2004**
Studio A: The Bob Dylan Reader. Trade Cloth. W. W. Norton & Company, Inc. New York, NY. 2004. 288p. ISBN:0-393-05844-1, ISBN13: 978-0-393-05844-4. Dewey:782.42164/092. LCCN:2004-013616.
Audience: **g,l,u,f.**

Formats: Web: ☐   Ebook: 🄴   CD/DVD-ROM: 💿   BCL3: 𝓑

Biographies and Studies of Composers and Performers > E > Europe, James Reese

Badger, R. Reid   **ML422.E87B2 1995**
A Life in Ragtime: A Biography of James Reese Europe. Trade Cloth. Oxford University Press, Inc. New York, NY. 1995. 338p. ISBN:0-19-506044-X, ISBN13: 978-0-19-506044-7. Dewey:781.65/092 B. LCCN:93-042407.
Audience: **g,l,u,f.** *Choice, 1995.*

Biographies and Studies of Composers and Performers > E > Evans, Bill

Pettinger, Peter   **ML417.E9P53 1998**
Bill Evans: How My Heart Sings. Cloth over Boards. Yale University Press. Cumberland, RI. 1998. 362p. ISBN:0-300-07193-0, ISBN13: 978-0-300-07193-1. Dewey:[B]. LCCN:97-049991.
Audience: **l,u,f.** *Choice, 1998.*

Biographies and Studies of Composers and Performers > E > Eisler, Hanns

Betz, Albrecht   **ML410.E37 B43 1982**
Hanns Eisler: Political Musician. Bill Hopkins (Translator). Trade Cloth. Cambridge University Press. New York, NY. 1982. 336p. ISBN:0-521-24022-0, ISBN13: 978-0-521-24022-2. Dewey:780/.92/4. LCCN:81-012260.
Audience: **u,f.**

Biographies and Studies of Composers and Performers > E > Elgar, Edward

Grimley, Daniel M. &   **ML410.E41C36 2004**
Rushton, Julian (Editors)
The Cambridge Companion to Elgar. Cloth Text. Cambridge University Press. New York, NY. 2005. 276p. Cambridge Companions to Music Ser. ISBN:0-521-82623-3, ISBN13: 978-0-521-82623-5. Dewey:780/.92 B. LCCN:2004-047286.
Audience: **u,f.** *Choice, 2005.*

Kennedy, Michael   **ML410.E41K48 2004**
The Life of Elgar. Cloth Text. Cambridge University Press. New York, NY. 2004. 238p. Musical Lives Ser. ISBN:0-521-81076-0, ISBN13: 978-0-521-81076-0. Dewey:780/.92 B. LCCN:2003-055733.
Audience: **u,f.**

Rushton, Julian (Author,   **ML410.E41 R87 1999**
Contribution by)
Elgar: Enigma Variations. Cloth Text. Cambridge University Press. New York, NY. 1999. 124p. Music Handbks. ISBN:0-521-63175-0, ISBN13: 978-0-521-63175-4. Dewey:784.2/1825. LCCN:98-022042.
Audience: **u,f.** *Choice, 1999.*

Biographies and Studies of Composers and Performers > E > Ellington, Duke

Ellington, Duke   **ML419.A75**
Music Is My Mistress. Trade Cloth. Doubleday Publishing. New York, NY. 1973. 544p. ISBN:0-385-02235-2, ISBN13: 978-0-385-02235-4. Dewey:785.4/2/0924 B. LCCN:73-083189.
Audience: **g,l,u,f.**

Lambert, Eddie &   **ML410.E44L33 1999**
Norsworthy, Elaine
Duke Ellington: A Listener's Guide. Trade Cloth. Scarecrow Press, Inc. Lanham, MD. 1998. 396p. Studies in Jazz, Vol. 26 ISBN:0-8108-3161-9, ISBN13: 978-0-8108-3161-2. Dewey:781.65/092. LCCN:98-036431.
Audience: **g,l,u,f.** *Choice, 1999.*

Nicholson, Stuart   **ML410.E44N53 1999**
Reminiscing in Tempo: A Portrait of Duke Ellington. Trade Cloth. Northeastern University Press. Boston, MA. 1999. 560p. ISBN:1-55553-380-9, ISBN13: 978-1-55553-380-9. Dewey:781.65/092 B. LCCN:99-010873.
Audience: **l,u,f.** *Choice, 1999.*

Rattenbury, Ken   **ML410.E44**
Duke Ellington, Jazz Composer. Trade Paper. Yale University Press. Cumberland, RI. 1993. 339p. ISBN:0-300-05507-2, ISBN13: 978-0-300-05507-8. Dewey:781.6/5/092. LCCN:89-016544.
Audience: **u,f.** *Choice, 1991.*

Tucker, Mark (Editor)   **ML410.E44**
The Duke Ellington Reader. Trade Paper. Oxford University Press, Inc. New York, NY. 1995. 560p. ISBN:0-19-509391-7, ISBN13: 978-0-19-509391-9. Dewey:781.6/5/092.
Audience: **g,l,u,f.** *Choice, 1994.*

Biographies and Studies of Composers and Performers > E > Eno, Brian

Tamm, Eric   **ML410.E58T3 1995**
Brian Eno: His Music and the Vertical Color of Sound. Trade Paper. Da Capo Press, Inc. Cambridge, MA. 1995. 246p. ISBN:0-306-80649-5, ISBN13: 978-0-306-80649-0. Dewey:780/.92/4 B. LCCN:95-021602.
Audience: **l,u,f.** *Choice, 1990.*

Biographies and Studies of Composers and Performers > F > Falla, Manuel de

Hess, Carol A. (Contribution by)   ML410.F215H48 2004

Sacred Passions: The Life and Music of Manuel de Falla. Trade Cloth. Oxford University Press, Inc. New York, NY. 2004. 368p. ISBN:0-19-514561-5, ISBN13: 978-0-19-514561-8. Dewey:780/.92 B. LCCN:2004-041472.

Audience: **u,f.** *Choice, 2005.*

Biographies and Studies of Composers and Performers > F > Farrenc, Louise

Friedland, Bea   ML0410.F227F7

Louise Farrenc, 1804-1875: Composer, Performer, Scholar. George J. Buelow (Editor). Trade Paper. Books on Demand. Ann Arbor, MI. 1980. 283p. Studies in Musicology, Vol. 32 ISBN:0-8357-1111-0, ISBN13: 978-0-8357-1111-1. Dewey:780/.92/4. LCCN:80-022465.

Audience: **l,u,f.**

Biographies and Studies of Composers and Performers > F > Faure, Gabriel

Caballero, Carlo   ML410.F27 C33 2001

Fauré and French Musical Aesthetics. Arnold Whittall (Contribution by). Trade Paper. Cambridge University Press. New York, NY. 2004. 345p. Music in the Twentieth Century Ser., Vol. 13 ISBN:0-521-54398-3, ISBN13: 978-0-521-54398-9. Dewey:780/.92.

Audience: **u,f.** *Choice, 2002.*

Nectoux, Jean-Michel   ML410.F27 N413 1991

Gabriel Fauré: A Musical Life. Roger Nichols (Translator). Trade Paper. Cambridge University Press. New York, NY. 2004. 672p. ISBN:0-521-61695-6, ISBN13: 978-0-521-61695-9. Dewey:780.92 B. LCCN:2005-280639.

Audience: **u,f.** *Choice, 1992.*

Biographies and Studies of Composers and Performers > F > Feldman, Morton

DeLio, Thomas   ML410

The Music of Morton Feldman. Book, Other. Greenwood Publishing Group, Inc. Portsmouth, NH. 1996. 260p. Contributions to the Study of Music and Dance Ser., Vol. 36 ISBN:0-313-29803-3, ISBN13: 978-0-313-29803-5. Dewey:780/.92. LCCN:95-024022.

Audience: **u,f.** *Choice, 1996.*

Feldman, Morton   ML410.M9

Give My Regards to Eighth Street: Collected Writings of Morton Feldman. B. H. Friedman (Editor), Frank O'Hara (Foreword by). Trade Paper. Exact Change. Cambridge, MA. 2003. 256p. ISBN:1-878972-31-6, ISBN13: 978-1-878972-31-6. Dewey:780.9/2.

Audience: **u,f.**

Biographies and Studies of Composers and Performers > F > Fitzgerald, Ella

Gourse, Leslie   ML420.F52

The Ella Fitzgerald Companion: Seven Decades of Commentary. Schirmer Books. 1998. ISBN:0-02-864625-8, ISBN13: 978-0-02-864625-1.

Audience: **u,f.**

Biographies and Studies of Composers and Performers > F > Foster, Stephen

Austin, William W.   ML410.F78A9 1989

Susanna, "Jeanie," and "The Old Folks at Home": The Songs of Stephen C. Foster from His Time to Ours. Ed. 2. Trade Cloth. University of Illinois Press. Champaign, IL. 1988. 456p. Music in American Life Ser. ISBN:0-252-01476-6, ISBN13: 978-0-252-01476-5. Dewey:784/.092/4. LCCN:87-013931.

Audience: **l,u,f.**

Emerson, Ken   ML410.F78E46 1997

Doo-Dah!: Stephen Foster and the Rise of American Popular Culture. Trade Cloth. Simon & Schuster. New York, NY. 1997. 400p. ISBN:0-684-81010-7, ISBN13: 978-0-684-81010-2. Dewey:782.42164/092 B. LCCN:96-029816.

Audience: **g,l,u,f.** *Choice, 1998.*

Biographies and Studies of Composers and Performers > F > Franklin, Aretha

Bego, Mark   ML420

Aretha Franklin: The Queen of Soul. Trade Paper. Da Capo Press, Inc. Cambridge, MA. 2001. 448p. ISBN:0-306-80935-4, ISBN13: 978-0-306-80935-4. Dewey:782.4/2/1644/092.

Audience: **g,l,u,f.**

Biographies and Studies of Composers and Performers > F > Frescobaldi, Girolamo

Hammond, Frederick ML0410.F85H3
Girolamo Frescobaldi. Trade Paper. Books on Demand. Ann Arbor, MI. 424p. ISBN:0-7837-6085-X, ISBN13: 978-0-7837-6085-8. Dewey:786.5/092/4. LCCN:82-011938.
Audience: **u,f.**

Biographies and Studies of Composers and Performers > G > Gabrieli, Giovanni

Arnold, Denis ML410.G11 A8
Giovanni Gabrieli and the Music of the Venetian High Renaissance. Trade Cloth. Oxford University Press, Inc. New York, NY. 1980. 334p. ISBN:0-19-315232-0, ISBN13: 978-0-19-315232-8. Dewey:780/.92/4. LCCN:77-030382.
Audience: **u,f.**

Biographies and Studies of Composers and Performers > G > Gershwin, George

Alpert, Hollis ML410.G288A35 1990
The Life and Times of Porgy and Bess: The Story of an American Classic. Trade Cloth. Alfred A. Knopf Inc. New York, NY. 1990. ISBN:0-394-58339-6, ISBN13: 978-0-394-58339-6. Dewey:782.1. LCCN:89-043367.
Audience: **g,l,u,f.**

Gilbert, Steven E. ML410.G288G55 1995
The Music of Gershwin. Cloth over Boards. Yale University Press. Cumberland, RI. 1995. 268p. Composers of the Twentieth Century Ser. ISBN:0-300-06233-8, ISBN13: 978-0-300-06233-5. Dewey:780.9/2. LCCN:95-012086.
Audience: **u,f.** *Choice, 1996.*

Hyland, William G. ML410
George Gershwin: A New Biography. Trade Cloth. Greenwood Publishing Group, Inc. Portsmouth, NH. 2003. 312p. ISBN:0-275-98111-8, ISBN13: 978-0-275-98111-2. Dewey:780/.92 B. LCCN:2003-046303.
Audience: **l,u,f.** *Choice, 2004.*

Jablonski, Edward ML410.G288J29 1998
Gershwin: A Biography. Trade Paper. Da Capo Press, Inc. Cambridge, MA. 1998. 460p. ISBN:0-306-80847-1, ISBN13: 978-0-306-80847-0. Dewey:780/.92 B. LCCN:98-011830.
Audience: **l,u,f.** *Choice, 1988.*

Jablonski, Edward & Stewart, Lawrence D. ML410.G288J3 1996
The Gershwin Years: George and Ira. Ed. 3. Trade Paper. Da Capo Press, Inc. Cambridge, MA. 1996. 400p. ISBN:0-306-80739-4, ISBN13: 978-0-306-80739-8. Dewey:780.9/22. LCCN:96-022950.
Audience: **u,f.**

Rosenberg, Deena ML410.G288R67 1997
Fascinating Rhythm: The Collaboration of George and Ira Gershwin. Trade Paper. University of Michigan Press. Chicago, IL. 1998. 560p. ISBN:0-472-08469-0, ISBN13: 978-0-472-08469-2. Dewey:780.922. LCCN:97-041926.
Audience: **l,u,f.** *Choice, 1992.*

Schiff, David ML410.G288 S27 1997
Gershwin: Rhapsody in Blue. Julian Rushton (Contribution by). Cloth Text. Cambridge University Press. New York, NY. 1997. 132p. Music Handbks. ISBN:0-521-55077-7, ISBN13: 978-0-521-55077-2. Dewey:784.2/62. LCCN:96-047439.
Audience: **l,u,f.**

Schneider, Wayne (Editor) ML410.G288.G49 1999
The Gershwin Style: New Looks at the Music of George Gershwin. Trade Cloth. Oxford University Press, Inc. New York, NY. 1999. 304p. ISBN:0-19-509020-9, ISBN13: 978-0-19-509020-8. Dewey:780.9/2. LCCN:97-050590.
Audience: **u,f.** *Choice, 1999.*

Wyatt, Robert & Johnson, John Andrew (Editors) ML410.G288G47 2004
The George Gershwin Reader. Trade Cloth. Oxford University Press, Inc. New York, NY. 2004. 368p. Readers on American Musicians Ser. ISBN:0-19-513019-7, ISBN13: 978-0-19-513019-5. Dewey:780/.92. LCCN:2003-016160.
Audience: **l,u,f.**

Biographies and Studies of Composers and Performers > G > Gershwin, Ira

Furia, Philip ML410.M9
Ira Gershwin: The Art of the Lyricist. Trade Paper. Oxford University Press, Inc. New York, NY. 1997. 288p. ISBN:0-19-511570-8, ISBN13: 978-0-19-511570-3. Dewey:780.9/2. LCCN:94-045715.
Audience: **u,f.** *Choice, 1996.*

Gershwin, Ira & Kimball, Robert PZ8.3
The Complete Lyrics of Ira Gershwin. Trade Cloth. Alfred A. Knopf Inc. New York, NY. 1993. 448p. ISBN:0-394-55651-8, ISBN13: 978-0-394-55651-2. Dewey:782.42. LCCN:93-012175.
Audience: **g,l,u,f.**

Jablonski, Edward & Stewart, Lawrence D. ML410.G288J3 1996
The Gershwin Years: George and Ira. Ed. 3. Trade Paper. Da

Audience: g=general, l=lower division undergraduate, u=upper division undergraduate, f=faculty.

325

Capo Press, Inc. Cambridge, MA. 1996. 400p.
ISBN:0-306-80739-4, ISBN13: 978-0-306-80739-8.
Dewey:780.9/22. LCCN:96-022950.

Audience: **u,f.**

Rosenberg, Deena   **ML410.G288R67 1997**
Fascinating Rhythm: The Collaboration of George and Ira
Gershwin. Trade Paper. University of Michigan Press. Chicago,
IL. 1998. 560p. ISBN:0-472-08469-0, ISBN13:
978-0-472-08469-2. Dewey:780.922. LCCN:97-041926.

Audience: **l,u,f.** *Choice, 1992.*

Biographies and Studies of Composers and Performers > G > Gesualdo, Carlo

Watkins, Glenn   **ML410.G29 W4 1991**
Gesualdo: The Man and His Music. Ed. 2. Igor Stravinsky
(Preface by). Trade Paper. Oxford University Press, Inc. New
York, NY. 1991. 438p. ISBN:0-19-816197-2, ISBN13:
978-0-19-816197-4. Dewey:782.430. LCCN:92-212547.

Audience: **l,u,f.**

Biographies and Studies of Composers and Performers > G > Getz, Stan

Maggin, Donald L.   **ML419.C645**
Stan Getz: A Life in Jazz. Trade Cloth. HarperCollins
Publishers. New York, NY. 1996. ISBN:0-614-95806-7, ISBN13:
978-0-614-95806-5. Dewey:788.7/165/092.

Audience: **g,l,u,f.**

Biographies and Studies of Composers and Performers > G > Gillespie, Dizzy

Gillespie, Dizzy & Fraser, Al   **ML419.G54.A3**
To Be or Not to Bop: Memoirs. Trade Cloth. Doubleday
Publishing. New York, NY. 1979. xix, 552p.
ISBN:0-385-12052-4, ISBN13: 978-0-385-12052-4.
Dewey:785.420924. LCCN:77-076237.

Audience: **g,l,u,f.**

Shipton, Alyn   **ML419.D39**
Groovin' High: The Life of Dizzy Gillespie. Trade Paper.
DIANE Publishing Company. Collingdale, PA. 2004. 422p.
ISBN:0-7567-7598-1, ISBN13: 978-0-7567-7598-8.
Dewey:788.9/2165/092 B.

Audience: **g,l,u,f.** *Choice, 2000.*

Biographies and Studies of Composers and Performers > G > Glass, Philip

Glass, Philip   **ML410.G398A3 1995**
Music by Philip Glass. Robert T. Jones (Editor). Paper Text. Da
Capo Press, Inc. Cambridge, MA. 1995. 432p.
ISBN:0-306-80636-3, ISBN13: 978-0-306-80636-0.
Dewey:780/.92/4 B. LCCN:95-005009.

Audience: **u,f.** *Choice, 1988.*

Kostelanetz, Richard   **ML410.G398**
Writings on Glass: Essays, Interviews, Criticism. New York:
Schirmer Books. 1997. ISBN:0-02-864657-6, ISBN13:
978-0-02-864657-2.

Audience: **u,f.**

Biographies and Studies of Composers and Performers > G > Gluck, Christoph Willibald

Howard, Patricia   **ML410.G5H668 1995**
Gluck: An Eighteenth-Century Portrait in Letters and
Documents. Trade Cloth. Oxford University Press, Inc. New
York, NY. 1995. 286p. ISBN:0-19-816385-1, ISBN13:
978-0-19-816385-5. Dewey:782.1/092. LCCN:95-017332.

Audience: **u,f.** *Choice, 1996.*

Howard, Patricia   **ML410.G5 C2 1981**
Orfeo. Richard Wagner (Contribution by). Trade Paper.
Cambridge University Press. New York, NY. 1981. 152p.
Cambridge Opera Handbooks Ser. ISBN:0-521-29664-1,
ISBN13: 978-0-521-29664-9. Dewey:782.1. LCCN:80-049734.

Audience: **l,u,f.**

Newman, Ernest   **ML410.G5 N3 1976**
Gluck and the Opera: A Study in Musical History. Trade Cloth.
Greenwood Publishing Group, Inc. Portsmouth, NH. 1976. 300p.
ISBN:0-8371-8849-0, ISBN13: 978-0-8371-8849-2.
Dewey:782.1/092/4. LCCN:76-007579.

Audience: **u,f.**

Biographies and Studies of Composers and Performers > G > Goodman, Benny

Firestone, Ross   **ML410.E44**
Swing, Swing, Swing: The Life and Times of Benny Goodman.
Trade Paper. W. W. Norton & Company, Inc. New York, NY.
1994. ISBN:0-393-31168-6, ISBN13: 978-0-393-31168-6.
Dewey:781.65092.

Audience: **g,l,u,f.** *Choice, 1993.*

Biographies and Studies of Composers and Performers > G > Gottschalk, Louis Moreau

Gottschalk, Louis M.   **ML410.C54**
Notes of a Pianist. Jeanne Behrend (Editor), Frederick S. Starr (Foreword by). Trade Paper. Princeton University Press. Princeton, NJ. 2006. 504p. ISBN:0-691-12716-6, ISBN13: 978-0-691-12716-3. Dewey:786.1/092/4.

Audience: **u,f.**

Starr, S. Frederick   **ML410.G68S7 2000**
Louis Moreau Gottschalk. Trade Paper. University of Illinois Press. Champaign, IL. 2000. 592p. Music in American Life Ser. ISBN:0-252-06876-9, ISBN13: 978-0-252-06876-8. Dewey:780/.92 B. LCCN:99-088040.

Audience: **l,u,f.**

Biographies and Studies of Composers and Performers > G > Gould, Glenn

Bazzana, Kevin   **ML417.G68B393 2004**
Wondrous Strange: The Life and Art of Glenn Gould. Trade Cloth. Oxford University Press, Inc. New York, NY. 2004. 558p. ISBN:0-19-517440-2, ISBN13: 978-0-19-517440-3. Dewey:786.2/092 B. LCCN:2004-300097.

Audience: **g,l,u,f.**

Biographies and Studies of Composers and Performers > G > Grainger, Percy

Bird, John   **ML410.M9**
Percy Grainger. Ed. 2. Trade Cloth. Oxford University Press, Inc. New York, NY. 1999. 404p. ISBN:0-19-816652-4, ISBN13: 978-0-19-816652-8. Dewey:780.9/2. LCCN:98-009603.

Audience: **u,f.** *Choice, 1999.*

Gillies, Malcolm & Pear,   **ML410.G75G55 2002**
  David (Editors)
Portrait of Percy Grainger. Trade Cloth. University of Rochester Press. Rochester, NY. 2002. 242p. Eastman Studies in Music ISBN:1-58046-087-9, ISBN13: 978-1-58046-087-3. Dewey:780/.92 B. LCCN:2001-048100.

Audience: **u,f.**

Biographies and Studies of Composers and Performers > G > Grappelli, Stephane

Balmer, Paul   **ML418.G7**
Stéphane Grappelli: With and Without Django. London : Sanctuary. 2003. ISBN:1-86074-453-2, ISBN13: 978-1-86074-453-2.

Audience: **g,l,u,f.**

Biographies and Studies of Composers and Performers > G > Grateful Dead

Dodd, David & Spaulding,   **ML421.B4**
  Diana (Editors)
The Grateful Dead Reader. Trade Paper. Oxford University Press, Inc. New York, NY. 2002. 353p. Readers on American Musicians Ser. ISBN:0-19-514706-5, ISBN13: 978-0-19-514706-3. Dewey:782.42166/092/2.

Audience: **g,l,u,f.**

Biographies and Studies of Composers and Performers > G > Grieg, Edvard

Benestad, Finn &   **ML410.G9B413 1988**
  Schjelderup-Ebbe, Dag
Edvard Grieg: The Man and the Artist. William H. Halverson & Leland B. Sateren (Translators). Trade Cloth. University of Nebraska Press. Lincoln, NE. 1988. 441p. ISBN:0-8032-1202-X, ISBN13: 978-0-8032-1202-2. Dewey:780/.92/4 B. LCCN:87-020608.

Audience: **g,l,u,f.** *Choice, 1989.*

Biographies and Studies of Composers and Performers > G > Griffes, Charles Tomlinson

Anderson, Donna K.   **ML410.G9134.A8 1993**
Charles T. Griffes: A Life in Music. Trade Cloth. Smithsonian Institution Press. Washington, DC. 1993. 272p. Studies of American Musicians ISBN:1-56098-191-1, ISBN13: 978-1-56098-191-6. Dewey:780.92. LCCN:92-021844.

Audience: **u,f.** *Choice, 1993.*

Biographies and Studies of Composers and Performers > G > Guthrie, Woody

Cray, Ed ML419.G852C73 2004
Ramblin Man: The Life and Times of Woody Guthrie. Trade Cloth. W. W. Norton & Company, Inc. New York, NY. 2004. 384p. ISBN:0-393-04759-8, ISBN13: 978-0-393-04759-2. Dewey:782.42162/13/0092 B. LCCN:2003-021071.
Audience: **g,l,u,f.** *Choice, 2004.*

Guthrie, Woody ML410
Pastures of Plenty: A Self-Portrait. Dave Marsh & Harold Leventhal (Editors). Trade Paper. HarperCollins Publishers. New York, NY. 1992. 288p. ISBN:0-06-098419-8, ISBN13: 978-0-06-098419-9. Dewey:781.62092. LCCN:89-046547.
Audience: **l,u,f.**

Biographies and Studies of Composers and Performers > H > Hamlisch, Marvin

Hamlisch, Marvin ML410.H1745 A3 1992
The Way I Was. Trade Cloth. Simon & Schuster. New York, NY. 1992. ISBN:0-684-19327-2, ISBN13: 978-0-684-19327-4. Dewey:780/.92. LCCN:92-020094.
Audience: **g,l,u,f.**

Biographies and Studies of Composers and Performers > H > Hammerstein, Oscar

Citron, Stephen ML403.C56 1995
The Wordsmiths: Oscar Hammerstein II and Alan Jay Lerner. Trade Cloth. Oxford University Press, Inc. New York, NY. 1995. 464p. The Great Songwriters Ser. ISBN:0-19-508386-5, ISBN13: 978-0-19-508386-6. Dewey:782.1/4/0922 B. LCCN:94-020279.
Audience: **u,f.**

Hammerstein, Oscar II ML49.H12H3 1985
(Lyrics by)
Lyrics by Oscar Hammerstein II. Ed. 2. Stephen Sondheim (Foreword by). Trade Cloth. Hal Leonard Corporation. Milwaukee, WI. 1985. 292p. Biographies and Commentary Ser., :Musicals/Classical/Folk/Religious Music Ser. ISBN:0-88188-379-4, ISBN13: 978-0-88188-379-4. Dewey:782.81/2. LCCN:85-050895.
Audience: **g,l,u,f.**

Rodgers, Richard & ML48
Hammerstein, Oscar II
Six Plays. Trade Cloth. Random House, Inc. New York, NY. 1959. ISBN:0-394-60200-5, ISBN13: 978-0-394-60200-4. Dewey:812.
Audience: **g,l,u,f.**

Biographies and Studies of Composers and Performers > H > Hampton, Lionel

Hampton, Lionel & Haskins, ML419.H26 A3 1993
James
Hamp: An Autobiography. Trade Paper. HarperCollins Publishers. New York, NY. 1999. 320p. ISBN:1-56743-019-8, ISBN13: 978-1-56743-019-6. Dewey:786.8/43/092. LCCN:93-000102.
Audience: **g,l,u,f.** *Choice, 1990.*

Biographies and Studies of Composers and Performers > H > Hancock, Herbie

Pond, Steven F. ML417.H23P66 2005
Head Hunters: The Making of Jazz's First Platinum Album. Trade Cloth. University of Michigan Press. Chicago, IL. 2005. 288p. Jazz Perspectives Ser. ISBN:0-472-11417-4, ISBN13: 978-0-472-11417-7. Dewey:781.65/7. LCCN:2005-014482.
Audience: **u,f.**

Biographies and Studies of Composers and Performers > H > Handel, George Frideric

Burrows, Donald ML410.H13
Handel. New York: Schirmer Books: Maxwell Macmillan International. 1994. The Master Musicians Ser.: Variation ISBN:0-02-870327-8, ISBN13: 978-0-02-870327-5.
Audience: **g,l,u,f.**

Burrows, Donald (Editor) ML410.H13 C2 1997
The Cambridge Companion to Handel. Jonathan Cross (Contribution by). Trade Paper. Cambridge University Press. New York, NY. 1997. 365p. Cambridge Companions to Music Ser. ISBN:0-521-45613-4, ISBN13: 978-0-521-45613-5. Dewey:780/.92 B. LCCN:96-050935.
Audience: **g,l,u,f.**

Burrows, Donald ML410.H13 B95 1991
Handel: Messiah. Julian Rushton (Contribution by). Trade Paper. Cambridge University Press. New York, NY. 1991. 137p. Music Handbks. ISBN:0-521-37620-3, ISBN13: 978-0-521-37620-4. Dewey:782.23. LCCN:90-002566.
Audience: **g,l,u,f.** *Choice, 1992.*

Dean, Winton ML410.B13
Handel's Dramatic Oratorios and Masques. Paper Text. Textbook Publishers. Temecula, CA. 2003. xii, 694p. ISBN:0-7581-7050-5, ISBN13: 978-0-7581-7050-7. Dewey:782.23.
Audience: **u,f.**

Formats: Web: ☐ Ebook: 🄴 CD/DVD-ROM: 🐝 BCL3: 𝐁

Dean, Winton & Knapp, John M.   ML410.H13D37 1987
Handel's Operas Seventeen Four to Seventeen Twenty-Six.
Trade Cloth. Oxford University Press, Inc. New York, NY. 1987.
772p. ISBN:0-19-315219-3, ISBN13: 978-0-19-315219-9.
Dewey:782.1/092/4. LCCN:85-011580.

Audience: **u,f.** *Choice, 1987.*

Deutsch, Otto Erich   ML0410.H13D4
Handel: A Documentary Biography. Trade Paper. Books on
Demand. Ann Arbor, MI. 1028p. ISBN:0-598-63419-3, ISBN13:
978-0-598-63419-1. Dewey:ML0410.H13D4. LCCN:55-006770.

Audience: **g,l,u,f.**

Hogwood, Christopher   ML410.M9
Handel. Trade Paper. Thames & Hudson. New York, NY. 1996.
312p. ISBN:0-500-27498-3, ISBN13: 978-0-500-27498-9.
Dewey:780.9/2. LCCN:84-072765.

Audience: **g,l,u,f.** *Choice, 1985.*

Larsen, Jens P.   ML410
Handel's Messiah: Origins, Composition, Sources. Ed. 2. Trade
Cloth. Greenwood Publishing Group, Inc. Portsmouth, NH.
1990. 336p. ISBN:0-313-24426-X, ISBN13: 978-0-313-24426-1.
Dewey:783.3/092/4. LCCN:88-010128.

Audience: **u,f.**

Mann, Alfred   ML410.H13M36 1996
Handel: The Orchestral Music. Cloth Text. Thomson
Wadsworth. Belmont, CA. 1995. 182p. Monuments of Western
Music Ser. ISBN:0-02-871382-6, ISBN13: 978-0-02-871382-3.
Dewey:784.2/092. LCCN:95-010441.

Audience: **u,f.** *Choice, 1996.*

Parker, Mary Ann   ML134.H16P37 2005
G. F. Handel: A Guide to Research. Ed. 2. Paper over Boards.
Routledge. New York, NY. 2005. 408p. Routledge Music
Bibliographies Ser. ISBN:0-415-94323-X, ISBN13:
978-0-415-94323-9. Dewey:016.78/092. LCCN:2005-006736.

Audience: **l,u,f.**

Biographies and Studies of Composers and Performers > H > Handy, William Christopher

Handy, W. C.   ML410.H18A3 1991
Father of the Blues: An Autobiography. Arna Bontemps (Editor),
Abbe Niles (Introduction by). Trade Paper. Da Capo Press, Inc.
Cambridge, MA. 1991. 340p. Quality Paperbacks Ser.
ISBN:0-306-80421-2, ISBN13: 978-0-306-80421-2.
Dewey:784.5/3/00924 B. LCCN:90-026262.

Audience: **g,l,u,f.**

Biographies and Studies of Composers and Performers > H > Harrison, Lou

Miller, Leta E. & Lieberman, Fredric   ML410.H2066M55 2004
Composing a World: Lou Harrison, Musical Wayfarer. Ed. 2.
Trade Paper. University of Illinois Press. Champaign, IL. 2004.
416p. Music in American Life Ser. ISBN:0-252-07188-3,
ISBN13: 978-0-252-07188-1. Dewey:780/.92 B.
LCCN:2004-042201.

Audience: **u,f.**

Biographies and Studies of Composers and Performers > H > Hart, Lorenz

Hart, Lorenz   ML54.6.H4H4 1995
The Complete Lyrics of Lorenz Hart. Dorothy Hart & Robert
Kimball (Editors). Trade Paper. Da Capo Press, Inc. Cambridge,
MA. 1995. 208p. ISBN:0-306-80667-3, ISBN13:
978-0-306-80667-4. Dewey:782.1/4/0268. LCCN:95-021606.

Audience: **g,l,u,f.**

Nolan, Fredrick   ML410.S6872
Lorenz Hart: A Poet on Broadway. Trade Paper. Oxford
University Press, Inc. New York, NY. 1995. 416p.
ISBN:0-19-510289-4, ISBN13: 978-0-19-510289-5.
Dewey:782.1/4/092.

Audience: **u,f.**

Biographies and Studies of Composers and Performers > H > Hawkins, Coleman

Chilton, John   ML419.H35C5 1990
The Song of the Hawk: The Life and Recordings of Coleman
Hawkins. Trade Paper. University of Michigan Press. Chicago,
IL. 1990. 460p. The American Music Ser. ISBN:0-472-08201-9,
ISBN13: 978-0-472-08201-8. Dewey:788.7/165/092 B.
LCCN:90-047644.

Audience: **u,f.** *Choice, 1991.*

Biographies and Studies of Composers and Performers > H > Haydn, Joseph

Brown, A. Peter   ML1255.B87
The First Golden Age of the Viennese Symphony: Haydn,
Mozart, Beethoven and Schubert. Trade Cloth. Indiana
University Press. Bloomington, IN. 2002. 816p.
ISBN:0-253-33487-X, ISBN13: 978-0-253-33487-9.
Dewey:784.2/184 s 784.2. LCCN:98-026549.

Audience: **g,l,u,f.** *Choice, 2003.*

Clark, Caryl (Editor)   ML410.H4C17 2005
The Cambridge Companion to Haydn. Jonathan Cross
(Contribution by). Cloth Text. Cambridge University Press. New
York, NY. 2005. 338p. Cambridge Companions to Music Ser.
ISBN:0-521-83347-7, ISBN13: 978-0-521-83347-9.
Dewey:780/.92 B. LCCN:2005-003945.
                              Audience: g,l u,f. *Choice, 2006.*

Grave, Floyd K. & Grave,   ML134.H272G74 1990
   Margaret G.
Franz Joseph Haydn: A Guide to Research. Cloth Text. Garland
Publishing, Inc. New York, NY. 1990. 464p. Composer
Resource Manuals Ser., Vol. 31 ISBN:0-8240-8487-X, ISBN13:
978-0-8240-8487-5. Dewey:016.78/092. LCCN:90-003533.
                              Audience: l,u,f. *Choice, 1991.*

Grave, Floyd K. & Grave,   ML410.H4G69 2006
   Margaret G.
The String Quartets of Joseph Haydn. Trade Cloth. Oxford
University Press, Inc. New York, NY. 2006. 492p.
ISBN:0-19-517357-0, ISBN13: 978-0-19-517357-4.
Dewey:785/.7194/092. LCCN:2005-047784.
                              Audience: u,f.

Haimo, Ethan   MT130.H4H35 1995
Haydn's Symphonic Forms: Essays in Compositional Logic.
Trade Cloth. Oxford University Press, Inc. New York, NY. 1995.
310p. Oxford Monographs on Music ISBN:0-19-816392-4,
ISBN13: 978-0-19-816392-3. Dewey:784.2/184/092.
LCCN:94-049097.
                              Audience: u,f. *Choice, 1996.*

Harrison, Bernard   ML410.H4 H314 1998
Haydn: The 'Paris' Symphonies. Julian Rushton (Contribution
by). Trade Paper. Cambridge University Press. New York, NY.
1998. 134p. Music Handbks. ISBN:0-521-47743-3, ISBN13:
978-0-521-47743-7. Dewey:784.2/184/092. LCCN:97-042606.
                              Audience: u,f. *Choice, 1999.*

Haydn, Joseph   ML410.H4
The Collected Correspondence and London Notebooks of Joseph
Haydn. Landon, Howard Chandler Robbins (Editor) (Translator).
London, Barrie and Rockliff. 1959.
                              Audience: u,f.

Heartz, Daniel   ML246.8.V6H4 1994
Haydn, Mozart and the Viennese School 1740-1780. Paper Text.
W. W. Norton & Company, Inc. New York, NY. 1994.
ISBN:0-393-96533-3, ISBN13: 978-0-393-96533-9.
Dewey:780/.9436/1309033. LCCN:93-047001.
                              Audience: u,f.

Landon, H. C. Robbins   ML410.H4
Haydn: The Early Years, 1732-1765. Trade Cloth. Thames &
Hudson. New York, NY. 1995. 656p. Haydn, :Chronicle and
Works ISBN:0-500-01169-9, ISBN13: 978-0-500-01169-0.
Dewey:780.924. LCCN:94-061473.
                              Audience: l,u,f.

Landon, H. C. Robbins   ML410.H4
Haydn: The Late Years, 1801-1809. Trade Cloth. Thames &

Hudson. New York, NY. 1995. 504p. Haydn, :Chronicle and
Works ISBN:0-500-01167-2, ISBN13: 978-0-500-01167-6.
Dewey:780/.92/4. LCCN:94-061478.
                              Audience: l,u,f.

Landon, H. C. Robbins   ML410.H4
Haydn: The Years of Creation, 1796-1800. Trade Cloth. Thames
& Hudson. New York, NY. 1995. 676p. Haydn, :Chronicle and
Works ISBN:0-500-01166-4, ISBN13: 978-0-500-01166-9.
Dewey:780/.92/4. LCCN:94-061477.
                              Audience: l,u,f.

Landon, H. C. Robbins   ML410.H4
Haydn at Eszterhaza, 1766-1790. Trade Cloth. Thames &
Hudson. New York, NY. 1995. 819p. Haydn, :Chronicle and
Works ISBN:0-500-01168-0, ISBN13: 978-0-500-01168-3.
Dewey:780/.92/4. LCCN:94-061475.
                              Audience: l,u,f.

Landon, H. C. Robbins   ML410.H4
Haydn in England, 1791-1795. Trade Cloth. Thames & Hudson.
New York, NY. 1995. 648p. Haydn, :Chronicle and Works
ISBN:0-500-01164-8, ISBN13: 978-0-500-01164-5.
Dewey:780/.92/4. LCCN:94-061476.
                              Audience: l,u,f.

Landon, H. C. Robbins   ML410.H4
The Symphonies of Joseph Haydn. Paper Text. Textbook
Publishers. Temecula, CA. 2003. xvii, 862p.
ISBN:0-7581-2881-9, ISBN13: 978-0-7581-2881-2.
Dewey:785.110924.
                              Audience: l,u,f.

Landon, H. C. & Wyn   ML410.H4L265 1988
   Jones, David
Haydn: His Life and Music. Cloth Text. Indiana University
Press. Bloomington, IN. 1988. 384p. ISBN:0-253-37265-8,
ISBN13: 978-0-253-37265-9. Dewey:780/.92/4 B.
LCCN:88-002685.
                              Audience: g,l,u,f. *Choice, 1989.*

MacIntyre, Bruce   ML410.H4M13 1998
Haydn: The Creation. Trade Cloth. Thomson Wadsworth.
Belmont, CA. 1997. Monuments of Western Music Ser.
ISBN:0-02-871375-3, ISBN13: 978-0-02-871375-5.
Dewey:782.23. LCCN:97-025759.
                              Audience: u,f.

Morrow, Mary S.   ML246.8.V6M87 1989
Concert Life in Haydn's Vienna: Aspects of a Developing
Musical and Social Institution. Library Binding. Pendragon
Press. Hillsdale, NY. 1989. 500p. Sociology of Music Ser., No.
7 ISBN:0-918728-83-5, ISBN13: 978-0-918728-83-8.
Dewey:780/.7/30943613. LCCN:88-023385.
                              Audience: u,f. *Choice, 1989.*

Rosen, Charles   ML195.R68 1997
Classical Style: Haydn, Mozart, Beethoven. Ed. 2. Trade Cloth.
W. W. Norton & Company, Inc. New York, NY. 1997. 548p.
ISBN:0-393-04020-8, ISBN13: 978-0-393-04020-3.
Dewey:780/.9/033. LCCN:96-027335.
                              Audience: l,u,f. *B* *Choice, 1997.*

Schroeder, David P.   ML410.H4S45 1997
Haydn and the Enlightenment: The Late Symphonies and Their
Audience. Trade Paper. Oxford University Press, Inc. New York,
NY. 1998. 230p. Oxford Monographs on Music
ISBN:0-19-816682-6, ISBN13: 978-0-19-816682-5.
Dewey:784.2/184/092. LCCN:97-025754.

Audience: **u,f.**

Temperley, Nicholas   ML410.H4 T36 1991
Haydn: The Creation. Julian Rushton (Contribution by). Trade
Paper. Cambridge University Press. New York, NY. 1991. 143p.
Music Handbks. ISBN:0-521-37865-6, ISBN13:
978-0-521-37865-9. Dewey:782.23. LCCN:90-001859.

Audience: **u,f.** *Choice, 1992.*

Wheelock, Gretchen A.   ML410.H4W47 1992
Haydn's Ingenious Jesting with Art: Contexts of Musical Wit
and Humor. Trade Cloth. Thomson Gale. Farmington Hills, MI.
1992. 269p. ISBN:0-02-872855-6, ISBN13: 978-0-02-872855-1.
Dewey:784/.092. LCCN:91-046730.

Audience: **u,f.** *Choice, 1993.*

Wyn Jones, David, et al.   ML410.H4
Haydn. Biba, Otto (Author). Oxford; New York: Oxford
University Press. 2002. Oxford Composer Companions
ISBN:0-19-866216-5, ISBN13: 978-0-19-866216-7.

Audience: **l,u,f.**

Biographies and Studies of Composers and Performers > H > Henderson, Fletcher

Magee, Jeffrey   ML422.H44M34 2004
The Uncrowned King of Swing: Fletcher Henderson and Big
Band Jazz. Trade Cloth. Oxford University Press, Inc. New
York, NY. 2005. 352p. ISBN:0-19-509022-5, ISBN13:
978-0-19-509022-2. Dewey:781.65/092 B. LCCN:2004-004727.

Audience: **u,f.**

Biographies and Studies of Composers and Performers > H > Hendrix, Jimi

Murray, Charles Shaar   ML410.H476
Crosstown Traffic: Jimi Hendrix and Post-War Pop. London:
Faber. 2001. ISBN:0-571-20749-9, ISBN13: 978-0-571-20749-7.

Audience: **g,l,u,f.**

Potash, Chris   ML420.P96
The Jimi Hendrix Companion: Three Decades of Commentary.
Trade Paper. Music Sales Corporation. New York, NY. 1996.
300p. ISBN:0-8256-7237-6, ISBN13: 978-0-8256-7237-8.
Dewey:782.4/2/166/092. LCCN:96-031526.

Audience: **g,l,u,f.**

Biographies and Studies of Composers and Performers > H > Hensel, Fanny Mendelssohn

Cooper, John Michael &   ML410
   Prandi, Julie D. (Editors)
The Mendelssohns: Their Music in History. Trade Cloth. Oxford
University Press, Inc. New York, NY. 2003. 404p.
ISBN:0-19-816723-7, ISBN13: 978-0-19-816723-5.
Dewey:780.922. LCCN:2003-275059.

Audience: **g,l,u,f.** *Choice, 2003.*

Tillard, Francoise   ML410.H482T513 1996
Fanny Mendelssohn. Camille Naish (Translator). Trade Cloth.
Hal Leonard Corporation. Milwaukee, WI. 1996. 402p.
ISBN:0-931340-96-9, ISBN13: 978-0-931340-96-3.
Dewey:786.2/092 B. LCCN:95-017336.

Audience: **l,u,f.** *Choice, 1996.*

Biographies and Studies of Composers and Performers > H > Henze, Hans Werner

Henze, Hans W. & Spencer,   ML410.H483A3 1998
   Stewart
Bohemian Fifths: An Autobiography. Cloth Text. Princeton
University Press. Princeton, NJ. 1999. 520p.
ISBN:0-691-00683-0, ISBN13: 978-0-691-00683-3.
Dewey:780/.92 B. LCCN:98-037783.

Audience: **u,f.**

Biographies and Studies of Composers and Performers > H > Herman, Jerry

Citron, Stephen   ML410.H5624C58 2004
Jerry Herman: Poet of the Showtune. Cloth over Boards. Yale
University Press. Cumberland, RI. 2004. 352p.
ISBN:0-300-10082-5, ISBN13: 978-0-300-10082-2.
Dewey:782.1/4/092 B. LCCN:2003-027632.

Audience: **g,l,u,f.**

Herman, Jerry & Stasio,   ML410.H5624H47 1996
   Marilyn
Showtune: A Memoir by Jerry Herman. Trade Cloth. Penguin
Group (USA) Inc. New York, NY. 1996. 288p.
ISBN:1-55611-502-4, ISBN13: 978-1-55611-502-8.
Dewey:782.1/4/092 B. LCCN:96-034210.

Audience: **g,l,u,f.**

Biographies and Studies of Composers and Performers > H > Herrmann, Bernard

Cooper, David   **ML410.H562C64 2005**
Bernard Herrmann's the Ghost and Mrs. Muir: A Film Score Guide. Trade Paper. Scarecrow Press, Inc. Lanham, MD. 2005. 192p. Scarecrow Film Score Guides Ser., No. 5 ISBN:0-8108-5679-4, ISBN13: 978-0-8108-5679-0. Dewey:781.5/42. LCCN:2005-007726.
Audience: **u,f.**

Cooper, David   **ML410**
Bernard Herrmann's Vertigo: A Film Score Handbook. Book, Other. Greenwood Publishing Group, Inc. Portsmouth, NH. 2001. 176p. Film Score Guides Ser., No. 2 ISBN:0-313-31490-X, ISBN13: 978-0-313-31490-2. Dewey:781.5/42. LCCN:00-049501.
Audience: **u,f.**

Smith, Steven C.   **ML410.H562S6 1991**
A Heart at Fire's Center: The Life and Music of Bernard Herrmann. Trade Cloth. University of California Press. Berkeley, CA. 1991. 400p. ISBN:0-520-07123-9, ISBN13: 978-0-520-07123-0. Dewey:780/.92 B. LCCN:90-036861.
Audience: **l,u,f.** *Choice, 1991.*

Biographies and Studies of Composers and Performers > H > Hildegard von Bingen

Flanagan, Sabina   **BX4700.J7**
Hildegard of Bingen: A Visionary Life. Ed. 2. Trade Paper. Routledge. New York, NY. 1998. 244p. ISBN:0-415-18551-3, ISBN13: 978-0-415-18551-6. Dewey:248.2/2/092. LCCN:98-012847.
Audience: **u,f.**

Biographies and Studies of Composers and Performers > H > Hindemith, Paul

Neumeyer, David   **ML410.H685N5 1986**
The Music of Paul Hindemith. Trade Cloth. Yale University Press. Cumberland, RI. 1986. 312p. ISBN:0-300-03287-0, ISBN13: 978-0-300-03287-1. Dewey:780/.92/4. LCCN:85-014495.
Audience: **u,f.** *Choice, 1986.*

Noss, Luther   **ML410.H685N7 1989**
Paul Hindemith in the United States. Trade Cloth. University of Illinois Press. Champaign, IL. 1989. 248p. Music in American Life Ser. ISBN:0-252-01563-0, ISBN13: 978-0-252-01563-2. Dewey:780/.92/4 B. LCCN:88-010694.
Audience: **u,f.** *Choice, 1989.*

Skelton, Geoffrey   **ML410.H685 S6**
Paul Hindemith: The Man Behind the Music. Trade Cloth. Taplinger Publishing Company, Inc. Marlboro, NJ. 1977. ISBN:0-87597-107-5, ISBN13: 978-0-87597-107-0. Dewey:780/.92/4.
Audience: **l,u,f.**

Biographies and Studies of Composers and Performers > H > Hines, Earl

Dance, Stanley   **ML417.H5 D4 1983**
The World of Earl Hines. Paper Text. Da Capo Press, Inc. Cambridge, MA. 1983. 262p. Quality Paperbacks Ser. ISBN:0-306-80182-5, ISBN13: 978-0-306-80182-2. Dewey:785.42/092/4. LCCN:82-025252.
Audience: **u,f.**

Biographies and Studies of Composers and Performers > H > Holiday, Billie

Gourse, Leslie   **ML420.H58**
The Billie Holiday Companion: 7 Decades of Commentary. Trade Paper. Music Sales Corporation. New York, NY. 1997. 300p. ISBN:0-8256-7165-5, ISBN13: 978-0-8256-7165-4. Dewey:782.42165/092. LCCN:96-031528.
Audience: **g,l,u,f.**

Biographies and Studies of Composers and Performers > H > Holst, Gustav

Greene, Richard   **ML410.H748 G74 1995**
Holst: The Planets. Julian Rushton (Contribution by). Cloth Text. Cambridge University Press. New York, NY. 1995. 110p. Music Handbks. ISBN:0-521-45000-4, ISBN13: 978-0-521-45000-3. Dewey:784.2/1858. LCCN:94-017175.
Audience: **u,f.** *Choice, 1995.*

Biographies and Studies of Composers and Performers > H > Horowitz, Vladimir

Schonberg, Harold C.   **ML417.H8S3 1992**
Horowitz: A Musical Biography. Trade Cloth. Simon & Schuster. New York, NY. 1992. 432p. ISBN:0-671-72568-8, ISBN13: 978-0-671-72568-6. Dewey:786.2/092 B. LCCN:92-024000.
Audience: **g,l,u,f.**

Biographies and Studies of Composers and Performers > I > Ives, Charles

Block, Geoffrey Holden ML410.I94
Ives, Concord Sonata: Piano Sonata No. 2. Cambridge University Press. 1996. Cambridge Music Handbooks ISBN:0-521-49656-X, ISBN13: 978-0-521-49656-8.
Audience: **u,f.**

Burkholder, J. Peter ML410.M9
All Made of Tunes: Charles Ives and the Uses of Musical Borrowing. Trade Paper. Yale University Press. Cumberland, RI. 2004. 568p. ISBN:0-300-10212-7, ISBN13: 978-0-300-10212-3. Dewey:780.9/2.
Audience: **u,f.** *Choice, 1996.*

Burkholder, J. Peter ML410.I94C33 1996
(Editor)
Charles Ives and His World. Cloth Text. Princeton University Press. Princeton, NJ. 1996. 464p. The Bard Music Festival Ser. ISBN:0-691-01164-8, ISBN13: 978-0-691-01164-6. Dewey:780.92. LCCN:96-021393.
Audience: **g,l,u,f.** *Choice, 1997.*

Debussy, Claude, et al. ML90
Three Classics in the Aesthetic of Music. Ferruccio Busoni & Charles Ives (Authors). Trade Paper. Dover Publications, Inc. Mineola, NY. 1962. 188p. ISBN:0-486-20320-4, ISBN13: 978-0-486-20320-1. Dewey:780.922.
Audience: **u,f.**

Feder, Stuart ML410.I94 F42 1999
The Life of Charles Ives. Cloth Text. Cambridge University Press. New York, NY. 1999. 214p. Musical Lives Ser. ISBN:0-521-59072-8, ISBN13: 978-0-521-59072-3. Dewey:780/.92 B. LCCN:98-049662.
Audience: **g,l,u,f.**

Kirkpatrick, John & Ives, ML410.M9
Charles
Charles E. Ives: Memos. Trade Paper. W. W. Norton & Company, Inc. New York, NY. 1991. 355p. ISBN:0-393-30756-5, ISBN13: 978-0-393-30756-6. Dewey:780.92.
Audience: **u,f.**

Lambert, Philip ML410.M9
The Music of Charles Ives. Trade Paper. Yale University Press. Cumberland, RI. 1997. 256p. Composers of the Twentieth Century Serie Ser. ISBN:0-300-10534-7, ISBN13: 978-0-300-10534-6. Dewey:780/.92 B.
Audience: **u,f.** *Choice, 1998.*

Perlis, Vivian ML410.I94P5 2002
Charles Ives Remembered: An Oral History. Trade Paper. University of Illinois Press. Champaign, IL. 2002. 264p. Music in American Life Ser. ISBN:0-252-07078-X, ISBN13: 978-0-252-07078-5. Dewey:780/.92 B. LCCN:2001-055532.
Audience: **l,u,f.**

Sherwood, Gayle ML134.I9S44 2002
Charles Ives: Guide to Research. Paper over Boards. Garland Publishing, Inc. New York, NY. 2002. 176p. Routledge Musical Bibliographies Ser. ISBN:0-8153-3821-X, ISBN13: 978-0-8153-3821-5. Dewey:016.780/92. LCCN:2002-075204.
Audience: **l,u,f.**

Biographies and Studies of Composers and Performers > J > Janacek, Leos

Beckerman, Michael Brim ML410
(Editor)
Janacek and His World. Trade Cloth. Princeton University Press. Princeton, NJ. 2003. 320p. The Bard Music Festival Ser. ISBN:0-691-11675-X, ISBN13: 978-0-691-11675-4. Dewey:780.9/2.
Audience: **g,l,u,f.**

Cheek, Timothy ML49.J36O62 2003
The Janacek Opera Libretti: Kat'a Kabanova Translations and Pronunciation. Trade Paper. Scarecrow Press, Inc. Lanham, MD. 2004. 280p. ISBN:0-8108-5014-1, ISBN13: 978-0-8108-5014-9. Dewey:782.1/0268. LCCN:2002-153032.
Audience: **u,f.**

Janacek, Leos & Cheek, ML49.J36J37 2003
Timothy
The Janacek Opera Libretti: Translations and Pronunciation. Trade Cloth. Scarecrow Press, Inc. Lanham, MD. 2003. 224p. ISBN:0-8108-4671-3, ISBN13: 978-0-8108-4671-5. Dewey:782.1/0268. LCCN:2002-153032.
Audience: **u,f.**

Tyrrell, John ML410.J18 A4 1992
Janacek Operas. Cloth Text. Princeton University Press. Princeton, NJ. 1992. 436p. ISBN:0-691-09148-X, ISBN13: 978-0-691-09148-8. Dewey:782.1/092. LCCN:92-016091.
Audience: **u,f.** *Choice, 1993.*

Tyrrell, John (Editor) ML410.J18 L49 1982
Leos Janacek: Kat'a Kabanova. Richard Wagner (Contribution by). Trade Paper. Cambridge University Press. New York, NY. 1982. 248p. Cambridge Opera Handbooks Ser. ISBN:0-521-29853-9, ISBN13: 978-0-521-29853-7. Dewey:782.1/092/4. LCCN:81-038505.
Audience: **u,f.**

Wingfield, Paul ML410.J18 W56 1992
Janacek: Glagolitic Mass. Julian Rushton (Contribution by). Cloth Text. Cambridge University Press. New York, NY. 1992. 146p. Music Handbks. ISBN:0-521-38013-8, ISBN13: 978-0-521-38013-3. Dewey:782.32/3. LCCN:91-016986.
Audience: **u,f.** *Choice, 1993.*

Zemanová, Mirka ML410.J18
Janáček. Boston : Northeastern University Press. 2002. ISBN:1-55553-549-6, ISBN13: 978-1-55553-549-0.
Audience: **l,u,f.**

Biographies and Studies of Composers and Performers > J > Jarrett, Keith

Carr, Ian　　　　　　　　**ML417.J35C4 1992**
Keith Jarrett: The Man and His Music. Trade Paper. Da Capo
Press, Inc. Cambridge, MA. 1992. 272p. ISBN:0-306-80478-6,
ISBN13: 978-0-306-80478-6. Dewey:786.2/165/092.
　　　　　　　　　　　　　　　　Audience: **g,l,u,f.**

Biographies and Studies of Composers and Performers > J > Johnson, James P.

Brown, Scott & Hilbert,　　　　**ML417.J62B76 1986**
　Robert
James P. Johnson: A Case of Mistaken Identity. Dan
Morgenstern (Foreword by). Trade Cloth. Scarecrow Press, Inc.
Lanham, MD. 1986. 522p. Studies in Jazz, No. 4
ISBN:0-8108-1887-6, ISBN13: 978-0-8108-1887-3.
Dewey:786.1/092/4 B. LCCN:86-003830.
　　　　　　　Audience: **g,l,u,f.**　*Choice, 1987.*

Biographies and Studies of Composers and Performers > J > Johnson, Robert

Guralnick, Peter　　　　　　**ML420.J735G8 1989**
Searching for Robert Johnson. Trade Cloth. Penguin Group
(USA) Inc. New York, NY. 1989. 9p. ISBN:0-525-24801-3,
ISBN13: 978-0-525-24801-9. Dewey:781.643092.
LCCN:89-007912.
　　　　　　　　　　　　　　　　Audience: **l,u,f.**

Pearson, Barry Lee &　　　　　**ML420.J735P4 2003**
　McCulloch, Bill
Robert Johnson: Lost and Found. Trade Cloth. University of
Illinois Press. Champaign, IL. 2003. 160p. Music in American
Life Ser. ISBN:0-252-02835-X, ISBN13: 978-0-252-02835-9.
Dewey:782.421643/092 B. LCCN:2002-012714.
　　　　　　　Audience: **l,u,f.**　*Choice, 2004.*

Schroeder, Patricia R.　　　　**ML420.J735S37 2004**
Robert Johnson, Mythmaking, and Contemporary American
Culture. Trade Cloth. University of Illinois Press. Champaign,
IL. 2004. 216p. Music in American Life Ser.
ISBN:0-252-02915-1, ISBN13: 978-0-252-02915-8.
Dewey:782.421643/092. LCCN:2003-020027.
　　　　　　　Audience: **g,l,u,f.**　*Choice, 2005.*

Wald, Elijah　　　　　　　**ML420.J735W35 2004**
Escaping the Delta: Robert Johnson and the Invention of the
Blues. Trade Cloth. HarperCollins Publishers. New York, NY.
2004. 368p. ISBN:0-06-052423-5, ISBN13: 978-0-06-052423-4.
Dewey:782.421643/092 B. LCCN:2003-052287.
　　　　　　　　　　　　　　　　Audience: **g,l,u,f.**

Biographies and Studies of Composers and Performers > J > Jones, Quincy

Jones, Quincy　　　　　　　　　**ML419.J7**
Q: The Autobiography of Quincy Jones. Trade Paper. Broadway
Books. New York, NY. 2002. 432p. ISBN:0-7679-0510-5,
ISBN13: 978-0-7679-0510-7. Dewey:781.64/092 B.
　　　　　　　　　　　　　　　　Audience: **g,l,u,f.**

Biographies and Studies of Composers and Performers > J > Joplin, Scott

Berlin, Edward A.　　　　　　　　**ML419.J7**
King of Ragtime: Scott Joplin and His Era. Trade Paper. Oxford
University Press, Inc. New York, NY. 1995. 352p.
ISBN:0-19-810408-1, ISBN13: 978-0-19-810408-7.
Dewey:781.6/4/092.
　　　　　　　　　　　　　　　　Audience: **g,l,u,f.**

Ping-Robbins, Nancy R. &　　　**ML134.J75P56 1998**
　Marco, Guy (Editors)
Scott Joplin: A Guide to Research. Cloth Text. Garland
Publishing, Inc. New York, NY. 1998. 426p. Composer
Resource Manuals Ser., Vol. 7 ISBN:0-8240-8399-7, ISBN13:
978-0-8240-8399-1. Dewey:016.78/092. LCCN:98-010988.
　　　　　　　Audience: **l,u,f.**　*Choice, 1999.*

Biographies and Studies of Composers and Performers > J > Josquin des Prez

Sherr, Richard (Editor)　　　　**ML410.J815J68 2000**
The Josquin Companion. Trade Cloth. Oxford University Press,
Inc. New York, NY. 2001. 732p. ISBN:0-19-816335-5, ISBN13:
978-0-19-816335-0. Dewey:782.2/2/092. LCCN:00-056654.
　　　　　　　Audience: **l,u,f.**　*Choice, 2001.*

Biographies and Studies of Composers and Performers > K > Kern, Jerome

Bordman, Gerald　　　　　　　**ML410.K385.B7**
Jerome Kern: His Life and Music. Trade Cloth. Oxford
University Press, Inc. New York, NY. 1980. 448p.
ISBN:0-19-502649-7, ISBN13: 978-0-19-502649-8.
Dewey:782.8/1/0924. LCCN:79-013826.
　　　　　　　　　　　　　　　　Audience: **l,u,f.**

Biographies and Studies of Composers and Performers > K > King, B. B.

King, B. B. & Ritz, David   ML420.K473
Blues All Around Me: The Autobiography of B. B. King. Trade Paper. HarperCollins Publishers. New York, NY. 1999. 360p. ISBN:0-380-80760-2, ISBN13: 978-0-380-80760-4. Dewey:781.643/092 B. LCCN:96-027773.
Audience: **g,l,u,f.**

Kostelanetz, Richard   ML420.K473B3 2005
  (Editor)
The B. B. King Reader: Six Decades of Commentary. Ed. 2. Trade Paper. Hal Leonard Corporation. Milwaukee, WI. 2005. 256p. ISBN:0-634-09927-2, ISBN13: 978-0-634-09927-4. Dewey:781.643/092 B. LCCN:2005-023200.
Audience: **g,l,u,f.**

Biographies and Studies of Composers and Performers > K > Kuti, Fela

Olaniyan, Tejumola   ML420.F333O43 2004
ⓔ Arrest the Music!: Fela and His Rebel Art and Politics. E-Book. Indiana University Press. Bloomington, IN. 2004. 248p. African Expressive Cultures Ser. ISBN:0-253-34461-1, ISBN13: 978-0-253-34461-8. Dewey:781.63/092 B. LCCN:2004-002138.
Audience: **g,l,u,f.** *Choice, 2005.*

Schoonmaker, Trevor   ML410.F2955F45 2003
  (Editor)
Fela: From West Africa to West Broadway. Cloth over Boards. Palgrave Macmillan. New York, NY. 2003. 224p. ISBN:1-4039-6209-X, ISBN13: 978-1-4039-6209-6. Dewey:781.63/092 B. LCCN:2003-545361.
Audience: **l,u,f.** *Choice, 2004.*

Biographies and Studies of Composers and Performers > L > La Rue, Pierre de

Meconi, Honey   ML410.L287
Pierre de la Rue and Musical Life at the Habsburg-Burgundian Court. Trade Cloth. Oxford University Press, Inc. New York, NY. 2003. 416p. ISBN:0-19-816554-4, ISBN13: 978-0-19-816554-5. Dewey:781.71/2/0092 B. LCCN:2002-038106.
Audience: **u,f.**

Biographies and Studies of Composers and Performers > L > Lawes, William

Ashbee, Andrew (Editor)   ML410.L334W55 1998
William Lawes (1602-1645): Essays on His Life, Times and Work. Trade Cloth. Ashgate Publishing, Ltd. Aldershot, 1998. 380p. ISBN:1-85928-354-3, ISBN13: 978-1-85928-354-7. Dewey:780/.92 B. LCCN:97-077628.
Audience: **u,f.**

Biographies and Studies of Composers and Performers > L > Leadbelly

Wolfe, Charles & Lornell,   ML420.L277W6 1999
  Kip
Life and Legend of Leadbelly. Trade Paper. Da Capo Press, Inc. Cambridge, MA. 1999. 360p. ISBN:0-306-80896-X, ISBN13: 978-0-306-80896-8. Dewey:782.42162/0092 B. LCCN:99-010989.
Audience: **l,u,f.**

Biographies and Studies of Composers and Performers > L > Led Zeppelin

Fast, Susan   ML421.L4F37 2001
In the Houses of the Holy: Led Zeppelin and the Power of Rock Music. Trade Paper. Oxford University Press, Inc. New York, NY. 2001. 258p. ISBN:0-19-514723-5, ISBN13: 978-0-19-514723-0. Dewey:782.42166/092/2. LCCN:00-048367.
Audience: **g,l,u,f.**

Biographies and Studies of Composers and Performers > L > Lennon, John

Thomson, Elizabeth, et al.   ML420.L38
The Lennon Companion: Twenty-Five Years of Comment. Gutman, David (Author). Cambridge, MA: Da Capo Press. 2004. ISBN:0-306-81270-3, ISBN13: 978-0-306-81270-5.
Audience: **g,l,u,f.**

Biographies and Studies of Composers and Performers > L > Lerner, Alan Jay

Citron, Stephen   ML403.C56 1995
The Wordsmiths: Oscar Hammerstein II and Alan Jay Lerner. Trade Cloth. Oxford University Press, Inc. New York, NY. 1995.

464p. The Great Songwriters Ser. ISBN:0-19-508386-5, ISBN13: 978-0-19-508386-6. Dewey:782.1/4/0922 B. LCCN:94-020279.

Audience: **u,f.**

Jablonski, Edward   **ML423.L3J3 1996**
Alan Jay Lerner: A Biography. Trade Cloth. Henry Holt & Company. New York, NY. 1996. 88p. ISBN:0-8050-4076-5, ISBN13: 978-0-8050-4076-0. Dewey:782.1/4/092 B. LCCN:95-037656.

Audience: **g,l,u,f.** *Choice, 1996.*

Lees, Gene   **ML410.L7986L4 1990**
Inventing Champagne: The Worlds of Lerner and Loewe. Trade Cloth. St. Martin's Press. Gordonville, VA. 1990. ISBN:0-312-05136-0, ISBN13: 978-0-312-05136-5. Dewey:782.1/4/0922 B. LCCN:90-037200.

Audience: **u,f.**

Lerner, Alan J.   **ML423.L3A3 1994**
Street Where I Live. Trade Paper. Da Capo Press, Inc. Cambridge, MA. 1994. 333p. ISBN:0-306-80602-9, ISBN13: 978-0-306-80602-5. Dewey:782.1/4/092. LCCN:94-012693.

Audience: **l,u,f.**

Lerner, Alan J. & Green,   **PS3523.E76H96 1987**
   Benny
A Hymn to Him: The Lyrics of Alan Jay Lerner. Al Hirschfeld (Illustrator). Trade Cloth. Hal Leonard Corporation. Milwaukee, WI. 1987. 319p. ISBN:0-87910-109-1, ISBN13: 978-0-87910-109-1. Dewey:782.81/2. LCCN:87-405427.

Audience: **g,l,u,f.**

Shaw, George Bernard &   **PR5363**
   Lerner, Alan Jay
Pygmalion and My Fair Lady. Ed. 50. Mass Market. Penguin Group (USA) Inc. New York, NY. 2006. 240p. ISBN:0-451-53009-8, ISBN13: 978-0-451-53009-7. Dewey:822.912.

Audience: **g,l,u,f.**

Biographies and Studies of Composers and Performers > L > Ligeti, Gyorgy

Griffiths, Paul   **ML410.M9**
Gyorgy Ligeti: Contemporary Composer. Trade Paper. Anova Books. London, 1997. 160p. ISBN:1-86105-058-5, ISBN13: 978-1-86105-058-8. Dewey:780.9/2.

Audience: **u,f.**

Steinitz, Richard   **ML410.L645S84 2003**
Gyorgy Ligeti: Music of the Imagination. Trade Cloth. Northeastern University Press. Boston, MA. 2005. 416p. ISBN:1-55553-551-8, ISBN13: 978-1-55553-551-3. Dewey:780/.92. LCCN:2002-035896.

Audience: **l,u,f.** *Choice, 2003.*

Toop, Richard   **ML410.L645T66 1999**
Gyorgy Ligeti. Trade Paper. Phaidon Press. London, 1999. 238p. Twentieth-Century Composers Ser. ISBN:0-7148-3795-4, ISBN13: 978-0-7148-3795-6. Dewey:780/.92 B. LCCN:00-363647.

Audience: **l,u,f.**

Biographies and Studies of Composers and Performers > L > Liszt, Franz

Hamilton, Kenneth (Editor)   **ML410.L7**
The Cambridge Companion to Liszt. Trade Paper, Perfect. Cambridge University Press. New York, NY. 2005. 300p. Cambridge Companions to Music Ser. ISBN:0-521-64462-3, ISBN13: 978-0-521-64462-4. Dewey:780/.92 B. LCCN:2004-040793.

Audience: **g,l,u,f.**

Hamilton, Kenneth & Liszt,   **ML410.L7 H258 1996**
   Franz
Liszt: Sonata in B Minor. Julian Rushton (Contribution by). Cloth Text. Cambridge University Press. New York, NY. 1996. 101p. Music Handbks. ISBN:0-521-46570-2, ISBN13: 978-0-521-46570-0. Dewey:786.2/183. LCCN:95-049839.

Audience: **u,f.**

Saffle, Michael   **ML134.L7S2 2003**
Franz Liszt: A Guide to Research. Ed. 2. Paper over Boards. Routledge. New York, NY. 2004. 536p. Routledge Music Bibliographies Ser. ISBN:0-415-94011-7, ISBN13: 978-0-415-94011-5. Dewey:016.78/092. LCCN:2003-026223.

Audience: **l,u,f.** *Choice, 1992.*

Walker, Alan   **ML410.L7**
Franz Liszt: The Final Years, 1861-1886. Ed. 2. Trade Paper. Cornell University Press. Ithaca, NY. 1997. 624p. ISBN:0-8014-8453-7, ISBN13: 978-0-8014-8453-7. Dewey:780.92.

Audience: **l,u,f.**

Walker, Alan   **ML410.L7W27 1987**
Franz Liszt: The Virtuoso Years, 1811-1847. Ed. 3. Trade Paper. Cornell University Press. Ithaca, NY. 1987. 512p. ISBN:0-8014-9421-4, ISBN13: 978-0-8014-9421-5. Dewey:780/.92/4 B. LCCN:82-047821.

Audience: **l,u,f.**

Walker, Alan   **ML410.L7 W27 1987**
Franz Liszt: The Weimar Years, 1848-1861. Ed. 2. Book, Other. Cornell University Press. Ithaca, NY. 1993. 656p. ISBN:0-8014-9721-3, ISBN13: 978-0-8014-9721-6. Dewey:780/.92/4.

Audience: **l,u,f.**

Walker, Alan   **ML410.L7W296 2005**
Reflections on Liszt. Book, Other. Cornell University Press. Ithaca, NY. 2005. 272p. ISBN:0-8014-4363-6, ISBN13: 978-0-8014-4363-3. Dewey:780/.92. LCCN:2004-030467.

Audience: **l,u,f.**

Williams, Adrian   ML410.L7W55 1990
Portrait of Liszt: By Himself and His Contemporaries. Cloth
Text. Oxford University Press, Inc. New York, NY. 1990. 784p.
ISBN:0-19-816150-6, ISBN13: 978-0-19-816150-9.
Dewey:780/.92 B. LCCN:89-009333.
       Audience: **l,u,f.** *Choice, 1991.*

Biographies and Studies of Composers and Performers > L > Lloyd Webber, Andrew

Black, Don & Hampton,   ML50.Z99
  Christopher
Sunset Boulevard. Trade Paper. Faber & Faber, Inc. New York,
NY. 1993. 128p. ISBN:0-571-17214-8, ISBN13:
978-0-571-17214-6. Dewey:782.140268.
       Audience: **g,l,u,f.**

Citron, Stephen   ML390.C586 2001
Stephen Sondheim and Andrew Lloyd Webber: The New
Musical. Trade Cloth. Oxford University Press, Inc. New York,
NY. 2001. 464p. The Great Songwriters Ser.
ISBN:0-19-509601-0, ISBN13: 978-0-19-509601-9.
Dewey:782.1/4/0922. LCCN:2001-031408.
       Audience: **u,f.**

Eliot, T. S.   ML50.L804
Cats: The Book of the Musical. John Napier (Photographer).
Trade Paper. Harcourt Trade Publishers. New York, NY. 1983.
112p. Harvest Book Ser. ISBN:0-15-615582-6, ISBN13:
978-0-15-615582-3. Dewey:782.81/2. LCCN:82-048026.
       Audience: **g,l,u,f.**

Ganzl, Kurt   ML410.L78
The Complete Aspects of Love. Clive Barda (Photographer).
Trade Cloth. Penguin Group (USA) Inc. New York, NY. 1990.
176p. ISBN:0-670-83192-1, ISBN13: 978-0-670-83192-0.
Dewey:782.1/4. LCCN:89-040452.
       Audience: **g,l,u,f.** *Choice, 1990.*

Lloyd Webber, Andrew &   ML50.L804
  Rice, Tim
Evita. Trade Cloth. Quite Specific Media Group, Ltd.
Hollywood, CA. 1979. 128p. ISBN:0-89676-030-8, ISBN13:
978-0-89676-030-1. Dewey:782.81/2. LCCN:79-053888.
       Audience: **g,l,u,f.**

Perry, George   ML1950
The Complete Phantom of the Opera. Clive Barda
(Photographer). Trade Paper. DIANE Publishing Company.
Collingdale, PA. 2005. 167p. ISBN:0-7567-8833-1, ISBN13:
978-0-7567-8833-9. Dewey:782.81.
       Audience: **g,l,u,f.**

Rice, Tim   ML50.Z99
Joseph and the Amazing Technicolor Dreamcoat. Quentin Blake
(Illustrator), Andrew Lloyd Webber (Composed by). Trade

Cloth. Henry Holt & Company. New York, NY. 1982. 48p.
ISBN:0-03-061517-8, ISBN13: 978-0-03-061517-7.
Dewey:782.81/2. LCCN:81-023722.
       Audience: **g,l,u,f.**

Snelson, John   ML410.L78S64 2004
Andrew Lloyd Webber. Geoffrey Holden Block (Foreword by).
Cloth over Boards. Yale University Press. Cumberland, RI.
2004. 288p. Yale Broadway Masters Ser. ISBN:0-300-10459-6,
ISBN13: 978-0-300-10459-2. Dewey:782.1/4/092.
LCCN:2004-004311.
       Audience: **g,l,u,f.** *Choice, 2005.*

Biographies and Studies of Composers and Performers > L > Loesser, Frank

Garebian, Keith   ML50.F49678
The Making of Guys and Dolls. Trade Paper. Mosaic Press.
Niagara Falls, NY. 2004. 154p. The Making of the Great
Broadway Musicals Ser. ISBN:0-88962-764-9, ISBN13:
978-0-88962-764-2. Dewey:782.1/4.
       Audience: **l,u,f.**

Loesser, Susan   ML410.L7984L6 1993
A Most Remarkable Fella: Frank Loesser and the Guys and
Dolls in His Life: A Portrait by His Daughter. Trade Cloth.
Penguin Group (USA) Inc. New York, NY. 1993. 320p.
ISBN:1-55611-364-1, ISBN13: 978-1-55611-364-2.
Dewey:782.1/4/092 B. LCCN:92-054985.
       Audience: **l,u,f.** *Choice, 1994.*

Biographies and Studies of Composers and Performers > L > Loewe, Frederick

Garebian, Keith   ML1711
The Making of My Fair Lady. Trade Paper. Mosaic Press.
Niagara Falls, NY. 2004. 160p. The Making of the Great
Broadway Musicals Ser. ISBN:0-88962-653-7, ISBN13:
978-0-88962-653-9. Dewey:782.1/4/0973.
       Audience: **l,u,f.**

Lees, Gene   ML410.L7986L4 1990
Inventing Champagne: The Worlds of Lerner and Loewe. Trade
Cloth. St. Martin's Press. Gordonville, VA. 1990.
ISBN:0-312-05136-0, ISBN13: 978-0-312-05136-5.
Dewey:782.1/4/0922 B. LCCN:90-037200.
       Audience: **u,f.**

Biographies and Studies of Composers and Performers > L > Lully, Jean Baptiste

Heyer, John Hajdu (Editor)   **ML410.L95 L96 2000**
Lully Studies. Trade Cloth. Cambridge University Press. New York, NY. 2000. 331p. Cambridge Composer Studies ISBN:0-521-62183-6, ISBN13: 978-0-521-62183-0. Dewey:780/.92. LCCN:00-020313.
Audience: **u,f.** *Choice, 2001.*

Biographies and Studies of Composers and Performers > L > Lutoslawski, Witold

Rae, Charles B.   **ML410.M9**
The Music of Lutoslawski. Ed. 3. Trade Cloth. Omnibus Press. New York, NY. 1999. 318p. ISBN:0-7119-6910-8, ISBN13: 978-0-7119-6910-0. Dewey:780.92.
Audience: **u,f.**

Biographies and Studies of Composers and Performers > M

Allanbrook, Wye J.   **ML410.M9**
Rhythmic Gesture in Mozart: "Le Nozze Di Figaro" and "Don Giovanni". Trade Cloth. University of Chicago Press. Chicago, IL. 1984. xii, 396p. ISBN:0-226-01403-7, ISBN13: 978-0-226-01403-6. Dewey:782.1/092/4. LCCN:83-009184.
Audience: **u,f.**

Biographies and Studies of Composers and Performers > M > MacDowell, Edward

Levy, Alan H.   **ML410.M12L48 1998**
Edward MacDowell: An American Master. Book, Other. Scarecrow Press, Inc. Lanham, MD. 1999. 281p. ISBN:0-8108-3463-4, ISBN13: 978-0-8108-3463-7. Dewey:780/.92 b. LCCN:98-007958.
Audience: **u,f.** *Choice, 1999.*

Biographies and Studies of Composers and Performers > M > Machaut, Giullaume de

Earp, Lawrence   **ML134.G956E3 1995**
Guillaume de Machaut: A Guide to Research. Library Binding. Garland Publishing, Inc. New York, NY. 1995. 696p. Composer Resource Manuals Ser., Vol. 36 ISBN:0-8240-2323-4, ISBN13: 978-0-8240-2323-2. Dewey:016.841/1. LCCN:95-035044.
Audience: **u,f.** *Choice, 1996.*

Leech-Wilkinson, Daniel   **ML410.G966L3 1990**
Machaut's Mass: An Introduction. Trade Cloth. Oxford University Press, Inc. New York, NY. 1990. 224p. ISBN:0-19-316333-0, ISBN13: 978-0-19-316333-1. Dewey:782.32/32. LCCN:89-023005.
Audience: **l,u,f.** *Choice, 1991.*

Reaney, Gilbert   **ML410.G966 R4**
Guillaume de Machaut. Trade Cloth. Oxford University Press, Inc. New York, NY. 1971. 76p. Oxford Studies of Composers ISBN:0-19-315218-5, ISBN13: 978-0-19-315218-2. Dewey:780/.924. LCCN:79-032092.
Audience: **u,f.**

Robertson, Anne W.   **ML410.G966.R63 2002**
Guillaume de Machaut and Reims: Context and Meaning in His Musical Works. Trade Cloth. Cambridge University Press. New York, NY. 2002. 476p. ISBN:0-521-41876-3, ISBN13: 978-0-521-41876-8. Dewey:782.2/6/092. LCCN:2001-043949.
Audience: **u,f.** *Choice, 2003.*

Biographies and Studies of Composers and Performers > M > Madonna

Fouz-Hernandez, Santiago   **ML420.M1387**
& Jarman-Ivens, Freya
Madonna's Drowned Worlds: New Approaches to Her Subcultural Transformations, 1983-2003. Trade Cloth. Ashgate Publishing, Ltd. Aldershot, 2004. 246p. Ashgate Popular and Folk Music Ser. ISBN:0-7546-3371-3, ISBN13: 978-0-7546-3371-6. Dewey:782.42166/092. LCCN:2003-062883.
Audience: **u,f.**

Metz, A. & Benson, C.   **ML420.P96**
The Madonna Companion: Two Decades of Commentary. Trade Paper. Music Sales Corporation. New York, NY. 1999. xiv, 346p. ISBN:0-8256-7194-9, ISBN13: 978-0-8256-7194-4. Dewey:782.4/2/166/092.
Audience: **g,l,u,f.**

Biographies and Studies of Composers and Performers > M > Mahler, Alma

Giroud, Francoise   **DB844.M34G5713 1991**
Alma Mahler: Or the Art of Being Loved. R. M. Stock (Editor, Translator). Trade Cloth. Oxford University Press, Inc. New York, NY. 1992. 176p. ISBN:0-19-816156-5, ISBN13: 978-0-19-816156-1. Dewey:780/.92 B. LCCN:91-003678.
Audience: **u,f.**

Biographies and Studies of Composers and Performers > M > Mahler, Gustav

de La Grange, Henry L.   **ML410.M23L3413 1995**
Gustav Mahler: Vienna: The Years of Challenge (1897-1904).
Trade Cloth. Oxford University Press, Inc. New York, NY. 1995.
912p. ISBN:0-19-315159-6, ISBN13: 978-0-19-315159-8.
Dewey:780/.92 B. LCCN:94-018322.

       Audience: **u,f.** *Choice, 1995.*

de La Grange, Henry L.   **ML410.M23L3413 1995**
Gustav Mahler: Vienna: Triumph and Disillusion (1904-1907).
Trade Cloth. Oxford University Press, Inc. New York, NY. 2000.
1,016p. ISBN:0-19-315160-X, ISBN13: 978-0-19-315160-4.
Dewey:780.9/2. LCCN:94-018322.

       Audience: **u,f.**

Franklin, Peter   **ML410.M23 F69 1997**
The Life of Mahler. Trade Paper. Cambridge University Press.
New York, NY. 1997. 238p. Musical Lives Ser.
ISBN:0-521-46761-6, ISBN13: 978-0-521-46761-2.
Dewey:780/.92 B. LCCN:96-025105.

       Audience: **g,l,u,f.**

Hefling, Stephen E.   **MT121.M34 H44 2000**
Mahler: Das Lied Von der Erde (The Song of the Earth). Cloth
Text. Cambridge University Press. New York, NY. 2000. 173p.
Music Handbks. ISBN:0-521-47534-1, ISBN13:
978-0-521-47534-1. Dewey:782.4/7. LCCN:99-023189.

       Audience: **u,f.**

La Grange, Henry-Louis de   **ML410.M23**
Mahler. London, Victor Gollancz Ltd. 1974.
ISBN:0-575-01672-8, ISBN13: 978-0-575-01672-9.

       Audience: **l,u,f.**

Mitchell, Donald   **ML410.M23M48 2002**
Gustav Mahler: Songs and Symphonies of Life and Death -
Interpretations and Annotations. Trade Paper. Boydell & Brewer,
Ltd. Woodbridge, 2005. 664p. ISBN:0-85115-908-7, ISBN13:
978-0-85115-908-9. Dewey:780.92. LCCN:2002-036674.

       Audience: **l,u,f.**

Mitchell, Donald   **ML410.B4978**
Gustav Mahler: the Wunderhorn Years: Chronicles and
Commentaries. Ed. 3. Trade Paper. Boydell & Brewer, Ltd.
Woodbridge, 2005. 528p. ISBN:1-84383-003-5, ISBN13:
978-1-84383-003-0. Dewey:780.92.

       Audience: **l,u,f.**

Mitchell, Donald   **ML410.M23**
Gustav Mahler: The Early Years. Ed. 3. Paul Banks & Donald
Matthews (Revised by). Trade Paper. Boydell & Brewer, Ltd.
Woodbridge, 2003. 372p. ISBN:1-84383-002-7, ISBN13:
978-1-84383-002-3. Dewey:780/.92 B. LCCN:2004-269960.

       Audience: **l,u,f.**

Mitchell, Donald (Author,   **ML410.M9**
   Editor)
The Mahler Companion. Andrew Nicholson (Editor). Trade
Paper. Oxford University Press, Inc. New York, NY. 2002. 668p.
ISBN:0-19-924965-2, ISBN13: 978-0-19-924965-7.
Dewey:780/.92.

       Audience: **g,l,u,f.** *Choice, 2000.*

Painter, Karen (Editor)   **ML410.M23**
Mahler and His World. Trade Paper. Princeton University Press.
Princeton, NJ. 2002. 408p. The Bard Music Festival Ser.
ISBN:0-691-09244-3, ISBN13: 978-0-691-09244-7.
Dewey:780/.92.

       Audience: **g,l,u,f.** *Choice, 2003.*

Zychowicz, James L.   **ML410.B42**
Mahler's Fourth Symphony. Trade Cloth. Oxford University
Press, Inc. New York, NY. 2000. 206p. Studies in Musical
Genesis, Structure, and Interpretation ISBN:0-19-816206-5,
ISBN13: 978-0-19-816206-3. Dewey:784.2/184.

       Audience: **u,f.**

Biographies and Studies of Composers and Performers > M > Mancini, Henry

Mancini, Henry   **ML410**
Did They Mention the Music?: The Autobiography of Henry
Mancini. Gene Lees (Author, Afterword by, Foreword by). Trade
Paper. Cooper Square Publishers, Inc. New York, NY. 2002.
312p. ISBN:0-8154-1175-8, ISBN13: 978-0-8154-1175-8.
Dewey:780.92.

       Audience: **g,l,u,f.**

Biographies and Studies of Composers and Performers > M > Marenzio, Luca

Bizzarini, Marco & Chater,   **ML410.M326B5813 2002**
   James (Translators)
Luca Marenzio: The Career of a Musician Between the
Renaissance and the Counter-Reformation. Trade Cloth. Ashgate
Publishing, Ltd. Aldershot, 2003. 400p. ISBN:0-7546-0516-7,
ISBN13: 978-0-7546-0516-4. Dewey:782.4/3/092 B.
LCCN:2002-027917.

       Audience: **u,f.**

Biographies and Studies of Composers and Performers > M > Marley, Bob

Bordowitz, Hank   **ML3532**
Every Little Thing Gonna Be Alright: The Bob Marley Reader.
Trade Paper. Da Capo Press, Inc. Cambridge, MA. 2004. 336p.
ISBN:0-306-81340-8, ISBN13: 978-0-306-81340-5.
Dewey:782.421646/092 B. LCCN:2004-009767.

Audience: **g,l,u,f.**

White, Timothy   **ML420.M3313**
Catch a Fire: The Life of Bob Marley. Ed. 4. Trade Paper.
Henry Holt & Company. New York, NY. 2006. 576p.
ISBN:0-8050-8086-4, ISBN13: 978-0-8050-8086-5.
Dewey:784.5/0092/4.

Audience: **g,l,u,f.**

Biographies and Studies of Composers and Performers > M > Marsalis, Wynton

Vigeland, Carl & Marsalis,   **ML419.D39**
  Wynton
Jazz in the Bittersweet Blues of Life. Trade Paper. Da Capo
Press, Inc. Cambridge, MA. 2002. 256p. ISBN:0-306-81127-8,
ISBN13: 978-0-306-81127-2. Dewey:788.9/2165/092.

Audience: **g,l,u,f.**

Biographies and Studies of Composers and Performers > M > Mascagni, Pietro

Mallach, Alan   **ML410.M39M25 2002**
Pietro Mascagni and His Operas. Trade Cloth. Northeastern
University Press. Boston, MA. 2002. 320p.
ISBN:1-55553-524-0, ISBN13: 978-1-55553-524-7.
Dewey:782.1/092 B. LCCN:2001-059191.

Audience: **l,u,f.**   *Choice, 2003, 2002.*

Stivender, David   **ML410.M393**
Mascagni: An Autobiography Compiled, Edited and Translated
from Original Sources. Trade Cloth. Bold Strummer, Limited,
The. Westport, CT. 1988. 388p. ISBN:0-912483-06-7, ISBN13:
978-0-912483-06-1. Dewey:782.1092.

Audience: **u,f.**   *Choice, 1989.*

Biographies and Studies of Composers and Performers > M > Massenet, Jules

Irvine, Demar   **ML410.M41I8 1994**
Massenet: A Chronicle of His Life and Times. Trade Cloth. Hal
Leonard Corporation. Milwaukee, WI. 1994. 400p.

ISBN:0-931340-63-2, ISBN13: 978-0-931340-63-5.
Dewey:782.1/092. LCCN:93-024443.

Audience: **u,f.**   *Choice, 1994.*

Biographies and Studies of Composers and Performers > M > McCartney, Paul

Giuliano, Geoffrey   **ML410.M115G58 1997**
Blackbird: The Life and Times of Paul McCartney. Ed. 2.
Denny Laine (Foreword by). Trade Paper. Da Capo Press, Inc.
Cambridge, MA. 1997. 440p. ISBN:0-306-80781-5, ISBN13:
978-0-306-80781-7. Dewey:782.42166/092 B. LCCN:97-021945.

Audience: **g,l,u,f.**

Biographies and Studies of Composers and Performers > M > Mendelssohn, Felix

Brown, Clive   **ML410.M5B76 2003**
A Portrait of Mendelssohn. Cloth over Boards. Yale University
Press. Cumberland, RI. 2003. 586p. ISBN:0-300-09539-2,
ISBN13: 978-0-300-09539-5. Dewey:780/.92 B.
LCCN:2002-012154.

Audience: **u,f.**   *Choice, 2004.*

Cooper, John M.   **ML134.M53C6 2001**
Felix Mendelssohn Bartholdy: Guide to Research with
Introduction to Research Concerning Fanny. Cloth Text. Garland
Publishing, Inc. New York, NY. 2001. 272p. Composer
Resource Manuals, Vol. 54 ISBN:0-8153-1513-9, ISBN13:
978-0-8153-1513-1. Dewey:016.78/092. LCCN:00-045737.

Audience: **l,u,f.**

Cooper, John Michael   **MT130.M35C66 2003**
Mendelssohn's 'Italian' Symphony. Trade Cloth. Oxford
University Press, Inc. New York, NY. 2003. 252p. Studies in
Musical Genesis and Structure ISBN:0-19-816653-2, ISBN13:
978-0-19-816653-5. Dewey:784.2/184. LCCN:2002-030842.

Audience: **u,f.**

Cooper, John Michael &   **ML410**
  Prandi, Julie D. (Editors)
The Mendelssohns: Their Music in History. Trade Cloth. Oxford
University Press, Inc. New York, NY. 2003. 404p.
ISBN:0-19-816723-7, ISBN13: 978-0-19-816723-5.
Dewey:780.922. LCCN:2003-275059.

Audience: **g,l,u,f.**   *Choice, 2003.*

Mercer-Taylor, Peter   **ML410.M5C36 2004**
  (Editor)
The Cambridge Companion to Mendelssohn. Jonathan Cross
(Contribution by). Trade Paper. Cambridge University Press.

New York, NY. 2004. 332p. Cambridge Companions to Music Ser. ISBN:0-521-53342-2, ISBN13: 978-0-521-53342-3. Dewey:780/.92 B. LCCN:2003-069735.

Audience: **g,l,u,f.** *Choice, 2005.*

Todd, R. Larry   **ML410**
Mendelssohn: A Life in Music. Trade Paper. Oxford University Press, Inc. New York, NY. 2005. 712p. ISBN:0-19-517988-9, ISBN13: 978-0-19-517988-0. Dewey:780/.92 B.

Audience: **l,u,f.**

Todd, R. Larry   **ML410.M5M47 1991**
Mendelssohn and His World by Todd. Trade Paper. Princeton University Press. Princeton, NJ. 1991. 428p. The Bard Music Festival Ser. ISBN:0-691-02715-3, ISBN13: 978-0-691-02715-9. LCCN:91-016124.

Audience: **g,l,u,f.** *Choice, 1992.*

Todd, R. Larry   **ML410.M5**
Mendelssohn: The Hebrides and Other Overtures. Julian Rushton (Contribution by). Trade Paper. Cambridge University Press. New York, NY. 1993. 129p. Music Handbks. ISBN:0-521-40764-8, ISBN13: 978-0-521-40764-9. Dewey:784.218926092. LCCN:92-036005.

Audience: **u,f.** *Choice, 1994.*

Biographies and Studies of Composers and Performers > M > Messiaen, Olivier

Hill, Peter (Editor)   **ML410.M595M48 1995**
The Messiaen Companion. Trade Paper. Hal Leonard Corporation. Milwaukee, WI. 1995. 584p. ISBN:0-931340-94-2, ISBN13: 978-0-931340-94-9. Dewey:780/.92. LCCN:95-170368.

Audience: **l,u,f.** *Choice, 1995.*

Hill, Peter & Simeone, Nigel   **ML410**
Messiaen. Saddle Stitched, Cloth over Boards, Dust Jacket. Yale University Press. Cumberland, RI. 2005. 352p. ISBN:0-300-10907-5, ISBN13: 978-0-300-10907-8. Dewey:780.92.

Audience: **u,f.** *Choice, 2006.*

Messiaen, Oliver   **MT6**
The Technique of My Musical Language. Library Binding. Reprint Services Company. Temecula, CA. 1987. ISBN:0-685-14827-0, ISBN13: 978-0-685-14827-3. Dewey:781.

Audience: **u,f.**

Messiaen, Olivier, et al.   **ML410.M595**
Music and Color: Conversations with Claude Samuel. Samuel, Claude (Author); Glasow, E. Thomas (Translator). Portland, Or.: Amadeus Press. 1994. ISBN:0-931340-67-5, ISBN13: 978-0-931340-67-3.

Audience: **u,f.**

Pople, Anthony   **ML410.M595 P58 1998**
Messiaen: Quatuor Pour la Fin du Temps. Julian Rushton (Contribution by). Cloth Text. Cambridge University Press. New York, NY. 1998. 126p. Music Handbks. ISBN:0-521-58497-3, ISBN13: 978-0-521-58497-5. Dewey:785/.24194. LCCN:98-023937.

Audience: **u,f.** *Choice, 1999.*

Rischin, Rebecca   **ML410.M595R57 2003**
For the End of Time: The Story of the Messiaen Quartet. Book, Other. Cornell University Press. Ithaca, NY. 2003. 184p. ISBN:0-8014-4136-6, ISBN13: 978-0-8014-4136-3. Dewey:785/.24194. LCCN:2003-011589.

Audience: **u,f.** *Choice, 2004.*

Biographies and Studies of Composers and Performers > M > Milhaud, Darius

Kelly, Barbara L.   **ML410.M674K45 2002**
Tradition and Style in the Works of Darius Milhaud 1912-1939. Trade Cloth. Ashgate Publishing, Ltd. Aldershot, 2003. 228p. ISBN:0-7546-3033-1, ISBN13: 978-0-7546-3033-3. Dewey:780/.92. LCCN:2002-074468.

Audience: **u,f.** *Choice, 2004.*

Milhaud, Darius   **ML410.M674A3 1994**
My Happy Life. Donald Evans (Translator), Christopher Palmer (Translator, Introduction by). Trade Paper. Marion Boyars Publishers, Inc. New York, NY. 1994. 380p. ISBN:0-7145-2957-5, ISBN13: 978-0-7145-2957-8. Dewey:780/.92 B. LCCN:94-009018.

Audience: **u,f.**

Biographies and Studies of Composers and Performers > M > Mingus, Charles

Mingus, Charles   **ML410.M6795**
Beneath the Underdog. Nel Kinh (Editor). Trade Paper. Penguin Group (USA) Inc. New York, NY. 1980. 272p. ISBN:0-14-003880-9, ISBN13: 978-0-14-003880-4. Dewey:781.6/5/092. LCCN:80-016132.

Audience: **g,l,u,f.**

Santoro, Gene   **ML410.E44**
Myself When I Am Real: The Life and Music of Charles Mingus. Ed. 2. Trade Paper. Oxford University Press, Inc. New York, NY. 2001. 462p. ISBN:0-19-514711-1, ISBN13: 978-0-19-514711-7. Dewey:781.65/092 B.

Audience: **l,u,f.** *Choice, 2001.*

Biographies and Studies of Composers and Performers > M > Mitchell, Joni

Luftig, Stacy   **ML420.S565**
The Joni Mitchell Companion: Four Decades of Commentary.
Trade Paper. Music Sales Corporation. New York, NY. 1999.
300p. Classic Rock Albums Ser. ISBN:0-8256-7190-6, ISBN13:
978-0-8256-7190-6. Dewey:782.42164/092.
                                                    Audience: **g,l,u,f.**

Biographies and Studies of Composers and Performers > M > Monk, Meredith

Jowitt, Deborah (Editor)   **ML410.M72M47 1997**
Meredith Monk. Trade Cloth. Johns Hopkins University Press.
Baltimore, MD. 1997. 224p. PAJ Bks., :Art and Performance
ISBN:0-8018-5539-X, ISBN13: 978-0-8018-5539-9.
Dewey:700/.92. LCCN:97-006597.
                                                    Audience: **l,u,f.**

Biographies and Studies of Composers and Performers > M > Monk, Thelonious

Gourse, Leslie   **ML417.M846**
Straight, No Chaser: The Life and Genius of Thelonious Monk.
Trade Paper. Music Sales Corporation. New York, NY. 1998.
400p. ISBN:0-8256-7229-5, ISBN13: 978-0-8256-7229-3.
Dewey:786.2/1/65/092. LCCN:97-010509.
                                                    Audience: **g,l,u,f.**

Van Der Bliek, Rob (Editor)   **ML417.M846T54 2001**
The Thelonious Monk Reader. Ed. 2. Trade Cloth. Oxford
University Press, Inc. New York, NY. 2001. 286p. Readers in
American Music Ser. ISBN:0-19-512166-X, ISBN13:
978-0-19-512166-7. Dewey:786.2165/092 B. LCCN:00-037475.
                                                    Audience: **g,l,u,f.**

Biographies and Studies of Composers and Performers > M > Monroe, Bill

Ewing, Tom   **ML420.M5595B55 2000**
The Bill Monroe Reader. Trade Cloth. University of Illinois
Press. Champaign, IL. 2000. 336p. Music in American Life Ser.
ISBN:0-252-02500-8, ISBN13: 978-0-252-02500-6.
Dewey:781.642/092. LCCN:00-008015.
                                        Audience: **g,l,u,f.** *Choice, 2001.*

Biographies and Studies of Composers and Performers > M > Monteverdi, Claudio

Carter, Tim   **ML410.M77C37 2002**
Monteverdi's Musical Theatre. Cloth over Boards. Yale
University Press. Cumberland, RI. 2002. 336p.
ISBN:0-300-09676-3, ISBN13: 978-0-300-09676-7.
Dewey:782.1/092. LCCN:2002-109930.
                                                    Audience: **u,f.**

Kiel, Dyke & Adams, K.   **ML134.M66A5 1989**
  Gary
Claudio Monteverdi: A Guide to Research. Cloth Text. Garland
Publishing, Inc. New York, NY. 1989. 292p. Composer
Resource Manuals Ser., Vol. 23 ISBN:0-8240-7743-1, ISBN13:
978-0-8240-7743-3. Dewey:016.782/0092. LCCN:89-033040.
                                        Audience: **l,u,f.** *Choice, 1989.*

Kurtzman, Jeffrey   **ML410.M77K87 1999**
The Monteverdi Vespers of 1610: Music, Context, and
Performance. Trade Cloth. Oxford University Press, Inc. New
York, NY. 2000. 624p. ISBN:0-19-816409-2, ISBN13:
978-0-19-816409-8. Dewey:782.32/4. LCCN:98-015026.
                                        Audience: **u,f.** *Choice, 2000.*

Monteverdi, Claudio   **ML410.V4**
Operas of Monteverdi: Includes Orfeo, Return of Ulysses,
Coronation of Poppea. Anne Ridler (Translator). Trade Paper.
Riverrun Press, Inc. Flemington, NJ. 1992. 208p. English
National Opera Guide Series: Bilingual Libretto, Articles, No.
45 ISBN:0-7145-4207-5, ISBN13: 978-0-7145-4207-2.
Dewey:782.1092.
                                                    Audience: **g,l,u,f.**

Stevens, Denis   **ML410.M77A4 1995**
The Letters of Claudio Monteverdi. Ed. 2. Cloth Text. Oxford
University Press, Inc. New York, NY. 1995. 480p.
ISBN:0-19-816414-9, ISBN13: 978-0-19-816414-2.
Dewey:782/.0092 B. LCCN:94-040349.
                                        Audience: **u,f.** *Choice, 1996.*

Tomlinson, Gary   **ML410.B4**
Monteverdi and the End of the Renaissance. Trade Paper.
University of California Press. Berkeley, CA. 1990. 292p.
ISBN:0-520-06980-3, ISBN13: 978-0-520-06980-0.
Dewey:780/.92/4.
                                        Audience: **u,f.** *Choice, 1987.*

Whenham, John   **ML410.M77**
Monteverdi, Vespers (1610). Cambridge University Press. 1997.
Cambridge music handbooks ISBN:0-521-45377-1, ISBN13:
978-0-521-45377-6.
                                                    Audience: **u,f.**

Whenham, John   **ML410.M77 C55 1986**
Claudio Monteverdi: Orfeo. Richard Wagner (Contribution by).
Trade Paper. Cambridge University Press. New York, NY. 1986.
230p. Cambridge Opera Handbooks Ser. ISBN:0-521-28477-5,

ISBN13: 978-0-521-28477-6. Dewey:782.1/092/4.
LCCN:85-009923.

Audience: **l,u,f.** *Choice, 1986.*

Biographies and Studies of Composers and Performers > M > Morton, Jelly Roll

Lomax, Alan   **ML410.M82 L6 2001**
Mister Jelly Roll: The Fortunes of Jelly Roll Morton, New
Orleans Creole and "Inventor of Jazz". Trade Paper. University
of California Press. Berkeley, CA. 2001. 368p.
ISBN:0-520-22530-9, ISBN13: 978-0-520-22530-5.
Dewey:781.65/092 B. LCCN:00-064430.

Audience: **g,l,u,f.**

Biographies and Studies of Composers and Performers > M > Mozart, Wolfgang Amadeus

Bauman, Thomas   **ML410.M9B185 1987**
W. A. Mozart: Die Entführung aus dem Serail. Richard Wagner
(Contribution by). Trade Paper. Cambridge University Press.
New York, NY. 1988. 156p. Cambridge Opera Handbooks Ser.
ISBN:0-521-31060-1, ISBN13: 978-0-521-31060-4.
Dewey:782.1/092/4. LCCN:87-010326.

Audience: **u,f.** *Choice, 1988.*

Branscombe, Peter   **ML410.M9 B76 1991**
W. A. Mozart: Die Zauberflöte. Richard Wagner (Contribution
by). Trade Paper. Cambridge University Press. New York, NY.
1991. 263p. Cambridge Opera Handbooks Ser.
ISBN:0-521-31916-1, ISBN13: 978-0-521-31916-4.
Dewey:782.1. LCCN:90-040403.

Audience: **u,f.**

Brown, A. Peter   **ML1255.B87**
The First Golden Age of the Viennese Symphony: Haydn,
Mozart, Beethoven and Schubert. Trade Cloth. Indiana
University Press. Bloomington, IN. 2002. 816p.
ISBN:0-253-33487-X, ISBN13: 978-0-253-33487-9.
Dewey:784.2/184 s 784.2. LCCN:98-026549.

Audience: **g,l,u,f.** *Choice, 2003.*

Brown, Bruce Alan   **ML410.M9B8191995**
W. A. Mozart: Così Fan Tutte. Richard Wagner (Contribution
by). Trade Paper. Cambridge University Press. New York, NY.
1995. 220p. Opera Handbooks Ser. ISBN:0-521-43735-0,
ISBN13: 978-0-521-43735-6. Dewey:782.1. LCCN:95-009885.

Audience: **u,f.** *Choice, 1997.*

Carter, Tim   **ML410.M9 C33 1987**
Le Nozze Di Figaro. Richard Wagner (Contribution by). Trade
Paper. Cambridge University Press. New York, NY. 1988. 192p.
Cambridge Opera Handbooks Ser. ISBN:0-521-31606-5,
ISBN13: 978-0-521-31606-4. Dewey:782.109.
LCCN:87-011597.

Audience: **u,f.** *Choice, 1988.*

Davidson, Michael   **MT220**
Mozart and the Pianist: A Guide for Performers and Teachers to
Mozart's Major Works for Solo Piano. Ed. 2. Trade Paper. Kahn
& Averill Publishers. London, 2001. 384p. ISBN:1-871082-76-5,
ISBN13: 978-1-871082-76-0. Dewey:786.2143.

Audience: **l,u,f.**

Deutsch, Otto Erich   **ML410.M9 D4782**
Mozart: A Documentary Biography. Trade Cloth. Stanford
University Press. Palo Alto, CA. 1965. xii, 680p.
ISBN:0-8047-0233-0, ISBN13: 978-0-8047-0233-1.
Dewey:780.924.

Audience: **g,l,u,f.**

Eisen, Cliff   **ML410.M9.D4782**
New Mozart Documents: A Supplement to O. E. Deutsch's
Documentary Biography. Trade Cloth. Stanford University Press.
Palo Alto, CA. 1991. 192p. ISBN:0-8047-1955-1, ISBN13:
978-0-8047-1955-1. Dewey:016.78/092. LCCN:91-065554.

Audience: **u,f.** *Choice, 1992.*

Glover, Jane   **ML410.M9G645 2004**
Mozart's Women: His Family, His Friends, His Music. Trade
Cloth. HarperCollins Publishers. New York, NY. 2006. 416p.
ISBN:0-06-056350-8, ISBN13: 978-0-06-056350-9.
Dewey:780/.92 B. LCCN:2005-052699.

Audience: **g,l,u,f.**

Grayson, David   **ML410.M9 G82 1998**
Mozart: Piano Concertos. Julian Rushton (Contribution by).
Cloth Text. Cambridge University Press. New York, NY. 1999.
155p. Cambridge Music Handbooks Ser. ISBN:0-521-48156-2,
ISBN13: 978-0-521-48156-4. Dewey:784.262092.
LCCN:97-050598.

Audience: **u,f.** *Choice, 1999.*

Halliwell, Ruth   **ML410.M91H35 1998**
The Mozart Family: Four Lives in a Social Context. Trade
Cloth. Oxford University Press, Inc. New York, NY. 1998. 784p.
ISBN:0-19-816371-1, ISBN13: 978-0-19-816371-8.
Dewey:780.9/22. LCCN:97-009676.

Audience: **u,f.** *Choice, 1998.*

Hastings, Baird   **ML134.M9H34 1989**
Wolfgang Amadeus Mozart: A Guide to Research. Trade Cloth.
Garland Publishing, Inc. New York, NY. 1989. 500p. Composer
Resource Manuals Ser. ISBN:0-8240-8347-4, ISBN13:
978-0-8240-8347-2. Dewey:016.78/092/4. LCCN:88-021294.

Audience: **l,u,f.** *Choice, 1989.*

Heartz, Daniel   **ML246.8.V6H4 1994**
Haydn, Mozart and the Viennese School 1740-1780. Paper Text.
W. W. Norton & Company, Inc. New York, NY. 1994.
ISBN:0-393-96533-3, ISBN13: 978-0-393-96533-9.
Dewey:780/.9436/1309033. LCCN:93-047001.

Audience: **u,f.**

Heartz, Daniel   **ML410.V4**
Mozart's Operas. Trade Paper. University of California Press.
Berkeley, CA. 1992. 382p. ISBN:0-520-07872-1, ISBN13:
978-0-520-07872-7. Dewey:782.1/092. LCCN:89-020435.

Audience: **u,f.** *Choice, 1991.*

Hutchings, Arthur   MT130.M8H8 1998
A Companion to Mozart's Piano Concertos. Ed. 2. Cliff Eisen
(Introduction by). Trade Paper. Oxford University Press, Inc.
New York, NY. 1999. 228p. ISBN:0-19-816708-3, ISBN13:
978-0-19-816708-2. Dewey:784.2/62/092. LCCN:98-039904.
Audience: **l,u,f.**

Irving, John   ML410.M9 I73 1998
Mozart: The 'Haydn' Quartets. Julian Rushton (Contribution
by). Cloth Text. Cambridge University Press. New York, NY.
1998. 113p. Music Handbks. ISBN:0-521-58475-2, ISBN13:
978-0-521-58475-3. Dewey:785/.7194/092. LCCN:97-007268.
Audience: **u,f.**

Keefe, Simon P. (Editor)   ML410.M9C255 2003
The Cambridge Companion to Mozart. Jonathan Cross
(Contribution by). Trade Paper. Cambridge University Press.
New York, NY. 2003. 312p. Cambridge Companions to Music
Ser. ISBN:0-521-00192-7, ISBN13: 978-0-521-00192-2.
Dewey:780/.92 B. LCCN:2002-034926.
Audience: **g,l,u,f.** *Choice, 2004.*

Kuster, Konrad   ML410.M9K9813 1996
Mozart: A Musical Biography. Mary Whittall (Translator). Trade
Cloth. Oxford University Press, Inc. New York, NY. 1996. 428p.
ISBN:0-19-816339-8, ISBN13: 978-0-19-816339-8.
Dewey:780.9/2. LCCN:95-035042.
Audience: **l,u,f.** *Choice, 1997.*

Köchel, Ludwig   ML134.M8
Chronologisch-thematisches Verzeichnis sämtlicher Tonwerke
Wolfgang Amadé Mozarts: nebst Angabe der
verlorengegangenen, angefangenen, von fremder Hand
bearbeiteten, zweifelhaften und unterschobenen Kompositionen.
Ed. 8. Geigling, Franz; Weinmann, Alexander; Sievers, Gerd.
Wiesbaden: Breitkopf & Härtel; New York: C. F. Peters, sole
agents in USA. 1983.
Audience: **u,f.**

Landon, H. C. Robbins   ML410.M9L236 1999
1791: Mozart's Last Year. Trade Paper. Thames & Hudson. New
York, NY. 1999. 240p. ISBN:0-500-28107-6, ISBN13:
978-0-500-28107-9. Dewey:780/.92 B. LCCN:98-061442.
Audience: **g,l,u,f.**

Lawson, Colin J.   ML410.M9 L26 1996
Mozart: Clarinet Concerto. Julian Rushton (Contribution by).
Cloth Text. Cambridge University Press. New York, NY. 1996.
123p. Music Handbks. ISBN:0-521-47384-5, ISBN13:
978-0-521-47384-2. Dewey:784.2/862. LCCN:95-022790.
Audience: **u,f.**

Mozart, Wolfgang Amadeus   ML49.M83 M42 1991
The Metropolitan Opera Book of Mozart Operas. Metropolitan
Opera Guild Staff & Paul Gruber (Editors), Judyth Schaubhut
Smith, David Stivender & Susan Webb (Translators). Trade
Paper. HarperCollins Publishers. New York, NY. 1991. 640p.
ISBN:0-06-273051-7, ISBN13: 978-0-06-273051-0.
Dewey:782.1/026/8. LCCN:91-055003.
Audience: **g,l,u,f.**

Mozart, Wolfgang Amadeus   ML134.M9A17 1990
Mozart's "Thematic Catalogue". Ed. 2. Albi Rosenthal & Alan
Tyson (Editors), Albi Rosenthal & Alan Tyson (Introduction by).
Book, Other. Cornell University Press. Ithaca, NY. 1990. 160p.
ISBN:0-8014-2545-X, ISBN13: 978-0-8014-2545-5.
Dewey:780/.92. LCCN:90-002486.
Audience: **l,u,f.** *Choice, 1992.*

Rosen, Charles   ML195.R68 1997
Classical Style: Haydn, Mozart, Beethoven. Ed. 2. Trade Cloth.
W. W. Norton & Company, Inc. New York, NY. 1997. 548p.
ISBN:0-393-04020-8, ISBN13: 978-0-393-04020-3.
Dewey:780/.9/033. LCCN:96-027335.
Audience: **l,u,f.** *B Choice, 1997.*

Rosselli, John   ML410.M9 R847 1998
The Life of Mozart. Trade Paper. Cambridge University Press.
New York, NY. 1998. 183p. Musical Lives Ser.
ISBN:0-521-58744-1, ISBN13: 978-0-521-58744-0.
Dewey:780/.92 B. LCCN:97-033013.
Audience: **g,l,u,f.** *Choice, 1998.*

Rushton, Julian   ML410.M9 R88 1981
Don Giovanni. Richard Wagner (Contribution by). Trade Paper.
Cambridge University Press. New York, NY. 1981. 176p.
Cambridge Opera Handbooks Ser. ISBN:0-521-29663-3,
ISBN13: 978-0-521-29663-2. Dewey:782.1/092/4.
LCCN:80-041534.
Audience: **l,u,f.**

Rushton, Julian   ML410.M9 R89 1993
W. A. Mozart: Idomeneo. Richard Wagner (Contribution by).
Trade Paper. Cambridge University Press. New York, NY. 1993.
197p. Cambridge Opera Handbooks Ser. ISBN:0-521-43741-5,
ISBN13: 978-0-521-43741-7. Dewey:782.1. LCCN:92-025833.
Audience: **u,f.**

Sisman, Elaine Rochelle   ML410.M9S561993
Mozart, the "Jupiter" Symphony, No. 41 in C Major, K. 551.
Julian Rushton (Editor, Contribution by). Trade Paper.
Cambridge University Press. New York, NY. 1993. 122p.
Cambridge Music Handbooks Ser. ISBN:0-521-40924-1,
ISBN13: 978-0-521-40924-7. Dewey:784.184092.
LCCN:92-039074.
Audience: **u,f.**

Solomon, Maynard   ML410.M9
Mozart: A Life. Trade Paper. HarperCollins Publishers. New
York, NY. 2006. 656p. ISBN:0-06-088344-8, ISBN13:
978-0-06-088344-7. Dewey:780.9/2.
Audience: **g,l,u,f.**

Spaethling, Robert (Editor,   ML410.M9A4 2000
Translator)
Mozart's Letters, Mozart's Life. Trade Cloth. W. W. Norton &
Company, Inc. New York, NY. 2000. 416p.
ISBN:0-393-04719-9, ISBN13: 978-0-393-04719-6.
Dewey:780/.92 B. LCCN:00-025530.
Audience: **u,f.** *Choice, 2001.*

Wolff, Christoph   **ML410.M9**
Mozart's Requiem: Historical and Analytical Studies, Documents, Score. Trade Paper. University of California Press. Berkeley, CA. 1998. 190p. ISBN:0-520-21389-0, ISBN13: 978-0-520-21389-0. Dewey:782.32/38.

         Audience: **u,f.**

Zaslaw, Neal (Editor)   **ML410.M9M875 1996**
Mozart's Piano Concertos: Text, Context, Interpretation. Trade Cloth. University of Michigan Press. Chicago, IL. 1997. 496p. ISBN:0-472-10314-8, ISBN13: 978-0-472-10314-0. Dewey:784.2/62/092. LCCN:96-004416.

         Audience: **l,u,f.**

Zaslaw, Neal   **ML410.B5**
Mozart's Symphonies: Context, Performance Practice, Reception. Paper Text. Oxford University Press, Inc. New York, NY. 1991. 642p. ISBN:0-19-816286-3, ISBN13: 978-0-19-816286-5. Dewey:785.1/1/0924.

         Audience: **l,u,f.** *Choice, 1990.*

Zaslaw, Neal & Cowdery,   **MT145.M7Z4 1990**
  William
The Compleat Mozart: A Guide to the Musical Works of Wolfgang Amadeus Mozart. Trade Cloth. W. W. Norton & Company, Inc. New York, NY. 1991. 368p. ISBN:0-393-02886-0, ISBN13: 978-0-393-02886-7. Dewey:780/.92. LCCN:90-030833.

         Audience: **g,l,u,f.** *Choice, 1991.*

Zaslaw, Neal & Fiel, Fiona   **ML134.M9M83 1991**
  M. (Editors)
The Mozart Repertory: A Guide for Musicians, Programmers, and Researchers. Book, Other. Cornell University Press. Ithaca, NY. 1991. 176p. ISBN:0-8014-9937-2, ISBN13: 978-0-8014-9937-1. Dewey:016.78/092. LCCN:91-007459.

         Audience: **g,l,u,f.**

Biographies and Studies of Composers and Performers > M > Mussorgsky, Modest

Brown, David   **ML410.M97B75 2002**
Musorgsky: His Life and Works. Trade Cloth. Oxford University Press, Inc. New York, NY. 2002. 410p. Master Musicians Ser. ISBN:0-19-816587-0, ISBN13: 978-0-19-816587-3. Dewey:780/.92 B. LCCN:2002-020154.

         Audience: **g,l,u,f.**

Emerson, Caryl   **ML410.M97 E42 1999**
The Life of Musorgsky. Trade Paper. Cambridge University Press. New York, NY. 1999. 216p. Musical Lives Ser. ISBN:0-521-48507-X, ISBN13: 978-0-521-48507-4. Dewey:780/.92 B. LCCN:98-047948.

         Audience: **g,l,u,f.** *Choice, 2000.*

Mussorgsky, Modest   **ML410.M97**
Boris Godunov. Nicholas John (Editor), David Lloyd-Jones (Translator). Trade Paper. Riverrun Press, Inc. Flemington, NJ. 1982. 128p. English National Opera Guide Ser., No. 11:Bilingual Libretto, Articles ISBN:0-7145-3922-8, ISBN13: 978-0-7145-3922-5. Dewey:782.1/092/4.

         Audience: **g,l,u,f.**

Orlova, Alexandra (Editor)   **ML410.M97M2213 1991**
Musorgsky Remembered. Veronique Zaytzeff & Frederick Morrison (Translators). Trade Cloth. Indiana University Press. Bloomington, IN. 1991. 212p. Russian Music Studies ISBN:0-253-34264-3, ISBN13: 978-0-253-34264-5. Dewey:780/.92 B. LCCN:90-025310.

         Audience: **u,f.** *Choice, 1992.*

Russ, Michael   **ML410.M97 R9 1992**
Musorgsky: Pictures at an Exhibition. Julian Rushton (Contribution by). Trade Paper. Cambridge University Press. New York, NY. 1992. 110p. Music Handbks. ISBN:0-521-38607-1, ISBN13: 978-0-521-38607-4. Dewey:786.21896. LCCN:91-032687.

         Audience: **l,u,f.** *Choice, 1993.*

Biographies and Studies of Composers and Performers > N > Nancarrow, Conlon

Gann, Kyle   **MT92.N36 G36 1995**
The Music of Conlon Nancarrow. Arnold Whittall (Contribution by). Trade Cloth. Cambridge University Press. New York, NY. 1995. 316p. Music in the Twentieth Century Ser., No. 7 ISBN:0-521-46534-6, ISBN13: 978-0-521-46534-2. Dewey:786.2/092. LCCN:94-029969.

         Audience: **u,f.**

Biographies and Studies of Composers and Performers > N > Nielsen, Carl

Lawson, Jack   **ML410.M9**
Carl Nielsen. Trade Paper. Phaidon Press. London, 1997. 240p. Twentieth-Century Composers Ser. ISBN:0-7148-3507-2, ISBN13: 978-0-7148-3507-5. Dewey:780.9/2.

         Audience: **u,f.**

Biographies and Studies of Composers and Performers > N > Nirvana

Berkenstadt, Jim & Cross,   **ML421.N57B4 2004**
  Charles R.
Nevermind: Nirvana. Trade Paper. Music Sales Corporation. New York, NY. 2004. 172p. ISBN:0-8256-7286-4, ISBN13: 978-0-8256-7286-6. Dewey:782.4/2166/0922. LCCN:97-051361.

         Audience: **g,l,u,f.**

Rocco, John   **ML421.N57**
The Nirvana Companion: Two Decades of Commentary. Trade
Paper. Music Sales Corporation. New York, NY. 1998. 300p.
ISBN:0-8256-7203-1, ISBN13: 978-0-8256-7203-3.
Dewey:782.42166/092/2. LCCN:98-016171.
> Audience: **g,l,u,f.**

Biographies and Studies of Composers and Performers > N > North, Alex

Shoilevska, Sanya   **ML410**
Alex North, Film Composer: A Biography. Cloth Text.
McFarland & Company, Incorporated Publishers. Jefferson, NC.
2003. 278p. ISBN:0-7864-1470-7, ISBN13: 978-0-7864-1470-3.
Dewey:781.5/42/092 B. LCCN:2003-007867.
> Audience: **u,f.**

Biographies and Studies of Composers and Performers > O > Offenbach, Jacques

Gammond, Peter   **ML410.O41**
Offenbach: His Life and Times. Tunbridge Wells, Kent: Midas
Books. 1980. ISBN:0-85936-231-0, ISBN13:
978-0-85936-231-3.
> Audience: **u,f.**

Biographies and Studies of Composers and Performers > O > Oliveros, Pauline

Oliveros, Pauline   **ML60**
Software for People. Trade Cloth. Printed Editions. West Glover,
VT. 1985. 320p. Music Ser. ISBN:0-914162-59-4, ISBN13:
978-0-914162-59-9. Dewey:780.
> Audience: **u,f.**

Von Gunden, Heidi   **ML410.O5834**
The Music of Pauline Oliveros. Trade Cloth. Scarecrow Press,
Inc. Lanham, MD. 1983. 195p. ISBN:0-8108-1600-8, ISBN13:
978-0-8108-1600-8. Dewey:780/.92/4. LCCN:82-021443.
> Audience: **u,f.**

Biographies and Studies of Composers and Performers > O > Obrecht, Jacob

Wegman, Rob C.   **ML410.O27W44 1996**
Born for the Muses: The Life and Masses of Jacob Obrecht.
Trade Paper. Oxford University Press, Inc. New York, NY. 1997.
432p. Oxford Monographs on Music ISBN:0-19-816650-8,
ISBN13: 978-0-19-816650-4. Dewey:780.9/2. LCCN:96-023052.
> Audience: **u,f.** *Choice, 1995.*

Biographies and Studies of Composers and Performers > P > Palestrina, Giovanni Pierluigi da

Jeppesen, Knud   **ML3003.J362 2005**
The Style of Palestrina and the Dissonance. Trade Paper. Dover
Publications, Inc. Mineola, NY. 2005. 320p.
ISBN:0-486-44268-3, ISBN13: 978-0-486-44268-6.
Dewey:782.2/2/092. LCCN:2004-065738.
> Audience: **u,f.**

Marvin, Clara   **ML134.P2M37 2001**
Giovanni Pierluigi da Palestrina: A Research Guide. Cloth Text.
Garland Publishing, Inc. New York, NY. 2002. 350p. Composer
Resource Manuals Ser., Vol. 56 ISBN:0-8153-2351-4, ISBN13:
978-0-8153-2351-8. Dewey:016.7822/2/092. LCCN:00-068435.
> Audience: **l,u,f.**

Biographies and Studies of Composers and Performers > P > Parker, Charlie

Koch, Lawrence O.   **ML156.7.P35K6 1999**
Yardbird Suite: A Compendium of the Music and Life of Charlie
Parker. Ed. 2. Cloth Text. Northeastern University Press. Boston,
MA. 1999. 416p. ISBN:1-55553-385-X, ISBN13:
978-1-55553-385-4. Dewey:788.7/3165/092. LCCN:99-019348.
> Audience: **u,f.** *Choice, 1999, 1989.*

Martin, Henry   **ML419.P4M37**
Charlie Parker and Thematic Improvisation. Trade Paper.
Scarecrow Press, Inc. Lanham, MD. 1996. 170p. Studies in
Jazz, No. 24 ISBN:0-8108-4155-X, ISBN13:
978-0-8108-4155-0. Dewey:781.6/136/092. LCCN:86-003830.
> Audience: **u,f.**

Woideck, Carl   **ML419.P4W65 2005**
Charlie Parker: His Music and Life. Trade Paper. University of
Michigan Press. Chicago, IL. 1998. 304p. The Michigan
American Music Ser. ISBN:0-472-08555-7, ISBN13:
978-0-472-08555-2. Dewey:788.7/165/092 B. LCCN:96-030211.
> Audience: **g,l,u,f.** *Choice, 1997.*

Woideck, Carl   **ML420.H58**
The Charlie Parker Companion: Six Decades of Commentary.
Trade Paper. Music Sales Corporation. New York, NY. 1998.
300p. ISBN:0-8256-7170-1, ISBN13: 978-0-8256-7170-8.
Dewey:782.4/2/165/092. LCCN:97-041859.
> Audience: **g,l,u,f.**

Biographies and Studies of Composers and Performers > P > Part, Arvo

Hillier, Paul   ML410.P1755H55 1997
Arvo Part. Trade Paper. Oxford University Press, Inc. New York, NY. 1997. 232p. Oxford Studies of Composers ISBN:0-19-816616-8, ISBN13: 978-0-19-816616-0. Dewey:780.9/2. LCCN:96-026035.

Audience: **u,f.**

Biographies and Studies of Composers and Performers > P > Partch, Harry

Gilmore, Bob   ML410.P176G55 1998
Harry Partch: A Biography. Cloth over Boards. Yale University Press. Cumberland, RI. 1998. 480p. ISBN:0-300-06521-3, ISBN13: 978-0-300-06521-3. Dewey:[B]. LCCN:97-039140.

Audience: **g,l,u,f.**

Partch, Harry   MT7
Genesis of a Music: An Account of a Creative Work, Its Roots, and Its Fulfillments. Ed. 2. Trade Paper. Da Capo Press, Inc. Cambridge, MA. 1979. 544p. Music Reprint Ser. ISBN:0-306-80106-X, ISBN13: 978-0-306-80106-8. Dewey:781. LCCN:76-087373.

Audience: **u,f.**

Partch, Harry   ML410.M9
Bitter Music: Collected Journals, Essays, Introductions and Librettos. Thomas McGeary (Editor, Introduction by). Trade Paper. University of Illinois Press. Champaign, IL. 2000. 520p. Music in American Life Ser. ISBN:0-252-06913-7, ISBN13: 978-0-252-06913-0. Dewey:780/.92 B.

Audience: **u,f.** *Choice, 1991.*

Biographies and Studies of Composers and Performers > P > Paul, Les

Shaughnessy, Mary Angela   ML419.P47S5 1993
Les Paul: An American Original. Trade Cloth. HarperCollins Publishers. New York, NY. 1993. 347p. ISBN:0-688-08467-2, ISBN13: 978-0-688-08467-7. Dewey:781.64/092. LCCN:92-035832.

Audience: **l,u,f.**

Biographies and Studies of Composers and Performers > P > Penderecki, Krzysztof

Schwinger, Wolfram   ML410.B4
Krzysztof Penderecki: His Life and Work. William Mann (Translator). Trade Paper. European American Music Distributors Corporation. New York, NY. 1989. 292p. ISBN:0-946535-11-6, ISBN13: 978-0-946535-11-8. Dewey:780/.92/4.

Audience: **u,f.**

Biographies and Studies of Composers and Performers > P > Peterson, Oscar

Peterson, Oscar   ML417.A46A3 2002
A Jazz Odyssey: The Life of Oscar Peterson. Richard Palmer (Editor). Trade Cloth. Continuum International Publishing Group, Ltd. London, 2002. 400p. ISBN:0-8264-5807-6, ISBN13: 978-0-8264-5807-0. Dewey:786.2/165/092 B. LCCN:2002-073362.

Audience: **l,u,f.** *Choice, 2003.*

Biographies and Studies of Composers and Performers > P > Piazzolla, Astor

Azzi, Maria Susana &   ML410.P579A99 2000
  Collier, Simon
Le Grand Tango: The Life and Music of Astor Piazzolla. Trade Cloth. Oxford University Press, Inc. New York, NY. 2000. 344p. ISBN:0-19-512777-3, ISBN13: 978-0-19-512777-5. Dewey:780/.92 B. LCCN:99-031795.

Audience: **g,l,u,f.**

Biographies and Studies of Composers and Performers > P > Porter, Cole

McBrien, William   ML410.P7844M33 1998
Cole Porter: A Biography. Trade Cloth. Alfred A. Knopf Inc. New York, NY. 1998. 480p. ISBN:0-394-58235-7, ISBN13: 978-0-394-58235-1. Dewey:782.1/4/092 B. LCCN:97-046116.

Audience: **l,u,f.** *Choice, 1999.*

Porter, Cole & Kimball,   ML50.Z99
  Robert
The Complete Lyrics of Cole Porter. John Updike (Foreword by). Trade Cloth. Alfred A. Knopf Inc. New York, NY. 1983. 354p. ISBN:0-394-53214-7, ISBN13: 978-0-394-53214-1. Dewey:782.1/4/0268. LCCN:83-048101.

Audience: **g,l,u,f.**

Biographies and Studies of Composers and Performers > P > Poulenc, Francis

Mellers, Wilfrid   **ML410.M9**
Francis Poulenc. Paper Text. Oxford University Press, Inc. New York, NY. 1995. 204p. Oxford Studies of Composers ISBN:0-19-816338-X, ISBN13: 978-0-19-816338-1. Dewey:780/.92.

Audience: **l,u,f.**   *Choice, 1994.*

Biographies and Studies of Composers and Performers > P > Powell, Bud

Groves, Alan & Shipton,   **ML417.P73G76 2001**
  Alyn
The Glass Enclosure: The Life of Bud Powell. Trade Paper. Continuum International Publishing Group, Ltd. London, 2001. 144p. A Bayou Book Ser. ISBN:0-8264-4746-5, ISBN13: 978-0-8264-4746-3. Dewey:786.2/165/092 B. LCCN:2001-028002.

Audience: **g,l,u,f.**

Biographies and Studies of Composers and Performers > P > Presley, Elvis

Bertrand, Michael T.   **ML3918.R63B47 2000**
Race, Rock and Elvis. Trade Cloth. University of Illinois Press. Champaign, IL. 2000. 352p. Music in American Life Ser. ISBN:0-252-02586-5, ISBN13: 978-0-252-02586-0. Dewey:781.66/0975. LCCN:99-050895.

Audience: **u,f.**   *Choice, 2001.*

Doss, Erika   **ML420.P96D68 1999**
Elvis Culture: Fans, Faith, and Image. Trade Cloth. University Press of Kansas. Lawrence, KS. 1999. xiv, 290p. CultureAmerica Ser. ISBN:0-7006-0948-2, ISBN13: 978-0-7006-0948-2. Dewey:782.42166/092. LCCN:97-034373.

Audience: **g,l,u,f.**   *Choice, 1999.*

Guralnick, Peter   **ML420.P96**
Last Train to Memphis: The Rise of Elvis Presley. Trade Cloth. DIANE Publishing Company. Collingdale, PA. 2000. 560p. ISBN:0-7881-9347-3, ISBN13: 978-0-7881-9347-7. Dewey:782.4/2/166/092.

Audience: **g,l,u,f.**   *Choice, 1995.*

Marsh, Dave   **ML420.S565**
Elvis. Trade Paper. Avalon Publishing Group. New York, NY. 1993. 272p. ISBN:1-56025-038-0, ISBN13: 978-1-56025-038-8. Dewey:784.5/0092/4.

Audience: **g,l,u,f.**

Quain, Kevin   **ML420.P96 E44 1992**
The Elvis Reader: Texts and Sources on the King of Rock 'n' Roll. Trade Paper. St. Martin's Press. Gordonville, VA. 1991. 352p. ISBN:0-312-06966-9, ISBN13: 978-0-312-06966-7. Dewey:782.42166/092. LCCN:91-033832.

Audience: **g,l,u,f.**

Biographies and Studies of Composers and Performers > P > Prince, Harold

Hirsch, Foster   **ML429.P78H6 2005**
Harold Prince and the American Musical Theater. Trade Paper. Applause Theatre Book Publishers. New York, NY. 2005. 288p. ISBN:1-55783-617-5, ISBN13: 978-1-55783-617-5. Dewey:792.602/3/092. LCCN:2005-003597.

Audience: **g,l,u,f.**   *Choice, 2005, 1989.*

Biographies and Studies of Composers and Performers > P > Prokofiev, Sergey

Jaffe, Daniel   **ML410.M9**
Sergey Prokofiev. Trade Paper. Phaidon Press. London, 1998. 240p. Twentieth-Century Composers Ser. ISBN:0-7148-3513-7, ISBN13: 978-0-7148-3513-6. Dewey:780.9/2.

Audience: **l,u,f.**

Minturn, Neil   **ML410.P865M56 1997**
The Music of Sergei Prokofiev. Cloth over Boards. Yale University Press. Cumberland, RI. 1997. 256p. Composers of the Twentieth Century Ser. ISBN:0-300-06366-0, ISBN13: 978-0-300-06366-0. Dewey:780.92. LCCN:96-027064.

Audience: **u,f.**   *Choice, 1998.*

Nice, David   **ML410.P865**
Prokofiev: A Biography: From Russia to the West, 1891-1935. Cloth over Boards. Yale University Press. Cumberland, RI. 2003. 416p. ISBN:0-300-09914-2, ISBN13: 978-0-300-09914-0. Dewey:780/.92 B. LCCN:2004-296430.

Audience: **u,f.**   *Choice, 2004.*

Prokofiev, Sergei   **ML410.P865**
Prokofiev by Prokofiev: A Composer's Memoir. Trade Cloth. Doubleday Publishing. New York, NY. 1979. ISBN:0-385-09960-6, ISBN13: 978-0-385-09960-8. Dewey:780/.92/4. LCCN:77-025605.

Audience: **l,u,f.**

Prokofiev, Sergei   **ML410.P865.A3 1992**
Soviet Diary, 1927 and Other Writings. Oleg Prokofiev & Christopher Palmer (Editors), Oleg Prokofiev (Translator). Cloth Text. Northeastern University Press. Boston, MA. 1992. 290p. ISBN:1-55553-120-2, ISBN13: 978-1-55553-120-1. Dewey:780.92. LCCN:91-045921.

Audience: **u,f.**   *Choice, 1993.*

Robinson, Harlow (Author,   ML410.P865R55 2002
   Foreword by, Afterword by)
Sergei Prokofiev: A Biography. Trade Paper. Northeastern
University Press. Boston, MA. 2005. 632p.
ISBN:1-55553-517-8, ISBN13: 978-1-55553-517-9.
Dewey:780/.92/4. LCCN:2002-070919.
                             Audience: **l,u,f.** *Choice, 1987.*

Biographies and Studies of Composers and Performers > P > Puccini, Giacomo

Ashbrook, William   MT100.P95A8 1985
The Operas of Puccini. Roger Parker (Foreword by). Trade
Paper. Cornell University Press. Ithaca, NY. 1985. 288p. Cornell
Paperbacks Ser. ISBN:0-8014-9309-9, ISBN13:
978-0-8014-9309-6. Dewey:782.1/092/4. LCCN:84-072674.
                             Audience: **g,l,u,f.**

Budden, Julian   ML410.V4
Puccini: His Life and Works. Trade Paper, Perfect. Oxford
University Press, Inc. New York, NY. 2005. 538p. Master
Musicians Ser. ISBN:0-19-517974-9, ISBN13:
978-0-19-517974-3. Dewey:782.1/092 B.
                             Audience: **g,l,u,f.**

Carner, Mosco   ML410.P89 C25 1985
Giacomo Puccini: Tosca. Cloth Text. Cambridge University
Press. New York, NY. 1985. 174p. Cambridge Opera Handbooks
Ser. ISBN:0-521-22824-7, ISBN13: 978-0-521-22824-4.
Dewey:782.1/092/4.
                        Audience: **u,f.** *Choice, 1986.*

Groos, Arthur & Parker,   ML410.P89 G76 1986
   Roger (Editors)
Giacomo Puccini: La Bohème. Trade Cloth. Cambridge
University Press. New York, NY. 1986. 224p. Cambridge Opera
Handbooks Ser. ISBN:0-521-26489-8, ISBN13:
978-0-521-26489-1. Dewey:782.1. LCCN:85-028076.
                        Audience: **u,f.** *Choice, 1987.*

Phillips-Matz, Mary Jane   ML410.P89P52 2002
Puccini: A Biography. William Weaver (Foreword by). Trade
Cloth. Northeastern University Press. Boston, MA. 2005. 384p.
ISBN:1-55553-530-5, ISBN13: 978-1-55553-530-8.
Dewey:782.1/092 B. LCCN:2002-009017.
                        Audience: **l,u,f.** *Choice, 2003.*

Puccini, Giacomo   ML410.P89.A23 1971
Letters of Giacomo Puccini. Ena Makin (Editor). Trade Cloth. A
M S Press, Inc. New York, NY. 1971. 335p.
ISBN:0-404-05149-9, ISBN13: 978-0-404-05149-5.
Dewey:782.1/0924. LCCN:71-140038.
                              Audience: **u,f.**

Puccini, Giacomo   ML49.P75
Seven Puccini Librettos. William Weaver (Translator). Trade

Paper. W. W. Norton & Company, Inc. New York, NY. 1981.
ISBN:0-393-00930-0, ISBN13: 978-0-393-00930-9.
Dewey:782.1/2.
                             Audience: **g,l,u,f.**

Weaver, William & Puccini,   ML410.P89
   Simonetta
The Puccini Companion. Ed. 1. New York: W.W. Norton. 1994.
ISBN:0-393-02930-1, ISBN13: 978-0-393-02930-7.
                             Audience: **g,l,u,f.**

Biographies and Studies of Composers and Performers > P > Puente, Tito

Loza, Steven J.   ML419.P82L6 1999
Tito Puente and the Making of Latin Music. Trade Paper.
University of Illinois Press. Champaign, IL. 1999. 312p. Music
in American Life Ser. ISBN:0-252-06778-9, ISBN13:
978-0-252-06778-5. Dewey:784.4/81888/092 B.
LCCN:98-025507.
                        Audience: **l,u,f.** *Choice, 2000.*

Biographies and Studies of Composers and Performers > P > Purcell, Henry

Burden, Michael (Editor)   ML410.P93P86 1995
The Purcell Companion. Trade Cloth. Hal Leonard Corporation.
Milwaukee, WI. 1995. 514p. ISBN:0-931340-93-4, ISBN13:
978-0-931340-93-2. Dewey:780/.92 B. LCCN:95-169070.
                      Audience: **g,l,u,f.** *Choice, 1995.*

Holman, Peter   ML410.P93H63 1994
Henry Purcell. Trade Paper. Oxford University Press, Inc. New
York, NY. 1995. 268p. Oxford Studies of Composers
ISBN:0-19-816341-X, ISBN13: 978-0-19-816341-1.
Dewey:780.9/2. LCCN:94-031870.
                        Audience: **u,f.** *Choice, 1995.*

Price, Curtis   ML410.P93
Henry Purcell and the London Stage. Trade Cloth. Cambridge
University Press. New York, NY. 1984. 394p.
ISBN:0-521-23831-5, ISBN13: 978-0-521-23831-1.
Dewey:780/.92/4. LCCN:83-015170.
                             Audience: **u,f.**

Zimmerman, Franklin B.   ML134.P95
Henry Purcell: A Guide to Research. New York : Garland Pub.
1989. Garland Composer Resource Manuals; Vol. 18
ISBN:0-8240-7786-5, ISBN13: 978-0-8240-7786-0.
                             Audience: **l,u,f.**

Biographies and Studies of Composers and Performers > R > Rachmaninoff, Sergei

Bertensson, Sergei & Leyda, Jay   ML410.R12B47 2001
Sergei Rachmaninoff: A Lifetime in Music. David Butler Cannata (Introduction by). Trade Paper. Indiana University Press. Bloomington, IN. 2001. 480p. Russian Music Studies ISBN:0-253-21421-1, ISBN13: 978-0-253-21421-8. Dewey:780/.92 B. LCCN:2001-016765.
Audience: **g,l,u,f.**

Norris, Geoffrey   ML410.R12N67 2000
Rachmaninoff. Ed. 2. Trade Paper. Oxford University Press, Inc. New York, NY. 2006. 216p. Master Musicians Ser. ISBN:0-19-816488-2, ISBN13: 978-0-19-816488-3. Dewey:780.9/2. LCCN:00-057115.
Audience: **u,f.** *Choice, 1994.*

Biographies and Studies of Composers and Performers > R > Rameau, Jean Philippe

Girdlestone, Cuthbert M.   ML410.R2 G5
Jean-Philippe Rameau: His Life and Work. Trade Paper. Dover Publications, Inc. Mineola, NY. 1990. 631p. ISBN:0-486-26200-6, ISBN13: 978-0-486-26200-0. Dewey:780/.924.
Audience: **g,l,u,f.**

Biographies and Studies of Composers and Performers > R > Ravel, Maurice

Mawer, Deborah (Editor)   ML410.R23 C36 2000
The Cambridge Companion to Ravel. Trade Paper. Cambridge University Press. New York, NY. 2000. 310p. Cambridge Companions to Music Ser. ISBN:0-521-64856-4, ISBN13: 978-0-521-64856-1. Dewey:780/.92 B. LCCN:99-047568.
Audience: **g,l,u,f.** *Choice, 2001.*

Orenstein, Arbie   ML410.R23O73 1991
Ravel: Man and Musician. Trade Paper. Dover Publications, Inc. Mineola, NY. 1991. 352p. ISBN:0-486-26633-8, ISBN13: 978-0-486-26633-6. Dewey:780/.92 B. LCCN:91-002789.
Audience: **g,l,u,f.**

Ravel, Maurice   ML410.R23A4 2003
A Ravel Reader: Correspondence, Articles, Interviews. Arbie Orenstein (Editor). Trade Paper. Dover Publications, Inc. Mineola, NY. 2003. 704p. ISBN:0-486-43078-2, ISBN13: 978-0-486-43078-2. Dewey:780/.92 B. LCCN:2003-047259.
Audience: **l,u,f.**

Biographies and Studies of Composers and Performers > R > Reich, Steve

Reich, Steve   ML60.R352 2002
Writings on Music, 1965-2000. Paul Hillier (Editor, Introduction by). Trade Paper. Oxford University Press, Inc. New York, NY. 2004. 270p. ISBN:0-19-515115-1, ISBN13: 978-0-19-515115-2. Dewey:789/.9/04. LCCN:2001-037477.
Audience: **l,u,f.**

Biographies and Studies of Composers and Performers > R > Reinhardt, Django

Dregni, Michael   ML419.R44D74 2004
Django: The Life and Music of a Gypsy Legend. Trade Cloth. Oxford University Press, Inc. New York, NY. 2004. 344p. ISBN:0-19-516752-X, ISBN13: 978-0-19-516752-8. Dewey:787.87/165/092 B. LCCN:2004-006214.
Audience: **u,f.**

Biographies and Studies of Composers and Performers > R > Rimsky-Korsakov, Nikolay

Abraham, Gerald E.   ML410.R52 A62 1976
Rimsky-Korsakov. Trade Cloth. A M S Press, Inc. New York, NY. BCL Ser., No. II ISBN:0-404-14500-0, ISBN13: 978-0-404-14500-2. Dewey:780/.92/4. LCCN:75-041002.
Audience: **l,u,f.**

Yastrebtsev, V. V. & Jonas, Florence   ML410.R52I233 1985
Reminiscences of Rimsky-Korsakov. Trade Cloth. Columbia University Press. New York, NY. 1985. 578p. ISBN:0-231-05260-X, ISBN13: 978-0-231-05260-3. Dewey:780/.92/4 B. LCCN:84-016967.
Audience: **l,u,f.** *Choice, 1986.*

Biographies and Studies of Composers and Performers > R > Rochberg, George

Rochberg, George   ML60.R62 2004
The Aesthetics of Survival: A Composer's View of Twentieth-Century Music. Trade Paper. University of Michigan Press. Chicago, IL. 2005. 288p. ISBN:0-472-03026-4, ISBN13: 978-0-472-03026-2. Dewey:780/.9/04. LCCN:2004-051645.
Audience: **u,f.**

Biographies and Studies of Composers and Performers > R > Rodgers, Richard

Block, Geoffrey   **ML410.S6872**
The Richard Rodgers Reader. Trade Paper. Oxford University Press, Inc. New York, NY. 2006. 368p. Readers on American Musicians Ser. ISBN:0-19-531343-7, ISBN13: 978-0-19-531343-7. Dewey:782.1/4/092.
Audience: **g,l,u,f.**

Block, Geoffrey Holden   **ML410.R6315B56 2003**
Richard Rodgers. Cloth over Boards. Yale University Press. Cumberland, RI. 2003. 336p. Yale Broadway Masters Ser. ISBN:0-300-09747-6, ISBN13: 978-0-300-09747-4. Dewey:782.1/4/092 B. LCCN:2003-002412.
Audience: **g,l,u,f.** *Choice, 2004.*

Rodgers, Richard &   **ML48**
 Hammerstein, Oscar II
Six Plays. Trade Cloth. Random House, Inc. New York, NY. 1959. ISBN:0-394-60200-5, ISBN13: 978-0-394-60200-4. Dewey:812.
Audience: **g,l,u,f.**

Rodgers, Richard   **ML410.S95**
Musical Stages: An Autobiography. Ed. 2. Mary Rodgers (Introduction by), John Lahr (Afterword by). Trade Paper. Da Capo Press, Inc. Cambridge, MA. 2002. 384p. ISBN:0-306-81134-0, ISBN13: 978-0-306-81134-0. Dewey:782.8/1/0924.
Audience: **g,l,u,f.**

Biographies and Studies of Composers and Performers > R > Rolling Stones

Perry, John   **ML421.R64**
Exile on Main Street: Rolling Stones. Trade Paper. Music Sales Corporation. New York, NY. 1999. 172p. Classic Rock Albums Ser. ISBN:0-8256-7180-9, ISBN13: 978-0-8256-7180-7. Dewey:782.42166/092/2.
Audience: **g,l,u,f.**

Rolling Stones   **ML421.R64**
According to the Rolling Stones. Dora Loewenstein & Philip Dodd (Editors). Trade Cloth. Chronicle Books LLC. San Francisco, CA. 2003. 360p. ISBN:0-8118-4060-3, ISBN13: 978-0-8118-4060-6. Dewey:782.42166092/2.
Audience: **g,l,u,f.**

Biographies and Studies of Composers and Performers > R > Rollins, Sonny

Nisenson, Eric   **ML419.C645**
Open Sky: Sonny Rollins and His World of Improvisation. Sonny Rollins (Foreword by). Trade Cloth. DIANE Publishing Company. Collingdale, PA. 2006. 216p. ISBN:1-4223-5032-0, ISBN13: 978-1-4223-5032-4. Dewey:788.7/165/092 B.
Audience: **u,f.**

Biographies and Studies of Composers and Performers > R > Rorem, Ned

Rorem, Ned   **ML60.R78425 2001**
A Ned Rorem Reader. Cloth over Boards. Yale University Press. Cumberland, RI. 2001. 320p. ISBN:0-300-08984-8, ISBN13: 978-0-300-08984-4. Dewey:780. LCCN:2001-033334.
Audience: **g,l,u,f.**

Biographies and Studies of Composers and Performers > R > Rossi, Salamone

Harran, Don   **ML410.R78H37 1999**
Salamone Rossi: Jewish Musician in Late Renaissance Mantua. Trade Cloth. Oxford University Press, Inc. New York, NY. 1999. 320p. Oxford Monographs on Music ISBN:0-19-816271-5, ISBN13: 978-0-19-816271-1. Dewey:780/.92 B. LCCN:98-007974.
Audience: **u,f.**

Biographies and Studies of Composers and Performers > R > Rossini, Gioacchino

Osborne, Charles   **ML390.O82 1994**
The Bel Canto Operas: A Guide to the Operas of Rossini, Bellini, and Donizetti. Trade Cloth. Hal Leonard Corporation. Milwaukee, WI. 1994. 378p. ISBN:0-931340-71-3, ISBN13: 978-0-931340-71-0. Dewey:782.1/0945/09034. LCCN:94-168756.
Audience: **g,l,u,f.** *Choice, 1994.*

Osborne, Richard   **ML410.R8O9 2001**
Rossini. Ed. 3. Trade Paper. Oxford University Press, Inc. New York, NY. 2002. 360p. Master Musicians Ser. ISBN:0-19-816490-4, ISBN13: 978-0-19-816490-6. Dewey:782.1/092/4. LCCN:00-057106.
Audience: **l,u,f.**

Rossini, Gioacchino Antonio　　　　**ML50.P965**
The Barber of Seville and Moses. Nicholas John (Editor),
Edward J. Dent, John Moody & Nell Moody (Translators).
Trade Paper. Riverrun Press, Inc. Flemington, NJ. 1986. 160p.
English National Opera Guide Ser., No. 36:Bilingual Libretto,
Articles ISBN:0-7145-4080-3, ISBN13: 978-0-7145-4080-1.
Dewey:782.1/2. LCCN:85-052162.

Audience: **g,l,u,f.**

Senici, Emanuele (Editor)　　　　**ML410.R8C17 2003**
The Cambridge Companion to Rossini. Trade Cloth. Cambridge
University Press. New York, NY. 2004. 280p. Cambridge
Companions to Music Ser. ISBN:0-521-80736-0, ISBN13:
978-0-521-80736-4. Dewey:782.1/092 B. LCCN:2003-048560.

Audience: **l,u,f.**

Biographies and Studies of Composers and Performers > S > Saint-Georges, Joseph Boulogne, Chevalier de

Guede, Alain　　　　**DC137.5.S35G8413**
Monsieur de Saint-George: Virtuoso, Swordsman,
Revolutionary: A Legendary Life Rediscovered. Gilda M.
Roberts (Translator). Cloth over Boards. Picador. New York,
NY. 2003. 240p. ISBN:0-312-30927-9, ISBN13:
978-0-312-30927-5. Dewey:944/.00496/0092 B.
LCCN:2003-049888.

Audience: **g,l,u,f.** *Choice, 2004.*

Biographies and Studies of Composers and Performers > S > Salieri, Antonio

Braunbehrens, Volkmar　　　　**ML410.S16B713 1992**
Maligned Master: The Real Story of Antonio Salieri. Eveline L.
Kanes (Translator). Trade Cloth. Fromm International Publishing
Corporation. New York, NY. 1993. 264p. ISBN:0-88064-140-1,
ISBN13: 978-0-88064-140-1. Dewey:780/.92. LCCN:92-028067.

Audience: **u,f.** *Choice, 1993.*

Biographies and Studies of Composers and Performers > S > Satie, Erik

Gillmor, Alan M.　　　　**ML410.S196G54 1988**
Erik Satie. Trade Cloth. Macmillan Publishing Company, Inc.
Old Tappan, NJ. 1988. 408p. Twayne's Music Ser.
ISBN:0-8057-9472-7, ISBN13: 978-0-8057-9472-4.
Dewey:780/.92/4 B. LCCN:87-037381.

Audience: **g,l,u,f.** *Choice, 1988.*

Orledge, Robert　　　　**ML410.M9**
Satie Remembered. Trade Cloth. Hal Leonard Corporation.
Milwaukee, WI. 1995. 272p. ISBN:1-57467-000-X, ISBN13:
978-1-57467-000-4. Dewey:780.9/2. LCCN:95-198285.

Audience: **u,f.** *Choice, 1996.*

Orledge, Robert　　　　**ML410.S196O74 1990**
Satie the Composer. Trade Cloth. Cambridge University Press.
New York, NY. 1990. 437p. Music in the Twentieth Century
Ser., No. 1 ISBN:0-521-35037-9, ISBN13: 978-0-521-35037-2.
Dewey:780/.92. LCCN:89-022309.

Audience: **u,f.** *Choice, 1991.*

Satie, Erik　　　　**ML410.M9**
A Mammal's Notebook: Collected Writings of Erik Satie.
Ornella Volta (Editor), Anthony Melville (Translator). Trade
Cloth. Atlas Press. London, 1997. 208p. Atlas Arkhive Ser., Vol.
5 ISBN:0-947757-92-9, ISBN13: 978-0-947757-92-2.
Dewey:780.92.

Audience: **u,f.**

Biographies and Studies of Composers and Performers > S > Scarlatti, Alessandro

Dent, Edward J.　　　　**ML410.S22**
Alessandro Scarlatti: His Life and Works. Paper Text. Classic
Textbooks. Murrieta, CA. 1960. 172p. ISBN:1-4047-0141-9,
ISBN13: 978-1-4047-0141-0. Dewey:927.8.

Audience: **u,f.**

Biographies and Studies of Composers and Performers > S > Scarlatti, Domenico

Boyd, Malcolm　　　　**ML410.S221B7 1987**
Domenico Scarlatti: Master of Music. Trade Cloth. Music Sales
Corporation. New York, NY. 1987. 302p. ISBN:0-02-870291-3,
ISBN13: 978-0-02-870291-9. Dewey:780/.92/4.
LCCN:86-021743.

Audience: **l,u,f.** *Choice, 1987.*

Kirkpatrick, Ralph　　　　**ML410.S221 K5 1983**
Domenico Scarlatti. Trade Paper. Princeton University Press.
Princeton, NJ. 1983. 496p. ISBN:0-691-02708-0, ISBN13:
978-0-691-02708-1. Dewey:[B]. LCCN:53-006387.

Audience: **l,u,f.**

Sutcliffe, W. Dean　　　　**ML410.S22S88 2003**
The Keyboard Sonatas of Domenico Scarlatti and
Eighteenth-Century Musical Style. Trade Cloth. Cambridge
University Press. New York, NY. 2003. 412p.
ISBN:0-521-48140-6, ISBN13: 978-0-521-48140-3.
Dewey:786/.183/092. LCCN:2002-035012.

Audience: **u,f.** *Choice, 2004.*

Biographies and Studies of Composers and Performers > S > Schikaneder, Emanuel

Honolka, Kurt   ML423.S346H613 1990
Papageno: Emanuel Schikaneder - Man of the Theater in
Mozart's Time. Jane M. Wilde (Translator). Trade Cloth. Hal
Leonard Corporation. Milwaukee, WI. 1990. 236p.
ISBN:0-931340-21-7, ISBN13: 978-0-931340-21-5.
Dewey:782.1/092 B. LCCN:89-017574.
                                    Audience: **u,f.** *Choice, 1990.*

Biographies and Studies of Composers and Performers > S > Schnittke, Alfred

Schnittke, Alfred   ML197.S2627 2002
⊙ A Schnittke Reader. John Goodliffe (Translator), Mstislav
Rostropovich (Preface by). E-Book. Indiana University Press.
Bloomington, IN. 2002. 352p. Russian Music Studies
ISBN:0-253-33818-2, ISBN13: 978-0-253-33818-1.
Dewey:780/.92. LCCN:2001-005133.
                                    Audience: **u,f.**

Biographies and Studies of Composers and Performers > S > Schoenberg, Arnold

Auner, Joseph Henry   ML410.S283A97 2003
A Schoenberg Reader: Documents of a Life. Cloth over Boards.
Yale University Press. Cumberland, RI. 2003. 460p.
ISBN:0-300-09540-6, ISBN13: 978-0-300-09540-1.
Dewey:780/.92. LCCN:2002-154114.
                                    Audience: **l,u,f.** *Choice, 2004.*

Dunsby, Jonathan   ML410.S283 D83 1992
Schoenberg: Pierrot Lunaire. Julian Rushton (Contribution by).
Trade Paper. Cambridge University Press. New York, NY. 1992.
94p. Music Handbks. ISBN:0-521-38715-9, ISBN13:
978-0-521-38715-6. Dewey:782.47. LCCN:91-036068.
                                    Audience: **u,f.**

Frisch, Walter (Editor)   ML410.S283S36 1999
Schoenberg and His World. Cloth Text. Princeton University
Press. Princeton, NJ. 1999. 350p. The Bard Music Festival Ser.
ISBN:0-691-04860-6, ISBN13: 978-0-691-04860-4.
Dewey:780/.92. LCCN:99-031792.
                                    Audience: **g,l,u,f.** *Choice, 2000.*

Haimo, Ethan   ML410.S283H33 1990
Schoenberg's Serial Odyssey: The Evolution of His
Twelve-Tone Method, 1914-1928. Trade Cloth. Oxford
University Press, Inc. New York, NY. 1990. 208p.
ISBN:0-19-315260-6, ISBN13: 978-0-19-315260-1.
Dewey:781.3. LCCN:88-019617.
                                    Audience: **u,f.** *Choice, 1991.*

Harris, Donald (Editor), et   ML410.B47A4 1987
al.
The Berg-Schoenberg Correspondence: Selected Letters.
Christopher Hailey & Juliane Brand (Editors). Trade Cloth. W.
W. Norton & Company, Inc. New York, NY. 1987. xxviii, 497p.
ISBN:0-393-01919-5, ISBN13: 978-0-393-01919-3.
Dewey:780/.92/2. LCCN:86-008346.
                                    Audience: **u,f.** *Choice, 1988.*

Kallir, Jane   NS511.5.S37
Arnold Schoenberg's Vienna. Trade Paper. Rizzoli International
Publications, Inc. New York, NY. 1985. 120p.
ISBN:0-8478-0580-8, ISBN13: 978-0-8478-0580-8.
Dewey:759.36.
                                    Audience: **l,u,f.**

Schoenberg, Arnold   ML60.S374S8 1985
Style and Idea: Selected Writings of Arnold Schoenberg.
Leonard Stein (Editor), Leo Black (Translator). Trade Paper.
University of California Press. Berkeley, CA. 1984. 560p.
ISBN:0-520-05294-3, ISBN13: 978-0-520-05294-9. Dewey:780.
LCCN:84-002604.
                                    Audience: **l,u,f.** *B*

Simms, Bryan R.   ML410.S283S45 2000
The Atonal Music of Arnold Schoenberg, 1908-1923. Trade
Cloth. Oxford University Press, Inc. New York, NY. 2000. 274p.
ISBN:0-19-512826-5, ISBN13: 978-0-19-512826-0.
Dewey:780/.92. LCCN:99-035938.
                                    Audience: **u,f.** *Choice, 2001.*

Stuckenschmidt, Hans Heinz   ML410.S283
Schoenberg: His Life, World, and Work. Searle, Humphrey
(Translator). New York: Schirmer Books. 1978.
ISBN:0-02-872480-1, ISBN13: 978-0-02-872480-5.
                                    Audience: **u,f.**

Biographies and Studies of Composers and Performers > S > Schubert, Franz

Brown, A. Peter   ML1255.B87
The First Golden Age of the Viennese Symphony: Haydn,
Mozart, Beethoven and Schubert. Trade Cloth. Indiana
University Press. Bloomington, IN. 2002. 816p.
ISBN:0-253-33487-X, ISBN13: 978-0-253-33487-9.
Dewey:784.2/184 s 784.2. LCCN:98-026549.
                                    Audience: **g,l,u,f.** *Choice, 2003.*

Daverio, John   ML390.D335 2002
Crossing Paths: Schubert, Schumann, and Brahms. Trade Cloth.
Oxford University Press, Inc. New York, NY. 2002. 328p.
ISBN:0-19-513296-3, ISBN13: 978-0-19-513296-0.
Dewey:780/.92/243. LCCN:2001-038744.
                                    Audience: **u,f.** *Choice, 2003.*

Deutsch, Otto Erich   **ML410.S3**
The Schubert Reader. Paper Text. Classic Textbooks. Murrieta, CA. 1947. 1039p. ISBN:1-4047-9618-5, ISBN13: 978-1-4047-9618-8. Dewey:927.8.

Audience: **g,l,u,f.**

Erickson, Raymond (Editor)   **ML410.S3S29975 1997**
Schubert's Vienna. Cloth over Boards. Yale University Press. Cumberland, RI. 1997. 304p. ISBN:0-300-07080-2, ISBN13: 978-0-300-07080-4. Dewey:780/.92 B. LCCN:97-010707.

Audience: **u,f.** *Choice, 1998.*

Gibbs, Christopher H.   **ML410.M9**
The Life of Schubert. Trade Paper. Cambridge University Press. New York, NY. 2000. 226p. Musical Lives Ser. ISBN:0-521-59512-6, ISBN13: 978-0-521-59512-4. Dewey:780/.92 B.

Audience: **g,l,u,f.** *Choice, 2000.*

Gibbs, Christopher H.   **ML410.S3 C18 1997**
(Editor)
The Cambridge Companion to Schubert. Jonathan Cross (Contribution by). Trade Paper. Cambridge University Press. New York, NY. 1997. 354p. Cambridge Companions to Music Ser. ISBN:0-521-48424-3, ISBN13: 978-0-521-48424-4. Dewey:780.9/2. LCCN:96-014260.

Audience: **g,l,u,f.** *Choice, 1998.*

Hall, Michael (Editor)   **MT121.S36H35 2003**
Schubert's Song Sets. Trade Cloth. Ashgate Publishing, Ltd. Aldershot, 2003. 300p. ISBN:0-7546-0798-4, ISBN13: 978-0-7546-0798-4. Dewey:782.4/7/092. LCCN:2001-099668.

Audience: **l,u,f.**

Newbould, Brian   **ML410.M9**
Schubert: The Music and the Man. Trade Paper. University of California Press. Berkeley, CA. 1999. 465p. ISBN:0-520-21957-0, ISBN13: 978-0-520-21957-1. Dewey:780.9/2. LCCN:96-049876.

Audience: **u,f.** *Choice, 1997.*

Reed, John   **ML410.S3R265 1997**
The Schubert Song Companion. Norma Deane & Celia Larner (Translators), Janet Baker (Foreword by). Trade Paper. Manchester University Press. Manchester, 1997. 528p. ISBN:1-901341-00-3, ISBN13: 978-1-901341-00-3. Dewey:784.3/0092/4. LCCN:98-179605.

Audience: **l,u,f.** *Choice, 1985.*

Wigmore, Richard   **ML54.6.S39.W53 1988**
(Translator)
Schubert: The Complete Song Texts. Trade Cloth. Thomson Gale. Farmington Hills, MI. 1988. 380p. ISBN:0-02-872911-0, ISBN13: 978-0-02-872911-4. Dewey:784.3/05. LCCN:88-011653.

Audience: **l,u,f.** *Choice, 1989.*

Youens, Susan   **ML410.S3**
Retracing a Winter's Journey: Schubert's Winterreise. Book, Other. Cornell University Press. Ithaca, NY. 1991. 320p.

ISBN:0-8014-9966-6, ISBN13: 978-0-8014-9966-1. Dewey:782.4/7. LCCN:91-055234.

Audience: **u,f.** *Choice, 1992.*

Youens, Susan   **ML410.S3 Y7 1992**
Schubert: Die Schone Mullerin. Julian Rushton (Contribution by). Trade Paper. Cambridge University Press. New York, NY. 1992. 129p. Music Handbks. ISBN:0-521-42279-5, ISBN13: 978-0-521-42279-6. Dewey:782.42168. LCCN:91-028960.

Audience: **u,f.**

Biographies and Studies of Composers and Performers > S > Schumann, Clara

Reich, Nancy B.   **ML417.S4R4 2001**
Clara Schumann: The Artist and the Woman. Ed. 2. Book, Other. Cornell University Press. Ithaca, NY. 2001. 408p. ISBN:0-8014-8637-8, ISBN13: 978-0-8014-8637-1. Dewey:786.2/092 B. LCCN:00-011932.

Audience: **l,u,f.** *Choice, 1985.*

Biographies and Studies of Composers and Performers > S > Schumann, Robert

Daverio, John   **ML390.D335 2002**
Crossing Paths: Schubert, Schumann, and Brahms. Trade Cloth. Oxford University Press, Inc. New York, NY. 2002. 328p. ISBN:0-19-513296-3, ISBN13: 978-0-19-513296-0. Dewey:780/.92/243. LCCN:2001-038744.

Audience: **u,f.** *Choice, 2003.*

Daverio, John   **ML410.S4D38 1997**
Robert Schumann: Herald of a New Poetic Age. Trade Cloth. Oxford University Press, Inc. New York, NY. 1997. 618p. ISBN:0-19-509180-9, ISBN13: 978-0-19-509180-9. Dewey:780/.92 B. LCCN:96-023177.

Audience: **g,l,u,f.** *Choice, 1997.*

Jensen, Eric Frederick   **ML410**
Schumann. Trade Paper. Oxford University Press, Inc. New York, NY. 2005. 408p. Master Musicians Ser. ISBN:0-19-518297-9, ISBN13: 978-0-19-518297-2. Dewey:780/.92 B. LCCN:00-027866.

Audience: **l,u,f.**

Krebs, Harald   **ML410.S4K68 1999**
Fantasy Pieces: Metrical Dissonance in the Music of Robert Schumann. Trade Cloth. Oxford University Press, Inc. New York, NY. 1999. 304p. ISBN:0-19-511623-2, ISBN13: 978-0-19-511623-6. Dewey:781.2/26/092. LCCN:98-012647.

Audience: **u,f.** *Choice, 2000.*

Marston, Nicholas   ML410.S4 M37 1992
Schumann: Fantasie, Op. 17. Julian Rushton (Contribution by).
Trade Paper. Cambridge University Press. New York, NY. 1992.
131p. Music Handbks. ISBN:0-521-39892-4, ISBN13:
978-0-521-39892-3. Dewey:786.2189. LCCN:91-039602.
Audience: **u,f.** *Choice, 1993.*

Miller, Richard   MT121.S38M55 1999
Singing Schumann: An Interpretive Guide for Performers. Trade
Cloth. Oxford University Press, Inc. New York, NY. 1999. 260p.
ISBN:0-19-511904-5, ISBN13: 978-0-19-511904-6.
Dewey:782.42168/092. LCCN:98-031645.
Audience: **u,f.** *Choice, 2000.*

Ostwald, Peter F.   ML410.S4
Schumann: The Inner Voices of a Musical Genius. Paper Text.
Northeastern University Press. Boston, MA. 1987. 390p.
ISBN:1-55553-014-1, ISBN13: 978-1-55553-014-3.
Dewey:780/.92/4.
Audience: **l,u,f.**

Reinhard, Thilo (Editor)   ML54.6.S4 R413 1989
The Singer's Schumann. Library Binding. Rosen Publishing
Group, Incorporated, The. New York, NY. 1989. 423p.
ISBN:0-8239-0673-6, ISBN13: 978-0-8239-0673-4.
Dewey:784.3/05. LCCN:88-028387.
Audience: **u,f.**

Sams, Eric   MT115.S38
The Songs of Robert Schumann. Ed. 3. Gerald Moore
(Foreword by). Bloomington: Indiana University Press. 1993.
ISBN:0-253-35065-4, ISBN13: 978-0-253-35065-7.
Audience: **l,u,f.**

Schumann, Robert   ML410.S4 A124 1983
On Music and Musicians. Konrad Wolff (Editor), Paul Rosenfeld
(Translator). Trade Paper. University of California Press.
Berkeley, CA. 1982. 274p. ISBN:0-520-04685-4, ISBN13:
978-0-520-04685-6. Dewey:780. LCCN:82-070650.
Audience: **g,l,u,f.**

Todd, Larry (Editor)   ML410.S4S323 1994
Schumann and His World. Trade Cloth. Princeton University
Press. Princeton, NJ. 1994. 408p. ISBN:0-691-03697-7, ISBN13:
978-0-691-03697-7. Dewey:780/.92. LCCN:94-009686.
Audience: **g,l,u,f.** *Choice, 1995.*

Biographies and Studies of Composers and Performers > S > Schutz, Heinrich

Smallman, Basil   ML410.S35S6 2000
Schutz. Cloth Text. Oxford University Press, Inc. New York,
NY. 2000. 236p. Master Musicians Ser. ISBN:0-19-816674-5,
ISBN13: 978-0-19-816674-0. Dewey:782.2/2/092 B.
LCCN:99-042131.
Audience: **l,u,f.** *Choice, 2001.*

Biographies and Studies of Composers and Performers > S > Scriabin, Aleksandr Nikolayevich

Baker, James M.   ML410.S5988B33 1986
The Music of Alexander Scriabin. Cloth over Boards. Yale
University Press. Cumberland, RI. 1986. 291p.
ISBN:0-300-03337-0, ISBN13: 978-0-300-03337-3.
Dewey:786.1/092/4. LCCN:85-002494.
Audience: **u,f.** *Choice, 1986.*

Schloezer, Boris   ML410.S5988S313 1987
Scriabin: Artist and Mystic. Nicolas Slonimsky (Translator),
Marina Scriabine (Introduction by). Trade Cloth. University of
California Press. Berkeley, CA. 1987. 336p.
ISBN:0-520-04384-7, ISBN13: 978-0-520-04384-8.
Dewey:780/.92/4 B. LCCN:86-040109.
Audience: **l,u,f.** *Choice, 1988.*

Biographies and Studies of Composers and Performers > S > Seeger, Pete

Dunaway, David K.   ML420.S445D8 1990
How Can I Keep from Singing: Pete Seeger. Trade Paper. Da
Capo Press, Inc. Cambridge, MA. 1990. 416p. Quality
Paperbacks Ser. ISBN:0-306-80399-2, ISBN13:
978-0-306-80399-4. Dewey:782.42162/0092 B.
LCCN:89-071394.
Audience: **u,f.**

Biographies and Studies of Composers and Performers > S > Seeger, Ruth Crawford

Straus, Joseph N.   ML410.S4446S77 1995
The Music of Ruth Crawford Seeger. Arnold Whittall
(Contribution by). Trade Paper. Cambridge University Press.
New York, NY. 2003. 272p. Music in the Twentieth Century
Ser., Vol. 6 ISBN:0-521-54818-7, ISBN13: 978-0-521-54818-2.
Dewey:780/.92.
Audience: **u,f.** *Choice, 1996.*

Tick, Judith   ML410.S4446T5 1997
Ruth Crawford Seeger: A Composer's Search for American
Music. Trade Cloth. Oxford University Press, Inc. New York,
NY. 1997. 472p. ISBN:0-19-506509-3, ISBN13:
978-0-19-506509-1. Dewey:780.9/2. LCCN:95-030085.
Audience: **l,u,f.** *Choice, 1998.*

Biographies and Studies of Composers and Performers > S > Sex Pistols

Heylin, Clinton   **ML421.S4**
Never Mind the Bollocks, Here's the Sex Pistols: The Sex Pistols. New York: Schirmer Books; London: Prentice Hall International. 1998. Classic Rock Albums ISBN:0-02-864726-2, ISBN13: 978-0-02-864726-5.

Audience: **g,l,u,f.**

Savage, Jon   **ML421.S47S3 2002**
England's Dreaming: Anarchy, Sex Pistols, Punk Rock, and Beyond. Trade Paper. St. Martin's Press. Gordonville, VA. 2002. 656p. ISBN:0-312-28822-0, ISBN13: 978-0-312-28822-8. Dewey:306.4/84. LCCN:2001-048360.

Audience: **g,l,u,f.**

Biographies and Studies of Composers and Performers > S > Shankar, Ravi

Shankar, Ravi   **ML1015.S6**
Raga Mala: The Autobiography of Ravi Shankar. Yehudi Menuhin (Afterword by), George Harrison (Foreword by). Trade Paper. Welcome Rain Publishers. New York, NY. 2001. 352p. ISBN:1-56649-217-3, ISBN13: 978-1-56649-217-1. Dewey:787.8/2.

Audience: **g,l,u,f.**

Biographies and Studies of Composers and Performers > S > Shorter, Wayne

Mercer, Michelle   **ML419.S55M47 2004**
Footprints: The Life and Music of Wayne Shorter. Trade Cloth. Penguin Group (USA) Inc. New York, NY. 2004. 320p. ISBN:1-58542-353-X, ISBN13: 978-1-58542-353-8. Dewey:788.7/165/092 B. LCCN:2004-058845.

Audience: **l,u,f.**

Biographies and Studies of Composers and Performers > S > Shostakovich, Dmitrii Dmitrievich

Brown, Malcolm Hamrick (Editor)   **ML410.S53S46 2004**
A Shostakovich Casebook. Trade Cloth. Indiana University Press. Bloomington, IN. 2004. 392p. ISBN:0-253-34364-X, ISBN13: 978-0-253-34364-2. Dewey:780/.92 B. LCCN:2003-017153.

Audience: **g,l,u,f.** *Choice, 2004.*

Fay, Laurel   **ML410.S53F39 2000**
Shostakovich: A Life. Trade Cloth. Oxford University Press, Inc. New York, NY. 1999. 480p. ISBN:0-19-513438-9, ISBN13: 978-0-19-513438-4. Dewey:780/.92 B. LCCN:99-025255.

Audience: **g,l,u,f.** *Choice, 2000.*

Fay, Laurel E. (Editor)   **ML410.S53**
Shostakovich and His World. Trade Cloth. Princeton University Press. Princeton, NJ. 2004. 432p. The Bard Music Festival Ser. ISBN:0-691-12068-4, ISBN13: 978-0-691-12068-3. Dewey:780.9/2. LCCN:2004-104803.

Audience: **g,l,u,f.**

Ho, Allan & Feofanov, Dmitry   **ML410.S53H58 1998**
Shostakovich Reconsidered. Allan Ho & Dmitry Feofanov (Editors), Vladimir Ashkenazy (Translator). Trade Cloth. Toccata Press. London, 1998. 788p. ISBN:0-907689-56-6, ISBN13: 978-0-907689-56-0. Dewey:780/.92. LCCN:98-221223.

Audience: **g,l,u,f.** *Choice, 1999.*

MacDonald, Ian   **ML410.S53**
The New Shostakovich. Cloth Text. Northeastern University Press. Boston, MA. 1990. 352p. ISBN:1-55553-089-3, ISBN13: 978-1-55553-089-1. Dewey:780/.92.

Audience: **l,u,f.** *Choice, 1991.*

Shostakovich, Dmitrii Dmitrievich   **ML410.S53**
Testimony: The Memoirs of Dmitri Shostakovich. Volkov, Solomon (Editor); Ashkenazy, Vladimir (Foreword by); Bouis, Antonina W. (Translator). New York: Limelight Editions. 2004. ISBN:0-87910-998-X, ISBN13: 978-0-87910-998-1.

Audience: **u,f.**

Biographies and Studies of Composers and Performers > S > Sibelius, Jean

Grimley, Daniel M. (Editor)   **ML410.S54C36 2003**
The Cambridge Companion to Sibelius. Cloth Text. Cambridge University Press. New York, NY. 2004. 294p. Cambridge Companions to Music Ser. ISBN:0-521-81552-5, ISBN13: 978-0-521-81552-9. Dewey:780/.92. LCCN:2003-051521.

Audience: **g,l,u,f.** *Choice, 2004.*

Hepokoski, James A.   **ML410.S54 H4 1993**
Sibelius: Symphony No. 5. Julian Rushton (Contribution by). Cloth Text. Cambridge University Press. New York, NY. 1993. 121p. Music Handbks. ISBN:0-521-40143-7, ISBN13: 978-0-521-40143-2. Dewey:784.2184. LCCN:92-021614.

Audience: **u,f.**

Pike, Lionel   **MT125 .P55**
Beethoven, Sibelius and "The Profound Logic": Studies in Symphonic Analysis. Cloth Text. Continuum International Publishing Group, Ltd. London, 1978. 240p. ISBN:0-485-11178-0, ISBN13: 978-0-485-11178-1. Dewey:785.1/1/0922. LCCN:79-309070.

Audience: **u,f.**

Rickards, Guy ML410.S54
Jean Sibelius. London: Phaidon Press. 1997.
ISBN:0-7148-3581-1, ISBN13: 978-0-7148-3581-5.

Audience: **l,u,f.**

Biographies and Studies of Composers and Performers > S > Simon, Paul

Luftig, Stacy ML420.S563
The Paul Simon Companion: 4 Decades of Commentary. Trade
Paper. Music Sales Corporation. New York, NY. 1997. 300p.
Companion Ser. ISBN:0-8256-7207-4, ISBN13:
978-0-8256-7207-1. Dewey:782.42164/092.

Audience: **g,l,u,f.**

Biographies and Studies of Composers and Performers > S > Sinatra, Frank

Ackelson, Richard W. ML156.7.S56
Frank Sinatra: A Complete Recording History of Technqiues,
Songs, Composers, Lyricists, Arrangers, Sessions and First-Issue
Albums, 1939-1984. Library Binding. McFarland & Company,
Incorporated Publishers. Jefferson, NC. 1991. 480p.
ISBN:0-89950-554-6, ISBN13: 978-0-89950-554-1.
Dewey:016.78242163092. LCCN:91-052629.

Audience: **u,f.**

Friedwald, Will ML420.S565F78 1997
Sinatra! The Song Is You: A Singer's Art. Trade Paper. Da Capo
Press, Inc. Cambridge, MA. 1997. 560p. ISBN:0-306-80742-4,
ISBN13: 978-0-306-80742-8. Dewey:782.4/2/164/092.
LCCN:96-043855.

Audience: **u,f.**

Petkov, Steven & Mustazza, ML420.S565F74 1995
  Leonard (Editors)
The Frank Sinatra Reader. Trade Cloth. Oxford University Press,
Inc. New York, NY. 1995. 336p. ISBN:0-19-509531-6, ISBN13:
978-0-19-509531-9. Dewey:782.4/2/164/092. LCCN:95-000197.

Audience: **g,l,u,f.**

Biographies and Studies of Composers and Performers > S > Smith, Bessie

Albertson, Chris ML420.S667A7 2003
Bessie. Ed. 2. Cloth over Boards. Yale University Press.
Cumberland, RI. 2003. 336p. ISBN:0-300-09902-9, ISBN13:
978-0-300-09902-7. Dewey:784/.092/4. LCCN:2002-155414.

Audience: **g,l,u,f.** *Choice, 2004.*

Biographies and Studies of Composers and Performers > S > Sondheim, Stephen

Citron, Stephen ML390.C586 2001
Stephen Sondheim and Andrew Lloyd Webber: The New
Musical. Trade Cloth. Oxford University Press, Inc. New York,
NY. 2001. 464p. The Great Songwriters Ser.
ISBN:0-19-509601-0, ISBN13: 978-0-19-509601-9.
Dewey:782.1/4/0922. LCCN:2001-031408.

Audience: **u,f.**

Furth, George ML50.S705C6 1996
Company: Music and Lyrics by Stephen Sondheim. Ed. 25.
Trade Paper. Theatre Communications Group, Inc. New York,
NY. 1995. 128p. ISBN:1-55936-108-5, ISBN13:
978-1-55936-108-8. Dewey:782.1/4. LCCN:95-045985.

Audience: **g,l,u,f.**

Lapine, James & Sondheim, ML50.S705I5 1989
  Stephen
Into the Woods. Trade Paper. Theatre Communications Group,
Inc. New York, NY. 1998. 160p. ISBN:0-930452-93-3, ISBN13:
978-0-930452-93-3. Dewey:782.81/2. LCCN:89-004402.

Audience: **g,l,u,f.**

Secrest, Meryle ML410.S6872S42 1999
Stephen Sondheim: A Life. Trade Paper. Dell Publishing. New
York, NY. 1999. 480p. ISBN:0-385-33412-5, ISBN13:
978-0-385-33412-9. Dewey:780.9/2.

Audience: **g,l,u,f.** *Choice, 1999.*

Sondheim, Stephen & ML50.S705F65 2001
  Goldman, James
Follies. Trade Paper. Theatre Communications Group, Inc. New
York, NY. 2000. 128p. ISBN:1-55936-196-4, ISBN13:
978-1-55936-196-5. Dewey:782.1/4/0268. LCCN:00-068276.

Audience: **g,l,u,f.**

Sondheim, Stephen & ML410.S6872A5 2002
  Horowitz, Mark Eden
Sondheim on Music: Minor Details and Major Decisions. Trade
Cloth. Scarecrow Press, Inc. Lanham, MD. 2003. 416p.
ISBN:0-8108-4437-0, ISBN13: 978-0-8108-4437-7.
Dewey:782.1/4/092. LCCN:2002-010564.

Audience: **l,u,f.** *Choice, 2003.*

Sondheim, Stephen (Lyrics ML50.Z99
  by, Music by)
Four by Sondheim: Wheeler, Lapine, Shevelove, Gelbart. Trade
Cloth. Applause Theatre Book Publishers. New York, NY. 2000.
772p. ISBN:1-55783-407-5, ISBN13: 978-1-55783-407-2.
Dewey:782.1/40268. LCCN:00-100279.

Audience: **g,l,u,f.**

Weidman, John & ML50.S705
  Sondheim, Stephen

Pacific Overtures. Trade Paper. Theatre Communications Group, Inc. New York, NY. 1991. 144p. ISBN:1-55936-026-7, ISBN13: 978-1-55936-026-5. Dewey:782.1/4/0268. LCCN:90-029041.

Audience: **g,l,u,f.**

Biographies and Studies of Composers and Performers > S > Sousa, John Philip

Bierley, Paul E.   **ML410.S688**
John Philip Sousa: American Phenomenon. Trade Cloth. Warner Bros. Publications. Miami, FL. 2001. 270p. ISBN:0-7579-0612-5, ISBN13: 978-0-7579-0612-1. Dewey:785/.092.

Audience: **g,l,u,f.**

Biographies and Studies of Composers and Performers > S > Springsteen, Bruce

Marsh, Dave   **ML420.S77M335 2003**
Bruce Springsteen: Two Hearts. Trade Paper. Routledge. New York, NY. 2003. 696p. ISBN:0-415-96928-X, ISBN13: 978-0-415-96928-4. Dewey:782.42166/092 B. LCCN:2003-054801.

Audience: **g,l,u,f.**

Sawyers, June Skinner   **ML420.S77R33 2004**
  (Author, Editor)
Racing in the Street: The Bruce Springsteen Reader. Martin Scorsese (Foreword by). Trade Paper. Penguin Group (USA) Inc. New York, NY. 2004. 464p. ISBN:0-14-200354-9, ISBN13: 978-0-14-200354-1. Dewey:782.42166/092 B. LCCN:2003-062414.

Audience: **g,l,u,f.**

Biographies and Studies of Composers and Performers > S > Still, William Grant

Smith, Catherine P.   **ML410.S855 S65 2000**
William Grant Still: A Study in Contradictions. D. G. Murchison & Willard Gatewood (Contribution by). Trade Cloth. University of California Press. Berkeley, CA. 2000. 384p. Music of the African Diaspora Ser., Vol. 2 ISBN:0-520-21542-7, ISBN13: 978-0-520-21542-9. Dewey:780/.92. LCCN:99-043232.

Audience: **l,u,f.**

Biographies and Studies of Composers and Performers > S > Stockhausen, Karlheinz

Kurtz, Michael   **ML410.M9**
Stockhausen: A Biography. Richard Toop (Translator). Trade Paper. Faber & Faber, Inc. New York, NY. 1994. 270p. ISBN:0-571-17146-X, ISBN13: 978-0-571-17146-0. Dewey:780.92.

Audience: **l,u,f.**

Maconie, Robin   **ML410.S858M29 2005**
Other Planets: The Music of Karlheinz Stockhausen. Book, Other. Scarecrow Press, Inc. Lanham, MD. 2005. 592p. ISBN:0-8108-5356-6, ISBN13: 978-0-8108-5356-0. Dewey:780/.92. LCCN:2004-062109.

Audience: **u,f.**   *Choice, 2005.*

Stockhausen, Karlheinz   **ML3845**
Stockhausen on Music: Lectures and Interviews. Robin Maconie (Compiled by). Trade Paper. Marion Boyars Publishers, Inc. New York, NY. 2000. 220p. ISBN:0-7145-2918-4, ISBN13: 978-0-7145-2918-9. Dewey:780.1.

Audience: **l,u,f.**   *Choice, 1989.*

Biographies and Studies of Composers and Performers > S > Stradella, Alessandro

Gianturco, Carolyn   **ML410.S87**
Alessandro Stradella, 1639-1682: His Life and Music. Oxford: Clarendon Press; New York: Oxford University Press. 1994. Oxford Monographs on Music ISBN:0-19-816138-7, ISBN13: 978-0-19-816138-7.

Audience: **u,f.**

Biographies and Studies of Composers and Performers > S > Stradivari, Antonio

Hill, William H., et al.   **ML424.S8**
Antonio Stradivari, His Life and Work (1644-1739). Ed. 2. Arthur F. Hill, Alfred E. Hill & Frances A. Davis (Authors). Trade Paper. Dover Publications, Inc. Mineola, NY. 1963. 315p. ISBN:0-486-20425-1, ISBN13: 978-0-486-20425-3. Dewey:787.12.

Audience: **g,l,u,f.**

Biographies and Studies of Composers and Performers > S > Strauss, Johann

Crittenden, Camille   ML410.S91 C75 2000
Johann Strauss and Vienna: Operetta and the Politics of Popular Culture. Trade Cloth. Cambridge University Press. New York, NY. 2000. 336p. Cambridge Studies in Opera ISBN:0-521-77121-8, ISBN13: 978-0-521-77121-4. Dewey:782.1/2/094361309034. LCCN:99-088871.

Audience: **u,f.**

Mayer, Anton   ML410.S91 M3913 1999
Johann Strauss: A Nineteenth Century Pop-Idol. Steblin, Rita. Wien: Bohlau. 1999. ISBN:3-205-99061-7, ISBN13: 978-3-205-99061-1.

Audience: **u,f.**

Biographies and Studies of Composers and Performers > S > Strauss, Richard

Gilliam, Bryan   ML410.S93 G53 1999
The Life of Richard Strauss. Trade Paper. Cambridge University Press. New York, NY. 1999. 210p. Musical Lives Ser. ISBN:0-521-57895-7, ISBN13: 978-0-521-57895-0. Dewey:780/.92 B. LCCN:98-047947.

Audience: **g,l,u,f.**   *Choice, 2000.*

Gilliam, Bryan (Editor)   ML410.S93 R44 1992
Richard Strauss and His World. Trade Paper. Princeton University Press. Princeton, NJ. 1992. 438p. Princeton Paperbacks Ser. ISBN:0-691-02762-5, ISBN13: 978-0-691-02762-3. Dewey:780.9/2. LCCN:92-015748.

Audience: **g,l,u,f.**   *Choice, 1993.*

Gilliam, Bryan   ML410.S93G54 1996
Richard Strauss's Elektra. Trade Paper. Oxford University Press, Inc. New York, NY. 1996. 284p. Studies in Musical Genesis and Structure ISBN:0-19-816602-8, ISBN13: 978-0-19-816602-3. Dewey:782.1/092. LCCN:95-049506.

Audience: **u,f.**   *Choice, 1992.*

Jefferson, Alan   ML410.S93
Richard Strauss, Der Rosenkavalier. Cambridge; New York: Cambridge University Press. 1985. Cambridge Opera Handbooks ISBN:0-521-26036-1, ISBN13: 978-0-521-26036-7.

Audience: **l,u,f.**

Kennedy, Michael   ML410.S93 K46 1999
Richard Strauss: Man, Musician, Enigma. Trade Cloth. Cambridge University Press. New York, NY. 1999. 472p. ISBN:0-521-58173-7, ISBN13: 978-0-521-58173-8. Dewey:780/.92 B. LCCN:98-035860.

Audience: **g,l,u,f.**   *Choice, 1999.*

Puffett, Derrick (Editor)   ML410.S93R485 1989
Richard Strauss: "Elektra". Cloth Text. Cambridge University Press. New York, NY. 1990. 187p. Cambridge Opera Handbooks Ser. ISBN:0-521-35173-1, ISBN13: 978-0-521-35173-7. Dewey:782.1/092/4. LCCN:89-000499.

Audience: **u,f.**   *Choice, 1990.*

Puffett, Derrick (Editor)   ML410.S93 R52 1989
Richard Strauss: Salome. Richard Wagner (Contribution by). Trade Paper. Cambridge University Press. New York, NY. 1989. 224p. Cambridge Opera Handbooks Ser. ISBN:0-521-35970-8, ISBN13: 978-0-521-35970-2. Dewey:782.109. LCCN:89-000500.

Audience: **u,f.**   *Choice, 1990.*

Strauss, Richard   ML50.S918S32 1988
Salome and Elektra. Nicholas John (Editor). Trade Paper. Riverrun Press, Inc. Flemington, NJ. 1989. 144p. English National Opera Guide Ser., No. 37:Bilingual Libretto, Articles ISBN:0-7145-4131-1, ISBN13: 978-0-7145-4131-0. Dewey:782.1/2. LCCN:88-006444.

Audience: **g,l,u,f.**

Strauss, Richard   ML50.M939
Der Rosenkavalier. Nicholas John (Editor), Alfred Kalisch (Translator). Trade Paper. Riverrun Press, Inc. Flemington, NJ. 1982. English National Opera Guide Series: Bilingual Libretto, Articles, No. 8 ISBN:0-7145-3851-5, ISBN13: 978-0-7145-3851-8. Dewey:782.10268.

Audience: **g,l,u,f.**

Williamson, John   ML410.S93 W55 1993
Strauss: Also Sprach Zarathustra. Julian Rushton (Contribution by). Cloth Text. Cambridge University Press. New York, NY. 1993. 136p. Music Handbks. ISBN:0-521-40076-7, ISBN13: 978-0-521-40076-3. Dewey:784.2184. LCCN:92-020457.

Audience: **u,f.**

Biographies and Studies of Composers and Performers > S > Stravinsky, Igor

Andriessen, Louis & Schonberger, Elmer   ML410.B4
The Apollonian Clockwork: On Stravinsky. Trade Paper. Amsterdam University Press. Amsterdam, 2006. ISBN:90-5356-856-5, ISBN13: 978-90-5356-856-9. Dewey:780/.92/4.

Audience: **u,f.**   *Choice, 1990.*

Craft, Robert   ML410.B4
Stravinsky: Selected Correspondence, Vol. II. Trade Cloth. Alfred A. Knopf Inc. New York, NY. 1984. 559p. ISBN:0-394-52813-1, ISBN13: 978-0-394-52813-7. Dewey:780/.92/4. LCCN:81-047495.

Audience: **u,f.**   *Choice, 1985.*

Craft, Robert ML410.S932C8 1994
Stravinsky: Chronicle of a Friendship. Ed. 2. Trade Cloth.
Vanderbilt University Press. Nashville, TN. 1994. 608p.
ISBN:0-8265-1258-5, ISBN13: 978-0-8265-1258-1.
Dewey:780/.92 B. LCCN:94-012666.
Audience: **u,f.** *Choice, 1995.*

Craft, Robert (Editor) ML410.B4
Stravinsky: Selected Correspondence, Vol. I. Trade Cloth. Alfred
A. Knopf Inc. New York, NY. 1982. 416p. ISBN:0-394-51870-5,
ISBN13: 978-0-394-51870-1. Dewey:780/.92/4.
LCCN:81-047495.
Audience: **u,f.** *Choice, 1985.*

Craft, Robert ML410.B4
Stravinsky: Selected Correspondence. Robert Gottlieb & Eva
Resnikova (Editors). Trade Cloth. Alfred A. Knopf Inc. New
York, NY. 1985. 521p. ISBN:0-394-54220-7, ISBN13:
978-0-394-54220-1. Dewey:780/.92/4. LCCN:81-047495.
Audience: **u,f.** *Choice, 1985.*

Cross, Jonathan (Editor) ML410.S932
The Cambridge Companion to Stravinsky. Cloth Text.
Cambridge University Press. New York, NY. 2003. 344p.
Cambridge Companions to Music Ser. ISBN:0-521-66330-X,
ISBN13: 978-0-521-66330-4. Dewey:780/.92.
LCCN:2003-279769.
Audience: **g,l,u,f.** *Choice, 2004.*

Cross, Jonathan ML410.S932 C87 1998
The Stravinsky Legacy. Arnold Whittall (Contribution by). Trade
Cloth. Cambridge University Press. New York, NY. 1998. 294p.
Music in the Twentieth Century Ser., No. 8
ISBN:0-521-56365-8, ISBN13: 978-0-521-56365-9.
Dewey:780/.92. LCCN:2006-562076.
Audience: **u,f.** *Choice, 1999.*

Forte, Allen MT100.S968 F7
The Harmonic Organization of the Rite of Spring. Trade Paper.
Yale University Press. Cumberland, RI. 1978. 160p.
ISBN:0-300-10537-1, ISBN13: 978-0-300-10537-7.
Dewey:782.9/5/0924.
Audience: **u,f.**

Hill, Peter ML410.S932 H55 2000
Stravinsky: The Rite of Spring. Julian Rushton (Contribution
by). Cloth Text. Cambridge University Press. New York, NY.
2000. 180p. Music Handbks. ISBN:0-521-62221-2, ISBN13:
978-0-521-62221-9. Dewey:784.2/1556. LCCN:00-023703.
Audience: **l,u,f.**

Joseph, Charles M. ML410.S932J665 2002
Stravinsky and Balanchine: A Journey of Invention. Cloth over
Boards. Yale University Press. Cumberland, RI. 2002. 464p.
ISBN:0-300-08712-8, ISBN13: 978-0-300-08712-3.
Dewey:781.5/56/092. LCCN:2001-007130.
Audience: **l,u,f.**

Joseph, Charles M. ML410.S932J68 2001
Stravinsky Inside Out. Cloth over Boards. Yale University Press.

Cumberland, RI. 2001. 352p. ISBN:0-300-07537-5, ISBN13:
978-0-300-07537-3. Dewey:780/.92 B. LCCN:2001-000913.
Audience: **l,u,f.** *Choice, 2002.*

Straus, Joseph N. ML410.S932 S72 2001
Stravinsky's Late Music. Ian Bent (Contribution by). Trade
Paper. Cambridge University Press. New York, NY. 2004. 278p.
Cambridge Studies in Music Theory and Analysis Ser., Vol. 16
ISBN:0-521-60288-2, ISBN13: 978-0-521-60288-4.
Dewey:780/.92.
Audience: **u,f.**

Stravinsky, Igor ML410.M9
Stravinsky: An Autobiography. Trade Paper. W. W. Norton &
Company, Inc. New York, NY. 1998. 192p.
ISBN:0-393-31856-7, ISBN13: 978-0-393-31856-2.
Dewey:780.92.
Audience: **u,f.**

Stravinsky, Igor, et al. ML410.S932
Conversations with Igor Stravinsky. Craft, Robert (Author).
Garden City, N.Y., Doubleday. 1977.
Audience: **u,f.**

Stravinsky, Igor, et al. ML410.S932
Themes and Episodes. Craft, Robert (Author). New York, A.A.
Knopf. 1966.
Audience: **u,f.**

Stravinsky, Igor & Craft, ML0410.S932A
Robert
Dialogues. Trade Paper. Books on Demand. Ann Arbor, MI.
152p. ISBN:0-7837-4848-5, ISBN13: 978-0-7837-4848-1.
Dewey:780/.92/4. LCCN:82-050247.
Audience: **u,f.**

Stravinsky, Igor & Craft, ML410.S932
Robert
Expositions and Developments. Trade Paper. University of
California Press. Berkeley, CA. 1981. ISBN:0-520-04403-7,
ISBN13: 978-0-520-04403-6. Dewey:784.092.
Audience: **u,f.**

Stravinsky, Igor & Craft, ML410.S932 A35
Robert
Memories and Commentaries, Vol. 1. Trade Paper. Faber &
Faber, Inc. New York, NY. 2003. 320p. ISBN:0-571-21163-1,
ISBN13: 978-0-571-21163-0. Dewey:780/.92/4.
Audience: **u,f.**

Stravinsky, Igor ML49.S77O32 1991
Oedipus Rex and the Rake's Progress. Nicholas John (Editor).
Trade Paper. Riverrun Press, Inc. Flemington, NJ. 1991. 112p.
English National Opera Guide Series: Bilingual Libretto,
Articles, No. 43 ISBN:0-7145-4193-1, ISBN13:
978-0-7145-4193-8. Dewey:782.1. LCCN:90-026770.
Audience: **g,l,u,f.**

Stravinsky, Igor MT7
Poetics of Music in the Form of Six Lessons. George Seferis
(Preface by). Trade Paper. Harvard University Press. Cambridge,
MA. 1993. 160p. The Charles Eliot Norton Lectures

ISBN:0-674-67856-7, ISBN13: 978-0-674-67856-9. Dewey:781. LCCN:79-099520.

Audience: **g,l,u,f.** *B*

Stravinsky, Vera & Craft,   **ML410.S932.S787**
  Robert
Stravinsky: In Pictures and Documents. Trade Cloth. Simon & Schuster. New York, NY. 1979. 688p. ISBN:0-671-24382-9, ISBN13: 978-0-671-24382-1. Dewey:780/.92/4. LCCN:78-015375.

Audience: **u,f.**

Taruskin, Richard F.   **ML410.S932.T38 1996**
Stravinsky and the Russian Traditions: A Biography of the Works Through "Mavra". Trade Cloth. University of California Press. Berkeley, CA. 1996. 1800p. ISBN:0-520-07099-2, ISBN13: 978-0-520-07099-8. Dewey:780/.92. LCCN:93-028500.

Audience: **l,u,f.** *Choice, 1997.*

Van den Toorn, Pieter C.   **ML410.S932**
The Music of Igor Stravinsky. Trade Cloth. Yale University Press. Cumberland, RI. 1987. 512p. Composers of the Twentieth Century Ser. ISBN:0-300-02693-5, ISBN13: 978-0-300-02693-1. Dewey:780/.92/4. LCCN:82-002560.

Audience: **l,u,f.**

Van den Toorn, Pieter C.   **ML410.S932.V38 1988**
Stravinsky and the "Rite of Spring": The Beginnings of a Musical Language. Trade Cloth. University of California Press. Berkeley, CA. 1987. 200p. ISBN:0-520-05958-1, ISBN13: 978-0-520-05958-0. Dewey:785.3/2/0924. LCCN:86-031778.

Audience: **l,u,f.** *Choice, 1988.*

Walsh, Stephen   **ML410.B4**
The Music of Stravinsky. Trade Paper. Oxford University Press, Inc. New York, NY. 1993. 326p. ISBN:0-19-816375-4, ISBN13: 978-0-19-816375-6. Dewey:780/.92/4. LCCN:87-012896.

Audience: **l,u,f.**

Walsh, Stephen   **ML410.S932W345 1999**
Stravinsky: A Creative Spring: Russia and France, 1882-1934. Trade Cloth. Alfred A. Knopf Inc. New York, NY. 1999. 720p. ISBN:0-679-41484-3, ISBN13: 978-0-679-41484-1. Dewey:780/.92 B. LCCN:99-462433.

Audience: **l,u,f.**

Walsh, Stephen   **ML410.S932W355 2006**
Stravinsky: The Second Exile: France and America, 1934-1971. Alfre. 2006. ISBN:0-375-40752-9, ISBN13: 978-0-375-40752-9.

Audience: **l,u,f.**

Walsh, Stephen   **ML410.S932 W35 1993**
Stravinsky: Oedipus Rex. Julian Rushton (Contribution by). Cloth Text. Cambridge University Press. New York, NY. 1993. 130p. Music Handbks. ISBN:0-521-40431-2, ISBN13: 978-0-521-40431-0. Dewey:782.1092. LCCN:92-030088.

Audience: **u,f.**

White, Eric W.   **ML410.B4**
Stravinsky: The Composer and His Works. Ed. 2. Trade Cloth.

University of California Press. Berkeley, CA. 1980. 656p. ISBN:0-520-03985-8, ISBN13: 978-0-520-03985-8. Dewey:780.9/2. LCCN:66-027667.

Audience: **l,u,f.**

Biographies and Studies of Composers and Performers > S > Strayhorn, Billy

Hajdu, David   **ML410.S9325H35 1996**
Lush Life: A Biography of Billy Strayhorn. Cloth over Boards. Farrar, Straus & Giroux. New York, NY. 1996. 305p. ISBN:0-374-19438-6, ISBN13: 978-0-374-19438-3. Dewey:781.6/55/092. LCCN:95-044707.

Audience: **u,f.** *Choice, 1996.*

van de Leur, Walter   **ML410.S9325L48 2002**
Something to Live For: The Music of Billy Strayhorn. Trade Paper. Oxford University Press, Inc. New York, NY. 2002. 352p. ISBN:0-19-512448-0, ISBN13: 978-0-19-512448-4. Dewey:781.65/092. LCCN:2001-037040.

Audience: **u,f.**

Biographies and Studies of Composers and Performers > S > Sullivan, Arthur

Ainger, Michael   **ML410.S95A77 2002**
Gilbert and Sullivan: A Dual Biography. Trade Cloth. Oxford University Press, Inc. New York, NY. 2002. 528p. ISBN:0-19-514769-3, ISBN13: 978-0-19-514769-8. Dewey:782.1/2/0922 B. LCCN:2001-056046.

Audience: **g,l,u,f.** *Choice, 2003.*

Bradley, Ian (Editor)   **ML49.S9A1 1996**
The Complete Annotated Gilbert and Sullivan. Trade Cloth. Oxford University Press, Inc. New York, NY. 1996. 1, 212p. ISBN:0-19-816503-X, ISBN13: 978-0-19-816503-3. Dewey:782.1/2/0268. LCCN:95-051813.

Audience: **g,l,u,f.** *Choice, 1997.*

Biographies and Studies of Composers and Performers > S > Sun Ra

Szwed, John F.   **ML410.S978S73 1998**
Space Is the Place: The Lives and Times of Sun Ra. Trade Paper. Da Capo Press, Inc. Cambridge, MA. 1998. 496p. ISBN:0-306-80855-2, ISBN13: 978-0-306-80855-5. Dewey:781.65/092 B. LCCN:98-015303.

Audience: **u,f.**

Biographies and Studies of Composers and Performers > S > Szymanowski, Karol

Wightman, Alistair   **ML410.S99W54 1999**
Karol Szymanowski: His Life and Work. Trade Cloth. Ashgate Publishing, Ltd. Aldershot, 1999. 492p. ISBN:1-85928-391-8, ISBN13: 978-1-85928-391-2. Dewey:780/.92 B. LCCN:99-022690.

Audience: **u,f.**

Biographies and Studies of Composers and Performers > T > Takemitsu, Toru

Burt, Peter   **ML410.T134 B87 2001**
The Music of Toru Takemitsu. Arnold Whittall (Contribution by). Trade Cloth. Cambridge University Press. New York, NY. 2001. 306p. Music in the Twentieth Century Ser. ISBN:0-521-78220-1, ISBN13: 978-0-521-78220-3. Dewey:780/.92. LCCN:00-045505.

Audience: **u,f.** *Choice, 2002.*

Takemitsu, Toru   **ML60.T258713 1995**
Confronting Silence: Selected Writings. Glenn Glasow & Yoshiko Kakudo (Translators), Seiji Ozawa (Foreword by), Glenn Glasow & Yoshiko Kakudo (Preface by). Trade Cloth. Scarecrow Press, Inc. Lanham, MD. 1995. 730p. Fallen Leaf Monographs on Contemporary Composers, No. 1 ISBN:0-914913-31-X, ISBN13: 978-0-914913-31-3. Dewey:780. LCCN:95-009884.

Audience: **u,f.**

Biographies and Studies of Composers and Performers > T > Tatum, Art

Lester, James   **ML417.M846**
Too Marvelous for Words: The Life and Genius of Art Tatum. Trade Paper. Oxford University Press, Inc. New York, NY. 1995. 254p. ISBN:0-19-509640-1, ISBN13: 978-0-19-509640-8. Dewey:786.2/165/092.

Audience: **u,f.** *Choice, 1995.*

Biographies and Studies of Composers and Performers > T > Tavener, John

Tavener, John   **ML410.M9**
The Music of Silence: A Composer's Testament. Brian Keeble (Editor). Trade Paper. Faber & Faber, Inc. New York, NY. 2000. 208p. ISBN:0-571-20088-5, ISBN13: 978-0-571-20088-7. Dewey:780.9/2.

Audience: **u,f.**

Biographies and Studies of Composers and Performers > T > Tchaikovsky, Peter Ilich

Brown, David   **ML390**
Tchaikovsky Remembered. Paper Text. DIANE Publishing Company. Collingdale, PA. 1999. 248p. ISBN:0-7881-6785-5, ISBN13: 978-0-7881-6785-0. Dewey:780/.92 B.

Audience: **u,f.**

Jackson, Timothy L.   **ML410.C4 J33 1999**
Tchaikovsky: Symphony No. 6 (Pathétique). Cloth Text. Cambridge University Press. New York, NY. 1999. 164p. Music Handbks. ISBN:0-521-64111-X, ISBN13: 978-0-521-64111-1. Dewey:784.2/184. LCCN:98-039930.

Audience: **u,f.**

Kearney, Leslie (Editor)   **ML410.C4T36 1998**
Tchaikovsky and His World. Cloth Text. Princeton University Press. Princeton, NJ. 1998. 350p. The Bard Music Festival Ser. ISBN:0-691-00429-3, ISBN13: 978-0-691-00429-7. Dewey:780/.92. LCCN:98-025777.

Audience: **g,l,u,f.** *Choice, 1999.*

Orlova, Alexandra   **ML410.C4.A3 1990**
Tchaikovsky: A Self-Portrait. R. M. Davison (Translator), David B. Brown (Foreword by). Trade Cloth. Oxford University Press, Inc. New York, NY. 1990. 476p. ISBN:0-19-315319-X, ISBN13: 978-0-19-315319-6. Dewey:780.92. LCCN:91-123364.

Audience: **u,f.** *Choice, 1991.*

Poznansky, Alexander   **ML410.C4P856 1996**
Tchaikovsky's Last Days: A Documentary Study. Trade Cloth. Oxford University Press, Inc. New York, NY. 1996. 254p. ISBN:0-19-816596-X, ISBN13: 978-0-19-816596-5. Dewey:780.9/2. LCCN:96-013332.

Audience: **l,u,f.** *Choice, 1997.*

Poznansky, Alexander & Langston, Brett   **ML134.C42P69 2001**
The Tchaikovsky Handbook: Catalogue of Letters, Bibliography. Trade Cloth. Indiana University Press. Bloomington, IN. 2002. 730p. Russian Music Studies ISBN:0-253-33947-2, ISBN13: 978-0-253-33947-8. Dewey:780/.92 B. LCCN:2001-039546.

Audience: **u,f.** *Choice, 2002.*

Poznansky, Alexander & Langston, Brett   **ML134.C42P69 2001**
The Tchaikovsky Handbook: Thematic Catalogue of Works, Catalogue of Photographs, Autobiography. Trade Cloth. Indiana University Press. Bloomington, IN. 2002. 730p. Russian Music Studies ISBN:0-253-33921-9, ISBN13: 978-0-253-33921-8. Dewey:780/.92 B. LCCN:2001-039546.

Audience: **u,f.** *Choice, 2002.*

Biographies and Studies of Composers and Performers > T > Theremin, Leon

Glinsky, Albert   ML429.T43G6 2000
Theremin: Ether Music and Espionage. Robert Moog (Foreword by). Trade Cloth. University of Illinois Press. Champaign, IL. 2000. 480p. Music in American Life Ser. ISBN:0-252-02582-2, ISBN13: 978-0-252-02582-2. Dewey:786.7/3 B. LCCN:00-008024.

Audience: **g,l,u,f** *Choice, 2001.*

Biographies and Studies of Composers and Performers > T > Thomson, Virgil

Kostelanetz, Richard   ML410.M9
  (Editor)
Virgil Thomson Reader: Selected Writings, 1924-1984. Paper over Boards. Routledge. New York, NY. 2002. 304p. ISBN:0-415-93795-7, ISBN13: 978-0-415-93795-5. Dewey:780.9/2.

Audience: **l,u,f**

Biographies and Studies of Composers and Performers > U > Umm Kulthum

Danielson, Virginia   ML420.U46D36 1997
The Voice of Egypt: Umm Kulthum, Arabic Song, and Egyptian Society in the Twentieth Century. Trade Paper. University of Chicago Press. Chicago, IL. 1998. 288p. Chicago Studies in Ethnomusicology ISBN:0-226-13612-4, ISBN13: 978-0-226-13612-7. Dewey:[B]. LCCN:96-045394.

Audience: **g,l,u,f**

Biographies and Studies of Composers and Performers > V > Varese, Edgard

Bernard, Jonathan W.   ML410.V27B5 1987
The Music of Edgard Varese. Trade Cloth. Yale University Press. Cumberland, RI. 1987. 304p. ISBN:0-300-03515-2, ISBN13: 978-0-300-03515-5. Dewey:780/.92/4. LCCN:86-022431.

Audience: **u,f** *Choice, 1987.*

MacDonald, Malcolm   ML410
Varese: Astronomer in Sound. Trade Paper. Kahn & Averill Publishers. London, 2003. 448p. ISBN:1-871082-79-X, ISBN13: 978-1-871082-79-1. Dewey:780.9/2.

Audience: **l,u,f**

Treib, Marc   NA6750.B7P497 1996
Space Calculated in Seconds: The Philips Pavilion, le Corbusier, Edgard Varese. Trade Cloth. Princeton University Press. Princeton, NJ. 1996. 302p. ISBN:0-691-02137-6, ISBN13: 978-0-691-02137-9. Dewey:725/.91/0949332. LCCN:96-004114.

Audience: **u,f**

Varese, Louise   ML410.V27 V272
Varese: A Looking-Glass Diary. Trade Cloth. W. W. Norton & Company, Inc. New York, NY. 1972. ISBN:0-393-07461-7, ISBN13: 978-0-393-07461-1. Dewey:785/.0924. LCCN:74-139392.

Audience: **u,f**

Biographies and Studies of Composers and Performers > V > Vaughan Williams, Ralph

Kennedy, Michael   ML410.B4
The Works of Ralph Vaughan Williams. Ed. 2. Paper Text. Oxford University Press, Inc. New York, NY. 1994. 464p. ISBN:0-19-816330-4, ISBN13: 978-0-19-816330-5. Dewey:780/.92/4.

Audience: **u,f**

Pike, Lionel   ML422.K22
Vaughan Williams and the Symphony. Cloth over Boards. Toccata Press. London, 2003. 352p. ISBN:0-907689-54-X, ISBN13: 978-0-907689-54-6. Dewey:784.2092.

Audience: **u,f**

Williams, Ralph Vaughan   ML60.V288 1996
National Music and Other Essays. Ed. 2. Ursula Vaughan Williams (Preface by), Michael Kennedy (Introduction by). Paper Text. Oxford University Press, Inc. New York, NY. 1996. 328p. ISBN:0-19-816593-5, ISBN13: 978-0-19-816593-4. Dewey:780/.9. LCCN:95-042483.

Audience: **u,f**

Biographies and Studies of Composers and Performers > V > Velvet Underground

Zak, Albin   ML421.V44
The Velvet Underground Companion: 4 Decades of Commentary. Trade Paper. Music Sales Corporation. New York, NY. 1997. 300p. Companion Ser. ISBN:0-8256-7242-2, ISBN13: 978-0-8256-7242-2. Dewey:782.42166/092/2. LCCN:97-009247.

Audience: **g,l,u,f**

Biographies and Studies of Composers and Performers > V > Verdi, Giuseppe

Abbate, Carolyn & Parker,   **MT95.A59 1989**
  Roger (Editors)
Analyzing Opera: Verdi and Wagner. Trade Cloth. University of California Press. Berkeley, CA. 1989. 250p. California Studies in 19th Century Music, No. 6 ISBN:0-520-06157-8, ISBN13: 978-0-520-06157-6. Dewey:782.1/092/2. LCCN:88-021072.
                                        Audience: **u,f.** *Choice, 1990.*

Balthazar, Scott L. (Editor)   **ML410**
The Cambridge Companion to Verdi. Jonathan Cross (Contribution by). Cloth Text. Cambridge University Press. New York, NY. 2004. 364p. Cambridge Companions to Music Ser. ISBN:0-521-63228-5, ISBN13: 978-0-521-63228-7. Dewey:782.1092 B. LCCN:2005-280590.
                                        Audience: **g,l,u,f.**

Budden, Julian   **ML410.V4**
The Operas of Verdi: From Il Trovatore to la Forza Del Destino, Vol. 2. Ed. 2. Trade Paper. Oxford University Press, Inc. New York, NY. 1992. 542p. ISBN:0-19-816262-6, ISBN13: 978-0-19-816262-9. Dewey:782.1/092.
                                        Audience: **g,l,u,f.**

Budden, Julian   **ML410.V4**
The Operas of Verdi: From Oberto to Rigoletto, Vol. 1. Ed. 2. Trade Paper. Oxford University Press, Inc. New York, NY. 1992. 538p. ISBN:0-19-816261-8, ISBN13: 978-0-19-816261-2. Dewey:782.1092.
                                        Audience: **g,l,u,f.**

Budden, Julian (Editor)   **ML410.V4 B88 1991**
The Operas of Verdi: From Don Carlos to Falstaff, Vol. 3. Ed. 2. Trade Paper. Oxford University Press, Inc. New York, NY. 1992. 550p. ISBN:0-19-816263-4, ISBN13: 978-0-19-816263-6. Dewey:782.1/092. LCCN:91-036272.
                                        Audience: **g,l,u,f.**

Budden, Julian   **ML410.V4**
Verdi. New York: Schirmer Books. 1996. Master Musicians Ser. ISBN:0-02-864616-9, ISBN13: 978-0-02-864616-9.
                                        Audience: **g,l,u,f.**

Harwood, Gregory W.   **ML134.V47H37 1998**
Giuseppe Verdi: A Guide to Research. Cloth Text. Garland Publishing, Inc. New York, NY. 1998. 426p. Composer Resource Manuals Ser., Vol. 42 ISBN:0-8240-4117-8, ISBN13: 978-0-8240-4117-5. Dewey:782.1/092. LCCN:98-012194.
                                        Audience: **l,u,f.** *Choice, 1998.*

Hepokoski, James A.   **ML410.V4 H46 1983**
Giuseppe Verdi: Falstaff. Richard Wagner (Contribution by). Trade Paper. Cambridge University Press. New York, NY. 1983. 192p. Cambridge Opera Handbooks Ser. ISBN:0-521-28016-8, ISBN13: 978-0-521-28016-7. Dewey:782.1/092/4. LCCN:83-023493.
                                        Audience: **u,f.**

Hepokoski, James A.   **ML410.V4 H48 1987**
Giuseppe Verdi: Otello. Richard Wagner (Contribution by). Trade Paper. Cambridge University Press. New York, NY. 1987. 226p. Cambridge Opera Handbooks Ser. ISBN:0-521-27749-3, ISBN13: 978-0-521-27749-5. Dewey:782.1/092/4. LCCN:86-017189.
                                        Audience: **u,f.**

Phillips-Matz, Mary J.   **ML410.V4P43 1993**
Verdi: A Biography. Andrew Porter (Foreword by). Trade Cloth. Oxford University Press, Inc. New York, NY. 1993. 994p. ISBN:0-19-313204-4, ISBN13: 978-0-19-313204-7. Dewey:782.1/092. LCCN:92-037841.
                                        Audience: **l,u,f.** *Choice, 1994.*

Rosen, David   **ML410.V4 R73 1995**
Verdi: Requiem. Julian Rushton (Contribution by). Trade Paper. Cambridge University Press. New York, NY. 1995. 125p. Music Handbks. ISBN:0-521-39767-7, ISBN13: 978-0-521-39767-4. Dewey:782.3/238. LCCN:94-033380.
                                        Audience: **u,f.** *Choice, 1996.*

Verdi, Giuseppe   **ML49.V45**
Seven Verdi Librettos. William Weaver (Translator). Trade Paper. W. W. Norton & Company, Inc. New York, NY. 1977. ISBN:0-393-00852-5, ISBN13: 978-0-393-00852-4. Dewey:782.5.
                                        Audience: **g,l,u,f.**

Weaver, William & Chusid,   **ML410.V4**
  Martin (Editors)
The Verdi Companion. Ed. 2. Trade Paper. W. W. Norton & Company, Inc. New York, NY. 1988. 384p. ISBN:0-393-30443-4, ISBN13: 978-0-393-30443-5. Dewey:782.1/092/4.
                                        Audience: **g,l,u,f.**

Biographies and Studies of Composers and Performers > V > Villa-Lobos, Heitor

Appleby, David P.   **ML410.V76A67 2002**
Heitor Villa-Lobos: A Life (1887-1959). Trade Cloth. Scarecrow Press, Inc. Lanham, MD. 2002. 288p. ISBN:0-8108-4149-5, ISBN13: 978-0-8108-4149-9. Dewey:780/.92 B. LCCN:2001-049887.
                                        Audience: **g,l,u,f.** *Choice, 2002.*

Biographies and Studies of Composers and Performers > V > Vivaldi, Antonio

Everett, Paul   **ML410.V82 E84 1996**
Vivaldi: The Four Seasons and Other Concertos, Op. 8. Julian Rushton (Contribution by). Cloth Text. Cambridge University

Press. New York, NY. 1996. 128p. Music Handbks.
ISBN:0-521-40499-1, ISBN13: 978-0-521-40499-0.
Dewey:780/.92. LCCN:95-018173.

Audience: **u,f.**

Talbot, Michael   **ML410.V82**
Vivaldi. New York: Schirmer Books: Maxwell Macmillan
International. 199. The Master Musicians ISBN:0-02-872665-0,
ISBN13: 978-0-02-872665-6.

Audience: **l,u,f.**

Biographies and Studies of Composers and Performers > W > Wagner, Richard

Abbate, Carolyn & Parker,   **MT95.A59 1989**
  Roger (Editors)
Analyzing Opera: Verdi and Wagner. Trade Cloth. University of
California Press. Berkeley, CA. 1989. 250p. California Studies
in 19th Century Music, No. 6 ISBN:0-520-06157-8, ISBN13:
978-0-520-06157-6. Dewey:782.1/092/2. LCCN:88-021072.

Audience: **u,f.** *Choice, 1990.*

Beckett, Lucy   **ML410.W17.B37**
Richard Wagner: "Parsifal". Cloth Text. Cambridge University
Press. New York, NY. 1981. 173p. Cambridge Opera Handbooks
Ser. ISBN:0-521-22825-5, ISBN13: 978-0-521-22825-1.
Dewey:782.1/092/4. LCCN:80-040870.

Audience: **u,f.**

Burbidge, Peter & Sutton,   **ML410.V4**
  Richard (Editors)
The Wagner Companion. Trade Cloth. Cambridge University
Press. New York, NY. 1979. ISBN:0-521-22787-9, ISBN13:
978-0-521-22787-2. Dewey:782.1/092/4. LCCN:79-050099.

Audience: **u,f.**

Dahlhaus, Carl   **ML410.W13**
Richard Wagner's Music Dramas. Mary Whittall (Translator).
Trade Cloth. Cambridge University Press. New York, NY. 1979.
174p. ISBN:0-521-22397-0, ISBN13: 978-0-521-22397-3.
Dewey:782.1092. LCCN:78-068359.

Audience: **u,f.**

Darcy, Warren   **MT100.W26D33 1996**
Wagner's das Rheingold. Paper Text. Oxford University Press,
Inc. New York, NY. 1996. 274p. Studies in Musical Genesis and
Structure ISBN:0-19-816603-6, ISBN13: 978-0-19-816603-0.
Dewey:782.1. LCCN:96-033659.

Audience: **u,f.**

Donington, Robert   **ML410.W15**
Wagner's 'Ring' and Its Symbols: The Music and the Myth. Ed.
3. Trade Paper. Faber & Faber, Inc. New York, NY. 1974. 304p.
ISBN:0-571-04818-8, ISBN13: 978-0-571-04818-2.
Dewey:782.154. LCCN:74-164583.

Audience: **u,f.**

Gregor-Dellin, Martin   **ML410.W1 G73413 1983**
Richard Wagner: His Life, His Work, His Century. J. Maxwell
Brownjohn (Translator). Trade Cloth. Harcourt Trade Publishers.
New York, NY. 1983. 592p. A Helen and Kurt Wolff Bk.
ISBN:0-15-177151-0, ISBN13: 978-0-15-177151-6.
Dewey:782.1/092/4. LCCN:82-015421.

Audience: **g,l,u,f.**

Grey, Thomas S. (Editor)   **ML410.W132 .R48 2000**
Richard Wagner: Der Fliegende Holländer. Trade Paper.
Cambridge University Press. New York, NY. 2000. 240p.
Cambridge Opera Handbooks Ser. ISBN:0-521-58763-8,
ISBN13: 978-0-521-58763-1. Dewey:782.1. LCCN:99-059951.

Audience: **u,f.**

Holman, J. K.   **ML1700**
Wagner's Ring: A Listener's Companion and Concordance.
Trade Paper. Hal Leonard Corporation. Milwaukee, WI. 2003.
440p. ISBN:1-57467-070-0, ISBN13: 978-1-57467-070-7.
Dewey:782.1.

Audience: **g,l,u,f.**

Katz, Jacob   **ML410.W19K3313 1986**
The Darker Side of Genius: Richard Wagner's Anti-Semitism.
Trade Cloth. University Press of New England. Lebanon, NH.
1986. 172p. Tauber Institute Ser., No. 5 ISBN:0-87451-368-5,
ISBN13: 978-0-87451-368-4. Dewey:782.1/092/4.
LCCN:85-040935.

Audience: **u,f.** *Choice, 1986.*

Kitcher, Philip & Schacht,   **ML410.W15K57 2004**
  Richard
Finding an Ending: Reflections on Wagner's Ring. Trade Cloth.
Oxford University Press, Inc. New York, NY. 2004. 253p.
ISBN:0-19-517359-7, ISBN13: 978-0-19-517359-8.
Dewey:782.1. LCCN:2004-041478.

Audience: **u,f.** *Choice, 2005.*

Kohler, Joachim   **ML410.W1K8313 2004**
Richard Wagner: The Last of the Titans. Stewart Spencer
(Translator). Cloth over Boards. Yale University Press.
Cumberland, RI. 2004. 704p. ISBN:0-300-10422-7, ISBN13:
978-0-300-10422-6. Dewey:782.1/092 B. LCCN:2004-110664.

Audience: **u,f.** *Choice, 2005.*

Magee, Bryan   **ML410.W19M14 2001**
The Tristan Chord: Wagner and Philosophy. Cloth over Boards.
Henry Holt & Company. New York, NY. 2001. 416p.
ISBN:0-8050-6788-4, ISBN13: 978-0-8050-6788-0.
Dewey:782.1/092. LCCN:2001-030779.

Audience: **u,f.**

Millington, Barry (Editor)   **ML410.M9**
The Wagner Compendium: A Guide to Wagner's Life and
Music. Trade Paper. Thames & Hudson. New York, NY. 2001.
432p. ISBN:0-500-28274-9, ISBN13: 978-0-500-28274-8.
Dewey:780.9/2.

Audience: **g,l,u,f.** *Choice, 1993.*

Muller, Ulrich (Editor), et al.   ML410.W131R41613
Wagner Handbook. Peter Wapnewski & John Deathridge
(Editors). Trade Cloth. Harvard University Press. Cambridge,
MA. 1992. 728p. ISBN:0-674-94530-1, ISBN13:
978-0-674-94530-2. Dewey:782.1/092. LCCN:91-042202.

Audience: **l,u,f.** *Choice, 1993.*

Newman, Ernest   ML410.W1
The Life of Richard Wagner. Trade Paper. Cambridge University
Press. New York, NY. 1976. ISBN:0-521-29149-6, ISBN13:
978-0-521-29149-1. Dewey:782.1/092/4. LCCN:76-022682.

Audience: **l,u,f.**

Osborne, Charles   ML410.V4
The Complete Operas of Richard Wagner. Trade Paper. Da Capo
Press, Inc. Cambridge, MA. 1993. 288p. ISBN:0-306-80522-7,
ISBN13: 978-0-306-80522-6. Dewey:782.1/092.
LCCN:92-034417.

Audience: **l,u,f.** *Choice, 1991.*

Sadie, Stanley (Editor)   ML410.W13W114 2000
Wagner and His Operas. Trade Cloth. St. Martin's Press.
Gordonville, VA. 2000. xv, 219p. The New Grove Composers
Ser. ISBN:0-333-79021-9, ISBN13: 978-0-333-79021-2.
Dewey:782.1/092. LCCN:00-701304.

Audience: **l,u,f.**

Saffle, Michael   ML134.W1S24 2002
Richard Wagner: A Guide to Research. Paper over Boards.
Garland Publishing, Inc. New York, NY. 2002. 352p. Routledge
Musical Bibliographies Ser. ISBN:0-8240-5695-7, ISBN13:
978-0-8240-5695-7. Dewey:016.7821/092. LCCN:2001-048162.

Audience: **l,u,f.**

Tanner, Michael   ML410.V4
Wagner. Trade Paper. Princeton University Press. Princeton, NJ.
2002. 248p. ISBN:0-691-10290-2, ISBN13: 978-0-691-10290-0.
Dewey:782.1/092.

Audience: **u,f.** *Choice, 1997.*

Von Westernhagen, Curt   ML410.W15
The Forging of the Ring: Richard Wagner's Composition
Sketches for Der Ring des Nibelungen. Arnold Whittall & Mary
Whittall (Translators). Trade Cloth. Cambridge University Press.
New York, NY. 1976. 248p. ISBN:0-521-21293-6, ISBN13:
978-0-521-21293-9. Dewey:782.1/092/4. LCCN:76-007140.

Audience: **u,f.**

Wagner, Richard   ML410.W1 A1434
The Art Work of the Future. Trade Paper. Kessinger Publishing,
LLC. Whitefish, MT. 2004. ISBN:1-4191-5273-4, ISBN13:
978-1-4191-5273-3. Dewey:700/.1.

Audience: **u,f.**

Wagner, Richard   ML410.V4
My Life. Library Binding. Reprint Services Company. Temecula,
CA. 1988. ISBN:0-7812-0537-9, ISBN13: 978-0-7812-0537-5.
Dewey:782.1/092 B.

Audience: **u,f.**

Wagner, Richard   ML410.W1A246 1989
Wagner on Conducting. Trade Paper. Dover Publications, Inc.
Mineola, NY. 1989. 128p. ISBN:0-486-25932-3, ISBN13:
978-0-486-25932-1. Dewey:781.6/35. LCCN:88-026827.

Audience: **u,f.**

Wagner, Richard   ML410.W1A1266 1995
Actors and Singers. William A. Ellis (Translator). Trade Cloth.
University of Nebraska Press. Lincoln, NE. 1995. 441p.
ISBN:0-8032-9773-4, ISBN13: 978-0-8032-9773-9. Dewey:780.
LCCN:95-030854.

Audience: **u,f.**

Wagner, Richard   ML410.W1A12663 1995
Art and Politics. William A. Ellis (Translator). Paper Text.
University of Nebraska Press. Lincoln, NE. 1995. 415p.
ISBN:0-8032-9774-2, ISBN13: 978-0-8032-9774-6. Dewey:780.
LCCN:95-024316.

Audience: **u,f.**

Wagner, Richard   ML410.W1A1268 1995
Opera and Drama. William Ashton Ellis (Translator). Trade
Paper. University of Nebraska Press. Lincoln, NE. 1995. 416p.
ISBN:0-8032-9765-3, ISBN13: 978-0-8032-9765-4.
Dewey:782.1. LCCN:95-005263.

Audience: **u,f.**

Wagner, Richard   ML50.M939
Lohengrin. Nicholas John (Editor). Trade Paper. Riverrun Press,
Inc. Flemington, NJ. 1994. 128p. English National Opera Guide
Series: Bilingual Libretto, Articles, No. 47 ISBN:0-7145-3852-3,
ISBN13: 978-0-7145-3852-5. Dewey:782.10268.

Audience: **g,l,u,f.**

Wagner, Richard   ML50.W14T22 1988
Tannhauser. Nicholas John (Editor). Trade Paper. Riverrun Press,
Inc. Flemington, NJ. 1988. 96p. English National Opera Guide
Series: Bilingual Libretto, Articles, No. 39 ISBN:0-7145-4147-8,
ISBN13: 978-0-7145-4147-1. Dewey:782.1/2. LCCN:88-006443.

Audience: **g,l,u,f.**

Wagner, Richard   ML410.W16
The Mastersingers of Nuremberg. Nicholas John (Editor), F.
Jameson & Feasey Kember (Translators). Trade Paper. Riverrun
Press, Inc. Flemington, NJ. 2003. 128p. English National Opera
Guide Ser., No. 19:Bilingual Libretto, Articles
ISBN:0-7145-3961-9, ISBN13: 978-0-7145-3961-4.
Dewey:782.1/092/4.

Audience: **g,l,u,f.**

Wagner, Richard   ML410.W17
Parsifal. Nicholas John (Editor), Andrew Porter (Translator).
Trade Paper. Riverrun Press, Inc. Flemington, NJ. 1986. 128p.
English National Opera Guide Series: Bilingual Libretto,
Articles, No. 34 ISBN:0-7145-4079-X, ISBN13:
978-0-7145-4079-5. Dewey:782.1/092/4. LCCN:85-052160.

Audience: **g,l,u,f.**

Wagner, Richard   ML50.B422
Tristan and Isolde. Nicholas John (Editor), Andrew Porter
(Translator). Trade Paper. Riverrun Press, Inc. Flemington, NJ.

1981. 96p. English National Opera Guide Ser., No. 6:Bilingual Libretto, Articles ISBN:0-7145-3849-3, ISBN13: 978-0-7145-3849-5. Dewey:782.1/2.

Audience: **g,l,u,f.**

Wagner, Richard   **ML50.W14**
The Ring of the Nibelung. Andrew Porter (Translator). Trade Paper. W. W. Norton & Company, Inc. New York, NY. 1977. ISBN:0-393-00867-3, ISBN13: 978-0-393-00867-8. Dewey:782.12.

Audience: **g,l,u,f.**

Warrack, John   **ML410.W1 A286 1994**
Richard Wagner: Die Meistersinger von Nürnberg. Richard Wagner (Contribution by). Cloth Text. Cambridge University Press. New York, NY. 1994. 185p. Opera Handbooks Ser. ISBN:0-521-44444-6, ISBN13: 978-0-521-44444-6. Dewey:782.1. LCCN:93-039615.

Audience: **u,f.**

Watson, Derek   **ML410.W1.W38 1981**
Richard Wagner: A Biography. Trade Cloth. Music Sales Corporation. New York, NY. 1981. 384p. ISBN:0-02-872700-2, ISBN13: 978-0-02-872700-4. Dewey:782.1/092/4. LCCN:81-001161.

Audience: **g,l,u,f.**

Weiner, Marc A.   **ML410.W19W23 1997**
Richard Wagner and the Anti-Semetic Imagination. Cloth Text. University of Nebraska Press. Lincoln, NE. 1995. 447p. Texts and Contexts Ser. ISBN:0-8032-4775-3, ISBN13: 978-0-8032-4775-8. Dewey:782.1/092. LCCN:94-012187.

Audience: **u,f.** *Choice, 1995.*

Biographies and Studies of Composers and Performers > W > Waller, Fats

Shipton, Alyn   **ML417.W15S5 2002**
Fats Waller: The Cheerful Little Earful. Ed. 2. Trade Cloth. Continuum International Publishing Group, Ltd. London, 2002. 192p. Bayou Jazz Lives Ser. ISBN:0-8264-5796-7, ISBN13: 978-0-8264-5796-7. Dewey:786.2/165/092 B. LCCN:2001-047404.

Audience: **l,u,f.** *Choice, 2002.*

Biographies and Studies of Composers and Performers > W > Weber, Carl Maria von

Warrack, John   **ML410.W3**
Carl Maria Von Weber. Ed. 2. Trade Cloth. Cambridge University Press. New York, NY. 1976. 411p. ISBN:0-521-21354-1, ISBN13: 978-0-521-21354-7. Dewey:780.92. LCCN:76-012915.

Audience: **u,f.**

Weber, Carl M.   **ML275.4**
Writings on Music. John Warrack (Editor), Martin Cooper (Translator). Trade Cloth. Cambridge University Press. New York, NY. 1981. 413p. ISBN:0-521-22892-1, ISBN13: 978-0-521-22892-3. Dewey:781.743. LCCN:76-012915.

Audience: **u,f.**

Biographies and Studies of Composers and Performers > W > Webern, Anton

Bailey, Kathryn   **ML410.W33 B32 1998**
The Life of Webern. Trade Paper. Cambridge University Press. New York, NY. 1998. 237p. Musical Lives Ser. ISBN:0-521-57566-4, ISBN13: 978-0-521-57566-9. Dewey:780/.92 B. LCCN:97-025751.

Audience: **g,l,u,f.** *Choice, 1998.*

Bailey, Kathryn   **ML410.U33**
The Twelve-Note Music of Anton Webern: Old Forms in a New Language. Arnold Whittall (Contribution by). Trade Paper. Cambridge University Press. New York, NY. 2004. 474p. Music in the Twentieth Century Ser., Vol. 2 ISBN:0-521-54796-2, ISBN13: 978-0-521-54796-3. Dewey:781.2/68092. LCCN:2006-277394.

Audience: **u,f.** *Choice, 1992.*

Forte, Allen   **ML410.W33F67 1998**
The Atonal Music of Anton Webern. Cloth over Boards. Yale University Press. Cumberland, RI. 1999. 416p. Composers of the Twentieth Century Ser. ISBN:0-300-07352-6, ISBN13: 978-0-300-07352-2. Dewey:780/.92. LCCN:97-049645.

Audience: **u,f.** *Choice, 1999.*

Moldenhauer, Hans &   **ML410.W33.M55 1979**
  Moldenhauer, Rosaleen
Anton Von Webern: A Chronicle of His Life and Work. Trade Cloth. Alfred A. Knopf Inc. New York, NY. 1979. 803p. ISBN:0-394-47237-3, ISBN13: 978-0-394-47237-9. Dewey:780/.92/4. LCCN:77-020370.

Audience: **u,f.**

Biographies and Studies of Composers and Performers > W > Weill, Kurt

Brecht, Bertolt   **PT2603.R397**
The Threepenny Opera. Eric Bentley & Desmond Vesey (Translators), Lotte Lenya (Foreword by). Trade Paper. Grove/Atlantic, Inc. New York, NY. 1964. ISBN:0-394-17472-0, ISBN13: 978-0-394-17472-3. Dewey:832/.912.

Audience: **g,l,u,f.**

Farneth, David   ML410.W395F37 1999
Kurt Weill: A Life in Pictures and Documents. Trade Cloth.
Overlook Press, The. New York, NY. 1999. 312p.
ISBN:0-87951-721-2, ISBN13: 978-0-87951-721-2.
Dewey:782.1/092 B. LCCN:99-033577.
> Audience: **g,l,u,f.** *Choice, 2000.*

Hinton, Stephen (Editor)   ML410.W395
Kurt Weill: "The Threepenny Opera". Trade Paper. Cambridge
University Press. New York, NY. 1990. 245p. Cambridge Opera
Handbooks Ser. ISBN:0-521-33888-3, ISBN13:
978-0-521-33888-2. Dewey:780/.92/4. LCCN:91-109557.
> Audience: **u,f.** *Choice, 1991.*

Schebera, Jurgen   ML410.W395S3513 1995
Kurt Weill: An Illustrated Life. Caroline Murphy (Translator).
Cloth over Boards. Yale University Press. Cumberland, RI.
1995. 400p. ISBN:0-300-06055-6, ISBN13: 978-0-300-06055-3.
Dewey:780.9/2. LCCN:94-041444.
> Audience: **l,u,f.** *Choice, 1996.*

Biographies and Studies of Composers and Performers > W > Whiteman, Paul

Berrett, Joshua   ML419.A75B46 2004
Louis Armstrong and Paul Whiteman: Two Kings of Jazz. Cloth
over Boards. Yale University Press. Cumberland, RI. 2004.
256p. ISBN:0-300-10384-0, ISBN13: 978-0-300-10384-7.
Dewey:781.65/092/2 B. LCCN:2004-004217.
> Audience: **u,f.**

Rayno, Don   ML422.W4R38 2003
Paul Whiteman: Pioneer in American Music, Vol. l. William H.
Youngren (Foreword by). Trade Cloth. Scarecrow Press, Inc.
Lanham, MD. 2003. 840p. Studies in Jazz, No. 43
ISBN:0-8108-4579-2, ISBN13: 978-0-8108-4579-4.
Dewey:784.4/8165/092 B. LCCN:2002-012943.
> Audience: **u,f.**

Biographies and Studies of Composers and Performers > W > Williams, Hank

Escott, Colin, et al.   ML420.W55E83 2004
Hank Williams: The Biography. George Merritt & William
MacEwen (Authors). Trade Paper. Little Brown & Company.
New York, NY. 2004. 388p. ISBN:0-316-73497-7, ISBN13:
978-0-316-73497-4. Dewey:782.42/1642/092 B.
LCCN:2003-026510.
> Audience: **g,l,u,f.**

Biographies and Studies of Composers and Performers > W > Williams, Mary Lou

Kernodle, Tammy L.   ML410.W7134K46 2004
Soul on Soul: The Life and Music of Mary Lou Williams. Trade
Cloth. Northeastern University Press. Boston, MA. 2005. 348p.
ISBN:1-55553-606-9, ISBN13: 978-1-55553-606-0.
Dewey:786.2/165/092 B. LCCN:2003-021871.
> Audience: **l,u,f.** *Choice, 2004.*

Biographies and Studies of Composers and Performers > W > Wolf, Hugo

Youens, Susan   ML410.W8.Y7 1992
Hugo Wolf: The Vocal Music. Cloth Text. Princeton University
Press. Princeton, NJ. 1992. 412p. ISBN:0-691-09145-5, ISBN13:
978-0-691-09145-7. Dewey:782.42168/092. LCCN:91-045446.
> Audience: **u,f.** *Choice, 1993.*

Biographies and Studies of Composers and Performers > XYZ > Xenakis, Iannis

Harley, James   ML410.X45H37 2004
Xenakis: His Life in Music. Paper over Boards. Routledge. New
York, NY. 2004. 296p. ISBN:0-415-97145-4, ISBN13:
978-0-415-97145-4. Dewey:780/.92 B. LCCN:2004-002283.
> Audience: **u,f.**

Xenakis, Iannis   ML3800.X4 1991
Formalized Music: Thought and Mathematics in Composition.
Library Binding. Pendragon Press. Hillsdale, NY. 1992. 402p.
Harmonologia Ser., No. 6 ISBN:0-945193-24-6, ISBN13:
978-0-945193-24-1. Dewey:781.3. LCCN:90-041022.
> Audience: **u,f.** *Choice, 1992.*

Biographies and Studies of Composers and Performers > XYZ > Young, La Monte

Duckworth, William & Fleming, Richard (Editors)   ML390
Sound and Light: La Monte Young Marian Zazeela. Trade
Cloth. Bucknell University Press. Cranbury, NJ. 1997. 232p.
Review Ser., Vol. 40, No. 1 ISBN:0-8387-5346-9, ISBN13:
978-0-8387-5346-0. Dewey:780.922. LCCN:55-058217.
> Audience: **u,f.**

Biographies and Studies of Composers and Performers > XYZ > Young, Lester

Porter, Lewis　　　　　　　**ML419.Y7P7 2005**
Lester Young. Trade Paper, Perfect. University of Michigan Press. Chicago, IL. 2005. 176p. Jazz Perspectives Ser. ISBN:0-472-08922-6, ISBN13: 978-0-472-08922-2. Dewey:788.7/165/092 B. LCCN:2004-065835.

Audience: **l,u,f.**　*Choice, 1986.*

Porter, Lewis (Editor)　　　　**ML419.Y7L47 1991**
A Lester Young Reader. Trade Cloth. Smithsonian Institution Press. Washington, DC. 1991. 344p. Smithsonian Readers in American Music Ser. ISBN:1-56098-064-8, ISBN13: 978-1-56098-064-3. Dewey:788.7/165/092 B. LCCN:90-024922.

Audience: **l,u,f.**　*Choice, 1992.*

Biographies and Studies of Composers and Performers > XYZ > Zappa, Frank

Kostelanetz, Richard　　　　　**ML420.P96**
The Frank Zappa Companion: Four Decades of Commentary. Trade Paper. Music Sales Corporation. New York, NY. 1997. 300p. Companion Ser. ISBN:0-8256-7181-7, ISBN13: 978-0-8256-7181-4. Dewey:782.4/2/166/092. LCCN:96-041352.

Audience: **g,l,u,f.**

Miles, Barry　　　　　　**ML410.Z285.M49 2004**
Zappa: A Biography. Trade Cloth. Grove/Atlantic, Inc. New York, NY. 2004. 464p. ISBN:0-8021-1783-X, ISBN13: 978-0-8021-1783-0. Dewey:782.42166/092 B. LCCN:2004-051805.

Audience: **l,u,f.**

Zappa, Frank　　　　　　　　**ML420.P96**
Real Frank Zappa Book. Trade Paper. Simon & Schuster. New York, NY. 1990. 352p. ISBN:0-671-70572-5, ISBN13: 978-0-671-70572-5. Dewey:784.5/4/00924 B.

Audience: **l,u,f.**

Music Theory and Composition

Agawu, V. K.　　　　　　　**ML3838.A317 1991**
Playing with Signs. Cloth Text. Princeton University Press. Princeton, NJ. 1991. 168p. ISBN:0-691-09138-2, ISBN13: 978-0-691-09138-9. Dewey:781.6/8111. LCCN:90-008569.

Audience: **u,f.**

Aldwell, Edward &　　　　　　**MT50**
　Schachter, Carl
Harmony and Voice Leading. Ed. 3. Cloth Text. Thomson Wadsworth. Belmont, CA. 2002. 672p. ISBN:0-15-506242-5, ISBN13: 978-0-15-506242-9. Dewey:781.2/5. LCCN:2002-537209.

Audience: **l,u,f.**

Ayotte, Benjamin　　　　　　**ML134.S25A95 2003**
Heinrich Schenker: A Guide to Research. Paper over Boards. Routledge. New York, NY. 2003. 368p. Routledge Music Bibliographies Ser. ISBN:0-415-94071-0, ISBN13: 978-0-415-94071-9. Dewey:016.78/092. LCCN:2003-008616.

Audience: **u,f.**

Barker, Paul　　　　　　　　　**MT67**
Composing for Voice: A Guide for Composers, Singers, and Teachers. Paper over Boards. Routledge. New York, NY. 2003. 208p. ISBN:0-415-94186-5, ISBN13: 978-0-415-94186-0. Dewey:783/.03. LCCN:2004-556867.

Audience: **l,u,f.**

Berry, Wallace　　　　　　　**MT58.B34 1986**
Form in Music. Ed. 2. Cloth Text. Prentice Hall PTR. Upper Saddle River, NJ. 1985. 464p. ISBN:0-13-329285-1, ISBN13: 978-0-13-329285-5. Dewey:781/.5. LCCN:85-003374.

Audience: **l,u,f.** 𝐁

Berry, Wallace　　　　　　**MT6.B465M9 1989**
Musical Structure and Performance. Cloth over Boards. Yale University Press. Cumberland, RI. 1989. 248p. ISBN:0-300-04327-9, ISBN13: 978-0-300-04327-3. Dewey:781. LCCN:97-006468.

Audience: **u,f.**　*Choice, 1990.*

Berry, Wallace　　　　　　　**MT6.B465S8 1987**
Structural Functions in Music. Trade Paper. Dover Publications, Inc. Mineola, NY. 1987. 480p. ISBN:0-486-25384-8, ISBN13: 978-0-486-25384-8. Dewey:781. LCCN:86-031912.

Audience: **u,f.**

Cadwallader, Allen &　　　　**MT6.C12A53 1998**
　Gagne, David
Analysis of Tonal Music: A Schenkerian Approach. Cloth Text. Oxford University Press, Inc. New York, NY. 1998. 432p. ISBN:0-19-510232-0, ISBN13: 978-0-19-510232-1. Dewey:781. LCCN:97-005752.

Audience: **u,f.**

Carter, Elliott　　　　　　　　**MT50**
Harmony Book. Nicholas Hopkins & J. F. Link (Arranged by). Trade Cloth. Carl Fischer LLC. New York, NY. 2002. ISBN:0-8258-4594-7, ISBN13: 978-0-8258-4594-9. Dewey:781.3.

Audience: **u,f.**

Christensen, Thomas　　　　　**ML3800 .C165 2001**
　(Editor)
The Cambridge History of Western Music Theory. Trade Paper. Cambridge University Press. New York, NY. 2006. 1024p. The Cambridge History of Music Ser. ISBN:0-521-68698-9, ISBN13: 978-0-521-68698-3. Dewey:781.09.

Audience: **u,f.**

Clendinning, Jane Piper　　　　**MT6.C57 2004**
Musician's Guide to Theory and Analysis. Trade Cloth. W. W. Norton & Company, Inc. New York, NY. 2004. xxxi, 759p. ISBN:0-393-97652-1, ISBN13: 978-0-393-97652-6. Dewey:781. LCCN:2004-049508.

Audience: **l,u,f.**

Cogan, Robert & Escot, Pozzi MT6.C63
Sonic Design: The Nature of Sound and Music. Ed. 4. Trade Paper. Publication Contact International. Cambridge, MA. 1985. 350p. ISBN:0-9634500-0-X, ISBN13: 978-0-9634500-0-5. Dewey:781.
Audience: l,u,f. *B*

Cone, Edward T. MT58
Musical Form and Musical Performance. Trade Paper. W. W. Norton & Company, Inc. New York, NY. 1968. 103p. ISBN:0-393-09767-6, ISBN13: 978-0-393-09767-2. Dewey:781.5. LCCN:68-011157.
Audience: l,u,f. *B*

Cook, Nicholas MT6.C775G8 1987
A Guide to Musical Analysis. Trade Cloth. George Braziller Inc. New York, NY. 1987. 377p. ISBN:0-8076-1172-7, ISBN13: 978-0-8076-1172-2. Dewey:781. LCCN:87-000727.
Audience: l,u,f. *Choice, 1987.*

Cooper, Grosvenor & Meyer, Leonard B. MT42
The Rhythmic Structure of Music. Trade Paper. University of Chicago Press. Chicago, IL. 1963. 221p. ISBN:0-226-11522-4, ISBN13: 978-0-226-11522-1. Dewey:781.62. LCCN:60-014068.
Audience: l,u,f. *B*

Cope, David MT40.C74 1997
Techniques of the Contemporary Composer. Paper Text. Thomson Wadsworth. Belmont, CA. 1997. 272p. ISBN:0-02-864737-8, ISBN13: 978-0-02-864737-1. Dewey:781.3. LCCN:97-005415.
Audience: l,u,f.

Cowell, Henry MT6.C7895 N4 1996
New Musical Resources. David Nicholls (Notes by). Cloth Text. Cambridge University Press. New York, NY. 1996. 195p. ISBN:0-521-49651-9, ISBN13: 978-0-521-49651-3. Dewey:784.1. LCCN:95-031529.
Audience: u,f.

Damschroder, David & Williams, David R. ML128.T5D27 1990
Music Theory from Zarlino to Schenker: A Bibliography and Guide. Library Binding. Pendragon Press. Hillsdale, NY. 1991. 550p. Harmonologia Ser., No. 4 ISBN:0-918728-99-1, ISBN13: 978-0-918728-99-9. Dewey:016.781. LCCN:90-006952.
Audience: u,f.

Duckworth, William MT7
A Creative Approach to Music Fundamentals. Ed. 9. Paper Text, CD-ROM. Thomson Learning. Independence, KY. 2006. 384p. ISBN:0-495-09093-X, ISBN13: 978-0-495-09093-9. Dewey:781. LCCN:2005-928009.
Audience: g,l,u,f.

Forte, Allan & Gilbert, Steve MT6
Introduction to Schenkerian Analysis: Form and Content in

Tonal Music. Trade Paper. W. W. Norton & Company, Inc. New York, NY. 1982. 350p. ISBN:0-393-95192-8, ISBN13: 978-0-393-95192-9. Dewey:781/.071. LCCN:81-022502.
Audience: l,u,f. *B*

Forte, Allen ML3811
The Structure of Atonal Music. Trade Paper. Yale University Press. Cumberland, RI. 1977. 208p. ISBN:0-300-02120-8, ISBN13: 978-0-300-02120-2. Dewey:781/.22. LCCN:72-091295.
Audience: u,f. *B*

Forte, Allen MT50.F713.T7 1979
Tonal Harmony. Ed. 3. Cloth Text. Holt, Rinehart & Winston. Austin, TX. 1979. 564p. ISBN:0-03-020756-8, ISBN13: 978-0-03-020756-3. Dewey:781.3. LCCN:78-012229.
Audience: l,u,f. *B*

Frisch, Walter ML410.M9
Brahms and the Principle of Developing Variation. Trade Paper. University of California Press. Berkeley, CA. 1984. 232p. California Studies in 19th Century Music, No. 2 ISBN:0-520-06958-7, ISBN13: 978-0-520-06958-9. Dewey:780.9/2. LCCN:82-013675.
Audience: u,f.

Fux, Johann J. MT55
Study of Counterpoint. Alfred Mann (Editor, Translator). Trade Paper. W. W. Norton & Company, Inc. New York, NY. 1965. 156p. ISBN:0-393-00277-2, ISBN13: 978-0-393-00277-5. Dewey:781.2/86.
Audience: l,u,f. *B*

Gauldin, Robert MT50.G286 2004
Harmonic Practice in Tonal Music. Ed. 2. Digital, Other. W. W. Norton & Company, Inc. New York, NY. 2004. xxxi, 771p. ISBN:0-393-10360-9, ISBN13: 978-0-393-10360-1. Dewey:781.2/5.
Audience: l,u,f.

Gedalge, Andre MT0059.G4
Treatise on the Fugue. Ferdinand Davis (Translator), Darius Milhaud (Foreword by). Trade Cloth. Books on Demand. Ann Arbor, MI. 442p. ISBN:0-8357-9744-9, ISBN13: 978-0-8357-9744-3. Dewey:781.42. LCCN:65-011241.
Audience: u,f. *B*

Harrison, Daniel ML444.H376 1994
Harmonic Function in Chromatic Music: A Renewed Dualist Theory and an Account of Its Precedents. Trade Cloth. University of Chicago Press. Chicago, IL. 1994. 336p. ISBN:0-226-31808-7, ISBN13: 978-0-226-31808-0. Dewey:781.25. LCCN:93-011540.
Audience: u,f.

Hasty, Christopher ML3850.H37 1997
Meter As Rhythm. Trade Cloth. Oxford University Press, Inc. New York, NY. 1997. 328p. ISBN:0-19-510066-2, ISBN13: 978-0-19-510066-2. Dewey:781.2/2. LCCN:96-024694.
Audience: u,f. *Choice, 1998.*

Formats: Web: ☐ Ebook: ⓔ CD/DVD-ROM: 🕮 BCL3: *B*

Hindemith, Paul   **MT40.H5**
The Craft of Musical Composition. Mendel, Arthur (Translator); Ortmann, Otto (Translator). New York : Schott Music Corp. : Distributor for U.S.A., Canada and Mexico, European American Music Distributors Corp. 1980. ISBN:0-901938-41-6, ISBN13: 978-0-901938-41-1.
Audience: **u,f.**

Horsley, Imogene   **ML448**
Fugue: History and Practice. New York: Free Press; London: Collier-Macmillan. 1966.
Audience: **u,f.**

Jeppesen, Knud   **MT55**
Counterpoint: The Polyphonic Vocal Style of the 16th Century. Trade Paper. Dover Publications, Inc. Mineola, NY. 1992. 320p. ISBN:0-486-27036-X, ISBN13: 978-0-486-27036-4. Dewey:781.286. LCCN:91-040595.
Audience: **l,u,f.** *B*

Jeppesen, Knud   **ML3003.J362 2005**
The Style of Palestrina and the Dissonance. Trade Paper. Dover Publications, Inc. Mineola, NY. 2005. 320p. ISBN:0-486-44268-3, ISBN13: 978-0-486-44268-6. Dewey:782.2/2/092. LCCN:2004-065738.
Audience: **u,f.**

Kennan, Kent   **MT55.K53 1999**
Counterpoint. Ed. 4. Trade Cloth. Prentice Hall PTR. Upper Saddle River, NJ. 1998. 292p. ISBN:0-13-080746-X, ISBN13: 978-0-13-080746-5. Dewey:781.2/86. LCCN:98-022174.
Audience: **l,u,f.** *B*

Kinderman, William & Krebs, Harald (Editors)   **ML3811.S43 1996**
The Second Practice of Nineteenth Century Tonality. Cloth Text. University of Nebraska Press. Lincoln, NE. 1996. 281p. ISBN:0-8032-2724-8, ISBN13: 978-0-8032-2724-8. Dewey:781.2/6/09034. LCCN:95-016160.
Audience: **u,f.**

Kopp, David   **MT50**
Chromatic Transformations in Nineteenth-Century Music. Ian Bent (Contribution by). Trade Paper. Cambridge University Press. New York, NY. 2006. 289p. Cambridge Studies in Music Theory and Analysis Ser. ISBN:0-521-02849-3, ISBN13: 978-0-521-02849-3. Dewey:781.2/52.
Audience: **u,f.**

Kostka, Stefan   **MT40.K8 2006**
Materials and Techniques of 20th Century Music. Ed. 3. Cloth Text. Prentice Hall PTR. Upper Saddle River, NJ. 2005. 368p. ISBN:0-13-193080-X, ISBN13: 978-0-13-193080-3. Dewey:781.3/09/04. LCCN:2005-047615.
Audience: **l,u,f.**

Kostka, Stefan   **MT50.K85**
Tonal Harmony. Ed. 5. Mixed Media, Trade Paper, CD-ROM. McGraw-Hill Higher Education. Burr Ridge, IL. 2003. ISBN:0-07-291896-9, ISBN13: 978-0-07-291896-0. Dewey:780.
Audience: **l,u,f.**

Kraft, Leo   **MT6.K877G72 1990**
Gradus II: The Second Year and After. Ed. 2. Trade Paper. W. W. Norton & Company, Inc. New York, NY. 1990. 534p. ISBN:0-393-95626-1, ISBN13: 978-0-393-95626-9. Dewey:781. LCCN:89-034460.
Audience: **l,u,f.**

Kramer, Jonathan D.   **ML3850.K72 1988**
The Time of Music: New Meanings, New Temporalities, New Listening Strategies. Trade Cloth. Thomson Wadsworth. Belmont, CA. 1988. 493p. ISBN:0-02-872590-5, ISBN13: 978-0-02-872590-1. Dewey:781. LCCN:88-004505.
Audience: **u,f.** *Choice, 1989.*

LaRue, Jan   **MT6.L146 G8 1992**
Guidelines for Style Analysis. Ed. 2. Trade Cloth. Harmonie Park Press. Sterling Heights, MI. 1992. xviii, 286p. Detroit Monographs in Musicology, No. 12 ISBN:0-89990-062-3, ISBN13: 978-0-89990-062-9. Dewey:781. LCCN:92-025439.
Audience: **l,u,f.**

Lerdahl, Fred & Jackendoff, Ray S.   **MT7**
A Generative Theory of Tonal Music. Trade Paper. MIT Press. Cambridge, MA. 1996. 368p. ISBN:0-262-62107-X, ISBN13: 978-0-262-62107-6. Dewey:781. LCCN:82-017104.
Audience: **u,f.** *B*

Lester, Joel   **MT6**
Analytical Approaches to 20th Century Music. Trade Cloth. W. W. Norton & Company, Inc. New York, NY. 1989. 320p. ISBN:0-393-95762-4, ISBN13: 978-0-393-95762-4. Dewey:781.
Audience: **u,f.**

Lester, Joel   **ML430**
Compositional Theory in the 18th Century. Trade Paper. Harvard University Press. Cambridge, MA. 1994. 368p. ISBN:0-674-15523-8, ISBN13: 978-0-674-15523-7. Dewey:781.
Audience: **u,f.**

Lester, Joel   **MT42.L48 1986**
The Rhythms of Tonal Music. Cloth Text. Southern Illinois University Press. Carbondale, IL. 1986. 300p. ISBN:0-8093-1282-4, ISBN13: 978-0-8093-1282-5. Dewey:781.6/2. LCCN:85-022293.
Audience: **u,f.** *Choice, 1987.*

Lewin, David   **ML3809.L39 1987**
Generalized Musical Intervals and Their Transformations. Trade Cloth. Yale University Press. Cumberland, RI. 1987. 288p. ISBN:0-300-03493-8, ISBN13: 978-0-300-03493-6. Dewey:781/.22. LCCN:86-029538.
Audience: **u,f.**

Mann, Alfred   **MT55**
The Study of Fugue. Paper Text. Textbook Publishers. Temecula, CA. 2003. x, 341p. ISBN:0-7581-4303-6, ISBN13: 978-0-7581-4303-7. Dewey:781.4/2.
Audience: **l,u,f.**

Messiaen, Oliver   **MT6**
The Technique of My Musical Language. Library Binding.
Reprint Services Company. Temecula, CA. 1987.
ISBN:0-685-14827-0, ISBN13: 978-0-685-14827-3. Dewey:781.
Audience: **u,f.**

Morris, Reginald O.   **MT224.M8**
Figured Harmony at the Keyboard, Pt. 1. Trade Paper. Oxford
University Press, Inc. New York, NY. 1968. 64p.
ISBN:0-19-321471-7, ISBN13: 978-0-19-321471-2.
Dewey:786.1/25/14.
Audience: **l,u,f.**

Morris, Reginald O.   **MT224.M8**
Figured Harmony at the Keyboard, Pt. 2. Trade Paper. Oxford
University Press, Inc. New York, NY. 1968. 32p.
ISBN:0-19-321472-5, ISBN13: 978-0-19-321472-9.
Dewey:786.1/25/14.
Audience: **l,u,f.**

Morris, Robert D.   **MT46.M67 1987**
Composition with Pitch-Classes: A Theory of Compositional
Design. Cloth over Boards. Yale University Press. Cumberland,
RI. 1987. 416p. ISBN:0-300-03684-1, ISBN13:
978-0-300-03684-8. Dewey:781.6/1. LCCN:87-015955.
Audience: **u,f.**

Nattiez, Jean-Jacques   **ML3797.N3713 1990**
Music and Discourse: Toward a Semiology of Music. Carolyn
Abbate (Translator). Trade Paper. Princeton University Press.
Princeton, NJ. 1990. 272p. ISBN:0-691-02714-5, ISBN13:
978-0-691-02714-2. Dewey:781/.1. LCCN:90-037225.
Audience: **u,f.**

Neumeyer, David, et al.   **MT6.N248**
A Guide to Schenkerian Analysis. Tepping, Susan (Author).
Englewood Cliffs, N.J.: Prentice Hall. 1992.
ISBN:0-13-497215-5, ISBN13: 978-0-13-497215-2.
Audience: **l,u,f.**

Perle, George   **MT40.P45 1991**
Serial Composition and Atonality: An Introduction to the Music
of Schoenberg, Berg, and Webern. Ed. 6. Trade Cloth.
University of California Press. Berkeley, CA. 1991. 178p.
ISBN:0-520-07430-0, ISBN13: 978-0-520-07430-9.
Dewey:781.2/67. LCCN:90-050902.
Audience: **u,f.** 𝐵

Persichetti, Vincent   **MT50.P455**
Twentieth-Century Harmony: Creative Aspects and Practice.
W.W. Norton. 1961. ISBN:0-393-09539-8, ISBN13:
978-0-393-09539-5.
Audience: **l,u,f.**

Piston, Walter   **MT55**
Counterpoint. Trade Cloth. W. W. Norton & Company, Inc. New
York, NY. 1947. ISBN:0-393-09728-5, ISBN13:
978-0-393-09728-3. Dewey:781.4.
Audience: **l,u,f.** 𝐵

Piston, Walter, et al.   **MT50.P665 1987**
Harmony. Ed. 5. Mark DeVoto & Arthur Jannery (Authors).
Cloth Text. W. W. Norton & Company, Inc. New York, NY.
1987. 500p. ISBN:0-393-95480-3, ISBN13: 978-0-393-95480-7.
Dewey:781.3. LCCN:86-023901.
Audience: **l,u,f.** 𝐵

Rahn, John   **MT40**
Basic Atonal Theory. Trade Cloth. Thomson Wadsworth.
Belmont, CA. 1987. 168p. ISBN:0-02-873160-3, ISBN13:
978-0-02-873160-5. Dewey:781.3.
Audience: **u,f.**

Rameau, Jean Philippe   **MT50**
A Treatise on Harmony. Philip Gossett (Translator). Trade Paper.
Dover Publications, Inc. Mineola, NY. 1971. 491p.
ISBN:0-486-22461-9, ISBN13: 978-0-486-22461-9.
Dewey:781.3. LCCN:79-122776.
Audience: **u,f.**

Rastall, Richard   **ML431.R27 1982**
The Notation of Western Music: An Introduction. Trade Cloth.
St. Martin's Press. Gordonville, VA. 1983. 320p.
ISBN:0-312-57963-2, ISBN13: 978-0-312-57963-0.
Dewey:781/.24. LCCN:83-009546.
Audience: **g,l,u,f.** 𝐵

Reti, Rudolph   **MT40**
The Thematic Process in Music. Paper Text. Textbook
Publishers. Temecula, CA. 2003. x, 362p. ISBN:0-7581-9107-3,
ISBN13: 978-0-7581-9107-6. Dewey:781.61.
Audience: **u,f.** 𝐵

Rimsky-Korsakov, Nikolay   **MT50**
Practical Manual of Harmony. Achron, Joseph (Translator);
Hopkins, Nicholas (Editor). C. Fischer. 2005.
ISBN:0-8258-5699-X, ISBN13: 978-0-8258-5699-0.
Audience: **u,f.**

Rothstein, William   **MT42.R84 1989**
Phrase Rhythm in Tonal Music. Trade Cloth. Thomson Gale.
Farmington Hills, MI. 1990. 349p. ISBN:0-02-872191-8,
ISBN13: 978-0-02-872191-0. Dewey:781.6/2. LCCN:88-039325.
Audience: **u,f.**

Russolo, Luigi   **ML3877.R8713 1986**
The Art of Noises. Barclay Brown (Translator). Library Binding.
Pendragon Press. Hillsdale, NY. 1987. 87p. Monographs in
Musicology, No. 6 ISBN:0-918728-57-6, ISBN13:
978-0-918728-57-9. Dewey:789.9/8. LCCN:85-028413.
Audience: **u,f.**

Salzer, Felix   **MT50**
Structural Hearing: Tonal Coherence in Music. Leopold Manners
(Foreword by). Trade Paper. Dover Publications, Inc. Mineola,
NY. 1962. 667p. ISBN:0-486-22275-6, ISBN13:
978-0-486-22275-2. Dewey:781.2/5.
Audience: **u,f.** 𝐵

Salzer, Felix & Schachter, Carl   MT55.S217 1989
Counterpoint in Composition: The Study of Voice Leading.
Trade Paper. Columbia University Press. New York, NY. 1989.
477p. ISBN:0-231-07039-X, ISBN13: 978-0-231-07039-3.
Dewey:781.2/86. LCCN:89-007258.

Audience: **u,f.**

Samson, Jim   ML3809
Music in Transition: A Study of Tonal Expansion and Atonality,
1900-1920. Paper Text. Oxford University Press, Inc. New York,
NY. 1995. 256p. ISBN:0-460-86150-6, ISBN13:
978-0-460-86150-2. Dewey:781/.22.

Audience: **u,f.**

Schenker, Heinrich   MT40
Free Composition: New Musical Theories and Fantasies = Der
freie Satz. Oster, Ernst (Translator). Pendragon Press. 2001.
Distinguished Reprints Ser.; Vol. 3; No. 2 ISBN:1-57647-074-1,
ISBN13: 978-1-57647-074-9.

Audience: **u,f.**

Schenker, Heinrich   MT6.S2874 M413 1994
Schenker: The Masterwork in Music, Vol. 2. William Drabkin
(Editor). Trade Cloth. Cambridge University Press. New York,
NY. 1996. 149p. Studies in Music Theory and Analysis, No. 8
ISBN:0-521-45542-1, ISBN13: 978-0-521-45542-8. Dewey:781.
LCCN:93-033355.

Audience: **u,f.**

Schenker, Heinrich   MT7
Schenker: The Masterwork in Music:1930. William Drabkin
(Editor). Trade Cloth. Cambridge University Press. New York,
NY. 1997. 135p. Studies in Music Theory and Analysis, No. 9
ISBN:0-521-45543-X, ISBN13: 978-0-521-45543-5. Dewey:781.

Audience: **u,f.**

Schenker, Heinrich   MT6.S2874T6513 2002
Der Tonwille: Pamphlets in Witness of the Immutable Laws of
Music: Issues 1-5 (1921-1923). William Drabkin (Editor). Trade
Cloth. Oxford University Press, Inc. New York, NY. 2004. 252p.
ISBN:0-19-512237-2, ISBN13: 978-0-19-512237-4. Dewey:781.
LCCN:2002-019636.

Audience: **u,f.**

Schenker, Heinrich   MT6.S2874T6513 2004
Der Tonwille: Pamphlets in Witness of the Immutable Laws of
Music. William Drabkin (Editor). Trade Cloth. Oxford
University Press, Inc. New York, NY. 2005. 192p.
ISBN:0-19-517518-2, ISBN13: 978-0-19-517518-9. Dewey:781.
LCCN:2002-019636.

Audience: **u,f.**

Schenker, Heinrich   MT6.S2874M413 1994
The Masterwork in Music: A Yearbook (1925). William Drabkin
(Editor), Ian D. Bent (Translator, Foreword by). Trade Cloth.
Cambridge University Press. New York, NY. 1994. 147p.
Studies in Music Theory and Analysis, No. 4
ISBN:0-521-45541-3, ISBN13: 978-0-521-45541-1. Dewey:781.
LCCN:93-003355.

Audience: **u,f.**

Schenker, Heinrich   MT40
Harmony. Oswald Jonas (Editor), Elisabeth M. Borgese
(Translator). Trade Paper. University of Chicago Press. Chicago,
IL. 1980. 394p. ISBN:0-226-73734-9, ISBN13:
978-0-226-73734-8. Dewey:781.3. LCCN:54-011213.

Audience: **u,f.** *B*

Schenker, Heinrich   MT55
Counterpoint: A Translation of Kontrapunkt. John Rothgeb
(Editor, Translator), Jurgen Thym (Translator). Trade Cloth.
Musicalia Press. Ann Arbor, MI. 2001. 396p.
ISBN:0-9678099-1-6, ISBN13: 978-0-9678099-1-5.
Dewey:781.286.

Audience: **u,f.**

Schenker, Heinrich   MT55
Counterpoint: A Translation of Kontrapunkt. John Rothgeb
(Editor, Translator), Jurgen Thym (Translator). Trade Cloth.
Musicalia Press. Ann Arbor, MI. 2001. 306p.
ISBN:0-9678099-2-4, ISBN13: 978-0-9678099-2-2.
Dewey:781.286.

Audience: **u,f.**

Schillinger, Joseph   MT40 .S315 1977
The Schillinger System of Musical Compsition. Paper Text. Da
Capo Press, Inc. Cambridge, MA. 1978. 1674p.
ISBN:0-306-77552-2, ISBN13: 978-0-306-77552-9.
Dewey:781.6/1. LCCN:77-021709.

Audience: **u,f.**

Schoenberg, Arnold   MT40
Theory of Harmony. Roy E. Carter (Translator). Trade Paper.
University of California Press. Berkeley, CA. 1983. California
Library Reprint Ser. ISBN:0-520-04944-6, ISBN13:
978-0-520-04944-4. Dewey:781.3.

Audience: **u,f.** *B*

Schoenberg, Arnold   MT50
Structural Function of Harmony. Leonard Stein (Editor). Trade
Cloth. W. W. Norton & Company, Inc. New York, NY. 1969.
ISBN:0-393-00478-3, ISBN13: 978-0-393-00478-6.
Dewey:781.2/5.

Audience: **u,f.**

Schoenberg, Arnold   MT40
Fundamentals of Musical Composition. Gerald Strang &
Leonard Stein (Editors). Trade Paper. Faber & Faber, Inc. New
York, NY. 1982. 240p. ISBN:0-571-09276-4, ISBN13:
978-0-571-09276-5. Dewey:781.6/1.

Audience: **u,f.**

Simoni, Mary   ML1380.A53 2005
Analytical Methods of Electroacoustic Music. Cloth Text.
Routledge. New York, NY. 2005. 312p. Studies on New Music
Research ISBN:0-415-97629-4, ISBN13: 978-0-415-97629-9.
Dewey:781.2. LCCN:2005-014484.

Audience: **u,f.**

Slonimsky, Nicolas   MT45
Thesaurus of Scales and Melodic Patterns. Trade Paper. Music

Sales Corporation. New York, NY. 1997. 256p.
ISBN:0-8256-1449-X, ISBN13: 978-0-8256-1449-1.
Dewey:781.246.

Audience: **u,f.**

Steblin, Rita   ML3838.S8 2002
A History of Key Characteristics in the 18th and Early 19th
Centuries. Ed. 2. Trade Cloth. University of Rochester Press.
Rochester, NY. 2005. 420p. ISBN:1-58046-041-0, ISBN13:
978-1-58046-041-5. Dewey:781.1/1/09033. LCCN:2002-020679.

Audience: **u,f.**

Straus, Joseph Nathan   MT6.S788E44 2003
Elements of Music. Trade Paper. Prentice Hall PTR. Upper
Saddle River, NJ. 2002. 446p. ISBN:0-13-034341-2, ISBN13:
978-0-13-034341-3. Dewey:781.2. LCCN:2002-025225.

Audience: **l,u,f.**

Straus, Joseph Nathan   MT40.S96 2005
Introduction to Post-Tonal Theory. Ed. 3. Cloth Text. Prentice
Hall PTR. Upper Saddle River, NJ. 2004. 288p.
ISBN:0-13-189890-6, ISBN13: 978-0-13-189890-5.
Dewey:781.2/67. LCCN:2004-050370.

Audience: **l,u,f.**

Tchaikovsky, Peter Ilyitch   MT50
Guide to the Practical Study of Harmony. Trade Paper, Perfect.
Dover Publications, Inc. Mineola, NY. 2005. 137p.
ISBN:0-486-44272-1, ISBN13: 978-0-486-44272-3.
Dewey:781.3.

Audience: **u,f.**

Thomson, Virgil   ML1406.T5 1989
Music with Words: A Composer's View. Cloth over Boards. Yale
University Press. Cumberland, RI. 1989. 112p.
ISBN:0-300-04505-0, ISBN13: 978-0-300-04505-5.
Dewey:784/.028. LCCN:89-030709.

Audience: **u,f.** *Choice, 1989.*

Vander Weg, etval.   ML128.T9
Serial Music and Serialism: A Research and Information Guide.
John Dean (Author). New York; London: Routledge. 2001.
ISBN:0-8153-3528-8, ISBN13: 978-0-8153-3528-3.

Audience: **u,f.**

Wittlich, Gary E. & Martin,   MT224.W58 1989
Deborah S.
Tonal Harmony at the Keyboard. Trade Cloth. Thomson Gale.
Farmington Hills, MI. 1988. 291p. ISBN:0-02-870130-5,
ISBN13: 978-0-02-870130-1. Dewey:786.1/01.
LCCN:88-004105.

Audience: **l,u,f.**

Xenakis, Iannis   ML3800.X4 1991
Formalized Music: Thought and Mathematics in Composition.
Library Binding. Pendragon Press. Hillsdale, NY. 1992. 402p.
Harmonologia Ser., No. 6 ISBN:0-945193-24-6, ISBN13:
978-0-945193-24-1. Dewey:781.3. LCCN:90-041022.

Audience: **u,f.** *Choice, 1992.*

Yasser, Joseph   ML3811.Y2 T4 1975
Theory of Evolving Tonality. Paper Text. Da Capo Press, Inc.
Cambridge, MA. 1975. x, 381p. Music Reprint Ser.
ISBN:0-306-70729-2, ISBN13: 978-0-306-70729-2.
Dewey:781/.22. LCCN:74-034376.

Audience: **u,f.** *B*

Yellin, Victor F.   ML444.Y45 1998
The Omnibus Idea. Trade Cloth. Harmonie Park Press. Sterling
Heights, MI. 1997. Detroit Monographs in Musicology/Studies
in Music, Vol. 22 ISBN:0-89990-081-X, ISBN13:
978-0-89990-081-0. Dewey:781.2/5. LCCN:97-045589.

Audience: **u,f.**

Physics of Music, Acoustics, and Tuning

Barbour, James Murray   ML3809.B234 2004
Tuning and Temperament: A Historical Survey. Trade Paper.
Dover Publications, Inc. Mineola, NY. 2004. 240p.
ISBN:0-486-43406-0, ISBN13: 978-0-486-43406-3.
Dewey:784.192/8. LCCN:2004-043835.

Audience: **u,f.**

Benade, Arthur H.   ML3805
Horns, Strings and Harmony. Trade Paper. Dover Publications,
Inc. Mineola, NY. 1992. 288p. ISBN:0-486-27331-8, ISBN13:
978-0-486-27331-0. Dewey:781.23. LCCN:92-025381.

Audience: **g,l,u,f.**

Cook, Perry R.   BF251
Music, Cognition, and Computerized Sound: An Introduction to
Psychoacoustics. Trade Paper, Mixed Media, Compact Disc.
MIT Press. Cambridge, MA. 2001. 384p. ISBN:0-262-53190-9,
ISBN13: 978-0-262-53190-0. Dewey:152.15. LCCN:98-016783.

Audience: **u,f.**

Fauvel, John (Editor), et al.   ML3800
Music and Mathematics: From Pythagoras to Fractals. Raymond
Flood & Robin Wilson (Editors). Trade Cloth. Oxford
University Press, Inc. New York, NY. 2003. 200p.
ISBN:0-19-851187-6, ISBN13: 978-0-19-851187-8.
Dewey:781.2. LCCN:2004-297544.

Audience: **g,l,u,f.** *Choice, 2004.*

Gann, Kyle
☐ Just Intonation Explained.
http://www.kylegann.com/tuning.html
Kyle Gann.

Audience: **u,f.**

Hall, Donald E.   ML3805.H153 2002
Musical Acoustics. Ed. 3. Cloth Text. Brooks/Cole. Pacific
Grove, CA. 2001. 496p. Physics Ser. ISBN:0-534-37728-9,
ISBN13: 978-0-534-37728-1. Dewey:781.2.
LCCN:2001-037422.

Audience: **g,l,u,f.**

Haynes, Bruce   ML3807.H39 2002
A History of Performing Pitch: The Story of "A". Trade Cloth.
Scarecrow Press, Inc. Lanham, MD. 2002. 632p.
ISBN:0-8108-4185-1, ISBN13: 978-0-8108-4185-7.
Dewey:781.2/32. LCCN:2002-075248.
                                        Audience: **u,f.**

Helmholtz, Hermann   ML3800
On the Sensations of Tone. Ed. 2. Henry Margenau
(Introduction by). Trade Paper. Dover Publications, Inc.
Mineola, NY. 1954. 576p. ISBN:0-486-60753-4, ISBN13:
978-0-486-60753-5. Dewey:781.1.
                                        Audience: **u,f.**

Howard, David & Angus,   ML3805.H77 2001
  James
Acoustics and Psychoacoustics. Ed. 2. Paper Text. Elsevier
Science & Technology Books. Saint Louis, MO. 2001. 385p.
Music Technology Ser. ISBN:0-240-51609-5, ISBN13:
978-0-240-51609-7. Dewey:152.1/5. LCCN:00-049494.
                                        Audience: **l,u,f.**

Jorgensen, Owen   MT165 .J67
Tuning the Historical Temperaments by Ear. Trade Cloth.
Northern Michigan University Press. Marquette, MI. 1977.
ISBN:0-918616-00-X, ISBN13: 978-0-918616-00-5.
Dewey:786.2/3. LCCN:77-070993.
                                        Audience: **u,f.**

Maconie, Robin   ML3800.M237 1997
The Science of Music. Trade Cloth. Oxford University Press,
Inc. New York, NY. 1997. 232p. ISBN:0-19-816648-6, ISBN13:
978-0-19-816648-1. Dewey:781. LCCN:96-043398.
                        Audience: **g,l,u,f.** *Choice, 1997.*

Pierce, John Robinson   ML3807
The Science of Musical Sound. W.H. Freeman. 1992.
ISBN:0-7167-6005-3, ISBN13: 978-0-7167-6005-4.
                                        Audience: **g,l,u,f.**

Schafer, R. Murray   ML3805
The Soundscape: Our Sonic Environment and the Tuning of the
World. Rochester, Vt.: Destiny Books. 1994.
ISBN:0-89281-455-1, ISBN13: 978-0-89281-455-8.
                                        Audience: **u,f.**

Psychology and Physiology of Music

Bamberger, Jeanne   ML3838
The Mind Behind the Musical Ear: How Children Develop
Musical Intelligence. Trade Paper. Harvard University Press.
Cambridge, MA. 1995. 304p. ISBN:0-674-57606-3, ISBN13:
978-0-674-57606-3. Dewey:780/.1/9.
                                        Audience: **u,f.**

Butler, David E.   ML3830.B95 1992
Musician's Guide to Perception and Cognition. CD-ROM, Trade
Cloth. Thomson Gale. Farmington Hills, MI. 1992. 265p.
ISBN:0-02-870341-3, ISBN13: 978-0-02-870341-1.
Dewey:781/.11. LCCN:91-017181.
                                        Audience: **l,u,f.**

Davies, John Booth   ML3830.D28 1978
The Psychology of Music. Trade Cloth. Stanford University
Press. Palo Alto, CA. 1978. 240p. ISBN:0-8047-0980-7,
ISBN13: 978-0-8047-0980-4. Dewey:781/.15. LCCN:77-092339.
                                Audience: **l,u,f.** *B*

Deliege, Irene & Sloboda,   ML3838.M95 1996
  John A. (Editors)
Musical Beginnings: Origins and Development of Musical
Competence. Paper Text. Oxford University Press, Inc. New
York, NY. 1996. 238p. ISBN:0-19-852332-7, ISBN13:
978-0-19-852332-1. Dewey:781/.11. LCCN:95-009599.
                                        Audience: **u,f.**

Deutsch, Diana (Editor)   ML3830.P9 1999
The Psychology of Music. Ed. 2. Paper Text. Elsevier Science
& Technology Books. Saint Louis, MO. 1998. 807p. Academic
Press Ser. ISBN:0-12-213565-2, ISBN13: 978-0-12-213565-1.
Dewey:781/.11. LCCN:98-085210.
                        Audience: **u,f.** *B Choice, 1999.*

Farnsworth, Paul R.   ML3830
Social Psychology of Music. Ed. 2. Trade Cloth. Blackwell
Publishing Professional. Ames, IA. 1969. 298p.
ISBN:0-8138-1548-7, ISBN13: 978-0-8138-1548-0.
Dewey:781.1/5.
                                        Audience: **u,f.**

Griffith, Niall & Todd, Peter   ML3838.M955 1999
  M. (Editors)
Musical Networks: Parallel Distributed Perception and
Performance. Trade Cloth. MIT Press. Cambridge, MA. 1999.
385p. Bradford Bks. ISBN:0-262-07181-9, ISBN13:
978-0-262-07181-9. Dewey:781/.11. LCCN:98-025671.
                                        Audience: **u,f.**

Hargreaves, David & North,   ML3830.S57 1997
  Adrian C. (Editors)
The Social Psychology of Music. Trade Paper. Oxford
University Press, Inc. New York, NY. 1997. 324p.
ISBN:0-19-852383-1, ISBN13: 978-0-19-852383-3.
Dewey:781.1/1. LCCN:96-045586.
                        Audience: **u,f.** *Choice, 1998.*

Jones, Mari R. & Holleran,   ML3830 .C58 1992
  Susan (Editors)
Cognitive Bases of Musical Communication. Trade Cloth.
American Psychological Association. Washington, DC. 1992.
284p. Science Ser. ISBN:1-55798-127-2, ISBN13:
978-1-55798-127-1. Dewey:781/.11. LCCN:91-023245.
                                        Audience: **u,f.**

Juslin, Patrik N. & Sloboda,   ML3830.M965 2001
  John A. (Editors)
Music and Emotion: Theory and Research. Trade Paper. Oxford
University Press, Inc. New York, NY. 2001. 498p. Series in
Affective Science ISBN:0-19-263188-8, ISBN13:
978-0-19-263188-6. Dewey:781/.11. LCCN:2001-036068.
                        Audience: **u,f.** *Choice, 2002.*

Kemp, Anthony E.   ML3838.K46 1996
The Musical Temperament: Psychology and Personality of
Musicians. Trade Paper. Oxford University Press, Inc. New
York, NY. 1996. 296p. ISBN:0-19-852362-9, ISBN13:
978-0-19-852362-8. Dewey:781/.11. LCCN:95-039981.
Audience: **u,f.** *Choice, 1997.*

Krumhansl, Carol L.   ML3830
Cognitive Foundations of Musical Pitch. Trade Paper. Oxford
University Press, Inc. New York, NY. 2001. 307p. Oxford
Psychology Ser. ISBN:0-19-514836-3, ISBN13:
978-0-19-514836-7. Dewey:781/.11. LCCN:89-009312.
Audience: **u,f.**

Lanza, Joseph   ML3920.L35 2003
Elevator Music: A Surreal History of Muzak, Easy-Listening,
and Other Moodsong; Revised and Expanded Edition. Trade
Paper. University of Michigan Press. Chicago, IL. 2004. 344p.
ISBN:0-472-08942-0, ISBN13: 978-0-472-08942-0.
Dewey:781.5. LCCN:2004-555153.
Audience: **u,f.** *Choice, 2005.*

MacDonald, Raymond R.   ML3830.M9823 2002
  (Editor), et al.
Musical Identities. David Hargreaves & Dorothy Miell (Editors).
Trade Paper. Oxford University Press, Inc. New York, NY. 2002.
224p. ISBN:0-19-850932-4, ISBN13: 978-0-19-850932-5.
Dewey:781/.11. LCCN:2002-025814.
Audience: **u,f.**

Miell, Dorothy (Editor), et   ML3830.M9822 2005
  al.
Musical Communication. Raymond MacDonald & David
Hargreaves (Editors). Trade Cloth. Oxford University Press, Inc.
New York, NY. 2005. 352p. ISBN:0-19-852935-X, ISBN13:
978-0-19-852935-4. Dewey:781/.11. LCCN:2005-007552.
Audience: **u,f.**

Parncutt, Richard &   ML3838.S385 2002
  McPherson, Gary (Editors)
The Science and Psychology of Music Performance: Creative
Strategies for Teaching and Learning. Trade Cloth. Oxford
University Press, Inc. New York, NY. 2002. 400p.
ISBN:0-19-513810-4, ISBN13: 978-0-19-513810-8.
Dewey:781.4. LCCN:2001-036292.
Audience: **u,f.**

Peretz, Isabelle (Editor)   ML3838
The Cognitive Neuroscience of Music. Zatorre, Robert J.
(Editor). Oxford University Press. 2003. ISBN:0-19-852519-2,
ISBN13: 978-0-19-852519-6.
Audience: **u,f.**

Perris, Arnold   ML3838
Music as Propaganda: Art to Persuade, Art to Control. Trade
Cloth. Greenwood Publishing Group, Inc. Portsmouth, NH.
1985. 256p. Contributions to the Study of Music and Dance
Ser., No. 8 ISBN:0-313-24505-3, ISBN13: 978-0-313-24505-3.
Dewey:781.15. LCCN:84-027969.
Audience: **u,f.**

Seashore, Carl E.   ML3830.S32
Psychology of Music. Trade Paper. Dover Publications, Inc.
Mineola, NY. 1967. 408p. ISBN:0-486-21851-1, ISBN13:
978-0-486-21851-9. Dewey:781.1/5.
Audience: **u,f.**

Sloboda, John (Editor)   ML3838.G38 2000
Generative Processes in Music: The Psychology of Performance,
Improvisation, and Composition. Trade Paper. Oxford University
Press, Inc. New York, NY. 2001. 316p. ISBN:0-19-850846-8,
ISBN13: 978-0-19-850846-5. Dewey:781.4/3111.
LCCN:2001-271717.
Audience: **u,f.** *Choice, 2001.*

Sloboda, John A.   ML3830.S52 2005
Exploring the Musical Mind: Cognition, Emotion, Ability,
Function. Trade Cloth. Oxford University Press, Inc. New York,
NY. 2005. 472p. ISBN:0-19-853012-9, ISBN13:
978-0-19-853012-1. Dewey:781/.11. LCCN:2005-560241.
Audience: **u,f.**

Sociology of Music

Adorno, Theodor W.   ML3797.1 .A3413
Introduction to the Sociology of Music. E. B. Ashton
(Translator). Trade Cloth. Continuum International Publishing
Group, Ltd. London, 1976. ISBN:0-8264-0119-8, ISBN13:
978-0-8264-0119-9. Dewey:780/.07. LCCN:75-033883.
Audience: **u,f.**

Attali, Jacques   ML3795.A913 1985
Noise. Brian Massumi (Translator), Fredric Jameson (Foreword
by), Susan McClary (Afterword by). Trade Paper. University of
Minnesota Press. Minneapolis, MN. 1985. 180p. Theory and
History of Literature Ser., Vol. 16 ISBN:0-8166-1287-0,
ISBN13: 978-0-8166-1287-1. Dewey:780/.07. LCCN:84-028069.
Audience: **u,f.** *Choice, 1985.*

Blacking, John & Nettl,   ML60.B63 1995
  Bruno
Music, Culture, and Experience: Selected Papers of John
Blacking. Reginald Byron (Editor). Trade Cloth. University of
Chicago Press. Chicago, IL. 1995. 277p. Chicago Studies in
Ethnomusicology ISBN:0-226-08829-4, ISBN13:
978-0-226-08829-7. Dewey:780/.89. LCCN:94-025598.
Audience: **u,f.**

Carroll, Mark   ML3795.C34 2003
Music and Ideology in Cold War Europe. Arnold Whittall
(Contribution by). Trade Cloth. Cambridge University Press.
New York, NY. 2003. 256p. Music in the Twentieth Century
Ser., Vol. 18 ISBN:0-521-82072-3, ISBN13: 978-0-521-82072-1.
Dewey:780/.9/04. LCCN:2002-031245.
Audience: **u,f.**

Cavicchi, Daniel & Keil,   ML3920
  Charles (Editors)
My Music: Explorations of Music in Daily Life. Susan D. Crafts
(Compiled by). Trade Paper. Wesleyan University Press.

Middletown, CT. 1993. 244p. Music Culture Ser.
ISBN:0-8195-6264-5, ISBN13: 978-0-8195-6264-7.
LCCN:92-056907.

Audience: **u,f.**

DeNora, Tia   **ML3795 .D343 2000**
Music in Everyday Life. Cloth Text. Cambridge University
Press. New York, NY. 2000. 196p. ISBN:0-521-62206-9,
ISBN13: 978-0-521-62206-6. Dewey:781.11. LCCN:99-052606.

Audience: **u,f.**

Eisenberg, Evan   **ML3916**
The Recording Angel: Music, Records and Culture from
Aristotle to Zappa. Ed. 2. Trade Paper. Yale University Press.
Cumberland, RI. 2005. 256p. ISBN:0-300-09904-5, ISBN13:
978-0-300-09904-1. Dewey:306.4842. LCCN:2004-117200.

Audience: **u,f.**

Eyerman, Ron & Jamison,   **ML3795 .E98 1998**
  Andrew
Music and Social Movements: Mobilizing Traditions in the
Twentieth Century. Jeffrey C. Alexander & Steven Seidman
(Contribution by). Trade Paper. Cambridge University Press.
New York, NY. 1998. 203p. Cultural Social Studies
ISBN:0-521-62966-7, ISBN13: 978-0-521-62966-9.
Dewey:306.4/84. LCCN:97-025752.

Audience: **u,f.** *Choice, 1998.*

Keil, Charles & Feld, Steven   **ML60.K26 1994**
Music Grooves: Essays and Dialogues. Trade Cloth. University
of Chicago Press. Chicago, IL. 1995. 410p.
ISBN:0-226-42956-3, ISBN13: 978-0-226-42956-4.
Dewey:780/.89. LCCN:94-008226.

Audience: **u,f.**

Kramer, Lawrence   **ML3880.K7 1990**
Music As Cultural Practice, 1800-1900. Trade Cloth. University
of California Press. Berkeley, CA. 1990. 241p. California
Studies in 19th Century Music, No. 8 ISBN:0-520-06857-2,
ISBN13: 978-0-520-06857-5. Dewey:780/.9/034.
LCCN:89-020445.

Audience: **u,f.** *Choice, 1991.*

Leppert, Richard D.   **ML3800.L6 1993**
The Sight of Sound: Music, Representation, and the History of
the Body. Trade Cloth. University of California Press. Berkeley,
CA. 1993. 345p. ISBN:0-520-08174-9, ISBN13:
978-0-520-08174-1. Dewey:781.11. LCCN:92-039075.

Audience: **u,f.** *Choice, 1994.*

Leppert, Richard D. &   **ML3795.M78 1987**
  McClary, Susan (Editors)
Music and Society: The Politics of Composition, Performance
and Reception. Trade Paper. Cambridge University Press. New
York, NY. 1989. 224p. ISBN:0-521-37977-6, ISBN13:
978-0-521-37977-9. Dewey:780/.07. LCCN:86-031672.

Audience: **u,f.** *Choice, 1988.*

Loesser, Arthur   **ML650.L64 1990**
Men, Women and Pianos: A Social History. Trade Paper. Dover

Publications, Inc. Mineola, NY. 1991. 672p.
ISBN:0-486-26543-9, ISBN13: 978-0-486-26543-8.
Dewey:786.2/09. LCCN:90-044829.

Audience: **g,l,u,f.**

Radano, Ronald M. &   **ML3795.M782 2000**
  Bohlman, Philip V. (Editors)
Music and the Racial Imagination. Trade Cloth. University of
Chicago Press. Chicago, IL. 2000. 703p. Chicago Studies in
Ethnomusicology ISBN:0-226-70199-9, ISBN13:
978-0-226-70199-8. Dewey:780/.89. LCCN:00-023672.

Audience: **u,f.**

Scott, Derek B. (Editor)   **ML60**
Music, Culture, and Society: A Reader. Trade Paper. Oxford
University Press, Inc. New York, NY. 2000. 248p.
ISBN:0-19-879012-0, ISBN13: 978-0-19-879012-9. Dewey:780.
LCCN:99-044502.

Audience: **u,f.**

Shepherd, John & Wicke,   **ML3795.S423 1997**
  Peter
Music and Cultural Theory. Trade Paper. Blackwell Publishing,
Inc. Malden, MA. 1997. 240p. ISBN:0-7456-0864-7, ISBN13:
978-0-7456-0864-8. Dewey:781/.1. LCCN:97-002730.

Audience: **u,f.**

Small, Christopher   **ML3795.S55 1996**
Music, Society, Education. Robert Walser (Foreword by). Trade
Paper. Wesleyan University Press. Middletown, CT. 1996. 248p.
Music Culture Ser. ISBN:0-8195-6307-2, ISBN13:
978-0-8195-6307-1. Dewey:780/.7. LCCN:96-020010.

Audience: **u,f.**

Sterne, Jonathan   **TK7881.4.S733 2002**
The Audible Past: Cultural Origins of Sound Reproduction.
Trade Cloth. Duke University Press. Durham, NC. 2003. 448p.
ISBN:0-8223-3004-0, ISBN13: 978-0-8223-3004-2.
Dewey:621.389/3/09. LCCN:2002-009196.

Audience: **l,u,f.** *Choice, 2003.*

Waksman, Steve   **ML1015.G9W24 1999**
Instruments of Desire: The Electric Guitar and the Shaping of
Musical Experience. Trade Cloth. Harvard University Press.
Cambridge, MA. 2000. 384p. ISBN:0-674-00065-X, ISBN13:
978-0-674-00065-0. Dewey:787.87/19. LCCN:99-039764.

Audience: **u,f.** *Choice, 2000.*

Gender and Sexuality Studies

Akenson, James E.   **ML394.W65 2003**
The Women of Country Music: A Reader. Charles K. Wolfe
(Editor). Trade Cloth. University Press of Kentucky. Lexington,
KY. 2003. 224p. ISBN:0-8131-2280-5, ISBN13:
978-0-8131-2280-9. Dewey:782.421642/082.
LCCN:2003-005310.

Audience: **u,f.**

Ammer, Christine ML82.A45 2001
Unsung: A History of Women in American Music. Ed. 2. Trade
Paper. Hal Leonard Corporation. Milwaukee, WI. 2003. 382p.
ISBN:1-57467-061-1, ISBN13: 978-1-57467-061-5.
Dewey:780/.82/0973. LCCN:00-042017.

Audience: **u,f.** *B*

Auslander, Philip ML3534.A9 2006
Performing Glam Rock: Gender and Theatricality in Popular
Music. Trade Cloth. University of Michigan Press. Chicago, IL.
2006. 272p. ISBN:0-472-09868-3, ISBN13: 978-0-472-09868-2.
Dewey:781.66. LCCN:2005-017928.

Audience: **u,f.**

Baldauf-Berdes, Jane J. ML82
Women Musicians of Venice: Musical Foundations, 1525-1855.
Ed. 2. Paper Text. Oxford University Press, Inc. New York, NY.
1996. 329p. Oxford Monographs on Music
ISBN:0-19-816604-4, ISBN13: 978-0-19-816604-7.
Dewey:780.8/2.

Audience: **u,f.**

Bernstein, Jane A. (Editor) ML82.W697 2003
Women's Voices Across Musical Worlds. Trade Paper.
Northeastern University Press. Boston, MA. 2005. 344p.
ISBN:1-55553-588-7, ISBN13: 978-1-55553-588-9.
Dewey:780/.82. LCCN:2003-008327.

Audience: **g,l,u,f.** *Choice, 2004.*

Block, Adrienne F. ML410.B36B56 1998
Amy Beach, Passionate Victorian: The Life and Works of an
American Composer, 1867-1944. Trade Cloth. Oxford
University Press, Inc. New York, NY. 1998. 426p.
ISBN:0-19-507408-4, ISBN13: 978-0-19-507408-6.
Dewey:780.9/2. LCCN:97-002710.

Audience: **g,l,u,f.** *Choice, 1999.*

Born, Georgina & ML3795 .W45 2000
Hesmondhalgh, David (Editors)
Western Music and Its Others: Difference, Representation, and
Appropriation in Music. Trade Paper. University of California
Press. Berkeley, CA. 2000. 374p. ISBN:0-520-22084-6, ISBN13:
978-0-520-22084-3. Dewey:781.6. LCCN:00-029871.

Audience: **u,f.**

Bowers, Jane & Tick, Judith ML82
(Editors)
Women Making Music: The Western Art Tradition, 1150-1950.
Trade Paper. University of Illinois Press. Champaign, IL. 1987.
424p. ISBN:0-252-01470-7, ISBN13: 978-0-252-01470-3.
Dewey:780/.88042. LCCN:85-008642.

Audience: **g,l,u,f.** *Choice, 1986.*

Brett, Philip (Editor), et al. ML55
Queering the Pitch: The New Gay and Lesbian Musicology.
Elizabeth Wood & Gary Thomas (Editors). Paper over Boards.
Routledge. New York, NY. 1994. 368p. ISBN:0-415-90753-5,
ISBN13: 978-0-415-90753-8. Dewey:780.8664.
LCCN:93-015025.

Audience: **u,f.** *Choice, 1995.*

Bufwack, Mary A. & ML3524.B83 2003
Oermann, Robert K.
Finding Her Voice: Women in Country Music, 1800-2000. Trade
Cloth. Vanderbilt University Press. Nashville, TN. 2003. 616p.
ISBN:0-8265-1432-4, ISBN13: 978-0-8265-1432-5.
Dewey:781.642/082. LCCN:2003-002519.

Audience: **u,f.** *Choice, 2004.*

Burns, Lori & Lafrance, MT146.B87 2001
Melisse
Disruptive Divas: Feminism, Identity, and Popular Music. Cloth
Text. Routledge. New York, NY. 2001. 248p. Studies in
Contemporary Music and Culture ISBN:0-8153-3553-9,
ISBN13: 978-0-8153-3553-5. Dewey:782.42164/092/273.
LCCN:2001-019249.

Audience: **u,f.** *Choice, 2002.*

Clement, Catherine ML1700
Opera: The Undoing of Women. Betsy Wing (Translator). Trade
Paper. University of Minnesota Press. Minneapolis, MN. 1999.
224p. ISBN:0-8166-3526-9, ISBN13: 978-0-8166-3526-9.
Dewey:782.1/09.

Audience: **u,f.** *Choice, 1989.*

Cook, Susan C. & Tsou, ML82 .C42 1994
Judy S. (Editors)
Cecilia Reclaimed: Feminist Perspectives on Gender and Music.
Susan McClary (Foreword by). Trade Paper. University of
Illinois Press. Champaign, IL. 1993. 256p. ISBN:0-252-06341-4,
ISBN13: 978-0-252-06341-1. Dewey:780/.82. LCCN:93-018463.

Audience: **u,f.** *Choice, 1994.*

Fuller, Sophie & Whitesell, ML63.Q44 2002
Lloyd (Editors)
Queer Episodes in Music and Modern Identity. Trade Cloth.
University of Illinois Press. Champaign, IL. 2002. 336p.
ISBN:0-252-02740-X, ISBN13: 978-0-252-02740-6.
Dewey:780/.86/64. LCCN:2001-005639.

Audience: **l,u,f.** *Choice, 2003.*

Gaar, Gillian G. ML394
She's a Rebel: The History of Women in Rock and Roll. Ed. 2.
Yoko Ono (Preface by). Trade Paper. Avalon Publishing Group.
New York, NY. 2002. 496p. ISBN:1-58005-078-6, ISBN13:
978-1-58005-078-4. Dewey:781.66/092/2 B.
LCCN:2003-267936.

Audience: **g,l,u,f.** *Choice, 1993.*

Gill, John ML63.G49 1995
Queer Noises: Male and Female Homosexuality in
Twentieth-Century Music. Cloth Text. University of Minnesota
Press. Minneapolis, MN. 1995. ISBN:0-8166-2718-5, ISBN13:
978-0-8166-2718-9. Dewey:780/.8/664. LCCN:94-043922.

Audience: **l,u,f.**

Giroud, Francoise DB844.M34G5713 1991
Alma Mahler: Or the Art of Being Loved. R. M. Stock (Editor,
Translator). Trade Cloth. Oxford University Press, Inc. New
York, NY. 1992. 176p. ISBN:0-19-816156-5, ISBN13:
978-0-19-816156-1. Dewey:780/.92 B. LCCN:91-003678.

Audience: **u,f.**

Glover, Jane   ML410.M9G645 2004
Mozart's Women: His Family, His Friends, His Music. Trade
Cloth. HarperCollins Publishers. New York, NY. 2006. 416p.
ISBN:0-06-056350-8, ISBN13: 978-0-06-056350-9.
Dewey:780/.92 B. LCCN:2005-052699.

Audience: **g,l,u,f.**

Green, Lucy   ML82 .G74 1997
Music, Gender, Education. Cloth Text. Cambridge University
Press. New York, NY. 1997. 294p. ISBN:0-521-55517-5,
ISBN13: 978-0-521-55517-3. Dewey:780.7. LCCN:96-024711.

Audience: **u,f.** *Choice, 1998.*

Hixon, Don L. & Hennessee,   ML105.H6 1993
  Don A.
Women in Music: An Encyclopedic Biobibliography. Ed. 2.
Trade Cloth. Scarecrow Press, Inc. Lanham, MD. 1993. 772p.
ISBN:0-8108-2769-7, ISBN13: 978-0-8108-2769-1.
Dewey:016.78/0922. LCCN:93-034731.

Audience: **g,l,u,f.**

Hubbs, Nadine   ML200.5 .H83 2004
The Queer Composition of America's Sound: Gay Modernists,
American Music, and National Identity. Trade Cloth. University
of California Press. Berkeley, CA. 2004. 288p.
ISBN:0-520-24184-3, ISBN13: 978-0-520-24184-8.
Dewey:780/.86/640973. LCCN:2004-003478.

Audience: **l,u,f.** *Choice, 2005.*

International Alliance for   ML128.W7
  Women in Music
⬜ IAWM = International Alliance for Women in Music.
http://www.iawm.org
International Alliance for Women in Music.

Audience: **g,l,u,f.**

Jezic, Diane P.   ML390.J37 1994
Women Composers: The Lost Tradition Found. Ed. 2. Elizabeth
Wood (Editor). Trade Cloth. Feminist Press at The City
University of New York. New York, NY. 1993. 272p. Diane
Peacock Jezic Series on Women and Music
ISBN:1-55861-073-1, ISBN13: 978-1-55861-073-6.
Dewey:780/.92/2 B. LCCN:94-039300.

Audience: **g,l,u,f.**

Kallberg, Jeffrey   ML410.C54
Chopin at the Boundaries: Sex, History, and Musical Genre.
Trade Paper. Harvard University Press. Cambridge, MA. 1998.
320p. Convergences Ser., :Inventories of the Present Ser.
ISBN:0-674-12791-9, ISBN13: 978-0-674-12791-3.
Dewey:786.2092.

Audience: **u,f.** *Choice, 1996.*

Kendrick, Robert L.   ML290.8.M4K46 1996
Celestial Sirens: Nuns and Their Music in Early Modern Milan.
Cloth Text. Oxford University Press, Inc. New York, NY. 1996.
577p. Monographs on Music ISBN:0-19-816408-4, ISBN13:
978-0-19-816408-1. Dewey:781.71/2/0082. LCCN:95-044937.

Audience: **u,f.** *Choice, 1997.*

Koestenbaum, Wayne   ML410.V4
The Queen's Throat: Opera, Homosexuality, and the Mystery of
Desire. Trade Paper. Da Capo Press, Inc. Cambridge, MA. 2001.
280p. ISBN:0-306-81008-5, ISBN13: 978-0-306-81008-4.
Dewey:782.1/092 B.

Audience: **g,l,u,f.**

McClary, Susan   ML82.M38 2002
Feminine Endings: Music, Gender, and Sexuality. Trade Paper.
University of Minnesota Press. Minneapolis, MN. 2002. 240p.
ISBN:0-8166-4189-7, ISBN13: 978-0-8166-4189-5.
Dewey:780/.82. LCCN:2002-072791.

Audience: **g,l,u,f.**

Mitchell, John Cameron &   ML50.T769H4 2003
  Trask, Stephen
Hedwig and the Angry Inch. Trade Paper. Dramatists Play
Service, Inc. New York, NY. 2003. 42p. ISBN:0-8222-1901-8,
ISBN13: 978-0-8222-1901-9. Dewey:782.1/4/0268.
LCCN:2005-560193.

Audience: **g,l,u,f.**

Moisala, Pirkko &   ML82.M74 2000
  Diamond, Beverley
Music and Gender. Trade Paper. University of Illinois Press.
Champaign, IL. 2000. 392p. ISBN:0-252-06865-3, ISBN13:
978-0-252-06865-2. Dewey:780/.82. LCCN:99-006791.

Audience: **u,f.** *Choice, 2001.*

Neuls-Bates, Carol (Editor)   ML82.W65 1996
Women in Music: An Anthology of Source Readings from the
Middle Ages to the Present. Ed. 2. Trade Paper. Northeastern
University Press. Boston, MA. 1995. 400p.
ISBN:1-55553-240-3, ISBN13: 978-1-55553-240-6.
Dewey:780/.88042. LCCN:95-017460.

Audience: **g,l,u,f.** **ℬ** *Choice, 1996.*

Pendle, Karin   ML82.W6 2001
Women and Music: A History. Ed. 2. Trade Paper. Indiana
University Press. Bloomington, IN. 2001. x, 516p.
ISBN:0-253-21422-X, ISBN13: 978-0-253-21422-5.
Dewey:780/.82. LCCN:00-044886.

Audience: **g,l,u,f.** *Choice, 2001, 1992.*

Pendle, Karin   ML128.W7P46 2005
Women in Music Guide to Research. Paper over Boards.
Routledge. New York, NY. 2005. 728p. Routledge Music
Bibliographies Ser. ISBN:0-415-94354-X, ISBN13:
978-0-415-94354-3. Dewey:016.78/082. LCCN:2005-023054.

Audience: **l,u,f.**

Peraino, Judith Ann   ML3838 .P365 2006
Listening to the Sirens: Musical Technologies of Queer Identity
from Homer to Hedwig. Trade Cloth. University of California
Press. Berkeley, CA. 2005. 358p. ISBN:0-520-21587-7, ISBN13:
978-0-520-21587-0. Dewey:780/.86/64. LCCN:2005-006234.

Audience: **l,u,f.** *Choice, 2006.*

Rhodes, Lisa L.   ML82.R54 2005
Electric Ladyland: Women and Rock Culture, 1965-1975. Book,

Other. University of Pennsylvania Press. Philadelphia, PA. 2005.
328p. ISBN:0-8122-1899-X, ISBN13: 978-0-8122-1899-2.
Dewey:781.66/082. LCCN:2004-043094.

Audience: **g,l,u,f.**

Sadie, Julie Anne & Samuel,   **ML105**
  Rhian (Editors)
New Grove Dictionary of Women Composers. Trade Cloth.
Oxford University Press, Inc. New York, NY. 1994. 592p.
ISBN:0-333-51598-6, ISBN13: 978-0-333-51598-3.
Dewey:780.9203.

Audience: **g,l,u,f.**

Schulman, Sarah   **ML410.L2857S38 1998**
Stagestruck: Theater, AIDS and Marketing of Gay America.
Trade Cloth. Duke University Press. Durham, NC. 1998. 152p.
ISBN:0-8223-2132-7, ISBN13: 978-0-8223-2132-3.
LCCN:98-012053.

Audience: **g,l,u,f.** *Choice, 1999.*

Smart, Mary Ann   **ML2100.S52 2000**
Siren Songs: Representations of Gender and Sexuality in Opera.
Cloth Text. Princeton University Press. Princeton, NJ. 2000.
288p. Princeton Studies in Opera ISBN:0-691-05814-8, ISBN13:
978-0-691-05814-6. Dewey:782.1. LCCN:00-038500.

Audience: **u,f.**

Solie, Ruth A. (Editor)   **ML82**
Musicology and Difference: Gender and Sexuality in Music
Scholarship. Trade Paper. University of California Press.
Berkeley, CA. 1995. 368p. ISBN:0-520-20146-9, ISBN13:
978-0-520-20146-0. Dewey:780.82.

Audience: **u,f.** *Choice, 1994.*

Wolf, Stacy   **ML2054.W65 2002**
A Problem Like Maria: Gender and Sexuality in the American
Musical. Trade Cloth. University of Michigan Press. Chicago,
IL. 2002. 312p. Triangulations Ser., :Lesbian - Gay - Queer
Theater - Drama - Performance ISBN:0-472-09772-5, ISBN13:
978-0-472-09772-2. Dewey:782.1/4/0820973.
LCCN:2001-008273.

Audience: **l,u,f.** *Choice, 2003.*

Yardley, Anne Bagnall   **ML3003**
Performing Piety: Musical Cultures in Medieval English
Nunneries. Cloth over Boards. Palgrave Macmillan. New York,
NY. 2006. 344p. The New Middle Ages Ser.
ISBN:1-4039-6299-5, ISBN13: 978-1-4039-6299-7.
Dewey:781.71/24200902. LCCN:2005-045614.

Audience: **u,f.**

Philosophy and Aesthetics of Music

Adorno, Theodor W.   **ML3845**
Philosophy of Modern Music. Trade Paper. Continuum
International Publishing Group, Ltd. London, 2003. 240p.
Athlone Contemporary European Thinkers Ser.
ISBN:0-8264-1490-7, ISBN13: 978-0-8264-1490-8.
Dewey:780/.9/04. LCCN:2003-276732.

Audience: **u,f.**

Adorno, Theodor W.   **ML423.A33 A63 2002**
Essays on Music. Susan H. Gillespie (Translator), Richard D.
Leppert (Commentaries by, Introduction by, Notes by). Trade
Cloth. University of California Press. Berkeley, CA. 2002. 752p.
ISBN:0-520-22672-0, ISBN13: 978-0-520-22672-2. Dewey:780.
LCCN:2001-044601.

Audience: **u,f.**

Bowman, Wayne D.   **ML3800.B79 1998**
Philosophical Perspectives on Music. Trade Cloth. Oxford
University Press, Inc. New York, NY. 1998. 496p.
ISBN:0-19-511296-2, ISBN13: 978-0-19-511296-2.
Dewey:780.1. LCCN:97-025601.

Audience: **u,f.** *Choice, 1998.*

Budd, Malcolm   **ML3845.B77 1985**
Music and the Emotions: The Philosophical Theories. Trade
Cloth. Routledge. New York, NY. 1985. 224p. International
Library of Philosophy, Psychology, and Scientific Method
ISBN:0-7102-0520-1, ISBN13: 978-0-7102-0520-9.
Dewey:781/.15. LCCN:85-001975.

Audience: **u,f.**

Burrows, David   **ML3845.B837 1990**
Sound, Speech, and Music. Trade Cloth. University of
Massachusetts Press. Amherst, MA. 1990. 152p.
ISBN:0-87023-685-7, ISBN13: 978-0-87023-685-3.
Dewey:780/.1. LCCN:89-004947.

Audience: **u,f.** *Choice, 1990.*

Clifton, Thomas   **ML3800**
Music As Heard: A Study in Applied Phenomenology. Trade
Cloth. Yale University Press. Cumberland, RI. 1983. 336p.
ISBN:0-300-02091-0, ISBN13: 978-0-300-02091-5.
Dewey:780/.1. LCCN:82-010944.

Audience: **u,f.** ℬ

Cook, Nicholas   **ML3845**
Music, Imagination, and Culture. Trade Paper. Oxford
University Press, Inc. New York, NY. 1992. 272p.
ISBN:0-19-816303-7, ISBN13: 978-0-19-816303-9.
Dewey:781.17. LCCN:89-003352.

Audience: **u,f.**

Dahlhaus, Carl   **ML3845 .D2913 1982**
Esthetics of Music. William Austin (Translator). Trade Paper.
Cambridge University Press. New York, NY. 1982. 128p.
ISBN:0-521-28007-9, ISBN13: 978-0-521-28007-5.
Dewey:780/.1. LCCN:81-010080.

Audience: **u,f.**

Dahlhaus, Carl   **ML3845**
The Idea of Absolute Music. Roger Lustig (Translator). Trade
Paper. University of Chicago Press. Chicago, IL. 1991. 186p.
ISBN:0-226-13487-3, ISBN13: 978-0-226-13487-1.
Dewey:781.1/7.

Audience: **u,f.** *Choice, 1990.*

Davies, Stephen   **ML3800.D25 1994**
Musical Meaning and Expression. Trade Paper. Cornell

University Press. Ithaca, NY. 1994. 400p. ISBN:0-8014-8151-1, ISBN13: 978-0-8014-8151-2. Dewey:781/.1. LCCN:93-039890.
Audience: **u,f.** *Choice, 1994.*

Debussy, Claude, et al.   **ML90**
Three Classics in the Aesthetic of Music. Ferruccio Busoni & Charles Ives (Authors). Trade Paper. Dover Publications, Inc. Mineola, NY. 1962. 188p. ISBN:0-486-20320-4, ISBN13: 978-0-486-20320-1. Dewey:780.922.
Audience: **u,f.**

DeNora, Tia   **ML3795.D3428 2003**
After Adorno: Rethinking Music Sociology. Cloth Text. Cambridge University Press. New York, NY. 2003. 192p. ISBN:0-521-83025-7, ISBN13: 978-0-521-83025-6. Dewey:780/.1. LCCN:2003-051525.
Audience: **u,f.**

Ferrara, Lawrence   **ML3845**
Philosophy and the Analysis of Music: Bridges to Musical Sound, Form, and Reference. Trade Cloth. Greenwood Publishing Group, Inc. Portsmouth, NH. 1991. 392p. Contributions to the Study of Music and Dance Ser., No. 24 ISBN:0-313-28345-1, ISBN13: 978-0-313-28345-1. Dewey:780/.1. LCCN:91-026022.
Audience: **u,f.**

Godwin, Joscelyn   **ML3800.H27 1993**
The Harmony of the Spheres: The Pythagotean Tradition in Music. Trade Cloth. Inner Traditions International, Ltd. Rochester, VT. 1992. 512p. ISBN:0-89281-265-6, ISBN13: 978-0-89281-265-3. Dewey:780/.1. LCCN:89-024741.
Audience: **u,f.**

Goehr, Lydia   **ML3845**
The Imaginary Museum of Musical Works: An Essay in the Philosophy of Music. Trade Paper. Oxford University Press, Inc. New York, NY. 1994. 324p. ISBN:0-19-823541-0, ISBN13: 978-0-19-823541-5. Dewey:780/.1.
Audience: **u,f.** *Choice, 1993.*

Hanslick, Eduard   **ML3847.H3 1986**
On the Musically Beautiful. Geoffrey Payzant (Editor, Translator, Introduction by). Trade Cloth. Hackett Publishing Company, Inc. Indianapolis, IN. 1986. 151p. HPC Classics Ser. ISBN:0-87220-015-9, ISBN13: 978-0-87220-015-9. Dewey:780/.1. LCCN:85-027249.
Audience: **u,f.** *Choice, 1987.*

Keil, Charles, et al.   **ML60**
Music Grooves: Essays and Dialogues. Ed. 2. Feld, Steven. Fenestra. 2005. ISBN:1-58736-412-3, ISBN13: 978-1-58736-412-9.
Audience: **u,f.**

Keil, Charles & Feld, Steven   **ML60.K26 1994**
Music Grooves: Essays and Dialogues. Trade Cloth. University of Chicago Press. Chicago, IL. 1995. 410p. ISBN:0-226-42956-3, ISBN13: 978-0-226-42956-4. Dewey:780/.89. LCCN:94-008226.
Audience: **u,f.**

Kivy, Peter   **ML457.K58 1995**
Authenticities: Philosophical Reflections on Musical Performance. Book, Other. Cornell University Press. Ithaca, NY. 1995. 296p. ISBN:0-8014-3046-1, ISBN13: 978-0-8014-3046-6. Dewey:781.4/3/01. LCCN:94-036842.
Audience: **u,f.** *Choice, 1995.*

Kivy, Peter   **ML3845.K584 2002**
Introduction to a Philosophy of Music. Trade Paper. Oxford University Press, Inc. New York, NY. 2002. 296p. ISBN:0-19-825048-7, ISBN13: 978-0-19-825048-7. Dewey:781/.1. LCCN:2001-058833.
Audience: **u,f.**

Kivy, Peter   **ML3845**
Music Alone: Philosophical Reflections on the Purely Musical Experience. Trade Paper. Cornell University Press. Ithaca, NY. 1991. 240p. ISBN:0-8014-9960-7, ISBN13: 978-0-8014-9960-9. Dewey:780/.1. LCCN:89-035570.
Audience: **u,f.** *Choice, 1990.*

Kivy, Peter   **ML3845.K595 1989**
Sound Sentiment: An Essay on the Musical Emotions. Joseph Margolis (Foreword by). Trade Paper. Temple University Press. Philadelphia, PA. 1989. 304p. The Arts and Their Philosophies Ser. ISBN:0-87722-677-6, ISBN13: 978-0-87722-677-2. Dewey:780/.1. LCCN:89-004336.
Audience: **u,f.**

Kramer, Lawrence   **ML3845**
Classical Music and Postmodern Knowledge. Trade Paper. University of California Press. Berkeley, CA. 1996. 316p. ISBN:0-520-20700-9, ISBN13: 978-0-520-20700-4. Dewey:781.6/8/01. LCCN:94-014391.
Audience: **u,f.** *Choice, 1996.*

Kramer, Lawrence   **ML3880.K7 1990**
Music As Cultural Practice, 1800-1900. Trade Cloth. University of California Press. Berkeley, CA. 1990. 241p. California Studies in 19th Century Music, No. 8 ISBN:0-520-06857-2, ISBN13: 978-0-520-06857-5. Dewey:780/.9/034. LCCN:89-020445.
Audience: **u,f.** *Choice, 1991.*

Kramer, Lawrence   **ML3845 .K814 2002**
Musical Meaning: Toward a Critical History. Trade Cloth. University of California Press. Berkeley, CA. 2001. 346p. ISBN:0-520-22824-3, ISBN13: 978-0-520-22824-5. Dewey:781.1/7. LCCN:2001-027819.
Audience: **u,f.**

Krausz, Michael (Editor)   **ML3845.I62 1993**
The Interpretation of Music: Philosophical Essays. Cloth Text. Oxford University Press, Inc. New York, NY. 1993. 298p. ISBN:0-19-823958-0, ISBN13: 978-0-19-823958-1. Dewey:781/.1. LCCN:92-016508.
Audience: **u,f.** *Choice, 1993.*

Liebert, Georges   **ML423.N56L5413 2004**
Nietzsche and Music. David Pellauer & Graham Parkes

(Translators). Trade Cloth. University of Chicago Press. Chicago, IL. 2004. 304p. ISBN:0-226-48087-9, ISBN13: 978-0-226-48087-9. Dewey:780/.92. LCCN:2003-012778.

Audience: **u,f.**

Lippman, Edward A.   **ML3845**
A History of Western Musical Aesthetics. Paper Text. University of Nebraska Press. Lincoln, NE. 1992. 551p. ISBN:0-8032-7951-5, ISBN13: 978-0-8032-7951-3. Dewey:781.17. LCCN:91-047076.

Audience: **u,f.** *Choice, 1993.*

Lippman, Edward A.   **ML3845 .M975**
(Editor)
Musical Aesthetics: A Historical Reader - The Twentieth Century. Library Binding. Pendragon Press. Hillsdale, NY. 1990. 350p. Aesthetics in Music Ser., No. 4, Vol. 3 ISBN:0-945193-10-6, ISBN13: 978-0-945193-10-4. Dewey:780/.1. LCCN:85-028415.

Audience: **u,f.**

Lippman, Edward A.   **ML3845.L567 1999**
(Contribution by)
The Philosophy and Aesthetics of Music. Chris Hatch (Introduction by). Cloth Text. University of Nebraska Press. Lincoln, NE. 1999. 249p. ISBN:0-8032-2912-7, ISBN13: 978-0-8032-2912-9. Dewey:781.1/7. LCCN:98-043967.

Audience: **u,f.** *Choice, 2000.*

Meyer, Leonard B.   **ML3845**
Emotion and Meaning in Music. Paper Text. Textbook Publishers. Temecula, CA. 2003. 307p. ISBN:0-7581-2590-9, ISBN13: 978-0-7581-2590-3. Dewey:781.1/7.

Audience: **g,l,u,f.** *B*

Meyer, Leonard B.   **ML160**
Explaining Music: Essays and Explorations. Paper Text. University of Chicago Press. Chicago, IL. 1994. xiii, 284p. ISBN:0-226-52142-7, ISBN13: 978-0-226-52142-8. Dewey:780. LCCN:77-090968.

Audience: **u,f.**

Meyer, Leonard B.   **ML3800.M633 1994**
Music, the Arts, and Ideas: Patterns and Predictions in Twentieth-Century Culture. Trade Paper. University of Chicago Press. Chicago, IL. 1994. 349p. ISBN:0-226-52143-5, ISBN13: 978-0-226-52143-5. Dewey:780/.9/04. LCCN:93-045855.

Audience: **u,f.** *B*

Meyer, Leonard B.   **ML60.M616S74 2000**
The Spheres of Music: A Gathering of Essays. Trade Cloth. University of Chicago Press. Chicago, IL. 2000. 328p. ISBN:0-226-52153-2, ISBN13: 978-0-226-52153-4. Dewey:780. LCCN:99-034400.

Audience: **u,f.**

Meyer, Leonard B.   **ML430.5.M5 1996**
Style and Music: Theory, History, and Ideology. Trade Paper. University of Chicago Press. Chicago, IL. 1997. 385p. ISBN:0-226-52152-4, ISBN13: 978-0-226-52152-7. Dewey:781. LCCN:96-017957.

Audience: **u,f.** *Choice, 1990.*

Paddison, Max   **ML3795**
Adorno, Modernism and Mass Culture: Essays in Critical Theory and Music. Ed. 2. Trade Paper. Kahn & Averill Publishers. London, 2004. 160p. ISBN:1-871082-81-1, ISBN13: 978-1-871082-81-4. Dewey:306.484.

Audience: **u,f.**

Raffman, Diana   **ML3800.R25 1993**
Language, Music, and Mind. Trade Cloth. MIT Press. Cambridge, MA. 1993. 183p. Bradford Bks. ISBN:0-262-18150-9, ISBN13: 978-0-262-18150-1. Dewey:781.11. LCCN:92-026560.

Audience: **u,f.** *Choice, 1993.*

Rahn, Jay   **ML3845.R18 1983**
A Theory for All Music: Problems and Solutions in the Analysis of Non-Western Forms. Trade Cloth. University of Toronto Press. Toronto, ON. 1983. 288p. ISBN:0-8020-5538-9, ISBN13: 978-0-8020-5538-5. Dewey:781. LCCN:83-226717.

Audience: **u,f.**

Schafer, R. Murray   **ML3805**
The Soundscape: Our Sonic Environment and the Tuning of the World. Rochester, Vt.: Destiny Books. 1994. ISBN:0-89281-455-1, ISBN13: 978-0-89281-455-8.

Audience: **u,f.**

Scher, Steven Paul (Editor)   **ML3849 .M935 1991**
Music and Text: Critical Inquiries. Trade Cloth. Cambridge University Press. New York, NY. 1992. 345p. ISBN:0-521-40158-5, ISBN13: 978-0-521-40158-6. Dewey:780/.08. LCCN:90-023762.

Audience: **u,f.** *Choice, 1992.*

Scruton, Roger   **ML3845.S3975 1999**
The Aesthetics of Music. Trade Paper. Oxford University Press, Inc. New York, NY. 1999. 552p. ISBN:0-19-816727-X, ISBN13: 978-0-19-816727-3. Dewey:781.1/7. LCCN:98-054066.

Audience: **u,f.** *Choice, 1998.*

Stravinsky, Igor   **MT7**
Poetics of Music in the Form of Six Lessons. George Seferis (Preface by). Trade Paper. Harvard University Press. Cambridge, MA. 1993. 160p. The Charles Eliot Norton Lectures ISBN:0-674-67856-7, ISBN13: 978-0-674-67856-9. Dewey:781. LCCN:79-099520.

Audience: **g,l,u,f.** *B*

Subotnik, Rose R.   **ML3800.S9 1990**
Developing Variations: Style and Ideology in Western Music. Trade Paper. University of Minnesota Press. Minneapolis, MN. 1991. 406p. ISBN:0-8166-1874-7, ISBN13: 978-0-8166-1874-3. Dewey:780.1. LCCN:90-042317.

Audience: **u,f.**

Sudnow, David   **MT68.S89 2001**
Ways of the Hand: A Rewritten Account. Ed. 2. Hubert L. Dreyfus (Foreword by). Trade Cloth. MIT Press. Cambridge, MA. 2001. 163p. ISBN:0-262-19467-8, ISBN13: 978-0-262-19467-9. Dewey:786.2/16593. LCCN:2001-044330.

Audience: **u,f.**

Treitler, Leo   **ML3845**
Music and the Historical Imagination. Trade Paper. Harvard
University Press. Cambridge, MA. 1990. 348p.
ISBN:0-674-59129-1, ISBN13: 978-0-674-59129-5.
Dewey:780/.1.
Audience: u,f. Choice, 1989.

Washburne, Christopher J.   **ML3800.B13 2004**
  & Derno, Maiken (Editors)
Bad Music: The Music We Love to Hate. Paper over Boards.
Routledge. New York, NY. 2004. 288p. ISBN:0-415-94365-5,
ISBN13: 978-0-415-94365-9. Dewey:781.1/7.
LCCN:2004-016591.
Audience: u,f.

Business and Industry of Music

                           ML3790
Recording Industry Sourcebook. Anscona Communications.
1990.
Audience: g,l,u,f.

Aczon, Michael   **KF4291 .A926**
The Professional Musician's Legal Companion. Trade Paper.
Thomson Course Technology. Boston, MA. 2005.
ISBN:1-59200-765-1, ISBN13: 978-1-59200-765-3.
Dewey:343/.7307878.
Audience: l,u,f.

Alderman, John   **ML74.7**
Sonic Boom: Napster, MP3, and the New Pioneers of Music.
Trade Paper. Basic Books. New York, NY. 2002. 224p.
ISBN:0-7382-0777-2, ISBN13: 978-0-7382-0777-3.
Dewey:780.2/85/4678.
Audience: g,l,u,f.

American Society of   **ML27.U5**
  Composers, Authors and Publishers
⬚ ASCAP: The American Society of Composers, Authors and
Publishers.
http://www.ascap.com/index.html
American Society of Composers, Authors and Publishers.
Audience: l,u,f.

Baskerville, David   **ML3795.B33 2006**
Music Business Handbook and Career Guide. Ed. 8. Cloth Text.
SAGE Publications, Inc. Thousand Oaks, CA. 2005. 640p.
ISBN:1-4129-0438-2, ISBN13: 978-1-4129-0438-4.
Dewey:780/.23/73. LCCN:2005-003608.
Audience: l,u,f. Choice, 1995.

Broadcast Music Inc.   **ML27.U5 B65**
⬚ BMI = Broadcast Music Inc.
http://www.bmi.com/
Broadcast Music Inc.
Audience: l,u,f.

Burnett, Robert   **ML3790.B85 1995**
The Global Jukebox: The International Music Industry. Paper
over Boards. Routledge. New York, NY. 1996. 192p.
Communication and Society Ser. ISBN:0-415-09275-2, ISBN13:
978-0-415-09275-3. Dewey:338.4/7/78164. LCCN:95-009247.
Audience: l,u,f.

Cohen, Rich   **ML405.C63 2004**
Machers and Rockers: Chess Records and the Business of Rock
and Roll. Trade Cloth. W. W. Norton & Company, Inc. New
York, NY. 2004. 160p. ISBN:0-393-05280-X, ISBN13:
978-0-393-05280-0. Dewey:781.66/0973. LCCN:2004-011792.
Audience: l,u,f.

Cohodas, Nadine   **ML405**
Spinning Blues into Gold: The Chess Brothers and the
Legendary Chess Records. Trade Paper. DIANE Publishing
Company. Collingdale, PA. 2004. 358p. ISBN:0-7567-8432-8,
ISBN13: 978-0-7567-8432-4. Dewey:781.643/149.
Audience: l,u,f. Choice, 2000.

Dannen, Fredric   **ML3790.D32 1991**
Hit Men: Power Brokers and Fast Money Inside the Music
Business. UK-Trade Paper. Knopf Publishing Group. New York,
NY. 1991. 432p. ISBN:0-679-73061-3, ISBN13:
978-0-679-73061-3. Dewey:338.4778163. LCCN:90-055680.
Audience: g,l,u,f.

Davis, Clive   **ML429.D36.A3**
Clive: Inside the Record Business. Trade Cloth. HarperCollins
Publishers. New York, NY. 1975. 300p. ISBN:0-688-02872-1,
ISBN13: 978-0-688-02872-5. Dewey:338.4/7/7899120924.
LCCN:74-012246.
Audience: l,u,f.

Day, Timothy   **ML156.9**
A Century of Recorded Music: Listening to Musical History.
Trade Paper. Yale University Press. Cumberland, RI. 2002.
336p. ISBN:0-300-09401-9, ISBN13: 978-0-300-09401-5.
Dewey:780/.26/6.
Audience: u,f. Choice, 2001.

Early, Gerald   **ML3477.E2 2004**
One Nation under a Groove: Motown and American Culture.
Trade Paper. University of Michigan Press. Chicago, IL. 2004.
248p. ISBN:0-472-08956-0, ISBN13: 978-0-472-08956-7.
Dewey:306.4/84244/0973. LCCN:2003-068714.
Audience: u,f.

Ertegun, Ahmet   **ML427.A85**
What'd I Say?: The Atlantic Story, 50 Years of Music. Greil
Marcus, Lenny Kaye & Robert Christgau (Contribution by).
Trade Cloth. Welcome Rain Publishers. New York, NY. 2001.
528p. ISBN:1-56649-048-0, ISBN13: 978-1-56649-048-1.
Dewey:781.660973.
Audience: l,u,f.

Frith, Simon & Marshall,   **K1420.5**
  Lee (Editors)

Music and Copyright. Ed. 2. Trade Cloth. Routledge. New York, NY. 2004. 256p. ISBN:0-415-97252-3, ISBN13: 978-0-415-97252-9. Dewey:346.04/82.

Audience: **u,f.**

Glixon, Beth Lise, et al.   ML1733.8.V4
Inventing the Business of Opera: The Impresario and His World in Seventeenth-Century Venice. Glixon, Jonathan Emmanuel (Author). Oxford University Press. 2006. AMS Studies in Music ISBN:0-19-515416-9, ISBN13: 978-0-19-515416-0.

Audience: **u,f.**

Gordy, Berry Jr.   ML429.G67A3 1994
To Be Loved: The Music, the Magic, the Memories of Motown an Autobiography. Trade Cloth. Warner Books. Inc. New York, NY. 1994. 448p. ISBN:0-446-51523-X, ISBN13: 978-0-446-51523-8. Dewey:781.644/092 B. LCCN:94-029067.

Audience: **l,u,f.**

Gronow, Pekka & Saunio, Ilpo   ML3790.G7813 1998
An International History of the Recording Industry. Ed. 2. Christopher Moseley (Translator). Trade Cloth. Continuum International Publishing Group, Ltd. London, 1998. 240p. ISBN:0-304-70173-4, ISBN13: 978-0-304-70173-5. Dewey:780.26/6. LCCN:97-041865.

Audience: **l,u,f.**

Gueraseva, Stacy   ML427.D44G84 2005
Def Jam, Inc.: Russell Simmons, Rick Rubin, and the Rise of Def Jam Records. Trade Cloth. Ballantine Books. New York, NY. 2005. 352p. ISBN:0-345-46804-X, ISBN13: 978-0-345-46804-8. Dewey:782.421649/092/2 B. LCCN:2004-066261.

Audience: **l,u,f.**

Harry Fox Agency
HFA = Harry Fox Agency.
http://www.harryfox.com/
Harry Fox Agency.

Audience: **u,f.**

Heylin, Clinton   ML3790
Bootleg: The Rise and Fall of the Secret Recording History. Trade Paper. Omnibus Press. New York, NY. 400p. ISBN:1-84449-151-X, ISBN13: 978-1-84449-151-3. Dewey:338.4/778149.

Audience: **g,l,u,f.**

Holzman, Jac & Daws, Gavan   ML3792.H65 1998
Follow the Music. Trade Paper. FirstMedia Books. Santa Monica, CA. 1998. 460p. ISBN:0-9661221-1-9, ISBN13: 978-0-9661221-1-4. Dewey:781.64/0973. LCCN:97-077539.

Audience: **u,f.**

Hull, Geoffrey P.   ML3790.H84 2004
The Recording Industry. Ed. 2. Paper over Boards. Routledge. New York, NY. 2004. 352p. ISBN:0-415-96802-X. ISBN13: 978-0-415-96802-7. Dewey:338.4/778149/0973. LCCN:2003-024594.

Audience: **l,u,f.**

Kennedy, Rick & McNutt, Randy   ML3792.K46 1999
Little Labels - Big Sound. Al Kooper (Foreword by). Cloth Text. Indiana University Press. Bloomington, IN. 1999. 183p. ISBN:0-253-33548-5, ISBN13: 978-0-253-33548-7. Dewey:781.64/0973. LCCN:98-049455.

Audience: **u,f.** *Choice, 1999.*

Kraft, James P.   ML3795.K82 2003
Stage to Studio: Musicians and the Sound Revolution, 1890-1950. Trade Paper. Johns Hopkins University Press. Baltimore, MD. 2003. 248p. Studies in Industry and Society Ser. ISBN:0-8018-7742-3, ISBN13: 978-0-8018-7742-1. Dewey:331/.04178/0973. LCCN:95-043923.

Audience: **u,f.**

Krasilovsky, M. William & Schemel, Sidney   ML3790.K72 2003
This Business of Music: The Definitive Guide to the Music Industry. Ed. 9. John M. Gross (Contribution by). Trade Cloth. Watson-Guptill Publications, Inc. New York, NY. 2003. 544p. Ser. ISBN:0-8230-7728-4, ISBN13: 978-0-8230-7728-1. Dewey:338.4/778/0973. LCCN:2003-103770.

Audience: **l,u,f.**

Krummel, Donald W. & Sadie, Stanley (Editors) ML112.M86 1990
Music Printing and Publishing. Trade Cloth. W. W. Norton & Company, Inc. New York, NY. 1990. xiv, 615p. Grove Handbooks in Music Ser. ISBN:0-393-02809-7, ISBN13: 978-0-393-02809-6. Dewey:070.5/794. LCCN:90-178838.

Audience: **u,f.**

MacLeod, Bruce A.   ML3795.M14 1993
Club Date Musicians: Playing the New York Party Circuit. Trade Cloth. University of Illinois Press. Champaign, IL. 1993. 232p. ISBN:0-252-01954-7, ISBN13: 978-0-252-01954-8. Dewey:780/.23/7471. LCCN:92-010010.

Audience: **u,f.** *Choice, 1994.*

Marshall, Lee   ML3916
Bootlegging: Romanticism and Copyright in the Music Industry. Cloth Text. SAGE Publications, Inc. Thousand Oaks, CA. 2005. 192p. ISBN:0-7619-4490-7, ISBN13: 978-0-7619-4490-4. Dewey:306.4842.

Audience: **g,l,u,f.**

Martland, Peter   ML3792.M37 1997
Since Records Began: EMI: the First Hundred Years. Trade Cloth. Hal Leonard Corporation. Milwaukee, WI. 1997. 359p. ISBN:1-57467-033-6, ISBN13: 978-1-57467-033-2. Dewey:338.7/6178/0266/0941. LCCN:97-002709.

Audience: **u,f.**

Music Library Association   ML3790
Copyright for Music Librarians.
http://www.lib.jmu.edu/org/mla/
Music Library Association.

Audience: **g,l,u,f.**

Music Publishers'   ML112 M73
  Association of the United States
☐ MPA = Music Publisher's Association of the United States.
http://www.mpa.org
Music Publisher's Association of the United States.

Audience: **u,f.**

National Music Publishers'   ML27
  Association
☐ NMPA = National Music Publishers' Association.
http://www.nmpa.org/
National Music Publishers' Association.

Audience: **u,f.**

Negus, Keith   ML3790.N4 1999
Music Genres and Corporate Cultures. Paper over Boards.
Routledge. New York, NY. 1999. 224p. ISBN:0-415-17399-X,
ISBN13: 978-0-415-17399-5. Dewey:781.64. LCCN:98-051909.

Audience: **u,f.** *Choice, 2000.*

Olmsted, Anthony   ML3792.F65O65 2003
Folkways Records: Moses Asch and His Encyclopedia of Sound.
Paper over Boards. Routledge. New York, NY. 2003. 256p.
ISBN:0-415-93708-6, ISBN13: 978-0-415-93708-5.
Dewey:781.62/13/0092 B. LCCN:2002-155714.

Audience: **u,f.**

Passman, Donald S.   ML3790.P35 2003
All You Need to Know about the Music Business. Ed. 5. Randy
Glass (Illustrator). Trade Cloth. Simon & Schuster. New York,
NY. 2003. 464p. ISBN:0-7432-4637-3, ISBN13:
978-0-7432-4637-8. Dewey:780/.23/73. LCCN:2003-049115.

Audience: **l,u,f.**

Prial, Dunstan   ML429.H26P75 2006
The Producer: John Hammond and the Soul of American Music.
Cloth over Boards. Farrar, Straus & Giroux. New York, NY.
2006. 368p. ISBN:0-374-11304-1, ISBN13: 978-0-374-11304-9.
Dewey:781.64/092 B. LCCN:2005-012666.

Audience: **u,f.**

Recording Industry   ML3790
  Association of America
☐ RIAA = Recording Industry Association of America.
http://www.riaa.com
Recording Industry Association of America.

Audience: **g,l,u,f.**

Rosselli, John   ML1733.R78 1984
The Opera Industry in Italy from Cimarosa to Verdi: The Role
of the Impresario. Trade Cloth. Cambridge University Press.
New York, NY. 1984. 224p. ISBN:0-521-25732-8, ISBN13:
978-0-521-25732-9. Dewey:782.1/0945. LCCN:83-007688.

Audience: **u,f.** *B*

Sanjek, Russell   ML200.S26 1988
American Popular Music and Its Business: The First Four
Hundred Years: From 1790 to 1909, Vol. II. Cloth Text. Oxford
University Press, Inc. New York, NY. 1988. 494p.

ISBN:0-19-504310-3, ISBN13: 978-0-19-504310-5.
Dewey:780/.42/0973. LCCN:87-018605.

Audience: **g,l,u,f.** *Choice, 1989.*

Sanjek, Russell   ML200.S26 1988
American Popular Music and Its Business: The First Four
Hundred Years, 1790-1909. Cloth Text. Oxford University Press,
Inc. New York, NY. 1988. 494p. ISBN:0-19-504028-7, ISBN13:
978-0-19-504028-9. Dewey:780/.42/0973. LCCN:87-018605.

Audience: **g,l,u,f.** *Choice, 1989.*

Sanjek, Russell   ML200.S26 1988
American Popular Music and Its Business: The First Four
Hundred Years, 1900-1984, Vol. 3. Cloth Text. Oxford
University Press, Inc. New York, NY. 1988. 750p.
ISBN:0-19-504311-1, ISBN13: 978-0-19-504311-2.
Dewey:780/.42/0973. LCCN:87-018605.

Audience: **g,l,u,f.** *Choice, 1989.*

Sanjek, Russell   ML3477.S2 1996
Pennies from Heaven: The American Popular Music Business in
the Twentieth Century. David Sanjek (Contribution by). Trade
Paper. Da Capo Press, Inc. Cambridge, MA. 1996. 790p.
ISBN:0-306-80706-8, ISBN13: 978-0-306-80706-0.
Dewey:338.4/778164/0973090. LCCN:96-023223.

Audience: **u,f.** *Choice, 1997.*

Scherer, F. M.   ML3795.S23835 2004
Quarter Notes and Bank Notes: The Economics of Music
Composition in the Eighteenth and Nineteenth Centuries. Trade
Cloth. Princeton University Press. Princeton, NJ. 2003. 256p.
The Princeton Economic History of the Western World Ser.
ISBN:0-691-11621-0, ISBN13: 978-0-691-11621-1.
Dewey:331.7/617813/09033. LCCN:2003-053645.

Audience: **u,f.** *Choice, 2004.*

Smith, Jeff   ML2075.S65 1998
The Sounds of Commerce: Marketing Popular Film Music.
Trade Paper. Columbia University Press. New York, NY. 1998.
304p. Film and Culture Ser. ISBN:0-231-10863-X, ISBN13:
978-0-231-10863-8. Dewey:781.5/42/0688. LCCN:98-017923.

Audience: **l,u,f.** *Choice, 1999.*

Smith, Suzanne E.   ML3792.S65 1999
Dancing in the Street: Motown and the Cultural Politics of
Detroit. Trade Cloth. Harvard University Press. Cambridge, MA.
2000. 336p. ISBN:0-674-00063-3, ISBN13: 978-0-674-00063-6.
Dewey:781.644/09774/34. LCCN:99-034399.

Audience: **u,f.**

Society of European Stage   Z653 .N2
  Authors and Composers
☐ SESAC = Society of European Stage Authors and
Composers.
http://www.sesac.com
Society of European Stage Authors and Composers.

Audience: **u,f.**

Symes, Colin   ML3790.S97 2004
Setting the Record Straight: A Material History of Classical
Recording. Trade Paper. Wesleyan University Press.

Middletown, CT. 2004. xiii, 313p. ISBN:0-8195-6722-1, ISBN13: 978-0-8195-6722-2. Dewey:781.49/09. LCCN:2004-017354.

Audience: **u,f.**

Welch, Walter L. & Stenzel　　　**TS2301.P3W36 1994**
Burt, Leah B.
From Tinfoil to Stereo: The Acoustic Years of the Recording Industry, 1877-1929. George L. Frow (Foreword by). Trade Cloth. University Press of Florida. Gainesville, FL. 1994. 232p. ISBN:0-8130-1317-8, ISBN13: 978-0-8130-1317-6. Dewey:621.389/3/09. LCCN:94-004823.

Audience: **l,■,f.** *Choice, 1995.*

Wexler, Jerry & Ritz, David　　　**ML429.W4A3 1994**
Rhythm and the Blues: A Life in American Music. Trade Paper. St. Martin's Press. Gordonville, VA. 1994. 352p. ISBN:0-312-11376-5, ISBN13: 978-0-312-11376-6. Dewey:781.643/092 B. LCCN:94-025583.

Audience: **l,u,f.**

Whitsett, Tim　　　　　　　　　　　**ML3790**
Dictionary of Music Business Terms. Sarah Jones (Editor). Trade Paper. artistpro.com, LLC. Vallejo, CA. 1998. 159p. ISBN:0-87288-684-0, ISBN13: 978-0-87288-684-1. Dewey:780.25. LCCN:98-067691.

Audience: **g,l,u,f.**

Music Technology

Axford, Elizabeth C.　　　　　　**ML74.7.A94 2004**
Song Sheets to Software: A Guide to Print Music, Software, and Web Sites for Musicians. Ed. 2. Trade Paper. Scarecrow Press, Inc. Lanham, MD. 2004. 274p. ISBN:0-8108-5027-3, ISBN13: 978-0-8108-5027-9. Dewey:780.26. LCCN:2004-002488.

Audience: **l,u,f** *Choice, 2005.*

Braun, Hans-Joachim　　　　　　**ML197.I2 2002**
Music and Technology in the Twentieth Century. International Committee for the History of Technology (Contribution by). Trade Cloth. Johns Hopkins University Press. Baltimore, MD. 2002. 256p. ISBN:0-8018-6885-8, ISBN13: 978-0-8018-6885-6. Dewey:780/.06. LCCN:2001-042490.

Audience: **u,f.**

Cary, Tristram　　　　　　　　　　**ML102**
Dictionary of Musical Technology. Cloth Text. Greenwood Publishing Group, Inc. Portsmouth, NH. 1992. 575p. ISBN:0-313-28694-9, ISBN13: 978-0-313-28694-0. Dewey:780/.3. LCCN:92-014583.

Audience: **g,l,u,f.** *Choice, 1993.*

Cope, David　　　　　　　　　　**MT56.C668 2000**
The Algorithmic Composer. Trade Cloth. A-R Editions, Inc. Middleton, WI. 2000. ISBN:0-89579-454-3, ISBN13: 978-0-89579-454-3. Dewey:781.3/4. LCCN:99-059109.

Audience: **u,f.**

Cope, David　　　　　　　　　　**MT56.C69 2004**
Virtual Music: Computer Synthesis of Musical Style. Trade Paper. MIT Press. Cambridge, MA. 2004. 584p. ISBN:0-262-53261-1, ISBN13: 978-0-262-53261-7. Dewey:781.3/4.

Audience: **u,f.** *Choice, 2001.*

Davis, Deta S.　　　　　　　　　　**ML128.C62D4 1988**
Computer Applications in Music: A Bibliography. Trade Cloth. A-R Editions, Inc. Middleton, WI. 1988. 537p. Computer Music and Digital Audio Ser., Vol. 4 ISBN:0-89579-225-7, ISBN13: 978-0-89579-225-9. Dewey:016.780285. LCCN:88-070079.

Audience: **u,f.** *Choice, 1989.*

Davis, Deta S.　　　　　　　　　　**ML128.C62**
Computer Applications in Music: A Bibliography, Supplement 1. John Strawn (Preface by). Trade Cloth. A-R Editions, Inc. Middleton, WI. 1993. 600p. Computer Music and Digital Audio Ser., Vol. 10 ISBN:0-89579-267-2, ISBN13: 978-0-89579-267-9. Dewey:016.780285. LCCN:92-013289.

Audience: **u,f.** *Choice, 1989.*

Day, Timothy　　　　　　　　　　**ML156.9**
A Century of Recorded Music: Listening to Musical History. Trade Paper. Yale University Press. Cumberland, RI. 2002. 336p. ISBN:0-300-09401-9, ISBN13: 978-0-300-09401-5. Dewey:780/.26/6.

Audience: **u,f.** *Choice, 2001.*

Dodge, Charles & Jerse,　　　　　**ML1092.D54 1997**
Thomas A.
Computer Music: Synthesis, Composition, and Performance. Ed. 2. Paper Text. Thomson Wadsworth. Belmont, CA. 1997. 480p. ISBN:0-02-864682-7, ISBN13: 978-0-02-864682-4. Dewey:780.2/85. LCCN:96-053478.

Audience: **l,u,f.**

Duckworth, William　　　　　　**ML74.7.D83 2005**
Virtual Music: How the Web Got Wired for Sound. Paper over Boards. Routledge. New York, NY. 2005. 232p. ISBN:0-415-96674-4, ISBN13: 978-0-415-96674-0. Dewey:781.3/4. LCCN:2005-005960.

Audience: **l,u,f.** *Choice, 2005.*

Eisenberg, Evan　　　　　　　　**ML3916**
The Recording Angel: Music, Records and Culture from Aristotle to Zappa. Ed. 2. Trade Paper. Yale University Press. Cumberland, RI. 2005. 256p. ISBN:0-300-09904-5, ISBN13: 978-0-300-09904-1. Dewey:306.4842. LCCN:2004-117200.

Audience: **u,f.**

Emmerson, Simon (Editor)　　　**ML1380.M86 2000**
Music, Electronic Media and Culture. Trade Cloth. Ashgate Publishing, Ltd. Aldershot, 2000. 262p. ISBN:0-7546-0109-9, ISBN13: 978-0-7546-0109-8. Dewey:786.7. LCCN:00-059415.

Audience: **l,u,f.**

Greene, Paul D. & Porcello,　　　**ML3545.W57 2004**
Thomas
Wired for Sound: Engineering and Technologies in Sonic Cultures. Library Binding. Wesleyan University Press.

Middletown, CT. 2004. 304p. Music/Culture Ser.
ISBN:0-8195-6516-4, ISBN13: 978-0-8195-6516-7.
Dewey:780/.9/05. LCCN:2004-016021.
                    Audience: **u,f.** *Choice, 2005.*

Hoffmann, Frank W.   **ML102.S67E5 2004**
  (Editor)
Encyclopedia of Recorded Sound. Ed. 2. Paper over Boards.
Routledge. New York, NY. 2004. 1320p. ISBN:0-415-93835-X,
ISBN13: 978-0-415-93835-8. Dewey:384. LCCN:2003-026491.
                    Audience: **g,l,u,f.** *Choice, 2005.*

Katz, Mark   **ML3790 .K277 2004**
Capturing Sound: How Technology Has Changed Music. Trade
Paper. University of California Press. Berkeley, CA. 2004. 288p.
A Roth Family Foundation Music in America Book Ser.
ISBN:0-520-24380-3, ISBN13: 978-0-520-24380-4.
Dewey:781.49. LCCN:2004-011383.
                    Audience: **g,l,u,f.** *Choice, 2005.*

Kefauver, Alan P.   **TK7881.K44 2001**
The Audio Recording Handbook. Trade Paper. A-R Editions,
Inc. Middleton, WI. 2001. xii + 606p. The Computer Music and
Digital Audio Ser., Vol. DAS 17 ISBN:0-89579-462-4, ISBN13:
978-0-89579-462-8. Dewey:621.389/3. LCCN:2001-022651.
                    Audience: **l,u,f.**

Lysloff, Rene T. A. & Gay,   **ML197.M78 2003**
  Leslie C. (Editors)
Music and Technoculture. Library Binding. Wesleyan University
Press. Middletown, CT. 2003. 416p. Music/Culture Ser.
ISBN:0-8195-6513-X, ISBN13: 978-0-8195-6513-6.
Dewey:780/.06. LCCN:2003-004628.
                    Audience: **u,f.** *Choice, 2004.*

Millard, Andre   **ML1055.M47 2005**
America on Record: A History of Recorded Sound. Ed. 2. Cloth
Text. Cambridge University Press. New York, NY. 2005. 474p.
ISBN:0-521-83515-1, ISBN13: 978-0-521-83515-2.
Dewey:621.389/3/0973. LCCN:2005-025304.
                    Audience: **l,u,f.** *Choice, 1996.*

Mitsui, Toru & Hosokawa,   **ML3795.K22 1998**
  Shuhei
Karaoke Around the World: Global Technology, Local Singing.
Paper over Boards. Routledge. New York, NY. 1998. 224p.
Research in Cultural and Media Studies ISBN:0-415-16371-4,
ISBN13: 978-0-415-16371-2. Dewey:306.4/84.
LCCN:97-019902.
                    Audience: **u,f.**

Moore, F. Richard   **MT723.M6 1990**
Elements of Computer Music. Ed. 1. Trade Paper. Prentice Hall
PTR. Upper Saddle River, NJ. 1990. 656p.
ISBN:0-13-252552-6, ISBN13: 978-0-13-252552-7.
Dewey:786.7/6. LCCN:89-008679.
                    Audience: **l,u,f.**

Moorefield, Virgil   **ML3470.M66 2005**
The Producer as Composer: Shaping the Sounds of Popular
Music. Trade Cloth. MIT Press. Cambridge, MA. 2005. 143p.

ISBN:0-262-13457-8, ISBN13: 978-0-262-13457-6.
Dewey:781.49. LCCN:2005-041588.
                    Audience: **l,u,f.** *Choice, 2006.*

Morton, David   **TK7881**
Sound Recording: The Life Story of a Technology. Cloth Text.
Greenwood Publishing Group, Inc. Portsmouth, NH. 2004. 240p.
Greenwood Technographies Ser. ISBN:0-313-33090-5, ISBN13:
978-0-313-33090-2. Dewey:621.389/3. LCCN:2004-047541.
                    Audience: **l,u,f.** *Choice, 2005.*

Olsen, Eric, et al.   **ML105.E53 1999**
The Encyclopedia of Record Producers. Carlo Wolff & Paul
Verna (Authors). Trade Paper. Watson-Guptill Publications, Inc.
New York, NY. 1999. 912p. ISBN:0-8230-7607-5, ISBN13:
978-0-8230-7607-9. Dewey:781.64/092/2 B. LCCN:99-032191.
                    Audience: **g,l,u,f.** *Choice, 2000.*

Philip, Robert   **ML457 .P5 1992**
Early Recordings and Musical Style: Changing Tastes in
Instrumental Performance, 1900-1950. Trade Paper. Cambridge
University Press. New York, NY. 2004. 284p.
ISBN:0-521-60744-2, ISBN13: 978-0-521-60744-5.
Dewey:781.4/30904. LCCN:2005-280641.
                    Audience: **u,f.** *Choice, 1993.*

Philip, Robert   **ML457**
Performing Music in the Age of Recording. Cloth over Boards.
Yale University Press. Cumberland, RI. 2004. 304p.
ISBN:0-300-10246-1, ISBN13: 978-0-300-10246-8.
Dewey:781.4/3/0904. LCCN:2004-100136.
                    Audience: **u,f.** *Choice, 2004.*

Roads, Curtis   **MT56.R6 1995**
The Computer Music Tutorial. Trade Paper. MIT Press.
Cambridge, MA. 1996. 904p. ISBN:0-262-68082-3, ISBN13:
978-0-262-68082-0. Dewey:780/.285. LCCN:94-019027.
                    Audience: **u,f.**

Roads, Curtis   **MT723**
The Music Machine: Selected Readings from Computer Music
Journal. Trade Paper. MIT Press. Cambridge, MA. 1992. 739p.
ISBN:0-262-68078-5, ISBN13: 978-0-262-68078-3.
Dewey:786.7/6.
                    Audience: **u,f.**

Ross, Ted   **ML112**
The Art of Music Engraving and Processing; A Complete
Manual, Reference and Text book on Preparing Music for
Reproduction and Print. Miami, Hansen Books. 1970.
                    Audience: **u,f.**

Rothstein, Joseph   **MT723.R68 1995**
MIDI: A Comprehensive Introduction, Vol. 7. Ed. 2. Trade
Paper. A-R Editions, Inc. Middleton, WI. 1995. xvii, 268p.
ISBN:0-89579-309-1, ISBN13: 978-0-89579-309-6.
Dewey:784.19/0285/46. LCCN:94-045738.
                    Audience: **u,f.** *Choice, 1992.*

Rowe, Robert   ML74.R68 2001
Machine Musicianship. Trade Cloth, CD-ROM. MIT Press.
Cambridge, MA. 2001. 416p. ISBN:0-262-18206-8, ISBN13:
978-0-262-18206-5. Dewey:780/.285. LCCN:00-038699.
                                         Audience: **u,f.** *Choice, 2001.*

Schloss, Joseph G.   ML3531.S35 2004
Making Beats: The Art of Sample-Based Hip-Hop. Library
Binding. Wesleyan University Press. Middletown, CT. 2004.
240p. Music/Culture Ser. ISBN:0-8195-6695-0, ISBN13:
978-0-8195-6695-9. Dewey:782.421649/149.
LCCN:2004-043013.
                                     Audience: **g,l,u,f.** *Choice, 2005.*

Schwanauer, Stephen &   ML74.3.M3 1993
   Levitt, David
Machine Models of Music. Trade Cloth. MIT Press. Cambridge,
MA. 1993. 556p. ISBN:0-262-19319-1, ISBN13:
978-0-262-19319-1. Dewey:781.34. LCCN:92-017179.
                                         Audience: **u,f.** *Choice, 1994.*

Selfridge-Field, Eleanor   ML74.B49 1997
   (Editor)
Beyond MIDI: The Handbook of Musical Codes. Trade Cloth.
MIT Press. Cambridge, MA. 1997. 630p. ISBN:0-262-19394-9,
ISBN13: 978-0-262-19394-8. Dewey:780/.285/572.
LCCN:97-002596.
                                                       Audience: **u,f.**

Shaughnessy, Mary Angela   ML419.P47S5 1993
Les Paul: An American Original. Trade Cloth. HarperCollins
Publishers. New York, NY. 1993. 347p. ISBN:0-688-08467-2,
ISBN13: 978-0-688-08467-7. Dewey:781.64/092.
LCCN:92-035832.
                                                     Audience: **l,u,f.**

Sterne, Jonathan   TK7881.4.S733 2002
The Audible Past: Cultural Origins of Sound Reproduction.
Trade Cloth. Duke University Press. Durham, NC. 2003. 448p.
ISBN:0-8223-3004-0, ISBN13: 978-0-8223-3004-2.
Dewey:621.389/3/09. LCCN:2002-009196.
                                     Audience: **l,u,f.** *Choice, 2003.*

Utz, Peter   TK7881.4.U89 2003
Introduction to Audio. Trade Cloth. A-R Editions, Inc.
Middleton, WI. 2003. 268p. Computer Music and Digital Audio
Ser., Vol. 20 ISBN:0-89579-512-4, ISBN13: 978-0-89579-512-0.
Dewey:621.389/3. LCCN:2002-151108.
                                                     Audience: **l,u,f.**

Wadhams, Wayne   ML102.M85W3 1988
Dictionary of Music Production and Engineering Terminology.
Cloth Text. Thomson Gale. Farmington Hills, MI. 1987. 288p.
ISBN:0-02-872691-X, ISBN13: 978-0-02-872691-5.
Dewey:338.4/778/0321. LCCN:87-030988.
                                     Audience: **g,l,u,f.** *Choice, 1989.*

Watkinson, John   TK7881.4.W3834 2002
Introduction to Digital Audio. Ed. 2. Paper Text. Elsevier

Science & Technology Books. Saint Louis, MO. 2002. 419p.
ISBN:0-240-51643-5, ISBN13: 978-0-240-51643-1.
Dewey:621.389/3. LCCN:2002-026543.
                                                     Audience: **l,u,f.**

Welch, Walter L. & Stenzel   TS2301.P3W36 1994
   Burt, Leah B.
From Tinfoil to Stereo: The Acoustic Years of the Recording
Industry, 1877-1929. George L. Frow (Foreword by). Trade
Cloth. University Press of Florida. Gainesville, FL. 1994. 232p.
ISBN:0-8130-1317-8, ISBN13: 978-0-8130-1317-6.
Dewey:621.389/3/09. LCCN:94-004823.
                                     Audience: **l,u,f.** *Choice, 1995.*

White, Glenn D. & Louie,   TK7881.4.W48 2004
   Gary J.
The Audio Dictionary. Ed. 3. Trade Paper, Perfect. University of
Washington Press. Seattle, WA. 2005. 516p.
ISBN:0-295-98498-8, ISBN13: 978-0-295-98498-8.
Dewey:621.389/3. LCCN:2004-029425.
                                  Audience: **g,l,u,f.** *Choice, 2005, 1992.*

Williams, David Brian &   ML74
   Webster, Peter Richard
Experiencing Music Technology. Ed. 3. Paper Text. Thomson
Wadsworth. Belmont, CA. 2005. 504p. ISBN:0-534-17672-0,
ISBN13: 978-0-534-17672-3. Dewey:ML74.
                                                     Audience: **l,u,f.**

Musical Instruments

Bachmann, Alberto   ML800.B13
An Encyclopedia of the Violin. Trade Cloth. Library Reprints,
Inc. Temecula, CA. 2001. 470p. ISBN:0-7222-5990-5, ISBN13:
978-0-7222-5990-0. Dewey:787.1.
                                                  Audience: **l,u,f.** *B*

Baines, Anthony   ML933.B33
Brass Instruments: Their History and Development. Trade Paper.
Dover Publications, Inc. Mineola, NY. 1993. 320p.
ISBN:0-486-27574-4, ISBN13: 978-0-486-27574-1.
Dewey:788/.01/09. LCCN:93-019988.
                                                  Audience: **l,u,f.** *B*

Baines, Anthony   ML102.I5B34 1992
The Oxford Companion to Musical Instruments. Trade Cloth.
Oxford University Press, Inc. New York, NY. 1992. 416p.
ISBN:0-19-311334-1, ISBN13: 978-0-19-311334-3.
Dewey:784.19/03. LCCN:92-008635.
                                     Audience: **g,l,u,f.** *Choice, 1993.*

Baines, Anthony   ML931.B3 1991
Woodwind Instruments and Their History. Ed. 3. Trade Paper.
Dover Publications, Inc. Mineola, NY. 1998. 384p.
ISBN:0-486-26885-3, ISBN13: 978-0-486-26885-9.
Dewey:788.2/19. LCCN:91-023745.
                                                  Audience: **l,u,f.** *B*

Bevan, Clifford   ML970
The Tuba Family. Ed. 2. Winchester : Piccolo. 2000.
ISBN:1-872203-30-2, ISBN13: 978-1-872203-30-0.
> Audience: **l,u,f.**

Blades, James   ML1030.B6 1992
Percussion Instruments and Their History. Ed. 4. Benjamin
Britten (Foreword by). Trade Paper. Bold Strummer, Limited,
The. Westport, CT. 1992. 512p. ISBN:0-933224-61-3, ISBN13:
978-0-933224-61-2. Dewey:789/.01/09. LCCN:93-162831.
> Audience: **l,u,f.** *B̶*

Boyden, David D.   ML850.B7 1990
The History of Violin Playing from Its Origins to 1761: And Its
Relationship to the Violin and Violin Music. Trade Paper.
Oxford University Press, Inc. New York, NY. 1990. 594p.
ISBN:0-19-816183-2, ISBN13: 978-0-19-816183-7.
Dewey:787.2/143/09. LCCN:89-016285.
> Audience: **l,u,f.**

Brown, Rachel   ML937.B76 2002
The Early Flute: A Practical Guide. Cloth Text. Cambridge
University Press. New York, NY. 2003. 198p. Cambridge
Handbooks to the Historical Performance of Music
ISBN:0-521-81391-3, ISBN13: 978-0-521-81391-4.
Dewey:788.3/09. LCCN:2001-052903.
> Audience: **u,f.** *Choice, 2003.*

Burgess, Geoffrey &   ML940
   Haynes, Bruce
The Oboe. Cloth over Boards. Yale University Press.
Cumberland, RI. 2004. 432p. The Yale Musical Instrument Ser.
ISBN:0-300-09317-9, ISBN13: 978-0-300-09317-9.
Dewey:788.5/2/09. LCCN:2003-114791.
> Audience: **l,u,f.** *Choice, 2004.*

Coelho, Victor Anand   ML1015.G9C23 2002
   (Editor)
The Cambridge Companion to the Guitar. Cloth Text.
Cambridge University Press. New York, NY. 2003. 278p.
Cambridge Companions to Music Ser. ISBN:0-521-80192-3,
ISBN13: 978-0-521-80192-8. Dewey:787.87.
LCCN:2002-025691.
> Audience: **l,u,f.**

Cole, Michael   ML655.C63 1998
The Pianoforte in the Classical Era. Trade Cloth. Oxford
University Press, Inc. New York, NY. 1998. 412p.
ISBN:0-19-816634-6, ISBN13: 978-0-19-816634-4.
Dewey:786.2/094/09033. LCCN:97-015105.
> Audience: **u,f.** *Choice, 1998.*

Diamond, Beverley, et al.   ML3557.D5 1994
Visions of Sound: Musical Instruments of First Nations
Communities in Northeastern America. M. Sam Cronk &
Franziska Von Rosen (Authors). Trade Paper. University of
Chicago Press. Chicago, IL. 1995. 240p. Chicago Studies in
Ethnomusicology ISBN:0-226-14476-3, ISBN13:
978-0-226-14476-4. Dewey:784.1974/08997. LCCN:94-010337.
> Audience: **g,l,u,f.**

Ehrlich, Cyril   ML652.E4 1990
The Piano: A History. Ed. 2. Trade Paper. Oxford University
Press, Inc. New York, NY. 1990. 262p. ISBN:0-19-816171-9,
ISBN13: 978-0-19-816171-4. Dewey:786.2/1/09.
LCCN:89-023161.
> Audience: **g,l,u,f.** *B̶ Choice, 1990.*

Good, Edwin M.   ML652
Giraffes, Black Dragons, and Other Pianos: A Technological
History from Cristofori to the Modern Concert Grand. Ed. 2.
Trade Paper. Stanford University Press. Palo Alto, CA. 2002.
400p. ISBN:0-8047-4549-8, ISBN13: 978-0-8047-4549-9.
Dewey:786.2/19/09.
> Audience: **g,l,u,f.** *Choice, 2001.*

Gregory, Robin   ML965.G74
The Trombone: The Instrument and Its Music. Praeger. 1973.
> Audience: **l,u,f.**

Gura, Philip F. & Bollman,   98-46164 [ML]
   James F.
America's Instrument: The Banjo in the Nineteenth Century.
Trade Cloth. University of North Carolina Press. Chapel Hill,
NC. 1999. 400p. ISBN:0-8078-2484-4, ISBN13:
978-0-8078-2484-9. Dewey:787.8/81973/09034.
LCCN:98-046164.
> Audience: **l,u,f.** *Choice, 2000.*

Haynes, Bruce   ML940.H39 2001
The Eloquent Oboe: A History of the Hautboy from 1640-1760.
Cloth Text. Oxford University Press, Inc. New York, NY. 2001.
544p. Oxford Early Music Ser. ISBN:0-19-816646-X, ISBN13:
978-0-19-816646-7. Dewey:788.5/2/09. LCCN:00-050419.
> Audience: **u,f.**

Herbert, Trevor   ML965
The Trombone. Cloth over Boards. Yale University Press.
Cumberland, RI. 2006. 336p. Yale Musical Instrument Ser.
ISBN:0-300-10095-7, ISBN13: 978-0-300-10095-2.
Dewey:788.9/3. LCCN:2005-930979.
> Audience: **l,u,f.** *Choice, 2006.*

Herbert, Trevor (Editor)   ML933.C36 1997
The Cambridge Companion to Brass Instruments. Wallace, John
(Editor). Cambridge University Press. 1997. Cambridge
Companions to Music ISBN:0-521-56343-7, ISBN13:
978-0-521-56343-7.
> Audience: **l,u,f.**

Hill, William H., et al.   ML424.S8
Antonio Stradivari, His Life and Work (1644-1739). Ed. 2.
Arthur F. Hill, Alfred E. Hill & Frances A. Davis (Authors).
Trade Paper. Dover Publications, Inc. Mineola, NY. 1963. 315p.
ISBN:0-486-20425-1, ISBN13: 978-0-486-20425-3.
Dewey:787.12.
> Audience: **g,l,u,f.**

Hinson, Maurice   ML102.P5H46 2004
The Pianist's Dictionary. Trade Paper. Indiana University Press.
Bloomington, IN. 2004. 160p. ISBN:0-253-21682-6, ISBN13:
978-0-253-21682-3. Dewey:786.2/03. LCCN:2003-025350.
> Audience: **g,l,u,f.** *Choice, 2004.*

Holland, James   ML1030 .H64

Percussion. Trade Paper. Kahn & Averill Publishers. London, 2001. 296p. Yehudi Menuhin Music Guides Ser. ISBN:1-871082-39-0, ISBN13: 978-1-871082-39-5. Dewey:789/.01/09.

Audience: **l,u,f.** 𝐵

Humphries, John   ML955 .H86 2000

The Early Horn: A Practical Guide. Colin Lawson & Robin Stowell (Contribution by). Cloth Text. Cambridge University Press. New York, NY. 2000. 146p. Handbooks to the Historical Performance of Music ISBN:0-521-63210-2, ISBN13: 978-0-521-63210-2. Dewey:788.9/4/09. LCCN:99-054036.

Audience: **u,f.** *Choice, 2001.*

Ingham, Richard (Editor)   ML975 .C36 1998

The Cambridge Companion to the Saxophone. Thomas Liley, Thomas Dryer-Beers, Kyle Horch, David Roach, Nick Turner, Stephen Trier, Gordon Lewin, Chris Davis & Jonathan Cross (Contribution by). Trade Paper. Cambridge University Press. New York, NY. 1999. 242p. Cambridge Companions to Music Ser. ISBN:0-521-59666-1, ISBN13: 978-0-521-59666-4. Dewey:788.7. LCCN:98-017404.

Audience: **l,u,f.** *Choice, 1999.*

Kartomi, Margaret J.   ML460.K36 1990

On Concepts and Classifications of Musical Instruments. Stephen Blum (Foreword by). Trade Paper. University of Chicago Press. Chicago, IL. 1990. 349p. Chicago Studies in Ethnomusicology ISBN:0-226-42549-5, ISBN13: 978-0-226-42549-8. Dewey:784.19/012. LCCN:90-031361.

Audience: **u,f.** *Choice, 1991.*

Katz, Mark   ML128.V4K38 2006

The Violin: A Research and Information Guide. Trade Cloth. Routledge. New York, NY. 2005. 336p. Music Research and Information Guides ISBN:0-8153-3637-3, ISBN13: 978-0-8153-3637-2. Dewey:016.7872. LCCN:2005-030659.

Audience: **u,f.**

Kottick, Edward L.   ML650.K68 2002

A History of the Harpsichord. Trade Cloth. Indiana University Press. Bloomington, IN. 2003. 592p. ISBN:0-253-34166-3, ISBN13: 978-0-253-34166-2. Dewey:786.4/19/09. LCCN:2002-006385.

Audience: **u,f.**

Kozinn, Allan, et al.   ML1015.G9 G845 1984

The Guitar: The History, the Music, the Players. Pete Welding, Dan Forte & Gene Santoro (Authors). Trade Cloth. HarperCollins Publishers. New York, NY. 1984. 200p. ISBN:0-688-01972-2, ISBN13: 978-0-688-01972-3. Dewey:787.6/1/09. LCCN:83-062354.

Audience: **g,l,u,f.**

Langwill, Lyndesay G.   ML:950

Bassoon and Contrabassoon. Trade Cloth. W. W. Norton & Company, Inc. New York, NY. 1966. ISBN:0-393-02098-3, ISBN13: 978-0-393-02098-4. Dewey:788.8.

Audience: **l,u,f.**

Lawson, Colin J. (Editor)   ML945 .C36 1995

The Cambridge Companion to the Clarinet. Jonathan Cross (Contribution by). Trade Paper. Cambridge University Press. New York, NY. 1995. 256p. Cambridge Companions to Music Ser. ISBN:0-521-47668-2, ISBN13: 978-0-521-47668-3. Dewey:788.6/2. LCCN:94-047624.

Audience: **l,u,f.**

Linn, Karen   ML1015.B3L5 1994

That Half-Barbaric Twang: The Banjo in American Popular Culture. Trade Paper. University of Illinois Press. Champaign, IL. 1994. 208p. Music in American Life Ser. ISBN:0-252-06433-X, ISBN13: 978-0-252-06433-3. Dewey:787.8/80973. LCCN:95-168823.

Audience: **u,f.** *Choice, 1992.*

Loesser, Arthur   ML650.L64 1990

Men, Women and Pianos: A Social History. Trade Paper. Dover Publications, Inc. Mineola, NY. 1991. 672p. ISBN:0-486-26543-9, ISBN13: 978-0-486-26543-8. Dewey:786.2/09. LCCN:90-044829.

Audience: **g,l,u,f.**

Millard, André (Editor)   ML1015.G9E43 2004

The Electric Guitar: A History of an American Icon. Trade Cloth. Johns Hopkins University Press. Baltimore, MD. 2004. 248p. ISBN:0-8018-7862-4, ISBN13: 978-0-8018-7862-6. Dewey:787.87/1973. LCCN:2003-016415.

Audience: **g,l,u,f.** *Choice, 2004.*

Montagu, Jeremy   ML1035.M66 2002

Timpani and Percussion. Cloth over Boards. Yale University Press. Cumberland, RI. 2002. 280p. Musical Instrument Ser. ISBN:0-300-09337-3, ISBN13: 978-0-300-09337-7. Dewey:786.8/09. LCCN:2002-102864.

Audience: **l,u,f.** *Choice, 2002.*

Music, David W.   ML3001.I57 1998

Instruments in Church: A Collection of Source Documents. Book, Other. Scarecrow Press, Inc. Lanham, MD. 1998. 232p. Studies in Liturgical Musicology, No. 7 ISBN:0-8108-3595-9, ISBN13: 978-0-8108-3595-5. Dewey:264/.2. LCCN:98-041678.

Audience: **u,f.**

Myers, Arnold, et al.   ML459

Musical Instruments: History, Technology, and Performance of Instruments of Western Music. Donald Murray Campbell & Clive Alan Greated (Authors). Trade Cloth. Oxford University Press, Inc. New York, NY. 2004. 518p. ISBN:0-19-816504-8, ISBN13: 978-0-19-816504-0. Dewey:784.19. LCCN:2004-303547.

Audience: **l,u,f.** *Choice, 2005.*

Ochse, Orpha C.   ML561

The History of the Organ in the United States. Trade Paper. Indiana University Press. Bloomington, IN. 1988. 512p. ISBN:0-253-20495-X, ISBN13: 978-0-253-20495-0. Dewey:786.6/273. LCCN:73-022644.

Audience: **u,f.**

Otterstedt, Annette   **ML927.V5**
The Viol: History of an Instrument. Reiners, Hans (Translator).
Kassel; London; New York: Bärenreiter. 2002.
ISBN:3-7618-1151-9, ISBN13: 978-3-7618-1151-1.
Audience: **u,f.**

Palmieri, Robert &   **ML102.P5E53 2003**
  Palmieri, Margaret W. (Editors)
The Piano: An Encyclopedia. Ed. 2. Paper over Boards.
Routledge. New York, NY. 2003. 576p. Encyclopedia of
Keyboard Instruments Ser. ISBN:0-415-93796-5, ISBN13:
978-0-415-93796-2. Dewey:786.203. LCCN:2003-002696.
Audience: **g,l,u,f.** *Choice, 2004.*

Pino, David   **MT380 .P56 1998**
The Clarinet and Clarinet Playing. Trade Paper. Dover
Publications, Inc. Mineola, NY. 1998. 320p.
ISBN:0-486-40270-3, ISBN13: 978-0-486-40270-3.
Dewey:788.6/219. LCCN:98-044312.
Audience: **l,u,f.**

Pollens, Stewart   **ML655.P64 1995**
The Early Pianoforte. Trade Cloth. Cambridge University Press.
New York, NY. 1995. 317p. Cambridge Musical Texts and
Monographs ISBN:0-521-41729-5, ISBN13: 978-0-521-41729-7.
Dewey:786.2/19/09. LCCN:93-041231.
Audience: **u,f.**

Powell, Ardal   **ML935.P69 2002**
The Flute. Cloth over Boards. Yale University Press.
Cumberland, RI. 2002. 352p. Musical Instrument Ser.
ISBN:0-300-09341-1, ISBN13: 978-0-300-09341-4.
Dewey:788.3209. LCCN:2002-102865.
Audience: **l,u,f.** *Choice, 2003.*

Rensch, Roslyn   **ML920**
Harps and Harpists. Trade Paper. Indiana University Press.
Bloomington, IN. 1998. 344p. ISBN:0-253-21209-X, ISBN13:
978-0-253-21209-2. Dewey:787/.5/09. LCCN:88-037609.
Audience: **l,u,f.** *Choice, 1990.*

Reynolds, Verne   **MT420.R49 1996**
The Horn Handbook. Trade Cloth. Hal Leonard Corporation.
Milwaukee, WI. 1997. 258p. ISBN:1-57467-016-6, ISBN13:
978-1-57467-016-5. Dewey:788.9/4/193. LCCN:96-013672.
Audience: **l,u,f.** *Choice, 1997.*

Roell, Craig H.   **ML661.R64 1989**
The Piano in America, 1890-1940. Cloth Text. University of
North Carolina Press. Chapel Hill, NC. 1991. xx, 396p.
ISBN:0-8078-1802-X, ISBN13: 978-0-8078-1802-2.
Dewey:381/.4568181621/0973. LCCN:88-014326.
Audience: **u,f.** *Choice, 1989.*

Rowland, David (Editor)   **ML650 .C3 1998**
The Cambridge Companion to the Piano. Kenneth Hamilton,
Rovert Philip, Bernard Richardson, Dorothy De Val, Cyril
Ehrlich, J. Barrie Jones, Mervyn Cooke, Brian Priestley &
Jonathan Cross (Contribution by). Trade Paper. Cambridge

University Press. New York, NY. 1998. 266p. Cambridge
Companions to Music Ser. ISBN:0-521-47986-X, ISBN13:
978-0-521-47986-8. Dewey:786.2. LCCN:97-041860.
Audience: **l,u,f.** *Choice, 1999.*

Rowland, David   **ML549 .R69 2001**
Early Keyboard Instruments: A Practical Guide. Colin Lawson
& Robin Stowell (Contribution by). Cloth Text. Cambridge
University Press. New York, NY. 2001. 166p. Handbooks to the
Historical Performance of Music ISBN:0-521-64366-X, ISBN13:
978-0-521-64366-5. Dewey:786.19. LCCN:00-062179.
Audience: **u,f.** *Choice, 2001.*

Sadie, Stanley   **ML102.I5**
The New Grove Dictionary of Musical Instruments. Trade Cloth.
Oxford University Press, Inc. New York, NY. 1985.
ISBN:0-333-37878-4, ISBN13: 978-0-333-37878-6.
Dewey:781.91/03/21.
Audience: **g,l,u,f.**

Schonberg, Harold C.   **ML397.S3 1987**
The Great Pianists. Trade Paper. Simon & Schuster. New York,
NY. 1987. 528p. ISBN:0-671-63837-8, ISBN13:
978-0-671-63837-5. Dewey:786.1/092/2 B. LCCN:87-000341.
Audience: **g,l,u,f.** *B*

Smith, Douglas Alton   **ML1010.S558 2002**
A History of the Lute from Antiquity to the Renaissance. Cloth
Text. Lute Society of America. Fort Worth, TX. 2002. 389p.
ISBN:0-9714071-0-X, ISBN13: 978-0-9714071-0-7.
Dewey:787.8/319/09. LCCN:2002-103414.
Audience: **l,u,f.** *Choice, 2003.*

Smithers, Don L.   **ML960.S63 1988**
The Music and History of the Baroque Trumpet Before 1721.
Cloth Text. Southern Illinois University Press. Carbondale, IL.
1989. 356p. ISBN:0-8093-1497-5, ISBN13: 978-0-8093-1497-3.
Dewey:788/.1/09. LCCN:88-023804.
Audience: **u,f.** *B*

Steele-Perkins, Crispian   **ML960**
Trumpet. Trade Paper. Kahn & Averill Publishers. London,
2001. 256p. ISBN:1-871082-69-2, ISBN13: 978-1-871082-69-2.
Dewey:788.92.
Audience: **u,f.**

Stimpson, Michael   **ML1015.G9**
The Guitar: A Guide for Students and Teachers. Oxford ; New
York : Oxford University Press. 1988. ISBN:0-19-317419-7,
ISBN13: 978-0-19-317419-1.
Audience: **l,u,f.**

Stowell, Robin (Editor)   **ML910 .C36 1999**
The Cambridge Companion to the Cello. Jonathan Cross
(Contribution by). Trade Paper. Cambridge University Press.
New York, NY. 1999. 286p. Cambridge Companions to Music
Ser. ISBN:0-521-62928-4, ISBN13: 978-0-521-62928-7.
Dewey:787.4. LCCN:98-030366.
Audience: **l,u,f.**

Stowell, Robin (Editor)   ML800 .C35 1992
The Cambridge Companion to the Violin. Jonathan Cross
(Contribution by). Trade Paper. Cambridge University Press.
New York, NY. 1992. 319p. Cambridge Companions to Music
Ser. ISBN:0-521-39923-8, ISBN13: 978-0-521-39923-4.
Dewey:787.2. LCCN:91-034017.

      Audience: **l,u,f.** *Choice, 1993.*

Stowell, Robin   ML855 .S79 2001
The Early Violin and Viola: A Practical Guide. Colin Lawson
(Contribution by). Cloth Text. Cambridge University Press. New
York, NY. 2001. 250p. Handbooks to the Historical Performance
of Music ISBN:0-521-62380-4, ISBN13: 978-0-521-62380-3.
Dewey:787.214309033. LCCN:00-065086.

      Audience: **u,f.**

Sumner, William L.   ML550 .S9
The Organ: Its Evolution, Principles of Construction and Use.
Library Binding. Reprint Services Company. Temecula, CA.
1988. ISBN:0-7812-0572-7, ISBN13: 978-0-7812-0572-6.
Dewey:786.6.

      Audience: **l,u,f.**

Tarr, Edward H.   ML960.T3713 1988
Trumpet. S. E. Plank (Translator). Trade Cloth. Hal Leonard
Corporation. Milwaukee, WI. 1988. 229p. ISBN:0-931340-13-6,
ISBN13: 978-0-931340-13-0. Dewey:788/.12/09.
LCCN:88-019280.

      Audience: **l,u,f.** *Choice, 1989.*

Thistlethwaite, Nicholas &   ML550 .C35 1998
   Webber, Geoffrey (Editors)
The Cambridge Companion to the Organ. Stephen Bicknell,
John Mainstone, Christopher Kent, Kimberly Marshall, Edward
Higginbottom, Christopher Stembridge, James Dalton &
Jonathan Cross (Contribution by). Trade Paper. Cambridge
University Press. New York, NY. 1999. 354p. Cambridge
Companions to Music Ser. ISBN:0-521-57584-2, ISBN13:
978-0-521-57584-3. Dewey:786.5. LCCN:97-041723.

      Audience: **l,u,f.** *Choice, 1999.*

Thomson, John Mansfield &   ML990.R4 C35 1995
   Rowland-Jones, Anthony (Editors)
The Cambridge Companion to the Recorder. Jonathan Cross
(Contribution by). Trade Paper. Cambridge University Press.
New York, NY. 1995. 62p. Cambridge Companions to Music
Ser. ISBN:0-521-35816-7, ISBN13: 978-0-521-35816-3.
Dewey:788.3/6. LCCN:94-031992.

      Audience: **l,u,f.**

Toff, Nancy   ML935.T65 1996
The Flute Book: A Complete Guide for Students and
Performers. Ed. 2. Trade Paper. Oxford University Press, Inc.
New York, NY. 1996. 484p. ISBN:0-19-510502-8, ISBN13:
978-0-19-510502-5. Dewey:788/.51/09. LCCN:96-023178.

      Audience: **l,u,f.** *B Choice, 1997, 1985.*

Tuckwell, Barry   ML955
Horn. Yehudi Menuhin (Preface by). Trade Paper. Kahn &

Averill Publishers. London, 2003. 224p. Yehudi Menuhin Music
Guides ISBN:1-871082-42-0, ISBN13: 978-1-871082-42-5.
Dewey:788/.41/0714.

      Audience: **l,u,f.**

Tyler, James & Sparks, Paul   ML1015.G9T96 2002
The Guitar and Its Music. Trade Cloth. Oxford University Press,
Inc. New York, NY. 2002. 348p. Oxford Early Music Ser.
ISBN:0-19-816713-X, ISBN13: 978-0-19-816713-6.
Dewey:787.87/09. LCCN:2001-058231.

      Audience: **l,u,f.**

Waksman, Steve   ML1015.G9W24 1999
Instruments of Desire: The Electric Guitar and the Shaping of
Musical Experience. Trade Cloth. Harvard University Press.
Cambridge, MA. 2000. 384p. ISBN:0-674-00065-X, ISBN13:
978-0-674-00065-0. Dewey:787.87/19. LCCN:99-039764.

      Audience: **u,f.** *Choice, 2000.*

Waterhouse, William   ML128.B26
Bassoon. Trade Paper. Kahn & Averill Publishers. London,
2001. 256p. ISBN:1-871082-68-4, ISBN13: 978-1-871082-68-5.
Dewey:788.58.

      Audience: **l,u,f.**

Whitener, Scott   ML933
A Complete Guide to Brass: Instruments and Techniques. Ed. 3.
Spiral. Thomson Wadsworth. Belmont, CA. 2006. 408p.
ISBN:0-534-50988-6, ISBN13: 978-0-534-50988-0.
Dewey:788.9/19. LCCN:2005-933211.

      Audience: **l,u,f.**

Williams, Peter   ML553.W54 1993
The Organ in Western Culture, 750-1250. Iain Fenlon, Thomas
Forrest Kelly & John Stevens (Contribution by). Trade Paper.
Cambridge University Press. New York, NY. 2005. 415p.
Cambridge Studies in Medieval and Renaissance Music Ser.
ISBN:0-521-61707-3, ISBN13: 978-0-521-61707-9.
Dewey:786.5/1909. LCCN:2005-284177.

      Audience: **u,f.**

Winternitz, Emanuel   ML0085.W58
Musical Instruments and Their Symbolism in Western Art:
Studies in Musical Iconology. Trade Paper. Books on Demand.
Ann Arbor, MI. 349p. ISBN:0-7837-3314-3, ISBN13:
978-0-7837-3314-2. Dewey:704.94978. LCCN:78-065482.

      Audience: **g,l,u,f.**

Orchestration, Orchestras, and Notation

      MT35
Standard Music Notation Practice. Music Publishers Association
(U.S.) ; Music Educators National Conference (U.S.). 1993.

      Audience: **l,u,f.**

Adler, Samuel   MT70
The Study of Orchestration. Ed. 3. Cloth Text. W. W. Norton &
Company, Inc. New York, NY. 2002. ISBN:0-393-94823-4,
ISBN13: 978-0-393-94823-3. Dewey:781.3/74.

      Audience: **u,f. *B***

Formats: Web: ▢   Ebook: **e**   CD/DVD-ROM: 🌣   BCL3: *B*

Bartolozzi, Bruno   MT339.5.B37 1982
New Sounds for Woodwind. Trade Cloth. Oxford University
Press, Inc. New York, NY. 1982. 113p. ISBN:0-19-318607-1,
ISBN13: 978-0-19-318607-1. Dewey:788/.05/0712.
LCCN:80-040519.

      Audience: **u,f.** *B*

Berlioz, Hector   MT70 .B4813 2002
Berlioz's Orchestration Treatise: A Translation and Commentary.
Hugh Macdonald (Editor), John Butt & Laurence Dreyfus
(Contribution by). Trade Cloth. Cambridge University Press.
New York, NY. 2002. 428p. Cambridge Musical Texts and
Monographs ISBN:0-521-23953-2, ISBN13: 978-0-521-23953-0.
Dewey:781.374. LCCN:2001-052619.

      Audience: **u,f.**

Boras, Tom   MT40.B72 2005
Jazz Composition and Arranging. Spiral. Thomson Wadsworth.
Belmont, CA. 2004. 396p. ISBN:0-534-25261-3, ISBN13:
978-0-534-25261-8. Dewey:781.65/13. LCCN:2004-106300.

      Audience: **l,u,f.**

Carse, Adam   ML469 .C3
The Orchestra from Beethoven to Berlioz. Library Binding.
Reprint Services Company. Temecula, CA. 1988.
ISBN:0-685-55956-4, ISBN13: 978-0-685-55956-7.
Dewey:785/.09/034.

      Audience: **l,u,f.**

Carse, Adam Von Ahn   ML455
The History of Orchestration. Trade Paper. Dover Publications,
Inc. Mineola, NY. 1964. 348p. ISBN:0-486-21258-0, ISBN13:
978-0-486-21258-6. Dewey:781.374.

      Audience: **l,u,f.** *B*

Dempster, Stuart   MT339.5
The Modern Trombone: A Definition of Its Idioms. Trade Cloth.
Accura Music, Inc. North Greece, NY. 1994.
ISBN:0-918194-27-X, ISBN13: 978-0-918194-27-5.
Dewey:788/.2/0712.

      Audience: **u,f.**

Heussenstamm, George   MT35.H55 1987
Norton Manual of Music Notation. Trade Cloth. W. W. Norton
& Company, Inc. New York, NY. 1987. 200p.
ISBN:0-393-95526-5, ISBN13: 978-0-393-95526-2.
Dewey:781/.24. LCCN:86-016449.

      Audience: **l,u,f.**

Inglefield, Ruth K, et al.   MT540
Writing for the Pedal Harp: A Standardized Manual for
Composers and Harpists. Neill, Lou Anne (Author). University
of California Press. 1985. ISBN:0-520-04832-6, ISBN13:
978-0-520-04832-4.

      Audience: **l,u,f.**

Lawson, Colin (Editor)   ML1255
The Cambridge Companion to the Orchestra. Cloth Text.
Cambridge University Press. New York, NY. 2003. 312p.
Cambridge Companions to Music Ser. ISBN:0-521-80658-5,

ISBN13: 978-0-521-80658-9. Dewey:784.2.
LCCN:2003-277276.

      Audience: **l,u,f.** *Choice, 2004.*

Read, Gardner-   MT170
Compendium of Modern Instrumental Techniques. Book, Other.
Greenwood Publishing Group, Inc. Portsmouth, NH. 1993. 296p.
ISBN:0-313-28512-8, ISBN13: 978-0-313-28512-7.
Dewey:784.193. LCCN:92-017854.

      Audience: **u,f.** *Choice, 1994.*

Read, Gardner-   MT38
Music Notation: A Manual of Modern Practice. Trade Paper.
Taplinger Publishing Company, Inc. Marlboro, NJ. 1997. 482p.
ISBN:0-8008-5453-5, ISBN13: 978-0-8008-5453-9.
Dewey:781/.24. LCCN:68-054213.

      Audience: **l,u,f.**

Read, Gardner-   MT70.R368 2004
Orchestral Combinations: The Science and Art of Instrumental
Tone-Color. Trade Cloth. Scarecrow Press, Inc. Lanham, MD.
2003. 304p. ISBN:0-8108-4814-7, ISBN13: 978-0-8108-4814-6.
Dewey:784.13/74. LCCN:2003-020719.

      Audience: **u,f.** *Choice, 2004.*

Read, Gardner-   ML431
Pictographic Score Notation: A Compendium. Cloth Text.
Greenwood Publishing Group, Inc. Portsmouth, NH. 1998. 296p.
ISBN:0-313-30469-6, ISBN13: 978-0-313-30469-9.
Dewey:780/.1/48. LCCN:97-049480.

      Audience: **u,f.**

Read, Gardner-   MT70
Thesaurus of Orchestral Devices. Trade Cloth. Greenwood
Publishing Group, Inc. Portsmouth, NH. 1969. 631p.
ISBN:0-8371-1884-0, ISBN13: 978-0-8371-1884-0.
Dewey:785/.0284. LCCN:69-014045.

      Audience: **u,f.** *B*

Read, Gardner-   MT35
Twentieth-Century Microtonal Notation. Trade Cloth.
Greenwood Publishing Group, Inc. Portsmouth, NH. 1990. 208p.
Contributions to the Study of Music and Dance Ser., No. 18
ISBN:0-313-27398-7, ISBN13: 978-0-313-27398-8.
Dewey:780/.148. LCCN:90-002782.

      Audience: **u,f.** *Choice, 1990.*

Rehfeldt, Phillip   ML945.R43 2004
New Directions for Clarinet. Trade Paper. Scarecrow Press, Inc.
Lanham, MD. 2003. 208p. ISBN:0-520-03379-5, ISBN13:
978-0-520-03379-5. Dewey:788.6/2193. LCCN:76-050259.

      Audience: **u,f.**

Rimsky-Korsakov, Nikolay   MT70.R62 1964
Principles of Orchestration : With Musical Examples Drawn
from His Own Works. Shteinberg, Maksimilian Oseevich
(Editor); Agate, Edward (Translator). Dover Publications. 1964.
Dover Books on Music

      Audience: **u,f.**

Russo, William   ML3506
Jazz Composition and Orchestration. Mixed Media. University
of Chicago Press. Chicago, IL. 1997. 843p.
ISBN:0-226-73208-8, ISBN13: 978-0-226-73208-4.
Dewey:781.6/513.

Audience: **u,f.** 𝐵

Sabina, Leslie M.   MT73
Jazz Arranging and Orchestration: A Concise Introduction with
Interactive CD-ROM. Schirmer/Thomson Learning. 2002.
ISBN:0-534-58590-6, ISBN13: 978-0-534-58590-7.

Audience: **u,f.**

Sebesky, Don   MT70
The Contemporary Arranger. Alfred Pub. Co.. 1994.
ISBN:0-88284-485-7, ISBN13: 978-0-88284-485-5.

Audience: **u,f.**

Spitzer, John & Zaslaw,   ML1200
  Neal
The Birth of the Orchestra: History of an Institution, 1650-1815.
Trade Paper, Perfect. Oxford University Press, Inc. New York,
NY. 2005. 640p. ISBN:0-19-518955-8, ISBN13:
978-0-19-518955-1. Dewey:784.2/09.

Audience: **u,f.** *Choice, 2005.*

Stone, Kurt   MT35.S87
Music Notation in the Twentieth Century: A Practical
Guidebook. Trade Cloth. W. W. Norton & Company, Inc. New
York, NY. 1980. 380p. ISBN:0-393-95053-0, ISBN13:
978-0-393-95053-3. Dewey:781/.24/0904. LCCN:79-023093.

Audience: **u,f.** 𝐵

Strange, Patricia & Strange,   ML857.S77 2001
  Allen
The Contemporary Violin: Extended Performance Techniques.
Trade Paper. Scarecrow Press, Inc. Lanham, MD. 2001. 350p.
New Instrumentation Ser., Vol. 7 ISBN:0-520-22409-4, ISBN13:
978-0-520-22409-4. Dewey:787.2/193. LCCN:00-029870.

Audience: **u,f.**

Turetzky, Bertram   MT320.T87 1989
The Contemporary Contrabass. Ed. 2. Trade Paper. University of
California Press. Berkeley, CA. 1989. 128p. New
Instrumentation Ser., Vol. 7 ISBN:0-520-06381-3, ISBN13:
978-0-520-06381-5. Dewey:787/.41/071. LCCN:87-035486.

Audience: **u,f.**

Van Cleve, Libby   MT360
Oboe Unbound: Contemporary Techniques. Scarecrow Press.
2004. The New Instrumentation Ser., Vol. 8; Variation
ISBN:0-8108-5031-1, ISBN13: 978-0-8108-5031-6.

Audience: **u,f.**

Performance Techniques and
Interpretation > Vocal

Adams, David   MT883.A23 1999
A Handbook of Diction for Singers: Italian, German, French.
Trade Paper. Oxford University Press, Inc. New York, NY. 1998.

192p. ISBN:0-19-512077-9, ISBN13: 978-0-19-512077-6.
Dewey:783/.043. LCCN:98-012204.

Audience: **l,u,f.** *Choice, 1999.*

Agricola, Johann Friedrich   MT892 .T6713 1995
  & Tosi, Pier Francesco
Introduction to the Art of Singing by Johann Friedrich Agricola.
John Butt & Laurence Dreyfus (Contribution by), Julianne C.
Baird (Edited and Translated by). Trade Cloth. Cambridge
University Press. New York, NY. 1995. 308p. Cambridge
Musical Texts and Monographs ISBN:0-521-45428-X, ISBN13:
978-0-521-45428-5. Dewey:783/.043. LCCN:94-011416.

Audience: **u,f.**

Bleiler, Ellen H. (Editor,   ML48.F3 1996
  Translator)
Famous Italian Opera Arias: A Dual-Language Book. Trade
Paper. Dover Publications, Inc. Mineola, NY. 1996. 144p.
ISBN:0-486-29158-8, ISBN13: 978-0-486-29158-1.
Dewey:782.1/026/8. LCCN:95-041475.

Audience: **l,u,f.**

Bunch, Meribeth & Vaughn,   MT820.B86 2004
  Cynthia
The Singing Book. Trade Paper. W. W. Norton & Company, Inc.
New York, NY. 2004. xi, 339p. ISBN:0-393-97994-6, ISBN13:
978-0-393-97994-7. Dewey:783. LCCN:2003-066238.

Audience: **l,u,f.**

Coffin, Berton   PE1128.A2R454 2002
Singer's Repertoire: Mezzo Soprano and Contralto. Ed. 2. Trade
Paper. Scarecrow Press, Inc. Lanham, MD. 2002. 234p.
ISBN:0-8108-4190-8, ISBN13: 978-0-8108-4190-1.
Dewey:428/.0071. LCCN:2001-054168.

Audience: **l,u,f.**

Coffin, Berton   ML128.V7 C67
Singer's Repertoire: Coloratura Soprano, Lyric Soprano, and
Dramatic Soprano. Ed. 2. Trade Paper. Scarecrow Press, Inc.
Lanham, MD. 2003. 313p. ISBN:0-8108-4526-1, ISBN13:
978-0-8108-4526-8. Dewey:781.97.

Audience: **u,f.**

Coffin, Berton   ML54.6 .W65
Word-by-Word Translations of Songs and Arias: German and
French. Trade Cloth. Scarecrow Press, Inc. Lanham, MD. 1966.
620p. ISBN:0-8108-0149-3, ISBN13: 978-0-8108-0149-3.
Dewey:781.96. LCCN:66-013746.

Audience: **l,u,f.**

Coffin, Berton & Singer,   ML128.V7 C67
  Werner
Program Notes for the Singer's Repertoire. Trade Cloth.
Scarecrow Press, Inc. Lanham, MD. 1962. 230p.
ISBN:0-8108-0169-8, ISBN13: 978-0-8108-0169-1.
Dewey:781.97. LCCN:60-007265.

Audience: **u,f.**

Coperman, Harold   **MT883**
Singing in Latin: Or Pronunciation Explor'd. Ed. 2. Oxford : H.
Copeman. 1996. ISBN:0-9515798-7-8, ISBN13:
978-0-9515798-7-9.
                                    Audience: **u,f.**

Elliott, Martha   **MT892**
Singing in Style: A Guide to Vocal Performance Practices. Yale
University Press. 2006. ISBN:0-300-10932-6, ISBN13:
978-0-300-10932-0.
                                    Audience: **u,f.**

Emmons, Shirlee &   **MT820.B383**
   Sonntag, Stanley
The Art of the Song Recital. Paper Text. Waveland Press, Inc.
Prospect Heights, IL. 2001. 595p. ISBN:1-57766-220-2,
ISBN13: 978-1-57766-220-4. Dewey:784.9/34.
                                    Audience: **u,f.**

Garcia, Manuel   **MT835**
A Complete Treatise on the Art of Singing : Complete and
Unabridged. Paschke, Donald V. (Editor). Da Capo Press. 1975.
Da Capo Press Music Reprint Series, Vol. 2.
ISBN:0-306-70660-1, ISBN13: 978-0-306-70660-8.
                                    Audience: **u,f.**

Garcia, Manuel   **MT835**
A Complete Treatise on the Art of Singing : Complete and
Unabridged. Paschke, Donald V. (Editor). Da Capo Press. 1975.
Da Capo Press Music Reprint Ser., Vol. 1. ISBN:0-306-76212-9,
ISBN13: 978-0-306-76212-3.
                                    Audience: **u,f.**

Gordon, Stewart   **ML457.G66 2006**
Mastering the Art of Performance: A Primer for Musicians.
Trade Paper. Oxford University Press, Inc. New York, NY. 2005.
240p. ISBN:0-19-517743-6, ISBN13: 978-0-19-517743-5.
Dewey:781.4/3. LCCN:2005-010152.
                         Audience: **l,u,f.** *Choice, 2006.*

Hagberg, Karen A.   **ML3795.H13 2003**
Stage Presence from Head to Toe: A Manual for Musicians.
Trade Paper. Scarecrow Press, Inc. Lanham, MD. 2003. 120p.
ISBN:0-8108-4777-9, ISBN13: 978-0-8108-4777-4.
Dewey:781.4/3. LCCN:2003-004846.
                         Audience: **l,u,f.** *Choice, 2004.*

Hylton, John   **MT875.H95 1995**
Comprehensive Choral Music Education. Trade Paper. Prentice
Hall PTR. Upper Saddle River, NJ. 1994. 300p.
ISBN:0-13-045287-4, ISBN13: 978-0-13-045287-0.
Dewey:782.5/07. LCCN:94-029344.
                                    Audience: **l,u,f.**

Johnson, Graham & Stokes,   **ML54.6.J76F74 2000**
   Richard
A French Song Companion. Cloth Text. Oxford University
Press, Inc. New York, NY. 2000. 568p. ISBN:0-19-816410-6,
ISBN13: 978-0-19-816410-4. Dewey:782.42168/0268.
LCCN:99-057524.
                         Audience: **l,u,f.** *Choice, 2001.*

Mabry, Sharon   **MT820.M129 2002**
Exploring Twentieth-Century Vocal Music: A Practical Guide to
Innovations in Performance and Repertoire. Trade Cloth. Oxford
University Press, Inc. New York, NY. 2002. 206p.
ISBN:0-19-514198-9, ISBN13: 978-0-19-514198-6.
Dewey:782/.009/04. LCCN:2001-052354.
                         Audience: **u,f.** *Choice, 2003.*

May, William V. & Tolin,   **MT883 .M39**
   Craig
Pronunciation Guide for Choral Literature: French, German,
Hebrew, Italian, Latin, Spanish. Trade Paper. Rowman &
Littlefield Education. Lanham, MD. 1987. 100p.
ISBN:0-940796-47-3, ISBN13: 978-0-940796-47-8. Dewey:418.
                                    Audience: **l,u,f.**

McKinney, James C.   **MT820**
The Diagnosis and Correction of Vocal Faults: A Manual for
Teachers of Singing and for Choir Directors. Paper Text,
CD-ROM. Waveland Press, Inc. Prospect Heights, IL. 2005.
213p. ISBN:1-57766-403-5, ISBN13: 978-1-57766-403-1.
Dewey:784.9/32.
                                    Audience: **u,f.**

McTyre, Ruthann B.   **ML128**
   (Compiled by)
Library Resources for Singers, Coaches and Accompanists: An
Annotated Bibliography, 1970-1997. Cloth Text. Greenwood
Publishing Group, Inc. Portsmouth, NH. 1998. 176p. Music
Reference Collection, Vol. 71 ISBN:0-313-30266-9, ISBN13:
978-0-313-30266-4. Dewey:016.783. LCCN:98-023959.
                         Audience: **l,u,f.** *Choice, 1998.*

Miller, Richard   **MT823.M55 1997**
National Schools of Singing: English, French, German and
Italian Techniques of Singing Revisited. Ed. 2. Trade Cloth.
Scarecrow Press, Inc. Lanham, MD. 2003. 304p.
ISBN:0-8108-3237-2, ISBN13: 978-0-8108-3237-4.
Dewey:783/.0094. LCCN:96-035557.
                         Audience: **u,f.** *Choice, 1997.*

Miller, Richard   **MT820.M599 1996**
On the Art of Singing. Cloth Text. Oxford University Press, Inc.
New York, NY. 1996. 336p. ISBN:0-19-509825-0, ISBN13:
978-0-19-509825-9. Dewey:782/.043. LCCN:95-030176.
                                    Audience: **l,u,f.**

Miller, Richard   **MT121.S38M55 1999**
Singing Schumann: An Interpretive Guide for Performers. Trade
Cloth. Oxford University Press, Inc. New York, NY. 1999. 260p.
ISBN:0-19-511904-5, ISBN13: 978-0-19-511904-6.
Dewey:782.42168/092. LCCN:98-031645.
                         Audience: **u,f.** *Choice, 2000.*

Miller, Richard   **MT820.M5993 2003**
Solutions for Singers: Tools for Performers and Teachers. Trade
Cloth. Oxford University Press, Inc. New York, NY. 2004. 308p.
ISBN:0-19-516005-3, ISBN13: 978-0-19-516005-5.
Dewey:783/.04. LCCN:2002-041661.
                         Audience: **l,u,f.** *Choice, 2004.*

Paton, John Glenn &   **MT825.C52 2006**
  Christy, Van A.
Foundations in Singing. Ed. 8. Spiral. McGraw-Hill Companies,
The. New York, NY. 2005. 320p. ISBN:0-07-298979-3, ISBN13:
978-0-07-298979-3. Dewey:782.4/142. LCCN:2005-047407.
                        Audience: **l,u,f.**

Plank, Steven Eric   **MT875.P53 2004**
Choral Performance: A Guide to Historical Practice. Trade
Paper. Scarecrow Press, Inc. Lanham, MD. 2004. 128p.
ISBN:0-8108-5141-5, ISBN13: 978-0-8108-5141-2.
Dewey:782.5/143. LCCN:2004-008272.
                 Audience: **u,f.** *Choice, 2005.*

Potter, John (Editor)   **ML1460 .C28 2000**
The Cambridge Companion to Singing. Trade Paper. Cambridge
University Press. New York, NY. 2000. 296p. Cambridge
Companions to Music Ser. ISBN:0-521-62709-5, ISBN13:
978-0-521-62709-2. Dewey:782/.009. LCCN:99-032948.
              Audience: **g,l,u,f.** *Choice, 2000.*

Reid, Cornelius L.   **ML102.V6 R4**
A Dictionary of Vocal Terminology. Cloth Text. Recital
Publications. Huntsville, TX. 1994. 480p. ISBN:0-9663862-0-5,
ISBN13: 978-0-9663862-0-2. Dewey:784.9/03/21.
                   Audience: **g,l,u,f.**

Schoep, Arthur & Harris,   **ML54.6 .W65**
  Daniel
Word-by-Word Translations of Songs and Arias: Italian. Trade
Cloth. Scarecrow Press, Inc. Lanham, MD. 1992. 584p.
Word-By-Word Translations of Songs and Arias Ser., Vol. 2
ISBN:0-8108-0463-8, ISBN13: 978-0-8108-0463-0.
Dewey:781.96. LCCN:66-013746.
                   Audience: **l,u,f.**

Scott, Michael   **ML1460**
The Record of Singing. Paper Text. Northeastern University
Press. Boston, MA. 1993. 505p. ISBN:1-55553-163-6, ISBN13:
978-1-55553-163-8. Dewey:783.009. LCCN:92-046984.
                   Audience: **u,f.**

Seaton, Douglas   **ML128.S3S33 1987**
The Art Song: A Reference and Information Guide. Library
Binding. Garland Publishing, Inc. New York, NY. 1987. 300p.
Reference Library of the Humanities ISBN:0-8240-8554-X,
ISBN13: 978-0-8240-8554-4. Dewey:016.7843.
LCCN:86-033553.
              Audience: **l,u,f.** *Choice, 1987.*

Sharp, Avery T. & Floyd,   **ML128.C48S53 2001**
  James Michael
Choral Music: A Research and Information Guide. Cloth Text.
Garland Publishing, Inc. New York, NY. 2001. 498p. Routledge
Music Bibliographies Ser. ISBN:0-8240-5944-1, ISBN13:
978-0-8240-5944-6. Dewey:016.7825. LCCN:2001-019115.
              Audience: **l,u,f.** *Choice, 2002.*

Steane, J. B.   **ML400.S83 1996**
Singers of the Century. Trade Cloth. Hal Leonard Corporation.
Milwaukee, WI. 2003. 288p. Singers of the Century Ser., Vol. 2

ISBN:1-57467-040-9, ISBN13: 978-1-57467-040-0.
Dewey:782/.00922. LCCN:96-016827.
              Audience: **u,f.** *Choice, 1997.*

Steane, J. B.   **ML400.S83 1996**
Singers of the Century. Trade Cloth. Hal Leonard Corporation.
Milwaukee, WI. 1996. 288p. ISBN:1-57467-009-3, ISBN13:
978-1-57467-009-7. Dewey:782/.00922. LCCN:96-016827.
              Audience: **u,f.** *Choice, 1997.*

Steane, J. B.   **ML400.S83 1996**
Singers of the Century. Trade Cloth. Hal Leonard Corporation.
Milwaukee, WI. 2003. 275p. Singers of the Century Ser., Vol. 3
ISBN:1-57467-057-3, ISBN13: 978-1-57467-057-8.
Dewey:782/.00922. LCCN:96-016827.
              Audience: **u,f.** *Choice, 1997.*

Stein, Deborah & Spillman,   **MT120.S74 1996**
  Robert
Poetry into Song: Performance and Analysis of Lieder. Trade
Cloth. Oxford University Press, Inc. New York, NY. 1996. 432p.
ISBN:0-19-509328-3, ISBN13: 978-0-19-509328-5.
Dewey:782.42168/0943. LCCN:95-005398.
              Audience: **u,f.** *Choice, 1996.*

Stoherer Sharon   **MT820**
Singer's Companion. Trade Cloth. Routledge. New York, NY.
2006. 224p. ISBN:0-415-97697-9, ISBN13: 978-0-415-97697-8.
Dewey:783. LCCN:2005-036480.
                   Audience: **l,u,f.**

Ware, Clifton   **MT820.W26 1998**
Basics of Vocal Pedagogy: The Foundations and Process of
Singing. Paper Text. McGraw-Hill Higher Education. Burr
Ridge, IL. 1997. 320p. ISBN:0-07-068289-5, ISBN13:
978-0-07-068289-4. Dewey:783/.04/071. LCCN:97-001281.
                   Audience: **u,f.**

Performance Techniques and Interpretation > Instrumental

Agay, Denes (Editor)   **MT220**
Art of Teaching Piano. Trade Paper. Music Sales Corporation.
New York, NY. 2004. 519p. ISBN:0-8256-8111-1, ISBN13:
978-0-8256-8111-0. Dewey:786.2/07.
                   Audience: **l,f.**

Bachelder, Daniel F. &   **MT418.H9 2002**
  Hunt, Norman J.
Guide to Teaching Brass. Ed. 6. Spiral. McGraw-Hill Higher
Education. Burr Ridge, IL. 2001. 224p. ISBN:0-07-241423-5,
ISBN13: 978-0-07-241423-3. Dewey:788.9/193/071.
LCCN:2001-030066.
                   Audience: **u,f.**

Bachmann, Alberto   **ML800.B13**
An Encyclopedia of the Violin. Trade Cloth. Library Reprints,
Inc. Temecula, CA. 2001. 470p. ISBN:0-7222-5990-5, ISBN13:
978-0-7222-5990-0. Dewey:787.1.
               Audience: **l,u,f.** *B*

Banowetz, Joseph   MT227 .B2
The Pianist's Guide to Pedaling. Trade Paper. Indiana University Press. Bloomington, IN. 1992. 320p. ISBN:0-253-20732-0, ISBN13: 978-0-253-20732-6. Dewey:786.3/5. LCCN:84-047534.
Audience: **l,u,f.** ℬ *Choice, 1985.*

Bartolozzi, Bruno   MT339.5.B37 1982
New Sounds for Woodwind. Trade Cloth. Oxford University Press, Inc. New York, NY. 1982. 113p. ISBN:0-19-318607-1, ISBN13: 978-0-19-318607-1. Dewey:788/.05/0712. LCCN:80-040519.
Audience: **u,f.** ℬ

Blades, James & Dean, Johnny   ML1035
How to Play Drums. Trade Paper. St. Martin's Press. Gordonville, VA. 1992. 112p. How-to-Play Ser. ISBN:0-312-08212-6, ISBN13: 978-0-312-08212-3. Dewey:789/.1. LCCN:92-007231.
Audience: **l,u,f.**

Boyden, David D.   ML850.B7 1990
The History of Violin Playing from Its Origins to 1761: And Its Relationship to the Violin and Violin Music. Trade Paper. Oxford University Press, Inc. New York, NY. 1990. 594p. ISBN:0-19-816183-2, ISBN13: 978-0-19-816183-7. Dewey:787.2/143/09. LCCN:89-016285.
Audience: **l,u,f.**

Campos, Frank Gabriel   MT440.C35 2004
Trumpet Technique. Trade Cloth. Oxford University Press, Inc. New York, NY. 2004. 208p. ISBN:0-19-516692-2, ISBN13: 978-0-19-516692-7. Dewey:788.9/2193. LCCN:2004-002576.
Audience: **l,u,f.** *Choice, 2005.*

Cavalli, Harriet   MT950.C38 2001
Dance and Music: A Guide to Dance Accompaniment for Musicians and Dance Teachers. Trade Cloth. University Press of Florida. Gainesville, FL. 2001. xvii, 425p. ISBN:0-8130-1887-0, ISBN13: 978-0-8130-1887-4. Dewey:781.5/54143. LCCN:2001-027588.
Audience: **l,u,f.**

Clementi, Muzio   MT222.C617 1974
Introduction to the Art of Playing on the Piano Forte; Containing the Elements of Music, Preliminary Notions on Fingering, and Fifty Fingered Lessons. Da Capo Press. 1974. Da Capo Press Music Reprint Series ISBN:0-385-41609-1, ISBN13: 978-0-385-41609-2.
Audience: **l,u,f.**

Colwell, Richard J. & Goolsby, Thomas W.   MT170.C64 2002
The Teaching of Instrumental Music. Ed. 3. Trade Paper. Prentice Hall PTR. Upper Saddle River, NJ. 2001. 464p. ISBN:0-13-020689-X, ISBN13: 978-0-13-020689-3. Dewey:784/.071. LCCN:2001-056021.
Audience: **u,f.**

Cook, Gary D.   MT655.C67 2006
Teaching Percussion, Set. Ed. 3. Spiral. Thomson Wadsworth. Belmont, CA. 2005. 512p. ISBN:0-534-50990-8, ISBN13: 978-0-534-50990-3. Dewey:789/.01/07. LCCN:2005-933546.
Audience: **u,f.**

Cooke, James Francis   MT220.G7815 1999
Great Pianists on Piano Playing: Godowsky, Hofmann, Lhevinne, Paderewski and 24 Other Legendary Pianists. Trade Paper. Dover Publications, Inc. Mineola, NY. 1999. 448p. ISBN:0-486-40845-0, ISBN13: 978-0-486-40845-3. Dewey:786.2/143. LCCN:99-038221.
Audience: **u,f.**

Cortot, Alfred   MT140
Alfred Cortot's Studies in Musical Interpretation. Jacques, Robert (Translator); Thieffry, Jeanne. Da Capo Press. 1989. ISBN:0-306-79715-1, ISBN13: 978-0-306-79715-6.
Audience: **u,f.**

Davidson, Michael   MT220
Mozart and the Pianist: A Guide for Performers and Teachers to Mozart's Major Works for Solo Piano. Ed. 2. Trade Paper. Kahn & Averill Publishers. London, 2001. 384p. ISBN:1-871082-76-5, ISBN13: 978-1-871082-76-0. Dewey:786.2143.
Audience: **l,u,f.**

Debost, Michel   MT340.D4313 2002
The Simple Flute: From A to Z. Trade Cloth. Oxford University Press, Inc. New York, NY. 2002. 282p. ISBN:0-19-514521-6, ISBN13: 978-0-19-514521-2. Dewey:788.3/2193. LCCN:2001-033831.
Audience: **l,u,f.** *Choice, 2002.*

Dempster, Stuart   MT339.5
The Modern Trombone: A Definition of Its Idioms. Trade Cloth. Accura Music, Inc. North Greece, NY. 1994. ISBN:0-918194-27-X, ISBN13: 978-0-918194-27-5. Dewey:788/.2/0712.
Audience: **u,f.**

Fraser, Alan   MT220.F8 2003
The Craft of Piano Playing: A New Approach to Piano Technique. Trade Paper. Scarecrow Press, Inc. Lanham, MD. 2003. 448p. ISBN:0-8108-4591-1, ISBN13: 978-0-8108-4591-6. Dewey:786.2/193. LCCN:2002-190802.
Audience: **l,u,f.** *Choice, 2003.*

Galamian, Ivan   MT260.G34 1999
Principles of Violin Playing and Teaching. Ed. 3. Trade Cloth. Shar Products Company. Ann Arbor, MI. 1999. 144p. ISBN:0-9621416-3-1, ISBN13: 978-0-9621416-3-8. Dewey:787.2/193. LCCN:99-062988.
Audience: **l,u,f.**

Gordon, Stewart   ML457.G66 2006
Mastering the Art of Performance: A Primer for Musicians. Trade Paper. Oxford University Press, Inc. New York, NY. 2005. 240p. ISBN:0-19-517743-6, ISBN13: 978-0-19-517743-5. Dewey:781.4/3. LCCN:2005-010152.
Audience: **l,u,f.** *Choice, 2006.*

Audience: g=general, l=lower division undergraduate, u=upper division undergraduate, f=faculty.   **397**

Hagberg, Karen A.   **ML3795.H13 2003**
Stage Presence from Head to Toe: A Manual for Musicians.
Trade Paper. Scarecrow Press, Inc. Lanham, MD. 2003. 120p.
ISBN:0-8108-4777-9, ISBN13: 978-0-8108-4777-4.
Dewey:781.4/3. LCCN:2003-004846.
          Audience: **l,u,f.** *Choice, 2004.*

Hinson, Maurice   **ML128.P3H5 2000**
ⓔ Guide to the Pianist's Repertoire. Ed. 3. E-Book. Indiana
University Press. Bloomington, IN. 2000. 992p.
ISBN:0-253-33646-5, ISBN13: 978-0-253-33646-0.
Dewey:016.7862/0263. LCCN:99-058594.
          Audience: **l,u,f.** *Choice, 1987.*

Hinson, Maurice   **ML128.P3H534 1998**
The Pianist's Bookshelf: A Practical Guide to Books, Videos,
and Other Resources. Trade Paper. Indiana University Press.
Bloomington, IN. 1998. 352p. ISBN:0-253-21145-X, ISBN13:
978-0-253-21145-3. Dewey:016.7862. LCCN:97-047307.
          Audience: **l,u,f.**

Hurford, Peter   **ML74.4C**
Making Music on the Organ. Trade Paper. Oxford University
Press, Inc. New York, NY. 1990. 176p. ISBN:0-19-816207-3,
ISBN13: 978-0-19-816207-0. Dewey:786.7. LCCN:88-005139.
          Audience: **l,u,f.** *Choice, 1989.*

Hutcheson, Ernest & Ganz,   **MT140**
  Rudolph
Literature of the Piano: A Guide for Amateur and Student. Trade
Cloth. Random House Children's Books. New York, NY. 1965.
ISBN:0-394-40830-6, ISBN13: 978-0-394-40830-9.
Dewey:786.4/09. LCCN:63-009130.
          Audience: **g,l,u,f.** **𝐵**

Inglefield, Ruth K, et al.   **MT540**
Writing for the Pedal Harp: A Standardized Manual for
Composers and Harpists. Neill, Lou Anne (Author). University
of California Press. 1985. ISBN:0-520-04832-6, ISBN13:
978-0-520-04832-4.
          Audience: **l,u,f.**

Mozart, Leopold   **MT262.M93 1985**
A Treatise on the Fundamental Principles of Violin Playing. Ed.
2. Editha Knocker (Translator). Paper Text. Oxford University
Press, Inc. New York, NY. 1985. 274p. Early Music Ser.
ISBN:0-19-318513-X, ISBN13: 978-0-19-318513-5.
Dewey:787.1/07/14. LCCN:85-002895.
          Audience: **u,f.** **𝐵**

Oddo, Vincent   **MT259.O3 1995**
Playing and Teaching the Strings. Ed. 2. Spiral. Thomson
Wadsworth. Belmont, CA. 1994. 208p. Music Ser.
ISBN:0-534-22971-9, ISBN13: 978-0-534-22971-9.
Dewey:787/.143/07. LCCN:94-035620.
          Audience: **u,f.**

Pino, David   **MT380 .P56 1998**
The Clarinet and Clarinet Playing. Trade Paper. Dover

Publications, Inc. Mineola, NY. 1998. 320p.
ISBN:0-486-40270-3, ISBN13: 978-0-486-40270-3.
Dewey:788.6/219. LCCN:98-044312.
          Audience: **l,u,f.**

Quantz, Johann J.   **MT342**
On Playing the Flute. Ed. 2. Edward R. Reilly (Editor). Trade
Cloth. Thomson Gale. Farmington Hills, MI. 1985. 412p.
ISBN:0-02-872920-X, ISBN13: 978-0-02-872920-6.
Dewey:788/.51/071.
          Audience: **u,f.**

Read, Gardner-   **MT170**
Compendium of Modern Instrumental Techniques. Book, Other.
Greenwood Publishing Group, Inc. Portsmouth, NH. 1993. 296p.
ISBN:0-313-28512-8, ISBN13: 978-0-313-28512-7.
Dewey:784.193. LCCN:92-017854.
          Audience: **u,f.** *Choice, 1994.*

Rehfeldt, Phillip   **ML945.R43 2004**
New Directions for Clarinet. Trade Paper. Scarecrow Press, Inc.
Lanham, MD. 2003. 208p. ISBN:0-520-03379-5, ISBN13:
978-0-520-03379-5. Dewey:788.6/2193. LCCN:76-050259.
          Audience: **u,f.**

Reynolds, Verne   **MT420.R49 1996**
The Horn Handbook. Trade Cloth. Hal Leonard Corporation.
Milwaukee, WI. 1997. 258p. ISBN:1-57467-016-6, ISBN13:
978-1-57467-016-5. Dewey:788.9/4/193. LCCN:96-013672.
          Audience: **l,u,f.** *Choice, 1997.*

Ritchie, George H. &   **MT182.R6 2000**
  Stauffer, George B.
Organ Technique: Modern and Early. Spiral. Oxford University
Press, Inc. New York, NY. 2000. 390p. ISBN:0-19-513745-0,
ISBN13: 978-0-19-513745-3. Dewey:786.5/193.
LCCN:00-021249.
          Audience: **l,u,f.**

Rosenblum, Sandra P.   **ML705.R67 1988**
Performance Practices in Classic Piano Music: Their Principles
and Applications. Malcolm Bilson (Foreword by). Trade Cloth.
Indiana University Press. Bloomington, IN. 1988. 544p. Music,
:Scholarship and Performance Ser. ISBN:0-253-34314-3,
ISBN13: 978-0-253-34314-7. Dewey:786.3/041.
LCCN:87-045437.
          Audience: **u,f.** *Choice, 1989.*

Rothwell, Evelyn   **MT360 .R8 1982**
Oboe Technique. Ed. 3. Paper Text. Oxford University Press,
Inc. New York, NY. 1983. 112p. ISBN:0-19-322333-3, ISBN13:
978-0-19-322333-2. Dewey:788/.7/0714. LCCN:84-102657.
          Audience: **l,u,f.**

Saucier, Gene A.   **MT339.5.S3 2002**
Woodwinds: Fundamental Performance Techniques. Ed. 2. Trade
Cloth. Opus 2 Publishing Company. Oxford, MS. 2002. xi,
271p. ISBN:0-9679765-0-2, ISBN13: 978-0-9679765-0-1.
Dewey:788.2/193/071. LCCN:00-091058.
          Audience: **l,u,f.**

Spillman, Robert   **MT68.S7 1985**
The Art of Accompanying: Master Lessons from the Repertoire.
Trade Cloth. Thomson Gale. Farmington Hills, MI. 1985. 384p.
ISBN:0-02-872380-5, ISBN13: 978-0-02-872380-8.
Dewey:781.6/6. LCCN:84-005418.

      Audience: **l,u,f.**

Strange, Patricia & Strange,   **ML857.S77 2001**
   Allen
The Contemporary Violin: Extended Performance Techniques.
Trade Paper. Scarecrow Press, Inc. Lanham, MD. 2001. 350p.
New Instrumentation Ser., Vol. 7 ISBN:0-520-22409-4, ISBN13:
978-0-520-22409-4. Dewey:787.2/193. LCCN:00-029870.

      Audience: **u,f.**

Taub, Robert   **MT145.B42T38 2002**
Playing the Beethoven Piano Sonatas. Trade Cloth. Hal Leonard
Corporation. Milwaukee, WI. 2003. 258p. ISBN:1-57467-071-9,
ISBN13: 978-1-57467-071-4. Dewey:786.2/183/092.
LCCN:2001-046126.

      Audience: **l,u,f.** *Choice, 2003, 2002.*

Toff, Nancy   **ML935.T65 1996**
The Flute Book: A Complete Guide for Students and
Performers. Ed. 2. Trade Paper. Oxford University Press, Inc.
New York, NY. 1996. 484p. ISBN:0-19-510502-8, ISBN13:
978-0-19-510502-5. Dewey:788/.51/09. LCCN:96-023178.

      Audience: **l,u,f.** *B Choice, 1997, 1985.*

Turetzky, Bertram   **MT320.T87 1989**
The Contemporary Contrabass. Ed. 2. Trade Paper. University of
California Press. Berkeley, CA. 1989. 128p. New
Instrumentation Ser., Vol. 7 ISBN:0-520-06381-3, ISBN13:
978-0-520-06381-5. Dewey:787/.41/071. LCCN:87-035486.

      Audience: **u,f.**

Turk, Daniel Gottlob   **MT0222.T8513**
School of Clavier Playing, or, Instructions in Playing the Clavier
for Teachers and Students. Trade Paper. Books on Demand. Ann
Arbor, MI. 427p. ISBN:0-598-04659-3, ISBN13:
978-0-598-04659-8. Dewey:786.3/041. LCCN:81-014626.

      Audience: **u,f.**

Van Cleve, Libby   **MT360**
Oboe Unbound: Contemporary Techniques. Scarecrow Press.
2004. The New Instrumentation Ser., Vol. 8; Variation
ISBN:0-8108-5031-1, ISBN13: 978-0-8108-5031-6.

      Audience: **u,f.**

Weisberg, Arthur   **MT75.W38 1993**
Performing Twentieth-Century Music: A Handbook for
Conductors and Instrumentalists. Trade Paper. Yale University
Press. Cumberland, RI. 1996. 152p. ISBN:0-300-06655-4,
ISBN13: 978-0-300-06655-5. Dewey:781.43.

      Audience: **u,f.** *Choice, 1994.*

Whitener, Scott   **ML933**
A Complete Guide to Brass: Instruments and Techniques. Ed. 3.
Spiral. Thomson Wadsworth. Belmont, CA. 2006. 408p.
ISBN:0-534-50988-6, ISBN13: 978-0-534-50988-0.
Dewey:788.9/19. LCCN:2005-933211.

      Audience: **l,u,f.**

Wick, Denis   **MT460**
Trombone Technique. Ed. 2. Oxford: Music Department, Oxford
University Press. 1996. ISBN:0-19-322378-3, ISBN13:
978-0-19-322378-3.

      Audience: **l,u,f.**

Performance Techniques and Interpretation > Historical Performance Practices

Agricola, Johann Friedrich   **MT892 .T6713 1995**
   & Tosi, Pier Francesco
Introduction to the Art of Singing by Johann Friedrich Agricola.
John Butt & Laurence Dreyfus (Contribution by), Julianne C.
Baird (Edited and Translated by). Trade Cloth. Cambridge
University Press. New York, NY. 1995. 308p. Cambridge
Musical Texts and Monographs ISBN:0-521-45428-X, ISBN13:
978-0-521-45428-5. Dewey:783/.043. LCCN:94-011416.

      Audience: **u,f.**

Arnold, F. T.   **ML442.A7 2003**
The Art of Accompaniment from a Thorough-Bass, Vol. 2. Trade
Paper. Dover Publications, Inc. Mineola, NY. 2003. 448p.
American Musicological Society-Music Library Association
Reprint ISBN:0-486-43195-9, ISBN13: 978-0-486-43195-6.
Dewey:781.47. LCCN:2003-048966.

      Audience: **u,f.**

Arnold, F. T.   **ML442.A7 2003**
The Art of Accompaniment from a Thorough-Bass, Vol. 1. Trade
Paper. Dover Publications, Inc. Mineola, NY. 2003. 512p.
American Musicological Society-Music Library Association
Reprint ISBN:0-486-43188-6, ISBN13: 978-0-486-43188-8.
Dewey:781.47. LCCN:2003-048966.

      Audience: **u,f.**

Bach, Carl Philipp Emanuel   **MT224.B132**
Essay on the True Art of Playing Keyboard Instruments.
William J. Mitchell (Editor). Trade Cloth. W. W. Norton &
Company, Inc. New York, NY. 1948. 449p.
ISBN:0-393-09716-1, ISBN13: 978-0-393-09716-0.
Dewey:786.193.

      Audience: **u,f.** *B*

Boyden, David D.   **ML850.B7 1990**
The History of Violin Playing from Its Origins to 1761: And Its
Relationship to the Violin and Violin Music. Trade Paper.
Oxford University Press, Inc. New York, NY. 1990. 594p.
ISBN:0-19-816183-2, ISBN13: 978-0-19-816183-7.
Dewey:787.2/143/09. LCCN:89-016285.

      Audience: **l,u,f.**

Brown, Clive   **ML457**
Classical and Romantic Performing Practice 1750-1900. Trade
Paper. Oxford University Press, Inc. New York, NY. 2004. 676p.
ISBN:0-19-516665-5, ISBN13: 978-0-19-516665-1.
Dewey:781.4309033. LCCN:97-050572.

      Audience: **u,f.**

Brown, Howard Mayer &   **ML5**
Sadie, Stanley (Editors)
Performance Practice: Music after 1600. Trade Cloth. W. W.
Norton & Company, Inc. New York, NY. 1990. xi, 533p. Grove
Handbooks in Music Ser. ISBN:0-393-02808-9, ISBN13:
978-0-393-02808-9. Dewey:780/.903. LCCN:91-110857.

                             Audience: **u,f.**

Brown, Howard Mayer &   **ML5**
Sadie, Stanley (Editors)
Performance Practice: Music Before 1600. Trade Cloth. W. W.
Norton & Company, Inc. New York, NY. 1990. Grove
Handbooks in Music Ser. ISBN:0-393-02807-0, ISBN13:
978-0-393-02807-2. Dewey:780/.903.

                             Audience: **u,f.**

Brown, Rachel   **ML937.B76 2002**
The Early Flute: A Practical Guide. Cloth Text. Cambridge
University Press. New York, NY. 2003. 198p. Cambridge
Handbooks to the Historical Performance of Music
ISBN:0-521-81391-3, ISBN13: 978-0-521-81391-4.
Dewey:788.3/09. LCCN:2001-052903.

           Audience: **u,f.** *Choice, 2003.*

Burton, Anthony (Editor)   **ML457**
A Performer's Guide to Music of the Classical Period. London:
Associated Board of the Royal Schools of Music. 2002.
Performer's Guides ISBN:1-86096-193-2, ISBN13:
978-1-86096-193-9.

                       Audience: **l,u,f.**

Burton, Anthony (Editor)   **ML457**
A Performer's Guide to Music of the Romantic Period. London;
Associated Board of the Royal Schools of Music. 2002.
Performer's Guides ISBN:1-86096-194-0, ISBN13:
978-1-86096-194-6.

                       Audience: **l,u,f.**

Butt, John   **ML457 .B92 2002**
Playing with History: The Historical Approach to Musical
Performance. Trade Cloth. Cambridge University Press. New
York, NY. 2002. 282p. Musical Performance and Reception Ser.
ISBN:0-521-81352-2, ISBN13: 978-0-521-81352-5.
Dewey:781.4311. LCCN:2001-043656.

           Audience: **u,f.** *Choice, 2003.*

Carter, Stewart   **ML457.P49 1997**
A Performer's Guide to Seventeenth-Century Music. Trade
Cloth. Thomson Wadsworth. Belmont, CA. 1997. Early Music
America Ser. ISBN:0-02-870492-4, ISBN13:
978-0-02-870492-0. Dewey:781.4/3/09032. LCCN:97-001310.

                       Audience: **u,f.**

Clementi, Muzio   **MT222.C617 1974**
Introduction to the Art of Playing on the Piano Forte;
Containing the Elements of Music, Preliminary Notions on
Fingering, and Fifty Fingered Lessons. Da Capo Press. 1974. Da
Capo Press Music Reprint Series ISBN:0-385-41609-1, ISBN13:
978-0-385-41609-2.

                       Audience: **l,u,f.**

Coelho, Victor Anand   **ML1003 .P47 1997**
(Editor)
Performance on Lute, Guitar, and Vihuela: Historical Practice
and Modern Interpretation. Trade Paper. Cambridge University
Press. New York, NY. 2005. 251p. Cambridge Studies in
Performance Practice Ser., Vol. 6 ISBN:0-521-01943-5, ISBN13:
978-0-521-01943-9. Dewey:787.8/143. LCCN:2006-272018.

                       Audience: **u,f.**

Duffin, Ross W.   **ML457.P475 2000**
A Performer's Guide to Medieval Music. Trade Cloth. Indiana
University Press. Bloomington, IN. 2000. xi, 599p. Publications
of the Early Music Institute ISBN:0-253-33752-6, ISBN13:
978-0-253-33752-8. Dewey:781.4/3/0902. LCCN:00-040968.

                       Audience: **u,f.**

Elliott, Martha   **MT892**
Singing in Style: A Guide to Vocal Performance Practices. Yale
University Press. 2006. ISBN:0-300-10932-6, ISBN13:
978-0-300-10932-0.

                       Audience: **u,f.**

Garcia, Manuel   **MT835**
A Complete Treatise on the Art of Singing : Complete and
Unabridged. Paschke, Donald V. (Editor). Da Capo Press. 1975.
Da Capo Press Music Reprint Series, Vol. 2.
ISBN:0-306-70660-1, ISBN13: 978-0-306-70660-8.

                       Audience: **u,f.**

Garcia, Manuel   **MT835**
A Complete Treatise on the Art of Singing : Complete and
Unabridged. Paschke, Donald V. (Editor). Da Capo Press. 1975.
Da Capo Press Music Reprint Ser., Vol. 1. ISBN:0-306-76212-9,
ISBN13: 978-0-306-76212-3.

                       Audience: **u,f.**

Gordon, Stewart   **ML457.G66 2006**
Mastering the Art of Performance: A Primer for Musicians.
Trade Paper. Oxford University Press, Inc. New York, NY. 2005.
240p. ISBN:0-19-517743-6, ISBN13: 978-0-19-517743-5.
Dewey:781.4/3. LCCN:2005-010152.

          Audience: **l,u,f.** *Choice, 2006.*

Hudson, Richard   **ML457.H83 1997**
Stolen Time: The History of Tempo Rubato. Trade Paper.
Oxford University Press, Inc. New York, NY. 1997. 488p.
ISBN:0-19-816667-2, ISBN13: 978-0-19-816667-2.
Dewey:781.4/32/09. LCCN:97-011322.

          Audience: **u,f.** *Choice, 1995.*

Humphries, John   **ML955 .H86 2000**
The Early Horn: A Practical Guide. Colin Lawson & Robin
Stowell (Contribution by). Cloth Text. Cambridge University
Press. New York, NY. 2000. 146p. Handbooks to the Historical
Performance of Music ISBN:0-521-63210-2, ISBN13:
978-0-521-63210-2. Dewey:788.9/4/09. LCCN:99-054036.

          Audience: **u,f.** *Choice, 2001.*

Jackson, Roland   **ML100.J29 2004**
Performance Practice: A Dictionary Guide for Musicians. Paper
over Boards. Routledge. New York, NY. 2005. 544p.

Formats: Web: ☐   Ebook: 🄴   CD/DVD-ROM: 🦋   BCL3: 𝓑

ISBN:0-415-94139-3, ISBN13: 978-0-415-94139-6.
Dewey:781.4/3/09. LCCN:2004-026541.

Audience: **g,l,u,f.** *Choice, 2005.*

Jorgensen, Owen   **MT165 .J67**
Tuning the Historical Temperaments by Ear. Trade Cloth.
Northern Michigan University Press. Marquette, MI. 1977.
ISBN:0-918616-00-X, ISBN13: 978-0-918616-00-5.
Dewey:786.2/3. LCCN:77-070993.

Audience: **u,f.**

Keller, Hermann   **MT49.K2952 1990**
Thoroughbass Method. Cloth Text. Columbia University Press.
New York, NY. 1990. 112p. A Morningside Bk.
ISBN:0-231-07320-8, ISBN13: 978-0-231-07320-2.
Dewey:781.47. LCCN:89-071221.

Audience: **u,f.**

Kenyon, Nicholas (Editor)   **ML457.A98 1988**
Authenticity and Early Music: A Symposium. Paper Text.
Oxford University Press, Inc. New York, NY. 1989. 234p.
ISBN:0-19-816153-0, ISBN13: 978-0-19-816153-0.
Dewey:781.6/3. LCCN:88-015464.

Audience: **u,f.** *Choice, 1989.*

Kite-Powell, Jeffery T.   **ML457.P48 1994**
(Editor)
A Performer's Guide to Renaissance Music. Trade Cloth.
Thomson Wadsworth. Belmont, CA. 1994. 400p. Performer's
Guides to Early Music Ser. ISBN:0-02-871231-5, ISBN13:
978-0-02-871231-4. Dewey:781.4/3/09031. LCCN:93-048544.

Audience: **u,f.** *Choice, 1995.*

Kivy, Peter   **ML457.K58 1995**
Authenticities: Philosophical Reflections on Musical
Performance. Book, Other. Cornell University Press. Ithaca, NY.
1995. 296p. ISBN:0-8014-3046-1, ISBN13: 978-0-8014-3046-6.
Dewey:781.4/3/01. LCCN:94-036842.

Audience: **u,f.** *Choice, 1995.*

Kroll, Mark   **MT252.K76 2004**
Playing the Harpsichord Expressively: A Practical and Historical
Guide. Trade Paper. Scarecrow Press, Inc. Lanham, MD. 2004.
112p. ISBN:0-8108-5032-X, ISBN13: 978-0-8108-5032-3.
Dewey:786.4/193. LCCN:2004-003439.

Audience: **u,f.**

Lawson, Colin J. & Stowell,   **ML457 .L39 1999**
Robin
The Historical Performance of Music: An Introduction. Colin J.
Lawson & Robin Stowell (Contribution by). Cloth Text.
Cambridge University Press. New York, NY. 1999. 233p.
Handbooks to the Historical Performance of Music
ISBN:0-521-62193-3, ISBN13: 978-0-521-62193-9.
Dewey:781.4/3/09. LCCN:98-042731.

Audience: **u,f.**

Mather, Betty B. & Karns,   **ML3427.M37 1987**
Dean M.
Dance Rhythms of the French Baroque: A Handbook for
Performance. Trade Cloth. Indiana University Press.

Bloomington, IN. 1988. 352p. Music, :Scholarship and
Performance Ser. ISBN:0-253-31606-5, ISBN13:
978-0-253-31606-6. Dewey:785.4/1/0944. LCCN:86-045991.

Audience: **u,f.**

Miller, Richard   **MT823.M55 1997**
National Schools of Singing: English, French, German and
Italian Techniques of Singing Revisited. Ed. 2. Trade Cloth.
Scarecrow Press, Inc. Lanham, MD. 2003. 304p.
ISBN:0-8108-3237-2, ISBN13: 978-0-8108-3237-4.
Dewey:783/.0094. LCCN:96-035557.

Audience: **u,f.** *Choice, 1997.*

Mozart, Leopold   **MT262.M93 1985**
A Treatise on the Fundamental Principles of Violin Playing. Ed.
2. Editha Knocker (Translator). Paper Text. Oxford University
Press, Inc. New York, NY. 1985. 274p. Early Music Ser.
ISBN:0-19-318513-X, ISBN13: 978-0-19-318513-5.
Dewey:787.1/07/14. LCCN:85-002895.

Audience: **u,f.** *B*

Musgrave, Michael &   **MT92**
Sherman, Bernard D. (Editors)
Performing Brahms: Early Evidence of Performance Style. John
Butt & Laurence Dreyfus (Contribution by). Trade Cloth.
Cambridge University Press. New York, NY. 2003. 412p.
Musical Performance and Reception Ser. ISBN:0-521-65273-1,
ISBN13: 978-0-521-65273-5. Dewey:781.4/3/09034.
LCCN:2004-272942.

Audience: **u,f.**

Newman, William S.   **ML410.C54**
Beethoven on Beethoven: Playing His Piano Music His Way.
Trade Paper. W. W. Norton & Company, Inc. New York, NY.
1991. 336p. ISBN:0-393-30719-0, ISBN13: 978-0-393-30719-1.
Dewey:786.1/092/4.

Audience: **l,u,f.** *Choice, 1989.*

Parrott, Andrew   **ML410.B13P29 2000**
The Essential Bach Choir. Trade Paper, Trade Cloth. Boydell &
Brewer, Ltd. Woodbridge, 2002. 240p. ISBN:0-85115-786-6,
ISBN13: 978-0-85115-786-3. Dewey:782.2/4/092.
LCCN:99-087035.

Audience: **u,f.** *Choice, 2000.*

Philip, Robert   **ML457 .P5 1992**
Early Recordings and Musical Style: Changing Tastes in
Instrumental Performance, 1900-1950. Trade Paper. Cambridge
University Press. New York, NY. 2004. 284p.
ISBN:0-521-60744-2, ISBN13: 978-0-521-60744-5.
Dewey:781.4/30904. LCCN:2005-280641.

Audience: **u,f.** *Choice, 1993.*

Philip, Robert   **ML457**
Performing Music in the Age of Recording. Cloth over Boards.
Yale University Press. Cumberland, RI. 2004. 304p.
ISBN:0-300-10246-1, ISBN13: 978-0-300-10246-8.
Dewey:781.4/3/0904. LCCN:2004-100136.

Audience: **u,f.** *Choice, 2004.*

Phillips, Elizabeth B. &   ML430.5.P52 1986
Jackson, John-Paul C.
Performing Medieval and Renaissance Music: An Introductory Guide. Trade Cloth. Thomson Gale. Farmington Hills, MI. 1986. 240p. ISBN:0-02-871790-2, ISBN13: 978-0-02-871790-6. Dewey:780/.902. LCCN:85-018419.

Audience: **u,f.**

Plank, Steven Eric   MT875.P53 2004
Choral Performance: A Guide to Historical Practice. Trade Paper. Scarecrow Press, Inc. Lanham, MD. 2004. 128p. ISBN:0-8108-5141-5, ISBN13: 978-0-8108-5141-2. Dewey:782.5/143. LCCN:2004-008272.

Audience: **u,f.** *Choice, 2005.*

Quantz, Johann J.   MT342
On Playing the Flute. Ed. 2. Edward R. Reilly (Editor). Trade Cloth. Thomson Gale. Farmington Hills, MI. 1985. 412p. ISBN:0-02-872920-X, ISBN13: 978-0-02-872920-6. Dewey:788/.51/071.

Audience: **u,f.**

Ritchie, George H. &   MT182.R6 2000
Stauffer, George B.
Organ Technique: Modern and Early. Spiral. Oxford University Press, Inc. New York, NY. 2000. 390p. ISBN:0-19-513745-0, ISBN13: 978-0-19-513745-3. Dewey:786.5/193. LCCN:00-021249.

Audience: **l,u,f.**

Rosenblum, Sandra P.   ML705.R67 1988
Performance Practices in Classic Piano Music: Their Principles and Applications. Malcolm Bilson (Foreword by). Trade Cloth. Indiana University Press. Bloomington, IN. 1988. 544p. Music, :Scholarship and Performance Ser. ISBN:0-253-34314-3, ISBN13: 978-0-253-34314-7. Dewey:786.3/041. LCCN:87-045437.

Audience: **u,f.** *Choice, 1989.*

Rowland, David   ML549 .R69 2001
Early Keyboard Instruments: A Practical Guide. Colin Lawson & Robin Stowell (Contribution by). Cloth Text. Cambridge University Press. New York, NY. 2001. 166p. Handbooks to the Historical Performance of Music ISBN:0-521-64366-X, ISBN13: 978-0-521-64366-5. Dewey:786.19. LCCN:00-062179.

Audience: **u,f.** *Choice, 2001.*

Stowell, Robin (Editor)   ML410.B42 P47 1994
Performing Beethoven. Trade Paper. Cambridge University Press. New York, NY. 2005. 260p. Cambridge Studies in Performance Practice Ser., Vol. 4 ISBN:0-521-02374-2, ISBN13: 978-0-521-02374-0. Dewey:780.92. LCCN:2006-276118.

Audience: **l,u,f.** *Choice, 1995.*

Stowell, Robin   ML855 .S79 2001
The Early Violin and Viola: A Practical Guide. Colin Lawson (Contribution by). Cloth Text. Cambridge University Press. New York, NY. 2001. 250p. Handbooks to the Historical Performance of Music ISBN:0-521-62380-4, ISBN13: 978-0-521-62380-3. Dewey:787.214309033. LCCN:00-065086.

Audience: **u,f.**

Taruskin, Richard F.   ML457.T37 1995
Text and Act: Essays on Music and Performance. Trade Paper. Oxford University Press, Inc. New York, NY. 1995. 390p. ISBN:0-19-509458-1, ISBN13: 978-0-19-509458-9. Dewey:781.4/3. LCCN:94-024903.

Audience: **u,f.** *Choice, 1996.*

Troeger, Richard   MT179.T76 2003
Playing Bach on the Keyboard: A Practical Guide. Trade Cloth. Hal Leonard Corporation. Milwaukee, WI. 2003. 300p. ISBN:1-57467-084-0, ISBN13: 978-1-57467-084-4. Dewey:786/.092. LCCN:2003-012791.

Audience: **l,u,f.** *Choice, 2004.*

Turk, Daniel Gottlob   MT0222.T8513
School of Clavier Playing, or, Instructions in Playing the Clavier for Teachers and Students. Trade Paper. Books on Demand. Ann Arbor, MI. 427p. ISBN:0-598-04659-3, ISBN13: 978-0-598-04659-8. Dewey:786.3/041. LCCN:81-014626.

Audience: **u,f.**

Performance Techniques and Interpretation > Conducting

Bowen, José Antonio   ML458.C36 2003
(Editor)
The Cambridge Companion to Conducting. Jonathan Cross (Contribution by). Cloth Text. Cambridge University Press. New York, NY. 2003. 366p. Cambridge Companions to Music Ser. ISBN:0-521-82108-8, ISBN13: 978-0-521-82108-7. Dewey:781.45. LCCN:2003-043813.

Audience: **u,f.** *Choice, 2004.*

Galkin, Elliott W.   ML457.G3 1988
The History of Orchestral Conducting: In Theory and Practice. Trade Cloth. Pendragon Press. Hillsdale, NY. 1989. 894p. ISBN:0-918728-47-9, ISBN13: 978-0-918728-47-0. Dewey:781.6/35. LCCN:85-028433.

Audience: **l,u,f.**

Garretson, Robert L.   MT85.G175C6 1998
Conducting Choral Music. Ed. 8. Cloth Text. Prentice Hall PTR. Upper Saddle River, NJ. 1998. 427p. ISBN:0-13-775735-2, ISBN13: 978-0-13-775735-0. Dewey:782.5/145. LCCN:97-036067.

Audience: **u,f.**

Labuta, Joseph A.   MT85.L24 2003
Basic Conducting Techniques. Ed. 5. Trade Paper. Prentice Hall PTR. Upper Saddle River, NJ. 2003. 400p. ISBN:0-13-112108-1, ISBN13: 978-0-13-112108-9. Dewey:781.45. LCCN:2002-044965.

Audience: **l,u,f.**

McElheran, Brock   MT85.M125 2004
Conducting Technique: For Beginners and Professionals. Ed. 3. Trade Cloth. Oxford University Press, Inc. New York, NY. 2004. xiv, 140p. ISBN:0-19-386854-7, ISBN13: 978-0-19-386854-0. Dewey:781.45. LCCN:2004-059512.

Audience: **l,u,f.**

Rudolf, Max MT85.R8 1993
The Grammar of Conducting: A Comprehensive Guide to Baton Technique and Interpretation. Ed. 3. Michael Stern (Contribution by). Paper Text. Thomson Wadsworth. Belmont, CA. 1995. 504p. ISBN:0-02-872221-3, ISBN13: 978-0-02-872221-4. Dewey:781.45. LCCN:93-012310.

Audience: **u,f.**

Schonberg, Harold C. ML402.S387
Great Conductors. Ed. 2. Trade Paper. Simon & Schuster. New York, NY. 1970. ISBN:0-671-20735-0, ISBN13: 978-0-671-20735-9. Dewey:780.922.

Audience: **g,l,u,f.**

Schuller, Gunther MT85
The Compleat Conductor. Trade Paper. Oxford University Press, Inc. New York, NY. 1998. 592p. ISBN:0-19-512661-0, ISBN13: 978-0-19-512661-7. Dewey:784.2/145.

Audience: **u,f.**

Wagar, Jeannine ML402.W23 1991
Conductors in Conversation: Fifteen Contemporary Conductors Discuss Their Lives and Profession. Trade Cloth. Macmillan Publishing Company, Inc. Old Tappan, NJ. 1991. 320p. ISBN:0-8161-8996-X, ISBN13: 978-0-8161-8996-0. Dewey:784.2/092/2. LCCN:90-024997.

Audience: **g,l,u,f.** *Choice, 1991.*

Wagner, Richard ML410.W1A246 1989
Wagner on Conducting. Trade Paper. Dover Publications, Inc. Mineola, NY. 1989. 128p. ISBN:0-486-25932-3, ISBN13: 978-0-486-25932-1. Dewey:781.6/35. LCCN:88-026827.

Audience: **u,f.**

Weisberg, Arthur MT75.W38 1993
Performing Twentieth-Century Music: A Handbook for Conductors and Instrumentalists. Trade Paper. Yale University Press. Cumberland, RI. 1996. 152p. ISBN:0-300-06655-4, ISBN13: 978-0-300-06655-5. Dewey:781.43.

Audience: **u,f.** *Choice, 1994.*

Performance Techniques and Interpretation > Jazz and Improvisation

Baker, David MT68 .B25 1988
Jazz Improvisation. Paper Text. Alfred Publishing Company, Inc. Van Nuys, CA. 1988. 132p. ISBN:0-88284-370-2, ISBN13: 978-0-88284-370-4. Dewey:781.65/136. LCCN:92-213873.

Audience: **l,u,f.**

Boras, Tom MT40.B72 2005
Jazz Composition and Arranging. Spiral. Thomson Wadsworth. Belmont, CA. 2004. 396p. ISBN:0-534-25261-3, ISBN13: 978-0-534-25261-8. Dewey:781.65/13. LCCN:2004-106300.

Audience: **l,u,f.**

Goldsby, John MT322
The Jazz Bass Book: Technique and Tradition. Trade Paper.

Backbeat Books. San Francisco, CA. 2002. 240p. ISBN:0-87930-716-1, ISBN13: 978-0-87930-716-5. Dewey:787.5/193165. LCCN:2002-066676.

Audience: **l,u,f.**

Levine, Mark MT239.L46 1989
The Jazz Piano Book. Trade Paper. Sher Music Company. Petaluma, CA. 1990. 307p. ISBN:0-9614701-5-1, ISBN13: 978-0-9614701-5-9. Dewey:786.3041. LCCN:93-704247.

Audience: **l,u,f.**

Mauleon, Rebeca ML417.S92
The Salsa Guidebook for Piano and Ensemble. Trade Paper. Sher Music Company. Petaluma, CA. 1993. 259p. ISBN:0-9614701-9-4, ISBN13: 978-0-9614701-9-7. Dewey:786.2162687291.

Audience: **l,u,f.**

Olmstead, Neil (Composed by) MT239
Solo Jazz Piano: The Linear Approach. Compact Disc, Book, Other. Berklee Press. 2003. 310p. ISBN:0-634-00761-0, ISBN13: 978-0-634-00761-3. Dewey:786.2.

Audience: **l,u,f.**

Reeves, Scott D. MT68
Creative Jazz Improvisation. Ed. 4. Trade Paper. Pearson Education. Boston, MA. 2006. 320p. ISBN:0-13-177639-8, ISBN13: 978-0-13-177639-5. Dewey:781.65/136. LCCN:2006-018669.

Audience: **l,u,f.**

Russell, George A. ML3811
George Russell's Lydian Chromatic Concept of Tonal Organization: The Art and Science of Tonal Gravity. Ed. 4. Cloth Text. Concept. Jamaica Plain, MA. 2001. "iv, 252"p. ISBN:0-9703739-0-2, ISBN13: 978-0-9703739-0-8. Dewey:781.258.

Audience: **u,f.**

Russo, William ML3506
Jazz Composition and Orchestration. Mixed Media. University of Chicago Press. Chicago, IL. 1997. 843p. ISBN:0-226-73208-8, ISBN13: 978-0-226-73208-4. Dewey:781.6/513.

Audience: **u,f.** ℬ

Sabina, Leslie M. MT73
Jazz Arranging and Orchestration: A Concise Introduction with Interactive CD-ROM. Schirmer/Thomson Learning. 2002. ISBN:0-534-58590-6, ISBN13: 978-0-534-58590-7.

Audience: **u,f.**

Sudnow, David MT68.S89 2001
Ways of the Hand: A Rewritten Account. Ed. 2. Hubert L. Dreyfus (Foreword by). Trade Cloth. MIT Press. Cambridge, MA. 2001. 163p. ISBN:0-262-19467-8, ISBN13: 978-0-262-19467-9. Dewey:786.2/16593. LCCN:2001-044330.

Audience: **u,f.**

Performance Techniques and Interpretation > Stage Production

Boland, Robert & Argentini, Paul   MT955.B6 1997

Musicals!: Directing School and Community Theatre. Trade Paper. Scarecrow Press, Inc. Lanham, MD. 1997. 224p. ISBN:0-8108-3323-9, ISBN13: 978-0-8108-3323-4. Dewey:792.6/0233. LCCN:97-011996.

Audience: **l,u,f.**

Citron, Stephen   MT67.C54 1997

The Musical from the Inside Out. Trade Paper. Ivan R. Dee Publisher. Blue Ridge Summit, PA. 1997. 305p. ISBN:1-56663-176-9, ISBN13: 978-1-56663-176-1. Dewey:782.1/4. LCCN:97-019905.

Audience: **l,u,f.** *Choice, 1992.*

Engel, Lehman   MT67 .E6 1986

The Making of a Musical. Trade Paper. Hal Leonard Corporation. Milwaukee, WI. 1985. 176p. ISBN:0-87910-049-4, ISBN13: 978-0-87910-049-0. Dewey:782.81. LCCN:85-018148.

Audience: **l,u,f.**

Frankel, Aaron   MT67.F78 2000

Writing the Broadway Musical. Trade Paper. Da Capo Press, Inc. Cambridge, MA. 2000. 196p. ISBN:0-306-80943-5, ISBN13: 978-0-306-80943-9. Dewey:782.1/413. LCCN:00-040490.

Audience: **u,f.**

Jones, Tom   MT67.J775 1997

Making Musicals: An Informal Introduction to the World of Musical Theater. Trade Paper. Hal Leonard Corporation. Milwaukee, WI. 1997. 189p. ISBN:0-87910-095-8, ISBN13: 978-0-87910-095-7. Dewey:782.1/4/0973. LCCN:97-013033.

Audience: **l,u,f.**

Radice, Mark A.   MT955.O54 1998

Opera in Context: Essays on Historical Staging from the Late Renaissance to the Time of Puccini. Trade Cloth. Hal Leonard Corporation. Milwaukee, WI. 2003. 410p. ISBN:1-57467-032-8, ISBN13: 978-1-57467-032-5. Dewey:792.5/023. LCCN:97-002712.

Audience: **u,f.** *Choice, 1998.*

Van Witsen, Leo   MT955

Costuming for Opera: Who Wears What and Why. Trade Cloth. Scarecrow Press, Inc. Lanham, MD. 1994. 256p. ISBN:0-8108-2933-9, ISBN13: 978-0-8108-2933-6. Dewey:792.5026. LCCN:93-029999.

Audience: **u,f.** *Choice, 1995.*

Warren, Raymond   ML1700.W3 1995

Opera Workshop. Trade Cloth. Ashgate Publishing, Ltd. Aldershot, 1995. 288p. ISBN:0-85967-970-5, ISBN13: 978-0-85967-970-1. Dewey:782.1/143. LCCN:94-013604.

Audience: **u,f.** *Choice, 1995.*

Ear Training and Musicianship

Benward, Bruce & Kolosick, J. Timothy   MT35.B478 2005

Ear Training: A Technique for Listening. Ed. 7. Trade Cloth. McGraw-Hill Companies, The. New York, NY. 2004. xi, 271p. ISBN:0-07-293675-4, ISBN13: 978-0-07-293675-9. Dewey:781.4/24. LCCN:2004-040194.

Audience: **l,u,f.**

Ghezzo, Marta Arkossy   MT6.G474S6 2004

Solfege, Ear Training, Rhythm, Dictation, and Music Theory: A Comprehensive Course. Ed. 3. Mel Powell (Preface by). Trade Paper, CD-ROM. University of Alabama Press. Tuscaloosa, AL. 2005. 464p. ISBN:0-8173-5147-7, ISBN13: 978-0-8173-5147-2. Dewey:781. LCCN:2004-001103.

Audience: **l,u,f.**

Hindemith, Paul   MT35

Elementary Training for Musicians. Ed. 2. Schott. 1967. ISBN:0-901938-16-5, ISBN13: 978-0-901938-16-9.

Audience: **l,u,f.**

Ottman, Robert & Rogers, Nancy   MT870 .O86

Music for Sight Singing. Ed. 7. Spiral. Prentice Hall PTR. Upper Saddle River, NJ. 2006. 432p. ISBN:0-13-187234-6, ISBN13: 978-0-13-187234-9. Dewey:783.0423.

Audience: **l,u,f.**

Teck, Katherine   ML3460 .T38 1994

Ear Training for the Body: A Dancer's Guide to Music. Trade Paper. Princeton Book Company Publishers. Hightstown, NJ. 1994. 321p. ISBN:0-87127-192-3, ISBN13: 978-0-87127-192-1. Dewey:781/.0247928. LCCN:94-004805.

Audience: **g,l,u,f.**

Music Education

Abeles, Harold F., et al.   MT1.A25 1994

Foundations of Music Education. Ed. 2. Charles R. Hoffer & Robert H. Klotman (Authors). Paper Text. Thomson Wadsworth. Belmont, CA. 1994. 424p. ISBN:0-02-870011-2, ISBN13: 978-0-02-870011-3. Dewey:780/.7. LCCN:93-001877.

Audience: **l,u,f.**

Bachmann, Marie-Laure   ML3809

Dalcroze Today: An Education Through and into Music. David Parlett (Translator). Trade Paper. Oxford University Press, Inc. New York, NY. 1993. 388p. ISBN:0-19-816400-9, ISBN13: 978-0-19-816400-5. Dewey:781.2/2.

Audience: **u,f.** *Choice, 1992.*

Boardman, Eunice (Editor, Compiled by)   MT1.D56 2002

Dimensions of Musical Learning and Teaching: A Different Kind of Classroom. Trade Paper. Rowman & Littlefield Education. Lanham, MD. 2002. 242p. ISBN:1-56545-146-5, ISBN13: 978-1-56545-146-9. Dewey:780/.71. LCCN:2002-283121.

Audience: **u,f.**

Campbell, Patricia Shehan,   **MT1.C226 2006**
et al.
Music in Childhood: From Preschool Through the Elementary
Grades. Ed. 3. Kirk Kassner & Carol Scott-Kassner (Authors).
Spiral, Compact Disc. Thomson Wadsworth. Belmont, CA.
2005. 480p. ISBN:0-534-59548-0, ISBN13: 978-0-534-59548-7.
Dewey:372.87. LCCN:2004-118217.
Audience: **l,u,f.**

Campbell, Patricia Shehan   **MT1**
& Wade, Bonnie C.
Teaching Music Globally. Trade Paper. Oxford University Press,
Inc. New York, NY. 2004. 286p. Global Music Ser.
ISBN:0-19-517143-8, ISBN13: 978-0-19-517143-3.
Dewey:780.7/1. LCCN:2003-054900.
Audience: **u,f.**

Choksy, Lois   **MT1.C5365 1999**
The Kodaly Method I: Comprehensive Music Education. Ed. 3.
Cloth Text. Prentice Hall PTR. Upper Saddle River, NJ. 1998.
303p. ISBN:0-13-949165-1, ISBN13: 978-0-13-949165-8.
Dewey:372.87. LCCN:98-036152.
Audience: **u,f.**

Choksy, Lois   **MT1.C5366 1999**
The Kodaly Method II: Folksong to Masterwork. Trade Paper.
Prentice Hall PTR. Upper Saddle River, NJ. 1998. 210p.
ISBN:0-13-949173-2, ISBN13: 978-0-13-949173-3.
Dewey:372.87. LCCN:98-010892.
Audience: **u,f.**

Choksy, Lois   **MT1**
Teaching Music in the Twenty-First Century. Ed. 2. Prentice
Hall. 2001. ISBN:0-13-028027-5, ISBN13: 978-0-13-028027-5.
Audience: **l,u,f.**

College Music Society   **ML13**
Directory of Music Faculties in Colleges and Universities, U.S.
and Canada. College Music Society. 2006.
Audience: **g,l,u,f.**

Colwell, Richard J. &   **MT170.C64 2002**
Goolsby, Thomas W.
The Teaching of Instrumental Music. Ed. 3. Trade Paper.
Prentice Hall PTR. Upper Saddle River, NJ. 2001. 464p.
ISBN:0-13-020689-X, ISBN13: 978-0-13-020689-3.
Dewey:784/.071. LCCN:2001-056021.
Audience: **u,f.**

Colwell, Richard &   **MT1.S44 2002**
Richardson, Carol P. (Editors)
The New Handbook of Research on Music Teaching and
Learning: A Project of the Music Educators National
Conference. Music Educators National Conference Staff
(Contribution by). Trade Cloth. Oxford University Press, Inc.
New York, NY. 2002. 1,248p. ISBN:0-19-513884-8, ISBN13:
978-0-19-513884-9. Dewey:780/.71. LCCN:2001-036516.
Audience: **u,f.**

Elliott, David J.   **MT1.E435 1995**
Music Matters: A New Philosophy of Music Education. Cloth

Text. Oxford University Press, Inc. New York, NY. 1995. 400p.
ISBN:0-19-509171-X, ISBN13: 978-0-19-509171-7.
Dewey:780/.7. LCCN:94-003815.
Audience: **u,f.**

Gordon, Edwin   **MT1**
Learning Sequences in Music. Trade Cloth. G I A Publications,
Inc. Chicago, IL. 2003. 398p. ISBN:1-57999-204-8, ISBN13:
978-1-57999-204-0. Dewey:780/.71.
Audience: **u,f.**

Green, Lucy   **MT3.E5G74 2001**
How Popular Musicians Learn: A Way Ahead for Music
Education. Trade Cloth. Ashgate Publishing, Ltd. Aldershot,
2001. 250p. Popular and Folk Music Ser. ISBN:0-7546-0338-5,
ISBN13: 978-0-7546-0338-2. Dewey:781.64/071.
LCCN:2001-033362.
Audience: **u,f.**

Labuta, Joseph A. & Smith,   **MT3.U5L23 1997**
Deborah
Music Education: Historical Contexts and Perspectives. Cloth
Text. Prentice Hall PTR. Upper Saddle River, NJ. 1996. 158p.
ISBN:0-13-489444-8, ISBN13: 978-0-13-489444-7.
Dewey:780/.71/073. LCCN:96-024983.
Audience: **l,u,f.**

Mark, Michael L. (Editor)   **MT2.M94 2002**
Music Education: Source Readings from Ancient Greece to
Today. Ed. 2. UK-B Format Paperback. Routledge. New York,
NY. 2002. 352p. ISBN:0-415-93679-9, ISBN13:
978-0-415-93679-8. Dewey:780/.71. LCCN:2001-048186.
Audience: **u,f.**

Mark, Michael L. & Gary,   **MT3.U5M325 1999**
Charles L.
A History of American Music Education. Ed. 2. Book, Other.
MENC - The National Association for Music Education. Reston,
VA. 1999. xxiv, 405p. ISBN:1-56545-115-5, ISBN13:
978-1-56545-115-5. Dewey:780/.7/073. LCCN:00-512458.
Audience: **u,f.**

McKinney, James C.   **MT820**
The Diagnosis and Correction of Vocal Faults: A Manual for
Teachers of Singing and for Choir Directors. Paper Text,
CD-ROM. Waveland Press, Inc. Prospect Heights, IL. 2005.
213p. ISBN:1-57766-403-5, ISBN13: 978-1-57766-403-1.
Dewey:784.9/32.
Audience: **u,f.**

Meadows, Eddie S.   **ML128.J3**
Jazz Scholarship and Pedagogy: A Research and Information
Guide. Ed. 3. Routledge. 2006. Routledge Music Bibliographies
ISBN:0-415-93965-8, ISBN13: 978-0-415-93965-2.
Audience: **l,u,f.**

MENC, the National   **MT1.M98725 2000**
Association for Music Education Staff (Contribution by)
Music Makes the Difference. Trade Paper. Rowman & Littlefield

Education. Lanham, MD. 2000. 152p. Music Makes the
Difference ISBN:1-56545-129-5, ISBN13: 978-1-56545-129-2.
Dewey:780.7. LCCN:00-699227.

Audience: **u,f.**

Music Library Association   **ML3790**
▢ Copyright for Music Librarians.
http://www.lib.jmu.edu/org/mla/
Music Library Association.

Audience: **g,l,u,f.**

Natvig, Mary (Editor)   **MT18.T38 2002**
Teaching Music History. Trade Cloth. Ashgate Publishing, Ltd.
Aldershot, 2002. 282p. ISBN:0-7546-0129-3, ISBN13:
978-0-7546-0129-6. Dewey:780/.71/1. LCCN:2001-053479.

Audience: **u,f.**

Nettl, Bruno   **ML3799**
Heartland Excursions: Ethnomusicological Reflections on
Schools of Music. Trade Paper. University of Illinois Press.
Champaign, IL. 1995. 192p. ISBN:0-252-06468-2, ISBN13:
978-0-252-06468-5. Dewey:780/.89.

Audience: **u,f.** *Choice, 1995.*

Oddo, Vincent   **MT259.O3 1995**
Playing and Teaching the Strings. Ed. 2. Spiral. Thomson
Wadsworth. Belmont, CA. 1994. 208p. Music Ser.
ISBN:0-534-22971-9, ISBN13: 978-0-534-22971-9.
Dewey:787/.143/07. LCCN:94-035620.

Audience: **u,f.**

Parncutt, Richard &   **ML3838.S385 2002**
 McPherson, Gary (Editors)
The Science and Psychology of Music Performance: Creative
Strategies for Teaching and Learning. Trade Cloth. Oxford
University Press, Inc. New York, NY. 2002. 400p.
ISBN:0-19-513810-4, ISBN13: 978-0-19-513810-8.
Dewey:781.4. LCCN:2001-036292.

Audience: **u,f.**

Phelps, Roger P., et al.   **MT1.P5 2005**
A Guide to Research in Music Education. Ed. 5. Ronald Sadoff,
Edward C. Warburton & Lawrence Ferrara (Authors). Trade
Cloth. Scarecrow Press, Inc. Lanham, MD. 2004. 288p.
ISBN:0-8108-5240-3, ISBN13: 978-0-8108-5240-2.
Dewey:780/.7. LCCN:2004-010739.

Audience: **u,f.**

Volk, Terese M.   **MT4**
Music Education, and Multiculturalism. Trade Paper. Oxford
University Press, Inc. New York, NY. 2004. 282p.
ISBN:0-19-517975-7, ISBN13: 978-0-19-517975-0.
Dewey:780.7/1/073.

Audience: **u,f.**

Ware, Clifton   **MT820.W26 1998**
Basics of Vocal Pedagogy: The Foundations and Process of
Singing. Paper Text. McGraw-Hill Higher Education. Burr
Ridge, IL. 1997. 320p. ISBN:0-07-068289-5, ISBN13:
978-0-07-068289-4. Dewey:783/.04/071. LCCN:97-001281.

Audience: **u,f.**

Music Therapy

Bruscia, Kenneth E. (Editor)   **ML3920 .C325 1991**
Case Studies in Music Therapy. Paper Text. Barcelona
Publishers. Gilsum, NH. 1991. 656p. ISBN:0-9624080-1-8,
ISBN13: 978-0-9624080-1-4. Dewey:615.8/5154.
LCCN:91-072288.

Audience: **u,f.**

Bruscia, Kenneth E.   **ML3920.B775 1998**
Defining Music Therapy. Ed. 2. Paper Text. Barcelona
Publishers. Gilsum, NH. 1998. 320p. ISBN:1-891278-07-X,
ISBN13: 978-1-891278-07-5. Dewey:615.8/5154.
LCCN:99-167032.

Audience: **l,u,f.**

Bruscia, Kenneth E.   **ML3920.B78 1987**
Improvisational Models of Music Therapy. Cloth Text. Charles
C Thomas Publisher, Ltd. Springfield, IL. 1987. 606p.
ISBN:0-398-05272-7, ISBN13: 978-0-398-05272-0.
Dewey:615.8/5154. LCCN:86-014389.

Audience: **u,f.** *Choice, 1987.*

Davis, William B., et al.   **ML3920 .D28 1999**
An Introduction to Music Therapy: Theory and Practice. Ed. 2.
Kate E. Gfeller & Michael H. Thaut (Authors). Paper Text.
McGraw-Hill Higher Education. Burr Ridge, IL. 1998. 384p.
ISBN:0-697-38860-3, ISBN13: 978-0-697-38860-5.
Dewey:615.8/5154. LCCN:98-029454.

Audience: **l,u,f.**

Dileo, Cheryl (Editor)   **ML3920**
Music Therapy and Medicine: Theoretical and Clinical
Approaches. Trade Cloth. American Music Therapy Association.
Silver Spring, MD. 1999. ISBN:1-884914-00-4, ISBN13:
978-1-884914-00-3. Dewey:615.85154.

Audience: **u,f.**

Horden, Peregrine (Editor)   **ML3920**
Music as Medicine: The History of Music Therapy Since
Antiquity. Aldershot ; Brookfield, USA : Ashgate. 2000.
ISBN:1-84014-299-5, ISBN13: 978-1-84014-299-0.

Audience: **u,f.**

Peters, Jacqueline S.   **ML3920.P383 2000**
Music Therapy: An Introduction. Ed. 2. Trade Cloth. Charles C
Thomas Publisher, Ltd. Springfield, IL. 2000. 486p.
ISBN:0-398-07042-3, ISBN13: 978-0-398-07042-7.
Dewey:615.8/5154. LCCN:99-088599.

Audience: **l,u,f.**

Wheeler, Barbara L.   **ML3920**
 (Editor)
Music Therapy Research: Second Edition. Ed. 2. Cloth Text.
Barcelona Publishers. Gilsum, NH. 2005. ISBN:1-891278-26-6,
ISBN13: 978-1-891278-26-6. Dewey:615.85154.

Audience: **u,f.**

Librettos to Operas and Musicals

Beethoven, Ludwig van   ML410.B4
Fidelio. Nicholas John (Editor), Tom Hammond (Translator).
Trade Paper. Riverrun Press, Inc. Flemington, NJ. 1981. 96p.
English National Opera Guide Ser., No. 4:Bilingual Libretto,
Articles ISBN:0-7145-3823-X, ISBN13: 978-0-7145-3823-5.
Dewey:782.1.

Audience: **g,l,u,f.**

Berg, Alban   ML50.B491W62 1990
Wozzeck. Nicholas John (Editor), Eric Blocknel & Vicki
Hartfold (Translators). Trade Paper. Beekman Books, Inc.
Wappingers Falls, NY. 1990. 116p. English National Opera
Guide Series: Bilingual Libretto, Articles, No. 42
ISBN:0-7145-4201-6, ISBN13: 978-0-7145-4201-0.
Dewey:782.1/0268. LCCN:90-044450.

Audience: **g,l,u,f.**

Bizet, Georges   ML50.B625C22 1982
Carmen. Nicholas John (Editor), Nell Moody & John Moody
(Translators). Trade Paper. Beekman Books, Inc. Wappingers
Falls, NY. 1982. 128p. English National Opera Guide Ser., No.
13:Bilingual Libretto, Articles ISBN:0-7145-3937-6, ISBN13:
978-0-7145-3937-9. Dewey:782.1/2. LCCN:83-107621.

Audience: **g,l,u,f.**

Black, Don & Hampton,   ML50.Z99
Christopher
Sunset Boulevard. Trade Paper. Faber & Faber, Inc. New York,
NY. 1993. 128p. ISBN:0-571-17214-8, ISBN13:
978-0-571-17214-6. Dewey:782.140268.

Audience: **g,l,u,f.**

Bradley, Ian (Editor)   ML49.S9A1 1996
The Complete Annotated Gilbert and Sullivan. Trade Cloth.
Oxford University Press, Inc. New York, NY. 1996. 1, 212p.
ISBN:0-19-816503-X, ISBN13: 978-0-19-816503-3.
Dewey:782.1/2/0268. LCCN:95-051813.

Audience: **g,l,u,f.** *Choice, 1997.*

Brecht, Bertolt   PT2603.R397
The Threepenny Opera. Eric Bentley & Desmond Vesey
(Translators), Lotte Lenya (Foreword by). Trade Paper.
Grove/Atlantic, Inc. New York, NY. 1964. ISBN:0-394-17472-0,
ISBN13: 978-0-394-17472-3. Dewey:832/.912.

Audience: **g,l,u,f.**

Cheek, Timothy   ML49.J36O62 2003
The Janacek Opera Libretti: Kat'a Kabanova Translations and
Pronunciation. Trade Paper. Scarecrow Press, Inc. Lanham, MD.
2004. 280p. ISBN:0-8108-5014-1, ISBN13: 978-0-8108-5014-9.
Dewey:782.1/0268. LCCN:2002-153032.

Audience: **u,f.**

Comden, Betty & Green,   ML48.N49 1997
Adolph
The New York Musicals of Comden and Green: On the Town,
Wonderful Town, Bells Are Ringing. Trade Cloth. Applause

Theatre Book Publishers. New York, NY. 1996. 298p.
ISBN:1-55783-242-0, ISBN13: 978-1-55783-242-9.
Dewey:782.1/4/0268. LCCN:96-032626.

Audience: **g,l,u,f.**

Coward, Noel   ML54.6.C83N64 1998
Noel Coward: The Complete Illustrated Lyrics. Barry Day
(Editor). Trade Cloth. Overlook Press, The. New York, NY.
1998. 367p. ISBN:0-87951-896-0, ISBN13: 978-0-87951-896-7.
Dewey:782.42164/0268. LCCN:98-017414.

Audience: **g,l,u,f.** *Choice, 1999.*

Darion, Joe & Wasserman,   ML50.L536M32
Dale
Man of La Mancha. Trade Paper. Random House, Inc. New
York, NY. 1966. 112p. ISBN:0-394-40619-2, ISBN13:
978-0-394-40619-0. Dewey:782.81028.

Audience: **g,l,u,f.**

Debussy, Claude   ML410.D28
Pelleas and Melisande. Nicholas John (Editor), Hugh
MacDonald (Translator). Trade Paper. Riverrun Press, Inc.
Flemington, NJ. 1982. 128p. English National Opera Guide Ser.,
No. 9:Bilingual Libretto, Articles ISBN:0-7145-3906-6, ISBN13:
978-0-7145-3906-5. Dewey:782.1/092/4.

Audience: **g,l,u,f.**

Eliot, T. S.   ML50.L804
Cats: The Book of the Musical. John Napier (Photographer).
Trade Paper. Harcourt Trade Publishers. New York, NY. 1983.
112p. Harvest Book Ser. ISBN:0-15-615582-6, ISBN13:
978-0-15-615582-3. Dewey:782.81/2. LCCN:82-048026.

Audience: **g,l,u,f.**

Finn, William & Lapine,   ML49.F55 R5 1993
James
Falsettos: In Trousers, Falsettoland and March of the Falsettos.
Frank Rich (Afterword by). Trade Paper. Penguin Group (USA)
Inc. New York, NY. 1993. 256p. Drama Ser.
ISBN:0-452-27072-3, ISBN13: 978-0-452-27072-5.
Dewey:782.1/4/0268.

Audience: **g,l,u,f.**

Furth, George   ML50.S705C6 1996
Company: Music and Lyrics by Stephen Sondheim. Ed. 25.
Trade Paper. Theatre Communications Group, Inc. New York,
NY. 1995. 128p. ISBN:1-55936-108-5, ISBN13:
978-1-55936-108-8. Dewey:782.1/4. LCCN:95-045985.

Audience: **g,l,u,f.**

Ganzl, Kurt   ML410.L78
The Complete Aspects of Love. Clive Barda (Photographer).
Trade Cloth. Penguin Group (USA) Inc. New York, NY. 1990.
176p. ISBN:0-670-83192-1, ISBN13: 978-0-670-83192-0.
Dewey:782.1/4. LCCN:89-040452.

Audience: **g,l,u,f.** *Choice, 1990.*

Gay, John   ML50.7.B43 1999
The Beggar's Opera. Trade Paper. Dover Publications, Inc.

Mineola, NY. 1999. 64p. Thrift Editions Ser.
ISBN:0-486-40888-4, ISBN13: 978-0-486-40888-0.
Dewey:782.1/40268. LCCN:99-015104.

Audience: **g,l,u,f.**

Gelbart, Larry, et al.   **ML50.C688C6 1990**
City of Angels. Cy Coleman & David Zippel (Authors). Trade
Paper. Applause Theatre Book Publishers. New York, NY. 1990.
204p. Applause Musical Library ISBN:1-55783-081-9, ISBN13:
978-1-55783-081-4. Dewey:782.1/4/0268. LCCN:90-001207.

Audience: **g,l,u,f.**

Gershwin, Ira & Kimball,   **PZ8.3**
  Robert
The Complete Lyrics of Ira Gershwin. Trade Cloth. Alfred A.
Knopf Inc. New York, NY. 1993. 448p. ISBN:0-394-55651-8,
ISBN13: 978-0-394-55651-2. Dewey:782.42. LCCN:93-012175.

Audience: **g,l,u,f.**

Hammerstein, Oscar II   **ML49.H12H3 1985**
  (Lyrics by)
Lyrics by Oscar Hammerstein II. Ed. 2. Stephen Sondheim
(Foreword by). Trade Cloth. Hal Leonard Corporation.
Milwaukee, WI. 1985. 292p. Biographies and Commentary Ser.,
:Musicals/Classical/Folk/Religious Music Ser.
ISBN:0-88188-379-4, ISBN13: 978-0-88188-379-4.
Dewey:782.81/2. LCCN:85-050895.

Audience: **g,l,u,f.**

Hart, Lorenz   **ML54.6.H4H4 1995**
The Complete Lyrics of Lorenz Hart. Dorothy Hart & Robert
Kimball (Editors). Trade Paper. Da Capo Press, Inc. Cambridge,
MA. 1995. 208p. ISBN:0-306-80667-3, ISBN13:
978-0-306-80667-4. Dewey:782.1/4/0268. LCCN:95-021606.

Audience: **g,l,u,f.**

Hausam, Wiley (Editor)   **ML48.N485 2001**
The New American Musical: An Anthology from the End of the
20th Century. Trade Paper. Theatre Communications Group, Inc.
New York, NY. 2001. 450p. ISBN:1-55936-200-6, ISBN13:
978-1-55936-200-9. Dewey:782.1/40268. LCCN:2001-027192.

Audience: **g,l,u,f.**

Houghton, Norris   **PR2831.A2**
Romeo and Juliet and West Side Story. Mass Market. Random
House Children's Books. New York, NY. 1965. 256p.
ISBN:0-440-97483-6, ISBN13: 978-0-440-97483-3.
Dewey:822.3/3.

Audience: **g,l,u,f.**

Janacek, Leos & Cheek,   **ML49.J36J37 2003**
  Timothy
The Janacek Opera Libretti: Translations and Pronunciation.
Trade Cloth. Scarecrow Press, Inc. Lanham, MD. 2003. 224p.
ISBN:0-8108-4671-3, ISBN13: 978-0-8108-4671-5.
Dewey:782.1/0268. LCCN:2002-153032.

Audience: **u,f.**

Kimball, Robert & Berlin,   **ML54.6.B464K55 2000**
  Irving
Complete Lyrics of Irving Berlin. Trade Cloth. Alfred A. Knopf

Inc. New York, NY. 2001. 560p. ISBN:0-679-41943-8, ISBN13:
978-0-679-41943-3. Dewey:782.42164/0268. LCCN:00-062890.

Audience: **g,l,u,f.**

Kimball, Robert & Nelson,   **ML54.6.L64 2003**
  Steve
The Complete Lyrics of Frank Loesser. Trade Cloth. David
McKay Company, Inc. New York, NY. 2003. 352p.
ISBN:0-679-45059-9, ISBN13: 978-0-679-45059-7.
Dewey:782.4216403. LCCN:2003-109481.

Audience: **g,l,u,f.**

Kirkwood, James, et al.   **ML50.H2397C5 1995**
A Chorus Line: The Complete Book of the Musical. Nicholas
Dante & Edward Kleban (Authors), Michael Bennett (Created
by). Trade Cloth. Applause Theatre Book Publishers. New York,
NY. 2000. 150p. Musical Library ISBN:1-55783-131-9, ISBN13:
978-1-55783-131-6. Dewey:782.1/4/0268. LCCN:95-021617.

Audience: **g,l,u,f.**

Kotis, Greg & Hollmann,   **ML50.K8785U75 2002**
  Mark
Urinetown: The Musical. David Auburn (Preface by). Trade
Paper. Faber & Faber, Inc. New York, NY. 2003. 144p.
ISBN:0-571-21182-8, ISBN13: 978-0-571-21182-1.
Dewey:782.1/4/0268. LCCN:2002-033875.

Audience: **g,l,u,f.**

Lapine, James & Sondheim,   **ML50.S705I5 1989**
  Stephen
Into the Woods. Trade Paper. Theatre Communications Group,
Inc. New York, NY. 1998. 160p. ISBN:0-930452-93-3, ISBN13:
978-0-930452-93-3. Dewey:782.81/2. LCCN:89-004402.

Audience: **g,l,u,f.**

Lerner, Alan J. & Green,   **PS3523.E76H96 1987**
  Benny
A Hymn to Him: The Lyrics of Alan Jay Lerner. Al Hirschfeld
(Illustrator). Trade Cloth. Hal Leonard Corporation. Milwaukee,
WI. 1987. 319p. ISBN:0-87910-109-1, ISBN13:
978-0-87910-109-1. Dewey:782.81/2. LCCN:87-405427.

Audience: **g,l,u,f.**

Lloyd Webber, Andrew &   **ML50.L804**
  Rice, Tim
Evita. Trade Cloth. Quite Specific Media Group, Ltd.
Hollywood, CA. 1979. 128p. ISBN:0-89676-030-8, ISBN13:
978-0-89676-030-1. Dewey:782.81/2. LCCN:79-053888.

Audience: **g,l,u,f.**

MacDermot, Galt, et al.   **ML50.M1229**
Hair: The American Tribal Love-Rock Musical. Ragni, Gerome;
Rado, James (Authors). Pocket Books. 1969.
ISBN:0-671-77060-8, ISBN13: 978-0-671-77060-0.

Audience: **g,l,u,f.**

Masteroff, Joe, et al.   **ML410.H1745**
Cabaret: The Illustrated Book and Lyrics. John Kander & Fred
Ebb (Authors), Linda Sunshine (Editor), Rivka Katvan & Joan

Marcus (Photographers). Trade Cloth. Newmarket Press. New York, NY. 2004. 128p. ISBN:1-55704-383-3, ISBN13: 978-1-55704-383-2. Dewey:792.6/42. LCCN:99-022945.

Audience: **g,l,u,f.**

Mitchell, John Cameron &   **ML50.T769H4 2003**
  Trask, Stephen
Hedwig and the Angry Inch. Trade Paper. Dramatists Play Service, Inc. New York, NY. 2003. 42p. ISBN:0-8222-1901-8, ISBN13: 978-0-8222-1901-9. Dewey:782.1/4/0268. LCCN:2005-560193.

Audience: **g,l,u,f.**

Monteverdi, Claudio   **ML410.V4**
Operas of Monteverdi: Includes Orfeo, Return of Ulysses, Coronation of Poppea. Anne Ridler (Translator). Trade Paper. Riverrun Press, Inc. Flemington, NJ. 1992. 208p. English National Opera Guide Series: Bilingual Libretto, Articles, No. 45 ISBN:0-7145-4207-5, ISBN13: 978-0-7145-4207-2. Dewey:782.1092.

Audience: **g,l,u,f.**

Mozart, Wolfgang Amadeus   **ML49.M83 M42 1991**
The Metropolitan Opera Book of Mozart Operas. Metropolitan Opera Guild Staff & Paul Gruber (Editors), Judyth Schaubhut Smith, David Stivender & Susan Webb (Translators). Trade Paper. HarperCollins Publishers. New York, NY. 1991. 640p. ISBN:0-06-273051-7, ISBN13: 978-0-06-273051-0. Dewey:782.1/026/8. LCCN:91-055003.

Audience: **g,l,u,f.**

Mussorgsky, Modest   **ML410.M97**
Boris Godunov. Nicholas John (Editor), David Lloyd-Jones (Translator). Trade Paper. Riverrun Press, Inc. Flemington, NJ. 1982. 128p. English National Opera Guide Ser., No. 11:Bilingual Libretto, Articles ISBN:0-7145-3922-8, ISBN13: 978-0-7145-3922-5. Dewey:782.1/092/4.

Audience: **g,l,u,f.**

Perry, George   **ML1950**
The Complete Phantom of the Opera. Clive Barda (Photographer). Trade Paper. DIANE Publishing Company. Collingdale, PA. 2005. 167p. ISBN:0-7567-8833-1, ISBN13: 978-0-7567-8833-9. Dewey:782.81.

Audience: **g,l,u,f.**

Porter, Cole & Kimball,   **ML50.Z99**
  Robert
The Complete Lyrics of Cole Porter. John Updike (Foreword by). Trade Cloth. Alfred A. Knopf Inc. New York, NY. 1983. 354p. ISBN:0-394-53214-7, ISBN13: 978-0-394-53214-1. Dewey:782.1/4/0268. LCCN:83-048101.

Audience: **g,l,u,f.**

Puccini, Giacomo   **ML49.P75**
Seven Puccini Librettos. William Weaver (Translator). Trade Paper. W. W. Norton & Company, Inc. New York, NY. 1981. ISBN:0-393-00930-0, ISBN13: 978-0-393-00930-9. Dewey:782.1/2.

Audience: **g,l,u,f.**

Rice, Tim   **ML50.Z99**
Joseph and the Amazing Technicolor Dreamcoat. Quentin Blake (Illustrator), Andrew Lloyd Webber (Composed by). Trade Cloth. Henry Holt & Company. New York, NY. 1982. 48p. ISBN:0-03-061517-8, ISBN13: 978-0-03-061517-7. Dewey:782.81/2. LCCN:81-023722.

Audience: **g,l,u,f.**

Richards, Stanley   **ML48.R5 1976**
Great Musicals of the American Theatre. Trade Cloth. Chilton Book Publishing Company. Southborough, MA. 1976. ISBN:0-8019-5731-1, ISBN13: 978-0-8019-5731-4. Dewey:782.8/1/2. LCCN:78-113020.

Audience: **g,l,u,f.**

Richards, Stanley   **ML48.G7**
Great Rock Musicals. Trade Cloth. Henry Holt & Company. New York, NY. 1979. x, 562p. ISBN:0-8128-2509-8, ISBN13: 978-0-8128-2509-1. Dewey:782.8/1/2. LCCN:78-007005.

Audience: **g,l,u,f.**

Rodgers, Richard &   **ML48**
  Hammerstein, Oscar II
Six Plays. Trade Cloth. Random House, Inc. New York, NY. 1959. ISBN:0-394-60200-5, ISBN13: 978-0-394-60200-4. Dewey:812.

Audience: **g,l,u,f.**

Rossini, Gioacchino Antonio   **ML50.P965**
The Barber of Seville and Moses. Nicholas John (Editor), Edward J. Dent, John Moody & Nell Moody (Translators). Trade Paper. Riverrun Press, Inc. Flemington, NJ. 1986. 160p. English National Opera Guide Ser., No. 36:Bilingual Libretto, Articles ISBN:0-7145-4080-3, ISBN13: 978-0-7145-4080-1. Dewey:782.1/2. LCCN:85-052162.

Audience: **g,l,u,f.**

Schmidt, Harvey & Jones,   **ML50.S347F42 1990**
  Tom
The Fantasticks. Ed. 30. Trade Cloth. Applause Theatre Book Publishers. New York, NY. 1990. 170p. Musical Library ISBN:1-55783-074-6, ISBN13: 978-1-55783-074-6. Dewey:782.1/4. LCCN:90-033931.

Audience: **g,l,u,f.** *Choice, 1990.*

Shaw, George Bernard &   **PR5363**
  Lerner, Alan Jay
Pygmalion and My Fair Lady. Ed. 50. Mass Market. Penguin Group (USA) Inc. New York, NY. 2006. 240p. ISBN:0-451-53009-8, ISBN13: 978-0-451-53009-7. Dewey:822.912.

Audience: **g,l,u,f.**

Smalls, Charlie (Music by,   **ML50.S618**
  Lyrics by)
The Wiz. L. Frank Baum & William F. Brown (Based on a book by). Trade Paper. Samuel French Inc. New York, NY. 1979. ISBN:0-573-68091-4, ISBN13: 978-0-573-68091-5. Dewey:782.81/2.

Audience: **g,l,u,f.**

Sondheim, Stephen &   **ML50.S705F65 2001**
Goldman, James
Follies. Trade Paper. Theatre Communications Group, Inc. New York, NY. 2000. 128p. ISBN:1-55936-196-4, ISBN13: 978-1-55936-196-5. Dewey:782.1/4/0268. LCCN:00-068276.

Audience: **g,l,u,f.**

Sondheim, Stephen &   **ML50.S955G9 1994**
Laurents, Arthur
Gypsy. Jules Styne (Contribution by). Trade Paper. Theatre Communications Group, Inc. New York, NY. 1994. 120p. ISBN:1-55936-086-0, ISBN13: 978-1-55936-086-9. Dewey:782.1/4/0268. LCCN:94-002588.

Audience: **g,l,u,f.**

Sondheim, Stephen (Lyrics   **ML50.Z99**
by, Music by)
Four by Sondheim: Wheeler, Lapine, Shevelove, Gelbart. Trade Cloth. Applause Theatre Book Publishers. New York, NY. 2000. 772p. ISBN:1-55783-407-5, ISBN13: 978-1-55783-407-2. Dewey:782.1/40268. LCCN:00-100279.

Audience: **g,l,u,f.**

Stein, Joseph, et al.   **ML50.B6745F52 1990**
Fiddler on the Roof: Based on Sholom Aleichem's Stories. Jerry Bock, Sheldon Harnick & Sholem Aleichem (Authors). Trade Paper. Hal Leonard Corporation. Milwaukee, WI. 1990. 154p. ISBN:0-87910-136-9, ISBN13: 978-0-87910-136-7. Dewey:782.1/4/0268. LCCN:89-049701.

Audience: **g,l,u,f.**

Strauss, Richard   **ML50.S918S32 1988**
Salome and Elektra. Nicholas John (Editor). Trade Paper. Riverrun Press, Inc. Flemington, NJ. 1989. 144p. English National Opera Guide Ser., No. 37:Bilingual Libretto, Articles ISBN:0-7145-4131-1, ISBN13: 978-0-7145-4131-0. Dewey:782.1/2. LCCN:88-006444.

Audience: **g,l,u,f.**

Strauss, Richard   **ML50.M939**
Der Rosenkavalier. Nicholas John (Editor), Alfred Kalisch (Translator). Trade Paper. Riverrun Press, Inc. Flemington, NJ. 1982. English National Opera Guide Series: Bilingual Libretto, Articles, No. 8 ISBN:0-7145-3851-5, ISBN13: 978-0-7145-3851-8. Dewey:782.10268.

Audience: **g,l,u,f.**

Stravinsky, Igor   **ML49.S77O32 1991**
Oedipus Rex and the Rake's Progress. Nicholas John (Editor). Trade Paper. Riverrun Press, Inc. Flemington, NJ. 1991. 112p. English National Opera Guide Series: Bilingual Libretto, Articles, No. 43 ISBN:0-7145-4193-1, ISBN13: 978-0-7145-4193-8. Dewey:782.1. LCCN:90-026770.

Audience: **g,l,u,f.**

Verdi, Giuseppe   **ML49.V45**
Seven Verdi Librettos. William Weaver (Translator). Trade Paper. W. W. Norton & Company, Inc. New York, NY. 1977. ISBN:0-393-00852-5, ISBN13: 978-0-393-00852-4. Dewey:782.5.

Audience: **g,l,u,f.**

Wagner, Richard   **ML50.M939**
Lohengrin. Nicholas John (Editor). Trade Paper. Riverrun Press, Inc. Flemington, NJ. 1994. 128p. English National Opera Guide Series: Bilingual Libretto, Articles, No. 47 ISBN:0-7145-3852-3, ISBN13: 978-0-7145-3852-5. Dewey:782.10268.

Audience: **g,l,u,f.**

Wagner, Richard   **ML50.W14T22 1988**
Tannhauser. Nicholas John (Editor). Trade Paper. Riverrun Press, Inc. Flemington, NJ. 1988. 96p. English National Opera Guide Series: Bilingual Libretto, Articles, No. 39 ISBN:0-7145-4147-8, ISBN13: 978-0-7145-4147-1. Dewey:782.1/2. LCCN:88-006443.

Audience: **g,l,u,f.**

Wagner, Richard   **ML410.W16**
The Mastersingers of Nuremberg. Nicholas John (Editor), F. Jameson & Feasey Kember (Translators). Trade Paper. Riverrun Press, Inc. Flemington, NJ. 2003. 128p. English National Opera Guide Ser., No. 19:Bilingual Libretto, Articles ISBN:0-7145-3961-9, ISBN13: 978-0-7145-3961-4. Dewey:782.1/092/4.

Audience: **g,l,u,f.**

Wagner, Richard   **ML410.W17**
Parsifal. Nicholas John (Editor), Andrew Porter (Translator). Trade Paper. Riverrun Press, Inc. Flemington, NJ. 1986. 128p. English National Opera Guide Series: Bilingual Libretto, Articles, No. 34 ISBN:0-7145-4079-X, ISBN13: 978-0-7145-4079-5. Dewey:782.1/092/4. LCCN:85-052160.

Audience: **g,l,u,f.**

Wagner, Richard   **ML50.B422**
Tristan and Isolde. Nicholas John (Editor), Andrew Porter (Translator). Trade Paper. Riverrun Press, Inc. Flemington, NJ. 1981. 96p. English National Opera Guide Ser., No. 6:Bilingual Libretto, Articles ISBN:0-7145-3849-3, ISBN13: 978-0-7145-3849-5. Dewey:782.1/2.

Audience: **g,l,u,f.**

Wagner, Richard   **ML50.W14**
The Ring of the Nibelung. Andrew Porter (Translator). Trade Paper. W. W. Norton & Company, Inc. New York, NY. 1977. ISBN:0-393-00867-3, ISBN13: 978-0-393-00867-8. Dewey:782.12.

Audience: **g,l,u,f.**

Weidman, John &   **ML50.S705**
Sondheim, Stephen
Pacific Overtures. Trade Paper. Theatre Communications Group,

Inc. New York, NY. 1991. 144p. ISBN:1-55936-026-7, ISBN13: 978-1-55936-026-5. Dewey:782.1/4/0268. LCCN:90-029041.

Audience: **g,l,u,f.**

Lyrics and Texts to Songs and Choral Works

Bach, Johann Sebastian   ML53.8.B33 2000
J. S. Bach: The Complete Cantatas. Richard Stokes (Translator). Trade Paper. Scarecrow Press, Inc. Lanham, MD. 2004. 404p. ISBN:0-8108-3933-4, ISBN13: 978-0-8108-3933-5. Dewey:782.2/40268. LCCN:00-046361.

Audience: **u,f.**

Bausano, William (Compiled   ML54
by)
Sacred Latin Texts and English Translations for the Choral Conductor and Church Musician: Propers of the Mass, 68. Cloth Text. Greenwood Publishing Group, Inc. Portsmouth, NH. 1998. 304p. Music Reference Collection, Vol. 68 ISBN:0-313-30636-2, ISBN13: 978-0-313-30636-5. Dewey:782.32/35/0268. LCCN:97-042485.

Audience: **u,f.**

Beatles, The (Performed by)   ML54.6.B4
The Beatles Lyrics: The Songs of Lennon, McCartney, Harrison and Starr. Trade Paper. Hal Leonard Corporation. Milwaukee, WI. 1992. 256p. Songwriting and Lyrics Ser. ISBN:0-7935-1537-8, ISBN13: 978-0-7935-1537-0. Dewey:782.42166.

Audience: **g,l,u,f.**

Bleiler, Ellen H. (Editor,   ML48.F3 1996
Translator)
Famous Italian Opera Arias: A Dual-Language Book. Trade Paper. Dover Publications, Inc. Mineola, NY. 1996. 144p. ISBN:0-486-29158-8, ISBN13: 978-0-486-29158-1. Dewey:782.1/026/8. LCCN:95-041475.

Audience: **l,u,f.**

Buchanan, Scott (Editor)   ML54.6.R58 1994
Rock 'n Roll: The Famous Lyrics. Trade Paper. HarperCollins Publishers. New York, NY. 1994. 320p. ISBN:0-06-273235-8, ISBN13: 978-0-06-273235-4. Dewey:782.42166/0268. LCCN:94-010112.

Audience: **g,l,u,f.**

Coffin, Berton   ML54.6 .W65
Word-by-Word Translations of Songs and Arias: German and French. Trade Cloth. Scarecrow Press, Inc. Lanham, MD. 1966. 620p. ISBN:0-8108-0149-3, ISBN13: 978-0-8108-0149-3. Dewey:781.96. LCCN:66-013746.

Audience: **l,u,f.**

Coward, Noel   ML54.6.C83N64 1998
Noel Coward: The Complete Illustrated Lyrics. Barry Day (Editor). Trade Cloth. Overlook Press, The. New York, NY.

1998. 367p. ISBN:0-87951-896-0, ISBN13: 978-0-87951-896-7. Dewey:782.42164/0268. LCCN:98-017414.

Audience: **g,l,u,f.** *Choice, 1999.*

Dylan, Bob   ML54.6.D94S62 2002
Lyrics: 1962-2001. Trade Cloth. Simon & Schuster. New York, NY. 2004. 624p. ISBN:0-7432-2827-8, ISBN13: 978-0-7432-2827-5. Dewey:782.42164/0268. LCCN:2002-042823.

Audience: **g,l,u,f.**

Gershwin, Ira & Kimball,   PZ8.3
Robert
The Complete Lyrics of Ira Gershwin. Trade Cloth. Alfred A. Knopf Inc. New York, NY. 1993. 448p. ISBN:0-394-55651-8, ISBN13: 978-0-394-55651-2. Dewey:782.42. LCCN:93-012175.

Audience: **g,l,u,f.**

Goldin, Frederick (Editor,   PC3322
Translator)
Lyrics of the Troubadours and Trouveres: An Anthology and a History. Trade Cloth. Peter Smith Publisher, Inc. Magnolia, MA. 1990. ISBN:0-8446-5036-6, ISBN13: 978-0-8446-5036-4. Dewey:849.104.

Audience: **u,f.**

Gottlieb, Robert & Kimball,   ML54.6.R39 2000
Robert
Reading Lyrics: More Than 1,000 of the Century's Finest--A Celebration of Our Greatest Songwriters,A Rediscovery of Forgotten Masters, and an Appreciation. Trade Cloth. Knopf Publishing Group. New York, NY. 2000. 736p. ISBN:0-375-40081-8, ISBN13: 978-0-375-40081-0. Dewey:782.42164/0268. LCCN:99-088811.

Audience: **g,l,u,f.** *Choice, 2001.*

Hammerstein, Oscar II   ML49.H12H3 1985
(Lyrics by)
Lyrics by Oscar Hammerstein II. Ed. 2. Stephen Sondheim (Foreword by). Trade Cloth. Hal Leonard Corporation. Milwaukee, WI. 1985. 292p. Biographies and Commentary Ser., :Musicals/Classical/Folk/Religious Music Ser. ISBN:0-88188-379-4, ISBN13: 978-0-88188-379-4. Dewey:782.81/2. LCCN:85-050895.

Audience: **g,l,u,f.**

Hart, Lorenz   ML54.6.H4H4 1995
The Complete Lyrics of Lorenz Hart. Dorothy Hart & Robert Kimball (Editors). Trade Paper. Da Capo Press, Inc. Cambridge, MA. 1995. 208p. ISBN:0-306-80667-3, ISBN13: 978-0-306-80667-4. Dewey:782.1/4/0268. LCCN:95-021606.

Audience: **g,l,u,f.**

Herder, Ronald (Editor)   PZ8.3
500 Best-Loved Song Lyrics. Trade Paper. Dover Publications, Inc. Mineola, NY. 1998. 208p. ISBN:0-486-29725-X, ISBN13: 978-0-486-29725-5. Dewey:782.421640268. LCCN:98-034608.

Audience: **g,l,u,f.**

Johnson, Graham & Stokes,   ML54.6.J76F74 2000
Richard
A French Song Companion. Cloth Text. Oxford University

Press, Inc. New York, NY. 2000. 568p. ISBN:0-19-816410-6,
ISBN13: 978-0-19-816410-4. Dewey:782.42168/0268.
LCCN:99-057524.

Audience: **l,u,f.** *Choice, 2001.*

Kimball, Robert & Berlin,   ML54.6.B464K55 2000
Irving
Complete Lyrics of Irving Berlin. Trade Cloth. Alfred A. Knopf
Inc. New York, NY. 2001. 560p. ISBN:0-679-41943-8, ISBN13:
978-0-679-41943-3. Dewey:782.42164/0268. LCCN:00-062890.

Audience: **g,l,u,f.**

Kimball, Robert & Nelson,   ML54.6.L64 2003
Steve
The Complete Lyrics of Frank Loesser. Trade Cloth. David
McKay Company, Inc. New York, NY. 2003. 352p.
ISBN:0-679-45059-9, ISBN13: 978-0-679-45059-7.
Dewey:782.4216403. LCCN:2003-109481.

Audience: **g,l,u,f.**

Miller, Philip L.   ML54.6.M5 R5 1973
(Introduction by)
The Ring of Words: An Anthology of Song Texts. Trade Paper.
W. W. Norton & Company, Inc. New York, NY. 1973. 544p.
Norton Library ISBN:0-393-00677-8, ISBN13:
978-0-393-00677-3. Dewey:781.9/6. LCCN:72-010270.

Audience: **g,l,u,f.**

Miller, Phillip L. (Editor), et   ML54.6.G275 1990
al.
German Lieder. Brahms & Gustav Mahler (Editors). Trade
Paper. Continuum International Publishing Group, Ltd. London,
1990. German Library, Vol. 42 ISBN:0-8264-0328-X, ISBN13:
978-0-8264-0328-5. Dewey:782.4/3/0943. LCCN:89-039980.

Audience: **g,l,u,f.**

Peters, Erskine   ML54.6
Lyrics of the Afro-American Spiritual: A Documentary
Collection. Cloth Text. Greenwood Publishing Group, Inc.
Portsmouth, NH. 1993. 480p. Encyclopedia of Black Music Ser.
ISBN:0-313-26238-1, ISBN13: 978-0-313-26238-8.
Dewey:782.25. LCCN:92-027574.

Audience: **g,l,u,f.**

Porter, Cole & Kimball,   ML50.Z99
Robert

The Complete Lyrics of Cole Porter. John Updike (Foreword
by). Trade Cloth. Alfred A. Knopf Inc. New York, NY. 1983.
354p. ISBN:0-394-53214-7, ISBN13: 978-0-394-53214-1.
Dewey:782.1/4/0268. LCCN:83-048101.

Audience: **g,l,u,f.**

Reinhard, Thilo (Editor)   ML54.6.S4 R413 1989
The Singer's Schumann. Library Binding. Rosen Publishing
Group, Incorporated, The. New York, NY. 1989. 423p.
ISBN:0-8239-0673-6, ISBN13: 978-0-8239-0673-4.
Dewey:784.3/05. LCCN:88-028387.

Audience: **u,f.**

Schoep, Arthur & Harris,   ML54.6 .W65
Daniel
Word-by-Word Translations of Songs and Arias: Italian. Trade
Cloth. Scarecrow Press, Inc. Lanham, MD. 1992. 584p.
Word-By-Word Translations of Songs and Arias Ser., Vol. 2
ISBN:0-8108-0463-8, ISBN13: 978-0-8108-0463-0.
Dewey:781.96. LCCN:66-013746.

Audience: **l,u,f.**

Stanley, Lawrence A.   ML3531
(Editor)
Rap - The Lyrics: The Words to Rap's 175 Greatest Hits.
Jefferson Morley (Introduction by). Trade Paper. Penguin Group
(USA) Inc. New York, NY. 1992. 400p. ISBN:0-14-014788-8,
ISBN13: 978-0-14-014788-9. Dewey:782.42164.
LCCN:91-047632.

Audience: **g,l,u,f.**

Taft, Michael   PS591.N4T35 2005
Talkin' to Myself: Blues Lyrics, 1921-1942. Trade Paper.
Routledge. New York, NY. 2005. 744p. ISBN:0-415-97378-3,
ISBN13: 978-0-415-97378-6. Dewey:811/.52080357.
LCCN:2005-006740.

Audience: **g,l,u,f.**

Wigmore, Richard   ML54.6.S39.W53 1988
(Translator)
Schubert: The Complete Song Texts. Trade Cloth. Thomson
Gale. Farmington Hills, MI. 1988. 380p. ISBN:0-02-872911-0,
ISBN13: 978-0-02-872911-4. Dewey:784.3/05.
LCCN:88-011653.

Audience: **l,u,f.** *Choice, 1989.*

PHILOSOPHY

The selections in Philosophy reflect primarily material that is classified by Library of Congress as belonging to Philosophy (i.e., has the classification "B", "BC", "BD", "BH" or "BJ" in the LC classification system). Some selections, however, were also made in "non-Philosophy" categories that involved philosophically oriented subjects of an interdisciplinary nature.

The taxonomy approaches the subject hierarchically starting with broad categories. Under "General Philosophy" are included Reference works—dictionaries, encyclopedias, yearbooks, handbooks, bibliographies and databases—dealing with the discipline as a whole, as well as books that discuss the general nature of philosophy. The historical perspective is presented under "History of Philosophy" with an emphasis on Ancient Greek Philosophy (Modern Philosophy is approached in greater detail under "Philosophy by Country"). The "Philosophy by Country" category emphasizes western civilization but includes material on Asian Philosophy (which can also be found under "History of Philosophy/Ancient Oriental Philosophy") and African Philosophy.

The section on "Divisions of Philosophy" includes the major divisions that are typically taught in undergraduate courses. Under "Philosophical Schools and Doctrines" are the major -isms and philosophical schools to which undergraduates are exposed.

The more recent editions, translations and commentaries of the major philosophers were generally preferred, but older editions were also included that are still widely used.

A majority of the selections would be useful for Philosophy majors, but many of the selections would also be appropriate at the introductory level. In general, the Philosophy section avoids textbooks but includes a fair number of general surveys, such as those in the "Cambridge Companions to Philosophy," "Blackwell Philosophy Guides," and the "Routledge Philosophy Guidebooks" series.

The selection of electronic resources was generally limited to a) ebooks in which the print format was unavailable, b) Philosopher's Index, and c) the Stanford Encyclopedia of Philosophy. For cost considerations I did not recommend the electronic versions of the Gale/MacMillan Encyclopedia of Philosophy, 2nd ed., or the Routledge Encyclopedia of Philosophy, but I assume the better endowed undergraduate colleges will afford one or the other of those databases and the less endowed institutions will settle for the print format.

— Blake Landor

Deleuze, Gilles   B2430.D453D4513 1994
Difference and Repetition. Paul Patton (Translator). Columbia University Press. 1995. ISBN:0-231-08159-6, ISBN13: 978-0-231-08159-7.

Audience: **g,u,f.**

General Philosophy > Reference Works > Databases

B52.68

⌨ Erratic Impact: Philosophy Research Base.
http://www.erraticimpact.com/default.htm

Audience: **l.**

B1.A1

⌨ The Philosopher's Index.
http://www.philinfo.org/
Philosopher's Information Center.

Audience: **g,l,u,f.**

Kemerling, Garth   BD21
⌨ Philosophy Pages.
http://www.philosophypages.com/index.htm

Audience: **g,l.**

Stone, Thomas Ryan   B52.68
⌨ Episteme Links.
http://www.epistemelinks.com/index.aspx

Audience: **l.**

General Philosophy > Reference Works > Dictionaries

Arrington, Robert L.   B72.C595 1999
(Editor)
A Companion to the Philosophers. Trade Cloth. Blackwell Publishing, Inc. Malden, MA. 1998. 720p. Companions to Philosophy Ser. ISBN:1-55786-845-X, ISBN13: 978-1-55786-845-9. Dewey:109/.2 B. LCCN:98-007599.

Audience: **g,l,u.**

Audi, Robert (Editor)   B41.C35
The Cambridge Dictionary of Philosophy. Ed. 2. Paper Text. Cambridge University Press. New York, NY. 1999. 1039p. ISBN:0-521-63722-8, ISBN13: 978-0-521-63722-0. Dewey:103. LCCN:99-012920.

Audience: **g,l,u.** *Choice, 2000, 1996.*

Blackburn, Simon   B41.B53 1996
The Oxford Dictionary of Philosophy. Trade Paper. Oxford University Press, Inc. New York, NY. 1996. 432p. Oxford Paperback Reference Ser. ISBN:0-19-283134-8, ISBN13: 978-0-19-283134-7. Dewey:103. LCCN:95-033025.

Audience: **g,l,u.** *Choice, 1995.*

Bunnin, Nicholas &   B21.B56 2003
Tsui-James, E. P. (Editors)
The Blackwell Companion to Philosophy. Ed. 2. Trade Cloth. Blackwell Publishing, Inc. Malden, MA. 2002. 976p. Blackwell Companions to Philosophy Ser. ISBN:0-631-21907-2, ISBN13: 978-0-631-21907-1. Dewey:100. LCCN:2002-023053.

Audience: **g,u.** *Choice, 1996.*

Bunnin, Nicholas & Yu,   B51
Jiyuan
The Blackwell Dictionary of Western Philosophy. Trade Cloth. Blackwell Publishing, Inc. Malden, MA. 2004. 776p. ISBN:1-4051-0679-4, ISBN13: 978-1-4051-0679-5. Dewey:190/.3. LCCN:2004-000107.

Audience: **g,l,u.** *Choice, 2005.*

Collinson, Diane (Editor)   B104.B56 1996
Biographical Dictionary of Twentieth-Century Philosophers. Paper over Boards. Routledge. New York, NY. 1995. 968p. World Reference Ser. ISBN:0-415-06043-5, ISBN13: 978-0-415-06043-1. Dewey:109/.2 B. LCCN:97-185841.

Audience: **g,l,u.** *Choice, 1996.*

Flew, Antony G.   B41 .D52 1984
A Dictionary of Philosophy. Ed. 2. Trade Paper. St. Martin's Press. Gordonville, VA. 1984. 388p. ISBN:0-312-20923-1, ISBN13: 978-0-312-20923-0. Dewey:103/.21. LCCN:78-068699.

Audience: **l,u.** *B*

Honderich, Ted (Editor)   B51
The Oxford Companion to Philosophy. Ed. 2. Trade Cloth. Oxford University Press, Inc. New York, NY. 2005. 1,076p. ISBN:0-19-926479-1, ISBN13: 978-0-19-926479-7. Dewey:109. LCCN:2005-275452.

Audience: **g,u.** *Choice, 1996.*

Iannone, A. Pablo   B41.I26 2001
ⓔ Dictionary of World Philosophy. E-Book. Routledge. New York, NY. 2001. ISBN:0-203-18596-X, ISBN13: 978-0-203-18596-4. Dewey:103.

Audience: **l,u.** *Choice, 2001.*

Lacey, Alan   B41
Dictionary of Philosophy. Ed. 3. Trade Paper. Routledge. New York, NY. 1996. 400p. ISBN:0-415-13332-7, ISBN13: 978-0-415-13332-6. Dewey:190.3.

Audience: **g,l,u.**

General Philosophy > Reference Works > Encyclopedias

B51

⌨ Stanford Encyclopedia of Philosophy.
http://plato.stanford.edu

Audience: **g,l,u,f.**

Borchert, Donald M.   **B51.E53 2005**
Encyclopedia of Philosophy, Set. Ed. 2. Trade Cloth. Thomson Gale. Farmington Hills, MI. 2005. 6200p. ISBN:0-02-865780-2, ISBN13: 978-0-02-865780-6. Dewey:103. LCCN:2005-018573.
Audience: **g,l,u,f.** *Choice, 2006.*

Craig, Edward (Editor)   **B51.R68 1998**
Routledge Encyclopedia of Philosophy, Set. Paper over Boards, Box or Slipcased. Routledge. New York, NY. 1998. 8680p. ISBN:0-415-07310-3, ISBN13: 978-0-415-07310-3. Dewey:100. LCCN:97-004549.
Audience: **g,l,u.** *Choice, 1998.*

Fieser, James   **B51**
⬜ The Internet Encyclopedia of Philosophy.
http://www.utm.edu/research/iep/
Dowden, Bradley.
Audience: **g,l.**

Horowitz, Maryanne Cline   **CB9.N49 2005**
New Dictionary of the History of Ideas. Trade Cloth. Thomson Gale. Farmington Hills, MI. 2004. ISBN:0-684-31382-0, ISBN13: 978-0-684-31382-5. Dewey:903. LCCN:2004-014731.
Audience: **g,l,u,f.** *Choice, 2005.*

Urmson, J. O. & Ree,   **B41**
  Jonathan (Editors)
The Concise Encyclopedia of Western Philosophy and Philosophers. Trade Paper. Routledge. New York, NY. 1990. 256p. ISBN:0-04-445342-6, ISBN13: 978-0-04-445342-0. Dewey:190/.3/21.
Audience: **g,l,u.**

General Philosophy > Reference Works > Yearbooks

Michon, Heather K.   **B935.D5 2004**
Directory of American Philosophers. Philosophy Documentation Center. 2004. ISBN:1-889680-34-6, ISBN13: 978-1-889680-34-7.
Audience: **g,u,f.**

General Philosophy > Reference Works > Bibliographies

Burr, John R. & Burr,   **B801**
  Charlotte A.
World Philosophy: A Contemporary Bibliography, No. 3. Cloth Text. Greenwood Publishing Group, Inc. Portsmouth, NH. 1993. 400p. Bibliographies and Indexes in Philosophy Ser., No. 3 ISBN:0-313-24032-9, ISBN13: 978-0-313-24032-4. Dewey:016.109047. LCCN:93-018031.
Audience: **u.** *Choice, 1994.*

Bynagle, Hans E.   **Z7125**
Philosophy: A Guide to Reference Literature. Ed. 2. James Rettig (Editor). Book, Other. Libraries Unlimited, Inc. Westport, CT. 1996. 233p. Reference Sources in the Humanities Ser. ISBN:1-56308-376-0, ISBN13: 978-1-56308-376-1. Dewey:016.1. LCCN:96-031379.
Audience: **u,f.** *Choice, 1997, 1986.*

Roth, John K. (Editor)   **B104.W67 2000**
World Philosophers and Their Works, 3 vols. Christian J. Moose (Editor-In-Chief), Rowena Wildin (Editorial Coordinator). Library Binding. Salem Press, Inc. Hackensack, NJ. 2000. 2066p. ISBN:0-89356-878-3, ISBN13: 978-0-89356-878-8. Dewey:109. LCCN:99-055143.
Audience: **g,l.** *Choice, 2001.*

General Philosophy > Nature, Methods, Scope of Philosophy

Appiah, Anthony   **BD21.A68 2003**
Thinking It Through: An Introduction to Contemporary Philosophy. Trade Cloth. Oxford University Press, Inc. New York, NY. 2003. 432p. ISBN:0-19-516028-2, ISBN13: 978-0-19-516028-4. Dewey:100. LCCN:2002-027437.
Audience: **g,l,u.** *Choice, 2003.*

Ayer, A. J.   **B1618.A91 1974**
The Central Questions of Philosophy. Trade Cloth. Holt, Rinehart & Winston. Austin, TX. 1974. x, 243p. ISBN:0-03-013116-2, ISBN13: 978-0-03-013116-5. Dewey:108. LCCN:74-004407.
Audience: **g,l,u.** 𝐵

Blackburn, Simon   **BD21.B47 1999**
Think: A Compelling Introduction to Philosophy. Trade Cloth. Oxford University Press, Inc. New York, NY. 1999. 320p. ISBN:0-19-210024-6, ISBN13: 978-0-19-210024-5. Dewey:101. LCCN:00-265286.
Audience: **g,l,u.** *Choice, 2000.*

Collingwood, R. G.   **BD241**
An Essay on Philosophical Method. Ed. 2. James Connelly & Giuseppina D'Oro (Editors). Trade Cloth. Oxford University Press, Inc. New York, NY. 2005. 492p. ISBN:0-19-928087-8, ISBN13: 978-0-19-928087-2. Dewey:101. LCCN:2005-299436.
Audience: **g,u.** 𝐵

Deleuze, Gilles & Guattari,   **B2430.D453Q4713**
  Félix
What Is Philosophy? Hugh Tomlinson & Graham Burchell III (Translators). Trade Paper. Columbia University Press. New York, NY. 1996. 256p. European Perspectives Ser., :A Series in Social Thought and Cultural Criticism Ser. ISBN:0-231-07989-3, ISBN13: 978-0-231-07989-1. Dewey:100.
Audience: **g,u.** *Choice, 1994.*

Ewing, Alfred C.   **B804**
The Fundamental Questions of Philosophy. Trade Paper.
Routledge. New York, NY. 1985. 260p. ISBN:0-7100-0586-5,
ISBN13: 978-0-7100-0586-1. Dewey:190/.9/04.
Audience: **g,l,u.**

Heidegger, Martin   **B53**
What Is Philosophy? Book, Other. Rowman & Littlefield
Publishers, Inc. Lanham, MD. 1956. 104p. ISBN:0-8084-0319-2,
ISBN13: 978-0-8084-0319-7. Dewey:101.
Audience: **g,u.** *B*

Jackson, Frank & Smith,   **B804**
 Michael (Editors)
The Oxford Handbook of Contemporary Philosophy. Trade
Cloth. Oxford University Press, Inc. New York, NY. 2005. 920p.
Oxford Handbooks Ser. ISBN:0-19-924295-X, ISBN13:
978-0-19-924295-5. Dewey:190/.9/05. LCCN:2005-019433.
Audience: **g,u.**

Nozick, Robert   **B53.N7**
Philosophical Explanations. Trade Cloth. Harvard University
Press. Cambridge, MA. 1981. 784p. ISBN:0-674-66448-5,
ISBN13: 978-0-674-66448-7. Dewey:191. LCCN:81-001369.
Audience: **g,u,f.** *B*

Papineau, David   **BD21.W434 2004**
Western Philosophy: An Illustrated Guide. Trade Cloth. Oxford
University Press, Inc. New York, NY. 2004. 224p.
ISBN:0-19-522143-5, ISBN13: 978-0-19-522143-5. Dewey:190.
LCCN:2004-010215.
Audience: **g,l,u.** *Choice, 2005.*

Piaget, Jean   **B67**
Insights and Illusions of Philosophy, Vol. 5. Routledge. 1998.
ISBN:0-415-16894-5, ISBN13: 978-0-415-16894-6.
Audience: **g,l,u.**

Reichenbach, Hans   **B53**
The Rise of Scientific Philosophy. Trade Cloth. University of
California Press. Berkeley, CA. 1951. 334p.
ISBN:0-520-01055-8, ISBN13: 978-0-520-01055-0. Dewey:100.
Audience: **g,u,f.** *B*

Rorty, Richard McKay   **B53.R68 1980**
Philosophy and the Mirror of Nature. Trade Paper. Princeton
University Press. Princeton, NJ. 1981. 418p.
ISBN:0-691-02016-7, ISBN13: 978-0-691-02016-7. Dewey:190.
LCCN:79-084013.
Audience: **g,u,f.** *B*

Tice, Terrence N. & Slavens,   **B52.T5**
 Thomas P.
Research Guide to Philosophy. Trade Paper. Books on Demand.
Ann Arbor, MI. 1983. 620p. Sources of Information in the
Humanities Ser., Vol. 3 ISBN:0-7837-7313-7, ISBN13:
978-0-7837-7313-1. Dewey:107. LCCN:83-011834.
Audience: **u.** *B*

Wisdom, J. O.   **B53.W57**
Philosophy and Its Place in Our Culture. Cloth Text. Gordon &
Breach Publishing Group. New York, NY. 1975. 270p. Current

Topics of Contemporary Thought Ser., Vol. 13
ISBN:0-677-05150-6, ISBN13: 978-0-677-05150-5. Dewey:190.
LCCN:74-079475.
Audience: **g,u.** *B*

History of Philosophy

Copleston, Frederick   **B72.C62**
A History of Philosophy. Library Binding, Trade Cloth.
Continuum International Publishing Group, Ltd. London, 2003.
ISBN:0-8264-6947-7, ISBN13: 978-0-8264-6947-2. Dewey:109.
Audience: **g,l,u.**

Kenny, Anthony (Editor)   **B72**
The Oxford Illustrated History of Western Philosophy. Trade
Paper. Oxford University Press, Inc. New York, NY. 2001. 420p.
Oxford Illustrated Histories Ser. ISBN:0-19-285440-2, ISBN13:
978-0-19-285440-7. Dewey:190.
Audience: **g,l,u.**

Parkinson, G. H. R. &   **B1.R68 1999**
 Shanker, S. G. (Editors)
Routledge History of Philosophy, Set. Paper over Boards.
Routledge. New York, NY. 1999. 5024p. ISBN:0-415-21371-1,
ISBN13: 978-0-415-21371-4. Dewey:109.
Audience: **g,u.**

Popkin, Richard H.   **B72.C593 1999**
The Columbia History of Western Philosophy. Trade Cloth.
Columbia University Press. New York, NY. 1998. 864p.
ISBN:0-231-10128-7, ISBN13: 978-0-231-10128-8. Dewey:190.
LCCN:98-015219.
Audience: **g,u,f.** *Choice, 1999.*

Russell, Bertrand   **B72.R8 2004**
History of Western Philosophy. Ed. 2. Trade Paper. Routledge.
New York, NY. 2004. 792p. Routledge Classics Ser.
ISBN:0-415-32505-6, ISBN13: 978-0-415-32505-9.
Dewey:190.9.
Audience: **g,u.**

Scharfstein, Ben-Ami   **B799.S37 1998**
A Comparative History of World Philosophy: From the
Upanishads to Kant. Paper Text. State University of New York
Press. Albany, NY. 1998. 670p. ISBN:0-7914-3684-5, ISBN13:
978-0-7914-3684-4. Dewey:109. LCCN:97-019489.
Audience: **u,f.** *Choice, 1998.*

History of Philosophy > Ancient Oriental Philosophy > Chinese Philosophy

Chuang Tzu   **BL1900.C5 W34**
The Complete Works of Chuang Tzu. Burton Watson
(Translator), W. T. De Barry (Foreword by). Trade Cloth.
Columbia University Press. New York, NY. 1968. 397p.
UNESCO Collection of Representative Works
ISBN:0-231-03147-5, ISBN13: 978-0-231-03147-9.
Dewey:181/.09514. LCCN:68-019000.
Audience: **g,u,f.**

Confucius & Slingerland,   **PL2478.L8 2003**
Edward
Analects. Trade Cloth. Hackett Publishing Company, Inc.
Indianapolis, IN. 2003. 279p. Hackett Classics Ser.
ISBN:0-87220-636-X, ISBN13: 978-0-87220-636-6.
Dewey:181/.112. LCCN:2003-047772.

Audience: **g,l,u.** *Choice, 2004.*

Csikszentmihalyi, Mark   **B126.R433 2006**
(Translator, Introduction by)
Readings in Han Chinese Thought. Trade Paper. Hackett
Publishing Company, Inc. Indianapolis, IN. 2006. 240p.
ISBN:0-87220-709-9, ISBN13: 978-0-87220-709-7.
Dewey:181/.11. LCCN:2006-001102.

Audience: **g,u.**

Fung, Yu-Lan   **B126 .F3413 1983**
History of Chinese Philosophy: The Period of the Philosophers
(from the Beginnings to Circa 100 B. C.). Derk Bodde
(Translator). Trade Paper. Princeton University Press. Princeton,
NJ. 1983. 800p. ISBN:0-691-02021-3, ISBN13:
978-0-691-02021-1. LCCN:92-245418.

Audience: **g,l,u.** *B*

Hinton, David   **N7369.P35A4**
Tao Te Ching: Lac Tzu. Trade Paper. Basic Books. New York,
NY. 2001. 128p. ISBN:1-58243-182-5, ISBN13:
978-1-58243-182-6. Dewey:700/.92.

Audience: **u,f.**

Holder, John J. (Editor,   **BQ1192.E53**
Translator)
Early Buddhist Discourses. Trade Cloth. Hackett Publishing
Company, Inc. Indianapolis, IN. 2006. 216p.
ISBN:0-87220-793-5, ISBN13: 978-0-87220-793-6.
Dewey:294.3/823.

Audience: **g,u.**

Kohn, Livia & LaFargue,   **BL1900.L351998**
Michael (Editors)
Lao-Tzu and the Tao-Te-Ching. Paper Text. State University of
New York Press. Albany, NY. 1998. 320p. ISBN:0-7914-3600-4,
ISBN13: 978-0-7914-3600-4. Dewey:299/.51482.
LCCN:97-007857.

Audience: **g,u,f.** *Choice, 1998.*

Liu, Xiusheng & Ivanhoe, P.   **B128.M324 2002**
J. (Editors)
Essays on the Moral Philosophy of Mengzi. Xiusheng Liu & P.
J. Ivanhoe (Introduction by). Trade Paper. Hackett Publishing
Company, Inc. Indianapolis, IN. 2002. 249p.
ISBN:0-87220-623-8, ISBN13: 978-0-87220-623-6.
Dewey:170/.92. LCCN:2002-068472.

Audience: **g,u,f.**

Mencius   **PL2478**
Mencius. D. C. Lau (Translator, Introduction by). Trade Paper.
Penguin Group (USA) Inc. New York, NY. 2005. 304p.
ISBN:0-14-044971-X, ISBN13: 978-0-14-044971-6.
Dewey:181.1/12.

Audience: **g,u,f.**

Michael, Thomas   **BL1920.M53 2005**
The Pristine Dao: Metaphysics in Early Daoist Discourse. Cloth
Text. State University of New York Press. Albany, NY. 2005.
224p. SUNY Series in Chinese Philosophy and Culture
ISBN:0-7914-6475-X, ISBN13: 978-0-7914-6475-5.
Dewey:181/.114. LCCN:2004-017949.

Audience: **g,u,f.**

Munro, Donald J.   **BD450**
The Concept of Man in Early China. Trade Cloth. Stanford
University Press. Palo Alto, CA. 1969. xiv, 224p.
ISBN:0-8047-0682-4, ISBN13: 978-0-8047-0682-7.
Dewey:128/.0931. LCCN:68-021288.

Audience: **g,u,f.**

Ronkin, Noa   **B162**
Early Buddhist Metaphysics: The Making of a Philosophical
Tradition. Trade Cloth. Routledge. New York, NY. 2005. 240p.
ISBN:0-415-34519-7, ISBN13: 978-0-415-34519-4.
Dewey:181/.043.

Audience: **g,u,f.**

Shun, Kwong-Loi   **B128.M324S48 1997**
Mencius and Early Chinese Thought. Trade Cloth. Stanford
University Press. Palo Alto, CA. 1997. xii, 295p.
ISBN:0-8047-2788-0, ISBN13: 978-0-8047-2788-4.
Dewey:181/.112. LCCN:96-012393.

Audience: **g,u,f.** *Choice, 1997.*

Tzu, Lao   **BL1900.L35 R628 2001**
Dao de Jing: The Book of the Way. Moss Roberts (Translator).
Trade Cloth. University of California Press. Berkeley, CA. 2001.
235p. ISBN:0-520-20555-3, ISBN13: 978-0-520-20555-0.
Dewey:299/.51482. LCCN:2001-005077.

Audience: **g,l,u.**

Waley, Arthur   **B126 .W3 1982**
Three Ways of Thought in Ancient China. Trade Paper. Stanford
University Press. Palo Alto, CA. 1939. 238p.
ISBN:0-8047-1169-0, ISBN13: 978-0-8047-1169-2.
Dewey:181/.11. LCCN:82-232832.

Audience: **g,u.** *B*

Yao, Xinzhong   **BL1852 .Y36 2000**
An Introduction to Confucianism. Cloth Text. Cambridge
University Press. New York, NY. 2000. 362p. Introduction to
Religion Ser. ISBN:0-521-64312-0, ISBN13:
978-0-521-64312-2. Dewey:181.112. LCCN:99-021094.

Audience: **g,l,u.** *Choice, 2000.*

History of Philosophy > Ancient Oriental Philosophy > Indian Philosophy

Beidler, W.   **B132.V3.B42 1975**
Vision of Self in Early Vedanta. Trade Cloth. Orient Book
Distributors. Livingston, NJ. 1975. xii, 266p.
ISBN:0-8426-0990-3, ISBN13: 978-0-8426-0990-6. Dewey:126.
LCCN:76-900890.

Audience: **g,u,f.** *B*

Deutsch, Eliot   B132.A3E77 2004
The Essential Vedanta: A New Source Book of Advaita Vedanta.
Trade Paper. World Wisdom, Inc. Bloomington, IN. 2004. 432p.
Treasures of the World's Religions Ser. ISBN:0-941532-52-6,
ISBN13: 978-0-941532-52-5. Dewey:181/.482.
LCCN:2004-015866.

Audience: **g,l,u.**

Ganeri, Jonardon   B131.G276 2001
Philosophy in Classical India: The Proper Work of Reason.
Trade Paper. Routledge. New York, NY. 2001. 216p.
ISBN:0-415-24035-2, ISBN13: 978-0-415-24035-2.
Dewey:181/.4. LCCN:2001-019222.

Audience: **g,l,u.**

King, Richard   B131 .K487 1999
Indian Philosophy: An Introduction to Hindu and Buddhist
Thought. Trade Cloth. Edinburgh University Press. Edinburgh,
1999. 288p. ISBN:0-7486-0954-7, ISBN13: 978-0-7486-0954-3.
Dewey:181.4. LCCN:99-488335.

Audience: **g,l,u.** *Choice, 2000.*

Mohanty, J. N.   B131.M54M63 2001
Explorations in Indian Philosophy: Indian Philosophy, Vol. 1.
Bina Gupta (Editor). Trade Cloth. Oxford University Press, Inc.
New York, NY. 2001. 268p. ISBN:0-19-565083-2, ISBN13:
978-0-19-565083-9. Dewey:181/.4. LCCN:00-440687.
Audience: **g,u,f.** *Choice, 2002.*

Mohanty, Jitendra N.   B131.M615 1992
Reason and Tradition in Indian Thought: An Essay on the
Nature of Indian Philosophical Thinking. Trade Cloth. Oxford
University Press, Inc. New York, NY. 1993. 316p.
ISBN:0-19-823960-2, ISBN13: 978-0-19-823960-4.
Dewey:181/.4. LCCN:91-023781.
Audience: **g,u,f.** *Choice, 1993.*

Mohanty, Jitendra N. &   B131.M54M64 2000
  Gupta, Bina
Classical Indian Philosophy: An Introductory Text. Book, Other.
Rowman & Littlefield Publishers, Inc. Lanham, MD. 2000.
192p. ISBN:0-8476-8932-8, ISBN13: 978-0-8476-8932-3.
Dewey:181/.4. LCCN:99-036603.
Audience: **g,l,u.** *Choice, 2000.*

Potter, Karl H. &   B131.E5 1977
  Bhattacharyya, Sibajiban (Editors)
Encyclopedia of Indian Philosophies: Nyaya-Vaisesika from
Gangesa to Raghunatha Siromani. Trade Cloth. Princeton
University Press. Princeton, NJ. 1994. 633p. Encyclopedia of
Indian Philosophies, Vol. VI ISBN:0-691-07384-8, ISBN13:
978-0-691-07384-2. Dewey:181/.4/03 s. LCCN:90-022379.
Audience: **g,u,f.**

Radhakrishnan, S.   B130.R3
A Source Book in Indian Philosophy. Paper Text. Textbook
Publishers. Temecula, CA. 2003. xxix, 683p.
ISBN:0-7581-5744-4, ISBN13: 978-0-7581-5744-7.
Dewey:181.4.

Audience: **g,u.**

History of Philosophy > Ancient Western Philosophy > Greek Philosophy

Annas, Julia   B111.A56 2000
Ancient Philosophy: A Very Short Introduction. Trade Paper.
Oxford University Press, Inc. New York, NY. 2001. 140p. Very
Short Introductions Ser., Vol. 26 ISBN:0-19-285357-0, ISBN13:
978-0-19-285357-8. Dewey:180. LCCN:00-058869.

Audience: **g,l,u.**

Annas, Julia (Editor)   B162.9.V65 2001
Voices of Ancient Philosophy: An Introductory Reader. Paper
Text. Oxford University Press, Inc. New York, NY. 2000. 478p.
ISBN:0-19-512695-5, ISBN13: 978-0-19-512695-2. Dewey:180.
LCCN:00-020531.

Audience: **g,l,u.**

Bell, Albert A. Jr. & Allis,   Z7125.B39 1991
  James B.
Resources in Ancient Philosophy: An Annotated Bibliography of
Scholarship in English, 1965-1989. Trade Cloth. Scarecrow
Press, Inc. Lanham, MD. 1991. 818p. ISBN:0-8108-2520-1,
ISBN13: 978-0-8108-2520-8. Dewey:016.18. LCCN:91-039912.
Audience: **u,f.** *Choice, 1992.*

Burnet, John   B395 .B85 1983
Platonism. Trade Cloth. Greenwood Publishing Group, Inc.
Portsmouth, NH. 1983. 130p. Sather Classical Lecture, Vol. 5
ISBN:0-313-23699-2, ISBN13: 978-0-313-23699-0. Dewey:184.
LCCN:83-001503.

Audience: **g,l,u.** *B*

Cornford, Francis   B171.C72
  Macdonald
Principium Sapientiae: The Origins of Greek Philosophical
Thought. Trade Paper. Books on Demand. Ann Arbor, MI. 280p.
ISBN:0-598-97116-5, ISBN13: 978-0-598-97116-6. Dewey:180.
LCCN:52-014534.

Audience: **g,l,u.** *B*

Furley, David (Editor)   B505.F76 1999
From Aristotle to Augustine. Paper over Boards. Routledge.
New York, NY. 1999. 480p. History of Philosophy Ser., Vol. 2
ISBN:0-415-06002-8, ISBN13: 978-0-415-06002-8. Dewey:185.
LCCN:98-008543.

Audience: **g,l,u.**

Furley, David (Editor)   B505.F76 2003
From Aristotle to Augustine. Trade Paper. Routledge. New York,
NY. 2003. 480p. History of Philosophy Ser., Vol. 2
ISBN:0-415-30874-7, ISBN13: 978-0-415-30874-8. Dewey:185.

Audience: **g,l,u.**

Furley, David (Author,   BD495 .F87 1987
  Contribution by)
The Greek Cosmologists: The Formation of the Atomic Theory
and Its Earliest Critics. Trade Cloth. Cambridge University
Press. New York, NY. 1987. 228p. The Greek Cosmologists Ser.

ISBN:0-521-33328-8, ISBN13: 978-0-521-33328-3.
Dewey:113/.0938. LCCN:86-026384.

Audience: **u,f.** *Choice, 1988.*

Gadamer, Hans Georg   **B187.5**
The Beginning of Philosophy. Trade Paper. Continuum
International Publishing Group, Ltd. London, 2000. 132p.
ISBN:0-8264-1225-4, ISBN13: 978-0-8264-1225-6. Dewey:182.
LCCN:98-034594.

Audience: **g,u.**

Guthrie, W. K. C.   **B171 .G83 1962**
A History of Greek Philosophy: The Presocratic Tradition from
Parmenides to Democritus, Vol. 2. Trade Cloth. Cambridge
University Press. New York, NY. 1965. 572p.
ISBN:0-521-05160-6, ISBN13: 978-0-521-05160-6. Dewey:180.

Audience: **g,l,u.**

Guthrie, W. K. C.   **B171**
A History of Greek Philosophy: Plato: The Man and His
Dialogues: Earlier Period. Trade Cloth. Cambridge University
Press. New York, NY. 1975. 621p. ISBN:0-521-20002-4,
ISBN13: 978-0-521-20002-8. Dewey:180/.938.
LCCN:62-052735.

Audience: **g,l,u.**

Guthrie, W. K. C.   **B171**
A History of Greek Philosophy: Aristotle: An Encounter. Trade
Paper. Cambridge University Press. New York, NY. 1990. 472p.
ISBN:0-521-38760-4, ISBN13: 978-0-521-38760-6.
Dewey:180/.938.

Audience: **g,l,u.**

Guthrie, W. K. C.   **B171**
A History of Greek Philosophy: The Earlier Presocratics and the
Pythagoreans. Trade Cloth. Cambridge University Press. New
York, NY. 1962. 558p. ISBN:0-521-05159-2, ISBN13:
978-0-521-05159-0. Dewey:180/.938.

Audience: **g,l,u.** *B*

Guthrie, W. K. C.   **B171**
A History of Greek Philosophy: The Fifth Century
Enlightenment. Trade Cloth. Cambridge University Press. New
York, NY. 1969. 560p. ISBN:0-521-07566-1, ISBN13:
978-0-521-07566-4. Dewey:182. LCCN:62-052735.

Audience: **g,l,u.**

Guthrie, W. K. C.   **B171.G83 1978**
A History of Greek Philosophy: The Later Plato and the
Academy. Trade Cloth. Cambridge University Press. New York,
NY. 1978. 556p. ISBN:0-521-20003-2, ISBN13:
978-0-521-20003-5. Dewey:180/.938. LCCN:62-052735.

Audience: **g,l,u.**

Irwin, Terence H.   **B171.I77 1989**
Classical Thought. Paper Text. Oxford University Press, Inc.
New York, NY. 1988. 288p. A History of Western Philosophy
Ser., No. 1 ISBN:0-19-289177-4, ISBN13: 978-0-19-289177-8.
Dewey:180. LCCN:88-012616.

Audience: **g,u.** *Choice, 1989.*

Kenny, Anthony John   **B72**
Patrick
Ancient Philosophy: A New History of Western Philosophy.
Trade Cloth. Oxford University Press, Inc. New York, NY. 2004.
364p. ISBN:0-19-875273-3, ISBN13: 978-0-19-875273-8.
Dewey:180. LCCN:2004-303627.

Audience: **g,l,u.**

Nussbaum, Martha C.   **BJ192 .N87 2001**
The Fragility of Goodness: Luck and Ethics in Greek Tragedy
and Philosophy. Ed. 2. Cambridge University Press. 2001.
ISBN:0-521-79126-X, ISBN13: 978-0-521-79126-7.

Audience: **g,u,f.**

Pellegrin, Pierre   **B111.C66 2005**
Companion to Ancient Philosophy. Mary Louise Gill (Editor).
Trade Cloth. Blackwell Publishing, Inc. Malden, MA. 2006.
832p. Blackwell Companions to Philosophy Ser.
ISBN:0-631-21061-X, ISBN13: 978-0-631-21061-0. Dewey:180.
LCCN:2005-014100.

Audience: **u,f.**

Reale, Giovanni   **B171.R4213 1985**
A History of Ancient Philosophy I: From the Origins to
Socrates. John R. Catan (Editor, Translator). Paper Text. State
University of New York Press. Albany, NY. 1987. 425p. SUNY
Series in Philosophy ISBN:0-88706-290-3, ISBN13:
978-0-88706-290-2. Dewey:180. LCCN:86-014559.

Audience: **g,l,u.**

Reale, Giovanni   **B171**
A History of Ancient Philosophy II: Plato and Aristotle. John R.
Catan (Editor, Translator). Paper Text. State University of New
York Press. Albany, NY. 1990. 437p. SUNY Series in
Philosophy ISBN:0-7914-0517-6, ISBN13: 978-0-7914-0517-8.
Dewey:184. LCCN:84-016310.

Audience: **g,l,u.** *Choice, 1991.*

Reale, Giovanni   **B171.R4213 1985**
A History of Ancient Philosophy III: Systems of the Hellenistic
Age. John R. Catan (Editor, Translator). Book, Other. State
University of New York Press. Albany, NY. 1985. 499p. SUNY
Series in Philosophy ISBN:0-88706-027-7, ISBN13:
978-0-88706-027-4. Dewey:180. LCCN:79-013867.

Audience: **g,l,u.** *Choice, 1986.*

Reale, Giovanni   **B171.R4213**
A History of Ancient Philosophy IV: The Schools of the
Imperial Age. John R. Catan (Editor, Translator). Cloth Text.
State University of New York Press. Albany, NY. 1990. 548p.
SUNY Series in Philosophy ISBN:0-7914-0128-6, ISBN13:
978-0-7914-0128-6. Dewey:180. LCCN:84-016310.

Audience: **l,u.**

Shields, Christopher   **B171.B65 2003**
(Editor)
The Blackwell Guide to Ancient Philosophy. Trade Paper.
Blackwell Publishing, Inc. Malden, MA. 2002. 352p. Blackwell
Philosophy Guides Ser., Vol. 13 ISBN:0-631-22215-4, ISBN13:
978-0-631-22215-6. Dewey:180. LCCN:2002-006209.

Audience: **g,u.**

Taylor, C. C. W. (Editor)   B187.5.R68 2003
From the Beginning to Plato. Trade Paper. Routledge. New York, NY. 2003. 520p. History of Philosophy Ser. ISBN:0-415-30873-9, ISBN13: 978-0-415-30873-1. Dewey:180.
                    Audience: **g,l,u.**

Vlastos, Gregory   B171.V538 1995
Studies in Greek Philosophy, Set. Daniel W. Graham (Editor). Trade Paper. Princeton University Press. Princeton, NJ. 1996. 800p. ISBN:0-691-01939-8, ISBN13: 978-0-691-01939-0. Dewey:180. LCCN:94-003112.
                    Audience: **u,f.** *Choice, 1995.*

Wardy, Robert   B177.W37 2005
Greek Philosophy. Paper over Boards. Routledge. New York, NY. 2006. x 150p. Classical Foundations Ser. ISBN:0-415-28234-9, ISBN13: 978-0-415-28234-5. Dewey:180. LCCN:2005-010473.
                    Audience: **l,u.**

Zeyl, Donald (Editor)   B171.E52 1997
Encyclopedia of Classical Philosophy. Trade Cloth. Fitzroy Dearborn Publishers, Inc. Chicago, IL. 1997. 614p. ISBN:1-884964-94-X, ISBN13: 978-1-884964-94-7. Dewey:180.3.
                    Audience: **g,l,u.**

History of Philosophy > Ancient Western Philosophy > Greek Philosophy > Pre-Socratic Philosophers

Barnes, Jonathan   B188
The Presocratic Philosophers. Trade Paper. Routledge. New York, NY. 1983. 728p. Arguments of the Philosophers Ser. ISBN:0-415-05079-0, ISBN13: 978-0-415-05079-1. Dewey:182.
                    Audience: **g,u,f.** *B*

Burkert, Walter   B243 .B813
Lore and Science in Ancient Pythagoreanism. Edwin L. Minar Jr. (Translator). Trade Cloth. Harvard University Press. Cambridge, MA. 1972. 544p. ISBN:0-674-53918-4, ISBN13: 978-0-674-53918-1. Dewey:182/.2. LCCN:70-162856.
                    Audience: **g,u,f.** *B*

Burnet, John   B188 .B9
Early Greek Philosophy. Trade Paper. Kessinger Publishing, LLC. Whitefish, MT. 2003. ISBN:0-7661-2826-1, ISBN13: 978-0-7661-2826-2. Dewey:182.
                    Audience: **g,l,u.** *B*

Cornford, F. M.   B188.C6 2004
From Religion to Philosophy: A Study in the Origins of Western Speculation. Trade Paper. Dover Publications, Inc. Mineola, NY. 2004. 288p. ISBN:0-486-43372-2, ISBN13: 978-0-486-43372-1. Dewey:180. LCCN:2004-041428.
                    Audience: **g,l,u.**

Curd, Patricia (Editor)   B187.5.P75 1996
A Presocratics Reader: Selected Fragments and Testimonia. Richard D. McKirahan Jr. (Translator), Patricia Curd (Introduction by). Trade Cloth. Hackett Publishing Company, Inc. Indianapolis, IN. 1996. 144p. ISBN:0-87220-327-1, ISBN13: 978-0-87220-327-3. Dewey:182. LCCN:95-039291.
                    Audience: **g,l,u.**

Freeman, Kathleen   B165
Ancilla to the Pre-Socratic Philosophers: A Complete Translation of the Fragments in Diels, Fragmente Der Vorsokratiker. Trade Paper. Harvard University Press. Cambridge, MA. 1983. 174p. ISBN:0-674-03501-1, ISBN13: 978-0-674-03501-0. Dewey:180.
                    Audience: **g,l,u.** *B*

Gallop, David   B235.P23.F7 1984
Parmenides of Elea Fragments. Cloth Text. University of Toronto Press. Toronto, ON. 1984. 160p. ISBN:0-8020-2443-2, ISBN13: 978-0-8020-2443-5. Dewey:182/.3. LCCN:85-123404.
                    Audience: **u,f.** *B*

Heidegger, Martin   B3279.H48P3713 1992
Parmenides. Richard Rojcewicz & Andre Schuwer (Translators). Cloth Text. Indiana University Press. Bloomington, IN. 1998. 192p. Studies in Continental Thought ISBN:0-253-32726-1, ISBN13: 978-0-253-32726-0. Dewey:182/.3. LCCN:91-019431.
                    Audience: **g,u.**

Heraclitus   B220.E5
The Art and Thought of Heraclitus: A New Arrangement and Translation of the Fragments with Literary and Philosophical Commentary. Charles H. Kahn (Editor). Trade Paper. Cambridge University Press. New York, NY. 1981. 368p. ISBN:0-521-28645-X, ISBN13: 978-0-521-28645-9. Dewey:182/.4. LCCN:77-082499.
                    Audience: **u,f.** *B*

Inwood, Brad (Editor)   B218.A4E6 2001
The Poem of Empedocles, Vol. 39. Trade Paper. University of Toronto Press. Toronto, ON. 2001. 514p. ISBN:0-8020-8353-6, ISBN13: 978-0-8020-8353-1. Dewey:182/.5. LCCN:2001-276583.
                    Audience: **u,f.**

Kahn, Charles H.   B243.K34 2001
Pythagoras and the Pythagoreans. Trade Cloth. Hackett Publishing Company, Inc. Indianapolis, IN. 2001. 193p. ISBN:0-87220-576-2, ISBN13: 978-0-87220-576-5. Dewey:182/.2. LCCN:2001-024119.
                    Audience: **g,u.**

Kingsley, Peter   B218.Z7
Ancient Philosophy, Mystery, and Magic: Empedocles and Pythagorean Tradition. Trade Paper. Oxford University Press, Inc. New York, NY. 1997. 432p. ISBN:0-19-815081-4, ISBN13: 978-0-19-815081-7. Dewey:182.
                    Audience: **g,u,f.**

Long, A. A. (Editor)   B188 .C35 1999
The Cambridge Companion to Early Greek Philosophy. Trade

Paper. Cambridge University Press. New York, NY. 1999. 460p. Cambridge Companions to Philosophy Ser. ISBN:0-521-44667-8, ISBN13: 978-0-521-44667-9. Dewey:182.

Audience: **g,l,u.**

Robinson, T. M.   **B220.E5**
Heraclitus - Fragments: A Text and Translation with a Commentary. Trade Paper. University of Toronto Press. Toronto, ON. 1991. 342p. Phoenix Supplementary Volumes, XXII Pre Ser., No. XXII: Pre-Socratics II ISBN:0-8020-6913-4, ISBN13: 978-0-8020-6913-9. Dewey:182/.4.

Audience: **u,f.**

Schofield, Malcolm   **B205.Z7 S36**
An Essay on Anaxagoras. P. E. Easterling, M. K. Hopkins, M. D. Reeve, A. M. Snodgrass, G. Striker, P. D. Garnsey, G. C. Horrocks, R. L. Hunter, M. Millett, R. G. Osborne & D. N. Sedley (Contribution by). Trade Cloth. Cambridge University Press. New York, NY. 1980. 200p. Cambridge Classical Studies ISBN:0-521-22722-4, ISBN13: 978-0-521-22722-3. Dewey:182/.8. LCCN:79-010348.

Audience: **u,f.** *B*

Schofield, Malcolm, et al.   **B188 .K5 1983**
The Presocratic Philosophers: A Critical History with a Selections of Texts. Ed. 2. G. S. Kirk & J. E. Raven (Authors). Trade Paper. Cambridge University Press. New York, NY. 1983. 520p. ISBN:0-521-27455-9, ISBN13: 978-0-521-27455-5. Dewey:180/.938. LCCN:82-023505.

Audience: **u,f.** *B*

Taylor, C. C. (Commentaries by)   **B225.E5L48 1999**
The Atomists: Leucippus and Democritus: Fragments. Trade Cloth. University of Toronto Press. Toronto, ON. 1999. 608p. Phoenix Presocractic Ser. ISBN:0-8020-4390-9, ISBN13: 978-0-8020-4390-0. Dewey:182.5.

Audience: **g,u,f.**

Wheelwright, Philip Ellis   **B223 .W5 1981**
Heraclitus. Trade Cloth. Greenwood Publishing Group, Inc. Portsmouth, NH. 1981. 181p. ISBN:0-313-23142-7, ISBN13: 978-0-313-23142-1. LCCN:81-012555.

Audience: **g,l,u.**

History of Philosophy > Ancient Western Philosophy > Greek Philosophy > Socrates

Bostock, David   **B379.B67 1986**
Plato's Phaedo. Paper Text. Oxford University Press, Inc. New York, NY. 1986. 236p. ISBN:0-19-824918-7, ISBN13: 978-0-19-824918-4. Dewey:184. LCCN:85-031961.

Audience: **u,f.** *Choice, 1986.*

Brickhouse, Thomas C. & Smith, Nicholas D.   **B317**
Plato's Socrates. Trade Paper. Oxford University Press, Inc.

New York, NY. 1996. 256p. ISBN:0-19-510111-1, ISBN13: 978-0-19-510111-9. Dewey:183.2.

Audience: **g,l,u.** *Choice, 1994.*

Brickhouse, Thomas C. & Smith, Nicholas D.   **B365.B73 2004**
Routledge Philosophy Guidebook to Plato and the Trial of Socrates. Trade Cloth. Routledge. New York, NY. 2004. 312p. Routledge Philosophy Guidebooks ISBN:0-415-15681-5, ISBN13: 978-0-415-15681-3. Dewey:184. LCCN:2003-022822.

Audience: **g,l,u.**

Brickhouse, Thomas C. & Smith, Nicholas D.   **B365.B74 1989**
Socrates on Trial. Trade Cloth. Princeton University Press. Princeton, NJ. 1989. 350p. ISBN:0-691-07332-5, ISBN13: 978-0-691-07332-3. Dewey:183/.2. LCCN:88-017971.

Audience: **g,l,u.**

Gomez-Lobo, Alfonso   **B318.E8G6513 1994**
The Foundations of Socratic Ethics. Trade Paper. Hackett Publishing Company, Inc. Indianapolis, IN. 2001. 149p. ISBN:0-87220-236-4, ISBN13: 978-0-87220-236-8. Dewey:170/.92. LCCN:94-025963.

Audience: **l,u,f.**

Kamtekar, Rachana   **B317**
Companion to Socrates. Sara Ahbel-Rappe (Editor). Trade Cloth. Blackwell Publishing, Inc. Malden, MA. 2006. 552p. Blackwell Companions to Philosophy Ser., Vol. 34 ISBN:1-4051-0863-0, ISBN13: 978-1-4051-0863-8. Dewey:183/.2. LCCN:2005-024158.

Audience: **u,f.** *Choice, 2006.*

McPherran, Mark L.   **B318.R45M38 1996**
The Religion of Socrates. Trade Cloth. Pennsylvania State University Press. University Park, PA. 1996. 690p. ISBN:0-271-01581-0, ISBN13: 978-0-271-01581-1. Dewey:292/.0092. LCCN:95-045059.

Audience: **g,l,u.** *Choice, 1997.*

Navia, Luis E.   **B317.N39 2002**
Socratic Testimonies. Ed. 2. Trade Paper. University Press of America, Inc. Lanham, MD. 2002. 302p. ISBN:0-7618-2333-6, ISBN13: 978-0-7618-2333-9. Dewey:183/.2. LCCN:2002-020376.

Audience: **g,u,f.**

Plato   **B358.J82 2000**
The Trial and Death of Socrates: Euthyphro, Apology, Crito, Death Scene from Phaedo. Ed. 3. John M. Cooper (Editor), G. M. A. Grube (Translator), John M. Cooper (Revised by). Trade Cloth. Hackett Publishing Company, Inc. Indianapolis, IN. 2001. 58p. ISBN:0-87220-555-X, ISBN13: 978-0-87220-555-0. LCCN:00-047208.

Audience: **l,u.**

Plato   **B365.A5**
Defence of Socrates, Euthyphro, Crito. David Gallop (Editor,

Translator). Trade Paper. Oxford University Press, Inc. New York, NY. 1999. 160p. Oxford World's Classics Ser. ISBN:0-19-283864-4, ISBN13: 978-0-19-283864-3. Dewey:184.

Audience: **g,l,u.**

Plato   **B385.A5N44 1989**
The Symposium. Paul Woodruff (Translator), Alexander Nehamas (Introduction by). Trade Cloth. Hackett Publishing Company, Inc. Indianapolis, IN. 1989. 110p. HPC Classics Ser. ISBN:0-87220-077-9, ISBN13: 978-0-87220-077-7. Dewey:184. LCCN:89-030960.

Audience: **g,u,f.** *Choice, 1989.*

Reeve, C. D.   **B365.R44 1989**
Socrates in the Apology: An Essay on Plato's Apology of Socrates. Trade Cloth. Hackett Publishing Company, Inc. Indianapolis, IN. 1989. 224p. ISBN:0-87220-089-2, ISBN13: 978-0-87220-089-0. Dewey:184. LCCN:89-033069.

Audience: **g,l,u.** *Choice, 1990.*

Rudebush, George   **B318.E8R83 1999**
Socrates, Pleasure, and Value. Cloth Text. Oxford University Press, Inc. New York, NY. 1999. 192p. ISBN:0-19-512855-9, ISBN13: 978-0-19-512855-0. Dewey:183/.2. LCCN:98-036534.

Audience: **u,f.** *Choice, 2000.*

Santas, Gerasimos X.   **B317.S28 1999**
Socrates. Paper over Boards. Routledge. New York, NY. 1999. 360p. Arguments of the Philosophers Ser. ISBN:0-415-20354-6, ISBN13: 978-0-415-20354-8. Dewey:183/.2. LCCN:00-268158.

Audience: **g,l,u,f.** *B*

Smith, Nicholas D. &   **B317.P68 2000**
  Brickhouse, Thomas C.
Philosophy of Socrates. Trade Paper. Westview Press. Boulder, CO. 1999. 304p. History of Ancient and Medieval Philosophy Ser. ISBN:0-8133-2085-2, ISBN13: 978-0-8133-2085-4. Dewey:183/.2. LCCN:99-036572.

Audience: **g,l,u,f.** *Choice, 2000.*

Taylor, Christopher   **B317 .T24 2000**
Socrates: A Very Short Introduction. Trade Paper. Oxford University Press, Inc. New York, NY. 2001. 134p. Very Short Introductions Ser. ISBN:0-19-285412-7, ISBN13: 978-0-19-285412-4. Dewey:183/.2. LCCN:2001-268264.

Audience: **g,l,u.**

Vlastos, Gregory   **B317.V56 1991**
Socrates, Ironist and Moral Philosopher. Trade Paper. Cornell University Press. Ithaca, NY. 1991. 500p. Cornell Studies in Classical Philology, Vol. 50 ISBN:0-8014-9787-6, ISBN13: 978-0-8014-9787-2. Dewey:183/.2. LCCN:90-037095.

Audience: **g,l,u,f.** *Choice, 1991.*

Vlastos, Gregory   **B317 .V57 1994**
Socratic Studies. Myles F. Burnyeat (Editor). Trade Paper. Cambridge University Press. New York, NY. 1993. 166p. ISBN:0-521-44735-6, ISBN13: 978-0-521-44735-5. Dewey:183.2. LCCN:92-047419.

Audience: **g,l,u,f.** *Choice, 1994.*

Xenophon   **B316.X2B66 1994**
Memorabilia. Amy L. Bonnette (Translator, Annotations by), Christopher J. Bruell (Introduction by). Trade Cloth. Cornell University Press. Ithaca, NY. 1994. 288p. Agora Editions Ser. ISBN:0-8014-2963-3, ISBN13: 978-0-8014-2963-7. Dewey:183/.2 B. LCCN:94-009351.

Audience: **g,l,u,f.**

History of Philosophy > Ancient Western Philosophy > Greek Philosophy > Plato

Annas, Julia   **JC71.P6 1981**
An Introduction to Plato's Republic. Paper Text. Oxford University Press, Inc. New York, NY. 1981. 384p. ISBN:0-19-827429-7, ISBN13: 978-0-19-827429-2. Dewey:321.07. LCCN:80-041901.

Audience: **g,l,u.** *B*

Blondell, Ruby   **B395 .B57 2002**
The Play of Character in Plato's Dialogues. Trade Cloth. Cambridge University Press. New York, NY. 2002. 464p. ISBN:0-521-79300-9, ISBN13: 978-0-521-79300-1. Dewey:184. LCCN:2001-052963.

Audience: **g,u,f.** *Choice, 2003.*

Brandwood, Leonard   **B351.B72**
A Word Index to Plato. Trade Cloth. Bow Historical Books. New Providence, NJ. 1976. xxxi, 1003p. ISBN:0-901286-09-5, ISBN13: 978-0-901286-09-3. Dewey:184. LCCN:76-380277.

Audience: **u,f.** *B*

Cornford, Francis   **B378.A2**
  Macdonald
Plato and Parmenides: Parmenides' Way of Truth and Plato's Parmenides. Paper over Boards. Routledge. New York, NY. 2000. 272p. ISBN:0-415-22517-5, ISBN13: 978-0-415-22517-5. Dewey:184.

Audience: **u,f.**

Cornford, Francis   **B387.A5 C65 1997**
  Macdonald
Plato's Cosmology. Trade Cloth. Hackett Publishing Company, Inc. Indianapolis, IN. 1997. 390p. ISBN:0-87220-387-5, ISBN13: 978-0-87220-387-7. Dewey:113. LCCN:97-074231.

Audience: **g,l,u.**

Fine, Gail (Editor)   **B395.P516 2000**
Plato. Cloth Text. Oxford University Press, Inc. New York, NY. 2000. 1008p. Oxford Readings in Philosophy Ser. ISBN:0-19-875207-5, ISBN13: 978-0-19-875207-3. Dewey:184. LCCN:99-013232.

Audience: **u,f.**

Gosling, J. C. B.   **B395**
Plato: Arguments of the Philosophers, Set. Paper over Boards. Routledge. New York, NY. 1999. 328p. ISBN:0-415-20349-X, ISBN13: 978-0-415-20349-4. Dewey:184.

Audience: **g,u,f.**

Grube, G. M.   **B395**
Plato's Thought. Ed. 2. Donald J. Zeyl (Introduction by). Trade Cloth. Hackett Publishing Company, Inc. Indianapolis, IN. 1980. 368p. ISBN:0-915144-79-4, ISBN13: 978-0-915144-79-2. Dewey:184. LCCN:80-014588.

Audience: **g,l,u.**

Gulley, Norman   **B398**
Plato's Theory of Knowledge. Trade Cloth. Greenwood Publishing Group, Inc. Portsmouth, NH. 1986. 211p. ISBN:0-313-25209-2, ISBN13: 978-0-313-25209-9. Dewey:121/.092/4. LCCN:86-004622.

Audience: **g,u.** *B*

Havelock, Eric A.   **B398.P6**
Preface to Plato. Trade Paper. Harvard University Press. Cambridge, MA. 1982. 342p. History of the Greek Mind Ser., Vol. L ISBN:0-674-69906-8, ISBN13: 978-0-674-69906-9. Dewey:808.1/092/4. LCCN:62-013859.

Audience: **g,u.**

Irwin, Terence   **B398.E8.I79X**
Plato's Moral Theory: The Early and Middle Dialogues. Trade Cloth. Oxford University Press, Inc. New York, NY. 1977. xvii, 376p. ISBN:0-19-824567-X, ISBN13: 978-0-19-824567-4. Dewey:170/.92/4. LCCN:78-300940.

Audience: **u,f.** *B*

Irwin, Terence H. (Editor)   **B171.C53 1995**
Plato's Ethics. Cloth Text. Garland Publishing, Inc. New York, NY. 1995. 432p. Classical Philosophy: Collected Papers, Vol. 3 ISBN:0-8153-1832-4, ISBN13: 978-0-8153-1832-3. Dewey:180. LCCN:95-005168.

Audience: **u,f.**

Kahn, Charles H.   **B395**
Plato and the Socratic Dialogue: The Philosophical Use of a Literary Form. Trade Paper. Cambridge University Press. New York, NY. 1998. 453p. ISBN:0-521-64830-0, ISBN13: 978-0-521-64830-1. Dewey:184.

Audience: **g,u,f.** *Choice, 1997.*

Kraut, Richard (Editor)   **B395 .C28 1992**
The Cambridge Companion to Plato. Cloth Text. Cambridge University Press. New York, NY. 1992. 576p. Cambridge Companions to Philosophy Ser. ISBN:0-521-43018-6, ISBN13: 978-0-521-43018-0. Dewey:184. LCCN:92-004991.

Audience: **g,u,f.** *Choice, 1993.*

McDowell, John   **BD161**
(Translator)
Theaetetus. Paper Text. Oxford University Press, Inc. New York, NY. 1977. 272p. Clarendon Plato Ser. ISBN:0-19-872083-1, ISBN13: 978-0-19-872083-6. Dewey:121.

Audience: **u,f.**

Murdoch, Iris   **B398.A4.M87**
The Fire and the Sun: Why Plato Banished the Artists. Trade Cloth. Oxford University Press, Inc. New York, NY. 1977. 89p. ISBN:0-19-824580-7, ISBN13: 978-0-19-824580-3. Dewey:184. LCCN:77-005827.

Audience: **g,l,u.** *B*

Pappas, Nickolas   **JC71.P6P36 2003**
Routledge Philosophy Guidebook to Plato and the Republic. Ed. 2. Paper over Boards. Routledge. New York, NY. 2003. 272p. Routledge Philosophy Guidebooks Ser. ISBN:0-415-29996-9, ISBN13: 978-0-415-29996-1. Dewey:321/.07. LCCN:2002-037171.

Audience: **l,u.**

Plato   **B358**
The Dialogues of Plato: Ion, Hippias Minor, Laches, Protagoras. R. E. Allen (Translator). Cloth over Boards. Yale University Press. Cumberland, RI. 1996. 248p. The Dialogues of Plato Ser. ISBN:0-300-06343-1, ISBN13: 978-0-300-06343-1. Dewey:184. LCCN:84-017349.

Audience: **g,l,u.**

Plato   **B358.A44**
The Dialogues of Plato: The Symposium. R. E. Allen (Translator, Commentaries by). Trade Paper. Yale University Press. Cumberland, RI. 1993. 192p. The Dialogues of Plato Ser. ISBN:0-300-05699-0, ISBN13: 978-0-300-05699-0. Dewey:184.

Audience: **g,l,u.**

Plato   **B358.A44 1984 VOL. 4**
Plato's Parmenides. Reginald E. Allen (Translator, Commentaries by). Cloth over Boards. Yale University Press. Cumberland, RI. 1997. 336p. Dialogues of Plato Ser., Vol. 4 ISBN:0-300-06616-3, ISBN13: 978-0-300-06616-6. Dewey:184. LCCN:97-128617.

Audience: **g,u,f.**

Plato   **B378.A5.A44**
Plato's Parmenides: Translation and Analysis. Reginald E. Allen (Translator, Commentaries by). Trade Paper. Yale University Press. Cumberland, RI. 1998. 336p. Dialogues of Plato Ser., Vol. 4 ISBN:0-300-07729-7, ISBN13: 978-0-300-07729-2. Dewey:184. LCCN:84-017349.

Audience: **g,l,u.** *B*

Plato   **B379.A5 G34 1999**
Phaedo. David Gallop (Editor). Trade Paper. Oxford University Press, Inc. New York, NY. 1999. 144p. Oxford World's Classics Ser. ISBN:0-19-283953-5, ISBN13: 978-0-19-283953-4. Dewey:184.

Audience: **u,f.** *B*

Plato   **B378.A5G5513 1996**
Parmenides. Mary L. Gill & Paul Ryan (Translators), Mary L. Gill (Introduction by). Trade Cloth. Hackett Publishing Company, Inc. Indianapolis, IN. 1996. 144p. ISBN:0-87220-329-8, ISBN13: 978-0-87220-329-7. Dewey:184. LCCN:95-048981.

Audience: **u,f.**

Plato   **B358**
The Collected Dialogues of Plato: Including the Letters. Edith Hamilton & Huntington Cairns (Editors). Cloth Text. Princeton University Press. Princeton, NJ. 1961. 1776p. Bollingen Ser., Vol. LXX, No. 1:LXXI Ser. ISBN:0-691-09718-6, ISBN13: 978-0-691-09718-3. Dewey:888. LCCN:61-011758.

Audience: **g,l,u,f.**

Plato   **BJ1012**
Gorgias. Terence H. Irwin (Translator). Paper Text. Oxford
University Press, Inc. New York, NY. 1980. 280p. Clarendon
Plato Ser. ISBN:0-19-872091-2, ISBN13: 978-0-19-872091-1.
Dewey:170. LCCN:79-040477.

                Audience: **l,u,f.** *B*

Plato   **B386.A5L48 1992**
Theaetetus. M. J. Levett (Translator), Bernard Williams
(Introduction by), Myles F. Burnyeat (Revised by). Trade Paper.
Hackett Publishing Company, Inc. Indianapolis, IN. 1992. 128p.
ISBN:0-87220-158-9, ISBN13: 978-0-87220-158-3. Dewey:121.
LCCN:92-028261.

                Audience: **g,l,u,f.** *B*

Plato   **BD161**
Theaetetus. John McDowell (Notes by). Trade Cloth. Oxford
University Press, Inc. New York, NY. 1973. 264p.
ISBN:0-19-872043-2, ISBN13: 978-0-19-872043-0. Dewey:121.
LCCN:74-164763.

                Audience: **u,f.** *B*

Plato   **B382.A5**
Protagoras. C. C. W. Taylor (Translator). Trade Paper. Oxford
University Press, Inc. New York, NY. 2002. 122p. Oxford
World's Classics Ser. ISBN:0-19-280401-4, ISBN13:
978-0-19-280401-3. Dewey:184.

                Audience: **g,l,u,f.** *B*

Plato   **B384.A5 1993**
The Sophist. Nicholas White (Translator, Introduction by). Trade
Cloth. Hackett Publishing Company, Inc. Indianapolis, IN. 1993.
128p. Hackett Classics Ser. ISBN:0-87220-203-8, ISBN13:
978-0-87220-203-0. Dewey:184. LCCN:93-005792.

                Audience: **g,l,u,f.** *Choice, 1991.*

Plato   **B372.A5**
Ion and Hippias Major: Two Comic Diaglogues. Paul Woodruff
(Translator). Trade Cloth. Hackett Publishing Company, Inc.
Indianapolis, IN. 1983. 93p. Hackett Classics Ser.
ISBN:0-915145-76-6, ISBN13: 978-0-915145-76-8. Dewey:184.
LCCN:83-000269.

                Audience: **u,f.**

Plato   **B385.A5N44 1989**
The Symposium. Paul Woodruff (Translator), Alexander
Nehamas (Introduction by). Trade Cloth. Hackett Publishing
Company, Inc. Indianapolis, IN. 1989. 110p. HPC Classics Ser.
ISBN:0-87220-077-9, ISBN13: 978-0-87220-077-7. Dewey:184.
LCCN:89-030960.

                Audience: **g,u,f.** *Choice, 1989.*

Raven, John E.   **B395**
Plato's Thought in the Making: A Study of the Development of
His Metaphysics. Trade Cloth. Greenwood Publishing Group,
Inc. Portsmouth, NH. 1985. 256p. ISBN:0-313-24958-X,
ISBN13: 978-0-313-24958-7. Dewey:184. LCCN:85-010074.

                Audience: **g,l,u.**

Santas, Gerasimos   **JC71.P6B58 2006**
  Xenophon (Editor)
The Blackwell Guide to Plato's Republic. Trade Cloth.
Blackwell Publishing, Inc. Malden, MA. 2006. 320p. Blackwell
Guides to Great Works ISBN:1-4051-1563-7, ISBN13:
978-1-4051-1563-6. Dewey:321/.07. LCCN:2005-004895.

                Audience: **g,l,u,f.**

Sayre, Kenneth M.   **B395**
Plato's Literary Garden: How to Read a Platonic Dialogue.
Trade Cloth. University of Notre Dame Press. Notre Dame, IN.
2002. 320p. ISBN:0-268-03876-7, ISBN13: 978-0-268-03876-2.
Dewey:184.

                Audience: **g,l,u,f.** *Choice, 1996.*

Tarrant, Harold   **B395.T22 2000**
Plato's First Interpreters. Trade Cloth. Cornell University Press.
Ithaca, NY. 2000. 224p. ISBN:0-8014-3792-X, ISBN13:
978-0-8014-3792-2. Dewey:184. LCCN:00-037677.

                Audience: **u,f.** *Choice, 2001.*

Taylor, A. E.   **B395.T25 2001**
Plato: The Man and His Work. Trade Paper. Dover Publications,
Inc. Mineola, NY. 2001. 574p. Dover Books on Western
Philosophy ISBN:0-486-41605-4, ISBN13: 978-0-486-41605-2.
Dewey:184 B. LCCN:00-065955.

                Audience: **g,l,u,f.**

Vlastos, Gregory (Editor)   **B395 .V57**
Plato: A Collection of Critical Essays, Vol. 1. Trade Paper.
Doubleday Publishing. New York, NY. 1970.
ISBN:0-385-09045-5, ISBN13: 978-0-385-09045-2.
Dewey:184/.08.

                Audience: **u,f.** *B*

Vlastos, Gregory   **ND237.I75 A4 1982**
Plato's Universe. Trade Paper. University of Washington Press.
Seattle, WA. 1975. 144p. Jessie and John Danz Lectures
ISBN:0-295-95390-X, ISBN13: 978-0-295-95390-8.
Dewey:759.13. LCCN:74-028489.

                Audience: **u,f.** *B*

White, Nicholas P.   **JC71.P6.W47**
A Companion to Plato's Republic. Trade Cloth. Hackett
Publishing Company, Inc. Indianapolis, IN. 1979. 283p.
ISBN:0-915144-56-5, ISBN13: 978-0-915144-56-3.
Dewey:321/.07. LCCN:78-070043.

                Audience: **l,u.** *B*

History of Philosophy > Ancient Western Philosophy > Greek Philosophy > Aristotle

Ackrill, J. L. (Editor)   **B485.A3**
Aristotle the Philosopher. Paper Text. Oxford University Press,
Inc. New York, NY. 1981. 168p. Oxford Paperbacks Ser.
ISBN:0-19-289118-9, ISBN13: 978-0-19-289118-1. Dewey:185.
LCCN:82-103501.

                Audience: **g,l,u.** *B*

Annas, Julia　　　　　　　　　　**B 434.A5**
Metaphysics: Books M and N. Trade Paper. Oxford University Press, Inc. New York, NY. 1988. 240p. Clarendon Aristotle Ser. ISBN:0-19-872133-1, ISBN13: 978-0-19-872133-8. Dewey:110.
Audience: **u,f.**

Aristotle　　　　　　　　　　**B407**
Complete Works of Aristotle: The Revised Oxford Translation. Jonathan Barnes (Editor). Trade Cloth. Princeton University Press. Princeton, NJ. 1984. 1264p. Bollingen Ser., Vol. 1:LXXI 2 Ser ISBN:0-691-01650-X, ISBN13: 978-0-691-01650-4.
Audience: **g,l,u,f.**

Aristotle　　　　　　　　　　**B441.A5**
Posterior Analytics. Ed. 2. Jonathan Barnes (Translator, Commentaries by). Paper Text. Oxford University Press, Inc. New York, NY. 1994. 324p. Clarendon Aristotle Ser. ISBN:0-19-824089-9, ISBN13: 978-0-19-824089-1. Dewey:160.
Audience: **u,f.**

Aristotle　　　　　　　　　　**B415.A5H28 1993**
De Anima, Bks. II-III. Ed. 2. David W. Hamlyn (Translator, Introduction by, Notes by), Christopher Shields (Contribution by). Trade Cloth. Oxford University Press, Inc. New York, NY. 1993. 212p. Clarendon Aristotle Ser. ISBN:0-19-824084-8, ISBN13: 978-0-19-824084-6. Dewey:128.1. LCCN:93-018647.
Audience: **u,f.** $\mathcal{B}$

Aristotle　　　　　　　　　　**BD100**
Physics, Bks. III and IV. Edward Hussey (Translator, Notes by). Paper Text. Oxford University Press, Inc. New York, NY. 1983. 276p. Clarendon Aristotle Ser. ISBN:0-19-872069-6, ISBN13: 978-0-19-872069-0. Dewey:530.01. LCCN:82-018996.
Audience: **u,f.** $\mathcal{B}$

Aristotle　　　　　　　　　　**B430.A5P29 1998**
The Nicomachean Ethics, Bks. VIII & IX. Michael Pakaluk (Translator, Commentaries by). Trade Cloth. Oxford University Press, Inc. New York, NY. 1999. 254p. Clarendon Aristotle Ser. ISBN:0-19-875103-6, ISBN13: 978-0-19-875103-8. Dewey:170. LCCN:98-037479.
Audience: **u,f.**

Aristotle　　　　　　　　　　**B440.A5S65 1989**
Prior Analytics. Robin Smith (Translator, Introduction by, Notes by, Commentaries by). Trade Cloth. Hackett Publishing Company, Inc. Indianapolis, IN. 1989. 320p. HPC Classics Ser. ISBN:0-87220-065-5, ISBN13: 978-0-87220-065-4. Dewey:160. LCCN:88-039877.
Audience: **g,u,f.** *Choice, 1990.*

Aristotle　　　　　　　　　　**B422.A5W66 1992**
Eudemian Ethics. Ed. 2. Michael Woods (Translator). Trade Paper. Oxford University Press, Inc. New York, NY. 1992. 224p. Clarendon Aristotle Ser., Bks. I, II, & VIII ISBN:0-19-824020-1, ISBN13: 978-0-19-824020-4. Dewey:171.3. LCCN:92-015172.
Audience: **u,f.** $\mathcal{B}$

Barnes, Jonathan (Editor)　　　　**B485 .C35 1995**
The Cambridge Companion to Aristotle. Cloth Text. Cambridge University Press. New York, NY. 1995. 432p. Cambridge Companions to Philosophy Ser. ISBN:0-521-41133-5, ISBN13: 978-0-521-41133-2. Dewey:185. LCCN:94-000516.
Audience: **u,f.** *Choice, 1995.*

Broadie, Sarah　　　　　　　　**B430**
Ethics with Aristotle. Paper Text. Oxford University Press, Inc. New York, NY. 1993. 476p. ISBN:0-19-508560-4, ISBN13: 978-0-19-508560-0. Dewey:171/.3. LCCN:90-033456.
Audience: **u,f.** *Choice, 1991.*

Cooper, John M.　　　　　　　　**B430**
Reason and Human Good in Aristotle. Trade Cloth. Hackett Publishing Company, Inc. Indianapolis, IN. 1986. 216p. ISBN:0-87220-115-5, ISBN13: 978-0-87220-115-6. Dewey:171/.3. LCCN:86-019468.
Audience: **u,f.** $\mathcal{B}$

Hughes, Gerard J.　　　　　　　**B430.H84 2001**
Routledge Philosophy Guidebook to Aristotle on Ethics. Trade Paper. Routledge. New York, NY. 2004. 248p. Philosophy Guidebooks ISBN:0-415-22187-0, ISBN13: 978-0-415-22187-0. Dewey:171/.3. LCCN:00-051835.
Audience: **g,u.**

Irwin, Terence H.　　　　　　　**B171.C53 1995**
Aristotle's Ethics. Cloth Text. Garland Publishing, Inc. New York, NY. 1995. 432p. Classical Philosophy: Collected Papers, Vol. 5 ISBN:0-8153-1834-0, ISBN13: 978-0-8153-1834-7. Dewey:180. LCCN:95-005168.
Audience: **g,u.**

Jaeger, Werner W.　　　　　　　**B485**
Aristotle: Fundamentals of the History of His Development. Ed. 2. Richard Robinson (Translator). Trade Cloth. A M S Press, Inc. New York, NY. ISBN:0-404-20131-8, ISBN13: 978-0-404-20131-9. Dewey:185.1. LCCN:83-045440.
Audience: **u,f.**

Kraut, Richard (Editor)　　　　　**B430.B53 2005**
Aristotle's Nicomachean Ethics. Trade Paper. Blackwell Publishing, Inc. Malden, MA. 2006. 384p. Blackwell Guides to Great Works ISBN:1-4051-2021-5, ISBN13: 978-1-4051-2021-0. Dewey:171/.3. LCCN:2005-014101.
Audience: **u,f.**

Lear, Jonathan　　　　　　　　**B485 .L43 1988**
Aristotle: The Desire to Understand. Trade Paper. Cambridge University Press. New York, NY. 1988. 352p. ISBN:0-521-34762-9, ISBN13: 978-0-521-34762-4. Dewey:185. LCCN:87-020284.
Audience: **g,u,f.** *Choice, 1988.*

McKeon, Richard &　　　　　　**B407.A2713 2001**
　Aristotle
The Basic Works of Aristotle. UK-Trade Paper. Random House Adult Trade Publishing Group. New York, NY. 2001. 1520p. Modern Library Classics ISBN:0-375-75799-6, ISBN13: 978-0-375-75799-0. Dewey:185. LCCN:2001-030607.
Audience: **g,l,u,f.**

Formats: Web: ▢　Ebook: 🄴　CD/DVD-ROM: 💿　BCL3: $\mathcal{B}$

Mure, Geoffrey R.   B485 .M8 1975
Aristotle. Trade Cloth. Greenwood Publishing Group, Inc.
Portsmouth, NH. 1975. 282p. ISBN:0-8371-8298-0, ISBN13:
978-0-8371-8298-8. Dewey:185. LCCN:75-017199.

Audience: **g,l,u.**

Nussbaum, Martha C. &   B415
   Rorty, Amelie O. (Editors)
Essays on Aristotle's de Anima. Paper Text. Oxford University
Press, Inc. New York, NY. 1995. 462p. ISBN:0-19-823600-X,
ISBN13: 978-0-19-823600-9. Dewey:128. LCCN:91-022833.

Audience: **u,f.**

Owens, Joseph   B434 .O85
The Doctrine of Being in the Aristotelian Metaphysics: A Study
in the Greek Background of Mediaeval Thought. Ed. 3. Trade
Paper. Pontifical Institute of Mediaeval Studies, Department of
Publications. Toronto, ON. 1978. 575p. ISBN:0-88844-409-5,
ISBN13: 978-0-88844-409-7. Dewey:111.

Audience: **u,f.** ℬ

Pakaluk, Michael   B491.E7
Aristotle's Nicomachean Ethics: An Introduction. Cloth Text.
Cambridge University Press. New York, NY. 2005. 358p.
Cambridge Introductions to Key Philosophical Texts
ISBN:0-521-81742-0, ISBN13: 978-0-521-81742-4.
Dewey:171/.3.

Audience: **g,l,u.**

Reeve, C. D.   B430
Practices of Reason: Aristotle's Nicomachean Ethics. Trade
Paper. Oxford University Press, Inc. New York, NY. 1995. 238p.
ISBN:0-19-823565-8, ISBN13: 978-0-19-823565-1. Dewey:170.

Audience: **g,u,f.** *Choice, 1993.*

Rorty, Amélie (Editor)   B430.A5R66
Essays on Aristotle's Ethics. Trade Cloth. University of
California Press. Berkeley, CA. 1981. 438p. Major Thinkers
Ser., No. 2 ISBN:0-520-04041-4, ISBN13: 978-0-520-04041-0.
Dewey:170. LCCN:78-062858.

Audience: **g,u.** ℬ

Ross, David (Editor)   B415 .A5
Aristotle: De Anima. Trade Cloth. Oxbow Books, Ltd. Oxford,
1999. ISBN:0-19-814155-6, ISBN13: 978-0-19-814155-6.
Dewey:128.2.

Audience: **g,u,f.**

Sorabji, Richard (Editor)   B485.A655 1990
Aristotle Transformed: The Ancient Commentators and Their
Influence. Trade Cloth. Cornell University Press. Ithaca, NY.
1990. 556p. ISBN:0-8014-2432-1, ISBN13: 978-0-8014-2432-8.
Dewey:185. LCCN:89-037190.

Audience: **u,f.** *Choice, 1990.*

Witt, Charlotte   B434.W58 1989
Substance and Essence in Aristotle: An Interpretation of
Metaphysics, VII-IX. Book, Other. Cornell University Press.
Ithaca, NY. 1989. 216p. ISBN:0-8014-2126-8, ISBN13:
978-0-8014-2126-6. Dewey:111/.1. LCCN:88-047913.

Audience: **u,f.**

History of Philosophy > Ancient Western Philosophy > Greek Philosophy > The Sophists

De Romilly, Jacqueline   B288
The Great Sophists in Periclean Athens. Janet Lloyd
(Translator). Trade Paper. Oxford University Press, Inc. New
York, NY. 1998. 276p. ISBN:0-19-823807-X, ISBN13:
978-0-19-823807-2. Dewey:183.1.

Audience: **g,l,u,f.**

Guthrie, W. K. C.   B288 .G86 1971
A History of Greek Philosophy: The Fifth Century
Enlightenment: The Sophists. Trade Paper. Cambridge
University Press. New York, NY. 1977. 356p.
ISBN:0-521-09666-9, ISBN13: 978-0-521-09666-9.
Dewey:183/.1. LCCN:72-177084.

Audience: **g,l,u.**

Kerferd, George B.   B288.K47
The Sophistic Movement. Trade Cloth. Cambridge University
Press. New York, NY. 1981. 192p. ISBN:0-521-23936-2,
ISBN13: 978-0-521-23936-3. Dewey:183/.1. LCCN:80-041934.

Audience: **g,l,u,f.** ℬ

Plato   B382.A5T3913 1992
Protagoras. Stanley Lombardo & Karen Bell (Translators),
Michael Frede & Micahel Frede (Introduction by). Trade Paper.
Hackett Publishing Company, Inc. Indianapolis, IN. 1992. 112p.
HPC Classics Ser. ISBN:0-87220-094-9, ISBN13:
978-0-87220-094-4. Dewey:184. LCCN:91-028322.

Audience: **u,f.** ℬ

Sprague, Rosamond Kent   B288.A4813 2001
   (Editor)
The Older Sophists. Trade Cloth. Hackett Publishing Company,
Inc. Indianapolis, IN. 2001. 348p. ISBN:0-87220-557-6,
ISBN13: 978-0-87220-557-4. Dewey:183/.1. LCCN:00-054191.

Audience: **u,f.**

History of Philosophy > Ancient Western Philosophy > Greco-Roman Philosophy

Algra, Keimpe (Editor), et   B171.C36 1999
al.
The Cambridge History of Hellenistic Philosophy. Jonathan
Barnes, Jaap Mansfeld & Malcolm Schofield (Editors). Cloth
Text. Cambridge University Press. New York, NY. 1999. 936p.
ISBN:0-521-25028-5, ISBN13: 978-0-521-25028-3. Dewey:180.
LCCN:98-036033.

Audience: **g,u,f.** *Choice, 2001.*

Annas, Julia   B105.M55
Hellenistic Philosophy of Mind. Trade Paper. University of
California Press. Berkeley, CA. 1994. 256p. Hellenistic Culture

---

and Society Ser., Vol. 8 ISBN:0-520-07659-1, ISBN13: 978-0-520-07659-4. Dewey:128/.2/0938. LCCN:91-010694.

Audience: **u,f.** *Choice, 1992.*

Branham, R. Bracht   **B508 .C94**
Cynics: The Cynic Movement in Antiquity and Its Legacy. Trade Paper. University of California Press. Berkeley, CA. 2000. 468p. Hellenistic Culture and Society Ser., Vol. XXIII ISBN:0-520-21645-8, ISBN13: 978-0-520-21645-7. Dewey:183/.4.

Audience: **g,u,f.**

Cicero, Marcus Tullius   **PA6308.D2 W66 2001**
Cicero: On Moral Ends. Julia Annas (Editor), Raphael Woolf (Translator), Karl Ameriks & Desmond M. Clarke (Contribution by). Trade Paper. Cambridge University Press. New York, NY. 2001. 200p. Texts in the History of Philosophy ISBN:0-521-66901-4, ISBN13: 978-0-521-66901-6. Dewey:171. LCCN:2002-265146.

Audience: **u,f.**

Copleston, Frederick   **B72**
Charles
History of Philosophy: Greece and Rome. Trade Cloth. Paulist Press. Mahwah, NJ. 1946. 534p. History of Philosophy Ser., I ISBN:0-8091-0065-7, ISBN13: 978-0-8091-0065-1. Dewey:109.

Audience: **g,l,u.**

Dudley, Donald R.   **B508 .D8**
A History of Cynicism, from Diogenes to the 6th Century A. D. Library Binding. Lubrecht & Cramer, Ltd. Port Jervis, NY. 1967. 224p. ISBN:3-487-05916-9, ISBN13: 978-3-487-05916-7. Dewey:183/.4.

Audience: **g,l,u.**

Inwood, Brad & Gerson,   **B505.H45 1997**
Lloyd P. (Editors)
Hellenistic Philosophy: Introductory Readings. Ed. 2. Brad Inwood & Lloyd P. Gerson (Translators). Trade Cloth. Hackett Publishing Company, Inc. Indianapolis, IN. 1998. 438p. ISBN:0-87220-379-4, ISBN13: 978-0-87220-379-2. Dewey:180. LCCN:97-026796.

Audience: **g,l,u.** *Choice, 1989.*

Long, A. A.   **B171**
Hellenistic Philosophy: Stoics, Epicureans, Sceptics. Ed. 2. Trade Cloth. University of California Press. Berkeley, CA. 1986. ISBN:0-520-05807-0, ISBN13: 978-0-520-05807-1. Dewey:180.

Audience: **g,l,u,f.** *B Choice, 1987.*

Long, A. A. & Sedley, D. N.   **B505 .L66 1987**
The Hellenistic Philosophers: Translations of the Principal Sources with Philosophical Commentary, Vol. 1. Trade Paper. Cambridge University Press. New York, NY. 1987. 528p. ISBN:0-521-27556-3, ISBN13: 978-0-521-27556-9. Dewey:186. LCCN:85-030956.

Audience: **g,l,u,f.** *Choice, 1987.*

Morford, Mark P. O.   **B505.M67 2002**
Roman Philosophers. Trade Paper. Routledge. New York, NY. 2002. 304p. ISBN:0-415-18852-0, ISBN13: 978-0-415-18852-4. Dewey:180/.937. LCCN:2002-068070.

Audience: **g,u,f.**

Nussbaum, Martha C.   **B505**
The Therapy of Desire: Theory and Practice in Hellenistic Ethics. Princeton University Press. 1996. Martin Classical Lectures ISBN:0-691-00052-2, ISBN13: 978-0-691-00052-7.

Audience: **g,l,u,f.**

Sedley, David (Editor)   **B111.C36 2003**
The Cambridge Companion to Greek and Roman Philosophy. Cloth Text. Cambridge University Press. New York, NY. 2003. 412p. Cambridge Companions to Philosophy Ser. ISBN:0-521-77285-0, ISBN13: 978-0-521-77285-3. Dewey:180. LCCN:2002-035188.

Audience: **u,f.** *Choice, 2004.*

Sharples, R. W.   **B505.S52 1996**
Stoics, Epicureans and Sceptics: Introduction to Hellenistic Philosophy. Paper over Boards. Routledge. New York, NY. 1996. 176p. ISBN:0-415-11034-3, ISBN13: 978-0-415-11034-1. Dewey:180. LCCN:95-026248.

Audience: **u,f.**

Zeller, Edward   **B505**
The Stoics, Epicureans and Skeptics. Trade Cloth. Gordon Press Publishers. New York, NY. 1973. ISBN:0-8490-1125-6, ISBN13: 978-0-8490-1125-2. Dewey:188.

Audience: **g,l,u,f.**

History of Philosophy > Ancient Western Philosophy > Greco-Roman Philosophy > Stoics

Aurelius, Marcus   **B580**
Meditations. Gregory Hays (Translator, Introduction by). Trade Paper. Random House Adult Trade Publishing Group. New York, NY. 2003. 256p. ISBN:0-8129-6825-5, ISBN13: 978-0-8129-6825-5. Dewey:188.

Audience: **g,l,u,f.**

Becker, Lawrence C.   **BJ1012**
A New Stoicism. Trade Paper. Princeton University Press. Princeton, NJ. 1999. 228p. ISBN:0-691-00964-3, ISBN13: 978-0-691-00964-3. Dewey:171/.2. LCCN:97-015847.

Audience: **g,u,f.**

Inwood, Brad (Editor)   **B528.C26 2003**
The Cambridge Companion to the Stoics. Trade Paper. Cambridge University Press. New York, NY. 2003. 448p. Cambridge Companions to Philosophy Ser. ISBN:0-521-77985-5, ISBN13: 978-0-521-77985-2. Dewey:188. LCCN:2002-031359.

Audience: **u,f.** *Choice, 2004.*

Inwood, Brad   **B618**
Reading Seneca. Trade Cloth. Oxford University Press, Inc.
New York, NY. 2005. 392p. ISBN:0-19-925089-8, ISBN13:
978-0-19-925089-9. Dewey:188. LCCN:2005-296403.
                                           Audience: **u,f.**

Long, A. A.   **B563.L66 2002**
Epictetus: A Stoic and Socratic Guide to Life. Trade Cloth.
Oxford University Press, Inc. New York, NY. 2002. 330p.
ISBN:0-19-924556-8, ISBN13: 978-0-19-924556-7. Dewey:188.
LCCN:2001-052070.
                       Audience: **g,u,f.** *Choice, 2003, 2002.*

Long, A. A.   **B528 .L65 1996**
Stoic Studies. Cloth Text. Cambridge University Press. New
York, NY. 1996. 325p. ISBN:0-521-48263-1, ISBN13:
978-0-521-48263-9. Dewey:188. LCCN:95-038497.
                                           Audience: **u,f.**

Rutherford, R. B.   **B583**
The Meditations of Marcus Aurelius: A Study. Trade Paper.
Oxford University Press, Inc. New York, NY. 1991. 300p.
Oxford Classical Monographs ISBN:0-19-814755-4, ISBN13:
978-0-19-814755-8. Dewey:188. LCCN:88-020834.
                       Audience: **u,f.** *Choice, 1990.*

Sandbach, F. H.   **B528.S27 1989**
The Stoics. Ed. 2. Trade Cloth. Hackett Publishing Company,
Inc. Indianapolis, IN. 1994. 192p. ISBN:0-87220-254-2,
ISBN13: 978-0-87220-254-2. Dewey:188. LCCN:93-081019.
                                 Audience: **g,u,f.** *B*

Sellars, John   **B528 .S298 2006**
Stoicism. Trade Cloth. University of California Press. Berkeley,
CA. 2006. 219p. Ancient Philosophies Ser., Vol. 1
ISBN:0-520-24907-0, ISBN13: 978-0-520-24907-3. Dewey:188.
LCCN:2005-034505.
                                         Audience: **g,u,f.**

Seneca, Lucius Annaeus   **PA6156.S4**
Moral Letters: Epistles 66-92. Trade Cloth. Harvard University
Press. Cambridge, MA. 1920. 496p. Loeb Classical Library, No.
75-77 ISBN:0-674-99085-4, ISBN13: 978-0-674-99085-2.
Dewey:188.
                                       Audience: **g,l,u,f.**

Seneca, Lucius Annaeus   **PA6156.S4**
Moral Letters: Epistles 1-65. Trade Cloth. Harvard University
Press. Cambridge, MA. 1917. 496p. Loeb Classical Library, No.
75-77 ISBN:0-674-99084-6, ISBN13: 978-0-674-99084-5.
Dewey:188.
                                       Audience: **g,l,u,f.**

Strange, Steven K. &   **B528.S6785 2004**
 Zupko, Jack (Editors)
Stoicism: Traditions and Transformations. Trade Cloth.

Cambridge University Press. New York, NY. 2004. 310p.
ISBN:0-521-82709-4, ISBN13: 978-0-521-82709-6. Dewey:188.
LCCN:2003-056919.
                                         Audience: **g,u,f.**

History of Philosophy > Ancient Western Philosophy > Greco-Roman Philosophy > Epicureans

Asmis, Elizabeth   **B573**
Epicurus' Scientific Method. Book, Other. Cornell University
Press. Ithaca, NY. 1983. 400p. Cornell Studies in Classical
Philology ISBN:0-8014-1465-2, ISBN13: 978-0-8014-1465-7.
Dewey:187. LCCN:83-045133.
                                           Audience: **u,f.**

De Witt, Norman W.   **B573 .D4 1973**
Epicurus and His Philosophy. Trade Cloth. Greenwood
Publishing Group, Inc. Portsmouth, NH. 1973. 388p.
ISBN:0-8371-6639-X, ISBN13: 978-0-8371-6639-1. Dewey:187.
LCCN:72-011234.
                                         Audience: **g,l,u.**

Epicurus   **B570.E5I582 1994**
The Epicurus Reader: Selected Writings and Testimonia. Brad
Inwood & Lloyd P. Gerson (Editors), Brad Inwood & Lloyd P.
Gerson (Translators), D. S. Hutchinson (Introduction by). Trade
Cloth. Hackett Publishing Company, Inc. Indianapolis, IN. 1994.
128p. HPC Classics Ser. ISBN:0-87220-242-9, ISBN13:
978-0-87220-242-9. Dewey:187. LCCN:93-044073.
                                         Audience: **g,l,u.**

Gordon, Pamela   **B557.D564G67 1996**
Epicurus in Lycia: The Second-Century World of Diogenes of
Oenoanda. Trade Cloth. University of Michigan Press. Chicago,
IL. 1997. 152p. ISBN:0-472-10461-6, ISBN13:
978-0-472-10461-1. Dewey:187. LCCN:96-042968.
                              Audience: **g,u.** *Choice, 1997.*

Jones, Howard   **B573.J57 1989**
The Epicurean Tradition. Trade Cloth. Routledge. New York,
NY. 1989. 288p. ISBN:0-415-02069-7, ISBN13:
978-0-415-02069-5. Dewey:187. LCCN:89-006226.
                              Audience: **g,u.** *Choice, 1990.*

Preuss, Peter   **B573.P74 1994**
Epicurean Ethics: Katastematic Hedonism. Trade Cloth. Edwin
Mellen Press, The. Lewiston, NY. 1994. 288p. Studies in the
History of Philosophy, Vol. 35 ISBN:0-7734-9124-4, ISBN13:
978-0-7734-9124-3. Dewey:171/.4. LCCN:93-048974.
                              Audience: **u,f.** *Choice, 1995.*

Rist, John M.   **B573**
Epicurus: An Introduction. Trade Paper. Books on Demand. Ann Arbor, MI. 199p. ISBN:0-608-12496-6, ISBN13: 978-0-608-12496-4. Dewey:187. LCCN:70-177939.

Audience: **g,l,u,f.**

History of Philosophy > Ancient Western Philosophy > Alexandrian and Early Christian Philosophy

Armstrong, D. M. (Editor)   **B171**
The Cambridge History of Later Greek and Early Medieval Philosophy. Trade Cloth. Cambridge University Press. New York, NY. 1967. 726p. ISBN:0-521-04054-X, ISBN13: 978-0-521-04054-9. Dewey:182.

Audience: **g,u,f.**

Augustine   **B655.C62E5 1995**
Against the Academicians and the Teacher. Peter King (Translator, Introduction by). Trade Cloth. Hackett Publishing Company, Inc. Indianapolis, IN. 1995. 208p. ISBN:0-87220-213-5, ISBN13: 978-0-87220-213-9. Dewey:189/.2. LCCN:95-032851.

Audience: **g,l,u.**

Augustine   **N/A**
Augustine: On the Trinity. Gareth B. Matthews (Editor), Stephen McKenna (Translator), Karl Ameriks & Desmond M. Clarke (Contribution by). Cloth Text. Cambridge University Press. New York, NY. 2002. 264p. Cambridge Texts in the History of Philosophy Ser. ISBN:0-521-79231-2, ISBN13: 978-0-521-79231-8. Dewey:231/.044. LCCN:2002-510790.

Audience: **g,u,f.**

Boethius   **B659.C2E52 2001**
The Consolation of Philosophy. Joel C. Relihan (Translator, Introduction by, Notes by). Trade Cloth. Hackett Publishing Company, Inc. Indianapolis, IN. 2001. 240p. Hackett Classics Ser. ISBN:0-87220-584-3, ISBN13: 978-0-87220-584-0. Dewey:100. LCCN:2001-026401.

Audience: **g,l,u,f.** *B*

Boethius   **B659.D582.E5 1978**
Boethius Is "De topicis Differentilis". Eleonore Stump (Editor, Translator). Book, Other. Cornell University Press. Ithaca, NY. 1978. 264p. ISBN:0-8014-1067-3, ISBN13: 978-0-8014-1067-3. Dewey:160. LCCN:77-017275.

Audience: **u,f.** *B*

Brown, Peter   **BR1720.A9B7 2000**
Augustine of Hippo: A Biography with a New Epilogue. Trade Paper. University of California Press. Berkeley, CA. 2000. 562p. ISBN:0-520-22757-3, ISBN13: 978-0-520-22757-6. LCCN:2001-268207.

Audience: **g,l,u,f.**

Chadwick, Henry   **B659.Z7C45**
e Boethius, the Consolations of Music, Logic, Theology, and Philosophy. E-Book. NetLibrary, Inc. Boulder, CO. 1981. ISBN:0-585-25951-8, ISBN13: 978-0-585-25951-2. Dewey:189.

Audience: **l,u.**

Dillon, John   **B517.D54 1996**
The Middle Platonists: 80 B.C. to A.D. 220. Trade Paper. Cornell University Press. Ithaca, NY. 1996. 430p. ISBN:0-8014-8316-6, ISBN13: 978-0-8014-8316-5. Dewey:184. LCCN:96-013942.

Audience: **u,f.**

Dzielska, Maria   **B667.H84D9513 1995**
Hypatia of Alexandria. F. Lyra (Translator). Trade Cloth. Harvard University Press. Cambridge, MA. 1995. 176p. Revealing Antiquity Ser., No. 8 ISBN:0-674-43775-6, ISBN13: 978-0-674-43775-3. Dewey:186.4. LCCN:94-024499.

Audience: **g,u.** *Choice, 1995.*

Gerson, Lloyd P.   **B693.Z7G47 1999**
Plotinus. Paper over Boards. Routledge. New York, NY. 1999. 356p. Arguments of the Philosophers Ser. ISBN:0-415-20352-X, ISBN13: 978-0-415-20352-4. Dewey:186/.4. LCCN:00-269051.

Audience: **u,f.**

Gilson, Etienne   **B655.Z7G52**
The Christian Philosophy of Saint Augustine. Paper Text. Textbook Publishers. Temecula, CA. 2003. xii, 398p. ISBN:0-7581-5030-X, ISBN13: 978-0-7581-5030-1. Dewey:189.2.

Audience: **g,l,u,f.** *B*

Gregory, John   **B517.G74 1998**
The Neoplatonists. Ed. 2. Paper over Boards. Routledge. New York, NY. 1998. 208p. ISBN:0-415-18784-2, ISBN13: 978-0-415-18784-8. Dewey:186/.4. LCCN:98-025045.

Audience: **g,l,u.**

MacKenna, Stephen   **B693.E59**
Plotinus: The Enneads. Trade Cloth. Larson Publications. Burdett, NY. 2004. 768p. ISBN:0-943914-55-8, ISBN13: 978-0-943914-55-8. Dewey:186/.4.

Audience: **g,l,u,f.**

O'Donnell, James J.   **BR1720.A9**
Augustine: A New Biography. Trade Paper. HarperCollins Publishers. New York, NY. 2006. 432p. P. S. Ser. ISBN:0-06-053538-5, ISBN13: 978-0-06-053538-4. Dewey:270.2/092 B.

Audience: **g,u,f.**

O'Meara, Dominic J.   **B693.E6**
Plotinus: An Introduction to the Enneads. Paper Text. Oxford University Press, Inc. New York, NY. 1995. 154p. ISBN:0-19-875147-8, ISBN13: 978-0-19-875147-2. Dewey:186.4.

Audience: **g,u.** *Choice, 1993.*

Philo & Lewy, Yochanan   **B689.A4E5 2004**
Selected Writings. Hans Lewy (Editor). Trade Paper. Dover
Publications, Inc. Mineola, NY. 2004. 112p.
ISBN:0-486-43734-5, ISBN13: 978-0-486-43734-7.
Dewey:181/.06. LCCN:2004-050044.

Audience: **g,u,f.**

Rist, John M.   **B693.Z7**
Plotinus: The Road to Reality. Trade Paper. Cambridge
University Press. New York, NY. 1977. 280p.
ISBN:0-521-29202-6, ISBN13: 978-0-521-29202-3.
Dewey:186/.4.

Audience: **g,l,u.** ℬ

Siorvanes, Lucas   **B701.Z7S56 1996**
Proclus: Neo-Platonic Philosophy and Science. Cloth over
Boards. Yale University Press. Cumberland, RI. 1997. 356p.
ISBN:0-300-06806-9, ISBN13: 978-0-300-06806-1.
Dewey:186/.4. LCCN:96-022687.

Audience: **u,f.** *Choice, 1997.*

Smith, Andrew   **B517.S65 2004**
Philosophy in Late Antiquity. Paper over Boards. Routledge.
New York, NY. 2004. 168p. ISBN:0-415-22510-8, ISBN13:
978-0-415-22510-6. Dewey:355.02/0938. LCCN:2004-000761.

Audience: **g,u,f.**

Stump, Eleonore &   **B655.Z7C35 2001**
  Kretzmann, Norman (Editors)
The Cambridge Companion to Augustine. Cloth Text.
Cambridge University Press. New York, NY. 2001. 324p.
Cambridge Companions to Philosophy Ser.
ISBN:0-521-65018-6, ISBN13: 978-0-521-65018-2.
Dewey:189/.2. LCCN:00-031173.

Audience: **g,l,u,f.** *Choice, 2002.*

Wolfson, Harry A.   **B689.Z7**
Philo: Foundations of Religious Philosophy in Judaism,
Christianity and Islam, Set. Trade Cloth. Harvard University
Press. Cambridge, MA. 1962. 1024p. ISBN:0-674-66450-7,
ISBN13: 978-0-674-66450-0. Dewey:181.3. LCCN:47-030635.

Audience: **g,l,u,f.**

History of Philosophy > Medieval Philosophy

Abelard, Peter   **BJ1240.A2313 1995**
Ethical Writings: The Complete Texts of Ethics and Dialogue
Between a Philosopher, a Jew, and a Christian. Paul V. Spade
(Translator), Marilyn M. Adams (Introduction by). Trade Cloth.
Hackett Publishing Company, Inc. Indianapolis, IN. 1995. 208p.
Hackett Classics Ser. ISBN:0-87220-323-9, ISBN13:
978-0-87220-323-5. Dewey:241. LCCN:95-024270.

Audience: **u,f.**

Afnan, Soheil M.   **B751.Z7 A6 1980**
Avicenna, His Life and Works. Trade Cloth. Greenwood

Publishing Group, Inc. Portsmouth, NH. 1980. 298p.
ISBN:0-313-22198-7, ISBN13: 978-0-313-22198-9.
Dewey:181/.5. LCCN:79-008705.

Audience: **u,f.**

Al-Ghazali   **B753.G33**
The Incoherence of the Philosophers. Ed. 2. Michael E.
Marmura (Translator). Trade Cloth. Brigham Young University.
Provo, UT. 2002. 580p. Islamic Translations Ser.
ISBN:0-8425-2466-5, ISBN13: 978-0-8425-2466-7.
Dewey:297.2/61. LCCN:97-021195.

Audience: **u,f.**

Ali Khalidi, Muhammad   **B741.M44 2004**
  (Editor)
Medieval Islamic Philosophical Writings. Cambridge University
Press. 2005. Cambridge Texts in the History of Philosophy Ser.
ISBN:0-521-52963-8, ISBN13: 978-0-521-52963-1.

Audience: **g,u,f.**

Anselm, Saint & Anselm of   **B765.A82 E58**
  Canterbury
Truth, Freedom, and Evil: Three Philosophical Dialogues. Jasper
Hopkins & Herbert W. Richardson (Editors). Trade Cloth.
Edwin Mellen Press, The. Lewiston, NY. 1989. 196p.
ISBN:0-88946-844-3, ISBN13: 978-0-88946-844-3.
Dewey:189/.4.

Audience: **g,l,u.**

Augustine   **BR65.A664E5 1993**
On Free Choice of the Will. Thomas Williams (Translator,
Introduction by). Trade Cloth. Hackett Publishing Company, Inc.
Indianapolis, IN. 1993. 192p. Hackett Classics Ser.
ISBN:0-87220-189-9, ISBN13: 978-0-87220-189-7.
Dewey:233.7. LCCN:93-022170.

Audience: **g,l,u,f.** ℬ

Copleston, Frederick   **B72**
  Charles
History of Philosophy: Ockham to Suarez. Trade Cloth. Paulist
Press. Mahwah, NJ. 1953. 496p. History of Philosophy Ser., III
ISBN:0-8091-0067-3, ISBN13: 978-0-8091-0067-5. Dewey:109.

Audience: **g,l,u.**

Copleston, Frederick   **B721.C57 2001**
  Charles
Medieval Philosophy: An Introduction. Trade Paper. Dover
Publications, Inc. Mineola, NY. 2001. 208p.
ISBN:0-486-42008-6, ISBN13: 978-0-486-42008-0. Dewey:189.
LCCN:2001-028590.

Audience: **g,l,u.**

Copleston, Frederick J.   **B72C62**
Late Medieval and Renaissance Philosophy: Ockham, Francis
Bacon and the Beginning of the Modern World, Vol. 3.
UK-Trade Paper. Doubleday Publishing. New York, NY. 1993.
496p. ISBN:0-385-46845-8, ISBN13: 978-0-385-46845-9.
Dewey:109. LCCN:92-034997.

Audience: **g,l,u.**

Audience: g=general, l=lower division undergraduate, u=upper division undergraduate, f=faculty.

431

Copleston, Frederick J.   **B72.C62 1993**
Medieval Philosophy: From Augustine to Duns Scotus.
UK-Trade Paper. Doubleday Publishing. New York, NY. 1993.
624p. ISBN:0-385-46844-X, ISBN13: 978-0-385-46844-2.
Dewey:190. LCCN:92-034997.

Audience: **g,l,u.**

Cullen, Christopher M.   **B765.B74C85 2005**
Bonaventure. Trade Paper. Oxford University Press, Inc. New
York, NY. 2006. 270p. Great Medieval Thinkers Ser.
ISBN:0-19-514926-2, ISBN13: 978-0-19-514926-5.
Dewey:189/.4. LCCN:2005-012591.

Audience: **u,f.**

Davies, Brian & Leftow,   **B765.A84C36 2004**
  Brian (Editors)
The Cambridge Companion to Anselm. Cloth Text. Cambridge
University Press. New York, NY. 2004. 338p. Cambridge
Companions to Philosophy Ser. ISBN:0-521-80746-8, ISBN13:
978-0-521-80746-3. Dewey:189/.4. LCCN:2004-047305.

Audience: **u,f.**

Dronke, Peter (Editor)   **B721.H58 1992**
A History of Twelfth-Century Western Philosophy. Trade Paper.
Cambridge University Press. New York, NY. 1992. 507p.
ISBN:0-521-42907-2, ISBN13: 978-0-521-42907-8. Dewey:189.

Audience: **g,u.**

Duhem, Pierre M.   **BD495.5**
Medieval Cosmology: Theories of Infinity, Place, Time, Void,
and the Plurality of Worlds. Roger Ariew (Translator). Trade
Paper. University of Chicago Press. Chicago, IL. 1987. 642p.
ISBN:0-226-16923-5, ISBN13: 978-0-226-16923-1.
Dewey:113/.09/02. LCCN:85-008115.

Audience: **u,f.**

Fakhry, Majid   **B741.F23 2004**
History of Islamic Philosophy. Ed. 3. Trade Cloth. Edinburgh
University Press. Edinburgh, 2004. 472p. ISBN:0-231-13220-4,
ISBN13: 978-0-231-13220-6. Dewey:181/.07.
LCCN:2004-051978.

Audience: **u,f.**

Gilson, Etienne   **B72 .G48**
History of Christian Philosophy in the Middle Ages. Paper Text.
Textbook Publishers. Temecula, CA. 2003. 829p.
ISBN:0-7581-5033-4, ISBN13: 978-0-7581-5033-2. Dewey:189.

Audience: **g,u.** 𝐵

Gilson, Etienne   **B721.G5714 1991**
The Spirit of Medieval Philosophy. Trade Cloth. University of
Notre Dame Press. Notre Dame, IN. 1991. 504p.
ISBN:0-268-01740-9, ISBN13: 978-0-268-01740-8. Dewey:189.
LCCN:90-050958.

Audience: **g,l,u,f.**

Goodman, Lenn E.   **B751.Z7**
Avicenna. Trade Paper. Cornell University Press. Ithaca, NY.
2005. 256p. ISBN:0-8014-7254-7, ISBN13: 978-0-8014-7254-1.
Dewey:181/.5. LCCN:2005-054845.

Audience: **g,u,f.** *Choice, 1993.*

Haren, Michael   **B721.H34 1992**
Medieval Thought: The Western Intellectual Tradition from
Antiquity to the Thirteenth Century. Ed. 2. Cloth Text.
University of Toronto Press. Toronto, ON. 1992. 530p.
ISBN:0-8020-2868-3, ISBN13: 978-0-8020-2868-6. Dewey:189.
LCCN:92-094449.

Audience: **g,u,f.** 𝐵 *Choice, 1985.*

Hartshorne, Charles   **BT102**
Anselm's Discovery: A Re-Examination of the Ontological
Proof for God's Existence. Trade Cloth. Open Court Publishing
Company. Chicago, IL. 1973. 349p. ISBN:0-87548-216-3,
ISBN13: 978-0-87548-216-3. Dewey:211. LCCN:65-020278.

Audience: **u,f.**

Hyman, Arthur & Walsh,   **B720.P5 1983**
  James J. (Editors)
Philosophy in the Middle Ages: The Christian, Islamic and
Jewish Traditions. Ed. 2. Trade Paper. Hackett Publishing
Company, Inc. Indianapolis, IN. 1983. 815p.
ISBN:0-915145-80-4, ISBN13: 978-0-915145-80-5. Dewey:189.
LCCN:82-023337.

Audience: **g,u.** 𝐵

Inglis, John (Editor)   **B721.M457 2003**
Medieval Philosophy and the Classical Tradition: In Islam,
Judaism and Christianity. Paper over Boards. Taylor & Francis
Group. Abingdon, 2001. 328p. ISBN:0-7007-1469-3, ISBN13:
978-0-7007-1469-8. Dewey:189. LCCN:2003-467178.

Audience: **g,l,u.** *Choice, 2003.*

John of Salisbury   **B765.J43 M43**
The Metalogicon of John of Salisbury. Daniel McGarry
(Translator). Trade Cloth. Peter Smith Publisher, Inc. Magnolia,
MA. 1990. ISBN:0-8446-0159-4, ISBN13: 978-0-8446-0159-5.
Dewey:160.

Audience: **u,f.**

Kenny, Anthony   **B72**
Medieval Philosophy: A New History of Western Philosophy.
Trade Cloth. Oxford University Press, Inc. New York, NY. 2005.
352p. ISBN:0-19-875275-X, ISBN13: 978-0-19-875275-2.
Dewey:180.

Audience: **g,l,u.**

Kretzmann, Norman   **B721**
  (Editor), et al.
The Cambridge History of Later Medieval Philosophy: From the
Rediscovery of Aristotle to the Disintegration of Scholasticism,
1100-1600. Anthony Kenny, Jan Pinborg & Eleonore Stump
(Editors). Trade Paper. Cambridge University Press. New York,
NY. 1988. 1056p. ISBN:0-521-36933-9, ISBN13:
978-0-521-36933-6. Dewey:189. LCCN:81-010086.

Audience: **g,u,f.**

Leaman, Oliver   **B759**
Moses Maimonides. Trade Paper. Taylor & Francis Group.
Abingdon, 1997. 212p. RoutledgeCurzon Jewish Philosophy Ser.
ISBN:0-7007-0676-3, ISBN13: 978-0-7007-0676-1.
Dewey:181/.06.

Audience: **g,u.** *Choice, 1990.*

Luscombe, David   B721.L87 1997
Medieval Thought. Paper Text. Oxford University Press, Inc.
New York, NY. 1997. 256p. A History of Western Philosophy
Ser., No. 2 ISBN:0-19-289179-0, ISBN13: 978-0-19-289179-2.
Dewey:189. LCCN:96-029604.
Audience: **g,u,f.** *Choice, 1997.*

Maimonides, Moses   **BM545**
The Guide for the Perplexed. Ed. 2. Trade Cloth. Kegan Paul
International, Ltd. London, 2005. 473p. ISBN:0-7103-1036-6,
ISBN13: 978-0-7103-1036-1. Dewey:181/.06.
Audience: **g,l,u,f.**

Marenbon, John   **B721**
Early Medieval Philosophy, 480-1150. Ed. 2. Trade Paper.
Routledge. New York, NY. 1988. 216p. ISBN:0-415-00070-X,
ISBN13: 978-0-415-00070-3. Dewey:189. LCCN:87-037106.
Audience: **g,u,f.**

Marenbon, John (Editor)   **B721**
Medieval Philosophy, Vol. 3. Trade Paper. Routledge. New York,
NY. 2003. 552p. History of Philosophy Ser., Vol. 3
ISBN:0-415-30875-5, ISBN13: 978-0-415-30875-5.
Dewey:109/.02.
Audience: **g,u,f.**

Maurer, Armand A.   B721 .M37 1982
Medieval Philosophy. Ed. 2. Etienne Gilson (Introduction by).
Paper Text. Pontifical Institute of Mediaeval Studies,
Department of Publications. Toronto, ON. 1982. 477p. The
Etienne Gilson Ser., Vol. 4 ISBN:0-88844-704-3, ISBN13:
978-0-88844-704-3. Dewey:189. LCCN:82-202212.
Audience: **g,u,f.** ℬ

McEvoy, James   B765.G74M34 2000
Robert Grosseteste. Trade Paper. Oxford University Press, Inc.
New York, NY. 2000. 240p. Great Medieval Thinkers Ser.
ISBN:0-19-511450-7, ISBN13: 978-0-19-511450-8.
Dewey:189/.4. LCCN:99-036238.
Audience: **u,f.**

McGrade, A. S. (Editor)   **B721**
The Cambridge Companion to Medieval Philosophy. Cloth Text.
Cambridge University Press. New York, NY. 2003. 424p.
Cambridge Companions to Philosophy Ser.
ISBN:0-521-80603-8, ISBN13: 978-0-521-80603-9. Dewey:189.
LCCN:2003-279243.
Audience: **u,f.** *Choice, 2004.*

Nicholas   B765.N53D63
Of Learned Ignorance. Paper Text. Textbook Publishers.
Temecula, CA. 2003. xxvii, 174p. ISBN:0-7581-0089-2,
ISBN13: 978-0-7581-0089-4. Dewey:189.5.
Audience: **u,f.** ℬ

Scotus, John D.   B765.D73L4313 1994
Contingency and Freedom: John Duns Scotus Lectura 139. A.
Vos Jaczn (Editor, Commentaries by, Introduction by). Trade
Cloth. Springer Dordrecht. Dordrecht, 1994. 216p. The New
Synthese Historical Library, Vol. 42 ISBN:0-7923-2707-1,
ISBN13: 978-0-7923-2707-3. Dewey:123. LCCN:94-000318.
Audience: **u,f.**

Scotus, John D.   B765.D72 E58 1987
Philosophical Writings: A Selection. Allan B. Wolter & Marilyn
M. Adams (Introduction by). Trade Paper. Hackett Publishing
Company, Inc. Indianapolis, IN. 1987. 400p. HPC Classics Ser.
ISBN:0-87220-018-3, ISBN13: 978-0-87220-018-0. Dewey:211.
LCCN:87-011990.
Audience: **g,u,f.**

St. Anselm   B765.A82 E54
Basic Writings: Proslogium; Monologium; Gaunilo's "In Behalf
of the Fool"; Cur Deus Homo. Ed. 2. Charles Hartshorne
(Foreword by). Trade Paper. Open Court Publishing Company.
Chicago, IL. 1962. 342p. ISBN:0-87548-109-4, ISBN13:
978-0-87548-109-8. Dewey:199.99.
Audience: **g,l,u,f.**

St. Bonaventure   BT100 .B5613 1993
The Journey of the Mind to God. Philotheus Boehner
(Translator), Stephen F. Brown (Introduction by). Trade Cloth.
Hackett Publishing Company, Inc. Indianapolis, IN. 1993. 96p.
Hackett Classics Ser. ISBN:0-87220-201-1, ISBN13:
978-0-87220-201-6. Dewey:248.2/2. LCCN:93-024136.
Audience: **g,l,u,f.**

Weinberg, Julius Rudolf   **B721**
A Short History of Medieval Philosophy. Trade Paper. Princeton
University Press. Princeton, NJ. 1967. 316p.
ISBN:0-691-01956-8, ISBN13: 978-0-691-01956-7. Dewey:189.
Audience: **g,l,u.** ℬ

William of Ockham   B765.T54
Philosophical Writings: A Selection. Philotheus Boehner
(Translator, Introduction by), Stephen F. Brown (Foreword by).
Trade Paper. Hackett Publishing Company, Inc. Indianapolis, IN.
1990. 315p. ISBN:0-87220-078-7, ISBN13: 978-0-87220-078-4.
Dewey:189/.4. LCCN:89-048587.
Audience: **u,f.**

William of Ockham   BC60.O25213 1998
Ockham's Theory of Terms: Summa Logicae. Michael J. Lonx
(Translator, Introduction by). Trade Cloth. Saint Augustine's
Press, Inc. South Bend, IN. 1998. 235p. ISBN:1-890318-50-7,
ISBN13: 978-1-890318-50-5. Dewey:160. LCCN:97-037876.
Audience: **g,u,f.**

History of Philosophy > Medieval Philosophy > Aquinas

Aquinas, Thomas   JC121.T42 2002
Aquinas: Political Writings. R. W. Dyson (Editor, Translator).
Cloth Text. Cambridge University Press. New York, NY. 2002.
360p. Cambridge Texts in the History of Political Thought Ser.
ISBN:0-521-37569-X, ISBN13: 978-0-521-37569-6. Dewey:320.
LCCN:2002-025748.
Audience: **g,u.**

Aquinas, Thomas   **B415**
A Commentary on Aristotle's De Anima. Kenelm Foster &
Silvester Humphries (Translators), Ralph McInerny (Introduction
by). Trade Cloth. Dumb Ox Books. South Bend, IN. 1995.
298p. Dumb Ox Books' Aristotelian Commentaries, xxii, 276
ISBN:1-883357-10-1, ISBN13: 978-1-883357-10-8. Dewey:128.
Audience: **u,f.**

Aquinas, Thomas, et al.   **B765.T51 2005**
Aquinas: Disputed Questions on the Virtues. Jeffrey Hause &
Claudia Murphy (Authors), Thomas Williams & Margaret Atkins
(Editors), Desmond M. Clarke & Karl Ameriks (Contribution
by). Cloth Text. Cambridge University Press. New York, NY.
2005. 344p. Cambridge Texts in the History of Philosophy Ser.
ISBN:0-521-77225-7, ISBN13: 978-0-521-77225-9.
Dewey:179/.9. LCCN:2004-062845.
Audience: **u,f.**

Aquinas, Thomas & King,   **B765.T53**
  Peter
On Being and Essence. Trade Cloth. Hackett Publishing
Company, Inc. Indianapolis, IN. 2006. 128p.
ISBN:0-87220-616-5, ISBN13: 978-0-87220-616-8. Dewey:111.
Audience: **u,f.**

Aquinas, Thomas   **B430**
Commentary on Aristotle's Nicomacheau Ethics. C. I. Litzinger
(Translator), Ralph McInerny (Foreword by). Trade Cloth.
Dumb Ox Books. South Bend, IN. 1993. 700p. Aristotelian
Commentaries Ser. ISBN:1-883357-50-0, ISBN13:
978-1-883357-50-4. Dewey:185.
Audience: **u,f.**

Aquinas, Thomas   **B765**
Selected Philosophical Writings. Timothy McDermott
(Translator, Selected by). Trade Paper. Oxford University Press,
Inc. New York, NY. 1998. 488p. Oxford World's Classics Ser.
ISBN:0-19-283585-8, ISBN13: 978-0-19-283585-7.
Dewey:189.4.
Audience: **g,l,u.**

Aquinas, Thomas   **B765.T53Q3413 1994**
Truth, 3 vols. Robert W. Mulligan, James V. McGlynn & Robert
W. Schmidt (Translators). Trade Cloth. Hackett Publishing
Company, Inc. Indianapolis, IN. 1994. 1525p.
ISBN:0-87220-270-4, ISBN13: 978-0-87220-270-2. Dewey:121.
LCCN:94-029598.
Audience: **u,f.**

Aquinas, Thomas   **BX1749 .T324**
Basic Writings of Saint Thomas Aquinas. Anton C. Pegis
(Editor). Trade Cloth. Hackett Publishing Company, Inc.

Indianapolis, IN. 1997. 2362p. Classics Ser.
ISBN:0-87220-385-9, ISBN13: 978-0-87220-385-3.
Dewey:230/.2. LCCN:97-026330.
Audience: **g,u.**

Aquinas, Thomas   **B434.T53 1995**
Commentary on Aristotle's Metaphysics. John P. Rowan
(Translator), Ralph McInerny (Preface by). Trade Cloth. Dumb
Ox Books. South Bend, IN. 1995. 870p. Dumb Ox Books'
Aristotelian Commentaries ISBN:1-883357-60-8, ISBN13:
978-1-883357-60-3. Dewey:110.
Audience: **u,f.**

Gilson, Etienne   **B765.T54G5 1994**
The Christian Philosophy of St. Thomas Aquinas: Philosophy.
Trade Paper. University of Notre Dame Press. Notre Dame, IN.
1994. 502p. ISBN:0-268-00801-9, ISBN13: 978-0-268-00801-7.
LCCN:94-010241.
Audience: **u,f.**

Goodman, J.   **BX1749**
Aquinas: Summa Theologiae, Questions on God. Brian Davies
& Brian Leftow (Editors), Karl Ameriks & Desmond M. Clarke
(Contribution by). Trade Paper. Cambridge University Press.
New York, NY. 2006. 344p. Cambridge Texts in the History of
Philosophy Ser. ISBN:0-521-52892-5, ISBN13:
978-0-521-52892-4. Dewey:231.
Audience: **g,u,f.**

Kretzmann, Norman &   **B765.T54 C29 1993**
  Stump, Eleonore (Editors)
The Cambridge Companion to Aquinas. Trade Paper. Cambridge
University Press. New York, NY. 1993. 312p. Cambridge
Companions to Philosophy Ser. ISBN:0-521-43769-5, ISBN13:
978-0-521-43769-1. Dewey:189.4. LCCN:92-031977.
Audience: **u,f.**

Leftow, Brian & Davies,   **BX1749**
  Brian (Editors)
Aquinas: Summa of Theology, Questions on God. Karl Ameriks
& Desmond M. Clarke (Contribution by). Cloth Text.
Cambridge University Press. New York, NY. 2006. 342p.
Cambridge Texts in the History of Philosophy Ser.
ISBN:0-521-82140-1, ISBN13: 978-0-521-82140-7. Dewey:231.
Audience: **g,l,u,f.**

Pegis, Anton C.   **BX1749.T7P4**
St. Thomas and Philosophy. Trade Cloth. Marquette University
Press. Milwaukee, WI. 1964. Aquinas Lectures
ISBN:0-87462-129-1, ISBN13: 978-0-87462-129-7.
Dewey:201.4. LCCN:64-017418.
Audience: **g,u,f.**

Stump, Eleonore   **B765.T54**
Aquinas. Ed. 2. Paper Text. Routledge. New York, NY. 2005. 640p. The Arguments of the Philosophers Ser. ISBN:0-415-37898-2, ISBN13: 978-0-415-37898-7. Dewey:189/.4.
                        Audience: **g,l,u,f.**

History of Philosophy > Renaissance Philosophy

Cassirer, Ernst   **B775.C313 2000**
The Individual and the Cosmos in Renaissance Philosophy. Trade Paper. Dover Publications, Inc. Mineola, NY. 2000. 214p. ISBN:0-486-41438-8, ISBN13: 978-0-486-41438-6. Dewey:189. LCCN:00-043044.
                       Audience: **u,f.** *B*

Copenhaver, Brian P.   **B775.C67 1992**
Renaissance Philosophy. Paper Text. Oxford University Press, Inc. New York, NY. 1992. 464p. A History of Western Philosophy Ser., No. 3 ISBN:0-19-289184-7, ISBN13: 978-0-19-289184-6. Dewey:190.9/031. LCCN:91-039554.
        Audience: **g,l,u,f.** *Choice, 1993.*

D'Aragona, Tullia   **BD436.D3713 1997**
Dialogue on the Infinity of Love. Rinaldina Russell & Bruce Merry (Translators). Trade Cloth. University of Chicago Press. Chicago, IL. 1997. 118p. The Other Voice in Early Modern Europe Ser. ISBN:0-226-13638-8, ISBN13: 978-0-226-13638-7. Dewey:128.46. LCCN:96-028841.
          Audience: **g,u,f.** *Choice, 1997.*

Koenigsberger, Dorothy   **B775.K6 1979**
Renaissance Man and Creative Thinking: A History of Concepts of Harmony, 1400-1700. Trade Cloth. Humanities Press International, Inc. Atlantic Highlands, NJ. 1979. xiii, 282p. ISBN:0-391-00851-X, ISBN13: 978-0-391-00851-9. Dewey:169/.094. LCCN:78-000956.
                    Audience: **g,u,f.** *B*

Kraye, Jill (Editor)   **BJ161 .C36 1997**
Cambridge Translations of Renaissance Philosophical Texts: Moral and Political Philosophy. Trade Paper. Cambridge University Press. New York, NY. 1997. 327p. ISBN:0-521-58757-3, ISBN13: 978-0-521-58757-0. Dewey:320/.01/09024. LCCN:96-035176.
                       Audience: **u,f.**

Kraye, Jill (Editor)   **BJ161 .C36 1997**
Cambridge Translations of Renaissance Philosophical Texts: Moral and Political Philosophy. Trade Paper. Cambridge University Press. New York, NY. 1997. 295p. ISBN:0-521-42604-9, ISBN13: 978-0-521-42604-6. Dewey:190/.9/031. LCCN:96-035176.
            Audience: **u,f.** *Choice, 1998.*

Kraye, Jill (Editor)   **BJ161 .C36 1997**
Cambridge Translations of Renaissance Philosophical Texts: Moral and Political Philosophy. Quantity Pack, Trade Paper. Cambridge University Press. New York, NY. 1998. 624p. ISBN:0-521-59772-2, ISBN13: 978-0-521-59772-2. Dewey:190/.9/031. LCCN:96-035176.
                       Audience: **u,f.**

Kristeller, Paul O.   **B776.I8K714**
Eight Philosophers of the Italian Renaissance. Trade Paper. Stanford University Press. Palo Alto, CA. 1964. 215p. ISBN:0-8047-0111-3, ISBN13: 978-0-8047-0111-2. Dewey:195.
                   Audience: **g,l,u,f.**

Parkinson, G. H. R. (Editor)   **B833**
The Renaissance and 17th Century Rationalism. Trade Paper. Routledge. New York, NY. 2003. 480p. History of Philosophy Ser., Vol. 4 ISBN:0-415-30876-3, ISBN13: 978-0-415-30876-2. Dewey:149.7.
                       Audience: **u,f.**

Popkin, Richard H.   **LA228.S3**
Philosophy of the Sixteenth and Seventeenth Centuries. Trade Paper. Simon & Schuster. New York, NY. 1966. 384p. Readings in the History of Philosophy Ser. ISBN:0-02-925490-6, ISBN13: 978-0-02-925490-5. Dewey:378.73. LCCN:66-010365.
                Audience: **g,u,f.** *B*

Schmitt, C. B. (Editor), et al.   **B775 .C25 1988**
The Cambridge History of Renaissance Philosophy. Quentin Skinner, Eckhard Kessler & Jill Kraye (Editors). Trade Cloth. Cambridge University Press. New York, NY. 1988. 922p. ISBN:0-521-25104-4, ISBN13: 978-0-521-25104-4. Dewey:190/.9/024. LCCN:87-005212.
            Audience: **u,f.** *Choice, 1988.*

History of Philosophy > Modern Philosophy

Beardsley, Monroe C.   **B790.E97 2002**
The European Philosophers from Descartes to Nietzsche. Book, Other. Random House, Inc. New York, NY. 2002. 944p. The Modern Library Classics ISBN:0-375-75804-6, ISBN13: 978-0-375-75804-1. Dewey:190. LCCN:2002-070263.
                  Audience: **g,u,f.** *B*

Bennett, Jonathan   **B790**
Learning from Six Philosophers: Descartes, Spinoza, Leibniz, Locke, Berkeley, Hume, Vol. 2. Trade Paper. Oxford University Press, Inc. New York, NY. 2003. 400p. ISBN:0-19-926629-8, ISBN13: 978-0-19-926629-6. Dewey:190.
           Audience: **g,u,f.** *Choice, 2002.*

Bennett, Jonathan   **B790**
Learning from Six Philosophers: Descartes, Spinoza, Leibniz, Locke, Berkeley, Hume, Vol. 1. Trade Paper. Oxford University Press, Inc. New York, NY. 2003. 424p. ISBN:0-19-926628-X, ISBN13: 978-0-19-926628-9. Dewey:190.
           Audience: **g,u,f.** *Choice, 2002.*

Emmanuel, Steven M.   **B791.B53 2000**
(Editor)
Blackwell Guide to the Modern Philosophers: Descartes to
Nietzsche. Trade Paper. Blackwell Publishing, Inc. Malden, MA.
2000. 440p. Philosophy Guides, Vol. 3 ISBN:0-631-21017-2,
ISBN13: 978-0-631-21017-7. Dewey:190. LCCN:00-022954.
Audience: **u,f.** *Choice, 2001.*

Garber, Daniel & Ayers,   **B801 .C35 1998**
Michael (Editors)
The Cambridge History of Seventeenth-Century Philosophy, Set.
Trade Cloth. Cambridge University Press. New York, NY. 1998.
1642p. ISBN:0-521-58864-2, ISBN13: 978-0-521-58864-5.
Dewey:190.9032. LCCN:96-025475.
Audience: **g,u,f.** *Choice, 1998.*

Garber, Daniel & Nadler,   **B791**
Steven (Editors)
Oxford Studies in Early Modern Philosophy. Trade Paper.
Oxford University Press, Inc. New York, NY. 2005. 272p.
Oxford Studies in Early Modern Philosophy Ser.
ISBN:0-19-927976-4, ISBN13: 978-0-19-927976-0. Dewey:190.
Audience: **u,f.**

Garber, Daniel & Nadler,   **B791**
Steven M.
Oxford Studies in Early Modern Philosophy. Daniel Garber &
Steven Nadler (Editors). Trade Paper. Oxford University Press,
Inc. New York, NY. 2004. 268p. Oxford Studies in Early
Modern Philosophy ISBN:0-19-926791-X, ISBN13:
978-0-19-926791-0. Dewey:190.
Audience: **u,f.**

Lennon, Thomas M.   **B1887.L46 1993**
The Battle of the Gods and Giants: The Legacies of Descartes
and Gassendi, 1655-1715. Trade Cloth. Princeton University
Press. Princeton, NJ. 1993. 456p. Studies in Intellectual History
and the History of Philosophy ISBN:0-691-07400-3, ISBN13:
978-0-691-07400-9. Dewey:194. LCCN:92-026088.
Audience: **g,u,f.** *Choice, 1993.*

Miller, Jon & Inwood, Brad   **B801.H45 2003**
(Editors)
Hellenistic and Early Modern Philosophy. Trade Cloth.
Cambridge University Press. New York, NY. 2003. 342p.
ISBN:0-521-82385-4, ISBN13: 978-0-521-82385-2. Dewey:190.
LCCN:2002-031073.
Audience: **u,f.**

Nadler, Steven (Editor)   **B801.C66 2002**
A Companion to Early Modern Philosophy. Trade Cloth.
Blackwell Publishing, Inc. Malden, MA. 2002. 672p. Blackwell
Companions to Philosophy Ser., Vol. 23 ISBN:0-631-21800-9,
ISBN13: 978-0-631-21800-5. Dewey:190/.9/032.
LCCN:2002-070947.
Audience: **u,f.**

Royce, Josiah   **B72**
The Spirit of Modern Philosophy. Trade Paper. Dover

Publications, Inc. Mineola, NY. 1983. 519p.
ISBN:0-486-24432-6, ISBN13: 978-0-486-24432-7.
Dewey:190/.9/03. LCCN:82-017724.
Audience: **g,l,u,f.**

Scruton, Roger   **B791.S29 2001**
A Short History of Modern Philosophy: From Descartes to
Wittgenstein. Ed. 3. Trade Paper. Routledge. New York, NY.
2001. 328p. Classics Ser. ISBN:0-415-26763-3, ISBN13:
978-0-415-26763-2. Dewey:190. LCCN:2001-034885.
Audience: **g,l,u.**

Sedgwick, Peter   **B791.S39 2001**
Descartes to Derrida: An Introduction to European Philosophy.
Trade Paper. Blackwell Publishing, Inc. Malden, MA. 2001.
328p. ISBN:0-631-20143-2, ISBN13: 978-0-631-20143-4.
Dewey:190. LCCN:00-057917.
Audience: **g,u,f.** *Choice, 2002.*

Taylor, Mark C.   **B4378.S4T38 2000**
Journeys to Selfhood: Hegel and Kierkegaard. Ed. 2. Trade
Paper. Fordham University Press. Bronx, NY. 2000. 298p.
Perspectives in Continental Philosophy Ser., Vol. 14
ISBN:0-8232-2059-1, ISBN13: 978-0-8232-2059-5.
Dewey:126/.092/2. LCCN:00-025099.
Audience: **g,l,u.** *Choice, 2001.*

Tlumak, Jeffrey   **B801.T58 2006**
Classical Modern Philosophy. Trade Paper. Routledge. New
York, NY. 2006. 320p. Routledge Contemporary Introductions to
Philosophy Ser. ISBN:0-415-27593-8, ISBN13:
978-0-415-27593-4. Dewey:190.9/032. LCCN:2006-008369.
Audience: **g,l,u.**

Yolton, John W.   **BD161.Y65 1996**
Perception and Reality: A History from Descartes to Kant. Trade
Cloth. Cornell University Press. Ithaca, NY. 1996. 248p.
ISBN:0-8014-3227-8, ISBN13: 978-0-8014-3227-9.
Dewey:121/.3. LCCN:95-049162.
Audience: **u,f.** *Choice, 1996.*

History of Philosophy > Modern Philosophy > 17th Century Philosophy

Ariew, Roger   **B1831.H57 2003**
Historical Dictionary of Descartes and Cartesian Philosophy.
Trade Cloth. Scarecrow Press, Inc. Lanham, MD. 2003. 320p.
Historical Dictionaries of Religions, Philosophies, and
Movements Ser., No. 46 ISBN:0-8108-4833-3, ISBN13:
978-0-8108-4833-7. Dewey:194. LCCN:2003-012223.
Audience: **g,u,f.**

Atherton, Margaret   **B801.W65 1994**
Women Philosophers of the Early Modern Period. Trade Paper.
Hackett Publishing Company, Inc. Indianapolis, IN. 1994. 176p.
ISBN:0-87220-259-3, ISBN13: 978-0-87220-259-7.
Dewey:190/.82. LCCN:94-027004.
Audience: **u,f.**

Garber, Daniel & Ayers,   **B801 .C35 1998**
  Michael (Editors)
The Cambridge History of Seventeenth-Century Philosophy, Set.
Trade Cloth. Cambridge University Press. New York, NY. 1998.
1642p. ISBN:0-521-58864-2, ISBN13: 978-0-521-58864-5.
Dewey:190.9032. LCCN:96-025475.

Audience: **g,u,f.** *Choice, 1998.*

Hampshire, Stuart   **B801.H3 1970**
The Age of Reason: The Seventeenth Century Philosophers.
Trade Cloth. Ayer Company Publishers, Inc. Manchester, NH.
1977. 186p. ISBN:0-8369-1833-9, ISBN13: 978-0-8369-1833-5.
Dewey:190. LCCN:70-117801.

Audience: **g,l,u.**

Kennington, Richard, et al.   **B801.K46 2004**
On Modern Origins: Essays in Early Modern Philosophy. Frank
Hunt & Pamela Kraus (Authors). Trade Paper. Lexington Books.
Lanham, MD. 2004. 304p. ISBN:0-7391-0815-8, ISBN13:
978-0-7391-0815-4. Dewey:190/.9/032. LCCN:2004-002884.

Audience: **g,u,f.**

Nadler, Steven (Editor)   **B801.C66 2002**
A Companion to Early Modern Philosophy. Trade Cloth.
Blackwell Publishing, Inc. Malden, MA. 2002. 672p. Blackwell
Companions to Philosophy Ser., Vol. 23 ISBN:0-631-21800-9,
ISBN13: 978-0-631-21800-5. Dewey:190/.9/032.
LCCN:2002-070947.

Audience: **u,f.**

Popkin, Richard H.   **LA228.S3**
Philosophy of the Sixteenth and Seventeenth Centuries. Trade
Paper. Simon & Schuster. New York, NY. 1966. 384p. Readings
in the History of Philosophy Ser. ISBN:0-02-925490-6, ISBN13:
978-0-02-925490-5. Dewey:378.73. LCCN:66-010365.

Audience: **g,u,f.** ℬ

History of Philosophy > Modern Philosophy > 18th Century Philosophy. Enlightenment

Lord Shaftesbury   **B1385.A3.S52 1999**
Shaftesbury: Characteristics of Men, Manners, Opinions, Times.
Lawrence E. Klein (Editor). Cambridge University Press. 1999.
Texts in the History of Philosophy ISBN:0-521-57892-2,
ISBN13: 978-0-521-57892-9.

Audience: **g,u,f.**

Berlin, Isaiah (Editor)   **B802.B45 1970**
The Age of Enlightenment. Trade Cloth. Ayer Company
Publishers, Inc. Manchester, NH. 1980. 282p. Essay Index
Reprint Ser. ISBN:0-8369-1822-3, ISBN13: 978-0-8369-1822-9.
Dewey:190/.9/033. LCCN:72-117760.

Audience: **g,l,u.**

Cassirer, Ernst   **B802**
The Philosophy of the Enlightenment. James P. Pettegrove

(Editor), Fritz C. A. Koelin (Translator). Trade Paper. Princeton
University Press. Princeton, NJ. 1968. 384p.
ISBN:0-691-01963-0, ISBN13: 978-0-691-01963-5. Dewey:190.

Audience: **u,f.** ℬ

Copleston, Frederick   **B72**
  Charles
History of Philosophy: Descartes to Leibniz. Trade Cloth.
Paulist Press. Mahwah, NJ. 1958. 384p. History of Philosophy
Ser., IV ISBN:0-8091-0068-1, ISBN13: 978-0-8091-0068-2.
Dewey:109.

Audience: **g,l,u.**

Copleston, Frederick   **B72**
  Charles
History of Philosophy: Wolff to Kant. Trade Cloth. Paulist Press.
Mahwah, NJ. 1960. 520p. History of Philosophy Ser., VI
ISBN:0-8091-0070-3, ISBN13: 978-0-8091-0070-5. Dewey:109.

Audience: **g,l,u.**

Haakonssen, Knud   **B802.C24 2005**
The Cambridge History of Eighteenth-Century Philosophy, Set.
Trade Cloth. Cambridge University Press. New York, NY. 2006.
1424p. ISBN:0-521-41854-2, ISBN13: 978-0-521-41854-6.
Dewey:190/.9/033. LCCN:2004-054878.

Audience: **g,u.**

Himmelfarb, Gertrude   **B802.H65 2003**
The Roads to Modernity: The British, French and American
Enlightenments. Trade Cloth. Alfred A. Knopf Inc. New York,
NY. 2004. 304p. ISBN:1-4000-4236-4, ISBN13:
978-1-4000-4236-4. Dewey:190.9033. LCCN:2003-060576.

Audience: **g,u.** *Choice, 2005.*

Kors, Alan Charles (Editor)   **B802.E53 2002**
Encyclopedia of the Enlightenment, Vol. 3. Trade Cloth. Oxford
University Press, Inc. New York, NY. 2002.
ISBN:0-19-510433-1, ISBN13: 978-0-19-510433-2.
Dewey:940.2/5. LCCN:2002-003766.

Audience: **g,l,u,f.**

Kors, Alan Charles (Editor)   **B802.E53 2002**
Encyclopedia of the Enlightenment, Vol. 1. Trade Cloth. Oxford
University Press, Inc. New York, NY. 2002.
ISBN:0-19-510431-5, ISBN13: 978-0-19-510431-8.
Dewey:940.2/5. LCCN:2002-003766.

Audience: **g,l,u,f.**

Kors, Alan Charles (Editor)   **B802.E53 2002**
Encyclopedia of the Enlightenment, Vol. 4. Trade Cloth. Oxford
University Press, Inc. New York, NY. 2002.
ISBN:0-19-510434-X, ISBN13: 978-0-19-510434-9.
Dewey:940.2/5. LCCN:2002-003766.

Audience: **g,l,u,f.**

Kors, Alan Charles (Editor)   **B802.E53 2002**
Encyclopedia of the Enlightenment, Vol. 2. Trade Cloth. Oxford
University Press, Inc. New York, NY. 2002.
ISBN:0-19-510432-3, ISBN13: 978-0-19-510432-5.
Dewey:940.2/5. LCCN:2002-003766.

Audience: **g,l,u,f.**

History of Philosophy > Modern Philosophy > 19th Century Philosophy.

Copleston, Frederick Charles   **B72**
History of Philosophy: Bentham to Russell. Trade Cloth. Paulist Press. Mahwah, NJ. 1966. 592p. History of Philosophy Ser., VIII ISBN:0-8091-0072-X, ISBN13: 978-0-8091-0072-9. Dewey:109.

Audience: **g,l,u.**

Gardiner, Patrick (Editor)   **B803**
Nineteenth-Century Philosophy. Trade Paper. Simon & Schuster. New York, NY. 1969. 464p. ISBN:0-02-911220-6, ISBN13: 978-0-02-911220-5. Dewey:190. LCCN:69-010325.

Audience: **g,u.**

Mead, George Herbert   **B803.M4**
Movements of Thought in the Nineteenth Century. Trade Cloth. University of Chicago Press. Chicago, IL. 1936. xxxix, 518p. ISBN:0-226-53638-6, ISBN13: 978-0-226-53638-5. Dewey:190. LCCN:36-009407.

Audience: **g,l,u.** *B*

Schacht, Richard   **B803**
Hegel and After: Studies in Continental Philosophy Between Kant and Sartre. Trade Cloth. University of Pittsburgh Press. Pittsburgh, PA. 1975. xviii, 297p. ISBN:0-8229-3287-3, ISBN13: 978-0-8229-3287-1. Dewey:190/.9/034. LCCN:74-004526.

Audience: **u,f.** *B*

Ten, C. L. (Editor)   **B803.N55 2003**
The Nineteenth Century. Trade Paper. Routledge. New York, NY. 2003. 496p. History of Philosophy Ser., Vol. 7 ISBN:0-415-30879-8, ISBN13: 978-0-415-30879-3. Dewey:190.9/034.

Audience: **g,l,u.**

History of Philosophy > Modern Philosophy > 20th and 21st Centuries

Ayer, Alfred Jules   **B804.A818 1982**
Philosophy in the Twentieth Century. Trade Cloth. Random House, Inc. New York, NY. 1982. 283p. ISBN:0-394-50454-2, ISBN13: 978-0-394-50454-4. Dewey:190/.9/04. LCCN:82-040131.

Audience: **g,l,u.** *B*

Burr, John R.   **B804**
Handbook of World Philosophy: Contemporary Developments since 1945. Cloth Text. Greenwood Publishing Group, Inc. Portsmouth, NH. 1980. 639p. ISBN:0-313-22381-5, ISBN13: 978-0-313-22381-5. Dewey:109/.04. LCCN:80-000539.

Audience: **g,l,u.** *B*

Canfield, John V. (Editor)   **B804**
Philosophy of Meaning, Knowledge and Value in the 20th Century. Trade Paper. Routledge. New York, NY. 2003. 504p. History of Philosophy Ser., Vol. 10 ISBN:0-415-30882-8, ISBN13: 978-0-415-30882-3. Dewey:190.9/04.

Audience: **u,f.**

D'Amico, Robert   **B804.D28 1998**
Contemporary Continental Philosophy. Trade Paper. Westview Press. Boulder, CO. 1998. 280p. Dimensions of Philosophy Ser. ISBN:0-8133-3222-2, ISBN13: 978-0-8133-3222-2. Dewey:190/.9/04. LCCN:98-037834.

Audience: **g,u,f.** *Choice, 1999.*

Floistad, Guttorm (Editor)   **B804**
Contemporary philosophy, a New Survey. Trade Cloth. Martinus-Nijhoff Publishers (N E). 2003. ix, 550p. ISBN:90-247-2436-8, ISBN13: 978-90-247-2436-9. Dewey:190/.9/047 19. LCCN:81-003972.

Audience: **g,u.** *B*

Kearney, Richard (Editor)   **B804.T884 2003**
Continental Philosophy in the 20th Century. Trade Paper. Routledge. New York, NY. 2003. 576p. History of Philosophy Ser., Vol. 8 ISBN:0-415-30880-1, ISBN13: 978-0-415-30880-9. Dewey:190/.9/04. LCCN:2004-445463.

Audience: **u,f.**

Sills, Chip & Jensen, George H. (Editors)   **B804.P536 1992**
The Philosophy of Discourse: The Rhetorical Turn in Twentieth-Century Thought. Paper Text. Heinemann. Portsmouth, NH. 1992. 270p. ISBN:0-86709-286-6, ISBN13: 978-0-86709-286-8. Dewey:149/.94. LCCN:91-14249.

Audience: **g,u,f.**

Sills, Chip & Jensen, George H.   **B804.P536 1992**
The Philosophy of Discourse: The Rhetorical Turn in Twentieth-Century Thought. Paper Text. Heinemann. Portsmouth, NH. 1992. 266p. ISBN:0-86709-287-4, ISBN13: 978-0-86709-287-5. Dewey:149/.94. LCCN:91-14249.

Audience: **g,u,f.**

Soames, Scott   **B808.5.S63 2005**
Philosophical Analysis in the Twentieth Century: The Age of Meaning. Trade Paper. Princeton University Press. Princeton, NJ. 2005. 504p. ISBN:0-691-12312-8, ISBN13: 978-0-691-12312-7. Dewey:146.4.

Audience: **g,l,u,f.**

Soames, Scott   **B808.5.S63 2005**
Philosophical Analysis in the Twentieth Century: The Dawn of Analysis. Trade Paper. Princeton University Press. Princeton, NJ. 2005. 432p. ISBN:0-691-12244-X, ISBN13: 978-0-691-12244-1. Dewey:146/.4.

Audience: **g,l,u,f.** *Choice, 2004.*

Philosophy by Country > American Philosophy

Flower, E. & Murphey, M. G. B851.F56 1977
A History of Philosophy in America, Vol. 1. Trade Cloth. Hackett Publishing Company, Inc. Indianapolis, IN. 1977. 480p. ISBN:0-399-11650-8, ISBN13: 978-0-399-11650-6. Dewey:191. LCCN:75-040254.

Audience: **g,l,u.** ℬ

Kuklick, Bruce B851.K85 2003
A History of Philosophy in America, 1720-2000. Trade Paper. Oxford University Press, Inc. New York, NY. 2003. 342p. ISBN:0-19-926016-8, ISBN13: 978-0-19-926016-4. Dewey:191.

Audience: **g,l,u,f.**

Marsoobian, Armen & Ryder, John B851.B49 2004
The Blackwell Guide to American Philosophy. Trade Cloth. Blackwell Publishing, Inc. Malden, MA. 2004. 432p. Blackwell Philosophy Guides Ser., Vol. 16 ISBN:0-631-21622-7, ISBN13: 978-0-631-21622-3. Dewey:191. LCCN:2003-020353.

Audience: **g,l,u,f.**

Smith, John B893 .S63 1983
The Spirit of American Philosophy. Paper Text. State University of New York Press. Albany, NY. 1983. 253p. SUNY Series in Philosophy ISBN:0-87395-651-6, ISBN13: 978-0-87395-651-2. Dewey:191. LCCN:82-005612.

Audience: **g,l,u.**

Philosophy by Country > American Philosophy > 19th Century

Bird, Graham B945.J24B39 1999
James. Paper over Boards. Routledge. New York, NY. 1999. 232p. Arguments of the Philosophers Ser. ISBN:0-415-20381-3, ISBN13: 978-0-415-20381-4. Dewey:191. LCCN:00-687930.

Audience: **g,u,f.**

Emerson, Ralph Waldo PS1602.A86 2000
The Essential Writings of Ralph Waldo Emerson. Brooks Atkinson (Editor). Random House Adult Trade Publishing Group. 2000. Modern Library Classics ISBN:0-679-78322-9, ISBN13: 978-0-679-78322-0.

Audience: **g,l,u.**

James, William B945.J23E7 2003
Essays in Radical Empiricism. Trade Paper. Dover Publications, Inc. Mineola, NY. 2003. 160p. ISBN:0-486-43094-4, ISBN13: 978-0-486-43094-2. Dewey:146/.44. LCCN:2003-053261.

Audience: **g,u,f.** ℬ

James, William B945.J23W5
Will to Believe and Other Essays in Popular Philosophy and

Human Immortality. Trade Cloth. Peter Smith Publisher, Inc. Magnolia, MA. 1990. ISBN:0-8446-2313-X, ISBN13: 978-0-8446-2313-9. Dewey:191.

Audience: **g,l,u,f.**

James, William (Editor), et al. B945.J2
The Correspondence of William James. John J. McDermott, Ignas K. Skrupskelis & Elizabeth M. Berkeley (Editors). Trade Cloth. University Press of Virginia. Charlottesville, VA. 2003. 800p. ISBN:0-8139-2149-X, ISBN13: 978-0-8139-2149-5. Dewey:191. LCCN:91-035923.

Audience: **g,u,f.**

Lachs, John B945.S24
On Santayana. Trade Paper, Perfect. Thomson Wadsworth. Belmont, CA. 2005. 112p. Wadsworth Philosophers Ser. ISBN:0-534-58382-2, ISBN13: 978-0-534-58382-8. Dewey:191. LCCN:2005-934289.

Audience: **g,l,u.**

Marcel, Gabriel B945
Royce's Metaphysics. Virginia Ringer & Gordon Ringer (Translators). Trade Cloth. Greenwood Publishing Group, Inc. Portsmouth, NH. 1975. 180p. ISBN:0-8371-7978-5, ISBN13: 978-0-8371-7978-0. Dewey:110/.92/4. LCCN:74-033746.

Audience: **g,u.** ℬ

Menand, Louis E169.1.M546 2001
The Metaphysical Club: A Story of Ideas in America. Cloth over Boards. Farrar, Straus & Giroux. New York, NY. 2001. 384p. ISBN:0-374-19963-9, ISBN13: 978-0-374-19963-0. Dewey:973.9. LCCN:00-066279.

Audience: **g,l,u,f.** *Choice, 2002.*

Perry, Ralph B. B945.J24P42 1996
The Thought and Character of William James. Charlene H. Seigfried (Introduction by). Trade Paper. Vanderbilt University Press. Nashville, TN. 1996. 424p. Vanderbilt Library of American Philosophy ISBN:0-8265-1279-8, ISBN13: 978-0-8265-1279-6. Dewey:191 B. LCCN:96-032306.

Audience: **g,u,f.**

Royce, Josiah B945.R63.M48 1998
Metaphysics. Richard Hocking, Frank Oppenheim & William Ernest Hocking (Editors). Cloth Text. State University of New York Press. Albany, NY. 1998. 352p. SUNY Series in Philosophy ISBN:0-7914-3865-1, ISBN13: 978-0-7914-3865-7. Dewey:110. LCCN:97-047449.

Audience: **g,u,f.** *Choice, 1999.*

Royce, Josiah B945
The Philosophy of Josiah Royce. John K. Roth (Editor, Introduction by). Trade Paper. Hackett Publishing Company, Inc. Indianapolis, IN. 1982. 429p. HPC Classics Ser. ISBN:0-915145-41-3, ISBN13: 978-0-915145-41-6. Dewey:191. LCCN:82-002932.

Audience: **g,u,f.** ℬ

Audience: g=general, l=lower division undergraduate, u=upper division undergraduate, f=faculty.

439

Santayana, George   **B945.S23L7 1998**
The Life of Reason. Trade Cloth. Prometheus Books, Publishers.
Amherst, NY. 1998. 512p. Great Books in Philosophy
ISBN:1-57392-210-2, ISBN13: 978-1-57392-210-4. Dewey:191.
LCCN:98-015125.
Audience: **g,l,u,f.**

Santayana, George   **BH39**
The Sense of Beauty. Trade Paper. Dover Publications, Inc.
Mineola, NY. 1955. 168p. ISBN:0-486-20238-0, ISBN13:
978-0-486-20238-9. Dewey:111/.85.
Audience: **g,u,f.**

Santayana, George   **B945.S23**
Skepticism and Animal Faith: Introduction to a System of
Philosophy. Trade Paper. Kessinger Publishing, LLC. Whitefish,
MT. 2005. ISBN:1-4179-0222-1, ISBN13: 978-1-4179-0222-4.
Dewey:149.7.
Audience: **g,u.**

Sprigge, Timothy L. S.   **B945.S24S65 1999**
Santayana. Ed. 2. Paper over Boards. Routledge. New York, NY.
1999. 272p. Arguments of the Philosophers Ser.
ISBN:0-415-20383-X, ISBN13: 978-0-415-20383-8. Dewey:191.
LCCN:00-268662.
Audience: **g,u,f.**

Talisse, Robert & Hester,   **B945.J24T35 2004**
 Micah
On James. Trade Paper. Thomson Wadsworth. Belmont, CA.
2003. 104p. Wadsworth Philosophers Ser. ISBN:0-534-58397-0,
ISBN13: 978-0-534-58397-2. Dewey:191. LCCN:2004-299957.
Audience: **u,f.**

Philosophy by Country > American Philosophy > 19th Century > Peirce

Brent, Joseph   **B945.P44B73 1993**
Charles Sanders Peirce: A Life. Trade Cloth. Indiana University
Press. Bloomington, IN. 1993. 412p. ISBN:0-253-31267-1,
ISBN13: 978-0-253-31267-9. Dewey:191 B. LCCN:92-019888.
Audience: **g,u,f.** *Choice, 1993.*

Corrington, Robert S.   **B945.P44 C67 1993**
An Introduction to C. S. Peirce: Philosopher, Semiotician, and
Ecstatic Naturalist. Trade Paper. Rowman & Littlefield
Publishers, Inc. Lanham, MD. 1993. 188p. ISBN:0-8476-7814-8,
ISBN13: 978-0-8476-7814-3. Dewey:191. LCCN:92-040976.
Audience: **g,u,f.**

de Waal, Cornelis   **B945.P44D493 2001**
On Peirce. Trade Paper. Thomson Wadsworth. Belmont, CA.
2000. 96p. Wadsworth Philosophers Ser. ISBN:0-534-58376-8,
ISBN13: 978-0-534-58376-7. Dewey:191. LCCN:2001-271345.
Audience: **g,l,u.**

Houser, Nathan & Kloesel,   **B945.P4125 1992**
 Christian J.
The Essential Peirce: Selected Philosophical Writings,
1867-1893. Trade Cloth. Indiana University Press. Bloomington,

IN. 1992. 446p. Essential Peirce Ser., Vol. 1
ISBN:0-253-32849-7, ISBN13: 978-0-253-32849-6. Dewey:191.
LCCN:91-032113.
Audience: **u,f.** *Choice, 1993.*

Misak, Cheryl (Editor)   **B945.P44C36 2004**
The Cambridge Companion to Peirce. Trade Cloth. Cambridge
University Press. New York, NY. 2004. 376p. Cambridge
Companions to Philosophy Ser. ISBN:0-521-57006-9, ISBN13:
978-0-521-57006-0. Dewey:191. LCCN:2003-061744.
Audience: **u,f.** *Choice, 2005.*

Peirce, Charles Sanders   **B945.P4**
Writings of Charles S. Peirce: A Chronological Edition, Vol. 4:
1879-1884. Trade Cloth. Indiana University Press. Bloomington,
IN. 1989. 768p. ISBN:0-253-37204-6, ISBN13:
978-0-253-37204-8. Dewey:191. LCCN:79-001993.
Audience: **g,u,f.**

Peirce, Charles Sanders   **B945.P43R43 1992**
Reasoning and the Logic of Things. Kenneth L. Ketner &
Hilary Putnam (Introduction by). Trade Paper. Harvard
University Press. Cambridge, MA. 1992. 312p.
ISBN:0-674-74967-7, ISBN13: 978-0-674-74967-2. Dewey:160.
LCCN:92-001038.
Audience: **u,f.** *Choice, 1993.*

Peirce, Charles Sanders   **B945.P4**
Writings of Charles S. Peirce: A Chronological Edition: Vol. 2,
1867-1871. Christian J. Kloesel, Max H. Fisch, Don Robers &
Lynn A. Ziegler (Editors). Trade Cloth. Indiana University Press.
Bloomington, IN. 1984. 704p. ISBN:0-253-37202-X, ISBN13:
978-0-253-37202-4. Dewey:191. LCCN:79-001993.
Audience: **g,u,f.**

Peirce, Charles Sanders   **B945.P4**
Writings of Charles S. Peirce: A Chronological Edition: Vol. 3,
1872-1878. Christian J. Kloesel, Max H. Fisch, Lynn A. Ziegler,
Don D. Roberts, Nathan Houser, Aleta House, Ursula Niklas &
Edward C. Moore (Editors). Trade Cloth. Indiana University
Press. Bloomington, IN. 1986. 672p. ISBN:0-253-37203-8,
ISBN13: 978-0-253-37203-1. Dewey:191. LCCN:79-001993.
Audience: **g,u,f.**

Peirce, Charles Sanders   **B945.P4 1982**
Writings of Charles S. Peirce: A Chronological Edition: Vol. 1,
1857-1866. Edward C. Moore, Max H. Fisch, Christian J.
Kloesel, Don D. Roberts, Lynn A. Ziegler & Norma P. Atkinson
(Editors). Trade Cloth. Indiana University Press. Bloomington,
IN. 1982. 738p. ISBN:0-253-37201-1, ISBN13:
978-0-253-37201-7. Dewey:191. LCCN:79-001993.
Audience: **g,u,f.** *B*

Peirce, Charles Sanders   **B945P37F5 1982**
Writings of Charles S. Peirce: A Chronological Edition, Vol. 5,
1884-1886. Peirce Edition Project Staff (Compiled by). Trade
Cloth. Indiana University Press. Bloomington, IN. 1993. 592p.
ISBN:0-253-37205-4, ISBN13: 978-0-253-37205-5. Dewey:191.
LCCN:79-001993.
Audience: **g,u,f.** *Choice, 1994.*

Peirce, Charles Sanders   **B945.P41**
Charles S. Peirce: Selected Writings. Philip P. Wiener (Editor).
Trade Paper. Dover Publications, Inc. Mineola, NY. 1966. 446p.
ISBN:0-486-21634-9, ISBN13: 978-0-486-21634-8. Dewey:191.

Audience: **g,u,f.**

Philosophy by Country > American Philosophy > 20th and 21st Centuries

Ben-Menahem, Yemina   **B945.P874H54 2004**
(Editor)
Hilary Putnam. Trade Paper. Cambridge University Press. New
York, NY. 2005. 284p. Contemporary Philosophy in Focus Ser.
ISBN:0-521-01254-6, ISBN13: 978-0-521-01254-6. Dewey:191.
LCCN:2004-048193.

Audience: **u,f.**

Brook, Andrew & Ross, Don   **B945.D394 D36 2002**
(Editors)
Daniel Dennett. Trade Cloth. Cambridge University Press. New
York, NY. 2002. 316p. Contemporary Philosophy in Focus Ser.
ISBN:0-521-80394-2, ISBN13: 978-0-521-80394-6. Dewey:191.
LCCN:2001-037489.

Audience: **u,f.**

Brook, Andrew & Ross, Don   **B945.D394 D36 2002**
(Editors)
Daniel Dennett. Trade Paper. Cambridge University Press. New
York, NY. 2002. 316p. Contemporary Philosophy in Focus Ser.
ISBN:0-521-00864-6, ISBN13: 978-0-521-00864-8. Dewey:191.
LCCN:2001-037489.

Audience: **u,f.**

Danto, Arthur C.   **D16.8 .D23 1968**
Analytical Philosophy of History. Cambridge University Press.
1965. ISBN:0-521-04768-4, ISBN13: 978-0-521-04768-5.

Audience: **u,f.**

Davidson, Donald   **B105.A35**
Essays on Actions and Events: Philosophical Essays Volume 1.
Trade Cloth. Oxford University Press, Inc. New York, NY. 1980.
320p. ISBN:0-19-824529-7, ISBN13: 978-0-19-824529-2.
Dewey:128/.4. LCCN:80-040064.

Audience: **u,f.** *B*

Davidson, Donald   **B105**
Essays on Actions and Events. Ed. 2. Trade Paper. Oxford
University Press, Inc. New York, NY. 2001. 346p. Philosophical
Essays Ser. ISBN:0-19-924627-0, ISBN13: 978-0-19-924627-4.
Dewey:128/.4. LCCN:2002-278425.

Audience: **u,f.**

Davidson, Donald   **B945.D381L47 2006**
The Essential Davidson. Trade Cloth. Oxford University Press,
Inc. New York, NY. 2006. 288p. ISBN:0-19-928885-2, ISBN13:
978-0-19-928885-4. Dewey:191. LCCN:2005-020560.

Audience: **u,f.**

Davidson, Donald   **BC177**
Problems of Rationality, Vo. 4. Trade Cloth. Oxford University
Press, Inc. New York, NY. 2004. 300p. ISBN:0-19-823754-5,
ISBN13: 978-0-19-823754-9. Dewey:192. LCCN:2004-299798.

Audience: **u,f.**

Davidson, D. & Hintikka, K.   **NK3634.A2W67 1991**
J. (Editors)
Words and Objections: Essays on the Work of W. V. Quine.
Trade Cloth. Springer. New York, NY. 1975. 381p. Synthese
Library, No. 21 ISBN:90-277-0074-5, ISBN13:
978-90-277-0074-2. Dewey:745.6/19951.

Audience: **u,f.**

Fotion, Nick   **B1649.S264F68 2000**
John Searle. Trade Cloth. Princeton University Press. Princeton,
NJ. 2001. 256p. Philosophy Now Ser. ISBN:0-691-05711-7,
ISBN13: 978-0-691-05711-8. Dewey:191. LCCN:00-107340.

Audience: **g,u,f.** *Choice, 2002.*

Guignon, Charles & Hiley,   **B945.R524R52 2003**
David (Editors)
Richard Rorty. Trade Cloth. Cambridge University Press. New
York, NY. 2003. 222p. Contemporary Philosophy in Focus Ser.
ISBN:0-521-80058-7, ISBN13: 978-0-521-80058-7. Dewey:191.
LCCN:2002-042908.

Audience: **u,f.**

Hahn, Lewis E. (Editor)   **B945.D384P45 1999**
The Philosophy of Donald Davidson. Donald Davidson
(Contribution by). Trade Cloth. Open Court Publishing
Company. Chicago, IL. 1999. 768p. Library of Living
Philosophers, Vol. 27 ISBN:0-8126-9398-1, ISBN13:
978-0-8126-9398-0. Dewey:191. LCCN:99-039735.

Audience: **u,f.**

Hook, Sidney   **JC571**
Philosophy and Public Policy. Southern Illinois University Press.
1981. ISBN:0-8093-1041-4, ISBN13: 978-0-8093-1041-8.

Audience: **g.**

Hook, Sidney   **B945.H683 Q47 1991**
The Quest for Being. Trade Cloth. Prometheus Books,
Publishers. Amherst, NY. 1991. 276p. Great Books in
Philosophy ISBN:0-87975-700-0, ISBN13: 978-0-87975-700-7.
Dewey:191. LCCN:91-061909.

Audience: **g,u,f.**

Langer, Susanne K.   **BF458**
Feeling and Form. Ed. 1. Paper Text. Longman Publishing
Group. White Plains, NY. 1977. 431p. ISBN:0-02-367500-4,
ISBN13: 978-0-02-367500-3. Dewey:153.

Audience: **g,l,u.**

Langer, Susanne K.   **B945.L273 P45 1979**
Philosophical Sketches. Trade Cloth. Ayer Company Publishers,
Inc. Manchester, NH. 1979. ISBN:0-405-10610-6, ISBN13:
978-0-405-10610-1. Dewey:191. LCCN:78-019265.

Audience: **g,u.**

Langer, Susanne K.   **BF458**
Philosophy in a New Key: A Study in the Symbolism of
Reason, Rite, and Art. Ed. 3. Trade Paper. Harvard University
Press. Cambridge, MA. 1957. 334p. ISBN:0-674-66503-1,
ISBN13: 978-0-674-66503-3. Dewey:153. LCCN:57-001386.
Audience: **g,u.**

Lepore, Ernest & Ludwig,   **B945.D384L47 2005**
  Kirk
Donald Davidson: Meaning, Truth, Language, and Reality. Trade
Cloth. Oxford University Press, Inc. New York, NY. 2005. 464p.
ISBN:0-19-925134-7, ISBN13: 978-0-19-925134-6. Dewey:191.
LCCN:2004-024979.
Audience: **u,f.** *Choice, 2005.*

Lovejoy, Arthur Oncken   **B945.L583 E7 1978**
Essays in the History of Ideas. Trade Cloth. Greenwood
Publishing Group, Inc. Portsmouth, NH. 1978. 359p.
ISBN:0-313-20504-3, ISBN13: 978-0-313-20504-0. Dewey:109.
LCCN:78-017473.
Audience: **g,u,f.**

Ludwig, Kirk (Editor)   **B945.D384D65 2003**
Donald Davidson. Trade Cloth. Cambridge University Press.
New York, NY. 2003. 254p. Contemporary Philosophy in Focus
Ser. ISBN:0-521-79043-3, ISBN13: 978-0-521-79043-7.
Dewey:191. LCCN:2002-035082.
Audience: **u,f.**

Malachowski, Alan   **B945.SR524**
Richard Rorty. Cloth Text. Princeton University Press.
Princeton, NJ. 2002. 200p. Philosophy Now Ser.
ISBN:0-691-05707-9, ISBN13: 978-0-691-05707-1. Dewey:191.
Audience: **g,u,f.** *Choice, 2003.*

Mead, George Herbert   **B945.M463P5 2002**
The Philosophy of the Present. Trade Paper. Prometheus Books,
Publishers. Amherst, NY. 2004. 240p. Great Books in
Philosophy ISBN:1-57392-948-4, ISBN13: 978-1-57392-948-6.
Dewey:191. LCCN:2001-048788.
Audience: **g,u,f.** *B*

Mead, George Herbert   **B945**
Selected Writings. Andrew J. Reck (Editor). Trade Paper.
University of Chicago Press. Chicago, IL. 1981. 488p.
ISBN:0-226-51671-7, ISBN13: 978-0-226-51671-4. Dewey:191.
LCCN:80-027048.
Audience: **g,l,u.** *B*

Pittman, John P.   **B944.A37C66 2002**
A Companion to African-American Philosophy. Tommy Lee Lott
(Editor). Trade Cloth. Blackwell Publishing, Inc. Malden, MA.
2003. 488p. Blackwell Companions to Philosophy Ser., Vol. 25

ISBN:1-55786-839-5, ISBN13: 978-1-55786-839-8.
Dewey:191/.089/96073. LCCN:2002-066640.
Audience: **u,f.** *Choice, 2003.*

Putnam, Hilary   **B808.5**
Words and Life. James Conant (Introduction by). Trade Paper.
Harvard University Press. Cambridge, MA. 1995. 608p.
ISBN:0-674-95607-9, ISBN13: 978-0-674-95607-0.
Dewey:146.4.
Audience: **g,u,f.** *Choice, 1994.*

Rorty, Richard McKay   **B945 .R52 1991 VOL.**
Essays on Heidegger and Others: Philosophical Papers, Vol. 2.
Cloth Text. Cambridge University Press. New York, NY. 1991.
212p. ISBN:0-521-35370-X, ISBN13: 978-0-521-35370-0.
Dewey:191. LCCN:90-020328.
Audience: **u,f.** *Choice, 1991.*

Rorty, Richard McKay   **B945 .R52 1991**
Objectivity, Relativism, and Truth: Philosophical Papers, Vol. 1.
Trade Paper. Cambridge University Press. New York, NY. 1990.
236p. ISBN:0-521-35877-9, ISBN13: 978-0-521-35877-4.
Dewey:191. LCCN:90-041632.
Audience: **g,u,f.** *Choice, 1991.*

Schmidtz, David (Editor)   **B945.N684 R63 2002**
Robert Nozick. Trade Paper. Cambridge University Press. New
York, NY. 2002. 240p. Contemporary Philosophy in Focus Ser.
ISBN:0-521-00671-6, ISBN13: 978-0-521-00671-2. Dewey:191.
LCCN:2001-035263.
Audience: **g,u,f.**

Searle, J. R. (Editor)   **B840.S38**
The Philosophy of Language. Paper Text. Oxford University
Press, Inc. New York, NY. 1971. 156p. Oxford Readings in
Philosophy Ser. ISBN:0-19-875015-3, ISBN13:
978-0-19-875015-4. Dewey:401. LCCN:70-027065.
Audience: **g,u,f.** *B*

Searle, John R.   **B840**
Speech Acts: An Essay in the Philosophy of Language. Trade
Paper. Cambridge University Press. New York, NY. 1969. 212p.
ISBN:0-521-09626-X, ISBN13: 978-0-521-09626-3.
Dewey:149.94. LCCN:68-024484.
Audience: **g,u,f.** *B*

Smith, Barry (Editor)   **B1649.S264J63 2003**
John Searle. Trade Paper. Cambridge University Press. New
York, NY. 2003. 304p. Contemporary Philosophy in Focus Ser.
ISBN:0-521-79704-7, ISBN13: 978-0-521-79704-7. Dewey:191.
LCCN:2002-038846.
Audience: **g,u,f.**

Wheeler, Darrell   B945.D384W44 2003
On Davidson. Trade Paper. Thomson Wadsworth. Belmont, CA.
2002. 104p. Wadsworth Philosophers Ser. ISBN:0-534-58395-4,
ISBN13: 978-0-534-58395-8. Dewey:191. LCCN:2002-514827.
                                        Audience: **g,l,u.**

Philosophy by Country > American Philosophy > 20th and 21st Centuries > Dewey

Bernstein, Richard J.   B945.D44 B43
John Dewey. Paper Text. Ridgeview Publishing Company.
Atascadero, CA. 1981. 214p. ISBN:0-917930-15-0, ISBN13:
978-0-917930-15-7. Dewey:191.
                                        Audience: **g,u,f.** *B*

Boisvert, Raymond D.   B945.D4B65 1998
John Dewey: Rethinking Our Time. Paper Text. State University
of New York Press. Albany, NY. 1997. 189p. Suny Series,
Philosophy of Education Ser. ISBN:0-7914-3530-X, ISBN13:
978-0-7914-3530-4. Dewey:191. LCCN:96-052291.
                                        Audience: **g,l,u.** *Choice, 1998.*

Dewey, John   B945.D41
The Early Works of John Dewey, 1882-1898. Jo Ann Boydston
(Editor). Trade Paper. Southern Illinois University Press.
Carbondale, IL. ISBN:0-318-55567-0, ISBN13:
978-0-318-55567-6. Dewey:150. LCCN:67-013938.
                                        Audience: **g,l,u,f.**

Dewey, John   B945 .D41
The Middle Works of John Dewey, 1899-1924. Jo Ann
Boydston (Editor). Trade Paper. Southern Illinois University
Press. Carbondale, IL. ISBN:0-318-55568-9, ISBN13:
978-0-318-55568-3. Dewey:370.1/092/4. LCCN:76-007231.
                                        Audience: **g,l,u,f.**

Dewey, John   B945
1933: Essays and "How We Think". Jo Ann Boydston (Editor),
Richard McKay Rorty (Introduction by). Trade Cloth. Southern
Illinois University Press. Carbondale, IL. 1986. 435p.
ISBN:0-8093-1246-8, ISBN13: 978-0-8093-1246-7. Dewey:191.
LCCN:80-027285.
                                        Audience: **g,l,u,f.** *Choice, 1986.*

Geiger, George Raymond   B945.D44C53
John Dewey in Perspective. Paper Text. Textbook Publishers.
Temecula, CA. 2003. 248p. ISBN:0-7581-6857-8, ISBN13:
978-0-7581-6857-3. Dewey:370.1.
                                        Audience: **g,u,f.** *B*

Hickman, Larry A. &   B945.D41H53 1998
 Alexander, Thomas M. (Editors)
The Essential Dewey: Ethics, Logic, Psychology. Trade Cloth.
Indiana University Press. Bloomington, IN. 1998. 488p.
ISBN:0-253-33391-1, ISBN13: 978-0-253-33391-9. Dewey:191.
LCCN:97-043936.
                                        Audience: **g,u,f.** *Choice, 1999.*

Hickman, Larry A. &   B945.D41H53 1998
 Alexander, Thomas M. (Editors)
The Essential Dewey: Pragmatism, Education, Democracy.
Trade Cloth. Indiana University Press. Bloomington, IN. 1998.
488p. ISBN:0-253-33390-3, ISBN13: 978-0-253-33390-2.
Dewey:191. LCCN:97-043936.
                                        Audience: **g,u,f.** *Choice, 1999.*

Schilpp, Paul Arthur   B945 .D41
The Philosophy of John Dewey. Paper Text. Textbook
Publishers. Temecula, CA. 2003. 718p. ISBN:0-7581-3058-9,
ISBN13: 978-0-7581-3058-7. Dewey:191.
                                        Audience: **g,u,f.** *B*

Tiles, Jim E.   B945.D44T55 1999
Dewey. Paper over Boards. Routledge. New York, NY. 1999.
276p. Arguments of the Philosophers Ser. ISBN:0-415-20384-8,
ISBN13: 978-0-415-20384-5. Dewey:191. LCCN:00-268663.
                                        Audience: **g,u,f.** *Choice, 1989.*

Philosophy by Country > American Philosophy > 20th and 21st Centuries > Quine

Gibson, Roger F. Jr. (Editor)   B945.Q54C36 2004
The Cambridge Companion to Quine. Cloth Text. Cambridge
University Press. New York, NY. 2004. 344p. Cambridge
Companions to Philosophy Ser. ISBN:0-521-63056-8, ISBN13:
978-0-521-63056-6. Dewey:191. LCCN:2003-055313.
                                        Audience: **u,f.** *Choice, 2004.*

Gibson, Roger F.   B945.Q54
The Philosophy of W. V. Quine: An Expository Essay. Willard
V. Quine (Foreword by). Trade Paper. University Press of
Florida. Gainesville, FL. 1986. 228p. ISBN:0-8130-0855-7,
ISBN13: 978-0-8130-0855-4. Dewey:191.
                                        Audience: **u,f.**

Hahn, Lewis E. & Schilpp,   B945.Q54P48 1986
 Paul Arthur (Editors)
The Philosophy of W. V. Quine. Ed. 2. Trade Paper. Open Court
Publishing Company. Chicago, IL. 1982. 728p. Library of
Living Philosophers, Vol. XVIII ISBN:0-8126-9010-9, ISBN13:
978-0-8126-9010-1. Dewey:191. LCCN:86-017980.
                                        Audience: **g,u,f.** *Choice, 1987.*

Hylton, P   B945
Quine. Cloth Text. Routledge. New York, NY. 1998. The
Arguments of the Philosophers Ser. ISBN:0-415-06398-1,
ISBN13: 978-0-415-06398-2. Dewey:191.
                                        Audience: **u,f.**

Quine, Willard V.   B945.Q54A3 1995
From Stimulus to Science. Trade Cloth. Harvard University
Press. Cambridge, MA. 1995. 124p. ISBN:0-674-32635-0,
ISBN13: 978-0-674-32635-4. Dewey:121. LCCN:95-014062.
                                        Audience: **g,u,f.**

Quine, Willard V.   B840.Q49
Ontological Relativity and Other Essays. Cloth Text. Columbia
University Press. New York, NY. 1977. viii, 165p. John Dewey
Lectures, No. 1 ISBN:0-231-03307-9, ISBN13:
978-0-231-03307-7. Dewey:110. LCCN:72-091121.

Audience: **u,f.** 𝓑

Quine, Willard V.   B945.Q53P87 1990
Pursuit of Truth. Trade Cloth. Harvard University Press.
Cambridge, MA. 1990. 128p. ISBN:0-674-73950-7, ISBN13:
978-0-674-73950-5. Dewey:121. LCCN:89-034224.

Audience: **g,u,f.** *Choice, 1990.*

Quine, Willard V.   BC51
The Ways of Paradox and Other Essays. Ed. 2. Trade Paper.
Harvard University Press. Cambridge, MA. 1976. 350p.
ISBN:0-674-94837-8, ISBN13: 978-0-674-94837-2. Dewey:160.
LCCN:75-019554.

Audience: **g,u,f.** 𝓑

Quine, Willard V.   B840
Word and Object. Trade Paper. MIT Press. Cambridge, MA.
1964. 309p. Studies in Communication ISBN:0-262-67001-1,
ISBN13: 978-0-262-67001-2. Dewey:149.94. LCCN:60-009621.

Audience: **g,u,f.**

Van Orman Quine, Willard   B945.P44
The Time of My Life: An Autobiography. Trade Paper. MIT
Press. Cambridge, MA. 2000. 499p. ISBN:0-262-67004-6,
ISBN13: 978-0-262-67004-3. Dewey:191 B.

Audience: **g,u,f.** *Choice, 1985.*

Philosophy by Country > Latin American Philosophy

Gracia, Jorge J. E. (Editor)   B29.L295 1986
Latin American Philosophy in the Twentieth Century: Man,
Values and the Search for Philosophical Identity. Trade Paper.
Prometheus Books, Publishers. Amherst, NY. 1986. 269p.
Frontiers of Philosophy Ser. ISBN:0-87975-333-1, ISBN13:
978-0-87975-333-7. Dewey:199/.8. LCCN:86-091551.

Audience: **g,l,u.** *Choice, 1987.*

Mendieta, Eduardo (Editor)   B1001.L38 2003
Latin American Philosophy: Currents, Issues, Debates. Trade
Cloth. Indiana University Press. Bloomington, IN. 2003. 256p.
ISBN:0-253-34180-9, ISBN13: 978-0-253-34180-8.
Dewey:199/.8. LCCN:2002-008760.

Audience: **g,l,u.** *Choice, 2003.*

Mendieta, Eduardo &   F1414.L277 2001
  Lange-Churion, Pedro (Editors)
Latin America and Postmodernity: A Contemporary Reader.
Trade Paper. Prometheus Books, Publishers. Amherst, NY. 2001.
317p. ISBN:1-57392-911-5, ISBN13: 978-1-57392-911-0.
Dewey:980.03/3. LCCN:2001-016831.

Audience: **g,u.**

Millán-Zaibert, Elizabeth &   B1001.R649 2005
  Salles, Arleen (Editors)
The Role of History in Latin American Philosophy:
Contemporary Perspectives. Cloth Text. State University of New
York Press. Albany, NY. 2005. 256p. SUNY Series in Latin
American and Iberian Thought and Culture
ISBN:0-7914-6427-X, ISBN13: 978-0-7914-6427-4.
Dewey:199/.8. LCCN:2004-016074.

Audience: **u,f.** *Choice, 2006.*

Nuccetelli, Susana   B1001
Latin American Thought: Philosophical Problems and
Arguments. Trade Paper. Westview Press. Boulder, CO. 2001.
292p. ISBN:0-8133-6553-8, ISBN13: 978-0-8133-6553-4.
Dewey:199.8.

Audience: **g,u,f.** *Choice, 2002.*

Zea, Leopoldo   B1018.P6
Positivism in Mexico. Josephine H. Schulte (Translator). Trade
Cloth. University of Texas Press. Austin, TX. 1974. 265p. Texas
Pan American Ser. ISBN:0-292-76413-8, ISBN13:
978-0-292-76413-2. Dewey:146/.4/0972. LCCN:74-000549.

Audience: **g,u,f.** 𝓑

Philosophy by Country > British Philosophy > 19th Century

Anschutz, R. P.   B1607
The Philosophy of J. S. Mill. Trade Cloth. Greenwood
Publishing Group, Inc. Portsmouth, NH. 1986. 196p.
ISBN:0-313-25040-5, ISBN13: 978-0-313-25040-8. Dewey:192.
LCCN:85-027075.

Audience: **u,f.**

Atkinson, Charles M.   B1574 .B34A7 1970
Jeremy Bentham: His Life and Work. Trade Cloth. Greenwood
Publishing Group, Inc. Portsmouth, NH. 1970. 247p.
ISBN:0-8371-3243-6, ISBN13: 978-0-8371-3243-3. Dewey:192.
LCCN:78-098208.

Audience: **g,u.**

August, Eugene R.   B1607.A95
John Stuart Mill: A Mind at Large. Trade Cloth. Simon &
Schuster. New York, NY. 1975. xii, 276p. ISBN:0-684-14232-5,
ISBN13: 978-0-684-14232-6. Dewey:192. LCCN:75-012649.

Audience: **g,l,u.** 𝓑

Bentham, Jeremy & Hart,   B1574.B33I5 1996
  H. L. A.
An Introduction to the Principles of Morals and Legislation. Ed.
2. J. H. Burns & H. L. Hart (Editors), F. Rosen (Introduction
by). Paper Text. Oxford University Press, Inc. New York, NY.
1996. 456p. The Collected Works of Jeremy Bentham Ser.
ISBN:0-19-820516-3, ISBN13: 978-0-19-820516-6.
Dewey:340/.112. LCCN:96-136001.

Audience: **g,u,f.**

Capaldi, Nicholas   **B1606.C36 2003**
John Stuart Mill: A Biography. Trade Cloth. Cambridge
University Press. New York, NY. 2004. 456p.
ISBN:0-521-62024-4, ISBN13: 978-0-521-62024-6. Dewey:192
B. LCCN:2003-051546.
                              Audience: **g,l,u.** *Choice, 2004.*

Crisp, Roger   **B1603.U873C75 1997**
Routledge Philosophy Guidebook to Mill on Utilitarianism.
Trade Paper. Routledge. New York, NY. 1997. 256p. Philosophy
Guidebooks ISBN:0-415-10978-7, ISBN13: 978-0-415-10978-9.
Dewey:171.5. LCCN:97-001476.
                                          Audience: **u,f.**

Donner, Wendy   **B1607.D58 1991**
The Liberal Self: John Stuart Mill's Moral and Political
Philosophy. Book, Other. Cornell University Press. Ithaca, NY.
1991. 256p. ISBN:0-8014-2629-4, ISBN13: 978-0-8014-2629-2.
Dewey:171/.5/092. LCCN:91-055065.
                              Audience: **g,u,f.** *Choice, 1992.*

Harrison, Ross   **B1574.B34H37 1999**
Bentham. Paper over Boards. Routledge. New York, NY. 1999.
312p. Arguments of the Philosophers Ser. ISBN:0-415-20362-7,
ISBN13: 978-0-415-20362-3. Dewey:192. LCCN:00-551809.
                                    Audience: **u,f.** *B*

Mill, James   **B1596**
The Collected Works of James Mill, Set. Library Binding.
Routledge. New York, NY. 1992. 2324p. Collected Works Ser.
ISBN:0-415-08105-X, ISBN13: 978-0-415-08105-4.
Dewey:181.3.
                                       Audience: **g,l,u,f.**

Mill, John Stuart   **JC585.M6 2002**
The Basic Writings of John Stuart Mill: On Liberty, the
Subjection of Women and Utilitarianism. J. B. Schneewind
(Introduction by). Trade Paper. Random House Adult Trade
Publishing Group. New York, NY. 2002. 400p.
ISBN:0-375-75918-2, ISBN13: 978-0-375-75918-5.
Dewey:323.44. LCCN:2002-066028.
                                       Audience: **g,l,u,f.**

Mill, John Stuart   **B1571.M6 2001**
Utilitarianism. Ed. 2. George Sher (Editor). Trade Cloth. Hackett
Publishing Company, Inc. Indianapolis, IN. 2002. 72p. Classics
Ser. ISBN:0-87220-606-8, ISBN13: 978-0-87220-606-9.
Dewey:171/.5. LCCN:2001-039619.
                               Audience: **g,l,u,f.** *B*

Skorupski, John (Editor)   **B1607 .C25 1998**
The Cambridge Companion to Mill. Trade Paper. Cambridge
University Press. New York, NY. 1998. 607p. Cambridge
Companions to Philosophy Ser. ISBN:0-521-42211-6, ISBN13:
978-0-521-42211-6. Dewey:192. LCCN:97-002968.
                               Audience: **g,u,f.** *Choice, 1998.*

Skorupski, John   **B1607.S56 1999**
Mill. Paper over Boards. Routledge. New York, NY. 1999. 448p.
Arguments of the Philosophers Ser. ISBN:0-415-20365-1,
ISBN13: 978-0-415-20365-4. Dewey:192. LCCN:00-269383.
                                       Audience: **g,u,f.**

Philosophy by Country > British Philosophy > 20th and 21st Centuries

Ambrose, Alice   **B1647.M74.A65**
G. E. Moore: Essays in Retrospect. Paper over Boards.
Routledge. New York, NY. 2004. 376p. Muirhead Library of
Philosophy Ser. ISBN:0-415-29537-8, ISBN13:
978-0-415-29537-6. Dewey:192.
                                    Audience: **u,f.** *B*

Austin, J. L.   **B3376.W564**
Philosophical Papers. Ed. 3. J. O. Urmson & Geoffrey J.
Warnock (Editors). Paper Text. Oxford University Press, Inc.
New York, NY. 1990. 316p. ISBN:0-19-283021-X, ISBN13:
978-0-19-283021-0. Dewey:192.
                                  Audience: **g,u,f.** *B*

Austin, J. L.   **P302**
How to Do Things with Words. Ed. 2. J. O. Urmsson & Marina
Sbisa (Editors). Trade Paper. Harvard University Press.
Cambridge, MA. 1975. 188p. ISBN:0-674-41152-8, ISBN13:
978-0-674-41152-4. Dewey:401/.41.
                                  Audience: **g,u,f.** *B*

Ayer, Alfred Jules   **B53**
Language, Truth and Logic. Trade Cloth. Peter Smith Publisher,
Inc. Magnolia, MA. 1990. ISBN:0-8446-1571-4, ISBN13:
978-0-8446-1571-4. Dewey:101.
                                       Audience: **g,l,u.**

Baldwin, Thomas   **B1647.M74B35 1999**
Moore. Paper over Boards. Routledge. New York, NY. 1999.
352p. Arguments of the Philosophers Ser. ISBN:0-415-20377-5,
ISBN13: 978-0-415-20377-7. Dewey:192. LCCN:00-268660.
                                       Audience: **g,u,f.**

Bradley, F. H.   **BD111.B8 1969**
Appearance and Reality: A Metaphysical Essay. Trade Cloth.
Oxford University Press, Inc. New York, NY. 1969. xxvi, 570p.
ISBN:0-19-881150-0, ISBN13: 978-0-19-881150-3. Dewey:110.
LCCN:79-405526.
                                  Audience: **g,u,f.** *B*

Corvi, Roberta   **B1649.P64C66613 1997**
Introduction to the Thought of Karl Popper. Patrick Camiller
(Translator). Paper over Boards. Routledge. New York, NY.
1996. 224p. ISBN:0-415-12956-7, ISBN13: 978-0-415-12956-5.
Dewey:192. LCCN:96-007922.
                                       Audience: **g,u,f.**

Foster, John L.   **B1618.A94F67 1999**
Ayer. Paper over Boards. Routledge. New York, NY. 1999.
324p. Arguments of the Philosophers Ser. ISBN:0-415-20389-9,
ISBN13: 978-0-415-20389-0. Dewey:192. LCCN:00-699838.
                               Audience: **g,u,f.** *Choice, 1986.*

Keuth, Herbert   **B1649.P64K4813 2004**
The Philosophy of Karl Popper. Cloth Text. Cambridge
University Press. New York, NY. 2004. 384p.

ISBN:0-521-83946-7, ISBN13: 978-0-521-83946-4. Dewey:192.
LCCN:2004-045179.

Audience: **u,f.** *Choice, 2005.*

Leclerc, Ivor   **B1674.W354 L38**
Relevance of Whitehead: Philosophical Essays in
Commemoration of the Centenary of the Birth of Alfred North
Whitehead. Paper over Boards. Routledge. New York, NY. 2004.
384p. Muirhead Library of Philosophy Ser.
ISBN:0-415-29598-X, ISBN13: 978-0-415-29598-7.
Dewey:192.1.

Audience: **g,u,f.** ℬ

Lewis, H. D.   **B1615**
Contemporary British Philosophy: Personal Statements Fourth
Series. Paper over Boards. Routledge. New York, NY. 2004.
352p. Muirhead Library of Philosophy Ser.
ISBN:0-415-29547-5, ISBN13: 978-0-415-29547-5. Dewey:192.

Audience: **g,u,f.**

Lewis, H. D.   **B1615 .C653**
Contemporary British Philosophy: Personal Statements Third
Series. Paper over Boards. Routledge. New York, NY. 2004.
520p. Muirhead Library of Philosophy Ser.
ISBN:0-415-29546-7, ISBN13: 978-0-415-29546-8. Dewey:192.

Audience: **g,u,f.**

Magee, Bryan   **B1649.P64**
Popper. Paper over Boards. Taylor & Francis Group.
Philadelphia, PA. 1974. 109p. ISBN:0-7130-0109-7, ISBN13:
978-0-7130-0109-9. Dewey:192.

Audience: **g,u,f.**

Mehta, Ved   **B1615.M43**
Fly and the Fly: Bottle. Paper Text. Textbook Publishers.
Temecula, CA. 2003. 269 pp. ISBN:0-7581-9649-0, ISBN13:
978-0-7581-9649-1. Dewey:192.

Audience: **g,l,u,f.** ℬ

Moore, G. E.   **B1647.M71 1993**
G. E. Moore: Selected Writings. Thomas Baldwin (Editor).
Paper over Boards. Routledge. New York, NY. 1993. 232p.
International Library of Philosophy, Psychology, and Scientific
Method ISBN:0-415-09853-X, ISBN13: 978-0-415-09853-3.
Dewey:192. LCCN:93-016366.

Audience: **u,f.**

Moore, G. E.   **B1647.M73 P74 1993**
Principia Ethica. Ed. 2. Thomas Baldwin (Editor). Trade Paper.
Cambridge University Press. New York, NY. 1993. 352p.
ISBN:0-521-44848-4, ISBN13: 978-0-521-44848-2.
Dewey:171/.2. LCCN:93-006493.

Audience: **g,u,f.** ℬ

Moore, G. E.   **BJ1011**
Ethics. William H. Shaw (Editor). Trade Cloth. Oxford
University Press, Inc. New York, NY. 2005. 224p. British Moral
Philosophers Ser. ISBN:0-19-927200-X, ISBN13:
978-0-19-927200-6. Dewey:170. LCCN:2005-019318.

Audience: **g,u,f.** ℬ

Moore, George Edward   **B1647.M73 P38**
Philosophical Papers. Paper over Boards. Routledge. New York,
NY. 2004. 328p. Muirhead Library of Philosophy Ser.
ISBN:0-415-29551-3, ISBN13: 978-0-415-29551-2. Dewey:108.

Audience: **u,f.**

Muirhead, J. H.   **B1615 .C6**
Contemporary British Philosophy: Personal Statements Second
Series. Paper over Boards. Routledge. New York, NY. 2004.
368p. Muirhead Library of Philosophy Ser.
ISBN:0-415-29555-6, ISBN13: 978-0-415-29555-0. Dewey:192.

Audience: **g,l,u,f.**

Muirhead, J. H.   **B1615**
Contemporary British Philosophy: Personal Statements First
Series. Paper over Boards. Routledge. New York, NY. 2004.
432p. Muirhead Library of Philosophy Ser.
ISBN:0-415-29554-8, ISBN13: 978-0-415-29554-3. Dewey:192.

Audience: **g,l,u,f.**

O'Hear, Anthony   **B1649.P64O35 1999**
Popper. Paper over Boards. Routledge. New York, NY. 1999.
232p. Arguments of the Philosophers Ser. ISBN:0-415-20388-0,
ISBN13: 978-0-415-20388-3. Dewey:192. LCCN:00-267876.

Audience: **u,f.**

Popper, Karl R.   **B1649.P63 P37 1984**
Popper Selections. David W. Miller (Editor). Trade Paper.
Princeton University Press. Princeton, NJ. 1985. 480p.
ISBN:0-691-02031-0, ISBN13: 978-0-691-02031-0. Dewey:192.
LCCN:83-043084.

Audience: **g,u,f.**

Ramsey, F. P.   **B1649.R252 R36 1990**
F. P. Ramsey: Philosophical Papers. David H. Mellor (Editor).
Trade Paper. Cambridge University Press. New York, NY. 1990.
285p. ISBN:0-521-37621-1, ISBN13: 978-0-521-37621-1.
Dewey:192. LCCN:89-038814.

Audience: **u,f.**

Ryle, Gilbert   **B1649.R961 1971**
Collected Papers. Trade Cloth. Barnes & Noble, Inc. New York,
NY. 1971. ISBN:0-389-04112-2, ISBN13: 978-0-389-04112-2.
Dewey:192. LCCN:70-028252.

Audience: **u,f.** ℬ

Schilpp, Paul Arthur   **B1647.M74**
 (Editor)
The Philosophy of G. E. Moore. Trade Cloth. Open Court
Publishing Company. Chicago, IL. 1942. 745p. Library of
Living Philosophers, Vol. IV ISBN:0-87548-136-1, ISBN13:
978-0-87548-136-4. Dewey:192. LCCN:68-057206.

Audience: **u,f.** ℬ

Strawson, P. F.   **B840**
Logico-Linguistic Papers. Ed. 2. Trade Cloth. Ashgate
Publishing, Ltd. Aldershot, 2004. 210p. ISBN:0-7546-3724-7,
ISBN13: 978-0-7546-3724-0. Dewey:149/.94.
LCCN:2003-043683.

Audience: **u,f.**

Formats: Web: ▢   Ebook: ℯ   CD/DVD-ROM: 🦋   BCL3: ℬ

Warnlock, Geoffrey   B1618.A84W37 1989
J. L. Austin. Trade Cloth. Routledge. New York, NY. 1989.
240p. ISBN:0-415-02962-7, ISBN13: 978-0-415-02962-9.
Dewey:192. LCCN:88-032338.

Audience: **g,u,f.** *Choice, 1989.*

Warnock, Geoffrey J.   B1615 .W3 1982
English Philosophy Since Nineteen Hundred. Ed. 2. Trade Cloth.
Greenwood Publishing Group, Inc. Portsmouth, NH. 1982. 126p.
ISBN:0-313-23545-7, ISBN13: 978-0-313-23545-0. Dewey:192.
LCCN:82-006123.

Audience: **g,l,u,f.**

Whitehead, Alfred North   B1674.W351
Alfred North Whitehead: An Anthology. Paper Text. Textbook
Publishers. Temecula, CA. 2003. 928p. ISBN:0-7581-9020-4,
ISBN13: 978-0-7581-9020-8. Dewey:192.9.

Audience: **g,l,u,f.** *B*

Whitehead, Alfred North   B1674.W353D5
Dialogues of Alfred North Whitehead. Paper Text. Textbook
Publishers. Temecula, CA. 2003. 396p. ISBN:0-7581-9689-X,
ISBN13: 978-0-7581-9689-7. Dewey:192.

Audience: **g,l,u,f.**

Whitehead, Alfred North   QB981
Process and Reality: An Essay in Cosmology. Ed. 2. Trade
Paper. Simon & Schuster. New York, NY. 1979. 448p. Gifford
Lectures ISBN:0-02-934570-7, ISBN13: 978-0-02-934570-2.
Dewey:523.1. LCCN:77-090011.

Audience: **g,u,f.** *B*

Philosophy by Country > British Philosophy > 20th and 21st Centuries > Russell

Ayer, Alfred Jules   B1649.R94A86 1988
Bertrand Russell. Trade Paper. University of Chicago Press.
Chicago, IL. 1988. 175p. ISBN:0-226-03343-0, ISBN13:
978-0-226-03343-3. Dewey:192. LCCN:87-034279.

Audience: **g,l,u.**

Grayling, A. C.   B1649.R94G743 2002
Russell: A Very Short Introduction. Trade Paper. Oxford
University Press, Inc. New York, NY. 2002. 144p. Very Short
Introductions Ser., Vol. 59 ISBN:0-19-280258-5, ISBN13:
978-0-19-280258-3. Dewey:192 B. LCCN:2002-514396.

Audience: **g,l,u.**

Griffin, Nicholas (Editor)   B1649.R94C36 2003
The Cambridge Companion to Bertrand Russell. Trade Cloth.
Cambridge University Press. New York, NY. 2003. 568p.
Cambridge Companions to Philosophy Ser.
ISBN:0-521-63178-5, ISBN13: 978-0-521-63178-5. Dewey:192.
LCCN:2002-031367.

Audience: **u,f.**

Russell, Bertrand   B1649.R94 A3 2000
The Autobiography of Bertrand Russell. Ed. 2. Trade Paper.
Routledge. New York, NY. 2000. 760p. ISBN:0-415-22862-X,
ISBN13: 978-0-415-22862-6. Dewey:192. LCCN:2001-272204.

Audience: **g,l,u,f.** *B*

Russell, Bertrand   B1649.R91
Basic Writings of Bertrand Russell. Trade Paper. Routledge.
New York, NY. 2001. 744p. ISBN:0-415-08301-X, ISBN13:
978-0-415-08301-0. Dewey:192.

Audience: **g,u,f.**

Russell, Bertrand   B1649.R94
Cambridge Essays, 1888-99. Kenneth Blackwell, Andrew Brink
& Nicholas Griffin (Editors). Paper over Boards. Routledge.
New York, NY. 1988. 600p. Collected Papers of Bertrand
Russell, Vol. 1 ISBN:0-04-920067-4, ISBN13:
978-0-04-920067-8. Dewey:192. LCCN:83-015865.

Audience: **u,f.**

Sainsbury, R. M.   B1649.R94S24 1999
Russell. Paper over Boards. Routledge. New York, NY. 1999.
364p. Arguments of the Philosophers Ser. ISBN:0-415-20379-1,
ISBN13: 978-0-415-20379-1. Dewey:192. LCCN:00-713436.

Audience: **g,u,f.**

Tait, Katharine   B1649.R94.T34
My Father, Bertrand Russell. Trade Cloth. Harcourt College
Publishers. Fort Worth, TX. 1975. xii, 211p.
ISBN:0-15-130432-7, ISBN13: 978-0-15-130432-5. Dewey:192.
LCCN:75-015719.

Audience: **g,l,u,f.** *B*

Philosophy by Country > British Philosophy > 17th Century

Ayers, Michael   B1294.A94 1999
Locke. Paper over Boards. Routledge. New York, NY. 1999.
700p. Arguments of the Philosophers Ser. ISBN:0-415-20359-7,
ISBN13: 978-0-415-20359-3. Dewey:192. LCCN:00-268312.

Audience: **g,l,u,f.** *Choice, 1992.*

Bacon, Francis   B11902001B
The Advancement of Learning. Trade Paper. Random House
Adult Trade Publishing Group. New York, NY. 2001. 254p.
ISBN:0-375-75846-1, ISBN13: 978-0-375-75846-1. Dewey:121.
LCCN:2001-030611.

Audience: **g,u,f.** *B*

Bacon, Francis   B1168.E5A5
The New Organon, and Related Writings. Paper Text. Classic
Books. Murrieta, CA. 2001. Collected Works of Sir Francis
Bacon ISBN:0-7426-7034-1, ISBN13: 978-0-7426-7034-1.
Dewey:112.

Audience: **g,l,u.** *B*

Bacon, Francis   PR2205
Francis Bacon: The Major Works. Brian Vickers (Editor). Trade

Paper. Oxford University Press, Inc. New York, NY. 2002. 862p. Oxford World's Classics Ser. ISBN:0-19-284081-9, ISBN13: 978-0-19-284081-3. Dewey:824/.3. LCCN:2002-727711.

Audience: **g,l,u.**

Chappell, Vere (Editor)   **B1297 .C29 1994**
The Cambridge Companion to Locke. Trade Paper. Cambridge University Press. New York, NY. 1994. 343p. Cambridge Companions to Philosophy Ser. ISBN:0-521-38772-8, ISBN13: 978-0-521-38772-9. Dewey:192. LCCN:93-033190.

Audience: **u,f.** *Choice, 1995.*

Conway, Anne   **B1201.C553 P7416 19**
Anne Conway: The Principles of the Most Ancient and Modern Philosophy. Allison P. Coudert (Editor). Cambridge University Press. 1996. Texts in the History of Philosophy ISBN:0-521-47335-7, ISBN13: 978-0-521-47335-4.

Audience: **g,u,f.**

Dunn, John   **B1296**
Locke: A Very Short Introduction. Ed. 2. Trade Paper. Oxford University Press, Inc. New York, NY. 2003. 136p. Very Short Introductions Ser. ISBN:0-19-280394-8, ISBN13: 978-0-19-280394-8. Dewey:192.

Audience: **g,l,u.**

Gaukroger, Stephen   **B1198 .G38 2001**
Francis Bacon and the Transformation of Early-Modern Philosophy. Trade Cloth. Cambridge University Press. New York, NY. 2001. 202p. ISBN:0-521-80154-0, ISBN13: 978-0-521-80154-6. Dewey:192. LCCN:00-063097.

Audience: **g,u,f.**

Hobbes, Thomas   **SF85.35.S88**
The English Works of Thomas Hobbes, Set. Trade Cloth. Library Reprints, Inc. Temecula, CA. 1962. ISBN:0-7222-2032-4, ISBN13: 978-0-7222-2032-0. Dewey:633.2.

Audience: **g,l,u.**

Hobbes, Thomas & Gaskin,   **JC153.H65 1998**
J. C. A.
e The Leviathan. E-Book. NetLibrary, Inc. Boulder, CO. 1998. ISBN:0-585-19328-2, ISBN13: 978-0-585-19328-1. Dewey:320.1.

Audience: **g,l,u,f.**

Jenkins, J. J.   **B1294**
Understanding Locke. Trade Paper. Edinburgh University Press. Edinburgh, 1983. 192p. ISBN:0-85224-449-5, ISBN13: 978-0-85224-449-4. Dewey:121. LCCN:83-151780.

Audience: **g,u.** *B*

Locke, John   **B1255.L49 2002**
Essays on the Law of Nature: The Latin Text with a Translation, Introduction and Notes, Together with Transcripts of Locke's Shorthand in His Journal for 1676. Ed. 2. Trade Paper. Oxford University Press, Inc. New York, NY. 2002. 306p. ISBN:0-19-925421-4, ISBN13: 978-0-19-925421-7. Dewey:192. LCCN:2002-029056.

Audience: **u,f.**

Locke, John   **B1291.L63 1996**
An Essay Concerning Human Understanding. Kenneth Winkler (Editor). Trade Cloth. Hackett Publishing Company, Inc. Indianapolis, IN. 1996. 416p. HPC Classics Ser. ISBN:0-87220-217-8, ISBN13: 978-0-87220-217-7. Dewey:121. LCCN:96-026935.

Audience: **u,f.** *B*

Locke, John   **BD161**
An Essay Concerning Human Understanding. Kenneth Winkler (Editor). Trade Paper. Hackett Publishing Company, Inc. Indianapolis, IN. 1996. 416p. HPC Classics Ser. ISBN:0-87220-216-X, ISBN13: 978-0-87220-216-0. Dewey:121. LCCN:96-026935.

Audience: **g,u,f.** *B*

Lowe, E. J.   **B1297.L69 2005**
Locke. Paper over Boards. Routledge. New York, NY. 2005. XIV, 226p. The Routledge Philosophers Ser. ISBN:0-415-28347-7, ISBN13: 978-0-415-28347-2. Dewey:192. LCCN:2004-017847.

Audience: **g,l,u,f.**

Lowe, E. J.   **B1294.L65 1995**
Locke on Human Understanding. Trade Paper. Routledge. New York, NY. 1995. 216p. Routledge Philosophy Guidebooks Ser. ISBN:0-415-10091-7, ISBN13: 978-0-415-10091-5. Dewey:121. LCCN:94-043131.

Audience: **l,u,f.**

Martinich, A. P.   **B1247.M38 2005**
Hobbes. Trade Cloth. Routledge. New York, NY. 2005. 14+266p. Routledge Philosophers Ser. ISBN:0-415-28327-2, ISBN13: 978-0-415-28327-4. Dewey:192 B. LCCN:2004-024124.

Audience: **g,u,f.**

Newey, Glen   **JA71**
Routledge Philosophy Guidebook to Hobbes and Leviathan. Trade Paper. Routledge. New York, NY. 2006. 224p. Routledge Philosophy Guidebooks ISBN:0-415-22435-7, ISBN13: 978-0-415-22435-2. Dewey:320/.01.

Audience: **g,u,f.**

Peltonen, Markku (Editor)   **B1198 .C265 1996**
The Cambridge Companion to Bacon. Trade Paper. Cambridge University Press. New York, NY. 1996. 392p. Cambridge Companions to Philosophy Ser. ISBN:0-521-43534-X, ISBN13: 978-0-521-43534-5. Dewey:192. LCCN:95-026405.

Audience: **u,f.**

Schouls, Peter A.   **B1297.S295 1992**
Reasoned Freedom: John Locke and Enlightenment. Book, Other. Cornell University Press. Ithaca, NY. 1992. 256p. ISBN:0-8014-8037-X, ISBN13: 978-0-8014-8037-9. Dewey:192. LCCN:92-052771.

Audience: **g,l,u,f.** *Choice, 1993.*

Sorell, Tom (Editor)   **B1247 .C26 1996**
The Cambridge Companion to Hobbes. Trade Paper. Cambridge University Press. New York, NY. 1996. 416p. Cambridge

Companions to Philosophy Ser. ISBN:0-521-42244-2, ISBN13: 978-0-521-42244-4. Dewey:192. LCCN:95-008796.

Audience: **u,f.** *Choice, 1996.*

Sorell, Tom   **B1247.S63 1999**
Hobbes. Paper over Boards. Routledge. New York, NY. 1999. 176p. Arguments of the Philosophers Ser. ISBN:0-415-20358-9, ISBN13: 978-0-415-20358-6. Dewey:192. LCCN:00-268522.

Audience: **g,u,f.**

Yolton, John W.   **B1253**
  (Introduction by)
Collected Works of John Locke: Collected Works. Library Binding. Routledge. New York, NY. 1997. 4640p. Collected Works Ser. ISBN:0-415-15384-0, ISBN13: 978-0-415-15384-3. Dewey:192.

Audience: **g,l,u,f.**

Yolton, John W.   **B1297.Y6 1968**
John Locke and the Way of Ideas. Trade Cloth. Oxford University Press, Inc. New York, NY. 1968. x, 235p. ISBN:0-19-824331-6, ISBN13: 978-0-19-824331-1. Dewey:121. LCCN:76-389586.

Audience: **g,u,f.** ℬ

Yolton, John W.   **B1294.Y66 2004**
The Two Intellectual Worlds of John Locke: Man, Person, and Spirits in the Essay. Book, Other. Cornell University Press. Ithaca, NY. 2004. 224p. ISBN:0-8014-4290-7, ISBN13: 978-0-8014-4290-2. Dewey:121. LCCN:2004-010282.

Audience: **g,u,f.** *Choice, 2005.*

Zagorin, Perez   **B1197**
Francis Bacon. Trade Paper. Princeton University Press. Princeton, NJ. 1999. 304p. ISBN:0-691-00966-X, ISBN13: 978-0-691-00966-7. Dewey:192. LCCN:97-041404.

Audience: **u,f.** *Choice, 1998.*

Philosophy by Country > British Philosophy > 18th Century

Atherton, Margaret   **B1302.E6E46 1998**
The Empiricists: Critical Essays on Locke, Berkeley, and Hume. Trade Cloth. Rowman & Littlefield Publishers, Inc. Lanham, MD. 1999. 278p. Critical Essays on the Classics Ser. ISBN:0-8476-8912-3, ISBN13: 978-0-8476-8912-5. Dewey:146/.44. LCCN:98-039077.

Audience: **u,f.**

Bennett, Jonathan   **B1111**
Locke, Berkeley, Hume: Central Themes. Paper Text. Oxford University Press, Inc. New York, NY. 1971. 372p. ISBN:0-19-875016-1, ISBN13: 978-0-19-875016-1. Dewey:192.

Audience: **g,l,u.**

Berkeley, George   **B1326.D36 1998**
Three Dialogues Between Hylas and Philonous. Jonathan Dancy (Editor). Paper Text. Oxford University Press, Inc. New York,

NY. 1998. 192p. Oxford Philosophical Texts ISBN:0-19-875149-4, ISBN13: 978-0-19-875149-6. Dewey:192. LCCN:97-012129.

Audience: **g,u,f.** ℬ

Berkeley, George   **B1331.D38 1998**
A Treatise Concerning the Principles of Human Knowledge. Jonathan Dancy (Editor). Paper Text. Oxford University Press, Inc. New York, NY. 1998. 244p. Oxford Philosophical Texts ISBN:0-19-875161-3, ISBN13: 978-0-19-875161-8. Dewey:121. LCCN:97-012131.

Audience: **g,l,u.** ℬ

Berkeley, George   **B1334 .B47 2000**
Berkeley's Principles and Dialogues: Background Source Materials. C. J. McCracken & I. C. Tipton (Editors), John Cottingham & Daniel Garber (Contribution by). Trade Paper. Cambridge University Press. New York, NY. 2000. 310p. Cambridge Philosophical Texts in Context Ser. ISBN:0-521-49806-6, ISBN13: 978-0-521-49806-7. Dewey:192. LCCN:99-059435.

Audience: **g,u,f.** *Choice, 2000.*

Berkeley, George   **B1305**
Works on Vision. Colin Murray Turbayne (Editor). Trade Cloth. Greenwood Publishing Group, Inc. Portsmouth, NH. 1981. 158p. Library of Liberal Arts, No. 83 ISBN:0-313-23186-9, ISBN13: 978-0-313-23186-5. Dewey:121/.3. LCCN:81-007160.

Audience: **u,f.** ℬ

Berkeley, George   **B1331.W56 1982**
A Treatise Concerning the Principles of Human Knowledge. Kenneth Winkler (Editor, Introduction by). Trade Cloth. Hackett Publishing Company, Inc. Indianapolis, IN. 1982. 156p. HPC Classics Ser. ISBN:0-915145-40-5, ISBN13: 978-0-915145-40-9. Dewey:121. LCCN:82-002876.

Audience: **g,u,f.** ℬ

Berkeley, George   **B1304**
The Works of George Berkeley, Vol. 2. G. N. Wright (Translator). Trade Paper. Kessinger Publishing, LLC. Whitefish, MT. 2004. ISBN:1-4179-2228-1, ISBN13: 978-1-4179-2228-4. Dewey:192.

Audience: **g,u,f.**

Berkeley, George   **B1304**
The Works of George Berkeley, Vol. 1. G. N. Wright (Translator). Trade Paper. Kessinger Publishing, LLC. Whitefish, MT. 2004. ISBN:1-4179-2227-3, ISBN13: 978-1-4179-2227-7. Dewey:192.

Audience: **g,u,f.**

Brown, Stuart (Editor)   **B1302.E65B68 2003**
British Philosophy in the Age of Enlightenment. Trade Paper. Routledge. New York, NY. 2003. 440p. History of Philosophy Ser., Vol. 5 ISBN:0-415-30877-1, ISBN13: 978-0-415-30877-9. Dewey:192.

Audience: **g,u,f.**

Burke, Edmund   **BH181**
Edmund Burke: A Philosophical Inquiry into the Origin of Our
Ideas of the Sublime and Beautiful. James T. Boulton (Editor).
Trade Paper. University of Notre Dame Press. Notre Dame, IN.
1968. 328p. ISBN:0-268-00085-9, ISBN13: 978-0-268-00085-1.
Dewey:111.8/5. LCCN:68-027583.

Audience: **g,u,f.**

Copleston, Frederick   **B 72.C62 2003**
British Philosophy: Hobbes to Hume, Vol. 5. Trade Paper.
Continuum International Publishing Group, Ltd. London, 2003.
448p. ISBN:0-8264-6899-3, ISBN13: 978-0-8264-6899-4.
Dewey:109.

Audience: **g,l,u.**

Cuneo, Terence & van   **B1537.C36 2004**
  Woudenberg, Rene
The Cambridge Companion to Thomas Reid. Cloth Text.
Cambridge University Press. New York, NY. 2004. 392p.
Cambridge Companions to Philosophy Ser.
ISBN:0-521-81270-4, ISBN13: 978-0-521-81270-2. Dewey:192.
LCCN:2003-051249.

Audience: **u,f.**

Darwall, Stephen   **B1131 .D37 1995**
The British Moralists and the Internal "Ought": 1640-1740.
Trade Cloth. Cambridge University Press. New York, NY. 1995.
368p. ISBN:0-521-45167-1, ISBN13: 978-0-521-45167-3.
Dewey:170/.941/09032. LCCN:94-021945.

Audience: **g,u,f.** *Choice, 1996.*

Fogelin, Robert J.   **B1334.F64 2001**
Routledge Philosophy Guidebook to Berkeley and the Principles
of Human Knowledge. Paper over Boards. Routledge. New
York, NY. 2001. 176p. Philosophy Guidebooks
ISBN:0-415-25010-2, ISBN13: 978-0-415-25010-8. Dewey:121.
LCCN:00-054869.

Audience: **g,u,f.**

Hutcheson, Francis   **BJ654**
A System of Moral Philosophy. Continuum International
Publishing Group, Ltd. 2005. ISBN:0-8264-8815-3, ISBN13:
978-0-8264-8815-2.

Audience: **g,u.**

Hutcheson, Francis   **BJ1005.H88 2004**
An Inquiry into the Original of Our Ideas of Beauty and Virtue:
In Two Treatises. Wolfgang Leidhold (Introduction by). Trade
Cloth. Liberty Fund, Inc. Indianapolis, IN. 2004. 258p. Natural
Law and Enlightenment Classics Ser. ISBN:0-86597-428-4,
ISBN13: 978-0-86597-428-9. Dewey:171/.2.
LCCN:2003-065286.

Audience: **g,u.** *B*

Hutcheson, Francis   **B1501 .O5 1993**
Hutcheson: Two Texts on Human Nature. Thomas Mautner
(Editor). Cloth Text. Cambridge University Press. New York,
NY. 1993. 208p. ISBN:0-521-43089-5, ISBN13:
978-0-521-43089-0. Dewey:171.2. LCCN:92-023820.
Audience: **g,l,u,f.** *Choice, 1994.*

Lehrer, Keith   **B1537.L44 1989**
Thomas Reid. Trade Cloth. Routledge. New York, NY. 1989.
400p. ISBN:0-415-03886-3, ISBN13: 978-0-415-03886-7.
Dewey:192. LCCN:88-032337.

Audience: **u,f.** *Choice, 1990.*

Penelhum, Terence   **B1363.Z7P46 1999**
Butler. Paper over Boards. Routledge. New York, NY. 1999.
232p. Arguments of the Philosophers Ser. ISBN:0-415-20364-3,
ISBN13: 978-0-415-20364-7. Dewey:192. LCCN:00-267239.
Audience: **u,f.** *Choice, 1986.*

Pitcher, George   **B1349.M47P57 1999**
Berkeley. Paper over Boards. Routledge. New York, NY. 1999.
292p. Arguments of the Philosophers Ser. ISBN:0-415-20356-2,
ISBN13: 978-0-415-20356-2. Dewey:192. LCCN:00-269386.
Audience: **g,u,f.** *B*

Porter, Roy   **B1302.E65P67 2000**
The Creation of the Modern World: The Untold Story of the
British Enlightenment. Trade Cloth. W. W. Norton & Company,
Inc. New York, NY. 2000. 608p. ISBN:0-393-04872-1, ISBN13:
978-0-393-04872-8. Dewey:941.07. LCCN:00-049632.
Audience: **l,u,f.** *Choice, 2001.*

Reid, Thomas   **B1532**
Inquiry and Essays. Ronald E. Beanblossom & Keith Lehrer
(Editors). Trade Paper. Hackett Publishing Company, Inc.
Indianapolis, IN. 1983. lxii, 430p. HPC Classics Ser.
ISBN:0-915145-85-5, ISBN13: 978-0-915145-85-0. Dewey:192.
LCCN:83-022864.

Audience: **u,f.**

Reid, Thomas   **BD450**
Essays on the Active Powers of Man. Rene Wellek (Editor).
Library Binding. Garland Publishing, Inc. New York, NY. 1977.
vii, 493p. British Philosophers and Theologians of the 17th and
18th Centuries Ser., Vol. 50 ISBN:0-8240-1802-8, ISBN13:
978-0-8240-1802-3. Dewey:128/.4. LCCN:75-011251.

Audience: **u,f.**

Smith, Adam   **BJ1005 .S6 2002**
Adam Smith: The Theory of Moral Sentiments. Knud
Haakonssen (Editor). Cambridge University Press. 2002.
ISBN:0-521-59847-8, ISBN13: 978-0-521-59847-7.

Audience: **g,u,f.**

Warnock   **B1348**
Berkeley. Trade Cloth. Ashgate Publishing Company. Williston,
VT. 1993. 240p. ISBN:0-7512-0118-9, ISBN13:
978-0-7512-0118-5. Dewey:192.

Audience: **g,u,f.**

Winkler, Kenneth P.   **B1348.W56 1989**
Berkeley: An Interpretation. Trade Cloth. Oxford University
Press, Inc. New York, NY. 1989. 332p. ISBN:0-19-824907-1,
ISBN13: 978-0-19-824907-8. Dewey:192. LCCN:88-025116.
Audience: **u,f.** *Choice, 1990.*

Philosophy by Country > British Philosophy > 18th Century > Hume

Ayer, Alfred Jules   **B1498.A95 2000**
Hume: A Very Short Introduction. Trade Paper. Oxford
University Press, Inc. New York, NY. 2001. 136p. Very Short
Introductions Ser., Vol. 33 ISBN:0-19-285406-2, ISBN13:
978-0-19-285406-3. Dewey:192. LCCN:2001-268448.
Audience: **g,l,u.**

Baier, Annette C.   **B1489.B35 1991**
A Progress of Sentiments: Reflections on Hume's Treatise.
Trade Cloth. Harvard University Press. Cambridge, MA. 1991.
352p. ISBN:0-674-71385-0, ISBN13: 978-0-674-71385-7.
Dewey:128. LCCN:90-005124.
Audience: **g,u,f.** *Choice, 1991.*

Beauchamp, Thomas L. &   **B1499.C38.B4**
  Rosenberg, Alexander
Hume and the Problem of Causation. Trade Cloth. Oxford
University Press, Inc. New York, NY. 1981. 366p.
ISBN:0-19-520236-8, ISBN13: 978-0-19-520236-6. Dewey:122.
LCCN:80-020259.
Audience: **u,f.** *B*

Bricke, John   **B1499.E8B67 1996**
Mind and Morality: An Examination of Hume's Moral
Psychology. Trade Cloth. Oxford University Press, Inc. New
York, NY. 1996. 274p. ISBN:0-19-823589-5, ISBN13:
978-0-19-823589-7. Dewey:192. LCCN:95-046828.
Audience: **u,f.** *Choice, 1997.*

Flew, Antony G.   **B1484**
Hume's Philosophy of Belief: A Study of His First Inquiry.
Trade Paper. Continuum International Publishing Group, Ltd.
London, 1997. 295p. Key Texts Ser. ISBN:1-85506-548-7,
ISBN13: 978-1-85506-548-2. Dewey:192.
Audience: **g,u,f.**

Hume, David   **B1480 2000**
An Enquiry Concerning Human Understanding. Thomas L.
Beauchamp (Editor). Cloth Text. Oxford University Press, Inc.
New York, NY. 2001. 452p. The Clarendon Edition of the
Works of David Hume Ser. ISBN:0-19-825060-6, ISBN13:
978-0-19-825060-9. Dewey:121. LCCN:00-035610.
Audience: **g,l,u,f.**

Hume, David   **B1455.L4**
Of the Standard of Taste and Other Essays. John W. Lenz
(Editor). Trade Paper. Macmillan Publishing Company, Inc. Old
Tappan, NJ. 1965. xxviii, 183p. ISBN:0-672-60269-5, ISBN13:
978-0-672-60269-6. Dewey:192. LCCN:64-066070.
Audience: **g,l,u,f.** *B*

Hume, David   **BL180.H78 1998**
Dialogues Concerning Natural Religion and the Natural History
of Religion. Ed. 2. Richard H. Popkin (Editor, Introduction by).

Trade Cloth. Hackett Publishing Company, Inc. Indianapolis, IN.
1998. 125p. Classics Ser. ISBN:0-87220-403-0, ISBN13:
978-0-87220-403-4. Dewey:210. LCCN:97-038335.
Audience: **g,l,u,f.**

Hume, David &   **BJ1012**
  Sayre-McCord, Geoffrey
Moral Philosophy. Trade Cloth. Hackett Publishing Company,
Inc. Indianapolis, IN. 2006. 432p. Hackett Classics Ser.
ISBN:0-87220-600-9, ISBN13: 978-0-87220-600-7. Dewey:170.
LCCN:2006-043572.
Audience: **g,l,u,f.**

Hume, David   **B1485 1978**
A Treatise of Human Nature. Ed. 2. L. A. Selby-Bigge & Peter
H. Nidditch (Editors). Paper Text. Oxford University Press, Inc.
New York, NY. 1978. 764p. ISBN:0-19-824588-2, ISBN13:
978-0-19-824588-9. Dewey:192. LCCN:77-030415.
Audience: **g,u,f.**

Jenkins, John J.   **B1498.U53 1992**
Understanding Hume. Trade Cloth. Rowman & Littlefield
Publishers, Inc. Lanham, MD. 1992. 224p. ISBN:0-389-20986-4,
ISBN13: 978-0-389-20986-7. Dewey:192. LCCN:92-001118.
Audience: **g,u.** *Choice, 1993.*

Livingston, Donald W.   **B1498.L58 1984**
Hume's Philosophy of Common Life. University of Chicago
Press. 1984. ISBN:0-226-48714-8, ISBN13: 978-0-226-48714-4.
Audience: **g,l,u,f.**

Mackie, J. L.   **B2799.E8**
Hume's Moral Theory. Trade Paper. Routledge. New York, NY.
1980. 176p. International Library of Philosophy, Psychology,
and Scientific Method ISBN:0-415-10436-X, ISBN13:
978-0-415-10436-4. Dewey:170/.92/4.
Audience: **g,l,u,f.** *B*

Mossner, E. C.   **B1497.M65 2001**
The Life of David Hume. Ed. 2. Trade Paper. Oxford University
Press, Inc. New York, NY. 2001. 730p. ISBN:0-19-924336-0,
ISBN13: 978-0-19-924336-5. Dewey:192 B. LCCN:00-053036.
Audience: **g,l,u,f.** *B*

Noonan, Harold W.   **B1489.N66 1999**
Routledge Philosophy Guidebook to Hume on Knowledge.
Paper over Boards. Routledge. New York, NY. 1999. 240p.
ISBN:0-415-15046-9, ISBN13: 978-0-415-15046-0. Dewey:128.
LCCN:99-014365.
Audience: **u,f.**

Norton, David Fate (Editor)   **B1498 .C26 1994**
The Cambridge Companion to Hume. Cloth Text. Cambridge
University Press. New York, NY. 1993. 416p. Cambridge
Companions to Philosophy Ser. ISBN:0-521-38273-4, ISBN13:
978-0-521-38273-1. Dewey:192. LCCN:92-047406.
Audience: **u,f.**

Noxon, James   **B1498 .N68**
Hume's Philosophical Development: A Study of His Methods.

Trade Cloth. Oxford University Press, Inc. New York, NY. 1973.
xiv, 197p. ISBN:0-19-824398-7, ISBN13: 978-0-19-824398-4.
Dewey:192. LCCN:73-159942.

Audience: **u,f.** 𝓑

O'Connor, David   **B3279.H49P39 2000**
Routledge Philosophy Guidebook to Hume on Religion. Paper
over Boards. Routledge. New York, NY. 2001. 248p. Philosophy
Guidebooks ISBN:0-415-20194-2, ISBN13: 978-0-415-20194-0.
Dewey:210. LCCN:00-051836.

Audience: **u,f.**

Penelhum, Terence   **B1498.P45 1991**
David Hume: An Introduction to His Philosophical System.
Trade Paper. Purdue University Press. West Lafayette, IN. 1992.
218p. Series in the History of Philosophy ISBN:1-55753-013-0,
ISBN13: 978-1-55753-013-4. Dewey:192. LCCN:91-009096.

Audience: **g,l,u,f.** *Choice, 1993.*

Sessions, William Lad   **B1493.D523S47 2002**
Reading Hume's Dialogues: A Veneration for True Religion.
Trade Cloth. Indiana University Press. Bloomington, IN. 2002.
x, 281p. Indiana Series in the Philosophy of Religion
ISBN:0-253-34116-7, ISBN13: 978-0-253-34116-7. Dewey:210.
LCCN:2001-006741.

Audience: **g,u,f.** *Choice, 2003.*

Stroud, Barry   **B1498.S85 1999**
Hume. Paper over Boards. Routledge. New York, NY. 1999.
292p. Arguments of the Philosophers Ser. ISBN:0-415-20363-5,
ISBN13: 978-0-415-20363-0. Dewey:192. LCCN:00-267240.

Audience: **g,u,f.** 𝓑

Philosophy by Country > French Philosophy > 17th Century

Brundell, Harry   **B1887.B84 1987**
Pierre Gassendi: From Aristotelianism to a New Natural
Philosophy. Trade Cloth. Springer London, Ltd. Guildford, 1987.
268p. Synthese Library, No. 30 ISBN:90-277-2428-8, ISBN13:
978-90-277-2428-1. Dewey:194. LCCN:86-031348.

Audience: **g,u,f.**

Davidson, Hugh M.   **B1903.D35 1983**
Blaise Pascal. Trade Cloth. Thomson Gale. Farmington Hills,
MI. 1983. 165p. World Authors Ser., No. 701
ISBN:0-8057-6548-4, ISBN13: 978-0-8057-6548-9.
Dewey:230/.2. LCCN:83-008438.

Audience: **g,l,u.** 𝓑

Hammond, Nicholas   **B1901.P43**
  (Editor)
The Cambridge Companion to Pascal. Cloth Text. Cambridge
University Press. New York, NY. 2003. 304p. Cambridge
Companions to Philosophy Ser. ISBN:0-521-80924-X, ISBN13:
978-0-521-80924-5. Dewey:194. LCCN:2003-273207.

Audience: **u,f.**

Malebranche, Nicolas   **B1893.E63 E5 1997**
Malebranche: Dialogues on Metaphysics and on Religion.
Nicholas Jolley (Editor), David Scott (Editor, Translator), Karl
Ameriks & Desmond M. Clarke (Contribution by). Trade Paper.
Cambridge University Press. New York, NY. 1997. 330p. Texts
in the History of Philosophy ISBN:0-521-57435-8, ISBN13:
978-0-521-57435-8. Dewey:110. LCCN:96-019806.

Audience: **g,u,f.**

Malebranche, Nicolas   **B1893.R332 E5 1997**
Malebranche: The Search after Truth: With Elucidations of the
Search after Truth. Thomas M. Lennon & Paul J. Olscamp
(Editors), Thomas M. Lennon & Paul J. Olscamp (Translators),
Karl Ameriks & Desmond M. Clarke (Contribution by). Trade
Paper. Cambridge University Press. New York, NY. 1997. 822p.
Texts in the History of Philosophy ISBN:0-521-58995-9,
ISBN13: 978-0-521-58995-6. Dewey:121. LCCN:96-023819.

Audience: **u,f.**

Nadler, Steven (Editor)   **B1897 .C36 2000**
The Cambridge Companion to Malebranche. Cloth Text.
Cambridge University Press. New York, NY. 2000. 332p.
Cambridge Companions to Philosophy Ser.
ISBN:0-521-62212-3, ISBN13: 978-0-521-62212-7. Dewey:194.
LCCN:00-022060.

Audience: **u,f.** *Choice, 2001.*

Pascal, Blaise & Ariew,   **B1901.P42.E5 2004**
  Roger
Pensées. Trade Cloth. Hackett Publishing Company, Inc.
Indianapolis, IN. 2005. 320p. ISBN:0-87220-718-8, ISBN13:
978-0-87220-718-9. Dewey:230/.2. LCCN:2004-021245.

Audience: **g,l,u,f.**

Pascal, Blaise   **B1903**
The Provincial Letters. A. J. Krailsheimer (Translator,
Introduction by). Trade Paper. Penguin Group (USA) Inc. New
York, NY. 1982. 304p. ISBN:0-14-044196-4, ISBN13:
978-0-14-044196-3. Dewey:194.

Audience: **g,l,u,f.**

Pyle, Andrew   **B1897.P95 2002**
Malebranche. Paper over Boards. Routledge. New York, NY.
2003. 320p. The Arguments of the Philosophers Ser.
ISBN:0-415-28911-4, ISBN13: 978-0-415-28911-5. Dewey:194.
LCCN:2002-032459.

Audience: **u,f.** *Choice, 2004.*

Sarasohn, Lisa T. &   **B1887.S27 1996**
  Gassendi, Pierre
Gassendi's Ethics: Freedom in a Mechanistic Universe. Book,
Other. Cornell University Press. Ithaca, NY. 1996. 256p.
ISBN:0-8014-2947-1, ISBN13: 978-0-8014-2947-7.
Dewey:170/.92. LCCN:96-018279.

Audience: **u,f.** *Choice, 1997.*

Philosophy by Country > French Philosophy > 17th Century > Descartes

Almog, Joseph   **BD418**
What Am I?: Descartes and the Mind-Body Problem. Trade
Paper. Oxford University Press, Inc. New York, NY. 2005. 158p.
ISBN:0-19-517719-3, ISBN13: 978-0-19-517719-0.
Dewey:128/.2.

Audience: **u,f.** *Choice, 2002.*

Ariew, Roger & Grene,   **B1875.D37 1995**
  Marjorie (Editors)
Descartes and His Contemporaries: Meditations, Objections, and
Replies. Trade Cloth. University of Chicago Press. Chicago, IL.
1995. 270p. ISBN:0-226-02629-9, ISBN13: 978-0-226-02629-9.
Dewey:194. LCCN:94-006453.

Audience: **g,u,f.** *Choice, 1996.*

Cottingham, John G.   **B1873 .C25 1992**
  (Editor)
The Cambridge Companion to Descartes. Trade Paper.
Cambridge University Press. New York, NY. 1992. 455p.
Cambridge Companions to Philosophy Ser.
ISBN:0-521-36696-8, ISBN13: 978-0-521-36696-0. Dewey:194.
LCCN:91-040483.

Audience: **g,u,f.** *Choice, 1994.*

Cottingham, John G.   **B1873.C67 1986**
Descartes. Trade Paper. Blackwell Publishing, Inc. Malden, MA.
1986. 192p. ISBN:0-631-15046-3, ISBN13: 978-0-631-15046-6.
Dewey:194. LCCN:86-006791.

Audience: **g,l,u,f.** *Choice, 1987.*

Cottingham, John G.   **B1831.C67 1993**
A Descartes Dictionary. Trade Paper. Blackwell Publishing, Inc.
Malden, MA. 1993. 196p. The Blackwell Philosopher
Dictionaries Ser. ISBN:0-631-18538-0, ISBN13:
978-0-631-18538-3. Dewey:194. LCCN:92-039483.

Audience: **g,l,u.**

Curley, E. M.   **B1878.S55.C87**
Descartes Against the Skeptics. Trade Cloth. Harvard University
Press. Cambridge, MA. 1978. 288p. ISBN:0-674-19826-3,
ISBN13: 978-0-674-19826-5. Dewey:194. LCCN:77-014366.

Audience: **u,f.** *B*

Descartes, René   **B1837.A75 2000**
Philosophical Essays and Correspondence. Roger Ariew (Editor).
Trade Cloth. Hackett Publishing Company, Inc. Indianapolis, IN.
2000. 320p. Hackett Classics Ser. ISBN:0-87220-503-7,
ISBN13: 978-0-87220-503-1. Dewey:194. LCCN:99-049303.

Audience: **g,u,f.**

Descartes, René   **B1837 .C67 1984**
The Philosophical Writings of Descartes, Vol. 1. John G.
Cottingham, Dugald Murdoch & Robert Stoothoff (Translators).
Trade Paper. Cambridge University Press. New York, NY. 1985.
432p. ISBN:0-521-28807-X, ISBN13: 978-0-521-28807-1.
Dewey:194. LCCN:84-009399.

Audience: **g,u,f.** *Choice, 1986.*

Descartes, René   **B1837 .C67 1984**
The Philosophical Writings of Descartes, Vol. 2. John G.
Cottingham, Dugald Murdoch & Robert Stoothoff (Translators).
Trade Paper. Cambridge University Press. New York, NY. 1985.
448p. ISBN:0-521-28808-8, ISBN13: 978-0-521-28808-8.
Dewey:194. LCCN:84-009399.

Audience: **g,u,f.** *Choice, 1986.*

Descartes, René   **B1848.E5C73 1998B**
A Discourse on Method and Meditations on First Philosophy.
Ed. 4. Donald Cress (Translator). Trade Cloth. Hackett
Publishing Company, Inc. Indianapolis, IN. 1999. 103p. Classics
Ser. ISBN:0-87220-421-9, ISBN13: 978-0-87220-421-8.
Dewey:194. LCCN:98-038149.

Audience: **g,l,u.**

Descartes, René   **B1863.E53M54 1983**
Rene Descartes: Principles of Philosophy. Valentine R. Miller &
Reese P. Miller (Translators). Trade Cloth. Springer London,
Ltd. Guildford, 1982. 353p. Synthese Library, No. 4
ISBN:90-277-1451-7, ISBN13: 978-90-277-1451-0. Dewey:194.
LCCN:82-018111.

Audience: **g,l,u.** *B*

Descartes, René   **B1858.E5V67 1989**
Passions of the Soul. Stephen H. Voss (Translator). Trade Cloth.
Hackett Publishing Company, Inc. Indianapolis, IN. 1989. 191p.
HPC Classics Ser. ISBN:0-87220-036-1, ISBN13:
978-0-87220-036-4. Dewey:128/.3. LCCN:87-023818.

Audience: **g,u,f.**

Descartes, René   **B1848.E5H35 1996**
A Discourse on Method and Meditations on First Philosophy.
David Weissman (Editor), William T. Bluhm (Contribution by).
Cloth over Boards. Yale University Press. Cumberland, RI.
1996. 400p. Rethinking the Western Tradition Ser.
ISBN:0-300-06772-0, ISBN13: 978-0-300-06772-9. Dewey:194.
LCCN:96-005885.

Audience: **g,l,u.**

Florka, Roger   **B1878.R37F58 2001**
Descartes's Metaphysical Reasoning. Cloth Text. Routledge.
New York, NY. 2001. 136p. Studies in Philosophy Ser.
ISBN:0-8153-4035-4, ISBN13: 978-0-8153-4035-5. Dewey:194.
LCCN:00-067370.

Audience: **g,u,f.**

Gaukroger, Stephen (Editor)   **B1854.B55 2005**
The Blackwell Guide to Descartes' Meditations. Trade Paper.
Blackwell Publishing, Inc. Malden, MA. 2006. 288p. Blackwell
Guides to Great Works ISBN:1-4051-1874-1, ISBN13:
978-1-4051-1874-3. Dewey:194. LCCN:2005-009842.

Audience: **u,f.** *Choice, 2006.*

Gaukroger, Stephen   **B1875.G38 1995**
Descartes: An Intellectual Biography. Trade Cloth. Oxford
University Press, Inc. New York, NY. 1995. 520p.
ISBN:0-19-823994-7, ISBN13: 978-0-19-823994-9. Dewey:194.
LCCN:94-031924.

Audience: **g,l,u,f.**

Gaukroger, Stephen, et al.   B1878.N3D47 2000
Descartes' Natural Philosophy. John A. Schuster & John Sutton
(Authors). Cloth Text. Routledge. New York, NY. 2000. 784p.
Studies in Seventeenth-Century Philosophy, Vol. 3
ISBN:0-415-21993-0, ISBN13: 978-0-415-21993-8.
Dewey:113/.092. LCCN:99-059525.

Audience: **u,f.**

Grene, Marjorie   B1875.G72 1998
Descartes. Trade Cloth. Hackett Publishing Company, Inc.
Indianapolis, IN. 1998. 236p. ISBN:0-87220-405-7, ISBN13:
978-0-87220-405-8. Dewey:194. LCCN:97-043979.

Audience: **g,l,u,f.** *Choice, 1986.*

Hatfield, Gary   B1854.H38 2002
Routledge Philosophy GuideBook to Descartes and Meditations.
Paper over Boards. Routledge. New York, NY. 2002. 384p.
Routledge Philosophy Guidebooks ISBN:0-415-11192-7,
ISBN13: 978-0-415-11192-8. Dewey:194. LCCN:2002-072752.

Audience: **g,l,u.**

Joachim, Harold H. &   B1868.R43 J6 1979
Harris, Errol E.
Descartes's Rules for the Direction of the Mind. David Ross
(Editor). Trade Cloth. Greenwood Publishing Group, Inc.
Portsmouth, NH. 1979. 122p. ISBN:0-313-21263-5, ISBN13:
978-0-313-21263-5. Dewey:160. LCCN:79-009958.

Audience: **u,f.** *B*

Rodis-Lewis, Genevieve   B2430.S34
Descartes: His Life and Thought. Book, Other. Cornell
University Press. Ithaca, NY. 1999. 288p. ISBN:0-8014-8627-0,
ISBN13: 978-0-8014-8627-2. Dewey:194 B. LCCN:97-038681.

Audience: **g,l,u,f.** *Choice, 1998.*

Sarkar, Husain   B1873.S37 2003
Descartes' Cogito: Saved from the Great Shipwreck. Trade
Cloth. Cambridge University Press. New York, NY. 2003. 326p.
ISBN:0-521-82166-5, ISBN13: 978-0-521-82166-7. Dewey:194.
LCCN:2002-073601.

Audience: **g,u,f.** *Choice, 2004.*

Sorell, Tom   B1875.S672 2005
Descartes Reinvented. Trade Cloth. Cambridge University Press.
New York, NY. 2005. 204p. ISBN:0-521-85114-9, ISBN13:
978-0-521-85114-5. Dewey:194. LCCN:2004-024990.

Audience: **u,f.** *Choice, 2006.*

Spinoza, Baruch   B1875 .S8
The Principles of Descartes' Philosophy. Paper Text. Textbook
Publishers. Temecula, CA. 2003. lxxxi, 177p.
ISBN:0-7581-7336-9, ISBN13: 978-0-7581-7336-2. Dewey:194.

Audience: **g,u,f.**

Williams, Bernard   B1875
Descartes: The Project of Pure Enquiry. Perfect, Paper over
Boards. Routledge. New York, NY. 2005. 308p.
ISBN:0-415-35626-1, ISBN13: 978-0-415-35626-8. Dewey:194.
LCCN:2004-029482.

Audience: **g,u,f.**

Wilson, Margaret Dauler   B1875.W58 1999
Descartes. Paper over Boards. Routledge. New York, NY. 1999.
264p. Arguments of the Philosophers Ser. ISBN:0-415-20357-0,
ISBN13: 978-0-415-20357-9. Dewey:194. LCCN:00-269398.

Audience: **g,u,f.**

Philosophy by Country > French Philosophy > 18th Century

Bertram, Christopher   JC179.R88B48 2003
  (Translator)
Routledge Philosophy Guidebook to Rousseau and the Social
Contract. Paper over Boards. Routledge. New York, NY. 2003.
224p. Philosophy Guidebooks ISBN:0-415-20198-5, ISBN13:
978-0-415-20198-8. Dewey:320.1/1. LCCN:2003-046655.

Audience: **g,l,u,f.**

Condillac, Etienne Bonnot   B1983.E82 E5 2001
  de
Condillac: Essay on the Origin of Human Knowledge. Hans
Aarsleff (Edited & Translated by). Cambridge University Press.
2001. Texts in the History of Philosophy ISBN:0-521-58467-1,
ISBN13: 978-0-521-58467-8.

Audience: **g,u,f.**

Dent, Nicholas   B2137.D46 2005
Rousseau. Perfect, Paper over Boards. Routledge. New York,
NY. 2005. XX, 252p. Routledge Philosophers Ser.
ISBN:0-415-28349-3, ISBN13: 978-0-415-28349-6. Dewey:194.
LCCN:2004-021177.

Audience: **g,u,f.**

O'Hagan, Timothy   B2137.O37 2003
Rousseau. Trade Paper. Routledge. New York, NY. 2003. 336p.
The Arguments of the Philosophers Ser. ISBN:0-415-30863-1,
ISBN13: 978-0-415-30863-2. Dewey:194.

Audience: **g,u,f.**

Riley, Patrick   B2137 .C27 2001
The Cambridge Companion to Rousseau. Trade Paper.
Cambridge University Press. New York, NY. 2001. 466p.
Companions to Philosophy Ser. ISBN:0-521-57615-6, ISBN13:
978-0-521-57615-4. Dewey:194. LCCN:2001-018430.

Audience: **g,u,f.**

Rousseau, Jean-Jacques   JC179.R7 2002
The Social Contract: And, the First and Second Discourses.
Susan Dunn (Editor, Introduction by), Gita May, Robert N.
Bellah, David Bromwich & Conor Cruise O'Brien (Contribution
by). Cloth over Boards. Yale University Press. Cumberland, RI.
2002. 328p. Rethinking the Western Tradition Ser.
ISBN:0-300-09140-0, ISBN13: 978-0-300-09140-3.
Dewey:320/.01. LCCN:2001-046557.

Audience: **g,l,u,f.**

Voltaire   B2173.T742 E5 2000
Voltaire: Treatise on Tolerance. Simon Harvey (Editor).
Cambridge University Press. 2000. Texts in the History of
Philosophy ISBN:0-521-64017-2, ISBN13: 978-0-521-64017-6.

Audience: **g,u.**

Philosophy by Country > French Philosophy > 19th Century

Comte, Auguste   **B808.5**
Introduction to Positive Philosophy. Frederick Ferre (Translator, Introduction by). Trade Cloth. Hackett Publishing Company, Inc. Indianapolis, IN. 1988. 86p. HPC Classics Ser. ISBN:0-87220-051-5, ISBN13: 978-0-87220-051-7. Dewey:146/.4. LCCN:87-034831.
Audience: **g,u.**

Copleston, Frederick   **B72**
    Charles
History of Philosophy: Maine de Bira to Sartre. Trade Cloth. Paulist Press. Mahwah, NJ. 1975. 504p. History of Philosophy Ser., IX ISBN:0-8091-0196-3, ISBN13: 978-0-8091-0196-2. Dewey:190.
Audience: **g,l,u.**

Scharff, Robert C.   **B2249.P6 S33 1995**
Comte after Positivism. Robert B. Pippin (Contribution by). Trade Cloth. Cambridge University Press. New York, NY. 1995. 247p. Modern European Philosophy Ser. ISBN:0-521-47488-4, ISBN13: 978-0-521-47488-7. Dewey:194. LCCN:94-044551.
Audience: **g,u,f.**

Wernick, Andrew   **B2249.P6 W47 2001**
Auguste Comte and the Religion of Humanity: The Post-Theistic Program of French Social Theory. Trade Cloth. Cambridge University Press. New York, NY. 2001. 290p. ISBN:0-521-66272-9, ISBN13: 978-0-521-66272-7. Dewey:194. LCCN:00-063093.
Audience: **g,u,f.**

Philosophy by Country > French Philosophy > 20th and 21st Centuries

Althusser, Louis   **B29.A48 1990**
Philosophy and the Spontaneous Philosophy of the Scientists: And Other Essays. Gregory Elliott (Introduction by). Cloth Text. Analytical Psychology Club of San Francisco, Inc. San Francisco, CA. 1990. 375p. ISBN:0-86091-244-2, ISBN13: 978-0-86091-244-6. Dewey:194. LCCN:89-038421.
Audience: **g,u,f.**

Bachelard, Gaston   **B2430.B253F5813 1990**
Fragments of a Poetics of Fire. Kenneth Haltman (Translator), Joanne H. Stroud (Foreword by). Trade Cloth. Dallas Institute Publications, The. Dallas, TX. 1991. 196p. Bachelard Translation Ser. ISBN:0-911005-17-X, ISBN13: 978-0-911005-17-2. Dewey:194. LCCN:90-039813.
Audience: **g,u,f.**

Bachelard, Gaston   **BD638**
Dialectic of Duration. Jones Mary McAllester (Translator), Cristina Chimisso (Introduction by). Trade Paper. Clinamen Press Ltd. Manchester, 2000. 218p. ISBN:1-903083-07-9, ISBN13: 978-1-903083-07-9. Dewey:115. LCCN:2001-369177.
Audience: **g,u,f.**

Bachelard, Gaston   **B2430.B253**
The Poetics of Space. John R. Stilgoe (Foreword by). Trade Paper. Beacon Press. Boston, MA. 1994. 288p. ISBN:0-8070-6473-4, ISBN13: 978-0-8070-6473-3. Dewey:114. LCCN:93-027874.
Audience: **g,u,f.** *B*

Badiou, Alain   **BZ430**
Infinite Thought: Truth and the Return of Philosophy. Trade Cloth. Continuum International Publishing Group, Ltd. London, 2003. 208p. ISBN:0-8264-6724-5, ISBN13: 978-0-8264-6724-9. Dewey:194. LCCN:2004-296006.
Audience: **g,u,f.**

Badiou, Alain, et al.   **B2430.B3**
Theoretical Writings. Ray Brassier & Alberto Toscano (Authors). Trade Cloth. Continuum International Publishing Group, Ltd. London, 2004. 256p. ACET Ser. ISBN:0-8264-6145-X, ISBN13: 978-0-8264-6145-2. Dewey:194. LCCN:2004-043822.
Audience: **g,u,f.**

Badiou, Alain   **B2430.B273M3713 1999**
Manifesto for Philosophy. Norman Madarasz (Translator). Trade Cloth. State University of New York Press. Albany, NY. 1999. 128p. SUNY Series, Intersections, :Philosophy and Critical Theory ISBN:0-7914-4219-5, ISBN13: 978-0-7914-4219-7. Dewey:101. LCCN:98-043903.
Audience: **g,u,f.**

Bataille, Georges   **B2430.B33952 2001**
The Unfinished System of Nonknowledge. Stuart Kendall (Editor, Translator, Introduction by). Book, Other. University of Minnesota Press. Minneapolis, MN. 2001. 296p. ISBN:0-8166-3504-8, ISBN13: 978-0-8166-3504-7. Dewey:848/.91209. LCCN:2001-000711.
Audience: **g,u,f.**

Baudrillard, Jean   **B2430.B33973E2513**
The Impossible Exchange. Chris Turner (Translator). Trade Cloth. Analytical Psychology Club of San Francisco, Inc. San Francisco, CA. 2001. 160p. ISBN:1-85984-647-5, ISBN13: 978-1-85984-647-6. Dewey:194. LCCN:2001-045420.
Audience: **g,u,f.**

Baudrillard, Jean   **B2430.B33973**
The Intelligence of Evil or the Lucidity Pact. Chris Turner (Translator). Cloth over Boards. Berg Publishers. Oxford, 2005. 208p. Talking Images Ser. ISBN:1-84520-327-5, ISBN13: 978-1-84520-327-6. Dewey:194. LCCN:2005-017087.
Audience: **g,u,f.**

Baudrillard, Jean   **B2430.B33973C7315**
The Perfect Crime. Chris Turner (Translator). Trade Cloth. Analytical Psychology Club of San Francisco, Inc. San Francisco, CA. 1996. 224p. ISBN:1-85984-919-9, ISBN13: 978-1-85984-919-4. Dewey:110. LCCN:96-015755.
Audience: **g,u,f.**

Benjamin, Andrew (Editor)   B2430.L962E5 1989
The Lyotard Reader. Trade Paper. Blackwell Publishing, Inc. Malden, MA. 1989. 370p. ISBN:0-631-16339-5, ISBN13: 978-0-631-16339-8. Dewey:194. LCCN:89-000110.
Audience: **g,u,f.** *Choice, 1990.*

Bergson, Henri   B2430.B4M313 2004
Matter and Memory. Trade Paper. Dover Publications, Inc. Mineola, NY. 2004. 368p. Dover Philosophical Classics Ser. ISBN:0-486-43415-X, ISBN13: 978-0-486-43415-5. Dewey:128/.3. LCCN:2004-041427.
Audience: **g,u,f.** *ℬ Choice, 1989.*

Bergson, Henri   B2430.B4I413 1999
An Introduction to Metaphysics. T. E. Hulme (Translator). Trade Cloth. Hackett Publishing Company, Inc. Indianapolis, IN. 1999. 62p. ISBN:0-87220-475-8, ISBN13: 978-0-87220-475-1. Dewey:110. LCCN:99-028080.
Audience: **g,u,f.** *ℬ*

Bergson, Henri   B2430.B4E72 1998
Creative Evolution. Arthur Mitchell (Translator). Trade Paper. Dover Publications, Inc. Mineola, NY. 1998. 432p. ISBN:0-486-40036-0, ISBN13: 978-0-486-40036-5. Dewey:113/.8. LCCN:97-046431.
Audience: **g,u,f.** *ℬ*

Carman, Taylor & Hansen, Mark (Editors)   B2430.M3764C36 2004
The Cambridge Companion to Merleau-Ponty. Cloth Text. Cambridge University Press. New York, NY. 2004. 406p. Cambridge Companions to Philosophy Ser. ISBN:0-521-80989-4, ISBN13: 978-0-521-80989-4. Dewey:194. LCCN:2003-069683.
Audience: **u,f.** *Choice, 2005.*

Deleuze, Gilles   B2430.D453D4513 1994
Difference and Repetition. Paul Patton (Translator). Columbia University Press. 1995. ISBN:0-231-08159-6, ISBN13: 978-0-231-08159-7.
Audience: **g,u,f.**

Deleuze, Gilles & Parnet, Claire   B2430.D453D4313 2002
Dialogues. Ed. 2. Hugh Tomlinson, Barbara Habberjam & Eliot Ross Albert (Translators). Trade Paper. Columbia University Press. New York, NY. 2002. 176p. ISBN:0-231-12669-7, ISBN13: 978-0-231-12669-4. Dewey:084/.1. LCCN:2002-020218.
Audience: **g,u,f.** *Choice, 1988.*

Descombes, Vincent   B2421 .D4413
Modern French Philosophy. L. Scott-Fox & J. M. Harding (Translators), Alan Montefiore (Foreword by). Trade Paper. Cambridge University Press. New York, NY. 1981. 208p. ISBN:0-521-29672-2, ISBN13: 978-0-521-29672-4. Dewey:194. LCCN:80-040768.
Audience: **g,u,f.** *ℬ*

Gutting, Gary   B2421 .G88 2001
French Philosophy in the Twentieth Century. Cloth Text. Cambridge University Press. New York, NY. 2001. 434p.

ISBN:0-521-66212-5, ISBN13: 978-0-521-66212-3. Dewey:194. LCCN:00-050241.
Audience: **g,u,f.** *Choice, 2001.*

Irigaray, Luce   B2430.I7
Luce Irigaray: Key Writings. Trade Paper. Continuum International Publishing Group, Ltd. London, 2004. 272p. ACET Ser. ISBN:0-8264-6940-X, ISBN13: 978-0-8264-6940-3. Dewey:194. LCCN:2004-301256.
Audience: **u,f.**

Kamber, Richard   B2430.C354K29 2002
On Camus. Trade Paper. Thomson Wadsworth. Belmont, CA. 2001. 104p. Wadsworth Philosophers Ser. ISBN:0-534-58381-4, ISBN13: 978-0-534-58381-1. Dewey:194. LCCN:2002-276834.
Audience: **g,l.**

Lacey, A. R.   B2430.B43L16 1989
Bergson. Trade Cloth. Routledge. New York, NY. 1989. 240p. ISBN:0-415-03007-2, ISBN13: 978-0-415-03007-6. Dewey:194. LCCN:88-032167.
Audience: **g,u,f.** *Choice, 1990.*

Levinas, Emmanuel   B2430.L483D5413 2000
God, Death and Time. Bettina Bergo (Translator), Jacques Rolland (Foreword by, Afterword by). Trade Cloth. Stanford University Press. Palo Alto, CA. 2000. xii, 296p. Meridian: Crossing Aesthetics Ser. ISBN:0-8047-3665-0, ISBN13: 978-0-8047-3665-7. Dewey:194. LCCN:00-059523.
Audience: **g,u,f.** *Choice, 2001.*

Levinas, Emmanuel   B2430.L482E6 1987
Collected Philosophical Papers. Alphonso Lingis (Editor). Library Binding. Martinus-Nijhoff Publishers (N E). 1987. 318p. ISBN:90-247-3272-7, ISBN13: 978-90-247-3272-2. Dewey:194. LCCN:85-028430.
Audience: **g,u,f.**

Levinas, Emmanuel   B2430.L483A8313 1998
Otherwise Than Being or Beyond Essence. Alphonso Lingis (Translator), Richard A. Cohen (Foreword by). Trade Paper. Duquesne University Press. Pittsburgh, PA. 1998. 205p. ISBN:0-8207-0299-4, ISBN13: 978-0-8207-0299-5. Dewey:111. LCCN:98-019597.
Audience: **g,u,f.**

Levinas, Emmanuel   B2430.L483I4613 2003
Unforeseen History. Nidra Poller (Translator), Don Ihde (Foreword by), Richard A. Cohen (Introduction by). Trade Cloth. University of Illinois Press. Champaign, IL. 2003. 184p. ISBN:0-252-02883-X, ISBN13: 978-0-252-02883-0. Dewey:194. LCCN:2003-008356.
Audience: **g,l,u.** *Choice, 2004.*

Levinas, Emmanuel   B2430.L483E5813 1998
Entre Nous: Essays on Thinking-of-the-Other. Michael B. Smith & Barbara Harshav (Translators). Cloth Text. Columbia University Press. New York, NY. 1998. 256p. European Perspectives, :Social Thought and Culturall Criticism Ser. ISBN:0-231-07910-9, ISBN13: 978-0-231-07910-5. Dewey:194. LCCN:97-051471.
Audience: **g,u,f.** *Choice, 1999.*

     Formats: Web: ☐   Ebook: 🄴   CD/DVD-ROM: 🐝   BCL3: ℬ

Lyotard, Jean-Francois   B2430.L963E2613 1993
The Libidinal Economy. Iain H. Grant (Translator). Cloth Text.
Indiana University Press. Bloomington, IN. 1993. 320p.
Theories of Contemporary Culture Ser. ISBN:0-253-33614-7,
ISBN13: 978-0-253-33614-9. Dewey:155.3. LCCN:91-032761.
                                        Audience: **g,u,f.**

Madison, G. B.   B2430.M3764 M3213
The Phenomenology of Merleau-ponty: A Search for the Limits
of Consciousness. Paul Ricoeur (Preface by). Trade Paper. Ohio
University Press. Athens, OH. 1981. 377p. Phenomenology of
Merleau-Ponty Ser., Vol. 3 ISBN:0-8214-0644-2, ISBN13:
978-0-8214-0644-1. Dewey:194. LCCN:81-004026.
                                        Audience: **g,u,f.**

Marcel, Gabriel   B2430.M253E513 2002
Awakenings: A Translation of Gabriel Marcel's Autobiography.
Trade Cloth. Marquette University Press. Milwaukee, WI. 2002.
262p. Marquette Studies in Philosophy, Vol. 30
ISBN:0-87462-653-6, ISBN13: 978-0-87462-653-7. Dewey:194
B. LCCN:2002-014652.
                                        Audience: **g,l,u,f.**

Marcel, Gabriel   B2430.M253H5813
Man Against Mass Society. Paper Text. Textbook Publishers.
Temecula, CA. 2003. 273p. ISBN:0-7581-4961-1, ISBN13:
978-0-7581-4961-9. Dewey:128.
                                        Audience: **g,l,u.** *B*

Maritain, Jacques   B2430.M32 E5
The Social and Political Philosophy of Jacques Maritain. Paper
Text. Textbook Publishers. Temecula, CA. 2003. 348p.
ISBN:0-7581-4018-5, ISBN13: 978-0-7581-4018-0. Dewey:194.
                                        Audience: **g,l,u,f.** *B*

Merleau-Ponty, Maurice   B2430
Phenomenology of Perception: An Introduction. Ed. 2. Trade
Paper. Routledge. New York, NY. 2002. 576p. Classics Ser.
ISBN:0-415-27841-4, ISBN13: 978-0-415-27841-6.
Dewey:142.7.
                                        Audience: **g,u,f.**

Merleau-Ponty, Maurice   B2430.M379.S43
Sense and Non-Sense. Herbert L. Dreyfus & Patrica A. Dreyfus
(Translators). Trade Cloth. Northwestern University Press.
Evanston, IL. 1964. 193p. Studies in Phenomenology and
Existential Philosophy ISBN:0-8101-0167-X, ISBN13:
978-0-8101-0167-8. Dewey:194.
                                        Audience: **g,u,f.** *B*

Merleau-Ponty, Maurice   B829.5
Phenomenology of Perception. Colin J. Smith (Translator).
Trade Paper. Routledge. New York, NY. 1981.
ISBN:0-391-02551-1, ISBN13: 978-0-391-02551-6.
Dewey:142.7.
                                        Audience: **g,u,f.**

Montefiore, Alan (Editor)   B29 .P5248 1983
Philosophy in France Today. Trade Paper. Cambridge University
Press. New York, NY. 1983. 223p. ISBN:0-521-29673-0,
ISBN13: 978-0-521-29673-1. Dewey:194. LCCN:82-009730.
                                        Audience: **g,l,u.** *B*

Priest, Stephen   B2430.M3764P74 2003
Merleau-Ponty. Trade Paper. Routledge. New York, NY. 2003.
322p. The Arguments of the Philosophers Ser.
ISBN:0-415-30864-X, ISBN13: 978-0-415-30864-9. Dewey:194.
                                        Audience: **g,u,f.**

Richardson, Michael   B2430.B33952E5 1998
Georges Bataille: Essential Writings. Cloth Text. SAGE
Publications, Inc. Thousand Oaks, CA. 1998. 256p. Sociology
Ser. ISBN:0-7619-5449-X, ISBN13: 978-0-7619-5449-1.
Dewey:194.
                                        Audience: **g,u,f.**

Ricoeur, Paul   PN212
Time and Narrative. Kathleen McLaughlin & David Pellauer
(Translators). Trade Paper. University of Chicago Press.
Chicago, IL. 1990. 216p. Time and Narrative Ser., Vol. 2
ISBN:0-226-71334-2, ISBN13: 978-0-226-71334-2.
Dewey:809.9/23. LCCN:83-017995.
                    Audience: **g,u,f.** *Choice, 1988, 1986.*

Ricoeur, Paul   BD241 .R484
Hermeneutics and the Human Sciences: Essays on Language,
Action and Interpretation. John B. Thompson (Edited and
Translated by). Trade Paper. Cambridge University Press. New
York, NY. 1981. 324p. ISBN:0-521-28002-8, ISBN13:
978-0-521-28002-0. Dewey:121/.68. LCCN:80-041546.
                                        Audience: **u,f.**

Ricoeur, Paul   B2430.R553
A Ricoeur Reader: Reflection and Imagination. Mario J. Valdes
(Editor). Trade Cloth. University of Toronto Press. Toronto, ON.
1991. 840p. ISBN:0-8020-5880-9, ISBN13: 978-0-8020-5880-5.
Dewey:121/.68.
                    Audience: **g,u,f.** *Choice, 1992.*

Simms, Karl   B2430.R554.S56 2003
Paul Ricoeur. Paper over Boards. Routledge. New York, NY.
2002. 176p. Critical Thinkers Ser. ISBN:0-415-23636-3,
ISBN13: 978-0-415-23636-2. Dewey:194. LCCN:2002-068223.
                                        Audience: **g,u,f.**

Stocker, Barry   B2430.D4
Routledge Philosophy Guidebook to Derrida on Deconstruction.
Paper over Boards. Routledge. New York, NY. 2006. 216p.
Routledge Philosophy Guidebooks ISBN:0-415-32501-3,
ISBN13: 978-0-415-32501-1. Dewey:194. LCCN:2005-026150.
                                        Audience: **g,u,f.**

Taylor, Victor E. &   B2430.L964J44 2005
Lambert, Gregg
Jean François Lyotard: Critical Evaluations in Cultural Theory.
Trade Cloth. Routledge. New York, NY. 2005.
ISBN:0-415-33820-4, ISBN13: 978-0-415-33820-2. Dewey:194.
LCCN:2005-050002.
                                        Audience: **g,u,f.**

Tiles, Mary   B2430.B254 T55 1984
Bachelard: Science and Objectivity. Trade Cloth. Cambridge
University Press. New York, NY. 1984. 264p. Modern European

Philosophy Ser. ISBN:0-521-24803-5, ISBN13:
978-0-521-24803-7. Dewey:121. LCCN:84-005001.

Audience: **g,u,f.** *B̶* *Choice, 1985.*

Weil, Simone   **B2430.W473A7713 2000**
Waiting for God. Trade Paper. HarperCollins Publishers. New
York, NY. 2001. 192p. Perennial Classics Ser.
ISBN:0-06-095970-3, ISBN13: 978-0-06-095970-8. Dewey:248.
LCCN:00-047271.

Audience: **g,l,u.** *B̶*

Weil, Simone   **B2430.W473 L3513**
Lectures on Philosophy. H. Price (Translator), Peter Winch
(Introduction by). Trade Paper. Cambridge University Press.
New York, NY. 1978. 240p. ISBN:0-521-29333-2, ISBN13:
978-0-521-29333-4. Dewey:194. LCCN:77-026735.

Audience: **g,u,f.** *B̶*

Wicks, Robert   **B2421**
Modern French Philosophy: From Existentialism to
Postmodernism. Trade Cloth. Oneworld Publications. Oxford,
2003. 352p. ISBN:1-85168-318-6, ISBN13: 978-1-85168-318-5.
Dewey:194. LCCN:2004-445465.

Audience: **g,l,u,f.** *Choice, 2004.*

Williams, Caroline   **B1809.S85W55 2001**
Contemporary French Philosophy: Modernity and the
Persistence of the Subject. Trade Cloth. Continuum International
Publishing Group, Ltd. London, 2001. 272p.
ISBN:0-485-00432-1, ISBN13: 978-0-485-00432-8. Dewey:194.
LCCN:2006-273036.

Audience: **g,u.**

Wood, David (Editor)   **B2430.R554O6 1991**
On Paul Ricoeur: Narrative and Interpretation. Paper over
Boards. Routledge. New York, NY. 1992. 224p. Warwick
Studies in Philosophy and Literature ISBN:0-415-07406-1,
ISBN13: 978-0-415-07406-3. Dewey:194. LCCN:91-028657.

Audience: **g,u,f.** *Choice, 1992.*

Philosophy by Country > French Philosophy > 20th and 21st Centuries > Sartre

Caws, Peter   **B2430.S34C38 1999**
Sarte. Paper over Boards. Routledge. New York, NY. 1999.
224p. Arguments of the Philosophers Ser. ISBN:0-415-20390-2,
ISBN13: 978-0-415-20390-6. Dewey:194. LCCN:00-266188.

Audience: **g,l,u.**

Howells, Christina (Editor)   **B2430.S34 C29 1992**
The Cambridge Companion to Sartre. Trade Paper. Cambridge
University Press. New York, NY. 1992. 407p. Cambridge
Companions to Philosophy Ser. ISBN:0-521-38812-0, ISBN13:
978-0-521-38812-2. Dewey:194. LCCN:91-030563.

Audience: **u,f.** *Choice, 1993.*

Sartre, Jean-Paul   **B819 .S267**
Of Human Freedom. Trade Cloth. Philosophical Library, Inc.
New York, NY. 1967. 176p. ISBN:0-8022-1488-6, ISBN13:
978-0-8022-1488-1. Dewey:142.7. LCCN:66-018816.

Audience: **g,u,f.**

Sartre, Jean-Paul   **B819**
Being and Nothingness. Hazel Barnes (Translator). Trade Paper.
Kensington Publishing Corporation. New York, NY. 2001. 640p.
ISBN:0-8065-2276-3, ISBN13: 978-0-8065-2276-0. Dewey:111.

Audience: **g,u,f.**

Sartre, Jean-Paul   **B2430.S31P75 2000**
Jean-Paul Sartre: Basic Writings. Stephen Priest (Introduction
by). Trade Paper. Routledge. New York, NY. 2000. 352p.
ISBN:0-415-21368-1, ISBN13: 978-0-415-21368-4. Dewey:194.
LCCN:00-056017.

Audience: **g,u,f.**

Schilpp, Paul Arthur   **B2430.S34**
(Editor)
The Philosophy of Jean-Paul Sartre. Trade Paper. Open Court
Publishing Company. Chicago, IL. 1981. 766p. Library of
Living Philosophers, Vol. XVI ISBN:0-8126-9150-4, ISBN13:
978-0-8126-9150-4. Dewey:194.

Audience: **g,u,f.**

Philosophy by Country > French Philosophy > 20th and 21st Centuries > Foucault

Dreyfus, Hubert L. &   **B2430.F724D73 1983**
Rabinow, Paul
Michel Foucault: Beyond Structuralism and Hermeneutics. Ed.
2. Michel Foucault (Afterword by). Trade Paper. University of
Chicago Press. Chicago, IL. 1983. 256p. ISBN:0-226-16312-1,
ISBN13: 978-0-226-16312-3. Dewey:194. LCCN:83-009316.

Audience: **g,u,f.**

Foucault, Michel   **B2430.F723A7313 2002**
Archaeology of Knowledge. Ed. 2. Trade Paper. Routledge. New
York, NY. 2002. 256p. Classics Ser. ISBN:0-415-28753-7,
ISBN13: 978-0-415-28753-1. Dewey:001.2.
LCCN:2002-067999.

Audience: **g,u,f.**

Foucault, Michel   **B2430**
Power, Vol. 3. Colin Gordon & Paul Rabinow (Editors), Robert
Hurley (Translator). Trade Cloth. New Press, The. New York,
NY. 2000. 528p. Essential Works of Michel Foucault, 1954-1984
ISBN:1-56584-257-X, ISBN13: 978-1-56584-257-1. Dewey:901.
LCCN:96-031819.

Audience: **g,u,f.** *Choice, 2001.*

Foucault, Michel   **B2430.F721 1984**
The Foucault Reader: An Introduction to Foucault's Thought.
Paul Rabinow (Editor). Trade Paper. Knopf Publishing Group.
New York, NY. 1984. 400p. ISBN:0-394-71340-0, ISBN13:
978-0-394-71340-3. Dewey:194. LCCN:83-019510.

Audience: **g,l,u.**

Gutting, Gary (Editor)   B2430.F724C36 2006
The Cambridge Companion to Foucault. Ed. 2. Cloth Text.
Cambridge University Press. New York, NY. 2005. 488p.
Cambridge Companions to Philosophy Ser.
ISBN:0-521-84082-1, ISBN13: 978-0-521-84082-8. Dewey:194.
LCCN:2005-005777.
                                    Audience: **u,f.** *Choice, 2006, 1994.*

Han, Beatrice   B2430.F724H3613 2002
Foucault's Critical Project: Between the Transcendental and the
Historical. Trade Paper. Stanford University Press. Palo Alto,
CA. 2002. 256p. ISBN:0-8047-3709-6, ISBN13:
978-0-8047-3709-8. Dewey:194. LCCN:2002-003858.
                                    Audience: **u,f.** *Choice, 2003.*

Hoy, David (Editor)   B2430.F724F68 1986
Foucault: A Critical Reader. Trade Paper. Blackwell Publishing,
Inc. Malden, MA. 1986. 256p. Critical Readers Ser.
ISBN:0-631-14043-3, ISBN13: 978-0-631-14043-6. Dewey:194.
LCCN:86-006786.
                                    Audience: **u,f.** *Choice, 1987.*

Mahon, Michael   B2430.F724 M334 1992
Foucault's Nietzschean Genealogy: Truth, Power, and the
Subject. Paper Text. State University of New York Press.
Albany, NY. 1992. 255p. SUNY Series in Contemporary
Continental Philosophy ISBN:0-7914-1150-8, ISBN13:
978-0-7914-1150-6. Dewey:194. LCCN:91-035092.
                                    Audience: **u,f.** *Choice, 1993.*

Mills, Sara   B2430.F724M555 2003
Michel Foucault. Paper over Boards. Routledge. New York, NY.
2004. 176p. Critical Thinkers Ser. ISBN:0-415-24568-0,
ISBN13: 978-0-415-24568-5. Dewey:194. LCCN:2002-154393.
                                    Audience: **u,f.**

Philosophy by Country > German, Austrian Philosophy > 17th Century

Hunter, Ian   B2535 .H86 2001
Rival Enlightenments: Civil and Metaphysical Philosophy in
Early Modern Germany. Quentin Skinner, Lorraine Daston,
Dorothy Ross & James Tully (Contribution by). Trade Paper.
Cambridge University Press. New York, NY. 2006. 425p. Ideas
in Context Ser. ISBN:0-521-02549-4, ISBN13:
978-0-521-02549-2. Dewey:193.
                                    Audience: **g,u,f.**

Ishiguro, Hide   B2599.L8I83 1990
Leibniz's Philosophy of Logic and Language. Ed. 2. Trade
Paper. Cambridge University Press. New York, NY. 1991. 256p.
ISBN:0-521-37781-1, ISBN13: 978-0-521-37781-2.
Dewey:160.92. LCCN:89-028814.
                                    Audience: **g,u,f.** *B*

Jolley, Nicholas (Editor)   B2598 .C335 1995
The Cambridge Companion to Leibniz. Cloth Text. Cambridge
University Press. New York, NY. 1994. 512p. Cambridge

Companions to Philosophy Ser. ISBN:0-521-36588-0, ISBN13:
978-0-521-36588-8. Dewey:193. LCCN:94-000515.
                                    Audience: **u,f.** *Choice, 1995.*

Leibniz, Gottfried Wilhelm   B2590 .E5 1985
Theodicy. Trade Cloth. Open Court Publishing Company.
Chicago, IL. 1985. 448p. ISBN:0-87548-437-9, ISBN13:
978-0-87548-437-2. Dewey:231/.8. LCCN:85-008833.
                                    Audience: **g,u,f.**

Leibniz, Gottfried Wilhelm   B2558.A75 1989
Philosophical Essays. Roger Ariew & Daniel Garber (Editors),
Roger Ariew & Daniel Garber (Translators). Trade Cloth.
Hackett Publishing Company, Inc. Indianapolis, IN. 1989. 386p.
HPC Classics Ser. ISBN:0-87220-063-9, ISBN13:
978-0-87220-063-0. Dewey:193. LCCN:88-038259.
                                    Audience: **g,u,f.**

Leibniz, Gottfried Wilhelm   B2597.A4 2000
& Clarke, Samuel
Correspondence. Roger Ariew (Editor). Trade Cloth. Hackett
Publishing Company, Inc. Indianapolis, IN. 2000. 112p.
ISBN:0-87220-525-8, ISBN13: 978-0-87220-525-3. Dewey:193.
LCCN:99-052339.
                                    Audience: **g,u,f.**

Leibniz, Gottfried Wilhelm   B2558.A74213 1991
Discourse on Metaphysics and Other Essays. Daniel Garber
(Editor), Roger Ariew & Daniel Garber (Translators), Roger
Ariew (Introduction by). Trade Cloth. Hackett Publishing
Company, Inc. Indianapolis, IN. 1991. 84p. HPC Classics Ser.
ISBN:0-87220-133-3, ISBN13: 978-0-87220-133-0. Dewey:110.
LCCN:91-024570.
                                    Audience: **g,u,f.**

Leibniz, Gottfried Wilhelm   B2581.E5 R45 1996
Leibniz: New Essays on Human Understanding. Ed. 2. Peter
Remnant & Jonathan Bennett (Editors), Karl Ameriks &
Desmond M. Clarke (Contribution by). Trade Paper. Cambridge
University Press. New York, NY. 1996. 648p. Texts in the
History of Philosophy ISBN:0-521-57660-1, ISBN13:
978-0-521-57660-4. Dewey:121. LCCN:96-005308.
                                    Audience: **g,l,u,f.**

Leibniz, Gottfried Wilhelm   B2558.F73 1998
Philosophical Texts. R. S. Woolhouse & Richard Francks
(Translators), R. S. Woolhouse (Introduction by, Notes by).
Paper Text. Oxford University Press, Inc. New York, NY. 1998.
320p. Oxford Philosophical Texts ISBN:0-19-875153-2,
ISBN13: 978-0-19-875153-3. Dewey:193. LCCN:97-028372.
                                    Audience: **g,u,f.**

Rescher, Nicholas   B2580.E5R47 1991
G. W. Leibniz's Monadology: An Edition for Students. Trade
Paper. University of Pittsburgh Press. Pittsburgh, PA. 1991.
480p. ISBN:0-8229-5449-4, ISBN13: 978-0-8229-5449-1.
Dewey:193. LCCN:90-024820.
                                    Audience: **g,l,u.**

Rescher, Nicholas   **B2598**
Leibniz: An Introduction to His Philosophy. Trade Cloth.
Ashgate Publishing, Ltd. Aldershot, 1994. 176p. Modern
Revivals in Philosophy Ser. ISBN:0-7512-0275-4, ISBN13:
978-0-7512-0275-5. Dewey:193.
     Audience: **g,l,u.**

Russell, Bertrand   **B2598.R83**
The Philosophy of Leibniz. Ed. 3. Trade Paper. Routledge. New
York, NY. 1992. 344p. The Collected Papers of Bertrand Russell
Ser. ISBN:0-415-08296-X, ISBN13: 978-0-415-08296-9.
Dewey:193. LCCN:95-006523.
     Audience: **g,l,u.**

Rutherford, Donald   **B2598**
Leibniz and the Rational Order of Nature. Trade Paper.
Cambridge University Press. New York, NY. 1998. 317p.
ISBN:0-521-59737-4, ISBN13: 978-0-521-59737-1. Dewey:193.
     Audience: **g,u,f.** *Choice, 1996.*

Savile, Anthony & Leibniz,   **B2599.M8S28 2000**
  Gottfried Wilhelm
Routledge Philosophy Guidebook to Leibniz and the
Monadology. Trade Cloth. Routledge. New York, NY. 2000. v,
247p. ISBN:0-415-16575-X, ISBN13: 978-0-415-16575-4.
Dewey:193. LCCN:00-027144.
     Audience: **u,f.**

Philosophy by Country > German, Austrian Philosophy > 18th Century

Altmann, Alexander   **B2693.A64 1998**
Moses Mendelssohn: A Biographical Study. Trade Paper.
Littman Library of Jewish Civilization, The. London, 1998.
914p. ISBN:1-874774-53-6, ISBN13: 978-1-874774-53-2.
Dewey:193. LCCN:99-160435.
     Audience: **g,u,f.** 𝓑

Arkush, Allan   **B2693.A75 1994**
Moses Mendelssohn and the Enlightenment. Cloth Text. State
University of New York Press. Albany, NY. 1994. 304p. SUNY
Series in Judaica, Hermeneutics, Mysticism, and Religion
ISBN:0-7914-2071-X, ISBN13: 978-0-7914-2071-3. Dewey:193.
LCCN:93-039401.
     Audience: **g,u,f.** *Choice, 1995.*

Beck, Lewis W.   **B2521**
Early German Philosophy: Kant and His Predecessors. Trade
Paper. Continuum International Publishing Group, Ltd. London,
1996. 567p. ISBN:1-85506-447-2, ISBN13: 978-1-85506-447-8.
Dewey:193.
     Audience: **g,u,f.** 𝓑

Fichte, Johann Gottlieb   **BJ1012**
Fichte: The System of Ethics. Gunter Zvller (Editor). Cambridge
University Press. 2005. Cambridge Texts in the History of
Philosophy Ser. ISBN:0-521-57140-5, ISBN13:
978-0-521-57140-1.
     Audience: **g,u,f.**

Fichte, Johann G.   **B2844.B52E5 1987**
The Vocation of Man. Peter Preuss (Translator). Trade Cloth.
Hackett Publishing Company, Inc. Indianapolis, IN. 1987. 139p.
HPC Classics Ser. ISBN:0-87220-038-8, ISBN13:
978-0-87220-038-8. Dewey:128. LCCN:87-003610.
     Audience: **g,u,f.** 𝓑

Holzhey, Helmut &   **B2751.H65 2005**
  Mudroch, Vilem
Historical Dictionary of Kant and Kantianism. Trade Cloth.
Scarecrow Press, Inc. Lanham, MD. 2005. 416p. Historical
Dictionaries of Religions, Philosophies, and Movements Ser.,
No. 60 ISBN:0-8108-5390-6, ISBN13: 978-0-8108-5390-4.
Dewey:193. LCCN:2005-004107.
     Audience: **g,u.** *Choice, 2005.*

Lessing, Gotthold Ephraim   **BT40.L4713 2005**
Philosophical and Theological Writings. Cambridge University
Press. 2005. ISBN:0-521-83120-2, ISBN13: 978-0-521-83120-8.
     Audience: **g,u,f.**

Mendelssohn, Moses   **B2690.E5 D34 1997**
Moses Mendelssohn: Philosophical Writings. Daniel O.
Dahlstrom (Editor), Karl Ameriks & Desmond M. Clarke
(Contribution by). Cloth Text. Cambridge University Press. New
York, NY. 1997. 362p. Texts in the History of Philosophy
ISBN:0-521-57383-1, ISBN13: 978-0-521-57383-2. Dewey:193.
LCCN:97-016141.
     Audience: **g,u,f.** *Choice, 1998.*

Schiller, Friedrich   **BH183.S25 2004**
On the Aesthetic Education of Man. Reginald Snell (Translator).
Trade Paper. Dover Publications, Inc. Mineola, NY. 2004. 160p.
ISBN:0-486-43739-6, ISBN13: 978-0-486-43739-2.
Dewey:111/.85. LCCN:2004-050046.
     Audience: **g,l,u,f.**

Philosophy by Country > German, Austrian Philosophy > 18th Century > Kant

Adorno, Theodor W.   **B2779**
Kant's "Critique of Pure Reason". Rolf Tiedemann (Editor),
Rodney Livingstone (Translator). Trade Paper. Stanford
University Press. Palo Alto, CA. 2001. 312p.
ISBN:0-8047-4426-2, ISBN13: 978-0-8047-4426-3. Dewey:121.
     Audience: **u,f.** *Choice, 2002.*

Ameriks, Karl   **B2799.M52A44 2000**
Kant's Theory of Mind: An Analysis of the Paralogisms of Pure
Reason. Ed. 2. Trade Cloth. Oxford University Press, Inc. New
York, NY. 2000. 390p. ISBN:0-19-823896-7, ISBN13:
978-0-19-823896-6. Dewey:128/.2/092.
     Audience: **u,f.** 𝓑

Beck, Lewis W.   **B2774**
A Commentary on Kant's Critique of Practical Reason. Trade

Paper. University of Chicago Press. Chicago, IL. 1996. 320p. ISBN:0-226-04075-5, ISBN13: 978-0-226-04075-2. Dewey:170.924. LCCN:60-005464.

Audience: **g,u,f.** ℬ

Beck, Lewis W.   **B2521**
Early German Philosophy: Kant and His Predecessors. Trade Paper. Continuum International Publishing Group, Ltd. London, 1996. 567p. ISBN:1-85506-447-2, ISBN13: 978-1-85506-447-8. Dewey:193.

Audience: **g,u,f.** ℬ

Cassirer, Ernst   **B2797**
Kant's Life and Thought. James Haden (Translator), Stephan Korner (Introduction by). Cloth over Boards. Yale University Press. Cumberland, RI. 1981. 430p. ISBN:0-300-02358-8, ISBN13: 978-0-300-02358-9. Dewey:193. LCCN:81-003354.

Audience: **u,f.** ℬ

Cassirer, H W   **B2779 .C3 1955A**
Kant's First Critique: An Appraisal of the Permanent Significance of Kant's Critique of Pure Reason. Paper over Boards. Routledge. New York, NY. 2004. 368p. Muirhead Library of Philosophy Ser. ISBN:0-415-29585-8, ISBN13: 978-0-415-29585-7. Dewey:121.

Audience: **g,u,f.**

Gardner, Sebastian   **B2779.G27 1999**
Routledge Philosophy Guidebook to Kant and "The Critique of Pure Reason". Trade Paper. Routledge. New York, NY. 1999. 392p. Philosophy Guidebooks ISBN:0-415-11909-X, ISBN13: 978-0-415-11909-2. Dewey:121. LCCN:98-042339.

Audience: **u,f.**

Guyer, Paul (Editor)   **B2798**
The Cambridge Companion to Kant and Modern Philosophy. Cloth Text. Cambridge University Press. New York, NY. 2006. 736p. Cambridge Companions to Philosophy Ser. ISBN:0-521-82303-X, ISBN13: 978-0-521-82303-6. Dewey:193. LCCN:2005-029335.

Audience: **u,f.**

Heidegger, Martin   **B2779.H4213 1997**
Phenomenological Interpretation of Kant's Critique of Pure Reason. Parvis Emad & Kenneth Maly (Translators). Trade Cloth. Indiana University Press. Bloomington, IN. 1997. 368p. Studies in Continental Thought ISBN:0-253-33258-3, ISBN13: 978-0-253-33258-5. Dewey:121. LCCN:96-044479.

Audience: **g,u,f.**

Heidegger, Martin   **B2799.M5F5513 1997**
Kant and the Problem of Metaphysics. Ed. 5. Richard Taft (Translator). Trade Cloth. Indiana University Press. Bloomington, IN. 1997. 256p. Studies in Continental Thought ISBN:0-253-33276-1, ISBN13: 978-0-253-33276-9. Dewey:110. LCCN:96-048023.

Audience: **g,u,f.** ℬ *Choice, 1991.*

Hoffe, Otfried   **B2798.H6313 1994**
Immanuel Kant. Marshall Farrier (Translator). Paper Text. State University of New York Press. Albany, NY. 1994. 290p. SUNY

Series in Ethical Theory ISBN:0-7914-2094-9, ISBN13: 978-0-7914-2094-2. Dewey:193. LCCN:93-045476.

Audience: **g,u,f.** *Choice, 1995.*

Holzhey, Helmut &   **B2751.H65 2005**
 Mudroch, Vilem
Historical Dictionary of Kant and Kantianism. Trade Cloth. Scarecrow Press, Inc. Lanham, MD. 2005. 416p. Historical Dictionaries of Religions, Philosophies, and Movements Ser., No. 60 ISBN:0-8108-5390-6, ISBN13: 978-0-8108-5390-4. Dewey:193. LCCN:2005-004107.

Audience: **g,u.** *Choice, 2005.*

Kant, Immanuel   **B2773.E5A2 2004**
Critique of Practical Reason. Trade Paper. Dover Publications, Inc. Mineola, NY. 2004. 176p. ISBN:0-486-43445-1, ISBN13: 978-0-486-43445-2. Dewey:170. LCCN:2003-067428.

Audience: **g,u,f.**

Kant, Immanuel   **B2791.E5**
Religion Within the Limits of Reason Alone. Trade Paper. HarperCollins Publishers. New York, NY. 1960. 352p. ISBN:0-06-130067-5, ISBN13: 978-0-06-130067-7. Dewey:193.

Audience: **g,u,f.** ℬ

Kant, Immanuel   **B2794.L43E5 1997**
Lectures on Metaphysics. Karl Ameriks & Steve Naragon (Edited and Translated by), Paul Guyer & Allen W. Wood (Contribution by). Trade Paper. Cambridge University Press. New York, NY. 2001. 692p. The Works of Immanuel Kant in Translation ISBN:0-521-00076-9, ISBN13: 978-0-521-00076-5. Dewey:110.

Audience: **g,u,f.**

Kant, Immanuel   **B2799.R4K3613 1996**
Religion and Rational Theology. George di Giovanni (Editor), Allen W. Wood & George Di Giovanni (Edited and Translated by), Paul Guyer (Contribution by). Trade Paper. Cambridge University Press. New York, NY. 2001. 544p. Cambridge Edition of the Works of Immanuel Kant ISBN:0-521-79998-8, ISBN13: 978-0-521-79998-0. Dewey:210.

Audience: **g,u,f.** *Choice, 1997.*

Kant, Immanuel   **BH39**
Observations on the Feeling of the Beautiful and Sublime. Ed. 2. John T. Goldthwait (Translator). Trade Paper. University of California Press. Berkeley, CA. 2004. 192p. ISBN:0-520-24078-2, ISBN13: 978-0-520-24078-0. Dewey:111.85.

Audience: **g,u,f.** ℬ

Kant, Immanuel   **B2766.E6 G7 1998**
Groundwork of the Metaphysics of Morals. Mary J. Gregor (Editor, Translator), Christine M. Korsgaard (Introduction by), Karl Ameriks, Desmond M. Clarke & Immanuel Kant (Contribution by). Trade Paper. Cambridge University Press. New York, NY. 1998. 120p. Texts in the History of Philosophy ISBN:0-521-62695-1, ISBN13: 978-0-521-62695-8. Dewey:170. LCCN:97-030153.

Audience: **g,u,f.** *Choice, 1998.*

Kant, Immanuel   **B2794.D42 E5**
Kant's Inaugural Dissertation and Early Writings on Space. John Handyside (Translator). Trade Cloth. Hyperion Press, Inc. Westport, CT. 1994. ISBN:0-88355-699-5, ISBN13: 978-0-88355-699-3. Dewey:115/.4. LCCN:78-059026.

Audience: **u,f.** *B*

Kant, Immanuel   **B2766**
Groundwork for the Metaphysics of Morals. Thomas E. Hill (Editor), Arnulf Zweig (Translator). Paper Text. Oxford University Press, Inc. New York, NY. 2003. 306p. Oxford Philosophical Texts ISBN:0-19-875180-X, ISBN13: 978-0-19-875180-9. Dewey:170. LCCN:2002-193019.

Audience: **g,u,f.**

Kant, Immanuel   **KZ2322.A3Z8613 2003**
To Perpetual Peace. Ted Humphrey (Translator). Trade Cloth. Hackett Publishing Company, Inc. Indianapolis, IN. 2003. 50p. ISBN:0-87220-692-0, ISBN13: 978-0-87220-692-2. Dewey:341.7/3. LCCN:2003-047180.

Audience: **g,u,f.**

Kant, Immanuel   **B2783.E5 G89 2000**
Critique of the Power of Judgment. Eric Matthews (Translator), Paul Guyer (Edited and Translated by, Contribution by), Allen W. Wood (Contribution by). Trade Cloth. Cambridge University Press. New York, NY. 2000. 416p. Cambridge Edition of the Works of Immanuel Kant ISBN:0-521-34447-6, ISBN13: 978-0-521-34447-0. Dewey:121. LCCN:99-088501.

Audience: **g,u,f.**

Kant, Immanuel   **B2778.E5M5 2003**
Critique of Pure Reason. J. M. D. Meiklejohn (Translator). Trade Paper. Dover Publications, Inc. Mineola, NY. 2003. 400p. Dover Philosophical Classics Ser. ISBN:0-486-43254-8, ISBN13: 978-0-486-43254-0. Dewey:121. LCCN:2003-048963.

Audience: **g,u,f.**

Kant, Immanuel   **B2783.E53 M47X 1980**
The Critique of Judgment: Containing Kant's Critique of Aesthetic Judgement and Critique of Teleological Judgement. J. C. Meredith (Translator). Paper Text. Oxford University Press, Inc. New York, NY. 1978. 140p. ISBN:0-19-824589-0, ISBN13: 978-0-19-824589-6. Dewey:121. LCCN:86-673058.

Audience: **g,u,f.** *B*

Kant, Immanuel   **B2794.V642**
Lectures on Philosophical Theology. Allen W. Wood & Gertrude M. Clark (Translators). Trade Paper. Cornell University Press. Ithaca, NY. 1986. 176p. ISBN:0-8014-9379-X, ISBN13: 978-0-8014-9379-9. Dewey:211/.01. LCCN:78-058034.

Audience: **g,u,f.** *B*

Louden, Robert B. &   **BD450**
  Kuehn, Manfred (Editors)
Kant: Anthropology from a Pragmatic Point of View. Karl Ameriks & Desmond M. Clarke (Contribution by). Cloth Text. Cambridge University Press. New York, NY. 2006. 288p. Cambridge Texts in the History of Philosophy Ser. ISBN:0-521-85556-X, ISBN13: 978-0-521-85556-3. Dewey:128.

Audience: **g,u,f.**

Murphy, Jeffrie G.   **B2799.E8M85 1994**
Kant: The Philosophy of Right. Trade Paper. Mercer University Press. Macon, GA. 1994. 143p. ISBN:0-86554-443-3, ISBN13: 978-0-86554-443-7. Dewey:170/.92. LCCN:94-004605.

Audience: **u,f.** *B*

Paton, Herbert J.   **B2799.E8**
The Categorical Imperative: A Study in Kant's Moral Philosophy. Book, Other. University of Pennsylvania Press. Philadelphia, PA. 1971. 288p. ISBN:0-8122-1023-9, ISBN13: 978-0-8122-1023-1. Dewey:193.

Audience: **u,f.**

Schonfeld, Martin   **B2798.S315 2000**
The Philosophy of the Young Kant: The Precritical Project. Trade Cloth. Oxford University Press, Inc. New York, NY. 2000. 364p. ISBN:0-19-513218-1, ISBN13: 978-0-19-513218-2. Dewey:193. LCCN:99-030602.

Audience: **g,u,f.** *Choice, 2001.*

Smith, Norman Kemp   **B2779**
A Commentary to Kant's Critique of Pure Reason. Trade Cloth. Prometheus Books, Publishers. Amherst, NY. 1991. 724p. ISBN:1-57392-482-2, ISBN13: 978-1-57392-482-5. Dewey:121.

Audience: **g,u,f.**

Strawson, Peter F.   **B2779**
The Bounds of Sense: An Essay on Kant's Critique of Pure Reason. UK-B Format Paperback. Routledge. New York, NY. 1990. 296p. ISBN:0-415-04030-2, ISBN13: 978-0-415-04030-3. Dewey:121.

Audience: **g,u,f.**

Sullivan, Roger J.   **B2799.E8 S84 1994**
An Introduction to Kant's Ethics. Trade Paper. Cambridge University Press. New York, NY. 1994. 191p. ISBN:0-521-46769-1, ISBN13: 978-0-521-46769-8. Dewey:170/.92. LCCN:93-040557.

Audience: **g,u.** *Choice, 1995.*

Sullivan, Roger J.   **B2799.E8 S83 1989**
Kant's Moral Theory. Trade Paper. Cambridge University Press. New York, NY. 1989. 432p. ISBN:0-521-36908-8, ISBN13: 978-0-521-36908-4. Dewey:170/.92/4. LCCN:88-010225.

Audience: **g,u,f.** *Choice, 1989.*

Walker, Ralph Charles   **B2798.W23 1999**
  Sutherland
Kant. Paper over Boards. Routledge. New York, NY. 1999. 216p. Arguments of the Philosophers Ser. ISBN:0-415-20367-8, ISBN13: 978-0-415-20367-8. Dewey:193. LCCN:00-269385.

Audience: **g,u,f.**

Zoller, Gunter   **B2787**
Prolegomena to Any Future Metaphysics That Will Be Able to Present Itself As Science: With Two Early Reviews of the Critique of Reason. Paper Text. Oxford University Press, Inc. New York, NY. 2004. 260p. Oxford Philosophical Texts ISBN:0-19-875151-6, ISBN13: 978-0-19-875151-9. Dewey:110. LCCN:2004-299758.

Audience: **u,f.**

Philosophy by Country > German, Austrian Philosophy > 18th Century > Hegel

Althaus, Horst   **B2947.A67 2000**
Hegel: An Intellectual Biography. Trade Cloth. Polity Press.
Cambridge, 2000. 304p. ISBN:0-7456-1781-6, ISBN13:
978-0-7456-1781-7. Dewey:193 B. LCCN:00-039957.
Audience: g,u,f. Choice, 2001.

Beiser, Frederick C. (Editor)   **B2948 .C28 1993**
The Cambridge Companion to Hegel. Trade Paper. Cambridge
University Press. New York, NY. 1993. 528p. Cambridge
Companions to Philosophy Ser. ISBN:0-521-38711-6, ISBN13:
978-0-521-38711-8. Dewey:193. LCCN:92-015572.
Audience: u,f. Choice, 1993.

Findlay, J. N.   **B2948**
Hegel: A Re-Examination. Paper over Boards. Routledge. New
York, NY. 2004. 376p. Muirhead Library of Philosophy Ser.
ISBN:0-415-29578-5, ISBN13: 978-0-415-29578-9. Dewey:193.
Audience: g,u,f. B

Hartnack, Justus   **B2948.H24513 1998**
An Introduction to Hegel's Logic. Kenneth R. Westphal
(Editor), Lars Aagaard-Mogensen (Translator). Trade Paper.
Hackett Publishing Company, Inc. Indianapolis, IN. 1998. 126p.
HPC Classics Ser. ISBN:0-87220-424-3, ISBN13:
978-0-87220-424-9. Dewey:160.92. LCCN:98-038163.
Audience: u,f.

Hegel, G. W. F.   **K230.H43G7813 2005**
Philosophy of Right. S. W. Dyde (Translator). Trade Paper,
Perfect. Dover Publications, Inc. Mineola, NY. 2005. 219p.
Dover Philosophical Classics Ser. ISBN:0-486-44563-1,
ISBN13: 978-0-486-44563-2. Dewey:320/.01/1.
LCCN:2005-040107.
Audience: g,u,f.

Hegel, Georg Wilhelm   **B2936.E5 H3**
Friedrich
Hegel's Lectures in the History of Philosophy, Vols. 1-3. Ed. 2.
Cloth Text. Brill Academic Publishers, Inc. Boston, MA. 1966.
ISBN:0-391-03883-4, ISBN13: 978-0-391-03883-7. Dewey:109.
LCCN:96-025490.
Audience: u,f.

Hegel, Georg Wilhelm   **B2908.G7 1997**
Friedrich
On Art, Religion, and the History of Philosophy: Introductory
Lectures. J. Glenn Gray (Editor), Tom Rockmore (Introduction
by). Trade Cloth. Hackett Publishing Company, Inc.
Indianapolis, IN. 1997. 342p. ISBN:0-87220-371-9, ISBN13:
978-0-87220-371-6. Dewey:193. LCCN:97-026470.
Audience: g,u,f.

Hegel, Georg Wilhelm   **JC336**
Friedrich
Philosophy of Right. T. M. Knox (Translator). Paper Text.

Oxford University Press, Inc. New York, NY. 1967. 400p.
ISBN:0-19-500276-8, ISBN13: 978-0-19-500276-8.
Dewey:320.1/1.
Audience: g,u,f. B

Hegel, Georg Wilhelm   **BD111**
Friedrich
Phenomenology of Spirit. A. V. Miller & J. N. Findlay
(Translators). Paper Text. Oxford University Press, Inc. New
York, NY. 1979. 630p. ISBN:0-19-824597-1, ISBN13:
978-0-19-824597-1. Dewey:110.
Audience: g,u,f.

Hegel, Georg Wilhelm   **D16.8 .H46 1975**
Friedrich
Lectures on the Philosophy of World History: Reason in History.
Hugh Barr Nisbet (Translator), Duncan Forbes (Introduction by).
Trade Cloth. Cambridge University Press. New York, NY. 1975.
290p. Cambridge Studies in the History and Theory of Politics
ISBN:0-521-20566-2, ISBN13: 978-0-521-20566-5. Dewey:901.
LCCN:74-079137.
Audience: g,u,f.

Hegel, Georg Wilhelm   **BD111**
Friedrich
Hegel's Logic: Being Part One of the Encyclopaedia of the
Philosophical Sciences (1830). Ed. 3. William Wallace
(Translator), John N. Findlay (Foreword by). Paper Text. Oxford
University Press, Inc. New York, NY. 1975. 386p.
ISBN:0-19-824512-2, ISBN13: 978-0-19-824512-4. Dewey:110.
Audience: u,f.

Heidegger, Martin   **B2929.H3513 1988**
Hegel's Phenomenology of Spirit. Cloth Text. Indiana
University Press. Bloomington, IN. 1988. 176p. Studies in
Phenomenology and Existential Philosophy
ISBN:0-253-32766-0, ISBN13: 978-0-253-32766-6. Dewey:193.
LCCN:87-045440.
Audience: g,u,f. Choice, 1989.

Hyppolite, Jean   **B2929 .H913**
Genesis and Structure of Hegel's Phenomenology of Spirit.
Samuel Cherniak & John Heckman (Translators). Trade Paper.
Northwestern University Press. Evanston, IL. 1979. 609p.
Studies in Phenomenology and Existential Philosophy
ISBN:0-8101-0594-2, ISBN13: 978-0-8101-0594-2. Dewey:193.
LCCN:73-094431.
Audience: u,f. B

Hyppolite, Jean   **D16.8.H913 1996**
Introduction to Hegel's Philosophy of History. Bond Harris &
Jacqueline B. Spurlock (Translators), Arkady Plotnitsky
(Foreword by). Trade Cloth. University Press of Florida.
Gainesville, FL. 1996. 128p. ISBN:0-8130-1458-1, ISBN13:
978-0-8130-1458-6. Dewey:901. LCCN:96-032322.
Audience: g,u,f. Choice, 1997.

Hyppolite, Jean   **B2949.L8H913 1997**
Logic and Existence. Leonard Lawlor & Amit Sen (Translators).
Cloth Text. State University of New York Press. Albany, NY.

1997. 212p. SUNY Series in Contemporary Continental
Philosophy ISBN:0-7914-3231-9, ISBN13: 978-0-7914-3231-0.
Dewey:193. LCCN:96-013009.

Audience: **g,u,f.**

Inwood, M. J.   **B2948.I56 1999**
Hegel. Paper over Boards. Routledge. New York, NY. 1999.
600p. Arguments of the Philosophers Ser. ISBN:0-415-20368-6,
ISBN13: 978-0-415-20368-5. Dewey:193. LCCN:00-267274.

Audience: **g,u,f.**

Inwood, Michael J.   **B2901.I58 1992**
A Hegel Dictionary. Trade Paper. Blackwell Publishing, Inc.
Malden, MA. 1992. 356p. Philosopher Dictionaries Ser.
ISBN:0-631-17533-4, ISBN13: 978-0-631-17533-9. Dewey:193.
LCCN:92-013463.

Audience: **g,u,f.** *Choice, 1993.*

Kojeve, Alexandre   **B2929 .K6213 1980**
Introduction to the Reading of Hegel: Lectures on the
Phenomenology of Spirit. James H. Nicholas Jr. (Translator).
Book, Other. Cornell University Press. Ithaca, NY. 1980. 304p.
Agora Editions Ser. ISBN:0-8014-9203-3, ISBN13:
978-0-8014-9203-7. Dewey:193. LCCN:80-066908.

Audience: **g,u,f.**

Lauer, Quentin   **B2929.L38 1993**
A Reading of Hegel's "Phenomenology of Spirit". Ed. 3. Trade
Cloth. Fordham University Press. Bronx, NY. 1993. 303p.
ISBN:0-8232-1354-4, ISBN13: 978-0-8232-1354-2. Dewey:193.
LCCN:92-009891.

Audience: **u,f.** *B*

Singer, Peter   **B2948.S57 2001**
Hegel: A Very Short Introduction. Ed. 2. Trade Paper. Oxford
University Press, Inc. New York, NY. 2001. 148p. Very Short
Introductions Ser., Vol. 49 ISBN:0-19-280197-X, ISBN13:
978-0-19-280197-5. Dewey:193. LCCN:2001-036444.

Audience: **g,l,u.**

Stern, Robert   **B2929**
Philosophy Guidebook to Hegel and Phenomenology of Spirit.
Paper over Boards. Routledge. New York, NY. 2001. 256p.
Philosophy Guidebooks ISBN:0-415-21787-3, ISBN13:
978-0-415-21787-3. Dewey:193. LCCN:2001-049064.

Audience: **u,f.**

Philosophy by Country > German,
Austrian Philosophy > 19th Century

Carver, Terrell (Editor)   **B3305.M74 C35 1991**
The Cambridge Companion to Marx. Trade Paper. Cambridge
University Press. New York, NY. 1991. 373p. Cambridge
Companions to Philosophy Ser. ISBN:0-521-36694-1, ISBN13:
978-0-521-36694-6. Dewey:335.4. LCCN:91-000682.

Audience: **u,f.** *Choice, 1992.*

Chisholm, Roderick M.   **B3212.Z7 C47 1986**
Brentano and Intrinsic Value. Robert B. Pippin (Contribution
by). Trade Paper. Cambridge University Press. New York, NY.
1986. 120p. Modern European Philosophy Ser.
ISBN:0-521-26989-X, ISBN13: 978-0-521-26989-6.
Dewey:121.809. LCCN:86-014756.

Audience: **g,u,f.** *Choice, 1987.*

Dilthey, Wilhelm   **B3216.D83E413 1988**
Introduction to the Human Sciences: An Attempt to Lay a
Foundation for the Study of Society and History. Ramon J.
Betanzos (Editor, Translator). Trade Paper. Wayne State
University Press. Detroit, MI. 1988. 388p. ISBN:0-8143-1898-3,
ISBN13: 978-0-8143-1898-0. Dewey:001.3. LCCN:88-000052.

Audience: **g,u,f.**

Dilthey, Wilhelm &   **B3216.D84 M26 1992**
  Makkreel, Rudolf A.
Dilthey: Philosopher of the Human Studies. Trade Paper.
Princeton University Press. Princeton, NJ. 1992. 494p.
ISBN:0-691-02097-3, ISBN13: 978-0-691-02097-6. Dewey:193.
LCCN:92-025042.

Audience: **g,u,f.**

Feuerbach, Ludwig   **B2971.W4 E5**
The Essence of Christianity. George Eliot (Translator). Trade
Cloth. Prometheus Books, Publishers. Amherst, NY. 1989. 363p.
Great Books in Philosophy ISBN:0-87975-559-8, ISBN13:
978-0-87975-559-1. Dewey:201. LCCN:89-062324.

Audience: **g,l,u.**

Feuerbach, Ludwig   **B2971.G392E5 1980**
Thoughts on Death and Immortality: From the Papers of a
Thinker, along with an Appendix of Theological Satirical
Epigrams, Edited by One of His Friends. James A. Massey
(Translator). Trade Paper. University of California Press.
Berkeley, CA. 1981. 263p. ISBN:0-520-04062-7, ISBN13:
978-0-520-04062-5. Dewey:129. LCCN:80-025259.

Audience: **g,u,f.** *B*

Feuerbach, Ludwig   **B2971.G72E5 1986**
Principles of the Philosophy of the Future. Manfred Vogel
(Translator), Thomas E. Wartenberg (Illustrator). Trade Cloth.
Hackett Publishing Company, Inc. Indianapolis, IN. 1986. 112p.
HPC Classics Ser. ISBN:0-915145-26-X, ISBN13:
978-0-915145-26-3. Dewey:101. LCCN:86-007699.

Audience: **g,u,f.** *B*

Grossmann, Reinhardt   **B3309.M24G76 1999**
Meinong. Paper over Boards. Routledge. New York, NY. 1999.
272p. Arguments of the Philosophers Ser. ISBN:0-415-20375-9,
ISBN13: 978-0-415-20375-3. Dewey:193. LCCN:00-268521.

Audience: **g,u,f.**

Hodges, H. A.   **B3216.D84**
The Philosophy of Wilhelm Dilthey. Paper over Boards.
Routledge. New York, NY. 2003. 396p. International Library of
Sociology Ser. ISBN:0-415-17514-3, ISBN13:
978-0-415-17514-2. Dewey:193.

Audience: **g,u,f.**

Jacquette, Dale (Editor) B3212.Z7C35 2004
The Cambridge Companion to Brentano. Cloth Text. Cambridge University Press. New York, NY. 2004. 344p. Cambridge Companions to Philosophy Ser. ISBN:0-521-80980-0, ISBN13: 978-0-521-80980-1. Dewey:193. LCCN:2003-053215.

Audience: **u,f.**

Marx, Karl HX273.M23713 1998
The German Ideology Including Theses on Feuerbach and Introduction to the Critique of Political Economy: With Friedrich Engels. Prometheus Books. 1998. Great Books in Philosophy ISBN:1-57392-258-7, ISBN13: 978-1-57392-258-6.

Audience: **g,u,f.**

Marx, Karl HX39.5.A224 1997
Writings of the Young Marx on Philosophy and Society. Loyd D. Easton (Editor). Hacket Publishing Co.. 1997. Hackett Classics Ser. ISBN:0-87220-369-7, ISBN13: 978-0-87220-369-3.

Audience: **g,u,f.**

Marx, Karl HB97.5
The Economic and Philosophic Manuscripts of 1844 and the Communist Manifesto: With Friedrich Engels. Martin Milligan (Translator). Prometheus Books. 1988. Great Books in Philosophy ISBN:0-87975-446-X, ISBN13: 978-0-87975-446-4.

Audience: **g,u,f.**

Rockmore, Tom B3305.M74R57 2002
Marx after Marxism: The Philosophy of Karl Marx. Trade Paper. Blackwell Publishing, Inc. Malden, MA. 2003. 248p. ISBN:0-631-23190-0, ISBN13: 978-0-631-23190-5. Dewey:193. LCCN:2001-052685.

Audience: **g,u,f.** *Choice, 2003, 2002.*

Schelling, Friedrich Wilhelm Joseph B2883
System of Transcendental Idealism. Peter Heath (Translator, Introduction by). Paper Text. University Press of Virginia. Charlottesville, VA. 1993. 248p. ISBN:0-8139-1458-2, ISBN13: 978-0-8139-1458-9. Dewey:141.3.

Audience: **u,f.**

Smith, Barry B3258.H324
Austrian Philosophy: The Legacy of Franz Brentano. Trade Cloth. Open Court Publishing Company. Chicago, IL. 1996. 393p. ISBN:0-8126-9307-8, ISBN13: 978-0-8126-9307-2. Dewey:193.

Audience: **g,u,f.** *Choice, 1995.*

Wood, Allen W. B3305.M74W63 2004
Karl Marx. Ed. 2. Paper over Boards. Routledge. New York, NY. 2004. 344p. Arguments of the Philosophers Ser. ISBN:0-415-31697-9, ISBN13: 978-0-415-31697-2. Dewey:335.4/11. LCCN:2003-058733.

Audience: **g,u,f.** *B*

Philosophy by Country > German, Austrian Philosophy > 19th Century > Schopenhauer

Atwell, John E. B3148.A892 1995
Schopenhauer on the Character of the World: The Metaphysics of Will. Trade Cloth. University of California Press. Berkeley, CA. 1995. 238p. ISBN:0-520-08770-4, ISBN13: 978-0-520-08770-5. Dewey:193. LCCN:94-018811.

Audience: **g,u,f.** *Choice, 1995.*

Hamlyn, D. W. B3148.H27 1999
Schopenhauer. Paper over Boards. Routledge. New York, NY. 1999. 192p. Arguments of the Philosophers Ser. ISBN:0-415-20369-4, ISBN13: 978-0-415-20369-2. Dewey:193. LCCN:00-269381.

Audience: **g,u,f.**

Janaway, Christopher (Editor) B3148 .C36 1999
The Cambridge Companion to Schopenhauer. Cloth Text. Cambridge University Press. New York, NY. 1999. 492p. Cambridge Companions to Philosophy Ser. ISBN:0-521-62106-2, ISBN13: 978-0-521-62106-9. Dewey:193. LCCN:99-011396.

Audience: **u,f.** *Choice, 2000.*

Magee, Bryan B3148.M27 1997
The Philosophy of Schopenhauer. Ed. 2. Trade Cloth. Oxford University Press, Inc. New York, NY. 1997. 476p. ISBN:0-19-823723-5, ISBN13: 978-0-19-823723-5. Dewey:193. LCCN:97-220691.

Audience: **g,u,f.** *B*

Schopenhauer, Arthur
The Psychological Significance of Art and Literature. Trade Cloth. American Classical College Press. Albuquerque, NM. 1985. 129p. ISBN:0-89266-506-8, ISBN13: 978-0-89266-506-8.

Audience: **g,l,u,f.**

Schopenhauer, Arthur B3118.E5 S492 1970
Studies in Pessimism. Trade Cloth. Scholarly Press, Inc. Saint Clair Shores, MI. 1970. ISBN:0-403-00044-0, ISBN13: 978-0-403-00044-9. Dewey:083/.1. LCCN:73-121311.

Audience: **g,l,u,f.** *B*

Schopenhauer, Arthur B3118.E5
Essays and Aphorisms. R. J. Hollingdale (Translator, Selected by). Trade Paper. Penguin Group (USA) Inc. New York, NY. 1973. 240p. Classics Ser. ISBN:0-14-044227-8, ISBN13: 978-0-14-044227-4. Dewey:193. LCCN:79-509016.

Audience: **g,l,u,f.**

Schopenhauer, Arthur B3144.U352E5 1985
On the Freedom of the Will. Konstantin Kolenda (Editor, Translator). Trade Paper. Blackwell Publishing, Inc. Malden, MA. 1985. 388p. ISBN:0-631-14552-4, ISBN13: 978-0-631-14552-3. Dewey:123/.5. LCCN:85-007406.

Audience: **g,u,f.**

Audience: g=general, l=lower division undergraduate, u=upper division undergraduate, f=faculty.

465

Schopenhauer, Arthur   B3138.E5 P32
The World As Will and Representation, Vol. 1. E. F. Payne
(Translator). Trade Paper. Dover Publications, Inc. Mineola, NY.
1966. 564p. 0 ISBN:0-486-21761-2, ISBN13:
978-0-486-21761-1. Dewey:792.0942. LCCN:70-011268.
Audience: **g,u,f.**

Schopenhauer, Arthur   PN2585.B7
The World As Will and Representation, Vol. 2. E. F. Payne
(Translator). Trade Paper. Dover Publications, Inc. Mineola, NY.
1966. 694p. 0 ISBN:0-486-21762-0, ISBN13:
978-0-486-21762-8. Dewey:792.0942.
Audience: **g,u,f.**

Schopenhauer, Arthur   B3118.E5P38 2000
Parerga and Paralipomena: Short Philosophical Essays, Vol. 1.
E. F. J. Payne (Translator). Trade Paper. Oxford University
Press, Inc. New York, NY. 2001. 514p. ISBN:0-19-924220-8,
ISBN13: 978-0-19-924220-7. Dewey:193. LCCN:00-059825.
Audience: **g,u,f.**

Schopenhauer, Arthur   B3118.E5 S485 1973
Religion: A Dialogue, and Other Essays. T. Bailey Saunders
(Translator). Trade Cloth. Greenwood Publishing Group, Inc.
Portsmouth, NH. 1973. 140p. ISBN:0-8371-6652-7, ISBN13:
978-0-8371-6652-0. Dewey:193. LCCN:72-011305.
Audience: **g,u,f.**

Schopenhauer, Arthur   B3108.S3 1994
Philosophical Writings. Wolfgang Schirmacher (Editor). Trade
Paper. Continuum International Publishing Group, Ltd. London,
1994. 324p. German Library, Vol. 27 ISBN:0-8264-0729-3,
ISBN13: 978-0-8264-0729-0. Dewey:193. LCCN:81-040469.
Audience: **g,u,f.**

Philosophy by Country > German, Austrian Philosophy > 19th Century > Nietzsche

Bataille, Georges   B3317
On Nietzsche. Trade Paper. Paragon House Publishers. Saint
Paul, MN. 1993. ISBN:1-55778-644-5, ISBN13:
978-1-55778-644-9. Dewey:193.
Audience: **g,u,f.** *Choice, 1993.*

Danto, Arthur C.   B3317.D3 2004
Nietzsche As Philosopher. Trade Paper. Columbia University
Press. New York, NY. 2005. 336p. Columbia Classics in
Philosophy Ser. ISBN:0-231-13519-X, ISBN13:
978-0-231-13519-1. Dewey:193. LCCN:2004-056186.
Audience: **g,l,u,f.**

Deleuze, Gilles   B3317.D413
Nietzsche and Philosophy. Hugh Tomlinson (Translator). Trade
Paper. Columbia University Press. New York, NY. 1985. 221p.
ISBN:0-231-05669-9, ISBN13: 978-0-231-05669-4. Dewey:193.
LCCN:82-017676.
Audience: **g,u,f.** 𝐵

Heidegger, Martin   B3279.H48N5413 1991
Nietzsche, Vols. 1&2. David F. Krell (Editor). Trade Paper.
HarperCollins Publishers. New York, NY. 1991. 608p.
ISBN:0-06-063841-9, ISBN13: 978-0-06-063841-2. Dewey:193.
LCCN:78-019509.
Audience: **g,u,f.**

Hollingdale, R. J.   B3317 .H557 1999
Nietzsche: The Man and his Philosophy. Ed. 2. Trade Paper.
Cambridge University Press. New York, NY. 2001. 284p.
ISBN:0-521-00295-8, ISBN13: 978-0-521-00295-0. Dewey:193
B.
Audience: **g,u,f.** 𝐵

Kaufmann, Walter A.   B3317
Nietzsche: Philosopher, Psychologist, Antichrist. Ed. 4. Paper
Text. Princeton University Press. Princeton, NJ. 1975. 532p.
ISBN:0-691-01983-5, ISBN13: 978-0-691-01983-3.
Dewey:193.9.
Audience: **g,u,f.**

Kautmann, Walter
(Translator)   B3313.F72E5 1974
The Gay Science: With a Prelude in Rhymes and an Appendix
of Songs. Friedrich Wilhelm Nietzsche (Contribution by), Walter
Kautmann (Commentaries by). Trade Cloth. Random House,
Inc. New York, NY. 1974. xviii, 396p. ISBN:0-394-48206-9,
ISBN13: 978-0-394-48206-4. Dewey:193. LCCN:73-010477.
Audience: **g,u,f.** 𝐵

Lampert, Laurence   B3317.L255
Nietzsche and Modern Times: A Study of Bacon, Descartes, and
Nietzsche. Trade Paper. Yale University Press. Cumberland, RI.
1995. 490p. ISBN:0-300-06510-8, ISBN13: 978-0-300-06510-7.
Dewey:193.
Audience: **g,u,f.** *Choice, 1994.*

Leiter, Brian   B3318.E9L45 2002
Routledge Philosophy Guidebook to Nietzsche on Morality.
Paper over Boards. Routledge. New York, NY. 2002. 352p.
Routledge Philosophy Guidebooks ISBN:0-415-15284-4,
ISBN13: 978-0-415-15284-6. Dewey:170/.92.
LCCN:2002-072609.
Audience: **g,u,f.**

Nietzsche, Friedrich
Wilhelm   B3312.E5R53 2005
Nietzsche: The Anti-Christ, Ecce Homo, Twilight of the Idols:
And Other Writings. Aaron Ridley (Editor). Cambridge
University Press. 2005. Cambridge Texts in the History of
Philosophy Ser. ISBN:0-521-01688-6, ISBN13:
978-0-521-01688-9.
Audience: **g,u,f.**

Nietzsche, Friedrich
Wilhelm   B3313.A43E5 2005
Thus Spoke Zarathustra: A Book for Everyone and Nobody.
Graham Parkes (Translator). Trade Paper, Perfect. Oxford
University Press, Inc. New York, NY. 2005. 384p. Oxford
World's Classics Ser. ISBN:0-19-280583-5, ISBN13:
978-0-19-280583-6. Dewey:193. LCCN:2005-019431.
Audience: **g,l,u.**

Nietzsche, Friedrich   **B3313.Z73E5 1998**
On the Genealogy of Morality. Maudemarie Clark & Alan
Swenson (Translators), Maudemarie Clark (Introduction by,
Notes by), Alan Swenson (Notes by). Trade Cloth. Hackett
Publishing Company, Inc. Indianapolis, IN. 1998. 177p. Classics
Ser. ISBN:0-87220-284-4, ISBN13: 978-0-87220-284-9.
Dewey:170. LCCN:98-037868.
                                                  Audience: **g,l,u.**

Nietzsche, Friedrich   **B3313.M52E5 2006**
Human, All-Too-Human, Vol. 2, Pts. 1&2. Paul V. Cohn &
Helen Zimmern (Translators), J. M. Kennedy (Introduction by).
Trade Paper. Dover Publications, Inc. Mineola, NY. 2006. 480p.
Dover Philosophical Classics Ser. ISBN:0-486-44566-6,
ISBN13: 978-0-486-44566-3. Dewey:128. LCCN:2005-052029.
                                                  Audience: **g,u,f.**

Nietzsche, Friedrich   **B3313.J43 E5 2002**
Nietzsche: Beyond Good and Evil. Rolf-Peter Horstmann
(Editor), Judith Norman (Edited and Translated by), Karl
Ameriks & Desmond M. Clarke (Contribution by). Cloth Text.
Cambridge University Press. New York, NY. 2001. 230p. Texts
in the History of Philosophy ISBN:0-521-77078-5, ISBN13:
978-0-521-77078-1. Dewey:193. LCCN:2001-035672.
                                                  Audience: **g,l,u.**

Nietzsche, Friedrich   **B3312.E5K3 2000**
Basic Writings of Nietzsche. Walter Kaufmann (Editor,
Translator), Peter Gay (Introduction by). Trade Paper. Random
House Adult Trade Publishing Group. New York, NY. 2000.
880p. Modern Library Classics ISBN:0-679-78339-3, ISBN13:
978-0-679-78339-8. Dewey:193. LCCN:00-064578.
                                                  Audience: **g,l,u.**

Nietzsche, Friedrich   **B3316.N54**
Ecce Homo: How One Becomes What One Is. Duncan Large
(Translator). Trade Paper. Oxford University Press, Inc. New
York, NY. 2006. 160p. Oxford World's Classics Ser.
ISBN:0-19-283228-X, ISBN13: 978-0-19-283228-3. Dewey:193.
                                                  Audience: **g,u,f.**

Nietzsche, Friedrich   **B3313.G6713 1997**
Twilight of the Idols. Richard Polt (Translator), Tracy B. Strong
(Introduction by). Trade Cloth. Hackett Publishing Company,
Inc. Indianapolis, IN. 1997. 128p. Classics Ser.
ISBN:0-87220-355-7, ISBN13: 978-0-87220-355-6. Dewey:193.
LCCN:96-040331.
                                                  Audience: **g,u,f.**

Nietzsche, Friedrich   **B3312.E5 G48 1999**
Nietzsche: The Birth of Tragedy and Other Writings. Ronald
Speirs & Raymond Geuss (Editors), Ronald Speirs (Translator),
Karl Ameriks & Desmond M. Clarke (Contribution by). Cloth
Text. Cambridge University Press. New York, NY. 1999. 204p.
Texts in the History of Philosophy ISBN:0-521-63016-9,
ISBN13: 978-0-521-63016-0. Dewey:193. LCCN:98-035097.
                                                  Audience: **g,l,u,f.**

Pippin, Robert (Editor)   **B3313.A43**
Nietzsche: Thus Spoke Zarathustra. Adrian Del Caro
(Translator), Karl Ameriks & Desmond M. Clarke (Contribution

by). Cloth Text. Cambridge University Press. New York, NY.
2006. 316p. Cambridge Texts in the History of Philosophy Ser.
ISBN:0-521-84171-2, ISBN13: 978-0-521-84171-9. Dewey:193.
                                                  Audience: **g,u,f.**

Ridley, Aaron (Editor)   **B3312.E5R53 2005**
Nietzsche: The Anti-Christ, Ecce Homo, Twilight of the
Idols:And Other Writings. Judith Norman (Translator), Karl
Ameriks & Desmond M. Clarke (Contribution by). Cloth Text.
Cambridge University Press. New York, NY. 2005. 338p.
Cambridge Texts in the History of Philosophy Ser.
ISBN:0-521-81659-9, ISBN13: 978-0-521-81659-5. Dewey:193.
LCCN:2005-005780.
                                                  Audience: **g,u,f.**

Safranski, Rudiger   **B3317.S2413 2001**
Nietzsche: A Philosophical Biography. Shelley Frisch
(Translator). Trade Cloth. W. W. Norton & Company, Inc. New
York, NY. 2001. 384p. ISBN:0-393-05008-4, ISBN13:
978-0-393-05008-0. Dewey:193 B. LCCN:2001-052130.
                                       Audience: **g,l,u,f.** *Choice, 2002.*

Schacht, Richard   **B3317.S36 1999**
Nietzsche. Paper over Boards. Routledge. New York, NY. 1999.
568p. Arguments of the Philosophers Ser. ISBN:0-415-20371-6,
ISBN13: 978-0-415-20371-5. Dewey:193. LCCN:00-267275.
                                                  Audience: **g,u,f.**

Schacht, Richard (Editor)   **B3313.Z73N54 1994**
Nietzsche, Genealogy, Morality: Essays on Nietzsche's
Genealogy of Morals. Trade Paper. University of California
Press. Berkeley, CA. 1994. 502p. Philosophical Traditions Ser.,
Vol. 5 ISBN:0-520-08318-0, ISBN13: 978-0-520-08318-9.
Dewey:170. LCCN:93-012082.
                                       Audience: **g,u,f.** *Choice, 1994.*

Sleinis, E. E.   **B3318.V25S57 1994**
Nietzsche's Revaluation of Values: A Study in Strategies. Trade
Paper. University of Illinois Press. Champaign, IL. 1994. 264p.
International Nietzsche Studies ISBN:0-252-06383-X, ISBN13:
978-0-252-06383-1. Dewey:121/.8/092. LCCN:93-040385.
                                       Audience: **g,u,f.** *Choice, 1995.*

Solomon, Robert C. &   **B3317**
  Higgins, Kathleen M.
Reading Nietzsche. Paper Text. Oxford University Press, Inc.
New York, NY. 1990. 272p. ISBN:0-19-506673-1, ISBN13:
978-0-19-506673-9. Dewey:193. LCCN:88-015609.
                                       Audience: **g,u.** *Choice, 1989.*

Philosophy by Country > German, Austrian Philosophy > 20th and 21st Centuries

Buber, Martin   **B3213.B83B43 2002**
Between Man and Man. Ed. 2. Paper over Boards. Routledge.
New York, NY. 2002. 288p. Routledge Classics Ser.
ISBN:0-415-27826-0, ISBN13: 978-0-415-27826-3. Dewey:193.
LCCN:2002-021964.
                                                  Audience: **g,l,u.**

Buber, Martin   **B2313**
I and Thou. Trade Cloth. Simon & Schuster. New York, NY.
2000. 128p. ISBN:0-7432-0133-7, ISBN13: 978-0-7432-0133-9.
Dewey:181/.06.

Audience: **g,u,f.** *B*

Carnap, Rudolf   **B840**
Meaning and Necessity: A Study in Semantics and Modal Logic.
Ed. 2. Trade Paper. University of Chicago Press. Chicago, IL.
1988. 266p. ISBN:0-226-09347-6, ISBN13: 978-0-226-09347-5.
Dewey:189.4.

Audience: **u,f.** *B*

Cassirer, Ernst   **B3216.C33L63**
The Logic of the Humanities. Paper Text. Textbook Publishers.
Temecula, CA. 2003. 217p. ISBN:0-7581-0031-0, ISBN13:
978-0-7581-0031-3. Dewey:193.

Audience: **g,u,f.** *B*

Cassirer, Ernst   **B3216.C33 P513**
The Philosophy of Symbolic Forms. Paper Text. Textbook
Publishers. Temecula, CA. 2003. ISBN:0-7581-0039-6, ISBN13:
978-0-7581-0039-9. Dewey:193.9.

Audience: **g,u,f.** *B*

Dostal, Robert J. (Editor)   **B3248.G34 C35 2002**
The Cambridge Companion to Gadamer. Trade Cloth.
Cambridge University Press. New York, NY. 2002. 332p.
Cambridge Companions to Philosophy Ser.
ISBN:0-521-80193-1, ISBN13: 978-0-521-80193-5. Dewey:193.
LCCN:2001-037367.

Audience: **u,f.**

Friedman, Maurice S.   **B3213.B84F7 2002**
Martin Buber: The Life of Dialogue. Ed. 4. Paper over Boards.
Taylor & Francis Group. Philadelphia, PA. 2002. 432p.
ISBN:0-415-28474-0, ISBN13: 978-0-415-28474-5.
Dewey:296.3/092. LCCN:2002-074327.

Audience: **g,l,u.**

Gadamer, Hans Georg   **BD241.G313**
Truth and Method. Garrett Barden & John Cumming (Editors),
Garrett Barden & John Cumming (Translators). Trade Cloth.
The Seabury Press, Inc. New York, NY. 1975. xxvi, 551p. A
Continuum Book Ser. ISBN:0-8164-9220-4, ISBN13:
978-0-8164-9220-6. Dewey:121.68. LCCN:75-002053.

Audience: **g,u,f.** *B*

Habermas, Jürgen   **B3258**
Philosophical Political Profiles. Frederick G. Lawrence
(Translator). Trade Paper. MIT Press. Cambridge, MA. 1985.
240p. Studies in Contemporary German Social Thought
ISBN:0-262-58071-3, ISBN13: 978-0-262-58071-7. Dewey:193.

Audience: **g,u,f.**

Hacker, P. M.   **B3376.W564H245 1997**
Wittgenstein's Place in Twentieth-Century Analytic Philosophy.
Trade Paper. Blackwell Publishing, Inc. Malden, MA. 1996.
368p. ISBN:0-631-20099-1, ISBN13: 978-0-631-20099-4.
Dewey:192. LCCN:95-042004.

Audience: **g,u.** *Choice, 1997.*

Hahn, Lewis E. (Editor)   **B3258.H324P47 2000**
Perspectives on Habermas. Trade Paper. Open Court Publishing
Company. Chicago, IL. 2000. 672p. ISBN:0-8126-9427-9,
ISBN13: 978-0-8126-9427-7. Dewey:193. LCCN:00-056961.

Audience: **u,f.**

Heidegger, Martin   **B3279.H48**
The Basic Problems of Phenomenology. Albert Hofstadter
(Translator, Introduction by). Trade Paper. Indiana University
Press. Bloomington, IN. 1988. 430p. Studies in Phenomenology
and Existential Philosophy ISBN:0-253-20478-X, ISBN13:
978-0-253-20478-3. Dewey:142.7. LCCN:80-008379.

Audience: **g,u,f.** *B*

Hook, Sidney   **B3305.M74H6 1994**
From Hegel to Marx: Studies in the Intellectual Development of
Karl Marx. Trade Cloth. Columbia University Press. New York,
NY. 1994. 335p. ISBN:0-231-09664-X, ISBN13:
978-0-231-09664-5. Dewey:335.4/092. LCCN:93-046389.

Audience: **g,u,f.** *B*

Horkheimer, Max   **B3279.H8473E3 2004**
Eclipse of Reason. Trade Paper. Continuum International
Publishing Group, Ltd. London, 2005. 144p.
ISBN:0-8264-7793-3, ISBN13: 978-0-8264-7793-4. Dewey:193.
LCCN:2005-276218.

Audience: **g,u,f.** *B*

Horkheimer, Max &   **B3279.H8473P513 2002**
  Adorno, Theodor W.
Dialectic of Enlightenment. Gunzelin Schmitt-Noerr (Editor),
Edmund Jephcott (Translator). Trade Cloth. Stanford University
Press. Palo Alto, CA. 2002. 304p. Cultural Memory in the
Present Ser. ISBN:0-8047-3632-4, ISBN13: 978-0-8047-3632-9.
Dewey:193. LCCN:2002-000073.

Audience: **g,u,f.**

Husserl, Edmund   **B3279.H93**
Idea of Phenomenology. W. P. Alston (Translator). Paper Text.
Martinus-Nijhoff Publishers (N E). 1973. 82p.
ISBN:90-247-0114-7, ISBN13: 978-90-247-0114-8.
Dewey:142.7.

Audience: **g,u,f.**

Jaspers, Karl   **BD171**
Truth and Symbol: The Apprehension and Consciousness of
Being. Book, Other. Rowman & Littlefield Publishers, Inc.
Lanham, MD. 1959. 79p. ISBN:0-8084-0303-6, ISBN13:
978-0-8084-0303-6. Dewey:111.

Audience: **g,l,u.**

Jaspers, Karl   **B3279.J32E52 1989**
Philosophy and the World. E. B. Ashton (Translator). Trade
Paper. Regnery Publishing, Incorporated, An Eagle Publishing
Company. Washington, DC. 1989. 288p. ISBN:0-89526-757-8,
ISBN13: 978-0-89526-757-3. Dewey:193. LCCN:88-032675.

Audience: **g,l,u.**

Noonan, Harold W.   **B3245.F24 N66**
Frege: A Critical Introduction. Trade Paper. Polity Press.

Cambridge, 2001. 256p. Key Contemporary Thinkers Ser. ISBN:0-7456-1673-9, ISBN13: 978-0-7456-1673-5. Dewey:193.

Audience: **g,u,f.** *Choice, 2001.*

Schilpp, Paul Arthur B3216.C34 S3
The Philosophy of Ernst Cassirer. Paper Text. Textbook Publishers. Temecula, CA. 2003. xviii, 936p. ISBN:0-7581-3059-7, ISBN13: 978-0-7581-3059-4. Dewey:193.

Audience: **g,u,f.** ℬ

Schilpp, Paul Arthur B945.C164 S3
(Editor)
The Philosophy of Rudolph Carnap, Vol. 11. Trade Paper. Open Court Publishing Company. Chicago, IL. 1963. 1104p. Library of Living Philosophers, Vol. XI ISBN:0-8126-9153-9, ISBN13: 978-0-8126-9153-5. Dewey:193. LCCN:62-009577.

Audience: **g,u,f.**

Sluga, Hans D. B3245.F24S58 1999
Frege. Paper over Boards. Routledge. New York, NY. 1999. 216p. Arguments of the Philosophers Ser. ISBN:0-415-20374-0, ISBN13: 978-0-415-20374-6. Dewey:193. LCCN:00-267879.

Audience: **u,f.**

Vaihinger, H. B3354.V5 P6
The Philosophy of As If: A System of the Theoretical, Practical and Religious Fictions of Mankind. Ed. 2. C. K. Ogden (Translator). Trade Cloth. Routledge. New York, NY. 1968. International Library of Philosophy, Psychology, and Scientific Method ISBN:0-685-04393-2, ISBN13: 978-0-685-04393-6. Dewey:149.9.

Audience: **g,l,u,f.**

Voegelin, Eric & Wizer, B3354.V88 1989 V. 23
James L.
ⓔ The Collected Works of Eric Voegelin. E-Book. University of Missouri Press. Columbia, MO. 1998. ISBN:0-8262-6193-0, ISBN13: 978-0-8262-6193-9. Dewey:193.

Audience: **g,u,f.**

White, Stephen K. (Editor) B3258.H324
The Cambridge Companion to Habermas. Trade Paper. Cambridge University Press. New York, NY. 1995. 366p. Cambridge Companions to Philosophy Ser. ISBN:0-521-44666-X, ISBN13: 978-0-521-44666-2. Dewey:193. LCCN:94-028826.

Audience: **u,f.** *Choice, 1996.*

Philosophy by Country > German, Austrian Philosophy > 20th and 21st Centuries > Husserl

Bell, David Andrew B3279.H94B39 1999
Husserl. Paper over Boards. Routledge. New York, NY. 1999. 266p. Arguments of the Philosophers Ser. ISBN:0-415-20376-7, ISBN13: 978-0-415-20376-0. Dewey:193. LCCN:00-268664.

Audience: **u,f.**

Findlay, J. N. & Husserl, B3279.H93L6413 2000
Edmund
Logical Investigations. Trade Cloth. Prometheus Books, Publishers. Amherst, NY. 2000. 913p. ISBN:1-57392-866-6, ISBN13: 978-1-57392-866-3. Dewey:160. LCCN:00-063460.

Audience: **g,u,f.**

Husserl, Edmund B3279.H93 I33
Ideas: General Introduction to Pure Phenomenology. Paper over Boards. Routledge. New York, NY. 2004. 464p. Muirhead Library of Philosophy Ser. ISBN:0-415-29544-0, ISBN13: 978-0-415-29544-4. Dewey:142/.7.

Audience: **g,u,f.** ℬ

Husserl, Edmund B3279.H93Z8413
On the Phenomenology of the Consciousness of Internal Time (1893-1917). Trade Cloth. Springer Dordrecht. Dordrecht, 1992. 468p. ISBN:0-7923-1536-7, ISBN13: 978-0-7923-1536-0. Dewey:115.

Audience: **g,u,f.**

Husserl, Edmund B3279.H93
Cartesian Meditations, 1. Dorion Cairns (Translator). Trade Paper. Martinus-Nijhoff Publishers (N E). 1977. 176p. ISBN:90-247-0068-X, ISBN13: 978-90-247-0068-4. Dewey:142.7.

Audience: **g,u,f.**

Husserl, Edmund BC177.N69
Crisis of European Sciences and Transcendental Phenomenology: An Introduction to Phenomenological Philosophy. David Carr (Translator). Trade Paper. Northwestern University Press. Evanston, IL. 1970. 405p. Studies in Phenomenology and Existential Philosophy ISBN:0-8101-0458-X, ISBN13: 978-0-8101-0458-7. Dewey:142.7. LCCN:77-082511.

Audience: **g,u,f.** ℬ

Husserl, Edmund B3279.H93 I3313
Phenomenology and the Foundations of the Sciences. Ted Klein & W. E. Pohl (Translators). Trade Paper. Springer. New York, NY. 2001. 152p. ISBN:1-4020-0256-4, ISBN13: 978-1-4020-0256-4. Dewey:142/.7.

Audience: **g,u,f.**

Kolakowski, Leszek B3279.H94K64 2001
Husserl and the Search for Certitude. Trade Paper. Saint Augustine's Press, Inc. South Bend, IN. 2001. 85p. ISBN:1-890318-29-9, ISBN13: 978-1-890318-29-1. Dewey:193. LCCN:2001-019390.

Audience: **g,u,f.** ℬ

Levinas, Emmanuel B3279.H94L413 1995
The Theory of Intuition in Husserl's Phenomenology. Ed. 2. Andre Orianne (Translator). Trade Paper. Northwestern University Press. Evanston, IL. 1995. 163p. Studies in Phenomenology and Existential Philosophy ISBN:0-8101-1281-7, ISBN13: 978-0-8101-1281-0. Dewey:121/.3. LCCN:95-014655.

Audience: **g,u,f.** ℬ

McCormick, Peter &   **B3279.H92.E5 1981**
Elliston, Frederick A. (Editors)
Husserl: Shorter Works. Cloth Text. University of Notre Dame
Press. Notre Dame, IN. 1982. 440p. ISBN:0-268-01703-4,
ISBN13: 978-0-268-01703-3. Dewey:193. LCCN:80-053178.

Audience: **g,u,f.** ℬ

Smith, Barry & Smith,   **B3279.H94 C28 1995**
David Woodruff (Editors)
The Cambridge Companion to Husserl. Cloth Text. Cambridge
University Press. New York, NY. 1995. 528p. Cambridge
Companions to Philosophy Ser. ISBN:0-521-43023-2, ISBN13:
978-0-521-43023-4. Dewey:193. LCCN:95-003957.

Audience: **g,u,f.** *Choice, 1996.*

Sokolowski, Robert   **B3279.H94 S624**
Husserlian Meditations: How Words Present Things. Trade
Paper. Northwestern University Press. Evanston, IL. 1974. 296p.
Studies in Phenomenology and Existential Philosophy
ISBN:0-8101-0623-X, ISBN13: 978-0-8101-0623-9. Dewey:193.
LCCN:73-091312.

Audience: **u,f.** ℬ

Stroker, Elisabeth   **B3279.H94S77413 1993**
Husserl's Transcendental Phenomenology. Lee Hardy
(Translator). Trade Cloth. Stanford University Press. Palo Alto,
CA. 1993. 268p. Stanford Series in Philosophy
ISBN:0-8047-2133-5, ISBN13: 978-0-8047-2133-2. Dewey:193.
LCCN:92-024003.

Audience: **g,u,f.** *Choice, 1993.*

Velarde-Mayol, Victor   **B3279.H94V45 2000**
On Husserl. Trade Paper. Thomson Wadsworth. Belmont, CA.
1999. 96p. Wadsworth Philosophers Ser. ISBN:0-534-57610-9,
ISBN13: 978-0-534-57610-3. Dewey:193. LCCN:00-551606.

Audience: **g,u,f.**

Philosophy by Country > German, Austrian Philosophy > 20th and 21st Centuries > Heidegger

Gelven, Michael   **B3279.H48S465 1989**
A Commentary on Heidegger's Being and Time. Trade Paper.
Northern Illinois University Press. DeKalb, IL. 2003. 243p.
ISBN:0-87580-544-2, ISBN13: 978-0-87580-544-3. Dewey:111.
LCCN:89-008585.

Audience: **u,f.**

Glazebrook, Trish   **B3279.H49G57 2000**
(Contribution by)
Heidegger's Philosophy of Science. Trade Cloth. Fordham
University Press. Bronx, NY. 2000. 278p. Perspectives in
Continental Philosophy Ser., Vol. 12 ISBN:0-8232-2037-0,
ISBN13: 978-0-8232-2037-3. Dewey:193. LCCN:00-025802.

Audience: **u,f.** *Choice, 2001.*

Guignon, Charles (Editor)   **B3279.H49C25 2006**
The Cambridge Companion to Heidegger. Ed. 2. Cloth Text.
Cambridge University Press. New York, NY. 2006. 456p.
Cambridge Companions to Philosophy Ser.
ISBN:0-521-82136-3, ISBN13: 978-0-521-82136-0. Dewey:193.
LCCN:2006-001151.

Audience: **u,f.**

Heidegger, Martin   **B3279.H48**
Being and Time. Trade Cloth. HarperCollins Publishers. New
York, NY. 1962. 592p. ISBN:0-06-063850-8, ISBN13:
978-0-06-063850-4. Dewey:111. LCCN:72-078334.

Audience: **g,u,f.** ℬ

Heidegger, Martin   **B3279.H47 E56**
The Question of Being. Book, Other. Rowman & Littlefield
Publishers, Inc. Lanham, MD. 1958. ISBN:0-8084-0258-7,
ISBN13: 978-0-8084-0258-9. Dewey:111.

Audience: **g,u,f.**

Heidegger, Martin   **B3279.H48B44513 1999**
Contributions to Philosophy: From Enowning. Parvis Emad &
Kenneth Maly (Translators). Trade Cloth. Indiana University
Press. Bloomington, IN. 2000. 464p. Studies in Continental
Thought ISBN:0-253-33606-6, ISBN13: 978-0-253-33606-4.
Dewey:193. LCCN:99-034597.

Audience: **g,u,f.** *Choice, 2000.*

Heidegger, Martin   **BD111.H42 2000**
Introduction to Metaphysics. Gregory Fried & Richard Polt
(Translators). Cloth over Boards. Yale University Press.
Cumberland, RI. 2000. 294p. ISBN:0-300-08327-0, ISBN13:
978-0-300-08327-9. Dewey:110. LCCN:99-088479.

Audience: **g,u,f.**

Heidegger, Martin   **BF455**
What Is Called Thinking? J. Glenn Gray & Fred D. Wieck
(Translators). Trade Paper. HarperCollins Publishers. New York,
NY. 1976. 272p. ISBN:0-06-090528-X, ISBN13:
978-0-06-090528-6. Dewey:111. LCCN:68-017591.

Audience: **g,u,f.**

Heidegger, Martin   **B3279.H48**
The Question Concerning Technology, and Other Essays.
William Lovitt (Translator). Trade Paper. HarperCollins
Publishers. New York, NY. 1982. 224p. ISBN:0-06-131969-4,
ISBN13: 978-0-06-131969-3. Dewey:193.

Audience: **g,u,f.** ℬ

Heidegger, Martin   **B3279.H48 W413 1998**
Pathmarks. William McNeil (Editor, Translator). Trade Cloth.
Cambridge University Press. New York, NY. 1998. 399p.
ISBN:0-521-43362-2, ISBN13: 978-0-521-43362-4. Dewey:193.
LCCN:97-022565.

Audience: **g,u,f.** *Choice, 1998.*

Heidegger, Martin   **BD236**
Identity and Difference. Joan Stambaugh (Translator). Trade
Paper. University of Chicago Press. Chicago, IL. 2002. 150p.
ISBN:0-226-32378-1, ISBN13: 978-0-226-32378-7. Dewey:111.

Audience: **g,u,f.**

Heidegger, Martin   **B3239.H47E55 2003**
The End of Philosophy. Joan Stambaugh (Translator,
Introduction by). Trade Paper. University of Chicago Press.
Chicago, IL. 2003. 124p. ISBN:0-226-32383-8, ISBN13:
978-0-226-32383-1. Dewey:110. LCCN:2003-040997.
                                     Audience: **g,u,f.**

Inwood, Michael   **B3279.H49 I594 2000**
Heidegger: A Very Short Introduction. Trade Paper. Oxford
University Press, Inc. New York, NY. 2002. 160p. Very Short
Introductions Ser. ISBN:0-19-285410-0, ISBN13:
978-0-19-285410-0. Dewey:193. LCCN:2003-267665.
                                     Audience: **g,l,u.**

Inwood, Michael J. (Editor)   **B3279.H48Z44 1999**
A Heidegger Dictionary. Trade Paper. Blackwell Publishing, Inc.
Malden, MA. 1999. 304p. The Philosopher Dictionaries Ser.
ISBN:0-631-19095-3, ISBN13: 978-0-631-19095-0. Dewey:193.
LCCN:99-017512.
                        Audience: **g,u.** *Choice, 2000.*

Kisiel, Theodore J.   **B3279.H48**
The Genesis of Heidegger's Being and Time. Trade Paper.
University of California Press. Berkeley, CA. 1995. 622p.
ISBN:0-520-20159-0, ISBN13: 978-0-520-20159-0. Dewey:111.
                        Audience: **u,f.** *Choice, 1994.*

Langan, Thomas   **B3279**
The Meaning of Heidegger: A Critical Study of an Existentialist
Phenomenology. Trade Cloth. Greenwood Publishing Group,
Inc. Portsmouth, NH. 1983. 247p. ISBN:0-313-24124-4,
ISBN13: 978-0-313-24124-6. Dewey:193. LCCN:83-012737.
                        Audience: **g,u,f.** *B*

McCumber, John   **B3279.H49M3754 1999**
Metaphysics and Oppression: Heidegger's Challenge to Western
Philosophy. Cloth Text. Indiana University Press. Bloomington,
IN. 1999. 525p. Studies in Continental Thought
ISBN:0-253-33473-X, ISBN13: 978-0-253-33473-2. Dewey:193.
LCCN:98-045926.
                        Audience: **u,f.** *Choice, 2000.*

Mulhall, Stephen   **B3279.H48S46654 2005**
Routledge Philosophy Guidebook to Heidegger and Being and
Time. Ed. 2. Perfect, Paper over Boards. Routledge. New York,
NY. 2005. 220p. Routledge Philosophy Guidebooks
ISBN:0-415-35719-5, ISBN13: 978-0-415-35719-7. Dewey:111.
LCCN:2005-004675.
                                     Audience: **g,u,f.**

Pattison, George   **B3279.H49**
Routledge Philosophy Guidebook to the Later Heidegger. Paper
over Boards. Routledge. New York, NY. 2000. 256p. Philosophy
Guidebooks ISBN:0-415-20196-9, ISBN13: 978-0-415-20196-4.
Dewey:193. LCCN:00-020572.
                                     Audience: **u,f.**

Phoggeler, Otto   **B3279.H49P63813 1998**
The Paths of Heidegger's Life and Thought. Trade Cloth.
Prometheus Books, Publishers. Amherst, NY. 1999. 374p.

Contemporary Studies in Philosophy and the Human Sciences
Ser. ISBN:1-57392-503-9, ISBN13: 978-1-57392-503-7.
Dewey:193. LCCN:99-010396.
                                     Audience: **g,u,f.**

Richardson, W. J.   **B3279.H49 R5**
Heidegger: Through Phenomenology to Thought. Ed. 3. Library
Binding. Martinus-Nijhoff Publishers (N E). 1974. 797p.
Phaenomenologica Ser., No. 13 ISBN:90-247-0246-1, ISBN13:
978-90-247-0246-6. Dewey:193.
                                     Audience: **g,u,f.**

Wrathall, Mark A.   **B3279.H49B583 2004**
A Companion to Heidegger. Hubert L. Dreyfus (Editor). Trade
Cloth. Blackwell Publishing, Inc. Malden, MA. 2005. 560p.
Blackwell Companions to Philosophy Ser. ISBN:1-4051-1092-9,
ISBN13: 978-1-4051-1092-1. Dewey:193. LCCN:2004-019151.
                        Audience: **u,f.** *Choice, 2005.*

Philosophy by Country > German, Austrian Philosophy > 20th and 21st Centuries > Wittgenstein

Ambrose, Alice &   **B3376.W564**
  Lazerowitz, Morris (Editors)
Ludwig Wittgenstein: Philosophy and Language. Trade Paper.
Continuum International Publishing Group, Ltd. London, 1996.
325p. Wittgenstein Studies ISBN:1-85506-488-X, ISBN13:
978-1-85506-488-1. Dewey:192.
                                     Audience: **g,u,f.**

Anscombe, G. E. M. & von   **B3376.W563.O5**
  Wright, G. H. (Editors)
On Certainty. G. E. M. Anscombe & Denis Paul (Translators),
Ludwig Wittgenstein (Contribution by). Trade Cloth. Blackwell
Publishing, Inc. Malden, MA. 1969. vii, 90p.
ISBN:0-631-12000-9, ISBN13: 978-0-631-12000-1.
Dewey:121/.6. LCCN:69-020428.
                                     Audience: **g,u,f.** *B*

Black, Max   **BC135.W52 B6**
A Companion to Wittgenstein's Tractatus. Trade Cloth. Cornell
University Press. Ithaca, NY. 1964. 466p. ISBN:0-8014-0039-2,
ISBN13: 978-0-8014-0039-1. Dewey:164.
                                     Audience: **u,f.** *B*

Fogelin, Robert J.   **B3376.W564**
Wittgenstein. Trade Paper. Routledge. New York, NY. 9999. xvi,
223p. Arguments of the Philosophers Ser. ISBN:0-7100-8347-5,
ISBN13: 978-0-7100-8347-0. Dewey:192.
                                     Audience: **u,f.** *B*

Glock, Hans Johann   **B3376.W563Z83 1996**
A Wittgenstein Dictionary. Trade Paper. Blackwell Publishing,
Inc. Malden, MA. 1996. 416p. The Blackwell Philosopher
Dictionaries Ser. ISBN:0-631-18537-2, ISBN13:
978-0-631-18537-6. Dewey:192. LCCN:95-018426.
                        Audience: **g,u,f.** *Choice, 1996.*

Hintikka, Jaakko   B3376.W564H56 2000
On Wittgenstein. Trade Paper. Thomson Wadsworth. Belmont, CA. 1999. 80p. Philosophy Ser. ISBN:0-534-57594-3, ISBN13: 978-0-534-57594-6. Dewey:192. LCCN:00-269010.

Audience: **u,f.**

Kenny, Anthony   B3376.W564K4 2006
Wittgenstein. Trade Paper. Blackwell Publishing, Inc. Malden, MA. 2005. 248p. ISBN:1-4051-3655-3, ISBN13: 978-1-4051-3655-6. Dewey:192. LCCN:2005-016890.

Audience: **g,l,u,f.** 𝓑

Kripke, Saul A.   B3376.W564.K74 1982
Wittgenstein on Rules and Private Language: An Elementary Exposition. Trade Cloth. Harvard University Press. Cambridge, MA. 1982. 160p. ISBN:0-674-95400-9, ISBN13: 978-0-674-95400-7. Dewey:401. LCCN:79-026088.

Audience: **u,f.** 𝓑

Malcolm, Norman   B3376
Ludwig Wittgenstein: A Memoir. Ed. 2. Trade Paper. Oxford University Press, Inc. New York, NY. 2001. 144p. ISBN:0-19-924759-5, ISBN13: 978-0-19-924759-2. Dewey:192 B. LCCN:2002-276852.

Audience: **g,l,u.**

McGinn, Marie &   B3376.W563.P53255
    Wittgenstein, Ludwig Josef Johann
Routledge Philosophy Guidebook to Wittgenstein and the Philosophical Investigations. Paper over Boards. Routledge. New York, NY. 1997. 240p. Philosophy Guidebooks ISBN:0-415-11190-0, ISBN13: 978-0-415-11190-4. Dewey:192. LCCN:96-027227.

Audience: **u,f.**

Nordmann, Alfred   B3376.W563T73543
Wittgenstein's Tractatus: An Introduction. Cloth Text. Cambridge University Press. New York, NY. 2005. 246p. Cambridge Introductions to Key Philosophical Texts ISBN:0-521-85086-X, ISBN13: 978-0-521-85086-5. Dewey:192. LCCN:2005-047005.

Audience: **g,u,f.**

Sluga, Hans D. & Stern,   B3376.W564 C345 1996
    David G. (Editors)
The Cambridge Companion to Wittgenstein. Trade Paper. Cambridge University Press. New York, NY. 1996. 523p. Cambridge Companions to Philosophy Ser. ISBN:0-521-46591-5, ISBN13: 978-0-521-46591-5. Dewey:193. LCCN:96-005300.

Audience: **u,f.** *Choice, 1997.*

Stern, David G.   B3376.W563P532 2004
Wittgenstein's Philosophical Investigations: An Introduction. Cloth Text. Cambridge University Press. New York, NY. 2004. 224p. Cambridge Introductions to Key Philosophical Texts ISBN:0-521-81442-1, ISBN13: 978-0-521-81442-3. Dewey:192. LCCN:2004-045823.

Audience: **g,u,f.**

Waismann, Friedrich   B3376.W564
Ludwig Wittgenstein and the Vienna Circle. J. Schulte & B. McGuinness (Translators). Trade Paper. Blackwell Publishing, Inc. Malden, MA. 266p. ISBN:0-631-13469-7, ISBN13: 978-0-631-13469-5. Dewey:192.

Audience: **g,l,u,f.**

Wittgenstein, Ludwig   B3376.W563
Philosophical Grammar. Ed. 2. Trade Paper. University of California Press. Berkeley, CA. 2005. 496p. ISBN:0-520-24502-4, ISBN13: 978-0-520-24502-0. Dewey:192.

Audience: **g,u,f.**

Wittgenstein, Ludwig Josef   B3376.W561A6
    Johann
Zettel. G. E. Anscombe & George H. Von Wright (Editors), G. E. Anscombe (Translator). Trade Paper. University of California Press. Berkeley, CA. 1970. ISBN:0-520-01635-1, ISBN13: 978-0-520-01635-4. Dewey:192.

Audience: **g,u,f.** 𝓑

Wittgenstein, Ludwig Josef   B3376.W562.E5 1993
    Johann
Philosophical Occasions, 1912-1951. James Klagge & Alfred Nordmann (Editors). Trade Cloth. Hackett Publishing Company, Inc. Indianapolis, IN. 1993. 542p. ISBN:0-87220-155-4, ISBN13: 978-0-87220-155-2. Dewey:192. LCCN:92-038232.

Audience: **g,u,f.** *Choice, 1994.*

Wittgenstein, Ludwig Josef   B3376.W563T7313 2001
    Johann
Tractatus Logico-Philosophicus. Ed. 2. David Francis Pears & Brian McGuinness (Translators). Paper over Boards. Routledge. New York, NY. 2001. 144p. Classics Ser. ISBN:0-415-25562-7, ISBN13: 978-0-415-25562-2. Dewey:192. LCCN:2001-041223.

Audience: **g,u,f.**

Wittgenstein, Ludwig Josef   B3376.W563
    Johann
Notebooks, 1914-1916. Ed. 2. George H. Von Wright & G. E. Anscombe (Editors). Trade Paper. University of Chicago Press. Chicago, IL. 1984. 234p. ISBN:0-226-90447-4, ISBN13: 978-0-226-90447-4. Dewey:192. LCCN:79-015685.

Audience: **g,u,f.**

Wittgenstein, Ludwig   B3376.W561 2001
Wittgenstein's Lectures: Cambridge, 1932-1935 from the Notes of Alice Ambrose and Margaret Macdonald. Alice Ambrose (Editor). Trade Paper. Prometheus Books, Publishers. Amherst, NY. 2004. 225p. Great Books in Philosophy ISBN:1-57392-875-5, ISBN13: 978-1-57392-875-5. Dewey:192. LCCN:2001-019037.

Audience: **g,u,f.**

Wittgenstein, Ludwig &   B3376.W563P53 1968B
    Anscombe, Gertrude Elizabeth Margaret
Philosophical Investigations. Ed. 3. Trade Cloth. Blackwell Publishing Ltd. Oxford, 1968. viii, 250p. ISBN:0-631-11900-0, ISBN13: 978-0-631-11900-5. Dewey:192. LCCN:69-020432.

Audience: **u,f.** 𝓑

Wittgenstein, Ludwig &   **B840**
  Docherty, Peter
Blue and Brown Books: Preliminary Studies for the
Philosophical Investigations. Ed. 2. Trade Paper. Blackwell
Publishing, Inc. Malden, MA. 2002. 180p. ISBN:0-631-14660-1,
ISBN13: 978-0-631-14660-5. Dewey:149/.94.

                          Audience: **g,u,f.**

Philosophy by Country > Italian Philosophy

Croce, Benedetto   **D13**
The Philosophy of History. Trade Cloth. Foundation for
Classical Reprints, The. Albuquerque, NM. 1983. 123p.
ISBN:0-89901-128-4, ISBN13: 978-0-89901-128-8.
Dewey:907.2.

                          Audience: **g,u,f.**

Croce, Benedetto   **B3614.C73B7413 1995**
Guide to Aesthetics. Ed. 2. Patrick Romanell (Translator). Trade
Cloth. Hackett Publishing Company, Inc. Indianapolis, IN. 1995.
128p. HPC Classics Ser. ISBN:0-87220-305-0, ISBN13:
978-0-87220-305-1. Dewey:111/.85. LCCN:94-043408.

                          Audience: **g,u,f.**

Croce, Benedetto   **B3583.C713 2001**
The Philosophy of Giambattista Vico. Alan Sica (Introduction
by). Trade Paper. Transaction Publishers. Somerset, NJ. 2002.
317p. ISBN:0-7658-0869-2, ISBN13: 978-0-7658-0869-1.
Dewey:195. LCCN:2001-048081.

                          Audience: **g,u,f.**

De Gennaro, Angelo A.   **B3614.C74 D4**
The Philosophy of Benedetto Croce. Trade Cloth. Philosophical
Library, Inc. New York, NY. 1961. 128p. ISBN:0-8022-0371-X,
ISBN13: 978-0-8022-0371-7. Dewey:195. LCCN:61-012620.

                          Audience: **g,u,f.**

Moss, M. E.   **B3614.C74M6**
Benedetto Croce Reconsidered: Truth and Error in Theories of
Art, Literature, and History. Maurice Mandelbaum (Foreword
by). Trade Paper. Books on Demand. Ann Arbor, MI. 1987.
164p. ISBN:0-608-02326-4, ISBN13: 978-0-608-02326-7.
Dewey:195. LCCN:86-022399.

                          Audience: **u,f.**

Pompa, Leon (Editor)   **B3581.P73 V53 2002**
Vico: The First New Science. Cloth Text. Cambridge University
Press. New York, NY. 2002. 366p. Cambridge Texts in the
History of Political Thought Ser. ISBN:0-521-38290-4, ISBN13:
978-0-521-38290-8. Dewey:195. LCCN:2002-073724.

                          Audience: **g,u,f.**

Verene, Donald Phillip   **B3583**
Vico's Science of Imagination. Book, Other. Cornell University
Press. Ithaca, NY. 1981. 248p. ISBN:0-8014-1391-5, ISBN13:
978-0-8014-1391-9. Dewey:195. LCCN:80-069828.

                    Audience: **g,u,f.** ℬ

Vico, Giambattista   **B3581.P72E5 1999**
New Science: Principles of the New Science Concerning the
Common Nat- ure of Nations. Ed. 3. David Marsh (Translator),
Anthony Grafton (Introduction by). Trade Paper. Penguin Group
(USA) Inc. New York, NY. 2000. 560p. Classics Ser.
ISBN:0-14-043569-7, ISBN13: 978-0-14-043569-6. Dewey:195.
LCCN:00-265320.

                          Audience: **g,u,f.**

Yates, Frances A.   **B783.Z7**
Selected Works of Frances Yates, Set. Library Binding.
Routledge. New York, NY. 1999. 3656p. ISBN:0-415-22043-2,
ISBN13: 978-0-415-22043-9. Dewey:192.

                          Audience: **g,u,f.**

Philosophy by Country > Russian Philosophy

Althusser, Louis   **B2430.A473L4613 2001**
Lenin and Philosophy and Other Essays. Trade Cloth. Monthly
Review Press. New York, NY. 2002. 288p.
ISBN:1-58367-038-6, ISBN13: 978-1-58367-038-5.
Dewey:335.43. LCCN:2001-052137.

                    Audience: **g,u,f.** ℬ

Berlin, Isaiah   **DK189**
Russian Thinkers. Henry Hardy & Aileen Kelly (Editors). Trade
Paper. Penguin Group (USA) Inc. New York, NY. 1979. 336p.
ISBN:0-14-013625-8, ISBN13: 978-0-14-013625-8.
Dewey:947/.07.

                          Audience: **g,l,u.**

Copleston, Frederick   **B72 .C62 2003**
Russian Philosophy, Vol. 10. Trade Paper. Continuum
International Publishing Group, Ltd. London, 2003. 464p.
ISBN:0-8264-6904-3, ISBN13: 978-0-8264-6904-5. Dewey:109.

                          Audience: **g,l,u.**

Scanlan, James P. & Zeldin,   **B4201 .E3 1976**
  Mary-Barbara
Russian Philosophy: The Beginning of Russian Philosophy: the
Slavophiles: the Weternizers. James M. Edie (Editor). Trade
Paper. University of Tennessee Press. Knoxville, TN. 1976.
456p. ISBN:0-87049-200-4, ISBN13: 978-0-87049-200-6.
Dewey:197. LCCN:77-352053.

                        Audience: **g,l,u,f.**

Scanlan, James P. (Editor),   **B4201 .E3**
  et al.
Russian Philosophy: Pre-Revolutionary Philosophy and
Theology: Philosiphers in Exile: Marxists and Communists, Vol.
3. Mary-Barbara Zeldin, James M. Edie & George L. Kline
(Editors). Trade Paper. University of Tennessee Press. Knoxville,
TN. 1976. 542p. ISBN:0-87049-716-2, ISBN13:
978-0-87049-716-2. Dewey:197. LCCN:64-010928.

                        Audience: **g,l,u,f.**

Scanlan, James P. & Zeldin,   B4201 .E3
  Mary-Barbara
Russian Philosophy: The Nihilists: the Populists: the Critics of
Religion and Culture, Vol. 2. James W. Edie (Editor). Trade
Paper. University of Tennessee Press. Knoxville, TN. 1976.
ISBN:0-87049-715-4, ISBN13: 978-0-87049-715-5. Dewey:197.
LCCN:64-010928.

Audience: **g,l,u,f.**

Shein, Louis J.   B4259.S54S54 1991
The Philosophy of Lev Shestov, 1866-1938: A Russian
Religious Existentialist. Trade Cloth. Edwin Mellen Press, The.
Lewiston, NY. 1991. 120p. Toronto Studies in Theology, Vol. 57
ISBN:0-7734-9662-9, ISBN13: 978-0-7734-9662-0.
Dewey:200.1. LCCN:91-023662.

Audience: **g,l,u.**

Shestov, Lev   B4259.S52 E55
Penultimate Words, and Other Essays. Trade Cloth. Ayer
Company Publishers, Inc. Manchester, NH. 1977. Essay Index
Reprint Ser. ISBN:0-8369-0876-7, ISBN13: 978-0-8369-0876-3.
Dewey:197/.2. LCCN:67-022117.

Audience: **g,l,u.**

Soloviev, Vladimir &   B4262.E5W69 2000
  Wozniuk, Vladimir (Editors)
Politics, Law and Morality: Essays by V. S. Soloviev. Cloth over
Boards. Yale University Press. Cumberland, RI. 2000. 368p.
Russian Literature and Thought Ser. ISBN:0-300-07995-8,
ISBN13: 978-0-300-07995-1. Dewey:197. LCCN:99-041463.
Audience: **g,u,f.** *Choice, 2000.*

Zenkovsky, V. V.   B4231
A History of Russian Philosophy, Set. Paper over Boards.
Routledge. New York, NY. 2003. 1008p. ISBN:0-415-30304-4,
ISBN13: 978-0-415-30304-0. Dewey:197.

Audience: **g,u,f.**

Philosophy by Country > Spanish Philosophy

Ferrater Mora, Jose   B4568.U54F43
Unamuno, a Philosophy of Tragedy. Paper Text. Textbook
Publishers. Temecula, CA. 2003. 136p. ISBN:0-7581-2685-9,
ISBN13: 978-0-7581-2685-6. Dewey:196.1.
Audience: **g,u,f.** *B*

Mora, Jose Ferrater   B4568.U54F3913 2003
Three Spanish Philosophers: Unamuno, Ortega, Ferrater Mora. J.
M. Terricabras (Editor). Paper Text. State University of New
York Press. Albany, NY. 2003. vii, 268p. SUNY Series in Latin
American and Iberian Thought and Culture
ISBN:0-7914-5714-1, ISBN13: 978-0-7914-5714-6.
Dewey:196/.1. LCCN:2002-030967.
Audience: **g,u,f.**

Ortega y Gasset, Jose   B92.O76513 2000
The Origin of Philosophy. Trade Paper. University of Illinois
Press. Champaign, IL. 2000. 128p. ISBN:0-252-06896-3,
ISBN13: 978-0-252-06896-6. Dewey:100. LCCN:99-056002.
Audience: **g,l,u,f.**

Ortega y Gasset, Jose   B4568.O73Q42 2001
What Is Knowledge? Jorge Garcia-Gomez (Editor). Cloth Text.
State University of New York Press. Albany, NY. 2001. 288p.
Series in Latin American and Iberian Thought and Culture
ISBN:0-7914-5171-2, ISBN13: 978-0-7914-5171-7. Dewey:121.
LCCN:2001-031186.
Audience: **g,u,f.**

Ortega y Gasset, José   B4568.O73.S6213 1984
Historical Reason. Philip W. Silver (Translator). Trade Cloth. W.
W. Norton & Company, Inc. New York, NY. 1984. 224p.
ISBN:0-393-01831-8, ISBN13: 978-0-393-01831-8.
Dewey:196/.1. LCCN:83-013139.
Audience: **g,u,f.** *B*

Unamuno, Miguel de   B4568.U53
Tragic Sense of Life. J. Crawford Flitch (Translator). Trade
Paper. Dover Publications, Inc. Mineola, NY. 1954. 367p.
ISBN:0-486-20257-7, ISBN13: 978-0-486-20257-0. Dewey:196.
Audience: **g,l,u,f.**

Philosophy by Country > Asian Philosophy

Baird, Forrest E. &   BD21
  Heimbeck, Raeburne S.
Philosophic Classics: Asian Philosophy. Trade Paper. Prentice
Hall PTR. Upper Saddle River, NJ. 2005. 608p.
ISBN:0-13-352329-2, ISBN13: 978-0-13-352329-4. Dewey:100.
Audience: **g,l,u.**

Bontekoe, Ron   B121.C664 1999
A Companion to World Philosophies. Eliot Deutsch (Editor).
Trade Paper. Blackwell Publishing, Inc. Malden, MA. 1999.
608p. Companions to Philosophy Ser. ISBN:0-631-21327-9,
ISBN13: 978-0-631-21327-7. Dewey:181. LCCN:00-269347.
Audience: **g,l,u.** *Choice, 1998.*

Carr, Brian & Mahalingam,   B121.C66 2000
  Indira
Companion Encyclopedia of Asian Philosophy. Trade Paper.
Routledge. New York, NY. 2001. 1168p. Companion
Encyclopedia Ser. ISBN:0-415-24038-7, ISBN13:
978-0-415-24038-3. Dewey:181/.003. LCCN:00-032831.
Audience: **g,l,u.** *Choice, 1997.*

Chan, Wing-Tsit   B125
  (Translator)
A Source Book in Chinese Philosophy. Trade Paper. Princeton
University Press. Princeton, NJ. 1969. 874p.
ISBN:0-691-01964-9, ISBN13: 978-0-691-01964-2.
Dewey:181.1.
Audience: **g,u,f.**

Chuang Tzu   **BL1900.C5 W34**
The Complete Works of Chuang Tzu. Burton Watson
(Translator), W. T. De Barry (Foreword by). Trade Cloth.
Columbia University Press. New York, NY. 1968. 397p.
UNESCO Collection of Representative Works
ISBN:0-231-03147-5, ISBN13: 978-0-231-03147-9.
Dewey:181/.09514. LCCN:68-019000.

Audience: **g,u,f.**

Clarke, J. J.   **B5010.C57 1997**
Oriental Enlightenment: The Encounter Between Asian and
Western Thought. Paper over Boards. Routledge. New York, NY.
1997. 288p. ISBN:0-415-13375-0, ISBN13: 978-0-415-13375-3.
Dewey:950/.07/01821. LCCN:96-041067.

Audience: **g,u,f.** *Choice, 1997.*

Collinson, Diane   **B5005.C645 2000**
Fifty Key Eastern Thinkers. Ed. 2. Trade Paper. Routledge. New
York, NY. 2000. 448p. Key Guides ISBN:0-415-20284-1,
ISBN13: 978-0-415-20284-8. Dewey:181. LCCN:00-701223.

Audience: **g,l,u.**

Creel, Herrlee G.   **B126**
Chinese Thought from Confucius to Mao Tse-Tung. Trade
Paper. University of Chicago Press. Chicago, IL. 1971. 304p.
ISBN:0-226-12030-9, ISBN13: 978-0-226-12030-0.
Dewey:181.11. LCCN:53-010054.

Audience: **g,l,u.**

Cua, Antonio S. (Editor)   **B126.E496 2002**
Encyclopedia of Chinese Philosophy. Paper over Boards.
Routledge. New York, NY. 2002. 1020p. ISBN:0-415-93913-5,
ISBN13: 978-0-415-93913-3. Dewey:181/.11/03.
LCCN:2002-010760.

Audience: **g,u,f.** *Choice, 2003.*

Dainian, Zhang   **B126.Z446 2003**
Key Concepts in Chinese Philosophy. Edmund Ryden
(Translator). Cloth over Boards. Yale University Press.
Cumberland, RI. 2002. 592p. Culture and Civilization of China
Ser. ISBN:0-300-09210-5, ISBN13: 978-0-300-09210-3.
Dewey:181.1/1.

Audience: **g,l,u.** *Choice, 2003.*

Feng Yu-Lan   **B126 .F43 1970**
Spirit of Chinese Philosophy. Ernest R. Hughes (Translator).
Trade Cloth. Greenwood Publishing Group, Inc. Portsmouth,
NH. 1970. 224p. ISBN:0-8371-2816-1, ISBN13:
978-0-8371-2816-0. Dewey:181/.1. LCCN:71-098757.

Audience: **g,l,u.** *B*

Feuerstein, Georg   **B132.Y6F4875 2003**
The Deeper Dimension of Yoga: Theory and Practice. UK-Trade
Paper. Shambhala Publications, Inc. Boston, MA. 2003. 432p.
ISBN:1-57062-935-8, ISBN13: 978-1-57062-935-8.
Dewey:181/.45. LCCN:2002-014201.

Audience: **g,l.** *Choice, 2004.*

Gandhi, Mohandas   **DS481.G3A17 2005**
Gandhi: Selected Writings. Alastair Duncan (Editor). Trade

Paper. Dover Publications, Inc. Mineola, NY. 2005. 256p.
ISBN:0-486-43766-3, ISBN13: 978-0-486-43766-8.
Dewey:954.03/5/092. LCCN:2004-056238.

Audience: **g,l,u.**

Hamilton, Sue   **B131.H285 2001**
Indian Philosophy: A Very Short Introduction. Trade Paper.
Oxford University Press, Inc. New York, NY. 2001. 168p. Very
Short Introductions Ser., Vol. 47 ISBN:0-19-285374-0, ISBN13:
978-0-19-285374-5. Dewey:181/.4. LCCN:2001-269146.

Audience: **g,l,u.**

Hochsmann, Hyun   **B126.H554 2004**
On Philosophy in China. Trade Paper. Thomson Wadsworth.
Belmont, CA. 2003. 208p. Wadsworth Philosophical Topics Ser.
ISBN:0-534-60995-3, ISBN13: 978-0-534-60995-5.
Dewey:181/.11. LCCN:2003-545431.

Audience: **g,l,u.**

Kupperman, Joel J.   **B121.K85 2001**
Classic Asian Philosophy: A Guide to the Essential Texts. Trade
Paper. Oxford University Press, Inc. New York, NY. 2001. 176p.
ISBN:0-19-513335-8, ISBN13: 978-0-19-513335-6. Dewey:181.
LCCN:00-020488.

Audience: **g,u,f.** *Choice, 2002.*

Leaman, Oliver   **B121.L43 2000**
Eastern Philosophy: The Key Readings. Paper over Boards.
Routledge. New York, NY. 2000. 328p. Key Texts
ISBN:0-415-17357-4, ISBN13: 978-0-415-17357-5. Dewey:181.
LCCN:00-710872.

Audience: **g,l,u,f.**

Leaman, Oliver (Editor)   **B121.E53 2001**
Encyclopedia of Asian Philosophy. Ed. 2. Paper over Boards.
Routledge. New York, NY. 2001. 704p. ISBN:0-415-17281-0,
ISBN13: 978-0-415-17281-3. Dewey:181/.003.
LCCN:00-032836.

Audience: **g,u,f.** *Choice, 2001.*

Leaman, Oliver   **B121.L43 1999**
Key Concepts in Eastern Philosophy. Paper over Boards.
Routledge. New York, NY. 1999. 352p. Key Concepts Ser.
ISBN:0-415-17362-0, ISBN13: 978-0-415-17362-9.
Dewey:181/.003. LCCN:00-700136.

Audience: **g,l,u,f.**

Richards, Glyn
The Philosophy of Gandhi: A Study of His Basic Ideas. Brill
Academic Publishers, Inc. 1981. ISBN:0-7007-0150-8, ISBN13:
978-0-7007-0150-6.

Audience: **g,u.** *B*

Sharma, C. D.   **B131**
A Critical Survey of Indian Philosophy. Trade Paper. Motilal
Banarsidass Publishers (Pvt. Ltd). New Delhi, 2000. 415p. Iib:
Philosophy Ser., :Modern Ser. ISBN:81-208-0365-5, ISBN13:
978-81-208-0365-7. Dewey:181.4.

Audience: **g,l,u.**

Smart, Ninian   **B131 .S62 1992**
Doctrine and Argument in Indian Philosophy. Ed. 2. Trade
Paper. Brill Academic Publishers, Inc. Boston, MA. 1992. x,
278p. Indian Thought Ser., Vol. 4 ISBN:90-04-09479-2,
ISBN13: 978-90-04-09479-6. Dewey:181/.4. LCCN:92-010917.
                              Audience: **g,u,f.** *Choice, 1993.*

Tian, Chenchan   **B809.82.C5T53 2005**
Chinese Dialectics: From Yijing to Marxism. Lexington Books.
2004. ISBN:0-7391-0922-7, ISBN13: 978-0-7391-0922-9.
                              Audience: **g,u,f.**

Watts, Alan   **B121**
The Philosophies of Asia. Trade Paper. Tuttle Publishing.
Boston, MA. 1999. 128p. ISBN:0-8048-3198-X, ISBN13:
978-0-8048-3198-7. Dewey:294.
                              Audience: **g,l,u.**

Philosophy by Country > Asian Philosophy > Japanese Philosophy

Dilworth, David A. &   **B5241**
  Viglielmo, Valdo H. (Editors)
Sourcebook for Modern Japanese Philosophy: Selected
Documents. David A. Dilworth, Valdo H. Viglielmo & Agustin
J. Zavala (Translators). Cloth Text. Greenwood Publishing
Group, Inc. Portsmouth, NH. 1998. 448p. Resources in Asian
Philosophy and Religion Ser. ISBN:0-313-27433-9, ISBN13:
978-0-313-27433-6. Dewey:181/.12. LCCN:97-012763.
                              Audience: **g,u,f.**

Fujisawa, Chikao   **B136**
Zen and Shinto: The Story of Japanese Philosophy. Trade Cloth.
Greenwood Publishing Group, Inc. Portsmouth, NH. 1971. 96p.
ISBN:0-8371-5749-8, ISBN13: 978-0-8371-5749-8.
Dewey:181/.12. LCCN:78-139133.
                              Audience: **g,u,f.** *B*

Heisig, James W.   **B5241.H47 2001**
Philosophers of Nothingness: An Essay on the Kyoto School.
Trade Cloth. University of Hawaii Press. Honolulu, HI. 2001.
392p. Nanzan Library of Asian Religion and Culture
ISBN:0-8248-2480-6, ISBN13: 978-0-8248-2480-8.
Dewey:181/.12. LCCN:2001-017133.
                              Audience: **g,u,f.** *Choice, 2002.*

Heisig, James W.   **B5241.H47 2001**
Philosophers of Nothingness: An Essay on the Kyoto School.
Trade Cloth. University of Hawaii Press. Honolulu, HI. 2001.
392p. Nanzan Library of Asian Religion and Culture
ISBN:0-8248-2481-4, ISBN13: 978-0-8248-2481-5.
Dewey:181/.12. LCCN:2001-017133.
                              Audience: **g,u,f.** *Choice, 2002.*

Nakamura, Hajime   **B5241.N2844 2002**
A History of the Development of Japanese Thought: From 1592
to 1868. Trade Cloth. Kegan Paul International, Ltd. London,
2002. 300p. ISBN:0-7103-0650-4, ISBN13: 978-0-7103-0650-0.
Dewey:181/.12. LCCN:2002-511574.
                              Audience: **g,u,f.** *B*

Starling, Christopher L. &   **B5241.B56 2001**
  Blocker, H. Gene
Japanese Philosophy. Cloth Text. State University of New York
Press. Albany, NY. 2001. 256p. ISBN:0-7914-5019-8, ISBN13:
978-0-7914-5019-2. Dewey:181/.12. LCCN:2001-020222.
                              Audience: **g,u,f.**

Suzuki, D. T.   **BQ9262.9.J3S9 1970**
Zen and Japanese Culture. Trade Paper. Princeton University
Press. Princeton, NJ. 1970. 502p. Bollingen Ser., Vol. 64
ISBN:0-691-01770-0, ISBN13: 978-0-691-01770-9.
Dewey:294.3/927.
                              Audience: **g,l,u,f.**

Yusa, Michiko   **B5244.N554Y86 2002**
Zen and Philosophy: An Intellectual Biography of Nishida
Kitaro. Trade Cloth. University of Hawaii Press. Honolulu, HI.
2002. 510p. ISBN:0-8248-2402-4, ISBN13: 978-0-8248-2402-0.
Dewey:181/.12 B. LCCN:2001-040662.
                              Audience: **g,u,f.** *Choice, 2003.*

Philosophy by Country > African Philosophy

Coetzee, P. H. & Roux, A. P.   **B5305**
  J. (Editors)
The African Philosophy Reader. Ed. 2. UK-B Format Paperback.
Routledge. New York, NY. 2003. 672p. ISBN:0-415-96809-7,
ISBN13: 978-0-415-96809-6. Dewey:199/.6.
                              Audience: **g,u.** *Choice, 1999.*

Hallen, B.   **B5305.H35 2002**
A Short History of African Philosophy. Trade Cloth. Indiana
University Press. Bloomington, IN. 2002. 144p.
ISBN:0-253-34106-X, ISBN13: 978-0-253-34106-8.
Dewey:199/.6. LCCN:2001-006883.
                              Audience: **g,l,u.** *Choice, 2003.*

Imbo, Samuel O.   **B5305.I43 1998**
An Introduction to African Philosophy. Book, Other. Rowman &
Littlefield Publishers, Inc. Lanham, MD. 1998. 175p.
ISBN:0-8476-8840-2, ISBN13: 978-0-8476-8840-1.
Dewey:199.6. LCCN:97-048810.
                              Audience: **g,l,u.** *Choice, 1999.*

Wiredu, Kwasi (Editor)   **B5305**
A Companion to African Philosophy. Trade Paper. Blackwell
Publishing, Inc. Malden, MA. 2006. 608p. ISBN:1-4051-4567-6,
ISBN13: 978-1-4051-4567-1. Dewey:199/.6.
LCCN:2006-280274.
                              Audience: **u,f.** *Choice, 2004.*

Philosophy by Country > Dutch Philosophy

Bennett, Jonathan   B3974 .B46 1984
A Study of Spinoza's Ethics. Trade Cloth. Hackett Publishing
Company, Inc. Indianapolis, IN. 1984. 406p.
ISBN:0-915145-82-0, ISBN13: 978-0-915145-82-9. Dewey:170.
LCCN:83-018568.

Audience: **g,u,f.** *B*

Curley, Edwin M.   B3974.C87 1988
Behind the Geometrical Method: A Reading of Spinoza's Ethics.
Trade Paper. Princeton University Press. Princeton, NJ. 1988.
200p. ISBN:0-691-02037-X, ISBN13: 978-0-691-02037-2.
Dewey:170/.92/4. LCCN:87-025850.

Audience: **g,u,f.** *Choice, 1989.*

Delahunty, R. J.   B3998.D37 1999
Spinoza. Paper over Boards. Routledge. New York, NY. 1999.
336p. Arguments of the Philosophers Ser. ISBN:0-415-20360-0,
ISBN13: 978-0-415-20360-9. Dewey:199/.492.
LCCN:00-688420.

Audience: **g,u,f.** *Choice, 1985.*

Garrett, Don (Editor)   B3998 .C32 1996
The Cambridge Companion to Spinoza. Trade Cloth. Cambridge
University Press. New York, NY. 1995. 479p. Cambridge
Companions to Philosophy Ser. ISBN:0-521-39235-7, ISBN13:
978-0-521-39235-8. Dewey:199.4/92. LCCN:95-011445.

Audience: **u,f.**

Goetschel, Willi   B3998.G63 2003
Spinoza's Modernity: Mendelssohn, Lessing, and Heine. Trade
Cloth. University of Wisconsin Press. Chicago, IL. 2003. 368p.
Studies in German Jewish Cultural History and Literature
ISBN:0-299-19080-3, ISBN13: 978-0-299-19080-4.
Dewey:199/.492. LCCN:2003-007693.

Audience: **u,f.** *Choice, 2004.*

Hampshire, Stuart   B3998
Spinoza and Spinozism. Trade Cloth. Oxford University Press,
Inc. New York, NY. 2005. 264p. ISBN:0-19-927953-5, ISBN13:
978-0-19-927953-1. Dewey:199.492. LCCN:2005-279971.

Audience: **g,u,f.**

Lloyd, Genevieve   B3974.L56 1994
Part of Nature: Self-Knowledge in Spinoza's Ethics. Book,
Other. Cornell University Press. Ithaca, NY. 1994. 200p.
ISBN:0-8014-2999-4, ISBN13: 978-0-8014-2999-6. Dewey:170.
LCCN:94-003195.

Audience: **g,u,f.** *Choice, 1995.*

Lloyd, Genevieve   B3974.L57 1996
Routledge Philosophy Guidebook to Spinoza and The Ethics.
Paper over Boards. Routledge. New York, NY. 1996. 176p.
Philosophy Guidebooks ISBN:0-415-10781-4, ISBN13:
978-0-415-10781-5. Dewey:199.4/92. LCCN:96-006392.

Audience: **u,f.**

Nadler, Steven   B3997
Spinoza: A Life. Trade Paper. Cambridge University Press. New
York, NY. 2001. 422p. ISBN:0-521-00293-1, ISBN13:
978-0-521-00293-6. Dewey:199/.492 B.

Audience: **g,l,u,f.** *Choice, 1999.*

Scruton, Roger   B3397
Spinoza: A Very Short Introduction. Trade Paper. Oxford
University Press, Inc. New York, NY. 2002. 142p. Very Short
Introductions Ser. ISBN:0-19-280316-6, ISBN13:
978-0-19-280316-0. Dewey:199.492. LCCN:2002-725610.

Audience: **g,l,u.**

Spinoza, Baruch   B3958.S55 2002
Spinoza: Complete Works. Michael L. Morgan (Editor), Samuel
Shirley (Translator), Michael L. Morgan (Introduction by). Trade
Cloth. Hackett Publishing Company, Inc. Indianapolis, IN. 2002.
966p. Hackett Classics Ser. ISBN:0-87220-620-3, ISBN13:
978-0-87220-620-5. Dewey:199/.492. LCCN:2002-068497.

Audience: **g,u,f.**

Spinoza, Baruch   B3973.E5P37 2000
Ethics. G. H. R. Parkinson (Editor). Paper Text. Oxford
University Press, Inc. New York, NY. 2000. 366p. Oxford
Philosophical Texts ISBN:0-19-875214-8, ISBN13:
978-0-19-875214-1. Dewey:170. LCCN:99-057765.

Audience: **g,u,f.**

Spinoza, Baruch   B3958.S45 1995
The Letters. Samuel Shirley (Translator), Steven Barbone, Lee
Rice & Jacob Adler (Introduction by, Notes by). Trade Cloth.
Hackett Publishing Company, Inc. Indianapolis, IN. 1995. 404p.
ISBN:0-87220-275-5, ISBN13: 978-0-87220-275-7.
Dewey:199/.492. LCCN:95-023700.

Audience: **g,u,f.** *Choice, 1996.*

Spinoza, Baruch   B1863.E53S487 1998
Principles of Cartesian Philosophy: With Metaphysical Thoughts
and Lodewijk Meyer's Inaugural Dissertation. Samuel Shirley
(Translator), Lee Rice & Steven Barbone (Introduction by, Notes
by). Trade Cloth. Hackett Publishing Company, Inc.
Indianapolis, IN. 1998. 192p. Classics Ser. ISBN:0-87220-401-4,
ISBN13: 978-0-87220-401-0. Dewey:199/.492.
LCCN:97-051491.

Audience: **g,u,f.**

Spinoza, Baruch & Spinoza,   B3985.E5E49 2004
 Benedict de
A Theologico-Political Treatise and a Political Treatise. R. H.
M. Elwes (Translator), Francesco Cordasco (Other Primary
Creator). Trade Paper. Dover Publications, Inc. Mineola, NY.
2004. 432p. Dover Philosophical Classics Ser.
ISBN:0-486-43722-1, ISBN13: 978-0-486-43722-4.
Dewey:199/.492. LCCN:2004-056123.

Audience: **g,u,f.**

Spinoza, Benedict de   B3958.C87 1994
A Spinoza Reader: The Ethics and Other Works. Edwin M.
Curley (Edited and Translated by). Trade Paper. Princeton
University Press. Princeton, NJ. 1994. 316p.

ISBN:0-691-00067-0, ISBN13: 978-0-691-00067-1.
Dewey:199.492. LCCN:93-001628.

Audience: **g,u,f.** *Choice, 1994.*

Spinoza, Benedictus De   **B3958 1985**
The Collected Works of Spinoza, Vol. 1. Edwin Curley (Editor).
Trade Cloth. Princeton University Press. Princeton, NJ. 1985.
752p. ISBN:0-691-07222-1, ISBN13: 978-0-691-07222-7.
Dewey:199/.492. LCCN:84-011716.

Audience: **g,u,f.** *B* *Choice, 1985.*

Philosophy by Country > Danish Philosophy

Evans, C. Stephen   **B4378.R44E83 1998**
Kierkegaard's Fragments and Postscript: The Religious
Philosophy of Johannes Climacus. Trade Cloth. Prometheus
Books, Publishers. Amherst, NY. 1998. 320p.
ISBN:1-57392-302-8, ISBN13: 978-1-57392-302-6.
Dewey:200/.1. LCCN:98-054285.

Audience: **g,u,f.** *B*

Garff, Joakim   **B4376.G28 2005**
Soren Kierkegaard: A Biography. Bruce H. Kirmmse
(Translator). Trade Cloth. Princeton University Press. Princeton,
NJ. 2004. 872p. ISBN:0-691-09165-X, ISBN13:
978-0-691-09165-5. Dewey:198/.9 B. LCCN:2004-044525.

Audience: **g,l,u,f.** *Choice, 2005.*

Hannay, Alastair   **B4377.H348 1999**
Kierkegaard. Paper over Boards. Routledge. New York, NY.
1999. 404p. Arguments of the Philosophers Ser.
ISBN:0-415-20370-8, ISBN13: 978-0-415-20370-8.
Dewey:198.9. LCCN:00-506124.

Audience: **g,u,f.**

Hong, Howard V. & Hong,   **B4372.E5 2000**
Edna H. (Editors)
The Essential Kierkegaard. Cloth Text. Princeton University
Press. Princeton, NJ. 2000. 544p. ISBN:0-691-03309-9, ISBN13:
978-0-691-03309-9. Dewey:198/.9. LCCN:99-039031.

Audience: **g,l,u,f.** *Choice, 2001.*

Kierkegaard, Soren   **B4373.O42**
The Concept of Irony, with Continual Reference to
Socrates/Notes of Schelling's Berlin Lectures. Howard V. Hong
& Edna H. Hong (Edited and Translated by). Trade Paper.
Princeton University Press. Princeton, NJ. 1992. 664p.
Kierkegaard's Writings ISBN:0-691-02072-8, ISBN13:
978-0-691-02072-3. Dewey:190. LCCN:89-003642.

Audience: **g,u,f.** *Choice, 1990.*

Kierkegaard, Soren   **B53**
Philosophical Fragments, or a Fragment of Philosophy/Johannes
Climacus, or de Omnibus Dubitandum Rst. Howard V. Hong &
Edna H. Hong (Edited and Translated by). Trade Paper.

Princeton University Press. Princeton, NJ. 1985. 399p.
Kierkegaard's Writings, No. VII ISBN:0-691-02036-1, ISBN13:
978-0-691-02036-5. Dewey:201. LCCN:85-003420.

Audience: **g,u,f.** *B* *Choice, 1986.*

Kierkegaard, Soren   **B4372.E5 1998**
The Point of View. Howard V. Hong & Edna H. Hong (Edited
and Translated by). Trade Cloth. Princeton University Press.
Princeton, NJ. 1998. 382p. Kierkegaard's Writings, Vol. 22
ISBN:0-691-05855-5, ISBN13: 978-0-691-05855-9.
Dewey:198.9. LCCN:97-034909.

Audience: **g,u,f.** *B*

Kierkegaard, Soren   **B4373.A472E5 1992**
Concluding Unscientific Postscripts to Philosophical Fragments,
Vol. I. Howard V. Hong & Edna H. Hong (Editors), Howard V.
Hong & Edna H. Hong (Translators). Trade Cloth. Princeton
University Press. Princeton, NJ. 1992. 650p. Kierkegaard's
Writings, XII, XII ISBN:0-691-07395-3, ISBN13:
978-0-691-07395-8. Dewey:230/.01. LCCN:91-004093.

Audience: **g,u,f.** *Choice, 1993.*

Kierkegaard, Soren   **BR100.K52 1982**
Fear and Trembling: Repetition. Howard V. Hong & Edna H.
Hong (Editors), Howard V. Hong & Edna H. Hong
(Translators). Paper Text. Princeton University Press. Princeton,
NJ. 1983. 464p. Kierkegaard's Writings, No. VI
ISBN:0-691-02026-4, ISBN13: 978-0-691-02026-6. Dewey:201.
LCCN:82-009006.

Audience: **g,u,f.**

Kierkegaard, Soren   **B4376**
Kierkegaard's Journals and Notebooks: Journals AA-DD. Bruce
H. Kirmmse, Niels Jorgen Cappelorn, Alastair Hannay, George
Pattison & Jon Stewart (Editors). Trade Cloth. Princeton
University Press. Princeton, NJ. 2006. 464p.
ISBN:0-691-09222-2, ISBN13: 978-0-691-09222-5.
Dewey:198.9.

Audience: **g,u,f.**

Kierkegaard, Soren   **B4376.I58**
The Sickness unto Death: A Christian Psychological Exposition
for Upbuilding and Awakening. Robert L. Perkins (Editor).
Trade Cloth. Mercer University Press. Macon, GA. 1987. 272p.
International Kierkegaard Commentary Ser., No. 19
ISBN:0-86554-271-6, ISBN13: 978-0-86554-271-6.
Dewey:241.3. LCCN:87-005614.

Audience: **g,u,f.** *Choice, 1988.*

Lippitt, John   **B4373.F793K54 2003**
Routledge Philosophy Guidebook to Kierkegaard and Fear and
Trembling. Paper over Boards. Routledge. New York, NY. 2003.
232p. Routledge Philosophy Guidebooks Ser.
ISBN:0-415-18046-5, ISBN13: 978-0-415-18046-7.
Dewey:198/.9. LCCN:2002-045500.

Audience: **g,u,f.**

Divisions of Philosophy > Aesthetics

Adorno, Theodor W.   **B3199.A33A813 1997**
Aesthetic Theory. Robert Hullot-Kentor, Rolf Tiedemann &
Gretel Adorno (Editors), Rolf Tiedemann (Translator), Robert
Hullot-Kentor (Introduction by). Trade Cloth. University of
Minnesota Press. Minneapolis, MN. 1996. 448p. Theory and
History of Literature Ser., Vol. 88 ISBN:0-8166-1799-6,
ISBN13: 978-0-8166-1799-9. Dewey:111.8/5. LCCN:96-007729.
Audience: **g,u,f.** ℬ *Choice, 1997.*

Ashfield, Andrew & de   **BH301.S7 S82 1996**
Bolla, Peter (Editors)
The Sublime: A Reader in British Eighteenth-Century Aesthetic
Theory. Trade Paper. Cambridge University Press. New York,
NY. 1996. 324p. ISBN:0-521-39582-8, ISBN13:
978-0-521-39582-3. Dewey:111.8/5. LCCN:95-043245.
Audience: **g,u,f.**

Beardsley, Monroe C.   **BH39**
Aesthetics: Problems in the Philosophy of Criticism. Ed. 2.
Trade Cloth. Hackett Publishing Company, Inc. Indianapolis, IN.
1981. 688p. ISBN:0-915145-09-X, ISBN13: 978-0-915145-09-6.
Dewey:111/.85. LCCN:80-028899.
Audience: **g,u,f.**

Berys, Gaut & Dominic,   **BH21.R6 2005**
Mover Lopes
The Routledge Companion to Aesthetics. Ed. 2. Trade Cloth.
Routledge. New York, NY. 2005. 736p. ISBN:0-415-32797-0,
ISBN13: 978-0-415-32797-8. Dewey:111/.85.
Audience: **g,u,f.**

Cazeaux, Clive   **BH201.C59 2000**
The Continental Aesthetics Reader. Paper over Boards.
Routledge. New York, NY. 2000. 640p. ISBN:0-415-20053-9,
ISBN13: 978-0-415-20053-0. Dewey:111/.85/094.
LCCN:00-032177.
Audience: **g,u.**

Danto, Arthur C.   **BH39**
The Transfiguration of the Commonplace: A Philosophy of Art.
Trade Paper. Harvard University Press. Cambridge, MA. 1981.
224p. ISBN:0-674-90346-3, ISBN13: 978-0-674-90346-3.
Dewey:700/.1.
Audience: **g,u,f.** ℬ

Derrida, Jacques   **BH39.D4513 1987**
The Truth in Painting. Geoffrey Bennington & Ian McLeod
(Translators). Trade Paper. University of Chicago Press.
Chicago, IL. 1987. 402p. ISBN:0-226-14324-4, ISBN13:
978-0-226-14324-8. Dewey:701/.1/7. LCCN:86-030914.
Audience: **g,u,f.** *Choice, 1988.*

Dickie, George, et al.   **BH21.A35 1989**
Aesthetics: A Critical Anthology. Ed. 2. Richard J. Sclafani &
Ronald Roblin (Authors). Cloth over Boards. Bedford/Saint
Martin's. New York, NY. 1989. 678p. ISBN:0-312-00309-9,
ISBN13: 978-0-312-00309-8. Dewey:111/.85. LCCN:88-060543.
Audience: **g,u.**

Dufrenne, Mikel   **BH301.E8 D8313**
The Phenomenology of Aesthetic Experience. Edward S. Casey
& Albert A. Anderson (Translators). Trade Paper. Northwestern
University Press. Evanston, IL. 1989. 578p. Studies in
Phenomenology and Existential Philosophy
ISBN:0-8101-0591-8, ISBN13: 978-0-8101-0591-1.
Dewey:111.8/5. LCCN:73-076806.
Audience: **u,f.** ℬ

Eagleton, Terry   **BH151.E2 1990**
The Ideology of the Aesthetic. Trade Paper. Blackwell
Publishing, Inc. Malden, MA. 1994. 432p. ISBN:0-631-16302-6,
ISBN13: 978-0-631-16302-2. Dewey:111/.85/0903.
LCCN:89-035824.
Audience: **g,u,f.** *Choice, 1990.*

Eldridge, Richard   **BH39.E535 2003**
An Introduction to the Philosophy of Art. Trade Paper.
Cambridge University Press. New York, NY. 2003. 296p.
Cambridge Introduction to Philosophy Ser.
ISBN:0-521-80521-X, ISBN13: 978-0-521-80521-6.
Dewey:111/.85. LCCN:2003-043501.
Audience: **g,l,u.** *Choice, 2004.*

Gilson, Etienne   **BH201.G55 2000**
The Arts of the Beautiful. Trade Paper. Dalkey Archive Press.
Normal, IL. 2000. 189p. ISBN:1-56478-250-6, ISBN13:
978-1-56478-250-2. Dewey:111/.85. LCCN:00-020954.
Audience: **g,u,f.** ℬ

Goldman, Alan H.   **BH39.G5815 1995**
Aesthetic Value. Trade Paper. Westview Press. Boulder, CO.
1995. 208p. Focus Ser. ISBN:0-8133-2019-4, ISBN13:
978-0-8133-2019-9. Dewey:111/.85. LCCN:95-017025.
Audience: **g,u,f.** *Choice, 1996.*

Goodman, Nelson   **BD241**
Languages of Art. Ed. 2. Trade Cloth. Hackett Publishing
Company, Inc. Indianapolis, IN. 1976. 288p.
ISBN:0-915144-35-2, ISBN13: 978-0-915144-35-8.
Dewey:121.6/8. LCCN:68-031825.
Audience: **g,u,f.**

Graham, Gordon   **BH39.G67 2000**
Philosophy of the Arts: An Introduction to Aesthetics. Ed. 2.
Trade Paper. Routledge. New York, NY. 2000. 240p.
ISBN:0-415-23564-2, ISBN13: 978-0-415-23564-8.
Dewey:111/.85. LCCN:00-036889.
Audience: **g,l,u.**

Kelly, Michael (Editor)   **BH56.E53 1998**
Encyclopedia of Aesthetics, Set. Trade Cloth. Oxford University
Press, Inc. New York, NY. 1998. 3,004p. ISBN:0-19-511307-1,
ISBN13: 978-0-19-511307-5. Dewey:111/.85/03.
LCCN:98-018741.
Audience: **l,u.** *Choice, 1999.*

Kivy, Peter (Editor)   **BH39.B556 2004**
The Blackwell Guide to Aesthetics. Trade Paper. Blackwell
Publishing, Inc. Malden, MA. 2004. 368p. Blackwell Philosophy

---

Guides Ser. ISBN:0-631-22131-X, ISBN13: 978-0-631-22131-9. Dewey:111/.85. LCCN:2003-010096.

Audience: **g,l,u,f.** *Choice, 2004.*

Manns, James   **BH39.M385 1998**
Aesthetics. Cloth Text. M. E. Sharpe Inc. Armonk, NY. 1997. 195p. Explorations in Philosophy Ser. ISBN:1-56324-953-7, ISBN13: 978-1-56324-953-2. Dewey:111/.85. LCCN:97-021723.

Audience: **g,l,u.** *Choice, 1998.*

Parker, DeWitt H.   **BH201 .P35**
The Principles of Aesthetics. Trade Paper. Kessinger Publishing, LLC. Whitefish, MT. 2004. ISBN:1-4191-7882-2, ISBN13: 978-1-4191-7882-5. Dewey:111.8/5.

Audience: **g,u.**

Pepper, Stephen C.   **BH201**
Aesthetic Quality: A Contextualistic Theory of Beauty. Trade Cloth. Greenwood Publishing Group, Inc. Portsmouth, NH. 1970. 255p. ISBN:0-8371-4437-X, ISBN13: 978-0-8371-4437-5. Dewey:111.8/5. LCCN:79-110052.

Audience: **g,u,f.** *ß*

Schaeffer, Jean-Marie   **BH151.S3313 2000**
Art of the Modern Age: Philosophy of Art from Kant to Heidegger. Steven Rendall (Translator). Trade Cloth. Princeton University Press. Princeton, NJ. 2000. 370p. New French Thought Ser. ISBN:0-691-01669-0, ISBN13: 978-0-691-01669-6. Dewey:111/.85/0903. LCCN:99-038862.

Audience: **g,u.** *Choice, 2001.*

Sheppard, Anne   **BH39.S5127 1987**
Aesthetics: An Introduction to the Philosophy of Art. Paper Text. Oxford University Press, Inc. New York, NY. 1987. 160p. ISBN:0-19-289164-2, ISBN13: 978-0-19-289164-8. Dewey:701. LCCN:87-011206.

Audience: **g,l,u.**

Townsend, Dabney   **BH39.T635 1997**
An Introduction to Aesthetics. Trade Cloth. Blackwell Publishing, Inc. Malden, MA. 1997. 256p. Introducing Philosophy Ser. ISBN:1-55786-730-5, ISBN13: 978-1-55786-730-8. Dewey:111.8/5. LCCN:96-038819.

Audience: **g,l,u.**

Wood, Robert E.   **BH81.W66 1999**
Placing Aesthetics: Reflections on the Philosophic Tradition. Trade Cloth. Ohio University Press. Athens, OH. 2000. 429p. Series in Continental Thought, Vol.26 ISBN:0-8214-1280-9, ISBN13: 978-0-8214-1280-0. Dewey:111/.85/09. LCCN:99-027142.

Audience: **g,u,f.** *Choice, 2000.*

Zuidervaart, Lambert   **BH301.T77Z85 2004**
Artistic Truth: Aesthetics, Discourse and Imaginative Disclosure. Trade Cloth. Cambridge University Press. New York, NY. 2004. 294p. ISBN:0-521-83903-3, ISBN13: 978-0-521-83903-7. Dewey:111/.85. LCCN:2004-040679.

Audience: **g,u,f.** *Choice, 2005.*

Divisions of Philosophy > Aesthetics > History of Aesthetics

Beardsley, Monroe C.   **BH81.B4**
Aesthetics from Classical Greece to the Present: A Short History. Trade Paper. University of Alabama Press. Tuscaloosa, AL. 1975. 416p. Studies in the Humanities: No. 13 ISBN:0-8173-6623-7, ISBN13: 978-0-8173-6623-0. Dewey:111.8/5. LCCN:75-020138.

Audience: **g,l,u.** *ß*

Bernstein, J. M. (Editor)   **BH221.G3**
Classic and Romantic German Aesthetics. Karl Ameriks, Desmond M. Clarke, S. R. Anderson, J. Bresnan, B. Comrie, W. Dressler & C. J. Ewen (Contribution by). Trade Paper. Cambridge University Press. New York, NY. 2002. 356p. Cambridge Texts in the History of Philosophy Ser. ISBN:0-521-00111-0, ISBN13: 978-0-521-00111-3. Dewey:111/.85/0943. LCCN:2003-271174.

Audience: **g,u,f.**

Breton, Andre   **NX600.S9**
Manifestoes of Surrealism. Richard Seaver & Helen R. Lane (Translators). Trade Paper. University of Michigan Press. Chicago, IL. 1969. 316p. Ann Arbor Paperbacks Ser. ISBN:0-472-06182-8, ISBN13: 978-0-472-06182-2. Dewey:709.0406.

Audience: **g,u,f.** *ß*

Burke, Edmund   **BH181**
Edmund Burke: A Philosophical Inquiry into the Origin of Our Ideas of the Sublime and Beautiful. James T. Boulton (Editor). Trade Paper. University of Notre Dame Press. Notre Dame, IN. 1968. 328p. ISBN:0-268-00085-9, ISBN13: 978-0-268-00085-1. Dewey:111.8/5. LCCN:68-027583.

Audience: **g,u,f.**

Croce, Benedetto   **B3614.C73B7413 1995**
Guide to Aesthetics. Ed. 2. Patrick Romanell (Translator). Trade Cloth. Hackett Publishing Company, Inc. Indianapolis, IN. 1995. 128p. HPC Classics Ser. ISBN:0-87220-305-0, ISBN13: 978-0-87220-305-1. Dewey:111/.85. LCCN:94-043408.

Audience: **g,u,f.**

Hammermeister, Kai   **BH221.G3H36 2002**
The German Aesthetic Tradition. Trade Cloth. Cambridge University Press. New York, NY. 2002. 278p. ISBN:0-521-78065-9, ISBN13: 978-0-521-78065-0. Dewey:111/.85/0943. LCCN:2002-073480.

Audience: **g,u,f.** *Choice, 2003.*

Kant, Immanuel   **BH39**
Observations on the Feeling of the Beautiful and Sublime. Ed. 2. John T. Goldthwait (Translator). Trade Paper. University of California Press. Berkeley, CA. 2004. 192p. ISBN:0-520-24078-2, ISBN13: 978-0-520-24078-0. Dewey:111.85.

Audience: **g,u,f.** *ß*

Kant, Immanuel   B2783.E53 M47X 1980
The Critique of Judgment: Containing Kant's Critique of
Aesthetic Judgement and Critique of Teleological Judgement. J.
C. Meredith (Translator). Paper Text. Oxford University Press,
Inc. New York, NY. 1978. 140p. ISBN:0-19-824589-0, ISBN13:
978-0-19-824589-6. Dewey:121. LCCN:86-673058.
Audience: **g,u,f.** ℬ

Kemal, Salim   B2799.A4K46 1997
Kant's Aesthetic Theory: An Introduction. Ed. 2. Trade Paper.
Palgrave Macmillan. New York, NY. 1997. 210p.
ISBN:0-312-12164-4, ISBN13: 978-0-312-12164-8.
Dewey:111.8/5. LCCN:97-012039.
Audience: **g,u.** *Choice, 1992.*

Krukowski, Lucian   BH191.K78 1992
Aesthetic Legacies. Trade Cloth. Temple University Press.
Philadelphia, PA. 1992. 264p. Arts and Their Philosophies Ser.
ISBN:0-87722-972-4, ISBN13: 978-0-87722-972-8.
Dewey:111/.85/09034. LCCN:92-019307.
Audience: **g,u,f.** *Choice, 1993.*

Lessing, Gotthold Ephraim   BH39
Laocoon: An Essay on the Limits of Painting and Poetry.
Edward A. McCormick (Translator). Trade Paper. Johns Hopkins
University Press. Baltimore, MD. 1984. 296p.
ISBN:0-8018-3139-3, ISBN13: 978-0-8018-3139-3.
Dewey:700/.1. LCCN:83-023880.
Audience: **g,u,f.**

Ortega y Gasset, José   BH0205.O713
The Dehumanization of Art: And Other Essays on Art, Culture,
and Literature. Trade Paper. Books on Demand. Ann Arbor, MI.
1968. 210p. Princeton Paperbacks Ser., Vol. 128
ISBN:0-7837-9281-6, ISBN13: 978-0-7837-9281-1.
Dewey:701.17. LCCN:68-008963.
Audience: **g,l,u,f.**

Schiller, Friedrich   BH183.S25 2004
On the Aesthetic Education of Man. Reginald Snell (Translator).
Trade Paper. Dover Publications, Inc. Mineola, NY. 2004. 160p.
ISBN:0-486-43739-6, ISBN13: 978-0-486-43739-2.
Dewey:111/.85. LCCN:2004-050046.
Audience: **g,l,u,f.**

Tolstoy, Leo   BH39.T62413 1996
What Is Art? Alymer Maude (Translator), Vincent Tomas
(Introduction by). Trade Paper. Hackett Publishing Company,
Inc. Indianapolis, IN. 1996. 232p. ISBN:0-87220-295-X,
ISBN13: 978-0-87220-295-5. Dewey:700.1. LCCN:96-077859.
Audience: **g,l,u.**

Divisions of Philosophy > Epistemology

Alcoff, Linda M. (Editor)   BD161.E63 1998
Epistemology: The Big Questions. Trade Cloth. Blackwell
Publishing, Inc. Malden, MA. 1998. 464p. Philosophy Ser., :The
Big Questions ISBN:0-631-20579-9, ISBN13:
978-0-631-20579-1. Dewey:121. LCCN:97-051452.
Audience: **g,u.**

Alston, William P.   BD214.A57 1993
The Reliability of Sense Perception. Book, Other. Cornell
University Press. Ithaca, NY. 1996. 168p. ISBN:0-8014-8101-5,
ISBN13: 978-0-8014-8101-7. Dewey:121.3. LCCN:92-054964.
Audience: **g,u,f.** *Choice, 1993.*

Austin, John Langshaw   B828.45
Sense and Sensibilia. Ed. 2. Geoffrey J. Warnock (Editor). Cloth
Text. Oxford University Press, Inc. New York, NY. 1964. 156p.
ISBN:0-19-500307-1, ISBN13: 978-0-19-500307-9.
Dewey:121/.3.
Audience: **g,u,f.**

Berkeley, George   B1331.D38 1998
A Treatise Concerning the Principles of Human Knowledge.
Jonathan Dancy (Editor). Paper Text. Oxford University Press,
Inc. New York, NY. 1998. 244p. Oxford Philosophical Texts
ISBN:0-19-875161-3, ISBN13: 978-0-19-875161-8. Dewey:121.
LCCN:97-012131.
Audience: **g,l,u.** ℬ

BonJour, Laurence & Sosa,   BD212.B66 2003
Ernest
Epistemic Justification: Internalism vs. Externalism, Foundations
vs. Virtues. Trade Paper. Blackwell Publishing, Inc. Malden,
MA. 2003. 248p. Great Debates in Philosophy Ser.
ISBN:0-631-18284-5, ISBN13: 978-0-631-18284-9.
Dewey:121/.2. LCCN:2002-015309.
Audience: **u,f.** *Choice, 2003.*

Brann, Eva T. H.   B105.I49B72 1990
The World of the Imagination: Sum and Substance. Book, Other.
Rowman & Littlefield Publishers, Inc. Lanham, MD. 1992.
824p. ISBN:0-8476-7650-1, ISBN13: 978-0-8476-7650-7.
Dewey:153.3. LCCN:90-048616.
Audience: **g,u,f.** *Choice, 1991.*

Burke, Peter   BD175.B86 2000
A Social History of Knowledge: From Gutenberg to Diderot.
Trade Paper. Polity Press. Cambridge, 2000. 268p.
ISBN:0-7456-2485-5, ISBN13: 978-0-7456-2485-3.
Dewey:306.4/2/0903. LCCN:00-039973.
Audience: **g,u,f.** *Choice, 2001.*

Cassirer, Ernst   BD163
Problem of Knowledge: Philosophy, Science, and History since
Hegel. William H. Woglom (Translator), Charles W. Hendel
(Translator, Preface by). Trade Paper. Yale University Press.
Cumberland, RI. 1969. 352p. ISBN:0-300-01098-2, ISBN13:
978-0-300-01098-5. Dewey:121.
Audience: **g,u,f.** ℬ

Collingwood, Robin George   B1618
Speculum Mentis: The Map of Knowledge. Trade Cloth.
Greenwood Publishing Group, Inc. Portsmouth, NH. 1982. 327p.
ISBN:0-313-23701-8, ISBN13: 978-0-313-23701-0. Dewey:192.
LCCN:82-015552.
Audience: **g,u,f.**

Dancy, Jonathan & Sosa, Ernest (Editors) BD161.C637
A Companion to Epistemology. Trade Paper. Blackwell Publishing, Inc. Malden, MA. 1994. 560p. Companions to Philosophy Ser. ISBN:0-631-19258-1, ISBN13: 978-0-631-19258-9. Dewey:121. LCCN:92-032205.

Audience: **u,f.** *Choice, 1993.*

Descartes, René B1848.E5H35 1996
A Discourse on Method and Meditations on First Philosophy. David Weissman (Editor), William T. Bluhm (Contribution by). Cloth over Boards. Yale University Press. Cumberland, RI. 1996. 400p. Rethinking the Western Tradition Ser. ISBN:0-300-06772-0, ISBN13: 978-0-300-06772-9. Dewey:194. LCCN:96-005885.

Audience: **g,l,u.**

Dewey, John BD161.D4
The Quest for Certainty: A Study of the Relation of Knowledge and Action. Trade Paper. Kessinger Publishing, LLC. Whitefish, MT. 2005. ISBN:1-4179-0845-9, ISBN13: 978-1-4179-0845-5. Dewey:121.

Audience: **g,u,f.** *B*

Fodor, Jerry A. BD418.3
A Theory of Content and Other Essays. MIT Press. 1992. Bradford Books ISBN:0-262-56069-0, ISBN13: 978-0-262-56069-6.

Audience: **u,f.**

Habermas BD163 .H2213 1971
Knowledge and Human Interests. Trade Cloth. Beacon Press. Boston, MA. 1971. viii, 356p. ISBN:0-8070-1540-7, ISBN13: 978-0-8070-1540-7. Dewey:121/.09/034. LCCN:72-136230.

Audience: **g,u,f.** *B*

Habermas, Jürgen B3258.H323W3413 2003
Truth and Justification. Barbara Fultner (Editor, Translator). Trade Cloth. MIT Press. Cambridge, MA. 2003. 368p. Studies in Contemporary German Social Thought ISBN:0-262-08318-3, ISBN13: 978-0-262-08318-8. Dewey:100. LCCN:2002-190859.

Audience: **g,u,f.** *Choice, 2004.*

Hetherington, Stephen Cade BD161.H45 1996
Knowledge Puzzles: An Introduction to Epistemology. Trade Paper. Westview Press. Boulder, CO. 1996. 224p. ISBN:0-8133-2487-4, ISBN13: 978-0-8133-2487-6. Dewey:121. LCCN:95-040996.

Audience: **u,f.** *Choice, 1996.*

Kirkham, Richard L. BC171
Theories of Truth: A Critical Introduction. Trade Paper. MIT Press. Cambridge, MA. 1995. 415p. Bradford Bks. ISBN:0-262-61108-2, ISBN13: 978-0-262-61108-4. Dewey:121.

Audience: **g,u,f.** *Choice, 1993.*

Lehrer, Keith BD161.L368 2000
Theory of Knowledge. Ed. 2. Trade Paper. Westview Press. Boulder, CO. 2000. 272p. Dimensions of Philosophy Ser. ISBN:0-8133-9053-2, ISBN13: 978-0-8133-9053-6. Dewey:121. LCCN:00-043263.

Audience: **g,u,f.** *Choice, 1990.*

Locke, John BD161
An Essay Concerning Human Understanding. Kenneth Winkler (Editor). Trade Paper. Hackett Publishing Company, Inc. Indianapolis, IN. 1996. 416p. HPC Classics Ser. ISBN:0-87220-216-X, ISBN13: 978-0-87220-216-0. Dewey:121. LCCN:96-026935.

Audience: **g,u,f.** *B*

Misak, C. J. B945.P44
Truth and the End of Inquiry: A Peircean Account of Truth. Trade Paper. Oxford University Press, Inc. New York, NY. 2004. 232p. Oxford Philosophical Monographs ISBN:0-19-927059-7, ISBN13: 978-0-19-927059-0. Dewey:121/.092.

Audience: **g,u,f.** *Choice, 1991.*

Moser, Paul K. (Editor) BD161.O96 2002
The Oxford Handbook of Epistemology. Trade Cloth. Oxford University Press, Inc. New York, NY. 2002. 608p. Oxford Handbooks ISBN:0-19-513005-7, ISBN13: 978-0-19-513005-8. Dewey:121. LCCN:2001-058016.

Audience: **g,u,f.** *Choice, 2003.*

Moser, Paul K., et al. BD161.M8485 1998
The Theory of Knowledge: A Thematic Introduction. Dwayne H. Mulder & J. D. Trout (Authors). Paper Text. Oxford University Press, Inc. New York, NY. 1997. 224p. ISBN:0-19-509466-2, ISBN13: 978-0-19-509466-4. Dewey:121. LCCN:96-052985.

Audience: **g,u,f.** *Choice, 1998.*

Plato B386.A5L48 1992
Theaetetus. M. J. Levett (Translator), Bernard Williams (Introduction by), Myles F. Burnyeat (Revised by). Trade Paper. Hackett Publishing Company, Inc. Indianapolis, IN. 1992. 128p. ISBN:0-87220-158-9, ISBN13: 978-0-87220-158-3. Dewey:121. LCCN:92-028261.

Audience: **g,l,u,f.** *B*

Popper, Karl R. BD161 .P727 1979
Objective Knowledge: An Evolutionary Approach. Ed. 2. Paper Text. Oxford University Press, Inc. New York, NY. 1972. 416p. ISBN:0-19-875024-2, ISBN13: 978-0-19-875024-6. Dewey:121. LCCN:79-318586.

Audience: **g,u,f.**

Reichenbach, Hans BD0163.R4
Experience and Prediction: An Analysis of the Foundations and the Structure of Knowledge. Trade Paper. Books on Demand. Ann Arbor, MI. 421p. Midway Reprint Ser. ISBN:0-608-12117-7, ISBN13: 978-0-608-12117-8. Dewey:121.

Audience: **g,u,f.** *B*

Rescher, Nicholas BD220.R49 1997
Objectivity: The Obligations of Impersonal Reason. Cloth Text. University of Notre Dame Press. Notre Dame, IN. 1997. 264p. ISBN:0-268-03701-9, ISBN13: 978-0-268-03701-7. Dewey:149/.7. LCCN:96-026431.

Audience: **g,u,f.** *Choice, 1997.*

Russell, Bertrand   **B1649.R93O8 1993**
Our Knowledge of the External World: As a Field for Scientific Method in Philosophy. Trade Paper. Routledge. New York, NY. 1993. 256p. ISBN:0-415-09605-7, ISBN13: 978-0-415-09605-8. Dewey:121. LCCN:93-016365.
           Audience: **g,l,u,f.**

Russell, Bertrand & Marsh,   **B1649.R9**
  Robert C. (Editors)
Logic and Knowledge. Trade Paper. Routledge. New York, NY. 1988. 400p. ISBN:0-415-09074-1, ISBN13: 978-0-415-09074-2. Dewey:160.
           Audience: **g,u,f.**

Sayre, Kenneth M.   **BD215.S28 1997**
Belief and Knowledge: Mapping the Cognitive Landscape. Trade Cloth. Rowman & Littlefield Publishers, Inc. Lanham, MD. 1997. 248p. Studies in Epistemology and Cognitive Theory, No. 35 ISBN:0-8476-8472-5, ISBN13: 978-0-8476-8472-4. Dewey:121/.6. LCCN:97-014921.
           Audience: **g,u,f.** *Choice, 1998.*

Smith, A. D.   **B835.S57 2002**
The Problem of Perception. Trade Cloth. Harvard University Press. Cambridge, MA. 2002. 336p. ISBN:0-674-00841-3, ISBN13: 978-0-674-00841-0. Dewey:121/. 34. LCCN:2002-017164.
           Audience: **g,u,f.** *Choice, 2003.*

Sosa, Ernest (Author,   **BD161 .S647 1991**
  Contribution by)
Knowledge in Perspective: Selected Essays in Epistemology. Jonathan Dancy, John Haldane, Gilbert Harman, Frank Jackson & William G. Lucan (Contribution by). Trade Paper. Cambridge University Press. New York, NY. 1991. 312p. Cambridge Studies in Philosophy Ser. ISBN:0-521-39643-3, ISBN13: 978-0-521-39643-1. Dewey:121. LCCN:90-044708.
           Audience: **u,f.** *Choice, 1991.*

Wilson, Edward O.   **B72.W54 1998**
Consilience: The Unity of Knowledge. Trade Cloth. Alfred A. Knopf Inc. New York, NY. 1998. 352p. ISBN:0-679-45077-7, ISBN13: 978-0-679-45077-1. Dewey:121. LCCN:97-002816.
           Audience: **g,u,f.** *Choice, 1999.*

Wittgenstein, Ludwig   **BD181**
On Certainty. Gertrude Elizabeth Margaret Anscombe, G. H. von Wright & Denis Paul (Editors), D. Paul & G. E. M. Anscombe (Translators). Trade Paper. Blackwell Publishing, Inc. Malden, MA. 1996. 208p. ISBN:0-631-16940-7, ISBN13: 978-0-631-16940-6. Dewey:121/.6.
           Audience: **u,f.** *B*

Divisions of Philosophy > Ethics

Annas, Julia   **BJ161**
The Morality of Happiness. Paper Text. Oxford University Press, Inc. New York, NY. 1995. 512p. ISBN:0-19-509652-5, ISBN13: 978-0-19-509652-1. Dewey:170/.938.
           Audience: **l,u,f.** *Choice, 1994.*

Badiou, Alain   **BJ319**
Ethics: An Essay on the Understanding of Evil. Verso Books. 2002. ISBN:1-85984-435-9, ISBN13: 978-1-85984-435-9.
           Audience: **u,f.**

Becker, Lawrence C. &   **BJ63.E45 2001**
  Becker, Charlotte B. (Editors)
Encyclopedia of Ethics, Set. Ed. 2. Paper over Boards. Routledge. New York, NY. 2001. 2032p. ISBN:0-415-93672-1, ISBN13: 978-0-415-93672-9. Dewey:170/.3. LCCN:2001-019657.
           Audience: **g.** *Choice, 2002, 1992.*

Bonhoeffer, Dietrich   **BJ1253.B61513 2005**
Ethics. Ilse Todt (Editor). Trade Cloth. Augsburg Fortress, Publishers. Minneapolis, MN. 2005. 608p. ISBN:0-8006-8306-4, ISBN13: 978-0-8006-8306-1. Dewey:241. LCCN:2004-019811.
           Audience: **g.** *B*

Brandt, Richard B.   **BJ37**
Ethical Theory: The Problems of Normative and Critical Ethics. Paper Text. Textbook Publishers. Temecula, CA. 2003. 538p. ISBN:0-7581-5896-3, ISBN13: 978-0-7581-5896-3. Dewey:170.
           Audience: **u,f.** *B*

Copp, David (Editor)   **BJ1012.C675 2005**
The Oxford Handbook of Ethical Theory. Trade Cloth. Oxford University Press, Inc. New York, NY. 2005. 672p. Oxford Handbooks Ser. ISBN:0-19-514779-0, ISBN13: 978-0-19-514779-7. Dewey:171. LCCN:2004-065411.
           Audience: **u.** *Choice, 2006.*

DesAutels, Peggy & Waugh,   **BJ1395.D47 2001**
  Joanne
Feminists Doing Ethics. Book, Other. Rowman & Littlefield Publishers, Inc. Lanham, MD. 2001. 280p. New Feminist Perspectives Ser. ISBN:0-7425-1210-X, ISBN13: 978-0-7425-1210-8. Dewey:170/.82. LCCN:2001-019407.
           Audience: **g,u.** *Choice, 2002.*

Dover, Kenneth J.   **BJ182.D68 1994**
Greek Popular Morality in the Time of Plato and Aristotle. Trade Cloth. Hackett Publishing Company, Inc. Indianapolis, IN. 1994. 352p. ISBN:0-87220-246-1, ISBN13: 978-0-87220-246-7. Dewey:170/.938. LCCN:93-042840.
           Audience: **g,l,u,f.** *B*

Edwards, Jonathan   **BJ1520.E3**
The Nature of True Virtue. Paper Text. Textbook Publishers. Temecula, CA. 2003. xiii, 107p. ISBN:0-7581-2090-7, ISBN13: 978-0-7581-2090-8. Dewey:170.
           Audience: **g.** *B*

Everson, Stephen (Editor)   **BJ161 .E84 1998**
Ethics. Susan S. Meyer, C. H. Kahn, C. C. Taylor, Julia Annas, John McDowell, David Sedley & T. H. Irwin (Contribution by). Trade Paper. Cambridge University Press. New York, NY. 1998. 308p. Companions to Ancient Thought Ser., Vol. 4 ISBN:0-521-38832-5, ISBN13: 978-0-521-38832-0. Dewey:170/.938. LCCN:97-008899.
           Audience: **l,u.** *Choice, 1999.*

Foot, Philippa   **BJ1012.F57 2002**
Virtues and Vices: And Other Essays in Moral Philosophy. Trade
Paper. Oxford University Press, Inc. New York, NY. 2003. 232p.
ISBN:0-19-925286-6, ISBN13: 978-0-19-925286-2. Dewey:170.
LCCN:2002-025813.
                                              Audience: **u,f.**

Fromm, Erich   **BJ45**
Man for Himself: An Inquiry into the Psychology of Ethics.
Library Binding. Routledge. New York, NY. 1999. 268p.
International Library of Psychology ISBN:0-415-21020-8,
ISBN13: 978-0-415-21020-1. Dewey:171.2.
                                  Audience: **g,l,u,f.** B

Hare, Richard M.   **BJ1012 .H3**
Freedom and Reason. Paper Text. Oxford University Press, Inc.
New York, NY. 1977. 236p. Oxford Paperbacks Ser., No. 92
ISBN:0-19-881092-X, ISBN13: 978-0-19-881092-6. Dewey:170.
                                              Audience: **u,f.**

Hinman, Lawrence M.   **LC251**
🖵 Ethics Updates.
http://ethics.acusd.edu/index.asp
                                               Audience: **l.**

Hutcheson, Francis   **BJ654**
A System of Moral Philosophy. Continuum International
Publishing Group, Ltd. 2005. ISBN:0-8264-8815-3, ISBN13:
978-0-8264-8815-2.
                                              Audience: **g,u.**

Hutcheson, Francis   **BJ1005.H88 2004**
An Inquiry into the Original of Our Ideas of Beauty and Virtue:
In Two Treatises. Wolfgang Leidhold (Introduction by). Trade
Cloth. Liberty Fund, Inc. Indianapolis, IN. 2004. 258p. Natural
Law and Enlightenment Classics Ser. ISBN:0-86597-428-4,
ISBN13: 978-0-86597-428-9. Dewey:171/.2.
LCCN:2003-065286.
                                  Audience: **g,u.** B

Huxley, Thomas Henry &   **BJ1311.H8 1971**
  Huxley, Julian S.
Touchstone for Ethics, 1893-1943. Trade Cloth. Ayer Company
Publishers, Inc. Manchester, NH. 1977. viii, 257p. Essay Index
Reprint Ser. ISBN:0-8369-2402-9, ISBN13: 978-0-8369-2402-2.
Dewey:171/.7. LCCN:74-156661.
                                    Audience: **g.** B

Kagan, Shelly   **BJ1012.K244 1998**
Normative Ethics. Trade Paper. Westview Press. Boulder, CO.
1997. 352p. Dimensions of Philosophy Ser.
ISBN:0-8133-0846-1, ISBN13: 978-0-8133-0846-3. Dewey:170.
LCCN:97-030631.
                              Audience: **g,u.** *Choice, 1998.*

Kant, Immanuel   **B2766.E6 G7 1998**
Groundwork of the Metaphysics of Morals. Mary J. Gregor
(Editor, Translator), Christine M. Korsgaard (Introduction by),
Karl Ameriks, Desmond M. Clarke & Immanuel Kant
(Contribution by). Trade Paper. Cambridge University Press.

New York, NY. 1998. 120p. Texts in the History of Philosophy
ISBN:0-521-62695-1, ISBN13: 978-0-521-62695-8. Dewey:170.
LCCN:97-030153.
                              Audience: **g,u,f.** *Choice, 1998.*

Korsgaard, Christine M.   **BJ1458.3 .K67 1996**
The Sources of Normativity. Onora O'Neill (Foreword by).
Trade Paper. Cambridge University Press. New York, NY. 1996.
289p. ISBN:0-521-55960-X, ISBN13: 978-0-521-55960-7.
Dewey:170. LCCN:95-012848.
                              Audience: **u,f.** *Choice, 1997.*

Lewis, C. S.   **BJ1401.L4 2000**
The Great Divorce. Trade Paper. HarperCollins Publishers. New
York, NY. 2001. 160p. ISBN:0-06-065295-0, ISBN13:
978-0-06-065295-1. Dewey:236/.2. LCCN:00-049859.
                                    Audience: **g.** B

Lippman, Walter   **BJ47 .L5**
A Preface to Morals. Trade Paper. Kessinger Publishing, LLC.
Whitefish, MT. 2005. ISBN:0-7661-9558-9, ISBN13:
978-0-7661-9558-5. Dewey:170.
                                               Audience: **g.**

MacIntyre, Alasdair   **BJ1012.M325 1984**
After Virtue: A Study in Moral Theory. Ed. 2. Trade Cloth.
University of Notre Dame Press. Notre Dame, IN. 1984. 320p.
ISBN:0-268-00611-3, ISBN13: 978-0-268-00611-2. Dewey:170.
LCCN:83-040601.
                                  Audience: **g,u.** B

MacIntyre, Alasdair   **BJ71.M3 1998**
A Short History of Ethics. Ed. 2. Trade Cloth. University of
Notre Dame Press. Notre Dame, IN. 1997. 304p.
ISBN:0-268-01759-X, ISBN13: 978-0-268-01759-0.
Dewey:170/.9. LCCN:97-022280.
                              Audience: **g,l,u.** *Choice, 1998.*

MacIntyre, Alasdair   **B105.J87M33 1988**
Whose Justice? Which Rationality? Cloth Text. University of
Notre Dame Press. Notre Dame, IN. 1989. 432p.
ISBN:0-268-01942-8, ISBN13: 978-0-268-01942-6. Dewey:172.
LCCN:87-040354.
                              Audience: **g,l,u,f.** *Choice, 1988.*

Mandeville, Bernard   **BJ1520.M4 1997**
The Fable of the Bees and Other Writings. E. J. Hundert
(Editor). Trade Cloth. Hackett Publishing Company, Inc.
Indianapolis, IN. 1997. 260p. Classics Ser. ISBN:0-87220-375-1,
ISBN13: 978-0-87220-375-4. Dewey:170. LCCN:97-029593.
                                               Audience: **g.**

Midgley, Mary   **BJ1401.M52 2001**
Wickedness. Ed. 2. Trade Paper. Routledge. New York, NY.
2001. 248p. Classics Ser. ISBN:0-415-25398-5, ISBN13:
978-0-415-25398-7. Dewey:170. LCCN:2001-041221.
                                               Audience: **g.**

Neiman, Susan   **BJ1401.N45 2002**
Evil in Modern Thought: An Alternative History of Philosophy.
Trade Cloth. Princeton University Press. Princeton, NJ. 2002.

304p. ISBN:0-691-09608-2, ISBN13: 978-0-691-09608-7. Dewey:170. LCCN:2002-070374.

Audience: **g,u.** *Choice, 2003.*

Niebuhr, Reinhold   **BJ1251 .N5 1987**
An Interpretation of Christian Ethics. Trade Paper. HarperCollins Publishers. New York, NY. 1986. ISBN:0-8164-2206-0, ISBN13: 978-0-8164-2206-7. Dewey:241. LCCN:86-031935.

Audience: **g.** *B*

Oakeshott, Michael   **BJ1581.2O2 1990**
On Human Conduct. Trade Paper. Oxford University Press, Inc. New York, NY. 1991. 340p. ISBN:0-19-827758-X, ISBN13: 978-0-19-827758-3. Dewey:320/.01. LCCN:90-007604.

Audience: **g,l,u.** *B*

Rachels, James & Rachels, Stuart   **BJ1012.R29 2006**
The Elements of Moral Philosophy. McGraw-Hill Higher Education. 2006. ISBN:0-07-312547-4, ISBN13: 978-0-07-312547-3.

Audience: **g,l.**

Russell, Bertrand   **BJ1481 .R75**
The Conquest of Happiness. Trade Paper. Liveright Publishing Corporation. New York, NY. 1996. 256p. ISBN:0-87140-162-2, ISBN13: 978-0-87140-162-5. Dewey:171.4. LCCN:74-149626.

Audience: **g.**

Scanlon, T. M.   **BJ1411.S36 1998**
What We Owe to Each Other. Trade Cloth. Harvard University Press. Cambridge, MA. 1999. 432p. ISBN:0-674-95089-5, ISBN13: 978-0-674-95089-4. Dewey:170. LCCN:98-023318.

Audience: **g,u,f.** *Choice, 2000.*

Sidgwick, Henry   **BJ71.S55 1988**
Outlines of the History of Ethics. Ed. 5. Trade Cloth. Hackett Publishing Company, Inc. Indianapolis, IN. 1988. 312p. HPC Classics Ser. ISBN:0-87220-061-2, ISBN13: 978-0-87220-061-6. Dewey:170/.9. LCCN:88-010986.

Audience: **u,f.**

Singer, Peter Albert David (Editor)   **BJ1012.C62**
A Companion to Ethics. Trade Paper. Blackwell Publishing, Inc. Malden, MA. 1993. 592p. Companions to Philosophy Ser. ISBN:0-631-18785-5, ISBN13: 978-0-631-18785-1. Dewey:170. LCCN:00-039772.

Audience: **g,l,u,f.** *Choice, 1992.*

Singer, Peter Albert David (Editor)   **BJ1012**
Ethics. Paper Text. Oxford University Press, Inc. New York, NY. 1994. 426p. Oxford Readers Ser. ISBN:0-19-289245-2, ISBN13: 978-0-19-289245-4. Dewey:170. LCCN:93-029249.

Audience: **g,l,u.**

Smith, Adam   **BJ1005 .S6 2002**
Adam Smith: The Theory of Moral Sentiments. Knud Haakonssen (Editor). Cambridge University Press. 2002. ISBN:0-521-59847-8, ISBN13: 978-0-521-59847-7.

Audience: **g,u,f.**

Williams, Bernard   **BJ1012 .W533**
Moral Luck: Philosophical Papers, 1973-1980. Trade Cloth. Cambridge University Press. New York, NY. 1981. 192p. ISBN:0-521-24372-6, ISBN13: 978-0-521-24372-8. Dewey:170. LCCN:81-010152.

Audience: **g,f.**

Divisions of Philosophy > Ethics > Applied Ethics

Beauchamp, Thomas L. & Bowie, Norman E. (Editors)   **HF5387**
Ethical Theory and Business. Ed. 5. Trade Cloth. Prentice Hall PTR. Upper Saddle River, NJ. 1997. ISBN:0-01-339852-0, ISBN13: 978-0-01-339852-3. Dewey:174/.4. LCCN:96-008098.

Audience: **g,u,f.**

Beauchamp, Thomas L. & Childress, James F.   **R724.B36 2001**
Principles of Biomedical Ethics. Ed. 5. Trade Paper. Oxford University Press, Inc. New York, NY. 2001. 468p. ISBN:0-19-514332-9, ISBN13: 978-0-19-514332-4. Dewey:174/.2. LCCN:00-062394.

Audience: **g,u,f.**

Beauchamp, Tom L.   **BJ1012 .M37 1986**
Matters of Life and Death: New Introductory Essays in Moral Philosophy. Ed. 2. Tom Regan (Editor). Trade Paper. Random House, Inc. New York, NY. 1986. xx, 437p. ISBN:0-394-34297-6, ISBN13: 978-0-394-34297-9. Dewey:179/.1. LCCN:85-018411.

Audience: **g,l,u.**

Boonin, David   **HQ767.15.B66 2002**
A Defense of Abortion. Douglas MacLean (Contribution by). Trade Paper. Cambridge University Press. New York, NY. 2002. 368p. Cambridge Studies in Philosophy and Public Policy ISBN:0-521-52035-5, ISBN13: 978-0-521-52035-5. Dewey:179.7/6. LCCN:2002-022282.

Audience: **g,u,f.** *Choice, 2003.*

Callahan, Daniel & Singer, Peter (Editors)   **BJ63.E44 1998**
Encyclopedia of Applied Ethics, Set. Ruth Chadwick (Editor-In-Chief). Trade Cloth. Elsevier Science & Technology Books. Saint Louis, MO. 1997. 3101p. ISBN:0-12-227065-7, ISBN13: 978-0-12-227065-9. Dewey:170/.3. LCCN:97-074395.

Audience: **g,l.** *Choice, 1998.*

DeGeorge, Richard   **HF5387.D38 2005**
Business Ethics with CD-ROM. Ed. 6. Mixed Media. Prentice Hall PTR. Upper Saddle River, NJ. 2005. 656p. ISBN:0-13-099163-5, ISBN13: 978-0-13-099163-8. Dewey:174/.4. LCCN:2004-025402.

Audience: **g,l,u.**

Frey, R. G., et al.   **R726 .D93 1998**
Euthanasia and Physician-Assisted Suicide. Gerald Dworkin & Sissela Bok (Authors), R. G. Frey (Contribution by). Cloth Text.

Cambridge University Press. New York, NY. 1998. 160p. For and Against Ser. ISBN:0-521-58246-6, ISBN13: 978-0-521-58246-9. Dewey:179.7. LCCN:98-022810.

Audience: **g,l,u.**

Glannon, Walter (Editor)   **QH332**
Biomedical Ethics. Trade Cloth. Oxford University Press, Inc. New York, NY. 2004. 188p. Fundamentals of Philosophy Ser. ISBN:0-19-514430-9, ISBN13: 978-0-19-514430-7. Dewey:174.2. LCCN:2004-050092.

Audience: **g,u,f.** *Choice, 2005.*

LaFollette, Hugh (Editor)   **BJ1031.O94 2003**
The Oxford Handbook of Practical Ethics. Trade Cloth. Oxford University Press, Inc. New York, NY. 2003. 790p. Oxford Handbooks ISBN:0-19-824105-4, ISBN13: 978-0-19-824105-8. Dewey:170. LCCN:2002-070167.

Audience: **g,l,u,f.** *Choice, 2006.*

Light, Andrew & Rolston,   **GE42.E573 2002**
Holmes (Editors)
Environmental Ethics: An Anthology. Trade Cloth. Blackwell Publishing, Inc. Malden, MA. 2002. 568p. Philosophy Anthologies Ser., Vol. 19 ISBN:0-631-22293-6, ISBN13: 978-0-631-22293-4. LCCN:2002-066429.

Audience: **g,u,f.**

Machan, Tibor R.; Cheser,   **HF5387.M3 2002**
James E.
A Primer on Business Ethics. Rowman & Littlefield Publishers, Inc. 2002. ISBN:0-7425-1388-2, ISBN13: 978-0-7425-1388-4.

Audience: **g,l,u.**

Mappes, Thomas A. &   **R724.B49 2005**
DeGrazia, David
Biomedical Ethics. Ed. 6. Paper Text. McGraw-Hill Higher Education. Burr Ridge, IL. 2005. 752p. ISBN:0-07-297644-6, ISBN13: 978-0-07-297644-1. Dewey:174.2. LCCN:2005-017337.

Audience: **g,l,u.**

McMahan, Jeff   **BJ1469**
The Ethics of Killing: Problems at the Margins of Life. Paper Text. Oxford University Press, Inc. New York, NY. 2003. 560p. Oxford Ethics Ser. ISBN:0-19-516982-4, ISBN13: 978-0-19-516982-9. Dewey:179.7. LCCN:2001-021768.

Audience: **g,u,f.**

Midgley, Mary   **BJ1012**
Animals and Why They Matter. Trade Paper. University of Georgia Press. Athens, GA. 1998. 160p. ISBN:0-8203-2041-2, ISBN13: 978-0-8203-2041-0. Dewey:179.3. LCCN:83-017933.

Audience: **g.** *B*

Miller, Richard B.   **B105.W3M55 1991**
Interpretations of Conflict: Ethics, Pacifism, and the Just-War Tradition. University of Chicago Press. 1991. ISBN:0-226-52796-4, ISBN13: 978-0-226-52796-3.

Audience: **g,l,u.**

Nagel, Thomas   **BD431.N32 1991**
Mortal Questions. Cambridge University Press. 1991. A Canto Book Ser. ISBN:0-521-40676-5, ISBN13: 978-0-521-40676-5.

Audience: **g,l,u.**

Nagel, Thomas & Scanlon,   **HQ767**
Thomas
Rights and Wrongs of Abortion: A Philosophy and Public Affairs Reader. Marshall Cohen (Editor). Trade Paper. Princeton University Press. Princeton, NJ. 1974. 127p. Philosophy and Public Affairs Reader Ser. ISBN:0-691-01979-7, ISBN13: 978-0-691-01979-6. Dewey:179/.7. LCCN:73-008268.

Audience: **l,u.**

Singer, Peter (Editor)   **HV4711.I6 2005**
In Defense of Animals: The Second Wave. Ed. 2. Trade Cloth. Blackwell Publishing, Inc. Malden, MA. 2005. 264p. ISBN:1-4051-1940-3, ISBN13: 978-1-4051-1940-5. Dewey:179/.3. LCCN:2005-009479.

Audience: **g,l,u,f.**

Singer, Peter Albert David   **BJ1012**
(Editor)
Applied Ethics. Paper Text. Oxford University Press, Inc. New York, NY. 1986. 272p. Oxford Readings in Philosophy Ser. ISBN:0-19-875067-6, ISBN13: 978-0-19-875067-3. Dewey:170. LCCN:86-016316.

Audience: **l,u.**

Singer, Peter   **R724.C616 1998**
A Companion to Bioethics. Helga Kuhse (Editor). Trade Cloth. Blackwell Publishing, Inc. Malden, MA. 1998. 528p. Companions to Philosophy Ser. ISBN:0-631-19737-0, ISBN13: 978-0-631-19737-9. Dewey:174/.2. LCCN:97-050242.

Audience: **g,l,u,f.**

Tuckerman, Nancy, et al.   **BJ1853.T83 1995**
The Amy Vanderbilt Complete Book of Etiquette. Ed. 50. Nancy Dunnan & Amy Vanderbilt (Authors). Trade Cloth. Doubleday Publishing. New York, NY. 1995. 800p. ISBN:0-385-41342-4, ISBN13: 978-0-385-41342-8. Dewey:395. LCCN:93-044452.

Audience: **g.**

Wenz, Peter S.   **GE42.W458 2001**
Environmental Ethics Today. Oxford University Press. 2000. ISBN:0-19-513384-6, ISBN13: 978-0-19-513384-4.

Audience: **g,l.**

Divisions of Philosophy > Ethics > Metaethics

Brandt, Richard B.   **BJ1012.B63 1998**
A Theory of the Good and the Right. Ed. 2. Trade Paper. Prometheus Books, Publishers. Amherst, NY. 1998. 381p. ISBN:1-57392-220-X, ISBN13: 978-1-57392-220-3. Dewey:171/.5. LCCN:98-017904.

Audience: **u,f.** *B*

Brink, David Owen   BJ1012 .B676 1989
Moral Realism and the Foundations of Ethics. Jonathan Dancy,
John Haldane, Gilbert Harman, Frank Jackson, William G.
Lucan & Ernest Sosa (Contribution by). Trade Paper. Cambridge
University Press. New York, NY. 1989. 352p. Cambridge
Studies in Philosophy ISBN:0-521-35937-6, ISBN13:
978-0-521-35937-5. Dewey:170. LCCN:88-016179.
Audience: **g,u,f.** *Choice, 1989.*

Donagan, Alan   BJ1012.D57
The Theory of Morality. Trade Paper. University of Chicago
Press. Chicago, IL. 1979. 294p. ISBN:0-226-15567-6, ISBN13:
978-0-226-15567-8. Dewey:170. LCCN:76-025634.
Audience: **u,f.**

Foot, Philippa R. (Editor)   BJ21
Theories of Ethics. Paper Text. Oxford University Press, Inc.
New York, NY. 1976. 192p. Oxford Readings in Philosophy Ser.
ISBN:0-19-875005-6, ISBN13: 978-0-19-875005-5.
Dewey:171/.08.
Audience: **l,u.**

Gewirth, Alan   BJ1012
Reason and Morality. Trade Paper. University of Chicago Press.
Chicago, IL. 1980. 401p. ISBN:0-226-28876-5, ISBN13:
978-0-226-28876-5. Dewey:170. LCCN:77-013911.
Audience: **u,f.** *B*

Hare, Richard M.   BJ1012 .H3
Freedom and Reason. Paper Text. Oxford University Press, Inc.
New York, NY. 1977. 236p. Oxford Paperbacks Ser., No. 92
ISBN:0-19-881092-X, ISBN13: 978-0-19-881092-6. Dewey:170.
Audience: **u,f.**

Hare, Richard M.   BJ1025
The Language of Morals. Paper Text. Oxford University Press,
Inc. New York, NY. 1991. 208p. ISBN:0-19-881077-6, ISBN13:
978-0-19-881077-3. Dewey:170.
Audience: **u,f.**

Harman, Gilbert   BJ1012.H317
The Nature of Morality: An Introduction to Ethics. Trade Cloth.
Oxford University Press, Inc. New York, NY. 1977. xiii, 165p.
ISBN:0-19-502142-8, ISBN13: 978-0-19-502142-4. Dewey:160.
LCCN:76-029806.
Audience: **u,f.** *B*

Lyons, David   BJ55 .L95 1984
Ethics and the Rule of Law. Trade Paper. Cambridge University
Press. New York, NY. 1983. 240p. ISBN:0-521-27712-4,
ISBN13: 978-0-521-27712-9. Dewey:340/.112.
LCCN:83-007687.
Audience: **g,l,u.** *B*

Moore, G. E.   B1647.M73 P74 1993
Principia Ethica. Ed. 2. Thomas Baldwin (Editor). Trade Paper.
Cambridge University Press. New York, NY. 1993. 352p.
ISBN:0-521-44848-4, ISBN13: 978-0-521-44848-2.
Dewey:171/.2. LCCN:93-006493.
Audience: **g,u,f.** *B*

Moore, G. E.   BJ1011
Ethics. William H. Shaw (Editor). Trade Cloth. Oxford
University Press, Inc. New York, NY. 2005. 224p. British Moral
Philosophers Ser. ISBN:0-19-927200-X, ISBN13:
978-0-19-927200-6. Dewey:170. LCCN:2005-019318.
Audience: **g,u,f.** *B*

Murdoch, Iris   BJ1012
The Sovereignty of Good. Ed. 2. Paper over Boards. Routledge.
New York, NY. 2001. 112p. Classics Ser. ISBN:0-415-25552-X,
ISBN13: 978-0-415-25552-3. Dewey:170.
Audience: **g.** *B*

Nielsen, Kai   BJ1012.N53 1990
Ethics Without God. Ed. 2. Trade Paper. Prometheus Books,
Publishers. Amherst, NY. 1990. 207p. ISBN:0-87975-552-0,
ISBN13: 978-0-87975-552-2. Dewey:171. LCCN:89-039720.
Audience: **g.** *B*

Ross, David   BJ1401.R6 2002
The Right and the Good. Ed. 2. Philip Stratton-Lake (Editor).
Trade Paper. Oxford University Press, Inc. New York, NY. 2003.
242p. British Moral Philosophers Ser. ISBN:0-19-925265-3,
ISBN13: 978-0-19-925265-7. Dewey:170. LCCN:2002-066234.
Audience: **g,u,f.**

Ross, W. David   BJ1012 .R63 2000
Foundations of Ethics: The Gifford Lectures Delivered in the
University of Aberdeen, 1935-1936. Cloth Text. Oxford
University Press, Inc. New York, NY. 2000. 348p. Oxford
Scholarly Classics Ser. ISBN:0-19-824162-3, ISBN13:
978-0-19-824162-1. Dewey:170. LCCN:2001-266314.
Audience: **u,f.**

Singer, Marcus George   BJ1011.S55
Generalization in Ethics: An Essay in the Logic of Ethics, with
the Rudiments of a System of Moral Philosophy. Paper Text.
Textbook Publishers. Temecula, CA. 2003. 351p.
ISBN:0-7581-4439-3, ISBN13: 978-0-7581-4439-3. Dewey:170.
Audience: **u,f.** *B*

Sullivan, Roger J.   B2799.E8 S84 1994
An Introduction to Kant's Ethics. Trade Paper. Cambridge
University Press. New York, NY. 1994. 191p.
ISBN:0-521-46769-1, ISBN13: 978-0-521-46769-8.
Dewey:170/.92. LCCN:93-040557.
Audience: **g,u.** *Choice, 1995.*

Toulmin, Stephen E.   BJ43 .T6
An Examination of the Place of Reason in Ethics. Trade Paper.
Books on Demand. Ann Arbor, MI. 240p. ISBN:0-608-12921-6,
ISBN13: 978-0-608-12921-1. Dewey:170.
Audience: **u,f.**

Williams, Bernard   BJ1012.W52 1985
Ethics and the Limits of Philosophy. Trade Cloth. Harvard
University Press. Cambridge, MA. 1985. 244p.
ISBN:0-674-26857-1, ISBN13: 978-0-674-26857-9.
Dewey:170/.42. LCCN:84-023479.
Audience: **g,f.** *Choice, 1985.*

Divisions of Philosophy > Metaphysics

Bergson, Henri B2430.B4I413 1999
An Introduction to Metaphysics. T. E. Hulme (Translator). Trade
Cloth. Hackett Publishing Company, Inc. Indianapolis, IN. 1999.
62p. ISBN:0-87220-475-8, ISBN13: 978-0-87220-475-1.
Dewey:110. LCCN:99-028080.

Audience: **g,u,f.** *B*

Bradley, F. H. BD111.B8 1969
Appearance and Reality: A Metaphysical Essay. Trade Cloth.
Oxford University Press, Inc. New York, NY. 1969. xxvi, 570p.
ISBN:0-19-881150-0, ISBN13: 978-0-19-881150-3. Dewey:110.
LCCN:79-405526.

Audience: **g,u,f.** *B*

Collingwood, Robin George B1618.C71M37 1998
An Essay on Metaphysics. Ed. 2. Rex Martin (Editor,
Introduction by). Trade Cloth. Oxford University Press, Inc.
New York, NY. 1998. 546p. ISBN:0-19-823561-5, ISBN13:
978-0-19-823561-3. Dewey:110. LCCN:98-015538.

Audience: **g,u,f.**

Dummett, Michael BC51
The Logical Basis of Metaphysics. Trade Cloth. Harvard
University Press. Cambridge, MA. 1991. 376p. The William
James Lectures ISBN:0-674-53785-8, ISBN13:
978-0-674-53785-9. Dewey:121.68. LCCN:90-039999.

Audience: **g,u,f.** *Choice, 1991.*

Gale, Richard M. (Editor) BD111.B57 2002
The Blackwell Guide to Metaphysics. Trade Paper. Blackwell
Publishing, Inc. Malden, MA. 2002. 360p. Blackwell Philosophy
Guides Ser., Vol. 7 ISBN:0-631-22121-2, ISBN13:
978-0-631-22121-0. Dewey:110. LCCN:2002-066443.

Audience: **u,f.**

Hoffman, Joshua & BD331 .H57 1994
Rosenkrantz, Gary S.
Substance among Other Categories. Trade Cloth. Cambridge
University Press. New York, NY. 1994. 208p. Cambridge
Studies in Philosophy ISBN:0-521-46101-4, ISBN13:
978-0-521-46101-6. Dewey:111/.1. LCCN:93-049101.

Audience: **u,f.** *Choice, 1995.*

Jubien, Michael BD111.J83 1997
An Introduction to Contemporary Metaphysics. Trade Paper.
Blackwell Publishing, Inc. Malden, MA. 1997. 224p.
Contemporary Philosophy Ser. ISBN:1-55786-859-X, ISBN13:
978-1-55786-859-6. Dewey:110. LCCN:96-052895.

Audience: **g,u,f.**

Kim, Jaegwon & Sosa, BD111.M55 1999
Ernest (Editors)
Metaphysics: An Anthology. Trade Cloth. Blackwell Publishing,
Inc. Malden, MA. 1999. 688p. Philosophy Anthologies Ser.
ISBN:0-631-20278-1, ISBN13: 978-0-631-20278-3. Dewey:110.
LCCN:98-008538.

Audience: **g,u.**

Koyre, Alexandre BD511
From the Closed World to the Infinite Universe. Trade Paper.
Johns Hopkins University Press. Baltimore, MD. 1994. 328p.
ISBN:0-8018-0347-0, ISBN13: 978-0-8018-0347-5. Dewey:113.
LCCN:57-007080.

Audience: **g,u,f.** *B*

Loux, Michael J. & BD111.L68 2003
Zimmerman, Dean W. (Editors)
The Oxford Handbook of Metaphysics. Trade Cloth. Oxford
University Press, Inc. New York, NY. 2003. 736p. Oxford
Handbooks ISBN:0-19-825024-X, ISBN13: 978-0-19-825024-1.
Dewey:110. LCCN:2004-273365.

Audience: **g,u,f.**

Lovejoy, Arthur Oncken B105.C5
The Great Chain of Being: A Study of the History of an Idea.
Trade Paper. Harvard University Press. Cambridge, MA. 1936.
400p. The William James Lectures ISBN:0-674-36153-9,
ISBN13: 978-0-674-36153-9. Dewey:119. LCCN:36-014264.

Audience: **g,l,u,f.**

Lowe, E. J. BD111.L685 2002
A Survey of Metaphysics. Paper Text. Oxford University Press,
Inc. New York, NY. 2002. 416p. ISBN:0-19-875253-9, ISBN13:
978-0-19-875253-0. Dewey:110. LCCN:2002-280736.

Audience: **g,u,f.** *Choice, 2003.*

Munitz, Milton K. BD331.M87
The Question of Reality. Trade Paper. Princeton University
Press. Princeton, NJ. 1992. 224p. ISBN:0-691-02091-4, ISBN13:
978-0-691-02091-4. Dewey:111. LCCN:89-010210.

Audience: **g,u,f.** *Choice, 1990.*

Murdoch, Iris BJ1012
Metaphysics As a Guide to Morals: Philosophical Reflections.
UK-B Format Paperback. Knopf Publishing Group. New York,
NY. 2003. 512p. ISBN:0-09-943355-9, ISBN13:
978-0-09-943355-2. Dewey:170.

Audience: **g,l,u.** *Choice, 1993.*

Owens, Joseph BD331.O93 1985
An Interpretation of Existence. Trade Cloth. University of Notre
Dame Press. Notre Dame, IN. 1987. 162p. ISBN:0-268-01157-5,
ISBN13: 978-0-268-01157-4. Dewey:111/.1. LCCN:84-023805.

Audience: **g,u,f.**

Sider, Theodore & Conee, BD111
Earl Brink
Riddles of Existence: A Guided Tour of Metaphysics. Trade
Cloth. Oxford University Press, Inc. New York, NY. 2005. 224p.
ISBN:0-19-928226-9, ISBN13: 978-0-19-928226-5. Dewey:110.

Audience: **g,u,f.** *Choice, 2006.*

Sosa, Ernest BD111.C626 1995
A Companion to Metaphysics. Jaegwon Kim (Editor). Trade
Paper. Blackwell Publishing, Inc. Malden, MA. 1996. 560p.
Companions to Philosophy Ser. ISBN:0-631-19999-3, ISBN13:
978-0-631-19999-1. Dewey:110/.3. LCCN:93-048296.

Audience: **u,f.** *Choice, 1995.*

Strawson, Peter F.   **BD111**
Individuals. Trade Paper. Routledge. New York, NY. 1959. 260p.
ISBN:0-415-05185-1, ISBN13: 978-0-415-05185-9. Dewey:110.
Audience: **u,f.**

Unger, Peter K.   **BD111.U54 2005**
All the Power in the World. Trade Cloth. Oxford University
Press, Inc. New York, NY. 2005. 670p. ISBN:0-19-515561-0,
ISBN13: 978-0-19-515561-7. Dewey:110. LCCN:2005-047274.
Audience: **g,u,f.**

Van Inwagen, Peter   **BD311.V35 1990**
Material Beings. Book, Other. Cornell University Press. Ithaca,
NY. 1990. 288p. ISBN:0-8014-1969-7, ISBN13:
978-0-8014-1969-0. Dewey:111. LCCN:90-055125.
Audience: **g,u,f.** *Choice, 1991.*

Van Inwagen, Peter   **BD111.V38 2002**
Metaphysics. Ed. 2. Trade Paper. Westview Press. Boulder, CO.
2002. 256p. Dimensions of Philosophy Ser.
ISBN:0-8133-9055-9, ISBN13: 978-0-8133-9055-0. Dewey:110.
LCCN:2002-002981.
Audience: **g,u,f.** *Choice, 1994.*

Whitehead, Alfred North   **QB981**
Process and Reality: An Essay in Cosmology. Ed. 2. Trade
Paper. Simon & Schuster. New York, NY. 1979. 448p. Gifford
Lectures ISBN:0-02-934570-7, ISBN13: 978-0-02-934570-2.
Dewey:523.1. LCCN:77-090011.
Audience: **g,u,f.** *B*

Divisions of Philosophy > Metaphysics > Ontology

Gilson, Etienne   **BD331 .G495**
Being and Some Philosophers. Ed. 2. Cloth Text. Pontifical
Institute of Mediaeval Studies, Department of Publications.
Toronto, ON. 1952. 247p. ISBN:0-88844-401-X, ISBN13:
978-0-88844-401-1. Dewey:111.
Audience: **g,u,f.** *B*

Heidegger, Martin   **B3279.H47 E56**
The Question of Being. Book, Other. Rowman & Littlefield
Publishers, Inc. Lanham, MD. 1958. ISBN:0-8084-0258-7,
ISBN13: 978-0-8084-0258-9. Dewey:111.
Audience: **g,u,f.**

Plato   **B378.A5G5513 1996**
Parmenides. Mary L. Gill & Paul Ryan (Translators), Mary L.
Gill (Introduction by). Trade Cloth. Hackett Publishing
Company, Inc. Indianapolis, IN. 1996. 144p.
ISBN:0-87220-329-8, ISBN13: 978-0-87220-329-7. Dewey:184.
LCCN:95-048981.
Audience: **u,f.**

Plato   **B384.A5 1993**
The Sophist. Nicholas White (Translator, Introduction by). Trade
Cloth. Hackett Publishing Company, Inc. Indianapolis, IN. 1993.

128p. Hackett Classics Ser. ISBN:0-87220-203-8, ISBN13:
978-0-87220-203-0. Dewey:184. LCCN:93-005792.
Audience: **g,l,u,f.** *Choice, 1991.*

Sellars, Wilfrid   **B29**
Naturalism and Ontology. Library Binding. Ridgeview
Publishing Company. Atascadero, CA. 1980. viii, 182p.
ISBN:0-917930-36-3, ISBN13: 978-0-917930-36-2. Dewey:111.
Audience: **g,u,f.**

Van Inwagen, Peter   **B945.V353 O58 2001**
Ontology, Identity, and Modality: Essays in Metaphysics.
Jonathan Dancy, John Haldane, Gilbert Harman, Frank Jackson,
William G. Lucan & Ernest Sosa (Contribution by). Trade
Cloth. Cambridge University Press. New York, NY. 2001. 272p.
Cambridge Studies in Philosophy ISBN:0-521-79164-2,
ISBN13: 978-0-521-79164-9. Dewey:110. LCCN:00-031180.
Audience: **g,u,f.**

Divisions of Philosophy > Philosophy of Language

Austin, J. L.   **P302**
How to Do Things with Words. Ed. 2. J. O. Urmsson & Marina
Sbisa (Editors). Trade Paper. Harvard University Press.
Cambridge, MA. 1975. 188p. ISBN:0-674-41152-8, ISBN13:
978-0-674-41152-4. Dewey:401/.41.
Audience: **g,u,f.** *B*

Black, Max   **B840 .B58 1981**
Language and Philosophy: Studies in Method. Trade Cloth.
Greenwood Publishing Group, Inc. Portsmouth, NH. 1981. 264p.
ISBN:0-313-23082-X, ISBN13: 978-0-313-23082-0.
Dewey:149/.94. LCCN:81-006206.
Audience: **g,u,f.** *B*

Burke, Kenneth   **B945.B77 G7**
A Grammar of Motives. Trade Cloth. University of California
Press. Berkeley, CA. 1969. 544p. ISBN:0-520-01544-4, ISBN13:
978-0-520-01544-9. Dewey:191. LCCN:69-016741.
Audience: **g,l,u.** *B*

Carnap, Rudolf   **B840**
Meaning and Necessity: A Study in Semantics and Modal Logic.
Ed. 2. Trade Paper. University of Chicago Press. Chicago, IL.
1988. 266p. ISBN:0-226-09347-6, ISBN13: 978-0-226-09347-5.
Dewey:189.4.
Audience: **u,f.** *B*

Collin, Finn & Guldmann,   **B840.C654 2004**
  Finn
Meaning, Use and Truth: The Philosophy of Natural Language.
Trade Paper. Ashgate Publishing, Ltd. Aldershot, 2005. 312p.
ISBN:0-7546-0759-3, ISBN13: 978-0-7546-0759-5.
Dewey:121/.68. LCCN:2004-005413.
Audience: **g,u,f.** *Choice, 2005.*

Davis, Wayne A.   B840.D36 2002
Meaning, Expression and Thought. Trade Cloth. Cambridge
University Press. New York, NY. 2002. 672p. Cambridge
Studies in Philosophy ISBN:0-521-55513-2, ISBN13:
978-0-521-55513-5. Dewey:121/.68. LCCN:2002-073478.
Audience: **u,f.** *Choice, 2003.*

Devitt, Michael & Hanley,   **P107**
  Richard (Editors)
Blackwell Guide to Philosophy of Language. Trade Cloth.
Blackwell Publishing, Inc. Malden, MA. 2006. 456p. Blackwell
Philosophy Guides, Vol. 19 ISBN:0-631-23141-2, ISBN13:
978-0-631-23141-7. Dewey:401. LCCN:2005-028555.
Audience: **u,f.**

Goodman, Nelson   **B29.G619**
Of Mind and Other Matters. Trade Paper. Harvard University
Press. Cambridge, MA. 1987. 224p. ISBN:0-674-63126-9,
ISBN13: 978-0-674-63126-7. Dewey:191. LCCN:83-012868.
Audience: **u,f.** *B*

Grice, Paul   B1641.G483S77 1989
Studies in the Way of Words. Trade Cloth. Harvard University
Press. Cambridge, MA. 1989. 406p. ISBN:0-674-85270-2,
ISBN13: 978-0-674-85270-9. Dewey:121/.68. LCCN:88-021400.
Audience: **g,u,f.** *Choice, 1989.*

Habermas, Jürgen   B831.5.H33 1998
On the Pragmatics of Communication. Trade Cloth. MIT Press.
Cambridge, MA. 1998. 416p. Studies in Contemporary German
Social Thought ISBN:0-262-08265-9, ISBN13:
978-0-262-08265-5. Dewey:306.4/4. LCCN:98-018171.
Audience: **g,u,f.** *Choice, 1999.*

Horwich, Paul   B840.H65 1998
Meaning. Trade Cloth. Oxford University Press, Inc. New York,
NY. 1999. 254p. ISBN:0-19-823728-6, ISBN13:
978-0-19-823728-0. Dewey:121.6/8. LCCN:98-037480.
Audience: **g,u,f.**

Kripke, Saul A.   **BD417 .K74**
Naming and Necessity. Trade Cloth. Harvard University Press.
Cambridge, MA. 1980. 184p. ISBN:0-674-59845-8, ISBN13:
978-0-674-59845-4. Dewey:160. LCCN:79-026088.
Audience: **g,u,f.**

Martinich, A. P.   P106.P455 2001
The Philosophy of Language. Ed. 4. Paper Text. Oxford
University Press, Inc. New York, NY. 2000. 608p.
ISBN:0-19-513543-1, ISBN13: 978-0-19-513543-5. Dewey:401.
LCCN:00-025522.
Audience: **l,u.**

Polanyi, Michael & Prosch,   **BD241**
  Harry
Meaning. Trade Paper. University of Chicago Press. Chicago,
IL. 1977. 260p. ISBN:0-226-67295-6, ISBN13:
978-0-226-67295-3. Dewey:121/.68. LCCN:75-005067.
Audience: **u,f.** *B*

Quine, Willard V.   **B840.Q49**
Ontological Relativity and Other Essays. Cloth Text. Columbia
University Press. New York, NY. 1977. viii, 165p. John Dewey
Lectures, No. 1 ISBN:0-231-03307-9, ISBN13:
978-0-231-03307-7. Dewey:110. LCCN:72-091121.
Audience: **u,f.** *B*

Quine, Willard V.   **B840**
Word and Object. Trade Paper. MIT Press. Cambridge, MA.
1964. 309p. Studies in Communication ISBN:0-262-67001-1,
ISBN13: 978-0-262-67001-2. Dewey:149.94. LCCN:60-009621.
Audience: **g,u,f.**

Richard, Mark (Editor)   B840.M445 2002
Meaning. Trade Paper. Blackwell Publishing, Inc. Malden, MA.
2003. 352p. Blackwell Readings in Philosophy Ser., Vol. 5
ISBN:0-631-22223-5, ISBN13: 978-0-631-22223-1.
Dewey:121/.68. LCCN:2002-066432.
Audience: **g,u,f.**

Rorty, Richard McKay   B840 .L528 1992
The Linguistic Turn: Essays in Philosophical Method. Trade
Paper. University of Chicago Press. Chicago, IL. 1992. 416p.
ISBN:0-226-72569-3, ISBN13: 978-0-226-72569-7.
Dewey:149/.94. LCCN:91-038851.
Audience: **g,u,f.**

Searle, J. R. (Editor)   **B840.S38**
The Philosophy of Language. Paper Text. Oxford University
Press, Inc. New York, NY. 1971. 156p. Oxford Readings in
Philosophy Ser. ISBN:0-19-875015-3, ISBN13:
978-0-19-875015-4. Dewey:401. LCCN:70-027065.
Audience: **g,u,f.** *B*

Searle, John R.   **B840**
Speech Acts: An Essay in the Philosophy of Language. Trade
Paper. Cambridge University Press. New York, NY. 1969. 212p.
ISBN:0-521-09626-X, ISBN13: 978-0-521-09626-3.
Dewey:149.94. LCCN:68-024484.
Audience: **g,u,f.** *B*

Strawson, P. F.   **B840**
Logico-Linguistic Papers. Ed. 2. Trade Cloth. Ashgate
Publishing, Ltd. Aldershot, 2004. 210p. ISBN:0-7546-3724-7,
ISBN13: 978-0-7546-3724-0. Dewey:149/.94.
LCCN:2003-043683.
Audience: **u,f.**

Divisions of Philosophy > Philosophy of Law

Aquinas, Thomas   JC121.T42 2002
Aquinas: Political Writings. R. W. Dyson (Editor, Translator).
Cloth Text. Cambridge University Press. New York, NY. 2002.
360p. Cambridge Texts in the History of Political Thought Ser.
ISBN:0-521-37569-X, ISBN13: 978-0-521-37569-6. Dewey:320.
LCCN:2002-025748.
Audience: **g,u.**

Bentham, Jeremy & Hart,   **B1574.B33I5 1996**
H. L. A.
An Introduction to the Principles of Morals and Legislation. Ed.
2. J. H. Burns & H. L. Hart (Editors), F. Rosen (Introduction
by). Paper Text. Oxford University Press, Inc. New York, NY.
1996. 456p. The Collected Works of Jeremy Bentham Ser.
ISBN:0-19-820516-3, ISBN13: 978-0-19-820516-6.
Dewey:340/.112. LCCN:96-136001.

Audience: **g,u,f.**

Cheng, Sinkwan   **K376.L376 2004**
Law, Justice, and Power: Between Reason and Will. Trade
Paper. Stanford University Press. Palo Alto, CA. 2004. 296p.
ISBN:0-8047-4891-8, ISBN13: 978-0-8047-4891-9.
Dewey:340/.1. LCCN:2003-025167.

Audience: **g,u,f.**

Feinberg, Joel   **K230.F44A2 2002**
Problems at the Roots of Law: Essays in Legal and Political
Theory. Trade Cloth. Oxford University Press, Inc. New York,
NY. 2002. 232p. ISBN:0-19-515526-2, ISBN13:
978-0-19-515526-6. Dewey:340/.1. LCCN:2002-025753.

Audience: **g,u,f.**

Golding, Martin &   **K235.B58 2004**
Edmundson, William (Editors)
Blackwell Guide to the Philosophy of Law and Legal Theory.
Trade Paper. Blackwell Publishing, Inc. Malden, MA. 2004.
368p. Blackwell Philosophy Guides Ser., Vol. 18
ISBN:0-631-22832-2, ISBN13: 978-0-631-22832-5.
Dewey:340/.1. LCCN:2004-012895.

Audience: **g,u.**   *Choice, 2005.*

Haakonssen, Knud   **K455 .H33 1996**
Natural Law and Moral Philosophy: From Grotius to the
Scottish Enlightenment. Trade Cloth. Cambridge University
Press. New York, NY. 1996. 396p. ISBN:0-521-49686-1,
ISBN13: 978-0-521-49686-5. Dewey:171.2. LCCN:95-009657.

Audience: **g,u.**

Hegel, G. W. F.   **K230.H43G7813 2005**
Philosophy of Right. S. W. Dyde (Translator). Trade Paper,
Perfect. Dover Publications, Inc. Mineola, NY. 2005. 219p.
Dover Philosophical Classics Ser. ISBN:0-486-44563-1,
ISBN13: 978-0-486-44563-2. Dewey:320/.01/1.
LCCN:2005-040107.

Audience: **g,u,f.**

Murphy, Mark   **K230.A3M87 2007**
The Philosophy of Law: The Fundamentals. Trade Cloth.
Blackwell Publishing, Inc. Malden, MA. 2006. 232p. Blackwell
Fundamentals of Philosophy Ser., Vol. 2 ISBN:1-4051-2946-8,
ISBN13: 978-1-4051-2946-6. Dewey:340/.1.
LCCN:2005-031980.

Audience: **g,u.**

Nussbaum, Martha Craven   **K346.N87 2006**
Hiding from Humanity: Disgust, Shame, and the Law. Trade
Paper. Princeton University Press. Princeton, NJ. 2006. 432p.
ISBN:0-691-12625-9, ISBN13: 978-0-691-12625-8.
Dewey:340/.1/9.

Audience: **u,f.**   *Choice, 2004.*

Ricoeur, Paul   **B2430.R553J8713 2003**
The Just. David Pellauer (Translator). Trade Paper. University of
Chicago Press. Chicago, IL. 2003. 192p. ISBN:0-226-71340-7,
ISBN13: 978-0-226-71340-3. Dewey:172/.2.

Audience: **g,u,f.**   *Choice, 2000.*

Tebbit, Mark   **K230**
Philosophy of Law: An Introduction. Ed. 2. Trade Cloth.
Routledge. New York, NY. 2005. 264p. ISBN:0-415-33440-3,
ISBN13: 978-0-415-33440-2. Dewey:340/.1.
LCCN:2005-000798.

Audience: **u.**

Wacks, Raymond   **K230.W29A37 2006**
The Philosophy of Law: A Very Short Introduction. Trade Paper.
Oxford University Press, Inc. New York, NY. 2006. 144p. Very
Short Introductions Ser. ISBN:0-19-280691-2, ISBN13:
978-0-19-280691-8. Dewey:340.1. LCCN:2006-000591.

Audience: **u.**

Divisions of Philosophy > Logic

Anscombe, G. E. M.   **BC199.I5.A5 2000**
Intention. Ed. 2. Trade Paper. Harvard University Press.
Cambridge, MA. 2000. 106p. ISBN:0-674-00399-3, ISBN13:
978-0-674-00399-6. Dewey:128/.4. LCCN:00-057521.

Audience: **u,f.** *B*

Bennett, Deborah J.   **BC177.B42 2004**
Logic Made Easy: How to Know When Language Deceives
You. Trade Cloth. W. W. Norton & Company, Inc. New York,
NY. 2004. 256p. ISBN:0-393-05748-8, ISBN13:
978-0-393-05748-5. Dewey:160. LCCN:2003-026910.

Audience: **l.**   *Choice, 2004.*

Blackburn, Patrick, et al.   **QA9.46 .B58 2001**
Modal Logic. Maarten De Rijke & Yde Venema (Authors), C. J.
van Rijsbergen, S. Abramsky, P. H. Aczel, Y. Gurevich, J. V.
Tucker & J. W. De Bakker (Contribution by). Trade Paper.
Cambridge University Press. New York, NY. 2002. 576p.
Cambridge Tracts in Theoretical Computer Science Ser.
ISBN:0-521-52714-7, ISBN13: 978-0-521-52714-9.
Dewey:511.3.

Audience: **u,f.**   *Choice, 2002.*

Boole, George   **BC135.B7 2003**
The Laws of Thought. John Corcoran (Introduction by). Trade
Paper. Prometheus Books, Publishers. Amherst, NY. 2004. 430p.
Great Books in Philosophy ISBN:1-59102-089-1, ISBN13:
978-1-59102-089-9. Dewey:160. LCCN:2003-053871.

Audience: **u,f.**

Carnap, Rudolf   **BC135**
Introduction to Symbolic Logic and Its Applications. Trade
Paper. Dover Publications, Inc. Mineola, NY. 1958. 241p.
ISBN:0-486-60453-5, ISBN13: 978-0-486-60453-4. Dewey:164.

Audience: **u,f.** *B*

Cohen, Morris R. & Nagel,   **BC108**
Ernest
An Introduction to Logic and Scientific Method. Laminated.
Simon Publications, Inc. 2002. 471p. ISBN:1-931541-91-4,
ISBN13: 978-1-931541-91-6. Dewey:160. LCCN:34-002513.
Audience: **l,u.** ℬ

Copi, Irving M. & Cohen,   **BC108.C69 2005**
Carl
Introduction to Logic. Ed. 12. Trade Cloth. Prentice Hall PTR.
Upper Saddle River, NJ. 2004. 704p. ISBN:0-13-189834-5,
ISBN13: 978-0-13-189834-9. Dewey:160. LCCN:2004-040147.
Audience: **l.**

Engel, Pascal   **BC71**
The Norm of Truth: An Introduction to the Philosophy of Logic.
Miriam Kochan (Translator). Cloth Text. University of Toronto
Press. Toronto, ON. 1992. 400p. Studies in Philosophy
ISBN:0-8020-2775-X, ISBN13: 978-0-8020-2775-7. Dewey:160.
Audience: **u,f.** *Choice, 1992.*

Fisher, Alec   **BC177.F57 2004**
The Logic of Real Arguments. Ed. 2. Cloth Text. Cambridge
University Press. New York, NY. 2004. 236p.
ISBN:0-521-65241-3, ISBN13: 978-0-521-65241-4. Dewey:168.
LCCN:2004-041847.
Audience: **l,u.** *Choice, 1989.*

Fogelin, Robert J. &   **BC50**
Sinnott-Armstrong, Walter
Understanding Arguments: An Introduction to Informal Logic.
Ed. 7. Paper Text. Thomson Wadsworth. Belmont, CA. 2004.
608p. ISBN:0-534-62586-X, ISBN13: 978-0-534-62586-3.
Dewey:168. LCCN:2004-105766.
Audience: **l.** ℬ

Forbes, Graeme   **BC135.F57 1994**
Modern Logic: A Text in Elementary Symbolic Logic. Paper
Text. Oxford University Press, Inc. New York, NY. 1994. 416p.
ISBN:0-19-508029-7, ISBN13: 978-0-19-508029-2. Dewey:160.
LCCN:93-017282.
Audience: **l,u.**

Goble, Lou (Editor)   **BC71.B565 2001**
The Blackwell Guide to Philosophical Logic. Trade Paper.
Blackwell Publishing, Inc. Malden, MA. 2001. 520p. Philosophy
Guides, Vol. 4 ISBN:0-631-20693-0, ISBN13:
978-0-631-20693-4. Dewey:160. LCCN:00-069788.
Audience: **u,f.** *Choice, 2002.*

Grayling, A. C.   **BC71**
An Introduction to Philosophical Logic. Ed. 3. Trade Paper.
Blackwell Publishing, Inc. Malden, MA. 1998. 352p.
ISBN:0-631-19982-9, ISBN13: 978-0-631-19982-3. Dewey:160.
Audience: **l,u.** ℬ

Hollis, Martin   **BC177 .H65 1987**
The Cunning of Reason. Trade Paper. Cambridge University
Press. New York, NY. 1988. 232p. ISBN:0-521-27039-1,
ISBN13: 978-0-521-27039-7. Dewey:128/.3. LCCN:87-014630.
Audience: **u,f.** *Choice, 1988.*

Hughes, G. E. & Cresswell,   **BC199.M6H85 1996**
Maxwell J.
A New Introduction to Modal Logic. Paper over Boards.
Routledge. New York, NY. 1996. 432p. ISBN:0-415-12599-5,
ISBN13: 978-0-415-12599-4. Dewey:160. LCCN:95-014723.
Audience: **u.**

Jacquette, Dale (Editor)   **BC71.C65 2002**
A Companion to Philosophical Logic. Trade Cloth. Blackwell
Publishing, Inc. Malden, MA. 2002. 832p. Companions to
Philosophy Ser., Vol. 22 ISBN:0-631-21671-5, ISBN13:
978-0-631-21671-1. Dewey:160. LCCN:2001-043236.
Audience: **u,f.** *Choice, 2002.*

Jeffrey, Richard   **BC128.J43 2004**
Formal Logic: Its Scope and Limits. Ed. 3. Trade Cloth. Hackett
Publishing Company, Inc. Indianapolis, IN. 2004. 156p.
ISBN:0-87220-749-8, ISBN13: 978-0-87220-749-3. Dewey:160.
LCCN:2004-042363.
Audience: **l,u.**

Martin, Robert M.   **BC199.P2M38 2002**
There Are Two Errors in the the Title of This Book: A
Sourcebook of Philosophical Puzzles, Problems and Paradoxes.
Ed. 2. Trade Paper. Broadview Press. Peterborough, ON. 2002.
xvi, 327p. ISBN:1-55111-493-3, ISBN13: 978-1-55111-493-4.
Dewey:165. LCCN:2002-284606.
Audience: **g,l.** *Choice, 2002.*

Mates, Benson   **BC135.M37 1972**
Elementary Logic. Ed. 2. Cloth Text. Oxford University Press.
Inc. New York, NY. 1972. 250p. ISBN:0-19-501491-X, ISBN13:
978-0-19-501491-4. Dewey:511/.3. LCCN:74-166004.
Audience: **l,u.** ℬ

McInerny, D. Q.   **BC71.M37**
Being Logical: A Guide to Good Thinking. Trade Paper.
Random House Adult Trade Publishing Group. New York, NY.
2005. 160p. ISBN:0-8129-7115-9, ISBN13: 978-0-8129-7115-6.
Dewey:160.
Audience: **g,l.** *Choice, 2005.*

Prior, Arthur N.   **BC135 .P775**
Past, Present and Future. Trade Cloth. Oxford University Press,
Inc. New York, NY. 1967. 228p. ISBN:0-19-824311-1, ISBN13:
978-0-19-824311-3. Dewey:164.
Audience: **u,f.** ℬ

Quine, Willard V.   **BC71.Q5 1982**
Methods of Logic. Ed. 4. Trade Paper. Harvard University Press.
Cambridge, MA. 1982. 344p. ISBN:0-674-57176-2, ISBN13:
978-0-674-57176-1. Dewey:160. LCCN:81-022929.
Audience: **u.** ℬ

Rescher, Nicholas   **QA9**
Many-Valued Logic. Trade Cloth. Ashgate Publishing, Ltd.
Aldershot, 1993. 376p. Modern Revivals in Philosophy Ser.
ISBN:0-7512-0274-6, ISBN13: 978-0-7512-0274-8.
Dewey:511/.3.
Audience: **u,f.** ℬ

Sainsbury, R. M.   **BC199.P2 S25 1995**
Paradoxes. Ed. 2. Trade Paper. Cambridge University Press. New York, NY. 1995. 175p. ISBN:0-521-48347-6, ISBN13: 978-0-521-48347-6. Dewey:165. LCCN:94-039587.
Audience: **u,f.** *Choice, 1988.*

Suppes, Patrick   **BC108.S85 1999**
Introduction to Logic. Trade Paper. Dover Publications, Inc. Mineola, NY. 1999. 330p. ISBN:0-486-40687-3, ISBN13: 978-0-486-40687-9. Dewey:160. LCCN:99-013623.
Audience: **g,l.** 𝕭

Toulmin, Stephen Edelston   **BC177.T6 2003**
The Uses of Argument. Ed. 2. Trade Cloth. Cambridge University Press. New York, NY. 2003. 262p. ISBN:0-521-82748-5, ISBN13: 978-0-521-82748-5. Dewey:168. LCCN:2003-043502.
Audience: **g,l,u.** 𝕭

Walton, Douglas   **BC175**
Slippery Slope Arguments. Library Binding. Vale Press. Newport News, VA. 1999. Studies in Critical Thinking and Informal Logic, Vol. 4 ISBN:0-916475-22-0, ISBN13: 978-0-916475-22-2. Dewey:168.
Audience: **l,u.** *Choice, 1993.*

Walton, Douglas N.   **BC177 .W324 1989**
Informal Logic: A Handbook for Critical Argument. Trade Cloth. Cambridge University Press. New York, NY. 1989. 302p. ISBN:0-521-37032-9, ISBN13: 978-0-521-37032-5. Dewey:168. LCCN:88-030762.
Audience: **l,u.** *Choice, 1990.*

Divisions of Philosophy > Logic > Philosophy of Logic

Barwise, Jon &   **BC61**
  Etchemendy, John
Language, Proof and Logic. Trade Paper. C S L I Publications/Center for the Study of Language & Information. Stanford, CA. 2002. 598p. ISBN:1-57586-374-X, ISBN13: 978-1-57586-374-0. Dewey:160. LCCN:99-041113.
Audience: **u,f.**

Frege, Gottlob   **BC135.F7 1980**
Translations from the Philosophical Writings of Gottlob Frege. Ed. 3. Trade Cloth. Blackwell Publishing Ltd. Oxford, 1980. x, 228p. ISBN:0-631-12901-4, ISBN13: 978-0-631-12901-1. Dewey:160. LCCN:82-124415.
Audience: **u,f.** 𝕭

Goodman, Nelson   **BC91**
Fact, Fiction, and Forecast. Ed. 4. Trade Paper. Harvard University Press. Cambridge, MA. 1983. 160p. ISBN:0-674-29071-2, ISBN13: 978-0-674-29071-6. Dewey:161. LCCN:82-015764.
Audience: **g,u,f.** 𝕭

Haack, Susan   **BC51**
Philosophy of Logics. Trade Paper. Cambridge University Press. New York, NY. 1978. 292p. ISBN:0-521-29329-4, ISBN13: 978-0-521-29329-7. Dewey:160. LCCN:77-017071.
Audience: **u,f.** 𝕭

Kirkham, Richard L.   **BC171**
Theories of Truth: A Critical Introduction. Trade Paper. MIT Press. Cambridge, MA. 1995. 415p. Bradford Bks. ISBN:0-262-61108-2, ISBN13: 978-0-262-61108-4. Dewey:121.
Audience: **g,u,f.** *Choice, 1993.*

Lepore, Ernest   **BC108.L44 2003**
Meaning and Argument: An Introduction to Logic Through Language. Ed. 2. Trade Paper. Blackwell Publishing, Inc. Malden, MA. 2003. 456p. ISBN:1-4051-0783-9, ISBN13: 978-1-4051-0783-9. Dewey:160. LCCN:2002-038482.
Audience: **l,u.**

Lewis, David   **BC199.C66L48 1973B**
Counterfactuals. Trade Cloth. Harvard University Press. Cambridge, MA. 1973. 160p. ISBN:0-674-17540-9, ISBN13: 978-0-674-17540-2. Dewey:160. LCCN:72-078430.
Audience: **u,f.** 𝕭

Nozick, Robert   **BC177.N69 1993**
The Nature of Rationality. Cloth Text. Princeton University Press. Princeton, NJ. 1993. 232p. ISBN:0-691-07424-0, ISBN13: 978-0-691-07424-5. Dewey:128.3. LCCN:92-046660.
Audience: **g,l,u,f.** *Choice, 1994.*

Plantinga, Alvin   **BC199.M6P55 1992**
The Nature of Necessity. Trade Paper. Oxford University Press, Inc. New York, NY. 1979. 268p. Clarendon Library of Logic and Philosophy ISBN:0-19-824414-2, ISBN13: 978-0-19-824414-1. Dewey:123/.7. LCCN:95-112582.
Audience: **u,f.** 𝕭

Putnam, Hilary   **BC51.P88 1971**
Philosophy of Logic. Trade Cloth. Harper & Row Ltd. London, 1971. 76p. ISBN:0-06-136042-2, ISBN13: 978-0-06-136042-8. Dewey:160. LCCN:71-149364.
Audience: **u,f.** 𝕭

Quine, Willard V.   **BC71 .Q48 1980**
From a Logical Point of View: Nine Logico-Philosophical Essays. Ed. 2. Trade Cloth. Harvard University Press. Cambridge, MA. 1980. 200p. ISBN:0-674-32350-5, ISBN13: 978-0-674-32350-6. Dewey:160. LCCN:79-092851.
Audience: **u,f.** 𝕭

Quine, Willard V.   **BC51.Q5 1986**
Philosophy of Logic. Ed. 2. Trade Paper. Harvard University Press. Cambridge, MA. 1986. 128p. ISBN:0-674-66563-5, ISBN13: 978-0-674-66563-7. Dewey:160. LCCN:85-024734.
Audience: **u,f.** 𝕭

Read, Stephen   **BC71.R43 1994**
Thinking about Logic: An Introduction to the Philosophy of Logic. Paper Text. Oxford University Press, Inc. New York, NY.

1995. 270p. ISBN:0-19-289238-X, ISBN13: 978-0-19-289238-6. Dewey:160. LCCN:94-005697.

Audience: **l,u,f.** *Choice, 1995.*

Robinson, Richard B.   **BC199.D4 R6**
Definition. Trade Cloth. Oxford University Press, Inc. New York, NY. 1950. 216p. ISBN:0-19-824160-7, ISBN13: 978-0-19-824160-7. Dewey:741.59.

Audience: **g,l,u,f.**

Russell, Bertrand   **B1649.R93M92 2004**
Mysticism and Logic. Trade Paper. Dover Publications, Inc. Mineola, NY. 2004. 192p. ISBN:0-486-43440-0, ISBN13: 978-0-486-43440-7. Dewey:192. LCCN:2004-042804.

Audience: **g,l,u.** *B*

Sanford, David H.   **BC199.C56S26 2003**
If P Then Q: Conditionals and the Foundations of Reasoning. Ed. 2. Paper over Boards. Routledge. New York, NY. 2003. 304p. ISBN:0-415-28368-X, ISBN13: 978-0-415-28368-7. Dewey:160. LCCN:2002-036920.

Audience: **u,f.**

Divisions of Philosophy > Logic > Metalogic

Carnap, Rudolf   **BC135**
Logical Syntax of Language. Paper over Boards. Taylor & Francis Group. Abingdon, 2002. 368p. ISBN:0-415-22553-1, ISBN13: 978-0-415-22553-3. Dewey:164.

Audience: **u,f.**

Dummett, Michael   **B29.D85**
Truth and Other Enigmas. Trade Cloth. Harvard University Press. Cambridge, MA. 1978. 528p. ISBN:0-674-91075-3, ISBN13: 978-0-674-91075-1. Dewey:192. LCCN:77-012777.

Audience: **u,f.** *B*

Etchemendy, John   **BC135**
The Concept of Logical Consequence. Trade Paper. C S L I Publications/Center for the Study of Language & Information. Stanford, CA. 1999. 176p. The David Hume Ser., :The Philosophy and Cognitive Science Reissues ISBN:1-57586-194-1, ISBN13: 978-1-57586-194-4. Dewey:160. LCCN:99-012538.

Audience: **u,f.** *Choice, 1991.*

Hunter, Geoffrey   **QA9**
Metalogic: An Introduction to the Metatheory of Standard First Order Logic. Trade Paper. University of California Press. Berkeley, CA. 1996. 302p. ISBN:0-520-02356-0, ISBN13: 978-0-520-02356-7. Dewey:511/.3. LCCN:71-131195.

Audience: **u,f.** *B*

Mackie, John L.   **BC171 .M24**
Truth, Probability, and Paradox: Studies in Philosophical Logic. Trade Cloth. Oxford University Press, Inc. New York, NY. 1973.

xii, 305p. Clarendon Library of Logic and Philosophy ISBN:0-19-824402-9, ISBN13: 978-0-19-824402-8. Dewey:160. LCCN:73-157025.

Audience: **u,f.** *B*

Tarski, Alfred   **BC135.T35 1983**
Logic, Semantics, Metamathematics. Ed. 2. John Corcoran (Editor), J. H. Woodger (Translator). Trade Cloth. Hackett Publishing Company, Inc. Indianapolis, IN. 1983. 520p. ISBN:0-915144-75-1, ISBN13: 978-0-915144-75-4. Dewey:160. LCCN:83-010850.

Audience: **u,f.** *B*

Divisions of Philosophy > Logic > History of Logic

Aristotle   **B440.A5S65 1989**
Prior Analytics. Robin Smith (Translator, Introduction by, Notes by, Commentaries by). Trade Cloth. Hackett Publishing Company, Inc. Indianapolis, IN. 1989. 320p. HPC Classics Ser. ISBN:0-87220-065-5, ISBN13: 978-0-87220-065-4. Dewey:160. LCCN:88-039877.

Audience: **g,u,f.** *Choice, 1990.*

Broadie, Alexander   **BC34.B76 1993**
Introduction to Medieval Logic. Ed. 2. Trade Cloth. Oxford University Press, Inc. New York, NY. 1993. 228p. ISBN:0-19-824026-0, ISBN13: 978-0-19-824026-6. Dewey:160/.9/023. LCCN:92-033382.

Audience: **u,f.** *Choice, 1988.*

Kneale, William & Kneale,   **BC15.K55 1984**
Martha
The Development of Logic. Paper Text. Oxford University Press, Inc. New York, NY. 1985. 790p. ISBN:0-19-824773-7, ISBN13: 978-0-19-824773-9. Dewey:160/.9. LCCN:84-014881.

Audience: **g,l,u,f.** *B*

Mates, Benson   **BC28 .M37**
Stoic Logic. Paper Text. Textbook Publishers. Temecula, CA. 2003. 148p. ISBN:0-7581-2696-4, ISBN13: 978-0-7581-2696-2. Dewey:188.

Audience: **u,f.** *B*

Mill, John Stuart   **MLCSC 89/2809**
System of Logic Ratiocinative and Induct. Trade Paper. Kessinger Publishing, LLC. Whitefish, MT. 2004. ISBN:0-7661-8874-4, ISBN13: 978-0-7661-8874-7. Dewey:160.

Audience: **g,l,u,f.**

Moody, Ernest A.   **BC171 .M65 1976**
Truth and Consequence in Medieval Logic. Trade Cloth. Greenwood Publishing Group, Inc. Portsmouth, NH. 1976. 113p. Studies in Logic and the Foundations of Mathematics ISBN:0-8371-9053-3, ISBN13: 978-0-8371-9053-2. Dewey:160. LCCN:76-044307.

Audience: **u,f.**

Sorensen, Roy   BC199.P2S67 2003
A Brief History of the Paradox: Philosophy and the Labyrinths
of the Mind. Trade Cloth. Oxford University Press, Inc. New
York, NY. 2003. 416p. ISBN:0-19-515903-9, ISBN13:
978-0-19-515903-5. LCCN:2003-048631.
Audience: **g,l.** *Choice, 2004.*

Divisions of Philosophy > Logic > Probability and Induction

Boolos, George S.   BC199.M6.B65
The Logic of Provability. Trade Paper. Cambridge University
Press. New York, NY. 1995. 314p. ISBN:0-521-48325-5,
ISBN13: 978-0-521-48325-4. Dewey:511.3.
Audience: **u,f.** *Choice, 1995.*

Broad, C. D.   B1618
Induction Probability and Causation: Selected Papers. Trade
Cloth. Springer. New York, NY. 1967. 307p. Synthese Library
ISBN:90-277-0012-5, ISBN13: 978-90-277-0012-4. Dewey:160.
Audience: **u,f.**

Carnap, Rudolf   BC135 .C312
The Continuum of Inductive Methods. Paper Text. Textbook
Publishers. Temecula, CA. 2003. v, 92p. ISBN:0-7581-2456-2,
ISBN13: 978-0-7581-2456-2. Dewey:161.
Audience: **u,f.** *B*

Jeffrey, Richard   BC141 .J44 1992
Probability and the Art of Judgment. Richard C. Jeffrey, Ernest
W. Adams, Ken Binmore, Jeremy Butterfield, Persi W. Diaconis,
William L. Harper, Brian Skyrms, John Harsanyi, Wolfgang
Spohn & Patrick Suppes (Contribution by). Cloth Text.
Cambridge University Press. New York, NY. 1992. 256p.
Cambridge Studies in Probability, Induction and Decision
Theory ISBN:0-521-39459-7, ISBN13: 978-0-521-39459-8.
Dewey:121.63. LCCN:91-034257.
Audience: **u,f.**

Josephson, John R. &   BC199.A26 J67 1994
  Josephson, Susan G. (Editors)
Abductive Inference: Computation, Philosophy, Technology.
Trade Cloth. Cambridge University Press. New York, NY. 1994.
316p. ISBN:0-521-43461-0, ISBN13: 978-0-521-43461-4.
Dewey:160. LCCN:93-016027.
Audience: **u,f.** *Choice, 1995.*

Keynes, John Maynard   BC141.K4 2003
A Treatise on Probability. Cloth over Boards. Dover
Publications, Inc. Mineola, NY. 2004. 480p. Dover Phoenix
Editions Ser. ISBN:0-486-49580-9, ISBN13: 978-0-486-49580-4.
Dewey:160. LCCN:2004-041359.
Audience: **u,f.** *B*

Leblanc, Hugues   BC141.L4 2006
Statistical and Inductive Probabilities. Trade Paper. Dover
Publications, Inc. Mineola, NY. 2006. 160p. Dover Books on
Mathematics ISBN:0-486-44980-7, ISBN13: 978-0-486-44980-7.
Dewey:160. LCCN:2005-053729.
Audience: **u,f.** *B*

Skyrms, Brian   BC91.S5 2000
Choice and Chance: An Introduction to Inductive Logic. Ed. 4.
Paper Text. Thomson Wadsworth. Belmont, CA. 1999. 184p.
Philosophy Ser. ISBN:0-534-55737-6, ISBN13:
978-0-534-55737-9. Dewey:161. LCCN:99-051889.
Audience: **g,l.** *B*

Divisions of Philosophy > Philosophy of Man

Adler, Mortimer J.   BD450 .A3 1993
The Difference of Man and the Difference It Makes. Deal
Hudson (Introduction by). Trade Paper. Fordham University
Press. Bronx, NY. 1993. 395p. ISBN:0-8232-1535-0, ISBN13:
978-0-8232-1535-5. Dewey:128. LCCN:93-026503.
Audience: **g,l,u.**

Cassirer, Ernst   B3216.C33 E8 1992
An Essay on Man: An Introduction to a Philosophy of Human
Culture. Trade Paper. Yale University Press. Cumberland, RI.
1962. 250p. ISBN:0-300-00034-0, ISBN13: 978-0-300-00034-4.
Dewey:901. LCCN:92-003163.
Audience: **g,l,u.**

Davidson, Donald   B105
Essays on Actions and Events. Ed. 2. Trade Paper. Oxford
University Press, Inc. New York, NY. 2001. 346p. Philosophical
Essays Ser. ISBN:0-19-924627-0, ISBN13: 978-0-19-924627-4.
Dewey:128/.4. LCCN:2002-278425.
Audience: **u,f.**

Foucault, Michel   B2430.F723A613 2003
Abnormal: Lectures at the College de France, 1974-1975.
Arnold I. Davidson (Introduction by). Cloth over Boards.
Picador. New York, NY. 2003. 368p. ISBN:0-312-20334-9,
ISBN13: 978-0-312-20334-4. Dewey:194. LCCN:2003-049892.
Audience: **g,l,u,f.**

Habermas, Jurgen   B3258.H323
The Future of Human Nature. Trade Paper. Polity Press.
Cambridge, 2004. 136p. ISBN:0-7456-2987-3, ISBN13:
978-0-7456-2987-2. Dewey:179.7.
Audience: **g,u,f.** *Choice, 2003.*

Olson, Eric T.   BD450
The Human Animal: Personal Identity Without Psychology.
Trade Paper. Oxford University Press, Inc. New York, NY. 1999.
200p. Philosophy of Mind Ser. ISBN:0-19-513423-0, ISBN13:
978-0-19-513423-0. Dewey:126.
Audience: **g,u,f.** *Choice, 1997.*

Taylor, Charles   BD450 .T265 1985
Philosophical Papers, Vol. 1: Human Agency and Language.
Cambridge University Press. 1985. ISBN:0-521-31750-9,
ISBN13: 978-0-521-31750-4.
Audience: **g,u,f.**

Taylor, Charles   B63 .T39 1985
Philosophical Papers. Philosophy and the Human Sciences, Vol.
2. Cambridge University Press. 1985. ISBN:0-521-31749-5,
ISBN13: 978-0-521-31749-8.

Audience: **g,u,f.**

Thomson, Judith J.   **BD450**
Acts and Other Events. Book, Other. Cornell University Press.
Ithaca, NY. 1977. 320p. Contemporary Philosophy Ser.
ISBN:0-8014-1050-9, ISBN13: 978-0-8014-1050-5.
Dewey:128/.4. LCCN:77-007639.

Audience: **g,u,f.** 𝓑

Divisions of Philosophy > Philosophy of Mind

Annas, Julia   **B105.M55**
Hellenistic Philosophy of Mind. Trade Paper. University of
California Press. Berkeley, CA. 1994. 256p. Hellenistic Culture
and Society Ser., Vol. 8 ISBN:0-520-07659-1, ISBN13:
978-0-520-07659-4. Dewey:128/.2/0938. LCCN:91-010694.

Audience: **u,f.** *Choice, 1992.*

Armstrong, David M.   **BF161.A72 1993**
A Materialist Theory of the Mind. Ed. 2. Trade Paper.
Routledge. New York, NY. 1993. 400p. International Library of
Philosophy, Psychology, and Scientific Method
ISBN:0-415-10031-3, ISBN13: 978-0-415-10031-1.
Dewey:128.2. LCCN:93-019013.

Audience: **g,u,f.**

Chalmers, David   **BD418.3**
▢ Contemporary Philosophy of Mind: An Annotated
Bibliography.
http://consc.net/biblio.html

Audience: **g,u,f.**

Chalmers, David J.   **BD418.3.C435 2002**
Philosophy of Mind: Classical and Contemporary Readings.
Cloth Text. Oxford University Press, Inc. New York, NY. 2002.
688p. ISBN:0-19-514580-1, ISBN13: 978-0-19-514580-9.
Dewey:128/.2. LCCN:2002-072403.

Audience: **u,f.**

Chalmers, David John   **BD418.3**
The Conscious Mind: In Search of a Fundamental Theory. Trade
Paper. Oxford University Press, Inc. New York, NY. 1997. 432p.
Philosophy of Mind Ser. ISBN:0-19-511789-1, ISBN13:
978-0-19-511789-9. Dewey:126.

Audience: **g,u,f.** *Choice, 1996.*

Churchland, Paul M.   **QP356**
The Engine of Reason, the Seat of the Soul: A Philosophical
Journey into the Brain. Trade Paper. MIT Press. Cambridge,
MA. 1996. 344p. Bradford Bks. ISBN:0-262-53142-9, ISBN13:
978-0-262-53142-9. Dewey:612.8/2/01.

Audience: **g,l,u,f.** *Choice, 1995.*

Dennett, Daniel Clement   **BD418.3**
Brainstorms: Philosophical Essays on Mind and Psychology.
Trade Cloth. MIT Press. Cambridge, MA. 2004. xxii, 353p.
ISBN:0-89706-002-4, ISBN13: 978-0-89706-002-8.
Dewey:128/.2. LCCN:78-013723.

Audience: **g,u,f.**

Dennett, Daniel Clement   **BD450**
Consciousness Explained. Trade Paper. Little Brown &
Company. New York, NY. 1992. 528p. ISBN:0-316-18066-1,
ISBN13: 978-0-316-18066-5. Dewey:126.

Audience: **g,l,u,f.**

Dretske, Fred I.   **BD418.3**
Naturalizing the Mind. Trade Paper. MIT Press. Cambridge,
MA. 1997. 222p. Jean Nicod Lectures ISBN:0-262-54089-4,
ISBN13: 978-0-262-54089-6. Dewey:128.2.

Audience: **u,f.** *Choice, 1996.*

Flanagan, Owen   **B808.9**
Consciousness Reconsidered. Trade Paper. MIT Press.
Cambridge, MA. 1993. 256p. Bradford Bks.
ISBN:0-262-56077-1, ISBN13: 978-0-262-56077-1. Dewey:126.
LCCN:92-010057.

Audience: **g,u,f.** *Choice, 1993.*

Geach, Peter T.   **BF441 .G4**
Mental Acts, 1971. Trade Paper. Continuum International
Publishing Group, Ltd. London, 1996. 148p. Key Texts Ser.,
:Classic Studies in the History of Ideas ISBN:1-85506-166-X,
ISBN13: 978-1-85506-166-8. Dewey:128/.3.

Audience: **g,u,f.**

Goldie, Peter   **B815.G65 2002**
The Emotions: A Philosophical Exploration. Oxford University
Press. 2002. ISBN:0-19-925304-8, ISBN13: 978-0-19-925304-3.

Audience: **u,f.**

Goldman, Alvin I.   **B945.G593P55 1993**
Philosophical Applications of Cognitive Science. Trade Paper.
Westview Press. Boulder, CO. 1993. 200p. Focus Ser.
ISBN:0-8133-8040-5, ISBN13: 978-0-8133-8040-7. Dewey:149.
LCCN:92-038143.

Audience: **g,u,f.** *Choice, 1994.*

Gregory, R. L. & Zangwill,   **BF31.O94 1987**
O. L.
🄴 The Oxford Companion to the Mind. E-Book. NetLibrary,
Inc. Boulder, CO. 1987. ISBN:0-585-15700-6, ISBN13:
978-0-585-15700-9. Dewey:128/.2.

Audience: **g,u.**

Guttenplan, Samuel (Editor)   **BD418.3.C62**
A Companion to the Philosophy of Mind. Trade Paper.
Blackwell Publishing, Inc. Malden, MA. 1996. 656p.
Companions to Philosophy Ser. ISBN:0-631-19996-9, ISBN13:
978-0-631-19996-0. Dewey:128.2. LCCN:93-039595.

Audience: **u,f.** *Choice, 1995.*

Harré, Rom   **BF311.H347 2002**
Cognitive Science: A Philosophical Introduction. Sage
Publications. 2002. ISBN:0-7619-4746-9, ISBN13:
978-0-7619-4746-2.
                                       Audience: **g,u,f.**

Heil, John & Mele, Alfred   **BD418.3.M45 1993**
R. (Editors)
Mental Causation. Trade Cloth. Oxford University Press, Inc.
New York, NY. 1993. 352p. ISBN:0-19-823929-7, ISBN13:
978-0-19-823929-1. Dewey:128/.2. LCCN:92-022764.
                        Audience: **u,f.** *Choice, 1993.*

Hurley, S. L.   **B808.9.H87 1998**
Consciousness in Action. Trade Cloth. Harvard University Press.
Cambridge, MA. 1998. 520p. ISBN:0-674-16420-2, ISBN13:
978-0-674-16420-8. Dewey:126. LCCN:98-012790.
                    Audience: **g,u,f.** *Choice, 1999.*

Kim, Jaegwon   **BD418.3.K53 1998**
Mind in a Physical World: An Essay on the Mind-Body Problem
and Mental Causation. Trade Cloth. MIT Press. Cambridge, MA.
1998. 156p. Representation and Mind Ser. ISBN:0-262-11234-5,
ISBN13: 978-0-262-11234-5. Dewey:128/.2. LCCN:98-024346.
                  Audience: **g,u,f.** *Choice, 1999.*

Kim, Jaegwon   **BD418.3.K54 2005**
Philosophy of Mind. Ed. 2. Trade Paper. Westview Press.
Boulder, CO. 2005. 352p. ISBN:0-8133-4269-4, ISBN13:
978-0-8133-4269-6. Dewey:128/.2. LCCN:2005-013315.
                   Audience: **u,f.** *Choice, 2006, 1996.*

Lowe, E. J.   **BD418.3 .L69 2000**
An Introduction to the Philosophy of Mind. Cloth Text.
Cambridge University Press. New York, NY. 2000. 332p.
Cambridge Introduction to Philosophy Ser. ISBN:0-521-65285-5,
ISBN13: 978-0-521-65285-8. Dewey:128.2. LCCN:99-021498.
                  Audience: **g,u.** *Choice, 2000.*

McGinn, Colin   **B105.I49M36 2004**
Mindsight: Image, Dream, Meaning. Harvard University Press.
2004. ISBN:0-674-01560-6, ISBN13: 978-0-674-01560-9.
                                  Audience: **l,u,f.**

Nussbaum, Martha C.   **BF531 .N87 2001**
Upheavals of Thought: The Intelligence of Emotions. Cambridge
University Press. 2003. ISBN:0-521-53182-9, ISBN13:
978-0-521-53182-5.
                                    Audience: **g,u,f.**

Papineau, David   **B808.9.P36 2002**
Thinking about Consciousness. Trade Cloth. Oxford University
Press, Inc. New York, NY. 2002. 220p. ISBN:0-19-924382-4,
ISBN13: 978-0-19-924382-2. Dewey:126. LCCN:2001-058066.
                      Audience: **u,f.** *Choice, 2003.*

Perry, John   **BD161.P43 2001**
Knowledge, Possibility and Consciousness. Ed. 2. Trade Cloth.
MIT Press. Cambridge, MA. 2001. 237p. Jean Nicod Lectures,
Vol. 1999 ISBN:0-262-16199-0, ISBN13: 978-0-262-16199-2.
Dewey:128.2. LCCN:00-048959.
                  Audience: **g,u,f.** *Choice, 2001.*

Pols, Edward   **BD418.3.P65 1998**
Mind Regained: How Mind Functions As a Real Cause in the
Material World. Trade Cloth. Cornell University Press. Ithaca,
NY. 1998. 176p. ISBN:0-8014-3531-5, ISBN13:
978-0-8014-3531-7. Dewey:128/.2. LCCN:98-009482.
                  Audience: **u,f.** *Choice, 1999.*

Robinson, William   **B808.9.R63 2004**
Understanding Phenomenal Consciousness. Jonathan Dancy,
John Haldane, Gilbert Harman, Frank Jackson, William G.
Lucan & Ernest Sosa (Contribution by). Trade Cloth. Cambridge
University Press. New York, NY. 2004. 276p. Cambridge
Studies in Philosophy Ser. ISBN:0-521-83463-5, ISBN13:
978-0-521-83463-6. Dewey:126. LCCN:2003-059539.
                  Audience: **g,u,f.** *Choice, 2005.*

Ryle, Gilbert   **BF161.R9 2002**
The Concept of Mind. Trade Paper. University of Chicago Press.
Chicago, IL. 2000. 348p. ISBN:0-226-73296-7, ISBN13:
978-0-226-73296-1. Dewey:128/.2. LCCN:2002-020496.
                              Audience: **g,l,u.**

Seager, William   **B808.9.S4 1998**
Theories of Consciousness: An Introduction. Paper over Boards.
Routledge. New York, NY. 1999. 320p. Philosophical Issues in
Science Ser. ISBN:0-415-18393-6, ISBN13: 978-0-415-18393-2.
Dewey:128. LCCN:98-034492.

                                       Audience: **g,u.**

Searle, John R.   **B105.I56 S43 1983**
Intentionality: An Essay in the Philosophy of Mind. Trade Paper.
Cambridge University Press. New York, NY. 1983. 288p.
ISBN:0-521-27302-1, ISBN13: 978-0-521-27302-2. Dewey:121.
LCCN:82-019849.
                          Audience: **g,u,f.** *B*

Searle, John R.   **BD418.3.S4 2004**
Mind: A Brief Introduction. Trade Cloth. Oxford University
Press, Inc. New York, NY. 2004. 336p. Fundamentals of
Philosophy Ser. ISBN:0-19-515733-8, ISBN13:
978-0-19-515733-8. Dewey:128/.2. LCCN:2004-049546.
                  Audience: **g,l,u,f.** *Choice, 2005.*

Sellars, Wilfrid, et al.   **BD418.3.S45 1997**
Empiricism and the Philosophy of Mind. Richard McKay Rorty
& Robert Brandom (Authors). Trade Cloth. Harvard University
Press. Cambridge, MA. 1997. 192p. ISBN:0-674-25154-7,
ISBN13: 978-0-674-25154-0. Dewey:128/.2. LCCN:96-051811.
                              Audience: **g,u,f.**

Smith, Peter & Jones, O. R.   **BD418.3 .S65 1986**
The Philosophy of Mind: An Introduction. Trade Cloth.
Cambridge University Press. New York, NY. 1986. 304p.
ISBN:0-521-32078-X, ISBN13: 978-0-521-32078-8.
Dewey:128.2. LCCN:86-009571.
                    Audience: **g,l,u.** *Choice, 1987.*

Solomon, Robert C.   **B105.E46S675 2006**
True to Our Feelings: What Our Emotions Are Really Telling
Us. Oxford University Press. 2006. ISBN:0-19-530672-4,
ISBN13: 978-0-19-530672-9.
                                  Audience: **g,l,u.**

Sorabji, Richard   **B105.E45S67 2002**
Emotion and Peace of Mind: From Stoic Agitation to Christian
Temptation. Trade Paper. Oxford University Press, Inc. New
York, NY. 2003. 512p. The Gifford Lectures
ISBN:0-19-925660-8, ISBN13: 978-0-19-925660-0.
Dewey:128/.37/09. LCCN:2002-030832.
                                   Audience: **g,u,f.** *Choice, 2001.*

Stich, Stephen P. &   **BD418.3.B57 2003**
Warfield, Ted A.
The Blackwell Guide to Philosophy of Mind. Trade Cloth.
Blackwell Publishing, Inc. Malden, MA. 2003. 432p. Blackwell
Philosophy Guides Ser., Vol. 9 ISBN:0-631-21774-6, ISBN13:
978-0-631-21774-9. Dewey:128/.2. LCCN:2002-071221.
                                               Audience: **u,f.**

Wollheim, Richard   **BD418.3.W65 1993**
The Mind and Its Depths. Trade Cloth. Harvard University
Press. Cambridge, MA. 1993. 224p. ISBN:0-674-57611-X,
ISBN13: 978-0-674-57611-7. Dewey:128.2. LCCN:92-012738.
                                   Audience: **g,u,f.** *Choice, 1993.*

Divisions of Philosophy > Philosophy of Nature

Armstrong, D. M.   **B105.U5**
What Is a Law of Nature? Jonathan Dancy, John Haldane,
Gilbert Harman, Frank Jackson, William G. Lucan & Ernest
Sosa (Contribution by). Trade Paper. Cambridge University
Press. New York, NY. 1985. 192p. Cambridge Studies in
Philosophy ISBN:0-521-31481-X, ISBN13: 978-0-521-31481-7.
Dewey:111/.2.
                                   Audience: **g,u,f.** B

Gaukroger, Stephen, et al.   **B1878.N3D47 2000**
Descartes' Natural Philosophy. John A. Schuster & John Sutton
(Authors). Cloth Text. Routledge. New York, NY. 2000. 784p.
Studies in Seventeenth-Century Philosophy, Vol. 3
ISBN:0-415-21993-0, ISBN13: 978-0-415-21993-8.
Dewey:113/.092. LCCN:99-059525.
                                               Audience: **u,f.**

Van Fraassen, Bas C.   **BD581.V27 1989**
Laws and Symmetry. Trade Paper. Oxford University Press, Inc.
New York, NY. 1990. 410p. ISBN:0-19-824860-1, ISBN13:
978-0-19-824860-6. Dewey:113. LCCN:89-030366.
                                   Audience: **u,f.** *Choice, 1990.*

Woodbridge, Frederick J.   **BD581**
An Essay on Nature. Trade Cloth. Greenwood Publishing
Group, Inc. Portsmouth, NH. 1982. 351p. ISBN:0-313-23445-0,
ISBN13: 978-0-313-23445-3. Dewey:113. LCCN:81-020182.
                                               Audience: **g,l,u,f.**

Divisions of Philosophy > Philosophy of Religion

Craig, William Lane &   **BD555.D64 2002**
Flew, Antony
Does God Exist?: The Craig-Flew Debate. Stan W. Wallace
(Editor). Trade Cloth. Ashgate Publishing, Ltd. Aldershot, 2003.
242p. ISBN:0-7546-3189-3, ISBN13: 978-0-7546-3189-7.
Dewey:212/.1. LCCN:2002-074437.
                                   Audience: **g,l,u.** *Choice, 2004.*

Feuerbach, Ludwig   **B2971.W4 E5**
The Essence of Christianity. George Eliot (Translator). Trade
Cloth. Prometheus Books, Publishers. Amherst, NY. 1989. 363p.
Great Books in Philosophy ISBN:0-87975-559-8, ISBN13:
978-0-87975-559-1. Dewey:201. LCCN:89-062324.
                                               Audience: **g,l,u.**

Gooch, Paul W.   **B317.G66 1996**
Reflections on Jesus and Socrates: Word and Silence. Cloth over
Boards. Yale University Press. Cumberland, RI. 1997. 320p.
ISBN:0-300-06695-3, ISBN13: 978-0-300-06695-1. Dewey:128.
LCCN:96-015792.
                                   Audience: **g,l,u,f.** *Choice, 1997.*

Kant, Immanuel   **B2791.E5**
Religion Within the Limits of Reason Alone. Trade Paper.
HarperCollins Publishers. New York, NY. 1960. 352p.
ISBN:0-06-130067-5, ISBN13: 978-0-06-130067-7. Dewey:193.
                                   Audience: **g,u,f.** B

Kant, Immanuel   **B2799.R4K3613 1996**
Religion and Rational Theology. George di Giovanni (Editor),
Allen W. Wood & George Di Giovanni (Edited and Translated
by), Paul Guyer (Contribution by). Trade Paper. Cambridge
University Press. New York, NY. 2001. 544p. Cambridge
Edition of the Works of Immanuel Kant ISBN:0-521-79998-8,
ISBN13: 978-0-521-79998-0. Dewey:210.
                                   Audience: **g,u,f.** *Choice, 1997.*

Mann, William Edward   **BR100.B49 2004**
The Blackwell Guide to the Philosophy of Religion. Trade
Cloth. Blackwell Publishing, Inc. Malden, MA. 2004. 352p.
Blackwell Philosophy Guides Ser., Vol. 17
ISBN:0-631-22128-X, ISBN13: 978-0-631-22128-9. Dewey:210.
LCCN:2003-026163.
                                   Audience: **g,l,u.** *Choice, 2005.*

Matthews, Gareth B.   **B655.Z7 A95 1999**
The Augustinian Tradition. Trade Paper. University of California
Press. Berkeley, CA. 1998. 420p. Philosophical Traditions Ser.,
Vol. 8 ISBN:0-520-21001-8, ISBN13: 978-0-520-21001-1.
Dewey:189/.2. LCCN:97-035854.
                                   Audience: **g,u,f.** *Choice, 1999.*

Mitchell, Basil (Editor)   **BL51 .M6553**
The Philosophy of Religion. Paper Text. Oxford University

Press, Inc. New York, NY. 1971. 206p. Oxford Readings in Philosophy Ser. ISBN:0-19-875018-8, ISBN13: 978-0-19-875018-5. Dewey:200/.1. LCCN:70-855551.

Audience: **g,l,u.**

Morris, Thomas V. (Editor)   **BD555.D58 1988**
Divine and Human Action: Essays in the Metaphysics of Theism. Book, Other. Cornell University Press. Ithaca, NY. 1988. 368p. ISBN:0-8014-2197-7, ISBN13: 978-0-8014-2197-6. Dewey:211/.3. LCCN:88-047738.

Audience: **g,u,f.** *Choice, 1989.*

Moser, Paul K. & Copan,   **BD555.R38 2003**
Paul (Editors)
The Rationality of Theism. Paper over Boards. Routledge. New York, NY. 2003. 304p. ISBN:0-415-26331-X, ISBN13: 978-0-415-26331-3. Dewey:211/.3. LCCN:2002-038166.

Audience: **g,u,f.** *Choice, 2004.*

Prevost, Robert   **BD555.P87 1990**
Probability and Theistic Explanation. Trade Cloth. Oxford University Press, Inc. New York, NY. 1990. 202p. Oxford Theological Monographs ISBN:0-19-826735-5, ISBN13: 978-0-19-826735-5. Dewey:211/.3. LCCN:90-033121.

Audience: **u,f.** *Choice, 1991.*

Swinburne, Richard   **BJ1451.S9 1989**
Responsibility and Atonement. Trade Paper. Oxford University Press, Inc. New York, NY. 1989. 220p. ISBN:0-19-824849-0, ISBN13: 978-0-19-824849-1. Dewey:241. LCCN:88-034613.

Audience: **g,u,f.** *Choice, 1990.*

Divisions of Philosophy > Philosophy of Science

Achinstein, Peter   **Q175**
Concepts of Science: A Philosophical Analysis. Trade Paper. Johns Hopkins University Press. Baltimore, MD. 1995. 279p. ISBN:0-8018-1273-9, ISBN13: 978-0-8018-1273-6. Dewey:501. LCCN:68-015451.

Audience: **g,u,f.** *B*

Clark, Peter & Hawley,   **Q175**
Katherine (Editors)
Philosophy of Science Today. Trade Cloth. Oxford University Press, Inc. New York, NY. 2003. 312p. ISBN:0-19-925054-5, ISBN13: 978-0-19-925054-7. Dewey:501. LCCN:2003-271821.

Audience: **u,f.**

Feyerabend, Paul K.   **Q174**
Problems of Empiricism: Philosophical Papers. Trade Paper. Cambridge University Press. New York, NY. 1985. 268p. ISBN:0-521-31641-3, ISBN13: 978-0-521-31641-5. Dewey:501.

Audience: **u,f.**

Feyerabend, Paul K.   **Q174 .F49 1985**
Realism, Rationalism and Scientific Method: Philosophical

Papers, Vol. 1. Trade Paper. Cambridge University Press. New York, NY. 1985. 368p. ISBN:0-521-31642-1, ISBN13: 978-0-521-31642-2. Dewey:501.

Audience: **u,f.**

Fuller, Steve   **Q175.46.F85 2004**
Kuhn vs. Popper: The Struggle for the Soul of Science. Trade Cloth. Columbia University Press. New York, NY. 2004. 160p. ISBN:0-231-13428-2, ISBN13: 978-0-231-13428-6. Dewey:501/.09/04. LCCN:2004-049393.

Audience: **g,u,f.** *Choice, 2005.*

Hempel, Carl G.   **Q175**
Aspects of Scientific Explanation. Trade Paper. Simon & Schuster. New York, NY. 1970. 504p. ISBN:0-02-914340-3, ISBN13: 978-0-02-914340-7. Dewey:501. LCCN:65-015441.

Audience: **g,u,f.**

Hickey, Thomas J.   **Q174.8 .H46 1995**
History of Twentieth-Century Philosophy of Science. Trade Paper. Thomas J. Hickey. Oak Park, IL. 1995. 502p. ISBN:0-9644665-0-3, ISBN13: 978-0-9644665-0-0. Dewey:501/.09/04. LCCN:94-096838.

Audience: **g,u,f.**

Kuhn, Thomas S.   **Q175.K95 1996**
The Structure of Scientific Revolutions. University of Chicago Press. 1996. ISBN:0-226-45807-5, ISBN13: 978-0-226-45807-6.

Audience: **g,u,f.**

Popper, Karl R.   **BD241.P65 2002**
Conjectures and Refutations: The Growth of Scientific Knowledge. Ed. 2. Trade Paper. Routledge. New York, NY. 2002. 608p. Classics Ser. ISBN:0-415-28594-1, ISBN13: 978-0-415-28594-0. Dewey:121. LCCN:2002-067998.

Audience: **g,u,f.**

Popper, Karl R.   **Q175**
The Logic of Scientific Discovery: 14th Printing. Ed. 2. Paper over Boards. Routledge. New York, NY. 2002. 544p. Classics Ser. ISBN:0-415-27843-0, ISBN13: 978-0-415-27843-0. Dewey:501.

Audience: **g,u,f.**

Potter, Elizabeth   **Q175**
Feminist Philosophy of Science: An Introduction. Routledge. 2006. Understanding Feminist Philosophy Ser. ISBN:0-415-26652-1, ISBN13: 978-0-415-26652-9.

Audience: **l,u.**

Sellars, Wilfrid   **B29.S49**
Science, Perception and Reality. Paper Text. Ridgeview Publishing Company. Atascadero, CA. 1991. 384p. ISBN:0-924922-00-1, ISBN13: 978-0-924922-00-8. Dewey:100.

Audience: **g,u,f.** *B*

Shanker, Stuart G. (Editor)   **Q174.8.P55 1996**
Philosophy of Science, Logic and Mathematics in the 20th Century, Vol. 9. Paper over Boards. Routledge. New York, NY.

1996. 504p. Routledge History of Philosophy Ser.
ISBN:0-415-05776-0, ISBN13: 978-0-415-05776-9. Dewey:501.
LCCN:96-010545.

Audience: **g,u,f.**

Divisions of Philosophy > Philosophy of Science > Cosmology

Cornford, Francis   **B387.A5 C65 1997**
  Macdonald
Plato's Cosmology. Trade Cloth. Hackett Publishing Company,
Inc. Indianapolis, IN. 1997. 390p. ISBN:0-87220-387-5,
ISBN13: 978-0-87220-387-7. Dewey:113. LCCN:97-074231.

Audience: **g,l,u.**

Curran, Noel   **BD632.C87 1994**
The Logical Universe: The Real Universe. Trade Cloth. Ashgate
Publishing, Ltd. Aldershot, 1994. 176p. Avebury Series in
Philosophy ISBN:1-85628-863-3, ISBN13: 978-1-85628-863-7.
Dewey:113. LCCN:94-013450.

Audience: **g,u.**

Duhem, Pierre M.   **BD495.5**
Medieval Cosmology: Theories of Infinity, Place, Time, Void,
and the Plurality of Worlds. Roger Ariew (Translator). Trade
Paper. University of Chicago Press. Chicago, IL. 1987. 642p.
ISBN:0-226-16923-5, ISBN13: 978-0-226-16923-1.
Dewey:113/.09/02. LCCN:85-008115.

Audience: **u,f.**

Furley, David (Author,   **BD495 .F87 1987**
  Contribution by)
The Greek Cosmologists: The Formation of the Atomic Theory
and Its Earliest Critics. Trade Cloth. Cambridge University
Press. New York, NY. 1987. 228p. The Greek Cosmologists Ser.
ISBN:0-521-33328-8, ISBN13: 978-0-521-33328-3.
Dewey:113/.0938. LCCN:86-026384.

Audience: **u,f.** *Choice, 1988.*

Le Poidevin, Robin   **BD620**
Travels in Four Dimensions: The Enigmas of Space and Time.
Trade Cloth. Oxford University Press, Inc. New York, NY. 2003.
294p. ISBN:0-19-875254-7, ISBN13: 978-0-19-875254-7.
Dewey:115. LCCN:2002-035583.

Audience: **g,u,f.** *Choice, 2004.*

MacBeath, Murray   **BD638.P49 1993**
The Philosophy of Time. Robin Le Poidevin (Editor). Paper
Text. Oxford University Press, Inc. New York, NY. 1993. 236p.
Readings in Philosophy Ser. ISBN:0-19-823999-8, ISBN13:
978-0-19-823999-4. Dewey:115. LCCN:92-026125.

Audience: **g,u,f.**

Matt, Daniel Chanan   **BM723**
God and the Big Bang: Discovering Harmony Between Science
and Spirituality. Trade Paper. Jewish Lights Publishing.
Woodstock, VT. 1998. 216p. ISBN:1-879045-89-3, ISBN13:
978-1-879045-89-7. Dewey:296.3/873. LCCN:96-006106.

Audience: **g,u,f.**

McLure, Roger   **BD638.M37 2004**
Philosophy of Time. Trade Cloth. Routledge. New York, NY.
2005. 224p. Routledge Studies in Twentieth Century Philosophy
ISBN:0-415-33178-1, ISBN13: 978-0-415-33178-4. Dewey:115.
LCCN:2004-050971.

Audience: **g,u,f.**

Nerlich, Graham   **BD632 .N45 1994**
The Shape of Space. Ed. 2. Cloth Text. Cambridge University
Press. New York, NY. 1994. 306p. ISBN:0-521-45014-4,
ISBN13: 978-0-521-45014-0. Dewey:114. LCCN:93-028935.

Audience: **g,u,f.**

Philoponus & Simplicius   **B485.P52 1991**
Place, Void, and Eternity. David Furley & Christian Wildberg
(Translators). Trade Cloth. Cornell University Press. Ithaca, NY.
1991. 160p. Ancient Commentators on Aristotle Ser.
ISBN:0-8014-2634-0, ISBN13: 978-0-8014-2634-6. Dewey:114.
LCCN:90-023732.

Audience: **g,u,f.** *Choice, 1991.*

Reichenbach, Hans   **BD632**
The Philosophy of Space and Time. Maria Reichenbach
(Translator). Trade Paper. Dover Publications, Inc. Mineola, NY.
1998. 295p. ISBN:0-486-60443-8, ISBN13: 978-0-486-60443-5.
Dewey:113.

Audience: **g,u,f.**

Toulmin, Stephen E. &   **BD638 .T67 1982**
  Goodfield, June
The Discovery of Time. Trade Paper. University of Chicago
Press. Chicago, IL. 1982. 280p. ISBN:0-226-80842-4, ISBN13:
978-0-226-80842-0. Dewey:115. LCCN:81-071398.

Audience: **g,u,f.**

Trusted, Jennifer   **BD632.T78 1991**
Physics and Metaphysics: Theories of Space and Time. Paper
over Boards. Routledge. New York, NY. 1991. 224p.
ISBN:0-415-05948-8, ISBN13: 978-0-415-05948-0. Dewey:113.
LCCN:90-046821.

Audience: **g,u,f.** *Choice, 1991.*

Wright, M. R.   **BD495.W75 1995**
Cosmology in Antiquity. Trade Paper. Routledge. New York,
NY. 1995. 216p. Sciences of Antiquity Ser.
ISBN:0-415-12183-3, ISBN13: 978-0-415-12183-5.
Dewey:113/.093. LCCN:94-045131.

Audience: **g,l,u.**

Divisions of Philosophy > Political and Social Philosophy

Collin, Finn   **BD331.C566 1997**
Social Reality. Paper over Boards. Routledge. New York, NY.
1997. 272p. The Problems of Philosophy Ser., :Their Past and
Present ISBN:0-415-14796-4, ISBN13: 978-0-415-14796-5.
Dewey:301/.01. LCCN:96-048387.

Audience: **g,u,f.**

Eagleton, Terry B823.3.I346 1994
(Introduction by)
Ideology: An Introduction. Ed. 1. Cloth Text. Addison-Wesley
Longman, Ltd. Harlow, 1994. 328p. Critical Readers Ser.
ISBN:0-582-23715-7, ISBN13: 978-0-582-23715-5. Dewey:140.
LCCN:93-048939.
Audience: **g,l,u.** *Choice, 1992.*

Freeden, Michael B823.3
Ideology: A Very Short Introduction. Trade Paper. Oxford
University Press, Inc. New York, NY. 2003. 160p. Very Short
Introductions Ser. ISBN:0-19-280281-X, ISBN13:
978-0-19-280281-1. Dewey:320.5.
Audience: **g,l,u.**

Gaus, Gerald F. BD232 .G38 1990
Value and Justification: The Foundations of Liberal Theory.
Jonathan Dancy, John Haldane, Gilbert Harman, Frank Jackson,
William G. Lucan & Ernest Sosa (Contribution by). Trade
Paper. Cambridge University Press. New York, NY. 1990. 558p.
Cambridge Studies in Philosophy ISBN:0-521-39733-2,
ISBN13: 978-0-521-39733-9. Dewey:121/.8. LCCN:89-027088.
Audience: **g,u,f.** *Choice, 1991.*

Nozick, Robert JC571
Anarchy, State, and Utopia. Blackwell Publishing. 2001.
ISBN:0-631-19780-X, ISBN13: 978-0-631-19780-5.
Audience: **g,u,f.**

Popper, Karl R. JA71
The Open Society and Its Enemies. Ed. 5. Other. Princeton
University Press. Princeton, NJ. 1966. ISBN:0-318-55362-7,
ISBN13: 978-0-318-55362-7. Dewey:320/.01.
Audience: **g,l,u.**

Rawls, John JC578.R38 1999
A Theory of Justice. Harvard University Press. 1999.
ISBN:0-674-00078-1, ISBN13: 978-0-674-00078-0.
Audience: **g,u,f.**

Rescher, Nicholas BD394
Pluralism: Against the Demand for Consensus. Paper Text.
Oxford University Press, Inc. New York, NY. 1995. 216p.
Clarendon Library of Logic and Philosophy
ISBN:0-19-823601-8, ISBN13: 978-0-19-823601-6.
Dewey:147.4.
Audience: **g,u,f.** *Choice, 1994.*

Searle, John R. BD175.S43 1995
The Construction of Social Reality. Trade Cloth. Simon &
Schuster. New York, NY. 1995. 241p. ISBN:0-02-928045-1,
ISBN13: 978-0-02-928045-4. Dewey:121. LCCN:94-041402.
Audience: **g,u,f.** *Choice, 1995.*

Thoreau, Henry David PS3051
Civil Disobedience and Other Essays. Dover Publications, Inc.
1993. ISBN:0-486-27563-9, ISBN13: 978-0-486-27563-5.
Audience: **g,l,u.**

Turner, Stephen P. & Roth, H61.B4774 2003
Paul Andrew (Editors)
The Blackwell Guide to the Philosophy of the Social Sciences.
Trade Cloth. Blackwell Publishing, Inc. Malden, MA. 2003.
400p. Blackwell Philosophy Guides Ser., Vol. 11
ISBN:0-631-21537-9, ISBN13: 978-0-631-21537-0.
Dewey:300/.1. LCCN:2002-004263.
Audience: **u,f.**

Zizek, Slavoj B823.3
The Sublime Object of Ideology. Verso. 1989.
ISBN:0-86091-256-6, ISBN13: 978-0-86091-256-9.
Audience: **g,l,u.**

Philosophical Schools and Doctrines > Altruism

Nagel, Thomas BJ1474
The Possibility of Altruism. Trade Paper. Princeton University
Press. Princeton, NJ. 1979. 156p. ISBN:0-691-02002-7, ISBN13:
978-0-691-02002-0. Dewey:171/.8. LCCN:78-004323.
Audience: **g,u,f.**

Post, Stephen G., et al. BJ1474.A472 2001
Altruism and Altruistic Love: Science, Philosophy, and Religion
in Dialogue. Lynn G. Underwood, Jeffrey P. Schloss & William
B. Hurlbut (Authors), Stephen Garrard Post (Editor). Trade
Cloth. Oxford University Press, Inc. New York, NY. 2002. 516p.
ISBN:0-19-514358-2, ISBN13: 978-0-19-514358-4.
Dewey:171/.8. LCCN:00-068140.
Audience: **g,l,u,f.** *Choice, 2003.*

Rescher, Nicholas BJ1474 .R47
Unselfishness: The Role of the Vicarious Affects in Moral
Philosophy and Social Theory. Cloth Text. University of
Pittsburgh Press. Pittsburgh, PA. 1975. 138p.
ISBN:0-8229-3308-X, ISBN13: 978-0-8229-3308-3.
Dewey:171/.8. LCCN:75-009123.
Audience: **u,f.**

Wyschogrod, Edith BJ1012.W97 1990
Saints and Postmodernism: Revisioning Moral Philosophy. Trade
Paper. University of Chicago Press. Chicago, IL. 1990. 326p.
Religion and Postmodernism Ser. ISBN:0-226-92043-7, ISBN13:
978-0-226-92043-6. Dewey:170. LCCN:90-036721.
Audience: **g,u,f.** *Choice, 1991.*

Philosophical Schools and Doctrines > Analytic philosophy

Ammerman, R. T. (Editor) B808.5.A4 1990
Classics of Analytic Philosophy. Trade Cloth. Hackett Publishing
Company, Inc. Indianapolis, IN. 1990. 424p. Hackett Classics
Ser. ISBN:0-87220-102-3, ISBN13: 978-0-87220-102-6.
Dewey:146/.4. LCCN:90-038344.
Audience: **g,u,f.**

Black, Max   **B808.5 .B55 1971**
Problems of Analysis: Philosophical Essays. Trade Cloth.
Greenwood Publishing Group, Inc. Portsmouth, NH. 1971. 304p.
ISBN:0-8371-5740-4, ISBN13: 978-0-8371-5740-5. Dewey:160.
LCCN:74-139124.

Audience: **g,u,f.** *B*

Dummett, Michael   **B808.5**
Origins of Analytical Philosophy. Trade Paper. Harvard
University Press. Cambridge, MA. 1996. 212p.
ISBN:0-674-64473-5, ISBN13: 978-0-674-64473-1.
Dewey:146.4.

Audience: **g,l,u,f.**

Hacker, P. M.   **B3376.W564H245 1997**
Wittgenstein's Place in Twentieth-Century Analytic Philosophy.
Trade Paper. Blackwell Publishing, Inc. Malden, MA. 1996.
368p. ISBN:0-631-20099-1, ISBN13: 978-0-631-20099-4.
Dewey:192. LCCN:95-042004.

Audience: **g,u.** *Choice, 1997.*

Hylton, Peter   **B1649.R94**
Russell, Idealism, and the Emergence of Analytic Philosophy.
Trade Paper. Oxford University Press, Inc. New York, NY. 1993.
438p. ISBN:0-19-824018-X, ISBN13: 978-0-19-824018-1.
Dewey:146.4. LCCN:89-038213.

Audience: **g,u,f.** *Choice, 1991.*

Lewis, David   **B841.4**
Convention: A Philosophical Study. Trade Paper. Blackwell
Publishing, Inc. Malden, MA. 2002. 232p. ISBN:0-631-23257-5,
ISBN13: 978-0-631-23257-5. Dewey:149/.9.

Audience: **u,f.**

Martinich, A. P. & Sosa,   **B808.5.A52 2001**
David (Editors)
Analytic Philosophy: An Anthology. Trade Paper. Blackwell
Publishing, Inc. Malden, MA. 2001. 528p. Philosophy
Anthologies Ser., Vol. 13 ISBN:0-631-21647-2, ISBN13:
978-0-631-21647-6. Dewey:146/.4. LCCN:00-069789.

Audience: **u.**

Sosa, David   **B808.5**
A Companion to Analytic Philosophy. A. P. Martinich (Editor).
Trade Paper, Perfect. Blackwell Publishing, Inc. Malden, MA.
2005. 512p. ISBN:1-4051-3346-5, ISBN13: 978-1-4051-3346-3.
Dewey:146/.4. LCCN:00-050770.

Audience: **u,f.**

Stevens, Graham   **B1649.R94S74 2005**
The Russellian Origins Of Analytical Philosophy. Paper over
Boards. Routledge. New York, NY. 2005. 208p. Routledge
Studies in Twentieth Century Philosophy Ser.
ISBN:0-415-36044-7, ISBN13: 978-0-415-36044-9. Dewey:192.
LCCN:2004-061401.

Audience: **g,u,f.**

Strawson, Peter F.   **B29.S8216 1992**
Analysis and Metaphysics: An Introduction to Philosophy. Trade
Paper. Oxford University Press, Inc. New York, NY. 1992. 152p.

ISBN:0-19-875118-4, ISBN13: 978-0-19-875118-2. Dewey:100.
LCCN:91-036879.

Audience: **g,l,u.** *Choice, 1993.*

Stroll, Avrum   **B808.5.S77**
Twentieth-Century Analytic Philosophy. Trade Paper. Columbia
University Press. New York, NY. 2001. 304p.
ISBN:0-231-11221-1, ISBN13: 978-0-231-11221-5.
Dewey:146/.4/0904.

Audience: **g,l,u,f.**

Philosophical Schools and Doctrines > Critical Theory

Adorno, Theodor W.   **B3199.A33N413 1983**
Negative Dialectics. Ed. 2. Trade Paper. Continuum International
Publishing Group, Ltd. London, 1983. 444p. Negative Dialectics
Ser., Vol. 1 ISBN:0-8264-0132-5, ISBN13: 978-0-8264-0132-8.
Dewey:110. LCCN:80-005339.

Audience: **g,u,f.** *B*

Bronner, Stephen Eric   **B809.3.B76 2002**
Of Critical Theory and Its Theorists. Ed. 2. Paper over Boards.
Routledge. New York, NY. 2002. 320p. ISBN:0-415-93262-9,
ISBN13: 978-0-415-93262-2. Dewey:142. LCCN:2001-058917.

Audience: **g,u,f.**

Ingram, David &   **BD175.C75 1991**
Simon-Ingram, Julia
Critical Theory: The Essential Readings. Trade Paper. Paragon
House Publishers. Saint Paul, MN. 1992. 388p. Issues in
Philosophy Ser. ISBN:1-55778-353-5, ISBN13:
978-1-55778-353-0. Dewey:142. LCCN:90-040648.

Audience: **g,l,u.**

Marcuse, Herbert &   **B945.M298 1998 V.2**
Kellner, Douglas
Towards a Critical Theory of Society. Paper over Boards.
Routledge. New York, NY. 2001. 256p. Collected Papers of
Herbert Marcuse, Vol. 2 ISBN:0-415-13781-0, ISBN13:
978-0-415-13781-2. Dewey:301/.01. LCCN:00-053357.

Audience: **g,l,u,f.**

Rasmussen, David M.   **B809.3.H36 1996**
(Editor)
The Handbook of Critical Theory. Trade Cloth. Blackwell
Publishing, Inc. Malden, MA. 1996. 432p. ISBN:0-631-18379-5,
ISBN13: 978-0-631-18379-2. Dewey:142. LCCN:95-049861.

Audience: **g,u.**

Rush, Fred (Editor)   **B809.3.C36 2004**
The Cambridge Companion to Critical Theory. Cloth Text.
Cambridge University Press. New York, NY. 2004. 396p.
Cambridge Companions to Philosophy Ser.
ISBN:0-521-81660-2, ISBN13: 978-0-521-81660-1. Dewey:142.
LCCN:2005-297203.

Audience: **u,f.** *Choice, 2005.*

Simons, Jon   **B809.3**
Contemporary Critical Theorists: From Lacan to Said. Trade
Paper. Edinburgh University Press. Edinburgh, 2005. 272p.
ISBN:0-7486-1720-5, ISBN13: 978-0-7486-1720-3. Dewey:142.
Audience: **g,u.**

Philosophical Schools and Doctrines > Determinism and Free Will

Augustine   **BR65.A664E5 1993**
On Free Choice of the Will. Thomas Williams (Translator,
Introduction by). Trade Cloth. Hackett Publishing Company, Inc.
Indianapolis, IN. 1993. 192p. Hackett Classics Ser.
ISBN:0-87220-189-9, ISBN13: 978-0-87220-189-7.
Dewey:233.7. LCCN:93-022170.
Audience: **g,l,u,f.** ℬ

Bishop, John Christopher   **B105.A35 B54 1989**
Natural Agency: An Essay on the Causal Theory of Action.
Jonathan Dancy, John Haldane, Gilbert Harman, Frank Jackson,
William G. Lucan & Ernest Sosa (Contribution by). Trade
Cloth. Cambridge University Press. New York, NY. 1990. 223p.
Cambridge Studies in Philosophy ISBN:0-521-37430-8,
ISBN13: 978-0-521-37430-9. Dewey:128/.4. LCCN:89-033231.
Audience: **u,f.** *Choice, 1990.*

Bok, Hilary   **BJ1461.B64 1998**
Freedom and Responsibility. Trade Cloth. Princeton University
Press. Princeton, NJ. 1998. 232p. ISBN:0-691-01566-X,
ISBN13: 978-0-691-01566-8. Dewey:123/.5. LCCN:98-021288.
Audience: **g,l,u.** *Choice, 1999.*

Campbell, Joseph Keim   **BJ1461.F755 2004**
(Editor), et al.
Freedom and Determinism. Michael O'Rourke & David Shier
(Editors). Trade Cloth. MIT Press. Cambridge, MA. 2004. 352p.
Topics in Contemporary Philosophy Ser. ISBN:0-262-03319-4,
ISBN13: 978-0-262-03319-0. Dewey:123/.5.
LCCN:2003-066491.
Audience: **g,u,f.**

Dennett, Daniel C.   **BJ1461.D427 2003**
Freedom Evolves. Trade Paper. Penguin Group (USA) Inc. New
York, NY. 2004. 368p. ISBN:0-14-200384-0, ISBN13:
978-0-14-200384-8. Dewey:123/.5. LCCN:2002-028085.
Audience: **g,u.** *Choice, 2004.*

Dennett, Daniel Clement   **BJ1461.D426 1984**
🄴 Elbow Room: The Varieties of Free Will Worth Wanting.
E-Book. NetLibrary, Inc. Boulder, CO. 1984.
ISBN:0-585-36508-3, ISBN13: 978-0-585-36508-4.
Dewey:123.5.
Audience: **g,l,u.**

Double, Richard   **BJ1461.D67 1991**
The Non-Reality of Free Will. Trade Cloth. Oxford University
Press, Inc. New York, NY. 1990. 258p. ISBN:0-19-506497-6,
ISBN13: 978-0-19-506497-1. Dewey:123/.5. LCCN:90-033531.
Audience: **g,u,f.** *Choice, 1991.*

Fischer, John M.   **BJ1461**
The Metaphysics of Free Will: An Essay on Control. Trade
Paper. Blackwell Publishing, Inc. Malden, MA. 1996. 288p.
Aristotelian Society Ser. ISBN:1-55786-857-3, ISBN13:
978-1-55786-857-2. Dewey:123.5.
Audience: **g,u,f.** *Choice, 1995.*

Honderich, Ted   **BJ1461.H57 2002**
How Free Are You?: The Determinism Problem. Ed. 2. Trade
Paper. Oxford University Press, Inc. New York, NY. 2002. 184p.
ISBN:0-19-925197-5, ISBN13: 978-0-19-925197-1.
Dewey:123/.5. LCCN:2002-024214.
Audience: **g,l,u.**

Kane, Robert (Editor)   **BJ1461**
The Oxford Handbook of Free Will. Trade Paper. Oxford
University Press, Inc. New York, NY. 2005. 658p. Oxford
Handbooks ISBN:0-19-517854-8, ISBN13: 978-0-19-517854-8.
Dewey:123.5.
Audience: **g,l,u.** *Choice, 2002.*

Midgley, Mary   **BJ1468.5.M53 1994**
The Ethical Primate: Humans, Freedom and Morality. Paper
over Boards. Routledge. New York, NY. 1994. 208p.
ISBN:0-415-09530-1, ISBN13: 978-0-415-09530-3. Dewey:170.
LCCN:94-008485.
Audience: **g,l,u.** *Choice, 1995.*

Pereboom, Derk (Editor)   **BJ1461.F75 1997**
Free Will. Trade Cloth. Hackett Publishing Company, Inc.
Indianapolis, IN. 1997. 312p. Hackett Classics Ser.
ISBN:0-87220-373-5, ISBN13: 978-0-87220-373-0.
Dewey:123/.5. LCCN:97-027677.
Audience: **g,l,u.**

Scotus, John D.   **B765.D73L4313 1994**
Contingency and Freedom: John Duns Scotus Lectura 139. A.
Vos Jaczn (Editor, Commentaries by, Introduction by). Trade
Cloth. Springer Dordrecht. Dordrecht, 1994. 216p. The New
Synthese Historical Library, Vol. 42 ISBN:0-7923-2707-1,
ISBN13: 978-0-7923-2707-3. Dewey:123. LCCN:94-000318.
Audience: **u,f.**

Van Inwagen, Peter   **BJ1461**
An Essay on Free Will. Paper Text. Oxford University Press,
Inc. New York, NY. 1986. 254p. ISBN:0-19-824924-1, ISBN13:
978-0-19-824924-5. Dewey:123.
Audience: **g,l,u,f.**

Wallace, R. Jay   **BJ1451.W27 1994**
Responsibility and the Moral Sentiments. Trade Cloth. Harvard
University Press. Cambridge, MA. 1994. 288p.
ISBN:0-674-76622-9, ISBN13: 978-0-674-76622-8.
Dewey:171.2. LCCN:94-017255.
Audience: **g,u,f.** *Choice, 1995.*

Wright, Georg H.   **BD0591.W74**
Causality and Determinism. Trade Paper. Books on Demand.
Ann Arbor, MI. 165p. Woodbridge Lectures Columbia
University, No. 10 ISBN:0-608-11070-1, ISBN13:
978-0-608-11070-7. Dewey:122. LCCN:74-011030.
Audience: **g,u,f.**

Philosophical Schools and Doctrines > Dualism

Baker, Gordon & Morris, Katherine   **B1878.M55 B35**
Descartes' Dualism. Paper over Boards. Routledge. New York, NY. 1995. 256p. ISBN:0-415-10121-2, ISBN13: 978-0-415-10121-9. Dewey:194.
Audience: **g,u,f.**

Foster, John L.   **BD418.3.F67 1991**
The Immaterial Self: A Defence of the Cartesian Dualist Conception of the Mind. Paper over Boards. Routledge. New York, NY. 1991. 308p. International Library of Philosophy, Psychology, and Scientific Method ISBN:0-415-02989-9, ISBN13: 978-0-415-02989-6. Dewey:128/.2. LCCN:90-026357.
Audience: **g,u.** *Choice, 1992.*

Gennaro, Rocco J.   **B812.G46 1996**
Mind and Brain: A Dialogue on the Mind-Body Problem. Trade Cloth. Hackett Publishing Company, Inc. Indianapolis, IN. 1996. 72p. ISBN:0-87220-333-6, ISBN13: 978-0-87220-333-4. Dewey:128/.2. LCCN:95-046249.
Audience: **g,l,u.**

Lovejoy, Arthur Oncken   **B945.L583R48 1996**
The Revolt Against Dualism: An Inquiry Concerning the Existence of Ideas. Ed. 3. Jonathan B. Imber (Introduction by). Trade Paper. Transaction Publishers. Somerset, NJ. 1995. 424p. ISBN:1-56000-847-4, ISBN13: 978-1-56000-847-7. Dewey:121/.4. LCCN:95-020118.
Audience: **g,l,u.**

Taliaferro, Charles   **BL182 .T35 1994**
Consciousness and the Mind of God. Trade Cloth. Cambridge University Press. New York, NY. 1994. 357p. ISBN:0-521-46173-1, ISBN13: 978-0-521-46173-3. Dewey:212/.1. LCCN:93-042897.
Audience: **g,u,f.** *Choice, 1995.*

Philosophical Schools and Doctrines > Egoism

Nielsen, Kai   **BJ1012.N54 1989**
Why Be Moral? Trade Paper. Prometheus Books, Publishers. Amherst, NY. 1989. 300p. ISBN:0-87975-519-9, ISBN13: 978-0-87975-519-5. Dewey:170. LCCN:89-003524.
Audience: **g,l,u.**

Paterson   **B3153.S75P37 1993**
Nihilistic Egoist. Trade Cloth. Ashgate Publishing Company. Williston, VT. 1993. 336p. ISBN:0-7512-0258-4, ISBN13: 978-0-7512-0258-8. Dewey:193. LCCN:94-183750.
Audience: **g,u.**

Rand, Ayn   **BJ1474**
The Virtue of Selfishness. Trade Paper. Penguin Group (USA) Inc. New York, NY. 1964. 152p. ISBN:0-451-16393-1, ISBN13: 978-0-451-16393-6. Dewey:171.9.
Audience: **g,l,u.**

Van Ingen, John F.   **BJ1474.V36 1994**
Why Be Moral?: The Egoist Challenge. Cloth Text. Peter Lang Publishing, Inc. New York, NY. 1994. VIII, 192p. American University Studies, Vol. 156:Philosophy ISBN:0-8204-2357-2, ISBN13: 978-0-8204-2357-9. Dewey:171/.9. LCCN:93-036873.
Audience: **g,l,u.** *Choice, 1995.*

Philosophical Schools and Doctrines > Empiricism

Fraassen, Bas C. van   **B816**
Empirical Stance. Trade Paper. Yale University Press. Cumberland, RI. 2004. 304p. The Terry Lectures Ser. ISBN:0-300-10306-9, ISBN13: 978-0-300-10306-9. Dewey:146.4/4.
Audience: **g,u,f.**

Garrett, Don & Barbanel, Edward (Editors)   **B816**
Encyclopedia of Empiricism. Trade Cloth. Fitzroy Dearborn Publishers, Inc. Chicago, IL. 1997. 455p. ISBN:1-57958-019-X, ISBN13: 978-1-57958-019-3. Dewey:146/.44/03.
Audience: **g,l,u.** *Choice, 1999.*

Misak, C. J.   **BD212.5.M57 1995**
Verificationism: Its History and Prospects. Trade Paper. Routledge. New York, NY. 1995. 272p. Philosophical Issues in Science Ser. ISBN:0-415-12598-7, ISBN13: 978-0-415-12598-7. Dewey:111/.8. LCCN:95-007728.
Audience: **g,u,f.** *Choice, 1996.*

Prinz, Jesse J.   **BD418.3.P77 2002**
Furnishing the Mind: Concepts and Their Perceptual Basis. Trade Cloth. MIT Press. Cambridge, MA. 2002. 375p. Representation and Mind Ser. ISBN:0-262-16207-5, ISBN13: 978-0-262-16207-4. Dewey:121/.4. LCCN:2001-056245.
Audience: **g,u,f.** *Choice, 2003.*

Van Fraassen, Bas C.   **B816.V36 2001**
The Empirical Stance. Cloth over Boards. Yale University Press. Cumberland, RI. 2002. 304p. Terry Lectures ISBN:0-300-08874-4, ISBN13: 978-0-300-08874-8. Dewey:146/.44. LCCN:2001-046649.
Audience: **g,u,f.** *Choice, 2003.*

Woolhouse, Roger S.   **B816.W66 1988**
The Empiricists. Paper Text. Oxford University Press, Inc. New York, NY. 1988. 190p. A History of Western Philosophy Ser., No. 5 ISBN:0-19-289188-X, ISBN13: 978-0-19-289188-4. Dewey:192. LCCN:87-007818.
Audience: **g,u,f.**

Philosophical Schools and Doctrines > Essentialism

Ellis, B. D.   **B105.E65E44 2002**
The Philosophy of Nature: A Guide to the New Essentialism.
Trade Paper. McGill-Queen's University Press. Montreal, PQ.
2002. 224p. ISBN:0-7735-2474-6, ISBN13: 978-0-7735-2474-3.
Dewey:113. LCCN:2003-272910.
Audience: **u,f.** *Choice, 2003.*

Salmon, Nathan U.   **B105.R25S24 2004**
Reference and Essence. Ed. 2. Trade Paper, Perfect. Prometheus
Books, Publishers. Amherst, NY. 2005. 320p. Studies in
Analytic Philosophy ISBN:1-59102-215-0, ISBN13:
978-1-59102-215-2. Dewey:110. LCCN:2004-040149.
Audience: **u,f.**

Wiggins, David   **BD236 .W53 2001**
Sameness and Substance Renewed. Ed. 2. Trade Cloth.
Cambridge University Press. New York, NY. 2001. 274p.
ISBN:0-521-45411-5, ISBN13: 978-0-521-45411-7. Dewey:110.
LCCN:00-065152.
Audience: **u,f.**

Witt, Charlotte   **B434.W58 1989**
Substance and Essence in Aristotle: An Interpretation of
Metaphysics, VII-IX. Book, Other. Cornell University Press.
Ithaca, NY. 1989. 216p. ISBN:0-8014-2126-8, ISBN13:
978-0-8014-2126-6. Dewey:111/.1. LCCN:88-047913.
Audience: **u,f.**

Philosophical Schools and Doctrines > Existentialism

Barrett, William E.   **B819.B34 1990**
Irrational Man: A Study in Existential Philosophy. UK-Trade
Paper. Doubleday Publishing. New York, NY. 1962. 320p.
ISBN:0-385-03138-6, ISBN13: 978-0-385-03138-7.
Dewey:142/.78. LCCN:58-008081.
Audience: **g,l,u.**

Cooper, David E.   **B819.C62 1999**
Existentialism: A Reconstruction. Ed. 2. Trade Cloth. Blackwell
Publishing, Inc. Malden, MA. 1999. 232p. Introducing
Philosophy Ser., Vol. 8 ISBN:0-631-21322-8, ISBN13:
978-0-631-21322-2. Dewey:142/.78. LCCN:98-052529.
Audience: **g,l,u.** *Choice, 1991.*

Golomb, Jacob J.   **B105.A8G65 1995**
In Search of Authenticity: Existentialism from Kierkegaard to
Camus. Trade Paper. Routledge. New York, NY. 1995. 232p.
Problems in Modern European Thought Ser.
ISBN:0-415-11947-2, ISBN13: 978-0-415-11947-4.
Dewey:142.7/8. LCCN:94-431030.
Audience: **g,l,u.** *Choice, 1996.*

Gordon, Haim (Editor)   **B819**
Dictionary of Existentialism. Cloth Text. Greenwood Publishing
Group, Inc. Portsmouth, NH. 1999. 552p. ISBN:0-313-27404-5,
ISBN13: 978-0-313-27404-6. Dewey:142.7/8/03.
LCCN:98-030495.
Audience: **g,l,u.** *Choice, 1999.*

Guignon, Charles B.   **B819.E9453 2003**
Existentialists. Book, Other. Rowman & Littlefield Publishers,
Inc. Lanham, MD. 2003. 192p. Critical Essays on the Classics
Ser. ISBN:0-7425-1413-7, ISBN13: 978-0-7425-1413-3.
Dewey:142/.78. LCCN:2003-011950.
Audience: **g,l,u.**

Jaspers, Karl   **B829.5**
Philosophy of Existence. Richard F. Grabau (Translator). Book,
Other. University of Pennsylvania Press. Philadelphia, PA. 1971.
128p. Works in Continental Philosophy ISBN:0-8122-1010-7,
ISBN13: 978-0-8122-1010-1. Dewey:142/.7. LCCN:79-133203.
Audience: **g,l,u.** ℬ

Kaufmann, Walter   **B819**
Existentialism from Dostoevsky to Sartre. Trade Cloth. Peter
Smith Publisher, Inc. Magnolia, MA. 1984.
ISBN:0-8446-6151-1, ISBN13: 978-0-8446-6151-3.
Dewey:142/.78.
Audience: **g,l,u.**

Marcel, Gabriel   **B819**
Philosophy of Existence. Manya Harai (Translator). Trade Cloth.
Ayer Company Publishers, Inc. Manchester, NH. 1977. Essay
Index Reprint Ser. ISBN:0-8369-1094-X, ISBN13:
978-0-8369-1094-0. Dewey:142/.7. LCCN:73-080390.
Audience: **g,l,u.** ℬ

Marino, Gordon (Editor,   **B819.B37 2004**
  Introduction by)
Basic Writings of Existentialism. Trade Paper. Random House
Adult Trade Publishing Group. New York, NY. 2004. 528p. The
Modern Library Classics ISBN:0-375-75989-1, ISBN13:
978-0-375-75989-5. Dewey:142/.78. LCCN:2003-061060.
Audience: **g,l,u.**

Sartre, Jean-Paul   **B2430.S33E813**
Being and Nothingness. Trade Cloth. Peter Smith Publisher, Inc.
Magnolia, MA. 1996. ISBN:0-8446-6912-1, ISBN13:
978-0-8446-6912-0. Dewey:111.
Audience: **g,l,u,f.**

Sartre, Jean-Paul   **B819 .S320**
Existentialism and Humanism. Library Binding. M. S. G.
Haskell House. Brooklyn, NY. 1977. Studies in Philosophy, No.
40 ISBN:0-8383-2148-8, ISBN13: 978-0-8383-2148-5.
Dewey:142/.7. LCCN:76-030584.
Audience: **g,l,u.** ℬ

Schmitt, Richard   **B808.2.S36 2002**
Alienation and Freedom. Trade Paper. Westview Press. Boulder,
CO. 2002. 160p. ISBN:0-8133-2853-5, ISBN13:
978-0-8133-2853-9. Dewey:128. LCCN:2002-009649.
Audience: **g,l,u.** *Choice, 2003.*

Solomon, Robert C.   **B819.E864 2005**
Existentialism. Ed. 2. Paper Text. Oxford University Press, Inc.
New York, NY. 2004. 400p. ISBN:0-19-517463-1, ISBN13:
978-0-19-517463-2. Dewey:142/.78. LCCN:2004-057576.

Audience: **g,l,u,f.**

Solomon, Robert C.   **B791**
From Hegel to Existentialism. Paper Text. Oxford University
Press, Inc. New York, NY. 1989. 320p. ISBN:0-19-506182-9,
ISBN13: 978-0-19-506182-6. Dewey:190.9. LCCN:86-012528.

Audience: **g,u,f.**   *Choice, 1987.*

Philosophical Schools and Doctrines > Feminist Philosophy

Calhoun, Cheshire (Editor)   **BJ1395.S48 2003**
Setting the Moral Compass: Essays by Women Philosophers.
Trade Cloth. Oxford University Press, Inc. New York, NY. 2003.
400p. Studies in Feminist Philosophy ISBN:0-19-515474-6,
ISBN13: 978-0-19-515474-0. Dewey:170/.82.
LCCN:2003-048636.

Audience: **g,u,f.**

Genevieve Lloyd (Editor)   **HQ1190.F46 2001**
Feminism and History of Philosophy. Oxford University Press.
2002. Oxford Readings in Feminism Ser. ISBN:0-19-924374-3,
ISBN13: 978-0-19-924374-7.

Audience: **g,u.**

Howells, Christina (Editor)   **B2421**
French Women Philosophers: A Contemporary Reader. Paper
over Boards. Routledge. New York, NY. 2004. 472p.
ISBN:0-415-26139-2, ISBN13: 978-0-415-26139-5.
Dewey:194/.082. LCCN:2003-047221.

Audience: **g,l,u.**

Kittay, Eva Feder & Alcoff,   **HQ1190**
 Linda (Editors)
Feminist Philosophy. Trade Cloth. Blackwell Publishing, Inc.
Malden, MA. 2006. 304p. Blackwell Philosophy Guides Ser.,
Vol. 20 ISBN:0-631-22427-0, ISBN13: 978-0-631-22427-3.
Dewey:305.4201. LCCN:2006-015949.

Audience: **g,u,f.**

Nye, Andrea   **B105.W59**
Feminism and Modern Philosophy. Trade Cloth. Routledge. New
York, NY. 2004. 168p. Understanding Feminist Philosophy Ser.
ISBN:0-415-26654-8, ISBN13: 978-0-415-26654-3.
Dewey:190/.82. LCCN:2003-026264.

Audience: **g,l,u.**

On, Bat-Ami Bar (Editor)   **B395.E64 1994**
Engendering Origins: Critical Feminist Readings in Plato and
Aristotle. Cloth Text. State University of New York Press.
Albany, NY. 1993. 247p. SUNY Series in Feminist Philosophy
ISBN:0-7914-1643-7, ISBN13: 978-0-7914-1643-3.
Dewey:184/.082. LCCN:92-036046.

Audience: **g,u.**   *Choice, 1994.*

On, Bat-Ami Bar (Editor)   **B791.M64 1994**
Modern Engendering: Critical Feminist Readings in Modern
Western Philosophy. Cloth Text. State University of New York
Press. Albany, NY. 1993. 280p. SUNY Series in Feminist
Philosophy ISBN:0-7914-1641-0, ISBN13: 978-0-7914-1641-9.
Dewey:190/.82. LCCN:92-036047.

Audience: **g,u,f.**   *Choice, 1994.*

Potter, Elizabeth   **Q175**
Feminist Philosophy of Science: An Introduction. Routledge.
2006. Understanding Feminist Philosophy Ser.
ISBN:0-415-26652-1, ISBN13: 978-0-415-26652-9.

Audience: **l,u.**

Prokhovnik, Raia   **B812.P77 1999**
Rational Woman: A Feminist Critique of Dualism. Paper over
Boards. Routledge. New York, NY. 1999. 208p. Routledge
Innovations in Political Theory Ser. ISBN:0-415-14618-6,
ISBN13: 978-0-415-14618-0. Dewey:305.4/01.
LCCN:98-047963.

Audience: **g,l,u.**   *Choice, 2000.*

Rooney, Phyllis   **BD175.5**
Feminism and Epistemology: An Introduction. Trade Paper.
Routledge. New York, NY. 2005. 160p. ISBN:0-415-26661-0,
ISBN13: 978-0-415-26661-1. Dewey:121.082.

Audience: **g,l,u.**

Philosophical Schools and Doctrines > Frankfurt School

Adorno, Theodor W., et al.   **B3183.5.G47 2000**
German Twentieth Century Philosophy: The Frankfurt School.
W. Benjamin & M. Horkheimer (Authors), Wolfgang
Schirmacher (Editor). Trade Paper. Continuum International
Publishing Group, Ltd. London, 2000. 324p. German Library,
Vol. 78 ISBN:0-8264-0967-9, ISBN13: 978-0-8264-0967-6.
Dewey:142. LCCN:98-022507.

Audience: **g,u,f.**

Bernstein, J. M.   **B3199.A34 B48 2001**
Adorno: Disenchantment and Ethics. Robert B. Pippin
(Contribution by). Trade Cloth. Cambridge University Press.
New York, NY. 2001. 478p. Modern European Philosophy Ser.
ISBN:0-521-62230-1, ISBN13: 978-0-521-62230-1.
Dewey:170/.92. LCCN:00-065175.

Audience: **u,f.**   *Choice, 2003, 2002.*

Huhn, Tom (Editor)   **B3199.A34C36 2004**
The Cambridge Companion to Adorno. Cloth Text. Cambridge
University Press. New York, NY. 2004. 442p. Cambridge
Companions to Philosophy Ser. ISBN:0-521-77289-3, ISBN13:
978-0-521-77289-1. Dewey:193. LCCN:2003-055910.

Audience: **u,f.**   *Choice, 2005.*

Philosophical Schools and Doctrines > Hedonism

Feldman, Fred   **BJ1491**
Pleasure and the Good Life: Concerning the Nature, Varieties, and Plausibility of Hedonism. Trade Cloth. Oxford University Press, Inc. New York, NY. 2004. 240p. ISBN:0-19-926516-X, ISBN13: 978-0-19-926516-9. Dewey:171/.4. LCCN:2004-274451.

Audience: **g,u.**

Moore, G. E.   **B1647.M73**
Hedonism and Naturalistic Ethics. Trade Cloth. Foundation for Classical Reprints, The. Albuquerque, NM. 1984. 133p. ISBN:0-89901-151-9, ISBN13: 978-0-89901-151-6.

Audience: **g,u,f.**

Rasdall, Hastings   **BJ1011**
The Hedonistic Approach to Life. Trade Cloth. Foundation for Classical Reprints, The. Albuquerque, NM. 1983. 138p. ISBN:0-685-42596-7, ISBN13: 978-0-685-42596-1. Dewey:170.

Audience: **g,l,u.**

Philosophical Schools and Doctrines > Hermeneutics

Gadamer, Hans Georg   **BD241.G313**
Truth and Method. Garrett Barden & John Cumming (Editors), Garrett Barden & John Cumming (Translators). Trade Cloth. The Seabury Press, Inc. New York, NY. 1975. xxvi, 551p. A Continuum Book Ser. ISBN:0-8164-9220-4, ISBN13: 978-0-8164-9220-6. Dewey:121.68. LCCN:75-002053.

Audience: **g,u,f.** ℬ

Gadamer, Hans Georg   **B3248.G343L6313 1998**
Praise of Theory: Speeches and Essays. Chris Dawson (Translator). Cloth over Boards. Yale University Press. Cumberland, RI. 1999. 234p. Yale Studies in Hermeneutics ISBN:0-300-07310-0, ISBN13: 978-0-300-07310-2. Dewey:193. LCCN:98-007115.

Audience: **g,u,f.** *Choice, 1999.*

Gadamer, Hans Georg   **BD241**
Philosophical Hermeneutics. David E. Linge (Editor, Translator). Trade Cloth. University of California Press. Berkeley, CA. 1976. lviii, 243p. ISBN:0-520-02953-4, ISBN13: 978-0-520-02953-8. Dewey:121. LCCN:74-030519.

Audience: **g,u,f.**

Grondin, Jean   **BD241.G69513 1994**
Introduction to Philosophical Hermeneutics. Joel C. Weinsheimer (Translator), Hans Georg Gadamer (Foreword by). Cloth over Boards. Yale University Press. Cumberland, RI. 1994. 252p. Yale Studies in Hermeneutics ISBN:0-300-05969-8, ISBN13: 978-0-300-05969-4. Dewey:121.6/86. LCCN:94-001236.

Audience: **g,u,f.** *Choice, 1995.*

Ormiston, Gayle L. &   **BD241.H355 1990**
  Schrift, Alan D. (Editors)
The Hermeneutic Tradition: From Ast to Ricoeur. Paper Text. State University of New York Press. Albany, NY. 1989. 380p. SUNY Series, Intersections, :Philosophy and Critical Theory ISBN:0-7914-0137-5, ISBN13: 978-0-7914-0137-8. Dewey:121/.68. LCCN:89-004173.

Audience: **g,u.** *Choice, 1990.*

Ricoeur, Paul   **PN212**
Time and Narrative. Kathleen McLaughlin & David Pellauer (Translators). Trade Paper. University of Chicago Press. Chicago, IL. 1990. 216p. Time and Narrative Ser., Vol. 2 ISBN:0-226-71334-2, ISBN13: 978-0-226-71334-2. Dewey:809.9/23. LCCN:83-017995.

Audience: **g,u,f.** *Choice, 1988, 1986.*

Ricoeur, Paul   **BD241 .R484**
Hermeneutics and the Human Sciences: Essays on Language, Action and Interpretation. John B. Thompson (Edited and Translated by). Trade Paper. Cambridge University Press. New York, NY. 1981. 324p. ISBN:0-521-28002-8, ISBN13: 978-0-521-28002-0. Dewey:121/.68. LCCN:80-041546.

Audience: **u,f.**

Todorov, Tzvetan   **BD241.T5813 1982**
Symbolism and Interpretation. Catherine Porter (Translator). Trade Cloth. Cornell University Press. Ithaca, NY. 1982. 176p. ISBN:0-8014-1269-2, ISBN13: 978-0-8014-1269-1. Dewey:121/.68. LCCN:82-005078.

Audience: **g,u,f.** ℬ

Wachterhauser, Brice R.   **BD241.H365 1986**
ⓔ Hermeneutics and Modern Philosophy. E-Book. NetLibrary, Inc. Boulder, CO. 1986. ISBN:0-585-06842-9, ISBN13: 978-0-585-06842-8. Dewey:149.

Audience: **g,l,u.** *Choice, 1987.*

Philosophical Schools and Doctrines > Humanism

Ehrenfeld, David W.   **B821**
The Arrogance of Humanism. Paper Text. Oxford University Press, Inc. New York, NY. 1981. 296p. ISBN:0-19-502890-2, ISBN13: 978-0-19-502890-4. Dewey:144. LCCN:78-001664.

Audience: **g,l,u.** ℬ

Janicaud, Dominique   **B2430.J283H6613 2005**
On the Human Condition. Eileen Brennan. Routledge. 2005. Thinking in Action Ser ISBN:0-415-32796-2, ISBN13: 978-0-415-32796-1.

Audience: **g,l,u.**

Lamont, Corliss   **B821 .L33**
The Philosophy of Humanism. Trade Cloth. Philosophical Library, Inc. New York, NY. 1958. 256p. ISBN:0-8022-0909-2, ISBN13: 978-0-8022-0909-2. Dewey:144 180*. LCCN:58-000633.

Audience: **g,l,u.**

Levinas, Emmanuel   B2430.L48H8413 2003
Humanism of the Other. Nidra Poller (Translator), Richard A. Cohen (Introduction by). Trade Cloth. University of Illinois Press. Champaign, IL. 2003. 136p. ISBN:0-252-02840-6, ISBN13: 978-0-252-02840-3. Dewey:144. LCCN:2002-151569.
Audience: **g,u,f.**

Todorov, Tzvetan   B778.T5613 2002
Imperfect Garden: The Legacy of Humanism. Trade Cloth. Princeton University Press. Princeton, NJ. 2002. 264p. ISBN:0-691-01047-1, ISBN13: 978-0-691-01047-2. Dewey:144/.0944. LCCN:2001-036868.
Audience: **g,l,u,f.** *Choice, 2002.*

Philosophical Schools and Doctrines > Idealism

Ameriks, Karl (Editor)   B2745 .C36 2000
The Cambridge Companion to German Idealism. Cloth Text. Cambridge University Press. New York, NY. 2000. 322p. Companions to Philosophy Ser. ISBN:0-521-65178-6, ISBN13: 978-0-521-65178-3. Dewey:193. LCCN:00-020469.
Audience: **u,f.** *Choice, 2001.*

Copleston, Frederick   B2741 .C67 1963
Charles
History of Philosophy: Fichte to Nietzsche. Trade Cloth. Paulist Press. Mahwah, NJ. 1963. 510p. History of Philosophy Ser., VIII ISBN:0-8091-0071-1, ISBN13: 978-0-8091-0071-2. Dewey:190. LCCN:92-194829.
Audience: **g,l,u.**

Higgins, Kathleen M. &   B2615.A35 2003
Solomon, Robert C. (Editors)
The Age of German Idealism. Trade Paper. Routledge. New York, NY. 2003. 440p. History of Philosophy Ser., Vol. 6 ISBN:0-415-30878-X, ISBN13: 978-0-415-30878-6. Dewey:141/.0943.
Audience: **g,l,u.**

Solomon, Robert C. &   B2615.A35 1993
Higgins, Kathleen M. (Editors)
The Age of German Idealism. Paper over Boards. Routledge. New York, NY. 1993. 440p. History of Philosophy Ser., Vol. 6 ISBN:0-415-05604-7, ISBN13: 978-0-415-05604-5. Dewey:141.0943. LCCN:92-032040.
Audience: **g,u,f.**

Philosophical Schools and Doctrines > Marxism

Gottlieb, Roger S. (Editor)   B809.8.A644 1989
An Anthology of Western Marxism: From Lukacs and Gramsci to Socialist-Feminism. Paper Text. Oxford University Press, Inc. New York, NY. 1989. 390p. ISBN:0-19-505569-1, ISBN13: 978-0-19-505569-6. Dewey:335.4. LCCN:88-010121.
Audience: **g,l,u.**

Kolakowski, Leszek   HX36
Main Currents of Marxism: The Founders the Golden Age the Breakdown. P.S. Falla (translator). W. W. Norton & Company, Inc. 2005. ISBN:0-393-06054-3, ISBN13: 978-0-393-06054-6.
Audience: **g,l,u,f.**

Lee, Wendy Lynne   B809.8.L4734 2001
On Marx. Trade Paper. Thomson Wadsworth. Belmont, CA. 2001. 104p. Philosophy Ser. ISBN:0-534-57602-8, ISBN13: 978-0-534-57602-8. Dewey:335.4/11. LCCN:2001-279196.
Audience: **g,l.**

Lefebvre, Henri   B809.8.L3413
Dialectical Materialism. Trade Cloth. Random House. London, 1968. 171p. ISBN:0-224-61507-6, ISBN13: 978-0-224-61507-5. Dewey:146/.32. LCCN:79-411276.
Audience: **g,u.** *B*

Lunn, Eugene   HB501.M37
Marxism and Modernism: An Historical Study of Lukacs, Brecht, Benjamin, and Adorno. Trade Cloth. University of California Press. Berkeley, CA. 1984. 344p. ISBN:0-520-05330-3, ISBN13: 978-0-520-05330-4. Dewey:335.4/1. LCCN:81-023169.
Audience: **g,u,f.** *B*

Merleau-Ponty, Maurice   B809.8.M4413
Adventures of the Dialectic. Joseph J. Bien (Translator). Trade Paper. Northwestern University Press. Evanston, IL. 1973. 237p. Studies in Phenomenology and Existential Philosophy ISBN:0-8101-0596-9, ISBN13: 978-0-8101-0596-6. Dewey:335.4/11. LCCN:72-096697.
Audience: **g,u,f.** *B*

Perry, Matt   B809.8.P37 2002
Marxism and History. Trade Paper. Palgrave Macmillan. New York, NY. 2002. 203p. Theory and History Ser. ISBN:0-333-92244-1, ISBN13: 978-0-333-92244-6. Dewey:901. LCCN:2001-053161.
Audience: **g,u.**

Roberts, Marcus   B809.8.R49 1997
Analytical Marxism: A Critique. Cloth Text. Analytical Psychology Club of San Francisco, Inc. San Francisco, CA. 1997. 320p. ISBN:1-85984-855-9, ISBN13: 978-1-85984-855-5. Dewey:335.4/1. LCCN:96-048950.
Audience: **g,u,f.**

Sartre, Jean-Paul   B809.8
Critique of Dialectical Reason, Vol. 1. Alan Sheridan-Smith (Translator), Fredric Jameson (Introduction by). Trade Paper. Verso Books. London, 2002. 480p. ISBN:1-85984-485-5, ISBN13: 978-1-85984-485-4. Dewey:335.4/112.
Audience: **g,u,f.**

Tian, Chenchan   B809.82.C5T53 2005
Chinese Dialectics: From Yijing to Marxism. Lexington Books. 2004. ISBN:0-7391-0922-7, ISBN13: 978-0-7391-0922-9.
Audience: **g,u,f.**

Volosinov, V. N.   **B809.8.V59413 1986**
Marxism and the Philosophy of Language. Ladislav Matejka &
Irwin R. Titunik (Translators). Paper Text. Harvard University
Press. Cambridge, MA. 1986. 216p. ISBN:0-674-55125-7,
ISBN13: 978-0-674-55125-1. Dewey:401. LCCN:85-027163.
Audience: **g,u,f.**

Philosophical Schools and Doctrines > Materialism

What Is Historical Materialism?: A Reader. Brill Academic
Publishers, Inc. 1997. ISBN:1-899438-18-1, ISBN13:
978-1-899438-18-1.
Audience: **g,l,u.**

Gillett, Carl & Loewer,   **B825 .P49 2001**
  Barry (Editors)
Physicalism and Its Discontents. Trade Cloth. Cambridge
University Press. New York, NY. 2001. 380p.
ISBN:0-521-80175-3, ISBN13: 978-0-521-80175-1.
Dewey:146/.3. LCCN:00-065155.
Audience: **g,u,f.**

Kim, Jaegwon   **BD418.3.K55 2005**
Physicalism, or Something near Enough. Trade Cloth. Princeton
University Press. Princeton, NJ. 2005. 200p. Princeton
Monographs in Philosophy ISBN:0-691-11375-0, ISBN13:
978-0-691-11375-3. Dewey:128/.2. LCCN:2004-053451.
Audience: **u,f.**

Melnyk, Andrew   **B825.M38 2003**
A Physicalist Manifesto: Thoroughly Modern Materialism. Trade
Cloth. Cambridge University Press. New York, NY. 2003. 340p.
Cambridge Studies in Philosophy ISBN:0-521-82711-6, ISBN13:
978-0-521-82711-9. Dewey:146/.3. LCCN:2003-041959.
Audience: **u,f.**

Moser, Paul K. & Trout, J.   **B825.C64 1995**
  D. (Editors)
Contemporary Materialism: A Reader. Paper over Boards.
Routledge. New York, NY. 1995. 400p. ISBN:0-415-10863-2,
ISBN13: 978-0-415-10863-8. Dewey:146/.3. LCCN:94-032686.
Audience: **g,l,u.**

Poland, Jeffrey   **B825.P63 1994**
Physicalism: The Philosophical Foundations. Trade Cloth.
Oxford University Press, Inc. New York, NY. 1994. 392p.
ISBN:0-19-824980-2, ISBN13: 978-0-19-824980-1.
Dewey:146.3. LCCN:93-005500.
Audience: **g,u,f.**

Rosenthal, David M.   **B825.M334 2000**
  (Editor)
Materialism and the Mind-Body Problem. Ed. 2. Trade Cloth.
Hackett Publishing Company, Inc. Indianapolis, IN. 2000. 296p.
Hackett Classics Ser. ISBN:0-87220-479-0, ISBN13:
978-0-87220-479-9. Dewey:128/.2. LCCN:00-033456.
Audience: **g,u.**

Philosophical Schools and Doctrines > Nihilism

Baudrillard, Jean   **B2430.B33973E2513**
The Impossible Exchange. Chris Turner (Translator). Trade
Cloth. Analytical Psychology Club of San Francisco, Inc. San
Francisco, CA. 2001. 160p. ISBN:1-85984-647-5, ISBN13:
978-1-85984-647-6. Dewey:194. LCCN:2001-045420.
Audience: **g,u,f.**

Carr, Karen L.   **B825.2.C37 1992**
The Banalization of Nihilism: Twentieth-Century Responses to
Meaninglessness. Cloth Text. State University of New York
Press. Albany, NY. 1992. 196p. ISBN:0-7914-0833-7, ISBN13:
978-0-7914-0833-9. Dewey:149/.8. LCCN:90-027104.
Audience: **g,l,u.**   *Choice, 1992.*

Cunningham, Conor   **B828.3.C86 2002**
A Genealogy of Nihilism: Philosophies of Nothing and the
Difference of Theology. Paper over Boards. Routledge. New
York, NY. 2002. 336p. Radical Orthodoxy Ser.
ISBN:0-415-27693-4, ISBN13: 978-0-415-27693-1.
Dewey:149/.8. LCCN:2002-072421.
Audience: **g,u.**

Heisig, James W.   **B5241.H47 2001**
Philosophers of Nothingness: An Essay on the Kyoto School.
Trade Cloth. University of Hawaii Press. Honolulu, HI. 2001.
392p. Nanzan Library of Asian Religion and Culture
ISBN:0-8248-2481-4, ISBN13: 978-0-8248-2481-5.
Dewey:181/.12. LCCN:2001-017133.
Audience: **g,u,f.**   *Choice, 2002.*

Nishitani, Keiji   **B828.3.N513 1990**
The Self-Overcoming of Nihilism. Graham Parkes & Setsuko
Aihara (Translators). Paper Text. State University of New York
Press. Albany, NY. 1990. 240p. SUNY Series in Modern
Japanese Philosophy ISBN:0-7914-0438-2, ISBN13:
978-0-7914-0438-6. Dewey:149/.8. LCCN:90-031631.
Audience: **g,l,u.**   *Choice, 1991.*

Young, Julian   **BD431.Y59 2003**
The Death of God and the Meaning of Life. Paper over Boards.
Routledge. New York, NY. 2003. 248p. ISBN:0-415-30789-9,
ISBN13: 978-0-415-30789-5. Dewey:128. LCCN:2002-037166.
Audience: **g,l,u.**

Philosophical Schools and Doctrines > Nominalism

Armstrong, D. M.   **B105.U5A74 1989**
Universals: An Opinionated Introduction. Trade Paper. Westview
Press. Boulder, CO. 1989. 160p. Focus Ser.
ISBN:0-8133-0772-4, ISBN13: 978-0-8133-0772-5.
Dewey:111/.2. LCCN:89-034723.
Audience: **g,u,f.**   *Choice, 1990.*

Armstrong, D. M.   **B105.U5**
Universals and Scientific Realism: Nominalism and Realism.
Cloth Text. Cambridge University Press. New York, NY. 1978.
164p. ISBN:0-521-21741-5, ISBN13: 978-0-521-21741-5.
Dewey:111/.2. LCCN:77-080824.
Audience: **g,u,f.** *B*

Loux, Michael J.   **BD352 .L68**
Substance and Attribute: A Study in Ontology. Trade Cloth.
Springer. New York, NY. 1978. 204p. Philosophical Studies, No.
14 ISBN:90-277-0926-2, ISBN13: 978-90-277-0926-4.
Dewey:111. LCCN:78-012989.
Audience: **u,f.**

Quine, Willard V.   **BC71 .Q48 1980**
From a Logical Point of View: Nine Logico-Philosophical
Essays. Ed. 2. Trade Cloth. Harvard University Press.
Cambridge, MA. 1980. 200p. ISBN:0-674-32350-5, ISBN13:
978-0-674-32350-6. Dewey:160. LCCN:79-092851.
Audience: **u,f.** *B*

Rodriguez-Pereyra, Gonzalo   **B731.R63 2002**
Resemblance Nominalism: A Solution to the Problem of
Universals. Trade Cloth. Oxford University Press, Inc. New
York, NY. 2002. 250p. ISBN:0-19-924377-8, ISBN13:
978-0-19-924377-8. Dewey:111/.2. LCCN:2001-058834.
Audience: **g,u,f.**

William of Ockham   **BC60.O25213 1998**
Ockham's Theory of Terms: Summa Logicae. Michael J. Lonx
(Translator, Introduction by). Trade Cloth. Saint Augustine's
Press, Inc. South Bend, IN. 1998. 235p. ISBN:1-890318-50-7,
ISBN13: 978-1-890318-50-5. Dewey:160. LCCN:97-037876.
Audience: **g,u,f.**

Philosophical Schools and Doctrines > Objectivism

Peikoff, Leonard   **B945.R234**
Objectivism: The Philosophy of Ayn Rand. Trade Paper. Penguin
Group (USA) Inc. New York, NY. 1993. 512p. Ayn Rand
Library Ser. ISBN:0-452-01101-9, ISBN13: 978-0-452-01101-4.
Dewey:191. LCCN:93-027923.
Audience: **g,l,u.**

Rand, Ayn   **B945**
The Voice of Reason: Essays in Objectivist Thought. Leonard
Peikoff (Editor, Introduction by). Trade Paper. Penguin Group
(USA) Inc. New York, NY. 1990. 368p. The Ayn Rand Library
Ser., Vol. V ISBN:0-452-01046-2, ISBN13: 978-0-452-01046-8.
Dewey:191. LCCN:88-018192.
Audience: **g,l,u,f.**

Smith, Tara   **B945.R234S65 2006**
Ayn Rand's Normative Ethics: The Virtuous Egoist. Cloth Text.
Cambridge University Press. New York, NY. 2006. 328p.
ISBN:0-521-86050-4, ISBN13: 978-0-521-86050-5.
Dewey:171/.9/092. LCCN:2005-018733.
Audience: **g,u.**

Philosophical Schools and Doctrines > Ordinary Language Philosophy

Austin, J. L.   **P302**
How to Do Things with Words. Ed. 2. J. O. Urmsson & Marina
Sbisa (Editors). Trade Paper. Harvard University Press.
Cambridge, MA. 1975. 188p. ISBN:0-674-41152-8, ISBN13:
978-0-674-41152-4. Dewey:401/.41.
Audience: **g,u,f.** *B*

Fleming, Richard   **B828.36.F57 2004**
First Word Philosophy: Wittgenstein-Austin-Cavell, Writings on
Ordinary Language. Trade Cloth. Bucknell University Press.
Cranbury, NJ. 2004. 150p. Philosophy Ser. ISBN:0-8387-5568-2,
ISBN13: 978-0-8387-5568-6. Dewey:149/.94.
LCCN:2003-012788.
Audience: **g,u.**

Hanfling, Oswald   **B828.36.H36 2003**
Philosophy and Ordinary Language: The Bent and Genius of
Our Tongue. Ed. 2. Trade Paper. Routledge. New York, NY.
2003. 288p. ISBN:0-415-32277-4, ISBN13: 978-0-415-32277-5.
Dewey:149.9/4.
Audience: **g,l,u.**

Philosophical Schools and Doctrines > Phenomenology

Critchley, Simon &   **B803**
  Schroeder, William (Editors)
Companion to Continental Philosophy. Trade Paper. Blackwell
Publishing, Inc. Malden, MA. 1999. 704p. Companions to
Philosophy Ser. ISBN:0-631-21850-5, ISBN13:
978-0-631-21850-0. Dewey:190.
Audience: **u,f.**

Dreyfuss, Hubert L. &   **B829.5.C557 2005**
  Wrathall, Mark A.
Companion to Phenomenology and Existentialism. Trade Cloth.
Blackwell Publishing, Inc. Malden, MA. 2006. 616p. Blackwell
Companions to Philosophy Ser., Vol. 35 ISBN:1-4051-1077-5,
ISBN13: 978-1-4051-1077-8. Dewey:142/.7.
LCCN:2005-017581.
Audience: **g,l,u.**

Embree, Lester (General   **B829.5.E53 1997**
  Editor)
Encyclopedia of Phenomenology. Elisabeth A. Behnke, David
Carr, J. Claude Evans, José Huertas-Jourda, J. J. Kockelmans Jr.,
W. Mckenna, Algis Mickunas, J. N. Mohanty, Thomas Nenon,
Thomas M. Seebohm & R. M. Zaner (Editorial Board
Members). Trade Cloth. Springer. New York, NY. 1996. 770p.
Contributions to Phenomenology Ser. ISBN:0-7923-2956-2,
ISBN13: 978-0-7923-2956-5. Dewey:142/.7/03.
LCCN:96-051040.
Audience: **g,l,u,f.**

Heidegger, Martin   **B3279.H48**
The Basic Problems of Phenomenology. Albert Hofstadter
(Translator, Introduction by). Trade Paper. Indiana University
Press. Bloomington, IN. 1988. 430p. Studies in Phenomenology
and Existential Philosophy ISBN:0-253-20478-X, ISBN13:
978-0-253-20478-3. Dewey:142.7. LCCN:80-008379.
                                    Audience: **g,u,f.** ℬ

Husserl, Edmund   **B3279.H93**
Idea of Phenomenology. W. P. Alston (Translator). Paper Text.
Martinus-Nijhoff Publishers (N E). 1973. 82p.
ISBN:90-247-0114-7, ISBN13: 978-90-247-0114-8.
Dewey:142.7.
                                    Audience: **g,u,f.**

Lyotard, Jean-Francois   **B829.5.L92 1991**
Phenomenology. Brian Beakley (Translator), Gayle L. Ormiston
(Foreword by, Introduction by). Cloth Text. State University of
New York Press. Albany, NY. 1991. 153p. SUNY Series in
Contemporary Continental Philosophy ISBN:0-7914-0805-1,
ISBN13: 978-0-7914-0805-6. Dewey:142/.7. LCCN:90-019828.
                            Audience: **g,u.**   *Choice, 1992.*

Merleau-Ponty, Maurice   **B829.5**
Phenomenology of Perception. Colin J. Smith (Translator).
Trade Paper. Routledge. New York, NY. 1981.
ISBN:0-391-02551-1, ISBN13: 978-0-391-02551-6.
Dewey:142.7.
                                    Audience: **g,u,f.**

Moran, Dermot   **B829.5.M647 2000**
Introduction to Phenomenology. Paper over Boards. Routledge.
New York, NY. 2000. 592p. ISBN:0-415-18372-3, ISBN13:
978-0-415-18372-7. Dewey:142/.7. LCCN:99-042071.
                            Audience: **g,l,u.**   *Choice, 2000.*

Moran, Dermot & Mooney,   **B829.5.R68 2002**
  Tim (Editors)
Phenomenology Reader. Paper over Boards. Routledge. New
York, NY. 2002. 624p. ISBN:0-415-22421-7, ISBN13:
978-0-415-22421-5. Dewey:142/.7. LCCN:2001-048693.
                                    Audience: **g,l,u.**

Sallis, John   **B829.5.S23 2003**
Phenomenology and the Return to Beginnings. Trade Paper.
Duquesne University Press. Pittsburgh, PA. 2003. 120p.
ISBN:0-8207-0338-9, ISBN13: 978-0-8207-0338-1.
Dewey:142/.7. LCCN:2003-005055.
                                    Audience: **g,l,u.** ℬ

Sokolowski, Robert   **B829.5 .S576 2000**
Introduction to Phenomenology. Cloth Text. Cambridge
University Press. New York, NY. 1999. 248p.
ISBN:0-521-66099-8, ISBN13: 978-0-521-66099-0.
Dewey:142/.7. LCCN:99-021499.
                        Audience: **g,l,u,f.**   *Choice, 2000.*

Solomon, Robert C. &   **B803.B57 2003**
  Sherman, David L. (Editors)
The Blackwell Guide to Continental Philosophy. Trade Cloth.

Blackwell Publishing, Inc. Malden, MA. 2003. 360p. Blackwell
Philosophy Guides Ser., Vol. 12 ISBN:0-631-22124-7, ISBN13:
978-0-631-22124-1. Dewey:190. LCCN:2002-006208.
                                    Audience: **g,u.**

Spiegelberg, Herbert   **B829.5**
The Phenomenological Movement. Ed. 3. Library Binding.
Martinus-Nijhoff Publishers (N E). 1981. 788p.
Phaenomenologica Ser. ISBN:90-247-2577-1, ISBN13:
978-90-247-2577-9. Dewey:142/.7/09.
                                    Audience: **g,u,f.** ℬ

Stewart, David   **B829.5.S67 1990**
Exploring Phenomenology: A Guide to the Field and Its
Literature. Ed. 2. Algis Mickunas (Contribution by). Trade
Cloth. Ohio University Press. Athens, OH. 1990. 196p.
ISBN:0-8214-0961-1, ISBN13: 978-0-8214-0961-9.
Dewey:142/.7. LCCN:89-049294.
                            Audience: **g,u.**   *Choice, 1991.*

Philosophical Schools and Doctrines > Positivism

Ayer, Alfred Jules   **B824**
Logical Positivism. Trade Paper. Simon & Schuster. New York,
NY. 1966. 464p. ISBN:0-02-901130-2, ISBN13:
978-0-02-901130-0. Dewey:146.4. LCCN:58-006467.
                                    Audience: **g,l,u.**

Bergmann, Gustav   **B824.6 .B4 1978**
The Metaphysics of Logical Positivism. Trade Cloth.
Greenwood Publishing Group, Inc. Portsmouth, NH. 1978. 340p.
ISBN:0-313-20235-4, ISBN13: 978-0-313-20235-3.
Dewey:146/.4. LCCN:77-028139.
                                    Audience: **u,f.**

Comte, Auguste   **B808.5**
Introduction to Positive Philosophy. Frederick Ferre (Translator,
Introduction by). Trade Cloth. Hackett Publishing Company, Inc.
Indianapolis, IN. 1988. 86p. HPC Classics Ser.
ISBN:0-87220-051-5, ISBN13: 978-0-87220-051-7.
Dewey:146/.4. LCCN:87-034831.
                                    Audience: **g,u.**

Copleston, Frederick   **B824.6**
Contemporary Philosophy: Studies of Logical Positivism and
Existentialism. Trade Paper. Continuum International Publishing
Group, Ltd. London, 2002. 240p. ISBN:0-8264-6507-2, ISBN13:
978-0-8264-6507-8. Dewey:146/.42. LCCN:2003-283220.
                                    Audience: **l,u.**

Mill, John Stuart   **PN6112**
Auguste Comte and Positivism. Trade Paper. Kessinger
Publishing, LLC. Whitefish, MT. 2003. ISBN:0-7661-5582-X,
ISBN13: 978-0-7661-5582-4. Dewey:808.82.
                                    Audience: **g,u,f.**

Nozick, Robert   B824.6.E438 1996
The Emergence of Logical Empiricism: From 1900 to the
Vienna Circle. Cloth Text. Garland Publishing, Inc. New York,
NY. 1996. 432p. Science and Philosophy in the Twentieth
Century Ser., Vol. 1 ISBN:0-8153-2262-3, ISBN13:
978-0-8153-2262-7. Dewey:146/.42. LCCN:95-026648.
                                            Audience: **g,u,f.**

Parrini, Paolo (Editor), et   B824.6.L6225 2003
al.
Logical Empiricism: Historical and Contemporary Perspectives.
Wesley C. Salmon & Merrilee H. Salmon (Editors). Trade
Cloth. University of Pittsburgh Press. Pittsburgh, PA. 2003.
368p. ISBN:0-8229-4194-5, ISBN13: 978-0-8229-4194-1.
Dewey:146/.42. LCCN:2002-155566.
                              Audience: **g,u,f.**   *Choice, 2004.*

Sarkar, Sahotra   B824.6.D37 1996
Decline and Obsolescence of Logical Empiricism: Carnap vs.
Quine and the Critics. Cloth Text. Garland Publishing, Inc. New
York, NY. 1996. 440p. Science and Philosophy in the Twentieth
Century Ser., Vol. 5 ISBN:0-8153-2266-6, ISBN13:
978-0-8153-2266-5. Dewey:146/.42. LCCN:95-052885.
                                            Audience: **g,u,f.**

Philosophical Schools and Doctrines >
Postmodernism

Caputo, John D. (Editor)   B809.6.D46 1997
Deconstruction in a Nutshell: A Conversation with Jacques
Derrida. Trade Paper. Fordham University Press. Bronx, NY.
1996. 215p. Perspectives in Continental Philosophy Ser., Vol. 1
ISBN:0-8232-1755-8, ISBN13: 978-0-8232-1755-7. Dewey:194.
LCCN:96-045189.
                              Audience: **g,l,u.**   *Choice, 1997.*

Connor, Steven (Editor)   B831.2.C36 2004
The Cambridge Companion to Postmodernism. Cloth Text.
Cambridge University Press. New York, NY. 2004. 254p.
Cambridge Companions to Literature Ser. ISBN:0-521-64052-0,
ISBN13: 978-0-521-64052-7. Dewey:149/.97.
LCCN:2003-065411.
                              Audience: **u,f.**   *Choice, 2005.*

Eagleton, Terry   B831.2.E18 1996
The Illusions of Postmodernism. Trade Paper. Blackwell
Publishing, Inc. Malden, MA. 1996. 160p. ISBN:0-631-20323-0,
ISBN13: 978-0-631-20323-0. Dewey:149. LCCN:96-008101.
                              Audience: **g,u,f.**   *Choice, 1997.*

Lechte, John   B804.L37 1994
Fifty Key Contemporary Thinkers: From Structuralism to
Postmodernity. Trade Paper. Routledge. New York, NY. 1994.
264p. Fifty Key Thinkers Ser. ISBN:0-415-07408-8, ISBN13:
978-0-415-07408-7. Dewey:190/.9/04. LCCN:94-000996.
                                            Audience: **g,l,u.**

Norris, Christopher   B831.2 .N67 1990
What's Wrong with Postmodernism?: Critical Theory and the
Ends of Philosophy. Trade Paper. Johns Hopkins University
Press. Baltimore, MD. 1978. 296p. Parallax Ser., :Re-Visions of
Culture and Society ISBN:0-8018-4137-2, ISBN13:
978-0-8018-4137-8. Dewey:909.82/8. LCCN:90-038438.
                              Audience: **g,u,f.**   *Choice, 1991.*

Sim, Stuart   B831.2.R68 2004
The Routledge Companion to Postmodernism. Ed. 2. Paper over
Boards. Routledge. New York, NY. 2004. 368p. The Routledge
Companions Ser. ISBN:0-415-33358-X, ISBN13:
978-0-415-33358-0. Dewey:149/.97. LCCN:2004-009640.
                                            Audience: **u.**

Winquist, Charles E. &   B831.2.E63 2000
  Taylor, Victor E. (Editors)
Encyclopedia of Postmodernism. Paper over Boards. Routledge.
New York, NY. 2000. 480p. ISBN:0-415-15294-1, ISBN13:
978-0-415-15294-5. Dewey:149/.97/03. LCCN:00-028239.
                              Audience: **g,l,u.**   *Choice, 2001.*

Philosophical Schools and Doctrines >
Poststcuturalism

Belsey, Catherine   B841.4.B45 2002
Poststructuralism: A Very Short Introduction. Trade Paper.
Oxford University Press, Inc. New York, NY. 2002. 126p. Very
Short Introductions Ser., Vol. 73 ISBN:0-19-280180-5, ISBN13:
978-0-19-280180-7. Dewey:149/.96. LCCN:2002-027057.
                                            Audience: **g,l,u.**

Colebrook, Claire   B841.4
Philosophy and Post-Structuralist Theory: From Kant to
Deleuze. Trade Paper. Edinburgh University Press. Edinburgh,
2005. 272p. ISBN:0-7486-2227-6, ISBN13: 978-0-7486-2227-6.
Dewey:190. LCCN:2005-432736.
                                            Audience: **g,u,f.**

Harland, Richard   B841.4
Superstructuralism: The Philosophy of Structuralism and
Post-Structuralism. Trade Paper. Routledge. New York, NY.
1987. 213p. ISBN:0-416-03242-7, ISBN13: 978-0-416-03242-0.
Dewey:149/.96. LCCN:86-023627.
                              Audience: **g,u,f.**   *Choice, 1988.*

Philosophical Schools and Doctrines >
Pragmatism

Gallie, W. B.   B945.P44 G3 1975
Peirce and Pragmatism. Trade Cloth. Greenwood Publishing
Group, Inc. Portsmouth, NH. 1975. 247p. ISBN:0-8371-8342-1,
ISBN13: 978-0-8371-8342-8. Dewey:191. LCCN:75-025534.
                                    Audience: **g,u,f.** *B*

Haack, Susan & Lane,   **B832.P767 2005**
  Robert (Editors)
Pragmatism, Old and New: Selected Writings. Trade Cloth.
Prometheus Books, Publishers. Amherst, NY. 2005. 560p.
ISBN:1-59102-359-9, ISBN13: 978-1-59102-359-3.
Dewey:144/.3. LCCN:2005-020530.

Audience: **g,u,f.**

James, William   **B945.J23M47 1997**
The Meaning of Truth. Trade Cloth. Prometheus Books,
Publishers. Amherst, NY. 1997. 334p. Great Books in
Philosophy ISBN:1-57392-138-6, ISBN13: 978-1-57392-138-1.
Dewey:144/.3. LCCN:97-004501.

Audience: **g,l,u,f.** *B*

James, William   **B832.J2 1995**
Pragmatism. Trade Paper. Dover Publications, Inc. Mineola, NY.
1995. 128p. ISBN:0-486-28270-8, ISBN13: 978-0-486-28270-1.
Dewey:144/.3. LCCN:94-040828.

Audience: **g,l,u,f.** *B*

Menand, Louis   **B832.P756 1997**
Pragmatism: A Reader. Trade Paper. Random House, Inc. New
York, NY. 1997. 560p. ISBN:0-679-77544-7, ISBN13:
978-0-679-77544-7. Dewey:144/.3. LCCN:97-009328.

Audience: **g,l,u.**

Moore, Edward C.   **B832**
American Pragmatism: Peirce, James and Dewey. Trade Cloth.
Greenwood Publishing Group, Inc. Portsmouth, NH. 1985. 285p.
ISBN:0-313-24740-4, ISBN13: 978-0-313-24740-8.
Dewey:144/.3/0973. LCCN:84-025291.

Audience: **g,u.** *B*

Peirce, Charles Sanders   **B945.P43P73 1997**
Pragmatism As a Principle and Method of Right Thinking: The
1903 Harvard Lectures on Pragmatism. Patricia Ann Turrisi
(Editor). Cloth Text. State University of New York Press.
Albany, NY. 1997. 305p. ISBN:0-7914-3265-3, ISBN13:
978-0-7914-3265-5. Dewey:144/.3. LCCN:96-014144.

Audience: **g,u,f.**

Putnam, Hilary   **B832.P94 1995**
Pragmatism: An Open Question. Trade Paper. Blackwell
Publishing, Inc. Malden, MA. 1995. 128p.
ISBN:0-631-19343-X, ISBN13: 978-0-631-19343-2.
Dewey:144/.3. LCCN:94-021503.

Audience: **g,u,f.** *Choice, 1995.*

Rescher, Nicholas   **BD161.R4695 2001**
Cognitive Pragmatism: The Theory of Knowledge in Pragmatic
Perspective. Trade Cloth. University of Pittsburgh Press.
Pittsburgh, PA. 2001. 140p. ISBN:0-8229-4153-8, ISBN13:
978-0-8229-4153-8. Dewey:121. LCCN:2001-002730.

Audience: **g,u,f.** *Choice, 2002.*

Rorty, Richard McKay   **B29 .R625 1982**
Consequences of Pragmatism: Essays 1972-1980. Trade Paper.
University of Minnesota Press. Minneapolis, MN. 1982. 239p.
ISBN:0-8166-1064-9, ISBN13: 978-0-8166-1064-8.
Dewey:144/.3. LCCN:82-002597.

Audience: **g,u,f.**

Thayer, H. Standish   **B832.T48 1981**
Meaning and Action: A Critical History of Pragmatism. Ed. 2.
Trade Cloth. Hackett Publishing Company, Inc. Indianapolis, IN.
1981. 638p. ISBN:0-915144-73-5, ISBN13: 978-0-915144-73-0.
Dewey:144/.3/09. LCCN:80-020890.

Audience: **g,l,u,f.** *B*

West, Cornel   **B944.P72W47 1989**
The American Evasion of Philosophy: A Genealogy of
Pragmatism. Trade Paper. University of Wisconsin Press.
Chicago, IL. 1989. 296p. Wisconsin Project on American
Writers Ser. ISBN:0-299-11964-5, ISBN13: 978-0-299-11964-5.
Dewey:191. LCCN:88-040446.

Audience: **g,u,f.** *Choice, 1989.*

Philosophical Schools and Doctrines > Process Philosophy

Browning, Douglas &   **BD372.P54 1998**
  Myers, William T. (Editors)
Philosophers of Process. Ed. 2. Trade Cloth. Fordham University
Press. Bronx, NY. 1998. 449p. ISBN:0-8232-1878-3, ISBN13:
978-0-8232-1878-3. Dewey:146/.7. LCCN:98-025568.

Audience: **u.**

Rescher, Nicholas   **BD372.R475 2000**
Process Philosophy: A Survey of Basic Issues. Trade Cloth.
University of Pittsburgh Press. Pittsburgh, PA. 2000. 144p.
ISBN:0-8229-4142-2, ISBN13: 978-0-8229-4142-2.
Dewey:146/.7. LCCN:00-011647.

Audience: **g,u.** *Choice, 2001.*

Weiss, Paul   **B 945 W436**
Philosophy in Process, Vol. 11. Cloth Text. State University of
New York Press. Albany, NY. 1988. 401p. SUNY Series in
Philosophy ISBN:0-88706-762-X, ISBN13: 978-0-88706-762-4.
Dewey:191. LCCN:63-014293.

Audience: **g,u,f.**

Philosophical Schools and Doctrines > Rationalism

Audi, Robert   **BC177**
The Architecture of Reason: The Structure and Substance of
Rationality. Trade Paper. Oxford University Press, Inc. New
York, NY. 2002. 302p. ISBN:0-19-515842-3, ISBN13:
978-0-19-515842-7. Dewey:128/.33.

Audience: **u,f.**

Cottingham, John G.   **B833**
The Rationalists. Paper Text. Oxford University Press, Inc. New
York, NY. 1988. 246p. A History of Western Philosophy Ser.,
No. 4 ISBN:0-19-289190-1, ISBN13: 978-0-19-289190-7.
Dewey:149.7.

Audience: **g,l,u.**

Davidson, Donald **BC177**
Problems of Rationality, Vo. 4. Trade Cloth. Oxford University Press, Inc. New York, NY. 2004. 300p. ISBN:0-19-823754-5, ISBN13: 978-0-19-823754-9. Dewey:192. LCCN:2004-299798.
Audience: **u,f.**

MacIntyre, Alasdair **B105.J87M33 1988**
Whose Justice? Which Rationality? Cloth Text. University of Notre Dame Press. Notre Dame, IN. 1989. 432p. ISBN:0-268-01942-8, ISBN13: 978-0-268-01942-6. Dewey:172. LCCN:87-040354.
Audience: **g,l,u,f.** *Choice, 1988.*

Nozick, Robert **BC177.N69**
The Nature of Rationality. Trade Paper. Princeton University Press. Princeton, NJ. 1994. 242p. ISBN:0-691-02096-5, ISBN13: 978-0-691-02096-9. Dewey:128.3.
Audience: **g,u,f.** *Choice, 1994.*

Parfit, Derek **BJ1012**
Reasons and Persons. Paper Text. Oxford University Press, Inc. New York, NY. 1986. 560p. ISBN:0-19-824908-X, ISBN13: 978-0-19-824908-5. Dewey:170. LCCN:83-015139.
Audience: **u,f.**

Stout, Rowland **B105.A35S76 1996**
Things That Happen Because They Should: A Teleological Approach to Action. Trade Cloth. Oxford University Press, Inc. New York, NY. 1996. 200p. Oxford Philosophical Monographs ISBN:0-19-824063-5, ISBN13: 978-0-19-824063-1. Dewey:124. LCCN:96-020124.
Audience: **g,u,f.** *Choice, 1997.*

Philosophical Schools and Doctrines > Realism

Alston, William P. (Editor) **B835.R315 2002**
Realism and Antirealism. Trade Cloth. Cornell University Press. Ithaca, NY. 2003. 304p. ISBN:0-8014-4028-9, ISBN13: 978-0-8014-4028-1. Dewey:149/.2. LCCN:2002-009210.
Audience: **g,u,f.**

Alston, William P. **BD171.A42**
A Realist Conception of Truth. Trade Paper. Cornell University Press. Ithaca, NY. 1997. 296p. ISBN:0-8014-8410-3, ISBN13: 978-0-8014-8410-0. Dewey:121.
Audience: **g,u,f.** *Choice, 1996.*

Brink, David Owen **BJ1012 .B676 1989**
Moral Realism and the Foundations of Ethics. Jonathan Dancy, John Haldane, Gilbert Harman, Frank Jackson, William G. Lucan & Ernest Sosa (Contribution by). Trade Paper. Cambridge University Press. New York, NY. 1989. 352p. Cambridge Studies in Philosophy ISBN:0-521-35937-6, ISBN13: 978-0-521-35937-5. Dewey:170. LCCN:88-016179.
Audience: **g,u,f.** *Choice, 1989.*

Chisholm, Roderick M. **B835**
  (Editor)
Realism and the Background of Phenomenology. Paper Text. Ridgeview Publishing Company. Atascadero, CA. 1981. vii, 308p. ISBN:0-917930-14-2, ISBN13: 978-0-917930-14-0. Dewey:149.2.
Audience: **g,u.** 𝕭

Nagel, Thomas **B945.N333L37 1997**
The Last Word. Trade Cloth. Oxford University Press, Inc. New York, NY. 1997. 156p. ISBN:0-19-510834-5, ISBN13: 978-0-19-510834-7. Dewey:128.3. LCCN:96-005509.
Audience: **g,l,u.** *Choice, 1997.*

Putnam, Hilary **B29.P87 1987**
The Many Faces of Realism. Trade Cloth. Open Court Publishing Company. Chicago, IL. 1987. 112p. Paul Carus Lectures, Vol. 16 ISBN:0-8126-9043-5, ISBN13: 978-0-8126-9043-9. Dewey:149/.2. LCCN:87-007817.
Audience: **g,u,f.** *Choice, 1988.*

Putnam, Hilary **B835.P87 1990**
Realism with a Human Face. James Conant (Introduction by). Trade Cloth. Harvard University Press. Cambridge, MA. 1990. 448p. ISBN:0-674-74950-2, ISBN13: 978-0-674-74950-4. Dewey:149/.2. LCCN:89-078131.
Audience: **g,u,f.** *Choice, 1991.*

Rorty, Richard McKay **B945 .R52 1991**
Objectivity, Relativism, and Truth: Philosophical Papers, Vol. 1. Trade Paper. Cambridge University Press. New York, NY. 1990. 236p. ISBN:0-521-35877-9, ISBN13: 978-0-521-35877-4. Dewey:191. LCCN:90-041632.
Audience: **g,u,f.** *Choice, 1991.*

Weiss, Bernhard **B1626.D854**
Michael Dummett. Cloth Text. Princeton University Press. Princeton, NJ. 2002. 224p. Philosophy Now Ser. ISBN:0-691-11329-7, ISBN13: 978-0-691-11329-6. Dewey:192.
Audience: **g,u,f.** *Choice, 2003.*

Philosophical Schools and Doctrines > Relativism

Baghramian, Maria **BD221**
Relativism. Trade Cloth. Routledge. New York, NY. 2004. 384p. The Problems of Philosophy Ser., :Their Past and Present ISBN:0-415-16149-5, ISBN13: 978-0-415-16149-7. Dewey:149. LCCN:2004-000297.
Audience: **g,u.**

Harman, Gilbert & **BJ1012.H316 1996**
  Thomson, Judith J.
Moral Relativism and Moral Objectivity, L. Trade Cloth. Blackwell Publishing, Inc. Malden, MA. 1996. 224p. Great Debates in Philosophy Ser. ISBN:0-631-19209-3, ISBN13: 978-0-631-19209-1. Dewey:171.7. LCCN:95-012472.
Audience: **g,u,f.** *Choice, 1996.*

Moser, Paul K. & Carson,   **BJ37.M8185 2001**
  Thomas L. (Editors)
Moral Relativism: A Reader. Paper Text. Oxford University
Press, Inc. New York, NY. 2000. 347p. ISBN:0-19-513130-4,
ISBN13: 978-0-19-513130-7. Dewey:171/.7. LCCN:99-055853.
                                            Audience: **g,l,u.**

Philosophical Schools and Doctrines > Structuralism

Caws, Peter   **B841.4.C39 1997**
Structuralism: A Philosophy for the Human Science. Trade
Paper. Brill Academic Publishers, Inc. Boston, MA. 1997.
Contemporary Studies in Philosophy and the Human Sciences
Ser. ISBN:0-391-04044-8, ISBN13: 978-0-391-04044-1.
Dewey:149/.96. LCCN:96-052015.
                                            Audience: **g,u,f.**

De George, Richard T. & De   **B841.4**
  George, Fernande M. (Editors)
The Structuralists. Trade Paper. Doubleday Publishing. New
York, NY. 1984. ISBN:0-385-00930-5, ISBN13:
978-0-385-00930-0. Dewey:108.
                                            Audience: **g,l,u.**

Dosse, Francois   **B841.4.D6713 1997**
History of Structuralism. Deborah Glassman (Translator). Trade
Cloth. University of Minnesota Press. Minneapolis, MN. 1997.
xxvi, 458p. ISBN:0-8166-2254-X, ISBN13: 978-0-8166-2254-2.
Dewey:149/.96/09. LCCN:96-051477.
                                 Audience: **g,l,u.** *Choice, 1997.*

Sturrock, John   **B841.4.S927 2003**
Structuralism. Ed. 2. Trade Cloth. Blackwell Publishing, Inc.
Malden, MA. 2002. 176p. ISBN:0-631-23238-9, ISBN13:
978-0-631-23238-4. Dewey:149/.96. LCCN:2002-028112.
                                            Audience: **g,l,u,f.**

Philosophical Schools and Doctrines > Subjectivism

Georgalis, Nicholas   **BD418.3.G46 2005**
The Primacy of the Subjective: Foundations for a Unified
Theory of Mind and Language. Trade Cloth. MIT Press.
Cambridge, MA. 2005. 336p. Bradford Bks.
ISBN:0-262-07265-3, ISBN13: 978-0-262-07265-6.
Dewey:128/.2. LCCN:2005-047473.
                                 Audience: **u,f.** *Choice, 2006.*

Siebers, Tobin Anthony   **BD438.5.S54 1998**
The Subject and Other Subjects: On Ethical, Aesthetic, and
Political Identity. Trade Cloth. University of Michigan Press.
Chicago, IL. 1998. 168p. ISBN:0-472-09673-7, ISBN13:
978-0-472-09673-2. Dewey:126. LCCN:97-033948.
                                 Audience: **g,u.** *Choice, 1999.*

Williams, Caroline   **B1809.S85W55 2001**
Contemporary French Philosophy: Modernity and the
Persistence of the Subject. Trade Cloth. Continuum International
Publishing Group, Ltd. London, 2001. 272p.
ISBN:0-485-00432-1, ISBN13: 978-0-485-00432-8. Dewey:194.
LCCN:2006-273036.
                                            Audience: **g,u.**

Philosophical Schools and Doctrines > Transcendentalism

Emerson, Ralph Waldo   **PS1602.A86 2000**
The Essential Writings of Ralph Waldo Emerson. Brooks
Atkinson (Editor). Random House Adult Trade Publishing
Group. 2000. Modern Library Classics ISBN:0-679-78322-9,
ISBN13: 978-0-679-78322-0.
                                            Audience: **g,l,u.**

Geldard, Richard   **B905.E87 2005**
Essential Transcendentalists. Trade Paper. Penguin Group (USA)
Inc. New York, NY. 2005. 272p. ISBN:1-58542-434-X, ISBN13:
978-1-58542-434-4. Dewey:141/.3/0973. LCCN:2005-044016.
                                            Audience: **g,l,u.**

Leighton, Walter L.   **B905**
French Philosophers and New England Transcendentalism. Trade
Cloth. Greenwood Publishing Group, Inc. Portsmouth, NH.
1970. 105p. ISBN:0-8371-0143-3, ISBN13: 978-0-8371-0143-9.
Dewey:141/.3/0974. LCCN:68-019289.
                                            Audience: **g,u.**

Miller, Perry G. (Editor)   **B905**
The Transcendentalists: An Anthology. Trade Paper. Harvard
University Press. Cambridge, MA. 1950. 540p.
ISBN:0-674-90333-1, ISBN13: 978-0-674-90333-3. Dewey:141.
LCCN:50-007360.
                                      Audience: **g,l,u.** *B*

Mott, Wesley T. (Editor)   **B905**
Biographical Dictionary of Transcendentalism. Cloth Text.
Greenwood Publishing Group, Inc. Portsmouth, NH. 1996. 336p.
ISBN:0-313-28836-4, ISBN13: 978-0-313-28836-4.
Dewey:810.9/384 B. LCCN:95-045187.
                                 Audience: **g,l,u.** *Choice, 1997.*

Philosophical Schools and Doctrines > Utilitarianism

Bentham, Jeremy & Mill,   **HB94.C428 2003**
  John Stuart
The Classical Utilitarians: Bentham and Mill. John Troyer
(Translator, Introduction by). Trade Cloth. Hackett Publishing
Company, Inc. Indianapolis, IN. 2003. 281p.
ISBN:0-87220-650-5, ISBN13: 978-0-87220-650-2.
Dewey:330.15/3/0922. LCCN:2002-191279.
                                            Audience: **g,l,u.**

Crisp, Roger   B1603.U873C75 1997
Routledge Philosophy Guidebook to Mill on Utilitarianism.
Paper over Boards. Routledge. New York, NY. 1997. 256p.
Philosophy Guidebooks ISBN:0-415-10977-9, ISBN13:
978-0-415-10977-2. Dewey:171.5. LCCN:97-001476.
                                    Audience: **g,u.**

Crisp, Roger   B1603.U873C75 1997
Routledge Philosophy Guidebook to Mill on Utilitarianism.
Trade Paper. Routledge. New York, NY. 1997. 256p. Philosophy
Guidebooks ISBN:0-415-10978-7, ISBN13: 978-0-415-10978-9.
Dewey:171.5. LCCN:97-001476.
                                    Audience: **u,f.**

Lyons, David   B1608.E8L96 1994
Rights, Welfare, and Mill's Moral Theory. Paper Text. Oxford
University Press, Inc. New York, NY. 1994. 198p.
ISBN:0-19-508218-4, ISBN13: 978-0-19-508218-0.
Dewey:171/.5/092. LCCN:93-034799.
                              Audience: **l,u.** *Choice, 1995.*

Mill, John Stuart   B1571.M6 2001
Utilitarianism. Ed. 2. George Sher (Editor). Trade Cloth. Hackett
Publishing Company, Inc. Indianapolis, IN. 2002. 72p. Classics
Ser. ISBN:0-87220-606-8, ISBN13: 978-0-87220-606-9.
Dewey:171/.5. LCCN:2001-039619.
                                 Audience: **g,l,u,f.** ℬ

Stephen, Leslie   B1571
The English Utilitarians. Trade Paper. Continuum International
Publishing Group, Ltd. London, 2005. 1264p. Continuum
Classic Texts Ser. ISBN:0-8264-8816-1, ISBN13:
978-0-8264-8816-9. Dewey:171.50942. LCCN:2006-273895.
                                    Audience: **g,l,u.** ℬ

West, Henry   B1608.E8W47 2003
An Introduction to Mill's Utilitarian Ethics. Cloth Text.
Cambridge University Press. New York, NY. 2003. 228p.
ISBN:0-521-82832-5, ISBN13: 978-0-521-82832-1.
Dewey:171/.5/092. LCCN:2003-051540.
                          Audience: **g,l,u.** *Choice, 2004.*

Philosophical Schools and Doctrines > Darwinianism

Cunningham, Suzanne   B818.C89 1996
ⓔ Philosophy and the Darwinian Legacy. E-Book. NetLibrary,
Inc. Boulder, CO. 1996. ISBN:0-585-24625-4, ISBN13:
978-0-585-24625-3. Dewey:116.
                              Audience: **g,l,u.** *Choice, 1996.*

Dennett, Daniel Clement   QH375.D45 1995
Darwin's Dangerous Idea: Evolution and the Meanings of Life.
Trade Cloth. Simon & Schuster. New York, NY. 1995. 592p.
ISBN:0-684-80290-2, ISBN13: 978-0-684-80290-9.
Dewey:146/.7. LCCN:94-049158.
                              Audience: **l,u,f.** *Choice, 1995.*

Ruse, Michael   B818.R87 1995
Evolutionary Naturalism: Selected Essays. Paper over Boards.
Routledge. New York, NY. 1995. 336p. ISBN:0-415-08997-2,
ISBN13: 978-0-415-08997-5. Dewey:146/.7. LCCN:94-018435.
                                    Audience: **g,u,f.**

Sober, Elliott   B818 .S64 1994
From a Biological Point of View: Essays in Evolutionary
Philosophy. Michael Ruse (Contribution by). Trade Paper.
Cambridge University Press. New York, NY. 1994. 267p.
Cambridge Studies in Philosophy and Biology
ISBN:0-521-47753-0, ISBN13: 978-0-521-47753-6.
Dewey:146/.7. LCCN:94-015745.
                                    Audience: **g,u,f.**

Philosophical Schools and Doctrines > Naturalism

French, Peter A. (Editor), et   B828.2.P48 1994
al.
Philosophical Naturalism. Theodore E. Uehling Jr. & Howard K.
Wettstein (Editors). Cloth Text. University of Notre Dame Press.
Notre Dame, IN. 1995. 608p. Midwest Studies in Philosophy,
Vol. 19 ISBN:0-268-01410-8, ISBN13: 978-0-268-01410-0.
Dewey:501. LCCN:94-015939.
                                    Audience: **u,f.**

Nielsen, Kai   B828.2.N54 1996
Naturalism Without Foundations. Trade Cloth. Prometheus
Books, Publishers. Amherst, NY. 1996. 608p. Prometheus
Lecture Ser. ISBN:1-57392-076-2, ISBN13: 978-1-57392-076-6.
Dewey:146. LCCN:96-008794.
                                    Audience: **u,f.**

Ryder, John (Editor)   B944.N3A44 1994
American Philosophic Naturalism in the Twentieth Century.
Trade Cloth. Prometheus Books, Publishers. Amherst, NY. 1994.
566p. ISBN:0-87975-894-5, ISBN13: 978-0-87975-894-3.
Dewey:146/.0973/0904. LCCN:94-018813.
                                    Audience: **g,u,f.**

Wagner, Steven J. &   B828.2.N37
Warner, Richard (Editors)
Naturalism: A Critical Appraisal. Trade Cloth. University of
Notre Dame Press. Notre Dame, IN. 1994. 342p.
ISBN:0-268-01473-6, ISBN13: 978-0-268-01473-5. Dewey:146.
LCCN:91-051119.
                              Audience: **g,u,f.** *Choice, 1994.*

Philosophical Schools and Doctrines > Skepticism

Barnes, Jonathan   B623 .B37 1990
The Toils of Scepticism. Trade Cloth. Cambridge University
Press. New York, NY. 1990. 174p. ISBN:0-521-38339-0,
ISBN13: 978-0-521-38339-4. Dewey:186/.1. LCCN:89-027951.
                              Audience: **u,f.** *Choice, 1991.*

DeRose, Keith & Warfield,   **B837.S566 1999**
  Ted A. (Editors)
Skepticism: A Contemporary Reader. Paper Text. Oxford
University Press, Inc. New York, NY. 1999. 320p.
ISBN:0-19-511827-8, ISBN13: 978-0-19-511827-8.
Dewey:149.7/3. LCCN:98-022393.

                               Audience: **g,u.**

Empiricus, Sextus   **B621.P972 E5 2000**
Sextus Empiricus: Outlines of Scepticism. Ed. 2. Julia Annas &
Jonathan Barnes (Editors), Karl Ameriks & Desmond M. Clarke
(Contribution by). Cloth Text. Cambridge University Press. New
York, NY. 2000. 286p. Texts in the History of Philosophy
ISBN:0-521-77139-0, ISBN13: 978-0-521-77139-9.
Dewey:186/.1. LCCN:99-015976.

                             Audience: **g,u,f.**

Hankinson, R. J.   **B525.H26**
Sceptics. Ed. 2. Trade Paper. Routledge. New York, NY. 1998.
384p. Arguments of the Philosophers Ser. ISBN:0-415-18446-0,
ISBN13: 978-0-415-18446-5. Dewey:186.

                             Audience: **g,u,f.**

Penelhum, Terence   **BT50**
God and Skepticism. Trade Cloth. Springer London, Ltd.
Guildford, 1983. 200p. ISBN:90-277-1550-5, ISBN13:
978-90-277-1550-0. Dewey:200/.1. LCCN:83-006791.

                        Audience: **g,l,u.** *B*

Popkin, Richard Henry   **B779.P65 2002**
The History of Scepticism: From Savonarola to Bayle. Ed. 3.
Trade Paper. Oxford University Press, Inc. New York, NY. 2003.
440p. ISBN:0-19-510768-3, ISBN13: 978-0-19-510768-5.
Dewey:149/.73. LCCN:2002-025769.

             Audience: **g,l,u,f.** *Choice, 2004.*

Popkin, Richard H. &   **B837.P67 2001**
  Stroll, Avrum
Skeptical Philosophy for Everyone. Trade Cloth. Prometheus
Books, Publishers. Amherst, NY. 2001. 342p.

ISBN:1-57392-936-0, ISBN13: 978-1-57392-936-3.
Dewey:149/.73. LCCN:2001-049237.

        Audience: **g,l,u.** *Choice, 2003, 2002.*

Popkin, Richard H.   **B1301.P67 1993**
The High Road to Pyrrhonism. Richard A. Watson & James E.
Force (Editors). Trade Cloth. Hackett Publishing Company, Inc.
Indianapolis, IN. 1989. 399p. ISBN:0-87220-252-6, ISBN13:
978-0-87220-252-8. Dewey:149/.73/09033. LCCN:93-038549.

                        Audience: **g,l,u,f.**

Richard Bett (Editor)   **B621.P682E5 2005**
Sextus Empiricus: Against the Logicians. Cambridge University
Press. 2005. Cambridge Texts in the History of Philosophy Ser.
ISBN:0-521-82497-4, ISBN13: 978-0-521-82497-2.

                        Audience: **g,u,f.**

Schofield, Malcolm (Editor),   **B525.D68**
  et al.
Doubt and Dogmatism: Studies in Hellenistic Epistemology.
Myles F. Burnyeat & Jonathan Barnes (Editors). Trade Cloth.
Oxford University Press, Inc. New York, NY. 1980. 356p.
ISBN:0-19-824601-3, ISBN13: 978-0-19-824601-5.
Dewey:121/.0938. LCCN:79-041044.

                      Audience: **u,f.** *B*

Stroud, Barry   **BD201**
The Significance of Philosophical Scepticism. Paper Text.
Oxford University Press, Inc. New York, NY. 1984. 294p.
ISBN:0-19-824761-3, ISBN13: 978-0-19-824761-6.
Dewey:149.7/3. LCCN:83-025244.

                      Audience: **g,u,f.** *B*

Williams, Michael   **BD161.W49 1996**
Unnatural Doubts: Epistemological Realism and the Basis of
Skepticism. Trade Paper. Princeton University Press. Princeton,
NJ. 1995. 410p. ISBN:0-691-01115-X, ISBN13:
978-0-691-01115-8. Dewey:121/.2. LCCN:95-040064.

                        Audience: **g,u,f.**

RELIGION

The Religion section, covering both theology and religious studies generally, provides a selection of titles appropriate for study at the undergraduate level. The world's major religions (Western and Eastern, ancient and modern) are covered, with emphasis on their history and intellectual traditions. Also included are works covering various religious institutions, cultural practices, and ethical and philosophical issues, as well as editions if major texts. The scope of this selection reflects the interdisciplinary nature of religious studies. Some consideration has been given to the rise of "new" or "alternative" religions.

Where possible, works are recommended in their newest, most reliable editions. Some works are available only as reprints, while a few are out of print, though still recommended.

— Emily Horning

BL1; Z7751

☐ ATLA Religion Database.
http://www.atla.com/products/catalogs/catalogs_rdb.html#general

Audience: **l,u,f.**

Religions. Mythology. Rationalism > General Works

Connolly, Peter (Editor)   **BL41**
Approaches to the Study of Religion. Trade Cloth. Continuum International Publishing Group, Ltd. London, 1998. 256p. ISBN:0-304-33710-2, ISBN13: 978-0-304-33710-1. Dewey:200.7/1. LCCN:97-180728.

Audience: **l,u,f.**

Derrida, Jacques & Vattimo,   **BL21.R39513 1998**
Gianni (Editors)
Religion. David Webb (Translator). Trade Cloth. Stanford University Press. Palo Alto, CA. 1998. 224p. Cultural Memory in the Present Ser. ISBN:0-8047-3486-0, ISBN13: 978-0-8047-3486-8. Dewey:210. LCCN:98-060374.

Audience: **u,f.** *Choice, 1999.*

Dewey, John   **BL48.D4 1991**
Common Faith. Trade Paper. Yale University Press. Cumberland, RI. 1960. 96p. Terry Lectures ISBN:0-300-00069-3, ISBN13: 978-0-300-00069-6. Dewey:200. LCCN:91-023976.

Audience: **g,l,u,f.**

Douglas, Mary   **GN452.5**
Natural Symbols: Explorations in Cosmology. Ed. 3. Trade Paper. Routledge. New York, NY. 2003. 240p. Classics Ser. ISBN:0-415-31454-2, ISBN13: 978-0-415-31454-1. Dewey:301.5/8. LCCN:2003-015374.

Audience: **g,l,u,f.**

Durkheim, Emile   **BL50.D85 1994**
Durkheim on Religion. W. S. F. Pickering (Editor). Paper Text. Oxford University Press, Inc. New York, NY. 1993. 386p. AAR Texts and Translations Ser., No. 6 ISBN:1-55540-981-4, ISBN13: 978-1-55540-981-4. Dewey:200. LCCN:94-015084.

Audience: **u,f.**

Ford, David F. & Soskice,   **BL41.F53 2004**
Janet M.
Fields of Faith: Theology and Religious Studies for the Twenty-First Century. David F. Ford, Ben Quash & Janet M. Soskice (Editors). Trade Cloth. Cambridge University Press. New York, NY. 2005. 248p. ISBN:0-521-84737-0, ISBN13: 978-0-521-84737-7. Dewey:200/.71/1. LCCN:2004-054643.

Audience: **u,f.**

Frankenberry, Nancy K.   **BL21.R33 2002**
(Editor)
Radical Interpretation in Religion. Trade Cloth. Cambridge University Press. New York, NY. 2002. 248p. ISBN:0-521-81686-6, ISBN13: 978-0-521-81686-1. Dewey:200/.7. LCCN:2002-024644.

Audience: **u,f.**

James, William (Editor)   **BL53.J36 2002**
The Varieties of Religious Experience. Trade Paper. Prometheus Books, Publishers. Amherst, NY. 2004. 552p. Great Books in Philosophy ISBN:1-57392-981-6, ISBN13: 978-1-57392-981-3. Dewey:204/.2. LCCN:2002-067965.

Audience: **g,l,u,f.**

Masuzawa, Tomoko   **BL60**
In Search of Dreamtime: The Quest for the Origin of Religion. Trade Paper. University of Chicago Press. Chicago, IL. 1993. 232p. Religion and Postmodernism Ser. ISBN:0-226-50985-0, ISBN13: 978-0-226-50985-3. Dewey:306.609. LCCN:93-000518.

Audience: **u,f.**

McCutcheon, Russell T.   **BL41.I46 1998**
(Editor)
The Insider/Outsider Problem in the Study of Religion: A Reader. Trade Cloth. Continuum International Publishing Group, Ltd. London, 1999. 448p. Controversies in the Study of Religion Ser. ISBN:0-304-70177-7, ISBN13: 978-0-304-70177-3. Dewey:306.6. LCCN:98-004479.

Audience: **g,l,u,f.**

Otto, Rudolf   **BL48.O82 1971**
The Idea of the Holy. Ed. 2. John W. Harvey (Translator). Paper Text. Oxford University Press, Inc. New York, NY. 1958. 254p. ISBN:0-19-500210-5, ISBN13: 978-0-19-500210-2. Dewey:211. LCCN:58-000776.

Audience: **u,f.**

Pals, Daniel L.   **BL41.P36 2005**
Eight Theories of Religion. Ed. 2. Trade Cloth. Oxford University Press, Inc. New York, NY. 2006. 368p. ISBN:0-19-530458-6, ISBN13: 978-0-19-530458-9. Dewey:200/.7. LCCN:2005-050238.

Audience: **g,l,u.**

Schleiermacher, Friedrich   **BL48 .S3313 1996**
Daniel Ernst
Schleiermacher: on Religion: Speeches to Its Cultured Despisers. Richard Crouter (Editor), Karl Ameriks & Desmond M. Clarke (Contribution by). Trade Paper. Cambridge University Press. New York, NY. 1996. 175p. Texts in the History of Philosophy ISBN:0-521-47975-4, ISBN13: 978-0-521-47975-2. Dewey:200. LCCN:95-022987.

Audience: **u,f.**

Smart, Ninian   **BL624**
Dimensions of the Sacred: An Anatomy of the World's Beliefs. Trade Paper. University of California Press. Berkeley, CA. 1999. 359p. ISBN:0-520-21960-0, ISBN13: 978-0-520-21960-1. Dewey:291.2.

Audience: **u,f.** *Choice, 1997.*

Smith, Jonathan Z.   **BL41.S65 2004**
Relating Religion: Essays in the Study of Religion. Trade Cloth. University of Chicago Press. Chicago, IL. 2004. 424p. ISBN:0-226-76386-2, ISBN13: 978-0-226-76386-6. Dewey:200/.71. LCCN:2004-045967.

Audience: **u,f.** *Choice, 2005.*

Stone, Jon R. (Editor)   BL41.C75 1998
The Craft of Religious Studies. Cloth over Boards. Palgrave
Macmillan. New York, NY. 1998. 352p. ISBN:0-312-17727-5,
ISBN13: 978-0-312-17727-0. Dewey:291. LCCN:97-022903.
                                        Audience: **u,f.** *Choice, 2001.*

Whitehead, Alfred North   BL48.W35 1996
Religion in the Making. Judith A. Jones (Introduction by). Trade
Paper. Fordham University Press. Bronx, NY. 1996. 256p.
ISBN:0-8232-1646-2, ISBN13: 978-0-8232-1646-8. Dewey:200.
LCCN:96-030783.
                                        Audience: **l,u,f.**

Religions. Mythology. Rationalism > General Works > Dictionaries. Encyclopedias.

American Academy of   BL31.H37 1995
Religion Staff, 1972 & 1973
The HarperCollins Dictionary of Religion. Jonathan Smith &
William S. Green (Editors). Trade Cloth. HarperCollins
Publishers. New York, NY. 1995. 1200p. ISBN:0-06-067515-2,
ISBN13: 978-0-06-067515-8. Dewey:200/.3. LCCN:95-037024.
                                        Audience: **g,l,u,f.** *Choice, 1996.*

Bowker, John (Editor)   BL31.O84 1997
The Oxford Dictionary of World Religions. Trade Cloth. Oxford
University Press, Inc. New York, NY. 1997. 1136p.
ISBN:0-19-213965-7, ISBN13: 978-0-19-213965-8.
Dewey:200/.3. LCCN:97-166787.
                                        Audience: **g,l,u,f.** *Choice, 1997.*

Crim, Keith R. (Editor), et   BL31.A24
al.
Abingdon Dictionary of Living Religions. Larry D. Shinn &
Roger A. Bullard (Editors). Trade Cloth. Abingdon Press.
Nashville, TN. 1981. 864p. ISBN:0-687-00409-8, ISBN13:
978-0-687-00409-6. Dewey:291/.03/21. LCCN:81-001465.
                                        Audience: **g,l,u,f.**

Hinnells, John R.   BL31.P38 1997
The Penguin Dictionary of Religions. Ed. 2. Trade Paper.
Penguin Group (USA) Inc. New York, NY. 1997. 800p.
Reference Ser. ISBN:0-14-051261-6, ISBN13:
978-0-14-051261-8. Dewey:200/.3. LCCN:97-228873.
                                        Audience: **g,l,u,f.**

Jones, Lindsay   BL31.E46 2005
Encyclopedia of Religion. Ed. 2. Trade Cloth. Thomson Gale.
Farmington Hills, MI. 2004. 13,500p. ISBN:0-02-865733-0,
ISBN13: 978-0-02-865733-2. Dewey:200/.3.
LCCN:2004-017052.
                                        Audience: **g,l,u,f.** *Choice, 2006.*

Religions. Mythology. Rationalism > Philosophy of Religion

Alston, William P.   BT102.A46 1991
Perceiving God: The Epistemology of Religious Experience.
Book, Other. Cornell University Press. Ithaca, NY. 1991. 336p.
ISBN:0-8014-2597-2, ISBN13: 978-0-8014-2597-4.
Dewey:248.2. LCCN:91-055068.
                                        Audience: **u,f.** *Choice, 1992.*

Audi, Robert & Wainwright,   BL51.R295 1986
William J. (Editors)
Rationality, Religious Belief, and Moral Commitment: New
Essays in the Philosophy of Religion. Book, Other. Cornell
University Press. Ithaca, NY. 1986. 352p. ISBN:0-8014-1856-9,
ISBN13: 978-0-8014-1856-3. Dewey:200/.1. LCCN:85-048200.
                                        Audience: **u,f.** *Choice, 1986.*

1957 ed. **Buber, Martin**   BL51.B8213 1988
Eclipse of God: Studies in the Relation Between Religion and
Philosophy. Robert M. Seltzer (Introduction by). Trade Paper.
Brill Academic Publishers, Inc. Boston, MA. 1988. 168p.
ISBN:0-391-03533-9, ISBN13: 978-0-391-03533-1.
Dewey:291.1/75. LCCN:87-019594.
                                        Audience: **u,f.** *B*

Delaney, C. F. (Editor)   BL51
Rationality and Religious Belief. Cloth Text. University of Notre
Dame Press. Notre Dame, IN. 1979. viii, 168p. Studies in the
Philosophy of Religion, No. 1 ISBN:0-268-01602-X, ISBN13:
978-0-268-01602-9. Dewey:200/.1. LCCN:79-063359.
                                        Audience: **u,f.**

Habermas, Jürgen   BL51.H23 2002
Religion and Rationality: Essays on Reason, God and
Modernity. Trade Cloth. MIT Press. Cambridge, MA. 2002.
184p. Studies in Contemporary German Social Thought
ISBN:0-262-08312-4, ISBN13: 978-0-262-08312-6.
Dewey:291.2. LCCN:2002-101841.
                                        Audience: **u,f.**

Hegel, Georg Wilhelm   BL51
Friedrich
3 vols Lectures on the Philosophy of Religion: One-Volume Edition.
The Lectures of 1827. Peter C. Hodgson (Editor). Trade Cloth.
University of California Press. Berkeley, CA. 1988. 569p.
ISBN:0-520-06126-8, ISBN13: 978-0-520-06126-2.
Dewey:200/.1. LCCN:83-009132.
                                        Audience: **g,l,u,f.**

Heschel, Abraham Joshua   BL51
Man Is Not Alone: A Philosophy of Religion. Trade Paper.
Farrar, Straus & Giroux. New York, NY. 1976. 320p.
ISBN:0-374-51328-7, ISBN13: 978-0-374-51328-3. Dewey:201.
                                        Audience: **g,l,u.** *B*

Hick, John   **BT50**
Faith and Knowledge. Ed. 2. Trade Paper. Macmillan Publishers Ltd. London, 1988. 268p. ISBN:0-333-41783-6, ISBN13: 978-0-333-41783-6. Dewey:200/.1.

Audience: **l,u.** *B*

Hume, David   **BL51.H963**
The Natural History of Religion. Trade Paper. Kessinger Publishing, LLC. Whitefish, MT. 2004. ISBN:1-4191-7520-3, ISBN13: 978-1-4191-7520-6. Dewey:210.

Audience: **g,l,u,f.**

Jaspers, Karl & Bultmann, Rudolf   **BS2378.J35132005**
Myth and Christianity: An Inquiry into the Possibility of Religion without Myth. Trade Paper, Perfect. Prometheus Books, Publishers. Amherst, NY. 2005. 120p. ISBN:1-59102-291-6, ISBN13: 978-1-59102-291-6. Dewey:230. LCCN:2005-001951.

Audience: **g,l.**

Kant, Immanuel   **B2799.R4K3613 1996**
Religion and Rational Theology. George di Giovanni (Editor), Allen W. Wood & George Di Giovanni (Edited and Translated by), Paul Guyer (Contribution by). Trade Paper. Cambridge University Press. New York, NY. 2001. 544p. Cambridge Edition of the Works of Immanuel Kant ISBN:0-521-79998-8, ISBN13: 978-0-521-79998-0. Dewey:210.

Audience: **g,u,f.** *Choice, 1997.*

Kierkegaard, Soren   **BL51.K487131985**
Philosophical Fragments, or a Fragment of Philosophy/Johannes Climacus, or de Omnibus Dubitandum Rst. Howard V. Hong & Edna H. Hong (Editors). Cloth Text. Princeton University Press. Princeton, NJ. 1985. 386p. New French Thought Ser., No. 7 ISBN:0-691-07273-6, ISBN13: 978-0-691-07273-9. Dewey:201. LCCN:85-003420.

Audience: **u,f.** *B Choice, 1986.*

Mackie, J. L.   **BT102**
The Miracle of Theism: Arguments for and Against the Existence of God. Paper Text. Oxford University Press, Inc. New York, NY. 1983. 276p. ISBN:0-19-824682-X, ISBN13: 978-0-19-824682-4. Dewey:212/.1. LCCN:82-003552.

Audience: **u,f.**

Marcel, Gabriel   **B2430.M253D813 2002**
Creative Fidelity. Robert Rosthal (Translator). Trade Cloth. Fordham University Press. Bronx, NY. 2002. 261p. ISBN:0-8232-2183-0, ISBN13: 978-0-8232-2183-7. Dewey:194. LCCN:2002-283397.

Audience: **u,f.** *B*

Mill, John Stuart   **BL51.M62 1998**
Three Essays on Religion: Nature, the Utility of Religion, and Theism. Trade Cloth. Prometheus Books, Publishers. Amherst, NY. 1998. 265p. Great Books in Philosophy ISBN:1-57392-212-9, ISBN13: 978-1-57392-212-8. Dewey:210. LCCN:98-015124.

Audience: **g,l,u,f.**

Plantinga, Alvin   **BT1102.P57 2000**
Warranted Christian Belief. Trade Cloth. Oxford University Press, Inc. New York, NY. 2000. 528p. ISBN:0-19-513192-4, ISBN13: 978-0-19-513192-5. Dewey:230/.01. LCCN:98-054362.

Audience: **u,f.** *Choice, 2000.*

Plantinga, Alvin & Wolterstorff, Nicholas (Editors)   **BT50**
Faith and Rationality: Reason and Belief in God. Trade Cloth. University of Notre Dame Press. Notre Dame, IN. 1984. 336p. ISBN:0-268-00965-1, ISBN13: 978-0-268-00965-6. Dewey:201. LCCN:83-014843.

Audience: **g,l,u,f.**

Pojman, Louis P.   **BL51.P532 2003**
Philosophy of Religion: An Anthology. Ed. 4. Paper Text. Thomson Wadsworth. Belmont, CA. 2002. 592p. Philosophy Ser. ISBN:0-534-54364-2, ISBN13: 978-0-534-54364-8. Dewey:210. LCCN:2002-282855.

Audience: **l,u.**

Scheler, Max Ferdinand   **BL51.S423 1972**
On the Eternal in Man. Bernard Noble (Translator). Trade Cloth. Shoe String Press, Inc. North Haven, CT. 1972. 480p. ISBN:0-208-01280-X, ISBN13: 978-0-208-01280-7. Dewey:100. LCCN:72-006599.

Audience: **g,l,u,f.** *B*

Senor, Thomas D. (Editor)   **BL51.R294 1995**
The Rationality of Belief and the Plurality of Faith. Book, Other. Cornell University Press. Ithaca, NY. 1996. 296p. ISBN:0-8014-3127-1, ISBN13: 978-0-8014-3127-2. Dewey:210. LCCN:95-024730.

Audience: **l,u,f.**

Swinburne, Richard   **BT102**
The Existence of God. Ed. 2. Trade Cloth. Oxford University Press, Inc. New York, NY. 2004. 376p. ISBN:0-19-927167-4, ISBN13: 978-0-19-927167-2. Dewey:212/.1. LCCN:2004-555474.

Audience: **u,f.** *B*

Trigg, Roger   **BL51.T65 1998**
Rationality and Religion: Does Faith Need Reason? Trade Cloth. Blackwell Publishing, Inc. Malden, MA. 1998. 232p. ISBN:0-631-19747-8, ISBN13: 978-0-631-19747-8. Dewey:210. LCCN:97-038754.

Audience: **u,f.** *Choice, 1998.*

Westphal, Merold   **BL51**
God, Guilt and Death: An Existential Phenomenology of Religion. Trade Paper. Indiana University Press. Bloomington, IN. 1987. 320p. Studies in Phenomenology and Existential Philosophy ISBN:0-253-20417-8, ISBN13: 978-0-253-20417-2. Dewey:200/.1. LCCN:83-048525.

Audience: **u,f.** *B*

Religions. Mythology. Rationalism > Psychology of Religion

Bagger, Matthew C.   **BL53 .B24 1999**
Religious Experience, Justification, and History. Trade Cloth.
Cambridge University Press. New York, NY. 1999. 248p.
ISBN:0-521-62255-7, ISBN13: 978-0-521-62255-4.
Dewey:291.42. LCCN:98-033302.

Audience: **u,f.**

Batson, C. Daniel, et al.   **BL53**
Religion and the Individual: A Social-Psychological Perspective.
Ed. 2. Patricia Schoenrade & W. Larry Ventis (Authors). Trade
Paper. Oxford University Press, Inc. New York, NY. 1993. 436p.
ISBN:0-19-506209-4, ISBN13: 978-0-19-506209-0.
Dewey:200.19. LCCN:92-028606.

Audience: **l,u,f.**

Fontana, David   **BL53.F57 2003**
Psychology, Religion and Spirituality. Trade Cloth. British
Psychological Society. Leicester, 2003. 272p.
ISBN:1-4051-0805-3, ISBN13: 978-1-4051-0805-8.
Dewey:200/.1/9. LCCN:2002-010324.

Audience: **l,u,f.** *Choice, 2003.*

Freud, Sigmund   **BL53.F67 1989**
The Future of an Illusion. James Strachey (Editor). Trade Paper.
W. W. Norton & Company, Inc. New York, NY. 1989. xxiii,
80p. ISBN:0-393-00831-2, ISBN13: 978-0-393-00831-9.
Dewey:302.

Audience: **g,l,u,f.** *B*

James, William   **BL624**
The Varieties of Religious Experience. Trade Paper. Kessinger
Publishing, LLC. Whitefish, MT. 2004. ISBN:1-4191-8661-2,
ISBN13: 978-1-4191-8661-5. Dewey:204/.2.

Audience: **g,l,u,f.**

Jung, C. G.   **BL53 .J8 1992**
Psychology and Religion. Trade Paper. Yale University Press.
Cumberland, RI. 1960. 138p. Terry Lectures
ISBN:0-300-00137-1, ISBN13: 978-0-300-00137-2.
Dewey:200/.1/9. LCCN:91-038405.

Audience: **l,u,f.** *B*

Tremlin, Todd   **BL53.T68 2006**
Minds and Gods: The Cognitive Foundations of Religion. Trade
Cloth. Oxford University Press, Inc. New York, NY. 2006. 242p.
ISBN:0-19-530534-5, ISBN13: 978-0-19-530534-0.
Dewey:200/.1/9. LCCN:2005-023088.

Audience: **u,f.**

Religions. Mythology. Rationalism > Religion: Relation to Other Subjects

Aldridge, Alan   **BL60.A53 1999**
Religion in the Contemporary World: A Sociological
Introduction. Trade Cloth. Polity Press. Cambridge, 1999. 240p.

ISBN:0-7456-2082-5, ISBN13: 978-0-7456-2082-4.
Dewey:306.6. LCCN:99-026047.

Audience: **l,u.** *Choice, 2000.*

Barnes, Linda L. & Sered,   **BL65.M4R4362004**
  Susan Starr (Editors)
Religion and Healing in America. Trade Cloth. Oxford
University Press, Inc. New York, NY. 2004. 552p.
ISBN:0-19-516795-3, ISBN13: 978-0-19-516795-5.
Dewey:203/.1/0973. LCCN:2003-022679.

Audience: **u,f.**

Cipriani, Roberto   **BL60.C5613 2000**
The Sociology of Religion: An Historical Introduction. Laura
Ferrarotti (Translator). Trade Cloth. Aldine Transaction.
Somerset, NJ. 2000. 278p. ISBN:0-202-30591-0, ISBN13:
978-0-202-30591-2. Dewey:306.6. LCCN:00-027071.

Audience: **g,l.**

Dowdy, Thomas E. &   **BL60.R35 1996**
  McNamara, Patrick H.
Religion: North American Style. Ed. 3. Cloth Text. Rutgers
University Press. Piscataway, NJ. 1997. 250p.
ISBN:0-8135-2343-5, ISBN13: 978-0-8135-2343-9.
Dewey:200/.973. LCCN:96-018514.

Audience: **g,l,u,f.**

Eagleton, Terry   **HV6431**
Holy Terror. Trade Cloth. Oxford University Press, Inc. New
York, NY. 2005. 160p. ISBN:0-19-928717-1, ISBN13:
978-0-19-928717-8. Dewey:201/.7. LCCN:2005-019762.

Audience: **u,f.**

Hunt, Stephen (Editor)   **BL60**
Religion and Everyday Life. Trade Paper. Routledge. New York,
NY. 2005. 208p. The New Sociology Ser. ISBN:0-415-35154-5,
ISBN13: 978-0-415-35154-6. Dewey:306.6.
LCCN:2005-017949.

Audience: **l.**

Insoll, Timothy (Editor)   **BL65.A72A73 2001**
Archaeology and World Religion. Paper over Boards. Routledge.
New York, NY. 2001. 240p. ISBN:0-415-22154-4, ISBN13:
978-0-415-22154-2. Dewey:200/.9. LCCN:00-059239.

Audience: **l,u,f.**

Juergensmeyer, Mark   **BL65.V55 J84 2003**
Terror in the Mind of God: The Global Rise of Religious
Violence. Ed. 3. Trade Paper. University of California Press.
Berkeley, CA. 2003. 320p. Comparative Studies in Religion and
Society, Vol. 13 ISBN:0-520-24011-1, ISBN13:
978-0-520-24011-7. Dewey:291.1/78331. LCCN:2003-008770.

Audience: **g,l,u,f.** *Choice, 2000.*

Martin, James A. Jr.   **BL65.A4M35 1990**
Beauty and Holiness: The Dialogue Between Aesthetics and
Religion. Trade Cloth. Princeton University Press. Princeton, NJ.
1990. 269p. ISBN:0-691-07357-0, ISBN13: 978-0-691-07357-6.
Dewey:200/.1. LCCN:89-012835.

Audience: **u,f.** *Choice, 1990.*

Formats: Web: ▢   Ebook: **e**   CD/DVD-ROM: ✍   BCL3: *B*

Sawyer, John F.　　　　　　　　**BL65.L2S25 1999**
Sacred Languages and Sacred Texts. Paper over Boards.
Routledge. New York, NY. 1999. 200p. Religion in the First
Christian Centuries Ser. ISBN:0-415-12546-4, ISBN13:
978-0-415-12546-8. Dewey:291.8/2. LCCN:98-054120.
　　　　　　　　　　　　　　　　Audience: **l,u,f.**

Sharot, Stephen　　　　　　　　　**BL60.S529 2001**
A Comparative Sociology of World Religions: Virtuosi, Priests,
and Popular Religion. Trade Cloth. New York University Press.
New York, NY. 2001. 352p. ISBN:0-8147-9804-7, ISBN13:
978-0-8147-9804-1. Dewey:306.6. LCCN:2001-000737.
　　　　　　　　　　　　　　　　Audience: **l,u,f.**

Simmel, Georg　　　　　　　　　　**BL60.S5477 1997**
Essays on Religion. Horst J. Helle (Editor, Translator), Ludwig
Nieder (Translator, Contribution by). Cloth over Boards. Yale
University Press. Cumberland, RI. 1997. 244p. Monograph Ser.,
Vol. 10 ISBN:0-300-06110-2, ISBN13: 978-0-300-06110-9.
Dewey:200. LCCN:95-051112.
　　　　　　　　　　　　　　　　Audience: **u,f.**

Smith, Anthony D.　　　　　　　　　　　　**JC311**
Chosen Peoples: Sacred Sources of National Identity. Trade
Cloth. Oxford University Press, Inc. New York, NY. 2004. 360p.
ISBN:0-19-210017-3, ISBN13: 978-0-19-210017-7.
Dewey:320.5/4. LCCN:2004-298484.
　　　　　　　　Audience: **g,l,u,f.** *Choice, 2004.*

Stark, Rodney　　　　　　　　　　**BL60.S677 2004**
Exploring the Religious Life. Trade Cloth. Johns Hopkins
University Press. Baltimore, MD. 2004. 232p.
ISBN:0-8018-7844-6, ISBN13: 978-0-8018-7844-2.
Dewey:306.6. LCCN:2003-010641.
　　　　　　　　　　　　　　　Audience: **g,l,u,f.**

Stark, Rodney & Finke,　　　　　　**BL60 .S675 2000**
　Roger
Acts of Faith: Explaining the Human Side of Religion. Trade
Cloth. University of California Press. Berkeley, CA. 2000. 343p.
ISBN:0-520-22201-6, ISBN13: 978-0-520-22201-4.
Dewey:306.6. LCCN:99-088220.
　　　　　　　　　　　　　　　Audience: **g,l,u,f.**

Temkin, Owsei　　　　　　　　　　　**BL65.M4**
Hippocrates in a World of Pagans and Christians. Trade Paper.
Johns Hopkins University Press. Baltimore, MD. 1975. 336p.
ISBN:0-8018-5129-7, ISBN13: 978-0-8018-5129-2.
Dewey:610/.9/015. LCCN:90-045564.
　　　　　　　　Audience: **u,f.** *Choice, 1992.*

Religions. Mythology. Rationalism >
Biography

Bowden, Henry W.　　　　　　　　　　　**BL72**
Dictionary of American Religious Biography. Ed. 2. Cloth Text.
Greenwood Publishing Group, Inc. Portsmouth, NH. 1993. 720p.
ISBN:0-313-27825-3, ISBN13: 978-0-313-27825-9.
Dewey:209/.2/2. LCCN:92-035524.
　　　　　　　　Audience: **g,l,u,f.** *Choice, 1993.*

Religions. Mythology. Rationalism >
Religions of the World

Brink, T. L. & Carmody,　　　　　　**BL80.3.C34 2006**
　Denise L.
Ways to the Center: An Introduction to World Religions. Ed. 6.
Paper Text. Thomson Wadsworth. Belmont, CA. 2005. 420p.
ISBN:0-534-52120-7, ISBN13: 978-0-534-52120-2. Dewey:291.
LCCN:2004-117062.
　　　　　　　　　　　　　　　Audience: **l.**

Corrigan, John, et al.　　　　　　　**BM561.R43 1998**
Readings in Judaism, Christianity and Islam. Martin S. Jaffee,
Frederick M. Denny & Carlos M. N. Eire (Authors). Trade
Paper. Prentice Hall PTR. Upper Saddle River, NJ. 1998. 376p.
ISBN:0-02-325098-4, ISBN13: 978-0-02-325098-9. Dewey:291.
LCCN:97-029976.
　　　　　　　　　　　　　　　Audience: **l,u.**

Partridge, Christopher　　　　　　　**BL80.3.I58 2005**
　(Editor)
Introduction to World Religions. Trade Cloth, CD-ROM.
Augsburg Fortress, Publishers. Minneapolis, MN. 2005. 496p.
ISBN:0-8006-3714-3, ISBN13: 978-0-8006-3714-9. Dewey:200.
LCCN:2006-615036.
　　　　　　　　Audience: **l,u.** *Choice, 2005.*

Smart, Ninian　　　　　　　　　　　　**BL80.2**
Atlas of the World's Religions. Trade Cloth. Oxford University
Press. Oxford, 2000. 240p. ISBN:0-19-866235-1, ISBN13:
978-0-19-866235-8. Dewey:291.
　　　　　　　　　　　　　　　Audience: **g,l,u,f.**

Religions. Mythology. Rationalism >
Natural Theology

Hartshorne, Charles　　　　　　　　**BL205.H37 1976**
The Divine Relativity: A Social Conception of God. Trade
Paper. Yale University Press. Cumberland, RI. 1982. 184p. Terry
Lectures ISBN:0-300-02880-6, ISBN13: 978-0-300-02880-5.
Dewey:211.2. LCCN:48-007802.
　　　　　　　　　　　　Audience: **g,l,u,f.** *B*

Hartshorne, Charles　　　　　　　　　**BL182 .H34**
A Natural Theology for Our Time. Trade Cloth. Open Court
Publishing Company. Chicago, IL. 1967. 145p.
ISBN:0-87548-238-4, ISBN13: 978-0-87548-238-5. Dewey:210.
LCCN:66-014722.
　　　　　　　　　　　　Audience: **u,f.** *B*

Mbiti, John Samuel　　　　　　　　　　**BT98 .M38**
Concepts of God in Africa. Trade Cloth. SPCK Publishing.
London, 1970. xv, 348p. ISBN:0-281-02434-0, ISBN13:
978-0-281-02434-6. Dewey:252.03. LCCN:75-487191.
　　　　　　　　　　　　　　　Audience: **u,f.**

Taliaferro, Charles   BD573.T35 2005
Evidence and Faith: Philosophy and Religion since the 17th
Century. Paul Guyer & Gary Hatfield (Contribution by). Trade
Cloth. Cambridge University Press. New York, NY. 2005. 470p.
The Evolution of Modern Philosophy Ser. ISBN:0-521-79027-1,
ISBN13: 978-0-521-79027-7. Dewey:210. LCCN:2004-054538.
Audience: **u,f.** *Choice, 2005.*

Religions. Mythology. Rationalism > Religion and the Sciences

Bowker, John   BC177
The Sacred Neuron: The Extraordinary New Discoveries
Linking Science and Religion. Cloth over Boards, Trade Cloth.
I. B. Tauris & Company, Ltd. London, 2005. 150p.
ISBN:1-85043-481-6, ISBN13: 978-1-85043-481-8.
Dewey:128.33. LCCN:2005-298945.
Audience: **u,f.** *Choice, 2005.*

Brown, Warren S. (Editor),   BT702.W43 1998
et al.
Whatever Happened to the Soul?: Scientific and Theological
Portraits of Human Nature. Nancey Murphy & H. Newton
Malony (Editors). Trade Paper. Augsburg Fortress, Publishers.
Minneapolis, MN. 1998. 272p. Theology and the Sciences Ser.
ISBN:0-8006-3141-2, ISBN13: 978-0-8006-3141-3.
Dewey:233/.5. LCCN:98-037943.
Audience: **u,f.**

1997 ed.
Clayton, Philip   BL240.2
God and Contemporary Science. Trade Cloth. Continuum
International Publishing Group, Ltd. London, 2005. 288p.
ISBN:0-567-04173-5, ISBN13: 978-0-567-04173-9.
Dewey:261.5/5.
Audience: **l,u,f.**

Crabbe, M. James C.   BD421.F76 1999
(Contribution by)
From Soul to Self. Paper over Boards. Routledge. New York,
NY. 1999. 176p. ISBN:0-415-17117-2, ISBN13:
978-0-415-17117-5. Dewey:128/.1. LCCN:98-041840.
Audience: **l,u,f.**

Grant, Edward   BL240
Science and Religion, 400 B. C. to A. D. 1550: From Aristotle
to Copernicus. Cloth Text. Greenwood Publishing Group, Inc.
Portsmouth, NH. 2004. 336p. Greenwood Guides to Science and
Religion Ser. ISBN:0-313-32858-7, ISBN13:
978-0-313-32858-9. Dewey:201/.65/09. LCCN:2004-017429.
Audience: **g,l,u.**

Gregersen, Niels Henrik   BD450
(Editor), et al.
The Human Person in Science and Theology. Willem B. Drees
& Ulf Gorman (Editors). Trade Paper. Continuum International
Publishing Group, Ltd. London, 2000. 240p.
ISBN:0-567-08692-5, ISBN13: 978-0-567-08692-1. Dewey:126.
Audience: **g,l,u,f.**

Jeeves, Malcolm (Editor)   BL240.3.F75 2004
From Cells to Souls and Beyond: Changing Portraits of Human
Nature. Trade Paper. William B. Eerdmans Publishing Company.
Grand Rapids, MI. 2004. 266p. ISBN:0-8028-0985-5, ISBN13:
978-0-8028-0985-8. Dewey:202/.2. LCCN:2004-040942.
Audience: **g,l,u,f.**

McGrath, Alister E.   BL240.2.M4 1998
Foundations of Dialogue in Science and Religion. Trade Cloth.
Blackwell Publishing, Inc. Malden, MA. 1998. 288p.
ISBN:0-631-20853-4, ISBN13: 978-0-631-20853-2.
Dewey:261.5/5. LCCN:98-009207.
Audience: **g,l,u,f.**

McGrath, Alister E.   BL240.2.M413 1999
Science and Christianity: An Introduction. Book, Other.
Blackwell Publishing, Inc. Malden, MA. 1998. 264p.
ISBN:0-631-20841-0, ISBN13: 978-0-631-20841-9. Dewey:215.
LCCN:98-023477.
Audience: **g,l,u.**

Polkinghorne, John   BL240.3.P64 2005
Exploring Reality: The Intertwining of Science and Religion.
Cloth over Boards. Yale University Press. Cumberland, RI.
2005. 208p. ISBN:0-300-11014-6, ISBN13: 978-0-300-11014-2.
Dewey:261.5/5. LCCN:2005-012580.
Audience: **g,u,f.**

Polkinghorne, John C.   BL241.P56 1998
Belief in God in an Age of Science. Cloth over Boards. Yale
University Press. Cumberland, RI. 1998. 150p. Terry Lectures
ISBN:0-300-07294-5, ISBN13: 978-0-300-07294-5.
Dewey:261.5/5. LCCN:97-030508.
Audience: **g,l,u,f.**

Waters, Brent &   QH442.2.G63 2003
Cole-Turner, Ronald (Editors)
God and the Embryo: Religious Voices on Stem Cells and
Cloning. Trade Paper. Georgetown University Press.
Washington, DC. 2003. 240p. ISBN:0-87840-998-X, ISBN13:
978-0-87840-998-3. Dewey:241/.64957. LCCN:2003-006470.
Audience: **u,f.** *Choice, 2004.*

Wilson, A. N.   BL245.W66 1999
God's Funeral: The Decline of Faith in Western Civilization.
Trade Cloth. W. W. Norton & Company, Inc. New York, NY.
1999. 512p. ISBN:0-393-04745-8, ISBN13: 978-0-393-04745-5.
Dewey:200/.94/034. LCCN:99-021306.
Audience: **l,u,f.**

Religions. Mythology. Rationalism > Myth. Comparative Mythology

Brunel, Pierre   PN56.M95D4813 1992
Companion to Literary Myths: Heroes and Archetypes. Trade
Cloth. Routledge. New York, NY. 1992. 864p.
ISBN:0-415-06460-0, ISBN13: 978-0-415-06460-6.
Dewey:809.93351. LCCN:92-028204.
Audience: **g,l,u,f.**

Campbell, Joseph   **BL312**

The Hero with a Thousand Faces. Ed. 2. Trade Paper. Princeton University Press. Princeton, NJ. 1972. 440p. Bollingen Ser., No. XVII ISBN:0-691-01784-0, ISBN13: 978-0-691-01784-6. Dewey:201/.3. LCCN:49-008590.

Audience: **g,l,u,f.**

Campbell, Joseph & Abadie,   **BL311**
M. J.

1974 ed. The Mythic Image. Trade Paper. Princeton University Press. Princeton, NJ. 1981. 564p. Princeton/Bollingen Paperbacks Ser., No. C ISBN:0-691-01839-1, ISBN13: 978-0-691-01839-3. Dewey:291.1/3. LCCN:79-166363.

Audience: **g,l,u,f.**

Coupe, Laurence   **BL304.C68 1997**

Myth. Paper over Boards. Routledge. New York, NY. 1998. 240p. The New Critical Idiom Ser. ISBN:0-415-13493-5, ISBN13: 978-0-415-13493-4. Dewey:291.1/3. LCCN:97-007292.

Audience: **l,u,f.**

Doty, William G.   **BL304.D58 2000**

Mythography: The Study of Myths and Rituals. Ed. 2. Trade Paper. University of Alabama Press. Tuscaloosa, AL. 2000. 552p. ISBN:0-8173-1006-1, ISBN13: 978-0-8173-1006-6. Dewey:291.1/3. LCCN:99-006781.

Audience: **l,u,f.** *Choice, 2000.*

Gimbutas, Marija   **GN803 .G55 1982B**

Goddesses and Gods of Old Europe, 7000 to 3500 B. C.: Myths, Legends, and Cult Images. Trade Paper. University of California Press. Berkeley, CA. 1982. 304p. ISBN:0-520-04655-2, ISBN13: 978-0-520-04655-9. Dewey:936.

Audience: **g,l,u,f.**

Leeming, David   **BL312.L44 2005**

The Oxford Companion to World Mythology. Trade Cloth. Oxford University Press, Inc. New York, NY. 2005. 507p. ISBN:0-19-515669-2, ISBN13: 978-0-19-515669-0. Dewey:201/.3. LCCN:2005-014216.

Audience: **g,l,u,f.**

Mercatante, Anthony S.   **BL303.M45 2003**

The Facts on File Encyclopedia of World Mythology and Legend. Ed. 2. James R. Dow (Revised by). Trade Cloth. Facts On File, Inc. New York, NY. 2004. 1120p. ISBN:0-8160-4708-1, ISBN13: 978-0-8160-4708-6. Dewey:291.1/3/03. LCCN:2003-040262.

Audience: **g,l,u.** *Choice, 2004, 1989.*

Sykes, Egerton   **BL303.S9 1993**

Who's Who in Non-Classical Mythology. Trade Paper. Oxford University Press, Inc. New York, NY. 1993. 256p. Who's Who Ser. ISBN:0-19-521032-8, ISBN13: 978-0-19-521032-3. Dewey:398.2/0922. LCCN:93-013818.

Audience: **l,u,f.**

Religions. Mythology. Rationalism > Religious Doctrines. Worship

Ahern, Emily M.   **BL467**

Cult of the Dead in a Chinese Village. Trade Cloth. Stanford University Press. Palo Alto, CA. 1973. 296p. ISBN:0-8047-0835-5, ISBN13: 978-0-8047-0835-7. Dewey:299/.5122/13. LCCN:72-097202.

Audience: **u,f.**

Albanese, Catherine L.   **BL2525.A4 1990**

Nature Religion in America: From the Algonkian Indians to the New Age. Martin E. Marty (Foreword by). Trade Cloth. University of Chicago Press. Chicago, IL. 1990. 284p. Chicago History of American Religion Ser. ISBN:0-226-01145-3, ISBN13: 978-0-226-01145-5. Dewey:291.2/12/0973. LCCN:89-039561.

Audience: **l,u,f.** *Choice, 1991.*

Andrews, Tamra   **BL435.A53 2000**

Dictionary of Nature Myths: Legends of the Earth, Sea, and Sky. Trade Paper. Oxford University Press, Inc. New York, NY. 2000. 304p. ISBN:0-19-513677-2, ISBN13: 978-0-19-513677-7. Dewey:291.2/12/03. LCCN:99-040342.

Audience: **g,l,u,f.**

Armstrong, Karen   **BL430.A76 2006**

The Great Transformation: The Beginning of Our Religious Traditions. Trade Cloth. Alfred A. Knopf Inc. New York, NY. 2006. 496p. ISBN:0-375-41317-0, ISBN13: 978-0-375-41317-9. Dewey:200.9/014. LCCN:2005-047536.

Audience: **g,l.**

Halbertal, Moshe &   **BL485.H34 1992**
Margalit, Avishai

Idolatry. Trade Cloth. Harvard University Press. Cambridge, MA. 1992. 312p. ISBN:0-674-44312-8, ISBN13: 978-0-674-44312-9. Dewey:291.218. LCCN:91-033312.

Audience: **g,u,f.**

Keller, Mary   **BL482.K45 2001**

The Hammer and the Flute: Women, Power, and Spirit Possession. Trade Cloth. Johns Hopkins University Press. Baltimore, MD. 2002. 304p. ISBN:0-8018-6787-8, ISBN13: 978-0-8018-6787-3. Dewey:291.4/2. LCCN:2001-002461.

Audience: **u,f.**

Kieckhefer, Richard &   **BL488.S32 1988**
Bond, George D. (Editors)

Sainthood: Its Manifestations in World Religions. Trade Cloth. University of California Press. Berkeley, CA. 1988. xii, 263p. ISBN:0-520-05154-8, ISBN13: 978-0-520-05154-6. Dewey:291.6/1. LCCN:88-006963.

Audience: **g,l,u,f.** *Choice, 1989.*

Melton, J. Gordon (Editor)   **BL2525.M449 1999**

1987 ed. The Encyclopedia of American Religions. Ed. 6. Trade Cloth.

Thomson Gale. Farmington Hills, MI. 1998. xxiv, 1243p.
ISBN:0-8103-8417-5, ISBN13: 978-0-8103-8417-0.
Dewey:200/.973. LCCN:00-702484.

Audience: **g,l,u,f.**

Religions. Mythology. Rationalism > Religious Doctrines. Worship > Woman: Comparative Religion

Atkinson, Clarissa W.   **BL458.I46 1985**
(Editor), et al.
Immaculate and Powerful: The Female in Sacred Image and
Social Reality. Constance H. Buchanan & Margaret R. Miles
(Editors). Trade Cloth. Beacon Press. Boston, MA. 1985. 272p.
Harvard Women's Studies in Religion Ser., Vol. 1
ISBN:0-8070-1004-9, ISBN13: 978-0-8070-1004-4.
Dewey:291.1/78344. LCCN:85-070448.

Audience: **u,f.** *Choice, 1986.*

Baring, Anne & Cashford,   **BL205**
Jules
The Myth of the Goddess: Evolution of an Image. Trade Cloth.
Penguin Group (USA) Inc. New York, NY. 1992. 800p.
ISBN:0-670-83564-1, ISBN13: 978-0-670-83564-5.
Dewey:291.211.

Audience: **u,f.** *Choice, 1992.*

Christ, Carol P.   **BL458.C47 1995**
1980 ed. Diving Deep and Surfacing: Women Writers on Spiritual Quest.
Ed. 3. Trade Paper. Beacon Press. Boston, MA. 1995. 208p.
ISBN:0-8070-6207-3, ISBN13: 978-0-8070-6207-4.
Dewey:291.4/082. LCCN:95-022312.

Audience: **g,l,u,f.**

Clément, Catherine &   **B2430.C634A42001**
Kristeva, Julia
The Feminine and the Sacred. Jane Marie Todd (Translator).
Trade Cloth. Columbia University Press. New York, NY. 2001.
224p. European Perspectives, :Social Thought and Cultural
Criticism Ser. ISBN:0-231-11578-4, ISBN13:
978-0-231-11578-0. Dewey:200/.82. LCCN:00-052307.

Audience: **u,f.**

Falk, Nancy Auer & Gross,   **BL458.U57 2001**
Rita M.
Unspoken Worlds: Women's Religious Lives. Ed. 3. Paper Text.
Thomson Wadsworth. Belmont, CA. 2000. 336p. Philosophy
Ser. ISBN:0-534-51570-3, ISBN13: 978-0-534-51570-6.
Dewey:200/.82. LCCN:00-033410.

Audience: **g,l,u,f.**

Franzmann, Majella   **BL458.F67 2000**
Women and Religion. Paper Text. Oxford University Press, Inc.
New York, NY. 1999. 204p. ISBN:0-19-510773-X, ISBN13:
978-0-19-510773-9. Dewey:200/.82. LCCN:99-026247.

Audience: **u,f.**

Gross, Rita M.   **BL458.G76 1996**
Feminism and Religion: An Introduction. Trade Paper. Beacon
Press. Boston, MA. 1996. 288p. ISBN:0-8070-6785-7, ISBN13:
978-0-8070-6785-7. Dewey:200/.82. LCCN:96-011472.

Audience: **g,l.**

Keller, Rosemary Skinner   **BL458.E52 2006**
(Editor), et al.
Encyclopedia of Women and Religion in North America.
Rosemary Radford Ruether & Marie Cantlon (Editors). Trade
Cloth. Indiana University Press. Bloomington, IN. 2006. 1296p.
ISBN:0-253-34685-1, ISBN13: 978-0-253-34685-8.
Dewey:200.82/0973. LCCN:2005-032429.

Audience: **g,l,u,f.**

King, Karen L. (Editor)   **BL458.W563 1997**
Women and Goddess Traditions: In Antiquity and Today. Trade
Paper. Continuum International Publishing Group, Ltd. London,
1998. 400p. Studies in Antiquity and Christianity
ISBN:0-8006-2919-1, ISBN13: 978-0-8006-2919-9.
Dewey:200/.82. LCCN:97-020399.

Audience: **g,l,u.**

Paper, Jordan   **BL458.P36 1997**
Through the Earth Darkly: Female Spirituality in Comparative
Perspective. Rita M. Gross (Foreword by), Catherine Keller
(Afterword by). Trade Paper. Continuum International
Publishing Group, Ltd. London, 1997. 320p.
ISBN:0-8264-1050-2, ISBN13: 978-0-8264-1050-4.
Dewey:200/.82. LCCN:97-023307.

Audience: **u,f.** *Choice, 1998.*

Plaskow, Judith   **BL625.7.W43 1989**
Weaving the Visions: New Patterns in Feminist Spirituality.
Carol P. Christ (Editor). Trade Paper. HarperCollins Publishers.
New York, NY. 1989. 368p. ISBN:0-06-061383-1, ISBN13:
978-0-06-061383-9. Dewey:291/.088042. LCCN:88-045697.

Audience: **g,l,u.**

Ruether, Rosemary Radford   **BL458**
1985 ed. Womanguides: Readings Toward a Feminist Theology. Ed. 2.
Trade Paper. Beacon Press. Boston, MA. 1996. 304p.
ISBN:0-8070-1235-1, ISBN13: 978-0-8070-1235-2.
Dewey:291.8/088042. LCCN:96-155352.

Audience: **u,f.** *Choice, 1985.*

Sered, Susan Starr   **BL458**
Priestess, Mother, Sacred Sister: Religions Dominated by
Women. Trade Paper. Oxford University Press, Inc. New York,
NY. 1996. 352p. ISBN:0-19-510467-6, ISBN13:
978-0-19-510467-7. Dewey:291/.082.

Audience: **u,f.**

Sharma, Arvind & Young,   **BL458.F455 1998**
Katherine K. (Editors)
Feminism and World Religions. Cloth Text. State University of
New York Press. Albany, NY. 1998. 352p. SUNY Series, McGill
Studies in the History of Religions ISBN:0-7914-4023-0,
ISBN13: 978-0-7914-4023-0. Dewey:2913.1/783442.
LCCN:98-010509.

Audience: **l,u,f.** *Choice, 1999.*

vols. 3-5

Sharma, Arvind (Editor)   **BL458.W5831987**
Women in World Religions. Katherine K. Young (Introduction by). Paper Text. State University of New York Press. Albany, NY. 1987. 302p. SUNY Series, McGill Studies in the History of Religions ISBN:0-88706-375-6, ISBN13: 978-0-88706-375-6. Dewey:291/.088042. LCCN:87-006475.

Audience: **l,u,f.**

Young, Katherine &   **BL458.H45 2004**
  Sharma, Arvind
Her Voice, Her Faith: Women Speak on World Religions. Trade Paper. Westview Press. Boulder, CO. 2004. 336p. ISBN:0-8133-4257-0, ISBN13: 978-0-8133-4257-3. Dewey:200/.82.

Audience: **l,u,f.** *Choice, 2003.*

Young, Serinity (Editor)   **BL458.E53 1999**
Encyclopedia of Women and World Religions, Set. Trade Cloth. Thomson Gale. Farmington Hills, MI. 1905. 1152p. ISBN:0-02-864608-8, ISBN13: 978-0-02-864608-4. Dewey:200.8/2. LCCN:98-039292.

Audience: **l,u,f.** *Choice, 1999.*

Religions. Mythology. Rationalism > Religious Doctrines. Worship > Gods. Demons

Frymer-Kensky, Tikva   **BL473.5.F78 1992**
In the Wake of the Goddesses: Women, Culture and the Biblical Transformation of Pagan Myth. Trade Cloth. Simon & Schuster. New York, NY. 1991. 250p. ISBN:0-02-910800-4, ISBN13: 978-0-02-910800-0. Dewey:220.92. LCCN:91-021860.

Audience: **g,l.**

Gimbutas, Marija   **BL473.5**
The Language of the Goddess. Ed. 2. Trade Paper. Thames & Hudson. New York, NY. 2001. 424p. ISBN:0-500-28249-8, ISBN13: 978-0-500-28249-6. Dewey:291.2114. LCCN:00-101120.

Audience: **u,f.**

Olson, Carl (Editor)   **BL473.5**
The Book of the Goddess Past and Present: An Introduction to Her Religion. Paper Text. Waveland Press, Inc. Prospect Heights, IL. 2002. 261p. ISBN:1-57766-273-3, ISBN13: 978-1-57766-273-0. Dewey:291.2.

Audience: **g,l.**

Russell, Jeffrey B.   **BL480**
The Devil: Perceptions of Evil from Antiquity to Primitive Christianity. Trade Paper. Cornell University Press. Ithaca, NY. 1987. 288p. ISBN:0-8014-9409-5, ISBN13: 978-0-8014-9409-3. Dewey:291.2/16. LCCN:77-003126.

Audience: **l,u,f.**

Russell, Jeffrey B.   **BT981**
Lucifer: The Devil in the Middle Ages. Trade Paper. Cornell University Press. Ithaca, NY. 1986. 356p. ISBN:0-8014-9429-X, ISBN13: 978-0-8014-9429-1. Dewey:235/.47. LCCN:84-045153.

Audience: **l,u,f.**

Russell, Jeffrey B.   **BT981.R865 1986**
Mephistopheles: The Devil in the Modern World. Book, Other. Cornell University Press. Ithaca, NY. 1986. 352p. ISBN:0-8014-1808-9, ISBN13: 978-0-8014-1808-2. Dewey:235/.4/0903. LCCN:86-047648.

Audience: **l,u,f.**

Religions. Mythology. Rationalism > Religious Doctrines. Worship > Eschatology

3 vols.

Collins, John J. (Editor)   **BL501.E531998**
The Encyclopedia of Apocalypticism: The Origins of Apocalypticism in Judaism and Christianity, Vol. 1. Cloth Text. Continuum International Publishing Group, Ltd. London, 1998. 500p. ISBN:0-8264-1071-5, ISBN13: 978-0-8264-1071-9. Dewey:291.2/3. LCCN:97-046016.

Audience: **g,l,u,f.**

Coward, Harold (Editor)   **BL535.L544 1997**
Life after Death in the World Religions. Trade Paper. Orbis Books. Maryknoll, NY. 1997. 125p. Faith Meets Faith Ser. ISBN:1-57075-119-6, ISBN13: 978-1-57075-119-6. Dewey:291.2/3. LCCN:96-051083.

Audience: **g,l,u,f.**

Kung, Hans   **BL535.K8613 1991**
Eternal Life?: Life after Death As a Medical, Philosophical, and Theological Problem. Trade Paper. Crossroad Publishing Company. New York, NY. 1991. 288p. ISBN:0-8245-1120-4, ISBN13: 978-0-8245-1120-3. Dewey:236/.2. LCCN:91-004091.

Audience: **g,l,u,f.**

McGinn, Bernard A.   **BL501**
  (Editor)
The Encyclopedia of Apocalypticism: Apocalypticism in Western History and Culture, Vol. 2. Trade Cloth. Continuum International Publishing Group, Ltd. London, 1998. 500p. The Encyclopedia of Apocalypticism Ser., Vol. 2 ISBN:0-8264-1072-3, ISBN13: 978-0-8264-1072-6. Dewey:291.2/3. LCCN:78-015807.

Audience: **g,l,u,f.**

Stein, Stephen J. (Editor)   **BL501**
The Encyclopedia of Apocalypticism: Apocalypticism in the Modern Period and the Contemporary Age, Vol. 3. Trade Cloth. Continuum International Publishing Group, Ltd. London, 1998. 500p. ISBN:0-8264-1073-1, ISBN13: 978-0-8264-1073-3. Dewey:291.2/3.

Audience: **g,l,u,f.**

Religions. Mythology. Rationalism > Religious Doctrines. Worship > Rites. Ceremonies

Bado-Fralick, Nikki   **BL615.B33 2005**
Coming to the Edge of the Circle: A Wiccan Initiation Ritual. Trade Cloth. Oxford University Press, Inc. New York, NY. 2005.

200p. An American Academy of Religion Book Ser.
ISBN:0-19-516645-0, ISBN13: 978-0-19-516645-3.
Dewey:299/.94. LCCN:2005-002176.

Audience: **l,u,f.**   *Choice, 2006.*

Bell, Catherine   **BL600.B46 1992**
Ritual Theory, Ritual Practice. Paper Text. Oxford University
Press, Inc. New York, NY. 1992. 288p. ISBN:0-19-507613-3,
ISBN13: 978-0-19-507613-4. Dewey:291.3/8. LCCN:91-016816.

Audience: **u,f.**

Burkert, Walter   **BL96**
Ancient Mystery Cults. Trade Paper. Harvard University Press.
Cambridge, MA. 1987. 192p. Carl Newell Jackson Lectures
ISBN:0-674-03387-6, ISBN13: 978-0-674-03387-0.
Dewey:291/.093.

Audience: **g,u,f.**   *Choice, 1988.*

Coakley, Sarah (Editor)   **BL604.B64 R44 1997**
Religion and the Body. John Clayton, Steven Collins, William
Graham & Nicholas de Lange (Contribution by). Cloth Text.
Cambridge University Press. New York, NY. 1997. 330p.
Cambridge Studies in Religious Traditions, No. 8
ISBN:0-521-36669-0, ISBN13: 978-0-521-36669-4.
Dewey:291.2/2. LCCN:96-006474.

Audience: **u,f.**

Coleman, Simon & Eade,   **BL619.P5**
John (Editors)
Reframing Pilgrimage: Cultures in Motion. Paper over Boards.
Routledge. New York, NY. 2004. 224p. European Association of
Social Anthropologists Ser. ISBN:0-415-30354-0, ISBN13:
978-0-415-30354-5. Dewey:203/.51. LCCN:2003-024747.

Audience: **u,f.**

Driver, Tom F.   **BL600**
The Magic of Ritual: Our Need for Liberating Rites That
Transform Our Lives and Our Communities. Trade Paper.
HarperCollins Publishers. New York, NY. 1992. 288p.
ISBN:0-06-061897-3, ISBN13: 978-0-06-061897-1.
Dewey:291.3/8. LCCN:91-055136.

Audience: **g,l.**   *Choice, 1992.*

Dubisch, Jill & Winkelman,   **BL619.P5P519 2005**
Michael
Pilgrimage and Healing. Saddle Stitched, Cloth over Boards,
Dust Jacket. University of Arizona Press. Tucson, AZ. 2005.
268p. ISBN:0-8165-2475-0, ISBN13: 978-0-8165-2475-4.
Dewey:203/.51. LCCN:2005-011397.

Audience: **g,l,u,f.**

Eliade, Mircea   **BL600**
Rites and Symbols of Initiation: The Mysteries of Birth and
Rebirth. Willard R. Trask (Translator), Michael Meade
(Foreword by). Trade Cloth. Spring Publications, Inc. Putnam,
CT. 1994. 175p. ISBN:0-88214-358-1, ISBN13:
978-0-88214-358-3. Dewey:291.38. LCCN:93-003049.

Audience: **g,l,u,f.**

Firth, Raymond   **BL600**
Symbols: Public and Private. Trade Paper. Cornell University

Press. Ithaca, NY. 1975. 469p. Symbol, Myth and Ritual Ser.
ISBN:0-8014-9150-9, ISBN13: 978-0-8014-9150-4.
Dewey:301.2/1. LCCN:72-011806.

Audience: **g,l,u,f.**

Grimes, Ronald L.   **BL600 .G745 2000**
Deeply into the Bone: Re-Inventing Rites of Passage. Trade
Cloth. University of California Press. Berkeley, CA. 2000. 396p.
Life Passages Ser., Vol. 1 ISBN:0-520-21533-8, ISBN13:
978-0-520-21533-7. Dewey:291.3/8. LCCN:99-053678.

Audience: **u,f.**

Muir, Edward   **BL600**
Ritual in Early Modern Europe. Ed. 2. William Beik, T. C. W.
Blanning & Brendan Simms (Contribution by). Cloth Text.
Cambridge University Press. New York, NY. 2005. 332p. New
Approaches to European History Ser. ISBN:0-521-84153-4,
ISBN13: 978-0-521-84153-5. Dewey:203/.8/094.
LCCN:2005-046998.

Audience: **u,f.**

Rappaport, Roy A.   **BL600 .R37 1999**
Ritual and Religion in the Making of Humanity. Keith Hart
(Foreword by), Meyer Fortes, Jack Goody, Edmund Leach &
Stanley Tambiah (Contribution by). Cloth Text. Cambridge
University Press. New York, NY. 1999. 562p. Studies in Social
and Cultural Anthropology, No. 110 ISBN:0-521-22873-5,
ISBN13: 978-0-521-22873-2. Dewey:291.38. LCCN:98-024494.

Audience: **l,u,f.**   *Choice, 1999.*

Religions. Mythology. Rationalism > Religious Life and Experience. Mysticism. Asceticism

Carmody, Denise L. &   **BL625.C33 1996**
Carmody, John T.
Mysticism: Holiness East and West. Paper Text. Oxford
University Press, Inc. New York, NY. 1996. 336p.
ISBN:0-19-508819-0, ISBN13: 978-0-19-508819-9.
Dewey:291.4/22. LCCN:95-014411.

Audience: **u,f.**

De Certeau, Michel   **BV5077.E85 C4713**
The Mystic Fable: The Sixteenth and Seventeenth Centuries,
Vol. 1. Michael B. Smith (Translator). Trade Paper. University
of Chicago Press. Chicago, IL. 1995. 384p. Religion and
Postmodernism Ser. ISBN:0-226-10037-5, ISBN13:
978-0-226-10037-1. Dewey:248.22094.

Audience: **u,f.**

Ellwood, Robert S.   **BL625.E44 1999**
Mysticism and Religion. Ed. 2. Paper Text. CQ Press.
Washington, DC. 1998. xiii, 201p. ISBN:1-889119-02-4,
ISBN13: 978-1-889119-02-1. Dewey:291.4/22.
LCCN:98-026078.

Audience: **l,u,f.**

Johnston, William M.   **BL631.E63 2000**
(Editor)
Encyclopedia of Monasticism, Set. Trade Cloth. Fitzroy
Dearborn Publishers, Inc. Chicago, IL. 2000. 1600p.
ISBN:1-57958-090-4, ISBN13: 978-1-57958-090-2.
Dewey:291.6/57/03. LCCN:00-712518.
           Audience: **g,l,u,f.** *Choice, 2001.*

Katz, Steven T. (Editor)   **BL625.M885 1992**
Mysticism and Language. Cloth Text. Oxford University Press,
Inc. New York, NY. 1992. 272p. ISBN:0-19-505455-5, ISBN13:
978-0-19-505455-2. Dewey:291.4/22/014. LCCN:91-031701.
           Audience: **u,f.**

Katz, Steven T.   **BL625 .M89 1978**
Mysticism and Philosophical Analysis. Paper Text. Oxford
University Press, Inc. New York, NY. 1978. 272p.
ISBN:0-19-520011-X, ISBN13: 978-0-19-520011-9.
Dewey:291.4/2. LCCN:78-005958.
           Audience: **u,f.** *B*

Katz, Steven T.   **BL625.M894 1983**
Mysticism and Religious Traditions. Trade Cloth. Oxford
University Press, Inc. New York, NY. 1983. 279p.
ISBN:0-19-503313-2, ISBN13: 978-0-19-503313-7.
Dewey:291.4/2. LCCN:82-022508.
           Audience: **u,f.** *B*

Katz, Steven T. (Editor)   **BL625.K37 2000**
Mysticism and Sacred Scripture. Trade Cloth. Oxford University
Press, Inc. New York, NY. 2000. 270p. ISBN:0-19-509703-3,
ISBN13: 978-0-19-509703-0. Dewey:291.4/22.
LCCN:99-028187.
           Audience: **u,f.** *Choice, 2001.*

Kraemer, Ross Shepard   **BL625.7**
Women's Religions in the Greco-Roman World: A Sourcebook.
Trade Cloth. Oxford University Press, Inc. New York, NY. 2004.
416p. ISBN:0-19-517065-2, ISBN13: 978-0-19-517065-8.
Dewey:200/.82/093. LCCN:2003-069777.
           Audience: **g,l,u,f.**

Suzuki, Daisetz Teitaro   **BL625.S85 2002**
Mysticism: Christian and Buddhist. Ed. 2. Trade Paper.
Routledge. New York, NY. 2002. 208p. Classics Ser.
ISBN:0-415-28586-0, ISBN13: 978-0-415-28586-5.
Dewey:291.4/22. LCCN:2002-067997.
           Audience: **g,l,u,f.**

Wimbush, Vincent L. &   **BL625**
   Valantasis, Richard (Editors)
Asceticism. Trade Paper. Oxford University Press, Inc. New
York, NY. 2002. 672p. ISBN:0-19-515138-0, ISBN13:
978-0-19-515138-1. Dewey:291.4/47.
           Audience: **u,f.** *Choice, 1996.*

Woods, Richard (Editor)   **BL625**
Understanding Mysticism. Trade Cloth. Continuum International
Publishing Group, Ltd. London, xi, 586p. ISBN:0-485-11219-1,
ISBN13: 978-0-485-11219-1. Dewey:149/.3.
           Audience: **u,f.** *B*

Religions. Mythology. Rationalism > History and Principles of Religion > European Religions

Dowden, Ken   **BL689**
European Paganism: Realities of Cult from Antiquity to Middle
Ages. Paper over Boards. Routledge. New York, NY. 1999.
392p. ISBN:0-415-12034-9, ISBN13: 978-0-415-12034-0.
Dewey:299/.094. LCCN:99-028007.
           Audience: **g,l,u.** *Choice, 2000.*

Gimbutas, Marija   **GN803**
The Civilization of the Goddess: The World of Old Europe.
Trade Paper. HarperCollins Publishers. New York, NY. 1997.
ISBN:0-06-251450-4, ISBN13: 978-0-06-251450-9. Dewey:936.
           Audience: **g,l.**

McLeod, Hugh   **BL695.M35 1997**
Religion and the People of Western Europe, 1789-1990. Ed. 2.
Paper Text. Oxford University Press, Inc. New York, NY. 1998.
196p. ISBN:0-19-289283-5, ISBN13: 978-0-19-289283-6.
Dewey:200/.94/0903. LCCN:97-012639.
           Audience: **l,u,f.**

Valantasis, Richard   **BL690.R46 2000**
Religions of Late Antiquity in Practice. Cloth Text. Princeton
University Press. Princeton, NJ. 2000. 527p. Princeton Readings
in Religions Ser. ISBN:0-691-05750-8, ISBN13:
978-0-691-05750-7. Dewey:200/.9/015. LCCN:99-049325.
           Audience: **l,u,f.** *Choice, 2001.*

Religions. Mythology. Rationalism > History and Principles of Religion > European Religions > Classical Religion and Mythology

Beard, Mary, et al.   **BL802 .B43 1998**
Religions of Rome: A History, Vol. 1. John North & Simon
Price (Authors). Cloth Text. Cambridge University Press. New
York, NY. 1998. 478p. ISBN:0-521-30401-6, ISBN13:
978-0-521-30401-6. Dewey:200/.937/6. LCCN:97-021302.
           Audience: **u,f.** *Choice, 1999.*

Beard, Mary, et al.   **BL802 .B43 1998**
Religions of Rome: A Sourcebook. John North & Simon Price
(Authors). Trade Paper. Cambridge University Press. New York,
NY. 1998. 430p. ISBN:0-521-45646-0, ISBN13:
978-0-521-45646-3. Dewey:200/.937/6. LCCN:97-021302.
           Audience: **u,f.**

Burkert, Walter   **BL96**
Ancient Mystery Cults. Trade Paper. Harvard University Press.
Cambridge, MA. 1987. 192p. Carl Newell Jackson Lectures
ISBN:0-674-03387-6, ISBN13: 978-0-674-03387-0.
Dewey:291/.093.
           Audience: **g,u,f.** *Choice, 1988.*

1985 ed **Burkert, Walter**   **BL782**
Greek Religion: Archaic and Classical. Trade Paper. Blackwell
Publishing, Inc. Malden, MA. 2002. 504p. ISBN:0-631-15624-0,
ISBN13: 978-0-631-15624-6. Dewey:292/.08.

Audience: **u,f.**

Burkert, Walter   **BL788.B8713**
Homo Necans: The Anthropology of Ancient Greek Sacrificial
Ritual and Myth. Peter Bing (Translator). Trade Cloth.
University of California Press. Berkeley, CA. 1986. 360p.
ISBN:0-520-05875-5, ISBN13: 978-0-520-05875-0.
Dewey:292/.38. LCCN:77-093473.

Audience: **u,f.**

Dowden   **BL820.J8D68 2005**
Zeus. Trade Cloth. Routledge. New York, NY. 2006. 192p.
ISBN:0-415-30502-0, ISBN13: 978-0-415-30502-0.
Dewey:292.2/113. LCCN:2005-009985.

Audience: **l,u,f.**

Dumézil, Georges & Eliade,   **BL802.D813 1996**
  Mircea
Archaic Roman Religion, Vol. 2. Philip Krapp (Translator).
Trade Paper. Johns Hopkins University Press. Baltimore, MD.
1996. 321p. ISBN:0-8018-5481-4, ISBN13: 978-0-8018-5481-1.
Dewey:292.07. LCCN:96-014884.

Audience: **u,f.**

Feeney, Denis (Author,   **PA6029.R4 F441998**
  Contribution by)
Literature and Religion at Rome: Cultures, Contexts, and
Beliefs. Stephen Hinds (Contribution by). Trade Cloth.
Cambridge University Press. New York, NY. 1998. 173p.
Roman Literature and Its Contexts Ser. ISBN:0-521-55104-8,
ISBN13: 978-0-521-55104-5. Dewey:870.9/382.
LCCN:97-006950.

Audience: **u,f.**

Gantz, Timothy   **BL782**
Early Greek Myth: A Guide to Literary and Artistic Sources.
Trade Paper. Johns Hopkins University Press. Baltimore, MD.
1996. 584p. ISBN:0-8018-5360-5, ISBN13: 978-0-8018-5360-9.
Dewey:292.1/3. LCCN:92-026010.

Audience: **g,u,f.** *Choice, 1994.*

Grant, Michael   **BL722.G7 1995**
Myths of the Greeks and Romans. Trade Paper. Penguin Group
(USA) Inc. New York, NY. 1995. 432p. ISBN:0-452-01162-0,
ISBN13: 978-0-452-01162-5. Dewey:292.1/3. LCCN:95-010012.

Audience: **g,l,u.**

1955 ed. **Guthrie, William K**   **BL782.G88 1985**
The Greeks and Their Gods. Beacon Press. 1971. Ariadne Ser.
ISBN:0-8070-5793-2, ISBN13: 978-0-8070-5793-3.

Audience: **g,l.**

Guthrie, William Keith   **BL820.O7**
  Chambers
Orpheus and Greek Religion: A Study of the Orphic Movement.
L. Alderlink (Editor). Trade Paper. Princeton University Press.

Princeton, NJ. 1993. 352p. Princeton Paperbacks Ser.
ISBN:0-691-02499-5, ISBN13: 978-0-691-02499-8.
Dewey:292.9. LCCN:92-041997.

Audience: **g,l,u,f.**

Harrison, Jane E.   **BL785**
Themis, a Study of the Social Origins of Greek Religion. Paper
Text. Textbook Publishers. Temecula, CA. 2003. xxxvi, 559p.
ISBN:0-7581-0221-6, ISBN13: 978-0-7581-0221-8. Dewey:292.

Audience: **u,f.**

1966 ed **Hesiod**   **PA4010**
Theogony and Works and Days. M. L. West (Editor). Trade
Paper. Oxford University Press, Inc. New York, NY. 1999. 106p.
Oxford World's Classics Ser. ISBN:0-19-283941-1, ISBN13:
978-0-19-283941-1. Dewey:881/.01.

Audience: **g,l,u.** *Choice, 1988.*

Jannot, Jean-Rene   **BL740.J3613 2005**
Religion in Ancient Etruria. Jane K. Whitehead (Translator).
Trade Cloth. University of Wisconsin Press. Chicago, IL. 2005.
252p. Wisconsin Studies in Classics ISBN:0-299-20840-0,
ISBN13: 978-0-299-20840-0. Dewey:299/.9294.
LCCN:2004-024545.

Audience: **u,f.** *Choice, 2006.*

Kerenyi, Carl   **BL781.K363**
The Gods of the Greeks. Trade Paper. Thames & Hudson. New
York, NY. 1980. 304p. ISBN:0-500-27048-1, ISBN13:
978-0-500-27048-6. Dewey:292/.08. LCCN:51-014117.

Audience: **g,l.**

Kerenyi, Carl   **BL820.T5**
The Heroes of the Greeks. Trade Paper. Thames & Hudson.
New York, NY. 1978. 440p. ISBN:0-500-27049-X, ISBN13:
978-0-500-27049-3. Dewey:398.2/2/0938. LCCN:77-099200.

Audience: **g,l.**

Kerenyi, Carl   **BL820.B2**
Dionysos: Archetypal Image of Indestructible Life. Ralph
Manheim (Translator). Trade Paper. Princeton University Press.
Princeton, NJ. 1996. 516p. Bollingen Ser. ISBN:0-691-02915-6,
ISBN13: 978-0-691-02915-3. Dewey:292.08.

Audience: **u,f.**

Kerényi, Karl & Holme,   **BL820.J88**
  Christopher
Zeus and Hera: Archetypal Image of Father, Husband, and Wife.
Trade Cloth. Routledge & Kegan Paul, Ltd. 1975. xvii, 211p.
ISBN:0-7100-7904-4, ISBN13: 978-0-7100-7904-6.
Dewey:292/.2/11.

Audience: **u,f.**

Larson, Jennifer   **BL820.N95L37 2001**
Greek Nymphs: Myth, Cult, Lore. Paper Text. Oxford
University Press, Inc. New York, NY. 2001. 392p.
ISBN:0-19-514465-1, ISBN13: 978-0-19-514465-9.
Dewey:292.2/114. LCCN:00-026246.

Audience: **u,f.**

Mikalson, Jon D.   BL783.M55 2004
Ancient Greek Religion. Trade Cloth. Blackwell Publishing, Inc.
Malden, MA. 2004. 240p. Blackwell Ancient Religions Ser.
ISBN:0-631-23222-2, ISBN13: 978-0-631-23222-3.
Dewey:292.08. LCCN:2003-021518.

Audience: **g,l,u,f.** *Choice, 2005.*

Newman, Harold &   BL785.N442003
Newman, Jon O. (Compiled by)
A Genealogical Chart of Greek Mythology. Trade Cloth.
University of North Carolina Press. Chapel Hill, NC. 2003.
252p. ISBN:0-8078-2790-8, ISBN13: 978-0-8078-2790-1.
Dewey:292.1/3. LCCN:2002-043574.

Audience: **g,l,u,f.** *Choice, 2003.*

O'Brien, Joan V.   PA4037
The Transformation of Hera: A Study of Ritual, Hero, and the
Goddess in the Iliad. Trade Cloth. Rowman & Littlefield
Publishers, Inc. Lanham, MD. 1993. 240p. Greek Studies,
:Interdisciplinary Approaches ISBN:0-8476-7807-5, ISBN13:
978-0-8476-7807-5. Dewey:883/.01. LCCN:92-037157.

Audience: **u,f.** *Choice, 1994.*

Otto, Walter F   BL820.B2
Dionysus: Myth and Cult. Ed. 2. Trade Cloth. Indiana
University Press. Bloomington, IN. 1995. 266p.
ISBN:0-253-34275-9, ISBN13: 978-0-253-34275-1.
Dewey:292.08. LCCN:65-011792.

Audience: **g,l,u,f.**

Price, Simon   BL782 .P73 1999
Religions of the Ancient Greeks. P. A. Cartledge & P. D. A.
Garnsey (Contribution by). Cloth Text. Cambridge University
Press. New York, NY. 1999. 230p. Key Themes in Ancient
History Ser. ISBN:0-521-38201-7, ISBN13: 978-0-521-38201-4.
Dewey:292.08. LCCN:98-039104.

Audience: **g,l,u.** *Choice, 2000.*

Price, Simon & Kearns,   BL723
Emily (Editors)
The Oxford Dictionary of Classical Myth and Religion. Trade
Cloth. Oxford University Press, Inc. New York, NY. 2003. 640p.
ISBN:0-19-280288-7, ISBN13: 978-0-19-280288-0.
Dewey:292/.003. LCCN:2004-298013.

Audience: **g,l,u,f.** *Choice, 2004.*

Rice, David G. &   BL782
Stambaugh, John E.
Sources for the Study of Greek Religion. Mass Market. Society
of Biblical Literature. Atlanta, GA. 1979. 292p. Resources for
Biblical Study Ser., No. 14 ISBN:0-89130-347-2, ISBN13:
978-0-89130-347-3. Dewey:292/.08. LCCN:79-018389.

Audience: **l,u,f.**

Roller, Lynn E.   BL820.C8 R65 1999
In Search of God the Mother: The Cult of Anatolian Cybele.
Trade Cloth. University of California Press. Berkeley, CA. 1999.
400p. ISBN:0-520-21024-7, ISBN13: 978-0-520-21024-0.
Dewey:291.2/114/093. LCCN:98-020627.

Audience: **u,f.**

Rose, H. J. & Hard, Robin   BL783.H37 2003
New Handbook of Greek Mythology. Ed. 7. Paper over Boards.
Routledge. New York, NY. 2003. 776p. ISBN:0-415-18636-6,
ISBN13: 978-0-415-18636-0. Dewey:292.1/3.
LCCN:2003-046672.

Audience: **g,l,u.**

Scheid, John   BL803.S3413 2003
An Introduction to Roman Religion. Janet Lloyd (Translator).
Trade Paper. Indiana University Press. Bloomington, IN. 2003.
240p. ISBN:0-253-21660-5, ISBN13: 978-0-253-21660-1.
Dewey:292.07. LCCN:2003-007470.

Audience: **g,l,u,f.** *Choice, 2004.*

Seznec, Jean   BR135
The Survival of the Pagan Gods: The Mythological Tradition
and Its Place in Renaissance Humanism and Art. Barbara F.
Sessions (Translator). Trade Paper. Princeton University Press.
Princeton, NJ. 1953. 396p. Mythos Ser. ISBN:0-691-02988-1,
ISBN13: 978-0-691-02988-7. Dewey:292.13.

Audience: **l,u,f.**

Turcan, Robert   BL805.T8713 1996
The Cults of the Roman Empire. Antonia Nevill (Translator).
Trade Cloth. Blackwell Publishing, Inc. Malden, MA. 1996.
416p. The Ancient World Ser. ISBN:0-631-20046-0, ISBN13:
978-0-631-20046-8. Dewey:292/.07. LCCN:96-007500.

Audience: **g,l,u,f.** *Choice, 1997.*

Veyne, Paul   BL782.V4713 1988
Did the Greeks Believe in Their Myths?: An Essay on the
Constitutive Imagination. Paula Wissing (Translator). Trade
Paper. University of Chicago Press. Chicago, IL. 1988. 169p.
ISBN:0-226-85434-5, ISBN13: 978-0-226-85434-2.
Dewey:292/.13. LCCN:87-025536.

Audience: **u,f.** *Choice, 1988.*

Willetts, R. F.   BL793.C7
Cretan Cults and Festivals. Trade Cloth. Greenwood Publishing
Group, Inc. Portsmouth, NH. 1980. 362p. ISBN:0-313-22050-6,
ISBN13: 978-0-313-22050-0. Dewey:292.3. LCCN:79-016739.

Audience: **g,l.**

Wiseman, T.P.   BL803
Myths of Rome. Trade Cloth. University of Exeter Press. Exeter,
2004. 480p. ISBN:0-85989-703-6, ISBN13: 978-0-85989-703-7.
Dewey:398.2'0937. LCCN:2005-274865.

Audience: **l,u,f.** *Choice, 2005.*

Religions. Mythology. Rationalism > History and Principles of Religion > European Religions > Germanic and Norse Mythology

Lindow, John   BL860.L56 2001
Handbook of Norse Mythology. Library Binding. ABC-CLIO,
Inc. Santa Barbara, CA. 2001. 365p. World Mythology Ser.

ISBN:1-57607-217-7, ISBN13: 978-1-57607-217-2.
Dewey:293/.13. LCCN:2001-001351.

Audience: **g,l,u,f.** *Choice, 2001.*

Sturluson, Snorri   **PT7313.E5**
Prose Edda: Tales from Norse Mythology. Jesse L. Byock
(Translator, Notes by). Trade Paper. Penguin Group (USA) Inc.
New York, NY. 2006. 220p. ISBN:0-14-044755-5, ISBN13:
978-0-14-044755-2. Dewey:839.61.

Audience: **g,l,u,f.**

Religions. Mythology. Rationalism > History and Principles of Religion > European Religions > Celtic Mythology. Druids

1965 ed. **Piggott, Stuart**   **BL900**
The Druids. Trade Paper. Thames & Hudson. New York, NY.
1985. 216p. Ancient Peoples and Places Ser.
ISBN:0-500-27363-4, ISBN13: 978-0-500-27363-0.
Dewey:299.1/6. LCCN:84-051870.

Audience: **g,l,u.**

Religions. Mythology. Rationalism > History and Principles of Religion > European Religions > Other

Dixon-Kennedy, Mike   **BL930.D58 1998**
Encyclopedia of Russian and Slavic Myth and Legend. Library
Binding. ABC-CLIO, Inc. Santa Barbara, CA. 1998. 392p.
ISBN:1-57607-063-8, ISBN13: 978-1-57607-063-5.
Dewey:398.2/0947. LCCN:98-020330.

Audience: **g,l,u,f.** *Choice, 1999.*

Warner, Elizabeth   **BL930.W37 2002**
Russian Myths. Trade Paper. University of Texas Press. Austin,
TX. 2002. 80p. Legendary Past Ser. ISBN:0-292-79158-5,
ISBN13: 978-0-292-79158-9. Dewey:299/.171.
LCCN:2002-102991.

Audience: **g,l.**

Religions. Mythology. Rationalism > History and Principles of Religion > Asian Religions

Lopez, Donald S. (Editor)   **BL1032.A85 1999**
Asian Religions in Practice: An Introduction. Trade Paper.
Princeton University Press. Princeton, NJ. 1999. 182p. Princeton
Readings in Religions Ser. ISBN:0-691-00513-3, ISBN13:
978-0-691-00513-3. Dewey:200/.95. LCCN:98-047112.

Audience: **g,l,u.**

Lopez, Donald S. (Editor)   **BL1015.R45 2002**
Religions of Asia in Practice: An Anthology. Trade Cloth.
Princeton University Press. Princeton, NJ. 2002. 760p. Princeton
Readings in Religions Ser. ISBN:0-691-09060-2, ISBN13:
978-0-691-09060-3. Dewey:200/.95. LCCN:2001-050015.

Audience: **g,l,u.**

Religions. Mythology. Rationalism > History and Principles of Religion > Asian Religions > Hinduism

BL1210.H49
✓Hinduism: New Essays in the History of Religions. Trade Cloth.
Brill Academic Publishers, Inc. Boston, MA. 1976. 231p.
ISBN:90-04-04495-7, ISBN13: 978-90-04-04495-1.
Dewey:294.5. LCCN:76-369439.

Audience: **u,f.** 𝓑

Acharya, Sabita   **BL1243.76.P87A24**
Pilgrimage in Indian Civilization. Trade Cloth. Manak
Publications Private, Ltd. Delhi, 1997. xv, 270p.
ISBN:81-86562-35-4, ISBN13: 978-81-86562-35-2.
Dewey:294.5351. LCCN:97-906047.

Audience: **l,u,f.**

other eds. **Anonymous**   **PK3633.B5 M35 1962**
The Bhagavad Gita. Juan Mascaro (Translator), Simon Brodbeck
(Introduction by). Trade Paper. Penguin Group (USA) Inc. New
York, NY. 2003. 160p. ISBN:0-14-044918-3, ISBN13:
978-0-14-044918-1. Dewey:294.592. LCCN:2003-267588.

Audience: **g,l,u,f.**

Aurobindo, Sri   **B133.G5**
The Life Divine. Ed. 5. Trade Cloth. Sri Aurobindo Ashram
Publication Department. Pondicherry, 1996. 1113p.
ISBN:81-7058-188-5, ISBN13: 978-81-7058-188-8.
Dewey:181.4. LCCN:89-063859.

Audience: **g,l,u,f.**

Avalon, Arthur   **BL1245.S4 W6 1978**
Shakti and Shakta. Trade Paper. Dover Publications, Inc.
Mineola, NY. 1978. 732p. ISBN:0-486-23645-5, ISBN13:
978-0-486-23645-2. Dewey:294.5/514. LCCN:77-093380.

Audience: **u,f.**

Babb, Lawrence A.   **BL1226.2**
The Divine Hierarchy: Popular Hinduism in Central India. Cloth
Text. Columbia University Press. New York, NY. 1975. 266p.
ISBN:0-231-03882-8, ISBN13: 978-0-231-03882-9.
Dewey:301.5/8/09543. LCCN:75-061693.

Audience: **l,u,f.** 𝓑

Banarsidass, Motilal   **F209**
Saivism in Philosophical Perspective: A Study of the Formative
Concepts, Problems and Methods of Saiva Siddhanta. Trade
Cloth. Motilal Banarsidass Publishers (Pvt. Ltd). New Delhi,
2001. xiv, v, 687p. Iia: Philosophy Ser., :Indian Ser.
ISBN:81-208-1771-0, ISBN13: 978-81-208-1771-5. Dewey:975.

Audience: **u,f.**

Bhardwaj, Surinder M.   **DS414**
Hindu Places of Pilgrimage in India: A Study in Cultural
Geography. Trade Cloth. University of California Press.
Berkeley, CA. 1973. xix, 258p. Center for South and Southeast
Asia Studies, UC Berkeley ISBN:0-520-02135-5, ISBN13:
978-0-520-02135-8. Dewey:301.5/8. LCCN:73-174454.

Audience: **u,f.** *B*

Bryant, Edwin & Ekstrand,   **BL1285.83.H37 2004**
Maria
The Hare Krishna Movement: The Postcharismatic Fate of a
Religious Transplant. Trade Cloth. Kegan Paul International,
Ltd. London, 2004. 496p. ISBN:0-231-12256-X, ISBN13:
978-0-231-12256-6. Dewey:294.5/512. LCCN:2003-055557.

Audience: **u,f.** *Choice, 2005.*

Chari, Srinivasa M.   **B132.A35**
Fundamentals of Vasistadvaita Vedanta: A Study Based on
Vedanta Desika's Tattva-Mukta-Kalapa. Trade Cloth. Motilal
Banarsidass Publishers (Pvt. Ltd). New Delhi, 1988.
ISBN:81-208-0266-7, ISBN13: 978-81-208-0266-7.
Dewey:181.483.

Audience: **u,f.**

Doniger, Wendy (Translator)   **BL1216**
Hindu Myths: A Sourcebook Translated from the Sanskrit. Trade
Paper. Penguin Group (USA) Inc. New York, NY. 1975. 368p.
Classics Ser. ISBN:0-14-044306-1, ISBN13: 978-0-14-044306-6.
Dewey:294.5/13. LCCN:75-323936.

Audience: **g,l,u,f.**

Eck, Diana L.   **BL1153.7.V36E24 1999**
Banaras: City of Light. Trade Paper. Columbia University Press.
New York, NY. 1999. 448p. ISBN:0-231-11447-8, ISBN13:
978-0-231-11447-9. Dewey:294.5/44/09542. LCCN:99-011349.

Audience: **g,l,u,f.** *B*

Eck, Diana L.   **BL1205.E25 1998**
Darsan: Seeing the Divine Image in India. Ed. 3. Trade Paper.
Columbia University Press. New York, NY. 1998. 97p.
Translations from the Asian Classics Ser. ISBN:0-231-11265-3,
ISBN13: 978-0-231-11265-9. Dewey:294.5/37.
LCCN:99-192162.

Audience: **u,f.**

1966 ed. **Embree, Ainslie T.**   **BL1145.5 .E5**
The Hindu Tradition: Readings in Oriental Thought. William
Theodore De Bary (Editor). Trade Paper. Knopf Publishing
Group. New York, NY. 1972. 384p. ISBN:0-394-71702-3,
ISBN13: 978-0-394-71702-9. Dewey:294.508.

Audience: **g,l.**

Feldhaus, Anne (Editor)   **BL1175.G775.D44 1984**
The Deeds of God in Rddhipur. Trade Cloth. Oxford University
Press, Inc. New York, NY. 1984. 222p. ISBN:0-19-503438-4,
ISBN13: 978-0-19-503438-7. Dewey:294.5/95.
LCCN:83-021949.

Audience: **u,f.** *B*

Feldhaus, Anne   **BL1215.R5F45 1995**
Water and Womanhood: Religious Meanings of Rivers in
Maharashtra. Cloth Text. Oxford University Press, Inc. New
York, NY. 1995. 288p. ISBN:0-19-509122-1, ISBN13:
978-0-19-509122-9. Dewey:294.5/212. LCCN:94-036158.

Audience: **u,f.**

Flood, Gavin   **BL1202.F56 1996**
An Introduction to Hinduism. Cloth Text. Cambridge University
Press. New York, NY. 1996. 359p. Introduction to Religion Ser.
ISBN:0-521-43304-5, ISBN13: 978-0-521-43304-4.
Dewey:294.5. LCCN:95-042755.

Audience: **g,l,u,f.** *Choice, 1997.*

Flood, Gavin   **BL1283.84**
The Tantric Body: The Secret Tradition of Hindu Religion.
Trade Paper. I. B. Tauris & Company, Ltd. London, 2005. 250p.
ISBN:1-84511-012-9, ISBN13: 978-1-84511-012-3.
Dewey:294.5/514. LCCN:2006-295549.

Audience: **u,f.**

Fuller, C. J.   **BL1150.F85 2004**
The Camphor Flame: Popular Hinduism and Society in India.
Trade Paper. Princeton University Press. Princeton, NJ. 2004.
360p. ISBN:0-691-12048-X, ISBN13: 978-0-691-12048-5.
Dewey:294.5/0954. LCCN:2004-044776.

Audience: **u,f.** *Choice, 1992.*

Fuller, C. J.   **BL1241.44.F83 2003**
The Renewal of the Priesthood: Modernity and Traditionalism in
a South Indian Temple. Trade Cloth. Princeton University Press.
Princeton, NJ. 2003. 224p. ISBN:0-691-11657-1, ISBN13:
978-0-691-11657-0. Dewey:294.5/61/095482.
LCCN:2003-040491.

Audience: **g,u,f.**

Goldman, R. P. & Goldman,   **PK4474**
S. S. (Translators)
The Ramayana of Valmiki: Sundarakanda. Trade Cloth.
Princeton University Press. Princeton, NJ. 1996. 576p. Princeton
Library of Asian Translations ISBN:0-691-06662-0, ISBN13:
978-0-691-06662-2. Dewey:294.5922. LCCN:96-037044.

Audience: **u,f.**

Goldman, Robert P. (Editor)   **PK4474**
The Ramayana of Valmiki: An Epic of Ancient India:
Kiskindhakanda. Rosalind Lefeber (Translator). Trade Cloth.
Princeton University Press. Princeton, NJ. 1994. 414p. Library
of Asian Translations ISBN:0-691-06661-2, ISBN13:
978-0-691-06661-5. Dewey:294.5/922. LCCN:93-037044.

Audience: **u,f.**

Goldman, Robert P. (Editor)   **PG3415.R4G87 1986**
1988 ed. The Ramayana of Valmiki: An Epic of Ancient India. Sheldon I.
Pollock (Translator). Cloth Text. Princeton University Press.
Princeton, NJ. 1986. 525p. Library of Asian Translations
ISBN:0-691-06654-X, ISBN13: 978-0-691-06654-7.
Dewey:891.73/3. LCCN:85-061364.

Audience: **u,f.** *Choice, 1987.*

Goldman, Robert P. (Editor)   BL1139.22.E54 1990
The Ramayana of Valmiki: An Epic of Ancient India, Aranyakanda. Sheldon I. Pollock (Introduction by). Cloth Text. Princeton University Press. Princeton, NJ. 1991. 448p. ISBN:0-691-06660-4, ISBN13: 978-0-691-06660-8. Dewey:294.5/922. LCCN:90-008510.

Audience: **u,f.**

Goldman, Robert P.   BL1139.22.E54 1984
   (Translator)
The Ramayana of Valmiki Balakanda. Sally Sutherland (Annotations by). Cloth Text. Princeton University Press. Princeton, NJ. 1985. 450p. Ramayana of Valmiki Balakanda Ser., Vol. I ISBN:0-691-06561-6, ISBN13: 978-0-691-06561-8. Dewey:294.5/922. LCCN:82-061364.

Audience: **u,f.**   ℬ   *Choice, 1985.*

Gonda, Jan   BL1220.G6
Aspects of Early Visnuism. Trade Paper. Books on Demand. Ann Arbor, MI. 280p. ISBN:0-598-83866-X, ISBN13: 978-0-598-83866-7. Dewey:294. LCCN:55-017775.

Audience: **u,f.**

Goudriaan,Teun   BL114.56
Hindu Tantric and Sakta Literature. Gupta, Sanjukta. O. Harrassowitz. 1981. A History of Indian literature; v. 2, fasc. 2 ISBN:3-447-02091-1, ISBN13: 978-3-447-02091-6.

Audience: **u,f.**

Haberman, David L.   BL1239.5.A25H33 1988
Acting as a Way of Salvation: A Study of Raganuga Bhakti Sadhana. Trade Cloth. Oxford University Press, Inc. New York, NY. 1988. 232p. ISBN:0-19-505321-4, ISBN13: 978-0-19-505321-0. Dewey:294.5/22. LCCN:87-033960.

Audience: **u,f.** *Choice, 1989.*

Harper, Katherine Anne &   BL1283.83.R66 2002
   Brown, Robert L. (Editors)
The Roots of Tantra. Cloth Text. State University of New York Press. Albany, NY. 2002. 288p. SUNY Series in Tantric Studies ISBN:0-7914-5305-7, ISBN13: 978-0-7914-5305-6. Dewey:294.5/514. LCCN:2001-054184.

Audience: **u,f.**

Hawley, John Stratton &   BL1225.R24.D58 1982
   Wulff, Donna Marie (Editors)
The Divine Consort: R-adh-a and the Goddesses of India. Trade Cloth. Jain Publishing Company, Inc. Fremont, CA. 1982. "xviii, 414"p. ISBN:0-89581-102-2, ISBN13: 978-0-89581-102-8. Dewey:294.5/211 19. LCCN:81-018128.

Audience: **u,f.** ℬ

Hopkins, E. Washburn   BL1130 .H6
Epic Mythology. Trade Cloth. Biblo & Tannen Booksellers & Publishers, Inc. Cheshire, CT. 1968. ISBN:0-8196-0228-0, ISBN13: 978-0-8196-0228-2. Dewey:294.5/922. LCCN:76-075358.

Audience: **g,l,u.**

Jones, Kenneth W.   BL1254.5.P86
Arya Dharm: Hindu Consciousness in Nineteenth-Century

Punjab. Trade Cloth. University of California Press. Berkeley, CA. 1976. 350p. ISBN:0-520-02919-4, ISBN13: 978-0-520-02919-4. Dewey:306/.6. LCCN:74-027290.

Audience: **u,f.**

Jordans   BL1255.D3.J67
Dayananda Sarasvati: His Life and Ideas. Trade Cloth. Oxford University Press, Inc. New York, NY. 1979. 386p. ISBN:0-19-560995-6, ISBN13: 978-0-19-560995-0. Dewey:294.5/6/4. LCCN:79-111204.

Audience: **u,f.** ℬ

Keith, A. B. (Editor)   BL1150.K43
1970 ed. The Religion and Philosophy of the Veda and Upanishads, Set. Trade Cloth. Motilal Banarsidass Publishers (Pvt. Ltd). New Delhi, 1998. xviii, 683p. Hinduism and Its Sources Ser., :Vedic Literature-Tradition and Mythology, Social and Religious Laws, Texts, Translations and Studies ISBN:81-208-0644-1, ISBN13: 978-81-208-0644-3. Dewey:294.5.

Audience: **u,f.**

Kinsley, David   BL1220.K538
Divine Player: A Study of Krsna Lila. Trade Paper. Motilal Banarsidass Publishers (Pvt. Ltd). New Delhi, 1999. 318p. ISBN:81-208-1313-8, ISBN13: 978-81-208-1313-7. Dewey:294.5/211.

Audience: **u,f.**

Kinsley, David   BL1261.2 .K56
Hindu Goddesses: Vision of the Divine Feminine in the Hindu Religious Tradition. Trade Cloth. Motilal Banarsidass Publishers (Pvt. Ltd). New Delhi, 1999. 289p. ISBN:81-208-0379-5, ISBN13: 978-81-208-0379-4. Dewey:294.52114.

Audience: **u,f.**

Kinsley, David R.   BL1202.K48 1993
Hinduism: A Cultural Perspective. Ed. 2. Trade Paper. Prentice Hall PTR. Upper Saddle River, NJ. 1993. 208p. ISBN:0-13-395732-2, ISBN13: 978-0-13-395732-7. Dewey:294.5. LCCN:92-031484.

Audience: **l,u.**

Kinsley, David R.   BL1220
Sword and the Flute; Kali and Krsna: Dark Visions of the Terrible and Sublime in Hindu Mythology. Trade Paper. University of California Press. Berkeley, CA. 2000. 178p. Hermeneutics, Studies in the History of Religions, Vol. 4 ISBN:0-520-22476-0, ISBN13: 978-0-520-22476-6. Dewey:294.52112. LCCN:73-091669.

Audience: **u,f.**

Klostermaier, Klaus K.   BL1105.K56 1998
A Concise Encyclopedia of Hinduism. Trade Paper. Oneworld Publications. Oxford, 1998. 288p. Concise Encyclopedia of World Faiths Ser. ISBN:1-85168-175-2, ISBN13: 978-1-85168-175-4. Dewey:294.5/03. LCCN:96-053522.

Audience: **g,l,u,f.**

Klostermaier, Klaus K.   BL1111.32.E5
Hindu Writings: A Short Introduction to the Major Sources. Trade Cloth. Oneworld Publications. Oxford, 2000. 208p. From

Buddhism to Sufism Ser., :Concise Introductions Ser.
ISBN:1-85168-230-9, ISBN13: 978-1-85168-230-0.
Dewey:294.5/92.

Audience: **g,l,u,f.**

Klostermaier, Klaus K.   **BL1202.K56 1994**
A Survey of Hinduism. Ed. 2. Trade Paper. State University of
New York Press. Albany, NY. 1994. 715p. ISBN:0-7914-2110-4,
ISBN13: 978-0-7914-2110-9. Dewey:294.5. LCCN:93-046778.

Audience: **g,l,u,f.** *Choice, 1995, 1989.*

Knott, Kim   **BL1202.K564 2000**
Hinduism: A Very Short Introduction. Trade Paper. Oxford
University Press, Inc. New York, NY. 1998. 160p. Very Short
Introductions Ser. ISBN:0-19-285341-4, ISBN13:
978-0-19-285341-7. Dewey:294.5. LCCN:98-010944.

Audience: **g,l,u.**

Lorenzen, David N.   **BL1245.S5 L67**
The Kapalikas and Kalamukhas: Two Lost Saivite Sects. Ed. 2.
Trade Paper. Motilal Banarsidass Publishers (Pvt. Ltd). New
Delhi, 1999. 256p. ISBN:81-208-0708-1, ISBN13:
978-81-208-0708-2. Dewey:294.5/513.

Audience: **u,f.**

Madan, T. N., et al.   **BL1202**
The Hinduism Omnibus. Madeleine Biardeau, Nirad C.
Chaudhuri & J. L. Brockington (Authors), T. N. Madan (Editor).
Trade Cloth. Oxford University Press, Inc. New York, NY. 2003.
948p. ISBN:0-19-566411-6, ISBN13: 978-0-19-566411-9.
Dewey:294.5. LCCN:2003-307507.

Audience: **g,l,u,f.**

Mani, Vettam   **BL1135.P88.M3613**
Puranic Encyclopaedia. Trade Cloth. Orient Book Distributors.
Livingston, NJ. 1979. viii, 922p. ISBN:0-8426-0822-2, ISBN13:
978-0-8426-0822-0. Dewey:294.5/92. LCCN:76-900024.

Audience: **g,l,u,f.**

Miller, David M. & Wertz,   **BL1175.A183**
  Dorothy C.
Hindu Monastic Life: The Monks and Monasteries of
Bhubaneswar. Ed. 2. Trade Cloth. Manohar Publications. New
Delhi, 1996. 262p. ISBN:81-7304-156-3, ISBN13:
978-81-7304-156-3. Dewey:294.5/6/5.

Audience: **u,f.** *B*

Muller, F. Max   **BL1010**
The Satapatha Brahmana. Library Binding. Taylor & Francis
Group. Philadelphia, PA. 2001. ISBN:0-7007-1534-7, ISBN13:
978-0-7007-1534-3. Dewey:294.538.

Audience: **u,f.**

Muller, F. Max (Editor)   **BL1115**
The Vedanta Sutras: The Sacred Books of the East Part
Thirty-Four. George Thibaut (Translator). Trade Paper. Kessinger
Publishing, LLC. Whitefish, MT. 2004. ISBN:1-4179-3030-6,
ISBN13: 978-1-4179-3030-2. Dewey:294.1.

Audience: **u,f.**

Muller, F. Max   **BL1115**
The Vedanta Sutras: The Sacred Books of the East Part
Thirty-Eight. George Thibaut (Translator). Trade Paper.
Kessinger Publishing, LLC. Whitefish, MT. 2004.
ISBN:1-4179-3033-0, ISBN13: 978-1-4179-3033-3.
Dewey:294.1.

Audience: **u,f.**

O'Flaherty, Wendy Doniger   **BL1218 .O34**
Asceticism and Eroticism in the Mythology of Siva. Trade
Cloth. Oxford University Press. Oxford, 1973. xiv, 386p.
ISBN:0-19-713573-0, ISBN13: 978-0-19-713573-0.
Dewey:294.5/2/11. LCCN:73-180569.

Audience: **u,f.** *B*

Olivelle, Patrick   **BL1228**
The Asrama System: The History and Hermeneutics of a
Religious Institution. Trade Cloth. Oxford University Press, Inc.
New York, NY. 1993. 288p. ISBN:0-19-508327-X, ISBN13:
978-0-19-508327-9. Dewey:294.5/44. LCCN:92-038998.

Audience: **u,f.**

Olivelle, Patrick (Editor)   **KNS125.D5313 1999**
Dharmasutras: The Law Codes of Ancient India. Trade Paper.
Oxford University Press, Inc. New York, NY. 1999. 480p.
Oxford World's Classics Ser. ISBN:0-19-283882-2, ISBN13:
978-0-19-283882-7. Dewey:294.5.

Audience: **u,f.**

Olivelle, Patrick   **KN5126**
  (Translator)
Law Lib. The Law Code of Manu. Trade Paper. Oxford University Press,
Inc. New York, NY. 2004. 366p. Oxford World's Classics Ser.
ISBN:0-19-280271-2, ISBN13: 978-0-19-280271-2.
Dewey:340.5/34. LCCN:2004-271886.

Audience: **u,f.**

Olivelle, Patrick   **BL1124.52.E5 1996**
  (Translator)
Upanisads. Trade Paper. Oxford University Press, Inc. New
York, NY. 1996. 510p. Oxford World's Classics Ser.
ISBN:0-19-282292-6, ISBN13: 978-0-19-282292-5.
Dewey:294.5/9218. LCCN:95-031976.

Audience: **u,f.**

Shulman, David D.   **BL1245.S5**
Tamil Temple Myths: Sacrifice and Divine Marriage in the
South Indian Saiva Tradition. Trade Cloth. Princeton University
Press. Princeton, NJ. 1980. 448p. ISBN:0-691-06415-6, ISBN13:
978-0-691-06415-4. Dewey:294.5/513. LCCN:79-017051.

Audience: **u,f.** *B*

Sullivan, Bruce M.   **BL1105.S85 1997**
Historical Dictionary of Hinduism. Trade Cloth. Scarecrow
Press, Inc. Lanham, MD. 1997. 368p. Religions, Philosophies,
and Movements Ser., Vol. 13 ISBN:0-8108-3327-1, ISBN13:
978-0-8108-3327-2. Dewey:294.5/03. LCCN:97-011325.

Audience: **g,l,u,f.** *Choice, 1998.*

Van Buitenen, J. A. &   **BL1135**
  Dimmet, Cornelia (Editors)
Classical Hindu Mythology: A Reader in the Sanskrit Puranas. J.

A. Van Buitenen & Cornelia Dimmet (Translators). Trade Cloth. Sri Satguru Publications. New Delhi, 1998. ISBN:81-7030-596-9, ISBN13: 978-81-7030-596-5. Dewey:294.5925.

Audience: **l,u,f.**

Waghorne, Joanne P., et al.   **BL1216.2.G63 1996**
Gods of Flesh/Gods of Stone: The Embodiment of Divinity in India. Norman Cutler & Vasudha Narayanan (Authors). Trade Paper. Columbia University Press. New York, NY. 1985. 208p. ISBN:0-231-10777-3, ISBN13: 978-0-231-10777-8. Dewey:294.5/211. LCCN:96-028517.

Audience: **u,f.** *B Choice, 1985.*

Woodroffe, John   **BL1245.S4 W618**
The World as Power. M. P. Pandit (Preface by). Trade Cloth. Auromere, Inc. Lodi, CA. 1981. ISBN:0-89744-119-2, ISBN13: 978-0-89744-119-3. Dewey:294.5/514.

Audience: **u,f.**

Wyatt, Thomas   **BL1112.54**
The Rig Veda: An Anthology of One Hundred Eight Hymns. Wendy Doniger O'Flaherty (Editor, Translator). Trade Paper. Penguin Group (USA) Inc. New York, NY. 1982. 352p. Classics Ser. ISBN:0-14-044402-5, ISBN13: 978-0-14-044402-5. Dewey:294.5/9212. LCCN:82-198997.

Audience: **g,l,u,f.**

Religions. Mythology. Rationalism > History and Principles of Religion > Asian Religions > Jainism

Cort, John E. (Editor)   **BL1320.O54 1998**
Open Boundaries: Jain Communities and Cultures in Indian History. Cloth Text. State University of New York Press. Albany, NY. 1998. 278p. SUNY Series in Hindu Studies ISBN:0-7914-3785-X, ISBN13: 978-0-7914-3785-8. Dewey:294.4. LCCN:97-046027.

Audience: **u,f.**

Dundas, Paul   **BL1351.3.D86 2002**
The Jains. Ed. 2. Trade Paper. Routledge. New York, NY. 2002. 368p. Library of Religious Beliefs and Practices ISBN:0-415-26606-8, ISBN13: 978-0-415-26606-2. Dewey:294.4. LCCN:2002-074329.

Audience: **g,u,f.** *Choice, 1993.*

Max-Muller, F. (Editor)   **BL1310.32.E5**
Jaina Sutras, Pt. 2. Hermann Jacobi (Translator). Trade Cloth. Motilal Banarsidass Publishers (Pvt. Ltd). New Delhi, 1989. 456p. ISBN:81-208-0146-6, ISBN13: 978-81-208-0146-2. Dewey:294.4.

Audience: **u,f.**

Oldenberg, H.   **BL1310.32.E5**
Jaina Sutras, Pt. 1. F.M. Muller & F. Max-Muller (Editors), Hermann Jacobi (Translator). Trade Cloth. Motilal Banarsidass

Publishers (Pvt. Ltd). New Delhi, 1989. 324p. ISBN:81-208-0123-7, ISBN13: 978-81-208-0123-3. Dewey:294.4.

Audience: **u,f.**

Religions. Mythology. Rationalism > History and Principles of Religion > Asian Religions > Zoroastrianism. Mithraism

Boyce, Mary   **BL1525**
Zoroastrians: Their Religious Beliefs and Practices. Ed. 2. Paper over Boards. Routledge. New York, NY. 2001. 280p. Library of Religious Beliefs and Practices ISBN:0-415-23902-8, ISBN13: 978-0-415-23902-8. Dewey:295/.09.

Audience: **u,f.**

Boyce, Mary (Editor,   **BL1571.T44 1990**
   Translator)
Textual Sources for the Study of Zoroastrianism. Trade Paper. University of Chicago Press. Chicago, IL. 1990. 176p. Textual Sources for the Study of Religion Ser. ISBN:0-226-06930-3, ISBN13: 978-0-226-06930-2. Dewey:295. LCCN:90-044072.

Audience: **u,f.**

Clark, Peter   **BL1571.C53 1998**
Zoroastrianism: An Introduction to Ancient Faith. Trade Paper. Sussex Academic Press. Eastbourne, 1998. 204p. ISBN:1-898723-78-8, ISBN13: 978-1-898723-78-3. Dewey:295. LCCN:98-027763.

Audience: **l,u.** *Choice, 1999.*

M, Clauss   **BL1585**
Roman Cult of Mithras: The God and His Mysteries. Paper over Boards. Routledge. New York, NY. 2001. 256p. ISBN:0-415-92977-6, ISBN13: 978-0-415-92977-6. Dewey:299.15.

Audience: **g,l,u.**

Religions. Mythology. Rationalism > History and Principles of Religion > Asian Religions > Semitic Religions

Bottero, Jean   **BL2350**
Religion in Ancient Mesopotamia. Teresa Lavender Fagan (Translator). Trade Paper. University of Chicago Press. Chicago, IL. 2004. 260p. ISBN:0-226-06718-1, ISBN13: 978-0-226-06718-6. Dewey:299/.21. LCCN:00-011052.

Audience: **u,f.** *Choice, 2002.*

Dalley, Stephanie (Editor)   **BL1620.M98 1989**
Myths from Mesopotamia: Creation, the Flood, Gilgamesh, and Others. Trade Cloth. Oxford University Press, Inc. New York, NY. 1989. 360p. ISBN:0-19-814397-4, ISBN13: 978-0-19-814397-0. Dewey:299/.21. LCCN:89-003108.

Audience: **u,f.** *Choice, 1990.*

Foster, Benjamin R.   **PJ3771.G5E5 2001**
The Epic of Gilgamesh. Trade Cloth. W. W. Norton &
Company, Inc. New York, NY. 2001. 252p. Critical Editions Ser.
ISBN:0-393-97516-9, ISBN13: 978-0-393-97516-1.
Dewey:892/.1. LCCN:00-038035.
             Audience: **g,l,u.**

Makarim, Sami N.   **BL1695 .M33**
Druze Faith. Trade Cloth. Caravan Books. Carefree, AZ. 1974.
168p. ISBN:0-88206-003-1, ISBN13: 978-0-88206-003-3.
Dewey:297/.85/09. LCCN:73019819.
             Audience: **u,f.** *B*

Roberts, Jimmy Jack   **BL1605.G/**
The Earliest Semitic Pantheon: A Study of the Semitic Deities
Attested in Mesopotamia Before Ur III. Trade Cloth. Johns
Hopkins University Press. Baltimore, MD. 1962. 192p. The
Johns Hopkins near Eastern Studies ISBN:0-8018-1388-3,
ISBN13: 978-0-8018-1388-7. Dewey:299/.2. LCCN:70-186515.
             Audience: **u,f.**

Wolkstein, Diane & Kramer,   **BL2615**
   Samuel N.
Inanna: Queen of Heaven and Earth. Trade Paper. HarperCollins
Publishers. New York, NY. 1983. 256p. ISBN:0-06-090854-8,
ISBN13: 978-0-06-090854-6. Dewey:299/.92. LCCN:80-008690.
             Audience: **g,l.** *B*

Religions. Mythology. Rationalism > History and Principles of Religion > Asian Religions > Asian Religions in China

Ching, Julia   **BL1802.C548 1993**
Chinese Religions. Trade Paper. Orbis Books. Maryknoll, NY.
1993. 300p. ISBN:0-88344-875-0, ISBN13: 978-0-88344-875-5.
Dewey:299.51. LCCN:93-002896.
         Audience: **l,u,f.** *Choice, 1994.*

Feuchtwang, Stephan   **BL1802**
Popular Religion in China: The Imperial Metaphor. Ed. 2. Paper
over Boards. Taylor & Francis Group. Philadelphia, PA. 2001.
283p. ISBN:0-7007-1421-9, ISBN13: 978-0-7007-1421-6.
Dewey:299.5/1.
         Audience: **u,f.** *Choice, 2002.*

Kohn, Livia   **BL1920.K64 2001**
Daoism and Chinese Culture. Trade Paper. Three Pines Press.
Waltham, MA. 2005. 218p. ISBN:1-931483-00-0, ISBN13:
978-1-931483-00-1. Dewey:299/.514. LCCN:2001-001409.
         Audience: **g,u,f.** *Choice, 2002.*

Lagerwey, John (Editor)   **PQ1888.E5D5**
Chinese Religion and Society: The Transformation of a Field.
Trade Cloth. Chinese University of Hong Kong, The. Hong
Kong SAR, 2004. 960p. ISBN:962-996-123-7, ISBN13:
978-962-996-123-7. Dewey:842.4.
         Audience: **u,f.** *Choice, 2005.*

Lopez, Donald S. Jr.   **BL1802.R43 1996**
   (Editor)
Religions of China in Practice. Cloth Text. Princeton University
Press. Princeton, NJ. 1996. 472p. Readings in Religions Ser.
ISBN:0-691-02144-9, ISBN13: 978-0-691-02144-7.
Dewey:299/.51. LCCN:95-041332.
             Audience: **g,u,f.**

Overmyer, Daniel L.   **BL1802.R428 2003**
   (Editor)
Religion in China Today. Richard Edmonds (Contribution by).
Trade Paper. Cambridge University Press. New York, NY. 2003.
244p. The China Quarterly Special Issues Ser., No. 3
ISBN:0-521-53823-8, ISBN13: 978-0-521-53823-7.
Dewey:200/.951/090511. LCCN:2003-055425.
             Audience: **g,l,u,f.**

Sommer, Deborah (Editor)   **BL1802.C5477 1995**
Chinese Religion: An Anthology of Sources. Paper Text. Oxford
University Press, Inc. New York, NY. 1995. 398p.
ISBN:0-19-508895-6, ISBN13: 978-0-19-508895-3.
Dewey:299/.51. LCCN:94-007557.
             Audience: **l,u,f.**

Weber, Max M.   **BL1801.W33 1964**
Religion of China. Trade Paper. Simon & Schuster. New York,
NY. 1968. 308p. ISBN:0-02-934450-6, ISBN13:
978-0-02-934450-7. Dewey:915.1. LCCN:68-005410.
             Audience: **g,l.**

Religions. Mythology. Rationalism > History and Principles of Religion > Asian Religions > Asian Religions in India. Southeast Asia

Babb, Lawrence A.   **BL1226.2**
The Divine Hierarchy: Popular Hinduism in Central India. Trade
Paper. Columbia University Press. New York, NY. 1989. 266p.
ISBN:0-231-08387-4, ISBN13: 978-0-231-08387-4.
Dewey:301.5/8/09543. LCCN:75-061693.
             Audience: **l,u,f.**

Copley, Antony   **BV3265.2**
Religions in Conflict: Ideology, Cultural Contact and Conversion
in Late-Colonial India. Trade Paper. Oxford University Press,
Inc. New York, NY. 2000. 296p. Oxford India Paperbacks Ser.
ISBN:0-19-564910-9, ISBN13: 978-0-19-564910-9.
Dewey:266/.02341054.
             Audience: **u,f.**

Eck, Diana L.   **BL1205.E25 1998**
Darsan: Seeing the Divine Image in India. Ed. 3. Trade Paper.
Columbia University Press. New York, NY. 1998. 97p.
Translations from the Asian Classics Ser. ISBN:0-231-11265-3,
ISBN13: 978-0-231-11265-9. Dewey:294.5/37.
LCCN:99-192162.
             Audience: **u,f.**

Feldhaus, Anne   DS485.M348F45 2003
Connected Places: Region, Pilgrimage, and Geographical
Imagination in India. Cloth over Boards. Palgrave Macmillan.
New York, NY. 2003. 340p. Religion/Culture/Critique Ser.
ISBN:1-4039-6323-1, ISBN13: 978-1-4039-6323-9.
Dewey:954/.7923. LCCN:2003-045977.
                                                       Audience: l,u,f.

1950 ed. **Fischer, Louis**   DS481.G3
The Life of Mahatma Gandhi. Trade Paper. HarperCollins
Publishers Ltd. London, 1997. 671p. ISBN:0-00-638887-6,
ISBN13: 978-0-00-638887-6. Dewey:954/.035/092.
                                                       Audience: g,l.

Gandhi, Mohandas K.   DS481.G3A25 1993
The Penguin Gandhi Reader. Rudrangshu Mukherjee (Editor).
Trade Paper. Penguin Group (USA) Inc. New York, NY. 1995.
320p. ISBN:0-14-023686-4, ISBN13: 978-0-14-023686-6.
Dewey:954.03/5/092. LCCN:95-129205.
                                                       Audience: g,l,u.

Geertz, Clifford   BL2120.J3G42
The Religion of Java. Trade Paper. University of Chicago Press.
Chicago, IL. 1976. 412p. ISBN:0-226-28510-3, ISBN13:
978-0-226-28510-8. Dewey:200.9/5982. LCCN:75-018746.
                                                       Audience: u,f. *B*

Gombrich, Richard F. &   BQ356
Obeyeskere, Gananth
Buddhism Transformed: Religious Change in Sri Lanka. Trade
Paper. Princeton University Press. Princeton, NJ. 1990. 500p.
ISBN:0-691-01901-0, ISBN13: 978-0-691-01901-7.
Dewey:294.3/095493.
                                                       Audience: u,f. *Choice, 1989.*

Gonda, Jan   N7445700
Change and Continuity in Indian Religion. Cloth Text.
Munshiram Manoharial Publishers Private, Ltd. New Delhi,
1984. ISBN:81-215-0312-4, ISBN13: 978-81-215-0312-9.
Dewey:700.
                                                       Audience: l,u,f.

Grewal, J. S.   DS436 .N47 1987 PT.
The Sikhs of the Punjab. C. A. Bayly, Gordon Johnson & John
F. Richards (Contribution by). Trade Paper. Cambridge
University Press. New York, NY. 1998. 302p. The New
Cambridge History of India Ser., No. II:3 ISBN:0-521-63764-3,
ISBN13: 978-0-521-63764-0. Dewey:954.500882946.
LCCN:99-158580.
                                                       Audience: u,f. *Choice, 1992.*

Hansen, Thomas B.   BL1215.P65 1999
The Saffron Wave: Democracy and Hindu Nationalism in
Modern India. Trade Paper. Princeton University Press.
Princeton, NJ. 1999. 300p. ISBN:0-691-00671-7, ISBN13:
978-0-691-00671-0. Dewey:294.5/5/0954. LCCN:98-033355.
                                                       Audience: g,l,u,f.

Hardy, Friedhelm   BL2001.2 .H37 1994
The Religious Culture of India: Power, Love and Wisdom. John
Clayton, Steven Collins, Nicholas de Lange & William Graham
(Contribution by). Trade Paper. Cambridge University Press.

New York, NY. 2005. 627p. Cambridge Studies in Religious
Traditions Ser., Vol. 4 ISBN:0-521-02344-0, ISBN13:
978-0-521-02344-3. Dewey:294.
                                                       Audience: g,l,u,f. *Choice, 1995.*

Hawley, John S. & Wulff,   BL1216.2
Donna M.
Devi: Goddesses of India. Trade Cloth. Motilal Banarsidass
Publishers (Pvt. Ltd). New Delhi, 1999. ISBN:81-208-1491-6,
ISBN13: 978-81-208-1491-2. Dewey:294.5/2114.
                                                       Audience: u,f. *Choice, 1996.*

Hiltebeitel, Alf & Erndl,   BL2015.G6I8 2000
Kathleen M. (Editors)
Is the Goddess a Feminist?: The Politics of South Asian
Goddesses. Trade Cloth. New York University Press. New York,
NY. 2000. 287p. ISBN:0-8147-3618-1, ISBN13:
978-0-8147-3618-0. Dewey:294.5/2114. LCCN:99-058589.
                                                       Audience: u,f.

Jaffrelot, Christophe   DS480.45
The Hindu Nationalist Movement in India. Trade Paper.
Columbia University Press. New York, NY. 1998. 536p.
ISBN:0-231-10335-2, ISBN13: 978-0-231-10335-0.
Dewey:324.254/082.
                                                       Audience: u,f.

King, Richard   BL2203.K561999
Orientalism and Religion: Postcolonial Theory, India and "the
Mystic East". Paper over Boards. Routledge. New York, NY.
1999. 296p. ISBN:0-415-20257-4, ISBN13: 978-0-415-20257-2.
Dewey:200/.7. LCCN:98-046343.
                                                       Audience: u,f.

Lopez, Donald S. Jr.   BL2001.2.R384 1995
(Editor)
Religions of India in Practice. Cloth Text. Princeton University
Press. Princeton, NJ. 1995. 648p. Princeton Readings in
Religions Ser. ISBN:0-691-04325-6, ISBN13:
978-0-691-04325-8. Dewey:294. LCCN:94-034695.
                                                       Audience: g,u,f. *Choice, 1995.*

Mann, Gurinder S.   BL2017.45.M369 2001
The Making of Sikh Scripture. Trade Cloth. Oxford University
Press, Inc. New York, NY. 2001. 206p. ISBN:0-19-513024-3,
ISBN13: 978-0-19-513024-9. Dewey:294.6/82.
LCCN:00-020857.
                                                       Audience: u,f.

Mann, Gurinder Singh   BL2018
Sikhism. Trade Paper. Prentice Hall PTR. Upper Saddle River,
NJ. 2004. 128p. ISBN:0-13-040977-4, ISBN13:
978-0-13-040977-5. Dewey:294.6.
                                                       Audience: l,u.

McLeod, W. H.   BL2017.9.N3
Guru Nanak and the Sikh Religion. Paper Text. Oxford
University Press, Inc. New York, NY. 1996. 272p.
ISBN:0-19-563735-6, ISBN13: 978-0-19-563735-9.
Dewey:294.5/53/0924.
                                                       Audience: u,f.

McLeod, W. H.   **BL2017.3.M35 2005**
Historical Dictionary of Sikhism. Ed. 2. Saddle Stitched, Cloth over Boards. Scarecrow Press, Inc. Lanham, MD. 2005. 297p. Historical Dictionaries of Religions, Philosophies, and Movements Ser., No. 59 ISBN:0-8108-5088-5, ISBN13: 978-0-8108-5088-0. Dewey:294.6/03. LCCN:2004-030461.

Audience: **g,l,u,f.**

Mittal, Sushil & Thursby,   **BL1055.R473 2006**
G. R.
Religions of South Asia: An Introduction. Trade Cloth. Routledge. New York, NY. 2006. ISBN:0-203-08776-3, ISBN13: 978-0-203-08776-3. Dewey:200/.954. LCCN:2005-025185.

Audience: **g,l,u.**

Ortner, Sherry B.   **DS493.9.S5**
Sherpas Through Their Rituals. Trade Paper. Cambridge University Press. New York, NY. 1978. 208p. Cambridge Studies in Cultural Systems ISBN:0-521-29216-6, ISBN13: 978-0-521-29216-0. Dewey:301.29/549/6. LCCN:76-062582.

Audience: **g,l,u,f.**

Peter, Van Der Veer   **BL65.S8V44 2001**
Imperial Encounters: Religion and Modernity in India and Britain. Trade Paper. Princeton University Press. Princeton, NJ. 2001. 216p. ISBN:0-691-07478-X, ISBN13: 978-0-691-07478-8. Dewey:200.9/54. LCCN:2001-275616.

Audience: **u,f.**

Sharma, Arvind   **BL2015.W6W66 2002**
Women in Indian Religions. Trade Cloth. Oxford University Press, Inc. New York, NY. 2002. 276p. ISBN:0-19-564634-7, ISBN13: 978-0-19-564634-4. Dewey:200/.82/0954. LCCN:2002-286793.

Audience: **g,l,u,f.** *Choice, 2003.*

Sircar, D. C.   **BL2010**
Studies in the Religious Life of Ancient and Medieval India. Trade Cloth. Orient Book Distributors. Livingston, NJ. 1971. ISBN:0-89684-326-2, ISBN13: 978-0-89684-326-4. Dewey:200/.954.

Audience: **u,f.**

Webster, John C. B.   **DS422.C3W435 2002**
Religion and Dalit Liberation: An Examination of Perspectives. Ed. 2. Trade Cloth. Manohar Publications. New Delhi, 1999. 159p. ISBN:81-7304-327-2, ISBN13: 978-81-7304-327-7. Dewey:305.568. LCCN:2002-314746.

Audience: **u,f.**

Winternitz, Maurice   **PK2903**
History of Indian Literature. Trade Cloth. Motilal Banarsidass Publishers (Pvt. Ltd). New Delhi, 1999. 2052p. ISBN:81-208-0263-2, ISBN13: 978-81-208-0263-6. Dewey:891.209.

Audience: **u,f.**

Religions. Mythology. Rationalism > History and Principles of Religion > Asian Religions > Asian Religions in Japan

Bellah, Robert N.   **BL2210**
Tokugawa Religion. Ed. 2. Trade Paper. Simon & Schuster. New York, NY. 1985. 272p. ISBN:0-02-902460-9, ISBN13: 978-0-02-902460-7. Dewey:291/.0952. LCCN:85-007035.

Audience: **u,f.**

Bowring, Richard   **BL2206**
The Religious Traditions of Japan, 500-1600. Trade Cloth. Cambridge University Press. New York, NY. 2005. 502p. ISBN:0-521-85119-X, ISBN13: 978-0-521-85119-0. Dewey:2200.952. LCCN:2006-295740.

Audience: **u,f.** *Choice, 2006.*

Hardacre, Helen   **BL2222.K884**
Kurozumikyo and the New Religions of Japan. Trade Paper. Princeton University Press. Princeton, NJ. 1988. 240p. ISBN:0-691-02048-5, ISBN13: 978-0-691-02048-8. Dewey:299/.5619. LCCN:85-043287.

Audience: **u,f.** *Choice, 1986.*

Hardacre, Helen   **BL65.P7**
Shinto and the State, 1868-1988. Trade Cloth. Princeton University Press. Princeton, NJ. 1991. 224p. Studies in Church and State Ser. ISBN:0-691-02052-3, ISBN13: 978-0-691-02052-5. Dewey:322/.1. LCCN:88-035665.

Audience: **u,f.** *Choice, 1990.*

1968 ed. **Hori, Ichiro**   **BL2202**
Folk Religion in Japan: Continuity and Change. Joseph M. Kitagawa & Alan L. Miller (Editors). Trade Paper. University of Chicago Press. Chicago, IL. 1994. 294p. The Haskell Lectures on History of Religions Ser. ISBN:0-226-35334-6, ISBN13: 978-0-226-35334-0. Dewey:291.0952. LCCN:67-030128.

Audience: **u,f.**

Kasahara, Kazuo   **BL2202.3.N5513 2001**
A History of Japanese Religion. Paul McCarthy & Gaynor Sekimori (Translators). Trade Paper. Kosei Publishing Company. Tokyo, 2002. 648p. ISBN:4-333-01917-6, ISBN13: 978-4-333-01917-5. Dewey:200/.952. LCCN:2002-428227.

Audience: **u,f.**

Nelson   **BL2225.N2552S883**
Year in Life of a Shinto Shrine. Trade Paper. University of Washington Press. Seattle, WA. 1996. 288p. ISBN:0-295-97500-8, ISBN13: 978-0-295-97500-9. Dewey:299/.56135/095224. LCCN:95-023257.

Audience: **u,f.** *Choice, 1996.*

Reader, Ian   **BL2209.R42 1990**
Religion in Contemporary Japan. Trade Cloth. University of Hawaii Press. Honolulu, HI. 1991. 294p. ISBN:0-8248-1354-5,

ISBN13: 978-0-8248-1354-3. Dewey:291/.0952.
LCCN:90-038407.

Audience: **u,f.** *Choice, 1992.*

Tanabe, George J. Jr.   **BL2202.R48 1999**
  (Editor)
Religions of Japan in Practice. Trade Cloth. Princeton University
Press. Princeton, NJ. 1999. 550p. Princeton Readings in
Religions Ser. ISBN:0-691-05788-5, ISBN13:
978-0-691-05788-0. Dewey:200/.952. LCCN:98-044252.

Audience: **u,f.**

Wheeler, Post (Editor,   **DS855**
  Translator)
1952
ed.
The Sacred Scriptures of the Japanese: With All Authoritative
Variants, Chronologically Arranged. Library Binding.
Greenwood Publishing Group, Inc. Portsmouth, NH. 1976. 562p.
ISBN:0-8371-8393-6, ISBN13: 978-0-8371-8393-0.
Dewey:952/.01. LCCN:75-031427.

Audience: **u,f.**

Religions. Mythology. Rationalism > History and Principles of Religion > Asian Religions > Shamanism

Eliade, Mircea   **BL2370.S5E413 2004**
Shamanism: Archaic Techniques of Ecstasy. Willard R. Trask
(Translator), Wendy Doniger (Foreword by). Trade Paper.
Princeton University Press. Princeton, NJ. 2004. 648p. Bollingen
Ser., Vol. 76 ISBN:0-691-11942-2, ISBN13: 978-0-691-11942-7.
Dewey:201/.44. LCCN:2003-064777.

Audience: **u,f.**

Kehoe, Alice Beck   **BL2370.S5K43 2000**
Shamans and Religion: An Anthropological Exploration in
Critical Thinking. Paper Text. Waveland Press, Inc. Prospect
Heights, IL. 2000. 125p. ISBN:1-57766-162-1, ISBN13:
978-1-57766-162-7. Dewey:291.1/44. LCCN:2001-268737.

Audience: **g,l,u,f.** *Choice, 2001.*

Religions. Mythology. Rationalism > History and Principles of Religion > African and Egyptian Religions

Brown, Karen McCarthy   **BL2490.K68 B76 2001**
Mama Lola: A Vodou Priestess in Brooklyn. Trade Paper.
University of California Press. Berkeley, CA. 2001. 448p.
Comparative Studies in Religion and Society, Vol. 4
ISBN:0-520-22475-2, ISBN13: 978-0-520-22475-9.
Dewey:299/.675/092 B. LCCN:2001-037028.

Audience: **u,f.**

Budge, E. A. Wallis   **BL2441.2**
The Egyptian Book of the Dead: The Papyrus of Ani. Trade
Paper. Kessinger Publishing, LLC. Whitefish, MT. 2004.
ISBN:1-4192-6068-5, ISBN13: 978-1-4192-6068-1.
Dewey:299/.31.

Audience: **u,f.**

Ellis, Stephen & ter Haar,   **BL2400.E45 2004**
  Gerrie
Worlds of Power: Religious Thought and Political Practice in
Africa. Trade Cloth. Oxford University Press, Inc. New York,
NY. 2004. 272p. Contemporary History of World Affairs Ser.,
Vol. 1 ISBN:0-19-522017-X, ISBN13: 978-0-19-522017-9.
Dewey:201/.72/096. LCCN:2004-000252.

Audience: **l,u,f.** *Choice, 2005.*

Frankfurter, David   **BL2455.F73 1998**
Religion in Roman Egypt: Assimilation and Resistance. Trade
Paper. Princeton University Press. Princeton, NJ. 2000. 332p.
Mythos Ser. ISBN:0-691-07054-7, ISBN13: 978-0-691-07054-4.
Dewey:200/.932/09015. LCCN:97-049576.

Audience: **u,f.**

Idowu, E. Bolaji   **BL2400**
African Traditional Religion: A Definition. Trade Cloth.
SCM-Canterbury Press Ltd. London, 1973. "xii, 228"p.
ISBN:0-334-00028-9, ISBN13: 978-0-334-00028-0.
Dewey:299/.6. LCCN:73-181014.

Audience: **l,u,f.**

Idowu, E. Bolasi   **BL2480.Y6**
Olodumare: God in Yoruba Belief. Ed. 2. Trade Paper. Original
Publications. Farmingdale, NY. 1995. 256p.
ISBN:0-942272-41-2, ISBN13: 978-0-942272-41-3.
Dewey:299.6833.

Audience: **u,f.**

Isichei, Elizabeth   **BL2400**
The Religious Traditions of Africa: A History. Trade Cloth.
Greenwood Publishing Group, Inc. Portsmouth, NH. 2004. 432p.
ISBN:0-325-07114-4, ISBN13: 978-0-325-07114-5.
Dewey:200/.96. LCCN:2004-017542.

Audience: **g,l.** *Choice, 2005.*

Mbiti, John S.   **BL2462.5.M36 1990**
1969
ed.
African Religions and Philosophy. Ed. 2. Trade Paper.
Heinemann. Portsmouth, NH. 1992. 288p. ISBN:0-435-89591-5,
ISBN13: 978-0-435-89591-4. Dewey:299.6. LCCN:89-48596.

Audience: **g,l,u.**

Mbiti, John S.   **BL2400.M383 1991**
Introduction to African Religion. Ed. 2. Trade Paper.
Heinemann. Portsmouth, NH. 1991. 216p. ISBN:0-435-94002-3,
ISBN13: 978-0-435-94002-7. Dewey:299/.6. LCCN:91-028675.

Audience: **g,l,u.**

Ranger, T. O. & Kimambo,   **BL2466**
  Isaria Ndelahiyosa
The Historical Study of African Religion: With Special

Reference to East and Central Africa. Trade Cloth. Harcourt Education. Oxford, 1972. ix, 307p. ISBN:0-435-32747-X, ISBN13: 978-0-435-32747-7. Dewey:200/.967.

Audience: **u,f.**

Redford, Donald B. (Editor)   BL2428.A53 2002
The Ancient Gods Speak: A Guide to Egyptian Religion. Trade Cloth. Oxford University Press, Inc. New York, NY. 2002. 428p. ISBN:0-19-515401-0, ISBN13: 978-0-19-515401-6. Dewey:299/.31/03. LCCN:2002-072411.

Audience: **g,l,u,f.**

Wilkinson, Richard H.   BL2450.G6
The Complete Gods and Goddesses of Ancient Egypt. Trade Cloth. Thames & Hudson. New York, NY. 2003. 256p. ISBN:0-500-05120-8, ISBN13: 978-0-500-05120-7. Dewey:299/.31211. LCCN:2002-110321.

Audience: **l,u,f.** *Choice, 2003.*

Zahan, Dominique   BL2400
The Religion, Spirituality, and Thought of Traditional Africa. Kate E. Martin & Lawrence M. Martin (Translators). Paper Text. University of Chicago Press. Chicago, IL. 1983. ISBN:0-226-97778-1, ISBN13: 978-0-226-97778-2. Dewey:299/.6. LCCN:78-023525.

Audience: **l,u,f.**

Religions. Mythology. Rationalism > History and Principles of Religion > Religions of the Americas

Allitt, Patrick   BL2525.A44 2003
Religion in America since 1945: A History. Trade Cloth. Chinese University of Hong Kong, The. Hong Kong SAR, 2003. 384p. Columbia Histories of Modern American Life Ser. ISBN:0-231-12154-7, ISBN13: 978-0-231-12154-5. Dewey:200/.973/09045. LCCN:2003-055288.

Audience: **g,l,u,f.**

Bastide, Roger   BL2590.B7
The African Religions of Brazil: Toward a Sociology of the Interpenetration of Civilizations. Helen Sebba (Translator). Trade Cloth. Johns Hopkins University Press. Baltimore, MD. 1978. 494p. Johns Hopkins Studies in Atlantic History and Culture Ser. ISBN:0-8018-2056-1, ISBN13: 978-0-8018-2056-4. Dewey:299/.6/0981. LCCN:78-005421.

Audience: **l,u,f.** *B*

Bonomi, Patricia U.   BL2525
Under the Cope of Heaven: Religion, Society, and Politics in Colonial America. Ed. 2. Trade Cloth. Oxford University Press, Inc. New York, NY. 2003. 328p. ISBN:0-19-516217-X, ISBN13: 978-0-19-516217-2. Dewey:277.3/07. LCCN:2004-271885.

Audience: **u,f.**

Brown, David H.   BL2532.S3B76 2003
Santeria Enthroned: Art, Ritual, and Innovation in an Afro-Cuban Religion. Trade Paper. University of Chicago Press.

Chicago, IL. 2003. 440p. ISBN:0-226-07610-5, ISBN13: 978-0-226-07610-2. Dewey:299/.674. LCCN:2002-073564.

Audience: **u,f.** *Choice, 2004.*

Butler, Jon   BL2525.B87 1990
Awash in a Sea of Faith: The Christianization of the American People 1550-1865. Trade Cloth. Harvard University Press. Cambridge, MA. 1990. 384p. Studies in Cultural History ISBN:0-674-05600-0, ISBN13: 978-0-674-05600-8. Dewey:200/.973. LCCN:89-035770.

Audience: **g,l,u,f.** *Choice, 1990.*

Butler, Jon & Stout, Harry   BL2525.R4655 1998
S. (Editors)
Religion in American History: A Reader. Trade Paper. Oxford University Press, Inc. New York, NY. 1997. 526p. ISBN:0-19-509776-9, ISBN13: 978-0-19-509776-4. Dewey:200/.973. LCCN:96-039446.

Audience: **g,l,u,f.**

Chidester, David   BP605.P46C48 2003
Salvation and Suicide: Jim Jones, the Peoples Temple, and Jonestown. Trade Cloth. Indiana University Press. Bloomington, IN. 2003. 224p. Religion in North America Ser. ISBN:0-253-34324-0, ISBN13: 978-0-253-34324-6. Dewey:289.9. LCCN:2003-007226.

Audience: **g,l,u,f.**

Choquette, Robert   BL2530.C2C46 2004
Canada's Religions. Trade Paper. University of Toronto Press. Toronto, ON. 2003. 464p. Religion and Beliefs Ser., No. 12 ISBN:0-7766-0557-7, ISBN13: 978-0-7766-0557-9. Dewey:200/.971. LCCN:2004-426312.

Audience: **g,l,u,f.** *Choice, 2004.*

Gaustad, Edwin S. & Noll,   BL2525.D63 2003
1982 **Mark A. (Editors)**
ed. A Documentary History of Religion in America since 1877. Ed. 3. Trade Paper. William B. Eerdmans Publishing Company. Grand Rapids, MI. 2003. 704p. ISBN:0-8028-2230-4, ISBN13: 978-0-8028-2230-7. Dewey:200/.973. LCCN:2003-049323.

Audience: **g,l,u.**

Herberg, Will   BL2525.H47 1983
Protestant--Catholic--Jew: An Essay in American Religious Sociology. Trade Paper. University of Chicago Press. Chicago, IL. 1983. 326p. ISBN:0-226-32734-5, ISBN13: 978-0-226-32734-1. Dewey:306.6. LCCN:83-009120.

Audience: **g,l,u,f.**

Jenkins, Philip   BL2500.J46 2004
Dream Catchers: How Mainstream America Discovered Native Spirituality. Trade Cloth. Oxford University Press, Inc. New York, NY. 2004. 320p. ISBN:0-19-516115-7, ISBN13: 978-0-19-516115-1. Dewey:299.7/93. LCCN:2003-026909.

Audience: **g,l,u,f.** *Choice, 2005.*

Keller, Rosemary Skinner, et   BL458.E52 2006
al.
The Encyclopedia of Women and Religion in North America. Rosemary Radford Ruether & Marie Cantlon (Authors). Trade

Cloth. Indiana University Press. Bloomington, IN. 2006. 1296p. ISBN:0-253-34686-X, ISBN13: 978-0-253-34686-5. Dewey:200.82/0973. LCCN:2005-032429.

Audience: **g,l,u,f.**

Martin, Joel W.   **E98.R3M333 2001**
The Land Looks after Us: A History of Native American Religion. Trade Paper. Oxford University Press, Inc. New York, NY. 2001. 172p. ISBN:0-19-514586-0, ISBN13: 978-0-19-514586-1. Dewey:299/.7/09. LCCN:00-066583.

Audience: **u,f.**

1ˢᵗ, 5ᵗʰ, 9ᵗʰ eds
Mead, Frank S.   **BL2525.M425 2001**
Handbook of Denominations in the United States. Ed. 11. Craig D. Atwood & Samuel S. Hill (Revised by). Trade Cloth. Abingdon Press. Nashville, TN. 2004. 384p. ISBN:0-687-06983-1, ISBN13: 978-0-687-06983-5. Dewey:200/.973. LCCN:2001-018872.

Audience: **g,l,u.**

Melton, J. Gordon   **BL72**
Biographical Dictionary of American Cult and Sect Leaders. Paper over Boards. Garland Publishing, Inc. New York, NY. 1986. 354p. Library of Social Sciences ISBN:0-8240-9037-3, ISBN13: 978-0-8240-9037-1. Dewey:291.6/03/21. LCCN:83-048226.

Audience: **g,l,u,f.** *Choice, 1986.*

2nd ed.
Melton, J. Gordon (Editor)   **BL2525.M449 1999**
The Encyclopedia of American Religions. Ed. 6. Trade Cloth. Thomson Gale. Farmington Hills, MI. 1998. xxiv, 1243p. ISBN:0-8103-8417-5, ISBN13: 978-0-8103-8417-0. Dewey:200/.973. LCCN:00-702484.

Audience: **g,l,u,f.**

1991 ed.
Melton, J. Gordon (Editor)   **BL72**
Religious Leaders of America: A Biographical Guide to Founders and Leaders of Religious Bodies, Churches and Spiritual Groups in North America. Ed. 2. Trade Cloth. Thomson Gale. Farmington Hills, MI. 1999. 724p. ISBN:0-8103-8878-2, ISBN13: 978-0-8103-8878-9. Dewey:200.973. LCCN:91-642355.

Audience: **g,l,u.**

Miller, Timothy (Editor)   **BL2525.A55 1995**
America's Alternative Religions. Cloth Text. State University of New York Press. Albany, NY. 1995. 474p. SUNY Series in Religious Studies ISBN:0-7914-2397-2, ISBN13: 978-0-7914-2397-4. Dewey:200/.973. LCCN:94-016605.

Audience: **g,l,u.**

Murphy, Larry G. (Editor),   **BR563.N4.E53 1993**
  et al.
Encyclopedia of African-American Religions. J. Gordon Melton & Gary L. Ward (Editors). Cloth Text. Taylor & Francis Group. Philadelphia, PA. 1993. 1008p. Religious Information Systems Ser., Vol. 9 ISBN:0-8153-0500-1, ISBN13: 978-0-8153-0500-2. Dewey:200.8996073. LCCN:93-007224.

Audience: **g,l,u,f.** *Choice, 1994.*

Orsi, Robert A.   **F128.9.I8**
The Madonna of 115th Street: Faith and Community in Italian Harlem, 1880-1950. Ed. 2. Trade Paper. Yale University Press. Cumberland, RI. 2002. 352p. ISBN:0-300-09135-4, ISBN13: 978-0-300-09135-9. Dewey:305.8/51/07471. LCCN:2001-098541.

Audience: **g,l,u,f.**

Simpson, George E.   **BL2520**
Black Religions in the New World. Trade Cloth. Columbia University Press. New York, NY. 1978. 415p. ISBN:0-231-04540-9, ISBN13: 978-0-231-04540-7. Dewey:291/.0899607. LCCN:78-016892.

Audience: **g,l,u,f.** *B*

Smith, Christian & Prokopy,   **BL2540.L37 1999**
  Joshua
Latin American Religion in Motion: Tracking Innovation, Unexpected Change, and Complexity. Trade Paper. Routledge. New York, NY. 1999. 272p. ISBN:0-415-92106-6, ISBN13: 978-0-415-92106-0. Dewey:200/.98. LCCN:98-028932.

Audience: **u,f.**

Religions. Mythology. Rationalism > History and Principles of Religion > Pacific Religions

Keesing, Roger M.   **BL2630.K85**
Kwaio Religion: The Living and the Dead in a Solomon Island Society. Trade Paper. Edinburgh University Press. Edinburgh, 1982. 257p. ISBN:0-231-05341-X, ISBN13: 978-0-231-05341-9. Dewey:299/.92. LCCN:82-004122.

Audience: **u,f.**

Swain, Tony & Trompf,   **BL2600.S92 1995**
  Garry
The Religions of Oceania. Trade Paper. Routledge. New York, NY. 1995. 256p. Library of Religious Beliefs and Practices ISBN:0-415-06019-2, ISBN13: 978-0-415-06019-6. Dewey:200/.99. LCCN:94-016171.

Audience: **g,l,u.**

Trompf, G. W.   **BL2620.M4 T76 1990**
Melanesian Religion. Trade Paper. Cambridge University Press. New York, NY. 2004. 303p. ISBN:0-521-60748-5, ISBN13: 978-0-521-60748-3. Dewey:299/.925. LCCN:2005-279286.

Audience: **u,f.**

Worsley, Peter   **BL2620.M4**
The Trumpet Shall Sound: A Study of Cargo Cults in Melanesia. Ed. 2. Trade Paper. Knopf Publishing Group. New York, NY. 1987. 300p. ISBN:0-8052-0156-4, ISBN13: 978-0-8052-0156-7. Dewey:299/.9. LCCN:67-026995.

Audience: **l,u,f.** *B*

Religions. Mythology. Rationalism > Rationalism. Atheism. Secularism

Allen, Ethan   **BL2773.A5**
Reason the Only Oracle of Man or A Compendious System of Natural Religion. Trade Paper. Kessinger Publishing, LLC. Whitefish, MT. 2003. ISBN:0-7661-6854-9, ISBN13: 978-0-7661-6854-1. Dewey:210.

Audience: **u,f.**

Chadwick, Owen   **BL2765.E85 C48 1990**
The Secularization of the European Mind in the Nineteenth Century. Trade Paper. Cambridge University Press. New York, NY. 1990. 292p. ISBN:0-521-39829-0, ISBN13: 978-0-521-39829-9. Dewey:940.2/8. LCCN:90-034449.

Audience: **u,f.**

Dennett, Daniel C.   **BL2775.3.D46 2006**
Breaking the Spell: Religion as a Natural Phenomenon. Trade Cloth. Penguin Group (USA) Inc. New York, NY. 2006. 464p. ISBN:0-670-03472-X, ISBN13: 978-0-670-03472-7. Dewey:200. LCCN:2005-042415.

Audience: **g,l,u,f.**

Fenn, Richard K.   **BL2747.8.F463 2001**
Beyond Idols: The Shape of a Secular Society. Trade Cloth. Oxford University Press, Inc. New York, NY. 2001. 224p. ISBN:0-19-514369-8, ISBN13: 978-0-19-514369-0. Dewey:306.6. LCCN:00-056684.

Audience: **u,f.**

Hunter, Michael & Wootton,   **BL2765.E85A84 1992**
   David (Editors)
Atheism from the Reformation to the Enlightenment. Trade Cloth. Oxford University Press, Inc. New York, NY. 1992. 314p. ISBN:0-19-822736-1, ISBN13: 978-0-19-822736-6. Dewey:211.8. LCCN:92-003324.

Audience: **u,f.**

Martin, Michael   **BL2747.3**
Atheism: A Philosophical Justification. Trade Paper. Temple University Press. Philadelphia, PA. 1992. 275p. ISBN:0-87722-943-0, ISBN13: 978-0-87722-943-8. Dewey:211/.8.

Audience: **u,f.** *Choice, 1990.*

Marty, Martin E.   **BL2747.8 .M37 1969B**
The Modern Schism: Three Paths to the Secular. Trade Cloth. SCM-Canterbury Press Ltd. London, 1969. 191p. ISBN:0-334-01030-6, ISBN13: 978-0-334-01030-2. Dewey:261. LCCN:70-460305.

Audience: **u,f.**

Marx, Karl & Engels,   **BL2775**
   Friedrich
On Religion. Reinhold Niebur (Introduction by). Trade Paper. Oxford University Press, Inc. New York, NY. 1963. 382p.

American Academy of Religion Classics in Religious Studies ISBN:0-89130-599-8, ISBN13: 978-0-89130-599-6. Dewey:200/.1. LCCN:82-017032.

Audience: **g,l,u,f.**

McGrath, Alister E.   **BL2747.3.M355 2004**
The Twilight of Atheism: The Rise and Fall of Disbelief in the Modern World. Trade Cloth. Doubleday Publishing. New York, NY. 2004. 320p. ISBN:0-385-50061-0, ISBN13: 978-0-385-50061-6. Dewey:211/.8/09. LCCN:2003-055531.

Audience: **g,l.** *Choice, 2004.*

Paine, Thomas   **BL2740.A1 2004**
The Age of Reason. Moncure Daniel Conway (Editor). Trade Paper. Dover Publications, Inc. Mineola, NY. 2004. 224p. ISBN:0-486-43393-5, ISBN13: 978-0-486-43393-6. Dewey:211/.5. LCCN:2003-070117.

Audience: **g,l,u,f.**

Sinclair, Upton   **BL2775.S54**
The Profits of Religion: An Essay in Economic Interpretation. Trade Paper. Kessinger Publishing, LLC. Whitefish, MT. 2004. ISBN:1-4179-4226-6, ISBN13: 978-1-4179-4226-8.

Audience: **u,f.**

Turner, James   **BL2757.T87 1985**
Without God, Without Creed: The Origins of Unbelief in America. Trade Cloth. Johns Hopkins University Press. Baltimore, MD. 1985. 336p. New Studies in American Intellectual and Cultural History ISBN:0-8018-2494-X, ISBN13: 978-0-8018-2494-4. Dewey:211/.8/0973. LCCN:84-015397.

Audience: **l,u,f.** *B*

Judaism

                                            Z6368
☐ RAMBI/Index of Articles on Jewish Studies.
http://jnul.huji.ac.il/rambi/

Audience: **g,l,u,f.**

Hirsch, S. R.   **BM45 .H4822**
Judaism Eternal. Dayan I. Grunfeld (Translator). Trade Cloth. Soncino Press. Brooklyn, NY. 1956. ISBN:0-900689-70-6, ISBN13: 978-0-900689-70-3. Dewey:296.04.

Audience: **u,f.**

Kook, Abraham Isaac   **BM601**
Abraham Isaac Kook: The Lights of Penitence, the Moral Principles, Lights of Holiness, Essays Letters and Poems. Trade Paper. SPCK Publishing. London, 1979. xxviii, 415p. ISBN:0-281-03652-7, ISBN13: 978-0-281-03652-3. Dewey:296.3.

Audience: **u,f.**

Satlow, Michael L.   **BM45**
Creating Judaism: History, Tradition, Practice. Trade Cloth. Columbia University Press. New York, NY. 2006. 384p. ISBN:0-231-13488-6, ISBN13: 978-0-231-13488-0. Dewey:296. LCCN:2006-018056.

Audience: **l,u,f.**

Werblowsky, Zvi &   **BM50.W45 1986**
   Wigoder, Geoffrey (Editors)
1966 ed. The Encyclopedia of the Jewish Religion. Trade Cloth. Lambda
Publishers, Inc. Brooklyn, NY. 1986. 478p.
ISBN:0-915361-53-1, ISBN13: 978-0-915361-53-3.
Dewey:296/.03/21. LCCN:86-010932.
           Audience: **g,l,u,f.** *B*

Wigoder, Geoffrey &   **DS102.8**
   Seckbach, Fern (Editors)
GVRL Encyclopedia Judaica. CD-ROM. Keter Publishing House.
Jerusalem, 1997. ISBN:965-07-0665-8, ISBN13:
978-965-07-0665-4. Dewey:909.
           Audience: **l,u,f.** *Choice, 1998.*

Judaism > Pre-Talmudic Jewish literature

Josephus, Flavius   **DS116.J7 1999**
The New Complete Works of Josephus. Trade Cloth. Kregel
Publications. Grand Rapids, MI. 1999. 1152p.
ISBN:0-8254-2924-2, ISBN13: 978-0-8254-2924-8.
Dewey:933/.05/092. LCCN:99-018852.
           Audience: **l,u,f.**

Stone, Michael E. (Editor)   **BM485.L57**
Jewish Writings of the Second Temple Period: Apocrypha,
Pseudepigrapha, Qumran, Sectarian Writings, Philo, Josephus.
Trade Cloth. Augsburg Fortress, Publishers. Minneapolis, MN.
1984. 656p. Compendia Rerum Iudaicarum Ad Novum
Testamentum Ser. ISBN:0-8006-0603-5, ISBN13:
978-0-8006-0603-9. Dewey:296.1. LCCN:83-048926.
           Audience: **u,f.** *B*

Yonge, C. D. (Translator)   **B689.A4E5 1993**
The Works of Philo. David M. Scholer (Foreword by, Notes by).
Trade Cloth. Hendrickson Publishers, Inc. Peabody, MA. 1993.
944p. ISBN:0-943575-93-1, ISBN13: 978-0-943575-93-3.
Dewey:181/.06. LCCN:94-168668.
           Audience: **u,f.**

Judaism > Pre-Talmudic Jewish literature > Dead Sea Scrolls

Magness, Jodi   **BM487**
The Archaeology of Qumran and the Dead Sea Scrolls. Trade
Paper. William B. Eerdmans Publishing Company. Grand
Rapids, MI. 2003. 284p. Studies in the Dead Sea Scrolls and
Related Literature ISBN:0-8028-2687-3, ISBN13:
978-0-8028-2687-9. Dewey:296.1/55.
           Audience: **g,l,u,f.** *Choice, 2003.*

Schiffman, Lawrence H. &   **BM487.E53 2000**
   VanderKam, James C. (Editors)
Encyclopedia of the Dead Sea Scrolls, Set. Trade Cloth. Oxford
University Press, Inc. New York, NY. 2000. 1,146p.
ISBN:0-19-508450-0, ISBN13: 978-0-19-508450-4.
Dewey:296.1/55/03. LCCN:99-055300.
           Audience: **l,u,f.** *Choice, 2000.*

VanderKam, James C. &   **BM487.V27 2002**
   Flint, Peter W.
The Meaning of the Dead Sea Scrolls: Their Significance for
Understanding the Bible, Judaism, Jesus, and Christianity. Trade
Paper. HarperCollins Publishers. New York, NY. 2004. 480p.
ISBN:0-06-068465-8, ISBN13: 978-0-06-068465-5.
Dewey:296.1/55. LCCN:2002-069730.
           Audience: **g,l,u,f.** *Choice, 2003.*

Vermes, Geza (Translator)   **BM487.A3D42 2004**
The Complete Dead Sea Scrolls in English. Ed. 6. Trade Paper.
Penguin Group (USA) Inc. New York, NY. 2004. 720p. Penguin
Classics Ser. ISBN:0-14-044952-3, ISBN13: 978-0-14-044952-5.
Dewey:296.1/55. LCCN:2004-275610.
           Audience: **g,l,u,f.**

Judaism > History

Biale, David (Editor)   **DS102.95.C85 2006**
Cultures of the Jews: Mediterranean Origins. Trade Paper.
Knopf Publishing Group. New York, NY. 2006. 352p.
ISBN:0-8052-1200-0, ISBN13: 978-0-8052-1200-6.
Dewey:909/.04924. LCCN:2005-049979.
           Audience: **u,f.**

Biale, David (Editor)   **DS102.95.C85 2006**
Cultures of the Jews: Diversities of Diaspora. Trade Paper.
Knopf Publishing Group. New York, NY. 2006. 480p.
ISBN:0-8052-1201-9, ISBN13: 978-0-8052-1201-3.
Dewey:909/.04924. LCCN:2005-049979.
           Audience: **u,f.**

Biale, David (Editor)   **DS102.95.C85 2006**
Cultures of the Jews: Modern Encounters. Trade Paper. Knopf
Publishing Group. New York, NY. 2006. 480p.
ISBN:0-8052-1202-7, ISBN13: 978-0-8052-1202-0.
Dewey:909/.04924. LCCN:2005-049979.
           Audience: **u,f.**

Buber, Martin   **BM198.B84213 1988**
The Origin and Meaning of Hasidism. David Burrell
(Introduction by). Trade Paper. Brill Academic Publishers, Inc.
Boston, MA. 1988. 264p. ISBN:0-391-03549-5, ISBN13:
978-0-391-03549-2. Dewey:296.8/33. LCCN:87-026192.
           Audience: **u,f.** *B*

Buber, Martin   **BM532.B7613 1991**
1947 ed. Tales of the Hasidim. Chaim Potok (Foreword by). Book, Other.
Knopf Publishing Group. New York, NY. 1991. 736p.
ISBN:0-8052-0995-6, ISBN13: 978-0-8052-0995-2.
Dewey:296.8/332. LCCN:90-052921.
           Audience: **l,u,f.** *B*

Epstein, Isidore   **BM155.2**
Judaism: A Historical Presentation. Trade Paper. Penguin Group
(USA) Inc. New York, NY. 1959. 352p. ISBN:0-14-013552-9,
ISBN13: 978-0-14-013552-7. Dewey:296.09.
           Audience: **g,l,u,f.** *B*

Glatzer, Nahum N.   BM157.G58
Essays in Jewish Thought. Trade Cloth. University of Alabama
Press. Tuscaloosa, AL. 1978. 304p. Judaic Studies, Vol. 8
ISBN:0-8173-6904-X, ISBN13: 978-0-8173-6904-0.
Dewey:296.3. LCCN:76-051044.

Audience: **u,f.** *B*

Meyer, Michael A.   BM316 .M41979
The Origins of the Modern Jew: Jewish Identity and European
Culture in Germany, 1749-1824. Trade Paper. Wayne State
University Press. Detroit, MI. 1972. 250p. Waynebooks Ser.,
No. 32 ISBN:0-8143-1470-8, ISBN13: 978-0-8143-1470-8.
Dewey:943/.004/924. LCCN:78-026528.

Audience: **u,f.** *B*

Peters, F. E.   BM157.P47 2004
The Children of Abraham: Judaism, Christianity, Islam. John L.
Esposito (Foreword by). Trade Cloth. Princeton University
Press. Princeton, NJ. 2004. 272p. ISBN:0-691-12041-2, ISBN13:
978-0-691-12041-6. Dewey:201/.4. LCCN:2004-040049.
Audience: **l,u,f.** *B* *Choice, 2005.*

Rabinowicz, Tzvi M.   BM198.E53 1996
(Editor)
The Encylopedia of Hasidism. Book, Other. Rowman &
Littlefield Publishers, Inc. Lanham, MD. 1996. 608p.
ISBN:1-56821-123-6, ISBN13: 978-1-56821-123-7.
Dewey:296.8/332.03. LCCN:94-003140.
Audience: **u,f.**

Schechter, Solomon   BM45
Studies in Judaism, Vol. 2. Ismar Schorsch (Introduction by).
Trade Cloth. Gorgias Press, LLC. Piscataway, NJ. 2003. 380p.
ISBN:1-59333-039-1, ISBN13: 978-1-59333-039-2. Dewey:296.
Audience: **u,f.** *B*

Schechter, Solomon   BM45
Studies in Judaism, Vol. 1. Ismar Schorsch (Introduction by).
Trade Cloth. Gorgias Press, LLC. Piscataway, NJ. 2003. 508p.
ISBN:1-59333-038-3, ISBN13: 978-1-59333-038-5. Dewey:296.
Audience: **l,u,f.** *B*

Schechter, Solomon   BM45
Studies in Judaism, Vol. 3. Ismar Schorsch (Introduction by).
Trade Cloth. Gorgias Press, LLC. Piscataway, NJ. 2003. 352p.
ISBN:1-59333-040-5, ISBN13: 978-1-59333-040-8. Dewey:296.
Audience: **l,u,f.** *B*

Scholem, Gershom Gerhard   BM199.S3 S3713 1989
Sabbatai Sevi: The Mystical Messiah, 1626-1676. R. J. Zwi
Werblowski (Translator). Trade Paper. Princeton University
Press. Princeton, NJ. 1976. 1027p. Bollingen Ser., Vol. 93
ISBN:0-691-01809-X, ISBN13: 978-0-691-01809-6.
Dewey:296.82. LCCN:75-166389.
Audience: **u,f.**

Silver, Daniel J. & Martin,   BM155.2 .H57
Bernard
History of Judaism. Cloth Text. Basic Books. New York, NY.
1974. ISBN:0-465-03008-4, ISBN13: 978-0-465-03008-8.
Dewey:296/.09. LCCN:73-090131.
Audience: **g,l,u,f.** *B*

Judaism > History > Ancient

Cohen, Shaye J. D.   BM176.C615
From the Maccabees to the Mishnah. Ed. 2. Trade Cloth.
Westminster John Knox Press. Louisville, KY. 2006. 272p.
ISBN:0-664-22743-0, ISBN13: 978-0-664-22743-2.
Dewey:296/.09/014.

Audience: **u,f.** *Choice, 1987.*

Collins, John J.   BM176.C64 2000
Between Athens and Jerusalem: Jewish Identity in the
Hellenistic Diaspora. Ed. 2. Trade Paper. William B. Eerdmans
Publishing Company. Grand Rapids, MI. 1999. 343p. Biblical
Resource Ser. ISBN:0-8028-4372-7, ISBN13:
978-0-8028-4372-2. Dewey:296/.09/014. LCCN:99-046739.
Audience: **u,f.** *Choice, 2000.*

Davies, W. D. & Finkelstein,   BM165
Louis (Editors)
The Hellenistic Age, Vol. 2. Cloth Text. Cambridge University
Press. New York, NY. 1990. 756p. The Cambridge History of
Judaism Ser. ISBN:0-521-21929-9, ISBN13: 978-0-521-21929-7.
Dewey:296/.0901. LCCN:77-085704.

Audience: **u,f.**

Davies, W. D. & Finkelstein,   BM155.2 .C35 1984
Louis (Editors)
Introduction: The Persian Period. W. D. Davies & L. Finkelstein
(Contribution by). Trade Cloth. Cambridge University Press.
New York, NY. 1984. 495p. The Cambridge History of Judaism
Ser. ISBN:0-521-21880-2, ISBN13: 978-0-521-21880-1.
Dewey:296/.0901. LCCN:77-085704.

Audience: **u,f.** *B*

Grabbe, Lester L.   BM176.G68 2000
Judaic Religion in the Second Temple Period: Belief and
Practice from the Exile to Yavneh. Paper over Boards.
Routledge. New York, NY. 2000. 448p. ISBN:0-415-21250-2,
ISBN13: 978-0-415-21250-2. Dewey:296/.09/014.
LCCN:00-023228.

Audience: **u,f.**

Horbury, William (Editor),   BM155.2
et al.
The Early Roman Period. W. D. Davies & John Sturdy
(Editors), Louis Finkelstein & W. D. Davies (Contribution by).
Cloth Text. Cambridge University Press. New York, NY. 1999.
1300p. The Cambridge History of Judaism Ser., Vol. 3
ISBN:0-521-24377-7, ISBN13: 978-0-521-24377-3.
Dewey:296/.0901. LCCN:77-085704.

Audience: **u,f.**

Kaufmann, Yehezkel   BM155
The Religion of Israel: From Its Beginnings to the Babylonian
Exile. Moshe Greenberg (Translator). Trade Paper. Knopf
Publishing Group. New York, NY. 1972. 304p.
ISBN:0-8052-0364-8, ISBN13: 978-0-8052-0364-6.
Dewey:296/.09. LCCN:60-005466.

Audience: **l,u,f.**

Moore, George Foot   **BM177**
1930 ed. Judaism in the First Centuries of the Christian Era: The Age of
the Tannaim. Other. Hendrickson Publishers, Inc. Peabody, MA.
1997. 1296p. ISBN:1-56563-286-9, ISBN13:
978-1-56563-286-8. Dewey:296.

Audience: **u,f.**

Neusner, Jacob   **BM177.S761992**
The Study of Ancient Judaism: The Palestinian and Babylonian
Talmuds, Vol. II. Trade Cloth. Scholars Press. Atlanta, GA.
1992. 244p. ISBN:1-55540-742-0, ISBN13: 978-1-55540-742-1.
Dewey:296.1/2/007. LCCN:92-019867.

Audience: **u,f.**

Neusner, Jacob (Editor)   **BM177**
The Study of Ancient Judaism: Mishnah, Midrash, Siddur. Trade
Cloth. Scholars Press. Atlanta, GA. 1992. 336p.
ISBN:1-55540-741-2, ISBN13: 978-1-55540-741-4.
Dewey:296.1/2/007. LCCN:92-019867.

Audience: **u,f.**

Sanders, E. P.   **BM177**
1977 ed. Paul and Palestinian Judaism: A Comparison of Patterns of
Religion. Trade Paper. Augsburg Fortress, Publishers.
Minneapolis, MN. 2003. 500p. ISBN:0-8006-1899-8, ISBN13:
978-0-8006-1899-5. Dewey:296.3/0933. LCCN:76-062612.

Audience: **u,f.** *B*

Schiffman, Lawrence H.   **BM176.T49 1998**
Texts and Traditions: A Source Reader for the Study of Second
Temple and Rabbinic Judaism. Trade Cloth. Ktav Publishing
House, Inc. Jersey City, NJ. 1997. xxvi, 777p.
ISBN:0-88125-434-7, ISBN13: 978-0-88125-434-1.
Dewey:296/.09/014. LCCN:97-035800.

Audience: **u,f.** *Choice, 1998.*

Judaism > History > Medieval and Renaissance

Cohen, Mark R.   **DS118**
Under Crescent and Cross: The Jews in the Middle Ages. Trade
Paper. Princeton University Press. Princeton, NJ. 1995. 302p.
ISBN:0-691-01082-X, ISBN13: 978-0-691-01082-3.
Dewey:909/.04924.

Audience: **l,u,f.** *Choice, 1994.*

Gerber, Jane S.   **DP17**
The Jews of Spain: A History of the Sephardic Experience.
Mishkenot Sha'ananim (Preface by). Trade Paper. Simon &
Schuster. New York, NY. 1994. 400p. ISBN:0-02-911574-4,
ISBN13: 978-0-02-911574-9. Dewey:946. LCCN:92-026941.

Audience: **g,l,u,f.** *Choice, 1993.*

Marcus, Jacob R.   **DS124**
Jew in the Medieval World: A Source Book, 315-1791. Ed.
1938. Trade Cloth. Wayne State University Press. Detroit, MI.
2000. 512p. ISBN:0-8143-2892-X, ISBN13: 978-0-8143-2892-7.
Dewey:296.

Audience: **l,u,f.**

Roth, Cecil   **DS113 .R66**
The Jews in the Renaissance. Trade Paper. Jewish Publication
Society. Dulles, VA. 1978. 378p. ISBN:0-8276-0103-4, ISBN13:
978-0-8276-0103-1. Dewey:945.05. LCCN:59-008516.

Audience: **l,u,f.**

Stillman, Norman A.   **DS118**
The Jews of Arab Lands: A History and Source Book. Trade
Paper. Jewish Publication Society. Dulles, VA. 416p.
ISBN:0-8276-0198-0, ISBN13: 978-0-8276-0198-7.
Dewey:909.04924. LCCN:78-070078.

Audience: **l,u,f.**

Judaism > History > Modern European Jewry

Dawidowicz, Lucy S.   **D810.J4D33 1986**
The War Against the Jews, 1933-1945. Trade Cloth. Simon &
Schuster. New York, NY. 1986. 496p. ISBN:0-02-908030-4,
ISBN13: 978-0-02-908030-6. Dewey:940.53/15/03924.
LCCN:86-006516.

Audience: **g,l,u,f.** *B*

Dubnow, Simon   **DS135.R9D77 2000**
History of the Jews in Russia and Poland. Israel Friedlaender
(Translator). Trade Cloth. Avotaynu, Inc. Bergenfield, NJ. 2000.
xii, 603p. ISBN:1-886223-11-4, ISBN13: 978-1-886223-11-0.
Dewey:947.004/924. LCCN:00-033175.

Audience: **u,f.** *B*

Hilberg, Raul   **D804.3.H548 2002**
1985 ed. The Destruction of the European Jews. Ed. 3. Cloth over
Boards. Yale University Press. Cumberland, RI. 2003. 1440p.
ISBN:0-300-09557-0, ISBN13: 978-0-300-09557-9.
Dewey:940.53/18. LCCN:2002-066369.

Audience: **g,l,u,f.** *B Choice, 2004.*

Meyer, Michael A.   **BM197.M48 1995**
1988 ed. Response to Modernity: A History of the Reform Movement in
Judaism. Trade Cloth. Wayne State University Press. Detroit,
MI. 1995. 508p. ISBN:0-8143-2555-6, ISBN13:
978-0-8143-2555-1. Dewey:296.8/346/09. LCCN:94-045560.

Audience: **u,f.** *Choice, 1989.*

Reinharz, Jehuda &   **DS102.J43 1995**
  Mendes-Flohr, Paul R. (Editors)
The Jew in the Modern World: A Documentary History. Ed. 2.
Paper Text. Oxford University Press, Inc. New York, NY. 1995.
766p. ISBN:0-19-507453-X, ISBN13: 978-0-19-507453-6.
Dewey:909/.04924. LCCN:94-009181.

Audience: **g,l,u,f.**

Sachar, Howard M.   **DS125.S28 1990**
1977 ed. Course of Modern Jewish History. Ed. 2. Trade Paper. Knopf
Publishing Group. New York, NY. 1990. 912p.
ISBN:0-679-72746-9, ISBN13: 978-0-679-72746-0.
Dewey:909/.04924. LCCN:89-040528.

Audience: **g,l,u,f.**

Judaism > History > American Judaism

Karp, Abraham J.   **E184.J5**
Haven and Home: A History of the Jews in America. Trade
Paper. Knopf Publishing Group. New York, NY. 1985. 416p.
ISBN:0-8052-0817-8, ISBN13: 978-0-8052-0817-7.
Dewey:973/.04924. LCCN:84-005530.

Audience: **l,u,f.** *B*

Marcus, Jacob R.   **E184.J5M199 1995**
The American Jew, 1545-1990: A History. Trade Cloth. Carlson
Publishing, Inc. Brooklyn, NY. 1995. viii, 475p.
ISBN:0-926019-89-9, ISBN13: 978-0-926019-89-8.
Dewey:973/.04924. LCCN:95-021034.

Audience: **u,f.** *Choice, 1996.*

Sarna, Jonathan D.   **BM205.S26 2004**
American Judaism: A History. Cloth over Boards. Yale
University Press. Cumberland, RI. 2004. 512p.
ISBN:0-300-10197-X, ISBN13: 978-0-300-10197-3.
Dewey:296/.0973. LCCN:2003-014464.

Audience: **l,u,f.** *Choice, 2004.*

Sorin, Gerald   **E184.J5S666 1997**
Tradition Transformed: The Jewish Experience in America.
Trade Paper. Johns Hopkins University Press. Baltimore, MD.
1997. 312p. The American Moment Ser. ISBN:0-8018-5447-4,
ISBN13: 978-0-8018-5447-7. Dewey:973/.04924.
LCCN:96-028303.

Audience: **l,u,f.** *Choice, 1997.*

Judaism > History > Israel and Zionism

Hertzberg, Arthur (Editor,   **DS149.Z675 1997**
Introduction by)
The Zionist Idea: A Historical Analysis and Reader. Trade Paper.
Jewish Publication Society. Dulles, VA. 1997. 656p.
ISBN:0-8276-0622-2, ISBN13: 978-0-8276-0622-7.
Dewey:320.54/095694. LCCN:96-049372.

Audience: **u,f.**

Laqueur, Walter   **DS149**
A History of Zionism: From the French Revolution to the
Establishment of the State of Israel. Trade Paper. Knopf
Publishing Group. New York, NY. 2003. 688p.
ISBN:0-8052-1149-7, ISBN13: 978-0-8052-1149-8.
Dewey:956.94/001. LCCN:2003-269536.

Audience: **u,f.**

Sachar, Howard Morley   **DS126.5**
A History of Israel: From the Rise of Zionism to Our Time. Ed.

2. Trade Paper. Random House, Inc. New York, NY. 1996.
1184p. ISBN:0-679-76563-8, ISBN13: 978-0-679-76563-9.
Dewey:956.94.

Audience: **g,l,u,f.**

Judaism > Judaism and Christianity

Chilton, Bruce D. &   **BM535.C5157 2004**
  Neusner, Jacob
Classical Christianity and Rabbinic Judaism: Comparing
Theologies. Trade Paper. Baker Academic. Ada, MI. 2004. 288p.
ISBN:0-8010-2787-X, ISBN13: 978-0-8010-2787-1.
Dewey:261.2/6. LCCN:2004-016943.

Audience: **u,f.** *Choice, 2005.*

Cohen, Arthur Allen   **BM535.C6 1971**
The Myth of the Judeo-Christian Tradition, and Other
Dissenting Essays. Trade Cloth. Knopf Publishing Group. New
York, NY. 1971. xx, 223p. ISBN:0-8052-0293-5, ISBN13:
978-0-8052-0293-9. Dewey:296.3/87/2. LCCN:77-152766.

Audience: **u,f.** *B*

Gager, John G.   **DS145**
The Origins of Anti-Semitism: Attitudes Toward Judaism in
Pagan and Christian Antiquity. Paper Text. Oxford University
Press, Inc. New York, NY. 1985. 312p. ISBN:0-19-503607-7,
ISBN13: 978-0-19-503607-7. Dewey:296.3/872.
LCCN:82-024523.

Audience: **u,f.** *B*

Jacobs, Andrew S.   **BM535.J26 2003**
Remains of the Jews: The Holy Land and Christian Empire in
Late Antiquity. Trade Cloth. Stanford University Press. Palo
Alto, CA. 2004. xiv, 249p. Divinations Ser.
ISBN:0-8047-4705-9, ISBN13: 978-0-8047-4705-9.
Dewey:261.2/6/095694. LCCN:2003-010165.

Audience: **u,f.**

Neusner, Jacob   **BM177.N475 1984**
Judaism in the Beginning of Christianity. Trade Paper. Augsburg
Fortress, Publishers. Minneapolis, MN. 2003. 112p.
ISBN:0-8006-1750-9, ISBN13: 978-0-8006-1750-9.
Dewey:296/.09/01. LCCN:83-048000.

Audience: **l,u,f.** *B*

Oberman, Heiko A.   **BM535.O2413 1984**
The Roots of Anti-Semitism: In the Age of Renaissance and
Reformation. James I. Porter (Translator). Trade Cloth. Sigler
Press. Mifflintown, PA. 1983. 163p. ISBN:0-8006-0709-0,
ISBN13: 978-0-8006-0709-8. Dewey:261.2/6. LCCN:83-005695.

Audience: **u,f.** *B*

Sandmel, Samuel   **BM155.2**
Judaism and Christian Beginnings. Trade Paper. Oxford
University Press, Inc. New York, NY. 1978. 526p.
ISBN:0-19-502282-3, ISBN13: 978-0-19-502282-7.
Dewey:296/.09.

Audience: **l,u.** *B*

Judaism > Judaism and Christianity > Sources of Judaism. Talmud

BM517.M6
1939 ed. Midrash Rabbah, Set. Trade Cloth. Soncino Press. Brooklyn,
NY. 1999. ISBN:0-900689-38-2, ISBN13: 978-0-900689-38-3.
Dewey:296.14.

Audience: **u,f.**

Blackman, Philip   **BM505.A1**
  (Translator)
The Mishnah. Trade Cloth. Judaica Press, Incorporated, The.
Brooklyn, NY. 1962. 4050p. ISBN:0-910818-00-2, ISBN13:
978-0-910818-00-1. Dewey:296.

Audience: **u,f.**

Braude, William G.   **BM511**
  (Translator)
The Midrash on Psalms. Cloth over Boards. Yale University
Press. Cumberland, RI. 1959. 1229p. Judaica Ser., No. 13
ISBN:0-300-00322-6, ISBN13: 978-0-300-00322-2.
Dewey:296.1/405/21. LCCN:58-006535.

Audience: **u,f.** *B*

Braude, William G. (Editor)   **BM601**
Pesikta Rabbati: Homiletical Discourses for Festal Days and
Special Sabbaths. Cloth over Boards. Yale University Press.
Cumberland, RI. 1968. 1015p. Judaica Ser., No. 18
ISBN:0-300-01071-0, ISBN13: 978-0-300-01071-8.
Dewey:296.3. LCCN:68-027748.

Audience: **u,f.**

Fine, Lawrence   **BM525.A2S24 1984**
Safed Spirituality: Rules of Mystical Piety, the Beginning of
Wisdom. Trade Cloth. Paulist Press. Mahwah, NJ. 1984. 224p.
Classics of Western Spirituality Ser. ISBN:0-8091-2612-5,
ISBN13: 978-0-8091-2612-5. Dewey:296.8/33.
LCCN:84-060735.

Audience: **u,f.** *B*

Freehof, Solomon B.   **F2423 .E7713**
The Responsa Literature and a Treasury of Responsa. Trade
Cloth. Ktav Publishing House, Inc. Jersey City, NJ. 1983.
ISBN:0-87068-212-1, ISBN13: 978-0-87068-212-4.
Dewey:988/.3/01. LCCN:73-001345.

Audience: **u,f.**

Ginzberg, Louis   **BM530.G513 2003**
ebook The Legends of the Jews, Vol. 1. Ed. 2. Trade Cloth, Prepack.
Jewish Publication Society. Dulles, VA. 2002. 1,650p.
ISBN:0-8276-0709-1, ISBN13: 978-0-8276-0709-5.
Dewey:296.1/9. LCCN:2003-047540.

Audience: **u,f.** *B*

Maimonides   **KBM520.84**
The Code of Maimonides, Bks. 5-6 & 8-14. Trade Cloth. Yale
University Press. Cumberland, RI. Judaica Ser.
ISBN:0-318-56512-9, ISBN13: 978-0-318-56512-5.
Dewey:296.1/72.

Audience: **u,f.**

Maimonides, Moses &   **BM700.M235132004**
  Kellner, Menachem Marc
The Code of Maimonides (Mishneh Torah): The Book of Love.
Cloth over Boards. Yale University Press. Cumberland, RI.
2004. 272p. Yale Judaica Ser., Vol. 32 ISBN:0-300-10348-4,
ISBN13: 978-0-300-10348-9. Dewey:296.1/812.
LCCN:2004-048078.

Audience: **u,f.**

Maimonides   **PQ145.6.T5**
The Code of Maimonides: The Book of Seasons. Solomon
Gandz & Hyman Klein (Translators), Leon Nemoy (Introduction
by). Cloth over Boards. Yale University Press. Cumberland, RI.
1961. 657p. Judaica Ser., No. 14 ISBN:0-300-00475-3, ISBN13:
978-0-300-00475-5. Dewey:840.9.

Audience: **u,f.**

Maimonides & Twersky,   **BM197**
  Isadore
Introduction to the Code of Maimonides (Mishneh Torah). Trade
Paper. Yale University Press. Cumberland, RI. 1982. 656p. Yale
Judaica Ser., No. XXII ISBN:0-300-02846-6, ISBN13:
978-0-300-02846-1. Dewey:296.1/8. LCCN:79-010347.

Audience: **l,u,f.** *B*

Matt, Daniel Chanan   **BM525.A52**
  (Introduction by)
2004 ed. Zohar: The Book of Enlightenment. Trade Paper. SPCK
Publishing. London, 1983. xvi, 320p. ISBN:0-281-04068-0,
ISBN13: 978-0-281-04068-1. Dewey:296.1/6.

Audience: **l,u,f**

Montefiore, C. G. & Loewe,   **BM516**
  H. (Editors)
1974 ed. A Rabbinic Anthology. Trade Paper. Knopf Publishing Group.
New York, NY. 1987. 854p. ISBN:0-8052-0442-3, ISBN13:
978-0-8052-0442-1. Dewey:296.142. LCCN:73-091340.

Audience: **u,f.** *B*

Neusner, Jacob   **BM496.5.N4797 1994**
1999 ed. Introduction to Rabbinic Literature. Trade Cloth. Doubleday
Publishing. New York, NY. 1994. 752p. The Anchor Bible
Reference Library Ser. ISBN:0-385-47093-2, ISBN13:
978-0-385-47093-3. Dewey:296.1. LCCN:93-028109.

Audience: **l,u,f.**

Neusner, Jacob   **BM506.M5**
The Mishnah: A New Translation. Trade Paper. Yale University
Press. Cumberland, RI. 1991. 1207p. ISBN:0-300-05022-4,
ISBN13: 978-0-300-05022-6. Dewey:296.1/2305.

Audience: **u,f.** *Choice, 1989.*

Neusner, Jacob &   **BM514.E53 2005**
  Avery-Peck, Alan J.
Encyclopaedia of Midrash: Biblical Interpretation in Formative

Judaism. Trade Cloth. Brill Academic Publishers, Inc. Boston, MA. 2005. xi, 1077p. ISBN:90-04-14334-3, ISBN13: 978-90-04-14334-0. Dewey:296.1/4/003. LCCN:2004-058219.

Audience: **u,f.**

Scholem, Gershom   **BM526**
Kabbalah. Trade Paper. Penguin Group (USA) Inc. New York, NY. 1978. 512p. ISBN:0-452-01007-1, ISBN13: 978-0-452-01007-9. Dewey:296.16.

Audience: **g,l,u,f.** *B*

Scholem, Gershom   **BM525.S3753 1996**
On the Kabbalah and Its Symbolism. Ralph Manheim (Translator), Bernard McGinn (Foreword by). Trade Paper. Knopf Publishing Group. New York, NY. 1996. 240p. ISBN:0-8052-1051-2, ISBN13: 978-0-8052-1051-4. Dewey:296.1/6. LCCN:95-031334.

Audience: **g,l,u,f.**

Stemberger, Gunter   **BM503.5 .S8713 1992**
Introduction to the Talmud and Midrash. Markus Bockmuehl & Jacob Neusner (Translators), Hermann L. Strack (Foreword by). Trade Paper. Augsburg Fortress, Publishers. Minneapolis, MN. 2003. 488p. ISBN:0-8006-2524-2, ISBN13: 978-0-8006-2524-5. Dewey:296.1/2061. LCCN:92-022974.

Audience: **u,f.**

Judaism > Principles of Judaism

Baeck, Leo   **BM560 .B32**
Essence of Judaism. Trade Paper. Knopf Publishing Group. New York, NY. 1987. 287p. ISBN:0-8052-0006-1, ISBN13: 978-0-8052-0006-5. Dewey:296. LCCN:61-008992.

Audience: **g,l.** *B*

Heschel, Abraham Joshua   **BM561**
God in Search of Man: A Philosophy of Judaism. Trade Cloth. Rowman & Littlefield Publishers, Inc. Lanham, MD. 1987. 478p. ISBN:0-87668-955-1, ISBN13: 978-0-87668-955-4. Dewey:296. LCCN:87-071336.

Audience: **g,l,u,f.** *B*

Rosenzweig, Franz   **BM45.R67213 1998**
God, Man and the World: Lectures and Essays. Barbara E. Galli (Editor, Translator), Michael Oppenheim (Introduction by). Trade Paper. Syracuse University Press. Syracuse, NY. 1998. 128p. Library of Jewish Philosophy ISBN:0-8156-2789-0, ISBN13: 978-0-8156-2789-0. Dewey:296.3. LCCN:98-027105.

Audience: **u,f.**

Steinberg, Milton   **BM560.S8 1987**
Basic Judaism. Trade Cloth. Rowman & Littlefield Publishers, Inc. Lanham, MD. 1987. 240p. ISBN:0-87668-975-6, ISBN13: 978-0-87668-975-2. Dewey:296. LCCN:87-026991.

Audience: **g,l,u,f.** *B*

Twersky, Isadore (Editor,   **BM545.A45T9 1972**
  Introduction by, Notes by)
A Maimonides Reader. Trade Cloth. Behrman House, Inc.

Springfield, NJ. 1972. "xvii, 494"p. Library of Jewish Studies ISBN:0-87441-200-5, ISBN13: 978-0-87441-200-0. Dewey:296.3. LCCN:76-160818.

Audience: **l,u,f.** *B*

Judaism > Dogmatic Judaism. Apologetics

Borowitz, Eugene B.   **BM601**
Renewing the Covenant: A Theology for the Postmodern Jew. Trade Paper. Jewish Publication Society. Dulles, VA. 1996. 320p. ISBN:0-8276-0627-3, ISBN13: 978-0-8276-0627-2. Dewey:296.3.

Audience: **g,u,f.**

Cohen, Hermann   **BM45 .C613 1993**
Reason and Hope: Selections from the Jewish Writings of Hermann Cohen. Eva Jospe (Translator, Introduction by). Trade Paper. Hebrew Union College Press. Cincinnati, OH. 1993. 237p. ISBN:0-87820-211-0, ISBN13: 978-0-87820-211-9. Dewey:296. LCCN:93-007895.

Audience: **u,f.**

Danzger, M. Herbert   **BM205 .D27**
Returning to Tradition: The Contemporary Revival of Orthodox Judaism. Trade Paper. Yale University Press. Cumberland, RI. 1989. 384p. ISBN:0-300-10559-2, ISBN13: 978-0-300-10559-9. Dewey:296.8/32/095694.

Audience: **u,f.** *Choice, 1990.*

Fackenheim, Emil L.   **BM561.F24 1999**
What Is Judaism?: An Interpretation for the Present Age. Paper Text. Syracuse University Press. Syracuse, NY. 1999. 328p. Library of Jewish Philosophy ISBN:0-8156-0623-0, ISBN13: 978-0-8156-0623-9. Dewey:296. LCCN:99-037825.

Audience: **g,l,u,f.**

Fishbane, Michael A.   **BM514.F57 1998**
The Exegetical Imagination: On Jewish Thought and Theology. Trade Cloth. Harvard University Press. Cambridge, MA. 1998. 460p. ISBN:0-674-27461-X, ISBN13: 978-0-674-27461-7. Dewey:296.3. LCCN:98-012599.

Audience: **u,f.**

Gillman, Neil   **BM197.5.G51993**
Conservative Judaism: The New Century. Trade Paper. Behrman House, Inc. Springfield, NJ. 1993. ISBN:0-87441-547-0, ISBN13: 978-0-87441-547-6. Dewey:296.8/342/09. LCCN:93-014637.

Audience: **u,f.**

Jacobs, Louis   **BM601**
Jewish Theology. Trade Paper. Behrman House, Inc. Springfield, NJ. 1973. 384p. ISBN:0-87441-226-9, ISBN13: 978-0-87441-226-0. Dewey:296.3. LCCN:73-017442.

Audience: **u,f.**

Kadushin, Max   **BM496.5 .K3 1972**
Rabbinic Mind. Ed. 3. Trade Paper. Bloch Publishing Company.
New York, NY. 1972. ISBN:0-8197-0007-X, ISBN13:
978-0-8197-0007-0. Dewey:296.1/4. LCCN:75-189016.
Audience: **u,f.**

Kellner, Menachem M   **BM603.K44 1986**
Dogma in Medieval Jewish Thought: From Maimonides to
Abravanel. Springer London, Ltd. 1986. The Littman Library of
Jewish Civilization ISBN:0-19-710044-9, ISBN13:
978-0-19-710044-8.

Plaut, W. Gunther & Meyer,   **BM197.R393 2000**
  Michael
The Reform Judaism Reader: North American Documents. Trade
Paper. URJ Press. New York, NY. 2004. xi, 228p.
ISBN:0-8074-0732-1, ISBN13: 978-0-8074-0732-5.
Dewey:296.8/341/0973. LCCN:00-041765.
Audience: **u,f.**

Scholem, Gershom   **BM615.S33 1995**
The Messianic Idea in Judaism: And Other Essays on Jewish
Spirituality. Arthur Herztberg (Introduction by). Book, Other.
Knopf Publishing Group. New York, NY. 1995. 400p.
ISBN:0-8052-1043-1, ISBN13: 978-0-8052-1043-9.
Dewey:296.3/3. LCCN:95-008425.
Audience: **l,u,f.**

Soloveitchik, Joseph B.   **BM723**
Halakhic Man. Lawrence Kaplan (Translator). Trade Paper.
Jewish Publication Society. Dulles, VA. 1984. 164p.
ISBN:0-8276-0397-5, ISBN13: 978-0-8276-0397-4.
Dewey:296.7.
Audience: **u,f.**

Judaism > Practical Judaism

Donin, Hayim H.   **BM700.D58 1991**
1972 ed. To Be a Jew: A Guide to Jewish Observance in Contemporary
Life. Norman Lamm (Introduction by). Trade Paper. Basic
Books. New York, NY. 1991. 368p. ISBN:0-465-08632-2,
ISBN13: 978-0-465-08632-0. Dewey:296.4. LCCN:72-089175.
Audience: **l,f.** *B*

Gaster, Theodor Herzl   **BM690**
Festivals of the Jewish Year: A Modern Interpretation and Guide
Theodor H. Gaster. Paper Text. Textbook Publishers. Temecula,
CA. 2003. 308p. ISBN:0-7581-3694-3, ISBN13:
978-0-7581-3694-7. Dewey:296.4.
Audience: **g,l,u,f.** *B*

Hertz, Joseph H., trans.   **BM675.D3**
Siddur. The Authorised Daily Prayer Book. New York: Bloch
Pub. Co.. 1948.
Audience: **g,l,u,f.**

Heschel, Abraham Joshua   **BM750.H48 1985**
The Circle of Baal Shem Tov: Studies in Hasidism. Samuel H.
Dresner (Editor). Trade Cloth. University of Chicago Press.
Chicago, IL. 1997. 280p. ISBN:0-226-32960-7, ISBN13:
978-0-226-32960-4. Dewey:296.8/33/0922 B. LCCN:84-016340.
Audience: **u,f.** *B Choice, 1985.*

Jacob, Walter (Editor)   **BM197 .J33 1987**
Contemporary American Reform Responsa. Trade Paper. Central
Conference of American Rabbis/ CCAR Press. New York, NY.
1988. 322p. ISBN:0-88123-003-0, ISBN13: 978-0-88123-003-1.
Dewey:296.1/8. LCCN:87-021339.
Audience: **u,f.**

Jacobs, Louis   **BM723**
Hasidic Prayer. Trade Paper. Littman Library of Jewish
Civilization, The. London, 1993. 222p. ISBN:1-874774-18-8,
ISBN13: 978-1-874774-18-1. Dewey:296.7/2. LCCN:93-027377.
Audience: **u,f.** *B*

Jacobs, Louis   **BM729.P7**
Jewish Mystical Testimonies. Trade Paper. Knopf Publishing
Group. New York, NY. 1987. 270p. ISBN:0-8052-0585-3,
ISBN13: 978-0-8052-0585-5. Dewey:296.7/1. LCCN:76-046644.
Audience: **l,u,f.** *B*

Klein, Isaac   **BM700 .K54**
A Guide to Jewish Religious Practice. Trade Cloth. Jewish
Theological Seminary of America. New York, NY. 1979.
Moreshet Ser., No. VI ISBN:0-317-64345-2, ISBN13:
978-0-317-64345-9. Dewey:296.4.
Audience: **l,u,f.**

Millgram, Abraham E.   **BM660**
Jewish Worship. Trade Cloth. Jewish Publication Society.
Dulles, VA. 1971. 674p. ISBN:0-8276-0003-8, ISBN13:
978-0-8276-0003-4. Dewey:296.4/09. LCCN:77-151316.
Audience: **g,l,u,f.** *B*

Satlow, Michael L.   **BM45**
Creating Judaism: History, Tradition, Practice. Trade Cloth.
Columbia University Press. New York, NY. 2006. 384p.
ISBN:0-231-13488-6, ISBN13: 978-0-231-13488-0. Dewey:296.
LCCN:2006-018056.
Audience: **l,u,f.**

Scholem, Gershom   **BM723.S35 1995**
1961 ed. Major Trends in Jewish Mysticism. Robert Alter (Introduction
by). Trade Paper. Knopf Publishing Group. New York, NY.
1995. 496p. ISBN:0-8052-1042-3, ISBN13: 978-0-8052-1042-2.
Dewey:296.8/33. LCCN:95-002182.
Audience: **u,f.**

Washofsky, Mark   **BM197.W37 2000**
Jewish Living: A Guide to Contemporay Reform Practice. Aron
Hirt-Manheimer (Editor). Trade Paper. URJ Press. New York,
NY. 2004. 320p. ISBN:0-8074-0702-X, ISBN13:
978-0-8074-0702-8. Dewey:296.8/341. LCCN:00-033770.
Audience: **u,f.**

Judaism > Practical Judaism > Women in Judaism

Baskin, Judith   BM729.W6J49 1999
Jewish Women in Historical Perspective. Ed. 2. Trade Cloth.
Wayne State University Press. Detroit, MI. 1999. 416p.
ISBN:0-8143-2713-3, ISBN13: 978-0-8143-2713-5.
Dewey:296/.082. LCCN:98-026374.
                                                Audience: **u,f.**

Goldman, Karla   BM729.W6G65 2000
Beyond the Synagogue Gallery: Finding a Place for Women in
American Judaism. Trade Cloth. Harvard University Press.
Cambridge, MA. 2000. 288p. ISBN:0-674-00221-0, ISBN13:
978-0-674-00221-0. Dewey:296/.082/0973. LCCN:00-021149.
                                                Audience: **u,f.**

Goldstein, Elyse (Editor)   BS1225.3.G578 2000
The Women's Torah Commentary: New Insights from Women
Rabbis on the 54 Weekly Torah Portions. Trade Cloth. Jewish
Lights Publishing. Woodstock, VT. 2000. 496p.
ISBN:1-58023-076-8, ISBN13: 978-1-58023-076-6.
Dewey:222/.107/082. LCCN:00-008694.
                                                Audience: **g,l,u,f.**

Greenberg, Blu   BM729.W6
On Women and Judaism: A View from Tradition. Trade Paper.
Jewish Publication Society. Dulles, VA. 1983. 178p.
ISBN:0-8276-0226-X, ISBN13: 978-0-8276-0226-7.
Dewey:296.3/878344. LCCN:81-011779.
                                                Audience: **g,l,u,f.**

Hauptman, Judith   BM509.W7
Rereading the Rabbis: A Woman's Voice. Trade Paper. Westview
Press. Boulder, CO. 1998. 304p. ISBN:0-8133-3406-3, ISBN13:
978-0-8133-3406-6. Dewey:296.1/2/0082.
                                                Audience: **u,f.** *Choice, 1998.*

1983
ed.
Heschel, Susannah   BM729.W6O6 1995
On Being a Jewish Feminist. Ed. 2. Trade Cloth. Knopf
Publishing Group. New York, NY. 1995. 352p.
ISBN:0-8052-1036-9, ISBN13: 978-0-8052-1036-1.
Dewey:296.3/878344. LCCN:95-234651.
                                                Audience: **g,l.** *B*

Hyman, Paula E. & Moore,   DS115.2.J49 1997
Deborah Dash (Editors)
Jewish Women in America: An Historical Encyclopedia, Set.
Paper over Boards. Routledge. New York, NY. 1997. 1800p.
ISBN:0-415-91936-3, ISBN13: 978-0-415-91936-4.
Dewey:920.72/089/924073 B. LCCN:97-026842.
                                                Audience: **g,l,u,f.** *Choice, 1998.*

Koltun, Elizabeth (Editor)   HQ1154
The Jewish Woman: New Perspectives. Trade Paper. Knopf
Publishing Group. New York, NY. 1987. 320p.
ISBN:0-8052-0532-2, ISBN13: 978-0-8052-0532-9.
Dewey:301.41/2. LCCN:75-035445.
                                                Audience: **l,u,f.** *B*

Islam

                                                Z7835.M6
☐ Index Islamicus Online.
http://www.indexislamicus.com/online.html
                                                Audience: **u,f.**

Abdullahi, Ahmed-An-Na'im   LAW
Toward an Islamic Reformation: Civil Liberties, Human Rights
and International Law. John Voll (Foreword by). Cloth Text.
Syracuse University Press. Syracuse, NY. 1990. 240p.
Contemporary Issues in the Middle East Ser.
ISBN:0-8156-2484-0, ISBN13: 978-0-8156-2484-4.
Dewey:340.5/9. LCCN:89-021828.
                                                Audience: **u,f.** *Choice, 1990.*

Ahmad, Aziz   DS36.85 .I8 NO. 7
An Intellectual History of Islamic India. Trade Cloth. Edinburgh
University Press. Edinburgh, 1979. x, 226p.
ISBN:0-85224-057-0, ISBN13: 978-0-85224-057-1.
Dewey:915.4/0976/7. LCCN:69-016010.
                                                Audience: **u,f.** *B*

Ahmad, Imtiaz (Editor)   BP63.I4R48
Ritual and Religion among Muslims in India. Trade Cloth.
Manohar Publications. New Delhi, 1982. ISBN:0-8364-0852-7,
ISBN13: 978-0-8364-0852-2. Dewey:306/.6/0954.
                                                Audience: **u,f.**

Ahmed, Akbar S.   BP52.A35 2002
Discovering Islam: Making Sense of Muslim History and
Society. Ed. 2. Paper over Boards. Routledge. New York, NY.
2002. 272p. ISBN:0-415-28524-0, ISBN13: 978-0-415-28524-7.
Dewey:297/.09. LCCN:2002-021320.
                                                Audience: **l,u,f.**

Ahmed, Akbar S.   BP161.2
Islam Today: A Short Introduction to the Muslim World. Trade
Paper. I. B. Tauris & Company, Ltd. London, 1999. 272p.
ISBN:1-86064-257-8, ISBN13: 978-1-86064-257-9. Dewey:297.
                                                Audience: **g,l,u,f.**

Bearman, P. (Editor)   DS35.53
☐ Encyclopedia of Islam Online.
http://www.brill.nl/product_id22380.htm
Bianquis, T. (Editor); Bosworth, C. E. (Editor); van Donzel, E.
(Editor); Heinrichs, W. P. (Editor).
                                                Audience: **g,l,u,f.**

Brill E   BP63.A4.S653 1983
Islam in South-East Asia. Trade Cloth. Brill Academic
Publishers, Inc. Boston, MA. 1983. viii, 262p.
ISBN:90-04-06844-9, ISBN13: 978-90-04-06844-5.
Dewey:297/.0959. LCCN:84-102654.
                                                Audience: **u,f.** *B*

Entelis, John P. (Editor)   BP64.A4N6428 1997
Islam, Democracy and the State in North Africa. Trade Cloth.

Indiana University Press. Bloomington, IN. 1997. 256p. Arab and Islamic Studies ISBN:0-253-33303-2, ISBN13: 978-0-253-33303-2. Dewey:320.961/09/048. LCCN:97-000410.

Audience: **u,f.**

Esposito, John L. (Editor)   BP60.P64 1997

Political Islam: Revolution, Radicalism, or Reform? Trade Cloth. Lynne Rienner Publishers, Inc. Boulder, CO. 1997. 310p. ISBN:1-55587-168-2, ISBN13: 978-1-55587-168-0. Dewey:320.5/5/0917671. LCCN:96-038160.

Audience: **u,f.** *Choice, 1998.*

Esposito, John L. (Editor)   BP52

Voices of Resurgent Islam. Paper Text. Oxford University Press, Inc. New York, NY. 1983. 304p. ISBN:0-19-503340-X, ISBN13: 978-0-19-503340-3. Dewey:297/.09/04. LCCN:82-024544.

Audience: **u,f.** *B*

Geertz, Clifford   BP63.I5

Islam Observed: Religious Development in Morocco and Indonesia. Trade Paper. University of Chicago Press. Chicago, IL. 1971. 144p. ISBN:0-226-28511-1, ISBN13: 978-0-226-28511-5. Dewey:297/.09598.

Audience: **u,f.** *B*

Goldziher, Ignac   BP25

Muslim Studies, Vol. 2. Stern,Samuel Miklos (Editor). Aldine Pub. Co.. 1971. Translation of Muhammedanische Studien

Audience: **u,f.**

Goldziher, Ignac   BP25.G6143

Muslim Studies. S. M. Stern (Editor, Translator), C. R. Barber (Translator). Cloth Text. State University of New York Press. Albany, NY. 1967. Muslim Studies, Vol. 1 ISBN:0-87395-234-0, ISBN13: 978-0-87395-234-7. Dewey:297. LCCN:72-011731.

Audience: **u,f.** *B*

Haddad, Yvonne Yazbeck &   D1056.2.M87M852 2002
Smith, Jane I. (Editors)

Muslim Minorities in the West: Visible and Invisible. Trade Cloth. AltaMira Press. Walnut Creek, CA. 2002. 328p. ISBN:0-7591-0217-1, ISBN13: 978-0-7591-0217-0. Dewey:305.6/97101821. LCCN:2001-045914.

Audience: **g,l,u,f.** *Choice, 2002.*

Hiskett, Mervyn   BP64.A4W4

Development of Islam in West Africa. Ed. 1. Paper Text. Longman Publishing Group. White Plains, NY. 1984. 353p. ISBN:0-582-64694-4, ISBN13: 978-0-582-64694-0. Dewey:297.0966. LCCN:82-006545.

Audience: **g,l,u,f.** *B*

Lapidus, Ira M.   DS35.63.L37 2002

A History of Islamic Societies. Ed. 2. Cloth Text. Cambridge University Press. New York, NY. 2002. 1000p. ISBN:0-521-77056-4, ISBN13: 978-0-521-77056-9. Dewey:909/.097671. LCCN:2002-074089.

Audience: **g,l,u,f.** *Choice, 1989.*

Martin, Richard C. (Editor)   BP40.E525 2003

Encyclopedia of Islam and the Muslim World. Trade Cloth. Thomson Gale. Farmington Hills, MI. 2003. xxxv, 823p. ISBN:0-02-865605-9, ISBN13: 978-0-02-865605-2. Dewey:909/.097671. LCCN:2003-009964.

Audience: **g,l,u,f.** *Choice, 2004.*

Martin, Richard C. (Editor)   BP40.E525 2003

Encyclopedia of Islam and the Muslim World. Trade Cloth. Thomson Gale. Farmington Hills, MI. 2003. xxxv, 823p. ISBN:0-02-865604-0, ISBN13: 978-0-02-865604-5. Dewey:909/.097671. LCCN:2003-009964.

Audience: **g,l,u,f.** *Choice, 2004.*

Noer, Deliar   BP63.I5

The Modernist Muslim Movement in Indonesia, 1900-1942. Trade Cloth. Oxford University Press. Oxford, 1973. xi, 390p. ISBN:0-19-638157-6, ISBN13: 978-0-19-638157-2. Dewey:301.45/29/710598.

Audience: **u,f.** *B*

Sanneh, Lamin   BP64.A4W367 1997

Crown and the Turban: Muslims and West African Pluralism. Trade Paper. Westview Press. Boulder, CO. 1996. 304p. ISBN:0-8133-3059-9, ISBN13: 978-0-8133-3059-4. Dewey:322.1/0966. LCCN:96-035598.

Audience: **l,u,f.** *Choice, 1997.*

Smith, Wilfred C.   BP25 .S6 1981

On Understanding Islam. Trade Cloth. Walter de Gruyter GmbH & Co. KG. Berlin, 1984. 352p. Religion and Reason Ser., No. 19 ISBN:90-279-3448-7, ISBN13: 978-90-279-3448-2. Dewey:297. LCCN:81-000871.

Audience: **g,l,u,f.** *B*

Trimingham, J. Spencer   BP64.A4.E27 1980

1964 ed Islam in East Africa. Library Binding. Ayer Company Publishers, Inc. Manchester, NH. 1980. xii, 198p. Islam Ser. ISBN:0-8369-9270-9, ISBN13: 978-0-8369-9270-0. Dewey:297/.0967. LCCN:79-052567.

Audience: **u,f.** *B*

Voll, John O.   BP60.V64 1994

Islam: Continuity and Change in the Modern World. Ed. 2. Trade Cloth. Syracuse University Press. Syracuse, NY. 1994. 400p. Contemporary Issues in the Middle East Ser. ISBN:0-8156-2639-8, ISBN13: 978-0-8156-2639-8. Dewey:297/.09/03. LCCN:94-022075.

Audience: **l,u,f.** *B*

Williams, John A. (Editor)   BP20

Themes of Islamic Civilization. Trade Paper. University of California Press. Berkeley, CA. 1971. 392p. ISBN:0-520-04514-9, ISBN13: 978-0-520-04514-9. Dewey:910.03/176/71.

Audience: **g,l,u,f.** *B*

Islam > Biography. Muhammad

Abbott, Nabia   **BP80.A3/**
Aishah: The Beloved of Mohammed. Box or Slipcased. Saqi
Books. London, 1985. xix, 230p. ISBN:0-86356-108-X,
ISBN13: 978-0-86356-108-5. Dewey:297/.64.

Audience: **u,f.**

1957 ed. **Andrae, Tor**   **BP75**
Mohammed: The Man and His Faith. Trade Paper. Kessinger
Publishing, LLC. Whitefish, MT. 2003. ISBN:0-7661-5958-2,
ISBN13: 978-0-7661-5958-7. Dewey:297/.63.

Audience: **g,l,u,f.**

Bennet, Clinton   **BP75.3.B461998**
In Search of Muhammad. Trade Cloth. Continuum International
Publishing Group, Ltd. London, 1998. 256p.
ISBN:0-304-33700-5, ISBN13: 978-0-304-33700-2.
LCCN:98-012243.

Audience: **l,u,f.**

Haykal, M. H.   **BP75**
The Life of Muhammad. R. I. Faruqi (Translator). Trade Cloth.
American Trust Publications. Burr Ridge, IN. 1976.
ISBN:0-89259-002-5, ISBN13: 978-0-89259-002-5.
Dewey:297.63. LCCN:76-003060.

Audience: **g,l,u,f.**

Ishaq, I.   **BP75.I2513 2001**
The Life of Muhammad. A. Guillaume (Translator). Trade
Cloth. Oxford University Press, Inc. New York, NY. 2002. 860p.
ISBN:0-19-636033-1, ISBN13: 978-0-19-636033-1.
Dewey:297.6/3 B. LCCN:2003-428555.

Audience: **g,l,u,f.**

Keddie, Nikki R.   **BP80.A45.K43**
Sayyid Jamal Ad-Din "Al-Afghani": A Political Biography.
Trade Cloth. University of California Press. Berkeley, CA. 1972.
520p. Near Eastern Center Series, UCLA, No. 10
ISBN:0-520-01986-5, ISBN13: 978-0-520-01986-7.
Dewey:297/.092/4. LCCN:74-159671.

Audience: **u,f.**

1983 ed. **Lings, Martin**   **BP75.L56 2001**
Muhammad: His Life Based on the Earliest Sources. Ed. 2.
Trade Cloth. Islamic Texts Society. Cambridge, 1991. 361p.
ISBN:0-946621-25-X, ISBN13: 978-0-946621-25-5.
Dewey:297.6/3 B. LCCN:2002-489449.

Audience: **g,l,u,f.**

Massignon, Louis   **BP80.H27.M3713 1982**
Hallaj: Mystic and Martyr. Herbert W. Mason (Translator). Cloth
Text. Princeton University Press. Princeton, NJ. 1983. 2010p.
Bollingen Ser., No. XCVIII ISBN:0-691-09910-3, ISBN13:
978-0-691-09910-1. Dewey:297/.6. LCCN:80-011085.

Audience: **u,f.**

Rodinson, Maxine   **BP75**
Muhammad. Ed. 2. Trade Paper. Penguin Books, Ltd. London,
1996. 384p. ISBN:0-14-024964-8, ISBN13: 978-0-14-024964-4.
Dewey:297.6/3.

Audience: **g,l.**

Smith, Margaret   **BP80.R3**
Rabi'a the Mystic and Her Fellow-Saints in Islam. Ed. 2. Trade
Cloth. Cambridge University Press. New York, NY. 1984. 256p.
ISBN:0-521-26779-X, ISBN13: 978-0-521-26779-3.
Dewey:297/.4/0924 B. LCCN:84-007655.

Audience: **u,f.**

Troll, Christian W.   **BP80.A485**
Sayyid Ahmad Khan: A Reinterpretation of Muslim Theology.
Vikas Publishing House. 1978.

Audience: **u,f.**

1953 ed. **Watt, W. Montgomery**   **BP75**
Muhammad at Mecca. Trade Cloth. Oxford University Press.
Don Mills, ON. 1991. 208p. ISBN:0-19-577278-4, ISBN13:
978-0-19-577278-4. Dewey:297.63.

Audience: **g,l,u,f.**

Watt, William M.   **BP77.6 .W37 1981**
Muhammad at Medina. Trade Cloth. Oxford University Press,
Inc. New York, NY. 1982. 432p. ISBN:0-19-577307-1, ISBN13:
978-0-19-577307-1. Dewey:297/.63. LCCN:82-184368.

Audience: **g,l,u,f.**

Islam > Islamic Civilization

Esposito, John L. (Author,   **DS35.53**
**   Editor)**
The Islamic World: Past and Present, Set. Trade Cloth. Oxford
University Press, Inc. New York, NY. 2004. 698p.
ISBN:0-19-516520-9, ISBN13: 978-0-19-516520-3.
Dewey:909/.09767/03. LCCN:2003-019665.

Audience: **g,l,u,f.** *Choice, 2004.*

Hodgson, Marshall G.   **DS36.85**
The Expansion of Islam in the Middle Periods. Trade Paper.
University of Chicago Press. Chicago, IL. 1977. 618p. Venture
of Islam Ser., Vol. 2 ISBN:0-226-34684-6, ISBN13:
978-0-226-34684-7. Dewey:909/.09/7671. LCCN:73-087243.

Audience: **u,f.**

Hodgson, Marshall G.   **DS36.85**
The Gunpower Empires and Modern Times, Vol. 3. Trade Paper.
University of Chicago Press. Chicago, IL. 1977. 476p. Venture
of Islam Vol. 3 Ser., Vol. 3 ISBN:0-226-34685-4, ISBN13:
978-0-226-34685-4. Dewey:909/.09/7671. LCCN:73-087243.

Audience: **u,f.**

Hodgson, Marshall G.   **DS36.85**
The Venture of Islam: The Classical Age of Islam. Trade Paper.
University of Chicago Press. Chicago, IL. 1977. 539p. Venture
of Islam Ser., Vol. 1 ISBN:0-226-34683-8, ISBN13:
978-0-226-34683-0. Dewey:909.097671. LCCN:73-087243.

Audience: **u,f.**

Islam > Sacred Books. Koran

Arberry, Arthur John   **BP109.A7 1996**

1986 ed

The Koran Interpreted: A Translation. Trade Paper. Simon &
Schuster. New York, NY. 1996. 708p. ISBN:0-684-82507-4,
ISBN13: 978-0-684-82507-6. Dewey:297.1/22521.

                Audience: **g,l,u,f.**

Ayoub, Mahmoud M.   **BP130.4.A835 1984**

The Qur'an and Its Interpreters: Surah Baqarah. Cloth Text.
State University of New York Press. Albany, NY. 1984. 450p.
ISBN:0-87395-727-X, ISBN13: 978-0-87395-727-4.
Dewey:297/.1226. LCCN:82-021713.

                Audience: **u,f.** *B*

Ayoub, Mahmoud M.   **BP130.4 .A835 1984**

The Qur'an and Its Interpreters: The House of 'Imran. Cloth
Text. State University of New York Press. Albany, NY. 1992.
444p. ISBN:0-7914-0993-7, ISBN13: 978-0-7914-0993-0.
Dewey:297/.1226. LCCN:82-021713.

                Audience: **u,f.**

Bosworth, C. E.   **DS35.7**

The Islamic Dynasties. Trade Paper. Edinburgh University Press.
Edinburgh, 1980. 243p. ISBN:0-85224-402-9, ISBN13:
978-0-85224-402-9. Dewey:909/.097671.

                Audience: **u,f.** *B*

Cragg, Kenneth   **BP130.4 .C7**

The Mind of the Qur'an: Chapters in Reflection. Trade Cloth.
Allen & Unwin, Ltd. London, 1973. ISBN:0-04-297030-X,
ISBN13: 978-0-04-297030-1. Dewey:297/.1226.
LCCN:73-160303.

                Audience: **u,f.** *B*

Guillaume, Alfred   **BP135.A1**

Traditions of Islam: An Introduction to the Study of the Hadith
Literature. Trade Paper. Kessinger Publishing, LLC. Whitefish,
MT. 2003. ISBN:0-7661-5959-0, ISBN13: 978-0-7661-5959-4.
Dewey:297.

                Audience: **g,l,u,f.**

Izutsu, Toshihiko   **BP134.E8I9 2002**

Ethico-Religious Concepts in the Qur'an. Trade Cloth.
McGill-Queen's University Press. Montreal, PQ. 2002. 292p.
ISBN:0-7735-2426-6, ISBN13: 978-0-7735-2426-2.
Dewey:297.1/226. LCCN:2003-267313.

                Audience: **u,f.**

Kassis, Hanna E.   **BP133.K37 1983**

A Concordance of the Qur'an. Fazlur Rahman (Foreword by).
Trade Cloth. University of California Press. Berkeley, CA. 1983.
1484p. ISBN:0-520-04327-8, ISBN13: 978-0-520-04327-5.
Dewey:297/.1225/21. LCCN:82-040100.

                Audience: **u,f.** *B*

Rahman, Fazlur   **BP132**

1990 ed

Major Themes of the Qur'an. Ed. 2. Trade Cloth. Bibliotheca
Islamica, Inc. Minneapolis, MN. 1994. ISBN:0-88297-051-8,
ISBN13: 978-0-88297-051-6. Dewey:297.2. LCCN:79-054189.

                Audience: **g,l,u,f.**

Robson, J. (Translator)   **BP135.A2 K43**

Mishkat al-Masabih, Set. Trade Cloth. Orientalia Art, Ltd. New
York, NY. ISBN:0-87902-068-7, ISBN13: 978-0-87902-068-2.
Dewey:297/.1240521.

                Audience: **l,u,f.**

Sells, Michael Anthony   **BP130.4 S43X 1999**

Approaching the Qur'an. White Cloud Press. 1999.
ISBN:1-883991-26-9, ISBN13: 978-1-883991-26-5.

                Audience: **g,l,u,f.**

Islam > Islamic law

Haddad, Yvonne Yazbeck &   **KBP144.I83 2004**
Stowasser, Barbara Freyer

Law

Islamic Law and the Challenges of Modernity. Book, Other.
AltaMira Press. Walnut Creek, CA. 2004. 274p.
ISBN:0-7591-0670-3, ISBN13: 978-0-7591-0670-3.
Dewey:340.5/9. LCCN:2003-021504.

            Audience: **u,f.** *Choice, 2005.*

Hallaq, Wael B.

Law

A History of Islamic Legal Theories: An Introduction to Sunni
Usul Al-fiqh. Trade Cloth. Cambridge University Press. New
York, NY. 1997. 304p. ISBN:0-521-59027-2, ISBN13:
978-0-521-59027-3. Dewey:340.5/9/09. LCCN:96-045194.

                Audience: **u,f.**

Schacht, Joseph   **KBP144**

The Origins of Muhammadan Jurisprudence. Trade Paper.
Oxford University Press, Inc. New York, NY. 1979. xii, 351p.
ISBN:0-19-825357-5, ISBN13: 978-0-19-825357-0.
Dewey:340.5/9. LCCN:79-040261.

                Audience: **u,f.** *B*

Weiss, Bernard G.

Law

The Spirit of Islamic Law. Cloth Text. University of Georgia
Press. Athens, GA. 1998. xiv, 211p. Spirit of the Laws Ser.
ISBN:0-8203-1977-5, ISBN13: 978-0-8203-1977-3.
Dewey:340.5/9. LCCN:98-010565.

                Audience: **u,f.**

Islam > Islam: General Works

Ash'ari, Abu al-Hasan 'Ali   **BP166**
ibn Isma'il & McCarthy, Richard Joseph

The Theology of al-Ash'ari : The Arabic Texts of al-Ash'ari's
Kitab al-luma' and Risalat istihsan al-khawd fi 'ilm al-kalam :
with Briefly Annotated Translations, and Appendices Containing
Material Pertinent to the Study of al-Ash'ari. Imprimerie
Catholique. 1953.

                Audience: **u,f.**

Black, Antony   **JC49.B58 2002**

The History of Islamic Political Thought: From the Prophet to
the Present. Trade Cloth. Routledge. New York, NY. 2002. 368p.
ISBN:0-415-93242-4, ISBN13: 978-0-415-93242-4.
Dewey:297.272. LCCN:2001-043364.

                Audience: **l,u,f.**

Cooper   **BP173.7**
Islam and Modernity. Cloth Text. I. B. Tauris & Company, Ltd.
London, 1998. 256p. ISBN:1-86064-175-X, ISBN13:
978-1-86064-175-6. Dewey:297.2/72.

Audience: **u,f.** *Choice, 1998.*

Cragg, Kenneth & Speight,   **BP161.2.I85**
   R. Marston (Editors)
Islam from Within: Anthology of a Religion. Trade Paper.
Thomson Wadsworth. Belmont, CA. 1980. 253p.
ISBN:0-87872-212-2, ISBN13: 978-0-87872-212-9. Dewey:297.
LCCN:78-024004.

Audience: **l,u,f.**

Esposito, John L.   **BP161.2.E85 2005**
Islam: The Straight Path Updated with New Epilogue. Ed. 3.
Paper Text. Oxford University Press, Inc. New York, NY. 2004.
336p. ISBN:0-19-518266-9, ISBN13: 978-0-19-518266-8.
Dewey:297. LCCN:2004-061688.

Audience: **g,l,u,f.**

Goldziher, Ignaz   **BP161.2**
Introduction to Islamic Theology and Law. Bernard Lewis
(Editor), Andras Hamori & Ruth Hamori (Translators). Trade
Paper. Princeton University Press. Princeton, NJ. 1981. 320p.
Modern Classics in Near Eastern Studies ISBN:0-691-10099-3,
ISBN13: 978-0-691-10099-9. Dewey:297. LCCN:80-007523.

Audience: **u,f.**

Kelly, Marjorie (Editor)   **BP161**
Islam: The Religious and Political Life of a World Community.
Trade Cloth. Greenwood Publishing Group, Inc. Portsmouth,
NH. 1984. 321p. ISBN:0-275-91204-3, ISBN13:
978-0-275-91204-8. Dewey:909/.097671. LCCN:84-013307.

Audience: **g,l,u.**

Mas'Ud Ibn Umar   **BP166.N263**
   Al-Taftazani
A Commentary on the Creed of Islam. Library Binding. Ayer
Company Publishers, Inc. Manchester, NH. 1980. Islam Ser.
ISBN:0-8369-9268-7, ISBN13: 978-0-8369-9268-7.
Dewey:297/.2. LCCN:79-052565.

Audience: **u,f.**

Mernissi, Fatima   **BP134.W6**
The Veil and the Male Elite: A Feminist Interpretation of
Women's Rights in Islam. Trade Paper. Basic Books. New York,
NY. 2000. 240p. ISBN:0-201-63221-7, ISBN13:
978-0-201-63221-7. Dewey:297.1/228/3054.

Audience: **u,f.** *Choice, 1992.*

Nasr, Seyyed Hossein   **BP170.8.N37 2004**
The Heart of Islam: Enduring Values for Humanity. Trade Paper.
HarperCollins Publishers. New York, NY. 2004. 352p.
ISBN:0-06-073064-1, ISBN13: 978-0-06-073064-2. Dewey:297.

Audience: **g,l,u,f.**

Rahman, Fazlur   **BP161.2.R29 1979**
Islam. Ed. 2. Trade Paper. University of Chicago Press. Chicago,
IL. 1979. 278p. ISBN:0-226-70281-2, ISBN13:
978-0-226-70281-0. Dewey:297. LCCN:78-068547.

Audience: **g,l,u,f.**

Rahnema, Ali (Editor)   **BP60.P56 2005**
Pioneers of Islamic Revival: With Major New Introduction. Ed.
2. Cloth over Boards. Zed Books, Ltd. London, 2006. 352p.
Studies in Islamic Society Ser. ISBN:1-84277-614-2, ISBN13:
978-1-84277-614-8. Dewey:297.2/72/0922. LCCN:2005-050261.

Audience: **l,u,f.**

Wensinck, Arent J.   **BP166.1 .W4**
The Muslim Creed: Its Genesis and Historical Development.
Cloth Text. Coronet Books. Philadelphia, PA. 1932. 311p.
ISBN:0-685-13805-4, ISBN13: 978-0-685-13805-2.
Dewey:297.2.

Audience: **g,l,u,f.**

Islam > Theology

Abduh, Muhammad   **BP166 .M7513 1980**
The Theology of Unity. Library Binding. Ayer Company
Publishers, Inc. Manchester, NH. 1980. Islam Ser.
ISBN:0-8369-9267-9, ISBN13: 978-0-8369-9267-0.
Dewey:297/.2. LCCN:79-052560.

Audience: **u,f.**

Ahmed, Leila   **HQ1170**
Women and Gender in Islam: Historical Roots of a Modern
Debate. Trade Paper. Yale University Press. Cumberland, RI.
1993. 304p. ISBN:0-300-05583-8, ISBN13: 978-0-300-05583-2.
Dewey:305.4/86971.

Audience: **l,u,f.** *Choice, 1992.*

Al-Jami, 'Abd al-Rahman   **BP166.2 .J3513**
The Precious Pearl. Nicholas L. Heer (Translator). Paper Text.
State University of New York Press. Albany, NY. 1992. 237p.
ISBN:0-7914-1490-6, ISBN13: 978-0-7914-1490-3.
Dewey:297/.211. LCCN:78-012607.

Audience: **u,f.**

Crone, Patricia & Hinds,   **DS234**
   Martin
God's Caliph: Religious Authority in the First Centuries of
Islam. Faculty of Oriental Studies Staff (Contribution by). Trade
Paper. Cambridge University Press. New York, NY. 2003. 163p.
University of Cambridge Oriental Publications, Vol. 37
ISBN:0-521-54111-5, ISBN13: 978-0-521-54111-4.
Dewey:297.6/1.

Audience: **u,f.**

Kurzman, Charles   **BP60 .L53 1998**
Liberal Islam: A Sourcebook. Trade Paper. Oxford University
Press, Inc. New York, NY. 1998. 360p. ISBN:0-19-511622-4,
ISBN13: 978-0-19-511622-9. Dewey:297.2/7. LCCN:97-030284.

Audience: **u,f.**

Kurzman, Charles   **BP60.M55 2002**
Modernist Islam, 1840-1940: A Sourcebook. Trade Paper.
Oxford University Press, Inc. New York, NY. 2002. 404p.
ISBN:0-19-515468-1, ISBN13: 978-0-19-515468-9.
Dewey:297/.09/04. LCCN:2002-022046.

Audience: **u,f.**

Montgomery, William   **BP55**
The Formative Period of Islamic Thought. Trade Cloth.
Oneworld Publications. Oxford, 1998. 442p.
ISBN:1-85168-152-3, ISBN13: 978-1-85168-152-5.
Dewey:297/.09021.

Audience: **u,f.**

Rahman, Fazlur   **B741**
Prophecy in Islam: Philosophy and Orthodoxy. Paper Text.
University of Chicago Press. Chicago, IL. 1992. Midway
Reprint Ser. ISBN:0-226-70282-0, ISBN13: 978-0-226-70282-7.
Dewey:297. LCCN:78-066082.

Audience: **u,f.** *B*

Rahman, Fazlur   **BP60.R36 2000**
Revival and Reform in Islam: A Study of Islamic
Fundamentalism. Ebrahim Moosa (Editor, Introduction by).
Trade Paper. Oneworld Publications. Oxford, 1999. 240p.
ISBN:1-85168-204-X, ISBN13: 978-1-85168-204-1.
Dewey:297/.09. LCCN:2003-467187.

Audience: **u,f.**

Sachedina, Abdulaziz A.   **BP166.93 .S22**
Islamic Messianism. Trade Paper. Kazi Publications, Inc.
Chicago, IL. 1996. 230p. ISBN:0-614-21435-1, ISBN13:
978-0-614-21435-2. Dewey:297/.23.

Audience: **l,u,f.**

Taymiya, Ibn   **BP170.I18913 1984**
A Muslim Theologian's Response to Christianity: A Translation
of Ibn Taymiyya's Jawab al-Sahih li-man Baddala din al-Masih.
Thomas F. Michel (Translator). Trade Cloth. Caravan Books.
Carefree, AZ. 1985. 480p. Studies in Islamic Philosophy and
Science ISBN:0-88206-058-9, ISBN13: 978-0-88206-058-3.
Dewey:297/.293. LCCN:83015430.

Audience: **g,l,u,f.** *B* *Choice, 1986.*

Watt, William M.   **BP166**
Islamic Philosophy and Theology. Ed. 2. Trade Paper. Edinburgh
University Press. Edinburgh, 1988. 175p. ISBN:0-85224-552-1,
ISBN13: 978-0-85224-552-1. Dewey:297.1.

Audience: **u,f.**

Wensinck, Arent J.   **BP166.1 .W4**
The Muslim Creed: Its Genesis and Historical Development.
Cloth Text. Coronet Books. Philadelphia, PA. 1932. 311p.
ISBN:0-685-13805-4, ISBN13: 978-0-685-13805-2.
Dewey:297.2.

Audience: **g,l,u,f.**

Islam > Islam and Other Religions

Cragg, Kenneth   **BP172**
Muhammad and the Christian: A Question of Response. Trade
Cloth. Oneworld Publications. Oxford, 1999. 192p.
ISBN:1-85168-179-5, ISBN13: 978-1-85168-179-2.
Dewey:261.2/7.

Audience: **u,f.** *B*

Daniel, Norman   **BP65.A1**
Islam and the West: The Making of an Image. Trade Paper.
Oneworld Publications. Oxford, 1994. 467p.
ISBN:1-85168-043-8, ISBN13: 978-1-85168-043-6.
Dewey:297/.094.

Audience: **g,l,u,f.** *B*

Esack, Farid   **JC49**
Qur'an, Liberation and Pluralism: An Islamic Perspective of
Interreligious Solidarity Against Oppression. Trade Paper.
Oneworld Publications. Oxford, 1997. 288p.
ISBN:1-85168-121-3, ISBN13: 978-1-85168-121-1.
Dewey:297.1/97/7.

Audience: **u,f.** *Choice, 1997.*

Gellner, Ernest   **HN768.A8 1983**
Muslim Society. Meyer Fortes, Jack Goody, Edmund Leach &
Stanley Tambiah (Contribution by). Trade Paper. Cambridge
University Press. New York, NY. 1983. 267p. Cambridge
Studies in Social and Cultural Anthropology, No. 32
ISBN:0-521-27407-9, ISBN13: 978-0-521-27407-4.
Dewey:909/.097671. LCCN:80-041103.

Audience: **u,f.** *B*

Haddad, Yvonne Yazbeck &   **BM729.W6D38 2000**
  Esposito, John L.
Daughters of Abraham: Feminist Thought in Judaism,
Christianity and Islam. Trade Cloth. University Press of Florida.
Gainesville, FL. 2001. 208p. ISBN:0-8130-2103-0, ISBN13:
978-0-8130-2103-4. Dewey:291.1/783442. LCCN:00-053662.

Audience: **u,f.**

Kritzeck, James   **BP171**
Sons of Abraham: Jews, Christians, and Moslems. Helicon,
Baltimore. 1965.

Audience: **l,u,f.**

Lewis, Bernard   **BP172**
The Jews of Islam. Trade Paper. Princeton University Press.
Princeton, NJ. 1987. 262p. ISBN:0-691-00807-8, ISBN13:
978-0-691-00807-3. Dewey:297/.1972. LCCN:84-042575.

Audience: **l,u,f.** *B*

Parrinder, Geoffrey   **BP134.S3**
Jesus in the Qur'an. Trade Paper. Oneworld Publications.
Oxford, 1995. 190p. ISBN:1-85168-094-2, ISBN13:
978-1-85168-094-8. Dewey:297/.1228.

Audience: **g,l,u,f.**

Piscatori, James P. (Editor)   **BP173.7**
Islam in the Political Process. Cloth Text. Cambridge University
Press. New York, NY. 1983. 256p. ISBN:0-521-24941-4,
ISBN13: 978-0-521-24941-6. Dewey:297/.1977.
LCCN:82-009745.

Audience: **u,f.** *B*

Siddiqui, Ataullah   **BP172.S53 1997**
Christian-Muslim Dialogue in the Twentieth Century. Trade
Cloth. Bow Historical Books. New Providence, NJ. 1997. 256p.
ISBN:0-333-67358-1, ISBN13: 978-0-333-67358-4.
Dewey:261.2/7. LCCN:96-017954.

Audience: **g,l,u,f.** *Choice, 1997.*

Southern, Richard W.   **BP172**
Western Views of Islam in the Middle Ages. Trade Cloth.
Harvard University Press. Cambridge, MA. 1962. 128p.
ISBN:0-674-95055-0, ISBN13: 978-0-674-95055-9.
Dewey:297.2/83/094/0902. LCCN:62-013270.
            Audience: **g,l,u,f.** *B*

Turner, Bryan S.   **BP173.25**
Weber and Islam: A Critical Study. Trade Paper. Routledge. New
York, NY. 1978. 222p. ISBN:0-7100-8942-2, ISBN13:
978-0-7100-8942-7. Dewey:306/.6.
            Audience: **u,f.**

Zebiri, Kate   **BP172.Z4 1997**
Muslims and Christians Face to Face. Trade Cloth. Oneworld
Publications. Oxford, 1997. 268p. ISBN:1-85168-133-7,
ISBN13: 978-1-85168-133-4. Dewey:261.2/7. LCCN:98-185624.
            Audience: **g,l,u,f.** *Choice, 1998.*

Islam > The Practice of Islam

Al-Hujwiri   **BP189**
The Kashf Al-Mahjub "The Revelation of the Veiled": An Early
Persian Treatise on Sufism. Ed. 2. Reynold A. Nicholson
(Translator). Trade Paper. Aris & Phillips. Oxford, 2000. 464p.
Gibb Memorial Ser., Vol. 17 ISBN:0-7189-0203-3, ISBN13:
978-0-7189-0203-2. Dewey:297/.4.
            Audience: **u,f.**

Arberry, Arthur John   **BP166**
The Doctrine of the Sufis. Trade Cloth. Kazi Publications, Inc.
Chicago, IL. 1986. ISBN:0-935782-76-1, ISBN13:
978-0-935782-76-9. Dewey:297/.2.
            Audience: **u,f.**

Arberry, Arthur John   **BP189.A7 2001**
Sufism: An Account of the Mystics of Islam. Trade Paper. Dover
Publications, Inc. Mineola, NY. 2001. 144p.
ISBN:0-486-41958-4, ISBN13: 978-0-486-41958-9.
Dewey:297.4. LCCN:2001-028671.
            Audience: **g,l,u,f.**

1985 ed. **Bouhdiba, Abdulwahab**   **HQ769.3**
Sexuality in Islam. Trade Paper. I. B. Tauris & Company, Ltd.
London, 1998. 288p. ISBN:0-86356-086-5, ISBN13:
978-0-86356-086-6. Dewey:297.5/77.
            Audience: **u,f.** *B*

Esack, Farid   **BP88.E83O52 1999**
On Being a Muslim: Finding a Religious Path in the World
Today. Trade Paper. Oneworld Publications. Oxford, 1999. 224p.
ISBN:1-85168-146-9, ISBN13: 978-1-85168-146-4. Dewey:297.
LCCN:99-488318.
            Audience: **g,l,u,f.** *Choice, 2000.*

Jenkins, Everett Jr.   **BP50.J46 1999**
The Muslim Diaspora: A Comprehensive Reference to the
Spread of Islam in Asia, Africa, Europe and the Americas. Cloth
Text. McFarland & Company, Incorporated Publishers. Jefferson,

NC. 1999. 437p. The Muslim Diaspora Ser.
ISBN:0-7864-0431-0, ISBN13: 978-0-7864-0431-5.
Dewey:297/.09. LCCN:98-49332.
            Audience: **g,l,u,f.**

Jenkins, Everett Jr.   **BP50**
The Muslim Diaspora: A Comprehensive Reference to the
Spread of Islam in Asia, Africa, Europe and the Americas,
1500-1799. Cloth Text. McFarland & Company, Incorporated
Publishers. Jefferson, NC. 2000. 423p. The Muslim Diaspora
Ser. ISBN:0-7864-0744-1, ISBN13: 978-0-7864-0744-6.
Dewey:297.5/0902. LCCN:98-49332.
            Audience: **g,l,u,f.** *Choice, 2000.*

Jenkins, Everett, Jr.   **BP50**
The Muslim Diaspora: A Comprehensive Reference to the
Spread of Islam in Asia, Africa, Europe, and the Americas, V. 1:
570-1500. McFarland. 1999. ISBN:0-7864-0431-0, ISBN13:
978-0-7864-0431-5.
            Audience: **g,l,u,f.**

Mayer, Ann Elizabeth   **LAW**
1991 ed Islam and Human Rights: Tradition and Politics. Ed. 3. Trade
Paper. Westview Press. Boulder, CO. 1998. 280p.
ISBN:0-8133-3504-3, ISBN13: 978-0-8133-3504-9.
Dewey:342/.085/0917671. LCCN:98-020762.
            Audience: **g,l,u,f.**

Peters, Rudolph (Author,   **BP182 .P48**
Translator)
Jihad in Classical and Modern Islam: Documentary
History-Updated Edition with a Section on Jihad in the 21st
Century. Cloth Text. Markus Wiener Publishers, Inc. Princeton,
NJ. 2005. 232p. ISBN:1-55876-381-3, ISBN13:
978-1-55876-381-4. Dewey:297.7/2. LCCN:2004-053426.
            Audience: **g,l,u,f.**

Razi, Najm A.   **BP188.9.N25413 1982**
The Path of God's Bondsmen: From Origin to Return. Hamid
Algar (Translator). Cloth Text. Bibliotheca Persica Press. New
York, NY. 1982. 537p. Persian Heritage Ser., Vol. 35
ISBN:0-88206-052-X, ISBN13: 978-0-88206-052-1.
Dewey:297/.4. LCCN:81-021780.
            Audience: **l,u,f.** *B*

Rippin, Andrew   **BP161.2.R53 2005**
Muslims: Their Religious Beliefs and Practices. Ed. 3. Perfect,
Paper over Boards. Routledge. New York, NY. 2005. 384p. The
Library of Religious Beliefs and Practices ISBN:0-415-34882-X,
ISBN13: 978-0-415-34882-9. Dewey:297. LCCN:2004-023465.
            Audience: **g,l,u,f.**

Schimmel, Annemarie   **73-16112**
Mystical Dimensions of Islam. Trade Paper. University of North
Carolina Press. Chapel Hill, NC. 1978. 527p.
ISBN:0-8078-1271-4, ISBN13: 978-0-8078-1271-6.
Dewey:297.4. LCCN:73-016112.
            Audience: **g,l,u,f.** *B*

Islam > The Practice of Islam > Jihad (Holy War). Terrorism

Akbar, M. J.   **BP182**
The Shade of Swords: Jihad and the Conflict Between Islam and Christianity. Paper over Boards. Routledge. New York, NY. 2002. 368p. ISBN:0-415-28470-8, ISBN13: 978-0-415-28470-7. Dewey:297.7/2/09.

Audience: **l,u,f.**

Bonney, Richard   **BP182.B66 2004**
Jihad: From Qu'ran to Bin Laden. Zaki Bedawi (Preface by). Cloth over Boards. Palgrave Macmillan. New York, NY. 2005. 500p. ISBN:1-4039-3372-3, ISBN13: 978-1-4039-3372-0. Dewey:297.7/2. LCCN:2004-051152.

Audience: **g,l,u,f.** *Choice, 2005.*

Cook, David   **BP182 .C66 2005**
Understanding Jihad. Trade Paper. University of California Press. Berkeley, CA. 2005. 288p. ISBN:0-520-24448-6, ISBN13: 978-0-520-24448-1. Dewey:297.7/2. LCCN:2004-026561.

Audience: **u,f.** *Choice, 2006.*

Firestone, Reuven   **BP182.F5 1999**
Jihad: The Origin of Holy War in Islam. Trade Paper. Oxford University Press, Inc. New York, NY. 2002. 208p. ISBN:0-19-515494-0, ISBN13: 978-0-19-515494-8. Dewey:297.7/2/09. LCCN:98-036384.

Audience: **u,f.**

Peters, Rudolph (Author, Translator)   **BP182 .P48**
Jihad in Classical and Modern Islam: Documentary History-Updated Edition with a Section on Jihad in the 21st Century. Cloth Text. Markus Wiener Publishers, Inc. Princeton, NJ. 2005. 232p. ISBN:1-55876-381-3, ISBN13: 978-1-55876-381-4. Dewey:297.7/2. LCCN:2004-053426.

Audience: **g,l,u,f.**

Rubin, Barry & Rubin, Judith Colp (Editors)   **HV6431**
Anti-American Terrorism and the Middle East: A Documentary Reader. Trade Paper. Oxford University Press, Inc. New York, NY. 2004. 408p. ISBN:0-19-517659-6, ISBN13: 978-0-19-517659-9. Dewey:303.6/25/0973.

Audience: **g,l,u,f.**

Islam > Branches. Sects

Cole, Juan R. & Keddie, Nikki R.   **BP192.7.N33S54 1986**
Shi'ism and Social Protest. Trade Cloth. Yale University Press. Cumberland, RI. 1986. 352p. ISBN:0-300-03550-0, ISBN13: 978-0-300-03550-6. Dewey:322/.1. LCCN:85-022780.

Audience: **u,f.** *B Choice, 1986.*

Daftary, Farhad   **BP195.I8**
A Short History of the Ismailis. Trade Cloth. Edinburgh University Press. Edinburgh, 1998. 256p. ISBN:0-7486-0904-0, ISBN13: 978-0-7486-0904-8. Dewey:297.8/22.

Audience: **g,l,u.**

Fuller, Graham E. & Francke, Rend Rahim   **BP192.7.A65F65 1999**
The Arab Shi'a: The Forgotten Muslims. Cloth over Boards. Palgrave Macmillan. New York, NY. 2000. 304p. ISBN:0-312-22178-9, ISBN13: 978-0-312-22178-2. Dewey:297.82109174927. LCCN:99-024292.

Audience: **u,f.** *Choice, 2000.*

ibn 'Ali Ibn Babawayh al-Qummi, Muhammad & Asaf Ali Asghar Fayzee   **BP193**
A Shi'ite Creed: A Translation of Risalatu'l-itiqadat of Muhammad b. 'Ali Ibn Babawayhi al-Qummi, known as Shaykh Saduq. Oxford University Press. 1942.

Audience: **u,f.**

Lincoln, C. Eric   **BP221**
The Black Muslims in America. Ed. 3. Trade Cloth. Africa World Press. Trenton, NJ. 1996. 307p. ISBN:0-86543-399-2, ISBN13: 978-0-86543-399-1. Dewey:297/.87.

Audience: **g,l,u.** *B*

Nasr, Seyyed Hossein (Editor), et al.   **BP193.5.S527 1988**
Shi'ism: Doctrines, Thought, and Spirituality. Hamid Dabashi & Seyyed Vali Reza Nasr (Editors), Seyyed Hossein Nasr, Hamid Dabashi & Seyyed Vali Reza Nasr (Introduction by). Cloth Text. State University of New York Press. Albany, NY. 1988. 401p. ISBN:0-88706-689-5, ISBN13: 978-0-88706-689-4. Dewey:297/.82. LCCN:87-010258.

Audience: **u,f.**

Tabataba'i, Muhammad Husayn   **BP193.5 .T3213 1975**
Shi'ite Islam. Seyyed Hossein Nasr (Introduction by, Notes by). Trade Cloth. Allen & Unwin, Ltd. London, 1975. xiv, 253p. ISBN:0-04-297033-4, ISBN13: 978-0-04-297033-2. Dewey:297/.82. LCCN:76-361457.

Audience: **u,f.**

Bahaism

Adamson, Hugh C. & Hainsworth, Philip   **BP327.A33 1998**
Historical Dictionary of the Bahai Faith. Trade Cloth. Scarecrow Press, Inc. Lanham, MD. 1997. 528p. Religions, Philosophies, and Movements Ser., No. 17 ISBN:0-8108-3353-0, ISBN13: 978-0-8108-3353-1. Dewey:297.9/3/03. LCCN:97-002610.

Audience: **u,f.** *Choice, 1998.*

Baha'u'llah; 'Abdu'l-Baha   **BP360**
Baha'i– World Faith: Selected Writings of Baha'u'llah and 'Abdu'l-Baha. Ed. 2. Baha'i– Pub. Trust. 1956.

Audience: **l,u,f.**

Hatcher, William S.   BP365.H335 1998
1984 ed.   Martin, Douglas J.
The Baha'i Faith: The Emerging Global Religion. Trade Paper.
Baha'i Publishing Trust, U.S.. Wilmette, IL. 1998. 253p.
ISBN:0-87743-264-3, ISBN13: 978-0-87743-264-7.
Dewey:297.9/3. LCCN:97-018936.

                         Audience: **l,u,f.**

Smith, Peter   BP330.S65 1987
The Babi and Baha'i Religions: From Messianic Sh'ism to a
World Religion. Trade Cloth. George Ronald Publisher, Ltd.
Saint Petersburg, FL. 1987. 272p. ISBN:0-521-30128-9,
ISBN13: 978-0-521-30128-2. Dewey:297/.88. LCCN:86-016781.
                  Audience: **l,u,f.** *Choice, 1988.*

Smith, Peter   BP330
The Baha'i Faith: A Short History. Trade Paper. Oneworld
Publications. Oxford, 1999. 176p. From Buddhism to Sufism
Ser., :Concise Introductions Ser. ISBN:1-85168-208-2, ISBN13:
978-1-85168-208-9. Dewey:297.9/3/09.

                         Audience: **l,u,f.**

Smith, Peter   BP327 .S65 2000
A Concise Encyclopedia of the Baha'i Faith. Trade Paper.
Oneworld Publications. Oxford, 1999. 416p. Concise
Encyclopedia of World Faiths Ser. ISBN:1-85168-184-1,
ISBN13: 978-1-85168-184-6. Dewey:297.9/3/03.
LCCN:00-273030.
                  Audience: **l,u,f.** *Choice, 2000.*

Buddhism > Collected Works. History. Biography

Blofeld, John E.   BQ942.L647A3 1988
The Wheel of Life: The Autobiography of a Western Buddhist.
Huston Smith (Foreword by). Trade Paper. Shambhala
Publications, Inc. Boston, MA. 1988. 305p. Shambhala Dragon
Editions Ser. ISBN:0-87773-034-2, ISBN13: 978-0-87773-034-7.
Dewey:294.3/092/4 B. LCCN:88-018219.

                         Audience: **g,l,u.**

Ch'en, Kenneth   BL1430
Buddhism in China: A Historical Survey. Trade Paper. Princeton
University Press. Princeton, NJ. 1972. 576p.
ISBN:0-691-00015-8, ISBN13: 978-0-691-00015-2.
Dewey:294.3.
                         Audience: **l,u,f.**

Conze, Edward   BQ336
Buddhist Thought in India: Three Phases of Buddhist
Philosophy. Trade Cloth. Munshiram Manoharial Publishers
Private, Ltd. New Delhi, 1996. ISBN:81-215-0722-7, ISBN13:
978-81-215-0722-6. Dewey:181.043.
                         Audience: **u,f.** *B*

1969 ed. Eliot, Charles   BQ674 .E58
Japanese Buddhism. Trade Cloth. Kegan Paul International, Ltd.

London, 2005. 486p. Kegan Paul Japan Library
ISBN:0-7103-0967-8, ISBN13: 978-0-7103-0967-9.
Dewey:294.32.

                         Audience: **g,l,u,f.**

Evans-Wentz, W. Y. &   BQ7800.T53 2000
   Lopez, Donald S.
The Tibetan Book of the Great Liberation: Or, the Method of
Realizing Nirvana Through Knowing the Mind. Ed. 2. Trade
Paper. Oxford University Press, Inc. New York, NY. 2000. 358p.
ISBN:0-19-513315-3, ISBN13: 978-0-19-513315-8.
Dewey:294.3/923. LCCN:00-022483.

                         Audience: **l,u,f.**

Gernet, Jacques   BQ638.G4713 1995
Buddhism in Chinese Society: An Economic History from the
Fifth to the Tenth Centuries. Franciscus Verellen (Translator).
Cloth Text. Columbia University Press. New York, NY. 1995.
448p. ISBN:0-231-07380-1, ISBN13: 978-0-231-07380-6.
Dewey:294.3/0951/09021. LCCN:94-042484.

                         Audience: **u,f.**

Gregory, Peter N. & Getz,   BQ640.B83 1999
   Daniel A. (Editors)
Buddhism in the Sung. Trade Cloth. University of Hawaii Press.
Honolulu, HI. 2002. 656p. Studies in East Asian Buddhism, Vol.
13 ISBN:0-8248-2155-6, ISBN13: 978-0-8248-2155-5.
Dewey:294.3/0951/09021. LCCN:99-034972.

                         Audience: **u,f.**

Heine, Steven & Prebish,   BQ316.B83 2003
   Charles S. (Editors)
Buddhism in the Modern World: Adaptations of an Ancient
Tradition. Trade Cloth. Oxford University Press, Inc. New York,
NY. 2003. 304p. ISBN:0-19-514697-2, ISBN13:
978-0-19-514697-4. Dewey:294.3/09/04. LCCN:2002-015649.

                         Audience: **l,u,f.**

Hirakawa, Akira   DS3.A2A82 NO. 36
A History of Indian Buddhism: From Sakyamuni to Early
Mahayana. Paul Groner (Editor, Translator). Trade Cloth.
University of Hawaii Press. Honolulu, HI. 1990. 424p. Asian
Studies at Hawaii, No. 36 ISBN:0-8248-1203-4, ISBN13:
978-0-8248-1203-4. Dewey:950 s. LCCN:89-020647.

                         Audience: **g,l,u,f.**

Lamotte, E.   BQ286 .L3613 1988
History of Indian Buddhism. Trade Paper. Peeters Publishers &
Booksellers. Leuven, Belgium, 1988. 870p.
ISBN:90-6831-100-X, ISBN13: 978-90-6831-100-6.
Dewey:294.3/0954. LCCN:88-208180.

                         Audience: **g,l,u,f.**

Lopez, Donald S. Jr.   BQ162.E85C87 1995
   (Editor)
Curators of the Buddha: The Study of Buddhism under
Colonialism. Trade Cloth. University of Chicago Press. Chicago,
IL. 1995. 304p. ISBN:0-226-49308-3, ISBN13:
978-0-226-49308-4. Dewey:294.3/07/04. LCCN:94-025130.

                         Audience: **u,f.**

McMullin, Neil   **BQ687.M4 1984**
Buddhism and the State in Sixteenth Century Japan. Trade
Cloth. Princeton University Press. Princeton, NJ. 1985. 408p.
ISBN:0-691-07291-4, ISBN13: 978-0-691-07291-3.
Dewey:322/.1/0952. LCCN:84-042572.
                              Audience: **u,f.** 𝕭 *Choice, 1985.*

Nanamoli, Bhikkhu   **BQ882**
The Life of Buddha: According to Pali Canon. Trade Cloth.
Buddhist Publication Society. Kandy, 1992. 400p.
ISBN:955-24-0063-5, ISBN13: 978-955-24-0063-6.
Dewey:294.363.
                                        Audience: **g,l,u,f.**

Overmyer, Daniel L.   **BQ628**
Folk Buddhist Religion: Dissenting Sects in Late Traditional
China. Trade Cloth. Harvard University Press. Cambridge, MA.
1976. 256p. East Asian Monographs, No. 83
ISBN:0-674-30705-4, ISBN13: 978-0-674-30705-6.
Dewey:301.5/8. LCCN:75-023467.
                                        Audience: **u,f.** 𝕭

Pande, Govind Chandra   **BQ288.P36**
Studies in the Origins of Buddhism. Trade Cloth. Motilal
Banarsidass Publishers (Pvt. Ltd). New Delhi, 1999. 604p.
ISBN:81-208-1016-3, ISBN13: 978-81-208-1016-7.
Dewey:294.3.
                                        Audience: **l,u,f.** 𝕭

Payne, Richard K. (Editor)   **BQ687.R48 1998**
Re-Visioning "Kamakura" Buddhism. Trade Cloth. University of
Hawaii Press. Honolulu, HI. 1998. 288p. Studies in East Asian
Buddhism, Vol. 11 ISBN:0-8248-2024-X, ISBN13:
978-0-8248-2024-4. Dewey:294.3/0952/0902. LCCN:98-009375.
                              Audience: **u,f.** *Choice, 1999.*

Reischauer, August Karl   **BL1440.R5**
Studies in Japanese Buddhism. Trade Paper. Kessinger
Publishing, LLC. Whitefish, MT. 2004. ISBN:1-4179-7737-X,
ISBN13: 978-1-4179-7737-6. Dewey:294.32.
                                        Audience: **l,u,f.**

Saddhatissa, H.   **BQ882**
The Life of the Buddha. Trade Cloth. Allen & Unwin Pty., Ltd.
Crows Nest, NSW. 1976. 3-89p. ISBN:0-04-294094-X, ISBN13:
978-0-04-294094-6. Dewey:294.3/63. LCCN:76-378879.
                                        Audience: **g,l,u,f.** 𝕭

Sarkisyanz, Manuel   **BL1443.1**
Buddhist Backgrounds of the Burmese Revolution. Mus, Paul
(pref. by). M. Nijhoff. 1965.
                                        Audience: **u,f.**

Smith, Bardwell L. (Editor)   **BQ359.R44**
Religion and Legitimation of Power in Sri Lanka. Trade Paper.
Columbia University Press. New York, NY. 1978. 254p.
ISBN:0-89012-008-0, ISBN13: 978-0-89012-008-8.
Dewey:294.3/3/77095493. LCCN:77-007449.
                                        Audience: **u,f.** 𝕭

Smith, B.L. (Editor)   **BL1055 .R435**
Religion and the Legitimation of Power in South Asia. Trade
Cloth. Brill Academic Publishers. Leiden, 1978. 196p.
ISBN:90-04-05674-2, ISBN13: 978-90-04-05674-9. Dewey:294.
LCCN:78-322677.
                                        Audience: **u,f.**

Spiro, Melford E.   **BL1443.1.S65**
Buddhism and Society: A Great Tradition and Its Burmese
Vicissitudes. Ed. 2. Trade Paper. University of California Press.
Berkeley, CA. 1996. 530p. ISBN:0-520-04672-2, ISBN13:
978-0-520-04672-6. Dewey:294.3/91/09591. LCCN:81-018522.
                                        Audience: **u,f.** 𝕭

Stone, Jacqueline I.   **BQ9118.6.S76 1999**
Original Enlightenment and the Transformation of Medieval
Japanese Buddhism. Trade Cloth. University of Hawaii Press.
Honolulu, HI. 2003. 600p. Studies in East Asian Buddhism, 12
ISBN:0-8248-2026-6, ISBN13: 978-0-8248-2026-8.
Dewey:294.3/92. LCCN:98-054333.
                                        Audience: **u,f.**

Strong, John S.   **BQ122.E97 2002**
The Experience of Buddhism: Sources and Interpretations. Ed.
2. Paper Text. Thomson Wadsworth. Belmont, CA. 2001. 400p.
Religion Ser. ISBN:0-534-54175-5, ISBN13:
978-0-534-54175-0. Dewey:294.3. LCCN:2001-026898.
                                        Audience: **g,l,u,f.**

Suzuki, D. T.   **BQ9262.9.J3S9 1970**
1959 ed. Zen and Japanese Culture. Trade Paper. Princeton University
Press. Princeton, NJ. 1970. 502p. Bollingen Ser., Vol. 64
ISBN:0-691-01770-0, ISBN13: 978-0-691-01770-9.
Dewey:294.3/927.
                                        Audience: **g,l,u,f.**

Tambiah, Stanley J.   **BQ554 .T35**
World Conqueror and World Renouncer. Trade Paper.
Cambridge University Press. New York, NY. 1977. 565p.
Cambridge Studies in Social and Cultural Anthropology, No. 15
ISBN:0-521-29290-5, ISBN13: 978-0-521-29290-0.
Dewey:294.3/3/7709593. LCCN:76-008290.
                                        Audience: **l,u,f.** 𝕭

Thomas, Edward J.   **BQ882.T45 2000**
The Life of Buddha As Legend and History. Trade Paper. Dover
Publications, Inc. Mineola, NY. 2000. 336p.
ISBN:0-486-41132-X, ISBN13: 978-0-486-41132-3.
Dewey:294.3/63 B. LCCN:99-088879.
                                        Audience: **g,l,u,f.**

Tsukamoto, Zenryv   **BQ636.T75713 1985**
A History of Early Chinese Buddhism: From Its Introduction to
the Death of Hui-Yuan, Set. Leon Hurvitz (Translator). Trade
Cloth, Box or Slipcased. Kodansha America, Inc. New York,
NY. 1985. 1332p. ISBN:0-87011-635-5, ISBN13:
978-0-87011-635-3. Dewey:294.3/0931. LCCN:83-048873.
                                        Audience: **g,l,u.** 𝕭

Warder, A. K.   BQ286
Indian Buddhism. Ed. 3. Trade Paper. Motilal Banarsidass
Publishers (Pvt. Ltd). New Delhi, 2000. xv, 627p. Buddhism
Ser., Vol. 6:Philosophy and Religion of All Schools Ser.
ISBN:81-208-1741-9, ISBN13: 978-81-208-1741-8.
Dewey:294.3/0954.

Audience: **g,l,u,f.**

Welch, Holmes   BQ647.W44
Buddhism under Mao. Trade Cloth. Harvard University Press.
Cambridge, MA. 1972. 690p. East Asian Ser., No. 69
ISBN:0-674-08565-5, ISBN13: 978-0-674-08565-7.
Dewey:294.3/0951. LCCN:72-078428.

Audience: **l,u,f.** *B*

Welch, Holmes H.   BL1430
Practice of Chinese Buddhism, 1900-1950. Trade Paper. Harvard
University Press. Cambridge, MA. 1967. 592p.
ISBN:0-674-69701-4, ISBN13: 978-0-674-69701-0.
Dewey:294.3. LCCN:67-013256.

Audience: **l,u,f.**

Wright, Arthur F.   BL1430
Buddhism in Chinese History. Trade Paper. Stanford University
Press. Palo Alto, CA. 1959. 182p. ISBN:0-8047-0548-8,
ISBN13: 978-0-8047-0548-6. Dewey:294.3. LCCN:59-007432.

Audience: **l,u,f.** *B*

Zürcher, Erik   BQ636
The Buddhist Conquest of China. The Spread and Adaptation of
Buddhism in Early Medieval China. Ed. 2. Brill. 1972. Sinica
Leidensia, V. 11

Audience: **u,f.**

Buddhism > Buddhist Literature: Sacred Texts

Buddhaghosa, Acaeiya   BQ2632.E5
The Path of Purification: Visuddhimagga. Bhikkhu Nanamoli
(Translator). Trade Cloth. Buddhist Publication Society. Kandy,
1991. 950p. ISBN:955-24-0023-6, ISBN13: 978-955-24-0023-0.
Dewey:294.3/82.

Audience: **u,f.**

Conze, Edward (Translator)   BQ1012
Buddhist Scriptures. Trade Paper. Penguin Group (USA) Inc.
New York, NY. 1959. 256p. Classics Ser. ISBN:0-14-044088-7.
ISBN13: 978-0-14-044088-1. Dewey:294.3. LCCN:00-002859.

Audience: **g,l,u,f.** *B*

1973 ed. **Conze, Edward (Translator)**   BQ1138
The Perfection of Wisdom in Eight Thousand Lines and Its
Verse Summary. Cloth Text. Sri Satguru Publications. New
Delhi, 1994. ISBN:81-7030-405-9, ISBN13: 978-81-7030-405-0.
Dewey:294.3/8.

Audience: **g,l,u,f.** *B*

Conze, Edward (Editor, Translator)   BQ1952.E5
The Large Sutra on Perfect Wisdom: With the Divisions of the
Abhisamayalankara. Trade Cloth. University of California Press.
Berkeley, CA. 1974. 697p. Center for South and Southeast Asia
Studies, UC Berkeley, No. 18 ISBN:0-520-05321-4, ISBN13:
978-0-520-05321-2. Dewey:294.3/8. LCCN:71-189224.

Audience: **l,u,f.**

Conze, Edward, et al.   BQ1
Buddhist Texts Through the Ages. I. B. Horner & David
Snellgrove (Authors). Trade Paper. Oneworld Publications.
Oxford, 1995. 324p. ISBN:1-85168-107-8, ISBN13:
978-1-85168-107-5. Dewey:294.3/82.

Audience: **g,l,u,f.**

Debary, William T. (Editor)   PS3507.U147Z85
The Buddhist Tradition: In India, China and Japan. Trade Paper.
Knopf Publishing Group. New York, NY. 1972. 448p.
ISBN:0-394-71696-5, ISBN13: 978-0-394-71696-1.
Dewey:303.48/4/092.

Audience: **g,l,u,f.**

Evans-Wentz, W. T. (Editor,   BQ4490.K3713 2000
1960 ed. **Compiled by)**
The Tibetan Book of the Dead: Or, the After-Death Experiences
on the Bardo Plane, According to Lama Kazi Dawa-Samdup's
English Rendering. Ed. 4. Donald S. Lopez Jr. (Foreword by,
Afterword by). Trade Cloth. Oxford University Press, Inc. New
York, NY. 2000. 370p. ISBN:0-19-513311-0, ISBN13:
978-0-19-513311-0. Dewey:294.3/423. LCCN:00-022529.

Audience: **g,l,u.**

Hakeda, Yoshito S.   BQ2992.E5 2006
The Awakening of Faith: Attributed to Asvaghosha. Ryuichi Abe
(Introduction by). Trade Cloth. Columbia University Press. New
York, NY. 2005. 136p. Translations from the Asian Classics Ser.
ISBN:0-231-13156-9, ISBN13: 978-0-231-13156-8.
Dewey:294.3/42042. LCCN:2005-049350.

Audience: **g,l,u,f.**

Hurvitz, Leon (Translator)   BQ1138
Scripture of the Lotus Blossom of the Fine Dharma: The Lotus
Sutra. Trade Paper. Columbia University Press. New York, NY.
1976. 421p. ISBN:0-231-03920-4, ISBN13: 978-0-231-03920-8.
Dewey:294.3/82. LCCN:75-045381.

Audience: **l,u,f.** *B*

Johnston, E. H.   BQ860
Buddhacarita or Acts of the Buddha. Trade Cloth. Motilal
Banarsidass Publishers (Pvt. Ltd). New Delhi, 1992. 130p.
ISBN:81-208-1029-5, ISBN13: 978-81-208-1029-7.
Dewey:294.3/63 B.

Audience: **u,f.**

Lopez, Donald S.   BQ1967.L66 1996
Elaborations on Emptiness: Uses of the Heart Sutra. Cloth Text.
Princeton University Press. Princeton, NJ. 1996. 280p.
ISBN:0-691-02732-3, ISBN13: 978-0-691-02732-6.
Dewey:294.3/85. LCCN:95-044449.

Audience: **g,l,u,f.**

Muller, F. Max   **BQ1192.E53D38**
Buddhist Suttas. Cloth Text. Taylor & Francis Group.
Philadelphia, PA. 2001. xlviii, 320p. ISBN:0-7007-1549-5,
ISBN13: 978-0-7007-1549-7. Dewey:294.3823.

Audience: **u,f.**

Muller, F. Max   **BL1411.M5**
The Questions of King Milinda. Cloth Text. Taylor & Francis
Group. Philadelphia, PA. 2001. ISBN:0-7007-1550-9, ISBN13:
978-0-7007-1550-3. Dewey:294.3.

Audience: **u,f.**

Muller, F. Max   **BQ2052.E5**
The Saddharma-Pundaraka or the Lotus of the True Law. Cloth
Text. Taylor & Francis Group. Philadelphia, PA. 2001.
ISBN:0-7007-1537-1, ISBN13: 978-0-7007-1537-4.
Dewey:294.3/85.

Audience: **u,f.**

1894 ed. **Muller, F. Max (Editor)**   **BQ1138**
Buddhist Mahayana Texts: The Sacred Books of the East Part
Forty-Nine. E. B. Cowell (Translator). Trade Paper. Kessinger
Publishing, LLC. Whitefish, MT. 2005. ISBN:1-4179-3008-X,
ISBN13: 978-1-4179-3008-1. Dewey:294.3/82.

Audience: **l,u,f.**

Nagarjuna   **BQ1138**
The Precious Garland and the Song of the Four Mindfulnesses.
Jeffrey Hopkins & Lati Rimpoche (Translators). Trade Paper.
Routledge. New York, NY. 1975. Wisdom of Tibet Ser.
ISBN:0-04-294089-3, ISBN13: 978-0-04-294089-2.
Dewey:294.3/82.

Audience: **u,f.** *B*

Prebish, Charles S.   **BQ2272.E5**
Buddhist Monastic Discipline: Sanskrit Pratimoksa Sutras of the
Mahasamghikas and Mulasarvastivadins. Trade Cloth. Motilal
Banarsidass Publishers (Pvt. Ltd). New Delhi, 1996. 156p.
ISBN:81-208-1339-1, ISBN13: 978-81-208-1339-7.
Dewey:294.3/822.

Audience: **u,f.**

Snellgrove, David L.   **BL1411.T3 E57**
Hevajra Tantra. Trade Cloth. Oxford University Press, Inc. New
York, NY. 1959. 366p. ISBN:0-19-713516-1, ISBN13:
978-0-19-713516-7. Dewey:294.3282.

Audience: **g,l,u,f.**

Suzuki, Diasetz Teitaro   **BL1411.L3**
Lankavatara Sutra. Trade Paper. Taylor & Francis Group.
Abingdon, 2004. ISBN:0-415-27399-4, ISBN13:
978-0-415-27399-2. Dewey:294.382.

Audience: **l,u,f.**

Thornton, John F. &   **BQ1962.E5T75 2001**
Varenne, Susan B. (Editors)
Buddhist Wisdom: The Diamond Sutra and the Heart Sutra.
Edward Conze (Translator, Commentaries by), Judith

Simmer-Brown (Preface by). Trade Paper. Knopf Publishing
Group. New York, NY. 2001. 160p. Vintage Spiritual Classics
Ser. ISBN:0-375-72600-4, ISBN13: 978-0-375-72600-2.
Dewey:294.3/85. LCCN:2001-022257.

Audience: **l,u,f.**

Thurman, Robert A.   **BQ1967**
(Translator)
The Holy Teaching of Vimalakirti: Mahayana Scripture. Trade
Paper. Pennsylvania State University Press. University Park, PA.
1976. 294p. Institute for Advanced Studies of World Religions
Ser. ISBN:0-271-00601-3, ISBN13: 978-0-271-00601-7.
Dewey:294.3/85. LCCN:75-027197.

Audience: **g,l,u,f.**

Warren, Henry Clarke   **BL1410; BQ1172.E5**
Buddhism in Translations: Passages Selec. Trade Paper.
Kessinger Publishing, LLC. Whitefish, MT. 2005.
ISBN:1-4179-6766-8, ISBN13: 978-1-4179-6766-7.
Dewey:294.3.

Audience: **l,u,f.**

Watson, Burton (Translator)   **BQ1967**
The Vimalakirti Sutra. Trade Paper. Columbia University Press.
New York, NY. 2000. 192p. Translations from the Asian
Classics ISBN:0-231-10657-2, ISBN13: 978-0-231-10657-3.
Dewey:294.3/85.

Audience: **u,f.**

Wayman, Alex & Wayman,   **BQ1967**
Hideko (Translators)
The Lion's Roar of Queen Srimala. Cloth Text. Columbia
University Press. New York, NY. 1974. 160p.
ISBN:0-231-03726-0, ISBN13: 978-0-231-03726-6.
Dewey:294.3/85. LCCN:73-009673.

Audience: **l,u,f.** *B*

Buddhism > Buddhism: General Works

Bechert, Heinz & Gombrich,   **BQ4012.W67 1991**
1984 ed. **Richard F. (Editors)**
The World of Buddhism. Trade Paper. Thames & Hudson. New
York, NY. 1991. 308p. ISBN:0-500-27628-5, ISBN13:
978-0-500-27628-0. Dewey:294.3. LCCN:91-065147.

Audience: **g,l,u,f.**

Conze, Edward   **BQ266**
Buddhism: A Short History. Trade Cloth. Oneworld Publications.
Oxford, 2000. 160p. From Buddhism to Sufism Ser., :Concise
Introductions Ser. ISBN:1-85168-221-X, ISBN13:
978-1-85168-221-8. Dewey:294.3/09.

Audience: **l,u,f.**

Conze, Edward   **BQ5612.C67 2003**
Buddhist Meditation. Trade Paper. Dover Publications, Inc.
Mineola, NY. 2003. 192p. Eastern Philosophy and Religion Ser.
ISBN:0-486-42716-1, ISBN13: 978-0-486-42716-4.
Dewey:294.3/4435. LCCN:2002-034888.

Audience: **g,l,u,f.** *B*

Gethin, Rupert   **BQ4012**
The Foundations of Buddhism. Paper Text. Oxford University Press, Inc. New York, NY. 1998. 350p. ISBN:0-19-289223-1, ISBN13: 978-0-19-289223-2. Dewey:294.3. LCCN:98-012246.
Audience: **g,l,u,f.**

Harvey, B. Peter   **BQ4022**
An Introduction to Buddhism: Teachings, History and Practices. Trade Cloth. Munshiram Manoharial Publishers Private, Ltd. New Delhi, 1990. 350p. ISBN:81-215-0493-7, ISBN13: 978-81-215-0493-5. Dewey:294.3.
Audience: **g,l,u,f.** *Choice, 1991.*

Harvey, B. Peter   **BQ4022 .H37 1990**
An Introduction to Buddhism: Teachings, History and Practices. Cloth Text. Cambridge University Press. New York, NY. 1990. 396p. Introduction to Religion Ser. ISBN:0-521-30815-1, ISBN13: 978-0-521-30815-1. Dewey:294.3. LCCN:89-007317.
Audience: **g,l,u,f.** *Choice, 1991.*

Lopez, Donald S. Jr. (Editor)   **BQ1012.B83 1995**
Buddhism in Practice. Trade Paper. Princeton University Press. Princeton, NJ. 1995. 624p. Princeton Readings in Religions Ser. ISBN:0-691-04441-4, ISBN13: 978-0-691-04441-5. Dewey:294.3. LCCN:94-048201.
Audience: **l,u,f.**

Prebish, Charles S. (Editor)   **BQ4012 .P73**
Buddhism: A Modern Perspective. Trade Paper. Pennsylvania State University Press. University Park, PA. 1973. 346p. ISBN:0-271-01195-5, ISBN13: 978-0-271-01195-0. Dewey:294.3. LCCN:74-300085.
Audience: **l,u,f.** *B*

Rahula, Walpola   **BL1451.2 .R3**
1962 ed. What the Buddha Taught. Trade Paper. Random House, Inc. New York, NY. 1974. ISBN:0-394-17236-1, ISBN13: 978-0-394-17236-1. Dewey:294.34.
Audience: **g,l,u,f.** *B*

Robinson, Richard H.   **BL1475.M3**
Early Madhyamika in India and China. University of Wisconsin Press. 1967.
Audience: **u,f.**

Swearer, Donald K.   **BL1478.6**
Secrets of the Lotus: Studies in Buddhist Meditation. Trade Paper. Macmillan Publishers Ltd. London, 1971. xii, 242p. ISBN:0-02-089610-7, ISBN13: 978-0-02-089610-4. Dewey:294.3/4/43. LCCN:75-150068.
Audience: **g,l,u.** *B*

Waley   **BQ8149.H787**
Real Tripitaka and Other Pieces V34. Trade Paper. RoutledgeCurzon. 2004. 296p. ISBN:0-415-36178-8, ISBN13: 978-0-415-36178-1. Dewey:294.361.
Audience: **u,f.**

Williams, Paul & Tribe, Anthony   **BQ286.W55 2000**
Buddhist Thought: Complete Introduction to the Indian Tradition. Paper over Boards. Routledge. New York, NY. 2000. 336p. ISBN:0-415-20700-2, ISBN13: 978-0-415-20700-3. Dewey:294.3.
Audience: **l,u,f.**

Buddhism > Doctrinal and Systematic Buddhism

Coleman, Graham & Jinpa, Thupten (Editors)   **BQ4490.K3713 2006**
Tibetan Book of the Dead. Gyurme Dorje (Translator). Trade Cloth. Penguin Group (USA) Inc. New York, NY. 2006. 592p. ISBN:0-670-85886-2, ISBN13: 978-0-670-85886-6. Dewey:294.3/423. LCCN:2005-042356.
Audience: **g,l,u,f.**

Guenther, Herbert V.   **BQ2495**
Philosophy and Psychology in the Abhidharma. Trade Paper. Motilal Banarsidass Publishers (Pvt. Ltd). New Delhi, 1999. 270p. ISBN:81-208-0773-1, ISBN13: 978-81-208-0773-0. Dewey:294.3/824.
Audience: **u,f.** *B*

Kalupahana, David J.   **BQ4150**
Buddhist Philosophy: A Historical Analysis. Trade Cloth. University of Hawaii Press. Honolulu, HI. 1976. 210p. ISBN:0-8248-0392-2, ISBN13: 978-0-8248-0392-6. Dewey:181/.04/3. LCCN:75-020040.
Audience: **l,u,f.** *B*

Morgan, Kenneth W.   **BL1420 .M6**
The Path of the Buddha: Buddhism Interpreted by Buddhists. Trade Cloth. Motilal Banarsidass Publishers (Pvt. Ltd). New Delhi, 1986. 432p. ISBN:0-317-60576-3, ISBN13: 978-0-317-60576-1. Dewey:294.3.
Audience: **l,u,f.**

Thomas, Edward J.   **BQ4090.T46 2002**
History of Buddhist Thought. Ed. 2. Trade Paper. Dover Publications, Inc. Mineola, NY. 2002. 338p. ISBN:0-486-42104-X, ISBN13: 978-0-486-42104-9. LCCN:2002-017468.
Audience: **g,l,u,f.**

Buddhism > Deities. Rituals. Folklore. Shrines

Beyer, Stephan V. (Editor)   **BQ4710.T34T53**
Magic and Ritual in Tibet: The Cult of Tara. Trade Cloth. Motilal Banarsidass Publishers (Pvt. Ltd). New Delhi, 1999. ISBN:81-208-0488-0, ISBN13: 978-81-208-0488-3. Dewey:294.3/4/38.
Audience: **u,f.**

Nakamura, Kyoko M.   BQ5775.J3 K4413 1997
(Translator, Annotations by, Introduction by)
Miraculous Stories from the Japanese Buddhist Tradition: The
Nihon Ryoiki of the Monk Kyokai. Paper over Boards. Taylor &
Francis Group. Abingdon, 1996. 344p. ISBN:0-7007-0449-3,
ISBN13: 978-0-7007-0449-1. Dewey:294.3/8. LCCN:97-128171.
Audience: **g,l,u,f.** *B*

Naquin, Susan & Yü,   BQ6450.C6P55 1989
Chün-fang (Editors)
Pilgrims and Sacred Sites in China. Trade Cloth. University of
California Press. Berkeley, CA. 1992. 456p. Studies on China,
Vol. 15 ISBN:0-520-07567-6, ISBN13: 978-0-520-07567-2.
Dewey:291.3/5/0951. LCCN:91-020671.
Audience: **g,l,u,f.**

Schopen, Gregory   BQ6160.I4S36 1997
Bones, Stones, and Buddhist Monks: Collected Papers on the
Archaeology, Epigraphy, and Texts of Monastic Buddhism in
India. Trade Cloth. University of Hawaii Press. Honolulu, HI.
1996. 344p. Studies in the Buddhist Tradition
ISBN:0-8248-1748-6, ISBN13: 978-0-8248-1748-0.
Dewey:294.3/657/0954. LCCN:96-030844.
Audience: **l,u,f.**

Strong, John   BQ924.S77 2004
Relics of the Buddha. Trade Cloth. Princeton University Press.
Princeton, NJ. 2004. 312p. Buddhisms Ser.
ISBN:0-691-11764-0, ISBN13: 978-0-691-11764-5.
Dewey:294.3/63. LCCN:2003-065642.
Audience: **g,l,u,f.** *Choice, 2005.*

Yü, Chün-fang   BQ4710.A8Y8 2000
Kuan-yin: The Chinese Transformation of Avalokitesvara. Trade
Cloth. Columbia University Press. New York, NY. 2001. 656p.
ISBN:0-231-12028-1, ISBN13: 978-0-231-12028-9.
Dewey:294.3/4211. LCCN:00-024015.
Audience: **u,f.**

Buddhism > Modifications of Buddhism > Mahayana Buddhism

Dutt, Nalinaksha   BQ7374 .D87
Mahayana Buddhism. Trade Cloth. Laurier Books, Ltd. Ottawa,
ON. 2003. 310p. ISBN:81-86050-95-7, ISBN13:
978-81-86050-95-8. Dewey:294.3/92.
Audience: **g,l,u,f.** *B*

Kiyota, Minoru   BQ7405.M34
Mahayana Buddhist Meditation: Theory and Practice. Cloth
Text. University of Hawaii Press. Honolulu, HI. 1978. 327p.
ISBN:0-8248-0556-9, ISBN13: 978-0-8248-0556-2.
Dewey:294.3/4/43. LCCN:78-060744.
Audience: **l,u,f.** *B*

Murti, T. R.   BQ7457
The Central Philosophy of Buddhism: A Study of the

Madhyamika System. Ed. 2. Trade Paper. Routledge. New York,
NY. 1988. 384p. Paperback Ser. ISBN:0-04-294108-3, ISBN13:
978-0-04-294108-0. Dewey:181/.04392. LCCN:80-504231.
Audience: **u,f.** *B*

Paul, Diana M.   BQ4570.W6P38 1985
Women in Buddhism: Images of the Feminine in the Mahayana
Tradition. Ed. 2. Trade Paper. University of California Press.
Berkeley, CA. 1985. 333p. ISBN:0-520-05428-8, ISBN13:
978-0-520-05428-8. Dewey:294.3/378344. LCCN:84-023960.
Audience: **l,u,f.**

Williams, Paul   BQ7405.W55 1989
Mahayana Buddhism: The Doctrinal Foundations. Trade Cloth.
Routledge. New York, NY. 1989. 272p. ISBN:0-415-02536-2,
ISBN13: 978-0-415-02536-2. Dewey:294.3/92.
LCCN:88-017635.
Audience: **u,f.** *Choice, 1989.*

Buddhism > Modifications of Buddhism > Lamaism

Allione, Tsultrim   BQ7920
Women of Wisdom. Trade Paper. Routledge. New York, NY.
1985. 224p. ISBN:0-7102-0240-7, ISBN13: 978-0-7102-0240-6.
Dewey:294.3/923/0922. LCCN:84-011440.
Audience: **g,l,u,f.** *B*

Dalai Lama XIV   BQ4022.B751975
The Buddhism of Tibet and the Key to the Middle Way. Trade
Cloth. Allen & Unwin, Ltd. London, 1975. 104p.
ISBN:0-04-294086-9, ISBN13: 978-0-04-294086-1.
Dewey:294.3/923. LCCN:77-350546.
Audience: **g,l,u,f.**

Dalai Lama XIV   BQ7935.B777A3 1997
My Land and My People: The Original Autobiography of His
Holiness the Dalai Lama of Tibet. Melissa Mathison Ford
(Foreword by). Trade Paper. Warner Books, Inc. New York, NY.
1997. 256p. ISBN:0-446-67421-4, ISBN13: 978-0-446-67421-8.
Dewey:[B]. LCCN:97-023849.
Audience: **g,u,f.**

Lopez, Donald S.   BQ7620.R45 1997
Religions of Tibet in Practice. Cloth Text. Princeton University
Press. Princeton, NJ. 1997. 560p. Princeton Readings in
Religions Ser. ISBN:0-691-01184-2, ISBN13:
978-0-691-01184-4. Dewey:294.3/923. LCCN:96-031592.
Audience: **g,u,f.** *Choice, 1997.*

Tucci, Giuseppe   BL1945.T5T815 2000
The Religions of Tibet. Ed. 3. Geoffrey Samuel (Translator).
Trade Cloth. Kegan Paul International, Ltd. London, 2001.
340p. The Kegan Paul Library of Religion and Mysticism
ISBN:0-7103-0674-1, ISBN13: 978-0-7103-0674-6.
Dewey:294.3/923. LCCN:2001-276228.
Audience: **g,l,u,f.** *B*

Buddhism > Modifications of Buddhism > Hua-Yen Buddhism

1983 ed. ebook

Cleary, Thomas BQ8218.3
Entry into the Inconceivable: An Introduction to Hua-yen Buddhism. Trade Cloth. University of Hawaii Press. Honolulu, HI. 1995. 232p. ISBN:0-8248-1697-8, ISBN13: 978-0-8248-1697-1. Dewey:294.392. LCCN:83-003613.

Audience: **l,u,f.**

Buddhism > Modifications of Buddhism > Nichiren

Daishonin, Nichiren & BQ8349.N573E5 1990
  Yampolsky, Philip B.
Selected Writings of Nichiren. Burton Watson (Translator). Trade Cloth. Columbia University Press. New York, NY. 1990. 508p. Translations from the Oriental Classics Ser. ISBN:0-231-07260-0, ISBN13: 978-0-231-07260-1. Dewey:294.3/928. LCCN:90-001367.

Audience: **u,f.**

Hardacre, Helen BQ8372
Lay Buddhism in Contemporary Japan. Trade Cloth. Princeton University Press. Princeton, NJ. 1984. 328p. ISBN:0-691-07284-1, ISBN13: 978-0-691-07284-5. Dewey:306/.6. LCCN:83-043075.

Audience: **l,u,f.** *B*

Buddhism > Modifications of Buddhism > Pure Land Buddhism

Blum, Mark L. BQ8512.2
The Origins and Development of Pure Land Buddhism: A Study and Translation of Gyonen's Jodo Homon Genrusho. Trade Cloth. Oxford University Press, Inc. New York, NY. 2002. 492p. ISBN:0-19-512524-X, ISBN13: 978-0-19-512524-5. Dewey:294.3/926. LCCN:99-049558.

Audience: **u,f.**

Payne, Richard K. & BQ4690.A74A44 2003
  Tanaka, Kenneth K. (Editors)
Approaching the Land of Bliss: Religious Praxis in the Cult of Amitabha. Trade Cloth. University of Hawaii Press. Honolulu, HI. 2003. 320p. Studies in East Asian Buddhism, Vol. 17 ISBN:0-8248-2578-0, ISBN13: 978-0-8248-2578-2. Dewey:294.3/926. LCCN:2003-009986.

Audience: **u,f.**

Buddhism > Modifications of Buddhism > Tantric Buddhism

Abé, Ryûichi BQ2910.M367
The Weaving of Mantra: Kûkai and the Construction of Esoteric Buddhist Discourse. Trade Paper. Columbia University Press. New York, NY. 2000. 620p. ISBN:0-231-11287-4, ISBN13: 978-0-231-11287-1. Dewey:294.3/92.

Audience: **u,f.**

Agehananda Bharati BQ8912.3
The Tantric Tradition. Library Binding. Greenwood Publishing Group, Inc. Portsmouth, NH. 1977. ISBN:0-8371-9660-4, ISBN13: 978-0-8371-9660-2. Dewey:294.3/925. LCCN:77-007204.

Audience: **g,l,u,f.** *B*

Davidson, Ronald M. BQ8912.9.I5D38 2002
Indian Esoteric Buddhism: A Social History of the Tantric Movement. Trade Cloth. Columbia University Press. New York, NY. 2002. 400p. ISBN:0-231-12618-2, ISBN13: 978-0-231-12618-2. Dewey:294.3/925/0954. LCCN:2002-067694.

Audience: **u,f.** *Choice, 2003.*

Flood, Gavin BL1283.84
The Tantric Body: The Secret Tradition of Hindu Religion. Cloth over Boards, Trade Cloth. I. B. Tauris & Company, Ltd. London, 2006. 250p. ISBN:1-84511-011-0, ISBN13: 978-1-84511-011-6. Dewey:294.5/514. LCCN:2006-295549.

Audience: **g,l,u,f.**

White, David Gordon BL1283.84.T36 2000
  (Editor)
Tantra in Practice. Trade Paper. Princeton University Press. Princeton, NJ. 2000. 654p. Princeton Readings in Religions Ser. ISBN:0-691-05779-6, ISBN13: 978-0-691-05779-8. Dewey:294.5/95. LCCN:00-022890.

Audience: **g,l,u,f.**

Buddhism > Modifications of Buddhism > Zen Buddhism

Dumoulin, Heinrich BQ9262.3.D8513
Zen Enlightenment: Origins and Meaning. Trade Paper. Shambhala Publications, Inc. Boston, MA. 1979. 192p. ISBN:0-8348-0141-8, ISBN13: 978-0-8348-0141-7. Dewey:294.3/927/09. LCCN:78-027310.

Audience: **g,l,u,f.** *B*

Kapleau, Roshi P. BQ9265.4.T48 2000
The Three Pillars of Zen. Ed. 25. Trade Paper. Doubleday Publishing. New York, NY. 1989. 480p. ISBN:0-385-26093-8, ISBN13: 978-0-385-26093-0. Dewey:294.3/927. LCCN:2001-272132.

Audience: **g,l,u,f.**

Kennett, Jiyu   BQ9415.4.K45
Selling Water by the River: A Manual of Zen Training. Trade
Cloth. Pantheon Books. New York, NY. 1972. xxv, 317p.
ISBN:0-394-46743-4, ISBN13: 978-0-394-46743-6.
Dewey:294.3/927. LCCN:70-038836.

Audience: **g,l,u,f.** *B*

Lai, Whalen & Lancaster,   BQ9262.9.C5.E27 1983
  Lewis R. (Editors)
Early Ch'an in China and Tibet. Trade Cloth. Jain Publishing
Company, Inc. Fremont, CA. 1983. 478p. ISBN:0-89581-152-9,
ISBN13: 978-0-89581-152-3. Dewey:294.3/927/0951.
LCCN:79-066989.

Audience: **u,f.** *B*

McRae, John R.   BQ9262.5 .M367 2003
Seeing Through Zen: Encounter, Transformation, and Genealogy
in Chinese Chan Buddhism. Trade Cloth. University of
California Press. Berkeley, CA. 2004. 237p.
ISBN:0-520-23797-8, ISBN13: 978-0-520-23797-1.
Dewey:294.3/927/0951. LCCN:2003-011741.

Audience: **u,f.** *Choice, 2004.*

Wu, John C. H.   BQ9262.5.W824 2004
The Golden Age of Zen: Zen Masters of the T'Ang Dynasty.
John C. H Wu Jr. (Foreword by), Thomas Merton & Kenneth
Kraft (Introduction by). Trade Cloth. World Wisdom, Inc.
Bloomington, IN. 2004. 280p. The Library of Perennial
Philosophy ISBN:0-941532-44-5, ISBN13: 978-0-941532-44-0.
Dewey:294.3/927/09. LCCN:2003-020214.

Audience: **g,l,u.**

Yokoi, Yuho & Victoria,   BQ9449.D652Y63
  Daizen
Zen Master Dogen: An Introduction with Selected Writings.
Trade Paper. Shambhala Publications, Inc. Boston, MA. 1976.
220p. ISBN:0-8348-0116-7, ISBN13: 978-0-8348-0116-5.
Dewey:294.3/927. LCCN:75-033200.

Audience: **g,l,u,f.** *B*

Christianity > Denominations > Church Unity. Ecumenical Movements

Briggs, John (Editor), et al.   BX6.5
A History of the Ecumenical Movement: 1968 to 2000. Mercy
A. Oduyoye & Georges Tsetsis (Editors). Trade Cloth. World
Council of Churches/Conseil Oecumenique des Eglises. Geneva,
2004. 697p. ISBN:2-8254-1355-0, ISBN13: 978-2-8254-1355-5.
Dewey:270.8/2.

Audience: **u,f.**

Brown, Robert McAfee   BX6
The ecumenical revolution; an interpretation of the
Catholic-Protestant dialogue. Garden City, N.Y., Doubleday.
1967.

Audience: **g,l,u.**

Fey, Harold E. (Editor)   BX6.5.H57 1986
2nd ed. A History of the Ecumenical Movement: 1948 to 1968. Ed. 4.
Trade Paper. World Council of Churches/Conseil Oecumenique
des Eglises. Geneva, 1993. 571p. ISBN:2-8254-0872-7, ISBN13:
978-2-8254-0872-8. Dewey:270.8/2. LCCN:89-189788.

Audience: **g,l,u.**

Lindbeck, George A.   BT77
The Nature of Doctrine: Religion and Theology in a Postliberal
Age. Trade Paper. Westminster John Knox Press. Louisville, KY.
1984. 142p. ISBN:0-664-24618-4, ISBN13: 978-0-664-24618-1.
Dewey:230. LCCN:83-027332.

Audience: **u,f.**

Outler, Albert Cook   BX8
The Christian Tradition and the Unity We Seek. Paper Text.
Textbook Publishers. Temecula, CA. 2003. 165p.
ISBN:0-7581-6940-X, ISBN13: 978-0-7581-6940-2.
Dewey:280.1.

Audience: **l,u.**

Randall, Ian & Hilborn,   BX3
  David
One Body in Christ: The History and Significance of the
Evangelical Alliance. Paper Text. Authentic Media. Waynesboro,
GA. 2001. 394p. ISBN:1-84227-089-3, ISBN13:
978-1-84227-089-9. Dewey:270.

Audience: **u,f.**

Rouse, Ruth & Neill,   BX6.5
  Stephen Charles (Editors)
2nd ed. A History of the Ecumenical Movement: 1517 to 1948. Ed. 4.
Trade Paper. World Council of Churches/Conseil Oecumenique
des Eglises. Geneva, 1993. 868p. ISBN:2-8254-0871-9, ISBN13:
978-2-8254-0871-1. Dewey:270.8/2.

Audience: **g,l,u.**

Wainwright, Geoffrey   BX6.3
  (Editor), et al.
Dictionary of the Ecumenical Movement. Ed. 2. Jose Miguez
Bonino, John S. Pobee, Tom Stransky, Pauline Webb &
Nicholas Lossky (Editors). Trade Cloth. World Council of
Churches/Conseil Oecumenique des Eglises. Geneva, 2002.
1296p. ISBN:2-8254-1354-2, ISBN13: 978-2-8254-1354-8.
Dewey:270.82. LCCN:2003-435502.

Audience: **g,l,u,f.** *Choice, 2003, 1991.*

Christianity > Denominations > Eastern Churches

Angold, Michael   BX300
Church and Society in Byzantium under the Comneni,
1081-1261. Trade Paper. Cambridge University Press. New
York, NY. 2000. 620p. ISBN:0-521-26986-5, ISBN13:
978-0-521-26986-5. Dewey:274.9/504. LCCN:94-012146.

Audience: **g,l,u,f.** *Choice, 1996.*

Angold, Michael (Editor)   **BX290**
Eastern Christianity. Cloth Text. Cambridge University Press.
New York, NY. 2006. 742p. Cambridge History of Christianity
Ser. ISBN:0-521-81113-9, ISBN13: 978-0-521-81113-2.
Dewey:281.9.

         Audience: **u,f.**

Baum, Wilhelm & Winkler, **BX153.3.B38 2003**
 Dietmar W.
The Apostolic Church of the East: A History of the Nestorian
Church. Paper over Boards. Routledge. New York, NY. 2003.
216p. Central Asian Studies Ser. ISBN:0-415-29770-2, ISBN13:
978-0-415-29770-7. Dewey:281/.8/09. LCCN:2002-036712.

         Audience: **u,f.**

Binns, John   **BX320.3 .B56 2002**
An Introduction to the Christian Orthodox Churches. Trade
Cloth. Cambridge University Press. New York, NY. 2002. 284p.
Introduction to Religion Ser. ISBN:0-521-66140-4, ISBN13:
978-0-521-66140-9. Dewey:281.5. LCCN:2002-073820.

         Audience: **g,l,u.**

Brock, Sebastian P.   **BR1713**
Holy Women of the Syrian Orient. Trade Paper. University of
California Press. Berkeley, CA. 1998. 218p. Transformation of
the Classical Heritage Ser., Vol. 13 ISBN:0-520-21366-1,
ISBN13: 978-0-520-21366-1. Dewey:275.6088042.
LCCN:86-011313.

         Audience: **u,f.**

Chryssavgis, John   **BX382.C493 2004**
Light Through Darkness: The Orthodox Tradition. Trade Paper.
Orbis Books. Maryknoll, NY. 2004. 128p. Traditions of
Christian Spirituality Ser. ISBN:1-57075-548-5, ISBN13:
978-1-57075-548-4. Dewey:281.9. LCCN:2004-010798.

         Audience: **g,l,u.**

Chryssavgis, John   **BX378.C6**
Repentance and Confession in the Orthodox Church. Trade
Paper. Holy Cross Orthodox Press. Brookline, MA. 1996. 102p.
ISBN:0-917651-56-1, ISBN13: 978-0-917651-56-4.
Dewey:265/.6.

         Audience: **u,f.**

Constantelos, Demetrios J. **BX320.2.C66 1998**
Understanding the Greek Orthodox Church Its Faith, History
and Life. Ed. 3. Trade Paper. Hellenic College Press. Brookline,
MA. 1998. 291p. ISBN:0-917653-50-5, ISBN13:
978-0-917653-50-6. Dewey:281.9/495. LCCN:97-045878.

         Audience: **g,u,f.**

Cunningham, Mary   **BX300.C86 2002**
Faith in the Byzantine World. Trade Paper. InterVarsity Press.
Downers Grove, IL. 2002. 192p. IVP Histories Ser.
ISBN:0-8308-2352-2, ISBN13: 978-0-8308-2352-9.
Dewey:281/.5. LCCN:2002-068744.

         Audience: **u,f.**

Davis, Stephen J.   **BX134.E3**
Early Coptic Papacy: The Egyptian Church and Its Leadership
in Late Antiquity. Trade Cloth. American University in Cairo

Press. New York, NY. 2005. 224p. ISBN:977-424-830-9,
ISBN13: 978-977-424-830-6. Dewey:262/.12172.
LCCN:2005-357452.

         Audience: **u,f.**

Dragon, Gilbert   **DF548**
Emperor and Priest: The Imperial Office in Byzantium. Trade
Cloth. Cambridge University Press. New York, NY. 2003. 354p.
Past and Present Publications ISBN:0-521-80123-0, ISBN13:
978-0-521-80123-2. Dewey:261.7/09. LCCN:2004-298378.

         Audience: **u,f.**

Erickson, John A.   **BX733.E75 1999**
Orthodox Christians in America. Cloth Text. Oxford University
Press, Inc. New York, NY. 1999. 144p. Religion in America Ser.
ISBN:0-19-510852-3, ISBN13: 978-0-19-510852-1.
Dewey:281.9/73. LCCN:99-019901.

         Audience: **l.**

Fennell, John   **BX485.F45 1995**
A History of the Russian Church to 1448. Cloth Text. Longman
Publishing. Boston, MA. 1995. 272p. ISBN:0-582-08068-1,
ISBN13: 978-0-582-08068-3. Dewey:281.947/09/02.
LCCN:94-016348.

    Audience: **g,l,u,f.** *Choice, 1995.*

Garsoian, Nina (Editor), et **DS57 .E18 1982**
 al.
East of Byzantium: Syria and Armenia in the Formative Period.
Thomas Mathews & Robert Thomson (Editors). Trade Cloth.
Dumbarton Oaks. Washington, DC. 1982. 266p. Dumbarton
Oaks Symposium ISBN:0-88402-104-1, ISBN13:
978-0-88402-104-9. Dewey:956. LCCN:82-009665.

         Audience: **u,f.**

Hussey, Joan M.   **BX324.3**
The Orthodox Church in the Byzantine Empire. Trade Paper.
Oxford University Press, Inc. New York, NY. 1990. 440p.
Oxford History of the Christian Church Ser.
ISBN:0-19-826456-9, ISBN13: 978-0-19-826456-9.
Dewey:281.9/09/02.

    Audience: **u,f.** *Choice, 1986.*

Kivelson, Valerie A. & **BX485.O77 2003**
 Greene, Robert H. (Editors)
Orthodox Russia: Belief and Practice under the Tsars and
Beyond. Trade Cloth. Pennsylvania State University Press.
University Park, PA. 2003. 304p. ISBN:0-271-02349-X,
ISBN13: 978-0-271-02349-6. Dewey:281.9/47.
LCCN:2002-153319.

    Audience: **u,f.** *Choice, 2004.*

Meinardus, Otto F.   **BX133.2**
Two Thousand Years of Coptic Christianity. Ed. 2. Trade Paper.
American University in Cairo Press. New York, NY. 2003. 368p.
ISBN:977-424-757-4, ISBN13: 978-977-424-757-6.
Dewey:281.72.

         Audience: **u,f.**

Melling, David J. & Griffith, **BX100.7.B53 2000**
 Sidney H.
The Blackwell Dictionary of Eastern Christianity. Ken Parry,

Dimitri Brady & John Healy (Editors). Trade Cloth. Blackwell Publishing, Inc. Malden, MA. 1999. 608p. ISBN:0-631-18966-1, ISBN13: 978-0-631-18966-4. Dewey:281/.5/03. LCCN:98-033150.

Audience: **g,l,u,f.**

Meyendorff, John   **B4238.B8**
Byzantine Theology: Historical Trends and Doctrinal Themes. Ed. 2. Trade Paper. Fordham University Press. Bronx, NY. 1987. 243p. ISBN:0-8232-0967-9, ISBN13: 978-0-8232-0967-5. Dewey:230/.19/0902. LCCN:72-094167.

Audience: **u,f.**

Meyendorff, John   **BX290**
The Orthodox Church: Its Past and Its Role in the World Today. Ed. 3. Trade Paper. Saint Vladimir's Seminary Press. Yonkers, NY. 1996. 196p. ISBN:0-913836-81-8, ISBN13: 978-0-913836-81-1. Dewey:281.9. LCCN:81-004978.

Audience: **u,f.**

Pospielovsky, Dimitry V.   **BX101**
The Russian Church under the Soviet Regime. Trade Paper. Saint Vladimir's Seminary Press. Yonkers, NY. 1984. 535p. ISBN:0-88141-033-0, ISBN13: 978-0-88141-033-4. Dewey:281.9/3. LCCN:84-005336.

Audience: **u,f.**

Quenot, Michael   **BX378.5.Q4613 1991**
The Icon: Window on the Kingdom. Trade Paper. Saint Vladimir's Seminary Press. Yonkers, NY. 1991. 176p. ISBN:0-88141-098-5, ISBN13: 978-0-88141-098-3. Dewey:246/.53. LCCN:91-021319.

Audience: **u,f.**

Runciman, Steven   **BX300**
The Byzantine Theocracy: The Weil Lectures, Cincinatti. Trade Paper. Cambridge University Press. New York, NY. 2004. 205p. ISBN:0-521-54591-9, ISBN13: 978-0-521-54591-4. Dewey:274.9/5.

Audience: **u,f.**

Tang, Li   **BX154.C4T36 2004**
A Study of the History of Nestorian Christianity in China and Its Literature in Chinese: Together with a New English Translation of the Dunhuang Nestorian Documents, Vol. 87. Ed. 2. Trade Cloth. Peter Lang Publishing, Inc. New York, NY. 2004. 230p. European University Studies, :Asian and African Studies ISBN:0-8204-6578-X, ISBN13: 978-0-8204-6578-4. Dewey:281/.8/0951. LCCN:2004-048420.

Audience: **u,f.**

Ware, Timothy   **BX106.W3 1993**
The Orthodox Church. Ed. 2. Trade Paper. Penguin Group (USA) Inc. New York, NY. 1993. 368p. ISBN:0-14-014656-3, ISBN13: 978-0-14-014656-1. Dewey:281.9. LCCN:93-241854.

Audience: **g,l,u.**

Wybrew, Hugh   **BX355.W92 1990**
The Orthodox Liturgy: The Development of the Eucharistic Liturgy in the Byzantine Rite. Trade Paper. Saint Vladimir's

Seminary Press. Yonkers, NY. 1990. 189p. ISBN:0-88141-100-0, ISBN13: 978-0-88141-100-3. Dewey:264/.019. LCCN:90-037967.

Audience: **u,f.**

Christianity > Denominations > Roman Catholic Church > Councils

Abbott, Walter M. (Editor)   **BX830 1962.A3G3 1989**
The Documents of Vatican II. Trade Cloth. Crossroad Publishing Company. New York, NY. 1989. 792p. ISBN:0-8245-0980-3, ISBN13: 978-0-8245-0980-4. Dewey:262/.52. LCCN:89-038818.

Audience: **g,l,u,f.**

Bellitto, Christopher M.   **BX825.B45 2002**
The General Councils: A History of the Twenty-One Church Councils from Nicaea to Vatican II. Trade Cloth. Paulist Press. Mahwah, NJ. 2002. 176p. ISBN:0-8091-4019-5, ISBN13: 978-0-8091-4019-0. Dewey:262/.52. LCCN:2002-005890.

Audience: **g,l,u.** *Choice, 2003.*

Flannery, Austin   **BX830.1962.A3**
Documents of the Vatican Council. Trade Paper. Costello Publishing Company, Inc. Northport, NY. 1996. ISBN:0-918344-37-9, ISBN13: 978-0-918344-37-3. Dewey:262.52.

Audience: **g,l,u,f.**

Flannery, Austin P.   **BX1751.2**
Vatican Council II: More Post-Conciliar Documents. Trade Paper. Pauline Books & Media. Boston, MA. 1988. 1034p. ISBN:0-918344-16-6, ISBN13: 978-0-918344-16-8. Dewey:230/.2. LCCN:82-074114.

Audience: **g,l,u,f.**

Lindbeck, George A.   **BX1751.2**
The Future of Roman Catholic Theology. Trade Cloth. SPCK Publishing. London, 1970. xiv, 125p. ISBN:0-281-02452-9, ISBN13: 978-0-281-02452-0. Dewey:230.2.

Audience: **u,f.**

O'Malley, John W.   **BX830**
Tradition and Transition: Historical Perspectives on Vatican II. Trade Paper. Liturgical Press. Collegeville, MN. 1989. 191p. Theology and Life Ser., Vol. 26 ISBN:0-8146-5769-9, ISBN13: 978-0-8146-5769-0. Dewey:262/.52.

Audience: **u,f.**

Rynne, Xavier   **BX830.1962**
Vatican Council II. Trade Paper. Orbis Books. Maryknoll, NY. 1999. 616p. ISBN:1-57075-293-1, ISBN13: 978-1-57075-293-3. Dewey:262/.52. LCCN:99-461982.

Audience: **u,f.** *Choice, 2000.*

Schroeder, H. J. (Translator)   **BX830.1545.A3**
Canons and Decrees of the Council of Trent. Trade Paper. TAN Books and Publishers, Inc. Rockford, IL. 1994. 293p. ISBN:0-89555-074-1, ISBN13: 978-0-89555-074-3. Dewey:262.9. LCCN:78-066132.

Audience: **u,f.**

Stump, Phillip H.   **BX830 1414.S78 1994**
The Reforms of the Council of Constance (1414-1418). Trade
Cloth. Brill Academic Publishers, Inc. Boston, MA. 1993. xv,
463p. Studies in the History of Christian Thought, Vol. 53
ISBN:90-04-09930-1, ISBN13: 978-90-04-09930-2.
Dewey:262/.52. LCCN:93-031994.

Audience: **u,f.**

Tanner, Norman P. (Editor)   **BX825.A1990**
Decrees of the Ecumenical Councils: From Nicea I to Vatican II.
Trade Cloth. Georgetown University Press. Washington, DC.
1990. 2,528p. ISBN:0-87840-490-2, ISBN13:
978-0-87840-490-2. Dewey:262/.52. LCCN:90-003209.

Audience: **u,f.**

Vatican Council Two   **BX830**
Declaration on the Relation of the Church to Non-Christian
Religions. Rene Laurentin & Joseph Neuner (Editors). Trade
Paper. Paulist Press. Mahwah, NJ. 1966. 104p.
ISBN:0-8091-1535-2, ISBN13: 978-0-8091-1535-8.
Dewey:261.2. LCCN:66-026208.

Audience: **u,f.**

Christianity > Denominations > Roman Catholic Church > Dictionaries. Encyclopedias. Documents

Catholic Church Staff   **BX860**
The Papal Encyclicals in Their Historical Context. Paper Text.
Textbook Publishers. Temecula, CA. 2003. 317p.
ISBN:0-7581-7836-0, ISBN13: 978-0-7581-7836-7.
Dewey:262.8.

Audience: **g,l,u.**

Catholic University of   **BX841.N44 2003**
America Staff (Contribution by)
e New Catholic Encyclopedia, Set. Ed. 2. E-Book. Thomson
Gale. Farmington Hills, MI. 2003. 12,000p.
ISBN:0-7876-4004-2, ISBN13: 978-0-7876-4004-0.
Dewey:282/.03. LCCN:2002-000924.

Audience: **g,l,u,f.** *Choice, 2003.*

Dwyer, Judith A. (Editor)   **BX1753.N497 1994**
The New Dictionary of Catholic Social Thought. Trade Cloth.
Liturgical Press. Collegeville, MN. 2005. 1,056p.
ISBN:0-8146-5526-2, ISBN13: 978-0-8146-5526-9.
Dewey:261.8/08/822. LCCN:94-004264.

Audience: **g,l,u,f.**

Glazier, Michael   **BX1406.2.E53 1997**
The Encyclopedia of American Catholic History. Thomas Shelly
(Editor). Trade Cloth. Liturgical Press. Collegeville, MN. 2005.
1,584p. ISBN:0-8146-5919-5, ISBN13: 978-0-8146-5919-9.
Dewey:282/.73/03. LCCN:97-041221.

Audience: **g,l,u,f.** *Choice, 1998.*

Christianity > Denominations > Roman Catholic Church > Collections

Aquinas, Thomas   **BX890.T62**
e The Collected Works of St. Thomas Aquinas. E-Book.
Intelex Corporation. Charlottesville, VA. Past Masters Ser.
ISBN:1-57085-201-4, ISBN13: 978-1-57085-201-5.
Dewey:230.2.

Audience: **g,l,u,f.**

Armstrong, Regis J. &   **BX890.F665 1982**
Brady, Ignatius C. (Editors)
Francis and Clare: The Complete Works. Trade Cloth. Paulist
Press. Mahwah, NJ. 1986. 272p. Classics of Western Spirituality
Ser. ISBN:0-8091-2446-7, ISBN13: 978-0-8091-2446-6.
Dewey:271/.3/022. LCCN:82-062693.

Audience: **g,l,u,f.**

Balthasar, Hans Urs Von   **BX1751.2**
The Von Balthasar Reader. Medard Kehl & Werner Loser
(Editors). Trade Paper. FaithWorks. Brentwood, TN. 1997. 456p.
ISBN:0-8245-0720-7, ISBN13: 978-0-8245-0720-6.
Dewey:230/.2.

Audience: **l,u.**

Cousins, Ewert (Editor)   **BX1751.2**
Bonaventure: The Soul's Journey into God: the Tree of Life, the
Life of Francis. Trade Cloth. Paulist Press. Mahwah, NJ. 1978.
384p. Classics of Western Spirituality Ser. ISBN:0-8091-2121-2,
ISBN13: 978-0-8091-2121-2. Dewey:230/.2. LCCN:78-060723.

Audience: **g,l,u.**

Kavanaugh, Kieran &   **BX890.J623313 1991**
Rodriguez, Otilio (Translators)
The Collected Works of St. John of the Cross. Trade Cloth. I C
S Publications. Washington, DC. 1991. 816p.
ISBN:0-935216-15-4, ISBN13: 978-0-935216-15-8.
Dewey:230/.2. LCCN:90-026713.

Audience: **g,l,u,f.**

Kavanaugh, Kieran &   **BV4501.2**
Rodriguez, Otilio (Translators)
The Collected Works of St. Teresa of Avila, Vol. 2. Trade Paper.
I C S Publications. Washington, DC. 1980. 560p.
ISBN:0-9600876-6-4, ISBN13: 978-0-9600876-6-2. Dewey:248.
LCCN:75-031305.

Audience: **g,l,u,f.**

Kavanaugh, Kieran &   **BV4501.2**
Rodriguez, Otilio (Translators)
The Collected Works of St. Teresa of Avila, Vol. 3. Sally J.
Bensusen (Illustrator). Trade Paper. I C S Publications.
Washington, DC. 1985. 504p. ISBN:0-935216-06-5, ISBN13:
978-0-935216-06-6. Dewey:248. LCCN:75-031305.

Audience: **g,l,u,f.**

Kavanaugh, Kieran   **BX890 .T353 1976**
The Collected Works of St. Teresa of Avila: The Book of Her
Life, Spiritual Testimonies, Soliloquies. Otillo Rodriquez

(Translator). Trade Paper. I C S Publications. Washington, DC. 1976. 504p. ISBN:0-9600876-2-1, ISBN13: 978-0-9600876-2-4. Dewey:248. LCCN:75-031305.

Audience: **g,l,u,f.**

Ker, Ian (Editor)   **BX890.N43 1989**
The Genius of John Henry Newman: Selections from His Writings. Cloth Text. Oxford University Press, Inc. New York, NY. 1990. 360p. ISBN:0-19-826682-0, ISBN13: 978-0-19-826682-2. Dewey:230/.2. LCCN:89-015946.

Audience: **g,l,u.**

O'Brien, David & Shannon,   **BX1753**
 Thomas A. (Editors)
Catholic Social Thought: The Documentary Heritage. Trade Paper. Orbis Books. Maryknoll, NY. 1992. 688p. ISBN:0-88344-787-8, ISBN13: 978-0-88344-787-1. Dewey:261.8. LCCN:92-003185.

Audience: **u,f.**

1949 ed. **Pegis, Anton Charles**   **BX880**
The Wisdom of Catholicism. Paper Text. Textbook Publishers. Temecula, CA. 2003. 988p. ISBN:0-7581-8069-1, ISBN13: 978-0-7581-8069-8. Dewey:208.2.

Audience: **l,u.**

Rahner, Karl & O'Hara,   **BX1751.2**
 William Joseph
A Rahner Reader. Trade Cloth. Darton, Longman & Todd, Ltd. Letchworth Garden City, 1975. xxix, 381p. ISBN:0-232-51325-2, ISBN13: 978-0-232-51325-7. Dewey:230/.2.

Audience: **g,l,u.**

Christianity > Denominations > Roman Catholic Church > History

Barraclough, Geoffrey   **BX955.2**
The Medieval Papacy. Trade Cloth. W. W. Norton & Company, Inc. New York, NY. 1979. 216p. Library of World Civilization ISBN:0-393-95100-6, ISBN13: 978-0-393-95100-4. Dewey:262.130902.

Audience: **g,l,u.** *B*

Bernard of Clairvaux   **BX953 .B47**
Bernard of Clairvaux: Five Books on Consideration - Advice to a Pope. Trade Cloth. Cistercian Publications, Inc. Kalamazoo, MI. 1989. 222p. Cistercian Fathers Ser., No. 37 ISBN:0-87907-737-9, ISBN13: 978-0-87907-737-2. Dewey:262/.13.

Audience: **u,f.**

Blumenthal, Uta-Renate   **BX1198.B5813 1988**
The Investiture Controversy: Church and Monarchy from the Ninth to the Twelfth Century. Trade Cloth. University of Pennsylvania Press. Philadelphia, PA. 1988. 212p. Middle Ages Ser. ISBN:0-8122-8112-8, ISBN13: 978-0-8122-8112-5. Dewey:262/.12. LCCN:88-010600.

Audience: **u,f.** *Choice, 1989.*

Bossy, John   **BX1492**
The English Catholic Community, 1570-1850. Trade Cloth. Darton, Longman & Todd, Ltd. Letchworth Garden City, 1975. xv, 446p. ISBN:0-232-51284-1, ISBN13: 978-0-232-51284-7. Dewey:282/.42.

Audience: **u,f.**

Bruneau, Thomas C.   **BX1466.2.B77 1982**
The Church in Brazil. Cloth Text. University of Texas Press. Austin, TX. 1982. 253p. Latin American Monographs, No. 56 ISBN:0-292-71071-2, ISBN13: 978-0-292-71071-9. Dewey:282/.81. LCCN:81-016391.

Audience: **u,f.**

Chadwick, Owen   **BX1361**
The Popes and European Revolution. Trade Cloth. Oxford University Press, Inc. New York, NY. 1981. 656p. Oxford History of the Christian Church Ser. ISBN:0-19-826919-6, ISBN13: 978-0-19-826919-9. Dewey:262/.13/09033. LCCN:80-040673.

Audience: **g,u,f.**

Chodorow, Stanley   **K447.G73**
Christian Political Theory and Church Politics in the Mid-Twelfth Century: The Ecclesiology of Gratian's Decretum. Trade Cloth. University of California Press. Berkeley, CA. 1972. UCLA Center for Medieval and Renaissance Studies ISBN:0-520-01850-8, ISBN13: 978-0-520-01850-1. Dewey:262.9/23. LCCN:71-138512.

Audience: **u,f.**

Cleary, Edward L. (Editor)   **BX1425.A2B67 1990**
Born of the Poor: The Latin American Church Since Medellin. Cloth Text. University of Notre Dame Press. Notre Dame, IN. 1990. 200p. ISBN:0-268-00683-0, ISBN13: 978-0-268-00683-9. Dewey:282/.8/09045. LCCN:89-040746.

Audience: **u,f.**

Cleary, Edward L.   **BX1426.2.C54 1985**
Crisis and Change: The Church in Latin America Today. Trade Paper. Orbis Books. Maryknoll, NY. 1985. 208p. ISBN:0-88344-149-7, ISBN13: 978-0-88344-149-7. Dewey:282.8. LCCN:84-016478.

Audience: **u,f.**

Davis, Cyprian   **BX1407.N4**
The History of Black Catholics in the United States. Trade Paper. FaithWorks. Brentwood, TN. 1995. 368p. ISBN:0-8245-1495-5, ISBN13: 978-0-8245-1495-2. Dewey:282/.73/08996073.

Audience: **l,u.**

Dolan, Jay P.   **BX1406.2**
The American Catholic Experience: A History from Colonial Times to the Present. Trade Cloth. University of Notre Dame Press. Notre Dame, IN. 1992. 504p. ISBN:0-268-00639-3, ISBN13: 978-0-268-00639-6. Dewey:282/.73. LCCN:92-050409.

Audience: **g,l,u,f.**

Dolan, Jay P.   BX1406.3
In Search of an American Catholicism: A History of Religion and Culture in Tension. Trade Paper. Oxford University Press, Inc. New York, NY. 2003. 320p. ISBN:0-19-516885-2, ISBN13: 978-0-19-516885-3. Dewey:282.7/3.
                    Audience: **g,l,u,f.** *Choice, 2003.*

Dolan, Jay P.   BX4603.N6
The Immigrant Church: New York's Irish and German Catholics, 1815-1865. Martin E. Marty (Foreword by). Trade Cloth. University of Notre Dame Press. Notre Dame, IN. 1983. 236p. ISBN:0-268-01151-6, ISBN13: 978-0-268-01151-2. Dewey:282/.747/1. LCCN:82-023827.
                    Audience: **u,f.**

Dominguez, Jorge I.   BX1426.2.R65 1994
  (Introduction by)
The Roman Catholic Church in Latin America. Cloth Text. Garland Publishing, Inc. New York, NY. 1994. 424p. Essays on Mexico Central South America Ser. ISBN:0-8153-1487-6, ISBN13: 978-0-8153-1487-5. Dewey:282/.8. LCCN:93-045525.
                    Audience: **u,f.**

Fisher, James T.   BX1406.3.F57 2002
Communion of Immigrants: A History of Catholics in America. Trade Paper. Oxford University Press, Inc. New York, NY. 2002. 200p. ISBN:0-19-515496-7, ISBN13: 978-0-19-515496-2. Dewey:282/.73. LCCN:2002-003386.
                    Audience: **g,l,u,f.**

Fogarty, Gerald P.   BS500.F64 2006
American Catholic Biblical Scholarship: A History from the Early Repbulic to Vatican II. Trade Paper. Society of Biblical Literature. Atlanta, GA. 2006. ISBN:1-58983-235-3, ISBN13: 978-1-58983-235-0. Dewey:220.088/28273. LCCN:2006-004219.
                    Audience: **u,f.**

Fox, Thomas C.   BX1615
Pentecost in Asia: A New Way of Being Church. Trade Paper. Orbis Books. Maryknoll, NY. 2003. 240p. ISBN:1-57075-492-6, ISBN13: 978-1-57075-492-0. Dewey:282/.5/09045.
                    Audience: **u,f.**

France, John   D157.F67 2005
The Crusades and the Expansion of Catholic Christendom, 1000-1714. Perfect, Paper over Boards. Routledge. New York, NY. 2005. 392p. ISBN:0-415-37127-9, ISBN13: 978-0-415-37127-8. Dewey:909.07. LCCN:2004-030018.
                    Audience: **u,f.**

Gillis, Chester   BX1406.2.G451999
Roman Catholicism in America. Trade Paper. Columbia University Press. New York, NY. 2000. 366p. Columbia Contemporary American Religion Ser. ISBN:0-231-10871-0, ISBN13: 978-0-231-10871-3. Dewey:282/.73. LCCN:99-017945.
                    Audience: **g,l,u,f.** *Choice, 2000.*

Greenleaf, Richard E.   BX1426.2.G73 1971
The Roman Catholic Church in Colonial Latin America. Trade

Cloth. Alfred A. Knopf Inc. New York, NY. 1971. xi, 272p. ISBN:0-394-30290-7, ISBN13: 978-0-394-30290-4. Dewey:282.8. LCCN:71-130774.
                    Audience: **u,f.**

Hastings, Adrian   BX1680.3.H37 1989
African Catholicism: Essays in Discovery. Trade Paper. Continuum International Publishing Group, Ltd. London, 1989. 224p. ISBN:0-334-00019-X, ISBN13: 978-0-334-00019-8. Dewey:282/.67. LCCN:89-004506.
                    Audience: **u,f.**

Hebblethwaite, Peter   BX1378
1985 ed. John XXIII: Pope of the Century. Ed. 2. Trade Paper. Continuum International Publishing Group, Ltd. London, 2000. 320p. ISBN:0-8264-4995-6, ISBN13: 978-0-8264-4995-5. Dewey:282.092.
                    Audience: **u,f.**

Kabasele, Francois L.   BX1977.A357K33 1998
Celebrating Jesus Christ in Africa: Liturgy and Inculturation. David N. Power (Foreword by). Trade Paper. Orbis Books. Maryknoll, NY. 1998. 128p. Faith and Cultures Ser. ISBN:0-88344-971-4, ISBN13: 978-0-88344-971-4. Dewey:264/.02/00967. LCCN:98-016478.
                    Audience: **u,f.**

Kenneally, James J.   BX1407.W65K43 1990
The History of American Catholic Women. Trade Cloth. Crossroad Publishing Company. New York, NY. 1990. 288p. ISBN:0-8245-1009-7, ISBN13: 978-0-8245-1009-1. Dewey:282/.082. LCCN:89-077880.
                    Audience: **u,f.** *Choice, 1991.*

Kung, Hans   BX945.3
The Catholic Church: A Short History. Trade Paper. Random House Adult Trade Publishing Group. New York, NY. 2003. 272p. Modern Library Chronicles ISBN:0-8129-6762-3, ISBN13: 978-0-8129-6762-3. Dewey:282/.09.
                    Audience: **g,l,u.** *Choice, 2001.*

Lawler, Justus George   BX1390.L39 2002
Popes and Politics: Reform, Resentment, and the Holocaust. Trade Cloth. Continuum International Publishing Group, Ltd. London, 2002. 256p. ISBN:0-8264-1385-4, ISBN13: 978-0-8264-1385-7. Dewey:262/.13/0904. LCCN:2001-052730.
                    Audience: **u,f.**

Levine, Daniel H.   BX1470.2
Religion and Politics in Latin America: The Catholic Church in Venezuela and Columbia. Trade Paper. Princeton University Press. Princeton, NJ. 1981. 356p. ISBN:0-691-02200-3, ISBN13: 978-0-691-02200-0. Dewey:282/.861. LCCN:80-007542.
                    Audience: **u,f.**

Lewy, Guenter   BX1536.L4 1999
1964 ed. The Catholic Church and Nazi Germany. Trade Paper. Da Capo Press, Inc. Cambridge, MA. 2000. 448p. ISBN:0-306-80931-1, ISBN13: 978-0-306-80931-6. Dewey:282/.43. LCCN:99-042093.
                    Audience: **u,f.** *B*

Mahoney, John   **BJ1249**
The Making of Moral Theology: A Study of the Roman Catholic
Tradition. Paper Text. Oxford University Press, Inc. New York,
NY. 1989. 382p. ISBN:0-19-826730-4, ISBN13:
978-0-19-826730-0. Dewey:241/.042. LCCN:86-019188.
Audience: **u,f.** *Choice, 1988.*

Massa, Mark S.   **BX1406.2.M38 1999**
Catholics and American Culture: Fulton Sheen, Dorothy Day
and the Notre Dame Football Team. Trade Cloth. Crossroad
Publishing Company. New York, NY. 1999. 288p.
ISBN:0-8245-1537-4, ISBN13: 978-0-8245-1537-9.
Dewey:305.6/2073. LCCN:98-031072.
Audience: **u,f.** *Choice, 1999.*

McBrien, Richard   **BX955.2**
2000 ed. Lives of the Popes: The Pontiffs from St. Peter to Benedict
XVI. Trade Paper. HarperCollins Publishers. New York, NY.
2006. 528p. ISBN:0-06-087807-X, ISBN13: 978-0-06-087807-8.
Dewey:282/.092/2.
Audience: **g,l,u.**

Noonan, John   **BX946.N66 2005**
A Church That Can and Cannot Change. Trade Cloth. University
of Notre Dame Press. Notre Dame, IN. 2005. 280p. Erasmus
Institute Books ISBN:0-268-03603-9, ISBN13:
978-0-268-03603-4. Dewey:241/.042. LCCN:2004-026983.
Audience: **u,f.** *Choice, 2005.*

Omenka, Nicholas I.   **LC508.N542E186 1989**
The School in the Service of Evangelization: The Catholic
Educational Impact in Eastern Nigeria 1886-1950. Trade Cloth.
Brill Academic Publishers, Inc. Boston, MA. 1989. xv, 317p.
Studies on Religion in Africa - Supplements to the Journal of
Religion in Africa, Vol. 6 ISBN:90-04-08632-3, ISBN13:
978-90-04-08632-6. Dewey:377/.82/669. LCCN:88-037555.
Audience: **u,f.**

Payne, Stanley G.   **BX1584**
Spanish Catholicism: An Historical Overview. Trade Paper.
University of Wisconsin Press. Chicago, IL. 2003. 263p.
ISBN:0-299-09804-4, ISBN13: 978-0-299-09804-9.
Dewey:282.46. LCCN:83-025946.
Audience: **u,f.**

Renouard, Yves & Bethell,   **BX1270**
  Denis
The Avignon Papacy, 1305-1403. Trade Cloth. Faber & Faber,
Ltd. London, 1970. ISBN:0-571-09159-8, ISBN13:
978-0-571-09159-1. Dewey:262/.13/09.
Audience: **u,f.**

Ricard, Robert   **BX1428.2**
1964 ed. The Spiritual Conquest of Mexico: An Essay on the Apostolate
and the Evangelizing Methods of the Mendicant Orders in New
Spain, 1523-1572. Lesley B. Simpson (Translator). Trade Cloth.
University of California Press. Berkeley, CA. 1974. 435p.
ISBN:0-520-02760-4, ISBN13: 978-0-520-02760-2.
Dewey:282/.72. LCCN:66-016286.
Audience: **u,f.**

Richards, Jeffrey   **BX965**
The Popes and the Papacy in the Early Middle Ages, 476-752.
Trade Cloth. Routledge. New York, NY. 1979. ix, 422p.
ISBN:0-7100-0098-7, ISBN13: 978-0-7100-0098-9.
Dewey:262/.13/09021. LCCN:78-041023.
Audience: **u,f.**

Robinson, Ian S.   **BX1535**
Authority and Resistance in the Investiture Contest. Trade Cloth.
Holmes & Meier Publishers, Inc. Teaneck, NJ. 1978. 189p.
ISBN:0-8419-0407-3, ISBN13: 978-0-8419-0407-1.
Dewey:262/.8. LCCN:78-009110.
Audience: **u,f.**

Rosales, Gaudencio &   **BX1615.F431992**
  Arevalo, Catalino (Editors)
For All the Peoples of Asia: Federation of Asian Bishops'
Conferences Documents from 1970 to 1991. Trade Cloth. Orbis
Books. Maryknoll, NY. 1992. 342p. ISBN:0-88344-837-8,
ISBN13: 978-0-88344-837-3. Dewey:282/.5/09045.
LCCN:92-005033.
Audience: **u,f.**

Tablino, Paolo   **BV3625.K4T33 2004**
Christianity among the Nomads: The Catholic Church in
Northern Kenya. Trade Cloth. Paulines Publications, Africa.
Nairobi, 2004. 312p. ISBN:9966-21-784-3, ISBN13:
978-9966-21-784-4. Dewey:266/.267622. LCCN:2004-360186.
Audience: **u,f.**

Ullmann, Walter   **BX955.2.U5 1970**
The Growth of Papal Government in the Middle Ages; a Study
in the Ideological Relation of Clerical to Lay Power. Ed. 3.
Trade Cloth. Methuen & Company, Ltd. London, 1970. xxiv,
496p. ISBN:0-416-15890-0, ISBN13: 978-0-416-15890-8.
Dewey:262/.13/09021. LCCN:72-476873.
Audience: **u,f.** *B*

Ullmann, Walter   **BX1301.U55 1972**
1948 ed. The Origins of the Great Schism. Trade Cloth. Shoe String
Press, Inc. North Haven, CT. 1972. xiii, 244p.
ISBN:0-208-01277-X, ISBN13: 978-0-208-01277-7.
Dewey:282/.09/023. LCCN:79-039365.
Audience: **u,f.**

Ullmann, Walter   **BX955.3.U45 2002**
1974 ed. A Short History of the Papacy in the Middle Ages. Ed. 2.
George Garnett (Introduction by). Trade Paper. Routledge. New
York, NY. 2003. 416p. ISBN:0-415-30227-7, ISBN13:
978-0-415-30227-2. Dewey:262/.13/0902. LCCN:2002-012456.
Audience: **u,f.**

Weaver, Mary J. & Appleby,   **BX1406.2.B45 1995**
  R. Scott (Editors)
Being Right: Conservative Catholics in America. Trade Cloth.
Indiana University Press. Bloomington, IN. 1995. 416p.
ISBN:0-253-32922-1, ISBN13: 978-0-253-32922-6.
Dewey:282/.73/09045. LCCN:95-006665.
Audience: **u,f.**

Whyte, John H.   BX1401.A1.W48 1981
Catholics in Western Democracies: A Study in Political
Behavior. Cloth Text. Palgrave Macmillan. New York, NY.
1981. 193p. ISBN:0-312-12446-5, ISBN13: 978-0-312-12446-5.
Dewey:322/.1/091713. LCCN:81-009375.

                                        Audience: **u,f.**

Zanca, Kenneth J.   HT917.C3A44 1994
American Catholics and Slavery, 1789-1866: An Anthology of
Primary Documents. Trade Cloth. University Press of America,
Inc. Lanham, MD. 1994. 322p. ISBN:0-8191-9565-0, ISBN13:
978-0-8191-9565-4. Dewey:261.8/34567/0973.
LCCN:94-011486.

                                        Audience: **g,l,u.**

Zoller, Michael   BX1406.2.Z6513 1999
Washington and Rome: The History of Catholicism in American
Culture. Albert Wimmer & Steven Rendall (Translators). Trade
Cloth. University of Notre Dame Press. Notre Dame, IN. 1999.
256p. ISBN:0-268-01952-5, ISBN13: 978-0-268-01952-5.
Dewey:282/.73. LCCN:98-003011.

                          Audience: **u,f.** *Choice, 2000.*

Christianity > Denominations > Roman Catholic Church > Theology. Doctrine. Sermons

Adam, Karl   BX1751.A4 1997
The Spirit of Catholicism. Justin McCann (Translator). Trade
Paper. FaithWorks. Brentwood, TN. 1997. 264p.
ISBN:0-8245-1718-0, ISBN13: 978-0-8245-1718-2. Dewey:282.
LCCN:97-028325.

                                        Audience: **g,l.**

Allsopp, Michael E. &   BJ1249.C19 1995
  O'Keefe, John J.
Veritatis Splendor: American Responses. Trade Paper. Rowman
& Littlefield Publishers, Inc. Lanham, MD. 1995. 313p.
ISBN:1-55612-760-X, ISBN13: 978-1-55612-760-1.
Dewey:241/.042. LCCN:94-023533.

                                        Audience: **l,u,f.**

Curran, Charles E.   BX1753
American Catholic Social Ethics: Twentieth-Century
Approaches. Paper Text. University of Notre Dame Press. Notre
Dame, IN. 1984. 353p. ISBN:0-268-00609-1, ISBN13:
978-0-268-00609-9. Dewey:261.8/0973. LCCN:82-004829.

                                        Audience: **l,u,f.**

DeBerri, Edward P., et al.   BX1753.H46 2003
Catholic Social Teaching: Our Best Kept Secret. Ed. 4. James E.
Hug, Peter J. Henroit & Michael J. Schultheis (Authors). Trade
Paper. Orbis Books. Maryknoll, NY. 2003. 224p.
ISBN:1-57075-485-3, ISBN13: 978-1-57075-485-2.
Dewey:261.8/088/22. LCCN:2003-049878.

                                        Audience: **g,l,u.**

Gaillardetz, Richard R.   BX1746.G326 1997
Teaching with Authority: A Theology of the Magisterium in the
Church. Trade Paper. Liturgical Press. Collegeville, MN. 2005.
312p. Theology and Life Ser., Vol. 4 ISBN:0-8146-5529-7,
ISBN13: 978-0-8146-5529-0. Dewey:262/.8. LCCN:96-036775.

                                        Audience: **u,f.**

Hollenbach, David   BJ1249 .H578 2002
The Common Good and Christian Ethics. Stephen R. L. Clark,
Robin Gill, Stanley Hauerwas & Robin W. Lovin (Contribution
by). Trade Paper. Cambridge University Press. New York, NY.
2002. 286p. New Studies in Christian Ethics, Vol. 22
ISBN:0-521-89451-4, ISBN13: 978-0-521-89451-7.
Dewey:241.042. LCCN:2002-073786.

                                        Audience: **g,u,f.**

Leftow, Brian & Davies,   BX1749
  Brian (Editors)
Aquinas: Summa of Theology, Questions on God. Karl Ameriks
& Desmond M. Clarke (Contribution by). Cloth Text.
Cambridge University Press. New York, NY. 2006. 342p.
Cambridge Texts in the History of Philosophy Ser.
ISBN:0-521-82140-1, ISBN13: 978-0-521-82140-7. Dewey:231.
                                        Audience: **g,l,u,f.**

Lubac, Henri De   BX1751
Catholicism: A Study of Dogma in Relation to the Corporate
Destiny of Mankind. Paper Text. Textbook Publishers.
Temecula, CA. 2003. 283p. ISBN:0-7581-3929-2, ISBN13:
978-0-7581-3929-0. Dewey:282.

                                        Audience: **l,u.**

McBrien, Richard P.   BX1751.2
Catholicism. Ed. 3. Trade Paper. Continuum International
Publishing Group, Ltd. London, 1994. 1328p.
ISBN:0-225-66743-6, ISBN13: 978-0-225-66743-1.
Dewey:230.2.

                                        Audience: **l,u.**

Newman, John Henry   BX5133.N4S352 1999
Selected Sermons, Prayers and Devotions. John F. Thornton &
Susan B. Varenne (Editors), Peter J. Gomes (Preface by). Trade
Paper. Alfred A. Knopf Inc. New York, NY. 1999. 432p. Vintage
Spiritual Classics Ser. ISBN:0-375-70551-1, ISBN13:
978-0-375-70551-9. Dewey:252/.03. LCCN:98-054136.

                                        Audience: **g,l,u,f.**

Rahner, Karl   BX1751.2
Foundations of Christian Faith: An Introduction to the Idea of
Christianity. Trade Paper. FaithWorks. Brentwood, TN. 1982.
470p. Foundations of Christian Faith Ser., Vol. 1
ISBN:0-8245-0523-9, ISBN13: 978-0-8245-0523-3.
Dewey:230/.2. LCCN:82-004663.

                                        Audience: **g,l,u.**

Segundo, Juan L.   BX1751.2.A1
The Community Called Church. John Drury (Translator). Trade
Paper. Orbis Books. Maryknoll, NY. 1973. 181p. A Theology for
Artisans of a New Humanity Ser., Vol. 1 ISBN:0-88344-487-9,
ISBN13: 978-0-88344-487-0. Dewey:230.2. LCCN:72-085795.

                                        Audience: **u,f.**

Traina, Cristina L.   BJ1395.T73 1999
Feminist Ethics and Natural Law: The End of the Anathemas.
Trade Cloth. Georgetown University Press. Washington, DC.
1999. 416p. Moral Traditions and Moral Arguments Ser.
ISBN:0-87840-726-X, ISBN13: 978-0-87840-726-2.
Dewey:170/.82. LCCN:98-044651.

Audience: **u,f.**

Christianity > Denominations > Roman Catholic Church > Catholic Church - Relations. Church and State. Church Government. Laity

Congar, Yves   BX1920
1957 ed Lay People in the Church: A Study for a Theology of the Laity.
Paper Text. Textbook Publishers. Temecula, CA. 2003. 447p.
ISBN:0-7581-7672-4, ISBN13: 978-0-7581-7672-1.
Dewey:262.2.

Audience: **u,f.**

Jenkins, Philip   BX1770.J46 2004
The New Anti-Catholicism: The Last Acceptable Prejudice.
Trade Paper. Oxford University Press, Inc. New York, NY. 2004.
268p. ISBN:0-19-517604-9, ISBN13: 978-0-19-517604-9.
Dewey:305.6/2073.

Audience: **u,f.** *Choice, 2003.*

Minus, Paul M.   BX1784
The Catholic Rediscovery of Protestantism. Trade Paper. Paulist
Press. Mahwah, NJ. 1976. 276p. ISBN:0-8091-1944-7, ISBN13:
978-0-8091-1944-8. Dewey:262/.001. LCCN:75-044804.

Audience: **u,f.**

Oakley, Francis & Russett, Bruce M.   BX1803.G68 2004
Governance, Accountability, and the Future of the Catholic
Church. Trade Cloth. Continuum International Publishing Group,
Ltd. London, 2004. 240p. ISBN:0-8264-1577-6, ISBN13:
978-0-8264-1577-6. Dewey:262/.02. LCCN:2003-019944.

Audience: **u,f.**

Quinn, John R.   BX1805.Q56 1999
Reform of the Papacy. Trade Paper. FaithWorks. Brentwood,
TN. 1999. 160p. ISBN:0-8245-1826-8, ISBN13:
978-0-8245-1826-4. Dewey:262/.13. LCCN:99-038951.

Audience: **g,l,u.**

Sigmund, Paul E. (Edited and Translated by)   BX1790.N5C613 1995
1963 ed Nicholas of Cusa: The Catholic Concordance. Raymond Guess
& Quentin Skinner (Contribution by). Trade Paper. Cambridge
University Press. New York, NY. 1996. 375p. Texts in the
History of Political Thought ISBN:0-521-56773-4, ISBN13:
978-0-521-56773-2. Dewey:261.7.

Audience: **u,f.**

Tellenbach, Gerd   BX1790
Church, State and Christian Society at the Time of the
Investiture Contest. R. F. Bennett (Translator). Trade Paper.
University of Toronto Press. Toronto, ON. 1991. 196p. Medieval
Academy Reprints for Teaching Ser., No. 27
ISBN:0-8020-6857-X, ISBN13: 978-0-8020-6857-6.
Dewey:261.709021. LCCN:92-120317.

Audience: **u,f.**

Tierney, B.   BX1806
1972 ed Origins of Papal Infallibility,1150-1350: A Study on the
Concepts of Infallibility, Sovereignty and Tradition in the
Middle Ages. Ed. 2. Trade Cloth. Brill Academic Publishers.
Leiden, 2004. x, 327p. ISBN:90-04-08884-9, ISBN13:
978-90-04-08884-9. Dewey:262/.131/0902.

Audience: **u,f.**

Christianity > Denominations > Roman Catholic Church > Creeds. Liturgy. Meditations. Sacraments

    BX1959.5
Catechism of the Catholic Church. Ed. 2. Trade Cloth. United
States Conference of Catholic Bishops. Washington, DC. 2000.
928p. ISBN:1-57455-109-4, ISBN13: 978-1-57455-109-9.
Dewey:238.2.

Audience: **g,l,u,f.**

    BX1961
1970 ed A New Catechism: Catholic Faith for Adults. Trade Paper.
Crossroad Publishing Company. New York, NY. 1977.
ISBN:0-8245-0332-5, ISBN13: 978-0-8245-0332-1.
Dewey:238/.2.

Audience: **g,l,u,f.**

Bouyer, Louis   BX1970.B68513 1985
1963 ed Rite and Man: Natural Sacredness and Christian Liturgy. Joseph
Costelloe (Translator). Trade Cloth. University Press of America,
Inc. Lanham, MD. 1985. 224p. ISBN:0-8191-4340-5, ISBN13:
978-0-8191-4340-2. Dewey:264/.001. LCCN:84-019650.

Audience: **u,f.**

De Sales, Francis   BX2179.F8.I5413 2001
Introduction to the Devout Life. Edward M. Egan (Preface by).
Trade Paper. Knopf Publishing Group. New York, NY. 2002.
288p. Vintage Spiritual Classics Ser. ISBN:0-375-72562-8,
ISBN13: 978-0-375-72562-3. Dewey:248.4/82.
LCCN:2001-045327.

Audience: **g,l,u,f.**

Francis de Sales   BX2179.F8
Treatise on the Love of God: Also Known Simply As: on the
Love of God. Henry B. Mackey (Translator). Trade Paper. TAN
Books and Publishers, Inc. Rockford, IL. 1997. 555p.
ISBN:0-89555-526-3, ISBN13: 978-0-89555-526-7.
Dewey:241/.4. LCCN:95-060646.

Audience: **g,l,u,f.**

Hardison, O. B. Jr.   **PN1751**
Christian Rite and Christian Drama in the Middle Ages: Essays in the Origin and Early History of Modern Drama. Trade Cloth. Greenwood Publishing Group, Inc. Portsmouth, NH. 1983. 328p. ISBN:0-313-24121-X, ISBN13: 978-0-313-24121-5. Dewey:809.202. LCCN:83-010864.

Audience: **u,f.**

Harvey, R. (Editor)   **PR119**
Richard Rolle: The Fire of Love and the Mending of Life. Trade Paper. Early English Text Society (E E T S). Woodbridge, Suffolk, 2006. 152p. Early English Text Society Original Ser. ISBN:0-85991-658-8, ISBN13: 978-0-85991-658-5. Dewey:820.99287.

Audience: **u,f.**

Hugh of Saint Victor   **BX2200**
Hugh of St. Victor: On the Sacraments of the Christian Faith. R. J. Deferrari (Translator). Trade Cloth. Medieval Academy of America. Cambridge, MA. 1976. Medieval Academy Bks., No. 58 ISBN:0-910956-32-4, ISBN13: 978-0-910956-32-1. Dewey:265.

Audience: **u,f.**

Mottola, Anthony & St.   **BX2179.L7**
Ignatius of Loyola Staff
Spiritual Exercises of St. Ignatius. R. W. Gleason (Introduction by). Trade Paper. Doubleday Publishing. New York, NY. 1964. 208p. ISBN:0-385-02436-3, ISBN13: 978-0-385-02436-5. Dewey:248.3. LCCN:64-012784.

Audience: **g,l,u,f.**

Rahner, Karl   **BV800**
Meditations on the Sacraments. Trade Paper. Continuum International Publishing Group, Ltd. London, 1999. 128p. ISBN:0-86012-053-8, ISBN13: 978-0-86012-053-7. Dewey:234/.16.

Audience: **u,f.**

Schillebeeckx, Edward   **BX2200**
Christ the Sacrament of the Encounter with God. Cornelius Ernest (Foreword by). Book, Other. Rowman & Littlefield Publishers, Inc. Lanham, MD. 1987. 222p. ISBN:0-934134-72-3, ISBN13: 978-0-934134-72-9. Dewey:265. LCCN:63-017144.

Audience: **u,f.**

Christianity > Denominations > Roman Catholic Church > Saints. Hagiography

Brown, Peter   **BX2333 .B74**
The Cult of the Saints: Its Rise and Function in Latin Christianity. Trade Paper. University of Chicago Press. Chicago, IL. 1982. 204p. The Haskell Lectures, Vol. 2 ISBN:0-226-07622-9, ISBN13: 978-0-226-07622-5. Dewey:270.2. LCCN:80-011210.

Audience: **u,f.**

Christianity > Denominations > Roman Catholic Church > Christian life. Monastic and Religious Life

Ashley, Benedict   **BX3506.2.A84 1990**
The Dominicans. Trade Cloth. Liturgical Press. Collegeville, MN. 1991. 280p. Religious Orders Ser. ISBN:0-8146-5723-0, ISBN13: 978-0-8146-5723-2. Dewey:271/.2. LCCN:90-062034.

Audience: **g,l,u.**

Barry, Patrick   **BX3004.E6 2004**
Saint Benedict's Rule. Ed. 2. Trade Cloth. Paulist Press. Mahwah, NJ. 2004. 176p. ISBN:1-58768-031-9, ISBN13: 978-1-58768-031-1. Dewey:255/.106. LCCN:2004-005737.

Audience: **l,u.**

Bitel, Lisa M.   **BX2600**
Isle of the Saints: Monastic Settlement and Christian Community in Early Ireland. Trade Paper. Cornell University Press. Ithaca, NY. 1993. 288p. ISBN:0-8014-8157-0, ISBN13: 978-0-8014-8157-4. Dewey:271/.009415/0902. LCCN:90-055118.

Audience: **u,f.** *Choice, 1991.*

Butler, Edward Cuthbert   **BX3002**
Benedictine Monachism: Studies in Benedictine Life and Rule. Paper Text. Textbook Publishers. Temecula, CA. 2003. 424p. ISBN:0-7581-3633-1, ISBN13: 978-0-7581-3633-6. Dewey:271.1.

Audience: **u,f.**

De Guibert, Joseph   **BX3703**
The Jesuits: Their Spiritual Doctrine and Practice. W. J. Young (Translator). Trade Paper. Institute of Jesuit Sources. Saint Louis, MO. 1964. xxviii, 692p. Modern Scholarly Studies about the Jesuits, in English Translations Series II, No. 1 ISBN:0-912422-09-2, ISBN13: 978-0-912422-09-1. Dewey:271.53. LCCN:64-021430.

Audience: **u,f.**

Durback, Robert   **BV4832.2**
Seeds of Hope: A Henri Nouwen Reader. Ed. 2. Trade Paper. Doubleday Publishing. New York, NY. 1997. 320p. ISBN:0-385-49049-6, ISBN13: 978-0-385-49049-8. Dewey:242.

Audience: **g,l,u.**

Harmless, William   **BR190.H37 2004**
Desert Christians: An Introduction to the Literature of Early Monasticism. Trade Paper. Oxford University Press, Inc. New York, NY. 2004. 440p. ISBN:0-19-516223-4, ISBN13: 978-0-19-516223-3. Dewey:271.009/015. LCCN:2004-000097.

Audience: **u,f.** *Choice, 2005.*

Knowles, David   **BX2592**
The Religious Orders in England: The Old Orders, Vol. 1. Cloth Text. Cambridge University Press. New York, NY. 1979. 368p. ISBN:0-521-05480-X, ISBN13: 978-0-521-05480-5. Dewey:271.0094203.

Audience: **u,f.**

Knowles, David   **BX2592**
The Religious Orders in England, Vol. 3. Trade Paper.
Cambridge University Press. New York, NY. 1979. 536p.
ISBN:0-521-29568-8, ISBN13: 978-0-521-29568-0.
Dewey:271.00942.

Audience: **u,f.**

Knowles, David, et al.   **BX2592 .K55 2001**
The Heads of Religious Houses: England and Wales, 940-1216.
Ed. 2. Christopher N. L. Brooke & Vera C. M. London
(Authors). Trade Cloth. Cambridge University Press. New York,
NY. 2001. 408p. ISBN:0-521-80452-3, ISBN13:
978-0-521-80452-3. Dewey:271.0092242. LCCN:2001-277135.

Audience: **u,f.**

Knowles, David & Hadcock,   **BX2592**
  R. Neville
Medieval Religious Houses in England and Wales. Ed. 2. Trade
Cloth. Longman Publishing Group. White Plains, NY. 1995.
584p. ISBN:0-582-11230-3, ISBN13: 978-0-582-11230-8.
Dewey:271/.00942.

Audience: **u,f.**

Lawrence, C. H.   **BX2470.L39 2001**
Medieval Monasticism: Forms of Religious Life in Western
Europe in the Middle Ages. Ed. 3. Trade Paper. Longman
Publishing. Boston, MA. 2000. 336p. ISBN:0-582-40427-4,
ISBN13: 978-0-582-40427-4. Dewey:271/.0094/0902.
LCCN:2001-268236.

Audience: **g,l,u,f.**

Leclercq, Jean   **BX2470.L413 1982**
Love of Learning and Desire for God: A Study of Monastic
Culture. Ed. 3. Trade Paper. Fordham University Press. Bronx,
NY. 1982. 282p. ISBN:0-8232-0407-3, ISBN13:
978-0-8232-0407-6. Dewey:255. LCCN:60-053004.

Audience: **u,f.** 🅑

Merton, Thomas   **BX2350.2.M4494 1978**
No Man Is an Island. Trade Paper. Harcourt Trade Publishers.
New York, NY. 2002. 288p. ISBN:0-15-602773-9, ISBN13:
978-0-15-602773-1. Dewey:248.4/82. LCCN:78-007108.

Audience: **g,l,u,f.**

O'Malley, John W.   **BX3706.2**
The First Jesuits. Trade Paper. Harvard University Press.
Cambridge, MA. 1993. 478p. ISBN:0-674-30313-X, ISBN13:
978-0-674-30313-3. Dewey:271.5/3/009031.

Audience: **g,l,u,f.**   *Choice, 1994.*

Schneiders, Sandra M.   **BX2435.S38 1986**
New Wineskins: Reimagining Religious Life Today. Trade
Paper. Paulist Press. Mahwah, NJ. 1986. 320p.
ISBN:0-8091-2765-2, ISBN13: 978-0-8091-2765-8.
Dewey:255/.9. LCCN:85-062865.

Audience: **u,f.**

Torres, Sergio & Eagleson,   **BX2347.72.L37.I57**
  John (Editors)
The Challenge of Basic Christian Communities. John Drury

(Translator), Jorge Lara-Braud (Preface by). Trade Paper. Orbis
Books. Maryknoll, NY. 1981. 283p. ISBN:0-88344-503-4,
ISBN13: 978-0-88344-503-7. Dewey:261.8. LCCN:81-038361.

Audience: **u,f.**

Weigle, Marta   **BX3653.U6**
Brothers of Light, Brothers of Blood: The Penitentes of the
Southwest. Trade Paper. Gibbs Smith, Publisher. Layton, UT.
1989. 320p. ISBN:0-941270-58-0, ISBN13: 978-0-941270-58-8.
Dewey:271.79. LCCN:88-072048.

Audience: **u,f.**

Woodward, G.W.O.   **BV2062.W66**
Dissolution of the Monasteries. Ed. 2. Trade Cloth. Pitkin
Unichrome, Ltd. Andover, 1993. 24p. ISBN:0-85372-617-5,
ISBN13: 978-0-85372-617-3. Dewey:262.240942.

Audience: **u,f.**

Christianity > Denominations > Roman Catholic Church > Biography

Bernard   **BX4700.B5**
The Letters of St. Bernard of Clairvaux. Trade Paper. Sutton
Publishing, Ltd. Stroud, 1998. xxx, 562p. ISBN:0-7509-1687-7,
ISBN13: 978-0-7509-1687-5. Dewey:271.1/2/02.

Audience: **g,u,f.**

Bredero, Adriaan H.   **BX4705.B5B813 1996**
Bernard of Clairvaux: Between Cult and History. Reinder
Bruinsma (Translator). Trade Cloth. William B. Eerdmans
Publishing Company. Grand Rapids, MI. 1996. 334p.
ISBN:0-8028-3796-4, ISBN13: 978-0-8028-3796-7.
Dewey:271/.1202 B. LCCN:96-014649.

Audience: **u,f.**   *Choice, 1997.*

Brenan, Gerald   **BX4700.J7**
St John of the Cross. Trade Paper. Cambridge University Press.
New York, NY. 1975. 245p. ISBN:0-521-09953-6, ISBN13:
978-0-521-09953-0. Dewey:861/.3. LCCN:72-083577.

Audience: **g,u,f.**

Butler, Alban   **BX4655.3.B88 2003**
Butler's Lives of the Saints. Paul Burns (Editor). Trade Cloth.
Liturgical Press. Collegeville, MN. 2005. 640p.
ISBN:0-8146-2903-2, ISBN13: 978-0-8146-2903-1.
Dewey:282/.092/2 B. LCCN:2003-041637.

Audience: **g,l,u,f.**

Caraman, Philip   **BX4700.L7**
Ignatius Loyola. Trade Paper. HarperCollins Publishers Ltd.
London, 1999. ix, 222p. ISBN:0-00-627487-0, ISBN13:
978-0-00-627487-2. Dewey:271.5302.

Audience: **g,l.**

Chapman, John   **BX4700**
St. Benedict and the Sixth Century. Trade Cloth. Greenwood
Publishing Group, Inc. Portsmouth, NH. 1971. 239p.
ISBN:0-8371-4209-1, ISBN13: 978-0-8371-4209-8.
Dewey:271/.1/024. LCCN:79-109719.

Audience: **g,l,u.**

Cross, Richard   B765.D74C75 1999
Duns Scotus. Trade Cloth. Oxford University Press, Inc. New
York, NY. 1999. 272p. Great Medieval Thinkers Ser.
ISBN:0-19-512552-5, ISBN13: 978-0-19-512552-8.
Dewey:189.4. LCCN:98-025710.
      Audience: **u,f.**

Cullen, Christopher M.   B765.B74C85 2005
Bonaventure. Trade Paper. Oxford University Press, Inc. New
York, NY. 2006. 270p. Great Medieval Thinkers Ser.
ISBN:0-19-514926-2, ISBN13: 978-0-19-514926-5.
Dewey:189/.4. LCCN:2005-012591.
      Audience: **u,f.**

De Voragine, Jacobus   BX4654.J33 1973
The Golden Legend: Readings on the Saints. F. S. Ellis (Editor),
William Caxton (Translator). Trade Cloth. A M S Press, Inc.
New York, NY. 1973. ISBN:0-404-06770-0, ISBN13:
978-0-404-06770-0. Dewey:270.0922. LCCN:76-170839.
      Audience: **g,l,u.**

Delehaye, Hippolyte   BR1700.2
The Legends of the Saints. Thomas O'Loughlin (Introduction
by). Trade Paper. Four Courts Press. Dublin 8, 1998. 252p.
ISBN:1-85182-370-0, ISBN13: 978-1-85182-370-3.
Dewey:270/.0922.
      Audience: **g,l,u.**

Eadmer   BX4700.A58
The Life of St Anselm, Archbishop of Canterbury. Paper Text.
Textbook Publishers. Temecula, CA. 2003. xxxvi, 171p.
ISBN:0-7581-3294-8, ISBN13: 978-0-7581-3294-9.
Dewey:282/.092.
      Audience: **l,u.**

Evans, Gillian R.   BX4700.B5E89 2000
Bernard of Clairvaux. Trade Paper. Oxford University Press, Inc.
New York, NY. 2000. 230p. Great Medieval Thinkers Ser.
ISBN:0-19-512526-6, ISBN13: 978-0-19-512526-9.
Dewey:271/.1202 B. LCCN:99-013708.
      Audience: **u,f.**

_4th ed._ **Farmer, David Hugh**   BR1710
The Oxford Dictionary of Saints. Ed. 5. Trade Paper. Oxford
University Press, Inc. New York, NY. 2004. 607p. Oxford
Paperback Reference Ser. ISBN:0-19-860949-3, ISBN13:
978-0-19-860949-0. Dewey:270/.092/2 B. LCCN:2005-272790.
      Audience: **g,l,u,f.**

Gregory I, Pope   BX4700.B3 G7213
Life and Miracles of St. Benedict. Trade Paper. Liturgical Press.
Collegeville, MN. 1987. 87p. ISBN:0-8146-0321-1, ISBN13:
978-0-8146-0321-5. Dewey:281/.4/0924.
      Audience: **g,l,u,f.**

Kenny, Anthony   DA334.M8
Thomas More. Trade Paper. Oxford University Press, Inc. New
York, NY. 1984. 112p. Past Masters Ser. ISBN:0-19-287573-6,
ISBN13: 978-0-19-287573-0. Dewey:942.05/2/0924.
      Audience: **u,f.**

Marenbon, John   B659.Z7M346 2002
Boethius. Trade Paper. Oxford University Press, Inc. New York,
NY. 2003. 268p. Great Medieval Thinkers Ser.
ISBN:0-19-513407-9, ISBN13: 978-0-19-513407-0. Dewey:189.
LCCN:2002-074896.
      Audience: **u,f.** _Choice, 2004._

Markus, R. A.   BX1076 .M37 1997
Gregory the Great and His World. Cloth Text. Cambridge
University Press. New York, NY. 1997. 265p.
ISBN:0-521-58430-2, ISBN13: 978-0-521-58430-2.
Dewey:270.2/092 B. LCCN:97-011308.
      Audience: **u,f.**

McBrien, Richard P.   BX4655.3.M33 2001
Lives of the Saints: From Mary and St. Francis of Assisi to
John XXIII and Mother Teresa. Trade Paper. HarperCollins
Publishers. New York, NY. 2003. 672p. ISBN:0-06-065341-8,
ISBN13: 978-0-06-065341-5. LCCN:00-053933.
      Audience: **g,l,u.**

McGreal, Wilfred   BX4700.J7
John of the Cross. Trade Paper. HarperCollins Publishers Ltd.
London, 1996. xiv, 80p. ISBN:0-00-627913-9, ISBN13:
978-0-00-627913-6. Dewey:271.7302.
      Audience: **g,l,u,f.**

Mews, C. J.   B765.A24M49 2004
Abelard and Heloise. Trade Paper. Oxford University Press, Inc.
New York, NY. 2005. 328p. Great Medieval Thinkers Ser.
ISBN:0-19-515689-7, ISBN13: 978-0-19-515689-8.
Dewey:189/.4 B. LCCN:2004-001243.
      Audience: **u,f.** _Choice, 2005._

other eds. **Newman, John Henry**   BX4705.N5A3 2005
Apologia Pro Vita Sua. Trade Paper, Perfect. Dover
Publications, Inc. Mineola, NY. 2005. 313p. Dover Giant Thrift
Editions Ser. ISBN:0-486-44213-6, ISBN13: 978-0-486-44213-6.
Dewey:282/.092 B. LCCN:2004-063466.
      Audience: **g,l,u,f.**

Nichols, Aidan   B765.T54N47 2003
Discovering Aquinas: An Introduction to His Life, Work, and
Influence. Trade Cloth. William B. Eerdmans Publishing
Company. Grand Rapids, MI. 2004. 224p. ISBN:0-8028-0514-0,
ISBN13: 978-0-8028-0514-0. Dewey:230/.2/092 B.
LCCN:2003-270275.
      Audience: **g,l,u.**

Rahner, Karl   BX4705.R287A342513
Karl Rahner in Dialogue. Trade Cloth. Crossroad Publishing
Company. New York, NY. 1986. 352p. ISBN:0-8245-0749-5,
ISBN13: 978-0-8245-0749-7. Dewey:230/.2. LCCN:86-008972.
      Audience: **u,f.** _Choice, 1987._

Rinehart, Mary Roberts   BX4700.F63 E5
other eds. The Little Flowers of St. Francis of Assisi. Trade Paper.
Kessinger Publishing, LLC. Whitefish, MT. 2004.
ISBN:1-4192-7022-2, ISBN13: 978-1-4192-7022-2.
      Audience: **g,l,u.**

Rosemann, Philipp W.   BX1749.P4R67 2003
Peter Lombard. Trade Cloth. Oxford University Press, Inc. New York, NY. 2004. 288p. Great Medieval Thinkers Ser. ISBN:0-19-515544-0, ISBN13: 978-0-19-515544-0. Dewey:230/.2/092. LCCN:2003-005370.

Audience: **u,f.**

Southern, Richard W.   BX4700.A58S59 1990
St. Anselm: A Portrait in a Landscape. Trade Paper. Cambridge University Press. New York, NY. 1992. 523p. ISBN:0-521-43818-7, ISBN13: 978-0-521-43818-6. Dewey:282/.092.

Audience: **u,f.** *Choice, 1991.*

Thomas of Celano   BX4700.F68E5 2004
Francis Trilogy: Life of Saint Francis... Trade Paper. New City Press. Hyde Park, NY. 2004. 392p. ISBN:1-56548-204-2, ISBN13: 978-1-56548-204-3. Dewey:271/.302 B. LCCN:2004-049859.

Audience: **g,l,u.**

Thérèse & Foley, Marc   BX4700.T5A5 2005
Story of a Soul: The Autobiography of Saint Thérèse of Lisieux. Trade Cloth. I C S Publications. Washington, DC. 2005. ISBN:0-935216-38-3, ISBN13: 978-0-935216-38-7. Dewey:282/.092 B. LCCN:2005-009446.

Audience: **g,l,u,f.**

Turner, Frank   BX4705
John Henry Newman: The Challenge to Evangelical Religion. Cloth over Boards. Yale University Press. Cumberland, RI. 2002. 752p. ISBN:0-300-09251-2, ISBN13: 978-0-300-09251-6. Dewey:282/.092. LCCN:2002-001086.

Audience: **u,f.** *Choice, 2003.*

Vorgrimler, Herbert   BX4705.R287V63213
Understanding Karl Rahner: An Introduction to His Life and Thought. Trade Cloth. Crossroad Publishing Company. New York, NY. 1986. 176p. ISBN:0-8245-0790-8, ISBN13: 978-0-8245-0790-9. Dewey:230/.2/0924 B. LCCN:86-011520.

Audience: **g,l,u.** *Choice, 1987.*

Weigel, George   BX1378.5.W45
Witness to Hope: The Biography of Pope John Paul II. Trade Paper. HarperCollins Publishers. New York, NY. 2005. 1056p. ISBN:0-06-073203-2, ISBN13: 978-0-06-073203-5. Dewey:282/.092. LCCN:99-026340.

Audience: **g,l,u,f.**

Christianity > Denominations > Protestantism

Hillerbrand, Hans J. (Editor)   BX4811.3.E53 2003
Encyclopedia of Protestantism. Paper over Boards. Routledge. New York, NY. 2003. 2048p. ISBN:0-415-92472-3, ISBN13: 978-0-415-92472-6. Dewey:280/.4/03. LCCN:2003-011582.

Audience: **g,l,u,f.** *Choice, 2004.*

Hutchison, William R.   BX1396
The Modernist Impulse in American Protestantism. Cloth Text. Duke University Press. Durham, NC. 1992. 367p. ISBN:0-8223-1237-9, ISBN13: 978-0-8223-1237-6. Dewey:273.9. LCCN:91-039184.

Audience: **u,f.**

Martin, David   306.6804098
Tongues of Fire: The Explosion of Protestantism in Latin America. Trade Paper. Blackwell Publishing, Inc. Malden, MA. 1993. 366p. ISBN:0-631-18914-9, ISBN13: 978-0-631-18914-5. Dewey:306.6/804/098. LCCN:93-015412.

Audience: **u,f.** *Choice, 1991.*

McGrath, Alister E. & Marks, Darren C. (Editors)   BX4811.3.B57 2003
The Blackwell Companion to Protestantism. Trade Cloth. Blackwell Publishing, Inc. Malden, MA. 2003. 528p. Blackwell Companions to Religion Ser. ISBN:0-631-23278-8, ISBN13: 978-0-631-23278-0. Dewey:280/.4. LCCN:2003-008185.

Audience: **u,f.** *Choice, 2004.*

Christianity > Denominations > Protestantism > Biography

Bonhoeffer, Dietrich   BX4827.B57 A43
Letters Papers from Prison. Trade Paper. Simon & Schuster. New York, NY. 1997. 448p. ISBN:0-684-83827-3, ISBN13: 978-0-684-83827-4. Dewey:230/.092/4.

Audience: **g,l,u,f.**

Bouwsma, William J.   BX9418
John Calvin: A Sixteenth-Century Portrait. Trade Paper. Oxford University Press, Inc. New York, NY. 1989. 320p. ISBN:0-19-505951-4, ISBN13: 978-0-19-505951-9. Dewey:284/.2/0924.

Audience: **g,l,u,f.** *Choice, 1988.*

Bremer, Francis J.   F67.W79B74 2005
John Winthrop: America's Forgotten Founding Father. Trade Paper. Oxford University Press, Inc. New York, NY. 2005. 496p. ISBN:0-19-517981-1, ISBN13: 978-0-19-517981-1. Dewey:974.402092.

Audience: **g,l,u,f.** *Choice, 2004.*

Bretall, Robert (Editor)   B4377
Kierkegaard Anthology. Trade Paper. Princeton University Press. Princeton, NJ. 1973. 516p. ISBN:0-691-01978-9, ISBN13: 978-0-691-01978-9. Dewey:198.9. LCCN:47-000827.

Audience: **l,u.**

Bushman, Richard Lyman   BX8695.S6B875 2005
Joseph Smith: Rough Stone Rolling. Trade Cloth. Alfred A. Knopf Inc. New York, NY. 2005. 768p. ISBN:1-4000-4270-4, ISBN13: 978-1-4000-4270-8. Dewey:289.3/092 B. LCCN:2004-061613.

Audience: **g,u,f.** *Choice, 2006.*

Garrow, David J.   E185.97.K5G36 2004
Bearing the Cross: Martin Luther King, Jr., and the Southern
Christian Leadership Conference. Trade Paper. HarperCollins
Publishers. New York, NY. 2004. 800p. Perennial Classics Ser.
ISBN:0-06-056692-2, ISBN13: 978-0-06-056692-0.
Dewey:323/.092 B. LCCN:2003-062226.

Audience: **g,l,u,f.**

Gerrish, B. A.   BX4827.S3
A Prince of the Church: Schleiermacher and the Beginnings of
Modern Theology. Trade Paper. Wipf & Stock Publishers.
Eugene, OR. 2001. 80p. ISBN:1-57910-780-X, ISBN13:
978-1-57910-780-2. Dewey:230/.044/0924.

Audience: **u,f.**

Graham, Billy   BV3785.G69
Just As I Am: The Autobiography of Billy Graham. Trade Paper.
HarperCollins Publishers. New York, NY. 1999. 784p.
ISBN:0-06-063392-1, ISBN13: 978-0-06-063392-9. Dewey:[B].
LCCN:97-000605.

Audience: **g,l.**

Hannay, Alastair & Marino,   B4377 .C29 1998
  Gordon Daniel (Editors)
The Cambridge Companion to Kierkegaard. Trade Cloth.
Cambridge University Press. New York, NY. 1997. 446p.
Cambridge Companions to Philosophy Ser.
ISBN:0-521-47151-6, ISBN13: 978-0-521-47151-0.
Dewey:198.9. LCCN:97-000617.

Audience: **u,f.** *Choice, 1998.*

Kegley, Charles W. Jr.   BX4827.N5
Reinhold Niebuhr: His Religious, Social, and Political Thought,.
Paper Text. Textbook Publishers. Temecula, CA. 2003. xiv,
486p. ISBN:0-7581-8914-1, ISBN13: 978-0-7581-8914-1.
Dewey:230/.092.

Audience: **l,u.**

Mariqa, Jacqueline (Editor)   BX4827.S3
The Cambridge Companion to Friedrich Schleiermacher. Cloth
Text. Cambridge University Press. New York, NY. 2005. 362p.
Cambridge Companions to Religion Ser. ISBN:0-521-81448-0,
ISBN13: 978-0-521-81448-5. Dewey:193. LCCN:2006-274285.

Audience: **u,f.**

Marsden, George M.   BX7260.E3M412 2003
Jonathan Edwards: A Life. Cloth over Boards. Yale University
Press. Cumberland, RI. 2003. 640p. ISBN:0-300-09693-3,
ISBN13: 978-0-300-09693-4. Dewey:285.8/092 B.
LCCN:2002-013611.

Audience: **g,l,u,f.** *Choice, 2003.*

Oberman, Heiko A.   BR325.O2713 1989
Luther: Man Between God and the Devil. Eileen
Walliser-Schwarzbart (Translator). Cloth over Boards. Yale
University Press. Cumberland, RI. 1990. 320p.
ISBN:0-300-03794-5, ISBN13: 978-0-300-03794-4.
Dewey:284.1092. LCCN:89-005747.

Audience: **u,f.** *Choice, 1990.*

Pauck, Wilhelm & Pauck,   BX4827.T53
Marion
Paul Tillich: His Life and Thought. Trade Cloth. HarperCollins
Publishers Ltd. London, 1977. xii, 340p. ISBN:0-00-216650-X,
ISBN13: 978-0-00-216650-8. Dewey:230/.092/4.

Audience: **g,l,u.**

Silverman, Kenneth   F67.M43
The Life and Times of Cotton Mather. Trade Cloth.
HarperCollins Publishers. New York, NY. 1984. 480p.
ISBN:0-06-015231-1, ISBN13: 978-0-06-015231-4.
Dewey:285.8/32/0924 B. LCCN:83-048385.

Audience: **g,l,u.**

Stephens, W. P.   BR346.S74 1992
Zwingli: An Introduction to His Thought. Trade Cloth. Oxford
University Press, Inc. New York, NY. 1992. 192p.
ISBN:0-19-826329-5, ISBN13: 978-0-19-826329-6.
Dewey:230/.42/092. LCCN:91-038083.

Audience: **u,f.** *Choice, 1992.*

Tillich, Paul   BJ1533.C8T5 2000
The Courage to Be. Ed. 2. Peter J. Gomes (Introduction by).
Trade Paper. Yale University Press. Cumberland, RI. 2000.
238p. Yale Nota Bene Ser. ISBN:0-300-08471-4, ISBN13:
978-0-300-08471-9. Dewey:179/.6. LCCN:00-102364.

Audience: **g,l,u,f.**

Webster, John B. (Editor)   BX4827.B3 C26 2000
The Cambridge Companion to Karl Barth. Trade Paper.
Cambridge University Press. New York, NY. 2000. 326p.
Companions to Religion Ser. ISBN:0-521-58560-0, ISBN13:
978-0-521-58560-6. Dewey:230/.044/092. LCCN:99-056882.

Audience: **u,f.** *Choice, 2001.*

Christianity > Denominations > Protestantism > Protestantism in Europe

Barnett, Victoria   BR856
For the Soul of the People: Protestant Protest Against Hitler.
Trade Paper. Oxford University Press, Inc. New York, NY. 1998.
368p. ISBN:0-19-512118-X, ISBN13: 978-0-19-512118-6.
Dewey:280.4/0943/09043.

Audience: **g,l,u,f.** *Choice, 1993.*

Bowen, Desmond   BX4839.B67 1995
History and the Shaping of Irish Protestantism, Vol. 4. Paper
Text. Peter Lang Publishing, Inc. New York, NY. 1995. XXI,
718p. Irish Studies ISBN:0-8204-2750-0, ISBN13:
978-0-8204-2750-8. Dewey:941.5/008/82. LCCN:94-047553.

Audience: **u,f.** *Choice, 1996.*

Todd, Margo   BX4840.T63 2002
The Culture of Protestantism in Early Modern Scotland. Cloth
over Boards. Yale University Press. Cumberland, RI. 2002.
480p. ISBN:0-300-09234-2, ISBN13: 978-0-300-09234-9.
Dewey:280/.4/09411. LCCN:2001-007254.

Audience: **u,f.**

Christianity > Denominations > Protestantism > Anglican Communion

BX2170.C55

Book of Common Prayer. Trade Cloth. Columba Press. Dublin, 2004. 800p. ISBN:1-85607-434-X, ISBN13: 978-1-85607-434-6. Dewey:242.3.

other eds

Audience: **g,l,u,f.**

Brooks, Nicholas   **BX5195.C3**
The Early History of the Church of Canterbury. Trade Paper. Continuum International Publishing Group, Ltd. London, 1996. 417p. ISBN:0-7185-0041-5, ISBN13: 978-0-7185-0041-2. Dewey:282.4/2234.

Audience: **u,f.**

Butler, Diana H.   **BX5925.B84 1995**
Standing Against the Whirlwind: Evangelical Episcopalians in Nineteenth-Century America. Trade Cloth. Oxford University Press, Inc. New York, NY. 1995. 286p. Religion in America Ser. ISBN:0-19-508542-6, ISBN13: 978-0-19-508542-6. Dewey:283/.73. LCCN:93-034323.

Audience: **u,f.** *Choice, 1996.*

Chadwick, Owen   **BX5099 .C45**
The Mind of the Oxford Movement. Paper Text. Textbook Publishers. Temecula, CA. 2003. 239p. ISBN:0-7581-3515-7, ISBN13: 978-0-7581-3515-5. Dewey:283.42.

Audience: **l,u.**

Communion, The Anglican   **BR115.H6**
Windsor Report. Saddle Stitched. Morehouse Publishing. Harrisburg, PA. 2004. 96p. ISBN:0-8192-2198-8, ISBN13: 978-0-8192-2198-8. Dewey:261.835766.

Audience: **u,f.**

Donne, John   **PR2246.C37 2000**
John Donne - the Major Works: Including Songs and Sonnets and Sermons. John Carey (Editor). Trade Paper. Oxford University Press, Inc. New York, NY. 2000. 528p. Oxford World's Classics Ser. ISBN:0-19-284041-X, ISBN13: 978-0-19-284041-7. Dewey:821/.3. LCCN:00-712822.

Audience: **g,l,u,f.**

Douglas, Iain T.   **BR115.H6D58 2005**
Understanding the Windsor Report. Paul F. M. Zahl (Based on a book by), Jan Nunley (Summary by). Trade Paper. Church Publishing, Inc. New York, NY. 2005. 200p. ISBN:0-89869-487-6, ISBN13: 978-0-89869-487-1. Dewey:261.835766. LCCN:2006-367130.

Audience: **g,u,f.**

Guelzo, Allen C.   **BX5199.N55**
For the Union of Evangelical Christendom: The Irony of the Reformed Episcopalians. Trade Paper. Pennsylvania State

1994 ed.

University Press. University Park, PA. 2005. 416p. ISBN:0-271-02732-0, ISBN13: 978-0-271-02732-6. Dewey:283/.3.

Audience: **u,f.** *Choice, 1995.*

Hefling, Charles &   **BX5145.O94 2006**
  Shattuck, Cynthia (Editors)
The Oxford Guide to the Book of Common Prayer: A Worldwide Survey. Trade Cloth. Oxford University Press, Inc. New York, NY. 2006. 630p. ISBN:0-19-529756-3, ISBN13: 978-0-19-529756-0. Dewey:264/.03009. LCCN:2005-031846.

Audience: **g,l,u,f.**

Hooker, Richard   **BX5037.A2**
Tractates and Sermons. W. Speed Hill (Editor). Trade Cloth. Harvard University Press. Cambridge, MA. 2002. 976p. Folger Library Edition of the Works of Richard Hooker, Vol. 5 ISBN:0-674-63217-6, ISBN13: 978-0-674-63217-2. Dewey:230/.3. LCCN:90-004818.

Audience: **u,f.**

Katerberg, William H.   **BX5610.K38 2001**
Modernity and the Dilemma of North American Anglican Identities, 1880-1950. Trade Cloth. McGill-Queen's University Press. Montreal, PQ. 2001. xii, 306p. McGill-Queen's Studies in the History of Religion ISBN:0-7735-2160-7, ISBN13: 978-0-7735-2160-5. Dewey:283/.71. LCCN:2002-421458.

Audience: **u,f.**

Moorman, John R.   **BR743.2.M6 1994**
A History of the Church in England. Ed. 3. Trade Paper. Morehouse Publishing. Harrisburg, PA. 1980. 512p. ISBN:0-8192-1406-X, ISBN13: 978-0-8192-1406-5. Dewey:274.2. LCCN:94-006111.

Audience: **u,f.**

Prelinger, Catherine M.   **BX5968**
  (Editor)
Episcopal Women: Gender, Spirituality, and Commitment in an American Mainline Denomination. Trade Paper. Oxford University Press, Inc. New York, NY. 1996. 376p. Religion in America Ser. ISBN:0-19-510465-X, ISBN13: 978-0-19-510465-3. Dewey:283.7/3/082. LCCN:91-046036.

Audience: **u,f.**

Rhoden, Nancy L.   **BX5881.R48 1999**
Revolutionary Anglicanism: The Colonial Church of England During the American Revolution. Trade Cloth. New York University Press. New York, NY. 1999. 280p. ISBN:0-8147-7519-5, ISBN13: 978-0-8147-7519-6. Dewey:283/.73/09033. LCCN:98-031403.

Audience: **u,f.** *Choice, 2000.*

Williams, Rowan   **BX5005.L6 2003**
Love's Redeeming Work: The Anglican Quest for Holiness.

Geoffrey Rowell & Kenneth E. Stevenson (Compiled by). Trade Paper. Oxford University Press, Inc. New York, NY. 2004. 818p. ISBN:0-19-107058-0, ISBN13: 978-0-19-107058-7. Dewey:283.

Audience: **u,f.**

Christianity > Denominations > Protestantism > Arminians

Bangs, Carl   **BX6196**

1971 ed

Arminius: A Study in the Dutch Reformation. Trade Paper. Wipf & Stock Publishers. Eugene, OR. 1998. 388p. ISBN:1-57910-150-X, ISBN13: 978-1-57910-150-3. Dewey:284/.9/0924 B.

Audience: **u,f.**

Christianity > Denominations > Protestantism > Baptists

George, Timothy &   **BX6331.2.B29 2001**
Dockery, David S. (Editors)
Theologians of the Baptist Tradition. Trade Cloth. B&H Publishing Group. Nashville, TN. 2001. xviii, 414p. ISBN:0-8054-1772-9, ISBN13: 978-0-8054-1772-2. Dewey:230/.6/0922. LCCN:2001-025126.

Audience: **u,f.**

Harrison, Paul Mansfield   **BX6207.A36**

1959 ed

Authority and Power in the Free Church Tradition: A Social Case Study of the American Baptist Convention. Paper Text. Textbook Publishers. Temecula, CA. 2003. 248p. ISBN:0-7581-5662-6, ISBN13: 978-0-7581-5662-4. Dewey:262.4.

Audience: **u,f.**

Harvey, Paul   **96-32882 [BX]**
Redeeming the South: Religious Cultures and Racial Identities among Southern Baptists, 1865-1925. Trade Paper. University of North Carolina Press. Chapel Hill, NC. 1997. 342p. Fred W. Morrison Series in Southern Studies ISBN:0-8078-4634-1, ISBN13: 978-0-8078-4634-6. Dewey:286/.175/089. LCCN:96-032882.

Audience: **u,f.** *Choice, 1997.*

Heyrman, Christine L.   **97-51487 [BR]**
Southern Cross: The Beginnings of the Bible Belt. Trade Paper. University of North Carolina Press. Chapel Hill, NC. 1998. 352p. ISBN:0-8078-4716-X, ISBN13: 978-0-8078-4716-9. Dewey:277.5/081. LCCN:97-051487.

Audience: **u,f.** *Choice, 1997.*

Juster, Susan   **BX6239**
Disorderly Women: Sexual Politics and Evangelicalism in Revolutionary New England. Trade Paper. Cornell University Press. Ithaca, NY. 1996. 224p. ISBN:0-8014-8388-3, ISBN13: 978-0-8014-8388-2. Dewey:286/.082.

Audience: **u,f.** *Choice, 1995.*

Leonard, Bill J.   **BX6231.L46 2003**
Baptist Ways: A History. Trade Cloth. Judson Press. Valley Forge, PA. 2003. 480p. ISBN:0-8170-1231-1, ISBN13: 978-0-8170-1231-1. Dewey:286/.09. LCCN:2003-047541.

Audience: **u,f.** *Choice, 2004.*

McBeth, Leon   **BX6231.M37 1987**
Baptist Heritage. Trade Cloth. B&H Publishing Group. Nashville, TN. 1987. 848p. ISBN:0-8054-6569-3, ISBN13: 978-0-8054-6569-3. Dewey:286/.09. LCCN:86-031667.

Audience: **u,f.**

McLoughlin, William G.   **BX6239**
New England Dissent, 1630-1833: The Baptists and the Separation of Church and State, Set. Trade Cloth. Harvard University Press. Cambridge, MA. 1971. 1346p. Center for the Study of the History of Liberty in America Ser. ISBN:0-674-61175-6, ISBN13: 978-0-674-61175-7. Dewey:322/.1. LCCN:70-131464.

Audience: **u,f.**

Christianity > Denominations > Protestantism > Christian Science

Eddy, Mary Baker   **BX6941.E85 2000**
Science and Health with Key to the Scriptures: Authorized Edition. Trade Cloth. The Writings of Mary Baker Eddy. Boston, MA. 2000. xii, 700p. ISBN:0-87952-260-7, ISBN13: 978-0-87952-260-5. Dewey:289.5/2. LCCN:00-105023.

Audience: **g,l,u,f.**

Peel, Robert   **BX6950.P44 1988**
Health and Medicine in the Christian Science Tradition. Trade Cloth. Crossroad Publishing Company. New York, NY. 1988. 160p. Health and Medicine in Faith Tradition Ser. ISBN:0-8245-0895-5, ISBN13: 978-0-8245-0895-1. Dewey:261.5/6. LCCN:88-020266.

Audience: **u,f.** *Choice, 1989.*

Silberger, Julius   **BX6995.S513**
Mary Baker Eddy: An Interpretive Biography of the Founder of Christian Science. Trade Cloth. Little Brown & Company. New York, NY. 1980. x, 274p. ISBN:0-316-79090-7, ISBN13: 978-0-316-79090-1. Dewey:289.5/092/4. LCCN:80-011098.

Audience: **g,l,u.**

Thomas, Robert D.   **BX6995**
With Bleeding Footsteps: Mary Baker Eddy's Path to Religious Leadership. Cloth Text. DIANE Publishing Company. Collingdale, PA. 1998. 363p. ISBN:0-7881-5640-3, ISBN13: 978-0-7881-5640-3. Dewey:289.5/092 B.

Audience: **g,l,u,f.** *Choice, 1995.*

Christianity > Denominations > Protestantism > Congregationalism

Conforti, Joseph A.
Jonathan Edwards, Religious Tradition, and American Culture from the Second Great Awakening to the Twentieth Century. Trade Paper. University of North Carolina Press. Chapel Hill, NC. 1995. 288p. ISBN:0-8078-4535-3, ISBN13: 978-0-8078-4535-6. Dewey:285.8/092. LCCN:94-049526.
Audience: **u,f.** *Choice, 1996.*

Cooper, James Fenimore   **BX7148.M4**
Tenacious of Their Liberties: The Congregationalists in Colonial Massachusetts. Trade Paper. Oxford University Press, Inc. New York, NY. 2002. 304p. Religion in America Ser. ISBN:0-19-515287-5, ISBN13: 978-0-19-515287-6. Dewey:285.8/744/09032.
Audience: **u,f.** *Choice, 2000.*

Edwards, Jonathan   **BX7117**
The Works of Jonathan Edwards. Sereno E. Dwight (Memoir by). Box or Slipcased. Hendrickson Publishers, Inc. Peabody, MA. 1998. 1952p. Works of Jonathan Edwards, Vol. 2 ISBN:1-56563-085-8, ISBN13: 978-1-56563-085-7. Dewey:230/.58.
Audience: **g,l,u,f.**

Fitzmier, John R.   **BX7260.D84F57 1998**
e New England's Moral Legislator: A Life of Timothy Dwight, 1752-1817. E-Book. Indiana University Press. Bloomington, IN. 1998. 272p. Religion in North America Ser. ISBN:0-253-33433-0, ISBN13: 978-0-253-33433-6. Dewey:285.8/092 B. LCCN:98-022498.
Audience: **g,u,f.** *Choice, 1999.*

Hall, David D.   **BR520**
The Faithful Shepherd: A History of the New England Ministry in the Seventeenth Century, with a New Introduction. Trade Paper. Harvard University Press. Cambridge, MA. 2006. 300p. Harvard Theological Studies ISBN:0-674-01959-8, ISBN13: 978-0-674-01959-1. Dewey:277.4/06. LCCN:2006-002433.
Audience: **u,f.**

Hambrick-Stowe, Charles E.   **BX7260.F47H35 1996**
Charles G. Finney and the Spirit of American Evangelicalism. George Weigel & Robert Royal (Editors). Trade Paper. William B. Eerdmans Publishing Company. Grand Rapids, MI. 1996. 335p. Library of Religious Biography ISBN:0-8028-0129-3, ISBN13: 978-0-8028-0129-6. Dewey:285.8/092 B. LCCN:96-016697.
Audience: **u,f.** *Choice, 1997.*

Lee, Sang Hyun (Editor)   **BX7260.E3P75 2005**
The Princeton Companion to Jonathan Edwards. Trade Cloth. Princeton University Press. Princeton, NJ. 2005. 344p. ISBN:0-691-12108-7, ISBN13: 978-0-691-12108-6. Dewey:230/.58/092. LCCN:2004-050560.
Audience: **u,f.**

Marsden, George M.   **BX7260.E3M412 2003**
Jonathan Edwards: A Life. Cloth over Boards. Yale University Press. Cumberland, RI. 2003. 640p. ISBN:0-300-09693-3, ISBN13: 978-0-300-09693-4. Dewey:285.8/092 B. LCCN:2002-013611.
Audience: **g,l,u,f.** *Choice, 2003.*

Mather, Cotton   **BX7117 .M25**
Selections from Cotton Mather. Trade Paper. Kessinger Publishing, LLC. Whitefish, MT. 2003. ISBN:0-7661-7171-X, ISBN13: 978-0-7661-7171-8. Dewey:230.58.
Audience: **g,l,u.**

Miller, Perry   **BX7260.E3M5 2005**
Jonathan Edwards. John F. Wilson (Introduction by). Trade Paper, Perfect. University of Nebraska Press. Lincoln, NE. 2005. 348p. ISBN:0-8032-8307-5, ISBN13: 978-0-8032-8307-7. Dewey:285.8/092 B. LCCN:2004-028365.
Audience: **u,f.**

Mullin, Robert Bruce   **BX7260.B9M79 2002**
The Puritan As Yankee: A Life of Horace Bushnell. Allen C. Guelzo (Foreword by). Trade Cloth. William B. Eerdmans Publishing Company. Grand Rapids, MI. 2004. 310p. Library of Religious Biography ISBN:0-8028-4252-6, ISBN13: 978-0-8028-4252-7. Dewey:285.8/092 B. LCCN:2002-067928.
Audience: **g,l,u,f.** *Choice, 2003.*

Von Rohr, John   **BX7135**
The Shaping of American Congregationalism. Trade Paper. Pilgrim Press, The/United Church Press. Cleveland, OH. 1992. 512p. ISBN:0-8298-0921-X, ISBN13: 978-0-8298-0921-3. Dewey:285.8/73. LCCN:92-029485.
Audience: **u,f.**

Christianity > Denominations > Protestantism > Restoration (Stone-Campbell) Movement

Foster, Douglas A. (Editor),   **BX7321.3.E53 2004**
et al.
The Encyclopedia of the Stone-Campbell Movement. Paul M. Blowers, Anthony L. Dunnavant & D. Newell Williams (Editors). Trade Cloth. William B. Eerdmans Publishing Company. Grand Rapids, MI. 2005. 894p. ISBN:0-8028-3898-7, ISBN13: 978-0-8028-3898-8. Dewey:286.6/03. LCCN:2004-056356.
Audience: **g,u,f.**

Noll, Mark   **BX7321.3.E83 2002**
Evangelicalism and the Stone-Campbell Movement. William R. Baker (Editor). Trade Paper. InterVarsity Press. Downers Grove, IL. 2002. 256p. ISBN:0-8308-2693-9, ISBN13: 978-0-8308-2693-3. Dewey:286.6. LCCN:2002-004046.
Audience: **u,f.**

Christianity > Denominations > Protestantism > Society of Friends. Quakers

Abbott, Margery Post, et al.   BX7611.A23 2003
Historical Dictionary of the Friends (Quakers). Mary Ellen Chijioke & Pink Dandelion (Authors). Trade Cloth. Scarecrow Press, Inc. Lanham, MD. 2003. 464p. Historical Dictionaries of Religions, Philosophies, and Movements Ser., No. 44 ISBN:0-8108-4483-4, ISBN13: 978-0-8108-4483-4. Dewey:289.6/03. LCCN:2002-012989.

Audience: **g,l,u,f.** *Choice, 2003.*

Barbour, Hugh (Editor)   BX7615
Early Quaker Writings. Perfect. Pendle Hill Publications. Wallingford, PA. 2004. 622p. ISBN:0-87574-942-9, ISBN13: 978-0-87574-942-6. Dewey:289.6/08.

Audience: **u,f.**

Booy, David   BX7793.A88 2004
Autobiographical Writings by Early Quaker Women. Trade Cloth. Ashgate Publishing, Ltd. Aldershot, 2004. 230p. The Early Modern Englishwoman 1500-1750 Ser., :Contemporary Editions Ser. ISBN:0-7546-0753-4, ISBN13: 978-0-7546-0753-3. Dewey:289.6/092/2 B. LCCN:2003-023473.

Audience: **u,f.**

Geiter, Mary K.   F152.2.G42 2000
William Penn. Trade Cloth. Longman Publishing Group. White Plains, NY. 2001. 224p. ISBN:0-582-29901-2, ISBN13: 978-0-582-29901-6. Dewey:974.8/02/092 B. LCCN:00-042826.

Audience: **g,l,u,f.** *Choice, 2001.*

Hamm, Thomas D.   BX7635.H26 2003
The Quakers in America. Trade Cloth. Chinese University of Hong Kong, The. Hong Kong SAR, 2003. 304p. Columbia Contemporary American Religion Ser. ISBN:0-231-12362-0, ISBN13: 978-0-231-12362-4. Dewey:289.6/73. LCCN:2002-041422.

Audience: **g,l,u.** *Choice, 2004.*

Hamm, Thomas D.   BX7637.H35 1988
The Transformation of American Quakerism: Orthodox Friends, 1800-1907. Cloth Text. Indiana University Press. Bloomington, IN. 1988. 288p. Religion in North America Ser. ISBN:0-253-36004-8, ISBN13: 978-0-253-36004-5. Dewey:289.6/3. LCCN:86-046236.

Audience: **u,f.** *Choice, 1988.*

HarperCollins Spiritual   BX7738.Q34 2005
  Classics Staff
Quaker Spirituality: Selected Writings. Trade Paper. HarperCollins Publishers. New York, NY. 2005. 176p. HarperCollins Spiritual Classics Ser. ISBN:0-06-057872-6, ISBN13: 978-0-06-057872-5. Dewey:248.4/896. LCCN:2004-060655.

Audience: **g,l,u,f.**

Ingle, H. Larry   BX7795.F7I54 1994
First among Friends: George Fox and the Creation of Quakerism. Trade Cloth. Oxford University Press, Inc. New York, NY. 1994. 424p. ISBN:0-19-507803-9, ISBN13: 978-0-19-507803-9. Dewey:289.6/092. LCCN:93-007660.

Audience: **u,f.** *Choice, 1994.*

Christianity > Denominations > Protestantism > Lutheran Church

Cimino, Richard (Editor)   BX8041.L88 2003
Lutherans Today: American Lutheran Identity in the Twenty-First Century. Trade Paper. William B. Eerdmans Publishing Company. Grand Rapids, MI. 2003. 224p. ISBN:0-8028-1365-8, ISBN13: 978-0-8028-1365-7. Dewey:284.1/73. LCCN:2003-059948.

Audience: **u,f.** *Choice, 2004.*

Gritsch, Eric W.   BX8018 .G75 1994
Fortress Introduction to Lutheranism. Trade Paper. Augsburg Fortress, Publishers. Minneapolis, MN. 2003. 144p. ISBN:0-8006-2780-6, ISBN13: 978-0-8006-2780-5. Dewey:284.1. LCCN:93-021891.

Audience: **g,u,f.**

Hendrix, Scott & Gassmann,   BX8068.G37 1999
  Gunther
Fortress Introduction to the Lutheran Confessions. Trade Paper. Augsburg Fortress, Publishers. Minneapolis, MN. 2003. 160p. ISBN:0-8006-3162-5, ISBN13: 978-0-8006-3162-8. Dewey:238/.41. LCCN:98-052258.

Audience: **g,l,u.**

Johnson, Jeff   BX8116.3.A37J64 1989
Black Christians: The Untold Lutheran Story. Trade Paper. Concordia Publishing House. Saint Louis, MO. 1991. 336p. Scholarship Today Ser. ISBN:0-570-04558-4, ISBN13: 978-0-570-04558-8. Dewey:284.1/089/96073. LCCN:91-012473.

Audience: **u,f.**

Kolb, Robert & Wengert,   BX8068.A3 2000
  Timothy J. (Editors)
The Book of Concord: The Confessions of the Evangelical Lutheran Church. Ed. 2. Trade Cloth. Augsburg Fortress, Publishers. Minneapolis, MN. 2003. xii, 774p. ISBN:0-8006-2740-7, ISBN13: 978-0-8006-2740-9. Dewey:238/.41. LCCN:99-053034.

Audience: **u,f.**

Lagerquist, L. DeAne   BX8041
The Lutherans, 9. Cloth Text. Greenwood Publishing Group, Inc. Portsmouth, NH. 1999. 272p. Denominations in America Ser. ISBN:0-313-27549-1, ISBN13: 978-0-313-27549-4. Dewey:284.1/73. LCCN:99-022099.

Audience: **g,l,u.**

Nelson, E. Clifford (Editor)   BX8041 .L87
Lutherans in North America. Trade Cloth. Augsburg Fortress,

Publishers. Minneapolis, MN. 2003. 576p. ISBN:0-8006-1409-7, ISBN13: 978-0-8006-1409-6. Dewey:284/.173. LCCN:74-026337.

Audience: **u,f.**

Christianity > Denominations > Protestantism > Anabaptist Traditions. Mennonites

Goertz, Hans-Jurgen   **BX4931.2.G6313 1996**
The Anabaptists. Ed. 2. Trevor Johnson (Translator). Paper over Boards. Routledge. New York, NY. 1996. 240p. Christianity and Society in the Modern World Ser. ISBN:0-415-08238-2, ISBN13: 978-0-415-08238-9. Dewey:284.3. LCCN:96-012032.

Audience: **u,f.**

1974 ed. **Hostetler, John A.**   **BX8129.H8H63 1997**
Hutterite Society. Trade Paper. Johns Hopkins University Press. Baltimore, MD. 1997. 424p. ISBN:0-8018-5639-6, ISBN13: 978-0-8018-5639-6. Dewey:305.6/87073. LCCN:97-178451.

Audience: **u,f.**

Kraybill, Donald B. &   **BX8129.H8K73 2001**
Bowman, Carl Desportes
On the Backroad to Heaven: Old Order Hutterites, Mennonites, Amish and Brethren. Trade Cloth. Johns Hopkins University Press. Baltimore, MD. 2001. 352p. Center Books in Anabaptist Studies ISBN:0-8018-6565-4, ISBN13: 978-0-8018-6565-7. Dewey:289.7/3. LCCN:00-010406.

Audience: **u,f.**

1995 ed. **Kraybill, Donald B. & Nolt,**   **BX8128.E36K73 2004**
Steven M.
Amish Enterprise: From Plows to Profits. Ed. 2. Trade Cloth. Johns Hopkins University Press. Baltimore, MD. 2004. 304p. Center Books in Anabaptist Studies ISBN:0-8018-7804-7, ISBN13: 978-0-8018-7804-6. Dewey:305.6/87074815. LCCN:2003-010637.

Audience: **g,l,u,f.** *Choice, 1996.*

Weaver-Zercher, David   **BX8129.A6W43 2001**
The Amish in the American Imagination. Trade Cloth. Johns Hopkins University Press. Baltimore, MD. 2001. 304p. Center Books in Anabaptist Studies ISBN:0-8018-6681-2, ISBN13: 978-0-8018-6681-4. Dewey:289.7/73. LCCN:00-011531.

Audience: **u,f.**

Christianity > Denominations > Protestantism > Methodists

Heitzenrater, Richard P.   **BX8495.W5H43 2003**
The Elusive Mr. Wesley. Ed. 2. Trade Cloth. Abingdon Press. Nashville, TN. 2003. 480p. ISBN:0-687-07461-4, ISBN13: 978-0-687-07461-7. Dewey:287/.092 B. LCCN:2003-004482.

Audience: **g,l,u.**

Heitzenrater, Richard P.   **BX8276.H4518 2001**
Wesley and the People Called Methodists. Trade Cloth. Abingdon Press. Nashville, TN. 2004. ISBN:0-687-05001-4, ISBN13: 978-0-687-05001-7. Dewey:287/.09/033. LCCN:2001-045775.

Audience: **g,l,u.**

Hempton, David   **BX8231.H46 2005**
Methodism: Empire of the Spirit. Cloth over Boards. Yale University Press. Cumberland, RI. 2005. 304p. ISBN:0-300-10614-9, ISBN13: 978-0-300-10614-5. Dewey:287/.09/033. LCCN:2004-024637.

Audience: **u,f.** *Choice, 2005.*

McEllhennery, John G.   **BX8235**
(Editor), et al.
United Methodism in America: A Compact History. Frederick E. Maser, Charles Yrigoyen Jr. & Kenneth E. Rowe (Editors). Trade Cloth. Abingdon Press. Nashville, TN. 1992. 160p. ISBN:0-687-43170-0, ISBN13: 978-0-687-43170-0. Dewey:287/.6/09. LCCN:92-004988.

Audience: **g,l,u.**

Norwood, Frederick A.   **BX8235**
The Story of American Methodism. Trade Cloth. Abingdon Press. Nashville, TN. 1974. 448p. ISBN:0-687-39641-7, ISBN13: 978-0-687-39641-2. Dewey:287/.673. LCCN:74-010621.

Audience: **g,l,u.**

Payne, Daniel A.   **BX8443**
History of the African Methodist Episcopal Church. Trade Cloth. Ayer Company Publishers, Inc. Manchester, NH. 1969. American Negro, :His History and Literature, Series 2 ISBN:0-405-01885-1, ISBN13: 978-0-405-01885-5. Dewey:287.83. LCCN:69-018573.

Audience: **g,l,u.**

Richey, Russell E. (Editor),   **BX8235.M43 2000**
et al.
The Methodist Experience in America: Sourcebook. Kenneth E. Rowe & Jean Miller-Schmidt (Editors). Trade Cloth. Abingdon Press. Nashville, TN. 2004. 720p. Methodist Experience in America Ser., Vol. 2 ISBN:0-687-24673-3, ISBN13: 978-0-687-24673-1. Dewey:287/.6/09. LCCN:00-042023.

Audience: **g,l,u.**

Stout, Harry S.   **BX9225.W4S74 1991**
The Divine Dramatist: George Whitefield and the Rise of Modern Evangelicalism. Nathan O. Hatch & Mark A. Noll (Editors). Trade Paper. William B. Eerdmans Publishing Company. Grand Rapids, MI. 1991. 325p. Library of Religious Biography ISBN:0-8028-0154-4, ISBN13: 978-0-8028-0154-8. Dewey:269/.2/092. LCCN:91-013549.

Audience: **u,f.**

Christianity > Denominations > Protestantism > Mormons

Arrington, Leonard J.   **BX8695.Y7A85 1986**
Brigham Young: American Moses. Trade Paper. University of
Illinois Press. Champaign, IL. 1986. 560p. ISBN:0-252-01296-8,
ISBN13: 978-0-252-01296-9. Dewey:289.3/32/0924 B.
LCCN:85-024533.

Audience: **u,f.** *Choice, 1985.*

Bagley, Will   **F826**
Blood of the Prophets: Brigham Young and the Massacre at
Mountain Meadows. Trade Paper. University of Oklahoma
Press. Norman, OK. 2004. 544p. ISBN:0-8061-3639-1, ISBN13:
978-0-8061-3639-4. Dewey:979.2/47.

Audience: **u,f.**

Barlow, Philip L.   **BS500.B33 1991**
Mormons and the Bible: The Place of the Latter-Day Saints in
American Religion. Trade Cloth. Oxford University Press, Inc.
New York, NY. 1991. 272p. Religion in America Ser.
ISBN:0-19-506233-7, ISBN13: 978-0-19-506233-5.
Dewey:289.3/73. LCCN:90-036034.

Audience: **l,u.** *Choice, 1992.*

Davies, Douglas James   **BX8635.3D38 2003**
An Introduction to Mormonism. Cloth Text. Cambridge
University Press. New York, NY. 2003. 284p. Introduction to
Religion Ser. ISBN:0-521-81738-2, ISBN13:
978-0-521-81738-7. Dewey:289.3. LCCN:2003-043582.

Audience: **g,u.** *Choice, 2004.*

Flake, Kathleen   **2003014536 [BX]**
The Politics of American Religious Identity: The Seating of
Senator Reed Smoot, Mormon Apostle. Trade Cloth. University
of North Carolina Press. Chapel Hill, NC. 2004. 256p.
ISBN:0-8078-2831-9, ISBN13: 978-0-8078-2831-1.
Dewey:328.73/092. LCCN:2003-014536.

Audience: **g,u,f.** *Choice, 2004.*

Gordon, Sarah Barringer   **2001041472 [KF]**
The Mormon Question: Polygamy and Constitutional Conflict in
Nineteenth-Century America. Trade Cloth. University of North
Carolina Press. Chapel Hill, NC. 2002. 352p. Studies in Legal
History ISBN:0-8078-2661-8, ISBN13: 978-0-8078-2661-4.
Dewey:342.73/0852. LCCN:2001-041472.

Audience: **u,f.**

Smith, Joseph (Translator)   **BX86232004**
The Book of Mormon: Another Testament of Jesus Christ. Trade
Cloth. Doubleday Publishing. New York, NY. 2004. 608p.
ISBN:0-385-51316-X, ISBN13: 978-0-385-51316-6.
Dewey:289.3/22. LCCN:2004-051982.

Audience: **g,l,u.**

Smith, Joseph   **BX8628**
Pearl of Great Price. Trade Paper. Kessinger Publishing, LLC.
Whitefish, MT. 2003. ISBN:0-7661-3653-1, ISBN13:
978-0-7661-3653-3. Dewey:289.32.

Audience: **g,l,u.**

1952 ed. **Smith, Joseph**   **BX8628**
Doctrine and Covenants of the Church of Jesus Christ of
Latter-Day Saints: Containing the Revelations Given to Joseph
Smith, Jun, the Prophet, for the Building up of the Kingdom of
God in the Last Days. Orson Pratt (Editor). Trade Cloth.
Greenwood Publishing Group, Inc. Portsmouth, NH. 1971. 503p.
ISBN:0-8371-4101-X, ISBN13: 978-0-8371-4101-5.
Dewey:289.3/2. LCCN:69-014082.

Audience: **g,l,u.**

Christianity > Denominations > Protestantism > Pentecostal Churches

Jacobsen, Douglas G.   **BR1644.5.U6J33 2003**
ⓔ Thinking in the Spirit: Theologies of the Early Pentecostal
Movement. E-Book. Indiana University Press. Bloomington, IN.
2003. 368p. ISBN:0-253-34320-8, ISBN13: 978-0-253-34320-8.
Dewey:230/.994. LCCN:2003-005879.

Audience: **u,f.** *Choice, 2004.*

Synan, Vinson   **BR1644.5.U6S86 1997**
The Holiness-Pentecostal Tradition: Charismatic Movements in
the Twentieth Century. Ed. 2. Trade Paper. William B. Eerdmans
Publishing Company. Grand Rapids, MI. 1997. 352p.
ISBN:0-8028-4103-1, ISBN13: 978-0-8028-4103-2.
Dewey:277.3/082. LCCN:97-010579.

Audience: **u,f.**

Wacker, Grant   **BX8762**
Heaven Below: Early Pentecostals and American Culture. Trade
Paper. Harvard University Press. Cambridge, MA. 2003. 384p.
ISBN:0-674-01128-7, ISBN13: 978-0-674-01128-1.
Dewey:289.9/4/097309041.

Audience: **g,l,u,f.** *Choice, 2002.*

Westmeier, Karl-Wilhelm   **BR1644.5.L29W47 1999**
Protestant Pentecostalism in Latin America: A Study in the
Dynamics of Change. Trade Cloth. Fairleigh Dickinson
University Press. Cranbury, NJ. 1999. 168p.
ISBN:0-8386-3834-1, ISBN13: 978-0-8386-3834-7.
Dewey:289.9/4/098. LCCN:99-032705.

Audience: **u,f.**

1984 ed. **Williams, Melvin D.**   **BR563.N4**
Community in a Black Pentecostal Church: An Anthropological
Study. Trade Cloth. University of Pittsburgh Press. Pittsburgh,
PA. 1974. xii, 202p. ISBN:0-8229-3290-3, ISBN13:
978-0-8229-3290-1. Dewey:306/.6. LCCN:74-005108.

Audience: **u,f.**

Christianity > Denominations > Protestantism > Presbyterians

Hart, D. G.   **BX8909.D53 1999**
Dictionary of the Presbyterian and Reformed Tradition in
America. Trade Cloth. InterVarsity Press. Downers Grove, IL.
1999. xxix + 286p. ISBN:0-8308-1453-1, ISBN13:
978-0-8308-1453-4. Dewey:285/.0973/03. LCCN:99-026699.

Audience: **g,l,u,f.**

Lingle, Walter L. &   BX8931.2 .L56 1978
  Kuykendall, John W.
Presbyterians, Their History and Beliefs. Trade Paper.
Westminster John Knox Press. Louisville, KY. 1958. 112p.
ISBN:0-8042-0985-5, ISBN13: 978-0-8042-0985-4. Dewey:285.
LCCN:77-015750.

Audience: **u,f.**

Longfield, Bradley J.   BX8937.L65 1991
The Presbyterian Controversy: Fundamentalists, Modernists, and
Moderates. Trade Cloth. Oxford University Press, Inc. New
York, NY. 1991. 352p. Religion in America Ser.
ISBN:0-19-506419-4, ISBN13: 978-0-19-506419-3.
Dewey:285/.1/09042. LCCN:90-033625.

Audience: **u,f.** *Choice, 1991.*

Marshall, Rosalind   BX9223.M37 2000
John Knox. Trade Paper. Birlinn, Ltd. Edinburgh, 2001. 244p.
ISBN:1-84158-091-0, ISBN13: 978-1-84158-091-3.
Dewey:285.20924. LCCN:2001-369156.

Audience: **u,f.** *Choice, 2001.*

Presbyterian Church Staff   BX8969.5.B66 1999
Book of Confessions: Study Edition. Trade Paper. Geneva Press.
Louisville, KY. 1999. 450p. ISBN:0-664-50012-9, ISBN13:
978-0-664-50012-2. Dewey:238/.5137. LCCN:98-048596.

Audience: **g,l,u.**

Rogers, J.   BX9183
Presbyterian Creeds: A Guide to the Book of Confessions. Trade
Paper. Westminster John Knox Press. Louisville, KY. 1991.
292p. ISBN:0-664-25496-9, ISBN13: 978-0-664-25496-4.
Dewey:238.51.

Audience: **u,f.**

Smylie, James H.   BX8935.S56 1996
A Brief History of the Presbyterians. Trade Paper. Geneva Press.
Louisville, KY. 1996. 176p. ISBN:0-664-50001-3, ISBN13:
978-0-664-50001-6. Dewey:285/.173. LCCN:96-024458.

Audience: **g,l,u.**

Christianity > Denominations > Protestantism > Puritans

Bremer, Francis J.   BX9358.B74 1994
Congregational Communion: Clerical Friendship in the
Anglo-American Puritan Community, 1610-1692. Cloth Text.
Northeastern University Press. Boston, MA. 1994. 352p. New
England Studies ISBN:1-55553-186-5, ISBN13:
978-1-55553-186-7. Dewey:285/.9/097409032.
LCCN:94-005620.

Audience: **u,f.**

1967 ed. **Collinson, Patrick**   BX9333.C62 1989
The Elizabethan Puritan Movement. Trade Paper. Oxford
University Press, Inc. New York, NY. 1990. 528p.
ISBN:0-19-822298-X, ISBN13: 978-0-19-822298-9.
Dewey:285/.9. LCCN:89-022977.

Audience: **u,f.**

Lake, Peter   BX9334.3.L34 1982
1982 ed. Moderate Puritans and the Elizabethan Church. Trade Paper.
Cambridge University Press. New York, NY. 2004. 366p.
ISBN:0-521-61187-3, ISBN13: 978-0-521-61187-9.
Dewey:285/.9/0922. LCCN:2005-274482.

Audience: **u,f.**

Miller, Perry G.   F7 .M54 1983
1953 ed. The New England Mind: From Colony to Province. Trade Paper.
Harvard University Press. Cambridge, MA. 1983. 528p.
ISBN:0-674-61301-5, ISBN13: 978-0-674-61301-0. Dewey:974.
LCCN:82-020740.

Audience: **u,f.**

Miller, Perry G.   F7 .M56 1983
1954 ed. The New England Mind: The Seventeenth Century. Trade Paper.
Harvard University Press. Cambridge, MA. 1983. 542p.
ISBN:0-674-61306-6, ISBN13: 978-0-674-61306-5.
Dewey:974/.02. LCCN:82-023291.

Audience: **u,f.**

Morgan, Edmund S.   BX9322.M6
Visible Saints: The History of a Puritan Idea. Trade Paper.
Cornell University Press. Ithaca, NY. 1965. 168p.
ISBN:0-8014-9041-3, ISBN13: 978-0-8014-9041-5.
Dewey:285.9. LCCN:63-009999.

Audience: **u,f.**

Stout, Harry S.   BV4208.U6
The New England Soul: Preaching and Religious Culture in
Colonial New England. Trade Paper. Oxford University Press,
Inc. New York, NY. 1988. 406p. ISBN:0-19-505645-0, ISBN13:
978-0-19-505645-7. Dewey:251/.00974. LCCN:85-029853.

Audience: **u,f.** *Choice, 1987.*

Christianity > Denominations > Protestantism > Reformed Church. Calvinism

Barth, Karl   BX9418.B15713 1995
The Theology of John Calvin. Geoffrey W. Bromiley
(Translator). Trade Paper. William B. Eerdmans Publishing
Company. Grand Rapids, MI. 1995. 448p. ISBN:0-8028-0696-1,
ISBN13: 978-0-8028-0696-3. Dewey:230/.42/092.
LCCN:95-033983.

Audience: **u,f.**

Benedict, Philip   BX9415.B47 2002
Christ's Churches Purely Reformed: A Social History of
Calvinism. Cloth over Boards. Yale University Press.
Cumberland, RI. 2002. 704p. ISBN:0-300-08812-4, ISBN13:
978-0-300-08812-0. Dewey:284/.24. LCCN:2002-002411.

Audience: **g,l,u,f.** *Choice, 2003.*

Bratt, James D.   BX7907
Dutch Calvinism in Modern America: A History of a
Conservative Subculture. Trade Paper. Wipf & Stock Publishers.
Eugene, OR. 2002. 368p. ISBN:1-59244-122-X, ISBN13:
978-1-59244-122-8. Dewey:285.7/73.

Audience: **u,f.**

Calvin, John   BX9422.3
Calvin: Institutes of the Christian Religion. John T. McNeill
(Editor). Trade Cloth. Westminster John Knox Press. Louisville,
KY. 2004. 1812p. Library of Christian Classics
ISBN:0-664-22028-2, ISBN13: 978-0-664-22028-0.
Dewey:230.42. LCCN:60-005379.

Audience: **g,l,u,f.**

Gerrish, Brian A.   BV825.2
Grace and Gratitude: The Eucharistic Theology of John Calvin.
Trade Paper. Continuum International Publishing Group, Ltd.
London, 1998. 224p. ISBN:0-567-29233-9, ISBN13:
978-0-567-29233-9. Dewey:234.163.

Audience: **u,f.**

McKim, Donald K. (Editor)   BX9418.C386 2004
The Cambridge Companion to John Calvin. Cloth Text.
Cambridge University Press. New York, NY. 2004. 370p.
Cambridge Companions to Religion Ser. ISBN:0-521-81647-5,
ISBN13: 978-0-521-81647-2. Dewey:230/.42/092.
LCCN:2003-063362.

Audience: **u,f.**   *Choice, 2005.*

McKim, Donald K.   BX9422.3.W47 2001
The Westminster Handbook to Reformed Theology. Trade Paper.
Westminster John Knox Press. Louisville, KY. 2001. 264p. The
Westminster Handbooks to Christian Theology
ISBN:0-664-22430-X, ISBN13: 978-0-664-22430-1.
Dewey:230/.42/03. LCCN:2003-266207.

Audience: **u,f.**

earlier eds. **McNeill, John Thomas**   BX9422
The History and Character of Calvinism. Paper Text. Textbook
Publishers. Temecula, CA. 2003. x, 466p. ISBN:0-7581-6994-9,
ISBN13: 978-0-7581-6994-5. Dewey:284.2.

Audience: **l,u.**

Parker, T. H.   BX9418.P33 1995
Calvin: An Introduction to His Thought. Trade Paper.
Westminster John Knox Press. Louisville, KY. 2003. 160p.
ISBN:0-664-25602-3, ISBN13: 978-0-664-25602-9.
Dewey:230/.42/092. LCCN:95-001055.

Audience: **g,l,u.**

Reid, J. K. (Editor)   BR85
Calvin: Theological Treatises. Trade Cloth. Westminster John
Knox Press. Louisville, KY. 2000. 355p. Library of Christian
Classics, Vol. 22 ISBN:0-664-22367-2, ISBN13:
978-0-664-22367-0. Dewey:230.044.

Audience: **u,f.**

Christianity > Denominations > Protestantism > Salvation Army

McKinley, Edward H.   BX9716.M32 1995
Marching to Glory: The History of the Salvation Army in the
United States, 1880-1992. Ed. 2. Trade Cloth. William B.

Eerdmans Publishing Company. Grand Rapids, MI. 1995. 440p.
ISBN:0-8028-3761-1, ISBN13: 978-0-8028-3761-5.
Dewey:287.9/6/0973. LCCN:95-017414.

Audience: **u,f.**

Winston, Diane H.   BX9718.N7
Red-Hot and Righteous: The Urban Religion of the Salvation
Army. Trade Paper. Harvard University Press. Cambridge, MA.
2000. 304p. ISBN:0-674-00396-9, ISBN13: 978-0-674-00396-5.
Dewey:287.9/6/097471. LCCN:98-047842.

Audience: **u,f.**   *Choice, 2000.*

Christianity > Denominations > Protestantism > Shakers

Morse, Flo   BX9766.M67 1987
The Shakers and the World's People. Trade Paper. University
Press of New England. Lebanon, NH. 1987. 399p.
ISBN:0-87451-426-6, ISBN13: 978-0-87451-426-1.
Dewey:289/.8. LCCN:87-008223.

Audience: **u,f.**

Stein, Stephen J.   BX9766.S74 1992
The Shaker Experience in America: A History of the United
Society of Believers. Cloth over Boards. Yale University Press.
Cumberland, RI. 1992. 576p. ISBN:0-300-05139-5, ISBN13:
978-0-300-05139-1. Dewey:289/.8/0973. LCCN:91-030836.

Audience: **g,l,u,f.**   *Choice, 1992.*

Christianity > Denominations > Protestantism > Unitarianism. Universalism

Grodzins, Dean   2002003832 [BX]
American Heretic: Theodore Parker and Transcendentalism.
Trade Cloth. University of North Carolina Press. Chapel Hill,
NC. 2002. 656p. ISBN:0-8078-2710-X, ISBN13:
978-0-8078-2710-9. Dewey:289.1/092 B. LCCN:2002-003832.

Audience: **u,f.**   *Choice, 2003.*

Harris, Mark W.   BX9809.H37 2004
Historical Dictionary of Unitarian Universalism. Trade Cloth.
Scarecrow Press, Inc. Lanham, MD. 2003. 616p. Historical
Dictionaries of Religions, Philosophies, and Movements Ser.,
No. 48 ISBN:0-8108-4869-4, ISBN13: 978-0-8108-4869-6.
Dewey:289.1/03. LCCN:2003-011871.

Audience: **g,l,u,f.**   *Choice, 2004.*

Howe, Daniel W.   BX9833.6.B68
The Unitarian Conscience. Trade Cloth. Harvard University
Press. Cambridge, MA. 1970. xi, 398p. ISBN:0-674-92121-6,
ISBN13: 978-0-674-92121-4. Dewey:001.2/09744/61.
LCCN:75-116737.

Audience: **u,f.**

Robinson, David (Editor)   **BX9815.C42 1985**
William Ellery Channing: Selected Writings. Trade Cloth.
Paulist Press. Mahwah, NJ. 1985. 320p. Sources of American
Spirituality Ser., Vol. 2 ISBN:0-8091-0359-1, ISBN13:
978-0-8091-0359-1. Dewey:230/.8. LCCN:84-062567.

Audience: **u,f.**

Wright, Conrad   **BX9833**
A Stream of Light: A Short History of American Unitarianism.
Trade Paper. Unitarian Universalist Association. Boston, MA.
1989. ISBN:1-55896-155-0, ISBN13: 978-1-55896-155-5.
Dewey:289.1.

Audience: **g,l,u,f.**

Christianity > Denominations > Protestantism > Pietistic Movements

Atwood, Craig D.   **BX8565**
Community of the Cross: Moravian Piety in Colonial
Bethlehem. Trade Cloth. Pennsylvania State University Press.
University Park, PA. 2004. 240p. Max Kade Institute Ser.
ISBN:0-271-02367-8, ISBN13: 978-0-271-02367-0.
Dewey:284/.674822. LCCN:2003-022440.

Audience: **u,f.** *Choice, 2004.*

Campbell, Ted A.   **BR440.C35 1991**
The Religion of the Heart: A Study of European Religious Life
in the Seventeenth and Eighteenth Centuries. Cloth Text.
University of South Carolina Press. Columbia, SC. 1991. 228p.
ISBN:0-87249-746-1, ISBN13: 978-0-87249-746-7.
Dewey:274/.07. LCCN:91-006913.

Audience: **u,f.**

Faull, Katherine M. (Editor,   **BX8591.M67**
  Translator)
Moravian Women's Memoirs: Their Related Lives, 1750-1820.
Trade Paper. Syracuse University Press. Syracuse, NY. 1997. xl,
166p. Women and Gender in North American Religions Ser.
ISBN:0-8156-0397-5, ISBN13: 978-0-8156-0397-9.
Dewey:284/.6/092274827. LCCN:96-021261.

Audience: **u,f.**

Christianity > Denominations > Protestantism > Evangelicalism

Cochran, Pamela   **BS521.4.C63 2004**
Evangelical Feminism: A History. Trade Cloth. New York
University Press. New York, NY. 2005. 253p.
ISBN:0-8147-1636-9, ISBN13: 978-0-8147-1636-6.
Dewey:230/.082. LCCN:2004-015011.

Audience: **u,f.** *Choice, 2005.*

Larsen, Timothy (Editor), et   **BV3780.B56 2003**
  al.
Biographical Dictionary of Evangelicals. David W. Bebbington
& Mark A. Noll (Editors). Trade Cloth. InterVarsity Press.

Downers Grove, IL. 2003. xviii + 789p. ISBN:0-8308-2925-3,
ISBN13: 978-0-8308-2925-5. Dewey:270.820922.
LCCN:2003-006847.

Audience: **g,l,u,f.** *Choice, 2004.*

Noll, Mark A.   **BR1640.N65 2004**
The Rise of Evangelicalism: The Age of Edwards, Whitefield
and the Wesleys. Trade Cloth. InterVarsity Press. Downers
Grove, IL. 2004. 330p. History of Evangelicalism Ser., Vol. 1
ISBN:0-8308-2581-9, ISBN13: 978-0-8308-2581-3.
Dewey:270.7. LCCN:2003-025927.

Audience: **u,f.**

Sweeney, Douglas A.   **BR1642.U5S94 2005**
The American Evangelical Story: A History of the Movement.
Paper Text. Baker Academic. Ada, MI. 2005. 208p.
ISBN:0-8010-2658-X, ISBN13: 978-0-8010-2658-4.
Dewey:277.3/082. LCCN:2004-029538.

Audience: **u,f.** *Choice, 2006.*

Ward, W. R.   **BV3777.E9 W37 1992**
The Protestant Evangelical Awakening. Trade Paper. Cambridge
University Press. New York, NY. 2002. 388p.
ISBN:0-521-89232-5, ISBN13: 978-0-521-89232-2.
Dewey:280.4/094/09033.

Audience: **u,f.**

Christianity > Early Christian Literature

Apostolic   **BR60.A62 2003**
The Apostolic Fathers: I Clement. II Clement. Ignatius.
Polycarp. Didache. Bart D. Ehrman (Editor, Translator). Trade
Cloth. Harvard University Press. Cambridge, MA. 2003. 464p.
Loeb Classical Library, Vols. 24-25 ISBN:0-674-99607-0,
ISBN13: 978-0-674-99607-6. Dewey:270.1.
LCCN:2002-032744.

Audience: **u,f.**

Barnard, Leslie W.   **BR65.J82A7413 1997**
St. Justin Martyr: The First and Second Apologies. Trade Cloth.
Paulist Press. Mahwah, NJ. 1996. 256p. Ancient Christian
Writers Ser., No. 56 ISBN:0-8091-0472-5, ISBN13:
978-0-8091-0472-7. Dewey:239/.1. LCCN:96-003012.

Audience: **u,f.**

Burghardt, Walter J. &   **BR60**
  Lawler, T. C. (Editors)
Rufinus: A Commentary of the Apostles' Creed. Trade Cloth.
Paulist Press. Mahwah, NJ. 1978. 176p. Ancient Christian
Writers Ser., No. 20 ISBN:0-8091-0257-9, ISBN13:
978-0-8091-0257-0. Dewey:270. LCCN:78-062468.

Audience: **u,f.**

Burghardt, Walter J.   **BR60.A35 NO. 23**
  (Editor), et al.
Athenagoras, Embassy for the Christians, the Resurrection of the
Dead. T. C. Lawler & J. Quasten (Editors). Trade Cloth. Paulist
Press. Mahwah, NJ. 1956. 200p. Ancient Christian Writers Ser.,
No. 23 ISBN:0-8091-0036-3, ISBN13: 978-0-8091-0036-1.
Dewey:239.1. LCCN:56-011421.

Audience: **u,f.**

Burghardt, Walter J.   **BR60.A35 NO.6**
(Editor), et al.
1948 ed. The Didache, the Epistle of Barnabas, the Epistle and
Martyrdom of St. Polycarp, the Fragments of Papias, the Epistle
of Diognetus. T. C. Lawler & J. Quasten (Editors). Trade Cloth.
Paulist Press. Mahwah, NJ. 1978. 248p. ACW Series: No. 6
Ser., No. 6 ISBN:0-8091-0247-1, ISBN13: 978-0-8091-0247-1.
Dewey:229.95. LCCN:78-062453.

Audience: **u,f.**

Burghardt, Walter J.   **BR60**
(Editor), et al.
Egeria, Diary of a Pilgrimage. T. C. Lawler & J. Quasten
(Editors). Trade Cloth. Paulist Press. Mahwah, NJ. 1970. 294p.
Ancient Christian Writers Ser., No. 38 ISBN:0-8091-0029-0,
ISBN13: 978-0-8091-0029-3. Dewey:263/.042394.
LCCN:70-119159.

Audience: **u,f.**

Burghardt, Walter J.   **BV65.O53**
(Editor), et al.
Origen, Prayer, Exhortation to Martyrdom. T. C. Lawler & J.
Quasten (Editors). Trade Cloth. Paulist Press. Mahwah, NJ.
1978. 264p. Ancient Christian Writers Ser., No. 19
ISBN:0-8091-0256-0, ISBN13: 978-0-8091-0256-3.
Dewey:264.1. LCCN:78-062467.

Audience: **u,f.**

Burghardt, Walter J.   **BR60**
(Editor), et al.
Tertullian, Treatise on Marriage and Remarriage: To His Wife,
an Exhortation to Chastity Monogamy. T. C. Lawler & J.
Quasten (Editors). Trade Cloth. Paulist Press. Mahwah, NJ.
1978. 208p. Ancient Christian Writers Ser., No. 13
ISBN:0-8091-0149-1, ISBN13: 978-0-8091-0149-8.
Dewey:265.5. LCCN:78-062462.

Audience: **u,f.**

Ehrman, Bart D. &   **BR60.A62 2003**
Apostolic
other eds The Apostolic Fathers: Epistle of Barnabas, Papias and
Quadratus, Epistle to Diognetus, the Shepherd of Hermas. Trade
Cloth. Harvard University Press. Cambridge, MA. 2003. 492p.
Loeb Classical Library ISBN:0-674-99608-9, ISBN13:
978-0-674-99608-3. Dewey:230.1/2.

Audience: **u,f.**

Greenslade, S. L.   **BR60E123**
Early Latin Theology. Trade Cloth. Westminster John Knox
Press. Louisville, KY. 1978. 412p. Library of Christian Classics
ISBN:0-664-24154-9, ISBN13: 978-0-664-24154-4.
Dewey:281.3. LCCN:56-005229.

Audience: **u,f.**

Gregg, Robert C. (Editor)   **BR1720.A6 A8313 1980**
Athanasius: The Life of Antony and the Letter to Marcellinus.
Trade Cloth. Paulist Press. Mahwah, NJ. 1979. 192p. Classics of
Western Spirituality Ser. ISBN:0-8091-2295-2, ISBN13:
978-0-8091-2295-0. Dewey:270.1/092/4. LCCN:79-056622.

Audience: **u,f.**

Holmes, Michael William   **BR60.A62 1999**
(Editor)
other eds The Apostolic Fathers: Greek Texts and English Translations.
Trade Paper. Baker Academic. Ada, MI. 1999. 640p.
ISBN:0-8010-2225-8, ISBN13: 978-0-8010-2225-8.
Dewey:270.1. LCCN:99-046353.

Audience: **u,f.**

Jefford, Clayton N.   **BR67.J44 2005**
Apostolic Fathers. Trade Cloth. Abingdon Press. Nashville, TN.
2005. 128p. Abingdon Essential Guides Ser.
ISBN:0-687-34204-X, ISBN13: 978-0-687-34204-4.
Dewey:270.1. LCCN:2005-017895.

Audience: **g,l,u.**

Lawler, Thomas C. &   **BR60; BT1116.M7**
Burghart, Johannes (Editors)
The Octavius of Marcus Minucius Felix. G. W. Clarke
(Translator). Trade Cloth. Paulist Press. Mahwah, NJ. 1974.
422p. Ancient Christian Writers Ser., No. 39
ISBN:0-8091-0189-0, ISBN13: 978-0-8091-0189-4.
Dewey:281/.08 s; 239/.1.

Audience: **u,f.**

Pamphilus, Eusebius   **BR160.E55**
Eusebius' Ecclesiastical History: A Third Century Historian
Looks at the Early Church. Trade Cloth. Hendrickson
Publishers, Inc. Peabody, MA. 1998. 528p.
ISBN:1-56563-371-7, ISBN13: 978-1-56563-371-1. Dewey:270.

Audience: **u,f.**

Petersen, William L.   **BP173.J8A33 1996**
Tatian's Diatessaron: Its Creation, Dissemination, Significance,
and History in Scholarship. Trade Cloth. Brill Academic
Publishers, Inc. Boston, MA. 1994. 320p. Supplements to
Vigiliae Christianae Ser., Vol. 25 ISBN:90-04-10034-2, ISBN13:
978-90-04-10034-3. Dewey:297/.1972. LCCN:94-002883.

Audience: **u,f.**

Ramsey, Boniface (Editor,   **BR60.A35 NO. 57**
Translator)
John Cassian: The Conferences. Trade Cloth. Paulist Press.
Mahwah, NJ. 1997. 912p. Ancient Christian Writers Ser., No. 57
ISBN:0-8091-0484-9, ISBN13: 978-0-8091-0484-0. Dewey:255.
LCCN:97-006523.

Audience: **u,f.**

Richardson, Cyril C.   **BR60.R5**
Early Christian Fathers. Trade Paper. Simon & Schuster. New
York, NY. 1995. 415p. ISBN:0-684-82951-7, ISBN13:
978-0-684-82951-7. Dewey:281.108.

Audience: **g,l,u.**

Roberts, Alexander &   **F213**
Donaldson, James (Editors)
The Ante-Nicene Fathers, Set. Trade Cloth. Hendrickson
Publishers, Inc. Peabody, MA. 1994. 6448p. The Early Church
Fathers Ser. ISBN:1-56563-082-3, ISBN13: 978-1-56563-082-6.
Dewey:975.

Audience: **u,f.**

Saint Cyprian of Carthage   **BR60**
St. Cyprian, the Lapsed, the Unity of the Catholic Church.
Walter J. Burghardt, T. C. Lawler & J. Quasten (Editors). Trade
Cloth. Paulist Press. Mahwah, NJ. 1957. 144p. Ancient Christian
Writers Ser., No. 25 ISBN:0-8091-0260-9, ISBN13:
978-0-8091-0260-0. Dewey:57-7364. LCCN:57-007364.

Audience: **u,f.**

Saint Gregory of Nyssa   **BR63**
St. Gregory the Great: Pastoral Care. Walter J. Burghardt & T.
C. Lawler (Editors). Trade Cloth. Paulist Press. Mahwah, NJ.
1978. 296p. Ancient Christian Writers Ser., No. 11
ISBN:0-8091-0251-X, ISBN13: 978-0-8091-0251-8. Dewey:253.

Audience: **u,f.**

Smith, Joseph P.   **BR65.I63**
St. Irenaeus: Proof of the Apostolic Preaching. Trade Cloth.
Paulist Press. Mahwah, NJ. 1978. 248p. Ancient Christian
Writers Ser., Vol. 16 ISBN:0-8091-0264-1, ISBN13:
978-0-8091-0264-8. Dewey:281.1.

Audience: **u,f.**

Christianity > Early Christian Literature > Augustine

Augustine, Saint, Bishop of   **BR65 A5**
Hippo.
in print ☐ The works of Saint Augustine [electronic resource] : a
translation for the 21st century.
http://pastmasters2000.nlx.com/display.cfm?&clientID=205144&
depth=2&infobase=pmauge2.nfo&softpage=GetClient42&
titleCategory=0&view=browse&toString=function%20()%20
%20else%20
%20%20%20%20%20%20%20%20result%20+=
%20prop%20+%20%22=
%22%20+%20this[prop];%20%20%20%20
%20%20%20%20return%20result;
Charlottesville, VA : InteLex Corp..

Audience: **g,l,u,f.**

Augustine (Editor)   **BR65.A6**
Confessions. Henry Chadwick (Translator, Introduction by,
Notes by). Trade Paper. Oxford University Press, Inc. New
York, NY. 1998. 340p. Oxford World's Classics Ser.
ISBN:0-19-283372-3, ISBN13: 978-0-19-283372-3.
Dewey:270.2092.

Audience: **g,l,u.**

Augustine   **BR65.A5**
City of God. Gill Evans (Editor), Henry Bettenson (Translator).
Trade Paper. Penguin Group (USA) Inc. New York, NY. 2004.
1168p. ISBN:0-14-044894-2, ISBN13: 978-0-14-044894-8.
Dewey:230/.01.

Audience: **g,l,u.**

Augustine   **BR65.A6552E5 1999**
On Christian Teaching. R. P. H. Green (Editor). Trade Paper.
Oxford University Press, Inc. New York, NY. 1999. 194p.
Oxford World's Classics Ser. ISBN:0-19-283928-4, ISBN13:
978-0-19-283928-2. Dewey:230/.14. LCCN:00-265519.

Audience: **g,l,u.**

Augustine   **BR65.A73E513 1999**
The Augustine Catechism: The Enchiridion on Faith, Hope, and
Love. Bruce Harbert (Translator), Boniface Ramsey
(Introduction by). Trade Paper. New City Press. Hyde Park, NY.
1999. 144p. Works of Saint Augustine ISBN:1-56548-124-0,
ISBN13: 978-1-56548-124-4. Dewey:230/.14. LCCN:99-018777.

Audience: **g,l,u.**

Augustine   **B655.C62E5 1995**
Against the Academicians and the Teacher. Peter King
(Translator, Introduction by). Trade Cloth. Hackett Publishing
Company, Inc. Indianapolis, IN. 1995. 208p.
ISBN:0-87220-213-5, ISBN13: 978-0-87220-213-9.
Dewey:189/.2. LCCN:95-032851.

Audience: **g,l,u.**

Augustine   **BR65.A5**
The Trinity. Ed. 4. John E. Rotelle (Editor), Edmund Hill
(Translator, Introduction by). Trade Paper. New City Press.
Hyde Park, NY. 1991. 472p. Trinity Ser., Vol. I
ISBN:0-911782-89-3, ISBN13: 978-0-911782-89-9.
Dewey:270.2.

Audience: **g,l,u.**

Augustine   **BR65.A664E5 1993**
On Free Choice of the Will. Thomas Williams (Translator,
Introduction by). Trade Cloth. Hackett Publishing Company, Inc.
Indianapolis, IN. 1993. 192p. Hackett Classics Ser.
ISBN:0-87220-189-9, ISBN13: 978-0-87220-189-7.
Dewey:233.7. LCCN:93-022170.

Audience: **g,l,u,f.** *B*

Fitzgerald, Allan D. (Editor)   **B655.Z69A84 1999**
Augustine through the Ages: An Encyclopedia. Trade Cloth.
William B. Eerdmans Publishing Company. Grand Rapids, MI.
1999. 952p. ISBN:0-8028-3843-X, ISBN13: 978-0-8028-3843-8.
Dewey:270.2/092. LCCN:99-012518.

Audience: **g,l,u,f.** *Choice, 2000.*

Stump, Eleonore &   **B655.Z7C35 2001**
Kretzmann, Norman (Editors)
The Cambridge Companion to Augustine. Cloth Text.
Cambridge University Press. New York, NY. 2001. 324p.
Cambridge Companions to Philosophy Ser.
ISBN:0-521-65018-6, ISBN13: 978-0-521-65018-2.
Dewey:189/.2. LCCN:00-031173.

Audience: **g,l,u,f.** *Choice, 2002.*

Christianity > Early Christian Literature > Others

Cyril of Alexandria   **BR65.C952E5 2000**
Cyril of Alexandria. Norman Russell (Translator). Paper over
Boards. Routledge. New York, NY. 2000. 288p. Early Church
Fathers Ser. ISBN:0-415-18250-6, ISBN13: 978-0-415-18250-8.
Dewey:270.2/092. LCCN:99-055830.

Audience: **u,f.**

Dunn, Geoffrey D.   **BR65.T7D86 2004**
Tertullian. Paper over Boards. Routledge. New York, NY. 2004.
208p. Early Church Fathers Ser. ISBN:0-415-28230-6, ISBN13:
978-0-415-28230-7. Dewey:230/.13/092. LCCN:2003-026276.

Audience: **u,f.**

Greer, Rowan A. (Editor)   **BR65**
Origen: Selected Writings. Hans Urs Von Balthasar (Preface by).
Trade Cloth. Paulist Press. Mahwah, NJ. 1979. 334p. Classics of
Western Spirituality Ser. ISBN:0-8091-0283-8, ISBN13:
978-0-8091-0283-9. Dewey:230/.1/3. LCCN:79-084886.

Audience: **u,f.**

Mayer, Wendy & Allen,   **BR65.C46M39 1999**
  Pauline
John Chrysostom. Paper over Boards. Routledge. New York,
NY. 1999. 240p. Early Church Fathers Ser.
ISBN:0-415-18252-2, ISBN13: 978-0-415-18252-2.
Dewey:270.2/092 B. LCCN:99-017709.

Audience: **u,f.**

Meredith, Anthony &   **BR65.G76M47 1999**
  Gregory
Gregory of Nyssa. Paper over Boards. Routledge. New York,
NY. 1999. 176p. Early Church Fathers Ser.
ISBN:0-415-11839-5, ISBN13: 978-0-415-11839-2.
Dewey:270.2/092. LCCN:98-024529.

Audience: **u,f.**

Moorhead, John   **BR65.G56M66 2005**
Gregory the Great. Perfect, Paper over Boards. Routledge. New
York, NY. 2005. 177p. The Early Church Fathers Ser.
ISBN:0-415-23389-5, ISBN13: 978-0-415-23389-7.
Dewey:270.2/092 B. LCCN:2004-017572.

Audience: **u,f.**

Yarnold, Edward S.   **BR65.C936Y37 2000**
Cyril of Jerusalem. Paper over Boards. Routledge. New York,
NY. 2000. 240p. Early Church Fathers Ser.
ISBN:0-415-19903-4, ISBN13: 978-0-415-19903-2.
Dewey:270.2/092. LCCN:00-036638.

Audience: **u,f.**

Young, Frances (Editor), et   **BR67.C25 2004**
  al.
The Cambridge History of Early Christian Literature. Lewis
Ayres & Andrew Louth (Editors), Augustine Casiday (Assisted
by). Cloth Text. Cambridge University Press. New York, NY.

2004. 566p. ISBN:0-521-46083-2, ISBN13: 978-0-521-46083-5.
Dewey:270.1. LCCN:2003-055726.

Audience: **u,f.** *Choice, 2005.*

Christianity > Literature of Later Periods

Bunyan, John   **PR3317**
The Pilgrim's Progress. Trade Cloth. Hendrickson Publishers,
Inc. Peabody, MA. 2004. 288p. ISBN:1-56563-134-X, ISBN13:
978-1-56563-134-2. Dewey:823/.4.

Audience: **g,l,u,f.**

Bunyan, John   **BR75.B73 1976**
The Miscellaneous Works of John Bunyan: The Doctrine of the
Law and Grace Unfolded and I Will Pray with the Spirit.
Richard L. Greaves (Editor). Trade Cloth. Oxford University
Press, Inc. New York, NY. 1976. 348p. Oxford English Texts
ISBN:0-19-811871-6, ISBN13: 978-0-19-811871-8.
Dewey:823/.4. LCCN:77-351855.

Audience: **u,f.** B

Bunyan, John   **BR75.B73 1976**
The Miscellaneous Works of John Bunyan: The Poems. E. G.
Midgley (Editor). Trade Cloth. Oxford University Press, Inc.
New York, NY. 1980. 408p. Oxford English Texts
ISBN:0-19-812734-0, ISBN13: 978-0-19-812734-5.
Dewey:823/.4. LCCN:79-040422.

Audience: **u,f.** B

Erasmus, Desiderius   **BX1749.E73 1983**
The Essential Erasmus. John P. Dolan (Translator). Trade Paper.
Penguin Group (USA) Inc. New York, NY. 1964. 400p.
Essentials Ser. ISBN:0-452-00972-3, ISBN13:
978-0-452-00972-1. Dewey:230/.2. LCCN:93-034751.

Audience: **g,l,u.**

Gardiner, Harold   **BV4832.2**
  (Photographer)
The Imitation of Christ. Thomas à Kempis (Contribution by).
Trade Cloth. Doubleday Publishing. New York, NY. 1976.
ISBN:0-385-12313-2, ISBN13: 978-0-385-12313-6. Dewey:242.

Audience: **g,l,u.**

Kierkegaard, Soren   **BR121**
Attack upon Christendom. Walter Lowrie (Translator), H. A.
Johnson (Introduction by). Trade Paper. Princeton University
Press. Princeton, NJ. 1968. 304p. ISBN:0-691-01950-9, ISBN13:
978-0-691-01950-5. Dewey:230.

Audience: **g,l,u,f.**

Christianity > Dictionaries. Encyclopedias

Bowden, John, John   **BR95.E47 2005**
  (Editor)
Encyclopedia of Christianity. Ed. 3. Saddle Stitched, Cloth over
Boards, Dust Jacket. Oxford University Press, Inc. New York,
NY. 2005. 1408p. ISBN:0-19-522393-4, ISBN13:
978-0-19-522393-4. Dewey:230/.003. LCCN:2005-048801.

Audience: **g,l,u,f.** *Choice, 2006.*

Cross, F. L. & Livingstone,   **BR95**
   E. A. (Editors)
The Oxford Dictionary of the Christian Church. Ed. 3. Trade
Cloth. Oxford University Press, Inc. New York, NY. 2005.
1,840p. ISBN:0-19-280290-9, ISBN13: 978-0-19-280290-3.
Dewey:270.03. LCCN:2005-282601.
                  Audience: **g,l,u,f.** *Choice, 2006.*

Fahlbusch, Erwin (Editor)   **BR95**
The Encyclopedia of Christianity, Vol. 4. Trade Cloth. Brill
Academic Publishers, Inc. Boston, MA. 2005.
ISBN:90-04-14595-8, ISBN13: 978-90-04-14595-5.
Dewey:230/.003.
                  Audience: **u,f.**

Fahlbusch, Erwin (Editor),   **BR95.E8913 1999**
   et al.
The Encyclopedia of Christianity: (A-D). Geoffrey W. Bromiley
& David B. Barrett (Editors). Trade Cloth. William B. Eerdmans
Publishing Company. Grand Rapids, MI. 1998. 912p. Eerdmans
Encyclopedia of Christianity Ser., Vol. 1 ISBN:0-8028-2413-7,
ISBN13: 978-0-8028-2413-4. Dewey:230/.003
LCCN:98-045953.
                  Audience: **u,f.** *Choice, 1999.*

Fahlbusch, Erwin (Editor),   **BR1**
   et al.
The Encyclopedia of Christianity: (J-O). Geoffrey W. Bromiley,
Jaroslav Pelikan, Jan Milie Lochman, John Mbiti, Lukas Vischer
& David B. Barrett (Editors), Geoffrey W. Bromiley
(Translator). Trade Cloth. William B. Eerdmans Publishing
Company. Grand Rapids, MI. 2003. 918p. Encyclopedia of
Christianity Ser., 3 ISBN:0-8028-2415-3, ISBN13:
978-0-8028-2415-8. Dewey:230/.003. LCCN:98-045953.
                  Audience: **u,f.**

Fahlbusch, Erwin (Editor),   **BR95**
   et al.
Encyclopedia of Christianity: E-I, Vol. 2. Jan Milic Lochman,
John S. Mbiti, Jaroslav Pelikan, Lukas Vischer, Geoffrey W.
Bromiley & David B. Barrett (Editors), Geoffrey W. Bromiley
(Translator). Trade Cloth. Brill Academic Publishers. Leiden,
2001. xxxii,788p. Biblical Studies and Religious Studies
ISBN:90-04-11695-8, ISBN13: 978-90-04-11695-5.
Dewey:230.003. LCCN:98-045953.
                  Audience: **u,f.**

Hastings, Adrian (Editor), et   **BR95.O94 2000**
   al.
The Oxford Companion to Christian Thought. Alistair Mason &
Hugh S. Pyper (Editors). Trade Cloth. Oxford University Press,
Inc. New York, NY. 2000. 808p. ISBN:0-19-860024-0, ISBN13:
978-0-19-860024-4. Dewey:230/.03. LCCN:2001-267818.
                  Audience: **u,f.** *Choice, 2001.*

McGrath, Alister E. (Editor,   **BR95.B58 1993**
   Introduction by)
The Blackwell Encyclopedia of Modern Christian Thought.
Trade Cloth. Blackwell Publishing, Inc. Malden, MA. 1993.
720p. ISBN:0-631-16896-6, ISBN13: 978-0-631-16896-6.
Dewey:230/.09/03. LCCN:93-012925.
                  Audience: **g,l,u,f.** *Choice, 1994.*

Rahner, Karl & Vorgrimler,   **BR95.R313 1981**
   Herbert
Dictionary of Theology. Ed. 2. Trade Cloth. Crossroad
Publishing Company. New York, NY. 1981. 500p.
ISBN:0-8245-0040-7, ISBN13: 978-0-8245-0040-5.
Dewey:230/.2/0321. LCCN:81-005492.
                  Audience: **g,l,u,f.** ℬ

Richardson, Alan &   **BR95.W494 1983**
   Bowden, John (Editors)
The Westminster Dictionary of Christian Theology. Trade Cloth.
Westminster John Knox Press. Louisville, KY. 1983. 632p.
ISBN:0-664-21398-7, ISBN13: 978-0-664-21398-5.
Dewey:230/.03. LCCN:83-014521.
                  Audience: **u,f.** ℬ

Christianity > Philosophy and Psychology

Feenstra, Ronald &   **BT113.T75 1989**
   Plantinga, Cornelius Jr.
Trinity, Incarnation, and Atonement: Philosophical and
Theological Essays. Cloth Text. University of Notre Dame
Press. Notre Dame, IN. 1990. Library of Religious Philosophy
ISBN:0-268-01870-7, ISBN13: 978-0-268-01870-2. Dewey:230.
LCCN:89-040386.
                  Audience: **u,f.**

Ganssle, Gregory E. &   **BT153.I47.G64 2002**
   Woodruff, David M. (Editors)
God and Time: Essays on the Divine Nature. Trade Cloth.
Oxford University Press, Inc. New York, NY. 2001. 268p.
ISBN:0-19-512965-2, ISBN13: 978-0-19-512965-6.
Dewey:212/.7. LCCN:00-068152.
                  Audience: **u,f.**

Howard-Snyder, Daniel   **BT160.E94 1996**
   (Editor)
The Evidential Argument from Evil. Trade Cloth. Indiana
University Press. Bloomington, IN. 1996. 384p. Indiana
University Series in the Philosophy of Religion
ISBN:0-253-32965-5, ISBN13: 978-0-253-32965-3. Dewey:214.
LCCN:95-011208.
                  Audience: **u,f.**

Jung, C. G.   **BR110.J84 1999**
Jung on Christianity. Murray Stein (Editor). Trade Paper.
Princeton University Press. Princeton, NJ. 1999. 292p.
Encountering Jung Ser. ISBN:0-691-00697-0, ISBN13:
978-0-691-00697-0. Dewey:230. LCCN:99-028902.
                  Audience: **u,f.**

Kierkegaard, Soren   **BR100.K52 2006**
Fear and Trembling. Alastair Hannay (Translator). Trade Paper.
Penguin Group (USA) Inc. New York, NY. 2006. 160p. Penguin
Great Ideas Ser. ISBN:0-14-303757-9, ISBN13:
978-0-14-303757-6. Dewey:498/.9. LCCN:2006-043992.
                  Audience: **g,l,u,f.**

Kierkegaard, Soren   **B4373.A472E5 1992**
Concluding Unscientific Postscripts to Philosophical Fragments,
Vol. II. Howard V. Hong & Edna H. Hong (Edited and
Translated by). Trade Paper. Princeton University Press.
Princeton, NJ. 1992. 376p. Kierkegaard's Writings, XII, XII
ISBN:0-691-02082-5, ISBN13: 978-0-691-02082-2.
Dewey:230/.01. LCCN:91-004093.
                                 Audience: **g,u,f.** *Choice, 1993.*

Kierkegaard, Soren   **B4373.A472E5 1992**
Concluding Unscientific Postscripts to Philosophical Fragments,
Vol. I. Howard V. Hong & Edna H. Hong (Editors), Howard V.
Hong & Edna H. Hong (Translators). Trade Cloth. Princeton
University Press. Princeton, NJ. 1992. 650p. Kierkegaard's
Writings, XII, XII ISBN:0-691-07395-3, ISBN13:
978-0-691-07395-8. Dewey:230/.01. LCCN:91-004093.
                                 Audience: **g,u,f.** *Choice, 1993.*

Leftow, Brian & Davies,   **BX1749**
  Brian (Editors)
Aquinas: Summa of Theology, Questions on God. Karl Ameriks
& Desmond M. Clarke (Contribution by). Cloth Text.
Cambridge University Press. New York, NY. 2006. 342p.
Cambridge Texts in the History of Philosophy Ser.
ISBN:0-521-82140-1, ISBN13: 978-0-521-82140-7. Dewey:231.
                                 Audience: **g,l,u,f.**

Moser, Paul K. & Copan,   **BD555.R38 2003**
  Paul (Editors)
The Rationality of Theism. Paper over Boards. Routledge. New
York, NY. 2003. 304p. ISBN:0-415-26331-X, ISBN13:
978-0-415-26331-3. Dewey:211/.3. LCCN:2002-038166.
                                 Audience: **g,u,f.** *Choice, 2004.*

Newman, John Henry   **BR100.N4 1984**
An Essay in Aid of a Grammar of Assent. Ian Ker (Editor,
Introduction by). Cloth Text. Oxford University Press, Inc. New
York, NY. 1985. 480p. ISBN:0-19-812751-0, ISBN13:
978-0-19-812751-2. Dewey:233. LCCN:84-007923.
                                 Audience: **g,u,f.** *Choice, 1986.*

Pascal, Blaise   **BX1751.2**
Pensees and Other Writings. Honor Levi (Translator), Anthony
Levi (Translator, Introduction by, Notes by). Trade Paper.
Oxford University Press, Inc. New York, NY. 1999. 312p.
Oxford World's Classics Ser. ISBN:0-19-283655-2, ISBN13:
978-0-19-283655-7. Dewey:230.2.
                                 Audience: **g,l,u,f.**

Plantinga, Alvin   **BT1102.P57 2000**
Warranted Christian Belief. Trade Cloth. Oxford University
Press, Inc. New York, NY. 2000. 528p. ISBN:0-19-513192-4,
ISBN13: 978-0-19-513192-5. Dewey:230/.01. LCCN:98-054362.
                                 Audience: **u,f.** *Choice, 2000.*

Swinburne, Richard   **BT102**
The Existence of God. Ed. 2. Trade Cloth. Oxford University
Press, Inc. New York, NY. 2004. 376p. ISBN:0-19-927167-4,
ISBN13: 978-0-19-927167-2. Dewey:212/.1.
LCCN:2004-555474.
                                 Audience: **u,f.**

Westphal, Merold   **BR128.A8W47 1998**
Suspicion and Faith: The Religious Uses of Modern Atheism.
Kelly J. Clark (Introduction by). Trade Paper. Fordham
University Press. Bronx, NY. 1999. 296p. ISBN:0-8232-1876-7,
ISBN13: 978-0-8232-1876-9. Dewey:261.2/1. LCCN:98-028456.
                                 Audience: **u,f.** *Choice, 1993.*

Christianity > Christianity: Relation to Other Topics

Bebbington, David   **D16.8**
Patterns in History: A Christian Perspective on Historical
Thought. Trade Paper. Regent College Publishing. Vancouver,
BC. 1990. 219p. ISBN:1-57383-153-0, ISBN13:
978-1-57383-153-6. Dewey:901.
                                 Audience: **g,l,u,f.**

Bradshaw, Timothy (Editor)   **BX5131.3.W39 2004**
The Way Forward?: Christian Voices on Homosexuality and the
Church. Ed. 2. Trade Paper. William B. Eerdmans Publishing
Company. Grand Rapids, MI. 2004. 256p. ISBN:0-8028-2777-2,
ISBN13: 978-0-8028-2777-7. Dewey:261.8/35766.
LCCN:2004-540794.
                                 Audience: **g,l,u,f.**

Cole-Turner, Ronald   **QH442.B49 2001**
  (Editor)
Beyond Cloning: Religion and the Remaking of Humanity.
Trade Paper. Continuum International Publishing Group, Ltd.
London, 2001. 160p. ISBN:1-56338-317-9, ISBN13:
978-1-56338-317-5. Dewey:261.5/5. LCCN:00-047680.
                                 Audience: **g,l,u,f.**

Colson, Charles W. &   **TP248.6.H85 2004**
  Cameron, Nigel M. de S. (Editors)
Human Dignity in the Biotech Century: A Christian Vision for
Public Policy. Trade Paper. InterVarsity Press. Downers Grove,
IL. 2004. 252p. ISBN:0-8308-2783-8, ISBN13:
978-0-8308-2783-1. Dewey:241/.64957. LCCN:2004-006654.
                                 Audience: **g,l,u,f.**

Gamwell, Franklin I.   **BR115.P7G315 2004**
Politics as a Christian Vocation: Faith and Democracy Today.
Trade Cloth. Cambridge University Press. New York, NY. 2004.
198p. ISBN:0-521-83876-2, ISBN13: 978-0-521-83876-4.
Dewey:261.7. LCCN:2004-045101.
                                 Audience: **g,l,u,f.** *Choice, 2005.*

Hill, Jonathan   **BR115.C5H54 2005**
What Has Christianity Ever Done for Us?: How It Shaped the
Modern World. Saddle Stitched, Cloth over Boards, Dust Jacket.
InterVarsity Press. Downers Grove, IL. 2005. 192p.
ISBN:0-8308-3328-5, ISBN13: 978-0-8308-3328-3. Dewey:270.
LCCN:2005-012103.
                                 Audience: **g,l,u,f.**

Lynch, Gordon   **BR115.C8L96 2004**
Understanding Theology and Popular Culture. Trade Cloth.
Blackwell Publishing, Inc. Malden, MA. 2004. 256p.

ISBN:1-4051-1747-8, ISBN13: 978-1-4051-1747-0. Dewey:261. LCCN:2004-009788.

Audience: **l,u,f.** *Choice, 2005.*

Maddox, Graham   **BR115.P7M3167 1996**
Religion and the Rise of Democracy. Paper over Boards. Routledge. New York, NY. 1996. 304p. ISBN:0-415-02603-2, ISBN13: 978-0-415-02603-1. Dewey:291.1/785. LCCN:95-019599.

Audience: **g,l,u,f.** *Choice, 1997.*

Manson, Neil A. (Editor)   **BD541.G63 2003**
God and Design: The Teleological Argument and Modern Science. Paper over Boards. Routledge. New York, NY. 2003. 400p. ISBN:0-415-26343-3, ISBN13: 978-0-415-26343-6. Dewey:212/.1. LCCN:2002-027548.

Audience: **u,f.**

McLellan, John   **BR115.P7**
Political Christianity - P. Trade Cloth. SPCK Publishing. London, 256p. ISBN:0-281-04921-1, ISBN13: 978-0-281-04921-9. Dewey:261.7.

Audience: **l,u,f.**

Newbigin, Lesslie   **BR115.C8N468 1989**
The Gospel in a Pluralist Society. Trade Paper. William B. Eerdmans Publishing Company. Grand Rapids, MI. 1989. 255p. ISBN:0-8028-0426-8, ISBN13: 978-0-8028-0426-6. Dewey:261. LCCN:89-035973.

Audience: **l,u,f.**

Niebuhr, Helmut Richard   **BR115.C8N5 2001**
Christ and Culture. Martin E. Marty (Foreword by), James Gustafson (Preface by). Trade Paper. HarperCollins Publishers. New York, NY. 1956. 320p. ISBN:0-06-130003-9, ISBN13: 978-0-06-130003-5. Dewey:261. LCCN:2002-284347.

Audience: **g,l,u,f.**

Polkinghorne, John   **BL240.3.P64 2005**
Exploring Reality: The Intertwining of Science and Religion. Cloth over Boards. Yale University Press. Cumberland, RI. 2005. 208p. ISBN:0-300-11014-6, ISBN13: 978-0-300-11014-2. Dewey:261.5/5. LCCN:2005-012580.

Audience: **g,u,f.**

Polkinghorne, John C.   **BL241.P563 2000**
Faith, Science and Understanding. Cloth over Boards. Yale University Press. Cumberland, RI. 2000. 224p. ISBN:0-300-08372-6, ISBN13: 978-0-300-08372-9. Dewey:261.5/5. LCCN:00-026934.

Audience: **u,f.**

Sanneh, Lamin   **BR115.C8S26 1993**
Encountering the West: Christianity and the Global Cultural Process. Trade Cloth. Orbis Books. Maryknoll, NY. 1993. 225p. World Christian Theology Ser. ISBN:0-88344-929-3, ISBN13: 978-0-88344-929-5. Dewey:261. LCCN:93-029939.

Audience: **u,f.**

Sedgwick, Peter H.   **BR115.C3 S43 1999**
The Market Economy and Christian Ethics. Stephen R. L. Clark, Robin Gill, Stanley Hauerwas & Robin W. Lovin (Contribution by). Trade Cloth. Cambridge University Press. New York, NY. 1999. 338p. New Studies in Christian Ethics, No. 14 ISBN:0-521-47048-X, ISBN13: 978-0-521-47048-3. Dewey:261.85. LCCN:98-053577.

Audience: **u,f.** *Choice, 2000.*

Tanner, Kathryn   **BT738**
The Politics of God: Christian Theologies and Social Justice. Trade Paper. Augsburg Fortress, Publishers. Minneapolis, MN. 2003. 272p. ISBN:0-8006-2613-3, ISBN13: 978-0-8006-2613-6. Dewey:261.8. LCCN:92-019360.

Audience: **l,u,f.**

Thiessen, Gesa Elsbeth   **BR115.A8**
  (Editor)
Theological Aesthetics: A Reader. Trade Cloth. William B. Eerdmans Publishing Company. Grand Rapids, MI. 2004. 416p. ISBN:0-8028-2888-4, ISBN13: 978-0-8028-2888-0. Dewey:261.57.

Audience: **l,u,f.**

older eds **Weber, Max M.**   **BR115.C3W413 2003**
The Protestant Ethic and the Spirit of Capitalism. Talcott Parsons (Translator). Trade Paper. Dover Publications, Inc. Mineola, NY. 2003. 320p. American Indians Ser. ISBN:0-486-42703-X, ISBN13: 978-0-486-42703-4. Dewey:306.6. LCCN:2002-041124.

Audience: **l,u,f.** *Choice, 2002.*

Wolterstorff, Nicholas   **BR115.A8**
Art in Action: Toward a Christian Aesthetic. Trade Paper. William B. Eerdmans Publishing Company. Grand Rapids, MI. 1987. 250p. ISBN:0-8028-1816-1, ISBN13: 978-0-8028-1816-4. Dewey:700/.1.

Audience: **g,l,u,f.**

Christianity > Christianity: General Works

Barth, Karl   **BR121**
The Word of God and the Word of Man. Douglas Horton (Translator). Trade Cloth. Peter Smith Publisher, Inc. Magnolia, MA. 1958. ISBN:0-8446-1599-4, ISBN13: 978-0-8446-1599-8. Dewey:230.04.

Audience: **g,l,u,f.** *B*

Chesterton, Gilbert K.   **BR121 .C5**
Orthodoxy. Trade Cloth. Hendrickson Publishers, Inc. Peabody, MA. 2006. 176p. ISBN:1-59856-051-4, ISBN13: 978-1-59856-051-0. Dewey:239.

Audience: **g,l,u,f.**

Jenkins, Philip   **BR121.3.J46 2002**
The Next Christendom: The Coming of Global Christianity. Trade Cloth. Oxford University Press, Inc. New York, NY. 2002.

288p. ISBN:0-19-514616-6, ISBN13: 978-0-19-514616-5. Dewey:270.8/30112. LCCN:2001-047554.

Audience: **g,l,u,f.** *Choice, 2003.*

Lewis, C. S.   **BR125.L67 2000**
The Screwtape Letters. Trade Cloth. HarperCollins Publishers. New York, NY. 2001. 160p. C. S. Lewis Signature Classics ISBN:0-06-065289-6, ISBN13: 978-0-06-065289-0. Dewey:248.4. LCCN:00-049860.

Audience: **g,l,u,f.**

Lewis, C. S. (Editor,   **BT77**
Compiled by)
Mere Christianity. Ed. 50. Trade Cloth. HarperCollins Publishers. New York, NY. 2001. 256p. ISBN:0-00-713186-0, ISBN13: 978-0-00-713186-0. Dewey:230/.

Audience: **g,l,u,f.** *B*

Locke, John   **BR120**
The Reasonableness of Christianity, with A Discourse of Miracles, and Part of a Third Letter Concerning Toleration. Paper Text. Textbook Publishers. Temecula, CA. 2003. 102p. ISBN:0-7581-3514-9, ISBN13: 978-0-7581-3514-8. Dewey:230.

Audience: **g,l,u,f.** *B*

McGrath, Alister E.   **BR121.3.M33 2006**
Christianity: An Introduction. Ed. 2. Trade Cloth. Blackwell Publishing, Inc. Malden, MA. 2006. 396p. ISBN:1-4051-0901-7, ISBN13: 978-1-4051-0901-7. Dewey:230. LCCN:2005-012639.

Audience: **g,l,u.**

McGrath, Alister E.   **BR121.3.M34 2001**
The Future of Christianity. Trade Paper. Blackwell Publishing, Inc. Malden, MA. 2001. 184p. Manifestos Ser. ISBN:0-631-22815-2, ISBN13: 978-0-631-22815-8. Dewey:270.8/3/0112. LCCN:2001-002624.

Audience: **g,l,u.** *Choice, 2002.*

Ward, Keith   **BT77**
Christianity: A Short Introduction. Trade Cloth. Oneworld Publications. Oxford, 2000. 192p. From Buddhism to Sufism Ser., :Concise Introductions Ser. ISBN:1-85168-229-5, ISBN13: 978-1-85168-229-4. Dewey:230.

Audience: **g,l,u.**

Christianity > Christianity and Other Religions

D'Costa, Gavin   **BR127.D39 2000**
The Meeting of Religions and the Trinity. Trade Paper. Orbis Books. Maryknoll, NY. 2000. 187p. Faith Meets Faith Ser. ISBN:1-57075-303-2, ISBN13: 978-1-57075-303-9. Dewey:261.2. LCCN:00-026620.

Audience: **u,f.**

Dupuis, Jacques   **BT83.85.D87 2002**
Christianity and the Religions: From Encounter to Dialogue. Phillip Berryman & Geraldine Tomlin (Translators). Trade

Paper. Orbis Books. Maryknoll, NY. 2002. 300p. ISBN:1-57075-440-3, ISBN13: 978-1-57075-440-1. Dewey:261.2. LCCN:2002-010234.

Audience: **l,u,f.**

Ferguson, Everett (Editor)   **BR128.G8C48 1999**
Christianity in Relation to Jews, Greeks and Romans. Cloth Text. Garland Publishing, Inc. New York, NY. 1999. 350p. Recent Studies in Early Christianity, Vol. 2 ISBN:0-8153-3069-3, ISBN13: 978-0-8153-3069-1. Dewey:261.2. LCCN:99-024676.

Audience: **l,u,f.**

Harris-Shapiro, Carol   **BR158**
Messianic Judaism: A Rabbi's Journey Through Religious Change in America. Trade Paper. Beacon Press. Boston, MA. 2000. 232p. ISBN:0-8070-1041-3, ISBN13: 978-0-8070-1041-9. Dewey:289.9. LCCN:98-054864.

Audience: **g,l,u,f.**

Hick, John   **BL48**
An Interpretation of Religion: Human Responses to the Transcendent. Ed. 2. Trade Paper. Yale University Press. Cumberland, RI. 2005. 464p. ISBN:0-300-10668-8, ISBN13: 978-0-300-10668-8. Dewey:200.

Audience: **u,f.** *Choice, 1989.*

Kraemer, H. (Hendrik   **BR121**
Why Christianity of all religions? Translated by Hubert Hoskins. Philadelphia, Westminster Press. 1962.

Audience: **g,l,u,f.**

Tennent, Timothy C.   **BR127.T46 2002**
Christianity at the Religious Roundtable: Evangelicalism in Conversation with Hinduism, Buddhism, and Islam. Trade Paper. Baker Academic. Ada, MI. 2002. 272p. ISBN:0-8010-2602-4, ISBN13: 978-0-8010-2602-7. Dewey:261.2. LCCN:2002-021569.

Audience: **g,l,u,f.**

Christianity > Church History > General History. Historiography

Bettenson, Henry &   **BR141.D63 1999**
Maunder, Chris (Editors)
1963 ed. Documents of the Christian Church. Ed. 3. Paper Text. Oxford University Press, Inc. New York, NY. 1999. 488p. ISBN:0-19-288071-3, ISBN13: 978-0-19-288071-0. Dewey:270. LCCN:00-267728.

Audience: **g,l,u,f.**

Bradley, James E. & Muller,   **BR138.B69 1995**
Richard A.
Church History: An Introduction to Research, Reference Works, and Methods. Trade Paper. William B. Eerdmans Publishing Company. Grand Rapids, MI. 1995. 252p. ISBN:0-8028-0826-3, ISBN13: 978-0-8028-0826-4. Dewey:270/.072. LCCN:94-040617.

Audience: **g,l,u,f.** *Choice, 1996.*

Chadwick, Owen   **BL2525**
A History of Christianity. Trade Paper. St. Martin's Press.
Gordonville, VA. 1998. 304p. ISBN:0-312-18723-8, ISBN13:
978-0-312-18723-1. Dewey:209.

Audience: **g,l.**

Day, Peter   **BR157**
Dictionary of Christian Denominations. Trade Cloth. Continuum
International Publishing Group, Ltd. London, 2003. 528p.
ISBN:0-8264-5745-2, ISBN13: 978-0-8264-5745-5.
Dewey:280/.03. LCCN:2003-273608.

Audience: **g,l,u,f.**

Dowley, Tim (Editor)   **BR145.3.I58 2002**
Introduction to the History of Christianity. Trade Cloth.
Augsburg Fortress, Publishers. Minneapolis, MN. 2004. 688p.
ISBN:0-8006-3496-9, ISBN13: 978-0-8006-3496-4. Dewey:270.
LCCN:2004-298883.

Audience: **g,l,u.**

González, Justo L.   **BR138.G66 2002**
The Changing Shape of Church History. Trade Cloth. Chalice
Press. Saint Louis, MO. 2005. vii, 159p. ISBN:0-8272-0490-6,
ISBN13: 978-0-8272-0490-4. Dewey:270/.7/2.
LCCN:2002-007782.

Audience: **u,f.**

González, Justo L.   **BR142.G66**
The Early Church to the Reformation. Trade Paper.
HarperCollins Publishers. New York, NY. 1984. 448p. Story of
Christianity Ser., Vol. 1 ISBN:0-06-063315-8, ISBN13:
978-0-06-063315-8. Dewey:270. LCCN:83-048430.

Audience: **g,l,u.**

González, Justo L.   **BR142.G66**
The Reformation to the Present Day. Trade Paper. HarperCollins
Publishers. New York, NY. 1985. 432p. Story of Christianity
Ser., Vol. II ISBN:0-06-063316-6, ISBN13: 978-0-06-063316-5.
Dewey:270. LCCN:83-049187.

Audience: **g,l,u.**

Hastings, Adrian (Editor)   **BR145.2**
A World History of Christianity. Trade Paper. William B.
Eerdmans Publishing Company. Grand Rapids, MI. 2000. 608p.
ISBN:0-8028-4875-3, ISBN13: 978-0-8028-4875-8. Dewey:270.

Audience: **g,l,u.**

Irvin, Dale T. & Sunquist,   **BR145.3.I78 2001**
  Scott W.
History of the World Christian Movement: Earliest Christianity
to 1453. Trade Paper. Orbis Books. Maryknoll, NY. 2001. 512p.
ISBN:1-57075-396-2, ISBN13: 978-1-57075-396-1. Dewey:270.
LCCN:2001-041424.

Audience: **g,l,u.** *Choice, 2002.*

McManners, John (Editor)   **BR145.2**
The Oxford History of Christianity. Ed. 2. Trade Paper. Oxford
University Press, Inc. New York, NY. 2002. 784p.
ISBN:0-19-280336-0, ISBN13: 978-0-19-280336-8. Dewey:270.
LCCN:2003-270086.

Audience: **g,l,u,f.**

Noll, Mark A.   **BR145.2.N65 2000**
Turning Points: Decisive Moments in the History of Christianity.
Ed. 2. Trade Paper. Baker Academic. Ada, MI. 2001. 352p.
ISBN:0-8010-6211-X, ISBN13: 978-0-8010-6211-7. Dewey:270.
LCCN:00-057212.

Audience: **u,f.**

Olson, Roger E.   **BT21.2.O57 1999**
The Story of Christian Theology: Twenty Centuries of Tradition
and Reform. Trade Cloth. InterVarsity Press. Downers Grove,
IL. 1999. 652p. ISBN:0-8308-1505-8, ISBN13:
978-0-8308-1505-0. Dewey:230/.09. LCCN:99-018734.

Audience: **u,f.** *Choice, 2000.*

Schaff, Philip   **BR145.S3 1996**
e-book History of the Christian Church, Set. Ed. 3. Box or Slipcased.
Hendrickson Publishers, Inc. Peabody, MA. 1996. 7120p.
ISBN:1-56563-196-X, ISBN13: 978-1-56563-196-0. Dewey:270.
LCCN:96-028348.

Audience: **u,f.** **B**

Williams, Rowan   **BV600.3 .W55**
Why Study the Past?: The Quest for the Historical Church.
Trade Paper, Perfect. William B. Eerdmans Publishing
Company. Grand Rapids, MI. 2005. 129p. ISBN:0-8028-2990-2,
ISBN13: 978-0-8028-2990-0. Dewey:270.

Audience: **u,f.**

Christianity > Church History > Origins to 600

Bock, Darrell L.   **BT1391.B63 2006**
The Missing Gospels: Unearthing the Truth Behind Alternative
Christianities. Trade Cloth. Thomas Nelson Inc. Nashville, TN.
2006. 256p. ISBN:0-7852-1294-9, ISBN13: 978-0-7852-1294-2.
Dewey:270.1. LCCN:2006-001318.

Audience: **g,l,u,f.**

Brown, Peter   **BR195.C45B76 1988**
The Body and Society: Men, Women, and Sexual Renunciation
in Early Christianity. Trade Cloth. Columbia University Press.
New York, NY. 1988. 504p. Lectures on the History of
Religions Ser., No. 13 ISBN:0-231-06100-5, ISBN13:
978-0-231-06100-1. Dewey:241.6/6. LCCN:87-030941.

Audience: **u,f.** *Choice, 1989.*

Brown, Peter   **BX2333 .B74**
The Cult of the Saints: Its Rise and Function in Latin
Christianity. Trade Paper. University of Chicago Press. Chicago,
IL. 1982. 204p. The Haskell Lectures, Vol. 2
ISBN:0-226-07622-9, ISBN13: 978-0-226-07622-5.
Dewey:270.2. LCCN:80-011210.

Audience: **u,f.**

Cameron, Averil   **BR67.C26 1991**
Christianity and the Rhetoric of Empire: The Development of
Christian Discourse. Trade Cloth. University of California Press.
Berkeley, CA. 1991. 275p. Sather Classical Lectures, No. 55

ISBN:0-520-07160-3, ISBN13: 978-0-520-07160-5.
Dewey:270.1. LCCN:90-039376.

Audience: **u,f.** *Choice, 1992.*

Chadwick, Henry   **BR145.2**
The Early Church. Trade Paper. Penguin Group (USA) Inc. New
York, NY. 1993. 320p. Hist of the Church Ser.
ISBN:0-14-023199-4, ISBN13: 978-0-14-023199-1. Dewey:270.

Audience: **g,l.**

Clark, Elizabeth Ann   **BR195.W6C574 1990**
Women in the Early Church. Thomas Halton (Editor). Trade
Paper. Liturgical Press. Collegeville, MN. 2005. 264p. Message
of the Fathers of the Church Ser., Vol. 13 ISBN:0-8146-5332-4,
ISBN13: 978-0-8146-5332-6. Dewey:261.8/344/09015.
LCCN:83-081477.

Audience: **g,l,u.**

Davis, Stephen J.   **BR1720.T33D38 2001**
The Cult of Saint Thecla: A Tradition of Women's Piety in Late
Antiquity. Trade Cloth. Oxford University Press, Inc. New York,
NY. 2001. 302p. Oxford Early Christian Studies
ISBN:0-19-827019-4, ISBN13: 978-0-19-827019-5.
Dewey:270.1/092. LCCN:00-040060.

Audience: **u,f.**

Ehrman, Bart D.   **BS2840.E4 2005**
Lost Christianities: The Battles for Scripture and the Faiths We
Never Knew. Trade Paper, Perfect. Oxford University Press, Inc.
New York, NY. 2005. 309p. ISBN:0-19-518249-9, ISBN13:
978-0-19-518249-1. Dewey:229/.9206.

Audience: **g,l,u,f.** *Choice, 2004.*

Ehrman, Bart D.   **BS2832.E37 2005**
Lost Scriptures: Books That Did Not Make It into the New
Testament. Trade Paper, Perfect. Oxford University Press, Inc.
New York, NY. 2005. 348p. ISBN:0-19-518250-2, ISBN13:
978-0-19-518250-7. Dewey:229.9205209.

Audience: **g,l,u,f.** *Choice, 2004.*

Ferguson, Everett   **BR129**
Backgrounds of Early Christianity. Ed. 3. Trade Paper. William
B. Eerdmans Publishing Company. Grand Rapids, MI. 2003.
648p. ISBN:0-8028-2221-5, ISBN13: 978-0-8028-2221-5.
Dewey:270.1. LCCN:2003-278233.

Audience: **g,l,u.**

Ferguson, Everett (Editor),   **BR162.2.E53 1997**
1990 **et al.**
ed Encyclopedia of Early Christianity. Ed. 2. Frederick W. Norris
& Michael P. McHugh (Editors). Trade Cloth. Garland
Publishing, Inc. New York, NY. 1997. 1212p.
ISBN:0-8153-1663-1, ISBN13: 978-0-8153-1663-3.
Dewey:270.1/03. LCCN:96-036865.

Audience: **g,l,u,f.** *Choice, 1997, 1990.*

Fioerenza, Elisabeth S.   **BR129.S365 1994**
In Memory of Her: A Feminist Theological Reconstruction of
Christian Origins. Ed. 10. Trade Paper. FaithWorks. Brentwood,
TN. 1994. 357p. ISBN:0-8245-1357-6, ISBN13:
978-0-8245-1357-3. Dewey:270.1/082. LCCN:94-003371.

Audience: **g,l,u.**

Frend, W. H.   **BR165**
The Rise of Christianity. Trade Paper. Augsburg Fortress,
Publishers. Minneapolis, MN. 1984. 1026p.
ISBN:0-8006-1931-5, ISBN13: 978-0-8006-1931-2.
Dewey:270.1. LCCN:83-048909.

Audience: **g,l,u.**

Gamble, Harry Y.   **BR67.2**
Books and Readers in the Early Church: A History of Early
Christian Texts. Trade Paper. Yale University Press. Cumberland,
RI. 1997. 352p. ISBN:0-300-06918-9, ISBN13:
978-0-300-06918-1. Dewey:002/.0901.

Audience: **g,l,u,f.** *Choice, 1996.*

Horsley, Richard A. (Editor)   **BR160.C47 2005**
Christian Origins: A People's History of Christianity. Trade
Paper. Augsburg Fortress, Publishers. Minneapolis, MN. 2005.
256p. A People's History of Christianity Ser., Vol. 1
ISBN:0-8006-3411-X, ISBN13: 978-0-8006-3411-7.
Dewey:270.1. LCCN:2005-024482.

Audience: **g,u,f.** *Choice, 2006.*

Kraemer, Ross S. &   **BR195.W6W63 1999**
D'Angelo, Mary R. (Editors)
Women and Christian Origins. Trade Paper. Oxford University
Press, Inc. New York, NY. 1999. 416p. ISBN:0-19-510396-3,
ISBN13: 978-0-19-510396-0. Dewey:270.1082.
LCCN:98-005780.

Audience: **u,f.**

Krautheimer, Richard   **NA950**
1965 Early Christian and Byzantine Architecture. Ed. 4. Trade Paper.
ed Yale University Press. Cumberland, RI. 1984. 553p. Pelican
History of Art Ser. ISBN:0-300-05294-4, ISBN13:
978-0-300-05294-7. Dewey:723.1.

Audience: **g,l,u,f.** *B*

MacMullen, Ramsay &   **BR128.R7**
Lane, Eugene N. (Editors)
Paganism and Christianity, 100-425 C. E.: A Sourcebook. Trade
Paper. Augsburg Fortress, Publishers. Minneapolis, MN. 2003.
224p. ISBN:0-8006-2647-8, ISBN13: 978-0-8006-2647-1.
Dewey:270.1. LCCN:92-003069.

Audience: **g,l,u.**

Mathews, Thomas F.   **N7832.M36 1999**
The Clash of Gods: A Reinterpretation of Early Christian Art.
Ed. 2. Trade Paper. Princeton University Press. Princeton, NJ.
1999. 250p. ISBN:0-691-00939-2, ISBN13: 978-0-691-00939-1.
Dewey:709.0212. LCCN:98-051583.

Audience: **u,f.** *Choice, 1994.*

Stevenson   **BR205**
Creeds, Councils, and Controversies. Ed. 2. Trade Cloth. SPCK
Publishing. London, 2000. 432p. ISBN:0-281-04327-2, ISBN13:
978-0-281-04327-9. Dewey:270.2.

Audience: **l,u.**

Stevenson   **BR165**
New Eusebius. Ed. 2. Trade Cloth. SPCK Publishing. London, 432p. ISBN:0-281-04268-3, ISBN13: 978-0-281-04268-5. Dewey:270.1.

Audience: **u,f.**

Wilken, Robert L.   **BL2756.W54 2003**
The Christians As the Romans Saw Them. Ed. 2. Trade Paper. Yale University Press. Cumberland, RI. 2003. 238p. ISBN:0-300-09839-1, ISBN13: 978-0-300-09839-6. Dewey:270.1. LCCN:2002-113908.

Audience: **u,f.**

Young, Frances & Mitchell,   **BR165.O66 2006**
   Margaret (Editors)
Cambridge History of Christianity: Origins to Constantine. Cloth Text. Cambridge University Press. New York, NY. 2006. 790p. Cambridge History of Christianity Ser., Vol. 1 ISBN:0-521-81239-9, ISBN13: 978-0-521-81239-9. Dewey:270.1. LCCN:2005-012926.

Audience: **u,f.**

Christianity > Church History > Medieval. Renaissance

Bouwsma, William J.   **CB361**
The Waning of the Renaissance, 1550-1640. Trade Paper. Yale University Press. Cumberland, RI. 2002. 304p. Yale Intellectual History of the West Se Ser. ISBN:0-300-09717-4, ISBN13: 978-0-300-09717-7. Dewey:940.2/1.

Audience: **u,f.** *Choice, 2001.*

Brady, Thomas A. Jr.   **D203.H36 1994**
   (Editor)
Handbook of European History, 1400-1600: Late Middle Ages, Renaissance, and Reformation. Trade Cloth. Brill Academic Publishers, Inc. Boston, MA. 1994. 600p. ISBN:90-04-09760-0, ISBN13: 978-90-04-09760-5. Dewey:940.2. LCCN:94-001290.

Audience: **u,f.** *Choice, 1995.*

Bynum, Caroline W.   **BV4509.5**
Holy Feast and Holy Fast: The Religious Significance of Food to Medieval Women. Trade Paper. University of California Press. Berkeley, CA. 1988. 300p. The New Historicism Ser., No. 1:Studies in Cultural Poetics ISBN:0-520-06329-5, ISBN13: 978-0-520-06329-7. Dewey:248.4/6. LCCN:85-028896.

Audience: **g,u,f.** *Choice, 1987.*

Cohn, Norman   **BR270**
The Pursuit of the Millennium: Revolutionary Millenarians and Mystical Anarchists of the Middle Ages. Trade Paper. Oxford University Press, Inc. New York, NY. 1970. 408p. ISBN:0-19-500456-6, ISBN13: 978-0-19-500456-4. Dewey:236/.3/094.

Audience: **u,f.**

Colish, Marcia   **CB351.C54**
Medieval Foundations of the Western Intellectual Tradition, 400-1400. Trade Paper. Yale University Press. Cumberland, RI.

1999. 400p. Yale Intellectual History of the West Se Ser. ISBN:0-300-07852-8, ISBN13: 978-0-300-07852-7. Dewey:940.

Audience: **u,f.** *Choice, 1998.*

Delumeau, Jean   **BT715.D443 1990**
Sin and Fear: The Emergence of a Western Guilt Culture 13th-18th Centuries. Eric Nicholson (Translator). Trade Cloth. Palgrave Macmillan. New York, NY. 1990. 677p. ISBN:0-312-03582-9, ISBN13: 978-0-312-03582-2. Dewey:241/.3/09. LCCN:89-012421.

Audience: **u,f.**

Huizinga, Johan   **DC33.2.H83 1996**
The Autumn of the Middle Ages. Ulrich H. Mammitzsch & Rodney J. Payton (Translators). Trade Cloth. University of Chicago Press. Chicago, IL. 1996. 490p. ISBN:0-226-35992-1, ISBN13: 978-0-226-35992-2. Dewey:944/.025. LCCN:95-000613.

Audience: **u,f.**

Lynch, Joseph H.   **BR252.L96 1992**
The Medieval Church: A Brief History. Trade Paper. Longman Publishing. Boston, MA. 1995. 400p. ISBN:0-582-49467-2, ISBN13: 978-0-582-49467-1. Dewey:270.094. LCCN:91-045261.

Audience: **l,u,f.**

McGinn, Bernard   **BT876.V58 1998**
Visions of the End: Apocalyptic Traditions in the Middle Ages. Trade Paper. Columbia University Press. New York, NY. 1998. 390p. Records of Civilization: Sources and Studies, Vol. XCVI ISBN:0-231-11257-2, ISBN13: 978-0-231-11257-4. Dewey:236/.09/02. LCCN:99-180823.

Audience: **u,f.**

Oakley, Francis   **BR252.O15 1985**
The Western Church in the Later Middle Ages. Book, Other. Cornell University Press. Ithaca, NY. 1979. 346p. ISBN:0-8014-1208-0, ISBN13: 978-0-8014-1208-0. Dewey:282/.09/023. LCCN:79-007621.

Audience: **f.** *B*

Ozment, Steven   **BR270**
The Age of Reform, 1250-1550: An Intellectual and Religious History of Late Medieval and Reformation Europe. Trade Paper. Yale University Press. Cumberland, RI. 1981. 458p. ISBN:0-300-02760-5, ISBN13: 978-0-300-02760-0. Dewey:274. LCCN:79-024162.

Audience: **u,f.** *B*

Rosenwein, Barbara H.   **D117.R67 2002**
A Short History of the Middle Ages. Trade Paper. Broadview Press. Peterborough, ON. 2002. 220p. ISBN:1-55111-290-6, ISBN13: 978-1-55111-290-9. Dewey:940.1. LCCN:2002-282702.

Audience: **l,u.** *Choice, 2002.*

Runciman, Steven   **BT1319 .R86 1982**
The Medieval Manichee: A Study of the Christian Dualist

Heresy. Trade Cloth. Cambridge University Press. New York, NY. 1982. 224p. ISBN:0-521-06166-0, ISBN13: 978-0-521-06166-7. Dewey:273. LCCN:82-004123.

Audience: **u,f.** ℬ

Tracy, James D. (Editor), et al.   **D203.H36 1994**
Handbook of European History, 1400-1600: Late Middle Ages, Renaissance, and Reformation. Heiko A. Oberman & James A. Brady (Editors). Trade Cloth. Brill Academic Publishers, Inc. Boston, MA. 1995. 722p. ISBN:90-04-09762-7, ISBN13: 978-90-04-09762-9. Dewey:940.2. LCCN:94-001290.

Audience: **u,f.**

Van Engen, John   **BR252**
Religion in the History of the Medieval West. Trade Cloth. Ashgate Publishing, Ltd. Aldershot, 2004. 344p. Variorum Collected Studies Ser., :Cs793 Ser. ISBN:0-86078-940-3, ISBN13: 978-0-86078-940-6. Dewey:274/.03. LCCN:2004-003232.

Audience: **u,f.**

Webb, Diana   **BX2320.5.E85W43 2002**
Medieval European Pilgrimage, C.700 - C.1500. Cloth over Boards. Palgrave Macmillan. New York, NY. 2002. 224p. European Culture and Society Ser. ISBN:0-333-76259-2, ISBN13: 978-0-333-76259-2. Dewey:263.04240902. LCCN:2001-056145.

Audience: **u,f.** *Choice, 2003.*

Christianity > Church History > Protestant Reformations

Baylor, Michael G. (Editor)   **BX4931.2 .R23 1991**
The Radical Reformation. Raymond Geuss & Quentin Skinner (Contribution by). Trade Paper. Cambridge University Press. New York, NY. 1991. 334p. Texts in the History of Political Thought ISBN:0-521-37948-2, ISBN13: 978-0-521-37948-9. Dewey:270.6. LCCN:90-020416.

Audience: **l,u,f.**

Benedict, Philip   **BX9415.B47 2002**
Christ's Churches Purely Reformed: A Social History of Calvinism. Cloth over Boards. Yale University Press. Cumberland, RI. 2002. 704p. ISBN:0-300-08812-4, ISBN13: 978-0-300-08812-0. Dewey:284/.24. LCCN:2002-002411.

Audience: **g,l,u,f.** *Choice, 2003.*

Cameron, Euan   **BR305.2.C35 1991**
The European Reformation. Paper Text. Oxford University Press, Inc. New York, NY. 1991. 580p. ISBN:0-19-873093-4, ISBN13: 978-0-19-873093-4. Dewey:274/.06. LCCN:90-047890.

Audience: **g,l,u,f.**

Chadwick, Owen   **BR300**
The Early Reformation on the Continent. Trade Paper. Oxford University Press, Inc. New York, NY. 2003. 456p. Oxford History of the Christian Church Ser. ISBN:0-19-926578-X, ISBN13: 978-0-19-926578-7. Dewey:274/.06.

Audience: **g,u,f.**

Collinson, Patrick   **BR305.3.C64 2004**
The Reformation: A History. Trade Cloth. Random House, Inc. New York, NY. 2004. 288p. Modern Library Chronicles, Vol. 19 ISBN:0-679-64323-0, ISBN13: 978-0-679-64323-4. Dewey:270.6. LCCN:2004-046667.

Audience: **g,l,u.**

Davis, Natalie Zemon   **DC33.D33**
Society and Culture in Early Modern France: Eight Essays by Natalie Zemon Davis. Trade Cloth. Stanford University Press. Palo Alto, CA. 1975. xx, 364p. ISBN:0-8047-0868-1, ISBN13: 978-0-8047-0868-5. Dewey:944/.027. LCCN:74-082777.

Audience: **u,f.** ℬ

Diefendorf, Barbara B. & Hesse, Carla (Editors)   **DC33.3**
Culture and Identity in Early Modern Europe (1500-1800): Essays in Honor of Natalie Zemon Davis. Trade Cloth. University of Michigan Press. Chicago, IL. 1994. 300p. ISBN:0-472-10470-5, ISBN13: 978-0-472-10470-3. Dewey:944.

Audience: **u,f.**

Eire, Carlos M. N.   **BR307.E57 1989**
War against the Idols: The Reformation of Worship from Erasmus to Calvin. Trade Paper. Cambridge University Press. New York, NY. 1989. 336p. ISBN:0-521-37984-9, ISBN13: 978-0-521-37984-7. Dewey:248.309409031.

Audience: **u,f.**

Forster, Marc R., et al.   **BV4647.P5**
Piety and Family in Early Modern Europe: Essays in Honour of Steven Ozment. Benjamin J. Kaplan & Steven Ozment (Authors). Trade Cloth. Ashgate Publishing, Ltd. Aldershot, 2005. 258p. St. Andrews Studies in Reformation History ISBN:0-7546-5248-3, ISBN13: 978-0-7546-5248-9. Dewey:274/.06. LCCN:2004-024644.

Audience: **u,f.**

Gregory, Brad S.   **BR307.G74 1999**
Salvation at Stake: Christian Martyrdom in Early Modern Europe. Trade Cloth. Harvard University Press. Cambridge, MA. 1999. 544p. Harvard Historical Studies, Vol. 134 ISBN:0-674-78551-7, ISBN13: 978-0-674-78551-9. Dewey:273.6. LCCN:99-029379.

Audience: **u,f.** *Choice, 2000.*

Huppert, George   **HN13.H86 1986**
After the Black Death: A Social History of Early Modern Europe. Ed. 2. Trade Cloth. Indiana University Press. Bloomington, IN. 1986. 190p. Interdisciplinary Studies in History ISBN:0-253-30446-6, ISBN13: 978-0-253-30446-9. Dewey:306/.094. LCCN:85-045580.

Audience: **u,f.** *Choice, 1987.*

Lindberg, Carter   **BR305.2.L486 1996**
The European Reformations. Trade Paper. Blackwell Publishing, Inc. Malden, MA. 1996. 464p. ISBN:1-55786-575-2, ISBN13: 978-1-55786-575-5. Dewey:274/.06. LCCN:95-022971.

Audience: **g,l,u,f.** *Choice, 1996.*

Lindberg, Carter (Editor)   BT27.R38 2001
The Reformation Theologians: An Introduction to Theology in
the Early Modern Period. Trade Paper. Blackwell Publishing,
Inc. Malden, MA. 2001. 416p. The Great Theologians Ser.
ISBN:0-631-21839-4, ISBN13: 978-0-631-21839-5.
Dewey:230/.092/2. LCCN:2001-037470.
                                   Audience: **u,f.** *Choice, 2002.*

McGrath, Alister E.   BT26.M37 1999
Reformation Thought: An Introduction. Ed. 3. Trade Paper.
Blackwell Publishing, Inc. Malden, MA. 1999. 344p.
ISBN:0-631-21521-2, ISBN13: 978-0-631-21521-9.
Dewey:270.6. LCCN:99-025163.
                                   Audience: **g,l,u.** *Choice, 1989.*

Moeller, Bernard   BR307 .M613 1982
Imperial Cities and the Reformation. H. C. Erik Midelfort &
Mark U. Edwards Jr. (Editors). Paper Text. Baker Books. Ada,
MI. 1982. 128p. ISBN:0-939464-04-7, ISBN13:
978-0-939464-04-3. Dewey:274.3/06. LCCN:82-006600.
                                   Audience: **u,f.**

Ozment, Steven   BR305.2
Protestants: The Birth of a Revolution. Trade Paper. Doubleday
Publishing. New York, NY. 1993. 284p. ISBN:0-385-47101-7,
ISBN13: 978-0-385-47101-5. Dewey:270.6. LCCN:93-016872.
                                   Audience: **g,l,u.**

Pettegree, Andrew (Editor)   BR309 .E37 1992
The Early Reformation in Europe. Cloth Text. Cambridge
University Press. New York, NY. 1992. 262p.
ISBN:0-521-39454-6, ISBN13: 978-0-521-39454-3.
Dewey:274.06. LCCN:91-046844.
                                   Audience: **u,f.**

Pettegree, Andrew   BR305.2.P48 2000
The Reformation World. Paper over Boards. Routledge. New
York, NY. 2000. 592p. ISBN:0-415-16357-9, ISBN13:
978-0-415-16357-6. Dewey:274/.06. LCCN:2001-044311.
                                   Audience: **u,f.** *Choice, 2000.*

Rice, Eugene F. Jr.   CB359 .R5
The Foundations of Early Modern Europe, 1460-1559, Vol. 1.
Trade Paper. W. W. Norton & Company, Inc. New York, NY.
1970. ISBN:0-393-09898-2, ISBN13: 978-0-393-09898-3.
Dewey:914/.03/21.
                                   Audience: **u,f.**

Thompson, Bard   CB359.T47 1996
Humanists and Reformers: A History of the Renaissance and
Reformation. Trade Cloth. William B. Eerdmans Publishing
Company. Grand Rapids, MI. 1996. 752p. ISBN:0-8028-3691-7,
ISBN13: 978-0-8028-3691-5. Dewey:940.21. LCCN:93-029076.
                                   Audience: **g,l,u.**

Tracy, James D.   BR290.T73 2005
Europe's Reformations, 1450-1650: Doctrine, Politics, and
Community. Ed. 2. Trade Cloth. Rowman & Littlefield
Publishers, Inc. Lanham, MD. 2006. 392p. Critical Issues in
History Ser. ISBN:0-7425-3788-9, ISBN13: 978-0-7425-3788-0.
Dewey:274/.06. LCCN:2005-009336.
                                   Audience: **u,f.**

Williams, George H.   BR307
The Radical Reformation. Ed. 3. Trade Cloth. Truman State
University Press. Kirksville, MO. 1992. 1516p. Sixteenth
Century Essays and Studies Ser., Vol. 15 ISBN:0-940474-15-8,
ISBN13: 978-0-940474-15-4. Dewey:270.6.
                                   Audience: **l,u.**

Williams, George H. &   BR301
  Mergal, Angel M. (Editors)
Spiritual and Anabaptist Writers. Trade Cloth. Westminster John
Knox Press. Louisville, KY. 1977. 418p. Library of Christian
Classics ISBN:0-664-24150-6, ISBN13: 978-0-664-24150-6.
Dewey:270.6. LCCN:57-005003.
                                   Audience: **u,f.**

Zuck, Lowell H. (Editor)   BR301
Christianity and Revolution: Radical Christian Testimonies,
1520-1650. Trade Paper. Temple University Press. Philadelphia,
PA. 1975. 324p. Documents in Free Church History Ser., No. 2
ISBN:0-87722-044-1, ISBN13: 978-0-87722-044-2.
Dewey:270.6.
                                   Audience: **l,u.**

Christianity > Church History > Protestant Reformations > Biography

Bainton, Roland H.   BR325.B26 1995
Here I Stand: A Life of Martin Luther. Trade Paper. Penguin
Group (USA) Inc. New York, NY. 1995. 336p.
ISBN:0-452-01146-9, ISBN13: 978-0-452-01146-5.
Dewey:284.1/092 B. LCCN:94-038811.
                                   Audience: **g,l,u.**

Bouwsma, William J.   BX9418
John Calvin: A Sixteenth-Century Portrait. Trade Paper. Oxford
University Press, Inc. New York, NY. 1989. 320p.
ISBN:0-19-505951-4, ISBN13: 978-0-19-505951-9.
Dewey:284/.2/0924.
                                   Audience: **g,l,u,f.** *Choice, 1988.*

Brecht, Martin   BR325
Martin Luther: The Preservation of the Church, 1532-1546.
Paper Text. Augsburg Fortress, Publishers. Minneapolis, MN.
2003. 578p. ISBN:0-8006-2815-2, ISBN13: 978-0-8006-2815-4.
Dewey:284.1/092/4.
                                   Audience: **u,f.**

Cottret, Bernard   BX9418
Calvin: A Biography. Trade Cloth. Continuum International
Publishing Group, Ltd. London, 2001. 368p.
ISBN:0-567-08757-3, ISBN13: 978-0-567-08757-7.
Dewey:284.2/092.
                                   Audience: **g,l,u,f.**

Ebeling, Gerhard   BR333.2
Luther: An Introduction to His Thought. R. A. Wilson
(Translator). Trade Paper. Augsburg Fortress, Publishers.
Minneapolis, MN. 1970. 288p. ISBN:0-8006-1162-4, ISBN13:
978-0-8006-1162-0. Dewey:230.410924. LCCN:77-099612.
                                   Audience: **g,l,u.**

Edwards, Mark U. Jr.   **BR325**
Luther and the False Brethren. Trade Cloth. Stanford University Press. Palo Alto, CA. 1975. xii, 242p. ISBN:0-8047-0883-5, ISBN13: 978-0-8047-0883-8. Dewey:270.6/092/4. LCCN:75-000181.

Audience: **u,f.**

Friesen, Abraham   **BX4946.M8F75 1990**
Thomas Muentzer, a Destroyer of the Godless: The Making of a Sixteenth-Century Religious Revolutionary. Trade Cloth. University of California Press. Berkeley, CA. 1990. 3320p. ISBN:0-520-06761-4, ISBN13: 978-0-520-06761-5. Dewey:284/.3/092 B. LCCN:90-032488.

Audience: **u,f.**

Gabler, Ulrich   **BR345**
Huldrych Zwingli: His Life and Work. Trade Cloth. Continuum International Publishing Group, Ltd. London, 1998. 208p. ISBN:0-567-09449-9, ISBN13: 978-0-567-09449-0. Dewey:284/.2/0924 B. LCCN:86-026033.

Audience: **u,f.**

Goertz, Hans-Jurgen   **BX4946.M8**
Thomas Muntzer: Apocalyptic Mystic and Revolutionary. Jocelyn Jaquiery (Translator). Trade Cloth. Continuum International Publishing Group, Ltd. London, 1993. 256p. ISBN:0-567-09606-8, ISBN13: 978-0-567-09606-7. Dewey:284.3092.

Audience: **u,f.** *Choice, 1994.*

Lull, Timothy F. & Russell,   **BR331.E5 3004**
William R. (Editors)
Martin Luther's Basic Theological Writings. Ed. 2. CD-ROM, Trade Paper. Augsburg Fortress, Publishers. Minneapolis, MN. 2004. 512p. ISBN:0-8006-3680-5, ISBN13: 978-0-8006-3680-7. Dewey:230/.41.

Audience: **g,l,u,f.** *Choice, 1990.*

McLaughlin, R. E.   **BX9749.S36**
Caspar Schwenckfeld, Reluctant Radical. Trade Cloth. Yale University Press. Cumberland, RI. 1986. 264p. ISBN:0-300-03367-2, ISBN13: 978-0-300-03367-0. Dewey:270.6/092/4. LCCN:85-020330.

Audience: **u,f.** *Choice, 1986.*

Muller, Richard A.   **BX9418**
The Unaccommodated Calvin: Studies in the Foundation of a Theological Tradition. Trade Paper. Oxford University Press, Inc. New York, NY. 2001. 320p. Oxford Studies in Historical Theology ISBN:0-19-515168-2, ISBN13: 978-0-19-515168-8. Dewey:230/.42/092.

Audience: **u,f.**

Oberman, Heiko A.   **BR325.O2713 1989**
Luther: Man Between God and the Devil. Eileen Walliser-Schwarzbart (Translator). Cloth over Boards. Yale University Press. Cumberland, RI. 1990. 320p. ISBN:0-300-03794-5, ISBN13: 978-0-300-03794-4. Dewey:284.1092. LCCN:89-005747.

Audience: **u,f.** *Choice, 1990.*

Pelikan, Jaroslav &   **BR330**
Lehmann, Helmut T. (Editors)
Luther's Works, Set. CD-ROM. Augsburg Fortress, Publishers. Minneapolis, MN. 2004. ISBN:0-8006-0359-1, ISBN13: 978-0-8006-0359-5. Dewey:230.41.

Audience: **g,l,u,f.**

Rummel, Erika   **B785.E64**
Erasmus of Rotterdam. Trade Cloth. Continuum International Publishing Group, Ltd. London, 2004. 192p. ISBN:0-8264-6813-6, ISBN13: 978-0-8264-6813-0. Dewey:199/.492. LCCN:2004-556881.

Audience: **u,f.**

Rupp, Gordon   **BR305.2**
Patterns of Reformation. Trade Cloth. Epworth Press, The. London, 1969. xxiii, 427p. ISBN:0-7162-0048-1, ISBN13: 978-0-7162-0048-2. Dewey:270.6.

Audience: **u,f.**

Snyder, C. Arnold   **BX4946.S29**
The Life and Thought of Michael Sattler. Trade Cloth. Herald Press. Scottdale, PA. 1984. 264p. Studies in Anabaptist and Mennonite History, Vol. 27 ISBN:0-8361-1264-4, ISBN13: 978-0-8361-1264-1. Dewey:284/.3. LCCN:83-022835.

Audience: **u,f.**

Stephens, W. P.   **BR346.S74 1992**
Zwingli: An Introduction to His Thought. Trade Cloth. Oxford University Press, Inc. New York, NY. 1992. 192p. ISBN:0-19-826329-5, ISBN13: 978-0-19-826329-6. Dewey:230/.42/092. LCCN:91-038083.

Audience: **u,f.** *Choice, 1992.*

Tracy, James D.   **B785.E6T73 1996**
Erasmus of the Low Countries. Trade Cloth. University of California Press. Berkeley, CA. 1997. 283p. ISBN:0-520-08745-3, ISBN13: 978-0-520-08745-3. Dewey:199/.492. LCCN:96-019335.

Audience: **u,f.** *Choice, 1997.*

Wright, D. F. (Editor)   **BR350.B93 M368 1994**
Martin Buber: Reforming Church and Community. Trade Paper. Cambridge University Press. New York, NY. 2002. 209p. ISBN:0-521-89252-X, ISBN13: 978-0-521-89252-0. Dewey:284.2/092.

Audience: **u,f.** *Choice, 1994.*

Christianity > Church History > Protestant Reformations > Reformations in Specific Countries

Cowan, Ian B.   **BR385.C76 1982**
The Scottish Reformation. Cloth Text. Palgrave Macmillan. New York, NY. 1982. 256p. ISBN:0-312-70519-0, ISBN13: 978-0-312-70519-0. Dewey:274.11/06. LCCN:82-005834.

Audience: **u,f.**

Dickens, A.G.   **BR375.D5 1991**

[handwritten: 1964 ed.] The English Reformation. Ed. 2. Trade Paper. Pennsylvania
State University Press. University Park, PA. 1991. 600p.
ISBN:0-271-00798-2, ISBN13: 978-0-271-00798-4.
Dewey:274.2/06. LCCN:91-013618.

Audience: **u,f.**

Duffy, Eamon   **BR742.D84 2005**

The Stripping of the Altars: Traditional Religion in England,
1400-1580. Ed. 2. Trade Paper. Yale University Press.
Cumberland, RI. 2005. 700p. ISBN:0-300-10828-1, ISBN13:
978-0-300-10828-6. Dewey:274.205.

Audience: **u,f.**

Gordon, Bruce   **BR410.G69 2002**

The Swiss Reformation. Cloth over Boards. Manchester
University Press. Manchester, 2003. 416p. New Frontiers in
History Ser. ISBN:0-7190-5117-7, ISBN13: 978-0-7190-5117-3.
Dewey:274.94/06. LCCN:2002-072472.

Audience: **u,f.** *Choice, 2003.*

Greengrass, Mark   **BR370.G74 1987**

The French Reformation. Trade Paper. Blackwell Publishing,
Inc. Malden, MA. 1987. 262p. ISBN:0-631-14516-8, ISBN13:
978-0-631-14516-5. Dewey:274.4/06. LCCN:86-021541.

Audience: **u,f.**

Haigh, Christopher   **DA315**

English Reformations: Religion, Politics, and Society under the
Tudors. Paper Text. Oxford University Press, Inc. New York,
NY. 1993. 384p. ISBN:0-19-822162-2, ISBN13:
978-0-19-822162-3. Dewey:942.05. LCCN:92-021515.

Audience: **u,f.** *Choice, 1994.*

Hsia, R. Po-chia (Editor)   **BR309.G37 1988**

The German People and the Reformation. Trade Paper. Cornell
University Press. Ithaca, NY. 1988. 296p. ISBN:0-8014-9485-0,
ISBN13: 978-0-8014-9485-7. Dewey:274.3/06.
LCCN:87-047863.

Audience: **u,f.**

Naphy, William G.   **BX9418.N27 2003**

Calvin and the Consolidation of the Genevan Reformation.
Trade Cloth. Westminster John Knox Press. Louisville, KY.
2003. 288p. ISBN:0-664-22662-0, ISBN13: 978-0-664-22662-6.
Dewey:274.94/5106. LCCN:2002-192268.

Audience: **u,f.** *Choice, 1995.*

Scribner, R. W. & Dixon, C.   **BR305.3.S37 2003**
  Scott

The German Reformation. Ed. 2. Trade Paper. Palgrave
Macmillan. New York, NY. 2003. 128p. Studies in European
History Ser. ISBN:0-333-66528-7, ISBN13: 978-0-333-66528-2.
Dewey:274.3/06. LCCN:2003-051168.

Audience: **g,u,f.**

Christianity > Church History > United States

Ahlstrom, Sydney E.   **BR515**

[handwritten: 1972 ed.] A Religious History of the American People. Ed. 2. Trade Paper.
Yale University Press. Cumberland, RI. 2004. 1216p.
ISBN:0-300-10012-4, ISBN13: 978-0-300-10012-9.
Dewey:200/.973. LCCN:2003-116918.

Audience: **g,l,u,f.**

Butler, Jon & Stout, Harry   **BL2525.R4655 1998**
  S. (Editors)

Religion in American History: A Reader. Trade Paper. Oxford
University Press, Inc. New York, NY. 1997. 526p.
ISBN:0-19-509776-9, ISBN13: 978-0-19-509776-4.
Dewey:200/.973. LCCN:96-039446.

Audience: **g,l,u,f.**

Corrigan, John S. &   **BL2525.C695 2004**
  Hudson, Winthrop S.

Religion in America. Ed. 7. Trade Paper. Prentice Hall PTR.
Upper Saddle River, NJ. 2003. 496p. ISBN:0-13-092389-3,
ISBN13: 978-0-13-092389-9. Dewey:200/.973.
LCCN:2003-002297.

Audience: **g,l,u.**

Dolan, Jay P.   **BX1406.3**

In Search of an American Catholicism: A History of Religion
and Culture in Tension. Trade Paper. Oxford University Press,
Inc. New York, NY. 2003. 320p. ISBN:0-19-516885-2, ISBN13:
978-0-19-516885-3. Dewey:282.7/3.

Audience: **g,l,u,f.** *Choice, 2003.*

Fowler, Robert Booth, et al.   **BL2525.F677 2004**

Religion and Politics in America. Ed. 3. Allen D. Hertzke, Laura
R. Olson & Kevin R. Den Dulk (Authors). Trade Paper.
Westview Press. Boulder, CO. 2004. 352p. ISBN:0-8133-4229-5,
ISBN13: 978-0-8133-4229-0. Dewey:322/.1/0973.

Audience: **g,l,u.**

Gaustad, Edwin S.   **BR516.G358 2003**

Church and State in America. Ed. 2. Book, Other. Oxford
University Press, Inc. New York, NY. 2003. 176p. Religion in
American Life Ser. ISBN:0-19-516738-4, ISBN13:
978-0-19-516738-2. Dewey:322/.1/0973. LCCN:2002-156396.

Audience: **l.**

Gaustad, Edwin S. &   **BR515.G3 2002**
  Schmidt, Leigh Eric

The Religious History of America: The Heart of the American
Story from Colonial Times to Today. Trade Paper. HarperCollins
Publishers. New York, NY. 2004. 464p. ISBN:0-06-063056-6,
ISBN13: 978-0-06-063056-0. Dewey:200/.973.
LCCN:2002-190208.

Audience: **g,l.**

Gillis, Chester   **BX1406.2.G451999**

Roman Catholicism in America. Trade Paper. Columbia
University Press. New York, NY. 2000. 366p. Columbia

Contemporary American Religion Ser. ISBN:0-231-10871-0, ISBN13: 978-0-231-10871-3. Dewey:282/.73. LCCN:99-017945.

Audience: **g,l,u,f.** *Choice, 2000.*

Handy, Robert T. BR515
A Christian America: Protestant Hopes and Historical Realities. Ed. 2. Paper Text. Oxford University Press, Inc. New York, NY. 1984. 284p. ISBN:0-19-503387-6, ISBN13: 978-0-19-503387-8. Dewey:280/.4/0973. LCCN:83-008177.

Audience: **u,f.**

Hatch, Nathan O. BR525
The Democratization of American Christianity. Trade Paper. Yale University Press. Cumberland, RI. 1991. 326p. ISBN:0-300-05060-7, ISBN13: 978-0-300-05060-8. Dewey:277.3/081.

Audience: **u,f.** *Choice, 1990.*

Holifield, E. Brooks BT30.U6H65 2005
Theology in America: Christian Thought from the Age of the Puritans to the Civil War. Trade Paper. Yale University Press. Cumberland, RI. 2005. 640p. ISBN:0-300-10765-X, ISBN13: 978-0-300-10765-4. Dewey:230/.0973.

Audience: **u,f.** *Choice, 2004.*

Keller, Rosemary Skinner BR515
In Our Own Voices: Four Centuries of American Women's Religious Writings. Trade Paper. Westminster John Knox Press. Louisville, KY. 2000. 552p. ISBN:0-664-22285-4, ISBN13: 978-0-664-22285-7. Dewey:200/.82.

Audience: **u,f.**

Keller, Rosemary Skinner, et al. BL458.E52 2006
The Encyclopedia of Women and Religion in North America. Rosemary Radford Ruether & Marie Cantlon (Authors). Trade Cloth. Indiana University Press. Bloomington, IN. 2006. 1296p. ISBN:0-253-34686-X, ISBN13: 978-0-253-34686-5. Dewey:200.82/0973. LCCN:2005-032429.

Audience: **g,l,u,f.**

Kenneally, James J. BX1407.W65K43 1990
The History of American Catholic Women. Trade Cloth. Crossroad Publishing Company. New York, NY. 1990. 288p. ISBN:0-8245-1009-7, ISBN13: 978-0-8245-1009-1. Dewey:282/.082. LCCN:89-077880.

Audience: **u,f.** *Choice, 1991.*

Marsden, George M. (Editor) BR1642.U5 E893 1984
Evangelicalism and Modern America. Trade Paper. William B. Eerdmans Publishing Company. Grand Rapids, MI. 1984. 212p. ISBN:0-8028-1993-1, ISBN13: 978-0-8028-1993-2. Dewey:280/.4.

Audience: **g,l,u,f.**

Marshall, Paul BR526.M345 2002
God and the Constitution: Christianity and American Politics. Trade Cloth. Rowman & Littlefield Publishers, Inc. Lanham, MD. 2002. 208p. ISBN:0-7425-2248-2, ISBN13: 978-0-7425-2248-0. Dewey:261.7/0973. LCCN:2002-002851.

Audience: **g,l,u,f.** *Choice, 2003.*

Marty, Martin E. BL2525
A Nation of Behavers. Trade Paper. University of Chicago Press. Chicago, IL. 1980. 247p. ISBN:0-226-50892-7, ISBN13: 978-0-226-50892-4. Dewey:306/.6/0973. LCCN:76-007997.

Audience: **g,l,u,f.**

Marty, Martin E. BR515.M324 1985
Pilgrims in Their Own Land: 500 Years of Religion in America. Trade Paper. Penguin Group (USA) Inc. New York, NY. 1985. 512p. ISBN:0-14-008268-9, ISBN13: 978-0-14-008268-5. Dewey:291/.0973. LCCN:85-003596.

Audience: **g,l,u,f.**

Marty, Martin E. BR515.M327 2004
The Protestant Voice in American Pluralism. Trade Cloth. University of Georgia Press. Athens, GA. 2004. 96p. George H. Shriver Lecture Series in Religion in American History, No. 2 ISBN:0-8203-2580-5, ISBN13: 978-0-8203-2580-4. Dewey:280/.4/0973. LCCN:2003-017196.

Audience: **g,l,u,f.**

Marty, Martin E. BR515.M328 1986
Protestantism in the United States: Righteous Empire. Ed. 2. Cloth Text. Prentice Hall PTR. Upper Saddle River, NJ. 1986. 320p. ISBN:0-02-376500-3, ISBN13: 978-0-02-376500-1. Dewey:280/.4/0973. LCCN:85-010475.

Audience: **g,l,u,f.**

Mead, Frank S. BL2525.M425 2001
Handbook of Denominations in the United States. Ed. 11. Craig D. Atwood & Samuel S. Hill (Revised by). Trade Cloth. Abingdon Press. Nashville, TN. 2004. 384p. ISBN:0-687-06983-1, ISBN13: 978-0-687-06983-5. Dewey:200/.973. LCCN:2001-018872.

Audience: **g,l,u.**

Melton, J. Gordon (Editor) BL2525.M449 1999
The Encyclopedia of American Religions. Ed. 6. Trade Cloth. Thomson Gale. Farmington Hills, MI. 1998. xxiv, 1243p. ISBN:0-8103-8417-5, ISBN13: 978-0-8103-8417-0. Dewey:200/.973. LCCN:00-702484.

Audience: **g,l,u,f.**

Melton, J. Gordon (Editor) BL72
Religious Leaders of America: A Biographical Guide to Founders and Leaders of Religious Bodies, Churches and Spiritual Groups in North America. Ed. 2. Trade Cloth. Thomson Gale. Farmington Hills, MI. 1999. 724p. ISBN:0-8103-8878-2, ISBN13: 978-0-8103-8878-9. Dewey:200.973. LCCN:91-642355.

Audience: **g,l,u.**

Noll, Mark A. PS3564.O42
America's God: From Jonathan Edwards to Abraham Lincoln. Trade Paper. Oxford University Press, Inc. New York, NY. 2005. 640p. ISBN:0-19-518299-5, ISBN13: 978-0-19-518299-6. Dewey:230/.0973.

Audience: **g,l,u,f.**

Noll, Mark A.   **BR500**
A History of Christianity in the United States and Canada. Trade
Paper. William B. Eerdmans Publishing Company. Grand
Rapids, MI. 1992. 592p. ISBN:0-8028-0651-1, ISBN13:
978-0-8028-0651-2. Dewey:277.

Audience: **g,l,u.**

Noll, Mark A.   **BR515.N745 2000**
Protestants in America. Book, Other. Oxford University Press,
Inc. New York, NY. 2000. 160p. Religion in America Ser.
ISBN:0-19-511034-X, ISBN13: 978-0-19-511034-0.
Dewey:280/.4/0973. LCCN:00-027271.

Audience: **l.**

Noll, Mark A. & Blumhofer,   **BV313.S56 2006**
  Edith L. (Editors)
Sing Them Over Again to Me: Hymns and Hymnbooks in
America. Trade Cloth. University of Alabama Press. Tuscaloosa,
AL. 2006. 376p. Religion and American Culture Ser.
ISBN:0-8173-1505-5, ISBN13: 978-0-8173-1505-4.
Dewey:264/.230973. LCCN:2005-027013.

Audience: **u,f.**

Noll, Mark A., et al.   **BR515.N75 1989**
The Search for Christian America. Nathan O. Hatch & George
M. Marsden (Authors). Trade Paper. Helmers & Howard,
Publishers, Inc. Colorado Springs, CO. 1989. 208p.
ISBN:0-939443-15-5, ISBN13: 978-0-939443-15-4.
Dewey:209/.73. LCCN:89-011052.

Audience: **g,l,u,f.**

Reid, Daniel G. (Editor), et   **BR515.D53 1990**
  al.
Dictionary of Christianity in America: A Comprehensive
Resource on the Religious Impulse That Shaped a Continent.
Harry S. Stout, Robert D. Linder & Bruce L. Shelley (Editors).
Trade Cloth. InterVarsity Press. Downers Grove, IL. 1990.
1305p. ISBN:0-8308-1776-X, ISBN13: 978-0-8308-1776-4.
Dewey:277.3/003. LCCN:89-029953.

Audience: **g,l,u,f.**

Wald, Kenneth D. &   **BL2525.W35 2006**
  Calhoun-Brown, Allison
Religion and Politics in the United States. Ed. 5. Trade Cloth.
Rowman & Littlefield Publishers, Inc. Lanham, MD. 2006.
ISBN:0-7425-4040-5, ISBN13: 978-0-7425-4040-8.
Dewey:322/.10973090511. LCCN:2006-007439.

Audience: **l,u.**

Christianity > Church History > United States > Special Periods

Butler, Jon   **BL2525.B87 1990**
Awash in a Sea of Faith: The Christianization of the American
People 1550-1865. Trade Cloth. Harvard University Press.
Cambridge, MA. 1990. 384p. Studies in Cultural History
ISBN:0-674-05600-0, ISBN13: 978-0-674-05600-8.
Dewey:200/.973. LCCN:89-035770.

Audience: **g,l,u,f.** *Choice, 1990.*

Carpenter, Joel A.   **BT82.2**
Revive Us Again: The Reawakening of American
Fundamentalism. Trade Paper. Oxford University Press, Inc.
New York, NY. 1999. 350p. ISBN:0-19-512907-5, ISBN13:
978-0-19-512907-6. Dewey:277.3/082.

Audience: **g,l,u,f.**

Carter, Paul A.   **BR525.C37**
Spiritual Crisis of the Gilded Age. Trade Cloth. Northern Illinois
University Press. DeKalb, IL. 1971. 295p. ISBN:0-87580-026-2,
ISBN13: 978-0-87580-026-4. Dewey:209/.73. LCCN:72-156938.

Audience: **u,f.**

Goen, C. C.   **BR525**
Broken Churches, Broken Nation: Denominational Schism and
the Coming of the American Civil War. Paper Text. Mercer
University Press. Macon, GA. 1985. 208p. ISBN:0-86554-187-6,
ISBN13: 978-0-86554-187-0. Dewey:277.3/081.
LCCN:85-007131.

Audience: **u,f.** *Choice, 1985.*

Jacobsen, Douglas G. &   **BR525.R35 1998**
  Trollinger, William Vance Jr. (Editors)
Re-Forming the Center: American Protestantism, 1900 to the
Present. Trade Paper. William B. Eerdmans Publishing
Company. Grand Rapids, MI. 1998. 508p. ISBN:0-8028-4298-4,
ISBN13: 978-0-8028-4298-5. Dewey:280/.4/09730904.
LCCN:98-006059.

Audience: **u,f.** *Choice, 1999.*

Marsden, George M.   **BT82.2.M37 2006**
Fundamentalism and American Culture: The Shaping of
Twentieth-Century Evangelicalism, 1870-1925. Ed. 2. Trade
Cloth. Oxford University Press, Inc. New York, NY. 2006. 468p.
ISBN:0-19-530051-3, ISBN13: 978-0-19-530051-2.
Dewey:277.3/082. LCCN:2005-053920.

Audience: **g,l,u,f.**

Moorhead, James H.   **E468.9**
American Apocalypse: Yankee Protestants and the Civil War,
1860-1869. Trade Cloth. Yale University Press. Cumberland, RI.
1978. xiv, 278p. ISBN:0-300-02152-6, ISBN13:
978-0-300-02152-3. Dewey:973.7. LCCN:77-014360.

Audience: **u,f.**

Noll, Mark A.   **PS3564.O42**
America's God: From Jonathan Edwards to Abraham Lincoln.
Trade Paper. Oxford University Press, Inc. New York, NY. 2005.
640p. ISBN:0-19-518299-5, ISBN13: 978-0-19-518299-6.
Dewey:230/.0973.

Audience: **g,l,u,f.**

Noll, Mark A. (Editor)   **BR525.G63 2002**
God and Mammon: Protestants, Money, and the Market,
1790-1860. Trade Paper. Oxford University Press, Inc. New
York, NY. 2001. 328p. ISBN:0-19-514801-0, ISBN13:
978-0-19-514801-5. Dewey:261.8/5/0973. LCCN:2001-023501.

Audience: **u,f.** *Choice, 2002.*

Stout, Harry S.   E468.9.S94 2005
Upon the Altar of the Nation: A Moral History of the Civil War.
Trade Cloth. Penguin Group (USA) Inc. New York, NY. 2006.
576p. ISBN:0-670-03470-3, ISBN13: 978-0-670-03470-3.
Dewey:973.7/1. LCCN:2005-042420.

Audience: **g,l,u,f.**

Stout, Harry S.   BX9225.W4S74 1991
The Divine Dramatist: George Whitefield and the Rise of
Modern Evangelicalism. Nathan O. Hatch & Mark A. Noll
(Editors). Trade Paper. William B. Eerdmans Publishing
Company. Grand Rapids, MI. 1991. 325p. Library of Religious
Biography ISBN:0-8028-0154-4, ISBN13: 978-0-8028-0154-8.
Dewey:269/.2/092. LCCN:91-013549.

Audience: **u,f.**

Swift, David E.   BR563.N4S97
Black Prophets of Justice: Activist Clergy Before the Civil War.
Trade Paper. Louisiana State University Press. Baton Rouge,
LA. 1989. 384p. ISBN:0-8071-2499-0, ISBN13:
978-0-8071-2499-4. Dewey:285.108. LCCN:88-030327.

Audience: **u,f.** *Choice, 1990.*

Weber, Timothy P.   BR525.W36 1987
Living in the Shadow of the Second Coming: American
Premillennialism, 1875-1982. Paper Text. University of Chicago
Press. Chicago, IL. 1993. xiv, 306p. ISBN:0-226-87732-9,
ISBN13: 978-0-226-87732-7. Dewey:236/.3/0973.
LCCN:86-030814.

Audience: **u,f.**

Westerkamp, Marilyn J.   BR520.W474 1999
Women and Religion in Early America, 1600-1850: The Puritan
and Evangelical Traditions. Paper over Boards. Routledge. New
York, NY. 1999. 240p. Christianity and Society in the Modern
World Ser. ISBN:0-415-09814-9, ISBN13: 978-0-415-09814-4.
Dewey:277.3/07/082. LCCN:98-030837.

Audience: **u,f.**

Christianity > Church History > United States > Special Regions

Heyrman, Christine L.   97-51487 [BR]
Southern Cross: The Beginnings of the Bible Belt. Trade Paper.
University of North Carolina Press. Chapel Hill, NC. 1998.
352p. ISBN:0-8078-4716-X, ISBN13: 978-0-8078-4716-9.
Dewey:277.5/081. LCCN:97-051487.

Audience: **u,f.** *Choice, 1997.*

Holifield, E. Brooks   BR535.H57
The Gentlemen Theologians: American Theology in Southern
Culture, 1795-1860. Cloth Text. Duke University Press. Durham,
NC. 1978. x, 262p. ISBN:0-8223-0414-7, ISBN13:
978-0-8223-0414-2. Dewey:277/.5. LCCN:78-059580.

Audience: **u,f.**

Longenecker, Stephen L.   BR555.P4L66 1994
Piety and Tolerance: Pennsylvania German Religion, 1700-1850.
Melvin Dieter (Foreword by). Trade Cloth. Scarecrow Press,
Inc. Lanham, MD. 1994. 216p. Pietist and Wesleyan Studies,
No. 6 ISBN:0-8108-2771-9, ISBN13: 978-0-8108-2771-4.
Dewey:277.48. LCCN:93-049988.

Audience: **u,f.** *Choice, 1994.*

Maffly-Kipp, Laurie R.   BR555.C2M34 1994
Religion and Society in Frontier California. Cloth over Boards.
Yale University Press. Cumberland, RI. 1994. 252p. Yale
Historical Publications ISBN:0-300-05377-0, ISBN13:
978-0-300-05377-7. Dewey:277.94/081. LCCN:93-024808.

Audience: **u,f.** *Choice, 1994.*

Mathews, Donald G.   BR535
Religion in the Old South. Martin E. Marty (Editor). Trade
Paper. University of Chicago Press. Chicago, IL. 1979. 294p.
Chicago History of American Religion Ser.
ISBN:0-226-51002-6, ISBN13: 978-0-226-51002-6.
Dewey:280/.4/0975. LCCN:77-000587.

Audience: **u,f.**

Mulder, Philip N.   BR515.M82 2002
A Controversial Spirit: Evangelical Awakenings in the South.
Trade Cloth. Oxford University Press, Inc. New York, NY. 2002.
244p. Religion in America Ser. ISBN:0-19-513163-0, ISBN13:
978-0-19-513163-5. Dewey:280/.4/0975. LCCN:2001-037044.

Audience: **u,f.** *Choice, 2002.*

Orsi, Robert A.   F128.9.I8
The Madonna of 115th Street: Faith and Community in Italian
Harlem, 1880-1950. Ed. 2. Trade Paper. Yale University Press.
Cumberland, RI. 2002. 352p. ISBN:0-300-09135-4, ISBN13:
978-0-300-09135-9. Dewey:305.8/51/07471.
LCCN:2001-098541.

Audience: **g,l,u,f.**

Christianity > Church History > United States > By race or Ethnic Group

Avalos, Hector   BR563.H57I57 2004
Introduction to the U. S. Latina and Latino Religious
Experience. Trade Cloth. Brill Academic Publishers, Inc.
Boston, MA. 2004. xiv, 322p. Religion in the Americas Ser.,
Vol. 2 ISBN:0-391-04149-5, ISBN13: 978-0-391-04149-3.
Dewey:200/.89/6872073. LCCN:2003-069591.

Audience: **l,u.** *Choice, 2005.*

Battle, Michael   BR563.N4
Black Church in America: African American Christian
Spirituality. Trade Cloth. Blackwell Publishing, Inc. Malden,
MA. 2006. 272p. Religious Life in America Ser.
ISBN:1-4051-1891-1, ISBN13: 978-1-4051-1891-0.
Dewey:277.3008996. LCCN:2005-017386.

Audience: **g,l,u,f.**

Hood, Robert E.   BT734.2.H62 1994
Begrimed and Black: Christian Traditions on Blacks and
Blackness. Trade Paper. Augsburg Fortress, Publishers.
Minneapolis, MN. 2003. 224p. ISBN:0-8006-2767-9, ISBN13:
978-0-8006-2767-6. Dewey:261.8/345196. LCCN:93-039510.
                                               Audience: **u,f.**

Lincoln, C. Eric & Mamiya,   BR563.N4L55 1990
Lawrence
The Black Church in the African American Experience. Trade
Paper. Duke University Press. Durham, NC. 1990. 536p.
ISBN:0-8223-1073-2, ISBN13: 978-0-8223-1073-0.
Dewey:277.3/08/08996073. LCCN:90-034050.
                          Audience: **g,l,u.**   *Choice, 1991.*

Phan, Peter C.   BR563.A82P43 2003
Christianity with an Asian Face: Asian-American Theology in
the Making. Trade Paper. Orbis Books. Maryknoll, NY. 2003.
256p. ISBN:1-57075-466-7, ISBN13: 978-1-57075-466-1.
Dewey:230/.089/95073. LCCN:2002-014159.
                          Audience: **u,f.**   *Choice, 2003.*

Raboteau, Albert J.   BR563.N4R237 2001
Canaan Land: A Religious History of African Americans. Trade
Paper. Oxford University Press, Inc. New York, NY. 2001. 164p.
ISBN:0-19-514585-2, ISBN13: 978-0-19-514585-4.
Dewey:200/.89/96073. LCCN:2001-035923.
                                               Audience: **u,f.**

Raboteau, Albert J.   BR563.N4
Slave Religion: The Invisible Institution in the Antebellum
South. Trade Paper. Oxford University Press, Inc. New York,
NY. 1980. 400p. ISBN:0-19-502705-1, ISBN13:
978-0-19-502705-1. Dewey:299.6/0975/09034.
LCCN:78-007275.
                                               Audience: **u,f.**

Yang, Fenggang   BR563.C45Y36 1999
Chinese Christians in America: Conversion, Assimilation and
Adhesive Identities. Trade Paper. Pennsylvania State University
Press. University Park, PA. 1999. 376p. ISBN:0-271-01917-4,
ISBN13: 978-0-271-01917-8. Dewey:280/.4/0899510753.
LCCN:98-037365.
                          Audience: **u,f.**   *Choice, 2000.*

Christianity > Church History > Latin America

Dussel, Enrique   BR600 .D8713
History of the Church in Latin America. Trade Paper. William
B. Eerdmans Publishing Company. Grand Rapids, MI. 2002.
388p. ISBN:0-8028-2131-6, ISBN13: 978-0-8028-2131-7.
Dewey:278.
                                               Audience: **u,f.**

Goodpasture, H. McKennie   BR600
Cross and Sword: An Eyewitness History of Christianity in
Latin America. Trade Paper. Wipf & Stock Publishers. Eugene,

OR. 2000. 338p. ISBN:1-57910-446-0, ISBN13:
978-1-57910-446-7. Dewey:278.
                          Audience: **u,f.**   *Choice, 1990.*

Christianity > Church History > Europe > Great Britain. Ireland

Acheson, Alan   BX5500.A24 1997
A History of the Church of Ireland. Trade Cloth. Columba
Press. Dublin, 1997. 304p. ISBN:1-85607-210-X, ISBN13:
978-1-85607-210-6. Dewey:283/.415. LCCN:97-224288.
                                               Audience: **g,u,f.**

Barlow, Frank   BR749.B3 1979
The English Church, 1000-1066: A History of the Later
Anglo-Saxon Church. Ed. 2. Trade Cloth. Longman Publishing
Group. White Plains, NY. 1979. xii, 354p. ISBN:0-582-49049-9,
ISBN13: 978-0-582-49049-9. Dewey:274.2. LCCN:78-040984.
                                               Audience: **u,f.**

Barlow, Frank   BR750.B37
The English Church, 1066-1154: A History of the
Anglo-Norman Church. Trade Cloth. Longman Publishing
Group. White Plains, NY. 1979. xii, 340p. ISBN:0-582-50236-5,
ISBN13: 978-0-582-50236-9. Dewey:274.2. LCCN:78-040458.
                                     Audience: **u,f.** ℬ

Bede   PA8260
The Ecclesiastical History of the English People; The Greater
Chronicle; Bede's Letter to Egbert. Trade Paper. Oxford
University Press, Inc. New York, NY. 1999. 484p. Oxford
World's Classics Ser. ISBN:0-19-283866-0, ISBN13:
978-0-19-283866-7. Dewey:274.2.
                                               Audience: **u,f.**

Bradley, Ian   BR759
Celtic Christianity: Making Myths and Chasing Dreams. Trade
Cloth. Edinburgh University Press. Edinburgh, 1999. 288p.
ISBN:0-7486-1047-2, ISBN13: 978-0-7486-1047-1.
Dewey:274.1.
                                               Audience: **u,f.**

Brown, Andrew   BR765.S25B76 1995
Popular Piety in Late Medieval England: The Diocese of
Salisbury, 1250-1550. Trade Cloth. Oxford University Press, Inc.
New York, NY. 1995. 308p. Oxford Historical Monographs
ISBN:0-19-820521-X, ISBN13: 978-0-19-820521-0.
Dewey:282/.42319/0902. LCCN:94-031782.
                                               Audience: **u,f.**

Clifton-Taylor, Alec   NA5461.C486 1989
The Cathedrals of England. Ed. 2. Trade Paper. Thames &
Hudson. New York, NY. 1989. 288p. World of Art Ser.
ISBN:0-500-20062-9, ISBN13: 978-0-500-20062-9.
Dewey:726/.6/0942. LCCN:79-066135.
                                               Audience: **g,l,u,f.**

Cowan, Ian B.   BR385.C76 1982
The Scottish Reformation. Cloth Text. Palgrave Macmillan. New York, NY. 1982. 256p. ISBN:0-312-70519-0, ISBN13: 978-0-312-70519-0. Dewey:274.11/06. LCCN:82-005834.

               Audience: **u,f.**

Davies, Oliver   BR794.C45 1999
Celtic Spirituality. Trade Cloth. Paulist Press. Mahwah, NJ. 2000. 576p. CWS Ser., No. 97 ISBN:0-8091-3894-8, ISBN13: 978-0-8091-3894-4. Dewey:270/.089/916. LCCN:99-041570.

               Audience: **u,f.**

De Paor, Liam   BR794
Saint Patrick's World: The Christian Culture of Ireland's Apostolic Age. Trade Cloth. Four Courts Press. Dublin 8, 1994. 336p. ISBN:1-85182-144-9, ISBN13: 978-1-85182-144-0. Dewey:274.15/02.

               Audience: **u,f.**

Deanesly, Margaret   BR743.2
The Pre-Conquest Church in England. Paper Text. Textbook Publishers. Temecula, CA. 2003. 374p. ISBN:0-7581-6993-0, ISBN13: 978-0-7581-6993-8. Dewey:274.2.

               Audience: **u.**

1964 ed. **Dickens, A.G.**   BR375.D5 1991
The English Reformation. Ed. 2. Trade Paper. Pennsylvania State University Press. University Park, PA. 1991. 600p. ISBN:0-271-00798-2, ISBN13: 978-0-271-00798-4. Dewey:274.2/06. LCCN:91-013618.

               Audience: **u,f.**

1992 ed. **Duffy, Eamon**   BR742.D84 2005
The Stripping of the Altars: Traditional Religion in England, 1400-1580. Ed. 2. Trade Paper. Yale University Press. Cumberland, RI. 2005. 700p. ISBN:0-300-10828-1, ISBN13: 978-0-300-10828-6. Dewey:274.205.

               Audience: **u,f.**

Gibson, William   BR758.R38 1998
Religion and Society in England and Wales, 1689-1800. Trade Cloth. Books International, Inc. Herndon, VA. 1998. 256p. Documents in Early Modern Social History Ser. ISBN:0-7185-0162-4, ISBN13: 978-0-7185-0162-4. Dewey:274.2/07. LCCN:97-047392.

               Audience: **u,f.**

Haigh, Christopher   DA315
English Reformations: Religion, Politics, and Society under the Tudors. Paper Text. Oxford University Press, Inc. New York, NY. 1993. 384p. ISBN:0-19-822162-2, ISBN13: 978-0-19-822162-3. Dewey:942.05. LCCN:92-021515.

         Audience: **u,f.** *Choice, 1994.*

Harrington, Christina   BR737.C4H37 2001
Women in the Celtic Church: Ireland C. 450-1150. Trade Cloth. Oxford University Press, Inc. New York, NY. 2002. 340p. ISBN:0-19-820823-5, ISBN13: 978-0-19-820823-5. Dewey:274.15/02/082. LCCN:2001-033969.

               Audience: **u,f.**

Knowles, David   BR754.A1
Saints and Scholars. Trade Paper. Cambridge University Press. New York, NY. 1966. 228p. ISBN:0-521-09172-1, ISBN13: 978-0-521-09172-5. Dewey:274.2/0092/2.

               Audience: **u,f.**

McLeod, Hugh   BR759.M37 1996
Religion and Society in England, 1850-1914. Trade Cloth. Palgrave Macmillan. New York, NY. 1996. 256p. Social History in Perspective Ser. ISBN:0-312-15798-3, ISBN13: 978-0-312-15798-2. Dewey:274.2/08. LCCN:95-031702.

         Audience: **u,f.** *Choice, 1996.*

Moorman, John R.   BR743.2.M6 1994
A History of the Church in England. Ed. 3. Trade Paper. Morehouse Publishing. Harrisburg, PA. 1980. 512p. ISBN:0-8192-1406-X, ISBN13: 978-0-8192-1406-5. Dewey:274.2. LCCN:94-006111.

               Audience: **u,f.**

Norman, E. R.   BR744.N67
Church and Society in England, 1770-1970: A Historical Survey. Trade Cloth. Oxford University Press, Inc. New York, NY. 1976. 507p. ISBN:0-19-826435-6, ISBN13: 978-0-19-826435-4. Dewey:261. LCCN:76-377182.

               Audience: **u,f.**

Rupp, Gordon   BR758.R87 1986
Religion in England, 1688-1791. Trade Cloth. Oxford University Press, Inc. New York, NY. 1987. 596p. History of the Christian Church Ser. ISBN:0-19-826918-8, ISBN13: 978-0-19-826918-2. Dewey:274.2/07. LCCN:85-023886.

         Audience: **u,f.** *Choice, 1988.*

Snyder, Graydon F.   BR737.C4S69 2002
Irish Jesus, Roman Jesus: The Formation of Early Irish Christianity. Trade Paper. Continuum International Publishing Group, Ltd. London, 2002. 288p. ISBN:1-56338-385-3, ISBN13: 978-1-56338-385-4. Dewey:274.15. LCCN:2002-009362.

               Audience: **u,f.**

Christianity > Church History > Europe > Other European Countries

1966 ed. **Billington, James H.**   DK32.7 .B5
The Icon and the Axe: An Interpretive History of Russian Culture. Trade Cloth. Peter Smith Publisher, Inc. Magnolia, MA. 1994. ISBN:0-8446-6754-4, ISBN13: 978-0-8446-6754-6. Dewey:914.703.

               Audience: **g,u,f.**

Ericksen, Robert P. &   DS146.G4B49 1999
  Heschel, Susannah (Editors)
Betrayal: German Churches and the Holocaust. Trade Paper. Augsburg Fortress, Publishers. Minneapolis, MN. 2003. 208p. ISBN:0-8006-2931-0, ISBN13: 978-0-8006-2931-1. Dewey:261.2/6/094309043. LCCN:99-011275.

         Audience: **u,f.** *Choice, 2000.*

Ginzburg, Carlo   **KKH3794**
The Cheese and the Worms: The Cosmos of a Sixteenth-Century
Miller. Trade Paper. Penguin Books, Ltd. London, 1997. xxvii,
177p. ISBN:0-14-016875-3, ISBN13: 978-0-14-016875-4.
Dewey:344.505/288.

Audience: **g,l,u,f.**

Helmreich, Ernst   **BR856.H443**
The German Churches under Hitler: Background, Struggle and
Epilogue. Trade Cloth. Wayne State University Press. Detroit,
MI. 1978. 617p. ISBN:0-8143-1603-4, ISBN13:
978-0-8143-1603-0. Dewey:261.7/0943. LCCN:78-017737.

Audience: **u,f.**

Holt, Mack P.   **DC111.3**
The French Wars of Religion, 1562-1629. Ed. 2. William Beik,
T. C. W. Blanning & Brendan Simms (Contribution by). Cloth
Text. Cambridge University Press. New York, NY. 2005. 258p.
New Approaches to European History Ser., Vol. 36
ISBN:0-521-83872-X, ISBN13: 978-0-521-83872-6.
Dewey:944.029. LCCN:2006-277383.

Audience: **u,f.**

Potter, David (Editor)   **DC111.A2F74 1997**
The French Wars of Religion: Selected Documents. Trade Cloth.
Palgrave Macmillan. New York, NY. 1998. 300p. Documents in
History Ser. ISBN:0-312-17545-0, ISBN13: 978-0-312-17545-0.
Dewey:944/.029. LCCN:97-009174.

Audience: **l,u.**

Zernov, Nicolas   **BX485**
The Russians and Their Church. Ed. 3. Trade Paper. Saint
Vladimir's Seminary Press. Yonkers, NY. 1977. 196p.
ISBN:0-913836-36-2, ISBN13: 978-0-913836-36-1.
Dewey:281.947.

Audience: **u,f.**

Christianity > Church History > Asia

Gillman, Ian & Klimkeit,   **BR1065**
Hans-Joachim
Christians in Asia Before 1500. Paper over Boards. Taylor &
Francis Group. Abingdon, 1998. 391p. ISBN:0-7007-1022-1,
ISBN13: 978-0-7007-1022-5. Dewey:275.

Audience: **u,f.**

Moffett, Samuel H.   **BR1065**
A History of Christianity in Asia: 1500 to Present. Trade Cloth.
HarperCollins Publishers. New York, NY. 1999.
ISBN:0-06-065880-0, ISBN13: 978-0-06-065880-9. Dewey:275.

Audience: **g,l,u,f.**

Moffett, Samuel H.   **BR1065.M63 1998**
A History of Christianity in Asia: Beginnings to 1500. Ed. 2.
Trade Paper. Orbis Books. Maryknoll, NY. 1998. 586p. History
of Christianity in Asia Ser., Vol. 1 ISBN:1-57075-162-5,
ISBN13: 978-1-57075-162-2. Dewey:275. LCCN:97-049236.

Audience: **g,l,u,f.**

Mullins, Mark R. (Editor)   **BR1305.H34 2003**
Handbook of Christianity in Japan. Trade Cloth. Brill Academic
Publishers. Leiden, 2003. x, 430p. Handbook of Oriental
Studies, Vol. 10 ISBN:90-04-13156-6, ISBN13:
978-90-04-13156-9. Dewey:275.2. LCCN:2003-050224.

Audience: **u,f.**

Neill, Stephen   **BR1155**
A History of Christianity in India: 1707-1858. Trade Paper.
Cambridge University Press. New York, NY. 2002. 596p.
ISBN:0-521-89332-1, ISBN13: 978-0-521-89332-9.
Dewey:275.4.

Audience: **u,f.**

Neill, Stephen   **BR1155**
A History of Christianity in India: The Beginnings to AD 1707.
Trade Paper. Cambridge University Press. New York, NY. 2004.
605p. ISBN:0-521-54885-3, ISBN13: 978-0-521-54885-4.
Dewey:209/.54.

Audience: **u,f.**

Standaert, Nicolas (Editor)   **BR1285.H36 2001**
Handbook of Christianity in China, 635-1800, Vol. 1. Trade
Cloth. Brill Academic Publishers. Leiden, 2001. xxviii, 964p.
Handbook of Oriental Studies, :China ISBN:90-04-11431-9,
ISBN13: 978-90-04-11431-9. Dewey:275.1.
LCCN:2001-267255.

Audience: **u,f.**

Sunquist, Scott W. (Editor),   **BR1065.D52 2001**
et al.
A Dictionary of Asian Christianity. David Wu Chu Sing &
Chew Hiang Chea (Editors). Trade Cloth. William B. Eerdmans
Publishing Company. Grand Rapids, MI. 2001. 989p.
ISBN:0-8028-3776-X, ISBN13: 978-0-8028-3776-9.
Dewey:275/.003. LCCN:2001-033224.

Audience: **g,l,u,f.**   *Choice, 2001.*

Christianity > Church History > Africa

Comaroff, Jean   **DT764.R65**
Body of Power, Spirit of Resistance: The Culture and History of
a South African People. Library Binding. University of Chicago
Press. Chicago, IL. 1985. 304p. ISBN:0-226-11422-8, ISBN13:
978-0-226-11422-4. Dewey:305.8/963. LCCN:84-024012.

Audience: **u,f.**   *Choice, 1986.*

Comaroff, Jean & Comaroff,   **DT1058.T78C66 1991**
John L.
Of Revelation and Revolution: Christianity, Colonialism, and
Consciousness in South Africa. Trade Paper. University of
Chicago Press. Chicago, IL. 1991. 434p. Of Revelation and
Revolution Ser., Vol. 1 ISBN:0-226-11442-2, ISBN13:
978-0-226-11442-2. Dewey:303.48/241/008996397.
LCCN:90-046753.

Audience: **u,f.**   *Choice, 1992.*

Comaroff, John L. &   **DT1058.T78C66 1991**
  Comaroff, Jean
Of Revelation and Revolution: The Dialectics of Modernity on a
South African Frontier. Trade Paper. University of Chicago
Press. Chicago, IL. 1997. 612p. Of Revelation and Revolution
Ser., Vol. 2 ISBN:0-226-11444-9, ISBN13: 978-0-226-11444-6.
Dewey:303.4824100899639775. LCCN:90-046753.

Audience: **u,f.**

Eide, Yvind   **BX8063.E85.E53 2000**
Revolution and Religion in Ethiopia: Growth and Persecution of
the Mekane Yesus Church, 1974-85. Ed. 2. Trade Cloth. Ohio
University Press. Athens, OH. 2000. 320p. Eastern African
Studies ISBN:0-8214-1365-1, ISBN13: 978-0-8214-1365-4.
Dewey:284.1/63. LCCN:00-034025.

Audience: **u,f.**

Etherington, Norman   **BR1450 .E83**
Preachers, Peasants and Politics in South East Africa,
1835-1880: African Communities in Natal, Pondoland and
Zululand. Trade Cloth. Royal Historical Society. London, 1970.
241p. Royal Historical Society Studies in History Ser.
ISBN:0-901050-48-2, ISBN13: 978-0-901050-48-9.
Dewey:276.8/4. LCCN:79-317272.

Audience: **u,f.**

Fields, K.   **DT3091.F54 1997**
Revival and Rebellion in Colonial Africa. Trade Paper.
Heinemann. Portsmouth, NH. 1997. 322p. ISBN:0-435-07418-0,
ISBN13: 978-0-435-07418-0. Dewey:968.9. LCCN:97-194591.

Audience: **u,f.**

Gifford, Paul   **BR1644.5.G4**
Ghana's New Christianity: Pentecostalism in a Globalising
African Economy. Trade Cloth. C. Hurst & Company,
Publishers, Ltd. London, 2003. xiv, 216p. ISBN:1-85065-718-1,
ISBN13: 978-1-85065-718-7. Dewey:276.67082.

Audience: **u,f.**

Isichei, Elizabeth   **BR1360.I75 1995**
A History of Christianity in Africa: From Antiquity to the
Present. Trade Paper. William B. Eerdmans Publishing
Company. Grand Rapids, MI. 1995. 432p. ISBN:0-8028-0843-3,
ISBN13: 978-0-8028-0843-1. Dewey:276. LCCN:94-046617.

Audience: **u,f.** *Choice, 1995.*

MacGaffey, Wyatt   **BL2470.Z2**
Modern Kongo Prophets: Religion in a Plural Society. Trade
Cloth. Indiana University Press. Bloomington, IN. 1983. 304p.
African Systems of Thought Ser., No. 307 ISBN:0-253-33865-4,
ISBN13: 978-0-253-33865-5. Dewey:299/.67. LCCN:82-048554.

Audience: **u,f.**

Sandgren, David P.   **BR1443**
Christianity and the Kikuyu: Religious Divisions and Social
Conflict. Trade Paper. Peter Lang Publishing, Inc. New York,
NY. 2000. xi, 193p. American University Studies, Vol.
IX:History ISBN:0-8204-4867-2, ISBN13: 978-0-8204-4867-1.
Dewey:276.762/082/08996395.

Audience: **u,f.**

Sanneh, Lamin O. &   **BR481.C47 2005**
  Carpenter, Joel A. (Editors)
Changing Face of Christianity. Trade Paper. Oxford University
Press, Inc. New York, NY. 2005. 256p. ISBN:0-19-517728-2,
ISBN13: 978-0-19-517728-2. Dewey:270.8/3.
LCCN:2004-008859.

Audience: **u,f.**

Sundkler, Bengt G.   **BR1367.Z8**
Bantu Prophets in South Africa. Ed. 2. Trade Cloth. Oxford
University Press, Inc. New York, NY. 1965. International
African Institute Ser. ISBN:0-19-724161-1, ISBN13:
978-0-19-724161-5. Dewey:276.8.

Audience: **u,f.** *B*

Tamrat, Taddesse   **BR1370**
Church and State in Ethiopia, 1270-1527. Trade Cloth. Oxford
University Press, Inc. New York, NY. 1972. xv, 327p.
ISBN:0-19-821671-8, ISBN13: 978-0-19-821671-1.
Dewey:322/.1/0963. LCCN:76-381840.

Audience: **u,f.** *B*

Christianity > Church History > Modern period

Brown, Stewart J. &   **DR470**
  Tackett, Timothy (Editors)
Cambridge History of Christianity: Enlightenment, Reawakening
and Revolution 1660-1815. Cloth Text. Cambridge University
Press. New York, NY. 2006. 688p. Cambridge History of
Christianity Ser. ISBN:0-521-81605-X, ISBN13:
978-0-521-81605-2. Dewey:270.7.

Audience: **u,f.**

Gilley, Sheridan & Stanley,   **BR477.W87 2005**
  Brian (Editors)
Cambridge History of Christianity: World Christianities C.
1815-C. 1914. Cloth Text. Cambridge University Press. New
York, NY. 2005. 698p. Cambridge History of Christianity Ser.,
Vol. 8 ISBN:0-521-81456-1, ISBN13: 978-0-521-81456-0.
Dewey:270.8. LCCN:2005-008392.

Audience: **u,f.** *Choice, 2006.*

Maclear, J. F.   **BR450.C48 1995**
Church and State in the Modern Age: A Documentary History.
Trade Cloth. Oxford University Press, Inc. New York, NY. 1995.
528p. ISBN:0-19-508681-3, ISBN13: 978-0-19-508681-2.
Dewey:322/.1/0903. LCCN:94-030051.

Audience: **g,l,u,f.** *Choice, 1996.*

McLeod, Hugh (Editor)   **BR477.W87 2005**
World Christianities C.1914-C.2000. Cloth Text. Cambridge
University Press. New York, NY. 2006. 736p. Cambridge
History of Christianity Ser., Vol. 9 ISBN:0-521-81500-2,
ISBN13: 978-0-521-81500-0. Dewey:270.8.
LCCN:2006-295954.

Audience: **u,f.**

Christianity > Church History > Catholic Reformation and Counter-Reformation

Hsia, R. Po-chia   **BX1304.H75 2005**
The World of Catholic Renewal, 1540-1770. Ed. 2. William
Beik & T. C. W. Blanning (Contribution by). Cloth Text.
Cambridge University Press. New York, NY. 2005. 282p. New
Approaches to European History Ser. ISBN:0-521-84154-2,
ISBN13: 978-0-521-84154-2. Dewey:282/.09/03.
LCCN:2004-062848.

Audience: **u,f.**

Monter, E. William   **BX1735**
Frontiers of Heresy: The Spanish Inquisition from the Basque
Lands to Sicily. John Elliott, Olwen Hufton, H. G.
Koenigsberger & H. M. Scott (Contribution by). Trade Paper.
Cambridge University Press. New York, NY. 2003. 362p.
Cambridge Studies in Early Modern History Ser.
ISBN:0-521-52259-5, ISBN13: 978-0-521-52259-5.
Dewey:272.2/0946.

Audience: **u,f.**

Mottola, Anthony & St.   **BX2179.L7**
Ignatius of Loyola Staff
Spiritual Exercises of St. Ignatius. R. W. Gleason (Introduction
by). Trade Paper. Doubleday Publishing. New York, NY. 1964.
208p. ISBN:0-385-02436-3, ISBN13: 978-0-385-02436-5.
Dewey:248.3. LCCN:64-012784.

Audience: **g,l,u,f.**

Olin, John C.   **BR305.2.O45 1990**
Catholic Reform from Cardinal Ximenes to the Council of
Trent, 1495-1563: An Essay with Illustrative Documents and a
Brief Study of St. Ignatius Loyola. Trade Paper. Fordham
University Press. Bronx, NY. 1990. 152p. ISBN:0-8232-1281-5,
ISBN13: 978-0-8232-1281-1. Dewey:282/.09/031.
LCCN:90-080702.

Audience: **u,f.**

O'Malley, John W.   **BR430.O45 2000**
Trent and All That: Renaming Catholicism in the Early Modern
Era. Trade Cloth. Harvard University Press. Cambridge, MA.
2000. 240p. ISBN:0-674-00087-0, ISBN13: 978-0-674-00087-2.
Dewey:282/.09/031. LCCN:99-041584.

Audience: **u,f.**

Christianity > Persecution. Toleration. Liberalism

Foxe, John   **BR1601.2**
Foxe's Book of Martyrs. Trade Cloth. Hendrickson Publishers,
Inc. Peabody, MA. 2004. 392p. ISBN:1-56563-504-3, ISBN13:
978-1-56563-504-3. Dewey:272.

Audience: **g,l,u,f.**

Frend, W. H.   **BR1604.2**
Martyrdom and Persecution in the Early Church. Trade Paper.
Baker Books. Ada, MI. 1981. 645p. Twin Brooks Ser.
ISBN:0-8010-3502-3, ISBN13: 978-0-8010-3502-9.
Dewey:272.1.

Audience: **u,f.**

Hefley, James & Hefley,   **BR1608.5.H44 2004**
Marti
By Their Blood: Christian Martyrs from the Twentieth Century
and Beyond. Ed. 3. Trade Paper. Baker Books. Ada, MI. 2004.
384p. ISBN:0-8010-6515-1, ISBN13: 978-0-8010-6515-6.
Dewey:272/.9/0922 B. LCCN:2004-003420.

Audience: **g,l,u,f.**

Christianity > Biography

Anatolios, Khaled   **BR1720.A7A53 2004**
Athananius. Paper over Boards. Routledge. New York, NY.
2004. 304p. The Early Church Fathers Ser.
ISBN:0-415-20202-7, ISBN13: 978-0-415-20202-2.
Dewey:270.2/092. LCCN:2003-026829.

Audience: **u,f.**

Athanasius Nikitin O Staff,   **BR1710**
et al.
Early Christian Lives. Gregory the Great Staff, Jerome &
Sulpicius Severus (Authors), Carolinne White (Translator). Trade
Paper. Penguin Group (USA) Inc. New York, NY. 1998. 288p.
Classics Ser. ISBN:0-14-043526-3, ISBN13: 978-0-14-043526-9.
Dewey:270/.0922. LCCN:98-166311.

Audience: **g,l,u.**

Brown, Peter   **BR1720.A9**
Augustine of Hippo. Ed. 2. Trade Paper. Faber & Faber, Inc.
New York, NY. 2000. 576p. ISBN:0-571-20495-3, ISBN13:
978-0-571-20495-3. Dewey:270.2/092.

Audience: **g,l,u,f.**

Farmer, David Hugh   **BR1710**
The Oxford Dictionary of Saints. Ed. 5. Trade Paper. Oxford
University Press, Inc. New York, NY. 2004. 607p. Oxford
Paperback Reference Ser. ISBN:0-19-860949-3, ISBN13:
978-0-19-860949-0. Dewey:270/.092/2 B. LCCN:2005-272790.

Audience: **g,l,u,f.**

Grant, Robert M.   **BR1720.I7G73 1997**
Irenaeus of Lyons. Paper over Boards. Routledge. New York,
NY. 1996. 224p. Early Church Fathers Ser.
ISBN:0-415-11837-9, ISBN13: 978-0-415-11837-8.
Dewey:230.2/092. LCCN:96-007705.

Audience: **u,f.**

Harvey, Susan (Translator)   **BR1070**
Holy Women of the Syrian Orient. Sebastian Brock & Susan
Harvey (Introduction by). Trade Cloth. University of California
Press. Berkeley, CA. 1987. 215p. The Transformation of the
Classical Heritage Ser., Vol. XIII ISBN:0-520-05705-8, ISBN13:
978-0-520-05705-0. Dewey:275.6. LCCN:86-011313.

Audience: **u,f.**

Head, Thomas   BR1710.M39 2000
Medieval Hagiography: An Anthology. Cloth Text. Garland
Publishing, Inc. New York, NY. 1999. xlix, 834p. Reference
Library of the Humanities, Vol. 26 ISBN:0-8153-2123-6,
ISBN13: 978-0-8153-2123-1. Dewey:270.3/092/2 B.
LCCN:99-045450.

Audience: **g,l,u,f.**

Kelly, J. N.   BR1720.C5K45 1995
Golden Mouth: The Story of John Chrysostom - Ascetic,
Preacher, Bishop. Trade Cloth. Cornell University Press. Ithaca,
NY. 1995. 320p. ISBN:0-8014-3189-1, ISBN13:
978-0-8014-3189-0. Dewey:270.2/092 B. LCCN:95-001444.

Audience: **g,l,u,f.** *Choice, 1996.*

Osborn, Eric   B666
Clement of Alexandria. Cloth Text. Cambridge University Press.
New York, NY. 2005. 342p. ISBN:0-521-83753-7, ISBN13:
978-0-521-83753-8. Dewey:261.51092. LCCN:2006-296288.

Audience: **u,f.**

Rebenich, Stefan   BR1720.J5R43 2002
Jerome. Paper over Boards. Routledge. New York, NY. 2002.
224p. Early Church Fathers Ser. ISBN:0-415-19905-0, ISBN13:
978-0-415-19905-6. Dewey:270.2/092. LCCN:2002-075143.

Audience: **u,f.**

Rousseau, Philip   BR1720.A9
Basil of Caesarea. Trade Cloth. University of California Press.
Berkeley, CA. 1995. 432p. The Transformation of the Classical
Heritage Ser., Vol. 20 ISBN:0-520-08238-9, ISBN13:
978-0-520-08238-0. Dewey:270.2092. LCCN:93-003552.

Audience: **u,f.**

Trigg, Joseph W.   BR1720.O7T75 1998
Origen. Paper over Boards. Routledge. New York, NY. 1998.
312p. Early Church Fathers Ser. ISBN:0-415-11835-2, ISBN13:
978-0-415-11835-4. LCCN:97-023338.

Audience: **u,f.**

Walsh, Michael J. (Editor)   BR1700.3.D53 2001
The Dictionary of Christian Biography. Trade Cloth. Liturgical
Press. Collegeville, MN. 2005. 1,264p. ISBN:0-8146-5921-7,
ISBN13: 978-0-8146-5921-2. Dewey:270/.092/2 B.
LCCN:2002-283697.

Audience: **g,l,u,f.** *Choice, 2002.*

Christianity > Bible > Texts and Versions

                                                   BS612
The Holy Bible, English Standard Version: Classic Reference -
Hardcover, Black Letter. Trade Cloth, CD-ROM. Crossway
Books. Wheaton, IL. 2005. 1328p. ISBN:1-58134-387-6,
ISBN13: 978-1-58134-387-8. Dewey:220.

Audience: **g,l,u,f.**

                                                   BS195
The Bible: Contemporary English Version. Trade Cloth.
HarperCollins Canada, Ltd. Scarborough, ON. 2001. 1344p.
ISBN:0-00-710299-2, ISBN13: 978-0-00-710299-0.
Dewey:220.5/208.

Audience: **g,l,u.**

                                                   BS195
Pew Bible - NKJV. Trade Cloth. Nelson Bibles. Nashville, TN.
1983. 690p. ISBN:0-8407-0055-5, ISBN13: 978-0-8407-0055-1.
Dewey:220.5.

Audience: **g,l,u.**

Coogan, Michael D.   BS191.5.A1 1991
(Editor), et al.
New Oxford Annotated Bible: New Revised Standard Version
with the Apocrypha. Ed. 3. Marc Zvi Brettler, Carol A. Newsom
& Pheme Perkins (Editors). Trade Cloth. Oxford University
Press, Inc. New York, NY. 2001. 2180p. ISBN:0-19-528478-X,
ISBN13: 978-0-19-528478-2. Dewey:220.520434.

Audience: **g,l,u,f.**

Hendrickson Publishers, Inc.   BS185 1992.O73
Staff
KJV Bible 1611 Edition. Leather. Alban Books Ltd. Edinburgh,
2006. ISBN:1-56563-808-5, ISBN13: 978-1-56563-808-2.
Dewey:220.5/2034.

Audience: **g,l,u,f.**

Jones, Alexander (Editor)   BS195
The Jerusalem Bible: Reader's Edition. Trade Cloth. Doubleday
Publishing. New York, NY. 2000. 1696p. ISBN:0-385-49918-3,
ISBN13: 978-0-385-49918-7. Dewey:220.5207.

Audience: **g,l,u.**

Kohlenberger, John R. III   BS2025 1995.K64 1995
(Editor)
The Precise Parallel New Testament. Leather. Oxford University
Press, Inc. New York, NY. 1995. 1472p. ISBN:0-19-528412-7,
ISBN13: 978-0-19-528412-6. Dewey:225.5/2. LCCN:97-208193.

Audience: **g,l,u,f.**

Lockman Foundation Staff   BS195
(Editor, Translator)
New American Standard Bible: Reader's Pew Edition. Ed. 2.
Trade Cloth. Foundation Publications. Anaheim, CA. 1997.
960p. ISBN:1-885217-68-4, ISBN13: 978-1-885217-68-4.
Dewey:220.5208.

Audience: **g,l,u.**

Peterson, Eugene   BS195
The Message. Trade Cloth. NavPress Publishing Group.
Colorado Springs, CO. 2006. 1728p. ISBN:1-57683-916-8,
ISBN13: 978-1-57683-916-4. Dewey:220.5/209.

Audience: **g,l,u.**

Phillips, J. B.   BS2095
New Testament in Modern English. Trade Cloth. World
Publishing. Nashville, TN. 2004. 576p. ISBN:0-88486-350-6,
ISBN13: 978-0-88486-350-2. Dewey:225.5/209.

Audience: **g,l,u.**

Zondervan   **BS195**
NIV Ministry/Pew Bible. Trade Cloth. Zondervan. Grand
Rapids, MI. 1989. 896p. Bibles Ser. ISBN:0-310-91291-1,
ISBN13: 978-0-310-91291-0.

Audience: **g,l,u.**

Christianity > Bible > Works about the Bible > Reference

Achtemeier, Paul J.   **BS440.H235 1996**
The HarperCollins Bible Dictionary. Trade Cloth. HarperCollins
Publishers. New York, NY. 1996. 1280p. ISBN:0-06-060037-3,
ISBN13: 978-0-06-060037-2. Dewey:220.3. LCCN:96-025424.

Audience: **g,l,u,f.**

1997 ed
Browning, W. R. F.   **BS440.B73 2004**
A Dictionary of the Bible. Ed. 2. Trade Paper. Oxford
University Press, Inc. New York, NY. 2004. 452p. Oxford
Paperback Reference Ser. ISBN:0-19-860890-X, ISBN13:
978-0-19-860890-5. Dewey:220.3. LCCN:2004-052060.

Audience: **g,l,u,f.**

Freedman, David Noel   **BS440.A54 1992**
The Anchor Bible Dictionary, Vol. 2. Trade Cloth. Doubleday
Publishing. New York, NY. 1992. 1136p. ISBN:0-385-19360-2,
ISBN13: 978-0-385-19360-3. Dewey:220.3. LCCN:91-008385.

Audience: **g,l,u,f.** *Choice, 1993.*

Freedman, David Noel   **BS440**
The Anchor Bible Dictionary, Vol. 5. Trade Cloth. Doubleday
Publishing. New York, NY. 1992. 1264p. ISBN:0-385-19363-7,
ISBN13: 978-0-385-19363-4. Dewey:220.3.

Audience: **g,l,u,f.** *Choice, 1993.*

Freedman, David Noel   **BS440**
The Anchor Bible Dictionary, Vol. 4. Trade Cloth. Doubleday
Publishing. New York, NY. 1992. 1200p. ISBN:0-385-19362-9,
ISBN13: 978-0-385-19362-7. Dewey:220.3.

Audience: **g,l,u,f.** *Choice, 1993.*

Freedman, David Noel   **BS440.A54 1992**
The Anchor Bible Dictionary, Vol. 1. Trade Cloth. Doubleday
Publishing. New York, NY. 1998. 1312p. ISBN:0-385-19351-3,
ISBN13: 978-0-385-19351-1. Dewey:220.3. LCCN:91-008385.

Audience: **g,l,u,f.** *Choice, 1993.*

Freedman, David Noel   **BS440**
The Anchor Bible Dictionary, Vol. 3. Trade Cloth. Doubleday
Publishing. New York, NY. 1992. 1168p. ISBN:0-385-19361-0,
ISBN13: 978-0-385-19361-0. Dewey:220.3.

Audience: **g,l,u,f.** *Choice, 1993.*

Freedman, David Noel   **BS440**
The Anchor Bible Dictionary, Vol. 6. Trade Cloth. Doubleday
Publishing. New York, NY. 1992. 1216p. ISBN:0-385-26190-X,
ISBN13: 978-0-385-26190-6. Dewey:220.3.

Audience: **g,l,u,f.** *Choice, 1993.*

Gentz, William H. (Editor)   **BR95.D46 1986**
The Dictionary of Bible and Religion. Trade Cloth. Abingdon
Press. Nashville, TN. 1986. 1152p. ISBN:0-687-10757-1,
ISBN13: 978-0-687-10757-5. Dewey:203/.21. LCCN:85-015011.

Audience: **g,l,u,f.** *Choice, 1987.*

Kohlenberger, John R. III &   **BS425.S8 2001**
  Strong, James
The Strongest Strong's Exhaustive Concordance. Trade Cloth.
Zondervan. Grand Rapids, MI. 2004. 1760p.
ISBN:0-310-25908-8, ISBN13: 978-0-310-25908-4.
Dewey:220.5/2033. LCCN:2001-026577.

Audience: **g,l,u,f.**

Metzger, Bruce M. &   **BS440.M434 1993**
  Coogan, Michael D. (Editors)
The Oxford Companion to the Bible. Trade Cloth. Oxford
University Press, Inc. New York, NY. 1993. 902p.
ISBN:0-19-504645-5, ISBN13: 978-0-19-504645-8.
Dewey:220.3. LCCN:93-019315.

Audience: **g,l,u,f.** *Choice, 1994.*

Rogerson, John (Editor)   **BS445.O94 2001**
The Oxford Illustrated History of the Bible. Trade Cloth. Oxford
University Press, Inc. New York, NY. 2001. 438p.
ISBN:0-19-860118-2, ISBN13: 978-0-19-860118-0.
Dewey:220/.09. LCCN:2001-272513.

Audience: **g,l,u,f.**

Wiseman, Donald J.   **BS440.N42 1996**
  (Editor), et al.
New Bible Dictionary. Ed. 3. J. I. Packer, I. Howard Marshall &
A. R. Millard (Editors). Trade Cloth. InterVarsity Press.
Downers Grove, IL. 1996. xix + 1,298p. ISBN:0-8308-1439-6,
ISBN13: 978-0-8308-1439-8. Dewey:220.3. LCCN:96-024002.

Audience: **g,l,u,f.**

Christianity > Bible > Works about the Bible > Introductions

Ackroyd, Peter R. & Evans,   **BS445**
  C. F. (Editors)
The Cambridge History of the Bible: From the Beginnings to
Jerome, Vol. 1. Trade Paper. Cambridge University Press. New
York, NY. 1975. 687p. The Cambridge History of the Bible Ser.
ISBN:0-521-09973-0, ISBN13: 978-0-521-09973-8.
Dewey:220/.09. LCCN:63-024435.

Audience: **g,l,u,f.**

Bruce, F. F.   **BS465.B78 1988**
The Canon of Scripture. Trade Cloth. InterVarsity Press.
Downers Grove, IL. 1988. 349p. ISBN:0-8308-1258-X, ISBN13:
978-0-8308-1258-5. Dewey:220.1/2. LCCN:88-029206.

Audience: **g,l,u,f.**

Bruce, Frederick Fyvie   **BS455**
History of the Bible in English. Trade Cloth. Lutterworth Press,
The. Cambridge, 2006. 288p. ISBN:0-7188-9032-9, ISBN13:
978-0-7188-9032-2. Dewey:220.52009.

Audience: **g,l,u,f.**

Greensdale, S. L. (Editor)   **BS445**
The West from the Reformation to the Present Day. Trade Cloth.
Cambridge University Press. New York, NY. 1963. 600p. The
Cambridge History of the Bible Ser., Vol. 3
ISBN:0-521-04254-2, ISBN13: 978-0-521-04254-3.
Dewey:220/.09. LCCN:63-024435.

Audience: **g,l,u,f.**

Kee, Howard Clark   **BS621**
The Cambridge Companion to the Bible. Trade Paper.
Cambridge University Press. Cambridge, 1997. vi, 616p.
ISBN:0-521-66981-2, ISBN13: 978-0-521-66981-8.
Dewey:220.9.

Audience: **g,l,u,f.** *Choice, 1997.*

Lampe, G. W. (Editor)   **BS612**
The West from the Fathers to the Reformation. Trade Cloth.
Cambridge University Press. New York, NY. 1969. 576p. The
Cambridge History of the Bible Ser., Vol. 2
ISBN:0-521-04255-0, ISBN13: 978-0-521-04255-0. Dewey:220.
LCCN:63-024435.

Audience: **g,l,u,f.**

Pelikan, Jaroslav   **BS445.P46 2004**
Whose Bible Is It?: A History of the Scriptures Through the
Ages. Trade Cloth. Penguin Group (USA) Inc. New York, NY.
2005. 288p. ISBN:0-670-03385-5, ISBN13: 978-0-670-03385-0.
Dewey:220/.09. LCCN:2004-058049.

Audience: **g,l,u,f.** *Choice, 2005.*

Ramsay, William M.   **BS475.2.R36 1994**
The Westminster Guide to the Books of the Bible. Trade Cloth.
Westminster John Knox Press. Louisville, KY. 1994. 608p.
ISBN:0-664-22061-4, ISBN13: 978-0-664-22061-7.
Dewey:220.6/1. LCCN:94-002706.

Audience: **g,l,u.**

Riches, John   **BS445.R53 2000**
The Bible: A Very Short Introduction. Trade Paper. Oxford
University Press, Inc. New York, NY. 2000. 164p. Very Short
Introductions Ser. ISBN:0-19-285343-0, ISBN13:
978-0-19-285343-1. Dewey:220.6/1. LCCN:99-059056.

Audience: **g,l,u.**

Von Campenhausen, Hans   **BS465**
The Formation of the Christian Bible. J. A. Baker (Translator).
Trade Paper. Sigler Press. Mifflintown, PA. 1997. 342p.
ISBN:1-888961-02-3, ISBN13: 978-1-888961-02-7.
Dewey:220.1/2.

Audience: **u,f.**

Christianity > Bible > Works about the Bible > Commentaries

Bergant, Dianne & Karris,   **BS491.2.C66 1989**
Robert J. (Editors)
Collegeville Bible Commentary. Trade Cloth. Liturgical Press.
Collegeville, MN. 2005. 1,344p. ISBN:0-8146-1484-1, ISBN13:
978-0-8146-1484-6. Dewey:220.7/7. LCCN:88-027356.

Audience: **g,l,u.**

Brown, Raymond E., et al.   **BS491.2.N485 1999**
The New Jerome Biblical Commentary. Ed. 3. Joseph A.
Fitzmyer & Roland E. Murphy (Authors). Trade Paper. Prentice
Hall PTR. Upper Saddle River, NJ. 1999. 1475p.
ISBN:0-13-859836-3, ISBN13: 978-0-13-859836-5.
Dewey:220.6. LCCN:99-040992.

Audience: **g,l,u.**

Dunn, James D. G. &   **BS491.3.E37 2003**
Rogerson, John (Editors)
Eerdmans Commentary on the Bible. Trade Cloth. William B.
Eerdmans Publishing Company. Grand Rapids, MI. 2004.
1649p. ISBN:0-8028-3711-5, ISBN13: 978-0-8028-3711-0.
Dewey:220.7. LCCN:2003-049524.

Audience: **g,l,u.**

Keck, Leander E. (Editor),   **BS491.2**
et al.
The New Interpreter's Bible, Vol. 11. Thomas G. Long, David
L. Petersen, Bruce C. Birch, John J. Collins, Katheryn Pfisterer
Daar, William L. Lane, James Earl Massey & Gail R. O'Day
(Editors). Trade Cloth, CD-ROM. Abingdon Press. Nashville,
TN. 2004. ISBN:0-687-01999-0, ISBN13: 978-0-687-01999-1.
Dewey:220.7.

Audience: **g,l,u.**

Mays, James L. & Gaventa,   **BS491.2.H37 2000**
Beverly R.
HarperCollins Bible Commentary. Ed. 2. Society of Biblical
Literature Staff (Editor). Trade Cloth. HarperCollins Publishers.
New York, NY. 2000. 1232p. ISBN:0-06-065548-8, ISBN13:
978-0-06-065548-8. Dewey:220.7. LCCN:00-020818.

Audience: **g,l,u.** *Choice, 2001.*

Christianity > Bible > Works about the Bible > Criticism and Interpretation

Barton, John (Editor)   **BS511.2 .C35 1998**
The Cambridge Companion to Biblical Interpretation. Trade
Paper. Cambridge University Press. New York, NY. 1998. 354p.
Companions to Religion Ser. ISBN:0-521-48593-2, ISBN13:
978-0-521-48593-7. Dewey:220.6/1. LCCN:97-027945.

Audience: **g,l,u.** *Choice, 1999.*

Davis, Ellen F. & Hays,   **BS476.A78 2003**
Richard B. (Editors)
The Art of Reading Scripture. Trade Cloth. William B.
Eerdmans Publishing Company. Grand Rapids, MI. 2004. 336p.
ISBN:0-8028-1269-4, ISBN13: 978-0-8028-1269-8.
Dewey:220.6/01. LCCN:2003-063072.

Audience: **f.**

Evans, Craig A. (Editor)   **BS500**
The Interpretation of Scripture in Early Judaism and
Christianity: Studies in Language and Tradition. Trade Cloth.
Continuum International Publishing Group, Ltd. London, 2000.

415p. Journal for the Study of the Pseudepigrapha Supplement Ser., Vol. 33 ISBN:1-84127-076-8, ISBN13: 978-1-84127-076-0. Dewey:220.6/09015.

Audience: **g,u,f.**

Hall, Christopher A.   **BS500.H27 1998**
Reading Scripture with the Church Fathers. Trade Paper. InterVarsity Press. Downers Grove, IL. 1998. 225p. ISBN:0-8308-1500-7, ISBN13: 978-0-8308-1500-5. Dewey:270.1. LCCN:98-023027.

Audience: **g,l,u.**

Hayes, John (Editor)   **BS500.D5 1999**
Dictionary of Biblical Interpretation. Trade Cloth. Abingdon Press. Nashville, TN. 2004. 704p. ISBN:0-687-05531-8, ISBN13: 978-0-687-05531-9. Dewey:220.6/03. LCCN:98-042795.

Audience: **g,l,u.**

Krentz, Edgar   **BS476**
The Historical-Critical Method. Trade Paper. Wipf & Stock Publishers. Eugene, OR. 2002. 96p. ISBN:1-57910-903-9, ISBN13: 978-1-57910-903-5. Dewey:220.6/7.

Audience: **l,u.**

McKnight, Edgar V. & Via,   **BS2555.2**
Dan O. Jr.
What Is Form Criticism? Trade Paper. Wipf & Stock Publishers. Eugene, OR. 1997. 96p. ISBN:1-57910-055-4, ISBN13: 978-1-57910-055-1. Dewey:226.0663.

Audience: **l,u.**

Morgan, Robert P. &   **BS511.2.M67 1988**
Barton, John
Biblical Interpretation. Paper Text. Oxford University Press, Inc. New York, NY. 1988. 352p. Oxford Bible Ser. ISBN:0-19-213257-1, ISBN13: 978-0-19-213257-4. Dewey:220.6/01. LCCN:88-005286.

Audience: **g,l,u.** *Choice, 1989.*

Perrin, Norman   **BS2553**
What Is Redaction Criticism? Dan O. Via Jr. (Editor). Trade Paper. Augsburg Fortress, Publishers. Minneapolis, MN. 1969. 96p. Guides to Biblical Scholarship ISBN:0-8006-0181-5, ISBN13: 978-0-8006-0181-2. Dewey:226. LCCN:72-081529.

Audience: **g,l,u.**

Vanhoozer, Kevin J.   **BS440.D495 2005**
(Editor), et al.
Dictionary for Theological Interpretation of the Bible. Craig G. Bartholomew, Daniel J. Treier & N. T. Wright (Editors). Saddle Stitched, Cloth over Boards, Dust Jacket. Baker Academic. Ada, MI. 2005. 896p. ISBN:0-8010-2694-6, ISBN13: 978-0-8010-2694-2. Dewey:220.3. LCCN:2005-015484.

Audience: **u,f.** *Choice, 2006.*

Christianity > Bible > Works about the Bible > Bible as Literature. Bible Biography

Alter, Robert   **BS535**
The Literary Guide to the Bible. Frank Kermode (Editor). Trade Paper. Harvard University Press. Cambridge, MA. 1990. 696p. ISBN:0-674-87531-1, ISBN13: 978-0-674-87531-9. Dewey:809/.93522.

Audience: **g,l,u,f.** *Choice, 1988.*

Barr, James   **BS480**
The Scope and Authority of the Bible. Trade Cloth. SCM-Canterbury Press Ltd. London, 2002. 170p. ISBN:0-334-02879-5, ISBN13: 978-0-334-02879-6. Dewey:220.1.

Audience: **l,u.**

Berlin, Adele   **BS535**
Poetics and Interpretation of Biblical Narrative. Trade Paper. Eisenbrauns, Inc. Winona Lake, IN. 1994. 180p. ISBN:1-57506-002-7, ISBN13: 978-1-57506-002-6. Dewey:220.6/6. LCCN:94-004841.

Audience: **u,f.**

Caird, George B.   **BS537.C33 1997**
The Language and Imagery of the Bible. N. T. Wright (Introduction by). Trade Paper. William B. Eerdmans Publishing Company. Grand Rapids, MI. 1997. 308p. ISBN:0-8028-4221-6, ISBN13: 978-0-8028-4221-3. Dewey:220.6/6. LCCN:96-016345.

Audience: **u,f.**

Craven, Toni & Kraemer,   **BS575**
Ross S. (Editors)
Women in Scripture: A Dictionary of Named and Unnamed Women in the Hebrew Bible, the Apocryphal/Deuterocanonical Books and New Testament. Carol L. Meyers (Photographer). Trade Paper. William B. Eerdmans Publishing Company. Grand Rapids, MI. 2001. 607p. ISBN:0-8028-4962-8, ISBN13: 978-0-8028-4962-5. Dewey:220.9/2/082.

Audience: **g,l,u,f.** *Choice, 2000.*

Fee, Gordon D.   **BS612**
How to Read the Bible for All Its Worth. Trade Cloth. Zondervan. Grand Rapids, MI. 2003. ISBN:0-310-24964-3, ISBN13: 978-0-310-24964-1. Dewey:220.

Audience: **g,l,u.**

Gabel, John B., et al.   **BS535.G25 2005**
The Bible As Literature: An Introduction. Ed. 5. Charles B. Wheeler, Anthony D. York & David Citino (Authors). Trade Paper. Oxford University Press, Inc. New York, NY. 2005. 432p. ISBN:0-19-517907-2, ISBN13: 978-0-19-517907-1. Dewey:809/.93522. LCCN:2005-052323.

Audience: **g,l,u.**

Gardner, Paul D. (Editor)   **220.92**
The Complete Who's Who in the Bible. Trade Cloth.

Zondervan. Grand Rapids, MI. 1996. 496p.
ISBN:0-310-21122-0, ISBN13: 978-0-310-21122-8.
Dewey:220.9/2.

Audience: **g,l,u,f.**

Johnson, Marshall D.   BS535.J64 2001
Making Sense of the Bible: Literary Type As an Approach to
Understanding. Trade Paper. William B. Eerdmans Publishing
Company. Grand Rapids, MI. 2002. 170p. ISBN:0-8028-4919-9,
ISBN13: 978-0-8028-4919-9. Dewey:809/.93522.
LCCN:2001-053865.

Audience: **g,l,u.**   *Choice, 2002.*

Christianity > Bible > Works about the Bible > Other Topics

Bartlett, John R. (Editor)   BS621.A68 1996
Archaeology and Biblical Interpretation. Paper over Boards.
Routledge. New York, NY. 1997. 192p. ISBN:0-415-14113-3,
ISBN13: 978-0-415-14113-0. Dewey:220.9/3. LCCN:96-013808.
Audience: **u,f.**

Brisco, Thomas V.   G2230
Holman Bible Atlas: A Complete Guide to the Expansive
Geography of Biblical History. Trade Cloth. B&H Publishing
Group. Nashville, TN. 2004. 304p. ISBN:1-55819-709-5,
ISBN13: 978-1-55819-709-1. Dewey:220.9/1/0223.
Audience: **g,l,u,f.**

Collins, John J.   BS646.C65 1998
The Apocalyptic Imagination: An Introduction to Jewish
Apocalyptic Literature. Ed. 2. Trade Paper. William B.
Eerdmans Publishing Company. Grand Rapids, MI. 1998. 350p.
Biblical Resource Ser. ISBN:0-8028-4371-9, ISBN13:
978-0-8028-4371-5. Dewey:229/.913. LCCN:97-049578.
Audience: **u,f.**

Coogan, Michael D.   BS635.2.O94 2001
The Oxford History of the Biblical World. Trade Cloth. Oxford
University Press, Inc. New York, NY. 1999. 656p.
ISBN:0-19-508707-0, ISBN13: 978-0-19-508707-9.
Dewey:220.9/5. LCCN:00-060612.
Audience: **g,l,u,f.**

Davis, Thomas W.   BS621.D38 2004
Shifting Sands: The Rise and Fall of Biblical Archaeology.
Trade Cloth. Oxford University Press, Inc. New York, NY. 2004.
192p. ISBN:0-19-516710-4, ISBN13: 978-0-19-516710-8.
Dewey:220.9/3/09. LCCN:2003-006652.
Audience: **g,l,u,f.**   *Choice, 2004.*

Dever, William G.   BS635.2
What Did the Biblical Writers Know and When Did They Know
It?: What Archaeology Can Tell Us about the Reality of Ancient
Israel. Trade Paper. William B. Eerdmans Publishing Company.
Grand Rapids, MI. 2002. 326p. ISBN:0-8028-2126-X, ISBN13:
978-0-8028-2126-3. Dewey:220.9/5.
Audience: **l,u,f.**   *Choice, 2001.*

Evans, Craig A.   DS111.9.E93 2003
Jesus and the Ossuaries. Trade Cloth. Baylor University Press.
Waco, TX. 2004. x, 168p. ISBN:0-918954-88-6, ISBN13:
978-0-918954-88-6. Dewey:933/.05. LCCN:2003-016223.
Audience: **g,l,u,f.**   *Choice, 2004.*

Finegan, Jack   BS637.2.F5 1998
Handbook of Biblical Chronology: Principles of Time
Reckoning in the Ancient World and Problems of Chronology in
the Bible. Ed. 2. Trade Cloth. Hendrickson Publishers, Inc.
Peabody, MA. 1998. 464p. ISBN:1-56563-143-9, ISBN13:
978-1-56563-143-4. Dewey:220.9. LCCN:95-030873.
Audience: **g,l,u.**

Harpur, James &   BS635.2H38 1998
Braybrooke, Marcus
The Collegeville Atlas of the Bible. Trade Cloth. Liturgical
Press. Collegeville, MN. 2005. 144p. ISBN:0-8146-2702-1,
ISBN13: 978-0-8146-2702-0. Dewey:220.9/5. LCCN:99-018653.
Audience: **g,l,u,f.**

Mazar, Amihai   BS621.M39 1990
Archaelogy of the Land of the Bible. Trade Cloth. Doubleday
Publishing. New York, NY. 1990. 608p. The Anchor Bible
Reference Library Ser. ISBN:0-385-23970-X, ISBN13:
978-0-385-23970-7. Dewey:220.9/3. LCCN:88-030999.
Audience: **g,l,u.**   *Choice, 1990.*

Meyers, Eric M. (Editor)   DS56.O9 1997
The Oxford Encyclopedia of Archaeology in the Near East, Set,
Vols. 1-4. American Schools of Oriental Research Staff
(Compiled by). Cloth Text. Oxford University Press, Inc. New
York, NY. 1996. 2608p. ISBN:0-19-506512-3, ISBN13:
978-0-19-506512-1. Dewey:939.4. LCCN:96-017152.
Audience: **g,l,u,f.**   *Choice, 1997.*

Negev, Avraham (Editor)   DS111
Archaeological Encyclopedia of the Holy Land. Trade Paper.
Continuum International Publishing Group, Ltd. London, 2003.
512p. ISBN:0-8264-1527-X, ISBN13: 978-0-8264-1527-1.
Dewey:913.33/03.
Audience: **g,l,u,f.**   *Choice, 2001.*

Rowland, Christopher   BT821.2
The Open Heaven: A Study of Apocalyptic in Judaism and Early
Christianity. Trade Paper. Wipf & Stock Publishers. Eugene,
OR. 2002. 576p. ISBN:1-59244-012-6, ISBN13:
978-1-59244-012-2. Dewey:236.
Audience: **l,u.**

Russell, Letty M. (Editor)   BS680.W7.F46 1985
Feminist Interpretation of the Bible. Trade Paper. Westminster
John Knox Press. Louisville, KY. 1985. 166p.
ISBN:0-664-24639-7, ISBN13: 978-0-664-24639-6.
Dewey:220.6. LCCN:84-017342.
Audience: **l,u.**   *Choice, 1985.*

Segovia, Fernando F.   BS511.3
(Editor)
Postcolonial Biblical Criticism: Interdisciplinary Intersections.
Perfect, Paper over Boards. Continuum International Publishing

Group, Ltd. London, 2005. 206p. The Bible and Postcolonialism Ser. ISBN:0-567-08439-6, ISBN13: 978-0-567-08439-2. Dewey:220.6. LCCN:2005-282541.

Audience: **u,f.**

Stern, Ephraim   **BS621**
Archaeology of the Land of the Bible: The Assyrian, Babylonian, and Persian Periods (782-332 B. C. E.). Trade Cloth. Doubleday Publishing. New York, NY. 2001. 704p. ISBN:0-385-42450-7, ISBN13: 978-0-385-42450-9. Dewey:220.93.

Audience: **g,l,u,f.** *Choice, 2001.*

Van der Toorn, Karel   **BS680.G57 D53 1999**
(Editor), et al.
Dictionary of Deities and Demons in the Bible. Ed. 2. Bob Becking & Pieter W. Van der Horst (Editors). Trade Cloth. William B. Eerdmans Publishing Company. Grand Rapids, MI. 1999. 998p. ISBN:0-8028-2491-9, ISBN13: 978-0-8028-2491-2. Dewey:220.3. LCCN:98-042505.

Audience: **g,l,u,f.** *Choice, 2000.*

Via, Dan O. & Gagnon,   **BS680.H67V53 2003**
Robert A. J.
Homosexuality and the Bible: Two Views. Trade Paper. Augsburg Fortress, Publishers. Minneapolis, MN. 2004. 117p. ISBN:0-8006-3618-X, ISBN13: 978-0-8006-3618-0. Dewey:220.8/306766. LCCN:2004-296135.

Audience: **g,l,u,f.**

Yamauchi, Edwin M.   **BS521.2.Y36 2004**
Africa and the Bible. Trade Cloth. Baker Academic. Ada, MI. 2004. 304p. ISBN:0-8010-2686-5, ISBN13: 978-0-8010-2686-7. Dewey:220.6/089/96. LCCN:2003-057906.

Audience: **u,f.**

Yamauchi, Edwin M.   **BR133.T9**
New Testament Cities in Western Asia Minor: Light from Archaeology on Cities of Paul and the Seven Churches of Revelation. Trade Paper. Wipf & Stock Publishers. Eugene, OR. 2003. 180p. ISBN:1-59244-230-7, ISBN13: 978-1-59244-230-0. Dewey:225.93.

Audience: **u,f.**

Yamauchi, Edwin M.   **BS680.I65Y35 1996**
Persia and the Bible. Trade Paper. Baker Publishing Group. Grand Rapids, MI. 1997. 584p. ISBN:0-8010-2108-1, ISBN13: 978-0-8010-2108-4. Dewey:220.9/3/0935. LCCN:89-048988.

Audience: **u,f.**

Christianity > Bible > Old Testament > Texts and Versions

Jewish Publication Society   **BS895.J4 1985**
Staff
Tanakh, the Holy Scriptures: The New Translation According to the Traditional Hebrew Text. Trade Cloth. Jewish Publication

Society. Dulles, VA. 1985. 1622p. Bible Titles Ser. ISBN:0-8276-0252-9, ISBN13: 978-0-8276-0252-6. Dewey:220.5/2. LCCN:88-004733.

Audience: **g,l,u.** *B*

Christianity > Bible > Old Testament > Works About the Old Testament

Alter, Robert   **BS1171.2.A45**
The Art of Biblical Narrative. Cloth Text. Basic Books. New York, NY. 1981. 464p. ISBN:0-465-00424-5, ISBN13: 978-0-465-00424-9. Dewey:221.4/4. LCCN:80-068958.

Audience: **g,l,u.** *B*

Barr, James   **BS1192.5**
The Concept of Biblical Theology: An Old Testament Perspective. Trade Paper. SCM-Canterbury Press Ltd. London, 1999. 608p. ISBN:0-334-02752-7, ISBN13: 978-0-334-02752-2. Dewey:230/.0411.

Audience: **u,f.**

Barton, John (Editor)   **BS511.2 .C35 1998**
The Cambridge Companion to Biblical Interpretation. Cloth Text. Cambridge University Press. New York, NY. 1998. 354p. Companions to Religion Ser. ISBN:0-521-48144-9, ISBN13: 978-0-521-48144-1. Dewey:220.6/1. LCCN:97-027945.

Audience: **g,l,u.** *Choice, 1999.*

Barton, John   **BS1171.2.B33 1996**
Reading the Old Testament: Method in Biblical Study. Trade Paper. Westminster John Knox Press. Louisville, KY. 1997. 294p. ISBN:0-664-25724-0, ISBN13: 978-0-664-25724-8. Dewey:221.601. LCCN:96-048556.

Audience: **l,u.**

Brueggemann, Walter   **BS1140.3.B78 2003**
Introduction to the Old Testament: The Canon and the Christian Imagination. Trade Cloth. Geneva Press. Louisville, KY. 2003. 352p. ISBN:0-664-22412-1, ISBN13: 978-0-664-22412-7. Dewey:230. LCCN:2004-296077.

Audience: **g,l,u.**

Brueggemann, Walter   **BS1192.5.B79 1997**
Theology of the Old Testament: Testimony, Dispute, Advocacy. Trade Cloth. Augsburg Fortress, Publishers. Minneapolis, MN. 2003. 800p. ISBN:0-8006-3087-4, ISBN13: 978-0-8006-3087-4. Dewey:221.6/01. LCCN:97-021888.

Audience: **u,f.** *Choice, 1998.*

Childs, Brevard S.   **BS1140.2.C48 1979**
Introduction to the Old Testament As Scripture. Trade Cloth. Augsburg Fortress, Publishers. Minneapolis, MN. 2003. 688p. ISBN:0-8006-0532-2, ISBN13: 978-0-8006-0532-2. Dewey:221.6. LCCN:78-014665.

Audience: **g,l,u.** *B*

Collins, John J.   **BS646.C65 1998**
The Apocalyptic Imagination: An Introduction to Jewish Apocalyptic Literature. Ed. 2. Trade Paper. William B.

Eerdmans Publishing Company. Grand Rapids, MI. 1998. 350p. Biblical Resource Ser. ISBN:0-8028-4371-9, ISBN13: 978-0-8028-4371-5. Dewey:229/.913. LCCN:97-049578.

Audience: **u,f.**

Collins, John J.   **BS1197**
Introduction to the Hebrew Bible. Trade Paper, CD-ROM. Augsburg Fortress, Publishers. Minneapolis, MN. 2004. 700p. ISBN:0-8006-2991-4, ISBN13: 978-0-8006-2991-5. Dewey:221.6/1. LCCN:2004-302478.

Audience: **g,l,u.**

Dever, William G.   **BS1180.D66 2001**
What Did the Biblical Writers Know and When Did They Know It?: What Archaeology Can Tell Us about the Reality of Ancient Israel. Trade Cloth. William B. Eerdmans Publishing Company. Grand Rapids, MI. 2001. 326p. ISBN:0-8028-4794-3, ISBN13: 978-0-8028-4794-2. Dewey:220.9/5. LCCN:00-067678.

Audience: **l,u,f.** *Choice, 2001.*

Finkelstein, Israel &   **BS621.F56 2001**
  Silberman, Neil Asher
The Bible Unearthed: Archaeology's New Vision of Ancient Israel and the Origin of Its Sacred Texts. Trade Cloth. Simon & Schuster. New York, NY. 2001. 400p. ISBN:0-684-86912-8, ISBN13: 978-0-684-86912-4. Dewey:221.9/5. LCCN:00-057311.

Audience: **g,l,u,f.**

Hayes, John H. & Miller, J.   **DS117.M6 1986**
  Maxwell
History of Ancient Israel and Judah. Trade Cloth. Westminster John Knox Press. Louisville, KY. 1986. 524p. ISBN:0-664-21262-X, ISBN13: 978-0-664-21262-9. Dewey:933. LCCN:85-011468.

Audience: **g,u.** *Choice, 1986.*

Levenson, Jon D.   **BS1192.5.L48 1985**
Sinai and Zion: An Entry into the Jewish Bible. Trade Cloth. HarperCollins Publishers. New York, NY. 1985. 240p. ISBN:0-86683-961-5, ISBN13: 978-0-86683-961-7. Dewey:221.6. LCCN:84-052138.

Audience: **g,l,u.**

Mays, James L., et al.   **BS1171.2.O43 1995**
Old Testament Interpretation: Past, Present, and Future: Essays in Honor of Gene M. Tucker. David L. Petersen & Kent Harold (Authors). Trade Cloth. Abingdon Press. Nashville, TN. 1995. 400p. ISBN:0-687-13871-X, ISBN13: 978-0-687-13871-5. Dewey:221.6/09/045. LCCN:95-020170.

Audience: **l,u.**

Overholt, Thomas W.   **BS661.O94 1996**
Cultural Anthropology and the Old Testament. Trade Paper. Augsburg Fortress, Publishers. Minneapolis, MN. 1996. 112p. Guides to Biblical Scholarship ISBN:0-8006-2889-6, ISBN13: 978-0-8006-2889-5. Dewey:221.6/7. LCCN:95-043457.

Audience: **g,l,u.** *Choice, 1997.*

Perdue, Leo G.   **BS1192.5.P48 2005**
Reconstructing OT Theology: After the Collapse of History. Trade Paper, Saddle Stitched. Augsburg Fortress, Publishers.

Minneapolis, MN. 2005. 399p. Overtures to Biblical Theology Ser. ISBN:0-8006-3716-X, ISBN13: 978-0-8006-3716-3. Dewey:230.0411. LCCN:2005-003316.

Audience: **u,f.**

Pritchard, James B. (Editor)   **BS1180**
Ancient near East in Pictures Relating to the Old Testament with Supplement. Ed. 2. Trade Cloth. Princeton University Press. Princeton, NJ. 1969. 372p. Princeton Studies on the near East Ser. ISBN:0-691-03502-4, ISBN13: 978-0-691-03502-4. Dewey:913.394.

Audience: **g,l,u,f.**

Pritchard, James B. (Editor)   **BS1180**
Ancient near Eastern Texts Relating to the Old Testament with Supplement, Set. Ed. 3. Trade Cloth. Princeton University Press. Princeton, NJ. 1969. 548p. Princeton Studies on the near East Ser. ISBN:0-691-03503-2, ISBN13: 978-0-691-03503-1.

Audience: **g,l,u,f.** *B*

Provan, Iain W., et al.   **BS1197.P76 2003**
A Biblical History of Israel. Philips V. Long & Tremper Longman III (Authors). Trade Cloth. Westminster John Knox Press. Louisville, KY. 2003. xiv, 426p. ISBN:0-664-22090-8, ISBN13: 978-0-664-22090-7. Dewey:221.9/5. LCCN:2003-050089.

Audience: **g,l,u.** *Choice, 2004.*

Sasson, Jack (Editor)   **DS57.C547 2000**
Civilizations of the Ancient Near East, set. Trade Cloth. Hendrickson Publishers, Inc. Peabody, MA. 2000. 3024p. ISBN:1-56563-607-4, ISBN13: 978-1-56563-607-1. Dewey:939/.4. LCCN:00-063144.

Audience: **u,f.**

Trible, Phyllis   **BS575**
Texts of Terror. Trade Cloth. SCM-Canterbury Press Ltd. London, 2003. 150p. ISBN:0-334-02900-7, ISBN13: 978-0-334-02900-7. Dewey:221.9/22.

Audience: **g,l,u.**

Trible, Phyllis   **BS1171.2.T74**
God and the Rhetoric of Sexuality. Trade Paper. Augsburg Fortress, Publishers. Minneapolis, MN. 1978. 224p. Overtures to Biblical Theology Ser., Vol. 2 ISBN:0-8006-0464-4, ISBN13: 978-0-8006-0464-6. Dewey:221.83067. LCCN:77-078647.

Audience: **u,f.** *B*

Tucker, Gene M. & Knight,   **BS1160.H43 1985**
  Douglas A.
The Hebrew Bible and Its Modern Interpreters. Trade Paper. Scholars Press. Atlanta, GA. 1985. 540p. ISBN:0-89130-784-2, ISBN13: 978-0-89130-784-6. Dewey:221.6/09/04. LCCN:83-049216.

Audience: **u,f.**

VanderKam, James C.   **BM487.V26 1994**
The Dead Sea Scrolls Today. Trade Paper. William B. Eerdmans Publishing Company. Grand Rapids, MI. 1994. 223p. ISBN:0-8028-0736-4, ISBN13: 978-0-8028-0736-6. Dewey:296.1/55. LCCN:94-005571.

Audience: **g,l,u,f.** *Choice, 1994.*

Vermes, Geza (Translator)   **BM487.A3D42 2004**
The Complete Dead Sea Scrolls in English. Ed. 6. Trade Paper.
Penguin Group (USA) Inc. New York, NY. 2004. 720p. Penguin
Classics Ser. ISBN:0-14-044952-3, ISBN13: 978-0-14-044952-5.
Dewey:296.1/55. LCCN:2004-275610.

Audience: **g,l,u,f.**

Von Rad, Gerhard   **BS1192.5 .R313**
Old Testament Theology. Walter Brueggemann (Introduction by).
Trade Paper. Westminster John Knox Press. Louisville, KY.
2003. Old Testament Library, Vol. 1 ISBN:0-664-22407-5,
ISBN13: 978-0-664-22407-3. Dewey:221.6.

Audience: **u,f.**

Christianity > Bible > Old Testament > Historical Books

Boling, Robert G.   **BS535**
Judges. Trade Cloth. Doubleday Publishing. New York, NY.
1974. 376p. Anchor Bible Ser., Vol. 6A ISBN:0-385-01029-X,
ISBN13: 978-0-385-01029-0. Dewey:220.6/6. LCCN:72-096229.

Audience: **g,l,u.**

Boling, Robert G. & Wright,   **BS1293**
Ernest
Joshua. Trade Cloth. Doubleday Publishing. New York, NY.
1982. 608p. Anchor Bible Ser., Vol. 6 ISBN:0-385-00034-0,
ISBN13: 978-0-385-00034-5. Dewey:220.7/7. LCCN:79-006583.

Audience: **g,l,u.**

Campbell   **PN2287.B4**
Ruth. Trade Paper. Doubleday Publishing. New York, NY. 2003.
214p. ISBN:0-385-51085-3, ISBN13: 978-0-385-51085-1.
Dewey:927.92.

Audience: **g,l.**

Childs   **BS1245.3**
Book of Exodus. Trade Cloth. Westminster John Knox Press.
Louisville, KY. ISBN:0-664-22968-9, ISBN13:
978-0-664-22968-9. Dewey:222.12/077.

Audience: **g,l,u.**

Cogan, Mordechai   **BS192.2.A1**
I Kings: A New Translation with Introduction and Commentary.
Trade Cloth. Doubleday Publishing. New York, NY. 2001. 576p.
The Anchor Bible Commentary Ser. ISBN:0-385-02992-6,
ISBN13: 978-0-385-02992-6. Dewey:220.7/7 s 222/.53077.
LCCN:00-043177.

Audience: **g,l,u.**

Cogan, Mordechai   **BS192.2.A1**
Kings II. Trade Cloth. Doubleday Publishing. New York, NY.
1988. 408p. Anchor Bible Ser., Vol. 11 ISBN:0-385-02388-X,
ISBN13: 978-0-385-02388-7. Dewey:220.7/7 s.
LCCN:86-016780.

Audience: **g,l,u.**

Knoppers, Gary   **BS192.2.A1 1964**
I Chronicles 10-29: A New Translation with Introduction and
Commentary. Trade Cloth. Doubleday Canada, Ltd. Toronto,
ON. 2004. 560p. ISBN:0-385-51288-0, ISBN13:
978-0-385-51288-6. Dewey:222.63.

Audience: **g,l,u.**

Knoppers, Gary N.   **BS192.2.A1**
I Chronicles: A New Translation with Introduction and
Commentary. Trade Cloth. Doubleday Publishing. New York,
NY. 2004. 544p. ISBN:0-385-46928-4, ISBN13:
978-0-385-46928-9. Dewey:222/.63077. LCCN:2003-055813.

Audience: **g,l,u.**

Levine, Baruch   **BS1263**
Numbers 1 to 20: A New Translation with Introduction and
Commentary. Trade Cloth. Doubleday Publishing. New York,
NY. 1993. 544p. Anchor Bible Ser., Vol. 4 ISBN:0-385-15651-0,
ISBN13: 978-0-385-15651-6. Dewey:220.7/7. LCCN:92-012262.

Audience: **g,l,u.**

Levine, Baruch A.   **BS192.2.A1**
Numbers 21-36. Trade Cloth. Doubleday Publishing. New York,
NY. 2000. 624p. Anchor Bible Ser., Vol. 4 ISBN:0-385-41256-8,
ISBN13: 978-0-385-41256-8. Dewey:220.7/7 s 222/.14077.
LCCN:99-028025.

Audience: **g,l,u.**

McCarter, P. Kyle Jr.   **BS192.2.A1 1964**
Samuel I: A New Translation with Introduction and
Commentary. Trade Cloth. Doubleday Publishing. New York,
NY. 1979. 504p. Anchor Bible Ser., Vol. 8 ISBN:0-385-06760-7,
ISBN13: 978-0-385-06760-7. Dewey:222.43. LCCN:79-007201.

Audience: **g,l,u.**

McCarter, P. Kyle Jr.   **BS1323**
Samuel II. Trade Cloth. Doubleday Publishing. New York, NY.
1984. 576p. Anchor Bible Ser., Vol. 9 ISBN:0-385-06808-5,
ISBN13: 978-0-385-06808-6. Dewey:220.7/7. LCCN:81-043919.

Audience: **g,l,u.**

Meyers, Jacob M.   **BS192.2.A1**
Chronicles II. Trade Paper. Doubleday Publishing. New York,
NY. 1995. 308p. ISBN:0-385-50907-3, ISBN13:
978-0-385-50907-7. Dewey:220.6/6.

Audience: **g,l,u.**

Milgrom, Jacob   **BS192.2.A1**
Leviticus 1-16, Vol. 3. Trade Cloth. Doubleday Publishing. New
York, NY. 1998. 1184p. Anchor Bible Ser. ISBN:0-385-11434-6,
ISBN13: 978-0-385-11434-9. Dewey:220.7/7 s.
LCCN:90-037069.

Audience: **g,l,u.**

Milgrom, Jacob   **BS192.2.A1**
Leviticus 17-22: A New Translation with Introduction and
Commentary. Trade Cloth. Doubleday Publishing. New York,
NY. 2000. 656p. The Anchor Bible Ser., Vol. 17
ISBN:0-385-41255-X, ISBN13: 978-0-385-41255-1.
Dewey:220.7/7 s 222/.13077. LCCN:99-089367.

Audience: **g,l,u.**

Milgrom, Jacob   **BS192.2.A1**
Leviticus 23-27: A New Translation with Introduction and
Commentary. Trade Cloth. Doubleday Publishing. New York,
NY. 2001. 848p. Anchor Bible Ser., Vol. 3 ISBN:0-385-50035-1,
ISBN13: 978-0-385-50035-7. Dewey:220.7/7 s 222/.13077.
LCCN:99-086528.
                                        Audience: **g,l,u.**

Moore, Carey A.   **BS192.2.A1**
Esther. Trade Paper. Doubleday Publishing. New York, NY.
1995. 192p. ISBN:0-385-50912-X, ISBN13: 978-0-385-50912-1.
Dewey:222/.9/077.
                                        Audience: **g,l,u.**

Myers, Jacob M. (Editor)   **BS192.2.A1**
Ezra and Nehemiah. Trade Cloth. Doubleday Publishing. New
York, NY. 1965. 360p. Anchor Bible Ser., Vol. 14
ISBN:0-385-04695-2, ISBN13: 978-0-385-04695-4.
Dewey:222.7. LCCN:65-023788.
                                        Audience: **g,l,u.**

Nelson, Richard D.   **BS1275.53.N45 2002**
Deuteronomy: A Commentary. Trade Cloth. Westminster John
Knox Press. Louisville, KY. 2002. xv, 424p. Old Testament
Library ISBN:0-664-21952-7, ISBN13: 978-0-664-21952-9.
Dewey:222/.15077. LCCN:2003-268165.
                                        Audience: **g,l,u.**

Propp, William H.   **BS192.2.A1**
Exodus 1-18: A New Translation with Notes and Comments.
Trade Cloth. Doubleday Publishing. New York, NY. 1999. 704p.
Anchor Bible Ser., Vol. 2 ISBN:0-385-14804-6, ISBN13:
978-0-385-14804-7. Dewey:220.7/7 s 222/.12077.
LCCN:97-037301.
                                        Audience: **g,l,u.**

Sarna   **BS1223**
Torah (New Translation). Trade Cloth. Jewish Publication
Society. Dulles, VA. 394p. Bible Titles Ser.
ISBN:0-8276-0015-1, ISBN13: 978-0-8276-0015-7.
Dewey:222.1.
                                        Audience: **g,l,u,f.**

Speiser, Ephraim A.   **BS192.2.A1**
Genesis, Vol. 1. Trade Cloth. Doubleday Publishing. New York,
NY. 1964. 456p. Anchor Bible Ser., Vol. 1 ISBN:0-385-00854-6,
ISBN13: 978-0-385-00854-9. Dewey:222.1107.
LCCN:64-021724.
                                        Audience: **g,l,u.**

Weinfeld, Moshe   **BS192.2.A1**
Deuteronomy 1-11. Trade Cloth. Doubleday Publishing. New
York, NY. 1991. 480p. Anchor Bible Ser., Vol. 5
ISBN:0-385-17593-0, ISBN13: 978-0-385-17593-7.
Dewey:222/.15077. LCCN:90-031508.
                                        Audience: **g,l,u.**

Christianity > Bible > Old Testament > Poetical Books. Psalms. Proverbs

Alter, Robert   **BS718**
Art of Biblical Poetry. Trade Paper. Basic Books. New York,
NY. 1987. 240p. ISBN:0-465-00431-8, ISBN13:
978-0-465-00431-7. Dewey:221.4/4. LCCN:85-047550.
                                        Audience: **g,l,u.**

Clifford, Richard J.   **BS1465.3.C57 1999**
Proverbs: A Commentary. Trade Cloth. Westminster John Knox
Press. Louisville, KY. 2003. 296p. Old Testament Library
ISBN:0-664-22131-9, ISBN13: 978-0-664-22131-7.
Dewey:223/.7077. LCCN:98-050850.
                                        Audience: **g,l,u.**

Clifford, Richard J.   **BS1455.C58 1998**
The Wisdom Literature. Trade Cloth. Abingdon Press. Nashville,
TN. 1998. 192p. Interpreting Biblical Texts Ser.
ISBN:0-687-00846-8, ISBN13: 978-0-687-00846-9.
Dewey:223/.06. LCCN:98-013825.
                                        Audience: **g,l,u.**

Dahood, Mitchell   **BS192.2**
Psalms I, 1-50. Trade Cloth. Doubleday Publishing. New York,
NY. 1966. 384p. Anchor Bible Ser., Vol. 16
ISBN:0-385-02765-6, ISBN13: 978-0-385-02765-6.
Dewey:66-11766.
                                        Audience: **g,l,u.**

Dahood, Mitchell   **BS0491.2**
Psalms II. Trade Paper. Doubleday Publishing. New York, NY.
1995. 430p. ISBN:0-385-50910-3, ISBN13: 978-0-385-50910-7.
Dewey:220.7.
                                        Audience: **g,l,u.**

Dahood, Mitchell   **BS192.2A1**
Psalms III. Trade Paper. Doubleday Publishing. New York, NY.
1995. 544p. ISBN:0-385-50908-1, ISBN13: 978-0-385-50908-4.
Dewey:222.13077.
                                        Audience: **g,l,u.**

Fox, Michael V.   **BS192.2.A1**
Proverbs 1-9. Trade Cloth. Doubleday Publishing. New York,
NY. 2000. 496p. Anchor Bible Ser., Vol. 1 ISBN:0-385-26437-2,
ISBN13: 978-0-385-26437-2. Dewey:220.7/7 s 223/.7077.
LCCN:99-030321.
                                        Audience: **g,l,u.**

Pope, Marvin H.   **BS192.2 .A1 1964**
Job. Trade Cloth. Doubleday Publishing. New York, NY. 1965.
504p. Anchor Bible Ser., Vol. 15 ISBN:0-385-00894-5, ISBN13:
978-0-385-00894-5. Dewey:223.1.
                                        Audience: **g,l,u.**

Pope, Marvin H.   **BS192.2.A1**
Song of Songs. Trade Paper. Doubleday Publishing. New York,
NY. 1995. 776p. ISBN:0-385-50906-5, ISBN13:
978-0-385-50906-0. Dewey:220.77.
                                        Audience: **g,l,u.**

Seow, Choon-Leong   **BS192.2.A1 1964**
Ecclesiastes: A New Translation with Introduction and
Commentary. Trade Cloth. Doubleday Publishing. New York,
NY. 1997. 448p. Anchor Bible Ser. ISBN:0-385-41114-6,
ISBN13: 978-0-385-41114-1. Dewey:223/.8077.
LCCN:96-008214.

Audience: **g,l,u.**

Christianity > Bible > Old Testament > Prophets

Andersen, Francis I.   **BS192.2.A1**
Habakkuk: A New Translation with Introduction and
Commentary. Trade Cloth. Doubleday Publishing. New York,
NY. 2001. 416p. The Anchor Bible Commentary Ser.
ISBN:0-385-08396-3, ISBN13: 978-0-385-08396-6.
Dewey:224/.95077. LCCN:00-031673.

Audience: **u,f.**

Andersen, Francis I.   **BS491.2**
Hosea. Trade Cloth. Doubleday Publishing. New York, NY.
1980. 720p. Anchor Bible Ser., Vol. 24 ISBN:0-385-00768-X,
ISBN13: 978-0-385-00768-9. Dewey:220.7/7. LCCN:73-009008.

Audience: **g,l,u.**

Andersen, Francis I. &   **BS192.2.A1**
Freedman, David Noel
Micah: A New Translation with Introduction and Commentary.
Trade Cloth. Doubleday Publishing. New York, NY. 2000. 664p.
The Anchor Bible Ser., Vol. 24 ISBN:0-385-08402-1, ISBN13:
978-0-385-08402-4. Dewey:220.7/7 s 224/.93077.
LCCN:99-022814.

Audience: **g,l,u.**

Andersen, Francis I.   **BS192.2.A1**
Amos: A New Translation. David N. Freedman (Editor,
Commentaries by). Trade Cloth. Doubleday Publishing. New
York, NY. 1989. 1024p. Anchor Bible Ser., Vol. 24A
ISBN:0-385-00773-6, ISBN13: 978-0-385-00773-3.
Dewey:220.7/7 s. LCCN:87-034494.

Audience: **g,l,u.**

Berlin, Adele   **BS192.2.A1**
Zephaniah: A New Translation with Introduction and
Commentary. Trade Cloth. Doubleday Publishing. New York,
NY. 1994. 160p. Anchor Bible Ser., Vol. 25A
ISBN:0-385-26631-6, ISBN13: 978-0-385-26631-4.
Dewey:220.7/7 s. LCCN:93-037736.

Audience: **g,l,u.**

Blenkinsopp, Joseph   **BS1198.B53 1996**
A History of Prophecy in Israel. Ed. 2. Trade Paper. Westminster
John Knox Press. Louisville, KY. 1996. 336p.
ISBN:0-664-25639-2, ISBN13: 978-0-664-25639-5.
Dewey:224/.06. LCCN:96-021402.

Audience: **u,f.**

Blenkinsopp, Joseph   **BS192.2.A1**
Isaiah 1-39: A New Translation with Introduction and
Commentary. Trade Cloth. Doubleday Publishing. New York,
NY. 2000. 544p. The Anchor Bible Ser., Vol. 19
ISBN:0-385-49716-4, ISBN13: 978-0-385-49716-9.
Dewey:224/.1077. LCCN:00-021326.

Audience: **g,l,u.**

Blenkinsopp, Joseph   **PR9199.3.W4984**
Isaiah 40-55: A New Translation with Introduction and
Commentary. Trade Cloth. Doubleday Publishing. New York,
NY. 2002. 432p. ISBN:0-385-49717-2, ISBN13:
978-0-385-49717-6. Dewey:813/.54.

Audience: **g,l,u.**

Blenkinsopp, Joseph   **BS192.2.A1**
Isaiah 56-66: A New Translation with Introduction and
Commentary. Trade Cloth. Doubleday Publishing. New York,
NY. 2003. 368p. ISBN:0-385-50174-9, ISBN13:
978-0-385-50174-3. Dewey:224/.1077. LCCN:2002-023737.

Audience: **g,l,u.**

Crenshaw, James L.   **BS192.2.A1**
Joel: A New Translation with Notes. Trade Cloth. Doubleday
Publishing. New York, NY. 1995. 272p. Anchor Bible Ser.
ISBN:0-385-41205-3, ISBN13: 978-0-385-41205-6.
Dewey:224/.7077. LCCN:94-034473.

Audience: **g,l,u.**

Greenberg, Moshe   **BS1543**
Ezekiel 1-20. Trade Paper. Doubleday Publishing. New York,
NY. 1995. 408p. ISBN:0-385-50913-8, ISBN13:
978-0-385-50913-8. Dewey:224/.4077.

Audience: **g,l,u.**

Greenberg, Moshe   **BS192.2.A1**
Ezekiel 21-37: A New Translation. Trade Paper. Doubleday
Publishing. New York, NY. 1995. 372p. ISBN:0-385-51276-7,
ISBN13: 978-0-385-51276-3. Dewey:224/.4077.

Audience: **g,l,u.**

Hartman, Louis F.   **BS192.2.A1**
The Book of Daniel. Trade Paper. Doubleday Publishing. New
York, NY. 1995. 360p. ISBN:0-385-51602-9, ISBN13:
978-0-385-51602-0. Dewey:220.6/6.

Audience: **g,l,u.**

Hill, Andrew E. (Editor)   **BS192.2.A1 1964**
Malachi: A New Translation with Introduction and Commentary.
Trade Paper. Doubleday Publishing. New York, NY. 1998. 480p.
Anchor Bible Ser., Vol. 25D ISBN:0-385-46892-X, ISBN13:
978-0-385-46892-3. Dewey:224/.99077. LCCN:96-050480.

Audience: **g,l,u.**

Hillers, Delbert R.   **BS192.2.A1**
Lamentations: A New Translation with Introduction and
Commentary. Ed. 2. Trade Cloth. Doubleday Publishing. New
York, NY. 1972. 168p. Anchor Bible Ser., Vol. 7A
ISBN:0-385-26407-0, ISBN13: 978-0-385-26407-5.
Dewey:220.7/7 s. LCCN:91-017533.

Audience: **g,l,u.**

Lundbom, Jack R.   BS192.2.A1
Jeremiah 1-20: A New Translation with Introduction and
Commentary. Trade Cloth. Doubleday Publishing. New York,
NY. 1999. 960p. Anchor Bible Ser. ISBN:0-385-41112-X,
ISBN13: 978-0-385-41112-7. Dewey:220.7/7 s 224/.2077.
LCCN:97-035473.

Audience: **g,l,u.**

Lundbom, Jack R.   BS1523
Jeremiah 21-36. Trade Cloth. Doubleday Publishing. New York,
NY. 2004. 672p. ISBN:0-385-41113-8, ISBN13:
978-0-385-41113-4. Dewey:220.7/7 s 224/.2077.
LCCN:2003-710250.

Audience: **g,l,u.**

Lundbom, Jack R.   BS192.2.A1 1964
Jeremiah 37-52: A New Translation with Introduction and
Commentary By. Trade Cloth. Doubleday Publishing. New York,
NY. 2004. 640p. ISBN:0-385-51160-4, ISBN13:
978-0-385-51160-5. Dewey:224.2077.

Audience: **g,l,u.**

Meyers, Carol L. & Meyers,   BS1663
Eric M.
Zechariah 9-14: A New Translation with Introduction and
Commentary. Trade Cloth. Doubleday Publishing. New York,
NY. 1998. 576p. Anchor Bible Ser., Vol. 25C
ISBN:0-385-14483-0, ISBN13: 978-0-385-14483-4.
Dewey:220.7/7. LCCN:92-034535.

Audience: **g,l,u.**

Meyers, Carol & Meyers,   BS192.2.A1
Eric
Haggai, Zechariah 1-8. Trade Paper. Doubleday Publishing. New
York, NY. 1995. 552p. ISBN:0-385-51446-8, ISBN13:
978-0-385-51446-0. Dewey:220.7/7.

Audience: **g,l,u.**

Petersen, David L.   BS1198.P46 2002
The Prophetic Literature: An Introduction. Trade Paper.
Westminster John Knox Press. Louisville, KY. 2002. 352p.
ISBN:0-664-25453-5, ISBN13: 978-0-664-25453-7.
Dewey:224/.061. LCCN:2003-266201.

Audience: **g,l,u,f.** *Choice, 2002.*

Raabe, Paul R.   BS192.2.A1 1964
Obadiah: A New Translation with Introduction and Commentary.
Trade Cloth. Doubleday Publishing. New York, NY. 1996. 336p.
Anchor Bible Ser. ISBN:0-385-41268-1, ISBN13:
978-0-385-41268-1. Dewey:224/.9106. LCCN:95-036913.

Audience: **g,l,u.**

Roberts, J. J.   BS1625.3.R62 1991
Nahum, Habakkuk and Zephaniah: A Commentary. Cloth Text.
Westminster John Knox Press. Louisville, KY. 1991. 224p. Old
Testament Library ISBN:0-664-21937-3, ISBN13:
978-0-664-21937-6. Dewey:224/.9. LCCN:90-024082.

Audience: **g,l,u.**

Sasson, Jack M.   BS192.2.A1 1964
Jonah. Trade Paper. Doubleday Publishing. New York, NY.
1995. 384p. ISBN:0-385-51005-5, ISBN13: 978-0-385-51005-9.
Dewey:224/.92077.

Audience: **g,l,u.**

Christianity > Bible > Old Testament > Apocrypha

Charlesworth, James H.   BS1830
Apocalyptic Literature and Testaments. Trade Cloth. Doubleday
Publishing. New York, NY. 1983. 1056p. Old Testament
Pseudepigrapha Ser., Vol. 1 ISBN:0-385-09630-5, ISBN13:
978-0-385-09630-0. Dewey:229. LCCN:80-002443.

Audience: **g,l,u,f.**

Charlesworth, James H.   BS1830 .A3 1983
Old Testament Pseudepigrapha: Expansions of the Old
Testament and Legends, Wisdom and Philosophical Literature,
Prayers, Psalms and Odes, Fragments of Lost Judeo-Hellenistic
Words, Vol. 2. Trade Cloth. Doubleday Publishing. New York,
NY. 1985. 1056p. ISBN:0-385-18813-7, ISBN13:
978-0-385-18813-5. Dewey:229. LCCN:80-002443.

Audience: **g,l,u,f.**

deSilva, David A.   BS1700
Introducing the Apocrypha: Message, Context, and Significance.
Trade Paper. Baker Academic. Ada, MI. 2004. 432p.
ISBN:0-8010-3103-6, ISBN13: 978-0-8010-3103-8.
Dewey:229/.061.

Audience: **l,u.**

Goldstein, Jonathan   BS192.2.A1
Maccabees II. Trade Paper. Doubleday Publishing. New York,
NY. 1995. 624p. ISBN:0-385-50918-9, ISBN13:
978-0-385-50918-3. Dewey:220.7/7 s 229/.73.

Audience: **g,l,u.**

Goldstein, Jonathan A.   BS1823
(Translator, Introduction by, Notes by)
I Maccabees. Trade Cloth. Doubleday Publishing. New York,
NY. 1976. 624p. Anchor Bible Ser., Vol. 41
ISBN:0-385-08533-8, ISBN13: 978-0-385-08533-5.
Dewey:220.6/6. LCCN:75-032719.

Audience: **g,l,u.**

Meyers, Jacob M.   RM671.A1
Esdras I and II. Trade Paper. Doubleday Publishing. New York,
NY. 1995. 416p. ISBN:0-385-50914-6, ISBN13:
978-0-385-50914-5. Dewey:613.28.

Audience: **g,l,u.**

Moore, Carey A.   BS192.2.A1
Judith. Trade Paper. Doubleday Publishing. New York, NY.
1995. 316p. ISBN:0-385-51168-X, ISBN13: 978-0-385-51168-1.
Dewey:229/.24077.

Audience: **g,l,u.** *Choice, 1986.*

Moore, Carey A.   **BS192.2.A1**
Tobit: A New Translation with Introduction and Commentary.
Trade Cloth. Doubleday Publishing. New York, NY. 1996. 368p.
Anchor Bible Ser., Vol. 40A ISBN:0-385-18913-3, ISBN13:
978-0-385-18913-2. Dewey:229/.22077. LCCN:95-042982.

Audience: **g,l,u.**

Skehan, Patrick W.   **BS1763**
Wisdom of Ben Shira. Trade Paper. Doubleday Publishing. New
York, NY. 1995. 644p. ISBN:0-385-51004-7, ISBN13:
978-0-385-51004-2. Dewey:229/.4077.

Audience: **g,l,u.**

Winston, David   **BS1753**
The Wisdom of Solomon. Trade Cloth. Doubleday Publishing.
New York, NY. 1979. 360p. Anchor Bible Ser., Vol. 43
ISBN:0-385-01644-1, ISBN13: 978-0-385-01644-5.
Dewey:220.7/7. LCCN:78-018148.

Audience: **g,l,u.**

Christianity > Bible > New Testament > Introductions

Brown, Raymond E.   **BS2330.2.B76 1997**
An Introduction to the New Testament. Trade Cloth. Doubleday
Publishing. New York, NY. 1997. 928p. Anchor Bible Ser.
ISBN:0-385-24767-2, ISBN13: 978-0-385-24767-2.
Dewey:225.6/1. LCCN:96-037742.

Audience: **g,l,u.** *Choice, 1998.*

Ehrman, Bart D.   **BS2330.3.E38 2003**
The New Testament: A Historical Introduction to the Early
Christian Writings. Ed. 3. Paper Text. Oxford University Press,
Inc. New York, NY. 2003. 560p. ISBN:0-19-515462-2, ISBN13:
978-0-19-515462-7. Dewey:225.6/7. LCCN:2003-047108.

Audience: **g,l,u,f.**

Fuller, R.   **BS2330.2**
Critical Introduction to the New Testament. Trade Paper. Gerald
Duckworth & Company, Ltd. London, 1998. 222p.
ISBN:0-7156-0582-8, ISBN13: 978-0-7156-0582-0.
Dewey:225.61.

Audience: **g,l,u.**

Johnson, Luke Timothy   **BS2395**
The Writings of the New Testament: An Interpretation.
CD-ROM, Trade Paper. Augsburg Fortress, Publishers.
Minneapolis, MN. 2001. 656p. ISBN:0-8006-3439-X, ISBN13:
978-0-8006-3439-1. Dewey:225.6.

Audience: **g,l,u.**

Kummel, Werner G.   **BS2330 .F413**
Introduction to the New Testament. Howard C. Kee (Translator).
Trade Cloth. Abingdon Press. Nashville, TN. 1996. 629p.
ISBN:0-687-05576-8, ISBN13: 978-0-687-05576-0.
Dewey:225.6. LCCN:74-026804.

Audience: **g,l,u.**

Martin, Ralph P.   **BS2330.2**
New Testament Foundations: A Guide for Christian Students.
Trade Paper. Wipf & Stock Publishers. Eugene, OR. 1999. 326p.
New Testament Foundations Vol. 1 Ser. ISBN:1-57910-310-3,
ISBN13: 978-1-57910-310-1. Dewey:225.61.

Audience: **g,l,u.**

Martin, Ralph P.   **BS2330.2**
New Testament Foundations: A Guide for Christian Students.
Trade Paper. Wipf & Stock Publishers. Eugene, OR. 1999. 470p.
New Testament Foundations Vol. 1 Ser. ISBN:1-57910-312-X,
ISBN13: 978-1-57910-312-5. Dewey:225.6/1.

Audience: **g,l,u.**

McDonald, Lee Martin &   **BS2330.2.M34 2000**
  Porter, Stanley E.
Early Christianity and Its Sacred Literature. Trade Cloth.
Hendrickson Publishers, Inc. Peabody, MA. 2000. 736p.
ISBN:1-56563-266-4, ISBN13: 978-1-56563-266-0.
Dewey:225.6/1. LCCN:00-039529.

Audience: **u.**

Metzger, Bruce M.   **BS2320**
The Canon of the New Testament: Its Origin, Development, and
Significance. Trade Paper. Oxford University Press, Inc. New
York, NY. 1997. 336p. ISBN:0-19-826954-4, ISBN13:
978-0-19-826954-0. Dewey:225.1/2.

Audience: **u,f.**

Robinson, John A. T.   **BS2315.5**
Redating the New Testament. Trade Paper. Wipf & Stock
Publishers. Eugene, OR. 2000. 384p. ISBN:1-57910-527-0,
ISBN13: 978-1-57910-527-3.

Audience: **l,u.**

Christianity > Bible > New Testament > Criticism. Interpretation. Theology

Aland, Kurt & Aland,   **BS1965**
  Barbara
The Text of the New Testament: An Introduction to the Critical
Editions and to the Theory and Practice of Modern Textual
Criticism. Ed. 2. Trade Paper. William B. Eerdmans Publishing
Company. Grand Rapids, MI. 1995. 384p. ISBN:0-8028-4098-1,
ISBN13: 978-0-8028-4098-1. Dewey:225.4/8. LCCN:89-027534.

Audience: **g,l,u.**

Aune, David E.   **BS2361.2**
The New Testament in Its Literary Environment. Trade Paper.
Westminster John Knox Press. Louisville, KY. 1985. 262p.
Library of Early Christianity, Vol. 8 ISBN:0-664-25018-1,
ISBN13: 978-0-664-25018-8. Dewey:225.66. LCCN:86-018949.

Audience: **l,u,f.** *Choice, 1987.*

Baird, William   **BS2350 .B35 1992**
History of New Testament Research: From Deism to Tubingen.
Trade Cloth. Augsburg Fortress, Publishers. Minneapolis, MN.

Early Christianity. Ed. 2. Trade Paper. Walter De Gruyter Inc. Ossining, NY. 2000. 375p. ISBN:3-11-014970-2, ISBN13: 978-3-11-014970-8. Dewey:225.9/5.

Audience: **g,l,u.**

Lohse, Edward   **BS2410**
The New Testament Environment. John E. Steely (Translator). Trade Cloth. Abingdon Press. Nashville, TN. 1976. 320p. ISBN:0-687-27944-5, ISBN13: 978-0-687-27944-9. Dewey:225.9/5. LCCN:75-043618.

Audience: **g,l,u.**

Meeks, Wayne A.   **BR166.M44 2003**
The First Urban Christians: The Social World of the Apostle Paul. Ed. 2. Trade Paper. Yale University Press. Cumberland, RI. 2003. 320p. ISBN:0-300-09861-8, ISBN13: 978-0-300-09861-7. Dewey:270.1. LCCN:2002-107884.

Audience: **u,f.**

Perrin, Norman   **BS2415**
Rediscovering the Teachings of Jesus. Trade Cloth. HarperCollins Publishers. New York, NY. 1976. ISBN:0-06-066493-2, ISBN13: 978-0-06-066493-0. Dewey:232.9/54. LCCN:67-011510.

Audience: **g,l,u.**

Sanders, E. P.   **BM177**
Paul and Palestinian Judaism: A Comparison of Patterns of Religion. Trade Paper. Augsburg Fortress, Publishers. Minneapolis, MN. 2003. 500p. ISBN:0-8006-1899-8, ISBN13: 978-0-8006-1899-5. Dewey:296.3/0933. LCCN:76-062612.

Audience: **u,f.** ℬ

Weiss, Johannes   **BS2410 .W2822**
Earliest Christianity: A History of the Period A.D. 30-150. F. C. Grant (Editor). Trade Cloth. Peter Smith Publisher, Inc. Magnolia, MA. 1979. ISBN:0-8446-0959-5, ISBN13: 978-0-8446-0959-1. Dewey:225.95.

Audience: **u,f.**

Christianity > Bible > New Testament > Historical Jesus

Bornkamm, Gunther   **BT301.2.B583 1995**
Jesus of Nazareth. Irene McLuskey & Fraser McLuskey (Translators). Trade Paper. Augsburg Fortress, Publishers. Minneapolis, MN. 2003. 256p. ISBN:0-8006-2887-X, ISBN13: 978-0-8006-2887-1. Dewey:232. LCCN:95-002155.

Audience: **g,l.**

Bultmann, Rudolf   **BS2415**
Jesus and the Word. Children's Board Books. Simon & Schuster. New York, NY. 1982. 396p. Hudson River Editions Ser. ISBN:0-684-17596-7, ISBN13: 978-0-684-17596-6. Dewey:232.9.

Audience: **g,l,u,f.**

Crossan, John Dominic   **BT202**
The Historical Jesus: The Life of a Mediterranean Jewish Peasant. Trade Paper. Continuum International Publishing Group, Ltd. London, 1998. 520p. ISBN:0-567-29229-0, ISBN13: 978-0-567-29229-2. Dewey:232.

Audience: **l,u,f.** *Choice, 1992.*

Dawes, Gregory W. (Editor)   **BT303.2**
The Historical Jesus: A Foundational Anthology. Trade Paper. Westminster John Knox Press. Louisville, KY. 2000. 320p. ISBN:0-664-22262-5, ISBN13: 978-0-664-22262-8. Dewey:232.908.

Audience: **g,l,u.**

Dunn, James D. G. &   **BT303.2.H485 2005**
 McKnight, Scot
The Historical Jesus in Recent Research. Trade Cloth. Eisenbrauns, Inc. Winona Lake, IN. 2005. xvi, 618p. Sources for Biblical and Theological Study Ser., Vol. 10 ISBN:1-57506-100-7, ISBN13: 978-1-57506-100-9. Dewey:232.9/08. LCCN:2005-024554.

Audience: **u,f.**

Meier, John P.   **BT302**
A Marginal Jew: Mentor, Message and Miracles. Trade Cloth. Doubleday Publishing. New York, NY. 1994. 1136p. Marginal Jew - Rethinking the Historical Jesus Vol. 2 Ser., Vol. 2 ISBN:0-385-46992-6, ISBN13: 978-0-385-46992-0. Dewey:232.9. LCCN:91-010538.

Audience: **g,l,u,f.**

Meier, John P.   **BT302**
A Marginal Jew: Rethinking the Historical Jesus. Trade Cloth. Doubleday Publishing. New York, NY. 2001. 720p. ISBN:0-385-46993-4, ISBN13: 978-0-385-46993-7. Dewey:232.9.

Audience: **g,l,u,f.** *Choice, 2002.*

Meier, John P.   **BT303.2.M465 1991**
A Marginal Jew: Roots of the Problem and the Person. Trade Cloth. Doubleday Publishing. New York, NY. 1991. 496p. Anchor Bible Reference Library, Vol. 1 ISBN:0-385-26425-9, ISBN13: 978-0-385-26425-9. Dewey:232.9. LCCN:91-010538.

Audience: **g,l,u,f.**

Sanders, E. P.   **BT202**
Jesus and Judaism. Trade Paper. Augsburg Fortress, Publishers. Minneapolis, MN. 2003. 448p. ISBN:0-8006-2061-5, ISBN13: 978-0-8006-2061-5. Dewey:232. LCCN:84-048806.

Audience: **u,f.** *Choice, 1985.*

Schweitzer, Albert   **BT303.S42 2005**
The Quest of the Historical Jesus. W. Montgomery (Translator), F. C Burkitt (Preface by). Trade Paper. Dover Publications, Inc. Mineola, NY. 2005. 416p. ISBN:0-486-44027-3, ISBN13: 978-0-486-44027-9. Dewey:232.9/08. LCCN:2004-058649.

Audience: **u,f.** *Choice, 2002.*

Witherington, Ben III   **BT301.9.W58 1997**
The Jesus Quest: The Third Search for the Jew of Nazareth. Ed.

2. Trade Paper. InterVarsity Press. Downers Grove, IL. 1997. 334p. ISBN:0-8308-1544-9, ISBN13: 978-0-8308-1544-9. Dewey:232. LCCN:97-002731.

Audience: **u,f.**

Christianity > Bible > New Testament > Other Topics

Ferguson, Everett   **BS2545.D5F47 1984**
Demonology of the Early Christian World. Trade Cloth. Edwin Mellen Press, The. Lewiston, NY. 1984. 191p. Symposium Ser., Vol. 12 ISBN:0-88946-703-X, ISBN13: 978-0-88946-703-3. Dewey:235/.4/09015. LCCN:84-016681.

Audience: **u,f.** *Choice, 1985.*

White, L. Michael &   **BS2545.S55S63 1995**
Yarbrough, O. Larry (Editors)
The Social World of the First Christians: Essays in Honor of Wayne A. Meeks. Trade Cloth. Augsburg Fortress, Publishers. Minneapolis, MN. 1995. 416p. ISBN:0-8006-2585-4, ISBN13: 978-0-8006-2585-6. Dewey:225.6/7. LCCN:95-002033.

Audience: **u,f.**

Christianity > Bible > New Testament > Gospels

Aland, Kurt (Editor)   **BS2560**
Synopsis of the Four Gospels. Ed. 10. Trade Cloth. Deutsche Bibelgesellschaft. Stuttgart, 1976. 361p. ISBN:3-438-05405-1, ISBN13: 978-3-438-05405-0. Dewey:226.1. LCCN:76-380511.

Audience: **g,l,u.**

Anderson, Janice C. &   **BS2585.2**
Moore, Stephen D. (Editors)
Mark and Method: New Approaches in Biblical Studies. Trade Paper. Augsburg Fortress, Publishers. Minneapolis, MN. 2003. 192p. ISBN:0-8006-2655-9, ISBN13: 978-0-8006-2655-6. Dewey:226.3/06/01. LCCN:92-017158.

Audience: **l,u,f.**

Ashton, John   **BS2615.2**
Understanding the Fourth Gospel. Trade Paper. Oxford University Press, Inc. New York, NY. 1993. 616p. ISBN:0-19-826353-8, ISBN13: 978-0-19-826353-1. Dewey:226.5/06. LCCN:90-043422.

Audience: **u,f.** *Choice, 1992.*

Bauckham, Richard   **BS2445.B38 2002**
Gospel Women: Studies of the Named Women in the Gospels. Trade Paper. William B. Eerdmans Publishing Company. Grand Rapids, MI. 2002. 368p. ISBN:0-8028-4999-7, ISBN13: 978-0-8028-4999-1. Dewey:226/.0922/082. LCCN:2001-059216.

Audience: **u,f.** *Choice, 2003.*

Black, David Alan & Beck,   **BS2555.2.R47 2001**
David R. (Editors)
Rethinking the Synoptic Problem. Trade Paper. Baker Academic. Ada, MI. 2001. 160p. ISBN:0-8010-2281-9, ISBN13: 978-0-8010-2281-4. Dewey:226/.066. LCCN:2001-035448.

Audience: **u,f.**

Bovon, Francois   **BS2595.53.B6813 2002**
Luke 1: A Commentary on the Gospel of Luke 1:1-9:50. Helmut Koester (Editor), Christine M. Thomas (Translator). Trade Cloth. Augsburg Fortress, Publishers. Minneapolis, MN. 2000. 480p. Hermeneia, :A Critical and Historical Commentary on the Bible Ser. ISBN:0-8006-6044-7, ISBN13: 978-0-8006-6044-4. Dewey:226.4/077. LCCN:2001-059786.

Audience: **g,l,u.**

Brown, Raymond E.   **BS2575.2**
The Birth of the Messiah: A Commentary on the Infancy Narratives in the Gospels of Matthew and Luke. Trade Paper. Doubleday Publishing. New York, NY. 1999. 752p. ISBN:0-385-49447-5, ISBN13: 978-0-385-49447-2. Dewey:226/.2/066.

Audience: **g,l,u.**

Brown, Raymond E.   **BT431.B74 1998**
The Death of the Messiah: From Gethsemane to the Grave: A Commentary on the Passion Narratives in the Four Gospels. Trade Paper. Doubleday Publishing. New York, NY. 1999. 912p. Anchor Bible Reference Library ISBN:0-385-49448-3, ISBN13: 978-0-385-49448-9. Dewey:226/.07. LCCN:98-024248.

Audience: **g,l,u.**

Brown, Raymond E.   **BS2615.52.B76 2003**
An Introduction to the Gospel of John. Francis J. Moloney (Editor). Trade Cloth. Doubleday Publishing. New York, NY. 2003. 384p. The Anchor Bible Reference Library ISBN:0-385-50722-4, ISBN13: 978-0-385-50722-6. Dewey:226.5/06. LCCN:2002-073475.

Audience: **g,l,u.**

Bultmann, Rudolf   **BS2615.3 .B7813 1971**
Gospel of John: A Commentary. Trade Cloth. Westminster John Knox Press. Louisville, KY. 1970. 758p. ISBN:0-664-20893-2, ISBN13: 978-0-664-20893-6. Dewey:226/.5/07. LCCN:70-125197.

Audience: **g,l,u.**

Bultmann, Rudolf   **BS2555.2**
History of the Synoptic Tradition. Trade Cloth. HarperCollins Publishers. New York, NY. 1976. ISBN:0-06-061172-3, ISBN13: 978-0-06-061172-9. Dewey:226. LCCN:62-007282.

Audience: **g,l,u,f.**

Dibelius, Martin   **BS2555.2**
From Tradition to Gospel. Bertram L. Wooff (Translator). Trade Cloth. James Clarke Company, Ltd. Cambridge, 1997. 328p. ISBN:0-227-67752-8, ISBN13: 978-0-227-67752-0. Dewey:226/.06.

Audience: **u,f.**

Dodd, C. H.   BS2615 .D57 1968
The Interpretation of the Fourth Gospel. Trade Paper. Cambridge University Press. New York, NY. 1968. 490p. ISBN:0-521-09517-4, ISBN13: 978-0-521-09517-4. Dewey:226.5.

Audience: **u,f.**

Donahue, John   BS2585.53.D66 2002
The Gospel of Mark. Trade Cloth. Liturgical Press. Collegeville, MN. 2005. 510p. Sacra Pagina Ser., No. 2 ISBN:0-8146-5804-0, ISBN13: 978-0-8146-5804-8. Dewey:226.3/077. LCCN:2001-038722.

Audience: **u,f.**

Dungan, David Laird   BS2555.2.D85 1999
A History of the Synoptic Problem: The Canon, the Text, the Composition, and the Interpretation of the Gospels. Trade Cloth. Doubleday Publishing. New York, NY. 1999. 544p. Biotechnology Annual Review Ser., Vol. 4 ISBN:0-385-47192-0, ISBN13: 978-0-385-47192-3. Dewey:226/.066. LCCN:97-049895.

Audience: **u,f.**

Goodacre, Mark S.   BS2555.52G66 2001
The Case Against Q: Studies in Markan Priority and the Synoptic Problem. Trade Paper. Continuum International Publishing Group, Ltd. London, 2001. 240p. ISBN:1-56338-334-9, ISBN13: 978-1-56338-334-2. Dewey:226/.066. LCCN:2001-048084.

Audience: **u,f.** *Choice, 2002.*

Green, Joel B. (Editor), et al.   BS2553
Dictionary of Jesus and the Gospels: A Compendium of Contemporary Biblical Scholarship. Scot McKnight & I. Howard Marshall (Editors). Trade Cloth. InterVarsity Press. Downers Grove, IL. 1992. xxv + 934p. ISBN:0-8308-1777-8, ISBN13: 978-0-8308-1777-1. Dewey:226.03. LCCN:91-032382.

Audience: **g,l,u,f.**

Harrington, Daniel J.   BS2575.3.H37 1991
The Gospel of Matthew. Trade Cloth. Liturgical Press. Collegeville, MN. 1991. 448p. Sacra Pagina Ser., No. 1 ISBN:0-8146-5803-2, ISBN13: 978-0-8146-5803-1. Dewey:226.2/077. LCCN:91-012955.

Audience: **g,l,u.**

Hengel, Martin   BS2555.2.H46 2000
The Four Gospels and the One Gospel of Jesus Christ. Trade Paper. Continuum International Publishing Group, Ltd. London, 2000. 370p. ISBN:1-56338-300-4, ISBN13: 978-1-56338-300-7. Dewey:226/.066. LCCN:00-029911.

Audience: **g,l,u.** *Choice, 2001.*

Johnson, Luke Timothy   BS2595.3.J64 1991
The Gospel of Luke. Trade Cloth. Liturgical Press. Collegeville, MN. 1991. 480p. Sacra Pagina Ser., No. 3 ISBN:0-8146-5805-9, ISBN13: 978-0-8146-5805-5. Dewey:226.4/077. LCCN:91-012956.

Audience: **g,l,u.**

Kingsbury, Jack D.   BS2575.2.K48 1988
Matthew As Story. Ed. 2. Trade Paper. Augsburg Fortress, Publishers. Minneapolis, MN. 2003. 192p. ISBN:0-8006-2099-2, ISBN13: 978-0-8006-2099-8. Dewey:226/.206. LCCN:88-003718.

Audience: **g,l,u.**

Kloppenborg, John S.   BS2555.2.K568 2000
The Formation of Q: Trajectories in Ancient Wisdom Collections. Trade Paper. Continuum International Publishing Group, Ltd. London, 2000. 400p. Studies in Antiquity and Christianity ISBN:1-56338-306-3, ISBN13: 978-1-56338-306-9. Dewey:226/.066. LCCN:99-057994.

Audience: **u,f.**

Luz, Ulrich   BS2575.5 .L8813 1995
The Theology of the Gospel of Matthew. J. Bradford Robinson (Translator), James D. G. Dunn (Contribution by). Trade Paper. Cambridge University Press. New York, NY. 1995. 180p. New Testament Theology Ser. ISBN:0-521-43576-5, ISBN13: 978-0-521-43576-5. Dewey:226.2/06. LCCN:94-030845.

Audience: **u,f.**

Marcus, Joel   BS192.2.A1
Mark 1-8: A New Translation with Introduction and Commentary. Trade Cloth. Doubleday Publishing. New York, NY. 2000. 592p. Anchor Bible Ser., Vol. 27 ISBN:0-385-42349-7, ISBN13: 978-0-385-42349-6. Dewey:220.7/7 s 226.3/077. LCCN:98-008741.

Audience: **g,l,u.**

Moloney, Francis J.   BS2615.3.M65 1998
The Gospel of John. Daniel J. Harrington (Editor). Trade Cloth. Liturgical Press. Collegeville, MN. 1998. 616p. Sacra Pagina Ser., No. 4 ISBN:0-8146-5806-7, ISBN13: 978-0-8146-5806-2. Dewey:226.5/077. LCCN:97-049883.

Audience: **g,l,u.**

Sanders, E. P. & Davies, Margaret   BS2555.2.S23 1989
Studying the Synoptic Gospels. Trade Paper. Continuum International Publishing Group, Ltd. London, 1989. 336p. ISBN:0-334-02342-4, ISBN13: 978-0-334-02342-5. Dewey:226/.061. LCCN:89-035754.

Audience: **l,u.**

Streeter, Burnett Hillman, 1874-1937   BS2555
The four Gospels; a study of origins, treating of the manuscript tradition, sources, authorship, & dates. Ed. 5. London : Macmillan. 1936.

Audience: **g,l,u.**

Christianity > Bible > New Testament > Acts of the Apostles

Bruce, F. F.   BS2625.3
The Book of the Acts. Ed. 2. Gordon D. Fee (Editor). Trade Cloth. William B. Eerdmans Publishing Company. Grand

Rapids, MI. 1988. 564p. New International Commentary on the
New Testament Ser. ISBN:0-8028-2505-2, ISBN13:
978-0-8028-2505-6. Dewey:226/.6077.

Audience: **g,l,u.**

Hengel, Martin   **BS2625.2**
Acts and the History of Earliest Christianity. Trade Paper. Wipf
& Stock Publishers. Eugene, OR. 2003. 160p.
ISBN:1-59244-190-4, ISBN13: 978-1-59244-190-7.
Dewey:226/.6/095.

Audience: **l,u.**

Johnson, Luke Timothy   **BS2625.3**
The Acts of the Apostles. Trade Cloth. Liturgical Press.
Collegeville, MN. 1992. 592p. Sacra Pagina Ser., No. 5
ISBN:0-8146-5807-5, ISBN13: 978-0-8146-5807-9.
Dewey:226.6/077. LCCN:92-036900.

Audience: **g,l,u.**

Christianity > Bible > New Testament > Epistles

Attridge, Harold W.   **BS2775.3.A88 1989**
Hebrews. Trade Cloth. Augsburg Fortress, Publishers.
Minneapolis, MN. 1988. 440p. Hermeneia, :A Critical and
Historical Commentary on the Bible Ser. ISBN:0-8006-6021-8,
ISBN13: 978-0-8006-6021-5. Dewey:227/.87077.
LCCN:87-046084.

Audience: **g,l,u.** *Choice, 1989.*

Barth, Karl   **BS2665 .B34**
The Epistle to the Romans. Ed. 6. Edwyn C. Hoskyns
(Translator). Paper Text. Oxford University Press, Inc. New
York, NY. 1968. 570p. ISBN:0-19-500294-6, ISBN13:
978-0-19-500294-2. Dewey:227/.1/077.

Audience: **g,l,u,f.**

Barth, Markus   **BS192.2.A1 1964**
Ephesians: Translation and Commentary on Chapters 4-6. Trade
Paper. Doubleday Publishing. New York, NY. 1998. 464p.
ISBN:0-385-51006-3, ISBN13: 978-0-385-51006-6.
Dewey:220.6/6.

Audience: **l,u.**

Barth, Roland & Barth,   **BS192.2.A1**
  Markus
Ephesians 1-3. Trade Cloth. Doubleday Publishing. New York,
NY. 1974. 464p. Anchor Bible Ser., Vol. 34
ISBN:0-385-04412-7, ISBN13: 978-0-385-04412-7.
Dewey:220.6/6. LCCN:72-079373.

Audience: **l,u.**

Bauckham, Richard J.   **BS2815.3**
2 Peter, Jude. Trade Cloth. Nelson Reference & Electronic
Publishing. Nashville, TN. 1983. 388p. Word Biblical
Commentary Ser., Vol. 50 ISBN:0-8499-0249-5, ISBN13:
978-0-8499-0249-9. Dewey:227.9.

Audience: **g,l,u.**

Betz, Hans D.   **BS2685.3.B47**
Galatians. Trade Cloth. Augsburg Fortress, Publishers.
Minneapolis, MN. 1979. 352p. Hermeneia, :A Critical and
Historical Commentary on the Bible Ser. ISBN:0-8006-6009-9,
ISBN13: 978-0-8006-6009-3. Dewey:227/.4077.
LCCN:77-078625.

Audience: **g,l,u.**

Bockmuehl, Markus   **BS2705.3**
Epistle to the Philippians. Trade Cloth. Hendrickson Publishers,
Inc. Peabody, MA. 1998. 352p. Black's New Testament
Commentary Ser., Vol. 11 ISBN:1-56563-350-4, ISBN13:
978-1-56563-350-6. Dewey:227.607. LCCN:98-011562.

Audience: **g,l,u.**

Cassidy, Richard J.   **BS2650.2.C35 2001**
Paul in Chains: Roman Imprisonment and the Letters of St.
Paul. Trade Paper. FaithWorks. Brentwood, TN. 2001. 352p.
ISBN:0-8245-1921-3, ISBN13: 978-0-8245-1921-6.
Dewey:227/.067. LCCN:2001-002048.

Audience: **g,l,u.**

Dibelius, Martin &   **BS2735.D513 1972**
  Conzelmann, Hans
The Pastoral Epistles. Helmut Koester (Editor), Philip Buttolph
& Adela Yarbro (Translators). Trade Cloth. Augsburg Fortress,
Publishers. Minneapolis, MN. 1972. 176p. Hermeneia, :A
Critical and Historical Commentary on the Bible Ser.
ISBN:0-8006-6002-1, ISBN13: 978-0-8006-6002-4.
Dewey:227/.8. LCCN:71-157549.

Audience: **g,u,f.**

Dibelius, Martin & Greeven,   **BS2785**
  Heinrich
James. Helmut Koester (Editor), Michael A. Williams
(Translator). Trade Cloth. Augsburg Fortress, Publishers.
Minneapolis, MN. 1975. 288p. Hermeneia, :A Critical and
Historical Commentary on the Bible Ser. ISBN:0-8006-6006-4,
ISBN13: 978-0-8006-6006-2. Dewey:227/.91/077.
LCCN:74-080428.

Audience: **g,u,f.**

Dunn, James D. G. (Editor)   **BS2650.52**
The Cambridge Companion to St. Paul. Trade Cloth. Cambridge
University Press. New York, NY. 2003. 324p. Cambridge
Companions to Religion Ser. ISBN:0-521-78155-8, ISBN13:
978-0-521-78155-8. Dewey:225.9/2. LCCN:2004-298479.

Audience: **u,f.**

Dunn, James D. G.   **BS491.2**
Romans 1-8. Trade Cloth. Nelson Reference & Electronic
Publishing. Nashville, TN. 1988. 592p. Word Biblical
Commentary Ser., Vol. 38A ISBN:0-8499-0237-1, ISBN13:
978-0-8499-0237-6. Dewey:220.7.

Audience: **g,l,u.**

Dunn, James D. G.   **BS491.2.W67 2003**
Romans 9-16. Trade Cloth. Nelson Reference & Electronic
Publishing. Nashville, TN. 1988. 502p. Word Biblical
Commentary Ser., Vol. 38B ISBN:0-8499-0252-5, ISBN13:
978-0-8499-0252-9. Dewey:220.77.

Audience: **g,l,u.**

Dunn, James D. G.   **BS580.A3**
The Theology of Paul the Apostle. Trade Paper. William B.
Eerdmans Publishing Company. Grand Rapids, MI. 2006. 844p.
ISBN:0-8028-4423-5, ISBN13: 978-0-8028-4423-1.
Dewey:227/.092.

Audience: **u,f.** *Choice, 1998.*

Elliott, John Hall   **BS192.2.A1**
I Peter: A New Translation with Introduction and Commentary.
Trade Cloth. Doubleday Publishing. New York, NY. 2001. 980p.
Anchor Bible Ser., Vol. 37 ISBN:0-385-41363-7, ISBN13:
978-0-385-41363-3. Dewey:220.7/7 s 227/.92077.
LCCN:00-021940.

Audience: **g,l,u.**

Fee, Gordon D.   **BS2675.3**
The First Epistle to the Corinthians. Ed. 2. Trade Cloth. William
B. Eerdmans Publishing Company. Grand Rapids, MI. 1987.
904p. New International Commentary on the New Testament
Ser. ISBN:0-8028-2507-9, ISBN13: 978-0-8028-2507-0.
Dewey:227/.2077.

Audience: **g,l,u.**

Furnish, Victor P.   **BS192.2.A1**
  (Introduction by)
II Corinthians. Trade Cloth. Doubleday Publishing. New York,
NY. 1984. 648p. Anchor Bible Ser., Vol. 32A
ISBN:0-385-11199-1, ISBN13: 978-0-385-11199-7.
Dewey:220.7/7. LCCN:83-002056.

Audience: **g,l,u.**

Hawthorne, Gerald F.   **BS2650.2.D53 1993**
  (Editor), et al.
Dictionary of Paul and His Letters: A Compendium of
Contemporary Biblical Scholarship. Daniel G. Reid & Ralph P.
Martin (Editors). Trade Cloth. InterVarsity Press. Downers
Grove, IL. 1993. xxix + 1038p. ISBN:0-8308-1778-6, ISBN13:
978-0-8308-1778-8. Dewey:227/.03. LCCN:93-036044.

Audience: **g,l,u,f.**

Johnson, Luke Timothy   **BS192.2.A1**
The Letter of James: A New Translation with Introduction and
Commentary. Trade Cloth. Doubleday Publishing. New York,
NY. 1995. 432p. Anchor Bible Ser., Vol. 37A
ISBN:0-385-41360-2, ISBN13: 978-0-385-41360-2.
Dewey:227/.91077. LCCN:94-040581.

Audience: **g,l,u.**

Lohse, Edward   **BS491.2**
Colossians and Philemon. Helmut Koester (Editor), William R.
Poehlman & Robert J. Karris (Translators). Trade Cloth.
Augsburg Fortress, Publishers. Minneapolis, MN. 1971. 240p.
Hermeneia, :A Critical and Historical Commentary on the Bible
Ser. ISBN:0-8006-6001-3, ISBN13: 978-0-8006-6001-7.
Dewey:220.7. LCCN:76-157550.

Audience: **g,l,u.**

Malherbe, Abraham J.   **227/.81077**
Letters to the Thessalonians. Trade Paper. Doubleday Publishing.
New York, NY. 2000. 528p. ISBN:0-385-51469-7, ISBN13:
978-0-385-51469-9. Dewey:BS192.2.A1 1964 .G3.

Audience: **g,l,u.**

Marshall, I.   **BS2735.53.M37 2004**
Pastoral Epistles. Trade Paper. Continuum International
Publishing Group, Ltd. London, 2004. 928p.
ISBN:0-567-08455-8, ISBN13: 978-0-567-08455-2.
Dewey:227/.83077. LCCN:2005-616632.

Audience: **u,f.**

Martyn, J. Louis   **BS192.2.A1 1964**
Galatians: A New Translation with Introduction and
Commentary. Trade Cloth. Doubleday Publishing. New York,
NY. 1997. 640p. Anchor Bible Ser. ISBN:0-385-08838-8,
ISBN13: 978-0-385-08838-1. Dewey:227/.4077.
LCCN:96-037760.

Audience: **g,l,u.**

Pauck, Wilhelm (Editor)   **BS2665 .L7613**
Luther: Lectures on Romans. Trade Cloth. Westminster John
Knox Press. Louisville, KY. 1977. 502p. Library of Christian
Classics, Vol. 20 ISBN:0-664-24151-4, ISBN13:
978-0-664-24151-3. Dewey:227.107. LCCN:61-013626.

Audience: **g,l,u.**

Porter, Stanley & Evans,   **BS2650.52.P38 2004**
  Craig
Pauline Writings. Trade Paper. Continuum International
Publishing Group, Ltd. London, 2005. 304p.
ISBN:0-567-04130-1, ISBN13: 978-0-567-04130-2.
Dewey:227/.06. LCCN:2005-280645.

Audience: **g,l,u.**

Sanders, E. P.   **BS2655.L35**
Paul, the Law and the Jewish People. Trade Paper. Augsburg
Fortress, Publishers. Minneapolis, MN. 2003. 240p.
ISBN:0-8006-1878-5, ISBN13: 978-0-8006-1878-0.
Dewey:241.2. LCCN:82-017487.

Audience: **u,f.**

Stowers, Stanley K.   **BS2665.2.S864 1994**
A Rereading of Romans: Justice, Jews, and Gentiles. Trade
Paper. Yale University Press. Cumberland, RI. 1997. 396p.
ISBN:0-300-07068-3, ISBN13: 978-0-300-07068-2.
Dewey:227.1/067. LCCN:94-001249.

Audience: **u,f.** *Choice, 1995.*

Strecker, Georg   **BS2805.3.S75513 1996**
The Johannine Letters: A Commentary on 1, 2, and 3 John.
Harold W. Attridge (Editor), Linda M. Maloney (Translator).
Trade Cloth. Augsburg Fortress, Publishers. Minneapolis, MN.
1995. 416p. Hermeneia, :A Critical and Historical Commentary
on the Bible Ser. ISBN:0-8006-6047-1, ISBN13:
978-0-8006-6047-5. Dewey:227/.94077. LCCN:95-036570.

Audience: **g,l,u.**

Wright, N. T.   **BS2651**
Paul. Trade Paper. Augsburg Fortress, Publishers. Minneapolis,
MN. 2005. 176p. ISBN:0-8006-3766-6, ISBN13:
978-0-8006-3766-8. Dewey:225.92.

Audience: **u,f.** *Choice, 2006.*

Christianity > Bible > New Testament > Revelation

Bauckham, Richard J.   BS2825.2 .B387 1993
The Theology of the Book of Revelation. James D. G. Dunn (Contribution by). Trade Paper. Cambridge University Press. New York, NY. 1993. 185p. New Testament Theology Ser. ISBN:0-521-35691-1, ISBN13: 978-0-521-35691-6. Dewey:228.06. LCCN:92-015805.

Audience: **u,f.**

Collins, Adela Yarbro   BS2825.2.C583 1984
Crisis and Catharsis: The Power of the Apocalypse. Trade Paper. Westminster John Knox Press. Louisville, KY. 1984. 179p. ISBN:0-664-24521-8, ISBN13: 978-0-664-24521-4. Dewey:228.06. LCCN:83-026084.

Audience: **g,u,f.**

Friesen, Steven J.   BS2825.6.E46 2001
Imperial Cults and the Apocalypse of John: Reading Revelation in the Ruins. Trade Cloth. Oxford University Press, Inc. New York, NY. 2001. 300p. ISBN:0-19-513153-3, ISBN13: 978-0-19-513153-6. Dewey:228/.067. LCCN:00-026806.

Audience: **u,f.**

Kermode, Frank   PN45.K44 2000
The Sense of an Ending: Studies in the Theory of Fiction. Ed. 2. Trade Paper. Oxford University Press, Inc. New York, NY. 2000. 218p. ISBN:0-19-513612-8, ISBN13: 978-0-19-513612-8. Dewey:801. LCCN:99-043613.

Audience: **g,l,u,f.** $\mathcal{B}$

Mounce, Robert H.   BS2825.3.M69 1998
The Book of Revelation. Ed. 3. Trade Cloth. William B. Eerdmans Publishing Company. Grand Rapids, MI. 1997. 448p. New International Commentary on the New Testament Ser. ISBN:0-8028-2537-0, ISBN13: 978-0-8028-2537-7. Dewey:228/.077. LCCN:97-025322.

Audience: **g,l,u.**

Murphy, Frederick J.   BS2825.3.M86 1998
Fallen Is Babylon: The Revelation to John. Trade Paper. Continuum International Publishing Group, Ltd. London, 1998. 496p. New Testament in Context Ser. ISBN:1-56338-152-4, ISBN13: 978-1-56338-152-2. Dewey:228/.07. LCCN:98-009598.

Audience: **g,l,u.**

Christianity > Bible > New Testament > Apocrypha

Elliott, J. K. (Editor)   BS2832
The Apocryphal New Testament: A Collection of Apocryphal Christian Literature in an English Translation. Trade Paper. Oxford University Press, Inc. New York, NY. 2005. 784p. ISBN:0-19-826181-0, ISBN13: 978-0-19-826181-0. Dewey:229.9205208.

Audience: **g,l,u,f.** *Choice, 1994.*

Schneemelcher, Wilhelm (Editor)   BS2832.S3 1991
New Testament Apocrypha: Gospels and Related Writings. R. M. Wilson (Translator). Cloth Text. Westminster John Knox Press. Louisville, KY. 1990. 2p. ISBN:0-664-21878-4, ISBN13: 978-0-664-21878-2. Dewey:229/.92052. LCCN:90-023504.

Audience: **g,l,u,f.**

Schneemelcher, Wilhelm   BS2832.S3 1991
New Testament Apocrypha: Writings Relating to the Apostles; Apocalypses and Related Topics. R. M. Wilson (Editor). Trade Cloth. Westminster John Knox Press. Louisville, KY. 1993. 896p. ISBN:0-664-21879-2, ISBN13: 978-0-664-21879-9. Dewey:229/.92052. LCCN:90-023504.

Audience: **g,l,u,f.**

Christianity > Doctrinal theology

Bultmann, Rudolf   BT80.B7813 1987
Faith and Understanding. Robert W. Funk (Editor), Louise P. Smith (Translator). Trade Paper. Augsburg Fortress, Publishers. Minneapolis, MN. 1987. 352p. Fortress Texts in Modern Theology Ser. ISBN:0-8006-3202-8, ISBN13: 978-0-8006-3202-1. Dewey:230. LCCN:86-045901.

Audience: **u,f.**

Hastings, Adrian (Editor), et al.   BR118
Key Thinkers in Christianity. Alistair Mason & Hugh Pyper (Editors). Trade Paper. Oxford University Press, Inc. New York, NY. 2003. 202p. ISBN:0-19-280279-8, ISBN13: 978-0-19-280279-8. Dewey:230/.092/2. LCCN:2003-273375.

Audience: **g,l,u,f.**

McGrath, Alister E.   BR118
The Genesis of Doctrine: A Study in the Foundation of Doctrinal Criticism. Trade Paper. Regent College Publishing. Vancouver, BC. 1995. 266p. ISBN:1-57383-072-0, ISBN13: 978-1-57383-072-0. Dewey:230/.01.

Audience: **u,f.**

Oberman, Heiko A.   BT26
Forerunners of the Reformation: The Shape of Late Medieval Thought. Paul L. Nyhus (Translator). Trade Cloth. James Clarke Company, Ltd. Cambridge, 2006. 344p. ISBN:0-227-17046-6, ISBN13: 978-0-227-17046-5. Dewey:230/.09/02.

Audience: **u,f.**

Tillich, Paul Johannes   BT75.2.T482 1999
The Essential Tillich: An Anthology of the Writings of Paul Tillich. F. Forrester Church (Editor). Trade Paper. University of Chicago Press. Chicago, IL. 1999. 304p. ISBN:0-226-80343-0, ISBN13: 978-0-226-80343-2. Dewey:230. LCCN:99-028156.

Audience: **l,u,f.**

Christianity > Doctrinal theology > Doctrine and Dogma

Ahlstrom, Sydney   BT30.U6T38 2003
Theology in America: The Major Protestant Voices from
Puritanism to Neo-Orthodoxy. Trade Cloth. Hackett Publishing
Company, Inc. Indianapolis, IN. 2003. 630p.
ISBN:0-87220-682-3, ISBN13: 978-0-87220-682-3.
LCCN:2003-054421.

Audience: **u,f.**

Anderson, Gerald H.   BT30.A8
(Editor)
Asian Voices in Christian Theology. Trade Cloth. Orbis Books.
Maryknoll, NY. 1976. 316p. ISBN:0-88344-017-2, ISBN13:
978-0-88344-017-9. Dewey:230/.095. LCCN:75-013795.

Audience: **u,f.**

Barth, Karl   BT30.G3B313 2002
Protestant Theology in the Nineteenth Century: Its Background
and History. Colin E. Gunton (Introduction by). Trade Paper.
William B. Eerdmans Publishing Company. Grand Rapids, MI.
2002. 672p. ISBN:0-8028-6078-8, ISBN13: 978-0-8028-6078-1.
Dewey:230.04409034. LCCN:2002-511442.

Audience: **u,f.**

Barth, Karl   BT28
Humanity of God. Thomas Weiser & John N. Thomas
(Translators). Trade Paper. Westminster John Knox Press.
Louisville, KY. 1960. ISBN:0-8042-0612-0, ISBN13:
978-0-8042-0612-9. Dewey:230.044. LCCN:60-003479.

Audience: **g,l,u,f.**

Chenu, M. D.   BT26
Nature, Man and Society in the 12th Century. Ed. 37. Trade
Paper. University of Toronto Press. Toronto, ON. 1997. 580p.
Medieval Academy Reprints for Teaching Ser., Vol. 37
ISBN:0-8020-7175-9, ISBN13: 978-0-8020-7175-0.
Dewey:230/.09/021.

Audience: **l,u.**

Cooper, John C.   BT28.C6 1988
The Roots of the Radical Theology. Trade Paper. University
Press of America, Inc. Lanham, MD. 1988. 174p.
ISBN:0-8191-7115-8, ISBN13: 978-0-8191-7115-3. Dewey:230.
LCCN:88-020461.

Audience: **u,f.**

Cunliffe-Jones, Hubert &   BT21.2
Drewery, Benjamin (Editors)
A History of Christian Doctrine. Trade Paper. Continuum
International Publishing Group, Ltd. London, 1997. 616p.
ISBN:0-567-08580-5, ISBN13: 978-0-567-08580-1.
Dewey:230/.09.

Audience: **u,f.**

Fackre, Gabriel   BT30.U6.F33 1982
The Religious Right and the Christian Faith. Trade Cloth.

William B. Eerdmans Publishing Company. Grand Rapids, MI.
1982. xiii, 126p. ISBN:0-8028-3566-X, ISBN13:
978-0-8028-3566-6. Dewey:230/.044. LCCN:82-002488.

Audience: **u,f.**

Ford, David & Muers,   BT28.M59 2005
Rachel (Editors)
Modern Theologians: An Introduction to Christian Theology
since 1918. Ed. 3. Trade Cloth. Blackwell Publishing, Inc.
Malden, MA. 2005. 832p. The Great Theologians Ser.
ISBN:1-4051-0276-4, ISBN13: 978-1-4051-0276-6.
Dewey:230/.09/04. LCCN:2004-029751.

Audience: **u,f.**

Harnack, Adolf   BT21 .H33
History of Dogma. Trade Paper. Wipf & Stock Publishers.
Eugene, OR. 1997. 2504p. ISBN:1-57910-067-8, ISBN13:
978-1-57910-067-4. Dewey:230.09.

Audience: **u,f.**

Haroutunian, Joseph   BX7250
Piety Versus Moralism: Passing of the New England Theology.
Trade Cloth. Peter Smith Publisher, Inc. Magnolia, MA. 1980.
ISBN:0-8446-0129-2, ISBN13: 978-0-8446-0129-8.
Dewey:285.874.

Audience: **u,f.**

Kelly, J. N. D.   BT25
Early Christian Doctrines. Ed. 5. Trade Paper. Continuum
International Publishing Group, Ltd. London, 2000. 528p.
ISBN:0-8264-5252-3, ISBN13: 978-0-8264-5252-8.
Dewey:230/.09/015.

Audience: **g,l,u.**

Lohse, Bernhard   BT21.2
A Short History of Christian Doctrine: From the First Century to
the Present. F. Ernest Stoeffer (Translator). Trade Paper.
Augsburg Fortress, Publishers. Minneapolis, MN. 2003. 320p.
ISBN:0-8006-1341-4, ISBN13: 978-0-8006-1341-9.
Dewey:230.09. LCCN:66-021732.

Audience: **g,l,u.**

McGuckin, John Anthony   BR162.3.M38 2004
The Westminster Handbook to Patristic Theology. Trade Cloth.
Westminster John Knox Press. Louisville, KY. 2004. 416p. The
Westminster Handbooks to Christian Theology
ISBN:0-664-22396-6, ISBN13: 978-0-664-22396-0.
Dewey:230/.11/03. LCCN:2003-060264.

Audience: **u,f.**

Musser, Donald W. & Price,   BR95.N393 2003
Joseph L. (Editors)
A New Handbook of Christian Theology. Trade Cloth. Abingdon
Press. Nashville, TN. 2004. 576p. ISBN:0-687-09112-8,
ISBN13: 978-0-687-09112-6. Dewey:230. LCCN:2003-005147.

Audience: **g,l,u.**

Oberman, Heiko A.   BT26
The Harvest of Medieval Theology: Gabriel Biel and Late

Medieval Nominalism. Trade Paper. Baker Academic. Ada, MI. 2001. 512p. ISBN:0-8010-2037-9, ISBN13: 978-0-8010-2037-7. Dewey:230.0902.

Audience: **u,f.**

Pelikan, Jaroslav J.   **BT21.2**
Christian Doctrine and Modern Culture (Since 1700), Vol. 5. Trade Paper. University of Chicago Press. Chicago, IL. 1991. 414p. The Christian Tradition Ser., :A History of the Development of Christian Doctrine Ser. ISBN:0-226-65380-3, ISBN13: 978-0-226-65380-8.

Audience: **u,f.**

Pelikan, Jaroslav J.   **BT21.2 .P42**
The Christian Tradition: A History of the Development of Doctrine: The Emergence of the Catholic Tradition (100-600), Vol. 1. Trade Paper. University of Chicago Press. Chicago, IL. 1975. 442p. The Christian Tradition Ser., :A History of the Development of Christian Doctrine Ser. ISBN:0-226-65371-4, ISBN13: 978-0-226-65371-6. Dewey:230. LCCN:79-142042.

Audience: **u,f.**

Pelikan, Jaroslav J.   **BT21.2.P42 VOL. 4**
The Christian Tradition: A History of the Development of Doctrine: Reformation of Church and Dogma (1300-1700). Trade Cloth. University of Chicago Press. Chicago, IL. 1984. 478p. Christian Tradition Ser., Vol. 4 ISBN:0-226-65376-5, ISBN13: 978-0-226-65376-1. Dewey:230/.09 s. LCCN:79-142042.

Audience: **u,f.**

Pelikan, Jaroslav J.   **BT26**
Growth of Medieval Theology (600-1300), Vol. 3. Trade Paper. University of Chicago Press. Chicago, IL. 1980. 364p. The Christian Tradition Ser., :A History of the Development of Christian Doctrine Ser. ISBN:0-226-65375-7, ISBN13: 978-0-226-65375-4. LCCN:78-001501.

Audience: **u,f.**

Pelikan, Jaroslav J.   **BT21.2**
The Spirit of Eastern Christendom (600-1700), Vol. 2. Trade Paper. University of Chicago Press. Chicago, IL. 1977. 358p. The Christian Tradition Ser., :A History of the Development of Christian Doctrine Ser. ISBN:0-226-65373-0, ISBN13: 978-0-226-65373-0. Dewey:230.2. LCCN:79-142042.

Audience: **u,f.**

Placher, William C.   **BT21.2.P57 1983**
A History of Christian Theology: An Introduction. Trade Paper. Westminster John Knox Press. Louisville, KY. 1983. 324p. ISBN:0-664-24496-3, ISBN13: 978-0-664-24496-5. Dewey:230/.09. LCCN:83-016778.

Audience: **u,f.**

Tracy, David   **BR118.T67 1996**
Blessed Rage for Order: The New Pluralism in Theology. Trade Paper. University of Chicago Press. Chicago, IL. 1996. 288p. ISBN:0-226-81129-8, ISBN13: 978-0-226-81129-1. Dewey:230. LCCN:95-038699.

Audience: **u,f.**

Welch, Claude   **BT28**
Protestant Thought in the Nineteenth Century: 1799-1870. Trade Paper. Wipf & Stock Publishers. Eugene, OR. 2003. 336p. ISBN:1-59244-439-3, ISBN13: 978-1-59244-439-7. Dewey:209/.034.

Audience: **u,f.**

Welch, Claude   **BT28**
Protestant Thought in the Nineteenth Century: 1870-1914. Trade Paper. Wipf & Stock Publishers. Eugene, OR. 2003. 328p. ISBN:1-59244-440-7, ISBN13: 978-1-59244-440-3. Dewey:209/.034.

Audience: **u,f.** *Choice, 1986.*

Wolfson, Harry A.   **BT25**
The Philosophy of the Church Fathers: Faith, Trinity, Incarnation. Ed. 3. Trade Cloth. Harvard University Press. Cambridge, MA. 1970. 668p. ISBN:0-674-66551-1, ISBN13: 978-0-674-66551-4. Dewey:230/.1/1. LCCN:70-119077.

Audience: **u,f.**

Christianity > Doctrinal theology > Philosophical Theology

Farrer, Austin & Conti,   **BT15**
  Charles Carl
Reflective Faith: Essays in Philosophical Theology. Trade Cloth. Colin Smythe Ltd. Gerrards Cross Bucks., 1972. xv, 234p. ISBN:0-281-02714-5, ISBN13: 978-0-281-02714-9. Dewey:230/.3.

Audience: **u,f.**

Tillich, Paul   **BT40**
Theology of Culture. Paper Text. Textbook Publishers. Temecula, CA. 2003. ix, 213p. ISBN:0-7581-6880-2, ISBN13: 978-0-7581-6880-1. Dewey:201.

Audience: **u,f.**

Christianity > Doctrinal theology > Doctrinal, Dogmatic, Systematic Theology

Aulen, Gustaf E.   **BT75 .A763**
The Faith of the Christian Church. Trade Paper. Wipf & Stock Publishers. Eugene, OR. 2002. 416p. ISBN:1-57910-944-6, ISBN13: 978-1-57910-944-8. Dewey:230.

Audience: **u,f.**

Barth, Karl   **BV4211.2**
Church Dogmatics. Trade Cloth. Continuum International Publishing Group, Ltd. London, 2004. ISBN:0-567-08384-5, ISBN13: 978-0-567-08384-5. Dewey:251.

Audience: **u,f.**

Barth, Karl   **BT77**
Evangelical Theology: An Introduction. Grover Foley (Translator). Trade Paper. William B. Eerdmans Publishing Company. Grand Rapids, MI. 1979. 219p. ISBN:0-8028-1819-6, ISBN13: 978-0-8028-1819-5. Dewey:230. LCCN:79-016735.

Audience: **l,u.**

Bonhoeffer, Dietrich   **BR45 .B6513 1996**
Act and Being. Wayne W. Floyd (Editor), H. Martin Rumscheidt (Translator). Trade Cloth. Augsburg Fortress, Publishers. Minneapolis, MN. 1996. 224p. Dietrich Bonhoeffer Works, Vol. 2 ISBN:0-8006-8302-1, ISBN13: 978-0-8006-8302-3. Dewey:230/.044. LCCN:95-038988.

Audience: **g,l,u,f.**

Cone, James H.   **BT82.7.C666 1990**
Black Theology of Liberation: Twentieth Anniversary with Critical Responses. Ed. 20. Trade Paper. Orbis Books. Maryknoll, NY. 1990. 214p. ISBN:0-88344-685-5, ISBN13: 978-0-88344-685-0. Dewey:230/.08996. LCCN:90-043041.

Audience: **u,f.**

Cone, James H.   **BT82.7**
Risks of Faith: The Emergence of a Black Theology of Liberation, 1968-1998. Trade Paper. Beacon Press. Boston, MA. 2000. 240p. ISBN:0-8070-0951-2, ISBN13: 978-0-8070-0951-2. Dewey:230.08996.

Audience: **u,f.**

Cone, James H. & Wilmore,   **BT82.7.B56 1993**
  Gayraud S.
Black Theology: A Documentary History, 1980-1992. Ed. 2. Trade Paper. Orbis Books. Maryknoll, NY. 1993. 400p. ISBN:0-88344-773-8, ISBN13: 978-0-88344-773-4. Dewey:230/.089/96. LCCN:92-044927.

Audience: **g,l,u,f.**

Cone, James H. & Wilmore,   **BT82.7**
  Gayraud S.
Black Theology: A Documentary History, 1966-1979. Ed. 2. Trade Paper. Orbis Books. Maryknoll, NY. 1993. 400p. Black Theology Ser., Vol. 1 ISBN:0-88344-853-X, ISBN13: 978-0-88344-853-3. Dewey:230/.089/96. LCCN:92-044927.

Audience: **g,l,u,f.**

Farley, Edward   **P99.4.S62F37 1996**
Deep Symbols: Their Postmodern Effacement and Reclamation. Trade Paper. Continuum International Publishing Group, Ltd. London, 1996. 160p. ISBN:1-56338-185-0, ISBN13: 978-1-56338-185-0. Dewey:302.2/22. LCCN:96-042949.

Audience: **u,f.**

Farley, Edward   **BT102.F29 1996**
Divine Empathy: A Theology of God. Trade Paper. Augsburg Fortress, Publishers. Minneapolis, MN. 2003. 336p. ISBN:0-8006-2976-0, ISBN13: 978-0-8006-2976-2. Dewey:231. LCCN:96-033148.

Audience: **u,f.**

Farley, Edward   **BT701.2.F37 1990**
Good and Evil: Interpreting a Human Condition. Trade Paper. Augsburg Fortress, Publishers. Minneapolis, MN. 2003. 320p. ISBN:0-8006-2447-5, ISBN13: 978-0-8006-2447-7. Dewey:233. LCCN:90-044380.

Audience: **u,f.**

Fiorenza, Francis S.   **BT75.2.F56 1984**
Foundational Theology: Jesus and the Church. Trade Cloth.

Crossroad Publishing Company. New York, NY. 1984. 320p. ISBN:0-8245-0494-1, ISBN13: 978-0-8245-0494-6. Dewey:230/.2. LCCN:84-007764.

Audience: **u,f.**

Ford, David & Muers,   **BT28.M59 2005**
  Rachel (Editors)
Modern Theologians: An Introduction to Christian Theology since 1918. Ed. 3. Trade Cloth. Blackwell Publishing, Inc. Malden, MA. 2005. 832p. The Great Theologians Ser. ISBN:1-4051-0276-4, ISBN13: 978-1-4051-0276-6. Dewey:230/.09/04. LCCN:2004-029751.

Audience: **u,f.**

Frei, Hans W.   **BS476**
The Eclipse of Biblical Narrative: A Study in Eighteenth and Nineteenth-Century Hermeneutics. Trade Paper. Yale University Press. Cumberland, RI. 1980. 365p. ISBN:0-300-02602-1, ISBN13: 978-0-300-02602-3. Dewey:220.6/01. LCCN:73-086893.

Audience: **u,f.**

Frei, Hans W.   **BT202**
The Identity of Jesus Christ. Trade Paper. Wipf & Stock Publishers. Eugene, OR. 1997. 206p. ISBN:1-57910-057-0, ISBN13: 978-1-57910-057-5. Dewey:232.

Audience: **u,f.**

Frei, Hans W.   **BR118**
Types of Christian Theology. George Hunsinger & William C. Placher (Editors). Trade Paper. Yale University Press. Cumberland, RI. 1994. 192p. ISBN:0-300-05945-0, ISBN13: 978-0-300-05945-8. Dewey:230.01. LCCN:91-034427.

Audience: **u,f.** *Choice, 1992.*

Green, Garrett   **BR115.I6**
Imagining God: Theology and Religious Imagination. Trade Paper. William B. Eerdmans Publishing Company. Grand Rapids, MI. 1998. 192p. ISBN:0-8028-4484-7, ISBN13: 978-0-8028-4484-2. Dewey:230/.01/9. LCCN:98-018075.

Audience: **u,f.**

Gunton, Colin E. (Editor)   **BT80 .C29 1997**
The Cambridge Companion to Christian Doctrine. Trade Paper. Cambridge University Press. New York, NY. 1997. 327p. Companions to Religion Ser. ISBN:0-521-47695-X, ISBN13: 978-0-521-47695-9. Dewey:230. LCCN:96-046023.

Audience: **u,f.** *Choice, 1998.*

Gunton, Colin E.   **BS651**
The Triune Creator: A Historical and Systematic Study. Trade Paper. William B. Eerdmans Publishing Company. Grand Rapids, MI. 1998. 256p. Edinburgh Studies in Constructive Theology ISBN:0-8028-4575-4, ISBN13: 978-0-8028-4575-7. Dewey:231.7/65.

Audience: **u,f.**

Haight, Roger   **BT202**
Jesus, Symbol of God. Trade Paper. Orbis Books. Maryknoll, NY. 2000. 520p. ISBN:1-57075-311-3, ISBN13: 978-1-57075-311-4. Dewey:232. LCCN:98-049921.

Audience: **u,f.** *Choice, 1999.*

Hodgson, Peter C. & King,   BT80.C49 1985
   Robert H. (Editors)
Christian Theology: An Introduction to Its Traditions and Tasks.
Ed. 2. Trade Paper. Augsburg Fortress, Publishers. Minneapolis,
MN. 1985. 432p. ISBN:0-8006-1848-3, ISBN13:
978-0-8006-1848-3. Dewey:230. LCCN:84-048720.

Audience: **l,u.**

Hutchison, William R.   BX1396
The Modernist Impulse in American Protestantism. Cloth Text.
Duke University Press. Durham, NC. 1992. 367p.
ISBN:0-8223-1237-9, ISBN13: 978-0-8223-1237-6.
Dewey:273.9. LCCN:91-039184.

Audience: **u,f.**

Jones, Serene   BT83.55J66 2001
Feminist Theory and Christian Theology: Cartographies of
Grace. Trade Paper. Augsburg Fortress, Publishers. Minneapolis,
MN. 2000. x, 214p. Guides to Theological Inquiry
ISBN:0-8006-2694-X, ISBN13: 978-0-8006-2694-5.
Dewey:230/.082. LCCN:00-035365.

Audience: **u,f.**

Lindbeck, George A.   BT77
The Nature of Doctrine: Religion and Theology in a Postliberal
Age. Trade Paper. Westminster John Knox Press. Louisville, KY.
1984. 142p. ISBN:0-664-24618-4, ISBN13: 978-0-664-24618-1.
Dewey:230. LCCN:83-027332.

Audience: **u,f.**

Macquarrie, John   BT77
Principles of Christian Theology. Ed. 2. Trade Paper. Prentice
Hall PTR. Upper Saddle River, NJ. 1997. 544p.
ISBN:0-02-374510-X, ISBN13: 978-0-02-374510-2. Dewey:230.
LCCN:76-023182.

Audience: **u.**

Marsden, George M.   BT82.2.M37 2006
Fundamentalism and American Culture: The Shaping of
Twentieth-Century Evangelicalism, 1870-1925. Ed. 2. Trade
Paper. Oxford University Press, Inc. New York, NY. 2006. 336p.
ISBN:0-19-530047-5, ISBN13: 978-0-19-530047-5.
Dewey:277.3/082. LCCN:2005-053920.

Audience: **g,l,u,f.**

Ogden, Schubert M.   BT80.O4 1992
The Reality of God and Other Essays. Paper Text. Southern
Methodist University Press. Dallas, TX. 1992. 238p.
ISBN:0-87074-318-X, ISBN13: 978-0-87074-318-4. Dewey:231.
LCCN:90-052663.

Audience: **u,f.**

Pannenberg, Wolfhart   BR85
Basic Questions in Theology: Collected Essays, Vol. II. Trade
Paper. Westminster John Knox Press. Louisville, KY. 1983.
258p. ISBN:0-664-24467-X, ISBN13: 978-0-664-24467-5.
Dewey:230/.044. LCCN:82-015984.

Audience: **u,f.**

Pannenberg, Wolfhart   BT80.P3413 1983
Basic Questions in Theology: Collected Essays, Vol. I. Trade
Paper. Westminster John Knox Press. Louisville, KY. 1983.
256p. ISBN:0-664-24466-1, ISBN13: 978-0-664-24466-8.
Dewey:230/.044. LCCN:82-015984.

Audience: **u,f.**

Pannenberg, Wolfhart (As   BT77
   told by)
Systematic Theology, Set. Trade Cloth. William B. Eerdmans
Publishing Company. Grand Rapids, MI. 2001.
ISBN:0-8028-3847-2, ISBN13: 978-0-8028-3847-6. Dewey:230.

Audience: **u,f.**

Placher, William C.   BT1102.P56 1989
Unapologetic Theology: A Christian Voice in a Pluralistic
Conversation. Trade Paper. Westminster John Knox Press.
Louisville, KY. 1989. 178p. ISBN:0-664-25064-5, ISBN13:
978-0-664-25064-5. Dewey:230/.01/8. LCCN:88-027706.

Audience: **u,f.** *Choice, 1990.*

Rahner, Karl   BX1751.2
Foundations of Christian Faith: An Introduction to the Idea of
Christianity. Trade Paper. FaithWorks. Brentwood, TN. 1982.
470p. Foundations of Christian Faith Ser., Vol. 1
ISBN:0-8245-0523-9, ISBN13: 978-0-8245-0523-3.
Dewey:230/.2. LCCN:82-004663.

Audience: **g,l,u.**

Roberts, J. Deotis   BT82.7.R577 2005
A Black Political Theology. Trade Paper. Westminster John
Knox Press. Louisville, KY. 2005. 240p. ISBN:0-664-22966-2,
ISBN13: 978-0-664-22966-5. Dewey:230/.089/96073.
LCCN:2005-042293.

Audience: **u,f.**

Sandeen, Ernest Robert   BT82.2
The Roots of Fundamentalism: British and American
Millenarianism, 1800-1930. Trade Cloth. University of Chicago
Press. Chicago, IL. 1970. xix, 328p. ISBN:0-226-73467-6,
ISBN13: 978-0-226-73467-5. Dewey:236/.3/0942.
LCCN:79-112739.

Audience: **u,f.**

Schleiermacher, Friedrich   BT77
The Christian Faith. H. R. Mackintosh (Translator), B. A.
Gerrish (Foreword by). Trade Paper. Continuum International
Publishing Group, Ltd. London, 2001. 776p.
ISBN:0-567-08709-3, ISBN13: 978-0-567-08709-6. Dewey:230.
Audience: **u,f.**

Tanner, Kathryn   BT65
Jesus, Humanity and the Trinity: A Brief Systematic Theology.
Trade Paper. Continuum International Publishing Group, Ltd.
London, 2001. 150p. SJT Current Issues in Theology Ser.
ISBN:0-567-08770-0, ISBN13: 978-0-567-08770-6. Dewey:230.

Audience: **u,f.**

Tanner, Kathryn E.   BR115.L25T36 1988
God and Creation in Christian Theology. Cloth Text. Blackwell
Publishing, Inc. Malden, MA. 1988. 288p. ISBN:0-631-15994-0,

ISBN13: 978-0-631-15994-0. Dewey:231/.014.
LCCN:87-033839.

Audience: **u,f.** *Choice, 1989.*

Tanner, Kathryn E. BR115.C8T36 1997
Theories of Culture: A New Agenda for Theology. Trade Paper.
Augsburg Fortress, Publishers. Minneapolis, MN. 1997. 128p.
Guides to Theological Inquiry ISBN:0-8006-3097-1, ISBN13:
978-0-8006-3097-3. Dewey:261/.01. LCCN:97-022497.

Audience: **u,f.**

Tillich, Paul BT77
Systematic Theology. Paper Text. Textbook Publishers.
Temecula, CA. 2003. ISBN:0-7581-2442-2, ISBN13:
978-0-7581-2442-5. Dewey:230.

Audience: **u,f.**

Tracy, David BT77
The Analogical Imagination. Trade Paper. FaithWorks.
Brentwood, TN. 1998. 467p. ISBN:0-8245-0694-4, ISBN13:
978-0-8245-0694-0. Dewey:230.

Audience: **u,f.**

Van Buren BT78
Theology of Jewish Christian Reality: Discerning the Way, Pt. 1.
Trade Paper. Continuum International Publishing Group, Ltd.
London, 1987. 208p. ISBN:0-06-068823-8, ISBN13:
978-0-06-068823-3. Dewey:231.7/6.

Audience: **u,f.**

Wainwright, Geoffrey BV15
Doxology: The Praise of God in Worship, Doctrine and Life: A
Systematic Theology. Trade Paper. Oxford University Press, Inc.
New York, NY. 1984. 622p. ISBN:0-19-520433-6, ISBN13:
978-0-19-520433-9. Dewey:264.

Audience: **u,f.**

Williams, Rowan BT75.2.W544 1999
On Christian Theology. Trade Paper. Blackwell Publishing, Inc.
Malden, MA. 1999. 328p. Challenges in Contemporary
Theology Ser. ISBN:0-631-21440-2, ISBN13:
978-0-631-21440-3. Dewey:230. LCCN:99-036585.

Audience: **u,f.**

Williams, Rowan BT481
Resurrection: Interpreting the Easter Gospel. Trade Cloth.
Pilgrim Press, The/United Church Press. Cleveland, OH. 2003.
144p. ISBN:0-8298-1541-4, ISBN13: 978-0-8298-1541-2.
Dewey:232/.5.

Audience: **u,f.**

Christianity > Doctrinal theology > Doctrinal, Dogmatic, Systematic Theology > Death of God. Theology. Liberation Theology. Process Theology. Secularization

Altizer, Thomas J. (Editor) BT83.5
Toward a New Christianity: Readings in the Death of God
Theology. Trade Cloth. Harcourt Trade Publishers. New York,
NY. 1967. ISBN:0-15-190902-4, ISBN13: 978-0-15-190902-5.
Dewey:231.08. LCCN:67-015377.

Audience: **g,l.**

Altizer, Thomas J. J. BT83.5.A427 2003
Godhead and the Nothing. Cloth Text. State University of New
York Press. Albany, NY. 2003. xiii, 192p. ISBN:0-7914-5795-8,
ISBN13: 978-0-7914-5795-5. Dewey:230. LCCN:2002-036481.

Audience: **u,f.**

Boff, Clodovis & Boff, BT83.57.B613 1984
Leonardo
Salvation and Liberation: In Search of a Balance Between Faith
and Politics. Robert R. Barr (Translator). Trade Paper. Orbis
Books. Maryknoll, NY. 1984. 128p. ISBN:0-88344-451-8,
ISBN13: 978-0-88344-451-1. Dewey:261.8/098.
LCCN:84-007220.

Audience: **u,f.**

Bonino, Jose M. BT83.57 .M53
Doing Theology in a Revolutionary Situation. William H.
Lazareth (Editor). Trade Paper. Augsburg Fortress, Publishers.
Minneapolis, MN. 1975. 208p. ISBN:0-8006-1451-8, ISBN13:
978-0-8006-1451-5. Dewey:261.8. LCCN:74-080424.

Audience: **u,f.**

Cobb, John B. Jr. & Griffin, BT83.6.C6
David R.
Process Theology: An Introductory Exposition. Trade Paper.
Westminster John Knox Press. Louisville, KY. 1976. 192p.
ISBN:0-664-24743-1, ISBN13: 978-0-664-24743-0. Dewey:230.
LCCN:76-010352.

Audience: **l,u.**

Ford, Lewis S. BT77
The Lure of God: A Biblical Background for Process Theism.
Trade Cloth. University Press of America, Inc. Lanham, MD.
1985. 158p. ISBN:0-8191-4902-0, ISBN13: 978-0-8191-4902-2.
Dewey:230.

Audience: **u,f.**

Gibellini, Rosino   **BT83.57**
Frontiers of Theology in Latin America. Trade Paper.
SCM-Canterbury Press Ltd. London, 1980. xii, 321p.
ISBN:0-334-00505-1, ISBN13: 978-0-334-00505-6.
Dewey:261.8.
                                    Audience: **u,f.**

Schillebeeckx, Edward   **BT83.7 .S3**
God the Future of Man. N.D. Smith (Translator). Trade Paper.
Continuum International Publishing Group, Ltd. London, 1977.
224p. ISBN:0-7220-7707-6, ISBN13: 978-0-7220-7707-8.
Dewey:260.
                                    Audience: **u,f.**

Segundo, Juan Luis   **BT83.57**
The Liberation of Theology. Trade Paper. Wipf & Stock
Publishers. Eugene, OR. 2002. 250p. ISBN:1-59244-096-7,
ISBN13: 978-1-59244-096-2. Dewey:230.
                                    Audience: **u,f.**

Witvliet, Theo   **BT83.57.W5713 1985**
A Place in the Sun: Liberation Theology in the Third World.
John Bowden (Translator). Trade Paper. Orbis Books.
Maryknoll, NY. 1985. 208p. ISBN:0-88344-404-6, ISBN13:
978-0-88344-404-7. Dewey:230. LCCN:84-027229.
                          Audience: **u,f.** *Choice, 1985.*

Christianity > Doctrinal theology > Authority. Kingdom of God

Buber, Martin   **BS1192.6.B8313 1990**
Kingship of God. Ed. 2. Richard Scheimann (Translator). Trade
Paper. Brill Academic Publishers, Inc. Boston, MA. 1990. 228p.
ISBN:0-391-03658-0, ISBN13: 978-0-391-03658-1.
Dewey:296.3/11. LCCN:90-032309.
                                    Audience: **g,l,u,f.**

Kelsey, David H.   **BT89.K44 1999**
Proving Doctrine: The Uses of Scripture in Modern Theology.
Trade Paper. Continuum International Publishing Group, Ltd.
London, 1999. 240p. ISBN:1-56338-283-0, ISBN13:
978-1-56338-283-3. Dewey:220.1/3. LCCN:99-021488.
                                    Audience: **u,f.**

Niebuhr, H. Richard   **BT94**
The Kingdom of God in America. Paper Text. Textbook
Publishers. Temecula, CA. 2003. 215p. ISBN:0-7581-3912-8,
ISBN13: 978-0-7581-3912-2. Dewey:277.3.
                                    Audience: **u,f.**

Pannenberg, Wolfhart   **BT94**
Theology and the Kingdom of God. Trade Paper. Westminster
John Knox Press. Louisville, KY. 1969. 144p.
ISBN:0-664-24842-X, ISBN13: 978-0-664-24842-0.
Dewey:231/.7. LCCN:69-012668.
                                    Audience: **u,f.**

Perrin, Norman   **BS2417.K5**
The Kingdom of God in the Teaching of Jesus. Trade Paper.
SCM-Canterbury Press Ltd. London, 1975. 215p.
ISBN:0-334-00838-7, ISBN13: 978-0-334-00838-5.
Dewey:231.7/2.
                                    Audience: **u,f.**

Schweitzer, Albert   **BT695.5**
The Kingdom of God and Primitive Christianity. Trade Cloth. A
& C Black. London, 1968. 193p. ISBN:0-7136-0909-5, ISBN13:
978-0-7136-0909-7. Dewey:231.7.
                                    Audience: **u,f.**

Tavard, Georges H.   **BT88.T35 1978**
Holy Writ or Holy Church: The Crisis of the Protestant
Reformation. Cloth Text. Greenwood Publishing Group, Inc.
Portsmouth, NH. 1978. 250p. ISBN:0-313-20584-1, ISBN13:
978-0-313-20584-2. Dewey:230. LCCN:78-017085.
                                    Audience: **u,f.**

Von Campenhausen, Hans   **BT91.C313 1997**
Ecclesiastical Authority and Spiritual Power in the Church of
the First Three Centuries. J. A. Baker (Translator). Trade Cloth.
Hendrickson Publishers, Inc. Peabody, MA. 1997. 320p.
ISBN:1-56563-272-9, ISBN13: 978-1-56563-272-1.
Dewey:262/.8/09015. LCCN:97-002500.
                                    Audience: **u,f.**

Christianity > Doctrinal theology > God

Bobik, Joseph (Translator)   **B765.T53**
Aquinas on Being and Essence: A Translation and Interpretation.
Trade Cloth. University of Notre Dame Press. Notre Dame, IN.
1988. 286p. ISBN:0-268-00617-2, ISBN13: 978-0-268-00617-4.
Dewey:111. LCCN:65-023516.
                                    Audience: **u,f.**

Burrell, David B.   **B765.T5**
Aquinas: God and Action. Trade Cloth. Routledge & Kegan
Paul, Ltd. 1979. xiii, 194p. ISBN:0-7100-0101-0, ISBN13:
978-0-7100-0101-6. Dewey:189/.4. LCCN:78-040837.
                                    Audience: **u,f.**

Evans, G. R.   **BT100.A57.E9**
Anselm and Talking about God. Trade Cloth. Oxford University
Press, Inc. New York, NY. 1978. 224p. ISBN:0-19-826647-2,
ISBN13: 978-0-19-826647-1. Dewey:230/.2/0924.
LCCN:78-040314.
                                    Audience: **u,f.**

Gilson, Etienne   **BT98**
God and Philosophy. Ed. 2. Jaroslav Pelikan (Foreword by).
Trade Paper. Yale University Press. Cumberland, RI. 2002.
182p. ISBN:0-300-09299-7, ISBN13: 978-0-300-09299-8.
Dewey:212.1.
                                    Audience: **g,l,u,f.**

Grant, Robert McQueen,   **BT98.G69**
 1917-
The early Christian doctrine of God. Charlottesville, University
Press of Virginia. 1966.

Audience: **u,f.**

Griffin, David Ray   **BT160**
God, Power, and Evil: A Process Theodicy. Trade Cloth.
Westminster John Knox Press. Louisville, KY. 2004. 366p.
ISBN:0-664-22906-9, ISBN13: 978-0-664-22906-1.
Dewey:231/.8. LCCN:2006-275044.

Audience: **u,f.**

Hartshorne, Charles   **BT102**
Anselm's Discovery: A Re-Examination of the Ontological
Proof for God's Existence. Trade Cloth. Open Court Publishing
Company. Chicago, IL. 1973. 349p. ISBN:0-87548-216-3,
ISBN13: 978-0-87548-216-3. Dewey:211. LCCN:65-020278.

Audience: **u,f.**

Hick, John Harwood   **BT160**
Evil God of Love. Ed. 3. Trade Paper. Palgrave Macmillan.
New York, NY. 1997. 406p. ISBN:0-333-39483-6, ISBN13:
978-0-333-39483-0. Dewey:231/.8.

Audience: **l,u.**

Jenson, Robert W.   **BT111.2**
The Triune Identity: God According to the Gospel. Trade Paper.
Wipf & Stock Publishers. Eugene, OR. 2002. 208p.
ISBN:1-57910-962-4, ISBN13: 978-1-57910-962-2.
Dewey:231/.044.

Audience: **u,f.**

Johnson, Elizabeth A.   **BT130**
She Who Is: The Mystery of God in Feminist Theological
Discourse. Trade Paper. FaithWorks. Brentwood, TN. 2002.
376p. ISBN:0-8245-1925-6, ISBN13: 978-0-8245-1925-4.
Dewey:231/.4.

Audience: **u,f.** *Choice, 1993.*

Kaufman, Gordon D.   **BT102 .K34**
God the Problem. Trade Paper. Harvard University Press.
Cambridge, MA. 1972. 276p. ISBN:0-674-35526-1, ISBN13:
978-0-674-35526-2. Dewey:211. LCCN:70-174543.

Audience: **u,f.**

Kaufman, Gordon D.   **BT77**
In Face of Mystery: A Constructive Theology. Trade Paper.
Harvard University Press. Cambridge, MA. 1995. 528p.
ISBN:0-674-44576-7, ISBN13: 978-0-674-44576-5. Dewey:230.

Audience: **u,f.** *Choice, 1993.*

Kenny, Anthony   **BL51**
The Five Ways: St. Thomas Aquinas' Proofs of God's
Existence, Vol. 5. Paper over Boards. Routledge. New York, NY.
2003. 144p. Studies in Ethics and Philosophy of Religion Ser..
Vol. 5 ISBN:0-415-31845-9, ISBN13: 978-0-415-31845-7.
Dewey:210.

Audience: **l,u,f.**

Kung, Hans   **BT102.K8213 1991**
Does God Exist?: An Answer for Today. Trade Paper. Crossroad
Publishing Company. New York, NY. 1994. 864p.
ISBN:0-8245-1119-0, ISBN13: 978-0-8245-1119-7. Dewey:231.
LCCN:91-004096.

Audience: **g,l,u,f.**

Lonergan, Bernard   **BT109.L6613**
The Way to Nicea: The Dialectical Development of Trinitarian
Theology. Trade Cloth. Westminster John Knox Press.
Louisville, KY. 1977. 176p. ISBN:0-664-21340-5, ISBN13:
978-0-664-21340-4. Dewey:231. LCCN:76-020792.

Audience: **u,f.**

Moltmann, Jurgen   **BT111.2**
The Trinity and the Kingdom: The Doctrine of God. Margaret
Kohl (Translator). Trade Paper. Augsburg Fortress, Publishers.
Minneapolis, MN. 2003. 272p. The Works of Jurgen Moltmann
ISBN:0-8006-2825-X, ISBN13: 978-0-8006-2825-3.
Dewey:231/.044. LCCN:93-029952.

Audience: **u,f.**

Niebuhr, Richa H.   **BT127.3 .N5**
The Meaning of Revelation: Library of Theological Terms.
Trade Cloth. Westminster John Knox Press. Louisville, KY.
2006. 120p. ISBN:0-664-22998-0, ISBN13: 978-0-664-22998-6.
Dewey:231.7/4.

Audience: **g,l,u,f.**

Plantinga, Alvin   **BT102 .P55 1990**
God and Other Minds: A Study of the Rational Justification of
Belief in God. Trade Paper. Cornell University Press. Ithaca,
NY. 1990. 288p. Cornell Paperbacks Ser. ISBN:0-8014-9735-3,
ISBN13: 978-0-8014-9735-3. Dewey:212/.1. LCCN:90-173100.

Audience: **u,f.**

Royce, Josiah   **BT101.R8 1971**
The Conception of God: A Philosophical Discussion Concerning
the Nature of the Divine Idea as a Demonstrable Reality. Trade
Cloth. Scholarly Press, Inc. Saint Clair Shores, MI. 1971.
xxxviii, 354p. ISBN:0-403-00309-1, ISBN13:
978-0-403-00309-9. Dewey:211. LCCN:79-107189.

Audience: **u,f.**

Rusch, William G. (Editor,   **BT109.T74**
 Translator)
The Trinitarian Controversy. Trade Paper. Augsburg Fortress,
Publishers. Minneapolis, MN. 1980. 182p. Sources of Early
Christian Thought Ser. ISBN:0-8006-1410-0, ISBN13:
978-0-8006-1410-2. Dewey:231/.044. LCCN:79-008889.

Audience: **u,f.**

Schillebeeckx, Edward &   **BX1751.2**
 Smith, David
Revelation and Theology. Trade Paper. Continuum International
Publishing Group, Ltd. London, 1979. xvi, 288p.
ISBN:0-7220-7956-7, ISBN13: 978-0-7220-7956-0. Dewey:230.

Audience: **u,f.**

Swinburne, Richard   **BT130.S94 1993**
The Coherence of Theism. Ed. 2. Trade Cloth. Oxford

University Press, Inc. New York, NY. 1993. 322p. Clarendon Library of Logic and Philosophy ISBN:0-19-824069-4, ISBN13: 978-0-19-824069-3. Dewey:211/.3. LCCN:92-030981.

Audience: **u,f.**

Swinburne, Richard   **BT102**
The Existence of God. Ed. 2. Trade Paper. Oxford University Press, Inc. New York, NY. 2004. 372p. ISBN:0-19-927168-2, ISBN13: 978-0-19-927168-9. Dewey:212/.1. LCCN:2004-555474.

Audience: **u,f.**

Christianity > Doctrinal theology > Jesus Christ > Christology

Fuller, Reginald Horace   **BT202**
The Foundations of New Testament Christology. Trade Paper. James Clarke Company, Ltd. Cambridge, 2002. 268p. ISBN:0-227-17075-X, ISBN13: 978-0-227-17075-5. Dewey:232.

Audience: **u,f.**

Grillmeier, Aloys   **BT198**
Christ in Christian Tradition: From the Apostolic Age to Chalcedon (451). Ed. 2. Trade Paper. Geneva Press. Louisville, KY. 1975. 599p. Christ in Christian Tradition Ser., Vol. 1 ISBN:0-664-22301-X, ISBN13: 978-0-664-22301-4. Dewey:232. LCCN:75-013456.

Audience: **u,f.**

Grillmeier, Aloys   **BT202**
Christ in Christian Tradition: From the Concil of Chalcedon (451) to Gregory the Great (590-604), Vol. 2. Paper Text. Westminster John Knox Press. Louisville, KY. 1986. 340p. Christ in Christian Tradition Ser., Vol. 2 ISBN:0-664-22160-2, ISBN13: 978-0-664-22160-7. Dewey:232. LCCN:75-013456.

Audience: **u,f.**

Grillmeier, Aloys &   **BT198**
  Hainthaler, Theresia
Christ in Christian Tradition: From the Council of Chalcedon (451) to Gregory the Great (590-604). Pauline Allen & John Cawte (Translators). Trade Cloth. Westminster John Knox Press. Louisville, KY. 1995. 544p. Christ in Christian Tradition Ser., Vol. 2, Pt. 2 ISBN:0-664-21997-7, ISBN13: 978-0-664-21997-0. Dewey:232.09. LCCN:75-013456.

Audience: **u,f.**

Grillmeier, S. J., et al.   **BT198 .G74313 1975B**
Christ in Christian Tradition: From the Council of Chalcedon (451) to Gregory the Great (590-604), Part 4: The Church of Alexandria with Nubia and Ethiopia after 451. Theresia Hainthaler & O. C. Dean Jr. (Authors). Trade Cloth. Westminster John Knox Press. Louisville, KY. 1996. 550p. The Church of Alexandria with Nubia and Ethiopia after 451 Ser., Vol. 2 Pt. 4 ISBN:0-664-21998-5, ISBN13: 978-0-664-21998-7. Dewey:232.

Audience: **u,f.**

Hardy, Edward R. (Editor)   **BT199**
Christology of the Later Fathers. Trade Cloth. Westminster John Knox Press. Louisville, KY. 1977. 396p. Library of Christian Classics, Vol. 3 ISBN:0-664-24152-2, ISBN13: 978-0-664-24152-0. Dewey:232. LCCN:54-009949.

Audience: **u,f.**

Hengel, Martin   **BT198**
Studies in Early Christology. Trade Paper. Continuum International Publishing Group, Ltd. London, 2005. 422p. ISBN:0-567-04280-4, ISBN13: 978-0-567-04280-4. Dewey:232.09/015.

Audience: **u,f.**

Hengel, Martin & Bowden,   **BS2651**
  John
The Son of God: The Origin of Christology and the History of Jewish-Hellenistic Religion. Trade Paper. SCM-Canterbury Press Ltd. London, 1976. xii, 100p. ISBN:0-334-01468-9, ISBN13: 978-0-334-01468-3. Dewey:232.

Audience: **u,f.**

Meyendorff, John   **BT202**
Christ in Eastern Christian Thought. Trade Paper. Saint Vladimir's Seminary Press. Yonkers, NY. 1975. 248p. ISBN:0-913836-27-3, ISBN13: 978-0-913836-27-9. Dewey:232. LCCN:75-031977.

Audience: **u,f.**

Norris, Richard A. Jr. &   **BT198**
  Rusch, William G. (Editors)
The Christological Controversy. Trade Paper. Augsburg Fortress, Publishers. Minneapolis, MN. 1980. 176p. Sources of Early Christian Thought Ser. ISBN:0-8006-1411-9, ISBN13: 978-0-8006-1411-9. Dewey:232/.09/015. LCCN:79-008890.

Audience: **u,f.**

Pelikan, Jaroslav   **BT198.P44 1999**
Jesus Through the Centuries: His Place in the History of Culture. Trade Paper. Yale University Press. Cumberland, RI. 1999. 304p. ISBN:0-300-07987-7, ISBN13: 978-0-300-07987-6. Dewey:232.9/04. LCCN:99-064259.

Audience: **g,l,u,f.**

Perrin, Norman   **BT198**
A Modern Pilgrimage in New Testament Christology. Trade Cloth. Augsburg Fortress, Publishers. Minneapolis, MN. 1974. 160p. ISBN:0-8006-0267-6, ISBN13: 978-0-8006-0267-3. Dewey:232/.09. LCCN:73-088352.

Audience: **u,f.**

Christianity > Doctrinal theology > Jesus Christ > General Works

Boff, Leonardo   **BT202.B5313**
Jesus Christ Liberator: A Critical Christology for Our Time. Patrick Hughes (Translator). Trade Paper. Orbis Books. Maryknoll, NY. 1978. 335p. ISBN:0-88344-236-1, ISBN13: 978-0-88344-236-4. Dewey:232. LCCN:78-000969.

Audience: **u,f.**

Formats: Web: ▢   Ebook: **℮**   CD/DVD-ROM: 🍥   BCL3: **ℬ**

Bonino, Jose Miguez   **BT202**
Faces of Jesus: Latin American Christologies. Trade Paper. Wipf
& Stock Publishers. Eugene, OR. 2002. 192p.
ISBN:1-59244-097-5, ISBN13: 978-1-59244-097-9.
Dewey:232/.098.

Audience: **u,f.**

Cobb, John B. Jr.   **BT202**
Christ in a Pluralistic Age. Trade Paper. Wipf & Stock
Publishers. Eugene, OR. 1999. 286p. ISBN:1-57910-300-6,
ISBN13: 978-1-57910-300-2. Dewey:232.

Audience: **u,f.**

Conzelmann, Hans.   **BT202**
Jesus; the classic article from RGG expanded and updated.
Translated by J. Raymond Lord. Edited with an introd. by John
Reumann.. Philadelphia, Fortress Press. 1973.
ISBN:0-8006-1000-8, ISBN13: 978-0-8006-1000-5.

Audience: **g,l,u.**

Jeremias, Joachim   **BT202.J3913**
New Testament Theology. Trade Cloth. Simon & Schuster. New
York, NY. 1971. ISBN:0-684-12363-0, ISBN13:
978-0-684-12363-9. Dewey:225.6/6. LCCN:70-143936.

Audience: **u,f.**

Kappen, Sebastian   **BT202.K27**
Jesus and Freedom. Francois Houtart (Introduction by). Trade
Cloth. Orbis Books. Maryknoll, NY. 1977. 186p.
ISBN:0-88344-232-9, ISBN13: 978-0-88344-232-6. Dewey:232.
LCCN:76-025927.

Audience: **u,f.**

Kasper, Walter   **BT202**
Jesus the Christ. Trade Cloth. Paulist Press. Mahwah, NJ. 1976.
290p. ISBN:0-8091-2081-X, ISBN13: 978-0-8091-2081-9.
Dewey:232. LCCN:76-020021.

Audience: **g,l,u.**

Machovec, Milan   **BT205**
A Marxist Looks at Jesus. Trade Paper. Darton, Longman &
Todd, Ltd. Letchworth Garden City, 1976. 231p.
ISBN:0-232-51260-4, ISBN13: 978-0-232-51260-1. Dewey:232.

Audience: **u,f.**

Moltmann, Jurgen   **BT202**
The Crucified God: The Cross of Christ as the Foundation and
Criticism of Christian Theology. R. A. Wilson & John Bowden
(Translators). Trade Paper. Augsburg Fortress, Publishers.
Minneapolis, MN. 2003. 346p. The Works of Jurgen Moltmann
ISBN:0-8006-2822-5, ISBN13: 978-0-8006-2822-2. Dewey:232.
LCCN:93-029953.

Audience: **u,f.**

Ogden, Schubert M.   **BT202**
The Point of Christology. Paper Text. Southern Methodist
University Press. Dallas, TX. 1992. 206p. ISBN:0-87074-331-7,
ISBN13: 978-0-87074-331-3. Dewey:232. LCCN:91-052783.

Audience: **u,f.**

Pannenberg, Wolfhart   **BT202**
Jesus - God and Man. Trade Cloth. SCM-Canterbury Press Ltd.
London, 2002. xxviii, 496p. ISBN:0-334-02897-3, ISBN13:
978-0-334-02897-0. Dewey:232.

Audience: **u,f.**

Schillebeeckx, Edward   **BT202**
Christ: The Experience of Jesus as Lord. Trade Paper. Crossroad
Publishing Company. New York, NY. 1983. 925p. Christ Ppr
Ser., Vol. 1 ISBN:0-8245-0605-7, ISBN13: 978-0-8245-0605-6.
Dewey:234.

Audience: **u,f.**

Schillebeeckx, Edward   **BT77.3**
Interim Report: On the Books Jesus & Christ. Trade Paper.
SCM-Canterbury Press Ltd. London, 1980. 151p.
ISBN:0-334-00756-9, ISBN13: 978-0-334-00756-2. Dewey:230.

Audience: **u,f.**

Schillebeeckx, Edward   **BT202.S33513 1979**
Jesus: An Experiment in Christology. Trade Cloth. The Seabury
Press, Inc. New York, NY. 1979. 767p. ISBN:0-8164-0345-7,
ISBN13: 978-0-8164-0345-5. Dewey:232. LCCN:78-010225.

Audience: **u,f.**

Sobrino, Jon   **BT202**
Christology at the Crossroads: A Latin American Approach.
Trade Paper. Wipf & Stock Publishers. Eugene, OR. 2002. 458p.
ISBN:1-59244-095-9, ISBN13: 978-1-59244-095-5. Dewey:232.

Audience: **u,f.**

Sykes, S. W. & Clayton, J.   **BT202**
P. (Editors)
Christ, Faith and History. Trade Paper. Cambridge University
Press. New York, NY. 1978. 280p. ISBN:0-521-29325-1,
ISBN13: 978-0-521-29325-9. Dewey:232. LCCN:70-176257.

Audience: **u,f.**

Vermes, Geza   **BT202**
Jesus the Jew: A Historian's Reading of the Gospels. Trade
Paper. Augsburg Fortress, Publishers. Minneapolis, MN. 2003.
288p. ISBN:0-8006-1443-7, ISBN13: 978-0-8006-1443-0.
Dewey:232. LCCN:80-002381.

Audience: **u,f.**

Christianity > Doctrinal theology > Jesus Christ > Special Topics

Aulen, Gustaf E.   **BT263**
Christus Victor: An Historical Study of the Three Main Types of
the Idea of Atonement. A. G. Herbert (Translator). Trade Paper.
Wipf & Stock Publishers. Eugene, OR. 2003. 182p.
ISBN:1-59244-330-3, ISBN13: 978-1-59244-330-7.
Dewey:232/.3/09.

Audience: **u,f.**

Pawlikowski, John T.   **BT701.2**
Christ in the Light of the Christian-Jewish Dialogue. Trade
Paper. Wipf & Stock Publishers. Eugene, OR. 2001. 174p.
ISBN:1-57910-726-5, ISBN13: 978-1-57910-726-0. Dewey:233.
                                            Audience: **u,f.**

Christianity > Doctrinal theology > Jesus Christ > Life of Christ

Bonhoeffer, Dietrich   **BT382**
The Cost of Discipleship. Paper Text. Textbook Publishers.
Temecula, CA. 2003. 285p. ISBN:0-7581-9235-5, ISBN13:
978-0-7581-9235-6. Dewey:241.5/3.
                                         Audience: **g,l,u,f.**

Crossan, John Dominic &   **BT303.2.C73 1998**
  Craig, William L.
Will the Real Jesus Please Stand Up?: A Debate Between
William Lane Craig and John Dominic Crossan. Paul Copan
(Editor), William F. Buckley Jr. (Contribution by). Trade Paper.
Baker Publishing Group. Grand Rapids, MI. 1999. 192p.
ISBN:0-8010-2175-8, ISBN13: 978-0-8010-2175-6.
Dewey:232.9/08. LCCN:98-037884.
                        Audience: **l,u,f.**   *Choice, 1999.*

Davies, W. D.   **BT380.2.D37 1989**
The Setting of the Sermon on the Mount. Trade Cloth. Brown
Judaic Studies. Atlanta, GA. 1961. 547p. ISBN:1-55540-403-0,
ISBN13: 978-1-55540-403-1. Dewey:226/.9067.
LCCN:89-039028.
                                            Audience: **u,f.**

Dodd, C. H.   **BT375**
The Parables of the Kingdom. Paper Text. Textbook Publishers.
Temecula, CA. 2003. 176p. ISBN:0-7581-4061-4, ISBN13:
978-0-7581-4061-6. Dewey:226.806.
                                            Audience: **l,u.**

Jeremias, Joachim   **BT375.2.J413 1972**
Parables of Jesus. Ed. 3. Trade Cloth. SCM-Canterbury Press
Ltd. London, 2002. 248p. ISBN:0-334-02917-1, ISBN13:
978-0-334-02917-5. Dewey:226/.806. LCCN:73-164900.
                                          Audience: **g,l,u.**

Schleiermacher, Friedrich   **BT301**
  Daniel Ernst
The Life of Jesus. Jack C. Verheyden & Leander E. Keck
(Editors), S. MacLean Gilmour (Translator). Trade Paper. Sigler
Press. Mifflintown, PA. 1997. 542p. ISBN:1-888961-04-X,
ISBN13: 978-1-888961-04-1. Dewey:232.901.
                                            Audience: **u,f.**

Wright, N. T.   **BT303.2.W75 1999**
The Challenge of Jesus: Rediscovering Who Jesus Was and Is.
Trade Cloth. InterVarsity Press. Downers Grove, IL. 1999. 202p.
ISBN:0-8308-2200-3, ISBN13: 978-0-8308-2200-3. Dewey:232.
LCCN:99-036481.
                                         Audience: **g,l,u,f.**

Christianity > Doctrinal theology > Mary. Mariology

Brown, Raymond E.   **BT611**
  (Editor), et al.
Mary in the New Testament. John E. Reumann, Joseph A.
Fitzmyer & Karl P. Donfried (Editors). Trade Cloth. Paulist
Press. Mahwah, NJ. 1978. 336p. ISBN:0-8091-2168-9, ISBN13:
978-0-8091-2168-7. Dewey:232.91. LCCN:78-008797.
                                            Audience: **u,f.**

Jones, F. Stanley (Editor)   **BS2485.W45 2002**
Which Mary?: The Marys of Early Christian Tradition. Trade
Cloth. Brill Academic Publishers. Leiden, 2003. x, 142p.
Symposium Ser. ISBN:90-04-12708-9, ISBN13:
978-90-04-12708-1. Dewey:232.91. LCCN:2002-011711.
                                            Audience: **u,f.**

Rahner, Karl & O'Hara,   **BT613**
  William Joseph
Mary, Mother of the Lord. Trade Paper. Source Books. Santa
Ana, CA. 1974. 107p. ISBN:0-85650-036-4, ISBN13:
978-0-85650-036-7. Dewey:232.91.
                                            Audience: **u,f.**

Shoemaker, Stephen J.   **BT630.S56 2002**
The Ancient Traditions of the Virgin Mary's Dormition and
Assumption. Trade Cloth. Oxford University Press, Inc. New
York, NY. 2003. 476p. Oxford Early Christian Studies
ISBN:0-19-925075-8, ISBN13: 978-0-19-925075-2.
Dewey:232.914. LCCN:2003-544636.
                                            Audience: **u,f.**

Christianity > Doctrinal theology > Creation. Doctrinal Anthropology and Sociology

Brunner, Emil   **BT701 .B72**
Man in Revolt: A Christian Anthropology. Olive Wyon
(Translator). Trade Paper. Lutterworth Press, The. Cambridge,
2003. 564p. ISBN:0-7188-9043-4, ISBN13: 978-0-7188-9043-8.
Dewey:233.
                                            Audience: **u,f.**

Clark, Elizabeth Ann   **BT704.C53 1996**
Women and Religion: The Original Sourcebook of Women in
Christian Thought. Herbert W. Richardson, Gary Brower &
Randall Styers (Editors). Trade Paper. HarperCollins Publishers.
New York, NY. 1997. 408p. ISBN:0-06-061409-9, ISBN13:
978-0-06-061409-6. Dewey:270/.082. LCCN:96-010959.
                                          Audience: **g,l,u.**

Cone, James H.   **BT734.2.C6 1997**
Black Theology and Black Power. Trade Paper. Orbis Books.
Maryknoll, NY. 1997. 200p. ISBN:1-57075-157-9, ISBN13:
978-1-57075-157-8. Dewey:230/.08996073. LCCN:97-220426.
                                    Audience: **g,l,u.** *B*

Ellul, Jacques & Kings,   **BR115.P7**
  Cecelia Gaul
Violence: Reflections from a Christian Perspective. Trade Paper.
A. R. Mowbray & Company, Ltd. Oxford, 1978. 179p.
ISBN:0-264-66530-9, ISBN13: 978-0-264-66530-6.
Dewey:261.8/3.

                Audience: **u,f.**

Gutierrez, Gustavo   **BT738**
Theology of Liberation. Trade Paper. Orbis Books. Maryknoll,
NY. 2004. ISBN:0-88344-478-X, ISBN13: 978-0-88344-478-8.
Dewey:230/.2.

                Audience: **u,f.**

Hengel, Martin   **BT736.15**
Victory Over Violence and Was Jesus a Revolutionist? Trade
Paper. Wipf & Stock Publishers. Eugene, OR. 2003. 158p.
ISBN:1-59244-144-0, ISBN13: 978-1-59244-144-0.
Dewey:261.8.

                Audience: **l,u.**

Innocent & Lewis, Robert   **BT701.2**
  E.
De Miseria Condicionis Humane. Trade Cloth. Scolar Press.
Aldershot, 1980. xiv, 303p. ISBN:0-85967-601-3, ISBN13:
978-0-85967-601-4. Dewey:233.

                Audience: **g,l,u,f.**

Kierkegaard, Soren   **B4376.I58**
The Concept of Anxiety. Robert L. Perkins (Editor). Trade
Cloth. Mercer University Press. Macon, GA. 2004. 203p.
International Kierkegaard Commentary Ser., Vol. 8
ISBN:0-86554-142-6, ISBN13: 978-0-86554-142-9.
Dewey:198/.9 s. LCCN:85-011571.

          Audience: **g,l,u,f.** *Choice, 1986.*

Lints, Richard S. (Editor),   **BT701.3.P46 2006**
  et al.
Personal Identity in Theological Perspective. Michael S. Horton
& Mark R. Talbot (Editors). Trade Paper. William B. Eerdmans
Publishing Company. Grand Rapids, MI. 2006. 232p.
ISBN:0-8028-2893-0, ISBN13: 978-0-8028-2893-4.
Dewey:233/.5. LCCN:2005-032085.

                Audience: **u,f.**

McFadyen, Alistair Iain   **BV4597.52 .M4 1990**
The Call to Personhood: A Christian Theory of the Individual in
Social Relationships. Trade Paper. Cambridge University Press.
New York, NY. 1990. 339p. ISBN:0-521-40929-2, ISBN13:
978-0-521-40929-2. Dewey:233.5. LCCN:90-032316.

                Audience: **u,f.**

McFadyen, Alistair I.   **BT715 .M376 2000**
Bound to Sin: Abuse, Holocaust and the Christian Doctrine of
Sin. Daniel W. Hardy (Contribution by). Cloth Text. Cambridge
University Press. New York, NY. 2000. 270p. Studies in
Christian Doctrine, Vol. 6 ISBN:0-521-43286-3, ISBN13:
978-0-521-43286-3. Dewey:241/.3. LCCN:99-058733.

                Audience: **u,f.**

Merton, Thomas   **BT736.15**
Faith and Violence: Christian Teaching and Christian Practice.
Trade Cloth. University of Notre Dame Press. Notre Dame, IN.
1968. 248p. ISBN:0-268-00094-8, ISBN13: 978-0-268-00094-3.
Dewey:261.8.

                Audience: **g,l,u,f.**

Merton, Thomas   **BX1753**
Seeds of Destruction. Trade Cloth. Peter Smith Publisher, Inc.
Magnolia, MA. 1983. ISBN:0-8446-5988-6, ISBN13:
978-0-8446-5988-6. Dewey:261.8.

                Audience: **g,l,u,f.**

Miles, Margaret R.   **BR115.A8**
Carnal Knowing: Female Nakedness and Religious Meaning in
the Christian West. Trade Cloth. Search Press, Ltd. Tunbridge
Wells, 1994. 272p. ISBN:0-86012-182-8, ISBN13:
978-0-86012-182-4. Dewey:246.

          Audience: **u,f.** *Choice, 1990.*

Niebuhr, Reinhold   **BT701.2**
The Self and the Dramas of History. Paper Text. Textbook
Publishers. Temecula, CA. 2003. ix, 246p. ISBN:0-7581-4023-1,
ISBN13: 978-0-7581-4023-4. Dewey:233.

                Audience: **u,f.**

Niebuhr, Reinhold   **BT701.N5213 1996**
The Nature and Destiny of Man: A Christian Interpretation, Vol.
2. Robin W. Lovin (Introduction by). Trade Cloth. Westminster
John Knox Press. Louisville, KY. 2004. 672p. Library of
Theological Ethics ISBN:0-664-25709-7, ISBN13:
978-0-664-25709-5. Dewey:233. LCCN:96-032259.

                Audience: **u,f.**

Pannenberg, Wolfhart   **BT701.2**
Anthropology in Theological Perspective. Matthew J. O'Connell
(Translator). Trade Paper. Continuum International Publishing
Group, Ltd. London, 1999. 818p. ISBN:0-567-08687-9, ISBN13:
978-0-567-08687-7. Dewey:233.

          Audience: **u,f.** *Choice, 1985.*

Plantinga, Cornelius Jr.   **BT715**
Not the Way It's Supposed to Be: A Breviary of Sin. Trade
Paper. William B. Eerdmans Publishing Company. Grand
Rapids, MI. 1996. 216p. ISBN:0-8028-4218-6, ISBN13:
978-0-8028-4218-3. Dewey:241/.3.

                Audience: **u,f.**

Plaskow, Judith   **BT704.P56**
Sex, Sin, and Grace: Women's Experience and the Theologies of
Reinhold Niebuhr and Paul Tillich. Trade Paper. University
Press of America, Inc. Lanham, MD. 2002. 224p.
ISBN:0-8191-0882-0, ISBN13: 978-0-8191-0882-1. Dewey:231.
LCCN:79-005434.

                Audience: **u,f.**

Rauschenbusch, Walter   **BR115.S6**
Christianity and the Social Crisis. Trade Paper. Wipf & Stock
Publishers. Eugene, OR. 2003. 446p. ISBN:1-59244-418-0,
ISBN13: 978-1-59244-418-2. Dewey:261.

                Audience: **u,f.**

Ricoeur, Paul BT715
The Symbolism of Evil. Trade Paper. Beacon Press. Boston, MA. 1986. ISBN:0-8070-1567-9, ISBN13: 978-0-8070-1567-4. Dewey:233.2. LCCN:67-011506.
Audience: **u,f.**

Ruether, Rosemary Radford BT738.3
The Radical Kingdom: The Western Experience of Messianic Hope. Trade Paper. Paulist Press. Mahwah, NJ. 1975. 324p. ISBN:0-8091-1860-2, ISBN13: 978-0-8091-1860-1. Dewey:261.8. LCCN:70-109080.
Audience: **u,f.**

Ruether, Rosemary Radford BT704
Sexism and God-Talk: Toward a Feminist Theology. Ed. 10. Trade Paper. Beacon Press. Boston, MA. 1993. 320p. ISBN:0-8070-1205-X, ISBN13: 978-0-8070-1205-5. Dewey:230/.088042. LCCN:92-033119.
Audience: **u,f.**

Russell, Frederick H. BT736.2
The Just War in the Middle Ages. Trade Paper. Cambridge University Press. New York, NY. 1977. 344p. Studies in Medieval Life and Thought ISBN:0-521-29276-X, ISBN13: 978-0-521-29276-4. Dewey:230. LCCN:74-025655.
Audience: **u,f.**

Smith, H. Shelton BT734.2.S56
In His Image, but: Racism in Southern Religion, 1780-1910. Trade Cloth. Duke University Press. Durham, NC. 1972. x, 318p. ISBN:0-8223-0273-X, ISBN13: 978-0-8223-0273-5. Dewey:261.8/34/5196073075. LCCN:72-091448.
Audience: **u,f.**

Stackhouse, Max L. BT738.S695 1972
Ethics and the Urban Ethos; an Essay in Social Theory and Theological Reconstruction. Trade Cloth. Beacon Press. Boston, MA. 1972. 220p. ISBN:0-8070-1136-3, ISBN13: 978-0-8070-1136-2. Dewey:261.1. LCCN:77-179155.
Audience: **u,f.**

White, Ronald C. Jr. & BT738
Hopkins, C. Howard
The Social Gospel: Religion and Reform in Changing America. Trade Paper. Temple University Press. Philadelphia, PA. 1975. 326p. ISBN:0-87722-084-0, ISBN13: 978-0-87722-084-8. Dewey:261/.0973. LCCN:75-034745.
Audience: **u,f.**

Christianity > Doctrinal theology > Salvation

Erasmus, Desiderius & BT810.3.D57 2005
Luther, Martin
Discourse on Free Will. Trade Paper. Continuum International Publishing Group, Ltd. London, 2005. 240p. ISBN:0-8264-7794-1, ISBN13: 978-0-8264-7794-1. Dewey:234/.9. LCCN:2005-273060.
Audience: **g,l,u,f.**

Gogarten, Friedrich BT771.2
Reality of Faith, the Problem of Subjectivism in Theology. Paper Text. Textbook Publishers. Temecula, CA. 2003. ISBN:0-7581-0570-3, ISBN13: 978-0-7581-0570-7. Dewey:234.2.
Audience: **l,u.**

Kung, Hans BT764.2.K7913 2004
Justification: The Doctrine of Karl Barth and a Catholic Reflection. Ed. 40. Trade Paper. Westminster John Knox Press. Louisville, KY. 2005. 400p. ISBN:0-664-22446-6, ISBN13: 978-0-664-22446-2. Dewey:234/.7. LCCN:2003-061153.
Audience: **u,f.**

McGrath, Alister E. BT764.2.M43 2005
Iustitia Dei: A History of the Christian Doctrine of Justification. Ed. 3. Cloth Text. Cambridge University Press. New York, NY. 2005. 462p. ISBN:0-521-82648-9, ISBN13: 978-0-521-82648-8. Dewey:234/.7/09. LCCN:2005-045379.
Audience: **u,f.**

Niebuhr, Helmut Richard BT771.2
Faith on Earth: An Inquiry into the Structure of Human Faith. Richard R. Niebuhr (Editor). Trade Paper. Yale University Press. Cumberland, RI. 1991. 160p. ISBN:0-300-05122-0, ISBN13: 978-0-300-05122-3. Dewey:234.2. LCCN:89-030178.
Audience: **u,f.** *Choice, 1990.*

Ruether, Rosemary Radford BT810.2
Liberation Theology. Trade Paper. Paulist Press. Mahwah, NJ. 1973. ISBN:0-8091-1744-4, ISBN13: 978-0-8091-1744-4. Dewey:230. LCCN:72-092263.
Audience: **u,f.**

Russell, Letty M. BR115.C8
Human Liberation in a Feminist Perspective: A Theology. Trade Paper. Westminster John Knox Press. Louisville, KY. 1995. 213p. ISBN:0-664-24991-4, ISBN13: 978-0-664-24991-5. Dewey:261.834. LCCN:74-010613.
Audience: **u,f.**

Tillich, Paul BT771.2.T54 2001
Dynamics of Faith. Trade Paper. HarperCollins Publishers. New York, NY. 2001. 176p. Perennial Classics Ser. ISBN:0-06-093713-0, ISBN13: 978-0-06-093713-3. Dewey:234/.23. LCCN:2001-024816.
Audience: **u,f.**

Weingart, Richard E. BT751.2.W4
The Logic of Divine Love: A Critical Analysis of the Soteriology of Peter Abailard. Trade Cloth. Oxford University Press, Inc. New York, NY. 1970. xiv, 220p. ISBN:0-19-826623-5, ISBN13: 978-0-19-826623-5. Dewey:230.2/0924. LCCN:78-521215.
Audience: **u,f.**

Wesley, John BT765
A Plain Account of Christian Perfection. Trade Cloth. Epworth Press, The. London, 2000. 116p. ISBN:0-7162-0081-3, ISBN13: 978-0-7162-0081-9. Dewey:234. LCCN:71-400150.
Audience: **g,l,u,f.**

Formats: Web: ▢ Ebook: ℮ CD/DVD-ROM: 🖊 BCL3: ℬ

Christianity > Doctrinal theology > Eschatology. Immortality

Barkun, Michael   **BS647.2**
Disaster and the Millennium. Paper Text. Syracuse University
Press. Syracuse, NY. 1986. 256p. ISBN:0-8156-2392-5, ISBN13:
978-0-8156-2392-2. Dewey:236/.3. LCCN:86-005979.
                                                          Audience: **u,f.**

Brunner, Emil   **BT821**
Eternal Hope. Paper Text. Textbook Publishers. Temecula, CA.
2003. 232p. ISBN:0-7581-0555-X, ISBN13: 978-0-7581-0555-4.
Dewey:236.
                                                          Audience: **g,l,u.**

Erickson, Millard J.   **BT891.E74 1998**
A Basic Guide to Eschatology: Making Sense of the
Millennium. Trade Paper. Baker Publishing Group. Grand
Rapids, MI. 1999. 200p. ISBN:0-8010-5836-8, ISBN13:
978-0-8010-5836-3. Dewey:236/.9. LCCN:77-089406.
                                                          Audience: **u,f.**

Helm, Paul   **BV4501.2**
The Last Things. Trade Paper. Banner of Truth, The. Carlisle,
PA. 1989. 160p. ISBN:0-85151-544-4, ISBN13:
978-0-85151-544-1. Dewey:248.4.
                                                          Audience: **g,l,u.**

Hoekema, Anthony A.   **BT821.2**
The Bible and the Future. Trade Paper. William B. Eerdmans
Publishing Company. Grand Rapids, MI. 1994. 354p.
ISBN:0-8028-0851-4, ISBN13: 978-0-8028-0851-6. Dewey:236.
LCCN:78-009966.
                                                          Audience: **u,f.**

Le Goff, Jacques   **BT842**
The Birth of Purgatory. Arthur Goldhammer (Translator). Trade
Paper. University of Chicago Press. Chicago, IL. 1986. 440p.
ISBN:0-226-47083-0, ISBN13: 978-0-226-47083-2.
Dewey:236/.5. LCCN:83-001108.
                                                          Audience: **u,f.**

McGinn, Bernard   **BT876.V58 1998**
Visions of the End: Apocalyptic Traditions in the Middle Ages.
Trade Paper. Columbia University Press. New York, NY. 1998.
390p. Records of Civilization: Sources and Studies, Vol. XCVI
ISBN:0-231-11257-2, ISBN13: 978-0-231-11257-4.
Dewey:236/.09/02. LCCN:99-180823.
                                                          Audience: **u,f.**

McGinn, Bernard   **BT821.2**
   (Translator)
Apocalyptic Spirituality. Marjorie Reeves (Preface by). Trade
Cloth. Paulist Press. Mahwah, NJ. 1979. 352p. Classics of
Western Spirituality Ser. ISBN:0-8091-2242-1, ISBN13:
978-0-8091-2242-4. Dewey:236. LCCN:79-090834.
                                                          Audience: **g,l,u.**

McGrath, Alister E.   **BT846.3.M34 2002**
A Brief History of Heaven. Trade Cloth. Blackwell Publishing,
Inc. Malden, MA. 2003. 216p. Blackwell Brief Histories of
Religion Ser. ISBN:0-631-23353-9, ISBN13:
978-0-631-23353-4. Dewey:236/.24/09. LCCN:2002-007251.
                                                          Audience: **g,l,u,f.**

Moltmann, Jurgen   **BT821.2**
Theology of Hope: On the Ground and the Implications of a
Christian Eschatology. James W. Leitch (Translator). Trade
Paper. Augsburg Fortress, Publishers. Minneapolis, MN. 2003.
352p. The Works of Jurgen Moltmann ISBN:0-8006-2824-1,
ISBN13: 978-0-8006-2824-6. Dewey:236. LCCN:93-029966.
                                                          Audience: **u,f.**

Pelikan, Jaroslav J.   **BT819**
The Shape of Death: Life, Death, and Immortality in the Early
Fathers. Trade Cloth. Greenwood Publishing Group, Inc.
Portsmouth, NH. 1978. 128p. ISBN:0-313-20458-6, ISBN13:
978-0-313-20458-6. Dewey:236. LCCN:78-006030.
                                                          Audience: **u,f.**

Rahner, Karl, 1904-   **BT825**
On the theology of death. Translated by Charles H. Henkey.
New York: Herder and Herder. 1964.
                                                          Audience: **u,f.**

Stannard, David E.   **BX9315**
The Puritan Way of Death: A Study in Religion, Culture, and
Social Change. Trade Paper. DIANE Publishing Company.
Collingdale, PA. 2004. 236p. ISBN:0-7567-8084-5, ISBN13:
978-0-7567-8084-5. Dewey:230/.5/9.
                                                          Audience: **u,f.**

Christianity > Doctrinal theology > Invisible World. Devil

Russell, Jeffrey B.   **BT981**
The Prince of Darkness: Radical Evil and the Power of Good in
History. Trade Paper. Cornell University Press. Ithaca, NY.
1992. 304p. ISBN:0-8014-8056-6, ISBN13: 978-0-8014-8056-0.
Dewey:235/.47. LCCN:88-047744.
                                                          Audience: **u,f.**

Christianity > Doctrinal theology > Creeds. Apologetics

Butler, Joseph   **BT1100 .B9**
Analogy of Religion, Natural and Reveale. Trade Paper.
Kessinger Publishing, LLC. Whitefish, MT. 2003.
ISBN:0-7661-5083-6, ISBN13: 978-0-7661-5083-6. Dewey:239.
                                                          Audience: **u,f.**

Geisler, Norman L.   **BT1102.G42 1999**
Baker Encyclopedia of Christian Apologetics. Trade Cloth.
Baker Academic. Ada, MI. 1998. 864p. Baker Reference Library
Ser. ISBN:0-8010-2151-0, ISBN13: 978-0-8010-2151-0.
Dewey:239/.03. LCCN:98-008735.
                                                          Audience: **g,l,u,f.** *Choice, 1999.*

Kelly, J. N.   **BT990**
Early Christian Creeds. Ed. 3. Trade Cloth. Longman Publishing
Group. White Plains, NY. 1989. 446p. ISBN:0-582-49219-X,
ISBN13: 978-0-582-49219-6. Dewey:238/.1. LCCN:72-169389.
Audience: **g,l,u.**

Kreeft, Peter & Tacelli,   **BT1102.K724 1994**
  Ronald K.
Handbook of Christian Apologetics. Trade Paper. InterVarsity
Press. Downers Grove, IL. 1994. 406p. ISBN:0-8308-1774-3,
ISBN13: 978-0-8308-1774-0. Dewey:239. LCCN:94-000415.
Audience: **u,f.**

Kung, Hans   **BL48**
On Being a Christian. Trade Paper. Doubleday Publishing. New
York, NY. 1984. 720p. ISBN:0-385-19286-X, ISBN13:
978-0-385-19286-6. Dewey:200. LCCN:83-016431.
Audience: **g,l,u,f.**

Pannenberg, Wolfhart   **BT993.2**
The Apostles' Creed in Light of Today's Questions. Trade
Paper. Wipf & Stock Publishers. Eugene, OR. 2000. 186p.
ISBN:1-57910-440-1, ISBN13: 978-1-57910-440-5.
Dewey:238/.11.
Audience: **u,f.**

Pelikan, Jaroslav &   **BT990**
  Hotchkiss, Valerie R. (Editors)
Creeds and Confessions of Faith in the Christian Tradition.
Cloth over Boards. Yale University Press. Cumberland, RI.
2003. 3344p. ISBN:0-300-09391-8, ISBN13:
978-0-300-09391-9. Dewey:238. LCCN:2003-043067.
Audience: **g,l,u,f.**

Young, Frances   **BT993.2**
The Making of the Creeds. Trade Cloth. SCM-Canterbury Press
Ltd. London, 2002. 130p. ISBN:0-334-02876-0, ISBN13:
978-0-334-02876-5. Dewey:238.1/1.
Audience: **u,f.**

Christianity > Doctrinal theology > Heterodox Movements

Bauer, Walter   **BR162.2**
Orthodoxy and Heresy in Earliest Christianity. Trade Cloth.
SCM-Canterbury Press Ltd. London, 1972. xxv, 326p.
ISBN:0-334-01189-2, ISBN13: 978-0-334-01189-7.
Dewey:230/.09/015.
Audience: **u,f.**

Evans, G. R.   **BT1315.3.E93 2002**
A Brief History of Heresy. Trade Cloth. Blackwell Publishing,
Inc. Malden, MA. 2002. 216p. Blackwell Brief Histories of
Religion Ser. ISBN:0-631-23525-6, ISBN13:
978-0-631-23525-5. Dewey:273. LCCN:2002-007334.
Audience: **u,f.**

Ferguson, Everett (Editor)   **BT1390**
Orthodoxy, Heresy, and Schism in Early Christianity. Library
Binding. Garland Publishing, Inc. New York, NY. 1993. 376p.
Studies in Early Christianity, Vol. 4 ISBN:0-8153-1064-1,
ISBN13: 978-0-8153-1064-8. Dewey:273.1. LCCN:92-041867.
Audience: **u,f.**

Frend, W. H.
The Rise of the Monophysite Movement: Chapters in the
History of the Church in the Fifth and Sixth Centuries. Trade
Cloth. Cambridge University Press. New York, NY. 1972. 422p.
ISBN:0-521-08130-0, ISBN13: 978-0-521-08130-6.
Dewey:273/.5. LCCN:72-075302.
Audience: **u,f.**

Frend, W. H. C.   **BT1370.F7 1985**
The Donatist Church: A Movement of Protest in Roman North
Africa. Trade Cloth. Oxford University Press, Inc. New York,
NY. 2000. 376p. Oxford Scholarly Classics Ser.
ISBN:0-19-826408-9, ISBN13: 978-0-19-826408-8.
Dewey:273/.4. LCCN:86-131188.
Audience: **u,f.**

Hultgren, Arland J.   **BT1313.E37 1996**
The Earliest Christian Heretics: Readings from Their Opponents.
Trade Paper. Augsburg Fortress, Publishers. Minneapolis, MN.
1996. 224p. ISBN:0-8006-2963-9, ISBN13: 978-0-8006-2963-2.
Dewey:273/.1. LCCN:96-024928.
Audience: **l,u.** *Choice, 1997.*

King, Karen L.   **BT1390**
What Is Gnosticism? Trade Cloth. Harvard University Press.
Cambridge, MA. 2003. 368p. ISBN:0-674-01071-X, ISBN13:
978-0-674-01071-0. Dewey:299/.932. LCCN:2003-041851.
Audience: **g,l,u.**

Lambert, Malcolm   **BT1319.L35 2002**
Medieval Heresy: Popular Movements from the Gregorian
Reform to the Reformation. Ed. 3. Trade Cloth. Blackwell
Publishing, Inc. Malden, MA. 2002. 504p. ISBN:0-631-22275-8,
ISBN13: 978-0-631-22275-0. Dewey:273/.6.
LCCN:2001-043102.
Audience: **g,u,f.**

Layton, Bentley   **BT1390**
The Gnostic Scriptures: A New Translation with Annotations
and Introductions. Trade Paper. Doubleday Publishing. New
York, NY. 1995. 576p. ISBN:0-385-47843-7, ISBN13:
978-0-385-47843-4. Dewey:273.1.
Audience: **g,l,u.**

Lieu, Samuel N.   **BT1390**
Manichaeism in the Later Roman Empire and Medieval China.
Trade Cloth. J. C. B. Mohr. 1992. 400p. WissUNT Neuen
Testament Ser., Vol. 63 ISBN:3-16-145820-6, ISBN13:
978-3-16-145820-0. Dewey:299/.932.
Audience: **u,f.** *Choice, 1986.*

Peters, Edward (Editor)   **BT1319 .P47**
Heresy and Authority in Medieval Europe. Book, Other.

University of Pennsylvania Press. Philadelphia, PA. 1980. 320p. Middle Ages Ser. ISBN:0-8122-1103-0, ISBN13: 978-0-8122-1103-0. Dewey:273/.6. LCCN:79-005262.

Audience: **u,f.**

Robinson, J.M. (Editor)   **BT1391**
Nag Hammadi Library: Definitive Translation of the Gnostic Scriptures. Ed. 4. Members Members of the Coptic Gnostic Library Project of the Institute for Antiquity and Christianity (Translator). Trade Cloth. Brill Academic Publishers. Leiden, 1996. "xiv, 549"p. ISBN:90-04-08856-3, ISBN13: 978-90-04-08856-6. Dewey:299/.932.

Audience: **g,l,u,f.**

Rudolph, Kurt   **BT1390**
Gnosis. Trade Paper. Continuum International Publishing Group, Ltd. London, 1998. 412p. ISBN:0-567-08640-2, ISBN13: 978-0-567-08640-2. Dewey:299.932.

Audience: **u,f.**

Williams, Rowan   **BT1350.W55 2002**
Arius: Heresy and Tradition. Trade Paper. William B. Eerdmans Publishing Company. Grand Rapids, MI. 2002. 384p. ISBN:0-8028-4969-5, ISBN13: 978-0-8028-4969-4. Dewey:273/.4. LCCN:2002-278294.

Audience: **u,f.**

Yamauchi, Edwin M.   **BT1390**
Pre-Christian Gnosticism: A Survey of the Proposed Evidences. Trade Paper. Wipf & Stock Publishers. Eugene, OR. 2003. 280p. ISBN:1-59244-396-6, ISBN13: 978-1-59244-396-3. Dewey:299/.932.

Audience: **u,f.**

Christianity > Practical Theology > Missions

Bosch, David J.   **BV2063.B649 1991**
Transforming Mission: Paradigm Shifts in Theology of Mission. Trade Paper. Orbis Books. Maryknoll, NY. 1991. 587p. American Society of Missiology Ser., Vol. 16 ISBN:0-88344-719-3, ISBN13: 978-0-88344-719-2. Dewey:266/.001. LCCN:90-021619.

Audience: **u,f.**

Costas, Orlando E.   **BV2063**
Christ Outside the Gate: Mission Beyond Christendom. Trade Paper. Orbis Books. Maryknoll, NY. 1982. 272p. ISBN:0-88344-147-0, ISBN13: 978-0-88344-147-3. Dewey:266/.001. LCCN:82-007892.

Audience: **u,f.**

Escobar, Samuel E.   **BV2063.E79 2003**
The New Global Mission: The Gospel from Everywhere to Everyone. Trade Paper. InterVarsity Press. Downers Grove, IL. 2003. 192p. Christian Doctrine in Global Perspective Ser. ISBN:0-8308-3301-3, ISBN13: 978-0-8308-3301-6. Dewey:266. LCCN:2003-016149.

Audience: **u,f.**

Jenkins, Philip   **BR121.3.J46 2004**
The Next Christendom: The Coming of Global Christianity. Trade Paper. Oxford University Press, Inc. New York, NY. 2003. 286p. ISBN:0-19-516891-7, ISBN13: 978-0-19-516891-4. Dewey:270.8/30112. LCCN:2001-047554.

Audience: **g,l,u,f.**   *Choice, 2003.*

McGavran, Donald A.   **BV652.25.M293 1990**
Understanding Church Growth. Ed. 3. C. Peter Wagner (Editor). Trade Paper. William B. Eerdmans Publishing Company. Grand Rapids, MI. 1990. 328p. ISBN:0-8028-0463-2, ISBN13: 978-0-8028-0463-1. Dewey:266. LCCN:89-039252.

Audience: **u,f.**

Neill, Stephen   **BV2100**
A History of Christian Missions. Ed. 2. Owen Chadwick (Revised by). Trade Paper. Penguin Group (USA) Inc. New York, NY. 1991. 528p. Hist of the Church Ser. ISBN:0-14-013763-7, ISBN13: 978-0-14-013763-7. Dewey:266.009.

Audience: **u,f.**

Robert, Dana L.   **BV2610.R63 1996**
American Women in Mission: A Social History of Their Thought and Practice. Paper Text. Mercer University Press. Macon, GA. 1997. 458p. ISBN:0-86554-549-9, ISBN13: 978-0-86554-549-6. Dewey:266/.02373/0082. LCCN:97-006439.

Audience: **u,f.**   *Choice, 1997.*

Ross, Andrew C.   **BV2061**
A Vision Betrayed: The Jesuits in Japan and China 1542-1742. Trade Paper. Orbis Books. Maryknoll, NY. 2003. ISBN:1-57075-480-2, ISBN13: 978-1-57075-480-7. Dewey:266.

Audience: **u,f.**

Sanneh, Lamin   **BV2063.S23 1989**
Translating the Message: The Missionary Impact on Culture. Trade Paper. Orbis Books. Maryknoll, NY. 1989. 310p. American Society of Missiology Ser., Vol. 13 ISBN:0-88344-361-9, ISBN13: 978-0-88344-361-3. Dewey:266. LCCN:88-036508.

Audience: **u,f.**

Thomas, Norman E.   **BV2061.C58 1995**
 (Editor)
Classic Texts in Mission and World Christianity. Trade Paper. Orbis Books. Maryknoll, NY. 1995. 368p. American Society of Missiology Ser., 20 ISBN:1-57075-006-8, ISBN13: 978-1-57075-006-9. Dewey:266. LCCN:94-044033.

Audience: **u,f.**

Thomas, Norman E.   **Z7817.I58**
 (Editor)
International Mission Bibliography, 1960-2000. Trade Cloth. Scarecrow Press, Inc. Lanham, MD. 2003. 896p. ATLA Bibliography Ser., No. 48 ISBN:0-8108-4785-X, ISBN13: 978-0-8108-4785-9. Dewey:016.266. LCCN:2003-045638.

Audience: **u,f.**   *Choice, 2004.*

Walls, Andrew F.   **BV2100.W257 2001**
The Cross-Cultural Process in Christian History: Studies in the

Transmission and Reception of Faith. Trade Paper. Orbis Books. Maryknoll, NY. 2001. 288p. ISBN:1-57075-373-3, ISBN13: 978-1-57075-373-2. Dewey:270. LCCN:2001-041425.

Audience: **u,f.**

Walls, Andrew F.   **BV2100.W26 1996**
The Missionary Movement in Christian History: Studies in the Transmission of Faith. Trade Paper. Orbis Books. Maryknoll, NY. 1996. 250p. ISBN:1-57075-059-9, ISBN13: 978-1-57075-059-5. Dewey:266/.009. LCCN:95-051175.

Audience: **u,f.**

Christianity > Practical Theology > Revivals

Bruns, Roger A.   **BV3785.S8B75 1992**
Preacher: Billy Sunday and Big-Time American Evangelism. Trade Cloth. W. W. Norton & Company, Inc. New York, NY. 1992. 416p. ISBN:0-393-03088-1, ISBN13: 978-0-393-03088-4. Dewey:269/.2/092 B. LCCN:91-027418.

Audience: **g,l.** *Choice, 1992.*

Conkin, Paul K.   **BV3774.K4C65 1991**
Cane Ridge: America's Pentecost. Cloth Text. University of Wisconsin Press. Chicago, IL. 1991. 198p. Curti Lectures ISBN:0-299-12720-6, ISBN13: 978-0-299-12720-6. Dewey:269/.24/09769423. LCCN:90-050081.

Audience: **g,u.** *Choice, 1991.*

Douglass-Chin, Richard J.   **BV3780.D68 2001**
Preacher Woman Sings the Blues: The Autobiographies of Nineteenth-Century African American Evangelists. Trade Paper. University of Missouri Press. Columbia, MO. 2001. 288p. ISBN:0-8262-1311-1, ISBN13: 978-0-8262-1311-2. Dewey:269/.2/092396073 B. LCCN:00-066596.

Audience: **u,f.**

Eslinger, Ellen   **BV3798.E75 1999**
Citizens of Zion: Social Origins of Camp Meeting Revivalism. Trade Cloth. University of Tennessee Press. Knoxville, TN. 1999. 328p. ISBN:1-57233-033-3, ISBN13: 978-1-57233-033-7. Dewey:269/.24/09769. LCCN:98-025485.

Audience: **u,f.** *Choice, 1999.*

Evensen, Bruce J. (Author, Editor)   **BV3785.M7E94 2003**
God's Man for the Gilded Age: D. L. Moody and the Rise of Modern Mass Evangelism. Trade Cloth. Oxford University Press, Inc. New York, NY. 2003. 240p. ISBN:0-19-516244-7, ISBN13: 978-0-19-516244-8. Dewey:269/.2/092. LCCN:2003-042041.

Audience: **u,f.**

Frady, Marshall   **BR1725.T35**
Billy Graham: A Parable of American Righteousness. Trade Paper. Simon & Schuster. New York, NY. 2006. 560p. ISBN:0-7432-9143-3, ISBN13: 978-0-7432-9143-9. Dewey:269/.2/0924.

Audience: **g,l.**

George, Timothy (Editor)   **BV3785.M7**
Mr. Moody and the Evangelical Tradition. Trade Cloth. Continuum International Publishing Group, Ltd. London, 2004. 200p. ISBN:0-567-08494-9, ISBN13: 978-0-567-08494-1. Dewey:269/.2/092. LCCN:2004-556822.

Audience: **u,f.**

Graham, Billy   **BV3785.G69A3 1997**
Just as I Am: The Autobiography of Billy Graham. Trade Cloth. HarperCollins Publishers. New York, NY. 1997. 760p. ISBN:0-06-063387-5, ISBN13: 978-0-06-063387-5. Dewey:269/.2/092 B. LCCN:97-000605.

Audience: **g,l.**

Harrell, David Edwin Jr.   **BV3773**
All Things Are Possible: The Healing and Charismatic Revivals in Modern America. Trade Paper. Indiana University Press. Bloomington, IN. 1979. 320p. ISBN:0-253-20221-3, ISBN13: 978-0-253-20221-5. Dewey:269/.24/0973. LCCN:75-001937.

Audience: **u,f.**

Krapohl, Robert H. & Lippy, Charles H.   **BV3773.K73 1999**
The Evangelicals: A Historical, Thematic and Biographical Guide. Cloth Text. Greenwood Publishing Group, Inc. Portsmouth, NH. 1999. 352p. ISBN:0-313-30103-4, ISBN13: 978-0-313-30103-2. Dewey:280/.4/0973. LCCN:98-030499.

Audience: **l,u,f.** *Choice, 1999.*

McClymond, Michael James   **BV3777.N56E46 2004**
Embodying the Spirit: New Perspectives on North American Revivalism. Trade Cloth. Johns Hopkins University Press. Baltimore, MD. 2004. 368p. ISBN:0-8018-7807-1, ISBN13: 978-0-8018-7807-7. Dewey:269/.24/097. LCCN:2003-015034.

Audience: **u,f.** *Choice, 2005.*

Noll, Mark A.   **BV3773.N65 2001**
American Evangelical Christianity: An Introduction. Trade Paper. Blackwell Publishing, Inc. Malden, MA. 2000. 328p. ISBN:0-631-22000-3, ISBN13: 978-0-631-22000-8. Dewey:277.3/082. LCCN:00-010082.

Audience: **g,l,u.** *Choice, 2001.*

Pope-Levison, Priscilla   **BV3780.P67 2004**
Turn the Pulpit Loose: Two Centuries of American Women Evangelists. Cloth over Boards. Palgrave Macmillan. New York, NY. 2004. 272p. ISBN:0-312-24022-8, ISBN13: 978-0-312-24022-6. Dewey:251/.0092/273 B. LCCN:2004-040098.

Audience: **u,f.**

Sensbach, Jon F.   **BV3785.P74S46 2005**
Rebecca's Revival: Creating Black Christianity in the Atlantic World. Trade Cloth. Harvard University Press. Cambridge, MA. 2005. 320p. ISBN:0-674-01689-0, ISBN13: 978-0-674-01689-7. Dewey:269/.2/092 B. LCCN:2004-054021.

Audience: **u,f.** *Choice, 2005.*

Shank, David A.   **BV3785.H348S43 1994**
Prophet Harris, the "Black Elijah" of West Africa. Jocelyn Murray (Editor). Trade Cloth. Brill Academic Publishers, Inc.

Boston, MA. 1994. xv, 309p. Studies of Religion in Africa, 10 ISBN:90-04-09980-8, ISBN13: 978-90-04-09980-7. Dewey:269/.2/092 B. LCCN:94-026022.

Audience: **u,f.**

Sims, Patsy   **BV3774.S68S56 1996**
Can Somebody Shout Amen!: Inside Tents and Tabernacles of American Revivalists. Trade Paper. University Press of Kentucky. Lexington, KY. 1996. 256p. Religion in the South Ser. ISBN:0-8131-0886-1, ISBN13: 978-0-8131-0886-5. Dewey:269/.24. LCCN:96-019642.

Audience: **u,f.**

Stout, Harry S.   **BX9225.W4S74 1991**
The Divine Dramatist: George Whitefield and the Rise of Modern Evangelicalism. Nathan O. Hatch & Mark A. Noll (Editors). Trade Paper. William B. Eerdmans Publishing Company. Grand Rapids, MI. 1991. 325p. Library of Religious Biography ISBN:0-8028-0154-4, ISBN13: 978-0-8028-0154-8. Dewey:269/.2/092. LCCN:91-013549.

Audience: **u,f.**

Ward, W. Reginald   **BV3777.E9 W37 1992**
The Protestant Evangelical Awakening. Trade Cloth. Cambridge University Press. New York, NY. 1992. 388p. ISBN:0-521-41491-1, ISBN13: 978-0-521-41491-3. Dewey:280.4094. LCCN:91-023665.

Audience: **u,f.** *Choice, 1993.*

Christianity > Practical Theology > Pastoral Theology

Baxter, Richard   **BX5175**
The Reformed Pastor. Ed. 5. Trade Paper. Banner of Truth, The. Carlisle, PA. 1979. 256p. Puritan Paperbacks Ser. ISBN:0-85151-191-0, ISBN13: 978-0-85151-191-7. Dewey:238.5. LCCN:74-189719.

Audience: **u,f.**

Bonhoeffer, Dietrich   **BV4010**
Spiritual Care. Jay C. Rochelle (Translator). Trade Paper. Augsburg Fortress, Publishers. Minneapolis, MN. 2003. 128p. ISBN:0-8006-1874-2, ISBN13: 978-0-8006-1874-2. Dewey:253. LCCN:85-047711.

Audience: **g,l,u,f.**

Evans, Gillian (Editor)   **BV4006.H57 2000**
A History of Pastoral Care. Trade Cloth. Continuum International Publishing Group, Ltd. London, 2000. 224p. ISBN:0-225-66840-8, ISBN13: 978-0-225-66840-7. Dewey:253/.09. LCCN:00-362318.

Audience: **u,f.**

Hunter, Rodney J. &   **BV4011.3.D53 2005**
  Ramsay, Nancy J.
Dictionary of Pastoral Care and Counseling. Trade Cloth. Abingdon Press. Nashville, TN. 2005. 1504p. ISBN:0-687-49751-5, ISBN13: 978-0-687-49751-5. Dewey:253/.03. LCCN:2005-005854.

Audience: **g,l,u,f.**

Lebacqz, Karen & Driskill,   **BV4011.5.L42 2000**
  Joseph D.
Ethics and Spiritual Care: A Guide for Pastors, Chaplains, and Spiritual Directors. Trade Cloth. Abingdon Press. Nashville, TN. 2004. 172p. ISBN:0-687-07156-9, ISBN13: 978-0-687-07156-2. Dewey:241/.641. LCCN:00-032287.

Audience: **u,f.**

Lischer, Richard   **BV4208.U6L57 1995**
The Preacher King: Martin Luther King, Jr. and the Word That Moved America. Trade Cloth. Oxford University Press, Inc. New York, NY. 1995. 360p. ISBN:0-19-508779-8, ISBN13: 978-0-19-508779-6. Dewey:251/.0092. LCCN:94-030029.

Audience: **g,l,u,f.** *Choice, 1995.*

Long, Thomas G.   **BV4211.3.L66 2005**
The Witness of Preaching. Ed. 2. Trade Paper, Perfect. Westminster John Knox Press. Louisville, KY. 2005. 267p. ISBN:0-664-22943-3, ISBN13: 978-0-664-22943-6. Dewey:251. LCCN:2005-042282.

Audience: **u,f.**

Miller-McLemore, Bonnie J.   **BV4011.F42 1999**
Feminist and Womanist Pastoral Theology. Trade Cloth. Abingdon Press. Nashville, TN. 1999. 240p. ISBN:0-687-08910-7, ISBN13: 978-0-687-08910-9. Dewey:253/.082. LCCN:99-030956.

Audience: **u,f.**

Pattison, Stephen   **BV4011.B54 2000**
Blackwell Reader in Pastoral and Practical Theology. James Woodward (Editor), John Patton (Contribution by). Trade Cloth. Blackwell Publishing, Inc. Malden, MA. 1999. 360p. Readings in Modern Theology Ser. ISBN:0-631-20744-9, ISBN13: 978-0-631-20744-3. Dewey:253. LCCN:99-036072.

Audience: **l,u.**

Patton, John   **BV4011.3.P367 2005**
Pastoral Care: An Essential Guide. Trade Paper. Abingdon Press. Nashville, TN. 2005. 144p. ISBN:0-687-05322-6, ISBN13: 978-0-687-05322-3. Dewey:253. LCCN:2004-022200.

Audience: **u,f.**

Phipps, William E.   **BX1912.85P48 2004**
Clerical Celibacy: The Heritage. Trade Cloth. Continuum International Publishing Group, Ltd. London, 2004. 288p. ISBN:0-8264-1617-9, ISBN13: 978-0-8264-1617-9. Dewey:253/.252. LCCN:2004-003704.

Audience: **g,u,f.**

Purves, Andrew   **BV4006.P87 2001**
Pastoral Theology in the Classical Tradition. Paper Text. Westminster John Knox Press. Louisville, KY. 2001. 160p. ISBN:0-664-22241-2, ISBN13: 978-0-664-22241-3. Dewey:253/.09. LCCN:2001-026567.

Audience: **u,f.**

Stout, Harry S.   **BV4208.U6S75 1986**
The New England Soul: Preaching and Religious Culture in Colonial New England. Trade Cloth. Oxford University Press,

Inc. New York, NY. 1986. 410p. ISBN:0-19-503958-0, ISBN13: 978-0-19-503958-0. Dewey:251/.00974. LCCN:85-029853.

Audience: **u,f.** *Choice, 1987.*

Taylor, Barbara B.   **BV4222**
When God Is Silent. Trade Cloth. Cowley Publications. Cambridge, MA. 1997. 129p. Lyman Beecher Lectures on Preaching ISBN:1-56101-157-6, ISBN13: 978-1-56101-157-5. Dewey:251. LCCN:98-004425.

Audience: **u,f.**

Warner, Michael (Editor)   **BV4241.A514 1999**
American Sermons: The Pilgrims to Martin Luther King Jr. Trade Cloth. Library of America, The. New York, NY. 1999. 939p. Library of America, Vol. 108 ISBN:1-883011-65-5, ISBN13: 978-1-883011-65-9. Dewey:252. LCCN:98-034295.

Audience: **g,l,u,f.**

Witham, Larry A.   **BV4011.3.W58 2005**
Who Shall Lead Them?: The Future of Ministry in America. Trade Cloth. Oxford University Press, Inc. New York, NY. 2005. 246p. ISBN:0-19-516697-3, ISBN13: 978-0-19-516697-2. Dewey:262/.1/0973. LCCN:2005-006364.

Audience: **u,f.** *Choice, 2005.*

Christianity > Practical Theology > Practical Religion. Christian Life

Bynum, Caroline W.   **BV4490**
Jesus As Mother: Studies in the Spirituality of the High Middle Ages. Trade Cloth. University of California Press. Berkeley, CA. 1982. 280p. Center for Medieval and Renaissance Studies, UCLA, No. 16:Contribution ISBN:0-520-04194-1, ISBN13: 978-0-520-04194-3. Dewey:248.4. LCCN:81-013137.

Audience: **u,f.**

Coffin, William Sloane   **BV4531.3.C54 2005**
Letters to a Young Doubter. Saddle Stitched, Cloth over Boards, Dust Jacket. Westminster John Knox Press. Louisville, KY. 2005. 200p. ISBN:0-664-22929-8, ISBN13: 978-0-664-22929-0. Dewey:230/.51. LCCN:2004-061243.

Audience: **g,l,u.**

Constable, Giles   **BV4490 .C65 1995**
Three Studies in Medieval Religious and Social Thought: The Interpretation of Mary and Martha, the Ideal of the Imitation of Christ, the Orders of Society. Cloth Text. Cambridge University Press. New York, NY. 1995. 443p. ISBN:0-521-30515-2, ISBN13: 978-0-521-30515-0. Dewey:274/.04. LCCN:94-008854.

Audience: **g,u,f.** *Choice, 1996.*

Dowling, Elizabeth M. &   **BV4571.3.E53 2006**
  Scarlett, W. George (Editors)
Encyclopedia of Religious and Spiritual Development. Trade Cloth. SAGE Publications, Inc. Thousand Oaks, CA. 2005. 544p. The SAGE Program on Applied Developmental Science Ser. ISBN:0-7619-2883-9, ISBN13: 978-0-7619-2883-6. Dewey:200/.83/03. LCCN:2005-012704.

Audience: **g,l,u,f.** *Choice, 2006.*

Dreyer, Elizabeth A. &   **BV4501.3.M558 2005**
  Burrows, Mark S.
Minding the Spirit: The Study of Christian Spirituality. Trade Cloth. Johns Hopkins University Press. Baltimore, MD. 2005. 416p. ISBN:0-8018-8076-9, ISBN13: 978-0-8018-8076-6. Dewey:248. LCCN:2004-013500.

Audience: **u,f.** *Choice, 2005.*

Edgell, Penny   **BV4526.3.E33 2006**
Religion and Family in a Changing Society. Trade Cloth. Princeton University Press. Princeton, NJ. 2005. 232p. Princeton Studies in Cultural Sociology ISBN:0-691-08674-5, ISBN13: 978-0-691-08674-3. Dewey:306.6/09747. LCCN:2004-058631.

Audience: **u,f.** *Choice, 2006.*

Heskins, Jeffrey   **BV4596.G38H47 2006**
Face to Face: Gay and Lesbian Clergy on Holiness and Life Together. Trade Paper. William B. Eerdmans Publishing Company. Grand Rapids, MI. 2006. 201p. ISBN:0-8028-6303-5, ISBN13: 978-0-8028-6303-4. Dewey:283.086/64. LCCN:2005-033763.

Audience: **u,f.**

Holder, Arthur G.   **BV4501.3.B535 2005**
The Blackwell Companion to Christian Spirituality. Trade Cloth. Blackwell Publishing, Inc. Malden, MA. 2006. 576p. Blackwell Companions to Religion Ser. ISBN:1-4051-0247-0, ISBN13: 978-1-4051-0247-6. Dewey:248. LCCN:2004-029753.

Audience: **u,f.**

Holt, Bradley P.   **BV4490.H67 2005**
Thirsty for God. Ed. 2. Trade Paper. Augsburg Fortress, Publishers. Minneapolis, MN. 2005. 240p. ISBN:0-8006-3709-7, ISBN13: 978-0-8006-3709-5. Dewey:248.09. LCCN:2004-026101.

Audience: **u,f.**

Jones, Cheslyn, et al.   **BV4501.2**
The Study of Spirituality. Geoffrey Wainwright & Edward S. Yarnold (Authors). Trade Cloth. Oxford University Press, Inc. New York, NY. 1986. 656p. ISBN:0-19-504169-0, ISBN13: 978-0-19-504169-9. Dewey:248.4.

Audience: **u,f.** *Choice, 1987.*

Kierkegaard, Soren   **BV4501.2**
Provocations: Spiritual Writings of Kierkegaard. Charles E. Moore (Editor). Trade Paper. Orbis Books. Maryknoll, NY. 2003. 460p. ISBN:1-57075-513-2, ISBN13: 978-1-57075-513-2. Dewey:248.4/841. LCCN:2004-271552.

Audience: **g,l,u,f.** *Choice, 1999.*

McGrath, Alister E.   **BV4501.2.M2357 1999**
Christian Spirituality: An Introduction. Trade Cloth. Blackwell Publishing, Inc. Malden, MA. 1999. 224p. ISBN:0-631-21280-9, ISBN13: 978-0-631-21280-5. Dewey:248. LCCN:98-033147.

Audience: **g,l,u.**

Norris, Kathleen   **BV4501.2.N63 1998**
Amazing Grace: A Vocabulary of Faith. Trade Paper. Penguin

Group (USA) Inc. New York, NY. 1998. 320p.
ISBN:1-57322-078-7, ISBN13: 978-1-57322-078-1.
Dewey:234.23092. LCCN:97-045211.

Audience: **g,l,u.**

Ochs, Carol   **BL625.7.O24 1997**
Women and Spirituality. Ed. 2. Trade Cloth. Rowman &
Littlefield Publishers, Inc. Lanham, MD. 1996. 256p. New
Feminist Perspectives Ser., No. 67 ISBN:0-8476-8329-X,
ISBN13: 978-0-8476-8329-1. Dewey:291.4/082.
LCCN:96-029291.

Audience: **u,f.**

Sheldrake, Philip   **BV4488.N49 2005**
The New Westminster Dictionary of Christian Spirituality.
Perfect, Paper over Boards, Dust Jacket. Westminster John Knox
Press. Louisville, KY. 2005. 680p. ISBN:0-664-23003-2,
ISBN13: 978-0-664-23003-6. Dewey:248/.03.
LCCN:2005-047932.

Audience: **g,l,u,f.** *Choice, 2006.*

Christianity > Practical Theology > Moral Theology. Love

Arendt, Hannah   **BV4639.A6513 1995**
Love and Saint Augustine. Joanna Vecchiarelli Scott & Judith
Chelius Stark (Editors), Joanna Vecchiarelli Scott & Judith
Chelius Stark (Contribution by). Trade Cloth. University of
Chicago Press. Chicago, IL. 1996. 254p. ISBN:0-226-02596-9,
ISBN13: 978-0-226-02596-4. Dewey:177/.7/092.
LCCN:95-012866.

Audience: **u,f.** *Choice, 1996.*

Brady, Bernard V.   **BV4639.B72 2003**
Christian Love. Trade Cloth. Georgetown University Press.
Washington, DC. 2003. 320p. ISBN:0-87840-894-0, ISBN13:
978-0-87840-894-8. Dewey:241/.4. LCCN:2002-015256.

Audience: **g,u,f.** *Choice, 2003.*

Geach, Peter T.   **BV4630**
The Virtues. Trade Cloth. Cambridge University Press. New
York, NY. 1977. 200p. ISBN:0-521-21350-9, ISBN13:
978-0-521-21350-9. Dewey:241/.4. LCCN:76-019627.

Audience: **u,f.**

Jackson, Timothy P.   **BV4639 .J33 1999**
Love Disconsoled: Meditations on Christian Charity. Trade
Cloth. Cambridge University Press. New York, NY. 1999. 268p.
Cambridge Studies in Religion and Critical Thought, No. 7
ISBN:0-521-55493-4, ISBN13: 978-0-521-55493-0.
Dewey:241/.4. LCCN:99-012129.

Audience: **u,f.**

Jackson, Timothy P.   **BV4639.J34 2003**
The Priority of Love: Christian Charity and Social Justice. Trade
Cloth. Princeton University Press. Princeton, NJ. 2002. 248p.
New Forum Bks. ISBN:0-691-05085-6, ISBN13:
978-0-691-05085-0. Dewey:241/.4. LCCN:2002-023666.

Audience: **u,f.**

Lewis, C. S.   **BV4639.L45 1991**
The Four Loves. Trade Cloth. Harcourt Trade Publishers. New
York, NY. 1991. 156p. HBJ Book Ser. ISBN:0-15-132916-8,
ISBN13: 978-0-15-132916-8. Dewey:241.4. LCCN:91-004033.

Audience: **g,l,u,f.**

Little, Lester K.   **BV4647.P6L57 1978**
Religious Poverty and the Profit Economy in Medieval Europe.
Trade Cloth. Cornell University Press. Ithaca, NY. 1978. xi,
267p. ISBN:0-8014-1213-7, ISBN13: 978-0-8014-1213-4.
Dewey:261.8/5. LCCN:78-058630.

Audience: **u,f.**

Murphy, Jeffrie G. &   **BJ1496**
  Hampton, Jean
Forgiveness and Mercy. Gerald Postema, Jules Coleman, Antony
Duff, David Lyons, Neil MacCormick, Stephen R. Munzer,
Philip Pettit, Joseph Raz & Jeremy Waldron (Contribution by).
Trade Paper. Cambridge University Press. New York, NY. 1990.
206p. Studies in Philosophy and Law ISBN:0-521-39567-4,
ISBN13: 978-0-521-39567-0. Dewey:179/.9.

Audience: **u,f.** *Choice, 1989.*

Outka, Gene   **BJ1278.A/**
Agape: An Ethical Analysis. Trade Paper. Yale University Press.
Cumberland, RI. 1977. 334p. Publications in Religion Ser., No.
17 ISBN:0-300-02122-4, ISBN13: 978-0-300-02122-6.
Dewey:241/.4. LCCN:78-088070.

Audience: **u,f.**

Tillich, Paul Johannes   **BV4633**
Love, Power, and Justice: Ontological Analysis and Ethical
Applications. Trade Paper. Oxford University Press, Inc. New
York, NY. 1960. 140p. ISBN:0-19-500222-9, ISBN13:
978-0-19-500222-5. Dewey:231.

Audience: **u,f.**

Vacek, Edward C.   **241/.4**
Love, Human and Divine: The Heart of Christian Ethics. Trade
Paper. Georgetown University Press. Washington, DC. 1996.
336p. Moral Traditions and Moral Arguments Ser.
ISBN:0-87840-627-1, ISBN13: 978-0-87840-627-2.
Dewey:BV4639 .V25. LCCN:93-037944.

Audience: **u,f.**

Wood, Rega   **BV4630.W66 1997**
Ockham on the Virtues. Cloth Text. Purdue University Press.

West Lafayette, IN. 1997. 296p. History of Philosophy Ser.
ISBN:1-55753-096-3, ISBN13: 978-1-55753-096-7.
Dewey:179/.9/092. LCCN:96-039436.

Audience: **u,f.**

Christianity > Practical Theology > Works of Meditation and Devotion. Consolation and Cheer

Donne, John   **BV4831.D6 1959**
Devotions upon Emergent Occasions and Death's Duel. Trade
Paper. University of Michigan Press. Chicago, IL. 1959. 246p.
Ann Arbor Paperbacks Ser. ISBN:0-472-06030-9, ISBN13:
978-0-472-06030-6. Dewey:242. LCCN:59-016355.

Audience: **g,l,u,f.**

Ford, David F.   **BV4817**
Living in Praise. Trade Paper. Darton, Longman & Todd, Ltd.
Letchworth Garden City, 2005. 240p. ISBN:0-232-52625-7,
ISBN13: 978-0-232-52625-7. Dewey:248.3.
LCCN:2006-272760.

Audience: **g,l,u.**

Julian of Norwich   **BV4831**
Revelations of Divine Love. Clifton Wolters (Translator,
Introduction by). Trade Paper. Penguin Group (USA) Inc. New
York, NY. 1982. 224p. Penguin Classics Ser.
ISBN:0-14-044177-8, ISBN13: 978-0-14-044177-2. Dewey:242.

Audience: **g,l,u,f.**

Kierkegaard, Soren   **BV4836.K5313 1997**
Without Authority. Howard V. Hong & Edna H. Hong (Edited
and Translated by). Trade Cloth. Princeton University Press.
Princeton, NJ. 1997. 340p. Kierkegaard's Writings, Vol. 18
ISBN:0-691-01239-3, ISBN13: 978-0-691-01239-1. Dewey:242.
LCCN:96-002929.

Audience: **g,l,u,f.**

Lewis, C. S.   **BT732.7.L48 2001**
The Problem of Pain. Trade Paper. HarperCollins Publishers.
New York, NY. 2001. 176p. C. S. Lewis Signature Classics
ISBN:0-06-065296-9, ISBN13: 978-0-06-065296-8.
Dewey:231/.8. LCCN:00-049861.

Audience: **g,l,u,f.**

Lewis, C. S.   **BV4905.2.L4 2001**
Grief Observed. Madeleine L'Engle (Foreword by). Trade Paper.
HarperCollins Publishers. New York, NY. 2001. 112p. C. S.
Lewis Signature Classics Ser. ISBN:0-06-065238-1, ISBN13:
978-0-06-065238-8. Dewey:242/.4. LCCN:00-063227.

Audience: **g,l,u,f.**

Sherley-Price, Leo   **BV4821**
  (Translator)
The Imitation of Christ. Thomas à Kempis (Contribution by),
Leo Sherley-Price (Introduction by). Trade Paper. Penguin
Group (USA) Inc. New York, NY. 1952. 224p. Classics Ser.
ISBN:0-14-044027-5, ISBN13: 978-0-14-044027-0. Dewey:242.

Audience: **g,l,u,f.**

Sittser, Jerry   **BV4905.3.S577 2004**
A Grace Disguised: How the Soul Grows Through Loss. Trade
Cloth. Zondervan. Grand Rapids, MI. 2005. 224p.
ISBN:0-310-25895-2, ISBN13: 978-0-310-25895-7.
Dewey:248.8/66. LCCN:2004-017824.

Audience: **g,l.**

Traherne, Thomas   **BV4831**
Thomas Traherne: Poetry and Prose. Denise Inge (Editor). Trade
Cloth. SPCK Publishing. London, 2002. 144p. The Golden Age
of Spiritual Writing Ser. ISBN:0-281-05468-1, ISBN13:
978-0-281-05468-8. Dewey:242.

Audience: **g,l,u,f.**

Weil, Simone   **B2430.W473A7713 2000**
Waiting for God. Trade Paper. HarperCollins Publishers. New
York, NY. 2001. 192p. Perennial Classics Ser.
ISBN:0-06-095970-3, ISBN13: 978-0-06-095970-8. Dewey:248.
LCCN:00-047271.

Audience: **g,l,u.** *B*

Wolterstorff, Nicholas   **BF575.G7W65 1987**
Lament for a Son. Trade Cloth. William B. Eerdmans Publishing
Company. Grand Rapids, MI. 1988. 111p. ISBN:0-8028-0294-X,
ISBN13: 978-0-8028-0294-1. Dewey:155.9/37.
LCCN:87-008990.

Audience: **g,l,u,f.**

Christianity > Practical Theology > Asceticism. Mysticism

Brown, Peter   **BR195.C45B76 1988**
The Body and Society: Men, Women, and Sexual Renunciation
in Early Christianity. Trade Cloth. Columbia University Press.
New York, NY. 1988. 504p. Lectures on the History of
Religions Ser., No. 13 ISBN:0-231-06100-5, ISBN13:
978-0-231-06100-1. Dewey:241.6/6. LCCN:87-030941.

Audience: **u,f.** *Choice, 1989.*

Butler, Dom Cuthbert   **BV5075.B8 2003**
Western Mysticism: Augustine, Gregory, and Bernard on
Contemplation and the Contemplative Life. Trade Paper. Dover
Publications, Inc. Mineola, NY. 2003. 304p.
ISBN:0-486-43142-8, ISBN13: 978-0-486-43142-0.
Dewey:248.2/2. LCCN:2003-055067.

Audience: **g,l,u,f.**

Colledge, Edmund &   **BV5080**
  McGinn, Bernard (Translators)
Meister Eckhart: The Essential Sermons, Commentaries,
Treatises and Defense. Edmund Colledge & Bernard McGinn
(Introduction by), Houston Smith (Preface by). Trade Cloth.
Paulist Press. Mahwah, NJ. 1981. 384p. Classics of Western
Spirituality Ser. ISBN:0-8091-2370-3, ISBN13:
978-0-8091-2370-4. Dewey:248.2/2.

Audience: **g,l,u,f.**

Danielou, Jean (Editor) BV5080
From Glory to Glory: Texts from Gregory of Nyssa's Mystical
Writings. Trade Paper. Saint Vladimir's Seminary Press.
Yonkers, NY. 1979. 304p. ISBN:0-913836-54-0, ISBN13:
978-0-913836-54-5. Dewey:248.2/2. LCCN:79-000038.
Audience: **u,f.**

De Catanzaro, C. J. BV5039.G7
Symeon, the New Theologian: The Discourses. Trade Cloth.
Paulist Press. Mahwah, NJ. 1980. 416p. Classics of Western
Spirituality Ser. ISBN:0-8091-2230-8, ISBN13:
978-0-8091-2230-1. Dewey:248.4/8140942. LCCN:80-082414.
Audience: **u,f.**

Duprbe, Louis K. & BV5072.L54 2001
Wiseman, James A.
Light from Light: An Anthology of Christian Mysticism. Ed. 2.
Trade Cloth. Paulist Press. Mahwah, NJ. 2001. 480p.
ISBN:0-8091-4013-6, ISBN13: 978-0-8091-4013-8.
Dewey:248.2/2. LCCN:00-068462.
Audience: **l,u.**

Elm, Susanna BV5023
Virgins of God: The Making of Asceticism in Late Antiquity.
Paper Text. Oxford University Press, Inc. New York, NY. 1996.
462p. Oxford Classical Monographs ISBN:0-19-815044-X,
ISBN13: 978-0-19-815044-2. Dewey:271/.9/0009015.
Audience: **u,f.**

Julian of Norwich BV4831.J813 1998
Revelations of Divine Love. Elizabeth Spearing & A. C.
Spearing (Translators). Trade Paper. Penguin Group (USA) Inc.
New York, NY. 1999. 240p. Classics Ser. ISBN:0-14-044673-7,
ISBN13: 978-0-14-044673-9. Dewey:242. LCCN:99-199182.
Audience: **g,l,u,f.**

Kempe, Margery B. PR2007.K4A3 1985
Book of Margery Kempe. Barry Windeatt (Translator,
Introduction by). Trade Paper. Penguin Group (USA) Inc. New
York, NY. 1986. 1p. Classics Ser. ISBN:0-14-043251-5,
ISBN13: 978-0-14-043251-0. Dewey:248.2/2/0924 B.
LCCN:86-116367.
Audience: **g,l.**

McGinn, Bernard BV5082.3.E87 2006
The Essential Writings of Christian Mysticism. Trade Paper.
Dell Publishing. New York, NY. 2006. 592p.
ISBN:0-8129-7421-2, ISBN13: 978-0-8129-7421-8.
Dewey:248.2/2. LCCN:2006-044877.
Audience: **g,l,u.**

McGinn, Bernard BV5075.M37 1994
The Flowering of Mysticism. Trade Cloth. FaithWorks.
Brentwood, TN. 1998. 526p. The Presence of God Ser., No. 3
ISBN:0-8245-1742-3, ISBN13: 978-0-8245-1742-7.
Dewey:248.2/2/09022. LCCN:97-052986.
Audience: **u,f.**

McGinn, Bernard BV5080
The Foundations of Mysticism: Origins to the Fifth Century.
Trade Paper. FaithWorks. Brentwood, TN. 1994. 494p.

ISBN:0-8245-1404-1, ISBN13: 978-0-8245-1404-4.
Dewey:248.2/2.
Audience: **u,f.** *Choice, 1992.*

McGinn, Bernard BV5075
The Growth of Mysticism: From Gregory the Great Through the
12th Century, Vol. 2. Trade Paper. FaithWorks. Brentwood, TN.
1996. 630p. Presence of God: A History of Christian Mysticism
Ser., Vol. 2 ISBN:0-8245-1628-1, ISBN13: 978-0-8245-1628-4.
Dewey:248.2/2/0902.
Audience: **u,f.** *Choice, 1995.*

McGinn, Bernard BV5077.G3
The Harvest of Mysticism in Medieval Germany (1300-1500).
Trade Paper, Perfect. Crossroad Publishing Company. New York,
NY. 2005. 480p. In the Presence of God Ser., Vol. IV
ISBN:0-8245-2345-8, ISBN13: 978-0-8245-2345-9.
Dewey:248.2/209 s 248.2. LCCN:2005-032733.
Audience: **u,f.**

McGinn, Bernard BV5095.E3M33 2003
The Mystical Thought of Meister Eckhart: The Man from
Whom God Hid Nothing. Trade Paper. FaithWorks. Brentwood,
TN. 2003. 320p. ISBN:0-8245-1996-5, ISBN13:
978-0-8245-1996-4. Dewey:230.2/092. LCCN:2001-001533.
Audience: **u,f.**

Ramsey, Boniface (Editor, BR60.A35 NO. 57
Translator)
John Cassian: The Conferences. Trade Cloth. Paulist Press.
Mahwah, NJ. 1997. 912p. Ancient Christian Writers Ser., No. 57
ISBN:0-8091-0484-9, ISBN13: 978-0-8091-0484-0. Dewey:255.
LCCN:97-006523.
Audience: **u,f.**

Rousseau, Philip BR1720
Pachomius: The Making of a Community in Fourth-Century
Egypt. Trade Paper. University of California Press. Berkeley,
CA. 1999. 250p. Transformation of the Classical Heritage Ser.,
Vol. 6 ISBN:0-520-21959-7, ISBN13: 978-0-520-21959-5.
Dewey:271/.0092.
Audience: **u,f.** *Choice, 1986.*

Walsh, James (Editor) BV5080.C5 1981
The Cloud of Unknowing. Simon Tugwell (Preface by). Trade
Cloth. Paulist Press. Mahwah, NJ. 1981. 320p. Classics of
Western Spirituality Ser. ISBN:0-8091-2332-0, ISBN13:
978-0-8091-2332-2. Dewey:248.2/2. LCCN:81-082201.
Audience: **g,l,u,f.**

Christianity > Practical Theology > Worship. Symbolism. Liturgies

Bradshaw, Paul F. & BV169.5 .M35
Hoffman, Lawrence A.
The Making of Jewish and Christian Worship. Cloth Text.
University of Notre Dame Press. Notre Dame, IN. 1991. 192p.

Two Liturgical Traditions Ser., Vol. 1 ISBN:0-268-01207-5, ISBN13: 978-0-268-01207-6. Dewey:264/.009. LCCN:90-070856.

Audience: **u,f.**

Camille, Michael   **BV153.E85**
The Gothic Idol: Ideology and Image-Making in Medieval Art. Trade Paper. Cambridge University Press. New York, NY. 1991. 441p. Cambridge New Art History and Criticism Ser. ISBN:0-521-42430-5, ISBN13: 978-0-521-42430-1. Dewey:246/.09/02. LCCN:88-011680.

Audience: **g,l,u,f.** *Choice, 1990.*

Davies, J. G. (Editor)   **BV173.N49 1986**
The New Westminster Dictionary of Liturgy and Worship. Trade Cloth. Westminster John Knox Press. Louisville, KY. 1986. 560p. ISBN:0-664-21270-0, ISBN13: 978-0-664-21270-4. Dewey:264/.003/21. LCCN:86-009219.

Audience: **g,l,u,f.** *Choice, 1987.*

Dawn, Marva J.   **BV15.D39 1999**
A Royal Waste of Time: The Splendor of Worshiping God and Being Church for the World. Trade Cloth. William B. Eerdmans Publishing Company. Grand Rapids, MI. 1999. 385p. ISBN:0-8028-4586-X, ISBN13: 978-0-8028-4586-3. Dewey:264. LCCN:99-019405.

Audience: **u,f.**

Dix, Gregory   **BV178 .D5**
Shape of the Liturgy. Trade Cloth. Continuum International Publishing Group, Ltd. London, 2005. 784p. ISBN:0-8264-7942-1, ISBN13: 978-0-8264-7942-6. Dewey:264/.36/09. LCCN:2006-620093.

Audience: **u,f.**

Heiler, Friedrich   **BV210.H3813 1997**
Prayer: A Study in the History and Psychology of Religion. Trade Cloth. Oneworld Publications. Oxford, 1997. 420p. ISBN:1-85168-143-4, ISBN13: 978-1-85168-143-3. Dewey:291.4/3. LCCN:98-187152.

Audience: **u,f.**

Jones, Cheslyn   **BV5**
The Study of Liturgy. Ed. 2. Paper Text. Oxford University Press, Inc. New York, NY. 1992. 646p. ISBN:0-19-520922-2, ISBN13: 978-0-19-520922-8. Dewey:264/.009. LCCN:91-044857.

Audience: **u,f.**

Jungmann   **BV207 .J813**
Christian Prayer Through the Centuries. Trade Paper. SPCK Publishing. London, ISBN:0-281-05759-1, ISBN13: 978-0-281-05759-7. Dewey:248/.3.

Audience: **u,f.**

Lang, Bernhard   **BV5.L36 1997**
Sacred Games: A History of Christian Worship. Cloth over Boards. Yale University Press. Cumberland, RI. 1997. 542p. ISBN:0-300-06932-4, ISBN13: 978-0-300-06932-7. Dewey:264/.009. LCCN:97-060406.

Audience: **u,f.** *Choice, 1998.*

Maag, Karin & Witvliet,   **BV8.W67 2004**
 John D.
Worship in Medieval and Early Modern Europe: Change and Continuity in Religious Practice. Trade Cloth. University of Notre Dame Press. Notre Dame, IN. 2004. 368p. ISBN:0-268-03474-5, ISBN13: 978-0-268-03474-0. Dewey:264/.0094. LCCN:2003-025294.

Audience: **u,f.**

Old, Hughes Oliphant   **BV226.O43 1995**
Leading in Prayer: A Workbook for Worship. Trade Paper. William B. Eerdmans Publishing Company. Grand Rapids, MI. 1995. 381p. ISBN:0-8028-0821-2, ISBN13: 978-0-8028-0821-9. Dewey:264/.1. LCCN:95-021725.

Audience: **u,f.**

Saliers, Don E.   **BV15.S25 1994**
Worship as Theology: Foretaste of Glory Divine. Ulrike Guthrie (Editor). Trade Cloth. Abingdon Press. Nashville, TN. 1994. 256p. ISBN:0-687-14693-3, ISBN13: 978-0-687-14693-2. Dewey:264/.001. LCCN:94-017519.

Audience: **u,f.**

Schoenborn, Christoph   **BV150.S3513 1994**
God's Human Face: The Christ Icon. Trade Paper. Ignatius Press. San Francisco, CA. 1994. 260p. ISBN:0-89870-514-2, ISBN13: 978-0-89870-514-0. Dewey:246/.53. LCCN:94-075957.

Audience: **u,f.**

Stringer, Martin D.   **BV5.S77 2005**
A Sociological History of Christian Worship. Trade Cloth. Cambridge University Press. New York, NY. 2005. 276p. ISBN:0-521-81955-5, ISBN13: 978-0-521-81955-8. Dewey:264/.009. LCCN:2004-057069.

Audience: **u,f.**

Viladesau, Richard   **BV160.V55 2005**
The Beauty of the Cross: The Passion of Christ in Theology and the Arts, from the Catacombs to the Eve of the Renaissance. Trade Cloth. Oxford University Press, Inc. New York, NY. 2005. 224p. ISBN:0-19-518811-X, ISBN13: 978-0-19-518811-0. Dewey:246/.558. LCCN:2005-008224.

Audience: **u,f.**

Wainwright, Geoffrey &   **BV15.O95 2005**
 Westerfield Tucker, Karen B. (Editors)
The Oxford History of Christian Worship. Trade Cloth. Oxford University Press, Inc. New York, NY. 2005. 936p. ISBN:0-19-513886-4, ISBN13: 978-0-19-513886-3. Dewey:264/.009. LCCN:2005-021054.

Audience: **u,f.** *Choice, 2006.*

Wannenwetsch, Bernd   **BV103**
Political Worship: Ethics for Christian Citizens. Margaret Kohl (Contribution by). Trade Cloth. Oxford University Press, Inc. New York, NY. 2004. 416p. Oxford Studies in Theological Ethics ISBN:0-19-925387-0, ISBN13: 978-0-19-925387-6. Dewey:264. LCCN:2004-556273.

Audience: **u,f.**

Watson, J. R.   BV312.W38 1997
The English Hymn: A Critical and Historical Study. Trade Cloth.
Oxford University Press, Inc. New York, NY. 1997. 564p.
ISBN:0-19-826762-2, ISBN13: 978-0-19-826762-1.
Dewey:264/.2/0942. LCCN:96-043077.

Audience: **u,f**. *Choice, 1998*

White, James F.   BV176.3.W48 2001
Introduction to Christian Worship. Ed. 3. Trade Cloth. Abingdon
Press. Nashville, TN. 2004. 318p. ISBN:0-687-09109-8,
ISBN13: 978-0-687-09109-6. Dewey:264. LCCN:00-063986.

Audience: **l,u**

Woolfenden, Gregory W.   BV207
Daily Liturgical Prayer: Origins and Theology. Trade Cloth.
Ashgate Publishing, Ltd. Aldershot, 2004. 338p. Liturgy,
Worship and Society Ser. ISBN:0-7546-1600-2, ISBN13:
978-0-7546-1600-9. Dewey:264/.15/09. LCCN:2003-063708.

Audience: **u,f**.

Christianity > Practical Theology > Ecclesiastical Theology

Abraham, William J.   BV600.3.A27 2003
The Logic of Renewal. Trade Paper. William B. Eerdmans
Publishing Company. Grand Rapids, MI. 2004. 182p.
ISBN:0-8028-2656-3, ISBN13: 978-0-8028-2656-5.
Dewey:262/.001/7. LCCN:2003-049469.

Audience: **u,f**.

Avis, Paul D. L.   BX5131.2 A94
Anglicanism and the Christian Church: Theological Resources in
Historical Perspective. Ed. 2. Trade Cloth. Continuum
International Publishing Group, Ltd. London, 2002. 384p.
ISBN:0-567-08849-9, ISBN13: 978-0-567-08849-9.
Dewey:262/.03.

Audience: **u,f**.

Barth, Karl   BV600.3.B378 2005
The Church and the Churches. William G. Rusch (Foreword
by). Trade Paper, Perfect. William B. Eerdmans Publishing
Company. Grand Rapids, MI. 2005. 59p. ISBN:0-8028-2970-8,
ISBN13: 978-0-8028-2970-2. Dewey:280/.042.
LCCN:2005-050060.

Audience: **g,l,u,f**.

Daly, Mary   HQ1394.D28 1985
The Church and the Second Sex. Trade Paper. Beacon Press.
Boston, MA. 1986. 240p. ISBN:0-8070-1101-0, ISBN13:
978-0-8070-1101-0. Dewey:261.8/344. LCCN:85-047519.

Audience: **l,u**. *B*

Dinan, Susan E. & Meyers,   BV639.W7W6153 2001
Debra (Editors)
Gender and Religion in Old and New Worlds. Paper over
Boards. Routledge. New York, NY. 2001. 240p.
ISBN:0-415-93034-0, ISBN13: 978-0-415-93034-5.
Dewey:270.6/082. LCCN:00-051710.

Audience: **u,f**.

Evans, G. R.   BV600.2 .E94 1994
The Church and the Churches: Toward an Ecumenical
Ecclesiology. Trade Cloth. Cambridge University Press. New
York, NY. 1994. 345p. ISBN:0-521-46286-X, ISBN13:
978-0-521-46286-0. Dewey:262/.001/1. LCCN:93-042441.

Audience: **u,f**. *Choice, 1995.*

Frankl, Razelle   BV656.3.F73 1987
Televangelism: The Marketing of Popular Religion. Trade Cloth.
Southern Illinois University Press. Carbondale, IL. 1986. 222p.
ISBN:0-8093-1299-9, ISBN13: 978-0-8093-1299-3.
Dewey:306/.6. LCCN:86-006584.

Audience: **l,u,f**. *Choice, 1987.*

Haight, Roger   BV600.3.H35 2004
Christian Community in History. Trade Cloth. Continuum
International Publishing Group, Ltd. London, 2004. 512p.
ISBN:0-8264-1630-6, ISBN13: 978-0-8264-1630-8.
Dewey:262/.009. LCCN:2004-004006.

Audience: **u,f**. *Choice, 2005.*

Healy, Nicholas M.   BV600.2 .H385 2000
Church, World and the Christian Life: Practical-Prophetic
Ecclesiology. Cloth Text. Cambridge University Press. New
York, NY. 2000. 212p. Studies in Christian Doctrine, No. 7
ISBN:0-521-78138-8, ISBN13: 978-0-521-78138-1. Dewey:262.
LCCN:99-089659.

Audience: **u,f**.

Hendershot, Heather   BV652.97.U6H46 2004
Shaking the World for Jesus: Media and Conservative
Evangelical Culture. Trade Cloth. University of Chicago Press.
Chicago, IL. 2004. 266p. ISBN:0-226-32679-9, ISBN13:
978-0-226-32679-5. Dewey:261.5/2/0973. LCCN:2003-014235.

Audience: **l,u,f**. *Choice, 2004.*

Jinkins, Michael   BV600.2.J53 1999
The Church Faces Death: Ecclesiology in a Post-Modern
Context. Trade Cloth. Oxford University Press, Inc. New York,
NY. 1999. 154p. ISBN:0-19-512840-0, ISBN13:
978-0-19-512840-6. Dewey:262. LCCN:98-036522.

Audience: **u,f**.

Kee, Howard C.   BV598.K425 1995
Who Are the People of God?: Early Christian Models of
Community. Cloth over Boards. Yale University Press.
Cumberland, RI. 1995. 288p. ISBN:0-300-05952-3, ISBN13:
978-0-300-05952-6. Dewey:270.1. LCCN:94-013883.

Audience: **u,f**. *Choice, 1995.*

Kung, Hans   BX1806
Infallible?: An Unresolved Enquiry. Trade Paper. Continuum
International Publishing Group, Ltd. London, 1994. 289p.
ISBN:0-8264-0678-5, ISBN13: 978-0-8264-0678-1.
Dewey:262/.131. LCCN:98-020738.

Audience: **u,f**.

McKinion, Steven A.   BV598.L54 2001
(Editor)
Life and Practice in the Early Church: A Documentary Reader.
Trade Cloth. New York University Press. New York, NY. 2001.

200p. ISBN:0-8147-5648-4, ISBN13: 978-0-8147-5648-5. Dewey:270.1. LCCN:2001-000564.

Audience: **l,u.** *Choice, 2002.*

Murray, Robert   **BV598**
Symbols of Church and Kingdom: A Study in Early Syriac Tradition. Ed. 2. Trade Paper. Continuum International Publishing Group, Ltd. London, 2006. 416p. ISBN:0-567-03082-2, ISBN13: 978-0-567-03082-5. Dewey:230.1.

Audience: **u,f.**

Ranft, Patricia   **BV639.W7R36 1998**
Women and Spirtual Equality in Christian Tradition. Cloth over Boards. Palgrave Macmillan. New York, NY. 1998. 321p. ISBN:0-312-15911-0, ISBN13: 978-0-312-15911-5. Dewey:270/.082. LCCN:97-050397.

Audience: **u,f.** *Choice, 1998.*

Schultze, Quentin J.   **BV652.97.U6S38 2003**
Christianity and the Mass Media in America: Toward a Democratic Accommodation. Trade Cloth. Michigan State University Press. East Lansing, MI. 2003. 512p. Rhetoric and Public Affairs Ser. ISBN:0-87013-696-8, ISBN13: 978-0-87013-696-2. Dewey:261.5/2/0973. LCCN:2003-020164.

Audience: **u,f.** *Choice, 2004.*

Tierney, Brian   **BX1790**
The Crisis of Church and State 1050-1300. Trade Paper. University of Toronto Press. Toronto, ON. 1988. 210p. Medieval Academy Reprints for Teaching Ser., Vol. 21 ISBN:0-8020-6701-8, ISBN13: 978-0-8020-6701-2. Dewey:261.709021. LCCN:89-124004.

Audience: **u,f.**

Vergara, Camilo Jose   **BV637**
How the Other Half Worships. Saddle Stitched, Cloth over Boards, Dust Jacket. Rutgers University Press. Piscataway, NJ. 2005. 286p. ISBN:0-8135-3682-0, ISBN13: 978-0-8135-3682-8. Dewey:277.3/009173/2.

Audience: **g,l,u,f.** *Choice, 2006.*

Westerhoff, John H.   **BV600.2**
Living the Faith Community: The Church That Makes a Difference. Trade Cloth. Church Publishing, Inc. New York, NY. 2005. ISBN:1-59628-003-4, ISBN13: 978-1-59628-003-8. Dewey:250.

Audience: **u,f.**

Williams, Rowan   **BR118**
Why Study the Past? Trade Paper. BPR Publishers. New Providence, NJ. 2005. 129p. Sarum Theological Lectures ISBN:0-232-52549-8, ISBN13: 978-0-232-52549-6. Dewey:270. LCCN:2005-363500.

Audience: **u,f.**

Christianity > Practical Theology > Ecclesiastical Theology > Freedom and Authority

Church, Forrest (Editor)   **BR516.S46 2004**
The Separation of Church and State: Writings on a Fundamental Freedom by America's Founders. Trade Cloth. Beacon Press. Boston, MA. 2004. 176p. ISBN:0-8070-7722-4, ISBN13: 978-0-8070-7722-1. Dewey:323.44/2/0973. LCCN:2004-006382.

Audience: **g,l,u.**

Cookson, Catharine (Editor)   **BV741.E47 2003**
Encyclopedia of Religious Freedom. Paper over Boards. Routledge. New York, NY. 2003. 512p. Religion and Society Ser., Vol. 4 ISBN:0-415-94181-4, ISBN13: 978-0-415-94181-5. Dewey:323.44/2/03. LCCN:2003-005354.

Audience: **g,l,u,f.** *Choice, 2003.*

Drinan, Robert F.   **K3258.D75 2004**
Can God and Caesar Coexist?: Balancing Religious Freedom and International Law. Cloth over Boards. Yale University Press. Cumberland, RI. 2004. 272p. ISBN:0-300-10086-8, ISBN13: 978-0-300-10086-0. Dewey:341.4/832. LCCN:2004-041977.

Audience: **g,l,u,f.** *Choice, 2005.*

Finkelman, Paul (Editor)   **KF4783.A68R45 2000**
Religion and American Law: An Encyclopedia. Trade Cloth. Garland Publishing, Inc. New York, NY. 1999. 624p. Reference Library of the Humanities, Vol. 1548 ISBN:0-8153-0750-0, ISBN13: 978-0-8153-0750-1. Dewey:342.73/0852. LCCN:99-057222.

Audience: **u,f.** *Choice, 2000.*

Helmstadter, Richard   **BV741.F79 1997**
  (Editor)
Freedom and Religion in the Nineteenth Century. Trade Cloth. Stanford University Press. Palo Alto, CA. 1997. 472p. The Making of Modern Freedom ISBN:0-8047-3087-3, ISBN13: 978-0-8047-3087-7. Dewey:323.44/2/09034. LCCN:96-054045.

Audience: **u,f.**

Kramnick, Isaac & Moore,   **BR516**
  R. Laurence
The Godless Constitution: A Moral Defense of the Secular State. Trade Paper, Perfect. W. W. Norton & Company, Inc. New York, NY. 2005. 208p. ISBN:0-393-32837-6, ISBN13: 978-0-393-32837-0. Dewey:323.4/42/0973. LCCN:2006-274845.

Audience: **g,l.**

Lee, Francis Graham   **KF4865**
Church-State Relations. Cloth Text. Greenwood Publishing Group, Inc. Portsmouth, NH. 2002. 456p. Major Issues in American History Ser. ISBN:0-313-31096-3, ISBN13: 978-0-313-31096-6. Dewey:342.73/0852. LCCN:2001-050112.

Audience: **g,l.** *Choice, 2002.*

McLaren, John & Coward,   **BV741.R428 1998**
  Harold (Editors)
Religious Conscience, the State, and the Law: Historical Contexts and Contemporary Significance. Cloth Text. State

Formats: Web: ☐   Ebook: **e**   CD/DVD-ROM: 🏵   BCL3: ***B***

University of New York Press. Albany, NY. 1998. 288p. SUNY Series in Religious Studies ISBN:0-7914-4001-X, ISBN13: 978-0-7914-4001-8. Dewey:323.44/2/09. LCCN:97-052270.

Audience: **g,l,u,f.**

Miller, William Lee　　　　　　**BR516.M543 2003**
The First Liberty: America's Foundation in Religious Freedom. Ed. 2. Box or Slipcased, Trade Cloth. Georgetown University Press. Washington, DC. 2003. 296p. ISBN:0-87840-899-1, ISBN13: 978-0-87840-899-3. Dewey:323.44/2/0973. LCCN:2002-033908.

Audience: **u,f.**

Noonan, John T. Jr.　　　　　　**BR516 .N59 1998**
The Lustre of Our Country: The American Experience of Religious Freedom. Trade Cloth. University of California Press Berkeley, CA. 1998. 436p. ISBN:0-520-20997-4, ISBN13: 978-0-520-20997-8. Dewey:323.44/2/0973. LCCN:97-049327.

Audience: **g,l,u,f.** *Choice, 1999.*

Christianity > Practical Theology > Ecclesiastical Theology > Sacraments

Beasley-Murray, George Raymond　　　　　　**BV811.2**
Baptism in the New Testament. Paper Text. William B. Eerdmans Publishing Company. Grand Rapids, MI. 1973. 432p. ISBN:0-8028-1493-X, ISBN13: 978-0-8028-1493-7. Dewey:234.161.

Audience: **u,f.**

Berkouwer, G. C.　　　　　　**BV800**
Sacraments. Paper Text. William B. Eerdmans Publishing Company. Grand Rapids, MI. 1969. 304p. Studies in Dogmatics ISBN:0-8028-4822-2, ISBN13: 978-0-8028-4822-2. Dewey:254. LCCN:66-027410.

Audience: **g,l,u.**

Holifield, E. Brooks　　　　　　**BV800**
The Covenant Sealed: The Development of Puritan Sacramental Theology in Old and New England, 1570-1720. Trade Paper. Wipf & Stock Publishers. Eugene, OR. 2002. 260p. ISBN:1-59244-854-2, ISBN13: 978-1-59244-854-8. Dewey:234/.16.

Audience: **u,f.**

Jeremias, Joachim　　　　　　**BT420**
The Eucharistic Words of Jesus. Norman Perrin (Translator). Trade Paper. Augsburg Fortress, Publishers. Minneapolis, MN. 1977. 280p. ISBN:0-8006-1319-8, ISBN13: 978-0-8006-1319-8. Dewey:232.957. LCCN:77-078633.

Audience: **u,f.**

1999 ed. **Johnson, Maxwell E.**　　　　　　**BV873.I54J 1999**
The Rites of Christian Initiation: Their Evolution and Interpretation. Trade Paper. Liturgical Press. Collegeville, MN. 2005. 440p. ISBN:0-8146-6011-8, ISBN13: 978-0-8146-6011-9. Dewey:265/.1/09. LCCN:98-002488.

Audience: **u,f.**

MacQuarrie, John　　　　　　**BV800.M28 1997**
A Guide to the Sacraments. Trade Cloth. Continuum International Publishing Group, Ltd. London, 1997. 256p. ISBN:0-8264-1027-8, ISBN13: 978-0-8264-1027-6. Dewey:234/.16. LCCN:96-051046.

Audience: **u,f.**

Mazza, Enrico　　　　　　**BV823.M38613 1999**
The Celebration of the Eucharist: The Origin of the Rite and the Development of Its Interpretation. Matthew J. O'Connell (Translator). Trade Paper. Liturgical Press. Collegeville, MN. 2005. 376p. ISBN:0-8146-6170-X, ISBN13: 978-0-8146-6170-3. Dewey:264/.02036/09. LCCN:98-037348.

Audience: **u,f.**

Reynolds, Philip L.　　　　　　**BV835.R485 1994**
Marriage in the Western Church: The Christianization of Marriage During the Patristic Medieval Periods. Trade Cloth. Brill Academic Publishers, Inc. Boston, MA. 1994. xxx, 436p. Supplements to Vigiliae Christianae Ser., Vol. 24 ISBN:90-04-10022-9, ISBN13: 978-90-04-10022-0. Dewey:234/.165/09. LCCN:94-000570.

Audience: **u,f.**

Rubin, Miri　　　　　　**BV823.R78 1991**
Corpus Christi: The Eucharist in Late Medieval Culture. Trade Paper. Cambridge University Press. New York, NY. 1992. 446p. ISBN:0-521-43805-5, ISBN13: 978-0-521-43805-6. Dewey:264/.02036/0940902.

Audience: **u,f.** *Choice, 1992.*

Tentler, T.　　　　　　**BV840**
Sin and Confession on the Eve of the Reformation. Trade Cloth. Princeton University Press. Princeton, NJ. 1977. 424p. ISBN:0-691-07219-1, ISBN13: 978-0-691-07219-7. Dewey:265/.6/09. LCCN:76-003022.

Audience: **u,f.**

White, James F.　　　　　　**BV800.W484**
The Sacraments in Protestant Practice and Faith. Trade Cloth. Abingdon Press. Nashville, TN. 1999. ISBN:0-687-36706-9, ISBN13: 978-0-687-36706-1. Dewey:234/.16/0882044. LCCN:99-015045.

Audience: **u,f.**

Christianity > Practical Theology > Ecclesiastical Theology > Women. Ordination

2005 ed. **Belleville, Linda L., et al.**　　　　　　**BV676.T96 2001**
Two Views on Women in Ministry. Craig S. Keener, Ann L. Bowman & Thomas R. Schreiner (Authors), Craig L. Blomberg & James R. Beck (Editors). Trade Paper. Zondervan. Grand Rapids, MI. 2001. 384p. ISBN:0-310-23195-7, ISBN13: 978-0-310-23195-0. Dewey:262/.14/082. LCCN:2001-017807.

Audience: **u,f.**

Chaves, Mark   **BV676**
Ordaining Women: Culture and Conflict in Religious
Organizations. Trade Paper. Harvard University Press.
Cambridge, MA. 1999. 249p. ISBN:0-674-64146-9, ISBN13:
978-0-674-64146-4. Dewey:262/.14/0820973.

Audience: **g,u,f.**

New Religious Movements

Lewis, James R. (Editor)   **BP603.H36 2003**
The Oxford Handbook of New Religious Movements. Cloth
Text. Oxford University Press, Inc. New York, NY. 2003. 550p.

Oxford Handbooks ISBN:0-19-514986-6, ISBN13:
978-0-19-514986-9. Dewey:200/.9/04. LCCN:2003-002013.

Audience: **l,u,f.** *Choice, 2004.*

Partridge, Christopher H.   **BP603.N492 2004**
(Editor)
New Religions: New Religious Movements, Sects and
Alternative Spiritualities. J. Gordon Melton (Foreword by).
Trade Cloth. Oxford University Press, Inc. New York, NY. 2004.
448p. ISBN:0-19-522042-0, ISBN13: 978-0-19-522042-1.
Dewey:200/.9/034. LCCN:2003-066204.

Audience: **u,f.** *Choice, 2004.*

VISUAL ARTS

The Visual Arts section of Resources for College Libraries identifies approximately 2,700 titles that contribute to a core collection supporting undergraduate majors in art, art history, architecture, and allied disciplines. Resources in this section complement titles included in the last edition of Books for College Libraries.

The arrangement of resources generally reflects the organization of academic programs in the visual arts. The primary subject categories are Visual Arts in General, Design, Drawing, Painting, Printmaking, Photography, Digital Arts and New Media, Sculpture, Architecture, Interior Design and Decoration, Landscape Architecture, Cultural Heritage, and Arts Management. Subcategories in each area generally cover reference sources, histories and handbooks, individual artists, materials and techniques. Some fields will have subcategories dealing with specialized topics relevant to that discipline. Title are rarely duplicated among categories to avoid redundancy. The largest grouping, Visual Arts in General, lists titles that treat more than one medium and topics that apply to all disciplines.

As with other disciplines, the research in the visual arts is increasingly interdisciplinary and draws upon resources in from a variety of subject areas. Designers in digital media, for example, will employ computer software and their explanatory manuals. Art historians will explore historical and literary resources outside of the visual arts, just as architects will make use of resources relevant to a building type beyond strictly design literature. To maintain focus, with the expectation that the collective RCL will enrich this interdisciplinary perspective, most titles in the Visual Arts section will likely have subject headings associated with art, architecture, or a closely allied field, and the majority of resources will fall into the Library of Congress "N" classification scheme.

An overarching consideration has been to keep the scale of this section in the range of 2,700 titles, approximately 10% more than the count in BCL3. The total number influenced how the counts in the constituent parts were apportioned. Freference for inclusion has been given to in-print academic titles ranked as 'outstanding' in Choice Magazine or rated as 'highly recommended' in Library Journal or other review sources. Titles which have been nominated for or have received an award,, such as ARLIS/NA's George Wittenborn Award, have been included. As another selection consideration, the database WorldCat was used to identify the most popular academic titles acquired annually in each subject area since 1988.

Most resources in this section were published after 1988 and are in the English language. While books are the predominant format, a large number of Web resources have been included, particularly if they are long-standing, hold original or professional content, or are rich sources of images. Periodicals have been excluded unless they were offered in the content of a selected website. A number of indexes or licensed databases provide arts information, but only five long-lived standards have been included here, ArtBibliographies Modern, Avery Index to Architectural Periodicals, Bibliography of the History of Art, Art Index Retrospective, and Art Full Tex. Some freely available databases or databases provided in selected Web resources have been included.

— Edward H. Teague

Visual Arts in General > Reference Works > Web Resources

N4000

American Memory.
http://memory.loc.gov/ammem/index.html
Library of Congress.

Audience: **g,l,u,f.**

AP63

Art.
http://lanic.utexas.edu/la/region/art/
Latin American Network Information Center, University of Texas.

Audience: **g,l,u,f.**

N33

Art and Architecture Thesaurus Online.
http://www.getty.edu/research/conducting_research/vocabularies/aat/
J. Paul Getty Trust.

Audience: **g,l,u,f.**

N

AskART ; the American Artists Bluebook.
http://www.askart.com
AskART.

Audience: **g,l,u,f.**

N

The Getty Provenance Index.
http://piweb.getty.edu/cgi-bin/starfinder/0?path=collab.txt&id=webber&pass=webber&OK=OK
J. Paul Getty Trust.

Audience: **g,l,u,f.**

N31

Grove Art Online.
http://www.groveart.com
Oxford University Press.

Audience: **g,l,u,f.**

AM11

MUSÉE.
http://www.musee-online.org/
MUSÉE, Inc.

Audience: **g,l,u,f.**

CD971

SIRIUS (Smithsonian Institution Research Information System): Archives, Manuscripts, Photographs Catalog.
http://siris-archives.si.edu/#focus
Smithsonian Institution.

Audience: **g,l,u,f.**

N4396

SIRIUS (Smithsonian Institution Research Information System): Art Inventories Catalog.

http://siris-artinventories.si.edu/
Smithsonian American Art Museum.

Audience: **g,l,u,f.**

N4396

SIRIUS (Smithsonian Institution Research Information System): Pre-1877 Art Exhibition Catalogue Index.
http://siris-artexhibition.si.edu/#focus
Smithsonian American Art Museum.

Audience: **g,l,u,f.**

N50

Union List of Artist Names Online.
http://www.getty.edu/research/conducting_research/vocabularies/ulan/
J. Paul Getty Trust.

Audience: **g,l,u,f.**

Delahunt, Michael   **N**
ArtLex - art dictionary.
http://www.artlex.com
Michael Delahunt.

Audience: **g,l,u,f.**

Visual Arts in General > Reference Works > Bibliographies and Research Guides

N59.

Art Full Text.
http://www.hwwilson.com/databases/artindex.htm

Audience: **g,l,u,f.**

N1.A12

Art Index Retrospective: 1929-1984.
http://www.hwwilson.com/databases/artretro.htm

Audience: **g,l,u,f.**

NA1.A12

Avery Index to Architectural Periodicals.
http://www.getty.edu/research/conducting_research/avery_index/
Getty Research Institute.

Audience: **g,l,u,f.**

N2450

Bibliography of the History of Art (BHA). Getty Research Institute and the Institut de l'Information Scientifique et Technique.

Audience: **g,l,u,f.**

Arntzen, Etta   **Z5931**
Guide to the Literature of Art History. Rainwater, Robert. American Library Association. 1980. ISBN:0-8389-0263-4, ISBN13: 978-0-8389-0263-9.

Audience: **g,l,u,f.**

Barnet, Sylvan   N7476.B37 2002
A Short Guide to Writing about Art. Longman. 2003. The Short Guide Series ISBN:0-321-10144-8, ISBN13: 978-0-321-10144-0.
Audience: g,l,u,f.

Burchett, Kenneth E.   QC495.8.B87 2005
A Bibliographical History of the Study and Use of Color from Aristotle to Kandinsky. Trade Cloth. Edwin Mellen Press, The. Lewiston, NY. 2005. 412p. ISBN:0-7734-6041-1, ISBN13: 978-0-7734-6041-6. Dewey:535.6/09. LCCN:2005-049270.
Audience: l,u,f.

Clement, Russell T.   N6853
Georges Braque: A Bio-Bibliography. Cloth Text. Greenwood Publishing Group, Inc. Portsmouth, NH. 1994. 256p. Bio-Bibliographies in Art and Architecture Ser., Vol. 3 ISBN:0-313-29235-3, ISBN13: 978-0-313-29235-4. Dewey:016.7/092. LCCN:93-045310.
Audience: g,l,u,f. *Choice, 1994.*

Clement, Russell T.   N6853
Henri Matisse: A Bio-Bibliography. Cloth Text. Greenwood Publishing Group, Inc. Portsmouth, NH. 1993. 416p. Bio-Bibliographies in Art and Architecture Ser., Vol. 2 ISBN:0-313-28127-0, ISBN13: 978-0-313-28127-3. Dewey:016.7594092. LCCN:93-021069.
Audience: g,l,u,f. *Choice, 1994.*

Crandall, Richard C. &   Z1210.E8C73 2001
  Crandall, Susan M.
An Annotated Bibliography of Inuit Art. Cloth Text. McFarland & Company, Incorporated Publishers. Jefferson, NC. 2001. 464p. ISBN:0-7864-1007-8, ISBN13: 978-0-7864-1007-1. Dewey:016.70403/9712. LCCN:2001-030517.
Audience: g,l,u,f. *Choice, 2001.*

Havlice, Patricia Pate   N40.H38 SUPPL.2
Index to Artistic Biography, Set. Trade Cloth. Scarecrow Press, Inc. Lanham, MD. 2002. 1834p. ISBN:0-8108-4062-6, ISBN13: 978-0-8108-4062-1. Dewey:016.709/2/2. LCCN:2001-049154.
Audience: g,l,u,f. *Choice, 2002.*

Igoe, Lynn M. & Igoe,   Z5956.A47
  James
Two Hundred Fifty Years of Afro-American Art: An Annotated Bibliography. Trade Paper. Books on Demand. Ann Arbor, MI. 1291p. ISBN:0-8357-8673-0, ISBN13: 978-0-8357-8673-7. Dewey:016.704/0396073. LCCN:81-012226.
Audience: g,l,u,f. *B*

Langmead, Donald   Z8245
Willem Marinus Dudok, a Dutch Modernist: A Bio-Bibliography. Cloth Text. Greenwood Publishing Group, Inc. Portsmouth, NH. 1996. 304p. Bio-Bibliographies in Art and Architecture Ser., No. 4 ISBN:0-313-29425-9, ISBN13: 978-0-313-29425-9. Dewey:016.72/092. LCCN:95-046113.
Audience: g,l,u,f.

Lerner, Loren R.   Z5961.C3
Art and Architecture in Canada: A Bibliography and Guide to the Literature to 1981 (Art et Archtiecture au Canada:

Bibliographie et Guide de la Documentation Jusqu'en 1981). Williamson, Mary F.. University of Toronto Press. 1991. ISBN:0-8020-5856-6, ISBN13: 978-0-8020-5856-0.
Audience: g,l,u,f.

Marmor, Max & Ross, Alex   Z5931.M374 2004
Guide to the Literature of Art History, Vol. 2. Trade Cloth. American Library Association. Chicago, IL. 2004. 168p. ISBN:0-8389-0878-0, ISBN13: 978-0-8389-0878-5. Dewey:016.7/09. LCCN:2004-016170.
Audience: l,u,f. *Choice, 2005.*

Robertson, Jack S.   NX456.R59 1996
Twentieth Century Artists on Art: An Index to Artists' Writings, Statements, and Interviews. Ed. 2. Trade Cloth. Thomson Gale. Farmington Hills, MI. 1996. 820p. ISBN:0-8161-9059-3, ISBN13: 978-0-8161-9059-1. Dewey:709.2/2. LCCN:95-033700.
Audience: g,l,u,f. *Choice, 1997.*

Visual Arts in General > Reference Works > Dictionaries, Encyclopedias

                                                          N43.P47
Dictionary of Women's Art Before 1900. Ed. 2. Trade Cloth. Thomson Gale. Farmington Hills, MI. 2002. ISBN:0-7838-8573-3, ISBN13: 978-0-7838-8573-5. Dewey:709/.2/2.
Audience: g,l,u,f.

                                                          N31
☐ Grove Art Online.
http://www.groveart.com
Oxford University Press.
Audience: g,l,u,f.

Atkins, Robert   N6490
Artspeak: A Guide to Contemporary Ideas, Movements and Buzzwords, 1945 to the Present. Ed. 2. Trade Cloth. Abbeville Press, Inc. New York, NY. 1997. 208p. ISBN:0-7892-0415-0, ISBN13: 978-0-7892-0415-8. Dewey:709/.04. LCCN:97-010858.
Audience: g,l,u,f.

Brigstocke, Hugh   N33.O923 2001
The Oxford Companion to Western Art. Trade Cloth. Oxford University Press, Inc. New York, NY. 2001. 840p. ISBN:0-19-866203-3, ISBN13: 978-0-19-866203-7. Dewey:703. LCCN:2002-265087.
Audience: g,l,u,f. *Choice, 2002.*

Caplan, H. H.   N45.C36 1987
The Classified Directory of Artists' Signatures, Symbols and Monograms: International and American Editions. Ed. 3. Trade Cloth. Editions Publisol. Wappingers Falls, NY. 1987. 608p. ISBN:0-9508893-1-8, ISBN13: 978-0-9508893-1-3. Dewey:760/.092/2. LCCN:89-124319.
Audience: g,l,u,f.

Caplan, H. H.   N45.C363 1999
Encyclopedia of Artists' Signatures, Symbols and Monograms:
North American, European Plus More. Old Masters to Modern.
Robert Fiallo (Editor), Bob Creps (Compiled by). Library
Binding. Dealer's Choice Books, Inc. Land O'Lakes, FL. 1999.
1050p. ISBN:0-9668526-0-5, ISBN13: 978-0-9668526-0-8.
Dewey:702/.78. LCCN:99-235656.

Audience: **g,l,u,f.**

Castagno, John   N45.C38 1990
European Artists: Signatures and Monograms, 1800-1990
Including Selected Artists from Other Parts of the World. Trade
Cloth. Scarecrow Press, Inc. Lanham, MD. 1990. 916p.
ISBN:0-8108-2313-6, ISBN13: 978-0-8108-2313-6.
Dewey:702/.78. LCCN:90-041504.

Audience: **g,l,u,f.** *Choice, 1991.*

Castagno, John   N45.C385 1997
Latin American Artists' Signatures and Monograms: Colonial
Era to 1996. Trade Cloth. Scarecrow Press, Inc. Lanham, MD.
1998. 688p. ISBN:0-8108-3293-3, ISBN13: 978-0-8108-3293-0.
Dewey:702/.78. LCCN:97-012178.

Audience: **g,l,u,f.**

Castagno, John   N45
Old Masters Signatures and Monograms, 1400-Born 1800. Trade
Cloth. Scarecrow Press, Inc. Lanham, MD. 1996. 396p.
ISBN:0-8108-3082-5, ISBN13: 978-0-8108-3082-0.
Dewey:702.7/8. LCCN:95-025561.

Audience: **g,l,u,f.**

Castagno, John   N45.C374 1991
Artists' Monograms and Indiscernible Signatures: An
International Directory, 1800-1991. Michael Findlay (Foreword
by). Trade Cloth. Scarecrow Press, Inc. Lanham, MD. 1991.
560p. Cartwheel Learning Bookshelf Ser. ISBN:0-8108-2415-9,
ISBN13: 978-0-8108-2415-7. Dewey:702/.78. LCCN:91-023003.
Audience: **g,l,u,f.** *Choice, 1992.*

Castagno, John   NC961.63.C37 1989
Artists as Illustrators: An International Directory with Signatures
and Monograms, 1800-Present. Judy Goffman (Foreword by).
Trade Cloth. Scarecrow Press, Inc. Lanham, MD. 1989. 645p.
ISBN:0-8108-2168-0, ISBN13: 978-0-8108-2168-2.
Dewey:741.6/092/2. LCCN:88-034832.
Audience: **g,l,u,f.** *Choice, 1990.*

Castagno, John   N45.C37 1990
American Artists: Signatures and Monograms, 1800-1989.
George J. Turak (Foreword by), Ann Horton (Preface by). Trade
Cloth. Scarecrow Press, Inc. Lanham, MD. 1990. 844p.
ISBN:0-8108-2249-0, ISBN13: 978-0-8108-2249-8.
Dewey:760/.0278. LCCN:89-028371.

Audience: **g,l,u,f.**

Chaturachinda, Gwyneth, et   N7300
al.
Dictionary of South and Southeast Asian Art. Pauline W.
Tabtiang & Sunanda Krishnamurty (Authors). Trade Paper. Silk
Worm Books. Bangkok, 2001. 144p. ISBN:974-7100-97-5,
ISBN13: 978-974-7100-97-6. Dewey:709.503.
Audience: **g,l,u,f.** *Choice, 2001.*

Clark, Andrew J., et al.   NK4645.C57 2002
Understanding Greek Vases: A Guide to Terms, Styles, and
Techniques. Maya Elston & Mary Louise Hart (Authors). Trade
Paper. Oxford University Press, Inc. New York, NY. 2002. 176p.
Looking at Ser. ISBN:0-89236-599-4, ISBN13:
978-0-89236-599-9. Dewey:738.3/82/0938. LCCN:2001-006214.
Audience: **g,l,u,f.** *Choice, 2003.*

Clarke, Michael   N33.C575 2001
The Concise Oxford Dictionary of Art Terms. Trade Paper.
Oxford University Press, Inc. New York, NY. 2001. 272p.
Oxford Paperback Reference Ser. ISBN:0-19-280043-4, ISBN13:
978-0-19-280043-5. Dewey:703. LCCN:2001-269472.
Audience: **g,l,u,f.**

Cole, Herbert & Turner,   N7380
Jane (Editors)
Encyclopedia of African Art. Library Binding. Groves
Dictionaries, Inc. New York, NY. 2001. 900p. Library of World
Art ISBN:1-884446-08-6, ISBN13: 978-1-884446-08-5.
Dewey:709.603.
Audience: **g,l,u,f.**

Collin, Simon (Editor)   N33
Dictionary of Art. Trade Cloth. Fitzroy Dearborn Publishers, Inc.
Chicago, IL. 2002. 240p. ISBN:1-57958-198-6, ISBN13:
978-1-57958-198-5. Dewey:703.
Audience: **g,l,u,f.**

Congdon, Kristin G. &   N6502
Hallmark, Kara Kelley
Artists from Latin American Cultures: A Biographical
Dictionary. Cloth Text. Greenwood Publishing Group, Inc.
Portsmouth, NH. 2002. 344p. ISBN:0-313-31544-2, ISBN13:
978-0-313-31544-2. Dewey:709/.2/368 B. LCCN:2001-058345.
Audience: **g,l,u,f.** *Choice, 2003.*

Darmon, Adrian M.   N7418.D3713 2003
Around Jewish Art: Encyclopaedia of Painters, Photographers,
and Sculptors. Trade Cloth. Carnot USA Books. New York, NY.
2004. 544p. ISBN:1-59209-042-7, ISBN13: 978-1-59209-042-6.
Dewey:704.03/924/003. LCCN:2003-016421.
Audience: **g,l,u,f.**

Dempsey, Amy   N6490.D4152002
Art in the Modern Era: A Guide to Styles, Schools, and
Movements. Trade Cloth. Harry N. Abrams, Inc. New York, NY.
2002. 304p. ISBN:0-8109-4172-4, ISBN13: 978-0-8109-4172-4.
Dewey:709/.04/03. LCCN:2001-046261.
Audience: **g,l,u,f.** *Choice, 2002.*

Dempsey, Amy   N6447.D46 2004
Styles, Schools and Movements: The Essential Encyclopaedic
Guide to Modern Art. Trade Paper. Thames & Hudson. New
York, NY. 2005. 304p. ISBN:0-500-28376-1, ISBN13:
978-0-500-28376-9. Dewey:709/.04. LCCN:2004-106362.
Audience: **g,l,u,f.**

Earls, Irene   N6415
Baroque Art: A Topical Dictionary. Cloth Text. Greenwood
Publishing Group, Inc. Portsmouth, NH. 1996. 352p.

ISBN:0-313-29406-2, ISBN13: 978-0-313-29406-8.
Dewey:709/.03/203. LCCN:95-051397.

Audience: **g,l,u,f.** *Choice, 1997.*

Earls, Irene   **N6370**
Renaissance Art: A Topical Dictionary. Cloth Text. Greenwood
Publishing Group, Inc. Portsmouth, NH. 1987. 366p.
ISBN:0-313-24658-0, ISBN13: 978-0-313-24658-6.
Dewey:709/.02/4. LCCN:87-000250.

Audience: **g,l,u,f.** *Choice, 1988.*

Editions Grund (Editor)   **N40.D5213**
Benezit Dictionary of Artists, Set. Library Binding. Librairie
Grund. Paris, 2006. 1465p. ISBN:2-7000-3070-2, ISBN13:
978-2-7000-3070-9. Dewey:709.22.

Audience: **g,l,u,f.**

Falk, Peter H. (Editor)   **N6536.W49 1999**
Who Was Who in American Art: 400 Years of Artists Active in
America, 1564-1975. Ed. 2. Trade Cloth. Falk Art Reference.
Madison, CT. 1999. 3750p. ISBN:0-932087-57-4, ISBN13:
978-0-932087-57-7. Dewey:709/.2/273. LCCN:2001-271878.

Audience: **g,l,u,f.** *Choice, 2000.*

Frick Art Reference Library   **N7112.S67 1993**
Staff
Spanish Artists from the Fourth to the Twentieth Century: A
Critical Dictionary, Set. Trade Cloth. Macmillan Publishing
Company, Inc. Old Tappan, NJ. 1997. 2700p.
ISBN:0-8161-0614-2, ISBN13: 978-0-8161-0614-1.
Dewey:709/.2/246. LCCN:94-174887.

Audience: **g,l,u,f.** *Choice, 1997.*

Gaze, Delia (Editor)   **N8354.D53 1997**
Dictionary of Women Artists, Set. Trade Cloth. Fitzroy Dearborn
Publishers, Inc. Chicago, IL. 1997. 1512p. ISBN:1-884964-21-4,
ISBN13: 978-1-884964-21-3. Dewey:709.2/2. LCCN:97-206872.

Audience: **g,l,u,f.** *Choice, 1998.*

Goldman, Paul   **N33.G65 1988**
Looking at Prints, Drawings and Watercolours: A Guide to
Technical Terms. Trade Paper. Oxford University Press, Inc.
New York, NY. 1989. 64p. Looking at Ser.
ISBN:0-89236-148-4, ISBN13: 978-0-89236-148-9.
Dewey:760/.03/21. LCCN:88-013241.

Audience: **g,l,u,f.**

Gowing, Lawrence (Editor)   **N31.F33 2005**
Facts on File Encyclopedia of Art, Set. Trade Cloth. Facts On
File, Inc. New York, NY. 2005. 1040p. ISBN:0-8160-5797-4,
ISBN13: 978-0-8160-5797-9. Dewey:703. LCCN:2005-040505.

Audience: **g,l,u,f.** *Choice, 2006.*

Hadden, Peggy   **PN6084.A8Q68 2002**
The Quotable Artist. Trade Cloth. Allworth Press. New York,
NY. 2002. 240p. ISBN:1-58115-226-4, ISBN13:
978-1-58115-226-5. Dewey:700. LCCN:2002-004234.

Audience: **g,l,u,f.**

Haslam, Malcolm   **N45.H37 1977**
Marks and Monograms of the Modern Movement, 1875-1930: A
Guide to the Marks of Artists, Designers, Retailers, and
Manufacturers, from the Period of the Aesthetic Movement to
Art Deco and Style Moderne. Trade Cloth. Simon & Schuster.
New York, NY. 1977. 192p. ISBN:0-684-14828-5, ISBN13:
978-0-684-14828-1. Dewey:702/.78. LCCN:76-026189.

Audience: **g,l,u,f.**

Heller, Jules & Heller,   **N40**
Nancy G. (Editors)
North American Women Artists of the Twentieth Century: A
Biographical Dictionary. Trade Paper. Garland Publishing, Inc.
New York, NY. 1997. 736p. Reference Library of the
Humanities, Vol. 1219 ISBN:0-8153-2584-3, ISBN13:
978-0-8153-2584-0. Dewey:709/.2/2 B. LCCN:94-049710.

Audience: **g,l,u,f.** *Choice, 1995.*

Hillstrom, Laurie Collier &   **N8354.C66 1999**
Hillstrom, Kevin
Contemporary Women Artists. Trade Cloth. Thomson Gale.
Farmington Hills, MI. 1999. xx, 760p. ISBN:1-55862-372-8,
ISBN13: 978-1-55862-372-9. Dewey:709/.2/2 B.
LCCN:99-010053.

Audience: **g,l,u,f.** *Choice, 1999.*

Impelluso, Lucia   **N7760.I47 2003**
Gods and Heroes in Art. Stefano Zuffi (Editor). Trade Paper.
Oxford University Press, Inc. New York, NY. 2003. 384p. A
Guide to Imagery Ser. ISBN:0-89236-702-4, ISBN13:
978-0-89236-702-3. Dewey:700/.415. LCCN:2002-013422.

Audience: **g,l,u,f.**

Jackson, Christine E.   **N40.J33 1999**
Dictionary of Bird Artists of the World. Trade Cloth. Antique
Collectors' Club. Easthampton, MA. 1999. 550p.
ISBN:1-85149-203-8, ISBN13: 978-1-85149-203-9.
Dewey:758.3. LCCN:00-300585.

Audience: **g,l,u,f.** *Choice, 2000.*

Jackson, Radway   **N45.J33 1991**
The Visual Index of Artists' Signatures and Monograms. Trade
Cloth. W. Foulsham Company, Ltd. Slough, 1991. 240p.
ISBN:0-572-01649-2, ISBN13: 978-0-572-01649-4.
Dewey:750/.278. LCCN:93-129209.

Audience: **g,l,u,f.**

Jiminez, Jill (Editor)   **N7574.D48 2001**
Dictionary of Artists' Models. Trade Cloth. Fitzroy Dearborn
Publishers, Inc. Chicago, IL. 2001. 624p. ISBN:1-57958-233-8,
ISBN13: 978-1-57958-233-3. Dewey:702/.8.
LCCN:2002-277125.

Audience: **g,l,u,f.** *Choice, 2002.*

Johnson, Jane & Greutzner,   **N6796.D531990**
A. (Compiled by)
The Dictionary of British Art: British Artists 1880-1940. Trade
Cloth. Antique Collectors' Club. Easthampton, MA. 1976. 572p.
ISBN:0-902028-36-7, ISBN13: 978-0-902028-36-4.
Dewey:709/.2/241 B. LCCN:92-136452.

Audience: **g,l,u,f.**

Langmuir, Erika & Lynton,   N33.L353 2000
  Norbert
The Yale Dictionary of Art and Artists. Trade Paper. Yale
University Press. Cumberland, RI. 2000. 768p.
ISBN:0-300-06458-6, ISBN13: 978-0-300-06458-2. Dewey:703.
LCCN:00-025800.
                                    Audience: **g,l,u,f.** *Choice, 2001.*

Lodwick, Marcus   N33.L632003
The Museum Companion: Understanding Western Art. Trade
Cloth. Harry N. Abrams, Inc. New York, NY. 2003. 224p.
ISBN:0-8109-4445-6, ISBN13: 978-0-8109-4445-9.
Dewey:700/.47/03. LCCN:2002-153178.
                                    Audience: **g,l,u,f.**

Lucie-Smith, Edward   N33
Thames and Hudson Dictionary of Art Terms. Ed. 2. Trade
Paper. Thames & Hudson. New York, NY. 2004. 240p. The
World of Art Ser. ISBN:0-500-20365-2, ISBN13:
978-0-500-20365-1. Dewey:703. LCCN:2003-100802.
                                    Audience: **g,l,u,f.** *Choice, 2004.*

Matuz, Roger (Editor)   E98.A7S81998
St. James Guide to Native North American Artists. Richard W.
Hill Sr. (Foreword by). Trade Cloth. Thomson Gale. Farmington
Hills, MI. 1997. 691p. ISBN:1-55862-221-7, ISBN13:
978-1-55862-221-0. Dewey:704.03/97. LCCN:97-018453.
                                    Audience: **g,l,u,f.**

McCulloch, Alan   N7400.M27 1994
The Encyclopedia of Australian Art. Susan McCulloch (Revised
by). Trade Cloth. University of Hawaii Press. Honolulu, HI.
1994. 880p. ISBN:0-8248-1688-9, ISBN13: 978-0-8248-1688-9.
Dewey:709/.94. LCCN:94-020404.
                                    Audience: **l,u,f.**

McEwan, Peter J.   N6772.M35 1994
Dictionary of Scottish Art and Architecture. Trade Cloth.
Antique Collectors' Club. Easthampton, MA. 1995. 626p.
ISBN:1-85149-134-1, ISBN13: 978-1-85149-134-6.
Dewey:709./2/2411 B. LCCN:93-247770.
                                    Audience: **g,l,u,f.** *Choice, 1995.*

McMann, Evelyn D.   N6548.M33 2003
  (Compiled by)
Biographical Index of Artists in Canada. Cloth over Boards.
University of Toronto Press. Toronto, ON. 1996. 240p.
ISBN:0-8020-2790-3, ISBN13: 978-0-8020-2790-0.
Dewey:709/.2/271. LCCN:2003-374624.
                                    Audience: **g,l,u,f.** *Choice, 2003.*

Milner, John   N6998.M55 1993
A Dictionary of Russian and Soviet Artists, 1420-1970. Trade
Cloth. Antique Collectors' Club. Easthampton, MA. 1993. 484p.
ISBN:1-85149-182-1, ISBN13: 978-1-85149-182-7.
Dewey:709/.2/247 B. LCCN:94-159262.
                                    Audience: **g,l,u,f.** *Choice, 1994.*

Murray, Linda & Murray,   N7825
  Peter (Editors)
Dictionary of Christian Art. Trade Paper. Oxford University

Press, Inc. New York, NY. 2004. 658p. Oxford Paperback
Reference Ser. ISBN:0-19-860966-3, ISBN13:
978-0-19-860966-7. Dewey:704.9/482/03. LCCN:2004-303063.
                                    Audience: **g,l,u,f.**

Murray, Peter & Murray,   N31.M8 1997
  Linda
Art and Artists. Ed. 7. Trade Paper. Penguin Group (USA) Inc.
New York, NY. 1998. 608p. Penguin Reference Bks.
ISBN:0-14-051300-0, ISBN13: 978-0-14-051300-4.
LCCN:98-130228.
                                    Audience: **g,l,u,f.** *B*

Naylor, Colin (Editor)   N6490.C65675 1991
Contemporary Masterworks. Trade Cloth. Thomson Gale.
Farmington Hills, MI. 1991. 933p. ISBN:1-55862-083-4,
ISBN13: 978-1-55862-083-4. Dewey:709.04. LCCN:92-233469.
                                    Audience: **g,l,u,f.**

Nelson, Robert S. & Shiff,   N34.C75 2003
  Richard (Editors)
Critical Terms for Art History. Ed. 2. Trade Paper. University of
Chicago Press. Chicago, IL. 2003. 540p. ISBN:0-226-57168-8,
ISBN13: 978-0-226-57168-3. Dewey:701/.4.
LCCN:2002-035978.
                                    Audience: **g,l,u,f.** *Choice, 1997.*

Onians, John (Editor)   N7425
Atlas of World Art. Trade Cloth. Oxford University Press, Inc.
New York, NY. 2004. 352p. ISBN:0-19-521583-4, ISBN13:
978-0-19-521583-0. Dewey:709.
                                    Audience: **g,l,u,f.** *Choice, 2004.*

Pendergast, Sara &   N6490.C6567 2001
  Pendergast, Tom (Editors)
Contemporary Artists. Ed. 5. Trade Cloth. Thomson Gale.
Farmington Hills, MI. 2001. 1400p. Contemporary Arts Ser.
ISBN:1-55862-407-4, ISBN13: 978-1-55862-407-8.
Dewey:709/.2/2 B. LCCN:2001-048443.
                                    Audience: **g,l,u,f.**

Pierce, James Smith   N33.P5 2003
From Abacus to Zeus: A Handbook of Art History. Ed. 7. Trade
Paper. Prentice Hall PTR. Upper Saddle River, NJ. 2003. 230p.
Art Basics Ser. ISBN:0-13-183051-1, ISBN13:
978-0-13-183051-6. Dewey:703. LCCN:2003-050880.
                                    Audience: **g,l,u,f.**

Read, Herbert & Stangos,   N33.T53 1994
  Nikos
The Thames and Hudson Dictionary of Art and Artists. Ed. 2.
Trade Paper. Thames & Hudson. New York, NY. 1994. 384p.
World of Art Ser. ISBN:0-500-20274-5, ISBN13:
978-0-500-20274-6. Dewey:703/.21. LCCN:93-061272.
                                    Audience: **g,l,u,f.** *B*

Riggs, Thomas   N40.S78 1997
St. James Guide to Black Artists. Trade Cloth. Thomson Gale.
Farmington Hills, MI. 1997. 625p. ISBN:1-55862-220-9,
ISBN13: 978-1-55862-220-3. Dewey:709/.2/396 B.
LCCN:97-003068.
                                    Audience: **g,l,u,f.** *Choice, 1998.*

Roberts, Helene E. (Editor)   **N7560.E53 1998**
Encyclopedia of Comparative Iconography: Themes Depicted in Works of Art, Set. Trade Cloth. Fitzroy Dearborn Publishers, Inc. Chicago, IL. 1998. 1120p. ISBN:1-57958-009-2, ISBN13: 978-1-57958-009-4. Dewey:704.9/03. LCCN:98-163033.
> Audience: **l,u,f.** *Choice, 1998.*

Room, Adrian   **N33.R56 2000**
A Dictionary of Art Titles: The Origins of the Names and Titles of 3,000 Works of Art. Cloth Text. McFarland & Company, Incorporated Publishers. Jefferson, NC. 2000. 294p. ISBN:0-7864-0770-0, ISBN13: 978-0-7864-0770-5. Dewey:703. LCCN:99-56537.
> Audience: **g,l,u,f.**

Ross, Leslie   **N7850**
Medieval Art: A Topical Dictionary. Cloth Text. Greenwood Publishing Group, Inc. Portsmouth, NH. 1996. 320p. ISBN:0-313-29329-5, ISBN13: 978-0-313-29329-0. Dewey:709/.02/03. LCCN:96-000160.
> Audience: **g,l,u,f.** *Choice, 1997.*

Schmied, Wieland &   **N33.P74 2000**
  Whitford, Frank
Prestel Dictionary of Art and Artists. Trade Cloth. Prestel Publishing. New York, NY. 2000. 384p. ISBN:3-7913-2325-3, ISBN13: 978-3-7913-2325-1. Dewey:709/.04/003. LCCN:99-069078.
> Audience: **g,l,u,f.** *Choice, 2001.*

Seymour, Nancy N.   **N7348.S481988**
An Index Dictionary of Chinese Artist, Collectors and Connoisseurs, with Character Identification by Modified Stroke Count: Including over 5,000 Chinese Names and Biographies from the T'ang Dynasty Through the Modern Period. Trade Cloth. Scarecrow Press, Inc. Lanham, MD. 1988. 987p. ISBN:0-8108-2091-9, ISBN13: 978-0-8108-2091-3. Dewey:700/.92/2 B. LCCN:87-028704.
> Audience: **l,u,f.**

Shipp, Steve   **N6502.4.S452002**
Latin American and Caribbean Artists of the Modern Era: A Biographical Dictionary of over 10,000 Persons. Cloth Text. McFarland & Company, Incorporated Publishers. Jefferson, NC. 2003. 916p. ISBN:0-7864-1057-4, ISBN13: 978-0-7864-1057-6. Dewey:704.03/68 B. LCCN:2002-013828.
> Audience: **g,l,u,f.** *Choice, 2003.*

Shorts, Don Allen   **N6558**
1200 Mexican Artists: An Identification Guide to Painters, Graphic Artist, Sculptors and Photographers. Trade Paper. Old California Press, The. Ventura, CA. 2002. 206p. ISBN:0-9720332-0-3, ISBN13: 978-0-9720332-0-6. Dewey:780.7.
> Audience: **g,l,u,f.**

Simon, Robin   **ND1314.S46 1987**
The Portrait in Britain and America with a Dictionary of Portrait Painters, 1680-1914. Trade Cloth. Macmillan Publishing Company, Inc. Old Tappan, NJ. 1987. 256p.

ISBN:0-8161-8795-9, ISBN13: 978-0-8161-8795-9. Dewey:757/.0941 B. LCCN:86-021750.
> Audience: **g,l,u,f.** *Choice, 1987.*

Snoddy, Theo   **N6796.S652002**
Dictionary of Irish Artists: 20th Century. Ed. 2. Cloth over Boards. Merlin Publishing, Dublin. Dublin 2, 2002. 1000p. ISBN:1-903582-17-2, ISBN13: 978-1-903582-17-6. Dewey:759.2/9/15/03. LCCN:00-056077.
> Audience: **g,l,u,f.** *Choice, 2003.*

Sokol, Stanley S.   **N7255.P6S65 2000**
The Artists of Poland: A Biographical Dictionary from the 14th Century to the Present. Cloth Text. McFarland & Company, Incorporated Publishers. Jefferson, NC. 2000. 271p. ISBN:0-7864-0697-6, ISBN13: 978-0-7864-0697-5. Dewey:709/.2/2438 B. LCCN:99-52118.
> Audience: **g,l,u,f.** *Choice, 2000.*

Soria, Regina   **N6917.5.R6 S67 1982**
The Dictionary of Nineteenth-Century American Artists in Italy, 1760-1914. Trade Cloth. Fairleigh Dickinson University Press. Cranbury, NJ. 1982. 336p. ISBN:0-8386-1310-1, ISBN13: 978-0-8386-1310-8. Dewey:709/.2/2. LCCN:74-004986.
> Audience: **g,l,u,f.**

Spalding, Francis & Collins,   **N6796.D531990**
  Judith
The Dictionary of British Art: 20th Century Painters and Sculptors. Trade Cloth. Antique Collectors' Club. Easthampton, MA. 1991. 484p. ISBN:1-85149-106-6, ISBN13: 978-1-85149-106-3. Dewey:709/.2/241 B. LCCN:92-136452.
> Audience: **g,l,u,f.** *Choice, 1991.*

Speake, Jennifer   **N7825.S68 1994**
The Dent Dictionary of Symbols in Christian Art. Trade Cloth. J. M. Dent & Sons. London, 1995. 192p. ISBN:0-460-86138-7, ISBN13: 978-0-460-86138-0. Dewey:704.9/482/03. LCCN:94-139747.
> Audience: **g,l,u,f.** *Choice, 1995.*

Strieter, Terry W.   **N6757**
Nineteenth-Century European Art: A Topical Dictionary. Cloth Text. Greenwood Publishing Group, Inc. Portsmouth, NH. 1999. 312p. ISBN:0-313-29898-X, ISBN13: 978-0-313-29898-1. Dewey:709/.03/403. LCCN:98-034720.
> Audience: **g,l,u,f.** *Choice, 1999.*

Summers, Claude J. (Editor)   **N72.H64Q44 2004**
The Queer Encyclopedia of the Visual Arts. Trade Paper. Cleis Press. San Francisco, CA. 2004. 400p. ISBN:1-57344-191-0, ISBN13: 978-1-57344-191-9. Dewey:704/.08664/03. LCCN:2004-004263.
> Audience: **g,l,u,f.** *Choice, 2005.*

Turner, Jane (Editor)   **N31.D5**
The Dictionary of Art. Trade Cloth. Oxford University Press, Inc. New York, NY. 2003. 32,600p. ISBN:0-19-517068-7, ISBN13: 978-0-19-517068-9. Dewey:703. LCCN:99-056537.
> Audience: **g,l,u,f.**

Turner, Jane (Editor)   **N6507.E532000**
The Encyclopedia of American Art Before 1914. Trade Cloth.
Oxford University Press, Inc. New York, NY. 2006. 752p. Grove
Encyclopedias of the Arts of the Americas Ser.
ISBN:1-884446-03-5, ISBN13: 978-1-884446-03-0.
Dewey:709.7/3/03. LCCN:99-041596.
    Audience: **g,l,u,f.** *Choice, 2000.*

Turner, Jane (Editor)   **N6502.E532000**
The Encyclopedia of Latin American and Caribbean Art. Trade
Cloth. Oxford University Press, Inc. New York, NY. 2000. 803p.
Grove Encyclopedias of the Arts of the Americas Ser.
ISBN:1-884446-04-3, ISBN13: 978-1-884446-04-7.
LCCN:99-041595.
    Audience: **g,l,u,f.** *Choice, 2000.*

Werness, Hope B.   **N5310.7**
The Continuum Encyclopedia of Native Art. Trade Paper.
Continuum International Publishing Group, Ltd. London, 2003.
370p. ISBN:0-8264-1465-6, ISBN13: 978-0-8264-1465-6.
Dewey:709/.011/03.
    Audience: **g,l,u,f.**

Wertkin, Gerard C. (Editor)   **NK805**
Encyclopedia of American Folk Art. Paper over Boards.
Routledge. New York, NY. 2003. 704p. ISBN:0-415-92986-5,
ISBN13: 978-0-415-92986-8. Dewey:745/.0973/03.
LCCN:2003-018051.
    Audience: **g,l,u,f.** *Choice, 2004.*

Wingfield, Mary A.   **N6796.W56 1992**
Dictionary of Sporting Artists. Trade Cloth. Antique Collectors'
Club. Easthampton, MA. 1992. 356p. ISBN:1-85149-140-6,
ISBN13: 978-1-85149-140-7. Dewey:760/.092/2 B.
LCCN:93-129387.
    Audience: **g,l,u,f.**

Wood, Christopher   **N6796.D531990**
The Dictionary of British Art: Victorian Painters. Ed. 3. Trade
Cloth. Antique Collectors' Club. Easthampton, MA. 1995. 476p.
Dictionary of British Art Ser., Vol. 2 ISBN:1-85149-172-4,
ISBN13: 978-1-85149-172-8. Dewey:759.2. LCCN:96-214374.
    Audience: **g,l,u,f.** *Choice, 1996.*

Wood, Christopher   **N6796.D531990**
The Dictionary of British Art: Victorian Painters. Ed. 3. Trade
Cloth. Antique Collectors' Club. Easthampton, MA. 1995. 596p.
Dictionary of British Art Ser., Vol. 1 ISBN:1-85149-171-6,
ISBN13: 978-1-85149-171-1. Dewey:759.2. LCCN:96-214374.
    Audience: **g,l,u,f.** *Choice, 1996.*

Visual Arts in General > Reference Works > Directories

    N50
American Art Directory 2005-2006. Ed. 60. Trade Cloth.
National Register Publishing. New Providence, NJ. 2004. 1004p.
ISBN:0-87217-846-3, ISBN13: 978-0-87217-846-5. Dewey:708.
    Audience: **g,l,u,f.**

    N50 .A77
Art Diary International 2004-2005: The World Art Directory.
Trade Paper. Giancarlo Politi Editore. Milano, 2003. 689p.
ISBN:88-7816-132-2, ISBN13: 978-88-7816-132-0.
Dewey:702/.5.
    Audience: **g,l,u,f.**

    AM11
☐ MUSÉE.
http://www.musee-online.org/
MUSÉE, Inc.
    Audience: **g,l,u,f.**

    AM11
The Official Museum Directory. Trade Cloth. National Register
Publishing. New Providence, NJ. 2004. ISBN:0-87217-805-6,
ISBN13: 978-0-87217-805-2. Dewey:69.0973.
    Audience: **g,l,u,f.**

Cox, Mary   **N7430.5**
2007 Artists and Graphic Designers Market. Trade Paper. F &
W Publications, Inc. Cincinnati, OH. 2006. 624p.
ISBN:1-58297-429-2, ISBN13: 978-1-58297-429-3. Dewey:760.
    Audience: **g,l,u,f.**

International Federation of   **Z675.A85**
   Library Associations. Section of Art Libraries
☐ International directory of art libraries.
http://artlibrary.vassar.edu/ifla-idal/
Hill, Thomas E. (Thomas Edward), 1952-. Poughkeepsie, NY :
Vassar College Libraries.
    Audience: **g,l,u,f.**

Visual Arts in General > Histories and Handbooks

Adams, Laurie Schneider   **N5300.A32006**
Art across Time Combined. Ed. 3. Paper Text. McGraw-Hill
Higher Education. Burr Ridge, IL. 2006. 1080p.
ISBN:0-07-296525-8, ISBN13: 978-0-07-296525-4. Dewey:709.
LCCN:2005-058443.
    Audience: **g,l,u,f.**

Belton, Robert   **N5300.A693 2002**
ART: The World of Art, from Aboriginal to American Pop,
Renaissance Masters to Postmodernism. Trade Cloth.
Watson-Guptill Publications, Inc. New York, NY. 2002. 512p.
Art Reference Essentials Ser. ISBN:0-8230-0342-6, ISBN13:
978-0-8230-0342-6. Dewey:709. LCCN:2002-109822.
    Audience: **g,l,u,f.** *Choice, 2003.*

Gardner, Helen, et al.   **N5300.G25 2006**
Gardner's Art Through the Ages: A Concise History. Fred S.
Kleiner & Christin J. Mamiya (Authors). Trade Cloth. Thomson
Wadsworth. Belmont, CA. 2006. xvi, 574p.
ISBN:0-534-63647-0, ISBN13: 978-0-534-63647-0. Dewey:709.
LCCN:2004-107969.
    Audience: **g,l,u,f.**

Gombrich, E. H.   N5300.G643 1995
The Story of Art. Ed. 16. Trade Cloth. Phaidon Press. London,
1995. 688p. ISBN:0-7148-3355-X, ISBN13: 978-0-7148-3355-2.
Dewey:709.
Audience: g,l,u,f.

Honour, Hugh & Fleming,   N5300.H68 2006
  John
The Visual Arts: A History. Ed. 7. Trade Paper. Prentice Hall
PTR. Upper Saddle River, NJ. 2005. 520p.
ISBN:0-13-155114-0, ISBN13: 978-0-13-155114-5. Dewey:709.
LCCN:2005-043185.
Audience: g,l,u,f. Choice, 2000.

Janson, Anthony   N5300.J3 2007
History of Art. Ed. 7. Davies Penelope (Editor). Trade Cloth.
Prentice Hall Art. Upper Saddle River, NJ. 2006. 1200p.
ISBN:0-13-193478-3, ISBN13: 978-0-13-193478-8. Dewey:709.
LCCN:2005-054647.
Audience: g,l,u,f.

Kampen-O'Riley, Michael   N5300
Art Beyond the West: The Arts of Africa, India and Southeast
Asia, China, Japan and Korea, the Pacific, and the Americas.
Saddle Stitched, Cloth over Boards, Dust Jacket. Prentice Hall
Art. Upper Saddle River, NJ. 2002. 344p. ISBN:0-13-183360-X,
ISBN13: 978-0-13-183360-9. Dewey:709.
Audience: g,l,u,f.

Spalding, Julian   N7477
The Art of Wonder: A History of Seeing. Saddle Stitched, Cloth
over Boards, Dust Jacket. Prestel Publishing. New York, NY.
2005. 287p. ISBN:3-7913-3150-7, ISBN13: 978-3-7913-3150-8.
Dewey:701.18. LCCN:2006-295598.
Audience: g,l,u,f. Choice, 2006.

Stokstad, Marilyn   N5300.S923 2007
All about Art. Ed. 3. Trade Cloth. Prentice Hall Art. Upper
Saddle River, NJ. 2006. 608p. ISBN:0-13-195442-3, ISBN13:
978-0-13-195442-7. Dewey:709. LCCN:2005-058680.
Audience: g,l,u,f.

Wilkins, David G., et al.   N5300.W64 2005
Art Past, Art Present. Ed. 5. Bernard Schultz & Katheryn M.
Linduff (Authors). Trade Cloth. Prentice Hall Art. Upper Saddle
River, NJ. 2004. 656p. ISBN:0-13-150546-7, ISBN13:
978-0-13-150546-9. Dewey:709. LCCN:2004-044482.
Audience: g,l,u,f.

Visual Arts in General > Histories and Handbooks > Periods and Styles > Prehistoric Art

Bahn, Paul G.   N5310 .B34 1998
The Cambridge Illustrated History of Prehistoric Art. Desmond
Morris (Foreword by). Trade Cloth. Cambridge University Press.
New York, NY. 1997. 334p. Illustrated Histories Ser.
ISBN:0-521-45473-5, ISBN13: 978-0-521-45473-5.
Dewey:709/.01/1. LCCN:96-051099.
Audience: g,l,u,f. Choice, 1998.

Campbell, Alec   GN861.C682001
African Rock Art: Paintings and Engravings on Stone. David
Coulson (Photographer). Trade Cloth. Harry N. Abrams, Inc.
New York, NY. 2001. 256p. ISBN:0-8109-4363-8, ISBN13:
978-0-8109-4363-6. Dewey:709/.01/13096. LCCN:99-053255.
Audience: g,l,u,f.

Caruana, Wally   N7401.C37 1993
Aboriginal Art. Trade Paper. Thames & Hudson. New York, NY.
1993. 216p. World of Art Ser. ISBN:0-500-20264-8, ISBN13:
978-0-500-20264-7. Dewey:704/.039915. LCCN:92-062140.
Audience: g,l,u,f. Choice, 1993.

Clottes, Jean   N5310.C5813 2002
World Rock Art. Trade Cloth. Oxford University Press, Inc.
New York, NY. 2002. 144p. Conservation and Cultural Heritage
Ser. ISBN:0-89236-682-6, ISBN13: 978-0-89236-682-8.
Dewey:709/.01/13. LCCN:2002-008893.
Audience: g,l,u,f.

Clottes, Jean   GN772.2.M3C57 2003
Chauvet Cave: The Art of Earliest Times. Paul G. Bahn
(Translator). Trade Cloth. University of Utah Press. Salt Lake
City, UT. 2003. 226p. ISBN:0-87480-758-1, ISBN13:
978-0-87480-758-5. Dewey:709/.0113/09449.
LCCN:2002-116011.
Audience: l,u,f. Choice, 2003.

Guthrie, R. Dale   GN772G87 2005
The Nature of Paleolithic Art. Trade Cloth. University of
Chicago Press. Chicago, IL. 2006. 520p. ISBN:0-226-31126-0,
ISBN13: 978-0-226-31126-5. Dewey:930.1/2.
LCCN:2004-014399.
Audience: g,l,u,f. Choice, 2006.

Hood, Sinclair   N5630
The Arts in Prehistoric Greece. Trade Paper. Yale University
Press. Cumberland, RI. 1992. 311p. Pelican History of Art Ser.
ISBN:0-300-05287-1, ISBN13: 978-0-300-05287-9.
Dewey:709.3/8.
Audience: g,l,u,f.

Kleinert, Sylvia & Neale,   NX590.A1O94 2000
  Margo (Editors)
The Oxford Companion to Aboriginal Art and Culture. Cloth
Text. Oxford University Press, Inc. New York, NY. 2001. 804p.
ISBN:0-19-550649-9, ISBN13: 978-0-19-550649-5.
Dewey:994.004/9915. LCCN:2001-269497.
Audience: l,u,f. Choice, 2002.

Lewis-Williams, David   N5310.L49 2002
The Mind in the Cave: Consciousness and the Origins of Art.
Trade Cloth. Thames & Hudson. New York, NY. 2002. 320p.
ISBN:0-500-05117-8, ISBN13: 978-0-500-05117-7.
Dewey:751.7/0901. LCCN:2002-102597.
Audience: g,l,u,f. Choice, 2003.

Metropolitan Museum of   N5330.A68 2003
  Art Staff (Contribution by)
Art of the First Cities: The Third Millennium B.C. from the
Mediterranean to the Indus. Trade Cloth. Metropolitan Museum

of Art, The. New York, NY. 2003. xxiv, 540p.
ISBN:1-58839-043-8, ISBN13: 978-1-58839-043-1.
Dewey:711/.4/0930747471. LCCN:2003-044482.

Audience: **g,l,u,f.**

Ruspoli, Mario N531.5
Cave of Lascaux: The Final Photographs. Harry N. Abrams.
1987. ISBN:0-8109-1267-8, ISBN13: 978-0-8109-1267-0.

Audience: **g,l,u,f.**

Sandars, Nancy K. GN772.2.A1
Prehistoric Art in Europe. Ed. 2. Trade Paper. Yale University
Press. Cumberland, RI. 1985. 508p. Pelican History of Art Ser.
ISBN:0-300-05286-3, ISBN13: 978-0-300-05286-2.
Dewey:709/.01/12094.

Audience: **g,l,u,f.**

Twohig, E. S. N531.5
Megalithic Art of Western Europe. Oxford University Press.
1981. ISBN:0-19-813193-3, ISBN13: 978-0-19-813193-9.

Audience: **g,l,u,f.**

White, Randall N5310.W48 2003
Prehistoric Art: The Symbolic Journey of Humankind. Trade
Cloth. Harry N. Abrams, Inc. New York, NY. 2003. 240p.
ISBN:0-8109-4262-3, ISBN13: 978-0-8109-4262-2.
Dewey:709/.01/1. LCCN:2002-014965.

Audience: **g,l,u,f.** *Choice, 2003.*

Visual Arts in General > Histories and Handbooks > Periods and Styles > Ancient World

N5350.E37 1999
Egyptian Art in the Age of the Pyramids. Metropolitan Museum
of Art, New York, NY; Distributed by H. N. Abrams. 1999.
ISBN:0-87099-906-0, ISBN13: 978-0-87099-906-2.

Audience: **g,l,u,f.**

Aldred, Cyril N5350
Egyptian Art. Trade Paper. Thames & Hudson. New York, NY.
1985. 252p. World of Art Ser. ISBN:0-500-20180-3, ISBN13:
978-0-500-20180-0. Dewey:709/.32. LCCN:84-051309.

Audience: **g,l,u,f.**

Aruz, Joan (Editor) N5335
Art of the First Cities: The Third Millennium B.C. from the
Mediterranean to the Indus. Ronald Wallenfels (Contribution
by). Cloth over Boards. Yale University Press. Cumberland, RI.
2003. 564p. Metropolitan Museum of Art Ser.
ISBN:0-300-09883-9, ISBN13: 978-0-300-09883-9.
Dewey:709.5/6/09013. LCCN:2003-044482.

Audience: **g,l,u,f.** *Choice, 2004.*

Bagley, Robert (Editor) DS793.S8A528 2001
Ancient Sichuan: Treasures from a Lost Civilization. Trade
Cloth. Princeton University Press. Princeton, NJ. 2001. 360p.
ISBN:0-691-08851-9, ISBN13: 978-0-691-08851-8. Dewey:931.
LCCN:00-068782.

Audience: **g,l,u,f.** *Choice, 2001.*

Beard, Mary & Henderson, John N5610.B295 2001
Classical Art: From Greece to Rome. Trade Paper. Oxford
University Press, Inc. New York, NY. 2001. 304p. Oxford
History of Art Ser. ISBN:0-19-284237-4, ISBN13:
978-0-19-284237-4. Dewey:709/.38. LCCN:2001-269631.

Audience: **g,l,u,f.**

Boardman, John NK4649.B624 1989
Athenian Red Figure Vases: The Classical Period. Trade Paper.
Thames & Hudson. New York, NY. 1989. 252p. World of Art
Ser. ISBN:0-500-20244-3, ISBN13: 978-0-500-20244-9.
Dewey:738.3/82/09385. LCCN:89-050539.

Audience: **g,l,u,f.**

Boardman, John N5630.B58 1996
Greek Art. Ed. 4. Trade Paper. Thames & Hudson. New York,
NY. 1996. 304p. The World of Art Ser. ISBN:0-500-20292-3,
ISBN13: 978-0-500-20292-0. Dewey:709/.38. LCCN:96-060184.

Audience: **g,l,u,f.**

Brendel, Otto J. N5750.B671995
Etruscan Art. Ed. 2. Trade Paper. Yale University Press.
Cumberland, RI. 1995. 536p. Pelican History of Art Ser.
ISBN:0-300-06446-2, ISBN13: 978-0-300-06446-9.
Dewey:709.3/75. LCCN:95-015894.

Audience: **g,l,u,f.** *B*

Clark, Andrew J., et al. NK4645.C57 2002
Understanding Greek Vases: A Guide to Terms, Styles, and
Techniques. Maya Elston & Mary Louise Hart (Authors). Trade
Paper. Oxford University Press, Inc. New York, NY. 2002. 176p.
Looking at Ser. ISBN:0-89236-599-4, ISBN13:
978-0-89236-599-9. Dewey:738.3/82/0938. LCCN:2001-006214.

Audience: **g,l,u,f.** *Choice, 2003.*

D'Ambra, Eve N5760 .D435 1998
Roman Art. Trade Paper. Cambridge University Press. New
York, NY. 1998. 176p. ISBN:0-521-64463-1, ISBN13:
978-0-521-64463-1. Dewey:709.3/7. LCCN:99-166514.

Audience: **g,l,u,f.** *Choice, 1999.*

D'Avennes, E. Prisse N5351
Atlas of Egyptian Art. Ed. 2. Trade Cloth. American University
in Cairo Press. New York, NY. 2002. 160p.
ISBN:977-424-584-9, ISBN13: 978-977-424-584-8.
Dewey:709.32.

Audience: **l,u,f.** *Choice, 2001.*

Elsner, J. R. N5760.E484 1998
Imperial Rome and Christian Triumph: The Art of the Roman
Empire AD 100-450. Trade Paper. Oxford University Press, Inc.
New York, NY. 1998. 320p. Oxford History of Art Ser.
ISBN:0-19-284201-3, ISBN13: 978-0-19-284201-5.
Dewey:709.3/7/09015. LCCN:99-189358.

Audience: **g,l,u,f.**

Fields, Virginia M. & Reents-Budet, Dorie F1435.3.A7
Lords of Creation: The Origins of Sacred Maya Kingship. Trade
Cloth. Scala Publishers, Ltd. London, 2005. 288p.

Audience: g=general, l=lower division undergraduate, u=upper division undergraduate, f=faculty.

669

ISBN:1-85759-386-3, ISBN13: 978-1-85759-386-0. Dewey:709.7281. LCCN:2005-482050.

Audience: **g,l,u,f.** *Choice, 2006.*

Frankfort, Henri A.   **N5345.F71996**
The Art and Architecture of the Ancient Orient. Ed. 5. Michael Roaf & Donald Matthews (Commentaries by, Notes by). Trade Paper. Yale University Press. Cumberland, RI. 1989. 500p. Pelican History of Art Ser. ISBN:0-300-06470-5, ISBN13: 978-0-300-06470-4. Dewey:709/.3. LCCN:95-015893.

Audience: **l,u,f.**

Fullerton, Mark D.   **N5630 .F85 2000**
Greek Art. Trade Paper. Cambridge University Press. New York, NY. 1999. 176p. ISBN:0-521-77973-1, ISBN13: 978-0-521-77973-9. Dewey:709/.38. LCCN:00-500521.

Audience: **l,u,f.** *Choice, 2000.*

Higgins, Reynold   **N5660.H5 1997**
Minoan and Mycenaean Art. Ed. 2. Lyvia Morgan (Revised by). Trade Paper. Thames & Hudson. New York, NY. 1997. 216p. World of Art Ser. ISBN:0-500-20303-2, ISBN13: 978-0-500-20303-3. Dewey:709.3/918. LCCN:97-060252.

Audience: **g,l,u,f.**

Holloway, R. Ross   **NA5620.A1H65 2004**
Constantine and Rome. Cloth over Boards. Yale University Press. Cumberland, RI. 2004. 208p. ISBN:0-300-10043-4, ISBN13: 978-0-300-10043-3. Dewey:722/.7. LCCN:2003-018712.

Audience: **u,f.** *Choice, 2004.*

Laing, Lloyd Robert &   **N5604.S65**
Laing, Jennifer
Art of the Celts: From 700 B.C. to the Celtic Revival. Trade Paper. Thames & Hudson. New York, NY. 1992. 216p. World of Art Ser. ISBN:0-500-20256-7, ISBN13: 978-0-500-20256-2. Dewey:709/.014. LCCN:91-066018.

Audience: **g,l,u,f.**

Markoe, Glenn, et al.   **N5335.C56C566 1996**
Mistress of the House, Mistress of Heaven: Women in Ancient Egypt. Anne K. Capel & Betsy M. Bryan (Authors). Trade Cloth. Hudson Hills Press LLC. Manchester, VT. 1997. 240p. ISBN:1-55595-129-5, ISBN13: 978-1-55595-129-0. Dewey:704.9/424/0932074771. LCCN:96-009376.

Audience: **l,u,f.** *Choice, 1997.*

Miller, Mary E.   **F1219.3.A7M551996**
The Art of MesoAmerica: From Olmec to Aztec. Ed. 2. Trade Paper. Thames & Hudson. New York, NY. 1996. 240p. The World of Art Ser. ISBN:0-500-20290-7, ISBN13: 978-0-500-20290-6. Dewey:709.7/2. LCCN:95-070510.

Audience: **g,l,u,f.**

Miller, Mary Ellen   **F1219.3.A7M55 2001**
The Art of Mesoamerica: From Olmec to Aztec. Ed. 3. Trade Paper. Thames & Hudson. New York, NY. 2001. 240p. World of Art Ser. ISBN:0-500-20345-8, ISBN13: 978-0-500-20345-3. Dewey:709.7/2. LCCN:2001-087365.

Audience: **g,l,u,f.**

Morris, Sarah P.   **N5633**
Daidalos and the Origins of Greek Art. Trade Cloth. Princeton University Press. Princeton, NJ. 1995. 484p. ISBN:0-691-00160-X, ISBN13: 978-0-691-00160-9. Dewey:700/.938. LCCN:91-023831.

Audience: **l,u,f.** *Choice, 1993.*

Osborne, Robin   **N5630.O83 1998**
Archaic and Classical Greek Art. Trade Paper. Oxford University Press, Inc. New York, NY. 1998. 278p. Oxford History of Art Ser. ISBN:0-19-284202-1, ISBN13: 978-0-19-284202-2. Dewey:709/.38. LCCN:99-177295.

Audience: **g,l,u,f.**

Pollitt, Jerome Jordan   **N5630 .P56 1990**
The Art of Ancient Greece: Sources and Documents. Ed. 2. Trade Paper. Cambridge University Press. New York, NY. 1990. 312p. ISBN:0-521-27366-8, ISBN13: 978-0-521-27366-4. Dewey:709.3/8. LCCN:90-001494.

Audience: **g,l,u,f.** *Choice, 1991.*

Preziosi, Donald &   **N5630**
Hitchcock, Louise
Aegean Art and Architecture. Trade Paper. Oxford University Press, Inc. New York, NY. 2000. 262p. Oxford History of Art Ser. ISBN:0-19-284208-0, ISBN13: 978-0-19-284208-4. Dewey:709.4/958/0901.

Audience: **g,l,u,f.** *Choice, 2000.*

Ramage, Nancy H. &   **N5760.R36 2005**
Ramage, Andrew
Roman Art: Romulus to Constantine. Ed. 4. Trade Cloth. Prentice Hall Art. Upper Saddle River, NJ. 2004. 368p. ISBN:0-13-189612-1, ISBN13: 978-0-13-189612-3. Dewey:709/.37. LCCN:2004-044585.

Audience: **l,u,f.**

Rasmussen, Tom & Spivey,   **NK4645 .L66 1991**
Nigel J. (Editors)
Looking at Greek Vases. Trade Paper. Cambridge University Press. New York, NY. 1991. 300p. ISBN:0-521-37679-3, ISBN13: 978-0-521-37679-2. Dewey:738.3/82/0938. LCCN:90-002568.

Audience: **g,l,u,f.** *Choice, 1992.*

Roehrig, Catharine H.   **DT87.15.H378 2005**
(Editor), et al.
Hatshepsut: From Queen to Pharaoh. Cathleen A. Keller & Renee Dreyfus (Editors). Saddle Stitched, Cloth over Boards, Dust Jacket. Yale University Press. Cumberland, RI. 2005. 356p. Metropolitan Museum of Art Ser. ISBN:0-300-11139-8, ISBN13: 978-0-300-11139-2. Dewey:932/.014/092. LCCN:2005-020286.

Audience: **g,l,u,f.**

Russmann, Edna R. (Editor)   **N5350**
Eternal Egypt: Masterworks of Ancient Art from the British Museum. Trade Cloth. University of California Press. Berkeley, CA. 2001. 288p. ISBN:0-520-23082-5, ISBN13: 978-0-520-23082-8. Dewey:709/.32/07442142.

Audience: **g,l,u,f.** *Choice, 2001.*

Schefold, Karl   N7760 .S27313 1992
Gods and Heroes in Late Archaic Greek Art. Alan Griffiths (Translator). Cloth Text. Cambridge University Press. New York, NY. 1992. 389p. ISBN:0-521-32718-0, ISBN13: 978-0-521-32718-3. Dewey:704.94/7/0938. LCCN:91-028560.
                 Audience: **u,f.** *Choice, 1993.*

Smith, W. Stevenson   N5350.S51998
The Art and Architecture of Ancient Egypt. William K. Simpson (Revised by). Trade Paper. Yale University Press. Cumberland, RI. 1999. 310p. Pelican History of Art Ser. ISBN:0-300-07747-5, ISBN13: 978-0-300-07747-6. Dewey:709/.32. LCCN:98-024893.
                 Audience: **g,l,u,f.**

Spivey, Nigel   N5750.S65 1997
Etruscan Art. Trade Paper. Thames & Hudson. New York, NY. 1997. 216p. The World of Art Ser. ISBN:0-500-20304-0, ISBN13: 978-0-500-20304-0. Dewey:709.3/75. LCCN:97-060250.
                 Audience: **g,l,u,f.** *Choice, 1998.*

Stone-Miller, Rebecca   F2230.1
Art of the Andes: From Chavin to Inca. Ed. 2. Trade Paper. Thames & Hudson. New York, NY. 2002. 224p. The World of Art Ser. ISBN:0-500-20363-6, ISBN13: 978-0-500-20363-7. Dewey:709.8. LCCN:2002-101747.
                 Audience: **g,l,f.**

Strong, Roy   N5760
Roman Art. Ed. 3. Roger Ling (Editor), Donald Strong (Revised by). Trade Paper. Yale University Press. Cumberland, RI. 1992. 408p. Pelican History of Art Ser. ISBN:0-300-05293-6, ISBN13: 978-0-300-05293-0. Dewey:709.3/7.
                 Audience: **g,l,u,f.** *B*

Tiradritti, Francesco   N5350
Egyptian Treasures from the Egyptian Museum in Cairo. Araldo De Luca (Photographer), Suzanne Mubarak (Introduction by). Trade Cloth. Harry N. Abrams, Inc. New York, NY. 1999. 416p. ISBN:0-8109-3276-8, ISBN13: 978-0-8109-3276-0. Dewey:709.32.
                 Audience: **g,l,u,f.**

Ward-Perkins, J. B.   NA310
Roman Imperial Architecture. Ed. 2. Trade Paper. Yale University Press. Cumberland, RI. 1981. 532p. Pelican History of Art Ser. ISBN:0-300-05292-8, ISBN13: 978-0-300-05292-3. Dewey:722/.7.
                 Audience: **g,l,u,f.**

Woodford, Susan   N5610.W6 2004
The Art of Greece and Rome. Ed. 2. Trade Paper. Cambridge University Press. New York, NY. 2004. 186p. ISBN:0-521-54037-2, ISBN13: 978-0-521-54037-7. Dewey:709/.38. LCCN:2003-069663.
                 Audience: **g,l,u,f.** *Choice, 2005.*

Woodford, Susan   N7760.W66 2002
Images of Myths in Classical Antiquity. Trade Paper. Cambridge University Press. New York, NY. 2002. 332p.

ISBN:0-521-78809-9, ISBN13: 978-0-521-78809-0. Dewey:704.9470938. LCCN:2002-073727.
                 Audience: **g,l,u,f.** *Choice, 2003.*

Visual Arts in General > Histories and Handbooks > Periods and Styles > Middle Ages

Beckwith, John   N5970.B43 1985
Early Medieval Art. Trade Paper. Thames & Hudson. New York, NY. 1985. 272p. World of Art Ser. ISBN:0-500-20019-X, ISBN13: 978-0-500-20019-3. Dewey:709/.02/1. LCCN:84-051844.
                 Audience: **g,l,u,f.**

Benton, Janetta Rebold   N5975.B46 2002
Art of the Middle Ages. Trade Paper. Thames & Hudson. New York, NY. 2002. 320p. World of Art Ser. ISBN:0-500-20350-4, ISBN13: 978-0-500-20350-7. Dewey:709/.02. LCCN:2001-092917.
                 Audience: **g,l,u,f.**

Bullen, J. B.   N6447
Byzantium Rediscovered. Trade Paper. Phaidon Press, Inc. New York, NY. 2006. 240p. ISBN:0-7148-4638-4, ISBN13: 978-0-7148-4638-5. Dewey:709.034.
                 Audience: **g,l,u,f.**

Camille, Michael   BV153.E85
The Gothic Idol: Ideology and Image-Making in Medieval Art. Trade Paper. Cambridge University Press. New York, NY. 1991. 441p. Cambridge New Art History and Criticism Ser. ISBN:0-521-42430-5, ISBN13: 978-0-521-42430-1. Dewey:246/.09/02. LCCN:88-011680.
                 Audience: **g,l,u,f.** *Choice, 1990.*

Cormack, Robin   N6250.C656 2000
Byzantine Art. Trade Paper. Oxford University Press, Inc. New York, NY. 2000. 256p. Oxford History of Art Ser. ISBN:0-19-284211-0, ISBN13: 978-0-19-284211-4. Dewey:709/.02/14. LCCN:00-036749.
                 Audience: **g,l,u,f.** *Choice, 2001.*

Dodwell, C. R.   N5970.D641993
The Pictorial Arts of the West, 800-1200. Cloth over Boards. Yale University Press. Cumberland, RI. 1993. 494p. Pelican History of Art Ser. ISBN:0-300-05348-7, ISBN13: 978-0-300-05348-7. Dewey:709/.021. LCCN:92-032502.
                 Audience: **g,l,u,f.** *Choice, 1994.*

Evans, Helen C. (Editor)   N6250.B962 2004
Byzantium: Faith and Power (1261-1557). Metropolitan Museum of Art Staff (Contribution by). Cloth over Boards. Yale University Press. Cumberland, RI. 2004. 680p. Metropolitan Museum of Art Ser. ISBN:0-300-10278-X, ISBN13: 978-0-300-10278-9. Dewey:709/.495/0747471. LCCN:2004-001565.
                 Audience: **l,u,f.** *Choice, 2004.*

Evans, Helen C. & Wixom,   **N6250.G55 1997**
William D. (Editors)
The Glory of Byzantium: Art and Culture of the Middle
Byzantine Era, A.D. 843-1261. Trade Paper. Metropolitan
Museum of Art, The. New York, NY. 1997.
ISBN:0-87099-778-5, ISBN13: 978-0-87099-778-5.
Dewey:709/.02/140747471. LCCN:96-045584.

Audience: **g,l,u,f.**

Folda, Jaroslav   **N6300.F655 2005**
Crusader Art in the Holy Land, from the Third Crusade to the
Fall of Acre, 1187-1291. Trade Cloth. Cambridge University
Press. New York, NY. 2005. 782p. ISBN:0-521-83583-6,
ISBN13: 978-0-521-83583-1. Dewey:709/.569/09022.
LCCN:2004-018634.

Audience: **l,u,f.**

Henderson, George   **N7943.A1 H46 1999**
Vision and Image in Early Christian England. Trade Cloth.
Cambridge University Press. New York, NY. 1999. 310p.
ISBN:0-521-55130-7, ISBN13: 978-0-521-55130-4.
Dewey:709/.42/09021. LCCN:98-020183.

Audience: **l,u,f.**   *Choice, 2000.*

Holt, Elizabeth G.   **N5303 .D6 1981**
A Documentary History of Art: The Middle Ages and the
Renaissance. Trade Paper. Princeton University Press. Princeton,
NJ. 1982. 380p. ISBN:0-691-00333-5, ISBN13:
978-0-691-00333-7. Dewey:709. LCCN:81-047281.

Audience: **l,u,f.**

Hourihane, Colum (Editor)   **N6784.F76 2001**
From Ireland Coming: Irish Art from the Early Christian to the
Late Gothic Period and Its European Context. Trade Paper.
Princeton University Press. Princeton, NJ. 2001. 392p.
Occasional Papers - Index of Christian Art, Vol. 4
ISBN:0-691-08825-X, ISBN13: 978-0-691-08825-9.
Dewey:709/.415. LCCN:00-062375.

Audience: **l,u,f.**

Kren, Thomas & Barstow,   **ND3159.K74 2005**
Kurt
Italian Illuminated Manuscripts in the J. Paul Getty Museum. J.
Paul Getty Museum Staff (Contribution by). Trade Paper. Getty
Conservation Institute. Los Angeles, CA. 2005. 96p.
ISBN:0-89236-820-9, ISBN13: 978-0-89236-820-4.
Dewey:745.6/7/094507479494. LCCN:2004-028795.

Audience: **g,l,u,f.**

Lasko, Peter   **N6245**
Ars Sacra, 800-1200. Ed. 2. Cloth over Boards. Yale University
Press. Cumberland, RI. 1995. 334p. Pelican History of Art Ser.
ISBN:0-300-06048-3, ISBN13: 978-0-300-06048-5.
Dewey:730/.094/09021.

Audience: **g,l,u,f.** ℬ *Choice, 1995.*

Martindale, Andrew   **N6310 .M3 1985**
Gothic Art. Trade Paper. Thames & Hudson. New York, NY.
1985. 288p. World of Art Ser. ISBN:0-500-20058-0, ISBN13:
978-0-500-20058-2. Dewey:709/.02/2. LCCN:84-051310.

Audience: **g,l,u,f.**

Nees, Lawrence   **N5970.N44 2002**
Early Medieval Art. Trade Paper. Oxford University Press, Inc.
New York, NY. 2002. 272p. Oxford History of Art Ser.
ISBN:0-19-284243-9, ISBN13: 978-0-19-284243-5.
Dewey:709.02. LCCN:2002-510289.

Audience: **g,l,u,f.**

Pacht, Otto   **ND2920 .P2313 1994**
Book Illumination in the Middle Ages: An Introduction. Trade
Paper. Harvey Miller Publishers. London, 1994. 224p. Otto
Pacht - the Collected Writings ISBN:1-872501-76-1, ISBN13:
978-1-872501-76-5. Dewey:745.67.

Audience: **g,l,u,f.**

Panayotova, S. & Binski,   **ND2893**
Paul
The Cambridge Illuminations: Ten Centuries of Book
Production. Trade Cloth. Harvey Miller Publishers. London,
2005. 416p. ISBN:1-872501-59-1, ISBN13: 978-1-872501-59-8.
Dewey:745.6707442659.

Audience: **g,l,u,f.**

Rice, David Talbot   **N6250**
Art of the Byzantine Era. Trade Paper. Thames & Hudson. New
York, NY. 1985. 288p. World of Art Ser. ISBN:0-500-20004-1,
ISBN13: 978-0-500-20004-9. Dewey:709.02.

Audience: **g,l,u,f.**

Rodley, Lyn   **N6250 .R59 1994**
Byzantine Art and Architecture: An Introduction. Trade Paper.
Cambridge University Press. New York, NY. 1996. 394p.
ISBN:0-521-35724-1, ISBN13: 978-0-521-35724-1.
Dewey:709/.0214. LCCN:92-033797.

Audience: **g,l,u,f.** *Choice, 1995.*

Ross, Leslie   **N7850**
Medieval Art: A Topical Dictionary. Cloth Text. Greenwood
Publishing Group, Inc. Portsmouth, NH. 1996. 320p.
ISBN:0-313-29329-5, ISBN13: 978-0-313-29329-0.
Dewey:709/.02/03. LCCN:96-000160.

Audience: **g,l,u,f.** *Choice, 1997.*

Sekules, Veronica   **N5970.S46 2001**
Medieval Art. Trade Paper. Oxford University Press, Inc. New
York, NY. 2001. 240p. Oxford History of Art Ser.
ISBN:0-19-284241-2, ISBN13: 978-0-19-284241-1.
Dewey:709/.02. LCCN:2001-273421.

Audience: **g,l,u,f.**

Snyder, James C.   **N5975.S581989**
Medieval Art: Painting, Sculpture, Architecture, 4th-14th
Century. Cloth Text. Harry N. Abrams, Inc. New York, NY.
1989. 512p. ISBN:0-8109-1532-4, ISBN13: 978-0-8109-1532-9.
Dewey:709/.02. LCCN:88-010394.

Audience: **g,l,u,f.** *Choice, 1989.*

Snyder, James   **N5975.S58 2006**
Art of the Middle Ages. Ed. 2. Henry Luttikhuizen & Dorothy
Verkerk (Revised by). Saddle Stitched, Cloth over Boards, Dust

Jacket. Prentice Hall Art. Upper Saddle River, NJ. 2005. 530p. ISBN:0-13-193825-8, ISBN13: 978-0-13-193825-0. Dewey:709/.02. LCCN:2004-060135.

Audience: **g,l,u,f.**

Stokstad, Marilyn   **N5970.S75 2004**
Medieval Art. Ed. 2. Trade Paper. Westview Press. Boulder, CO. 2004. 432p. ISBN:0-8133-4114-0, ISBN13: 978-0-8133-4114-9. Dewey:709/.02 19. LCCN:2003-006643.

Audience: **g,l,u,f.**

White, John   **N6915.W451993**
Art and Architecture in Italy: 1250-1400. Ed. 3. Trade Paper. Yale University Press. Cumberland, RI. 1973. 688p. Pelican History of Art Ser. ISBN:0-300-05585-4, ISBN13: 978-0-300-05585-6. Dewey:709/.45/09022. LCCN:93-193815.

Audience: **g,l,u,f.**

Visual Arts in General > Histories and Handbooks > Periods and Styles > Islamic Arts

Behrens-Abouseif, Doris &   **N6260.I828 2005**
    Vernoit, Stephen
Islamic Art in the 19th Century: Tradition, Innovation and Eclecticism. Trade Cloth. Brill Academic Publishers. Leiden, 2005. viii, 464p. Islamic History and Civilization Ser., Vol. 60 ISBN:90-04-14442-0, ISBN13: 978-90-04-14442-2. Dewey:709/.17/6709034. LCCN:2005-047218.

Audience: **l,u,f.**

Blair, Sheila S. & Bloom,   **N6260**
    Jonathan
The Art and Architecture of Islam, 1250-1800. Trade Paper. Yale University Press. Cumberland, RI. 1996. 368p. Pelican History of Art Ser. ISBN:0-300-06465-9, ISBN13: 978-0-300-06465-0. Dewey:709.1/7671. LCCN:93-049561.

Audience: **g,l,u,f.** *Choice, 1995.*

Bohrer, Frederick N.   **NX650.E85B64 2003**
Orientalism and Visual Culture: Imagining Mesopotamia in Nineteenth-Century Europe. Trade Cloth. Cambridge University Press. New York, NY. 2003. 398p. ISBN:0-521-80657-7, ISBN13: 978-0-521-80657-2. Dewey:704.9/49935/00744. LCCN:2002-031208.

Audience: **l,u,f.** *Choice, 2004.*

Brend, Barbara   **N6250.B76 1991**
Islamic Art. Trade Paper. Harvard University Press. Cambridge, MA. 1992. 240p. ISBN:0-674-46866-X, ISBN13: 978-0-674-46866-5. Dewey:709.1/7671. LCCN:90-025589.

Audience: **g,l,u,f.** *Choice, 1991.*

Carboni, Stefano, et al.   **NK5108.9.C37 2001**
Glass of the Sultans: Twelve Centuries of Islamic Masterworks. David Whitehouse & William Gudenrath (Authors). Cloth over Boards. Yale University Press. Cumberland, RI. 2001. 340p.

Metropolitan Museum of Art Ser. ISBN:0-300-08851-5, ISBN13: 978-0-300-08851-9. Dewey:748/.0917. LCCN:00-069544.

Audience: **g,l,u,f.** *Choice, 2002.*

Denny, Walter B.   **NK4340.I9D462004**
Iznik: The Artistry of Ottoman Ceramics. Trade Cloth. Thames & Hudson. New York, NY. 2004. 240p. ISBN:0-500-51192-6, ISBN13: 978-0-500-51192-3. Dewey:738.309561. LCCN:2004-103073.

Audience: **g,l,u,f.** *Choice, 2005.*

Derman, M. Ugur   **NK3636.5.A2**
Letters in Gold: Ottoman Calligraphy from the Sakip Sabanci Collection, Istanbul. Cloth over Boards. Yale University Press. Cumberland, RI. 1998. 208p. Metropolitan Museum of Art Ser. ISBN:0-300-08632-6, ISBN13: 978-0-300-08632-4. Dewey:745.6/19927/0956.

Audience: **g,l,u,f.** *Choice, 1999.*

Dodds, Jerrilynn D. (Editor)   **N7103.A41992**
Al-Andalus: The Art of Islamic Spain. Metropolitan Museum of Art Staff & Patronato de la Alhambra (Contribution by). Trade Cloth. Metropolitan Museum of Art, The. New York, NY. 1992. 432p. ISBN:0-87099-636-3, ISBN13: 978-0-87099-636-8. Dewey:709/.46/80747471 20. LCCN:91-041335.

Audience: **g,l,u,f.**

Ettinghausen, Richard, et al.   **N6260.E792001**
Islamic Art and Architecture, 650-1250. Ed. 2. Oleg Grabar & Marilyn Jenkins-Madina (Authors). Cloth over Boards. Yale University Press. Cumberland, RI. 2002. 352p. Pelican History of Art Ser. ISBN:0-300-08867-1, ISBN13: 978-0-300-08867-0. Dewey:709.1767109021. LCCN:00-043769.

Audience: **g,l,u,f.** *Choice, 2002.*

Ferrier, R. W. (Editor)   **N7280.A89 1989**
The Arts of Persia. Cloth over Boards. Yale University Press. Cumberland, RI. 1989. 344p. ISBN:0-300-03987-5, ISBN13: 978-0-300-03987-0. Dewey:709/.43/074435954. LCCN:89-031890.

Audience: **g,l,u,f.** *Choice, 1990.*

Grabar, Oleg   **N6260.G688 2005**
Early Islamic Art, 650-1100: Constructing the Study of Islamic Art. Trade Cloth. Ashgate Publishing, Ltd. Aldershot, 2005. 364p. Variorum Collected Studies Ser. ISBN:0-86078-921-7, ISBN13: 978-0-86078-921-5. Dewey:709/.17/6709021. LCCN:2004-011462.

Audience: **g,l,u,f.**

Grabar, Oleg   **N6260**
Islamic Visual Culture, 1100-1800, Vol. 2. Trade Cloth. Ashgate Publishing, Ltd. Aldershot, 2006. 488p. ISBN:0-86078-922-5, ISBN13: 978-0-86078-922-2. Dewey:709/.17/67. LCCN:2005-053079.

Audience: **g,l,u,f.**

Grube, Ernst J; Sims,
    Eleanor G; Bayani, Manijeh; Nassar, Nahla
Islamic Art V: Studies on the Art and Culture of the Muslim World. Ernst J. Grube (Editor) ; Eleanor G. Sims (Editor) ;

Manijeh Bayani (Editor) ; Nahla Nassar (Editor). Oxford
University Press, Inc. 2005. ISBN:0-19-924768-4, ISBN13:
978-0-19-924768-4.

Audience: **g,l,u,f.**

Hillenbrand, Robert   **N6260.H551999**
Islamic Art and Architecture. Thames & Hudson. 1999. World
of Art Ser. ISBN:0-500-20305-9, ISBN13: 978-0-500-20305-7.

Audience: **g,l,u,f.**

Komaroff, Linda &   **N7283.L44 2002**
  Carboni, Stefano (Editors)
The Legacy of Genghis Khan: Courtly Art and Culture in
Western Asia, 1256-1353. Cloth over Boards. Yale University
Press. Cumberland, RI. 2002. 336p. Metropolitan Museum of
Art Ser. ISBN:0-300-09691-7, ISBN13: 978-0-300-09691-0.
Dewey:709/.55/0747471. LCCN:2002-027893.

Audience: **g,l,u,f.**   *Choice, 2003.*

Roxburgh, David J.   **N7283.R68 2004**
The Persian Album, 1400-1600: From Dispersal to Collection.
Cloth over Boards. Yale University Press. Cumberland, RI.
2005. 392p. ISBN:0-300-10325-5, ISBN13: 978-0-300-10325-0.
Dewey:709/.55/09024. LCCN:2004-021251.

Audience: **g,l,u,f.**   *Choice, 2005.*

Ruggles, Fairchild D.   **SB457.8.R845 2000**
Gardens, Landscape and Vision in the Palaces of Islamic Spain.
Trade Cloth. Pennsylvania State University Press. University
Park, PA. 1999. 1334p. ISBN:0-271-01851-8, ISBN13:
978-0-271-01851-5. Dewey:712/.0917/671. LCCN:98-018914.

Audience: **g,l,u,f.**   *Choice, 2000.*

Zygulski, Zdzislaw Jr.   **NK1011.Z94 1991**
Ottoman Art in the Service of Empire. Trade Cloth. New York
University Press. New York, NY. 1991. 192p. Hagop Kevorkian
Series on Near Eastern Art and Civilization
ISBN:0-8147-9671-0, ISBN13: 978-0-8147-9671-9.
Dewey:745/.09561. LCCN:91-004446.

Audience: **g,l,u,f.**   *Choice, 1992.*

Visual Arts in General > Histories and Handbooks > Periods and Styles > Renaissance and Baroque

Bazin, Germain   **N6410**
Baroque and Rococo. Trade Paper. Thames & Hudson. New
York, NY. 1985. 288p. World of Art Ser. ISBN:0-500-20018-1,
ISBN13: 978-0-500-20018-6. Dewey:709.032.
LCCN:84-051843.

Audience: **g,l,u,f.**

Bell, Janis & Willette,   **N7483.B375B45 2002**
  Thomas (Editors)
Art History in the Age of Bellori: Scholarship and Cultural
Politics in Seventeenth-Century Rome. Trade Cloth. Cambridge

University Press. New York, NY. 2002. 412p.
ISBN:0-521-78248-1, ISBN13: 978-0-521-78248-7.
Dewey:709/.2 B. LCCN:2001-035675.

Audience: **l,u,f.**   *Choice, 2003.*

Bowron, Edgar Peters   **N6920**
Art in Rome in the Eighteenth Century. Rishel, Joseph J..
Rizzoli International Publications. 2000. ISBN:1-85894-098-2,
ISBN13: 978-1-85894-098-4.

Audience: **l,u,f.**

Brown, Patricia Fortini   **NK1452.V4B76 2004**
Private Lives in Renaissance Venice: Art, Architecture, and the
Family. Cloth over Boards. Yale University Press. Cumberland,
RI. 2004. 320p. ISBN:0-300-10236-4, ISBN13:
978-0-300-10236-9. Dewey:306.4/7/08621094531.
LCCN:2003-018889.

Audience: **g,l,u,f.**   *Choice, 2005.*

Campbell, Gordon   **N6370**
Renaissance Art and Architecture. Trade Cloth. Oxford
University Press, Inc. New York, NY. 2004. 319p.
ISBN:0-19-860985-X, ISBN13: 978-0-19-860985-8.
Dewey:709'.024. LCCN:2004-275931.

Audience: **g,l,u,f.**

Campbell, Stephen &   **N6915.A743 2004**
  Milner, Stephen (Editors)
Artistic Exchange and Cultural Translation in the Italian
Renaissance City. Trade Cloth. Cambridge University Press.
New York, NY. 2004. 386p. ISBN:0-521-82688-8, ISBN13:
978-0-521-82688-4. Dewey:709/.45/09024. LCCN:2003-062976.

Audience: **l,u,f.**   *Choice, 2005.*

Careri, Giovanni   **N6415.B3C3613 2003**
Baroques. Ferrante Ferrani (Photographer). Trade Cloth.
Princeton University Press. Princeton, NJ. 2003. 224p.
ISBN:0-691-11690-3, ISBN13: 978-0-691-11690-7.
Dewey:709/.03/2. LCCN:2003-050431.

Audience: **l,u,f.**   *Choice, 2004.*

Delaforce, Angela   **N6846 .D34 2002**
Art and Patronage in Eighteenth-Century Portugal. Trade Cloth.
Cambridge University Press. New York, NY. 2002. 532p.
ISBN:0-521-57130-8, ISBN13: 978-0-521-57130-2.
Dewey:707/.9/469. LCCN:2001-025426.

Audience: **l,u,f.**   *Choice, 2002.*

Earls, Irene   **N6415**
Baroque Art: A Topical Dictionary. Cloth Text. Greenwood
Publishing Group, Inc. Portsmouth, NH. 1996. 352p.
ISBN:0-313-29406-2, ISBN13: 978-0-313-29406-8.
Dewey:709/.03/203. LCCN:95-051397.

Audience: **g,l,u,f.**   *Choice, 1997.*

Earls, Irene   **N6370**
Renaissance Art: A Topical Dictionary. Cloth Text. Greenwood
Publishing Group, Inc. Portsmouth, NH. 1987. 366p.
ISBN:0-313-24658-0, ISBN13: 978-0-313-24658-6.
Dewey:709/.02/4. LCCN:87-000250.

Audience: **g,l,u,f.**   *Choice, 1988.*

Hall, Marcia B. (Editor, Contribution by)   N6920.R657 2005
Rome. Trade Cloth. Cambridge University Press. New York, NY. 2005. 398p. Artistic Centers of the Italian Renaissance Ser. ISBN:0-521-62445-2, ISBN13: 978-0-521-62445-9. Dewey:709/.45/63. LCCN:2004-054607.
Audience: **l,u,f.** *Choice, 2005.*

Harbison, Craig   N6370
Northern Renaissance Art. Trade Cloth. Prentice Hall PTR. Upper Saddle River, NJ. 2007. 500p. ISBN:0-13-118291-9, ISBN13: 978-0-13-118291-2. Dewey:709/.02/4.
Audience: **g,l,u,f.**

Hartt, Frederick   N6915
History of Italian Renaissance Art. Ed. 5. Trade Cloth. Prentice Hall Art. Upper Saddle River, NJ. 2002. 696p. ISBN:0-13-183251-4, ISBN13: 978-0-13-183251-0. Dewey:709.45/09024.
Audience: **g,l,u,f.**

Holt, Elizabeth G.   N5300
A Documentary History of Art: Michelangelo and the Mannerists, the Baroque and the Eighteenth Century. Trade Paper. Princeton University Press. Princeton, NJ. 1982. 386p. ISBN:0-691-00344-0, ISBN13: 978-0-691-00344-3. Dewey:709. LCCN:81-047281.
Audience: **l,u,f.**

Holt, Elizabeth G.   N5303 .D6 1981
A Documentary History of Art: The Middle Ages and the Renaissance. Trade Paper. Princeton University Press. Princeton, NJ. 1982. 380p. ISBN:0-691-00333-5, ISBN13: 978-0-691-00333-7. Dewey:709. LCCN:81-047281.
Audience: **l,u,f.**

Huse, Norbert & Wolters, Wolfgang   N6921.V5
The Art of Renaissance Venice: Architecture, Sculpture, and Painting, 1460-1590. Edmund Jephcott (Translator). Trade Paper. University of Chicago Press. Chicago, IL. 1993. 390p. ISBN:0-226-36109-8, ISBN13: 978-0-226-36109-3. Dewey:709.4531.
Audience: **l,u,f.**

Keyes, George S. (Editor)   N8230 .K49 1990
Mirror of Empire: Dutch Marine Art of the Seventeenth Century. Cloth Text. Cambridge University Press. New York, NY. 1990. 458p. ISBN:0-521-39328-0, ISBN13: 978-0-521-39328-7. Dewey:760/.04437/094920747. LCCN:90-001492.
Audience: **l,u,f.** *Choice, 1991.*

Koerner, Joseph L.   ND588.D9K82
The Moment of Self-Portraiture in German Renaissance Art. Trade Paper. University of Chicago Press. Chicago, IL. 1997. 564p. ISBN:0-226-44999-8, ISBN13: 978-0-226-44999-9. Dewey:759.3.
Audience: **l,u,f.** *Choice, 1994.*

Martineau, Jane & Robison, Andrew (Editors)   N6921.V5G57 1994
The Glory of Venice: Art in the Eighteenth Century. Trade Paper. Yale University Press. Cumberland, RI. 1997. 528p. ISBN:0-300-06186-2, ISBN13: 978-0-300-06186-4. Dewey:709/.45/3107442132. LCCN:94-061010.
Audience: **g,l,u,f.**

Minor, Vernon H   N6410.M56 1999
Baroque and Rococo: Art and Culture. Prentice Hall PTR. 1999. ISBN:0-8109-4108-2, ISBN13: 978-0-8109-4108-3.
Audience: **g,l,u,f.**

Murray, Linda   N6374 .M87 1977B
High Renaissance and Mannerism: Italy, the North and Spain, 1500-1600. Trade Paper. Thames & Hudson. New York, NY. 1985. 288p. World of Art Library ISBN:0-500-20162-5, ISBN13: 978-0-500-20162-6. Dewey:709/.03/1. LCCN:78-322258.
Audience: **g,l,u,f.**

Murray, Peter & Murray, Linda   N6370.M97 1985
The Art of the Renaissance. Trade Paper. Thames & Hudson. New York, NY. 1985. 288p. World of Art Ser. ISBN:0-500-20008-4, ISBN13: 978-0-500-20008-7. Dewey:709/.02/4. LCCN:84-051305.
Audience: **g,l,u,f.**

Paoletti, John T. & Radke, Gary M.   N6915.P26 2005
Art in Renaissance Italy. Ed. 3. Trade Paper. Prentice Hall PTR. Upper Saddle River, NJ. 2005. 544p. ISBN:0-13-193510-0, ISBN13: 978-0-13-193510-5. Dewey:709/.45/09024. LCCN:2005-043146.
Audience: **g,l,u,f.**

Shearman, John   N6915.S54 1992
Only Connect...: Art and the Spectator in the Italian Renaissance. Trade Cloth. Princeton University Press. Princeton, NJ. 1992. 300p. A. W. Mellon Lectures in the Fine Arts, No. XXXV: 37 ISBN:0-691-09972-3, ISBN13: 978-0-691-09972-9. Dewey:709/.45/09024. LCCN:91-027246.
Audience: **l,u,f.** *Choice, 1993.*

Smith, Jeffrey Chipps   N6370
The Northern Renaissance. Trade Paper. Phaidon Press. London, 2004. 448p. Art & Ideas Ser. ISBN:0-7148-3867-5, ISBN13: 978-0-7148-3867-0. Dewey:709/.17/5309024. LCCN:2004-303735.
Audience: **g,l,u,f.** *Choice, 2005.*

Snyder, James   N6370.S6 2005
Northern Renaissance Art: Painting, Sculpture, the Graphic Arts from 1350 to 1575. Ed. 2. Trade Cloth. Prentice Hall Art. Upper Saddle River, NJ. 2004. 592p. ISBN:0-13-150547-5, ISBN13: 978-0-13-150547-6. Dewey:709.024. LCCN:2004-044701.
Audience: **g,l,u,f.**

Snyder, James, et al.   N6370.S62005
Northern Renaissance Art: Painting, Sculpture, the Graphic Arts from 1350 to 1575. Ed. 2. Henry Luttikhuizen & Larry Silver

(Authors). Trade Paper. Prentice Hall PTR. Upper Saddle River, NJ. 2004. 592p. ISBN:0-13-189564-8, ISBN13: 978-0-13-189564-5. Dewey:709.024. LCCN:2004-044701.

Audience: **g,l,u,f.**

Vasari, Giorgio   **N6923.V32 V37 1998**
Vasari's Florence: Artists and Literati at the Medicean Court. Philip Jacks (Editor). Trade Cloth. Cambridge University Press. New York, NY. 1998. 336p. ISBN:0-521-58088-9, ISBN13: 978-0-521-58088-5. Dewey:709/.2. LCCN:96-046902.

Audience: **g,l,u,f.** *Choice, 1999.*

Vlieghe, Hans   **N6935.V581998**
Flemish Art and Architecture, 1585-1700. Cloth over Boards. Yale University Press. Cumberland, RI. 1999. 348p. Pelican History of Art Ser. ISBN:0-300-07038-1, ISBN13: 978-0-300-07038-5. Dewey:709/.493/09032. LCCN:98-004163.

Audience: **g,l,u,f.** *Choice, 1999.*

Von der Osten, Gert & Vey,   **N6925.O813**
  Horst
Painting and Sculpture in Germany and the Netherlands, 1500-1600. Trade Cloth. Yale University Press. Cumberland, RI. 1979. 296p. Pelican History of Art Ser. ISBN:0-300-05311-8, ISBN13: 978-0-300-05311-1. Dewey:759.3.

Audience: **g,l,u,f.**

Von Kalnein, Wend   **NA1046.K351995**
Architecture in France in the Eighteenth Century. David Britt (Translator). Cloth over Boards. Yale University Press. Cumberland, RI. 1995. 308p. Pelican History of Art Ser. ISBN:0-300-06013-0, ISBN13: 978-0-300-06013-3. Dewey:720/.944/09033. LCCN:94-049720.

Audience: **g,l,u,f.** *Choice, 1995.*

Warburg, Aby M.   **N6370.W3313 1999**
The Renewal of Pagan Antiquity. Trade Paper. Oxford University Press, Inc. New York, NY. 1999. 868p. Texts and Documents Ser. ISBN:0-89236-537-4, ISBN13: 978-0-89236-537-1. Dewey:709/.02/4. LCCN:98-025943.

Audience: **u,f.** *Choice, 2000.*

Welch, Evelyn   **N6915**
Art in Renaissance Italy: 1350-1500. Trade Paper. Oxford University Press, Inc. New York, NY. 2001. 354p. Oxford History of Art Ser. ISBN:0-19-284279-X, ISBN13: 978-0-19-284279-4. Dewey:709.4/5/09024.

Audience: **g,l,u,f.**

Wittkower, Rudolf, et al.   **N6916.W51999**
Art and Architecture in Italy, 1600-1750. Ed. 6. Jennifer Montagu & John A. Pinto (Authors). Trade Paper. Yale University Press. Cumberland, RI. 1999. 392p. Pelican History of Art Ser. ISBN:0-300-07889-7, ISBN13: 978-0-300-07889-3. Dewey:759.5. LCCN:98-049066.

Audience: **g,l,u,f.** *Choice, 2000.*

Wohl, Hellmut   **N6915 .W565 1999**
The Aesthetics of Italian Renaissance Art: A Reconsideration of Style. Trade Cloth. Cambridge University Press. New York, NY.

1999. 390p. ISBN:0-521-57064-6, ISBN13: 978-0-521-57064-0. Dewey:709/.45/09024. LCCN:98-034998.

Audience: **g,l,u,f.** *Choice, 2000.*

Wolfflin, Heinrich   **N6915.W5713 1994**
Classic Art: An Introduction to the Italian Renaissance. Ed. 5. Trade Paper. Phaidon Press. London, 1994. 294p. ISBN:0-7148-2974-9, ISBN13: 978-0-7148-2974-6. Dewey:709.45. LCCN:95-148652.

Audience: **l,u,f.** *B*

Visual Arts in General > Histories and Handbooks > Periods and Styles > Modern Era

Ades, Dawn (Editor)   **N6502.4.A3 1989**
Art in Latin America: The Modern Era, 1820-1980. Guy Brett, Stanton L. Catlin & Rosemary O'Neill (Contribution by). Trade Paper. Yale University Press. Cumberland, RI. 1993. 384p. Art - Latin American Studies ISBN:0-300-04561-1, ISBN13: 978-0-300-04561-1. Dewey:709/.8/09034. LCCN:89-050603.

Audience: **g,l,u,f.** *Choice, 1990.*

Anfam, David   **N6512.5.A25A89 1990**
Abstract Expressionism. Trade Paper. Thames & Hudson. New York, NY. 1990. 216p. World of Art Ser. ISBN:0-500-20243-5, ISBN13: 978-0-500-20243-2. Dewey:759.0652. LCCN:89-050635.

Audience: **g,l,u,f.**

Antliff, Mark & Leighten,   **N6494.C8A58 2001**
  Patricia
Cubism and Culture. Trade Paper. Thames & Hudson. New York, NY. 2001. 224p. World of Art Ser. ISBN:0-500-20342-3, ISBN13: 978-0-500-20342-2. Dewey:709/.04/032. LCCN:2001-086844.

Audience: **g,l,u,f.**

Archer, Michael   **N6490.A669 2002**
Art since 1960. Ed. 2. Trade Paper. Thames & Hudson. New York, NY. 2002. 256p. World of Art Ser. ISBN:0-500-20351-2, ISBN13: 978-0-500-20351-4. Dewey:709/.04/5. LCCN:2001-092919.

Audience: **g,l,u,f.** *Choice, 1997.*

Arnason, H. Horvard   **N6490**
History of Modern Art: Painting, Sculpture, Architecture, Photography. Ed. 5. Trade Cloth. Prentice Hall Art. Upper Saddle River, NJ. 2003. 848p. ISBN:0-13-184105-X, ISBN13: 978-0-13-184105-5. Dewey:709.04.

Audience: **g,l,u,f.**

Bailey, Gauvin Alexander   **N6502**
The Art of Colonial Latin America. Trade Paper. Phaidon Press. London, 2005. 448p. Art and Ideas Ser. ISBN:0-7148-4157-9, ISBN13: 978-0-7148-4157-1. Dewey:709.80903. LCCN:2006-531006.

Audience: **g,l,u,f.** *Choice, 2005.*

Baker, Kenneth   **N6512.5.M5B35 1988**
Minimalism: Art of Circumstance. Trade Cloth. Abbeville Press,
Inc. New York, NY. 1989. 144p. Abbeville Modern Art
Movements Ser. ISBN:0-89659-887-X, ISBN13:
978-0-89659-887-4. Dewey:709/.73/09045. LCCN:89-163713.
                              Audience: **g,l,u,f.** *Choice, 1989.*

Bann, Stephen   **NE647.3.B36 2001**
Parallel Lines: Printmakers, Painters and Photographers in 19th
Century France. Cloth over Boards. Yale University Press.
Cumberland, RI. 2001. 264p. ISBN:0-300-08932-5, ISBN13:
978-0-300-08932-5. Dewey:769.944/09/034. LCCN:00-048588.
                              Audience: **g,l,u,f.** *Choice, 2002.*

Barron, Stephanie   **N6512.E8871997**
Exiles and Emigres: The Flight of European Artists from Hitler.
Trade Cloth. Harry N. Abrams, Inc. New York, NY. 1997. 384p.
ISBN:0-8109-3271-7, ISBN13: 978-0-8109-3271-5.
Dewey:704/.03/034073. LCCN:96-078500.
                              Audience: **g,l,u,f.** *Choice, 1997.*

Battcock, Gregory (Editor)   **N6512.5.M5M56 1995**
Minimal Art: A Critical Anthology. Anne Wagner (Introduction
by). Trade Paper. University of California Press. Berkeley, CA.
1995. 470p. ISBN:0-520-20147-7, ISBN13: 978-0-520-20147-7.
Dewey:709.046. LCCN:94-032628.
                              Audience: **g,l,u,f.** B

Bohrer, Frederick N.   **NX650.E85B64 2003**
Orientalism and Visual Culture: Imagining Mesopotamia in
Nineteenth-Century Europe. Trade Cloth. Cambridge University
Press. New York, NY. 2003. 398p. ISBN:0-521-80657-7,
ISBN13: 978-0-521-80657-2. Dewey:704.9/49935/00744.
LCCN:2002-031208.
                              Audience: **l,u,f.** *Choice, 2004.*

Bowness, Alan   **N6450**
Modern European Art: Impressionism to Abstract Art. Trade
Paper. Thames & Hudson. New York, NY. 1995. 224p. The
World of Art Ser. ISBN:0-500-20205-2, ISBN13:
978-0-500-20205-0. Dewey:709/.034. LCCN:95-060189.
                              Audience: **g,l,u,f.**

Brettell, Richard   **N6757.B74 1999**
Modern Art, 1851-1929: Capitalism and Representation. Trade
Paper. Oxford University Press, Inc. New York, NY. 1999. 268p.
Oxford History of Art Ser. ISBN:0-19-284220-X, ISBN13:
978-0-19-284220-6. Dewey:760/.09/034. LCCN:00-500970.
                              Audience: **l,u,f.**

Brougher, Kerry   **ML3849**
Visual Music: Synaesthesia in Art and Music since 1900. Trade
Cloth. Thames & Hudson. New York, NY. 2005. 272p.
ISBN:0-500-51217-5, ISBN13: 978-0-500-51217-3.
Dewey:704.94978. LCCN:2004-113471.
                              Audience: **g,l,u,f.** *Choice, 2005.*

Caws, Mary Ann (Editor)   **PQ1170.E6S8 2001**
Surrealist Painters and Poets: An Anthology. Trade Cloth. MIT
Press. Cambridge, MA. 2001. 564p. ISBN:0-262-03275-9,

ISBN13: 978-0-262-03275-9. Dewey:700/.41163.
LCCN:00-032888.
                              Audience: **g,l,u,f.** *Choice, 2001.*

Chu, Petra ten-Doesschate   **N6757.C484 2006**
Nineteenth-Century European Art. Ed. 2. Trade Paper. Prentice
Hall PTR. Upper Saddle River, NJ. 2006. 560p.
ISBN:0-13-188643-6, ISBN13: 978-0-13-188643-8.
Dewey:709/.034. LCCN:2005-048290.
                              Audience: **g,l,u,f.** *Choice, 2003.*

Clayson, Hollis   **N6847.5.I4C58 2003**
Painted Love: Prostitution in French Art of the Impressionist
Era. Trade Paper. Oxford University Press, Inc. New York, NY.
2003. 224p. Texts and Documents Ser. ISBN:0-89236-729-6,
ISBN13: 978-0-89236-729-0. Dewey:757/.4/094409034.
LCCN:2003-108454.
                              Audience: **l,u,f.** *Choice, 1992.*

Clegg, Elizabeth   **N6757.C622006**
From Secession to Reinvention: Art, Design, and Architecture in
Central Europe 1890-1920. Cloth over Boards. Yale University
Press. Cumberland, RI. 1959. 356p. Pelican History of Art Ser.
ISBN:0-300-11120-7, ISBN13: 978-0-300-11120-0.
Dewey:709/.436/09034. LCCN:2005-017837.
                              Audience: **l,u,f.**

Codell, Julie F.   **N6767.5.V52C632003**
The Victorian Artist: Artists' Lifewritings in Britain, c.
1870-1910. Trade Cloth. Cambridge University Press. New
York, NY. 2003. 392p. ISBN:0-521-81757-9, ISBN13:
978-0-521-81757-8. Dewey:709/.41/09034. LCCN:2002-074196.
                              Audience: **l,u,f.** *Choice, 2004.*

Cumming, Elizabeth &   **NK1140.C85 1991**
  Kaplan, Wendy
The Arts and Crafts Movement. Trade Paper. Thames &
Hudson. New York, NY. 1991. 216p. World of Art Ser.
ISBN:0-500-20248-6, ISBN13: 978-0-500-20248-7.
Dewey:745/.09034. LCCN:90-070199.
                              Audience: **g,l,u,f.**

Dawkins, Heather   **N6847 .D34 2002**
The Nude in French Art and Culture, 1870-1910. Trade Cloth.
Cambridge University Press. New York, NY. 2002. 244p.
ISBN:0-521-80755-7, ISBN13: 978-0-521-80755-5.
Dewey:757/.4/094409034. LCCN:2001-025499.
                              Audience: **l,u,f.**

Dean, Tacita & Millar,   **N8236.P46**
  Jeremy
Art Works Place. Trade Paper. Thames & Hudson. New York,
NY. 2005. 208p. Art Works ISBN:0-500-93007-4, ISBN13:
978-0-500-93007-6. Dewey:700.42. LCCN:2004-112875.
                              Audience: **g,l,u,f.**

Dempsey, Amy   **N6490.D4152002**
Art in the Modern Era: A Guide to Styles, Schools, and
Movements. Trade Cloth. Harry N. Abrams, Inc. New York, NY.
2002. 304p. ISBN:0-8109-4172-4, ISBN13: 978-0-8109-4172-4.
Dewey:709/.04/03. LCCN:2001-046261.
                              Audience: **g,l,u,f.** *Choice, 2002.*

Dempsey, Amy   **N6447.D46 2004**
Styles, Schools and Movements: The Essential Encyclopaedic
Guide to Modern Art. Trade Paper. Thames & Hudson. New
York, NY. 2005. 304p. ISBN:0-500-28376-1, ISBN13:
978-0-500-28376-9. Dewey:709/.04. LCCN:2004-106362.
                                               Audience: **g,l,u,f.**

Doss, Erika   **N6512.D598 2002**
Twentieth-Century American Art. Trade Paper. Oxford
University Press, Inc. New York, NY. 2002. 288p. Oxford
History of Art Ser. ISBN:0-19-284239-0, ISBN13:
978-0-19-284239-8. Dewey:709.7/3/0904. LCCN:2002-283528.
                                               Audience: **g,l,u,f.**

Draguet, Michel   **N6757.5.A78D73 1999**
Treasures of Art Nouveau: Through the Collections of
Anne-Marie Gillion Crowet. Trade Cloth. Skira Editore. Milano,
1999. 304p. ISBN:88-8118-324-2, ISBN13: 978-88-8118-324-1.
Dewey:709/.03/49. LCCN:99-510598.
                                               Audience: **g,l,u,f.**

Dube, Wolf-Dieter   **N6868.5.E9D8213**
The Expressionists. Trade Paper. Thames & Hudson. New York,
NY. 1985. 216p. World of Art Library. History of Art
ISBN:0-500-20123-4, ISBN13: 978-0-500-20123-7.
Dewey:759.3. LCCN:87-050465.
                                               Audience: **g,l,u,f.**

Duncan, Alastair   **N6465.A7D86 1994**
Art Nouveau. Trade Paper. Thames & Hudson. New York, NY.
1994. 216p. World of Art Ser. ISBN:0-500-20273-7, ISBN13:
978-0-500-20273-9. Dewey:709/.03/49. LCCN:93-061372.
                                               Audience: **g,l,u,f.**

Durozoi, Gerard   **NX456.5.S8D8713 2001**
History of the Surrealist Movement. Alison Anderson
(Translator). Trade Paper. University of Chicago Press. Chicago,
IL. 2005. 816p. ISBN:0-226-17412-3, ISBN13:
978-0-226-17412-9. Dewey:709/.04/063. LCCN:2001-037743.
                        Audience: **l,u,f.** *Choice, 2003, 2002.*

Durozoi, Gerard   **NX456.5.S8D8713 2002**
History of the Surrealist Movement. Alison Anderson
(Translator). Trade Cloth. University of Chicago Press. Chicago,
IL. 2002. 816p. ISBN:0-226-17411-5, ISBN13:
978-0-226-17411-2. Dewey:709/.04/063. LCCN:2001-037743.
                        Audience: **g,l,u,f.** *Choice, 2003, 2002.*

Edwards, Holly (Editor)   **NX503.7.E355 2000**
Noble Dreams, Wicked Pleasures: Orientalism in America,
1870-1930. Trade Paper. Princeton University Press. Princeton,
NJ. 2000. 256p. ISBN:0-691-05004-X, ISBN13:
978-0-691-05004-1. Dewey:704.9/4995. LCCN:00-036685.
                              Audience: **l,u,f.** *Choice, 2001.*

Eisenman, Stephen F.   **N6450.E39 2001**
Nineteenth Century Art: A Critical History. Ed. 2. Trade Cloth.
Thames & Hudson. New York, NY. 2002. 428p.
ISBN:0-500-23793-X, ISBN13: 978-0-500-23793-9.
Dewey:709/.034. LCCN:2001-093467.
                            Audience: **g,l,u,f.** *Choice, 1994.*

Elder, Alan C. & Thom, Ian   **N6547.V3M63 2004**
M.
A Modern Life: Art and Design in British Columbia, 1945-1960.
Vancouver Art Gallery Staff (Contribution by). Trade Paper,
With Flaps. Arsenal Pulp Press. Vancouver, BC. 2005. 176p.
ISBN:1-55152-171-7, ISBN13: 978-1-55152-171-8.
Dewey:709/.711/07471133. LCCN:2004-484293.
                            Audience: **g,l,u,f.** *Choice, 2005.*

Facos, Michelle & Hirsh,   **N72.N38A77 2003**
  Sharon (Editors)
Art, Culture and National Identity in Fin-de-Siecle Europe.
Trade Cloth. Cambridge University Press. New York, NY. 2003.
314p. ISBN:0-521-81565-7, ISBN13: 978-0-521-81565-9.
Dewey:704.9/4932054. LCCN:2002-031394.
                              Audience: **l,u,f.** *Choice, 2004.*

Fineberg, Jonathan David   **N6490**
Art since 1940: Strategies of Being. Ed. 2. Trade Cloth. Prentice
Hall Art. Upper Saddle River, NJ. 2000. 528p.
ISBN:0-13-183321-9, ISBN13: 978-0-13-183321-0.
Dewey:709/.045.
                            Audience: **g,l,u,f.** *Choice, 1995.*

Francis, Mark & Foster, Hal   **N6494.P6**
Pop. Trade Cloth. Phaidon Press. London, 2005. 304p.
ISBN:0-7148-4363-6, ISBN13: 978-0-7148-4363-6.
Dewey:709.04071.
                            Audience: **g,l,u,f.** *Choice, 2006.*

Gibson, Michael   **N6465.S9G53131988**
The Symbolists. Trade Cloth. Harry N. Abrams, Inc. New York,
NY. 1988. 192p. ISBN:0-8109-1516-2, ISBN13:
978-0-8109-1516-9. Dewey:760/.09/0347. LCCN:87-030747.
                            Audience: **g,l,u,f.** *Choice, 1988.*

Goldstein, Ann &   **N6512.5.M5M5626 2004**
  Diederichsen, Diedrich
A Minimal Future?: Art As Object 1958-1968. Lisa Mark
(Editor), Museum of Contemporary Art, Los Angeles Staff
(Contribution by). Trade Cloth. MIT Press. Cambridge, MA.
2004. 452p. ISBN:0-262-07251-3, ISBN13: 978-0-262-07251-9.
LCCN:2003-066481.
                                               Audience: **g,l,u,f.**

Grant, Kim   **N6494.S8G73 2005**
Surrealism and the Visual Arts: Theory and Reception. Trade
Cloth. Cambridge University Press. New York, NY. 2005. 416p.
ISBN:0-521-83655-7, ISBN13: 978-0-521-83655-5.
Dewey:709/.04/063. LCCN:2004-052119.
                              Audience: **l,u,f.** *Choice, 2005.*

Green, Christopher   **N6848.G732000**
Art in France, 1900-1940. Cloth over Boards. Yale University
Press. Cumberland, RI. 2001. 336p. Pelican History of Art Ser.
ISBN:0-300-08401-3, ISBN13: 978-0-300-08401-6.
Dewey:709.44/09041. LCCN:99-089522.
                                               Audience: **g,l,u,f.**

Hamilton, George H.   **N6757.5.M63H361993**
Painting and Sculpture in Europe: 1880-1940. Ed. 4. Trade
Paper. Yale University Press. Cumberland, RI. 1989. 610p.

Pelican History of Art Ser. ISBN:0-300-05649-4, ISBN13: 978-0-300-05649-5. Dewey:759.94. LCCN:94-119000.

Audience: **g,l,u,f.** *B*

Hochman, Elaine S.   **N332.G33B4455 1997**
Bauhaus: Crucible of Modernism. Trade Cloth. Fromm International Publishing Corporation. New York, NY. 1997. 384p. ISBN:0-88064-175-4, ISBN13: 978-0-88064-175-3. Dewey:707/.1/143155. LCCN:96-037073.

Audience: **g,l,u,f.** *Choice, 1997.*

Hoffmann, Jens   **NX600.P47**
Art Works: Perform. Trade Paper. Thames & Hudson. New York, NY. 2005. 208p. Art Works ISBN:0-500-93006-6, ISBN13: 978-0-500-93006-9. Dewey:709/.04/9. LCCN:2004-110962.

Audience: **g,l,u,f.**

Holt, Elizabeth G. (Editor)   **N5300**
From the Classicists to the Impressionists: Art and Architecture in the Nineteenth Century. Ed. 2. Cloth over Boards. Yale University Press. Cumberland, RI. 1986. 555p. Documentary History of Art Ser., Vol. III ISBN:0-300-03358-3, ISBN13: 978-0-300-03358-8. Dewey:709/.03/4. LCCN:85-051918.

Audience: **l,u,f.**

Hopkins, David   **N6512.H657 2000**
After Modern Art, 1945-2000. Trade Paper. Oxford University Press, Inc. New York, NY. 2000. 290p. Oxford History of Art Ser. ISBN:0-19-284234-X, ISBN13: 978-0-19-284234-3. Dewey:709.045. LCCN:00-036750.

Audience: **g,l,u,f.** *Choice, 2001.*

Hunter, Sam, et al.   **N6447.H86 2005**
Modern Art. Ed. 3. John M. Jacobus & Daniel Wheeler (Authors). Trade Cloth. Prentice Hall Art. Upper Saddle River, NJ. 2004. 472p. ISBN:0-13-150519-X, ISBN13: 978-0-13-150519-3. Dewey:709/.04. LCCN:2004-046659.

Audience: **l,u,f.**

Joselit, David   **N6512**
American Art since 1945. Trade Paper. Thames & Hudson. New York, NY. 2003. 256p. World of Art Ser. ISBN:0-500-20368-7, ISBN13: 978-0-500-20368-2. Dewey:709.7/3/09045. LCCN:2002-109021.

Audience: **g,l,u,f.**

Kantor, Sybil Gordon   **N620.M9K36 2001**
Alfred H. Barr, Jr. and the Intellectual Origins of the Museum of Modern Art. Trade Cloth. MIT Press. Cambridge, MA. 2001. 496p. ISBN:0-262-11258-2, ISBN13: 978-0-262-11258-1. Dewey:708.1471. LCCN:2001-044034.

Audience: **g,l,u,f.** *Choice, 2003, 2002.*

Karnouk, Liliane   **N7381.7**
Modern Egyptian Art 1910-2003. Perfect, Paper over Boards, Dust Jacket. American University in Cairo Press. New York, NY. 2005. 274p. ISBN:977-424-859-7, ISBN13: 978-977-424-859-7. Dewey:709/.62.

Audience: **g,l,u,f.** *Choice, 2006.*

Kasfir, Sidney Littlefield   **N7380.K36 2000**
Contemporary African Art. Trade Paper. Thames & Hudson. New York, NY. 2000. 224p. World of Art Ser. ISBN:0-500-20328-8, ISBN13: 978-0-500-20328-6. Dewey:709/.6/09045. LCCN:99-070939.

Audience: **l,u,f.** *Choice, 2000.*

Kastner, Jeffrey   **N6494.E27L36 1998**
Land and Environmental Art. Trade Cloth. Phaidon Press. London, 1998. 304p. Themes and Movements Ser. ISBN:0-7148-3514-5, ISBN13: 978-0-7148-3514-3. Dewey:709/.04076. LCCN:2006-531008.

Audience: **g,l,u,f.**

Kuspit, Donald   **N6490.K864 2004**
The End of Art. Trade Cloth. Cambridge University Press. New York, NY. 2004. 224p. ISBN:0-521-83252-7, ISBN13: 978-0-521-83252-6. Dewey:701/.17/09045. LCCN:2003-055123.

Audience: **u,f.** *Choice, 2004.*

Levey, Michael   **N6846.L461993**
Painting and Sculpture in France, 1700-1789. Cloth over Boards. Yale University Press. Cumberland, RI. 1993. 332p. Pelican History of Art Ser. ISBN:0-300-05344-4, ISBN13: 978-0-300-05344-9. Dewey:759.4/09033. LCCN:92-032503.

Audience: **g,l,u,f.** *Choice, 1993.*

Livingstone, Marco   **N6494.P6**
Pop Art: A Continuing History. Ed. 2. Trade Paper. Thames & Hudson. New York, NY. 2000. 272p. ISBN:0-500-28240-4, ISBN13: 978-0-500-28240-3. Dewey:709/.04071. LCCN:00-100788.

Audience: **g,l,u,f.** *Choice, 1991.*

Lucie-Smith, Edward   **N72.H64**
Art Today. Trade Paper. Phaidon Press. London, 1999. 512p. ISBN:0-7148-3888-8, ISBN13: 978-0-7148-3888-5. Dewey:709/.049.

Audience: **g,l,u,f.**

Lucie-Smith, Edward   **N6502.5**
Latin American Art of the 20th Century. Ed. 2. Trade Paper. Thames & Hudson. New York, NY. 2004. 224p. World of Art Ser. ISBN:0-500-20356-3, ISBN13: 978-0-500-20356-9. Dewey:709.8/0904. LCCN:2002-109034.

Audience: **g,l,u,f.** *Choice, 1993.*

Lucie-Smith, Edward   **N6489.L83 1999**
Lives of Great 20th Century Artists. Ed. 2. Trade Cloth. Thames & Hudson. New York, NY. 1999. 352p. ISBN:0-500-23739-5, ISBN13: 978-0-500-23739-7. Dewey:709/.2/2 B. LCCN:98-075076.

Audience: **g,l,u,f.** *Choice, 2000.*

Lucie-Smith, Edward   **N6490.L79 2001**
Movements in Art since 1945. Ed. 5. Trade Paper. Thames & Hudson. New York, NY. 2001. 304p. World of Art Ser. ISBN:0-500-20344-X, ISBN13: 978-0-500-20344-6. Dewey:709.04. LCCN:00-109243.

Audience: **g,l,u,f.**

Lucie-Smith, Edward   **N6465.S9**
Symbolist Art. Trade Paper. Thames & Hudson. New York, NY.
1985. 216p. World of Art Ser. ISBN:0-500-20125-0, ISBN13:
978-0-500-20125-1. Dewey:760/.094.

Audience: **g,l,u,f.**

Lucie-Smith, Edward   **N6490.L792 1997**
Visual Arts in the Twentieth Century. Prentice Hall PTR. 1997.
ISBN:0-8109-3934-7, ISBN13: 978-0-8109-3934-9.

Audience: **g,l,u,f.**

Lynton, Norbert   **N6490**
The Story of Modern Art. Ed. 2. Trade Paper. Phaidon Press.
London, 1994. 400p. ISBN:0-7148-2422-4, ISBN13:
978-0-7148-2422-2. Dewey:709/.04.

Audience: **g,l,u,f.** *B*

Mansbach, S. A.   **N6758.M3521999**
Modern Art in Eastern Europe: From the Baltic to the Balkans,
ca. 1890-1939. Ronald H. Wainscott (Contribution by). Cloth
Text. Cambridge University Press. New York, NY. 1998. 400p.
ISBN:0-521-45085-3, ISBN13: 978-0-521-45085-0.
Dewey:709/.47/0904. LCCN:97-042894.

Audience: **g,u,f.** *Choice, 1999.*

McCloskey, Barbara   **N9160**
Artists of World War II. Trade Cloth. Greenwood Publishing
Group, Inc. Portsmouth, NH. 2005. 248p. Artists of an Era Ser.
ISBN:0-313-32153-1, ISBN13: 978-0-313-32153-5.
Dewey:940.54/88. LCCN:2004-026938.

Audience: **g,l,u,f.** *Choice, 2006.*

Meyer, James S.   **N6490**
Minimalism. Trade Cloth. Phaidon Press. London, 2000. 306p.
ISBN:0-7148-3460-2, ISBN13: 978-0-7148-3460-3.
Dewey:709/.04.

Audience: **g,l,u,f.**

Moszynska, Anna   **N6494.A2M57 1990**
Abstract Art. Trade Paper. Thames & Hudson. New York, NY.
1990. 240p. World of Art Ser. ISBN:0-500-20237-0, ISBN13:
978-0-500-20237-1. Dewey:709.04. LCCN:89-051347.

Audience: **g,l,u,f.**

Osborne, Peter (Author,   **N6494.C63C587 2002**
  Editor)
Conceptual Art. Trade Cloth. Phaidon Press. London, 2002.
304p. Themes and Movements Ser. ISBN:0-7148-3930-2,
ISBN13: 978-0-7148-3930-1. Dewey:709.04075.
LCCN:2002-728040.

Audience: **g,l,u,f.**

Pendergast, Sara &   **N6490.C6567 2001**
  Pendergast, Tom (Editors)
Contemporary Artists. Ed. 5. Trade Cloth. Thomson Gale.
Farmington Hills, MI. 2001. 1400p. Contemporary Arts Ser.
ISBN:1-55862-407-4, ISBN13: 978-1-55862-407-8.
Dewey:709/.2/2 B. LCCN:2001-048443.

Audience: **g,l,u,f.**

Perl, Jed   **N6535.N5P46 2005**
New Art City: The Painters and Sculptors of Manhattan,
1950-1965. Trade Cloth. Alfred A. Knopf Inc. New York, NY.
2005. 641p. ISBN:1-4000-4131-7, ISBN13: 978-1-4000-4131-2.
Dewey:700/.9747/109045. LCCN:2004-048846.

Audience: **g,l,u,f.** *Choice, 2006.*

Richter, Hans   **N6494.D3R5213 1997**
Dada: Art and Anti-Art. David Britt (Translator). Trade Paper.
Thames & Hudson. New York, NY. 1997. 302p. The World of
Art Ser. ISBN:0-500-20039-4, ISBN13: 978-0-500-20039-1.
Dewey:709/.04062. LCCN:96-061461.

Audience: **g,l,u,f.**

Rogoff, Irit (Editor)   **N6868.5.M63 D58 1990**
The Divided Heritage: Themes and Problems in German
Modernism. Trade Cloth. Cambridge University Press. New
York, NY. 1991. 406p. ISBN:0-521-34553-7, ISBN13:
978-0-521-34553-8. Dewey:709.43/09/04. LCCN:89-035777.

Audience: **u,f.** *Choice, 1992.*

Rosemont, Penelope (Editor)   **NX456.5.S8S92 1998**
Surrealist Women: An International Anthology. Trade Paper.
University of Texas Press. Austin, TX. 1998. 576p. Surrealist
Revolution Ser. ISBN:0-292-77088-X, ISBN13:
978-0-292-77088-1. Dewey:700/.41163/082. LCCN:97-035357.

Audience: **l,u,f.** *Choice, 1999.*

Rosenblum, Robert &   **N6450.R67 2005**
  Janson, H. W.
19th Century Art. Ed. 2. Trade Cloth. Prentice Hall Art. Upper
Saddle River, NJ. 2004. 544p. ISBN:0-13-189614-8, ISBN13:
978-0-13-189614-7. Dewey:709/.034. LCCN:2004-046660.

Audience: **g,l,u,f.**

Sandler, Irving   **N6490**
Art of the Postmodern Era: From the Late 1960s to the Early
1990s. Trade Paper. Westview Press. Boulder, CO. 1997. 680p.
ISBN:0-8133-3433-0, ISBN13: 978-0-8133-3433-2.
Dewey:709/.045. LCCN:96-033877.

Audience: **g,l,u,f.** *Choice, 1997.*

Selz, Peter   **N6494.M64 S43 1997**
Beyond the Mainstream: Essays on Modern and Contemporary
Art. Donald Kuspit (Contribution by). Trade Paper. Cambridge
University Press. New York, NY. 1998. 346p. Contemporary
Artists and Their Critics Ser. ISBN:0-521-55624-4, ISBN13:
978-0-521-55624-8. Dewey:709/.04. LCCN:96-046613.

Audience: **l,u,f.** *Choice, 1998.*

Siegel, Jonah   **NX454.S54 2000**
Desire and Excess: The Nineteenth-Century Culture of Art.
Trade Paper. Princeton University Press. Princeton, NJ. 2000.
380p. ISBN:0-691-04914-9, ISBN13: 978-0-691-04914-4.
Dewey:709/.03/4. LCCN:00-020897.

Audience: **g,l,u,f.**

Spalding, Frances   **N6767**
British Art since 1900. Trade Paper. Thames & Hudson. New
York, NY. 1986. 252p. World of Art Ser. ISBN:0-500-20204-4,
ISBN13: 978-0-500-20204-3. Dewey:709/.41. LCCN:85-051119.

Audience: **g,l,u,f.**

Spector, Jack J.   **NX542.A1 S68 1997**
Surrealist Art and Writing, 1919-1939: The Gold of Time.
Donald Kuspit (Contribution by). Trade Paper. Cambridge
University Press. New York, NY. 1999. 332p. Contemporary
Artists and Their Critics Ser. ISBN:0-521-65739-3, ISBN13:
978-0-521-65739-6. Dewey:700.9/4/09041.
Audience: **l,u,f.** *Choice, 1997.*

Stallabrass, Julian   **NA6490**
Art Incorporated: The Story of Contemporary Art. Trade Cloth.
Oxford University Press, Inc. New York, NY. 2005. 256p.
ISBN:0-19-280165-1, ISBN13: 978-0-19-280165-4.
Dewey:709/.04/9. LCCN:2004-054785.
Audience: **g,l,u,f.**

Stangos, Nikos (Editor)   **N6490.C65617 1994**
Concepts of Modern Art. Ed. 3. Trade Paper. Thames &
Hudson. New York, NY. 1994. 424p. World of Art Ser.
ISBN:0-500-20268-0, ISBN13: 978-0-500-20268-5.
Dewey:709/.04. LCCN:89-052177.
Audience: **g,l,u,f.** *B*

Stiles, Kristine   **N6490.T492 1996**
Theories and Documents of Contemporary Art: A Sourcebook of
Artists' Writings. Peter H. Selz (Editor). Trade Cloth. University
of California Press. Berkeley, CA. 1995. 1026p. California
Studies in the History of Art, Vol. XXXV ISBN:0-520-20251-1,
ISBN13: 978-0-520-20251-1. Dewey:709/.04. LCCN:94-046530.
Audience: **g,l,u,f.**

Stiles, Kristine & Selz, Peter   **N6490.T492 1996**
H.
Theories and Documents of Contemporary Art: A Sourcebook of
Artists' Writings. Trade Paper. University of California Press.
Berkeley, CA. 1996. 1026p. California Studies in the History of
Art, Vol. XXXV ISBN:0-520-20253-8, ISBN13:
978-0-520-20253-5. Dewey:709/.04. LCCN:94-046530.
Audience: **g,l,u,f.**

Sullivan, Michael   **N7345.S79 1996**
Art and Artists of Twentieth-Century China. Trade Cloth.
University of California Press. Berkeley, CA. 1996. 386p. An
Ahmanson Murphy Fine Arts Bk. ISBN:0-520-07556-0,
ISBN13: 978-0-520-07556-6. Dewey:709/.51/0904.
LCCN:95-025673.
Audience: **g,l,u,f.** *Choice, 1997.*

Tisdall, Caroline & Bozollo,   **NX600.F8**
Angelo
Futurism. Trade Cloth. Thames & Hudson. New York, NY.
1985. 216p. World of Art Ser. ISBN:0-500-18162-4, ISBN13:
978-0-500-18162-1. Dewey:700/.945. LCCN:78-313205.
Audience: **g,l,u,f.** *B*

Varnedoe, Kirk   **N6490**
High and Low: Modern Art and Popular Culture. Trade Cloth.
Harry N. Abrams, Inc. New York, NY. 1990. 464p.
ISBN:0-8109-6002-8, ISBN13: 978-0-8109-6002-2.
Dewey:709.04. LCCN:90-000006.
Audience: **g,l,u,f.** *Choice, 1991.*

Weber, Nicholas Fox   **NX504.W431995**
Patron Saints: Five Rebels Who Opened America to a New Art,
1928-1943. Trade Paper. Yale University Press. Cumberland, RI.
1995. 416p. ISBN:0-300-06448-9, ISBN13: 978-0-300-06448-3.
Dewey:700/.973/09041. LCCN:95-061164.
Audience: **g,l,u,f.**

Welish, Marjorie   **N6512 .W39 1999**
Signifying Art: Essays on Art after 1960. Donald Kuspit
(Contribution by). Cloth Text. Cambridge University Press. New
York, NY. 1999. 335p. Contemporary Artists and Their Critics
Ser. ISBN:0-521-63301-X, ISBN13: 978-0-521-63301-7.
Dewey:709/.73/09045. LCCN:99-014189.
Audience: **u,f.** *Choice, 2000.*

Visual Arts in General > Histories and Handbooks > Cultures, Regions, Nationalities > United States, Canada

Baigell, Matthew   **N6512 .B25 2001**
Artist and Identity in Twentieth-Century America. Trade Paper.
Cambridge University Press. New York, NY. 2001. 304p.
Contemporary Artists and Their Critics Ser.
ISBN:0-521-77601-5, ISBN13: 978-0-521-77601-1.
Dewey:709/.73/0904. LCCN:00-023664.
Audience: **g,l,u,f.** *Choice, 2001.*

Baigell, Matthew   **N6505.B338 1996**
Concise History of American Painting and Sculpture. Trade
Paper. Westview Press. Boulder, CO. 1996. 462p. Icon Editions
Ser. ISBN:0-06-430986-X, ISBN13: 978-0-06-430986-8.
Dewey:709/.73. LCCN:96-220575.
Audience: **g,l,u,f.**

Berlo, Janet Catherine &   **E98.A7B47 1998**
Phillips, Ruth
Native North American Art. Trade Paper. Oxford University
Press, Inc. New York, NY. 1998. 302p. Oxford History of Art
Ser. ISBN:0-19-284218-8, ISBN13: 978-0-19-284218-3.
Dewey:704.03/97. LCCN:99-177938.
Audience: **g,l,u,f.**

Bishop, Robert & Atkins,   **NK805**
Jacqueline M.
Folk Art in American Life. Cloth Text. DIANE Publishing
Company. Collingdale, PA. 2000. 228p. ISBN:0-7881-9094-6,
ISBN13: 978-0-7881-9094-0. Dewey:745/.0973.
Audience: **g,l,u,f.**

Bjelajac, David & Laurence,   **N72.S6B55 2005**
King
American Art: A Cultural History. Ed. 2. Trade Cloth. Prentice
Hall Art. Upper Saddle River, NJ. 2004. 512p.
ISBN:0-13-145579-6, ISBN13: 978-0-13-145579-5.
Dewey:701/.03/0973. LCCN:2004-044483.
Audience: **g,l,u,f.** *Choice, 2000.*

Burns, Sarah　　　　　　　　　**N6510.B87 1996**
Inventing the Modern Artist: Art and Culture in Gilded Age America. Cloth over Boards. Yale University Press. Cumberland, RI. 1996. 392p. ISBN:0-300-06445-4, ISBN13: 978-0-300-06445-2. Dewey:759.1/3/0904. LCCN:96-005929.
Audience: **l,u,f.** *Choice, 1997.*

Cooper, Wendy A.　　　　　　**N6510.5.N4C66 1993**
Classical Taste in America, 1800-1840. Richard L. Bushman (Introduction by). Trade Cloth. Abbeville Press, Inc. New York, NY. 1993. 256p. ISBN:1-55859-385-3, ISBN13: 978-1-55859-385-5. Dewey:709.73. LCCN:93-009784.
Audience: **l,u,f.** *Choice, 1993.*

Craven, Wayne　　　　　　　　**N6505.C7 2003**
American Art: History and Culture. Cloth Text. McGraw-Hill Professional Publishing. New York, NY. 2003. 688p. ISBN:0-07-141524-6, ISBN13: 978-0-07-141524-8. Dewey:709/.73. LCCN:2002-035777.
Audience: **g,l,u,f.** *Choice, 1994.*

Doezema, Marianne &　　　　　**N6505.R4 1998**
　Milroy, Elizabeth (Editors)
Reading American Art. Trade Paper. Yale University Press. Cumberland, RI. 1998. 480p. ISBN:0-300-06998-7, ISBN13: 978-0-300-06998-3. Dewey:709/.73. LCCN:97-018004.
Audience: **l,u,f.**

Doss, Erika　　　　　　　　　**N6512.D598 2002**
Twentieth-Century American Art. Trade Paper. Oxford University Press, Inc. New York, NY. 2002. 288p. Oxford History of Art Ser. ISBN:0-19-284239-0, ISBN13: 978-0-19-284239-8. Dewey:709.7/3/0904. LCCN:2002-283528.
Audience: **g,l,u,f.**

Edwards, Holly (Editor)　　　　**NX503.7.E355 2000**
Noble Dreams, Wicked Pleasures: Orientalism in America, 1870-1930. Trade Paper. Princeton University Press. Princeton, NJ. 2000. 256p. ISBN:0-691-05004-X, ISBN13: 978-0-691-05004-1. Dewey:704.9/4995. LCCN:00-036685.
Audience: **l,u,f.** *Choice, 2001.*

Elder, Alan C. & Thom, Ian　　　**N6547.V3M63 2004**
M.
A Modern Life: Art and Design in British Columbia, 1945-1960. Vancouver Art Gallery Staff (Contribution by). Trade Paper, With Flaps. Arsenal Pulp Press. Vancouver, BC. 2005. 176p. ISBN:1-55152-171-7, ISBN13: 978-1-55152-171-8. Dewey:709/.711/07471133. LCCN:2004-484293.
Audience: **g,l,u,f.** *Choice, 2005.*

Feest, Christian F.　　　　　　　**E98.A7F44 1992**
Native Arts of North America. Ed. 2. Trade Paper. Thames & Hudson. New York, NY. 1992. 216p. World of Art Ser. ISBN:0-500-20262-1, ISBN13: 978-0-500-20262-3. Dewey:704.0397. LCCN:92-082579.
Audience: **g,l,u,f.**

Forbes, David W.　　　　　　　**N6530.H3F67 1992**
Encounters with Paradise: Views of Hawaii and Its People, 1778-1941. Trade Cloth. University of Hawaii Press. Honolulu,

HI. 1992. 278p. ISBN:0-8248-1440-1, ISBN13: 978-0-8248-1440-3. Dewey:758/.99969/007496931. LCCN:91-032265.
Audience: **g,l,u,f.**

Harris, Mary E.　　　　　　　　**NX311**
The Arts at Black Mountain College. Trade Paper. MIT Press. Cambridge, MA. 2002. 343p. ISBN:0-262-58212-0, ISBN13: 978-0-262-58212-4. Dewey:700.7/1175688.
Audience: **g,l,u,f.**

Hughes, Robert　　　　　　　　**N6505.H84 1997**
American Visions: The Epic History of Art in America. Trade Cloth. Alfred A. Knopf Inc. New York, NY. 1997. 648p. ISBN:0-679-42627-2, ISBN13: 978-0-679-42627-1. Dewey:709/.73. LCCN:96-045111.
Audience: **g,l,u,f.** *Choice, 1997.*

Joselit, David　　　　　　　　**N6512**
American Art since 1945. Trade Paper. Thames & Hudson. New York, NY. 2003. 256p. World of Art Ser. ISBN:0-500-20368-7, ISBN13: 978-0-500-20368-2. Dewey:709.7/3/09045. LCCN:2002-109021.
Audience: **g,l,u,f.**

Lewis, Michael J.　　　　　　　**N6505**
American Art and Architecture. Trade Paper. Thames & Hudson. New York, NY. 2006. 336p. ISBN:0-500-20391-1, ISBN13: 978-0-500-20391-0. Dewey:709.73.
Audience: **g,l,u,f.**

Lovell, Margaretta M.　　　　　**N6515.L68 2004**
Art in a Season of Revolution: Painters, Artisans and Patrons in Early America. Trade Cloth. University of Pennsylvania Press. Philadelphia, PA. 2004. 352p. Early American Studies ISBN:0-8122-3842-7, ISBN13: 978-0-8122-3842-6. Dewey:306.4/7/097409033. LCCN:2004-043099.
Audience: **g,l,u,f.** *Choice, 2005.*

Lucie-Smith, Edward　　　　　**ND205.5.R42L83 2002**
American Realism. Trade Paper. Thames & Hudson. New York, NY. 2002. 240p. ISBN:0-500-28356-7, ISBN13: 978-0-500-28356-1. Dewey:759.13/09/034. LCCN:2001-096298.
Audience: **g,l,u,f.**

Newlands, Anne　　　　　　　**N6540.N49 2000**
Canadian Art: From Its Beginnings to 2000. Trade Cloth. Firefly Books, Ltd. Tonawanda, NY. 2000. 352p. ISBN:1-55209-450-2, ISBN13: 978-1-55209-450-1. Dewey:709/.71. LCCN:00-455037.
Audience: **g,l,u,f.** *Choice, 2001.*

Perl, Jed　　　　　　　　　　**N6535.N5P46 2005**
New Art City: The Painters and Sculptors of Manhattan, 1950-1965. Trade Cloth. Alfred A. Knopf Inc. New York, NY. 2005. 641p. ISBN:1-4000-4131-7, ISBN13: 978-1-4000-4131-2. Dewey:700/.9747/109045. LCCN:2004-048846.
Audience: **g,l,u,f.** *Choice, 2006.*

Pohl, Frances K.　　　　　　　**N6512.P59 2002**
Framing America: A Social History of American Art. Trade Cloth. Thames & Hudson. New York, NY. 2002. 560p.

ISBN:0-500-23792-1, ISBN13: 978-0-500-23792-2.
Dewey:709/.73. LCCN:2001-093466.
Audience: **g,l,u,f.** *Choice, 2003.*

Poon, Irene   **N6538.A83P66 2001**
Leading the Way: Asian American Artists of the Older
Generation. Trade Paper. Gordon College. Wenham, MA. 2001
108p. ISBN:0-9707487-0-1, ISBN13: 978-0-9707487-0-6.
Dewey:704.03/95073. LCCN:2001-368910.
Audience: **g,l,u,f.** *Choice, 2002.*

Power, Susan C.   **E99.W84P69 2004**
Early Art of the Southeastern Indians: Feathered Serpents and
Winged Beings. Trade Cloth. University of Georgia Press.
Athens, GA. 2004. 288p. ISBN:0-8203-2501-5, ISBN13:
978-0-8203-2501-9. Dewey:704.03/97075. LCCN:2003-011151.
Audience: **g,l,u,f.** *Choice, 2004.*

Price, B. Byron   **TS1032.P73 2004**
Fine Art of the West. Trade Cloth. Abbeville Press, Inc. New
York, NY. 2004. 276p. ISBN:0-7892-0659-5, ISBN13:
978-0-7892-0659-6. Dewey:685/.1. LCCN:2004-047745.
Audience: **g,l,u,f.**

Rushing, W. Jackson   **NX512.3.A35**
(Editor)
Native American Art in the Twentieth Century: Makers,
Meanings and Histories. Trade Paper. Routledge. New York, NY.
1999. 252p. ISBN:0-415-13748-9, ISBN13: 978-0-415-13748-5.
Dewey:700.8/9. LCCN:98-048803.
Audience: **u,f.** *Choice, 2000.*

Simpson, Georgiana   **E99.N3S56 2003**
Kennedy
Navajo Ceremonial Baskets: Sacred Symbols, Sacred Space.
Trade Paper. Book Publishing Company, The. Summertown, TN.
2004. 160p. ISBN:1-57067-118-4, ISBN13: 978-1-57067-118-0.
Dewey:746.41/20899726. LCCN:2003-025512.
Audience: **g,l,u,f.** *Choice, 2004.*

Smithsonian American Art   **N6505.S55 2005**
Museum Staff & Slowik, Theresa J.
America's Art: Masterpieces from the Smithsonian American Art
Museum. Trade Cloth. Smithsonian American Art Museum.
Washington, DC. 2006. 324p. ISBN:0-8109-5532-6, ISBN13:
978-0-8109-5532-5. Dewey:709/.73/074753.
LCCN:2005-017164.
Audience: **g,l,u,f.**

Updike, John   **N6505.U54 2005**
Still Looking: Essays on American Art. Trade Cloth. Alfred A.
Knopf Inc. New York, NY. 2005. 240p. ISBN:1-4000-4418-9,
ISBN13: 978-1-4000-4418-4. Dewey:709/.73.
LCCN:2004-061568.
Audience: **g,l,u,f.** *Choice, 2005.*

Wardwell, Allen   **E78.N78W283 1996**
Tangible Visions: Northwest Coast Indian Shamanism and Its
Art. Trade Cloth. Monacelli Press, Inc. New York, NY. 1996.
352p. ISBN:1-885254-16-4, ISBN13: 978-1-885254-16-0.
Dewey:704/.03972. LCCN:95-024157.
Audience: **g,l,u,f.**

Weber, Nicholas Fox   **NX504.W431995**
Patron Saints: Five Rebels Who Opened America to a New Art,
1928-1943. Trade Paper. Yale University Press. Cumberland, RI.
1995. 416p. ISBN:0-300-06448-9, ISBN13: 978-0-300-06448-3.
Dewey:700/.973/09041. LCCN:95-061164.
Audience: **g,l,u,f.**

Visual Arts in General > Histories and Handbooks > Cultures, Regions, Nationalities > Latin America

                                         AP63
☐ Art.
http://lanic.utexas.edu/la/region/art/
Latin American Network Information Center, University of
Texas.
Audience: **g,l,u,f.**

Ades, Dawn (Editor)   **N6502.4.A3 1989**
Art in Latin America: The Modern Era, 1820-1980. Guy Brett,
Stanton L. Catlin & Rosemary O'Neill (Contribution by). Trade
Paper. Yale University Press. Cumberland, RI. 1993. 384p. Art -
Latin American Studies ISBN:0-300-04561-1, ISBN13:
978-0-300-04561-1. Dewey:709/.8/09034. LCCN:89-050603.
Audience: **g,l,u,f.** *Choice, 1990.*

Bailey, Gauvin Alexander   **N6502**
The Art of Colonial Latin America. Trade Paper. Phaidon Press.
London, 2005. 448p. Art and Ideas Ser. ISBN:0-7148-4157-9,
ISBN13: 978-0-7148-4157-1. Dewey:709.80903.
LCCN:2006-531006.
Audience: **g,l,u,f.** *Choice, 2005.*

Barnitz, Jacqueline   **N6502.5.B36 2001**
Twentieth-Century Art of Latin America. Trade Cloth.
University of Texas Press. Austin, TX. 2001. 424p.
ISBN:0-292-70857-2, ISBN13: 978-0-292-70857-0.
Dewey:709/.8/0904. LCCN:99-050871.
Audience: **g,l,u,f.** *Choice, 2001.*

Bay'on, Dami'an   **N6620.B3913 1992**
History of South American Colonial Art and Architecture:
Spanish South American and Brazil. Marx, Murillo. Rizzoli.
1992. ISBN:0-8478-1555-2, ISBN13: 978-0-8478-1555-5.
Audience: **g,l,u,f.**

Boone, Elizabeth Hill   **F1219.54.A98B66 2000**
Stories in Red and Black: Pictorial Histories of the Aztec and
Mixtec. Trade Cloth. University of Texas Press. Austin, TX.
2000. 312p. ISBN:0-292-70876-9, ISBN13: 978-0-292-70876-1.
Dewey:972/.01. LCCN:99-006214.
Audience: **l,u,f.** *Choice, 2000.*

Braun, Barbara & Roe,   **F2519.1.A6A77 1995**
Peter
Arts of the Amazon. Trade Paper. Thames & Hudson. New
York, NY. 1995. 128p. ISBN:0-500-27824-5, ISBN13:
978-0-500-27824-6. Dewey:745/.089/980811. LCCN:94-061400.
Audience: **g,l,u,f.**

Camnitzer, Luis   **N6603.C26 2003**
New Art of Cuba. Ed. 2. Trade Paper. University of Texas Press. Austin, TX. 2003. 456p. Joe R. and Teresa Lozano Long Series in Latin American and Latino Art and Culture ISBN:0-292-70517-4, ISBN13: 978-0-292-70517-3. Dewey:709/.7291/09048. LCCN:2002-032061.
Audience: **g,l,u,f.** *Choice, 1994.*

Congdon, Kristin G. &   **N6502**
Hallmark, Kara Kelley
Artists from Latin American Cultures: A Biographical Dictionary. Cloth Text. Greenwood Publishing Group, Inc. Portsmouth, NH. 2002. 344p. ISBN:0-313-31544-2, ISBN13: 978-0-313-31544-2. Dewey:709/.2/368 B. LCCN:2001-058345.
Audience: **g,l,u,f.** *Choice, 2003.*

Craven, David   **N6502.C735 2002**
Art and Revolution in Latin America, 1910-1990. Cloth over Boards. Yale University Press. Cumberland, RI. 2002. 240p. ISBN:0-300-08211-8, ISBN13: 978-0-300-08211-1. Dewey:709/.8/0904. LCCN:2001-006900.
Audience: **g,l,u,f.**

Durand, Jorge & Massey,   **ND1432.M46D87 1995**
Douglas S.
Miracles on the Border: Retablos of Mexican Migrants to the United States. Library Binding. University of Arizona Press. Tucson, AZ. 1995. 216p. ISBN:0-8165-1471-2, ISBN13: 978-0-8165-1471-7. Dewey:755/.2. LCCN:94-032080.
Audience: **u,f.** *Choice, 1995.*

Fernandez De Calderon,   **NK844**
Candida
Great Masters of Mexican Folk Art. Alberto Sarmiento (Editor). Trade Cloth. Harry N. Abrams, Inc. New York, NY. 2001. 552p. ISBN:0-8109-6745-6, ISBN13: 978-0-8109-6745-8. Dewey:745/.0972/0904. LCCN:2001-090194.
Audience: **g,l,u,f.** *Choice, 2002.*

Fields, Virginia M. &   **F1435.3.A7**
Reents-Budet, Dorie
Lords of Creation: The Origins of Sacred Maya Kingship. Trade Cloth. Scala Publishers, Ltd. London, 2005. 288p. ISBN:1-85759-386-3, ISBN13: 978-1-85759-386-0. Dewey:709.7281. LCCN:2005-482050.
Audience: **g,l,u,f.** *Choice, 2006.*

Frank, Patrick (Editor)   **N6502.5.R43 2004**
Readings in Latin American Modern Art. Trade Paper. Yale University Press. Cumberland, RI. 2004. 288p. ISBN:0-300-10255-0, ISBN13: 978-0-300-10255-0. Dewey:709/.8/0904. LCCN:2003-023857.
Audience: **l,u,f.**

Lucie-Smith, Edward   **N6502.5**
Latin American Art of the 20th Century. Ed. 2. Trade Paper. Thames & Hudson. New York, NY. 2004. 224p. World of Art Ser. ISBN:0-500-20356-3, ISBN13: 978-0-500-20356-9. Dewey:709.8/0904. LCCN:2002-109034.
Audience: **g,l,u,f.** *Choice, 1993.*

McMenamin, Donna   **NK844.M383 1996**
Popular Arts of Mexico: 1850-1950. Trade Cloth. Schiffer Publishing, Ltd. Atglen, PA. 1996. 240p. ISBN:0-7643-0026-1, ISBN13: 978-0-7643-0026-4. Dewey:745/.0972/075. LCCN:96-017798.
Audience: **g,l,u,f.**

Miller, Mary E.   **F1219.3.A7M551996**
The Art of MesoAmerica: From Olmec to Aztec. Ed. 2. Trade Paper. Thames & Hudson. New York, NY. 1996. 240p. The World of Art Ser. ISBN:0-500-20290-7, ISBN13: 978-0-500-20290-6. Dewey:709.7/2. LCCN:95-070510.
Audience: **g,l,u,f.**

Miller, Mary Ellen   **F1219.3.A7M55 2001**
The Art of Mesoamerica: From Olmec to Aztec. Ed. 3. Trade Paper. Thames & Hudson. New York, NY. 2001. 240p. World of Art Ser. ISBN:0-500-20345-8, ISBN13: 978-0-500-20345-3. Dewey:709.7/2. LCCN:2001-087365.
Audience: **g,l,u,f.**

Mulryan, Lenore Hoag   **NK4031.M849 2003**
Ceramic Trees of Life: Popular Art from Mexico. Delia A. Cosentino (Contribution by). Trade Cloth. University of California Los Angeles, Fowler Museum of Cultural History. Los Angeles, CA. 2004. 168p. ISBN:0-930741-96-X, ISBN13: 978-0-930741-96-9. Dewey:738.8. LCCN:2003-042621.
Audience: **g,l,u,f.** *Choice, 2004.*

Paz, Octavio (Introduction   **N6550.M48 1990**
by)
Mexico: Splendors of Thirty Centuries. Trade Cloth. Bulfinch Press. Boston, MA. 1990. 728p. ISBN:0-8212-1797-6, ISBN13: 978-0-8212-1797-9. Dewey:709/.72/0747471. LCCN:90-038083.
Audience: **g,l,u,f.**

Poupeye, Veerle   **N6591.P68 1998**
Caribbean Art. Trade Paper. Thames & Hudson. New York, NY. 1998. 224p. World of Art Ser. ISBN:0-500-20306-7, ISBN13: 978-0-500-20306-4. Dewey:709/.729. LCCN:97-060254.
Audience: **g,l,u,f.** *Choice, 1998.*

Schele, Linda & Miller,   **F1435.3.A7 S34**
Mary Ellen
Blood of Kings: Dynasty and Ritual in Maya Art. Trade Paper. George Braziller Inc. New York, NY. 1992. 336p. ISBN:0-8076-1278-2, ISBN13: 978-0-8076-1278-1. Dewey:704.9097281. LCCN:86-080193.
Audience: **g,l,u,f.**

Scott, John F.   **N6502.S367 1999**
Latin American Art: Ancient to Modern. Trade Cloth. University Press of Florida. Gainesville, FL. 1999. 488p. ISBN:0-8130-1645-2, ISBN13: 978-0-8130-1645-0. Dewey:709/.8. LCCN:98-046535.
Audience: **g,l,u,f.** *Choice, 2000.*

Shipp, Steve   **N6502.4.S452002**
Latin American and Caribbean Artists of the Modern Era: A Biographical Dictionary of over 10,000 Persons. Cloth Text. McFarland & Company, Incorporated Publishers. Jefferson, NC.

2003. 916p. ISBN:0-7864-1057-4, ISBN13: 978-0-7864-1057-6. Dewey:704.03/68 B. LCCN:2002-013828.

Audience: **g,l,u,f.** *Choice, 2003.*

Shorts, Don Allen N6558
1200 Mexican Artists: An Identification Guide to Painters, Graphic Artist, Sculptors and Photographers. Trade Paper. Old California Press, The. Ventura, CA. 2002. 206p. ISBN:0-9720332-0-3, ISBN13: 978-0-9720332-0-6. Dewey:780.7.

Audience: **g,l,u,f.**

Stone-Miller, Rebecca F2230.1
Art of the Andes: From Chavin to Inca. Ed. 2. Trade Paper. Thames & Hudson. New York, NY. 2002. 224p. The World of Art Ser. ISBN:0-500-20363-6, ISBN13: 978-0-500-20363-7. Dewey:709.8. LCCN:2002-101747.

Audience: **g,l,f.**

Visual Arts in General > Histories and Handbooks > Cultures, Regions, Nationalities > Europe

Arnold, Bruce N6782 .A8
Concise History of Irish Art. Trade Cloth. Thames & Hudson. New York, NY. 1985. 216p. ISBN:0-500-18090-3, ISBN13: 978-0-500-18090-7. Dewey:709.415.

Audience: **g,l,u,f.**

Arnold, Bruce N6782
Irish Art. Ed. 2. Trade Paper. Thames & Hudson. New York, NY. 1989. 180p. World of Art Ser. ISBN:0-500-20148-X, ISBN13: 978-0-500-20148-0. Dewey:709/.415. LCCN:89-051262.

Audience: **g,l,u,f.**

Bann, Stephen NE647.3.B36 2001
Parallel Lines: Printmakers, Painters and Photographers in 19th Century France. Cloth over Boards. Yale University Press. Cumberland, RI. 2001. 264p. ISBN:0-300-08932-5, ISBN13: 978-0-300-08932-5. Dewey:769.944/09/034. LCCN:00-048588.

Audience: **g,l,u,f.** *Choice, 2002.*

Beard, Mary & Henderson, N5610.B295 2001
John
Classical Art: From Greece to Rome. Trade Paper. Oxford University Press, Inc. New York, NY. 2001. 304p. Oxford History of Art Ser. ISBN:0-19-284237-4, ISBN13: 978-0-19-284237-4. Dewey:709/.38. LCCN:2001-269631.

Audience: **g,l,u,f.**

Bell, Janis & Willette, N7483.B375B45 2002
Thomas (Editors)
Art History in the Age of Bellori: Scholarship and Cultural Politics in Seventeenth-Century Rome. Trade Cloth. Cambridge University Press. New York, NY. 2002. 412p. ISBN:0-521-78248-1, ISBN13: 978-0-521-78248-7. Dewey:709/.2 B. LCCN:2001-035675.

Audience: **l,u,f.** *Choice, 2003.*

Blunt, Anthony N6845.B591999
Art and Architecture in France, 1500-1700. Ed. 5. Richard Beresford (Revised by). Trade Paper. Yale University Press. Cumberland, RI. 1999. 332p. Pelican History of Art Ser. ISBN:0-300-07748-3, ISBN13: 978-0-300-07748-3. Dewey:709/.44. LCCN:98-023229.

Audience: **g,l,u,f.**

Boardman, John N5630.B58 1996
Greek Art. Ed. 4. Trade Paper. Thames & Hudson. New York, NY. 1996. 304p. The World of Art Ser. ISBN:0-500-20292-3, ISBN13: 978-0-500-20292-0. Dewey:709/.38. LCCN:96-060184.

Audience: **g,l,u,f.**

Boehm, Barbara Drake & N6833.P72P73 2005
Fajt, Jiri (Editors)
Prague, the Crown of Bohemia, 1347-1437. Saddle Stitched, Cloth over Boards, Dust Jacket. Yale University Press. Cumberland, RI. 2005. 384p. Metropolitan Museum of Art Ser. ISBN:0-300-11138-X, ISBN13: 978-0-300-11138-5. Dewey:709/.4371/20747471. LCCN:2005-022954.

Audience: **g,l,u,f.** *Choice, 2006.*

Borsi, Franco NA1010.V5
Vienna, 1900. Trade Paper. Harry N. Abrams, Inc. New York, NY. 1998. 264p. ISBN:0-8109-6106-7, ISBN13: 978-0-8109-6106-7. Dewey:720/.9436/13.

Audience: **g,l,u,f.**

Bowness, Alan N6450
Modern European Art: Impressionism to Abstract Art. Trade Paper. Thames & Hudson. New York, NY. 1995. 224p. The World of Art Ser. ISBN:0-500-20205-2, ISBN13: 978-0-500-20205-0. Dewey:709/.034. LCCN:95-060189.

Audience: **g,l,u,f.**

Bowron, Edgar Peters N6920
Art in Rome in the Eighteenth Century. Rishel, Joseph J.. Rizzoli International Publications. 2000. ISBN:1-85894-098-2, ISBN13: 978-1-85894-098-4.

Audience: **l,u,f.**

Brendel, Otto J. N5750.B671995
Etruscan Art. Ed. 2. Trade Paper. Yale University Press. Cumberland, RI. 1995. 536p. Pelican History of Art Ser. ISBN:0-300-06446-2, ISBN13: 978-0-300-06446-9. Dewey:709.3/75. LCCN:95-015894.

Audience: **g,l,u,f.** *B*

Brown, Patricia Fortini NK1452.V4B76 2004
Private Lives in Renaissance Venice: Art, Architecture, and the Family. Cloth over Boards. Yale University Press. Cumberland, RI. 2004. 320p. ISBN:0-300-10236-4, ISBN13: 978-0-300-10236-9. Dewey:306.4/7/08621094531. LCCN:2003-018889.

Audience: **g,l,u,f.** *Choice, 2005.*

Bruyn, J., et al. N6945.D3313 1993
Dawn of the Golden Age: Northern Netherlandish Art, 1580-1620. Wouter T. Kloek, G. Luijten, Hessel Miedema, Marten J. Bok, Nadine M. Orenstein, Huigen Leetland & Christian Schuckman (Authors). Cloth over Boards. Yale

University Press. Cumberland, RI. 1994. 718p.
ISBN:0-300-06016-5, ISBN13: 978-0-300-06016-4.
Dewey:709/.492/074492352. LCCN:94-231874.

Audience: **g,l,u,f.** *Choice, 1994.*

Bullen, J. B.   **N6447**
Byzantium Rediscovered. Trade Paper. Phaidon Press, Inc. New
York, NY. 2006. 240p. ISBN:0-7148-4638-4, ISBN13:
978-0-7148-4638-5. Dewey:709.034.

Audience: **g,l,u,f.**

Campbell, Stephen &   **N6915.A743 2004**
  Milner, Stephen (Editors)
Artistic Exchange and Cultural Translation in the Italian
Renaissance City. Trade Cloth. Cambridge University Press.
New York, NY. 2004. 386p. ISBN:0-521-82688-8, ISBN13:
978-0-521-82688-4. Dewey:709/.45/09024. LCCN:2003-062976.

Audience: **l,u,f.** *Choice, 2005.*

Chu, Petra ten-Doesschate   **N6757.C484 2006**
Nineteenth-Century European Art. Ed. 2. Trade Paper. Prentice
Hall PTR. Upper Saddle River, NJ. 2006. 560p.
ISBN:0-13-188643-6, ISBN13: 978-0-13-188643-8.
Dewey:709/.034. LCCN:2005-048290.

Audience: **g,l,u,f.** *Choice, 2003.*

Clayson, Hollis   **N6847.5.I4C58 2003**
Painted Love: Prostitution in French Art of the Impressionist
Era. Trade Paper. Oxford University Press, Inc. New York, NY.
2003. 224p. Texts and Documents Ser. ISBN:0-89236-729-6,
ISBN13: 978-0-89236-729-0. Dewey:757/.4/094409034.
LCCN:2003-108454.

Audience: **l,u,f.** *Choice, 1992.*

Clegg, Elizabeth   **N6757.C622006**
From Secession to Reinvention: Art, Design, and Architecture in
Central Europe 1890-1920. Cloth over Boards. Yale University
Press. Cumberland, RI. 1959. 356p. Pelican History of Art Ser.
ISBN:0-300-11120-7, ISBN13: 978-0-300-11120-0.
Dewey:709/.436/09034. LCCN:2005-017837.

Audience: **l,u,f.**

Codell, Julie F.   **N6767.5.V52C632003**
The Victorian Artist: Artists' Lifewritings in Britain, c.
1870-1910. Trade Cloth. Cambridge University Press. New
York, NY. 2003. 392p. ISBN:0-521-81757-9, ISBN13:
978-0-521-81757-8. Dewey:709/.41/09034. LCCN:2002-074196.

Audience: **l,u,f.** *Choice, 2004.*

Craske, Matthew   **N6756.C73 1997**
Art in Europe, 1700-1830. Trade Paper. Oxford University
Press, Inc. New York, NY. 1997. 320p. Oxford History of Art
Ser. ISBN:0-19-284206-4, ISBN13: 978-0-19-284206-0.
Dewey:709.409033. LCCN:96-037917.

Audience: **g,l,u,f.** *Choice, 1997.*

D'Ambra, Eve   **N5760 .D435 1998**
Roman Art. Trade Paper. Cambridge University Press. New
York, NY. 1998. 176p. ISBN:0-521-64463-1, ISBN13:
978-0-521-64463-1. Dewey:709.3/7. LCCN:99-166514.

Audience: **g,l,u,f.** *Choice, 1999.*

Dawkins, Heather   **N6847 .D34 2002**
The Nude in French Art and Culture, 1870-1910. Trade Cloth.
Cambridge University Press. New York, NY. 2002. 244p.
ISBN:0-521-80755-7, ISBN13: 978-0-521-80755-5.
Dewey:757/.4/094409034. LCCN:2001-025499.

Audience: **l,u,f.**

De Montclos, Jean-Marie   **N6850.P44513 2003**
  Pérouse
Paris, City of Art. Trade Cloth. Vendome Press, The. New York,
NY. 2003. 708p. ISBN:0-86565-226-0, ISBN13:
978-0-86565-226-2. Dewey:709/.44/361. LCCN:2003-053498.

Audience: **g,l,u,f.** *Choice, 2004.*

Delaforce, Angela   **N6846 .D34 2002**
Art and Patronage in Eighteenth-Century Portugal. Trade Cloth.
Cambridge University Press. New York, NY. 2002. 532p.
ISBN:0-521-57130-8, ISBN13: 978-0-521-57130-2.
Dewey:707/.9/469. LCCN:2001-025426.

Audience: **l,u,f.** *Choice, 2002.*

Dodds, Jerrilynn D. (Editor)   **N7103.A41992**
Al-Andalus: The Art of Islamic Spain. Metropolitan Museum of
Art Staff & Patronato de la Alhambra (Contribution by). Trade
Cloth. Metropolitan Museum of Art, The. New York, NY. 1992.
432p. ISBN:0-87099-636-3, ISBN13: 978-0-87099-636-8.
Dewey:709/.46/80747471 20. LCCN:91-041335.

Audience: **g,l,u,f.**

Elsner, J. R.   **N5760.E484 1998**
Imperial Rome and Christian Triumph: The Art of the Roman
Empire AD 100-450. Trade Paper. Oxford University Press, Inc.
New York, NY. 1998. 320p. Oxford History of Art Ser.
ISBN:0-19-284201-3, ISBN13: 978-0-19-284201-5.
Dewey:709.3/7/09015. LCCN:99-189358.

Audience: **g,l,u,f.**

Evans, Helen C. (Editor)   **N6250.B962 2004**
Byzantium: Faith and Power (1261-1557). Metropolitan
Museum of Art Staff (Contribution by). Cloth over Boards. Yale
University Press. Cumberland, RI. 2004. 680p. Metropolitan
Museum of Art Ser. ISBN:0-300-10278-X, ISBN13:
978-0-300-10278-9. Dewey:709/.495/0747471.
LCCN:2004-001565.

Audience: **l,u,f.** *Choice, 2004.*

Facos, Michelle & Hirsh,   **N72.N38A77 2003**
  Sharon (Editors)
Art, Culture and National Identity in Fin-de-Siecle Europe.
Trade Cloth. Cambridge University Press. New York, NY. 2003.
314p. ISBN:0-521-81565-7, ISBN13: 978-0-521-81565-9.
Dewey:704.9/4932054. LCCN:2002-031394.

Audience: **l,u,f.** *Choice, 2004.*

Foister, Susan & Holbein,   **N6888.H664F65 2004**
  Hans
Holbein and England. Cloth over Boards. Yale University Press.
Cumberland, RI. 2005. 320p. Studies in British Art Ser.
ISBN:0-300-10280-1, ISBN13: 978-0-300-10280-2.
Dewey:759.3. LCCN:2004-002274.

Audience: **l,u,f.** *Choice, 2005.*

Fullerton, Mark D.   N5630 .F85 2000
Greek Art. Trade Paper. Cambridge University Press. New York, NY. 1999. 176p. ISBN:0-521-77973-1, ISBN13: 978-0-521-77973-9. Dewey:709/.38. LCCN:00-500521.
Audience: **l,u,f.** *Choice, 2000.*

Green, Christopher   N6848.G73200
Art in France, 1900-1940. Cloth over Boards. Yale University Press. Cumberland, RI. 2001. 336p. Pelican History of Art Ser. ISBN:0-300-08401-3, ISBN13: 978-0-300-08401-6. Dewey:709.44/09041. LCCN:99-089522.
Audience: **g,l,u,l**

Hall, Marcia B. (Editor,   N6920.R657 2005
   Contribution by)
Rome. Trade Cloth. Cambridge University Press. New York, NY. 2005. 398p. Artistic Centers of the Italian Renaissance Ser. ISBN:0-521-62445-2, ISBN13: 978-0-521-62445-9. Dewey:709/.45/63. LCCN:2004-054607.
Audience: **l,u,f.** *Choice, 2005.*

Hamilton, George H.   N6988
The Art and Architecture of Russia. Ed. 3. Trade Paper. Yale University Press. Cumberland, RI. 1992. 482p. Pelican History of Art Ser. ISBN:0-300-05327-4, ISBN13: 978-0-300-05327-2. Dewey:709/.47.
Audience: **g,l,u,f.** *B*

Hamilton, George H.   N6757.5.M63H3C1993
Painting and Sculpture in Europe: 1880-1940. Ed. 4. Trade Paper. Yale University Press. Cumberland, RI. 1989. 610p. Pelican History of Art Ser. ISBN:0-300-05649-4, ISBN13: 978-0-300-05649-5. Dewey:759.94. LCCN:94-119000.
Audience: **g,l,u,l** *B*

Harbison, Craig   N6370
Northern Renaissance Art. Trade Cloth. Prentice Hall PTR. Upper Saddle River, NJ. 2007. 500p. ISBN:0-13-118291-5, ISBN13: 978-0-13-118291-2. Dewey:709/.02/4.
Audience: **g,l,u,f.**

Hartt, Frederick   N6915
History of Italian Renaissance Art. Ed. 5. Trade Cloth. Prentice Hall Art. Upper Saddle River, NJ. 2002. 696p. ISBN:0-13-183251-4, ISBN13: 978-0-13-183251-0. Dewey:709.45/09024.
Audience: **g,l,u,f.**

Henderson, George   N7943.A1 H46 1999
Vision and Image in Early Christian England. Trade Cloth. Cambridge University Press. New York, NY. 1999. 310p. ISBN:0-521-55130-7, ISBN13: 978-0-521-55130-4. Dewey:709/.42/09021. LCCN:98-020183.
Audience: **l,u,f.** *Choice, 2000.*

Higgins, Reynold   N5660.H5 1997
Minoan and Mycenaean Art. Ed. 2. Lyvia Morgan (Revised by). Trade Paper. Thames & Hudson. New York, NY. 1997. 216p. World of Art Ser. ISBN:0-500-20303-2, ISBN13: 978-0-500-20303-3. Dewey:709.3/918. LCCN:97-060252.
Audience: **g,l,u,f.**

Holloway, R. Ross   NA5620.A1H65 2004
Constantine and Rome. Cloth over Boards. Yale University Press. Cumberland, RI. 2004. 208p. ISBN:0-300-10043-4, ISBN13: 978-0-300-10043-3. Dewey:722/.7. LCCN:2003-018712.
Audience: **u,f.** *Choice, 2004.*

Holt, Elizabeth G. (Editor)   N5300
From the Classicists to the Impressionists: Art and Architecture in the Nineteenth Century. Ed. 2. Cloth over Boards. Yale University Press. Cumberland, RI. 1986. 555p. Documentary History of Art Ser., Vol. III ISBN:0-300-03358-3, ISBN13: 978-0-300-03358-8. Dewey:709/.03/4. LCCN:85-051918.
Audience: **l,u,f.**

Hood, Sinclair   N5630
The Arts in Prehistoric Greece. Trade Paper. Yale University Press. Cumberland, RI. 1992. 311p. Pelican History of Art Ser. ISBN:0-300-05287-1, ISBN13: 978-0-300-05287-9. Dewey:709.3/8.
Audience: **g,l,u,f.**

Hourihane, Colum (Editor)   N6784.F76 2001
From Ireland Coming: Irish Art from the Early Christian to the Late Gothic Period and Its European Context. Trade Paper. Princeton University Press. Princeton, NJ. 2001. 392p. Occasional Papers - Index of Christian Art, Vol. 4 ISBN:0-691-08825-X, ISBN13: 978-0-691-08825-9. Dewey:709/.415. LCCN:00-062375.
Audience: **l,u,f.**

Huse, Norbert & Wolters,   N6921.V5
   Wolfgang
The Art of Renaissance Venice: Architecture, Sculpture, and Painting, 1460-1590. Edmund Jephcott (Translator). Trade Paper. University of Chicago Press. Chicago, IL. 1993. 390p. ISBN:0-226-36109-8, ISBN13: 978-0-226-36109-3. Dewey:709.4531.
Audience: **l,u,f.**

Kaufmann, Thomas   N6754.K38 1995
   DaCosta
Court, Cloister, and City: The Art and Culture of Central Europe, 1450-1800. Trade Cloth. University of Chicago Press. Chicago, IL. 1995. 576p. ISBN:0-226-42729-3, ISBN13: 978-0-226-42729-4. Dewey:709/.43/0903. LCCN:95-010237.
Audience: **g,l,u,f.** *Choice, 1996.*

Kent, Neil   N7006.K4
The Triumph of Light and Nature: Nordic Art 1740-1940. Trade Paper. Thames & Hudson. New York, NY. 1992. 240p. ISBN:0-500-27659-5, ISBN13: 978-0-500-27659-4. Dewey:709.48. LCCN:87-050060.
Audience: **g,l,u,f.** *Choice, 1988.*

Keyes, George S. (Editor)   N8230 .K49 1990
Mirror of Empire: Dutch Marine Art of the Seventeenth Century. Cloth Text. Cambridge University Press. New York, NY. 1990. 458p. ISBN:0-521-39328-0, ISBN13: 978-0-521-39328-7. Dewey:760/.04437/094920747. LCCN:90-001492.
Audience: **l,u,f.** *Choice, 1991.*

Koerner, Joseph L.   ND588.D9K82

The Moment of Self-Portraiture in German Renaissance Art.
Trade Paper. University of Chicago Press. Chicago, IL. 1997.
564p. ISBN:0-226-44999-8, ISBN13: 978-0-226-44999-9.
Dewey:759.3.

                              Audience: **l,u,f.** *Choice, 1994.*

Laing, Lloyd Robert &   N5604.S65
  Laing, Jennifer

Art of the Celts: From 700 B.C. to the Celtic Revival. Trade
Paper. Thames & Hudson. New York, NY. 1992. 216p. World of
Art Ser. ISBN:0-500-20256-7, ISBN13: 978-0-500-20256-2.
Dewey:709/.014. LCCN:91-066018.

                              Audience: **g,l,u,f.**

Levey, Michael   N6846.L461993

Painting and Sculpture in France, 1700-1789. Cloth over
Boards. Yale University Press. Cumberland, RI. 1993. 332p.
Pelican History of Art Ser. ISBN:0-300-05344-4, ISBN13:
978-0-300-05344-9. Dewey:759.4/09033. LCCN:92-032503.

                              Audience: **g,l,u,f.** *Choice, 1993.*

Male, Emile   N7949.A1M3513 2000

Religious Art in France of the 13th Century. Trade Paper. Dover
Publications, Inc. Mineola, NY. 2000. 442p.
ISBN:0-486-41061-7, ISBN13: 978-0-486-41061-6.
Dewey:704.9/482/094409022. LCCN:00-026393.

                              Audience: **g,l,u,f.**

Mansbach, S. A.   N6758.M3521999

Modern Art in Eastern Europe: From the Baltic to the Balkans,
ca. 1890-1939. Ronald H. Wainscott (Contribution by). Cloth
Text. Cambridge University Press. New York, NY. 1998. 400p.
ISBN:0-521-45085-3, ISBN13: 978-0-521-45085-0.
Dewey:709/.47/0904. LCCN:97-042894.

                              Audience: **g,u,f.** *Choice, 1999.*

Martineau, Jane & Robison,   N6921.V5G57 1994
  Andrew (Editors)

The Glory of Venice: Art in the Eighteenth Century. Trade
Paper. Yale University Press. Cumberland, RI. 1997. 528p.
ISBN:0-300-06186-2, ISBN13: 978-0-300-06186-4.
Dewey:709/.45/3107442132. LCCN:94-061010.

                              Audience: **g,l,u,f.**

Moffitt, John F.   NX562.A1M65 1999

The Arts of Spain: From Prehistory to Postmodernism. Trade
Paper. Thames & Hudson. New York, NY. 1999. 240p. World of
Art Ser. ISBN:0-500-20315-6, ISBN13: 978-0-500-20315-6.
Dewey:709/.46. LCCN:98-060192.

                              Audience: **g,l,u,f.** *Choice, 1999.*

Murray, Linda   N6374 .M87 1977B

High Renaissance and Mannerism: Italy, the North and Spain,
1500-1600. Trade Paper. Thames & Hudson. New York, NY.
1985. 288p. World of Art Library ISBN:0-500-20162-5,
ISBN13: 978-0-500-20162-6. Dewey:709/.03/1.
LCCN:78-322258.

                              Audience: **g,l,u,f.**

Murray, Peter & Murray,   N6370.M97 1985
  Linda

The Art of the Renaissance. Trade Paper. Thames & Hudson.
New York, NY. 1985. 288p. World of Art Ser.
ISBN:0-500-20008-4, ISBN13: 978-0-500-20008-7.
Dewey:709/.02/4. LCCN:84-051305.

                              Audience: **g,l,u,f.**

Olson, Roberta J. M. &   N6766 .O45 1998
  Pasachoff, Jay M.

Fire in the Sky: Comets and Meteors, the Decisive Centuries, in
British Art and Science. Colin T. Pillinger (Epilogue by). Trade
Cloth. Cambridge University Press. New York, NY. 1998. 383p.
ISBN:0-521-63060-6, ISBN13: 978-0-521-63060-3.
Dewey:704.9/49/52360941. LCCN:97-046513.

                              Audience: **g,l,u,f.** *Choice, 1998.*

Paoletti, John T. & Radke,   N6915.P26 2005
  Gary M.

Art in Renaissance Italy. Ed. 3. Trade Paper. Prentice Hall PTR.
Upper Saddle River, NJ. 2005. 544p. ISBN:0-13-193510-0,
ISBN13: 978-0-13-193510-5. Dewey:709/.45/09024.
LCCN:2005-043146.

                              Audience: **g,l,u,f.**

Rogoff, Irit (Editor)   N6868.5.M63 D58 1990

The Divided Heritage: Themes and Problems in German
Modernism. Trade Cloth. Cambridge University Press. New
York, NY. 1991. 406p. ISBN:0-521-34553-7, ISBN13:
978-0-521-34553-8. Dewey:709.43/09/04. LCCN:89-035777.

                              Audience: **u,f.** *Choice, 1992.*

Rosenberg, Jakob, et al.   ND646

Dutch Art and Architecture: 1600-1800. Ed. 3. Seymour Slive &
E. H. Ter Kuile (Authors). Trade Paper. Yale University Press.
Cumberland, RI. 1987. 502p. Pelican History of Art Ser.
ISBN:0-300-05312-6, ISBN13: 978-0-300-05312-8.
Dewey:709.492.

                              Audience: **g,l,u,f.**

Salomon, Nanette   ND1452.N43S24 2004

Shifting Priorities: Gender and Genre in Seventeenth-Century
Dutch Painting. Trade Cloth. Stanford University Press. Palo
Alto, CA. 2004. 280p. Cultural Memory in the Present Ser.
ISBN:0-8047-4476-9, ISBN13: 978-0-8047-4476-8.
Dewey:754/.09492/09032. LCCN:2003-025165.

                              Audience: **g,l,u,f.**

Sarabianov, Dmitri V.   N6987.S271990

Russian Art from Neoclassicism to the Avant-Garde, 1800-1917:
Painting, Sculpture, Architecture. Trade Cloth. Harry N. Abrams,
Inc. New York, NY. 1990. 320p. ISBN:0-8109-3750-6, ISBN13:
978-0-8109-3750-5. Dewey:709.47/09/034. LCCN:89-035254.

                              Audience: **g,l,u,f.** *Choice, 1990.*

Snyder, James   N6370.S6 2005

Northern Renaissance Art: Painting, Sculpture, the Graphic Arts
from 1350 to 1575. Ed. 2. Trade Cloth. Prentice Hall Art. Upper
Saddle River, NJ. 2004. 592p. ISBN:0-13-150547-5, ISBN13:
978-0-13-150547-6. Dewey:709.024. LCCN:2004-044701.

                              Audience: **g,l,u,f.**

Spalding, Frances   **N676**
British Art since 1900. Trade Paper. Thames & Hudson. New
York, NY. 1986. 252p. World of Art Ser. ISBN:0-500-20204-4,
ISBN13: 978-0-500-20204-3. Dewey:709/.41. LCCN:85-05111.
Audience: **g,l,u,f**

Vasari, Giorgio   **N6923.V32 V37 1998**
Vasari's Florence: Artists and Literati at the Medicean Court.
Philip Jacks (Editor). Trade Cloth. Cambridge University Press.
New York, NY. 1998. 336p. ISBN:0-521-58088-9, ISBN13:
978-0-521-58088-5. Dewey:709/.2. LCCN:96-046902.
Audience: **g,l,u,f**. *Choice, 1999.*

Vlieghe, Hans   **N6935.V581998**
Flemish Art and Architecture, 1585-1700. Cloth over Boards.
Yale University Press. Cumberland, RI. 1999. 348p. Pelican
History of Art Ser. ISBN:0-300-07038-1, ISBN13:
978-0-300-07038-5. Dewey:709/.493/09032. LCCN:98-00413.
Audience: **g,l,u,f**. *Choice, 1999.*

Von der Osten, Gert & Vey,   **N6925.O813**
  Horst
Painting and Sculpture in Germany and the Netherlands,
1500-1600. Trade Cloth. Yale University Press. Cumberland, RI.
1979. 296p. Pelican History of Art Ser. ISBN:0-300-05311-3,
ISBN13: 978-0-300-05311-1. Dewey:759.3.
Audience: **g,,u,f**

Von Kalnein, Wend   **NA1046.K351995**
Architecture in France in the Eighteenth Century. David Britt
(Translator). Cloth over Boards. Yale University Press.
Cumberland, RI. 1995. 308p. Pelican History of Art Ser.
ISBN:0-300-06013-0, ISBN13: 978-0-300-06013-3.
Dewey:720/.944/09033. LCCN:94-049720.
Audience: **g,l,u,f**. *Choice, 1995.*

Welch, Evelyn   **N6915**
Art in Renaissance Italy: 1350-1500. Trade Paper. Oxford
University Press, Inc. New York, NY. 2001. 354p. Oxford
History of Art Ser. ISBN:0-19-284279-X, ISBN13:
978-0-19-284279-4. Dewey:709.4/5/09024.
Audience **g,l,u,f**

White, John   **N6915.V451993**
Art and Architecture in Italy: 1250-1400. Ed. 3. Trade Paper.
Yale University Press. Cumberland, RI. 1973. 688p. Pelican
History of Art Ser. ISBN:0-300-05585-4, ISBN13:
978-0-300-05585-6. Dewey:709/.45/09022. LCCN:93-93815.
Audience: **g,l,u,f**

Woodford, Susan   **N5610.W6 2004**
The Art of Greece and Rome. Ed. 2. Trade Paper. Cambridge
University Press. New York, NY. 2004. 186p.
ISBN:0-521-54037-2, ISBN13: 978-0-521-54037-7.
Dewey:709/.38. LCCN:2003-069663.
Audience: **g,l,u,f**. *Choice, 2005.*

Visual Arts in General > Histories and Handbooks > Cultures, Regions, Nationalities > Africa

                                        N5350.E37 1999
Egyptian Art in the Age of the Pyramids. Metropolitan Museum
of Art, New York, NY; Distributed by H. N. Abrams. 1999.
ISBN:0-87099-906-0, ISBN13: 978-0-87099-906-2.
Audience: **g,l,u,f**

Abiodun, Rowland, et al.   **N7380.H54 2001**
A History of Art in Africa. Monica Blackmun Visoná, Suzanne
Preston Blier, Herbert M. Cole, Michael D. Harris & Robin
Poynor (Authors). Trade Paper. Prentice Hall PTR. Upper
Saddle River, NJ. 2000. 448p. ISBN:0-13-442187-6, ISBN13:
978-0-13-442187-2. Dewey:709/.6. LCCN:00-022796.
Audience: **g,l,u,f**

Aldred, Cyril   **N5350**
Egyptian Art. Trade Paper. Thames & Hudson. New York, NY.
1985. 252p. World of Art Ser. ISBN:0-500-20180-3, ISBN13:
978-0-500-20180-0. Dewey:709/.32. LCCN:84-051309.
Audience: **g,l,u,f**

Bacquart, Jean-Baptiste   **N7380.B28 1998**
The Tribal Arts of Africa. Trade Cloth. Thames & Hudson. New
York, NY. 1998. 240p. ISBN:0-500-01870-7, ISBN13:
978-0-500-01870-5. Dewey:709/.6. LCCN:98-060234.
Audience: **g,l,u,f**. *Choice, 1999.*

Bassani, Ezio (Editor)   **N7380**
Arts of Africa: 7000 Years of African Art. Trade Cloth. Skira
Editore. Milano, 2005. 412p. ISBN:88-7624-284-8, ISBN13:
978-88-7624-284-7. Dewey:709.6/07444949.
Audience: **g,l,u,f**. *Choice, 2006.*

Blier, Suzanne Preston   **N7380**
Royal Arts of Africa: The Majesty of Form. Trade Paper.
Prentice Hall Art. Upper Saddle River, NJ. 1998. 272p.
ISBN:0-13-183343-X, ISBN13: 978-0-13-183343-2.
Dewey:709.6.
Audience: **g,l,u,f**

Campbell, Alec   **GN861.C682001**
African Rock Art: Paintings and Engravings on Stone. David
Coulson (Photographer). Trade Cloth. Harry N. Abrams, Inc.
New York, NY. 2001. 256p. ISBN:0-8109-4363-8, ISBN13:
978-0-8109-4363-6. Dewey:709/.01/13096. LCCN:99-053255.
Audience: **g,l,u,f**

Cole, Herbert & Turner,   **N7380**
  Jane (Editors)
Encyclopedia of African Art. Library Binding. Groves
Dictionaries, Inc. New York, NY. 2001. 900p. Library of World
Art ISBN:1-884446-08-6, ISBN13: 978-1-884446-08-5.
Dewey:709.603.
Audience: **g,l,u,f**

D'Avennes, E. Prisse   **N5351**
Atlas of Egyptian Art. Ed. 2. Trade Cloth. American University
in Cairo Press. New York, NY. 2002. 160p.
ISBN:977-424-584-9, ISBN13: 978-977-424-584-8.
Dewey:709.32.

Audience: **l,u,f.**   *Choice, 2001.*

Drewal, Henry J., et al.   **N7399.N52.Y681989**
Yoruba: Nine Centuries of African Art and Thought. John
Pemberton III & Rowland Abiodun (Authors), Allen Wardwell
(Editor). Trade Paper. Museum for African Art. Long Is City,
NY. 1989. 256p. ISBN:0-945802-04-8, ISBN13:
978-0-945802-04-4. Dewey:730/.089/96333. LCCN:89-022182.

Audience: **g,l,u,f.**   *Choice, 1990.*

Garlake, Peter   **N7380.G37 2002**
Early Art and Architecture of Africa. Trade Paper. Oxford
University Press, Inc. New York, NY. 2002. 214p. Oxford
History of Art Ser. ISBN:0-19-284261-7, ISBN13:
978-0-19-284261-9. Dewey:709/.6. LCCN:2002-283854.

Audience: **g,l,u,f.**

Garlake, Peter   **N5310.5.Z55G36 1995**
The Hunter's Vision: The Prehistoric Rock Art of Zimbabwe.
Trade Cloth. University of Washington Press. Seattle, WA. 1995.
192p. ISBN:0-295-97480-X, ISBN13: 978-0-295-97480-4.
Dewey:759.01/13/096891. LCCN:95-016323.

Audience: **g,l,u,f.**   *Choice, 1996.*

Geoffroy-Schneiter, Berenice   **N5311.G44 2000**
Tribal Art: Africa, Oceania, Southeast Asia. Trade Cloth.
Vendome Press, The. New York, NY. 2000.
ISBN:0-86565-215-5, ISBN13: 978-0-86565-215-6.
Dewey:709/.01/1. LCCN:00-038146.

Audience: **g,l,u,f.**

Karnouk, Liliane   **N7381.7**
Modern Egyptian Art 1910-2003. Perfect, Paper over Boards,
Dust Jacket. American University in Cairo Press. New York,
NY. 2005. 274p. ISBN:977-424-859-7, ISBN13:
978-977-424-859-7. Dewey:709/.62.

Audience: **g,l,u,f.**   *Choice, 2006.*

Kasfir, Sidney Littlefield   **N7380.K36 2000**
Contemporary African Art. Trade Paper. Thames & Hudson.
New York, NY. 2000. 224p. World of Art Ser.
ISBN:0-500-20328-8, ISBN13: 978-0-500-20328-6.
Dewey:709/.6/09045. LCCN:99-070939.

Audience: **l,u,f.**   *Choice, 2000.*

Loup Pivin, Jean (Editor)   **N7391.65A5713 2002**
An Anthology of African Art: The Twentieth Century. Elikia
M'Bokolo, Simon Njami & George Kyeyune (Contribution by).
Trade Cloth. D. A. P./Distributed Art Publishers. New York, NY.
2003. 408p. ISBN:1-891024-38-8, ISBN13: 978-1-891024-38-2.
Dewey:709/.6/0904. LCCN:2002-001449.

Audience: **g,l,u,f.**   *Choice, 2003.*

Markoe, Glenn, et al.   **N5335.C56C566 1996**
Mistress of the House, Mistress of Heaven: Women in Ancient
Egypt. Anne K. Capel & Betsy M. Bryan (Authors). Trade
Cloth. Hudson Hills Press LLC. Manchester, VT. 1997. 240p.

ISBN:1-55595-129-5, ISBN13: 978-1-55595-129-0.
Dewey:704.9/424/0932074771. LCCN:96-009376.

Audience: **l,u,f.**   *Choice, 1997.*

McClusky, Pamela &   **N7391.65.M28 2002**
Thompson, Robert Farris
Art from Africa: Long Steps Never Broke a Back. Seattle Art
Museum Staff (Contribution by). Trade Cloth. Princeton
University Press. Princeton, NJ. 2002. 304p.
ISBN:0-691-09275-3, ISBN13: 978-0-691-09275-1.
Dewey:709.6. LCCN:2001-049735.

Audience: **g,l,u,f.**

Phillips, Tom (Editor)   **N7380.5.A37 1995**
Africa: The Art of a Continent. John Mack (Contribution by).
Trade Cloth. Prestel Publishing. New York, NY. 1995. 620p.
ISBN:3-7913-1603-6, ISBN13: 978-3-7913-1603-1.
Dewey:709/.6. LCCN:97-229396.

Audience: **g,l,u,f.**

Roehrig, Catharine H.   **DT87.15.H378 2005**
(Editor), et al.
Hatshepsut: From Queen to Pharaoh. Cathleen A. Keller &
Renee Dreyfus (Editors). Saddle Stitched, Cloth over Boards,
Dust Jacket. Yale University Press. Cumberland, RI. 2005. 356p.
Metropolitan Museum of Art Ser. ISBN:0-300-11139-8, ISBN13:
978-0-300-11139-2. Dewey:932/.014/092. LCCN:2005-020286.

Audience: **g,l,u,f.**

Ross, Doran H. (Editor)   **NK5989.E44 1992**
Elephant: The Animal and Its Ivory in African Culture. Trade
Cloth. University of California Los Angeles, Fowler Museum of
Cultural History. Los Angeles, CA. 1992. 424p.
ISBN:0-930741-25-0, ISBN13: 978-0-930741-25-9.
Dewey:730/.096/07479494. LCCN:92-073840.

Audience: **g,l,u,f.**   *Choice, 1995.*

Russmann, Edna R. (Editor)   **N5350**
Eternal Egypt: Masterworks of Ancient Art from the British
Museum. Trade Cloth. University of California Press. Berkeley,
CA. 2001. 288p. ISBN:0-520-23082-5, ISBN13:
978-0-520-23082-8. Dewey:709/.32/07442142.

Audience: **g,l,u,f.**   *Choice, 2001.*

Steiner, Christopher B.   **N7399.I8 S74 1994**
African Art in Transit. Trade Paper. Cambridge University Press.
New York, NY. 1994. 236p. ISBN:0-521-45752-1, ISBN13:
978-0-521-45752-1. Dewey:382.457096668. LCCN:92-047387.

Audience: **l,u,f.**

Willet, Frank   **N7380.W5 1993**
African Art. Ed. 2. Trade Paper. Thames & Hudson. New York,
NY. 1993. 288p. World of Art Ser. ISBN:0-500-20267-2,
ISBN13: 978-0-500-20267-8. Dewey:709/.6. LCCN:93-060124.

Audience: **g,l,u,f.**

Visual Arts in General > Histories and Handbooks > Cultures, Regions, Nationalities > Middle East

Canby, Sheila R.   **N7283.C36200**
The Golden Age of Persian Art, 1501-1722. Trade Cloth. Harry
N. Abrams, Inc. New York, NY. 2000. 192p.
ISBN:0-8109-4144-9, ISBN13: 978-0-8109-4144-1.
Dewey:709/.55/0903. LCCN:99-076377.
Audience: **g,l,u,f.**   *Choice, 2000.*

Ettinghausen, Richard, et al.   **N6260.E79200I**
Islamic Art and Architecture, 650-1250. Ed. 2. Oleg Grabar &
Marilyn Jenkins-Madina (Authors). Cloth over Boards. Yale
University Press. Cumberland, RI. 2002. 352p. Pelican History
of Art Ser. ISBN:0-300-08867-1, ISBN13: 978-0-300-08867-C.
Dewey:709.1767109021. LCCN:00-043769.
Audience: **g,l,u,f.**   *Choice, 2002.*

Faraj, Maysaloun (Editor)   **N7267.S76 2001**
Strokes of Genius: Contemporary Iraqi Art. Trade Paper. Saqi
Books. London, 2006. 248p. ISBN:0-86356-563-8, ISBN13:
978-0-86356-563-2. Dewey:709/.567/09045.
LCCN:2002-318430.
Audience: **l,u,f.**   *Choice, 2002.*

Ferrier, R. W. (Editor)   **N7280.A89 1989**
The Arts of Persia. Cloth over Boards. Yale University Press.
Cumberland, RI. 1989. 344p. ISBN:0-300-03987-5, ISBN13:
978-0-300-03987-0. Dewey:709/.43/074435954.
LCCN:89-031890.
Audience: **g,l,u,f.**   *Choice, 1990.*

Grabar, Oleg   **ND3241.G671 2000**
Mostly Miniatures: An Introduction to Persian Painting. Trade
Cloth. Princeton University Press. Princeton, NJ. 2000. 175p.
ISBN:0-691-04941-6, ISBN13: 978-0-691-04941-0.
Dewey:745.6/749155. LCCN:00-035961.
Audience: **g,l,u,f.**   *Choice 2001.*

Grube, Ernst J; Sims, Eleanor G; Bayani, Manijeh; Nassar, Nahla
Islamic Art V: Studies on the Art and Culture of the Muslim
World. Ernst J. Grube (Editor) ; Eleanor G. Sims (Editor) ;
Manijeh Bayani (Editor) ; Nahla Nassar (Editor). Oxford
University Press, Inc. 2005. ISBN:0-19-924768-4, ISBN13:
978-0-19-924768-4.
Audience: **g,l,u,f.**

Hillenbrand, Robert   **N6260.H551999**
Islamic Art and Architecture. Thames & Hudson. 1999. World
of Art Ser. ISBN:0-500-20305-9, ISBN13: 978-0-500-20305-7.
Audience: **g,l,u,f.**

Komaroff, Linda & Carboni, Stefano (Editors)   **N7283.L44 2002**
The Legacy of Genghis Khan: Courtly Art and Culture in
Western Asia, 1256-1353. Cloth over Boards. Yale University

Press. Cumberland, RI. 2002. 336p. Metropolitan Museum of
Art Ser. ISBN:0-300-09691-7, ISBN13: 978-0-300-09691-0.
Dewey:709/.55/0747471. LCCN:2002-027893.
Audience: **g,l,u,f.**   *Choice, 2003.*

Michell, George & Zebrowski, Mark   **DS436.N471987 PT.**
Architecture and Art of the Deccan Sultanates. C. A. Bayly,
Gordon Johnson & John F. Richards (Contribution by). Trade
Cloth. Cambridge University Press. New York, NY. 1999. 324p.
The New Cambridge History of India Ser., Vol. I, 7
ISBN:0-521-56321-6, ISBN13: 978-0-521-56321-5. Dewey:954
s. LCCN:98-024737.
Audience: **l,u,f.**   *Choice, 2000.*

Roxburgh, David J.   **N7283.R68 2004**
The Persian Album, 1400-1600: From Dispersal to Collection.
Cloth over Boards. Yale University Press. Cumberland, RI.
2005. 392p. ISBN:0-300-10325-5, ISBN13: 978-0-300-10325-0.
Dewey:709/.55/09024. LCCN:2004-021251.
Audience: **g,l,u,f.**   *Choice, 2005.*

Visual Arts in General > Histories and Handbooks > Cultures, Regions, Nationalities > India and South Asia

Chaturachinda, Gwyneth, et al.   **N7300**
Dictionary of South and Southeast Asian Art. Pauline W.
Tabtiang & Sunanda Krishnamurty (Authors). Trade Paper. Silk
Worm Books. Bangkok, 2001. 144p. ISBN:974-7100-97-5,
ISBN13: 978-974-7100-97-6. Dewey:709.503.
Audience: **g,l,u,f.**   *Choice, 2001.*

Craven, Roy C.   **N7301.C7 1997**
Indian Art. Ed. 2. Thames & Hudson. 1997. World of Art
ISBN:0-500-20302-4, ISBN13: 978-0-500-20302-6.
Audience: **g,l,u,f.**

Dehejia, Vidya   **NA6007.S6D44 1990**
Art of the Imperial Cholas. Trade Cloth. Columbia University
Press. New York, NY. 1990. 160p. ISBN:0-231-07188-4,
ISBN13: 978-0-231-07188-8. Dewey:726/.145/09548.
LCCN:89-078065.
Audience: **l,u,f.**   *Choice, 1991.*

Fisher, Robert E.   **N7346.T5F57 1997**
Art of Tibet. Trade Paper. Thames & Hudson. New York, NY.
1998. 224p. World of Art Ser. ISBN:0-500-20308-3, ISBN13:
978-0-500-20308-8. Dewey:709.5/15. LCCN:97-060253.
Audience: **g,l,u,f.**   *Choice, 1998.*

Fisher, Robert E.   **N8193.A4**
Buddhist Art and Architecture. Trade Paper. Thames & Hudson.
New York, NY. 1993. 216p. World of Art Ser.
ISBN:0-500-20265-6, ISBN13: 978-0-500-20265-4.
Dewey:704.9/48943. LCCN:92-062141.
Audience: **g,l,u,f.**

Geoffroy-Schneiter, Berenice N5311.G44 2000
Tribal Art: Africa, Oceania, Southeast Asia. Trade Cloth.
Vendome Press, The. New York, NY. 2000.
ISBN:0-86565-215-5, ISBN13: 978-0-86565-215-6.
Dewey:709/.01/1. LCCN:00-038146.
Audience: **g,l,u,f.**

Hamilton, Roy W. GR265.H352003
The Art of Rice: Spirit and Sustenance in Asia. Aurora
Ammayao (Translator), University of California Staff
(Contribution by). Trade Cloth. University of California Los
Angeles, Fowler Museum of Cultural History. Los Angeles, CA.
2004. 552p. ISBN:0-930741-98-6, ISBN13: 978-0-930741-98-3.
Dewey:398/.36849/095. LCCN:2003-058024.
Audience: **g,l,u,f.** *Choice, 2005.*

Harle, J. C. N7301.H231994
Art and Architecture of the Indian Subcontinent. Ed. 2. Trade
Paper. Yale University Press. Cumberland, RI. 1986. 616p.
Pelican History of Art Ser. ISBN:0-300-06217-6, ISBN13:
978-0-300-06217-5. Dewey:709/.54. LCCN:95-125417.
Audience: **g,l,u,f.**

Jessup, Helen Ibbitson N7315
Art and Architecture of Cambodia. Trade Paper. Thames &
Hudson. New York, NY. 2004. 224p. World of Art Ser.
ISBN:0-500-20375-X, ISBN13: 978-0-500-20375-0.
Dewey:720/.9596/0901. LCCN:2003-108925.
Audience: **g,l,u,f.**

Kerolgue, Fiona NX577
Arts of Southeast Asia. Trade Paper. Thames & Hudson. New
York, NY. 2004. 224p. World of Art Ser. ISBN:0-500-20381-4,
ISBN13: 978-0-500-20381-1. Dewey:700.9/59.
LCCN:2004-102646.
Audience: **g,l,u,f.** *Choice, 2005.*

Mannikka, Eleanor DS554.98.A5M36 1996
Angkor Wat: Time, Space, and Kingship. Trade Cloth.
University of Hawaii Press. Honolulu, HI. 2000. 360p.
ISBN:0-8248-1720-6, ISBN13: 978-0-8248-1720-6.
Dewey:959.6. LCCN:96-004368.
Audience: **g,l,u,f.** *Choice, 1997.*

Michell, George N8195.A4M53 2000
Hindu Art and Architecture. Trade Paper. Thames & Hudson.
New York, NY. 2000. 224p. World of Art Ser.
ISBN:0-500-20337-7, ISBN13: 978-0-500-20337-8.
Dewey:704.9/48945. LCCN:00-100590.
Audience: **g,l,u,f.** *Choice, 2001.*

Mitter, Partha N7301.M48 2001
Indian Art. Trade Paper. Oxford University Press, Inc. New
York, NY. 2001. 272p. Oxford History of Art Ser.
ISBN:0-19-284221-8, ISBN13: 978-0-19-284221-3.
Dewey:709/.54. LCCN:2001-273423.
Audience: **g,l,u,f.**

Pal, Pratapaditya N8199.J36I46 1994
The Peaceful Liberators: Jain Art from India. Trade Cloth.
Thames & Hudson. New York, NY. 1994. 280p.

ISBN:0-500-01650-X, ISBN13: 978-0-500-01650-3.
Dewey:700.4/82944. LCCN:94-061006.
Audience: **g,l,u,f.** *Choice, 1995.*

Rawson, Philip S. N5877.A8 R3 1990
The Art of Southeast Asia: Cambodia, Vietnam, Thailand, Laos,
Burma, Java and Bali. Trade Paper. Thames & Hudson. New
York, NY. 1990. 288p. World of Art Ser. ISBN:0-500-20060-2,
ISBN13: 978-0-500-20060-5. Dewey:709/.59. LCCN:89-052204.
Audience: **g,l,u,f.**

Roveda, Vittorio NB1280
Images of the Gods: Khmer Mythology in Cambodia, Laos and
Thailand. Trade Cloth. Floating World Editions. Warren, NY.
2005. 840p. ISBN:1-891640-29-1, ISBN13: 978-1-891640-29-2.
Dewey:732.4.
Audience: **l,u,f.**

Shearer, Alistair BQ4022.S34 1992
The Buddha. Trade Paper. Thames & Hudson. New York, NY.
1992. 96p. Art and Imagination Ser. ISBN:0-500-81038-9,
ISBN13: 978-0-500-81038-5. Dewey:294.3. LCCN:91-067309.
Audience: **g,l,u,f.**

Visual Arts in General > Histories and Handbooks > Cultures, Regions, Nationalities > China, Japan, Korea

Bagley, Robert (Editor) DS793.S8A528 2001
Ancient Sichuan: Treasures from a Lost Civilization. Trade
Cloth. Princeton University Press. Princeton, NJ. 2001. 360p.
ISBN:0-691-08851-9, ISBN13: 978-0-691-08851-8. Dewey:931.
LCCN:00-068782.
Audience: **g,l,u,f.** *Choice, 2001.*

Barnhart, Richard M., et al. ND1040.T48 1997
Three Thousand Years of Chinese Painting. Yang Xin, Nie
Chongzheng, James Cahill, Lang Shaojun & Wu Hung
(Authors). Trade Paper. Yale University Press. Cumberland, RI.
2002. 416p. Culture and Civilization of China Ser.
ISBN:0-300-09447-7, ISBN13: 978-0-300-09447-3.
Dewey:759.9/51. LCCN:97-011152.
Audience: **g,l,u,f.**

Calza, Gian Carlo NE1321.8
Ukiyo-E. Trade Cloth. Phaidon Press, Inc. New York, NY. 2005.
520p. ISBN:0-7148-4538-8, ISBN13: 978-0-7148-4538-8.
Dewey:769.952.
Audience: **g,l,u,f.**

Calza, Gian Carlo & N7359.K37H65
Carpenter, John T. (Editors)
Hokusai and His Age. Trade Cloth. Hotei Publishing. Leiden,
2005. 300p. ISBN:90-74822-57-6, ISBN13: 978-90-74822-57-2.
Dewey:759.952. LCCN:2005-530010.
Audience: **l,u,f.** *Choice, 2006.*

Formats: Web: ☐ Ebook: **ⓔ** CD/DVD-ROM: 💥 BCL3: **ℬ**

Clunas, Craig   N7340.C59 1997
Art in China. Trade Paper. Oxford University Press, Inc. New
York, NY. 1997. 256p. Oxford History of Art Ser.
ISBN:0-19-284207-2, ISBN13: 978-0-19-284207-7.
Dewey:709.5/1. LCCN:96-047595.
                             Audience: **g,l,u,f.** *Choice, 1997.*

Clunas, Craig & Wen,   N7349.Z485C57 2003
  Zhengming
Elegant Debts: The Social Art of Wen Zhengming. Trade Cloth.
University of Hawaii Press. Honolulu, HI. 2004. 232p.
ISBN:0-8248-2772-4, ISBN13: 978-0-8248-2772-4.
Dewey:700/.92. LCCN:2003-001143.
                             Audience: **l,u,f.** *Choice, 2005.*

Earle, Joe   N7354
Splendors of Imperial Japan: Arts of the Meiji Period from the
Khalili Collection. Trade Paper. I. B. Tauris & Company, Ltd.
London, 2005. 468p. Emirates Center for Strategic Studies and
Research Ser. ISBN:1-874780-19-6, ISBN13:
978-1-874780-19-9. Dewey:709.5209034.
                             Audience: **g,l,u,f.**

Fisher, Robert E.   N8195.A4
Buddhist Art and Architecture. Trade Paper. Thames & Hudson.
New York, NY. 1993. 216p. World of Art Ser.
ISBN:0-500-20265-6, ISBN13: 978-0-500-20265-4.
Dewey:704.9/48943. LCCN:92-062141.
                             Audience: **g,l,u,f.**

Fong, Wen C. & Watt,   N3750.T32A87 1996
  James C.
Possessing the Past: Treasures from the National Palace
Museum, Taipei. Richard M. Barnhart (Contribution by). Trade
Cloth. Metropolitan Museum of Art, The. New York, NY. 1996.
600p. ISBN:0-87099-765-3, ISBN13: 978-0-87099-765-5.
Dewey:708.9/51. LCCN:95-049102.
                             Audience: **g,l,u,f.** *Choice, 1997.*

Frankfort, Henri A.   N5345.F71996
The Art and Architecture of the Ancient Orient. Ed. 5. Michael
Roaf & Donald Matthews (Commentaries by, Notes by). Trade
Paper. Yale University Press. Cumberland, RI. 1989. 500p.
Pelican History of Art Ser. ISBN:0-300-06470-5, ISBN13:
978-0-300-06470-4. Dewey:709/.3. LCCN:95-015893.
                             Audience: **l,u,f.**

Hickman, Money L. (Editor)   N7353.4.J39 1996
Japan's Golden Age: Momoyama. Cloth over Boards. Yale
University Press. Cumberland, RI. 1996. 320p.
ISBN:0-300-06897-2, ISBN13: 978-0-300-06897-9.
Dewey:709/.52/0747642812. LCCN:96-017758.
                             Audience: **g,l,u,f.** *Choice, 1997.*

Ho, Chimei & Bronson,   N7343.5
  Bennet (Editors)
Splendors of China's Forbidden City: The Glorious Reign of
Emperor Qianlong. Trade Paper. Merrell Publishers Ltd.
London, 2005. 272p. ISBN:1-85894-203-9, ISBN13:
978-1-85894-203-2. Dewey:709.5/1/09033.
                             Audience: **l,u,f.** *Choice, 2004.*

Hung, Chang-tai   DS721
War and Popular Culture: Resistance in Modern China,
1937-1945. Trade Cloth. University of California Press.
Berkeley, CA. 1994. 448p. ISBN:0-520-08236-2, ISBN13:
978-0-520-08236-6. Dewey:306.40951. LCCN:93-004738.
                             Audience: **l,u,f.** *Choice, 1994.*

Jackson, Anna & Jaffer,   N7260
  Amin
Encounters: The Meeting of Asia and Europe 1500 - 1800.
Trade Cloth. V & A Publications. London, 2004. 408p.
ISBN:1-85177-432-7, ISBN13: 978-1-85177-432-6.
Dewey:709.5/0903. LCCN:2004-103252.
                             Audience: **l,u,f.** *Choice, 2005.*

Lee, Sherman E
History of Far Eastern Art. Ed. 5. Prentice Hall PTR. 1994.
ISBN:0-8109-3414-0, ISBN13: 978-0-8109-3414-6.
                             Audience: **g,l,u,f.**

Little, Stephen, et al.   N8199.T3 L58 2000
Taoism and the Arts of China. Kristofer Shipper & Wu Hung
(Authors). Trade Cloth. University of California Press. Berkeley,
CA. 2000. 415p. ISBN:0-520-22784-0, ISBN13:
978-0-520-22784-2. Dewey:704.9/4899514/0951.
LCCN:00-034377.
                             Audience: **g,l,u,f.** *Choice, 2001.*

Mason, Penelope   N7350.M26 2004
History of Japanese Art. Ed. 2. Trade Cloth. Prentice Hall Art.
Upper Saddle River, NJ. 2004. 432p. ISBN:0-13-117602-1,
ISBN13: 978-0-13-117602-7. Dewey:709.52.
LCCN:2004-044653.
                             Audience: **g,l,u,f.** *Choice, 1993.*

Portal, Jane   N7360.P67 2000
Korea: Art and Archaeology. Trade Paper. Thames & Hudson.
New York, NY. 2000. 240p. ISBN:0-500-28202-1, ISBN13:
978-0-500-28202-1. Dewey:709.5/19. LCCN:99-066554.
                             Audience: **g,l,u,f.** *Choice, 2000.*

Shearer, Alistair   BQ4022.S34 1992
The Buddha. Trade Paper. Thames & Hudson. New York, NY.
1992. 96p. Art and Imagination Ser. ISBN:0-500-81038-9,
ISBN13: 978-0-500-81038-5. Dewey:294.3. LCCN:91-067309.
                             Audience: **g,l,u,f.**

Sickman, Laurence & Soper,   N7340
  Alexander C.
The Art and Architecture of China. Ed. 3. Trade Paper. Yale
University Press. Cumberland, RI. 1992. 527p. Pelican History
of Art Ser. ISBN:0-300-05334-7, ISBN13: 978-0-300-05334-0.
Dewey:709.5/1.
                             Audience: **g,l,u,f.** *B*

Singer, Robert T.   N7353.5.S656
Edo: Art in Japan, 1615-1868. Cloth over Boards. Yale
University Press. Cumberland, RI. 1998. 480p.
ISBN:0-300-07796-3, ISBN13: 978-0-300-07796-4.
Dewey:709.52074753. LCCN:98-029138.
                             Audience: **g,l,u,f.** *Choice, 1999.*

Soper, Alexander C. &   **N7350**
  Paine, Robert T.
The Art and Architecture of Japan. Ed. 3. Trade Paper. Yale
University Press. Cumberland, RI. 1981. 522p. Pelican History
of Art Ser. ISBN:0-300-05333-9, ISBN13: 978-0-300-05333-3.
Dewey:709.5/2. LCCN:75-309148.

Audience: **g,l,u,f.**

Stanley-Baker, Joan   **N7350.S7 2000**
Japanese Art. Ed. 2. Trade Paper. Thames & Hudson. New York,
NY. 2000. 224p. World of Art Ser. ISBN:0-500-20326-1,
ISBN13: 978-0-500-20326-2. Dewey:709/.52. LCCN:99-070841.

Audience: **g,l,u,f.**

Sullivan, Michael   **N7345.S79 1996**
Art and Artists of Twentieth-Century China. Trade Cloth.
University of California Press. Berkeley, CA. 1996. 386p. An
Ahmanson Murphy Fine Arts Bk. ISBN:0-520-07556-0,
ISBN13: 978-0-520-07556-6. Dewey:709/.51/0904.
LCCN:95-025673.

Audience: **g,l,u,f.** *Choice, 1997.*

Sullivan, Michael   **N7340.S92 1999**
The Arts of China. Ed. 4. Trade Paper. University of California
Press. Berkeley, CA. 2000. 348p. ISBN:0-520-21877-9, ISBN13:
978-0-520-21877-2. Dewey:709/.51. LCCN:98-049596.

Audience: **g,l,u,f.** *B*

Tregear, Mary   **N7340.T73 1997**
Chinese Art. Ed. 2. Trade Paper. Thames & Hudson. New York,
NY. 1997. 216p. The World of Art Ser. ISBN:0-500-20299-0,
ISBN13: 978-0-500-20299-9. Dewey:709.5/1. LCCN:96-061015.

Audience: **g,l,u,f.**

Watson, William   **N7343**
The Arts of China to A.D. 900. Trade Paper. Yale University
Press. Cumberland, RI. 2000. 288p. Pelican History of Art Ser.
ISBN:0-300-08284-3, ISBN13: 978-0-300-08284-5.
Dewey:709.5/1/0901. LCCN:94-049679.

Audience: **g,l,u,f.** *Choice, 1996.*

Wu, Hung   **N7343.2.W8 1995**
Monumentality in Early Chinese Art and Architecture. Trade
Cloth. Stanford University Press. Palo Alto, CA. 1997. 396p.
ISBN:0-8047-2428-8, ISBN13: 978-0-8047-2428-9.
Dewey:709.5/1/0901. LCCN:94-018434.

Audience: **u,f.** *Choice, 1996.*

Yonemura, Ann, et al.   **N7352.T891997**
Twelve Centuries of Japanese Art from the Imperial Collections.
Moritoku Hirabayashi, Freer Gallery of Art Staff & Arthur M.
Sackler Museum Staff (Authors). Trade Cloth. Smithsonian
Institution Press. Washington, DC. 1998. 224p.
ISBN:1-56098-893-2, ISBN13: 978-1-56098-893-9.
Dewey:709.52/074/753. LCCN:97-041676.

Audience: **g,l,u,f.**

Visual Arts in General > Histories and Handbooks > Cultures, Regions, Nationalities > Australasia and Pacific Islands

Allen, Christopher   **N7400.A451997**
Art in Australia: From Colonization to Postmodernism. Trade
Paper. Thames & Hudson. New York, NY. 1997. 224p. The
World of Art Ser. ISBN:0-500-20301-6, ISBN13:
978-0-500-20301-9. Dewey:709.9/4. LCCN:96-061173.

Audience: **g,l,u,f.**

Anderson, Christopher, et   **N7401.D73 1988**
  al.
Dreamings: The Art of Aboriginal Australia. Philip Jones,
Francoise Dussart & Steven Hemming (Authors), Peter Sutton
(Editor). Trade Cloth. George Braziller Inc. New York, NY.
1988. 266p. ISBN:0-8076-1201-4, ISBN13: 978-0-8076-1201-9.
Dewey:750/.899915. LCCN:88-010435.

Audience: **g,l,u,f.** *Choice, 1989.*

Forbes, David W.   **N6530.H3F67 1992**
Encounters with Paradise: Views of Hawaii and Its People,
1778-1941. Trade Cloth. University of Hawaii Press. Honolulu,
HI. 1992. 278p. ISBN:0-8248-1440-1, ISBN13:
978-0-8248-1440-3. Dewey:758/.99969/007496931.
LCCN:91-032265.

Audience: **g,l,u,f.**

Geoffroy-Schneiter, Berenice   **N5311.G44 2000**
Tribal Art: Africa, Oceania, Southeast Asia. Trade Cloth.
Vendome Press, The. New York, NY. 2000.
ISBN:0-86565-215-5, ISBN13: 978-0-86565-215-6.
Dewey:709/.01/1. LCCN:00-038146.

Audience: **g,l,u,f.**

Kaeppler, Adrienne L., et al.   **N7410.K341997**
Oceanic Art. Christian Kaufmann & Douglas Newton (Authors).
Trade Cloth. Harry N. Abrams, Inc. New York, NY. 1997. 642p.
ISBN:0-8109-3693-3, ISBN13: 978-0-8109-3693-5.
Dewey:709/.9. LCCN:97-008127.

Audience: **g,l,u,f.** *Choice, 1998.*

Kjellgren, Eric & Ivory,   **N7411.M3K44 2005**
  Carol
Adorning the World: Art of the Marquesas Islands. Trade Paper.
Yale University Press. Cumberland, RI. 2005. 140p.
ISBN:0-300-10712-9, ISBN13: 978-0-300-10712-8.
Dewey:745/.089/9942. LCCN:2005-000844.

Audience: **g,l,u,f.** *Choice, 2005.*

Kleinert, Sylvia & Neale,   **NX590.A1O94 2000**
  Margo (Editors)
The Oxford Companion to Aboriginal Art and Culture. Cloth
Text. Oxford University Press, Inc. New York, NY. 2001. 804p.
ISBN:0-19-550649-9, ISBN13: 978-0-19-550649-5.
Dewey:994.004/9915. LCCN:2001-269497.

Audience: **l,u,f.** *Choice, 2002.*

Mallon, Sean   **NX596.S26M35 2002**
Samoan Art and Artists. Trade Paper. University of Hawaii
Press. Honolulu, HI. 2002. 216p. ISBN:0-8248-2675-2, ISBN13:
978-0-8248-2675-8. Dewey:745/.09961/3. LCCN:2002-026628.
                                   Audience: **g,l,u,f.** *Choice, 2003.*

Sayers, Andrew   **N7400.S29 2001**
Australian Art. Trade Paper. Oxford University Press, Inc. New
York, NY. 2001. 266p. Oxford History of Art Ser.
ISBN:0-19-284214-5, ISBN13: 978-0-19-284214-5.
Dewey:709/.94. LCCN:2001-269768.
                                   Audience: **g,l,u,f.**

Visual Arts in General > Individual Artists

Prelinger, Elizabeth   **N6888.K62**
Kathe Kollwitz. Yale University Press, Cumberland, RI. 1993.
ISBN:0-300-06168-4, ISBN13: 978-0-300-06168-0.
                                   Audience: **g,l,u,f.**

Ades, Dawn   **N7113.D3A84 1995**
Dali. Ed. 2. Trade Paper. Thames & Hudson. New York, NY.
1995. 216p. World of Art Ser. ISBN:0-500-20280-X, ISBN13:
978-0-500-20280-7. Dewey:759.6. LCCN:94-061060.
                                   Audience: **g,l,u,f.**

Ades, Dawn, et al.   **N6853.D8A83 1999**
Marcel Duchamp. Neil Cox & David Hopkins (Authors). Trade
Paper. Thames & Hudson. New York, NY. 1999. 224p. Black
Enterprise Bks. ISBN:0-500-20322-9, ISBN13:
978-0-500-20322-4. Dewey:709/.2. LCCN:98-061434.
                                   Audience: **g,l,u,f.** *Choice, 1999.*

Baldassari, Anne, et al.   **N6853.M33A42002B**
Matisse/Picasso. Elizabeth Cowling, John Elderfield, John
Golding, Isabelle Monod-Fontaine & Kirk Varnedoe (Authors).
Trade Cloth. Museum of Modern Art. New York, NY. 2003.
400p. ISBN:0-87070-008-1, ISBN13: 978-0-87070-008-8.
Dewey:759.4.
                                   Audience: **g,l,u,f.** *Choice, 2003.*

Baxter, Marty   **N6953.M64A4 2001**
Complete Mondrian. Trade Paper. Ashgate Publishing Company.
Williston, VT. 2001. 592p. ISBN:0-85331-822-0, ISBN13:
978-0-85331-822-4. Dewey:759.9492. LCCN:2001-092685.
                                   Audience: **g,l,u,f.** *Choice, 2002.*

Beccaria, Marcella   **N6537**
Vanessa Beecroft: Performances 1993-2003. Trade Cloth. Skira
Editore. Milano, 2004. 400p. ISBN:88-8491-572-4, ISBN13:
978-88-8491-572-6. Dewey:709.2. LCCN:2005-476141.
                                   Audience: **g,l,u,f.**

Becker, Edwin   **N6797.R58**
Dante Gabriel Rossetti. Trade Cloth. Thames & Hudson. New
York, NY. 2003. 248p. ISBN:0-500-09316-4, ISBN13:
978-0-500-09316-0. Dewey:759.2. LCCN:2003-103604.
                                   Audience: **g,l,u,f.** *Choice, 2004.*

Bellosi, Luciano   **ND623.C65B45 1998**
Cimabue. Trade Cloth. Abbeville Press, Inc. New York, NY.
1998. 304p. ISBN:0-7892-0466-5, ISBN13: 978-0-7892-0466-0.
Dewey:759.5. LCCN:98-017963.
                                   Audience: **g,l,u,f.**

Bentley, Gerald Eades   **PR4146**
The Stranger from Paradise: A Biography of William Blake.
Paul Mellon Centre for Studies in British Art Staff (Contribution
by). Trade Paper. Yale University Press. Cumberland, RI. 2003.
632p. Paul Mellon Centre for Studies in Britis Ser.
ISBN:0-300-10030-2, ISBN13: 978-0-300-10030-3.
Dewey:821.7.
                                   Audience: **g,l,u,f.**

Blackburn, Julia   **N7113.G68**
Old Man Goya. Trade Paper. Knopf Publishing Group. New
York, NY. 2003. 256p. ISBN:0-375-70579-1, ISBN13:
978-0-375-70579-3. Dewey:760/.092 B.
                                   Audience: **g,l,u,f.**

Boggs, Jean Sutherland   **N6853.P5**
Degas. Trade Cloth. Metropolitan Museum of Art, The. New
York, NY. 1988. 640p. ISBN:0-87099-519-7, ISBN13:
978-0-87099-519-4. Dewey:709.2.
                                   Audience: **g,l,u,f.** *Choice, 1989.*

Buhler-Lynes, Barbara   **N6537.O39A4 1999**
Georgia O'Keeffe: Catalogue Raisonne. Cloth over Boards. Yale
University Press. Cumberland, RI. 1999. 1198p.
ISBN:0-300-08176-6, ISBN13: 978-0-300-08176-3.
Dewey:759.13. LCCN:99-065972.
                                   Audience: **g,l,u,f.** *Choice, 2000.*

Calza, Gian Carlo &   **N7359.K37H65**
  Carpenter, John T. (Editors)
Hokusai and His Age. Trade Cloth. Hotei Publishing. Leiden,
2005. 300p. ISBN:90-74822-57-6, ISBN13: 978-90-74822-57-2.
Dewey:759.952. LCCN:2005-530010.
                                   Audience: **l,u,f.** *Choice, 2006.*

Carr, Gerald L.   **N6537.C4977 A4 1994**
Frederic Edwin Church: Catalogue Raisonné of Works of Art at
Olana State Historic Site. Cloth Text. Cambridge University
Press. New York, NY. 1994. 635p. ISBN:0-521-38540-7,
ISBN13: 978-0-521-38540-4. Dewey:759.13. LCCN:91-046222.
                                   Audience: **g,l,u,f.** *Choice, 1995.*

Chagall, Marc   **N6999.C46H37 2003**
Marc Chagall and His Times: A Documentary Narrative.
Benjamin Harshav & Barbara Harshav (Translators). Trade
Paper. Stanford University Press. Palo Alto, CA. 2003. 1056p.
ISBN:0-8047-4214-6, ISBN13: 978-0-8047-4214-6.
Dewey:709/.2 B. LCCN:2003-007566.
                                   Audience: **g,l,u,f.** *Choice, 2004.*

Clark, Carol, et al.   **N6537.P68A41990**
Maurice Brazil Prendergast - Charles Prendergast: A Catalogue
Raisonne. Nancy M. Mathews & Gwendolyn Owens (Authors).

Trade Cloth. Prestel Publishing. New York, NY. 1990. 812p. ISBN:3-7913-0965-X, ISBN13: 978-3-7913-0965-1. Dewey:760/.092. LCCN:89-022575.

Audience: **g,l,u,f.**

Clement, Russell T.   **N6853**
Georges Braque: A Bio-Bibliography. Cloth Text. Greenwood Publishing Group, Inc. Portsmouth, NH. 1994. 256p. Bio-Bibliographies in Art and Architecture Ser., Vol. 3 ISBN:0-313-29235-3, ISBN13: 978-0-313-29235-4. Dewey:016.7/092. LCCN:93-045310.

Audience: **g,l,u,f.**   *Choice, 1994.*

Clement, Russell T.   **N6853**
Henri Matisse: A Bio-Bibliography. Cloth Text. Greenwood Publishing Group, Inc. Portsmouth, NH. 1993. 416p. Bio-Bibliographies in Art and Architecture Ser., Vol. 2 ISBN:0-313-28127-0, ISBN13: 978-0-313-28127-3. Dewey:016.7594092. LCCN:93-021069.

Audience: **g,l,u,f.**   *Choice, 1994.*

Cogeval, Guy   **N6853**
Edouard Vuillard. Cloth over Boards. Yale University Press. Cumberland, RI. 2003. 520p. ISBN:0-300-09737-9, ISBN13: 978-0-300-09737-5. Dewey:759.4. LCCN:2002-151120.

Audience: **g,l,u,f.**   *Choice, 2003.*

Cumbers, Pauline   **N6853**
  (Translator)
Jean Dubuffet: Trace of an Adventure. Agnes Husslein (Foreword by). Trade Cloth. Prestel Publishing. New York, NY. 2003. 296p. ISBN:3-7913-2998-7, ISBN13: 978-3-7913-2998-7. Dewey:709.2.

Audience: **l,u,f.**   *Choice, 2004.*

Darger, Henry   **NX512.D37A4 2000**
Henry Darger: Art and Selected Writings. Trade Cloth. Rizzoli International Publications, Inc. New York, NY. 2001. 256p. ISBN:0-8478-2284-2, ISBN13: 978-0-8478-2284-3. Dewey:700/.92. LCCN:00-101339.

Audience: **g,l,u,f.**

Delacroix, Eugene &   **ND553.M7**
  Wellington, Hubert
Journal of Delacroix. Ed. 3. Lucy Norton (Translator). Trade Paper. Phaidon Press. London, 1995. 570p. Arts and Letters Ser. ISBN:0-7148-3359-2, ISBN13: 978-0-7148-3359-0. Dewey:759.4.

Audience: **g,l,u,f.**

Dobke, Dirk & Kellein,   **N6797.R67**
  Thomas
Dieter Roth: Books + Multiples: Catalogue Raisonné. Trade Cloth. Thames & Hudson. New York, NY. 2004. 352p. ISBN:0-500-97630-9, ISBN13: 978-0-500-97630-2. Dewey:709.2.

Audience: **g,l,u,f.**   *Choice, 2004.*

Druick, Douglas W. (Editor)   **N6853.R38A4 1994**
Odilon Redon: Prince of Dreams. Trade Paper. Art Institute of

Chicago. Chicago, IL. 1994. 472p. ISBN:0-86559-126-1, ISBN13: 978-0-86559-126-4. Dewey:760/.092. LCCN:94-010379.

Audience: **g,l,u,f.**

Ekserdjian, David   **N6923.C638E39 1997**
Correggio. Cloth over Boards. Yale University Press. Cumberland, RI. 1998. 344p. ISBN:0-300-07299-6, ISBN13: 978-0-300-07299-0. Dewey:759.5. LCCN:97-015696.

Audience: **l,u,f.**   *Choice, 1998.*

Elderfield, John   **N6853.M33 A4 1992**
Henri Matisse: A Retrospective. Trade Paper. Museum of Modern Art. New York, NY. 1992. 480p. ISBN:0-87070-433-8, ISBN13: 978-0-87070-433-8. Dewey:709/.2. LCCN:92-081515.

Audience: **g,l,u,f.**   *Choice, 1993.*

Elzea, Betty   **N6797.S33 E492001**
Frederick Sandys: A Catalogue Raisonné. Trade Cloth. Antique Collectors' Club. Easthampton, MA. 2001. 366p. ISBN:1-85149-397-2, ISBN13: 978-1-85149-397-5. Dewey:759.2.

Audience: **g,l,u,f.**

Evans, John   **N6537.E896A4 2004**
Collages of John Evans. Robert M. Murdock (Introduction by). Trade Cloth. Quantuck Lane Press & The Mill Road Collaborative, The. New York, NY. 2004. 384p. ISBN:1-59372-009-2, ISBN13: 978-1-59372-009-4. Dewey:709/.2. LCCN:2004-010322.

Audience: **g,l,u,f.**   *Choice, 2005.*

Finkelstein, Haim   **ND813.D3 F56 1996**
Salvador Dalí's Art and Writing, 1927-1942: The Metamorphosis of Narcissus. Trade Paper. Cambridge University Press. New York, NY. 1998. 352p. RES Monographs on Anthropology and Aesthetics ISBN:0-521-63925-5, ISBN13: 978-0-521-63925-5. Dewey:709.2.

Audience: **g,l,u,f.**   *Choice, 1997.*

Gibson, Ian   **N7113.D3G53 1998**
The Shameful Life of Salvador Dali. Trade Cloth. W. W. Norton & Company, Inc. New York, NY. 1998. 736p. ISBN:0-393-04624-9, ISBN13: 978-0-393-04624-3. Dewey:759.6. LCCN:97-046707.

Audience: **g,l,u,f.**

Gilot, Francoise (Text by)   **ND553.G565**
Francoise Gilot: Monograph, 1940-2000. Dina Vierny (Foreword by), Mel Yoakum (Contribution by). Trade Cloth. Acatos, Editions. Lausanne, 2001. 450p. ISBN:2-940033-36-6, ISBN13: 978-2-940033-36-2. Dewey:759.4.

Audience: **g,l,u,f.**   *Choice, 2001.*

Gimferrer, Pere   **N7113.M54G561993**
Roots of Miró. Trade Cloth. Rizzoli International Publications, Inc. New York, NY. 1993. 440p. ISBN:0-8478-1768-7, ISBN13: 978-0-8478-1768-9. Dewey:709/.2. LCCN:93-083944.

Audience: **g,l,u,f.**   *Choice, 1994.*

Goldsworthy, Andy   **N6797.G65A42001**
Midsummer Snowballs. Judith Collins (Introduction by). Trade Cloth. Harry N. Abrams, Inc. New York, NY. 2001. 158p. ISBN:0-8109-0624-4, ISBN13: 978-0-8109-0624-2. Dewey:709/.2. LCCN:2001-092639.

            Audience: **g,l,u,f.**

Gouma-Peterson, Thalia   **N6537.S34G681999**
Miriam Schapiro: Shaping the Fragments of Art and Life. Linda Nochlin (Foreword by). Trade Cloth. Harry N. Abrams, Inc. New York, NY. 1999. 160p. ISBN:0-8109-4377-8, ISBN13: 978-0-8109-4377-3. Dewey:709/.2. LCCN:99-018149.

            Audience: **g,l,u,f.** *Choice, 2000.*

Hall, Marcia (Editor)   **N6923.R3C36 2005**
The Cambridge Companion to Raphael. Trade Cloth. Cambridge University Press. New York, NY. 2005. 468p. Cambridge Companions to the History of Art Ser. ISBN:0-521-80809-X, ISBN13: 978-0-521-80809-5. Dewey:759.5. LCCN:2004-051921.

            Audience: **g,l,u,f.** *Choice, 2005.*

Hartigan, Lynda Roscoe, et al.   **N6537.C66**
Joseph Cornell: Shadowplay . . . Eterniday. Walter Hopps, Richard Vine & Robert Lehrman (Authors). Trade Cloth. Thames & Hudson. New York, NY. 2003. 256p. ISBN:0-500-97628-7, ISBN13: 978-0-500-97628-9. Dewey:709.2. LCCN:2002-117474.

            Audience: **g,l,u,f.** *Choice, 2004.*

Hassrick, Peter H. & Webster, Melissa J.   **N6537.R4A4**
Frederic Remington: A Catalogue Raisonné of Paintings, Watercolors and Drawings. Trade Cloth. Buffalo Bill Historical Center. Cody, WY. 1996. 932p. ISBN:0-931618-56-8, ISBN13: 978-0-931618-56-7. Dewey:759.13.

            Audience: **g,l,u,f.**

Herrera, Hayden   **ND237.O5**
Arshile Gorky: His Life and Work. Trade Paper. Farrar, Straus & Giroux. New York, NY. 2005. 784p. ISBN:0-374-52972-8, ISBN13: 978-0-374-52972-7. Dewey:759.13 B.

            Audience: **g,l,u,f.** *Choice, 2004.*

Hickey, Dave, et al.   **N6537**
Andy Warhol. Steven Bluttal & Andy Warhol (Authors), Phaidon Press Editors (Editor). Trade Cloth. Phaidon Press, Inc. New York, NY. 2006. 624p. ISBN:0-7148-4540-X, ISBN13: 978-0-7148-4540-1. Dewey:709.2.

            Audience: **g,l,u,f.**

Hughes, Robert   **N7113.G63H83 2003**
Goya. Trade Cloth. Alfred A. Knopf Inc. New York, NY. 2003. 448p. ISBN:0-394-58028-1, ISBN13: 978-0-394-58028-9. Dewey:760/.092. LCCN:2002-043281.

            Audience: **g,l,u,f.**

Joosten, Joop M. & Welsh, Robert P.   **N6953.M64A41998**
Piet Mondrian: Catalogue Raisonné. Trade Cloth. Harry N.

Abrams, Inc. New York, NY. 1996. 1008p. ISBN:0-8109-4287-9, ISBN13: 978-0-8109-4287-5. Dewey:759.9/492. LCCN:96-012348.

            Audience: **g,l,u,f.**

Kandinsky, Wassily, et al.   **N6490.K293 1994**
Kandinsky: The Complete Writings on Art. Ed. 2. Peter Vergo & Kenneth C. Lindsay (Authors). Trade Paper. Da Capo Press, Inc. Cambridge, MA. 1994. 972p. ISBN:0-306-80570-7, ISBN13: 978-0-306-80570-7. Dewey:700. LCCN:93-033694.

            Audience: **g,l,u,f.**

Kotz, Mary Lynn   **N6537.R27K672004**
Rauschenberg: Art and Life. Trade Cloth. Harry N. Abrams, Inc. New York, NY. 2004. 352p. ISBN:0-8109-5588-1, ISBN13: 978-0-8109-5588-2. Dewey:700/.92 B. LCCN:2004-012639.

            Audience: **g,l,u,f.** *Choice, 2005, 1991.*

Lanchner, Carolyn   **N7113.M54.A41993**
Joan Miró. Trade Cloth. Museum of Modern Art. New York, NY. 1993. 464p. ISBN:0-87070-434-6, ISBN13: 978-0-87070-434-5. Dewey:709/.2. LCCN:93-078390.

            Audience: **g,l,u,f.** *Choice, 1994.*

Langmead, Donald   **Z8245**
Willem Marinus Dudok, a Dutch Modernist: A Bio-Bibliography. Cloth Text. Greenwood Publishing Group, Inc. Portsmouth, NH. 1996. 304p. Bio-Bibliographies in Art and Architecture Ser., No. 4 ISBN:0-313-29425-9, ISBN13: 978-0-313-29425-9. Dewey:016.72/092. LCCN:95-046113.

            Audience: **g,l,u,f.**

Laughton, Bruce   **N6853.D3L391996**
Honoré Daumier. Yale University Press, Cumberland, RI. 1996. ISBN:0-300-06945-6, ISBN13: 978-0-300-06945-7.

            Audience: **g,l,u,f.**

Leeman, Richard   **N6537**
Cy Twombly: A Monograph. Trade Cloth. Flammarion et Cie. Paris, 2005. 328p. ISBN:2-08-030483-6, ISBN13: 978-2-08-030483-4. Dewey:769.92. LCCN:2005-278325.

            Audience: **g,l,u,f.** *Choice, 2005.*

Levin, Gail   **N6537.H6A41995**
The Edward Hopper: A Catalogue Raisonné. Trade Cloth, Mixed Media, Compact Disc. W. W. Norton & Company, Inc. New York, NY. 1995. 1056p. ISBN:0-393-03786-X, ISBN13: 978-0-393-03786-9. Dewey:760/.092. LCCN:95-007059.

            Audience: **g,l,u,f.**

Liedtke, Walter, et al.   **N6946.5.D45L54 2001**
Vermeer and the Delft School. Michiel Plomp & Axel Ruger (Authors). Cloth over Boards. Yale University Press. Cumberland, RI. 2001. 640p. Metropolitan Museum of Art Ser. ISBN:0-300-08848-5, ISBN13: 978-0-300-08848-9. Dewey:759.9492/38 LCCN:00-049550.

            Audience: **l,u,f.**

Lightbown, Ronald   ND623.B7L53 1989
Botticelli: Life and Work. Trade Cloth. Abbeville Press, Inc.
New York, NY. 1989. 336p. ISBN:0-89659-931-0, ISBN13:
978-0-89659-931-4. Dewey:759.5 B. LCCN:89-006979.
                                        Audience: **g,l,u,f.**

Livingstone, Marco   N6797.H57L58 1996
David Hockney. Ed. 3. Trade Paper. Thames & Hudson. New
York, NY. 1996. 280p. The World of Art Ser.
ISBN:0-500-20291-5, ISBN13: 978-0-500-20291-3.
Dewey:759.2. LCCN:95-061697.
                                        Audience: **g,l,u,f.**

Livingstone, Marco   N6537.G72G76 2004
Red Grooms: A Retrospective. Arthur C. Danto (Introduction
by), Timothy Hyman (Contribution by). Trade Cloth. Rizzoli
International Publications, Inc. New York, NY. 2004. 240p.
ISBN:0-8478-2635-X, ISBN13: 978-0-8478-2635-3.
Dewey:709.2.
                            Audience: **g,l,u,f.** *Choice, 2005.*

Lucie-Smith, Edward &   N6537.C48L83 2000
  Chicago, Judy
Judy Chicago: An American Vision. Trade Cloth. Watson-Guptill
Publications, Inc. New York, NY. 2000. 192p.
ISBN:0-8230-2585-3, ISBN13: 978-0-8230-2585-5.
Dewey:709.2. LCCN:99-055367.
                                        Audience: **g,l,u,f.**

Marquis, Alice G.   N6853.D8 M3682 2002
Marcel Duchamp: The Bachelor Stripped Bare: A Biography.
Trade Cloth. Museum of Fine Arts, Boston. Boston, MA. 2003.
368p. ISBN:0-87846-644-4, ISBN13: 978-0-87846-644-3.
Dewey:759.4. LCCN:2002-104333.
                            Audience: **g,l,u,f.** *Choice, 2003.*

Marshall, Richard D.   N6537.R87
Ed Ruscha. Trade Cloth. Phaidon Press. London, 2003. 272p.
ISBN:0-7148-3908-6, ISBN13: 978-0-7148-3908-0.
Dewey:709.2. LCCN:2004-274549.
                            Audience: **g,l,u,f.** *Choice, 2004.*

Mercurio, Gianni &   N6537.W28
  Morera, Danila (Editors)
The Andy Warhol Show. Trade Cloth. Skira Editore. Milano,
2005. 332p. ISBN:88-7624-028-4, ISBN13: 978-88-7624-028-7.
Dewey:709.2.
                            Audience: **g,l,u,f.** *Choice, 2005.*

Murray, Linda   N6923.B9
Michelangelo. Trade Cloth. Thames & Hudson. New York, NY.
1985. 216p. World of Art Ser. ISBN:0-500-18175-6, ISBN13:
978-0-500-18175-1. Dewey:709/.2/4.
                                        Audience: **g,l,u,f.**

Nadler, Steven   N6953.R4N33 2003
Rembrandt's Jews. Trade Cloth. University of Chicago Press.
Chicago, IL. 2003. 280p. ISBN:0-226-56736-2, ISBN13:
978-0-226-56736-5. Dewey:759.9492. LCCN:2003-004088.
                                        Audience: **g,l,u,f.**

Nagel, Alexander &   N6923.B9 N34 2000
  Buonarroti, Michelangelo
Michelangelo and the Reform of Art. Trade Cloth. Cambridge
University Press. New York, NY. 2000. 320p.
ISBN:0-521-66292-3, ISBN13: 978-0-521-66292-5.
Dewey:709/.2. LCCN:99-055668.
                            Audience: **u,f.** *Choice, 2001.*

Naumann, Francis M. &   N6853.D8N391999
  Duchamp, Marcel
Marcel Duchamp. Trade Cloth. Harry N. Abrams, Inc. New
York, NY. 1999. 331p. ISBN:0-8109-6334-5, ISBN13:
978-0-8109-6334-4. Dewey:709/.2. LCCN:99-029063.
                            Audience: **g,l,u,f.** *Choice, 2000.*

Nicholl, Charles   N6923.L33N52 2004
Leonardo Da Vinci: Flights of the Mind. Trade Cloth. Penguin
Group (USA) Inc. New York, NY. 2004. 640p.
ISBN:0-670-03345-6, ISBN13: 978-0-670-03345-4.
Dewey:709/.2 B. LCCN:2004-057190.
                                        Audience: **g,l,u,f.**

Nitz, Genoveva & Berta   N6888.H825
  Hummel Museum Staff
Berta Hummel Catalogue Raisonné 1927-1931: Student Days in
Munich. Trade Cloth. Prestel Publishing. New York, NY. 2003.
160p. ISBN:3-7913-2824-7, ISBN13: 978-3-7913-2824-9.
Dewey:709.2. LCCN:2004-268096.
                                        Audience: **l,u,f.**

O'Connor, Francis V.   N6537.P57A4
  (Editor)
Jackson Pollock: Supplement Number 1 to a Catalogue
Raisonné of Paintings, Drawings, and Other Works. Trade Cloth.
Pollock-Krasner Foundation, Inc. New York, NY. 1995. 114p.
ISBN:0-9644639-0-3, ISBN13: 978-0-9644639-0-5.
Dewey:759.13. LCCN:95-067846.
                                        Audience: **g,l,u,f.**

Parry, Ellwood C. III   N6537.C593P37 1988
The Art of Thomas Cole: Ambition and Imagination. Trade
Cloth. University of Delaware Press. Newark, DE. 1989. 424p.
ISBN:0-87413-214-2, ISBN13: 978-0-87413-214-4.
Dewey:759.13. LCCN:85-040511.
                            Audience: **g,l,u,f.** *Choice, 1990.*

Parton, Anthony   N6537.W28
Mikhail Larionov and the Russian Avant-Garde. Trade Paper.
Princeton University Press. Princeton, NJ. 1996. 278p.
ISBN:0-691-02620-3, ISBN13: 978-0-691-02620-6.
Dewey:700/.92.
                            Audience: **g,u,f.** *Choice, 1994.*

Pivar, Stuart   NB553.B4P59
The Barye Bronzes: A Catalogue Raisonné. Ed. 2. Trade Cloth.
Antique Collectors' Club. Easthampton, MA. 1990. 308p.
ISBN:1-85149-142-2, ISBN13: 978-1-85149-142-1.
Dewey:730.92.
                                        Audience: **l,u,f.**

Price, Renee (Editor)   **N6811.5.S34**
Egon Schiele. Trade Cloth. Prestel Publishing. New York, NY.
2005. 320p. ISBN:3-7913-3390-9, ISBN13: 978-3-7913-3390-8.
Dewey:759.36. LCCN:2006-295040.
                                   Audience: **l,u,f.** *Choice, 2006.*

Prideaux, Sue   **N7073.M8P75 2005**
Edvard Munch: Behind the Scream. Saddle Stitched, Cloth over
Boards, Dust Jacket. Yale University Press. Cumberland, RI.
2005. 391p. ISBN:0-300-11024-3, ISBN13: 978-0-300-11024-1.
Dewey:709/.2 B. LCCN:2005-012040.
                                   Audience: **g,l,u,f.** *Choice, 2006.*

Rinder, Lawrence   **N6537.H377A42005**
Tim Hawkinson. Whitney Museum of American Art; Los
Angeles County Museum of Art. Distributed by Harry N.
Abrams. 2005. ISBN:0-87427-144-4, ISBN13:
978-0-87427-144-7.
                                              Audience: **g,l,u,f.**

Rosenthal, T. G.   **N7405.N65R67 2002**
Sidney Nolan. Trade Cloth. Thames & Hudson. New York, NY.
2002. 304p. ISBN:0-500-09304-0, ISBN13: 978-0-500-09304-7.
Dewey:759.994. LCCN:2001-096305.
                                   Audience: **g,l,u,f.** *Choice, 2003, 2002.*

Schmalenbach, Werner   **N6853.P5**
Amedeo Modigliani: Paintings, Sculptures, Drawings. Trade
Cloth. Prestel Publishing. New York, NY. 1990. 228p.
ISBN:3-7913-1095-X, ISBN13: 978-3-7913-1095-4.
Dewey:709.2. LCCN:91-150858.
                                   Audience: **l,u,f.** *Choice, 1991.*

Schmied, Wieland & Fuerst,   **ND511.5.H8H852000**
Andrea
Catalogue Raisonné: Friedensreich Hundertwasser, 1928-2000.
Trade Cloth, Box or Slipcased. Taschen America, LLC. Los
Angeles, CA. 2001. 1792p. Artists' Editions
ISBN:3-8228-6220-7, ISBN13: 978-3-8228-6220-9.
Dewey:709.2.
                                              Audience: **g,l,u,f.**

Schmied, Wieland & Fuerst,   **ND511.5.H8H852000**
Andrea
Catalogué Raisonne Friedensreich Hundertwasser. Trade Cloth.
Taschen America, LLC. Los Angeles, CA. 2000. 1392p.
ISBN:3-8228-6014-X, ISBN13: 978-3-8228-6014-4.
Dewey:709.2.
                                              Audience: **g,l,u,f.**

Schnabel, Julian   **NX512.S35A42004**
Julian Schnabel. Trade Cloth. Harry N. Abrams, Inc. New York,
NY. 2003. 370p. ISBN:0-8109-4633-5, ISBN13:
978-0-8109-4633-0. Dewey:709/.2. LCCN:2003-004498.
                                   Audience: **g,l,u,f.** *Choice, 2004.*

Schwitters, Kurt   **N6888.S42**
Kurt Schwitters: Catalogue Raisonné 1905-1922. Trade Cloth.
Hatje Cantz Verlag GmbH & Co KG. Ostfildern-Ruit, 2000.
552p. ISBN:3-7757-0926-6, ISBN13: 978-3-7757-0926-2.
Dewey:709.2.
                                              Audience: **g,l,u,f.**

Sewell, Darrel   **N6537.T35A4 1991**
Henry Ossawa Tanner. Trade Cloth. Philadelphia Museum of
Art. Philadelphia, PA. 1991. 308p. ISBN:0-87633-086-3,
ISBN13: 978-0-87633-086-9. Dewey:759.13. LCCN:90-024849.
                                   Audience: **g,l,u,f.** *Choice, 1991.*

Sewell, Darrel (Editor)   **N6537.E3A4 2001**
Thomas Eakins. Cloth over Boards. Yale University Press.
Cumberland, RI. 2001. 488p. ISBN:0-300-09111-7, ISBN13:
978-0-300-09111-3. Dewey:759.13. LCCN:2001-053142.
                                   Audience: **g,l,u,f.** *Choice, 2002.*

Shadbolt, Doris   **E99.H2R457 1999**
Bill Reid. Trade Cloth. University of Washington Press. Seattle,
WA. 1998. 200p. ISBN:0-295-97750-7, ISBN13:
978-0-295-97750-8. Dewey:730/.92. LCCN:98-025897.
                                   Audience: **g,l,u,f.** *Choice, 1999, 1987.*

Shiff, Richard, et al.   **N6537.N48A42004**
Barnett Newman: A Catalogue Raisonné. Barnett Newman,
Carol Mancusi-Ungaro, Heidemarie Colsman-Freyberger, Ellyn
Childs Allison & Heidi Colsman-Freyberger (Authors), Bruce
M. White (Photographer). Cloth over Boards. Yale University
Press. Cumberland, RI. 2004. 664p. ISBN:0-300-10167-8,
ISBN13: 978-0-300-10167-6. Dewey:709/.2.
LCCN:2004-052132.
                                   Audience: **g,l,u,f.** *Choice, 2005.*

Slive, Seymour   **N6953.R8A4 2001**
Jacob Van Ruisdael: A Complete Catalogue of His Paintings,
Drawings, and Etchings. Cloth over Boards. Yale University
Press. Cumberland, RI. 2002. 800p. ISBN:0-300-08972-4,
ISBN13: 978-0-300-08972-1. Dewey:760/.092.
LCCN:00-012466.
                                   Audience: **g,l,u,f.** ℬ *Choice, 2002.*

Spies, Werner & Rewald,   **N6888.E7A4 2005**
Sabine (Editors)
Max Ernst: A Retrospective. Cloth over Boards. Yale University
Press. Cumberland, RI. 2005. 328p. ISBN:0-300-10718-8,
ISBN13: 978-0-300-10718-0. Dewey:709/.2.
LCCN:2005-000843.
                                   Audience: **g,l,u,f.** *Choice, 2005, 1991.*

Spurling, Hilary   **N6853.M33S678 2005**
Matisse the Master: A Life of Henri Matisse, the Conquest of
Colour, 1909-1954. Trade Cloth. Alfred A. Knopf Inc. New
York, NY. 2005. 544p. ISBN:0-679-43429-1, ISBN13:
978-0-679-43429-0. Dewey:759.4 B. LCCN:2004-051074.
                                   Audience: **g,l,u,f.** *Choice, 2006.*

Spurling, Hilary   **N6853.M33S681998**
The Unknown Matisse: A Life of Henri Matisse: the Early
Years, 1869-1908. Trade Cloth. Alfred A. Knopf Inc. New York,
NY. 1998. 512p. Unknown Matisse Ser. ISBN:0-679-43428-3,
ISBN13: 978-0-679-43428-3. Dewey:[B]. LCCN:97-046816.
                                              Audience: **g,l,u,f.**

Staiti, Paul J.   **N6537.M66 A4 1989**
Samuel F. B. Morse. Cloth Text. Cambridge University Press.
New York, NY. 1990. 320p. Cambridge Monographs on

American Artists ISBN:0-521-32218-9, ISBN13: 978-0-521-32218-8. Dewey:759.13. LCCN:88-036918.

Audience: **g,l,u,f.** *Choice, 1990.*

Staller, Natasha E.   **N6853.P5S73 2001**
A Sum of Destructions: Picasso's Cultures and the Creation of Cubism. Cloth over Boards. Yale University Press. Cumberland, RI. 2002. 438p. ISBN:0-300-07242-2, ISBN13: 978-0-300-07242-6. Dewey:759.4. LCCN:00-043968.

Audience: **g,l,u,f.** *Choice, 2003, 2002.*

Stebbins, Theodore E.   **ND237.H39S682000**
The Life and Work of Martin Johnson Heade: A Critical Analysis and Catalogue Raisonné. Ed. 2. Cloth over Boards. Yale University Press. Cumberland, RI. 2000. 400p. ISBN:0-300-08183-9, ISBN13: 978-0-300-08183-1. Dewey:759.13 B. LCCN:99-036424.

Audience: **g,l,u,f.**

Stevens, Mark & Swan,   **N6537.D43S74 2004**
  Annalyn
De Kooning: An American Master. Trade Cloth. Knopf Publishing Group. New York, NY. 2004. 752p. ISBN:1-4000-4175-9, ISBN13: 978-1-4000-4175-6. Dewey:709/.2 B. LCCN:2004-048297.

Audience: **g,l,u,f.**

Storr, Robert   **N6537.C54S75 1998**
Chuck Close: A Retrospective. Kirk Varnedoe & Deborah Wye (Contribution by). Trade Cloth. Museum of Modern Art. New York, NY. 2003. 224p. ISBN:0-87070-066-9, ISBN13: 978-0-87070-066-8. Dewey:759.1/3. LCCN:97-075612.

Audience: **g,l,u,f.** *Choice, 1998.*

Szeemann, Harald (Editor)   **N6853.P5**
Marcel Duchamp. Museum Jen Tinguely, Basel Staff (Contribution by). Trade Cloth. Hatje Cantz Verlag GmbH & Co KG. Ostfildern-Ruit, 2002. 232p. ISBN:3-7757-1195-3, ISBN13: 978-3-7757-1195-1. Dewey:709.2.

Audience: **g,l,u,f.** *Choice, 2003.*

Teynard, Felix   **DT60.T48131992**
Felix Teynard, Calotypes of Egypt: A Catalogue Raisonné. Hans P. Kraus Jr. (Editor), Catharine H. Roehrig (Translator), Kathleen Stewart Howe (Contribution by). Trade Cloth. Hans P. Kraus Junior, Inc. New York, NY. 1993. 208p. ISBN:0-9621096-2-2, ISBN13: 978-0-9621096-2-1. Dewey:932. LCCN:92-061649.

Audience: **g,l,u,f.**

Thompson Wylder, Vicki D.,   **N6537.C48A4 2002**
  et al.
Judy Chicago. Lucy R. Lippard & Edward Lucie-Smith (Authors), Elizabeth A. Sackler (Editor). Trade Cloth. Watson-Guptill Publications, Inc. New York, NY. 2002. 144p. ISBN:0-8230-2587-X, ISBN13: 978-0-8230-2587-9. Dewey:700/.92. LCCN:2002-003740.

Audience: **g,l,u,f.** *Choice, 2003.*

Thomson, Richard, et al.   **N6853.T6A4 2005**
Toulouse-Lautrec and Montmartre. Phillip Dennis Cate & Mary

Weaver Chapin (Authors). Trade Cloth. Princeton University Press. Princeton, NJ. 2005. 320p. ISBN:0-691-12337-3, ISBN13: 978-0-691-12337-0. Dewey:760/.092. LCCN:2004-022870.

Audience: **g,l,u,f.**

Tomlinson, Janis A.   **ND813.G7**
Francisco Goya y Lucientes, 1746-1828. Phaidon Press. 1994. ISBN:0-7148-2912-9, ISBN13: 978-0-7148-2912-8.

Audience: **g,l,u,f.**

Tuttle, Richard   **N6537.T8A4 2005**
Richard Tuttle: A Retrospective. Madeleine Grynzstejn (Editor). Trade Cloth. D. A. P./Distributed Art Publishers. New York, NY. 2005. 388p. ISBN:1-933045-00-0, ISBN13: 978-1-933045-00-9. Dewey:709/.2. LCCN:2005-004159.

Audience: **g,l,u,f.** *Choice, 2005.*

Verdi, Richard   **ND553.C33V43 1992**
Cezanne. Trade Paper. Thames & Hudson. New York, NY. 1992. 216p. World of Art Ser. ISBN:0-500-20258-3, ISBN13: 978-0-500-20258-6. Dewey:759.4. LCCN:92-080596.

Audience: **g,l,u,f.**

Wright, Alison   **N6923.P6W74 2004**
The Pollaiuolo Brothers: The Arts of Florence and Rome. Saddle Stitched, Cloth over Boards, Dust Jacket. Yale University Press. Cumberland, RI. 2005. 584p. ISBN:0-300-10625-4, ISBN13: 978-0-300-10625-1. Dewey:709/.45/09024. LCCN:2004-004100.

Audience: **g,l,u,f.** *Choice, 2005.*

Visual Arts in General > Other Topics > Historiography

Belting, Hans   **N380.B4413 2002**
Art History after Modernism. Caroline Saltzwedel, Mitch Cohen & Kenneth J. Northcott (Translators). Trade Cloth. University of Chicago Press. Chicago, IL. 2003. 236p. ISBN:0-226-04184-0, ISBN13: 978-0-226-04184-1. Dewey:709/.04/5. LCCN:2001-006547.

Audience: **u,f.** *Choice, 2004.*

Bryson, Norman (Editor), et   **N72.S6**
  al.
Visual Culture: Images and Interpretations. Michael A. Holly & Keith Moxey (Editors). Trade Paper. Wesleyan University Press. Middletown, CT. 1994. 461p. ISBN:0-8195-6267-X, ISBN13: 978-0-8195-6267-8. Dewey:701/.03. LCCN:93-013614.

Audience: **g,l,u,f.** *Choice, 1995.*

Carter, Miranda   **UB271.R92**
Anthony Blunt: His Lives. Trade Paper. Picador. New York, NY. 2003. 608p. ISBN:0-312-42146-X, ISBN13: 978-0-312-42146-5. Dewey:327.1247/041/092 B.

Audience: **g,l,u,f.**

Elkins, James   N380.E44 2002
Stories of Art. Paper over Boards. Routledge. New York, NY.
2002. 160p. ISBN:0-415-93942-9, ISBN13: 978-0-415-93942-3
Dewey:707/.22. LCCN:2002-009624.

Audience: l,u f

Hatt, Michael & Klonk,   N7450
  Charlotte
Art History: A Critical Introduction to Its Methods. Cloth over
Boards. Manchester University Press. Manchester, 2006. 256p.
ISBN:0-7190-6958-0, ISBN13: 978-0-7190-6958-1.
Dewey:701.18.

Audience: l,u,f.

Preziosi, Donald (Editor)   N7480.A79 1998
The Art of Art History: A Critical Anthology. Trade Paper.
Oxford University Press, Inc. New York, NY. 1998. 608p.
Oxford History of Art Ser. ISBN:0-19-284242-0, ISBN13:
978-0-19-284242-8. Dewey:701/.18. LCCN:98-193489.

Audience: u,f. *Choice, 1998.*

Reid, Donna K.   N380.R438 2004
Thinking and Writing about Art History. Ed. 3. Trade Paper.
Prentice Hall PTR. Upper Saddle River, NJ. 2003. 43p. Art
Basics Ser. ISBN:0-13-183050-3, ISBN13: 978-0-13-183050-9.
Dewey:707/.2. LCCN:2003-048661.

Audience: l,u,f.

Wollheim, Richard   N66.W652001
Richard Wollheim on the Art of Painting: Art as Representation
and Expression. Rob van Gerwen (Editor). Trade Cloth.
Cambridge University Press. New York, NY. 2001. 300p.
ISBN:0-521-80174-5, ISBN13: 978-0-521-80174-4.
Dewey:750/.1. LCCN:00-052952.

Audience: l,u,f. *Choice, 2002.*

Zimmermann, Michael F.   N380
  (Editor)
The Art Historian: National Traditions and Institutional
Practices. Mieke Ball, Stephen Bann, Horst Bredekamp, H.
Perry Chapman, Georges Didi-Huberman, Eric Fernie, Francoise
Forster-Hahn & Carlo Ginzburg (Contribution by). Trade Paper.
Yale University Press. Cumberland, RI. 2003. 240p. Clark
Studies in the Visual Arts ISBN:0-300-09791-3, ISBN13:
978-0-300-09791-7. Dewey:701/.18. LCCN:2003-045593.

Audience: u,f.

Visual Arts in General > Other Topics > Pictorial Humor

Banerji, Christiane &   NC1479.G5G561999
  Donald, Diana (Edited and Translated by)
Gillray Observed: The Earliest Account of His Caricatures in
London and Paris. Trade Cloth. Cambridge University Press.
New York, NY. 1999. 290p. ISBN:0-521-58075-7, ISBN13:
978-0-521-58075-5. Dewey:769.92. LCCN:98-026521.

Audience: l,u,f. *Choice, 1999.*

Bryant, Mark   NC1476.B79 2000
Dictionary of Twentieth-Century British Cartoonists and
Caricaturists. Trade Cloth. Ashgate Publishing, Ltd. Aldershot,
2000. 224p. ISBN:1-84014-286-3, ISBN13: 978-1-84014-286-0.
Dewey:741.5/092/241 B. LCCN:99-045326.

Audience: g,l,u,f. *Choice, 2000.*

Bryant, Mark & Heneage,   NC1470
  Simon
Dictionary of British Cartoonists and Caricaturists. Trade Cloth.
Ashgate Publishing, Ltd. Aldershot, 1994. 250p.
ISBN:0-85967-976-4, ISBN13: 978-0-85967-976-3.
Dewey:741.5/0922/41. LCCN:93-021363.

Audience: g,l,u,f. *Choice, 1995.*

Carlin, John   NC1426.M342005
Masters of American Comics. Paul Karasik & Brian Walker
(Editors), Stanley Crouch, Cynthia Burlingham, Tom DeHaven
& Dave Eggers (Contribution by). Saddle Stitched, Cloth over
Boards. Yale University Press. Cumberland, RI. 2005. 328p.
ISBN:0-300-11317-X, ISBN13: 978-0-300-11317-4.
Dewey:741.5/973/07479494. LCCN:2005-019449.

Audience: g,l,u,f.

Clark, Alan   NC1470.C63 1998
Dictionary of British Comic Artists, Writers and Editors. Trade
Cloth. University of Toronto Press. Toronto, ON. 1997. 790p.
ISBN:0-7123-4521-3, ISBN13: 978-0-7123-4521-7.
Dewey:741.5/0922/41. LCCN:98-108283.

Audience: g,l,u,f.

Heller, Steven & Anderson,   NC998.5.A1H44 1991
  Gail
Graphic Wit: The Art of Humor in Design. Trade Paper.
Watson-Guptill Publications, Inc. New York, NY. 1991. 160p.
ISBN:0-8230-2161-0, ISBN13: 978-0-8230-2161-1.
Dewey:741.6. LCCN:91-017686.

Audience: g,l,u,f.

Henisch, Heinz K. &   TR679.5.H46 1998
  Henisch, Bridget A.
Positive Pleasures: Early Photography and Humor. Trade Cloth.
Pennsylvania State University Press. University Park, PA. 1998.
1146p. ISBN:0-271-01671-X, ISBN13: 978-0-271-01671-9.
Dewey:770/.2/07. LCCN:97-018490.

Audience: g,l,u,f. *Choice, 1998.*

Hirschfeld, Al   NC1429.H527
Hirschfeld on Line: Over 400 Drawings, Paintings and Photos.
Trade Cloth. Applause Theatre Book Publishers. New York, NY.
2000. 346p. Ser. ISBN:1-55783-356-7, ISBN13:
978-1-55783-356-3. Dewey:741.5973. LCCN:98-088469.

Audience: g,l,u,f. *Choice, 1999.*

Ryan, Allan J.   E78.C2R93 1999
The Trickster Shift: Humour and Irony in Contemporary Native
Art. Trade Cloth. University of Washington Press. Seattle, WA.
1999. 320p. ISBN:0-295-97816-3, ISBN13: 978-0-295-97816-1.
Dewey:704.03/97071. LCCN:99-017663.

Audience: l,u,f. *Choice, 2000.*

Smith, Joel NC139.S65S582005
Steinberg at the New Yorker. Ian Frazier (Introduction by).
Trade Cloth. Harry N. Abrams, Inc. New York, NY. 2005. 240p.
ISBN:0-8109-5901-1, ISBN13: 978-0-8109-5901-9.
Dewey:741.5/092 B. LCCN:2004-019498.
Audience: **g,l,u,f.** *Choice, 2005.*

Walker, Brian PN6725.W232004
The Comics Before 1945. Trade Cloth. Harry N. Abrams, Inc.
New York, NY. 2004. 336p. ISBN:0-8109-4970-9, ISBN13:
978-0-8109-4970-6. Dewey:741.5/0973/09041.
LCCN:2004-009514.
Audience: **g,l,u,f.** *Choice, 2005.*

Visual Arts in General > Other Topics > Theory, Philosophy, Aesthetics

Andrews, Malcolm N8213.A53 1999
Landscape and Western Art. Trade Paper. Oxford University
Press, Inc. New York, NY. 2000. 256p. Oxford History of Art
Ser. ISBN:0-19-284233-1, ISBN13: 978-0-19-284233-6.
Dewey:758/.1/091821. LCCN:00-267839.
Audience: **g,l,u,f.** *Choice, 2000.*

Banham, Reyner NK1390 .B28 1996
A Critic Writes: Essays by Reyner Banham. Sutherland Lyall
(Editor). Trade Paper. University of California Press. Berkeley,
CA. 1999. 368p. A Centennial Bk. ISBN:0-520-21944-9,
ISBN13: 978-0-520-21944-1. Dewey:745.2.
Audience: **g,l,u,f.**

Benjamin, Andrew (Editor) PT2603.E455K868 2004
Walter Benjamin and Art. Trade Cloth. Continuum International
Publishing Group, Ltd. London, 2005. 304p. Walter Benjamin
Studies ISBN:0-8264-6729-6, ISBN13: 978-0-8264-6729-4.
Dewey:834/.912. LCCN:2004-056178.
Audience: **g,l,u,f.** *Choice, 2005.*

Carey, John BH39.C373 2006
What Good Are the Arts? Trade Cloth. Oxford University Press,
Inc. New York, NY. 2006. 304p. ISBN:0-19-530554-X, ISBN13:
978-0-19-530554-8. Dewey:700/.1. LCCN:2005-018494.
Audience: **l,u,f.**

Clark, Timothy J. N6490.C584 1999
Farewell to an Idea: Episodes from a History of Modernism.
Cloth over Boards. Yale University Press. Cumberland, RI.
1999. 464p. ISBN:0-300-07532-4, ISBN13: 978-0-300-07532-8.
Dewey:709/.04. LCCN:98-049433.
Audience: **l,u,f.** *Choice, 1999.*

Dormer, Peter TT145.C84 1996
The Culture of Craft. Cloth over Boards. Manchester University
Press. Manchester, 1997. 224p. ISBN:0-7190-4618-1, ISBN13:
978-0-7190-4618-6. Dewey:745.5. LCCN:96-031364.
Audience: **g,l,u,f.**

Eck, Caroline van & N70
Winters, Edward
Dealing with the Visual: Art History, Aesthetics and Visual
Culture. Trade Cloth. Ashgate Publishing, Ltd. Aldershot, 2005.
256p. Histories of Vision Ser. ISBN:0-7546-3428-0, ISBN13:
978-0-7546-3428-7. Dewey:701/.17. LCCN:2004-049316.
Audience: **l,u,f.**

Eco, Umberto BD331
History of Beauty. Alastair McEwen (Translator). Trade Cloth.
Rizzoli International Publications, Inc. New York, NY. 2004.
432p. ISBN:0-8478-2646-5, ISBN13: 978-0-8478-2646-9.
Dewey:111. LCCN:2004-092388.
Audience: **g,l,u,f.** *Choice, 2005.*

Elkins, James (Editor) N7480.A776 2005
Art History Versus Aesthetics, Vol. 1. Saddle Stitched, Cloth
over Boards. Routledge. New York, NY. 2005. 306p. The Art
Seminar Ser., Vol. 1 ISBN:0-415-97688-X, ISBN13:
978-0-415-97688-6. Dewey:701/.17. LCCN:2005-013494.
Audience: **l,u,f.**

Emerling, Jae N7480.E46 2005
Theory for Art History. Paper over Boards. Routledge. New
York, NY. 2005. 264p. Theory4 Ser. ISBN:0-415-97363-5,
ISBN13: 978-0-415-97363-2. Dewey:701/.18.
LCCN:2005-011243.
Audience: **l,u,f.**

Emmer, Michele (Editor) N72.M3V58 2005
The Visual Mind II. Trade Cloth. MIT Press. Cambridge, MA.
2005. 712p. Leonardo Bks. ISBN:0-262-05076-5, ISBN13:
978-0-262-05076-0. Dewey:701/.5. LCCN:2004-057850.
Audience: **l,u,f.** *Choice, 2006.*

Freedberg, David N71.F65
The Power of Images: Studies in the History and Theory of
Response. Trade Paper. University of Chicago Press. Chicago,
IL. 1991. 560p. ISBN:0-226-26146-8, ISBN13:
978-0-226-26146-1. Dewey:701.1. LCCN:88-027638.
Audience: **l,u,f.** *Choice, 1990.*

Freeman, Mark P. N71 .F655 1993
Finding the Muse: A Sociopsychological Inquiry into the
Conditions of Artistic Creativity. Trade Cloth. Cambridge
University Press. New York, NY. 1994. 340p.
ISBN:0-521-39218-7, ISBN13: 978-0-521-39218-1.
Dewey:709.7309046. LCCN:93-003468.
Audience: **u,f.** *Choice, 1994.*

Gombrich, E. H. N71
Art and Illusion: A Study in the Psychology of Pictorial
Representation. Ed. 6. Trade Paper. Phaidon Press, Inc. New
York, NY. 2004. 412p. ISBN:0-7148-4208-7, ISBN13:
978-0-7148-4208-0. Dewey:701.1/5.
Audience: **l,u,f.** *B*

Gombrich, E. H. N7445.2
Meditations on a Hobby Horse and Other Essays on the Theory

of Art. Ed. 4. Trade Paper. Phaidon Press. London, 1994. 145p.
ISBN:0-7148-3245-6, ISBN13: 978-0-7148-3245-6.
Dewey:700.1.

Audience: **g,l,u,f.**

Gombrich, E. H.   **N5311.G643 2002**
The Preference for the Primitive: Episodes in the History of
Western Taste and Art. Trade Cloth. Phaidon Press. London,
2002. 324p. ISBN:0-7148-4154-4, ISBN13: 978-0-7148-4154-0.
Dewey:709. LCCN:2003-274005.

Audience: **l,u,f.** *Choice, 2003.*

Harris, Jonathan   **N7480.H37 2001**
The New Art History: A Critical Introduction. Paper over
Boards. Routledge. New York, NY. 2001. 320p.
ISBN:0-415-23007-1, ISBN13: 978-0-415-23007-0.
Dewey:707/.22. LCCN:2001-019752.

Audience: **l,u,f.**

Harrison, Charles & Wood,   **N6490.A7167 2002**
Paul (Editors)
Art in Theory, 1900-2000: An Anthology of Changing Ideas. Ed.
2. Trade Paper. Blackwell Publishing, Inc. Malden, MA. 2002.
1288p. ISBN:0-631-22708-3, ISBN13: 978-0-631-22708-3.
Dewey:709/.04. LCCN:2002-018490.

Audience: **g,l,u,f.**

Hearn, Fil   **NA2500.H379 2003**
Ideas That Shaped Buildings. Trade Paper. MIT Press.
Cambridge, MA. 2003. 312p. ISBN:0-262-58227-9, ISBN13:
978-0-262-58227-8. Dewey:720/.1. LCCN:2003-051206.

Audience: **g,l,u,f.** *Choice, 2004.*

Hocks, Mary E. &   **P93.5.E56 2005**
Kendrick, Michelle R. (Editors)
Eloquent Images: Word and Image in the Age of New Media.
Trade Paper. MIT Press. Cambridge, MA. 2005. 376p.
ISBN:0-262-58261-9, ISBN13: 978-0-262-58261-2.
Dewey:302.23.

Audience: **l,u,f.**

Kandinsky, Wassily   **N66**
Concerning the Spiritual in Art. Adrian Glew & Michael T. H.
Sadler (Contribution by). Trade Cloth. Museum of Fine Arts,
Boston. Boston, MA. 2006. 192p. ISBN:0-87846-702-5,
ISBN13: 978-0-87846-702-0. Dewey:701.17.

Audience: **g,l,u,f.**

Kemal, Salim & Gaskell,   **N5303.L35**
Ivan (Editors)
The Language of Art History. Salim Kemal & Ivan Gaskell
(Contribution by). Trade Paper. Cambridge University Press.
New York, NY. 1992. 255p. Cambridge Studies in Philosophy
and the Arts ISBN:0-521-44598-1, ISBN13: 978-0-521-44598-6.
Dewey:709.

Audience: **l,u,f.** *Choice, 1992.*

Komar, Vitaly, et al.   **ND1140 .P26 1999**
Painting by Numbers: Komar and Melamid's Scientific Guide to
Art. Aleksandr Melamid & Joann Wypijewski (Authors). Trade

Paper. University of California Press. Berkeley, CA. 1998. 206p.
ISBN:0-520-21861-2, ISBN13: 978-0-520-21861-1.
Dewey:750/.1. LCCN:98-028904.

Audience: **g,l,u,f.**

Kress, Gunther & Leeuwen,   **NK1510**
Theo Van
Reading Images: The Grammar of Visual Design. Ed. 2. Trade
Paper. Routledge. New York, NY. 2006. 320p.
ISBN:0-415-31915-3, ISBN13: 978-0-415-31915-7. Dewey:701.

Audience: **g,l,u,f.** *Choice, 1996.*

Leach, Neil   **NA2500.L47 1996**
Rethinking Architecture: A Reader in Cultural Theory. Paper
over Boards. Routledge. New York, NY. 1997. 432p.
ISBN:0-415-12825-0, ISBN13: 978-0-415-12825-4.
Dewey:720/.1. LCCN:96-019406.

Audience: **g,l,u,f.**

Livingstone, Margaret S.   **N7430.5.L542002**
Vision and Art: The Biology of Seeing. David Hubel (Foreword
by). Trade Cloth. Harry N. Abrams, Inc. New York, NY. 2002.
208p. ISBN:0-8109-0406-3, ISBN13: 978-0-8109-0406-4.
Dewey:750.1/8. LCCN:2001-046508.

Audience: **g,l,u,f.** *Choice, 2003, 2002.*

Mallgrave, Harry   **NA2500.M28 2005**
Modern Architectural Theory: A Historical Survey, 1673-1968.
Trade Cloth. Cambridge University Press. New York, NY. 2005.
522p. ISBN:0-521-79306-8, ISBN13: 978-0-521-79306-3.
Dewey:720/.1. LCCN:2004-045916.

Audience: **l,u,f.** *Choice, 2006.*

Mann, Vivian B. (Editor)   **N7415 .J49 2000**
Jewish Texts on the Visual Arts. Trade Cloth. Cambridge
University Press. New York, NY. 2000. 256p.
ISBN:0-521-65217-0, ISBN13: 978-0-521-65217-9.
Dewey:704.03/924. LCCN:99-014938.

Audience: **g,u,f.** *Choice, 2000.*

Margolin, Victor (Editor)   **NK1505.D47 1989**
Design Discourse: History, Theory, Criticism. Trade Paper.
University of Chicago Press. Chicago, IL. 1989. 302p.
ISBN:0-226-50514-6, ISBN13: 978-0-226-50514-5.
Dewey:745.4. LCCN:89-033920.

Audience: **g,l,u,f.**

Newman, Amy   **N1.A8143N49 2000**
Challenging Art: Artforum 1962-1974. Trade Cloth. Soho Press,
Inc. New York, NY. 2001. xi, 559p. ISBN:1-56947-207-6,
ISBN13: 978-1-56947-207-1. Dewey:709.7/3/09046.
LCCN:00-034422.

Audience: **l,u,f.**

Prettejohn, Elizabeth   **N66.P74 2005**
Beauty and Art 1750-2000. Trade Paper, Perfect. Oxford
University Press, Inc. New York, NY. 2005. 224p. Oxford
History of Art Ser. ISBN:0-19-280160-0, ISBN13:
978-0-19-280160-9. Dewey:701/.17/0903. LCCN:2004-061707.

Audience: **g,l,u,f.**

Proto, Francesco (Editor)   NA2543.S6B347 2003
Mass Identity Architecture: Architectural Writings of Jean
Baudrillard. Trade Cloth. John Wiley & Sons, Inc. Hoboken, NJ.
2004. 160p. ISBN:0-470-09019-7, ISBN13: 978-0-470-09019-0.
Dewey:720.1/03. LCCN:2004-299543.

Audience: **l,u,f.**

Rampley, Matthew (Editor)   P93.5 .E96 2005
Exploring Visual Culture: Definitions, Concepts, Contexts. Trade
Paper, Perfect. Edinburgh University Press. Edinburgh, 2005.
224p. ISBN:0-7486-1845-7, ISBN13: 978-0-7486-1845-3.
Dewey:302.2/3.

Audience: **g,l,u,f.**

Schefer, Jean Louis   NX640 .S34 1995
The Enigmatic Body: Essays on the Arts. Paul Smith (Editor),
Norman Bryson (Contribution by). Trade Cloth. Cambridge
University Press. New York, NY. 1995. 250p. Cambridge
Studies in New Art History and Criticism ISBN:0-521-37204-6,
ISBN13: 978-0-521-37204-6. Dewey:700. LCCN:94-023722.

Audience: **l,u,f.**

Shiner, Larry E.   NX440.S5 2001
The Invention of Art: A Cultural History. Trade Cloth.
University of Chicago Press. Chicago, IL. 2001. 352p.
ISBN:0-226-75342-5, ISBN13: 978-0-226-75342-3.
Dewey:700/.9. LCCN:00-053247.

Audience: **g,l,u,f.** *Choice, 2002.*

Solso, Robert L.   NX165
The Psychology of Art and the Evolution of the Conscious
Brain. Trade Paper. MIT Press. Cambridge, MA. 2005. 294p.
Bradford Bks. ISBN:0-262-69332-1, ISBN13:
978-0-262-69332-5. Dewey:701/.15.

Audience: **g,l,u,f.** *Choice, 2004.*

Sontag, Susan   PS3569.O6547R44 2003
Regarding the Pain of Others. Cloth over Boards. Farrar, Straus
& Giroux. New York, NY. 2003. 144p. ISBN:0-374-24858-3,
ISBN13: 978-0-374-24858-1. Dewey:303.6.
LCCN:2002-192527.

Audience: **g,l,u,f.** *Choice, 2003.*

Viollet-le-Duc,   NA1053.V7V471990
Eugène-Emmanuel
The Architectural Theory of Viollet-le-Duc: Readings and
Commentaries. M. F. Hearn (Editor). Trade Paper. MIT Press.
Cambridge, MA. 1990. 306p. ISBN:0-262-72013-2, ISBN13:
978-0-262-72013-7. Dewey:720. LCCN:89-034629.

Audience: **g,l,u,f.**

Washburn, Dorothy Koster   NK1570.S96 2004
& Crowe, Donald W. (Editors)
Symmetry Comes of Age: The Role of Pattern in Culture. Trade
Cloth. University of Washington Press. Seattle, WA. 2004. 392p.
ISBN:0-295-98366-3, ISBN13: 978-0-295-98366-0.
Dewey:745.4. LCCN:2003-054894.

Audience: **g,l,u,f.** *Choice, 2005.*

Wood, Paul & Gaiger, Jason   N6420.A78 2001
Art in Theory, 1648-1815: An Anthology of Changing Ideas.

Charles Harrison (Editor). Trade Paper. Blackwell Publishing,
Inc. Malden, MA. 2001. 1248p. ISBN:0-631-20064-9, ISBN13:
978-0-631-20064-2. LCCN:00-034312.

Audience: **g,l,u,f.**

Wood, Paul & Gaiger, Jason   N6450.A779 2001
Art in Theory, 1815-1900: An Anthology of Changing Ideas.
Charles Harrison (Editor). Trade Paper. Blackwell Publishing,
Inc. Malden, MA. 1998. 1120p. ISBN:0-631-20066-5, ISBN13:
978-0-631-20066-6. Dewey:709/.03/4. LCCN:97-020185.

Audience: **g,l,u,f.**

Visual Arts in General > Other Topics > African American Art

Arnett, William, et al.   NK9112 .Q54 2002
The Quilts of Gee's Bend: Masterpieces from a Lost Place. John
Beardsley, Jane Livingston & Alvia J. Wardlaw (Authors). Trade
Cloth. Tinwood Books. Atlanta, GA. 2002. 140p.
ISBN:0-9653766-4-8, ISBN13: 978-0-9653766-4-8.
Dewey:746.460976138. LCCN:2002-022468.

Audience: **g,l,u,f.** *Choice, 2003.*

Dunitz, Robin J. & Prigoff,   ND2639.3.A35P75 2000
James
Walls of Heritage, Walls of Pride: African American Murals.
Trade Cloth. Pomegranate Communications, Inc. Petaluma, CA.
2003. 280p. ISBN:0-7649-1339-5, ISBN13: 978-0-7649-1339-6.
Dewey:751.7/3/08996073. LCCN:00-029133.

Audience: **g,l,u,f.**

Farrington, Lisa E.   N6538.N5F27 2004
Creating Their Own Image: The History of African-American
Women Artists. Trade Cloth. Oxford University Press, Inc. New
York, NY. 2004. 368p. ISBN:0-19-516721-X, ISBN13:
978-0-19-516721-4. Dewey:704/.042/08996073.
LCCN:2003-066171.

Audience: **g,l,u,f.** *Choice, 2005.*

Honour, Hugh   N7625.5
The Image of the Black in Western Art: From the American
Revolution to World War I, Vol. IV, Pt. 2: Black Models &
White Myths. Trade Cloth. Harvard University Press.
Cambridge, MA. 1989. 306p. Menil Foundation Ser.
ISBN:0-939594-18-8, ISBN13: 978-0-939594-18-4.
Dewey:704.9/42. LCCN:76-025772.

Audience: **l,u,f.**

Igoe, Lynn M. & Igoe,   Z5956.A47
James
Two Hundred Fifty Years of Afro-American Art: An Annotated
Bibliography. Trade Paper. Books on Demand. Ann Arbor, MI.
1291p. ISBN:0-8357-8673-0, ISBN13: 978-0-8357-8673-7.
Dewey:016.704/0396073. LCCN:81-012226.

Audience: **g,l,u,f.** *B*

Jezierski, John Vincent   TR139.J48 2000
Enterprising Images: The Goodridge Brothers, African American
Photographers, 1847-1922. Trade Cloth. Wayne State University
Press. Detroit, MI. 2000. xv, 346p. Great Lakes Bks.

ISBN:0-8143-2451-7, ISBN13: 978-0-8143-2451-6.
Dewey:770/.92/273 B. LCCN:99-039386.

         Audience: **g,l,u,f.**   *Choice, 2001.*

Ketner, Joseph D.   **ND1839.D85**
The Emergence of the African-American Artist: Roberts S.
Duncanson, 1821-1872. Trade Paper. University of Missouri
Press. Columbia, MO. 1994. 248p. ISBN:0-8262-0974-2,
ISBN13: 978-0-8262-0974-0. Dewey:759.13.

         Audience: **g,l,u,f.**

Lewis, Samella S.   **N6538.N5 L38 2003**
African American Art and Artists. Ed. 3. Trade Cloth. University
of California Press. Berkeley, CA. 2003. 360p.
ISBN:0-520-23929-6, ISBN13: 978-0-520-23929-6.
Dewey:704.03/96073. LCCN:2002-041369.

         Audience: **g,l,u,f.**   *Choice, 2003.*

Patton, Sharon F.   **N6538.N5P38 1998**
African-American Art. Trade Paper. Oxford University Press,
Inc. New York, NY. 1998. 320p. Oxford History of Art Ser.
ISBN:0-19-284213-7, ISBN13: 978-0-19-284213-8.
Dewey:704.03/96/073. LCCN:98-190459.

         Audience: **g,l,u,f.**   *Choice, 1998.*

Powell, Richard J.   **N6538.N5P69 2002**
Black Art: A Cultural History. Ed. 2. Trade Paper. Thames &
Hudson. New York, NY. 2003. 272p. The World of Art Ser.
ISBN:0-500-20362-8, ISBN13: 978-0-500-20362-0.
Dewey:704.03/96073. LCCN:2002-102604.

         Audience: **g,l,u,f.**

Powell, Richard J.   **N6538.N5P64 1997**
Black Art and Culture in the 20th Century. Trade Paper. Thames
& Hudson. New York, NY. 1997. 256p. The World of Art Ser.
ISBN:0-500-20295-8, ISBN13: 978-0-500-20295-1.
Dewey:709/.04/008996. LCCN:96-060366.

         Audience: **g,l,u,f.**

Powell, Richard J. &   **N6538.N5P68 1999**
  Reynolds, Jock
To Conserve a Legacy: American Art from Historically Black
Colleges and Universities. Kinshasha Holman Conwill
(Introduction by). Trade Paper. MIT Press. Cambridge, MA.
1999. 200p. ISBN:0-262-66151-9, ISBN13: 978-0-262-66151-5.
Dewey:704.03/96073/0074. LCCN:98-050539.

         Audience: **g,l,u,f.**   *Choice, 1999.*

Riggs, Thomas   **N40.S78 1997**
St. James Guide to Black Artists. Trade Cloth. Thomson Gale.
Farmington Hills, MI. 1997. 625p. ISBN:1-55862-220-9,
ISBN13: 978-1-55862-220-3. Dewey:709/.2/396 B.
LCCN:97-003068.

         Audience: **g,l,u,f.**   *Choice, 1998.*

Willis, Deborah   **TR23.W55 2000**
Reflections in Black: A History of Black Photographers, 1840 to
the Present. Robin D. G. Kelley (Introduction by). Trade Cloth.
W. W. Norton & Company, Inc. New York, NY. 2000. 368p.
ISBN:0-393-04880-2, ISBN13: 978-0-393-04880-3.
Dewey:770/.8996/073. LCCN:99-055185.

         Audience: **g,l,u,f.**   *Choice, 2001.*

Wilson, Dreck Spurlock   **NA736.A47 2003**
  (Editor)
African American Architects: A Biographical Dictionary,
1865-1945. Paper over Boards. Routledge. New York, NY. 2004.
576p. ISBN:0-415-92959-8, ISBN13: 978-0-415-92959-2.
Dewey:720/.92/396073 B. LCCN:2003-009675.

         Audience: **g,l,u,f.**   *Choice, 2004.*

Wood, Marcus   **N8243.S576W66 2000**
Blind Memory: Visual Representations of Slavery in England
and America. Cloth Text. Routledge. New York, NY. 2000.
400p. ISBN:0-415-92697-1, ISBN13: 978-0-415-92697-3.
Dewey:704.9/49326. LCCN:00-020839.

         Audience: **g,l,u,f.**

Visual Arts in General > Other Topics > Art and Gender

         N43.P47
Dictionary of Women's Art Before 1900. Ed. 2. Trade Cloth.
Thomson Gale. Farmington Hills, MI. 2002.
ISBN:0-7838-8573-3, ISBN13: 978-0-7838-8573-5.
Dewey:709/.2/2.

         Audience: **g,l,u,f.**

Bartra, Eli (Editor,   **NK802.C7 2003**
  Translator)
Crafting Gender: Women and Folk Art in Latin America and the
Caribbean. Trade Cloth. Duke University Press. Durham, NC.
2003. 248p. ISBN:0-8223-3182-9, ISBN13: 978-0-8223-3182-7.
Dewey:745/.082. LCCN:2003-007677.

         Audience: **g,l,u,f.**   *Choice, 2004.*

Bernardin, Susan, et al.   **E77.5.T73 2003**
Trading Gazes: Euro-American Women Photographers and
Native North Americans, 1880-1940. Melody Graulich, Lisa
MacFarlane & Nicole Tonkovich (Authors), Louis Owens
(Afterword by). Trade Cloth. Rutgers University Press.
Piscataway, NJ. 2003. 240p. ISBN:0-8135-3169-1, ISBN13:
978-0-8135-3169-4. Dewey:970/.00497. LCCN:2002-070503.

         Audience: **g,l,u,f.**   *Choice, 2003.*

Borzello, Frances   **N8354.B672000**
A World of Our Own: Women as Artists since the Renaissance.
Trade Cloth. Watson-Guptill Publications, Inc. New York, NY.
2000. 224p. ISBN:0-8230-5874-3, ISBN13: 978-0-8230-5874-7.
Dewey:700.8/2. LCCN:00-103117.

         Audience: **g,l,u,f.**   *Choice, 2001.*

Brennan, Marcia   **N6512.5.S75B74 2001**
Painting Gender, Constructing Theory: The Alfred Stieglitz
Circle and American Formalist Aesthetics. Trade Cloth. MIT
Press. Cambridge, MA. 2001. 390p. ISBN:0-262-02488-8,
ISBN13: 978-0-262-02488-4. Dewey:709/.73/09042.
LCCN:00-046060.

         Audience: **u,f.**

Broude, Norma & Garrard,
Mary D. (Editors)
N72.F45 E96 1992

Expanding Discourse: Feminism and Art History. Trade Paper. Westview Press. Boulder, CO. 1992. 528p. ISBN:0-06-430207-5, ISBN13: 978-0-06-430207-4. Dewey:704/.042. LCCN:91-058341.

Audience: **g,l,u,f.**

Chadwick, Whitney
N8354

Women, Art, and Society. Ed. 3. Trade Paper. Thames & Hudson. New York, NY. 2002. 496p. World of Art Ser. ISBN:0-500-20354-7, ISBN13: 978-0-500-20354-5. Dewey:704/.042. LCCN:2001-092911.

Audience: **g,l,u,f.**

Deepwell, Katy (Editor)
N72.F45N45 1995

New Feminist Art Criticism: Critical Strategies. Trade Paper. Manchester University Press. Manchester, 1995. 201p. ISBN:0-7190-4258-5, ISBN13: 978-0-7190-4258-4. Dewey:701/.03. LCCN:94-005414.

Audience: **l,u,f.**

Farrington, Lisa E.
N6538.N5F27 2004

Creating Their Own Image: The History of African-American Women Artists. Trade Cloth. Oxford University Press, Inc. New York, NY. 2004. 368p. ISBN:0-19-516721-X, ISBN13: 978-0-19-516721-4. Dewey:704/.042/08996073. LCCN:2003-066171.

Audience: **g,l,u,f.** *Choice, 2005.*

Farris, Phoebe M. (Editor)
N8354

Women Artists of Color: A Bio-Critical Sourcebook to 20th Century Artists in the Americas. Cloth Text. Greenwood Publishing Group, Inc. Portsmouth, NH. 1999. 520p. ISBN:0-313-30374-6, ISBN13: 978-0-313-30374-6. Dewey:709/.2/39 B. LCCN:98-047134.

Audience: **l,u,f.**

Fernandez, Dominique
N8217.H67F4713 2001

A Hidden Love: Art and Homosexuality. David Radzinowicz (Translator). Trade Cloth. Prestel Publishing. New York, NY. 2001. 320p. ISBN:3-7913-2704-6, ISBN13: 978-3-7913-2704-4. Dewey:704.9/49306766. LCCN:2002-100141.

Audience: **g,l,u,f.** *Choice, 2002.*

Gaze, Delia (Editor)
N8354.D53 1997

Dictionary of Women Artists, Set. Trade Cloth. Fitzroy Dearborn Publishers, Inc. Chicago, IL. 1997. 1512p. ISBN:1-884964-21-4, ISBN13: 978-1-884964-21-3. Dewey:709.2/2. LCCN:97-206872.

Audience: **g,l,u,f.** *Choice, 1998.*

Hawass, Zahi
HQ1137.E3H39 2000

Silent Images: Women in Pharaonic Egypt. Trade Cloth. Harry N. Abrams, Inc. New York, NY. 2000. 207p. ISBN:0-8109-4478-2, ISBN13: 978-0-8109-4478-7. Dewey:305.4/0932. LCCN:99-069858.

Audience: **l,u,f.**

Heller, Jules & Heller,
Nancy G. (Editors)
N40

North American Women Artists of the Twentieth Century: A Biographical Dictionary. Trade Paper. Garland Publishing, Inc.

New York, NY. 1997. 736p. Reference Library of the Humanities, Vol. 1219 ISBN:0-8153-2584-3, ISBN13: 978-0-8153-2584-0. Dewey:709/.2/2 B. LCCN:94-049710.

Audience: **g,l,u,f.** *Choice, 1995.*

Hillstrom, Laurie Collier &
Hillstrom, Kevin
N8354.C66 1999

Contemporary Women Artists. Trade Cloth. Thomson Gale. Farmington Hills, MI. 1999. xx, 760p. ISBN:1-55862-372-8, ISBN13: 978-1-55862-372-9. Dewey:709/.2/2 B. LCCN:99-010053.

Audience: **g,l,u,f.** *Choice, 1999.*

Kirkham, Pat (Editor)
NK1404.W662000

Women Designers in the U.S.A., 1900-2000: Diversity and Difference. Cloth over Boards. Yale University Press. Cumberland, RI. 2000. 464p. ISBN:0-300-08734-9, ISBN13: 978-0-300-08734-5. Dewey:745.4/082/0973. LCCN:00-108610.

Audience: **g,l,u,f.** *Choice, 2001.*

Krauss, Rosalind E.
NX180.F4K73 1999

Bachelors: Essays on Nine Women "Bachelors" Who Challenged Masculinist Aesthetics. Trade Cloth. MIT Press. Cambridge, MA. 1999. 232p. October Bks. ISBN:0-262-11239-6, ISBN13: 978-0-262-11239-0. Dewey:704/.042. LCCN:98-040301.

Audience: **l,u,f.**

Lucie-Smith, Edward
N8217.E6L83 1991

Sexuality in Western Art. Ed. 2. Trade Paper. Thames & Hudson. New York, NY. 1991. 288p. World of Art Ser. ISBN:0-500-20252-4, ISBN13: 978-0-500-20252-4. Dewey:704.9/428. LCCN:90-071871.

Audience: **g,l,u,f.**

Mahon, Alyce
N8217.E6

Eroticism and Art. Trade Cloth. Oxford University Press, Inc. New York, NY. 2006. 336p. ISBN:0-19-280187-2, ISBN13: 978-0-19-280187-6. Dewey:704.9428. LCCN:2006-295852.

Audience: **l,u,f.**

Markoe, Glenn, et al.
N5335.C56C566 1996

Mistress of the House, Mistress of Heaven: Women in Ancient Egypt. Anne K. Capel & Betsy M. Bryan (Authors). Trade Cloth. Hudson Hills Press LLC. Manchester, VT. 1997. 240p. ISBN:1-55595-129-5, ISBN13: 978-1-55595-129-0. Dewey:704.9/424/0932074771. LCCN:96-009376.

Audience: **l,u,f.** *Choice, 1997.*

McEuen, Melissa A.
TR139.M3952000

Seeing America: Women Photographers Between the Wars. Trade Cloth. University Press of Kentucky. Lexington, KY. 1999. 360p. ISBN:0-8131-2132-9, ISBN13: 978-0-8131-2132-1. Dewey:770/.92/273 B. LCCN:99-017219.

Audience: **g,l,u,f.** *Choice, 2000.*

Nochlin, Linda
N72.S6

Women, Art, and Power and Other Essays. Trade Paper. Westview Press. Boulder, CO. 1989. 208p. ISBN:0-06-430183-4, ISBN13: 978-0-06-430183-1. Dewey:701/.03. LCCN:88-045118.

Audience: **g,l,u,f.** *Choice, 1989.*

Formats: Web: ☐ Ebook: 🄴 CD/DVD-ROM: 💿 BCL3: 𝓑

Owen, Nancy E.   NK4340.R7O95 2001
Rookwood and the Industry of Art: Women, Culture and
Commerce, 1880-1913. Trade Paper. Ohio University Press.
Athens, OH. 2001. 349p. ISBN:0-8214-1338-4, ISBN13:
978-0-8214-1338-8. Dewey:338.7/617383/0977178.
LCCN:00-040631.
                          Audience: **l,u,f.** *Choice, 2001.*

Rosenblum, Naomi   TR139.R67 2000
A History of Women Photographers. Ed. 2. Trade Cloth.
Abbeville Press, Inc. New York, NY. 2000. 400p.
ISBN:0-7892-0658-7, ISBN13: 978-0-7892-0658-9.
Dewey:770/.82. LCCN:00-036249.
                          Audience: **g,l,u,f.** *Choice, 1995.*

Rosenthal, Lisa   ND673.R9R67 2006
Gender, Politics, and Allegory in the Art of Rubens. Trade
Cloth. Cambridge University Press. New York, NY. 2005. 328p.
ISBN:0-521-84244-1, ISBN13: 978-0-521-84244-0.
Dewey:759.9493. LCCN:2005-010514.
                          Audience: **l,u,f.** *Choice, 2006.*

Salomon, Nanette   ND1452.N43S24 2004
Shifting Priorities: Gender and Genre in Seventeenth-Century
Dutch Painting. Trade Cloth. Stanford University Press. Palo
Alto, CA. 2004. 280p. Cultural Memory in the Present Ser.
ISBN:0-8047-4476-9, ISBN13: 978-0-8047-4476-8.
Dewey:754/.09492/09032. LCCN:2003-025165.
                          Audience: **g,l,u,f.**

Saslow, James M.   N8217.H67S27 1999
Pictures and Passions: A History of Homosexuality in the Visual
Arts. Penguin Group (USA) Inc. 1999. ISBN:0-670-85953-2,
ISBN13: 978-0-670-85953-5.
                          Audience: **g,l,u,f.**

Slatkin, Wendy   N43.S57 2001
Women Artists in History: From Antiquity to the Present. Ed. 4.
Trade Paper. Prentice Hall PTR. Upper Saddle River, NJ. 2000.
306p. ISBN:0-13-027319-8, ISBN13: 978-0-13-027319-2.
Dewey:704/.042. LCCN:00-026345.
                          Audience: **g,l,u,f.**

Solnit, Rebecca   NX456.5.E6S65 2001
As Eve Said to the Serpent: On Landscape, Gender, and Art.
Trade Cloth. University of Georgia Press. Athens, GA. 2001.
234p. ISBN:0-8203-2215-6, ISBN13: 978-0-8203-2215-5.
Dewey:704.9/436/01. LCCN:00-044726.
                          Audience: **g,l,u,f.**

Summers, Claude J. (Editor)   N72.H64Q44 2004
The Queer Encyclopedia of the Visual Arts. Trade Paper. Cleis
Press. San Francisco, CA. 2004. 400p. ISBN:1-57344-191-0,
ISBN13: 978-1-57344-191-9. Dewey:704/.08664/03.
LCCN:2004-004263.
                          Audience: **g,l,u,f.** *Choice, 2005.*

Vincentelli, Moira   NK3780.V56 1999
Women and Ceramics: Gendered Vessels. Trade Cloth.
Manchester University Press. Manchester, 2000. 273p. Studies

in Design and Material Culture ISBN:0-7190-3839-1, ISBN13:
978-0-7190-3839-6. Dewey:738/.082. LCCN:99-043120.
                          Audience: **g,l,u,f.** *Choice, 2000.*

Weinberg, Jonathan   N72.H64W452005
Male Desire: The Homoerotic in American Art. Trade Cloth.
Harry N. Abrams, Inc. New York, NY. 2005. 208p.
ISBN:0-8109-5894-5, ISBN13: 978-0-8109-5894-4.
Dewey:704.9/423/0866420973. LCCN:2004-023749.
                          Audience: **g,l,u,f.**

Weisman, Leslie K.   NA2543.W65
Discrimination by Design: A Feminist Critique of the Man-Made
Environment. Trade Paper. University of Illinois Press.
Champaign, IL. 1994. 200p. ISBN:0-252-06399-6, ISBN13:
978-0-252-06399-2. Dewey:720/.82.
                          Audience: **u,f.** *Choice, 1992.*

Visual Arts in General > Other Topics > Art and Society

Alexander, Victoria D.   NX180.S6A435 2003
Sociology of the Arts: Exploring Fine and Popular Forms. Trade
Cloth. Blackwell Publishing, Inc. Malden, MA. 2003. 392p.
ISBN:0-631-23039-4, ISBN13: 978-0-631-23039-7.
Dewey:306.4/7. LCCN:2002-006550.
                          Audience: **g,l,u,f.** *Choice, 2003.*

Avena, Thomas (Editor)   NX180.A36L54 1994
Life Sentences: Writers, Artists, and AIDS. Trade Paper.
Mercury House. San Francisco, CA. 1994. 284p.
ISBN:1-56279-051-X, ISBN13: 978-1-56279-051-6.
Dewey:700/.1/03. LCCN:93-038922.
                          Audience: **g,l,u,f.** *Choice, 1994.*

Boime, Albert   N6757.B561993
Art in an Age of Bonapartism, 1800-1815. Trade Paper.
University of Chicago Press. Chicago, IL. 1993. 734p. Social
History of Modern Art Ser., Vol. 2 ISBN:0-226-06336-4,
ISBN13: 978-0-226-06336-2. Dewey:709/.034.
LCCN:89-020201.
                          Audience: **g,l,u,f.**

Boime, Albert   N6757.B642004
Art in an Age of Counterrevolution (1815-1848). Trade Cloth.
University of Chicago Press. Chicago, IL. 2004. 736p. Social
History of Modern Art Ser., Vol. 3 ISBN:0-226-06337-2,
ISBN13: 978-0-226-06337-9. Dewey:701/.03/09034.
LCCN:2003-023130.
                          Audience: **g,l,u,f.** *Choice, 2005.*

Boime, Albert   N6425.N4B61987
Art in an Age of Revolution, 1750-1800. Trade Paper.
University of Chicago Press. Chicago, IL. 1990. 550p. Social
History of Modern Art Ser., Vol. 1 ISBN:0-226-06334-8,
ISBN13: 978-0-226-06334-8. Dewey:709/.033.
LCCN:87-005944.
                          Audience: **g,l,u,f.**

Greenfeld, Liah   N72.S6 G74 1989
Different Worlds: A Sociological Study of Taste, Choice and
Success in Art. Ernest Q. Campbell (Contribution by). Trade
Cloth. Cambridge University Press. New York, NY. 1989. 216p.
ASA Rose Monographs ISBN:0-521-36064-1, ISBN13:
978-0-521-36064-7. Dewey:306/.47/095694. LCCN:88-011901.
                                   Audience: **l,u,f**. *Choice, 1990.*

Harrington, Austin   NX180.S6H324 2004
Art and Social Theory: Sociological Arguments in Aesthetics.
Trade Paper. Polity Press. Cambridge, 2004. 248p.
ISBN:0-7456-3039-1, ISBN13: 978-0-7456-3039-7.
Dewey:306.4/7. LCCN:2003-013220.
                                        Audience: **l,u,f**.

Hauser, Arnold   N72.S6H3613 1999
The Social History of Art. Ed. 3. Trade Paper. Routledge. New
York, NY. 1999. 1007p. ISBN:0-415-21386-X, ISBN13:
978-0-415-21386-8. Dewey:709. LCCN:98-054602.
                      Audience: **l,u,f**. *B* *Choice, 2000.*

Ibson, John   TR681.M4I26 2002
Picturing Men: A Century of Male Relationships in Everyday
American Photography. Trade Cloth. Smithsonian Institution
Press. Washington, DC. 2002. 272p. ISBN:1-58834-055-4,
ISBN13: 978-1-58834-055-9. Dewey:779/.23.
LCCN:2002-021014.
                                     Audience: **g,l,u,f**.

Johnston, Patricia A.   N72.S6 S36 2006
Seeing High and Low: Representing Social Conflict in American
Visual Culture. Trade Paper. University of California Press.
Berkeley, CA. 2006. 353p. ISBN:0-520-24188-6, ISBN13:
978-0-520-24188-6. Dewey:701/.03. LCCN:2005-023951.
                                        Audience: **u,f**.

Morphy, Howard & Perkins,   N72.A56A67 2005
  Morgan
Anthropology of Art: A Reader. Trade Cloth. Blackwell
Publishing, Inc. Malden, MA. 2006. 576p. Blackwell
Anthologies in Social and Cultural Anthropology Ser.
ISBN:1-4051-0561-5, ISBN13: 978-1-4051-0561-3.
Dewey:709/.01.1. LCCN:2005-013067.
                                        Audience: **l,u,f**.

Newton, Stephen James   ND1158.P74 N48 2001
Painting, Psychoanalysis and Spirituality. Donald Kuspit
(Contribution by). Trade Cloth. Cambridge University Press.
New York, NY. 2001. 288p. Contemporary Artists and Their
Critics Ser. ISBN:0-521-66134-X, ISBN13: 978-0-521-66134-8.
Dewey:750/.1/9. LCCN:00-023602.
                                   Audience: **u,f**. *Choice, 2001.*

Pohl, Frances K.   N6512.P59 2002
Framing America: A Social History of American Art. Trade
Cloth. Thames & Hudson. New York, NY. 2002. 560p.
ISBN:0-500-23792-1, ISBN13: 978-0-500-23792-2.
Dewey:709/.73. LCCN:2001-093466.
                                 Audience: **g,l,u,f**. *Choice, 2003.*

West, Shearer   N7575
Portraiture. Trade Paper. Oxford University Press, Inc. New
York, NY. 2004. 256p. Oxford History of Art Ser.
ISBN:0-19-284258-7, ISBN13: 978-0-19-284258-9.
Dewey:704.942. LCCN:2004-558274.
                                     Audience: **g,l,u,f**.

White, Edmund (Editor)   NX180.A36L672001
Loss Within Loss: Artists in the Age of AIDS. Trade Cloth.
University of Wisconsin Press. Chicago, IL. 2001. vi, 303p.
Living Out Ser. ISBN:0-299-17070-5, ISBN13:
978-0-299-17070-7. Dewey:700/.87. LCCN:00-011012.
                                     Audience: **g,l,u,f**.

Zolberg, Vera L.   N72.S6 Z65 1990
Constructing a Sociology of the Arts. Trade Paper. Cambridge
University Press. New York, NY. 1990. 264p. Contemporary
Sociology Ser. ISBN:0-521-35959-7, ISBN13:
978-0-521-35959-7. Dewey:701/.03. LCCN:89-038446.
                                 Audience: **g,l,u,f**. *Choice, 1990.*

Visual Arts in General > Other Topics > Art Sales

                                                          N
☐ The Getty Provenance Index.
http://piweb.getty.edu/cgi-bin/starfinder/0?path=collab.txt&id=
webber&pass=webber&OK=OK
J. Paul Getty Trust.
                                     Audience: **g,l,u,f**.

                                                        TR6.5
Gordon's Photography Price Annual International 2005. Trade
Cloth. LTB Gordonsart, Inc. Phoenix, AZ. 2005. 600p.
ISBN:1-933295-00-7, ISBN13: 978-1-933295-00-8.
Dewey:779.075.
                                     Audience: **g,l,u,f**.

                                                         NE85
Gordon's Print Price Annual 2005. Trade Cloth. LTB
Gordonsart, Inc. Phoenix, AZ. 2005. 2050p.
ISBN:1-933295-02-3, ISBN13: 978-1-933295-02-2.
Dewey:760.075.
                                     Audience: **g,l,u,f**.

Frederickson, Burton B.   ND47.I51988
  (Editor), et al.
Index of Paintings Sold in the British Isles During the
Nineteenth Century: 1801-1805, Vol. 1. Julia I. Armstrong &
Doris A. Mendenhall (Editors). Trade Cloth. Getty Publications.
Los Angeles, CA. 1988. 1047p. ISBN:0-87436-526-0, ISBN13:
978-0-87436-526-9. Dewey:750/.75/0941. LCCN:88-003369.
                                 Audience: **l,u,f**. *Choice, 1989.*

Moneta, Howard (Editor)   N8675
Davenport's Art Reference and Price Guide 2006/2007 Book.
Trade Cloth. LTB Gordonsart, Inc. Phoenix, AZ. 2005. 2424p.
ISBN:1-933295-07-4, ISBN13: 978-1-933295-07-7.
Dewey:707.5.
                                     Audience: **g,l,u,f**.

Passantino, Erika D. &   **N858.P4A87 1999**
 Scott, David W. (Editors)
The Eye of Duncan Phillips: A Collection in the Making. Cloth over Boards. Yale University Press. Cumberland, RI. 1999. 840p. ISBN:0-300-08090-5, ISBN13: 978-0-300-08090-2. Dewey:750/.74/753. LCCN:99-015182.
Audience: **g,l,u,f.** *Choice, 2000.*

Secrest, Meryle   **N8660.D82S43 2004**
Duveen: A Life in Art. Trade Cloth. Knopf Publishing Group. New York, NY. 2004. 544p. ISBN:0-375-41042-2, ISBN13: 978-0-375-41042-0. Dewey:709/.2 B. LCCN:2004-046521.
Audience: **g,l,u,f.** *Choice, 2005.*

Visual Arts in General > Other Topics > Iconography and Symbolism

Battistini, Matilde   **N7740**
Symbols and Allegories in Art. Trade Paper. Getty Publications. Los Angeles, CA. 2005. 384p. ISBN:0-89236-818-7, ISBN13: 978-0-89236-818-1. Dewey:704.946.
Audience: **g,l,u,f.** *Choice, 2005.*

Bunce, Fredrick W.   **N8193.A4B86 1997**
Dictionary of Buddhist and Hindu Iconography: Objects, Devices, Concepts, Rites and Related Terms. G. X. Capdi (Illustrator). Trade Cloth. D. K. Publishers India. Delhi, 1997. xxviii, 473p. ISBN:81-246-0061-9, ISBN13: 978-81-246-0061-0. Dewey:704.948943. LCCN:97-901206.
Audience: **g.l,u,f.**

Cavallo, Adolfo   **NK3049.U5C38 2005**
The Unicorn Tapestries at the Metropolitan Museum of Art. Trade Paper. Yale University Press. Cumberland, RI. 2005. 128p. ISBN:0-300-10630-0, ISBN13: 978-0-300-10630-5. Dewey:746.3944.
Audience: **g,l,u,f.**

De Capoa, Chiara   **N8020.D4 2004**
Old Testament Figures in Art: A Guide to Imagery. Stefano Zuffi (Editor). Trade Paper. Getty Publications. Los Angeles, CA. 2004. 352p. A Guide to Imagery Ser. ISBN:0-89236-745-8, ISBN13: 978-0-89236-745-0. Dewey:755/.4. LCCN:2003-016254.
Audience: **g,l,u,f.** *Choice, 2004.*

Dixon, Laurinda S. &   **N8223.I5 2004**
 Weisberg, Gabriel P.
In Sickness and in Health: Disease As Metaphor in Art and Popular Wisdom. Trade Cloth. University of Delaware Press. Newark, DE. 2004. 224p. ISBN:0-87413-857-4, ISBN13: 978-0-87413-857-3. Dewey:704.9/49616. LCCN:2003-023518.
Audience: **g,l,u,f.**

Drury, John   **ND1432.E85D78 1999**
Painting the Word: Christian Pictures and Their Meanings. Cloth over Boards. Yale University Press. Cumberland, RI. 1999. 220p. National Gallery London Publications

ISBN:0-300-07777-7, ISBN13: 978-0-300-07777-3. Dewey:246. LCCN:99-025840.
Audience: **g,l,u,f.** *Choice, 2000.*

Egan, Martha   **NK1650 .E34 1993**
Relicarios: Devotional Miniatures from the Americas. Trade Paper. Museum of New Mexico Press. Albuquerque, NM. 1996. 130p. ISBN:0-89013-254-2, ISBN13: 978-0-89013-254-8. Dewey:739.278. LCCN:93-078896.
Audience: **g,l,u,f.**

Gibson, Michael   **N6465.S9G53131988**
The Symbolists. Trade Cloth. Harry N. Abrams, Inc. New York, NY. 1988. 192p. ISBN:0-8109-1516-2, ISBN13: 978-0-8109-1516-9. Dewey:760/.09/0347. LCCN:87-030747.
Audience: **g,l,u,f.** *Choice, 1988.*

Hirsh, Sharon   **N6465.S9H57 2004**
Symbolism and Modern Urban Society. Trade Cloth. Cambridge University Press. New York, NY. 2004. 384p. ISBN:0-521-81096-5, ISBN13: 978-0-521-81096-8. Dewey:709/.03/47. LCCN:2003-056909.
Audience: **l,u,f.** *Choice, 2005.*

Impelluso, Lucia   **N7680.I4713 2004**
Nature and Its Symbols. Stephen Sartarelli (Translator). Trade Paper. Getty Publications. Los Angeles, CA. 2004. 384p. A Guide to Imagery Ser. ISBN:0-89236-772-5, ISBN13: 978-0-89236-772-6. Dewey:704.9/46. LCCN:2004-014355.
Audience: **g,l,u,f.**

Muchembled, Robert   **NX652.D48M8313 2004**
Damned: An Illustrated History of the Devil. Trade Cloth. Editions du Seuil. Paris, 2004. 200p. ISBN:2-02-062929-1, ISBN13: 978-2-02-062929-4. Dewey:700/.4820216/09. LCCN:2003-023887.
Audience: **g,l,u,f.**

Preziosi, Donald   **N380.P68 1989**
Rethinking Art History: Meditations on a Coy Science. Trade Paper. Yale University Press. Cumberland, RI. 1991. 285p. ISBN:0-300-04983-8, ISBN13: 978-0-300-04983-1. Dewey:707/.2.
Audience: **u,f.** *Choice, 1990.*

Roberts, Helene E. (Editor)   **N7560.E53 1998**
Encyclopedia of Comparative Iconography: Themes Depicted in Works of Art, Set. Trade Cloth. Fitzroy Dearborn Publishers, Inc. Chicago, IL. 1998. 1120p. ISBN:1-57958-009-2, ISBN13: 978-1-57958-009-4. Dewey:704.9/03. LCCN:98-163033.
Audience: **l,u,f.** *Choice, 1998.*

Ross, Leslie   **N7850**
Medieval Art: A Topical Dictionary. Cloth Text. Greenwood Publishing Group, Inc. Portsmouth, NH. 1996. 320p. ISBN:0-313-29329-5. ISBN13: 978-0-313-29329-0. Dewey:709/.02/03. LCCN:96-000160.
Audience: **g,l,u,f.** *Choice, 1997.*

Shearer, Alistair   BQ4022.S34 1992
The Buddha. Trade Paper. Thames & Hudson. New York, NY.
1992. 96p. Art and Imagination Ser. ISBN:0-500-81038-9,
ISBN13: 978-0-500-81038-5. Dewey:294.3. LCCN:91-067309.
                                    Audience: **g,l,u,f.**

Speake, Jennifer   N7825.S68 1994
The Dent Dictionary of Symbols in Christian Art. Trade Cloth.
J. M. Dent & Sons. London, 1995. 192p. ISBN:0-460-86138-7,
ISBN13: 978-0-460-86138-0. Dewey:704.9/482/03.
LCCN:94-139747.
                          Audience: **g,l,u,f.**   *Choice, 1995.*

Tresidder, Jack   AZ108
The Complete Dictionary of Symbols. Trade Paper. Chronicle
Books LLC. San Francisco, CA. 2005. 544p.
ISBN:0-8118-4767-5, ISBN13: 978-0-8118-4767-4.
Dewey:302.222303.
                          Audience: **g,l,u,f.**   *Choice, 2005.*

Womack, Mari   N8250
Sport as Symbol: Images of the Athlete in Art, Literature and
Song. Ed. 2. Cloth Text. McFarland & Company, Incorporated
Publishers. Jefferson, NC. 2003. 252p. ISBN:0-7864-1579-7,
ISBN13: 978-0-7864-1579-3. Dewey:704.9/49796.
LCCN:2003-012455.
                          Audience: **g,l,u,f.**   *Choice, 2004.*

Zuffi, Stefano   N8030.Z8413 2003
Gospel Figures in Art. Trade Paper. Oxford University Press,
Inc. New York, NY. 2003. 384p. A Guide to Imagery Ser.
ISBN:0-89236-727-X, ISBN13: 978-0-89236-727-6.
Dewey:755/.4. LCCN:2003-005585.
                                    Audience: **g,l,u,f.**

Visual Arts in General > Other Topics > Color

Ball, Philip   N7432.7.B35 2003
Bright Earth: Art and the Invention of Color. Trade Paper.
University of Chicago Press. Chicago, IL. 2003. 434p.
ISBN:0-226-03628-6, ISBN13: 978-0-226-03628-1.
Dewey:701/.85. LCCN:2002-035981.
                                    Audience: **g,l,u,f.**

Burchett, Kenneth E.   QC495.8.B87 2005
A Bibliographical History of the Study and Use of Color from
Aristotle to Kandinsky. Trade Cloth. Edwin Mellen Press, The.
Lewiston, NY. 2005. 412p. ISBN:0-7734-6041-1, ISBN13:
978-0-7734-6041-6. Dewey:535.6/09. LCCN:2005-049270.
                                    Audience: **l,u,f.**

Byrne, Alexander & Hilbert,   QC495.R32 1997
  David R. (Editors)
The Philosophy of Color. Trade Paper. MIT Press. Cambridge,
MA. 1997. 340p. Readings on Color Ser., Vol. 1
ISBN:0-262-52230-6, ISBN13: 978-0-262-52230-4.
Dewey:152.14/5. LCCN:96-044539.
                          Audience: **g,l,u,f.**   *Choice, 1998.*

Byrne, Alexander   QC495.R32 1997
The Science of Color. David R. Hilbert (Editor). Trade Paper.
MIT Press. Cambridge, MA. 1997. 465p. Readings on Color
Ser., Vol. 2 ISBN:0-262-52231-4, ISBN13: 978-0-262-52231-1.
Dewey:152.14/5. LCCN:96-044539.
                          Audience: **g,l,u,f.**   *Choice, 1998.*

Hills, Paul   N6921.V5H56 1999
Venetian Colour: Marble, Mosaic and Glass, 1250-1550. Cloth
over Boards. Yale University Press. Cumberland, RI. 1999.
260p. ISBN:0-300-08135-9, ISBN13: 978-0-300-08135-0.
Dewey:701/.85/094531. LCCN:99-020880.
                          Audience: **g,l,u,f.**   *Choice, 2000.*

Kuehni, Rolf G.   ND1488.K82 2004
Color: An Introduction to Practice and Principles. Ed. 2. Trade
Cloth. John Wiley & Sons, Inc. Hoboken, NJ. 2004. 216p.
ISBN:0-471-66006-X, ISBN13: 978-0-471-66006-4.
Dewey:535.6. LCCN:2004-006024.
                          Audience: **g,l,u,f.**   *Choice, 2005.*

Kuehni, Rolf G.   QP483.K84 2003
Color Space and Its Divisions: Color Order from Antiquity to
the Present. Trade Cloth. John Wiley & Sons, Inc. Hoboken, NJ.
2003. 408p. ISBN:0-471-32670-4, ISBN13: 978-0-471-32670-0.
Dewey:152.14/5. LCCN:2002-014045.
                          Audience: **g,l,u,f.**   *Choice, 2003.*

Riley, Charles A. II   N7432.7
Color Codes: Modern Theories of Color in Philosophy, Painting
and Architecture, Literature, Music, and Psychology. Trade
Paper. University Press of New England. Lebanon, NH. 1996.
373p. ISBN:0-87451-742-7, ISBN13: 978-0-87451-742-2.
Dewey:701.8/5. LCCN:94-009733.
                          Audience: **g,l,u,f.**   *Choice, 1995.*

Zelanski, Paul & Fisher,   QC495.Z45 2006
  Mary Pat
Color. Ed. 5. Trade Paper. Prentice Hall PTR. Upper Saddle
River, NJ. 2006. 200p. ISBN:0-13-195864-X, ISBN13:
978-0-13-195864-7. Dewey:535.6. LCCN:2005-051339.
                                    Audience: **g,l,u,f.**

Visual Arts in General > Image Sources

                                                       NC845
☐ AIGA Design Archives.
http://designarchives.aiga.org/
American Institute of Graphic Arts.
                                    Audience: **g,l,u,f.**

                                                       N4000
☐ American Memory.
http://memory.loc.gov/ammem/index.html
Library of Congress.
                                    Audience: **g,l,u,f.**

N7520
☐ Art Museum Image Gallery.
http://www.hwwilson.com/Databases/artmuseum.htm
H. W. Wilson.

Audience: **g,l,u,f.**

N7520
☐ ARTstor.
http://www.artstor.org

Audience: **g,l,u,f.**

NA
☐ Built in America; Historic American Buildings
Survey/Historic American Engineering Record, 1933-Present.
http://memory.loc.gov/ammem/collections/habs_haer/
Washington, D. C. : Library of Congress.

Audience: **g,l,u,f.**

N7520
☐ CAMIO ; Catalog of Art Museum Images Online.
http://camio.rlg.org/
Research Libraries Group.

Audience: **g,l,u,f.**

NA200
☐ Historic American Buildings Survey / Historic American
Engineering Survey.
http://www.cr.nps.gov/habshaer/
Washington, D. C. : Department of the Interior, National Park
Service, HABS/HAER/HALS Division.

Audience: **g,l,u,f.**

NA
☐ International Architecture Database.
http://www.archinform.net
Berlin: archINFORM.

Audience: **g,l,u,f.**

N7520
☐ NYPL Digital Gallery.
http://digitalgallery.nypl.org/
New York Public Library.

Audience: **g,l,u,f.**

NA63.5
☐ Structurae; International Database and Gallery of Structures.
http://en.structurae.de/index.cfm
Nicolas Janberg.

Audience: **g,l,u,f.**

Bryce, Betty K.   **NE508.B76 1999**
American Printmakers, 1946-1996: An Index to Reproductions
and Biocritical Information. Trade Cloth. Scarecrow Press, Inc.
Lanham, MD. 1999. 606p. ISBN:0-8108-3586-X, ISBN13:
978-0-8108-3586-3. Dewey:016.76992/273. LCCN:98-043773.
Audience: **g,l,u,f.** *Choice, 2000.*

Culbertson, Margaret   **NA7207**
(Compiled by)
American House Designs: An Index to Popular and Trade

Periodicals 1850-1915. Cloth Text. Greenwood Publishing
Group, Inc. Portsmouth, NH. 1994. 360p. Art Reference
Collection Ser. ISBN:0-313-29202-7, ISBN13:
978-0-313-29202-6. Dewey:016.728/022/2. LCCN:94-030280.
Audience: **l,u,f.** *Choice, 1995.*

Havlice, Patricia P.   **ND45**
World Painting Index, 1973-1980, Set. Trade Cloth. Scarecrow
Press, Inc. Lanham, MD. 1982. 1233p. ISBN:0-8108-1531-1,
ISBN13: 978-0-8108-1531-5. Dewey:016.75. LCCN:82-003355.
Audience: **g,l,u,f.**

Havlice, Patricia P.   **ND45.H38 SUPPL. 2**
World Painting Index, 1980-1989. Trade Cloth. Scarecrow Press,
Inc. Lanham, MD. 1995. 1890p. ISBN:0-8108-3020-5, ISBN13:
978-0-8108-3020-2. Dewey:016.75. LCCN:95-002326.
Audience: **g,l,u,f.**

Havlice, Patricia Pate   **ND45.H38**
World Painting Index, 1990-1999. Trade Cloth. Scarecrow Press,
Inc. Lanham, MD. 2003. 2096p. ISBN:0-8108-4472-9, ISBN13:
978-0-8108-4472-8. Dewey:016.75. LCCN:2002-026813.
Audience: **g,l,u,f.** *Choice, 2003.*

Kren, Emil; Marx, Daniel   **ND450**
☐ Web Gallery of Art.
http://www.wga.hu/

Audience: **g,l,u,f.**

Laing, Ellen J.   **ND1045.L35 1998**
An Index to Reproductions of Paintings by Twentieth-Century
Chinese Artists. Trade Cloth. Center for Chinese Studies
Publications. Ann Arbor, MI. 1998. 550p. Michigan Monographs
in Chinese Studies, Vol. 76 ISBN:0-89264-126-6, ISBN13:
978-0-89264-126-0. Dewey:759.951. LCCN:98-002855.
Audience: **g,l,u,f.**

Teague, Edward H.   **NA202**
(Compiled by)
World Architecture Index: A Guide to Illustrations, 12. Cloth
Text. Greenwood Publishing Group, Inc. Portsmouth, NH. 1991.
472p. Art Reference Collection Ser., No. 12
ISBN:0-313-22552-4, ISBN13: 978-0-313-22552-9.
Dewey:016.72. LCCN:91-007565.
Audience: **g,l,u,f.** *Choice, 1991.*

Thomison, Dennis   **N6538.N5.T46 1991**
The Black Artist in America: An Index to Reproductions. Trade
Cloth. Scarecrow Press, Inc. Lanham, MD. 1991. 456p.
ISBN:0-8108-2503-1, ISBN13: 978-0-8108-2503-1.
Dewey:016.7040396073. LCCN:91-033050.
Audience: **g,l,u,f.** *Choice, 1992.*

Williams, Lynn B.   **NE507.W53 1993**
American Printmakers, 1880-1945: An Index to Reproductions
and Biocritical Information. Trade Cloth. Scarecrow Press, Inc.
Lanham, MD. 1993. 479p. ISBN:0-8108-2786-7, ISBN13:
978-0-8108-2786-8. Dewey:016.76992/273. LCCN:93-041591.
Audience: **g,l,u,f.** *Choice, 1994.*

Design > Reference Works

NC845

⬜ AIGA Design Archives.
http://designarchives.aiga.org/
American Institute of Graphic Arts.

Audience: **g,l,u,f.**

Cox, Mary   **N7430.5**
2007 Artists and Graphic Designers Market. Trade Paper. F &
W Publications, Inc. Cincinnati, OH. 2006. 624p.
ISBN:1-58297-429-2, ISBN13: 978-1-58297-429-3. Dewey:760.
Audience: **g,l,u,f.**

Edwards, David J.   **N33.E38 2003**
The Handbook of Art and Design Terms. Trade Paper. Prentice
Hall PTR. Upper Saddle River, NJ. 2003. 86p. Art Basics Ser.
ISBN:0-13-098991-6, ISBN13: 978-0-13-098991-8. Dewey:703.
LCCN:2003-046012.
Audience: **g,l,u,f.** *Choice, 2004.*

Horne, Alan   **NC978.H63 1994**
The Dictionary of 20th Century British Book Illustrators. Trade
Cloth. Antique Collectors' Club. Easthampton, MA. 1994. 456p.
ISBN:1-85149-108-2, ISBN13: 978-1-85149-108-7.
Dewey:741.6/4/092241 B. LCCN:94-105005.
Audience: **g,l,u,f.**

Houfe, Simon   **NC978.H65 1996**
The Dictionary of 19th Century British Book Illustrators. Ed. 2.
Trade Cloth. Antique Collectors' Club. Easthampton, MA. 1996.
380p. ISBN:1-85149-193-7, ISBN13: 978-1-85149-193-3.
Dewey:741.6/4/092. LCCN:95-137048.
Audience: **g,l,u,f.** *Choice, 1997.*

Lebenson, Richard &   **AP1**
  Creighton, Kathleen (Editors)
RSVP.01 - The Directory of Illustration and Design. Trade
Paper. R S V P. Brooklyn, NY. 2001. ISBN:1-878118-10-2,
ISBN13: 978-1-878118-10-3. Dewey:700.2573.
Audience: **g,l,u,f.**

Livingston, Alan &   **Z246**
  Livingston, Isabella
The Thames and Hudson Dictionary of Graphic Design. Ed. 2.
Trade Paper. Thames & Hudson. New York, NY. 2003. 240p.
The World of Art Ser. ISBN:0-500-20353-9, ISBN13:
978-0-500-20353-8. Dewey:741.603. LCCN:2003-495754.
Audience: **g,l,u,f.**

Naylor, Colin (Editor)   **NK1166 .C66 1990**
Contemporary Designers. Ed. 2. Trade Cloth. Thomson Gale.
Farmington Hills, MI. 1990. 641p. ISBN:0-912289-69-4,
ISBN13: 978-0-912289-69-4. Dewey:745.4492.
Audience: **g,l,u,f.** *Choice, 1991.*

Pendergast, Sara   **NK1390.C655 1997**
Contemporary Designers. Ed. 3. Trade Cloth. Thomson Gale.

Farmington Hills, MI. 1996. 981p. ISBN:1-55862-184-9,
ISBN13: 978-1-55862-184-8. Dewey:745.209.
LCCN:96-048898.
Audience: **g,l,f.**

Woodham, Jonathan   **NK1165**
A Dictionary of Modern Design. Trade Cloth. Oxford University
Press, Inc. New York, NY. 2005. 538p. ISBN:0-19-280097-3,
ISBN13: 978-0-19-280097-8. Dewey:745.4/09/0403.
LCCN:2004-024897.
Audience: **g,l,u,f.** *Choice, 2005.*

Design > Histories and Handbooks > Periods and Styles

Aav, Marianne &   **NK1471.F5**
  Stritzler-Levine, Nina (Editors)
Finnish Modern Design: Utopian Ideals and Everyday Realities,
1930-97. Trade Paper. Yale University Press. Cumberland, RI.
2000. 412p. ISBN:0-300-08280-0, ISBN13: 978-0-300-08280-7.
Dewey:745.4/494897/0747471.
Audience: **g,l,u,f.** *Choice, 1998.*

Bloemink, Barbara &   **NK1396**
  Cunningham, Joseph
Design Art: Functional Objects from Donald Judd to Rachel
Whiteread. Trade Cloth. Merrell Publishers Ltd. London, 2005.
224p. ISBN:1-85894-266-7, ISBN13: 978-1-85894-266-7.
Dewey:745.4/09045.
Audience: **g,l,u,f.** *Choice, 2005.*

Caban, Geoffrey (Editor)   **NC997**
World Graphic Design: Contemporary Graphics from Africa, the
Arab World, the Far East and Latin America. Trade Cloth.
Merrell Publishers Ltd. London, 2005. 160p.
ISBN:1-85894-219-5, ISBN13: 978-1-85894-219-3.
Dewey:741.6.
Audience: **g,l,u,f.** *Choice, 2004.*

Celant, Germano   **NA680**
Architecture and Arts 1900-2004: A Century of Creative Projects
in Building, Design, Cinema, Painting, Photography, Sculpture.
Trade Cloth. Skira Editore. Milano, 2005. 784p.
ISBN:88-7624-009-8, ISBN13: 978-88-7624-009-6.
Dewey:724.6. LCCN:2005-277341.
Audience: **g,l,u,f.**

Doordan, Dennis P. (Editor)   **NK1525.D43 1995**
Design History: An Anthology. Trade Paper. MIT Press.
Cambridge, MA. 1996. 288p. Design Issues Reader Ser.
ISBN:0-262-54076-2, ISBN13: 978-0-262-54076-6.
Dewey:745.4/4. LCCN:95-024677.
Audience: **g,l,u,f.**

Dormer, Peter   **NK1390**
Design since 1945. Trade Paper. Thames & Hudson. New York,
NY. 1993. 216p. World of Art Ser. ISBN:0-500-20261-3,
ISBN13: 978-0-500-20261-6. Dewey:745.4/442.
LCCN:92-080335.
Audience: **g,l,u,f.**

Forty, Adrian   **TS57 .F67 1992**
Objects of Desire: Design and Society, 1750-1980. Trade Paper.
Thames & Hudson. New York, NY. 1992. 256p.
ISBN:0-500-27412-6, ISBN13: 978-0-500-27412-5.
Dewey:745.2/0941/0903. LCCN:91-067302.
Audience: **g,l,u,f.** *Choice, 1986.*

Heller, Steven & Ballance,   **NC998.4.G667 2001**
  Georgette (Editors)
Graphic Design History. Trade Paper. Allworth Press. New York,
NY. 2001. 352p. ISBN:1-58115-094-6, ISBN13:
978-1-58115-094-0. Dewey:741.6/09/04. LCCN:2001-022588.
Audience: **g,l,u,f.** *Choice, 2001.*

Hiesinger, Kathryn B. &   **T180.P47P475 1994**
  Fischer, Felice
Japanese Design: A Survey since 1950. Trade Paper.
Philadelphia Museum of Art. Philadelphia, PA. 1994. 236p.
ISBN:0-87633-092-8, ISBN13: 978-0-87633-092-0.
Dewey:745.4/4952/09045. LCCN:94-067907.
Audience: **g,l,u,f.** *Choice, 1995.*

Margolin, Victor (Editor)   **NK1505.D47 1989**
Design Discourse: History, Theory, Criticism. Trade Paper.
University of Chicago Press. Chicago, IL. 1989. 302p.
ISBN:0-226-50514-6, ISBN13: 978-0-226-50514-5.
Dewey:745.4. LCCN:89-033920.
Audience: **g,l,u,f.**

McQuiston, Liz   **NC997**
Graphic Agitation 2: Social and Political Graphics in the Digital
Age. Trade Cloth. Phaidon Press. London, 2004. 240p.
ISBN:0-7148-4177-3, ISBN13: 978-0-7148-4177-9.
Dewey:741.6/09/0511. LCCN:2005-533986.
Audience: **g,l,u,f.**

Poynor, Rick   **NC998.45.P67P69 2003**
No More Rules: Graphic Design and Postmodernism. Trade
Paper. Yale University Press. Cumberland, RI. 2003. 192p.
ISBN:0-300-10034-5, ISBN13: 978-0-300-10034-1.
Dewey:741.6. LCCN:2003-104780.
Audience: **g,l,u,f.** *Choice, 2004.*

Raizman, David   **NK1175**
History of Modern Design. Prentice Hall Art. 2003.
ISBN:0-13-184266-8, ISBN13: 978-0-13-184266-3.
Audience: **g,l,u,f.**

Ryan, William E. &   **Z246.C58 2004**
  Conover, Theodore E.
Graphic Communications Today. Ed. 4. Paper Text. Thomson
Delmar Learning. Albany, NY. 2003. 672p.
ISBN:0-7668-2075-0, ISBN13: 978-0-7668-2075-3.
Dewey:686.2/252. LCCN:2004-298682.
Audience: **g,l,u,f.**

Scher, Paula   **NC998.5.A1S34 2005**
Make It Bigger. Trade Paper. Princeton Architectural Press. New
York, NY. 2005. 272p. ISBN:1-56898-548-7, ISBN13:
978-1-56898-548-0. Dewey:741.6/023/73. LCCN:2005-009938.
Audience: **g,l,u,f.**

Schwartz, Frederic J.   **NK951.S375 1996**
The Werkbund: Design Theory and Mass Culture before the
First World War. Cloth over Boards. Yale University Press.
Cumberland, RI. 1996. 272p. ISBN:0-300-06898-0, ISBN13:
978-0-300-06898-6. Dewey:720.9/43. LCCN:96-014708.
Audience: **l,u,f.** *Choice, 1997.*

Stern, Jewel   **NK7112**
Modernism in American Silver: 20th-Century Design. Kevin W.
Tucker & Charles L. Venable (Editors). Saddle Stitched, Cloth
over Boards, Dust Jacket. Yale University Press. Cumberland,
RI. 2005. 392p. ISBN:0-300-10927-X, ISBN13:
978-0-300-10927-6. Dewey:739.2309730904.
LCCN:2005-927185.
Audience: **l,u,f.** *Choice, 2006.*

Trilling, James   **NK1175.T549 2001**
Language of Ornament. Trade Paper. Thames & Hudson. New
York, NY. 2001. 224p. World of Art Ser. ISBN:0-500-20343-1,
ISBN13: 978-0-500-20343-9. Dewey:745. LCCN:00-109244.
Audience: **g,l,u,f.**

Whitford, Frank   **N332.G33B47**
Bauhaus. Trade Paper. Thames & Hudson. New York, NY. 1984.
216p. World of Art Ser. ISBN:0-500-20193-5, ISBN13:
978-0-500-20193-0. Dewey:707/.1143. LCCN:83-050527.
Audience: **g,l,u,f.** *B*

Woodham, Jonathan M.   **NK1390.W59 1997**
Twentieth-Century Design. Trade Paper. Oxford University
Press, Inc. New York, NY. 1997. 288p. Oxford History of Art
Ser. ISBN:0-19-284204-8, ISBN13: 978-0-19-284204-6.
Dewey:745.4/442. LCCN:96-047594.
Audience: **g,l,u,f.** *Choice, 1997.*

Design > Histories and Handbooks > Cultures, Regions, Nationalities

Aynsley, Jeremy   **NC998.6.G4A96 2000**
Graphic Design in Germany 1890-1945. Trade Cloth. University
of California Press. Berkeley, CA. 2000. 240p. Weimar and
Now Ser., Vol. 28:German Cultural Criticism
ISBN:0-520-22796-4, ISBN13: 978-0-520-22796-5.
Dewey:741.6/0943/09041. LCCN:00-034379.
Audience: **g,l,u,f.** *Choice, 2001.*

Friedman, Mildred &   **NC998.5.A1G651989**
  Giovannini, Joseph (Editors)
Graphic Design in America: A Visual Language History. Trade
Cloth. Harry N. Abrams, Inc. New York, NY. 1989. 248p.
ISBN:0-8109-1036-5, ISBN13: 978-0-8109-1036-2.
Dewey:741.6/0973/074. LCCN:89-000445.
Audience: **g,l,u,f.** *Choice, 1990.*

Hanks, David & Hoy, Anne   **NK1404**
American Streamlined Design: The World of Tomorrow. Trade
Cloth. Flammarion et Cie. Paris, 2005. 312p.
ISBN:2-08-030499-2, ISBN13: 978-2-08-030499-5.
Dewey:745.40973.
Audience: **g,l,u,f.** *Choice, 2006.*

Hiesinger, Kathryn B. &   T180.P47P475 1994
  Fischer, Felice
Japanese Design: A Survey since 1950. Trade Paper.
Philadelphia Museum of Art. Philadelphia, PA. 1994. 236p.
ISBN:0-87633-092-8, ISBN13: 978-0-87633-092-0.
Dewey:745.4/4952/09045. LCCN:94-067907.

Audience: **g,l,u,f.** *Choice, 1995.*

Kirkham, Pat (Editor)   NK1404.W662000
Women Designers in the U.S.A., 1900-2000: Diversity and
Difference. Cloth over Boards. Yale University Press.
Cumberland, RI. 2000. 464p. ISBN:0-300-08734-9, ISBN13:
978-0-300-08734-5. Dewey:745.4/082/0973. LCCN:00-108610.

Audience: **g,l,u,f.** *Choice, 2001.*

Levi, Vicki Gold & Heller,   NC998.5.N72N488 2004
  Steven
Times Square: Graphics from the Great White Way. Trade Paper.
Princeton Architectural Press. New York, NY. 2004. 168p.
ISBN:1-56898-490-1, ISBN13: 978-1-56898-490-2.
Dewey:741.6/097471. LCCN:2004-303791.

Audience: **g,l,u,f.**

Lupton, Ellen   NC998.5.A1L86 1996
Mixing Messages: Graphic Design in Contemporary American
Culture. Trade Paper. Princeton Architectural Press. New York,
NY. 1996. 176p. ISBN:1-56898-099-X, ISBN13:
978-1-56898-099-7. Dewey:741.6/0973/0747471.
LCCN:96-018695.

Audience: **g,l,u,f.**

Marling, Karal Ann   NC998.5.M5M37 2003
Looking North: Royal Canadian Mounted Police Illustrations,
the Potlach Collection. Trade Cloth. Afton Historical Society
Press. Afton, MN. 2004. 160p. ISBN:1-890434-54-X, ISBN13:
978-1-890434-54-0. Dewey:757/.3. LCCN:2002-152832.

Audience: **g,l,u,f.** *Choice, 2003.*

Meikle, Jeffrey L.   TS23 .M4496 2005
Design in the USA. Trade Paper, Perfect. Oxford University
Press, Inc. New York, NY. 2005. 252p. Oxford History of Art
Ser. ISBN:0-19-284219-6, ISBN13: 978-0-19-284219-0.
Dewey:745.2/0973. LCCN:2004-065438.

Audience: **g,l,u,f.**

Poynor, Rick (Editor)   NC998.6.G7
Communicate: Independent British Graphic Design since the
Sixties. David Crowley, Nico MacDonald & John O'Reilly
(Contribution by). Trade Paper. Yale University Press.
Cumberland, RI. 2005. 256p. ISBN:0-300-10684-X, ISBN13:
978-0-300-10684-8. Dewey:741.6.

Audience: **g,l,u,f.** *Choice, 2005.*

Sharp, Charles Dee   NK9509.65.U6S53 2002
The Wonder of American Toys: 1920-1950. Trade Cloth.
Collectors Press, Inc. Portland, OR. 2004. 336p.
ISBN:1-888054-70-0, ISBN13: 978-1-888054-70-5.
Dewey:688.7/2/0973075. LCCN:2002-006521.

Audience: **g,l,u,f.**

Sprigg, June   NK807
Shaker Design. Trade Paper. W. W. Norton & Company, Inc.
New York, NY. 1988. 228p. ISBN:0-393-30544-9, ISBN13:
978-0-393-30544-9. Dewey:973.

Audience: **g,l,u,f.** *Choice, 1986.*

Trowell, Margaret   NK1488.75.T76 2003
African Design: An Illustrated Survey of Traditional Craftwork.
Ed. 2. Trade Paper. Dover Publications, Inc. Mineola, NY. 2003.
160p. Fine Art, History of Art Ser. ISBN:0-486-42714-5,
ISBN13: 978-0-486-42714-0. Dewey:745.4/4967.
LCCN:2002-035175.

Audience: **g,l,u,f.**

Votolato, Gregory   NK1404.V68 1998
American Design in the 20th Century. Cloth over Boards.
Manchester University Press. Manchester, 1998. 320p. Studies
in Design and Material Culture ISBN:0-7190-4530-4, ISBN13:
978-0-7190-4530-1. Dewey:745.2/0973/0904. LCCN:98-012712.

Audience: **g,l,u,f.** *Choice, 1999.*

Washburn, Dorothy Koster   NK1570.S96 2004
  & Crowe, Donald W. (Editors)
Symmetry Comes of Age: The Role of Pattern in Culture. Trade
Cloth. University of Washington Press. Seattle, WA. 2004. 392p.
ISBN:0-295-98366-3, ISBN13: 978-0-295-98366-0.
Dewey:745.4. LCCN:2003-054894.

Audience: **g,l,u,f.** *Choice, 2005.*

Design > Histories and Handbooks >
Topics > Advertising Arts

Berger, Warren   HF5823
Advertising Today. Trade Paper. Phaidon Press. London, 2004.
512p. ISBN:0-7148-4387-3, ISBN13: 978-0-7148-4387-2.
Dewey:659.1. LCCN:2004-304321.

Audience: **g,l,u,f.**

Heller, Steven (Editor)   HF5821
Sex Appeal: The Art of Allure in Graphic and Advertising
Design. Trade Paper. Allworth Press. New York, NY. 2000.
288p. ISBN:1-58115-048-2, ISBN13: 978-1-58115-048-3.
Dewey:659.1/042. LCCN:00-022194.

Audience: **g,l,u,f.**

Heon, Laura S., et al.   N8217.A35H46 1999
Billboard: Art on the Road. Peggy Diggs, Joseph Thompson &
Lisa Dorin (Authors). Trade Paper. MIT Press. Cambridge, MA.
1999. 100p. ISBN:0-262-58177-9, ISBN13: 978-0-262-58177-6.
Dewey:741.6/7. LCCN:99-060345.

Audience: **g,l,u,f.**

Hoffman, Barry   NC998.5.A1H642003
The Fine Art of Advertising. Trade Cloth. Stewart, Tabori &
Chang. New York, NY. 2003. 144p. ISBN:1-58479-222-1,
ISBN13: 978-1-58479-222-2. Dewey:741.6/7/09730904.
LCCN:2003-041502.

Audience: **g,l,u,f.**

Formats: Web: ☐   Ebook: 🄴   CD/DVD-ROM: 🐾   BCL3: 𝓑

Jakle, John A. & Sculle,   HF5841.J35 2004
Keith A.
Signs in America's Auto Age: Signatures of Landscape and
Place. Trade Paper. University of Iowa Press. Iowa City, IA.
2004. 256p. American Land and Life Ser. ISBN:0-87745-890-1,
ISBN13: 978-0-87745-890-6. Dewey:659.13/42/0973.
LCCN:2003-063364.

     Audience: **g,l,u,f.** *Choice, 2004.*

Messaris, Paul   HF5822.M415 1996
Visual Persuasion: The Role of Images in Advertising. Paper
Text. SAGE Publications, Inc. Thousand Oaks, CA. 1996. 320p.
ISBN:0-8039-7246-6, ISBN13: 978-0-8039-7246-9.
Dewey:659.1/042. LCCN:96-025184.

     Audience: **g,l,u,f.**

One Club Staff   NC997.A1
Advertising's Best Print, Design, Radio, and TV. Printed Dust
Jacket. One Club Publishing. New York, NY. 2006. 480p. One
Show Annual Ser., Vol. 27 ISBN:0-929837-27-4, ISBN13:
978-0-929837-27-7. Dewey:741.605.

     Audience: **g,l,u,f.**

Poynor, Rick (Editor)   NC998.6.G7
Communicate: Independent British Graphic Design since the
Sixties. David Crowley, Nico MacDonald & John O'Reilly
(Contribution by). Trade Paper. Yale University Press.
Cumberland, RI. 2005. 256p. ISBN:0-300-10684-X, ISBN13:
978-0-300-10684-8. Dewey:741.6.

     Audience: **g,l,u,f.** *Choice, 2005.*

Design > Histories and Handbooks > Topics > Fashion and Ornament

Atchley, Virginia G.   NK6050.R39 2003
The Raymond and Frances Bushell Collection of Netsuke: A
Legacy at the Los Angeles County Museum of Art. Los Angeles
County Museum of Art Staff (Contribution by). Trade Cloth. Art
Media Resources, Inc. Chicago, IL. 2004. 520p.
ISBN:1-58886-034-5, ISBN13: 978-1-58886-034-7.
Dewey:736/.68/07479494. LCCN:2003-041931.

     Audience: **g,l,u,f.**

Ayres, Dianne & Hansen,   NK8812.A472002
Timothy
American Arts and Crafts Textiles. Trade Cloth. Harry N.
Abrams, Inc. New York, NY. 2002. 248p. ISBN:0-8109-0434-9,
ISBN13: 978-0-8109-0434-7. Dewey:746/.0973/09034.
LCCN:2001-006012.

     Audience: **g,l,u,f.**

Bartsch, Joel A.   NK7403.G67K742000
Kremlin Gold: 1000 Years of Russian Gems and Jewels. Trade
Cloth. Harry N. Abrams, Inc. New York, NY. 2000. 206p.
ISBN:0-8109-6695-6, ISBN13: 978-0-8109-6695-6.
Dewey:739.2/0947. LCCN:00-698028.

     Audience: **g,l,u,f.** *Choice, 2001.*

Bossan, Marie-Josephe   GT2130
The Art of the Shoe. Trade Cloth. Parkstone Press USA, Ltd.
New York, NY. 2004. 272p. Temporis Collection
ISBN:1-85995-803-6, ISBN13: 978-1-85995-803-2.
Dewey:391.4/13.

     Audience: **g,l,u,f.**

Breward, Christopher   TT504
Fashion. Ed. 1. Trade Paper. Oxford University Press, Inc. New
York, NY. 2003. 272p. Oxford History of Art Ser.
ISBN:0-19-284030-4, ISBN13: 978-0-19-284030-1. Dewey:391.
LCCN:2003-273453.

     Audience: **g,l,u,f.**

Chung, Young Yang   NK9272.C482004
Silken Threads: A History of Embroidery in China, Korea,
Japan, and Vietnam. Trade Cloth. Harry N. Abrams, Inc. New
York, NY. 2005. 464p. ISBN:0-8109-4330-1, ISBN13:
978-0-8109-4330-8. Dewey:746.44/095. LCCN:2004-009510.

     Audience: **g,l,u,f.**

Keene, Manuel & Kaoukji,   NK7376.A1K44 2001
Salam
Treasury of the World: Jeweled Arts of India in the Age of the
Mughals. Trade Paper. Thames & Hudson. New York, NY. 2001.
160p. ISBN:0-500-97608-2, ISBN13: 978-0-500-97608-1.
Dewey:739.27/095/074. LCCN:00-108913.

     Audience: **g,l,u,f.** *Choice, 2001.*

Koda, Harold   GT503
Extreme Beauty: The Body Transformed. Cloth over Boards.
Yale University Press. Cumberland, RI. 2001. 192p.
Metropolitan Museum of Art Ser. ISBN:0-300-09117-6,
ISBN13: 978-0-300-09117-5. Dewey:391/.074/7471.
LCCN:2001-044709.

     Audience: **g,l,u,f.**

Kunz, George Frederick &   NK7680.K8
Stevenson, Charles Hugh
The Book of Pearl: Its History, Art, Science and Industry. Trade
Paper. Dover Publications, Inc. Mineola, NY. 2001. 672p.
ISBN:0-486-42276-3, ISBN13: 978-0-486-42276-3.
Dewey:639/.412. LCCN:2001-047559.

     Audience: **g,l,u,f.**

Laver, James   GT511.L39 2002
Costume and Fashion: A Concise History. Ed. 4. Trade Paper.
Thames & Hudson. New York, NY. 2002. 304p. World of Art
Ser. ISBN:0-500-20348-2, ISBN13: 978-0-500-20348-4.
Dewey:391/.009. LCCN:2001-087366.

     Audience: **g,l,u,f.**

Le Van, Marthe   TT212.P462005
The Penland Book of Jewelry: Master Classes in Jewelry
Techniques. Saddle Stitched, Cloth over Boards, Dust Jacket.
Lark Books. Asheville, NC. 2005. 232p. ISBN:1-57990-698-2,
ISBN13: 978-1-57990-698-6. Dewey:739.27.
LCCN:2005-006162.

     Audience: **g,l,u,f.**

M'Closkey, Kathy E99.N3M315 2002
Swept under the Rug: A Hidden History of Navajo Weaving.
University of Arizona, Southwest Center Staff (Contribution by).
Trade Cloth. University of New Mexico Press. Albuquerque,
NM. 2002. 320p. ISBN:0-8263-2831-8, ISBN13:
978-0-8263-2831-1. Dewey:381/.45746/089972.
LCCN:2002-009369.
Audience: **u,f.** *Choice, 2003.*

Meyer, George H. NK9712.M49 1992
American Folk Art Canes: Personal Sculpture. Trade Cloth.
University of Washington Press. Seattle, WA. 1992. 252p.
ISBN:0-295-97200-9, ISBN13: 978-0-295-97200-8.
Dewey:736/.4. LCCN:92-009714.
Audience: **g,l,u,f.** *Choice, 1993.*

Paterek, Josephine E98.C8
Encyclopedia of American Indian Costume. Trade Paper. W. W.
Norton & Company, Inc. New York, NY. 1996. 536p.
ISBN:0-393-31382-4, ISBN13: 978-0-393-31382-6.
Dewey:391/.008997.
Audience: **g,l,u,f.** *Choice, 1994.*

Phillips, Clare NK7304.P48 1996
Jewelry: From Antiquity to the Present. Trade Paper. Thames &
Hudson. New York, NY. 1996. 224p. The World of Art Ser.
ISBN:0-500-20287-7, ISBN13: 978-0-500-20287-6.
Dewey:739.2/7/09. LCCN:95-060284.
Audience: **g,l,u,f.**

Prior, Katherine & NK7376.P65 2000
Adamson, John
Maharaja's Jewels. Trade Cloth. Vendome Press, The. New
York, NY. 1999. 208p. ISBN:0-86565-218-X, ISBN13:
978-0-86565-218-7. Dewey:739.27/0954. LCCN:00-033378.
Audience: **g,l,u,f.**

Sherrow, Victoria TT957
Encyclopedia of Hair: A Cultural History. Trade Cloth.
Greenwood Publishing Group, Inc. Portsmouth, NH. 2006. 488p.
ISBN:0-313-33145-6, ISBN13: 978-0-313-33145-9.
Dewey:391.5/09. LCCN:2005-020995.
Audience: **g,l,u,f.** *Choice, 2006.*

Sieber, Roy & Herreman, GT2295.A35H352000
Frank
Hair in African Art and Culture. Niangi Batulukisi (Contribution
by). Trade Paper. Museum for African Art. Long Is City, NY.
2000. 192p. ISBN:0-945802-26-9, ISBN13: 978-0-945802-26-6.
Dewey:391.5/096. LCCN:99-068113.
Audience: **g,l,u,f.**

Steele, Valerie GT615.S74 1997
Fifty Years of Fashion: From New Look to Now. Cloth over
Boards. Yale University Press. Cumberland, RI. 1997. 176p.
ISBN:0-300-07132-9, ISBN13: 978-0-300-07132-0.
Dewey:391/.00973/0904. LCCN:97-026413.
Audience: **g,l,u,f.**

Warner, Pamela NK9206
Embroidery: A History. Trafalgar Square. 1991.
ISBN:0-7134-6106-3, ISBN13: 978-0-7134-6106-0.
Audience: **g,l,u,f.**

Design > Histories and Handbooks > Topics > Illustration

Blake, William PR4142.B78 2000
William Blake: The Complete Illuminated Books. David
Bindman (Introduction by). Trade Cloth. Thames & Hudson.
New York, NY. 2000. 480p. ISBN:0-500-51014-8, ISBN13:
978-0-500-51014-8. Dewey:821/.7. LCCN:00-101383.
Audience: **g,l,u,f.**

Harthan, John NC960
The History of the Illustrated Book: The Western Tradition.
Trade Paper. Thames & Hudson. New York, NY. 1997. 288p.
ISBN:0-500-27946-2, ISBN13: 978-0-500-27946-5.
Dewey:741.6/4/09. LCCN:81-050283.
Audience: **g,l,u,f.**

Heller, Steven & Pomeroy, NC975.H4 1990
Karen
Designing with Illustration. Trade Paper. John Wiley & Sons,
Inc. Hoboken, NJ. 1990. 224p. ISBN:0-442-23277-2, ISBN13:
978-0-442-23277-1. Dewey:741.6/092/273. LCCN:89-014723.
Audience: **g,l,u,f.** *Choice, 1990.*

Kren, Thomas & Barstow, ND3159.K74 2005
Kurt
Italian Illuminated Manuscripts in the J. Paul Getty Museum. J.
Paul Getty Museum Staff (Contribution by). Trade Paper. Getty
Conservation Institute. Los Angeles, CA. 2005. 96p.
ISBN:0-89236-820-9, ISBN13: 978-0-89236-820-4.
Dewey:745.6/7/094507479494. LCCN:2004-028795.
Audience: **g,l,u,f.**

Reed, Walt NC975 .R4
Illustrator in America, 1860-2000. Trade Cloth. Madison Square
Press. New York, NY. 2001. 464p. ISBN:0-942604-80-6,
ISBN13: 978-0-942604-80-1. Dewey:741.6092273.
Audience: **g,l,u,f.**

Schwarcz, Joseph & NC965.S281990
Schwarcz, Chava
The Picture Book Comes of Age: Looking at Childhood
Through the Art of Illustration. Betsy Hearne (Introduction by).
Paper Text. American Library Association. Chicago, IL. 1990.
217p. ISBN:0-8389-0543-9, ISBN13: 978-0-8389-0543-2.
Dewey:741.6/42/09045. LCCN:90-037809.
Audience: **g,l,u,f.**

Wyeth, N. C. N6512.V57 2000
Visions of Adventure: N. C. Wyeth and the Brandywine Artists.
John Edward Dell (Editor). Trade Cloth. Watson-Guptill
Publications, Inc. New York, NY. 2000. 128p.
ISBN:0-8230-5608-2, ISBN13: 978-0-8230-5608-8.
Dewey:759.13. LCCN:00-023010.
Audience: **g,l,u,f.** *Choice, 2000.*

Design > Histories and Handbooks > Topics > Industrial Design

Adamson, Glenn TS23
Industrial Strength Design: How Brooks Stevens Shaped Your World. Trade Paper. MIT Press. Cambridge, MA. 2005. 300p. ISBN:0-262-51186-X, ISBN13: 978-0-262-51186-5. Dewey:745.2/092. LCCN:2003-104427.
Audience: **g,l,u,f.** *Choice, 2004.*

Fiell, Charlotte & Fiell, Peter TS171.4 .F54 2000
Industrial Design. Trade Cloth. Taschen America, LLC. Los Angeles, CA. 2000. 768p. Klotz Ser. ISBN:3-8228-6310-6, ISBN13: 978-3-8228-6310-7. Dewey:745.2/09. LCCN:2001-274164.
Audience: **g,l,u,f.** *Choice, 2001.*

Guidot, Raymond (Editor) TS171
Industrial Design Techniques and Materials. Jean-Baptiste Touchard, Jean Grenier & Jean Jacques Salomon (Contribution by). Trade Cloth. Flammarion et Cie. Paris, 2006. 352p. ISBN:2-08-030519-0, ISBN13: 978-2-08-030519-0. Dewey:745.2.
Audience: **g,l,u,f.**

Helfand, Jessica N7431.5.H45 2002
Reinventing the Wheel. Andrei Cordescu (Editor), Robert Kronenburg (Introduction by). Trade Cloth. Princeton Architectural Press. New York, NY. 2002. 160p. ISBN:1-56898-338-7, ISBN13: 978-1-56898-338-7. Dewey:701/.8. LCCN:2002-000532.
Audience: **g,l,u,f.**

Heskett, John TS171.H49 2002
Toothpicks and Logos: Design in Everyday Life. Trade Cloth. Oxford University Press, Inc. New York, NY. 2002. 224p. ISBN:0-19-280321-2, ISBN13: 978-0-19-280321-4. Dewey:745.2. LCCN:2001-055716.
Audience: **g,l,u,f.** *Choice, 2003.*

Slack, Laura
What Is Product Design? Paper over Boards. RotoVision SA. Hove, 2006. Essential Design Handbooks Ser. ISBN:2-940361-24-X, ISBN13: 978-2-940361-24-3.
Audience: **g,l,u,f.**

Design > Histories and Handbooks > Topics > Logos, Trademarks

Carter, David E. NC1002.L63
The Big Book of Logos. Trade Paper. HarperCollins Publishers. New York, NY. 2003. 384p. ISBN:0-06-055808-3, ISBN13: 978-0-06-055808-6. Dewey:741.6.
Audience: **g,l,u,f.**

Carter, David E. NC1002.L63B542003
The Big Book of Logos 3. Trade Paper. HarperCollins

Publishers. New York, NY. 2004. 384p. ISBN:0-06-059688-0, ISBN13: 978-0-06-059688-0. Dewey:741.6. LCCN:2003-110290.
Audience: **g,l,u,f.**

Carter, David E. NC1002.L63
The Big Book of Logos 4. Trade Cloth. HarperCollins Publishers. New York, NY. 2005. 400p. ISBN:0-06-074806-0, ISBN13: 978-0-06-074806-7. Dewey:741.6.
Audience: **g,l,u,f.**

Carter, David E. NC1002.L63N48 2003
The New Big Book of Logos. Trade Paper. HarperCollins Publishers. New York, NY. 2003. 384p. ISBN:0-06-056755-4, ISBN13: 978-0-06-056755-2. Dewey:929.9/5/0973. LCCN:2003-047807.
Audience: **g,l,u,f.**

Chapman, Giles TL275
Car Emblems: The Ultimate Guide to Automotive Logos Worldwide. Saddle Stitched, Cloth over Boards. Merrell Publishers Ltd. London, 2005. 320p. ISBN:1-85894-317-5, ISBN13: 978-1-85894-317-6. Dewey:629.262.
Audience: **g,l,u,f.**

Chermayeff, Ivan, et al. NC1003.C547 2000
TM: Trademarks Designed by Chermayeff and Geismar Inc. Tom Geismar & Steff Geissbuhler (Authors), Stefan Sagmeister (Introduction by). Trade Cloth. Princeton Architectural Press. New York, NY. 2000. 288p. ISBN:1-56898-256-9, ISBN13: 978-1-56898-256-4. Dewey:929.9/5. LCCN:00-041641.
Audience: **g,l,u,f.**

Design > Histories and Handbooks > Topics > Package Design

Calver, Giles TS195.4
What Is Packaging Design?: Essential Design Handbook. Trade Cloth. RotoVision SA. Hove, 2004. 256p. Essential Design Handbooks ISBN:2-88046-618-0, ISBN13: 978-2-88046-618-3. Dewey:658.5/64.
Audience: **g,l,u,f.**

Drate, Spencer NC1882.A15 2002
45 RPM: A Visual History of the Seven-Inch Record. Chuck Granata (Introduction by). Trade Paper. Princeton Architectural Press. New York, NY. 2002. 168p. ISBN:1-56898-358-1, ISBN13: 978-1-56898-358-5. Dewey:741.6/6. LCCN:2002-008638.
Audience: **g,l,u,f.** *Choice, 2003.*

Fishel, Catherine TS195.4
Perfect Package: How to Add Value Through Graphic Design. Trade Paper. Quayside. Chanhassen, MN. 2003. 160p. ISBN:1-59253-012-5, ISBN13: 978-1-59253-012-0. Dewey:741.6/92.
Audience: **g,l,u,f.**

Groth, Chuck   TS195.4.G76 2006
Exploring Package Design. Trade Paper. Thomson Delmar
Learning. Albany, NY. 2005. 256p. ISBN:1-4018-7217-4,
ISBN13: 978-1-4018-7217-5. Dewey:741.6.
LCCN:2005-053831.
Audience: **g,l,u,f.**

Jankowski, Jerry   HF5770 .J363
Shelf Space: Modern Package Design 1945-1965. Grant Kessler
(Photographer). Trade Paper. DIANE Publishing Company.
Collingdale, PA. 2004. 118p. ISBN:0-7567-7374-1, ISBN13:
978-0-7567-7374-8. Dewey:688.8.
Audience: **g,l,u,f.**

Roojen, Pepin Van   TS198.3.P3
Structural Package Designs. Trade Cloth, CD-ROM. Pepin
Press, The. Amsterdam, 2005. 424p. ISBN:90-5768-044-0,
ISBN13: 978-90-5768-044-1. Dewey:676.3/2.
Audience: **g,u,f.**

Roth, László & Wybenga,   TS195.4.R683 2006
  George L.
The Packaging Designer's Book of Patterns. Ed. 3. Trade Paper.
John Wiley & Sons, Inc. Hoboken, NJ. 2005. 656p.
ISBN:0-471-77146-5, ISBN13: 978-0-471-77146-3.
Dewey:688.8. LCCN:2005-030958.
Audience: **g,l,u,f.**

Design > Histories and Handbooks > Topics > Posters

Aulich, James &   DJK38
  Sylvestrova, Marta
Political Posters in Central and Eastern Europe 1945-1995:
Signs of the Times. Cloth over Boards. Manchester University
Press. Manchester, 2000. 300p. ISBN:0-7190-5418-4, ISBN13:
978-0-7190-5418-1. Dewey:943/.000904.
Audience: **g,l,u,f.**   *Choice, 2000.*

Bird, William L. &   D743.25.B57 1998
  Rubenstein, Harry R.
Design for Victory: World War II Posters on the American
Home Front. Trade Paper. Princeton Architectural Press. New
York, NY. 1998. 120p. ISBN:1-56898-140-6, ISBN13:
978-1-56898-140-6. Dewey:940.53/022/2. LCCN:97-048361.
Audience: **g,l,u,f.**   *Choice, 1999.*

Gundel, Marc   NC1827.G3H4542000
Picasso: The Art of the Poster, Catalogue Raisonné. Trade Cloth.
Prestel Publishing. New York, NY. 2000. 96p.
ISBN:3-7913-2277-X, ISBN13: 978-3-7913-2277-3.
Dewey:769.92. LCCN:99-069117.
Audience: **g,l,u,f.**   *Choice, 2001.*

Heyman, Theresa Thau   NC998.5.A1
Posters American Style. Trade Cloth. Harry N. Abrams, Inc.
New York, NY. 2000. 192p. ISBN:0-8109-8202-1, ISBN13:
978-0-8109-8202-4. Dewey:741.6/7/0973.
Audience: **g,l,u,f.**

King, Emily   PN1995.9.P5K56 2003
A Century of Movie Posters: From Silent to Art House. Trade
Cloth. Barron's Educational Series, Inc. Hauppauge, NY. 2003.
224p. ISBN:0-7641-5599-7, ISBN13: 978-0-7641-5599-4.
Dewey:791.43/75. LCCN:2003-102236.
Audience: **g,l,u,f.**   *Choice, 2004.*

Mann, James (Editor)   DS79.76
Peace Signs: The Anti-War Movement Illustrated. Howard Zinn
(Foreword by). Trade Paper. Georg Olms Verlag AG. Zurich,
2004. 208p. ISBN:3-283-00487-0, ISBN13: 978-3-283-00487-3.
Dewey:324.730207.
Audience: **g,l,u,f.**   *Choice, 2004.*

Muller-Brockmann, Josef &   NC1810
  Muller-Brockmann, Shizuko
History of the Poster. Trade Paper. Phaidon Press. London,
2004. 244p. ISBN:0-7148-4403-9, ISBN13: 978-0-7148-4403-9.
Dewey:741.6/74/09.
Audience: **g,l,u,f.**

Purvis, Alston W. & Le   NC1806.8.C68 2002
  Coultre, Martijn F.
A Century of Posters. Trade Paper. Ashgate Publishing
Company. Williston, VT. 2002. 448p. ISBN:0-85331-863-8,
ISBN13: 978-0-85331-863-7. Dewey:741.6/74/0904.
LCCN:2002-100640.
Audience: **g,l,u,f.**

Rawls, Walton   D522.25.R38 1988
Wake up, America!: World War I and the American Poster.
Maurice Rickards (Foreword by). Trade Cloth. Abbeville Press,
Inc. New York, NY. 2001. 288p. ISBN:0-89659-888-8, ISBN13:
978-0-89659-888-1. Dewey:741.67/0973/09041.
LCCN:88-014638.
Audience: **g,l,u,f.**   *Choice, 1989.*

Rothschild, Deborah, et al.   NC997.A4W487 1998
Graphic Design in the Mechanical Age: Selections from the
Merrill C. Berman Collection. Ellen Lupton & Darra Goldstein
(Authors). Cloth over Boards. Yale University Press.
Cumberland, RI. 1998. 222p. ISBN:0-300-07494-8, ISBN13:
978-0-300-07494-9. Dewey:741.6/074. LCCN:97-081268.
Audience: **g,l,u,f.**   *Choice, 1998.*

Schnapp, Jeffrey T.   JC491.S363 2005
Revolutionary Tides: The Art of the Political Poster, 1914-1989.
Iris & B. Gerald Cantor Center for Visual Arts at Stanford
University Staff & Wolfsonian-Florida International University
Staff (Contribution by). Trade Paper. Skira Editore. Milano,
2005. 158p. ISBN:88-7624-236-8, ISBN13: 978-88-7624-236-6.
Dewey:944.04/074. LCCN:2005-042495.
Audience: **g,l,u,f.**   *Choice, 2006.*

Villard, Henry Serrano &   NC1849.A35V55 2000
  Allen, Willis M. Jr.
Loop the Loop: Posters of Flight. Trade Cloth. Kales Press.
Carlsbad, CA. 2003. 159p. ISBN:0-9670076-2-3, ISBN13:
978-0-9670076-2-5. Dewey:741.6/74. LCCN:99-080208.
Audience: **g,l,u,f.**   *Choice, 2001.*

Zega, Michael E. & Gruber,   NC1849.R34Z44 2002
  John E.
Travel by Train: The American Railroad Poster, 1870-1950.
Trade Cloth, Poster. Indiana University Press. Bloomington, IN.
2002. 122p. ISBN:0-253-34152-3, ISBN13: 978-0-253-34152-5.
Dewey:741.6/74/0973. LCCN:2002-002516.
                         Audience: **g,l,u,f.**

Design > Histories and Handbooks > Topics > Publication Design

Crowley, David   **NC974**
Magazine Covers. Trade Cloth. Phaidon Press, Inc. New York,
NY. 2003. 144p. ISBN:1-84000-698-6, ISBN13:
978-1-84000-698-8. Dewey:741.652. LCCN:2004-401919.
                         Audience: **g,l,u,f.**

Heller, Steven & Chwast,   NC1883.U6H45 1995
  Seymour
Jackets Required: An Illustrated History of the American Book
Jacket 1920-1950. Trade Paper. Chronicle Books LLC. San
Francisco, CA. 1995. 144p. ISBN:0-8118-0396-1, ISBN13:
978-0-8118-0396-0. Dewey:741.6/4/097309041.
LCCN:94-013260.
             Audience: **g,l,u,f.** *Choice, 1995.*

Nelson, Roy P.   **Z246.N44 1991**
Publication Design. Ed. 5. Cloth Text. Brown & Benchmark.
Madison, WI. 1990. 336p. ISBN:0-697-08620-8, ISBN13:
978-0-697-08620-4. Dewey:686.2/24. LCCN:90-080171.
                         Audience: **g,l,u,f.**

The Society of Publication   **Z246**
  Designers Staff (Editor)
40th Publication Design Annual. Ed. 40. Paper over Boards.
Quayside. Chanhassen, MN. 2005. 272p. ISBN:1-59253-181-4,
ISBN13: 978-1-59253-181-3. Dewey:741.6505.
                         Audience: **g,l,u,f.**

Vidaling, Raphaelle;   **NC974**
  McLuhan, Marshall
Front Page: Covers of the Twentieth-Century. Marshall
McLuhan (Editor). Weidenfeld & Nicolson, Ltd. 2003.
ISBN:0-297-82971-8, ISBN13: 978-0-297-82971-3.
                         Audience: **g,l,u,f.**

Design > Histories and Handbooks > Topics > Typography and Letter Arts

Bo, Shi   NK3634.A2S53413 2003
Between Heaven and Earth: A History of Chinese Writing.
Trade Paper. Shambhala Publications, Inc. Boston, MA. 2003.
128p. ISBN:1-59030-050-5, ISBN13: 978-1-59030-050-3.
LCCN:2003-002497.
                         Audience: **g,l,u,f.**

Derman, M. Ugur   **NK3636.5.A2**
Letters in Gold: Ottoman Calligraphy from the Sakip Sabanci
Collection, Istanbul. Cloth over Boards. Yale University Press.
Cumberland, RI. 1998. 208p. Metropolitan Museum of Art Ser.
ISBN:0-300-08632-6, ISBN13: 978-0-300-08632-4.
Dewey:745.6/19927/0956.
             Audience: **g,l,u,f.** *Choice, 1999.*

Friedl, Friedrich, et al.   **Z250.A2**
Creative Type: A Sourcebook of Classic and Contemporary
Letterforms. Alston W. Purvis & Cees W. De Jong (Authors).
Saddle Stitched, Cloth over Boards, Dust Jacket. Thames &
Hudson. New York, NY. 2005. 399p. ISBN:0-500-51229-9,
ISBN13: 978-0-500-51229-6. Dewey:686.224.
             Audience: **g,l,u,f.** *Choice, 2005.*

Jury, David   **Z250**
What Is Typography? Printed Dust Jacket. RotoVision SA.
Hove, 2006. 256p. Essential Design Handbooks Ser.
ISBN:2-88046-822-1, ISBN13: 978-2-88046-822-4.
Dewey:686.22.
                         Audience: **g,l,u,f.**

Kendrick, Laura   **NK3610.K46 1999**
Animating the Letter: The Figurative Embodiment of Writing
from Late Antiquity to the Renaissance. Trade Cloth. Ohio State
University Press. Columbus, OH. 1999. 336p.
ISBN:0-8142-0822-3, ISBN13: 978-0-8142-0822-9.
Dewey:302.2/244/0902. LCCN:99-019159.
             Audience: **g,l,u,f.** *Choice, 2000.*

Kraus, Richard C.   **NK3634.A2K73 1991**
Brushes with Power: Modern Politics and the Chinese Art of
Calligraphy. Trade Cloth. University of California Press.
Berkeley, CA. 1991. 220p. ISBN:0-520-07285-5, ISBN13:
978-0-520-07285-5. Dewey:745.6/19951. LCCN:90-023590.
             Audience: **g,l,u,f.** *Choice, 1992.*

Lovett, Patricia   **Z43.L862000**
Calligraphy and Illumination: A History and Practical Guide.
Trade Cloth. Harry N. Abrams, Inc. New York, NY. 2000. 320p.
ISBN:0-8109-4119-8, ISBN13: 978-0-8109-4119-9.
Dewey:745.6/1. LCCN:00-031318.
             Audience: **g,l,u,f.** *Choice, 2001.*

Spencer, Herbert   **Z116.A3S6 2004**
Pioneers of Modern Typography. Rick Poynor (Foreword by).
Trade Paper. MIT Press. Cambridge, MA. 2004. 164p.
ISBN:0-262-69303-8, ISBN13: 978-0-262-69303-5.
Dewey:686.2/24/09. LCCN:2003-111972.
                         Audience: **g,l,u,f.**

Weingart, Wolfgang   **Z246.W472000**
My Way to Typography. Trade Cloth. Lars Muller. Schweiz,
2000. 528p. ISBN:3-907044-86-X, ISBN13: 978-3-907044-86-5.
Dewey:686.22. LCCN:2001-415745.
                         Audience: **g,l,u,f.**

Design > Individual Designers

Abercrombie, Stanley   NK1412.W75
George Nelson: The Design of Modern Design. Ettore Sottsaas
Jr. (Foreword by). Trade Paper. MIT Press. Cambridge, MA.
2000. 376p. ISBN:0-262-51116-9, ISBN13: 978-0-262-51116-2.
Dewey:745.4/492 B.

Audience: **g,l,u,f.** *Choice, 1995.*

Adamson, Jeremy Elwell   NK2439.M28A83 2001
The Furniture of Sam Maloof. Trade Cloth. W. W. Norton &
Company, Inc. New York, NY. 2001. 272p.
ISBN:0-393-73080-8, ISBN13: 978-0-393-73080-7.
Dewey:749.213 B. LCCN:2001-003691.

Audience: **g,l,u,f.** *Choice, 2002.*

Brindle, Steven   TA140
Brunel: The Man Who Built the World. Dan Cruickshank
(Introduction by). Trade Cloth. Weidenfeld & Nicolson, Ltd.
London, 2005. 288p. ISBN:0-297-84408-3, ISBN13:
978-0-297-84408-2. Dewey:624.092.

Audience: **g,l,u,f.** *Choice, 2006.*

Böhm, Florian,   TS140.G734 K453 2005
KGID: Konstantin Grcic Industrial Design. Phaidon Press. 2005.
ISBN:0-7148-4431-4, ISBN13: 978-0-7148-4431-2.

Audience: **g,l,u,f.**

Deschodt, Anne-Marie &   NK1535.F675D4813
Davanzo Poli, Doretta
Fortuny. Anthony Roberts (Translator). Trade Cloth. Harry N.
Abrams, Inc. New York, NY. 2001. 188p. ISBN:0-8109-1133-7,
ISBN13: 978-0-8109-1133-8. Dewey:700/.92 B.
LCCN:2001-022406.

Audience: **g,l,u,f.**

Fox Weber, Nicholas &   NK1412
Filler, Martin
Josef and Anni Albers: Designs for Living. Trade Cloth. Merrell
Publishers Ltd. London, 2005. 160p. ISBN:1-85894-264-0,
ISBN13: 978-1-85894-264-3. Dewey:745.4/0922.
LCCN:2005-357344.

Audience: **g,l,u,f.** *Choice, 2005.*

Glaser, Milton   NC999.4.G55A4 2000
Art Is Work: Graphic Design, Interiors, Objects and Illustration.
Trade Cloth. Overlook Press, The. New York, NY. 2000. 272p.
ISBN:1-58567-069-3, ISBN13: 978-1-58567-069-7.
Dewey:741.6/092. LCCN:00-057986.

Audience: **g,l,u,f.**

Gundel, Marc   NC1850.H34 A4 2002
Keith Haring - Short Messages: Posters Catalogue Raisonné.
Trade Cloth. Prestel Publishing. New York, NY. 2002. 96p.
ISBN:3-7913-2780-1, ISBN13: 978-3-7913-2780-8.
Dewey:741.6/74/092. LCCN:2003-268577.

Audience: **g,l,u,f.**

Jackson, Lesley   NK1447.6.D39
Robin and Lucienne Day: Pioneers of Modern Design. Trade

Cloth. Princeton Architectural Press. New York, NY. 2001. 192p.
ISBN:1-56898-271-2, ISBN13: 978-1-56898-271-7. Dewey:709.

Audience: **g,l,u,f.** *Choice, 2001.*

L'Enfant, Julie   NC975.5.G34L46 2002
The Gag Family: German-Bohemian Artists in America. Phil
Freshman (Editor). Trade Cloth. Afton Historical Society Press.
Afton, MN. 2004. 204p. ISBN:1-890434-50-7, ISBN13:
978-1-890434-50-2. Dewey:700/.92/39186073.
LCCN:2002-000902.

Audience: **l,u,f.** *Choice, 2002.*

Ludwig, Coy   NC975.5.P37L82 1993
Maxfield Parrish. Trade Cloth. Schiffer Publishing, Ltd. Atglen,
PA. 1993. 224p. ISBN:0-88740-527-4, ISBN13:
978-0-88740-527-3. Dewey:741.0924. LCCN:73-005691.

Audience: **g,l,u,f.**

Noever, Peter (Editor)   NK946.H63 A4
Josef Hoffmann Designs: MAK- Austrian Museum of Applied
Arts. Paper Text. Prestel Verlag, Germany. Munchen, 1997.
230p. ISBN:3-7913-1370-3, ISBN13: 978-3-7913-1370-2.
Dewey:745.4/492.

Audience: **l,u,f.** *Choice, 1993.*

Parry, Linda   NK1535.M67.A41996
William Morris. Trade Cloth. Harry N. Abrams, Inc. New York,
NY. 1996. 394p. ISBN:0-8109-4282-8, ISBN13:
978-0-8109-4282-0. Dewey:709.2. LCCN:95-051845.

Audience: **g,l,u,f.**

Purvis, Alston W.   N7113.G68
H. N. Werkman. Trade Paper, Perfect. Yale University Press.
Cumberland, RI. 2004. 112p. Monographics Ser.
ISBN:0-300-10290-9, ISBN13: 978-0-300-10290-1.
Dewey:760/.092.

Audience: **g,l,u,f.** *Choice, 2005.*

Sturgis, Matthew   NC242.B3S78 1999
Aubrey Beardsley: A Biography. Trade Cloth. Overlook Press,
The. New York, NY. 1999. 405p. ISBN:0-87951-910-X,
ISBN13: 978-0-87951-910-0. Dewey:760/.092 B.
LCCN:98-048817.

Audience: **g,l,u,f.** *Choice, 2000.*

Tatham, David   NC975.5.H65T38 1992
Winslow Homer and the Illustrated Book. Trade Cloth. Syracuse
University Press. Syracuse, NY. 1992. 366p.
ISBN:0-8156-2550-2, ISBN13: 978-0-8156-2550-6.
Dewey:741.6/4/092. LCCN:91-013534.

Audience: **g,l,u,f.** *Choice, 1992.*

Design > Materials and Techniques

Le Van, Marthe   TT212.P462005
The Penland Book of Jewelry: Master Classes in Jewelry
Techniques. Saddle Stitched, Cloth over Boards, Dust Jacket.
Lark Books. Asheville, NC. 2005. 232p. ISBN:1-57990-698-2,
ISBN13: 978-1-57990-698-6. Dewey:739.27.
LCCN:2005-006162.

Audience: **g,l,u,f.**

Lipton, Ronnie   NC998.5.A1L562002
Designing Across Cultures: How to Create Effective Graphics
for Diverse Ethnic Groups. Trade Cloth. F & W Publications,
Inc. Cincinnati, OH. 2002. 96p. ISBN:1-58180-194-7, ISBN13:
978-1-58180-194-1. Dewey:741.6/0973. LCCN:2001-051522.

Audience: **g,l,u,f.**

Martin, Diana & Haller,   NC998.5.A1M27 1997
  Lynn
Graphic Design Inspirations and Innovations. Ed. 2. Trade
Cloth. F & W Publications, Inc. Cincinnati, OH. 1997. 144p.
ISBN:0-89134-773-9, ISBN13: 978-0-89134-773-6. Dewey:760.
LCCN:96-006553.

Audience: **g,l,u,f.**

Smith, Paul J.   NK808.O252001
Objects for Use: Handmade by Design. Akiko Busch
(Contribution by). Trade Cloth. Harry N. Abrams, Inc. New
York, NY. 2001. 336p. ISBN:0-8109-0611-2, ISBN13:
978-0-8109-0611-2. Dewey:745/.0973/0747471.
LCCN:2001-001343.

Audience: **g,l,u,f.** *Choice, 2002.*

Tufte, Edward R.   P93.5
Envisioning Information. Trade Cloth. Graphics Press. Cheshire,
CT. 1990. 128p. ISBN:0-9613921-1-8, ISBN13:
978-0-9613921-1-6. Dewey:302.23.

Audience: **g,l,u,f.** *Choice, 1990.*

Washburn, Dorothy K. &   NK1510
  Crowe, Donald W.
Symmetries of Culture: Theory and Practice of Plane Pattern
Analysis. Trade Paper. University of Washington Press. Seattle,
WA. 1991. 304p. ISBN:0-295-97084-7, ISBN13:
978-0-295-97084-4. Dewey:745.4. LCCN:87-027924.

Audience: **g,l,u,f.**

Drawing > Reference Works > Dictionaries and Encyclopedias

Bryant, Mark   NC1476.B79 2000
Dictionary of Twentieth-Century British Cartoonists and
Caricaturists. Trade Cloth. Ashgate Publishing, Ltd. Aldershot,
2000. 224p. ISBN:1-84014-286-3, ISBN13: 978-1-84014-286-0.
Dewey:741.5/092/241 B. LCCN:99-045326.

Audience: **g,l,u,f.** *Choice, 2000.*

Bryant, Mark & Heneage,   NC1470
  Simon
Dictionary of British Cartoonists and Caricaturists. Trade Cloth.
Ashgate Publishing, Ltd. Aldershot, 1994. 250p.
ISBN:0-85967-976-4, ISBN13: 978-0-85967-976-3.
Dewey:741.5/0922/41. LCCN:93-021363.

Audience: **g,l,u,f.** *Choice, 1995.*

Goldman, Paul   N33.G65 1988
Looking at Prints, Drawings and Watercolours: A Guide to
Technical Terms. Trade Paper. Oxford University Press, Inc.

New York, NY. 1989. 64p. Looking at Ser.
ISBN:0-89236-148-4, ISBN13: 978-0-89236-148-9.
Dewey:760/.03/21. LCCN:88-013241.

Audience: **g,l,u,f.**

Drawing > Histories and Handbooks

Avery, Kevin J., et al.   NC139.G63
American Drawings and Watercolors in the Metropolitan
Museum of Art: A Catalogue of Works by Artists Born Before
1835. Claire A. Conway & Marjorie Shelley (Authors). Cloth
over Boards. Yale University Press. Cumberland, RI. 2002.
424p. The Metropolitan Museum of Art Ser.
ISBN:0-300-09372-1, ISBN13: 978-0-300-09372-8.
Dewey:741.9/73. LCCN:2002-067772.

Audience: **g,l,u,f.** *Choice, 2003.*

Bomford, David (Editor)   ND653.R4
Art in the Making: Underdrawings in Renaissance Paintings.
Rachel Billinge, Lorne Campbell, Jill Dunkerton, Susan Foister
& Jo Kirby (Contribution by). Trade Paper. Yale University
Press. Cumberland, RI. 2002. 192p. National Gallery London
Publications ISBN:0-300-09225-3, ISBN13: 978-0-300-09225-7.
Dewey:759.9492.

Audience: **g,l,u,f.** *Choice, 2003.*

Butts, Barbara & Hendrix,   N7433.5.B88 2000
  Lee
Painting on Light: Drawings and Stained Glass in the Age of
Durer and Holbein. Trade Paper. Oxford University Press, Inc.
New York, NY. 2001. 342p. Drawings Ser.
ISBN:0-89236-579-X, ISBN13: 978-0-89236-579-1.
Dewey:748.593/09. LCCN:99-059416.

Audience: **g,l,u,f.** *Choice, 2001.*

Cazort, Mimi   NC255.P5 2004
Italian Master Drawings at the Philadelphia Museum of Art.
Philadelphia Museum of Art Staff (Contribution by), Ann Percy
(Introduction by). Trade Paper. Philadelphia Museum of Art.
Philadelphia, PA. 2004. 287p. ISBN:0-87633-179-7, ISBN13:
978-0-87633-179-8. Dewey:741.945/074/74811.
LCCN:2004-040074.

Audience: **g,l,u,f.** *Choice, 2005.*

Clark, Alvin L. Jr. (Editor),   NC246.M38 1998
  et al.
Mastery and Elegance: Two Centuries of French Drawings from
the Collection of Jeffrey E. Horvitz. Margaret M. Grasselli,
Jean-Francois Mejanes & William W. Robinson (Editors), Pierre
Rosenberg (Foreword by). Trade Paper. Harvard University Art
Museums. Cambridge, MA. 1998. 492p. ISBN:1-891771-02-7,
ISBN13: 978-1-891771-02-6. Dewey:741.944/09/032074744.
LCCN:98-045920.

Audience: **g,l,u,f.** *Choice, 2000.*

Davis, B.   N6868.5.E9 R6
German Expressionist Prints and Drawings. Trade Cloth. Prestel
Publishing. New York, NY. 1989. 846p. ISBN:3-7913-0959-5,
ISBN13: 978-3-7913-0959-0. Dewey:759.3.

Audience: **g,l,u,f.** *Choice, 1990.*

Dexter, Emma   **NC95**
Vitamin D: New Perspectives in Drawing. Phaidon Press Editors
(Created by). Trade Cloth. Phaidon Press, Inc. New York, NY.
2005. 352p. ISBN:0-7148-4545-0, ISBN13: 978-0-7148-4545-6.
Dewey:741.9242.

Audience: **g,l,u,f.**

Fisher, Jay M., et al.   **NC246.E88 2005**
Essence of Line: French Drawings from Ingres to Degas.
William R. Johnston & Kimberly Schenck (Authors). Trade
Cloth. Pennsylvania State University Press. University Park, PA.
2005. 416p. ISBN:0-271-02682-0, ISBN13: 978-0-271-02682-4.
Dewey:741.944/074/7526. LCCN:2005-009563.

Audience: **g,l,u,f.** *Choice, 2006.*

Foster, Carter E., et al.   **NC246.F665 2001**
French Master Drawings from the Collection of Muriel Butkin.
Sylvain Bellenger & Patrick Shaw Cable (Authors). Trade Cloth.
Hudson Hills Press LLC. Manchester, VT. 2002. 160p.
ISBN:0-940717-67-0, ISBN13: 978-0-940717-67-1.
Dewey:741.944/074/77132. LCCN:2001-092438.

Audience: **g,l,f.** *Choice, 2002.*

Getty, J. Paul, Museum   **NC225.J25 1997**
Staff
Masterpieces of the J. Paul Getty Museum - Drawings. Trade
Cloth. Oxford University Press, Inc. New York, NY. 1997. 128p.
Drawings Ser. ISBN:0-89236-437-8, ISBN13:
978-0-89236-437-4. Dewey:741.94/074/79493.
LCCN:96-023151.

Audience: **g,l,u,f.** *Choice, 1998.*

Goldfarb, Hilliard T.   **NC246.G65 1989**
From Fontainebleau to the Louvre: French Drawing from the
Seventeenth Century. Trade Cloth. Cleveland Museum of Art.
Cleveland, OH. 1990. 232p. ISBN:0-910386-96-X, ISBN13:
978-0-910386-96-8. Dewey:741.944/074/7. LCCN:89-022051.

Audience: **g,l,u,f.** *Choice, 1990.*

Goldfinger, Eliot   **NC760.G67 1991**
Human Anatomy for Artists: The Elements of Form. Trade
Cloth. Oxford University Press, Inc. New York, NY. 1991. 368p.
ISBN:0-19-505206-4, ISBN13: 978-0-19-505206-0.
Dewey:702/.8. LCCN:91-002891.

Audience: **g,l,u,f.** *Choice, 1992.*

Meij, Bram (Contribution   **NC258.M86 2001**
by), et al.
Rubens, Jordaens, Van Dyck: 17th Century Flemish Drawings.
Maartje de Haan, Hans Vlieghe, Bert W. Meijer & Roger
Baetens (Contribution by). Trade Cloth. D. A. P./Distributed Art
Publishers. New York, NY. 2001. 381p. ISBN:90-5662-212-9,
ISBN13: 978-90-5662-212-1. Dewey:741.9493/1/074492385.
LCCN:2001-449723.

Audience: **l,u,f.** *Choice, 2002.*

Myers, Mary L.   **NC246.M94 1991**
French Architectural and Ornament Drawings of the Eighteenth
Century. Trade Cloth. Bow Historical Books. New Providence,
NJ. 1991. xxx, 224p. ISBN:0-87099-625-8, ISBN13:

978-0-87099-625-2. Dewey:741.944/09/033074747.
LCCN:91-023492.

Audience: **g,l,u,f.** *Choice, 1992.*

Rosenberg, Pierre   **NC246.R673 2000**
From Drawing to Painting: Poussin, Watteau, Fragonard, David,
and Ingres. Trade Cloth. Princeton University Press. Princeton,
NJ. 2000. 256p. Bollingen Ser., Vol. 47 ISBN:0-691-00918-X,
ISBN13: 978-0-691-00918-6. Dewey:741/.092/244.
LCCN:99-088620.

Audience: **g,l,u,f.** *Choice, 2000.*

Stein, Perrin   **NC246.S751999**
Eighteenth-Century French Drawings in New York Collections.
Trade Cloth. Metropolitan Museum of Art, The. New York, NY.
1999. 243p. ISBN:0-87099-892-7, ISBN13: 978-0-87099-892-8.
Dewey:741.944/09. LCCN:98-047341.

Audience: **g,l,u,f.** *Choice, 1999.*

Drawing > Individual Artists

Alexej Von Jawlensky   **ND699.J3**
Archive Staff
Alexej von Jawlensky, 1890-1938: Catalogue Raisonné of the
Watercolours and Drawings. Cloth over Boards. Philip Wilson
Publishers, Ltd. London, 1998. 504p. The Alexej von Jawlensky
Archive Ser. ISBN:0-85667-486-9, ISBN13: 978-0-85667-486-0.
Dewey:[B].

Audience: **g,l,u,f.**

Altcappenberg,   **ND623.R2**
Hein-Thomas Schulze, et al.
Sandro Botticelli: The Drawings for Dante's Divine Comedy.
Peter Keller, Julia Schewski, Horst Bredekamp, Damian
Dombrowski, Andreas Kablitz, Giovanni Morello, Robert S.
Fuchs & Doris Oltrogge (Authors). Trade Cloth. Harry N.
Abrams, Inc. New York, NY. 2000. 360p. ISBN:0-8109-6633-6,
ISBN13: 978-0-8109-6633-8. Dewey:759.5.

Audience: **g,l,u,f.** *Choice, 2001.*

Banerji, Christiane &   **NC1479.G5G561999**
Donald, Diana (Edited and Translated by)
Gillray Observed: The Earliest Account of His Caricatures in
London and Paris. Trade Cloth. Cambridge University Press.
New York, NY. 1999. 290p. ISBN:0-521-58075-7, ISBN13:
978-0-521-58075-5. Dewey:769.92. LCCN:98-026521.

Audience: **l,u,f.** *Choice, 1999.*

Boggs, Jean S. & Maheux,   **NC248.D38.A4 1992**
Anne F.
Degas Pastels. Trade Cloth. George Braziller Inc. New York,
NY. 1992. 200p. ISBN:0-8076-1276-6, ISBN13:
978-0-8076-1276-7. Dewey:741.944. LCCN:91-044423.

Audience: **g,l,u,f.** *Choice, 1993.*

Bohn, Babette   **NC257**
Ludovico Carracci and the Art of Drawing. Trade Cloth. Harvey
Miller Publishers. London, 2005. 450p. L' Arte del Disegno Ser.
ISBN:1-872501-18-4, ISBN13: 978-1-872501-18-5.
Dewey:741.092.

Audience: **l,u,f.** *Choice, 2005.*

Chapman, Hugo   NC257.L4
Michelangelo Drawings: Closer to the Master. Saddle Stitched,
Cloth over Boards, Dust Jacket. Yale University Press.
Cumberland, RI. 2005. 320p. ISBN:0-300-11147-9, ISBN13:
978-0-300-11147-7. Dewey:741.945.
                              Audience: **g,l,u,f.** *Choice, 2006.*

Cox-Rearick, Janet, et al.   NC257.R5748A4 1999
Giulio Romano, Master Designer: An Exhibition of Drawings in
Celebration of the 500th Anniversary of His Birth. Richard Aste,
Chris Begley, Elsa Homberg-Pinassi, Michael McAuliffe,
Margaret Schwartz & Valerie Taylor (Authors). Trade Paper.
Hunter College Art Galleries. New York, NY. 2000. 168p.
ISBN:1-885998-21-X, ISBN13: 978-1-885998-21-7.
Dewey:720.945. LCCN:99-073766.
                              Audience: **g,l,u,f.** *Choice, 2000.*

da Vinci, Leonardo, et al.   NC257.L4A42003
Leonardo da Vinci, Master Draftsman. Rachel Stern & Alison
Manges (Authors), Carmen Bambach (Editor), Metropolitan
Museum of Art Staff, Alessandro Cecchi, Claire J. Farago,
Varena Forcione & Martin Kemp (Contribution by). Cloth over
Boards. Yale University Press. Cumberland, RI. 2003. 800p.
Metropolitan Museum of Art Ser. ISBN:0-300-09878-2,
ISBN13: 978-0-300-09878-5. Dewey:741.945.
LCCN:2002-191234.
                              Audience: **g,l,u,f.** *Choice, 2003.*

Fleming-Williams, Ian   NC242.C5
Constable and His Drawings. Cloth over Boards. Philip Wilson
Publishers, Ltd. London, 1991. 328p. ISBN:0-85667-380-3,
ISBN13: 978-0-85667-380-1. Dewey:741.942.
                              Audience: **g,l,u,f.** *Choice, 1991.*

Forrer, Matthi   NE1325.K3 A4 1991
Hokusai: Prints and Drawings. Trade Paper. Prestel Publishing.
New York, NY. 2004. 219p. ISBN:3-7913-2490-X, ISBN13:
978-3-7913-2490-6. Dewey:769.92.
                              Audience: **g,l,u,f.** *Choice, 1992.*

Foye, Raymond & Percy,   NC257.C575A4 1990
  Ann
Francesco Clemente: Three Worlds. Trade Paper. Philadelphia
Museum of Art. Philadelphia, PA. 1990. 192p.
ISBN:0-87633-084-7, ISBN13: 978-0-87633-084-5.
Dewey:709/.2. LCCN:90-045673.
                              Audience: **g,l,u,f.** *Choice, 1991.*

Fumaroli, Marc   N6679.B6
Botero: Drawings. Benjamin Villegas (Editor), German Tellez
(Translator), Fernando Botero (Illustrator). Cloth over Boards.
Villegas Editores Ltda. Bogota, 1999. 240p.
ISBN:958-9393-73-X, ISBN13: 978-958-9393-73-4.
Dewey:759.9861.
                              Audience: **g,l,u,f.**

Garrould, Ann (Editor)   NC242.M7A41994
Henry Moore, Complete Drawings: A Catalogue Raisonné,
1916-83. Trade Cloth. Ashgate Publishing, Ltd. Aldershot, 1994.
200p. A Lund Humphries Ser. ISBN:0-85331-604-X, ISBN13:
978-0-85331-604-6. Dewey:709.2. LCCN:93-102221.
                              Audience: **g,l,u,f.**

Gealt, Adelheid M., et al.   NC257.T5A4 1996
Domenico Tiepolo: Master Draftsman. George Knox, Giovanni
B. Tiepolo & Indiana University Art Museum Staff (Authors).
Trade Cloth. Indiana University Press. Bloomington, IN. 1997.
253p. ISBN:0-253-33330-X, ISBN13: 978-0-253-33330-8.
Dewey:741.945. LCCN:97-002504.
                              Audience: **g,l,u,f.** *Choice, 1997.*

Getscher, Robert H.   NC139.W45A4 1991
James Abbott McNeill Whistler: Pastels. Trade Cloth. George
Braziller Inc. New York, NY. 1991. 200p. ISBN:0-8076-1266-9,
ISBN13: 978-0-8076-1266-8. Dewey:741.973.
LCCN:91-016530.
                              Audience: **g,l,u,f.** *Choice, 1992.*

Hirst, Michael   NC242.B3
Michelangelo and His Drawings. Trade Paper. Yale University
Press. Cumberland, RI. 1990. 304p. ISBN:0-300-04796-7,
ISBN13: 978-0-300-04796-7. Dewey:741/.092/4.
LCCN:88-050431.
                              Audience: **g,l,u,f.** *Choice, 1989.*

Kushner, Tony   NC975.5.S44K872003
The Art of Maurice Sendak: 1980 to the Present. Trade Cloth.
Harry N. Abrams, Inc. New York, NY. 2003. 224p.
ISBN:0-8109-4448-0, ISBN13: 978-0-8109-4448-0.
Dewey:741.6/092. LCCN:2003-009293.
                              Audience: **g,l,u,f.** *Choice, 2004.*

MacDonald, Margaret F.   NC139.W45A41994
James McNeill Whistler: Watercolors, Pastels, and Drawings: A
Catalogue Raisonné¡. Cloth over Boards. Yale University Press.
Cumberland, RI. 1995. 684p. Paul Mellon Centre for Studies in
British Art ISBN:0-300-05987-6, ISBN13: 978-0-300-05987-8.
Dewey:741.973. LCCN:94-010253.
                              Audience: **g,l,u,f.** *Choice, 1995.*

MacDonald, Margaret F.   NC139.W45A4 2001
Palaces in the Night: Whistler in Venice. Trade Cloth.
University of California Press. Berkeley, CA. 2001. 160p.
ISBN:0-520-23049-3, ISBN13: 978-0-520-23049-1.
Dewey:741/.092. LCCN:2001-269912.
                              Audience: **g,l,u,f.** *Choice, 2001.*

Munhall, Edgar   NC312.F53
Grueze the Draftsman. Irina Novosselskaya (Contribution by).
Trade Cloth. Merrell Publishers Ltd. London, 2005. 284p.
ISBN:1-85894-158-X, ISBN13: 978-1-85894-158-5.
Dewey:741/.092.
                              Audience: **g,l,u,f.** *Choice, 2003.*

Murphy, Alexandra R., et al.   NC248.M55A41999
Jean-Francois Millet: Drawn into the Light. Brian Allen, James
A. Ganz & Richard Rand (Authors). Cloth over Boards. Yale
University Press. Cumberland, RI. 1999. 150p.
ISBN:0-300-07925-7, ISBN13: 978-0-300-07925-8.
Dewey:741.944. LCCN:99-011142.
                              Audience: **g,l,u,f.** *Choice, 1999.*

Audience: **g**=general, **l**=lower division undergraduate, **u**=upper division undergraduate, **f**=faculty.   **723**

Rosenberg, Pierre & Prat,   NC248.W3A4
  Louis-Antoine
Antoine Watteau 1684-1721: Catalogue Raisonné des Dessins.
Trade Cloth. Art Books International. London, 1996. 1516p.
ISBN:88-7813-703-0, ISBN13: 978-88-7813-703-5.
Dewey:741.944.
                                        Audience: **g,l,u,f.**

Schaaf, Larry John   NC242.H45A4 1989
Tracings of Light: Sir John Herschel and the Camera Lucida.
Graham Howe (Preface by). Trade Cloth. Friends of
Photography, The. San Francisco, CA. 1989. 120p.
ISBN:0-933286-55-4, ISBN13: 978-0-933286-55-9.
Dewey:741.942. LCCN:89-085802.
                              Audience: **g,l,u,f.** *Choice, 1990.*

Spoerri, Elka, et al.   NC293.W65A4 2003
The Art of Adolf Wolfli: St. Adolf-Giant-Creation. Daniel
Baumann & Edward M. Gomez (Authors), Gerard C. Wertkin
(Foreword by). Trade Cloth. Princeton University Press.
Princeton, NJ. 2003. 112p. ISBN:0-691-11498-6, ISBN13:
978-0-691-11498-9. Dewey:741.9494. LCCN:2002-112249.
                              Audience: **g,l,u,f.** *Choice, 2003.*

Spring, Justin & Skolnick,   NC139.C32
  Arnold
Paul Cadmus: The Male Nude. Arnold Spring (Introduction by).
Trade Cloth. Universe Publishing. New York, NY. 2002. 160p.
ISBN:0-7893-0589-5, ISBN13: 978-0-7893-0589-3.
Dewey:741.973.
                                        Audience: **g,l,u,f.**

Taylor, Ina   NC978.5.G7.T37 1991
The Art of Kate Greenaway: A Nostalgic Portrait of Childhood.
Trade Cloth. Pelican Publishing Company, Inc. Gretna, LA.
1991. 128p. ISBN:0-88289-867-1, ISBN13: 978-0-88289-867-4.
Dewey:741.9/42. LCCN:91-060404.
                              Audience: **g,l,u,f.** *Choice, 1991.*

Tsai, Eugenie   N6537.S6184A4 1991
Robert Smithson Unearthed: Drawings, Collages, Writings.
Cloth Text. Columbia University Press. New York, NY. 1991.
192p. ISBN:0-231-07258-9, ISBN13: 978-0-231-07258-8.
Dewey:700/.92. LCCN:91-019698.
                              Audience: **g,l,u,f.** *Choice, 1992.*

Wilson-Bareau, Juliet   NC287.G65A4 2001
Goya: Drawings from His Private Albums. Trade Cloth. Ashgate
Publishing Company. Williston, VT. 2001. 192p.
ISBN:0-85331-804-2, ISBN13: 978-0-85331-804-0.
Dewey:741.946. LCCN:00-112061.
                              Audience: **g,l,u,f.** *Choice, 2001.*

Drawing > Materials and Techniques

Bermingham, Ann   NC228.B47 2000
Learning to Draw: Studies in the Cultural History of a Polite
and Useful Art. Cloth over Boards. Yale University Press.
Cumberland, RI. 2000. 320p. Paul Mellon Centre for Studies in

British Art ISBN:0-300-08039-5, ISBN13: 978-0-300-08039-1.
Dewey:306.4/7. LCCN:99-059794.
                              Audience: **g,l,u,f.** *Choice, 2000.*

Civardi, Giovanni   NC765.C45413 2001
Drawing the Human Body: An Anatomical Guide. Trade Paper.
Sterling Publishing Co., Inc. New York, NY. 2001. 168p.
ISBN:0-8069-5891-X, ISBN13: 978-0-8069-5891-0.
Dewey:743.4. LCCN:00-053191.
                                        Audience: **g,l,u,f.**

Eakins, Thomas   NC730.E232005
A Drawing Manual by Thomas Eakins. Kathleen A. Foster &
Amy Beth Werbel (Editors), Kathleen A. Foster & Amy Beth
Werbel (Introduction by). Trade Cloth. Philadelphia Museum of
Art. Philadelphia, PA. 2005. 125p. Primary Sources in American
Art Ser., No. 1 ISBN:0-87633-176-2, ISBN13:
978-0-87633-176-7. Dewey:741.2. LCCN:2004-058508.
                              Audience: **g,l,u,f.** *Choice, 2005.*

Garcia, Claire Watson   NC730
Drawing for the Absolute and Utter Beginner. Trade Paper.
Watson-Guptill Publications, Inc. New York, NY. 2003. 160p.
ISBN:0-8230-1395-2, ISBN13: 978-0-8230-1395-1.
Dewey:741.2. LCCN:2004-298828.
                                        Audience: **g,l,u,f.**

Steinhart, Peter   NC720.S73 2004
The Undressed Art: Why We Draw. Trade Cloth. Alfred A.
Knopf Inc. New York, NY. 2004. 272p. ISBN:1-4000-4184-8,
ISBN13: 978-1-4000-4184-8. Dewey:741.2.
LCCN:2003-065652.
                              Audience: **g,l,u,f.** *Choice, 2005.*

Painting > Reference Works

Wood, Christopher   N6796.D531990
The Dictionary of British Art: Victorian Painters. Ed. 3. Trade
Cloth. Antique Collectors' Club. Easthampton, MA. 1995. 596p.
Dictionary of British Art Ser., Vol. 1 ISBN:1-85149-171-6,
ISBN13: 978-1-85149-171-1. Dewey:759.2. LCCN:96-214374.
                              Audience: **g,l,u,f.** *Choice, 1996.*

Painting > Reference Works > Web Resources

                                                  CD971
☐ SIRIUS (Smithsonian Institution Research Information
System): Archives, Manuscripts, Photographs Catalog.
http://siris-archives.si.edu/#focus
Smithsonian Institution.
                                        Audience: **g,l,u,f.**

Painting > Reference Works > Bibliographies and Research Guides

Clement, Russell T., et al. **Z5961**
The Women Impressionists: A Sourcebook. Annick Houze &
Christiane Erbolato-Ramsey (Authors). Cloth Text. Greenwood
Publishing Group, Inc. Portsmouth, NH. 2000. 216p. Art
Reference Collection Ser., Vol. 24 ISBN:0-313-30848-9,
ISBN13: 978-0-313-30848-2. Dewey:016.7594.
LCCN:99-059411.

Audience: **g,l,u,f.**

Puniello, Francoise S. & **Z5949.U5P86 1996**
Rusak, Halina R.
Abstract Expressionist Women Painters: An Annotated
Bibliography: Elaine de Kooning, Helen Frankenthaler, Grace
Hartigan, Lee Krasner, Joan Mitchell, Ethel Schwabacher. Trade
Cloth. Scarecrow Press, Inc. Lanham, MD. 1996. 372p.
ISBN:0-8108-2998-3, ISBN13: 978-0-8108-2998-5.
Dewey:016.7/590652/082. LCCN:95-021924.

Audience: **g,l,u,f.** *Choice, 1997.*

Wilson, Raymond L. **ND1808.W56 1994**
Index of American Watercolor Exhibitions, 1900-1945. Trade
Cloth. Scarecrow Press, Inc. Lanham, MD. 1994. 790p.
ISBN:0-8108-2829-4, ISBN13: 978-0-8108-2829-2.
Dewey:759.13/09/04107473. LCCN:93-045541.

Audience: **g,l,u,f.**

Witt Library of the **ND35**
Courtauld Institute Staff
A Checklist of Painters from c.1200. Ed. 2, illustrate.
Continuum International Publishing Group, Ltd. 1995.

Audience: **g,l,u,f.**

Painting > Reference Works > Dictionaries and Encyclopedias

Archibald, E. H. **ND1374.A72 2000**
The Dictionary of Sea Painters of Europe and America. Ed. 3.
Trade Cloth. Antique Collectors' Club. Easthampton, MA. 1999.
632p. ISBN:1-85149-269-0, ISBN13: 978-1-85149-269-5.
Dewey:758/.2/03. LCCN:2001-347190.

Audience: **g,l,u,f.**

Blattel, Harry **ND1336.B63 1992**
International Dictionary Miniature Painters, Porcelain Printers,
and Silhouettists. Trade Cloth. Munich, Edition, Verlag,
Handels- und Dienstleistungskontor GmbH. Munchen, 1997.
1424p. ISBN:3-928263-11-0, ISBN13: 978-3-928263-11-5.
Dewey:757/.7/09409024. LCCN:94-160237.

Audience: **g,l,u,f.**

Cahill, James **ND1043.3**
An Index of Early Chinese Painters and Paintings: T'ang, Sung,
Yuan. Ed. 2. Trade Paper. Floating World Editions. Warren, NY.
2005. 402p. ISBN:1-891640-10-0, ISBN13: 978-1-891640-10-0.
Dewey:759.951/016.

Audience: **g,l,u,f.**

Foskett, Daphne **ND1337.G7**
Miniatures: Dictionary and Guide. Trade Cloth. Antique
Collectors' Club. Easthampton, MA. 1987. 704p.
ISBN:1-85149-063-9, ISBN13: 978-1-85149-063-9.
Dewey:757/.7/0941. LCCN:88-132478.

Audience: **g,l,u,f.**

Gealt, Adelheid M. **ND456**
Painters of the Golden Age: A Biographical Dictionary of
Seventeenth-Century European Painting. Cloth Text. Greenwood
Publishing Group, Inc. Portsmouth, NH. 1993. 800p.
ISBN:0-313-24310-7, ISBN13: 978-0-313-24310-3.
Dewey:759.046. LCCN:92-040223.

Audience: **g,l,u,f.** *Choice, 1994.*

Halsby, Julian, et al. **ND496.H35 1998**
The Dictionary of Scottish Painters, 1600 to the Present. Ed. 2.
Paul Harris & Bourne Fine Art Staff (Authors). Trade Cloth.
Canongate Books. Edinburgh, 1998. 240p. ISBN:0-86241-778-3,
ISBN13: 978-0-86241-778-9. Dewey:759.2/911.
LCCN:99-488536.

Audience: **g,l,u,f.**

Hardouin-Fugier, Elisabeth, **ND1403.F85H3 1989**
et al.
French Flower Painters: Eighteen Hundred to Nineteen Hundred
- A Dictionary. Etienne Grafe & Peter Mitchell (Authors). Trade
Cloth. Sotheby's Publications. New York, NY. 1989. 404p.
ISBN:0-85667-348-X, ISBN13: 978-0-85667-348-1.
Dewey:758/.42/094409034 B. LCCN:89-060470.

Audience: **g,l,u,f.**

Harris, Paul; Halsby, Julian **ND475**
Dictionary of Scottish Painters 1600-1960. Trafalgar Square.
1991. ISBN:0-86241-328-1, ISBN13: 978-0-86241-328-6.

Audience: **g,l,u,f.**

Lester, Patrick D. (Editor) **ND203.L47 1995**
The Biographical Directory of Native American Painters. Trade
Cloth. University of Oklahoma Press. Norman, OK. 1995. 720p.
ISBN:0-8061-9936-9, ISBN13: 978-0-8061-9936-8.
Dewey:759.1308997. LCCN:95-069012.

Audience: **g,l,u,f.** *Choice, 1996.*

Mallalieu, H. L. **ND1928 .M27 2002**
The Dictionary of Watercolour Artists: Up to 1920, Vol. 2. Ed.
3. Trade Cloth. Antique Collectors' Club. Easthampton, MA.
304p. ISBN:1-85149-427-8, ISBN13: 978-1-85149-427-9.
Dewey:759.2. LCCN:2004-351915.

Audience: **g,l,u,f.**

Mallalieu, H. L. **ND1928**
The Dictionary of Watercolour Artists: Up to 1920. Ed. 3. Trade
Cloth. Antique Collectors' Club. Easthampton, MA. 376p.
ISBN:1-85149-426-X, ISBN13: 978-1-85149-426-2.
Dewey:759.2.

Audience: **g,l,u,f.**

Stewart, Brian **ND1314.S7**
The Dictionary of Portrait Painters in Britain up to 1920. Trade

Cloth. Antique Collectors' Club. Easthampton, MA. 1997. 500p. ISBN:1-85149-173-2, ISBN13: 978-1-85149-173-5. Dewey:759.2/03. LCCN:97-121593.

Audience: **g,l,u,f.**

Walpole, Josephine   **ND497**
A History and Dictionary of British Flower Painters 1650-1950. Trade Cloth. Antique Collectors' Club. Easthampton, MA. 2006. 224p. ISBN:1-85149-504-5, ISBN13: 978-1-85149-504-7. Dewey:759.2.

Audience: **g,l,u,f.**

Waterhouse, Ellis   **N6796.D53**
The Dictionary of British Art: British 18th Century Painters, Vol. 2. Trade Cloth. Antique Collectors' Club. Easthampton, MA. 1981. 444p. ISBN:0-902028-93-6, ISBN13: 978-0-902028-93-7. Dewey:759.2. LCCN:96-214373.

Audience: **g,l,u,f.**

Wood, Christopher   **N6796.D531990**
The Dictionary of British Art: Victorian Painters. Ed. 3. Trade Cloth. Antique Collectors' Club. Easthampton, MA. 1995. 476p. Dictionary of British Art Ser., Vol. 2 ISBN:1-85149-172-4, ISBN13: 978-1-85149-172-8. Dewey:759.2. LCCN:96-214374.

Audience: **g,l,u,f.** *Choice, 1996.*

Painting > Reference Works > Directories

Nahum, Peter   **N6767**
Victorian Painters' Monograms: Identify Almost 2000 Signatures. Trade Paper. W. Foulsham Company, Ltd. Slough, 2005. 224p. ISBN:0-572-03070-3, ISBN13: 978-0-572-03070-4. Dewey:750.2/78.

Audience: **g,l,u,f.**

Wilder, Frank Van (Editor)   **PS3529.P54**
Artist's Signatures and Monograms of the 19th and 20th Centuries. Trade Cloth. Editions Van Wilder. Saint-Ouen, 484p. ISBN:2-85299-023-7, ISBN13: 978-2-85299-023-4. Dewey:811.52.

Audience: **g,l,u,f.**

Wright, Christopher   **ND40.W75 1991**
The World's Master Paintings: Catalogue and Location Index, Set. Library Binding. Routledge. New York, NY. 1992. 2032p. ISBN:0-415-02240-1, ISBN13: 978-0-415-02240-8. Dewey:750/.74. LCCN:91-031694.

Audience: **g,l,u,f.** *Choice, 1992.*

Painting > Histories and Handbooks

Hand, John Oliver   **N856.H36 2004**
National Gallery of Art: Master Paintings from the Collection. Trade Cloth. Harry N. Abrams, Inc. New York, NY. 2004. 492p. ISBN:0-8109-5619-5, ISBN13: 978-0-8109-5619-3. Dewey:750/.74/753. LCCN:2004-012473.

Audience: **g,l,u,f.** *Choice, 2005.*

Levey, Michael   **ND160 .L45 1984**
From Giotto to Cezanne: A Concise History of Painting. Trade Paper. Thames & Hudson. New York, NY. 1985. 324p. World of Art Ser. ISBN:0-500-20024-6, ISBN13: 978-0-500-20024-7. Dewey:759. LCCN:84-050479.

Audience: **g,l,u,f.**

Painting > Histories and Handbooks > Periods and Styles

Anfam, David   **N6512.5.A25A89 1990**
Abstract Expressionism. Trade Paper. Thames & Hudson. New York, NY. 1990. 216p. World of Art Ser. ISBN:0-500-20243-5, ISBN13: 978-0-500-20243-2. Dewey:759.0652. LCCN:89-050635.

Audience: **g,l,u,f.**

Apollinaire, Guillaume   **ND196.C8 A6613 2004**
The Cubist Painters. Trade Paper. University of California Press. Berkeley, CA. 2004. 248p. Documents of Twentieth-Century Art Ser. ISBN:0-520-24354-4, ISBN13: 978-0-520-24354-5. Dewey:759.06/32. LCCN:2004-051784.

Audience: **g,l,u,f.** *Choice, 2005.*

Bell, Julian   **ND1140.B45 1999**
What Is Painting?: Representation and Modern Art. Trade Paper. Thames & Hudson. New York, NY. 1999. 256p. ISBN:0-500-28101-7, ISBN13: 978-0-500-28101-7. Dewey:750/.1. LCCN:98-061188.

Audience: **g,l,u,f.** *Choice, 1999.*

Boardman, John   **NK4645.B5491998**
Early Greek Vase Painting: 11th to 6th Centuries B.C. Trade Paper. Thames & Hudson. New York, NY. 1998. 288p. World of Art Ser. ISBN:0-500-20309-1, ISBN13: 978-0-500-20309-5. Dewey:738.3/82/0938/09012. LCCN:97-061112.

Audience: **g,l,u,f.** *Choice, 1998.*

Boskovits, Miklos & Brown,   **ND615.N3832003**
David Alan
Italian Paintings of the Fifteenth Century. National Gallery of Art (U.S.) Staff (Contribution by). Trade Cloth. Oxford University Press, Inc. New York, NY. 2004. 800p. A Publication of the National Gallery of Art, Washington Ser. ISBN:0-89468-305-5, ISBN13: 978-0-89468-305-3. Dewey:759.5/09/024. LCCN:2003-015691.

Audience: **g,l,u,f.** *Choice, 2004.*

Brown, Jonathan   **ND805.B761998**
Painting in Spain, 1500-1700. Cloth over Boards. Yale University Press. Cumberland, RI. 1999. 290p. Pelican History of Art Ser. ISBN:0-300-06472-1, ISBN13: 978-0-300-06472-8. Dewey:759.6/09/03. LCCN:98-023228.

Audience: **g,l,u,f.**

Denvir, Bernard   **ND552**
The Impressionists at First Hand. Trade Paper. Thames &

Hudson. New York, NY. 1987. 296p. World of Art Ser. ISBN:0-500-20209-5, ISBN13: 978-0-500-20209-8. Dewey:759.4. LCCN:86-051261.

Audience: **g,l,f.**

Derbes, Anne   ND613 .D48 1996
Picturing the Passion in Late Medieval Italy: Narrative Painting, Franciscan Ideologies, and the Levant. Trade Paper. Cambridge University Press. New York, NY. 1998. 288p. ISBN:0-521-63926-3, ISBN13: 978-0-521-63926-2. Dewey:704.9/4853/0945.

Audience: **l,u,f.** *Choice, 1997.*

Dodwell, C. R.   N5970.D641993
The Pictorial Arts of the West, 800-1200. Cloth over Boards. Yale University Press. Cumberland, RI. 1993. 494p. Pelican History of Art Ser. ISBN:0-300-05348-7, ISBN13: 978-0-300-05348-7. Dewey:709/.021. LCCN:92-032502.

Audience: **g,l,u,f.** *Choice, 1994.*

Doxiadis, Euphrosyne   ND1327.E3D68 1995
Mysterious Fayum Portraits: Faces from Ancient Egypt. Dorothy J. Thompson (Foreword by). Trade Cloth. Harry N. Abrams, Inc. New York, NY. 1995. 256p. ISBN:0-8109-3331-4, ISBN13: 978-0-8109-3331-6. Dewey:759.9/32. LCCN:95-009506.

Audience: **g,l,u,f.** *Choice, 1996.*

Dunkerton, Jill, et al.   ND144 .N38 1991
Giotto to Durer: Early Renaissance Painting in the National Gallery. Susan Foister, Dillian Gordon & Nicholas Penny (Authors). Trade Paper. Yale University Press. Cumberland, RI. 1994. 408p. National Gallery London Publications ISBN:0-300-05082-8, ISBN13: 978-0-300-05082-0. Dewey:759.02/2/07442132. LCCN:91-065547.

Audience: **g,l,u,f.** *Choice, 1992.*

Dunkerton, Jill, et al.   ND170.D86 1999
Durer to Veronese: Sixteenth-Century Painting in the National Gallery. Susan Foister & Nicholas Penny (Authors). Cloth over Boards. Yale University Press. Cumberland, RI. 1999. 330p. National Gallery London Publications ISBN:0-300-07220-1, ISBN13: 978-0-300-07220-4. Dewey:759/.03/074421. LCCN:99-025852.

Audience: **g,l,u,f.** *Choice, 2000.*

Dunning, William V.   ND1475.D86 1991
Changing Images of Pictorial Space: A History of Spatial Illusion in Painting. Trade Paper. Syracuse University Press. Syracuse, NY. 1992. 272p. ISBN:0-8156-2508-1, ISBN13: 978-0-8156-2508-7. Dewey:750/.1/8. LCCN:90-010211.

Audience: **g,l,u,f.** *Choice, 1991.*

Ebert-Schifferer, Sybille   ND1390.E23131998
Still Life. Russell Stockman (Translator). Trade Cloth. Harry N. Abrams, Inc. New York, NY. 1999. 420p. ISBN:0-8109-4190-2, ISBN13: 978-0-8109-4190-8. Dewey:758/.4. LCCN:98-003888.

Audience: **g,l,u,f.** *Choice, 1999.*

Eitner, Lorenz   ND457.E38 2002
19th Century European Painting: David to Cezanne. Ed. 2.

Trade Paper. Westview Press. Boulder, CO. 2002. 768p. Icon Editions Ser. ISBN:0-8133-6570-8, ISBN13: 978-0-8133-6570-1. Dewey:759.05. LCCN:2002-003021.

Audience: **g,l,u,f.**

Frascina, Francis, et al.   ND547.5.I4M64 1993
Modernity and Modernism: French Painting in the Nineteenth Century. Nigel Blake, Briony Fer, Tamar Garb & Charles Harrison (Authors). Trade Paper. Yale University Press. Cumberland, RI. 1993. 304p. Modern Art - Practices and Debates Ser. ISBN:0-300-05514-5, ISBN13: 978-0-300-05514-6. Dewey:759.4. LCCN:92-035017.

Audience: **l,u,f.** *Choice, 1994.*

Fraser, Sarah Elizabeth   ND2849.D86F73 2003
Performing the Visual: The Practice of Buddhist Wall Painting in China and Central Asia, 618-960. Trade Cloth. Stanford University Press. Palo Alto, CA. 2003. 392p. ISBN:0-8047-4533-1, ISBN13: 978-0-8047-4533-8. Dewey:755/.943/095145. LCCN:2003-010278.

Audience: **l,u,f.** *Choice, 2004.*

Freedberg, Sydney J.   ND615.F661993
Painting in Italy, 1500-1600. Ed. 3. Trade Paper. Yale University Press. Cumberland, RI. 1971. 767p. Pelican History of Art Ser. ISBN:0-300-05587-0, ISBN13: 978-0-300-05587-0. Dewey:759.5/09/31. LCCN:93-237078.

Audience: **g,l,u,f.**

Friedlaender, Walter   ND615 .F7
Mannerism and Anti-Mannerism in Italian Painting. Trade Cloth. Columbia University Press. New York, NY. 1990. 89p. ISBN:0-231-02024-4, ISBN13: 978-0-231-02024-4. Dewey:759.5/09/031.

Audience: **g,l,u,f.** *B*

Gerdts, William H.   ND210.5.I4
American Impressionism. Trade Cloth. Abbeville Press, Inc. New York, NY. 2000. 288p. ISBN:0-7892-0612-9, ISBN13: 978-0-7892-0612-1. Dewey:759.13/09/034.

Audience: **g,l,u,f.** *B*

Golding, John   ND196.C8G6 1988
Cubism: A History and Analysis, Nineteen Hundred Seven to Nineteen Fourteen. Ed. 3. Trade Cloth. Harvard University Press. Cambridge, MA. 1988. 368p. ISBN:0-674-17929-3, ISBN13: 978-0-674-17929-5. Dewey:759.06/32. LCCN:88-009435.

Audience: **g,l,u,f.**

Hand, John Oliver & Wolff,   ND669.F5
Martha
Early Netherlandish Painting. Cloth Text. Cambridge University Press. New York, NY. 1997. 288p. The Collections of the National Gallery of Art Systematic Catalogue ISBN:0-521-34016-0, ISBN13: 978-0-521-34016-8. Dewey:759.9493/074. LCCN:86-012418.

Audience: **g,l,u,f.**

Herbert, Robert   **ND550.H47 1988**
Impressionism: Art, Leisure and Parisian Society. Cloth over
Boards. Yale University Press. Cumberland, RI. 1988. 312p.
ISBN:0-300-04262-0, ISBN13: 978-0-300-04262-7.
Dewey:759.4/361. LCCN:87-024967.

Audience: **g,l,u,f.**

Herskovic, Marika Jr.   **N6512.5.A25A64 2003**
  (Editor)
American Abstract Expressionism of the 1950s: An Illustrated
Survey. Trade Cloth. New York School Press LLC. Franklin
Lakes, NJ. 2003. 372p. ISBN:0-9677994-1-4, ISBN13:
978-0-9677994-1-4. Dewey:709/.73/09045. LCCN:2002-011270.
Audience: **g,l,u,f.** *Choice, 2003.*

Hickey, Dave, et al.   **N6537**
Andy Warhol. Steven Bluttal & Andy Warhol (Authors),
Phaidon Press Editors (Editor). Trade Cloth. Phaidon Press, Inc.
New York, NY. 2006. 624p. ISBN:0-7148-4540-X, ISBN13:
978-0-7148-4540-1. Dewey:709.2.

Audience: **g,l,u,f.**

Hiesinger, Ulrich W.   **ND210.5.I4 H531991**
Impressionism in America: The Ten American Painters. Trade
Cloth. Prestel Verlag, Germany. Munchen, 1991. 256p.
ISBN:3-7913-1142-5, ISBN13: 978-3-7913-1142-5.
Dewey:759.147/1/0747471. LCCN:92-120587.
Audience: **g,l,f.** *Choice, 1991.*

Immerwahr, Sara A.   **ND2570.I45 1990**
Aegean Painting in the Bronze Age. Trade Cloth. Pennsylvania
State University Press. University Park, PA. 1990. 1400p.
ISBN:0-271-00628-5, ISBN13: 978-0-271-00628-4.
Dewey:751.7/3/093918. LCCN:87-043123.
Audience: **u,f.** *Choice, 1990.*

Kleimann, Julian &   **ND2755.K572413 2004**
  Rohlmann, Michael
Italian Frescoes: High Renaissance to the Baroque, 1510-1600.
Trade Cloth. Abbeville Press, Inc. New York, NY. 2004. 464p.
Italian Frescoes Ser., Vol. 3 ISBN:0-7892-0831-8, ISBN13:
978-0-7892-0831-6. Dewey:751.7/3/094509031.
LCCN:2004-052908.

Audience: **g,l,u,f.**

Kostenevich, Albert   **ND547.K6831995**
  Grigor'evich
Hidden Treasures Revealed: Impressionist Masterpieces and
Other Important French Paintings Preserved by the State
Hermitage Museum, St. Petersburg. Trade Cloth. Harry N.
Abrams, Inc. New York, NY. 1995. 272p. ISBN:0-8109-3432-9,
ISBN13: 978-0-8109-3432-0. Dewey:709/.034.
LCCN:94-073477.

Audience: **g,l,u,f.** *Choice, 1995.*

Lambourne, Lionel   **ND467.L36 1999**
Victorian Painting. Trade Cloth. Phaidon Press. London, 1999.
512p. ISBN:0-7148-3776-8, ISBN13: 978-0-7148-3776-5.
Dewey:759/.05. LCCN:00-361504.
Audience: **g,l,u,f.** *Choice, 2000.*

Lavin, Marilyn A.   **ND2755.L38 1990**
The Place of Narrative: Mural Decoration in Italian Churches,
431-1600. Trade Cloth. University of Chicago Press. Chicago,
IL. 1990. 426p. ISBN:0-226-46956-5, ISBN13:
978-0-226-46956-0. Dewey:751.7/3/0945. LCCN:89-049474.
Audience: **l,u,f.** *Choice, 1991.*

Leach, Eleanor W.   **ND2575.L43 2004**
The Social Life of Painting in Ancient Rome and on the Bay of
Naples. Cloth Text. Cambridge University Press. New York, NY.
2004. 370p. ISBN:0-521-82600-4, ISBN13: 978-0-521-82600-6.
Dewey:751.7/3/09377. LCCN:2003-055282.
Audience: **l,u,f.** *Choice, 2005.*

Lemoine, Serge   **ND553.P9 D32513 2002**
Toward Modern Art: From Puvis de Chavennes to Matisse and
Picasso. Trade Cloth. Rizzoli International Publications, Inc.
New York, NY. 2002. 568p. ISBN:0-8478-2477-2, ISBN13:
978-0-8478-2477-9. Dewey:709.4.
Audience: **g,l,u,f.** *Choice, 2003.*

Lemoine, Serge   **ND547.P424132004**
Paintings in the Musée D'Orsay. Toula Ballas (Translator),
Musée d'Orsay Staff (Contribution by). Trade Cloth. Harry N.
Abrams, Inc. New York, NY. 2004. 768p. ISBN:0-8109-5608-X,
ISBN13: 978-0-8109-5608-7. Dewey:709/.0344/07444361.
LCCN:2004-010028.

Audience: **g,l,u,f.**

Levey, Michael   **ND186 .L48 1985**
Rococo to Revolution. Trade Paper. Thames & Hudson. New
York, NY. 1985. 252p. World of Art Ser. ISBN:0-500-20050-5,
ISBN13: 978-0-500-20050-6. Dewey:759.04/7.
LCCN:84-050569.

Audience: **g,l,u,f.**

Ling, Roger   **ND120 .L56 1990**
Roman Painting. Trade Paper. Cambridge University Press. New
York, NY. 1991. 261p. ISBN:0-521-31595-6, ISBN13:
978-0-521-31595-1. Dewey:759.937. LCCN:89-036871.
Audience: **g,l,u,f.** *Choice, 1991.*

Lucie-Smith, Edward   **ND196.A7**
Art Deco Painting. Trade Paper. Phaidon Press. London, 1996.
160p. ISBN:0-7148-3576-5, ISBN13: 978-0-7148-3576-1.
Dewey:759/.0612. LCCN:91-213396.

Audience: **g,l,u,f.**

Novotny, Fritz   **ND457**
Painting and Sculpture in Europe: 1780-1880. Ed. 3. Trade
Paper. Yale University Press. Cumberland, RI. 1992. 483p.
Pelican History of Art Ser. ISBN:0-300-05321-5, ISBN13:
978-0-300-05321-0. Dewey:759/.05.

Audience: **g,l,u,f.**

Palladino, Pia   **ND3159**
Treasures of a Lost Art: Italian Manuscript Painting of the
Middle Ages and Renaissance. Cloth over Boards. Yale
University Press. Cumberland, RI. 2003. 204p. Metropolitan

Museum of Art Ser. ISBN:0-300-09879-0, ISBN13: 978-0-300-09879-2. Dewey:745.67094507473. LCCN:2002-035987.

Audience: **g,l,u,f.** *Choice, 2003.*

Penny, Nicholas   **ND615**
The Sixteenth-Century Italian Paintings: Brescia, Bergamo and Cremona. Cloth over Boards. Yale University Press. Cumberland, RI. 2004. 448p. National Gallery London Publications ISBN:1-85709-908-7, ISBN13: 978-1-85709-908-9. Dewey:759.509/031. LCCN:2001-095566.

Audience: **l,u,f.** *Choice, 2005.*

Polizzotti, Mark   **ND196.S8**
  (Introduction by)
Andre Breton: Surrealism and Painting. Trade Paper. Museum of Fine Arts, Boston. Boston, MA. 2003. 448p. ISBN:0-87846-628-2, ISBN13: 978-0-87846-628-3. Dewey:709.04063.

Audience: **g,l,u,f.**

Prettejohn, Elizabeth   **ND467.5.P7P75 2000**
The Art of the Pre-Raphaelites. Cloth Text. Princeton University Press. Princeton, NJ. 2000. 304p. ISBN:0-691-07057-1, ISBN13: 978-0-691-07057-5. Dewey:759.2. LCCN:00-103168.

Audience: **g,l,u,f.** *Choice, 2001.*

Rathbone, Eliza E. &   **ND1393.F85I472001**
  Shackelford, George M.
Impressionist Still Life. Jeannene Mari Przyblyski, John W. McCoubrey, Richard Shiff, Phillips Collection Staff & Museum of Fine Arts, Boston Staff (Contribution by). Trade Cloth. Harry N. Abrams, Inc. New York, NY. 2001. 240p. ISBN:0-8109-0613-9, ISBN13: 978-0-8109-0613-6. Dewey:758/.4/0944074753. LCCN:2001-022629.

Audience: **g,l,u,f.** *Choice, 2002.*

Read, Herbert E.   **ND195**
Concise History of Modern Painting. Ed. 2. Trade Paper. Thames & Hudson. New York, NY. 1985. 396p. World of Art Ser. ISBN:0-500-20141-2, ISBN13: 978-0-500-20141-1. Dewey:759/.06. LCCN:84-051313.

Audience: **g,l,u,f.**

Robertson, Martin   **NK4645 .R7 1992**
The Art of Vase-Painting in Classical Athens. Cloth Text. Cambridge University Press. New York, NY. 1992. 362p. ISBN:0-521-33010-6, ISBN13: 978-0-521-33010-7. Dewey:738.3/82/09385. LCCN:91-021355.

Audience: **l,u,f.** *Choice, 1993.*

Rosand, David   **ND205.R67 2004**
The Invention of Painting in America. Trade Cloth. Kegan Paul International, Ltd. London, 2004. 246p. University Seminars/Leonard Hastings Schoff Memorial Lectures ISBN:0-231-13296-4, ISBN13: 978-0-231-13296-1. Dewey:759.13/09. LCCN:2004-047829.

Audience: **g,l,u,f.** *Choice, 2005.*

Rosenberg, Jakob & Slive,   **ND646.S4951995**
  Seymour
Dutch Painting, 1600-1800. Cloth over Boards. Yale University

Press. Cumberland, RI. 1995. 390p. Pelican History of Art Ser. ISBN:0-300-06418-7, ISBN13: 978-0-300-06418-6. Dewey:759.9/492. LCCN:95-014215.

Audience: **g,l,u,f.** *Choice, 1996.*

Rubin, James Henry   **ND192.I4R831999**
Impressionism. London : Phaidon. 1999. Art & Ideas ISBN:0-7148-3826-8, ISBN13: 978-0-7148-3826-7.

Audience: **g,l,u,f.**

Seitz, William C.   **ND212.5.A25**
Abstract Expressionist Painting in America. Dore Ashton (Introduction by), Robert Motherwell (Foreword by). Trade Cloth. Harvard University Press. Cambridge, MA. 1983. 514p. The Aisla Mellon Bruce Studies in American Art ISBN:0-674-00215-6, ISBN13: 978-0-674-00215-9. Dewey:753/.5/0973. LCCN:82-018734.

Audience: **g,l,u,f.**

Shapiro, David & Shapiro,   **N6512.5.A25 A25 1990**
  Cecile
Abstract Expressionism: A Critical Record. Trade Paper. Cambridge University Press. New York, NY. 1990. 456p. ISBN:0-521-36733-6, ISBN13: 978-0-521-36733-2. Dewey:759.147/1/0904. LCCN:89-015691.

Audience: **g,l,u,f.**

Slive, Seymour   **ND653.G7**
Dutch Painting, 1600-1800. Trade Paper. Yale University Press. Cumberland, RI. 1998. 392p. Pelican History of Art Ser. ISBN:0-300-07451-4, ISBN13: 978-0-300-07451-2. Dewey:759.9/492. LCCN:95-014215.

Audience: **g,l,u,f.**

Waterhouse, Ellis K.   **ND464**
Painting in Britain: 1530-1790. Ed. 5. Cloth over Boards. Yale University Press. Cumberland, RI. 1988. 387p. Pelican History of Art Ser. ISBN:0-300-05832-2, ISBN13: 978-0-300-05832-1. Dewey:759.2. LCCN:77-019107.

Audience: **g,l,u,f.**

Waterhouse, Ellis K.   **ND464**
Painting in Britain: 1530-1790. Ed. 5. Trade Paper. Yale University Press. Cumberland, RI. 1988. 387p. Pelican History of Art Ser. ISBN:0-300-05833-0, ISBN13: 978-0-300-05833-8. Dewey:759.2.

Audience: **g,l,u,f.**

Whitfield, Sarah   **ND548.5**
Fauvism. Trade Paper. Thames & Hudson. New York, NY. 1996. 216p. The World of Art Ser. ISBN:0-500-20227-3, ISBN13: 978-0-500-20227-2. Dewey:709/.04043. LCCN:87-051293.

Audience: **g,l,u,f.**

Wieck, Roger S.   **ND3363.H57W54 2000**
The Hours of Henry VIII: A Renaissance Masterpiece by Jean Poyet. Trade Cloth. George Braziller Inc. New York, NY. 2000. 176p. ISBN:0-8076-1477-7, ISBN13: 978-0-8076-1477-8. Dewey:745.6/7/092. LCCN:00-039758.

Audience: **l,u,f.**

Wine, Humphrey   **ND546 .N34**
The Seventeenth Century French Paintings: National Gallery
Catalogues. Cloth over Boards. Yale University Press.
Cumberland, RI. 2002. 472p. The National Gallery London Ser.
ISBN:0-300-08729-2, ISBN13: 978-0-300-08729-1.
Dewey:759.04/6/074753. LCCN:2001-095555.
       Audience: **g,l,u,f.**

Painting > Histories and Handbooks > Cultures, Regions, Nationalities

Allen, Christopher   **ND546**
French Painting in the Golden Age. Trade Paper. Thames &
Hudson. New York, NY. 2003. 224p. The World of Art Ser.
ISBN:0-500-20370-9, ISBN13: 978-0-500-20370-5.
Dewey:759.4/09032. LCCN:2003-101349.
       Audience: **g,l,u,f.**

Auping, Michael   **ND212.5.A25.A221987**
Abstract Expressionism: The Critical Developments. Trade
Cloth. Harry N. Abrams, Inc. New York, NY. 1987. 304p.
ISBN:0-8109-1866-8, ISBN13: 978-0-8109-1866-5.
Dewey:759.13/074/014797. LCCN:86-032071.
       Audience: **g,l,u,f.** *Choice, 1988.*

Avery, Kevin J., et al.   **NC139.G63**
American Drawings and Watercolors in the Metropolitan
Museum of Art: A Catalogue of Works by Artists Born Before
1835. Claire A. Conway & Marjorie Shelley (Authors). Cloth
over Boards. Yale University Press. Cumberland, RI. 2002.
424p. The Metropolitan Museum of Art Ser.
ISBN:0-300-09372-1, ISBN13: 978-0-300-09372-8.
Dewey:741.9/73. LCCN:2002-067772.
       Audience: **g,l,u,f.** *Choice, 2003.*

Avery, Kevin   **ND1351.5.A491987**
American Paradise: The World of the Hudson River School.
Oswaldo R. Roque, John K. Howat, Doreen B. Burke &
Catherine H. Voorsaner (Contribution by). Trade Cloth. Harry N.
Abrams, Inc. New York, NY. 1987. 448p. ISBN:0-8109-1165-5,
ISBN13: 978-0-8109-1165-9. Dewey:758/.1/097473.
LCCN:87-015417.
       Audience: **g,l,u,f.** *Choice, 1988.*

Bailey, Colin, et al.   **ND1452.F84A44 2003**
The Age of Watteau, Chardin, and Fragonard: Masterpieces of
French Genre Painting. Philip Conisbee & Thomas W.
Gaehtgens (Authors), Colin Bailey (Editor). Cloth over Boards.
Yale University Press. Cumberland, RI. 2003. 420p.
ISBN:0-300-09946-0, ISBN13: 978-0-300-09946-1.
Dewey:754/.0944/0747468. LCCN:2003-000024.
       Audience: **l,u,f.** *Choice, 2003.*

Baker, Ian & Laird, Thomas   **ND2850.L48B35 2000**
The Dalai Lama's Secret Temple: Tantric Wall Paintings from
Tibet. Dalai Lama XIV (Introduction by). Trade Cloth. Thames
& Hudson. New York, NY. 2000. 216p. ISBN:0-500-51003-2,
ISBN13: 978-0-500-51003-2. Dewey:751.7/3/09515.
LCCN:00-100630.
       Audience: **l,u,f.**

Barnhart, Richard M., et al.   **ND1040.T48 1997**
Three Thousand Years of Chinese Painting. Yang Xin, Nie
Chongzheng, James Cahill, Lang Shaojun & Wu Hung
(Authors). Trade Paper. Yale University Press. Cumberland, RI.
2002. 416p. Culture and Civilization of China Ser.
ISBN:0-300-09447-7, ISBN13: 978-0-300-09447-3.
Dewey:759.9/51. LCCN:97-011152.
       Audience: **g,l,u,f.**

Beach, Milo Cleveland   **DS436.N471987**
Mughal and Rajput Painting. C. A. Bayly, Gordon Johnson &
John F. Richards (Contribution by). Trade Cloth. Cambridge
University Press. New York, NY. 1992. 288p. The New
Cambridge History of India Ser., Vol. I: 3 ISBN:0-521-40027-9,
ISBN13: 978-0-521-40027-5. Dewey:954 s. LCCN:91-026573.
       Audience: **l,u,f.** *Choice, 1993.*

Bird, Alan F.   **ND681.B57 1987**
A History of Russian Painting. Trade Cloth. Macmillan
Publishing Company, Inc. Old Tappan, NJ. 1987. 304p.
ISBN:0-8161-8911-0, ISBN13: 978-0-8161-8911-3.
Dewey:759.7. LCCN:86-022145.
       Audience: **g,l,u,f.** *Choice, 1988.*

Blunt, Anthony   **ND615.B655 1994**
Artistic Theory in Italy. Trade Paper. Oxford University Press,
Inc. New York, NY. 1962. 180p. ISBN:0-19-881050-4, ISBN13:
978-0-19-881050-6. Dewey:759.5/09/024. LCCN:94-003411.
       Audience: **g,l,u,f.**

Bochert, Till Holger   **ND635.B649 2002**
The Age of Van Eyck: The Mediterranean World and Early
Netherlandish Painting, 1430-1530. Trade Cloth. Thames &
Hudson. New York, NY. 2002. 272p. ISBN:0-500-23795-6,
ISBN13: 978-0-500-23795-3. Dewey:759.9/492/09024.
LCCN:2001-099215.
       Audience: **g,l,u,f.** *Choice, 2003.*

Boskovits, Miklos & Brown,   **ND615.N3832003**
David Alan
Italian Paintings of the Fifteenth Century. National Gallery of
Art (U.S.) Staff (Contribution by). Trade Cloth. Oxford
University Press, Inc. New York, NY. 2004. 800p. A Publication
of the National Gallery of Art, Washington Ser.
ISBN:0-89468-305-5, ISBN13: 978-0-89468-305-3.
Dewey:759.5/09/024. LCCN:2003-015691.
       Audience: **g,l,u,f.** *Choice, 2004.*

Brody, J. J.   **E99.P9B732 1991**
Anasazi and Pueblo Painting. Trade Cloth. University of New
Mexico Press. Albuquerque, NM. 1991. 272p.
ISBN:0-8263-1236-5, ISBN13: 978-0-8263-1236-5.
Dewey:750/.89/974. LCCN:90-023678.
       Audience: **u,f.** *Choice, 1991.*

Brody, J. J.   **E99.P9B744 1997**
Pueblo Indian Painting: Tradition and Modernism in New
Mexico, 1900-1930. Trade Cloth. School of American Research
Press. Santa Fe, NM. 1997. 238p. ISBN:0-933452-45-4,
ISBN13: 978-0-933452-45-9. Dewey:759.189/089/974.
LCCN:96-050100.
       Audience: **u,f.** *Choice, 1997.*

Brown, Jonathan ND0804.B74
The Golden Age of Painting in Spain. Trade Paper. Books on Demand. Ann Arbor, MI. 1991. 339p. ISBN:0-608-07881-6, ISBN13: 978-0-608-07881-6. Dewey:759.6/09/03. LCCN:90-012564.

Audience: **g,l,u,f.**

Brown, Jonathan ND805.B761998
Painting in Spain, 1500-1700. Cloth over Boards. Yale University Press. Cumberland, RI. 1999. 290p. Pelican History of Art Ser. ISBN:0-300-06472-1, ISBN13: 978-0-300-06472-8. Dewey:759.6/09/03. LCCN:98-023228.

Audience: **g,l,u,f.**

Burns, Sarah ND210 .B87 2004
Painting the Dark Side: Art and the Gothic Imagination in Nineteenth-Century America. Trade Cloth. University of California Press. Berkeley, CA. 2004. 320p. The Ahmanson Murphy Fine Arts Imprint Ser. ISBN:0-520-23821-4, ISBN13: 978-0-520-23821-3. Dewey:759.13/09/034. LCCN:2003-013276.

Audience: **g,l,u,f.** *Choice, 2004.*

Cahill, James ND1043.5.C35
The Painter's Practice: How Artists Lived and Worked in Traditional China. Trade Paper. Columbia University Press. New York, NY. 1995. 187p. ISBN:0-231-08181-2, ISBN13: 978-0-231-08181-8. Dewey:305.9750951.

Audience: **g,l,u,f.** *Choice, 1994.*

Chotner, Deborah (Editor) ND205.5.P74N37 1992
American Naive Paintings. Julie Aronson, Sarah Cash & Laurie Weitzenkorn (Contribution by). Trade Cloth. Cambridge University Press. New York, NY. 1993. 688p. The Collections of the National Gallery of Art Systematic Catalogue ISBN:0-521-44301-6, ISBN13: 978-0-521-44301-2. Dewey:759.13/074/753. LCCN:92-004780.

Audience: **g,l,u,f.** *Choice, 1994.*

Christiansen, Keith & ND669.F5M471998
Arnsworth, Maryan W. (Editors)
From Van Eyck to Bruegel: Early Netherlandish Painting in the Metropolitan Museum of Art. Trade Cloth. Harry N. Abrams, Inc. New York, NY. 1998. 452p. ISBN:0-8109-6528-3, ISBN13: 978-0-8109-6528-7. Dewey:759.9493/074/7471. LCCN:98-022196.

Audience: **l,u,f.** *Choice, 1999.*

Crookshank, Anne & ND485.C759 2002
Knight of Glin
Ireland's Painters, 1600-1940. Cloth over Boards. Yale University Press. Cumberland, RI. 2002. 356p. Paul Mellon Centre for Studies in British Art ISBN:0-300-09765-4, ISBN13: 978-0-300-09765-8. Dewey:759.2/915. LCCN:2002-004497.

Audience: **g,l,u,f.** *Choice, 2003.*

Fuchs, R. H. ND653.G7
Dutch Painting. Trade Paper. Thames & Hudson. New York, NY. 1985. 216p. World of Art Ser. ISBN:0-500-20167-6, ISBN13: 978-0-500-20167-1. Dewey:759.9/492. LCCN:86-051573.

Audience: **g,l,u,f.**

Fuhrer, Ronald ND977.F85 1998
Israeli Painting: From Post-Impressionism to Post Zionism. Trade Cloth. Overlook Press, The. New York, NY. 1998. 260p. ISBN:0-87951-822-7, ISBN13: 978-0-87951-822-6. Dewey:759.95694. LCCN:98-018716.

Audience: **g,l,u,f.** *Choice, 1999.*

Gaunt, William ND461 .G3 1985
English Painting: A Concise History. Trade Paper. Thames & Hudson. New York, NY. 1985. 288p. World of Art Ser. ISBN:0-500-20016-5, ISBN13: 978-0-500-20016-2. Dewey:759.2. LCCN:85-050608.

Audience: **g,l,u,f.**

Gerdts, William H. ND210.5.I4
American Impressionism. Trade Cloth. Abbeville Press, Inc. New York, NY. 2000. 288p. ISBN:0-7892-0612-9, ISBN13: 978-0-7892-0612-1. Dewey:759.13/09/034.

Audience: **g,l,u,f.** *B*

Gerdts, William H. ND212.G47 1990
Art Across America: Two Centuries of Regional Painting, Set. Trade Paper. Abbeville Press, Inc. New York, NY. 1990. 1224p. ISBN:1-55859-033-1, ISBN13: 978-1-55859-033-5. Dewey:759.13. LCCN:90-000598.

Audience: **g,l,u,f.** *Choice, 1991.*

Goswami, B. N. & Fischer, ND1337.I5G67813 1997
Eberhard
Pahari Masters: Court Painters of Northern India. Trade Paper. Oxford University Press, Inc. New York, NY. 1997. 392p. ISBN:0-19-564014-4, ISBN13: 978-0-19-564014-4. Dewey:759.9/541. LCCN:97-167772.

Audience: **g,l,u,f.** *Choice, 1997.*

Grabar, Oleg ND3241.G6713 2000
Mostly Miniatures: An Introduction to Persian Painting. Trade Cloth. Princeton University Press. Princeton, NJ. 2000. 176p. ISBN:0-691-04941-6, ISBN13: 978-0-691-04941-0. Dewey:745.6/749155. LCCN:00-035961.

Audience: **g,l,u,f.** *Choice, 2001.*

Gray, Mary Lackritz ND2638.C4G73 2001
A Guide to Chicago's Murals. Franz Schulze (Foreword by). Trade Paper. University of Chicago Press. Chicago, IL. 2001. 520p. ISBN:0-226-30599-6, ISBN13: 978-0-226-30599-8. Dewey:751.7/3/0977311. LCCN:00-041167.

Audience: **g,l,u,f.**

Grijzenhout, Frans (Editor), ND646 .G6313 1999
et al.
The Golden Age of Dutch Painting in Historical Perspective. Henk Van Veen & Henk van der Veen (Editors), Andrew McCormick (Translator). Trade Cloth. Cambridge University Press. New York, NY. 1999. 348p. ISBN:0-521-49621-7, ISBN13: 978-0-521-49621-6. Dewey:759.9/492/09032. LCCN:98-011644.

Audience: **l,u,f.** *Choice, 2000.*

Haak, Bob ND646.H3
The Golden Age: Dutch Painters of the Seventeenth Century. Elizabeth Willems-Treeman (Translator). Saddle Stitched, Cloth

over Boards. Waanders B. V., Uitgeverij. 8013 PH Zwolle, 2005. 536p. ISBN:90-400-8792-X, ISBN13: 978-90-400-8792-9. Dewey:759.9492.

Audience: **g,l,u,f.** *B*

Harrist, Robert E. & Fong,   NK3634.A2H3751999
Wen C.
Embodied Image. Trade Cloth. Harry N. Abrams, Inc. New York, NY. 1999. 600p. ISBN:0-8109-6377-9, ISBN13: 978-0-8109-6377-1. Dewey:745.6/19951. LCCN:98-088465.

Audience: **g,l,u,f.**

Hearn, Maxwell K.   ND1366.7H43 2002
Cultivated Landscapes: Chinese Paintings from the Collection of Marie-Helene and Guy Weill. Metropolitan Museum of Art Staff (Contribution by). Trade Cloth. Metropolitan Museum of Art, The. New York, NY. 2002. xv, 204p. ISBN:1-58839-055-1, ISBN13: 978-1-58839-055-4. Dewey:759.951/074/7471. LCCN:2002-067780.

Audience: **l,u,f.** *Choice, 2003.*

Hurlburt, Laurence P.   ND2608.H84 1989
The Mexican Muralists in the United States. Trade Cloth. University of New Mexico Press. Albuquerque, NM. 1989. 343p. ISBN:0-8263-1134-2, ISBN13: 978-0-8263-1134-4. Dewey:759.13. LCCN:88-030000.

Audience: **g,l,u,f.** *Choice, 1990.*

Jones, Caroline   N6535.S3
Bay Area Figurative Art: 1950-1965. Trade Paper, Mixed Media, Trade Cloth. University of California Press. Berkeley, CA. 1989. 250p. ISBN:0-520-06842-4, ISBN13: 978-0-520-06842-1. Dewey:709/.794/607473. LCCN:89-040571.

Audience: **g,l,u,f.** *Choice, 1990.*

Kiers, Judikje & Tissink,   N6946.K45 2000
Fieke
The Golden Age of Dutch Art: Painting, Sculpture, Decorative Art. Trade Cloth. Thames & Hudson. New York, NY. 2000. 368p. ISBN:0-500-23774-3, ISBN13: 978-0-500-23774-8. Dewey:709/.492/074492352. LCCN:2001-347624.

Audience: **l,u,f.** *Choice, 2000.*

King, Ross   ND547.K47 2006
The Judgment of Paris: The Revolutionary Era that Gave the World Impressionism. Cloth over Boards. Walker & Company. New York, NY. 2006. 464p. ISBN:0-8027-1466-8, ISBN13: 978-0-8027-1466-4. Dewey:759.409/034. LCCN:2005-031089.

Audience: **g,l,u,f.** *Choice, 2006.*

Kleimann, Julian &   ND2755.K572413 2004
Rohlmann, Michael
Italian Frescoes: High Renaissance to the Baroque, 1510-1600. Trade Cloth. Abbeville Press, Inc. New York, NY. 2004. 464p. Italian Frescoes Ser., Vol. 3 ISBN:0-7892-0831-8, ISBN13: 978-0-7892-0831-6. Dewey:751.7/3/094509031. LCCN:2004-052908.

Audience: **g,l,u,f.**

Kossak, Steven & Singer,   ND1432.C58
Jane Casey
Sacred Visions: Early Paintings from Central Tibet. Cloth over

Boards. Yale University Press. Cumberland, RI. 1999. 240p. Metropolitan Museum of Art Ser. ISBN:0-300-08665-2, ISBN13: 978-0-300-08665-2. Dewey:759.9515/0747471.

Audience: **g,l,u,f.** *Choice, 1999.*

Kren, Thomas &   ND3171.K742003
McKendrick, Scot
Illuminating the Renaissance: The Triumph of Flemish Manuscript Painting in Europe. J. Paul Getty Museum Staff & Royal Academy of Arts, Great Britain Staff (Contribution by). Trade Cloth. Oxford University Press, Inc. New York, NY. 2003. 592p. Manuscripts ISBN:0-89236-703-2, ISBN13: 978-0-89236-703-0. Dewey:745.6/7. LCCN:2003-001611.

Audience: **l,u,f.** *Choice, 2003.*

Lavin, Marilyn A.   ND2755.L38 1990
The Place of Narrative: Mural Decoration in Italian Churches, 431-1600. Trade Cloth. University of Chicago Press. Chicago, IL. 1990. 426p. ISBN:0-226-46956-5, ISBN13: 978-0-226-46956-0. Dewey:751.7/3/0945. LCCN:89-049474.

Audience: **l,u,f.** *Choice, 1991.*

Leksukhum, Santi   ND1021.S268132000
Temples of Gold: Seven Centuries of Thai Buddhist Painting. George Braziller. 2000. ISBN:0-8076-1476-9, ISBN13: 978-0-8076-1476-1.

Audience: **g,l,u,f.**

Lillehoj, Elizabeth (Editor)   ND1053.5.C75 2004
Critical Perspectives on Classicism in Japanese Painting, 1600-1700. Trade Cloth. University of Hawaii Press. Honolulu, HI. 2004. 288p. ISBN:0-8248-2699-X, ISBN13: 978-0-8248-2699-4. Dewey:759.952/09/032. LCCN:2003-009998.

Audience: **l,u,f.** *Choice, 2004.*

Lovell, Charles M.   ND1432.M45A78 2001
Art and Faith in Mexico: The Nineteenth-Century Retablo Tradition. Elizabeth Netto Calil Zarur (Editor). Trade Paper. University of New Mexico Press. Albuquerque, NM. 2004. 360p. ISBN:0-8263-2324-3, ISBN13: 978-0-8263-2324-8. Dewey:755/.2/097207478961. LCCN:00-011009.

Audience: **g,l,u,f.** *Choice, 2001.*

Miles, Ellen G.   ND207
American Paintings of the Eighteenth Century. Patricia Burda, Leslie Kaye Reinhardt & Cynthia J. Mills (Contribution by). Cloth Text. Oxford University Press, Inc. New York, NY. 1996. 440p. USA Publication Ser. ISBN:0-89468-210-5, ISBN13: 978-0-89468-210-0. Dewey:759.13/09/033074753. LCCN:94-037473.

Audience: **l,u,f.**

Moffett, Charles S.   ND553.M7
The New Painting: Impressionism 1874-1886. Trade Paper. University of Washington Press. Seattle, WA. 1986. ISBN:0-295-96367-0, ISBN13: 978-0-295-96367-9. Dewey:759.4.

Audience: **g,l,u,f.** *Choice, 1986.*

Murase, Miyeko & Tosa,   **ND1059.6.G4T35 2001**
Mitsuoki
The Tale of Genji: Legends and Paintings. Trade Cloth. George
Braziller Inc. New York, NY. 2001. 144p. ISBN:0-8076-1500-5,
ISBN13: 978-0-8076-1500-3. Dewey:759.9/52/09032.
LCCN:2001-035321.
                              Audience: **g,l,u,f.** *Choice, 2002.*

Penny, Nicholas   **ND615**
The Sixteenth-Century Italian Paintings: Brescia, Bergamo and
Cremona. Cloth over Boards. Yale University Press.
Cumberland, RI. 2004. 448p. National Gallery London
Publications ISBN:1-85709-908-7, ISBN13: 978-1-85709-908-9.
Dewey:759.509/031. LCCN:2001-095566.
                              Audience: **l,u,f.** *Choice, 2005.*

Redgrave, Richard &   **ND466.R4 1981**
Redgrave, Samuel
A Century of British Painters. Ruthven Todd (Editor). Trade
Paper. Cornell University Press. Ithaca, NY. 1981. 622p.
Landmarks in Art History Ser. ISBN:0-8014-9217-3, ISBN13:
978-0-8014-9217-4. Dewey:759.2. LCCN:80-069737.
                              Audience: **g,l,u,f.** *B*

Roque, Alfredo Vilchis   **ND1432.M45R6713 2004**
Infinitas Gracias: Contemporary Mexican Votive Painting. Pierre
Schwartz (Photographer), Victoire Di Rosa & Herve Di Rosa
(Foreword by). Trade Paper. Editions du Seuil. Paris, 2004.
256p. ISBN:2-02-061861-3, ISBN13: 978-2-02-061861-8.
Dewey:755/.2/097209045. LCCN:2003-016172.
                              Audience: **g,l,u,f.**

Rosand, David   **ND205.R67 2004**
The Invention of Painting in America. Trade Cloth. Kegan Paul
International, Ltd. London, 2004. 246p. University
Seminars/Leonard Hastings Schoff Memorial Lectures
ISBN:0-231-13296-4, ISBN13: 978-0-231-13296-1.
Dewey:759.13/09. LCCN:2004-047829.
                              Audience: **g,l,u,f.** *Choice, 2005.*

Rosenberg, Jakob & Slive,   **ND646.S4951995**
Seymour
Dutch Painting, 1600-1800. Cloth over Boards. Yale University
Press. Cumberland, RI. 1995. 390p. Pelican History of Art Ser.
ISBN:0-300-06418-7, ISBN13: 978-0-300-06418-6.
Dewey:759.9/492. LCCN:95-014215.
                              Audience: **g,l,u,f.** *Choice, 1996.*

Shackelford, George T. M.   **ND1356.5.S492002**
& Wissman, Fronia E.
Impressions of Light: The French Landscape from Corot to
Monet. Trade Cloth. Museum of Fine Arts, Boston. Boston, MA.
2003. 292p. ISBN:0-87846-646-0, ISBN13: 978-0-87846-646-7.
Dewey:759.4. LCCN:2002-104337.
                              Audience: **g,l,u,f.** *Choice, 2003.*

Smith, Bernard, et al.   **ND1100.S553 2001**
Australian Painting, 1788-2000. Ed. 4. Terry Smith &
Christopher Heathcote (Authors). Paper Text. Oxford University

Press, Inc. New York, NY. 2002. 644p. ISBN:0-19-551554-4,
ISBN13: 978-0-19-551554-1. Dewey:759.994.
LCCN:2002-327681.
                              Audience: **g,l,u,f.**

Strehlke, Carl Brandon   **ND615.P468 2004**
Italian Paintings, 1250-1450, in the John G. Johnson Collection
and the Philadelphia Museum of Art. Philadelphia Museum of
Art Staff & John G. Johnson Collection (Philadelphia, Pa.) Staff
(Contribution by). Trade Paper. Philadelphia Museum of Art.
Philadelphia, PA. 2004. xi, 556p. ISBN:0-87633-184-3, ISBN13:
978-0-87633-184-2. Dewey:759.5/09/0207474811.
LCCN:2004-050517.
                              Audience: **g,l,u,f.** *Choice, 2005.*

Tinterow, Gary &   **ND544.T5 2003**
Lacambre, Genevieve
Manet/Velazquez: The French Taste for Spanish Painting.
Metropolitan Museum of Art Staff (Contribution by). Trade
Cloth. Metropolitan Museum of Art, The. New York, NY. 2003.
xvi, 592p. ISBN:1-58839-038-1, ISBN13: 978-1-58839-038-7.
Dewey:759.4/074/7471. LCCN:2003-042016.
                              Audience: **g,l,u,f.** *Choice, 2003.*

Torchia, Robert Wilson, et   **ND210 .K45 1996**
al.
American Paintings of the Nineteenth Century, Pt. II. Deborah
Chotner & Ellen G. Miles (Authors). Trade Cloth. Oxford
University Press, Inc. New York, NY. 1999. 384p. National
Gallery of Art USA Publication ISBN:0-89468-254-7, ISBN13:
978-0-89468-254-4. Dewey:759.13/074/753. LCCN:96-021655.
                              Audience: **g,l,u,f.**

Troccoli, Joan C. & Hunt,   **ND1441.5.T76 2000**
Sarah Anschutz
Painters and the American West: The Anschutz Collection. Cloth
over Boards. Yale University Press. Cumberland, RI. 2000.
220p. ISBN:0-300-08722-5, ISBN13: 978-0-300-08722-2.
Dewey:758.9978/007478883. LCCN:00-030329.
                              Audience: **g,l,u,f.** *Choice, 2001.*

Tyler, Ron, et al.   **N8214.5.U6A44 1987**
American Frontier Life: Early Western Painting and Prints.
Carol Clark, Linda Ayres, Warder H. Cadbury, Herman J. Viola,
Bernard Reilly Jr. & Peter H. Hassrick (Authors). Trade Cloth.
Abbeville Press, Inc. New York, NY. 1987. 204p.
ISBN:0-89659-691-5, ISBN13: 978-0-89659-691-7.
Dewey:760/.0449978. LCCN:86-028750.
                              Audience: **g,l,u,f.** *Choice, 1987.*

Vaughan, William   **ND466.V38 1999**
British Painting: The Golden Age. Trade Paper. Thames &
Hudson. New York, NY. 1999. 256p. World of Art Ser.
ISBN:0-500-20319-9, ISBN13: 978-0-500-20319-4.
Dewey:759.2. LCCN:98-060042.
                              Audience: **g,l,u,f.** *Choice, 1999.*

Verma, Som Prakash   **ND1002**
Painting the Mughal Experience. Trade Cloth. Oxford University

---

Press, Inc. New York, NY. 2005. 320p. ISBN:0-19-566756-5, ISBN13: 978-0-19-566756-1. Dewey:759.9/54. LCCN:2005-386885.

Audience: **l,u,f.**

Wilton, Andrew　　　　　　　　　**ND464.W7452001**
Five Centuries of British Painting: From Holbein to Hodgkin. Trade Paper. Thames & Hudson. New York, NY. 2002. 256p. World of Art Ser. ISBN:0-500-20349-0, ISBN13: 978-0-500-20349-1. Dewey:759.2. LCCN:2001-087396.

Audience: **g,l,u,f.**

Windsor, Alan　　　　　　　　　　**N6768.H26 1998**
Handbook of Modern British Painting and Printmaking, 1900-1990. Ed. 2. Trade Cloth. Ashgate Publishing, Ltd. Aldershot, 2002. 334p. ISBN:1-85928-427-2, ISBN13: 978-1-85928-427-8. Dewey:760/.0942. LCCN:98-009977.

Audience: **g,l,u,f.**

Wyckoff, Lydia & Jones,　　　　**ND238.A4 P45 1996**
Ruthe B.
Visions and Voices: Native American Painting from the Philbrook Museum of Art. Marla Redcorn & Andrea Rogers-Henry (Compiled by), Carol Haralson (Designed by). Trade Paper. Philbrook Museum of Art, The. Tulsa, OK. 1996. 304p. ISBN:0-86659-013-7, ISBN13: 978-0-86659-013-6. Dewey:750.8997. LCCN:97-142894.

Audience: **g,l,u,f.** *Choice, 1997.*

Yang, Hsin, et al.　　　　　　　　**ND1040.T48 1997**
Three Thousand Years of Chinese Painting. Richard Barnhart, James Cahill, Hung Wu, Xin Yang, Nie Chongzheng, Lang Shaojun & Yang Xin (Authors). Cloth over Boards. Yale University Press. Cumberland, RI. 1997. 416p. The Culture and Civilization of China Ser. ISBN:0-300-07013-6, ISBN13: 978-0-300-07013-2. Dewey:759.951. LCCN:97-011152.

Audience: **g,l,u,f.** *Choice, 1998.*

Painting > Histories and Handbooks > Types of Painting

Finch, Christopher　　　　　　　　**ND1797.F56 1991**
Nineteenth-Century Watercolors. Trade Cloth. Abbeville Press, Inc. New York, NY. 1991. 320p. ISBN:1-55859-019-6, ISBN13: 978-1-55859-019-9. Dewey:759.05. LCCN:91-021463.

Audience: **g,l,u,f.** *Choice, 1992.*

Kren, Thomas &　　　　　　　　　**ND3171.K742003**
McKendrick, Scot
Illuminating the Renaissance: The Triumph of Flemish Manuscript Painting in Europe. J. Paul Getty Museum Staff & Royal Academy of Arts, Great Britain Staff (Contribution by). Trade Cloth. Oxford University Press, Inc. New York, NY. 2003. 592p. Manuscripts ISBN:0-89236-703-2, ISBN13: 978-0-89236-703-0. Dewey:745.6/7. LCCN:2003-001611.

Audience: **l,u,f.** *Choice, 2003.*

Painting > Individual Painters

Abramowicz, Janet &　　　　　　**N6923.M6A84 2004**
Morandi, Giorgio
Giorgio Morandi: The Art of Silence. Cloth over Boards. Yale University Press. Cumberland, RI. 2005. 288p. ISBN:0-300-10036-1, ISBN13: 978-0-300-10036-5. Dewey:760/.092 B. LCCN:2004-023263.

Audience: **g,l,u,f.** *Choice, 2005.*

Adams, Henry　　　　　　　　　　**N6537.E3A84 2005**
Eakins Revealed. Trade Cloth. Oxford University Press, Inc. New York, NY. 2005. 608p. ISBN:0-19-515668-4, ISBN13: 978-0-19-515668-3. Dewey:759.13 B. LCCN:2004-023284.

Audience: **g,l,u,f.** *Choice, 2005.*

Adelson, Warren, et al.　　　　　**ND237.H345A84 1999**
Childe Hassam, Impressionist. Jay Cantor & William H. Gerdts (Authors). Trade Cloth. Abbeville Press, Inc. New York, NY. 1999. 256p. ISBN:0-7892-0587-4, ISBN13: 978-0-7892-0587-2. Dewey:759.13 B. LCCN:99-019610.

Audience: **g,l,u,f.**

Adler, Kathleen & Garb,　　　　　　　**ND553.M7**
Tamar
Berthe Morisot. Trade Paper. Phaidon Press. London, 1995. 128p. ISBN:0-7148-3479-3, ISBN13: 978-0-7148-3479-5. Dewey:759.4.

Audience: **g,l,u,f.** *Choice, 1987.*

Adriani, Gotz　　　　　　　　　　**ND553.R67A4 2001**
Henri Rousseau. Cloth over Boards. Yale University Press. Cumberland, RI. 2001. 282p. ISBN:0-300-09055-2, ISBN13: 978-0-300-09055-0. Dewey:759.4. LCCN:2001-091773.

Audience: **g,l,u,f.** *Choice, 2002.*

Ahl, Diane C.　　　　　　　　　　**ND623.G8A86 1996**
Benozzo Gozzoli. Cloth over Boards. Yale University Press. Cumberland, RI. 1996. 350p. ISBN:0-300-06699-6, ISBN13: 978-0-300-06699-9. Dewey:759.5. LCCN:96-060714.

Audience: **g,l,u,f.** *Choice, 1997.*

Ahl, Diane Cole (Editor)　　　　**ND623.M43 C36 2002**
The Cambridge Companion to Masaccio. Trade Paper. Cambridge University Press. New York, NY. 2002. 312p. Cambridge Companion to the History of Art Ser. ISBN:0-521-66941-3, ISBN13: 978-0-521-66941-2. Dewey:759.5. LCCN:2001-037496.

Audience: **l,u,f.**

Alexej Von Jawlensky　　　　　　　　**ND699.J3**
Archive Staff
Alexej von Jawlensky, 1890-1938: Catalogue Raisonné of the Watercolours and Drawings. Cloth over Boards. Philip Wilson Publishers, Ltd. London, 1998. 504p. The Alexej von Jawlensky Archive Ser. ISBN:0-85667-486-9, ISBN13: 978-0-85667-486-0. Dewey:[B].

Audience: **g,l,u,f.**

Anderson, Nancy K.   ND237.R36
Frederic Remington: The Color of Night. Alexander Nemerov &
William Sharpe (Contribution by). Trade Cloth. Princeton
University Press. Princeton, NJ. 2003. 224p.
ISBN:0-691-11554-0, ISBN13: 978-0-691-11554-2.
Dewey:759.13. LCCN:2002-154297.
                              Audience: **g,l,u,f.** *Choice, 2003.*

Anfam, David   ND237.R725A41998
Mark Rothko: The Works on Canvas: A Catalogue Raisonné.
Mark Rothko (Illustrator). Cloth over Boards. Yale University
Press. Cumberland, RI. 1998. 708p. ISBN:0-300-07489-1,
ISBN13: 978-0-300-07489-5. Dewey:759.13. LCCN:98-025970.
                              Audience: **g,l,u,f.** *Choice, 1999.*

Arasse, Daniel   N6888.K43A95132001
Anselm Kiefer. Trade Cloth. Harry N. Abrams, Inc. New York,
NY. 2001. 327p. ISBN:0-8109-0384-9, ISBN13:
978-0-8109-0384-5. Dewey:709/.2. LCCN:2001-045188.
                              Audience: **g,l,u,f.** *Choice, 2002.*

Athanassoglou-Kallmyer,   ND553.C33A88 2003
   Nina Maria
Cezanne and Provence: The Painter in His Culture. Trade Cloth.
University of Chicago Press. Chicago, IL. 2003. 337p.
ISBN:0-226-42308-5, ISBN13: 978-0-226-42308-1.
Dewey:759.4. LCCN:2002-007083.
                              Audience: **g,l,u,f.** *Choice, 2004.*

Auping, Michael (Editor)   ND237.G8A4 2003
Philip Guston. Trade Cloth. Thames & Hudson. New York, NY.
2003. 272p. ISBN:0-500-09308-3, ISBN13: 978-0-500-09308-5.
Dewey:759.13. LCCN:2002-015962.
                              Audience: **g,l,u,f.**

Baal-Teshuva, Jacob   ND699.C5B33 1998
Marc Chagall, 1887-1985. Trade Cloth. Taschen America, LLC.
Los Angeles, CA. 1998. 280p. ISBN:3-8228-8271-2, ISBN13:
978-3-8228-8271-9. Dewey:709/.2. LCCN:00-500990.
                              Audience: **g,l,u,f.** *Choice, 1999.*

Bailey, Colin B. (Author,   ND553.M7
   Contribution by)
Renoir's Portraits: Impressions of an Age. Linda Nochlin &
Anne Distel (Contribution by). Trade Paper. Yale University
Press. Cumberland, RI. 1998. 400p. ISBN:0-300-07134-5,
ISBN13: 978-0-300-07134-4. Dewey:759.4. LCCN:97-060428.
                              Audience: **g,l,u,f.**

Barcham, William L.   ND623.T5B37 1989
The Religious Paintings of Giambattista Tiepolo: Piety and
Tradition in Eighteenth-Century Venice. Cloth Text. Oxford
University Press, Inc. New York, NY. 1990. 280p. Clarendon
Studies in the History of Art ISBN:0-19-817501-9, ISBN13:
978-0-19-817501-8. Dewey:759.5. LCCN:88-003996.
                              Audience: **g,l,u,f.** *Choice, 1991.*

Barme, Geremie R.   ND1049.F45B372002
An Artistic Exile: A Life of Feng Zikai (1898-1975). Trade
Cloth. University of California Press. Berkeley, CA. 2002. 558p.
Asia Ser., No. 9:Local Studies/Global Themes

ISBN:0-520-20832-3, ISBN13: 978-0-520-20832-2.
Dewey:759.951. LCCN:2001-005019.
                              Audience: **g,l,u,f.** *Choice, 2003.*

Barnes, Susan J., et al.   ND673.D9
Van Dyck: A Complete Catalogue of the Paintings. Oliver
Millar, Horst Vey & Nora De Poorter (Authors), Anthony van
Dyck (Illustrator). Cloth over Boards. Yale University Press.
Cumberland, RI. 2004. 704p. Paul Mellon Centre for Studies in
British Art ISBN:0-300-09928-2, ISBN13: 978-0-300-09928-7.
Dewey:759.9493. LCCN:2003-009655.
                              Audience: **g,l,u,f.** *Choice, 2004.*

Barnett, Vivian E. (Editor)   ND1978.K3A41992
Kandinsky Watercolours: Catalogue Raisonné, 1900-1921. Trade
Cloth. Cornell University Press. Ithaca, NY. 1992. 600p.
ISBN:0-8014-2690-1, ISBN13: 978-0-8014-2690-2.
Dewey:759.7. LCCN:91-027618.
                              Audience: **g,l,u,f.** *Choice, 1992.*

Barnett, Vivian E.   ND1978.K3A41992
Kandinsky Watercolours: Catalogue Raisonné, 1922-1944. Trade
Cloth. Cornell University Press. Ithaca, NY. 1994. 600p.
ISBN:0-8014-2927-7, ISBN13: 978-0-8014-2927-9.
Dewey:759.7. LCCN:91-027618.
                              Audience: **g,l,u,f.** *Choice, 1994.*

Barratt, Carrie Rebora &   ND237.S8A42004
   Miles, Ellen G.
Gilbert Stuart. Metropolitan Museum of Art Staff & National
Gallery of Art (U.S.) Staff (Contribution by). Cloth over Boards.
Yale University Press. Cumberland, RI. 2004. 352p. The
Metropolitan Museum of Art Ser. ISBN:0-300-10495-2,
ISBN13: 978-0-300-10495-0. Dewey:759.13.
LCCN:2004-011647.
                              Audience: **g,l,u,f.** *Choice, 2005.*

Barter, Judith A.   N6537.C35A41998
Mary Cassatt: Modern Woman. Erica E. Hirshler, George T.
Shackelford, Kevin Sharp, Andrew J. Walker & Mary Cassatt
(Editors). Trade Cloth. Harry N. Abrams, Inc. New York, NY.
1998. 376p. ISBN:0-8109-4089-2, ISBN13: 978-0-8109-4089-5.
Dewey:760/.092. LCCN:98-007306.
                              Audience: **g,l,u,f.** *Choice, 1999.*

Bell, Adrienne Baxter   ND237.I5A4 2003
George Innes and the Visionary Landscape. Trade Cloth. George
Braziller Inc. New York, NY. 2003. 174p. ISBN:0-8076-1525-0,
ISBN13: 978-0-8076-1525-6. Dewey:759.13.
LCCN:2003-055060.
                              Audience: **g,l,u,f.** *Choice, 2004.*

Belting, Hans   ND653.B65
Hieronymus Bosch: Garden of Earthly Delights. Ed. 2. Trade
Cloth. Prestel Publishing. New York, NY. 2005. 128p.
ISBN:3-7913-3320-8, ISBN13: 978-3-7913-3320-5.
Dewey:759.9492.
                              Audience: **g,l,u,f.** *Choice, 2002.*

Berend-Corinth, Charlotte   **ND588.C5**
& Hernad, Beatrice
Lovis Corinth, the Paintings, a Catalogue Raisonné¡: Die
Gemaelde, Werkverzeichnis. Ed. 2. Lovis Corinth (Illustrator).
Trade Cloth, Box or Slipcased. Alan Wofsy Fine Arts. San
Francisco, CA. 1992. 960p. ISBN:1-55660-197-2, ISBN13:
978-1-55660-197-2. Dewey:759.3.

                           Audience: **g,l,u,f.**

Bissell, R. Ward   **ND623.G364B581999**
Artemisia Gentileschi and the Authority of Art: Critical Reading
and Catalogue Raisonné. Trade Cloth. Pennsylvania State
University Press. University Park, PA. 1999. 446p.
ISBN:0-271-01787-2, ISBN13: 978-0-271-01787-7.
Dewey:759.5. LCCN:97-048437.

                  Audience: **g,l,u,f.** *Choice, 1999.*

Bloch, E. Maurice   **ND237.B59A41986**
The Paintings of George Caleb Bingham: A Catalogue Raisonné.
Cloth Text. University of Missouri Press. Columbia, MO. 1986.
328p. ISBN:0-8262-0461-9, ISBN13: 978-0-8262-0461-5.
Dewey:759.13. LCCN:85-029013.

                  Audience: **g,l,u,f.** *Choice, 1987.*

Brambilla Barcilon, Pinin &   **ND623.L5.A683 2001**
Marani, Pietro C.
Leonardo, the Last Supper. Harlow Tighe (Translator). Trade
Cloth. University of Chicago Press. Chicago, IL. 2001. 458p.
ISBN:0-226-50427-1, ISBN13: 978-0-226-50427-8.
Dewey:759.5. LCCN:00-011655.

                          Audience: **g,l,u,f.**

Braun, Emily   **N6923.B587**
Boccioni's Materia: A Futurist Masterpiece and the European
Avant-Garde. Solomon R. Guggenheim Museum Staff
(Contribution by). Trade Cloth. Solomon R. Guggenheim
Museum. New York, NY. 2003. 232p. ISBN:0-89207-303-9,
ISBN13: 978-0-89207-303-0. Dewey:759.5.

                    Audience: **l,u,f.** *Choice, 2004.*

Brettell, Richard R. &   **ND553**
Fonsmark, Anne-Birgitte
Gauguin and Impressionism. Saddle Stitched, Cloth over
Boards, Dust Jacket. Yale University Press. Cumberland, RI.
2005. 288p. ISBN:0-300-11003-0, ISBN13: 978-0-300-11003-6.
Dewey:759.4.

                    Audience: **l,u,f.** *Choice, 2006.*

Brombert, Beth A.   **ND553.M3B76 1995**
Edouard Manet: Rebel in a Frock Coat. Trade Cloth. Little
Brown & Company. New York, NY. 1996. 528p.
ISBN:0-316-10947-9, ISBN13: 978-0-316-10947-5.
Dewey:759.4. LCCN:94-045881.

                          Audience: **g,l,u,f.**

Brown, David A.   **ND623.L5B78 1998**
Leonardo da Vinci: Origins of a Genius. Cloth over Boards.
Yale University Press. Cumberland, RI. 1998. 248p.
ISBN:0-300-07246-5, ISBN13: 978-0-300-07246-4.
Dewey:759.5. LCCN:98-015164.

                  Audience: **g,l,u,f.** *Choice, 1999.*

Buck, Stephanie & Sander,   **ND5883.H7**
Jochen
Hans Holbein the Younger: Painter at the Court of Henry VIII.
Trade Cloth. Thames & Hudson. New York, NY. 2004. 184p.
ISBN:0-500-09318-0, ISBN13: 978-0-500-09318-4.
Dewey:759.3. LCCN:2003-109214.

                  Audience: **g,l,u,f.** *Choice, 2004.*

Buckley, Laurene   **ND237.T35B83 2001**
Edmund C. Tarbell: Poet of Domesticity. Trade Cloth. Hudson
Hills Press LLC. Manchester, VT. 2001. 144p.
ISBN:1-55595-212-7, ISBN13: 978-1-55595-212-9.
Dewey:759.13 B. LCCN:2001-024470.

                  Audience: **g,l,u,f.** *Choice, 2002.*

Bullock, Margaret E.   **ND237.H37A4 2004**
Childe Hassam: Impressionist in the West. Portland Art Museum
(Or.) Staff (Contribution by). Trade Cloth. Portland Art Museum.
Portland, OR. 2005. 112p. ISBN:1-883124-19-0, ISBN13:
978-1-883124-19-9. Dewey:759.13. LCCN:2004-015742.

                  Audience: **g,l,u,f.** *Choice, 2005.*

Carbone, Teresa A.   **ND237.J7A4 1999**
Eastman Johnson : painting America. New York : Brooklyn
Museum of Art, in association with Rizzoli International. 1999.
ISBN:0-8478-2214-1, ISBN13: 978-0-8478-2214-0.

                          Audience: **g,l,u,f.**

Carr, Gerald L.   **ND237.C52 A4 2000**
In Search of the Promised Land: Paintings by Frederic Edwin
Church. Trade Paper. University Press of New England.
Lebanon, NH. 2000. 204p. ISBN:1-58465-126-1, ISBN13:
978-1-58465-126-0. Dewey:759.13. LCCN:00-131748.

                  Audience: **g,l,u,f.** *Choice, 2001.*

Chevlowe, Susan   **ND237.S465A4 1998**
Common Man, Mythic Vision: The Paintings of Ben Shahn.
Trade Cloth. Princeton University Press. Princeton, NJ. 1998.
208p. ISBN:0-691-00406-4, ISBN13: 978-0-691-00406-8.
Dewey:759.13. LCCN:98-024384.

                  Audience: **g,l,u,f.** *Choice, 1999.*

Chipp, Herschel B.   **ND553.P5A66**
Picasso's Guernica: History, Transformations, Meanings. Trade
Paper. University of California Press. Berkeley, CA. 1993. xii,
261p. California Studies in the History of Art Ser.
ISBN:0-520-07947-7, ISBN13: 978-0-520-07947-2.
Dewey:759.4. LCCN:87-030893.

                  Audience: **g,l,u,f.** *Choice, 1989.*

Christiansen, Keith, et al.   **ND623.G366A4 2001**
Orazio and Artemisia Gentileschi. Judith Walker Mann, Orazio
Gentileschi & Artemisia Gentileschi (Authors), Museo di
Palazzo Venezia Staff, Metropolitan Museum of Art Staff & St.
Louis Art Museum Staff (Contribution by). Cloth over Boards.
Yale University Press. Cumberland, RI. 2001. 472p.
Metropolitan Museum of Art Ser. ISBN:0-300-09077-3,
ISBN13: 978-0-300-09077-2. Dewey:759.5/09/032074.
LCCN:2001-044343.

                  Audience: **g,l,u,f.** *Choice, 2002.*

Christov-Bakargiev,   ND237.K56
  Carolyn, et al.
Franz Kline (1910-1962). David Anfam & W. Oechslin
(Authors), Carolyn Christov-Bakargiev, David Anfam & Dore
Eshton (Editors). Trade Cloth. Skira Editore. Milano, 2004.
424p. ISBN:88-7624-141-8, ISBN13: 978-88-7624-141-3.
Dewey:759.13.
                      Audience: **g,l,u,f.** *Choice, 2005.*

Cikovsky, Nicolai Jr.   ND237.H7C541990
Winslow Homer. Trade Cloth. Harry N. Abrams, Inc. New York,
NY. 1990. 160p. Library of American Art ISBN:0-8109-1193-0,
ISBN13: 978-0-8109-1193-2. Dewey:759.13. LCCN:89-017839.
                 Audience: **g,l,u,f.** *Choice, 1996, 1990.*

Clair, Jean   ND553.M7
Balthus. Trade Cloth. Rizzoli International Publications, Inc.
New York, NY. 2001. 386p. ISBN:0-8478-2410-1, ISBN13:
978-0-8478-2410-6. Dewey:759.4.
                            Audience: **g,l,u,f.**

Claridge, Laura   ND237.O5
Norman Rockwell: A Life. Trade Paper. Random House Adult
Trade Publishing Group. New York, NY. 2003. 592p.
ISBN:0-8129-6723-2, ISBN13: 978-0-8129-6723-4.
Dewey:759.13 B.
                     Audience: **g,l,u,f.** *Choice, 2002.*

Conisbee, Philip &   ND553
  Coutagne, Denis
Cezanne in Provence. Cloth over Boards. Yale University Press.
Cumberland, RI. 2006. 350p. ISBN:0-300-11338-2, ISBN13:
978-0-300-11338-9. Dewey:759.4. LCCN:2005-022838.
                          Audience: **g,l,u,f.**

Conrads, Margaret C.   ND237.H7A4 2001
Winslow Homer and the Critics: Forging a National Art in the
1870s. Trade Cloth. Princeton University Press. Princeton, NJ.
2001. 264p. ISBN:0-691-07099-7, ISBN13: 978-0-691-07099-5.
Dewey:759.13. LCCN:00-064257.
                     Audience: **g,l,u,f.** *Choice, 2001.*

Cooper, Douglas   N6853.T6A42004
Toulouse-Lautrec. Trade Paper. Harry N. Abrams, Inc. New
York, NY. 2005. 128p. ISBN:0-8109-9204-3, ISBN13:
978-0-8109-9204-7. Dewey:760.092. LCCN:2005-283924.
                         Audience: **g,l,u,f.**

Cormack, Malcolm   ND497.G2 A4 1991
The Paintings of Thomas Gainsborough. Trade Paper.
Cambridge University Press. New York, NY. 1993. 198p.
ISBN:0-521-38887-2, ISBN13: 978-0-521-38887-0.
Dewey:759.2. LCCN:90-019802.
                     Audience: **g,l,u,f.** *Choice, 1992.*

Courthion, Pierre   ND553.M3C682004
Manet. Trade Paper. Harry N. Abrams, Inc. New York, NY.
2004. 128p. Masters of Art Ser. ISBN:0-8109-9145-4, ISBN13:
978-0-8109-9145-3. Dewey:759.4. LCCN:2003-022521.
                         Audience: **g,l,u,f.**

Davies, David & Elliott,   ND813.T4A42003
  John H.
El Greco. Xavier Bray, Keith Christiansen, Gabriele Finaldi &
Ashok Roy (Contribution by). Trade Paper. Yale University
Press. Cumberland, RI. 2005. 320p. ISBN:1-85709-938-9,
ISBN13: 978-1-85709-938-6. Dewey:759.6.
LCCN:2003-105497.
                     Audience: **l,u,f.** *Choice, 2004.*

Davies, David & Elliott,   ND813.T4
  John
El Greco. Xavier Bray, Keith Christiansen & Gabriele Finaldi
(Contribution by). Cloth over Boards. National Gallery
Publications Ltd. London, 2003. 320p. ISBN:1-85709-933-8,
ISBN13: 978-1-85709-933-1. Dewey:759.6.
LCCN:2003-105497.
                     Audience: **g,l,u,f.** *Choice, 2004.*

Davies, David &   ND813.V4A4 1996
  Parke-Taylor, Michael
Velazquez in Seville. Enriqueta Harris & Michael Clarke
(Editors). Cloth over Boards. Yale University Press.
Cumberland, RI. 1996. 192p. ISBN:0-300-06949-9, ISBN13:
978-0-300-06949-5. Dewey:759.6. LCCN:96-060915.
                 Audience: **g,l,u,f.** *Choice, 1997.*

De Dos, Dirk   ND673.M5A41994
Hans Memling: The Complete Oeuvre. Trade Cloth. Harry N.
Abrams, Inc. New York, NY. 1994. 448p. ISBN:0-8109-3649-6,
ISBN13: 978-0-8109-3649-2. Dewey:759/.9493.
LCCN:94-003048.
                         Audience: **l,u,f.**

De Vecchi, Pierluigi &   ND623.B7
  Arasse, Daniel
Botticelli: From Lorenzo the Magnificent to Savonarola. Trade
Cloth. Skira Editore. Milano, 2004. 336p. ISBN:88-8491-565-1,
ISBN13: 978-88-8491-565-8. Dewey:759.5.
                 Audience: **g,l,u,f.** *Choice, 2004.*

DeLue, Rachael Ziady &   ND237.I5D45 2004
  Inness, George Jr.
George Inness and the Science of Landscape. Trade Cloth.
University of Chicago Press. Chicago, IL. 2005. 352p.
ISBN:0-226-14229-9, ISBN13: 978-0-226-14229-6.
Dewey:759.13. LCCN:2004-004953.
                 Audience: **l,u,f.** *Choice, 2006.*

Demetrion, James T.   ND237.S78A4 2001
  (Editor)
Clyfford Still: Paintings 1944-1960. David Anfam, Brooks
Adams & Neal Benezra (Contribution by). Cloth over Boards.
Yale University Press. Cumberland, RI. 2001. 160p.
ISBN:0-300-08969-4, ISBN13: 978-0-300-08969-1.
Dewey:759.13. LCCN:2001-016885.
                 Audience: **g,l,u,f.** *Choice, 2002.*

Denizeau, Gerard   ND553.L97A41998
Jean Lurcat: Monograph and Catalogue Raisonné, 1910-1965.

Trade Cloth. Acatos, Editions. Lausanne, 1998. 450p. ISBN:2-940033-22-6, ISBN13: 978-2-940033-22-5. Dewey:750. LCCN:2001-418018.

Audience: **g,l,u,f.**

Dixon, Laurinda   **ND653.B65**
Bosch. Trade Paper. Phaidon Press. London, 2003. 352p. Art & Ideas Ser. ISBN:0-7148-3974-4, ISBN13: 978-0-7148-3974-5. Dewey:759.9492. LCCN:2004-269384.

Audience: **g,l,u,f.** *Choice, 2004.*

Dobkins, Rebecca J., et al.   **E99.M18D393 1997**
Memory and Imagination: The Legacy of Maidu Indian Artist Frank Day. Frank R. LaPena & Carey T. Caldwell (Authors). Trade Paper. University of Washington Press. Seattle, WA. 1997. 120p. ISBN:0-295-97612-8, ISBN13: 978-0-295-97612-9. Dewey:759.13 B. LCCN:96-049341.

Audience: **g,l,u,f.** *Choice, 1997.*

Doezema, Marianne   **ND237.B45D6 1991**
George Bellows and Urban America. Cloth over Boards. Yale University Press. Cumberland, RI. 1992. 288p. ISBN:0-300-05043-7, ISBN13: 978-0-300-05043-1. Dewey:759.13. LCCN:91-019375.

Audience: **l,u,f.** *Choice, 1992.*

Drohojowska-Philip, Hunter   **ND237.O5D76 2004**
Full Bloom: The Art and Life of Georgia O'Keeffe. Trade Cloth. W. W. Norton & Company, Inc. New York, NY. 2004. 480p. ISBN:0-393-05853-0, ISBN13: 978-0-393-05853-6. Dewey:759.13 B. LCCN:2003-026071.

Audience: **g,l,u,f.** *Choice, 2005.*

Druick, Douglas W.   **ND553.R45D741997**
Renoir Art Institute of Chicago. Britt Salvesen (Editor). Trade Cloth. Harry N. Abrams, Inc. New York, NY. 1997. 112p. Artists in Focus Ser. ISBN:0-8109-6325-6, ISBN13: 978-0-8109-6325-2. Dewey:759.4. LCCN:97-073867.

Audience: **g,l,u,f.**

Druick, Douglas W. &   **ND653.G7D76 2001**
Zegers, Peter
Van Gogh and Gauguin: The Studio of the South. Trade Cloth. Thames & Hudson. New York, NY. 2001. 432p. ISBN:0-500-51054-7, ISBN13: 978-0-500-51054-4. Dewey:759.9492 B. LCCN:2001-037695.

Audience: **g,l,u,f.** *Choice, 2002.*

Edmonds, Martin   **ND1108.C58E36 1999**
The Resurrection of Philip Clairmont. Trade Paper. Auckland University Press. Auckland, 1999. 280p. ISBN:1-86940-195-6, ISBN13: 978-1-86940-195-5. Dewey:759.9931. LCCN:00-273460.

Audience: **g,l,u,f.**

Eldredge, Charles C.   **ND237.O5E431991**
Georgia O'Keeffe: Library of American Art. Trade Cloth. Harry N. Abrams, Inc. New York, NY. 1991. 160p. Library of American Art ISBN:0-8109-3657-7, ISBN13: 978-0-8109-3657-7. Dewey:759.13. LCCN:90-048459.

Audience: **g,l,u,f.** *Choice, 1991.*

Elzea, Rowland   **ND237.S57A4**
John Sloan's Oil Paintings: A Catalogue Raisonné. Trade Cloth. University of Delaware Press. Newark, DE. 1992. ISBN:0-318-68501-9, ISBN13: 978-0-318-68501-4. Dewey:759.13.

Audience: **g,l,u,f.**

Fairbrother, Trevor   **ND237.S3F334 2000**
John Singer Sargent: The Sensualist. Cloth over Boards. Yale University Press. Cumberland, RI. 2000. 228p. ISBN:0-300-08744-6, ISBN13: 978-0-300-08744-4. Dewey:759.13. LCCN:00-057405.

Audience: **g,l,u,f.** *Choice, 2001.*

Feaver, William   **ND1329.F74A42002**
Lucian Freud. Trade Cloth. Harry N. Abrams, Inc. New York, NY. 2002. 240p. ISBN:0-8109-6267-5, ISBN13: 978-0-8109-6267-5. Dewey:760/.092. LCCN:2002-105078.

Audience: **g,l,u,f.** *Choice, 2002.*

Fleming, G.   **ND497.M6.F58 1998**
John Everett Millais: A Biography. Trade Cloth. Constable & Robinson Ltd. London, 1999. 318p. ISBN:0-09-478560-0, ISBN13: 978-0-09-478560-1. Dewey:759.2.

Audience: **l,u,f.** *Choice, 1999.*

Foister, Susan & Holbein,   **N6888.H664F65 2004**
Hans
Holbein and England. Cloth over Boards. Yale University Press. Cumberland, RI. 2005. 320p. Studies in British Art Ser. ISBN:0-300-10280-1, ISBN13: 978-0-300-10280-2. Dewey:759.3. LCCN:2004-002274.

Audience: **l,u,f.** *Choice, 2005.*

Forge, Andrew   **ND553.M7A41995**
Monet: Art Institute of Chicago. Ed. 2. Susan F. Rossen (Editor), James N. Wood (Foreword by). Trade Cloth. Harry N. Abrams, Inc. New York, NY. 1995. 112p. Artists in Focus Ser. ISBN:0-8109-4290-9, ISBN13: 978-0-8109-4290-5. Dewey:759.4. LCCN:95-010039.

Audience: **g,l,u,f.**

Franits, Wayne E. (Editor)   **ND653.V5 C36 2001**
The Cambridge Companion to Vermeer. Cloth Text. Cambridge University Press. New York, NY. 2001. 266p. Cambridge Companions to the History of Art Ser. ISBN:0-521-65330-4, ISBN13: 978-0-521-65330-5. Dewey:759.9492. LCCN:00-052953.

Audience: **l,u,f.**

Franklin, David   **ND623.P255**
The Art of Parmigianino. Cloth over Boards. Yale University Press. Cumberland, RI. 2004. 302p. ISBN:0-300-10357-3, ISBN13: 978-0-300-10357-1. Dewey:759.5. LCCN:2003-495981.

Audience: **l,u,f.** *Choice, 2004.*

Fraser, Elisabeth A.   **ND553.D33F73 2004**
Delacroix, Art and Patrimony in Post-Revolutionary France. Trade Cloth. Cambridge University Press. New York, NY. 2004.

286p. ISBN:0-521-82829-5, ISBN13: 978-0-521-82829-1. Dewey:759.4. LCCN:2003-053290.
Audience: **l,u,f.** *Choice, 2004.*

Gemin, Massimo   **ND623.T5**
Giambattista Tiepolo: A Catalogue Raisonné, Paintings. Trade Cloth. Arsenale Editrice SRL. 30172 Venezia, 1994. 552p. ISBN:88-7743-133-4, ISBN13: 978-88-7743-133-2. Dewey:759.5.
Audience: **g,l,u,f.**

Gerdts, William H.   **ND1839.S33A4 2001**
Alice Schille. Trade Cloth. Hudson Hills Press LLC. Manchester, VT. 2001. 216p. ISBN:1-55595-181-3, ISBN13: 978-1-55595-181-8. Dewey:759.13. LCCN:00-054094.
Audience: **g,l,u,f.** *Choice, 2001.*

Gilbert, Creighton E.   **ND623.C26G53 1995**
Caravaggio and His Two Cardinals: Method and Meaning. Trade Cloth. Pennsylvania State University Press. University Park, PA. 1995. 1446p. ISBN:0-271-01312-5, ISBN13: 978-0-271-01312-1. Dewey:759.5. LCCN:93-044381.
Audience: **g,l,u,f.** *Choice, 1995.*

Gilbert, Creighton &   **ND623.S5A66 2001**
Signorelli, Luca
How Fra Angelico and Signorelli Saw the End of the World. Trade Cloth. Pennsylvania State University Press. University Park, PA. 2002. 336p. ISBN:0-271-02140-3, ISBN13: 978-0-271-02140-9. Dewey:759.5/09/024. LCCN:2001-021479.
Audience: **g,l,u,f.** *Choice, 2003.*

Ginzburg, Carlo   **ND623.F78G513 2000**
Enigma of Piero: Piero Della Francesca. Ed. 2. Trade Cloth. Analytical Psychology Club of San Francisco, Inc. San Francisco, CA. 2000. xxxiv, 158p. ISBN:1-85984-731-5, ISBN13: 978-1-85984-731-2. Dewey:759.5. LCCN:2001-265785.
Audience: **l,u,f.** *Choice, 2001.*

Goff, Robert & Abrams,   **ND813.D3G581998**
Harry N., Staff
The Essential Salvador Dali. Trade Cloth. Harry N. Abrams, Inc. New York, NY. 1998. 112p. Essential Ser. ISBN:0-8109-5800-7, ISBN13: 978-0-8109-5800-5. Dewey:759.6. LCCN:98-071952.
Audience: **g,l,u,f.**

Goffen, Rona   **ND623.B39G64 1989**
Giovanni Bellini. Cloth over Boards. Yale University Press. Cumberland, RI. 1989. 352p. ISBN:0-300-04334-1, ISBN13: 978-0-300-04334-1. Dewey:759.5. LCCN:89-033263.
Audience: **g,l,u,f.** *Choice, 1990.*

Golding, John   **ND553.B86A4 1997**
Braque: The Late Works. Sophie Bowness & Isabelle Monod-Fontaine (Contribution by). Cloth over Boards. Yale University Press. Cumberland, RI. 1997. 144p. ISBN:0-300-07159-0, ISBN13: 978-0-300-07159-7. Dewey:759.4. LCCN:96-051627.
Audience: **g,l,u,f.** *Choice, 1997.*

Goldwater, Robert   **ND553.G27G652004**
Gauguin. Trade Paper. Harry N. Abrams, Inc. New York, NY. 2004. 128p. Masters of Art Ser. ISBN:0-8109-9147-0, ISBN13: 978-0-8109-9147-7. Dewey:759.4. LCCN:2003-022520.
Audience: **g,l,u,f.**

Gordon, Dillian & Syson,   **N6923.P497S97 2001**
Luke
Pisanello: Painter to the Renaissance Court. Cloth over Boards. Yale University Press. Cumberland, RI. 2001. 276p. National Gallery London Publications ISBN:0-300-09108-7, ISBN13: 978-0-300-09108-3. Dewey:759.5. LCCN:2001-095569.
Audience: **g,l,u,f.**

Gould, Cecil   **ND623.P255G68 1994**
Parmigianino. Trade Cloth. Abbeville Press, Inc. New York, NY. 1995. 214p. ISBN:1-55859-892-8, ISBN13: 978-1-55859-892-8. Dewey:760/.092. LCCN:94-039742.
Audience: **g,l,u,f.** *Choice, 1995.*

Gouveia, Georgette   **ND237.C3G682001**
Mary Cassat. Trade Cloth. Harry N. Abrams, Inc. New York, NY. 2001. 112p. Essential Ser. ISBN:0-8109-5814-7, ISBN13: 978-0-8109-5814-2. Dewey:759.13. LCCN:2001-088662.
Audience: **g,l,u,f.**

Gowing, Lawrence   **ND653.V5G61997**
Vermeer. Trade Paper. University of California Press. Berkeley, CA. 1997. 240p. ISBN:0-520-21276-2, ISBN13: 978-0-520-21276-3. Dewey:759.9/492. LCCN:97-020774.
Audience: **g,l,u,f.**

Gray, John, et al.   **N6797**
Jenny Saville. Linda Nochlin, David Sylvester, Simon Schama & Gagosian Gallery Staff (Authors), Rizzoli Publications (Created by). Trade Cloth. Rizzoli International Publications, Inc. New York, NY. 2005. 160p. ISBN:0-8478-2757-7, ISBN13: 978-0-8478-2757-2. Dewey:759.2. LCCN:2005-900780.
Audience: **g,l,u,f.** *Choice, 2006.*

Green, Christopher   **ND813.G75.A4 1992**
Juan Gris. Christian Derouet & Karin Von Maur (Contribution by). Cloth over Boards. Yale University Press. Cumberland, RI. 1993. 312p. ISBN:0-300-05374-6, ISBN13: 978-0-300-05374-6. Dewey:759.6. LCCN:92-056394.
Audience: **g,l,u,f.** *Choice, 1993.*

Greenfeld, Howard   **N7113.G68**
Ben Shahn: An Artist's Life. Trade Paper. Random House, Inc. New York, NY. 1998. 384p. ISBN:0-679-78312-1, ISBN13: 978-0-679-78312-1. Dewey:760/.092 B. LCCN:97-046748.
Audience: **g,l,u,f.** *Choice, 1999.*

Hahl-Koch, Jelena   **N6999.K33.H34 1993**
Kandinsky. Trade Cloth. Rizzoli International Publications, Inc. New York, NY. 1994. 432p. ISBN:0-8478-1404-1, ISBN13: 978-0-8478-1404-6. Dewey:759.4. LCCN:91-052769.
Audience: **g,l,u,f.** *Choice, 1994.*

Hall, Edwin   **ND673.E9W44 1994**
[e] The Arnolfini Betrothal: Medieval Marriage and the Enigma
of Van Eyck's Double Portrait. E-Book. NetLibrary, Inc.
Boulder, CO. 1994. ISBN:0-585-36622-5, ISBN13:
978-0-585-36622-7. Dewey:759.9493.
                                   Audience: **l,u,f**. *Choice, 1995.*

Hall, Marcia (Editor)   **ND623.B9A69 2004**
Michelangelo's 'Last Judgment'. Trade Cloth. Cambridge
University Press. New York, NY. 2004. 208p. Masterpieces of
Western Painting Ser. ISBN:0-521-78002-0, ISBN13:
978-0-521-78002-5. Dewey:759.5. LCCN:2004-051846.
                                   Audience: **l,u,f**. *Choice, 2005.*

Hammacher, Abraham   **ND673.M35H35131995**
  Marie
Magritte. James Brockway (Translator). Trade Cloth. Harry N.
Abrams, Inc. New York, NY. 1995. 167p. ISBN:0-8109-8137-8,
ISBN13: 978-0-8109-8137-9. Dewey:759.9493.
LCCN:94-037476.

                                   Audience: **g,l,u,f**.

Hand, John Oliver   **ND673.C5555H352004**
Joos Van Cleve: The Complete Paintings. Cloth over Boards.
Yale University Press. Cumberland, RI. 2005. 240p.
ISBN:0-300-10578-9, ISBN13: 978-0-300-10578-0.
Dewey:759.9492. LCCN:2004-002258.
                                   Audience: **g,l,u,f**. *Choice, 2005.*

Harr, Jonathan   **ND623.C26H37 2005**
The Lost Painting: The Quest for a Caravaggio Masterpiece.
Trade Cloth. Random House Adult Trade Publishing Group.
New York, NY. 2005. 288p. ISBN:0-375-50801-5, ISBN13:
978-0-375-50801-1. Dewey:759.5. LCCN:2005-048593.
                                   Audience: **g,l,u,f**. *Choice, 2006.*

Hartt, Frederick   **ND623.B9H32004**
Michelangelo. Trade Paper. Harry N. Abrams, Inc. New York,
NY. 2004. 128p. Masters of Art Ser. ISBN:0-8109-9144-6,
ISBN13: 978-0-8109-9144-6. Dewey:759.5.
LCCN:2003-022522.
                                   Audience: **g,l,u,f**.

Hauptman, William   **ND853.G5H381996**
Charles Gleyre, 1806-1874: Biography and Catalogue Raisonné.
Trade Cloth. Princeton University Press. Princeton, NJ. 1997.
988p. ISBN:0-691-04448-1, ISBN13: 978-0-691-04448-4.
Dewey:759.9494 B. LCCN:95-019298.
                                   Audience: **g,l,u,f**. *Choice, 1997.*

Hennessey, Maureen Hart &   **ND237.R68H461999**
  Larson, Judy L.
Norman Rockwell: Pictures for the American People. Anne
Knutson (Editor). Trade Cloth. Harry N. Abrams, Inc. New
York, NY. 1999. 200p. ISBN:0-8109-6392-2, ISBN13:
978-0-8109-6392-4. Dewey:759.13. LCCN:99-073071.
                                   Audience: **g,l,u,f**. *Choice, 2000.*

Herbert, Robert L.   **ND553.M7H43 1994**
Monet on the Normandy Coast: Tourism and Painting,
1867-1886. Cloth over Boards. Yale University Press.

Cumberland, RI. 1994. 168p. ISBN:0-300-05973-6, ISBN13:
978-0-300-05973-1. Dewey:759.4. LCCN:94-013913.
                                   Audience: **g,l,u,f**. *Choice, 1995.*

Herrera, Hayden   **ND237.G613H47 2003**
Arshile Gorky: His Life and Work. Cloth over Boards. Farrar,
Straus & Giroux. New York, NY. 2003. 784p.
ISBN:0-374-11323-8, ISBN13: 978-0-374-11323-0.
Dewey:759.13 B. LCCN:2002-033881.
                                   Audience: **l,u,f**. *Choice, 2004.*

Hirst, Michael, et al.   **ND623.B9C2913**
Sistine Chapel: A Glorious Restoration. Gianluigi Colalicci,
Fabrizio Mancinelli & John Shearman (Authors), Diana Murphy
(Editor). Trade Cloth. Harry N. Abrams, Inc. New York, NY.
1999. 271p. ISBN:0-8109-8176-9, ISBN13: 978-0-8109-8176-8.
Dewey:759.5. LCCN:93-039787.

                                   Audience: **l,u,f**.

Hobbs, Robert   **ND237.K677H63**
Lee Krasner. Trade Cloth. Harry N. Abrams, Inc. New York,
NY. 1999. 224p. ISBN:0-8109-6395-7, ISBN13:
978-0-8109-6395-5. Dewey:759.1/3. LCCN:99-071500.
                                   Audience: **g,l,u,f**. *Choice, 1994.*

Hobbs, Robert Carleton   **ND237.A85A42001**
Milton Avery: The Late Paintings. American Federation of Arts
Staff, Milwaukee Art Museum Staff & Norton Museum of Art
Staff (Contribution by). Trade Cloth. Harry N. Abrams, Inc.
New York, NY. 2001. 112p. ISBN:0-8109-4274-7, ISBN13:
978-0-8109-4274-5. Dewey:759.13. LCCN:00-068928.
                                   Audience: **g,l,u,f**. *Choice, 2001.*

Hoberg, Annegret & Friedel,   **ND588**
  Helmut (Editors)
Franz Marc: The Retrospective. Trade Cloth. Prestel Publishing.
New York, NY. 2006. 336p. ISBN:3-7913-3578-2, ISBN13:
978-3-7913-3578-0. Dewey:759.3.

                                   Audience: **g,l,u,f**.

Hofmann, Werner   **ND588.F75H629 2000**
Caspar David Friedrich. Trade Cloth. Thames & Hudson. New
York, NY. 2000. 300p. ISBN:0-500-09295-8, ISBN13:
978-0-500-09295-8. Dewey:759.3. LCCN:00-101621.
                                   Audience: **g,l,u,f**. *Choice, 2001.*

Holmes, Megan   **ND623.L7H65 1999**
Fra Filippo Lippi: The Carmelite Painter. Cloth over Boards.
Yale University Press. Cumberland, RI. 1999. 312p.
ISBN:0-300-08104-9, ISBN13: 978-0-300-08104-6.
Dewey:759.5. LCCN:99-014918.
                                   Audience: **l,u,f**. *Choice, 2000.*

Homer, William I.   **N6537.E3.H65 1992**
Thomas Eakins: His Life and Art. Trade Cloth. Abbeville Press,
Inc. New York, NY. 1992. 276p. ISBN:1-55859-281-4, ISBN13:
978-1-55859-281-0. Dewey:759.73. LCCN:92-010163.
                                   Audience: **g,l,u,f**. *Choice, 1993.*

Homer, William I. &   ND237.R8H661989
  Goodrich, Lloyd
Albert Pinkham Ryder: Painter of Dreams. Trade Cloth. Harry
N. Abrams, Inc. New York, NY. 1989. 256p.
ISBN:0-8109-1599-5, ISBN13: 978-0-8109-1599-2.
Dewey:759.13 B. LCCN:89-000227.
                              Audience: **g,l,u,f.** *Choice, 1990.*

Hood, William   ND623.F5H66 1993
Fra Angelico at San Marco. Trade Cloth. Yale University Press.
Cumberland, RI. 1993. 354p. ISBN:0-300-05734-2, ISBN13:
978-0-300-05734-8. Dewey:759.5. LCCN:92-014504.
                              Audience: **g,l,u,f.** *Choice, 1993.*

Hopps, Walter & Bois,   ND237
  Yve-Alain
Edward Ruscha: Catalogue Raisonné of the Paintings. Gagosian
Gallery Staff (Contribution by). Trade Cloth. Gerhard Steidl
Druckerei und Verlag. Gottingen, 2004. 446p.
ISBN:3-88243-972-6, ISBN13: 978-3-88243-972-4.
Dewey:759.1/3. LCCN:2003-010329.
                              Audience: **g,l,u,f.**

Housley, Kathleen L.   ND237.F4313
Tranquil Power: The Art and Life of Perle Fine. Trade Paper.
Midmarch Arts Press. New York, NY. 2005. 256p.
ISBN:1-877675-54-7, ISBN13: 978-1-877675-54-6.
Dewey:759.13.
                              Audience: **l,u,f.**

Hughes, Robert   ND497.A86.H84
Frank Auerbach. Trade Paper. Thames & Hudson. New York,
NY. 1992. 240p. ISBN:0-500-27675-7, ISBN13:
978-0-500-27675-4. Dewey:759.2. LCCN:90-070337.
                              Audience: **u,f.** *Choice, 1991.*

Humfrey, Peter (Editor)   ND623.B39C36 2003
The Cambridge Companion to Giovanni Bellini. Cloth Text.
Cambridge University Press. New York, NY. 2003. 384p.
Cambridge Companions to the History of Art Ser.
ISBN:0-521-66296-6, ISBN13: 978-0-521-66296-3.
Dewey:759..5 B B. LCCN:2002-041535.
                              Audience: **l,u,f.** *Choice, 2004.*

Hungerford, Constance Cain   ND553.M5 H86 1999
Ernst Meissonier and Art for the French Bourgeoisie: Master in
His Genre. Trade Cloth. Cambridge University Press. New York,
NY. 1999. 288p. ISBN:0-521-63240-4, ISBN13:
978-0-521-63240-9. Dewey:709/.2 B. LCCN:98-036615.
                              Audience: **l,u,f.** *Choice, 1999.*

Hunter, Sam   ND237.H667A42002
Hans Hofmann. Trade Cloth. Rizzoli International Publications,
Inc. New York, NY. 2006. 282p. ISBN:0-8478-2380-6, ISBN13:
978-0-8478-2380-2. Dewey:759.13. LCCN:2002-102942.
                              Audience: **g,l,u,f.**

Hurlburt, Laurence P.   ND2608.H84 1989
The Mexican Muralists in the United States. Trade Cloth.
University of New Mexico Press. Albuquerque, NM. 1989.

343p. ISBN:0-8263-1134-2, ISBN13: 978-0-8263-1134-4.
Dewey:759.13. LCCN:88-030000.
                              Audience: **g,l,u,f.** *Choice, 1990.*

Hutton Turner, Elizabeth   ND237.O5A4 1999
Georgia O'Keeffe: The Poetry of Things. Cloth over Boards.
Yale University Press. Cumberland, RI. 1999. 160p.
ISBN:0-300-07935-4, ISBN13: 978-0-300-07935-7.
Dewey:759.13. LCCN:98-032429.
                              Audience: **g,l,u,f.** *Choice, 1999.*

Hyman, Timothy   ND553.B65H96 1998
Bonnard. Trade Paper. Thames & Hudson. New York, NY. 1998.
224p. World of Art Ser. ISBN:0-500-20310-5, ISBN13:
978-0-500-20310-1. Dewey:760/.092. LCCN:97-061113.
                              Audience: **g,l,u,f.**

Jawlensky, Angelica, et al.   ND699.J3 A41991
Alexej Von Jawlensky: Catalogue Raisonné of the Oil Paintings.
Alexej Von Jawlensky, Lucia Pieroni-Jawlensky & Maria
Jawlensky (Authors). Saddle Stitched, Cloth over Boards, Dust
Jacket. Philip Wilson Publishers, Ltd. London, 1991. 552p.
ISBN:0-85667-398-6, ISBN13: 978-0-85667-398-6.
Dewey:759.7. LCCN:91-060245.
                              Audience: **g,l,u,f.**

Jawlensky, Maria, et al.   ND699.J3
Alexej Von Jawlensky: Catalogue Raisonné of the Oil Paintings,
1934-1937. Lucia Jawlensky & Angelica Jawlensky (Authors).
Cloth over Boards. Philip Wilson Publishers, Ltd. London, 1993.
504p. ISBN:0-85667-420-6, ISBN13: 978-0-85667-420-4.
Dewey:759.7. LCCN:91-060245.
                              Audience: **g,l,u,f.**

Jawlensky, Maria, et al.   ND699.J3
Alexej Von Jawlensky: Catalogue Raisonné of the Oil Paintings
1914-1933. Lucia Pieroni-Jawlensky & Angelica Jawlensky
(Authors). Saddle Stitched, Cloth over Boards, Dust Jacket.
Philip Wilson Publishers, Ltd. London, 1992. 558p.
ISBN:0-85667-406-0, ISBN13: 978-0-85667-406-8.
Dewey:759.7. LCCN:92-080371.
                              Audience: **g,l,u,f.**

Jobert, Barthelemy   ND553.D33
Delacroix. Princeton. 1997.
                              Audience: **g,l,u,f.**

Johnson, Lee   ND553.D33A4 2002
The Paintings of Eugene Delacroix: Fourth Supplement and
Reprint of Third Supplement. Trade Cloth. Oxford University
Press, Inc. New York, NY. 2003. 362p. ISBN:0-19-925266-1,
ISBN13: 978-0-19-925266-4. Dewey:759.4.
                              Audience: **g,l,u,f.** *Choice, 2003.*

Joll, Evelyn (Author, Editor)   ND497.T8O94 2001
The Oxford Companion to J. M. W. Turner. Martin Butlin &
Luke Herrmann (Editors). Trade Cloth. Oxford University Press,
Inc. New York, NY. 2001. 448p. ISBN:0-19-860025-9, ISBN13:
978-0-19-860025-1. Dewey:759.2. LCCN:2001-267993.
                              Audience: **g,l,u,f.** *Choice, 2001.*

Junker, Patricia   ND237.C88A4 1998
John Steuart Curry: Inventing the Middle West. Henry Adams,
Thomas Hart Benton, Charles C. Eldredge, Robert L. Gambone,
M. Sue Kendall, Lucy J. Mathiak & Theodore F. Wolff
(Contribution by). Trade Cloth. Hudson Hills Press LLC.
Manchester, VT. 1998. 252p. ISBN:1-55595-139-2, ISBN13:
978-1-55595-139-9. Dewey:759.13. LCCN:97-049621.
                                      Audience: **g,l,u,f.** *Choice, 1998.*

Kahlo, Frida & Lozano,   ND259.K33F695132000
  Luis-Martin
Frida Kahlo. Trade Cloth. Bulfinch Press. Boston, MA. 2001.
260p. ISBN:0-8212-2766-1, ISBN13: 978-0-8212-2766-4.
Dewey:759.972. LCCN:2001-089093.
                                                Audience: **g,l,u,f.**

Kallir, Jane   ND237.O5
Grandma Moses in the Twenty-First Century. Roger Cardinal,
Michael D. Hall & Lynda Roscoe Hartigan (Contribution by).
Cloth over Boards. Yale University Press. Cumberland, RI.
2001. 264p. ISBN:0-300-08927-9, ISBN13: 978-0-300-08927-1.
Dewey:759.1/3.
                                                Audience: **g,l,u,f.**

Kammen, Michael G.   98-48441 [N]
Robert Gwathmey: The Life and Art of a Passionate Observer.
Trade Cloth. University of North Carolina Press. Chapel Hill,
NC. 1999. 272p. ISBN:0-8078-2495-X, ISBN13:
978-0-8078-2495-5. Dewey:759.13. LCCN:98-048441.
                                      Audience: **g,l,f.** *Choice, 2000.*

Kanter, Laurence &   ND623.F5A4 2005
  Palladino, Pia
Fra Angelico. Victor M. Schmidt, Magnolia Scudieri & Carl B.
Strehlke (Contribution by). Cloth over Boards. Yale University
Press. Cumberland, RI. 2005. 348p. Metropolitan Museum of
Art Ser. ISBN:0-300-11140-1, ISBN13: 978-0-300-11140-8.
Dewey:759.5. LCCN:2005-023349.
                                                Audience: **g,l,u,f.**

Kaplan, Rachel & Marani,   ND623.L5M324132000
  Pietro C.
Leonardo da Vinci: The Complete Paintings. A. Lawrence
Jenkens (Translator). Trade Cloth. Harry N. Abrams, Inc. New
York, NY. 2000. 384p. ISBN:0-8109-3581-3, ISBN13:
978-0-8109-3581-5. Dewey:759.5. LCCN:00-027556.
                                      Audience: **g,l,u,f.** *Choice, 2001.*

Karmel, Pepe   ND553.P5K265 2002
Picasso and the Invention of Cubism. Cloth over Boards. Yale
University Press. Cumberland, RI. 2003. 248p.
ISBN:0-300-09436-1, ISBN13: 978-0-300-09436-7.
Dewey:759.4. LCCN:2002-013603.
                                      Audience: **g,l,u,f.** *Choice, 2004.*

Kemp, Martin   ND623.L5
Leonardo. Trade Paper. Oxford University Press, Inc. New York,
NY. 2006. 304p. ISBN:0-19-280644-0, ISBN13:
978-0-19-280644-4. Dewey:709/.2.
                                                Audience: **g,l,u,f.**

Kendall, Richard   ND653.G7A41998
Van Gogh's Van Goghs. John Leighton (Contribution by). Trade
Cloth. Harry N. Abrams, Inc. New York, NY. 1998. 160p.
ISBN:0-8109-6366-3, ISBN13: 978-0-8109-6366-5.
Dewey:759.9492. LCCN:98-021871.
                                      Audience: **g,l,u,f.** *Choice, 1999.*

King, Ross   ND623.B9.K55 2003
Michelangelo and the Pope's Ceiling. Trade Paper. Penguin
Group (USA) Inc. New York, NY. 2003. 384p.
ISBN:0-14-200369-7, ISBN13: 978-0-14-200369-5.
Dewey:759.5. LCCN:2003-283284.
                                                Audience: **g,l,u,f.**

Klein, Mason & Berger,   ND623.M67A42004
  Maurice
Modigliani: Beyond the Myth. Jewish Museum (New York,
N.Y.) Staff, Art Gallery of Ontario Staff & Phillips Collection
Staff (Contribution by). Trade Cloth. Yale University Press.
Cumberland, RI. 2004. xiii, 241p. ISBN:0-300-10573-8,
ISBN13: 978-0-300-10573-5. Dewey:759.5.
LCCN:2003-026696.
                                      Audience: **g,l,u,f.** *Choice, 2004.*

Knutson, Anne Classen   ND237.W93A42005
Andrew Wyeth: Memory and Magic. John Wilmerding
(Introduction by), Christopher Crosman, Kathleen A. Foster &
Michael R. Taylor (Contribution by). Saddle Stitched, Cloth
over Boards, Dust Jacket. Rizzoli International Publications, Inc.
New York, NY. 2005. 223p. ISBN:0-8478-2771-2, ISBN13:
978-0-8478-2771-8. Dewey:759.13. LCCN:2005-012837.
                                      Audience: **g,l,u,f.** *Choice, 2006.*

Kornhauser, Elizabeth &   ND237.H3435A4 2003
  McDonnell, Patricia
Marsden Hartley: American Modernist. Cloth over Boards. Yale
University Press. Cumberland, RI. 2002. 352p.
ISBN:0-300-09767-0, ISBN13: 978-0-300-09767-2.
Dewey:759.13. LCCN:2002-008215.
                                      Audience: **g,l,u,f.** *Choice, 2003.*

Kosinski, Dorothy M.   ND553.L58.A4 1994
  (Editor)
Fernand Leger, 1911-1924: The Rhythm of Modern Life. Trade
Cloth. Prestel Publishing. New York, NY. 1994. 256p.
ISBN:3-7913-1372-X, ISBN13: 978-3-7913-1372-6.
Dewey:759.4. LCCN:96-109202.
                                      Audience: **g,l,u,f.** *Choice, 1994.*

Krell, Alan   ND553.M3K74 1996
Manet: And the Painters of Contemporary Life. Trade Paper.
Thames & Hudson. New York, NY. 1996. 208p. The World of
Art Ser. ISBN:0-500-20289-3, ISBN13: 978-0-500-20289-0.
Dewey:759.4. LCCN:95-060470.
                                                Audience: **g,l,u,f.**

Landau, Ellen G.   N6537.K69A41995
Lee Krasner: A Catalogue Raisonné. Eugene V. Thaw (Preface
by), Jeffrey D. Grove (Contribution by). Trade Cloth. Harry N.
Abrams, Inc. New York, NY. 1995. 336p. ISBN:0-8109-3513-9,
ISBN13: 978-0-8109-3513-6. Dewey:759.13. LCCN:94-041535.
                                      Audience: **g,l,u,f.** *Choice, 1996.*

Landauer, Susan   ND237.B59364L36
Elmer Bischoff: The Ethics of Paint. Trade Cloth. University of
California Press. Berkeley, CA. 2001. 230p.
ISBN:0-520-23041-8, ISBN13: 978-0-520-23041-5.
Dewey:759.13. LCCN:00-065794.
                    Audience: **g,l,u,f.** *Choice, 2002.*

Lee, Simon   ND553.D25L44 1999
David. Trade Paper. Phaidon Press. London, 1999. 352p. Art and
Ideas Ser. ISBN:0-7148-3804-7, ISBN13: 978-0-7148-3804-5.
Dewey:759.4. LCCN:99-233997.
                    Audience: **g,l,u,f.** *Choice, 1999.*

Leopold, Rudolf (Editor)   ND511.5
Egon Schiele: Landscapes. Trade Cloth. Prestel Publishing. New
York, NY. 2004. 208p. ISBN:3-7913-3213-9, ISBN13:
978-3-7913-3213-0. Dewey:759.36. LCCN:2006-530052.
                    Audience: **g,l,u,f.** *Choice, 2005.*

Levin, Gail   ND237.H75A4 2001
The Complete Oil Paintings of Edward Hopper. Trade Cloth. W.
W. Norton & Company, Inc. New York, NY. 2001. 367p.
ISBN:0-393-04996-5, ISBN13: 978-0-393-04996-1.
Dewey:759.13. LCCN:00-056616.
                    Audience: **g,l,u,f.**

Levin, Gail   ND1839.H63A4 2001
The Complete Watercolors of Edward Hopper. Trade Cloth. W.
W. Norton & Company, Inc. New York, NY. 2001. 350p.
ISBN:0-393-04995-7, ISBN13: 978-0-393-04995-4.
Dewey:759.13. LCCN:00-056617.
                    Audience: **g,l,u,f.**

Levine, Steven Z.   ND553.M7L49 1994
Monet, Narcissus, and Self-Reflection: The Modernist Myth of
the Self. Trade Cloth. University of Chicago Press. Chicago, IL.
1995. 388p. ISBN:0-226-47543-3, ISBN13: 978-0-226-47543-1.
Dewey:759.4. LCCN:94-001105.
                    Audience: **g,l,u,f.** *Choice, 1995.*

Linfert, Carl   N6953.B66L562003
Bosch. Trade Paper. Harry N. Abrams, Inc. New York, NY.
2003. 128p. Masters of Art Ser. ISBN:0-8109-9132-2, ISBN13:
978-0-8109-9132-3. Dewey:759.9492. LCCN:2003-013679.
                    Audience: **g,l,u,f.**

Links, J. G.   ND623.C2L49 1994
Canaletto. Ed. 2. Trade Paper. Phaidon Press. London, 1999.
256p. ISBN:0-7148-3843-8, ISBN13: 978-0-7148-3843-4.
Dewey:759.5. LCCN:00-500222.
                    Audience: **g,l,u,f.** **B** *Choice, 1990.*

Livingston, Jane, et al.   ND237.M58 A4 2002
The Paintings of Joan Mitchell. Joan Mitchell, Linda Nochlin &
Yvette Lee (Authors), Whitney Museum of American Art Staff
(Contribution by). Trade Paper. University of California Press.
Berkeley, CA. 2002. 240p. ISBN:0-520-23570-3, ISBN13:
978-0-520-23570-0. Dewey:759.13. LCCN:2001-058514.
                    Audience: **g,l,u,f.** *Choice, 2002.*

Locke, Nancy   ND553.M3.L63 2001
Manet and the Family Romance. Trade Cloth. Princeton
University Press. Princeton, NJ. 2001. 224p.
ISBN:0-691-05060-0, ISBN13: 978-0-691-05060-7.
Dewey:759.4. LCCN:00⁵064265.
                    Audience: **g,l,u,f.** *Choice, 2001.*

Lucie-Smith, Edward   ND237.L278
Julio Larraz. Trade Cloth. Skira Editore. Milano, 2003. 256p.
ISBN:88-8491-347-0, ISBN13: 978-88-8491-347-0.
Dewey:759.1/3.
                    Audience: **g,l,u,f.**

Ludman, Joan, et al.   N6537.P63A42001
Fairfield Porter: A Catalogue Raisonné of the Paintings,
Watercolors, and Pastels. William C. Agee, Rackstraw Downes
& John T. Spike (Authors). Trade Cloth. Hudson Hills Press
LLC. Manchester, VT. 2001. 400p. ISBN:1-55595-165-1,
ISBN13: 978-1-55595-165-8. Dewey:759.13. LCCN:00-054095.
                    Audience: **g,l,u,f.** *Choice, 2001.*

Lynes, Barbara Buhler, et   ND237.O5A4 2004
al.
Georgia O'Keeffe and New Mexico: A Sense of Place. Lesley
Poling-Kempes & Frederick W. Turner (Authors), Georgia
O'Keeffe Museum Staff, Columbus Museum of Art Staff &
Delaware Art Museum Staff (Contribution by). Trade Cloth.
Princeton University Press. Princeton, NJ. 2004. 144p.
ISBN:0-691-11659-8, ISBN13: 978-0-691-11659-4.
Dewey:759.13. LCCN:2003-062202.
                    Audience: **g,l,u,f.**

Maloon, Terence & Art   ND553.M7
Gallery of New South Wales Staff
Camille Pissarro. Trade Paper. Yale University Press.
Cumberland, RI. 2006. 259p. ISBN:0-300-11552-0, ISBN13:
978-0-300-11552-9. Dewey:759.4.
                    Audience: **g,l,u,f.** *Choice, 2006.*

Mancoff, Debra N. (Editor)   ND497.M6J64 2001
John Everett Millais: Beyond the Pre-Raphaelite Brotherhood.
Cloth over Boards. Yale University Press. Cumberland, RI.
2001. 260p. Studies in British Art, Vol. 7 ISBN:0-300-09119-2,
ISBN13: 978-0-300-09119-9. Dewey:759.2.
LCCN:2001-088448.
                    Audience: **g,l,u,f.** *Choice, 2002.*

Mann, Carol   ND623.M67M26 1991
Modigliani. Trade Paper. Thames & Hudson. New York, NY.
1991. 216p. World of Art Ser. ISBN:0-500-20176-5, ISBN13:
978-0-500-20176-3. Dewey:759.5. LCCN:90-072012.
                    Audience: **g,l,u,f.**

Mannings, David   ND497.R4A4 2000
Sir Joshua Reynolds: A Complete Catalogue of His Paintings.
Martin Postle (Contribution by). Cloth over Boards. Yale
University Press. Cumberland, RI. 2000. 1264p. Paul Mellon
Centre for Studies in British Art ISBN:0-300-08533-8, ISBN13:
978-0-300-08533-4. Dewey:759.2. LCCN:00-106557.
                    Audience: **l,u,f.** *Choice, 2001.*

Marnham, Patrick   N7639.P66G662000
Dreaming with His Eyes Open: A Life of Diego Rivera. Trade
Paper. University of California Press. Berkeley, CA. 2000. 368p.
Discovery Ser. ISBN:0-520-22408-6, ISBN13:
978-0-520-22408-7. Dewey:759.9/72. LCCN:99-041133.
           Audience: **g,l,u,f.**

Mauner, George   ND553.M3A42000
Manet: The Still Life Paintings. Trade Cloth. Harry N. Abrams,
Inc. New York, NY. 2001. 200p. ISBN:0-8109-4391-3, ISBN13:
978-0-8109-4391-9. Dewey:759.4. LCCN:00-042009.
           Audience: **g,l,u,f.** *Choice, 2001.*

Meilman, Patricia (Editor)   N6923.T57C36 2003
The Companion to Titian. Trade Cloth. Cambridge University
Press. New York, NY. 2003. 388p. Cambridge Companions to
the History of Art Ser. ISBN:0-521-79180-4, ISBN13:
978-0-521-79180-9. Dewey:759.5. LCCN:2002-041242.
           Audience: **l,u,f.** *Choice, 2004.*

Mello, Renato Gonzalez &   ND259.O7A4 2002
  Ades, Dawn
Jose Clemente Orozco in the United States. Trade Cloth. W. W.
Norton & Company, Inc. New York, NY. 2002. 288p.
ISBN:0-393-04176-X, ISBN13: 978-0-393-04176-7.
Dewey:759.972. LCCN:2001-039692.
           Audience: **g,l,u,f.**

Merot, Alain   ND553.P8M4413 1990
Nicolas Poussin. Trade Cloth. Abbeville Press, Inc. New York,
NY. 1990. 256p. ISBN:1-55859-120-6, ISBN13:
978-1-55859-120-2. Dewey:759.4. LCCN:90-039623.
           Audience: **g,l,u,f.** *Choice, 1991.*

Messer, Thomas M.   ND699.K3M471997
Kandinsky. Trade Cloth. Harry N. Abrams, Inc. New York, NY.
1997. 128p. Masters of Art Ser. ISBN:0-8109-1228-7, ISBN13:
978-0-8109-1228-1. Dewey:759.7. LCCN:96-037573.
           Audience: **g,l,u,f.** *Choice, 1998.*

Messinger, Lisa Mintz   N6537.O39M48 2001
Georgia O'Keeffe. Trade Paper. Thames & Hudson. New York,
NY. 2001. 192p. World of Art Ser. ISBN:0-500-20340-7,
ISBN13: 978-0-500-20340-8. Dewey:759.13 B.
LCCN:00-107990.
           Audience: **g,l,u,f.** *Choice, 2001.*

Milosch, Jane C. (Editor)   ND237
Grant Wood's Studio: Birthplace of American Gothic. Wanda M.
Corn, James M. Dennis, Joni L. Kinsey & Deba Foxley Leach
(Contribution by). Saddle Stitched, Cloth over Boards, Dust
Jacket. Prestel Publishing. New York, NY. 2005. 143p.
ISBN:3-7913-3325-9, ISBN13: 978-3-7913-3325-0.
Dewey:759.13. LCCN:2005-296177.
           Audience: **g,l,u,f.** *Choice, 2006.*

Moir, Alfred   ND623.C26M591989
Caravaggio. Trade Cloth. Harry N. Abrams, Inc. New York, NY.
1989. 128p. Masters of Art Ser. ISBN:0-8109-3150-8, ISBN13:
978-0-8109-3150-3. Dewey:759.5 B. LCCN:89-000298.
           Audience: **g,l,u,f.**

Motherwell, Robert;   ND237.M852A35 1992
  Terenzio, Stephania
The Collected Writings of Robert Motherwell. Stephania
Terenzio (Editor). Oxford University Press, Inc. 1993.
ISBN:0-19-507700-8, ISBN13: 978-0-19-507700-1.
           Audience: **g,l,u,f.**

Naifeh, Steven & Smith,   ND237.P73
  Gregory W.
Jackson Pollock: An American Saga. Trade Paper.
Woodward/White, Inc. Aiken, SC. 1998. ISBN:0-913391-19-0,
ISBN13: 978-0-913391-19-8. Dewey:759.13.
           Audience: **g,l,u,f.**

Nash, Steven A. (Editor)   ND553.P5A4 1998
Picasso and the War Years, 1937-1945. Trade Cloth. Thames &
Hudson. New York, NY. 1998. 256p. ISBN:0-500-09274-5,
ISBN13: 978-0-500-09274-3. Dewey:759.4. LCCN:98-060335.
           Audience: **g,l,u,f.** *Choice, 1999.*

Neff, Emily Ballew &   ND237.R36A4 2000
  Phelan, Wynne H.
Frederic Remington: The Hogg Brothers Collection of the
Museum of Fine Arts, Houston. Trade Cloth. Princeton
University Press. Princeton, NJ. 2000. 160p.
ISBN:0-691-04928-9, ISBN13: 978-0-691-04928-1.
Dewey:709/.2. LCCN:99-039063.
           Audience: **g,l,u,f.** *Choice, 2000.*

Nesbett, Peter T. & DuBois,   ND237.O5
  Michelle
The Complete Jacob Lawrence: Painting, Drawings, and Murals
(1935-1999), A Catalogue Raisonné. Trade Cloth, Box or
Slipcased. University of Washington Press. Seattle, WA. 2003.
360p. ISBN:0-295-97963-1, ISBN13: 978-0-295-97963-2.
Dewey:759.1/3.
           Audience: **g,l,u,f.** *Choice, 2001.*

Nigro, Salvatore S.   ND623.P8P54131994
Pontormo: Paintings. Trade Cloth. Harry N. Abrams, Inc. New
York, NY. 1994. 160p. ISBN:0-8109-3727-1, ISBN13:
978-0-8109-3727-7. Dewey:759.5. LCCN:93-031283.
           Audience: **g,l,u,f.** *Choice, 1994.*

Nodelman, Sheldon   ND237.R725N63 1997
The Rothko Chapel Paintings: Origins, Structure, Meaning.
Trade Cloth. University of Texas Press. Austin, TX. 1997. 359p.
ISBN:0-939594-36-6, ISBN13: 978-0-939594-36-8.
Dewey:759.13. LCCN:96-048538.
           Audience: **g,l,u,f.** *Choice, 1997.*

Nordland, Gerald   ND237.D465N67 2001
Richard Diebenkorn. Ed. 2. Trade Cloth. Rizzoli International
Publications, Inc. New York, NY. 2001. 280p.
ISBN:0-8478-2348-2, ISBN13: 978-0-8478-2348-2.
Dewey:759.13. LCCN:00-068841.
           Audience: **g,l,u,f.**

North, John David   ND588.H7A64 2002
The Ambassadors' Secret: Holbein and the World of the
Renaissance. Trade Cloth. Continuum International Publishing

Group, Ltd. London, 2003. 368p. ISBN:1-85285-330-1, ISBN13: 978-1-85285-330-3. Dewey:759.3. LCCN:2002-190232.

Audience: **l,u,f.** *Choice, 2003.*

Ollinger-Zinqu, Gisèle   **ND673.M35A4 1998**
Magritte, 1898-1967. Harry N. Abrams, Inc. 1998.
ISBN:0-8109-6359-0, ISBN13: 978-0-8109-6359-7.

Audience: **g,l,f.**

Ormond, Richard &   **ND237.S3A4 1998**
  Kilmurray, Elaine
John Singer Sargent: The Early Portraits. Cloth over Boards.
Yale University Press. Cumberland, RI. 1998. 304p. Complete
Paintings Ser., Vol. 1 ISBN:0-300-07245-7, ISBN13:
978-0-300-07245-7. Dewey:759.13. LCCN:97-027380.

Audience: **g,l,u,f.** *Choice, 1998.*

Ormond, Richard, et al.   **ND237.S3A4 2002**
John Singer Sargent: Portraits of the 1890s Complete Paintings.
Elaine Kilmurray & Warren Adelson (Authors). Cloth over
Boards. Yale University Press. Cumberland, RI. 2002. 240p.
Paul Mellon Centre for Studies in British Art
ISBN:0-300-09067-6, ISBN13: 978-0-300-09067-3.
Dewey:759.1/3. LCCN:2002-110823.

Audience: **g,l,u,f.** *Choice, 2003.*

Pach, Walter   **ND553.R45P282003**
Renoir. Trade Paper. Harry N. Abrams, Inc. New York, NY.
2003. 128p. ISBN:0-8109-9135-7, ISBN13: 978-0-8109-9135-4.
Dewey:759.4. LCCN:2003-013702.

Audience: **g,l,u,f.**

Pantazzi, Michael, et al.   **ND553**
Corot. Vincent Pomarede & Gary Tinterow (Authors). Trade
Cloth. Harry N. Abrams, Inc. New York, NY. 1996. 540p.
ISBN:0-8109-6501-1, ISBN13: 978-0-8109-6501-0.
Dewey:759.4. LCCN:96-006768.

Audience: **g,l,u,f.** *Choice, 1997.*

Picasso Project Staff   **ND553.P5 A4 2000**
  (Author, Introduction by)
Picasso's Paintings, Watercolors, Drawings and Sculpture - A
Comprehensive Illustrated Catalogue: Liberation and Post-War
Years, 1944-1949. Trade Cloth. Alan Wofsy Fine Arts. San
Francisco, CA. 2000. 288p. ISBN:1-55660-237-5, ISBN13:
978-1-55660-237-5. Dewey:759.6.

Audience: **g,l,u,f.** *Choice, 2000.*

Platzman, Steven   **ND553.C33P5582001**
Cézanne: The Self-Portraits. Trade Cloth. University of
California Press. Berkeley, CA. 2001. 224p.
ISBN:0-520-23291-7, ISBN13: 978-0-520-23291-4.
Dewey:759.4. LCCN:2001-027740.

Audience: **l,u,f.** *Choice, 2002.*

Pollock, Griselda   **ND237.C3P65 1998**
Mary Cassatt: Painter of Modern Women. Trade Paper. Thames
& Hudson. New York, NY. 1998. 224p. World of Art Ser.
ISBN:0-500-20317-2, ISBN13: 978-0-500-20317-0.
Dewey:759.13. LCCN:98-060039.

Audience: **g,l,u,f.** *Choice, 1999.*

Rewald, John   **ND553.S5R4371990**
Seurat: A Biography. Trade Cloth. Harry N. Abrams, Inc. New
York, NY. 1990. 240p. ISBN:0-8109-3814-6, ISBN13:
978-0-8109-3814-4. Dewey:759.4 B. LCCN:90-030519.

Audience: **g,l,u,f.** *Choice, 1991.*

Rewald, John, et al.   **ND553.C33R461996**
Paintings of Paul Cezanne: A Catalogue Raisonné. Walter
Feilchenfeldt & Jayne Warman (Authors). Trade Cloth, Box or
Slipcased. Harry N. Abrams, Inc. New York, NY. 1996. 880p.
ISBN:0-8109-4044-2, ISBN13: 978-0-8109-4044-4.
Dewey:759.4. LCCN:96-010853.

Audience: **l,u,f.**

Rhodes, Richard   **QL31.A9R524 2004**
John James Audubon: The Making of an American. Trade Cloth.
Alfred A. Knopf Inc. New York, NY. 2004. 528p.
ISBN:0-375-41412-6, ISBN13: 978-0-375-41412-1.
Dewey:598/.092 B. LCCN:2003-069489.

Audience: **g,l,u,f.** *Choice, 2005.*

Richter, Gerhard   **ND588.R48**
Gerhard Richter: Catalogue Raisonné. Trade Cloth. Edition
Cantz. Ostfildern, 1997. ISBN:3-89322-554-4, ISBN13:
978-3-89322-554-5. Dewey:759.3.

Audience: **g,l,u,f.**

Ridolfi, Carlo   **ND623.T7R52131996**
The Life of Titian. Julia C. Bondanella, Peter Bondanella, Bruce
Cole & Jody R. Shiffman (Editors), Julia C. Bondanella & Peter
Bondanella (Translators). Trade Cloth. Pennsylvania State
University Press. University Park, PA. 1996. 168p.
ISBN:0-271-01547-0, ISBN13: 978-0-271-01547-7.
Dewey:759.5 B. LCCN:95-038040.

Audience: **g,l,u,f.** *Choice, 1997.*

Robb, Peter   **ND623.C26R62 2000**
M: The Man Who Became Carravagio. Cloth over Boards.
Henry Holt & Company. New York, NY. 2000. 560p.
ISBN:0-8050-6356-0, ISBN13: 978-0-8050-6356-1.
Dewey:759.5. LCCN:99-043576.

Audience: **g,l,u,f.** *Choice, 2000.*

Roberts, Leonard &   **ND497 .H89 1997**
  Wildman, Stephen
Arthur Hughes: His Life and Works. Trade Cloth. Antique
Collectors' Club. Easthampton, MA. 1997. 304p.
ISBN:1-85149-262-3, ISBN13: 978-1-85149-262-6.
Dewey:759.2.

Audience: **g,l,u,f.**

Roberts, Warren   **ND553.D25R54 2000**
Jacques-Louis David and Jean-Louis Prieur, Revolutionary
Artists: The Public, the Populace, and Images of the French
Revolution. Cloth Text. State University of New York Press.
Albany, NY. 1999. 384p. ISBN:0-7914-4287-X, ISBN13:
978-0-7914-4287-6. Dewey:759.4 B. LCCN:99-037078.

Audience: **g,l,u,f.** *Choice, 2000.*

Rose, Ingrid & Quiroz,   **NE2312.T39**
   Roderick S. (Editors)
The Lithographs of Prentiss Taylor: A Catalogue Raisonné.
Trade Cloth. Fordham University Press. Bronx, NY. 1996. 132p.
ISBN:0-8232-1672-1, ISBN13: 978-0-8232-1672-7.
Dewey:769.92.
                      Audience: **g,l,u,f.** *Choice, 1996.*

Rosenblum, Robert   **ND553.I5R631990**
Ingres. Trade Cloth. Harry N. Abrams, Inc. New York, NY.
1990. 128p. Masters of Art Ser. ISBN:0-8109-3451-5, ISBN13:
978-0-8109-3451-1. Dewey:759.4. LCCN:90-000351.
                      Audience: **g,l,u,f.**

Rosenthal, Lisa   **ND673.R9R67 2006**
Gender, Politics, and Allegory in the Art of Rubens. Trade
Cloth. Cambridge University Press. New York, NY. 2005. 328p.
ISBN:0-521-84244-1, ISBN13: 978-0-521-84244-0.
Dewey:759.9493. LCCN:2005-010514.
                      Audience: **l,u,f.** *Choice, 2006.*

Rosenthal, Michael   **ND497.C7R67 1987**
Constable. Trade Paper. Thames & Hudson. New York, NY.
1987. 216p. World of Art Ser. ISBN:0-500-20211-7, ISBN13:
978-0-500-20211-1. Dewey:759.2. LCCN:86-050221.
                      Audience: **g,l,u,f.**

Rosenthal, Michael &   **N6797.G34A42002**
   Myrone, Martin
Thomas Gainsborough. Trade Cloth. Harry N. Abrams, Inc. New
York, NY. 2003. 296p. ISBN:0-8109-4440-5, ISBN13:
978-0-8109-4440-4. Dewey:759.2. LCCN:2002-112084.
                      Audience: **g,l,u,f.**

Ross, Doran H. & Marzio,   **NK7415.G45M87 2002**
   Frances
Gold of the Akan from the Glassell Collection. Museum of Fine
Arts, Houston Staff (Contribution by). Trade Cloth. Museum of
Fine Arts, Houston. Houston, TX. 2003. 296p.
ISBN:0-89090-115-5, ISBN13: 978-0-89090-115-1.
Dewey:739.2/2/089963385. LCCN:2002-033702.
                      Audience: **g,l,u,f.** *Choice, 2003.*

Rothko, Mark   **ND237.R725A35 2004**
The Artist's Reality: Philosophies of Art. Christopher Rothko
(Editor), Kate Prizel Rothko (Contribution by). Cloth over
Boards. Yale University Press. Cumberland, RI. 2004. 176p.
ISBN:0-300-10253-4, ISBN13: 978-0-300-10253-6.
Dewey:759.13. LCCN:2004-011574.
                      Audience: **l,u,f.** *Choice, 2005.*

Rubin, James Henry   **ND553.M3R8 1994**
Manet's Silence and the Poetics of Bouquets. Trade Cloth.
Harvard University Press. Cambridge, MA. 1994. 256p. Essays
in Art and Culture Ser. ISBN:0-674-54802-7, ISBN13:
978-0-674-54802-2. Dewey:759.4. LCCN:93-038505.
                      Audience: **g,l,u,f.** *Choice, 1994.*

Russell, John   **ND497.B16R8 1993**
Francis Bacon. Ed. 2. Trade Paper. Thames & Hudson. New
York, NY. 1993. 208p. World of Art Ser. ISBN:0-500-20271-0,

ISBN13: 978-0-500-20271-5. Dewey:759.9415.
LCCN:93-060306.
                      Audience: **g,l,u,f.** *B*

Sagner-Duchting, Karin   **ND553.M7.A4 2001**
Monet and Modernism. Trade Cloth. Prestel Publishing. New
York, NY. 2002. 312p. ISBN:3-7913-2615-5, ISBN13:
978-3-7913-2615-3. Dewey:759.06. LCCN:2002-277230.
                      Audience: **g,l,u,f.** *Choice, 2002.*

Sagner-Duchting, Karin   **ND553.M7S244 1994**
Monet at Giverny. Trade Cloth. Prestel Publishing. New York,
NY. 1994. 120p. Pegasus Library ISBN:3-7913-1384-3, ISBN13:
978-3-7913-1384-9. Dewey:759.4. LCCN:95-157090.
                      Audience: **g,l,u,f.** *Choice, 1995.*

Saunders, Richard H.   **ND1329.S63S28 1995**
John Smibert: Colonial America's First Portrait Painter. Cloth
over Boards. Yale University Press. Cumberland, RI. 1995.
294p. Barra Foundation Bks. ISBN:0-300-04258-2, ISBN13:
978-0-300-04258-0. Dewey:759.13 B. LCCN:94-042682.
                      Audience: **g,l,u,f.** *Choice, 1996.*

Saunders, Richard H.   **ND1329.S63S281995**
John Smibert: Colonial America's First Portrait Painter. Yale
University Press. 1996. ISBN:0-300-04258-2, ISBN13:
978-0-300-04258-0.
                      Audience: **g,l,u,f.**

Schaffner, Ingrid & Abrams,   **ND553.P5S3841999**
   Harry N., Staff
Pablo Picasso. Trade Cloth. Harry N. Abrams, Inc. New York,
NY. 1999. 112p. Essential Ser. ISBN:0-8109-5820-1, ISBN13:
978-0-8109-5820-3. Dewey:759.6. LCCN:98-074609.
                      Audience: **g,l.**

Schapiro, Meyer   **ND553.C33S382004**
Cezanne. Trade Paper. Harry N. Abrams, Inc. New York, NY.
2004. 128p. Masters of Art Ser. ISBN:0-8109-9146-2, ISBN13:
978-0-8109-9146-0. Dewey:759.4. LCCN:2003-022518.
                      Audience: **g,l,u,f.**

Schapiro, Meyer   **ND653.G7S3772003**
Van Gogh. Trade Paper. Harry N. Abrams, Inc. New York, NY.
2003. 128p. ISBN:0-8109-9134-9, ISBN13: 978-0-8109-9134-7.
Dewey:759.9492 B. LCCN:2003-013776.
                      Audience: **g,l,u,f.**

Schmied, Wieland   **ND237.H75S361995**
Edward Hopper: Portraits of America. Trade Cloth. Prestel
Verlag, Germany. Munchen, 1995. 126p. Pegasus Library
ISBN:3-7913-1480-7, ISBN13: 978-3-7913-1480-8.
Dewey:759.13. LCCN:98-149566.
                      Audience: **g,l,u,f.** *Choice, 1996.*

Scott, Katie & Warwick,   **ND553.P8 C58 1999**
   Genevieve (Editors)
Commemorating Poussin: Reception and Interpretation of the
Artist. Trade Cloth. Cambridge University Press. New York, NY.
1999. 254p. ISBN:0-521-64004-0, ISBN13: 978-0-521-64004-6.
Dewey:759.4. LCCN:98-029499.
                      Audience: **l,u,f.** *Choice, 2000.*

Seitz, William C.   ND553.M7S42003
Monet. Trade Paper. Harry N. Abrams, Inc. New York, NY.
2003. 128p. ISBN:0-8109-9131-4, ISBN13: 978-0-8109-9131-6.
Dewey:759.4. LCCN:2003-013701.
> Audience: **g,l,u,f.**

Sheriff, Mary D.   ND553.F7S53 1990
Fragonard: Art and Eroticism. Trade Cloth. University of
Chicago Press. Chicago, IL. 1990. 253p. ISBN:0-226-75273-9,
ISBN13: 978-0-226-75273-0. Dewey:759.4. LCCN:89-004783.
> Audience: **g,l,u,f.** *Choice, 1990.*

Shiff, Richard   N6537.N48A42002
Barnett Newman. Ann Temkin (Editor). Cloth over Boards. Yale
University Press. Cumberland, RI. 2002. 248p.
ISBN:0-300-09429-9, ISBN13: 978-0-300-09429-9.
Dewey:709/.2. LCCN:2001-059841.
> Audience: **g,l,u,f.** *Choice, 2003, 2002.*

Silcox, David P.   ND245.5.S4S55 2003
The Group of Seven and Tom Thomson. Trade Cloth. Firefly
Books, Ltd. Tonawanda, NY. 2003. 448p. ISBN:1-55297-605-X,
ISBN13: 978-1-55297-605-0. Dewey:759. LCCN:2003-363860.
> Audience: **g,l,u,f.** *Choice, 2004.*

Simon, Joan   ND237.R72484S551999
Susan Rothenberg. Trade Paper. Harry N. Abrams, Inc. New
York, NY. 2000. 206p. ISBN:0-8109-2748-9, ISBN13:
978-0-8109-2748-3. Dewey:759.13 B.
> Audience: **g,l,u,f.** *Choice, 1992.*

Slive, Seymour   N6953.R8
Jacob Van Ruisdael: Master of Landscape. Cloth over Boards.
Yale University Press. Cumberland, RI. 2005. 296p.
ISBN:1-903973-24-4, ISBN13: 978-1-903973-24-0. Dewey:706.
LCCN:2006-276766.
> Audience: **g,l,u,f.** *Choice, 2006.*

Smith, Elise L.   ND653.L85S631992
The Paintings of Lucas van Leyden: A New Appraisal, with
Catalogue Raisonné. Cloth Text. University of Missouri Press.
Columbia, MO. 1992. 408p. ISBN:0-8262-0824-X, ISBN13:
978-0-8262-0824-8. Dewey:759.9492. LCCN:92-018250.
> Audience: **g,l,u,f.** *Choice, 1993.*

Solomon, Deborah   ND237.P73S65 2001
Jackson Pollock: A Biography. Trade Paper. Cooper Square
Publishers, Inc. New York, NY. 2001. 312p.
ISBN:0-8154-1182-0, ISBN13: 978-0-8154-1182-6.
Dewey:759.13 B. LCCN:2001-028915.
> Audience: **g,l,u,f.**

Spate, Virginia   ND553.M7
Claude Monet: The Color of Time. Ed. Reprint, illustrated.
Thames and Hudson. 2001. ISBN:0-500-28273-0, ISBN13:
978-0-500-28273-1.
> Audience: **g,l,u,f.**

Spicer, Joaneath (Editor)   ND651.U88S671997
Masters of Light: Dutch Painters in Utrecht During the Golden
Age. Lynn Federle-Orr (Illustrator). Cloth over Boards. Yale
University Press. Cumberland, RI. 1997. 400p.

ISBN:0-300-07339-9, ISBN13: 978-0-300-07339-3.
Dewey:759.9/49232/09032. LCCN:97-061810.
> Audience: **g,l,u,f.** *Choice, 1998.*

Spike, John T.   ND623.F5A4 1997
Fra Angelico. Trade Cloth. Abbeville Press, Inc. New York, NY.
1997. 280p. ISBN:0-7892-0322-7, ISBN13: 978-0-7892-0322-9.
Dewey:759.5. LCCN:96-051128.
> Audience: **g,l,u,f.** *Choice, 1997.*

Spring, Justin   N6537.P63S66 2000
Fairfield Porter: A Life in Art. Cloth over Boards. Yale
University Press. Cumberland, RI. 1999. 400p.
ISBN:0-300-07637-1, ISBN13: 978-0-300-07637-0.
Dewey:700/.92 B. LCCN:99-030563.
> Audience: **g,l,u,f.** *Choice, 2000.*

Spring, Justin & Abrams,   ND237.H75S681998
  Harry N., Staff
Edward Hopper. Trade Cloth. Harry N. Abrams, Inc. New York,
NY. 1998. 112p. Essential Ser. ISBN:0-8109-5805-8, ISBN13:
978-0-8109-5805-0. Dewey:759.13. LCCN:98-071937.
> Audience: **g,l,u,f.**

Spring, Justin & Abrams,   ND237.P73S681998
  Harry N., Staff
Jackson Pollock. Trade Cloth. Harry N. Abrams, Inc. New York,
NY. 1998. 112p. ISBN:0-8109-5809-0, ISBN13:
978-0-8109-5809-8. Dewey:759.13. LCCN:98-071936.
> Audience: **g,l,u,f.**

Spurling, Hilary   N6853.M33S678 2005
Matisse the Master: A Life of Henri Matisse, the Conquest of
Colour, 1909-1954. Alfred A. Knopf Inc. 2005.
ISBN:0-679-43429-1, ISBN13: 978-0-679-43429-0.
> Audience: **g,l,u,f.**

Stebbins, Theodore E.   ND237.H39S682000
The Life and Work of Martin Johnson Heade: A Critical
Analysis and Catalogue Raisonné. Ed. 2. Cloth over Boards.
Yale University Press. Cumberland, RI. 2000. 400p.
ISBN:0-300-08183-9, ISBN13: 978-0-300-08183-1.
Dewey:759.13 B. LCCN:99-036424.
> Audience: **g,l,u,f.**

Stechow, Wolfgang   ND673.B73A41990
Bruegel. Trade Cloth. Harry N. Abrams, Inc. New York, NY.
1990. 128p. Masters of Art Ser. ISBN:0-8109-3103-6, ISBN13:
978-0-8109-3103-9. Dewey:759.9493. LCCN:89-035780.
> Audience: **g,l,u,f.**

Steinberg, Leo   ND623.L5A683 2001
Leonardo's Incessant Last Supper. Trade Cloth. Zone Books.
Brooklyn, NY. 2001. 312p. ISBN:1-890951-18-8, ISBN13:
978-1-890951-18-4. Dewey:759.5. LCCN:00-028315.
> Audience: **g,l,u,f.** *Choice, 2002.*

Storr, Robert   ND588.R48A4 2002
Gerhard Richter: Forty Years of Painting. Trade Cloth. Museum
of Modern Art. New York, NY. 2002. 340p.

ISBN:0-87070-357-9, ISBN13: 978-0-87070-357-7.
Dewey:759.3. LCCN:2001-099460.

          Audience: **g,l,u,f.** *Choice, 2002.*

Storr, Robert   **ND588.R48**
Gerhard Richter: Forty Years of Painting. Trade Cloth. D. A.
P./Distributed Art Publishers. New York, NY. 2003. 336p.
ISBN:1-891024-37-X, ISBN13: 978-1-891024-37-5.
Dewey:759.3.

          Audience: **g,l,u,f.** *Choice, 2002.*

Stratton-Pruitt, Suzanne L.   **ND813.V4 C337 2002**
   (Editor)
The Cambridge Companion to Velázquez. Trade Paper.
Cambridge University Press. New York, NY. 2002. 256p.
Cambridge Companions to the History of Art Ser.
ISBN:0-521-66940-5, ISBN13: 978-0-521-66940-5.
Dewey:759.6. LCCN:2001-037495.

          Audience: **g,l,u,f.**

Sullivan, Edward J. &   **E664.A19A22**
   Tasset, Jean-Marie (Text by)
Botero: Catalogue Raisonné: Paintings 1975-1990. Trade Cloth.
Acatos, Editions. Lausanne, 2000. 450p. ISBN:2-940033-40-4,
ISBN13: 978-2-940033-40-9. Dewey:385/.092/4.

          Audience: **g,l,u,f.**

Sultan, Terrie, et al.   **ND237.M24623A352000**
Kerry James Marshall. Arthur Jafa & Kerry James Marshall
(Authors). Trade Cloth. Harry N. Abrams, Inc. New York, NY.
2000. 128p. ISBN:0-8109-3527-9, ISBN13: 978-0-8109-3527-3.
Dewey:759.13. LCCN:00-020916.

          Audience: **g,l,u,f.**

Sutton, Peter & Wieseman,   **ND673.R9**
   Marjorie
Drawn by the Brush: Oil Sketches by Peter Paul Rubens. Nico
Van Hout (Contribution by). Cloth over Boards. Yale University
Press. Cumberland, RI. 2004. 272p. ISBN:0-300-10626-2,
ISBN13: 978-0-300-10626-8. Dewey:759.9/493.

          Audience: **g,l,u,f.** *Choice, 2005.*

Sylvester, David   **ND497.B16S923 2000**
Looking Back at Francis Bacon. Trade Cloth. Thames &
Hudson. New York, NY. 2000. 272p. ISBN:0-500-01994-0,
ISBN13: 978-0-500-01994-8. Dewey:759.2. LCCN:99-069757.

          Audience: **g,l,u,f.** *Choice, 2001.*

Thom, Ian & Hill, Charles   **N6853.P5**
   (Editors)
Emily Carr: New Perspectives. Cloth over Boards. Douglas &
McIntyre, Ltd. Vancouver, BC. 2006. 320p.
ISBN:1-55365-173-1, ISBN13: 978-1-55365-173-4.
Dewey:709.2.

          Audience: **g,l,u,f.**

Tinterow, Gary & Conisbee,   **ND1329.I53A41999**
   Philip (Editors)
Portraits by Ingres: Image of an Epoch. Trade Cloth. Harry N.
Abrams, Inc. New York, NY. 1999. 596p. ISBN:0-8109-6536-4,
ISBN13: 978-0-8109-6536-2. Dewey:759.4. LCCN:98-048508.

          Audience: **g,l,u,f.**

Tinterow, Gary & Conisbee,   **ND1329.I53A4**
   Phillip (Editors)
Portraits by Ingres: Image of an Epoch. Cloth over Boards. Yale
University Press. Cumberland, RI. 1999. 608p. Metropolitan
Museum of Art Ser. ISBN:0-300-08653-9, ISBN13:
978-0-300-08653-9. Dewey:759.4.

          Audience: **g,l,u,f.**

Townsend, Joyce H. (Editor)   **ND1942.B55 W55 2003**
William Blake: The Painter at Work. Cloth Text. Princeton
University Press. Princeton, NJ. 2004. 192p.
ISBN:0-691-11910-4, ISBN13: 978-0-691-11910-6.
Dewey:769.92. LCCN:2003-110696.

          Audience: **g,l,u,f.** *Choice, 2004.*

Tricot, Xavier   **ND673.E6**
Ensor: Catalogue Raisonné of the Oil Paintings. Trade Cloth.
Philip Wilson Publishers, Ltd. London, 1993. 732p.
ISBN:0-9566742-9-1, ISBN13: 978-0-9566742-9-6.
Dewey:759.949306.

          Audience: **g,l,u,f.**

Trippi, Peter   **ND497.W265**
J. W. Waterhouse. Trade Paper. Phaidon Press. London, 2005.
240p. ISBN:0-7148-4518-3, ISBN13: 978-0-7148-4518-0.
Dewey:759.2.

          Audience: **g,l,u,f.** *Choice, 2003.*

Tsujimoto, Karen   **ND237.T5515A4 1985**
Wayne Thiebaud. Henry Hopkins (Foreword by), Donna Graves
(Contribution by). Trade Paper. San Francisco Museum of
Modern Art. San Francisco, CA. 1985. 208p.
ISBN:0-295-96269-0, ISBN13: 978-0-295-96269-6.
Dewey:759.13. LCCN:85-040351.

          Audience: **g,l,u,f.** *Choice, 1986.*

Tucker, Paul H.   **ND553.M7.T83 1989**
Monet in the '90's: The Series Paintings. Cloth over Boards.
Yale University Press. Cumberland, RI. 1990. 340p.
ISBN:0-300-04659-6, ISBN13: 978-0-300-04659-5.
Dewey:759.4. LCCN:89-063207.

          Audience: **g,l,u,f.** *Choice, 1990.*

Tucker, Paul   **ND553.M7.A41998**
Monet in the 20th Century. Paul H. Tucker & George
Shackelford (Editors), MaryAnne Stevens, Romy Golan, John
House & Michael Leja (Contribution by). Cloth over Boards.
Yale University Press. Cumberland, RI. 1998. 410p. The
Renaissance in Europe Ser., :A Cultural Enquiry
ISBN:0-300-07749-1, ISBN13: 978-0-300-07749-0.
Dewey:759.4. LCCN:98-086163.

          Audience: **g,l,u,f.** *Choice, 1999.*

Urban, Martin   **ND588.N6A41990**
Emil Nolde: Catalogue Raisonné of the Oil Paintings: Volume
Two 1915-1951, Vol. 2. Gudran Parsons (Translator). Cloth over
Boards. Philip Wilson Publishers, Ltd. London, 1990. 648p.
ISBN:0-85667-377-3, ISBN13: 978-0-85667-377-1.
Dewey:759.3. LCCN:2004-463688.

          Audience: **g,l,u,f.**

Van Alphen, Ernst   ND497.B16A9 1993
Francis Bacon and the Loss of Self. Trade Cloth. Harvard
University Press. Cambridge, MA. 1992. 208p. Essays in Art
and Culture Ser. ISBN:0-674-31762-9, ISBN13:
978-0-674-31762-8. Dewey:759.2. LCCN:92-010641.
                        Audience: **g,l,u,f.** *Choice, 1993.*

Van Gogh, Vincent   ND653.G7
Complete Letters of Vincent Van Gogh. Trade Cloth. Little
Brown & Company. New York, NY. 2000. 1896p.
ISBN:0-8212-2630-4, ISBN13: 978-0-8212-2630-8.
Dewey:759.9492.

                        Audience: **g,l,u,f.**

Varnedoe, Kirk   ND237.P73A4 1998
Jackson Pollock. Pepe Karmel (Contribution by). Trade Cloth.
Museum of Modern Art. New York, NY. 2003. 336p.
ISBN:0-87070-068-5, ISBN13: 978-0-87070-068-2.
Dewey:759.13. LCCN:98-067140.
                        Audience: **g,l,u,f.** *Choice, 1999.*

Vaughn, William   ND497.G2V38 2002
Gainsborough. Trade Paper. Thames & Hudson. New York, NY.
2002. 224p. World of Art Ser. ISBN:0-500-20358-X, ISBN13:
978-0-500-20358-3. Dewey:759.2. LCCN:2001-094768.
                        Audience: **g,l,u,f.**

Vettriano, Jack   ND497
Vettriano: A Life. Trade Cloth. Anova Books. London, 2005.
192p. ISBN:1-86205-646-3, ISBN13: 978-1-86205-646-6.
Dewey:759.2/911. LCCN:2005-362703.
                        Audience: **g,l,u,f.**

Vidal, Mary   ND553.W3V53 1992
Watteau's Painted Conversations: Art, Literatura, and Talk in
Seventeenth- and Eighteenth-Century France. Cloth over Boards.
Yale University Press. Cumberland, RI. 1992. 248p.
ISBN:0-300-05480-7, ISBN13: 978-0-300-05480-4.
Dewey:759.4. LCCN:92-009695.
                        Audience: **g,l,u,f.** *Choice, 1993.*

Vigne, Georges   ND553.I5V5413 1995
Ingres. John Goodman (Translator). Trade Cloth. Abbeville
Press, Inc. New York, NY. 1995. 352p. ISBN:0-7892-0060-0,
ISBN13: 978-0-7892-0060-0. Dewey:759.4. LCCN:95-022529.
                        Audience: **g,l,u,f.** *Choice, 1996.*

Wasserman, Jack   ND623.L5W342003
Leonardo da Vinci. Trade Paper. Harry N. Abrams, Inc. New
York, NY. 2003. 128p. Masters of Art Ser. ISBN:0-8109-9130-6,
ISBN13: 978-0-8109-9130-9. Dewey:709/.2 B.
LCCN:2003-013703.
                        Audience: **g,l,u,f.**

Weinberg, H. Barbara   N6537.H367A4 2004
Childe Hassam, American Impressionist. Elizabeth E. Barker
(Contribution by). Trade Cloth. Metropolitan Museum of Art,
The. New York, NY. 2004. xi, 425p. ISBN:1-58839-119-1,
ISBN13: 978-1-58839-119-3. Dewey:759.13.
LCCN:2004-004299.
                        Audience: **g,l,u,f.** *Choice, 2005.*

Wheelock, Arthur K.   ND653.V5W4732004
Vermeer. Trade Paper. Harry N. Abrams, Inc. New York, NY.
2005. 128p. Masters of Art Ser. ISBN:0-8109-9205-1, ISBN13:
978-0-8109-9205-4. Dewey:759.9492.
                        Audience: **g,l,u,f.**

Wheelock, Arthur K. Jr.   ND653.V5W48 1995
Vermeer and the Art of Painting. Cloth over Boards. Yale
University Press. Cumberland, RI. 1995. 218p.
ISBN:0-300-06239-7, ISBN13: 978-0-300-06239-7.
Dewey:759.9492. LCCN:94-040119.
                        Audience: **g,l,u,f.** *Choice, 1995.*

Wheelock, Arthur K. Jr. &   ND653.V5A4 1995
  Broos, Ben
Johannes Vermeer. Cloth over Boards. Yale University Press.
Cumberland, RI. 1995. 232p. ISBN:0-300-06558-2, ISBN13:
978-0-300-06558-9. Dewey:759.9492. LCCN:95-023917.
                        Audience: **l,u,f.** *Choice, 1996.*

Wheelock, Arthur K. Jr.   ND1329.B63A42004
Gerard Ter Borch. National Gallery of Art (U.S.) Staff, Detroit
Institute of Arts Staff, Alison Kettering, Arie Wallert & Marjorie
Wieseman (Contribution by). Cloth over Boards. Yale University
Press. Cumberland, RI. 2004. 240p. ISBN:0-300-10639-4,
ISBN13: 978-0-300-10639-8. Dewey:759.9492.
LCCN:2004-008762.
                        Audience: **l,u,f.** *Choice, 2005.*

Whitfield, Sarah, et al.   ND673.M35A41998
Magritte, 1898-1998. David Sylvester & Harry Torczyner
(Authors). Trade Cloth. Harry N. Abrams, Inc. New York, NY.
1998. 335p. ISBN:0-8109-6359-0, ISBN13: 978-0-8109-6359-7.
Dewey:759.9493. LCCN:98-156454.
                        Audience: **g,l,u,f.** *Choice, 1998.*

Whitford, Frank   N6811.5.K55W47 1990
Klimt. Trade Paper. Thames & Hudson. New York, NY. 1990.
216p. World of Art Ser. ISBN:0-500-20246-X, ISBN13:
978-0-500-20246-3. Dewey:759.36. LCCN:90-070177.
                        Audience: **g,l,u,f.**

Wieck, Roger S.   ND3363.H57W54 2000
The Hours of Henry VIII: A Renaissance Masterpiece by Jean
Poyet. Trade Cloth. George Braziller Inc. New York, NY. 2000.
176p. ISBN:0-8076-1477-7, ISBN13: 978-0-8076-1477-8.
Dewey:745.6/7/092. LCCN:00-039758.
                        Audience: **l,u,f.**

Wildenstein, Daniel   ND553.G27.W52002
Gaugin: Catalogue Raisonné of the Paintings, 1873-1888. Trade
Cloth, Box or Slipcased. Skira Editore. Milano, 2002. 648p.
ISBN:88-8491-137-0, ISBN13: 978-88-8491-137-7.
Dewey:759.4.
                        Audience: **g,l,u,f.**

Wildenstein, Daniel   ND553.M7
Monet, Complete Paintings.: Catalogue Raisonné, 1885-1901.
Claude Monet (Illustrator). Trade Cloth. Wittenborn Art Books.
San Francisco, CA. 1996. ISBN:0-8150-0062-6, ISBN13:
978-0-8150-0062-4. Dewey:759.4.
                        Audience: **g,l,u,f.**

Wildenstein, Daniel   ND553.M7
Monet. Complete Paintings.: Catalogue Raisonné, 1858-1885.
Claude Monet (Illustrator). Trade Cloth. Wittenborn Art Books.
San Francisco, CA. 1996. ISBN:0-8150-0061-8, ISBN13:
978-0-8150-0061-7. Dewey:759.4.
                                        Audience: **g,l,u,f.**

Wilson, James   ND237.H915A4 1988
Clementine Hunter: American Folk Artist. Trade Cloth. Pelican
Publishing Company, Inc. Gretna, LA. 1988. 160p.
ISBN:0-88289-658-X, ISBN13: 978-0-88289-658-8.
Dewey:759.1/3. LCCN:88-002068.
                                        Audience: **g,l,u,f.**

Wong, Rita   ND1049.C3365A42001
Sanyu: Catalogue Raisonné Oil Paintings. Trade Paper. Yah
Tung Book Company, Ltd. Taipei, 2001. 368p.
ISBN:957-744-411-3, ISBN13: 978-957-744-411-0.
Dewey:759.9/51. LCCN:2001-368627.
                                 Audience: **g,l,u,f.** *Choice, 2002.*

Wood, Jeryldene M. (Editor)   ND623.F78 C26 2002
The Cambridge Companion to Piero Della Francesca. Trade
Paper. Cambridge University Press. New York, NY. 2002. 284p.
Cambridge Companions to the History of Art Ser.
ISBN:0-521-65472-6, ISBN13: 978-0-521-65472-2.
Dewey:759.5. LCCN:2001-043485.
                                        Audience: **g,l,u,f.**

Yount, Sylvia   ND237
Maxfield Parrish: 1870-1966. Trade Cloth. Harry N. Abrams,
Inc. New York, NY. 2003. 160p. ISBN:0-8109-8229-3, ISBN13:
978-0-8109-8229-1. Dewey:759.1/3.
                                 Audience: **g,l,u,f.** *Choice, 2000.*

Ziermann, Horst   ND588.G7Z5 2001
Matthias Grunewald. Trade Cloth. Prestel Publishing. New York,
NY. 2001. 208p. ISBN:3-7913-2500-0, ISBN13:
978-3-7913-2500-2. Dewey:759.3. LCCN:2001-089185.
                                 Audience: **l,u,f.** *Choice, 2001.*

Painting > Materials and Techniques

Albus, Anita   ND673.E9A8413 2001
The Art of Arts: Rediscovering Painting. Trade Paper. University
of California Press. Berkeley, CA. 2001. 398p.
ISBN:0-520-22964-9, ISBN13: 978-0-520-22964-8.
Dewey:750/.1. LCCN:00-059001.
                                 Audience: **u,f.** *Choice, 2001.*

Benjamin, Roger   N6853.M33 B46 1987
Matisse's Notes of a Painter: Criticism, Theory, and Context,
1891-1908. Trade Paper. Books on Demand. Ann Arbor, MI.
367p. Studies in the Fine Arts. Criticism, Vol. 21
ISBN:0-8357-1743-7, ISBN13: 978-0-8357-1743-4.
Dewey:709/.2/4. LCCN:86-025056.
                                 Audience: **g,l,u,f.** *Choice, 1987.*

Bird, William Larry Jr.   ND1471.5.B57 2001
Paint by Number: The How-to Craze That Swept the Nation.
Trade Paper. Princeton Architectural Press. New York, NY.
2001. 144p. ISBN:1-56898-282-8, ISBN13: 978-1-56898-282-3.
Dewey:306.4/7. LCCN:00-011279.
                                 Audience: **g,l,u,f.** *Choice, 2001.*

Boas, Nancy   ND1351.6.B63 1998
The Society of Six: California Colorists. Charles C. Eldredge
(Foreword by). Trade Paper. University of California Press.
Berkeley, CA. 1997. 224p. ISBN:0-520-21055-7, ISBN13:
978-0-520-21055-4. Dewey:758/.1/09794. LCCN:96-037048.
                                 Audience: **g,l,u,f.** *Choice, 1988.*

Bober, Phyllis Pray;
  Rubenstein, Ruth; Woodford, Susan
Renaissance Artists and Antique Sculpture: A Handbook of
Sources. Oxford University Press, Inc. 1991. A Harvey Miller
Publication ISBN:0-905203-96-8, ISBN13: 978-0-905203-96-6.
                                        Audience: **g,l,u,f.**

Bomford, David (Editor)   ND653.R4
Art in the Making: Underdrawings in Renaissance Paintings.
Rachel Billinge, Lorne Campbell, Jill Dunkerton, Susan Foister
& Jo Kirby (Contribution by). Trade Paper. Yale University
Press. Cumberland, RI. 2002. 192p. National Gallery London
Publications ISBN:0-300-09225-3, ISBN13: 978-0-300-09225-7.
Dewey:759.9492.
                                 Audience: **g,l,u,f.** *Choice, 2003.*

Callen, Anthea   ND1482.I6C35 2000
The Art of Impressionism: Painting Technique and the Making
of Modernity. Cloth over Boards. Yale University Press.
Cumberland, RI. 2000. 256p. ISBN:0-300-08402-1, ISBN13:
978-0-300-08402-3. Dewey:751.4. LCCN:00-108612.
                                 Audience: **g,l,u,f.** *Choice, 2001.*

Callen, Anthea   ND547.5 .I4 C34 1982
Techniques of the Impressionists. Trade Cloth. Book Sales, Inc.
Edison, NJ. 1997. 192p. ISBN:0-89009-545-0, ISBN13:
978-0-89009-545-4. Dewey:759.4.
                                        Audience: **g,l,u,f.**

Chalfant, Henry & Prigoff,   ND2590.C46 1987
James
Spraycan Art. Trade Paper. Thames & Hudson. New York, NY.
1987. 96p. ISBN:0-500-27469-X, ISBN13: 978-0-500-27469-9.
Dewey:751.7/3/09048. LCCN:87-050389.
                                 Audience: **g,l,u,f.** *Choice, 1988.*

Chesterman, Sandra   N7574.5.N45C49 2002
Figure Work: The Nude and Life Modelling in New Zealand
Art. Dorothy Page (Editor). Trade Paper. Otago University
Press. Dunedin, 2002. 160p. ISBN:1-877276-37-5, ISBN13:
978-1-877276-37-8. Dewey:704.9421. LCCN:2003-386456.
                                 Audience: **g,l,u,f.** *Choice, 2003.*

Eastlake, Charles L.   ND50.E2 2001
Methods and Materials of Painting of the Great Schools and

Masters. Trade Paper. Dover Publications, Inc. Mineola, NY. 2001. 1024p. ISBN:0-486-41726-3, ISBN13: 978-0-486-41726-4. Dewey:751.45/09. LCCN:00-052303.

Audience: **g,l,u,f.**

Hammond, Nicholas   **ND1383.E85.H36 1998**
Modern Wildlife Painting. Cloth over Boards. Yale University Press. Cumberland, RI. 1999. 240p. ISBN:0-300-07458-1, ISBN13: 978-0-300-07458-1. Dewey:758/.3. LCCN:98-088106.

Audience: **g,l,u,f.** *Choice, 1999.*

Hockney, David   **ND1471.H63 2001**
Secret Knowledge: Rediscovering the Lost Techniques of the Old Masters. Trade Cloth. Penguin Group (USA) Inc. New York, NY. 2001. 296p. ISBN:0-670-03026-0, ISBN13: 978-0-670-03026-2. Dewey:751.4. LCCN:2001-026022.

Audience: **g,l,u,f.**

Kirsh, Andrea & Levenson,   **ND1635.K572000**
  Rustin S.
Seeing Through Paintings: Physical Examination in Art Historical Studies. Cloth over Boards. Yale University Press. Cumberland, RI. 2000. 344p. Materials and Meaning in the Fine Arts Ser., Vol. 1 ISBN:0-300-08046-8, ISBN13: 978-0-300-08046-9. Dewey:751.6/2. LCCN:99-051835.

Audience: **g,l,u,f.** *Choice, 2000.*

Marinjnissen, R. H.   **ND1635 .M368 1985**
Paintings - Genuine, Fraud, Fake: Modern Methods of Examining Paintings. Cloth Text. Greenwood Publishing Group, Inc. Portsmouth, NH. 1987. 415p. ISBN:0-313-25874-0, ISBN13: 978-0-313-25874-9. Dewey:751.6/2. LCCN:87-140460.

Audience: **g,l,u,f.** *Choice, 1987.*

Roy, Ashok
Artists' Pigments: A Handbook of Their History and Characteristics. Ashok Roy (Editor). Oxford University Press, Inc. 1994. A National Gallery of Art U. S. A. Publication ISBN:0-89468-189-3, ISBN13: 978-0-89468-189-9.

Audience: **g,l,u,f.**

Seligman, Patricia   **ND2550.S45**
Painting Murals. Trade Paper. F & W Publications, Inc. Cincinnati, OH. 2003. 168p. ISBN:1-58180-470-9, ISBN13: 978-1-58180-470-6. Dewey:747.3.

Audience: **g,l,u,f.**

Spandorfer, Merle, et al.   **RC963.6.A78.S62 1993**
Making Art Safely: Alternatives in Drawing, Painting, Printmaking, Graphic Design, and Photography. Deborah Curtiss & Jack W. Snyder (Authors). Cloth Text. John Wiley & Sons, Inc. Hoboken, NJ. 1993. xvi, 255p. ISBN:0-442-23489-9, ISBN13: 978-0-442-23489-8. Dewey:363.1197. LCCN:92-004841.

Audience: **g,l,u,f.** *Choice, 1993.*

Turner, Jacques   **N8543 .T8**
Brushes: A Handbook for Artists and Artisans. Trade Paper. Globe Pequot Press, The. Guilford, CT. 1992. 104p. ISBN:1-55821-501-8, ISBN13: 978-1-55821-501-6. Dewey:751.3.

Audience: **g,l,u,f.**

Van Briessen, Fritz   **ND1040**
The Way of the Brush: Painting Techniques of China and Japan. Trade Paper. Tuttle Publishing. Boston, MA. 1999. 332p. ISBN:0-8048-3194-7, ISBN13: 978-0-8048-3194-9. Dewey:759.95. LCCN:62-014119.

Audience: **g,l,u,f.**

Wallert, Arie (Editor), et al.   **ND1500.H57 1995**
Historical Painting Techniques, Materials and Studio Practice: University of Leiden, Netherlands, June 1995 Preprints. Erma Hermens & Marja F. Peek (Editors). Trade Paper. Oxford University Press, Inc. New York, NY. 1995. 240p. Symposium Preprints Ser. ISBN:0-89236-322-3, ISBN13: 978-0-89236-322-3. Dewey:751/.09. LCCN:95-009805.

Audience: **g,l,u,f.**

Printmaking > Reference Works

Wilson, Raymond L.   **NE507.W55 1988**
Index of American Print Exhibitions, 1882-1940. Trade Cloth. Scarecrow Press, Inc. Lanham, MD. 1988. 906p. ISBN:0-8108-2139-7, ISBN13: 978-0-8108-2139-2. Dewey:769.973. LCCN:88-015640.

Audience: **g,l,u,f.**

Printmaking > Reference Works > Bibliographies and Research Guides

Bryce, Betty K.   **NE508.B76 1999**
American Printmakers, 1946-1996: An Index to Reproductions and Biocritical Information. Trade Cloth. Scarecrow Press, Inc. Lanham, MD. 1999. 606p. ISBN:0-8108-3586-X, ISBN13: 978-0-8108-3586-3. Dewey:016.76992/273. LCCN:98-043773.

Audience: **g,l,u,f.** *Choice, 2000.*

Smith, Donald E.   **NE508.S56 2004**
American Printmakers of the Twentieth Century: A Bibliography. Trade Cloth. Saint Johann Press. Haworth, NJ. 2004. iii, 363p. ISBN:1-878282-28-X, ISBN13: 978-1-878282-28-6. Dewey:016.76992/273. LCCN:2003-066822.

Audience: **g,l,u,f.** *Choice, 2004.*

Williams, Lynn B.   **NE507.W53 1993**
American Printmakers, 1880-1945: An Index to Reproductions and Biocritical Information. Trade Cloth. Scarecrow Press, Inc. Lanham, MD. 1993. 479p. ISBN:0-8108-2786-7, ISBN13: 978-0-8108-2786-8. Dewey:016.76992/273. LCCN:93-041591.

Audience: **g,l,u,f.** *Choice, 1994.*

Printmaking > Reference Works > Dictionaries and Encyclopedias

Engen, Rodney K.   **NE1143.E5 1985**
Dictionary of Victorian Wood Engravers. Trade Cloth. Ashgate Publishing, Ltd. Aldershot, 1985. 320p. ISBN:0-85964-139-2, ISBN13: 978-0-85964-139-5. Dewey:769.92/2 B. LCCN:85-208961.

Audience: **g,l,u,f.**

Engen, Rodney K.   NE628.3
Dictionary of Victorian Engravers, Print Publishers and Their
Works. Teaneck, N. J.: Somerset House. 1979.
ISBN:0-914146-86-6, ISBN13: 978-0-914146-86-5.

Audience: **g,l,u,f.**

Gascoigne, Bamber   NE400
How to Identify Prints. Ed. 2. Trade Paper. Thames & Hudson.
New York, NY. 2004. 208p. ISBN:0-500-28480-6, ISBN13:
978-0-500-28480-3. Dewey:760.2/8. LCCN:2003-112372.

Audience: **g,l,u,f.**

Goldman, Paul   N33.G65 1988
Looking at Prints, Drawings and Watercolours: A Guide to
Technical Terms. Trade Paper. Oxford University Press, Inc.
New York, NY. 1989. 64p. Looking at Ser.
ISBN:0-89236-148-4, ISBN13: 978-0-89236-148-9.
Dewey:760/.03/21. LCCN:88-013241.

Audience: **g,l,u,f.**

Hunnisett, Basil   NE625.H86 1988
An Illustrated Dictionary of British Steel Engravers. Cloth Text.
Ashgate Publishing, Ltd. Aldershot, 1989. 130p.
ISBN:0-85967-740-0, ISBN13: 978-0-85967-740-0.
Dewey:769.92/2 B. LCCN:88-004696.

Audience: **g,l,u,f.**

Lister, Raymond   NE628.3
Prints and Printmaking: A Dictionary and Handbook of the Art
in Nineteenth-Century Britaiin. Methuen. 1984.
ISBN:0-413-40130-8, ISBN13: 978-0-413-40130-4.

Audience: **g,l,u,f.**

Mackenzie, Ian   NE628.M24 1987
British Prints: Dictionary and Price Guide. Trade Cloth. Antique
Collectors' Club. Easthampton, MA. 1988. 360p.
ISBN:0-902028-96-0, ISBN13: 978-0-902028-96-8.
Dewey:769.92/2. LCCN:93-178114.

Audience: **g,l,u,f.**

Martin, Judy   NE850.M375 2002
The Encyclopedia of Printmaking Techniques: A Comprehensive
Visual Guide to Traditional and Contemporary Techniques.
Trade Paper. Sterling Publishing Co., Inc. New York, NY. 2002.
176p. ISBN:0-8069-9300-6, ISBN13: 978-0-8069-9300-3.
Dewey:760/.28. LCCN:2003-270614.

Audience: **g,l,u,f.**

Newland, Amy Reigle   NE1310
Hotei Encyclopedia of Japanese Woodblock Prints. Hotei
Publishing. 2005. ISBN:90-74822-65-7, ISBN13:
978-90-74822-65-7.

Audience: **g,l,u,f.**

Printmaking > Reference Works > Directories

NE85
Gordon's Print Price Annual 2005. Trade Cloth. LTB
Gordonsart, Inc. Phoenix, AZ. 2005. 2050p.
ISBN:1-933295-02-3, ISBN13: 978-1-933295-02-2.
Dewey:760.075.

Audience: **g,l,u,f.**

Printmaking > Histories and Handbooks > Periods and Styles

Castleman, Riva   NE508
American Impressions: Prints since Pollock. Alfred A. Knopf
Inc. 1985. ISBN:0-394-53683-5, ISBN13: 978-0-394-53683-5.

Audience: **g,l,u,f.**

Castleman, Riva   NE490
Prints of the 20th Century: A History. Ed. 2. Trade Paper.
Thames & Hudson. New York, NY. 1988. 192p. World of Art
Ser. ISBN:0-500-20228-1, ISBN13: 978-0-500-20228-9.
Dewey:769.9/04. LCCN:87-051289.

Audience: **g,l,u,f.**

Clark, Timothy A. R., et al.   NE1321.85.K38.C53
The Actor's Image: Print Makers of the Katsukawa School.
Donald Jenkins & Osamu Ueda (Authors), Naomi N. Richard
(Editor). Trade Cloth. Art Institute of Chicago. Chicago, IL.
1994. 504p. ISBN:0-86559-097-4, ISBN13: 978-0-86559-097-7.
Dewey:769.952. LCCN:93-006382.

Audience: **g,l,u,f.** *Choice, 1994.*

Dackerman, Susan &   NE625.D332002
   Primeau, Thomas
Painted Prints: The Revelation of Color in Northern Renaissance
and Baroque Engravings, Etchings, and Woodcuts. Trade Cloth.
Pennsylvania State University Press. University Park, PA. 2002.
312p. ISBN:0-271-02234-5, ISBN13: 978-0-271-02234-5.
Dewey:769.943/074/7526. LCCN:2002-005463.

Audience: **l,u,f.** *Choice, 2003.*

Dackerman, Susan &   NE625.D332002
   Primeau, Thomas
Painted Prints: The Revelation of Color in Northern Renaissance
and Baroque Engravings, Etchings, and Woodcuts. Trade Paper.
Pennsylvania State University Press. University Park, PA. 2002.
312p. ISBN:0-271-02235-3, ISBN13: 978-0-271-02235-2.
Dewey:769.943/074/7526. LCCN:2002-005463.

Audience: **g,l,u,f.** *Choice, 2003.*

Davis, B.   N6868.5.E9 R6
German Expressionist Prints and Drawings. Trade Cloth. Prestel
Publishing. New York, NY. 1989. 846p. ISBN:3-7913-0959-5,
ISBN13: 978-3-7913-0959-0. Dewey:759.3.
                              Audience: **g,l,u,f.** *Choice, 1990.*

Dunthorne, Gordon   NE953
Flower and Fruit Prints of the 18th and Early 19th Centuries:
Their History, Makers and Uses, with a Catalogue Raisonné of
the Works in Which They Are Found. Trade Cloth. Martino
Publishing. Mansfield Centre, CT. 1996. 289p.
ISBN:1-888262-05-2, ISBN13: 978-1-888262-05-6.
Dewey:016.58204600222; 769.
                              Audience: **g,l,u,f.**

Goldman, Judith   N6494.P6G65 1994
The Pop Image: Prints and Multiples. Trade Paper. D. A.
P./Distributed Art Publishers. New York, NY. 1995. 128p.
ISBN:0-89797-104-3, ISBN13: 978-0-89797-104-1.
Dewey:709/.04/0710747471. LCCN:94-072896.
                              Audience: **g,l,u,f.**

Grasselli, Margaret Morgan,   NE647.2
  et al.
Colorful Impressions: The Printmaking Revolution in
Eighteenth-Century France. Kristel Smentek & Judith G. Walsh
(Authors). Trade Cloth. Ashgate Publishing Company. Williston,
VT. 2003. 200p. ISBN:0-85331-892-1, ISBN13:
978-0-85331-892-7. Dewey:769.944/09/033074753.
LCCN:2003-013301.
                              Audience: **g,l,u,f.** *Choice, 2004.*

Griffiths, Antony   NE400.G74 1996
Prints and Printmaking: An Introduction to the History and
Techniques. Trade Paper. University of California Press.
Berkeley, CA. 1996. 152p. ISBN:0-520-20714-9, ISBN13:
978-0-520-20714-1. Dewey:760. LCCN:96-012571.
                              Audience: **g,l,u,f.** *Choice, 1996.*

Hind, Arthur M.   NE143.H55
Engraving in England in the Reign of James I: A Catalogue
Raisonné. Trade Cloth. Alan Wofsy Fine Arts. San Francisco,
CA. 2001. 702p. ISBN:1-55660-181-6, ISBN13:
978-1-55660-181-1. Dewey:769.942.
                              Audience: **g,l,u,f.**

Hind, Arthur M.   NE143
Engraving in England in the Tudor Period: A Catalogue
Raisonné. Trade Cloth. Alan Wofsy Fine Arts. San Francisco,
CA. 2000. 524p. ISBN:1-55660-180-8, ISBN13:
978-1-55660-180-4. Dewey:769.942.
                              Audience: **g,l,u.**

Hind, Arthur M.   ND621.F7M4
History of Engraving and Etching: From the 15th Century to the
Year 1914. Ed. 3. Trade Paper. Dover Publications, Inc.
Mineola, NY. 1963. 505p. ISBN:0-486-20954-7, ISBN13:
978-0-486-20954-8. Dewey:759.5.
                              Audience: **g,l,u,f.**

Hults, Linda C.   NE400.H79 1996
The Print in the Western World: An Introductory History. Trade
Cloth. University of Wisconsin Press. Chicago, IL. 1996. 968p.
ISBN:0-299-13700-7, ISBN13: 978-0-299-13700-7.
Dewey:769.9. LCCN:95-007231.
                              Audience: **g,l,u,f.** *Choice, 1996.*

Kaplan, Gilbert E. (Editor)   NE625.6.S8S871997
Surrealist Prints. Timothy Baum & Robert Rainwater (Text by),
Riva Castleman (Foreword by). Trade Cloth. Harry N. Abrams,
Inc. New York, NY. 1997. 160p. ISBN:0-8109-6339-6, ISBN13:
978-0-8109-6339-9. Dewey:769.94/074/79494.
LCCN:96-052626.
                              Audience: **g,l,u,f.** *Choice, 1997.*

Landau, David & Parshall,   N6370
  Peter W.
The Renaissance Print, 1470-1550. Trade Paper. Yale University
Press. Cumberland, RI. 1996. 448p. ISBN:0-300-06883-2,
ISBN13: 978-0-300-06883-2. Dewey:760/.09024.
                              Audience: **g,l,u,f.**

Lincoln, Evelyn   NE659.L56 2000
The Invention of the Italian Renaissance Printmaker. Cloth over
Boards. Yale University Press. Cumberland, RI. 2000. 216p.
ISBN:0-300-08041-7, ISBN13: 978-0-300-08041-4.
Dewey:769.945/09/031. LCCN:99-087337.
                              Audience: **g,l,u,f.** *Choice, 2000.*

Maidment, Brian   NE962.M35
Reading Popular Prints 1790-1870. Ed. 2. Trade Paper.
Manchester University Press. Manchester, 2001. 232p.
ISBN:0-7190-3371-3, ISBN13: 978-0-7190-3371-1.
Dewey:769.9/034.
                              Audience: **l,u,f.**

Melot, Michel   NE647.6.I4M4413 1996
The Impressionist Print. Caroline Beamish (Translator). Cloth
over Boards. Yale University Press. Cumberland, RI. 1997.
296p. ISBN:0-300-06792-5, ISBN13: 978-0-300-06792-7.
Dewey:769.9/44/09034. LCCN:95-050606.
                              Audience: **g,l,u,f.** *Choice, 1997.*

Merritt, Helen & Yamada,   NE1323
  Nanako
Guide to Modern Japanese Woodblock Prints, 1900-1975. Trade
Cloth. University of Hawaii Press. Honolulu, HI. 1992. 376p.
ISBN:0-8248-1732-X, ISBN13: 978-0-8248-1732-9.
Dewey:769.952/09/04. LCCN:91-040576.
                              Audience: **g,l,u,f.** *Choice, 1992.*

Moxey, Keith   NE958.3.G3M68 1989
Peasants, Warriors, and Wives: Popular Imagery in the
Reformation. Trade Cloth. University of Chicago Press.
Chicago, IL. 1989. 180p. ISBN:0-226-54391-9, ISBN13:
978-0-226-54391-8. Dewey:769.4/994332. LCCN:88-037668.
                              Audience: **l,u,f.** *Choice, 1990.*

Parshall, Peter W. &   NE1142.P37 2005
  Schoch, Rainer
Origins of European Printmaking: Fifteenth-Century Woodcuts
and Their Public. National Gallery of Art (U.S.) Staff &

Germanisches Nationalmuseum Nürnberg Staff (Contribution by). Trade Cloth. National Gallery of Art. Washington, DC. 2005. ix, 371p. ISBN:3-936688-08-7, ISBN13: 978-3-936688-08-5. Dewey:769.94/09/024074753. LCCN:2005-014244.

Audience: **g,l,u,f.**

Parshall, Peter W., et al. NE440
The Unfinished Print. Stacey Sell & Judith Brodie (Authors). Trade Cloth. Ashgate Publishing Company. Williston, VT. 2001. 100p. ISBN:0-85331-820-4, ISBN13: 978-0-85331-820-0. Dewey:760/.74/753.

Audience: **g,l,u,f.** *Choice, 2002.*

Tallman, Susan NE490.T35 1996
The Contemporary Print: Pre-Pop to Postmodernism. Trade Cloth. Thames & Hudson. New York, NY. 1996. 304p. ISBN:0-500-23684-4, ISBN13: 978-0-500-23684-0. Dewey:769.9. LCCN:95-060477.

Audience: **g,l,u,f.**

Printmaking > Histories and Handbooks > Cultures, Regions, Nationalities

E183.3.R45 1991
Catalog of American Political Prints in the Library of Congress, 1766-1876. Gale Group. 1991. Library Reference Ser. ISBN:0-8161-0444-1, ISBN13: 978-0-8161-0444-4.

Audience: **g,l,u,f.**

Clark, Timothy A. R., et al. ND1053.5.D382001
The Dawn of the Floating World: Early Ukiyo-E Treasures from the Museum of Fine Arts, Boston. Anne Nishimura Morse, Louise E. Virgin & Allen Hockley (Authors). Trade Cloth. Harry N. Abrams, Inc. New York, NY. 2002. 333p. ISBN:0-8109-6644-1, ISBN13: 978-0-8109-6644-4. Dewey:769.952.

Audience: **g,l,u,f.** *Choice, 2002.*

Garton, Robin (Editor) NE628.3.B751992
British Printmakers 1855-1955: A Century of Printmaking from the Etching Revival to St. Ives. Trade Paper. Ashgate Publishing, Ltd. Aldershot, 2000. 336p. ISBN:0-7546-0231-1, ISBN13: 978-0-7546-0231-6. Dewey:769.9/41/09034.

Audience: **g,l,f.**

Godfrey, Richard T. NE628
Printmaking in Britain: A General History from Its Beginnings to the Present Day. New York University Press. 1978. ISBN:0-8147-2973-8, ISBN13: 978-0-8147-2973-1.

Audience: **g,l,u,f.**

Newland, Amy Reigle NE1310
Hotei Encyclopedia of Japanese Woodblock Prints. Hotei Publishing. 2005. ISBN:90-74822-65-7, ISBN13: 978-90-74822-65-7.

Audience: **g,l,u,f.**

Reed, Sue W.; Wallace, Richard NE2052.2.R41989
Italian Etchers of the Renaissance and Baroque. Museum of Fine Arts, Boston. 1989. ISBN:0-87846-305-4, ISBN13: 978-0-87846-305-3.

Audience: **g,l,u,f.**

Seigle, Cecilia S., et al. NE1326.5.W65C68 2004
A Courtesan's Day. Tim Clark, Alfred Marks & Amy Reigle Newland (Authors). Trade Paper. Hotei Publishing. Leiden, 2004. 160p. Famous Japanese Prints Ser., Vol. 2 ISBN:90-74822-59-2, ISBN13: 978-90-74822-59-6. Dewey:769.952. LCCN:2004-547994.

Audience: **l,u,f.** *Choice, 2005.*

Stauffer, David M., et al. NE505.S8 1994
American Engravers upon Copper and Steel, Set. Mantle Fielding & Thomas H. Gage (Authors). Trade Cloth. Oak Knoll Press. New Castle, DE. 1994. 1520p. ISBN:0-938768-47-6, ISBN13: 978-0-938768-47-0. Dewey:769.92/273 B. LCCN:93-085898.

Audience: **g,l,u,f.**

Watrous, James NE507
A Century of American Printmaking, 1880-1980. University of Wisconsin Press. 1984. ISBN:0-299-09680-7, ISBN13: 978-0-299-09680-9.

Audience: **g,u,f.**

Windsor, Alan N6768.H26 1998
Handbook of Modern British Painting and Printmaking, 1900-1990. Ed. 2. Trade Cloth. Ashgate Publishing, Ltd. Aldershot, 2002. 334p. ISBN:1-85928-427-2, ISBN13: 978-1-85928-427-8. Dewey:760/.0942. LCCN:98-009977.

Audience: **g,l,u,f.**

Printmaking > Histories and Handbooks > Types of Printmaking

Castleman, Riva N6490
A Century of Artists Books. Trade Paper. Harry N. Abrams, Inc. New York, NY. 1997. 264p. ISBN:0-8109-6181-4, ISBN13: 978-0-8109-6181-4. Dewey:709/.04.

Audience: **g,l,u,f.** *Choice, 1995.*

Gilmour, Pat NE2295.L371988
Lasting Impressions: Lithography as Art. Trade Cloth. University of Pennsylvania Press. Philadelphia, PA. 1988. 416p. ISBN:0-8122-8126-8, ISBN13: 978-0-8122-8126-2. Dewey:763/.09. LCCN:88-001304.

Audience: **g,l,u,f.** *Choice, 1989.*

Slater, Rebecca NE1310
Japanese Woodblock Printing. University of Hawaii Press. 2002. ISBN:0-8248-2553-5, ISBN13: 978-0-8248-2553-9.

Audience: **g,l,f.**

Printmaking > Individual Printmakers

Axsom, Richard   NE2312.K38A4 2005
Drawn from Nature: The Plant Lithographs of Ellsworth Kelly.
Cloth over Boards. Yale University Press. Cumberland, RI.
2005. 124p. ISBN:0-300-10321-2, ISBN13: 978-0-300-10321-2.
Dewey:769.92. LCCN:2004-026207.

Audience: **g,l,u,f.** *Choice, 2005.*

Axsom, Richard H. &   NE539.O43A41997
  Platzker, David
Printed Stuff: Prints, Posters, and Ephemera by Claes
Oldenburg: A Catalogue Raisonné 1958-1996. Stephen
Fleischman (Foreword by). Trade Cloth. Hudson Hills Press
LLC. Manchester, VT. 1997. 368p. ISBN:1-55595-123-6,
ISBN13: 978-1-55595-123-8. Dewey:769.92. LCCN:96-039970.

Audience: **l,u,f.**

Baskett, Mary W.   NE2012.T88A41999
John Henry Twachtman, American Impressionist Painter as
Printmaker: A Catalogue Raisonné of His Prints. Trade Cloth.
M. Hausberg. Lake Forest, IL. 1999. 153p.
ISBN:0-9628234-3-0, ISBN13: 978-0-9628234-3-5.
Dewey:769.92. LCCN:99-071680.

Audience: **g,l,u,f.**

Beyer, Carl   NE2050.5.K55
Max Klinger: The Late Graphic Work 1909-1919, Catalogue
Raisonné. Bernd Estabrook (Translator), Max Klinger
(Illustrator). Trade Cloth. Alan Wofsy Fine Arts. San Francisco,
CA. 1997. 288p. ISBN:1-55660-170-0, ISBN13:
978-1-55660-170-5. Dewey:769.924.

Audience: **g,l,u,f.**

Black, Peter & Moorhead,   NE2054.5.R4
  Desiree
The Prints of Stanley William Hayter. Trade Cloth. Phaidon
Press. London, 1994. 400p. ISBN:0-7148-8078-7, ISBN13:
978-0-7148-8078-5. Dewey:769.92.

Audience: **g,l,u,f.**

Bocher, E. & Mahérault, J.   NC1499.G4
  Armelhault
Gavarni. Catalogue Raisonné of the Graphic Work: L'oeuvre de
Gavarni. Paul Gavarni (Illustrator), Robert J. Wickenden &
Gordon Ray (Introduction by). Trade Cloth. Alan Wofsy Fine
Arts. San Francisco, CA. 2004. 700p. ISBN:1-55660-314-2,
ISBN13: 978-1-55660-314-3. Dewey:741.

Audience: **g,l,u,f.**

Bolling, G. Fredric &   N6797.K63A41993
  Withington, Valerie A.
The Graphic Work of Dame Laura Knight: Including a
Catalogue Raisonné of Her Prints. Trade Cloth. Ashgate
Publishing, Ltd. Aldershot, 1993. 168p. ISBN:0-85967-939-X,
ISBN13: 978-0-85967-939-8. Dewey:760.092.
LCCN:92-028272.

Audience: **g,l,u,f.**

Bromberg, Ruth   NE2052.5.C25
Canaletto's Etchings: Catalogue Raisonné. Trade Cloth. Alan
Wofsy Fine Arts. San Francisco, CA. 1993. 244p.
ISBN:1-55660-214-6, ISBN13: 978-1-55660-214-6.
Dewey:769/.92/4.

Audience: **g,l,u,f.** *Choice, 1994.*

Bromberg, Ruth   NE642.S52A42000
Walter Sickert: The Prints: A Catalogue Raisonné. Cloth over
Boards. Yale University Press. Cumberland, RI. 2000. 312p.
Paul Mellon Centre for Studies in British Art
ISBN:0-300-08161-8, ISBN13: 978-0-300-08161-9.
Dewey:769.92. LCCN:99-059502.

Audience: **g,l,u,f.** *Choice, 2001.*

Callier, Pierre   NE650.D47
Maurice Denis: A Catalogue Raisonné of the Etchings and
Lithographs. Maurice Denis (Illustrator). Trade Cloth. Alan
Wofsy Fine Arts. San Francisco, CA. 1999. 200p.
ISBN:1-55660-299-5, ISBN13: 978-1-55660-299-3.
Dewey:759.4.

Audience: **g,l,u,f.**

Carpenter, Elizabeth   NE539.D5A42002
Jim Dine Prints, 1985-2000: A Catalogue Raisonné. Evan M.
Maurer & Richard Campbell (Foreword by), Joseph Ruzicka
(Contribution by). Trade Cloth. D. A. P./Distributed Art
Publishers. New York, NY. 2002. 255p. ISBN:0-912964-86-3,
ISBN13: 978-0-912964-86-7. Dewey:741.973.
LCCN:2001-099184.

Audience: **g,l,u,f.**

Castleman, Riva   NE539.J57A4 1986
Jasper Johns: A Print Retrospective. Trade Cloth. Museum of
Modern Art. New York, NY. 1990. 148p. ISBN:0-87070-401-X,
ISBN13: 978-0-87070-401-7. Dewey:769.92/4.
LCCN:85-063733.

Audience: **g,l,u,f.**

Chagall, Mark   NE2356.5.C45
Marc Chagall: The Lithographs; La Collection Sorlier. Ulrike
Gauss (Editor), Christofer Conrad, Henri DesChamps & Hans
Kinkel (Contribution by). Trade Cloth. D. A. P./Distributed Art
Publishers. New York, NY. 1999. 415p. ISBN:1-891024-07-8,
ISBN13: 978-1-891024-07-8. Dewey:759.7.

Audience: **g,l,u,f.**

Coppel, Stephan   NE1336.F55A4 1995
Linocuts of the Machine Age: Claude Flight and His Followers.
Trade Cloth. Ashgate Publishing, Ltd. Aldershot, 1995. 184p.
ISBN:0-85967-945-4, ISBN13: 978-0-85967-945-9.
Dewey:782.2/92. LCCN:95-015901.

Audience: **l,u,f.**

D'Oench, Ellen G.   NE642.S6D64 1999
Copper into Gold: Prints by John Raphael Smith (1751-1812).
Yale University Press. 1999. ISBN:0-300-07630-4, ISBN13:
978-0-300-07630-1.

Audience: **u,f.**

Delteil, Loys   NE650.D457
Delacroix - The Graphic Work: Catalogue Raisonné. Susan E.
Strauber (Translator), Eugene Delacroix (Illustrator), Susan E.
Strauber (Revised by). Trade Cloth. Alan Wofsy Fine Arts. San
Francisco, CA. 1997. 398p. ISBN:1-55660-252-9, ISBN13:
978-1-55660-252-8. Dewey:769.

Audience: **l,u,f.**

Dickey, Stephanie   NE2054.5.R4D45 2004
Rembrandt: Portraits in Print. Trade Cloth. John Benjamins
Publishing Company. Philadelphia, PA. 2004. 368p. OCULI
Studies in the Arts of the Low Countries, 9
ISBN:1-58811-498-8, ISBN13: 978-1-58811-498-3.
Dewey:769.92. LCCN:2004-005302.

Audience: **g,l,u,f.** *Choice, 2004.*

Duckers, Alexander   NE654.G76
George Grosz - The Graphic Work: Catalogue Raisonné. Ed. 2.
Steve Connell (Translator), George Grosz (Illustrator). Trade
Cloth. Alan Wofsy Fine Arts. San Francisco, CA. 1996. 416p.
ISBN:1-55660-213-8, ISBN13: 978-1-55660-213-9.
Dewey:769.92.

Audience: **g,l,u,f.**

Engberg, Siri & Banach,   NE539.M67A42002
   Joan
Robert Motherwell: The Complete Prints 1940-1991: A
Catalogue Raisonné. Ed. 4. Trade Cloth. Hudson Hills Press
LLC. Manchester, VT. 2003. 384p. ISBN:1-55595-163-5,
ISBN13: 978-1-55595-163-4. Dewey:769.92.
LCCN:2002-006167.

Audience: **g,l,u,f.** *Choice, 2003.*

Fath, Creekmore   NE2415.C417
The Lithographs of Thomas Hart Benton: Catalogue Raisonné.
Ed. 3. Thomas Hart Benton (Illustrator), Alan Hyman
(Afterword by). Trade Cloth. Alan Wofsy Fine Arts. San
Francisco, CA. 2001. 248p. ISBN:1-55660-306-1, ISBN13:
978-1-55660-306-8. Dewey:769.924.

Audience: **g,l,u,f.**

Feldman, Frayda &   NE539.W35A4 1989
   Schellmann, Jorg (Editors)
Andy Warhol Prints. Henry Geldzahler & Roberta Bernstein
(Contribution by). Trade Cloth. Abbeville Press, Inc. New York,
NY. 1989. 160p. ISBN:1-55859-050-1, ISBN13:
978-1-55859-050-2. Dewey:769.92. LCCN:89-006638.

Audience: **g,l,u,f.** *Choice, 1985.*

Ficacci, Luigi   NE2052.5.P5
Giovanni Batista Piranesi: The Complete Etchings. Trade Paper.
Taschen America, LLC. Los Angeles, CA. 2000. 800p.
ISBN:3-8228-6620-2, ISBN13: 978-3-8228-6620-7.
Dewey:767.2/092.

Audience: **g,l,u,f.** *Choice, 2001.*

Forrer, Matthi   NE1325.K3 A4 1991
Hokusai: Prints and Drawings. Trade Paper. Prestel Publishing.
New York, NY. 2004. 219p. ISBN:3-7913-2490-X, ISBN13:
978-3-7913-2490-6. Dewey:769.92.

Audience: **g,l,u,f.** *Choice, 1992.*

Friedlaender, Johnny   NE2049.5.F7
Friedlaender's Etchings, 1988-1992: Catalogue Raisonné. Felicia
Rupp (Editor), Johnny Friedlaender (Illustrator), Werner Schmidt
(Introduction by). Trade Cloth. Alan Wofsy Fine Arts. San
Francisco, CA. 1999. 48p. ISBN:1-55660-208-1, ISBN13:
978-1-55660-208-5. Dewey:769.92.

Audience: **g,l,u,f.**

Guastalla, Giorgio &   NE662.M34
   Guastalla, Guido
Marino Marini: Catalogue Raisonné of the Graphic Work,
1919-1980. Trade Cloth. Alan Wofsy Fine Arts. San Francisco,
CA. 1993. 280p. ISBN:1-55660-146-8, ISBN13:
978-1-55660-146-0. Dewey:769.92.

Audience: **g,l,u,f.**

Hardie, Martin & Carter,   NE2210.M3 A41997
   Charles
James McBey - Etchings and Drypoints: A Catalogue Raisonné.
James McBey (Illustrator), Malcolm Salaman (Introduction by).
Trade Cloth. Alan Wofsy Fine Arts. San Francisco, CA. 1997.
328p. ISBN:1-55660-179-4, ISBN13: 978-1-55660-179-8.
Dewey:769.92.

Audience: **g,l,u,f.**

Harrison, Pegram   NE539.F68A41996
Frankenthaler: A Catalog Raisonné, Prints 1961-1994. Suzanne
Boorsch (Introduction by). Trade Cloth. Harry N. Abrams, Inc.
New York, NY. 1996. 480p. ISBN:0-8109-3332-2, ISBN13:
978-0-8109-3332-3. Dewey:769.9/2. LCCN:95-049020.

Audience: **g,l,u,f.**

Hazard, Nicolas Auguste &   NE2349.5.D37A42001
   Delteil, Loys
Catalogue Raisonné de l'Oeuvre Lithographie de Honoré
Daumier. Trade Cloth. Martino Publishing. Mansfield Centre,
CT. 2002. 844p. ISBN:1-57898-347-9, ISBN13:
978-1-57898-347-6. Dewey:769.92. LCCN:2001-044864.

Audience: **g,l,u,f.**

Heenk, Liesbeth   NE539
Howard Hodgkin Prints: A Catalogue Raisonné. Nan Rosenthal
(Introduction by). Trade Cloth. Thames & Hudson. New York,
NY. 2003. 240p. ISBN:0-500-09309-1, ISBN13:
978-0-500-09309-2. Dewey:769.9/2. LCCN:2002-111487.

Audience: **g,l,u,f.** *Choice, 2003.*

Hinterding, Erik (Editor), et   DA682
   al.
Rembrandt the Printmaker. Martin Royaltonkisch & Ger Luijten
(Editors). Trade Cloth. Fitzroy Dearborn Publishers, Inc.
Chicago, IL. 2000. 384p. ISBN:1-57958-304-0, ISBN13:
978-1-57958-304-0. Dewey:942.107/2/07442142.

Audience: **g,l,u,f.** *Choice, 2001.*

Howe, A. Elizabeth   NE2237.5.K74H69 2003
Lynwood Kreneck, Printmaker. Lynwood Kreneck (Illustrator).
Trade Cloth. Texas Tech University Press. Lubbock, TX. 2003.
144p. ISBN:0-89672-505-7, ISBN13: 978-0-89672-505-8.
Dewey:769.92. LCCN:2002-155308.

Audience: **g,l,u,f.**

Jansen, Marije   NE1325.A5A73 2004
Hiroshige's Journey in the 60 Odd Provinces. Trade Paper.
Hotei Publishing. Leiden, 2004. 160p. Famous Japanese Prints
Ser., Vol. 1 ISBN:90-74822-60-6, ISBN13: 978-90-74822-60-2.
Dewey:769.92. LCCN:2004-282595.

Audience: **l,u,f.** *Choice, 2005.*

Johnson, Robert F. &   N40.1.O475Y
Bertazzoni, Giovanna
Variations in Time: Nathan Oliveira, Monotypes and
Monoprints. Trade Paper. University of Washington Press.
Seattle, WA. 1998. 64p. ISBN:0-295-97669-1, ISBN13:
978-0-295-97669-3. Dewey:769.92.

Audience: **g,l,u,f.**

Jones, Dan Burne   NE642.B5
The Prints of Rockwell Kent: Catalogue Raisonné. Ed. 2.
Rockwell Kent (Illustrator), Carl Zigrosser (Introduction by),
Robert Rightmire (Revised by). Trade Cloth. Alan Wofsy Fine
Arts. San Francisco, CA. 2002. 414p. ISBN:1-55660-307-X,
ISBN13: 978-1-55660-307-5. Dewey:769/.92/4.

Audience: **g,l,u,f.** *Choice, 2003.*

Katz, Vincent   NE539.G74A42001
Red Grooms: The Graphic Work. Abrams. 2001.
ISBN:0-8109-6733-2, ISBN13: 978-0-8109-6733-5.

Audience: **g,l,u,f.**

Kenney, George C.   NE539
Bol (Ferdinand), a Catalogue Raisonné of the Graphic Work.
Trade Cloth. Alan Wofsy Fine Arts. San Francisco, CA. 1998.
300p. ISBN:1-55660-247-2, ISBN13: 978-1-55660-247-4.
Dewey:769.92.

Audience: **g,l,u,f.**

Kraeft, Norman & Kraeft,   NE539.L29A41994
June K.
Armin Landeck: The Catalogue Raisonné of His Prints. Ed. 2.
Trade Cloth. Southern Illinois University Press. Carbondale, IL.
1994. 240p. ISBN:0-8093-1740-0, ISBN13: 978-0-8093-1740-0.
Dewey:769.92. LCCN:91-046827.

Audience: **g,l,u,f.**

Lafond, Paul   ND653.B65L3132
Hieronymus Bosch - The Complete Prints: Catalogue Raisonné.
Hieronymus Bosch (Illustrator), Susan Gilchrist (Revised by).
Trade Cloth. Alan Wofsy Fine Arts. San Francisco, CA. 2001.
176p. ISBN:0-614-26236-4, ISBN13: 978-0-614-26236-0.
Dewey:759.9492.

Audience: **g,l,u,f.**

Levinson, Orde (Compiled   NE1336.M83A4
by)
I Was Loneliness: The Complete Graphic Works of John
Muafangejo, A Catalogue Raisonné, 1968-1987. Trade Cloth.
George Braziller Inc. New York, NY. 1993. 428p.
ISBN:0-8076-1307-X, ISBN13: 978-0-8076-1307-8.
Dewey:769.92.

Audience: **g,l,u,f.**

Locker, J. L.   N6953.E82A42000
Magic of M. C. Escher. Joost Elffers & Andreas Landshoff
(Created by). Trade Cloth. Harry N. Abrams, Inc. New York,
NY. 2000. 200p. ISBN:0-8109-6720-0, ISBN13:
978-0-8109-6720-5. Dewey:769.92. LCCN:00-032286.

Audience: **g,l,u,f.** *Choice, 2001.*

Lowe, Ian   NE2047.6.F35L681990
Etchings of Wilfred Fairclough: A Catalogue Raisonné. Trade
Cloth. Ashgate Publishing, Ltd. Aldershot, 1990. 112p.
ISBN:0-85967-846-6, ISBN13: 978-0-85967-846-9.
Dewey:769.92.

Audience: **g,l,u,f.**

Lust, Herbert C.   NE650.G5
Alberto Giacometti: The Complete Graphics, Catalogue
Raisonné. Alberto Giacometti (Illustrator), John Lloyd Taylor
(Introduction by), Alan Wofsy (Revised by). Trade Cloth. Alan
Wofsy Fine Arts. San Francisco, CA. 1991. 240p.
ISBN:1-55660-093-3, ISBN13: 978-1-55660-093-7.
Dewey:741.6.

Audience: **g,l,u,f.** *Choice, 1992.*

Malbert, Roger & White,   NE647
Jessica (Editors)
Picasso and Printmaking in Paris. Susan Ferleger Brades
(Foreword by). Trade Paper. DIANE Publishing Company.
Collingdale, PA. 2002. 127p. ISBN:0-7567-5615-4, ISBN13:
978-0-7567-5615-4. Dewey:769.904074.

Audience: **g,l,u,f.**

Mason, Lauris & Ludman,   NE2312.B44
Joan
George Bellows, the Lithographs: Catalogue Raisonné. George
Bellows (Illustrator). Trade Cloth. Alan Wofsy Fine Arts. San
Francisco, CA. 1992. 300p. ISBN:1-55660-141-7, ISBN13:
978-1-55660-141-5. Dewey:16.76992.

Audience: **g,l,u,f.**

Mellerio, Andre   NE650.R4
Redon's Etchings and Lithographs: A Catalogue Raisonné. Alan
Hyman (Editor), Odilon Redon (Illustrator), Alfred Werner &
Daniel Rich (Introduction by). Trade Cloth. Alan Wofsy Fine
Arts. San Francisco, CA. 2001. 520p. ISBN:1-55660-309-6,
ISBN13: 978-1-55660-309-9. Dewey:759.4.

Audience: **l,u,f.** *Choice, 2002.*

Morse, Peter   NE539.S55
John Sloan's Prints: A Catalogue Raisonné of the Etchings,
Lithographs and Posters. Ed. 2. John Sloan (Illustrator), Jacob
Kainen (Introduction by). Trade Cloth. Alan Wofsy Fine Arts.
San Francisco, CA. 2001. 416p. ISBN:1-55660-308-8, ISBN13:
978-1-55660-308-2. Dewey:769/.924.

Audience: **g,l,u,f.**

Nesbett, Peter T.   NE539
Jacob Lawrence: The Complete Prints (1963-2000) - A
Catalogue Raisonné. Ed. 2. Trade Cloth. University of
Washington Press. Seattle, WA. 2001. 96p.
ISBN:0-295-97955-0, ISBN13: 978-0-295-97955-7.
Dewey:769.92. LCCN:2001-131677.

Audience: **g,l,u,f.** *Choice, 2002.*

Patten, Robert L.   N6797.C78 P3 1992
George Cruikshank's Life, Times and Art: 1835-1878. Trade
Cloth. Rutgers University Press. Piscataway, NJ. 1996. 500p.
ISBN:0-8135-1814-8, ISBN13: 978-0-8135-1814-5.
Dewey:741.6/092. LCCN:91-040344.
                              Audience: **g,l,u,f.** *Choice, 1996.*

Patten, Robert L.   N6797.C78.P3 1992
George Cruikshank's Life, Times and Art: 1792-1835. Trade
Cloth. Rutgers University Press. Piscataway, NJ. 1992. 550p.
ISBN:0-8135-1813-X, ISBN13: 978-0-8135-1813-8.
Dewey:741.6/092. LCCN:91-040344.
                              Audience: **g,l,u,f.** *Choice, 1993.*

Robinson, Susan B. & Pirog,   NE2312.D9A41997
 John
Mabel Dwight: A Catalogue Raisonné of the Lithographs. Trade
Cloth. Smithsonian Institution Press. Washington, DC. 1996.
344p. ISBN:1-56098-646-8, ISBN13: 978-1-56098-646-1.
Dewey:769.92. LCCN:95-048281.
                                           Audience: **g,l,u,f.**

Schellmann, Jorg, et al.   N6888.B463A41997
Joseph Beuys - The Multiples: Catalogue Raisonné of Multiples
and Prints. Ed. 8. Dirk Stemmler, Joan Rothfuss & Peter Nisbet
(Authors). Trade Cloth. Walker Art Center. Minneapolis, MN.
1997. 565p. ISBN:0-935640-57-6, ISBN13: 978-0-935640-57-1.
Dewey:709/.2. LCCN:97-037933.
                                           Audience: **g,l,u,f.**

Schulz, Andrew   NE2062.5.G6S355 2005
Goya's Caprichos: Aesthetics, Perception, and the Body. Trade
Cloth. Cambridge University Press. New York, NY. 2005. 272p.
ISBN:0-521-82105-3, ISBN13: 978-0-521-82105-6.
Dewey:769.92. LCCN:2004-051841.
                                           Audience: **l,u,f.**

Singer, Hans   NE654.K5
Max Klinger's Graphic Work: Catalogue Raisonné, 1878-1903.
Bernd Estabrook (Translator), Max Klinger (Illustrator). Trade
Cloth. Alan Wofsy Fine Arts. San Francisco, CA. 1991. 400p.
ISBN:1-55660-078-X, ISBN13: 978-1-55660-078-4.
Dewey:769.92.
                                           Audience: **g,l,u,f.**

Spink, Nesta, et al.   NE2312.W45A41998
The Lithographs of James McNeill Whistler: A Catalogue
Raisonné; Correspondence and Technical Studies. Harriet Stratis,
Martha Tedeschi & Katharine Lochnan (Authors). Trade Cloth,
Box or Slipcased. Hudson Hills Press LLC. Manchester, VT.
1998. 1000p. ISBN:0-86559-150-4, ISBN13:
978-0-86559-150-9. Dewey:769.92. LCCN:97-015806.
                                           Audience: **g,l,u,f.**

Sultan, Terrie   NE539.C56A42003
Chuck Close Prints: Process and Collaboration. Richard Shiff &
Blaffer Gallery Staff (Contribution by). Trade Cloth. Princeton
University Press. Princeton, NJ. 2003. 160p.
ISBN:0-691-11576-1, ISBN13: 978-0-691-11576-4.
Dewey:769.92. LCCN:2003-048297.
                              Audience: **g,l,u,f.** *Choice, 2004.*

Taylor, Welford Dunaway   NE1112.L37T381995
The Woodcut Art of J. J. Lankes. D. R. Godine. 1999.
ISBN:1-56792-049-7, ISBN13: 978-1-56792-049-9.
                                           Audience: **g,l,u,f.**

Turner, Silvie, et al.   NE642.T74A41998
Julian Trevelyan: Catalogue Raisonné of Prints. Julian
Trevelyan, Norman Ackroyd & Bohun Gallery Staff (Authors).
Trade Cloth. Ashgate Publishing Company. Williston, VT. 1998.
184p. ISBN:1-84014-662-1, ISBN13: 978-1-84014-662-2.
Dewey:769.92. LCCN:99-187806.
                                           Audience: **g,l,u,f.**

Webb, Marilynn & Lonie,   NE792.L66 2003
 Bridie
Marilynn Webb: Prints and Pastels. Trade Paper. Otago
University Press. Dunedin, 2003. 128p. ISBN:1-877276-36-7,
ISBN13: 978-1-877276-36-1. Dewey:769.9293.
LCCN:2004-380356.
                              Audience: **g,l,u,f.** *Choice, 2004.*

Winnan, Audur H.   NE539.G34A41999
Wanda Gag: A Catalogue Raisonné of the Prints. Trade Paper.
University of Minnesota Press. Minneapolis, MN. 1999. 336p.
ISBN:0-8166-3497-1, ISBN13: 978-0-8166-3497-2.
Dewey:769.92. LCCN:99-029637.
                              Audience: **g,l,u,f.** *Choice, 1994.*

Witthoft, Brucia   NE2012.S58A41992
The Fine-Arts Etchings of James David Smillie, 1833-1909: A
Catalogue Raisonné. Trade Cloth. Edwin Mellen Press, The.
Lewiston, NY. 1992. 324p. ISBN:0-7734-9520-7, ISBN13:
978-0-7734-9520-3. Dewey:769.92. LCCN:92-006379.
                                           Audience: **g,l,u,f.**

Woll, Gerd   NE694.M8A42001
Edvard Munch: The Complete Graphic Works. Trade Cloth.
Harry N. Abrams, Inc. New York, NY. 2001. 493p.
ISBN:0-8109-0874-3, ISBN13: 978-0-8109-0874-1.
Dewey:769.92. LCCN:2001-027924.
                              Audience: **g,l,u,f.** *Choice, 2002.*

Wuerth, Louis A.   NE2415.P41
Joseph Pennell - the Lithographs and Etchings: A Catalogue
Raisonné. Joseph Pennell (Illustrator). Trade Cloth. Alan Wofsy
Fine Arts. San Francisco, CA. 1992. 272, 334p.
ISBN:1-55660-220-0, ISBN13: 978-1-55660-220-7. Dewey:763.
                                           Audience: **g,l,u,f.**

Printmaking > Materials and Techniques

                                                   NE538.B6
Proof in Print: A Community of Printmaking Studios. Cloth
Text. Boston Public Library. Boston, MA. 2001. 155p.
ISBN:0-89073-121-7, ISBN13: 978-0-89073-121-5.
Dewey:769.904.
                                           Audience: **g,l,u,f.**

Ayres, Julia   **NE2242**
Monotype: Mediums and Methods for Painterly Printmaking.
Watson-Guptill Books. 2001. ISBN:0-8230-3128-4, ISBN13:
978-0-8230-3128-3.

Audience: **g,l,u,f.**

Banister, Manly   **NE1625.B36 1986**
Practical Guide to Etching and Other Intaglio Printmaking
Techniques. Trade Paper. Dover Publications, Inc. Mineola, NY.
1986. 128p. ISBN:0-486-25165-9, ISBN13: 978-0-486-25165-3.
Dewey:765. LCCN:86-008809.

Audience: **g,l,u,f.**

Barker, David   **NE1300.8.C6**
Traditional Techniques in Contemporary Chinese Printmaking.
Trade Paper. University of Hawaii Press. Honolulu, HI. 2005.
221p. ISBN:0-8248-2991-3, ISBN13: 978-0-8248-2991-9.
Dewey:769.9/51.

Audience: **g,l,u,f.**

Bodman, Sarah   **N7433.3.B63 2005**
Creating Artists' Books. Trade Paper, Perfect. Watson-Guptill
Publications, Inc. New York, NY. 2005. 128p. Printmaking
Handbooks ISBN:0-8230-1012-0, ISBN13: 978-0-8230-1012-7.
Dewey:702.81.

Audience: **g,l,u,f.**

Booth, John   **NE850**
Looking at Old Prints. Marquess of Bath Staff (Foreword by).
Trade Cloth. DIANE Publishing Company. Collingdale, PA.
2004. 202p. ISBN:0-7567-7475-6, ISBN13: 978-0-7567-7475-2.
Dewey:760/.28.

Audience: **g,l,u,f.**

Carr, Kathleen T.   **TR280.C35 1997**
Polaroid Transfers: A Complete Visual Guide to Creating Image
and Emulsion Transfers. Trade Cloth. Watson-Guptill
Publications, Inc. New York, NY. 1997. 144p.
ISBN:0-8174-5554-X, ISBN13: 978-0-8174-5554-5.
Dewey:771/.4. LCCN:97-001132.

Audience: **g,l,u,f.**

Dahl, Carolyn A.   **NE1338.D342002**
Natural Impressions: Taking an Artistic Path Through Nature.
Trade Cloth. Watson-Guptill Publications, Inc. New York, NY.
2002. 112p. ISBN:0-8230-3149-7, ISBN13: 978-0-8230-3149-8.
Dewey:769/.434. LCCN:2002-003466.

Audience: **g,l,u,f.**

Devon, Marjorie & Walch,   **NE304**
  Peter (Introduction by)
Tamarind Lithography Workshop Inc. Catalog Raisonné,
1960-1970. Trade Paper. University of New Mexico, Art
Museum. Albuquerque, NM. 1989. 284p. ISBN:0-944282-08-3,
ISBN13: 978-0-944282-08-3. Dewey:769.922.

Audience: **g,l,u,f.**

Eichenberg, Fritz   **NE400**
The Art of the Print: Masterpieces, History, Techniques. Trade
Cloth. Harry N. Abrams, Inc. New York, NY. 1975. 608p.

ISBN:0-8109-0103-X, ISBN13: 978-0-8109-0103-2.
Dewey:769/.9. LCCN:74-018024.

Audience: **g,l,u,f.** *B*

Erickson, Janet D. &   **NE0860.E7**
  Sproul, Adelaide
Print Making Without a Press. Trade Paper. Books on Demand.
Ann Arbor, MI. 123p. ISBN:0-608-11277-1, ISBN13:
978-0-608-11277-0. Dewey:761.028. LCCN:65-019672.

Audience: **g,l,u,f.**

Gascoigne, Bamber   **NE400**
How to Identify Prints. Ed. 2. Trade Paper. Thames & Hudson.
New York, NY. 2004. 208p. ISBN:0-500-28480-6, ISBN13:
978-0-500-28480-3. Dewey:760.2/8. LCCN:2003-112372.

Audience: **g,l,u,f.**

Green, Phil   **Z258**
Understanding Digital Color. Ed. 2. Trade Cloth. GATFPress.
Sewickley, PA. 1999. 400p. ISBN:0-88362-233-5, ISBN13:
978-0-88362-233-9. Dewey:686.2/3042. LCCN:99-064453.

Audience: **g,l,u,f.**

Grey, Christopher   **TR495.G74**
Photographer's Guide to Polaroid Transfer: Step-by-Step. Ed. 2.
Trade Cloth. Amherst Media, Inc. Buffalo, NY. 2001. 128p.
ISBN:1-58428-064-6, ISBN13: 978-1-58428-064-4.
Dewey:771.44.

Audience: **g,l,u,f.**

Griffiths, Antony   **NE400.G74 1996**
Prints and Printmaking: An Introduction to the History and
Techniques. Trade Paper. University of California Press.
Berkeley, CA. 1996. 152p. ISBN:0-520-20714-9, ISBN13:
978-0-520-20714-1. Dewey:760. LCCN:96-012571.

Audience: **g,l,u,f.** *Choice, 1996.*

Hausberg, Margaret D.   **ND553.R73**
The Prints of Theodore Roussel: A Catalogue Raisonné. Trade
Cloth. M. Hausberg. Lake Forest, IL. 1991. 264p.
ISBN:0-9628234-0-6, ISBN13: 978-0-9628234-0-4.
Dewey:760.3. LCCN:91-174199.

Audience: **g,l,u,f.**

Lambert, Susan   **NE850.L352001**
Prints: Art and Techniques. Trade Cloth. Harry N. Abrams, Inc.
New York, NY. 2001. 96p. Victoria and Albert Museum
Catalogues Ser. ISBN:0-8109-6577-1, ISBN13:
978-0-8109-6577-5. Dewey:769. LCCN:00-107863.

Audience: **g,l,u,f.** *Choice, 2002.*

Martin, Judy   **NE850.M375 2002**
The Encyclopedia of Printmaking Techniques: A Comprehensive
Visual Guide to Traditional and Contemporary Techniques.
Trade Paper. Sterling Publishing Co., Inc. New York, NY. 2002.
176p. ISBN:0-8069-9300-6, ISBN13: 978-0-8069-9300-3.
Dewey:760/.28. LCCN:2003-270614.

Audience: **g,l,u,f.**

Mayor, A. Hyatt   **NE400**
Prints and People: A Social History of Printed Pictures. Paper
Text. Princeton University Press. Princeton, NJ. 1981. 248p.
ISBN:0-691-00326-2, ISBN13: 978-0-691-00326-9.
Dewey:769.9. LCCN:80-007817.
                                              Audience: **g,l,u,f.**

McKnight, Thomas   **ND237.O5**
Thomas McKnight: Windows on Paradise. Trade Cloth.
Abbeville Press, Inc. New York, NY. 1997. 200p.
ISBN:0-89660-088-2, ISBN13: 978-0-89660-088-1.
Dewey:759.1/3.
                                              Audience: **g,l,u,f.**

Ogden Nature Center Staff   **NE1338.N3852004**
& Sterling Publishing Company Staff
Nature Printing. Trade Paper. Sterling Publishing Co., Inc. New
York, NY. 2004. 128p. ISBN:1-4027-0724-X, ISBN13:
978-1-4027-0724-7. Dewey:761. LCCN:2003-019006.
                                              Audience: **g,l,u,f.**

Platzker, David & Wyckoff,   **NE400.P58 2000**
Elizabeth
Hard Pressed: 600 Years of Prints and Process. Trade Cloth.
Hudson Hills Press LLC. Manchester, VT. 2000. 128p.
ISBN:1-55595-192-9, ISBN13: 978-1-55595-192-4.
Dewey:769.9. LCCN:00-040935.
                              Audience: **g,l,u,f.** *Choice, 2001.*

Rainbird, Sean   **NE642**
Print Matters: The Kenneth E. Tyler Gift. Pat Gilmour
(Contribution by). Trade Paper, Saddle Stitched, Dust Jacket.
Tate Gallery Publishing, Ltd. London, 2005. 128p.
ISBN:1-85437-558-X, ISBN13: 978-1-85437-558-2.
Dewey:769.9/2. LCCN:2004-111325.
                                              Audience: **g,l,u,f.**

Roberts, Adam &   **NE1843**
Robertson, Carol
Screenprinting. Trade Paper. Thames & Hudson. New York, NY.
2004. 208p. ISBN:0-500-28425-3, ISBN13: 978-0-500-28425-4.
Dewey:764.8. LCCN:2002-116936.
                                              Audience: **g,l,u,f.**

Ross, John, et al.   **NE850.R59 1990**
The Complete Printmaker: Techniques - Traditions -
Innovations. Ed. 2. Clare Romano & Tim Ross (Authors). Trade
Paper. Simon & Schuster. New York, NY. 1991. 352p.
ISBN:0-02-927372-2, ISBN13: 978-0-02-927372-2.
Dewey:760/.28. LCCN:89-011900.
                                              Audience: **g,l,u,f.**

Rumelin, Christian   **NE830**
Techniques of Printmaking. Ashmolean Museum Staff
(Contribution by). Trade Paper. Ashmolean Museum. Oxford,
2004. 24p. ISBN:1-85444-186-8, ISBN13: 978-1-85444-186-7.
Dewey:769.9/22.
                                              Audience: **g,l,u,f.**

Saff, Donald & Sacilotto,   **NE850**
Deli
Printmaking: History and Process. Trade Cloth. Holt, Rinehart &

Winston. Austin, TX. 1978. xii, 436p. ISBN:0-03-042106-3,
ISBN13: 978-0-03-042106-8. Dewey:760/.28. LCCN:76-054995.
                                    Audience: **g,l,u,f.** $\mathcal{B}$

Spandorfer, Merle, et al.   **RC963.6.A78.S62 1993**
Making Art Safely: Alternatives in Drawing, Painting,
Printmaking, Graphic Design, and Photography. Deborah Curtiss
& Jack W. Snyder (Authors). Cloth Text. John Wiley & Sons,
Inc. Hoboken, NJ. 1993. xvi, 255p. ISBN:0-442-23489-9,
ISBN13: 978-0-442-23489-8. Dewey:363.1197.
LCCN:92-004841.
                              Audience: **g,l,u,f.** *Choice, 1993.*

Stewart-Howe, Kathleen   **NE2250.T35 VOL. 17**
(Editor)
Intersections Lithography: Lithography, Photography, and the
Traditions of Printmaking. Trade Cloth. University of New
Mexico Press. Albuquerque, NM. 1998. 109p. The Tamarind
Papers ISBN:0-8263-1845-2, ISBN13: 978-0-8263-1845-9.
Dewey:763. LCCN:97-040483.
                                              Audience: **g,l,u,f.**

Stromquist, Annie   **TT273**
Simple Screenprinting: Basic Techniques and Creative Projects.
Trade Paper, Perfect. Lark Books. Asheville, NC. 2005. 128p.
ISBN:1-57990-664-8, ISBN13: 978-1-57990-664-1.
Dewey:745.73. LCCN:2004-004991.
                                              Audience: **g,l,u,f.**

Tyler, Ron (Editor)   **NC135.T4N67 1994**
Prints and Printmakers of Texas: Proceedings of the Twentieth
Annual North American Print Conference. Trade Cloth. Texas
State Historical Association. Austin, TX. 1996. 370p.
ISBN:0-87611-137-1, ISBN13: 978-0-87611-137-6.
Dewey:760/.09764. LCCN:94-013907.
                                              Audience: **g,l,u,f.**

Walker, George A.   **NE1223**
The Woodcut Artist's Handbook: Techniques and Tools for
Relief Printmaking. Trade Paper. Firefly Books, Ltd. Tonawanda,
NY. 2005. 168p. ISBN:1-55407-045-7, ISBN13:
978-1-55407-045-9. Dewey:761/.2. LCCN:2006-276608.
                                              Audience: **g,l,u,f.**

Welden, Dan & Muir,   **NE863.W45 2001**
Pauline
Printmaking in the Sun. Trade Cloth. Watson-Guptill
Publications, Inc. New York, NY. 2001. 144p.
ISBN:0-8230-4292-8, ISBN13: 978-0-8230-4292-0.
Dewey:766/.7. LCCN:00-049420.
                                              Audience: **g,l,u,f.**

Westley, A.   **NE850.W47 2002**
Relief Printmaking. Trade Cloth. Watson-Guptill Publications,
Inc. New York, NY. 2002. 128p. Printmaking Handbooks
ISBN:0-8230-4524-2, ISBN13: 978-0-8230-4524-2. Dewey:761.
LCCN:2001-091522.
                                              Audience: **g,l,u,f.**

White, Lucy Mueller　　　　　　　　**RC489.A7W476 2002**
Printmaking for Art Therapists. Trade Paper. Jessica Kingsley
Ltd. London, 2002. 240p. ISBN:1-84310-708-2, ISBN13:
978-1-84310-708-8. Dewey:615.8/5156. LCCN:2002-021895.
　　　　　　　　　　　　　　　　Audience: **g,l,u,f.**

Wilson, Daniel G.　　　　　　　　**Z252.5.O5W552005**
Lithography Primer. Ed. 3. Perfect. GATFPress. Sewickley, PA.
2005. 163p. ISBN:0-88362-521-0, ISBN13: 978-0-88362-521-7.
Dewey:686.2/315. LCCN:2004-114703.
　　　　　　　　　　　　　　　　Audience: **g,l,u,f.**

Printmaking > Other Topics

Cushing, Lincoln　　　　　　　　**NC1807.C8C872003**
Revolución: Cuban Poster Art. Trade Paper. Chronicle Books
LLC. San Francisco, CA. 2003. 132p. ISBN:0-8118-3582-0,
ISBN13: 978-0-8118-3582-4. Dewey:741.6/74/09729109046.
LCCN:2002-035092.
　　　　　　　　　Audience: **g,l,u,f.**　*Choice, 2004.*

Printmaking > Other Topics > Artists' Books

Drucker, Johanna　　　　　　　　**N7433.3**
The Century of Artists Books. Trade Paper. Granary Books, Inc.
New York, NY. 2004. 392p. ISBN:1-887123-69-5, ISBN13:
978-1-887123-69-3. Dewey:702.81.
　　　　　　　　　　　　　　　　Audience: **g,l,u,f.**

LaFerla, Jane & Gunter,　　　　　　**Z271.P452004**
Veronika A. (Editors)
The Penland Book of Handmade Books: Master Classes in
Bookmaking Techniques. Cloth over Boards. Lark Books.
Asheville, NC. 2004. 232p. ISBN:1-57990-474-2, ISBN13:
978-1-57990-474-6. Dewey:686.3. LCCN:2004-007419.
　　　　　　　　　　　　　　　　Audience: **g,l,u,f.**

Lyons, Joan (Editor)　　　　　　**N7433.3.A751985**
Artists' Books: A Critical Anthology and Sourcebook. Ed. 3.
Dick Higgins (Preface by). Paper Text. Visual Studies
Workshop. Rochester, NY. 1993. 274p. Research, Fine Arts Ser.
ISBN:0-89822-041-6, ISBN13: 978-0-89822-041-4.
Dewey:700/.9/04. LCCN:85-003180.
　　　　　　　　　Audience: **g,l,u,f.**　*Choice, 1986.*

Photography > Reference Works > Bibliographies and Research Guides

Kreisel, Martha　　　　　　　　**Z7134**
American Women Photographers: A Selected and Annotated
Bibliography. Cloth Text. Greenwood Publishing Group, Inc.
Portsmouth, NH. 1999. 368p. Art Reference Collection Ser., 18
ISBN:0-313-30478-5, ISBN13: 978-0-313-30478-1.
Dewey:016.77/082/0973. LCCN:98-048654.
　　　　　　　　　Audience: **g,l,u,f.**　*Choice, 1999.*

Roosens, Laurent P.　　　　　　**Z7134.R66 1989**
History of Photography: A Bibliography of Books, Vol. 2. Trade
Cloth. Continuum International Publishing Group, Ltd. London,
1994. 192p. ISBN:0-7201-2152-3, ISBN13: 978-0-7201-2152-0.
Dewey:016.77/09. LCCN:89-033758.
　　　　　　　Audience: **g,l,u,f.**　*Choice, 1995, 1990.*

Roosens, Laurent P.　　　　　　**Z7134.R66 1989**
History of Photography: A Bibliography of Books. Trade Cloth.
Continuum International Publishing Group, Ltd. London, 1996.
444p. ISBN:0-7201-2310-0, ISBN13: 978-0-7201-2310-4.
Dewey:016.7/7/09. LCCN:89-033758.
　　　　　　　　　　　　　　　　Audience: **g,l,u,f.**

Roosens, Laurent P. & Salu,　　　**Z7134.R661989TR15**
Luc
History of Photography: A Bibliography of Books. Trade Cloth.
Continuum International Publishing Group, Ltd. London, 1999.
448p. ISBN:0-7201-2354-2, ISBN13: 978-0-7201-2354-8.
Dewey:016.77/09. LCCN:89-033758.
　　　　　　　　　　　　　　　　Audience: **g,l,u,f.**

Rudisill, Richard, et al.　　　　　　　**TR15**
Photographers: A Sourcebook for Historical Research. Ed. 2.
Peter Palmquist & Jeremy Rowe (Authors), Martha A.
Sandweiss (Foreword by). Trade Paper. Carl Mautz Publishing.
Nevada City, CA. 2000. 154p. ISBN:1-887694-18-8, ISBN13:
978-1-887694-18-6. Dewey:929.1072. LCCN:99-070538.
　　　　　　　Audience: **g,l,u,f.**　*Choice, 2001.*

Photography > Reference Works > Dictionaries and Encyclopedias

Ang, Tom　　　　　　　　　　**TR9.A53 2002**
Dictionary of Photography and Digital Imaging: The Essential
Reference for the Modern Photographer. Trade Cloth.
Watson-Guptill Publications, Inc. New York, NY. 2002. 388p.
ISBN:0-8174-3789-4, ISBN13: 978-0-8174-3789-3.
Dewey:770/.3. LCCN:2001-094987.
　　　　　　　　　Audience: **g,l,u,f.**　*Choice, 2002.*

Bajac, Quentin & Caujolle,　　　　**TR9.P48132004**
Christian
The Abrams Encyclopedia of Photography. Trade Cloth. Harry
N. Abrams, Inc. New York, NY. 2004. 288p.
ISBN:0-8109-5609-8, ISBN13: 978-0-8109-5609-4.
Dewey:770/.3. LCCN:2004-007710.
　　　　　　　　　Audience: **g,l,u,f.**　*Choice, 2005.*

Baldwin, Gordon　　　　　　　**TR9.B35 1991**
Looking at Photographs: A Guide to Technical Terms. Trade
Paper. Oxford University Press, Inc. New York, NY. 1991. 88p.
Looking at Ser. ISBN:0-89236-192-1, ISBN13:
978-0-89236-192-2. Dewey:770/.3. LCCN:90-028861.
　　　　　　　　　　　　　　　　Audience: **g,l,u,f.**

Cope, Peter　　　　　　　　　　**TR267.C67 2002**
The Digital Photographer's Pocket Encyclopedia: 3000 Terms

Explained. Trade Paper. Tiffen Company LLC, The. Hauppauge, NY. 2002. 192p. ISBN:1-883403-90-1, ISBN13: 978-1-883403-90-4. Dewey:778.3. LCCN:2001-049499.

Audience: **g,l,u,f.**

Jeffrey, Ian   **TR147**
The Photography Book. Trade Cloth. Phaidon Press. London, 2005. 512p. ISBN:0-7148-4488-8, ISBN13: 978-0-7148-4488-6. Dewey:770. LCCN:2006-530401.

Audience: **g,l,u,f.**

Lenman, Robin (Editor)   **TR9**
The Oxford Companion to the Photograph. Trade Cloth. Oxford University Press, Inc. New York, NY. 2005. 792p. ISBN:0-19-866271-8, ISBN13: 978-0-19-866271-6. Dewey:770.3. LCCN:2006-295475.

Audience: **g,l,u,f.**

McDarrah, Timothy S., et   **TR9.M39 1999**
al.
The Photography Encyclopedia. Gloria S. McDarrah & Fred W. McDarrah (Authors). Trade Cloth. Thomson Gale. Farmington Hills, MI. 1998. 689p. ISBN:0-02-865025-5, ISBN13: 978-0-02-865025-8. Dewey:770.3. LCCN:98-046084.

Audience: **g,l,u,f.** *Choice, 1999.*

Naylor, Colin (Editor)   **TR139.C663 1988**
Contemporary Photographers. Ed. 2. Trade Cloth. Thomson Gale. Farmington Hills, MI. 1988. x, 1145p. ISBN:0-912289-79-1, ISBN13: 978-0-912289-79-3. Dewey:770/.92/2 B. LCCN:88-158445.

Audience: **g,l,u,f.** *Choice, 1988.*

Stroebel, Leslie & Zakia,   **TR9.F6 1993**
Richard D. (Editors)
Focal Encyclopedia of Photography. Ed. 3. Trade Paper. Elsevier Science & Technology Books. Saint Louis, MO. 1996. 928p. ISBN:0-240-51417-3, ISBN13: 978-0-240-51417-8. Dewey:770.3. LCCN:92-044267.

Audience: **g,l,u,f.**

Warren, Lynne (Editor)   **TR642.E5 2005**
Encyclopedia of Twentieth-Century Photography. Cloth Text. Routledge. New York, NY. 2005. 2048p. ISBN:1-57958-393-8, ISBN13: 978-1-57958-393-4. Dewey:770/.9/0403. LCCN:2005-046287.

Audience: **g,l,u,f.** *Choice, 2006.*

Photography > Reference Works > Directories

                                                                                    TR6.5
Gordon's Photography Price Annual International 2005. Trade Cloth. LTB Gordonsart, Inc. Phoenix, AZ. 2005. 600p. ISBN:1-933295-00-7, ISBN13: 978-1-933295-00-8. Dewey:779.075.

Audience: **g,l,u,f.**

Photography > Histories and Handbooks > Periods and Styles

Ades, Dawn   **TR685**
Photomontage. Trade Paper. Thames & Hudson. New York, NY. 1986. 180p. World of Art Ser. ISBN:0-500-20208-7, ISBN13: 978-0-500-20208-1. Dewey:778.8. LCCN:86-050313.

Audience: **g,l,u,f.**

Clarke, Graham   **TR15.C566 1997**
The Photograph. Trade Paper. Oxford University Press, Inc. New York, NY. 1997. 246p. Oxford History of Art Ser. ISBN:0-19-284200-5, ISBN13: 978-0-19-284200-8. Dewey:770.9. LCCN:96-047645.

Audience: **g,l,u,f.** *Choice, 1997.*

Cravens, R. H.   **TR654.C715 2002**
Photography Past and Forward: Aperture at Fifty. Melissa Harris (Editor). Trade Cloth. Aperture Foundation, Inc. New York, NY. 2002. 160p. ISBN:0-89381-996-4, ISBN13: 978-0-89381-996-5. Dewey:770. LCCN:2002-107716.

Audience: **g,l,u,f.** *Choice, 2003.*

Crawford, Alistair   **TR820.5**
Erich Lessing: Arresting Time - Reportage Photography 1948-1973. Erich Lessing (Photographer). Trade Cloth. Quantuck Lane Press & The Mill Road Collaborative, The. New York, NY. 2005. 456p. ISBN:1-59372-020-3, ISBN13: 978-1-59372-020-9. Dewey:779/.092.

Audience: **g,l,u,f.**

Elwall, Robert (Editor)   **TR659**
Building with Light: An International History of Architectural Photography. Trade Cloth. Merrell Publishers Ltd. London, 2005. 240p. ISBN:1-85894-215-2, ISBN13: 978-1-85894-215-5. Dewey:778.9/4/09.

Audience: **g,l,u,f.**

Goldberg, Vicki   **TR185.P49 1988**
Photography in Print: Writings from 1816 to Present. Trade Paper. University of New Mexico Press. Albuquerque, NM. 1988. 570p. ISBN:0-8263-1091-5, ISBN13: 978-0-8263-1091-0. Dewey:770. LCCN:88-014299.

Audience: **g,l,u,f.**

Hambourg, Maria Morris   **TR646.U6**
The New Vision: Photography Between the World Wars-The Ford Motor Company Collection at the Metropolitan Museum of Art. Ed. 2. Christopher Phillips (Contribution by). Trade Paper. Yale University Press. Cumberland, RI. 1989. 328p. Metropolitan Museum of Art Ser. ISBN:0-300-08642-3, ISBN13: 978-0-300-08642-3. Dewey:779/.09/0420747471.

Audience: **g,l,u,f.** *Choice, 1990.*

Henisch, Heinz K. &   **TR485.H46 1996**
Henisch, Bridget A.
The Painted Photograph, 1839-1914: Origins, Techniques, Aspirations. Trade Cloth. Pennsylvania State University Press.

University Park, PA. 1996. 1324p. ISBN:0-271-01507-1,
ISBN13: 978-0-271-01507-1. Dewey:771/.44. LCCN:95-022821.

Audience: **g,l,u,f.** *Choice, 1997.*

Henisch, Heinz K. &   **TR15.H46 1994**
   Henisch, Bridget A.
The Photographic Experience, 1839-1914: Images and Attitudes.
Trade Cloth. Pennsylvania State University Press. University
Park, PA. 1994. 2164p. ISBN:0-271-00930-6, ISBN13:
978-0-271-00930-8. Dewey:770/.9. LCCN:92-036781.

Audience: **g,l,u,f.** *Choice, 1994.*

Hunter, Jefferson   **PN56.P46H8 1987**
Image and Word: The Interaction of Twentieth-Century
Photographs and Texts. Trade Cloth. Harvard University Press.
Cambridge, MA. 1987. 264p. ISBN:0-674-44405-1, ISBN13:
978-0-674-44405-8. Dewey:770. LCCN:86-018298.

Audience: **l,u,f.** *Choice, 1987.*

Mulligan, Therese &   **TR650.I65 1999**
   Wooters, David (Editors)
Photography from 1839 to Today: George Eastman House,
Rochester, NY. Trade Cloth. Taschen America, LLC. Los
Angeles, CA. 1999. 768p. Klotz Ser. ISBN:3-8228-7073-0,
ISBN13: 978-3-8228-7073-0. Dewey:779.

Audience: **g,l,u,f.** *Choice, 2000.*

Rosenblum, Naomi   **TR15.R67 1997**
A World History of Photography. Ed. 3. Trade Cloth. Abbeville
Press, Inc. New York, NY. 1997. 696p. ISBN:0-7892-0028-7,
ISBN13: 978-0-7892-0028-0. Dewey:770/.9. LCCN:96-036153.

Audience: **g,l,u,f.** *B*

Schaaf, Larry John   **TR144 .S35 1996**
Records of the Dawn of Photography: Talbot's Notebooks P and
Q. Trade Cloth. Cambridge University Press. New York, NY.
1996. 449p. ISBN:0-521-44051-3, ISBN13: 978-0-521-44051-6.
Dewey:770/.92. LCCN:95-010540.

Audience: **l,u,f.**

Spira, S. F.   **TR15.S662001**
The History of Photography: As Seen Through the Spira
Collection. Eaton S. Lothrop Jr. & Jonathan B. Spira
(Contribution by). Trade Cloth. Aperture Foundation, Inc. New
York, NY. 2001. 192p. ISBN:0-89381-953-0, ISBN13:
978-0-89381-953-8. Dewey:770/.9. LCCN:2001-092554.

Audience: **g,l,u,f.** *Choice, 2002.*

Wood, John (Editor)   **TR365.W66 1995**
The Scenic Daguerreotype: Romanticism and Early
Photography. John R. Stilgoe (Foreword by). Trade Cloth.
University of Iowa Press. Iowa City, IA. 1995. 238p.
ISBN:0-87745-511-2, ISBN13: 978-0-87745-511-0.
Dewey:778.9/36/09034. LCCN:94-049126.

Audience: **g,l,u,f.** *Choice, 1996.*

Photography > Histories and Handbooks > Cultures, Regions, Nationalities

Bendavid-Val, Leah (Editor)   **TR790.T47 2003**
Through the Lens: National Geographic Greatest Photographs.
National Geographic Society Staff (Contribution by). Trade
Cloth. National Geographic Society. Washington, DC. 2003.
504p. ISBN:0-7922-6164-X, ISBN13: 978-0-7922-6164-3.
Dewey:779. LCCN:2003-052757.

Audience: **g,l,u,f.**

Bernardin, Susan, et al.   **E77.5.T73 2003**
Trading Gazes: Euro-American Women Photographers and
Native North Americans, 1880-1940. Melody Graulich, Lisa
MacFarlane & Nicole Tonkovich (Authors), Louis Owens
(Afterword by). Trade Cloth. Rutgers University Press.
Piscataway, NJ. 2003. 240p. ISBN:0-8135-3169-1, ISBN13:
978-0-8135-3169-4. Dewey:970/.00497. LCCN:2002-070503.

Audience: **g,l,u,f.** *Choice, 2003.*

Birgus, Vladimir   **TR65.3.C4713 2002**
Czech Photographic Avant-Garde, 1918-1948. Trade Cloth. MIT
Press. Cambridge, MA. 2002. 311p. ISBN:0-262-02516-7,
ISBN13: 978-0-262-02516-4. Dewey:779/.074/437.
LCCN:2001-094719.

Audience: **g,l,u,f.** *Choice, 2003.*

Debroise, Olivier   **TR28.D4313 2001**
Mexican Suite: A History of Photography in Mexico. Stella de
Sá Rego (Editor, Translator). Trade Cloth. University of Texas
Press. Austin, TX. 2001. 300p. ISBN:0-292-71611-7, ISBN13:
978-0-292-71611-7. Dewey:770/.972. LCCN:00-039295.

Audience: **g,l,u,f.** *Choice, 2001.*

Falconer, John   **TR652 .F35 2001**
India: Pioneering Photographers, 1850-1900. Trade Paper.
British Library, The. London, 2002. 144p. ISBN:0-7123-4746-1,
ISBN13: 978-0-7123-4746-4. Dewey:770.95409034.
LCCN:2003-313890.

Audience: **g,l,u,f.**

Fleischhauer, Carl &   **E806.D616 1988**
   Brannan, Beverly W. (Editors)
Documenting America, 1935-1943. Trade Paper. University of
California Press. Berkeley, CA. 1988. 300p. Approaches to
American Culture Ser., No. 2 ISBN:0-520-06221-3, ISBN13:
978-0-520-06221-4. Dewey:973.917. LCCN:87-024598.

Audience: **g,l,u,f.** *Choice, 1989.*

Foresta, Merry A.   **TR645.W18N37 1996**
American Photographs: The First Century. Charles Isaacs
(Afterword by). Trade Cloth. Smithsonian Institution Press.
Washington, DC. 1996. 172p. ISBN:1-56098-718-9, ISBN13:
978-1-56098-718-5. Dewey:779/.0973/074753.
LCCN:96-025338.

Audience: **g,l,u,f.** *Choice, 1997.*

FotoFest   **TR27.5.I451997**
Image and Memory: Photography from Latin America,
1866-1994. Wendy Watriss & Lois Parkinson Zamora (Editors),

Audience: g=general, l=lower division undergraduate, u=upper division undergraduate, f=faculty.

763

Fernando Castro, Boris Kossoy & Marta Sánchez Philippe (Other Primary Creators). Trade Cloth. University of Texas Press. Austin, TX. 1998. 464p. ISBN:0-292-79118-6, ISBN13: 978-0-292-79118-3. Dewey:779/.098. LCCN:94-035532.

Audience: **g,l,u,f.** *Choice, 1998.*

Garner, Gretchen   **TR23.G37 2003**
Disappearing Witness: Change in Twentieth-Century American Photography. Trade Cloth. Johns Hopkins University Press. Baltimore, MD. 2003. 328p. ISBN:0-8018-7167-0, ISBN13: 978-0-8018-7167-2. Dewey:770/.973/0904. LCCN:2002-006243.

Audience: **g,l,u,f.** *Choice, 2004.*

Geller, Peter L.   **F1090.5**
Northern Exposures: Photographing and Filming the Canadian North, 1920-45. Trade Cloth. University of British Columbia Press. Vancouver, BC. 2004. 256p. ISBN:0-7748-0927-2, ISBN13: 978-0-7748-0927-6. Dewey:971.9/02.

Audience: **u,f.**

Johnson, Tim (Editor)   **E77.5.S65 1998**
Spirit Capture: Photographs from the National Museum of the American Indian. Trade Cloth. Smithsonian Institution Press. Washington, DC. 1998. 205p. ISBN:1-56098-924-6, ISBN13: 978-1-56098-924-0. Dewey:779.997000497. LCCN:98-004173.

Audience: **g,l,u,f.** *Choice, 1999.*

Kozloff, Max   **TR645.N72K68 2002**
New York: Capital of Photography. Karen Levitov, Johanna Goldfeld & Jewish Museum, New York, N.Y. Staff (Contribution by). Cloth over Boards. Yale University Press. Cumberland, RI. 2002. 208p. ISBN:0-300-09332-2, ISBN13: 978-0-300-09332-2. Dewey:770/.9747/1. LCCN:2001-006947.

Audience: **g,l,u,f.** *Choice, 2003, 2002.*

Marien, Mary Warner   **TR15**
Photography: A Cultural History. Trade Cloth. Prentice Hall Art. Upper Saddle River, NJ. 2002. 544p. ISBN:0-13-183297-2, ISBN13: 978-0-13-183297-8. Dewey:770/.9.

Audience: **g,l,u,f.** *Choice, 2003.*

Marien, Mary Warner   **TR187 .M37 1997**
Photography and Its Critics: A Cultural History, 1839-1900. Trade Cloth. Cambridge University Press. New York, NY. 1997. 240p. Perspectives on Photography Ser. ISBN:0-521-55043-2, ISBN13: 978-0-521-55043-7. Dewey:770.7/22. LCCN:96-031557.

Audience: **g,l,u,f.** *Choice, 1997.*

McDannell, Colleen   **BL2525.M395 2005**
Picturing Faith: Photography and the Great Depression. Cloth over Boards. Yale University Press. Cumberland, RI. 2004. 336p. ISBN:0-300-10430-8, ISBN13: 978-0-300-10430-1. Dewey:200/.973/09043. LCCN:2004-007820.

Audience: **g,l,u,f.** *Choice, 2005.*

McEuen, Melissa A.   **TR139.M3952000**
Seeing America: Women Photographers Between the Wars. Trade Cloth. University Press of Kentucky. Lexington, KY. 1999. 360p. ISBN:0-8131-2132-9, ISBN13: 978-0-8131-2132-1. Dewey:770/.92/273 B. LCCN:99-017219.

Audience: **g,l,u,f.** *Choice, 2000.*

Nickel, Douglas R. &   **TR647.C3594 2002**
  Carroll, Lewis
Dreaming in Pictures: The Photography of Lewis Carroll. San Francisco Museum of Modern Art Staff (Contribution by). Cloth over Boards. Yale University Press. Cumberland, RI. 2002. 172p. ISBN:0-300-09169-9, ISBN13: 978-0-300-09169-4. Dewey:779/.092. LCCN:2002-006539.

Audience: **g,l,u,f.**

Orvell, Miles   **TR23**
American Photography. Trade Paper. Oxford University Press, Inc. New York, NY. 2003. 256p. Oxford History of Art Ser. ISBN:0-19-284271-4, ISBN13: 978-0-19-284271-8. Dewey:770/.973. LCCN:2003-273142.

Audience: **g,l,u,f.**

Rinhart, Floyd, et al.   **TR375.R56 1999**
The American Tintype. Marion Rinhart & Robert W. Wagner (Authors), W. Robert Nix (Foreword by). Cloth Text. Ohio State University Press. Columbus, OH. 1999. 392p. ISBN:0-8142-0806-1, ISBN13: 978-0-8142-0806-9. Dewey:772/.14/097309034. LCCN:98-049828.

Audience: **g,l,u,f.** *Choice, 2000.*

Romer, Grant B.   **TR365.Y682005**
Young America: The Daguerreotypes of Southworth & Hawes. Wallis, Brian (Editors). International Center of Photography, Rochester, NY; George Eastman House; Steidl. 2005. ISBN:3-86521-066-X, ISBN13: 978-3-86521-066-1.

Audience: **g,l,u,f.**

Rosenblum, Naomi   **TR139.R67 2000**
A History of Women Photographers. Ed. 2. Trade Cloth. Abbeville Press, Inc. New York, NY. 2000. 400p. ISBN:0-7892-0658-7, ISBN13: 978-0-7892-0658-9. Dewey:770/.82. LCCN:00-036249.

Audience: **g,l,u,f.** *Choice, 1995.*

Ryan, James   **DA16.R93 1997**
Picturing Empire: Photography and the Visualization of the British Empire. Trade Cloth. University of Chicago Press. Chicago, IL. 1998. 272p. ISBN:0-226-73233-9, ISBN13: 978-0-226-73233-6. Dewey:941.08. LCCN:97-026401.

Audience: **g,l,u,f.** *Choice, 1998.*

Sandweiss, Martha A.   **TR23.6.S25 2002**
Print the Legend: Photography and the American West. Cloth over Boards. Yale University Press. Cumberland, RI. 2002. 416p. ISBN:0-300-09522-8, ISBN13: 978-0-300-09522-7. Dewey:770/.978. LCCN:2002-007038.

Audience: **g,l,u,f.** *Choice, 2003.*

Savedoff, Barbara E.   **TR183.S29 2000**
Transforming Images: How Photography Complicates the Picture. Trade Cloth. Cornell University Press. Ithaca, NY. 2000. 256p. ISBN:0-8014-3375-4, ISBN13: 978-0-8014-3375-7. Dewey:770/.1. LCCN:99-037650.

Audience: **g,l,u,f.** *Choice, 2000.*

Formats: Web: ☐   Ebook: **e**   CD/DVD-ROM: ✦   BCL3: **B**

Talbot, William Henry Fox,   **TR651.T3397 2002**
et al.
First Photographs: William Henry Fox Talbot and the Birth of
Photography. Michael Gray, Arthur Ollman & Carol McCusker
(Authors). Trade Cloth. powerHouse Cultural Entertainment, Inc.
Brooklyn, NY. 2005. 144p. ISBN:1-57687-153-3, ISBN13:
978-1-57687-153-9. Dewey:770/.92 B. LCCN:2002-068437.

             Audience: **g,l,u,f.**

Tucker, Anne, et al.   **TR105.T832003**
The History of Japanese Photography. Dana Friis-Hansen,
Ryauichi Kaneko & Takeba Joe (Authors), Museum of Fine
Arts, Houston Staff & Kokusai Kaoryau Kikin Staff
(Contribution by). Cloth over Boards. Yale University Press.
Cumberland, RI. 2003. 432p. ISBN:0-300-09925-8, ISBN13:
978-0-300-09925-6. Dewey:770/.952. LCCN:2002-013593.

             Audience: **g,l,u,f.**

Tucker, Susan (Editor), et   **TR465.S393453 2005**
al.
The Scrapbook in American Life. Karherine Ott & Patricia P.
Buckler (Editors). Trade Paper. Temple University Press.
Philadelphia, PA. 2006. 344p. ISBN:1-59213-478-5, ISBN13:
978-1-59213-478-6. Dewey:973. LCCN:2005-052875.

             Audience: **g,l,u,f.**

Vettel-Becker, Patricia   **TR183.V48 2005**
Shooting from the Hip: Photography, Masculinity, and Postwar
America. Trade Paper. University of Minnesota Press.
Minneapolis, MN. 2005. 224p. ISBN:0-8166-4302-4, ISBN13:
978-0-8166-4302-8. Dewey:770/.973/09045.
LCCN:2004-021031.

             Audience: **g,l,u,f.**

Wexler, Laura   **TR139**
Tender Violence: Domestic Visions in an Age of U.S.
Imperialism. Trade Cloth. University of North Carolina Press.
Chapel Hill, NC. 2000. 384p. Cultural Studies of the United
States ISBN:0-8078-2570-0, ISBN13: 978-0-8078-2570-9.
Dewey:770/.9/73/09041. LCCN:00-039251.

             Audience: **g,l,u,f.** *Choice, 2001.*

Photography > Individual Photographers

Alinder, Mary Street   **TR140.A3A79 1996**
Ansel Adams: A Biography. Cloth over Boards. Henry Holt &
Company. New York, NY. 1996. 512p. ISBN:0-8050-4116-8,
ISBN13: 978-0-8050-4116-3. Dewey:770/.92 B.
LCCN:95-044741.

             Audience: **g,l,u,f.**

Assouline, Pierre   **TR140.C295**
Henri Cartier-Bresson: The Biography. Trade Cloth. Thames &
Hudson. New York, NY. 2005. 280p. ISBN:0-500-51223-X,
ISBN13: 978-0-500-51223-4. Dewey:770.92 B.
LCCN:2004-118015.

             Audience: **g,l,u,f.** *Choice, 2006.*

Avedon, Richard   **TR647**
An Autobiography. Trade Cloth. Random House, Inc. New York,
NY. 1993. ISBN:0-679-40921-1, ISBN13: 978-0-679-40921-2.
Dewey:779/.092. LCCN:93-000440.

             Audience: **g,l,u,f.**

Avedon, Richard (Editor)   **TR654.H56 1999**
Hiro: Photographs. Mark Holborn (Afterword by). Trade Cloth.
Little Brown & Company. New York, NY. 1999. 144p.
ISBN:0-8212-2592-8, ISBN13: 978-0-8212-2592-9.
Dewey:779/.092. LCCN:98-068373.

             Audience: **g,l,u,f.**

Barberie, Peter   **TR647.A827B372005**
Looking at Atget. Beth A. Price, Ken Sutherland & Philadelphia
Museum of Art Staff (Contribution by). Trade Cloth.
Philadelphia Museum of Art. Philadelphia, PA. 2005. ix, 125p.
ISBN:0-87633-189-4, ISBN13: 978-0-87633-189-7.
Dewey:770/.92. LCCN:2005-004920.

             Audience: **g,l,u,f.** *Choice, 2006.*

Beaton, Cecil   **TR140.B4.A3 2004**
Beaton in the Sixties: The Cecil Beaton Diaries As He Wrote
Them, 1965-1969. Hugo Vickers (Introduction by). Trade Cloth.
Knopf Publishing Group. New York, NY. 2004. 544p.
ISBN:1-4000-4297-6, ISBN13: 978-1-4000-4297-5.
Dewey:770/.92 B. LCCN:2004-048296.

             Audience: **g,l,u,f.**

Becher, Bernd & Becher,   **TR706.B429713 2002**
Hilla
Industrial Landscapes. Trade Cloth. MIT Press. Cambridge, MA.
2002. 270p. ISBN:0-262-02507-8, ISBN13: 978-0-262-02507-2.
Dewey:779/.967/0922. LCCN:2001-059622.

             Audience: **g,l,u,f.** *Choice, 2003.*

Benson, Harry   **TR820.B4262005**
Harry Benson's America. Trade Cloth. Harry N. Abrams, Inc.
New York, NY. 2005. 224p. ISBN:0-8109-5896-1, ISBN13:
978-0-8109-5896-8. Dewey:779/.9973. LCCN:2004-023440.

             Audience: **g,l,u,f.**

Blumenfeld, Erwin   **TR140.B53A3 1999**
Eye to I: The Autobiography of a Photographer. Mike Mitchell
& Brian Murdoch (Translators). Trade Cloth. Thames &
Hudson. New York, NY. 1999. 384p. ISBN:0-500-01907-X,
ISBN13: 978-0-500-01907-8. Dewey:770/.92 B.
LCCN:98-075140.

             Audience: **g,l,u,f.** *Choice, 2000.*

Breakey, Kate   **TR654.B71932001**
Small Deaths: Photographs. A. D. Coleman (Introduction by).
Trade Cloth. University of Texas Press. Austin, TX. 2001. 168p.
Wittliff Gallery Ser. ISBN:0-292-70901-3, ISBN13:
978-0-292-70901-0. Dewey:779/.3. LCCN:00-054520.

             Audience: **g,l,u,f.**

Buchanan, William (Editor)   **TR140.A557A25 1994**
J. Craig Annan: Selected Texts and Bibliography. Trade Cloth.
Thomson Gale. Farmington Hills, MI. 1994. 212p. World
Photographers Reference Ser., No. 6 ISBN:0-8161-0617-7,

ISBN13: 978-0-8161-0617-2. Dewey:770/.92 B.
LCCN:93-037065.
Audience: **l,u,f.** *Choice, 1994.*

Bunnell, Peter C.   **TR647.W458 1989**
Minor White: The Eye That Shapes. Jill Guthrie (Editor), Minor
White (Photographer). Paper Text. Princeton University Art
Museum. Princeton, NJ. 1989. 310p. ISBN:0-943012-09-0,
ISBN13: 978-0-943012-09-4. Dewey:779/.092.
LCCN:88-083824.
Audience: **g,l,u,f.** *Choice, 1989.*

Calvocoressi, Richard   **TR680**
Lee Miller: Portraits from a Life. Trade Cloth. Thames &
Hudson. New York, NY. 2002. 160p. ISBN:0-500-54260-0,
ISBN13: 978-0-500-54260-6. Dewey:779/.092.
LCCN:2002-101757.
Audience: **g,l,u,f.** *Choice, 2003.*

Conkelton, Sheryl (Editor)   **TR140.S635A6 1995**
Frederick Sommer: Selected Texts and Bibliography. Trade
Cloth. Thomson Gale. Farmington Hills, MI. 1995. 175p. World
Photographers Reference Ser., Vol. 7 ISBN:0-8161-0619-3,
ISBN13: 978-0-8161-0619-6. Dewey:770/.92. LCCN:94-045124.
Audience: **g,l,u,f.**

Cox, Julian & Ford, Colin   **TR652.C692003**
Julia Margaret Cameron: The Complete Photographs. Joanne
Lukitsh & Philippa Wright (Contribution by). Trade Cloth.
Oxford University Press, Inc. New York, NY. 2003. 576p. Getty
Trust Publications: J. Paul Getty Museum Ser.
ISBN:0-89236-681-8, ISBN13: 978-0-89236-681-1.
Dewey:770/.92 B. LCCN:2002-011369.
Audience: **g,l,u,f.** *Choice, 2003.*

Cunningham, Imogen   **TR575**
(Photographer)
Imogen Cunningham: Portraiture. Richard Lorenz (Text by).
Trade Cloth. Little Brown & Company. New York, NY. 1998.
200p. ISBN:0-8212-2437-9, ISBN13: 978-0-8212-2437-3.
Dewey:778.9/2. LCCN:97-071948.
Audience: **g,l,u,f.**

Curtis, Verna P. (Editor), et   **TR140.D37D37 1995**
al.
F. Holland Day: Selected Texts and Bibliography. Jane Van
Nimmen & Gedrim (Editors). Trade Cloth. Thomson Gale.
Farmington Hills, MI. 1996. 161p. World Photographers
Reference Ser., Vol. 8 ISBN:0-8161-0618-5, ISBN13:
978-0-8161-0618-9. Dewey:770/.92. LCCN:95-025681.
Audience: **g,l,u,f.** *Choice, 1996.*

Danly, Susan & Leibold,   **TR652.P46 1994**
Cheryl
Eakins and the Photograph: Works by Thomas Eakins and His
Circle in the Collection of the Pennsylvania Academy of the
Fine Arts. Elizabeth Johns, Anne McCauley & Mary Panzer
(Contribution by). Trade Cloth. Smithsonian Institution Press.
Washington, DC. 1994. 236p. ISBN:1-56098-352-3, ISBN13:
978-1-56098-352-1. Dewey:779/.092. LCCN:93-032940.
Audience: **g,l,u,f.**

Doisneau, Robert   **DC707**
Paris. Francine Derondille (Editor). Trade Cloth. Flammarion et
Cie. Paris, 2005. 400p. ISBN:2-08-030491-7, ISBN13:
978-2-08-030491-9. Dewey:779.9944361. LCCN:2006-278386.
Audience: **g,l,u,f.** *Choice, 2006.*

Evans, Walker &   **TR647.E9 2000**
Hambourg, Maria Morris
Walker Evans. San Francisco Museum of Modern Art Staff &
Museum of Fine Arts, Houston Staff (Contribution by). Trade
Cloth. Metropolitan Museum of Art, The. New York, NY. 2000.
xiii, 318p. ISBN:0-87099-937-0, ISBN13: 978-0-87099-937-6.
Dewey:779/.092/4. LCCN:99-055746.
Audience: **g,l,u,f.**

Foresta, Merry A.   **TR645.W18N37 1996**
American Photographs: The First Century. Charles Isaacs
(Afterword by). Trade Paper. Smithsonian Institution Press.
Washington, DC. 1996. 172p. ISBN:1-56098-719-7, ISBN13:
978-1-56098-719-2. Dewey:779/.0973/074753.
LCCN:96-025338.
Audience: **g,l,u,f.** *Choice, 1997.*

Galassi, Peter   **TR647.G352001**
Andreas Gursky. Trade Cloth. Harry N. Abrams, Inc. New York,
NY. 2001. 196p. A Museum of Modern Art Book Ser.
ISBN:0-8109-6215-2, ISBN13: 978-0-8109-6215-6.
Dewey:779/.092. LCCN:00-110690.
Audience: **g,l,u,f.**

Getty, J. Paul, Museum   **TR139**
Staff
In Focus: Photographs from the J. Paul Getty Museum. Trade
Paper. Oxford University Press, Inc. New York, NY. 1999. 430p.
In Focus Ser. ISBN:0-89236-568-4, ISBN13:
978-0-89236-568-5. Dewey:770.9/22.
Audience: **g,l,u,f.**

Greenough, Sarah   **TR653.N382002**
Alfred Stieglitz: The Key Set: The Alfred Stieglitz Collection of
Photographs. National Gallery of Art Staff (Contribution by).
Box or Slipcased. National Gallery of Art. Washington, DC.
2002. lxiii, 1012p. ISBN:0-89468-290-3, ISBN13:
978-0-89468-290-2. Dewey:770/.92. LCCN:2002-005066.
Audience: **g,l,u,f.** *Choice, 2003.*

Grossfeld, Stan   **TR647.A7**
Diane Arbus: An Aperture Monograph. Ed. 25. Marvin Israel &
Doon Arbus (Editors). Trade Paper. Aperture Foundation, Inc.
New York, NY. 1997. 184p. Monographs ISBN:0-89381-694-9,
ISBN13: 978-0-89381-694-0. Dewey:779/.2/092.
Audience: **g,l,u,f.**

Hammond, Anne   **TR140.A3H362002**
Ansel Adams: Divine Performance. Cloth over Boards. Yale
University Press. Cumberland, RI. 2002. 192p.
ISBN:0-300-09241-5, ISBN13: 978-0-300-09241-7.
Dewey:770/.92 B. LCCN:2001-046909.
Audience: **g,l,u,f.** *Choice, 2002.*

Hammond, Anne (Editor)   TR140.E9 F74 1992
Frederick H. Evans: Selected Texts and Bibliography. Trade
Cloth. Thomson Gale. Farmington Hills, MI. 1992. 200p. World
Photographers Reference Ser., Vol. 1 ISBN:0-8161-0577-4,
ISBN13: 978-0-8161-0577-9. Dewey:770/.92. LCCN:92-016967.
                                        Audience: **g,l,u,f.**

Hoffman, Katherine   TR140.S7H64 2004
Stieglitz: A Beginning Light. Cloth over Boards. Yale University
Press. Cumberland, RI. 2004. 398p. ISBN:0-300-10239-9,
ISBN13: 978-0-300-10239-0. Dewey:770/.92.
LCCN:2003-019486.
                          Audience: **g,l,u,f.** *Choice, 2005.*

Hopps, Walter, et al.   TR647.C47W55 2006
William Christenberry. Howard N. Fox & Andy Grundberg
(Authors), William Christenberry (Photographer). Trade Cloth.
Aperture Foundation, Inc. New York, NY. 2006. 204p.
ISBN:1-931788-89-8, ISBN13: 978-1-931788-89-2.
Dewey:779.092. LCCN:2005-025408.
                                        Audience: **g,l,u,f.**

Jacobs, Philip Walker   TR140.U426J33 2001
The Life and Photography of Doris Ulmann. Trade Cloth.
University Press of Kentucky. Lexington, KY. 2001. xxiii, 325p.
ISBN:0-8131-2175-2, ISBN13: 978-0-8131-2175-8.
Dewey:770/.92 B. LCCN:00-036337.
                          Audience: **g,l,u,f.** *Choice, 2001.*

Jezierski, John Vincent   TR139.J48 2000
Enterprising Images: The Goodridge Brothers, African American
Photographers, 1847-1922. Trade Cloth. Wayne State University
Press. Detroit, MI. 2000. xv, 346p. Great Lakes Bks.
ISBN:0-8143-2451-7, ISBN13: 978-0-8143-2451-6.
Dewey:770/.92/273 B. LCCN:99-039386.
                          Audience: **g,l,u,f.** *Choice, 2001.*

Kao, Deborah Martin, et al.   TR820.5.S4797 2000
Ben Shahn's New York: The Photography of Modern Times.
Laura Katzman & Jenna Webster (Authors), Ben Shahn
(Photographer). Cloth over Boards. Yale University Press.
Cumberland, RI. 2000. 352p. ISBN:0-300-08315-7, ISBN13:
978-0-300-08315-6. Dewey:770/.92. LCCN:99-053647.
                          Audience: **g,l,u,f.** *Choice, 2000.*

Keller, Judith   TR653.U44 1996
In Focus - Doris Ulmann: Photographs from the J. Paul Getty
Museum. Trade Paper. Oxford University Press, Inc. New York,
NY. 1996. 144p. In Focus Ser. ISBN:0-89236-373-8, ISBN13:
978-0-89236-373-5. Dewey:779/.092. LCCN:95-041084.
                                        Audience: **g,l,u,f.**

Kogan, Deborah Copaken   TR820
ⓔ Shutterbabe: Adventures in Love and War. E-Book. Adobe
Systems, Inc. Burlington, MA. ISBN:1-58945-589-4, ISBN13:
978-1-58945-589-4. Dewey:070.4/9/092 B.
                                        Audience: **g,l,u,f.**

Krase, Andreas   TR653 .A8433 2000
Eugene Atget. Hans Christian Adam (Editor). Trade Cloth.
Taschen America, LLC. Los Angeles, CA. 2000. 256p. FO Ser.

ISBN:3-8228-6215-0, ISBN13: 978-3-8228-6215-5.
Dewey:779/.9944/36. LCCN:2001-269813.
                          Audience: **g,l,u,f.** *Choice, 2001.*

Lee, Anthony W. & Pultz,   TR681.F28L44 2003
John
Diane Arbus: Family Albums. Trade Paper. Yale University
Press. Cumberland, RI. 2003. 168p. ISBN:0-300-10146-5,
ISBN13: 978-0-300-10146-1. Dewey:779/.2/092.
LCCN:2003-050065.
                          Audience: **g,l,u,f.** *Choice, 2004.*

Leibovitz, Annie & Sontag,   TR681.W6L34 1999
Susan
Women. Trade Cloth. Random House, Inc. New York, NY.
1999. 248p. ISBN:0-375-50020-0, ISBN13: 978-0-375-50020-6.
Dewey:305.4. LCCN:99-024968.
                          Audience: **g,l,u,f.** *Choice, 2000.*

Levi-Strauss, David   TR185.S77 2003
Between the Eyes: Essays on Photography and Politics. John
Berger (Introduction by). Cloth over Boards. Aperture
Foundation, Inc. New York, NY. 2003. 224p.
ISBN:1-931788-10-3, ISBN13: 978-1-931788-10-6.
Dewey:770/.1. LCCN:2002-110816.
                                        Audience: **g,l,u,f.**

Light, Michael   U264.3.L53 2003
100 Suns: 1945-1962. Trade Cloth. Knopf Publishing Group.
New York, NY. 2003. 208p. ISBN:1-4000-4113-9, ISBN13:
978-1-4000-4113-8. Dewey:779/.962345119/0973.
LCCN:2003-106275.
                                        Audience: **g,l,u,f.**

Lorenz, Richard   TR654.C8624 2001
Imogen Cunningham. Trade Cloth. Taschen America, LLC. Los
Angeles, CA. 2001. 251p. ISBN:3-8228-7182-6, ISBN13:
978-3-8228-7182-9. Dewey:779/.092. LCCN:2001-273397.
                                        Audience: **g,l,u,f.**

Lottman, Herbert R.   N6537.R3L672001
Man Ray's Montparnasse. Trade Cloth. Harry N. Abrams, Inc.
New York, NY. 2001. 264p. ISBN:0-8109-4333-6, ISBN13:
978-0-8109-4333-9. Dewey:709/.2 B. LCCN:2001-000633.
                          Audience: **l,u,f.** *Choice, 2002.*

Mann, Sally   TR654.M32352 2003
What Remains. Trade Cloth. Little Brown & Company. New
York, NY. 2003. 132p. ISBN:0-8212-2843-9, ISBN13:
978-0-8212-2843-2. Dewey:779/.092. LCCN:2003-049636.
                                        Audience: **g,l,u,f.**

Marien, Mary Warner   TR15.M273 2002
Photography: A Cultural History. Prentice Hall Art. 2002.
ISBN:0-8109-0559-0, ISBN13: 978-0-8109-0559-7.
                                        Audience: **g,l,u,f.**

Mark, Mary Ellen   TR820.5.M368 1999
Mary Ellen Mark: American Odyssey, 1963-1999. Maya

Angelou (Contribution by). Trade Cloth. Aperture Foundation, Inc. New York, NY. 1999. 152p. ISBN:0-89381-880-1, ISBN13: 978-0-89381-880-7. Dewey:779/.092. LCCN:99-064609.

Audience: **g,l,u,f.**

Moholy-Nagy, László   **TR653.M6291995**
In Focus - Lészló Moholy-Nagy: Photographs from the J. Paul Getty Museum. Trade Paper. Oxford University Press, Inc. New York, NY. 1995. 128p. In Focus Ser. ISBN:0-89236-324-X, ISBN13: 978-0-89236-324-7. Dewey:779/.092. LCCN:94-042443.

Audience: **g,l,u,f.**

Morrisroe, Patricia   **TR140.M347M67 1997**
Mapplethorpe: A Biography. Trade Paper. Da Capo Press, Inc. Cambridge, MA. 1997. 480p. ISBN:0-306-80766-1, ISBN13: 978-0-306-80766-4. Dewey:770.9/2. LCCN:96-043819.

Audience: **g,l,u,f.**

O'Donnell, Joe   **TR820.6.O362005**
Japan 1945: A U.S. Marine's Photographs from Ground Zero. Mark Seldon (Foreword by). Trade Cloth. Vanderbilt University Press. Nashville, TN. 2005. 120p. ISBN:0-8265-1467-7, ISBN13: 978-0-8265-1467-7. Dewey:779/.99405352. LCCN:2004-017367.

Audience: **g,l,u,f.** *Choice, 2005.*

Parks, Gordon Jr.   **TR140.P35P35 1997**
Half Past Autumn: A Retrospective. Trade Cloth. Little Brown & Company. New York, NY. 1997. 360p. ISBN:0-8212-2298-8, ISBN13: 978-0-8212-2298-0. Dewey:770.9/2. LCCN:97-019797.

Audience: **g,l,u,f.**

Perez, Nissan   **TR640**
Revelation: Representations of Christ in Photography. Muze'on Yisrael Staff (Contribution by). Trade Cloth. Merrell Publishers Ltd. London, 2005. 192p. ISBN:1-85894-225-X, ISBN13: 978-1-85894-225-4. Dewey:779.8/53.

Audience: **g,l,u,f.**

Reed, Eli   **TR820.R37 1997**
Black in America. Trade Cloth. W. W. Norton & Company, Inc. New York, NY. 1997. 176p. ISBN:0-393-03995-1, ISBN13: 978-0-393-03995-5. Dewey:779/.99730496073. LCCN:96-054490.

Audience: **g,l,u,f.**

Rexer, Lyle   **TR642.R4932002**
Photography's Antiquarian Avant-Garde: The New Wave in Old Processes. Trade Cloth. Harry N. Abrams, Inc. New York, NY. 2002. 160p. ISBN:0-8109-0402-0, ISBN13: 978-0-8109-0402-6. Dewey:770. LCCN:2001-005354.

Audience: **g,l,u,f.**

Roberts, Pam   **TR6.G72L666 2000**
PhotoHistorica, Landmarks in Photography: Rare Images from the Collection of the Royal Photographic Society. Royal Photographic Society Staff (Photographer). Trade Cloth. Artisan. New York, NY. 2000. 336p. ISBN:1-57965-169-0, ISBN13: 978-1-57965-169-5. Dewey:779/.074421. LCCN:00-038615.

Audience: **g,l,u,f.**

Rule, Amy & Lorenz,   **TR140.C78I49 1992**
  Richard (Editors)
Imogen Cunningham: Selected Texts and Bibliography. Trade Cloth. Thomson Gale. Farmington Hills, MI. 1993. 200p. World Photographers Reference Ser. ISBN:0-8161-0575-8, ISBN13: 978-0-8161-0575-5. Dewey:770/.92. LCCN:92-025360.

Audience: **g,l,u,f.**

Salgado, Sebastiao   **TR647.S23 1990**
An Uncertain Grace. Eduardo Galeano & Fred Ritchin (Text by). Trade Cloth. Aperture Foundation, Inc. New York, NY. 1990. 156p. ISBN:0-89381-421-0, ISBN13: 978-0-89381-421-2. Dewey:779/.092. LCCN:90-081487.

Audience: **g,l,u,f.** *Choice, 1991.*

Sayag, Alain, et al.   **TR647.L372003**
Lartigue: Album of a Century. Quentin Bajac & Martine d'Astier (Authors). Trade Cloth. Harry N. Abrams, Inc. New York, NY. 2003. 400p. ISBN:0-8109-4620-3, ISBN13: 978-0-8109-4620-0. Dewey:779/.092. LCCN:2003-103788.

Audience: **g,l,u,f.** *Choice, 2004.*

Sayag, Alain, et al.   **TR647.B732000**
Brassaï: The Monograph. Annick Lionel-Marie, Jean-Jacques Aillagon & Brassaï (Authors). Trade Cloth. Little Brown & Company. New York, NY. 2000. 320p. ISBN:0-8212-2668-1, ISBN13: 978-0-8212-2668-1. Dewey:770/.92. LCCN:00-103087.

Audience: **g,l,u,f.** *Choice, 2001.*

Schaaf, Larry J.   **TR651.S332000**
The Photographic Art of William Henry Fox Talbot. Cloth Text. Princeton University Press. Princeton, NJ. 2000. 264p. ISBN:0-691-05000-7, ISBN13: 978-0-691-05000-3. Dewey:770/.92. LCCN:00-032618.

Audience: **g,l,u,f.** *Choice, 2001.*

Scheler, Max Ferdinand   **TR647**
Herbert List: The Monograph. Ulrich Pohlmann, Gunter Metken, Matthias Harder, Edmund White & Wilfriend Wiegand (Text by). Trade Cloth. Monacelli Press, Inc. New York, NY. 2000. 320p. ISBN:1-58093-058-1, ISBN13: 978-1-58093-058-1. Dewey:770/.92. LCCN:99-085911.

Audience: **l,u.** *Choice, 2000.*

Sherbell, Shepard   **DK18.5.S482001**
Soviets: Pictures from the End of the U.S.S.R. Serge Schmemann (Introduction by). Cloth over Boards. Yale University Press. Cumberland, RI. 2001. 272p. ISBN:0-300-09112-5, ISBN13: 978-0-300-09112-0. Dewey:947.085/4/0222. LCCN:2001-003264.

Audience: **g,l,u,f.**

Shore, Stephen   **TR654**
Uncommon Places: The Complete Works. Stephan Schmidt-Wulffen & Lynn Tillman (Contribution by). Trade Cloth. Aperture Foundation, Inc. New York, NY. 2004. 180p. ISBN:1-931788-34-0, ISBN13: 978-1-931788-34-2. Dewey:779.092. LCCN:2003-116950.

Audience: **g,l,u,f.**

Sieverding, Katharina   **TR680**
Katharina Sieverding: Close-Ups. Sabeth Buchmann
(Contribution by). Trade Cloth. D. A. P./Distributed Art
Publishers. New York, NY. 2003. 548p. ISBN:3-9804265-5-6,
ISBN13: 978-3-9804265-5-8. Dewey:779.0924.
                        Audience: **g,l,u,f.**

Smith, Joel   **TR653.S595 1999**
Edward Steichen: The Early Years. Trade Cloth. Princeton
University Press. Princeton, NJ. 1999. 168p.
ISBN:0-691-04873-8, ISBN13: 978-0-691-04873-4.
Dewey:779/.092. LCCN:99-026617.
            Audience: **g,l,u,f.** *Choice, 2000.*

Steichen, Joanna   **TR653.S744 2000**
Steichen's Legacy: Photographs, 1895-1973. Trade Cloth. Alfred
A. Knopf Inc. New York, NY. 2000. 408p. ISBN:0-679-45076-9,
ISBN13: 978-0-679-45076-4. Dewey:770/.92. LCCN:00-020095.
            Audience: **g,l,u,f.** *Choice, 2001.*

Szarkowski, John   **TR647.A2362001**
Ansel Adams at 100. Trade Cloth, Box or Slipcased. Little
Brown & Company. New York, NY. 2001. 192p.
ISBN:0-8212-2515-4, ISBN13: 978-0-8212-2515-8.
Dewey:770/.92. LCCN:00-069941.
                        Audience: **g,l,u,f.**

Time-Life Books Editors   **TR820.5.B687 1998**
Margaret Bourke-White: Photographer. Margaret Bourke-White
(Photographer), Sean Callahan (Contribution by). Trade Cloth.
Little Brown & Company. New York, NY. 1998. 160p.
ISBN:0-8212-2490-5, ISBN13: 978-0-8212-2490-8.
Dewey:779/.092. LCCN:98-071654.
                        Audience: **g,l,u,f.**

Travis, David   **TR647.W44 2001**
Edward Weston: The Last Years in Carmel. Edward Weston
(Photographer). Trade Cloth. Art Institute of Chicago. Chicago,
IL. 2001. 144p. ISBN:0-86559-192-X, ISBN13:
978-0-86559-192-9. Dewey:770/.92 B. LCCN:2001-087121.
                        Audience: **g,l,u,f.**

Turner, Evan H.   **TR660.5.T872000**
Ray K. Metzker: Landscapes. Trade Cloth. Aperture Foundation,
Inc. New York, NY. 2000. 168p. ISBN:0-89381-911-5, ISBN13:
978-0-89381-911-8. Dewey:779/.36/092. LCCN:00-101113.
                        Audience: **g,l,u,f.**

Warburton, Nigel (Editor)   **TR140.B73A25 1993**
Bill Brandt: Selected Texts and Bibliography. Trade Cloth.
Thomson Gale. Farmington Hills, MI. 1994. 180p. World
Photographers Reference Ser., No. 5 ISBN:0-8161-0616-9,
ISBN13: 978-0-8161-0616-5. Dewey:770/.92. LCCN:93-033541.
                        Audience: **g,l,u,f.**

Watts, Jennifer A.   **TR647**
Edward Weston: A Legacy. Henry E. Huntington Library and
Art Gallery Staff (Contribution by). Trade Cloth. Merrell
Publishers Ltd. London, 2005. 288p. ISBN:1-85894-206-3,
ISBN13: 978-1-85894-206-3. Dewey:779/.092.
LCCN:2005-360920.
            Audience: **g,l,u,f.** *Choice, 2003.*

Weaver, Mike (Editor)   **TR140.T3A25 1992**
Henry Fox Talbot: Selected Texts and Bibliography. Trade
Cloth. Macmillan Publishing Company, Inc. Old Tappan, NJ.
1993. 189p. ISBN:0-8161-0576-6, ISBN13: 978-0-8161-0576-2.
Dewey:779.092. LCCN:92-028426.
                        Audience: **g,l,u,f.**

Willis, Deborah   **TR23.W55 2000**
Reflections in Black: A History of Black Photographers, 1840 to
the Present. Robin D. G. Kelley (Introduction by). Trade Cloth.
W. W. Norton & Company, Inc. New York, NY. 2000. 368p.
ISBN:0-393-04880-2, ISBN13: 978-0-393-04880-3.
Dewey:770/.8996/073. LCCN:99-055185.
            Audience: **g,l,u,f.** *Choice, 2001.*

Willumson, Glenn G.   **TR820.W53 1992**
W. Eugene Smith and the Photographic Essay. Cloth Text.
Cambridge University Press. New York, NY. 1992. 367p.
ISBN:0-521-41464-4, ISBN13: 978-0-521-41464-7.
Dewey:770/.92. LCCN:91-030529.
            Audience: **g,l,u,f.** *Choice, 1992.*

Woodward, Richard B.   **TR647**
An-My Le: Small Wars. An-My Le (Photographer). Perfect,
Paper over Boards, Dust Jacket. D. A. P./Distributed Art
Publishers. New York, NY. 2005. 128p. ISBN:1-931788-82-0,
ISBN13: 978-1-931788-82-3. Dewey:779.9959704.
                        Audience: **g,l,u,f.**

Photography > Materials and Techniques

Folts, James A., et al.   **TR146.H19 2001**
Handbook of Photography. Ed. 5. Fred C. Zwahlen & Ronald P.
Lovell (Authors). Trade Paper. Thomson Delmar Learning.
Albany, NY. 2001. 416p. ISBN:0-7668-2073-4, ISBN13:
978-0-7668-2073-9. Dewey:770. LCCN:2001-028303.
                        Audience: **g,l,u,f.**

Freeman, Michael   **TR267.F74 2005**
The Complete Guide to Digital Photography. Ed. 3. Trade Paper,
Perfect. Lark Books. Asheville, NC. 2005. 224p. A Lark
Photography Book Ser. ISBN:1-57990-759-8, ISBN13:
978-1-57990-759-4. Dewey:775. LCCN:2005-016031.
                        Audience: **g,l,u,f.**

Hedgecoe, John   **TR146.H417**
John Hedgecoe's Complete Guide to Black and White
Photography. Trade Paper, Perfect. Sterling Publishing Co., Inc.
New York, NY. 2005. 160p. ISBN:1-4027-2812-3, ISBN13:
978-1-4027-2812-9. Dewey:771.
                        Audience: **g,l,u,f.**

James, Christopher   **TR350.J35 2001**
The Book of Alternative Photographic Processes. Trade Paper.
Thomson Delmar Learning. Albany, NY. 2001. 400p.
ISBN:0-7668-2077-7, ISBN13: 978-0-7668-2077-7. Dewey:771.
LCCN:2001-028615.
                        Audience: **g,l,u,f.**

Wignall, Jeff   **TR267.W54 2004**
The Joy of Digital Photography. Cloth over Boards. Lark Books.
Asheville, NC. 2004. 304p. A Lark Photography Book Ser.
ISBN:1-57990-578-1, ISBN13: 978-1-57990-578-1. Dewey:775.
LCCN:2004-001116.

Audience: **g,l,u,f.**

Digital Art > Reference Works > Web Resources

            TR7433.8

☐ Media Art Net.
http://www.mediaartnet.org

Audience: **g,l,u,f.**

            TR7433.8

☐ Renderosity.
http://www.renderosity.com/
Nashville, TN : Bondware, Inc.

Audience: **g,l,u,f.**

            TK5105.888

☐ Rhizome.org.
http://rhizome.org
The New Museum of Contemporary Art, New York.

Audience: **g,l,u,f.**

Digital Art > Reference Works > Bibliographies and Research Guides

Horsfield, Kate &   **N6494.V53F42 2006**
   Hilderbrand, Lucas (Editors)
Feedback: The Video Data Bank Catalog of Video Art and Artist
Interviews. Trade Cloth. Temple University Press. Philadelphia,
PA. 2006. 360p. Wide Angle Bks. ISBN:1-59213-182-4,
ISBN13: 978-1-59213-182-2. Dewey:016.77859.
LCCN:2005-055962.

Audience: **g,l,u,f.**

Digital Art > Reference Works > Dictionaries and Encyclopedias

Ang, Tom   **TR9.A53 2002**
Dictionary of Photography and Digital Imaging: The Essential
Reference for the Modern Photographer. Trade Cloth.
Watson-Guptill Publications, Inc. New York, NY. 2002. 388p.
ISBN:0-8174-3789-4, ISBN13: 978-0-8174-3789-3.
Dewey:770/.3. LCCN:2001-094987.

Audience: **g,l,u,f.** *Choice, 2002.*

Cope, Peter   **TR267.C67 2002**
The Digital Photographer's Pocket Encyclopedia: 3000 Terms
Explained. Trade Paper. Tiffen Company LLC, The. Hauppauge,
NY. 2002. 192p. ISBN:1-883403-90-1, ISBN13:
978-1-883403-90-4. Dewey:778.3. LCCN:2001-049499.

Audience: **g,l,u,f.**

Hansen, Brad   **QA76.15.H318 2002**
The Dictionary of Multimedia Terms and Acronyms. Ed. 4.
Trade Paper, Perfect. Franklin, Beedle & Associates, Inc.
Wilsonville, OR. 2004. 611p. ISBN:1-887902-73-2, ISBN13:
978-1-887902-73-1. Dewey:004.003. LCCN:2002-071262.

Audience: **g,l,u,f.** *Choice, 2005.*

Digital Art > Histories and Handbooks

Barnett, Paul, et al.   **N7433.8.B37 2004**
Digital Art for the 21st Century: Renderosity. Malcolm Couch,
John Grant & Audre Vysniauskas (Authors). Trade Paper.
HarperCollins Publishers. New York, NY. 2004. 160p.
ISBN:0-06-073037-4, ISBN13: 978-0-06-073037-6. Dewey:776.
LCCN:2003-026550.

Audience: **g,l,u,f.**

Benjamin, Andrew (Editor)   **PT2603.E455K868 2004**
Walter Benjamin and Art. Trade Cloth. Continuum International
Publishing Group, Ltd. London, 2005. 304p. Walter Benjamin
Studies ISBN:0-8264-6729-6, ISBN13: 978-0-8264-6729-4.
Dewey:834/.912. LCCN:2004-056178.

Audience: **g,l,u,f.** *Choice, 2005.*

Bishop, Claire   **N6494.I56**
Installation Art. UK-B Format Paperback. Routledge. New York,
NY. 2005. 144p. ISBN:0-415-97412-7, ISBN13:
978-0-415-97412-7. Dewey:709/.04.

Audience: **g,l,u,f.**

Bolter, Jay David &   **TK5103.7.B65 2005**
   Gromala, Diane
Windows and Mirrors: Interaction Design, Digital Art, and the
Myth of Transparency. Trade Paper, Perfect. MIT Press.
Cambridge, MA. 2005. 208p. Leonardo Bks.
ISBN:0-262-52449-X, ISBN13: 978-0-262-52449-0.
Dewey:700/.285.

Audience: **g,l,u,f.**

Boomgaard, Jeroen &   **N6948.5.V53M34 2003**
   Rutten, Bart (Editors)
The Magnetic Era: Video Art in the Netherlands 1970-1985.
Trade Paper. NAi Uitgevers/Publishers. Rotterdam, 2004. 192p.
ISBN:90-5662-299-4, ISBN13: 978-90-5662-299-2.
Dewey:778.59/09492. LCCN:2003-461740.

Audience: **g,l,u,f.**

Cashen, Trish, et al.   **N7433.8**
Digital Art History: Computers and the History of Art. Anna
Bentkowska-Kafel & Hazel Gardiner (Authors). Trade Paper.
Intellect, Ltd. Bristol, 2005. 123p. ISBN:1-84150-116-6,
ISBN13: 978-1-84150-116-1. Dewey:776/.09.

Audience: **g,l,u,f.**

Resources for College Libraries   **VISUAL ARTS**

Darley, Andrew   GV1469.17.S63D27
Visual Digital Culture. Trade Paper. Routledge. New York, NY.
2000. 240p. Sussex Studies in Culture and Communication
ISBN:0-415-16555-5, ISBN13: 978-0-415-16555-6.
Dewey:306.4/87. LCCN:00-057632.

Audience: **g,l,u,f.**

De Oliveira, Nicolas   N6494.I56O45 2004
Installation Art in the New Millennium: The Empire of the
Senses. Trade Paper. Thames & Hudson. New York, NY. 2004.
208p. ISBN:0-500-28451-2, ISBN13: 978-0-500-28451-3.
Dewey:709/.05.

Audience: **g,l,u,f.**

De Oliveira, Nicolas, et al.   N6494.I56O44 1994
Installation Art. Nicola Oxley, Michael Petry & Michael Archer
(Authors). Trade Cloth. Smithsonian Institution Press.
Washington, DC. 1994. 208p. ISBN:1-56098-347-7, ISBN13:
978-1-56098-347-7. Dewey:709/.04. LCCN:93-086159.

Audience: **g,l,u,f.**

Elwes, Catherine   N6494.V53
Video Art: A Guided Tour. Trade Paper. I. B. Tauris &
Company, Ltd. London, 2005. 168p. ISBN:1-85043-546-4,
ISBN13: 978-1-85043-546-4. Dewey:702.8'1.
LCCN:2005-295114.

Audience: **g,l,u,f.**

Frieling, Rudolf & Daniels,   N 7433.92 .M43 2004
   Dieter (Editors)
Media Art Net 2: Topical Highlights. Trade Cloth. Springer
Wien. Wien, 2005. 320p. ISBN:3-211-23871-9, ISBN13:
978-3-211-23871-4. Dewey:709.04.

Audience: **g,l,u,f.**

Goriunova, Olga & Shulgin,   N7433.8
   Alexei (Editors)
Read Me: Software Art and Cultures. Trade Paper. Aarhus
Universitetsforlag. DK-8200 Aarhus N, 2005. 397p.
ISBN:87-988440-4-0, ISBN13: 978-87-988440-4-4. Dewey:760.
Audience: **g,l,u,f.**

Grau, Oliver   N7436.5.G7313 2004
Virtual Art: From Illusion to Immersion. Trade Paper. MIT
Press. Cambridge, MA. 2004. 430p. Leonardo Bks.
ISBN:0-262-57223-0, ISBN13: 978-0-262-57223-1.
Dewey:751.7/4/01. LCCN:2002-067829.

Audience: **g,l,u,f.**

Greene, Rachel   N7433.8
Internet Art. Trade Paper. Thames & Hudson. New York, NY.
2004. 224p. World of Art Ser. ISBN:0-500-20376-8, ISBN13:
978-0-500-20376-7. Dewey:776. LCCN:2003-108926.
Audience: **g,l,u,f.** *Choice, 2004.*

Hall, Doug & Fifer, Sally Jo   N6494.V53I4 1990
   (Editors)
Illuminating Video: An Essential Guide to Video Art. David
Ross (Foreword by), David Bolt (Preface by). Trade Paper.

Aperture Foundation, Inc. New York, NY. 1991. 576p.
ISBN:0-89381-390-7, ISBN13: 978-0-89381-390-1.
Dewey:778.599. LCCN:90-081584.

Audience: **g,l,u,f.**

Hocks, Mary E. &   P93.5.E56 2005
   Kendrick, Michelle R. (Editors)
Eloquent Images: Word and Image in the Age of New Media.
Trade Paper. MIT Press. Cambridge, MA. 2005. 376p.
ISBN:0-262-58261-9, ISBN13: 978-0-262-58261-2.
Dewey:302.23.

Audience: **l,u,f.**

Iles, Chrissie & Zummer,   N6512.5.V53I432001
   Thomas
Into the Light: The Projected Image in American Art,
1964-1977. Trade Cloth. Harry N. Abrams, Inc. New York, NY.
2001. 183p. ISBN:0-8109-6830-4, ISBN13: 978-0-8109-6830-1.
Dewey:709/.73/0747471. LCCN:2001-026965.

Audience: **g,l,u,f.**

Leopoldseder, Hannes   N6494.V53
   (Editor), et al.
Ars Electronica 1979-2004: The Network for Art, Technology
and Society: the First 25 Years. Christine Schöpf & Gerfried
Stocker (Editors). Trade Cloth. Hatje Cantz Verlag GmbH & Co
KG. Ostfildern-Ruit, 2005. 374p. ISBN:3-7757-1525-8, ISBN13:
978-3-7757-1525-6. Dewey:776.7.

Audience: **g,l,u,f.**

Lovejoy, Margot   NX180.M3L68 2004
Digital Currents: Art in the Electronic Age. Ed. 3. Trade Cloth.
Routledge. New York, NY. 2004. 376p. ISBN:0-415-30780-5,
ISBN13: 978-0-415-30780-2. Dewey:700/.1/05.
LCCN:2003-025226.

Audience: **g,l,u,f.**

Lovejoy, Margot   NX180.M3L68 1997
Postmodern Currents: Art and Artists in the Age of Electronic
Media. Ed. 2. Trade Paper. Prentice Hall PTR. Upper Saddle
River, NJ. 1996. 319p. ISBN:0-13-158759-5, ISBN13:
978-0-13-158759-5. Dewey:700/.1/05. LCCN:96-015913.
Audience: **g,l,u,f.**

Lunenfeld, Peter   QA76.9.C66L86 2000
Snap to Grid: A User's Guide to Digital Arts, Media, and
Cultures. Trade Cloth. MIT Press. Cambridge, MA. 2000. 240p.
ISBN:0-262-12226-X, ISBN13: 978-0-262-12226-9.
Dewey:006.7. LCCN:99-040216.

Audience: **g,l,u,f.** *Choice, 2000.*

Mealing, Stuart (Editor)   N72.E53
Computers and Art. Ed. 2. Trade Paper. Intellect, Ltd. Bristol,
2002. 159p. ISBN:1-84150-062-3, ISBN13: 978-1-84150-062-1.
Dewey:702.85. LCCN:2004-272224.

Audience: **g,l,u,f.**

Morgan, Jessica, et al.   N6494.V53
Time Zones: Recent Film and Video. Sylviane Agachinski &

Gregor Muir (Authors). Trade Paper. Tate Gallery Publishing, Ltd. London, 2004. 112p. ISBN:1-85437-549-0, ISBN13: 978-1-85437-549-0. Dewey:776.6.

Audience: **g,l,u,f.**

Nalven, Joseph & Jarvis, J.   **N7433.8**
D.
Going Digital: The Practice and Vision of Digital Artists. Trade Paper, Perfect. Thomson Course Technology. Boston, MA. 2005. 432p. ISBN:1-59200-918-2, ISBN13: 978-1-59200-918-3. Dewey:760.

Audience: **g,l,u,f.**

Paul, Christiane   **N7433.8**
Digital Art. Trade Paper. Thames & Hudson. New York, NY. 2003. 224p. World of Art Ser. ISBN:0-500-20367-9, ISBN13: 978-0-500-20367-5. Dewey:709.04. LCCN:2002-109024.

Audience: **g,l,u,f.**

Popper, Frank   **N7433.92.P67 2005**
From Technological to Virtual Art. Trade Cloth. MIT Press. Cambridge, MA. 2006. 504p. Leonardo Bks. ISBN:0-262-16230-X, ISBN13: 978-0-262-16230-2. Dewey:776/.7. LCCN:2004-062532.

Audience: **g,l,u,f.**

Rosenthal, Mark   **N6494.I56**
Understanding Installation Art: From Duchamp to Holzer. Trade Paper. Prestel Publishing. New York, NY. 2003. 96p. ISBN:3-7913-2984-7, ISBN13: 978-3-7913-2984-0. Dewey:709.04. LCCN:2003-107833.

Audience: **g,l,u,f.** *Choice, 2004.*

Rush, Michael   **N6494.M78**
New Media in Art. Ed. 2. Trade Paper. Thames & Hudson. New York, NY. 2005. 248p. World of Art Ser. ISBN:0-500-20378-4, ISBN13: 978-0-500-20378-1. Dewey:709.0407. LCCN:2003-108927.

Audience: **g,l,u,f.**

Wignall, Jeff   **TR267.W54 2004**
The Joy of Digital Photography. Cloth over Boards. Lark Books. Asheville, NC. 2004. 304p. A Lark Photography Book Ser. ISBN:1-57990-578-1, ISBN13: 978-1-57990-578-1. Dewey:775. LCCN:2004-001116.

Audience: **g,l,u,f.**

Digital Art > Individual Artists

Abramovic´, Marina   **N7253.A25A42001**
(Text by)
Marina Abramovic´: Installations and Objects 1965-2001. Germano Celant (Contribution by). Trade Cloth. Charta. Milano, 2002. 495p. ISBN:88-8158-295-3, ISBN13: 978-88-8158-295-2. Dewey:702.8/1/092. LCCN:2001-421885.

Audience: **g,l,u,f.**

Arden, Roy, et al.   **TR647.A715 2002**
Roy Arden: Selected Works 1985-2000. Shep Steiner & Marnie Fleming (Authors), Oakville Galleries Staff (Contribution by). Trade Cloth. Oakville Galleries. Oakville, ON. 2002. 48p. ISBN:1-894707-07-9, ISBN13: 978-1-894707-07-7. Dewey:779/.092. LCCN:2002-491811.

Audience: **g,l,u,f.**

Batschmann, Oskar &   **N6999.K23**
Groys, Boris
Ilya Kabakov - Installations: Catalogue Raisonné, 1983-2000. Toni Stoos (Editor), Kabakov Ilya (Illustrator). Trade Cloth. Richter Verlag. Dusseldorf, 2004. 1008p. ISBN:3-933807-28-X, ISBN13: 978-3-933807-28-1. Dewey:709.2.

Audience: **g,l,u,f.**

Berger, Maurice   **N6537.P47 A4 1999**
Adrian Piper - A Retrospective, 1965-2000: Issues in Cultural Theory. Paper Text. University of Maryland Baltimore County, Fine Arts Gallery. Catonsville, MD. 1999. 200p. ISBN:1-890761-02-8, ISBN13: 978-1-890761-02-8. Dewey:700.92.

Audience: **g,l,u,f.**

Birnbaum, Daniel, et al.   **N7053**
Olafur Eliasson. Madeleine Rynsztejn & Michael Speaks (Authors). Trade Paper. Phaidon Press. London, 2002. 160p. Contemporary Artists Ser. ISBN:0-7148-4036-X, ISBN13: 978-0-7148-4036-9. Dewey:709.2. LCCN:2003-271673.

Audience: **g,l,u,f.**

Chalet, Francois   **N7153.C448 A4 2000**
Chalet. Trade Cloth. Die Gestalten Verlag. Berlin, 2003. 192p. ISBN:3-931126-39-0, ISBN13: 978-3-931126-39-1. Dewey:741.59494. LCCN:2002-501377.

Audience: **g,l,u,f.**

Davila, Thierry, et al.   **N6853**
Pierre Bismuth. Michael Newman & Raimar Stange (Authors). Trade Cloth. Flammarion et Cie. Paris, 2006. 208p. ISBN:2-08-030514-X, ISBN13: 978-2-08-030514-5. Dewey:709.2.

Audience: **g,l,u,f.**

Ferguson, Russell (Editor)   **N6797.G66A4 2001**
Douglas Gordon. Michael Darling, Francis McKee & Nancy Spector (Contribution by). Trade Cloth. MIT Press. Cambridge, MA. 2001. 200p. ISBN:0-262-06222-4, ISBN13: 978-0-262-06222-0. Dewey:709/.2. LCCN:2001-041066.

Audience: **g,l,u,f.**

Fineberg, Jonathan David   **TT504.E33 2003**
Christo and Jeanne-Claude: On the Way to the Gates, Central Park, New York City. Wolfgang Volz (Photographer). Cloth over Boards. Yale University Press. Cumberland, RI. 2004. 224p. Metropolitan Museum of Art Ser. ISBN:0-300-10138-4, ISBN13: 978-0-300-10138-6. Dewey:709/.2/2. LCCN:2003-025145.

Audience: **g,l,u,f.** *Choice, 2004.*

Fuchs, Rudi, et al.   N6537.J83
Donald Judd. David Batchelor, Richard Schiff, Nicholas Serota,
David Raskin & John Jervis (Authors), Donald Judd
(Photographer). Trade Cloth. D. A. P./Distributed Art Publishers.
New York, NY. 2004. 288p. ISBN:1-891024-89-2, ISBN13:
978-1-891024-89-4. Dewey:709.73.

Audience: **g,l,u,f.** *Choice, 2004.*

Goldberg, Roselee &   N6494.V53S55 2002
  Verzotti, Giorgio (Contribution by)
Shirin Neshat. Trade Cloth. Charta. Milano, 2003. 160p.
ISBN:88-8158-360-7, ISBN13: 978-88-8158-360-7.
Dewey:709.2.

Audience: **g,l,u,f.**

Jonas, Joan   NX512.J66A4X 2003
Joan Jonas: Five Works. Valerie Smith & Warren Niesluchowski
(Editors). Trade Cloth. Queens Museum of Art. Queens, NY.
2005. 176p. ISBN:1-929641-03-6, ISBN13: 978-1-929641-03-1.
Dewey:709.2.

Audience: **g,l,u,f.**

Kogler, Peter   N6811.5.K557
Peter Kogler. Stephan Berg (Editor), Boris Groys (Contribution
by). Trade Paper. Hatje Cantz Verlag GmbH & Co KG.
Ostfildern-Ruit, 2004. 192p. ISBN:3-7757-1422-7, ISBN13:
978-3-7757-1422-8. Dewey:709.0407.

Audience: **g,l,u,f.**

Marclay, Christian   N6537
Christian Marclay: The First ICP Triennial of Photography and
Video. Russell Ferguson (Editor), Miwon Kwon (Contribution
by). Trade Paper. Gerhard Steidl Druckerei und Verlag.
Gottingen, 2004. 200p. ISBN:3-88243-931-9, ISBN13:
978-3-88243-931-1. Dewey:709.2.

Audience: **g,l,u,f.**

Melhus, Bjorn (Editor), et   N6888.M4418
  al.
You Are Not Alone: Bjorn Melhus. Katja Blomberg & Bernd
Schulz (Editors). Trade Cloth, CD-ROM. Kehrer Verlag
Heidelberg, Klaus Kehrer. Heidelberg, 2003. 112p.
ISBN:3-933257-55-7, ISBN13: 978-3-933257-55-0.
Dewey:702/.8/1.

Audience: **g,l,u,f.**

Morgan, Robert C.   N6537.N38B775 2002
Bruce Nauman. Trade Paper. Johns Hopkins University Press.
Baltimore, MD. 2002. 432p. PAJ Bks. ISBN:0-8018-6906-4,
ISBN13: 978-0-8018-6906-8. Dewey:700/.92.
LCCN:2001-050728.

Audience: **g,l,u,f.**

Munroe, Alexandra, et al.   N6537.O56A42000
Yes Yoko Ono. Jon Hendricks, Murray Sayle, David A. Ross &
Jann S. Wenner (Authors), Joan Rothfuss, Chrissie Iles &
Kristine Stiles (Contribution by). Trade Cloth, Compact Disc.
Harry N. Abrams, Inc. New York, NY. 2000. 352p.
ISBN:0-8109-4587-8, ISBN13: 978-0-8109-4587-6.
Dewey:700/.92. LCCN:00-040146.

Audience: **g,l,u,f.**

Paik, Nam June   QC173.B48
The Worlds of Nam June Paik. John G. Hanhardt (Editor). Trade
Cloth. Solomon R. Guggenheim Museum. New York, NY. 2004.
276p. ISBN:0-89207-291-1, ISBN13: 978-0-89207-291-0.
Dewey:539.7.

Audience: **g,l,u,f.**

Quasha, George (Text by)   N6537.H533.A42002
Gary Hill: Language Willing. Gary Hill (Composed by). Trade
Paper. further/art. Barrytown, NY. 2002. 64p.
ISBN:0-9727005-0-1, ISBN13: 978-0-9727005-0-4.
Dewey:709/.2. LCCN:2002-155022.

Audience: **g,l,u,f.**

Rugoff, Ralph & Storr,   N6537.M39626A42004A
  Robert
Paul McCarthy: Piccadilly Circus/Bunker Basement. Trade
Cloth. Scalo Verlag. Zurich, 2005. 348p. ISBN:3-908247-89-6,
ISBN13: 978-3-908247-89-0. Dewey:709.2.

Audience: **g,l,u,f.**

Schwartz, Sheila (Editor), et   N6537.F55A42004
  al.
Dan Flavin: The Complete Lights, 1961-1996. Michelle Piranio
& Mary DelMonico (Editors), Michael Govan (Text by,
Foreword by), Tiffany Bell (Text by, Compiled by), Brydon
Smith (Text by), Jeffrey Weiss (Preface by). Trade Cloth. Dia
Center for the Arts. New York, NY. 2004. 416p.
ISBN:0-944521-51-7, ISBN13: 978-0-944521-51-9.
Dewey:709/.2. LCCN:2004-052686.

Audience: **g,l,u,f.**   *Choice, 2005.*

Smith, Marquard (Editor)   NX590.Z9S7372005
Stelarc: The Monograph. William Gibson (Foreword by). Trade
Cloth. MIT Press. Cambridge, MA. 2005. 224p. Electronic
Culture Ser., :History, Theory, and Practice Ser.
ISBN:0-262-19518-6, ISBN13: 978-0-262-19518-8.
Dewey:700/.92. LCCN:2004-057926.

Audience: **g,l,u,f.**

Viola, Bill   N6537.V56
Bill Viola: Going Forth by Day. John G. Hanhardt (Contribution
by). Trade Cloth. Solomon R. Guggenheim Museum. New York,
NY. 2004. 152p. ISBN:0-89207-255-5, ISBN13:
978-0-89207-255-2. Dewey:700.924.

Audience: **g,l,u,f.**

Viola, Bill, et al.   N6537.V56A4 2003
Bill Viola: The Passions. Peter Sellars, John Walsh & Hans
Belting (Authors), J. Paul Getty Museum Staff (Contribution
by). Trade Paper. Oxford University Press, Inc. New York, NY.
2003. 308p. Getty Trust Publications: J. Paul Getty Museum Ser.
ISBN:0-89236-720-2, ISBN13: 978-0-89236-720-7.
Dewey:700/.92. LCCN:2002-152393.

Audience: **g,l,u,f.**

Waplington, Nick   N6797.W33A4 2002
Learn How to Die the Easy Way. Trade Cloth. Trolley. London,
2004. 128p. ISBN:0-9542079-7-1, ISBN13: 978-0-9542079-7-7.
Dewey:709.42. LCCN:2003-282049.

Audience: **g,l,u,f.**

Wolf, Sylvia   **TR654.W6363 2002**
Michal Rovner: The Space Between. Michal Rovner & Whitney
Museum of American Art Staff (Contribution by). Trade Cloth.
Gerhard Steidl Druckerei und Verlag. Gottingen, 2002. 288p.
ISBN:3-88243-828-2, ISBN13: 978-3-88243-828-4.
Dewey:779/.092. LCCN:2002-004796.

Audience: **g,l,u,f.**

Sculpture > Reference Works > Directories

McCarthy, Jane & Epstein,   **NB205.M33 1996**
  Laurily K.
A Guide to the Sculpture Parks and Gardens of America. Trade
Paper. Michael Kesend Publishing, Ltd. New York, NY. 1996.
224p. ISBN:0-935576-51-7, ISBN13: 978-0-935576-51-1.
Dewey:730/.973. LCCN:96-017393.

Audience: **g,l,u,f.**

Sculpture > Reference Works > Web Resources

                       NK3760
☐ CeramicsWeb.
http://grafik.sdsu.edu/ceramicsweb//ceramicsweb.html
University of California, San Diego.

Audience: **g,l,u,f.**

                       N857.6
☐ Hirshhorn Museum and Sculpture Garden.
http://hirshhorn.si.edu/index.asp
Washington, D. C. : Hirshhorn Museum and Sculpture Garden,
Smithsonian Institution.

Audience: **g,l,u,f.**

                       NB198
☐ International Sculpture Center.
http://www.sculpture.org/
Hamilton, N. J., : International Sculpture Center.

Audience: **g,l,u,f.**

                       CD971
☐ SIRIUS (Smithsonian Institution Research Information
System): Archives, Manuscripts, Photographs Catalog.
http://siris-archives.si.edu/#focus
Smithsonian Institution.

Audience: **g,l,u,f.**

                       NB230.V8
☐ SOS! Save Outdoor Sculpture.
http://www.heritagepreservation.org/PROGRAMS/SOS/sosmain.htm
Washington, D. C. : Heritage Preservation; the National Institute
for Conservation.

Audience: **g,l,u,f.**

Sculpture > Reference Works > Dictionaries and Encyclopedias

Bostrvm, Antonia et al.   **NB198.E53 2004**
Encyclopedia of 20th Century Sculpture. Fitzroy Dearborn
Publishers, Inc. 2004. ISBN:1-57958-428-4, ISBN13:
978-1-57958-428-3.

Audience: **g,l,u,f.**

Kjellberg, Pierre   **NB1230.K5713 1994**
Bronzes of the 19th Century: Dictionary of Sculptors. Leslie
Bockol, Alison Levie & Kate Dooner (Translators). Trade Cloth.
Schiffer Publishing, Ltd. Atglen, PA. 1994. 685p.
ISBN:0-88740-629-7, ISBN13: 978-0-88740-629-4.
Dewey:730/.92/244 B. LCCN:94-066376.

Audience: **g,l,u,f.**

Mackay, James   **NB1115.M27 1995**
The Dictionary of Sculptors in Bronze. Trade Cloth. Antique
Collectors' Club. Easthampton, MA. 1992. 414p.
ISBN:1-85149-110-4, ISBN13: 978-1-85149-110-0.
Dewey:730.922. LCCN:96-175047.

Audience: **g,l,u,f.**

McHam, Sarah Blake   **NB615 .L66 1998**
  (Editor, Contribution by)
Looking at Italian Renaissance Sculpture. G. M. Helms, H. W.
Janson, Irving Lavin, John T. Paoletti, Christine Klapisch-Zuber,
Joy Kenseth & Paul Barolsky (Contribution by). Cloth Text.
Cambridge University Press. New York, NY. 1998. 303p.
ISBN:0-521-47366-7, ISBN13: 978-0-521-47366-8.
Dewey:730/.945/09024. LCCN:97-014906.

Audience: **g,l,u,f.** *Choice, 1998.*

Opitz, Glenn B. (Editor)   **NB236.O64 1984**
Dictionary of American Sculptors: Eighteenth Century to the
Present. Trade Cloth. Dealer's Choice Books, Inc. Land
O'Lakes, FL. 1984. 656p. ISBN:0-938290-03-7, ISBN13:
978-0-938290-03-2. Dewey:730/.92/2 B. LCCN:84-203245.

Audience: **g,l,u,f.**

Watson-Jones, Virginia   **NB212.W37 1985**
Contemporary American Women Sculptors. Cloth Text.
Greenwood Publishing Group, Inc. Portsmouth, NH. 1986. 680p.
ISBN:0-89774-139-0, ISBN13: 978-0-89774-139-2.
Dewey:730/.92/2 B. LCCN:84-042713.

Audience: **g,l,u,f.** *Choice, 1986.*

Windsor, Alan   **NB468.B66 2002**
British Sculptors of the Twentieth Century. Ashgate Publishing,
Ltd. 2003. ISBN:1-85928-456-6, ISBN13: 978-1-85928-456-8.

Audience: **g,l,u,f.**

Sculpture > Histories and Handbooks > Periods and Styles

Baudez, Claude-François   **F1435.1.C7B381994**
Maya Sculpture of Copan: The Iconography. Trade Cloth.
University of Oklahoma Press. Norman, OK. 1994. 320p.

ISBN:0-8061-2594-2, ISBN13: 978-0-8061-2594-7.
Dewey:730/.97283/84. LCCN:93-043681.
Audience: **g,l,u,f.** *Choice, 1995.*

Boardman, John   **NB94.B63 1995**
Greek Sculpture: The Late Classical Period and Sculpture in
Colonies and Overseas. Trade Paper. Thames & Hudson. New
York, NY. 1995. 248p. World of Art Ser. ISBN:0-500-20285-0,
ISBN13: 978-0-500-20285-2. Dewey:733.3. LCCN:95-060279.
Audience: **g,l,u,f.**

Boettger, Suzaan   **N6494.E27**
Earthworks: Art and the Landscape of the Sixties. Trade Paper.
University of California Press. Berkeley, CA. 2004. 316p.
ISBN:0-520-24116-9, ISBN13: 978-0-520-24116-9.
Dewey:709/.04/076. LCCN:2002-002316.
Audience: **g,l,u,f.** *Choice, 2003.*

Boucher, Bruce   **NB615.B64 1998**
Italian Baroque Sculpture. Trade Paper. Thames & Hudson. New
York, NY. 1998. 224p. World of Art Ser. ISBN:0-500-20307-5,
ISBN13: 978-0-500-20307-1. Dewey:730.945.
LCCN:97-060251.
Audience: **g,l,u,f.** *Choice, 1998.*

Causey, Andrew   **NB198 .C35 1998**
Sculpture since 1945. Trade Paper. Oxford University Press, Inc.
New York, NY. 1998. 300p. Oxford History of Art Ser.
ISBN:0-19-284205-6, ISBN13: 978-0-19-284205-3.
Dewey:735/.235. LCCN:98-188405.
Audience: **g,l,u,f.** *Choice, 1998.*

Cole, Michael Wayne   **NB623.C28C65 2002**
Cellini and the Principles of Sculpture. Trade Cloth. Cambridge
University Press. New York, NY. 2002. 262p.
ISBN:0-521-81321-2, ISBN13: 978-0-521-81321-1.
Dewey:730/.92. LCCN:2001-043355.
Audience: **l,u,f.** *Choice, 2003.*

Conlin, Diane A.   **96-41830 [NB]**
The Artists of the Ara Pacis: The Process of Hellenization in
Roman Relief Sculpture. Trade Cloth. University of North
Carolina Press. Chapel Hill, NC. 1997. 360p. Studies in the
History of Greece and Rome ISBN:0-8078-2343-0, ISBN13:
978-0-8078-2343-9. Dewey:733/.5/09376. LCCN:96-041830.
Audience: **u,f.** *Choice, 1997.*

Curtis, Penelope   **NB198 .C87**
Sculpture 1900-1945. Trade Paper. Oxford University Press, Inc.
New York, NY. 1999. 304p. Oxford History of Art Ser.
ISBN:0-19-284228-5, ISBN13: 978-0-19-284228-2.
Dewey:730.94.
Audience: **g,l,u,f.**

de Waal, Edmund   **NK3930**
20th-Century Ceramics. Trade Paper. Thames & Hudson. New
York, NY. 2003. 224p. The World of Art Ser.
ISBN:0-500-20371-7, ISBN13: 978-0-500-20371-2.
Dewey:738/.0904/075. LCCN:2003-100124.
Audience: **g,l,u,f.**

Hallett, Christopher H.   **NB1296.3**
The Roman Nude: Heroic Portrait Statuary 200 BC-AD 300.
Trade Cloth. Oxford University Press, Inc. New York, NY. 2005.
416p. Oxford Studies in Ancient Culture and Representation Ser.
ISBN:0-19-924049-3, ISBN13: 978-0-19-924049-4.
Dewey:733/.5. LCCN:2005-048832.
Audience: **l,u,f.** *Choice, 2006.*

Jacoff, Michael (Editor)   **NK7952.V38.J33 1993**
The Horses of San Marco and The Quadriga of the Lord. Trade
Cloth. Princeton University Press. Princeton, NJ. 1993. 224p.
ISBN:0-691-03270-X, ISBN13: 978-0-691-03270-2.
Dewey:731/.832. LCCN:93-016276.
Audience: **l,u,f.** *Choice, 1994.*

Kleiner, Diana E.   **NB115.K57**
Roman Sculpture. Trade Paper. Yale University Press.
Cumberland, RI. 1994. 489p. Yale Publications in the History of
Art Ser. ISBN:0-300-05948-5, ISBN13: 978-0-300-05948-9.
Dewey:733.5.
Audience: **g,l,u,f.** *Choice, 1993.*

Lynn, Martha Drexler   **NB1270.G4L96 2005**
Sculpture, Glass, and American Museums. Saddle Stitched,
Cloth over Boards, Dust Jacket. University of Pennsylvania
Press. Philadelphia, PA. 2005. 223p. ISBN:0-8122-3896-6,
ISBN13: 978-0-8122-3896-9. Dewey:748/.09/045.
LCCN:2005-011654.
Audience: **g,l,u,f.** *Choice, 2006.*

Mattusch, Carol C.   **NB135.M38 1996**
Classical Bronzes: The Art and Craft of Greek and Roman
Statuary. Trade Cloth. Cornell University Press. Ithaca, NY.
1996. 280p. ISBN:0-8014-3182-4, ISBN13: 978-0-8014-3182-1.
Dewey:733. LCCN:95-036843.
Audience: **l,u,f.** *Choice, 1996.*

McHam, Sarah Blake   **NB615 .L66 1998**
 (Editor, Contribution by)
Looking at Italian Renaissance Sculpture. G. M. Helms, H. W.
Janson, Irving Lavin, John T. Paoletti, Christine Klapisch-Zuber,
Joy Kenseth & Paul Barolsky (Contribution by). Cloth Text.
Cambridge University Press. New York, NY. 1998. 303p.
ISBN:0-521-47366-7, ISBN13: 978-0-521-47366-8.
Dewey:730/.945/09024. LCCN:97-014906.
Audience: **g,l,u,f.** *Choice, 1998.*

Montagu, Jennifer   **NB620.M66 1989**
Roman Baroque Sculpture: The Industry of Art. Cloth over
Boards. Yale University Press. Cumberland, RI. 1989. 256p.
ISBN:0-300-04392-9, ISBN13: 978-0-300-04392-1.
Dewey:730/.945/632. LCCN:88-030482.
Audience: **l,u,f.** *Choice, 1990.*

Neils, Jenifer   **NA2965 .N45 2001**
The Parthenon Frieze. Trade Paper. Cambridge University Press.
New York, NY. 2006. 316p. ISBN:0-521-68402-1, ISBN13:
978-0-521-68402-6. Dewey:733/.3/09385.
Audience: **g,l,u,f.** *Choice, 2002.*

Olson, Roberta J. M.   NB615.O48 1992
Italian Renaissance Sculpture. Trade Paper. Thames & Hudson.
New York, NY. 1992. 216p. World of Art Ser.
ISBN:0-500-20253-2, ISBN13: 978-0-500-20253-1.
Dewey:730.945. LCCN:91-065310.

Audience: **g,l,u,f.**

Palagia, Olga (Editor)   NB90.A655 2005
Greek Sculpture: Function, Materials, and Techniques in the
Archaic and Classical Periods. Trade Cloth. Cambridge
University Press. New York, NY. 2006. 342p.
ISBN:0-521-77267-2, ISBN13: 978-0-521-77267-9.
Dewey:733/.3. LCCN:2005-002856.

Audience: **l,u,f.**

Payne, Christopher   NK7906
Animals in Bronze Reference and Price Guide. Trade Cloth.
Antique Collectors' Club. Easthampton, MA. 1993. 424p.
ISBN:0-907462-45-6, ISBN13: 978-0-907462-45-3.
Dewey:731/.832.

Audience: **g,l,u,f.**

Read, Herbert E.   NB198 .R4 1983
Modern Sculpture. Trade Paper. Thames & Hudson. New York,
NY. 1985. 312p. World of Art Ser. ISBN:0-500-20014-9,
ISBN13: 978-0-500-20014-8. Dewey:735/.23. LCCN:87-170396.
Audience: **g,l,u,f.**

Ridgway, Brunilde   NB94.R535
Sismondo
Hellenistic Sculpture I: The Styles of ca. 331-200 B.C. Trade
Paper. University of Wisconsin Press. Chicago, IL. 2001. 288p.
ISBN:0-299-11824-X, ISBN13: 978-0-299-11824-2.
Dewey:733.3. LCCN:89-040266.

Audience: **u,f.**

Ridgway, Brunilde   NB94
Sismondo
Hellenistic Sculpture II: The Styles of ca. 200-100 B.C. Trade
Cloth. University of Wisconsin Press. Chicago, IL. 2000. 576p.
ISBN:0-299-16710-0, ISBN13: 978-0-299-16710-3.
Dewey:733.3. LCCN:89-040266.

Audience: **u,f.** *Choice, 2001.*

Ridgway, Brunilde   NB94.R5351990
Sismondo
Hellenistic Sculpture III: The Styles of ca. 100-31 B.C. Trade
Cloth. University of Wisconsin Press. Chicago, IL. 2002. 400p.
Studies in Classics ISBN:0-299-17710-6, ISBN13:
978-0-299-17710-2. Dewey:733.3. LCCN:89-040266.

Audience: **u,f.** *Choice, 2003.*

Ridgway, Brunilde   NA3350.R53 1999
Sismondo
Prayers in Stone: Greek Architectural Sculpture 600-100 BC.
Trade Cloth. University of California Press. Berkeley, CA. 1999.
316p. Sather Classical Lectures, Vol. 63 ISBN:0-520-21556-7,
ISBN13: 978-0-520-21556-6. Dewey:733/.3. LCCN:98-003583.

Audience: **l,u,f.** *Choice, 2000.*

Russmann, Edna R. & Finn,   NB1296.2.R87 1989
David
Egyptian Sculpture: Cairo and Luxor. Trade Cloth. University of
Texas Press. Austin, TX. 1989. 242p. ISBN:0-292-70402-X,
ISBN13: 978-0-292-70402-2. Dewey:732/.8. LCCN:89-005315.

Audience: **g,l,u,f.** *Choice, 1990.*

Smith, R. R.   NB94.S631991
Hellenistic Sculpture. Trade Paper. Thames & Hudson. New
York, NY. 1991. 288p. World of Art Ser. ISBN:0-500-20249-4,
ISBN13: 978-0-500-20249-4. Dewey:733/.3. LCCN:90-063385.

Audience: **g,l,u,f.** *Choice, 1991.*

Stewart, Andrew   NB94
Greek Sculpture: An Exploration. Trade Paper. Yale University
Press. Cumberland, RI. 1993. 800p. ISBN:0-300-05208-1,
ISBN13: 978-0-300-05208-4. Dewey:733/.3. LCCN:89-009024.

Audience: **g,l,u,f.** *Choice, 1990.*

Williamson, Paul   NB180
Gothic Sculpture, 1140-1300. Trade Paper. Yale University
Press. Cumberland, RI. 1998. 316p. Pelican History of Art Ser.
ISBN:0-300-07452-2, ISBN13: 978-0-300-07452-9.
Dewey:734.2/5. LCCN:94-049678.

Audience: **g,l,u,f.** *Choice, 1996.*

Sculpture > Histories and Handbooks > Cultures, Regions, Nationalities

Bai, Su, et al.   NB1912.B83R82
Return of the Buddha: The Qingzhou Discoveries. Helmut
Brinker, Alexander L. Mayer, Lukas Nickel & Zhang Zonghu
(Authors). Trade Cloth. Harry N. Abrams, Inc. New York, NY.
2002. 176p. ISBN:0-8109-6643-3, ISBN13: 978-0-8109-6643-7.
Dewey:732.71.

Audience: **g,l,u,f.** *Choice, 2003, 2002.*

Benton, Charlotte   NB458
Figuration/Abstraction: Strategies for Public Sculpture in Europe
1945-1968. Henry Moore Institute Staff (Contribution by). Trade
Cloth. Ashgate Publishing, Ltd. Aldershot, 2004. 356p.
Subject/Object--New Studies in Sculpture ISBN:0-7546-0693-7,
ISBN13: 978-0-7546-0693-2. Dewey:735/.235.
LCCN:2004-043653.

Audience: **u,f.**

Conner, Janis &   NB210.C66 1989
Rosenkrantz, Joel
Rediscoveries in American Sculpture: Studio Works, 1893-1939.
David Finn (Illustrator). Trade Cloth. University of Texas Press.
Austin, TX. 1989. 216p. ISBN:0-292-70401-1, ISBN13:
978-0-292-70401-5. Dewey:730/.973. LCCN:88-020652.

Audience: **g,l,u,f.** *Choice, 1990.*

Dabakis, Melissa   NB1952.L33 D23 1998
Visualizing Labor in American Sculpture: Monuments,
Manliness, and the Work Ethic, 1880-1935. Albert Boime,
Patricia Hills, Garnett McCoy, Terry Smith, Roger Stein &
Lowery Stokes Sims (Contribution by). Trade Cloth. Cambridge

University Press. New York, NY. 1999. 312p. Studies in American Visual Culture ISBN:0-521-46147-2, ISBN13: 978-0-521-46147-4. Dewey:730/.973. LCCN:98-045452.
                                    Audience: **g,l,u,f.** *Choice, 1999.*

Dehejia, Vidya   NA6007.S6D44 1990
Art of the Imperial Cholas. Trade Cloth. Columbia University Press. New York, NY. 1990. 160p. ISBN:0-231-07188-4, ISBN13: 978-0-231-07188-8. Dewey:726/.145/09548. LCCN:89-078065.
                                    Audience: **l,u,f.** *Choice, 1991.*

Fontein, Jan   NB1026
The Sculpture of Indonesia. R. Soekmono & Edi Sedyawati (Contribution by). Trade Paper. Harry N. Abrams, Inc. New York, NY. 1992. 312p. ISBN:0-8109-2503-6, ISBN13: 978-0-8109-2503-8. Dewey:730/.9598/07473.
                                    Audience: **g,l,u,f.** *Choice, 1991.*

Howard, Angela Falco, et al.   NB1040.C516 2003
Chinese Sculpture. Yang Hongxun, Wu Hung, Li Song & Hong Yang (Authors). Cloth over Boards. Yale University Press. Cumberland, RI. 2006. 536p. The Culture and Civilization of China Ser. ISBN:0-300-10065-5, ISBN13: 978-0-300-10065-5. Dewey:730/.951. LCCN:2003-002733.
                                    Audience: **g,l,u,f.** *Choice, 2006.*

Jopek, Norbert   NB565.J67
German Sculpture, 1430-1540: A Catalogue of the Collection in the Victoria and Albert Museum. Trade Cloth. Harry N. Abrams, Inc. New York, NY. 2002. 176p. ISBN:0-8109-6592-5, ISBN13: 978-0-8109-6592-8. Dewey:730.943. LCCN:2001-095101.
                                    Audience: **g,l,u,f.** *Choice, 2002.*

Kerchache, Jacques, et al.   NB1098.K47131993
Art of Africa. Jean-Louis Paudrat & Lucien Stephan (Authors). Trade Cloth. Harry N. Abrams, Inc. New York, NY. 1993. 620p. ISBN:0-8109-0628-7, ISBN13: 978-0-8109-0628-0. Dewey:730/.0967. LCCN:92-027689.
                                    Audience: **g,l,u,f.** *Choice, 1993.*

Koplos, Janet   NB1055.K66 1991
Contemporary Japanese Sculpture. Trade Cloth. Abbeville Press, Inc. New York, NY. 1991. 148p. ISBN:1-55859-012-9, ISBN13: 978-1-55859-012-0. Dewey:730/.952/09045. LCCN:90-027482.
                                    Audience: **g,l,u,f.** *Choice, 1992.*

LaGamma, Alisa   NB1080.5.L34 2002
Genesis: Ideas of Origin in African Sculpture. Metropolitan Museum of Art Staff (Contribution by). Trade Paper. Metropolitan Museum of Art, The. New York, NY. 2002. viii, 128p. ISBN:1-58839-074-8, ISBN13: 978-1-58839-074-5. Dewey:730/.966/0747471. LCCN:2002-032554.
                                    Audience: **g,l,u,f.** *Choice, 2003.*

Mannikka, Eleanor   DS554.98.A5M36 1996
Angkor Wat: Time, Space, and Kingship. Trade Cloth. University of Hawaii Press. Honolulu, HI. 2000. 360p. ISBN:0-8248-1720-6, ISBN13: 978-0-8248-1720-6. Dewey:959.6. LCCN:96-004368.
                                    Audience: **g,l,u,f.** *Choice, 1997.*

McHam, Sarah Blake   NB615 .L66 1998
(Editor, Contribution by)
Looking at Italian Renaissance Sculpture. G. M. Helms, H. W. Janson, Irving Lavin, John T. Paoletti, Christine Klapisch-Zuber, Joy Kenseth & Paul Barolsky (Contribution by). Cloth Text. Cambridge University Press. New York, NY. 1998. 303p. ISBN:0-521-47366-7, ISBN13: 978-0-521-47366-8. Dewey:730/.945/09024. LCCN:97-014906.
                                    Audience: **g,l,u,f.** *Choice, 1998.*

Menair, Peter, et al.   E78.N78M32 1998
Down from the Shimmering Sky: Masks of the Northwest Coast. Robert Joseph & Bruce Grenville (Authors). Paper Text. University of Washington Press. Seattle, WA. 1998. 192p. ISBN:0-295-97709-4, ISBN13: 978-0-295-97709-6. Dewey:731/.75/089970795. LCCN:98-015997.
                                    Audience: **g,l,u,f.** *Choice, 1999.*

Muller, Theodor   R709
Sculpture in the Netherlands, Germany, France, and Spain: 1400-1500. Cloth over Boards. Yale University Press. Cumberland, RI. 1976. 262p. Pelican History of Art Ser. ISBN:0-300-05309-6, ISBN13: 978-0-300-05309-8. Dewey:734.25.
                                    Audience: **g,l,u,f.**

Mulryan, Lenore Hoag   NK4031.M849 2003
Ceramic Trees of Life: Popular Art from Mexico. Delia A. Cosentino (Contribution by). Trade Cloth. University of California Los Angeles, Fowler Museum of Cultural History. Los Angeles, CA. 2004. 168p. ISBN:0-930741-96-X, ISBN13: 978-0-930741-96-9. Dewey:738.8. LCCN:2003-042621.
                                    Audience: **g,l,u,f.** *Choice, 2004.*

Norton, Derek & Reading,   E99.E7N68 2005
Nigel
Cape Dorset Sculpture. Trade Cloth. University of Washington Press. Seattle, WA. 2005. 144p. ISBN:0-295-98478-3, ISBN13: 978-0-295-98478-0. Dewey:730/.89/9712071952. LCCN:2004-023553.
                                    Audience: **g,l,u,f.** *Choice, 2005.*

Robbins, Warren M. &   NB1091.65
Nooter, Nancy Ingram
African Art in American Collections. Ed. 2. Trade Cloth. Schiffer Publishing, Ltd. Atglen, PA. 2004. 616p. ISBN:0-7643-2005-X, ISBN13: 978-0-7643-2005-7. Dewey:730/.0967/074013. LCCN:2003-112278.
                                    Audience: **l,u,f.** *Choice, 1990.*

Rubinstein, Charlotte S.   NB236.R8 1990
American Women Sculptors: A History of Women Working in Three Dimensions. Trade Cloth. Thomson Gale. Farmington Hills, MI. 1990. 600p. Monographs ISBN:0-8161-8732-0, ISBN13: 978-0-8161-8732-4. Dewey:730/.82. LCCN:89-026846.
                                    Audience: **g,l,u,f.** *Choice, 1991.*

Sheehy, Colleen J.   NK808.S53 1997
The Flamingo in the Garden: American Yard Art and the Vernacular Landscape. Cloth Text. Garland Publishing, Inc. New

York, NY. 1998. 232p. Studies in American Popular History and Culture ISBN:0-8153-2914-8, ISBN13: 978-0-8153-2914-5. Dewey:645/.8. LCCN:97-023689.

Audience: **g,l,u,f.**

Stewart, Hilary　　　　　　　　　　　　　**E98.T65S74 1993**
Looking at Totem Poles. Trade Cloth. University of Washington Press. Seattle, WA. 2005. 192p. ISBN:0-295-97259-9, ISBN13: 978-0-295-97259-6. Dewey:731.7. LCCN:93-014724.

Audience: **g,l,u,f.**

Tolles, Thayer (Editor)　　　　　　　　　**NB210.M48 1999**
American Sculpture in the Metropolitan Museum of Art. Lauretta Dimmick & Donna J. Hassler (Contribution by). Trade Cloth. Metropolitan Museum of Art, The. New York, NY. 1999. 451p. ISBN:0-87099-914-1, ISBN13: 978-0-87099-914-7. Dewey:730.9/73. LCCN:99-024636.

Audience: **g,l,u,f.**　*Choice, 2000.*

Tunick, Susan　　　　　　　　　　　　　**NA3511.N48T86 1997**
Terra Cotta Skyline: New York's Architectural Ornament. Trade Cloth. Princeton Architectural Press. New York, NY. 1997. 176p. ISBN:1-56898-105-8, ISBN13: 978-1-56898-105-5. Dewey:729/.5. LCCN:96-052343.

Audience: **g,l,u,f.**　*Choice, 1998.*

Wagner, Anne Middleton　　　　　　　　**NB468.W34 2005**
Mother Stone: The Vitality of Modern British Sculpture. Saddle Stitched, Cloth over Boards, Dust Jacket. Yale University Press. Cumberland, RI. 2005. 256p. Studies in British Art Ser. ISBN:0-300-10685-8, ISBN13: 978-0-300-10685-5. Dewey:730/.941/0904. LCCN:2004-023972.

Audience: **u,f.**　*Choice, 2006.*

Whinney, Margaret　　　　　　　　　　　**NB464.W5**
Sculpture in Britain: 1530-1830. Ed. 2. John Physick (Revised by). Trade Paper. Yale University Press. Cumberland, RI. 1992. 522p. Pelican History of Art Ser. ISBN:0-300-05318-5, ISBN13: 978-0-300-05318-0. Dewey:730/.941.

Audience: **g,l,u,f.**

Wu Hung　　　　　　　　　　　　　　　**NB1280.W77 1989**
The Wu Liang Shrine: The Ideology of Early Chinese Pictorial Art. Trade Cloth. Stanford University Press. Palo Alto, CA. 1989. 440p. ISBN:0-8047-1529-7, ISBN13: 978-0-8047-1529-4. Dewey:732/.71/14. LCCN:88-036893.

Audience: **u,f.**　*Choice, 1990.*

Sculpture > Individual Sculptors

Andrews, Julian　　　　　　　　　　　**NB497.N37A85 1999**
The Sculpture of David Nash. Trade Paper. University of California Press. Berkeley, CA. 1999. 180p. British Sculptors and Sculpture Ser. ISBN:0-520-22044-7, ISBN13: 978-0-520-22044-7. Dewey:730.9/2. LCCN:97-145687.

Audience: **g,l,u,f.**

Ashton, Dore　　　　　　　　　　　　　**N6853.P5**
Noguchi East and West. Denise B. Hare (Photographer). Trade Paper. University of California Press. Berkeley, CA. 1993. 342p. ISBN:0-520-08340-7, ISBN13: 978-0-520-08340-0. Dewey:709/.2 B. LCCN:92-036450.

Audience: **g,l,u,f.**

Ayral-Clause, Odile　　　　　　　　　**NB553.C44A972002**
Camille Claudel: A Life. Trade Cloth. Harry N. Abrams, Inc. New York, NY. 2002. 280p. ISBN:0-8109-4077-9, ISBN13: 978-0-8109-4077-2. Dewey:730/.92 B. LCCN:2001-046507.

Audience: **g,l,u,f.**　*Choice, 2002.*

Bann, Stephen　　　　　　　　　　　　**NB497.C69A4 1995**
The Sculpture of Stephen Cox. Trade Cloth. Ashgate Publishing, Ltd. Aldershot, 1995. 144p. The British Sculptors and Sculpture Ser. ISBN:0-85331-675-9, ISBN13: 978-0-85331-675-6. Dewey:730.92. LCCN:95-211301.

Audience: **g,l,u,f.**

Benezra, Neal　　　　　　　　　　　　**NB553.R7**
Martin Puryear. Robert Storr (Contribution by). Trade Paper. Thames & Hudson. New York, NY. 1993. 160p. ISBN:0-500-27702-8, ISBN13: 978-0-500-27702-7. Dewey:730.9/2. LCCN:91-065308.

Audience: **g,l,u,f.**

Bergstein, Mary　　　　　　　　　　　**NB623.N3B47 2000**
The Sculpture of Nanni di Banco. Trade Cloth. Princeton University Press. Princeton, NJ. 2000. 240p. ISBN:0-691-00982-1, ISBN13: 978-0-691-00982-7. Dewey:730/.92. LCCN:99-047383.

Audience: **g,l,u,f.**　*Choice, 2000.*

Bilski, Emily　　　　　　　　　　　　**NK1412.K34B55 2004**
Ritual and the Art of Tobi Kahn: Objects of the Spirit. Nessa Rapoport (Contribution by). Trade Cloth. Hudson Hills Press LLC. Manchester, VT. 2004. 176p. ISBN:1-55595-247-X, ISBN13: 978-1-55595-247-1. Dewey:709/.2. LCCN:2004-041037.

Audience: **g,l,u,f.**　*Choice, 2004.*

Bowness, Alan　　　　　　　　　　　　**NB553.R7**
Bernard Meadows: Sculpture and Drawings. Trade Cloth. Ashgate Publishing, Ltd. Aldershot, 1995. 160p. British Sculptors and Sculpture Ser., Vol. 4 ISBN:0-85331-644-9, ISBN13: 978-0-85331-644-2. Dewey:730.9/2.

Audience: **g,l,u,f.**

Bryant, Julius　　　　　　　　　　　　**NB497.C35**
Anthony Caro: A Life in Sculpture. Trade Cloth. Merrell Publishers Ltd. London, 2005. 96p. ISBN:1-85894-259-4, ISBN13: 978-1-85894-259-9. Dewey:730.92. LCCN:2005-279377.

Audience: **g,l,u,f.**　*Choice, 2005.*

Butler, Ruth　　　　　　　　　　　　　**NB553.R7**
Rodin: The Shape of Genius. Trade Paper. Yale University Press. Cumberland, RI. 1996. 608p. ISBN:0-300-06498-5, ISBN13: 978-0-300-06498-8. Dewey:730.9/2. LCCN:92-043552.

Audience: **g,l,u,f.**　*Choice, 1994.*

Caranfa, Angelo   NB553.C44C36 1999
Camille Claudel: A Sculpture of Interior Solitude. Trade Cloth.
Bucknell University Press. Cranbury, NJ. 1999. 214p.
ISBN:0-8387-5391-4, ISBN13: 978-0-8387-5391-0.
Dewey:730/.92 B. LCCN:98-028188.
                              Audience: **g,l,u,f.** *Choice, 2000.*

Chapuis, Julien   NB588.R5A4 1999
Tilman Riemenschneider: Master Sculptor of the Late Middle
Ages. Michael Baxandall, Till-Holger Borchet & Timothy B.
Husband (Contribution by). Cloth over Boards. Yale University
Press. Cumberland, RI. 1999. 352p. National Gallery London
Publications ISBN:0-300-08162-6, ISBN13: 978-0-300-08162-6.
Dewey:730/.92. LCCN:99-025450.
                              Audience: **g,l,u,f.** *Choice, 2000.*

Compton, Ann   NB553.R7
Sculpture of Charles Sargeant Jagger. Trade Cloth. Ashgate
Publishing, Ltd. Aldershot, 2004. 144p. The British Sculptors
and Sculpture Ser. ISBN:0-85331-864-6, ISBN13:
978-0-85331-864-4. Dewey:730.92.
                              Audience: **g,l,u,f.**

Cooper, Edward S.   NB237.R38A4 2004
Vinnie Ream: An American Sculptor. Trade Cloth. Academy
Chicago Publishers, Ltd. Chicago, IL. 2002. 300p.
ISBN:0-89733-505-8, ISBN13: 978-0-89733-505-8.
Dewey:730/.92. LCCN:2003-022106.
                              Audience: **g,l,u,f.** *Choice, 2004.*

Crone, Rainer & Salzmann,   N6853.R63A4 1997
Siegfried (Editors)
Rodin: Eros and Creativity. Trade Paper. Prestel Publishing.
New York, NY. 1997. 236p. ISBN:3-7913-1809-8, ISBN13:
978-3-7913-1809-7. Dewey:730.9/2. LCCN:97-003599.
                              Audience: **g,l,u,f.** *Choice, 1992.*

Davidson, Amanda   NB461
The Sculpture of William Turnbull. Trade Cloth. Ashgate
Publishing, Ltd. Aldershot, 2005. 208p. The British Sculptors
and Sculpture Ser. ISBN:0-85331-891-3, ISBN13:
978-0-85331-891-0. Dewey:730.9/2.
                              Audience: **g,l,u,f.** *Choice, 2006.*

De Caso, Jacques   NB553.D3D413 1992
David d'Angers: Sculptural Communication in the Age of
Romanticism. Dorothy Johnson (Translator). Trade Cloth.
Princeton University Press. Princeton, NJ. 1992. 210p.
ISBN:0-691-04078-8, ISBN13: 978-0-691-04078-3.
Dewey:730/.92. LCCN:91-010881.
                              Audience: **u,f.** *Choice, 1992.*

Draper, James D.   NB623.B528D731992
Bertoldo di Giovanni, Sculptor of the Medici Household:
Critical Reappraisal and Catalogue Raisonné. Trade Cloth.
University of Missouri Press. Columbia, MO. 1992. 320p.
ISBN:0-8262-0819-3, ISBN13: 978-0-8262-0819-4.
Dewey:730.92. LCCN:91-046987.
                              Audience: **g,l,u,f.** *Choice, 1992.*

Duthuit, Claude & Bois,   NB553.M39
Yve-Alain
Henri Matisse: Catalogue Raisonné de l'Oeuvre Sculpte Etabli
avec la Collaboration de Wanda de Guebriant. Trade Cloth.
Claude/Duthuit. Paris, 1997. 416p. ISBN:2-904852-04-2,
ISBN13: 978-2-904852-04-6. Dewey:730.944.
                              Audience: **g,l,u,f.**

Duus, Masayo   NB237.N6D88132004
The Life of Isamu Noguchi: Journey Without Borders. Peter
Duus (Translator). Trade Cloth. Princeton University Press.
Princeton, NJ. 2004. 432p. ISBN:0-691-12096-X, ISBN13:
978-0-691-12096-6. Dewey:709/.2 B. LCCN:2004-044532.
                              Audience: **g,l,u,f.** *Choice, 2005.*

Fath, Manfred & Selz, Peter   N6888.Z38
H.
Bruce Beasley: Sculpture. Trade Paper. University of
Washington Press. Seattle, WA. 1995. 176p.
ISBN:3-89165-098-1, ISBN13: 978-3-89165-098-1.
Dewey:709.24.
                              Audience: **g,l,u,f.**

Fermon, An Jo   NB497
Clive Barker Sculpture: Catalogue Raisonné, 1958-2000. Paola
Gribaudo (Editor), Marco Livingstone (Contribution by). Trade
Cloth. Skira Editore. Milano, 2003. 212p. ISBN:88-8491-380-2,
ISBN13: 978-88-8491-380-7. Dewey:730.9/2.
                              Audience: **g,l,u,f.**

Goldsworthy, Andy   NB497.G64A42004
Passage. Trade Cloth. Harry N. Abrams, Inc. New York, NY.
2004. 168p. ISBN:0-8109-5586-5, ISBN13: 978-0-8109-5586-8.
Dewey:730.9/2. LCCN:2004-010344.
                              Audience: **g,l,u,f.** *Choice, 2005.*

Goldsworthy, Andy &   NB497.G64A42000
Thompson, Jerry L. (Photographers)
Wall. Trade Cloth. Harry N. Abrams, Inc. New York, NY. 2000.
92p. ISBN:0-8109-4559-2, ISBN13: 978-0-8109-4559-3.
Dewey:709/.04/076. LCCN:00-709610.
                              Audience: **g,l,u,f.**

Graham, Dan   N6537.G674
Dan Graham: Catalogue Raisonné. Trade Cloth. Richter Verlag.
Dusseldorf, 2001. 384p. ISBN:3-933807-31-X, ISBN13:
978-3-933807-31-1. Dewey:709.2.
                              Audience: **g,l,u,f.**

Grieve, Alastair   NB497.A33G75 1992
The Sculpture of Robert Adams. Trade Cloth. Ashgate
Publishing, Ltd. Aldershot, 1992. 280p. British Sculptors and
Sculpture Ser. ISBN:0-85331-624-4, ISBN13:
978-0-85331-624-4. Dewey:730/.92. LCCN:93-179720.
                              Audience: **g,l,u,f.** *Choice, 1993.*

Hamilton, James   NB497.W75H36 1994
The Sculpture of Austin Wright. Trade Cloth. Ashgate
Publishing, Ltd. Aldershot, 1994. 144p. The British Sculptors
and Sculpture Ser. ISBN:0-85331-651-1, ISBN13:
978-0-85331-651-0. Dewey:730.92. LCCN:95-148291.
                              Audience: **g,l,u,f.**

Hammacher, A. M.   **NB497.H4H413 1998**
Barbara Hepworth. Ed. 2. Trade Paper. Thames & Hudson. New York, NY. 1998. 216p. World of Art Ser. ISBN:0-500-20218-4, ISBN13: 978-0-500-20218-0. Dewey:730.9/2. LCCN:97-061660.
Audience: **g,l,u,f.**

Hanson, Duane, et al.   **NB237.H254A4 2000**
Duane Hanson: Virtual Reality. Christine Giles, Elizabeth Hayt & Katherine Plake Hough (Authors). Trade Paper. University of Washington Press. Seattle, WA. 2000. 80p. ISBN:0-295-98036-2, ISBN13: 978-0-295-98036-2. Dewey:730/.92. LCCN:00-044138.
Audience: **g,l,u,f.**

Hedgecoe, John   **NB497.M6**
A Monumental Vision: The Sculpture of Henry Moore. Trade Paper. Anova Books. London, 2003. 256p. ISBN:1-84340-046-4, ISBN13: 978-1-84340-046-2. Dewey:730.92.
Audience: **g,l,u,f.**

Hilton, Tim   **NB497.K5A4 1992**
The Sculpture of Phillip King. Trade Cloth. Ashgate Publishing, Ltd. Aldershot, 1992. 128p. British Sculptors and Sculpture Ser. ISBN:0-85331-622-8, ISBN13: 978-0-85331-622-0. Dewey:730.92. LCCN:92-229475.
Audience: **g,l,u,f.** *Choice, 1992.*

Jason, Neville   **NB497.D6J38 1994**
The Sculpture of Frank Dobson. Trade Cloth. Ashgate Publishing, Ltd. Aldershot, 1994. 168p. British Sculptors and Sculpture Ser. ISBN:0-85331-641-4, ISBN13: 978-0-85331-641-1. Dewey:730/.92. LCCN:95-140387.
Audience: **g,l,u,f.**

Kosinski, Dorothy (Editor)   **N6797.M5A4 2001**
Henry Moore: Sculpting the Twentieth Century. Cloth over Boards. Yale University Press. Cumberland, RI. 2001. 320p. ISBN:0-300-08992-9, ISBN13: 978-0-300-08992-9. Dewey:730/.92. LCCN:00-065687.
Audience: **g,l,u,f.** *Choice, 2001.*

Lampard, Marie Turbow   **NB699.K6U53 2001**
  (Editor), et al.
The Uncommon Vision of Sergei Konenkov, 1874-1971: A Russian Sculptor and His Times. John E. Bowlt & Wendy R. Salmond (Editors). Trade Cloth. Rutgers University Press. Piscataway, NJ. 2001. xiv, 223p. ISBN:0-8135-2854-2, ISBN13: 978-0-8135-2854-0. Dewey:730/.92 B. LCCN:00-039038.
Audience: **u,f.** *Choice, 2001.*

Lisle, Laurie   **N6853.P5**
Louise Nevelson: A Passionate Life. Trade Paper. iUniverse, Inc. Lincoln, NE. 2001. 356p. ISBN:0-595-19069-3, ISBN13: 978-0-595-19069-0. Dewey:709/.2 B.
Audience: **g,l,u,f.**

Long, Richard   **N6797.L65**
Walking the Line. Trade Paper. Thames & Hudson. New York, NY. 2005. 328p. ISBN:0-500-28409-1, ISBN13: 978-0-500-28409-4. Dewey:709.2.
Audience: **g,l,u,f.**

Lord, James   **NB553.G4L68 2004**
Mythic Giacometti. Cloth over Boards. Farrar, Straus & Giroux. New York, NY. 2004. 144p. ISBN:0-374-21880-3, ISBN13: 978-0-374-21880-5. Dewey:730/.92. LCCN:2003-060262.
Audience: **g,l,u,f.** *Choice, 2004.*

Lorquin, Bertrand   **N6853.M16**
Aristide Maillol. Skira. 2002. ISBN:88-8491-043-9, ISBN13: 978-88-8491-043-1.
Audience: **g,l,u,f.**

Lucie-Smith, Edward   **NB237.B43L82**
Fletcher Benton. Trade Cloth. Harry N. Abrams, Inc. New York, NY. 1990. 358p. ISBN:0-8109-3110-9, ISBN13: 978-0-8109-3110-7. Dewey:730.92.
Audience: **g,l,u,f.** *Choice, 1991.*

Madoff, Steven Henry   **NB237.W523M33 2004**
Christopher Wilmarth: Light and Gravity. Nancy Milford & Edward Saywell (Contribution by). Trade Cloth. Princeton University Press. Princeton, NJ. 2004. 184p. ISBN:0-691-11359-9, ISBN13: 978-0-691-11359-3. Dewey:730/.92 B. LCCN:2004-041464.
Audience: **g,l,u,f.**

Marter, Joan M.   **NB553.R7**
Alexander Calder. Trade Paper. Cambridge University Press. New York, NY. 1997. 318p. ISBN:0-521-58717-4, ISBN13: 978-0-521-58717-4. Dewey:730.9/2.
Audience: **g,l,u,f.** *Choice, 1992.*

Masson, Raphael, et al.   **NB553.R7**
Rodin. Veronique Mattiussi & Jacques Vilain (Authors). Trade Cloth. Flammarion et Cie. Paris, 2004. 248p. ISBN:2-08-030445-3, ISBN13: 978-2-08-030445-2. Dewey:730.9/2.
Audience: **g,l,u,f.** *Choice, 2005.*

McEwen, John   **NB497.S29M38 2001**
The Sculpture of Michael Sandle. Trade Cloth. Ashgate Publishing, Ltd. Aldershot, 2002. 144p. The British Sculptors and Sculpture Ser. ISBN:0-85331-817-4, ISBN13: 978-0-85331-817-0. Dewey:730/.92. LCCN:2001-039181.
Audience: **g,l,u,f.** *Choice, 2003, 2002.*

Mitchinson, David   **N6797.M57A4 1998**
Celebrating Moore: Works from the Collection of the Henry Moore Foundation. Trade Cloth. University of California Press. Berkeley, CA. 1998. 360p. ISBN:0-520-21670-9, ISBN13: 978-0-520-21670-9. Dewey:730.9/2. LCCN:98-203032.
Audience: **g,l,u,f.** *Choice, 1999.*

Moriarty, Catherine   **NB497**
The Sculpture of Gilbert Ledward. Trade Cloth. Ashgate Publishing, Ltd. Aldershot, 2003. 136p. The British Sculptors and Sculpture Ser. ISBN:0-85331-831-X, ISBN13: 978-0-85331-831-6. Dewey:730.92. LCCN:2002-117385.
Audience: **g,l,u,f.**

Nicolson, Vanessa &   NB497.L33A4 2002
   Panourgias, Klio K.
The Sculpture of Maurice Lambert. Trade Cloth. Ashgate
Publishing, Ltd. Aldershot, 2002. 128p. The British Sculptors
and Sculpture Ser. ISBN:0-85331-834-4, ISBN13:
978-0-85331-834-7. Dewey:730.92. LCCN:2002-020797.
                                        Audience: **g,l,u,f.**

Palmedo, Philip F.   NB237.B355P35 2003
Bill Barrett: The Evolution of a Sculptor. Trade Cloth. Hudson
Hills Press LLC. Manchester, VT. 2003. 144p. Ser.
ISBN:1-55595-223-2, ISBN13: 978-1-55595-223-5.
Dewey:730/.92. LCCN:2003-005017.
                              Audience: **g,l,u,f.** *Choice, 2004.*

Pope-Hennessy, John W.   NB623.D7P631993
Donatello: Sculptor. Trade Cloth. Abbeville Press, Inc. New
York, NY. 1993. 368p. ISBN:1-55859-645-3, ISBN13:
978-1-55859-645-0. Dewey:730.92. LCCN:93-019726.
                              Audience: **g,l,u,f.** *Choice, 1994.*

Proctor, Alexander   NB237.P74A42003
   Phimister & Hassrick, Peter H. (Translators)
Wildlife and Western Heroes: Alexander Phimister Proctor,
Sculptor. Alexander Phimister Proctor & Peter H. Hassrick
(Memoir by), Amon Carter Museum of Western Art Staff &
Proctor Museum Staff (Contribution by). Trade Cloth. Third
Millennium Publishing. London, 2003. 256p.
ISBN:1-903942-22-5, ISBN13: 978-1-903942-22-2.
Dewey:730/.92. LCCN:2003-013800.
                                        Audience: **g,l,u,f.**

Read, Bendict (Editor)   NB467.5.P7
Pre-Raphaelite Sculpture: Nature and Imagination in British
Sculpture 1848-1914. Trade Cloth. Ashgate Publishing, Ltd.
Aldershot, 1991. 176p. British Sculptors and Sculpture Ser.
ISBN:0-85331-609-0, ISBN13: 978-0-85331-609-1.
Dewey:735.074.
                                        Audience: **g,l,u,f.**

Rewald, John   NB553.D4
Degas's Complete Sculpture: A Catalogue Raisonné. Edgar
Degas (Illustrator). Trade Cloth. Alan Wofsy Fine Arts. San
Francisco, CA. 1990. 216p. ISBN:1-55660-045-3, ISBN13:
978-1-55660-045-6. Dewey:730.92.
                                        Audience: **g,l,u,f.**

Rushing, W. Jackson III   NB237.H62R872004
Allan Houser: An American Master - Chiricahua Apache
1914-1994. Trade Cloth. Harry N. Abrams, Inc. New York, NY.
2004. 256p. ISBN:0-8109-4326-3, ISBN13: 978-0-8109-4326-1.
Dewey:730/.92. LCCN:2003-021491.
                              Audience: **g,l,u,f.** *Choice, 2005.*

Sandler, Irving   NB237.D57A41996
Mark Di Suvero: At Storm King Art Center. Jerry L. Thompson
(Photographer). Trade Paper. Harry N. Abrams, Inc. New York,
NY. 1996. 128p. ISBN:0-8109-2614-8, ISBN13:
978-0-8109-2614-1. Dewey:730.9/2. LCCN:94-035360.
                                        Audience: **g,l,u,f.**

Scigliano, Eric   NB623.B9S39 2005
Michelangelo's Mountain: The Quest for Perfection in the
Marble Quarries of Carrara. Trade Cloth. Simon & Schuster.
New York, NY. 2005. 256p. ISBN:0-7432-5477-5, ISBN13:
978-0-7432-5477-9. Dewey:709.2 B. LCCN:2005-040150.
                                        Audience: **g,l,u,f.**

Sharp, Lewis I.   NB237.W2A4 1985
John Quincy Adams Ward. Trade Cloth. University of Delaware
Press. Newark, DE. 1985. 304p. ISBN:0-87413-253-3, ISBN13:
978-0-87413-253-3. Dewey:730/.92/4. LCCN:84-008664.
                              Audience: **u,f.** *Choice, 1985.*

Sherwood, Dolly   NB237.H6S53 1991
Harriet Hosmer, American Sculptor, 1830-1908. Trade Cloth.
University of Missouri Press. Columbia, MO. 1991. 392p.
ISBN:0-8262-0766-9, ISBN13: 978-0-8262-0766-1.
Dewey:730/.92 B. LCCN:91-015632.
                              Audience: **g,l,u,f.** *Choice, 1992.*

Spies, Werner   NB553.P45
Pablo Picasso: The Sculptures. Trade Cloth. Hatje Cantz Verlag
GmbH & Co KG. Ostfildern-Ruit, 2000. 400p.
ISBN:3-7757-0909-6, ISBN13: 978-3-7757-0909-5. Dewey:730.
                              Audience: **g,l,u,f.** *Choice, 2001.*

Stephens, Chris   NB497.D34S74 1999
The Sculpture of Hubert Dalwood. Trade Cloth. Ashgate
Publishing, Ltd. Aldershot, 1999. 144p. The British Sculptors
and Sculpture Ser. ISBN:0-85331-786-0, ISBN13:
978-0-85331-786-9. Dewey:730/.92. LCCN:00-700110.
                                        Audience: **g,l,u,f.**

Stoddard, Whitney S.   NB551.C45S76 1987
Sculptors of the West Portals of Chartres Cathedral. Trade Cloth.
W. W. Norton & Company, Inc. New York, NY. 1987. xvii,
252p. ISBN:0-393-02365-6, ISBN13: 978-0-393-02365-7.
Dewey:730/.944/51. LCCN:85-021702.
                              Audience: **l,u,f.** *Choice, 1987.*

Stone, Jonathan   NB497.W87A4 1993
The Sculpture of David Wynne, 1974-1992. Trade Cloth.
Ashgate Publishing, Ltd. Aldershot, 1993. 176p. The British
Sculptors and Sculpture Ser. ISBN:0-85331-638-4, ISBN13:
978-0-85331-638-1. Dewey:730/.92. LCCN:94-109741.
                                        Audience: **g,l,u,f.**

Varia, Radu   NB1115
Brancusi. Trade Cloth. Rizzoli International Publications, Inc.
New York, NY. 2003. 228p. ISBN:0-8478-2525-6, ISBN13:
978-0-8478-2525-7. Dewey:730.9/2.
                                        Audience: **g,l,u,f.**

Verderame, Lori   NB237.L55A4 2000
Seymour Lipton: An American Sculptor. Irving Sandler
(Introduction by). Trade Cloth. Hudson Hills Press LLC.
Manchester, VT. 2000. 128p. ISBN:1-55595-190-2, ISBN13:
978-1-55595-190-0. Dewey:730/.92. LCCN:99-075215.
                              Audience: **g,l,u,f.** *Choice, 2001.*

Warmus, William, et al.   **NB237.P35A4 2004**
Tom Patti: Illuminating the Invisible. Donald B. Kuspit & Tom
Patti (Authors), Museum of Glass: International Center for
Contemporary Art Staff (Contribution by). Trade Cloth.
University of Washington Press. Seattle, WA. 2005. 128p.
ISBN:0-295-98473-2, ISBN13: 978-0-295-98473-5.
Dewey:748/.092. LCCN:2004-020085.

Audience: **g,l,u,f.** *Choice, 2005.*

Whiteley, Gillian   **NB553.R7**
Assembling the Absurd: Sculpture of George Fullard. Trade
Cloth. Ashgate Publishing, Ltd. Aldershot, 1998. 160p. The
British Sculptors and Sculpture Ser. ISBN:0-85331-736-4,
ISBN13: 978-0-85331-736-4. Dewey:730.9/2.

Audience: **g,l,u,f.**

Whitworth, Ben   **NK4210.S367**
The Sculpture of Leon Underwood. Trade Cloth. Ashgate
Publishing, Ltd. Aldershot, 2000. 152p. The British Sculptors
and Sculpture Ser. ISBN:0-85331-774-7, ISBN13:
978-0-85331-774-6. Dewey:730.092. LCCN:00-107095.

Audience: **g,l,u,f.**

Wilkin, Karen   **NB237.W58W56 1998**
Isaac Witkin. Trade Cloth. Hudson Hills Press LLC. Manchester,
VT. 1998. 120p. ISBN:1-55595-153-8, ISBN13:
978-1-55595-153-5. Dewey:730/.92. LCCN:98-017811.

Audience: **g,l,u,f.** *Choice, 1999.*

Wilkin, Karen   **NB497.C35.A4 1991**
Anthony Caro: Explorations in Sculpture. John Riddy
(Photographer). Trade Cloth. Prestel Verlag, Germany. Munchen,
1991. 160p. ISBN:3-7913-1137-9, ISBN13: 978-3-7913-1137-1.
Dewey:730/.92. LCCN:93-179841.

Audience: **g,l,u,f.** *Choice, 1992.*

Woollcombe, Tamsyn   **NB553.R7**
The Sculpture of Kenneth Armitage. Trade Cloth. Ashgate
Publishing, Ltd. Aldershot, 1997. 160p. The British Sculptors
and Sculpture Ser. ISBN:0-85331-702-X, ISBN13:
978-0-85331-702-9. Dewey:730.92.

Audience: **g,l,u,f.**

Sculpture > Materials and Techniques

Jensen, Vickie   **E99.N734J44 1992**
Totem Pole Carving: Bringing a Log to Life. Trade Cloth.
University of Washington Press. Seattle, WA. 2004. 176p.
ISBN:0-295-98368-X, ISBN13: 978-0-295-98368-4.
Dewey:731/.7. LCCN:2003-055734.

Audience: **g,l,u,f.**

Langland, Tuck   **NB1230.L36 1999**
From Clay to Bronze: A Studio Guide to Figurative Sculpture.
Trade Cloth. Watson-Guptill Publications, Inc. New York, NY.
1999. 208p. ISBN:0-8230-0638-7, ISBN13: 978-0-8230-0638-0.
Dewey:731.4/56. LCCN:99-022169.

Audience: **g,l,u,f.**

Liebson, Milt   **TT199.7.L55 2001**
Direct Wood Sculpture: Technique, Innovation, Creativity. Trade
Cloth. Schiffer Publishing, Ltd. Atglen, PA. 2001. 160p.
ISBN:0-7643-1299-5, ISBN13: 978-0-7643-1299-1.
Dewey:736/.4. LCCN:00-012436.

Audience: **g,l,u,f.**

Penny, Nicholas   **NB1170**
The Materials of Sculpture. Trade Paper. Yale University Press.
Cumberland, RI. 1996. 328p. ISBN:0-300-06581-7, ISBN13:
978-0-300-06581-7. Dewey:731/.028.

Audience: **g,l,u,f.** *Choice, 1994.*

Tourtillott, Suzanne J. E.   **NK4235.T682005**
The Figure in Clay: Contemporary Sculpting Techniques by
Master Artists. Saddle Stitched, Cloth over Boards, Dust Jacket.
Lark Books. Asheville, NC. 2005. 176p. A Lark Ceramics Book
Ser. ISBN:1-57990-611-7, ISBN13: 978-1-57990-611-5.
Dewey:731/.82. LCCN:2004-028210.

Audience: **g,l,u,f.** *Choice, 2005.*

Architecture > Reference Works > Web Resources

▢ Architecture.com.
http://architecture.com
Royal Institute of British Architects.

Audience: **g,l,u,f.**

NA63.5

▢ BuildingGreen.com.
http://www.buildinggreen.com/

Audience: **g,l,u,f.**

NA200

▢ Historic American Buildings Survey / Historic American
Engineering Survey.
http://www.cr.nps.gov/habshaer/
Washington, D. C. : Department of the Interior, National Park
Service, HABS/HAER/HALS Division.

Audience: **g,l,u,f.**

NA

▢ International Architecture Database.
http://www.archinform.net
Berlin: archINFORM.

Audience: **g,l,u,f.**

TH455

▢ McGraw-Hill Construction.
http://www.construction.com/
McGraw-Hill.

Audience: **l,u,f.**

NA63.5
☐ Structurae; International Database and Gallery of Structures.
http://en.structurae.de/index.cfm
Nicolas Janberg.
Audience: **g,l,u,f.**

Brown, Jeanne　　　　　　　　　　　　　　**NA63.5**
☐ Architecture and Building.
http://library.nevada.edu/arch/rsrce/webrsrce/contents.html
University of Nevada, Las Vegas.
Audience: **g,l,u,f.**

Tasman, Dan　　　　　　　　　　　　　　**HT166**
☐ Cyburbia ; the Planning Portal.
http://www.cyburbia.org/
Audience: **g,l,u,f.**

Architecture > Reference Works > Bibliographies and Research Guides

NA1.A12
☐ Avery Index to Architectural Periodicals.
http://www.getty.edu/research/conducting_research/avery_index/
Getty Research Institute.
Audience: **g,l,u,f.**

Culbertson, Margaret　　　　　　　　**NA7207**
(Compiled by)
American House Designs: An Index to Popular and Trade
Periodicals 1850-1915. Cloth Text. Greenwood Publishing
Group, Inc. Portsmouth, NH. 1994. 360p. Art Reference
Collection Ser. ISBN:0-313-29202-7, ISBN13:
978-0-313-29202-6. Dewey:016.728/022/2. LCCN:94-030280.
Audience: **l,u,f.** *Choice, 1995.*

Langmead, Donald　　　　　　　　　　**Z8648**
J. J. P. Oud and the International Style: A Bio-Bibliography.
Cloth Text. Greenwood Publishing Group, Inc. Portsmouth, NH.
1999. 304p. Bio-Bibliographies in Art and Architecture Ser., Vol.
5 ISBN:0-313-30100-X, ISBN13: 978-0-313-30100-1.
Dewey:016.72092. LCCN:98-041648.
Audience: **g,l,u,f.** *Choice, 1999.*

Wayne, Kathryn M.　　　　　　　　　**NA2750**
Architecture Sourcebook: A Guide to Resources on the History
and Practice of Architecture. Library Binding. Omnigraphics,
Inc. Detroit, MI. 1997. Design Reference Ser., Vol. 2
ISBN:0-7808-0197-0, ISBN13: 978-0-7808-0197-4.
Dewey:016.72.
Audience: **g,l,u,f.** *Choice, 1997.*

Architecture > Reference Works > Dictionaries and Encyclopedias

Arnold, Dieter　　　　　　　　**NA215.A74513 2003**
The Encyclopedia of Ancient Egyptian Architecture. Cloth Text.
Princeton University Press. Princeton, NJ. 2003. 288p.

ISBN:0-691-11488-9, ISBN13: 978-0-691-11488-0.
Dewey:722.203. LCCN:2002-112371.
Audience: **g,l,u,f.** *Choice, 2003.*

Burden, Ernest E.　　　　　　　　　　**TH9**
Illustrated Dictionary of Building Design and Construction.
Trade Paper. McGraw-Hill Companies, The. New York, NY.
2004. 296p. ISBN:0-07-144506-4, ISBN13: 978-0-07-144506-1.
Dewey:690.03. LCCN:2004-275924.
Audience: **g,l,u,f.** *Choice, 2005.*

Ching, Francis D. K.　　　　　　　**NA31.C44 1995**
A Visual Dictionary of Architecture. Cloth Text. John Wiley &
Sons, Inc. Hoboken, NJ. 1995. 448p. Architecture Ser.
ISBN:0-442-00904-6, ISBN13: 978-0-442-00904-5.
Dewey:720.3. LCCN:95-001476.
Audience: **g,l,u,f.** *Choice, 1995.*

Colvin, Howard　　　　　　　　　**NA996.C6 1995**
A Biographical Dictionary of British Architects, 1600-1840. Ed.
3. Cloth over Boards. Yale University Press. Cumberland, RI.
1995. 1264p. Paul Mellon Centre for Studies in British Art
ISBN:0-300-06091-2, ISBN13: 978-0-300-06091-1.
Dewey:720.9/22. LCCN:94-039135.
Audience: **g,l,u,f.**

Cowan, Henry J. & Smith,　　　　　**NA31.C63 2004**
Peter R.
Dictionary of Architectural and Building Technology. Ed. 4. W.
K. Chow (Contribution by). Paper over Boards. Routledge. New
York, NY. 2004. 352p. ISBN:0-415-31233-7, ISBN13:
978-0-415-31233-2. Dewey:720/.3. LCCN:2003-023444.
Audience: **g,l,u,f.** *Choice, 1986.*

Curl, James Stevens　　　　　　　**NA260.C87 2003**
Classical Architecture: An Introduction to Its Vocabulary and
Essentials, with Special Terms Glossary. Ed. 2. Trade Paper. W.
W. Norton & Company, Inc. New York, NY. 2003. 232p.
ISBN:0-393-73119-7, ISBN13: 978-0-393-73119-4.
Dewey:720/.9. LCCN:2002-041073.
Audience: **g,l,u,f.**

Curl, James Stevens　　　　　　　　　**NA31**
Dictionary of Architecture and Landscape Architecture. Ed. 2.
Trade Cloth. Oxford University Press, Inc. New York, NY. 2006.
912p. Oxford Paperback Reference Ser. ISBN:0-19-280630-0,
ISBN13: 978-0-19-280630-7. Dewey:720.3.
LCCN:2006-040248.
Audience: **g,l,u,f.**

Curl, James Stevens　　　　　　　　**NA31.C86**
A Dictionary of Architecture. John Sambrook (Illustrator). Trade
Paper. Oxford University Press, Inc. New York, NY. 2000. 848p.
Oxford Paperback Reference Ser. ISBN:0-19-280017-5, ISBN13:
978-0-19-280017-6. Dewey:720/.3. LCCN:00-713457.
Audience: **g,l,u,f.**

Harris, Cyril M.　　　　　　　　　　**NA31**
Dictionary of Architecture and Construction. Ed. 4. Trade Cloth.
McGraw-Hill Professional Publishing. New York, NY. 2005.

1040p. ISBN:0-07-145237-0, ISBN13: 978-0-07-145237-3. Dewey:720/.3. LCCN:2005-042340.

Audience: **g,l,u,f.** *Choice, 2006, 1993.*

Harvey, John　　　　　　　　**NA963 .H37 1984**
English Mediaeval Architects: A Biographical Dictionary to 1550. Cloth Text. Sutton Publishing, Ltd. Stroud, 1993. 544p. ISBN:0-86299-034-3, ISBN13: 978-0-86299-034-3. Dewey:720/.92/2. LCCN:84-225086.

Audience: **g,l,u,f.**

Howe, Jeffrey　　　　　　　**NA5205.H69 2003**
Houses of Worship: An Identification Guide to the History and Style of American Religious Architecture. Trade Cloth. Advantage Publishers Group. San Diego, CA. 2003. 448p. ISBN:1-57145-970-7, ISBN13: 978-1-57145-970-1. Dewey:726/.0973. LCCN:2003-058403.

Audience: **l,u,f.** *Choice, 2004.*

Leick, Gwendolyn　　　　　　**NA212.L451988**
A Dictionary of Ancient Near Eastern Architecture. Paper over Boards. Routledge. New York, NY. 1988. 286p. ISBN:0-415-00240-0, ISBN13: 978-0-415-00240-0. Dewey:722/.5. LCCN:87-023375.

Audience: **g,l,u,f.** *Choice, 1989.*

Lounsbury, Carl R.　　　　　**NA727.I44 1999**
An Illustrated Glossary of Early Southern Architecture and Landscape. Trade Paper. University Press of Virginia. Charlottesville, VA. 1999. 448p. ISBN:0-8139-1923-1, ISBN13: 978-0-8139-1923-2. Dewey:720/.975/03. LCCN:99-030063.

Audience: **g,l,u,f.** *Choice, 1994.*

Morgan, Ann L. (Editor)　　　**NA680 .C625 1987**
Contemporary Architects. Ed. 2. Trade Cloth. Thomson Gale. Farmington Hills, MI. 1987. 1038p. ISBN:0-912289-26-0, ISBN13: 978-0-912289-26-7. Dewey:720/.92/2. LCCN:88-140209.

Audience: **g,l,u,f.**

Morgan, William　　　　　**NA7205.M67932004**
The Abrams Guide to American House Styles. Trade Paper. Harry N. Abrams, Inc. New York, NY. 2004. ISBN:0-8109-8241-2, ISBN13: 978-0-8109-8241-3. Dewey:728/.37/0973. LCCN:2004-000111.

Audience: **g,l,u,f.**

Oliver, Paul　　　　　　　**NA208.E531997**
Encyclopedia of Vernacular Architecture of the World. Cambridge University Press. 1997. ISBN:0-521-56422-0, ISBN13: 978-0-521-56422-9.

Audience: **g,l,u,f.**

Petersen, Andrew　　　　　　**NA380.P43**
Dictionary of Islamic Architecture. Trade Paper. Routledge. New York, NY. 1999. 352p. ISBN:0-415-21332-0, ISBN13: 978-0-415-21332-5. Dewey:720.8/8297/03. LCCN:96-018777.

Audience: **g,l,u,f.** *Choice, 1996.*

Pevsner, Nikolaus, et al.　　　　**NA31.F55 1999**
The Penguin Dictionary of Architecture and Landscape Architecture. Ed. 5. John Fleming & Hugh Honour (Authors). Trade Paper. Penguin Group (USA) Inc. New York, NY. 2000. 656p. Penguin Reference Bks. ISBN:0-14-051323-X, ISBN13: 978-0-14-051323-3. Dewey:720/.3. LCCN:00-267917.

Audience: **g,l,u,f.**

Phaidon Press Editors　　　　　**NA687**
The Phaidon Atlas of Contemporary World Architecture. Trade Cloth. Phaidon Press. London, 2004. 824p. ISBN:0-7148-4312-1, ISBN13: 978-0-7148-4312-4. Dewey:724.7. LCCN:2005-533910.

Audience: **g,l,u,f.**

R. S. Means Company Staff　　　**TH6010.M4582002**
Mechanical Estimating Methods: Standards and Procedures. Ed. 3. Trade Cloth. R. S. Means Company, Inc. Kingston, MA. 2002. 800p. ISBN:0-87629-574-X, ISBN13: 978-0-87629-574-8. Dewey:696. LCCN:2003-266589.

Audience: **g,l,u,f.**

Sennott, R. Stephen (Editor)　　　**NA680**
Encyclopedia of 20th-Century Architecture. Library Binding. Fitzroy Dearborn Publishers, Inc. Chicago, IL. 2003. 1568p. ISBN:1-57958-243-5, ISBN13: 978-1-57958-243-2. Dewey:724/.6/03. LCCN:2003-015674.

Audience: **g,l,u,f.** *Choice, 2004.*

Van Vynckt, Randall　　　　　**NA40.I48 1993**
(Editor)
International Dictionary of Architects and Architecture, Set. Doreen Yarwood & Suhail Butt (Contribution by). Trade Cloth. Thomson Gale. Farmington Hills, MI. 1993. 2161p. ISBN:1-55862-089-3, ISBN13: 978-1-55862-089-6. Dewey:720.9. LCCN:93-013431.

Audience: **g,l,u,f.** *Choice, 1994.*

Wilson, Dreck Spurlock　　　　**NA736.A47 2003**
(Editor)
African American Architects: A Biographical Dictionary, 1865-1945. Paper over Boards. Routledge. New York, NY. 2004. 576p. ISBN:0-415-92959-8, ISBN13: 978-0-415-92959-2. Dewey:720/.92/396073 B. LCCN:2003-009675.

Audience: **g,l,u,f.** *Choice, 2004.*

Architecture > Reference Works > Directories

　　　　　　　　　　　　　　TH455
McGraw-Hill Construction. http://www.construction.com/ McGraw-Hill.

Audience: **l,u,f.**

　　　　　　　　　　　　　　TH455
Sweets Product Marketplace. http://sweets.construction.com/ McGraw-Hill Companies.

Audience: **u,f.**

Spiegel, Ross & Meadows, Dru   TH455.S65 2006

Green Building Materials: A Guide to Product Selection and Specification. Ed. 2. Trade Cloth. John Wiley & Sons, Inc. Hoboken, NJ. 2006. 368p. ISBN:0-471-70089-4, ISBN13: 978-0-471-70089-0. Dewey:691. LCCN:2005-020000.

Audience: **g,l,u,f.**

Architecture > Reference Works > Codes and Standards

             KF

☐ ADA Home Page; Americans with Disabilities Act.
http://www.ada.gov/
Washington, D. C. : U. S. Dept. of Justice.

Audience: **g,l,u,f.**

           TH9115

☐ National Fire Protection Association (NFPA).
http://www.nfpa.org/
National Fire Protection Association.

Audience: **g,l,u,f.**

Crosbie, Michael J. & Watson, Donald   TH151.T55 2004

Time-Saver Standards for Architectural Design. Ed. 8. Mixed Media, Trade Cloth, CD-ROM. McGraw-Hill Professional Publishing. New York, NY. 2004. 640p. ISBN:0-07-143205-1, ISBN13: 978-0-07-143205-4. Dewey:721. LCCN:2004-053873.

Audience: **g,l,u,f.**

De Chiara, Joseph   NA2760.D42 2001

Time-Saver Standards for Building Types. Ed. 4. Cloth Text. McGraw-Hill Professional Publishing. New York, NY. 2001. 1005p. Time-Saver Standards Concise Ser. ISBN:0-07-016387-1, ISBN13: 978-0-07-016387-4. Dewey:721/.0218. LCCN:2001-030275.

Audience: **l,u,f.**

Dines, Nicholas T. & Harris, Charles W.   SB475.9.S72T55 1998

Time-Saver Standards for Landscape Architecture. Ed. 2. Trade Cloth. McGraw-Hill Professional Publishing. New York, NY. 1997. 928p. Time-Saver Standards Concise Ser. ISBN:0-07-017027-4, ISBN13: 978-0-07-017027-8. Dewey:712/.02/18. LCCN:97-031842.

Audience: **g,l,u,f.**

International Code Council   HF5351

International Building Code 2006: Softcover Version. Paper Text. Thomson Delmar Learning. Albany, NY. 2006. ISBN:1-58001-251-5, ISBN13: 978-1-58001-251-5. Dewey:650.

Audience: **g,l,u,f.**

International Code Council   KF3975.I58 2006

International Fire Code 2006: Softcover Version. Paper Text. Thomson Delmar Learning. Albany, NY. 2006. ISBN:1-58001-255-8, ISBN13: 978-1-58001-255-3. Dewey:344.730537.

Audience: **g,l,u,f.**

International Code Council   KFN5035

International Residential Code 2006: Softcover Version. Paper Text. Thomson Delmar Learning. Albany, NY. 2006. ISBN:1-58001-253-1, ISBN13: 978-1-58001-253-9. Dewey:690.837.

Audience: **g,l,u,f.**

Ramsey, Charles George, et al.   TH2031.R35

Architectural Graphic Standards. Ed. 10. Harold Reeve Sleeper & John Ray Hoke Jr. (Authors). Trade Cloth. John Wiley & Sons, Inc. Hoboken, NJ. 2000. 1072p. ISBN:0-471-39186-7, ISBN13: 978-0-471-39186-9. Dewey:721.0284.

Audience: **l,u,f.**

Architecture > Histories and Handbooks

Fletcher, Banister   NA200.F63 1996

Banister Fletcher's A History of Architecture: Centenary Edition. Ed. 20. Dan Cruickshank (Editor). Trade Cloth. Elsevier Science & Technology Books. Saint Louis, MO. 1996. 1696p. ISBN:0-7506-2267-9, ISBN13: 978-0-7506-2267-7. Dewey:720.9. LCCN:96-035511.

Audience: **g,l,u,f.**

Kostof, Spiro   NA200.K65

A History of Architecture: Settings and Rituals. Ed. 2. Gregory Castillo (Revised by). Paper Text. Oxford University Press, Inc. New York, NY. 1995. 800p. ISBN:0-19-508379-2, ISBN13: 978-0-19-508379-8. Dewey:720.9. LCCN:94-038787.

Audience: **g,l,u,f.** ℬ *Choice, 1986.*

Trachtenberg, Marvin   NA200 .T7

Architecture: From Prehistory to Postmodernism. Ed. 2. Trade Cloth. Prentice Hall Art. Upper Saddle River, NJ. 2002. 648p. ISBN:0-13-183365-0, ISBN13: 978-0-13-183365-4. Dewey:720/.9.

Audience: **g,l,u,f.**

Architecture > Histories and Handbooks > Periods and Styles

Binney, Marcus   NA7520.B56 1998

Town Houses: Urban Houses from 1200 to the Present Day. Trade Paper. Watson-Guptill Publications, Inc. New York, NY. 1998. 176p. ISBN:0-8230-6962-1, ISBN13: 978-0-8230-6962-0. Dewey:728/.312/09. LCCN:98-004148.

Audience: **l,u,f.** *Choice, 1999.*

Calkins, Robert G.   NA5453.C351998

Medieval Architecture in Western Europe: From A.D. 300 to 1500. Trade Cloth. Oxford University Press, Inc. New York, NY. 1998. 352p. ISBN:0-19-511241-5, ISBN13: 978-0-19-511241-2. Dewey:726.5/09/02. LCCN:97-008135.

Audience: **l,u,f.** *Choice, 1998.*

Clarke, Georgia   NA7514.6.C58 2003
Roman House - Renaissance Palaces: Inventing Antiquity in
Fifteenth-Century Italy. Nicholas Adams & Paul Davies
(Contribution by). Cloth Text. Cambridge University Press. New
York, NY. 2003. 412p. Architecture in Early Modern Italy Ser.
ISBN:0-521-77008-4, ISBN13: 978-0-521-77008-8.
Dewey:720/.945/09024. LCCN:2002-073602.
                                        Audience: l,u,f. *Choice, 2004.*

Clausen, Meredith L.   NA6233.N5P363 2004
The Pan Am Building and the Shattering of the Modernist
Dream. Trade Cloth. MIT Press. Cambridge, MA. 2004. 416p.
ISBN:0-262-03324-0, ISBN13: 978-0-262-03324-4.
Dewey:725/.23/097471. LCCN:2004-045468.
                                        Audience: g,l,u,f. *Choice, 2005.*

Coldstream, Nicola   NA350.C65 2002
Medieval Architecture. Trade Paper. Oxford University Press,
Inc. New York, NY. 2002. 256p. Oxford History of Art Ser.
ISBN:0-19-284276-5, ISBN13: 978-0-19-284276-3. Dewey:723.
LCCN:2002-283650.
                                        Audience: g,l,u,f.

Colquhoun, Alan   NA680.C593 2002
Modern Architecture. Trade Paper. Oxford University Press, Inc.
New York, NY. 2002. 288p. Oxford History of Art Ser.
ISBN:0-19-284226-9, ISBN13: 978-0-19-284226-8.
Dewey:724.6. LCCN:2002-510839.
                                        Audience: g,l,u,f.

Conant, Kenneth J.   NA350
Carolingian and Romanesque Architecture: 800-1200. Ed. 4.
Trade Paper. Yale University Press. Cumberland, RI. 1959.
352p. Pelican History of Art Ser. ISBN:0-300-05298-7, ISBN13:
978-0-300-05298-5. Dewey:723.4.
                                        Audience: g,l,u,f.

Crossley, Paul & Frankl,   NA5453.C772001
   Paul
Gothic Architecture. Ed. 2. Trade Paper. Yale University Press.
Cumberland, RI. 2001. 480p. Pelican History of Art Ser.
ISBN:0-300-08799-3, ISBN13: 978-0-300-08799-4.
Dewey:726.5/094/0902. LCCN:00-043517.
                                        Audience: g,l,u,f. *B*

Frampton, Kenneth   NA500.F75 1992
Modern Architecture. Ed. 3. Trade Paper. Thames & Hudson.
New York, NY. 1992. 376p. World of Art Ser.
ISBN:0-500-20257-5, ISBN13: 978-0-500-20257-9.
Dewey:724.6. LCCN:91-066733.
                                        Audience: g,l,u,f.

Ghirardo, Diane   NA682.P67G49 1996
Architecture after Modernism. Trade Paper. Thames & Hudson.
New York, NY. 1996. 240p. The World of Art Ser.
ISBN:0-500-20294-X, ISBN13: 978-0-500-20294-4.
Dewey:724/.6. LCCN:96-060260.
                                        Audience: g,l,u,f. *Choice, 1997.*

Godwin, E. W., et al.   NA997.G6A41999
Aesthetic Movement Architect and Designer. Susan W. Soros,
Bard Graduate Center for Studies in the Decorative Arts Staff &
Catherine Arbuthnott (Authors). Trade Cloth. Yale University
Press. Cumberland, RI. 1999. 431p. ISBN:0-300-08009-3,
ISBN13: 978-0-300-08009-4. Dewey:720/.92. LCCN:99-024645.
                                        Audience: g,l,u,f.

Hearn, Fil   NA2500.H379 2003
Ideas That Shaped Buildings. Trade Paper. MIT Press.
Cambridge, MA. 2003. 312p. ISBN:0-262-58227-9, ISBN13:
978-0-262-58227-8. Dewey:720/.1. LCCN:2003-051206.
                                        Audience: g,l,u,f. *Choice, 2004.*

Henderson, Paula   NA965.H46 2005
The Tudor House and Garden: Architecture and Landscape in
the Sixteenth and Early Seventeenth Centuries. Cloth over
Boards. Yale University Press. Cumberland, RI. 2005. 296p.
Studies in British Art Ser. ISBN:0-300-10687-4, ISBN13:
978-0-300-10687-9. Dewey:728/.37/094209031.
LCCN:2004-024093.
                                        Audience: l,u,f. *Choice, 2005.*

Heydenreich, Ludwig H.   NA1115.H49 1996
Architecture in Italy, 1400-1500. Ed. 2. Paul Davies
(Introduction by). Trade Paper. Yale University Press.
Cumberland, RI. 1996. 196p. Yale University Press Pelican
History of Art Ser. ISBN:0-300-06467-5, ISBN13:
978-0-300-06467-4. Dewey:720.9/45. LCCN:95-036474.
                                        Audience: g,l,u,f. *Choice, 1996.*

Hitchcock, Henry Russell   NA645
Architecture: Nineteenth and Twentieth Centuries. Ed. 4. Trade
Paper. Yale University Press. Cumberland, RI. 1989. 696p.
Pelican History of Art Ser. ISBN:0-300-05320-7, ISBN13:
978-0-300-05320-3. Dewey:724.
                                        Audience: g,l,u,f. *B*

Hopkins, Andrew   NA1115.H66 2002
Italian Architecture: From Michelangelo to Borromini. Trade
Paper. Thames & Hudson. New York, NY. 2002. 224p. World of
Art Ser. ISBN:0-500-20361-X, ISBN13: 978-0-500-20361-3.
Dewey:720.94509031. LCCN:2001-099496.
                                        Audience: g,l,u,f.

Jencks, Charles   NA682.P67J38 2002
The New Paradigm in Architecture: The Language of
Post-Modernism. Ed. 7. Cloth over Boards. Yale University
Press. Cumberland, RI. 2002. 288p. ISBN:0-300-09512-0,
ISBN13: 978-0-300-09512-8. Dewey:720/.9/045.
LCCN:2002-106785.
                                        Audience: l,u,f.

Kentgens-Craig, Margret   N332.G33B447513
The Bauhaus and America: First Contacts, 1919-1936. Trade
Paper. MIT Press. Cambridge, MA. 2001. 303p.
ISBN:0-262-61171-6, ISBN13: 978-0-262-61171-8.
Dewey:724.6. LCCN:99-018804.
                                        Audience: g,l,u,f. *Choice, 2000.*

King, Ross   NA5621.F7K56 2000
Brunelleschi's Dome: How a Renaissance Genius Reinvented
Architecture. Cloth over Boards. Walker & Company. New
York, NY. 2000. 192p. ISBN:0-8027-1366-1, ISBN13:
978-0-8027-1366-7. Dewey:726.6/0945/51. LCCN:2001-280068.
Audience: **g,l,u,f.** *Choice, 2001.*

Lane, Barbara Miller   NA1067.5.N38 L35 20
National Romanticism and Modern Architecture in Germany and
the Scandinavian Countries. Richard A. Etlin (Contribution by).
Trade Cloth. Cambridge University Press. New York, NY. 2000.
432p. Modern Architecture and Cultural Identity Ser.
ISBN:0-521-58309-8, ISBN13: 978-0-521-58309-1.
Dewey:724/.6. LCCN:99-043685.
Audience: **l,u,f.** *Choice, 2001.*

Lawrence, A. W.   NA270.L361996
Greek Architecture. Ed. 5. R. A. Tomlinson (Revised by). Cloth
over Boards. Yale University Press. Cumberland, RI. 1996.
264p. Pelican History of Art Ser. ISBN:0-300-06491-8, ISBN13:
978-0-300-06491-9. Dewey:722.8. LCCN:95-053785.
Audience: **g,l,u,f.** *B*

Lewis, Michael J.   NA610.L48 2002
The Gothic Revival. Trade Paper. Thames & Hudson. New
York, NY. 2002. 208p. World of Art Ser. ISBN:0-500-20359-8,
ISBN13: 978-0-500-20359-0. Dewey:724/.3.
LCCN:2001-094769.
Audience: **g,l,u,f.**

Lotz, Wolfgang   NA1115.L6661995
Architecture in Italy, 1500-1600. Ed. 2. Deborah Howard
(Revised by). Trade Paper. Yale University Press. Cumberland,
RI. 1995. 214p. Pelican History of Art Ser.
ISBN:0-300-06469-1, ISBN13: 978-0-300-06469-8.
Dewey:720.9/45/09031. LCCN:95-009124.
Audience: **g,l,u,f.** *Choice, 1996.*

Mallgrave, Harry   NA2500.M28 2005
Modern Architectural Theory: A Historical Survey, 1673-1968.
Trade Cloth. Cambridge University Press. New York, NY. 2005.
522p. ISBN:0-521-79306-8, ISBN13: 978-0-521-79306-3.
Dewey:720/.1. LCCN:2004-045916.
Audience: **l,u,f.** *Choice, 2006.*

Necipoglu, Gulru   NA1373.S5
Age of Sinan: Architectural Culture in the Ottoman Empire.
Arben N. Arapi & Reha Gunay (Other Primary Creators). Trade
Cloth. Princeton University Press. Princeton, NJ. 2005. 480p.
ISBN:0-691-12326-8, ISBN13: 978-0-691-12326-4.
Dewey:720.92.
Audience: **g,l,u,f.**

Paperny, Vladimir   NA1188 .P313 2002
Architecture in the Age of Stalin: Culture Two. Trade Cloth.
Cambridge University Press. New York, NY. 2002. 400p.
Cambridge Studies in New Art History and Criticism
ISBN:0-521-45119-1, ISBN13: 978-0-521-45119-2.
Dewey:720/.947/09043. LCCN:2001-037358.
Audience: **l,u,f.** *Choice, 2003.*

Proto, Francesco (Editor)   NA2543.S6B347 2003
Mass Identity Architecture: Architectural Writings of Jean
Baudrillard. Trade Cloth. John Wiley & Sons, Inc. Hoboken, NJ.
2004. 160p. ISBN:0-470-09019-7, ISBN13: 978-0-470-09019-0.
Dewey:720.1/03. LCCN:2004-299543.
Audience: **l,u,f.**

Roth, Leland M.   NA7207.R681999
Shingle Styles: Innovation and Tradition in American
Architecture, 1874-1984. Bret Morgan (Photographer). Trade
Cloth. Harry N. Abrams, Inc. New York, NY. 1999. 240p.
ISBN:0-8109-4477-4, ISBN13: 978-0-8109-4477-0.
Dewey:728/.0973. LCCN:99-014102.
Audience: **g,l,u,f.** *Choice, 2000.*

Schultz, Juergen   NA7514.623.V46S33
The New Palaces of Medieval Venice. Trade Cloth.
Pennsylvania State University Press. University Park, PA. 2004.
412p. ISBN:0-271-02351-1, ISBN13: 978-0-271-02351-9.
Dewey:728.8/0945/310902. LCCN:2003-026259.
Audience: **l,u,f.** *Choice, 2005.*

Scott, Robert A., 1935-   NA440
The Gothic Enterprise: A Guide to Understanding the Medieval
Cathedral. University of California Press. 2003.
ISBN:0-520-23177-5, ISBN13: 978-0-520-23177-1.
Audience: **g,l,u,f.**

Scully, Vincent   NA27
Modern Architecture and Other Essays. Neil Levine (Editor,
Introduction by). Trade Cloth. Princeton University Press.
Princeton, NJ. 2003. 416p. ISBN:0-691-07441-0, ISBN13:
978-0-691-07441-2. Dewey:724/.6. LCCN:2002-019005.
Audience: **g,l,u,f.** *Choice, 2003.*

Service, Alastair   NA967 .S47
Edwardian Architecture. Trade Cloth. Thames & Hudson. New
York, NY. 1985. 216p. World of Art Ser. ISBN:0-500-18158-6,
ISBN13: 978-0-500-18158-4. Dewey:720/.941.
LCCN:78-312155.
Audience: **g,l,u,f.**

Stalley, Roger   NA350 .S78
Early Medieval Architecture. Trade Paper. Oxford University
Press, Inc. New York, NY. 1999. 272p. Oxford History of Art
Ser. ISBN:0-19-284223-4, ISBN13: 978-0-19-284223-7.
Dewey:723.
Audience: **g,l,u,f.** *Choice, 2000.*

Summerson, John N.   NA956.S86 1986
The Architecture of the 18th Century. Trade Paper. Thames &
Hudson. New York, NY. 1986. 176p. World of Art Ser.
ISBN:0-500-20202-8, ISBN13: 978-0-500-20202-9.
Dewey:724/.1. LCCN:85-050749.
Audience: **g,l,u,f.**

Viollet-le-Duc,   NA1053.V7V471990
  Eugène-Emmanuel
The Architectural Theory of Viollet-le-Duc: Readings and

Commentaries. M. F. Hearn (Editor). Trade Paper. MIT Press. Cambridge, MA. 1990. 306p. ISBN:0-262-72013-2, ISBN13: 978-0-262-72013-7. Dewey:720. LCCN:89-034629.

Audience: **g,l,u,f.**

Watkin, David   **NA961.W37 2001**
English Architecture. Ed. 2. Trade Paper. Thames & Hudson. New York, NY. 2000. 224p. World of Art Ser. ISBN:0-500-20338-5, ISBN13: 978-0-500-20338-5. Dewey:720/.942. LCCN:00-101438.

Audience: **g,l,u,f.**

Watkin, David   **NA200**
A History of Western Architecture. Ed. 4. Perfect. Watson-Guptill Publications, Inc. New York, NY. 2005. 720p. ISBN:0-8230-2277-3, ISBN13: 978-0-8230-2277-9. Dewey:720/.9182/1.

Audience: **g,l,u,f.** *Choice, 2006, 1987.*

Whitford, Frank   **N332.G33B47**
Bauhaus. Trade Paper. Thames & Hudson. New York, NY. 1984. 216p. World of Art Ser. ISBN:0-500-20193-5, ISBN13: 978-0-500-20193-0. Dewey:707/.1143. LCCN:83-050527.

Audience: **g,l,u,f.** *B*

Wines, James   **NA2542.35**
Green Architecture: The Art of Architecture in the Age of Ecology. Philip Jodidio (Editor). Trade Cloth. Taschen America, LLC. Los Angeles, CA. 2000. 240p. Architecture and Design Ser. ISBN:3-8228-6303-3, ISBN13: 978-3-8228-6303-9. Dewey:720.4/7.

Audience: **g,l,u,f.**

Wittkower, Rudolf   **NA1115.W56 1998**
Architectural Principles in the Age of Humanism. Ed. 2. Trade Paper. John Wiley & Sons, Inc. Hoboken, NJ. 1999. 160p. ISBN:0-471-97763-2, ISBN13: 978-0-471-97763-6. Dewey:724/.12. LCCN:99-188944.

Audience: **l,u,f.**

Çakmak, Ahmet S. &   **NA1370.C352004**
  Freely, John
Byzantine Monuments of Istanbul. Trade Cloth. Cambridge University Press. New York, NY. 2004. 342p. ISBN:0-521-77257-5, ISBN13: 978-0-521-77257-0. Dewey:720/.94961/80902. LCCN:2003-058438.

Audience: **l,u,f.** *Choice, 2004.*

Architecture > Histories and Handbooks > Cultures, Regions, Nationalities

Adams, Michael Henry   **NA735.N5A33 2002**
Harlem: Lost and Found. Paul Rocheleau (Photographer). Trade Cloth. Monacelli Press, Inc. New York, NY. 2001. 240p. ISBN:1-58093-070-0, ISBN13: 978-1-58093-070-3. Dewey:974.7/1. LCCN:2002-005823.

Audience: **g,l,u,f.**

Asher, Catherine B.   **DS436 .N47 1987 PT.**
Architecture of Mughal India. C. A. Bayly, Gordon Johnson & John F. Richards (Contribution by). Trade Cloth. Cambridge University Press. New York, NY. 1992. 402p. The New Cambridge History of India Ser., Vol. I: 4 ISBN:0-521-26728-5, ISBN13: 978-0-521-26728-1. Dewey:954 s. LCCN:91-031572.

Audience: **g,l,u,f.** *Choice, 1993.*

Bergdoll, Barry   **NA956.B47 2000**
European Architecture 1750-1890. Trade Paper. Oxford University Press, Inc. New York, NY. 2000. 332p. Oxford History of Art Ser. ISBN:0-19-284222-6, ISBN13: 978-0-19-284222-0. Dewey:724/.19. LCCN:00-036747.

Audience: **g,l,u,f.** *Choice, 2001.*

Berliner, Nancy   **NA7449.H85B47 2003**
Yin Yu Tang: The Architecture and Daily Life of a Chinese House. Peabody Essex Museum Staff (Contribution by). Trade Cloth. Tuttle Publishing. Boston, MA. 2003. 192p. ISBN:0-8048-3487-3, ISBN13: 978-0-8048-3487-2. Dewey:728/.372/0951222. LCCN:2002-041621.

Audience: **g,l,u,f.** *Choice, 2004.*

Bernier, Ronald M.   **NA1510.8.H56B47 1997**
Himalayan Architecture. Dalai Lama XIV (Foreword by). Trade Cloth. Fairleigh Dickinson University Press. Cranbury, NJ. 1997. 208p. ISBN:0-8386-3602-0, ISBN13: 978-0-8386-3602-2. Dewey:720/.95496. LCCN:95-035280.

Audience: **g,l,u,f.** *Choice, 1997.*

Brumfield, William Craft   **NA1181.B72 2004**
A History of Russian Architecture. Trade Paper. University of Washington Press. Seattle, WA. 2004. 752p. ISBN:0-295-98393-0, ISBN13: 978-0-295-98393-6. Dewey:720/.947. LCCN:2003-064515.

Audience: **g,l,u,f.**

Cavalcanti, Lauro   **NA855.5.M63C38 2003**
When Brazil Was Modern: A Guide to Architecture, 1928-1960. Jon M. Tolman (Translator). Trade Paper. Princeton Architectural Press. New York, NY. 2003. 184p. ISBN:1-56898-341-7, ISBN13: 978-1-56898-341-7. Dewey:720/.972/0904. LCCN:2002-151544.

Audience: **g,l,u,f.**

Chambers, S. Allen   **NA730**
Buildings of West Virginia: With support from the West Virginia Humanities Council. Trade Cloth. Oxford University Press, Inc. New York, NY. 2004. 688p. Buildings of the United States Ser. ISBN:0-19-516548-9, ISBN13: 978-0-19-516548-7. Dewey:720/.9754. LCCN:2003-023135.

Audience: **g,l,u,f.** *Choice, 2004.*

Chambers, S. Allen, et al.   **NA705.P6 1983**
What Style Is It?: A Guide to American Architecture. Ed. 2. John C. Poppeliers & Nancy B. Schwartz (Authors). Trade Paper. National Trust for Historic Preservation. Washington, DC. 1984. 112p. Building Watchers Ser. ISBN:0-89133-116-6, ISBN13: 978-0-89133-116-2. Dewey:720/.973. LCCN:83-019278.

Audience: **g,l,u,f.**

Clifton-Taylor, Alec   NA5461.C486 1989
The Cathedrals of England. Ed. 2. Trade Paper. Thames &
Hudson. New York, NY. 1989. 288p. World of Art Ser.
ISBN:0-500-20062-9, ISBN13: 978-0-500-20062-9.
Dewey:726/.6/0942. LCCN:79-066135.
                                          Audience: **g,l,u,f.**

Concina, Ennio   NA1121.V4 C65613 19
A History of Venetian Architecture. Judith Landry (Translator).
Cloth Text. Cambridge University Press. New York, NY. 1998.
362p. ISBN:0-521-57338-6, ISBN13: 978-0-521-57338-2.
Dewey:720/.945/31. LCCN:97-019201.
                                Audience: **l,u,f.** *Choice, 1998.*

De Borja, Riquer i   NX562.B37M6313 2003
 Permanier
Modernismo: Architecture and Design in Spain. Trade Cloth.
Monacelli Press, Inc. New York, NY. 2003. 448p.
ISBN:1-58093-111-1, ISBN13: 978-1-58093-111-3.
Dewey:700/.946/709034. LCCN:2003-017001.
                                          Audience: **g,l,u,f.**

De Visser, John   NA7243.T67C78 2003
Old Toronto Houses. Tom Cruickshank (Text by). Trade Cloth.
Firefly Books, Ltd. Tonawanda, NY. 2003. 304p.
ISBN:1-55297-731-5, ISBN13: 978-1-55297-731-6.
Dewey:971.3/541. LCCN:2003-363168.
                                          Audience: **g,l,u,f.**

Decker, Julie & Chiei, Chris   NA8480.Q662005
 (Editors)
Quonset Hut: Metal Living for a Modern Age. Trade Cloth.
Princeton Architectural Press. New York, NY. 2005. 165p.
ISBN:1-56898-519-3, ISBN13: 978-1-56898-519-0.
Dewey:720.48. LCCN:2004-024738.
                                Audience: **g,l,u,f.** *Choice, 2006.*

Deckker, Zilah Quezado   NA855.5.M63Q47 2000
Brazil Built: The Architecture of the Modern Movement in
Brazil. UK-B Format Paperback. Routledge. New York, NY.
2004. 280p. ISBN:0-415-23178-7, ISBN13: 978-0-415-23178-7.
Dewey:720/.981/0904. LCCN:00-030082.
                                          Audience: **g,l,u,f.**

Donnelly, Marian C.   NA1201.D66 1992
Architecture in the Scandinavian Countries. Trade Cloth. MIT
Press. Cambridge, MA. 1991. 413p. ISBN:0-262-04118-9,
ISBN13: 978-0-262-04118-8. Dewey:720/.948.
LCCN:90-024720.
                                Audience: **g,l,u,f.** *Choice, 1992.*

Eckert, Kathryn Bishop   NA730.M5E28 1993
Buildings of Michigan. Trade Cloth. Oxford University Press,
Inc. New York, NY. 1993. 624p. Buildings of the United States
Ser. ISBN:0-19-506149-7, ISBN13: 978-0-19-506149-9.
Dewey:720.9774. LCCN:92-007096.
                                          Audience: **g,l,u,f.**

Fu, Xinian, et al.   NA1540.H574 2002
A History of Chinese Architecture. Daiheng Guo, Xujie Liu &
Guxi Pan (Authors), Nancy Shatzman Steinhardt (Editor). Cloth
over Boards. Yale University Press. Cumberland, RI. 2002.

384p. The Culture and Civilization of China Ser.
ISBN:0-300-09559-7, ISBN13: 978-0-300-09559-3.
Dewey:720/.951. LCCN:2001-007638.
                                Audience: **g,l,u,f.** *Choice, 2003.*

Gebhard, David &   NA730.I8
 Mansheim, Gerald
Buildings of Iowa. Trade Paper. Oxford University Press, Inc.
New York, NY. 1995. 592p. Buildings of the United States Ser.
ISBN:0-19-509378-X, ISBN13: 978-0-19-509378-0.
Dewey:720/.9777.
                                Audience: **g,l,u,f.** *Choice, 1993.*

Goldberger, Paul   NA6233.N5W6745 2004
Up from Zero: Politics, Architecture, and the Rebuilding of New
York. Trade Cloth. Random House Adult Trade Publishing
Group. New York, NY. 2004. 288p. ISBN:1-4000-6017-6,
ISBN13: 978-1-4000-6017-7. Dewey:725/.23/097471.
LCCN:2004-046769.
                                          Audience: **g,l,u,f.**

Gowans, Alan   NA703.G691991
Styles and Types of North American Architecture: Social
Function and Cultural Expression. Icon Editions. 1991.
ISBN:0-06-433276-4, ISBN13: 978-0-06-433276-7.
                                          Audience: **g,l,u,f.**

Handlin, David P.   NA705
American Architecture: A Critical History. Ed. 2. Trade Paper.
Thames & Hudson. New York, NY. 2004. 304p. World of Art
Ser. ISBN:0-500-20373-3, ISBN13: 978-0-500-20373-6.
Dewey:720/.973. LCCN:2003-102189.
                                          Audience: **g,l,u,f.**

Hoagland, Alison K.   NA730.A4H63
Buildings of Alaska. Trade Paper. Oxford University Press, Inc.
New York, NY. 1995. 352p. Buildings of the United States Ser.
ISBN:0-19-509380-1, ISBN13: 978-0-19-509380-3.
Dewey:720.9798. LCCN:92-046463.
                                Audience: **g,l,u,f.** *Choice, 1994.*

Hubka, Thomas C.   NA4690.H84 2003
Resplendent Synagogue: Architecture and Worship in an
Eighteenth-Century Polish Community. Trade Cloth. University
Press of New England. Lebanon, NH. 2005. 288p. Tauber
Institute for the Study of European Jewry Ser.
ISBN:1-58465-216-0, ISBN13: 978-1-58465-216-8.
Dewey:726/.3/094779. LCCN:2003-002101.
                                          Audience: **g,l,u,f.**

Isozaki, Arata, et al.   NA7758.K94
Katsura: Imperial Villa. Yoshihara Matsumura, Manfred Speidel,
Bruno Taut, Walter Gropius, Kenzo Tange & Francesco Dal Co
(Authors), Virginia Ponciroli (Editor). Trade Cloth. Electra
Architecture. London, 2005. 400p. ISBN:1-904313-37-X,
ISBN13: 978-1-904313-37-3. Dewey:728.8209521864.
                                          Audience: **g,l,u,f.**

Jordy, William H.   NA730.R5J67 2004
Buildings of Rhode Island. Trade Cloth. Oxford University
Press, Inc. New York, NY. 2004. 736p. Buildings of the United

States Ser. ISBN:0-19-506147-0, ISBN13: 978-0-19-506147-5. Dewey:720/.9745. LCCN:2003-022935.

Audience: **g,l,u,f**. *Choice, 2004.*

Jowitt, Glenn & Shaw, Peter   NA7475.A1J69 2000
Pacific Island Style. Trade Cloth. Thames & Hudson. New York, NY. 2000. 192p. ISBN:0-500-23772-7, ISBN13: 978-0-500-23772-4. Dewey:720/.995. LCCN:99-065178.

Audience: **g,l,u,f.**

Kalman, Harold D.   NA740 .K35 1994
A History of Canadian Architecture, Set. Trade Cloth. Oxford University Press, Inc. New York, NY. 1994. 956p. ISBN:0-19-541103-X, ISBN13: 978-0-19-541103-4. Dewey:720/.971. LCCN:95-112707.

Audience: **g,l,u,f.** *Choice, 1995.*

Kingsley, Karen   NA730.L8K55 2003
Buildings of Louisiana. Trade Cloth. Oxford University Press, Inc. New York, NY. 2003. 544p. Buildings of the United States Ser. ISBN:0-19-515999-3, ISBN13: 978-0-19-515999-8. Dewey:720/.9763. LCCN:2002-155947.

Audience: **g,l,u,f.** *Choice, 2003.*

Lejeune, Jean-Francois   NA702.C7813 2005
Cruelty and Utopia. Centre international pour la ville, l'architecture et le paysage Staff (Contribution by). Trade Paper. Princeton Architectural Press. New York, NY. 2005. 263p. ISBN:1-56898-489-8, ISBN13: 978-1-56898-489-6. Dewey:720/.98/091732. LCCN:2004-015433.

Audience: **u,f.** *Choice, 2005.*

Lemoine, Bertrand   NA1047.L4713 1998
Architecture in France, 1800-1900. Bonfante-Warren, Alexandra. New York: Harry N. Abrams. 1998. ISBN:0-8109-4090-6, ISBN13: 978-0-8109-4090-1.

Audience: **l,u,f.**

Lillie, Amanda   NA7594.L55 2004
Florentine Villas in the Fifteenth-Century: An Architectural and Social History. Trade Cloth. Cambridge University Press. New York, NY. 2005. 370p. ISBN:0-521-77047-5, ISBN13: 978-0-521-77047-7. Dewey:728/.0945/5109031. LCCN:2004-045674.

Audience: **l,u,f.** *Choice, 2006.*

Liscombe, Rhodri W.   NA747.V3L58 1997
The New Spirit: Modern Architecture in Vancouver, 1938-1963. Trade Paper. MIT Press. Cambridge, MA. 1997. 208p. ISBN:0-262-62115-0, ISBN13: 978-0-262-62115-1. Dewey:720.971133. LCCN:97-142734.

Audience: **g,l,u,f.** *Choice, 1997.*

Lobo Montalvo, Maria Luisa   F1799.H357L63 2000
Havana: History and Architecture of a Romantic City. Lorna S. Fox (Translator), Hugh Thomas (Prologue by). Trade Cloth. Monacelli Press, Inc. New York, NY. 2000. 320p. ISBN:1-58093-052-2, ISBN13: 978-1-58093-052-9. Dewey:972.91/23/00222. LCCN:00-106279.

Audience: **g,l,u,f.**

Maynard, W. Barksdale   NA710.M39 2002
Architecture in the United States, 1800-1850. New Haven: Yale University Press. 2002. ISBN:0-300-09383-7, ISBN13: 978-0-300-09383-4.

Audience: **g,l,u,f.**

Newhouse, Victoria   NA6695.N49 1998
Towards a New Museum. Trade Paper. Monacelli Press, Inc. New York, NY. 1998. 208p. ISBN:1-885254-60-1, ISBN13: 978-1-885254-60-3. Dewey:727/.7/09045. LCCN:98-004584.

Audience: **l,u,f.** *Choice, 1999.*

Nicoletta, Julie   NA730.N3N53 2000
Buildings of Nevada. Bret Morgan (Photographer). Trade Cloth. Oxford University Press, Inc. New York, NY. 2000. 336p. Buildings of the United States Ser. ISBN:0-19-514139-3, ISBN13: 978-0-19-514139-9. Dewey:720/.9793. LCCN:00-044609.

Audience: **g,l,u,f.**

Noel, Thomas J.   NA730.C6N64
Buildings of Colorado. Trade Paper. Oxford University Press, Inc. New York, NY. 2002. 688p. Buildings of the United States Ser. ISBN:0-19-515247-6, ISBN13: 978-0-19-515247-0. Dewey:720.9/788. LCCN:92-046463.

Audience: **g,l,u,f.**

Okrent, Daniel   F128.64.L6
Great Fortune: The Epic of Rockefeller Center. Trade Paper. DIANE Publishing Company. Collingdale, PA. 2006. 512p. ISBN:0-7567-9810-8, ISBN13: 978-0-7567-9810-9. Dewey:974.7/1.

Audience: **g,l,u,f.**

Pevsner, Nikolaus   NA950
An Outline of European Architecture. Paper Text. Textbook Publishers. Temecula, CA. 2003. 740p. ISBN:0-7581-6600-1, ISBN13: 978-0-7581-6600-5. Dewey:720/.94.

Audience: **g,l,u,f.**

Rigau, Jorge   NA812.R5 1991
Puerto Rico 1900: Turn-of-the-Century Architecture in the Hispanic Caribbean, 1890-1930. Leon Krier (Introduction by). Trade Cloth. Rizzoli International Publications, Inc. New York, NY. 1992. 232p. ISBN:0-8478-1400-9, ISBN13: 978-0-8478-1400-8. Dewey:720/.97295/09041. LCCN:91-011264.

Audience: **g,l,u,f.**

Roth, Leland   NA705
American Architecture: A History. Ed. 2. Trade Paper. Westview Press. Boulder, CO. 2003. 608p. ISBN:0-8133-3662-7, ISBN13: 978-0-8133-3662-6. Dewey:720.9/73.

Audience: **g,l,u,f.**

Scott, Pamela & Lee, Antoinette J.   NA735.W3S36 1993
Buildings of the District of Columbia. Trade Cloth. Oxford University Press, Inc. New York, NY. 1993. 480p. Buildings of the United States Ser. ISBN:0-19-506146-2, ISBN13: 978-0-19-506146-8. Dewey:720.9753. LCCN:93-009187.

Audience: **g,l,u,f.**

Smith, G. E. Kidder   **NA705**
Source Book of American Architecture: 500 Notable Buildings
from the 10th Century to the Present. Paul Goldberger
(Introduction by). Trade Paper. Princeton Architectural Press.
New York, NY. 2000. 688p. ISBN:1-56898-254-2, ISBN13:
978-1-56898-254-0. Dewey:720/.973. LCCN:95-049186.
                          Audience: **g,l,u,f**. *Choice, 1997.*

Stern, Robert A. M., et al.   **NA735.N5S727 1999**
New York 1880: Architecture and Urbanism in the Gilded Age.
Thomas Mellins & David Fishman (Authors). Trade Cloth.
Monacelli Press, Inc. New York, NY. 1999. 1008p.
ISBN:1-58093-027-1, ISBN13: 978-1-58093-027-7.
Dewey:720/.9747/109034. LCCN:99-017892.
                          Audience: **g,l,u,f**. *Choice, 2000.*

Sthapitanonda, N.   **NA1521**
Architecture of Thailand: A Guide to Traditional and
Contemporary Forms. Trade Cloth. Thames & Hudson. New
York, NY. 2006. 256p. ISBN:0-500-34223-7, ISBN13:
978-0-500-34223-7. Dewey:720.9593.
                          Audience: **g,l,u,f**.

Szabo, Albert & Barfield,   **NA7424.6.A1S94 1991**
   Thomas J.
Afghanistan: An Atlas of Indigenous Domestic Architecture.
Eduard F. Sekler (Foreword by). Trade Cloth. University of
Texas Press. Austin, TX. 1991. 288p. ISBN:0-292-70419-4,
ISBN13: 978-0-292-70419-0. Dewey:728/.09581.
LCCN:90-012528.
                          Audience: **l,u,f**. *Choice, 1992.*

Upton, Dell   **NA705.U78 1998**
Architecture in the United States. Trade Paper. Oxford
University Press, Inc. New York, NY. 1998. 336p. Oxford
History of Art Ser. ISBN:0-19-284217-X, ISBN13:
978-0-19-284217-6. Dewey:720.9/73. LCCN:98-186318.
                          Audience: **g,l,u,f**. *Choice, 1998.*

Wilson, Richard Guy   **NA730.V8B85 2002**
Buildings of Virginia: Tidewater and Piedmont. Trade Cloth.
Oxford University Press, Inc. New York, NY. 2002. 592p.
Buildings of the United States Ser. ISBN:0-19-515206-9,
ISBN13: 978-0-19-515206-7. Dewey:720/.9755.
LCCN:2002-001454.
                          Audience: **g,l,u,f**.

Zukowsky, John & Thorne,   **NA735.C45**
   Martha
Masterpieces of Chicago Architecture. Stanley Tigerman
(Preface by). Trade Cloth. Rizzoli International Publications,
Inc. New York, NY. 2004. 240p. ISBN:0-8478-2596-5, ISBN13:
978-0-8478-2596-7. Dewey:720.9/77311/0904.
                          Audience: **g,l,u,f**. *Choice, 2004.*

Architecture > Individual Architects

                          NA997.F65A42005
Catalogue: Foster and Partners. Ed. 2. Trade Paper, Saddle
Stitched. Prestel Publishing. New York, NY. 2005. 316p.

ISBN:3-7913-3298-8, ISBN13: 978-3-7913-3298-7.
Dewey:720.92. LCCN:2005-900731.
                          Audience: **g,l,u,f**. *Choice, 2006.*

Anderson, Stanford   **NA1088.B4A827 2000**
Peter Behrens and a New Architecture for the Twentieth
Century. Trade Cloth. MIT Press. Cambridge, MA. 2000. 443p.
ISBN:0-262-01176-X, ISBN13: 978-0-262-01176-1.
Dewey:720/.92. LCCN:99-049154.
                          Audience: **g,l,u,f**. *Choice, 2000.*

Argan, Carlo Giulio &   **NA1123.B9.A87131993**
   Contardi, Bruno
Michelangelo: Architect. Marion L. Grayson (Translator). Trade
Cloth. Harry N. Abrams, Inc. New York, NY. 1993. 388p.
ISBN:0-8109-3638-0, ISBN13: 978-0-8109-3638-6.
Dewey:720/.92. LCCN:92-038117.
                          Audience: **g,l,u,f**. *Choice, 1993.*

Baker, Geoffrey H.   **NA1053.J4B34 1996**
Le Corbusier: The Creative Search. Cloth Text. John Wiley &
Sons, Inc. Hoboken, NJ. 1996. 320p. Architecture Ser.
ISBN:0-442-02128-3, ISBN13: 978-0-442-02128-3.
Dewey:720.92. LCCN:94-066155.
                          Audience: **g,l,u,f**.

Beck, Haig & Cooper,   **NA1605.M87A42002**
   Jackie (Editors)
Glenn Murcutt: A Singular Architectural Practice. Trade Cloth.
Images Publishing Group Pty, Ltd. Mulgrave, VIC. 2004. 256p.
ISBN:1-876907-75-4, ISBN13: 978-1-876907-75-4.
LCCN:2002-483178.
                          Audience: **g,l,u,f**.

Bognar, Botond   **NA1559.H33A4 2001**
Hiroshi Hara: The 'Floating World' of his Architecture. Trade
Cloth. John Wiley & Sons, Inc. Hoboken, NJ. 2001. 272p.
ISBN:0-471-87730-1, ISBN13: 978-0-471-87730-1.
Dewey:720/.92. LCCN:2001-431685.
                          Audience: **g,l,u,f**.

Borsi, Franco & Portoghesi,   **NA1173.H6B613 1991**
   Paolo
Horta. Trade Cloth. Rizzoli International Publications, Inc. New
York, NY. 1991. 388p. ISBN:0-8478-1290-1, ISBN13:
978-0-8478-1290-5. Dewey:720/.92. LCCN:90-053176.
                          Audience: **g,l,u,f**. *Choice, 1992.*

Boutelle, Sara H.   **NA737**
Julia Morgan, Architect. Richard Barnes (Photographer). Trade
Cloth. Abbeville Press, Inc. New York, NY. 1995. 272p.
ISBN:0-7892-0019-8, ISBN13: 978-0-7892-0019-8.
Dewey:720/.92/4 B. LCCN:87-029008.
                          Audience: **g,l,u,f**. *Choice, 1989.*

Brooks, Michael   **NA967.5.V53B76 1987**
John Ruskin and Victorian Architecture. Cloth Text. Rutgers
University Press. Piscataway, NJ. 1987. 356p.
ISBN:0-8135-1205-0, ISBN13: 978-0-8135-1205-1. Dewey:720.
LCCN:86-015452.
                          Audience: **g,l,u,f**. *Choice, 1987.*

Bruegmann, Robert   **NA737.H558B78 1997**
The Architects and the City: Holabird and Roche of Chicago,
1880-1918. Trade Cloth. University of Chicago Press. Chicago,
IL. 1997. 562p. Chicago Architecture and Urbanism Ser.
ISBN:0-226-07695-4, ISBN13: 978-0-226-07695-9.
Dewey:720/.92/277311. LCCN:96-022151.
                              Audience: **g,l,u,f.** *Choice, 1998.*

Bruegmann, Robert (Editor)   **NA737.H558A4 1991**
Holabird and Roche and Root: An Illustrated Catalogue of
Works, 1880-1940. Cloth Text. Garland Publishing, Inc. New
York, NY. 1991. 1300p. ISBN:0-8240-3974-2, ISBN13:
978-0-8240-3974-5. Dewey:720/.92/2. LCCN:90-019652.
                              Audience: **g,l,u,f.** *Choice, 1991.*

Cappellato, Gabriele   **NA1353.B67**
   (Editor)
Mario Botta: Light and Gravity. Trade Cloth. Prestel Publishing.
New York, NY. 2004. 272p. ISBN:3-7913-3186-8, ISBN13:
978-3-7913-3186-7. Dewey:720.9/7. LCCN:2005-299153.
                              Audience: **g,l,u,f.** *Choice, 2005.*

Chappell, Sally Anderson   **NA737.G7C48 1992**
   Kitt
Architecture and Planning of Graham, Anderson, Probst and
White, 1912-1936: Transforming Tradition. Trade Cloth.
University of Chicago Press. Chicago, IL. 1992. 352p. Chicago
Architecture and Urbanism Ser. ISBN:0-226-10134-7, ISBN13:
978-0-226-10134-7. Dewey:720/.92/2. LCCN:91-009162.
                              Audience: **g,l,u,f.** *Choice, 1992.*

Christen, Barbara S.   **NA737.G5C37 2001**
Cass Gilbert: Life and Work. Trade Cloth. W. W. Norton &
Company, Inc. New York, NY. 2001. 304p.
ISBN:0-393-73065-4, ISBN13: 978-0-393-73065-4.
Dewey:720/.92 B. LCCN:00-069946.

                              Audience: **g,l,u,f.**

Clausen, Meredith L.   **NA737.W7**
Pietro Belluschi: Modern American Architect. Trade Paper. MIT
Press. Cambridge, MA. 1999. 480p. ISBN:0-262-53167-4,
ISBN13: 978-0-262-53167-2. Dewey:720.9/2. LCCN:94-020789.
                              Audience: **g,l,u,f.** *Choice, 1995.*

Constant, Caroline   **NA1053.G73C66 2000**
Eileen Gray. Trade Cloth. Phaidon Press. London, 2000. 256p.
ISBN:0-7148-3905-1, ISBN13: 978-0-7148-3905-9.
Dewey:720/.92. LCCN:2001-409293.

                              Audience: **g,l,u,f.**

Crawford, Alan   **N6797.M23C73 1995**
Charles Rennie Mackintosh. Trade Paper. Thames & Hudson.
New York, NY. 1995. 216p. World of Art Ser.
ISBN:0-500-20283-4, ISBN13: 978-0-500-20283-8.
Dewey:709/.2 B. LCCN:94-062072.

                              Audience: **g,l,u,f.**

Dal Co, Francesco &   **NA1053.J4**
   Mazzariol, Giuseppe
Carlo Scarpa: The Complete Works. Trade Paper. Rizzoli
International Publications, Inc. New York, NY. 2002. 320p.

ISBN:0-8478-0591-3, ISBN13: 978-0-8478-0591-4.
Dewey:720/.92/4. LCCN:84-043106.
                              Audience: **l,u,f.** *Choice, 1986.*

Darley, Gillian   **NA997.S7D37 1999**
John Soane: An Accidental Romantic. Cloth over Boards. Yale
University Press. Cumberland, RI. 1999. 368p.
ISBN:0-300-08165-0, ISBN13: 978-0-300-08165-7.
Dewey:720/.92. LCCN:99-062198.
                              Audience: **g,l,u,f.** *Choice, 2000.*

Dean, Andrea Oppenheimer   **NA2300.A9D43 2002**
   & Hursley, Timothy
Rural Studio: Samuel Mockbee and the Architecture of Decency.
Trade Paper. Princeton Architectural Press. New York, NY.
2002. 192p. ISBN:1-56898-292-5, ISBN13: 978-1-56898-292-2.
Dewey:720/.71/176143. LCCN:2001-003805.
                              Audience: **g,l,u,f.** *Choice, 2002.*

Frampton, Kenneth   **NA1053.J4F69 2001**
Le Corbusier. Trade Paper. Thames & Hudson. New York, NY.
2001. 240p. World of Art Ser. ISBN:0-500-20341-5, ISBN13:
978-0-500-20341-5. Dewey:720/.92. LCCN:00-107873.
                              Audience: **g,l,u,f.**

Frampton, Kenneth &   **NA1605.S4.A4 1992**
   Drew, Philip
Harry Seidler. Trade Cloth. Thames & Hudson. New York, NY.
1992. 432p. ISBN:0-500-97838-7, ISBN13: 978-0-500-97838-2.
Dewey:720.92. LCCN:92-080804.
                              Audience: **g,l,u,f.** *Choice, 1993.*

Frampton, Kenneth   **NA1053.J4F6932002**
Le Corbusier: Architect of the Twentieth Century. Roberto
Schezen (Photographer). Trade Cloth. Harry N. Abrams, Inc.
New York, NY. 2002. 208p. ISBN:0-8109-3494-9, ISBN13:
978-0-8109-3494-8. Dewey:720/.92. LCCN:2002-002252.
                              Audience: **g,l,u,f.**

Fromonot, Francoise   **NA1605**
Glenn Murcutt: Buildings and Projects, 1962-2003. Ed. 2. Trade
Cloth. Thames & Hudson. New York, NY. 2003. 326p.
ISBN:0-500-34193-1, ISBN13: 978-0-500-34193-3.
Dewey:720/.92. LCCN:2002-113523.

                              Audience: **g,l,u,f.**

Gehry, Frank O.   **NA737.G44**
Frank Gehry, Architect. J. Fiona Ragheb (Editor). Trade Cloth.
Solomon R. Guggenheim Museum. New York, NY. 2004. 390p.
ISBN:0-89207-277-6, ISBN13: 978-0-89207-277-4.
Dewey:720.92.

                              Audience: **g,l,u,f.**

Glanz, James & Lipton,   **NA6233.N5W6742 2003**
   Eric
City in the Sky: The Rise and Fall of the World Trade Center.
Trade Cloth. Henry Holt & Company. New York, NY. 2003.
448p. ISBN:0-8050-7428-7, ISBN13: 978-0-8050-7428-4.
Dewey:720/.483/097471. LCCN:2003-061081.
                              Audience: **g,l,u,f.**

Godwin, E. W.   NA997.G6A41999
E. W. Godwin: Aesthetic Movement Architect and Designer.
Susan W. Soros (Editor). Cloth over Boards. Yale University
Press. Cumberland, RI. 1999. 432p. ISBN:0-300-08008-5,
ISBN13: 978-0-300-08008-7. LCCN:99-024645.
Audience: **g,l,u,f.** *Choice, 2000.*

Goldhagen, Sarah Williams   NA737.K32G652001
Louis Kahn's Situated Modernism. Cloth over Boards. Yale
University Press. Cumberland, RI. 2001. 336p.
ISBN:0-300-07786-6, ISBN13: 978-0-300-07786-5.
Dewey:720/.92. LCCN:00-043677.
Audience: **g,l,u,f.** *Choice, 2001.*

Guidolotti, Pino   NA1123.P2A4 2001
Andrea Palladio: The Complete Illustrated Works. Universe
Publishing. 2001. ISBN:0-7893-0661-1, ISBN13:
978-0-7893-0661-6.
Audience: **g,l,u,f.**

Hewitt, Mark Allen   NA7238.P25H482001
Gustave Stickley's Craftsman Farms: The Quest for an Arts and
Crafts Utopia. Trade Cloth. Syracuse University Press. Syracuse,
NY. 2001. xviii, 248p. ISBN:0-8156-0689-3, ISBN13:
978-0-8156-0689-5. Dewey:728/.092. LCCN:00-050511.
Audience: **g,l,u,f.** *Choice, 2001.*

Huxtable, Ada Louise   NA737.W7H89 2004
Frank Lloyd Wright. Trade Cloth. Penguin Group (USA) Inc.
New York, NY. 2004. 272p. ISBN:0-670-03342-1, ISBN13:
978-0-670-03342-3. Dewey:720/.92 B. LCCN:2004-046477.
Audience: **g,l,u,f.** *Choice, 2005.*

Hyman, Isabelle   NA737.B68H972001
Marcel Breuer, Architect: The Career and the Buildings. Trade
Cloth. Harry N. Abrams, Inc. New York, NY. 2001. 395p.
ISBN:0-8109-4265-8, ISBN13: 978-0-8109-4265-3.
Dewey:720/.92 B. LCCN:2001-022593.
Audience: **g,l,u,f.** *Choice, 2002.*

Irish, Sharon   NA737.G5I74 1999
Cass Gilbert, Architect. Trade Paper. Monacelli Press, Inc. New
York, NY. 1999. 224p. Sources of American Architecture Ser.
ISBN:1-885254-90-3, ISBN13: 978-1-885254-90-0.
Dewey:720/.92. LCCN:98-020358.
Audience: **g,l,u,f.**

Isozaki, Arata   NA1559.I79A4 1991
Arata Isozaki: Architecture, 1960-1990. David B. Stewart
(Contribution by). Trade Paper. Rizzoli International
Publications, Inc. New York, NY. 1993. 304p.
ISBN:0-8478-1319-3, ISBN13: 978-0-8478-1319-3.
Dewey:720/.92. LCCN:90-050795.
Audience: **g,l,u,f.** *Choice, 1991.*

Ivy, Robert A. Jr.   NA737.J64 I88 1992
Fay Jones. Trade Cloth. American Institute of Architects Press.
Washington, DC. 1993. 224p. ISBN:1-55835-075-6, ISBN13:
978-1-55835-075-5. Dewey:720/.92.
Audience: **g,l,u,f.**

John Gorman, Michael   TA140.F9
Buckminster Fuller: Designing for Mobility. Trade Cloth. Skira
Editore. Milano, 2005. 208p. ISBN:88-7624-265-1, ISBN13:
978-88-7624-265-6. Dewey:620.0092. LCCN:2005-283974.
Audience: **g,l,u,f.** *Choice, 2006.*

Johnson, Philip, et al.   NA737.J6A4 2002
The Architecture of Philip Johnson. Richard Payne & Hillary
Lewis (Authors). Trade Cloth. Bulfinch Press. Boston, MA.
2002. 336p. ISBN:0-8212-2788-2, ISBN13: 978-0-8212-2788-6.
Dewey:720/.92. LCCN:2002-102356.
Audience: **g,l,u,f.**

Kastner, Victoria   NA7615.H43K372000
Hearst Castle: The Biography of a Country House. Victoria
Garagliano (Photographer), George Plimpton (Foreword by).
Trade Cloth. Harry N. Abrams, Inc. New York, NY. 2000. 240p.
ISBN:0-8109-3415-9, ISBN13: 978-0-8109-3415-3.
Dewey:728.8/09794/78. LCCN:00-021506.
Audience: **g,l,u,f.**

King, David   NA997.A4A4 2001
Complete Works of Robert and James Adam and Unbuilt Adam.
Ed. 2. Trade Cloth. Elsevier Science & Technology Books. Saint
Louis, MO. 2001. 768p. ISBN:0-7506-4468-0, ISBN13:
978-0-7506-4468-6. Dewey:720/.92/2. LCCN:2001-280244.
Audience: **g,l,u,f.**

Lambert, Phyllis & Van der   NA1088
Rohe, Ludwig Mies
Mies in America. Werner Oechslin (Translator), Whitney
Museum of American Art Staff (Contribution by). Trade Paper.
Harry N. Abrams, Inc. New York, NY. 2003. 792p.
ISBN:0-920785-69-7, ISBN13: 978-0-920785-69-0.
Dewey:720/.92.
Audience: **g,l,u,f.** *Choice, 2002.*

Landau, Sarah B.   NA737.P64L36 1998
George B. Post, Architect: Picturesque Designer and Determined
Realist. Trade Paper. Monacelli Press, Inc. New York, NY. 1998.
224p. Sources of American Architecture Ser.
ISBN:1-885254-92-X, ISBN13: 978-1-885254-92-4.
Dewey:720/.92. LCCN:98-020359.
Audience: **g,l,u,f.**

Langmead, Donald   Z8648
J. J. P. Oud and the International Style: A Bio-Bibliography.
Cloth Text. Greenwood Publishing Group, Inc. Portsmouth, NH.
1999. 304p. Bio-Bibliographies in Art and Architecture Ser., Vol.
5 ISBN:0-313-30100-X, ISBN13: 978-0-313-30100-1.
Dewey:016.72092. LCCN:98-041648.
Audience: **g,l,u,f.** *Choice, 1999.*

Libeskind, Daniel &   NA1123.T4
Terragni, Attilio
The Terragni Atlas: Built Architecture. Paolo Rosselli
(Photographer). Trade Cloth, Pictures or Photographs. Skira
Editore. Milano, 2005. 276p. ISBN:88-8491-732-8, ISBN13:
978-88-8491-732-4. Dewey:720.92. LCCN:2005-534399.
Audience: **u,f.** *Choice, 2005.*

Mallgrave, Harry F.   **NA1353.S45M36 1996**
Gottfried Semper: Architect of the Nineteenth Century: A
Personal and Intellectual Biography. Cloth over Boards. Yale
University Press. Cumberland, RI. 1996. 448p.
ISBN:0-300-06624-4, ISBN13: 978-0-300-06624-1.
Dewey:720.9/2. LCCN:95-047561.
> Audience: **g,l,u,f.** *Choice, 1996.*

Mansbridge, Michael   **NA997**
John Nash: A Complete Catalogue. Trade Paper. Phaidon Press.
London, 2004. 336p. ISBN:0-7148-4380-6, ISBN13:
978-0-7148-4380-3. Dewey:720/.92. LCCN:2005-272776.
> Audience: **g,l,u,f.** *Choice, 1992.*

Marder, T. A.   **NA1123.B5M369 1998**
Bernini and the Art of Architecture. Joseph Martin
(Photographer). Trade Cloth. Abbeville Press, Inc. New York,
NY. 1998. 344p. ISBN:0-7892-0115-1, ISBN13:
978-0-7892-0115-7. Dewey:720/.92. LCCN:98-017964.
> Audience: **g,l,u,f.**

Maxwell, Robert &   **NA997.J34A4 1994**
  Muirhead, Thomas
James Stirling and Michael Wilford: Buildings and Projects,
1975-1992. Trade Cloth. Thames & Hudson. New York, NY.
1994. 306p. ISBN:0-500-34126-5, ISBN13: 978-0-500-34126-1.
Dewey:720/.92/2. LCCN:93-060420.
> Audience: **l,u,f.** *Choice, 1994.*

Mayne, Thom   **NA737.M72**
Morphosis. Trade Paper. Phaidon Press, Inc. New York, NY.
2006. 288p. ISBN:0-7148-4625-2, ISBN13: 978-0-7148-4625-5.
Dewey:720/.92/2.
> Audience: **g,l,u,f.**

McCarter, Robert   **NA737.W7**
Frank Lloyd Wright. Trade Cloth. Phaidon Press, Inc. New
York, NY. 2002. ISBN:0-7148-9313-7, ISBN13:
978-0-7148-9313-6. Dewey:720.9/2.
> Audience: **g,l,u,f.** *Choice, 1998.*

McCarter, Robert   **NA680**
Louis I. Kahn. Trade Cloth. Phaidon Press. London, 2005. 512p.
ISBN:0-7148-4045-9, ISBN13: 978-0-7148-4045-1.
Dewey:720.92. LCCN:2005-415959.
> Audience: **g,l,u,f.** *Choice, 2005.*

Meier, Richard & Allen,   **NA737.M44A4 1999**
  Stan
Richard Meier Architect. Trade Cloth. Monacelli Press, Inc.
New York, NY. 2000. 336p. ISBN:1-58093-061-1, ISBN13:
978-1-58093-061-1. Dewey:720.9/2. LCCN:99-035830.
> Audience: **g,l,u,f.**

Meister, Maureen (Editor)   **NA737.R5H2 1999**
H. H. Richardson: The Architect, His Peers, and Their Era.
Trade Cloth. MIT Press. Cambridge, MA. 1999. 155p.
ISBN:0-262-13356-3, ISBN13: 978-0-262-13356-2.
Dewey:720/.92. LCCN:99-026903.
> Audience: **g,l,u,f.** *Choice, 2000.*

Merkel, Jayne   **NA737**
Eero Saarinen. Trade Cloth. Phaidon Press. London, 2005. 256p.
ISBN:0-7148-4277-X, ISBN13: 978-0-7148-4277-6.
Dewey:720.92. LCCN:2006-531004.
> Audience: **g,l,u,f.**

Mertins, Detlef   **NA1088.M65A4 1994**
Presence of Mies. Trade Paper. Princeton Architectural Press.
New York, NY. 1996. 272p. ISBN:1-56898-013-2, ISBN13:
978-1-56898-013-3. Dewey:720/.92. LCCN:94-016259.
> Audience: **u,f.** *Choice, 1995.*

Nerdinger, Winfried (Editor)   **NA1455.F53A2314 1999**
Alvar Aalto: Toward a Human Modernism. Trade Cloth. Prestel
Publishing. New York, NY. 1999. 168p. ISBN:3-7913-2049-1,
ISBN13: 978-3-7913-2049-6. Dewey:720/.92. LCCN:99-018300.
> Audience: **g,l,u,f.** *Choice, 2000.*

Nerdinger, Winfried (Editor)   **NA1088.O78**
Frei Otto: The Complete Works. Mirjana Grdanjski, Irene
Meissner & Eberhard Möller (Contribution by). Trade Cloth.
Birkhauser Boston. Cambridge, MA. 2006.
ISBN:3-7643-7233-8, ISBN13: 978-3-7643-7233-0.
Dewey:720.92.
> Audience: **g,l,u,f.**

Quantrill, Malcolm   **NA1455.F53A237 1989**
Alvar Aalto: A Critical Study. Trade Paper. Ivan R. Dee
Publisher. Blue Ridge Summit, PA. 1990. 307p.
ISBN:0-941533-35-2, ISBN13: 978-0-941533-35-5.
Dewey:720/.92/4. LCCN:89-039755.
> Audience: **g,l,u,f.**

Ragheb, J. Fiona   **NA737.G44**
Frank Gehry, Architect. Guggenheim Museum Publications.
2001. ISBN:0-8109-6929-7, ISBN13: 978-0-8109-6929-2.
> Audience: **g,l,u,f.**

Ray, Nicholas   **NA1455.F53A26 2005**
Alvar Aalto. Saddle Stitched, Cloth over Boards, Dust Jacket.
Yale University Press. Cumberland, RI. 2005. 224p.
ISBN:0-300-10749-8, ISBN13: 978-0-300-10749-4.
Dewey:720/.92 B. LCCN:2005-012043.
> Audience: **g,l,u,f.**

Richardson, Margaret &   **NA997.S7A4 2000**
  Stevens, Mary Anne (Editors)
John Soane, Architect: Master of Space and Light. Cloth over
Boards. Yale University Press. Cumberland, RI. 2000. 302p.
ISBN:0-300-08195-2, ISBN13: 978-0-300-08195-4.
Dewey:720.92. LCCN:99-066155.
> Audience: **g,l,u,f.** *Choice, 2000.*

Riley, Terence & Bergdoll,   **NA1088.M65A42001**
  Barry (Editors)
Mies Van der Rohe in Berlin. Trade Cloth. Harry N. Abrams,
Inc. New York, NY. 2001. 368p. A Museum of Modern Art
Book Ser. ISBN:0-8109-6216-0, ISBN13: 978-0-8109-6216-3.
Dewey:720/.92. LCCN:2001-088553.
> Audience: **l,u,f.** *Choice, 2002.*

Román, Antonio   NA737.S28R66 2003
Eero Saarinen : an architecture of multiplicity. New York :
Princeton Architectural Press. 2003. ISBN:1-56898-340-9,
ISBN13: 978-1-56898-340-0.
                                        Audience: **g,l,u,f.**

Rybczynski, Witold   NA1123.P2R932002
The Perfect House: A Journey with the Renaissance Architect
Andrea Palladio. Scribner. 2002. ISBN:0-7432-0586-3, ISBN13:
978-0-7432-0586-3.
                                        Audience: **g,l,u,f.**

Rykwert, Joseph   NA737.K32R942001
Louis Kahn. Roberto Schezen (Photographer). Trade Cloth.
Harry N. Abrams, Inc. New York, NY. 2001. 224p.
ISBN:0-8109-4226-7, ISBN13: 978-0-8109-4226-4.
Dewey:720/.92. LCCN:2001-001354.
                          Audience: **l,u,f.**   *Choice, 2002.*

Schulze, Franz   NA737.J6S381996
Philip Johnson: Life and Work. Trade Paper. University of
Chicago Press. Chicago, IL. 1996. 479p. ISBN:0-226-74058-7,
ISBN13: 978-0-226-74058-4. Dewey:720/.92 B.
LCCN:95-043299.
                          Audience: **g,l,u,f.**   *Choice, 1995.*

Snodin, Michael (Editor)   NA1088.S3.A4 1991
Karl Friedrich Schinkel: A Universal Man. Cloth over Boards.
Yale University Press. Cumberland, RI. 1991. 230p.
ISBN:0-300-05165-4, ISBN13: 978-0-300-05165-0.
Dewey:720.92. LCCN:91-050586.
                          Audience: **g,l,u,f.**   *Choice, 1992.*

Sola-Morales, Ignasi De   NA1313.G3S64132003
Antoni Gaudi. Rafael Vargas (Photographer). Trade Cloth. Harry
N. Abrams, Inc. New York, NY. 2003. 144p.
ISBN:0-8109-4625-4, ISBN13: 978-0-8109-4625-5.
Dewey:720/.92. LCCN:2003-007534.
                                        Audience: **g,l,u,f.**

Steele, James   NA1479.8
Rasem Badran. Trade Cloth. Thames & Hudson. New York, NY.
2005. 256p. ISBN:0-500-34206-7, ISBN13: 978-0-500-34206-0.
Dewey:720.92. LCCN:2004-110958.
                          Audience: **g,l,u,f.**   *Choice, 2006.*

Storrer, William A.   NA737.W7A4 1993
The Frank Lloyd Wright Companion. Trade Cloth. University of
Chicago Press. Chicago, IL. 1994. 508p. ISBN:0-226-77624-7,
ISBN13: 978-0-226-77624-8. Dewey:720.92.
LCCN:2006-044502.
                          Audience: **g,l,u,f.**   *Choice, 1994.*

Taniguchi, Yoshio   NA1559.T35A41999
Architecture of Yoshio Taniguchi. Fumihiko Maki (Contribution
by). Trade Cloth. Harry N. Abrams, Inc. New York, NY. 1999.
280p. ISBN:0-8109-1997-4, ISBN13: 978-0-8109-1997-6.
Dewey:720/.92. LCCN:98-074033.
                          Audience: **l,u,f.**   *Choice, 1999.*

Taylor, John   NA1605.H38T39 2000
Between Devotion and Design: The Architecture of John Cyril
Hawes. Trade Cloth. University of Western Australia Press.
Crawley, W.A.. 2000. 432p. ISBN:1-876268-16-6, ISBN13:
978-1-876268-16-9. Dewey:720/.92. LCCN:2001-430149.
                          Audience: **g,l,u,f.**   *Choice, 2001.*

Tinniswood, Adrian   NA997.W8T56 2001
His Invention So Fertile: A Life of Christopher Wren. Trade
Cloth. Oxford University Press, Inc. New York, NY. 2001. 504p.
ISBN:0-19-514989-0, ISBN13: 978-0-19-514989-0.
Dewey:720/.92 B. LCCN:2001-133026.
                                        Audience: **l,u,f.**

Toker, Franklin   NA737.W7T65 2003
Fallingwater Rising: Frank Lloyd Wright, E. J. Kaufmann, and
America's Most Extraordinary House. Trade Paper. Alfred A.
Knopf Inc. New York, NY. 2005. 496p. ISBN:0-375-71015-9,
ISBN13: 978-0-375-71015-5. Dewey:728/.372/092.
LCCN:2003-056181.
                          Audience: **g,l,u,f.**   *Choice, 2004.*

Tournikiotis, Panayotis   NA1011.5.L6T6813
Adolf Loos. Trade Cloth. Princeton Architectural Press. New
York, NY. 1996. 208p. ISBN:1-878271-80-6, ISBN13:
978-1-878271-80-8. Dewey:720/.92. LCCN:94-021141.
                          Audience: **g,l,u,f.**   *Choice, 1995.*

Twombly, Robert C.   NA2707.S94A4 2000
Louis Sullivan: The Poetry of Architecture. Trade Cloth. W. W.
Norton & Company, Inc. New York, NY. 2000. 416p.
ISBN:0-393-04823-3, ISBN13: 978-0-393-04823-0.
Dewey:720/.92. LCCN:00-020746.
                          Audience: **g,l,u,f.**   *Choice, 2001.*

Watkin, David (Editor)   NA966.5.N4 S54 2000
Sir John Soane: The Royal Academy Lectures. Ed. 2. Cloth
Text. Cambridge University Press. New York, NY. 2000. 336p.
ISBN:0-521-77082-3, ISBN13: 978-0-521-77082-8. Dewey:720.
LCCN:99-028761.
                          Audience: **g,l,u,f.**   *Choice, 2000.*

Weston, Richard   NA737.W7
Alvar Aalto. Trade Paper. Phaidon Press. London, 1997. 240p.
ISBN:0-7148-3710-5, ISBN13: 978-0-7148-3710-9.
Dewey:720.9/2.
                                        Audience: **g,l,u,f.**

Wiseman, Carter   NA737.P365W572001
I. M. Pei: A Profile in American Architecture. Trade Cloth.
Harry N. Abrams, Inc. New York, NY. 2001. 340p.
ISBN:0-8109-3477-9, ISBN13: 978-0-8109-3477-1.
Dewey:720/.92 B. LCCN:2001-018904.
                          Audience: **g,l,u,f.**   *Choice, 2002, 1991.*

Woodbridge, Sally B.   NA737.M435W66
Bernard Maybeck: Visionary Architect. Richard Barnes
(Photographer). Trade Paper. Abbeville Press, Inc. New York,
NY. 2006. 248p. ISBN:0-7892-0132-1, ISBN13:
978-0-7892-0132-4. Dewey:720.92. LCCN:92-012633.
                                        Audience: **g,l,u,f.**

Architecture > Materials and Techniques

TJ163.5.D86

Green Building Guidelines: Meeting the Demand for
Low-Energy, Resource-Efficient Homes. Ed. 4. Perfect.
Sustainable Buildings Industry Council. Washington, DC. 2004.
182p. ISBN:0-9762073-2-X, ISBN13: 978-0-9762073-2-0.
Dewey:696.

Audience: **l,u,f.**

TH455

☐ Sweets Product Marketplace.
http://sweets.construction.com/
McGraw-Hill Companies.

Audience: **u,f.**

Allen, Edward & Iano,   **TH145.A417 2004**
  Joseph
Fundamentals of Building Construction: Materials and Methods.
Ed. 4. Trade Cloth. John Wiley & Sons, Inc. Hoboken, NJ.
2003. 912p. ISBN:0-471-21903-7, ISBN13: 978-0-471-21903-3.
Dewey:690. LCCN:2003-011398.

Audience: **l,u,f.**

American Institute of   **NA1996.A726 2001**
  Architects Staff & Demkin, Joseph A.
The Architect's Handbook of Professional Practice. Ed. 13.
Trade Cloth, CD-ROM. John Wiley & Sons, Inc. Hoboken, NJ.
2001. 1008p. ISBN:0-471-41969-9, ISBN13:
978-0-471-41969-3. Dewey:720/.68. LCCN:2001-026131.

Audience: **l,u,f.**

Campbell, James W. P.   **NA4120**
Brick: A World History. Will Pryce (Photographer). Trade Cloth.
Thames & Hudson. New York, NY. 2003. 320p.
ISBN:0-500-34195-8, ISBN13: 978-0-500-34195-7.
Dewey:721/.04421. LCCN:2003-101343.

Audience: **g,l,u,f.** *Choice, 2004.*

Coldstream, Nicola   **TH5401.C76 1991**
Masons and Sculptors. Trade Paper. University of Toronto Press.
Toronto, ON. 1991. 72p. Medieval Craftsmen Ser.
ISBN:0-8020-6916-9, ISBN13: 978-0-8020-6916-0.
Dewey:693.1.

Audience: **l,u,f.**

Elizabeth, Lynne & Adams,   **TH146.A48 2005**
  Cassandra (Editors)
Alternative Construction: Contemporary Natural Building
Methods. Ed. 2. Trade Paper. John Wiley & Sons, Inc. Hoboken,
NJ. 2005. 416p. ISBN:0-471-71938-2, ISBN13:
978-0-471-71938-0. Dewey:691. LCCN:2004-061232.

Audience: **l,u,f.**

Heyman, Jacques   **TA676.H49**
The Stone Skeleton: Structural Engineering of Masonry
Architecture. Trade Paper. Cambridge University Press. New
York, NY. 1997. 170p. ISBN:0-521-62963-2, ISBN13:
978-0-521-62963-8. Dewey:693.1.

Audience: **l,u,f.** *Choice, 1996.*

Kibert, Charles   **TH880.K53 2005**
Sustainable Construction: Green Building Design and Delivery.
Trade Cloth. John Wiley & Sons, Inc. Hoboken, NJ. 2005. 448p.
ISBN:0-471-66113-9, ISBN13: 978-0-471-66113-9.
Dewey:720/.47. LCCN:2004-014938.

Audience: **g,l,u,f.**

Taylor, Rabun M.   **TH16.T38 2003**
Roman Builders: A Study in Architectural Process. Trade Paper.
Cambridge University Press. New York, NY. 2003. 320p.
ISBN:0-521-00583-3, ISBN13: 978-0-521-00583-8.
Dewey:690/.0937. LCCN:2002-073306.

Audience: **l,u,f.** *Choice, 2003.*

Watson, Donald   **TA404.5.T56 2000**
Time-Saver Standards for Building Materials and Systems:
Design Criteria and Selection Data. Cloth Text. McGraw-Hill
Professional Publishing. New York, NY. 2000. 784p. Time-Saver
Standards Concise Ser. ISBN:0-07-135692-4, ISBN13:
978-0-07-135692-3. Dewey:691/.02/18. LCCN:00-703158.

Audience: **l,u,f.**

Architecture > City Planning

Alexander, Christopher   **NA2760.A445 2002**
The Nature of Order: An Essay on the Art of Building and the
Nature of the Universe, Set. Quantity Pack. Center For
Environmental Structure. Berkeley, CA. 2005. 2158p. The
Center for Environmental Structure Ser., Vol. 12
ISBN:0-9726529-0-6, ISBN13: 978-0-9726529-0-2.
Dewey:720/.1. LCCN:2002-154268.

Audience: **g,l,u,f.**

Bruegmann, Robert   **HT371.B74 2005**
Sprawl: A Compact History. Trade Cloth. University of Chicago
Press. Chicago, IL. 2005. 306p. ISBN:0-226-07690-3, ISBN13:
978-0-226-07690-4. Dewey:307.76. LCCN:2005-007591.

Audience: **g,l,u,f.**

Cleary, Richard L.   **NA9070 .C49 1998**
The Place Royale and Urban Design in the Ancien Régime.
Trade Cloth. Cambridge University Press. New York, NY. 1998.
320p. ISBN:0-521-57268-1, ISBN13: 978-0-521-57268-2.
Dewey:711/.55. LCCN:98-003572.

Audience: **l,u,f.** *Choice, 2000.*

Duany, Andres (Editor)   **NA9030**
The New Civic Art: Elements of Town Planning. Stefanos
Polyzoides & Rocco Ceo (Contribution by). Trade Cloth. Rizzoli
International Publications, Inc. New York, NY. 2003. 384p.
ISBN:0-8478-2186-2, ISBN13: 978-0-8478-2186-0.
Dewey:711.4. LCCN:00-101283.

Audience: **l,u,f.** *Choice, 2004.*

Escobar, Jesus   **NA9072.M33P563 2003**
The Plaza Mayor and the Shaping of Baroque Madrid. Trade
Cloth. Cambridge University Press. New York, NY. 2003. 376p.
ISBN:0-521-81507-X, ISBN13: 978-0-521-81507-9.
Dewey:711/.4/094641. LCCN:2002-041459.

Audience: **l,u,f.** *Choice, 2004.*

Gause, Jo Allen   HT169.55
Great Planned Communities. Alexander Garvin (Introduction by). Trade Cloth. Urban Land Institute. Washington, DC. 2002. 280p. ISBN:0-87420-892-0, ISBN13: 978-0-87420-892-4. Dewey:711.4/0973.
                                        Audience: **g,l,u,f.**

Gillespie, Angus K.   NA6233.N5W674 1999
Twin Towers: The Life of New York City's World Trade Center. Trade Cloth. Rutgers University Press. Piscataway, NJ. 1999. 288p. ISBN:0-8135-2742-2, ISBN13: 978-0-8135-2742-0. Dewey:725/.23/097471. LCCN:99-015068.
                            Audience: **g,l,u,f.** *Choice, 2000.*

Girling, Cynthia L. &   HT166
  Helphand, Kenneth I.
Yard, Street, Park: The Design of Suburban Open Space. Ed. 1. Trade Paper. John Wiley & Sons, Inc. Hoboken, NJ. 1996. 256p. Professional Ser. ISBN:0-471-17844-6, ISBN13: 978-0-471-17844-6. Dewey:307.1/214/0973. LCCN:93-049454.
                                        Audience: **l,u,f.**

Goldberger, Paul   NA6233.N5
Up from Zero: Politics, Architecture, and the Rebuilding of New York. Trade Paper. Random House Adult Trade Publishing Group. New York, NY. 2005. 320p. ISBN:0-8129-6795-X, ISBN13: 978-0-8129-6795-1. Dewey:725/.23/097471.
                                        Audience: **g,l,u,f.**

Habel, Dorothy   NA9204.R7M46 2002
The Urban Development of Rome in the Age of Alexander VII. Trade Cloth. Cambridge University Press. New York, NY. 2002. 446p. ISBN:0-521-77264-8, ISBN13: 978-0-521-77264-8. Dewey:711/.4/0945632. LCCN:2001-037675.
                            Audience: **g,l,u,f.** *Choice, 2003.*

Hall, Kenneth B. &   HT167.H29 2001
  Porterfield, Gerald A.
Community by Design: New Urbanism for Suburbs and Small Communities. Cloth Text. McGraw-Hill Professional Publishing. New York, NY. 2001. 296p. ISBN:0-07-134523-X, ISBN13: 978-0-07-134523-1. Dewey:307.1/216/0973. LCCN:00-050049.
                                        Audience: **g,l,u,f.**

Jakle, John A. & Sculle,   TL175.J34 2004
  Keith A.
Lots of Parking: Land Use in a Car Culture. Trade Cloth. University Press of Virginia. Charlottesville, VA. 2004. 288p. ISBN:0-8139-2266-6, ISBN13: 978-0-8139-2266-9. Dewey:711/.73. LCCN:2003-021181.
                            Audience: **g,l,u,f.** *Choice, 2005.*

Koolhaas, Rem   NA735.N5K66 1994
Delirious New York: A Retroactive Manifesto for Manhattan. Trade Paper. Monacelli Press, Inc. New York, NY. 1997. 320p. ISBN:1-885254-00-8, ISBN13: 978-1-885254-00-9. Dewey:720/.9747/1. LCCN:94-076577.
                                        Audience: **l,u,f.**

Koolhaas, Rem & Mau,   NA1153.K64S63 1995
  Bruce
S, M, L, XL: Small, Medium, Large, Extra Large. Jennifer

Sigler (Editor), Hans Werlemann (Photographer). Trade Cloth. Monacelli Press, Inc. New York, NY. 1995. 1376p. ISBN:1-885254-01-6, ISBN13: 978-1-885254-01-6. Dewey:720.7. LCCN:94-076578.
                                        Audience: **g,l,u,f.**

Kostof, Spiro   HT111.K6251992
The City Assembled: The Elements of Urban Form Through History. Richard Tobias (Illustrator). Trade Cloth. Little Brown & Company. New York, NY. 1992. 320p. ISBN:0-8212-1930-8, ISBN13: 978-0-8212-1930-0. Dewey:711.4. LCCN:92-053424.
                                        Audience: **l,u,f.**

Leccese, Michael &   HT334.U5C4782000
  McCormick, Kathleen (Editors)
Charter of the New Urbanism. Paper Text. McGraw-Hill Professional Publishing. New York, NY. 1999. 320p. ISBN:0-07-135553-7, ISBN13: 978-0-07-135553-7. Dewey:307.76/0973. LCCN:99-051560.
                                        Audience: **l,u,f.**

LeGates, Richard T. &   HT151.C586 2003
  Stout, Frederic (Editors)
The City Reader. Ed. 3. Trade Paper. Routledge. New York, NY. 2003. 592p. Routledge Urban Readers Ser. ISBN:0-415-27173-8, ISBN13: 978-0-415-27173-8. Dewey:307.76. LCCN:2003-002134.
                                        Audience: **g,l,u,f.**

Levy, John M.   HT167.L38 2006
Contemporary Urban Planning. Ed. 7. Trade Paper, Perfect. Prentice Hall PTR. Upper Saddle River, NJ. 2005. 370p. ISBN:0-13-193068-0, ISBN13: 978-0-13-193068-1. Dewey:307.1/216/0973. LCCN:2005-018793.
                                        Audience: **g,l,u,f.**

Nobel, Philip   NA6233.N5W674882005
Sixteen Acres: Architecture and the Outrageous Struggle for the Future of Ground Zero. Metropolitan Books, Henry Holt and Co.. 2005. ISBN:0-8050-7494-5, ISBN13: 978-0-8050-7494-9.
                                        Audience: **g,l,u,f.**

Perlman, Dan L. & Milder,   GF75.P47 2004
  Jeffrey C.
Practical Ecology for Planners, Developers, and Citizens. Lincoln Institute of Land Policy Staff (Other Primary Creator). Trade Cloth. Island Press. Washington, DC. 2004. 328p. ISBN:1-55963-634-3, ISBN13: 978-1-55963-634-6. Dewey:304.2. LCCN:2004-012441.
                                        Audience: **g,l,u,f.**

Peterson, Jon A.   HT167.P47 2003
The Birth of City Planning in the United States: 1840-1917. Trade Cloth. Johns Hopkins University Press. Baltimore, MD. 2003. 464p. Creating the North American Landscape Ser. ISBN:0-8018-7210-3, ISBN13: 978-0-8018-7210-5. Dewey:307.76/0973. LCCN:2002-009870.
                            Audience: **l,u,f.** *Choice, 2004.*

Stein, Jay M. (Editor)   HT167.C565 2004
Classic Readings in Urban Planning. Ed. 2. Paper Text.

American Planning Association. Chicago, IL. 2004. 432p.
ISBN:1-884829-90-2, ISBN13: 978-1-884829-90-1.
Dewey:307.1/216/0973. LCCN:2003-115360.

Audience: **l,u,f.**

Tasman, Dan   **HT166**
☐ Cyburbia ; the Planning Portal.
http://www.cyburbia.org/

Audience: **g,l,u,f.**

Watson, Donald, et al.   **HT166.T47 2002**
Time-Saver Standards for Urban Design. Alan J. Plattus &
Robert G. Shibley (Authors). Trade Cloth. McGraw-Hill
Professional Publishing. New York, NY. 2003. 960p. Time-Saver
Standards Ser. ISBN:0-07-068507-X, ISBN13:
978-0-07-068507-9. Dewey:307.1/2. LCCN:2002-038067.

Audience: **l,u,f.**

Interior Design and Decoration > Reference Works > Bibliographies and Research Guides

NA1.A12
☐ Avery Index to Architectural Periodicals.
http://www.getty.edu/research/conducting_research/avery_index/
Getty Research Institute.

Audience: **g,l,u,f.**

Interior Design and Decoration > Reference Works > Dictionaries and Encyclopedias

Atterbury, Paul & Batkin, Maureen   **NK4210.M55A88 1998**
The Dictionary of Minton. Ed. 2. Trade Cloth. Antique
Collectors' Club. Easthampton, MA. 1999. 368p.
ISBN:1-85149-272-0, ISBN13: 978-1-85149-272-5.
Dewey:738/.09424/63. LCCN:00-302596.

Audience: **g,l,u,f.**

Coysh, A. W. & Henrywood, R. K.   **NK4277**
The Dictionary of Blue and White Printed Pottery, 1780-1880.
Trade Cloth. Antique Collectors' Club. Easthampton, MA. 1982.
424p. ISBN:0-907462-06-5, ISBN13: 978-0-907462-06-4.
Dewey:738.3/7. LCCN:81-195375.

Audience: **g,l,u,f.**

Hiesinger, Kathryn B. & Marcus, George H.   **NK30.H56 1997**
Antiquespeak: A Guide to the Styles, Techniques and Materials
of the Decorative Arts from the Renaissance to Art Deco. Trade
Cloth. Abbeville Press, Inc. New York, NY. 1997. 224p.
ISBN:0-7892-0337-5, ISBN13: 978-0-7892-0337-3.
Dewey:745.1/03. LCCN:97-010513.

Audience: **g,l,u,f.**

Kane, Patricia E.   **ND237.E15C66 1996**
Colonial Massachusetts Silversmiths and Jewelers: A
Biographical Dictionary Based on the Notes of Francis Hill
Bigelow and John Marshall Phillips. Library Binding. University
Press of New England. Lebanon, NH. 1998. 1265p.
ISBN:0-89467-077-8, ISBN13: 978-0-89467-077-0.
Dewey:759.13. LCCN:97-029813.

Audience: **g,l,u,f.**

Kaplan, Wendy   **NK805**
The Encyclopedia of Arts and Crafts. Trade Paper.
Knickerbocker Press. Edison, NJ. 1998. 192p.
ISBN:1-57715-048-1, ISBN13: 978-1-57715-048-0.
Dewey:745/.09.

Audience: **g,l,u,f.**

Kowalsky, Arnold A. & Kowalsky, Dorothy E.   **NK4007.K69 1999**
Encyclopedia of American, English, and European Earthenware,
Ironstone, Stoneware, 1780-1980: Makers, Marks, and Patterns
in Blue and White, Historic Blue, Flow Blue, Mulberry,
Romantic Transferware, Tea Leaf, and White Ironstone. Saddle
Stitched, Cloth over Boards, Dust Jacket. Schiffer Publishing,
Ltd. Atglen, PA. 1999. 688p. A Schiffer Book for Collectors Ser.
ISBN:0-7643-0731-2, ISBN13: 978-0-7643-0731-7.
Dewey:738.09034. LCCN:99-026188.

Audience: **g,l,u,f.**

Rickards, Maurice   **NC1280.R52 2000**
Encyclopedia of Ephemera: A Guide to the Fragmentary
Documents of Everyday Life for the Collector, Curator and
Historian. Michael Twyman (Editor). Trade Cloth. Routledge.
New York, NY. 2000. 416p. ISBN:0-415-92648-3, ISBN13:
978-0-415-92648-5. Dewey:769.5/03. LCCN:00-062569.

Audience: **g,l,u,f.** *Choice, 2001.*

Sandon, John   **NK4395.S15 1993**
The Dictionary of Worcester Porcelain, 1751-1851, Vol. 1. Trade
Cloth. Antique Collectors' Club. Easthampton, MA. 1993. 384p.
ISBN:1-85149-156-2, ISBN13: 978-1-85149-156-8.
Dewey:738.2/09424/48. LCCN:93-226655.

Audience: **g,l,u,f.**

Speel, Erika   **NK4998.5.S6 1998**
Dictionary of Enamelling. Trade Cloth. Ashgate Publishing, Ltd.
Aldershot, 1998. 288p. ISBN:1-85928-272-5, ISBN13:
978-1-85928-272-4. Dewey:738.4. LCCN:97-023088.

Audience: **g,l,u,f.** *Choice, 1998.*

Trench, Lucy (Editor)   **NK30.M38 2000**
Materials and Techniques in the Decorative Arts: An Illustrated
Dictionary. Trade Cloth. University of Chicago Press. Chicago,
IL. 2000. 576p. ISBN:0-226-81200-6, ISBN13:
978-0-226-81200-7. Dewey:745/.028. LCCN:00-029865.

Audience: **g,l,u,f.** *Choice, 2001.*

Interior Design and Decoration > Histories and Handbooks

Blakemore, Robbie G.   **NK1710.B57 2005**
History of Interior Design and Furniture: From Ancient Egypt to Nineteenth-Century Europe. Ed. 2. Trade Cloth. John Wiley & Sons, Inc. Hoboken, NJ. 2005. 448p. ISBN:0-471-46433-3, ISBN13: 978-0-471-46433-4. Dewey:747/.09. LCCN:2004-063824.
Audience: **g,l,u,f.**

Gray, Susan Kimberly   **NK1980.G73 2003**
Designers on Designers. Trade Cloth. McGraw-Hill Professional Publishing. New York, NY. 2003. 240p. ISBN:0-07-142160-2, ISBN13: 978-0-07-142160-7. Dewey:747. LCCN:2003-056211.
Audience: **g,l,u,f.**

Pile, John   **NK1710.P55 2004**
A History of Interior Design. Ed. 2. Trade Cloth. John Wiley & Sons, Inc. Hoboken, NJ. 2004. 464p. ISBN:0-471-46434-1, ISBN13: 978-0-471-46434-1. Dewey:747/.09. LCCN:2004-009411.
Audience: **g,l,u,f.**

Interior Design and Decoration > Histories and Handbooks > Periods and Styles

Bony, Anne   **NK2399**
Furniture and Interiors of the 1960s. Trade Cloth, Pictures or Photographs. Flammarion et Cie. Paris, 2004. 240p. ISBN:2-08-030446-1, ISBN13: 978-2-08-030446-9. Dewey:749/.09046.
Audience: **g,l,u,f.**

Bony, Anne   **NK1980**
Furniture and Interiors of the 1940s. Eric Philippe (Preface by). Trade Cloth. Flammarion et Cie. Paris, 2003. 240p. ISBN:2-08-011158-2, ISBN13: 978-2-08-011158-6. Dewey:747.2/049.
Audience: **g,l,u,f.**

Cornforth, John   **NK2043.A1C67 2004**
Early Georgian Interiors. Cloth over Boards. Yale University Press. Cumberland, RI. 2005. 372p. Paul Mellon Centre for Studies in British Art ISBN:0-300-10330-1, ISBN13: 978-0-300-10330-4. Dewey:747/.0942/09033. LCCN:2004-002599.
Audience: **g,l,u,f.** *Choice, 2005.*

Cumming, Elizabeth &   **NK1140.C85 1991**
Kaplan, Wendy
The Arts and Crafts Movement. Trade Paper. Thames & Hudson. New York, NY. 1991. 216p. World of Art Ser. ISBN:0-500-20248-6, ISBN13: 978-0-500-20248-7. Dewey:745/.09034. LCCN:90-070199.
Audience: **g,l,u,f.**

Fiell, Charlotte & Fiell,   **NK1390**
Peter
Decorative Art 1970s. Trade Paper. Taschen America, LLC. Los Angeles, CA. 2000. 576p. Architecture and Design Ser. ISBN:3-8228-6406-4, ISBN13: 978-3-8228-6406-7. Dewey:745.4/442.
Audience: **g,l,u,f.**

Fiell, Charlotte & Fiell,   **NK1390**
Peter
Decorative Art, 1950's. Trade Paper. Taschen America, LLC. Los Angeles, CA. 2000. 576p. Architecture and Design Ser. ISBN:3-8228-6619-9, ISBN13: 978-3-8228-6619-1. Dewey:745.4/442.
Audience: **g,l,f.**

Fiell, Charlotte & Fiell,   **NK1390**
Peter
Decorative Art, 1960's. Trade Paper. Taschen America, LLC. Los Angeles, CA. 2000. 576p. Architecture and Design Ser. ISBN:3-8228-6405-6, ISBN13: 978-3-8228-6405-0. Dewey:745.4/442.
Audience: **g,l,u,f.**

Fiell, Charlotte & Fiell,   **NK1390**
Peter
Decorative Arts 1900s-1910s. Trade Paper. Taschen America, LLC. Los Angeles, CA. 2000. 576p. Architecture and Design Ser. ISBN:3-8228-6050-6, ISBN13: 978-3-8228-6050-2. Dewey:745.4/442.
Audience: **g,l,f.**

Fiell, Charlotte & Fiell,   **NK1390**
Peter
Decorative Arts, 1920s. Trade Paper. Taschen America, LLC. Los Angeles, CA. 2000. 576p. Architecture and Design Ser. ISBN:3-8228-6051-4, ISBN13: 978-3-8228-6051-9. Dewey:745.4/442.
Audience: **g,l,u,f.**

Fiell, Charlotte & Fiell,   **NK1390**
Peter
Decorative Arts, 1930s-1940s. Trade Paper. Taschen America, LLC. Los Angeles, CA. 2000. 576p. Architecture and Design Ser. ISBN:3-8228-6052-2, ISBN13: 978-3-8228-6052-6. Dewey:745.4/442.
Audience: **g,l,u,f.**

Gere, Charlotte   **NK2043.G451989**
Nineteenth-Century Decoration: The Art of the Interior. Trade Cloth. Harry N. Abrams, Inc. New York, NY. 1989. 384p. ISBN:0-8109-1382-8, ISBN13: 978-0-8109-1382-0. Dewey:747.2/048. LCCN:89-000158.
Audience: **g,l,u,f.** *Choice, 1989.*

Greenhalgh, Paul   **NK775.5.A7A7852000**
Art Nouveau, 1890-1914. Trade Cloth. Harry N. Abrams, Inc. New York, NY. 2000. 496p. ISBN:0-8109-4219-4, ISBN13: 978-0-8109-4219-6. Dewey:709/.0349. LCCN:00-028027.
Audience: **g,l,u,f.** *Choice, 2001.*

Massey, Anne   NK1980.M3 2001
Interior Design in the 20th Century. Ed. 2. Trade Paper. Thames & Hudson. New York, NY. 2001. 224p. World of Art Ser. ISBN:0-500-20346-6, ISBN13: 978-0-500-20346-0. Dewey:747.2/049. LCCN:2001-087250.
                                Audience: **g,l,u,f.**

Morley, John   NK1355.M651993
Regency Design, 1790-1840: Gardens, Buildings, Interiors, Furniture. Trade Cloth. Harry N. Abrams, Inc. New York, NY. 1993. 448p. ISBN:0-8109-3768-9, ISBN13: 978-0-8109-3768-0. Dewey:709.033. LCCN:92-028364.
                            Audience: **g,l,u,f.** *Choice, 1993.*

Trapp, Kenneth R. (Editor)   NK1141.A78 1993
The Arts and Crafts Movement in California: Living the Good Life. Leslie G. Bowman (Contribution by). Trade Cloth. Abbeville Press, Inc. New York, NY. 1993. 328p. ISBN:1-55859-393-4, ISBN13: 978-1-55859-393-0. Dewey:745.09794. LCCN:92-028352.
                            Audience: **g,l,u,f.** *Choice, 1993.*

Weisman, Leslie K.   NA2543.W65
Discrimination by Design: A Feminist Critique of the Man-Made Environment. Trade Paper. University of Illinois Press. Champaign, IL. 1994. 200p. ISBN:0-252-06399-6, ISBN13: 978-0-252-06399-2. Dewey:720/.82.
                            Audience: **u,f.** *Choice, 1992.*

Interior Design and Decoration > Histories and Handbooks > Cultures, Regions, Nationalities

Aav, Marianne &   NK1471.F5
  Stritzler-Levine, Nina (Editors)
Finnish Modern Design: Utopian Ideals and Everyday Realities, 1930-97. Trade Paper. Yale University Press. Cumberland, RI. 2000. 412p. ISBN:0-300-08280-0, ISBN13: 978-0-300-08280-7. Dewey:745.4/494897/0747471.
                            Audience: **g,l,u,f.** *Choice, 1998.*

Ayres, James   NK2043
Domestic Interiors: The British Tradition 1500-1850. Ed. 2. Cloth over Boards. Yale University Press. Cumberland, RI. 2003. 272p. ISBN:0-300-08445-5, ISBN13: 978-0-300-08445-0. Dewey:728/.37/0941. LCCN:2003-005824.
                            Audience: **g,l,u,f.** *Choice, 2004.*

Cooper, Wendy   NK805.C678 2002
An American Vision: Henry Francis du Pont's Winterthur Museum. Trade Cloth. Ashgate Publishing, Ltd. Aldershot, 2002. 240p. ISBN:0-85331-859-X, ISBN13: 978-0-85331-859-0. Dewey:745/.0973/0747511. LCCN:2002-022114.
                            Audience: **g,l,u,f.** *Choice, 2002.*

Fehervari, Geza   NK3880 .F44
Ceramics of the Islamic World. Cloth over Boards. I. B. Tauris & Company, Ltd. London, 2000. 448p. ISBN:1-86064-430-9, ISBN13: 978-1-86064-430-6. Dewey:738.09176710745367.
                            Audience: **g,l,u,f.** *Choice, 2000.*

Fischer, Joseph   NK1060.J3F57 1994
The Folk Art of Java. Cloth Text. Oxford University Press, Inc. New York, NY. 1995. 152p. The Asia Collection ISBN:967-65-3041-7, ISBN13: 978-967-65-3041-7. Dewey:745/.09598/2. LCCN:94-000909.
                            Audience: **g,l,u,f.** *Choice, 1995.*

Harrod, Tanya   NK928.H375 1999
The Crafts in Britain in the Twentieth Century. Cloth over Boards. Yale University Press. Cumberland, RI. 1999. 496p. ISBN:0-300-07780-7, ISBN13: 978-0-300-07780-3. Dewey:745/.0941/0904. LCCN:98-045805.
                            Audience: **g,l,u,f.** *Choice, 2000.*

Hollander, Stacy C. &   NK805.A6442001
  Anderson, Brook Davis
American Anthem: Masterworks from the American Folk Art Museum. John Parnell & Gavin Ashworth (Photographers), American Folk Art Museum Staff & Lee Kogan (Contribution by). Trade Cloth. Harry N. Abrams, Inc. New York, NY. 2002. 431p. ISBN:0-8109-6740-5, ISBN13: 978-0-8109-6740-3. Dewey:745/.0973/0747471. LCCN:2001-027922.
                         Audience: **g,l,u,f.** *Choice, 2003, 2002.*

Krill, Rosemary Troy &   NK806.K75 2001
  Eversmann, Pauline K.
Early American Decorative Arts, 1620-1860: A Handbook for Interpreters. Trade Paper. AltaMira Press. Walnut Creek, CA. 2000. 320p. American Association for State and Local History Book Ser. ISBN:0-7425-0314-3, ISBN13: 978-0-7425-0314-4. Dewey:745/.0973. LCCN:00-036219.
                            Audience: **l,u,f.**

Lane, Terrance & Serk,   NK2090.A1.L36 1990
  Jessie
Australians at Home: A Documentary History of Australian Domestic Interiors from 1788-1914. Trade Cloth. Oxford University Press, Inc. New York, NY. 1991. 464p. ISBN:0-19-553128-0, ISBN13: 978-0-19-553128-2. Dewey:747.2994. LCCN:91-162858.
                            Audience: **g,l,u,f.** *Choice, 1991.*

Lubbock, Jules   NK1443.A1L8 1995
The Tyranny of Taste: The Politics of Architecture and Design in Britain, 1550-1960. Cloth over Boards. Yale University Press. Cumberland, RI. 1995. 430p. Paul Mellon Centre for Studies in British Art ISBN:0-300-05889-6, ISBN13: 978-0-300-05889-5. Dewey:720/.1/030942. LCCN:94-026853.
                            Audience: **u,f.** *Choice, 1995.*

Phillips, Betty Lou   NK2003.P53 2002
Villa Decor: Distinctively French and Italian Style. Ed. 4. Trade Cloth. Gibbs Smith, Publisher. Layton, UT. 2002. 160p. ISBN:1-58685-174-8, ISBN13: 978-1-58685-174-3. Dewey:747.213. LCCN:2002-007224.
                            Audience: **g,l,u,f.**

Ramljak, Suzanne   NK808.P495 2002
Crafting a Legacy: Contemporary American Crafts at the Philadelphia Museum of Art. Darrel Sewell (Introduction by), Philadelphia Museum of Art Staff (Contribution by). Trade

Cloth. Rutgers University Press. Piscataway, NJ. 2002. 196p.
ISBN:0-8135-3203-5, ISBN13: 978-0-8135-3203-5.
Dewey:745.5/0973/07474811. LCCN:2002-072705.
Audience: **g,l,u,f.** *Choice, 2003.*

Shifman, Barry & Walton,   NK512.I53G542001
Guy
Gifts to the Tzars 1500-1700: Treasures from the Kremlin. Trade
Cloth. Harry N. Abrams, Inc. New York, NY. 2001. 336p.
ISBN:0-8109-0600-7, ISBN13: 978-0-8109-0600-6.
Dewey:745.0940744731. LCCN:2001-022185.
Audience: **g,l,u,f.**

Snodin, Michael & Styles,   NK928.S632001
John
Design and the Decorative Arts: Britain 1500-1900. Christopher
Wilk (Foreword by). Trade Cloth. Harry N. Abrams, Inc. New
York, NY. 2001. 488p. ISBN:0-8109-6586-0, ISBN13:
978-0-8109-6586-7. Dewey:745.4/0941/07442134.
LCCN:2001-088704.
Audience: **l,u,f.** *Choice, 2002.*

Troy, Nancy J.   NK947.T76 1991
Modernism and the Decorative Arts in France: Art Nouveau to
le Corbusier. Cloth over Boards. Yale University Press.
Cumberland, RI. 1991. 336p. Yale Publications in the History of
Art Ser. ISBN:0-300-04554-9, ISBN13: 978-0-300-04554-3.
Dewey:745/.0944/09041. LCCN:90-040881.
Audience: **g,l,u,f.** *Choice, 1991.*

Wainwright, Clive   NK2043.A1W35 1989
Romantic Interior: The British Collector at Home, 1750-1850.
Cloth over Boards. Yale University Press. Cumberland, RI.
1989. 288p. Paul Mellon Centre for Studies in British Art
ISBN:0-300-04225-6, ISBN13: 978-0-300-04225-2.
Dewey:747/.888/094109033. LCCN:89-033705.
Audience: **g,l,u,f.** *Choice, 1990.*

Warren, David B. &   NK805.A675 1998
Museum of Fine Arts Staff
American Decorative Arts and Paintings in the Bayou Bend
Collection. Cloth Text. Princeton University Press. Princeton,
NJ. 1998. 520p. ISBN:0-691-05962-4, ISBN13:
978-0-691-05962-4. Dewey:709.730747641411.
LCCN:98-017179.
Audience: **g,l,u,f.** *Choice, 1999.*

Watson, Oliver   NK3880
Ceramics from Islamic Lands. Trade Cloth. Thames & Hudson.
New York, NY. 2004. 512p. ISBN:0-500-97629-5, ISBN13:
978-0-500-97629-6. Dewey:738.30917671. LCCN:2003-101345.
Audience: **l,u,f.** *Choice, 2004.*

White, Bruce   NK2438.W37M66 2000
(Photographer)
The White House: Its Historic Furnishings and First Families.
Betty C. Monkman (Text by), Wendell Garrett (Introduction by).
Trade Cloth. Abbeville Press, Inc. New York, NY. 2000. 320p.
ISBN:0-7892-0624-2, ISBN13: 978-0-7892-0624-4.
Dewey:917.5304/41. LCCN:00-027085.
Audience: **g,l,u,f.** *Choice, 2001.*

Zygulski, Zdzislaw Jr.   NK1011.Z94 1991
Ottoman Art in the Service of Empire. Trade Cloth. New York
University Press. New York, NY. 1991. 192p. Hagop Kevorkian
Series on Near Eastern Art and Civilization
ISBN:0-8147-9671-0, ISBN13: 978-0-8147-9671-9.
Dewey:745/.09561. LCCN:91-004446.
Audience: **g,l,u,f.** *Choice, 1992.*

Interior Design and Decoration > Histories and Handbooks > Types of Project

Susanka, Sarah &   NA7125.S87 1998
Obolensky, Kira
The Not So Big House: A Blueprint for the Way We Really
Live. Trade Cloth. Taunton Press, Inc. Newtown, CT. 1998.
208p. ISBN:1-56158-130-5, ISBN13: 978-1-56158-130-6.
Dewey:728/.37. LCCN:98-023080.
Audience: **g,l,u,f.**

Interior Design and Decoration > Histories and Handbooks > General Works

Piotrowski, Christine M.   NK2116.2.P57 2002
The Professional Practice for Interior Designers. Ed. 3. Trade
Cloth. John Wiley & Sons, Inc. Hoboken, NJ. 2001. 672p.
ISBN:0-471-38401-1, ISBN13: 978-0-471-38401-4.
Dewey:729/.068. LCCN:2001-022370.
Audience: **u,f.**

Interior Design and Decoration > Individual Designers

Berry, John D.   TT196
Herman Miller: The Purpose of Design. Trade Cloth. Rizzoli
International Publications, Inc. New York, NY. 2004. 272p.
ISBN:0-8478-2654-6, ISBN13: 978-0-8478-2654-4.
Dewey:745.4.
Audience: **g,l,u,f.** *Choice, 2005.*

Bradford, Peter   NK2439.Z64B73 2000
The Design Art of Nicos Zographos. George Lois (Introduction
by). Trade Cloth. Monacelli Press, Inc. New York, NY. 2000.
208p. ISBN:1-58093-066-2, ISBN13: 978-1-58093-066-6.
Dewey:749.213. LCCN:00-023794.
Audience: **g,l,u,f.** *Choice, 2001.*

Brush, Daniel, et al.   NK7198.B75D361998
Daniel Brush Gold Without Boundaries. Donald B. Kuspit &
Ralph Esmerian (Authors). Trade Cloth. Harry N. Abrams, Inc.
New York, NY. 1998. 276p. ISBN:0-8109-4018-3, ISBN13:
978-0-8109-4018-5. Dewey:739.2/272. LCCN:97-051377.
Audience: **g,l,u,f.** *Choice, 1999.*

Delaporte, Gillemette　　　　　　　　**NK1535.J33**
Rene Herbst: Pioneer of Modernism. Trade Cloth. Flammarion
et Cie. Paris, 2004. 224p. ISBN:2-08-010892-1, ISBN13:
978-2-08-010892-0. Dewey:749/.092.
　　　　　　　　　　　　　　　Audience: **g,l,u,f.**

Delaporte-Idrissi,　　　　　　　　　　**NK2550**
　Guillemette
René Herbst: Pioneer of Modernism. Trade Cloth. Flammarion
et Cie. Paris, 2004. 224p. ISBN:2-08-030467-4, ISBN13:
978-2-08-030467-4. Dewey:749/.092.
　　　　　　　　　　　Audience: **g,l,u,f.** *Choice, 2005.*

Denenberg, Thomas Andrew　　　**NK2439.N87D46 2003**
Wallace Nutting and the Invention of Old America. Cloth over
Boards. Yale University Press. Cumberland, RI. 2003. 240p.
ISBN:0-300-09683-6, ISBN13: 978-0-300-09683-5.
Dewey:770/.92 B. LCCN:2002-014448.
　　　　　　　　　　　Audience: **g,l,u,f.** *Choice, 2003.*

Dolan, Brian　　　　　　　　　**NK4210.W4D65 2004**
Wedgwood: The First Tycoon. Trade Cloth. Penguin Group
(USA) Inc. New York, NY. 2004. 416p. ISBN:0-670-03346-4,
ISBN13: 978-0-670-03346-1. Dewey:338.7/665/092 B.
LCCN:2004-049633.
　　　　　　　　　　　　　　　Audience: **g,l,u,f.**

Jackson, Lesley　　　　　　　　　**NK1447.6.D39**
Robin and Lucienne Day: Pioneers of Modern Design. Trade
Cloth. Princeton Architectural Press. New York, NY. 2001. 192p.
ISBN:1-56898-271-2, ISBN13: 978-1-56898-271-7. Dewey:709.
　　　　　　　　　　　Audience: **g,l,u,f.** *Choice, 2001.*

Kenny, Peter M., et al.　　　　　**NK2439.L24A41998**
Honoré Lannuier, Cabinet Maker from Paris: The Life and Work
of a French Ebeniste in Federal New York. Charles H. Lannuier,
Frances F. Bretter, Metropolitan Museum of Art Staff & Ulrich
Leben (Authors). Trade Cloth. Harry N. Abrams, Inc. New York,
NY. 1998. 340p. ISBN:0-8109-6517-8, ISBN13:
978-0-8109-6517-1. Dewey:749.213. LCCN:97-039012.
　　　　　　　　　　　Audience: **g,l,u,f.** *Choice, 1999.*

Kuspit, Donald B.　　　　　　　**NK5198.C43K871997**
Chihuly. Ed. 2. Trade Cloth. Harry N. Abrams, Inc. New York,
NY. 1999. 368p. ISBN:0-8109-6373-6, ISBN13:
978-0-8109-6373-3. Dewey:748/.092. LCCN:98-228833.
　　　　　　　　　　　　　　　Audience: **g,l,u,f.**

Lewis, Adam　　　　　　　　　**NK2004.3.H33L49 2005**
Albert Hadley: The Story of America's Preeminent Interior
Designer. Saddle Stitched, Cloth over Boards, Dust Jacket.
Rizzoli International Publications, Inc. New York, NY. 2005.
271p. ISBN:0-8478-2742-9, ISBN13: 978-0-8478-2742-8.
Dewey:747/.092 B. LCCN:2005-007724.
　　　　　　　　　　　　　　　Audience: **g,l,u,f.**

Loring, John　　　　　　　　　**NK839.T53A42002**
Louis Comfort Tiffany at Tiffany and Co. Trade Cloth. Harry N.
Abrams, Inc. New York, NY. 2002. 256p. ISBN:0-8109-3288-1,
ISBN13: 978-0-8109-3288-3. Dewey:709/.2.
LCCN:2002-005145.
　　　　　　　　　　　Audience: **g,l,u,f.** *Choice, 2003.*

Makinson, Randell & Heinz,　　　　　**NA737.G7**
　Thomas
Greene and Greene: Creating a Style. Trade Cloth. Gibbs Smith,
Publisher. Layton, UT. 2004. 96p. ISBN:1-58685-116-0,
ISBN13: 978-1-58685-116-3. Dewey:728/.370922794.
LCCN:2004-107724.
　　　　　　　　　　　　　　　Audience: **g,l,u,f.**

Marston, Gwen　　　　　　　**NK9198.S33M368 2004**
Mary Schafer, American Quilt Maker. Trade Cloth. University of
Michigan Press. Chicago, IL. 2004. 240p. ISBN:0-472-09855-1,
ISBN13: 978-0-472-09855-2. Dewey:746.46/092 B.
LCCN:2003-018071.
　　　　　　　　　　　Audience: **g,l,u,f.** *Choice, 2005.*

McLeod, Mary & Aujame,　　　**NK2049.Z9P47332003**
　Roger
Charlotte Perriand: An Art of Living. Trade Cloth. Harry N.
Abrams, Inc. New York, NY. 2003. 304p. ISBN:0-8109-4503-7,
ISBN13: 978-0-8109-4503-6. Dewey:747.2.
LCCN:2002-151490.
　　　　　　　　　　　Audience: **g,l,u,f.** *Choice, 2004.*

Menz, Christopher　　　　　　**NK1447.6.M6A4 2002**
Morris and Co. Trade Cloth. Art Gallery of South Australia.
Adelaide, SA. 2004. 188p. Ser. ISBN:0-7308-3029-2, ISBN13:
978-0-7308-3029-0. Dewey:745/.0942/07494231.
LCCN:2003-427404.
　　　　　　　　　　　　　　　Audience: **g,l,u,f.**

Parry, Linda　　　　　　　　　**NK1535.M67.A41996**
William Morris. Trade Cloth. Harry N. Abrams, Inc. New York,
NY. 1996. 394p. ISBN:0-8109-4282-8, ISBN13:
978-0-8109-4282-0. Dewey:709.2. LCCN:95-051845.
　　　　　　　　　　　　　　　Audience: **g,l,u,f.**

Salny, S. M.　　　　　　　　　**NK2004.3.E54A4 2005**
Frances Elkins - Interior Design. Trade Cloth. W. W. Norton &
Company, Inc. New York, NY. 2005. 192p.
ISBN:0-393-73146-4, ISBN13: 978-0-393-73146-0.
Dewey:747/.092. LCCN:2004-063597.
　　　　　　　　　　　Audience: **g,l,u,f.** *Choice, 2005.*

Soros, Susan W.　　　　　　　**NK2542.G64A41999**
Secular Furniture of E. W. Godwin: With Catalogue Raisonné.
Cloth over Boards. Yale University Press. Cumberland, RI.
1999. 300p. ISBN:0-300-08159-6, ISBN13: 978-0-300-08159-6.
Dewey:749.22. LCCN:99-033079.
　　　　　　　　　　　Audience: **g,l,u,f.** *Choice, 2000.*

Interior Design and Decoration >
Materials, Techniques, and Practices

Alderman, Robert L.　　　　　　**NK2116.2.A391997**
How to Prosper as an Interior Designer: A Business and Legal
Guide. Trade Cloth. John Wiley & Sons, Inc. Hoboken, NJ.
1997. 288p. ISBN:0-471-16223-X, ISBN13: 978-0-471-16223-0.
Dewey:729/.068. LCCN:96-043760.
　　　　　　　　　　　　　　　Audience: **g,l,u,f.**

Ander, Gregg D. NA2794.A53 2002
Daylighting Performance and Design. Ed. 2. Trade Cloth. John
Wiley & Sons, Inc. Hoboken, NJ. 2003. 335p.
ISBN:0-471-26299-4, ISBN13: 978-0-471-26299-2.
Dewey:729/.28. LCCN:2002-033187.
Audience: **l,u,f.**

DeChiara, Joseph, et al. NK2110.T48 2001
Time-Saver Standards for Interior Design and Space Planning.
Ed. 2. Julius Panero & Martin Zelnik (Authors). Trade Cloth.
McGraw-Hill Professional Publishing. New York, NY. 2001.
1689p. Time-Saver Standards Ser. ISBN:0-07-134616-3,
ISBN13: 978-0-07-134616-0. Dewey:729. LCCN:2001-030504.
Audience: **l,u,f.**

Goodwin, Elaine M. NA3750.G63 2004
Encyclopedia of Mosaics: Techniques, Materials and Designs.
Trade Cloth. Trafalgar Square. North Pomfret, VT. 2004. 192p.
ISBN:1-57076-266-X, ISBN13: 978-1-57076-266-6.
Dewey:751.48. LCCN:2003-110887.
Audience: **g,l,u,f.** *Choice, 2004.*

Gordon, Gary TK4188
Interior Lighting for Designers. Ed. 4. Gregory F. Day
(Illustrator). Trade Cloth. John Wiley & Sons, Inc. Hoboken, NJ.
2003. 304p. ISBN:0-471-44118-X, ISBN13: 978-0-471-44118-2.
Dewey:729/.28. LCCN:2002-152368.
Audience: **l,u,f.**

Knackstedt, Mary V. NK2002.K57 2001
The Interior Design Business Handbook: A Complete Guide to
Profitability. Ed. 3. Trade Cloth. John Wiley & Sons, Inc.
Hoboken, NJ. 2001. 416p. ISBN:0-471-41232-5, ISBN13:
978-0-471-41232-8. Dewey:729/.068. LCCN:2001-026894.
Audience: **u,f.**

McGowan, Maryrose TH2031 .I55
McGowan/Interior Graphic Standards and Interior Graphic
Standards, Set. CD-ROM, Trade Cloth, Mixed Media. John
Wiley & Sons, Inc. Hoboken, NJ. 2004. 720p.
ISBN:0-471-68033-8, ISBN13: 978-0-471-68033-8.
Dewey:721/.028/4.
Audience: **g,l,u,f.**

Rompilla, Ethel NK2115.5.C6R662005
Color for Interior Design. New York School of Interior Design
Staff (Contribution by). Trade Cloth. Harry N. Abrams, Inc.
New York, NY. 2005. 224p. ISBN:0-8109-5888-0, ISBN13:
978-0-8109-5888-3. Dewey:747/.94. LCCN:2004-021040.
Audience: **g,l,u,f.**

Steffy, Gary R. TH7703.S78 2002
Architectural Lighting Design. Ed. 2. Trade Cloth. John Wiley
& Sons, Inc. Hoboken, NJ. 2001. 288p. ISBN:0-471-38638-3,
ISBN13: 978-0-471-38638-4. Dewey:621.32.
LCCN:2001-023736.
Audience: **l,u,f.**

Trench, Lucy (Editor) NK30.M38 2000
Materials and Techniques in the Decorative Arts: An Illustrated
Dictionary. Trade Cloth. University of Chicago Press. Chicago,

IL. 2000. 576p. ISBN:0-226-81200-6, ISBN13:
978-0-226-81200-7. Dewey:745/.028. LCCN:00-029865.
Audience: **g,l,u,f.** *Choice, 2001.*

Whitehead, Randall TH7975.D8W49 2003
Residential Lighting: A Practical Guide. Trade Cloth. John
Wiley & Sons, Inc. Hoboken, NJ. 2003. 256p.
ISBN:0-471-45055-3, ISBN13: 978-0-471-45055-9.
Dewey:747/.92. LCCN:2003-019195.
Audience: **l,u,f.**

Interior Design and Decoration > Furniture > Histories and Handbooks

Adamson, Jeremy Elwell NK2439.M28A83 2001
The Furniture of Sam Maloof. Trade Cloth. W. W. Norton &
Company, Inc. New York, NY. 2001. 272p.
ISBN:0-393-73080-8, ISBN13: 978-0-393-73080-7.
Dewey:749.213 B. LCCN:2001-003691.
Audience: **g,l,u,f.** *Choice, 2002.*

Becksvoort, Christian NK2407
The Shaker Legacy: Perspectives on an Enduring Furniture
Style. UK-Trade Paper. Taunton Press, Inc. Newtown, CT. 2000.
240p. ISBN:1-56158-357-X, ISBN13: 978-1-56158-357-7.
Dewey:749.213/088/288.
Audience: **g,l,u,f.** *Choice, 1999.*

Bueno, Patricia NK2715.B84132004
Just Chairs: Over 600 Designs from Around the World. Trade
Paper. HarperCollins Publishers. New York, NY. 2004. 320p.
ISBN:0-06-059846-8, ISBN13: 978-0-06-059846-4.
Dewey:749/.32/0904. LCCN:2003-021260.
Audience: **g,l,u,f.**

Cooke, Edward S. Jr., et al. NK2408.C58
The Maker's Hand: American Studio Furniture 1940-1990.
Gerald W. R. Ward & Kelly H. L'Ecuyer (Authors), Pat Warner
(Contribution by). Trade Cloth. Museum of Fine Arts, Boston.
Boston, MA. 2004. 208p. ISBN:0-87846-662-2, ISBN13:
978-0-87846-662-7. Dewey:749/.0973/09045.
Audience: **g,l,u,f.** *Choice, 2004.*

D'Ambrosio, Anna Tobin NK2407.M86 1999
(Editor)
Masterpieces of American Furniture from the Munson-Williams-
Proctor Institute. Trade Cloth. Syracuse University Press.
Syracuse, NY. 1999. 171p. ISBN:0-8156-8127-5, ISBN13:
978-0-8156-8127-4. Dewey:749.213/09/034074747.
LCCN:98-045261.
Audience: **g,l,u,f.** *Choice, 2000.*

Edwards, Clive D. TS880.E39 1994
Twentieth-Century Furniture: Materials, Manufacture, and
Markets. Trade Cloth. Manchester University Press. Manchester,
1994. xii, 228p. Studies in Design and Material Culture
ISBN:0-7190-4066-3, ISBN13: 978-0-7190-4066-5.
Dewey:338.4/76841/00904. LCCN:93-044612.
Audience: **g,l,u,f.** *Choice, 1995.*

Ellison, Michael & Pina, Leslie A.   NK2579.A1E44 2002

Scandinavian Modern Furnishing, 1930-1970: Designed for Life. Trade Cloth. Schiffer Publishing, Ltd. Atglen, PA. 2001. 240p. A Schiffer Book for Designers and Collectors Ser. ISBN:0-7643-1492-0, ISBN13: 978-0-7643-1492-6. Dewey:749.28/09/04. LCCN:2001-005102.

Audience: **g,l,u,f.**

Fiell, Charlotte & Fiell, Peter   NK2395.F54 2001

Modern Furniture Classics: Postwar to Postmodern. Trade Paper. Thames & Hudson. New York, NY. 2001. 192p. ISBN:0-500-28300-1, ISBN13: 978-0-500-28300-4. Dewey:749.2/049. LCCN:2001-086846.

Audience: **g,l,u,f.**

Gilbert, Christopher   NK2528.G45 1991

English Vernacular Furniture, 1750-1900. Cloth over Boards. Yale University Press. Cumberland, RI. 1991. 534p. Paul Mellon Centre for Studies in British Art ISBN:0-300-04762-2, ISBN13: 978-0-300-04762-2. Dewey:749.22/09/033. LCCN:90-012754.

Audience: **g,l,u,f.** *Choice, 1991.*

Greene, Jeffrey P.   NK2406.G74 1996

American Furniture of the 18th Century: History, Technique, and Structure. Trade Cloth. Taunton Press, Inc. Newtown, CT. 1996. 320p. ISBN:1-56158-104-6, ISBN13: 978-1-56158-104-7. Dewey:749.2/13/09034. LCCN:96-012859.

Audience: **g,l,u,f.** *Choice, 1997.*

Handler, Sarah   NK2668 .H36 2001

Austere Luminosity of Chinese Classical Furniture. Trade Cloth. University of California Press. Berkeley, CA. 2001. 428p. ISBN:0-520-21484-6, ISBN13: 978-0-520-21484-2. Dewey:749.2951. LCCN:00-061992.

Audience: **g,l,u,f.** *Choice, 2002.*

Hurst, Ronald L., et al.   NK2411.H871997

Southern Furniture 1680-1830: The Colonial Williamsburg Collection. Jonathan Prown & Colonial Williamsburg Foundation Staff (Authors). Trade Cloth. Harry N. Abrams, Inc. New York, NY. 1997. 639p. Williamsburg Decorative Arts Ser. ISBN:0-8109-4175-9, ISBN13: 978-0-8109-4175-5. Dewey:749.215/074755/4252. LCCN:97-011154.

Audience: **g,l,u,f.** *Choice, 1998.*

Kassay, John   NK2406.K35 1998

The Book of American Windsor Furniture: Styles and Technologies. Trade Cloth. University of Massachusetts Press. Amherst, MA. 1998. 208p. ISBN:1-55849-137-6, ISBN13: 978-1-55849-137-3. Dewey:749.214. LCCN:97-039207.

Audience: **g,l,u,f.** *Choice, 1999.*

Katz, Sali B.   NK2435.A6K38 1986

Hispanic Furniture: An American Collection. Trade Cloth. Hastings House Daytrips Publishers. Winter Park, FL. 1986. 224p. ISBN:0-8038-3064-5, ISBN13: 978-0-8038-3064-6. Dewey:749.2191/074/0191. LCCN:86-071077.

Audience: **g,l,u,f.** *Choice, 1987.*

Kenny, Peter M., et al.   NK2439.L24A41998

Honoré Lannuier, Cabinet Maker from Paris: The Life and Work of a French Ebeniste in Federal New York. Charles H. Lannuier, Frances F. Bretter, Metropolitan Museum of Art Staff & Ulrich Leben (Authors). Trade Cloth. Harry N. Abrams, Inc. New York, NY. 1998. 340p. ISBN:0-8109-6517-8, ISBN13: 978-0-8109-6517-1. Dewey:749.213. LCCN:97-039012.

Audience: **g,l,u,f.** *Choice, 1999.*

Kirk, John T.   NK2405.K572000

American Furniture: Understanding Styles, Construction and Quality. Trade Cloth. Harry N. Abrams, Inc. New York, NY. 2000. 236p. ISBN:0-8109-4220-8, ISBN13: 978-0-8109-4220-2. Dewey:749.213. LCCN:00-027157.

Audience: **g,l,u,f.**

Lessard, Michel   NK2442.Q3L4813 2002

Antique Furniture of Quebec: Four Centuries of Furniture Making. Janet Macaulay (Translator). Trade Cloth. McClelland & Stewart/Tundra Books. Plattsburgh, NY. 2002. 544p. ISBN:0-7710-4670-7, ISBN13: 978-0-7710-4670-4. Dewey:749.211/4/09. LCCN:2002-318947.

Audience: **g,l,u,f.**

Linley, David   NK2231.L561996

Extraordinary Furniture. Trade Cloth. Harry N. Abrams, Inc. New York, NY. 1996. 192p. ISBN:0-8109-3257-1, ISBN13: 978-0-8109-3257-9. Dewey:749.1. LCCN:96-010862.

Audience: **g,l,u,f.**

Lo, Kai-yin   NK2220

Classical and Vernacular Chinese Furniture in the Living Environment. Trade Cloth. Art Media Resources, Inc. Chicago, IL. 1998. 200p. ISBN:1-878529-47-1, ISBN13: 978-1-878529-47-3. Dewey:749.2951.

Audience: **g,l,u,f.** *Choice, 1999.*

Rieman, Timothy D. & Burks, Jean M.   NK2407.R541993

Complete Book of Shaker Furniture. Trade Cloth. Harry N. Abrams, Inc. New York, NY. 1993. 400p. ISBN:0-8109-3841-3, ISBN13: 978-0-8109-3841-0. Dewey:749.213/088/288. LCCN:92-047357.

Audience: **g,l,u,f.** *Choice, 1994.*

Rodel, Kevin P. & Binzen, Jonathan   NK2394.A77R63 2003

Arts and Crafts Furniture: From Classic to Contemporary. Trade Cloth. Taunton Press, Inc. Newtown, CT. 2003. 240p. ISBN:1-56158-359-6, ISBN13: 978-1-56158-359-1. Dewey:749.2/04. LCCN:2003-008779.

Audience: **g,l,u,f.** *Choice, 2004.*

Royka, Paul A.   NK2407 .R69 1997

Mission Furniture: From the American Arts and Crafts Movement. Trade Cloth. Schiffer Publishing, Ltd. Atglen, PA. 1997. 256p. ISBN:0-88740-987-3, ISBN13: 978-0-88740-987-5. Dewey:749.213. LCCN:97-080044.

Audience: **g,l,u,f.**

Sassone, Adriana Boidi, et al.   NK2235 .F87 2000
Furniture: From Rococo to Art Deco. Elisabeth Cozzi, Andrea
Disertori & Massimo Griffo (Authors). Trade Cloth. Taschen
America, LLC. Los Angeles, CA. 2000. 813p. Evergreen Ser.
ISBN:3-8228-6517-6, ISBN13: 978-3-8228-6517-0.
Dewey:749.209.

>   Audience: **g,l,u,f.**   *Choice, 2001.*

Soros, Susan W.   NK2542.G64A41999
Secular Furniture of E. W. Godwin: With Catalogue Raisonné.
Cloth over Boards. Yale University Press. Cumberland, RI.
1999. 300p. ISBN:0-300-08159-6, ISBN13: 978-0-300-08159-6.
Dewey:749.22. LCCN:99-033079.

>   Audience: **g,l,u,f.**   *Choice, 2000.*

Umstattd, William D. & Davis, Charles W.   TT197.U47 2000
Modern Cabinetmaking. Ed. 3. Trade Cloth. Goodheart-Willcox
Publisher. Tinley Park, IL. 2000. 912p. ISBN:1-56637-503-7,
ISBN13: 978-1-56637-503-0. Dewey:684.1/6. LCCN:98-044628.

>   Audience: **g,l,u,f.**

Interior Design and Decoration > Furniture > Reference Works

Boyce, Charles   NK2205
Dictionary of Furniture. Ed. 2. Joseph T. Butler (Foreword by).
Trade Paper. DIANE Publishing Company. Collingdale, PA.
2001. 378p. ISBN:0-7567-6707-5, ISBN13: 978-0-7567-6707-5.
Dewey:749/.03.

>   Audience: **g,l,u,f.**   *Choice, 2001, 1986.*

Crochet, Treena M.   NK2235.C76 2004
Designer's Guide to Furniture Styles. Ed. 2. Cloth Text. Prentice
Hall PTR. Upper Saddle River, NJ. 2003. 368p.
ISBN:0-13-044757-9, ISBN13: 978-0-13-044757-9. Dewey:749.
LCCN:2003-042880.

>   Audience: **g,l,u,f.**

Edwards, Clive   NK2205.E34 2000
Encyclopedia of Furniture Materials, Trades and Techniques.
Trade Cloth. Ashgate Publishing, Ltd. Aldershot, 2001. 288p.
ISBN:1-84014-639-7, ISBN13: 978-1-84014-639-4.
Dewey:749/.03. LCCN:00-025076.

>   Audience: **g,l,u,f.**   *Choice, 2001.*

Edwards, Ralph   NK2529 .M3 1986
The Dictionary of English Furniture, Set. Ed. 2. Trade Paper,
Box or Slipcased. Antique Collectors' Club. Easthampton, MA.
1986. 350;384;376p. ISBN:1-85149-037-X, ISBN13:
978-1-85149-037-0. Dewey:749.22/03. LCCN:88-137893.

>   Audience: **g,l,u,f.**

Gloag, John   NK2205.G541991
A Complete Dictionary of Furniture. Clive Edwards (Revised
by). Trade Cloth. Overlook Press, The. New York, NY. 1991.
868p. ISBN:0-87951-414-0, ISBN13: 978-0-87951-414-3.
Dewey:749. LCCN:90-043798.

>   Audience: **g,l,u,f.**

Habegger, Jerryll   NK2395.H34 2004
Sourcebook of Modern Furniture. Ed. 3. Trade Cloth. W. W.
Norton & Company, Inc. New York, NY. 2005. 792p.
ISBN:0-393-73170-7, ISBN13: 978-0-393-73170-5.
Dewey:749/.09/04. LCCN:2004-057560.

>   Audience: **g,l,u,f.**   *Choice, 2005, 1989.*

MacQuoid, Percy & Edwards, Ralph   NK2529.M32
The Dictionary of English Furniture, Vol. 2. Ed. 2. Trade Paper.
Books on Demand. Ann Arbor, MI. 416p. ISBN:0-598-45052-1,
ISBN13: 978-0-598-45052-4. Dewey:749.22. LCCN:54-003800.

>   Audience: **g,l,u,f.**

MacQuoid, Percy & Edwards, Ralph   NK2529.M32
The Dictionary of English Furniture, Vol. 3. Ed. 2. Trade Paper.
Books on Demand. Ann Arbor, MI. 401p. ISBN:0-598-45053-X,
ISBN13: 978-0-598-45053-1. Dewey:749.22. LCCN:54-003800.

>   Audience: **g,l,u,f.**

MacQuoid, Percy & Edwards, Ralph   NK2529.M32
The Dictionary of English Furniture, Vol. 1. Ed. 2. Trade Paper.
Books on Demand. Ann Arbor, MI. 391p. ISBN:0-598-45050-5,
ISBN13: 978-0-598-45050-0. Dewey:749.22. LCCN:54-003800.

>   Audience: **g,l,u,f.**

Payne, Christopher (Editor)   NK2235.S68
Sotheby's Concise Encyclopedia of Furniture. Trade Cloth.
Octopus Publishing Group. London, 1995. 208p.
ISBN:1-85029-649-9, ISBN13: 978-1-85029-649-2.
Dewey:749.2/003/21.

>   Audience: **g,l,u,f.**

Rieman, Timothy D. & Burks, Jean M.   NK2407.R54 2003
The Encyclopedia of Shaker Furniture. Trade Cloth. Schiffer
Publishing, Ltd. Atglen, PA. 2003. 576p. ISBN:0-7643-1928-0,
ISBN13: 978-0-7643-1928-0. Dewey:749.213/088/288.
LCCN:2003-014164.

>   Audience: **g,l,u,f.**

White, Elizabeth   NK2529 .W53 1990
Pictorial Dictionary of British 18th Century Furniture Design.
Trade Cloth. Antique Collectors' Club. Easthampton, MA. 1992.
700p. ISBN:1-85149-105-8, ISBN13: 978-1-85149-105-6.
Dewey:749.2/2/09033. LCCN:91-191181.

>   Audience: **g,l,u,f.**

Interior Design and Decoration > Interior Objects and Decoration > Basketry

Bates, Craig D. & Lee, Martha J.   E78.C15B28 1990
Tradition and Innovation: A Basket History of the Indians of the
Yosemite- Mono Lake Area. Trade Cloth. Yosemite Association.

El Portal, CA. 1994. 225p. ISBN:0-939666-54-5, ISBN13: 978-0-939666-54-6. Dewey:746.41/2/08997079447. LCCN:90-012420.

Audience: **g,l,u.** *Choice, 1992.*

Busby, Sharon   **E99.H2B87 2003**
Spruce Root Basketry of the Haida and Tlingit. Trade Cloth. University of Washington Press. Seattle, WA. 2003. 160p. ISBN:0-295-98317-5, ISBN13: 978-0-295-98317-2. Dewey:746.41/2/089972. LCCN:2002-155165.

Audience: **u,f.** *Choice, 2003.*

Hill, Sarah H.   **96-47882 [E]**
Weaving New Worlds: Southeastern Cherokee Women and Their Basketry. Trade Cloth. University of North Carolina Press. Chapel Hill, NC. 1997. 440p. ISBN:0-8078-2345-7, ISBN13: 978-0-8078-2345-3. Dewey:746.41/2/0899755. LCCN:96-047882.

Audience: **g,l,u,f.** *Choice, 1997.*

Porter, Frank W. III   **E98**
  (Editor)
The Art of Native American Basketry: A Living Legacy. Trade Cloth. Greenwood Publishing Group, Inc. Portsmouth, NH. 1990. 368p. Contributions to the Study of Anthropology Ser., No. 5 ISBN:0-313-26716-2, ISBN13: 978-0-313-26716-1. Dewey:746.41/2/08997. LCCN:89-026008.

Audience: **g,l,u,f.** *Choice, 1991.*

Schlick, Mary D.   **E78.C64S35 1994**
Columbia River Basketry: Gift of the Ancestors, Gift of the Earth. Trade Cloth. University of Washington Press. Seattle, WA. 2003. 248p. Samuel and Althea Stroum Bks. ISBN:0-295-97289-0, ISBN13: 978-0-295-97289-3. Dewey:746.4/12/089974. LCCN:93-030658.

Audience: **g,l,u,f.** *Choice, 1994.*

Sentance, Bryan   **NK3649.5.S462001**
The Art of the Basket: Traditional Basketry from Around the World. Trade Cloth. Thames & Hudson. New York, NY. 2001. 216p. ISBN:0-500-51048-2, ISBN13: 978-0-500-51048-3. Dewey:746.41/2. LCCN:2002-442654.

Audience: **g,l,u,f.**

Simpson, Georgiana   **E99.N3S56 2003**
  Kennedy
Navajo Ceremonial Baskets: Sacred Symbols, Sacred Space. Trade Paper. Book Publishing Company, The. Summertown, TN. 2004. 160p. ISBN:1-57067-118-4, ISBN13: 978-1-57067-118-0. Dewey:746.41/20899726. LCCN:2003-025512.

Audience: **g,l,u,f.** *Choice, 2004.*

Interior Design and Decoration > Interior Objects and Decoration > Metalwork

Ball, Robert W. D.   **NK7500.S53B35 1999**
American Shelf and Wall Clocks: A Pictorial History for Collectors. Ed. 2. Trade Cloth. Schiffer Publishing, Ltd. Atglen,

PA. 1999. 272p. A Schiffer Book for Collectors Ser. ISBN:0-7643-0905-6, ISBN13: 978-0-7643-0905-2. Dewey:681.1/13/0973. LCCN:99-063175.

Audience: **g,l,u,f.**

Barquist, David L.   **NK7198.M9A4 2001**
Myer Myers: Jewish Silversmith in Colonial New York. Cloth over Boards. Yale University Press. Cumberland, RI. 2001. 336p. ISBN:0-300-09057-9, ISBN13: 978-0-300-09057-4. Dewey:739.2/372. LCCN:2002-265746.

Audience: **g,l,u,f.** *Choice, 2002.*

Braunstein, Susan L.   **BM657.H3J48 2004**
Five Centuries of Hannukah Lamps from the Jewish Museum: A Catalogue Raisonné. Jewish Museum (New York, N.Y.) Staff (Contribution by). Cloth over Boards. Yale University Press. Cumberland, RI. 2005. 416p. ISBN:0-300-10623-8, ISBN13: 978-0-300-10623-7. Dewey:296.4/61. LCCN:2004-056751.

Audience: **g,l,u,f.** *Choice, 2005.*

Loring, John   **NK7198.T5L672001**
Magnificent Tiffany Silver. Trade Cloth. Harry N. Abrams, Inc. New York, NY. 2001. 272p. ISBN:0-8109-4273-9, ISBN13: 978-0-8109-4273-8. Dewey:739.2/377471. LCCN:2001-001267.

Audience: **g,l,u,f.**

Muller, Hans W.   **NK7107.15.M8513 1999**
Gold of the Pharaohs. Eberhard Thiem (Photographer). Trade Cloth. Cornell University Press. Ithaca, NY. 1999. 256p. ISBN:0-8014-3725-3, ISBN13: 978-0-8014-3725-0. Dewey:739.2/2732. LCCN:99-034191.

Audience: **g,l,u,f.** *Choice, 2000.*

Stern, Jewel   **NK7112**
Modernism in American Silver: 20th-Century Design. Kevin W. Tucker & Charles L. Venable (Editors). Saddle Stitched, Cloth over Boards, Dust Jacket. Yale University Press. Cumberland, RI. 2005. 392p. ISBN:0-300-10927-X, ISBN13: 978-0-300-10927-6. Dewey:739.2309730904. LCCN:2005-927185.

Audience: **l,u,f.** *Choice, 2006.*

Interior Design and Decoration > Interior Objects and Decoration > Paper Arts

Kreisel, Martha   **Z6153.P35K74 1994**
Papercutting: An International Bibliography and Selected Guide to U. S. Collections. Trade Cloth. Scarecrow Press, Inc. Lanham, MD. 1994. 277p. ISBN:0-8108-2856-1, ISBN13: 978-0-8108-2856-8. Dewey:016.736/98. LCCN:94-002516.

Audience: **g,l,u,f.**

Matisse, Henri &   **N6797.T64**
  Castleman, Riva
Jazz. Sophie Hawkes (Translator). Trade Paper. George Braziller Inc. New York, NY. 1992. 96p. ISBN:0-8076-1291-X, ISBN13: 978-0-8076-1291-0. Dewey:741.6/4/092. LCCN:92-019148.

Audience: **g,l,u,f.**

Shadur, Joseph & Shadur, Yehudity   NK8553.2.E85S525
Traditional Jewish Papercuts: An Inner World of Art and Symbol. Trade Cloth. University Press of New England. Lebanon, NH. 2002. 272p. ISBN:1-58465-165-2, ISBN13: 978-1-58465-165-9. Dewey:736/.98/089924. LCCN:2001-004318.

Audience: **g,l,u,f.**

Tcherviakov, Alexander F.   NK4890.H34
Fans: From the 18th to the Beginning of the 20th Century. Trade Cloth. New Line Books. New York, NY. 2005. 216p. Temporis Ser. ISBN:1-59764-016-6, ISBN13: 978-1-59764-016-9. Dewey:391.4/4.

Audience: **g,l,u,f.**

Interior Design and Decoration > Interior Objects and Decoration > Pottery and Porcelain

Atterbury, Paul & Batkin, Maureen   NK4210.M55A88 1998
The Dictionary of Minton. Ed. 2. Trade Cloth. Antique Collectors' Club. Easthampton, MA. 1999. 368p. ISBN:1-85149-272-0, ISBN13: 978-1-85149-272-5. Dewey:738/.09424/63. LCCN:00-302596.

Audience: **g,l,u,f.**

Blumer, Thomas John   E99.C24B58 2004
Catawba Indian Pottery: The Survival of a Folk Tradition. Trade Cloth. University of Alabama Press. Tuscaloosa, AL. 2004. 240p. Contemporary American Indian Studies ISBN:0-8173-1383-4, ISBN13: 978-0-8173-1383-8. Dewey:738/.089/9752. LCCN:2003-012348.

Audience: **g,l,u,f.** *Choice, 2004.*

Boardman, John   NK4649.B624 1989
Athenian Red Figure Vases: The Classical Period. Trade Paper. Thames & Hudson. New York, NY. 1989. 252p. World of Art Ser. ISBN:0-500-20244-3, ISBN13: 978-0-500-20244-9. Dewey:738.3/82/09385. LCCN:89-050539.

Audience: **g,l,u,f.**

Chappell, James   TT921.5.C48 1991
The Potter's Complete Book of Clay and Glazes: A Comprehensive Guide to Formulating, Mixing, Applying and Firing Clay Bodies and Glazes. Ed. 2. Trade Cloth. Watson-Guptill Publications, Inc. New York, NY. 1991. 400p. ISBN:0-8230-4203-0, ISBN13: 978-0-8230-4203-6. Dewey:738.1. LCCN:90-027708.

Audience: **g,l,u,f.**

Chavarria, Joaquim   NK4225.C4313 1994
The Big Book of Ceramics: A Guide to the History, Materials, Equipment and Techniques of Hand-Building, Throwing, Molding, Kiln-Firing and Glazing Pottery and Other Ceramic Objects. Trade Cloth. Watson-Guptill Publications, Inc. New York, NY. 1994. 192p. ISBN:0-8230-0508-9, ISBN13: 978-0-8230-0508-6. Dewey:738.1. LCCN:94-011057.

Audience: **g,l,u,f.**

Clark, Andrew J., et al.   NK4645.C57 2002
Understanding Greek Vases: A Guide to Terms, Styles, and Techniques. Maya Elston & Mary Louise Hart (Authors). Trade Paper. Oxford University Press, Inc. New York, NY. 2002. 176p. Looking at Ser. ISBN:0-89236-599-4, ISBN13: 978-0-89236-599-9. Dewey:738.3/82/0938. LCCN:2001-006214.

Audience: **g,l,u,f.** *Choice, 2003.*

Clark, Garth   NK4007.C561987
American Ceramics: 1876 to the Present. Trade Cloth. Abbeville Press, Inc. New York, NY. 1988. 352p. ISBN:0-89659-743-1, ISBN13: 978-0-89659-743-3. Dewey:738/.0973. LCCN:87-001177.

Audience: **g,l,u,f.** *Choice, 1989.*

Clark, Garth   NK4085.C53 1995
The Potter's Art. Trade Cloth. Phaidon Press. London, 1995. 240p. ISBN:0-7148-3202-2, ISBN13: 978-0-7148-3202-9. Dewey:738.0941. LCCN:95-236742.

Audience: **g,l,u,f.**

Clark, Garth, et al.   NK4210.O42C5 1989
The Mad Potter of Biloxi: The Art and Life of George E. Ohr. Robert A. Ellison & Eugene Hecht (Authors), John White (Photographer). Trade Cloth. Abbeville Press, Inc. New York, NY. 1989. 192p. ISBN:0-89659-927-2, ISBN13: 978-0-89659-927-7. Dewey:738/.092. LCCN:89-006978.

Audience: **g,l,u,f.** *Choice, 1990.*

Cook, Robert M.   NK4645.C6 1997
Greek Painted Pottery. Ed. 3. Trade Paper. Routledge. New York, NY. 1997. 408p. ISBN:0-415-13860-4, ISBN13: 978-0-415-13860-4. Dewey:738.3/0938. LCCN:96-018748.

Audience: **g,l,u,f.** **B**

Cooper, Emmanuel   NK3780.C663 1999
Ten Thousand Years of Pottery. Ed. 4. Trade Cloth. University of Pennsylvania Press. Philadelphia, PA. 2000. 320p. ISBN:0-8122-3554-1, ISBN13: 978-0-8122-3554-8. Dewey:738/.09. LCCN:99-049100.

Audience: **g,l,u,f.** *Choice, 2000.*

Coutts, Howard   NK4083.C68 2001
The Art of Ceramics: European Ceramic Design 1500-1830. Cloth over Boards. Yale University Press. Cumberland, RI. 2001. 320p. ISBN:0-300-08387-4, ISBN13: 978-0-300-08387-3. Dewey:738/.094/0903. LCCN:00-054077.

Audience: **g,l,u,f.** *Choice, 2003.*

Coysh, A. W. & Henrywood, R. K.   NK4277
The Dictionary of Blue and White Printed Pottery, 1780-1880. Trade Cloth. Antique Collectors' Club. Easthampton, MA. 1982. 424p. ISBN:0-907462-06-5, ISBN13: 978-0-907462-06-4. Dewey:738.3/7. LCCN:81-195375.

Audience: **g,l,u,f.**

de Waal, Edmund   NK3930
20th-Century Ceramics. Trade Paper. Thames & Hudson. New

York, NY. 2003. 224p. The World of Art Ser.
ISBN:0-500-20371-7, ISBN13: 978-0-500-20371-2.
Dewey:738/.0904/075. LCCN:2003-100124.

Audience: **g,l,u,f.**

Ganz, Cheryl & Strobel,   NK4028.3.M4M48 2004
   Margaret (Editors)
Pots of Promise: Mexicans and Pottery at Hull-House, 1920-40.
Vicki L. Ruiz (Foreword by). Trade Cloth. University of Illinois
Press. Champaign, IL. 2004. 168p. Latinos in Chicago and the
Midwest Ser. ISBN:0-252-02894-5, ISBN13:
978-0-252-02894-6. Dewey:738/.089/6872077311.
LCCN:2003-009573.

Audience: **g,l,u,f.** *Choice, 2004.*

Harlow, Francis Harvey &   E99.Z52H37 2003
   Lanmon, Dwight P.
The Pottery of Zia Pueblo. Trade Paper. School of American
Research Press. Santa Fe, NM. 2003. 386p.
ISBN:1-930618-26-3, ISBN13: 978-1-930618-26-8.
Dewey:738/.089/974. LCCN:2003-007899.

Audience: **l,u,f.**

Honda, Hiromu, et al.   NK4154.H6313 1997
The Beauty of Fired Clay: Ceramics from Burma, Cambodia,
Laos, and Thailand. Noriki Shimazu & Dawn F. Rooney
(Authors). Trade Cloth. Oxford University Press, Inc. New York,
NY. 1997. 282p. ISBN:983-56-0020-1, ISBN13:
978-983-56-0020-3. Dewey:738/.0959. LCCN:96-031774.

Audience: **g,l,u,f.** *Choice, 1998.*

Lewis, Griselda   NK4085.L38 1999
Collector's History of English Pottery. Ed. 4. Trade Cloth.
Antique Collectors' Club. Easthampton, MA. 1999. 384p.
ISBN:1-85149-291-7, ISBN13: 978-1-85149-291-6.
Dewey:738/.0942. LCCN:99-230173.

Audience: **g,l,u,f.**

McErlain, Alex   NK4225 .M37 2002
Art of Throwing. Trade Cloth. Crowood Press, Limited, The.
Wiltshire, 2002. 176p. ISBN:1-86126-484-4, ISBN13:
978-1-86126-484-8. Dewey:738.14. LCCN:2004-478821.

Audience: **g,l,u,f.**

Mohr, Richard D.   NK4210.O42M64 2003
Pottery, Politics, Art: George Ohr and the Brothers Kirkpatrick.
Trade Cloth. University of Illinois Press. Champaign, IL. 2003.
256p. ISBN:0-252-02789-2, ISBN13: 978-0-252-02789-5.
Dewey:738/.092/273. LCCN:2002-007566.

Audience: **g,l,u,f.** *Choice, 2003.*

Nelson, Glenn C. & Burkett,   TP807.N363 2002
   Richard
Ceramics: A Potter's Handbook. Ed. 6. Paper Text. Thomson
Wadsworth. Belmont, CA. 2001. 456p. ISBN:0-03-028937-8,
ISBN13: 978-0-03-028937-8. Dewey:738. LCCN:2001-096329.

Audience: **g,l,u,f.**

Owen, Nancy E.   NK4340.R7O95 2001
Rookwood and the Industry of Art: Women, Culture and
Commerce, 1880-1913. Trade Paper. Ohio University Press.
Athens, OH. 2001. 349p. ISBN:0-8214-1338-4, ISBN13:

978-0-8214-1338-8. Dewey:338.7/617383/0977178.
LCCN:00-040631.

Audience: **l,u,f.** *Choice, 2001.*

Peterson, Susan   NK4225
The Craft and Art of Clay. Ed. 4. Trade Cloth. Overlook Press,
The. New York, NY. 2003. 432p. ISBN:1-58567-476-1, ISBN13:
978-1-58567-476-3. Dewey:738. LCCN:2004-269332.

Audience: **g,l,u,f.**

Peterson, Susan   E98.P8P37 1997
Pottery by American Indian Women: The Legacy of
Generations. Trade Cloth. Abbeville Press, Inc. New York, NY.
1997. 224p. ISBN:0-7892-0353-7, ISBN13: 978-0-7892-0353-3.
Dewey:738/.082. LCCN:97-012628.

Audience: **g,l,u,f.**

Rasmussen, Tom & Spivey,   NK4645 .L66 1991
   Nigel J. (Editors)
Looking at Greek Vases. Trade Paper. Cambridge University
Press. New York, NY. 1991. 300p. ISBN:0-521-37679-3,
ISBN13: 978-0-521-37679-2. Dewey:738.3/82/0938.
LCCN:90-002568.

Audience: **g,l,u,f.** *Choice, 1992.*

Rice, Prudence M.   NK3780
Pottery Analysis: A Sourcebook. Trade Paper. University of
Chicago Press. Chicago, IL. 2006. 584p. ISBN:0-226-71116-1,
ISBN13: 978-0-226-71116-4. Dewey:738.

Audience: **g,l,u,f.** *Choice, 1988.*

Richards, Dick   NK4154.A78 1995
South-East Asian Ceramics: Thai, Khmer, and Vietnamese from
the Collection of the Art Gallery of South Australia, Adelaide.
Trade Cloth. Oxford University Press, Inc. New York, NY. 1995.
210p. The Asia Collection ISBN:967-65-3075-1, ISBN13:
978-967-65-3075-2. Dewey:738/.0959/07494231.
LCCN:94-047273.

Audience: **g,l,u,f.** *Choice, 1996.*

Robertson, Martin   NK4645 .R7 1992
The Art of Vase-Painting in Classical Athens. Cloth Text.
Cambridge University Press. New York, NY. 1992. 362p.
ISBN:0-521-33010-6, ISBN13: 978-0-521-33010-7.
Dewey:738.3/82/09385. LCCN:91-021355.

Audience: **l,u,f.** *Choice, 1993.*

Sandon, John   NK4395.S15 1993
The Dictionary of Worcester Porcelain, 1751-1851, Vol. 1. Trade
Cloth. Antique Collectors' Club. Easthampton, MA. 1993. 384p.
ISBN:1-85149-156-2, ISBN13: 978-1-85149-156-8.
Dewey:738.2/09424/48. LCCN:93-226655.

Audience: **g,l,u,f.**

Wilson, Richard L.   NK4167
The Potter's Brush: The Kenzan Style in Japanese Ceramics.
Trade Cloth. Merrell Publishers Ltd. London, 2005. 256p.
ISBN:1-85894-156-3, ISBN13: 978-1-85894-156-1.
Dewey:738/.0952/074753.

Audience: **g,l,u,f.** *Choice, 2002.*

Interior Design and Decoration > Interior Objects and Decoration > Textile Arts

Aav, Marianne (Editor) NK1700
Marimekko: Fabrics, Fashion, Architecture. Cloth over Boards. Yale University Press. Cumberland, RI. 2003. 336p. ISBN:0-300-10183-X, ISBN13: 978-0-300-10183-6. Dewey:338.7/67702/094897. LCCN:2003-017532.
Audience: **g,l,u,f.** *Choice, 2004.*

Arnett, William, et al. NK9112 .Q54 2002
The Quilts of Gee's Bend: Masterpieces from a Lost Place. John Beardsley, Jane Livingston & Alvia J. Wardlaw (Authors). Trade Cloth. Tinwood Books. Atlanta, GA. 2002. 140p. ISBN:0-9653766-4-8, ISBN13: 978-0-9653766-4-8. Dewey:746.460976138. LCCN:2002-022468.
Audience: **g,l,u,f.** *Choice, 2003.*

Ayres, Dianne & Hansen, Timothy NK8812.A472002
American Arts and Crafts Textiles. Trade Cloth. Harry N. Abrams, Inc. New York, NY. 2002. 248p. ISBN:0-8109-0434-9, ISBN13: 978-0-8109-0434-7. Dewey:746/.0973/09034. LCCN:2001-006012.
Audience: **g,l,u,f.**

Chung, Young Yang NK9272.C482004
Silken Threads: A History of Embroidery in China, Korea, Japan, and Vietnam. Trade Cloth. Harry N. Abrams, Inc. New York, NY. 2005. 464p. ISBN:0-8109-4330-1, ISBN13: 978-0-8109-4330-8. Dewey:746.44/095. LCCN:2004-009510.
Audience: **g,l,u,f.**

Delmarcel, Guy NK3055.A1D44132000
Flemish Tapestry. Trade Cloth. Harry N. Abrams, Inc. New York, NY. 2000. 383p. ISBN:0-8109-3345-4, ISBN13: 978-0-8109-3345-3. Dewey:746.3/9492. LCCN:00-694538.
Audience: **g,l,u,f.** *Choice, 2000.*

Gibbs, Jenny NK3242.G53 1994
Curtains and Draperies: History, Design and Inspiration. Trade Cloth. Overlook Press, The. New York, NY. 1994. 224p. ISBN:0-87951-539-2, ISBN13: 978-0-87951-539-3. Dewey:747/.3. LCCN:93-040333.
Audience: **g,l,u,f.**

Harris, Jennifer NK8806.T451993
Textiles: 5000 Years. Trade Cloth. Harry N. Abrams, Inc. New York, NY. 1993. 320p. ISBN:0-8109-3875-8, ISBN13: 978-0-8109-3875-5. Dewey:746/.09. LCCN:93-016980.
Audience: **g,l,u,f.** *Choice, 1993.*

Jenkins, David (Editor) NK8906.C36 2002
The Cambridge History of Western Textiles, Set. Quantity Pack, Trade Cloth. Cambridge University Press. New York, NY. 2003. 1400p. ISBN:0-521-34107-8, ISBN13: 978-0-521-34107-3. Dewey:338.4/7677/009. LCCN:2001-052958.
Audience: **g,l,u,f.** *Choice, 2004.*

Johnson, Mary Elizabeth & Kiracofe, Roderick NK9112.K57 2005
The American Quilt: A History of Cloth and Comfort 1750-1950. Trade Paper. Crown Publishing Group. New York, NY. 2004. 304p. ISBN:1-4000-8096-7, ISBN13: 978-1-4000-8096-0. Dewey:746.460973.
Audience: **g,l,u,f.**

Marston, Gwen NK9198.S33M368 2004
Mary Schafer, American Quilt Maker. Trade Cloth. University of Michigan Press. Chicago, IL. 2004. 240p. ISBN:0-472-09855-1, ISBN13: 978-0-472-09855-2. Dewey:746.46/092 B. LCCN:2003-018071.
Audience: **g,l,u,f.** *Choice, 2005.*

M'Closkey, Kathy E99.N3M315 2002
Swept under the Rug: A Hidden History of Navajo Weaving. University of Arizona, Southwest Center Staff (Contribution by). Trade Cloth. University of New Mexico Press. Albuquerque, NM. 2002. 320p. ISBN:0-8263-2831-8, ISBN13: 978-0-8263-2831-1. Dewey:381/.45746/089972. LCCN:2002-009369.
Audience: **u,f.** *Choice, 2003.*

Meller, Susan & Elffers, Joost NK9500.M451991
Textile Designs: Two Hundred Years of European and American Patterns for Printed Fabrics. Trade Cloth. Harry N. Abrams, Inc. New York, NY. 1991. 464p. ISBN:0-8109-3853-7, ISBN13: 978-0-8109-3853-3. Dewey:746.6/2041. LCCN:90-048073.
Audience: **g,l,u,f.** *Choice, 1992.*

Warner, Pamela NK9206
Embroidery: A History. Trafalgar Square. 1991. ISBN:0-7134-6106-3, ISBN13: 978-0-7134-6106-0.
Audience: **g,l,u,f.**

Interior Design and Decoration > Interior Objects and Decoration > Woodworking

Fendelman, Helaine & Taylor, Jonathan NK9950.F46 1999
Tramp Art: A Folk Art Phenomenon. Trade Paper. Stewart, Tabori & Chang. New York, NY. 1999. 160p. ISBN:1-55670-905-6, ISBN13: 978-1-55670-905-0. Dewey:745/.0973. LCCN:99-018438.
Audience: **g,l,u,f.**

Ramond, Pierre NK9920.R3613 2002
Marquetry. Jacqueline Derenne, Claire Emili & Brian Considine (Translators). Trade Cloth. Oxford University Press, Inc. New York, NY. 2003. 240p. Getty Trust Publications ISBN:0-89236-685-0, ISBN13: 978-0-89236-685-9. Dewey:745.51/2. LCCN:2002-069511.
Audience: **g,l,u,f.**

Audience: g=general, l=lower division undergraduate, u=upper division undergraduate, f=faculty.

809

Sentance, Bryan   **TT180**
Wood: World of Woodwork and Carving. Trade Cloth. Thames
& Hudson. New York, NY. 2003. 208p. ISBN:0-500-51120-9,
ISBN13: 978-0-500-51120-6. Dewey:736/.4.
LCCN:2003-100224.

Audience: **g,l,f.**

Interior Design and Decoration > Interior Objects and Decoration > Glass Arts

Carboni, Stefano, et al.   **NK5108.9.C37 2001**
Glass of the Sultans: Twelve Centuries of Islamic Masterworks.
David Whitehouse & William Gudenrath (Authors). Cloth over
Boards. Yale University Press. Cumberland, RI. 2001. 340p.
Metropolitan Museum of Art Ser. ISBN:0-300-08851-5,
ISBN13: 978-0-300-08851-9. Dewey:748/.0917.
LCCN:00-069544.

Audience: **g,l,u,f.** *Choice, 2002.*

Cheshire, Jim   **NK5343.A1**
Stained Glass and the Victorian Gothic Revival. Cloth over
Boards. Manchester University Press. Manchester, 2005. 240p.
Studies in Design and Material Culture Ser.
ISBN:0-7190-6346-9, ISBN13: 978-0-7190-6346-6.
Dewey:748.50/942/09034. LCCN:2005-297312.

Audience: **g,l,u,f.**

Chihuly, Dale, et al.   **NK5198.C43.A42000**
Chihuly Projects. Barbara Rose & Dale M. Lanzone (Authors).
Trade Cloth. Harry N. Abrams, Inc. New York, NY. 2000. 364p.
ISBN:0-8109-6708-1, ISBN13: 978-0-8109-6708-3.
Dewey:748.2/9. LCCN:00-103955.

Audience: **g,l,u,f.** *Choice, 2001.*

Farnsworth, Jean M.   **NK5312.S73 2002**
(Editor), et al.
Stained Glass in Catholic Philadelphia. Carmen R. Croce &
Joseph F. Chorpenning (Editors). Trade Cloth. Saint Joseph's
University Press. Philadelphia, PA. 2002. 528p.
ISBN:0-916101-43-6, ISBN13: 978-0-916101-43-5.
Dewey:726.5/28/0974811. LCCN:2002-014875.

Audience: **g,l,u,f.** *Choice, 2003.*

Frelinghuysen, Alice Cooney,   **NK5198.T52A4 2005**
et al.
The Lamps of Louis Comfort Tiffany. Martin Eidelberg, Nancy
A. McClelland & Lars Rachen (Authors), Colin Cooke
(Photographer). Trade Cloth. Vendome Press, The. New York,
NY. 2005. 224p. ISBN:0-86565-163-9, ISBN13:
978-0-86565-163-0. Dewey:749/.63. LCCN:2005-002323.

Audience: **g,l,u,f.**

Goldstein, Sidney M.   **N6264.G7L667 2005**
Glass: From Sassanian Antecedents to European Imitations. Jens
Kroger, Melanie Gibson & Nahla Avinoam Shalem
(Contribution by). Cloth over Boards. I. B. Tauris & Company,
Ltd. London, 2005. 352p. ISBN:1-874780-50-1, ISBN13:
978-1-874780-50-2. Dewey:748.2091767. LCCN:2006-295673.

Audience: **g,l,u,f.**

Jones, Robert O. (Compiled   **NK5312.J66 2002**
by)
Biographical Index of Historic American Stained Glass Makers.
Perfect. Stained Glass Association of America, The. Raytown,
MO. 2002. 139p. ISBN:0-9619640-2-2, ISBN13:
978-0-9619640-2-3. Dewey:748.5. LCCN:2003-535319.

Audience: **l,u,f.**

Klein, Dan   **NB1270.G4K58 2001**
Artists in Glass: Late Twentieth Century Masters in Glass. Trade
Cloth. Phaidon Press, Inc. New York, NY. 2001. 240p.
ISBN:1-84000-340-5, ISBN13: 978-1-84000-340-6.
Dewey:748/.09/045. LCCN:2002-421113.

Audience: **g,l,u,f.**

Kuspit, Donald B.   **NK5198.C43K871997**
Chihuly. Ed. 2. Trade Cloth. Harry N. Abrams, Inc. New York,
NY. 1999. 368p. ISBN:0-8109-6373-6, ISBN13:
978-0-8109-6373-3. Dewey:748/.092. LCCN:98-228833.

Audience: **g,l,u,f.**

Layton, Peter   **NK5110.L38 1996**
Glass Art. Trade Cloth. University of Washington Press. Seattle,
WA. 1996. 224p. ISBN:0-295-97565-2, ISBN13:
978-0-295-97565-8. Dewey:748. LCCN:96-015718.

Audience: **g,l,u,f.**

Lynn, Martha Drexler   **NK5112.L97 2004**
American Studio Glass: 1960-1990. Trade Cloth. Hudson Hills
Press LLC. Manchester, VT. 2004. 168p. ISBN:1-55595-239-9,
ISBN13: 978-1-55595-239-6. Dewey:748/.0973/09045.
LCCN:2003-027582.

Audience: **g,l,u,f.**

Madigan, Mary Jean   **NK5198.S7M32003**
Steuben Glass: An American Tradition in Crystal. Ed. 2. Trade
Cloth. Harry N. Abrams, Inc. New York, NY. 2003. 384p.
ISBN:0-8109-3492-2, ISBN13: 978-0-8109-3492-4.
Dewey:748.29147/83. LCCN:2002-015972.

Audience: **g,l,u,f.** *Choice, 2004.*

McConnell, Andy   **NK5440.D4**
The Decanter: An Illustrated History 1650-1950. Trade Cloth.
Antique Collectors' Club. Easthampton, MA. 2004. 576p.
ISBN:1-85149-428-6, ISBN13: 978-1-85149-428-6.
Dewey:748.8/2.

Audience: **g,l,u,f.**

Mentasti, Rosa Barovier   **NK5104**
Glass Throughout Time: The History and Technology of
Glassmaking from the Ancient World to the Present. Trade
Cloth. Skira Editore. Milano, 2003. 288p. ISBN:88-8491-345-4,
ISBN13: 978-88-8491-345-6. Dewey:748. LCCN:2004-432699.

Audience: **g,l,u,f.**

Moor, Andrew   **NK5304.M654 1997**
Architectural Glass Art: Form and Technique in Contemporary
Glass. Trade Cloth. Rizzoli International Publications, Inc. New
York, NY. 1998. 160p. ISBN:0-8478-2073-4, ISBN13:
978-0-8478-2073-3. Dewey:721/.04496. LCCN:97-068145.

Audience: **g,l,u,f.**

Oldknow, Tina   NK5112.O43 1996
Pilchuck: A Glass School. Trade Cloth. University of
Washington Press. Seattle, WA. 1996. 296p.
ISBN:0-295-97559-8, ISBN13: 978-0-295-97559-7.
Dewey:748/.09797/71. LCCN:96-016615.
           Audience: **g,l,u,f.**

Opie, Jennifer Hawkins   NK5104
Contemporary International Glass. Trade Cloth. V & A
Publications. London, 2004. 144p. ISBN:1-85177-426-2,
ISBN13: 978-1-85177-426-5. Dewey:748.2.
LCCN:2004-103249.
           Audience: **g,l,u,f.**

Ricke, Helmut   NK5102.5.G3D88713
Glass Art: Reflections of the Centuries. Trade Cloth. Prestel
Publishing. New York, NY. 2002. 384p. ISBN:3-7913-2793-3,
ISBN13: 978-3-7913-2793-8. Dewey:748.2/074/435534.
LCCN:2003-544861.
           Audience: **g,l,u,f.** *Choice, 2004.*

Ricke, Helmut & Schmitt,   NK5309.85.A7
  Eva
Art Nouveau Glass: The Gerda Koepff Collection. Glasmuseum
Hentrich Staff (Contribution by). Trade Cloth. Prestel
Publishing. New York, NY. 2004. 336p. ISBN:3-7913-3021-7,
ISBN13: 978-3-7913-3021-1. Dewey:748.2/0944/09034.
           Audience: **g,l,u,f.** *Choice, 2004.*

Interior Design and Decoration > Other Topics

Ling, Roger   NA3760.L46 1998
Ancient Mosaics. Trade Paper. Princeton University Press.
Princeton, NJ. 1998. 144p. ISBN:0-691-00404-8, ISBN13:
978-0-691-00404-4. Dewey:738.5/2. LCCN:98-066086.
           Audience: **g,l,u,f.** *Choice, 1999.*

Landscape Architecture > Reference Works > Web Resources

           SB469
American Society of Landscape Architects.
http://www.asla.org
Washington, D. C. : American Society of Landscape Architects.
           Audience: **g,l,u,f.**

           SB450.97
GardenWeb : the internets garden community.
http://www.gardenweb.com
iVillage, Inc.
           Audience: **g,l,u,f.**

           E159
National Register of Historic Places, National Park Service.
http://www.cr.nps.gov/nr/
           Audience: **g,l,u,f.**

           QK95
Virtual Herbarium.
http://sciweb.nybg.org/science2/VirtualHerbarium.asp
International Plant Science Center, New York Botanical Garden.
           Audience: **g,l,u,f.**

Landscape Architecture > Reference Works > Bibliographies and Research Guides

           NA1.A12
Avery Index to Architectural Periodicals.
http://www.getty.edu/research/conducting_research/avery_index/
Getty Research Institute.
           Audience: **g,l,u,f.**

Vogelsong, Diana L.   Z5996.5.U6L36 1997
Landscape Architecture Sourcebook: A Guide to Resources on
the History and Practice of Landscape Architecture. Library
Binding. Omnigraphics, Inc. Detroit, MI. 1996. Design
Reference Ser., Vol. 1 ISBN:0-7808-0196-2, ISBN13:
978-0-7808-0196-7. Dewey:016.712. LCCN:96-034507.
           Audience: **g,l,u,f.** *Choice, 1997.*

Landscape Architecture > Reference Works > Dictionaries and Encyclopedias

Adams, Denise Wiles   SB453.A32 2004
Restoring American Gardens: An Encyclopedia of Heirloom
Ornamental Plants, 1640-1940. Trade Cloth. Timber Press, Inc.
Portland, OR. 2004. 420p. ISBN:0-88192-619-1, ISBN13:
978-0-88192-619-4. Dewey:635.9/0973. LCCN:2003-057274.
           Audience: **g,l,u,f.**

Aitken, Richard & Looker,   SB457.534
  Michael (Editors)
The Oxford Companion to Australian Gardens. Trade Cloth.
Oxford University Press, Inc. New York, NY. 2002. 728p.
ISBN:0-19-553644-4, ISBN13: 978-0-19-553644-7.
Dewey:635/.0994. LCCN:2003-386239.
           Audience: **g,l,u,f.** *Choice, 2003.*

Curl, James Stevens   NA31
Dictionary of Architecture and Landscape Architecture. Ed. 2.
Trade Cloth. Oxford University Press, Inc. New York, NY. 2006.
912p. Oxford Paperback Reference Ser. ISBN:0-19-280630-0,
ISBN13: 978-0-19-280630-7. Dewey:720.3.
LCCN:2006-040248.
           Audience: **g,l,u,f.**

Geist, Helmut (Editor)   **GF90**
Our Earth's Changing Land: An Encyclopedia of Land-Use and
Land-Cover Change. Cloth Text. Greenwood Publishing Group,
Inc. Portsmouth, NH. 2005. 792p. ISBN:0-313-32704-1,
ISBN13: 978-0-313-32704-9. Dewey:333.7.
LCCN:2005-019212.

Audience: **g,l,u,f.** *Choice, 2006.*

Nicolin, Pierluigi &   **SB472.45**
  Repishti, Francesco
Dictionary of Today's Landscape Designers. Trade Cloth. Skira
Editore. Milano, 2003. 336p. ISBN:88-8491-420-5, ISBN13:
978-88-8491-420-0. Dewey:712/.03. LCCN:2004-624526.

Audience: **g,l,u,f.**

Pevsner, Nikolaus, et al.   **NA31.F55 1999**
The Penguin Dictionary of Architecture and Landscape
Architecture. Ed. 5. John Fleming & Hugh Honour (Authors).
Trade Paper. Penguin Group (USA) Inc. New York, NY. 2000.
656p. Penguin Reference Bks. ISBN:0-14-051323-X, ISBN13:
978-0-14-051323-3. Dewey:720/.3. LCCN:00-267917.

Audience: **g,l,u,f.**

Russell, John   **SB466.U6**
Gardens Across America, Vol. 2. Trade Paper. Taylor Trade
Publishing. Blue Ridge Summit, PA. 2006. 288p.
ISBN:1-58979-296-3, ISBN13: 978-1-58979-296-8.
Dewey:712/.5/0973. LCCN:2005-002525.

Audience: **g,l,u,f.**

Shoemaker, Candace   **SB450.95.E49 2001**
  (Editor)
Encyclopedia of Gardens: History and Design, Set. Chicago
Botanical Gardens Staff (Produced by). Trade Cloth. Fitzroy
Dearborn Publishers, Inc. Chicago, IL. 1999. 1590p.
ISBN:1-57958-173-0, ISBN13: 978-1-57958-173-2.
Dewey:712/.03. LCCN:2003-267339.

Audience: **g,l,u,f.** *Choice, 2002.*

Spencer, Thomas S. &   **SB466.U6S642005**
  Russell, John J.
Gardens Across America: The American Horticultural Society's
Guide to American Public Gardens and Arboreta. Trade Paper,
Perfect. Taylor Trade Publishing. Blue Ridge Summit, PA. 2005.
416p. ISBN:1-58979-102-9, ISBN13: 978-1-58979-102-2.
Dewey:712/.5/0973. LCCN:2005-002525.

Audience: **g,l,u,f.**

Tenenbaum, Frances   **SB403.2.T39 2003**
  (Editor)
Taylor's Encyclopedia of Garden Plants: The Most Authoritative
Guide to the Best Flowers, Trees, and Shrubs for North
American Gardens. Dust Jacket. Houghton Mifflin Company
Trade & Reference Division. Boston, MA. 2003. 464p. Taylor's
Guides ISBN:0-618-22644-3, ISBN13: 978-0-618-22644-3.
Dewey:635.9/03. LCCN:2002-027630.

Audience: **g,l,u,f.** *Choice, 2004.*

Landscape Architecture > Reference Works > Directories

Cockshutt, Nicholas R.   **SB466.U62**
  (Editor)
The Edens of Florida: A Guide to Florida's Gardens, Preserves
and Nature Centers. Trade Cloth. National Tropical Botanical
Garden. Lawai Kauai, HI. 1997. 16p. ISBN:0-915809-24-9,
ISBN13: 978-0-915809-24-0. Dewey:712.60973.

Audience: **g,l,u,f.**

Joyce, Alice   **SB466.U65N76 2006**
Gardenwalks in the Pacific Northwest: Beautiful Gardens along
the Coast from Oregon to British Columbia. Trade Paper. Globe
Pequot Press, The. Guilford, CT. 2006. 256p. Gardenwalks Ser.
ISBN:0-7627-3818-9, ISBN13: 978-0-7627-3818-2.
Dewey:712.09795. LCCN:2005-055248.

Audience: **g,l,u,f.**

McCarthy, Jane & Epstein,   **NB205.M33 1996**
  Laurily K.
A Guide to the Sculpture Parks and Gardens of America. Trade
Paper. Michael Kesend Publishing, Ltd. New York, NY. 1996.
224p. ISBN:0-935576-51-7, ISBN13: 978-0-935576-51-1.
Dewey:730/.973. LCCN:96-017393.

Audience: **g,l,u,f.**

Proctor, Rob (Photographer)   **SB466.U65C654 1998**
Colorado's Great Gardens: Plains, Mountains and Plateaus.
Georgia Garnsey & Gaylynn Long (Text by). Trade Cloth.
Westcliffe Publishers. Englewood, CO. 1998. 144p.
ISBN:1-56579-284-X, ISBN13: 978-1-56579-284-5.
Dewey:712/.09788. LCCN:98-015965.

Audience: **g,l,u,f.**

Landscape Architecture > Histories and Handbooks

       SB469.386.G3E942003
Event Landscape?: Contemporary German Landscape
Architecture. Trade Cloth. Birkhauser Verlag AG. CH-4010
Basel, 2003. 167p. ISBN:3-7643-7016-5, ISBN13:
978-3-7643-7016-9. Dewey:709.04074.

Audience: **g,l,u,f.**

Alanen, Arnold R. &   **E159.P746 2000**
  Melnick, Robert
Preserving Cultural Landscapes in America. Dolores Hayden
(Foreword by). Trade Paper. Johns Hopkins University Press.
Baltimore, MD. 2000. 264p. Center Books on Contemporary
Landscape Design Ser., : ISBN:0-8018-6264-7, ISBN13:
978-0-8018-6264-9. Dewey:333.7/2. LCCN:99-038598.

Audience: **g,l,u,f.** *Choice, 2000.*

Amidon, Jane   **SB470.V34M53 2005**
Michael Van Valkenburgh Associates: Allegheny Riverfront
Park. Trade Paper, Perfect. Princeton Architectural Press. New

York, NY. 2005. 160p. Source Books in Landscape Architecture, Vol. 1 ISBN:1-56898-504-5, ISBN13: 978-1-56898-504-6. Dewey:712/.092. LCCN:2005-003475.

Audience: **l,u,f.**

Engler, Mira   **TD788.E54 2004**
Designing America's Waste Landscapes. Center for American Places Staff (Contribution by). Trade Cloth. Johns Hopkins University Press. Baltimore, MD. 2004. 312p. Center Books on Contemporary Landscape Design ISBN:0-8018-7803-9, ISBN13: 978-0-8018-7803-9. Dewey:711/.8. LCCN:2003-010634.

Audience: **l,u,f.** *Choice, 2005.*

Goldstein, Claire   **SB457.65.T7252002**
Tradition and Innovation in French Garden Art: Chapters of a New History. John Dixon Hunt & Michel Conan (Editors). Trade Cloth. University of Pennsylvania Press. Philadelphia, PA. 2002. 280p. Penn Studies in Landscape Architecture ISBN:0-8122-3634-3, ISBN13: 978-0-8122-3634-7. Dewey:712/.0944/09033. LCCN:2001-057520.

Audience: **u,f.** *Choice, 2003.*

Grove, Carol   **QK31.S47G76 2006**
Henry Shaw's Victorian Landscapes: The Missouri Botanical Garden and Tower Grove Park. Cloth Text. University of Massachusetts Press. Amherst, MA. 2005. 232p. ISBN:1-55849-508-8, ISBN13: 978-1-55849-508-1. Dewey:580.73778/66. LCCN:2005-011749.

Audience: **g,l,u,f.** *Choice, 2006.*

Helphand, Kenneth I.   **SB470.55.I75H46 2002**
Dreaming Gardens: Landscape Architecture and the Making of Modern Israel. Trade Cloth. Center for American Places, Inc. Staunton, VA. 2002. xiv, 239p. Center Books on the International Scene ISBN:1-930066-06-6, ISBN13: 978-1-930066-06-9. Dewey:712/.095694. LCCN:2002-073864.

Audience: **g,l,u,f.** *Choice, 2003.*

Hough, Michael   **GF90.H68**
Out of Place: Restoring Identity to the Regional Landscape. Trade Paper. Yale University Press. Cumberland, RI. 1992. 239p. ISBN:0-300-05223-5, ISBN13: 978-0-300-05223-7. Dewey:712.

Audience: **l,u,f.** *Choice, 1990.*

Hyde, Elizabeth   **SB457.65.H94 2005**
Cultivated Power: Flowers, Culture, and Politics in the Reign of Louis XIV. Saddle Stitched, Cloth over Boards, Dust Jacket. University of Pennsylvania Press. Philadelphia, PA. 2005. 330p. Penn Studies in Landscape Architecture ISBN:0-8122-3826-5, ISBN13: 978-0-8122-3826-6. Dewey:712.09440903. LCCN:2004-043089.

Audience: **l,u,f.** *Choice, 2006.*

Jenkins, Virginia S.   **SB433.J46 1994**
The Lawn: A History of an American Obsession. Trade Paper. Smithsonian Institution Press. Washington, DC. 2000. 272p. ISBN:1-56098-406-6, ISBN13: 978-1-56098-406-1. Dewey:716. LCCN:93-028003.

Audience: **g,l,u,f.** *Choice, 1994.*

Keeney, Gavin   **SB470.53.K44 2000**
On the Nature of Things: Contemporary American Landscape Architecture. John Dixon Hunt & Allen S. Weiss (Foreword by). Trade Cloth. Birkhauser Verlag AG. CH-4010 Basel, 2000. 184p. ISBN:3-7643-6192-1, ISBN13: 978-3-7643-6192-1. Dewey:712/.0973. LCCN:00-049356.

Audience: **u,f.**

Kienast, Dieter   **SB484.G4K44 2002**
Kienast Vogt: Parks and Cemeteries. F. Gloth (Translator), C. Vogt (Photographer), P. Bauer, T. Koenigs, K. Louafi & W. Prigge (Contribution by). Trade Cloth. Birkhauser Verlag AG. CH-4010 Basel, 2002. CCXCVIIIp. ISBN:3-7643-6434-3, ISBN13: 978-3-7643-6434-2. Dewey:7712/.0943/022. LCCN:2002-023218.

Audience: **g,l,u,f.**

Koolhaas, Rem   **SB470.B78A3 1996**
Yves Brunier: Landscape Architect. Trade Paper. Birkhauser Verlag AG. CH-4010 Basel, 1996. 128p. ISBN:3-7643-5436-4, ISBN13: 978-3-7643-5436-7. Dewey:712. LCCN:96-209039.

Audience: **g,l,u,f.**

Lassus, Bernard   **SB472.L3751998**
The Landscape Approach. Trade Cloth. University of Pennsylvania Press. Philadelphia, PA. 1998. 216p. Studies in Landscape Architecture ISBN:0-8122-3450-2, ISBN13: 978-0-8122-3450-3. Dewey:712.6. LCCN:98-026259.

Audience: **g,l,u,f.** *Choice, 1999.*

Leatherbarrow, David   **SB472.45.L43 2004**
Topographical Stories: Studies in Landscape and Architecture. Trade Cloth. University of Pennsylvania Press. Philadelphia, PA. 2004. 296p. Penn Studies in Landscape Architecture ISBN:0-8122-3809-5, ISBN13: 978-0-8122-3809-9. Dewey:712. LCCN:2004-041892.

Audience: **l,u,f.**

Loidl, Hans-Wolfgang &   **SB472.L69 2003**
  Bernard, Stefan
Opening Spaces: Design As Landscape Architecture. Trade Cloth. Birkhauser Verlag AG. CH-4010 Basel, 2003. 191p. ISBN:3-7643-7013-0, ISBN13: 978-3-7643-7013-8. Dewey:712. LCCN:2003-062865.

Audience: **g,l,u,f.**

Nadenicek, Daniel J.   **SB470.53**
What Do We Expect to Learn from Our History?: The First Symposium on History in Landscape Architecture. Eliza Pennypacker (Editor). Trade Paper. Penn State University, Center for Studies in Landscape History. University Park, PA. 1996. 156p. ISBN:1-888901-00-4, ISBN13: 978-1-888901-00-9. Dewey:712.09.

Audience: **g,l,u,f.**

Ndubisi, Forster   **SB472.45.N48 2002**
Ecological Planning: A Historical and Comparative Synthesis. Trade Cloth. Johns Hopkins University Press. Baltimore, MD. 2002. 304p. Center Books on Contemporary Landscape Design Ser., : ISBN:0-8018-6801-7, ISBN13: 978-0-8018-6801-6. Dewey:333.73. LCCN:2001-001744.

Audience: **l,u,f.** *Choice, 2003.*

Nolen, John NA9105.N6 2005
New Towns for Old: Achievements in Civic Improvement in Some American Small Towns and Neighborhoods. Charles D. Warren (Introduction by). Trade Cloth. University of Massachusetts Press. Amherst, MA. 2005. 328p. ISBN:1-55849-480-4, ISBN13: 978-1-55849-480-0. Dewey:711/.4/0973. LCCN:2005-000058.
Audience: **g,l,u,f.** *Choice, 2005.*

Prigann, Herman, et al. SB472.E25 2004
Aesthetics of Ecology. Heike Strelow & Vera David (Authors). Trade Cloth. Birkhauser Verlag AG. CH-4010 Basel, 2004. 255p. ISBN:3-7643-2424-4, ISBN13: 978-3-7643-2424-7. Dewey:712. LCCN:2004-301181.
Audience: **l,u,f.**

Reed, Peter SB472.45.R437 2005
Groundswell: Constructing the Contemporary Landscape. Trade Paper. Birkhauser Verlag AG. CH-4010 Basel, 2006. 176p. ISBN:3-7643-7240-0, ISBN13: 978-3-7643-7240-8. Dewey:712.5. LCCN:2004-117647.
Audience: **g,l,u,f.**

Ruggles, Fairchild D. SB457.8.R845 2000
Gardens, Landscape and Vision in the Palaces of Islamic Spain. Trade Cloth. Pennsylvania State University Press. University Park, PA. 1999. 1334p. ISBN:0-271-01851-8, ISBN13: 978-0-271-01851-5. Dewey:712/.0917/671. LCCN:98-018914.
Audience: **g,l,u,f.** *Choice, 2000.*

Saunders, William S. (Editor) SB466.U7B58 1998
Richard Haag: Bloedel Reserve and Gasworks Park. Trade Paper. Princeton Architectural Press. New York, NY. 1997. 64p. Landscape Views Ser. ISBN:1-56898-117-1, ISBN13: 978-1-56898-117-8. Dewey:712/.092. LCCN:97-024470.
Audience: **g,l,u,f.**

Schama, Simon HN17.5
Landscape and Memory. Trade Paper. Alfred A. Knopf Inc. New York, NY. 1996. 672p. ISBN:0-679-73512-7, ISBN13: 978-0-679-73512-0. Dewey:306/.09.
Audience: **l,u,f.** *Choice, 1995.*

Schröder, Thies (Volume Editor) SB470.55.E85S3613
Changes in Scenery: Contemporary Landscape Architecture in Europe. C. Girot (Preface by). Trade Cloth. Birkhauser Boston. Cambridge, MA. 2001. 183p. ISBN:3-7643-6428-9, ISBN13: 978-3-7643-6428-1. Dewey:712/.094. LCCN:2001-035381.
Audience: **l,u,f.**

Seddon, George QH45.2.S434 1998
Landprints: Reflections on Place and Landscape. Gustav J. V. Nossal (Foreword by). Trade Cloth. Cambridge University Press. New York, NY. 1997. 272p. ISBN:0-521-58501-5, ISBN13: 978-0-521-58501-9. Dewey:508. LCCN:97-027550.
Audience: **g,l,u,f.**

Simo, Melanie Louise SB470.53.S56 2003
Forest and Garden: Traces of Wildness in a Modernizing Land, 1897-1949. Trade Cloth. University Press of Virginia.

Charlottesville, VA. 2003. xix, 302p. ISBN:0-8139-2159-7, ISBN13: 978-0-8139-2159-4. Dewey:712/.0973. LCCN:2002-010189.
Audience: **l,u,f.** *Choice, 2003.*

Southam, Jem (Author, Photographer) TR660.5.S64 2005
Landscape Stories. Gerry Badger & Andy Grundberg (Contribution by). Trade Cloth. Princeton Architectural Press. New York, NY. 2005. 156p. ISBN:1-56898-517-7, ISBN13: 978-1-56898-517-6. Dewey:779/.36423/092. LCCN:2004-025877.
Audience: **l,u,f.**

Spirn, Anne Whiston SB472.S685 1998
The Language of Landscape. Cloth over Boards. Yale University Press. Cumberland, RI. 1998. 334p. ISBN:0-300-07745-9, ISBN13: 978-0-300-07745-2. Dewey:712. LCCN:98-007487.
Audience: **g,l,u,f.** *Choice, 1999.*

Swaffield, Simon R. (Editor) SB472.T44 2002
Theory in Landscape Architecture: A Reader. Trade Paper. University of Pennsylvania Press. Philadelphia, PA. 2002. xii, 265p. Penn Studies in Landscape Architecture ISBN:0-8122-1821-3, ISBN13: 978-0-8122-1821-3. Dewey:712.2. LCCN:2002-019461.
Audience: **l,u,f.**

Tishler, William H. (Editor) SB470.54.M54M55 2004
Midwestern Landscape Architecture. Trade Paper. University of Illinois Press. Champaign, IL. 2004. 272p. ISBN:0-252-07214-6, ISBN13: 978-0-252-07214-7. Dewey:712/.0977.
Audience: **g,l,u,f.** *Choice, 2001.*

Topos - European Landscape Magazine Staff SB470.55.E85T48 2003
About Landscape: Essays on Design, Style, Time and Space. Trade Paper. Birkhauser Verlag AG. CH-4010 Basel, 2003. 144p. ISBN:3-7643-6977-9, ISBN13: 978-3-7643-6977-4. Dewey:712/.094. LCCN:2003-057824.
Audience: **l,u,f.**

Topos - European Landscape Magazine Staff SB469.35.S34
Landscape Architecture in Scandinavia: Projects from Denmark, Sweeden, Norway, Finland and Iceland. Trade Paper. Birkhauser Verlag AG. CH-4010 Basel, 2002. 144p. ISBN:3-7643-6732-6, ISBN13: 978-3-7643-6732-9. Dewey:720.
Audience: **l,u,f.**

Topos - European Landscape Magazine Staff SB472.8.N48 2002
Netherlands in Focus: Exemplary Ideas and Concepts for Town and Landscape. Trade Paper. Birkhauser Verlag AG. CH-4010 Basel, 2002. 128p. ISBN:3-7643-6671-0, ISBN13: 978-3-7643-6671-1. Dewey:711.409492.
Audience: **g,l,u,f.**

Topos - European Landscape Magazine Staff SB484.E8P375 2002
Parks: Green Spaces in European Cities. L. Baljon, R. Burdett

& J. Dettmar (Contribution by). Trade Paper. Birkhauser Verlag AG. CH-4010 Basel, 2002. 128p. ISBN:3-7643-6731-8, ISBN13: 978-3-7643-6731-2. Dewey:712.5094.

Audience: **g,l,u,f.**

Treib, Marc (Editor)   **SB470.5.A7252002**
The Architecture of Landscape, 1940-1960. Trade Cloth. University of Pennsylvania Press. Philadelphia, PA. 2002. 328p. Penn Studies in Landscape Architecture ISBN:0-8122-3623-8, ISBN13: 978-0-8122-3623-1. Dewey:712/.09/044. LCCN:2001-057387.

Audience: **l,u,f.** *Choice, 2003.*

Vogt, Christian   **SB466.E9K54 2004**
  (Photographer)
Dieter Kienast. Udo Weilacher, Martin R. Dean, Thomas Göbel-Gross, Dieter Kienast, Erika Kienast, German Ritz & Arthur Ruegg (Contribution by). Trade Paper. Birkhauser Verlag AG. CH-4010 Basel, 2004. 304p. ISBN:3-7643-6847-0, ISBN13: 978-3-7643-6847-0. Dewey:712.

Audience: **g,l,u,f.**

Weilacher, Udo   **SB472.W545 1999**
Between Landscape Architecture and Land Art. Trade Cloth. Birkhauser Boston. Cambridge, MA. 1999. ISBN:0-8176-6119-0, ISBN13: 978-0-8176-6119-9. Dewey:712. LCCN:99-029959.

Audience: **l,u,f.**

Weilacher, Udo   **SB470.C73W4513 2001**
Visionary Gardens: The Modern Landscapes of Ernst Cramer. M. Robinson (Translator), P. Latz (Foreword by). Trade Cloth. Birkhauser Verlag AG. CH-4010 Basel, 2001. 287p. ISBN:3-7643-6567-6, ISBN13: 978-3-7643-6567-7. Dewey:712/.092. LCCN:2002-283460.

Audience: **g,l,u,f.**

Weltman-Aron, Brigitte   **SB470.55.G7W46 2001**
On Other Grounds: Landscape Gardening and Nationalism in Eighteenth-Century England and France. Cloth Text. State University of New York Press. Albany, NY. 2000. x, 190p. SUNY Series, The Margins of Literature ISBN:0-7914-4805-3, ISBN13: 978-0-7914-4805-2. Dewey:712/.0942/09033. LCCN:00-026554.

Audience: **g,l,u,f.**

Landscape Architecture > Individual Landscape Architects

American Society of   **SB469.9**
  Landscape Architects Staff
Profiles in Landscape Architecture. Trade Cloth. American Society of Landscape Architects. Washington, DC. 1992. 104p. ISBN:0-941236-18-8, ISBN13: 978-0-941236-18-8. Dewey:712.

Audience: **g,u,f.**

Amidon, Jane   **SB470.S57K46 2005**
Ken Smith Landscape Architects. Trade Paper. Princeton Architectural Press. New York, NY. 2005. 176p. Source Books

in Landscape Architecture, Vol. 2 ISBN:1-56898-510-X, ISBN13: 978-1-56898-510-7. Dewey:712/.092. LCCN:2005-013766.

Audience: **l,u,f.**

Amidon, Jane   **SB472.A472005**
Moving Horizons: The Landscape Architecture of Kathryn Gustafson and Partners. Aaron Betsky (Introduction by). Trade Cloth. Birkhauser Verlag AG. CH-4010 Basel, 2005. 208p. ISBN:3-7643-2425-2, ISBN13: 978-3-7643-2425-4. LCCN:2005-045283.

Audience: **g,l,u,f.**

Berrizbeitia, Anita   **SB470.B87B47 2004**
Roberto Burle Marx in Caracas: Parque Del Este, 1956-1961. Book, Other. University of Pennsylvania Press. Philadelphia, PA. 2004. 136p. Penn Studies in Landscape Architecture ISBN:0-8122-3804-4, ISBN13: 978-0-8122-3804-4. Dewey:712/.092. LCCN:2004-041894.

Audience: **u,f.** *Choice, 2005.*

Beveridge, Charles E. &   **SB470.O5**
  Olmsted, Frederick Law
The Papers of Frederick Law Olmsted: Creating Central Park, 1857-1861, Vol. 3. David Schuyler (Editor). Trade Cloth. Johns Hopkins University Press. Baltimore, MD. 1995. 504p. Papers of Frederick Law Olmsted, Vol. 3 ISBN:0-8018-2751-5, ISBN13: 978-0-8018-2751-8. Dewey:712/.092/4. LCCN:82-004701.

Audience: **l,u,f.**

Bisgrove, Richard   **SB470.J38B57**
Gardens of Gertrude Jekyll. Trade Cloth. Lincoln Frances Ltd. London, 1998. 192p. ISBN:0-7112-0746-1, ISBN13: 978-0-7112-0746-2. Dewey:712.60942.

Audience: **g,l,u,f.** *Choice, 1993.*

Cooper, Guy, et al.   **SB470.C43C66 2000**
Mirrors of Paradise: The Gardens of Fernando Caruncho. Gordon Taylor & Dan Kiley (Authors). Trade Cloth. Monacelli Press, Inc. New York, NY. 2000. 224p. ISBN:1-58093-071-9, ISBN13: 978-1-58093-071-0. Dewey:712/.092 B. LCCN:00-057867.

Audience: **g,l,u,f.** *Choice, 2001.*

Daniels, Stephen   **SB470.R4D35 1999**
Humphrey Repton: Landscape Gardening and the Geography of Georgian England. Cloth over Boards. Yale University Press. Cumberland, RI. 1999. 328p. Paul Mellon Centre for Studies in British Art ISBN:0-300-07964-8, ISBN13: 978-0-300-07964-7. Dewey:712/.092. LCCN:98-052787.

Audience: **g,l,u,f.** *Choice, 2000.*

Eggener, Keith L.   **NA759.B36E35 2001**
Luis Barragan's Gardens of El Pedregal. Mark Treib (Foreword by). Trade Cloth. Princeton Architectural Press. New York, NY. 2001. 256p. Building Studies ISBN:1-56898-267-4, ISBN13: 978-1-56898-267-0. Dewey:728/.37/092. LCCN:2001-000170.

Audience: **g,l,u,f.** *Choice, 2002.*

Eliot, Charles W.   SB470.E6E6 1999
Charles Eliot, Landscape Architect. Keith N. Morgan
(Introduction by). Cloth Text. University of Massachusetts Press.
Amherst, MA. 1999. 826p. American Society of Landscape
Architects Reprints Ser. ISBN:1-55849-212-7, ISBN13:
978-1-55849-212-7. Dewey:712/.092 B. LCCN:99-021373.
       Audience: **g,l,u,f.**

Helfrich, Kurt Gerard   SB470.G74H45 2005
   Frederick
Isabelle Greene: Shaping Place in the Landscape. Isabelle Clara
Greene & University of California, Santa Barbara, University
Art Museum Staff (Contribution by). Trade Paper. University of
California, Santa Barbara, Art Museum. Santa Barbara, CA.
2005. 96p. ISBN:0-942006-73-9, ISBN13: 978-0-942006-73-5.
Dewey:712/.092. LCCN:2005-004210.
       Audience: **g,l,u,f.**

Jackson, Faith R.   SB470.P48J33 1997
Pioneer of Tropical Landscape Architecture: William Lyman
Phillips in Florida. Trade Cloth. University Press of Florida.
Gainesville, FL. 1997. 304p. ISBN:0-8130-1516-2, ISBN13:
978-0-8130-1516-3. Dewey:[B]. LCCN:96-037166.
       Audience: **g,l,u,f.**

Karson, Robin   SB470.S65K37 2003
Fletcher Steele, Landscape Architect: An Account of the
Gardenmaker's Life, 1885-1971. Ed. 2. Trade Paper. University
of Massachusetts Press. Amherst, MA. 2003. 368p.
ISBN:1-55849-413-8, ISBN13: 978-1-55849-413-8.
Dewey:712/.092 B. LCCN:2003-016247.
       Audience: **g,l,u,f.**

Mesquita, Ivo, et al.   SB470.O5
Roberto Burle Marx: Landscape Architecture. Isabel Duprat &
Milton Hatoum (Authors). Trade Cloth. Birkhauser Verlag AG.
CH-4010 Basel, 2004. 228p. ISBN:3-7643-7103-X, ISBN13:
978-3-7643-7103-6. Dewey:712.092.
       Audience: **g,l,u,f.**

Montero, Marta Iris &   SB470.B87 M6613 2001
   Burle Marx, Roberto
Roberto Burle Marx: The Lyrical Landscape. Trade Cloth.
University of California Press. Berkeley, CA. 2001. 208p.
ISBN:0-520-23290-9, ISBN13: 978-0-520-23290-7.
Dewey:712/.092. LCCN:2001-027618.
       Audience: **g,l,u,f.** *Choice, 2002.*

Olin, Laurie   SB469.78.U6O45 1996
Transforming the Common-Place: Selections from Laurie Olin's
Sketchbooks. Trade Cloth. Princeton Architectural Press. New
York, NY. 1997. 72p. ISBN:1-878271-88-1, ISBN13:
978-1-878271-88-4. Dewey:712. LCCN:96-076087.
       Audience: **g,l,u,f.**

Olmsted, Frederick Law   SB470.O5
The Papers of Frederick Law Olmsted: Slavery and the South,
1852-1857. Charles E. Beveridge & Charles C. McLaughlin
(Editors). Trade Cloth. Johns Hopkins University Press.

Baltimore, MD. 1981. 528p. Papers of Frederick Law Olmsted
ISBN:0-8018-2242-4, ISBN13: 978-0-8018-2242-1.
Dewey:712/.092/4. LCCN:80-008881.
       Audience: **l,f.**

Olmsted, Frederick Law   SB470.O5A2
The Papers of Frederick Law Olmsted: Defending the Union:
the Civil War and the U. S. Sanitary Commission, 1861-1863.
Jane T. Censer (Editor). Trade Cloth. Johns Hopkins University
Press. Baltimore, MD. 1986. 782p. Papers of Frederick Law
Olmsted, Vol. 4 ISBN:0-8018-3067-2, ISBN13:
978-0-8018-3067-9. Dewey:973.7/77. LCCN:85-024044.
       Audience: **l,u,f.** *Choice, 1987.*

Olmsted, Frederick Law, et   SB470.O5
   al.
The Papers of Frederick Law Olmsted: The Formative Years,
1822-1853. Carolyn R. Hoffman & Charles E. Beveridge
(Authors), Charles C. McLaughlin (Editor). Trade Cloth. Johns
Hopkins University Press. Baltimore, MD. 1977. 448p. Papers
of Frederick Law Olmsted ISBN:0-8018-1798-6, ISBN13:
978-0-8018-1798-4. Dewey:712/.092/4. LCCN:76-047378.
       Audience: **l,u,f.**

Olmsted, Frederick Law   SB470.O5A2 1977 V.6
The Papers of Frederick Law Olmsted: The Years of Olmsted,
Vaux and Company, 1865-1874. David Schuyler & Jane T.
Censer (Editors). Trade Cloth. Johns Hopkins University Press.
Baltimore, MD. 1974. 760p. The Papers of Frederick Law
Olmsted Ser. ISBN:0-8018-4198-4, ISBN13:
978-0-8018-4198-9. Dewey:712.092.
       Audience: **l,u,f.**

Ranney, Victoria P. (Editor),   SB470.O5A2
   et al.
The Papers of Frederick Law Olmsted: The California Frontier,
1863-1865. Gerard J. Rauluk, Carolyn F. Hoffman & Frederick
Law Olmsted (Editors). Trade Cloth. Johns Hopkins University
Press. Baltimore, MD. 1990. 848p. Papers of Frederick Law
Olmsted, Vol. 5 ISBN:0-8018-3885-1, ISBN13:
978-0-8018-3885-9. Dewey:712 s. LCCN:89-015315.
       Audience: **l,u,f.**

Richardson, Tim (Editor)   SB472.45
Vanguard Landscapes and Gardens. Trade Cloth. Thames &
Hudson. New York, NY. 2004. 224p. ISBN:0-500-51131-4,
ISBN13: 978-0-500-51131-2. Dewey:712.092.
LCCN:2003-101332.
       Audience: **l,u,f.**

Rybczynski, Witold   SB470.O5R93 1999
A Clearing in the Distance: Frederick Law Olmsted and
America in the 19th Century. Trade Cloth. Simon & Schuster.
New York, NY. 1999. 480p. ISBN:0-684-82463-9, ISBN13:
978-0-684-82463-5. Dewey:712/.092 B. LCCN:99-018094.
       Audience: **g,l,u,f.**

Schnadelbach, R. Terry   SB470.V58S36 2001
Ferruccio Vitale: Landscape Architect of the Country Place

ERA. Trade Cloth. Princeton Architectural Press. New York, NY. 2001. 336p. ISBN:1-56898-290-9, ISBN13: 978-1-56898-290-8. Dewey:712/.092. LCCN:2001-001155.

Audience: **g,l,u,f.**

Tatum, George B. &   **SB470.D68D86 1987**
MacDougall, Elisabeth B. (Editors)
Prophet with Honor: The Career of Andrew Jackson Downing, 1815-1852. Trade Cloth. Dumbarton Oaks. Washington, DC. 1990. 332p. Dumbarton Oaks Colloquium on the History of Landscape Architecture Ser., No. 11 ISBN:0-88402-178-5, ISBN13: 978-0-88402-178-0. Dewey:712/.09. LCCN:88-013943.

Audience: **u,f.**

Treib, Marc & Imbert,   **SB470.E26T74 1997**
Dorothee
Garrett Eckbo: Modern Landscapes for Living. Trade Cloth. University of California Press. Berkeley, CA. 1997. 208p. ISBN:0-520-20779-3, ISBN13: 978-0-520-20779-0. Dewey:306/.09794. LCCN:96-031620.

Audience: **g,l,u,f.**

Walker, Peter   **SB470.W34**
Peter Walker and Partners: Defining the Craft. Jane Brown Gillette (Editor). Trade Cloth. D. A. P./Distributed Art Publishers. New York, NY. 2005. 232p. ISBN:0-9746800-1-X, ISBN13: 978-0-9746800-1-9. Dewey:712.092.

Audience: **g,l,u,f.**

Weller, Richard   **SB472.W45 2004**
Room 4.1.3: Innovations in Landscape Architecture. Trade Cloth. University of Pennsylvania Press. Philadelphia, PA. 2004. 288p. Penn Studies in Landscape Architecture ISBN:0-8122-3784-6, ISBN13: 978-0-8122-3784-9. Dewey:712. LCCN:2003-070549.

Audience: **g,l,u,f.**

Landscape Architecture > Materials, Techniques, Practices

Birnbaum, Charles A. &   **SB472.8.D47 2005**
Hughes, Mary V.
Design with Culture: Claiming America's Landscape Heritage. Trade Cloth. University Press of Virginia. Charlottesville, VA. 2001. 216p. ISBN:0-8139-2329-8, ISBN13: 978-0-8139-2329-1. Dewey:712/.0973. LCCN:2004-017412.

Audience: **g,l,u,f.**

Dines, Nicholas T. & Harris,   **SB475.9.S72T55 1998**
Charles W.
Time-Saver Standards for Landscape Architecture. Ed. 2. Trade Cloth. McGraw-Hill Professional Publishing. New York, NY. 1997. 928p. Time-Saver Standards Concise Ser. ISBN:0-07-017027-4, ISBN13: 978-0-07-017027-8. Dewey:712/.02/18. LCCN:97-031842.

Audience: **g,l,u,f.**

Duerksen, Christopher J. &   **QH76.D84 2005**
Snyder, Cara
Nature-Friendly Communities: Habitat Protection and Land Use Planning. Trade Cloth. Island Press. Washington, DC. 2005. 421p. ISBN:1-55963-593-2, ISBN13: 978-1-55963-593-6. Dewey:333.95/16. LCCN:2005-003191.

Audience: **g,u,f.** *Choice, 2006.*

Earth Pledge   **SB419.5.E29 2005**
Green Roofs: Ecological Design and Construction. William McDonough (Foreword by). Trade Cloth. Schiffer Publishing, Ltd. Atglen, PA. 2004. 240p. ISBN:0-7643-2189-7, ISBN13: 978-0-7643-2189-4. Dewey:635.9/671. LCCN:2004-025679.

Audience: **g,l,u,f.**

Melby, Pete & Cathcart,   **SB472.45.M45 2002**
Tom
Regenerative Design Techniques: Practical Applications in Landscape Design. Trade Cloth. John Wiley & Sons, Inc. Hoboken, NJ. 2002. 416p. ISBN:0-471-41472-7, ISBN13: 978-0-471-41472-8. Dewey:712. LCCN:2002-006388.

Audience: **u,f.**

Motloch, John L.   **SB472.M68 2001**
Introduction to Landscape Design. Ed. 2. Trade Cloth. John Wiley & Sons, Inc. Hoboken, NJ. 2000. 384p. ISBN:0-471-35291-8, ISBN13: 978-0-471-35291-4. Dewey:712. LCCN:00-026081.

Audience: **g,l,u,f.**

Simonds, John Ormsbee &   **SB472**
Starke, Barry W.
Landscape Architecture: A Manual of Site Planning and Design. Ed. 4. Trade Cloth. McGraw-Hill Professional Publishing. New York, NY. 2006. 396p. ISBN:0-07-146120-5, ISBN13: 978-0-07-146120-7. Dewey:712. LCCN:2006-015597.

Audience: **g,l,u,f.**

Stocklein, Marc C.   **SB408.S82 2001**
The Complete Plant Selection Guide for Landscape Design. Trade Cloth. Purdue University Press. West Lafayette, IN. 2001. 747p. ISBN:1-55753-139-0, ISBN13: 978-1-55753-139-1. Dewey:715. LCCN:00-051769.

Audience: **g,l,u,f.**

Strom, Steven, et al.   **TH375**
Site Engineering for Landscape Architects. Ed. 4. Kurt Nathan, David Lamm & Jake Woland (Authors). Trade Cloth. John Wiley & Sons, Inc. Hoboken, NJ. 2004. 352p. ISBN:0-471-27394-5, ISBN13: 978-0-471-27394-3. Dewey:624. LCCN:2004-013110.

Audience: **l,u,f.**

Trowbridge, Peter J. &   **SB436.T86 2004**
Bassuk, Nina L.
Trees in the Urban Landscape: Site Assessment, Design, and Installation. Trade Cloth. John Wiley & Sons, Inc. Hoboken, NJ. 2004. 224p. ISBN:0-471-39246-4, ISBN13: 978-0-471-39246-0. Dewey:715/.2. LCCN:2003-017375.

Audience: **g,l,u,f.**

Winterbottom, Daniel M.   TH4961.W557 2000
Wood in the Landscape: A Practical Guide to Specification and Design. Trade Cloth. John Wiley & Sons, Inc. Hoboken, NJ. 2000. 216p. Material in Landscape Architecture and Site Design Ser., Vol. 2 ISBN:0-471-29419-5, ISBN13: 978-0-471-29419-1. Dewey:624. LCCN:99-045536.

Audience: **l,u,f.**

Landscape Architecture > Gardens, Parks

Aitken, Richard & Looker,   SB457.534
   Michael (Editors)
The Oxford Companion to Australian Gardens. Trade Cloth. Oxford University Press, Inc. New York, NY. 2002. 728p. ISBN:0-19-553644-4, ISBN13: 978-0-19-553644-7. Dewey:635/.0994. LCCN:2003-386239.

Audience: **g,l,u,f.** *Choice, 2003.*

Baratay, Eric &   QL76.B3713 2002
   Hardouin-Fugier, Elisabeth
Zoo: A History of Zoological Gardens in the West. Oliver Welsh (Translator). Trade Cloth. Reaktion Books, Ltd. London, 2004. 356p. ISBN:1-86189-111-3, ISBN13: 978-1-86189-111-2. Dewey:590.73. LCCN:2004-426245.

Audience: **g,l,u,f.** *Choice, 2003.*

Bowe, Patrick (Translator)   SB458.55.B68 2004
Gardens of the Roman World. Trade Cloth. Oxford University Press, Inc. New York, NY. 2004. 176p. ISBN:0-89236-740-7, ISBN13: 978-0-89236-740-5. Dewey:712/.0937. LCCN:2003-017143.

Audience: **g,l,u,f.** *Choice, 2005.*

Brown, Jane   SB465
The Modern Garden. Sofia Brignone & Alan Ward (Text by). Trade Cloth. Princeton Architectural Press. New York, NY. 2000. 224p. ISBN:1-56898-238-0, ISBN13: 978-1-56898-238-0. Dewey:712.6/0904.

Audience: **g,l,u,f.** *Choice, 2001.*

Conan, Michel (Editor)   SB470.53.E58 2000
Environmentalism in Landscape Architecture: History of Landscape Architecture Colloquium. Trade Cloth. Dumbarton Oaks. Washington, DC. 2001. 292p. Dumbarton Oaks Colloquium on the History of Landscape Architecture Ser., Vol. 22 ISBN:0-88402-278-1, ISBN13: 978-0-88402-278-7. Dewey:712/.0973. LCCN:00-041375.

Audience: **u,f.**

Cothran, James R.   SB466.U6C58 2003
Gardens and Historic Plants of the Antebellum South. Trade Cloth. University of South Carolina Press. Columbia, SC. 2004. 344p. ISBN:1-57003-501-6, ISBN13: 978-1-57003-501-2. Dewey:712/.6/0975. LCCN:2003-000799.

Audience: **g,l,u,f.** *Choice, 2004.*

Cunningham, Anne S.   NA8360.C86 2000
Crystal Palaces: American Garden Conservatories. Paul Bennett (Introduction by). Trade Cloth. Princeton Architectural Press.

New York, NY. 2000. xiii, 178p. ISBN:1-56898-242-9, ISBN13: 978-1-56898-242-7. Dewey:728/.924/0973. LCCN:00-008825.

Audience: **g,l,u,f.** *Choice, 2001.*

de Jongh, Edward   SB457.58.J66132001
Nature and Art: Dutch Garden and Landscape Architecture 1650-1740. Ann Langenakens (Translator). Trade Cloth. University of Pennsylvania Press. Philadelphia, PA. 2001. 264p. Studies in Landscape Architecture ISBN:0-8122-3543-6, ISBN13: 978-0-8122-3543-2. Dewey:712/.09492. LCCN:00-062860.

Audience: **l,u,f.** *Choice, 2002.*

Grusin, Richard   SB484.A4G78 2003
Culture, Technology, and the Creation of America's National Parks. Albert Gelpi & Ross Posnock (Contribution by). Trade Cloth. Cambridge University Press. New York, NY. 2004. 232p. Cambridge Studies in American Literature and Culture Ser. ISBN:0-521-82649-7, ISBN13: 978-0-521-82649-5. Dewey:333.78/3/0973. LCCN:2003-043507.

Audience: **g,l,u,f.** *Choice, 2005.*

Helmreich, Anne   SB466.G7H45 2002
The English Garden and National Identity: The Competing Styles of Garden Design, 1870-1914. Trade Cloth. Cambridge University Press. New York, NY. 2002. 302p. Modern Architecture and Cultural Identity Ser. ISBN:0-521-59293-3, ISBN13: 978-0-521-59293-2. Dewey:712/.6/0942. LCCN:2001-043777.

Audience: **l,u,f.**

Hirschfeld, Christian C.   SB454.3.P45H572001
Theory of Garden Art. Linda B. Parshall (Translator). Trade Cloth. University of Pennsylvania Press. Philadelphia, PA. 2001. 504p. Studies in Landscape Architecture ISBN:0-8122-3584-3, ISBN13: 978-0-8122-3584-5. Dewey:712/.01. LCCN:00-045574.

Audience: **g,l,u,f.** *Choice, 2001.*

Hunt, John D. (Editor)   SB457.58.D86 1988
Dutch Garden in the Seventeenth Century. Trade Cloth. Dumbarton Oaks. Washington, DC. 1990. 214p. Dumbarton Oaks Colloquium on the History of Landscape Architecture Ser., No. 12 ISBN:0-88402-187-4, ISBN13: 978-0-88402-187-2. Dewey:712/.09492/09032. LCCN:89-023831.

Audience: **u,f.**

Hunt, John D. (Editor)   SB451.D85 1989
Garden History: Issues, Approaches, Methods. Trade Cloth. Dumbarton Oaks. Washington, DC. 1992. 404p. Dumbarton Oaks Colloquium on the History of Landscape Architecture Ser., No. 13 ISBN:0-88402-197-1, ISBN13: 978-0-88402-197-1. Dewey:712/.09. LCCN:91-023299.

Audience: **u,f.**

Hunt, John D.   SB457.6.H865
Gardens and the Picturesque: Studies in the History of Landscape Architecture. Trade Paper. MIT Press. Cambridge, MA. 1994. 408p. ISBN:0-262-58131-0, ISBN13: 978-0-262-58131-8. Dewey:712.609.

Audience: **u,f.** *Choice, 1992.*

Hunt, Lord   SB472.H83 2004
Afterlife of Gardens. Book, Other. University of Pennsylvania
Press. Philadelphia, PA. 2004. 256p. Penn Studies in Landscape
Architecture ISBN:0-8122-3846-X, ISBN13: 978-0-8122-3846-4.
Dewey:712. LCCN:2005-273270.
Audience: **l,u,f.**

Imbert, Dorothee   SB470.55.F8.I43 1993
The Modernist Garden in France. Cloth over Boards. Yale
University Press. Cumberland, RI. 1993. 400p.
ISBN:0-300-04716-9, ISBN13: 978-0-300-04716-5.
Dewey:712.0944. LCCN:92-030514.
Audience: **l,u,f.** *Choice, 1993.*

Kuitert, Wybe   SB458.K85 2002
Themes in the History of Japanese Garden Art. Trade Cloth.
University of Hawaii Press. Honolulu, HI. 2002. 304p.
ISBN:0-8248-2312-5, ISBN13: 978-0-8248-2312-2.
Dewey:712/.6/0952. LCCN:2001-052823.
Audience: **l,u,f.** *Choice, 2003.*

Laird, Mark   SB457.6.L3491999
Flowering of the Landscape Garden: English Pleasure Grounds,
1720-1800. Trade Cloth. University of Pennsylvania Press.
Philadelphia, PA. 1999. 448p. Studies in Landscape Architecture
ISBN:0-8122-3457-X, ISBN13: 978-0-8122-3457-2.
Dewey:712/.0942/09034. LCCN:98-022949.
Audience: **u,f.** *Choice, 1999.*

Littlewood, Antony R., et al. SB457.547.B97 2001
Byzantine Garden Culture. Henry Maguire & Joachim
Wolschke-Bulmahn (Authors). Trade Paper. Dumbarton Oaks.
Washington, DC. 2002. 280p. ISBN:0-88402-280-3, ISBN13:
978-0-88402-280-0. Dewey:712/.09495. LCCN:00-060020.
Audience: **u,f.**

MacDougall, Elizabeth B. &   SB458.55.D85 1984
 Jashemski, Wilhelmina Feemster (Editors)
Ancient Roman Villa Gardens. Trade Cloth. Dumbarton Oaks.
Washington, DC. 1987. 260p. Dumbarton Oaks Colloquium on
the History of Landscape Architecture Ser., No. 10
ISBN:0-88402-162-9, ISBN13: 978-0-88402-162-9.
Dewey:712/.6/0937. LCCN:86-024255.
Audience: **u,f.** *Choice, 1987.*

McClelland, Linda F.   SB482.A4M3 1998
Building the National Parks: The Historic Landscape Design and
Construction. John S. Reynolds (Foreword by). Trade Paper.
Johns Hopkins University Press. Baltimore, MD. 1997. 624p.
ISBN:0-8018-5583-7, ISBN13: 978-0-8018-5583-2.
Dewey:353.7/8. LCCN:97-012664.
Audience: **g,l,u,f.**

Moore, Charles W., et al.   SB472.M64
The Poetics of Gardens. William J. Mitchell & William Turnbull
Jr. (Authors). Trade Paper. MIT Press. Cambridge, MA. 1993.
272p. ISBN:0-262-63153-9, ISBN13: 978-0-262-63153-2.
Dewey:712.
Audience: **l,u,f.** *Choice, 1989.*

Morris, Alistair   SB473.5.M67 1996
Antiques from the Garden. Ed. 2. Trade Cloth. Garden Art
Press. Woodbridge, 1999. 288p. Antique Collectors' Club Ser.
ISBN:1-870673-33-6, ISBN13: 978-1-870673-33-4.
Dewey:635/.028. LCCN:99-494994.
Audience: **g,l,u,f.**

Olin, Laurie   SB470.55.G7O442000
Across the Open Field: Essays Drawn from English Landscapes.
Trade Cloth. University of Pennsylvania Press. Philadelphia, PA.
1999. 384p. Studies in Landscape Architecture
ISBN:0-8122-3531-2, ISBN13: 978-0-8122-3531-9.
Dewey:712/.0942. LCCN:99-015965.
Audience: **g,l,u,f.** *Choice, 2000.*

O'Malley, Therese & Treib,   SB457.53.R44 1995
 Marc (Editors)
Regional Garden Design in the United States. Trade Cloth.
Dumbarton Oaks. Washington, DC. 1995. 328p. Colloquium on
the History of Landscape Architecture Ser., No. 15
ISBN:0-88402-223-4, ISBN13: 978-0-88402-223-7.
Dewey:712/.0973. LCCN:93-023720.
Audience: **g,l,u,f.** *Choice, 1996.*

Pigeat, Jean-Paul   SB451
Gardens of the World: Two Thousand Years of Garden Design.
Susan Pickford (Translator). Trade Cloth, Pictures or
Photographs. Flammarion et Cie. Paris, 2004. 224p.
ISBN:2-08-011272-4, ISBN13: 978-2-08-011272-9.
Dewey:712.6/09.
Audience: **g,l,u,f.** *Choice, 2004.*

Porter, Yves & Thevenart,   SB466.I6
 Arthur
Palaces and Gardens of Persia. Trade Cloth. Flammarion et Cie.
Paris, 2004. 240p. ISBN:2-08-011257-0, ISBN13:
978-2-08-011257-6. Dewey:712.6/0955.
Audience: **g,l.** *Choice, 2004.*

Rosenzweig, Roy &   F128.65.C3R67
 Blackmar, Elizabeth
The Park and the People: A History of Central Park. Trade
Cloth. Cornell University Press. Ithaca, NY. 1998. 640p.
ISBN:0-8014-9751-5, ISBN13: 978-0-8014-9751-3.
Dewey:974.71. LCCN:92-007062.
Audience: **g,l,u,f.** *Choice, 1993.*

Ross, Stephanie   SB457.6
What Gardens Mean. Trade Paper. University of Chicago Press.
Chicago, IL. 2001. 302p. ISBN:0-226-72807-2, ISBN13:
978-0-226-72807-0. Dewey:712/.2/094209033.
Audience: **g,l,u,f.** *Choice, 1998.*

Shoemaker, Candace   SB450.95.E49 2001
 (Editor)
Encyclopedia of Gardens: History and Design, Set. Chicago
Botanical Gardens Staff (Produced by). Trade Cloth. Fitzroy
Dearborn Publishers, Inc. Chicago, IL. 1999. 1590p.
ISBN:1-57958-173-0, ISBN13: 978-1-57958-173-2.
Dewey:712/.03. LCCN:2003-267339.
Audience: **g,l,u,f.** *Choice, 2002.*

Smienk, Gerrit &   NA7594 .R44 1992
Steenbergen, Clemens
Italian Villas and Gardens. Ed. 2. Paul Van der Ree (Editor).
Trade Paper. Prestel Publishing. New York, NY. 1992. 298p.
ISBN:3-7913-1181-6, ISBN13: 978-3-7913-1181-4.
Dewey:728.8/0945/09024. LCCN:92-245857.
                                   Audience: **g,l,u,f.** *Choice, 1992.*

Steenbergen, Clemens &   SB470.55.E85R44 2003
Reh, Wouter
Architecture and Landscape: The Design Experiment of the
Great European Gardens and Landscapes. Trade Cloth.
Birkhauser Verlag AG. CH-4010 Basel, 2003. 399p.
ISBN:3-7643-0335-2, ISBN13: 978-3-7643-0335-8.
Dewey:712/.094/0903. LCCN:2003-062784.
                                                Audience: **g,l,u,f.**

Strong, Roy   ND1460.G37S77 2000
The Artist and the Garden. Cloth over Boards. Yale University
Press. Cumberland, RI. 2000. 288p. Paul Mellon Centre for
Studies in British Art ISBN:0-300-08520-6, ISBN13:
978-0-300-08520-4. Dewey:758/.9635. LCCN:00-035922.
                                   Audience: **g,l,u,f.** *Choice, 2001.*

Stuart, David C.   SB407.S795 2002
The Plants That Shaped Our Gardens. Trade Cloth. Harvard
University Press. Cambridge, MA. 2002. 208p.
ISBN:0-674-00790-5, ISBN13: 978-0-674-00790-1.
Dewey:712.6. LCCN:2001-047077.
                                   Audience: **g,l,u,f.** *Choice, 2002.*

Tamulevich, Susan, et al.   SB466.U65D868 2001
Dumbarton Oaks. Ping Amranand & Philip Johnson (Authors).
Trade Cloth. Monacelli Press, Inc. New York, NY. 2002. 224p.
ISBN:1-58093-069-7, ISBN13: 978-1-58093-069-7.
Dewey:712/.6/09753. LCCN:2001-044068.
                                   Audience: **g,l,u,f.** *Choice, 2002.*

Tankard, Judith B.   SB454.3.A76T362004
Gardens of the Arts and Crafts Movement: Reality and
Imagination. Trade Cloth. Harry N. Abrams, Inc. New York, NY.
2004. 216p. ISBN:0-8109-4965-2, ISBN13: 978-0-8109-4965-2.
Dewey:712.6/0942. LCCN:2004-000877.
                                   Audience: **l,u,f.** *Choice, 2005.*

Watelet, Claude-Henri   SB466.F8W38132003
Essay on Gardens: A Chapter in the French Picturesque
Translated into English for the First Time. Samuel Danon
(Editor, Translator). Trade Cloth. University of Pennsylvania
Press. Philadelphia, PA. 2003. 104p. Penn Studies in Landscape
Architecture ISBN:0-8122-3722-6, ISBN13: 978-0-8122-3722-1.
Dewey:712/.6/094409033. LCCN:2002-040932.
                                                Audience: **u,f.**

Wescoat, James L. Jr.   SB458.4.M84 1996
Mughal Gardens: Sources, Places, Representations, and
Prospects. Joachim Wolschke-Bulmahn (Editor). Trade Cloth.
Dumbarton Oaks. Washington, DC. 1996. 294p. Colloquium on
the History of Landscape Architecture Ser., No. 16
ISBN:0-88402-235-8, ISBN13: 978-0-88402-235-0.
Dewey:712/.0954. LCCN:94-042690.
                                                Audience: **u,f.**

Westmacott, Richard   SB457.527.W47 1992
African-American Gardens and Yards in the Rural South. Trade
Paper. University of Tennessee Press. Knoxville, TN. 1992.
216p. ISBN:0-87049-762-6, ISBN13: 978-0-87049-762-9.
Dewey:635/.089/96073075. LCCN:92-016555.
                                   Audience: **l,u,f.** *Choice, 1993.*

Wolschke-Bulmahn,   SB439.N431997
Joachim (Editor)
Nature and Ideology: Nature and Garden Design in the
Twentieth Century. Trade Cloth. Dumbarton Oaks. Washington,
DC. 1997. 284p. Colloquium on the History of Landscape
Architecture Ser., Vol. 18 ISBN:0-88402-246-3, ISBN13:
978-0-88402-246-6. Dewey:712/.01. LCCN:96-046176.
                                   Audience: **u,f.** *Choice, 1998.*

Wong, Young-Tsu   SB466.C53W66 2001
A Paradise Lost: The Imperial Garden Yuanming Yuan. Trade
Paper. University of Hawaii Press. Honolulu, HI. 2000. 238p.
Nanzan Library of Asian Religion and Culture
ISBN:0-8248-2328-1, ISBN13: 978-0-8248-2328-3.
Dewey:712/.6/0951156. LCCN:00-036879.
                                   Audience: **g,l,u,f.** *Choice, 2001.*

Young, Terence   SB482.C22S268 2004
Building San Francisco's Parks, 1850-1930. Trade Cloth. Johns
Hopkins University Press. Baltimore, MD. 2004. 280p. Creating
the North American Landscape Ser. ISBN:0-8018-7432-7,
ISBN13: 978-0-8018-7432-1. Dewey:712/.5/0979461.
LCCN:2003-006247.
                                   Audience: **g,l,u,f.** *Choice, 2004.*

Young, Terence & Riley,   SB481.A2D86 2002
Robert B. (Editors)
Theme Park Landscapes: Antecedents and Variations.
Dumbarton Oaks Staff (Contribution by). Trade Cloth.
Dumbarton Oaks. Washington, DC. 2002. 308p. Dumbarton
Oaks Colloquium on the History of Landscape Architecture Ser.,
20 ISBN:0-88402-285-4, ISBN13: 978-0-88402-285-5.
Dewey:712/.09. LCCN:2002-019400.
                                                Audience: **l,u,f.**

Cultural Heritage > Reference Works > Web Resources

                                                              G140.5
⬜ BCIN, the Bibliographic Database of the Conservation
Information Network.
http://www.bcin.ca
Canadian Heritage Information Network.
                                                Audience: **l,u,f.**

                                                                 NA
⬜ Built in America; Historic American Buildings
Survey/Historic American Engineering Record, 1933-Present.
http://memory.loc.gov/ammem/collections/habs_haer/
Washington, D. C. : Library of Congress.
                                                Audience: **g,l,u,f.**

G140.5

☐ eCultural Resources ; Cultural Resource Network.
http://www.eculturalresources.com/index.php
Cultural Resource Network.

Audience: **g,l,u,f.**

NA200

☐ Historic American Buildings Survey / Historic American
Engineering Survey.
http://www.cr.nps.gov/habshaer/
Washington, D. C. : Department of the Interior, National Park
Service, HABS/HAER/HALS Division.

Audience: **g,l,u,f.**

E159

☐ National Register of Historic Places, National Park Service.
http://www.cr.nps.gov/nr/

Audience: **g,l,u,f.**

NB230.V8

☐ SOS! Save Outdoor Sculpture.
http://www.heritagepreservation.org/PROGRAMS/SOS/sosmain.htm
Washington, D. C. : Heritage Preservation; the National Institute
for Conservation.

Audience: **g,l,u,f.**

G140.5

☐ World Heritage.
http://whc.unesco.org/
United Nations Educational, Scientific and Cultural Organization
(UNESCO).

Audience: **g,l,u,f.**

Cultural Heritage > Reference Works > Bibliographies and Research Guides

AM1

☐ AATA Online ; Abstracts of International Conservation
Literature.
http://aata.getty.edu/NPS

Audience: **g,l,u,f.**

NA1.A12

☐ Avery Index to Architectural Periodicals.
http://www.getty.edu/research/conducting_research/avery_index/
Getty Research Institute.

Audience: **g,l,u,f.**

Cultural Heritage > Reference Works > Dictionaries and Encyclopedias

Adams, Denise Wiles   **SB453.A32 2004**
Restoring American Gardens: An Encyclopedia of Heirloom
Ornamental Plants, 1640-1940. Trade Cloth. Timber Press, Inc.
Portland, OR. 2004. 420p. ISBN:0-88192-619-1, ISBN13:
978-0-88192-619-4. Dewey:635.9/0973. LCCN:2003-057274.

Audience: **g,l,u,f.**

Bucher, Ward (Editor)   **NA31.D55 1996**
Dictionary of Building Preservation. Ed. 1. Trade Cloth. John
Wiley & Sons, Inc. Hoboken, NJ. 1996. 576p.
ISBN:0-471-14413-4, ISBN13: 978-0-471-14413-7.
Dewey:720.2/88/03. LCCN:96-019947.

Audience: **g,l,u,f.** *Choice, 1997.*

Burden, Ernest   **NA105.B87 2003**
Illustrated Dictionary of Architectural Preservation. Trade Paper.
McGraw-Hill Professional Publishing. New York, NY. 2004.
280p. ISBN:0-07-142838-0, ISBN13: 978-0-07-142838-5.
Dewey:720/.28/8. LCCN:2003-066611.

Audience: **g,l,u,f.** *Choice, 2004.*

Colin, Amery & Curran,   **CC135.A54 2001**
Brian A.
Vanishing Histories: 100 Endangered Sites from the World
Monuments Watch. John Berendt (Foreword by). Trade Cloth.
Harry N. Abrams, Inc. New York, NY. 2001. 207p.
ISBN:0-8109-1435-2, ISBN13: 978-0-8109-1435-3.
Dewey:363.6/9. LCCN:2001-022622.

Audience: **g,l,u,f.** *Choice, 2002.*

Oliver, Paul   **NA208.E531997**
Encyclopedia of Vernacular Architecture of the World.
Cambridge University Press. 1997. ISBN:0-521-56422-0,
ISBN13: 978-0-521-56422-9.

Audience: **g,l,u,f.**

Phillips, Steven J.   **NA7205.P48 1996**
Old-House Dictionary: An Illustrated Guide to American
Domestic Architecture (1600-1940). Trade Paper. John Wiley &
Sons, Inc. Hoboken, NJ. 1992. 240p. ISBN:0-471-14407-X,
ISBN13: 978-0-471-14407-6. Dewey:728/.0973.
LCCN:96-023062.

Audience: **g,l,u,f.**

Cultural Heritage > Histories and Handbooks

Alanen, Arnold R. &   **E159.P746 2000**
Melnick, Robert
Preserving Cultural Landscapes in America. Dolores Hayden
(Foreword by). Trade Paper. Johns Hopkins University Press.
Baltimore, MD. 2000. 264p. Center Books on Contemporary
Landscape Design Ser., : ISBN:0-8018-6264-7, ISBN13:
978-0-8018-6264-9. Dewey:333.7/2. LCCN:99-038598.

Audience: **g,l,u,f.** *Choice, 2000.*

Birnbaum, Charles A. &   **SB472.8.D47 2005**
  Hughes, Mary V.
Design with Culture: Claiming America's Landscape Heritage.
Trade Cloth. University Press of Virginia. Charlottesville, VA.
2001. 216p. ISBN:0-8139-2329-8, ISBN13: 978-0-8139-2329-1.
Dewey:712/.0973. LCCN:2004-017412.

Audience: **g,l,u,f.**

Caple, Chris   **CC135.C29 2000**
Conservation Skills: Judgement, Method and Decision Making.
Trade Paper. Routledge. New York, NY. 2004. 256p.
ISBN:0-415-18881-4, ISBN13: 978-0-415-18881-4.
Dewey:363.6/9. LCCN:00-032183.

Audience: **l,u,f.** *Choice, 2001.*

Carter, Thomas & Cromley,   **NA705.C38 2005**
  Elizabeth C.
Invitation to Vernacular Architecture: A Guide to the Study of
Ordinary Buildings and Landscapes. Trade Paper. University of
Tennessee Press. Knoxville, TN. 2005. 248p. Vernacular
Architecture Studies ISBN:1-57233-331-6, ISBN13:
978-1-57233-331-4. Dewey:720/.973. LCCN:2004-024528.

Audience: **g,l,u,f.** *Choice, 2006.*

Corzo, Miguel A. (Editor)   **N6485.M67 1999**
Mortality Immortality?: The Legacy of 20th-Century Art. Arthur
C. Danto & Judy Chicago (Contribution by). Trade Paper.
Oxford University Press, Inc. New York, NY. 1999. 212p. Getty
Conservation Institute Ser. ISBN:0-89236-528-5, ISBN13:
978-0-89236-528-9. Dewey:709/.04/00288. LCCN:98-038695.

Audience: **g,l,u,f.**

Dubrow, Gail Lee   **HQ1410.R472002**
Restoring Women's History Through Historic Preservation.
Jennifer Goodman (Editor). Trade Cloth. Johns Hopkins
University Press. Baltimore, MD. 2003. 464p. Center Books on
Contemporary Landscape Design Ser., : ISBN:0-8018-7052-6,
ISBN13: 978-0-8018-7052-1. Dewey:305.4/0973.
LCCN:2001-007988.

Audience: **l,u,f.** *Choice, 2003.*

Gulliford, Andrew   **E159.5**
Sacred Objects and Sacred Places: Preserving Tribal Traditions.
Trade Cloth. University Press of Colorado. Boulder, CO. 2000.
307p. ISBN:0-87081-579-2, ISBN13: 978-0-87081-579-9.
Dewey:973/.1.

Audience: **g,l,u,f.** *Choice, 2001.*

Heath, Kingston William   **HD7304.N35H4 2001**
The Patina of Place: The Cultural Weathering of a New England
Industrial Landscape. Trade Cloth. University of Tennessee
Press. Knoxville, TN. 2002. 288p. ISBN:1-57233-138-0,
ISBN13: 978-1-57233-138-9. Dewey:728/.314/0974485.
LCCN:2001-001841.

Audience: **l,u,f.** *Choice, 2002.*

Highsmith, Carol M. &   **E159.H65 1994**
  Landphair, Ted
America Restored. Trade Cloth. National Trust for Historic
Preservation. Washington, DC. 1994. 320p.

ISBN:0-89133-228-6, ISBN13: 978-0-89133-228-2. Dewey:973.
LCCN:93-032365.

Audience: **g,l,u,f.** *Choice, 1994.*

Holleran, Michael   **F73.37**
Boston's "Changeful Times": Origins of Preservation and
Planning in America. Trade Paper. Johns Hopkins University
Press. Baltimore, MD. 2001. 352p. Creating the North American
Landscape Ser. ISBN:0-8018-6644-8, ISBN13:
978-0-8018-6644-9. Dewey:974.4/61.

Audience: **g,l,u,f.** *Choice, 1999.*

Howell, Benita J. (Editor)   **F217.A65C85 2002**
Culture, Environment, and Conservation in the Appalachian
South. Trade Cloth. University of Illinois Press. Champaign, IL.
2002. 216p. ISBN:0-252-02705-1, ISBN13: 978-0-252-02705-5.
Dewey:363.6/9/0974. LCCN:2001-003340.

Audience: **g,l,u,f.** *Choice, 2003, 2002.*

Johnson, Ronald W. &   **E159.C89 1987**
  Schene, Michael G.
Cultural Resources Management. Cloth Text. Krieger Publishing
Company. Melbourne, FL. 1987. 270p. ISBN:0-89874-880-1,
ISBN13: 978-0-89874-880-2. Dewey:973. LCCN:85-027024.

Audience: **l,u,f.** *Choice, 1987.*

Jokilehto, Jukka   **NA105**
History of Architectural Conservation. Paper Text. Elsevier
Science & Technology Books. Saint Louis, MO. 2002. 368p.
Conservation and Museology Ser. ISBN:0-7506-5511-9,
ISBN13: 978-0-7506-5511-8. Dewey:720.2/88.

Audience: **l,u,f.**

Jones, Janna   **NA6846.U6J66 2003**
The Southern Movie Place: Rise, Fall, and Resurrection. Trade
Cloth. University Press of Florida. Gainesville, FL. 2003. 285p.
ISBN:0-8130-2605-9, ISBN13: 978-0-8130-2605-3.
Dewey:725/.823/0975028. LCCN:2002-040905.

Audience: **l,u,f.** *Choice, 2003.*

Koshar, Rudy   **97-36877 [DD]**
Germany's Transient Pasts: Preservation and National Memory
in the Twentieth Century. Trade Paper. University of North
Carolina Press. Chapel Hill, NC. 1998. 440p.
ISBN:0-8078-4701-1, ISBN13: 978-0-8078-4701-5.
Dewey:363.690943. LCCN:97-036877.

Audience: **g,l,u,f.** *Choice, 1998.*

Lee, Antoinette J.   **E159.P34 1992**
Past Meets Future: Saving America's Historic Environment.
Trade Cloth. National Trust for Historic Preservation.
Washington, DC. 1992. 384p. ISBN:0-89133-198-0, ISBN13:
978-0-89133-198-8. Dewey:363.6/9/0973. LCCN:92-025913.

Audience: **g,l,u,f.** *Choice, 1993.*

Leepson, Marc   **E332.74.L44 2003**
Saving Monticello: The Levy Family's Epic Quest to Rescue the
House That Jefferson Built. Trade Paper. University Press of
Virginia. Charlottesville, VA. 2003. 303p. ISBN:0-8139-2219-4,
ISBN13: 978-0-8139-2219-5. Dewey:975.5/482.
LCCN:2002-040863.

Audience: **g,l,u,f.**

Little, Barbara J. (Editor)   CC77.H5P83 2002
Public Benefits of Archaeology. Trade Cloth. University Press of
Florida. Gainesville, FL. 2002. xix, 277p. ISBN:0-8130-2455-2,
ISBN13: 978-0-8130-2455-4. Dewey:973. LCCN:2001-043730.
                              Audience: **g,l,u,f.** *Choice, 2002.*

Lloyd, Sandra Mackenzie, et   E159.L488 2001
  al.
Great Tours!: Thematic Tours and Guide Training for Historic
Sites. Barbara A. Levy & Susan R. Schreiber (Authors). Trade
Cloth. AltaMira Press. Walnut Creek, CA. 2002. 176p. American
Association for State and Local History Book Ser.
ISBN:0-7591-0098-5, ISBN13: 978-0-7591-0098-5.
Dewey:917.304/068/3. LCCN:2001-034313.
                                            Audience: **l,u,f.**

Mansfield, Howard   E159.M37 2000
The Same Ax, Twice: Restoration and Renewal in a Throwaway
Age. Library Binding. University Press of New England.
Lebanon, NH. 2000. 304p. ISBN:1-58465-028-1, ISBN13:
978-1-58465-028-7. Dewey:973. LCCN:99-056170.
                                    Audience: **g,l,u,f.**

McCabe, Marsha &   F74.N5M371996
  Thomas, Joseph D.
Not Just Anywhere: The Story of W.H.A.L.E. and New
Bedford's Waterfront Historic District. Arthur Bennett & Clara
Stites (Editors). Trade Cloth. Spinner Publications, Inc. New
Bedford, MA. 1995. 128p. ISBN:0-932027-29-6, ISBN13:
978-0-932027-29-0. Dewey:974.4/85. LCCN:95-071046.
                              Audience: **g,l,u,f.** *Choice, 1996.*

Miele, Chris   NA109.G7
From William Morris: Building Conservation and the Arts and
Crafts Cult of Authenticity, 1877-1939. Cloth over Boards. Yale
University Press. Cumberland, RI. 2005. 364p. Studies in British
Art Ser. ISBN:0-300-10730-7, ISBN13: 978-0-300-10730-2.
Dewey:711.4094257.

                              Audience: **l,u,f.** *Choice, 2006.*

Murtagh, William J.   E159.M875 2005
Keeping Time: The History and Theory of Preservation in
America. Ed. 3. Trade Paper. John Wiley & Sons, Inc. Hoboken,
NJ. 2005. 272p. ISBN:0-471-47377-4, ISBN13:
978-0-471-47377-0. Dewey:363.6/9/0973. LCCN:2004-061237.
                                    Audience: **g,l,u,f.**

New Mexico Architectural   F797.R43 2001
  Foundation Staff & American Institute of Architects Staff
  (Editors)
Recording a Vanishing Legacy: The Historic American
Buildings Survey in New Mexico, 1933-today. Trade Paper.
Museum of New Mexico Press. Albuquerque, NM. 2001. 166p.
ISBN:0-89013-380-8, ISBN13: 978-0-89013-380-4.
Dewey:720/.9789. LCCN:00-048943.
                              Audience: **g,l,u,f.** *Choice, 2001.*

Nicholas, Lynn H.   N6750
The Rape of Europa: The Fate of Europe's Treasures in the
Third Reich and the Second World War. Trade Paper. Knopf
Publishing Group. New York, NY. 1995. 512p.

ISBN:0-679-75686-8, ISBN13: 978-0-679-75686-6.
Dewey:709.4.
                              Audience: **g,l,u,f.** *Choice, 1994.*

Page, Max & Mason,   NA105.G48 2003
  Randall (Editors)
Giving Preservation a History: Histories of Historic Preservation
in the United States. Trade Paper. Routledge. New York, NY.
2003. 336p. ISBN:0-415-93443-5, ISBN13: 978-0-415-93443-5.
Dewey:363.6/9. LCCN:2003-010962.
                              Audience: **l,u,f.** *Choice, 2004.*

Pickard, Robert   KJC6405.P65 2000
Policy and Law in Heritage Conservation. UK-B Format
Paperback. Routledge. New York, NY. 2001. 368p. Conservation
of the European Built Heritage Ser., Vol. 1
ISBN:0-419-23280-X, ISBN13: 978-0-419-23280-3.
Dewey:344.4/094. LCCN:00-044057.
                              Audience: **l,u,f.** *Choice, 2001.*

Quincy, John Jr.   F73.8.Q56Q56 2003
Quincy's Market: A Boston Landmark. Trade Cloth.
Northeastern University Press. Boston, MA. 2005. 256p.
ISBN:1-55553-552-6, ISBN13: 978-1-55553-552-0.
Dewey:711/.552/0974461. LCCN:2002-015422.
                              Audience: **l,u,f.** *Choice, 2004.*

Scarpaci, Joseph L.   F1408.5.S37 2004
Plazas and Barrios: Heritage Tourism and Globalization in the
Latin American Centro Historico. Trade Cloth. University of
Arizona Press. Tucson, AZ. 2004. 260p. Society, Environment,
and Place Ser. ISBN:0-8165-1631-6, ISBN13:
978-0-8165-1631-5. Dewey:980. LCCN:2004-008527.
                              Audience: **l,u,f.** *Choice, 2005.*

Schuster, Angela M. H. &   DS79.76.L66 2005
  Polk, Milbry
The Looting of the Iraq Museum, Baghdad: The Lost Legacy of
Ancient Mesopotamia. Trade Cloth. Harry N. Abrams, Inc. New
York, NY. 2005. 256p. ISBN:0-8109-5872-4, ISBN13:
978-0-8109-5872-2. Dewey:935/.0074/56747.
LCCN:2004-023525.
                              Audience: **g,l,u,f.** *Choice, 2005.*

Serageldin, Ismail (Editor),   CC135.H4672001
  et al.
Historic Cities and Sacred Sites: Cultural Roots for Urban
Futures. Joan Martin-Brown & Ephim Shluger (Editors). Trade
Paper. World Bank Publications. Washington, DC. 2001. 44p.
Bks. ISBN:0-8213-4904-X, ISBN13: 978-0-8213-4904-5.
Dewey:363.6/9. LCCN:00-069698.
                              Audience: **u,f.** *Choice, 2001.*

Stille, Alexander   CC135.S76 2002
The Future of the Past. Cloth over Boards. Farrar, Straus &
Giroux. New York, NY. 2002. 364p. ISBN:0-374-15977-7,
ISBN13: 978-0-374-15977-1. Dewey:303.4.
LCCN:2001-054348.
                                    Audience: **g,l,u,f.**

Tung, Anthony Max   NA9053.C6T86 2001
Preserving the World's Great Cities: The Destruction and
Renewal of the Historic Metropolis. Trade Cloth. Crown
Publishing Group. New York, NY. 2001. 480p.
ISBN:0-517-70148-0, ISBN13: 978-0-517-70148-5.
Dewey:711.4. LCCN:2001-021276.
                                        Audience: **g,l,u,f.**

Wasowski, Andy; Wasowski,   TH4812.W36 2000
Sally; Morrison, Darrel G
Building Inside Nature's Envelope: How New Construction and
Landscape Preservation Can Work Together. Andy Wasowski
(Contribution by) ; Sally Wasowski (Contribution by) ; Darrel
G. Morrison (Foreword by). Oxford University Press, Inc. 2000.
ISBN:0-19-513176-2, ISBN13: 978-0-19-513176-5.
                                        Audience: **g,l,u,f.**

Weyenth, Robert   F279.C447W49 2000
Historic Preservation for a Living City: Historic Charleston
Foundation, 1947-1997. Trade Cloth. University of South
Carolina Press. Columbia, SC. 2000. xxii, 256p. Historic
Charleston Foundation Ser. ISBN:1-57003-353-6, ISBN13:
978-1-57003-353-7. Dewey:975.7/915. LCCN:00-008146.
                                Audience: **g,l,u,f.** *Choice, 2000.*

Zenzen, Joan M.   E472.183.Z46 1998
Battling for Manassas: The Fifty-Year Preservation Struggle at
Manassas National Battlefield Park. Trade Cloth. Pennsylvania
State University Press. University Park, PA. 1998. 288p.
ISBN:0-271-01721-X, ISBN13: 978-0-271-01721-1.
Dewey:363.6/9/097552732. LCCN:96-053534.
                                Audience: **g,l,u,f.** *Choice, 1998.*

Cultural Heritage > Materials, Techniques, Practices

Burns, John A. (Editor)   E159.R425 2004
Recording Historic Structures. Ed. 2. Historic American
Buildings Survey Staff, Historic American Engineering Record
Staff, Historic American Landscapes Survey Staff, National Park
Service Staff & U. S. Department of the Interior Staff
(Contribution by). Trade Cloth. John Wiley & Sons, Inc.
Hoboken, NJ. 2003. 320p. ISBN:0-471-27380-5, ISBN13:
978-0-471-27380-6. Dewey:363.6/9/0973. LCCN:2003-007941.
                                        Audience: **g,l,u,f.**

Hull, Brent   TH2270.H85 2003
Historic Millwork: A Guide to Restoring and Re-Creating
Doors, Windows, and Moldings of the Late Nineteenth Through
Mid-Twentieth Centuries. Trade Cloth. John Wiley & Sons, Inc.
Hoboken, NJ. 2003. 224p. ISBN:0-471-41622-3, ISBN13:
978-0-471-41622-7. Dewey:684/.08. LCCN:2002-013661.
                                        Audience: **l,u,f.**

Jenrette, Richard Hampton   NA7207.J45 2000
Adventures with Old Houses. John M. Hall (Photographer).
Trade Cloth. Gibbs Smith, Publisher. Layton, UT. 2000. 224p.
ISBN:0-941711-46-3, ISBN13: 978-0-941711-46-3.
Dewey:728/.37/0973028. LCCN:99-045641.
                                        Audience: **g,l,u,f.**

Lavidrine, Bertrand, et al.   TR465.L39 2003
A Guide to the Preventative Conservation of Photograph
Collections. Jean-Paul Gandolfo & Sibylle Monod (Authors),
Getty Conservation Institute Staff (Contribution by). Trade
Paper. Oxford University Press, Inc. New York, NY. 2003. 304p.
Multicultural Art Print Series (Maps) Ser. ISBN:0-89236-701-6,
ISBN13: 978-0-89236-701-6. Dewey:770/.74.
LCCN:2003-004070.
                                        Audience: **g,l,u,f.**

MacLeish, A. Bruce   NK1127.5 .G8 1995
The Care of Antiques and Historical Collections. Ed. 2. Book,
Other. AltaMira Press. Walnut Creek, CA. 1985. 250p. American
Association for State and Local History Book Ser.
ISBN:0-7619-9135-2, ISBN13: 978-0-7619-9135-9.
Dewey:069/.5. LCCN:95-046056.
                                        Audience: **g,l,u,f.**

Newton, Roy & Davison,   NK5104.5
Sandra
Conservation and Restoration of Glass. Ed. 2. Trade Cloth.
Elsevier Science & Technology Books. Saint Louis, MO. 2003.
392p. ISBN:0-7506-4341-2, ISBN13: 978-0-7506-4341-2.
Dewey:748.2/0288.
                                        Audience: **l,u,f.**

Nylander, Jane C. &   TS1767.N93 2005
Nylander, Richard C.
Fabrics and Wallpapers for Historic Buildings. Trade Cloth.
John Wiley & Sons, Inc. Hoboken, NJ. 2005. 568p. Historic
Interiors Ser. ISBN:0-471-70655-8, ISBN13:
978-0-471-70655-7. Dewey:747/.5. LCCN:2004-043116.
                                        Audience: **l,u,f.**

Rabun, J. Stanley   TA645.R32 2000
Structural Analysis of Historic Buildings: Restoration,
Preservation, and Adaptive Reuse Applications for Architects
and Engineers. Trade Cloth. John Wiley & Sons, Inc. Hoboken,
NJ. 2000. 512p. ISBN:0-471-31545-1, ISBN13:
978-0-471-31545-2. Dewey:690/.24. LCCN:99-036214.
                                        Audience: **g,l,u,f.**

Schweidler, Max   NE380.S35132005
The Restoration of Engravings, Drawings, Books, and Other
Works on Paper. Roy Perkinson (Editor, Translator, Introduction
by). Trade Cloth. Getty Publications. Los Angeles, CA. 2006.
316p. Getty Trust Publications: Getty Conservation Institute Ser.
ISBN:0-89236-835-7, ISBN13: 978-0-89236-835-8.
Dewey:760.028/8. LCCN:2005-042449.
                                        Audience: **g,l,u,f.**

Von Rosenstiel, Helene &   NK2115.5.F55V66 1996
Winkler, Gail Caskey
Floor Coverings for Historic Buildings: A Guide to Selecting
Reproductions. Trade Paper. John Wiley & Sons, Inc. Hoboken,
NJ. 1995. 288p. Historic Interiors Ser., Vol. 2
ISBN:0-471-14382-0, ISBN13: 978-0-471-14382-6.
Dewey:747.4. LCCN:87-022310.
                                        Audience: **l,u,f.**

Arts Management > Reference Works

PN1584

▢ Americans for the Arts.
http://www.artsusa.org/

Audience: **g,l,u,f.**

Porter, Robert A. (Editor)   **NX711.U5.G84 1987**
Guide to Corporate Giving in the Arts 4. Ed. 4. Trade Cloth.
Americans for the Arts. Washington, DC. 1987. 481p.
ISBN:0-915400-56-1, ISBN13: 978-0-915400-56-0.
Dewey:700/.79. LCCN:87-018738.

Audience: **l,u,f.**   *Choice, 1988.*

Arts Management > Histories and Handbooks

Chong, Derrick   **NX760.C48 2002**
About Arts Management. Trade Paper. Routledge. New York,
NY. 2002. 168p. ISBN:0-415-23682-7, ISBN13:
978-0-415-23682-9. Dewey:706/.8. LCCN:2002-068287.

Audience: **g,l,u,f.**

Dreeszen, Craig, et al.   **NX22.F86 1994**
Fundamentals of Local Arts Management. Pam Korza, Barbara
S. Bacon, Tina Burdett, Halsey M. North & Alice H. North
(Authors), Jack Cavacco (Illustrator). Trade Paper. University of
Massachusetts, Arts Extension Service. Amherst, MA. 1998.
310p. ISBN:0-945464-07-X, ISBN13: 978-0-945464-07-5.
Dewey:706/.8. LCCN:94-071905.

Audience: **l,u,f.**

Heartney, Eleanor &   **N6535.N5**
 Gopnik, Adam
City Art: New York's Percent for Art Program. Michael
Bloomberg (Produced by). Trade Paper. Merrell Publishers Ltd.
London, 2005. 240p. ISBN:1-85894-290-X, ISBN13:
978-1-85894-290-2. Dewey:709.747/109045.
LCCN:2005-280754.

Audience: **g,l,u,f.**   *Choice, 2005.*

Reiss, Alvin H.   **NX760 .R45 1979**
Arts Management Reader. Paper over Boards. Marcel Dekker
Inc. New York, NY. 1979. 704p. ISBN:0-8247-6850-7, ISBN13:
978-0-8247-6850-8. Dewey:658/.91/7. LCCN:79-019330.

Audience: **l,u,f.**

Shore, Harvey   **NK765**
Arts Administration and Management: A Guide for
Administrators and Their Staffs. Trade Cloth. Greenwood
Publishing Group, Inc. Portsmouth, NH. 1987. 225p.
ISBN:0-89930-072-3, ISBN13: 978-0-89930-072-6.
Dewey:700.68. LCCN:86-030603.

Audience: **l,u,f.**

Straight, Michael   **NX768.H36S7 1988**
Nancy Hanks: An Intimate Portrait: The Creation of a National

Commitment to the Arts. Cloth Text. Duke University Press.
Durham, NC. 1988. xiii, 400p. ISBN:0-8223-0869-X, ISBN13:
978-0-8223-0869-0. Dewey:700/.92/4 B. LCCN:88-016956.

Audience: **g,l,u,f.**

Tschirhart, Mary   **NX765.T73 1996**
Artful Leadership: Managing Stakeholder Problems in Nonprofit
Arts Organizations. Cloth Text. Indiana University Press.
Bloomington, IN. 1996. 144p. Indiana University Center on
Philanthropy Series in Governance ISBN:0-253-33234-6,
ISBN13: 978-0-253-33234-9. Dewey:700/.68. LCCN:96-031852.

Audience: **l,u,f.**

Yeoman, Ian (Editor), et al.   **GT3405**
Festival and Events Management: An International Arts and
Culture Perspective. Jane Ali-Knight, Siobhan Drummond, Una
McMahon-Beattie & Martin Robertson (Editors). Paper Text.
Elsevier Science & Technology Books. Saint Louis, MO. 2003.
448p. ISBN:0-7506-5872-X, ISBN13: 978-0-7506-5872-0.
Dewey:394.2/068.

Audience: **g,l,u,f.**

Arts Management > Business and Art

Abbott, Susan & Webb,   **N8600.A2 1991**
 Barbara
Fine Art Publicity: The Complete Guide for Galleries and
Artists. Trade Paper. Art Business News. New York, NY. 1991.
189p. ISBN:1-879466-00-7, ISBN13: 978-1-879466-00-5.
Dewey:659/.02/47. LCCN:90-086153.

Audience: **g,l,u,f.**

Alberro, Alexander   **N6512.5.C64A43 2004**
Conceptual Art and the Politics of Publicity. Trade Paper. MIT
Press. Cambridge, MA. 2004. 248p. ISBN:0-262-51184-3,
ISBN13: 978-0-262-51184-1. Dewey:709/.73/09045.
LCCN:2002-075392.

Audience: **l,u,f.**

Bjorkegren, Dag   **NX634.B56 1996**
The Culture Business: Management Strategies for the
Arts-Related Business. Trade Paper. Thomson Learning.
Independence, KY. 1996. 216p. ISBN:0-415-12234-1, ISBN13:
978-0-415-12234-4. Dewey:700/.68. LCCN:95-032342.

Audience: **g,l,u,f.**

Bourdieu, Pierre & Johnson,   **NX180.S6B681993**
 Randal
The Field of Cultural Production: Essays on Art and Literature.
Lawrence D. Kritzman & Richard Wolin (Editors). Trade Paper.
Columbia University Press. New York, NY. 1994. 322p.
European Perspectives, :Social Thought and Culturall Criticism
Ser. ISBN:0-231-08287-8, ISBN13: 978-0-231-08287-7.
Dewey:700/.1/030944. LCCN:92-033843.

Audience: **l,u,f.**

Byrnes, William J.   **NX765.B87 2003**
Management and the Arts. Ed. 3. Paper Text. Elsevier Science

& Technology Books. Saint Louis, MO. 2003. 352p.
ISBN:0-240-80537-2, ISBN13: 978-0-240-80537-5.
Dewey:700/.68. LCCN:2002-043078.

Audience: **g,l,u,f.**

Caves, Richard E.   **NX705.5.U6C382000**
Creative Industries: Contracts Between Art and Commerce.
Trade Cloth. Harvard University Press. Cambridge, MA. 2000.
464p. ISBN:0-674-00164-8, ISBN13: 978-0-674-00164-0.
Dewey:338.4/77/00973. LCCN:99-086569.

Audience: **l,u,f.** *Choice, 2000.*

Cowen, Tyler   **NX634.C68 1998**
In Praise of Commercial Culture. Trade Cloth. Harvard
University Press. Cambridge, MA. 1998. 288p.
ISBN:0-674-44591-0, ISBN13: 978-0-674-44591-8.
Dewey:700/.68/8. LCCN:97-040445.

Audience: **l,u,f.** *Choice, 1998.*

Fine, Gary Alan   **N7432.5.A78F56 2004**
Everyday Genius: Self-Taught Art and the Culture of
Authenticity. Trade Cloth. University of Chicago Press. Chicago,
IL. 2004. 344p. ISBN:0-226-24950-6, ISBN13:
978-0-226-24950-6. Dewey:709/.04/07. LCCN:2003-023042.

Audience: **l,u,f.** *Choice, 2005.*

Fitzgibbon, Marian   **NX760**
Managing Innovation in the Arts: Making Art Work. Trade
Cloth. Greenwood Publishing Group, Inc. Portsmouth, NH.
2001. 232p. ISBN:1-56720-434-1, ISBN13: 978-1-56720-434-6.
Dewey:700/.68/8. LCCN:2001-019183.

Audience: **l,u,f.**

Hill, Elizabeth, et al.   **NX760**
Creative Arts Marketing. Ed. 2. Terry O'Sullivan & Catherine
O'Sullivan (Authors). Trade Paper. Elsevier Science &
Technology Books. Saint Louis, MO. 2003. 384p.
ISBN:0-7506-5737-5, ISBN13: 978-0-7506-5737-2.
Dewey:706/.8/8. LCCN:2003-051960.

Audience: **l,u,f.**

Kemp, Roger L. (Editor)   **NX634.C54 2004**
Cities and the Arts: A Handbook for Renewal. Paper Text.
McFarland & Company, Incorporated Publishers. Jefferson, NC.
2004. 300p. ISBN:0-7864-2007-3, ISBN13: 978-0-7864-2007-0.
Dewey:307.3/416. LCCN:2004-022365.

Audience: **l,u,f.**

Klein, Ulrike   **N8600.K53513 1994**
The Business of Art Unveiled: New York Art Dealers Speak Up.
Trade Paper. Peter Lang Publishing, Inc. New York, NY. 1994.
VII, 247p. ISBN:3-631-46364-2, ISBN13: 978-3-631-46364-2.
Dewey:381/.457/097471. LCCN:94-042331.

Audience: **l,u,f.**

Kurin, Richard   **GN36.U62D5775 1997**
Reflections of a Culture Broker: A View from the Smithsonian.
Trade Cloth. Smithsonian Institution Press. Washington, DC.
1997. xv, 315p. ISBN:1-56098-789-8, ISBN13:
978-1-56098-789-5. Dewey:069/.09753. LCCN:97-006974.

Audience: **g,l,u,f.**

Martorella, Rosanne   **N5207.M37 1990**
Corporate Art. Trade Cloth. Rutgers University Press.
Piscataway, NJ. 1990. 240p. ISBN:0-8135-1525-4, ISBN13:
978-0-8135-1525-0. Dewey:707/.9/73. LCCN:89-039325.

Audience: **l,u,f.** *Choice, 1990.*

Owen, Nancy E.   **NK4340.R7O95 2001**
Rookwood and the Industry of Art: Women, Culture and
Commerce, 1880-1913. Trade Paper. Ohio University Press.
Athens, OH. 2001. 349p. ISBN:0-8214-1338-4, ISBN13:
978-0-8214-1338-8. Dewey:338.7/617383/0977178.
LCCN:00-040631.

Audience: **l,u,f.** *Choice, 2001.*

Reiss, Alvin H.   **NX765 .R44 1992**
Arts Management: A Guide to Finding Funds and Winning
Audiences. Trade Cloth. Fund Raising Institute. Detroit, MI.
1992. 267p. ISBN:0-930807-32-4, ISBN13: 978-0-930807-32-0.
Dewey:700.68. LCCN:91-077426.

Audience: **l,u,f.**

Shell, Marc   **N8600.S53 1995**
Art and Money: Visual and Economic Representation. Trade
Cloth. University of Chicago Press. Chicago, IL. 1995. 230p.
ISBN:0-226-75213-5, ISBN13: 978-0-226-75213-6.
Dewey:701.03. LCCN:93-029238.

Audience: **l,u,f.**

Siegel, Katy & Mattick,   **N8225.M56**
Paul
Art Works: Money. Trade Paper. Thames & Hudson. New York,
NY. 2004. 208p. Art Works ISBN:0-500-93004-X, ISBN13:
978-0-500-93004-5. Dewey:704.9/49332. LCCN:2004-102814.

Audience: **g,l,u,f.**

Smith, Constance   **N8353.S63 1997**
Art Marketing 101: A Handbook for the Fine Artist. Ed. 2.
Trade Paper. ArtNetwork. Nevada City, CA. 1998. 64p.
ISBN:0-940899-32-9, ISBN13: 978-0-940899-32-2.
Dewey:700.68. LCCN:97-116792.

Audience: **l,u,f.**

Yamey, Basil S.   **N8217.B58Y36 1989**
Art and Accounting. Cloth over Boards. Yale University Press.
Cumberland, RI. 1989. 165p. ISBN:0-300-04227-2, ISBN13:
978-0-300-04227-6. Dewey:758/.96572. LCCN:88-027782.

Audience: **l,u,f.** *Choice, 1989.*

Arts Management > Art Law

Atwood, Roger   **CC135.A85 2004**
Stealing History: Tomb Raiders, Smugglers, and the Looting of
the Ancient World. Cloth over Boards. St. Martin's Press.
Gordonville, VA. 2004. 352p. ISBN:0-312-32406-5, ISBN13:
978-0-312-32406-3. Dewey:364.16/2. LCCN:2004-050862.

Audience: **g,l,u,f.**

Childs, Elizabeth C. (Editor)   **N8740.S87 1997**
Suspended License: Censorship and the Visual Arts. Trade
Paper. University of Washington Press. Seattle, WA. 1997. 413p.
Samuel and Althea Stroum Bks. ISBN:0-295-97627-6, ISBN13:
978-0-295-97627-3. Dewey:701/.03. LCCN:97-016469.
     Audience: **g,l,u,f.** *Choice, 1998.*

Corsane, Gerard (Editor)   **AM7.H465 2005**
Heritage, Museums and Galleries: An Introductory Reader.
Trade Paper. Routledge. New York, NY. 2005. 400p.
ISBN:0-415-28946-7, ISBN13: 978-0-415-28946-7. Dewey:069.
LCCN:2004-012159.
     Audience: **g,l,u,f.**

DuBoff, Leonard D.   **KF390.A69**
The Law in Plain English for Crafts. Ed. 6. Trade Paper,
Perfect. Allworth Press. New York, NY. 2005. 215p.
ISBN:1-58115-424-0, ISBN13: 978-1-58115-424-5.
Dewey:349.73/02/4745. LCCN:2005-014096.
     Audience: **g,l,u,f.**

Gerstenblith, Patty   **KF4288.A7G47 2004**
Art, Cultural Heritage, and the Law. Cloth Text. Carolina
Academic Press. Durham, NC. 2004. 932p.
ISBN:1-59460-099-6, ISBN13: 978-1-59460-099-9. Dewey:344.
LCCN:2004-112835.
     Audience: **g,l,u,f.**

Harvey, Archer St. Clair &   **K1**
  O'Keefe, Patrick J. (Editors)
Art, Antiquity and the Law: Preserving Our Global Cultural
Heritage. Trade Paper. Rutgers University Press. Piscataway, NJ.
2000. 304p. ISBN:0-8135-2849-6, ISBN13: 978-0-8135-2849-6.
Dewey:340.05.
     Audience: **g,l,u,f.**

Hoffman, Barbara T.   **K3791.A97 2005**
  (Editor)
Art and Cultural Heritage: Law, Policy and Practice. Trade
Cloth. Cambridge University Press. New York, NY. 2005. 600p.
ISBN:0-521-85764-3, ISBN13: 978-0-521-85764-2.
Dewey:344/.09. LCCN:2005-012017.
     Audience: **g,l,u,f.**

Kaufman, Roy S.   **KF4288.A9482000**
Art Law Handbook. Trade Cloth, Box or Slipcased. Aspen
Publishers, Inc. New York, NY. 2000. 1,164p.
ISBN:0-7355-1641-3, ISBN13: 978-0-7355-1641-0.
Dewey:344.73/097. LCCN:00-056558.
     Audience: **g,l,f.**

Kaufman, Roy S.   **KF4288**
Art Law Handbook: 2002 Supplement. Trade Paper. Aspen
Publishers, Inc. New York, NY. 2002. ISBN:0-7355-2955-8,
ISBN13: 978-0-7355-2955-7. Dewey:344.73087.
     Audience: **g,l,u,f.**

Lester, Robert (Editor)   **N9160.A77 2002**
Art Looting and Nazi Germany: Records of the Fine Arts and
Monuments Adviser, Ardelia Hall, 1945-1961. Trade Cloth.
University Publications of America. Bethesda, MD. 2002.

Holocaust Era Research Collection ISBN:1-55655-875-9,
ISBN13: 978-1-55655-875-7. Dewey:940.54/05.
LCCN:2002-022621.
     Audience: **g,l,u,f.**

Mason, Christopher   **HF5477.G74S6746 2004**
The Art of the Steal: Inside the Sotheby's-Christie's Auction
House Scandal. Trade Cloth. Penguin Group (USA) Inc. New
York, NY. 2004. 416p. ISBN:0-399-15093-5, ISBN13:
978-0-399-15093-7. Dewey:364.16/8. LCCN:2004-040041.
     Audience: **g,l,u,f.**

Salvesen, Magda &   **N6505.A85 2005**
  Cousineau, Diane
Artists' Estates: Reputations in Trust. Trade Cloth. Rutgers
University Press. Piscataway, NJ. 2005. 384p.
ISBN:0-8135-3604-9, ISBN13: 978-0-8135-3604-0.
Dewey:709/.2/273. LCCN:2004-021708.
     Audience: **g,l,u,f.**

Stokes, Simon   **KD1320.S76 2003**
Art and Copyright. Ed. 2. Trade Paper. Hart Publishing Ltd.
Oxford, 2003. 284p. ISBN:1-84113-385-X, ISBN13:
978-1-84113-385-0. Dewey:346.4104/82. LCCN:2004-268196.
     Audience: **g,l,u,f.**

Wienand, Peter, et al.   **KD1320.W53 2000**
A Guide to Copyright for Museums and Galleries. Anna Booy
& Robin Fry (Authors). Trade Paper. Routledge. New York, NY.
2000. 168p. ISBN:0-415-21721-0, ISBN13: 978-0-415-21721-7.
Dewey:346.4104/82. LCCN:99-053485.
     Audience: **g,l,u,f.**

Yeide, Nancy H., et al.   **N3999.Y45 2001**
The AAM Guide to Provenance Research. Amy Walsh &
Konstantin Akinsha (Authors), American Association of
Museums Staff (Contribution by). Trade Paper. American
Association of Museums. Washington, DC. 2001. 304p.
ISBN:0-931201-73-X, ISBN13: 978-0-931201-73-8.
Dewey:069/.4. LCCN:2001-022688.
     Audience: **g,l,u,f.** *Choice, 2002.*

Arts Management > Museum Studies

     AM11
☐ MUSÉE.
http://www.musee-online.org/
MUSÉE, Inc.
     Audience: **g,l,u,f.**

American Association of   **AM122.S58 2003**
  Museums Staff (Contribution by)
Slaying the Financial Dragon: Strategies for Museums. Trade
Cloth. American Association of Museums. Washington, DC.
2003. v, 122p. ISBN:0-931201-84-5, ISBN13:
978-0-931201-84-4. Dewey:069/.068/1. LCCN:2003-001951.
     Audience: **l,u,f.**

Buck, Rebecca A. &   AM151.B83 2003
  Gilmore, Jean Allman
On the Road Again: Developing and Managing Traveling
Exhibitions. Trade Cloth. American Association of Museums.
Washington, DC. 2003. vii, 158p. ISBN:0-931201-85-3,
ISBN13: 978-0-931201-85-1. Dewey:069/.5.
LCCN:2003-007528.

                                          Audience: **l,u,f.**

Eichstedt, Jennifer & Small,   F220.A1E37 2002
  Stephen
Representations of Slavery: Race and Ideology in Southern
Plantation Museums. Book, Other. Smithsonian Institution Press.
Washington, DC. 2002. 312p. ISBN:1-58834-071-6, ISBN13:
978-1-58834-071-9. Dewey:975.043/092. LCCN:2001-057730.
                        Audience: **l,u,f.** *Choice, 2003.*

Falk, John H. & Dierking,   AM7.F34 2000
  Lynn D.
Learning from Museums: Visitor Experiences and the Making of
Meaning. Trade Cloth. AltaMira Press. Walnut Creek, CA. 2000.
xv, 272p. American Association for State and Local History
Book Ser. ISBN:0-7425-0294-5, ISBN13: 978-0-7425-0294-9.
Dewey:069/.134. LCCN:00-021113.

                                          Audience: **l,u,f.**

Genoways, Hugh H. &   AM121.G465 2003
  Ireland, Lynne M.
Museum Administration: An Introduction. Trade Cloth. AltaMira
Press. Walnut Creek, CA. 2003. 416p. American Association for
State and Local History Book Ser. ISBN:0-7591-0293-7,
ISBN13: 978-0-7591-0293-4. Dewey:069/.068.
LCCN:2003-002004.

                                          Audience: **g,l,u,f.**

Lloyd, Sandra Mackenzie, et   E159.L488 2001
  al.
Great Tours!: Thematic Tours and Guide Training for Historic
Sites. Barbara A. Levy & Susan R. Schreiber (Authors). Trade
Cloth. AltaMira Press. Walnut Creek, CA. 2002. 176p. American
Association for State and Local History Book Ser.
ISBN:0-7591-0098-5, ISBN13: 978-0-7591-0098-5.
Dewey:917.304/068/3. LCCN:2001-034313.

                                          Audience: **l,u,f.**

Lord, Barry & Dexter, Gail   AM151.M34 2001
  (Editors)
The Manual of Museum Exhibitions. Trade Cloth. AltaMira
Press. Walnut Creek, CA. 2002. 576p. ISBN:0-7591-0233-3,
ISBN13: 978-0-7591-0233-0. Dewey:069/.5.
LCCN:2001-053954.

                                          Audience: **l,u,f.**

Lord, Barry & Lord, Gail   AM7
  Dexter
The Manual of Museum Management. Ed. 2. Trade Paper.
AltaMira Press. Walnut Creek, CA. 2002. 276p.
ISBN:0-7591-0249-X, ISBN13: 978-0-7591-0249-1. Dewey:069.
                                          Audience: **l,u,f.**

Marstine, Janet   AM151.N49 2005
New Museum Theory and Practice: An Introduction. Trade
Cloth. Blackwell Publishing, Inc. Malden, MA. 2005. 352p.
ISBN:1-4051-0558-5, ISBN13: 978-1-4051-0558-3.
Dewey:069/.5. LCCN:2005-013098.

                                          Audience: **l,u,f.**

Odegaard, Nancy &   AM145.O34 2005
  Sadongei, Alyce
Old Poisons, New Problems: A Museum Resource for Managing
Contaminated Cultural Materials. Trade Paper. AltaMira Press.
Walnut Creek, CA. 2005. 160p. ISBN:0-7591-0515-4, ISBN13:
978-0-7591-0515-7. Dewey:069/.53. LCCN:2004-017104.
                                          Audience: **l,u,f.**

Sherman, Daniel J.   N2010.S57 1989
Worthy Monuments: Art Museums and the Politics of Culture in
Nineteenth-Century France. Trade Cloth. Harvard University
Press. Cambridge, MA. 1989. 352p. ISBN:0-674-96230-3,
ISBN13: 978-0-674-96230-9. Dewey:708.4. LCCN:88-007939.
                        Audience: **l,u,f.** *Choice, 1990.*

Skramstad, Harold &   AM11.S58 2003
  Skramstad, Susan
A Handbook for Museum Trustees. American Association of
Museums Staff (Contribution by). Trade Cloth. American
Association of Museums. Washington, DC. 2003. xii, 209p.
ISBN:0-931201-83-7, ISBN13: 978-0-931201-83-7. Dewey:069.
LCCN:2003-000300.

                                          Audience: **l,u,f.**

Spalding, Julian   AM7.S74 2002
The Poetic Museum: Reviving Historic Collections. Trade Cloth.
Prestel Publishing. New York, NY. 2003. 192p.
ISBN:3-7913-2678-3, ISBN13: 978-3-7913-2678-8. Dewey:069.
LCCN:2001-096182.

                        Audience: **l,u,f.** *Choice, 2002.*

Sullivan, Martin E., et al.   AM133.A22 2004
The AAM Guide to Collections Planning. James B. Gardner &
Elizabeth E. Merritt (Authors), American Association of
Museums Staff (Contribution by). Trade Cloth. American
Association of Museums. Washington, DC. 2004. viii, 93p.
ISBN:0-931201-88-8, ISBN13: 978-0-931201-88-2.
Dewey:069/.5. LCCN:2004-002443.

                                          Audience: **l,u,f.**

Talboys, Graeme K.   AM7.T35 2005
Museum Educator's Handbook. Ed. 2. Trade Cloth. Ashgate
Publishing Company. Williston, VT. 2005. 192p.
ISBN:0-7546-4492-8, ISBN13: 978-0-7546-4492-7.
Dewey:069/.15. LCCN:2005-018438.

                                          Audience: **g,l,u,f.**

Theobald, Mary Miley   HF5429
Museum Store Management. Ed. 2. Trade Cloth. AltaMira Press.
Walnut Creek, CA. 2000. 288p. ISBN:0-7425-0430-1, ISBN13:
978-0-7425-0430-1. Dewey:658.8/7.

                                          Audience: **l,u,f.**

Thomas, Catherine (Editor)   N408.E34 2002
The Edge of Everything: Reflections on Curatorial Practice.
Trade Paper. Banff Centre Press. Banff, AB. 2002. 190p.
ISBN:0-920159-92-3, ISBN13: 978-0-920159-92-7.
Dewey:708/.0092. LCCN:2003-386698.

                   Audience: **l,u,f.**

Weil, Stephen E.   AM7.W3925 2002
Making Museums Matter. Trade Cloth. Smithsonian Institution
Press. Washington, DC. 2002. 288p. Museum Studies
ISBN:1-58834-025-2, ISBN13: 978-1-58834-025-2. Dewey:069.
LCCN:2001-042037.

                   Audience: **l,u,f.**

Zemans, Joyce   AM151
Museums after Modernism: Strategies of Engagement. Griselda
Pollock (Editor). Trade Cloth. Blackwell Publishing, Inc.
Malden, MA. 2006. 264p. New Interventions in Art History Ser.
ISBN:1-4051-3627-8, ISBN13: 978-1-4051-3627-3.
Dewey:708.001. LCCN:2006-016597.

                   Audience: **l,u,f.**

Zimmerman, Larry J.   CC175.E825 2003
Ethical Issues in Archaeology. Karen D. Vitelli & Julie
Hollowell-Zimmer (Editors). Trade Paper. AltaMira Press.
Walnut Creek, CA. 2003. 320p. ISBN:0-7591-0271-6, ISBN13:
978-0-7591-0271-2. Dewey:174/.993. LCCN:2002-151888.

                Audience: **l,u,f.** *Choice, 2003.*

Author Index

E

N

U

V

W

X

Y

Title Index

B

D

E

F

H

L

O

Q

R

S

T

U

W

Numeric Title